Heinemann Educational Publishers
Halley Court, Jordan Hill, Oxford OX2 8EJ
Part of Harcourt Education

Heinemann is the registered trademark of
Harcourt Education limited

© Heinemann Educational Publishers, 1979
New material © Heinemann Educational Publishers, 1992
New editions, 1989, 1993, 1995, 2001
This revised and updated edition first published 2001

All rights reserved. No part of this publication may be reproduced
in any material form (including photocopying or storing it in any
medium by electronic means and whether or not transiently or
incidentally to some other use of this publication) without the prior
written permission of the copyright owner, except in accordance
with the provisions of the Copyright, Designs and Patents Act 1988
or under the terms of a licence issued by the Copyright Licensing
Agency Ltd, 90 Tottenham Court Road, London W1P 0LP.
Applications for the copyright owner's written permission to
reproduce any part of this publication should be addressed in the
first instance to the publisher.

04
10 9 8 7 6

ISBN: 0435 10424 1

Heinemann English Dictionary
1. English Language Dictionaries
I. Harber, Katherine II. Payton, Geoffrey

Note: Words in this dictionary which we believe to be trademarks
ve been acknowledged as such. The presence or absence of such
knowledgement should not be regarded as affecting the legal
status of any trademark or proprietary name.

Typeset by LazerType (UK) Ltd., Colchester
Printed and bound in the UK by CPI Bath

Tel: 01865 888058   www.heinemann.co.uk

KT-490-767

palate (**pal**-it) *noun* — part of speech
1 *Anatomy* the roof of the mouth, hard at
the front and soft at the rear.
2 the sense of taste: *She has a sophisticated
palate.*
Figurative *Romantic novels just do not suit
my palate* (= liking, mental taste). — figurative usage with explanation of particular sense
3 the flavour of wine or beer.
Word Family palatal *adjective*.
[from Latin]

> **Pretty** is an example of a word whose
> meaning has moved far from its origins.
> It derives from Old English *praetig*
> (clever, wily), which came from Old
> English *praett* (a trick or wile). From
> this it came to mean 'clever' in a
> positive sense, then 'cleverly made', and
> then 'beautiful'.

language study box highlights point of spelling, history or language change

primary colour *noun*
any colour having no trace of another
colour: red, yellow, green and blue, plus
the pair black and white. Compare
SECONDARY COLOUR.

cross-reference to related entries

prime minister *noun*
the minister leading the government.

prime mover *noun*
1 the originator or chief promoter of a
scheme of action.
2 the initial source of power, e.g. a
windmill or stationary engine.

compounds as separate entries

prime number *noun*
Maths a positive integer that is exactly
divisible only by itself and one: *Prime
numbers include 5, 7 and 11.*

primer¹ (**pry**-ma) *noun*
a simple book of instruction or learning.

primer² *noun*
1 an undercoat of paint, varnish, etc. on a
surface.
2 a part of a cartridge containing a
substance which explodes when struck by
the firing pin, thus firing the main powder
charge.

numbered headwords of different meaning and/or derivation

primeval (pry-**mee**-v'l) *adjective* also
primaeval
of or relating to prehistoric times.
Word Family primevally *adverb*.
[Latin *primus* first + *aevum* age]

alternative spellings

HEINEM...
ENGLISH
DICTIONARY

Fifth Edition

PREFACE

This fifth edition of the **Heinemann English Dictionary** has been extensively edited and revised for the English curriculum, while keeping the distinctive features of layout and presentation which have made previous editions so popular. Hundreds of words and phrases now in current use have been added.

The dictionary is designed to be as clear, easy and fast to use as possible. Every aspect of its layout has been carefully planned to help you find the information you need without difficulty.

Firstly, the entries are well-spaced on the page, which enables the eye to find the one needed easily. Then, within each entry, the major subsections start a new line, allowing you to see all the possible definitions at a glance.

Perhaps the most distinctive and popular feature of the **Heinemann English Dictionary** is that all parts of speech, etymological derivations and usages are given in full, which makes the entries completely comprehensible at first sight.

The pronunciation guides provided for all irregular words are also immediately self-explanatory. We have used a simple re-spelling system, backed up occasionally by rhyming comparisons, which can be followed clearly without reference to tables or explanations.

The **How to Use the Dictionary** section provides a clear guide to its layout and content. The **Story of English** essay describes the development of English over the centuries.

At the back of the dictionary you will find the **Reference Section** that gives useful lists of **Abbreviations and Acronyms, Grammatical Terms, Punctuation, Prefixes, Suffixes, English Words Borrowed from Other Languages, Common Spellings** and **Periodic Table of Chemical Elements**.

CONTENTS

CONTENTS

For the Fifth Edition

Managing Editor

Martin Manser

Editors

Jessica Feinstein   Rosalind Fergusson
Alice Grandison   Fiona McIntosh

Assistant Editor

Gloria Wren

Subject Specialists

Malcolm Chandler	History
John Hopkin	Geography
Kath Howard	English and Drama
Ann Lovelace	Religious Education
Fred Norton	Mathematics
Jenny Ridgwell	Food Technology and Textiles
Steve Turner	Graphics and Resistant Materials
Sharon Young	Science

The Story of English

Ron Norman

On previous editions
Chief Editors

Katherine Harber   Geoffrey Payton

Adviser

Dr W. A. Gatherer, Chief Adviser, Lothian

Editors

Nicholas Hudson	Keith Nettle	Leonie Bennett
Sarah Dawson	Richard Tarrant	Jack Baldwin
Peter Adams	Andrew Nickson	Julie Chapman
Tim Bass	Helen Heacock	

Adviser for the Fourth Edition

Betty Kirkpatrick

HOW TO USE THE DICTIONARY

Headwords

Most of the words defined in the dictionary are called **headwords** or entry-words. These appear at the start of each entry and they are printed in bold or black type so that they are easy to pick out. This is important if you are in a hurry to find the meaning of a word or even to check the spelling of a word.

Some words in English have the same spelling but different meanings and derivations, for example **converse**, which can mean either 'to talk informally' or 'the opposite of something'. In such cases separate entries have been given to each of the headwords and these have been numbered.

> *Example:* **converse**[1]
> **converse**[2]

Not all headwords are single words. Some of them consist of two or more words.

> *Example:* **costume drama**
> **cost of living**

Alternative Spellings

Alternative spellings are given at headwords and sub-headwords where more than one spelling is common.

> *Example:* **emphasize, emphasise**
> **pictograph** also **pictogram**

Pronunciation

Pronunciation guides are given in brackets immediately after the headwords. They are given for any words which it is thought might present problems with regard to pronunciation or stress.

A simple respelling scheme using the ordinary letters of the Roman alphabet has been used in order to make the scheme easy to use.

> *Example:* **photosynthesis** (fo-toe-**sin**-tha-sis).

The bold type for **sin** shows that this is where the stress falls in this word. Hyphens are used to separate the syllables.

Sometimes a familiar rhyming word has been given if this is the clearest way of indicating the pronunciation.

Example: **ochre** (*rhymes with poker*).

There are a few sounds which cannot be unambiguously indicated by the methods outlined above. For these sounds the following conventions are used.

(') An apostrophe is used to indicate the unstressed vowel common in English and known technically as the schwa.

Example: **oxidation** (ok-si-**day**-sh'n).

When 'th' is pronounced as in **think** it is printed in ordinary or Roman type. When it is pronounced as in **this** it is printed in italic type.

Examples: **thief** (theef); **thine** (*th*ine).

When 'u' is pronounced as in **cup** it is printed in ordinary or Roman type. When it is pronounced as in **bull** it is printed in italic type.

Examples: **muscle** (**muss**-'l); **ombudsman** (**om**-*budz*-man).

The letters 'zh' are printed in italic to indicate the sound common to **measure** and **adhesion**.

Example: **treasure** (**tre***zh*-a).

Parts of Speech

The part of speech, showing whether a headword is a noun, verb, adjective, adverb, preposition, conjunction, article, contraction, interjection or pronoun, is given in italic type immediately after the headword or immediately after the pronunciation guide where this exists.

Example: **converse**[1] *verb*; **converse**[2] *noun*.

A change in the part of speech of the headword is shown by a bullet (•).

Example: **idle** (**eye**-d'l) *adjective*
             1 not busy, working or in use: *The machine had been idle since the workers went on strike.*
             2 useless, worthless: *Ignore their idle gossip.*
             3 weak, groundless: *an idle threat.*
             • **idle** *verb*
             1 to move or pass time in an idle manner.
             2 (of machinery, engines, etc.) to move or turn at minimum speed.

A headword consisting of two or more words which are not joined by a hyphen has been given a part of speech, for example **cable television** and **cost of living**.

Plurals

Plural forms likely to cause difficulty are given in bold type in brackets after the part of speech.

Example: **potato** *noun* (*plural* **potatoes**)
stadium *noun* (*plural* **stadiums** or **stadia**)

Parts of Verbs

Parts of irregular verbs are given in bold type in brackets after the part of speech. In each case the third person singular of the present tense, the present participle and the past tense (and past participle when this is different) are shown.

Example: **dig** *verb* (**digs; digging; dug**)
creep *verb* (**creeps; creeping; crept**)
drive *verb* (**drives; driving; drove; driven**)

Comparatives and Superlatives of Adjectives

The comparative and superlative forms of adjectives are shown when they might cause difficulty.

Example: **happy** *adjective* (**happier; happiest**)

Definitions and Examples

Definitions appear on a new line after the part of speech. Where a word has more than one meaning the definitions are numbered, for example:

> **ice-breaker** *noun*
> 1 a ship with a reinforced hull used for clearing or channelling through ice.
> 2 a person or thing that helps to relax the atmosphere.

Sometimes after the definition a short example phrase or sentence is given to show how a particular word or meaning is used in context. These are separated from the definition by a colon (:) and are printed in italic type.

Example: **ilk** *noun*
a type or kind: *People of his ilk are never happy.*

If there is more than one example, the examples are separated by an open square □.

Example: **evidence** (ev-i-d'nce) *noun*
1 anything which provides a basis for belief: *I don't think you have any evidence for that statement.* □ *There was little evidence of suffering in her face.*

Where a particular definition is used with the word printed with an initial capital letter or in the plural this is shown after the definition number.

Examples: **dame** *noun*
1 (**Dame**) a form of address for a woman of rank.
2 (*informal*) a woman.

damage (dam-ij) *noun*
1 any injury which causes loss of usefulness or value.
2 (**damages**) *Law* a sum of money claimed because of a loss, e.g. when a contract has been broken.
3 (*informal*) the cost.

Figurative Usages

Figurative is given in front of an example when a word, instead of being used in its ordinary way, is used in a more imaginative way that extends its meaning. Usually this applies when a word is used metaphorically or in a figure of speech.

Example: **artificial** (ar-ti-**fish**-'l) *adjective*
made as an imitation, as distinct from being natural: *They only sell artificial flowers.*
Figurative Her artificial smile did not fool any of us (= false, affected).

Word Family

Words directly related to the headword, or words formed directly from it, are not usually given separate definitions. They are grouped under the label *Word Family*.

Example: **idle** (**eye**-d'l) *adjective*
1 not busy, working or in use: *The machine had been idle since the workers went on strike.*
2 useless, worthless: *Ignore their idle gossip.*
3 weak, groundless: *an idle threat.*
● **idle** *verb*
1 to move or pass time in an idle manner.
2 (of machinery, engines, etc.) to move or turn at minimum speed.
Word Family **idleness** *noun*; **idly** *adverb*; **idler** *noun* a lazy person.

Where necessary, a pronunciation guide is provided in the *Word Family* list, together with irregular plurals or verb forms, or extensions in meaning.

Phrases

Phrases in which the headword is the most important word are listed under the headword.

> *Example:* **evidence** (ev-i-d'nce) *noun*
> 1 anything which provides a basis for belief: *I don't think you have any evidence for that statement.* □ *There was little evidence of suffering in her face.*
> 2 *Law* the statements, documents or objects presented in a court to prove disputed facts.
> *Phrase* **in evidence** very clear to see: *Her talent was very much in evidence during the play.*

Labels

Labels are given to indicate words or meanings used in a specialized area of language.

> *Example:* **icon** *noun*
> 3 *Computers* a picture or symbol in a graphic display on a VDU screen, especially one that represents a particular facility available to users.

They are also given to indicate words or meanings which are common in other countries.

> *Example:* **sidewalk** *noun*
> *American* a pavement.

The label (*informal*) is used to indicate words or meanings which are not used in formal situations or contexts but should be restricted to informal situations or colloquial contexts. This label also covers slang words.

The label (*used with singular verb*) indicates that a noun which is plural in form is to be used with a singular verb.

> *Example:* **economics** (ee-ka-**nom**-iks *or* ek-a-**nom**-iks) *plural noun*
> 1 (*used with singular verb*) the study of the production and distribution of goods, services and wealth.

The label (*formerly*) is used to indicate a former meaning of a word which is not commonly found nowadays.

> *Example:* **guinea** (**ginn**-ee) *noun*
> (*formerly*) a sum of money equal to £1·05.

Cross-references

Where the definition of a word is given at another entry an arrow (⇨) is given to show you where to look, followed by the word to be referred to in small capital letters.

> *Example:* **ice rink** ⇨ RINK (definition 1).

Where there is important information given at another entry which relates to a particular entry, a cross-reference may be given at the end of the definition introduced by the word 'Compare'.

> *Example:*   **planet** (**plan**-it) *noun*
> 1 *Astronomy* any body that does not
> produce light and revolves around a star,
> especially the nine planets of our solar
> system. Compare SATELLITE
> (definition 1).

If the definition of a word for some reason is not found in its alphabetical position a cross-reference is given to the headword where it is to be found.

Etymologies

Etymologies are given within square brackets at the end of entries wherever they throw light on the origin, evolution or modern meaning of the word. This applies particularly to words deriving from Greek, Latin and modern foreign languages. Etymologies are not generally given for words of Old English origin where the word and meaning have not significantly changed; nor are they given in cases where the etymology is so complex that a brief summary would cause confusion. Where no English equivalent is given for a classical or foreign word cited in the etymology it may be assumed that the word means essentially the same as the headword. Where the headword is a foreign word adopted into English only the language of origin is given.

See also the **Reference Section** at the back of the dictionary for lists of prefixes, suffixes and examples of English words borrowed from other languages.

Common Errors

In cases where one headword is likely to be confused with another of similar spelling, function, usage or pronunciation, a brief note beginning '!' distinguishes the words.

> **its** *possessive adjective* (*plural* **their**)
> belonging to it: *Has the house got its own*
> *garden?*

- **its** *possessive pronoun* (*plural* **theirs**) belonging to it.

> ❗ Note that there is no apostrophe in the possessive adjective and pronoun *its*, meaning 'belonging to it', as in *The dog wagged its tail*. Do not confuse *its* with the contraction *it's*, meaning 'it is', as in *It's too late* or 'it has', as in *It's been cold today*.

Language Boxes

These appear at intervals throughout the text and cover a wide spread of aspects of English, including extended etymologies, development of words and modern usage.

> The word **candidate** comes from the Latin word for 'white'. In ancient Rome, people who were standing as *candidates* for positions of public service had to dress in white, the colour associated with purity and honesty. Since the Latin for 'white' is *candidus*, the Roman *candidate* standing for office was called a *candidatus*, literally 'one clothed in white'.

THE STORY OF ENGLISH

This dictionary gives us a clear picture of the words and their meanings which make up the English language at the beginning of the 21st century. English is a remarkable language. Nowadays, it is not just spoken by the people of England, Britain, or even the United States. Apart from the millions of people who learn it as their native language, it is learnt as a second language throughout the world. Some estimates suggest over one billion people worldwide speak English.

The history of the rise of English is a fascinating story of the growth of an obscure and unimportant northern European dialect into what is virtually a world language. In the 1500 years it has taken for English to develop into the language we speak today, it has seen many changes – if there had been a *Heinemann English Dictionary* at the beginning of the 6th century it would have appeared very different from the current edition.

The story of English begins in the part of northern Europe which today we know as Germany and Denmark.

5th – 8th centuries A.D.: the triumph of 'Old English'

If we could travel back to 5th century Britain, we would find our ancestors speaking in an unfamiliar tongue. We may have a hope of recognizing some of its sounds or meanings – but only if we were speakers of Welsh, or one of the other 'Celtic' languages such as Scots or Irish Gaelic or Irish. There are many reasons why most British speakers in the 21st century speak English instead of Welsh or Gaelic, but a major factor was the arrival in large numbers of people from northern Germany and Denmark between the 5th and 7th centuries.

These new arrivals were the Angles, Saxons and Jutes – so called after the areas of northern Europe they came from. The violent struggles between them and the native Britons were to drag on over a couple of centuries, but there was no stopping the advance of the Germanic tribes. Even today, a linguistic map of the British Isles illustrates the extent of their triumph, as the Celtic languages – Welsh, Scots Gaelic, Irish, and the now defunct Cornish and Manx* – are confined to the

* The languages of Cornwall and the Isle of Man officially 'died' but attempts are being made to preserve and revive these ancient tongues.

extreme fringes of the kingdom, showing how the ancient Britons were forced back in the face of the German advance.

This triumph was inevitably reflected in the progress of their language, which eventually displaced the Celtic tongues in most of Britain. Although there were significant differences between the dialects which the new arrivals spoke, the term **Anglo-Saxon** is used to describe what evolved in this period as the dominant language. This, then, was the true beginning of English – the name itself derived from the tribe (the Angles) who originated it.

Anglo-Saxon, or **Old English** as it is also known, survives in a rich body of literature, and this has enabled us to learn a great deal about the language. We can even speculate with some confidence about what it may have sounded like, as the rhymes and rhythms of the verse in which this literature was written provides many helpful clues. To modern eyes, Anglo-Saxon seems as unfamiliar as a foreign language. Its alphabet included letters which we do not now recognize and much of its vocabulary may seem strange. However, if English speakers look at Anglo-Saxon more closely, we can begin to pick out some familiar words, even if the spellings have changed. These are often the very basic, everyday words, such as *is*, *was*, *this*, *that*, *in*, or everyday things and people like *man*, *wife*, *child* or *house*. In fact, the more down-to-earth and basic is the English that someone uses, the more likely it is that he or she is using a high proportion of Anglo-Saxon words.

8th – 9th centuries A.D.: enter the Vikings

What happens when a language becomes separated from the land it comes from and people who originally spoke it? To answer this question, we have only to look at the differences between modern American English and modern British English. In the space of three of four centuries, they have grown apart so that although we can still understand each other, there are marked differences of vocabulary, pronunciation and even grammar on either side of the Atlantic Ocean. In just the same way, Old English gradually became distinct from the Germanic language spoken in mainland Europe. As the two languages drifted apart, modern English was always going to emerge as a very different language from modern German – but this difference was to be increased by a number of major historical events.

The first of these was the arrival of the next wave of invaders – the Vikings. Over a period of nearly 200 years, visitors from Scandinavia arrived and settled throughout the eastern parts of the country. It does seem that the language they spoke – Old Norse – was similar enough to Anglo-Saxon for the invaders and the Anglo-Saxons to understand each other. However, many distinctive Viking words (such as days of the week) were absorbed by Anglo-Saxon, and in the north and east of England, place names such as those ending in *-thorp* and *-by* record their presence. Some scholars also believe that the effect of Old Norse and Anglo-Saxon coming into such close contact was to simplify the extremely complex grammar of Old English, which was an important step along the road to English as we know it.

Although the impact of the Vikings certainly helped move English Anglo-Saxon away from the mainland Germanic language from which it had sprung, this influence was slight compared to that of the next party of uninvited guests who arrived on English shores – the Normans.

1066 – the coming of the Normans and Middle English

For all the gradual changes which had affected Anglo-Saxon over 500 years, it was still recognizably a Germanic language, and still seems like a foreign language to our modern eyes (and ears). However, the next 500 years were to transform Old English into one which is much closer to the language we speak today. This was the language of the poet Geoffrey Chaucer, a language that we modern English speakers can – with a little effort – understand and enjoy. The trigger for this transformation was the Norman Conquest of 1066.

The Normans who accompanied William the Conqueror spoke a French dialect of the time – Norman French. As the victors in the Battle of Hastings, William's supporters not only seized control of the country, but also installed Norman French as the language of law, government and power.

For perhaps 200 or 300 years after William's victory, English went 'underground'. It ceased to be used for official documents, and all the business of government and law was carried out in French. However, where French was the official language of the rich and powerful, English continued to be used as the 'common' language of ordinary people. If the Norman lords wished to communicate less formally or officially with the English people they ruled over, they had to resort to English. What is more, there is evidence that some of the descendants of William the Conqueror were, within a couple of generations, growing up with English as their *first* language, and learning French as a second.

The result of all this was that in due time, English re-emerged as the official language of the English – but this was a very different English from the Anglo-Saxon spoken before William's arrival. The impact of the French had been huge. Even before the Normans came, the influence of the Christian Church – whose business was carried out in Latin – had introduced many Latin words into the language. After 1066, the influence of French, itself a language grown from Latin roots, intensified this process. The vocabulary of our language expanded as French, Latin-based equivalents took their place alongside Anglo-Saxon originals. We already had *cow* – but the French gave us *beef*. We already had *pig* – the French gave us *pork*. Where we once said *take*, we could now choose *receive*. This enrichment of the vocabulary coincided with major changes in the grammar of the language to produce the **Middle English** illustrated by these opening lines of Geoffrey Chaucer's *Canterbury Tales*, written in the 1380s.

Whan that aprill with his shoures soote
  The droghte of march hath perced to the roote,
And bathed every veyne in swich licour
  Of which vertu engendred is the flour;

We can almost sum up this transformation as an equation: Anglo-Saxon + Norman French = Middle English.

In the extract above, some of Chaucer's words may look familiar, but the spellings clearly do not. One of the reasons for this is that they reflect patterns of pronunciation which were to change hugely in the 200 years or so between his lifetime and that of William Shakespeare. The large amount of surviving Middle English literature – as with Anglo-Saxon, much of it written in rhythmical and rhyming verse – helps us work out these older pronunciations. What is not quite as clear is just how, and why, such a tremendous change in English pronunciation took place in a relatively short period. Whatever the reasons, within 150 years of Chaucer's death there seems little doubt that his descendants were speaking English in a very different way. This was to be the English of Shakespeare.

Begging, stealing and borrowing: Shakespeare and Early Modern English

There were to be no more military invasions of Britain by unwelcome guests, but the so-called Early Modern period of English was still a period of huge expansion and development. This was a complex process, but we can pick out four important elements of it:

1 The invention of printing in the 15th century led to a vast increase in the written material available, and a lot of this literature attempted to translate into English the works of the 'classic' authors of ancient Greece and Rome. Many translators used this opportunity to introduce words from Greek and Latin into English, claiming that the existing English words did not convey their meanings accurately or precisely enough.

2 Meanwhile, this was an age of geographical, as well as intellectual exploration. As traders and explorers encountered different cultures and languages, large-scale 'borrowings' of words from many other languages (European and beyond) took place.

3 This was a period of great creative activity in literature and drama. Shakespeare is the most well-known of a whole host of writers who were creative not just in their storytelling but in their language, often inventing words of their own where they felt the need. Shakespeare, famously, seems to have contributed hundreds of new words to English.

4 Some people increasingly felt that English was becoming chaotic. There were great disputes about what was 'good' and 'bad' English, what words meant and how they should be spelt. Until the 1700s, there was no standard dictionary or grammar of English to settle these arguments. As a result, when looking at English written before this time it is not unusual to find the same word spelt differently even in the same sentence. Several dictionaries appeared, the most famous of which was written by Dr Samuel Johnson. Grammar books were also published, laying down rules about good or correct usage – which we have been breaking ever since. English was being modernized and standardized. If the same thing happened today, we might even have called it 'New English'. In practice, the English of 1800 had become recognizably our English, or simply **Modern English**.

An ever-changing language: Modern English

Some of the writers in the 18th century who laboured long and hard over their dictionaries and grammars thought English was in a confused state and aimed to put a stop to its constant change. But this was, and is, a futile hope. A living language *must* change, or die. Most obviously, its vocabulary and meanings change in response to the changing needs of its speakers and the different ways they live their lives. Rather harder to spot are the ways in which even our grammar and our pronunciation continue to change. These changes are often more subtle and difficult to see in just a few years, but when we listen to old radio broadcasts or examine old texts we can more easily see the differences.

Although the changes in English in the last 200 years have sometimes been less obvious than the huge transformations of the more distant past, there have still been powerful forces at work. In this period, the ways people live have changed unimaginably, and our language has had to reflect these changes. Since the 19th century, the rapid advance of industry and technology has driven bewildering expansions in English vocabulary. Most recently, the development of computer technology has led to the creation of an entirely new set of English words and phrases. For example, *this article is being written on a PC, saved onto hard disk and CD-ROM, then emailed via the Internet*. Fifty years ago this last sentence could not have been written, and if it had, it would have seemed like a piece of nonsense.

An equally important influence on our ever-changing English is its increasing use across the world. In the 19th century, it was the British Empire that established English in places such as North America, Australia, Africa and many parts of Asia. Nowadays, the English spoken in these parts of the world has developed its own distinctive qualities and British English continues to 'borrow' new words from these sources. In the 20th and 21st centuries the increasing enormous economic power of the United States in the world has meant that it is American English which is becoming most influential. Some British speakers have always regarded 'Americanisms' with hostility, but many such terms have taken root in British English. Some American spellings (as in computer *program*) have also been accepted in British English, and the slang generated by a series of music and youth cults has often made the short hop across the Atlantic to British streets. However, worldwide English extends far beyond the United States; wherever English is spoken – in Asia, Africa, America or Australia – it takes on its own distinctive character, reflecting the culture of the people who use it.

So there is not one single language we can call 'Modern English', but many variations, each of them rubbing off continuously onto the others and constantly renewing the words and phrases of their everyday speech.

English today

Modern English is indeed bewildering in its variety. Even if we concentrate on the language spoken within the British Isles, there are still widespread differences, many of which can be heard just by listening to the characters and voices broadcast on TV and radio. The most noticeable of these are differences in the way speakers pronounce words, phrases and sentences – their accents, in other words – according to where in the country they come from. This may be a matter of how they say words like *bath* or *butter*, of how they say the sounds in the middle of *bottle*, or of how their voices go up, or down (their intonation), as they speak a sentence.

Then there are differences in the actual words used for everyday things; a child may be a *bairn*, a back alley a *ginnel*, a cigarette a *tab* or a gooseberry a *goosegog*. For a dictionary like ours, these dialect words pose a problem – how many such words deserve to be included in a Dictionary of English? For they belong to a speaker's dialect rather than the 'Standard English' that we have grown to accept as the 'normal' or 'correct' version of our language. Many dialect speakers will also use constructions which are not regarded as 'correct' English – such as *I seen him do it, he never did nothing wrong, innit* or *the lad done good.*

To some people, these non-standard expressions represent 'bad' English, and like the dictionary and grammar writers of the 1700s, they may see them as evidence of chaos. There have been many arguments in the field of education about what some people see as the 'poor' English used by some children, and regular calls for the strict 'grammar' of Standard English to be enforced. Others say that it is important for students to learn about the differences between Standard English and other forms of English, and to use whichever is suitable, according to the situation.

It certainly seems as if non-standard accents and dialects are here to stay. True, some traditional countryside dialects seem to be disappearing as fewer and fewer people remain in the villages in which they were born and move to the big towns and cities. However, the dialects of these towns and cities show no signs of fading away, and the popularity of soap operas such as *Coronation Street*, *EastEnders* and *Brookside*, in which such regional speech figures prominently, indicates the broad appeal of such language.

In some ways, it is surprising that these local variations continue to survive; travel and telecommunications have made the world a small place, and the 'official' voices of the major broadcast networks use Standard English. There seem to be lots of reasons why we should be using such a standardized speech in large numbers – so why aren't we?

The reasons are tied up with complicated social factors. We don't just use language to send information from person to person; as with our clothes, the style of language we use also tells the rest of the world something about ourselves and the groups of people we belong to and identify with. Many people feel a strong sense of pride in and loyalty to the places they come from, or the people they associate with. By using a regional accent or dialect they announce this sense of belonging, even if they know that in 'official' terms, the language is 'incorrect'. Many types of slang work in this way. We may choose to use a particular kind of slang to fit in with friends or identify with people who like similar kinds of music. Some slang has a very short 'shelf life' and can disappear along with the short-lived craze with which it is associated; other slang terms can take root and become an established part of the language.

In fact, many speakers of English are now able to switch between different styles or dialects of English according to the situation they are in. So, it is unlikely that a wholly 'Standard' English can ever completely triumph. Perhaps we should celebrate the rich diversity of English throughout the world and its endless capacity to reinvent itself.

DICTIONARY

Aa

a *article*
Grammar an indefinite article ⇨ ARTICLE.

aback *adverb*
Phrase **taken aback** *She was taken aback by his rudeness* (= startled).

abacus (**abb**-a-kus) *noun* (*plural* **abacuses**)
a device used for counting by sliding beads along thin rods set in a frame.
[Greek *abax*]

abaft *adverb, preposition*
Nautical at or towards the stern.

abandon *verb*
1 to leave something without intending to return to it: *We had to abandon all our possessions and flee.*
2 to stop going on with: *We abandoned the search after four days with no results.*
Figurative *The boy abandoned himself to grief* (= surrendered).
• **abandon** *noun* a freedom from restraint: *The class cheered with great abandon.*
Word Family **abandonment** *noun*.

abase *verb*
to humble or degrade: *The prisoner abased himself before the judge.*
Word Family **abasement** *noun*.

abashed *adjective*
ashamed or embarrassed.
Word Family **abash** *verb*.

abate *verb*
to lessen in amount or intensity.
Word Family **abatement** *noun*.

abattoir (**abb**-a-twar) *noun*
a place where cattle, sheep, etc. are killed for food.
[French]

abbey (**abb**-ee) *noun*
1 a monastery or convent.
2 a church or house that was once part of an abbey, such as Westminster Abbey.
Word Family **abbot** *noun* the male head of an abbey; **abbess** *noun* (*plural* **abbesses**) a female abbot.

abbreviate (a-**bree**-vi-ate) *verb*
to shorten or contract, especially a word or phrase.
Word Family **abbreviation** (a-bree-vi-ay-sh'n) *noun* 1 the act of abbreviating.
2 a shortened form of a word, especially one using only the first letter or letters: '*PTO' is an abbreviation for 'please turn over'.* Compare CONTRACTION (definition 2).
[*ab-* + Latin *brevis* short]

abdicate *verb*
1 to renounce the throne.
2 to give up a claim, position, privilege, etc.
Word Family **abdication** *noun*.

abdomen (**ab**-da-m'n) *noun* also called **belly**.
Anatomy the lower front part of the body, which is separated from the chest by the diaphragm. The abdomen contains the organs of digestion and excretion and, in women, the uterus and ovaries.
Word Family **abdominal** (ab-**domm**-i-n'l) *adjective*.
[Latin]

abduct *verb*
to take away a person, illegally or by force. Compare KIDNAP.
Word Family **abduction** *noun*; **abductor** *noun*.
[Latin *abductus* led away]

abeam (a-**beem**) *adverb*
Nautical opposite to the middle of a ship.

aberration (abb-a-**ray**-sh'n) *noun*
a deviation from the normal course: *He destroyed his own work in a moment of aberration.*
Word Family **aberrant** (a-**berr**-ent) *adjective*.
[Latin *aberrare* to wander away]

abet (a-**bet**) *verb* (**abets; abetting; abetted**)
to encourage or assist someone to commit a crime.
Word Family **abetter, abettor** (*Law*) *noun*.

abeyance (a-**bay**-'nce) *noun*
a state of temporary inactivity: *The project is in abeyance because of a lack of support.*

abhor (ab-**hor**) *verb* (**abhors; abhorring; abhorred**)
to regard with hatred or disgust.
Word Family **abhorrent** (ab-**horr**-ent) *adjective* causing disgust or horror; **abhorrently** *adverb*; **abhorrence** *noun*.
[Latin *abhorrere* to shrink back]

abide *verb* (**abides; abiding; abided** or **abode**)
1 to continue or remain.
2 an old word for **dwell**.
3 to tolerate: *I can't abide fools.*
Phrase **abide by** *He abided by his decision* (= kept to).

ability *noun* (*plural* **abilities**)
the quality of being able to do something.
[Latin *habilitas* aptitude]

abiogenesis (ay-by-o-**jen**-i-sis) ⇨
SPONTANEOUS GENERATION.
[*a-* + Greek *bios* life + *genesis* creation]

abject (**ab**-jekt) *adjective*
1 contemptible: *an abject coward.*
2 humble: *an abject apology.*
3 wretched: *He lived in abject poverty.*
Word Family **abjectly** *adverb*; **abjection** *noun.*
[*ab-* + Latin *jactus* thrown]

abjure *verb*
to renounce publicly a belief, opinion, etc.
[Latin *abjurare* to deny on oath]

ablaze *adverb, adjective*
on fire or lit up: *The town was ablaze with lights.*

able *adjective*
1 having the skill to do something: *Are you able to drive a car?*
2 having the opportunity or permission to do something: *Will you be able to start work tomorrow?*
3 clever: *He is an able man.*
Word Family **ably** *adverb.*
[Latin *habilis* fit, apt]

able-bodied *adjective*
healthy or strong.

abled *adjective*
able-bodied, not disabled.

ableism, ablism *noun*
discrimination in favour of able-bodied people.

able rating *noun*
Navy the lowest rank of sailor in the service.

ablution (a-**bloo**-sh'n) *noun*
(*usually* **ablutions**) the act of washing oneself.

abnegate (**ab**-ni-gate) *verb*
1 to renounce: *I will not abnegate my rights in this matter.*
2 to give up.
Word Family **abnegation** *noun.*
[Latin *abnegare* to deny]

abnormal *adjective*
different from what is normal or expected.
Word Family **abnormally** *adverb*;

abnormality *noun* (*plural* **abnormalities**).

aboard *adverb, preposition*
on a ship, aircraft, etc.

abode (a-**bode**) *noun*
the place where one lives.
• **abode** *verb* a past tense and past participle of **abide**.

abolish (a-**bol**-ish) *verb*
to put an end to: *It took many years to abolish the slave trade.*
Word Family **abolition** (abb-a-**lish**-'n), **abolishment** *noun.*
[Latin *abolere*]

A-bomb *noun*
short form of **atom bomb**.

abominable (a-**bomm**-in-a-b'l) *adjective*
dreadful or shocking.
Word Family **abominably** *adverb*; **abomination** *noun* a person or thing that is abominable.

Abominable Snowman ⇨ YETI.

aborigines (abb-a-**rijj**-i-neez) *plural noun*
the original inhabitants of a country.
Word Family **Aborigine** *noun* an original inhabitant of Australia; **Aboriginal** (abb-a-**rijj**-i-n'l) *noun* 1 any of the original inhabitants of Australia. 2 any of their languages; **aboriginal, Aboriginal** *adjective.*
[Latin *ab origine* from the beginning]

> **Aboriginal** is now the preferred term for a person of a race originally inhabiting Australia. It is the term advocated by the Australian government and by the Aboriginals themselves in preference to *Aborigine*, the previously usual term. In general, people are now much more sensitive about what they call members of other races. It is important to avoid really offensive words such as *Abo*.

abortion (a-**bore**-sh'n) *noun*
1 the expulsion or removal of a human fetus from the uterus before the fetus is capable of independent survival.
2 anything which is a failure.
3 a monstrous creature or thing.
Word Family **abort** *verb*; **abortive** *adjective* unsuccessful; **abortionist** *noun.*
[Latin *abortus* a miscarriage]

abound *verb*
to be plentiful.

about *preposition, adverb*
1 around: *He looked about as he walked.*
2 on the subject of: *What is the book about?*
3 approximately: *She ate about 14 cakes.*

4 engaged in doing: *What are you about?*
Phrase about to *He is about to jump*
(= just going to).

about-face *verb* also **about-turn**
to turn so as to face the opposite direction.
• **about-face, about-turn** *noun* a sudden
reversal.

above *adverb, preposition*
1 in a higher position: *The sun rose above
the horizon.*
2 more than: *above average.*
Word Family above *adjective.*

above board *adverb, adjective*
open and honest.

abracadabra (ab-ra-ka-**dab**-ra)
interjection
an exclamation used as a magic spell.

abrade *verb*
to scrape off or wear away by rubbing.
[Latin *abradere* to scrape off]

abrasion *noun*
1 the act or process of abrading.
2 a place where something has been
rubbed away.
3 *Geography* the wearing away of rocks by
particles thrown against them by water in
a river or waves. Compare ATTRITION
(definition 2); CORROSION (definition 2).

abrasive *adjective*
1 serving to abrade.
2 (of a personality, etc.) harsh, irritating or
annoying.
• **abrasive** *noun* something which
abrades.

abreast *adverb*
side by side.

abridge *verb*
to shorten: *The book was abridged for
publication in serial form.*
**Word Family abridgement,
abridgment** *noun.*

abroad *adverb*
1 in or to another country: *We went abroad
for our holidays.*
2 an old word for outside: *He did not
venture abroad all day.*
Figurative *Vicious rumours are abroad*
(= circulating).

abrogate (**ab**-ra-gate) *verb*
to repeal or annul.
Word Family abrogation (ab-ra-**gay**-
sh'n) *noun.*
[Latin *abrogare* to repeal]

abrupt *adjective*
1 sudden or unexpected.
2 discourteous or brief, especially in
manner.

Word Family abruptly *adverb;*
abruptness *noun.*
[Latin *abruptus* broken off]

abscess (**ab**-sess) *noun* (*plural*
abscesses)
an acute local bacterial infection
containing pus, such as a boil.
[Latin *abscessus* a going away]

abscissa (ab-**siss**-a) *noun* (*plural*
abscissae (ab-**siss**-ee) or **abscissas**))
Maths the horizontal distance of a point
from the origin of a graph; the *x*-
coordinate. Compare ORDINATE.

abscond (ab-**skond**) *verb*
to leave suddenly or secretly, especially
after doing wrong: *She absconded with the
money.*
[Latin *abscondere* to hide away]

abseil (**ab**-sail) *verb*
to slide down a cliff or mountain, using a
rope.
• **abseil** *noun.*

absent (**ab**-s'nt) *adjective*
1 away: *She was absent from school.*
2 inattentive or preoccupied: *He had an
absent look about him.*
Word Family absent (ab-**sent**) *verb* to
take or keep (oneself) away; **absently**
adverb; **absence** *noun;* **absentee** (ab-s'n-
tee) *noun* a person who is absent;
absenteeism *noun* the practice of staying
away from one's place of work, study, etc.,
habitually or without good excuse or
permission.
[Latin *absens* being away]

absent-minded *adjective*
vague or forgetful.
Word Family absent-mindedly *adverb;*
absent-mindedness *noun.*

absinth *noun* also **absinthe**
a strong drink made with wormwood.

absolute (**ab**-sa-loot) *adjective*
complete, perfect or unlimited: *The day
was an absolute success.* □ *The dictator had
absolute power.*
Word Family absolutely *adverb.*
[Latin *absolutus* freed]

absolute majority *noun*
a winning number of votes which is more
than the combined votes received by all
other candidates or parties in an election.

absolute zero *noun*
the lowest temperature possible, which is
equal to 0 kelvin (−273·15°C).

absolve *verb*
to pardon or release from guilt, blame, etc.

Word Family **absolution** (ab-sa-**loo**-sh'n) *noun*.
[Latin *absolvere* to acquit]

absorb *verb*
to take in or soak up: *The sponge absorbed the water.*
Figurative She was completely absorbed by the book (= engrossed). □ *The international corporation absorbed its competitors* (= took over). □ *A black surface tends to absorb heat, whereas a white surface tends to reflect it* (= retain).
Word Family **absorbent** *adjective*; **absorption** *noun*.
[*ab-* + Latin *sorbere* to suck in]

abstain *verb*
to refrain voluntarily from doing something: *Some people abstain from drinking alcohol.* □ *He abstained from voting.*
Word Family **abstinence** (**ab**-sti-nence) *noun* self-restraint; **abstention** *noun* the act of abstaining.
[Latin *abstinere* to keep away from]

abstemious (ab-**stee**-mi-us) *adjective*
tending to eat and drink sparingly.
[Latin *abstemius*]

abstract (**ab**-strakt) *adjective*
1 concerning things which have no real or physical existence, such as ideas.
2 based on theory: *abstract arguments.*
3 *Art* not representing people or things, but relying on colour, form, etc.
• **abstract** *noun*
1 the state of being abstract.
2 a summary.
• **abstract** (ab-**strakt**) *verb* to remove or take away.
Figurative She had a vague abstracted look (= preoccupied, withdrawn).
Word Family **abstractly** *adverb*; **abstraction** *noun*.
[Latin *abstractus* drawn away]

abstract noun *noun*
a noun which refers to thoughts, feelings and ideas, which cannot be touched.
Compare CONCRETE NOUN.

abstruse (ab-**strewce**) *adjective*
obscure or difficult to understand: *I couldn't follow the lawyer's abstruse argument.*
[Latin *abstrusus* hidden]

> **!** Do not confuse *abstruse* with *obtuse*: *abstruse* means 'difficult to understand' (*an abstruse academic debate*), whereas *obtuse* means 'slow to understand' (*an obtuse student*).

absurd *adjective*
foolish or illogical.
Word Family **absurdly** *adverb*; **absurdity** *noun* (*plural* **absurdities**) 1 the quality of being absurd. 2 something which is absurd.
[Latin *absurdus* out of tune]

abundance (a-**bun**-d'nce) *noun*
a full or ample supply or amount.
Word Family **abundant** *adjective*; **abundantly** *adverb*.
[Latin *abundare* to overflow]

abuse (a-**bewz**) *verb*
1 to use wrongly or maltreat: *Never abuse a chisel by using it as a screwdriver.*
2 to speak insultingly to: *The drunk abused the barman.*
3 to ill-treat, especially physically or sexually.
• **abuse** (a-**bewce**) *noun*
1 wrong or improper use.
2 insulting remarks.
3 ill-treatment or maltreatment, especially physical or sexual: *child abuse.*
4 excessive or illegal use: *alcohol abuse.*
□ *drug abuse.*
Word Family **abusive** *adjective*; **abusively** *adverb*; **abuser** *noun*.
[*ab-* + USE]

abut (a-**but**) *verb* (**abuts**; **abutting**; **abutted**)
to border on or be next to: *His farm abuts on the park.*

abysmal (a-**biz**-m'l) *adjective*
1 of, like or as deep as an abyss: *Your abysmal ignorance appals me.*
2 very bad: *I thought the performance was abysmal.*
Word Family **abysmally** *adverb*.
[Greek *abyssos* bottomless]

abyss (a-**biss**) *noun* (*plural* **abysses**)
1 an immeasurable depth or chasm.
2 anything very profound or deep: *She wept in an abyss of grief.*

acacia (a-**kay**-sha) *noun*
any of a large group of trees or shrubs, mostly tropical or subtropical, usually thorny, some yielding gum arabic.
[Greek *akakia* a thorny tree]

academic (akk-a-**demm**-ik) *adjective*
1 of or relating to learning or studies, especially in a university or similar institution.
2 theoretical rather than practical: *That is just an academic quibble.*
• **academic** *noun* a person who teaches or does research in a university or other advanced institution.
Word Family **academically** *adverb*.

academy (a-**kadd**-a-mee) *noun* (*plural* **academies**)
1 a scientific or artistic association: *the Royal Academy.*
2 a specialized college: *the Royal Military Academy.*
3 *Scottish* a secondary school.
[Greek *Akademeia* the garden where Plato taught]

accede (ak-**seed**) *verb*
1 to agree: *I accede to your request.*
2 to attain a position, office, etc.: *The prince acceded to the throne.*
[Latin *accedere* to go towards]

accelerate (ak-**sell**-a-rate) *verb*
to move or cause to move faster: *The car accelerated and passed the van.*
Word Family acceleration (ak-sell-a-**ray**-sh'n) *noun* 1 an increase in swiftness of movement. 2 *Science* a change in the speed of an object.

accelerator (ak-**sell**-a-ray-ta) *noun*
a device to increase or control speed, especially the device in a motor vehicle which controls the throttle.

accent (**ak**-s'nt) *noun*
1 a particular way of pronouncing a language: *She speaks French with an American accent.*
2 any of the marks used above or below letters in some languages.
3 any stress or emphasis.
Word Family accent (ak-**sent**) *verb*.
[*ad-* + Latin *cantus* tone]

> **Accents** are the marks used above or below letters in some languages, to change their sound or to indicate stress:
> 1 an **acute** may indicate stress or pronunciation: *attaché* (a-**tash**-ay).
> 2 a **grave** (grahv) generally flattens the vowel sound, as in French: *père* (pair).
> 3 a **circumflex** indicates a dropped s, as in French: *arrêter* (= to arrest or stop).
> 4 a **tilde** (**til**-da) introduces the sound of a y, as in Spanish: *señor* (sen-**yor**).
> 5 a **cedilla** (si-**dill**-a) softens a hard c(k) to a soft c(s), as in French: *façade* (fa-**sahd**).
> 6 a **diaeresis** (die-**err**-i-sis), placed over the second of two adjacent vowels, indicates that both vowel sounds should be pronounced: *noël* (no-**el**).
> 7 an **umlaut** (**um**-lout) indicates a change from the normal vowel sound, as in German: *Köln* (kerln).

accentuate (ak-**sen**-choo-ate) *verb*
to emphasize.

accept (ak-**sept**) *verb*
to receive, especially with approval: *Please accept my apologies.*
Word Family acceptable *adjective* welcome or worthy of being accepted; **acceptably** *adverb*.
[Latin *acceptus* received]

> ⚠ Do not confuse *accept* with *except*. *Accept* means 'to receive, especially with approval': *to accept an offer.* *Except* means 'with the exception of', as in *He likes all sports except cricket.*

acceptance *noun*
the act of taking or receiving something offered.

access (**ak**-sess) *noun*
1 a means of entry or approach: *The only access to the island is by boat.* □ *The town has good access to the motorway network.*
2 the right or opportunity of reaching, approaching, etc., such as the right of a divorced parent to visit the children.
● **access** *verb*
1 to gain access to.
2 to obtain information.
Word Family accessible (ak-**sess**-i-b'l) *adjective* able to be reached or obtained; **accessibility** (ak-sess-i-**bill**-i-tee) *noun*.
[Latin *accesus* an approach]

> ⚠ Do not confuse *access* with *excess*. The noun *access* is used to describe an means of approach or the right to approach: *gain access to a building.* *Excess* means 'more than is needed or usual', as in *an excess of fat.*

accession *noun*
1 the act of acceding: *the king's accession to the throne.*
2 an addition or increase: *Numbers rose with the accession of new members.*

accessory (ak-**sess**-a-ree) *noun* (*plural* **accessories**)
1 any extra non-essential item: *Many cars today have air bags as an accessory.*
2 (*usually* **accessories**) any additional item of clothing, such as shoes, a handbag, etc. to complement one's dress.
3 *Law* any person who helps a criminal before or after a crime.
[Latin *accessio* an addition]

accident (**ak**-si-d'nt) *noun*
1 anything which is unexpected or unintentional: *I met him by accident.*

2 any unfortunate event, especially one involving injury: *a car accident*.
[Latin *accidere* to happen suddenly]

accidental *adjective*
occurring by chance.
• **accidental** *noun Music* a sign used before a note to indicate change to a sharp, flat or natural.
Word Family **accidentally** *adverb*.

> [!] The words *accidental* and *incidental* have related but separate meanings: *accidental* describes something which happens unexpectedly or unintentionally (*a verdict of accidental death*), while *incidental* refers to something which accompanies an event or is of secondary importance (*incidental details*).

acclaim (a-**claim**) *verb*
to applaud or express loud approval.
Word Family **acclaim** *noun*;
acclamation *noun*.
[Latin *acclamare* to shout approval]

acclimatize, acclimatise (a-**klime**-a-tize) *verb*
to make or become used to something new: *It took a month to become acclimatized to the tropical heat*.
Word Family **acclimatization** (a-klime-a-tie-**zay**-sh'n) *noun*.

accolade (**akk**-a-lade) *noun*
1 a special recognition of, or praise for, merit.
2 a ceremonial touching of the shoulder with a sword, a symbol of the award of a knighthood.
[*ac-* + Latin *collum* neck]

accommodate (a-**komm**-a-date) *verb*
1 to have rooms or beds for: *The hotel accommodates 14 guests*.
2 (*formal*) to do a favour for, especially by providing something: *Can you accommodate me with a loan?*
3 (*formal*) to adapt: *It takes a few minutes for my eyes to accommodate to the dark*.
[*ac-* + Latin *commodus* convenient]

accommodation (a-komm-a-**day**-sh'n) *noun*
1 any rooms provided for visitors or paying guests, such as in a hotel.
2 the act of accommodating.

> [!] Note the spelling of *accommodation*: it has two *c*'s and two *m*'s.

accompaniment (a-**kump**-ni-m'nt) *noun*
anything which goes with or adds to another: *There was no piano accompaniment for the singer*.
Word Family **accompanist** *noun* a person who plays a musical accompaniment.

accompany (a-**kum**-pa-nee) *verb*
(**accompanies; accompanying; accompanied**)
1 to go with: *We will accompany you to the airport*.
2 to be or provide an accompaniment to.

accomplice (a-**kum**-pliss) *noun*
a partner in crime or wrongdoing.

accomplish (a-**kum**-plish) *verb*
to bring about or complete successfully: *He accomplished his task ahead of time*.
Word Family **accomplished** *adjective*
1 already done: *My task is accomplished*.
2 skilled: *an accomplished skier*;
accomplishment *noun* **1** something achieved. **2** an acquired skill: *His many accomplishments include horseriding and operatic singing*.
[*ac-* + Latin *complere* to complete]

accord (a-**kord**) *verb*
1 to agree or be in harmony: *What he said today doesn't accord with what he said yesterday*.
2 to give or grant: *He was accorded a warm welcome*.
• **accord** *noun* an agreement or harmony.
Phrases **of one's own accord** *She did it quite of her own accord* (= voluntarily).
with one accord *The whole crowd cheered with one accord* (= spontaneously together).
Word Family **accordance** *noun*.
[*ac-* + Latin *cordis* of the heart]

according *adverb*
Phrase **according to 1** in relation to: *We sorted the fruit according to size*. **2** as stated by: *According to all reports she's quite mad*.

accordingly *adverb*
therefore or for that reason.

accordion *noun*
a portable keyed musical instrument with bellows and two sets of metal reeds.
Word Family **accordionist** *noun*.

accost (a-**kost**) *verb*
to greet or approach, often offensively: *The beggar accosted me in the street*.
[*ac-* + Latin *costa* side]

account *noun*
1 any statement which lists, describes or explains: *The radio gave a full account of the match.* □ *The clerk kept the financial accounts.*
2 an agreement allowing one to buy goods on credit, of which a record is kept.
3 ⇨ BANK ACCOUNT.
Phrase **of no account** of no importance: *He's a man of no account.*
• **account** *verb*
Phrase **account for** to explain: *There's no accounting for taste.*

accountable *adjective*
1 able to be explained.
2 responsible: *I'm not accountable for your debts.*
Word Family **accountability** (a-kownt-a-**bill**-i-ti) *noun.*

accountant *noun*
a person who keeps the accounts and draws up the balance sheets for a business.
Word Family **accounting** *noun;* **accountancy** *noun.*

accoutrements (a-**koo**-tra-m'nts)
plural noun
equipment.
[French]

accredit *verb*
1 to give credit for: *He is accredited with several inventions.*
2 to authorize or recognize officially: *An ambassador is the accredited representative of his country.*

accretion (a-**kree**-sh'n) *noun*
any growth or increase by addition.
[Latin *accretio* an increasing]

accrue (a-**kroo**) *verb*
to occur as a natural increase or addition: *Interest accrues at 8 per cent a year.*

accrued interest *noun* ⇨ INTEREST *noun.*

accumulate (a-**kew**-mew-late) *verb*
to gather or pile up.
Word Family **accumulation** (a-kew-mew-**lay**-sh'n) *noun* 1 the act of accumulating. 2 a number of things collected together; **accumulative** (a-**kew**-mew-la-tiv) *adjective.*
[Latin *accumulare* to heap up]

accumulator *noun*
1 a person or thing that accumulates.
2 *Electricity* any rechargeable battery.

accurate (**ak**-yoo-rit) *adjective*
free from error or deviation: *My new watch is more accurate than my old one.* □ *She made an accurate guess.*

Word Family **accurately** *adverb;* **accuracy** *noun.*
[Latin *accuratus* prepared with care]

accursed (a-**kerst** or a-**ker**-sid) *adjective*
1 (*informal*) hateful or irritating.
2 under a curse.

accusative case (a-**kew**-za-tiv case)
noun
a grammatical case expressing the direct object of a verb or of certain prepositions.

accuse (a-**kewz**) *verb*
to blame with having done wrong: *I accuse you of stealing the money.*
Word Family **accusation** (ak-yoo-**zay**-sh'n) *noun;* **accusatory** *adjective;* **accused** *noun* the defendant in a criminal court case; **accuser** *noun.*
[Latin *accusare*]

accustom *verb*
to become familiar with through use or habit: *You'll have to accustom yourself to our strange ways.*
Word Family **accustomed** *adjective*
1 familiar with. 2 usual or customary.

ace *noun*
1 a playing card with a single pip, the highest or lowest card in its suit.
2 a person who excels in a particular field, such as a fighter pilot.
3 *Tennis* a service which one's opponent cannot even touch: *She served an ace.*
• **ace** *adjective* (*informal*) wonderful or excellent: *an ace snooker player.*
[Latin *as* a unit]

acerbic (a-**ser**-bik) *adjective*
sharp or bitter.
Word Family **acerbity** *noun.*
[Latin *acerbus* bitter]

acetic acid (a-see-tik **ass**-id) *noun*
a colourless liquid, the principal part of vinegar and producing its characteristic smell.

acetylene (a-**sett**-i-leen) *noun*
a colourless poisonous inflammable gas used in making organic compounds and in welding.

ache (*rhymes with* take) *noun*
any dull continuous pain.
• **ache** *verb.*

achieve (a-**cheev**) *verb*
to attain or accomplish something.
Word Family **achievement** *noun;* **achiever** *noun.*

Achilles heel (a-**kill**-eez **heel**) *noun*
a person's vulnerable point.
[after *Achilles*, a hero in Greek mythology, who was vulnerable only in the heel]

Achilles tendon *noun*
a tendon attaching the heel to the calf.

acid (**ass**-id) *noun*
1 a substance which liberates hydrogen ions when dissolved in water and which has a pH value of between pH1 and pH6 on the pH scale.
2 (*informal*) lysergic acid diethylamide (LSD).
• **acid** *adjective* sharp or bitter: *an acid taste.* □ *an acid comment.*
Word Family **acidly** *adverb*; **acidity** (a-**sidd**-i-tee) *noun*; **acidic** (a-**sidd**-ik) *adjective*.
[Latin *acidus* sour]

acid rain *noun*
rain containing high levels of acids discharged into the atmosphere by the effluent from factories and industrial processes and harmful to crops, etc.

acid test *noun*
any decisive or crucial test.

acknowledge (ak-**noll**-ij) *verb*
1 to confess or accept responsibility for: *Will you acknowledge your mistake?*
2 to mention having received something, etc.: *I'd like to acknowledge your letter.*
Word Family **acknowledgement, acknowledgment** *noun*.

acme (**ak**-mee) *noun*
the peak or highest point: *the acme of perfection.*
[Greek *akmé*]

acne (**ak**-nee) *noun*
an inflammation of the skin, common in adolescence, causing pimples.

acolyte (**akk**-a-lite) *noun*
1 *Christianity* a person who assists the priest at religious services, especially at the Eucharist.
2 any assistant or helper.
[Greek *akolouthos* follower]

acorn (**ay**-korn) *noun*
the fruit of an oak tree, consisting of a nut with a cup-shaped base.

acoustic (a-**koo**-stik) *adjective* also **acoustical**
1 (of a musical instrument) whose sound is not electronically operated.
2 of or relating to hearing.
3 of or relating to the study of sound.
Word Family **acoustically** *adverb*; **acoustics** *plural noun* 1 (*used with singular verb*) a branch of physics which studies sound. 2 the properties of a particular space which determine the quality of sound.
[Greek *akouein* to hear]

acquaint (a-**kwaint**) *verb*
to make familiar: *Who will acquaint him with the facts?*
Word Family **acquaintance** *noun* 1 a person known slightly, as distinct from a friend. 2 familiarity: *I have no acquaintance with the French language.*

acquiesce (ak-wee-**ess**) *verb*
to agree or submit passively: *I insisted that she should leave the building, and she acquiesced.*
Word Family **acquiescent** *adjective*; **acquiescence** *noun*.
[*ac-* + Latin *quiescere* to keep quiet]

acquire (a-**kwire**) *verb*
to get or obtain.
Word Family **acquisition** (ak-wi-**zish**-'n) *noun* 1 the act of acquiring. 2 something which is acquired.

acquisitive (a-**kwizz**-i-tiv) *adjective*
having a liking for or habit of acquiring or collecting things.

acquit (a-**kwit**) *verb* (**acquits; acquitting, acquitted**)
to declare a person free of guilt, especially in a court of law.
Phrase **acquit oneself** to perform: *She acquitted herself well in the exam.*
Word Family **acquittal** *noun*.
[*ac-* + QUIT]

acre (**ay**-ka) *noun*
a unit of area equal to 4840 square yards, or about 0·4 hectare.
Word Family **acreage** *noun* an area expressed in acres.

acrid *adjective*
sharp or biting: *an acrid smell of burning rubber.*
[Latin *acer, acris* pungent]

acrimonious (ak-ra-**mo**-nee-us) *adjective*
bitter or resentful.
Word Family **acrimony** (**ak**-ri-ma-nee) *noun*.
[Latin *acrimonia* pungency]

acrobat (**ak**-ra-bat) *noun*
a skilled entertainer who performs tricks on a tightrope or trapeze.
Word Family **acrobatic** (ak-ra-**bat**-ik) *adjective*; **acrobatics** *plural noun* 1 the feats of an acrobat. 2 any elaborate or agile behaviour.
[Greek *akrobatos* walking on tiptoe]

acronym (**ak**-ra-nim) *noun*
a word formed from the first letter or letters of several words, such as NATO from *North Atlantic Treaty Organization*.
[Greek *akros* top + *onyma* name]

across *preposition, adverb*
1 from one side to the other: (as a preposition) *a track across the desert.*
□ (as an adverb) *The river is nearly a mile across.*
2 on the opposite side of: (as a preposition) *the house across the street.*
□ (as an adverb) *Are you across yet?*
Phrase **across the board** applying in all cases.

acrostic (a-kross-tik) *noun*
a poem or puzzle in which the first or last letters of each line form a word.
[Greek *akron* end + *stikhos* row]

acrylic (a-krill-ik) *noun*
1 a kind of quick-drying paint which is soluble in water.
2 a kind of synthetic cloth.

act *noun*
1 anything done: *an act of great bravery.*
2 the process of doing: *She was caught in the act.*
3 a law or decree, especially one passed by a parliament.
4 *Theatre* a main division in a play or opera.
5 a single item in a programme: *The next act will be a juggler.*
● **act** *verb*
1 to do or perform: *He acted wisely.*
2 to take part in a play or film, especially imitating or representing a particular character.
Phrase **act up** to misbehave: *Without its teacher, this class always acts up.*
Word Family **acting** *adjective* being a substitute for: *He is the acting Prime Minister;* **acting** *noun* the profession of being an actor.
[Latin *actus*]

action (ak-sh'n) *noun*
1 the process of acting or doing: *Is the machine in action yet?*
Figurative The soldiers saw no action abroad (= fighting, combat).
2 the manner of acting or operating: *That racehorse has a very graceful action.*
3 any legal proceedings: *They started an action against the company.*
4 (*informal*) lively or exciting occurrences: *Where's the action in this town?*

activate *verb*
to put into action or operation: *Press this button to activate the alarm.*

active *adjective*
1 being in action: *Only one engine is active.*
2 busy or lively: *She leads an active life.*
3 *Grammar* ⇨ VOICE *noun* (definition 4).
4 (of a volcano) which has recently erupted. Compare DORMANT (definition 3); EXTINCT (definition 2).
Word Family **actively** *adverb.*

activist *noun*
a person who encourages and practises direct action, especially in politics.
Word Family **activism** *noun.*

activity *noun* (*plural* **activities**)
1 the state of being active: *Her life was one of constant activity.*
2 a pastime or occupation: *Swimming is usually a summer activity.*

act of God *noun* (*plural* **acts of God**)
an event for which no person is responsible, such as an earthquake, a flood, etc.

actor *noun*
a person who performs a role in a play, film, etc.
Word Family **actress** *noun* (*plural* **actresses**) a female actor.

actual (ak-tew-'l) *adjective*
real or existing.
Word Family **actually** *adverb;* **actuality** (ak-tew-all-it-ee) *noun* (*plural* **actualities**).

actuary (ak-tew-a-ree) *noun* (*plural* **actuaries**)
a person who calculates insurance risks, rates, etc., based on recorded facts.
Word Family **actuarial** (ak-tew-air-i-al) *adjective.*
[Latin *actuarius* a bookkeeper]

actuate (ak-tew-ate) *verb*
to cause to act or move: *This button actuates the engine.*

acuity (a-kew-it-ee) *noun*
sharpness: *He has great acuity of vision.*
[Latin *acuere* to sharpen]

acumen (ak-yoo-men) *noun*
a quickness of mind or perception.
[Latin, *acuteness*]

acupressure (ak-yoo-presh-er) *noun* also called **shiatsu**.
the Japanese technique in which pressure is applied to specific pressure points on the body to relieve symptoms.

acupuncture (ak-yoo-punk-cher) *noun*
the Chinese technique of puncturing the skin with needles to reach the nerve areas, used as an anaesthetic or to treat and cure illness.
Word Family **acupuncturist** *noun.*
[Latin *acus* needle + PUNCTURE]

acute *adjective*
1 sharp or keen.
2 (of an angle) being less than 90°.

3 intense, severe and usually short-term: *A boil is an acute local infection.* □ *Since the floods there has been an acute shortage of tomatoes.*
• **acute** *noun* ⇨ ACCENT.
Word Family **acutely** *adverb*; **acuteness** *noun*.
[Latin *acutus* sharp]

ad *noun*
(*informal*) an advertisement.
Word Family **adman** *noun* (*plural* **admen**) a person involved in advertising.

adage (add-ij) *noun*
a proverb.

adagio (a-dah-jee-o) *adverb*
Music slowly or in a leisurely manner.
[Italian]

adamant (add-a-m'nt) *adjective*
stubborn or inflexible: *She was adamant in her opinion.*
Word Family **adamantly** *adverb*.
[Greek *adamantinos* invincible]

Adam's apple *noun*
the larynx.

adapt (a-dapt) *verb*
to alter or adjust: *One must adapt to change.*
Word Family **adaptable** (a-dap-ta-b'l) *adjective* easily or able to be adapted; **adaptability** (a-dap-ta-bill-it-ee) *noun*; **adaptation** (add-ap-tay-sh'n) *noun* **1** the act of adapting. **2** anything which has been adapted: *This film is an adaptation of a novel.*
[*ad-* + Latin *aptus* suited]

adaptor *noun*
1 any device which fits together parts of different sizes, etc.
2 any device which modifies a machine or tool.
3 a person or thing that adapts.

add *verb*
1 to find the sum of two or more numbers.
2 to join one thing to another: *We added an extension to the house.* □ *I'd like to add some advice.*
Phrase **add up 1** to add numbers together. **2** to make sense: *Your explanation does not add up.*

addendum *noun* (*plural* **addenda**)
anything added, such as an appendix to a book.
[Latin]

adder *noun*
any of various kinds of snake, mostly poisonous, including the common European viper.

addict (add-ikt) *noun*
a person who cannot free himself or herself from a particular habit, such as smoking.
Word Family **addicted** (a-dikt-ed) *adjective*; **addiction** *noun*; **addictive** *adjective* causing addiction.
[Latin *addictus* surrendered]

addition *noun*
1 the act of adding.
2 something which is added.
Word Family **additional** *adjective*; **additionally** *adverb*.

additive (add-it-iv) *noun*
anything which is added, such as a preservative or colouring to canned or other foods.

addled *adjective*
(of eggs) rotten.
Figurative *He has an addled mind* (= confused, muddled).

address *noun* (*plural* **addresses**)
1 the place where someone lives or may be contacted: *I'll give you my home address.* □ *an email address.*
2 the destination of a letter, parcel, etc., written on it.
3 a formal talk made to an audience.
4 any adroit or skilful behaviour: *She handled the matter with great address.*
• **address** *verb*
1 to write an address on: *She addressed the letter.*
2 to speak to: *In a debate speakers must address the chair.*
3 to direct attention or energy: *He addressed himself to the task.*
Word Family **addressee** (ad-ress-ee) *noun* a person to whom something is addressed.

adduce (a-dewce) *verb*
to offer or present in argument: *He adduced several reasons for his behaviour.*
[Latin *adducere* to lead to]

adenoids (add-a-noyds) *plural noun*
Anatomy the lymphatic tissue, similar to the tonsils, in the cavity at the back of the nose, which may affect breathing and speech.
Word Family **adenoidal** (add-a-noy-d'l) *adjective*.
[Greek *aden* a gland]

adept (a-dept) *adjective*
highly skilled or clever.
Word Family **adeptly** *adverb*; **adept** (add-ept) *noun* a person who is skilled.
[Latin *adeptus* having attained]

adequate (**add**-i-kwit) *adjective*
sufficient or enough.
Word Family adequately *adverb*;
adequacy (**add**-i-kwa-see) *noun*.
[*ad-* + Latin *aequus* equal]

adhere *verb*
to stick: *The label must adhere to the bottle.*
□ *We must adhere to our plans.*
Word Family adhesion (ad-**hee**-*zh*'n)
noun 1 the act of adhering, such as the
growing together of living tissues which
are not usually joined. 2 the state of being
adhered; **adhesive** *noun* any substance,
such as cement, etc., used for sticking two
surfaces together; **adhesive** *adjective*;
adhesiveness *noun*; **adherent** *noun* a
person who follows or supports a cause,
etc.; **adherence** *noun*.
[Latin *adhaerere* to stick to]

ad hoc *adjective*
for a special purpose: *We will set up an ad
hoc committee to deal with the matter.*
[Latin]

> The expression **ad hoc** is one of many
> English phrases that have come straight
> from Latin. Some of the phrases, such
> as *ad hoc*, are more usually found in
> formal English, while words such as
> *status quo* are used more generally.
> Legal terms have been much influenced
> by Latin and phrases such as *sub judice*
> are common in legal contexts. Some
> Latin phrases appear in English in an
> abbreviated form, e.g. *ad-lib* is a short
> form of *ad libitum*.

adieu (ad-**yer** *or* a-**dew**) *interjection*
goodbye.
[French *à Dieu* to God]

ad infinitum (ad in-fi-**nite**-um) *adverb*
without end.
[Latin, to infinity]

adipose *adjective*
fatty.
[Latin *adipis* of fat]

adjacent (a-**jay**-s'nt) *adjective*
next to or near.
[Latin *adjectus* something added]

adjective *noun*
a word that gives more information about
a noun or pronoun, describing what a
person or thing is like, such as *tall*, *new* or
red.

adjoin *verb*
to be connected or next to: *The bedroom
adjoins the balcony.*
[*ad-* + Latin *jungere* to join]

adjourn (a-**jern**) *verb*
to break off or postpone: *The meeting was
adjourned until the next day.*
Word Family adjournment *noun* 1 the
act of adjourning. 2 the state or time of
being adjourned.
[*ad-* + Latin *diurnus* daily]

adjudicate (a-**joo**-di-kate) *verb*
to judge or settle a dispute, etc.
Word Family adjudication (a-joo-di-
kay-sh'n) *noun*; **adjudicator** *noun* a
person who adjudicates.

adjunct (**aj**-unkt) *noun*
something added or attached.
[Latin *adjunctum* something connected]

adjure (a-**joor**) *verb*
to solemnly command or request.
Word Family adjuration *noun*.
[*ad-* + Latin *jurare* to swear]

adjust (a-**just**) *verb*
1 to change the shape, form or position of
something, so that it fits.
2 to change oneself to match particular
circumstances: *It is hard to adjust to a new
way of life.*
Word Family adjustment *noun*;
adjustable *adjective*.

adjutant (**ajj**-oo-t'nt) *noun*
an officer acting as an administrative
assistant to a commanding officer.
[Latin *adjutare* to help]

ad-lib *adverb*
freely, or as one pleases.
• **ad-lib** *verb* (**ad-libs**; **ad-libbing**;
ad-libbed) to improvise.
[Latin *ad libitum* at pleasure]

adman ⇨ AD.

administer *verb*
1 to manage or have charge of: *The park is
administered by the local council.*
2 to give or apply: *The doctor administered
first aid to the patient.*
3 to give help: *The nurses administered to the
wounded.*
[Latin *administrare*]

administration (ad-minn-i-**stray**-sh'n)
noun
1 the act of administering.
2 a group of people appointed to govern,
manage or have charge.
Word Family administrator (ad-**minn**-
i-stray-ter) *noun*; **administrative** (ad-
minn-i-stra-tiv) *adjective*.

admiral (**ad**-ma-r'l) *noun*
Navy a commissioned officer ranking
between vice admiral and Admiral of the
Fleet.

Word Family **Admiralty** *noun* the department that administers the navy.
[Arabic *amir al-* commander]

Admiral of the Fleet *noun* (*plural* **Admirals of the Fleet**)
Navy a commissioned officer of the highest rank.

admire *verb*
to have a high regard or respect for.
Word Family **admirable** (ad-mer-a-b'l) *adjective* worthy or deserving to be admired; **admirably** *adverb*; **admiration** (ad-ma-**ray**-sh'n) *noun*; **admiring** *adjective*; **admiringly** *adverb*; **admirer** *noun*.
[Latin *admirari* to wonder at]

admissible *adjective*
capable or worthy of being allowed or considered: *A letter is admissible evidence.*

admission *noun*
1 the act of entering.
2 the state of being allowed to enter.
3 to give entrance to: *Dogs not admitted.*
4 the act of admitting something: *He made an admission of guilt to his lawyer.*

admit *verb* (**admits**; **admitting**; **admitted**)
1 to say that one is responsible for something: *Will you admit to breaking the cup?*
2 to agree that something is true or valid: *Will you admit that the dog is lost?*
Phrase **admit of** (*formal*) to have: *The problem admits of no easy solution.*
Word Family **admittance** *noun* the right to enter; **admittedly** *adverb* without denial.
[Latin *admittere*]

admixture *noun*
1 the act of mixing.
2 a mixture or its ingredients.

admonish *verb*
to advise or warn.
Word Family **admonition** (ad-ma-**nish**-'n) *noun*.
[Latin *admonere* to warn]

ad nauseam (ad **naw**-zi-am) *adverb*
to a sickening or boring length or extent.
[Latin]

ado (a-**doo**) *noun*
any bustle, excitement or fuss.

adolescence (add-a-**less**-'nce) *noun*
the period between puberty and adulthood.
Word Family **adolescent** *noun*, *adjective*.
[Latin *adolescere* to grow up]

adopt *verb*
1 to make a child a member of one's family by legal means.
2 to make one's own: *They adopted the customs of their new country.*
3 to accept by vote: *The committee adopted both suggestions.*
Word Family **adoption** *noun*; **adoptive** *adjective* related by adoption.
[Latin *adoptare*]

adore *verb*
1 to worship or love devotedly.
2 (*informal*) to like very much: *I adore ice cream.*
Word Family **adorable** *adjective* enchanting or lovable: *What an adorable puppy!*; **adoration** (add-a-**ray**-sh'n) *noun*; **adoringly** *adverb*.
[Latin *adorare*]

adorn *verb*
to decorate or make beautiful: *The crown was adorned with jewels.* □ *His speech was adorned with elaborate phrases.*
Word Family **adornment** *noun* 1 the act of adorning. 2 something which adorns.

adrenalin (a-**drenn**-a-lin) *noun* also **adrenaline**
a hormone secreted by the **adrenal gland** which stimulates the heart at times of emotional stress.

adrift *adverb*
loose or drifting.

adroit (a-**droyt**) *adjective*
skilful or clever.
Word Family **adroitly** *adverb*; **adroitness** *noun*.
[French *à droit* rightly]

adulation (ad-yoo-**lay**-sh'n) *noun*
any excessive praise or flattery.
Word Family **adulatory** *adjective*.
[Latin *adulare* to fawn like a dog]

adult *noun*
a fully-grown mature animal or plant.
Word Family **adulthood** *noun*.
[Latin *adultus*]

adulterate (a-**dul**-ta-rate) *verb*
to lower the quality or make impure, especially by adding inferior substances: *This milk is adulterated with water.*
Word Family **adulteration** (a-dul-ta-**ray**-sh'n) *noun* 1 the act of adulterating. 2 an adulterated substance or condition.
[Latin *adulterare* to defile or alter]

adultery (a-**dul**-ta-ree) *noun*
the act of a married person having sexual intercourse with a person other than his or her spouse.

Word Family **adulterer** *noun* a person who commits adultery; **adulteress** *noun* (*plural* **adulteresses**) a female adulterer; **adulterous** *adjective*.
[Latin *adulterare*]

advance *verb*
to move forward: *The troops advanced towards the enemy.* □ *How far have you advanced with your music lessons?*
Figurative *The bank advanced me £100* (= lent). □ *Being rude will not advance your cause* (= assist). □ *The shares advanced on the stock exchange* (= rose in price).
● **advance** *noun*
1 a forward movement or progress: *Have you made any advance in your inquiries?*
2 something done or given before it is actually due, such as a loan or an early payment of a wage.
Figurative *The boy encouraged her advances* (= attempts to establish friendly relations).
Phrase **in advance** ahead: *Rent must be paid one month in advance.*
Word Family **advancement** *noun*.

advantage (ad-**vahn**-tij) *noun*
1 anything which is favourable or profitable: *You will not gain any advantage by shouting.*
2 short form is **van** *Tennis* the first point after a score of deuce.
Phrase **take advantage of** 1 to make use of: *We took advantage of the shelter.* 2 to exploit: *She always takes advantage of his weakness.*
● **advantage** *verb* to help.
Word Family **advantageous** (ad-ven-**tay**-jus) *adjective*; **advantageously** *adverb*.

advent *noun*
1 a coming or arrival: *We'll have to buy warm clothes with the advent of winter.*
2 (**Advent**) *Christianity* the festival which includes the four Sundays immediately preceding Christmas.
[Latin *adventus* coming]

adventitious (ad-ven-**tish**-us) *adjective*
occurring by chance or accident.

adventure *noun*
a dangerous or exciting activity or experience.
Word Family **adventure** *verb*; **adventurer** *noun*; **adventurous** *adjective*
1 exciting. 2 willing to seek or risk danger: *an adventurous young explorer*; **adventurously** *adverb*

adventure playground *noun*
an area of land, especially in a city, equipped with wooden structures, tyres, ropes, etc. with which children can play imaginatively.

adverb *noun*
a word that gives more information about a verb, an adjective or another adverb, answering the questions when?, why?, how?, etc. *Yesterday*, *quickly*, and *there* are examples of adverbs.

adverse *adjective*
unfavourable or opposing one's interests: *Adverse weather prevented the picnic.*
Word Family **adversary** (ad-ver-ser-ee) *noun* (*plural* **adversaries**) an opponent.
[Latin *adversus* opposite]

> ⚠ The words *adverse* and *averse* both describe opposition, but *adverse* refers to something which is different from what is expected or desired and suggests misfortune (*adverse weather conditions*), whereas *averse* means unwilling or reluctant to do something (*not averse to staying longer*).

adversity *noun* (*plural* **adversities**)
any hardship or misfortune.

advertise *verb*
to promote or make known to the public, especially through the media: *The job was advertised in several newspapers.*
Word Family **advertisement** (ad-vert-is-m'nt) *noun* short form is **ad** or **advert** (ad-vert) a public notice offering a service, goods for sale, etc.; **advertising** *noun*
1 the use of advertisements. 2 the business of creating, producing and circulating advertisements; **advertiser** *noun*.

advice *noun*
1 an opinion or suggestion: *We need an expert's advice to solve this problem.*
2 information.

> ⚠ Do not confuse the noun *advice* with the verb *advise*. *Advise* means 'to give advice to', as in *I advise you to go to the police.*

advisable (ad-**vize**-a-b'l) *adjective*
being the sensible or recommended thing to do: *It is advisable to wear a life-jacket when sailing in a small boat.*
Word Family **advisability** (ad-vize-a-bill-it-ee) *noun*.

advise (ad-**vize**) *verb*
to give advice to.
Word Family **advisedly** (ad-**vize**-id-li) *adverb* after careful thought; **adviser** *noun*; **advisory** *adjective* 1 of or giving advice:

She said a few advisory words. **2** having the
duty or power to advise: *We will appoint an
advisory committee.*

> ⚠ Do not confuse *advise* with
> ADVICE.

advocate (**ad**-va-kit) *noun*
1 a person who recommends or supports a
particular cause: *She is an advocate of
abortion reform.*
2 a person, especially a barrister, who
speaks on behalf of another.
• **advocate** (**ad**-va-kate) *verb* to urge or
support, especially by argument.
Word Family **advocacy** (**ad**-va-kiss-ee)
noun.
[Latin *advocare* to call in as legal adviser]

aegis (**ee**-jis) *noun*
any protection or patronage: *Under the
aegis of the King the subjects grew extremely
prosperous.*
[after *aigis*, the shield of Zeus in Greek
mythology]

aeon (**ee**-on) *noun* also **eon**
an immensely long period of time.
[Greek *aion* an age]

aerate (**air**-ate) *verb*
to add air or gas to a liquid under
pressure, as in making lemonade.

aerial (**air**-i-al) *noun* also called **antenna**.
a device which receives or sends out radio
waves.
• **aerial** *adjective*
1 of or existing in the air: *This tree has
aerial roots.*
2 from the air: *aerial bombardment.*
[Greek *aër* air]

aerobatics (air-a-**batt**-iks) *plural noun*
any acrobatics carried out by an
aeroplane, such as loops or dives.
Word Family **aerobatic** *adjective.*
[AERO(plane) + (acro)BATICS]

aerobe (**air**-robe) *noun*
an organism that requires oxygen to live.
Compare ANAEROBE.
Word Family **aerobic** (air-**ro**-bik)
adjective.

aerobics (air-**ro**-biks) *plural noun*
(*used with singular verb*) a system of
vigorous physical exercises performed to
music which improves body fitness
through increased oxygen consumption.
Word Family **aerobic** *adjective.*

aerodrome (**air**-a-drome) *noun*
an airport, especially a small one.
[AERO(plane) + Greek *dromos* a running
track]

aerodynamics (air-o-die-**namm**-iks)
plural noun
(*used with singular verb*) the study of the
motion of gases, especially in relation to
moving or flying objects.
Word Family **aerodynamic** *adjective.*

aerofoil (**air**-o-foil) *noun*
any surface on an aircraft, such as a wing
or tail, which deflects the passing
airstream to provide lift or control.

aerogramme ⇨ AIR LETTER.

aeronautics (air-a-**naw**-tiks) *plural noun*
(*used with singular verb*) the study of flight,
especially of aircraft.
Word Family **aeronautical** *adjective.*
[AERO(plane) + NAUTIC(al)]

aeroplane (**air**-a-plane) *noun*
an aircraft which is driven by jet engines or
propellers.
[Greek *aër* air + *planos* wandering]

aerosol (**air**-a-sol) *noun*
a can or container with a substance, such
as perfume, stored under pressure and
released as a spray.
[Greek *aër* air + SOL(ution)]

aerospace *adjective*
of or relating to the earth's atmosphere
and the space outside it, in which
spacecraft travel.

aesthetic (ees-**thett**-ik) *adjective*
(*American* **esthetic**)
of or relating to the appreciation of beauty:
*The old building was saved for aesthetic rather
than practical reasons.*
Word Family **aesthetically** *adverb*;
aesthetics *plural noun* (*used with singular
verb*) a branch of philosophy dealing with
the principles and judgements of art and
beauty; **aesthete** (**ees**-theet) *noun* **1** a
person who cultivates sensitivity and a love
of beauty. **2** a person whose sensitivity is
considered to be affected or excessive.
[Greek *aisthetikos* concerning the senses]

> ⚠ Do not confuse *aesthetic* with
> ASCETIC.

aether ⇨ ETHER (definitions 2, 3).

aetiology (ee-ti-**oll**-a-jee) *noun* also
etiology
the study of causes, especially the causes
of disease.
Word Family **aetiologist** *noun.*

afar *adverb*
far away: *We could see the city from afar.*

affable (aff-a-b'l) *adjective*
friendly or pleasant.
Word Family **affably** *adverb*; **affability**
(aff-a-**bill**-it-ee) *noun*.
[Latin *affabilis* that can be easily spoken
to]

affair *noun*
1 (*usually* **affairs**) any particular interests:
The affairs of state must be dealt with first.
2 a particular event or matter: *Have you
heard any details of that kidnapping affair?*
3 short form of **love affair** a sexual
relationship between two people who are
not married to each other.

affect[1] *verb*
to act on or influence: *The sight of the
accident did not affect me at all.*
Word Family **affecting** *adjective* moving.
[Latin *afficere* to do something to]

> ! Do not confuse *affect* with *effect*.
> *Effect* when used as a verb is a
> rather formal word meaning 'to bring
> about', as in *to effect a change*.

affect[2] *verb*
to pretend or imitate: *He affected complete
innocence about the trick.* □ *Sally affects the
manners of a princess.*
Word Family **affectation** (aff-ek-**tay**-
sh'n) *noun* a pretended or artificial manner
etc.; **affected** *adjective*.

affection *noun*
any liking or warm feeling: *She greeted her
daughter with affection.*
Word Family **affectionate** *adjective*
showing affection; **affectionately** *adverb*.
[Latin *affectio* goodwill]

affiance (a-**fie**-'nce) *verb*
an old word meaning 'to betroth'.

affidavit (aff-i-**day**-vit) *noun*
Law a written statement made under oath.
[Latin, he has sworn]

affiliate (a-**fill**-i-ate) *verb*
to join or unite, especially as part of
something larger: *The local associations are
now affiliated with the national body.*
Word Family **affiliation** (a-fill-i-**ay**-sh'n)
noun.
[Latin *affiliare* to adopt as a son]

affinity *noun* (*plural* **affinities**)
a mutual attraction or resemblance.
[Latin *affinitas*]

affinity card *noun*
a credit card which is linked to a particular
charity, the charity receiving a donation
for each card issued and also a proportion
of the money spent by the card user on
purchases.

affirm *verb*
1 to firmly declare or confirm: *I affirm my
right to decide for myself.*
2 *Law* to solemnly promise to tell the
truth, as distinct from making a formal
oath.
Word Family **affirmative** *adjective* being
in agreement: *He gave an affirmative
answer;* **affirmatively** *adverb*;
affirmation (aff-a-**may**-sh'n) *noun*.
[Latin *affirmare* to make firm]

affirmative action *noun*
a series of positive steps taken to avoid
discrimination such as racism, sexism, etc.

affix (a-**fix**) *verb*
to attach or fasten: *He affixed two stamps to
the envelope.*
● **affix** (**aff**-ix) *noun* (*plural* **affixes**)
1 *Grammar* any of various forms which can
be added to a word to change its meaning.
⇨ PREFIX; SUFFIX.
2 something which is added or attached.
[Latin *affixus* fastened]

afflict *verb*
to trouble or cause distress: *He is afflicted
with gout.*
Word Family **affliction** *noun*.
[Latin *afflictus* distressed]

affluence (**aff**-loo-'nce) *noun*
any wealth or abundance, especially of
possessions: *The size of their house is one
indication of their affluence.*
Word Family **affluent** *adjective.*
[Latin *affluens* abounding in]

> ! Do not confuse *affluence* with
> *effluence*. *Effluence* means 'an
> outward flow', as in *the effluence of waste
> from a sewer*.

afford *verb*
1 to have enough of something for a
particular purpose: *I cannot afford a new
coat this winter.* □ *No one can afford to miss
the next lecture.*
2 (*formal*) to give: *It affords me great
pleasure.*

afforestation (af-forr-is-**tay**-sh'n) *noun*
the planting of trees to form forests.

affray *noun*
(*formal*) a noisy quarrel or brawl.

affront (a-**frunt**) *verb*
to upset or offend: *I was affronted by his
rudeness.*
● **affront** *noun*.

Afghan (**af**-gan) *noun*
any of a breed of large long-haired
hounds, originally from Afghanistan.

aficionado (a-fish-ya-**nah**-doe) *noun*
an enthusiastic follower.
[Spanish]

afield (a-**feeld**) *adverb*
away, especially from home: *Do not go too
far afield.*

afire *adverb, adjective*
on fire.

aflame *adverb, adjective*
flaming or glowing: *Her face was aflame
with delight.*

afloat *adverb, adjective*
floating or carried on water: *The lifeboat
stayed afloat for several days.*
Figurative *The government has provided
loans to keep the corporation afloat* (= in
business).

afoot *adverb, adjective*
in progress: *There is trouble afoot.*

aforesaid *adjective* also **aforementioned**
Law said or mentioned earlier.

aforethought (a-**for**-thawt) *adjective*
premeditated: *The crime was committed with
malice aforethought.*

afraid *adjective*
feeling fear or apprehension: *I'm afraid of
the dark.*
Phrase be afraid to regret: *I'm afraid we
cannot come tonight.*

afresh *adverb*
again: *You must start afresh.*

African-American *noun* also **Afro-American**
a black American.
• **African-American** *adjective*.

Afro *noun*
a bushy hairstyle with frizzy curls, based
on an African style.

aft *adverb, adjective*
Nautical towards the stern of a boat.
Compare FORE.

after *preposition, adverb, conjunction,
adjective*
later or behind: (as a preposition) *He came
after me.* □ (as an adverb) *The dog trotted
after.* □ (as a conjunction) *after we left.* □ (as
an adjective) *the after parts of a boat.*
Figurative *They asked after you* (= about).
□ *a man after my own heart* (= in agreement
with). □ *He paints after Hockney's style* (= in
imitation of). □ *Who are you named after?*
(= in honour of).
Phrase after all in spite of everything: *We
are able to come after all.*

afterbirth *noun*
the placenta expelled from the uterus after
birth.

after-effect *noun*
the delayed result of something: *The
operation has had no after-effects.*

afterlife *noun*
life after death.

aftermath *noun*
the time or conditions after something:
*They discovered a lot of damage in the
aftermath of the storm.*

> The word **aftermath** refers to a
> situation that occurs following
> something else, usually something bad
> or unfortunate, such as a war or a
> storm. *Math* comes from an Old
> English word *maeth* meaning 'mowing'.
> Originally *aftermath* was an agricultural
> term referring to a second crop of grass
> or other grazing crop grown after an
> earlier crop had been mown or
> harvested.

afternoon *noun*
the time of day between noon and sunset.

aftershave *noun*
a perfumed liquid applied after shaving.

aftertaste *noun*
a taste or sensation which lingers.

afterthought *noun*
an idea or reflection which comes to mind
after an event: *That outhouse was added as
an afterthought.*

afterwards *adverb*
later: *I'm in a meeting now, but I'll speak to
you afterwards.*

Aga (**ar**-ga) *noun*
(*trademark*) a type of stove.

again *adverb*
1 once more or another time: *Let us try
again.*
2 besides or on the other hand: *We may
come, but then again we may not.*

against *preposition*
1 not in favour of: *I'm against the idea of
Saturday morning school.*
2 in collision with: *He fell heavily against the
chair.*
3 in preparation for: *We must save against
the possibility of no work.*
4 in contrast with: *The trees stood out
against the sky.*

agape (a-**gape**) *adverb*
with the mouth wide open: *He stood agape
in horror at the sight.*

agar (ay-gar) *noun*
short form of **agar-agar** a substance
obtained from seaweed, used in cooking
and to make jellies of liquid nutrient
material on which micro-organisms are
grown.
[Malay]

agate (agg-it) *noun*
a variegated form of quartz used as a semi-
precious gemstone.
[Greek *Akhates*, a river in Sicily where this
stone was first found]

age *noun*
1 the length of time during which
something has existed: *She is 12 years of
age.*
2 a particular period of time in history: *the
Ice Age.* □ *the Middle Ages.*
Figurative I've been waiting here for ages
(= a long time).
• **age** *verb* (**ages**; **ageing** or **aging**; **aged**)
1 to become or appear older: *He has aged a
lot since we last saw him.*
2 to allow wine, etc. to stand so that it
matures or becomes mellow.
Word Family **aged** *adjective* 1 (ayjd)
having the age of: *a boy aged 13.* 2 (ay-jid)
old: *an aged grandparent;* **ageless** *adjective*
1 not growing or seeming to grow old.
2 without definable age.

ageism (ay-jizm) *noun* also **agism**
discrimination on the grounds of age,
especially old age.
Word Family **ageist** *noun.*

agency (ay-j'n-see) *noun* (*plural*
agencies)
1 a business organization which provides a
particular service: *an employment agency.*
2 anything which acts or produces a result:
*It was achieved through the agency of his
friends.*

agenda (a-jen-da) *noun*
any matters to be dealt with or introduced,
usually in the form of a list: *An agenda has
been prepared for the meeting.*

> The word **agenda** is now treated as a
> singular noun, its plural being *agendas.*
> Strictly speaking, it is a plural noun
> meaning, literally, 'things to be done',
> *agendum* being its singular form.
> *Agendum* is now found only in very
> formal contexts.

agent (ay-j'nt) *noun*
1 a person who has authority to act
for another person, a company or a
government.

2 anything which produces an effect or
result: *Storms can be agents of destruction.*
3 *Chemistry* any substance causing a
reaction.
[Latin *agens* acting]

agent provocateur (ar-zhon
pro-vokk-a-ter) *noun* (*plural* **agents
provocateurs**)
a person paid, especially by a government,
to tempt people to do illegal acts in order
to unmask possible troublemakers.
[French *agent* agent + *provocateur*
provoking]

age of consent *noun*
Law the age at which it is legal for a person
to marry, or for a person to have sexual
intercourse.

agglomerate (a-glomm-a-rate) *verb*
to collect into a mass or cluster.
Word Family **agglomeration** (a-glomm-
a-ray-sh'n) *noun.*
[*ag-* + Latin *glomeris* of a ball]

aggrandizement, aggrandisement
(a-gran-diz-m'nt) *noun*
an increase in size, strength, wealth,
importance, etc.: *He is ambitious and seeks
personal aggrandizement.*

aggravate (ag-ra-vate) *verb*
1 to make more intense or worse: *That will
aggravate the pain.*
2 (*informal*) to annoy or irritate: *They like
to aggravate the teacher with their noise.*
Word Family **aggravating** *adjective;*
aggravation (ag-ra-vay-sh'n) *noun.*
[*ag-* + Latin *gravis* heavy]

aggregate (ag-ri-git) *noun*
1 a number of separate things brought
together in a group.
2 a total.
3 a mixture of different minerals used in
making concrete, etc.
Word Family **aggregate** (ag-ri-gate)
verb; **aggregation** (ag-ri-gay-sh'n) *noun*
any collection or total forming a unified
whole.
[*ag-* + Latin *gregis* of a flock]

aggression (a-gresh-'n) *noun*
1 the tendency to attack or be hostile.
2 a hostile act, especially if unprovoked.
Word Family **aggressive** *adjective* feeling
or showing aggression; **aggressor** *noun* a
person or thing that is aggressive;
aggressively *adverb;* **aggressiveness**
noun.
[Latin *aggressio*]

aggrieve (a-**greev**) *verb*
to cause someone to feel pain or
resentment: *Mother was aggrieved by the
rareness of our visits home.*

aggro *noun*
(*informal*) any aggressiveness, especially if
deliberate or for perverse excitement.

aghast (a-**gahst**) *adjective*
amazed and horrified: *I'm aghast at your
suggestion.*

agile (**ajj**-ile) *adjective*
quick or nimble.
Word Family agility (a-**jill**-it-ee) *noun*;
agilely *adverb*.
[Latin *agilis* nimble]

agism ⇨ AGEISM.

agitate (**ajj**-i-tate) *verb*
1 to shake or move rapidly from side to
side: *The clothes in the washing machine were
agitated in the soapy water.*
2 to disturb or excite: *She became agitated
after the accident.*
3 to arouse public feelings about an issue,
such as a political or social reform.
Word Family agitation (ajj-i-**tay**-sh'n)
noun; **agitator** *noun* 1 a person who
agitates: *The student was well-known as a
political agitator.* 2 a machine or device for
stirring or shaking.
[Latin *agitare* to shake]

aglow (a-**glo**) *adverb*
glowing: *Her cheeks were aglow with health.*

agnostic (ag-**noss**-tik) *noun*
a person who believes that one cannot
know whether God exists. Compare
ATHEIST.
Word Family agnosticism (ag-**noss**-ti-
sizm) *noun*.
[*a-* + Greek *gnostikos* knowing]

ago *adverb*
in the past: *It happened long ago.*

agog *adverb*
eager or excited: *We are all agog for news.*

agony (**agg**-a-nee) *noun* (*plural* **agonies**)
a state of extreme pain or anguish: *The
injury caused him great agony.*
Word Family agonize, agonise *verb* to
suffer agony or intense worry: *Do not
agonize over your mistake*; **agonizing**
adjective; **agonizingly** *adverb*.
[Greek *agonia* a struggle, anguish]

agora (**agg**-a-ra) *noun*
an open marketplace or place of assembly
in ancient Greece.
[Greek]

agoraphobia (agg-ra-**fo**-be-a) *noun*
an abnormal fear of open spaces.
Word Family agoraphobic *adjective*.
[AGORA + PHOBIA]

agrarian (a-**grair**-i-un) *adjective*
relating to farming land or agriculture.
[Latin *ager* field]

agree *verb*
1 to decide in favour of a request,
suggestion, etc.: *I agreed to help.*
2 to hold or come to the same idea, etc.:
We all agreed that the film was good.
3 to exist without difference or friction:
The children rarely agree. □ *Your story agrees
with what your sister said.*
Phrase agree with to suit: *Spicy foods
don't agree with me.*
Word Family agreement *noun* 1 the fact
of thinking the same things or in the same
way: *Everyone was in agreement about the
quality of the film.* 2 an arrangement: *We
came to an agreement with the landlord about
the repairs.* 3 a contract.

agreeable *adjective*
1 to one's liking: *She has an agreeable smile.*
□ *Do you find your new job agreeable?*
2 willing or ready to agree: *I'm agreeable to
either plan.*
Word Family agreeably *adverb*.

agriculture (**ag**-ri-kul-cher) *noun*
the use of land for planting and growing
crops, and raising animals.
Word Family agricultural *adjective*;
agriculturist, agriculturalist *noun*.
[Latin *ager* field + *cultura* a tilling]

aground *adverb*
(of a boat) touching the ground in shallow
water, so that it is stranded.

ague (**ay**-gew) *noun*
1 malaria.
2 a fever accompanied by chills and
shivering.
[as for ACUTE (fever)]

ahead *adverb*
in front or forward: *Walk ahead of us.*
Phrase go ahead to continue: *The
building work went ahead despite the bad
weather.*

ahimsa (a-**him**-sar) *noun*
(in Hindu, Buddhist and Jainist teaching)
the law of non-violence and respect for all
life.
[Sanskrit *a* without + *himsa* violence].

ahoy *interjection*
Nautical a call to attract attention.

aid *noun*
  1 any help or assistance: *We must have the aid of a doctor.*
  2 something which helps: *films, maps and other teaching aids.*
  Phrase in aid of for: *What is all this noise in aid of?*
  ● **aid** *verb*.

aide *noun*
  an assistant.
  [French]

aide-de-camp (ayd-der-**kom**) *noun*
  (*plural* **aides-de-camp**) (ayd-der-**kom**)
  an officer acting as personal assistant and secretary to a general, governor, etc.
  [AIDE + French *de camp* at camp]

Aids (aydz) *noun* also **AIDS**
  a serious viral disease which hinders the production of the body's antibodies and so lessens immunity to infection.
  [A(cquired) i(mmune) d(eficiency) s(yndrome)]

ail *verb*
  an old word meaning 'to trouble': *What ails you?*

aileron (**ayl**-a-ron) *noun*
  a movable hinged section mounted near the trailing edge of an aeroplane wing and used to control balance.
  [French, small wing]

ailment *noun*
  any mild illness: *A cold is a common ailment.*

aim *verb*
  1 to point or direct towards something: *He carefully aimed his gun at the target.*
  2 to have a purpose or intention: *Where do you aim to go first?*
  Word Family aim *noun*; **aimless** *adjective* without purpose; **aimlessness** *noun*; **aimlessly** *adverb*.

air *noun*
  1 the gases surrounding the earth.
  2 a simple tune or melody.
  3 a particular manner or appearance: *She has the air of a kind, gentle person.*
  Phrases clear the air to remove emotional differences or tension. **off the air** (of a radio station) no longer broadcasting. **on the air** (of a radio station) broadcasting. **put on airs, put on airs and graces** to behave affectedly: *He put on airs to impress us.* **up in the air** uncertain: *The decision is still up in the air.* **vanish into thin air** to vanish completely.
  ● **air** *verb* to expose to the air: *We must air the spare room to get rid of the smell.*

Figurative *He airs his new ideas at parties* (= circulates, tests).
  [Greek *aēr*]

air bag *noun*
  a safety device in a car which inflates on impact.

airbase *noun*
  an airfield used as a base for military aircraft.

air-bed *noun*
  an inflatable mattress.

airborne *adjective*
  being in the air.

air brake *noun*
  1 a brake operated by air pressure.
  2 also called **flap**. a hinged panel set in the wing or body of an aeroplane, used to reduce its speed.

airbrush *noun* (*plural* **airbrushes**)
  an atomizer capable of producing a fine spray of paint.
  ● **airbrush** *verb* to apply paint using an airbrush.

Airbus *noun* (*plural* **Airbuses**)
  (*trademark*) a wide-bodied passenger aeroplane on regular service.

air chief marshal *noun*
  Air force a commissioned officer ranking between air marshal and marshal of the RAF.

air commodore *noun*
  Air force a commissioned officer ranking between group captain and air vice-marshal.

air conditioning *noun*
  the process of controlling temperature, moisture and dust content of air in a building or vehicle.
  Word Family air-condition *verb*; **air conditioner** *noun*.

aircraft *noun* (*plural* **aircraft**)
  any vehicle which is capable of flight, such as an aeroplane or a helicopter.

aircraft carrier *noun*
  a warship with a very large upper deck (the **flight deck**), for carrying, launching or receiving aircraft.

aircraftman *noun* (*plural* **aircraftmen**)
  Air force a member of an aircrew of the lowest rank.

aircraftwoman *noun* (*plural* **aircraftwomen**)
  Air force a female member of an aircrew of the lowest rank.

aircrew *noun*
the personnel in an aircraft.

air cushion *noun*
the layer of high-pressure air, produced by fans, which supports a hovercraft, etc.

airdrop *noun*
the dropping of troops or supplies by parachute from an aircraft.

Airedale *noun*
any of a breed of large wire-haired terriers. [first bred in the district of Airedale in Yorkshire]

airer *noun*
a frame for drying clothes on.

airfield *noun*
a large open level area with runways, buildings, etc. for the operation and maintenance of aircraft.

air force *noun*
the armed forces of a country which are concerned with fighting in the air.

airfreight (**air**-frate) *noun*
1 any cargo carried by aircraft.
2 its cost: *What is the airfreight to Sydney?*

air-freshener *noun*
a spray, powder, etc. used to make a room, car, etc. smell pleasant.

air guitar *noun*
(*informal*) an imaginary guitar: *He's playing air guitar in his bedroom.*

air gun *noun*
a gun using compressed air to fire pellets or darts.

airhead *noun*
(*informal*) an empty-headed person, a fool.

air hostess *noun* (*plural* **air hostesses**)
an old name for a female flight attendant.

airily *adverb*
in a light or carefree manner.

airing *noun*
1 exposure to fresh air.
2 an occasion when an idea is first expressed in public.

airless *adjective*
1 having no air.
2 having no fresh air.
Word Family **airlessness** *noun.*

air letter *noun* also called **aerogramme**.
a letter consisting of a single sheet of paper which is folded and sent by airmail without an envelope.

airlift *noun*
the transporting of large numbers of people or goods by aircraft, often in an emergency.

airline *noun*
any organization which provides scheduled air transport between specified points.
Word Family **airliner** *noun* any large passenger- or cargo-carrying aircraft.

airlock *noun*
1 an airtight compartment at the entrance of a pressure chamber, to prevent loss of pressure or gases when the chamber is entered.
2 a stoppage of the flow of liquid in a pipe, caused by an air bubble.

airmail *noun*
the carrying of post in aircraft. Compare SURFACE MAIL.
● **airmail** *adjective.*

airman *noun* (*plural* **airmen**)
a pilot or member of the crew of an aircraft.

air marshal *noun*
Air force a commissioned officer ranking between air vice-marshal and air chief marshal.

airplay *noun*
broadcasting on the radio: *Their new CD received a lot of airplay.*

air pocket *noun*
a downward current of air causing an aircraft to drop suddenly.

airport *noun*
a large airfield with runways, hangars, workshops and one or more passenger terminals.

air raid *noun*
an attack by enemy aircraft, especially bombers.

air resistance *noun*
a force acting on anything moving through the air, such as a falling object, which slows it down.

airscrew *noun*
an aeroplane propeller.

airship *noun*
any aircraft lighter than air, with a rigid structure containing hydrogen or helium gas, driven by propellers and able to be steered.

air show *noun*
a show of aircraft involving flying displays.

airside *noun*
the part of an airport complex nearest the aircraft, reached after going through security checks and passport control.

airspace *noun*
the space above an area or country.

airspeed *noun*
the speed of an aircraft relative to the air around it. Compare GROUND SPEED.

airstream *noun*
1 a flow of air, especially past a flying aeroplane.
2 a wind, especially at high altitude.

airstrip *noun*
1 a runway.
2 an airfield for small aircraft, especially if in a remote area or privately owned.

air terminal *noun*
a building, including offices, where aircraft passengers assemble.

airtight *adjective*
not allowing the passage of air.

air vice-marshal *noun*
Air force a commissioned officer ranking between air commodore and air marshal.

airwaves *plural noun*
radio waves.

airway *noun*
a tube through which air can go into the lungs.

airwoman *noun* (*plural* **airwomen**)
a female pilot or member of the crew of an aircraft.

airworthy *adjective*
(of an aircraft) meeting certain safety requirements for flight.
Word Family **airworthiness** *noun*.

airy *adjective* (**airier; airiest**)
1 open to the passage of air: *This is a very airy room.*
2 light or carefree: *She apologized in an airy manner.*
Word Family **airiness** *noun*.

airy-fairy *adjective*
(*informal*) light or fanciful: *He is full of airy-fairy ideas.*

aisle (ile) *noun*
any passage between blocks of seats, as in a church or theatre.

ajar (a-**jar**) *adverb, adjective*
(of a door) partly open.

akimbo *adverb*
having the hands on the hips, with the elbows pointed outwards.

akin (a-**kin**) *adjective*
similar or related: *Your fears are akin to superstition.*

alabaster *noun*
a white or tinted fine-grained gypsum, used for ornaments and statues.
• **alabaster** *adjective*
1 made of alabaster.
2 smooth, white or cold like alabaster.
[Greek *alabastos*]

à la carte (ah la **kart**) *adjective*
(of a menu) giving a choice for each course of a meal. Compare TABLE D'HÔTE.
[French]

alacrity (a-**lak**-ra-tee) *noun*
(*formal*) a prompt and cheerful willingness: *She accepted the invitation with alacrity.*
[Latin *alacritas* briskness]

à la mode (ah la **mode**) *adjective*
fashionable: *That new suit is very à la mode.*
[French]

alar (**ay**-la) *adjective*
1 of or having wings.
2 wing-shaped.
[Latin *ala* wing]

alarm *noun*
1 any noise or signal used as a warning.
2 a sudden fear or apprehension caused by an awareness of danger: *She felt great alarm at the sight of the huge dog.*
• **alarm** *verb* to cause or feel alarm.
Word Family **alarming** *adjective*.
[Italian *all' arme!* to arms!]

alarm clock *noun*
a clock with a bell which can be set to ring at a certain time.

alarmist *noun*
a person with a habit of causing alarm, especially with little reason.

alas (a-**lass**) *interjection*
a cry of sorrow, grief or pity.

alb *noun*
a full-length white robe worn by Christian priests during celebration of the Eucharist.
[Latin *albus* white]

albatross *noun* (*plural* **albatrosses**)
1 a large long-winged seabird related to the petrel, found especially in the Pacific regions.
2 an inescapable burden: *The mortgage proved to be an albatross round his neck.*
[Portuguese]

albeit (awl-**bee**-it) *conjunction*
although: *It was a brave, albeit foolish, act.*

albinism (al-bin-izm) *noun*
Biology the failure, usually inherited, to develop pigment in the skin, hair, eyes, etc.

albino (al-bee-no) *noun*
a person or animal suffering from albinism.
[Latin *albus* white]

album *noun*
1 a book or similar container for storing stamps, photographs, etc.
2 a long-playing CD or record.

The word **album** comes from the Latin word for a blank white stone tablet on which things such as public notices were inscribed in ancient Rome. This in turn comes from *albus*, a Latin word for 'white'. *Album* then came to mean a book with completely blank pages. It was used in the 17th century as an *album amicorum*, Latin for an 'album of friends', a book in which people collected the signatures of friends as a souvenir — the forerunner of our autograph *album*. Later, the idea of an *album* as a book for a collection of things spread to photograph *albums*, stamp *albums*, etc.

albumen ⇨ EGG WHITE.
[Latin, the white of egg]

albumin (al-bew-min) *noun*
any of a group of water-soluble proteins found in animals and plants.

alchemy (al-ka-mee) *noun (plural* **alchemies)**
1 a medieval science which attempted to change ordinary metals into gold.
2 any strange or magical process, change, etc.
Word Family **alchemist** *noun* a person who practises alchemy.
[Arabic *al-* the + CHEM(istr)Y]

alcohol (al-ka-hol) *noun*
1 a colourless liquid that is the intoxicating part of drinks such as beer, wine, etc., and is also used in fuels, solvents, etc.
2 *Chemistry* any of a class of organic compounds (general formula ROH where R is any alkyl radical).
[Arabic]

alcoholic (al-ka-**holl**-ik) *noun*
a person who compulsively drinks alcohol.
● **alcoholic** *adjective*
1 of or containing alcohol.
2 of or relating to an alcoholic.
Word Family **alcoholism** (al-ka-hol-izm) *noun*.

alcopop (al-ko-pop) *noun*
(*informal*) a commercially prepared soft drink containing alcohol.

alcove *noun*
a section of a room or other space which is set back from the main part.
[Arabic, the vault]

alder (awl-da) *noun*
a small deciduous tree related to the birch, found especially by river-sides.

alderman (awl-da-m'n) *noun (plural* **aldermen)**
a senior co-opted member of a county, borough or city council.
[from Old English for elder man]

ale *noun*
any of various types of beer, as pale ale, brown ale, etc.

alert *adjective*
wide awake or attentive: *He fought to stay alert despite his tiredness.*
● **alert** *noun*
1 a state of readiness or caution: *You must be on the alert for trouble.*
2 a warning or alarm, as before an air raid or attack.
● **alert** *verb* to warn of a danger.
Word Family **alertness** *noun*.
[Italian *all' erta!* to the watchtower]

alfalfa ⇨ LUCERNE.
[Arabic *al-fasfasah* the best sort of fodder]

alfresco *adjective, adverb*
outside or in the open air: *Lunch will be served alfresco.*
[Italian *al fresco* in the cool]

alga (al-gah) *noun (plural* **algae**) (al-jee)
any of a group of simple plants with single-celled reproductive structures, growing in fresh water, seawater or damp places and varying in size from microscopic to several metres long.
Word Family **algal** (al-g'l) *adjective*.
[Latin, seaweed]

algebra (al-ji-bra) *noun*
the branch of maths which studies the properties and relationships of quantities by the use of symbols such as letters of the alphabet.
Word Family **algebraic** (al-ji-**bray**-ik) *adjective*; **algebraically** *adverb*.
[Arabic *al-jabr* bone-setting, the reunion of broken parts]

Algol *noun*
a computer language mainly used in maths and science.
[ALGO(rithmic) + L(anguage)]

algorithm 23 allegory

algorithm (al-ga-rith-'m) *noun*
a clearly defined sequence of operations for solving a particular mathematical problem.
Word Family **algorithmic** (al-go-rith-mik) *adjective*.
[from the name of a Persian mathematician]

alias (ay-lee-us) *noun* (*plural* **aliases**)
an assumed or false name: *The criminal travelled under an alias*.
• **alias** *adverb* also or otherwise called: *Dawson, alias Bass, was soon captured.*
[Latin, at another time or place]

alibi (al-i-by) *noun*
1 a defence by an accused person that he or she was elsewhere at the time the crime was committed.
2 (*informal*) any excuse: *I hope you have a good alibi for being away from work.*
[Latin, elsewhere]

alien (ay-li-an) *noun*
1 a foreigner or non-naturalized citizen.
2 in science fiction, a being from another planet or world.
3 any person or thing that is strange or unfamiliar.
• **alien** *adjective* foreign or strange: *His ideas are alien to us.*
[Latin *alienus* belonging to another]

alienate (ay-lee-a-nate) *verb*
to turn away or make hostile: *That attitude will alienate many of your friends.*
Word Family **alienation** (ay-lee-a-nay-sh'n) *noun*.

alight[1] (a-lite) *verb*
(*formal*) to get out of or down from a vehicle: *A ramp was provided for us to alight from the train.*

alight[2] (a-lite) *adverb, adjective*
lit up or burning: *Is your pipe alight?*

align (a-line) *verb*
to arrange in a line: *These posts are not quite aligned.*
Figurative *His ambitions do not align with his family's hopes* (= match, agree).
Word Family **alignment** *noun*.

alike *adverb, adjective*
similar or in the same way: *I think all politicians are alike.*

alimentary (ali-ment-a-ree) *adjective*
relating to food, nutrition and digestion.
[Latin *alimentum* food]

alimentary canal *noun*
the system within the body, including the mouth, oesophagus, stomach, intestines and anus, which receives food, digests it and expels the remains.

alimony (al-imm-a-nee) *noun*
any regular payment of money due to a separated or divorced person from his or her spouse.
[Latin *alimonia* sustenance]

alive (*rhymes with* arrive) *adjective*
living or active.
Figurative *His eyes were alive with excitement* (= lively, full).
Phrase **alive to** aware of : *She is not alive to the danger.*

alkali (al-ka-lie) *noun*
Chemistry a base that is soluble in water. When an alkali dissolves, it produces hydroxide ions, OH⁻.
Word Family **alkaline** *adjective*;
alkalinity (al-ka-linn-i-tee) *noun*.
[Arabic, ashes]

alkaloid (al-ka-loyd) *noun*
any of a group of complex organic bases derived from plants and containing nitrogen, such as morphine, codeine and quinine.

all (awl) *adjective, adverb, pronoun*
being the whole quantity or number of anything: (as an adjective) *All men are equal*. □ (as an adverb) *He sat all alone.*
□ (as a pronoun) *We all laughed.*
Figurative *Come with all speed* (= the greatest possible).
Phrases **above all** most importantly: *Above all, remember my advice.* **all in** exhausted: *We were all in after the game.* **all in all** altogether: *All in all it was a great success.* **at all** in any way: *I cannot agree at all.*

Allah *noun*
the Muslim name for God, the supreme ruler and creator of the universe.
[Arabic *al-ilah* the God]

allay (a-lay) *verb*
to relieve or reduce: *The pilot tried to allay their fears.*

allege (a-lej) *verb*
to declare or assert, often without actual proof: *He still alleges his innocence.*
Word Family **allegation** (al-i-gay-sh'n) *noun*; **allegedly** (a-lejj-id-lee) *adverb*.

allegiance (a-lee-j'nce) *noun*
a loyalty or duty, especially to a government or ruler of a country.

allegory (al-i-gree) *noun* (*plural* **allegories**)
a literary form which presents, through its characters, events or qualities, other corresponding but unstated characters, events or qualities.

Word Family **allegorical** (al-i-**gor**-ik'l) *adjective*.
[Greek *allegoria* another speaking]

allegro (a-**lay**-gro) *adverb*
Music fast and lively.
[Italian]

alleluia ⇨ HALLELUJAH.

allergy (**al**-a-jee) *noun* (*plural* **allergies**)
an abnormal physical sensitivity to any substance, such as to certain fruits, plants, etc.
Word Family **allergic** (a-**ler**-jik) *adjective*
1 having an allergy: *I am allergic to pollen.*
2 caused by an allergy: *an allergic reaction*;
allergen *noun* any substance which can cause an allergy.
[Greek *allos* other + *ergon* work]

alleviate (a-**lee**-vi-ate) *verb*
to lessen or make easier to bear: *Nothing could alleviate her misery.*
Word Family **alleviation** (a-lee-vi-**ay**-sh'n) *noun*.
[*al-* + Latin *levare* to relieve]

alley (**al**-ee) *noun*
1 short form of **alleyway** a narrow path or street, usually between buildings.
2 a long narrow enclosed lane with a polished wooden floor, used for bowling.

alliance (a-**lie**-'nce) *noun*
an association or union, usually made by formal agreement.
[*al-* + Latin *ligare* to bind]

allied the past tense and past participle of **ally**.

alligator (**al**-i-gay-ta) *noun*
any of various large amphibian freshwater reptiles with a broad rounded snout and growing up to about 5 m long.
[Spanish *el lagarto* the lizard]

alliteration (a-litt-a-**ray**-sh'n) *noun*
the commencement of two or more closely connected words with the same letter or sound, especially a consonant, as in *five miles meandering with a mazy motion* (Samuel Taylor Coleridge).
Word Family **alliterative** (a-**litt**-a-ra-tiv) *adjective*.
[*al-* + Latin *littera* letter]

allocate (**al**-a-kate) *verb*
to set aside for a particular purpose: *The city council has allocated money for public transport.*
Word Family **allocation** (a-la-**kay**-sh'n) *noun*.
[*al-* + Latin *locus* a place]

allot (a-**lot**) *verb* (**allots; allotting; allotted**)
to share out or distribute: *You have been allotted several tickets.*
Word Family **allotment** *noun* 1 the act of allotting: *There will be an allotment of shares.*
2 a person's share of anything: *What was the teacher's allotment of classes last term?*
3 a plot of land: *a vacant allotment.*
[*al-* + LOT]

allow (*rhymes with* a cow) *verb*
1 to permit or agree to: *You are not going out tonight. I won't allow it.*
2 to give the right to enter: *My dogs are allowed in the house.*
3 to give: *She is allowed £15 a week for clothes.*
4 (*formal*) to admit: *I allow I was wrong.*
Phrase **allow for** to take into consideration: *You have not allowed for train fares.*
Word Family **allowable** *adjective*.

allowance *noun*
1 the act of allowing: *the allowance of a claim.*
2 a sum of money, etc. given for particular needs: *Many salesmen receive a travelling allowance.*
Phrase **make allowance for 1** to make provision for. **2** to make concession or excuse for.

alloy (**al**-oy) *noun*
a mixture of a metal with other metals or non-metals, in specific proportions, prepared when they are molten. For example, bronze is an alloy of the metals copper and tin, and steel is an alloy of the metal iron and the non-metal carbon.
• **alloy** (a-**loy**) *verb*
to mix metals to form an alloy.
[*al-* + Latin *ligare* to bind]

all right *adjective*
satisfactory or in good order: *Are you all right? □ Is it all right if I leave early today?*

> **!** The spelling *all right* is correct; the spelling *alright* is thought by many people to be wrong.

all-rounder *noun*
a person with equal ability in many different things, especially in sport.

allspice *noun* also called **pimento**.
a sweet-smelling sharp spice made from a dried berry.
[ALL + SPICE]

all-terrain bike *noun*
a mountain bike.

all-time *adjective*
never exceeded: *an all-time record.*

allude (a-lood) *verb*
Phrase **allude to** to refer to something indirectly: *Several times he alluded to his past.*
Word Family **allusion** (a-loo-zh'n) *noun*; **allusive** *adjective*.
[Latin *alludere* to play with]

allure (al-yoor) *verb*
to attract or entice: *Many gimmicks were used to allure customers.*
Word Family **alluring** *adjective*.

alluvium (a-loo-vi-um) *noun*
the silt carried by a river and deposited in its valley or delta.
Word Family **alluvial** *adjective*.
[Latin *alluvio* an overflowing]

ally (al-eye) *noun (plural* **allies***)*
1 a person or group united with another, especially by formal agreement: *Britain's trade allies.*
2 any close friend or supporter.
• **ally** *verb* (**allies; allying; allied**)
1 to unite by formal agreement etc.
2 to connect or associate.
[*al-* + Latin *ligare* to bind]

alma mater (al-ma **may**-ta) *noun*
a person's former school, college or university.
[Latin *alma* bounteous + *mater* mother]

almanac (awl-ma-nak) *noun*
a yearly calendar giving information about the sun, moon, tides, etc.

almighty (awl-my-tee) *adjective*
1 having absolute power.
2 (*informal*) very great: *What an almighty noise!*
Phrase **the Almighty** God.

almond (ah-m'nd) *noun*
1 an edible oval nut with a mild taste.
2 a pale creamish-brown colour.
Word Family **almond** *adjective*.

almoner (ah-m'n-a *or* al-m'n-a) *noun*
(*formerly*) a medically trained social worker attached to a hospital.

almost (awl-most) *adverb*
very nearly: *We are almost there.*

alms (ahms) *plural noun*
(*formerly*) any money or gifts given to the poor.

aloe (al-o) *noun*
1 a large African plant with long cactus-like leaves.
2 (**aloes**) a bitter drug extracted from this plant, used as a laxative.
[Greek]

aloe vera (al-o **vee**-ra) *noun*
a jelly-like substance obtained from aloe and used in shampoos, cosmetics, etc.

aloft *adverb*
high up or in the air: *The glider stayed aloft for several hours.*

alone *adjective, adverb*
1 by oneself: *Do not leave me penniless and alone.*
2 only: *It was anger alone which drove him on.*
Phrases **let alone** not to mention: *He can hardly walk, let alone run.* **let well alone** to be satisfied with the situation as it is: *He won't change his mind, so let well alone.*

along *preposition, adverb*
1 following the length of: *The guide asked us to move along the path.*
2 on or onwards: *They went along together.*
3 together with oneself: *I thought I'd bring my dog along.*
Phrases **all along** all the time: *I knew that all along.* **get along 1** to like each other: *They get along well.* **2** to leave: *I must be getting along now.*

alongside *adverb*
beside or at the side of anything: *The car drew up alongside.*

aloof *adverb, adjective*
apart or at a distance, especially from people: (as an adverb) *He stands aloof from family quarrels.* □ (as an adjective) *She seems aloof, but I know she is only shy.*
Word Family **aloofness** *noun*.

aloud *adverb*
1 in a voice to be heard: *Recite the poem aloud.*
2 loudly: *She cried aloud for joy.*

alp *noun*
a high mountain.

alpaca *noun*
a long-haired South American mammal related to the llama.

alpha (al-fa) *noun*
1 the first letter of the Greek alphabet.
2 the beginning of anything. Compare OMEGA.

alphabet (al-fa-bet) *noun*
1 the letters or signs of a particular language, set in an established order.
2 the basic principles of anything: *the alphabet of survival.*
Word Family **alphabetical** (al-fa-**bett**-i-k'l) *adjective* being in the order of the alphabet, as in a dictionary; **alphabetically** *adverb*; **alphabetize, alphabetise** *verb* to make alphabetical.
[Greek *alpha* A + *beta* B]

alpine (**al**-pine) *adjective*
of or growing on the alps.

already (awl-**redd**-i) *adverb*
by or before a particular time.

> [!] Do not confuse *already*, meaning
> 'by a particular time', as in *They
> had already gone home*, with *all ready*,
> meaning 'all prepared', as in *Are you all
> ready for the exam?*

Alsatian (al-**say**-sh'n) ⇨ GERMAN
SHEPHERD.
[from *Alsace*, a region of France]

also (**awl**-so) *adverb*
as well or in addition: *We also bought you a
present.*

also-ran *noun*
the loser of a race, competition, etc.

altar (**awl**-ta) *noun*
a raised structure where sacrifices are
offered or religious rites are performed.

altarpiece *noun*
a painting or other work of art behind the
altar of a church.

alter (**awl**-ta) *verb*
to make or become different: *We must alter
our plans.*
Word Family **alteration** (awl-ta-**ray**-
sh'n) *noun* 1 the act of altering: *The house
needs a lot of alteration to make it
comfortable.* 2 a change or modification:
The alterations to the law have been accepted.
[Latin, other]

altercation (awl-ta-**kay**-sh'n) *noun*
an angry or noisy quarrel: *There was a long
altercation between the two drivers.*
[Latin *altercatio* a dispute]

alter ego *noun*
1 another part of oneself: *My alter ego
warned me not to do it.*
2 a very close or faithful friend: *She has
always been my alter ego.*
[Latin *alter* another + *ego* I]

alternate (**awl**-ta-nate) *verb*
to replace each other by turns: *Her moods
alternate between joy and depression.*
● **alternate** (awl-**ter**-nit) *adjective*
1 (of two things) first one and then the
other.
2 every second: *We play squash on alternate
Saturdays.*
Word Family **alternately** *adverb*;
alternation (awl-ter-**nay**-sh'n) *noun*.
[Latin *alternare* to do one thing and then a
second thing]

> [!] *Alternate* and *alternative* have
> related but separate meanings:
> *alternate* means in turn, or every second
> part of a series (*on alternate weekends*),
> whereas *alternative* refers to choosing
> between two or more possibilities
> (*follow an alternative route*).

alternating current ⇨ ELECTRIC
CURRENT.

alternative (awl-**ter**-na-tiv) *noun*
a choice between two or more available
possibilities: *Is there no alternative to your
method?*
● **alternative** *adjective*
1 offering a choice between two or more
possibilities: *an alternative plan.*
2 offering or following a different
approach from the conventional or
established one: *alternative medicine.*
□ *alternative theatre.*
Word Family **alternatively** *adverb*.

> [!] Do not confuse *alternative* with
> ALTERNATE.

alternative medicine *noun*
a form of treatment using such methods as
acupuncture, osteopathy and homeopathy
rather than the methods and drugs used in
conventional medicine.

alternator (**awl**-ta-nayta) *noun*
Electricity a generator used to produce
alternating current. Compare DYNAMO
(definition 1).

although (awl-**tho**) *conjunction*
even though: *I will go, although I would
prefer not to.*

altimeter (**al**-ti-mee-ta) *noun*
an instrument similar to a barometer, used
to measure altitude by the decrease of
atmospheric pressure.

altitude *noun*
1 the height of anything, especially above
sea level.
2 ⇨ ELEVATION.
[Latin *altitudo* height]

alto (**al**-toe) *noun*
1 *Music* the range between tenor and
soprano.
2 *Music* any instrument having this range.
3 *Music* a contralto, the lowest female
singing voice.
4 *Music* a countertenor, a high, adult male
singing voice.
[Italian, high]

altogether (awl-ta-**geth**-a) *adverb*
1 in total: *Altogether it adds up to £400.*
2 entirely or completely: *That is altogether out of the question.*
Phrase in the altogether (*informal*)
nude: *The children swam in the altogether.*

> [!] Do not confuse *altogether*, meaning 'completely', as in *He gave up football altogether when he broke his leg*, with *all together*, meaning 'everyone together', as in *I'd like the class to recite the poem all together.*

altruism (al-troo-izm) *noun*
an unselfish generosity to, or concern for, other people.
Word Family altruistic (al-troo-**ist**-ik) *adjective.*
[Italian *altrui* somebody else]

aluminium (al-yoo-**min**-y'm) *noun*
(*American* **aluminum**) a light soft abundant metal which is ductile, malleable and a good conductor of electricity. It is used extensively in alloys, lightweight utensils, etc.
[Latin *aluminis* of alum]

aluminium foil *noun* also called **silver foil; tinfoil**.
a thin sheet of aluminium or a similar substance, used for wrapping, etc.

alumnus (a-**lum**-nus) *noun* (*plural* **alumni**) (a-**lum**-nie)
a former male student of a college or university.
Word Family (*plural* **alumnae** (a-**lum**-nee)) *noun* a former female student of a college or university.
[Latin, a foster-son]

always (awl-ways) *adverb*
at all times or continually. *Has the earth always been round? □ The bus is always late.*

> [!] Do not confuse *always*, meaning 'at all times', as in *I always wear my glasses*, with *all ways*, meaning '(in) every way', as in *I have tried all ways to persuade her to come.*

alyssum (a-**liss**-'m) *noun*
a low garden plant with small white or yellow flowers.

Alzheimer's disease (alts-high-merz diz-eez) *noun*
a form of premature senility affecting the mental processes.

am the first person singular present tense of **be**.

amalgam (a-**mal**-g'm) *noun*
1 any alloy of mercury and another metal, particularly gold.
2 a mixture or combination.
[Greek *malagma* an ointment]

amalgamate (a-**mal**-ga-mate) *verb*
to combine or mix: *The three companies amalgamated last month.*
Word Family amalgamation (a-mal-ga-**may**-sh'n) *noun.*

amanuensis (a-man-yoo-**en**-sis) *noun* (*plural* **amanuenses**)
a secretary or person employed to take dictation, especially for a writer.
[Latin, a secretary]

amass *verb*
to collect or heap together, especially for oneself: *The Duke had amassed a great fortune.*

amateur (**amm**-a-ter) *noun*
1 a person who engages in any activity for enjoyment as distinct from making money.
2 a person who lacks skill or ability.
Word Family amateurish *adjective* unskilled; **amateurishly** *adverb.*
[Latin *amator* lover]

amatory (**amm**-a-tree) *adjective*
relating to love or love-making: *His intentions were obviously amatory.*

amaze *verb*
to surprise or astonish: *His wide knowledge amazed us.*
Word Family amazement *noun*; **amazing** *adjective*; **amazingly** *adverb.*

amazon (**amm**-a-zon) *noun*
1 (**Amazon**) *Ancient mythology* a member of a race of female warriors and hunters who excluded men from their country.
2 a physically strong or powerful woman.

> **Amazon** is most commonly found nowadays as the name of a river in South America. However, it first appeared as the name given to a mythical race of fierce female warriors in Scythia who frequently went to war with the Greeks. The origin of the word is uncertain, but it may derive from Greek *a* (without) and *mazos* (breast), since the Amazons were said to be so intent on winning that they cut off their right breasts so that they could pull their bows back further. It is possible that Orellana, a Spanish explorer, named the River Amazon after seeing female warriors on the bank.

ambassador *noun*
Politics the chief representative of a government, sent to a foreign country. Compare CONSUL.
Word Family **ambassadorial** (am-bass-a-**daw**-ree-'l) *adjective*.
[from French]

amber *noun*
1 the yellow, reddish or brown fossilized resin of coniferous trees, used in jewellery.
2 an orange to yellowish-brown colour.
[Arabic *anbar* ambergris]

ambergris (**am**-ba-griss) *noun*
a grey waxy substance obtained from the intestine of the sperm whale and used in making perfume.
[Arabic *anbar* + French *gris* grey]

ambidextrous *adjective*
able to use both hands equally well.
Word Family **ambidexterity** (am-bi-deks-**terr**-it-ee) *noun*.
[*ambi-* + Latin *dextera* the right hand]

ambience *noun*
an environment or atmosphere: *The country has a peaceful ambience.*
Word Family **ambient** *adjective*.
[Latin *ambire* to go round]

ambient temperature *noun*
Physics the temperature of the area surrounding a body.

ambiguous (am-**big**-yew-us) *adjective*
having two or more possible meanings: *The adjective 'wicked' is ambiguous: it is used either to mean 'bad, evil' or as a slang term to mean 'wonderful, excellent'.*
Word Family **ambiguity** (am-bi-**gew**-it-ee) *noun*; **ambiguously** *adverb*.
[Latin *ambiguus* changing sides]

ambit *noun*
the boundary or range of anything: *Ancient history was not within the ambit of his knowledge.*
[Latin *ambire* to go round]

ambition *noun*
a strong desire for success, fame, etc.
Word Family **ambitious** *adjective*; **ambitiously** *adverb*.
[Latin *ambitio* striving for honour]

ambivalent (am-**bivv**-a-l'nt) *adjective*
having opposite and conflicting feelings about something: *She loves him but is ambivalent about marriage.*
Word Family **ambivalence** *noun*; **ambivalently** *adverb*.
[*ambi-* + Latin *valens* strong]

amble *verb*
to walk at a relaxed or easy pace: *The cattle ambled across the field.*
● **amble** *noun*.
[Latin *ambulare* to walk]

ambrosia (am-**bro**-zee-a) *noun*
1 *Greek mythology* the food of the gods.
2 anything delightfully pleasing or delicious to taste or smell.
[Greek *ambrotos* immortal]

ambulance (**am**-bew-l'nce) *noun*
a vehicle equipped to carry sick or injured people.
[Latin *ambulare* to walk]

ambulant (**am**-bew-l'nt) *adjective*
(*formal*) moving from place to place.

ambulatory (am-bew-**lay**-ta-ree) *adjective*
related to or capable of walking.
Word Family **ambulation** (am-bew-**lay**-sh'n) *noun*.

ambush (**am**-bush) *verb* also **ambuscade**
to lie in wait in order to make a surprise attack.
Word Family **ambush** *noun* (*plural* **ambushes**).

ameer (a-**meer**) *noun* ➩ AMIR.

ameliorate (a-**mee**-li-a-rate) *verb*
(*formal*) to make or become better: *Prison conditions may be ameliorated by the new law.*
Word Family **amelioration** (a-mee-li-a-**ray**-sh'n) *noun*.
[Latin *melior* better]

amen (ah-**men** *or* ay-**men**) *interjection*
a word meaning 'so be it', usually said at the end of a prayer.
[Hebrew, certainly or true]

amenable (a-**mee**-na-b'l) *adjective*
willing or agreeable: *He was not amenable to the suggestion.*
Word Family **amenability** (a-mee-na-**bill**-it-ee) *noun*; **amenableness** *noun*; **amenably** *adverb*.
[French *amener* to lead to]

amend *verb*
1 to make changes in a law etc.: *The committee has amended the rule.*
2 to correct or improve: *Here is an amended version of the original document.*
Word Family **amendment** *noun* 1 the act of amending: *The amendment of the Bill took several hours.* 2 the change or correction made: *a list of amendments to the document*; **amends** *plural noun*; **make amends** to compensate: *How can I make amends for my carelessness?*
[Latin *emendare* to remove faults from]

> **!** Do not confuse *amend* with *emend*. *Emend* means 'to remove errors from a text', as in *The scholar emended the variant readings*.

amenity (a-**menn**-i-tee *or* a-**mee**-ni-tee) *noun* (*plural* **amenities**)
1 (*usually* **amenities**) anything which adds to comfort, ease or pleasure: *The cooking amenities in this flat are excellent.*
2 any pleasantness: *The amenity of the holiday resort made them want to stay longer.*
[Latin *amoenitas* a pleasing sight]

amethyst (**amm**-a-thist) *noun*
a purple or violet quartz, used as a gem.
[Greek *amethystos* not drunk, because the stone was believed to remedy the effects of drink]

amiable (ay-mi-a-b'l) *adjective*
friendly or kind.
Word Family **amiably** *adverb*; **amiability** (ay-mi-a-**bill**-it-ee) *noun*.

amicable (**amm**-ik-a-b'l) *adjective*
peaceful and friendly: *It was an amicable agreement.*
Word Family **amicably** *adverb*; **amicability** (am-ik-a-**bill**-it-ee) *noun*.
[Latin *amicabilis* friendly]

amid *preposition* also **amidst**
among or in the middle of: *She disappeared amid the crowd.*

amidships *adverb*
being in, or referring to, the middle part of a ship.

amir (a-**meer**) *noun* also **ameer**
1 a title given to certain Turkish officials.
2 an emir.
[Arabic, a commander]

amiss *adverb, adjective*
wrong or faulty: *Something must have gone amiss with their plans.*
Phrase **take something amiss** to resent something: *Do not take his comments amiss.*

amity (**amm**-a-tee) *noun*
a state of friendship and harmony: *The peace treaty led to greater amity between the nations.*
[Latin *amicus* friend]

ammeter (**amm**-it-a) *noun*
an instrument used to measure the length of electric current in ampere.
[AM(pere) + METER]

ammonia (a-mo-nee-a) *noun*
a colourless strong-smelling gas (formula NH₃), which is very soluble in water, where it produces an alkaline solution. It is used in refrigerators, cleaning mixtures, explosives and fertilizers.
[from the Temple of *Ammon* in Libya, where first found]

ammunition (am-yoo-**nish**-'n) *noun*
any of the materials, e.g. shot, shells, etc. used in firing guns.
[from MUNITIONS]

amnesia (am-**nee**-zi-a) *noun*
a loss of memory.
[*a-* + Greek *mnestis* recollection]

amnesty (**am**-na-stee) *noun* (*plural* **amnesties**)
a general pardon, especially for crimes against a government.
[Greek *amnestia* forgetting a wrong]

amniocentesis (am-ni-o-sen-**tee**-sis) *noun* (*plural* **amniocenteses**)
removal of some of the amniotic fluid especially as a test for fetal abnormality.

amnion *noun*
the sac containing the unborn offspring of a reptile, bird or mammal.
Word Family **amniotic** (am-ni-**ott**-ik) *adjective*.
[Greek]

amniotic fluid *noun*
the watery fluid which surrounds the embryo in the amnion and is expelled before birth.

amoeba (a-**mee**-ba) *noun* (*plural* **amoebae** (a-**mee**-bee) *or* **amoebas**)
a microscopic unicellular animal which moves by changing its shape and reproduces by simple division into two parts.
Word Family **amoebic** *adjective*.
[Greek *amoibé* change]

amok (a-**mok** *or* a-**muk**) *adverb* also **amuck**
Phrase **run amok** to rush about wildly or violently.
[Malay]

among (a-**mung**) *preposition* also **amongst**
1 surrounded by: *He stood among the crowd.*
2 each of: *The chocolates were divided among the children.*
3 between: *The family dispute must be settled among themselves.*
4 within the group of: *I number him among my friends.*
5 one of: *She is among the best known pop stars.*
[Old English *on* in + *gemang* the crowd]

amoral (ay-**morr**-'l) *adjective*
of or relating to behaviour which is not
based on any moral standards.
Word Family **amorally** *adverb*;
amorality (ay-mo-**rall**-a-tee) *noun*.
[*a-* + MORAL]

> ❗ The words *amoral* and *immoral*
> have related but separate
> meanings: *amoral* describes behaviour
> which is not based on any moral
> standards and may therefore not be
> judged by such standards, whereas
> *immoral* refers to actions which offend
> against an accepted moral law or
> standard.

amorous (**amm**-a-rus) *adjective*
1 of or showing love: *an amorous glance*.
2 inclined or disposed to love: *His
intentions were clearly amorous*.
Word Family **amorously** *adverb*.
[Latin *amor* love]

amorphous (a-**mor**-fus) *adjective*
having no definite form or shape.
[*a-* + Greek *morphé* a shape]

amount *noun*
the extent or total of anything: *The amount
of effort required is minimal*.
• **amount** *verb*
Phrase **amount to** to add up to or be equal
to: *Her debts amounted to £1500*.
[Old French *amont* upward or to the
mountain]

amour (a-**moor**) *noun*
an old word for a love affair.
[French, love]

amour-propre (amm-oor-**prop**-ra) *noun*
self-esteem.
[French]

ampere (**am**-pair) *noun*
short form is **amp** the base SI unit of
electric current. *abbrev.* A.

ampersand *noun*
the sign (**&**), meaning *and*.

amphetamine (am-**fett**-a-meen) *noun*
a drug used to relieve congestion or
stimulate the nervous system.

amphibian (am-**fibb**-ee-an) *noun*
1 any of a group of animals with a
backbone, able to live in water and on
land, usually developing in water but
spending most of its adult life on land.
2 an aircraft which can take off and land
on land or water.
3 a vehicle which can travel on land or
water.

Word Family **amphibian, amphibious**
adjective.
[Greek *amphibios* living a double life]

amphitheatre (am-fi-**theer**-ta) *noun*
a circular or oval area with sloping sides
rising around it, such as a theatre gallery,
sports arena, etc.

amphora (**am**-for-a) *noun* (*plural*
amphorae (**am**-for-ee))
a two-handled vessel with a narrow neck,
used by ancient Greeks and Romans.
[*amphi-* + Greek *phoreus* carried]

ample *adjective*
large or plentiful: *The house has ample room
for all of us*.
Word Family **amply** *adverb*.
[Latin *amplus* spacious]

amplifier (**am**-pli-fire) *noun*
Electricity any device which uses power
from another source to increase the
strength of a signal fed into it, such as that
used in a stereo system to increase volume.

amplify (**am**-pli-fie) *verb* (**amplifies;
amplifying; amplified**)
1 to enlarge, extend or increase: *Could you
amplify that statement?*
2 *Physics* to increase the amplitude of.
Word Family **amplification** (am-pli-fi-
kay-sh'n) *noun*.
[Latin *amplificare* to widen]

amplitude (**am**-pli-tewd) *noun*
1 the extent, breadth or fullness of
anything.
2 *Physics* the height of a vibration. For a
water wave, the amplitude is the height of
the wave: half the distance from peak to
trough. For a sound wave, the amplitude
determines how loud the sound will be,
e.g. a sound with a big amplitude has a
loud sound.

amplitude modulation *noun*
a method of radio broadcasting, in which
the amplitude of the transmitted wave is
varied, producing long-range but low-
fidelity reception. Compare FREQUENCY
MODULATION.

ampoule (**am**-pool) *noun*
a small sealed glass container for sterile
liquids or solids.
[Latin *ampulla* a bottle]

amputate (**am**-pew-tate) *verb*
to cut off a diseased or injured limb, etc.
by surgical operation.
Word Family **amputation** (am-pew-**tay**-
sh'n) *noun*; **amputee** (am-pew-**tee**) *noun*
a person who has had a limb amputated.
[*ambi-* + Latin *putare* to prune]

amrit (**um**-rit) *noun* also **amrita** (**um**-ree-ta)
Sikhism nectar made from sugar and water.
[Sanskrit, immortal]

amuck ⇨ AMOK.

amulet (**am**-yoo-let) *noun*
an ornament or charm believed to protect the wearer from misfortune.

amuse (a-**mewz**) *verb*
1 to cause to smile or laugh.
2 to make time pass pleasantly: *Can you amuse yourself until we return?*
Word Family **amused** adjective; **amusement** *noun* 1 the state of being amused. 2 anything which amuses; **amusingly** *adverb*.
[Old French *amuser* to waste time]

amusement arcade *noun*
a building containing coin-operated gambling machines and electronic games machines.

an *article*
Grammar an indefinite article ⇨ ARTICLE.

anabolic steroid *noun*
one of a group of synthetic steroid hormones used to stimulate muscle size and strength in athletes and for therapeutic purposes.

anachronism (a-**nak**-ra-nizm) *noun*
1 the assigning of something to a wrong, especially an earlier, date.
2 something chronologically out of place: *Horse-drawn transport is an anachronism in large modern cities.*
Word Family **anachronistic** (a-nak-ra-**nist**-ik) *adjective*.
[Greek *ana-* against + *khronos* time]

anaconda (ann-a-**kon**-da) *noun*
a very large South American snake related to the boa, reaching at least 10 m in length.

anaemia (a-**nee**-mi-a) *noun* (*American* **anemia**)
a shortage of red blood cells due to loss of blood or reduced production of cells causing weakness and pale skin colouring.
Word Family **anaemic** *adjective*
1 suffering from anaemia. 2 colourless or weak: *an anaemic complexion.*
[Greek *an-* without + *haima* blood]

anaerobe (**ann**-a-robe) *noun*
an organism that does not require oxygen to live. Compare AEROBE.
Word Family **anaerobic** (ann-a-**ro**-bik) *adjective*.
[Greek *an-* without + AEROBE]

anaesthesia (ann-is-**theez**-ya) *noun* (*American* **anesthesia**)
a general loss of feeling, especially of pain.
Word Family **anaesthetic** (ann-is-**thett**-ik) *noun* any substance, such as ether or chloroform, producing a general or local loss of feeling, pain, etc.; **anaesthetize** (a-**nees**-tha-tize), **anaesthetise** *verb*; **anaesthetist** (a-**nees**-tha-tist) *noun* a person trained to give anaesthetics.
[Greek *an-* without + AESTHETIC]

anagram (**ann**-a-gram) *noun*
a word formed by rearranging the letters of another word: *'March' is an anagram of 'charm'.*
[Greek *ana* again + *gramma* a letter]

anal (**ay**-n'l) *adjective*
Anatomy of or relating to the anus.

analgesia (ann-al-**jeez**-ya) *noun*
an inability to feel pain.
Word Family **analgesic** (ann-al-**jee**-zik) *noun* any substance which relieves pain.
[Greek *an-* without + *algos* pain]

analogue watch *noun* (*plural* **analogue watches**) also **analogue clock**
a watch or clock which indicates the time by means of a pointer moving round a numbered dial. Compare DIGITAL WATCH.

> The term **analogue watch** has been introduced only relatively recently. Until the invention, in the second half of the 20th century, of the *digital watch*, which displays the time by means of numbers only, the dial and pointers version was simply known as a *watch*. The term *analogue watch* came into being to differentiate between the two types of watch. Such words and phrases are called *retronyms*, another example being 'acoustic guitar'.

analogy (a-**nall**-a-jee) *noun* (*plural* **analogies**)
a comparison between two things that are alike in some ways: *We can draw an analogy between the heart and a pump.*
Word Family **analogize, analogise** *verb* to use or explain by analogy; **analogous** (a-**nall**-a-gus) *adjective* comparable in several respects; **analogously** *adverb*.
[Greek *analogos* proportionate]

analyse (**ann**-a-lize) *verb* (*American* **analyze**)
1 to examine critically or establish the essential features of: *to analyse one's motives.*
2 to divide into the constituent parts and examine each element: *to analyse a chemical compound.*

analysis (a-**nall**-a-sis) *noun* (*plural* **analyses**) (a-**nall**-a-seez)
1 the process of separating something into its constituent parts, so as to examine or describe it. Compare SYNTHESIS.
2 *Maths* the branch of maths which uses algebraic and calculus methods.
3 *Maths* the exposition of the principles involved in solving a problem.
4 *Psychology* ⇨ PSYCHOANALYSIS.
Word Family **analyst** (**ann**-al-ist) *noun* a person skilled in analysis, especially psychoanalysis; **analytic** (ann-a-**litt**-ik) **analytical** *adjective*; **analytically** *adverb*.
[Greek, a breaking up]

anarchy (**ann**-a-kee) *noun*
1 a lack of established government or control, usually leading to disorder.
2 a general state of disorder or uproar: *Anarchy reigned in the school during the teachers' strike.*
Word Family **anarchist** (**ann**-a-kist) *noun* a person who believes that all organized authority should be abolished in the interest of individual freedom; **anarchism** *noun*; **anarchic** (a-**nar**-kik), **anarchical** *adjective*.
[Greek *an*- without + *arkhos* a ruler]

anathema (a-**nath**-em-a) *noun*
1 a curse by God or the Church.
2 anything which is detested or loathed: *Wedding receptions are anathema to him.*
[Greek, a curse]

anatomy (a-**natt**-a-mee) *noun* (*plural* **anatomies**)
1 the internal structure of anything.
2 *Biology* the study of the structure of an organism. Compare PHYSIOLOGY (definition 1).
Word Family **anatomist** *noun*; **anatomical** (ann-a-**tomm**-ik'l) *adjective*; **anatomically** *adverb*.
[Greek *anatomé* a cutting up]

ancestor (**an**-sess-ta) *noun*
a person from whom descent can be traced through either of one's parents.
Word Family **ancestral** (an-**sess**-tr'l) *adjective*.
[*ante*- + Latin *cedere* to go]

ancestry (**an**-sess-tree) *noun* (*plural* **ancestries**)
1 a line of descent.
2 all one's ancestors.

anchor (**an**-ka) *noun*
Nautical a heavy object attached to a ship by a rope or chain and lowered into the seabed to prevent the ship drifting.
● **anchor** *verb*

1 to lower an anchor.
2 to hold or be held fast by an anchor.
Figurative Fear anchored her to the spot (= firmly fixed).
Word Family **anchorage** *noun* 1 an area where ships may anchor. 2 the fee paid for this.

anchorman *noun* (*plural* **anchormen**)
1 the person at the end of a tug-of-war rope.
2 the final runner in a relay.
3 a compère.

anchovy (**an**-cha-vee) *noun* (*plural* **anchovies**)
any of a group of small edible oily fish, related to the herring.
[Spanish]

ancient (**ane**-sh'nt) *adjective*
1 existing or occurring in times long past, especially before the fall of the Western Roman Empire in A.D. 476.
2 (*informal*) very old: *an ancient pensioner.*
● **ancient** *noun*
1 a person who lived in ancient times.
2 a very old person.

ancillary (an-**sill**-a-ree) *adjective*
auxiliary.
[Latin *ancilla* a servant]

and *conjunction*
1 a word used to indicate connection or joining of ideas, etc.: *We ate dinner and then we left.*
2 a word used to indicate continuation: *We talked and talked for hours.*
3 a word used to indicate addition: *Seven and eight equals fifteen.*
4 as well as: *The house was dark and cold.*
5 (*informal*) to: *Please try and find it.*

andante (an-**dan**-tee) *adverb*
Music slowly.
[Italian]

andiron ⇨ FIREDOG.

androgen (**an**-dra-j'n) *noun*
any of various hormones which control the appearance and development of masculine characteristics.
[Greek *andros* of a man + GEN(esis)]

androgynous (an-**drojj**-i-nus) *adjective*
having male and female characteristics.
[Greek *andros* of a man + *gyne* woman]

anecdote (**ann**-ek-dote) *noun*
a short interesting or amusing story about a particular person or event: *He told us an anecdote about losing his dog.*
Word Family **anecdotal** (ann-ek-**doe**-t'l) *adjective*.
[Greek *anekdotos* unpublished]

anemone (a-**nemm**-a-nee) *noun*
1 a small garden flower growing from a corm and resembling a poppy.
2 ⇨ SEA ANEMONE.
[Greek *anemos* wind]

aneroid barometer (anna-royd ba-**romm**-it-a) *noun*
an instrument for measuring air-pressure by the movement of the elastic top of a box which has been emptied of air.
[*a-* + Greek *neros* wet + *-oid*]

aneurysm (**an**-yoo-rizm) *noun* also **aneurism**
a disorder of the heart or arteries in which the wall bulges outwards at an area of weakness.
[Greek *aneurysma* a widening]

anew *adverb*
(*formal*) once more or again: *We will start anew.*

angel (ane-j'l) *noun*
1 a divine or spiritual being, usually pictured as having wings, who is an attendant or messenger of God.
2 (*informal*) any beautiful or kind person: *You're an angel for doing my shopping.*
Word Family angelic (an-**jell**-ik) *adjective*.
[Greek *aggelos* messenger]

angelica (an-**jell**-i-ka) *noun*
a fragrant plant, the crystallized stalks of which are used in cooking as a decoration.

angelus (**an**-ju-lus) *noun*
Roman Catholicism a prayer to the Virgin Mary in remembrance of the Annunciation, said daily at 6 a.m., noon and 6 p.m.,
angelus bell the bell tolled at these times.

anger *noun*
a strong feeling of displeasure and often hostility: *Her clumsy apology only made his anger greater.*
● **anger** *verb* to make angry.

angina pectoris (an-jie-na **pek**-ta-ris) *noun*
short form is **angina** brief severe pain in the heart due to the blockage of a coronary artery and a lack of oxygen reaching the heart muscle.
[Latin *angina* spasm + *pectoris* of the chest]

angle¹ *noun*
1 the space between two lines or planes which diverge from a point.
2 the inclination to each other of such lines or planes, measured in degrees

(360 making a revolution) or in radians (2π making a revolution).
3 an aspect or point of view: *We must consider all angles of the matter.*
● **angle** *verb* to move or direct at an angle: *The roof was angled steeply to allow snow to slide off.*
Figurative The question was angled so that only one answer was possible (= biased, slanted).
[Latin *angulus*]

angle² *verb*
to fish.
Figurative She angled for an invitation to the party (= schemed, tried).
Word Family angler *noun* a fisherman.

Anglican Church ⇨ CHURCH OF ENGLAND.
Word Family Anglican *noun*.

Anglicism (**an**-gli-sizm) *noun*
an English expression or idiom.
[Late Latin *Anglice* in English]

anglicize, anglicise (**an**-gli-size) *verb*
to make or become English in character, habits, etc.: *the anglicized pronunciation of a foreign word.*

Anglo-Catholic ⇨ HIGH CHURCH.

Anglophile (**an**-glo-file) *noun*
a person who has an admiration for England or Britain.
Word Family Anglophilia (an-glo-**fill**-ee-a) *noun*.

angora (an-**gaw**-ra) *noun*
1 a cat, goat or rabbit with long silky hair.
2 the yarn or fabric made from the coat of such an animal.
[from *Angora* Ankara, the capital of Turkey]

angry *adjective* (**angrier; angriest**)
full of anger: *He was unabashed by her angry glare.*
Word Family angrily *adverb*.

angst *noun*
(*often ironical*) a morbid anxiety, especially about the state of the modern world.
[German, anguish]

angstrom *noun*
a unit of length equal to 10^{-10} m.
[after *A. J. Angstrom*, 1814–1874, a Swedish physicist]

anguish (**an**-gwish) *noun*
extreme pain or suffering: *She was in anguish over his death.*
Word Family anguished *adjective*.

angular (**an**-gyoo-la) *adjective*
1 having, consisting of, or forming an angle.
2 *Physics* measured by an angle: *the angular distance.*
3 (of a person) bony or awkward.
Word Family: **angularity** (an-gyoo-**larr**-it-ee) *noun*.

aniline (**ann**-i-leen) *noun*
Chemistry an oily liquid (formula $C_6H_5NH_2$), prepared from benzene. It is the basis of many dyes, plastics and resins.
[from Arabic *anil* indigo]

animal *noun*
1 any living organism which is able to move about for at least part of its life, but cannot make its own food from chemical elements or simple compounds. Compare PLANT (definition 1).
2 any beast-like or uncivilized person.
• **animal** *adjective*
1 of or relating to animals.
2 of the physical rather than intellectual nature of humankind: *Food is an animal need.*
[Latin, a living being]

animal rights *plural noun*
the rights of animals not to be abused by human beings.

animate (**ann**-i-mate) *verb*
to make alive or lively: *Her face was animated by her smile.*
• **animate** (**ann**-i-mit) *adjective* alive or possessing life.
Word Family **animation** (ann-i-**may**-sh'n) *noun*.

animatronics (ann-i-ma-**tron**-iks) *plural noun*
(*used with singular verb*) the technique of making lifelike robots in the shape of people or animals, programmed electronically to make lifelike movements and noises.

animosity (ann-i-**moss**-it-ee) *noun*
a feeling of hostility or aggression.
[Latin *animosus* spirited]

animus *noun*
1 animosity.
2 a moving or animating force.
[Latin, spirit]

aniseed *noun*
the strong-smelling seed of a plant called **anise**, used in medicine and cooking.
[Greek *anison* anise + SEED]

ankle *noun*
1 the joint connecting the lower leg to the foot, made up of seven bones called **tarsal bones**.
2 the slender part of the leg immediately above the foot.

anklet *noun*
an ornamental band or chain worn around the ankle.

annals *plural noun*
1 a history of events recorded year by year.
2 the books containing such records.
Word Family **annalist** *noun*.
[Latin *annales* chronicles]

anneal (a-**neel**) *verb*
to heat and then carefully cool a material, such as glass, to remove any structural weaknesses and hence toughen it.

annelid (**an**-ell-id) *noun*
any of a group of segmented worms, e.g. the earthworm.
[Latin *anulus* a ring]

annex (a-**neks**) *verb*
1 to attach or join to something larger: *The farm was annexed to the neighbouring estate.*
2 to take over or attach land to one's own: *The empire annexed several small territories during the short war.*
Word Family **annexation** (ann-eks-**ay**-sh'n) *noun*.
[*an-* + Latin *nexus* tied to]

annexe (**an**-eks) *noun* also **annex**
1 a building or structure added to or situated near a larger one.
2 anything which has been added or joined.

annihilate (a-**nigh**-a-late) *verb*
to completely destroy or defeat.
Word Family **annihilation** (a-nigh-a-**lay**-sh'n) *noun*.
[*ad-* + Latin *nihil* nothing]

anniversary (ann-i-**ver**-sa-ree) *noun*
(*plural* **anniversaries**)
1 the annual return of the date of an event: *a wedding anniversary.*
2 the celebration of this.
[Latin *annus* year + *versus* turning]

Anno Domini (ann-o **domm**-in-eye) *adverb*
in the year of the Lord: used in dates to show how long after the birth of Christ something happened. *abbrev.* A.D.
[Latin]

annotate *verb*
to supply or add notes, e.g. in explanation, criticism, etc.: *This book is annotated in the margins.*

Word Family annotation (ann-oh-**tay**-sh'n) *noun;* **annotator** *noun.*
[*an-* + Latin *notare* to record]

announce *verb*
1 to state or make known publicly: *The Prime Minister announced the new policies.*
2 to introduce: *Snow announced the beginning of winter.*
Word Family announcement *noun;*
announcer *noun* a person who announces or narrates, especially on the radio or on television.
[*an-* + Latin *nuntius* a messenger]

annoy (a-**noy**) *verb*
to displease or irritate: *She was annoyed by the delay.*
Word Family annoyance *noun*
1 something which annoys. 2 the act of annoying. 3 the feeling of being annoyed.

annual *adjective*
1 occurring once a year: *an annual race meeting.*
2 happening over the course of a year: *the annual journey of the planets.*
• **annual** *noun*
1 a book published once a year.
2 *Biology* any plant which completes its life cycle within one season or one year.
[Latin *annus* a year]

annuity (a-**new**-it-ee) *noun (plural* **annuities***)*
Insurance a sum of money paid as a regular yearly income from an insurance policy.

annul (a-**null**) *verb* (**annuls; annulling, annulled***)*
to abolish or make void, e.g. a law or marriage.
Word Family annulment *noun.*
[*an-* + Latin *nullus* none]

Annunciation (a-nun-see-ay-sh'n) *noun*
1 *Christianity* the angel Gabriel's announcement to the Virgin Mary that she would give birth to Christ.
2 *Christianity* the festival celebrating this.
[Latin, announcement]

anode (**an**-ode) *noun*
a positive electrode. Compare CATHODE.
[Greek *ana* up + *hodos* a way]

anodyne (**ann**-a-dine) *adjective*
bland: *a rather anodyne speech.*
• **anodyne** *noun* any drug which relieves pain.
[Greek *an-* without + *odyné* pain]

anoint *verb*
to put oil on as a sign of consecration, especially in a religious ceremony.

anomaly (a-**nomm**-a-lee) *noun (plural* **anomalies***)*
anything which is irregular or different from what is normal: *A flightless bird is an anomaly.*
Word Family anomalous *adjective.*
[Greek *anomalos* uneven]

anon *adverb*
an old word for **soon.**

anonymous (a-**nonn**-i-mus) *adjective*
having no known or acknowledged name or authorship: *an anonymous poem.*
Figurative *an anonymous face which she could not recall* (= lacking individuality).
Word Family anonymously *adverb;*
anonymity (ann-a-**nimm**-i-tee) *noun.*
[Greek *an-* without + *onyma* name]

anorak (**ann**-a-rak) *noun*
1 a waterproof jacket, usually with a hood.
2 (*informal*) a socially inept person who is preoccupied by a particular interest.
[Eskimo]

anorexia (ann-a-**rek**-si-a) *noun*
short for **anorexia nervosa** a medical condition characterized by undereating or complete loss of appetite.
Word Family anorexic *adjective.*
[Greek *an-* without + *orexis* appetite]

another (a-**nuth**-a) *adjective*
1 an additional: *Pass me another cake.*
2 a different: *Come another day.*
• **another** *pronoun*
1 an additional one: *Choose another.*
2 a different one: *going from one place to another.*
3 a similar or identical one.

Anschluss (**an**-shlus) *noun*
the union of Germany and Austria carried out by Hitler in March 1938.
[German *anschliessen* to join]

answer (**ahn**-sa) *noun*
1 a reply or response: *Please give me an answer to my request.*
2 a solution to a problem: *What answer did you get for that maths problem?*
• **answer** *verb*
1 to respond.
2 to suit, serve: *This should answer our purpose.*
3 to correspond: *This man answers to your description.*
Phrase answer for 1 to accept responsibility for: *Who will answer for the damage?* 2 to pay for, suffer the consequences of: *He must answer for such cruel violence.*

Word Family **answerable** *adjective*
1 responsible or accountable: *Who is answerable for this child's behaviour?* **2** able to be answered.

answering machine *noun*
a device attached to a telephone which accepts incoming calls and records messages.

ant *noun*
any of a group of very small insects which form, and live in, communities.

antacid (an-**tass**-id) *noun*
any substance which neutralizes or counteracts acids, e.g. in the stomach.

antagonism (an-**tagg**-a-nizm) *noun*
any active opposition or hostility: *He feels great antagonism towards his ex-wife.*
Word Family **antagonist** *noun* a person actively opposed to, or in competition with, another; **antagonize, antagonise** *verb* to make hostile; **antagonistic** (an-tagg-a-**nist**-ik) *adjective*.
[*anti-* + Greek *agon* a contest]

Antarctic *adjective*
at or near the South Pole.
● **Antarctic** *noun* the Antarctic regions.
[Greek *antarktikos* opposite the north]

Antarctic Circle *noun*
a line drawn on a map showing the most northerly point at which the sun does not set on one day a year, at about 66°30′ south.

ante (**an**-ti) *noun*
1 *Cards* a minimum bet placed before the first card is dealt, e.g. in poker.
2 (*informal*) an amount to be paid, a price: *We had to up the ante for the house.*
[from *ante-*]

anteater *noun*
any of various animals which live on ants and termites.

antecedent (an-ti-**see**-d'nt) *noun*
1 (**antecedents**) one's ancestors or past history.
2 *Grammar* the word or phrase in a sentence to which a pronoun refers: *In the sentence 'Have you seen the book that I bought yesterday?' 'book' is the antecedent of 'that'.*
● **antecedent** *adjective* occurring before or earlier.
[*ante-* + Latin *cedere* to go]

antechamber ➪ ANTEROOM.

antediluvian (an-ti-de-**loo**-vi-an) *adjective*
before the biblical Flood.

Figurative primitive, outdated: *That is a very antediluvian belief.*
[*ante-* + Latin *diluvium* deluge]

antelope (**an**-ti-lope) *noun*
any of various horned ruminant mammals similar to deer, such as the chamois, gnu and gazelle.

> The word **antelope** (from Greek *antholops*) usually makes us think of a gentle animal but in the Middle Ages it was applied to a mythical animal which was very savage, being able to cut down trees with its horns, and which inhabited the banks of the River Euphrates. Later the name was used to describe an animal depicted by heraldry, along with other mythical animals such as unicorns. Today's *antelope* was first given its name by the naturalist, Edward Topsell. Despite its lack of aggression, it does bear some resemblance to its mythical forerunner, being horned and swift-moving.

ante meridiem (an-ti mer-**ridd**-i-em) *adverb*
the time before midday. *abbrev.* a.m. Compare POST MERIDIEM.
[*ante-* + Latin *meridiem* midday]

antenatal (an-ti-**nay**-t'l) *adjective*
during pregnancy but before birth: *an antenatal clinic.* Compare POST-NATAL.
[*ante-* + Latin *natus* born]

antenna (an-**tenn**-a) *noun* (*plural* **antennae** (an-**tenn**-ee) or **antennas**)
1 *Biology* either of the pair of jointed outgrowths occurring on the heads of insects and some other animals.
2 *Electronics* ➪ AERIAL.
[Latin, spar of a sail]

anterior (an-**teer**-i-a) *adjective*
1 situated before or to the front: *an anterior room.* Compare POSTERIOR *adjective* (definition 1).
2 preceding in time.
[Latin, earlier, before]

anteroom *noun* also **antechamber**
a waiting room outside a larger room.

anthem *noun*
a short solemn song of praise. Compare NATIONAL ANTHEM.

anther *noun*
Biology the end of a stamen containing the pollen.
[Greek *anthos* a flower]

anthology (an-**tholl**-a-jee) *noun* (*plural* **anthologies**)
a collection of poems or literary extracts.

Word Family **anthologist** *noun*.
[Greek *anthos* a flower + *legein* to collect]

anthracite (**an**-thra-site) *noun* also called
hard coal.
a coal which is almost pure carbon.
[Greek *anthrakos* of coal]

anthrax *noun*
an often fatal bacterial infection of cattle
and man, often causing severe carbuncles.
[Greek, coal, carbuncle]

anthropoid *adjective*
of or resembling man.
• **anthropoid** *noun* an ape which
resembles man, such as a gorilla.
[*anthropo-* + *-oid*]

anthropology (an-thra-**poll**-a-jee) *noun*
the study of man and the customs,
characteristics, etc. of human societies.
Word Family **anthropological**
(an-thra-pa-**lojj**-i-k'l) *adjective*;
anthropologist *noun*.
[*anthropo-* + *-logy*]

anthropometric (an-throp-a-**met**-rik)
adjective
relating to or using measurements of the
human body.
[*anthropo-* + Greek *metron* measure]

anthropomorphic (an-throp-a-**mor**-fik)
adjective
attributing human characteristics to
something which is non-human, such as a
god.
[*anthropo-* + Greek *morphe* a shape]

anti-aircraft *adjective*
of or relating to weapons and equipment
used against enemy aircraft.

antibiotic (an-ti-by-**ott**-ik) *noun*
a substance, such as penicillin, produced
by living organisms, which will kill or
prevent the growth of other organisms,
and is widely used to treat disease.

antibody (**an**-ti-bod-ee) *noun* (*plural*
antibodies)
Medicine a protein that is made by certain
white blood cells (lymphocytes), in the
body, in response to the invasion of a
foreign substance (an **antigen**) such as
bacteria, foreign tissue grafts, inhaled
pollen grains and dust. By combining with
and neutralizing antigens, antibodies
provide immunity to disease.

antic *noun*
(*often* **antics**) any ludicrous or absurd
behaviour: *Journalists love the antics of
politicians*.

anticipate (an-**tiss**-i-pate) *verb*
1 to expect or realize beforehand:
I anticipated a better response.
2 to forestall: *The general successfully
anticipated the enemy's strategy* .
3 to foresee: *Jules Verne anticipated modern
technology by 50 years.*
Word Family **anticipation** (an-tiss-i-
pay-sh'n) *noun*; **anticipatory** *adjective*.
[Latin *anticipare* to take before]

anticlimax (an-ti-**klie**-maks) *noun* (*plural*
anticlimaxes)
1 a disappointing outcome or conclusion.
2 the weakening of an effect, especially in a
literary work.
Word Family **anticlimactic** (an-ti-klie-
mak-tik) *adjective*.

anticlockwise *adjective, adverb*
in a direction opposite to the movement of
the hands of a clock. Compare CLOCKWISE.

anticyclone ⇨ HIGH *noun* (definition 3).

antidepressant (an-ti-de-**press** 'nt) *noun*
any of a group of drugs used to prevent or
relieve depression.

antidote *noun*
1 *Medicine* any substance that will
counteract the effects of a poison, disease,
etc.
2 any remedy: *Time is the only antidote for a
broken heart.*
[*anti* + Greek *dotos* given]

antifreeze *noun*
a substance added to the water in car
radiators, etc. to prevent freezing.

antigen ⇨ ANTIBODY.

anti-hero *noun* (*plural* **anti-heroes**)
a character who is cast as the hero of a
modern novel or play, but who has no
heroic qualities.

antihistamine (an-ti-**hist**-a-meen) *noun*
any of a group of drugs which neutralize
substances released in animal and plant
tissues in allergic reactions. Antihistamines
are used to treat allergies such as hay fever.

antilogarithm ⇨ LOGARITHM.

antimacassar (an-ti-ma-**kass**-a) *noun*
a decorative cover for the back and arms of
a chair.
[*anti-* + *Macassar* oil, a hair oil]

antimony (an-**timm**-a-nee) *noun*
a brittle metal which expands on
solidifying, used in alloys and in medicine.

antinomy (an-**tinn**-a-mee) *noun*
an opposition or contradiction.
[*anti-* + Greek *nomos* a law]

antioxidant *noun*
any substance that inhibits or prevents retardation by oxidation, as of fats, oils, foods, petroleum products, etc.

antipasto (an-ti-**pas**-to) *noun* (*plural* **antipasti** (an-ti-**pas**-tee))
an appetizer.
[Italian *anti* before + *pasto* a meal]

antipathy (an-**tipp**-a-thee) *noun* (*plural* **antipathies**)
a strong fixed dislike or aversion: *My antipathy towards him is entirely instinctive.*
[*anti-* + Greek *pathos* feeling]

antiperspirant (an-ti-**pers**-pi-r'nt) *noun*
any substance which is used to prevent or decrease sweating.

Antipodes (an-**tipp**-a-deez) *plural noun*
Australia and New Zealand.
Word Family **Antipodean** (an-tipp-a-**dee**-an) *adjective, noun.*
[*anti-* + Greek *podos* of a foot]

antiquarian (an-ti-**kwair**-i-an) *adjective*
of or relating to the study of antiquities.
Word Family **antiquarian, antiquary** (an-ti-**kwerr**-ee) *noun* (*plural* **antiquaries**) an expert on, or dealer in, antiquities.

antiquated (an-ti-**kway**-tid) *adjective*
old-fashioned, quaint or obsolete: *Antiquated machinery is often valued as a collector's item.*

antique (an-**teek**) *noun*
any rare or valued object from the past, especially one more than l00 years old.
● **antique** *adjective*
1 of or relating to antiques.
2 of or relating to the distant past: *The fountain gave the courtyard an antique charm.*
Word Family **antiquity** (an-**tik**-wi-tee) *noun* (*plural* **antiquities**) 1 any ancient time or remote period: *The origins of the legend are lost in antiquity.* 2 the quality of being ancient: *It is a city of great antiquity.* 3 (*usually* **antiquities**) any works of art or ruins from the distant past: *We studied the Greek antiquities in the museum.*
[Latin *antiquus* ancient]

anti-Semitism (an-ti-**sem**-it-izm) *noun*
a dislike or ill-treatment of Jews.
Word Family **anti-Semitic** (an-ti-si-**mitt**-ik) *adjective*; **anti-Semite** (an-ti-**see**-mite *or* an-ti-**sem**-ite) *noun.*

antiseptic (an-ti-**sep**-tik) *adjective*
of or relating to the killing of micro-organisms.
● **antiseptic** *noun* a substance which kills micro-organisms.

antiserum (**an**-ti-seer-'m) *noun*
a serum containing antibodies.

antisocial (an-ti-**so**-sh'l) *adjective*
withdrawn from or actively hostile to others or to social institutions.

antithesis (an-**tith**-a-sis) *noun* (*plural* **antitheses**) (an-**tith**-a-seez)
the direct opposite of something: *Certainty is the antithesis of doubt.*
Word Family **antithetical** (an-ti-**thett**-i-k'l) *adjective.*
[*anti-* + THESIS]

antitoxin *noun*
an antibody produced by the body in order to counteract a poison.

antler *noun*
either of the bony growths on the skull of deer, covered by soft velvety skin during growth and shed and renewed annually.
Compare HORN (definition 1).

antonym (**an**-ta-nim) *noun*
a word opposite in meaning to another: *'Good' is an antonym of 'bad'.* Compare SYNONYM.
[*anti-* + Greek *onyma* name]

antrum *noun* (*plural* **antra**)
either of two large sinuses within the bones of the upper jaw.
[Greek *antron* a cave]

anus (**ay**-nus) *noun* (*plural* **anuses**)
Anatomy the ring of muscle at the lower end of the alimentary canal, connecting the rectum to the exterior, through which solid waste matter is excreted.
[Latin]

anvil *noun*
a heavy iron block, often with a horn-like projection on one end, on which metals are hammered into shape.

anxiety (ang-**zie**-a-tee) *noun* (*plural* **anxieties**)
a state of worry or apprehension: *His anxiety about public speaking is hard to understand.*

anxious (**ang**-shus) *adjective*
1 suffering from or causing anxiety: *I can't help being anxious about the examination.* □ *His illness was an anxious time for all of us.*
2 eager: *She was anxious to please.*
Word Family **anxiously** *adverb*; **anxiousness** *noun.*
[Latin *anxius*]

any (**enn**-ee) *adjective*
1 one or some: *Do you have any friends?*
2 every: *Any fool knows that.*

3 a great or unlimited amount: *Any number of things could still go wrong.*
● **any** *pronoun* any person: *Do any of you know him?*
● **any** *adverb* at all: *Are you feeling any better?*
Word Family anybody, anyone *pronoun* any person: *Didn't anybody help you?*; **anyhow** *adverb* **1** in any case: *Anyhow, the contract was already signed.* **2** in a careless manner: *The table was put together anyhow;* **anything** *pronoun* any thing whatever: *Did anything strange happen last night?*; **anyway** *adverb* however or in any case: *Anyway, I'll see you tomorrow;* **anywhere** *adverb* in, at or to any place: *We can't find it anywhere.*

aorta (ay-**or**-ta) *noun*
Anatomy the largest artery in the body, arching out of the heart and down through the diaphragm into the abdomen.

apace *adverb*
(*formal*) quickly or rapidly.

apart *adverb*
separated or at a distance: *Let's take the engine apart.* □ *Joking apart, what did you think of my speech?*
● **apart** *adjective* separate or independent.

apartheid (a-**par**-tite *or* a-**par**-tate) *noun*
(*formerly*) a policy or law segregating racial groups in South Africa.
[Afrikaans *apart* apart + *heid* -hood]

apartment *noun*
1 a single room.
2 a suite of furnished rooms in a very large house.
3 *American* a flat.

apathy (**app**-a-thee) *noun*
a lack of interest or energy: *The appeal for funds met with general apathy.*
Word Family apathetic (ap-a-**thett**-ik) *adjective;* **apathetically** *adverb.*
[Greek *apatheia* insensibility]

apatosaurus (a-pat-a-**saw**-rus) *noun*
a long-extinct plant-eating reptile, one of the largest animals ever known.
[Greek *apaté* deceit + *sauros* lizard]

ape *noun*
any of the tailless primates closest to man in evolutionary development, such as the chimpanzee, gorilla and orang-utan.
Compare MONKEY.
● **ape** *verb* to imitate or mimic: *Children frequently ape their teachers.*

aperitif (a-perr-i-**teef**) *noun*
an alcoholic drink taken before a meal to stimulate the appetite.
[French]

aperture (**app**-a-cher) *noun*
1 a gap or opening.
2 *Photography* the size of the adjustable diaphragm in a camera.
[Latin *apertura* an opening]

apex (**ay**-peks) *noun* (*plural* **apexes** or **apices** (**ay**-pi-seez))
1 the highest point or summit: *The apex of a triangle is opposite its base.*
2 the culminating point, climax.
[Latin, point or summit]

aphasia (a-**faze**-ya) *noun*
the loss of the ability to use language, caused by lesions in the brain.
Word Family aphasiac *noun* a person suffering from aphasia; **aphasic** *adjective.*
[*a-* + Greek *phasis* speech]

aphid (**ay**-fid) *noun* also **aphis**
any of a group of small insects which suck plant juices.

aphorism (**aff**-a-rizm) *noun*
a short pithy saying expressing a truth.
[Greek *aphorismos* a definition]

aphrodisiac (af-ra-**dizz**-i-ak) *noun*
any food, drink or drug arousing sexual desire.
[from APHRODITE]

Aphrodite (af-ra-**die**-tee) *noun*
Greek mythology the goddess of beauty, fertility and sexual love, identified with the Roman goddess Venus.

apiary (**ape**-y'-ree) *noun* (*plural* **apiaries**)
an area in which bees are kept.
Word Family apiarist *noun* a person who keeps bees.
[Latin *apis* a bee]

apical (**app**-i-k'l) *adjective*
of, at or forming the apex.

apices
the plural of **apex**.

apiculture (**ay**-pi-kul-cher) *noun*
the breeding and care of bees.

apiece (a-**peece**) *adverb*
each, or for each one: *The chairs at the sale were £10 apiece.*

aplomb (a-**plom**) *noun*
poise or self-possession.
[French]

apocalypse (a-**pokk**-a-lips) *noun*
1 any revelation or remarkable disclosure.
2 (**Apocalypse**) *Christianity* the revelation described in the Bible in the Book of Revelation.
Word Family apocalyptic (a-pokk-a-**lip**-tik) *adjective;* **apocalyptically** *adverb.*
[Greek]

The word **apocalypse** is now often found meaning 'an event of tremendous importance', frequently an event of catastrophic or disastrous importance. It can also mean 'a disclosure or revelation', usually unexpected or surprising. The connection between these meanings is that the revelations referred to were originally of the kind made by the prophets who foretold important events, including disasters. *Apocalypse* was originally an alternative name for the *Book of Revelation* in the Bible which describes a vision of the future given to St John on the island of Patmos and comes from the Greek *apokaluptein* (to reveal).

apocrypha (a-**pok**-ri-fa) *plural noun*
any writings or works considered not to be genuine or authentic.
Word Family apocryphal *adjective* doubtful or false.
[Greek *apokryphos* hidden]

apogee (**app**-a-jee) *noun*
1 *Astronomy* the point in the orbit of the moon, a planet or an artificial satellite when it is furthest from the earth. Compare PERIGEE.
2 the highest point or climax.
[Greek *apogaion* from the earth]

Apollo *noun*
Greek mythology the god of youth, light, archery, healing, prophecy and music.

apology (a-**poll**-a-jee) *noun* (*plural* **apologies**)
an expression of regret for some wrong or injury: *Please accept my apologies for being so late.* □ *I expect an apology from that rude child.*
Figurative *Do you call that apology for a horse a thoroughbred?* (= poor substitute).
Word Family apologize, apologise *verb*; **apologetic** (a-poll-a-**jett**-ik) *adjective*; **apologetically** *adverb*; **apologia** (app-a-**lo**-ja) *noun* a formal justification or defence.
[Greek *apologia* a speech in defence]

apoplexy (**app**-a-pleks-i) *noun* (*plural* **apoplexies**)
1 *Medicine* a sudden loss of a bodily function, such as speech, due to a brain haemorrhage.
2 (*informal*) a fit of rage: *Merely mentioning the subject gives him apoplexy.*
Word Family apoplectic (app-a-**plek**-tik) *adjective*.
[Greek *apoplexia* a stroke]

apostasy (a-**post**-a-see) *noun*
the desertion of a religious faith, political principle, cause, etc.
Word Family apostate *noun*.
[Greek *apostasis* a standing away from]

a posteriori (ay pos-terr-i-**aw**-rye) *adverb, adjective*
based on experience and observation rather than theory; by induction. Compare A PRIORI.
[Latin, from what comes after]

apostle (a-**poss**-'l) *noun*
1 any of the early Christian disciples, missionaries and teachers.
2 the founder of the Christian faith in any region or country.
3 any reformer, pioneer or leader of a cause: *He was respected as an apostle of freedom.*
Word Family apostolic (app-a-**stoll**-ik) *adjective* 1 *Christianity* of or relating to an apostle or apostles. 2 *Roman Catholicism* of or relating to the Pope, as successor to St Peter.
[Greek *apostolos* one sent forth]

apostrophe *noun*
a punctuation mark ('), which has two uses: to show that something belongs to someone, e.g. *Paul's pen*, or to show when letters have been missed out, e.g. *haven't* (= have not).

apothecaries' weight *noun*
a system of units of weight formerly used for drugs.

apothecary (a-**poth**-a-ka-ree) *noun* (*plural* **apothecaries**)
an old word for a chemist or pharmacist.

apotheosis (a-poth-i-o-sis) *noun* (*plural* **apotheoses**) (a-poth-i-o-seez)
1 the act of raising a person to the status of a god or saint.
2 the essence or perfect example of something: *She thinks table manners are the apotheosis of good breeding.*
[Greek *apo* from + *theos* a god]

appal (a-**pawl**) *verb* (**appals; appalling; appalled**)
to shock or fill with horror: *I was appalled at the news of her death.*
[Old French *apallir* to make or become pale]

apparatus (app-a-**ray**-tus) *noun* (*plural* **apparatuses**)
a set of instruments, machinery or appliances for a particular task.
Figurative *The apparatus of government is*

both costly and unwieldy (= organization, administration).
[Latin, instruments]

apparel (a-**parr**-'l) *noun*
any clothing or dress.

apparent (a-**parr**-'nt) *adjective*
1 clearly seen or understood: *It is quite apparent that you don't want to come.*
2 seeming: *Her confidence is apparent rather than real.*
Word Family **apparently** *adverb*.
[Latin *apparens* becoming visible]

apparition (app-a-**rish**-'n) *noun*
a sudden or frightening vision, especially of a ghost.

appeal (a-**peel**) *verb*
1 to call upon or make an earnest or desperate plea: *He appealed for help.*
2 to offer interest or attraction: *Does that book appeal to you?*
3 *Law* to apply for a case to be heard again by a higher court.
• **appeal** *noun*.
[Latin *appellare* to address, call by name]

appear (a-**peer**) *verb*
1 to become clear or visible: *The sun appeared at last.*
2 to seem to be: *Try not to appear frightened.*
3 to come or perform before the public: *The orchestra has appeared in several countries.*
[Latin *apparere* to become visible]

appearance *noun*
1 the act of appearing.
2 (**appearances**) any outward signs or indications: *You shouldn't judge by appearances.*
Phrases **keep up appearances** to maintain an acceptable outward show. **to all appearances** as far as could be seen: *He was to all appearances a wealthy man.*

appease (a-**peez**) *verb*
to quiet or calm, especially to placate someone who is hostile: *The employers tried to appease the workers by offering a bonus.*
Word Family **appeasement** *noun* 1 the act of appeasing. 2 *History* the policy used by Britain and France to deal with Hitler in the late 1930s.
[Old French *à pais* to peace]

appellation (app-a-**lay**-sh'n) *noun*
1 a name or title: *The official appellation is Your Excellency.*
2 the act of naming.
[Latin *appellare* to address, call by name]

append *verb*
(*formal*) to add, join or attach: *I hereby append my signature.*
Word Family **appendage** *noun* a subordinate or subsidiary part: *Only a biologist would refer to an arm as an appendage.* □ *He regarded his secretary as a mere appendage.*
[*ap-* + Latin *pendere* to hang]

appendectomy (app-en-**dek**-ta-mee) *noun* (*plural* **appendectomies**)
an operation to remove the appendix.
[APPENDIX + Greek *ektomé* a cutting out]

appendicitis (a-pen-di-**sigh**-tis) *noun*
an inflammation of the appendix causing severe abdominal pain, which may require the removal of the appendix.
[APPENDIX + *-itis*]

appendix *noun* (*plural* **appendices** (a-**pen**-di-seez) or **appendixes**)
1 *Anatomy* a small tube which is closed at one end and opens at the point where the small intestine joins the colon.
2 any material added at the end of a book, such as lists or tables.
[Latin, something added on]

appertain (app-a-**tane**) *verb*
to pertain, belong or relate to: *The facts appertaining to his dismissal were not mentioned.*
[*ap-* + PERTAIN]

appetite (**app**-i-tite) *noun*
a desire or craving, especially for food.
[Latin *appetitio* a desire]

appetizer, appetiser *noun*
any food or drink served before a meal to stimulate the appetite.

appetizing *adjective*
stimulating or appealing to the appetite: *an appetizing smell from the kitchen.*

applaud (a-**plawd**) *verb*
to express approval or praise by clapping.
Word Family **applause** *noun* clapping to show approval.
[*ap-* + Latin *plaudere* to clap hands]

apple *noun*
a round fruit with crisp firm flesh and a green, yellow or red skin.
Phrases **in apple-pie order** neatly arranged. **the apple of one's eye** a person specially loved by one: *John's youngest daughter is the apple of his eye.* **upset the apple cart** to spoil the plans: *Be careful not to upset the applecart.*

appliance (a-**ply**-ance) *noun*
a device designed for a special use,
especially a domestic device such as an
iron.

applicable (a-**plikk**-a-b'l) *adjective*
suitable or relevant: *That rule is not
applicable in this case.*
Word Family applicability (a-plik-a-
bill-it-ee) *noun*.

applicant (**ap**-li-k'nt) *noun*
a candidate or person who applies:
*Applicants for the position must supply
references.*

application *noun*
1 a request: *Further information will be
supplied on application to the organizers.*
□ *We regret to inform you that your
application has been unsuccessful.*
2 a thing applied, especially a preparation:
This application will soothe your sunburn.
3 the act of applying: *An application of this
cream will soothe your sunburn.*
4 any sustained effort or concentration:
She shows little application in science subjects.
5 *Computers* a piece of software for a
particular purpose.

applicator (**ap**-li-kay-ta) *noun*
an instrument for applying something,
such as a sponge used to apply make-up.

appliqué (a-**plee**-kay) *noun*
needlework that is ornamented by
applying pieces of material, etc. to a
surface.
[French, put on]

apply (a-**ply**) *verb* (**applies; applying;
applied**)
1 to put onto a surface: *Apply the glue
sparingly.*
2 to put into use: *I solved it by applying
common sense.*
3 to request or ask to be given: *20 people
have applied for the job.*
4 to have reference to: *The pay rise applies
to all employees.*
Phrase apply oneself to devote oneself:
He applied himself to the task with gusto.
Word Family applied *adjective* put into
or designed for practical use: *applied
maths.* Compare PURE (definition 2).
[Latin *applicare*]

appoint *verb*
1 to select for a post.
2 to equip: *a well-appointed study.*
Word Family appointee (a-poyn-**tee**)
noun a person who is appointed.

appointment *noun*
1 an arrangement to meet or visit: *I have
an appointment with the dentist at 2.30 p.m.*
2 an office or position to which a person is
appointed: *His new appointment is with the
Department of Trade.*

apportion (a-**por**-sh'n) *verb*
to divide or distribute evenly.
Word Family apportionment *noun*.

apposite (**app**-a-zit) *adjective*
particularly relevant or pertinent.
[Latin *appositus* appropriate]

appraise (a-**praze**) *verb*
to estimate the value, quality or price of
something.
Word Family appraisal *noun*.

appreciate (a-**pree**-shi-ate) *verb*
1 to value something highly: *I appreciate
your help more than I can say.*
2 to understand: *We appreciate your
reluctance to supply names.*
3 to rise in value: *This property has
appreciated greatly in the past year.*
Compare DEPRECIATE (definition 1).
Word Family appreciation (a-pree-shi-
ay-sh'n) *noun*; **appreciative** *adjective*;
appreciable *adjective* 1 noticeable.
2 fairly large.
[*ap-* + Latin *pretium* price]

apprehend (ap-ree-**hend**) *verb*
1 to arrest or seize a person: *He was
apprehended a week after the robbery.*
2 (*formal*) to grasp the meaning of
something: *She was quick to apprehend my
statement.*
Word Family apprehension *noun*
1 anxious anticipation: *We waited with some
apprehension.* 2 (*formal*) understanding.
3 (*formal*) the act of arresting someone.
[Latin *apprehendere* to seize]

apprehensive (ap-ree-**hen**-siv) *adjective*
fearful about something which may
happen.
Word Family apprehensively *adverb*.

apprentice (a-**pren**-tis) *noun*
1 a person who undertakes to work in a
trade for a specified period, in return for
instruction.
2 any learner or beginner.
Word Family apprentice *verb*;
apprenticeship *noun*.
[French *apprendre* to learn]

apprise (a-**prize**) *verb*
(*formal*) to inform: *He apprised me of the
fact that legal action would be taken.*
[French *appris* taught]

approach *verb*
1 to move nearer or draw near: *Approach the house cautiously.* □ *As dawn approached we made ready to leave.*
2 to make a request: *You should approach your local Member of Parliament about this problem.*
3 to begin or set about something: *I wouldn't approach the problem like that.*
● **approach** *noun* (*plural* **approaches**)
1 the act of approaching: *the approach of winter.*
2 (*often* **approaches**) an advance made to a person to gain interest or attention: *He has made approaches about buying the house.*
3 any way or means of access: *The approach to the camp site was densely overgrown.* □ *A practical approach is usually best.*
Word Family **approachable** *adjective*;
approachability *noun*.
[French *approcher*]

approbation (ap-ro-**bay**-sh'n) *noun*
(*formal*) approval: *He gave the scheme his approbation upon certain conditions.*
[*ap-* + Latin *probare* to approve]

appropriate (a-**pro**-pree-it) *adjective*
suitable or fitting: *an appropriate speech for the occasion.*
● **appropriate** (a-**pro**-pree-ate) *verb*
1 to set aside for a special purpose: *Funds for the new project have already been appropriated.*
2 to take, especially without permission: *His book, far from being original, merely appropriates my ideas.*
Word Family **appropriately** *adverb*,
appropriateness *noun*; **appropriation**
(a-pro-pree-**ay**-sh'n) *noun* **1** the act of appropriating. **2** something which has been appropriated.
[Latin *appropriatus* made one's own]

approval (a-**proo**-v'l) *noun*
1 any agreement or confirmation.
2 the act of approving.

approve (a-**proov**) *verb*
to agree to or consider as worthy, correct, etc.: *I do not approve of such behaviour.*
□ *The committee has officially approved the minutes.*
[*ap-* + Latin *probare* to approve]

approximate (a-**prok**-si-mit) *adjective*
nearly correct or accurate: *Just tell me the approximate price.*
● **approximate** (a-**prok**-si-mate) *verb* to approach or be nearly equal to.
Word Family **approximation** (a-prok-si-**may**-sh'n) *noun*; **approximately** *adverb*.
[*ap-* + Latin *proximus* nearest]

appurtenance (a-**per**-tin-ance) *noun*
something attached or belonging to another, more important, thing.

apricot (**ay**-pri-kot) *noun*
1 a small round fruit with orange flesh and a hard stone.
2 a yellowish-orange colour.
Word Family **apricot** *adjective*.

April *noun*
the fourth month of the year, after March and before May.
[Latin *Aprilis* the month of opening buds, from *aperire* to open]

a priori (ay pry-**aw**-rye) *adverb, adjective*
not based on fact, observation or study; deduced or presumed. Compare A POSTERIORI.
[Latin, from something prior]

apron (**ay**-pr'n) *noun*
1 a loose piece of clothing worn over clothes to protect them, usually tied at the back.
2 a paved area, especially on an airfield.
Phrase **tied to the apron strings** emotionally dependent.
[alteration of *a napron*, from Old French *nape* a tablecloth]

apropos (ap-ra-**po**) *adverb*
to the purpose: *That's hardly apropos to this discussion.*
Phrase **apropos of** with reference to: *Apropos of Judy Garland, who was her last husband?*
Word Family **apropos** *adjective*.
[French *à propos* to the purpose]

apse *noun*
Architecture a recess in a church, usually vaulted and semicircular.
[Greek *hapsis* an arch]

apt *adjective*
1 relevant or appropriate: *I think his criticism of the novel is very apt.*
2 having a tendency to: *She is apt to talk too much.*
3 intelligent or quick to learn: *an apt student in all subjects.*
Word Family **aptly** *adverb*; **aptness** *noun*.
[Latin *aptus* fitting]

aptitude *noun*
a natural ability or skill: *He has a great aptitude for maths.*

aqua ⇨ AQUAMARINE (definition 1).
[Latin, water]

aqualung (**ak**-wa-lung) *noun* also called **scuba**.
an apparatus of one or more cylinders of compressed air, used by a diver to breathe

underwater by means of a tube attached to a mouthpiece.

aquamarine (ak-wa-ma-**reen**) *noun*
1 short form is **aqua** a light bluish-green colour.
2 *Geology* a translucent pale blue or green variety of beryl, used as a gem.
Word Family **aquamarine** *adjective*.
[Latin *aqua marina* seawater]

aquanaut (ak-wa-nawt) *noun*
a skin-diver.
[Latin *aqua* water + *nauta* a sailor]

aquaplane (ak-wa-plane) *noun*
a single wide board used as a waterski.
• **aquaplane** *verb*.

aquarium (a-kwair-i-um) *noun* (*plural*
aquariums or **aquaria**)
a pond, tank or building in which living aquatic animals and plants are kept and displayed.

Aquarius (a-**kwair**-i-us) *noun*
Astrology a group of stars, the eleventh sign of the Zodiac; the sign of the Water Bearer.
[Latin, water carrier]

aquatic *adjective*
living or growing in or near water: *Seaweed is an aquatic plant.*
[Latin *aquaticus* watery]

aquatint (ak-wa-tint) *noun*
1 an etching process which gives an effect like a watercolour.
2 a print made by this process.
[Latin *aqua* water + TINT]

aqueduct (ak-wi-dukt) *noun*
an artificial channel for carrying water, e.g. on a bridge across a valley.
[Latin *aqua* water + *ductus* led]

aqueous (ay-kwee-us) *adjective*
relating to or containing water.

aqueous humour *noun*
Anatomy the thin clear fluid which fills the space at the front of the eye between the lens and the cornea. Compare VITREOUS HUMOUR.

aquiline *adjective*
(of a nose) curved or hooked like the beak of an eagle.
[Latin *aquila* eagle]

Arab *noun*
any of a breed of horses, originally from Arabia, noted for their speed and intelligence.
• **Arab** *adjective*.

arabesque (arr-a-besk) *noun*
1 *Ballet* a position with one leg raised backwards in the air and held straight.

2 an ornamental design of leaves, flowers and geometric figures, used in some Eastern architecture.

Arabic numerals *plural noun* also called
Arabic figures.
the numerical symbols, 1, 2, 3, 4, 5, 6, 7, 8, 9 and 0.

arable (arr-a-b'l) *adjective*
(of land) suitable for growing crops.
Compare PASTORAL *adjective* (definition **1**).
arable farming farming of arable land.
[Latin *arare* to plough]

arachnid (a-rak-nid) *noun*
any of various arthropods, such as spiders, mites, etc., with the body divided into two parts and having four pairs of walking legs.
Word Family **arachnoid** *adjective*.
[Greek *arachné* spider]

arbiter (ar-bitt-a) *noun*
1 a person who leads, decides or establishes: *French designers are the arbiters of fashion.*
2 an arbitrator.
[Latin]

arbitrary (ar-bit-ra-ree) *adjective*
1 based on personal opinion or whim rather than reason, etc.: *an arbitrary choice.*
2 despotic or tyrannical: *the arbitrary rule of a dictator.*
Word Family **arbitrarily** *adverb*;
arbitrariness *noun*.

arbitrate *verb*
to judge or decide, especially in order to settle a dispute.
Word Family **arbitrator, arbiter** *noun* a person appointed to settle disputes;
arbitration *noun*.
[Latin *arbitrari*]

arboreal (ar-baw-ri-ul) *adjective*
of, like or adapted to living in trees:
A squirrel is an arboreal rodent.

arbour (ar-ba) *noun* (*American* **arbor**)
a shady place among trees, especially in a garden.
[Latin *arbor* a tree]

arc (ark) *noun*
1 any part of the circumference of a circle or other curved line.
2 anything shaped like an arc.
3 *Electricity* a continuous electric discharge across a gap, producing an intense light, as in an arc lamp.
• **arc** *verb* to form an electric arc.
[Latin *arcus* a bow or arch]

arcade *noun*
1 a series of arches.
2 a covered hall or passage, often with shops on one or both sides.
3 ⇨ AMUSEMENT ARCADE.

Arcadian (ar-**kay**-dee-an) *adjective*
simple, peaceful or innocent.
[after *Arcadia*, a region in ancient Greece regarded as the ideal of rural contentment]

arcane *adjective*
secret or mysterious.
[Latin *arcanus* hidden]

arch¹ *noun* (*plural* **arches**)
1 a curved supporting structure over an opening.
2 something with the shape or function of an arch, such as the curved lower part of the human foot.
3 *Geography* an opening in a rock, often produced by erosion by the sea or wind.
• **arch** *verb*
1 to form an arch or curve.
2 to supply with an arch.
[Latin *arcus* an arch]

arch² *adjective*
1 chief or most important: *an arch enemy*.
2 mischievous or cunning in a playful way: *He gave her an arch glance.*
Word Family **archly** *adverb* slyly.
[Greek *arkhos* chief]

archaeology (ar-ki-**oll**-a-jee) *noun*
the study of history, especially ancient cultures, by digging up and describing remains, such as buildings, coins, etc.
Word Family **archaeologist** *noun*
archaeological (ar-ki-a-**lojj**-i-k'l)
adjective.
[Greek *arkhaios* ancient + *-logy*]

archaic (ar-**kay**-ik) *adjective*
being from long ago and therefore not in modern use: *Alarum is an archaic word.*
Word Family **archaism** (ar-**kay**-izm)
noun.
[Greek *arkhaios* ancient]

archangel (**ark**-ane-j'l) *noun*
an angel of the highest rank.
[ARCH² + ANGEL]

archbishop *noun*
Christianity a bishop of the highest rank.

archdeacon *noun*
Christianity a church administrative official next below a bishop.

archdiocese (arch-**die**-a-sis) *noun*
Christianity the area under the control of an archbishop.

archduke *noun*
History a supreme prince in Austria.
Word Family **archduchess** *noun* (*plural* **archduchesses**) 1 a female archduke.
2 the wife of an archduke.

archer *noun*
a person who shoots with a bow and arrow, especially for sport.
[Latin *arcus* a bow]

archery *noun*
the sport of shooting with bows and arrows.

archetype (**ar**-ki-tipe) *noun*
a first perfect type or form from which copies, usually inferior, may be made.
Word Family **archetypal** (ar-ki-**tie**-p'l)
adjective.
[ARCH² + TYPE]

archipelago (ar-ki-**pell**-a-go) *noun* (*plural* **archipelagos** or **archipelagoes**)
1 a large group of islands.
2 a sea which contains a large group of islands.
[ARCH² + Greek *pelagos* sea]

architect (**ar**-ki-tekt) *noun*
1 a person trained in architecture.
2 a person who plans, designs or constructs: *the architect of the revolution.*

architecture (**ar**-ki-tek-cher) *noun*
1 the art or science of designing buildings.
2 a particular style of building: *Gothic architecture.*
Word Family **architectural** (ar-ki-**tek**-cher-'l) *adjective;* **architecturally** *adverb.*
[ARCH² + Greek *tekton* a builder]

architrave (**ar**-ki-trave) *noun*
a decorative moulding around an opening, such as a doorway.
[ARCH² + Latin *trabs* a beam]

archives (**ar**-kives) *plural noun*
1 any public documents or historical records relating to a particular organization or country.
2 the place where such records are kept.
Word Family **archivist** (**ar**-ki-vist) *noun.*
[Greek *arkheion* a law court]

archway *noun*
1 the passage beneath an arch.
2 an arch forming an entrance, etc.

arc lamp *noun*
a lamp which uses an electric arc as its source of light.

Arctic *adjective*
at or near the North Pole.
● **Arctic** *noun* the Arctic regions.
[Greek *arktos* the (Great) Bear]

Arctic Circle *noun*
a line drawn on a map showing the most
southerly point at which the sun does not
set on one day of the year, at about 66°30′
north.

ardent (**ar**-d'nt) *adjective*
full of ardour or enthusiasm.
Word Family **ardently** *adverb*.

ardour (**ar**-da) *noun* (*American* **ardor**)
an eagerness or passion: *She has a great
ardour for work.*
[Latin *ardor* fire]

arduous (**ard**-yew-us) *adjective*
requiring great effort or energy.
Word Family **arduously** *adverb*.
[Latin *arduus* steep, laborious]

are[1] (ar) *verb*
1 the second person singular present tense
of **be**: *You are a doctor, aren't you?*
2 the plural present tense of **be**: *We are
Irish.*

are[2] (ar) *noun*
a unit of area, equal to 100 m².

area (**air**-i-a) *noun*
1 the surface measurement: *What is the
area of the paddock?*
2 a particular extent or piece of land: *This
is a rural area.*
3 the scope of an activity, operation or
concept: *His skills cover a wide area of
human accomplishments.*
[Latin]

arena (a-**ree**-na) *noun*
1 a field or space set aside for sports,
contests, etc.
2 any area of activity, conflict, etc.:
He entered the arena of politics.

> The word **arena** is associated with
> competition. In its literal sense it refers
> to an enclosure for sports contests. In
> its figurative sense it deals with areas
> involving some dispute, such as 'the
> political arena'. This association
> between competition and contest goes
> back to ancient Rome when gladiators
> fought each other in amphitheatres.
> The centre of the amphitheatre, where
> the gladiators fought, was covered in
> sand to soak up the blood shed in the
> fight. *Arena* is the Latin for 'sand' and
> the contest area came to be called *arena*
> as well. Later it came to mean the
> whole enclosure.

aren't *contraction*
a short form of **are not**: *These shoes aren't
mine.*

areola (a-**ree**-a-la) *noun* (*plural* **areolae**)
(a-**ree**-a-lee)
Anatomy a darkened circle around a
centre, e.g. around the human nipple.
[Latin, a small area]

arête (a-**rate**) *noun*
a sharp mountain ridge.
[French, a fish-bone or ridge]

argent (**arj**-'nt) *adjective*
an old word for silver.
[Latin *argentum*]

argon *noun*
a colourless odourless inert gas found in
the earth's atmosphere and used in electric
light bulbs, fluorescent tubes, etc.
[Greek *argos* idle]

argosy (**ar**-ga-see) *noun* (*plural* **argosies**)
1 a large merchant ship.
2 a fleet of such ships.

argot (**ar**-go) *noun*
the particular language or vocabulary of a
group, especially of thieves or vagabonds.
[French]

arguable (**ar**-gew-a-b'l) *adjective*
1 capable of being maintained or asserted.
2 open to dispute or argument.
Word Family **arguably** *adverb*.

argue (**ar**-gew) *verb* (**argues; arguing;
argued**)
1 to give reasons for or against something:
*They argued about the method they should
use.*
2 to exchange angry words: *They argued
about the money.*
[Latin *argutari* to prattle]

argument (**ar**-gew-m'nt) *noun*
1 the act of arguing.
2 a series of reasons given to explain or
prove.
3 a theme or subject: *The introduction sets
out the book's argument.*
Word Family **argumentative** (ar-gew-
men-ta-tiv) *adjective* fond of arguing;
argumentatively *adverb*.

aria (**ar**-ee-a) *noun*
an opera song for one person.
[Italian]

arid (**arr**-id) *adjective*
very dry: *the arid Sahara desert.*
*Figurative What an arid and unrewarding
task!* (= dull, uninteresting).
Word Family **aridity** (a-**ridd**-i-tee),
aridness *noun*.
[Latin *aridus* parched]

Aries (air-eez) *noun*
Astrology a group of stars, the first sign of the Zodiac; the sign of the Ram.
[Latin, ram]

aright *adverb*
an old word meaning 'properly' or 'correctly'.

arise *verb* (**arises; arising; arose** (a-**rose**); **arisen** (a-**rizz**-'n))
1 to appear or come into existence, especially as a result of something: *New problems may arise during your investigations.*
2 to get up or move upwards.

aristocracy (arr-iss-**tok**-ra-see) *noun* (*plural* **aristocracies**)
1 the upper or privileged classes, usually hereditary.
2 the governing of a state or country by the aristocracy.
3 any superior group or class.
Word Family **aristocrat** (**arr**-is-ta-krat) *noun* **1** a member of the aristocracy.
2 a person who has the tastes, manners, etc. considered characteristic of the aristocracy; **aristocratic** (arr-is-ta-**kratt**-ik) *adjective*; **aristocratically** *adverb*
[Greek *aristos* best + *kratia* rule]

arithmetic (a-**rith**-ma-tik) *noun*
the branch of maths which studies numbers and their combination, using addition, subtraction, multiplication and division.
Word Family **arithmetic** (arr-ith-**mett**-ik) *adjective*, **arithmetical** *adjective*, **arithmetician** (arr-ith-ma-**tish**-'n) *noun*.
[Greek *arithmos* number]

ark *noun*
(*often* **Ark**) the boat built by Noah in order to survive the biblical Flood.
[Latin *arca* cupboard]

arm¹ *noun*
1 *Anatomy* the part of the body between the elbow and the shoulder.
2 *Anatomy* the entire limb from the wrist to the shoulder.
3 the part of a garment covering the arm.
4 something which has the shape or function of an arm: *the arm of a chair.*
Figurative An arm of the sea flows inland (= branch, division).
Phrases **at arm's length** *She kept him at arm's length* (= at a distance, from undue familiarity). **twist someone's arm** to put pressure on someone to do as one wishes.

arm² *noun*
1 (*usually* **arms**) any weapons.
2 ⇨ COAT OF ARMS.

Phrase **up in arms** (*informal*) protesting very strongly.
● **arm** *verb* to equip with weapons.
Figurative You must arm yourself against boredom (= prepare; equip).

armada (ar-**mah**-da) *noun*
a large fleet of warships.
[Spanish *armata* navy]

armadillo (arm-a-**dill**-o) *noun*
a burrowing South American mammal which is covered with bony plates like armour.
[Spanish, the little armoured thing]

Armageddon (arm-a-**ged**-'n) *noun*
1 *Christianity* the site of the final battle between good and evil which will mark the end of the world.
2 any large-scale international war.

armament (**arm**-a-m'nt) *noun*
(*often* **armaments**) the weapons with which a military unit, vehicle, etc. is equipped.

armature (**arm**-a-cher) *noun*
1 *Electricity* a piece of metal connecting the poles of a magnet.
2 *Electricity* the movable part of a dynamo or electric motor, consisting essentially of coils of wire wound around an iron core.
3 *Sculpture* a framework used as a support for wet clay.
[Latin *armatura* equipment]

armchair *noun*
a comfortable chair with supports for the arms.
● **armchair** *adjective* lacking direct or active involvement: *an armchair critic.*

armed *adjective*
having a weapon, especially a gun: *armed guards.*

armistice (**arm**-i-stis) *noun*
a temporary peace agreement between countries.
[Latin *arma* arms + *sistere* to stop]

armorial *adjective*
of or relating to heraldry.
[Latin *arma* arms]

armour (**ar**-ma) *noun* (*American* **armor**)
1 any protective covering, such as chain mail for the body, steel plating on battleships, etc.
2 anything which protects or keeps something safe.
Word Family **armour** *verb* to fit with armour; **armourer** *noun* a person who makes or sells armour or weapons.
[Latin *arma* arms]

armour plate *noun*
a sheet of hardened steel used on vehicles for protection.

armoury (**arm**-a-ree) *noun* (*plural* **armouries**) (*American* **armory**)
a place where weapons and military equipment are stored.

armpit *noun* also called **axilla**.
Anatomy the hollow beneath the shoulder, where the arm joins the trunk.

army *noun* (*plural* **armies**)
1 an organized group trained and equipped to fight on land.
2 any large organized group: *We need an army of cleaners.*

aroma (a-**ro**-ma) *noun*
a sweet or pleasant smell.
Word Family aromatic (arr-a-**matt**-ik) *adjective* having a sweet or pleasant smell.
[Greek, spice]

aromatherapy (a-roam-a-**therr**-a-pee) *noun*
the use of essential oils and plant extracts, in massage, inhalation or baths, to promote physical and mental well-being.
Word Family aromatherapist *noun*.

arose (a-**rose**) the past tense of **arise**.

around *adverb, preposition*
1 on all sides of: *There were people all around us.*
2 from one place to another of: *We walked around the city.*
3 at approximately: *I'll meet you around one o'clock.*
4 near: *We had to stay around the camp site.*

arouse (a-**rowze**) *verb*
to wake or stir up: *His behaviour aroused her suspicions.*
Word Family arousal *noun*.

arpeggio (ar-**pejj**-ee-o) *noun*
Music the playing of the notes of a chord in quick succession instead of at the same time.
[Italian]

arraign (a-**rane**) *verb*
to accuse or put on trial.
Word Family arraignment *noun*.
[French *arraigner*]

arrange (a-**range**) *verb*
1 to set in a certain or proper order: *Arrange those chairs around the table.*
2 to prepare, organize: *Who will arrange the details of the trip?*
3 to agree or settle: *We arranged to meet later.*

4 *Music* to adapt: *He arranged this composition for an orchestra.*
Word Family arrangement *noun* 1 the act of arranging. 2 something which has been arranged: *a flower arrangement.* □ *party arrangements.*

arrant (**arr**-'nt) *adjective*
(*formal*) complete or thorough: *arrant nonsense.*

arras *noun* (*plural* **arrases**)
a tapestry, often used as a wall hanging.
[after *Arras*, France, where first made]

array (a-**ray**) *verb*
1 to place in order or position: *The tribes arrayed themselves against the army.*
2 to clothe or adorn: *The bride was arrayed in white.*
● **array** *noun* a large number: *an array of toys.*

arrears (a-**reerz**) *plural noun*
1 something which still remains to be paid, fulfilled, etc.
2 the state of being behind with something which is owing or due: *Our rent is three months in arrears.*

arrest (a-**rest**) *verb*
1 to take a person into legal charge or keeping.
2 to stop or catch: *Her words arrested our attention.*
● **arrest** *noun*.

arrive (a-**rive**) *verb*
to reach or be reached: *The hour of reckoning arrived.* □ *At last we arrived at a decision.*
Word Family arrival *noun* 1 the act of arriving or reaching. 2 something which has arrived.

arrogant (**arr**-a-g'nt) *adjective*
overbearingly proud: *His arrogant manner made him unpopular.*
Word Family arrogantly *adverb*; **arrogance** *noun*.

arrogate (**arr**-a-gate) *verb*
to assume or claim without right: *He arrogated to himself the position of leader.*
[Latin *arrogare* to claim by right]

arrow *noun*
1 a long slender shaft with a point at one end and often feathers at the other, shot from a bow as a missile.
2 something with the shape of an arrow, especially a sign used to indicate direction.

arrowroot *noun*
a starch derived from the roots of an American plant, used in cooking.

arsenal (ar-sa-n'l) *noun*
a place where weapons and ammunition are manufactured or stored.
[from Arabic, factory]

arsenic (ar-s'n-ik) *noun*
a brittle metal which is highly poisonous and whose compounds are used in insecticides and weedkillers.
[Arabic]

arson (ar-s'n) *noun*
Law the act of deliberately burning or setting fire to something, especially a building.
Word Family **arsonist** *noun*.

art[1] *noun*
1 any objects or activities in which people express feelings and ideas about life by giving them some imaginative form.
2 a particular skill or ability: *the art of diplomacy*.
3 (**arts**) ⇨ HUMANITIES.
[Latin *ars* skilled work]

art[2] the old form of the second person singular present tense of **be**.

art deco (art dek-oh) *noun*
a style of art, architecture, and design which is characterized by geometric shapes. Art deco was particularly popular in the 1930s.
[from French *art décoratif* decorative art]

artefact (art-i-fakt) *noun* also **artifact**
anything made by people for their own use.
[Latin *arte* by skill + *factus* made]

arteriosclerosis (ar-tee-ri-o-skla-**ro**-sis) *noun*
a disease of the arteries causing a reduced flow of blood due to a thickening of vessel walls.
[ARTERY + SCLEROSIS]

artery (art-a-ree) *noun* (*plural* **arteries**)
1 *Anatomy* any of the thick-walled tubes carrying oxygenated blood away from the heart to other parts of the body. Compare CAPILLARY; VEIN (definition 1).
2 a major road or similar part in a system of communication or transport.
Word Family **arterial** (ar-tee-ri-al) *adjective*.
[Greek *arteria* the windpipe]

artesian well (ar-tee-*zh*'n well) *noun*
a well in which water rises, under pressure, above the level of the water-bearing rock to the earth's surface.
[Latin *Artesium* Artois, the region of France where the Romans sank wells]

artful *adjective*
sly or crafty.
Word Family **artfully** *adverb*; **artfulness** *noun*.

art house *noun*
a cinema which shows artistic films rather than mainstream films.

arthritis (ar-**thry**-tis) *noun*
an inflammation of the joints causing pain and difficulty in movement.
Word Family **arthritic** (ar-**thritt**-ik) *adjective, noun*.
[Greek *arthron* joint + -*itis*]

arthropod (ar-thra-pod) *noun*
any of a large group of segmented invertebrate animals, such as insects and spiders, with jointed legs and sometimes a hard external skeleton.
[Greek *arthron* joint + *podos* of a foot]

artichoke ⇨ GLOBE ARTICHOKE, JERUSALEM ARTICHOKE.
[Arabic]

article *noun*
1 an individual thing or object.
2 *Grammar* any of three words (*a, an* or *the*) used before a noun.
3 a piece of writing which gives information or an opinion and forms part of a magazine, newspaper, etc.: *an article on paragliding*.
4 *Law* a section of a document.
5 (**articles**) *Law* a document, especially a contract: *the articles of apprenticeship*.
definite article *Grammar* the word *the*, used before a noun to indicate a particular person or thing: *The boy was happy*.
indefinite article *Grammar* the word *a* or *an*, used before a noun without specifying which particular thing: *I would like a new car*.
• **article** *verb Law* to bind by articles.

articled clerk *noun*
a person training in a solicitor's office.

articulate (ar-**tik**-yoo-lit) *adjective*
1 clear in one's speech or expression.
2 able to speak.
• **articulate** (ar-**tik**-yoo-late) *verb*
1 to pronounce words distinctly.
2 to unite by a joint or joints.
Word Family **articulateness** *noun* the quality of being articulate; **articulately** *adverb*; **articulation** (ar-tik-yoo-**lay**-sh'n) *noun* the act of articulating.
[Latin *articulare* to divide into joints]

artifact ⇨ ARTEFACT.

artifice (ar-ti-fis) *noun*
1 a clever trick or device.
2 trickery.
[Latin *arte* by skill + *facere* to make]

artificial (ar-ti-**fish**-'l) *adjective*
made as an imitation, as distinct from
being natural: *They only sell artificial
flowers.*
Figurative *Her artificial smile did not fool
any of us* (= false, affected).
Word Family artificially *adverb*;
artificiality (ar-ti-fish-i-**al**-i-tee) *noun.*

artificial insemination *noun*
the placing of sperm in a female to make
her pregnant without direct sexual
contact.

artificial intelligence *noun*
Computers the ability to imitate intelligent
human behaviour.

artillery (ar-**till**-a-ree) *noun*
1 any large-calibre guns, such as cannons,
howitzers, etc.
2 the branch of an army which uses such
guns.
• **artillery** *adjective*.
[from Old French, equipment]

artisan (ar-ti-**zan** *or* ar-ti-zan) *noun*
a trained or skilled manual worker.

artist *noun*
1 a painter, sculptor or other person who
creates works of art.
2 also **artiste** (ar-**teest**) an entertainer,
especially a singer or dancer.
Word Family artistic (ar-**tist**-ik)
adjective of or characteristic of art or
artists; **artistically** *adverb*.

artistry *noun*
the degree of skill in practising an art.

artless *adjective*
free from deceit or cunning.
Word Family artlessly *adverb*;
artlessness *noun.*

art nouveau (ar noo-**vo**) *noun*
a decorative art style used from about
1890 to 1910.
[French, new art]

artwork *noun*
any illustrations or extra material to be
added to the text of a book, magazine, etc.

arty *adjective* (**artier; artiest**)
(*informal*) interested in the arts.

arvo *noun*
Australian afternoon.

as *adverb*
1 to the amount or degree that: *Hard as he
tries, he never wins.*
2 for example: *cities such as London and
Paris.*
• **as** *conjunction*
1 when or while: *As we approached, the door
opened.*

2 because: *As he was late, we could not start.*
3 like or in the manner of: *quick as
lightning.*
• **as** *preposition* in the function or position
of: *Let this serve as a warning.*
Phrases as for, as to with regard to:
As for his work, nothing more can be said.
as it were in some way.

asbestos (az-**best**-os) *noun*
a heat-resistant fibrous mineral used to
make fireproof and heatproof articles.
[from Greek]

ascend (a-**send**) *verb*
to rise or climb: *He carefully ascended the
ladder.*
Word Family ascent *noun* 1 the act of
ascending. 2 an upward slope or gradient;
Ascension *noun* the event, believed by
Christians, of Jesus' ascent to heaven 40
days after his resurrection.
[Latin *ascendere* to climb]

ascendant (a-**sen**-d'nt) *noun* also
ascendent
1 a position of influence, control, etc.: *By
now Socialism was in the ascendant.*
2 *Astrology* the sign of the zodiac which is
above the horizon at the time of a person's
birth.
• **ascendant** *adjective*
1 having influence, power or control.
2 rising: *an ascendant star.*
Word Family ascendance, ascendancy
noun a governing or controlling influence.

ascertain (ass-a-**tane**) *verb*
to find out: *We must ascertain the true facts.*
Word Family ascertainable *adjective.*

ascetic (a-**sett**-ik) *adjective*
severely strict and self-denying.
• **ascetic** *noun* a person who practises
strict self-denial.
Word Family ascetically *adverb*;
asceticism (a-**sett**-i-sizm) *noun.*
[Greek *asketes* a hermit]

> ! Do not confuse *ascetic* with
> *aesthetic*. *Aesthetic* means 'relating
> to the appreciation of beauty', as in *the
> aesthetic appeal of the scene.*

ascorbic acid (a-**skaw**-bik **ass**-id) *noun*
vitamin C.
[*a*- + medieval Latin *scorbutus* scurvy]

ascribe (a-**scribe**) *verb*
to attribute: *That discovery is ascribed to a
German scientist.*
Word Family ascribable *adjective*;
ascription (a-**skrip**-sh'n) *noun.*
[Latin *ascribere*]

aseptic (ay-**sep**-tik) *adjective*
free from living germs, etc.
[*a-* + SEPTIC]

asexual (ay-**seks**-yoo-al) *adjective*
1 having no sex or sexual organs.
2 unrelated to sex or sexual processes.
Word Family asexually *adverb*;
asexuality (ay-seks-yoo-**al**-it-ee) *noun*.
[*a-* + SEXUAL]

ash¹ *noun* (*plural* **ashes**)
1 the powdery remains of anything which
has been burnt: *cigarette ash*.
2 *Geology* the fine particles sent up by an
erupting volcano.
3 (**ashes**) any ruins or remains, especially
of a human body after cremation.
Ash Wednesday *Christianity* the first day
of Lent. In some churches penitents
receive the sign of the cross in ashes on
their foreheads.
Word Family ashy *adjective*.

ash² *noun* (*plural* **ashes**)
any of a group of trees with grey bark and
hard tough wood used for timber.

ashamed *adjective*
1 feeling shame or guilt.
2 unwilling through fear of shame: *Don't be
ashamed to confess your mistakes*.
Word Family ashamedly (a-**shame**-id-
lee) *adverb*.

ashen (**ash**-'n) *adjective*
grey or pale: *Her face was ashen with fear*.

ashore (a-**shore**) *adverb*
on or to land: *They went ashore from the
boat*.

ashtray *noun*
a small dish or bowl for tobacco ash.

aside *adverb*
on or to one side: *Put aside some money for
the holiday*.
• **aside** *noun* a word or words spoken so
that only certain people will hear.

asinine (**ass**-i-nine) *adjective*
silly or stupid.
Word Family asininity (ass-i-**ninn**-i-tee)
noun; **asininely** *adverb*.
[Latin *asinus* ass]

ask *verb*
1 to seek a reply or response from or
concerning: *Don't ask me!* □ *May I ask how
old you are?*
2 to invite: *We asked them to come tomorrow*.
3 to require: *This job will ask for all your
concentration*.
4 to act in such a way as to bring: *He is
asking for trouble*.

askance (a-**skance**) *adverb*
with a sideways glance.
Figurative *Our sister looked askance at our
plan* (= with disapproval or mistrust).

askew (a-**skew**) *adverb*
crooked or out of position.

asleep (a-**sleep**) *adverb*, *adjective*
in or into a state of sleep.
Figurative *My foot is asleep* (= numb).

asp *noun*
any of various small poisonous snakes,
such as the Egyptian viper.
[Greek *aspis*]

asparagus (a-**sparr**-a-gus) *noun*
the long edible soft-tipped shoots of a
plant related to the lily.
[Greek *aspharagos*]

aspect (**ass**-pekt) *noun*
1 a particular view of a subject, situation,
etc.: *We must consider all aspects of the
matter*.
2 the view or direction to which something
faces: *The front rooms have a northerly
aspect*.
3 (*formal*) the appearance of something.
4 also called **configuration**. *Astrology* the
position of a star or group of stars in
relation to others, which affects its
influence on events.
5 *Grammar* the way a verb changes to show
whether the action is complete or in
progress.
[Latin *aspectus* a view]

aspen *noun*
a kind of poplar tree whose leaves quiver
even in a light breeze.

asperity (a-**sperr**-i-tee) *noun*
a harshness or severity: *She spoke with
asperity*.
[Latin *asper* rough, biting]

aspersion (a-**sper**-sh'n) *noun*
(*often* **aspersions**) any unkind or
damaging criticism: *Do not cast aspersions
on his character*.
[Latin *aspersus* bespattered]

asphalt (**ass**-falt) *noun* also called
tarmac.
a black sticky substance which is a mixture
of bitumen and small stones, used for road
surfaces, etc.
• **asphalt** *verb*.
[Greek *asphaltos* bitumen]

asphyxiate (ass-**fik**-si-ate) *verb*
to produce difficulty in breathing,
unconsciousness or death through a lack
of oxygen.

Word Family asphyxia *noun* the severe condition caused by a lack of oxygen; **asphyxiation** (ass-fik-si-**ay**-sh'n) *noun*.
[Greek *asphyxia* a stopping of the pulse]

aspic *noun*
a clear savoury jelly made of meat, fish or vegetable stock, and often gelatine.
[French]

aspidistra (asp-i-**dist**-ra) *noun*
an evergreen Chinese plant with broad pointed leaves, usually grown indoors.

aspirate (**asp**-a-rate) *verb*
Language to begin a word or syllable with an *h* sound, as in *hiss* or *hit*.
• **aspirate** (**asp**-a-rit) *noun* the sound of the letter *h*.

aspiration (asp-a-**ray**-sh'n) *noun*
1 an eager desire or ambition: *His greatest aspiration is to become a politician.*
2 the act of aspirating.
Word Family aspirational *adjective*.

aspire (a-**spire**) *verb*
to seek or desire ambitiously: *She aspires after wealth.*
Word Family aspirant *noun* a person who aspires to or seeks a position.
[Latin *aspirare* to pant after]

aspirin (**ass**-prin) *noun*
a white crystalline drug, used to relieve pain, fever, etc.

ass *noun* (*plural* **asses**)
1 a donkey.
2 (*informal*) a stupid person.

assail (a-**sail**) *verb*
to attack or overcome: *She was assailed by doubts.*

assailant *noun*
an attacker: *The victim of the attack could not identify her assailant.*
Word Family assailable *adjective*.
[Latin *assilire* to leap upon]

The word **assassin** has moved quite far away from its origin. It is derived from the Arabic word *hashshashin* meaning 'eaters of the drug hashish or cannabis'. They were a fanatical sect of Muslims who conducted a campaign of terror in Persia and Syria against their enemies during the Crusades. Before going out to commit murders they are said to have drugged themselves with cannabis. The *hashshashin* tended to commit murders for political rather than personal reasons, which is often true of modern assassins also.

assassin (a-**sass**-in) *noun*
a person who murders another, especially for political reasons.
Word Family assassinate *verb* to kill deliberately and violently, especially for political reasons; **assassination** (a-sass-i-**nay**-sh'n) *noun*.

assault (a-**sawlt**) *verb*
1 to attack violently.
2 *Law* to threaten or attempt to injure another person.
• **assault** *noun* the act of assaulting.

assay (a-**say**) *verb*
1 to analyse a mixture, especially to estimate the metal content in ores.
2 to test: *He assayed his strength.*
• **assay** *noun*.
[French *essai* a trial or sample]

assegai (**ass**-i-guy) *noun*
a light spear or javelin used by the Bantu peoples of southern Africa.
[from Arabic, spear]

assemblage (a-**sem**-blij) *noun*
a collection of people or things.

assemble (a-**sem**-b'l) *verb*
1 to meet or gather: *Let's assemble outside the hall.*
2 to put together: *to assemble a model aeroplane.*

assembly (a-**sem**-blee) *noun* (*plural* **assemblies**)
1 a group of people gathered together for a particular purpose: *a legislative assembly.*
2 the putting together of something, especially parts of machines, etc.

assembly line *noun*
a line of workers, machines, etc. in a factory, along which a product passes to be assembled in stages.

assent (a-**sent**) *verb*
to agree.
• **assent** *noun*.
[Latin *assentiri* to agree with]

assert (a-**sert**) *verb*
to claim positively: *He still asserts his innocence.*
Phrase assert oneself to insist on one's rights, put oneself forward: *You must assert yourself in business matters.*
Word Family assertion (a-**ser**-sh'n) *noun*; **assertive** *adjective* dogmatic; **assertively** *adverb*; **assertiveness** *noun*.
[Latin *assertus* claimed]

assess (a-**sess**) *verb*
1 to estimate or judge: *Let's assess the situation.*

2 to work out or estimate an amount to be paid, a value, etc.
Word Family assessor *noun* a person appointed to assess or advise; **assessment** *noun.*
[Latin *assessor* one who sits by]

asset (ass-et) *noun*
1 anything which is useful or valuable: *An alert mind is a great asset.*
2 (*usually* **assets**) any property with money value.
[*ad-* + Latin *satis* enough]

asset-stripping *noun*
the selling off of a company's assets so as to make maximum profit, without concern for the future of the company.

assiduous (a-sid-yew-us) *adjective*
diligent or hard-working.
Word Family assiduity (ass-i-**dew**-i-tee), **assiduousness** *noun*; **assiduously** *adverb.*
[Latin *assiduus* continually present]

assign (a-sine) *verb*
1 to appoint or allocate: *We must assign a day for the next meeting.*
2 *Law* to transfer property, or property rights.

assignation (ass-ig-**nay**-sh'n) *noun*
an appointment to meet, especially between lovers.
[Latin *assignare* to allot]

assignment (a-sine-m'nt) *noun*
1 the act of assigning.
2 a particular task or duty: *a homework assignment.*

assimilate (a-simm-i-late) *verb*
to absorb, especially into a system: *The immigrants were assimilated into their new society.*
Word Family assimilation (a-simm-i-**lay**-sh'n) *noun*; **assimilable** *adjective.*
[*ad-* + Latin *similis* similar]

assist *verb*
to help or support.
Word Family assistant *noun* a helper; **assistant** *adjective*; **assistance** *noun* help.
[Latin *assidere* to sit by]

assize (a-size) *noun*
(*usually* **assizes**) *Law* a court in session.
[Latin *assidere* to sit by]

associate (a-so-she-ate) *verb*
1 to connect, as in the mind: *I associate swimming with summer.*
2 to spend one's time: *He associates with some odd people.*
● **associate** (a-**so**-she-it *or* a-**so**-see-ut) *noun*

1 a partner or colleague.
2 a person who is granted partial membership of an organization.
[*ad-* + Latin *socius* an ally]

association *noun*
1 a group of people joined or organized together for a common purpose.
2 the act of associating: *the association of ideas.*
3 the state of being associated: *working in close association with my publisher.*

assonance (ass-a-n'nce) *noun*
a similarity between sounds, especially the repeating of vowel sounds in the words of a line of poetry, etc., as in *dream team.*
[*ad-* + Latin *sonus* sound]

assort (a-sort) *verb*
to arrange or classify according to size, kind, etc.
Word Family assorted *adjective* of different sorts or kinds: *assorted chocolates*; **assortment** *noun* 1 the act of assorting.
2 a mixed collection.

assuage (a-swayj) *verb*
to satisfy or make less severe: *What will assuage my thirst?*
[*ad-* + Latin *suavis* pleasant]

assume *verb*
1 to suppose to be a fact, especially without proof: *Let us assume you are right.*
2 to take on: *He assumed command of the group.*
Word Family assumption (a-**sump**-sh'n) *noun* 1 the act of assuming.
2 something which is assumed: *That is an assumption, not a fact.*

assurance (a-sure-'nce) *noun*
1 a positive declaration that something will be done, etc.: *He has given his assurance of payment.*
2 a confidence or courage, especially in oneself.
3 insurance, especially life insurance.

assure (a-sure) *verb*
1 to convince or tell earnestly: *He assured us that he would return.*
2 to make sure or secure: *Our victory is assured.*
Word Family assuredly (a-sure-id-lee) *adverb.*

astatine (as-ta-teen) ⇨ HALOGEN.

aster *noun*
any of a large group of flowering plants, of which the best known is the Michaelmas daisy.
[Greek, star]

asterisk (**ass**-ta-risk) *noun*
a mark (*) used beside a word in writing or printing, to refer the reader to a footnote, etc.
[Greek *asteriskos* small star]

astern (a-stern) *adverb, adjective*
Nautical behind or at the back.

asteroid (**ast**-a-royd) *noun*
1 also called **planetoid**. any of a vast number of small planetary bodies all less than 500 km in diameter orbiting the sun.
2 any organism with a body shaped like a star, such as a starfish.
[Greek *aster* a star + -*oid*]

asthma (**ass**-ma) *noun*
a disorder due to narrowing of air passages, causing shortness of breath and wheezing.
Word Family **asthmatic** (ass-**mat**-ik) *adjective* of or suffering from asthma; **asthmatic** *noun*; **asthmatically** *adverb*.
[Greek, panting]

astigmatism (a-**stig**-ma-tizm) *noun*
a faulty deflection of light rays producing poor focusing or vision in an eye, lens, etc.
Word Family **astigmatic** (a-stig-**mat**-tik) *adjective*.
[*a*- + Greek *stigmatos* of a point]

astir (a-**ster**) *adjective, adverb*
moving or in motion: *The village was astir with excitement.*
Figurative He was astir very early (= out of bed).

astonish *verb*
to surprise greatly: *We were astonished at the news.*
Word Family **astonishment** *noun*; **astonishing** *adjective*; **astonishingly** *adverb*.

astound *verb*
to overcome with amazement.
Word Family **astounding** *adjective*; **astoundingly** *adverb*.

astrakhan (**ast**-ra-kan) *noun*
the fur-like woolly skin of the young lamb of a Central Asian breed of sheep.
[a region and city in Russia]

astral *adjective*
of or relating to the stars.

astray (a-**stray**) *adverb, adjective*
away from the right path: *He was led astray by criminals.*

astride (a-**stride**) *preposition*
with one leg on each side of: *He sat astride the chair.*
• **astride** *adverb*.

astringent (a-**strin**-j'nt) *adjective*
causing skin or tissue to contract.
Figurative His astringent comments made us flinch (= harsh, severe).
• **astringent** *noun* any of various substances which cause skin or tissue to contract, used in medicine, cosmetics, etc.
Word Family **astringently** *adverb*; **astringency** *noun*.
[Latin *adstringere* to compress]

astrology (a-**stroll**-a-jee) *noun*
the study of the possible influence of the stars on human events. Compare ASTRONOMY.
Word Family **astrologer** *noun*; **astrological** (ast-ra-**lojj**-i-k'l) *adjective*; **astrologically** *adverb*.
[Greek *aster* a star + -*logy*]

astronaut (**ast**-ra-nawt) *noun* also called **cosmonaut**.
a person trained to operate and travel in spacecraft.
Word Family **astronautics** (ast-ra-**naw**-tiks) *plural noun* (*used with singular verb*) the study of flight outside the earth's atmosphere.
[Greek *aster* a star + *nautes* a sailor]

astronomical unit *noun*
the average distance between the sun and the earth, about 149 600 000 km, used as the unit of distance within the solar system.

astronomy (a-**stronn**-a-mee) *noun*
the study of planets and stars, their movements, relative positions and composition. Compare ASTROLOGY.
Word Family **astronomer** *noun*; **astronomical** (ast-ra-**nomm**-ik-'l), **astronomic** *adjective* 1 of or relating to astronomy. 2 immensely large or numerous: *an astronomical rise in prices*; **astronomically** *adverb*.
[Greek *aster* a star + *nomos* an arrangement, law]

astrophysics (ast-ro-**fizz**-iks) *noun*
the study of the physical properties of the planets and stars, a branch of astronomy.
Word Family **astrophysicist** (as-tro-**fizz**-i-sist) *noun*.

AstroTurf *noun*
(*trademark*) artificial turf used for football pitches, etc.

astute (a-**stewt**) *adjective*
shrewd or mentally alert: *Her comments are always astute.*
Word Family **astutely** *adverb*; **astuteness** *noun*.

asunder (a-**sun**-da) *adverb*
apart or into separate pieces: *The roof was torn asunder in the storm.*

asylum (a-**sigh**-l'm) *noun*
1 the protection given by one country to a political refugee from another.
2 any place of shelter or refuge.
3 an old word for a hospital or home for people with mental disorders, etc.

> The word **asylum** is an example of how society's attitude can change towards language. Today it is generally avoided — in the 'hospital' sense people prefer to use the term 'mental hospital'. In the 15th century, when it first appeared in English, *asylum* simply meant 'a place of safety or sanctuary', for hunted criminals or others. In the mid-18th century *asylum* came to be applied to mental hospitals, often in the form *lunatic asylum*. Attitudes to the mentally ill then were extremely cruel and *asylum* became a derogatory term in the same way that *madhouse* did.

asymmetrical (ay-sim-**met**-ri-k'l) *adjective* also **asymmetric**
not symmetrical.
Word Family **asymmetry** (ay-**simm**-a-tree) *noun.*

at *preposition*
1 used to indicate place: *We will meet at home.*
2 used to indicate time: *Be there at noon.*
3 on: *The car started at the second push.*
4 during: *The crickets chirp mostly at night.*
5 used to indicate action, state or manner: *Set your mind at rest.* □ *He came at a run.*
6 because of: *I was horrified at the news.*

atavism (**att**-a-vizm) *noun*
1 *Biology* the reappearance of a feature or character after it has not been evident for several generations.
2 a reversion to primitive instincts.
Word Family **atavistic** (att-a-**vist**-ik) *adjective.*
[Latin *atavus* a forefather]

ate (*rhymes with* get *or* gate) the past tense of **eat**.

atheist (**ay**-thee-ist) *noun*
a person who does not believe in the existence of a god or gods. Compare AGNOSTIC.
Word Family **atheism** *noun*; **atheistic** (ay-thee-**ist**-ik) *adjective*; **atheistically** *adverb.*
[a- + Greek *theos* a god]

athlete (**ath**-leet) *noun*
a person trained to take part in competitive sports, especially athletics.
[Greek *athletes* a contender for a prize]

athlete's foot *noun*
a fungal infection of the skin between the toes.

athletic *adjective*
1 of or relating to physical sports or activities.
2 physically strong and active: *He is quite athletic despite his age.*
Word Family **athletics** *plural noun*
1 physical sports or activities such as running, jumping, etc. 2 (*used with singular verb*) the system or principles of training for such activities.

athwart (a-**thwawt**) *preposition*
across or from side to side of.

atlas *noun* (*plural* **atlases**)
a book of maps.
[after *Atlas*, a giant in Greek mythology who was condemned to support the heavens on his shoulders as a punishment for rebellion against Zeus]

atmosphere (**at**-mos-feer) *noun*
1 a layer of gases that surround a planet, star or moon.
2 the dominant feeling or mood of a situation, etc.: *The atmosphere at the meeting was hostile.*
3 a unit of pressure equal to the average atmospheric pressure at sea level (equal to 1.01×10^5 pascal).
Word Family **atmospheric** (at-mos-**ferr**-ik), **atmospherical** *adjective.*
[Greek *atmos* smoke, vapour + SPHERE]

atmospheric pressure *noun* also called **pressure.**
the pressure at a particular place, caused by the weight of the earth's atmosphere. The atmospheric pressure on top of a mountain is less than at sea level.

atoll (**att**-ol) *noun*
a circular coral reef, usually forming one or more islands around a lagoon.

atom (**at**-'m) *noun*
1 *Physics* the smallest part of an element that retains its chemical identity. Atoms are electrically neutral and consist of negatively charged electrons that surround a central positively-charged nucleus. ⇨ ION.
2 anything which is extremely small.
Word Family **atomic** (a-**tom**-ik) *adjective.*
[Greek *atomos* indivisible]

atom bomb *noun* also **atomic bomb**
short form is **A-bomb** ⇨ NUCLEAR WEAPON
(definition 1).

atomic energy ⇨ NUCLEAR ENERGY.

atomic number *noun*
Physics the number used to classify an
element, equal to the number of protons
in its nucleus. Compare MASS NUMBER.

atomic pile ⇨ NUCLEAR REACTOR.

atomizer, atomiser *noun*
a device for converting a liquid, such as
perfume, into a fine spray under pressure.

atone (a-**tone**) *verb*
to make amends, especially for a sin or
offence: *You must atone for your mistake.*
Word Family **atonement** *noun*.
[AT + ONE]

atop *preposition*
on or at the top of: *atop the mountain.*

atrium (**ay**-tree-um) *noun* (*plural* **atria**)
(**ay**-tree-a)
1 a courtyard, usually at the centre of a
building, common in ancient Rome.
2 *Anatomy* either of the two chambers in
the heart which receive blood from the
veins.
[Latin, central court]

atrocious (a-**tro**-shus) *adjective*
1 extremely cruel or wicked: *an atrocious
act.*
2 (*informal*) very bad.
Word Family **atrocity** (a-**tross**-i-tee)
noun (*plural* **atrocities**) 1 the quality of
being atrocious. 2 an atrocious act;
atrociously *adverb*.
[Latin *atrox, atrocis* cruel]

atrophy (**at**-ra-fee) *noun* (*plural*
atrophies)
a wasting away or diminishing, especially
of all or part of an organism.
Word Family **atrophy** *verb* (**atrophies;**
atrophying; atrophied).
[*a-* + Greek *trophé* nourishment]

atropine *noun*
a poisonous drug obtained from
belladonna.

attach *verb*
to connect or fasten: *The cupboards are
attached to the wall.*
Figurative *She is very attached to her cat*
(= bound by affection). □ *I attach little
importance to it* (= give).
Word Family **attachment** *noun* 1 the act
of attaching. 2 a bond of affection

between people. 3 something which is
attached, such as an extra part or device.
4 something which attaches, such as a
strap, fastener, etc.

attaché (a-**tash**-ay) *noun*
a member of an embassy or legation:
a press attaché.
[French]

attaché case *noun*
a small rectangular case for carrying
documents or papers.

attack *verb*
to set upon with force: *The enemy attacked
the fort at nightfall.*
Figurative *The newspaper was attacked for
its biased editorial* (= strongly criticized).
□ *We all hungrily attacked our meal* (=
began eating energetically).
• **attack** *noun* the act of attacking.
Figurative *an attack of measles* (=
occurrence). □ *We must make an attack on
the dishes* (= start). □ *Their performance was
full of attack* (= vigour).
Word Family **attacker** *noun*.

attain *verb*
to reach or accomplish by one's efforts:
He finally attained his ambition.
Word Family **attainment** *noun* 1 the act
of attaining. 2 something attained;
attainable *adjective*.
[*at-* + Latin *tangere* to touch]

attar *noun*
a sweet-smelling oil obtained from petals,
especially rose petals.
[Arabic, the perfume]

attempt *noun*
1 an effort to achieve something: *She made
several attempts before she succeeded.*
2 an attack: *An attempt was made on the
princess's life.*
• **attempt** *verb*.
[*at-* + Latin *temptare* to attempt]

attend *verb*
1 to be present at: *Did you attend the
meeting?*
2 to accompany: *The President was attended
by his bodyguards.* □ *Her cold was attended by
fever.*
3 to help, look after: *A doctor attended the
victims.*
Phrase **attend to** to pay attention to, deal
with: *Please attend to your work.*
Word Family **attendance** *noun* 1 the
act of attending. 2 the number of

people present; **attendant** *adjective* accompanying; **attendant** *noun* a person or thing that attends.
[Latin *attendere* to turn the mind to]

attention *noun*
1 the act of concentrating or directing one's thoughts: *One must pay attention when driving.*
Figurative Your letter will receive early attention (= consideration).
2 (*often* **attentions**) any courtesy or helpfulness.
Phrase **at attention, to attention** standing with one's heels together and arms at one's sides.
Word Family **attentive** *adjective* helpful or giving attention; **attentively** *adverb*; **attentiveness** *noun*.

attention deficit hyperactive disorder *noun*
a behavioural disorder of children which causes hyperactivity and inability to concentrate.

attenuate (a-ten-yew-ate) *verb*
to weaken or reduce in size or intensity
Word Family **attenuation** (a-ten-yew-ay-sh'n) *noun*.
[*at-* + Latin *tenuis* slender]

attest (a-test) *verb*
to declare to be true or genuine: *Will you attest to the truth of this statement?*
Word Family **attestation** (att-es-tay-sh'n) *noun*
[*at-* + Latin *testari* to attest]

attic *noun*
the room or space immediately under the roof of a house.

attire (a-tire) *noun*
(*formal*) any clothes.
● **attire** *verb* to dress.

attitude *noun*
1 a physical or mental position: *He stood in a menacing attitude.* □ *What is your attitude to gambling?*
2 (*informal*) a readiness to argue and a rather defiant pattern of behaviour.
Word Family **attitudinize, attitudinise** (att-i-tew-di-nize) *verb* to assume affected attitudes.

attorney (a-ter-ni) *noun*
any person, such as a lawyer, appointed by another to act on his or her behalf.
[Old French *atorner* to assign]

attract (a-trakt) *verb*
1 to arouse interest or attention in: *The speech attracted a large audience.*

2 to pull or cause to move towards.
Word Family **attraction** (a-trak-sh'n) *noun* 1 the act or power of attracting: *magnetic attraction.* 2 something which attracts, such as a public event; **attractive** *adjective* having the power to attract or please; **attractively** *adverb*; **attractiveness** *noun*.
[*at-* + Latin *tractus* drawn towards]

attribute (a-trib-yewt) *verb*
to consider as belonging to or created by: *Although unsigned, this painting is attributed to Raphael.*
● **attribute** (att-rib-yewt) *noun* a quality or characteristic: *She has the attributes of intelligence and beauty.*
Word Family **attribution** (att-ri-bew-sh'n) *noun*; **attributable** *adjective* to be attributed to; **attributive** (a-trib-yew-tiv) *adjective* of or expressing an attribute.
[Latin *attribuere*]

attrition (a-trish-'n) *noun*
1 a wearing away, as by friction or rubbing.
2 *Geography* wearing down or erosion of materials by friction or rubbing, e.g. where boulders on a beach rub against one another to become smaller pebbles. Compare ABRASION (definition 3); CORROSION (definition 2).
[*at-* + Latin *tritus* worn out]

attune *verb*
to bring into tune or harmony: *His ideas are not attuned to ours.*

atypical (ay-tipp-i-k'l) *adjective*
not typical or normal.
Word Family **atypically** *adverb*.
[*a-* + TYPICAL]

aubergine (o-ber-zheen) *noun* also called eggplant.
a pear-shaped fruit with a dark purple skin and pale firm flesh, used as a vegetable.
[Arabic]

auburn (aw-b'n) *noun*
a rich reddish-brown colour.
● **auburn** *adjective*.
[Late Latin *alburnus* whitish]

auction (awk-sh'n) *noun*
a public sale at which goods are sold to the highest bidder.
auction bridge ⇨ BRIDGE².
Word Family **auction** *verb*; **auctioneer** *noun* a person who conducts an auction.
[Latin *auctio*]

audacious (aw-**day**-shus) *adjective*
daring or recklessly bold.
Word Family **audacity** (aw-**dass**-i-tee)
noun; **audaciously** *adverb*.
[Latin *audax, audacis* daring]

audible (aw-di-b'l) *adjective*
loud enough to be heard.
Word Family **audibly** *adverb*; **audibility**
(aw-di-**bill**-it-ee) *noun*.

audience (aw-di-'nce) *noun*
1 the people attending or listening to
something, especially a play, concert or
lecture.
2 a formal meeting held by a high official
or ruler: *He asked for an audience with the
Pope.*

audio *adjective*
of or relating to sound, especially the
devices, etc. used to transmit, receive or
reproduce sound waves, such as tape
recorders or CD players.
[Latin *audire* to hear].

audio frequency *noun* (*plural* **audio
frequencies**)
any frequency at which vibrations can be
heard by the human ear.

audiotape *noun*
1 a sound tape recording.
2 a cassette tape.

audio-visual *adjective*
involving the use of both sight and
hearing, as in television, etc.: *audio-visual
teaching aids.*

audit *noun*
an official examination of financial records
and statements.
Word Family **audit** *verb*; **auditor** *noun*
1 a person appointed to make an audit.
2 (*formal*) a listener.

audition (aw-**dish**-'n) *noun*
Theatre a trial performance to test
suitability for a part in a play, etc.
• **audition** *verb*.

auditorium (aw-di-**taw**-ri-um) *noun*
(*plural* **auditoriums** or **auditoria** (aw-di-
taw-ri-a))
1 a large theatre, concert hall, etc.
2 the area in such a building where the
audience sits.

auditory (aw-da-tree) *adjective*
relating to hearing: *the auditory nerve.*

au fait (o *fay*)
well informed about something: *au fait
with the latest gossip.*
[French, to the fact]

Augean (aw-**jee**-an) *adjective*
filthy or dirty.

> **Augean stables** is a term for
> something very dirty. It is most
> commonly found in the phrase *to
> cleanse the Augean stables* meaning 'to
> clear up' — either physical dirt or moral
> corruption — or 'to do something
> virtually impossible'. It was one of the
> twelve tasks of similar difficulty
> imposed on the Greek hero Hercules,
> by King Eurystheus when Hercules was
> made to serve the king for twelve years
> as a punishment for killing his own wife
> and children. King Augeas kept 3000
> oxen in stables which had not been
> cleaned for 30 years; Hercules diverted
> the River Alpheus through the stables
> and cleaned them in a day.

auger (aw-ga) *noun*
a tool, such as a small gimlet, for drilling.

aught (awt) *noun*
an old word meaning 'anything whatever'.

augment (awg-ment) *verb*
to increase or add to.
Word Family **augmentation** (awg-men-
tay-sh'n) *noun*.
[Latin *augmen* an increase]

au gratin (o **grat**-an) *adjective*
topped with breadcrumbs or grated cheese
and browned.
[French, by grating]

augur (aw-ga) *noun*
any prophet or soothsayer.
• **augur** *verb* to foretell or be a sign of: *The
weather augurs well for our holiday.*
Word Family **augury** (aw-gyoo-ree)
noun (*plural* **auguries**).
[Latin]

august (aw-**gust**) *adjective*
imposing or majestic: *The king had an
august manner.*
Word Family **augustly** *adverb*.
[Latin *augustus* majestic]

August (aw-gust) *noun*
the eighth month of the year, after July and
before September.
[after the Roman Emperor *Augustus*]

auk (*rhymes with* hawk) *noun*
any of various black and white saltwater
diving birds with short wings, e.g. the
guillemot and puffin.

aum (ah-oom) *noun*
Hinduism the sacred symbol and sound
representing the ultimate; the most sacred
of Hindu words.

aunt (ahnt) *noun*
1 the sister of one's parent.
2 the wife of one's uncle.
3 (*informal*) used as a title for an older female friend of a child's parents: *Say hello to Aunt Madge.*
[Latin *amita*]

au pair (o **pair**) *noun*
a young foreigner, usually female, who lives with a family, minds the children, etc., and often studies the language.
[French, on equal terms]

aura (**or**-a) *noun* (*plural* **auras** or **aurae** (**or**-ee))
a distinct air or atmosphere surrounding someone or something: *an aura of wisdom.*
[Greek, breath]

aural (**or**-'l or **ow**-r'l) *adjective*
of or perceived by the ear.
Word Family **aurally** *adverb*.
[Latin *auris* ear]

aureole (**aw**-ree-ole) *noun* also **aureola**
a halo.
[Latin *aureolus* golden]

au revoir (o-ri-**vwah**) *interjection*
goodbye for now.
[French, until we see each other again]

auricle (**aw**-ri-k'l) *noun*
1 the outer part of the ear.
2 either of the two upper chambers of the heart which receive blood from the veins.
Word Family **auricular** (aw-**rik**-yew-la) *adjective*.

auriferous (aw-**riff**-er-us) *adjective*
yielding or containing gold.
[Latin *aurum* gold + *ferre* to carry]

aurora (aw-**raw**-ra) *noun* (*plural* **auroras** or **aurorae** (aw-**raw**-ree))
a glowing display in the upper layers of the atmosphere near the poles, caused by fast charged particles from the sun.

aurora australis (aw-raw-ra oss-**trah**-liss) *noun*
the aurora which occurs near the South Pole.

aurora borealis (aw-raw-ra borr-ee-**ah**-liss) *noun*
the aurora which occurs near the North Pole.

auspices (**aw**-spiss-iz) *plural noun*
any help or patronage: *research carried out under the auspices of the government.*
[Latin *auspicium* divination]

auspicious (aw-**spish**-us) *adjective*
fortunate or favourable.
Word Family **auspiciously** *adverb*.

austere (aw-**steer**) *adjective*
1 morally strict or self-restrained: *the austere life of a monk.*
2 lacking comfort or ornament: *an austere building.*
Word Family **austerely** *adverb*;
austerity (os-**terr**-i-tee) *noun*.
[Greek *austeros* severe]

autarchy (**aw**-tar-kee) *noun* (*plural* **autarchies**)
despotism; absolute rule.
[*auto-* + Greek *arkhos* a leader]

autarky (**aw**-tar-kee) *adjective*
economic self-sufficiency.

authentic (aw-**then**-tik) *adjective*
genuine or believable: *Her French accent sounds quite authentic.*
Word Family **authentically** *adverb*;
authenticity (aw-then-**tiss**-i-tee) *noun*.
[Greek *authentikos* genuine]

authenticate (aw-**then**-ti-kate) *verb*
to make or prove to be authentic.
Word Family **authentication** (aw-thent-i-**kay**-sh'n) *noun*.

author (**aw**-tha) *noun*
1 a person who writes a book, essay, etc.
2 any person who originates something: *Who was the author of this scheme?*
Word Family **authorship** *noun*;
authorial (aw-**thaw**-ree-al) *adjective*.
[Latin *auctor* originator]

authoritarian (aw-thorr-i-**tair**-i-an) *adjective*
in favour of obedience to authority, rather than the exercise of individual freedom.
• **authoritarian** *noun* a person who has an authoritarian manner.
Word Family **authoritarianism** *noun*.

authority (aw-**thorr**-i-tee) *noun* (*plural* **authorities**)
1 the power or right to give orders and make others obey.
2 permission: *Who gave you authority to act?*
3 an expert or reliable source: *He is an authority on road safety.*
4 an organization or group having control over public affairs.
Word Family **authoritative** *adjective*
having authority; **authoritatively** *adverb*.
[Latin *auctoritas* responsibility]

authorize, authorise (aw-tha-rize) *verb*
to give authority to or for: *You must authorize your solicitor to act for you.*
Word Family **authorization** (aw-tha-rie-zay-sh'n) *noun*.

autism (aw-tizm) *noun*
an abnormal tendency to withdraw into a private world to such an extent that normal human communication is impossible.
Word Family **autistic** (aw-**tis**-tik) *adjective*.
[Greek *autos* self + *-ism*]

autobiography (aw-toe-by-**og**-ra-fee) *noun* (*plural* **autobiographies**)
the life story of a person written by himself or herself. Compare BIOGRAPHY.
Word Family **autobiographical** (aw-toe-by-a-**graff**-i-k'l) *adjective*; **autobiographically** *adverb*; **autobiographer** *noun*.

autoclave *noun*
a closed vessel for sterilizing equipment by using steam under pressure.
[*auto-* + Latin *clavis* a key]

autocracy (aw-**tok**-ra-see) *noun* (*plural* **autocracies**)
despotism.
Word Family **autocrat** (aw-ta-krat) *noun* a person having or using absolute power; **autocratic** *adjective*; **autocratically** *adverb*.
[*auto-* + Greek *kratia* rule]

Autocue *noun*
(*trademark*) a device from which television presenters, newsreaders, etc. can read a script.

auto-da-fé (aw-to-dah-**fay**) *noun* (*plural* **autos-da-fé**) (aw-toze-dah-**fay**)
the burning of a heretic after sentence by the Inquisition.
[Portuguese, act of the Faith]

autograph (aw-ta-graf) *noun*
1 a person's signature or handwriting.
2 an original manuscript in a person's own handwriting.
[*auto-* + Greek *graphein* to write]

automatic *adjective*
1 done without thought or conscious effort: *Breathing is an automatic process.*
2 (of a machine) operating without direct human control.
3 (of a gun) using the pressure of the exploding cartridge to operate a mechanism which reloads the chamber for repeated firing.
• **automatic** *noun* an automatic washing machine, gun, etc.
Word Family **automatically** *adverb*.
[Greek *automatos* self-moving]

automatic pilot *noun*
an automatic steering device in an aeroplane.

automatic teller machine *noun*
a device, often set in a wall, provided by a financial institution such as a bank, for the withdrawal and deposit of money both during and after normal business hours.

automation (aw-ta-**may**-sh'n) *noun*
the process of replacing manpower by machinery, especially in industry.
Word Family **automate** (**aw**-ta-mate) *verb* to apply the principles of automation.

automaton (aw-**tomm**-a-t'n) *noun* (*plural* **automatons** or **automata**)
1 a person who acts in an automatic or unthinking way.
2 an automatic device or machine, such as a robot.

automobile (**aw**-ta-mo-beel) *noun*
(*especially American*) a motor car.
[*auto-* + Latin *mobilis* movable]

automotive (aw-ta-**mo**-tiv) *adjective*
1 self-propelled.
2 of or relating to motor vehicles: *the automotive industry.*

autonomic nervous system ⇨ NERVOUS SYSTEM.

autonomy (aw-**tonn**-a-mee) *noun*
1 the ruling of a country by its own people.
2 any independence or freedom.
Word Family **autonomous** *adjective* independent.
[*auto-* + Greek *nomos* law]

autopsy (**aw**-top-see) *noun* (*plural* **autopsies**) ⇨ POST-MORTEM (definition 1).

autosuggestion (awto-suj-**jess**-ch'n) *noun*
Psychology a change in a person's outlook or attitude, caused by his or her own thoughts or belief.

autumn (**aw**-t'm) *noun*
the season of the year between summer and winter.
Word Family **autumnal** (aw-**tum**-n'l) *adjective*.

auxiliary (awg-**zill**-i-a-ree) *adjective*
giving support or aid: *auxiliary troops.*
• **auxiliary** *noun* (*plural* **auxiliaries**)
a person or thing that gives aid of any kind.
[Latin *auxilium* assistance]

auxiliary verb *noun*
a verb that is used with other verbs to form tenses, voices, negatives and questions. Examples of auxiliary verbs are: *be, have, do, may, can, shall, must.*

avail (a-**vale**) *noun*
usefulness or advantage: *It is of little avail to shout.*
• **avail** *verb* to be of use or value.
Phrase **avail oneself of** to make use of: *You should avail yourself of this chance.*

available (a-**vay**-la-b'l) *adjective*
suitable or ready for use: *No more seats available for the concert.*
Word Family **availability** (a-vay-la-**bill**-i-tee) *noun*; **availably** *adverb*.

avalanche (**avv**-a-lahnch) *noun*
1 a sudden fall or movement of a mass of snow, rock or mud down a slope.
2 something which has the force or movement of an avalanche: *an avalanche of angry questions.*
[French]

avant-garde (avv-on-**gard**) *adjective*
in the forefront of modern trends, in the arts, etc.
Word Family **avant-garde** *noun*.
[French]

avarice (**avv**-a-ris) *noun*
an extreme greed for wealth, possessions, etc.
Word Family **avaricious** (avv-a-**rish**-us) *adjective*; **avariciously** *adverb*; **avariciousness** *noun*.
[Latin *avarus* greedy]

avatar (**a**-va-tar) *noun*
Hinduism a manifestation or incarnation of a Hindu deity in human, superhuman or animal form.

avenge (a-**venj**) *verb*
to take revenge for.
Word Family **avenger** *noun*.

> [!] Do not confuse *avenge* with *revenge*. You *avenge* a wrong that someone has done to someone else, as in *He wanted to avenge his wife's murder.* You *revenge* yourself on someone who has caused you harm, as in *She revenged herself on her cheating partner.* *Revenge* is also a noun, as in *He took revenge on those who had criticized him.*

avenue (**avv**-a-new) *noun*
1 a street or road, originally a wide tree-lined street.
2 a means: *to search for avenues of escape.*

aver (a-**ver**) *verb* (**avers; averring; averred**)
to declare in a positive way.

average (**av**-rij) *noun*
1 the result obtained by dividing the sum of several quantities by the number of quantities added.

2 the most common or usual amount, quality, kind, etc.
• **average** *verb*
1 to calculate the average of.
2 to be or obtain an average.
Word Family **average** *adjective*; **averagely** *adverb*.
[from Arabic]

averse (a-**verse**) *adjective*
opposed or reluctant: *I'm not averse to hard work.*
[Latin *aversus* turned round]

> [!] Do not confuse *averse* with ADVERSE.

aversion (a-**ver**-sh'n) *noun*
1 an extreme dislike: *I have an aversion to spiders.*
2 a person or thing that is disliked.

avert (a-**vert**) *verb*
to turn away: *She averted her eyes.*
Figurative *It was too late to avert the disaster* (= avoid).

aviary (**ave**-y'ree) *noun* (*plural* **aviaries**)
a large cage or enclosure in which birds are kept.
[Latin *avis* a bird]

aviation (ay-vee-**ay**-sh'n) *noun*
the science or skill of flying aircraft.
Word Family **aviator** (**ay**-vee-ate-or) *noun* a pilot.
[Latin *avis* a bird]

avid (**avv**-id) *adjective*
1 greedy: *avid for power.*
2 very enthusiastic or keen: *He is an avid collector of old guns.*
Word Family **avidly** *adverb*; **avidity** (a-**vidd**-i-tee) *noun*.
[Latin *avidus* desirous]

avocado (avv-a-**kah**-do) *noun*
1 short form of **avocado pear** an edible tropical fruit with a dark green or black skin, creamy yellowish flesh and a large seed.
2 a pale yellowish-green colour.
Word Family **avocado** *adjective*.
[an Aztec name]

avocet (**avv**-a-set) *noun*
a large wading bird with a long up-curved beak and blue legs.

avoid (a-**voyd**) *verb*
to keep away from: *Most people try to avoid danger.*
Word Family **avoidable** *adjective*; **avoidably** *adverb* **avoidance** *noun*.

avoirdupois (av-wah-dew-**pwah**) *noun*
a system of mass in which one pound
equals 16 ounces. The units are the grain,
dram, ounce, pound, stone, quarter,
hundredweight and ton. Compare TROY.
[French, goods of weight]

avow (a-**vow**) *verb*
to acknowledge or confess.
Word Family **avowal** *noun*.

avuncular (a-**vunk**-yew-la) *adjective*
of or like an uncle: *Children love his kindly
avuncular manner.*
[Latin *avunculus* uncle]

await *verb*
to wait for or expect: *We will await your
decision.*

awake *adjective*
not asleep.
Figurative I think he is awake to the danger
(= alert).
• **awake** *verb* (awakes; awaking; awoke;
awoken) also **awaken** to wake from sleep.
Word Family **awakening** *noun* 1 the act
of waking from sleep. 2 an arousing of
interest, etc.

award *verb*
to officially give or grant: *He was awarded
several prizes.*
• **award** *noun*
1 any prize or token which is awarded.
2 the minimum legal rate of pay for a
particular type of work.
3 *Law* a decision, e.g. of an arbitrator.

aware *adjective*
having knowledge or understanding of:
He was aware of the danger.
Word Family **awareness** *noun*.

awash *adjective, adverb*
covered by water.

away *adverb, adjective*
1 towards or at a different place, etc.:
Please go away!
2 into a cupboard, etc. for storage: *I put the
plates away.*
3 continuously: *They worked away all
morning.*
4 out of existence: *The water has boiled
away.*
5 (of a sports event) not at the home club's
ground: *The team plays away next week.*

awe (*rhymes with* paw) *noun*
respect mixed with fear.
Word Family **awe** *verb*.

aweigh (a-**way**) *adverb*
Nautical (of an anchor) raised just clear of
the bottom of the sea.

awesome *adjective*
1 inspiring awe, impressive: *an awesome
sight.*
2 (*informal*) excellent, marvellous: *an
awesome performance.*

awful (aw-f'l) *adjective*
1 (*informal*) extremely bad or unpleasant:
What an awful day!
2 very great: *He has an awful lot of money.*
3 inspiring fear or dread.
Word Family **awfully** *adverb*; **awfulness**
noun.

awhile (a-**wile**) *adverb*
for a short time: *Let us rest awhile.*

awkward *adjective*
1 lacking grace or skill: *He is very awkward
with his hands.*
2 causing problems or embarrassment: *Ten
o'clock is an awkward time for me to come.*
3 difficult or dangerous: *He is an awkward
person to deal with.*
Word Family **awkwardly** *adverb*;
awkwardness *noun*.

awl *noun*
a small pointed tool for piercing holes in
wood or leather.

awning *noun*
a roof-like cover, usually canvas, for
protecting doorways or windows.

awoke the past tense of **awake**.

awoken the past participle of **awake**.

awry (a-**rye**) *adverb, adjective*
1 crooked or turned to one side.
2 wrong or off the right course: *Our plans
went awry.*

axe *noun* (American **ax**)
a tool with a long wooden handle and a
sharp wedge-shaped metal head, used for
chopping wood, etc.
Phrase **have an axe to grind** to have a
private grievance.
• **axe** *verb* (*informal*) to reduce or abolish.

axel (**ak**-s'l) *noun*
in ice skating, a jump from one skate to the
other with one and a half turns in the air.
[after *Axel* Paulsen, Norwegian skater]

axes
1 the plural of **axe**.
2 the plural of **axis**.

axial *adjective*
relating to or situated at an axis.

axilla ⇨ ARMPIT.
[Latin]

axiom (aks-ee-um) *noun*
an established or accepted truth, such as a general statement which is used as a basis for reasoning or argument: *to challenge the axiom that full employment is desirable*.
Word Family **axiomatic** (ak-see-a-**mat**-tik) *adjective*.
[Greek *axioma* a self-evident principle]

axis *noun* (*plural* **axes**) (**ak**-seez)
1 the line around which a rotating body turns.
2 a line which divides something such as a flat geometrical shape in half.
3 *Maths* a fixed line chosen as a reference, e.g. for a graph.
[Latin, axle]

axle (**ak**-s'l) *noun*
a supporting shaft on which a wheel or wheels turn.

ayatollah (eye-a-**toll**-a) *noun*
a title for an Islamic religious leader.

aye (eye) *noun* also **ay**
a vote in favour of something.
● **aye** *interjection* yes.
Phrase **aye aye** *Nautical* a reply to an order indicating that it will be done: *'Go below!'* *'Aye aye, captain!'*

azalea (a-**zay**-lee-a) *noun*
any of a group of garden shrubs which are smaller, often scented, forms of rhododendron and have bright decorative flowers.
[Greek *azaleos* dry (soil)]

azimuth (**azz**-i-m'th) *noun*
Astronomy the angle made between a vertical circle through a planet or star and the observer's meridian.
[Arabic, the directions]

azure (**azh**-er) *noun*
a clear sky-blue colour.
Word Family **azure** *adjective*.
[from Persian, lapis lazuli]

Bb

babble *verb*
1 to utter incoherent or meaningless
sounds: *The baby babbled happily in its cot.*
2 to talk continuously or thoughtlessly:
Knowing him, he'll babble on for hours.
3 (of flowing water) to make a continuous
murmuring or rippling sound.
Word Family **babble** *noun* a babbling
sound; **babbler** *noun*.

babel (*rhymes with* table) *noun*
a confused mixture of many different
sounds.
[from the *Tower of Babel* in the Bible]

baboon (ba-**boon**) *noun*
a large monkey from Africa and Arabia
with a muzzle rather like a dog's.
[Old French *babuin* a stupid person]

baby *noun* (*plural* **babies**)
1 a very young child or animal.
2 the youngest member of a group: *She is
the baby of her class.*
3 an inexperienced or naive person: *He's
only a baby when it comes to business matters.*
4 (*informal*) an affectionate term for a
woman or man.
5 (*informal*) an invention or creation: *As
the plan is your baby, you present it at the
meeting.*
Word Family **baby** *verb* (**babies;
babying; babied**) to pamper or coddle;
babyhood *noun*.

babysit *verb* (**babysits; babysitting;
babysat**)
to look after children when their parents
are out.
Word Family **babysitter** *noun*.

bacchanalian (bakk-a-**nay**-li-an) *adjective*
drunken, wild and unrestrained, like the
festivals in honour of Bacchus.

Bacchus *noun*
Roman mythology the god of wine and
fertility.

bachelor (**batch**-a-la) *noun*
1 an unmarried man.

2 a person who holds the first degree
awarded by a university: *a Bachelor of Arts.*
[Old French *bacheler* a young man aspiring
to knighthood]

bacillus (ba-**sill**-us) *noun* (*plural* **bacilli**)
(ba-**sil**-eye)
Biology any of a group of rod-shaped
bacteria, especially one causing disease.
[Latin *baculus* rod]

back *noun*
1 the rear part of the human body between
the shoulders and the buttocks.
2 the corresponding part of any animal's
body.
3 the rear side or part of anything: *at the
back of the shop.*
4 the keel of a boat: *The ship broke its back
on the reef.*
5 *Sport* a player in a defensive position.
Phrases **break the back of** *Another two
hours' work should break the back of it*
(= deal with the hardest part of). **get off
one's back** *Get off my back!* (= stop
criticizing or pestering). **get, put one's
back up** *She always gets his back up*
(= annoys him). **turn one's back on** *You
can't turn your back on family responsibilities*
(= ignore, neglect).
● **back** *verb*
1 to move or cause to move backwards: *He
backed the truck skilfully.*
2 to support or bet on: *We should back that
horse in today's race.*
3 to be placed at the rear or to form a
background: *The workshop backs onto
a lane.* □ *The view is backed by rising
foothills.*
Phrases **back down** to retreat. **back out**
to withdraw or refuse. **back up 1** *Do you
have any witnesses who can back up your
story?* (= corroborate). **2** to assist or
support. **3** to make an extra copy of: *Don't
forget to back up your work regularly.*
Word Family **back-up** *noun*.
● **back** *adjective*
1 placed behind or in the rear: *Enter by the
back door.*
2 of or for a date earlier than the present:
back issues of a periodical.
Phrase **on the back burner** awaiting
attention, in reserve.
● **back** *adverb*
1 at, to or towards the rear: *Move back,
please, and let the doctor near.*
2 in, to or towards a former place, time
or condition: *to go back home.* □ *My
cold has come back.* □ *She remembers back
50 years.*

Word Family **backer** *noun* a person who supports an enterprise, especially with money; **backless** *adjective*.

back-bencher *noun*
Parliament a member of the House of Commons who is not entitled to occupy the front benches, which are reserved for ministers and shadow ministers. Compare FRONTBENCHER.

backbone *noun*
1 ⇨ SPINE (definition 1).
2 strength of character: *He didn't have the backbone to admit he was wrong.*

backchat *noun*
any impertinent answering back: *I won't put up with any more backchat.*

backdate *verb*
to date or apply at an earlier date than the present: *Your pay rise will be backdated two months.*

backdrop *noun* also called **backcloth**
Theatre a painted curtain or hanging at the back of a stage, forming part of the set.

backfire *verb*
(of an internal-combustion engine) to explode through the exhaust pipe, owing to the accumulation of unburnt fuel.
Figurative Our plans backfired at the last moment (= went wrong).

backgammon *noun*
a board game for two people, each with 15 pieces which move according to the throw of dice.
[BACK + Middle English *gamen* a game, because sometimes the pieces must return to the start]

background *noun*
1 the remoter part of a scene or setting, against which things are seen or represented: *The view overlooks the lake with the mountains in the background.*
2 the events surrounding or causing something: *My essay is on the background of the French Revolution.*
3 experience and training: *Smith's background in science makes him ideal for the job.*

backhand *noun*
Tennis a stroke made across the body with the back of the hand facing forward. Compare FOREHAND.

backhanded *adjective*
(of a stroke or blow) delivered or made with the back of the hand, or the back of the hand facing forward.
Phrase **backhanded compliment** an ambiguous double-edged compliment.

Word Family **backhandedly** *adverb*; **backhander** *noun* a backhanded blow or stroke.

backing *noun*
1 any support, promotion or assistance: *The enterprise will never succeed without proper backing.*
2 a supporting or strengthening back part: *The backing on this furniture isn't very strong.*

backlash *noun*
a hostile reaction to something considered to be a threat.

backless ⇨ **backless** under BACK.

backlog *noun*
an accumulation of work, etc.: *There is a huge backlog of mail to answer.*

backpack *noun*
a bag carried on the back.

back-pedal *verb* (**back-pedals; back-pedalling; back-pedalled**)
1 to pedal backwards.
2 also **backtrack** to retreat or abandon one's position in an argument, commitment, etc.

back seat *noun*
a seat at or towards the back.
Phrases **back-seat driver** *noun* (*informal*) anyone who interferes or gives unwanted advice, such as a car passenger who constantly corrects the driver. **take a back seat** *She took a back seat in the discussion* (= played an inconspicuous part).

backside *noun*
(*informal*) the buttocks.

backslide *verb* (**backslides; backsliding; backslid**)
to fall back into error or wrongdoing.
Word Family **backslider** *noun*.

backstage *noun*
Theatre the area behind or at the sides of the stage, containing the dressing-rooms, props and other equipment.
Word Family **backstage** *adjective* private or behind the scenes.

backstreet *noun*
a small out-of-the-way street in a city or town.
● **backstreet** *adjective* illegal or underhand: *a backstreet enterprise.*

backstroke *noun*
a swimming style in which the swimmer lies on his or her back, reaching back and pulling alternately with each arm.

backtrack ⇨ BACK-PEDAL (definition 2).

back-up ⇨ **back-up** under BACK.

backward *adjective*
1 towards the back or in reverse: *She left without a backward glance.*
2 retarded or showing no progress: *a backward child.*
3 shy or retiring: *He isn't backward in making his opinions known.*
• **backwards, backward** *adverb* towards the back or in reverse: *He leant backwards in his chair.*
Phrase **bend, fall** or **lean over backwards** *They bent over backwards to help her* (= went to great trouble).
Word Family **backwardly** *adverb*; **backwardness** *noun.*

backwash *noun*
Geography the return of a wave down a beach, after it has broken. Compare SWASH.

backwater *noun*
1 a stagnant stretch of a river or a still pool fed by a river.
2 a backward or unprogressive place: *She was bored living in such a backwater.*

backwoods *plural noun*
1 uncleared land away from settled areas.
2 any obscure or remote area.

bacon (**bay-k'n**) *noun*
a cut of pork from the back or sides of a pig, usually salted or smoked.
Phrases **bring home the bacon** to succeed in an enterprise. **save one's bacon** *A good alibi might save his bacon* (= get him out of trouble).

bacteria (bak-**teer**-i-a) *plural noun* (*singular* **bacterium**)
a large group of micro-organisms which display both plant and animal characteristics. Bacteria are important in the decay of plant and animal tissue, providing food, such as nitrates, for higher plants, and assisting in processes such as the fermentation of wines and the maturing of cheese. Some bacteria cause severe diseases, such as typhoid and diphtheria.
Word Family **bacterial** *adjective.*
[Greek *bakterion* a small stick]

bacteriology (bak-teer-i-**oll**-a-jee) *noun*
the study of bacteria.
Word Family **bacteriologist** *noun.*

Bactrian camel (back-tree-'n **kamm**-'l) *noun*
a camel with two humps.
[*Bactria*, ancient country in Asia]

bad *adjective* (**worse; worst**)
1 having unpleasant or disagreeable qualities: *a bad dream.*
2 faulty: *This car has bad brakes.*
3 naughty or mischievous: *You bad boy!*
4 malicious: *She is selfish, but she's not a bad person.*
5 sour or spoilt: *The milk will go bad if you leave it out.*
6 incompetent: *He is a bad tennis player.*
7 severe or serious: *He has bad toothache.*
8 harmful: *Reading by a poor light is bad for your eyes.*
9 (*informal*) very good, excellent.
Phrase **not bad** rather good.
Word Family **badly** *adverb* 1 poorly, inadequately. 2 very much; **badness** *noun.*

> The word **bad** is an example of how meanings change as it now has an additional meaning which is the very opposite of its original meaning. The new meaning has come to us from slang used by blacks, originally black jazz musicians, in America. Many of our slang terms have come from America and now black culture is having an increasing effect on the language. A similar example is *wicked.*

bad debt ⇨ DEBT.

bade (bad) an old past tense of **bid**.

badge (baj) *noun*
an emblem signifying rank or membership in an organization: *a Boy Scout badge.*

badger (**baj**-a) *noun*
a small burrowing flesh-eating mammal which hunts at night.
• **badger** *verb* to pester or harass: *Stop badgering me with questions.*

badinage (**badd**-i-nah*zh*) *noun*
any playful or witty exchange in conversation.
[French *badiner* to jest]

badminton *noun*
a game similar to tennis but using a high net and a light shuttlecock which does not bounce.
[invented at the Duke of Beaufort's home at *Badminton*, Gloucestershire]

bad-mouth *verb*
(*informal*) to speak about unfavourably or maliciously.

badness ⇨ BAD.

baffle *verb*
to confuse or puzzle: *Why does my remark baffle you?*

- **baffle** noun any of various devices used to control flow or movement, as in a car silencer (to control hot gases) or in a loudspeaker (to control soundwaves). *Word Family* **bafflingly** adverb.

bag noun
1 any of various containers made from paper, cloth, leather, etc., such as a mailbag or a travelling bag.
2 (**bags**)(*informal*) a large quantity: *He has bags of money.*
3 (*informal*) an unattractive woman.
Phrase **in the bag** a business deal which is in the bag (= assured, secured).
- **bag** verb (**bags; bagging; bagged**)
1 to put into a bag: *to bag wheat.*
2 to sag or hang loosely: *His trousers bagged at the knees.*
3 to catch or kill, especially game: *We bagged an elephant first day out.*
Word Family **bags** interjection (*informal*) a claim for first use of, right to, etc.: *Bags I have the top bunk!*

bagatelle ⇨ PINBALL.

bagel (**bay-g'l**) noun
a hard ring-shaped bread roll.
[Yiddish *beygel*]

baggage (**baggg-ij**) noun
luggage for taking on a journey.

baggy adjective (**baggier; baggiest**)
bulging or hanging in folds: *baggy trousers.*

bag lady noun (*plural* **bag ladies**)
a homeless woman who carries all her possessions in carrier bags.

bagpipes plural noun
Music any of several reed instruments for which wind from the mouth or bellows is stored in a bag, and expelled through a number of pipes.

ball¹ noun
1 *Law* the sum of money given to a court as a guarantee that an accused person, who is freed until his or her trial, will return to court for the trial.
2 *Law* temporary release granted on this basis.
Phrase **jump bail** to abscond while on bail.
[Old French, power or custody]

bail² verb also **bale**
to remove water from the bottom of a boat.
Phrase **bail out 1** to parachute from an aircraft. **2** to help out of a difficult or awkward situation: *We ran out of money and our parents had to bail us out.*

bail³ noun
a small piece of wood on the top of cricket stumps.

bailiff noun
Law a person employed by a sheriff to serve writs and carry out court orders.
[Latin *bajulus* a porter or manager]

bairn noun
Scottish a child.

Baisakhi (**by-sah-kee**) noun
a major Sikh festival celebrating the formation of the Sikh community of the Khalsa.
[Sanskrit]

bait noun
a lure in the form of food, used to attract fish, game, etc.
Figurative They offered him a salary rise as a bait to stop him resigning (= enticement).
- **bait** verb
1 to prepare a fishhook, trap, etc. by attaching bait.
2 to anger or torment deliberately.

baize (**baze**) noun
a woollen felt-like fabric, usually green, used as a cover for billiard tables, etc.

bake verb
1 to cook or heat in an oven.
2 to harden by heating.

Bakelite (**bay-k'l-ite**) noun
(*trademark*) an early type of plastic.

baker noun
a person who bakes and sells bread, cakes, etc.

baker's dozen noun
thirteen.
[after the former practice among bakers of adding an extra loaf to each dozen to ensure full weight]

bakery noun (*plural* **bakeries**)
a place where bread, cakes, buns, etc. are baked or sold.

baking powder noun
a raising agent used in making cakes and biscuits.

baking soda noun
bicarbonate of soda.

balaclava (**bal-a-klah-va**) noun
a woollen hood which covers the head, ears and neck.
[as worn at the battle of *Balaclava* in the Crimean War]

balalaika (**bal-a-lie-ka**) noun
Music a triangular Russian instrument related to the guitar, with three strings.

balance *noun*
1 an equal distribution of weight, amount, etc.: *The balance of the load must be carefully arranged.*
2 a condition of steadiness, especially when two opposing forces, influences, etc. are equal: *Don't lose your balance on that bike.*
3 an instrument for measuring mass, especially one with two pans on an arm which pivots about a central point.
4 (in bookkeeping) the difference between the debit and credit sides of an account.
5 the remainder: *She promised to pay the balance by the end of the month.*
Phrases **balance of payments** the difference between the amount a country spends abroad on imports, etc. and the amount it earns through its exports, etc.
balance of power 1 the condition in which no single nation or group of nations is stronger than any other. **2** the power to decide or determine: *Which party holds the balance of power in parliament?*
hang in the balance to be or remain undecided.
strike a balance to find a solution that is considered to be fair to all.
• **balance** *verb*
1 to bring into or keep in a steady condition or position: *Can you balance a book on your head?* □ *The acrobat balanced on one hand.*
2 to make or be equal in weight, amount, force, etc.: *His good points probably balance his bad.*
3 (in bookkeeping) to make the necessary adjustments so that the debit and credit sides of an account are equal.
[Latin *bilanx* having two scales]

balcony (**bal**-ka-nee) *noun* (*plural* **balconies**)
1 a platform projecting from a building, usually with a railing or balustrade.
2 ⇨ GALLERY (definition 3).

bald (bawld) *adjective*
1 lacking hair on the scalp.
2 blunt or plain: *a bald lie.* □ *He gave a bald statement of the facts.*
Word Family **baldly** *adverb*; **baldness** *noun*.

balderdash (**bawl**-da-dash) *noun*
nonsense or words jumbled illogically together.

bale[1] *noun*
a large compact package or bundle held together by wires, cord or cloth: *a bale of hay.*

bale[2] ⇨ BAIL[2].

baleful *adjective*
menacing or evil.
Word Family **balefully** *adverb*; **balefulness** *noun*.

balk ⇨ BAULK.

ball[1] (bawl) *noun*
1 a spherical object, either hollow or solid, such as that used in cricket, tennis, etc.
2 a rounded protuberance or part of something: *He balanced on the balls of his feet.*
Phrases **on the ball** alert or in touch.
play ball to cooperate.

ball[2] *noun*
a large social gathering, usually formal, with dancing, eating and drinking.
Phrase **have a ball** to enjoy oneself thoroughly.
[Old French *baler* to dance]

ballad *noun*
1 a simple poem which tells a story. It has short regular verses with a rhyme scheme.
2 a slow romantic pop song.

ballast (**bal**-ast) *noun*
any heavy material, such as lead or bags of sand, placed in the hold of a ship, etc. to ensure stability.

ball bearing *noun*
1 a bearing which moves on small steel balls placed in a ring-shaped groove.
2 one of the small steel balls.

ballet (**bal**-ay) *noun*
1 an artistic dance form characterized by stylized steps, movements and gestures.
2 a performance of such a dance, usually with a musical accompaniment, scenery and theatrical effects, acting out a story or theme.
Word Family **ballet dancer** *noun*; **ballerina** (bal-a-**ree**-na) *noun* a female ballet dancer.

ball game *noun*
1 a game played with a ball.
2 (*informal*) a state of affairs: *If she's coming as well, that's a whole new ball game.*

ballistic missile *noun*
a missile which is propelled and guided only in the first stages of its flight.
Compare GUIDED MISSILE.

ballistics (ba-**list**-iks) *plural noun*
(*used with singular verb*) the study of the motion of projectiles, such as bullets or missiles.
[Greek *ballein* to throw]

balloon (ba-**loon**) *noun*
1 an inflatable rubber bag, usually coloured, used as a toy or for decoration.
2 an aircraft which is lighter than air and consists of a large bag filled with hydrogen, helium or hot air, and a basket or harness to carry the crew.
Word Family **balloon** *verb* to swell up like a balloon; **balloonist** *noun*.
[French *ballon*]

ballot *noun*
a system of secret voting in an election, in which the voter is given a paper printed with the names of candidates, on which he or she indicates the chosen candidate, before placing it in the ballot box.
• **ballot** *verb* to vote by ballot.
[Italian *ballotta* a little ball, because originally votes were cast by dropping a ball into a box]

ballpark *noun*
1 *American* a baseball stadium.
2 (*informal*) an approximate range: *The price is in the right ballpark.*

ballpoint pen *noun*
a pen containing a supply of ink and a point consisting of a metal ball which turns on contact with paper and releases a small amount of ink onto the paper.

ballroom *noun*
a large room or hall in which balls are held.

ballyhoo *noun*
an uproar or outcry.

balm (*rhymes with* calm) *noun*
1 any of various ointments made from the resin of certain trees.
2 anything which heals or soothes: *sleep, the balm of troubled minds.*
Word Family **balmy** *adjective* (**balmier; balmiest**) (of weather) mild or warm.
[Latin *balsamum* balsam]

baloney (ba**lo**nee) *noun also* **boloney**
(*informal*) nonsense.

balsa (**bawl**-sa) *noun*
a tropical South American tree with extremely light soft wood, used for timber in rafts, model aircraft, etc.
[Spanish]

balsam (**bawl**-s'm) *noun*
any of various secretions from plants, used as a balm.
[Latin *balsamum*]

balustrade (**bal**-a-strade) *noun*
a series of upright supports joined at the top by a rail, as in a stone balcony, etc.

Word Family **baluster** *noun* an upright support that is part of a balustrade.
[Greek *balaustion* the pomegranate flower, because a baluster supposedly resembles it in shape]

bamboo *noun*
a tall tropical woody grass with long hollow jointed stems.

> **Bamboo** shows how a word that appears in English can have changed quite considerably from the foreign language word from which it comes. The word was originally *mambu*, a Malay word brought to Europe by Portuguese explorers. It appeared in this form in English in the 17th century and 18th century but for some reason not now known the letter *b* was substituted for the *m* and an *s* was added to the end of the word making *bambus* or alternatively *bambos*. This was later taken wrongly to be a plural, and the word *bamboo* was born.

bamboozle *verb*
1 to trick or deceive: *The con man bamboozled the woman out of £100.*
2 to puzzle or mystify. *I was completely bamboozled by the time he'd finished explaining it to me.*

ban *verb* (**bans; banning; banned**)
to prohibit: *I can't see why that book was banned.*
• **ban** *noun* an official order or prohibition: *There is a ban on fires in the open today.*
[Old English *bannan* to summon]

banal (ba-**nahl**) *adjective*
hackneyed, ordinary or trivial: *a banal conversation about the weather.*
Word Family **banally** *adverb*; **banality** (ba-**nal**-i-tee) *noun* (*plural* **banalities**)
1 the quality of being banal. 2 something which is banal.
[French]

banana (ba-**nah**-na) *noun*
a long curved tropical fruit with a yellow skin, growing in bunches called hands.
[Spanish]

band[1] *noun*
1 a group of musicians playing brass and percussion instruments: *the Salvation Army Band.*
2 a pop group.
3 a group of people acting together: *A small band of soldiers led the expedition.*
Word Family **band** *verb* 1 to unite or join together. 2 to arrange in bands or

categories. **bandsman** noun (plural **bandsmen**) a musician who plays in a brass band.

band² noun
1 a flat strip of any material for binding, trimming, etc.: *The box was strengthened with metal bands.*
2 a broad stripe crossing any surface: *The fish had bands of red and silver.*
3 *Radio* a waveband.
Word Family **band** verb to stripe or mark with bands.

bandage (**ban**-dij) noun
a strip of fabric, etc. used to bind a wound.
Word Family **bandage** verb.

bandanna noun
a large coloured handkerchief or cotton scarf.

bandicoot noun
any of a group of rat-like Australian marsupials with long pointed snouts.
[Hindi]

bandit noun
a robber or outlaw.
[Italian *bandito* outlawed or banished]

bandolier (ban-da-**leer**) noun also **bandoleer**
Military a belt worn over one shoulder and fitted with small loops for carrying cartridges.

bandsman ⇨ BAND¹.

bandstand noun
a platform, e.g. in a park, where a band can play outdoors.

bandwagon noun
Phrase **climb, jump on the bandwagon** to follow or join a popular movement, fashion, etc. because it appears likely to succeed.

bandy verb (**bandies**; **bandying**; **bandied**)
to pass back and forth: *Don't bandy words with me.* □ *The story was bandied about but she didn't believe it.*
• **bandy** adjective (**bandier**; **bandiest**)
bandy-legged.

bandy-legged adjective
having the legs curved outwards at the knees.

bane noun
anything which causes annoyance: *Those dogs are the bane of my life.*

bang noun
1 a sudden loud noise.
2 any violent blow or knock: *a nasty bang on the head.*

3 (**bangs**) *American* a fringe of hair.
Phrase **bang on** (informal) absolutely accurate.
Word Family **bang** verb; **bang** adverb with a bang.

banger noun
1 (informal) a sausage.
2 (informal) an old car.
3 a firework that explodes with a bang.

bangle noun
an ornamental band or chain without a clasp, worn around the arm.
[Hindi *bangri* a glass bracelet]

banian ⇨ BANYAN.

banish verb
1 to send a person into exile.
2 to put or drive something away: *to banish fear.*
Word Family **banishment** noun.

banister noun also **bannister**
1 one of the supports of a stair rail.
2 (**banisters**) a stair rail with its supports.

banjo noun (plural **banjos** or **banjoes**)
Music a fretted stringed instrument plucked with fingers or a plectrum.
[Greek *pandoura* a three-stringed lute]

bank¹ noun
1 a slope or area of raised ground: *The river has steep banks.*
2 a pile or solid mass: *a bank of clouds.*
3 a set of objects arranged in a line: *a bank of spotlights.*
• **bank** verb
1 to form into a bank: *The earth is banked up near the construction site.*
2 to tilt an aircraft laterally in flight.

bank² noun
1 *Commerce* an organization whose business is the safe keeping of money and valuables, lending and borrowing money, and in some cases issuing and exchanging foreign money.
2 a storage place, such as a blood bank.
3 a reserve or fund to or from which money may be paid, as in various card or gambling games.
• **bank** verb to deposit in a bank: *I banked the cheque.*
Phrase **bank on** to rely on: *We are banking on you to do a good job.*
Word Family **banker** noun 1 a person who manages or owns a bank. 2 a person in charge of the bank in a game.

bank account noun
short form is **account** the money kept by a customer at a bank, from which withdrawals may be made in cash or by

cheque and to which deposits may be
added.

bank holiday *noun*
a public holiday, originally a day when the
banks were closed by law.

banknote *noun*
a piece of paper money.

bankrupt *noun*
Law a person who cannot pay his or her
debts and whose possessions are given to a
trustee to be distributed among the people
to whom he or she owes money.
• **bankrupt** *adjective*
1 legally declared a bankrupt.
2 destitute: *He is morally bankrupt.*
Word Family **bankrupt** *verb* to make
bankrupt; **bankruptcy** (**bank**-rup-see)
noun the state of being bankrupt.
[BANK² + Latin *ruptus* broken]

banner *noun*
1 a piece of cloth, etc. held up on a pole in
a procession.
2 a flag, especially of a country, army, etc.:
the star-spangled banner.
3 a headline in a newspaper which extends
the full width of the page.

bannister ⇨ BANISTER.

banns *plural noun*
an announcement made in a church on
three successive Sundays, declaring that
two people intend to be married, so that
any legal objection to the marriage may be
made known.
[the old plural of *ban*]

banquet (**bang**-kwit) *noun*
a feast or ceremonial public dinner.
Word Family **banquet** *verb*.

banshee *noun*
(in Scottish and Irish mythology) a
supernatural being, believed to wail
around a house if someone is about to die.
[Irish *bean sidhe* a woman of the fairies]

bantam (**ban**-t'm) *noun*
a small domestic fowl, the male having
brightly coloured feathers.
[probably from *Bantam*, Indonesia]

bantamweight *noun*
a weight division in boxing, equal to about
8½ stone (54 kg).

banter *noun*
any playfully teasing or mocking talk.
Word Family **banter** *verb*; **banteringly**
adverb.

banyan *noun* also **banian**
an Indian fig tree whose branches send
down roots which develop into new
trunks.
[Sanskrit, a trader]

baobab (**bay**-o-bab) *noun*
a large African and Australian tree with a
very thick trunk.

baptism *noun*
Religion a ritual washing or bath, especially
as a sign of spiritual rebirth, purification or
initiation.
Phrase **baptism of fire** 1 a soldier's first
experience of battle. 2 any severe or
crucial test.
Word Family **baptismal** (bap-**tiz**-m'l)
adjective; **baptismally** *adverb*.
[Greek *baptizein* to dip]

Baptist *noun*
Christianity a member of any Protestant
sect teaching that only adult believers
should be baptized.

baptize, baptise *verb*
to perform the ritual of baptism.

bar *noun*
1 a piece of some solid material, usually
longer than it is wide: *the bars of a railing.*
□ *a bar of chocolate.*
2 a room or small establishment where
alcohol is served.
3 a counter where drinks are served.
4 *Music* a group of beats, of which the first
usually has an accent, marked off from
similar groups of beats.
5 *Music* short form of **bar line** the line
dividing groups of beats.
6 any barrier or obstruction: *Traditional
attitudes are a bar to reform.*
7 a stripe or band: *a bar of colour.*
8 an underwater ridge of sand or pebbles
which obstructs a river mouth or
harbour.
9 *Geography* a low narrow tongue of sand
or pebbles which has grown right across a
bar or inlet. Bars are formed by longshore
drift. Compare SPIT² *noun* (definition 2).
Phrase **be called to the bar** to be
admitted as a barrister.
• **bar** *verb* (**bars; barring; barred**)
1 to fasten or shut with or as if with a bar:
Don't forget to bar the gate.
2 to block, prohibit or obstruct: *Police
barred access to the building.* □ *He barred any
discussion of politics.*
• **bar** *preposition* except or omitting.

barb *noun*
1 a sharp backward point at the end of a
fish hook, harpoon, etc.

2 a sharp or cutting remark: *Barbs or taunts rarely anger her.*
[Latin *barba* a beard]

barbarian (bar-**bair**-i-an) *noun*
a person who is crude, coarse, brutal or uncivilized.
Word Family **barbarian, barbaric** (bar-**barr**-ik), **barbarous** (**bar**-ber-us) *adjective*; **barbarically, barbarously** *adverb*; **barbarize, barbarise** (**bar**-ber-ize) *verb*.
[Greek *barbaros* foreign, having unintelligible speech]

> ⚠ **Barbaric, barbarous** and **barbarian** all mean 'uncivilized', but *barbaric* suggests crudeness or wildness (*the barbaric grandeur of the symphony*), *barbarous* stresses cruelty or brutality (*the barbarous practice of torturing prisoners*) and *barbarian* is more neutral in tone (*barbarian tribes*).

barbarism (**bar**-ba-rizm) *noun*
a primitive or early stage of civilization: *living in a state of barbarism.*

barbarity (bar-**barr**-i-tee) *noun*
brutal or cruel behaviour: *The development of modern weapons is sheer barbarity.*

barbecue (**bar**-bi-kew) *noun*
1 an outdoor meal at which meat is grilled.
2 the structure or device on which the meat is grilled.
• **barbecue** *verb* (**barbecues; barbecuing; barbecued**).

> The word **barbecue** came to us from America, which acquired it from *barbacoa*, a word from Haiti in the West Indies meaning a wooden framework set on posts. The framework had several purposes. It could, for example, be a bed. However it was its other use as a framework for smoking or roasting meat that gave us our modern *barbecue*. Soon *barbecue* came to be used not only for the cooking apparatus but also for the gathering at which the cooking is done.

barbed wire *noun*
a type of wire with barbs at intervals, used for fences.

barbell *noun*
a steel bar about 2 m long, with weighted discs attached to each end, and used in weightlifting.

barber *noun*
a person who cuts or shaves men's hair as a trade.
[Latin *barba* a beard]

barbican *noun*
a watchtower guarding a town or castle gate.

barbiturate (bar-**bit**-yoo-rit) *noun*
any of a group of drugs used as sedatives.

bar chart *noun* also called **bar graph**.
a statistical diagram of bars with lengths proportional to the frequency each represents. Unlike a histogram, it can be used when one axis is not numerical, e.g. to show how many black, red, white, etc. cars pass a point in a given time interval. Compare HISTOGRAM.

bar code *noun*
a set of parallel lines and spaces of varying thicknesses used on a label to help speed up the recording of product sales on a computer.

bard *noun*
an old word for a poet or singer.

bare *adjective*
1 without clothing or covering: *bare feet.* □ *bare trees.*
2 empty or plain: *bare floorboards.* □ *The room was bare.*
3 basic, simple: *the bare facts.*
4 just sufficient: *He earned a bare living as a writer.*
• **bare** *verb* to make bare.
Word Family **barely** *adverb*; **bareness** *noun*.

bareback *adjective, adverb*
without a saddle: *a bareback rider.* □ *riding bareback.*

barefaced *adjective*
shameless or insolent: *He told a barefaced lie.*

barf *verb*
(*especially American informal*) to vomit.

bargain (**bar**-gin) *noun*
1 an agreement between two parties about how a transaction is to be conducted, especially with regard to buying and selling.
2 an item bought or offered for sale at a low price: *There are always good bargains in the shops after Christmas.*
Phrase **into the bargain** *She tripped and broke her watch into the bargain* (= in addition).
• **bargain** *verb* to arrive at an agreement, especially by haggling: *She enjoys bargaining with the greengrocer.*
Phrase **bargain for, bargain on** to expect: *The strong competition was more than we bargained for.*

barge (*rhymes with* large) *noun*
a flat-bottomed boat, sometimes without
an engine, used for loading and unloading
ships, or for transporting goods.
• **barge** *verb*
1 to move clumsily or heavily.
2 to rush in or intrude: *Don't barge into the
room without knocking.*
[Greek *baris* an Egyptian boat]

bar graph ⇨ BAR CHART.

baritone (**barr**-i-tone) *noun*
1 *Music* the male singing voice between
tenor and bass.
2 *Music* an instrument having this range.
[Greek *barys* deep + *tonos* tone]

barium (**bair**-i-um) *noun*
a soft poisonous metal. Its compounds are
used in making glass and fireworks, and in
medicine.
[Greek *baros* weight]

barium meal *noun*
barium sulphate fed to a patient so that
any obstruction in the intestines will show
up on an X-ray photograph.

bark[1] *noun*
the harsh abrupt sound made by a dog or
other animal.
• **bark** *verb*
1 to make the harsh abrupt sound of a dog
or other animal.
2 to speak sharply or gruffly: *The general
barked out his orders.*

bark[2] *noun*
the outer covering of the trunk and
branches of a tree.
• **bark** *verb*
1 to remove the bark from a tree.
2 to scrape or skin: *He barked his shins.*

bark[3] ⇨ BARQUE.

barley (**bar**-lee) *noun*
a cereal plant used as food and in making
malt and beer.

barley sugar *noun*
a sweet made from sugar boiled until it is
hard and brittle.

bar line ⇨ BAR (definition 5).

barmaid *noun*
a woman who serves drinks in a bar.

barman *noun* (*plural* **barmen**)
a man who serves drinks in a bar.

bar mitzvah (bar-**mits**-vah) *noun*
Judaism a religious ceremony for a boy at
the age of 13, showing that he is now an
adult. Compare BAT MITZVAH.
[Hebrew *bar mitzvah* son of the
commandment]

barmy *adjective* (**barmier; barmiest**)
(*informal*) silly, stupid or mad.
[from *barm*, a froth which forms on the
top of fermenting malt liquors]

barn *noun*
a simple farm building used to store hay,
etc.
[Old English *bere* barley + *aern* house]

barnacle (**bar**-na-k'l) *noun*
a small marine shellfish which clings
firmly to rocks, floating timber and the
bottoms of ships.

barnacle goose *noun* (*plural* **barnacle
geese**)
a medium-sized black and white goose
which breeds in the Arctic and visits
Europe in winter.

barney *noun* (*plural* **barneys**)
(*informal*) an argument or quarrel.

barnstorming *adjective*
exciting and full of energy: *a barnstorming
performance.*

barnyard *noun*
American the central yard of farm
buildings, partly surrounded by barns.

barometer (ba-**rom**-i-ta) *noun*
1 an instrument for measuring
atmospheric pressure.
2 anything which indicates change:
*Opinion polls are not true barometers of public
opinion.*
Word Family barometric (barr-a-**met**-
rik), **barometrical** *adjective*.
[Greek *baros* weight + METER]

baron *noun*
1 *History* a feudal lord who held power and
lands under the authority of the king.
2 a nobleman ranking below a viscount,
occupying the lowest rank of the peerage.
3 a magnate or powerful person in
industry or big business.
Word Family baroness *noun* **1** a female
baron **2** the wife of a baron; **baronial**
(ba-**ro**-nee-al) *adjective*.

baronet (**barr**-a-net) *noun*
a member of the lowest hereditary titled
British order.
Word Family baronetcy (**barr**-a-net-
see) *noun* the rank of a baronet.

baroque (ba-**rok**) *noun*
1 a style of art and architecture developed
in Europe during the 17th century,
characterized by bold and contorted
forms, exaggeration and theatrical effects.
2 the ornate style characteristic of some
17th-century music.

Word Family **baroque** *adjective*
overwrought, florid or extravagantly
ornamental in style.
[Portuguese *barroco* an irregular pearl]

barouche (ba-**roosh**) *noun*
an open four-wheeled carriage, with two
seats facing each other and a hood over the
back seat.
[Latin *birotus* two-wheeled]

barque (bark) *noun also* **bark**
1 *Nautical* a sailing vessel with three or
more masts, having square sails on all but
the mast furthest to the stern.
2 an old word for any boat or sailing vessel.
[Latin *barca* a boat]

barrack (**barr**-uk) *verb*
to shout against or jeer at, especially a
sporting team.
[Aboriginal *borak* banter]

barracks (**barr**-uks) *plural noun*
a group of buildings that are used as living
quarters for soldiers.
[Italian *baracca* a soldier's tent]

barracuda (barr-a-**koo**-da) *noun*
a savage fast-swimming fish, found in the
West Indies, and usually with one sharp
tooth near the tip of the lower jaw.
[Spanish]

barrage (**barr**-ah*zh*) *noun*
1 *Military* a concentration of artillery fire.
2 an overwhelming number: *The Prime
Minister faced a barrage of questions from
reporters.*
3 an artificial barrier in a river to regulate
the flow of water.

barrel *noun*
1 a large cylindrical container with flat
ends, made of curved wooden strips
bound together with hoops.
2 the tube-like part of a gun through
which a projectile is discharged.
3 any of various units of volume for
liquids, such as an oil barrel that is equal
to about 159 litres.
4 the part of a lock into which a key is
inserted.
Phrases **over a barrel** *We've got him over
a barrel* (= at our mercy). **scrape the
barrel** *The TV schedulers have really been
scraping the barrel this Christmas* (= using
the worst that is available).
• **barrel** *verb* (**barrels; barrelling;
barrelled**) (*informal*) to move fast:
barrelling along in the fast lane.

barrel organ *noun*
a hand-turned musical instrument in
which pins projecting from a rotating

barrel work a small row of organ pipes to
produce a tune.

barren *adjective*
sterile or unfruitful: *a barren woman.* □ *The
country is dry and barren.*

barricade *noun*
a temporary barrier or obstruction, usually
across a street.
• **barricade** *verb* to obstruct, enclose or
defend with or as if with a barricade.
[Spanish *barrica* a cask]

barrier *noun*
1 anything which obstructs or restrains:
Police installed barriers to control the crowd.
□ *The Canadian Rockies were the barrier
which delayed exploration.*
2 anything which separates: *a language
barrier.*

barrier reef ⇨ REEF¹ (definition 2).

barrister *noun*
Law a lawyer who is permitted to practise
as advocate in the higher courts, such as
the High Court. Compare LAWYER;
SOLICITOR.

barrow¹ *noun*
a handcart, such as a wheelbarrow, or a
street cart where vegetables, fruit, etc. are
sold.

barrow² *noun*
a mound of earth or stones built over a
grave, usually dating from prehistoric
times.

barter *verb*
to trade goods in return for other goods
rather than for money: *The farmer bartered
his best horse for ten cattle.*
• **barter** *noun.*

basalt (**bass**-awlt) *noun*
a basic dark-coloured igneous rock with
small even grains, formed by the rapid
cooling of lava on the earth's surface, and
used mainly for buildings and road metal.
Word Family **basaltic** (ba-**sawl**-tik)
adjective.
[Latin *basaltes* a touchstone]

base¹ *noun*
1 the bottom part of something, especially
the part which provides physical support:
a vase with a narrow base.
2 the fundamental part: *The base of this
soup is meat.*
3 *Baseball* any of the four fixed stations
around which the player must run.
4 a place from which work, operations, etc.
proceed and where equipment, etc. is
located: *a military base.*

5 *Maths* the line or surface on which a figure stands.

6 ⇨ LOGARITHM.

7 *Maths* the number which, when raised to various powers, forms the main counting units of a system.

8 *Chemistry* anything which reacts with an acid. A base which dissolves in water is called an alkali.

• **base** *verb* to establish or build upon: *His theory is based on careful research.*

Word Family **baseless** *adjective* having no base or support.

[Greek *basis* a step or pedestal]

base² *adjective*
low or contemptible: *a base crime.*
Word Family **basely** *adverb*; **baseness** *noun.*

baseball *noun*
1 a ball game played between two teams of nine on a diamond formed by four bases. Having hit the ball, the striker tries to score by running round the four bases before the ball is thrown home.
2 the ball used in this game.

baseball mitt ⇨ MITT (definition 3).

baseline *noun* also called **service line**.
Tennis the boundary line at each end of the court, behind which a player must stand when serving.

basement *noun*
the lowest level of a building, usually below ground level.

bases
the plural of **basis**.

bash *verb*
(*informal*) to strike violently.
• **bash** *noun* (*plural* **bashes**)
1 (*informal*) a crushing blow.
2 (*informal*) a try: *Tim will have a bash at anything.*

bashful *adjective*
timid or easily embarrassed.
Word Family **bashfully** *adverb*; **bashfulness** *noun.*
[same origin as *abash*]

basic (**bay**-sik) *adjective*
1 essential: *The basic principles of chess are easy to learn.*
2 plain, simple: *basic accommodation.*
3 *Chemistry* relating to or having the properties of a base.
Word Family **basically** *adverb* essentially; **basics** *plural noun* the facts or skills that are needed for something.

BASIC *noun*
Computers a widely used language with many applications.
[B(eginners') A(ll)-purpose S(ymbolic) I(nstruction) C(ode)]

basil (**baz**-il) *noun*
an aromatic herb used in cooking.
[Greek *basilikos* royal]

basilica (ba-**sil**-i-ka) *noun*
Christianity an oblong church with colonnades, a wide nave, side aisles, and an apse at one end.
[Greek *basiliké* royal (palace)]

basilisk *noun*
1 *Mythology* a reptile whose gaze and breath are fatal.
2 a small American lizard.
[Greek *basileus* king (of reptiles)]

basin (**bay**-sin) *noun*
1 a deep round container with sloping sides, used to hold liquids.
2 a similar vessel for mixing, cooking, etc.
3 *Geography* an area in which the strata dip from all directions towards a common central point.

basis (**bay**-sis) *noun* (*plural* **bases**) (**bay**-seez)
the foundation or fundamental principle, constituent, etc. of something: *The basis of my argument is this.*
[Greek, a step or pedestal]

bask (*rhymes with* ask) *verb*
1 to enjoy a pleasant warmth: *to bask in the sun.*
2 to enjoy: *She basked in his approval.*

basket *noun*
1 a container, usually with handles, made of woven reeds, straw, twigs, etc.
2 anything which has the shape or function of a basket, such as the net in the game of basketball.
Word Family **basketry, basketwork** *noun.*

basketball *noun*
1 a game played on a rectangular court between two teams of five, six or seven players. The aim is to throw an inflated leather ball through the basket suspended from an iron ring at either end of the court.
2 the ball used in this game.

basmati rice (baz-**mah**-ti) *noun*
a type of long-grain rice with a delicate aroma and flavour, used especially in Indian cooking.
[Hindi]

bas-relief (bass-re-**leef**) *noun*
a sculpture in low relief.
[Italian *basso relievo* low relief]

bass¹ (base) *adjective*
Music deep-sounding or low in pitch:
a rich bass voice. □ *a bass guitar.*
• **bass** *noun* (*plural* **basses**)
1 the lowest male singing voice.
2 an instrument having this range.
[Italian *basso*]

bass² (bass) *noun* (*plural* **bass** or **basses**)
a marine or freshwater fish related to the
perch.

bass clef ⇨ CLEF.

basset hound *noun*
a medium-sized hound with short legs,
originally used to hunt small animals.
[French *bas* low]

bassinet *noun*
a basket, sometimes with a hood, used as a
baby's cradle.
[French *bassin* a basin]

bassoon (ba-**soon**) *noun*
Music a wind instrument with a deep rich
tone, made from a long wooden tube
which doubles back on itself and played
with a double reed.
Word Family **bassoonist** *noun*.
[Italian]

bastard (**bah**-st'd *or* **bass**-t'd) *noun*
1 a child whose parents were not married
at the time of his or her birth.
2 (*informal*) a selfish or unscrupulous
person.
3 (*informal*) any person: *The poor bastard
lost his job.*
Word Family **bastardy** *noun* the state of
being a bastard.

bastardize, bastardise *verb*
1 to debase or corrupt.
2 an old word meaning 'to declare or prove
someone a bastard'.
Word Family **bastardization** *noun*.

baste¹ (*rhymes with* taste) *verb*
Cooking to pour liquid, especially melted
fat, over meat which is being roasted.

baste² *verb*
Needlework to tack with long loose stitches.

bastion (**bast**-i-on) *noun*
1 a protecting part of a rampart in a
fortification.
2 a person or thing that provides strong
defence or support: *They consider
themselves bastions of democracy.*
[Italian *bastione* bulwark]

bat¹ *noun*
an implement, usually wooden, used to hit
the ball in games such as cricket, baseball,
etc.
Phrase **off one's own bat** independently
or without assistance.
• **bat** *verb* (**bats; batting; batted**)
1 to hit the ball with a bat, as in table
tennis or cricket.
2 to be on the batting team: *We'll bat first.*

bat² *noun*
a flying mammal with membranes joining
the front and hind legs to form wings.
Phrase **have bats in the belfry** to have
mad or crazy ideas.

bat³ *verb* (**bats; batting; batted**)
to blink: *She admitted lying without batting
an eye.*

batch *noun* (*plural* **batches**)
a number of things produced or dealt with
together: *a batch of scones.* □ *batch
production.*
[Old English *bacan* to bake]

bate *verb*
Phrase **with bated breath** *She waited
for the decision with bated breath* (= in
suspense).
[shortening of ABATE]

bath (*rhymes with* path) *noun*
1 a large vessel containing water in which
one sits to wash.
2 an occasion of washing one's body in a
bath.
3 (**baths**) a public swimming pool.
4 a preparation in which something is
immersed: *The printing plates were placed in
an acid bath.*
• **bath** *verb*.

bathe (bayth) *verb*
1 to immerse or wash in liquid: *Bathe the
wound with antiseptic.* □ *Her eyes were bathed
with tears.*
2 to cover or envelop: *streets bathed in
sunlight.*
3 to swim in the sea, a river, lake, etc.
• **bathe** *noun*.

bathos (**bay**-thos) *noun*
a sudden change of mood or tone from
dignity or intensity to an absurd
anticlimax, especially in literature.
Compare PATHOS.
Word Family **bathetic** (ba-**thet**-ik)
adjective.
[Greek, depth]

bathroom *noun*
1 a room for washing in, usually having a basin, shower, bath, etc.
2 *American* a toilet.

> The word **bathroom** in Britain is usually used of a room with a bath or washing facilities in it. In America, it is commonly used for what we would call a toilet, WC or loo. British and American English are sometimes far apart in meaning as well as in spelling and pronunciation. Often the same word will have quite a different meaning in each. For example, in America *purse* means 'handbag' and the American word for the British 'purse' is *wallet*.

bathysphere (bath-a-sfeer) *noun*
a spherical device from which marine life, etc. may be observed in deep-sea diving.
[Greek *bathys* deep + SPHERE]

batik (ba-teek *or* bat-ik) *noun*
1 a method of printing on fabric using wax and dyes to make a pattern.
2 a fabric printed in this way.
[Malay]

bat mitzvah (bat-mits-vah) *noun*
Judaism a religious ceremony for a girl at the age of twelve, showing that she is now an adult. Compare BAR MITZVAH.

baton (batt-on) *noun*
a short stick or rod: *The conductor raised his baton and the orchestra began to play.* □ *She passed the baton to the next runner.*
[French *bâton*]

batsman *noun* (*plural* **batsmen**)
Cricket the player using the bat.

battalion (ba-tal-y'n) *noun*
1 *Military* a basic infantry unit consisting of several companies.
2 a large group.
[Italian *battaglia* a battle]

batten[1] *verb*
to prosper or grow fat, especially at the expense of others: *The landlord battened on his unfortunate tenants.*

batten[2] *noun*
1 *Nautical* a thin strip of wood or plastic slipped into a sail to keep it flat.
2 a light strip of wood for fastening or joining items such as fence wires.
• **batten** *verb*
Phrase **batten down** to fasten a ship's hatches with battens.

batter[1] *verb*
to damage by repeatedly striking or beating: *The ship was battered against the rocks.*

batter[2] *noun*
Cooking a beaten mixture of water or milk with flour, eggs, etc. used to coat foods for frying, make pancakes, etc.

batter[3] *noun*
Sport the player using the bat in a game of baseball, softball, etc.

battering ram *noun*
a long heavy beam, formerly used as a weapon for breaking down walls or gates.

battery *noun* (*plural* **batteries**)
1 *Electricity* a group of cells connected together in order to produce a higher electric current or voltage.
2 *Engineering* a set of similar machines or parts: *a battery of printing presses.*
3 a group of guns on a warship.
4 *Military* a tactical unit of artillery, equivalent to an infantry company.
5 *Military* a platform or other structure supporting guns.
6 *Law* an attack on a person by striking or wounding: *He was charged with assault and battery.*

battery hen *noun*
a hen kept with others in a battery of cages and mechanically fed throughout its life, to promote high egg production. Compare FREE-RANGE HEN.

battle *noun*
1 a fight, especially between organized forces.
2 any struggle: *the battle against poverty.*
Word Family battle *verb*; **battler** *noun* a person who battles or struggles, often unsuccessfully.
[Latin *battuere* to strike]

battleaxe *noun*
1 a large broad-headed axe, formerly used as a weapon.
2 (*informal*) a domineering woman.

battledress *noun*
the uniform worn by soldiers in battle.

battlefield *noun* also called **battleground**.
the place where a battle is or was fought.

battlement *noun*
(*often* **battlements**) the upper edge of a wall containing a series of openings and used for defence.

battleship *noun*
a powerful and heavily armoured warship.

batty *adjective* (**battier; battiest**)
(*informal*) mad.

bauble (baw-b'l) *noun*
a pretty but worthless object.

Bauhaus (*rhymes with* cow-house) *noun*
a style of architecture and design in which
form is influenced by function. It
originated in Germany in 1919.
[German *Bau* building + *Haus* house]

baulk (*rhymes with* walk) *verb* also **balk**
1 to stop and refuse to continue: *The horse
baulked at the gate.*
2 to object to: *She baulked at the idea of
marriage.*
3 to prevent or thwart: *a publicity campaign
baulked by a newspaper strike.*

bauxite (bawk-site) *noun*
the main ore of aluminium, being a rock
composed mainly of aluminium oxide or
hydroxide.
[from *Les Baux*, France, where first found]

bawdy *adjective* (**bawdier; bawdiest**)
crudely or coarsely humorous: *a bawdy
joke.*
Word Family **bawdily** *adverb*;
bawdiness *noun*.

bawl *verb*
1 to shout or yell out loudly: *He bawled out
my name from across the street.*
2 to cry or sob noisily: *She broke down on
the spot and just bawled.*
Phrase **bawl out** *She was bawled out for
cheating* (= scolded severely).
• **bawl** *noun*.
[Latin *baulare* to bark]

bay¹ *noun*
1 a curved section of the coast which
partly surrounds an area of sea.
2 the body of water partly surrounded in
this way.

bay² *noun*
1 *Architecture* the part of a wall between
two columns or arches.
2 a recess or area set back or apart from
another: *a parking bay.*

bay³ *verb*
(of a hound) to utter a deep drawn-out
bark, especially when hunting.
• **bay** *noun*
Phrases **bring to bay** *The criminal was
finally brought to bay* (= forced into a last
stand). **hold at bay, keep at bay** *This
medicine will hold the pain at bay* (= keep it
at a distance).

bay⁴ *noun*
a European or West Indian tree related to
the laurel.

bay⁵ *noun*
a dark brown horse, usually with a black
mane and tail.

bay leaf *noun* (*plural* **bay leaves**)
the dried leaf of a bay tree, used as a herb.

bayonet (bay-o-net) *noun*
a sharp blade attached to the end of a rifle,
used to stab or slash.
• **bayonet** *verb* (**bayonets; bayoneting;
bayoneted**).
[French, from *Bayonne* where first made]

bayou (by-yoo) *noun*
American a small marshy tributary of a
lake or river.
[Amerindian *bayuk* a small stream]

bay window *noun*
a window projecting from a building.

bazaar (ba-zar) *noun*
1 an Eastern marketplace or street of
shops.
2 a sale of miscellaneous objects, especially
to aid a charity.
[Persian]

bazooka (ba-zoo-ka) *noun*
a portable rocket launcher firing a small
armour-piercing rocket, used by infantry
against tanks.
[American slang *bazoo* mouth]

be *verb*
(I **am**; he, she, it **is**; we, you, they **are**;
being; I, he, she, it **was**; we, you, they
were; **been**; *old forms:* thou **art**; thou **wast**
or **wert**)
1 to exist or live.
2 to take place or occur: *When is your
birthday?*
3 to become: *What will you be when you
grow up?*
4 special use joining subject and predicate:
You are late. □ *Today is Wednesday.*
5 special use with other verbs to form
present continuous, past and future tenses
and the passive voice: *He is playing outside.*
□ *You were walking too fast.* □ *She is coming
later.* □ *We were left alone.*
Phrases **be-all and end-all** *To win the
championship was the be-all and end-all for
him* (= the most important aim). **for the
time being** *I have finished for the time being*
(= for the present). **-to-be** *her husband-to-
be* (= future).

beach *noun* (*plural* **beaches**)
the gently sloping land at the water's edge,
composed of sand, pebbles, etc. formed by
the waves.
• **beach** *verb* to bring a boat, etc. up onto a
beach from the water.

beachcomber (**beech**-ko-ma) *noun*
a person who collects articles washed up
onto beaches, often for a living.

beachhead *noun*
an area on an enemy shore occupied by an
advance force, before support troops and
supplies are landed.

beacon (**bee**-k'n) *noun*
1 a signal used as a guide or warning, such
as a fire on a hilltop, a flashing light from a
lighthouse or a radio signal.
2 anything which serves as or shines like a
beacon.
[Old English *beacn* a sign]

bead *noun*
1 a small ball of glass, wood or similar
material, pierced so that it may be put on
a string.
2 a drop or bubble: *beads of sweat.*
3 (**beads**) a rosary.
• **bead** *verb* to decorate or form with
beads.
[Middle English *bede* a prayer or rosary
bead]

beading *noun*
1 a narrow strip of rounded wood used to
trim joints or corners.
2 also called **beadwork**. the threading of
beads into patterns or designs for
decoration, etc.

beadle *noun*
the leader of a ceremonial procession at a
university, official function, etc.

beady *adjective* (**beadier; beadiest**)
small and bright like a bead: *beady eyes.*
Word Family **beadily** *adverb.*

beagle *noun*
a small smooth-haired hound used for
hunting hares, etc.
[Old French *beegueule* a noisy person]

beak *noun*
1 also called **bill**. the horny mouthparts of
a bird.
2 (*informal*) a magistrate.
3 (*informal*) a headmaster.

beaker *noun*
1 a flat-bottomed cylindrical vessel,
usually with a beak for pouring liquids,
used in laboratories.
2 a wide-mouthed drinking vessel, usually
made of plastic or glass.

beam *noun*
1 a long thick piece of wood, steel or
concrete, used as a horizontal support,
such as a joist.
2 a bundle of parallel light rays or other
radiation.

3 *Nautical* the widest part of a ship.
4 *Nautical* the side of a ship.
5 the crossbar of a balance, supporting the
pans.
6 a radiant smile.
Phrase **broad in the beam** overweight,
especially having broad hips.

bean *noun*
1 a long thin green or yellow vegetable
which grows on a vine and contains small
seeds.
2 the seed of a coffee, cocoa, etc. plant.
Phrases **full of beans** energetic or
cheerful. **not have a bean** to have no
money at all. **spill the beans** to let out
secret information.

beanbag *noun*
1 a small cloth bag filled with beans and
used as a toy.
2 a large bag made of leather, cloth, etc.,
filled with small soft objects and able to be
formed into a comfortable seat.

bean curd ⇨ TOFU.

beanpole *noun*
(*informal*) a tall thin person.

bean sprouts *plural noun*
the germinated seeds of millet, used as a
vegetable and especially popular in Asian
cookery.

bear[1] (bair) *verb* (**bears; bearing; bore;
borne**)
1 to support: *Will that branch bear my
weight?* □ *I am willing to bear the blame for
my mistakes.*
2 to carry or give birth to an offspring: *She
bore him three sons.*
3 to convey: *The carriage bore us to our
destination.*
4 to put up with or suffer: *I cannot bear
pain.* □ *Bear with me until I've finished.*
5 to move or lie in a certain direction: *We
must bear hard right at the next intersection.*
6 (of a tree or plant) to produce fruit or
flowers
7 to possess: *He bears the unlikely name of
Blake Fox.*
8 to harbour: *Do not bear grudges.*
9 to conduct: *She bore herself well during
that difficult time.*
Phrases **bear down on 1** to press hard
upon. **2** to approach: *The ship bore down on
the raft.* **bear out** to confirm: *His story
bears out what you said.* **bear up** to keep up
one's spirits or strength when under strain.
bring to bear to apply: *Pressure was
brought to bear on him to resign.*
Word Family **bearable** *adjective*
endurable; **bearably** *adverb.*

**bear² ** *noun*
1 a large mammal with a shaggy coat and a short tail, such as the brown **grizzly bear** of America or the white **polar bear** of the arctic regions.
2 *Stock Exchange* a person who sells, for future delivery, shares he or she does not possess, hoping to buy at a lower price before he or she has to deliver. Compare BULL¹ (definition 3).
Word Family **bearish** *adjective* 1 like a bear. 2 *Stock Exchange* causing or characterized by falling prices: *a bearish market*.

bear-baiting *noun*
History a cruel sport in which dogs attacked a captive bear.

beard (beerd) *noun*
the coarse hair on the face of adult males, especially on or below the chin.
● **beard** *verb* to oppose or defy: *to beard the lion in his den*.
Word Family **bearded** *adjective* having a beard.

bearer (**bair**-a) *noun*
1 a person who brings or carries something: *Please pay the bearer of this letter*.
2 *Commerce* a person who presents a cheque, money order, etc. at a bank.

bearing (**bair**-ing) *noun*
1 a person's posture, manner, etc: *He has a dignified bearing*.
2 a relevance or relation: *That evidence has little bearing on the case*.
3 (*usually* **bearings**) the direction or relative position of anything: *I cannot find my bearings*.
4 *Engineering* a part which supports a rotating part in a machine.
5 a direction measured as an angle from one position to another: *a compass bearing*.

beast *noun*
1 a four-footed animal.
2 a wild, cruel or inhuman person.

beastly *adjective* (**beastlier; beastliest**)
(*informal*) nasty or unpleasant: *What beastly weather!*
Word Family **beastliness** *noun*.
[Latin *bestia*]

beat *verb* (**beats; beating; beat; beaten**)
1 to hit or strike repeatedly: *The rain beat against the windows*.
2 to flap: *The trapped bird was frantically beating its wings*.
3 to stir or mix thoroughly: *Beat six eggs*.

4 to defeat: *The team was beaten by two points*.
5 to make by trampling: *The animals had beaten a track to the waterhole*.
6 to mark or measure: *The conductor was beating time with her baton*.
7 (*informal*) to baffle: *It beats me!*
Phrases **beat down** to bargain with to lower a price: *We beat him down to £6.* **beat hollow** to defeat decisively or thoroughly. **beat it** (*informal*) to leave: *Beat it before I call the police!* **beat up** to attack or assault with violence.
● **beat** *noun*
1 a regular repeated stroke or sound.
2 *Music* a pulse or rhythm.
3 a regular route or area: *The policeman's beat covered most of the suburb*.
4 *Hunting* the flushing out of game by moving noisily through scrub, etc.
Word Family **beat** *adjective* (*informal*) worn out or defeated; **beater** *noun* a person or thing that beats.

beatific (bee-a-**tiff**-ik) *adjective*
1 blissful.
2 making blessed.
Word Family **beatifically** *adverb*.

beatification
(bee-att-i-fik-**ay**-sh'n) *noun*
Roman Catholicism the Pope's official statement that a dead person is in heavenly bliss, as a step towards declaring that person a saint.
Word Family **beatify** (bee-**att**-i-fie) *verb* (**beatifies; beatifying; beatified**).
[Latin *beatus* blessed + *facere* to make]

beatitude (bee-**att**-i-tewd) *noun*
a state of bliss or blessedness.

beatnik *noun*
a person who avoids or rejects conventional standards of behaviour, dress, etc.
[probably from BEAT (rhythm) + Yiddish suffix *-nik* person]

beau (bo) *noun* (*plural* **beaux** (bo) or **beaus** (boze))
1 (*dated*) a boyfriend or lover.
2 (*dated*) a man who is extremely concerned with his clothes and appearance, a dandy.
[French, handsome]

Beaufort scale (**bo**-fort skale) *noun*
Weather a scale and description of wind in which 0 is calm and force 12 is a hurricane.
[after its inventor, *Sir Francis Beaufort*, 1774-1857, a British admiral]

beauteous (bew-ti-us) *adjective*
a poetic word for **beautiful**.

beautician (bew-**tish**-'n) *noun*
a person whose work is to care for the body, chiefly with massage, manicure and facials.

beautiful (bew-ti-full) *adjective*
giving pleasure or delight to the senses: *a beautiful face*.
Word Family **beautifully** *adverb*;
beautify *verb* (**beautifies; beautifying; beautified**) to adorn or make beautiful.

beauty (bew-tee) *noun* (*plural* **beauties**)
1 the quality of being pleasing and exciting to the senses.
2 anything which is beautiful or particularly pleasing.

beauty salon *noun* also called **beauty parlour**.
a shop which provides services such as hairdressing, manicures, massage or skin care.

beaux
a plural of **beau**.

beaver *noun*
1 a small amphibious North American dam-building mammal with webbed hind feet, thick fur and a paddle-like tail.
2 the fur of this animal.

becalmed (bi-**kahmd**) *adjective*
being unable to move because there is no wind: *The ship was becalmed*.
Word Family **becalm** *verb*

because (bi-**koz**) *conjunction, adverb*
for the reason that: *We could not see because it was dark.*

beck[1] *noun*
Phrase **at the beck and call of** *He is at the beck and call of his mother* (= obedient to the slightest wish of).

beck[2] *noun*
a small mountain stream or brook.

beckon *verb*
to signal or summon by a gesture: *He beckoned us to follow.*

become (bi-**kum**) *verb* (**becomes; becoming; became; become**)
1 to come to be: *It has become a habit.*
□ *What will become of you?*
2 to suit well: *That that becomes you.*

becoming *adjective*
1 proper or suitable: *Such behaviour is not becoming to your position.*
2 attractive: *What a becoming dress.*
Word Family **becomingly** *adverb*.

bed *noun*
1 a fixture or surface for sleeping on, usually with a frame, mattress, pillow and coverings.
2 a place to sleep for the night.
3 a flat base on which something rests: *The benches in the park were set into a bed of concrete.*
4 the ground or surface beneath something: *The sunken ship rested on the seabed.*
5 *Geology* a layer of sedimentary rock of varying thickness.
6 an area of soil in a garden in which plants are grown.
● **bed** *verb* (**beds; bedding; bedded**)
1 to provide with or put into a bed.
2 (*informal*) to go to bed with for the purpose of sexual intercourse: *to bed a wench.*

bed and breakfast *noun*
short form is **b & b** overnight accommodation as provided by hotels, boarding houses, etc.

bedclothes *plural noun*
the blankets and sheets for a bed.

bedding *noun*
materials used to form a bed, such as straw for animals.

bedeck (bi-**dek**) *verb*
to decorate or adorn: *The hall was bedecked with flowers.*

bedevil (bi-**dev**-il) *verb* (**bedevils; bedevilling; bedevilled**)
to confuse or torment: *He was bedevilled by questions.*

bedlam *noun*
a scene of noisy uproar and confusion: *There was bedlam in the school after the fire.*

> **Bedlam** is one of many words in English which have their origins in proper names. *Bedlam* is named after a place, the Hospital of St Mary of *Bethlehem*, a mental hospital in Bishopsgate in London. *Bethlehem* was shortened to *bedlam* – *bedlam* was in fact the Middle English word for *Bethlehem* – and the hospital became known as that. Because many of the patients were badly disturbed and often noisy, the hospital became known for its noise and confusion. Thus *bedlam* became a word for a scene of uproar and confusion.

bedlinen *noun*
the sheets and pillowcases for a bed.

bedpan *noun*
a pan used as a toilet by people confined to bed.

bedraggled (bi-**dragg**-'ld) *adjective*
limp, wet and dirty: *She was bedraggled after her fall in the river.*

bedridden *adjective*
forced to remain in bed because of illness, old age, etc.

bedrock *noun*
1 *Geology* the solid rock under the soil and subsoil.
2 underlying ideas, facts or principles: *a relationship built on the bedrock of trust.*

bedroom *noun*
a room for sleeping in.

bedsit *noun* also called **bedsitter** or **bed-sitting room**.
a flat consisting of one room for living and sleeping in, often without a separate kitchen.

bedsore *noun*
a sore caused by a prolonged stay in bed.

bedspread *noun*
a decorative cloth cover for a bed.

bedstead (**bed**-sted) *noun*
a framework of wood or metal, supporting the springs and mattress of a bed.

bee *noun*
1 a stinging insect with licking mouthparts for gathering nectar. Bees live in large groups and produce honey.
2 a meeting for work, entertainment, etc.: *a spelling bee.*
Phrase **have a bee in one's bonnet** *She has a bee in her bonnet about health foods* (= is obsessed).

beech *noun*
a large deciduous tree found in the northern hemisphere, with shiny leaves, small triangular nuts and smooth bark, and timber which is used for furniture.

beef *noun*
1 the flesh of a cow, bull or ox.
2 (*informal*) a complaint: *She went to the management with her beefs.*
• **beef** *verb* (*informal*) to complain.
Phrase **beef up** to strengthen or reinforce.
[Latin *bovis* of an ox]

beefburger ⇨ HAMBURGER.

beefeater *noun*
a Yeoman of the Guard.

beehive *noun*
1 a natural or artificial structure housing bees.
2 a colony of bees living in a hive.

beeline *noun*
Phrase **make a beeline for** *We all made a beeline for the birthday cake* (= went directly to).

Beelzebub (bee-**el**-zi-bub) *noun*
the Devil.
[Hebrew *ba'alzebub* lord of the flies]

been the past participle of **be**.

beep *verb* to produce a short high-pitched sound: *The machine beeped every 20 seconds.*
• **beep** *noun.*

beeper ⇨ PAGER.

beer *noun*
1 an alcoholic drink brewed and fermented from malt and flavoured with hops.
2 a non-alcoholic drink made from roots, sugar and yeast, such as ginger beer.
small beer a person or thing of no importance.

beeswax *noun*
a wax secreted by bees and often used for polishing wood.

beet *noun*
a biennial plant with an edible root and leaves. **Beet sugar** is made from the roots of the sugar beet.

beetle *noun*
a flying insect with biting mouthparts and hard forewings which protect the hindwings.
[Old English *bitula* a biting thing]

beetroot *noun*
a round dark red root of a variety of beet, used as food.
• **beetroot** *adjective* crimson like beetroot: *Her face was beetroot with embarrassment.*

befall (bi-**fall**) *verb* (**befalls; befalling; befell; befallen**)
to happen or occur: *Whatever befalls, let us remain friends.*

befit (bi-**fit**) *verb* (**befits; befitting; befitted**)
to be suitable or appropriate for: *It does not befit your position to talk like that.*
Word Family **befittingly** *adverb*.

before *adverb*
1 previously or earlier: *Has he been here before?* □ *Start when I say and not before.*
2 ahead: *He rode before to show us the way home.*
• **before** *preposition*

1 ahead of or in advance of: *We stood before the door.*
2 earlier or sooner than: *before the war.*
3 in the presence of: *I get tongue-tied before an audience.*
4 under consideration by: *The issue before us is this.*
• **before** *conjunction*
1 previously to the time when: *before we leave.*
2 rather than: *Death before dishonour!*

beforehand *adverb*
earlier or in advance: *I know about it beforehand.*

befriend (bi-**frend**) *verb*
to become a friend of: *She befriended her new neighbours.*

befuddle *verb*
to make stupid or confused: *His mind was befuddled with alcohol.*

beg *verb* (**begs; begging; begged**)
1 to ask for charity: *He had to beg for his meals.*
2 to ask for earnestly: *to beg forgiveness.*
3 to take the liberty of: *I beg to differ with you there.*
Phrases beg the question to take for granted the very matter which is in question. **go begging** to be unwanted and therefore available: *Is that sandwich going begging?*

beget *verb* (**begets; begetting; begot; begotten**)
an old word meaning 'to generate or produce': *He has begotten four sons.*
□ *Poverty begets hardship.*

beggar *noun*
1 a person who lives by begging.
2 any poor person.
3 a wretched or roguish person: *What a naughty little beggar.*
• **beggar** *verb* to reduce to poverty.
Phrase beggar belief, beggar description to be extraordinary or unbelievable.
Word Family beggary *noun* the state of being a beggar.

begin *verb* (**begins; beginning; began; begun**)
1 to start: *We will begin work after lunch.*
2 (of an action or state) to come into existence: *It began to rain.*
Word Family beginner *noun* a person who is learning or has little experience.

beginning *noun*
the start or first part of anything: *Have you read the beginning of that story?*

begone (bi-**gon**) *interjection*
an old exclamation meaning 'go away!'

begonia (bi-**go**-ni-a) *noun*
a garden plant with brightly coloured flowers and leaves.
[after *M. Bégon*, 1638-1710, a French patron of botany]

begrudge (bi-**gruj**) *verb*
to be envious of: *I do not begrudge him his wealth.*
Word Family begrudgingly *adverb.*

beguile (bi-**gile**) *verb*
1 to charm or amuse: *We beguiled the child with fairy stories.*
2 to get or take by dishonesty or tricks: *She was beguiled out of her savings.*
Word Family beguiling *adjective*;
beguilement *noun.*

behalf *noun*
interest or part: *On whose behalf are you acting?*

behave (bi-**hayv**) *verb*
1 to act, especially in relation to what is accepted or expected: *How did she behave today?*
2 to behave well: *He promised to behave at school.*

behaviour (bi-**hayv**-y'r) *noun* (*American* **behavior**)
any actions or manner of acting: *His behaviour at home is dreadful.*

behaviourism (bi-**hayv**-y'r-izm) *noun* (*American* **behaviorism**)
the belief that psychology, sociology, etc. should study only actual behaviour as distinct from unobservable qualities like the mind, and that behaviour is mainly determined by emotions of fear, anger or content.

behead (bi-**hed**) *verb*
to cut off the head of.

behest *noun*
a command or bidding: *You must do it at the law's behest.*

behind *preposition, adverb*
1 at the back of: (as a preposition) *behind the house.* (as an adverb) *The children walked behind.*
2 supporting: *We're all behind you in this matter.*
3 less advanced: *He's behind in Maths.*
4 late, in arrears: *You're behind with the rent.*
• **behind** *noun* (*informal*) the hindquarters of a person or animal.

behindhand *adverb, adjective*
late or behind in progress: *She's behindhand in her studies.*

behold *verb* (**beholds; beholding; beheld**)
an old word meaning 'to see or look at'.
Word Family beholder *noun*.

beholden *adjective*
bound by gratitude or in debt: *We are beholden to the government for the wage increase.*

behove *verb*
(*formal*) to be right and fitting: *It behoves you to make a speech.*

beige (bay*zh*) *noun*
a light brownish-yellow colour.
• **beige** *adjective*.
[French]

being *noun*
1 a creature which exists or lives: *a human being.*
2 existence or life: *When did the Labour Party come into being?*

belabour (bi-**lay**-b'r) *verb* (*American* **belabor**)
to beat or strike hard: *He was belaboured with clubs.*

belated (bi-**lay**-tid) *adjective*
late: *A belated happy birthday for last week.*
Word Family belatedly *adverb*; **belatedness** *noun*.

belay (*verb*s; **belays; belaying; belayed**)
to fasten a rope around an object without using a knot.

belch *verb*
1 to eject gas or wind noisily from the stomach through the mouth.
2 to gush or burst out: *The volcano belched out lava and smoke.*
• **belch** *noun* (*plural* **belches**).

beleaguer (bi-**lee**-g'r) *verb*
to besiege or surround: *The lecturer was beleaguered with questions.*

belfry (**bel**-free) *noun* (*plural* **belfries**)
a bell tower.

belie (bi-**lie**) *verb* (**belies; belying; belied**)
1 to give a false or wrong idea of: *His words belied his actual feelings.*
2 to fail to justify or fulfil: *You have belied our faith in you.*

belief (bi-**leef**) *noun*
1 the feeling or confidence that something is real, true or worthwhile: *They laughed at his belief in ghosts.* □ *Her claim was beyond belief.*

2 something which is taught or accepted as true: *a religious belief.*

believe (bi-**leev**) *verb*
1 to accept as real or true: *Do you believe in U.F.O.s?*
2 to have faith or trust in: *You must believe in me.*
Phrase **make believe** *Let's make believe we are pirates* (= imagine).
Word Family believable *adjective*; **believably** *adverb*; **believer** *noun* a person who believes, especially one belonging to a particular religious faith.

Belisha beacon (bi-leesh-a bee-k'n) *noun*
a pole with an amber flashing light, indicating a zebra crossing.
[after *Leslie Hore-Belisha*, Minister of Transport when they were introduced in 1934]

belittle *verb*
to make something seem unimportant or less valuable: *Do not belittle his efforts.*
Word Family belittlement *noun*.

bell *noun*
1 a hollow metal cup, usually with a tongue or hammer inside, which makes a ringing sound when hit.
2 the sound made by a bell.
3 any device which produces a ringing sound: *an electric doorbell.*
4 something which has the shape of a bell, such as the flared end of a brass musical instrument.
5 *Nautical* the stroke of the bell that marks off each half-hour of the watch, so that a four-hour watch ends at eight bells.
Phrase **ring a bell** to sound familiar: *Does his name ring a bell?*

belladonna (bel-a-**don**-a) *noun* also called **deadly nightshade; nightshade**.
a poisonous plant with red flowers and black berries from which a drug (atropine) is made.
[Italian *bella* beautiful + *donna* woman]

bell-bottomed *adjective*
widening into a bell-shape at the bottom: *bell-bottomed jeans.*

bellboy *noun*
(*especially American*) a boy servant in a hotel, etc.

belle (bel) *noun*
a beautiful girl or woman: *She was the belle of the ball.*
[French, beautiful]

bellhop *noun*
American a bellboy.

bellicose (**bell**-i-kose) *adjective*
warlike or eager to fight: *The ill-treated inhabitants became bellicose.*
Word Family bellicosity (bel-i-**kos**-i-tee) *noun*.
[Latin *bellum* war]

belligerent (bi-**lij**-a-r'nt) *adjective*
1 aggressive or hostile: *We were shocked at her belligerent reply.*
2 engaged in war: *a belligerent nation.*
Word Family belligerent *noun* a person or group engaged in a war; **belligerently** *adverb*; **belligerence, belligerency** *noun*.
[Latin *belligerare* to wage war]

bell jar *noun*
a bell-shaped glass vessel, used for protecting delicate instruments, holding gases, etc. in laboratory experiments.

bellow (**bel**-o) *verb*
to make a loud animal-like cry or roar: *He bellowed with rage and pain.*
• **bellow** *noun*.

bellows (**bel**-oze) *plural noun*
a device for pumping a stream of air, e.g. to kindle a fire or to produce sound from the pipes of an organ or similar musical instrument.

bell tower *noun*
a tower containing a bell.

belly *noun* (*plural* **bellies**)
1 the lower part of the body containing the stomach and intestines. ⇨ ABDOMEN.
2 the lower or inner part of anything: *the belly of a ship.*
3 any bulging or rounded part or surface: *the belly of a guitar.*

bellyache *verb*
(*informal*) to grumble or complain.
• **bellyache** *noun*
1 (*informal*) a pain in the stomach.
2 (*informal*) a complaint.

belly button *noun*
(*informal*) the navel.

belly dance *noun*
a solo dance consisting of movements of the stomach muscles and the hips.

bellyflop *noun*
(*Swimming informal*) an awkward dive in which one lands forwards flat on the water.

bellyful *noun* (*plural* **bellyfuls**)
1 enough food to eat.
2 (*informal*) far more than enough of something: *I'd had a bellyful of their complaining.*

belly landing *noun*
the landing of an aeroplane on its fuselage when its landing gear fails to operate.

belly laugh *noun*
a deep loud laugh.

belong *verb*
to have a correct, proper or usual place: *Where do these books belong?*
Phrase belong to 1 *That house belongs to my aunt* (= is owned by). 2 *She belongs to the golf club* (= is a member of).

belongings *plural noun*
possessions, especially personal ones.

beloved (bi-**luvd** or bi-**luv**-id) *adjective*
much loved.
• **beloved** *noun*.

below *preposition, adverb*
1 in or to a lower place or position: (as a preposition) *The sun sank below the horizon.* (as an adverb) *The lift descended to the floor below.*
2 at a later point on a page: *See the footnote below.*
3 downstream from: *the tree just below the bridge.*
4 lower than the deck of a ship: *The passengers stayed below during the storm.*
5 beneath: *She thought it below her to travel by bus.*

belt *noun*
1 a band worn around the waist to attach objects or keep clothes in place.
2 a large strip of land with common features or characteristics: *the wheat belt.*
3 a flexible band passing around two or more pulleys: *a conveyor belt.*
Phrase below the belt *That remark was a bit below the belt* (= unfair).
• **belt** *verb*
1 (*informal*) to thrash or hit.
2 (*informal*) to go very quickly: *He belted down the road.*
3 to fasten with a belt: *a loosely belted jacket.*
Phrase belt up (*informal*) *Belt up before your mother hears* (= be quiet).

belvedere (**bel**-va-deer) *noun*
an ornamental tower on an estate, commanding a view.
[Italian *bel* beautiful + *vedere* to see]

belying the present participle of **belie**.

bemoan *verb*
to mourn or show sorrow for: *They bemoaned the loss of their leader.*

bemused (bi-**mewzd**) *adjective*
confused or perplexed: *a bemused frown.*
Word Family bemuse *verb*.

ben *noun*
Scottish a mountain.

bench *noun* (*plural* **benches**)
1 a long seat for several people.
2 a long heavy worktable: *a carpenter's
bench.*
3 *Geography* a raised strip of relatively level
earth or rock.
4 *Parliament* the seat occupied by certain
ranks of members: *the Opposition bench.*
5 *Law* the judge or judges of a court: *The
bench will now pass sentence.*
6 *Law* the seat or position of a judge: *The
prisoner will stand before the bench.*

benchmark *noun*
a standard to compare a product
against its specification.

bend *verb* (**bends; bending; bent**)
1 to turn or force into a particular shape or
direction: *He bent the wire into a loop.*
□ *The road bends sharply here.* □ *We bent our
steps towards home.*
*Figurative The prisoner still didn't bend
after weeks of torture* (= yield, submit).
2 to stoop: *She bent to go under the arch.*
● **bend** *noun*
1 a turn or change in direction.
2 (**the bends**) ⇨ DECOMPRESSION SICKNESS.
Phrase **round the bend** mad.

bender *noun*
(*informal*) a drinking spree.

beneath *adverb, preposition*
under or below: *They sat beneath the oak
tree.* □ *It is beneath my dignity to comment.*

benediction (ben-i-**dik**-sh'n) *noun*
a grace or blessing.
[*bene-* + Latin *dictio* a declaration]

benefactor (**ben**-i-fakt-a) *noun*
a person giving kindly help or support,
especially financial aid.
Word Family **benefactress** *noun* a
female benefactor; **benefaction** (ben-i-
fak-sh'n) *noun* (*formal*) a good deed or
charitable gift.
[*bene-* + Latin *factor* a doer]

benefice (**ben**-i-fis) *noun*
the church property from which a minister
earns a living.

beneficial (ben-i-**fish**-'l) *adjective*
having a good or helpful effect: *A balanced
diet is beneficial to one's health.*
Word Family **beneficially** *adverb.*

beneficiary (ben-i-**fish**-a-ree) *noun*
(*plural* **beneficiaries**)
a person who receives a benefit or
advantage, such as an inheritance.

benefit *noun*
1 a thing which is helpful or favourable: *I
hope the money will be of benefit to you.*
2 a payment or assistance given by an
institution, government, etc.:
unemployment benefit.
3 an entertainment held to raise money for
charity.
● **benefit** *verb* (**benefits; benefiting** or
benefitting; benefited or **benefitted**).

benevolent (bi-**nev**-a-l'nt) *adjective*
1 kind or wishing well to others: *a
benevolent attitude.*
2 formed for charitable purposes rather
than profit: *a benevolent society.*
Word Family **benevolence** *noun*;
benevolently *adverb.*
[*bene-* + Latin *volens* wishing]

benighted (bi-**nigh**-tid) *adjective*
ignorant.

benign (bi-**nine**) *adjective*
1 gentle and kind: *a benign smile.*
2 not threatening life: *a benign tumour.*
Compare MALIGNANT.
3 favourable: *The climate has a benign effect
on the vegetation.*
Word Family **benignly** *adverb*
[Latin *benignus* kind-hearted]

benison (**ben**-i-s'n) *noun*
an old word for **blessing**.
[same origin as *benediction*]

bent *noun*
a natural liking or bias: *He has always had a
bent for writing.*
● **bent** *adjective*
1 out of the true shape or course.
2 (*informal*) dishonest: *The accountant is
bent.*
Phrase **bent on** being determined to or
set on.
● **bent** the past tense and past participle of
bend.

benumb (bi-**num**) *verb*
to stupefy or make numb: *Her fingers were
benumbed with cold.*

benzene (**ben**-zeen) *noun*
a colourless liquid hydrocarbon used as a
solvent, in motor fuel, and in making a
wide variety of organic compounds.
[from *benzoin* an aromatic gum]

benzine (**ben**-zeen) *noun*
Chemistry a colourless liquid mixture of
hydrocarbons of the paraffin series, with a
boiling-point range of 50–60°C, and used
for dry-cleaning and as a solvent.

bequeath (bi-**kwee**th) *verb*
to hand down or leave to those who come
after, as in a will: *This knowledge was
bequeathed to us by the ancient Greeks.*

bequest (bi-**kwest**) *noun*
a legacy.

berate (bi-**rate**) *verb*
to scold: *She was berated for losing her coat.*

bereave (bi-**reev**) *verb* (**bereaves;
bereaving; bereaved** or **bereft**)
to make sad through loss or death.
Word Family **bereavement** *noun* a loss,
especially by death.

bereft *adjective*
missing or deprived of something: *bereft of
hope.*

beret (**berr**-ay) *noun*
a soft round flat cap, such as worn by some
soldiers.
[French]

beribori (berr-i-**berr**-i) *noun*
a disease due to lack of vitamin B_1 in the
diet, causing weakness and loss of function
of the nerves and the heart muscles.
[Sinhalese, weakness]

berry *noun* (*plural* **berries**)
a small juicy stoneless fruit, such as the
strawberry, blackberry, etc.

berserk (ber-**zerk**) *adverb, adjective*
Phrase **go berserk** to become
uncontrollable.

> The word **berserk** has come into
> English from the Icelandic word
> *berserkr*, a member of a tribe of Norse
> warriors who worked themselves into a
> fury before a battle and then fought
> with great fierceness and recklessness.
> *Berserkr* is thought to come from the
> Icelandic words *björn* (bear), and *serkr*
> (shirt), as the warriors of the tribe
> dressed themselves for battle in the
> skins of fierce animals.

berth *noun*
1 a bunk in a ship, train, etc.
2 a place where a ship may be moored.
Phrase **give a wide berth to** to avoid.
• **berth** *verb* to come to a mooring.

beryl (**berr**-il) *noun*
Geology a hard crystalline silicate mineral,
used as a gem.
[Greek *beryllos* a sea-green gem]

beseech *verb* (**beseeches; beseeching;
besought** or **beseeched**)
to implore or ask earnestly and urgently:

We beseech you not to be angry.
Word Family **beseechingly** *adverb.*

beset *verb* (**besets; besetting; beset**)
to attack or harass: *The family was beset by
financial worries.*

besetting *adjective*
continually attacking or tempting:
Overeating is one of my besetting sins.

beside *preposition*
1 at the side of or close to: *Sit beside me.*
2 compared with: *Her plate looked quite full
beside mine.*
Phrase **beside oneself** *He is still beside
himself with grief* (= greatly affected).

besides *adverb, preposition*
1 in addition to: *Who else came besides you?*
□ *The dress was too expensive, besides which it
didn't fit.*
2 other than: *She has no other possessions
besides her motorbike.*

besiege (bi-**seej**) *verb*
to surround or crowd in upon, especially
with troops: *The enemy besieged the city for
four months.*
*Figurative The stranger was besieged with
questions.*

besmirch *verb*
1 to damage: *The family's name was
besmirched by the scandal.*
2 a poetic word meaning 'to make dirty': *a
face besmirched with mud.*

besotted *adjective*
completely in love: *He was besotted by her.*

besought a past tense and past participle
of **beseech**.

bespatter *verb*
to soil by spattering: *His trousers were all
bespattered with mud.*

bespeak *verb* (**bespeaks; bespeaking;
bespoke; bespoken**)
an old word meaning 'to reserve or order
something in advance'.

bespoke suit *noun*
a specially made, not ready-made, suit.

best *adjective*
the superlative of **good**.
• **best** *adverb* the superlative of **well**[1].
Phrase **had best** would be wiser to: *We
had best not answer.*
• **best** *noun* the best quality, thing or part:
nothing but the best.
Phrases **at best** on the most hopeful view.
make the best of to do as well as possible
in circumstances which are unfavourable.
• **best** *verb* to outdo or defeat.

best-before date *noun*
a date on a food package indicating the date by which the contents should be used to ensure perfect quality.

bestial *adjective*
of or like a beast: *a bestial crime*.
Word Family **bestiality** (bes-ti-al-i-tee) *noun* brutal or beastly behaviour.

bestir *verb* (**bestirs; bestirring; bestirred**)
to rouse up or exert: *Bestir yourselves, for there is much work to be done*.

best man *noun*
the chief attendant of the groom at a wedding.

bestow (bi-sto) *verb*
to give or present: *Many gifts were bestowed on him*.
Word Family **bestowal** *noun*.

bestride *verb* (**bestrides; bestriding; bestrode; bestridden**)
1 to be on both sides of: *The city bestrides the river*.
2 to have one leg on each side of: *She bestrode her horse*.

best-seller *noun*
a book of which many copies are sold, especially in a short time.

bet *noun*
1 a promise made between two or more people on the probable outcome of an uncertain fact or event, usually in the form of money.
2 the thing or event on which one makes a bet: *That horse is not a good bet at all*.
Phrase **hedge one's bets** to avoid the risk of failure or loss by having more than one possible course of action.
● **bet** *verb* (**bets; betting; bet** or **betted**)
1 to make a bet.
2 (*informal*) to be certain: *I bet I'm right*.

beta (bee-ta) *noun*
the second letter of the Greek alphabet.

betake *verb* (**betakes; betaking; betook; betaken**)
Phrase **betake oneself** to go: *She betook herself to London*.

betel (bee-t'l) *noun*
an Asian climbing plant, the leaves of which are chewed as a stimulant.

betel nut *noun*
the seed of the orange or scarlet fruit of an Asian palm tree, chewed with lime or betel leaves as a stimulant.

bête noire (bate **nwah**) *noun* (*plural* **bêtes noires**) (bate **nwah**)
a person or thing that one particularly dreads or dislikes.
[French *bête* beast + *noire* black]

betide *verb*
a poetic word meaning 'to happen'.

betoken *verb*
a poetic word meaning 'to indicate or be a sign of': *These gems betoken great wealth*.

betray *verb*
1 to act disloyally or treacherously towards: *He has betrayed our trust*.
2 to reveal unintentionally: *Extreme nervousness betrayed his guilt*.
Word Family **betrayal** *noun*; **betrayer** *noun* a person who betrays.

betrothed (bi-**trothd**) *adjective*
engaged to be married.
Word Family **betroth** *verb*; **betrothal** *noun*.

better¹ *adjective*
the comparative of **good**.
● **better** *adverb* the comparative of **well¹**.
Phrases **better off** in a better position: *You would be better off without her*. **had better** would be wiser to: *You had better obey him*. **think better of** decide against: *We were going to throw a stone at the window but thought better of it*.
● **better** *verb* to surpass: *Her record had never been bettered*.
Phrase **better oneself** to improve one's circumstances.
● **better** *noun*
1 something which is better.
2 (**betters**) one's superiors.
Word Family **betterment** *noun* improvement.

better² *noun* also **bettor**
a person who bets.

between *preposition, adverb*
a word used to indicate the following:
1 (within the given limits): *Come between 1 p.m. and 2 p.m.* □ *a mountain range between here and the sea*.
2 (connection): *love between two people*. □ *a similarity between two things*.
3 (sharing): *We own the house between us*.
4 (distinction): *There is little difference between raisins and sultanas*.
Phrase **between ourselves, between you and me** in confidence.

> [!] On *between you and I* and *between you and me* ⇨ ME¹.

betwixt *preposition, adverb*
an old word for **between**.

bevel (bevv-'l) *noun*
1 the sloping angle which one line or surface makes with another, when not at right angles.
2 a tool for cutting such an angle.
• **bevel** *verb* (**bevels; bevelling; bevelled**).

beverage (bev-a-rij) *noun*
a drink.
[Latin *bibere* to drink]

bevy (bev-ee) *noun* (*plural* **bevies**)
a gathering or group: *a bevy of girls*.

bewail *verb*
to express great sorrow or grief: *She bewailed the loss of her husband*.

beware *verb*
be cautious or careful of: *Beware the Ides of March!*

bewilder *verb*
to puzzle or make uncertain: *The strange language bewildered her*.
Word Family **bewilderment** *noun*.

bewitch *verb*
1 to put a charm or magic spell on: *The sorcerer bewitched the animals*.
2 to fascinate: *The children were bewitched by the puppets*.
Word Family **bewitchingly** *adverb*.

bey (bay) *noun*
(*formerly*) a title of respect, used in Turkey.

beyond *preposition, adverb*
1 further on than: *Beyond us lay the desert.* □ *Don't stay beyond midnight*.
2 outside the limits of: *It is beyond understanding*.
3 except: *The police found nothing beyond some fingerprints*.

Bhagavadgita (bug-a-vad-**gee**-ta) *noun*
a sacred Hindu scripture containing the teachings of the deity Krishna.
[Sanskrit, song of the Blessed One]

bhaji (bah-jee) *noun*
a kind of Indian savoury consisting of deep-fried vegetables in a batter.
[Hindi]

bhangra (bahng-gra) *noun*
a type of pop music which combines elements of Punjabi folk music with elements of Western pop and disco music.
[Punjabi, a traditional folk dance]

biannual (by-**an**-yew-'l) *adjective*
occurring twice a year.
Word Family **biannually** *adverb*.

bias (by-us) *noun* (*plural* **biases**)
1 a movement or prejudice in a particular direction: *The teacher had a bias against boys.* □ *The ball spun with a bias towards the left*.
2 a slanting or diagonal cut: *a skirt cut on the bias*.
• **bias** *verb* (**biases; biasing** or **biassing; biased** or **biassed**) to prejudice or influence unfairly.
Word Family **biased, biassed** *adjective*
prejudiced.

bib *noun*
1 a piece of cloth tied around the neck of a child to protect clothes while eating.
2 the upper part of an apron.

Bible *noun*
1 *Christianity* the sacred writings, consisting of the Old and New Testaments.
2 (**bible**) (*informal*) a text or book considered as an authority: *That encyclopedia is his bible*.
Word Family **biblical** (**bib**-li k'l) *adjective*.
[Greek *biblos* book]

bibliography (bib-li-**og**-ra-fee) *noun* (*plural* **bibliographies**)
1 a list of books or sources for a particular topic, sometimes printed at the end of a book.
2 the description, history or classification of books, etc.
Word Family **bibliographical** (bib-li-o-**graff**-i-k'l), **bibliographic** *adjective*.
[Greek *biblion* book + *graphein* to write]

bibliophile (**bib**-li-o-file) *noun*
a lover of books.
[Greek *biblion* book + *philos* loving]

bibulous (**bib**-yoo-lus) *adjective*
(*formal*) addicted to drinking alcohol.
[Latin *bibulus*]

bicameral (by-**kam**-a-r'l) *adjective*
Parliament having two chambers, e.g. the House of Commons and the House of Lords. Compare UNICAMERAL.
[*bi-* + Latin *camera* chamber]

bicarbonate of soda *noun* also called **baking soda**.
sodium bicarbonate (formula $NaHCO_3$), a white crystalline solid used as a medicine, and in cooking as a raising agent.

bicentenary (by-sen-**tee**-na-ree) *noun* (*plural* **bicentenaries**)
a 200th anniversary.
Word Family **bicentennial** (by-sen-**ten**-i-al) *adjective*.

biceps (by-seps) *noun* (*plural* **biceps**)
Anatomy a large muscle in two parts, controlling movement of the elbow and forearm.
[Latin, two-headed]

bicker *verb*
to quarrel over petty things.

bicuspid (by-kusp-id) *noun* also called **premolar**.
a two-pointed tooth.
Word Family **bicuspid, bicuspidate** *adjective* having two points.

bicycle (by-si-k'l) *noun*
a two-wheeled vehicle with one wheel in front of the other, for one person, and propelled by the feet turning pedals.

bid *verb* (**bids; bidding; bid**, *old form* **bade; bid**, *old form* **bidden**)
1 to make an offer to buy, especially at an auction: *Shall I bid for that chair?*
2 to command or tell: *We bid the travellers farewell.*
3 *Cards* to declare the number of tricks a player thinks he or she will win.
Word Family **bid** *noun*; **bidding** *noun* an order or command.

biddy *noun* (*plural* **biddies**)
(*informal*) an old woman.
[diminutive of *Bridget*]

bide *verb*
Phrase **bide one's time** to wait for a favourable opportunity.

bidet (bee-day) *noun*
a low basin on which one sits to wash one's genitals and bottom.
[French, a small horse]

biennial (by-en-i-al) *adjective*
1 occurring every two years.
2 taking two years to complete its life cycle: *a biennial plant.*
Word Family **biennial** *noun*; **biennially** *adverb*.

bier (beer) *noun*
a stand on which a corpse, or the coffin containing it, is placed before burial.

bifocals (by-fo-k'ls) *plural noun*
a pair of spectacles in which the lenses are in two sections, the upper half for seeing distant objects, the lower half for reading.

bifurcate (by-fir-kate) *verb*
to divide into two branches.
Word Family **bifurcate** *adjective*; **bifurcation** (by-fir-kay-sh'n) *noun*.
[*bi-* + Latin *furca* a fork]

big *adjective* (**bigger; biggest**)
1 large in size, importance, etc.: *She has big ambitions but no drive.*
2 elder: *He's my big brother.*
3 (*informal*) generous: *It was big of you to pay for us.*
Phrase **big talk** boastful exaggerated talk. **big with young** an old phrase meaning 'pregnant'.
● **big** *adverb*.
Word Family **bigness** *noun*.

bigamy (big-a-mee) *noun*
Law the crime of going through a marriage ceremony with one person when already married to another.
Word Family **bigamist** *noun*; **bigamous** *adjective*.
[*bi-* + Greek *gamos* marriage]

big bang *noun*
1 the explosion of a small dense mass held by some scientists to have originated the universe.
2 (**Big Bang**) the deregulation of the London Stock Exchange in 1986 which opened it to a greater number of participants and abolished many of its restrictions.
3 any major change.

big cat ⇨ CAT (definition 2).

big dipper ⇨ ROLLER COASTER.

big end *noun*
the end of a connecting rod attached to the crankshaft of a piston engine.

big game *noun*
large animals hunted for sport.

big-headed *adjective*
(*informal*) conceited.

big-hearted *adjective*
generous or kind.

bight (bite) *noun*
1 a bend in the coastline.
2 a body of water bounded by such a bend: *the Great Australian Bight.*
3 the part of a rope between the ends.

bigness ⇨ BIG.

bigot (big-ut) *noun*
a person who is intolerant or prejudiced in matters of religion, race, etc.
Word Family **bigoted** *adjective*; **bigotry** *noun*.

big time *noun*
(*informal*) the top or most important level: *She had made the big time.*

big top *noun*
1 the main tent in a circus.
2 the circus itself.

bigwig *noun*
(*informal*) an important person.

bike *noun*
(*informal*) a bicycle.
Phrase **on your bike** go away, get on with
it.

biker *noun*
1 (*informal*) a motorcyclist, especially a
member of a group or gang.
2 (*informal*) a cyclist.

bikini (be-**kee**-nee) *noun*
a two-piece swimsuit, consisting of a bra
and pants.
[name of the Pacific atoll laid bare by
atomic bomb tests]

bilateral (by-**lat**-a-r'l) *adjective*
of or affecting two sides or parties: *a
bilateral trade agreement*.
Word Family **bilaterally** *adverb*.

bilberry *noun* (*plural* **bilberries**) also
called **whortleberry**.
a small round edible dark purple berry
with a firm skin.

bile *noun*
1 *Biology* the bitter yellow secretion of the
liver, which is stored in the gall bladder
and is essential for fat digestion.
2 bad temper or irritability.
[Latin *bilis* gall, bile, anger]

bilge (bilj) *noun*
1 *Nautical* the lowest parts of the inside of
a boat.
2 *Nautical* the water which collects in these
parts.
3 (*informal*) nonsense.

bilingual (by-**ling**-gw'l) *adjective*
able to speak two languages with equal
ease.
Word Family **bilingually** *adverb*;
bilingualism *noun*.

bilious (**bil**-yus) *adjective*
1 feeling nauseous.
2 sickly: *a bilious green*.
3 bad-tempered.
4 of or relating to bile.
Word Family **biliousness** *noun*.

bilk *verb*
(*informal*) to cheat or defraud.

bill¹ *noun*
1 a statement of money owed for goods
supplied or services rendered.
2 a suggested or proposed law which has
not yet been passed by parliament.
3 a notice, advertisement or poster.
4 *American* a banknote.
• **bill** *verb*

1 to send a bill to: *Bill me for the goods*.
2 to advertise or proclaim: *He is billed as a
top star*.

bill² ⇨ BEAK.

billabong *noun*
Australian a branch of a river which flows
away from the main stream and forms a
separate pool.

billboard ⇨ HOARDING.

billet¹ *verb* (**billets; billeting; billeted**)
to assign to a lodging: *The soldiers were
billeted at private homes in the town*.
• **billet** *noun*.

billet² *noun*
1 a stick of firewood.
2 a solid block of metal suitable for rolling
or extrusion.

billet-doux (bil-ay-**doo**) *noun* (*plural*
billets-doux) (bil-ay-**dooz**)
(*dated*) a love letter.
[French *billet* note + *doux* sweet]

billfold *noun*
American a wallet.

billhook *noun*
a long-handled tool with a hooked blade
for trimming or pruning trees.

billiards *noun*
a game for two played on a rectangular
table using a long rod and three balls. The
aim is to hit balls into pockets at the side,
or to hit two other balls in succession.
[French *billard*]

billion *noun* (*plural* **billions** or **billion**)
a cardinal number, traditionally 1 000 000
000 000 or 10^{12} (a million million), but
the American usage, 1 000 000 000 or 10^9
(a thousand million), is now general.
Compare TRILLION.
Word Family **billion** *adjective*; **billionth**
noun, adjective; **billionaire** *noun* a person
who has a billion dollars or pounds.
[*bi-* + (mi)LLION]

bill of fare *noun* (*plural* **bills of fare**)
(*dated*) a menu.

bill of rights *noun* (*plural* **bills of rights**)
Politics an official statement of the rights of
citizens in a country.

bill of sale *noun* (*plural* **bills of sale**)
a document transferring property from
one person to another.

billow *verb*
1 to swell out with air: *sheets billowing on
the line*.
2 to move outward in waves: *billowing smoke*.

Word Family **billow** *noun*; **billowy**
adjective.

billy *noun* (*plural* **billies**)
short form of **billycan** a tin-plated pot
with a lid and a handle, used over open
fires to boil water, etc.
[Aboriginal *billa* water]

billy goat *noun*
a male goat. Compare NANNY GOAT.

biltong *noun*
strips of sun-dried meat used as iron
rations on trek.
[Afrikaans]

bimbo *noun* (*plural* **bimbos**)
an attractive but unintelligent young
woman.
[Italian, little child]

bimonthly (by-**munth**-lee) *adjective*
1 occurring once every two months.
2 occurring twice every month.

bin *noun*
a container, usually with a lid, for holding
foods, rubbish, etc.

binary (**by**-na-ree) *adjective*
of or relating to two.
[Latin *bini* a pair]

binary number system *noun* also called
binary code; **binary notation**; **binary
scale**.
a number system to the base 2, using only
0 and 1 and often used in computers: *In the
binary number system 10 means 2, 11 means
3, 100 means 4, 101 means 5, etc*. Compare
DENARY SYSTEM.

binary star *noun* also called **double star**.
any pair of stars which revolve around
each other.

bind (*rhymes with* kind) *verb* (**binds**;
binding; **bound**)
1 to tie or secure: *His hands were bound
together with rope*.
2 to stick together: *Bind the cake mixture
with eggs*.
3 to cover: *an old manuscript bound in
leather*.
Word Family **bind** *noun* 1 (*informal*) a
nuisance. 2 (*informal*) a difficult situation.
binding *noun* a book cover.

binder *noun*
anything which binds, such as a cover for
several issues of a magazine or a machine
which ties cut grain.

bindweed ⇨ CONVOLVULUS.

binge (binj) *noun*
(*informal*) a wild or prolonged bout of
drinking, eating, etc.

• **binge** *verb* (*informal*) to eat or drink too
much.
[Lincolnshire dialect *binge* to soak]

bingo *noun*
a game in which contestants match
numbers on a card with those drawn at
random.

binnacle (**bin**-i-k'l) *noun*
a case which contains a ship's compass.

binoculars (bin-**nok**-yoo-larz)
plural noun also called **field glasses**.
an instrument with lenses for both eyes,
used for making distant objects appear
closer.
[Latin *bini* a pair + *oculus* an eye]

binomial (by-**no**-mee-ul) *adjective*
Maths of or relating to an expression
containing two terms, e.g. $x + y$.
[*bi-* + Greek *nomos* a part]

biochemistry (by-o-**kem**-iss-tree) *noun*
the study of the chemical substances and
processes in living things.
Word Family **biochemical** *adjective*;
biochemically *adverb*; **biochemist** *noun*.

biodata (by-o-**day**-ta) *plural noun*
(*used with singular verb*) biographical
information.

biodegradable
(by-o-de-**grade**-a-b'l) *adjective*
able to be broken down into natural
substances by organisms, especially
bacteria, in the environment: *packaging
made of cardboard and other biodegradable
materials*.

biodiversity *noun*
the richness of the variety of the biosphere,
under threat from intensive cultivation of
particular species.

bioethics (**by**-o-eth-iks) *plural noun*
(*used with singular verb*) the study of ethical
problems arising from scientific and
medical advances.

biofeedback *noun*
a technique in which a person controls his
or her bodily response by monitoring
changes in pulse rate, temperature, blood
pressure, etc.

biogenesis (by-o-**jen**-i-sis) *noun*
Biology the principle that living matter is
produced only from other living matter.
Compare SPONTANEOUS GENERATION.

biography (by-**og**-ra-fee) *noun* (*plural*
biographies)
the life story of a person written by
another. Compare AUTOBIOGRAPHY.

Word Family biographical (by-o-**graf**-i-k'l) *adjective*; **biographer** *noun*.
[*bio-* + Greek *graphein* to write]

biohazard *noun*
a risk to mankind or to the environment, especially one that arises out of biological or medical work.

biological warfare *noun*
any warfare using poisons, bacteria, etc. to destroy human, animal or plant life.

biology (by-**ol**-a-jee) *noun*
the study of living things.
Word Family biological (by-o-**loj**-i-k'l) *adjective*; **biologist** *noun*.
[*bio-* + *-logy*]

bionic *adjective*
1 relating to artificial body parts, such as limbs, which are electronically or mechanically powered.
2 (*informal*) showing superhuman strength.

biophysics (by-o-**fiz**-iks) *plural noun*
(*used with singular verb*) the application of the science of physics to the study of biological processes.

biopsy (**by**-op-see) *noun* (*plural* **biopsies**)
Medicine the removal and study of a sample of body tissue, usually to aid in diagnosis.
[*bio-* + Greek *opsis* sight]

biosphere (**by**-o-sfeer) *noun*
the part of the earth where living organisms are found.

biostatistics *plural noun*
(*used with singular verb*) the study of biological data, especially those relating to mortality and life expectancy.

biotechnology (by-o-tek-**nol**-a-jee) *noun*
the use of living cells such as bacteria in industrial processes to produce useful materials.

biotextiles *plural noun*
textile products which are given a biological finish for a specific use.

biotic *adjective*
pertaining to life.

bipartisan (by-**part**-i-zan) *adjective*
involving the agreement of two parties, especially political parties.

bipartite (by-**par**-tite) *adjective*
divided into or involving two parts.

biped (**by**-ped) *adjective*
having two feet.
• **biped** *noun*.
[*bi-* + Latin *pedis* of a foot]

biplane (**by**-plane) *noun*
an old type of aeroplane with two pairs of wings, one above the other.

birch *noun* (*plural* **birches**)
1 a deciduous tree with slender branches and smooth bark, used for timber.
2 a rod or bundle of birch twigs, used as a whip.
• **birch** *verb* to punish with a birch.

bird *noun*
1 a warm-blooded feathered vertebrate animal with wings. Most birds can fly.
2 (*informal*) a person, especially one with some peculiarity.
3 (*informal*) a girl or young woman. This term is often considered offensive to women.
Phrase **kill two birds with one stone** in reaching one objective, to gain another satisfactorily.

birdie *noun*
Golf a score of one stroke less than par for a hole. Compare EAGLE (definition 2).

birdlime *noun*
a sticky substance which is smeared on branches, to catch small birds.

bird of paradise *noun* (*plural* **birds of paradise**)
a tropical bird with brilliantly coloured feathers, found especially in New Guinea.

bird sanctuary *noun* (*plural* **bird sanctuaries**)
an area where wild birds are protected.

bird's-eye view *noun*
a view from above.

biretta *noun*
a square cap worn by certain members of the Roman Catholic and Anglican clergy.
[Spanish *birreta*]

biriani (bir-ee-**ah**-nee) *noun* also **biryani**
an Indian dish made of rice, spices and meat, vegetables, etc.
[Urdu]

> The word **biriani** can be spelt in two ways. In English, spelling is usually standardized and there is only one correct spelling of a particular word. There are exceptions to this and among these are several words that have recently come into English from languages which use alphabets which are different from the Roman alphabet used in English. People have tried to write these words down as they are pronounced and different spellings (*biriani, biryani*) have resulted.

Biro *noun*
(*trademark*) a ballpoint pen.

birth *noun*
1 the act, time or process of being born.
2 a beginning: *the birth of Islam.*
3 one's descent or origin.

birth control *noun*
contraception.

birthday *noun*
the day or date of one's birth.

birthday suit *noun*
Phrase **in one's birthday suit** naked.

birthmark *noun*
a congenital mark on the body.

birth mother *noun*
the woman who has given birth to a child.

birth rate *noun*
the number of births in proportion to the
total population at a given time, expressed
per 1000 people. Compare DEATH RATE.

birthright *noun*
something to which one is entitled by
birth.

biryani ⇨ BIRIANI.

biscuit (**bis**-kit) *noun*
a small flat cake made from flour, fat and
flavourings.

bisect (by-**sekt**) *verb*
to divide into two, usually equal, parts.
Word Family **bisection** *noun;* **bisector**
noun something which bisects.
[*bi-* + Latin *sectus* cut]

bisexual *adjective*
1 sexually attracted to both sexes.
2 *Biology* containing both male and female
reproductive organs.
Word Family **bisexual** *noun;* **bisexually**
adverb.

bishop *noun*
1 *Christianity* a member of the clergy of
high rank in charge of a diocese.
2 *Chess* a piece that may move any number
of squares diagonally.
Word Family **bishopric** *noun* the office
or diocese of a bishop.
[Greek *episkopos* overseer]

bison (by-s'n) *noun* (*plural* **bison**)
a large-hoofed American mammal with a
shaggy mane and short curved horns.

bisque (bisk *or* beesk) *noun*
a rich soup made from lobster or shellfish.
[French]

bistro (**bee**-stro) *noun*
a small informal restaurant with a bar.
[French]

bit[1] *noun*
1 a bar of metal or rubber passing through
a horse's mouth and attached to the reins
to help control the horse.
2 the cutting part of certain tools,
especially drills.
Phrase **take the bit between one's
teeth** to act boldly and independently.

bit[2] *noun*
1 a small piece or amount.
2 a short time: *Wait a bit.*
Phrases **bit by bit** *He built his home bit by
bit* (= slowly, in stages). **do one's bit** *We
felt obliged to do our bit* (= make a
contribution). **not a bit of it** not at all, by
no means.

bit[3] *noun*
Computers a unit of information fed into a
computer.
[B(inary) + (dig)IT]

bitch *noun* (*plural* **bitches**)
1 a female dog, wolf or fox.
2 (*informal*) a malicious or unpleasant
woman.
3 (*informal*) a complaint.
• **bitch** *verb*
1 (*informal*) to complain.
2 (*informal*) to talk maliciously about
someone.
Word Family **bitchy** *adjective* (**bitchier;
bitchiest**) (*informal*) spiteful or malicious.

bite *verb* (**bites; biting; bit; bitten**)
1 to cut or cut into with or as if with the
teeth.
2 (of acid) to corrode.
3 (of a fish) to take the lure.
4 (*informal*) to annoy or worry: *What's
biting him?*
Phrase **bite off more than one can
chew** to take on more than one can cope
with.
• **bite** *noun*
1 the act of biting.
2 an injury resulting from biting.
3 a mouthful.
4 a small meal or snack.

biting (**by**-ting) *adjective*
1 keen or piercing: *a biting wind.*
2 sarcastic or cutting: *a biting comment.*

bit part *noun*
a small or unimportant role in a play, film
or opera.

bitter *adjective*
1 being harsh or disagreeable in taste.
2 distressing, hard to bear: *bitter sorrow.*
3 sarcastic, cutting: *He had only bitter words
for her.*

4 very cold: *a bitter wind.*
● **bitter** *noun* a strong draught beer with a sharp taste.
Word Family **bitterly** *adverb*; **bitterness** *noun.*

bittern *noun*
a long-legged tawny marshbird which emits a unique booming call.

bitters *plural noun*
a liquid obtained from herbs, used in small amounts to flavour drinks.

bitumen (**bit-**yoo-min) *noun*
a black sticky mixture of hydrocarbons obtained from natural deposits or by distilling petroleum.
Word Family **bituminous** (bit-**yoom**-i-nus) *adjective.*
[Latin, asphalt]

bivalve (**by-**valv) *noun*
Biology a mollusc having a shell with two hinged parts, such as an oyster. Compare UNIVALVE.

bivouac (**biv-**oo-ak) *noun*
a temporary camp in the open.
● **bivouac** *verb* (**bivouacs; bivouacking; bivouacked**) to camp in the open.

biweekly *adjective*
1 occurring every two weeks.
2 occurring twice a week.

bizarre (biz-**ar**) *adjective*
very strange or odd.
Word Family **bizarrely** *adverb*; **bizarreness** *noun.*

blab *verb* (**blabs; blabbing; blabbed**)
1 (*informal*) to reveal a secret.
2 (*informal*) to tell tales.
Word Family **blabbermouth** *noun*
(*informal*) a person who blabs.

black *noun*
1 the darkest achromatic colour, reflecting virtually no light.
2 something which has this colour: *dressed in black.*
3 a member of a dark-skinned race of people.
Phrase **in the black** having money or capital. Compare IN THE RED under RED *noun.*
● **black** *adjective*
1 having the colour black.
2 without milk or cream: *a black coffee.*
3 pessimistic or gruesome: *a black comedy.*
4 sullen or angry: *a black look.*
5 belonging or relating to a dark-skinned race of people.

● **black** *verb* to impose a ban on a firm, product or country, in a trade union dispute.
Phrase **black out** to lose consciousness for a short period.
Word Family **blackish** *adjective*; **blackly** *adverb*; **blackness** *noun.*

blackball *verb*
to deny a person membership of something, usually by voting against him or her.

black beetle *noun*
(*informal*) the common house cockroach, which is neither black nor a beetle.

black belt *noun*
a sign of rank awarded to a grade of mastership in judo, karate, etc.

blackberry *noun* (*plural* **blackberries**)
an edible dark purple berry which grows on a thorny bush.

blackbird *noun*
a songbird related to the thrush, the male being black and the female brown.

blackboard *noun*
a board painted black, suitable for writing on with chalk.

black box *noun* (*plural* **black boxes**)
a specially protected electronic device installed in an aircraft to record any information about its flight which may be useful if there is a crash.

blackcock *noun* also called **black grouse; black game.**
a black and white grouse of northern Europe; the female is called a **greyhen.**

black comedy ⇨ COMEDY.

blackcurrant *noun*
a small black edible fruit growing on a shrub.

Black Death *noun*
History the bubonic plague which spread from Asia to Europe in the 14th century.

black economy *noun*
the part of a nation's economy dealing with earned income that is illegally not declared for tax purposes.

blacken *verb*
1 to make or become black.
2 to defame, malign: *The gossip began as an attempt to blacken his character.*

blackguard (**blag-**ard) *noun*
(*dated*) a scoundrel.

blackhead *noun*
a blocked skin pore having a dark greasy head.

black hole *noun*
Astrophysics a theoretically possible region of space where matter is so condensed by gravitation that no radiation can escape from it and anything approaching it will disappear.

blacking *noun*
a preparation, such as polish, for blackening shoes, stoves, etc.

blackjack ⇨ PONTOON².

blacklead (blak-led) *noun*
graphite.

blackleg *noun*
1 also called **scab**. a worker who refuses to join a trade union or take part in a strike.
2 an infectious disease of cattle and sheep which causes swellings in the legs and is usually fatal.

blacklist *noun*
a list of people who are suspected or disapproved of.
• **blacklist** *verb*.

black magic *noun*
magic which is used for evil purposes.

blackmail *noun*
the crime of demanding payment in return for not revealing damaging information.
Word Family **blackmail** *verb*;
blackmailer *noun*.

Black Maria (blak ma-**rye**-a) *noun*
(*informal*) a police patrol wagon for carrying prisoners.

black market *noun*
the illegal buying and selling of commodities, ignoring price controls, rationing, etc.
Word Family **black marketeer** *noun* a person who operates on the black market.

blackout *noun*
1 the extinguishing or concealment of lights in a city or district, as a result of power failure or during enemy air attacks at night.
2 (*informal*) a sudden temporary loss of consciousness.
3 concealment of information: *The government ordered a news blackout during the war.*

black out ⇨ BLACK *verb*.

black pudding *noun* also called **blood pudding**.
a dark sausage made from blood, fat, flour and seasonings packed into a skin and boiled.

black sheep *noun*
(*informal*) a person regarded as worthless or inferior by his or her family, group, etc.

blacksmith *noun*
a person who forges iron objects, such as horseshoes, with a hammer and anvil.

blackthorn *noun*
a thorny deciduous shrub with white blossoms and purple plum-like fruit (sloes).

black tie *noun*
a black bow tie worn on formal occasions with a dinner jacket.

black widow *noun*
a very poisonous American spider, the female of which eats its mate.

bladder *noun*
1 *Biology* an elastic sac in the abdomen for storing urine.
2 an inflatable bag.

bladderwrack (blad-a-rak) *noun*
a large branched brown seaweed with many air bladders, usually found attached to rocks in shallow water.

blade *noun*
1 the flat cutting part of a sword, knife, etc.
2 a sword.
3 a thin broad flat part of anything: *the blade of an oar.* □ *a blade of grass.*
3 (*informal dated*) a smart dashing young fellow.

blame *verb*
to find fault with or hold responsible for a wrong or error.
Phrase **to blame** *Who's to blame for this awful mess?* (= responsible).
Word Family **blame** *noun*;
blameworthy *adjective* deserving blame;
blameless *adjective* innocent or free from blame.

blanch (*rhymes with* branch) *verb*
1 to make or become pale or white: *to blanch with fear.*
2 to immerse in boiling water, in order to remove skins.
[French *blanc* white]

blancmange (bla-**monj**) *noun*
a flavoured jelly-like dessert.
[French *blanc* white + *manger* to eat]

bland *adjective*
1 mild, smooth or non-stimulating: *a bland diet.*
2 not showing emotion: *a bland smile.*
Word Family **blandly** *adverb*; **blandness** *noun*.
[Latin *blandus* smooth-tongued]

blandishments *plural noun*
flattering or coaxing words.

blank *adjective*
1 unmarked: *Put your name in the blank space.*
2 empty: *a blank cartridge.*
3 expressionless: *a blank look.*
4 utter: *Her behaviour was blank stupidity.*
● **blank** *noun*
1 an empty space: *blanks in a document.*
□ *The accident is a blank in her memory.*
2 an empty or unmarked object, such as a form to be filled in, or a sheet of metal to be stamped into a finished article.
3 a cartridge containing powder but no bullet and therefore harmless.
Phrase **draw a blank** to fail.
Word Family **blankly** *adverb* 1 without expression or understanding. 2 directly; **blankness** *noun*.

blanket *noun*
1 a piece of soft woollen or other material, especially used as a bedcovering.
2 a layer: *a blanket of smog.*
● **blanket** *verb* (**blankets; blanketing; blanketed**) to cover with or as if with a blanket.
● **blanket** *adjective* being general or covering a whole group.

blank verse ⇨ VERSE.

blare *verb*
to make a prolonged harsh loud noise: *The hi-fi next door was blaring all night.*
● **blare** *noun*: *the blare of the TV.*

blarney (**blar**-nee) *noun*
talk which is smooth and flattering but obviously deceptive.
[after a stone in *Blarney Castle*, Ireland, said to give the gift of persuasive speech]

blasé (**blah**-zay) *adjective*
indifferent to or bored by something, especially because it is not new.
[French *blaser* to exhaust]

blaspheme (blas-**feem**) *verb*
to speak disrespectfully about a deity or sacred things.
Word Family **blasphemer** *noun* a person who blasphemes; **blasphemy** (**blas**-fa-mee) *noun* (*plural* **blasphemies**); **blasphemous** (**blas**-fa-mus) *adjective*.
[Greek *blasphemia* slander]

blast (blahst) *noun*
1 a strong gust of wind, jet of air, etc.: *The furnace gave out a blast of hot air.* □ *a blast of sound.*
2 an explosive charge.
3 the ignition of an explosive charge.

4 the shock wave caused by an explosion.
Phrase **full blast** at top speed or full power: *a stereo playing full blast.*
● **blast** *verb*
1 to explode or blow up: *The bomb blasted three city blocks.*
2 to blow a trumpet, car horn, etc.
3 (*informal*) to criticize.
4 to strike hard: *I blasted the ball past the goalie.*
5 a poetic word meaning 'to wither, shrivel or destroy'.
6 to damn.
Phrase **blast off** (of a rocket) to take off.

blast furnace *noun*
a vertical cylindrical furnace heated from the bottom by a blast of hot air, and used to extract iron from its ores.

blast-off *noun*
the launching or lift-off of a space vehicle.

blatant (**blay**-t'nt) *adjective*
extremely obvious or conspicuous: *blatant advertisements.* □ *a blatant lie.*
Word Family **blatantly** *adverb*.

> **!** Both *blatant* and *flagrant* mean 'obvious', but *flagrant* suggests that somebody is doing something bad in a deliberate way: *flagrant disobedience.*

blather (**blath**-a) *noun*
stupid or babbling talk.
Word Family **blather** *verb*; **blatherskite** *noun* (*especially Scottish, American*) a babbling or foolish person.

blaze¹ *noun*
1 a bright flame or fire: *Firemen rushed to the blaze.*
2 a bright display of light or colour.
3 (**blazes**) (*informal*) hell.
Phrase **like blazes** very energetically.
● **blaze** *verb*
1 to burn or shine brightly.
2 to fire: *The battleship's guns blazed away.*

blaze² *noun*
1 a mark made on a tree by removing a patch of bark, to indicate a path, boundary, etc.
2 a white mark on the face of a horse, cow, etc.
● **blaze** *verb* to mark a tree with blazes.
Phrase **blaze a trail** 1 to mark a trail with blazes. 2 to pioneer or be the first.

blazer *noun*
a coloured lightweight jacket, usually with a school or club badge on the breast pocket.

blazon (blay-z'n) *verb*
to proclaim publicly or in a conspicuous manner: *Headlines blazoned the outbreak of war.*

bleach *verb*
to make or become white, pale or colourless: *His hair was bleached by the sun.*
• **bleach** *noun* a chemical agent used to bleach clothes and clean drains.

bleak *adjective*
1 cold or windswept: *a bleak hillside.*
2 cheerless, dismal or dreary: *The future seemed bleak to her.*
Word Family **bleakly** *adverb;* **bleakness** *noun.*

bleary (bleer-ee) *adjective* (**blearier; bleariest**)
blurred and watery: *bleary eyes.*
Word Family **blearily** *adverb;* **bleariness** *noun.*

bleat *verb*
1 to cry like a sheep or goat.
2 to complain: *I wish you'd stop bleating about being misunderstood.*
• **bleat** *noun.*

bleed *verb* (**bleeds; bleeding; bled**)
1 to lose blood from an artery or vein.
2 to ooze: *The sap bled from the tree.*
3 to run: *The new shirt bled in the wash.*
4 (*informal*) to get money from someone: *The blackmailer bled him for years.*

bleeding *adjective*
(*informal*) bloody: *Mind the bleeding cat!*

bleep *noun*
a short high-pitched sound, especially that made by electronic or radio equipment.
• **bleep** *verb.*

blemish *noun*
a stain, mark or defect: *There were no blemishes on her skin.* □ *A parking fine is not a blemish on one's driving record.*
• **blemish** *verb.*

blench *verb*
to shrink back or draw away: *She blenched at the idea.*

blend *verb*
to join different things together so that they can no longer be separately distinguished: *This wine was blended from local and imported wines.* □ *The rabbit's colouring blended with that of the dry grass.*
Word Family **blend** *noun* a mixture of several things; **blender** *noun* an electrical device in which foods can be finely chopped to an even texture.

bless *verb* (**blesses; blessing; blessed,** *old form* **blest**)
1 to make or pronounce holy: *The archbishop blessed the new church.*
2 to ask divine favour for: *Bless this house.*
Phrases **blessed with** favoured or endowed with: *She is blessed with a sense of humour.* **bless oneself** *Christianity* to make the sign of the cross.

blessed (bless-id *or* blest) *adjective*
1 holy or sacred.
2 divinely favoured or fortunate.
3 (*informal*) damned: *This blessed machine won't work.*
4 (*informal*) a word used for emphasis: *He spent every blessed cent on gambling.*
Word Family **blessedly** *adverb;* **blessedness** *noun* the state of being blessed.

blessing *noun*
1 the words or ceremony used to bless.
2 anything which leads to happiness, favour, etc.: *The legacy was a blessing to the impoverished family.*

blew the past tense of **blow²**.

blight *noun*
1 a plant disease, usually caused by fungi.
2 a destructive influence.
• **blight** *verb* to destroy, ruin or cause to decay.

blighter *noun*
(*informal*) a person, often one who is disliked or pitied.

blind *adjective*
1 lacking the sense of sight.
2 unquestioning: *He has blind faith in doctors.*
3 hard to see round: *a blind corner.*
4 uncontrolled: *She murdered him in a fit of blind passion.*
Phrases **blind drunk** very drunk. **blind to** unable or unwilling to see: *He is blind to his own faults.*
• **blind** *verb* to make blind or as if blind: *He was blinded by the explosion.* □ *The headlights blinded her for a moment.*
Figurative He was blinded by success (= deprived of common sense).
• **blind** *noun*
1 a strip of cloth or other material pulled down over a window to keep light out.
2 something that hides or conceals one's intentions: *The import business was a blind for a smuggling racket.*
Word Family **blindly** *adverb;* **blindness** *noun.*

blind alley *noun*
1 an alley closed at one end.
2 a place from where it is not possible to proceed: *The false clue was just another blind alley in the investigation.*

blind date *noun*
a date with a person whom one has not met before.

blindfold *verb*
to cover the eyes with a cloth or bandage to prevent sight.
• **blindfold** *noun.*

blinding *adjective*
1 very bright: *a blinding light.*
2 obvious: *It came to him in a blinding flash.*
3 (*informal*) exciting: *He played a blinding shot and scored.*
Word Family **blindingly** *adverb.*

blind man's buff *noun*
a children's game in which a blindfolded player tries to catch and identify other players.

blind spot *noun*
1 *Anatomy* the small spot on the eye which has no light-sensitive cells, where the optic nerve attaches to the retina.
2 a subject about which a person cannot think or judge clearly.

blindworm ⇨ SLOW-WORM.

blink *verb*
1 to open and shut the eyes rapidly.
2 (of lights) to shine intermittently.
3 to hesitate: *He wouldn't blink at using violence.*
• **blink** *noun* the act of blinking.
Phrase **on the blink** not working, out of order.
Word Family **blinking** *adjective* (*informal*) confounded: *The blinking key is stuck in the lock.*

blinkers *plural noun*
two stiff leather flaps attached to a bridle on a horse's head to stop it seeing sideways.

blip *noun*
1 a short high-pitched sound.
2 a spot of light on a radar screen, representing a particular object.
3 a sudden unexpected short-lived rise or fall in some form of statistics such as inflation figures.
4 an unexpected temporary problem or hitch.

bliss *noun*
a state of ecstatic happiness and contentment.
Word Family **blissful** *adjective*; **blissfully** *adverb.*

blister *noun*
1 a thin-walled swelling on the skin containing a watery liquid, usually due to rubbing or a burn.
2 a similar swelling, as in old paint.
Word Family **blister** *verb* to raise or cause to raise blisters; **blistering** *adjective* severely critical or scathing.

blister pack *noun*
a transparent plastic dome on a firm backing for packaging small articles for sale.

blithe (bly*th*) *adjective*
cheerful or carefree.
Word Family **blithely** *adverb.*

blithering *adjective*
(*informal*) complete: *You blithering fool!*

blitz *noun* (*plural* **blitzes**)
1 a sudden attack in a military offensive, especially using aircraft and heavy bombing.
2 an intense attack or campaign: *a blitz against untidiness.*
• **blitz** *verb.*

> The word **blitz** comes from modern German and is the German word for lightning. To the British it was short for *Blitzkrieg*, lightning war, the nickname given to the swift movement of Hitler's troops across western Europe in the Second World War. In English, *blitz* came to mean specifically the intensive air raids on Britain, particularly London. In recent times it has lost some of its bad associations and can even be a swift course of action to bring about something good.

blizzard *noun*
a fierce storm of wind and snow.

bloat *verb*
to swell out or puff up, especially with a gas or liquid.

bloater *noun*
a salted and smoked herring.

blob *noun*
1 a small round mass, drop or spot.
2 a shapeless mass.

bloc (blok) *noun*
a group of parties or countries joining together for a particular purpose.

block *noun*
1 a solid mass or piece, especially of wood, stone, etc. and usually flat-sided or cube-like.
2 a large building containing flats, offices, etc.

3 an area in a city bounded by four roads: *The chemist is in the next block.*
4 anything which obstructs: *Police have set up a roadblock.*
5 *Printing* a metal plate with a raised image from which an illustration is printed.
6 a quantity, number or section taken as a whole: *a block of cinema tickets.*
7 *Athletics* a starting block.
● **block** *verb*
1 to hinder or prevent the movement of: *A large dog blocked the way.* □ *The Opposition blocked the bill in Parliament.*
2 to stop: *The batsman blocked the ball with his bat.*

blockade *noun*
1 the blocking of sea or land communications by an armed force in an attempt to starve the inhabitants.
2 the blocking or obstruction of progress, movement, etc.
● **blockade** *verb*.

blockage (**blok**-ij) *noun*
an obstruction or blocking.

block and tackle *noun*
a set of ropes and pulleys with a hook, used for lifting.

blockbuster *noun*
(*informal*) an outstanding or exceptionally successful book, film or show.

blockhead *noun*
(*informal*) a person who is stupid.

blockhouse *noun*
a fortified building with small openings for shooting through.

blockish *adjective*
1 like a block.
2 stupid.

bloke *noun*
(*informal*) a man.

blond *adjective* also **blonde**
light in colour: *blond hair.*
Word Family **blonde** *noun* a woman with blond hair; **blondness** *noun*.

blood (blud) *noun*
1 *Biology* the red fluid, a mixture of cells and liquid plasma, pumped by the heart throughout the body.
2 a person's descent or ancestry: *They are related by blood.*
Phrases **bad blood** hostility or ill feeling. **in cold blood** deliberately and without feeling. **new blood** new people or a new person in a group: *We need a bit of new blood in this office.* **out for blood** looking for revenge or violence. **sweat blood** to work very hard.

● **blood** *verb*
to give hunting dogs their first taste of blood.
Word Family **bloodless** *adjective*
1 without bloodshed. 2 pale: *a bloodless face.* 3 cold or unfeeling.

blood bank *noun*
a store of blood plasma of different types, kept for use in blood transfusions.

bloodbath *noun*
a massacre or slaughter.

blood brother *noun*
a person who has sworn brotherhood, especially by the ceremonial mingling of blood.

blood count *noun*
a count of the number of red or white cells in a specific volume of blood.

blood-curdling *adjective*
terrifying or horrible.

blood donor *noun*
someone who gives blood.

blood feud *noun*
a murderous feud between families or clans.

blood group *noun*
any of several classes into which blood is grouped depending on its reactions with specific antibodies.

bloodhound *noun*
a large strong smooth-haired hound with a good sense of smell, used for tracking and hunting.

bloodily ⇨ BLOODY.

bloodiness ⇨ BLOODY.

bloodless ⇨ BLOOD.

blood money *noun*
money gained at the cost of another's life.

blood poisoning *noun*
an infection caused by micro-organisms or toxins in the blood.

blood pressure *noun*
the pressure exerted by the blood on the inner walls of blood vessels, arteries, etc. which varies in different parts of the body.

blood pudding ⇨ BLACK PUDDING.

blood relation *noun*
a person related by birth, not marriage.

bloodshed *noun*
slaughter or the shedding of blood.

bloodshot *adjective*
being red because of dilated blood vessels: *bloodshot eyes.*

blood sport *noun*
any sport where blood is shed, such as
hunting.

bloodstained *adjective*
stained with blood.

bloodstock *noun*
thoroughbred horses.

bloodstone *noun*
a greenish variety of chalcedony with small
scattered red spots.

bloodstream *noun*
Anatomy the blood flowing through the
body.

bloodthirsty *adjective* (**bloodthirtier;
bloodthirstiest**)
violent or murderous.
Word Family **bloodthirstily** *adverb*;
bloodthirstiness *noun*.

blood transfusion *noun*
the transfer of blood from one person or
animal to another.

blood vessel *noun*
Anatomy a tube or vessel which contains or
transports blood within the body.

bloody (**blud-ee**) *adjective* (**bloodier;
bloodiest**)
1 marked or stained with blood: *a bloody
handkerchief.*
2 violent or accompanied by bloodshed: *a
bloody battle.*
3 (*informal*) damned: *You bloody idiot!*
4 (*informal*) very: *A bloody big piece of
timber just missed him.*
• **bloody** *verb* (**bloodies; bloodying;
bloodied**) to mark or stain with blood.
Word Family **bloodily** *adverb*;
bloodiness *noun*.

bloody-minded *adjective*
(*informal*) deliberately obstructive or
unhelpful.
Word Family **bloody-mindedness** *noun*.

bloom *noun*
1 a flower.
2 the time or state of flowering: *The roses
are in bloom early this year.*
3 a white powdery coating on a surface, as
on certain fruits, metals, etc.
4 a healthy glow on the face.
• **bloom** *verb*
1 to flower.
2 to flourish or grow vigorous and healthy.

bloomer *noun*
(*informal dated*) a silly or embarrassing
blunder.

bloomers *plural noun*
1 loose knee-length underpants for
women.
2 (*formerly*) women's loose trousers worn
for cycling, etc.
[after *Amelia Bloomer*, 1818-1894, an
American feminist]

blooming *adjective*
(*informal*) damned: *She's a blooming
nuisance!*

blossom (**blos-om**) *noun*
1 a flower, especially the flower of a fruit
tree.
2 the time or state of flowering: *The apple
trees are in blossom.*
• **blossom** *verb*
1 to flower.
2 to flourish or develop fully.
Word Family **blossomy** *adjective*.

blot *noun*
1 a spot or stain, especially of ink.
2 a blemish: *The allegations were a blot on
his character.*
• **blot** *verb* (**blots; blotting; blotted**)
1 to spot or stain.
2 to dry or soak up.
Phrase **blot out**
1 to hide: *The clouds blotted out the sun.*
2 to destroy, wipe out: *She had blotted out
the memory.*

blotch *noun* (*plural* **blotches**)
a large irregular spot.
Word Family **blotchy** *adjective*
(**blotchier; blotchiest**).

blotting paper *noun*
thick absorbent paper used to dry ink.

blotto *adjective*
(*informal*) drunk.

blouse (*rhymes with* cows) *noun*
a shirt, especially a loose or decorative one
worn by girls or women.

blouson (**blooz-on**) *noun*
a short loose jacket fitted or belted at the
waist.
[French]

blow¹ (*rhymes with* slow) *noun*
1 a hard sudden stroke with the hand, a
weapon, etc.: *a painful blow on the head.*
2 a shock or setback: *Her death was a great
blow to the family.*

blow² (*rhymes with* slow) *verb* (**blows;
blowing; blew; blown**)
1 (of air) to be in motion: *The winter wind
blows hard in this climate.*
2 to produce or emit a current of air: *She
blew on her cold hands.*

3 to move something by a current of air:
The wind blew the tree down.
4 to produce sound by a current of air:
blowing a trumpet.
5 (*informal*) to squander: *She blew £500 at
the races.*
6 to burn out: *The fuse has blown.*
7 (*informal*) to fail or bungle: *He's blown his
only chance now.*
Phrases **blow in** to arrive unexpectedly.
blow one's own trumpet to praise
oneself. **blow out** to extinguish. **blow
over** to subside, be forgotten. **blow up**
1 to explode. **2** to enlarge a photograph,
etc. **3** to inflate.

blower (blo-er) *noun*
1 a device which forces air through a fire,
etc.
2 (*informal*) a telephone.

blowfly *noun* (*plural* **blowflies**)
a fly that lays its eggs on meat, on which
the larvae feed.

blowhole *noun*
a hole on the top of the head of a whale or
dolphin, through which it breathes.

blowout *noun*
1 a sudden bursting of a tyre on a motor
vehicle.
2 an escape of oil or gas from a well, due to
a sudden surge of high pressure below
ground which forces the oil through the
safety devices which normally contain it.

blowpipe *noun*
1 also called **blowgun**. a weapon
consisting of a tube through which a dart
or pellet is blown.
2 a pipe through which a stream of gas is
directed at a flame to increase its heat.

blowsy (*rhymes with* drowsy) *adjective*
(**blowsier; blowsiest**) also **blowzy**
(**blowzier; blowziest**)
1 untidy or dishevelled.
2 having a ruddy complexion.

blowtorch *noun* also called **blowlamp**.
a torch which burns paraffin under
pressure to produce a very hot flame, used
for burning off old paint, etc.

blow-up *noun*
a large copy of a print or negative.

blowy (blo-ee) *adjective* (**blowier;
blowiest**)
windy: *a blowy winter's day.*

blub *verb* (**blubs; blubbing; blubbed**)
(*informal*) to weep or sob noisily.

blubber¹ *noun*
Biology a thick layer of fat under the skin of
aquatic mammals, such as whales and
seals, which provides insulation and is a
source of oil.

blubber² *verb*
to weep noisily.

bludgeon (bluj-'n) *noun*
a short heavy club.
● **bludgeon** *verb*
1 to hit with a club.
2 to bully or threaten: *He bludgeoned me
into agreeing.*

blue (bloo) *noun*
1 a primary colour like that of a clear sky.
2 the colour between green and indigo in
the spectrum.
3 something which has this colour: *dressed
in blue.*
4 a blue powder used to whiten laundry.
5 a person who has played for his or her
university in certain sports.
Phrase **out of the blue** suddenly or
unexpectedly.
● **blue** *adjective*
1 of or having the colour blue.
2 (*informal*) depressed, unhappy: *feeling
blue.*
3 (*informal*) obscene, pornographic: *a blue
movie.*
● **blue** *verb* (**blues; bluing** or **blueing;
blued**) (*informal dated*) to squander: *He
blued all his money on drink.*
Word Family **blueness** *noun*; **bluish,
blueish** *adjective.*

bluebell *noun*
1 a small European plant with spikes of
blue bell-shaped flowers, growing from a
bulb.
2 *Scottish* the harebell.

blueberry *noun* (*plural* **blueberries**)
a small smooth edible bluish berry which
grows on a shrub.

blue blood *noun*
aristocratic descent.
Word Family **blue-blooded** *adjective.*

bluebottle *noun*
a large blue and green fly.

blue cheese *noun*
cheese with a greenish-blue mould
through it.

blue-chip *adjective*
Stock Exchange of a share regarded as
almost as safe an investment as gilt-edged
securities.

blue-collar worker *noun*
a person employed in a trade or manual work, and receiving a wage. Compare WHITE-COLLAR WORKER.

blue ensign ⇨ ENSIGN.

blue-eyed boy *noun*
(*informal*) a favourite who can do no wrong: *Jim is his boss's blue-eyed boy.*

blue flag *noun*
a flag allowed to be flown at a seaside resort that meets European Union standards of cleanliness of beaches and lack of pollution of water.

bluegrass *noun*
1 a meadow grass used as fodder.
2 traditional country music, especially from the southern states of America.

bluejacket *noun*
(*informal*) a seaman of the British or American Navy.

Blue Peter *noun*
a blue flag with a white square, flown by a ship about to sail.

blueprint *noun*
1 a photographic copy of an architect's plan, printed in white on blue paper.
2 a detailed outline or plan.

blues *plural noun*
1 *Music* a style of jazz which developed from the slow sad songs of the early black Americans.
2 (*informal*) a state of depression or melancholy.
[from *blue devils*, an old phrase for melancholia]

blue-sky *adjective*
(*informal*) purely theoretical: *blue-sky research.*

blue tit *noun*
a small bird with blue feathers on the top of its head and on its back, wings and tail.

blue whale *noun*
a whale found in arctic and antarctic waters. It is the largest mammal which has ever lived, growing from 21–30 m in length and weighing up to 100 tonne.

bluff¹ *noun*
a prominent steep headland or cliff.
[German *blaf* flat]

bluff² *verb*
to mislead or deceive by a display of confidence.
● **bluff** *noun*.

bluff³ *adjective*
abrupt, frank.

Word Family **bluffly** *adverb*; **bluffness** *noun*.

bluish ⇨ BLUE.

blunder *noun*
a stupid mistake.
● **blunder** *verb*
1 to make a stupid mistake.
2 to move or act awkwardly.

blunderbuss *noun* (*plural* **blunderbusses**)
a large musket having a short barrel with a wide muzzle which scatters shot at close range.
[Dutch *donder* thunder + *buss* gun]

blunt *adjective*
1 having a dull rounded edge or tip: *a blunt knife.*
2 abrupt and straightforward in manner.
Word Family **blunt** *verb*; **bluntly** *adverb*; **bluntness** *noun*.

blur *verb* (**blurs; blurring; blurred**)
to make or become indistinct: *The tears in her eyes blurred her vision.*
Word Family **blur** *noun*; **blurry** *adjective* (**blurrier; blurriest**).

blurb *noun*
1 information about a book, designed to attract readers, printed on its jacket.
2 an advertisement or description of a product.

blurt *verb*
to speak impulsively: *He blurted out the secret.*

blush *verb*
1 to become red in the face, from embarrassment or shame.
2 to be ashamed: *She blushed to admit her mistake.*
● **blush** *noun* (*plural* **blushes**).

bluster *verb*
1 to speak noisily and indignantly.
2 (of wind) to blow in loud violent gusts.
Word Family **bluster** *noun*; **blustering**, **blustery** *adjective*.

boa (bo-a) *noun*
1 a large non-poisonous snake, such as the South American **boa constrictor**, noted for coiling around its prey and crushing it to death.
2 a long thin scarf made of feathers, fur, etc. worn around the neck.

boar (bore) *noun* (*plural* **boar** or **boars**)
a male pig.

board (bawd) *noun*
1 a long flat piece of timber, used in building.

2 a thin flat slab of wood, card, etc. used for a special purpose: *an ironing-board.*
□ *a chess board.*
3 a group of people appointed to manage the affairs of a company, etc.
4 daily meals, especially when paid for: *bed and board.*
Phrases **go by the board** to be discarded or neglected. **on board** on or in a ship, aeroplane, etc. **tread the boards** to be an actor.
• **board** *verb*
1 to enter a ship, aeroplane, etc.
2 to be supplied with meals, and usually accommodation, in exchange for payment.
Word Family **boarder** *noun* a person who pays for food and lodgings.

boarding house *noun*
a building with accommodation for paying guests.

boarding school *noun*
a school which provides some or all students with board and lodgings.

boardsailing ⇨ WINDSURFING.

boast (*rhymes with* post) *verb*
1 to speak with excessive pride, especially about oneself.
2 to possess something which one is proud of: *This city boasts the oldest church in the country.*
Word Family **boast** *noun*; **boaster** *noun* a person who boasts.

boastful *adjective*
tending to boast.
Word Family **boastfully** *adverb*; **boastfulness** *noun*.

boat *noun*
1 a vessel built to float and travel on water.
2 something with the shape or function of a boat: *a gravy boat.*
Phrases **burn one's boats** to commit oneself to a course of action from which there is no turning back. **in the same boat** all in the same situation, especially an unfortunate one.
• **boat** *verb*.

boater *noun*
a light straw hat with a flat round crown and brim.

boathouse *noun*
a shed built near or over the water for storing small boats.

boatswain (**bo-**s'n) *noun* also **bo'sun;**
bosun
a sailor in charge of a ship's rigging, boats and anchors.

bob[1] *verb* (**bobs; bobbing; bobbed**)
1 to move up and down: *We could see the ball bobbing in the water.*
2 to curtsy.
Phrase **bob up** to appear suddenly.
• **bob** *noun*.

bob[2] *noun*
1 a haircut for women, styled so that the hair is the same length all round.
2 a small dangling object, such as the weight on a pendulum.
• **bob** *verb* (**bobs; bobbing; bobbed**) to cut short, as a horse's tail.

bob[3] *noun* (*plural* **bob**)
(*informal*) an old word for a shilling (five pence).

bobbin *noun*
an object around which thread or yarn is wound for use in weaving, sewing, etc.

bobble *noun*
a small ball which dangles, as on a hat.

bobby *noun* (*plural* **bobbies**)
(*informal*) a policeman.
[after *Sir Robert Peel* 1788-1850, who was Home Secretary in Britain when the Metropolitan Police were created]

bobby socks *plural noun*
American short socks.

bobcat *noun*
a wildcat common in America.

bobsleigh (**bob-**slay) *noun*
a racing sledge carrying two or more people and having two sets of runners, the front set of which is used to steer the vehicle.

bobtail *noun*
a short or docked tail.

bod *noun*
(*informal*) a person: *an odd bod.*
[shortening of BODY]

bode *verb*
to be an omen of: *These results do not bode well for his future.*

bodice (**bod-**iss) *noun*
1 the top part of a dress, excluding the sleeves.
2 (*formerly*) a laced piece of clothing worn as underwear by women.

bodice-ripper *noun*
(*informal*) a romantic novel involving sex and violence.

bodkin *noun*
a blunt needle for sewing with tape, cord, etc.

body *noun* (*plural* **bodies**)
1 the structure of bones, flesh, etc. of an animal.
2 the trunk of an animal: *He was wounded in the leg and body.*
3 a corpse: *A body was found in the boot of the car.*
4 the main part: *the body of a poem.*
5 a group or quantity of things or matter: *a body of troops.* □ *a body of water.*
6 a distinct object or piece of matter: *celestial bodies.*
7 strength or consistency in wine.
8 fullness: *This shampoo will give your hair more body.*
9 a bodysuit.
Word Family **bodily** *adjective.*

bodybuilding *noun*
the performing of regular physical exercises designed to increase the power of muscles and make them more conspicuous.
Word Family **bodybuilder** *noun.*

bodyguard *noun*
a personal or private guard, e.g. for an important person.

body language *noun*
gestures, unconscious bodily movements, etc that function as a means of communication.

body politic *noun*
a nation or society forming a single unit under its government.

body-popping *noun*
a type of popular dance featuring jerky robot-like movements.

bodysuit *noun*
a woman's close fitting piece of clothing made of stretch material.

bodywarmer *noun*
a sleeveless padded garment worn as a jacket.

bodywork *noun*
the outer shell of a motor vehicle.

boffin *noun*
(*informal*) an inventor, originally of airforce equipment.

bog *noun*
an area of permanently wet spongy ground, formed especially by decaying plants.
• **bog** *verb* (**bogs; bogging; bogged**)
Phrase **bog down** to slow down or cause to become stuck.
Word Family **boggy** *adjective* (**boggier; boggiest**).
[Irish, soft]

bogey¹ (**bo-gee**) *noun* also **bogy** (*plural* **bogies**)
1 an evil spirit, or something which causes fear.
2 (*informal*) a piece of mucus from the nose.

bogey² *noun*
Golf a score of one more than par.

boggle *verb*
(*informal*) to be startled or hesitate in fear: *The mind boggles at the idea.* □ *The horse boggled at the high jump.*

bogie (**bo-gee**) *noun*
a trolley or truck, e.g. one supporting a railway locomotive.

bogus *adjective*
counterfeit or sham.

Bohemian *noun*
an artistic or intellectual person who disregards conventional standards of behaviour.
• **bohemian** *adjective.*
[French *bohémien* a gipsy from Bohemia (now in the Czech Republic)]

boil¹ *verb*
1 to change a liquid to a vapour by applying heat.
2 to cook in boiling water, etc.: *boiled potatoes.*
3 to be very agitated: *She boiled with fury at the insult.*
Phrase **boil down 1** to reduce by boiling.
2 to add up: *It all boils down to this.*

boil² *noun*
an infection of the skin, causing a swelling with a small pus-filled centre.

boiler *noun*
1 a vessel in which water is stored, heated and circulated, to be used for heating or power.
2 (*informal*) a chicken suitable for boiling.

boiler suit *noun*
a piece of clothing consisting of trousers and a long-sleeved shirt in one piece.

boiling *adjective*
1 at boiling point.
2 (*informal*) very hot: *I'm boiling!*

boiling point *noun*
1 *Physics* the temperature at which the vapour pressure of a liquid is equal to the external pressure, and bubbles of vapour freely form within the liquid.
2 the peak of anger or vexation.

boisterous (**boy-sta-rus**) *adjective*
noisy, rough or unrestrained.
Word Family **boisterously** *adverb*; **boisterousness** *noun.*

bolas (bo-lus) *plural noun*
a throwing weapon consisting of balls attached to cords, used in South America to catch cattle, etc.

bold *adjective*
1 fearless and courageous.
2 impudent: *Her bold reply shocked us all.*
3 clear and distinct.
4 *Printing* having thick dark lines, as in **bold** typeface.
Word Family **boldly** *adverb*; **boldness** *noun*.

bole *noun*
Biology the trunk of a tree.

bolero *noun*
1 (**bol**-a-ro) a very short jacket, usually sleeveless.
2 (ba-**lair**-o) a lively dance from Spain, usually accompanied by singing and castanets.
3 (ba-**lair**-o) the music for such a dance.

boll (bole) *noun*
Biology a rounded seed pod of some plants, such as cotton.

bollard *noun*
a short strong post, e.g. one to which a ship may be tied at a dock, or one on a kerb or traffic island for the guidance of vehicles.

boloney ⇨ BALONEY.

Bolshevik (**bol**-sha-vik) *noun*
1 a Russian communist in the early 20th century.
2 a revolutionary person.
Word Family **Bolshevik** *adjective*; **bolshie, bolshy** *adjective* (*informal*) rebellious or awkward.

bolster (**bole**-sta) *noun*
a long narrow pillow or cushion.
• **bolster** *verb* to reinforce or support: *to bolster up one's courage.*

bolt *noun*
1 a sliding device for fastening a door, etc.
2 the part of a lock moved forward or withdrawn when the key is turned.
3 a heavy metal pin with a thread at one end, used with a nut for holding things together.
4 a sliding metal bar which closes the breech of a rifle or artillery piece.
5 a short heavy arrow used with a crossbow.
6 a flash of lightning.
Phrases **bolt from the blue** a complete surprise. **bolt upright** stiffly erect. **make a bolt** to make a sudden swift dash: *I left the hutch open and the rabbit made a bolt for freedom.*

• **bolt** *verb*
1 to fasten with a bolt.
2 to move or escape hurriedly or without control: *The horse bolted after its jockey fell.*
3 to eat hurriedly: *bolting his cereal.*

bolt hole *noun*
a place or means of escape.

bomb (bom) *noun*
a destructive device containing an explosive or incendiary charge.
Phrase **go like a bomb** to be a great success: *The party went like a bomb.*
• **bomb** *verb*
1 to attack or destroy with bombs.
2 (*informal*) to fail: *The play bombed.*
[Latin *bombus* a booming sound]

bombard *verb*
1 to attack with bombs or other artillery weapons.
2 to attack with questions or pieces of information.
3 *Physics* to send a stream of particles towards something.
Word Family **bombardment** *noun*.

bombastic *adjective*
pompous in speech or writing.
Word Family **bombastically** *adverb*; **bombast** *noun* pompous words.

bomber (**bom**-a) *noun*
1 a type of aircraft designed to carry and drop bombs.
2 someone who plants a bomb.

bombshell *noun*
1 a bomb.
2 a sudden or shocking surprise: *The news came as a bombshell.*

bona fide (bo-na **fie**-dee) *adjective*
sincere or without fraud: *He is a bona fide representative of that company.*
[Latin, in good faith]

bona fides (bo-na **fie**-deez) *noun*
evidence that someone is sincere and honest: *She established her bona fides.*
[Latin, good faith]

bonanza *noun*
a source of good luck or wealth: *That mineral strike was a bonanza.*
[Spanish, fair weather, prosperity]

bonbon *noun*
a small sweet.
[French]

bond *noun*
1 something which binds or holds things together: *a prisoner in bonds.* □ *a bond of affection.*

2 a formal promise to perform or not to perform certain actions, etc.

3 a sum of money paid as a security: *The tenants must pay a bond in case of damage.*

4 *Commerce* a certificate of debt from a government, etc. and offering repayment with interest by a fixed date.

5 *Building* the arrangement of bricks or stones in a wall in overlapping layers to make the structure stronger.

• **bond** *verb*

1 to join or hold together firmly.

2 to place under a bond.

3 to provide with a bond.

bondage (**bon**-dij) *noun*
the state of being subjected or enslaved to some force, power or control.

bonding *noun*
the process by which people form a relationship with one another, especially parent and child.

bone *noun*

1 a piece forming the rigid framework of the body of a vertebrate.

2 the hard substance of which this framework is composed, consisting of strands of protein in a bed of calcium phosphate.

3 a piece of this substance with meat attached: *a juicy bone for the dog.*

4 a substance or object which resembles or is made of bone.

Phrases **feel in one's bones** to know instinctively. **have a bone to pick** to have a complaint. **make no bones about** to have no difficulty in doing something awkward: *He made no bones about asking us to leave.* **bare bones** the essentials.

• **bone** *verb* to remove the bones from.

Phrase **bone up, bone up on** to study in a hurry.

Word Family **boneless** *adjective.*

bone china *noun*

1 an especially translucent type of porcelain made with calcium phosphate from bone ash. Bone china was developed and is still mostly produced in England.

2 cups, plates, etc. made of this.

bone dry *adjective*
very dry.

bone idle *adjective*
extremely lazy.

bone marrow ⇨ MARROW (definition 1).

bonemeal *noun*
a coarse powder of ground bones, used as fertilizer.

boneshaker *noun*
(*informal*) a decrepit old bike.
[the nickname of an 1870 bicycle with steel tyres]

bonfire *noun*
a large fire built in the open.

A **bonfire** was originally a fire where bones were burnt. Animal bones would be burnt both to get rid of the remains of a meal and as a means of providing fuel. These bone-burning fires tended to be situated in the open air and after the practice of burning bones was discontinued the name *bonfire* remained to describe an outdoor fire. It came to describe either rubbish fires or celebratory fires, the most famous being those burnt on 5 November with effigies of Guy Fawkes, who tried to blow up the Houses of Parliament.

bongos *plural noun* also **bongoes**
a pair of small drums struck with the hands.
[Spanish-American]

bonhomie (bon-a-**mee**) *noun*
a pleasant good-natured manner.
[French *bonhomme* a good sort]

bonkers *adjective*
(*informal*) crazy.

bon mot (bon mo) *noun* (*plural* **bons mots**) (bon mo *or* bon moze)
a witty remark.
[French *bon* good + *mot* word]

bonnet *noun*

1 a baby's or woman's soft hat, with its sides pulled down over the ears and tied under the chin.

2 a cover or protective device, such as the hinged or detachable cover for the engine of a motor vehicle.

bonny *adjective* also **bonnie** (**bonnier; bonniest**)
looking healthy and pretty: *a bonny girl.*

bonsai (**bon**-sigh) *noun*

1 the art of growing miniature decoratively shaped trees.

2 a tree grown in this way.
[Japanese *bon* pot + *sai* plant]

bonus *noun* (*plural* **bonuses**)
something which is given in addition to what is usual or expected, such as extra money given to an employee as well as his or her salary.
[Latin, good]

bon voyage (bon voy-**ahzh**) *interjection*
a wish for a pleasant trip.
[French]

bony *adjective* (**bonier; boniest**)
1 of or like bones.
2 containing many bones: *a bony piece of fish.*
3 very thin: *He's very bony.*

boo *interjection*
a shout expressing disapproval or contempt, or used to frighten someone.
• **boo** *verb* (**boos; booing; booed**).

boob¹ *noun*
1 (*informal*) a foolish mistake.
2 (*American informal*) a fool.
Word Family **boob** *verb* (*informal*) to make a foolish mistake; **boo-boo** *noun* (*informal*) a mistake.

boob² *noun*
(*informal*) a woman's breast.

booby *noun* (*plural* **boobies**)
a fool.

booby prize *noun*
a prize given in consolation or as a joke to the worst competitor.

booby trap *noun*
a device or situation which catches a person off guard.
Word Family **booby-trap** *verb* (**booby-traps; booby-trapping; booby-trapped**).

boogie *noun*
1 also called **boogie-woogie**. an early style of blues piano music dominated by a continuous bass accompaniment.
2 (*informal*) a dance to pop music.
• **boogie** *verb* (**boogies; boogieing; boogied**) (*informal*) to dance.

book (buk) *noun*
1 a group of sheets of paper bound or fastened together between covers: *a storybook.* □ *a chequebook.*
2 a written or printed work in this form, especially a literary composition.
3 a division of a larger written or printed work.
4 a record of bets, accounts or similar transactions.
Phrases **bring to book** to call to account. **by the book** absolutely correctly: *He does everything by the book.* **in someone's bad books** out of favour with someone. **in someone's good books** in favour with someone. **throw the book at** to make every possible charge against.
• **book** *verb*

1 to write or enter in a book or other record.
2 to reserve in advance: *We booked tickets for the play.*
3 to record a charge against: *She was booked for speeding.*
Word Family **booking** *noun* an advance reservation.

bookcase *noun*
a series of shelves, usually in a frame, for storing books.

bookend *noun*
a support for keeping books upright on a shelf.

bookie *noun*
(*informal*) a bookmaker.

bookish *adjective*
fond of reading and study, especially to an extreme degree.

bookkeeping *noun*
the art or process of recording financial transactions, accounts, etc.
Word Family **bookkeeper** *noun*

booklet *noun*
a small book or pamphlet.

bookmaker *noun*
a person who takes bets on races, competitions, etc.

bookmark *noun*
a slip of paper or material inserted between the pages of a book to mark one's place.

bookworm *noun*
(*informal*) a person who reads or studies a lot.

boom¹ *verb*
to make a loud hollow sound, such as the echo of an explosion.
• **boom** *noun* a loud hollow sound.

boom² *noun*
1 a long pole attached to the bottom of a sail and often by one end to the mast.
2 a long pole, chain, etc. which can be held across an area of land or water to prevent movement of traffic, etc.
3 a device with a movable arm from which a microphone, light or camera can be hung during filming.

boom³ *verb*
to flourish or progress vigorously: *Business was booming.*
• **boom** *noun*
1 a sudden increase or growth, as of business, popularity, etc.
2 a period of economic expansion, as in America in the 1920s.

boomerang *noun*
Australian a curved wooden Aboriginal throwing device which returns to the thrower.
• **boomerang** *verb* to rebound with harmful effects upon the originator.

boon[1] *noun*
a benefit or thing to be enjoyed.

boon[2] *adjective*
Phrase **boon companion** a good friend.

boondocks *plural noun*
(*American informal*) uninhabited or remote country.
[Tagalog *bundok* mountain]

boor *noun*
a person who is rude, surly and ill-mannered.
Word Family **boorish** *adjective*; **boorishly** *adverb*.
[Dutch *boer* peasant]

boost *verb*
1 to raise by pushing from behind or below.
2 to increase, promote: *The advertising campaign boosted sales.*
Word Family **boost** *noun* 1 an upward lift. 2 an increase; **booster** *noun* something which boosts or increases, such as an extra injection which prolongs immunity to a disease, or a device which increases power.

boot[1] *noun*
1 a heavy shoe, usually reaching above the ankle.
2 a compartment in the front or rear of a motor car for carrying luggage, etc.
3 (*informal*) a kick.
Phrases **get the boot** to be dismissed, **put the boot in** to kick someone who is on the ground. **the boot is on the other foot** the situation is reversed.
• **boot** *verb*
1 to kick.
2 to start a computer program running.

boot[2] *noun*
Phrase **to boot** in addition.

booth (booth) *noun*
a small enclosed structure or stall: *a telephone booth.*

bootleg *adjective*
traded, smuggled or made illegally: *bootleg liquor.*
Word Family **bootleg** *noun* a tape or CD which has been copied illegally; **bootlegger** *noun*; **bootlegging** *noun*

bootless *adjective*
an old word for **unprofitable**.

booty *noun*
anything stolen or captured in war or by robbery, etc.

booze *noun*
(*informal*) alcohol.
Word Family **booze** *verb* (*informal*) to drink heavily; **boozy** *adjective* (**boozier**; **booziest**); **boozer** *noun* 1 (*informal*) a pub. 2 (*informal*) someone who drinks a large amount of alcohol.

borax (baw-raks) *noun*
sodium borate, a white crystalline solid used in making glass and in cleaning agents.
[Arabic *burak*]

border *noun*
1 a part or line which forms the end or furthest sides of something.
2 the line or area which separates one country, state or place from another.
• **border** *verb*
1 to form or provide with a border.
2 to lie on the border of: *Italy borders France and Austria.*
Phrase **border on** 1 *Spain borders on France* (= adjoins). 2 *His fits of temper border on madness* (= are close to).

borderline *adjective*
close to a given limit, margin or condition: *a borderline pass in the exam.*

bore[1] *verb*
to make a hole by digging, drilling, etc.
• **bore** *noun*
1 a hole made by drilling.
2 the internal diameter of a cylinder, especially that of a gun barrel.

bore[2] *verb*
to tire by being dull and tedious: *He bored us with his long tales.*
Word Family **bore** *noun* a person or thing that bores; **boredom** *noun* the state of being bored.

bore[3] *noun*
a tidal wave in a river or estuary.

bore[4] the past tense of **bear**[1].

borer *noun*
a person or thing that bores holes, especially an insect which burrows into trees, wood, etc.

boring *adjective*
dull and tedious.

born *adjective*
having an innate quality or talent: *a born writer.*

Phrases **be born** to be brought into the world. **born and bred** born and having grown up.

> [!] Do not confuse *born* with *borne*. *Borne* is the past participle of the verb *bear*, meaning 'to carry or give birth to', as in *She had borne him three sons*. *Born* is only used in the passive sense of having been brought into the 'world: *I was born in 1989*.

born-again *adjective*
1 having undergone conversion, especially to evangelical Christianity.
2 showing the enthusiasm of someone newly converted to a cause: *a born-again socialist*.

borne the past participle of **bear**[1].

> [!] Do not confuse *borne* with BORN.

boron *noun*
a brown brittle metal used for hardening steel and in enamels and glass.
[BOR(ax) + (carb)ON]

borough (**burr**-a) *noun*
1 a town, especially one founded on a charter from a monarch.
2 a town or district with its own local government.
[Middle English *burgh* town]

borrow *verb*
to obtain on loan with a promise to return: *May I borrow £5 until tomorrow?*
Figurative He has borrowed my idea (= adopted for his own use).
Word Family **borrower** *noun*.

> [!] Do not confuse *borrow* with *lend*: *borrow* means 'to take and give back later', as in *Jack borrowed a pen from Megan*, while *lend* means 'to give and take back later', as in *Megan lent a pen to Jack*.

borscht (borsht) *noun* also **borsch**
a Russian soup made from beetroot and served hot or cold.

borstal *noun*
(*formerly*) a reformatory for young offenders.
[after the first, instituted in 1902 at *Borstal*, Kent]

borzoi (**bor**-zoy) *noun*
a large long-legged hound with a pointed head and a soft coat, formerly used to hunt wolves.
[Russian, swift]

bosh *noun*
(*informal*) nonsense.

bosom (**buz**-um) *noun*
1 the breasts of a woman.
Figurative in the bosom of my family (= affectionate centre).
2 the part of a piece of clothing covering the bosom.
Word Family **bosom** *adjective* close or intimate; **bosomy** *adjective* having large breasts.

boss[1] *noun* (*plural* **bosses**)
(*informal*) a person who has charge or control, especially over workers.
• **boss** *verb* (*informal*) to act in a domineering manner.
Word Family **bossy** *adjective* (**bossier**; **bossiest**) (*informal*) domineering; **bossily** *adverb*; **bossiness** *noun*.
[Dutch *baas* master]

boss[2] *noun* (*plural* **bosses**)
a knob-like projection.

bossa nova *noun*
1 a rhythmic jazz-style dance originally from Brazil.
2 the music for such a dance.
[Portuguese, new movement]

bosun ⇨ BOATSWAIN.

bo'sun ⇨ BOATSWAIN.

botanical garden *noun*
a public park displaying a wide variety of plants.

botany (**bot**-a-nee) *noun*
the study of plants.
Word Family **botanist** *noun*; **botanic** (ba-**tan**-ik), **botanical** *adjective*.
[Greek *botané* plant]

botch *verb*
(*informal*) to spoil through poor work or clumsiness.
• **botch** *noun* (*plural* **botches**).

botfly (**bot**-fly) *noun* (*plural* **botflies**)
a fly with parasitic larvae which feed beneath the skin of mammals.

both *adjective*
the two together: *Use both hands!*
• **both** *pronoun* the two: *Both of us will go.*
• **both** *conjunction* equally: *There is pollution in both Auckland and New York.*

bother (**both**-a) *verb*
1 to cause trouble or annoyance: *Stop bothering me while I'm reading.*
2 to concern oneself: *He didn't bother to reply.*
• **bother** *noun*
1 something which bothers or troubles.

2 a worried or agitated state: *She got into a real bother over it.*
Word Family **bothersome** *adjective*
giving or causing bother.

bottle *noun*
1 a glass or plastic container for liquid, usually with a narrow neck and an opening which may be sealed.
2 (*informal*) nerve, courage: *She was going to jump, but she lost her bottle.*
Phrase **hit the bottle** to drink alcohol excessively.
• **bottle** *verb* to put into a bottle.
Phrase **bottle up** *She bottled up her emotions* (= confined or restrained).

bottle green *noun*
a deep green colour.
Word Family **bottle-green** *adjective*.

bottleneck *noun*
a narrow congested area: *The street is a bottleneck for traffic.*

bottom *noun*
1 the lowest part of anything, as compared with the top: *the bottom of the cupboard.*
□ *the bottom of the sea.*
2 the buttocks.
3 (**bottoms**) the bottom part of a piece of clothing with two parts: *pyjama bottoms.*
Phrase **get to the bottom of** to find out the cause of.
Word Family **bottom** *adjective*; **bottom** *verb* to reach or touch the bottom; **bottomless** *adjective*.

bottom line *noun*
1 (*informal*) the last line of a firm's financial statement which indicates the net profit or loss.
2 (*informal*) the final outcome or conclusion of a discussion, etc.

The phrase **bottom line** is one of an increasing number of expressions which have entered the general language from a more specialized area. It is a term used by accountants for the last line of a profit and loss account which shows whether a profit or loss has been made. In the general language it is used more loosely as many users do not know its original meaning. Its meanings vary from 'final outcome' to 'the most important point of something', or even 'the last straw'.

botulism (bot-yoo-liz-um) *noun*
a disease of the nervous system due to eating contaminated food, and causing double vision and paralysis.
[Latin *botulus* a sausage]

bouclé (boo-klay) *noun*
a yarn with loops which produces a fabric with a rough appearance.
[French, curled]

boudoir (boo-dwar) *noun*
a woman's bedroom.
[French *bouder* to pout or sulk)

bouffant (boo-fon) *adjective*
puffed out: *a bouffant hairstyle.*
[French]

bougainvillea (boo-gan-**vil**-i-a) *noun* also
bougainvillaea
a climbing tropical American plant, now common in Australia, New Zealand and other warm countries.
[after *Admiral de Bougainville*, 1729-1811, a French navigator]

bough (*rhymes with* cow) *noun*
a large branch of a tree, usually starting at the trunk.

bought the past tense and past participle of **buy**.

> ! Do not confuse *bought* with *brought*. *Bought* is the past tense of *buy*, as in *I bought a new pair of shoes*, whereas *brought* is the past tense of *bring*: *I brought my camera to school.*

bouillabaisse (boo-ya-base) *noun*
a rich spicy fish stew.

bouillon (boo-yon) *noun*
a thin clear soup.

bouldor (bole-da) *noun*
a large stone.

boulevard (bool-a-vahd) *noun*
a wide street lined with trees.
[French]

bounce *verb*
1 to spring or cause to spring back after hitting something: *The ball bounced on the concrete.*
2 to move in a lively manner: *She bounced into the room.*
3 (*informal*) (of a cheque) to be returned unpaid from a bank.
Word Family **bounce** *noun*; **bouncy** *adjective* (**bouncier; bounciest**).

bouncer *noun*
1 a person hired to remove disorderly persons from a dance, club, etc.
2 *Cricket* a fast ball which bounces up dangerously at the batsman.

bouncing *adjective*
strong and healthy: *a bouncing baby.*

bound¹ *adjective*
1 certain or determined: *Their plan is bound to fail.*

2 (*used in compound words*) unable to operate, progress, etc. due to: *snowbound*.
3 (*used in compound words*) restricted to: *housebound*.
• **bound** the past tense and past participle of **bind**.

bound² *verb*
to move in leaps: *He bounded energetically into the room*.
• **bound** *noun*.

bound³ *noun*
a limit or boundary: *There are no bounds to his ambition*.
Phrase **out of bounds** forbidden.
Word Family **bound** *verb* to limit or form the limit of; **boundless** *adjective* unlimited: *boundless enthusiasm*.

bound⁴ *adjective*
on the way or intending to go: *homeward bound*.

boundary *noun* (*plural* **boundaries**)
1 a line which indicates the edge: *This is the boundary of our property*.
2 *Cricket* a strike which reaches the boundary and scores four or six.

bounteous *adjective*
an old word for **bountiful**: *a bounteous harvest*.
Word Family **bounteously** *adverb*; **bounteousness** *noun*.

bountiful *adjective*
1 generous: *a bountiful giver*.
2 plentiful: *a bountiful supply*.
Word Family **bountifully** *adverb*.

bounty *noun* (*plural* **bounties**)
1 a bonus or reward, especially one given by a government.
2 generosity.
[Latin *bonitas* goodness]

bouquet (bo-**kay** *or* boo-**kay**) *noun*
1 a bunch of flowers.
2 the characteristic smell of wines, liqueurs or perfumes.
[Old French *bosquet* little wood]

bourbon (**ber**-b'n) *noun*
a whisky made from maize.
[first made in *Bourbon County*, America]

bourgeois (boor-*zh*wa) *adjective*
of or thought to be characteristic of the middle class.
Word Family **bourgeois** *noun* (*plural* **bourgeois**) a member of the middle class; **bourgeoisie** (boor-*zh*wa-**zee**) *noun* the middle class, often with implications that it is conventional.
[French, townsman]

bout *noun*
1 a period of time in some activity, work, etc.
2 a period of illness.
3 a wrestling or boxing contest.

boutique (boo-**teek**) *noun*
a small fashionable shop usually selling women's clothing or gifts.
[French]

bovine (**bo**-vine) *adjective*
of, like or relating to cows, oxen, etc.
[Latin *bovis* of a bull]

bovine spongiform encephalopathy (bo-vine sponge-i-fawm en-sef-a-**lop**-a-thee) *noun*
short form is **BSE** a fatal disease of cattle involving the nervous system.

bow¹ (*rhymes with* cow) *verb*
1 to bend down or sideways: *The branches bowed in the wind.* □ *He bowed courteously to the princess*.
2 to yield, submit: *She bowed to their wishes*.
• **bow** *noun*.

bow² (*rhymes with* go) *noun*
1 a weapon made from a length of wood or other flexible material with a string tightly stretched between the two ends, used to shoot arrows.
2 a bend or curve.
3 a decorative looped knot.
4 *Music* a stick with horsehairs stretched along it, used to sound the strings of a violin or similar instrument.
Word Family **bow** *verb* to play with a bow.

bow³ (*rhymes with* cow) *noun*
Nautical (*often* **bows**) the front end of a boat. Compare STERN² (definition 1).

bowdlerize, bowdlerise (**bowd**-la-rize) *verb*
to censor words in a book which are believed to be unsuitable for certain readers.
Word Family **bowdlerization** (bowd-la-rye-**zay**-sh'n) *noun*.
[after *Dr T. Bowdler*, 1734-1825, who published a censored version of Shakespeare's plays in the 19th century]

bowel (*rhymes with* towel) *noun*
1 *Anatomy* ⇨ INTESTINE.
2 (**bowels**) the innermost part: *in the bowels of the earth*.

bower (*rhymes with* flower) *noun*
a shady leafy shelter.

bowerbird *noun*
an Australian bird which lives in scrub.
The male builds an elaborate walled
enclosure to attract the female.

bowie knife (**bo**-ee nife) *noun* (*plural*
bowie knives)
a sheath knife which has a long blade and
one cutting edge.
[after *James Bowie*, 1796-1836, an
American pioneer]

bowl[1] (bole) *noun*
1 a deep round dish.
2 a rounded hollow object or area: *the bowl
of a pipe*.

bowl[2] *noun*
1 a ball made of wood, rubber or a
synthetic material, used in the game of
bowls, tenpin bowling, etc.
2 a roll or delivery of the bowl.
• **bowl** *verb*
1 to throw or roll a ball.
2 *Cricket* to pitch the ball towards the
batsman, with the arm held straight using
a circular overarm motion.
3 to move along smoothly and rapidly.
Word Family **bowler** *noun*

bow-legged (bo-leg-id) *adjective*
having legs which bend outwards so that
the knees are separated when the ankles
are close together.

bowler *noun*
short form of **bowler hat** a man's hat with
a rounded crown and narrow brim, usually
made of felt.

bowline (**bo**-lin) *noun*
a non-slipping knot which forms a loop.

bowling alley *noun*
a long indoor wooden alley for tenpin
bowling or skittles.

bowls *noun*
a game played on a green by two to eight
players who aim to place their bowls which
are biased (weighted on one side), as close
as possible to a small white ball, called the
jack.

bowsprit (**bo**-sprit or **bough**-sprit) *noun*
Nautical a spar projecting from the bow of
a boat and holding the forestay.

bow tie *noun*
a tie made into a bow at the neck.

bow window *noun*
a curved bay window.

box[1] *noun* (*plural* **boxes**)
1 a container, usually rectangular, and
with a lid, made of cardboard, wood, etc.

2 a separate compartment, container or
enclosure: *the glovebox of a car.* □ *witness
box*.
3 *Soccer* the penalty area.
4 *Baseball* the place where the batter
stands to face the pitcher.
5 (*formerly*) a small raised seat in a horse-
drawn vehicle, for the driver.
6 (*informal*) television: *watching the box*.
• **box** *verb* to enclose in or as if in a box.

box[2] *verb*
to fight with the fists.
Word Family **boxing** *noun* the art or
sport of a person who boxes.

box[3] *noun* (*plural* **boxes**) also called **box
tree**.
a small evergreen tree, often used for
ornamental hedging and having hard fine-
grained timber.
[Latin *buxus*]

boxcar *noun*
American a large enclosed and covered
railway freight van.

boxer *noun*
1 a person who boxes, especially in
competitions.
2 a large short-haired dog of the bulldog
type, usually tan or brindled.

boxer shorts *plural noun*
men's underpants in the shape of shorts.

Boxing Day *noun*
the day after Christmas Day.
[when tradespeople were given Christmas
boxes]

box number *noun*
a number given in a newspaper
advertisement to which replies are sent.

box office *noun*
a place where one can buy tickets in or for
a theatre.

box tree *noun* ⊃ BOX[3].

boy *noun*
a male child.
Word Family **boyish** *adjective*; **boyishly**
adverb; **boyhood** *noun*.

boycott *verb*
to refuse to use or deal with, as a method
of protest or threat: *to boycott imported
goods*.
• **boycott** *noun*.
[after *Captain Boycott*, 1832-1897, an
English land agent who was boycotted by
Irish workers]

boyfriend *noun*
a person's chosen male companion,
especially in a romantic or sexual sense.

bra *noun*
short form of **brassiere** a close-fitting support for the breasts.

brace *noun*
1 something which holds parts together or acts as a support.
2 an arrangement of wires and bands fitted against teeth to straighten them.
3 (**braces**) the straps worn over the shoulders to hold up trousers.
4 a pair: *a brace of rabbits.*
5 also called **brace and bit**. a drill with a U-shaped crank handle which turns the bit.
• **brace** *verb* to support, fix or strengthen with or as if with a brace.
Phrase **brace oneself** to prepare oneself: *Brace yourself for some bad news.*
Word Family **bracing** *adjective* invigorating.

bracelet (**brace**-lit) *noun*
1 a decorative band, chain, etc. worn on the arm.
2 (**bracelets**) (*informal*) handcuffs.

bracken *noun*
a large coarse fern or clump of ferns.

bracket *noun*
1 a frame-like support for a shelf, rack, etc.
2 a punctuation mark used in pairs ( ) or [ ], to indicate that the enclosed word or words are to be treated as a separate unit.
3 *Maths* a mark used in pairs ( ), [ ] or { }, to indicate that the enclosed figures are to be treated separately.
4 a grouping or category: *the high income bracket.*
• **bracket** *verb*
1 to support with a bracket.
2 to enclose in or as if in brackets.

brackish *adjective*
slightly salty: *brackish water.*

bract *noun*
a leaf-like part at the base of a flower.

brad *noun*
a small fine nail with little or no head.

bradawl *noun*
an awl for making small holes in wood, etc.

brag *verb* (**brags**; **bragging**; **bragged**)
to boast.
Word Family **braggart** *noun* a person who boasts or brags.

Brahman *noun* also **Brahmin**
1 a member of the highest Hindu caste, originally priests.
2 the ultimate reality or supreme being in Hindu belief.

Brahmin ⇨ ZEBU.

braid *noun*
1 a decorative band of fabric made of various woven threads and used for trimming, decoration, etc.
2 a plait.
• **braid** *verb* to weave or plait.

Braille (brale) *noun*
a system of printing for blind people, using raised symbols which are identified by touch.
[invented by *Louis Braille*, 1809-1852]

brain *noun*
1 the mass of nerve tissue which controls the functions of the body in most forms of animal life.
2 (*usually* **brains**) intelligence.
Phrases **have something on the brain** to be obsessed or concerned about something. **pick someone's brains** to use someone else's ideas.
• **brain** *verb* (*informal*) to hit on the head.

brainchild *noun*
(*informal*) an original plan or thought.

brain drain *noun*
(*informal*) the departure of large numbers of highly qualified professional people from a country.

brainless *adjective*
stupid or unintelligent.

brainstorming *noun*
producing ideas quickly without stopping to discuss details: *The design team had a brainstorming session.*

brainwashing *noun*
a systematic indoctrination to change a person's beliefs or attitudes.
Word Family **brainwash** *verb*.

brainwave *noun*
(*informal*) a sudden inspiration.

brainy *adjective* (**brainier**; **brainiest**)
(*informal*) clever.

braise *verb*
to cook by browning in fat and then stewing with little moisture.

brake[1] *noun*
a device for slowing the motion of a wheel, motor or vehicle.
• **brake** *verb* to slow down or stop by a brake.

brake[2] *noun*
an old or poetic word meaning 'a small area or thicket of dense undergrowth'.

brake horsepower *noun*
the horsepower developed by an engine measured by the resistance offered by a brake.

bramble *noun*
a coarse prickly shrub, especially the blackberry bush.

bran *noun*
the husks of corn after the flour has been removed.

branch *noun* (*plural* **branches**)
1 a division or offshoot of the stem of a tree or other plant.
2 a small division or section: *the suburban branch of a bank.* □ *Botany is a branch of biology.*
• **branch** *verb* to split into separate paths: *a road branching off to the right.*

branchiae (**brang**-ki-ee) *plural noun*
(*singular* **branchia**) (**brang**-ki-a)
the gills of a fish.
[Latin]

brand *noun*
1 a trademark or name used to identify a product: *Which brand of soap is best?*
2 something which indicates type, quality, etc., such as a mark burnt onto cattle as a sign of ownership.
3 a tool or iron used for branding.
4 a piece of burning wood.
• **brand** *verb* to label accusingly: *She was branded a thief.*

brandish *verb*
to wave about: *He brandished a sword.*

brand new *adjective*
completely new.

brandy *noun* (*plural* **brandies**)
an alcoholic drink made by distilling wine or fermented fruit juice.

brash *adjective*
impertinent, rash or bold.

brass (*rhymes with* grass) *noun* (*plural* **brasses**)
1 a malleable ductile alloy composed of zinc and over 50 per cent copper.
2 something which is made of brass.
3 *Music* metal instruments, such as trumpets, horns, etc., in which sound is produced by blowing through a mouthpiece.
4 *Music* the section of an orchestra having these instruments.
5 (*informal*) short form of **top brass** important officials, especially military officers.
6 (*informal*) money.
• **brass** *adjective*.

brassiere ⇨ BRA.

brassy *adjective* (**brassier; brassiest**)
1 harsh or metallic: *a brassy noise.*
2 bold or vulgar: *a brassy woman.*

brat *noun*
(*informal*) a child, especially an irritating one.

bravado (bra-**vah**-do) *noun*
a display of bravery or courage, especially false bravery.
[Spanish *bravata*]

brave *adjective*
having or displaying courage: *a brave deed.*
• **brave** *noun* (*dated*) a Native American warrior.
• **brave** *verb* to meet or face courageously: *We decided to brave the winter weather.*
Word Family **bravely** *adverb*; **bravery** *noun* brave spirit or conduct.

bravo (brah-**vo**) *interjection*
well done!

bravura (brav-**yor**-a) *noun*
daring or brilliant performance.
[Italian, bravery]

brawl *noun*
a noisy quarrel or fight.
• **brawl** *verb*.

brawn *noun*
1 muscles, or muscular strength.
2 boiled and moulded meat from a pig's or calf's head.
Word Family **brawny** *adjective* (**brawnier; brawniest**) muscular or strong.

bray *noun*
1 the harsh noisy cry of a donkey.
2 a similar sound.
• **bray** *verb*.

braze *verb*
to join metals by drawing a molten metal, usually a brass alloy, between them.

brazen *adjective*
1 bold or shameless.
2 a poetic word meaning 'made of brass'.

brazier¹ (**braze**-ya) *noun*
a person who works with brass.

brazier² (**braze**-i-a) *noun*
a metal container for holding burning fuels such as coal.

brazil *noun* also called **Brazil nut**.
a large oily edible nut.
[originally from *Brazil*, South America]

breach *noun* (*plural* **breaches**)
1 a break, rupture or gap.

2 the act of breaking: *They sued him for breach of promise.*
• **breach** *verb*
1 to make a break in.
2 to break: *She had breached their agreement.*

bread (bred) *noun*
1 a shaped baked food made of flour, liquid and yeast or another raising agent.
2 (*informal*) money.

breadfruit *noun*
a large round tropical fruit commonly grown in the Pacific Islands.

breadline *noun*
a subsistence level of living.

breadth (bredth) *noun*
1 width.
2 extent: *He showed great breadth of feeling.*

breadwinner *noun*
a person who earns the money for a family or household.

break (*rhymes with* cake) *verb* (**breaks; breaking; broke; broken**)
1 to divide into parts, usually by force: *The vase broke when it fell to the floor.*
2 to interrupt or discontinue: *It's hard to break a habit.*
3 to force one's way: *He broke out of their grip.*
4 to fail to keep: *She broke her promise.*
5 to ruin: *broken by gambling losses.*
6 to outdo: *breaking a world record.*
7 to train by weakening the resistance of: *breaking a colt.*
8 (of a voice) to change in range or tone.
Phrases **break down** 1 to cease to function. 2 to be overcome physically or emotionally. **break up** 1 to separate: *I was shocked to hear that they had broken up.* 2 to end: *When does school break up?* 3 to laugh uncontrollably.
• **break** *noun*
1 the act of breaking.
2 an opening etc. made by breaking: *a break in the wall.*
3 a rest or interruption: *I needed a break.*
4 a holiday: *a weekend break.*
5 (*informal*) a chance: *a lucky break.*
6 *Billiards, Snooker* a series of successful shots.
Word Family **breakable** *adjective;* **breakage** *noun* 1 the act of breaking.
2 the amount which is broken.

break-dancing *noun*
a form of street dancing involving acrobatic movements often performed to rap music.

breakdown *noun*
1 a collapse or failure to function: *a mental breakdown.*
2 an analysis or summary of important points.
3 *Science* the act of separating into constituent parts.

breaker *noun*
1 a wave which breaks into foam when it reaches shallow water.
2 a person or thing that breaks.

breakfast (brek-f'st) *noun*
the first meal of the day.
• **breakfast** *verb*.
[Middle English *brek* break + *faste* a fast]

breakneck (brake-nek) *adjective*
dangerous.

breakthrough (brake-throo) *noun*
a new discovery, development or success which increases progress.

breakwater (brake-waw-ta) *noun*
a jetty built out from a beach or river bank, to prevent movement or erosion of the beach.

bream *noun* (*plural* **bream**)
an edible fish with a compressed body and silvery scales.

breast (brest) *noun*
1 *Anatomy* a human mammary gland.
2 the chest.
Phrase **make a clean breast of** to confess.

breastbone ⇨ STERNUM.

breastfeed *verb* (**breastfeeds; breastfeeding; breastfed**)
to feed a baby by allowing it to suck milk from the nipple of a woman's breast.

breastplate *noun*
1 a piece of armour covering the chest.
2 the part of a harness which crosses the horse's chest.

breaststroke *noun*
Swimming a style in which the swimmer lies on his or her front in the water with both arms extended forward and pulls them out sideways in horizontal arcs.

breath (breth) *noun*
1 the air that is taken in and given out during respiration.
2 the act of taking in and giving out such air: *Take a deep breath.*
3 the smallest amount of air: *a breath of wind.*
Phrases **below, under one's breath** in a whisper. **in the same breath** at the same time. **out of breath** unable to breathe

freely. **take one's breath away** to astonish one.
Word Family **breathless** *adjective* **1** out of breath. **2** holding the breath, as in fear, excitement, etc.; **breathlessly** *adverb*; **breathlessness** *noun*.

> [!] Do not confuse *breath* with *breathe*: *breath* is a noun (*Take a deep breath*) and *breathe* is a verb (*She breathed the fresh air*).

breathalyser (breth-a-lize-a) *noun*
an instrument which measures the amount of alcohol in exhaled breath.

breathe (breeth) *verb*
to take in and give out air.
Phrase **breathe freely** to relax.
Word Family **breather** *noun* (*informal*) a pause or rest.

> [!] Do not confuse *breathe* with BREATH.

breathtaking (breth-tay-king) *adjective*
inspiring awe and admiration: *The view was breathtaking.*

breech (breech) *noun* (*plural* **breeches**)
the lower or rear part of something, such as the part of a gun behind the barrel.

breech birth *noun* also called **breech delivery**.
a birth in which the baby's buttocks appear first.

breeches (brit-chiz) *plural noun*
trousers, especially ones reaching to or just below the knee.

breed *verb* (**breeds**; **breeding**; **bred**)
1 to produce offspring: *Many animals breed in the spring.*
2 to produce and raise crops, livestock, etc.: *He breeds bantams.*
3 to cause: *Hatred breeds violence.*
• **breed** *noun* a group of animals within a species, which has a common origin: *a breed of dog.*
Word Family **breeder** *noun*.

breeze *noun*
a light steady wind.
• **breeze** *verb* (*informal*) to move lightly and easily: *He breezed into the room.*
Word Family **breezily** *adverb*; **breezy** *adjective* (**breezier**; **breeziest**); **breeziness** *noun*.

Bren gun *noun*
a light machine gun.
[from BR(no) in the Czech Republic, where originally made + EN(field), where made in England]

brethren
an old plural of **brother**.

breve (breev) *noun*
Music the longest note, equal to two whole notes.

breviary (breev-ya-ree) *noun* (*plural* **breviaries**)
Roman Catholicism a book containing the services for each day.
[Latin *breviarium* a summary]

brevity (brev-i-tee) *noun*
the fact of being short or brief.
[Latin *brevis* short]

brew (broo) *verb*
1 to make a drink by soaking, boiling or fermenting: *to brew beer.*
2 to form, develop: *There is trouble brewing.*
• **brew** *noun* a drink made by brewing.
Word Family **brewer** *noun* a person who brews; **brewery** *noun* (*plural* **breweries**) a place where beer and similar drinks are brewed.

briar[1] *noun* also **brier**
a prickly bush, especially a rose.

briar[2] *noun* also **brier**; **briar pipe**
a tobacco pipe made from the hard woody root of a shrub.

bribe *noun*
something offered or given to persuade a person to do something, usually dishonest.
Word Family **bribe** *verb*; **bribery** *noun*.

bric-a-brac *noun*
odd items of furniture, jewellery or ornaments of decorative or antique interest.
[Old French *à bric et à brac* at random]

brick *noun*
1 a block made of baked clay or a similar substance, used to build walls, etc.
2 a shaped block of a substance: *a brick of vanilla ice cream.*
3 (*informal dated*) a kind or generous person.
Phrase **drop a brick** to make a clumsy or indiscreet mistake.

bricklayer *noun*
a person whose work is to build structures with bricks.

bride *noun*
a woman who is about to be or is newly married.
Word Family **bridal** *adjective* relating to a bride or wedding.

bridegroom ⇨ GROOM *noun* (definition 1).

bridesmaid *noun*
a girl or woman who attends the bride at a wedding.

bridge¹ *noun*
1 a structure built over and across something, usually to provide passage: *a wooden bridge across the river*.
2 something which has the shape or function of a bridge, such as a thin support for the strings of a musical instrument.
3 *Anatomy* the bony upper line of the nose.
4 an artificial tooth or teeth, usually supported on either side by the natural teeth.
5 a raised platform over the deck of a ship, used by the captain or officers.
Phrase **burn one's bridges** to commit oneself to a course of action from which there is no turning back.
• **bridge** *verb* to cross or extend across.

bridge² *noun*
a card game for four players in which one pair attempts to win the number of rounds specified by bids.
auction bridge a form of bridge in which all tricks won count towards the score.
contract bridge a form of bridge in which only the winning tricks which were bid for count towards the game.

bridgehead *noun*
a fortified area established in enemy territory, especially on the enemy side of a river, etc.

bridle *noun*
an arrangement of leather strips, with a bit and reins, fitted around the head of a horse to guide or control it.
• **bridle** *verb*
1 to put a bridle on.
2 to control: *She had to bridle her resentment.*
3 to draw back in pride and scorn: *He bridled with indignation.*

bridleway *noun* also called **bridle path**.
a path or track for horses.

Brie (bree) *noun*
a soft white cheese with a mild taste.

brief (breef) *adjective*
short: *a brief weather forecast*. □ *a brief skirt.*
• **brief** *noun* an outline or instructions given concerning a project, duty, etc., e.g. to a barrister concerning a case.
Phrase **in brief** *Here is today's news in brief* (= in a few words).
Word Family **brief** *verb* to give a briefing to; **briefly** *adverb*; **briefness** *noun*.
[Latin *brevis* short]

briefcase *noun*
a case, often leather, for carrying books, papers, etc.

briefing *noun*
instructions, especially those given to a military unit before an operation.

briefs *plural noun*
short underpants.

brier¹ ⇨ BRIAR¹.

brier² ⇨ BRIAR².

brigade *noun*
1 an organized group of people, usually in uniform, who perform special duties: *a fire brigade*.
2 *Military* a tactical army unit consisting of three battalions or armoured units.
[Italian *brigata* a troop]

brigadier (brig-a-**deer**) *noun*
Army a commissioned officer ranking between colonel and major general.

brigand (**brig**-and) *noun*
a bandit or robber.

bright *adjective*
1 shining or giving out much light: *a bright star*.
2 vivid: *bright red*.
3 clever, intelligent: *a bright pupil*.
4 cheerful: *a bright voice*.
5 optimistic: *a bright future*.
Word Family **brightly** *adverb*; **brightness** *noun*.

brighten *verb*
to make more bright or cheerful.

brill¹ *noun*
an edible European flatfish resembling and related to the turbot.

brill² *adjective*
(*informal*) very good, excellent.
[from *brilliant*]

brilliant *adjective*
1 very bright or sparkling: *brilliant sunshine*.
2 very clever: *a brilliant mathematician*.
3 (*informal*): excellent: *It was a brilliant game*.
• **brilliant** *noun* a cut diamond or other gem which sparkles.
Word Family **brilliance** *noun*; **brilliantly** *adverb*.

brim *noun*
the upper or outer edge of anything: *a hat brim*.
• **brim** *verb* (**brims**; **brimming**; **brimmed**) to be full to overflowing: *Her eyes brimmed with tears*.
Word Family **brimful** *adjective* completely full.

brimstone *noun*
an old word for **sulphur**.

brindle *adjective* also **brindled**
brown or grey with dark streaks or spots: *a brindle dog.*

brine *noun*
1 water which contains or is saturated with salt, used for preserving meat, etc.
2 seawater.
Word Family **briny** *adjective* (**brinier; briniest**); **briny** *noun* (*informal*) the sea.

bring *verb* (**brings; bringing; brought**)
1 to take, convey: *Did you bring your book?*
2 to cause: *Her accident brought a change of heart.*
3 to cause to be: *Bring the soup to a simmer.*
4 to sell for: *Did the house bring a decent price?*
Phrases **bring about** to cause: *His recklessness had brought about the tragedy.*
bring off to do successfully. **bring on** to cause: *Running upstairs brought on a coughing fit.* **bring round, bring to** to restore to consciousness. **bring up 1** to raise, educate. 2 to mention. 3 to vomit.

brink *noun*
the very edge: *the brink of a cliff.*

brinkmanship *noun*
the practice of tempting disaster or danger to achieve one's aims.

brioche (**bree-**osh) *noun*
a type of soft bread roll made from a sweet yeast dough.
[French]

briquette (bri-**ket**) *noun* also **briquet**
a small block of compressed coal dust, used for fuel.
[French, a small brick]

brisk *adjective*
1 quick or lively: *a brisk walk.*
2 abrupt or blunt.
Word Family **briskly** *adverb*; **briskness** *noun*.

brisket *noun*
a cut of meat from the breast of a cow.

bristle (**bris-**'l) *noun*
a short coarse stiff hair.
• **bristle** *verb*
1 to stand on end like a bristle: *Her hair bristled.*
2 to react in horror or anger: *She bristled at the suggestion.*
3 to be full of: *The house was bristling with police.*
Word Family **bristly** (**bris-**lee) *adjective* like or covered with bristles.

British Commonwealth ⇨
COMMONWEALTH (definition 1).

British Standards *plural noun*
standards which set requirements for product performance and reliability.

British Summer Time *noun*
a time one hour ahead of Greenwich Mean Time, used in Britain from late March to late October.

British thermal unit *noun*
a unit of energy, equal to about 1060 joules.

brittle *adjective*
hard but fragile and easily broken: *Glass is brittle.*
• **brittle** *noun* a sweet made of burnt sugar, nuts, etc.: *peanut brittle.*
Word Family **brittleness** *noun*.

broach (*rhymes with* coach) *verb*
1 to begin to talk about: *Please do not broach the subject again.*
2 to pierce, especially to draw liquid out of a cask.

broad (brawd) *adjective*
1 wide or large: *a broad smile.* □ *a person of broad experience.*
2 general: *a broad outline.*
3 obvious: *a broad hint.*
4 strong, noticeable: *a broad Liverpudlian accent.*
Phrase **broad daylight** full daylight.
• **broad** *noun* (*American informal*) a woman.
Word Family **broadly** *adverb*; **broaden** *verb*.

broad bean *noun*
a variety of bean with large flat edible seeds and a thick pod.

broadcast *verb* (**broadcasts; broadcasting; broadcast; broadcast** or **broadcasted**)
1 to send out by television or radio.
2 to spread: *His secret was broadcast round the school.*
• **broadcast** *noun* a programme which is sent out by television or radio.

broad-minded *adjective*
having an open or tolerant mind.
Word Family **broad-mindedly** *adverb*; **broad-mindedness** *noun*.

broadsheet *noun*
1 a large single sheet of paper, originally having a ballad or song printed on one side.
2 a newspaper twice the size of a tabloid, dealing with news in depth and in a formal tone. Compare TABLOID.

broadside *noun*
1 the whole side of a ship which is above the waterline.
2 the simultaneous firing of all the guns on one side of a ship.
3 a strong verbal attack.

brocade (bro-**kade**) *noun*
a woven cloth, originally of silk, but now of cotton or fibre, patterned with areas of different weaves, giving raised or shiny effects.
Word Family **brocaded** *adjective*.

broccoli (**brok**-a-lee) *noun*
a vegetable with tightly bunched green heads, resembling a cauliflower.
[Italian, cabbage sprouts]

brochure (**bro**-sher) *noun*
a booklet or commercial pamphlet.

brogue¹ (*rhymes with* rogue) *noun*
a strong leather shoe with small decorative holes on the upper surface.
[Irish *brog* shoe]

brogue² *noun*
an accent, especially an Irish one.

broil *verb*
(*especially American*) to grill.
[Old French *bruler* to burn]

broke *adjective*
(*informal*) having no money.
● **broke** *verb* the past tense of **break**.

broken the past participle of **break**.
Phrase **broken home** a family in which the parents are divorced.

broker *noun*
a person who buys and sells goods or securities, on behalf of others, for a commission.
Word Family **brokerage** *noun* the commission charged by a broker.

brolly *noun* (*plural* **brollies**)
(*informal*) an umbrella.

bromide (**bro**-mide) *noun*
1 *Chemistry* a salt containing the univalent Br⁻ ion.
2 *Photography* a print made on paper containing light-sensitive silver bromide.

bromine (**bro**-meen) *noun*
a dark red poisonous non-metal liquid with a choking irritating smell, used in making organic chemicals. Its compounds are used in photography and medicine.
⇨ HALOGEN.
[Greek *bromos* stench]

bronchiole (**bronk**-i-ole) *noun*
Anatomy any of the numerous fine tube-like extensions of a bronchus.

bronchitis (bron-**kie**-tis) *noun*
an inflammation of the membranes lining the bronchial tubes.
[BRONCH(us) + -*itis*]

bronchus (**bronk**-us) *noun* (*plural* **bronchi**) (**bronk**-eye)
Anatomy either of the two branched tubes of the trachea leading to the lungs.
Word Family **bronchial** *adjective*.
[Latin]

bronco *noun* (*plural* **broncos**)
a horse which has not been broken in.
[Spanish, rough or wild]

brontosaurus (bron-ta-**saw**-rus) *noun* (*plural* **brontosauruses**) also **brontosaur**
an apatosaurus.
[Greek *bronté* thunder + *sauros* lizard]

bronze *noun*
1 an alloy of copper (more than 80 per cent) and other metals such as tin or aluminium.
2 an object, such as a statue, made from bronze.
3 a bronze medal.
4 a lustrous yellowish or reddish-brown colour.
● **bronze** *verb*
1 to provide with a bronze or bronze-like surface.
2 to tan: *bronzed sunbathers*.

Bronze Age *noun*
a period in history between the Stone Age and the Iron Age, when tools and weapons were first made of bronze.

bronze medal *noun*
a medal made of bronze or bronze in colour awarded to the person or team coming third in a race or competition.

brooch (*rhymes with* coach) *noun* (*plural* **brooches**)
a decorative clasp which fastens by a pin at the back.

brood (*rhymes with* food) *noun*
a group of young animals, especially birds, hatched at the same time.
● **brood** *verb*
1 (of birds) to sit over eggs or young offspring.
2 to dwell moodily on something: *The prisoner brooded on his fate*.
Word Family **brooding** *adjective*.

broody *adjective* (**broodier; broodiest**)
1 ready to sit on eggs: *a broody hen*.
2 (*informal*) keen to have a baby.
3 thoughtful.
Word Family **broodily** *adverb*; **broodiness** *noun*.

brook¹ (*rhymes with* book) *noun*
a small stream.

brook² *verb*
(*formal*) to put up with: *He is a stern man who will brook no opposition.*

broom *noun*
1 a long-handled brush for sweeping floors.
2 a European shrub with small leaves and yellow flowers.

broomstick *noun*
the handle of a broom.

broth *noun*
a thin soup made with meat, fish or vegetable juices.

brothel *noun*
a house where prostitutes work.

brother (bru*th*-a) *noun* (*plural* **brothers**, *old form* **brethren**)
1 a son of the same parents as another child.
2 a man belonging to a religious order, who has not taken vows or who is not a priest.
Word Family **brotherly** *adjective*;
brotherhood, brotherliness *noun*.

brother-in-law *noun* (*plural* **brothers-in-law**)
1 the brother of one's husband or wife.
2 the husband of one's sister or sister-in-law.

brougham (broo-um) *noun*
an enclosed four-wheeled carriage for two or four passengers with the driver's seat outside.
[after *Lord Brougham*, 1778-1868, a British statesman who designed it]

brought the past tense and past participle of **bring**.

> ⚠️ Do not confuse *brought* with BOUGHT.

brouhaha (broo-ha-ha) *noun*
a hubbub or uproar.
[French, imitating the confused noise of a marketplace]

brow (*rhymes with* cow) *noun*
1 the eyebrow.
2 the forehead.
3 the top of a hill.

browbeat *verb* (**browbeats**; **browbeating**; **browbeat**; **browbeaten**)
to bully or domineer: *They tried to browbeat him into signing the contract.*

brown *noun*
a dark colour formed by mixing such colours as red, black and yellow.
Word Family **brown** *adjective*; **brown** *verb* to make or become brown;
brownness *noun*.

brown ale *noun*
a bottled beer which is milder and sweeter than pale ale.

browned off *adjective*
(*informal*) bored or fed up.

brownie *noun*
1 *Folklore* a friendly elf or goblin.
2 a small square soft chocolate cake containing nuts.
3 (**Brownie**) also **Brownie Guide** a girl belonging to a junior section of the Guide Association.

browse (*rhymes with* cows) *verb*
1 (of animals) to graze or nibble on grass.
2 to glance or look at random: *browsing in a bookshop.*
• **browse** *noun*.

browser *noun*
Computers a program used for searching the World Wide Web.

brucellosis (broo-sa-lo-sis) *noun*
a bacterial disease of cattle, pigs and goats, occasionally transmitted to people.
[after *Sir David Bruce*, 1855-1931, a Scottish physician]

bruise (brooz) *noun*
a discoloured area on the skin, due to an injury which did not break the skin but damaged the underlying blood vessels.
• **bruise** *verb* to cause or develop a bruise.
Word Family **bruiser** *noun* (*informal*) a strong or tough person.

brunch *noun* (*plural* **brunches**)
a late morning meal which replaces breakfast and lunch.
[BR(eakfast) + (l)UNCH]

brunette (broo-net) *noun*
a girl or woman with dark hair.

brunt *noun*
the main strength or force of something:
The children bore the brunt of his temper.

brush¹ *noun* (*plural* **brushes**)
1 an object used for painting, smoothing the hair, sweeping, etc., usually made of hair or bristles set into a solid base.
2 a touch: *the brush of her fingers on my face.*
3 a short fight or hostile encounter: *The demonstrators had a brush with the police.*
4 the bushy tail of an animal, especially a fox.

Phrase **tarred with the same brush**
thought of as having the same faults.
• **brush** *verb*
1 to use a brush on.
2 to touch lightly in passing: *He brushed
past the staring children.*
Phrases **brush off** to dismiss. **brush up**
to revise: *He brushed up his French before the
holiday.*

brush² *noun*
(*especially American, Australian*) a dense
growth of bushes or shrubs.

brusque (broosk) *adjective*
blunt or abrupt in speech or manner: *a
brusque reply.*
Word Family **brusquely** *adverb*;
brusqueness *noun*.
[Italian *brusco* sour]

Brussels sprout *noun* also **Brussel
sprout**
a small green vegetable like a tiny cabbage
growing in clusters on a stalk.

brutal (broo-t'l) *adjective*
savage or cruel: *a brutal attack.*
Word Family **brutally** *adverb*; **brutalize,
brutalise** *verb* to make or become brutal;
brutality (broo-**tal**-i-tee) *noun*: *We were
shocked by his brutality.*

brute *noun*
1 a four-legged animal or beast.
2 a strong or cruel person.
Word Family **brute** *adjective* 1 like an
animal. 2 strong: *brute force*; **brutish**
adjective.
[Latin *brutus* dull, stupid]

bubble *noun*
1 a small ball of gas in or rising through a
liquid.
2 a light transparent ball of liquid
containing gas.
• **bubble** *verb*
1 to rise in or make the sound of bubbles:
The stew bubbled on the stove.
2 to be filled with: *children bubbling with
excitement.*

bubble and squeak *noun*
cabbage and potato cooked and fried
together.

bubblegum *noun*
chewing gum which can be blown into
bubbles.

bubbly *adjective* (**bubblier; bubbliest**)
like or containing bubbles.
• **bubbly** *noun* (*informal*) champagne.

bubonic plague (bew-bon-ik **playg**) *noun*
an often fatal infectious bacterial disease
causing swelling of the lymph glands, chills
and fevers.
[Greek *boubon* groin]

buccal (buk-'l) *adjective*
of or relating to the cheeks or mouth.
[Latin *bucca* cheek]

buccaneer (buk-a-**neer**) *noun*
1 a pirate or bold adventurer.
2 *History* a pirate of Spanish and American
ships, especially in the 17th and 18th
centuries.
[French *boucanier* to barbecue]

buck¹ *noun*
a male deer, rabbit, etc. Compare DOE.
• **buck** *verb* (of an animal) to leap in the
air with the head down, back arched and
all four feet off the ground.
Phrases **buck up** 1 *Buck up or we'll be late*
(= hurry). 2 *She bucked up after we gave her
an ice cream* (= cheered up).

buck² *noun*
(*American informal*) a dollar.

buck³ *noun*
Phrase **pass the buck** to shift
responsibility or blame onto another
person.

bucket *noun*
an open container with a handle for
holding or carrying liquids.
Phrase **kick the bucket** (*informal*) to die.
Word Family **bucketful** *noun*.

The phrase **kick the bucket** is one of
several which have more than one
suggested origin. The word *bucket* may
be from an old word for a beam on
which animals were hung by the heels
in slaughterhouses; alternatively, the
phrase may refer to a bucket on which a
suicide stands to hang himself or
herself, the bucket then being knocked
over by the swinging feet.

bucket seat *noun*
a seat for one person in a motor vehicle,
which is slightly curved to give support at
the sides.

bucket shop *noun*
1 (*informal*) the office of an unofficial firm
of stockbrokers that speculates dishonestly
with clients' money.
2 a shop selling cheap airline tickets.

buckle *noun*
a clasp with a movable pin set in a frame
through which a strap is passed and held
in place by the pin, e.g. on a belt.

• buckle *verb*
1 to fasten with a buckle.
2 to bend or give way suddenly, owing to pressure, heat, etc.
Phrase **buckle down** *We must buckle down to work now* (= set to).

buckler *noun*
a small round shield.

buckram (buk-r'm) *noun*
a stiff cotton fabric used for interlining, binding books, etc.

buckshot *noun*
a large size of lead shot used for hunting big game.

buckskin *noun*
1 a soft pale leather formerly made from deerskin but now made from sheepskin.
2 *American* a greyish-brown horse.

buck-tooth *noun* (*plural* **buck-teeth**)
a projecting tooth.
Word Family **buck-toothed** *adjective*.

bucolic (bew-kol-ik) *adjective*
of rural life or the country.

bud *noun*
1 *Biology* a tightly folded undeveloped shoot of a plant.
2 *Biology* a subsidiary growth from a simple animal, such as a hydra or yeast cell, which forms another individual.
Phrase **nip in the bud** to stop something before it has really started or developed.
• bud *verb* (**buds; budding; budded**)
1 to produce buds.
2 to graft a single bud onto a plant.
Word Family **budding** *adjective*
promising: *a budding footballer*.

Buddhism (bud-izm) *noun*
a religion stressing that human existence is pain, caused by desire, which may be overcome by contemplation and a right way of life.
Word Family **Buddhist** *adjective, noun*.
[Sanskrit *Buddha* the enlightened one, the title given to an Indian teacher living in the 5th century B.C., on whose ideas Buddhism is based]

buddleia (bud-lee-a) *noun*
a shrub with spikes of scented mauve, white or yellow flowers.
[after *Adam Buddle, c*.1660-1715, an English botanist]

buddy *noun* (*plural* **buddies**)
(*informal*) a friend.

budge *verb*
to move or give way slightly.

budgerigar (buj-a-ree-gar) *noun*
1 a small green Australian parakeet living in open country.
2 a bird of this species kept as a pet, with specially bred colours, usually blue, yellow or white.
[Aboriginal *budgeri* good + *garor kaar* cockatoo]

budget (buj-it) *noun*
1 a plan or summary giving details of expected income and expenditure.
2 the sum of money allotted for a particular purpose: *a film made on a small budget*.
3 (**Budget**) the annual financial statement of a government.
• budget *verb* (**budgets; budgeting; budgeted**) to plan the use of money in advance.

budgie *noun*
(*informal*) a budgerigar.

buff[1] *noun*
1 a pale brownish-yellow colour.
2 a thick light brownish-yellow leather, first made from buffalo skins, used for belts, etc.
Phrase **in the buff** naked.
• buff *verb* to polish or shine.
Word Family **buff** *adjective*.

buff[2] *noun*
(*informal*) an enthusiast: *a film buff*.

buffalo (buf-a-lo) *noun* (*plural* **buffalos** or **buffaloes**)
1 a large-hoofed African or Asian mammal, like an ox, with broad flat horns which curve downwards.
2 *American* a bison.

buffer[1] *noun*
something which absorbs or neutralizes shock, especially between opposing forces, such as a projecting bumper bar on the end of a railway vehicle.

buffer[2] *noun*
(*informal*) a silly old man.

buffet[1] (buff-it) *verb* (**buffets; buffeting; buffeted**)
to strike or knock, especially repeatedly: *The plane was buffeted by the winds*.

buffet[2] (buf-ay *or* buf-ay) *noun*
1 an informal meal at which guests stand and serve themselves.
2 a refreshment bar at a railway station or on a train.
[Old French *bufet* a stool]

buffoon *noun*
a person who stupidly acts the fool.
Word Family **buffoonery** *noun*.
[Italian *buffone* jester]

bug *noun*
1 (*informal*) any insect.
2 (*informal*) an illness or infection caused by a micro-organism: *a tummy bug*.
3 a hidden microphone.
4 a fault in a computer program.
• **bug** *verb* (**bugs; bugging; bugged**)
1 (*informal*) to irritate.
2 to install or use a hidden microphone in: *They bugged his hotel room.*

bugbear *noun*
a thing which causes needless fear, irritation, etc.

buggery *noun*
anal intercourse.

Buggins's turn *noun*
(*informal*) the system of automatically awarding a post or appointment to the person who is next in line in terms of seniority, irrespective of talent.
[*Buggins*, a typical surname]

buggy *noun* (*plural* **buggies**)
1 a light four-wheeled passenger vehicle pulled by one or two horses.
2 a light pushchair.

bugle (bew-g'l) *noun*
Music a simple brass instrument used by armies to signal movements, etc.
Word Family **bugler** *noun*.

build (bild) *verb* (**builds; building; built**)
1 to join or assemble parts to make a whole structure.
2 to establish or develop: *building a business from nothing.*
Word Family **build** *noun* body shape: *a slim build;* **builder** *noun* a person who builds or makes things.

building *noun*
a thing which is built or constructed, especially for a particular use, such as a house, office, etc.

building society *noun* (*plural* **building societies**)
a business organization which lends money to people buying or building houses, etc. and offers interest to those investing in the company.

build-up *noun*
a progressive increase, e.g. of military troops for a particular battle.

built-up area *noun*
a length of road with street lights, dense housing, etc. along which speed restrictions are enforced.

bulb *noun*
1 *Biology* a modified bud of a plant, usually underground, which is an organ of vegetative reproduction.
2 *Biology* a plant which is grown from a bulb, such as an onion.
3 a light bulb.
4 a rounded or pear-shaped object.
Word Family **bulbous** *adjective* having the bulging or rounded shape of a bulb.
[Greek *bolbos* onion]

bulgar wheat *noun* also **bulgur wheat**
a type of dried cracked wheat used in Turkish and Middle Eastern cooking.
[Turkish]

bulge (bulj) *noun*
a rounded swelling or part.
• **bulge** *verb*.
[Latin *bulga* bag]

bulimia (bull-**im**-i-a) *noun*
short for **bulimia nervosa** a medical condition characterized by alternately overeating and vomiting.
Word Family **bulimic** *adjective, noun*.
[Greek *boulimia* great hunger]

bulk *noun*
1 the size or volume of anything.
2 the main part.
Phrase **in bulk** in large quantities.
Word Family **bulky** *adjective* (**bulkier; bulkiest**) very large or awkward; **bulkiness** *noun*.

bulkhead *noun*
a partition or wall in a boat or aircraft.

bull[1] (bull) *noun*
1 an uncastrated male bovine mammal, especially of beef or dairy cattle.
2 the male of various other mammals, especially the elephant. Compare COW[1] (definition 2).
3 *Stock Exchange* a person who buys, for future delivery, shares he or she hopes to sell at a profit before he or she has to take delivery. Compare BEAR[2] (definition 2).
Word Family **bullish** *adjective*
1 confident or aggressive. 2 *Stock Exchange* causing or characterized by rising prices: *a bullish market*.

bull[2] *noun*
a formal letter or instruction from a pope.

bull[3] *noun*
(*informal*) nonsense.

bulldog *noun*
a sturdy short-haired dog, originally bred in England for baiting bulls.

Bulldog clip *noun*
(*trademark*) a large clip operated by a spring.

bulldozer *noun*
a powerful tractor with a vertical blade at the front for moving earth, etc.
• **bulldoze** *verb*
1 to use a bulldozer.
2 to bully or intimidate.

bullet (**bull**-it) *noun*
a small cylindrical projectile fired from a rifle, pistol, etc.

bulletin (**bull**-a-tin) *noun*
1 a public statement giving news or a report.
2 a magazine, especially of a society or organization.
[French, a daily or official report]

bullfight *noun*
a ritual fighting sport between a person and a bull, held in an arena.
Word Family **bullfighter** *noun* a person trained to bullfight; **bullfighting** *noun*.

bullfinch *noun* (*plural* **bullfinches**)
a vividly coloured finch, beautiful but a garden pest.

bullfrog *noun*
a large frog with a very deep voice.

bullheaded *adjective*
very obstinate or determined.

bullion (**bull**-y'n) *noun*
gold or silver, especially in bars, etc.

bullish ⇨ BULL¹.

bullock *noun* also called **steer**.
a castrated bull reared for beef.

bullring *noun*
an arena for bullfights.

bullseye *noun*
the centre of a target.

bull terrier *noun*
a cross-breed of bulldog and terrier, thickset and short-haired.

bully¹ (*rhymes with* woolly) *noun* (*plural* **bullies**)
a person who takes pleasure in hurting or intimidating weaker people.
• **bully** *verb* (**bullies; bullying; bullied**).

bully² *noun* (*plural* **bullies**)
short form of **bully off** *Hockey* the start or restart of a game, where two players, with the ball between them, must alternately tap the ground and each other's stick three times before trying to hit the ball.
• **bully** *verb* (**bullies; bullying; bullied**).

bully³ *noun* also called **bully beef**.
(*informal*) corned beef.

bulrush (**bull**-rush) *noun* (*plural* **bulrushes**) also **bullrush** (*plural* **bullrushes**)
a large reed found in swampy areas. The leaves are used to make mats, etc.

bulwark (**bull**-w'k) *noun*
1 a mound or wall of earth used as protection.
Figurative The police force is a bulwark of society.
2 (*usually* **bulwarks**) the part of a ship's side which extends above the deck.

bum¹ *noun*
(*informal*) the buttocks.

bum² *noun*
1 a lazy or worthless person.
2 *American* a tramp.
• **bum** *verb* (**bums; bumming; bummed**)
1 to lead a lazy or worthless life.
2 to cadge.
• **bum** *adjective* of poor quality.

bumbag *noun*
(*informal*) a pouch with a zip worn at the front or the back of the body on a belt round the waist and used for carrying money or small personal belongings.

bumble *verb*
to act or speak in a clumsy way: *She bumbled nervously through the speech.*

bumblebee *noun*
a large bee with a loud buzz.

bump *verb*
1 to strike or collide with: *The car bumped into the fence.*
2 to move with jolts or jerks: *The motorcycle bumped over the paddock.*
Phrases **bump off** to kill. **bump up** to increase.
• **bump** *noun*
1 the act or sound of bumping: *There was a loud bump as she fell off the chair.*
2 the raised mark left by a collision or blow: *a large bump on her forehead.*
Word Family **bumpy** *adjective* (**bumpier; bumpiest**).

bumper *adjective*
unusually large or full: *a bumper crop of tomatoes.*
• **bumper** *noun* a horizontal rounded bar at the front of a motor vehicle, to protect the body in collisions.

bumpkin *noun*
an awkward or unsophisticated person.

bumptious (**bump**-shus) *adjective*
unpleasantly conceited: *an annoyingly
bumptious young man.*
Word Family bumptiously *adverb*;
bumptiousness *noun.*

bun *noun*
1 a type of sweet bread roll, usually round
and containing spices or fruit.
2 a long bunch of hair wound into a coil at
the back of the head.

bunch *noun* (*plural* **bunches**)
1 a group of things attached or collected
together: *a bunch of grapes.*
2 (**bunches**) a hairstyle in which the hair
is separated and tied at each side of the
head.
Word Family bunch *verb* to form into
bunches or folds.

buncombe ⇨ BUNKUM.

bundle *noun*
a number of things fastened or carried
together: *a bundle of firewood.*
• **bundle** *verb*
1 to carry or tie in a bundle: *Bundle these
parcels together.*
2 (*informal*) to put hastily: *He bundled her
into the car.*
Phrase bundle up to dress warmly.

bung *noun*
a stopper for closing a hole in a barrel, etc.
• **bung** *verb* to block or close with or as if
with a bung.

bungalow (**bung**-ga-lo) *noun*
a house with one storey.

> **Bungalow** is now a very British word
> for a house with one storey, but it
> comes from a Hindi word *bangla*,
> meaning 'Bengali, of or belonging to
> Bengal'. English borrowed it in the
> sense of 'house in the Bengal style'.
> Europeans in India often lived in such
> houses – simple lightly-built one-storey
> structures with a verandah – and the
> word was brought back to Britain
> although only the one-storey element
> survives. The long British presence in
> India brought to English many words
> from the Indian subcontinent.

bungle *verb*
to do something clumsily or without
success: *You have bungled the job.*
Word Family bungle *noun* a bungled
attempt; **bungler** *noun*; **bunglingly**
adverb.

bunion (**bun**-y'n) *noun*
a swelling at the base of the big toe due to
an inflammation.

bunk[1] *noun*
a simple bed, often built-in and having
another bed set above it.

bunk[2] *noun*
(*informal dated*) bunkum.

bunk[3] *noun*
Phrase do a bunk *The culprits had done a
bunk and could not be found* (= run away).

bunker *noun*
1 a large container, such as a coal
compartment on a ship.
2 an underground shelter.
3 *Golf* an obstacle consisting of a pit filled
with sand, backed by a grassy ridge.

bunkum *noun* also **buncombe**
(*informal dated*) meaningless talk or
nonsense.
[from a long-winded congressman, in the
1820s, from *Buncombe County*, America]

bunny *noun* (*plural* **bunnies**)
(*informal*) a rabbit.

Bunsen burner *noun*
a gas burner used in scientific laboratories.
[after *R. W. Bunsen*, 1811-1899, a German
chemist]

bunting *noun*
a collection of flags.

bunyip *noun*
a mythical Australian monster supposed to
inhabit swamps and lagoons.
[Aboriginal]

buoy (boy) *noun*
Nautical a fixed floating object marking a
channel or obstruction in the water.
• **buoy** *verb* to sustain or support: *She was
buoyed up by the hope of victory.*

buoyant (**boy**-ant) *adjective*
1 able to float: *The boat remained buoyant
despite its damage.*
2 lively or cheerful: *Her spirits were buoyant
when she passed her exams.*
Word Family buoyancy *noun*;
buoyantly *adverb.*

bur ⇨ BURR.

burble *verb*
to make a gurgling or bubbling sound: *a
burbling stream.*

burden *noun*
a heavy or difficult load to carry.
Figurative *The burden of responsibility is on
your shoulders.*

Phrase **burden of proof** *The burden of proof remains with us* (= duty to prove a claim).

Word Family **burden** *verb*; **burdensome** *adjective*.

burdock *noun*
a roadside wild flower with prickly flower heads and foliage resembling dock leaves. [BUR(r) + DOCK⁴]

bureau (bure-o) *noun* (*plural* **bureaux** or **bureaus**)
1 an office or department with particular duties: *the weather bureau.*
2 a writing desk with drawers.
3 *American* a chest of drawers.
[French, desk or office]

bureaucracy (bure-ok-ra-see) *noun* (*plural* **bureaucracies**)
1 rule by departmental civil servants rather than by elected politicians.
2 an official organization with too much power or having too many rules.
Word Family **bureaucrat** (bure-o-krat) *noun* a member of the bureaucracy; **bureaucratic** (bure-o-krat-ik) *adjective* too official or attached to rules; **bureaucratically** *adverb.*

> The word **bureaucracy** is usually used in a derogatory way. In other words, it is used by people for something which they do not like. It comes from the French word *bureaucratie*, meaning 'government by officials' and many people feel that too many administrators slow proceedings down. The word *bureaucratie* comes from *bureau*, French for an office and also for a type of writing desk. *Bureau* has been borrowed from the French into English directly in both these senses.

burette (bew-ret) *noun*
a graduated glass tube with a tap at the bottom, used for accurate measurement of small amounts of liquid. [French]

burgeon (ber-j'n) *verb*
to begin to grow or blossom: *the burgeoning area of electronic shopping.*

burger ⇨ HAMBURGER.

burgher (ber-ga) *noun*
an old word meaning 'a person who lives in a town'.

burghul (ber-gool) *noun*
bulgar wheat.

burglar *noun*
a person who breaks into a house in order to steal.
Word Family **burgle** *verb*; **burglary** *noun* (*plural* **burglaries**) the crime of breaking into a house in order to steal.

burgundy (ber-g'n-dee) *noun*
1 a rich red French wine made from grapes grown in Burgundy.
2 a deep red colour.
• **burgundy** *adjective*.

burial (berr-i-ul) *noun*
the act or ceremony of burying.

burlap ⇨ HESSIAN.

burlesque (ber-lesk) *noun*
a ridiculous parody or caricature. [Italian *burla* mockery]

burly *adjective* (**burlier; burliest**)
big and strong: *a burly policeman.*

burn¹ *verb* (**burns; burning; burnt** or **burned**)
1 to produce fire or be on fire: *These wet matches will not burn.*
2 to injure or mark with extreme heat, cold, chemicals, etc.
3 to use as a fuel.
4 (of the skin) to be damaged by the sun
5 to feel hot: *His cheeks burnt.*
6 to feel emotional or passionate: *burning with hatred.*
7 (of lights) to be on.
• **burn** *noun* an injury produced by extreme heat, cold, chemicals, etc.

burn² *noun*
Scottish a small stream.

burnish *verb*
to polish or make smooth by rubbing, etc.
Word Family **burnished** *adjective* shiny, glossy.

burnout *noun*
1 *Aerospace* the dying out of the flame in a rocket engine because of its fuel being used up or shut off.
2 extreme mental fatigue caused by a prolonged period of intensive work.

burp *verb*
1 (*informal*) to belch.
2 (*informal*) to cause a baby to belch after feeding.
• **burp** *noun* (*informal*).

burr *noun*
1 a low or muffled buzzing or whirring sound.
2 a rough or indistinct pronunciation, especially of the letter *r*.

3 also **bur** a rough edge left on a metal surface by drilling or cutting.

4 also **bur** *Biology* a round prickly case covering a seed.

• **burr** *verb*

1 to make a buzzing or whirring sound.

2 to form a rough edge on.

burrow *noun*

a hole made in the ground by a rabbit or similar animal.

• **burrow** *verb*

1 to dig into.

Figurative He burrowed into his mother's lap (= snuggled).

2 to search: *I burrowed in my pockets for some change.*

bursa *noun* (*plural* **bursae** (ber-see) or **bursas**)

Anatomy a sac or pouch, especially near a joint.

Word Family **bursal** *adjective*; **bursitis** *noun* an inflammation of a bursa.

[Latin, bag, purse]

bursar *noun*

a person who manages the finances in a school or college.

bursary (ber-sa-ree) *noun* (*plural* **bursaries**)

a scholarship given by a school or college.

burst *verb* (**bursts; bursting; burst**)

1 to explode or break open suddenly: *The balloon burst loudly.*

2 to be full to overflowing: *Their pockets were bursting with chestnuts.*

3 to be full of: *The children were bursting with excitement.*

4 to enter loudly or suddenly: *He burst into the room.*

• **burst** *noun*

1 a sudden or violent explosion: *a burst of gunfire.*

2 a sudden display of energy or activity: *He cleaned the car in a burst of enthusiasm.*

bury (berr-ee) *verb* (**buries; burying; buried**)

1 to place a dead body in a grave.

2 to put underground or cover from view: *The dog has buried his bone in the garden.* □ *She buried her face in her hands.*

Phrase **bury oneself in** *The children buried themselves in their books* (= gave their attention to).

bus *noun* (*plural* **buses**)

a public motor vehicle with a long body, containing seats for many passengers.

Phrase **miss the bus** to miss an opportunity.

• **bus** *verb* (**buses** or **busses; busing** or **bussing; bused** or **bussed**) to transport by bus.

[shortening of OMNIBUS]

busby (buz-bee) *noun* (*plural* **busbies**)

a tall fur hat worn by hussar regiments.

bush¹ (bush) *noun* (*plural* **bushes**)

1 a small woody shrub with branches which begin near the ground.

2 *Australian, African* the natural countryside, especially where it is uncleared or uncultivated.

Phrase **beat about the bush, beat around the bush** to avoid or take too long coming to the point or issue.

Word Family **bushy** *adjective* (**bushier; bushiest**)

bush² *noun* (*plural* **bushes**)

a cylindrical metal lining placed in a hole to reduce wear.

bushbaby *noun* (*plural* **bushbabies**)

a small African lemur which lives in trees and feeds at night.

bushel (bush-'l) *noun*

1 a unit of volume for grain, fruit, etc. equal to 8 gallons, or 36·4 litres. *abbrev.* bu.

2 *American* a unit of volume equal to 8 American gallons, or 35·2 litres *abbrev.* bu.

bush fire *noun*

a fire in uncleared or forest land.

bushman *noun* (*plural* **bushmen**)

a person who lives or travels in the Australian bush and is knowledgeable about it.

bush telegraph *noun*

a line of communication along which information or rumour spreads.

bushy ⇨ BUSH¹.

busily ⇨ BUSY.

business (biz-niss) *noun* (*plural* **businesses**)

1 a person's occupation or work.

2 something that needs to be done: *I had some unfinished business to attend to.*

3 trading or trade: *He wouldn't be doing business with them again.*

4 an event or matter: *The robbery was a mysterious business.*

Phrases **mean business** to be in earnest. **mind one's own business** to keep out of matters that don't concern one.

Word Family **businesslike** *adjective* methodical, efficient and practical; **businessman, businesswoman** *noun* (*plural* **businessmen, businesswomen**).

busker noun
a street entertainer.

busman's holiday noun
a holiday during which one does one's regular work or similar activities.

bust¹ noun
1 a sculpture of the head and shoulders.
2 the bosom, especially of a woman.

bust² verb (**busts; busting; busted** or **bust**)
1 (informal) to break.
2 (informal) to arrest: They were busted for possessing heroin.
Phrase **go bust** to become bankrupt.
• **bust** noun (informal) an arrest.

bustard (rhymes with custard) noun
a large shy fast-running brown and white bird living in open country in Europe, Australia and Africa.

bustle¹ (buss-'l) verb
to move or act with energy or fuss: The waiters bustled about amongst the guests.
• **bustle** noun.

bustle² noun
a frame set under the back of an old-fashioned skirt to support or shape it.

bust-up noun
(informal) a serious fight or quarrel.

busy (biz-ee) adjective (**busier; busiest**)
1 fully or continuously engaged in work, etc.
2 full of activity: the busy city.
3 being used: The phone is busy at the moment.
4 cluttered: busy paintings.
• **busy** verb (**busies; busying; busied**) to keep busy: He busied himself putting the crockery away.
Word Family **busily** adverb; **busyness** noun.

busybody noun (plural **busybodies**)
a person who interferes or meddles in the affairs of others.

but conjunction
except or on the contrary: I will take all but the last two. □ They laughed but we didn't.
Phrase **but for** He would not be here but for you (= without).
• **but** adverb only: We have but one choice left.
Phrase **all but** The game is all but over (= almost).
• **but** noun an objection or restriction: There were many ifs and buts to the suggestion.
• **but** preposition except.

butane (bew-tane) noun
Chemistry a colourless inflammable gas (formula C_4H_{10}). It is used as a fuel and in making synthetic rubber.

butch (butch) adjective
(informal) having aggressive or masculine characteristics.

butcher noun
1 a person who cuts up and sells animal flesh for food.
2 a person who slaughters animals and prepares the flesh to be sold.
• **butcher** verb
1 to kill and prepare animal flesh for food.
2 to kill cruelly or needlessly.
Word Family **butchery** noun.

butcher-bird noun
a black and grey shrike, with a white breast and brown wings, living in forests and woodland areas.
[so called because it hangs its prey on thorns or small branches before eating it]

butler noun
the head male servant of a household.
[Old French bouteillier a bottler]

butt¹ noun
1 also called **butt end**, the end of something, especially the thicker end: a rifle butt.
2 also called **butt-end**, a cigarette stub.
3 (American informal) the buttocks.
• **butt** verb to join or be joined at the ends: a property butting on to a lane.

butt² noun
1 a person who is an object of ridicule. She is the butt of all their jokes.
2 either of two banks of earth beneath and behind the targets on a rifle range, used to stop bullets safely.

butt³ verb
to hit with the head or horns: The goat butted the boy in the back.
Phrase **butt in** to interrupt or interfere.
• **butt** noun a blow with the head.

butt⁴ noun
a large cask or barrel.

butte (bewt) noun
a hill with a flat top and steep sides, similar to, but smaller than, a mesa.

butter noun
1 the fatty part of milk which separates when cream is churned.
2 this substance solidified for use as a food or spread and used in cooking.
3 a similar spread: peanut butter. □ brandy butter.

• **butter** *verb* to spread with butter: *Butter a baking dish.*
Phrase **butter up** to flatter.
[Greek *boutyron*]

butter bean *noun*
a type of small edible yellow bean.

buttercup *noun*
a wild plant with yellow cup-shaped flowers.

butterfingers *noun* (*plural* **butterfingers**)
(*informal*) a clumsy person who drops things.

butterfly *noun* (*plural* **butterflies**)
1 an insect with short antennae and large wings, often brightly coloured.
2 *Swimming* a style in which the swimmer lifts both arms simultaneously out of the water, bringing them strongly forwards and down.

butterfly fish *noun* (*plural* **butterfly fish** or **butterfly fishes**)
a brightly coloured carnivorous fish living among coral reefs.

buttermilk *noun*
the liquid which remains when butter is separated from cream or milk.

butterscotch *noun* (*plural* **butterscotches**)
Cooking a flavouring, sauce or toffee made with brown sugar, vanilla essence and butter.

buttery *adjective*
like or containing butter.

butt joint *noun*
a joint made by putting the ends of two things together.

buttock *noun*
Anatomy either of the two rounded fleshy areas at the base of the trunk.

button *noun*
1 a small disc or knob attached to clothing as a decoration or passed through a hole as a fastener.
2 something which has the shape or function of a button, especially a knob or switch for an electrical appliance.
• **button** *verb* to fasten with a button or buttons.

buttonhole *noun*
1 a slit in clothing through which a button is passed.
2 a single flower worn as a decoration on the lapel.
• **buttonhole** *verb* (*informal*) to stop and detain a person: *She buttonholed me and lectured me for an hour.*

buttress *noun* (*plural* **buttresses**)
a structure built into or against a wall to support or strengthen it. Compare FLYING BUTTRESS.
• **buttress** *verb* to support with a buttress.
Figurative He buttressed his argument with several quotations.

buxom (**buk-s'm**) *adjective*
large, especially having large breasts.

buy (by) *verb* (**buys; buying; bought**)
1 to get in exchange for payment, especially money: *We are buying a new car.*
2 (*informal*) to accept the truth of: *I can't buy that story.*
Phrases **buy off** to bribe in order to get rid of opposition, etc. **buy out** to obtain ownership by buying all other shares, etc.
• **buy** *noun* (*informal*) something bought.

buyer *noun*
1 a person who buys.
2 a person who selects, orders and buys stock for a department store, etc.

buzz *verb*
1 to make a low humming sound: *Flies buzzed noisily in the kitchen.*
2 to move rapidly or busily: *People buzzed around the scene of the accident.*
3 to communicate by telephone or an intercom system: *I will buzz his office.*
4 (*informal*) to fly an aircraft very low to attract attention.
Phrase **buzz off** (*informal*) to leave.
• **buzz** *noun* (*plural* **buzzes**).

buzzard *noun*
a large heavy bird of the falcon family.

buzzer *noun*
an electrical device, such as a doorbell, which produces a buzzing sound.

buzzword *noun*
(*informal*) a word of technical or specialist origin which becomes a vogue word and so overused in general language.

by *preposition, adverb*
1 near: *Sit by me.*
2 past: *He walked by.*
3 through: *You learn by doing.*
4 using: *We went by car.*
5 during: *travelling by day.*
6 not later than: *Be home by midnight.*
7 to the extent of: *It missed us by miles.*
8 per: *paid by the hour.*
9 according to: *She's late, by my reckoning.*
Phrases **by and by** before long. **by and large** on the whole. **by the way, by the by, by the bye** incidentally.

bye *noun*
1 *Sport* the state of having no opponent for a particular round in a contest and therefore entering automatically into the next.
2 *Cricket* a run scored when a ball passes the batsman and the wicket without touching either of them.
3 *Golf* any holes which remain unplayed at the end of a match.

bye-bye *interjection*
(*informal*) goodbye.

by-election ⇨ ELECTION.

bygone (by-gon) *adjective*
being in the past: *In bygone days people believed the world was flat.*
● **bygone** *noun*
Phrase **let bygones be bygones** to forgive and forget a past disagreement, offence, etc.

by-law *noun* also **bye-law**
a law or rule having effect in a local area only, and generally made by a local council.

byline *noun*
an author's name printed above or below an article he or she has written for a newspaper or magazine.

bypass *noun* (*plural* **bypasses**)
1 a road which passes around or avoids a busy area such as a city centre.
2 a surgical procedure to create a permanent alternative pathway for a blood vessel, artery, etc., created by transplanting a vessel from elsewhere in the body or by inserting an artificial one.
● **bypass** *verb* to avoid or ignore: *The officials bypassed normal procedures.*

byplay *noun*
action or speech carried on apart from the main action: *The byplay at the back of the stage brought much laughter from the audience.*

by-product *noun*
a thing or effect which is produced during another process or by an event.

bystander *noun*
a person who sees or watches an event but does not take part in it.

byte (bite) *noun*
Computers a group of bits, usually eight, used to represent a character.

byway *noun*
a minor road or path.

byword *noun*
something which represents or characterizes a quality, type, etc.: *In our office Keith is a byword for efficiency.*

Cc

cab *noun*
1 a taxi.
2 short form of **cabin** the part of a lorry, bus or train where the driver sits.
3 (*formerly*) a horse-drawn carriage for public hire.

> **Cab** is a short form of *cabriolet*, a light horse-drawn carriage. This comes via French and Italian from the Latin *capreolus* a wild goat. The connection between this and *cabriolet* and *cab* is that the suspension of the vehicle was so springy that it seemed to jump up and down, in the way goats do, as it was driven along.

cabal (ka-**bahl**) *noun*
a group of people working towards a common aim, especially by secret methods.

cabaret (**kabb**-a-ray) *noun*
a form of entertainment consisting of songs and dances, usually performed in a restaurant or nightclub.
[French, a tavern]

cabbage *noun*
a large vegetable that has broad leaves arranged in a tight head.

cabby *noun* (*plural* **cabbies**)
(*informal*) a taxi driver.

caber (**kay**-ber) *noun*
a long heavy pole which is lifted at one end and tossed in Scottish Highland games.

cabin *noun*
1 a small simple house, often in the country.
2 a room where passengers on a ship sleep.
3 the space available for passengers or crew on an aircraft.
4 ⇨ CAB (definition **2**).

cabin boy *noun*
a boy who works on a passenger ship.

cabinet *noun*
1 a piece of furniture with shelves and drawers for storage or display.

2 (**Cabinet**) *Parliament* a group of ministers from the ruling political party, which advises the Prime Minister on policy and each of whom leads a government department.

cable *noun*
1 a thick strong rope or chain.
2 a bundle of insulated wires for carrying electricity.
3 (*formerly*) short form of **cablegram** a message sent along wires using electricity.
4 ⇨ CABLE TELEVISION.
• **cable** *verb* to send a message along wires using electricity.

cable car *noun*
a vehicle suspended from an overhead cable which takes people up and down mountains.

cable stitch *noun*
a form of knitting which produces a pattern of twisted raised bands.

cable television *noun*
a commercial television system which carries television signals by cable to subscribers' homes.

caboodle (ka-**boo**-d'l) *noun*
Phrase **the whole caboodle** (*informal*) the whole lot.

cacao (ka-**kay**-o) *noun*
the seeds from a small tropical tree, from which cocoa, chocolate, etc. are made.

cache (kash) *noun*
1 a supply of things hidden or stored.
2 *Computers* a temporary file storage space which may be accessed quickly. The cache is used by the computer to store the most frequently accessed files.
[French *cacher* to hide]

cachet (**kash**-ay) *noun*
1 prestige or status.
2 a distinctive sign: *Her music has the cachet of genius.*
[French, a seal]

cachou (**kash**-oo *or* ka-**shoo**) *noun*
a tablet for sweetening the breath.

cack-handed *adjective*
(*informal*) clumsy.

cackle *verb*
1 to make a shrill broken sound similar to that of a hen after it lays an egg.
2 to laugh or chatter noisily.
• **cackle** *noun*.

cacophony (ka-**koff**-a-nee) *noun* (*plural* **cacophonies**)
a harsh discordant sound.

Word Family cacophonous (ka-**koff**-a-nus) *adjective*.
[Greek *kakos* bad + *phoné* sound]

cactus *noun* (*plural* **cacti** or **cactuses**)
any of various desert plants which store water in their fleshy spike-covered stems.
[Greek *kaktos*]

cad *noun*
(*informal*) a man who does not behave decently towards other people.
Word Family caddish *adjective*.
[short form of Scots *caddie*, a gentleman who joined the lowest ranks of the army]

cadaver (ka-**dah**-va *or* ka-**davv**-a) *noun*
a human corpse, especially one used for dissection.
Word Family cadaverous (ka-**davv**-er-us) *adjective* pale and haggard.
[Latin *cadere* to fall]

caddie *noun* also **caddy** (*plural* **caddies**)
Golf a person assisting a player by carrying his or her golf bag or selecting the clubs used.
Word Family caddie *verb* (**caddies; caddying; caddied**).

caddy *noun* (*plural* **caddies**)
a small airtight tin or box for holding food, especially tea.

cadence (**kay**-d'nce) *noun*
the rise and fall of sounds in the pitch of a voice, a line of poetry, etc.
[Latin *cadens* falling]

cadenza (ka-**den**-za) *noun*
Music an elaborate passage for a solo instrument towards the end of a concerto, etc.
[Italian]

cadet *noun*
a young person being trained to serve in the armed forces, police, etc.

cadge *verb*
to beg or borrow without intending to repay.
Word Family cadger *noun*.

cadmium *noun*
a metal used as a pigment, for protective plating and in alloys.

cadre (**kah**-da *or* **kah**-dra) *noun*
a special group of trained people in a political or military organization.
[French]

Caesarean section *noun* also **Caesarian section**
short form is **Caesarean** an operation to deliver a baby by cutting open the wall of the mother's uterus.

[after the Roman emperor *Julius Caesar*, at whose birth such an operation was supposedly performed]

caesium (**seez**-i-um) *noun* (*American* **cesium**)
a rare metal used in photoelectric cells.

caesura (siz-**yoor**-a) *noun*
a pause in the middle of a line of poetry.
[Latin *caesus* cut]

cafe (**kaff**-ay) *noun* also **café**
a restaurant where coffee, tea, etc. and light meals are served.
[French *café* coffee]

cafeteria (kaff-a-**teer**-i-a) *noun*
a self-service restaurant, especially in an office building, department store, etc.
[Spanish, a coffee shop]

cafetière (kaf-'t-**yair**) *noun*
a kind of coffee pot into which boiling water is poured and a plunger is pressed down, pushing the coffee grounds to the bottom of the pot.
[French]

caffeine (**kaff**-een) *noun*
a bitter drug found in tea, coffee, etc. which acts as a stimulant.

caftan ⇨ KAFTAN.

cage *noun*
1 a box-like enclosure with wires or bars in which birds, animals, etc. are kept: *opening the cage door*.
Figurative *To the bored patient the hospital was a cage.*
2 a structure resembling a cage, such as an enclosed lift in a coal mine.
• **cage** *verb*.

cagey (**kay**-jee) *adjective* also **cagy** (**cagier; cagiest**)
(*informal*) secretive or cautious.
Word Family cagily *adverb*; **caginess** *noun*.

cagoule (k'-**gool**) *noun*
a light waterproof coat with a hood attached, worn by walkers and mountain climbers.

cahoots (ka-**hoots**) *plural noun*
Phrase **in cahoots** (*informal*) in a secret partnership.

Cain *noun*
Phrase **raise Cain** to make a violent fuss.

cairn *noun*
a pile of stones erected as a landmark, monument, etc.

caisson disease (**kay**-s'n diz-eez) ⇨
DECOMPRESSION SICKNESS.

cajole (ka-**jole**) *verb*
to coax or persuade by flattery, promises,
etc.

Cajun (**kay**-jun) *noun*
a descendant of the French Canadians
who settled in Louisiana in America in the
18th century.
● **Cajun** *adjective* relating to the language,
music or food of the Cajuns: *Cajun dishes*.

cake *noun*
1 a sweet food made by baking flour, eggs,
etc.
2 a compressed block of any substance:
a cake of soap.
Phrases **a piece of cake** (*informal*)
something which is very easy to do. **take
the cake** (*informal*) to be more foolish
than anything else.
Word Family **cake** *verb* to form into or
cover with a compact mass: *Her shoes were
caked with mud*.

calabash *noun* (*plural* **calabashes**)
a large fruit whose dried shell can be used
as a bowl or a musical instrument.

calamine lotion *noun*
a soothing pink liquid used on the skin for
sunburn, rashes, etc.

calamity (ka-**lamm**-a-tee) *noun* (*plural*
calamities)
a disaster.
Word Family **calamitous** *adjective*.
[Latin *calamitas*]

calcify (**kal**-si-fie) *verb* (**calcifies;
calcifying; calcified**)
to harden by changing into a calcium
compound.
Word Family **calcification** (kal-si-fi-
kay-sh'n) *noun*.

calcium (**kal**-si-um) *noun*
a soft metal whose compounds are found
in limestone, chalk, teeth and bones.
[Latin *calcis* of limestone]

calculate (**kal**-kew-late) *verb*
to solve a problem using mathematical
methods: *We calculated how long our trip
would take*.
Phrase **be calculated to** to be
deliberately intended to: *Her indifference
was calculated to irritate me*.
Word Family **calculation** (kal-kew-**lay**-
sh'n) *noun* **1** the act of calculating. **2** the
result of calculating; **calculator** *noun* a
machine that calculates; **calculating**
adjective shrewd or slyly clever.
[Latin *calculus* a pebble (used in
counting)]

calculus (**kal**-kew-lus) *noun* (*plural*
calculuses)
1 *Maths* a branch of analysis which studies
the properties of functions using
derivatives and integrals.
2 (*plural* **calculi** (**kal**-kew-lie))
Medicine ⇨ STONE *noun* (definition **9**).

caldera (kal-**dair**-a) *noun*
a deep, often lake-filled, cavity at the
summit of a volcano.
[Spanish, cauldron]

calendar (**kal**-en-da) *noun*
1 a list of the days, weeks and months of a
particular year.
2 any system of dividing time into fixed
periods and marking the beginning and
end of a year. ⇨ GREGORIAN CALENDAR.
3 a list of important dates: *one of the
highlights of her social calendar*.
[Latin *kalendae* (first day of) a month]

> [!] The words *calendar, calender* and
> *colander* are similar in spelling and
> pronunciation but very different in
> meaning. *Calendar* ends in *ar* and
> means 'a list of dates'; *calender* ends in
> *er* and means 'a machine with rollers';
> *colander* begins with *col* and means 'a
> bowl used for draining liquid from food'.

calendar year ⇨ YEAR.

calender *noun*
a machine with rollers, used to smooth
cloth, paper, etc. or to convert a soft
material into a thin sheet.
Word Family **calender** *verb*.

> [!] Do not confuse *calender* with
> CALENDAR.

calf¹ *noun*
1 (*plural* **calves**) a young cow, whale, seal,
etc.
2 leather made from the skin of a calf.
Phrase **in calf** *Seven of my cows are in calf*
(= pregnant).

calf² *noun* (*plural* **calves**)
the fleshy muscular area at the back of the
leg below the knee.

calibrate (**kal**-i-brate) *verb*
to mark the scale on a measuring instrument.
Word Family **calibration** (kal-i-**bray**-
sh'n) *noun*.

calibre (**kal**-i-ba) *noun* (*American* **caliber**)
1 the diameter of a bullet, shell, etc.
2 the quality or worth of a person or thing.
[Arabic *kalib* mould]

calico *noun*
a coarse cotton fabric, usually off-white in
colour.
[first made in *Calicut*, India]

caliper ⇨ CALLIPER.

caliph (**kay**-lif, **kal**-if) *noun*
a Muslim leader believed to be a successor to Muhammad.
[Arabic *khalifah* successor]

call (cawl) *verb*
1 to say in a loud clear voice: '*Come here,*' *she called.* □ *Someone was calling for help.*
2 to ask for the presence of: *Quick – call a doctor!*
3 to use a telephone to try to speak to: *He's called six times today.* □ *I'll call you back – I'm busy just now.*
4 to make a visit: *Ben called in on his way to school.*
5 to make happen by an official demand: *The Prime Minister called an election.*
6 to name: *They called the boat 'Hopper'.* □ *What's your rabbit called?*
7 to consider as: *I don't think you could call the party a success.*
8 *Cards* to bid or to demand to see another player's cards.
Phrases **call for 1** to collect. **2** to need or demand: *This calls for a celebration!* **call off** to cancel. **call on 1** to visit. **2** to ask formally: *He called on the Prime Minister to take immediate action.* **call up 1** to summon to be a soldier, sailor, etc.: *He was called up in 1914.* **2** to bring onto a computer screen.
• **call** *noun*
1 a shout: *her calls for help.*
2 the sound a bird or animal makes.
3 an attempt to speak to someone using a telephone.
4 a visit.
5 a need or demand: *There's not much call for this type of program.*
6 *Cards* a bid.
Phrases **call of nature** a need to go to the toilet. **close call** a narrow escape. **on call** available for work if necessary: *Which doctor is on call this evening?*
Word Family **caller** *noun.*

callbox *noun* (*plural* **callboxes**)
a telephone box.

call girl *noun*
a female prostitute who makes appointments by telephone.

calligram (**kal**-i-gram) *noun*
a poem in which the formation of the letters or the font represents an aspect of the poem's subject.

calligraphy (ka-**lig**-ra-fee) *noun*
the art of fine handwriting.
[Greek *kallos* beauty + *graphein* to write]

calling *noun*
1 an inner urge or impulse: *He felt a strong calling to help the poor.*
2 a person's profession.

calliper *noun* also **caliper**
1 a support worn to straighten a deformed leg.
2 (*usually* **callipers**) an instrument with two arms hinged at one end, used to measure curved surfaces.

callisthenics (kal-iss-**thenn**-iks)
plural noun
(*used with singular verb*) a series of exercises performed to improve gracefulness, suppleness and control of the muscles.
Word Family **callisthenic** *adjective.*
[Greek *kallos* beauty + *sthenos* strength]

callous *adjective*
cruel and insensitive: *His callous treatment of animals shocked us.*
Word Family **callously** *adverb*;
callousness *noun.*
[Latin *callosus* thick-skinned]

callow *adjective*
inexperienced or immature.

call sign *noun*
a series of letters or numbers used by radio operators in order to identify themselves.

callus *noun* (*plural* **calluses**)
Medicine a hard thickened area of skin, caused by continual pressure.

calm *adjective*
1 quiet or undisturbed.
2 not windy.
Word Family **calm** *verb* to make or become calm; **calmly** *adverb*; **calm**, **calmness** *noun.*

Calor gas *noun*
(*trademark*) liquefied butane in metal containers, used for light and heat in caravans, boats, etc.

calorie (**kal**-a-ree) *noun*
1 a unit used to measure how much energy a food will produce.
2 the quantity of heat required to raise the temperature of one gram of water one degree Celsius, equal to about 4.19 joules.
Word Family **calorific** (kal-a-**rif**-ik)
adjective relating to calories or conversion into heat.
[Latin *calor* heat]

calumny (**kal**-um-nee) *noun* (*plural* **calumnies**)
a false or malicious statement.
[Latin *calumnia* trickery]

calve (karv) *verb*
to give birth to a calf.

calves
the plural of **calf**[1] (definition 1) and **calf**[2].

Calvinist *noun*
a follower of a religious movement which emphasizes strict church discipline and the theory of predestination.
Word Family **Calvinism** *noun* the beliefs or practices of Calvinists; **Calvinist, Calvinistic** *adjective*.
[after *John Calvin*, 1509-1564, on whose system of theology the movement is based]

calypso (ka-**lip**-so) *noun*
a type of music from the West Indies which has topical words and a strong rhythm.

calyx (**kay**-lix *or* **kal**-ix) *noun* (*plural* **calyces** (**kay**-li-seez) *or* **calyxes**)
Biology the sepals or outermost group of floral parts.
[Greek *kalyx* husk]

cam *noun*
a device in a machine for changing circular motion into movement back and forth.

camaraderie (kam-a-**rah**-da-ree) *noun*
comradeship.
[French]

camber *noun*
a slight upward curve or arch in the middle, e.g. on a road to allow drainage.

Cambrian ⇨ PALAEOZOIC.

camcorder *noun*
a video camera and a recorder in one portable unit.

came the past tense of **come**.

camel *noun*
a large mammal with one or two humps on its back for storing food. It is found in the desert regions of Africa and Asia and is valued for its milk, wool, meat and as a pack animal.

camellia (ka-**meel**-i-a) *noun*
a garden shrub with large white, pink or red flowers.

Camembert (**kam**-em-bair) *noun*
a soft French cheese.

cameo (**kam**-i-o) *noun*
1 a raised engraving on a background of a different colour, usually on a brooch.
2 a short appearance in a film or play, especially by a famous actor.

camera (**kam**-ra) *noun*
a device for taking photographs.
Phrases **off camera, on camera** (not) while being filmed.
[Greek *kamara* a (vaulted) room]

camisole (**kam**-i-sole) *noun*
a decorative woman's undergarment for the upper part of the body.

camomile (**kam**-o-mile) *noun*
a fragrant plant whose flowers are used in medicine and cooking.

camouflage (**kam**-a-flah*zh*) *noun*
a method of disguise in which something assumes the colour, texture, etc. of its surroundings and thus appears to be a part of them.
Word Family **camouflage** *verb* to disguise or deceive by means of camouflage.

camp[1] *noun*
1 a group of tents, caravans or other kinds of temporary shelter in one place.
2 a place where such shelters are situated: *a refugee camp*.
3 a group of people who share the same ideals, etc.
Phrase **break camp** to take down tents and leave a site.
Word Family **camp** *verb* to pitch tents or live temporarily in tents, etc.; **camper** *noun* 1 a person who camps. 2 also **camper van** a large drivable caravan.

camp[2] *adjective*
1 exaggerated or artificial in style.
2 homosexual.
Phrase **camp up** (*informal*) to do something with exaggerated movements, and usually an artificial voice.
[possibly from American police abbreviation *KAMP* Known As Male Prostitute]

campaign (kam-**pane**) *noun*
1 *Military* the active operations of an army, especially during one season or period.
2 any organized set of operations for a particular purpose: *a political campaign*.
Word Family **campaign** *verb*; **campaigner** *noun*.

campanile (kam-pa-**nee**-li) *noun*
the bell tower of an Italian church, usually a completely separate building.
[Italian *campana* a bell]

camp bed *noun*
a small folding bed.

camp follower *noun*
1 a civilian who provides services to a military camp.
2 a supporter of a political party, etc. who is not a member of the main group.

camphor (**kam**-fer) *noun*
a strong-smelling substance used in mothballs, medicine and industry.

campion *noun*
any of various plants, typically with pink or scarlet flowers.

campus *noun* (*plural* **campuses**)
the grounds and buildings of a university or college.
[Latin, a level space]

campus university *noun* (*plural* **campus universities**)
a university which has all its buildings in one area, often outside a town.

can¹ *verb* (**could**)
an auxiliary verb indicating:
1 power or ability to do something: *Can you lift it?* □ *I think I can see him.*
2 permission: *You can only enter if you have a pass.* □ *Can I go now?*
3 a tendency: *She can be very nasty.*

can² *noun*
1 any metal container, such as one in which food or drink is sealed by the manufacturer.
2 (*American informal*) the toilet.
Phrase **can of worms** an extremely difficult situation. **carry the can** to take the blame.
Word Family **can** *verb* (**cans; canning; canned**) to preserve food in a can by heating and sealing in a vacuum; **canned** *adjective* **1** packed or preserved in cans. **2** *Radio, Television* pre-recorded: *canned laughter;* **canning** *noun.*

canal (ka-**nal**) *noun*
1 an artificial waterway.
2 *Biology* a long tubular passage in an animal or plant, e.g. for carrying food.
[Latin *canalis* a channel]

canapé (**kan** a **pay**) *noun*
a thin piece of bread or toast spread with cheese, caviar, etc.
[French, a couch]

canary (ka-**nair**-ee) *noun* (*plural* **canaries**)
a small yellow bird, often kept in a cage as a pet.
[originally from the *Canary Islands*]

canasta (ka-**nas**-ta) *noun*
a card game played by two to six people.
[Spanish, basket]

cancan *noun*
a lively French stage dance involving fast high kicks.
[French]

cancel (**kan**-s'l) *verb* (**cancels; cancelling; cancelled**)
1 to give up an activity: *The match was cancelled because of rain.*

2 to make invalid or ineffective: *I've cancelled my order.*
3 to cross out or mark: *to cancel a postage stamp.*
Phrase **cancel out** to balance: *Your help cancels out your earlier rudeness.*
Word Family **cancellation** (kan-s'l-**ay**-sh'n) *noun* the act or an instance of cancelling: *The restaurant will let us know if they get a cancellation.*

cancer (**kan**-sa) *noun*
1 any of various diseases in which a group of cells grows and multiplies rapidly, destroying nearby tissue. Pieces of the growth may break off and spread throughout the body.
Figurative Apathy is the cancer at the heart of the school system.
2 (**Cancer**) *Astrology* a group of stars, the fourth sign of the Zodiac; the sign of the Crab.
Word Family **cancerous** *adjective.*

candela (kan-**dee**-la) *noun*
the base SI unit of luminous intensity. *abbrev.* cd.

candelabrum *noun* (*plural* **candelabra**)
an ornamental holder for candles.

candid *adjective*
frank or honest: *a candid opinion.*
Word Family **candidly** *adverb;* **candidness** *noun.*
[Latin *candidus* dazzling white]

candidate (**kand**-i-date) *noun*
1 a person who seeks or is nominated for a certain position, prize, etc.: *He is the new parliamentary candidate.*
2 a person who takes an examination.
Word Family **candidacy, candidature** *noun.*

> The word **candidate** comes from the Latin word for 'white'. In ancient Rome, people who were standing as *candidates* for positions of public service had to dress in white, the colour associated with purity and honesty. Since the Latin for 'white' is *candidus*, the Roman *candidate* standing for office was called a *candidatus*, literally 'one clothed in white'.

candied *adjective*
covered in sugar.

candle *noun*
a stick of wax or fat containing a length of thread which provides light when burned.
Phrases **burn the candle at both ends** to attempt to do more than one's energy

allows. **cannot hold a candle to**
(*informal*) is very much inferior to.
[Latin *candela*]

candlestick *noun*
a holder for a candle or candles.

candour (**kan**-da) *noun* (*American*
candor)
the quality of being candid or honest.

candy *noun* (*plural* **candies**)
American a sweet or sweets.
[Persian *kand* sugar]

candyfloss *noun*
a fluffy kind of sweet made from coloured
spun sugar, usually held on a stick.

cane *noun*
1 the long hollow jointed stems of certain
grass-like plants such as bamboo, used to
make furniture, etc.
2 a stick used to beat someone with.
3 a walking stick.
• **cane** *verb* to hit with a stick as a
punishment.
[Greek *kanna* a reed]

cane sugar ⇨ SUCROSE.

canine (**kay**-nine) *noun*
1 any animal in the dog family.
2 also **canine tooth** *Dentistry* any of four
pointed teeth, one on each side of each jaw
next to the incisors.
• **canine** *adjective* of or relating to dogs.
[Latin *canis* dog]

canister (**kan**-iss-ta) *noun*
an airtight tin or jar for storing tea, flour,
etc.

canker *noun*
a nasty sore area of flesh.

cannabis *noun*
a drug made from the hemp plant which
is usually smoked as a narcotic. Its use is
illegal in Britain.
[Greek *kannabis* hemp]

cannelloni (can-na-**lo**-nee) *noun*
tubular rolls of pasta filled with a savoury
mixture of meat or vegetables.
[Italian]

cannery *noun* (*plural* **canneries**)
a factory where food is put into tins or
cans.

cannibal *noun*
any animal, especially a human being,
which eats its own species.
Word Family cannibalism *noun* the
practice of eating the flesh of one's own
species; **cannibalistic** *adjective*;
cannibalize, cannibalise *verb* to take

parts from damaged machinery for use in
the repair of other equipment.
[Spanish *Canibales* peoples of the
Caribbean]

cannon *noun*
1 any of various large mounted guns. The
old type fired a solid metal ball, called a
cannonball.
2 *Billiards* a shot in which a ball hits two
other balls in succession.
• **cannon** *verb* to collide heavily.

> [!] The words *cannon* and *canon*
> sound the same but have different
> spellings and meanings. *Cannon* has
> two *n*'s and means 'a large gun'; *canon*
> has one *n* and means 'a law or
> standard', 'a type of song or musical
> composition' or 'a clergyman'.

cannonade *noun*
a continuous firing of guns, especially in a
battle.

cannot *verb*
can not: *The sound cannot be heard by the
human ear.*

canny *adjective* (**cannier; canniest**)
cautiously shrewd and wary.
Word Family cannily *adverb*; **canniness**
noun.

canoe (ka-**noo**) *noun*
any light narrow boat which is moved
using paddles.
Phrase paddle one's own canoe to be
independent and manage on one's own.
Word Family canoe *verb*; **canoeist** *noun*.
[Haitian]

canon¹ (**kan**-'n) *noun*
1 any law or rule, especially a religious one.
2 a basic standard by which something is
judged.
3 *Music* any music in which the melody is
repeated by different instruments or voices
which overlap.
4 a list of works considered to be genuinely
by a certain writer.
Word Family canonical (ka-**nonn**-i-k'l)
adjective; **canonize, canonise** *verb* to
declare to be a saint; **canonization** (kan-
na-nize-**ay**-sh'n) *noun*.

canon² *noun*
Religion a clergyman who works in a
cathedral.

> [!] Do not confuse *canon* with
> CANNON.

canopy (**kan**-a-pee) *noun* (*plural*
canopies)
1 a hanging roof-like cover, e.g. for a bed.

2 the transparent covering of the cockpit of an aircraft.
[Greek *konopeion* a mosquito net]

cant (*rhymes with* pant) *noun*
1 any hypocritically pious language.
2 the jargon used by a particular group of people.

can't (kahnt) *contraction*
a short form of **cannot**: *You can't go in there!*

cantaloup (**kan**-ta-loop *or* **kan**-ta-lope) *noun also* **cantaloupe**
a round melon with sweet orange flesh.
[first grown in Europe at *Cantalupo*, Italy]

cantankerous (kan-**tank**-er-us) *adjective*
bad-tempered or quarrelsome.
Word Family **cantankerously** *adverb*; **cantankerousness** *noun*.

cantata (kan-**tah**-ta) *noun*
a long musical composition for soloists, chorus and often an orchestra.
[Italian, sung]

canteen (kan-**teen**) *noun*
1 a place in a school, factory, etc. where people eat meals.
2 a box containing a set of cutlery.
3 the eating and drinking utensils of a soldier, especially a water-bottle.

canter *noun*
a gait of a horse between a trot and a gallop.
• **canter** *verb*.
[from *Canterbury gallop*, the pace at which pilgrims supposedly travelled to Canterbury]

canticle (**kan**-ti-k'l) *noun*
Christianity a short hymn or chant with words taken from the Bible.

cantilever (**kan**-ti-lee-va) *noun*
a projecting part, such as the bracket supporting a balcony or a horizontal beam supporting a bridge.

canto *noun*
one of the divisions of a long poem.

canton *noun*
a small district, especially in Switzerland.

cantor *noun*
Religion the main singer or person who leads the singing in a service.
[Latin, singer]

canvas (**kan**-v's) *noun* (*plural* **canvases**)
1 a heavy fabric made from flax or cotton and used for tents, sails, etc.
2 anything made of canvas, such as a piece of canvas used by an artist as a painting surface.

3 *Boxing* the covering over the floor of the ring.
Phrase **under canvas** in a tent or tents.
[Greek *kannabis* hemp]

canvass (**kan**-v's) *verb*
1 to campaign for support, donations, etc., e.g. for a charity or a political candidate.
2 to try to find out the views of electors in a forthcoming election.
Word Family **canvasser** *noun* a person who canvasses.

canyon *noun*
a narrow steep-sided river valley.
[Spanish *cañon*]

cap *noun*
1 a soft round hat with no brim, usually with a peak at the front.
2 the removable top of a pen, jar, etc.
3 something resembling a cap, such as the top curved part of a mushroom.
4 a small explosive used to make a noise in a toy gun.
5 an upper limit: *a cap on the department's spending.*
6 ⇨ DIAPHRAGM (definition 3).
Phrases **cap in hand** humbly. **set one's cap at** to try to capture the affections of.
• **cap** *verb* (**caps**; **capping**; **capped**)
1 to cover with or as if with a cap: *cap an oil well.*
2 to improve on: *I got 80%. Cap that!*
3 to impose an upper limit on.
4 to choose as a member of a national sports team: *He was capped 30 times for England.*

capable (**kay**-pa-b'l) *adjective*
able, competent or efficient.
Phrase **be capable of** to have the ability to do, become, etc.: *Do you really think he is capable of murder?*
Word Family **capability** (kay-pa-**bill**-i-tee) *noun* (*plural* **capabilities**); **capably** *adverb*

capacious (ka-**pay**-shus) *adjective*
able to hold a large amount.
[Latin *capax*, *capacis* spacious]

capacitor (ka-**pas**-i-ta) *noun also called* **condenser**.
Electricity any device for storing electric charge, consisting in its simplest form of two conducting surfaces with an insulator between them.

capacity (ka-**pas**-i-tee) *noun* (*plural* **capacities**)
1 the maximum amount that something can hold, contain or produce: *The theatre*

was filled to capacity. □ *a container with a capacity of five litres.*
2 ability: *the capacity of elastic to be stretched.*
3 a position or function: *in his capacity as leader.*

cape[1] *noun*
a short sleeveless cloak fastened at the neck and hanging around the shoulders.

cape[2] *noun*
Geography a piece of land jutting out into the sea.

caper[1] *noun*
1 a playful leap or skip.
2 a prank.
• **caper** *verb* to leap about.
[Latin *caper* a goat]

caper[2] *noun*
a flower bud used in sauces, etc.

capillary (ka-**pill**-a-ree) *noun* (*plural* **capillaries**)
Anatomy any of the smallest blood vessels which connect the arteries to the veins. Compare ARTERY (definition 1); VEIN (definition 1).
• **capillary** *adjective* relating to or occurring in a narrow tube.
[Latin *capillus* a hair]

capital[1] *noun*
1 the city or town which is the official seat of government in a country, state, etc.
2 ⇨ CAPITAL LETTER.
3 money or property owned, used or invested.
Phrase **make capital out of** to get an advantage from.
• **capital** *adjective*
1 of or relating to capital.
2 involving the loss of life: *a capital offence.*
3 (*dated informal*) splendid or excellent.
[Latin *capitalis* chief]

capital[2] *noun*
Architecture the top of a column.

capitalism *noun*
an economic and political system where industry, trade, etc. are owned and controlled by private individuals or groups. Compare COMMUNISM.
Word Family **capitalist** *noun, adjective.*

capitalize, capitalise *verb*
Phrase **capitalize on** to get an advantage from: *You must capitalize on this marvellous piece of luck.*

capital letter *noun* also called **capital**.
a large form of a letter, e.g. A, B, C.

capital punishment *noun*
punishment by execution.

capitulate (ka-**pit**-yoo-late) *verb*
to surrender, usually on stated conditions.
Word Family **capitulation** (ka-pit-yoo-lay-sh'n) *noun.*

cappuccino (kap-pa-**chee**-no) *noun*
an Italian coffee made with frothy milk.
[Italian]

capricious (ka-**prish**-us) *adjective*
tending to change suddenly, and so not reliable.
Word Family **capriciously** *adverb;* **capriciousness** *noun.*

Capricorn *noun*
Astrology a group of stars, the tenth sign of the Zodiac; the sign of the Goat.
[Latin *caper* goat + *cornus* horned]

capsize *verb*
1 to turn over into water: *The boat capsized.*
2 to overturn anything floating.

capstan (**kap**-st'n) *noun*
Nautical an upright post on a dock or ship which can be turned to pull in a rope.

capsule (**kaps**-yool) *noun*
1 a small soluble container for a dose of medicine.
2 the part of a spacecraft where the crew works and lives.
[Latin *capsula* little box]

captain *noun*
1 a person appointed to have leadership or authority over others: *the team captain.*
2 *Army* a commissioned officer ranking between lieutenant and major.
3 *Navy* a commissioned officer ranking between commander and commodore.
Word Family **captain** *verb* to lead; **captaincy** *noun* (*plural* **captaincies**) the position or period of being a captain.
[Latin *caput* head]

caption (**kap**-sh'n) *noun*
a heading, description or short explanation, e.g. one accompanying a cartoon or illustration.

captivate (**kap**-ti-vate) *verb*
to enthral: *He was captivated by her beauty.*
Word Family **captivation** (kap-ti-**vay**-sh'n) *noun.*

captive (**kap**-tiv) *noun*
a person who is captured.
Word Family **captivity** (kap-**tivv**-i-tee) *noun* the state of being a captive; **captive** *adjective.*
[Latin *captivus* caught]

capture (**kap**-cher) *verb*
1 to seize as a prisoner.

Figurative His tale captured their imaginations.
2 to store data in a computer.
Word Family capture noun the act of capturing; **captor** noun a person who captures another.

car noun
1 a road vehicle used by individuals and families to travel around.
2 a railway carriage.
[Latin *carrus* a four-wheeled wagon]

carafe (ka-**rahf** or ka-**raff**) noun
a decanter which does not have a stopper.
[Arabic *gharraf* a drinking vessel]

carambola (karr-am-**bole**-a)
⇨ STARFRUIT.

caramel (**karr**-a-mel) noun
1 sugar cooked to a dark brown colour, used as a flavouring in desserts, etc.
2 a sweet with this taste.

carapace (**karr**-a-pace) noun
Biology a shell or hard covering on the back of some animals, such as a crab, tortoise, etc.

carat (**karr**-'t) noun
1 a unit of mass for jewels, equal to 200 mg.
2 a unit used in expressing how pure gold is; *a ring of 18-carat gold.*

caravan (**karr**-a-van) noun
1 a vehicle designed to be drawn by a car or horses, in which people can live.
2 a group of people travelling together, usually with camels across a desert.
[Persian *karwan*]

caraway (**karr**-a-way) noun
a herb whose strong-smelling seed-like fruits are used in cooking and medicine.

carbide noun
Chemistry a compound of carbon and one other element, especially a metal.

carbine noun
a light short rifle.

carbohydrate (kar-bo-**high**-drate) noun
1 *Biology* an organic compound, such as sugar, starch, cellulose, etc., which only contains the elements carbon, hydrogen and oxygen.
2 (*informal*) food that contains such compounds, e.g. rice, bread and potatoes.

carbon noun
a non-metallic element found in the pure state in graphite and diamond. It forms the large molecules which are the basis of living tissue and is also found in petroleum, coal, etc.
[Latin *carbonis* of charcoal]

carbonated (**kar**-b'n-ay-tid) adjective
having had carbon dioxide added.

carbon copy noun (plural **carbon copies**)
1 a copy made by using carbon paper.
2 any exact copy.

carbon dating noun
short form of **radiocarbon dating** a method of estimating the age of very old animal or plant products by measuring their radioactive carbon content.

carbon dioxide noun
a compound (formula CO_2) which is a gas at room temperature. It is a waste product of respiration and one of the reactants of photosynthesis. It is widely used in industry as dry ice, in fizzy drinks, etc.

carbon fibre noun
a very strong but relatively light material made from carbon.

Carboniferous (kar-b'n-**iff**-er-us) ⇨ PALAEOZOIC.

carbon monoxide noun
a colourless odourless poisonous gas (formula CO) which forms when carbon burns in an insufficient supply of oxygen.

carbon paper noun
a chemically treated paper placed between pages so that anything marked on the top sheet will be reproduced on the others.

car boot sale noun
a sale at which people sell second-hand goods from their car boots.

carborundum (kar-ba-**run**-d'm) noun
Metallurgy a dark crystalline solid which is nearly as hard as diamond and is used as an abrasive.

carbuncle noun
1 a large area of infection in the skin, producing pus.
2 a red jewel.
[Latin *carbunculus* a live coal]

carburettor (karb-ya-**rett**-a) noun
(*American* **carburetor**)
a device in an internal combustion engine for mixing fuel and air in the correct proportions.

carcass (**kar**-k's) noun (plural **carcasses**)
also **carcase**
1 the dead body of an animal.
2 the framework of a ship, piece of furniture, etc.

carcinogen (kar-**sin**-a-j'n) noun
any substance producing a cancer in an organism.

Word Family **carcinogenic** (kar-sin-na-jenn-ik) *adjective*.

carcinoma (kar-si-**no**-ma) *noun*
Medicine a form of cancer.
[Greek *karkinos* crab + *-oma* a tumour]

card¹ *noun*
1 a piece of stiff paper, often printed for a particular purpose: *a Christmas card.* □ *a business card.*
2 a postcard.
3 short form of **playing card** any of a set of 52 small pieces of stiff paper printed with numbers and pictures of four suits (clubs, diamonds, hearts and spades) and used in various games: *a pack of cards.*
4 a piece of stiff plastic used instead of cash, e.g. a credit card or a debit card.
5 a strong argument or trick: *Don't worry – I've still got a few cards up my sleeve!*
6 (*dated informal*) an amusing person.
7 (**cards**) a game or games using playing cards: *We played cards all afternoon.*
Phrases **be given one's cards** (*dated*) to lose one's job. **on the cards** possible. **put one's cards on the table** to be completely truthful about one's intentions.
[Greek *khartes* a papyrus leaf]

card² *verb*
to disentangle fibres of wool, etc. before spinning.

cardamom (**kar**-da-mum) *noun* also **cardamum**
the seed of an Asian plant, used in cooking.
[Greek]

cardboard *noun*
a stiff material like very thick paper.
• **cardboard** *adjective*
1 of or relating to cardboard.
2 unnatural: *cardboard characters in a novel.*

cardboard city *noun* (*plural* **cardboard cities**)
an area of a city, particularly London, where the homeless gather to sleep in makeshift shelters made from cardboard boxes.

cardholder *noun*
a person whose name is on a credit card, cheque card, etc.

cardiac *adjective*
of or relating to the heart: *a cardiac arrest.*
[Greek *kardia* the heart]

cardigan *noun*
a knitted jacket which fastens down the front.

Cardigan is what is called an *eponymous* word, that is, it is named after a person. *Eponymous* is the adjective from *eponym*, a word derived from Greek, meaning 'a person who gives his or her name to a thing or place'. It was James Thomas Brudenell, 7th Earl of Cardigan, who gave his name to the *cardigan*. He was one of the first people to wear such a woollen jacket.

cardinal (**kar**-di-n'l) *noun*
Roman Catholicism a member of the council called the Sacred College which elects and advises the Pope.
• **cardinal** *adjective* extremely important: *one of the cardinal rules of sailing.*
[Latin *cardo, cardinis* that on which all depends]

cardinal number *noun*
Maths any whole number as used for counting, e.g. 1, 2, 3, etc. Compare
ORDINAL NUMBER.

cardinal points *plural noun*
the four main directions of the compass: north, south, east and west.

cardiology (kar-di-**oll**-a-jee) *noun*
the study of the heart and its functions.
Word Family **cardiologist** *noun*.

cardiovascular (kar-di-o-**vass**-kew-la) *adjective*
relating to the heart and the blood vessels.

card phone *noun*
a phone box that only takes phonecards.

card sharp *noun*
a person, especially a professional gambler, who cheats at cards.

care (*rhymes with* hair) *noun*
1 looking after: *hair care.*
2 supervision: *She left the children in my care.*
3 worry or mental distress: *without a care in the world.*
4 serious attention: *Handle with care.*
Phrases **care of** at the address of: *Write to me care of my aunt.* **take care of** to look after. **take into care** to put under supervision in a special home run by an official authority: *His children were taken into care.*
• **care** *verb*
1 to be concerned or interested.
2 to want: *Would you care to step inside, sir?*
Phrase **care for 1** to look after. **2** to like.

career (ka-**reer**) *noun*
a chosen pursuit or occupation.
• **career** *verb* to move rapidly: *The car careered down the hill.*

carefree *adjective*
free of worry or anxiety.

careful *adjective*
1 cautious: *He's very careful about what he says in public.*
2 thorough: *a careful worker.*
Word Family carefully *adverb*;
carefulness *noun*.

care label *noun*
a label on a textile item showing how the product should be washed or treated.

careless *adjective*
resulting from or showing a lack of care, attention, thought, etc.: *a careless remark.*
□ *careless work.*
Word Family carelessly *adverb*;
carelessness *noun*.

carer *noun*
a person who looks after someone, especially a sick, elderly or disabled relative in the home.

caress (ka-**ress**) *verb*
to touch or embrace affectionately.
• **caress** *noun* (*plural* **caresses**).
[Latin *carus* dear]

caretaker *noun*
a person employed to look after a building, goods, etc.
• **caretaker** *adjective* holding office temporarily until a new appointment is made: *a caretaker Prime Minister.*

careworn *adjective*
tired and troubled with worries.

cargo *noun* (*plural* **cargoes** or **cargos**)
the goods carried on a ship, aircraft, etc.
[Spanish]

caribou (**karr**-i-boo) *noun* (*plural* **caribou**)
a North American reindeer with large antlers.

caricature (**karr**-i-ka-chaw) *noun*
a sketch or description of a person which exaggerates a predominant or peculiar feature, as in a cartoon.
• **caricature** *verb*.
[Italian *caricare* to exaggerate]

carillon (ka-**ril**-y'n) *noun*
1 a set of bells in a tower.
2 a tune played on such bells.
[French]

carmine *adjective*
having a deep purplish-red colour.

carnage (**kar**-nij) *noun*
a massive slaughter or massacre.

carnal *adjective*
sensual or sexual.
[Latin *carnis* of flesh]

carnation (kar-**nay**-sh'n) *noun*
1 a garden plant with sweet-smelling rose-like flowers growing on long stems.
2 a strong pink colour.
[Latin *carnatio* fleshiness]

carnelian (kar-**nee**-lee-an) *noun* also **cornelian**
a semi-transparent reddish stone, used in jewellery, etc.

carnival *noun*
1 a festive occasion with noisy merrymaking, dancing and processions.
2 a fair or amusement show, especially a temporary one.

carnivorous (kar-**nivv**-er-us) *adjective*
of or relating to an organism which eats flesh, especially an animal which primarily eats meat. A few plants are described as carnivorous, although they only supplement their diet with insects.
Word Family carnivore (**kar**-ni-vor) *noun*.
[Latin *carnis* of flesh + *vorare* to swallow]

carob (**karr**-'b) *noun*
the edible pod of a Mediterranean tree, often used as a substitute for chocolate.

carol (**karr**-'l) *noun*
a song for Christmas or other religious festivals.
• **carol** *verb* (**carols; carolling; carolled**)
to sing joyously.

carotene (**karr**-a-teen) *noun*
Biology a yellow pigment found in plants and changed into vitamin A in the liver.
[same origin as CARROT]

carousal (ka-**rouse**-'l) *noun*
a noisy or drunken gathering, celebration, etc.
Word Family carouse *verb*.

carousel (karr-a-**sel**) *noun*
a merry-go-round.

carp[1] *verb*
to find fault or complain unreasonably.
Word Family carpingly *adverb*.

carp[2] *noun* (*plural* **carp**)
any of a group of freshwater fish used as food and often bred in ponds.

carpel *noun*
the female reproductive organ of a flower.

carpenter *noun*
a person who builds or fixes wooden parts or structures.
Word Family **carpentry** *noun*.
[Latin *carpentarius*]

carpet (**kar**-pit) *noun*
a thick fabric covering for the floor, often patterned.
Phrases **on the carpet** being reprimanded by a person in authority.
sweep under the carpet to conceal or cover up a problem, incident, etc.
• **carpet** *verb*
1 to cover with carpet.
2 (*informal*) to reprimand.

carpet bag *noun*
an oblong travelling bag made of a heavy fabric.

carport *noun*
an open-sided shelter for cars, with a roof supported by posts.

carriage (**karr**-ij) *noun*
1 a wheeled vehicle, usually horse-drawn, for carrying passengers.
2 a railway vehicle.
3 a part, e.g. of a machine, designed to hold or carry something: *a gun carriage*.
4 the manner of holding the head and body.
5 the act or cost of transporting.

carriageway *noun*
the part of a road for use by vehicles.

carrier *noun*
1 a person or thing that carries or conveys.
2 short form of **carrier bag** a paper or plastic bag for carrying shopping.
3 *Medicine* a person who transmits a disease without contracting it himself or herself.

carrion *noun*
any dead or decaying flesh.

carrot *noun*
a plant with a cone-shaped orange root which is eaten as a vegetable.
Word Family **carroty** *adjective*
resembling a carrot in colour.
[Greek *karoton*]

carry *verb* (**carries; carrying; carried**)
1 to hold in the arms, especially while moving.
2 to transport: *This train carries about 500 people.*
3 to be able to support: *That branch won't carry your weight.*
4 to have on the body: *The American police carry guns.*

5 to contain: '*The Times' did not carry the story.*
6 to have for sale: *shops carrying a wide range of goods.*
7 to move or travel in a particular way: *He carries himself like a soldier.* □ *Her voice carried well.*
8 to approve: *The motion was carried by 287 votes to 16.*
9 *Maths* to transfer a number into the next column: *5 into 31 goes 6 and carry 1.*
Phrases **carry away** to affect strongly: *She got rather carried away when the Queen came out, and screamed with excitement.*
carry off 1 to perform successfully: *He carried off the deception brilliantly.* 2 to win: *She carried off all the prizes.* **carry on** 1 to continue. 2 (*informal*) to behave in an excited or foolish way. **carry out** to do or complete: *I need to carry out a few repairs to my car.* □ *She'll never carry out her threat!*
carry through to perform successfully.

cart *noun*
1 a wheeled vehicle used to carry goods or passengers.
2 any small vehicle pulled by hand.
Phrase **put the cart before the horse** to reverse the natural order of things.
Word Family **cart** *verb* to carry, especially in a cart; **cart away**, **cart off** to remove forcefully or unceremoniously; **carter** *noun*.

carte blanche (kart **blonsh**) *noun*
full or unconditional power, authority, etc.
[French *carte* card + *blanche* white]

cartel (kar-**tel**) *noun*
a group of companies which agrees to control output or prices of products, in order to increase profits.

cartilage (**kar**-ta-lij) *noun*
Anatomy the tough elastic tissue forming the ends of the bones and also found in the ears and nose.

cartography (kar-**tog**-ra-fee) *noun*
the drawing and study of maps and charts.
Word Family **cartographer** *noun*.

carton (**kar**-t'n) *noun*
a cardboard box or container.
[French]

cartoon *noun*
1 a drawing or series of drawings which comment in an amusing and often exaggerated way on a person or event.
2 ⇨ COMIC STRIP.
3 a film consisting of a series of drawings which form continuous movement when shown through a projector.

4 *Art* a preliminary sketch for a painting, etc.
Word Family cartoonist *noun*.

cartridge (**kar**-trij) *noun*
1 a cylindrical case containing the charge of powder, primer and bullet or shot for a gun.
2 any similar object, such as a disposable ink container for a fountain pen.

cartridge paper *noun*
a rough paper used for drawing or printing.

cartwheel *noun*
1 the wheel of a cart.
2 a somersault performed sideways with hands and legs extended.

carve *verb*
1 to cut into a shape: *a statue carved from stone*.
2 to cut into pieces: *Who will carve the roast?*
3 also **carve out** to make by a lot of effort: *She has carved out a place in history*.
Word Family carver *noun* a person or thing that carves; **carving** *noun* a carved object or sculpture.

cascade (kass-**kade**) *noun*
1 a waterfall or series of waterfalls.
2 something resembling a waterfall.
• **cascade** *verb*.
[Italian *cascare* to fall]

case¹ *noun*
1 an instance, event or example: *I hear she doesn't want me there – in that case, I won't come.* □ *It was a case of mistaken identity.*
2 a set of facts and opinions forming an argument: *She made out a very good case for being allowed to come with us.*
3 an issue that is decided in a court: *The case is expected to take several months.*
4 a person being dealt with by someone professional: *The doctor has several urgent cases to see this morning.*
5 *Grammar* the relationship of a word or pronoun to another word in a sentence: *In 'he threw the ball', 'he' is in the nominative case.*
Phrases in any case 1 in any circumstances: *He wasn't hurt. In any case, he hit me first!* **in case of** in the event of: *In case of fire, break the glass.* **just in case** in order to be all right if something happens: *She won't ring, but I'll take my mobile phone, just in case.*

case² *noun*
1 a large container or box.
2 a suitcase.

3 a covering, e.g. a pillowcase.
4 *Printing* either of the two forms a letter can have in writing or printing. ⇨ LOWER CASE; UPPER CASE.
• **case** *verb* (*informal*) to watch or examine a house, etc. when planning a crime.

case history *noun* (*plural* **case histories**)
all relevant information about a person, used to help doctors, social workers, etc. diagnose or solve problems.

casement *noun*
a window which opens outwards on hinges attached at one side of it.

case study *noun* (*plural* **case studies**)
1 a particular example of something in reality rather than theory.
2 an account of the way somebody or something being studied has developed over a period of time.

cash *noun*
any money in the form of banknotes or coins, rather than cheques, credit cards, etc.
• **cash** *verb* to give or get cash in exchange for: *Can you cash a cheque for me?*
Phrase cash in on (*informal*) to gain a profit or advantage from.

cash card *noun*
a plastic card used in a cash dispenser.

cash crop *noun*
a crop grown for sale rather than for the use of the farmer and his family.

cash dispenser *noun* also called **cash machine; cashpoint**.
a machine from which one can withdraw money from a bank, etc., using a cash card.

cashew (**kash**-oo) *noun*
a kidney-shaped edible nut.

cash flow *noun*
Economics the flow of money into and out of a business.

cashier (kash-**eer**) *noun*
a person who receives and pays out money in a bank, shop, etc.

cashmere (**kash**-meer) *noun*
a soft woollen fabric.
[first made from the hair of goats from *Kashmir*, India]

cash register *noun*
a machine used to record cash sales, equipped with a drawer to keep banknotes and coins.

casing *noun*
any outer case or covering.

casino (ka-**see**-no) *noun*
a place where gambling and other amusements are provided.

cask (*rhymes with* ask) *noun*
a barrel.

casket (*rhymes with* basket) *noun*
1 a small decorative box for storing jewels, letters, etc.
2 a coffin.

cassava (ka-**sah**-va) *noun*
a fleshy root grown in the tropics and made into flour or tapioca.

casserole (**kass**-a-role) *noun*
1 a deep ovenproof dish, often with a lid, used for baking.
2 any food cooked in such a dish, usually a mixture of meat and vegetables.

cassette (ka-**set**) *noun*
a small plastic box containing a tape, used in an electrical apparatus to record or play back sounds and/or images.

cassock *noun*
a long robe, usually black, worn by Christian priests.

cassowary (**kass**-a-wair-ee) *noun* (*plural* **cassowaries**)
a large blue-black flightless bird of Australia and New Guinea.
[Malay]

cast (*rhymes with* fast) *verb* (**casts; casting; cast**)
1 to throw or direct: *The searchlight cast strong shadows on the wall.*
2 to remove or get rid of: *The horse cast a shoe.*
3 to pour liquid into a mould and allow it to set: *to cast a statue in bronze.*
4 *Theatre* to choose actors for the roles in a play, film, etc.
Phrases **cast about** to search in all directions. **cast a vote** to vote. **cast off**
1 to reject or discard. 2 to let go, e.g. as a ship from its mooring. 3 to remove the last row of stitches from the needle in knitting.
cast on to place the first row of stitches on the needle in knitting.
• **cast** *noun*
1 the act of casting, especially a fishing line.
2 *Theatre* all the actors in a play, film, etc.
3 something shaped into a mould while in a fluid state, such as plaster for a broken limb.
4 a sort or kind: *He is a different cast of person.*
5 a small pile of earth thrown up by a worm.

castanets (kass-ta-**nets**) *plural noun*
Music a percussion instrument used in Spanish dances, etc., made from two hollow round pieces of wood which are clicked together by the fingers.
[Spanish *castañetas* little chestnuts]

castaway (**kahst**-a-way) *noun*
a person who has been shipwrecked.

caste (kahst) *noun*
a hereditary social group defined by occupation or trade, wealth, religion and marriage laws, such as the Hindu castes in India.
[Spanish *casta* lineage]

caster *noun* ⇨ CASTOR.

caster sugar *noun* also **castor sugar**
a fine sugar used in cooking.

castigate (**kass**-ti-gate) *verb*
to punish or criticize severely.
Word Family **castigation** (kass-ti-**gay**-sh'n) *noun*.
[Latin *castigare* to chastise]

casting vote *noun*
the vote of the chairperson, used to decide an issue when both sides have the same number of votes.

cast iron *noun*
any hard brittle alloy of iron and carbon which can be cast into shape.
• **cast-iron** *adjective* made of cast iron.
Figurative The witness had a cast-iron excuse (= unquestionable).

castle (**kah**-s'l) *noun*
1 a large fortified building.
2 *Chess* ⇨ ROOK².
• **castle** *verb Chess* to move the king two squares towards a rook, then place the rook on the first square passed by the king.
[Latin *castellum* fort]

castle in the air *noun* (*plural* **castles in the air**)
a daydream.

cast-off *noun*
a person or thing that has been rejected or discarded, especially an item of clothing.

castor (**kah**-sta) *noun* also **caster**
1 a small wheel or roller made to swivel in any direction, such as that used on furniture legs.
2 a container with holes in the top for sprinkling sugar, salt or flour.

castor oil *noun*
a thick oil obtained from the seeds of a tall Indian plant and used as a laxative.

castor sugar ⇨ CASTER SUGAR.

castrate (kass-**trate**) *verb*
to remove the testicles to make sterile or prevent fertilization. Compare SPAY; STERILIZE (definition 1).
Word Family **castration** *noun*.
[Latin]

casual (**kazh**-yew-'l) *adjective*
1 careless or unconcerned: *Her casual attitude towards work made her parents angry.*
2 informal: *casual dress.*
3 happening by chance: *a casual meeting.*
4 irregular or occasional: *casual employment.*
Word Family **casually** *adverb*; **casualness** *noun*.
[Latin *casus* a chance]

casualty (**kazh**-yew-'l-tee) *noun* (*plural* **casualties**)
1 a person injured or killed.
Figurative My job was a casualty of the company's reorganization.
2 (**Casualty**) the accident and emergency department of a hospital.

cat *noun*
1 a small mammal with soft fur kept as a pet.
2 also **big cat** any of a family of flesh-eating mammals including lions, tigers, etc.
3 a gossipy spiteful woman.
4 (*informal*) a cat-o'-nine-tails.
5 *Nautical* ⇨ CATAMARAN.
Phrases **let the cat out of the bag** to reveal information, usually unintentionally. **play cat and mouse with** to tease in an unpleasant way. **rain cats and dogs** to rain very heavily.

cataclysm (**kat**-a-klizm) *noun*
any sudden upheaval or change.
Word Family **cataclysmic** (kat-a-**kliz**-mik) *adjective*.
[Greek *kataklysmos* deluge]

catacomb (**kat**-a-koom *or* **kat**-a-kome) *noun*
(*usually* **catacombs**) an underground cemetery consisting of tunnels with recesses for graves.

catafalque (**kat**-a-falk) *noun*
a temporary stand on which a corpse lies in state.

catalogue (**kat**-a-log) *noun* (*American* **catalog**)
a list of items, names, goods, etc., often in alphabetical order.

• **catalogue** *verb* (**catalogues; cataloguing; catalogued**).
[Greek *katalogos* list]

catalyst (**kat**-a-list) *noun*
1 *Science* a substance which causes or increases the rate of a chemical reaction, but remains unchanged itself at the end of the reaction: *An enzyme is a biological catalyst.*
2 any person or thing that causes or accelerates change.

> The word **catalyst** is an example of how everyday language is affected by technical language. *Catalyst* is a chemical term for a substance that accelerates the rate of a chemical reaction while itself remaining unchanged. In the general language *catalyst* is used very loosely and can simply mean 'someone or something that causes a change', whether or not the person or thing remains unchanged. This shows how language is constantly developing and how words can acquire new or changed meanings from the misunderstanding of technical terms.

catalytic converter *noun*
a device that is fitted to a car's exhaust pipe to reduce the amount of poisonous gases it emits.

catamaran (kat-a-m'-**ran**) *noun*
short form is **cat** a boat or raft with two parallel hulls which are joined above the water. Compare TRIMARAN.
[Tamil]

catapult (**kat**-a-pult) *noun*
1 a device for throwing objects, e.g. a Y-shaped device for shooting stones.
2 a mechanical device for launching gliders or other aircraft.
• **catapult** *verb* to hurl from or as if from a catapult.
[Greek *katapeltes*]

cataract *noun*
1 a waterfall or series of waterfalls.
2 a condition in which the lens of the eye becomes increasingly opaque.
[Greek *katarrhaktes* rushing down]

catarrh (ka-**tar**) *noun*
an inflammation of the mucous membranes which produces excess mucus, especially in the respiratory tract.
[Greek *katarrhein* to run down]

catastrophe (ka-**tast**-ra-fee) *noun*
a sudden widespread disaster.

Word Family **catastrophic** (kat-a-**stroff**-ik) *adjective*; **catastrophically** *adverb*.
[Greek *katastrophé* the turning point of a play]

catatonic (kat-a-**tonn**-ik) *adjective* (*informal*) in a stupor and with one's arms and legs rigid.
[Greek *kata* down + *tonos* tension]

cat burglar *noun*
a burglar who enters a house by climbing.

catcall (**kat**-kawl) *noun*
a cry or sound used to express disapproval, disgust, etc.

catch *verb* (**catches; catching; caught**)
1 to stop and hold a moving object: *Throw the ball, and I'll catch it.*
2 to be in time to get on a bus, train, etc.
3 to trap: *Our cat caught a bird.* □ *My dad caught him stealing.* □ *I caught my jumper on a branch.*
4 to become trapped or stuck: *My jumper caught in the branches.*
5 to become infected with: *She caught a bad cold.*
6 to attract: *The play caught the children's imagination.*
7 to get briefly: *The fox caught sight of his prey.*
8 to understand or hear: *I didn't quite catch what you said.*
9 to begin to burn: *The fire caught first time.*
10 *Sport* to get a player out by catching a ball before it lands: *The batsman was caught first ball.*
11 to hit: *The stick caught him a glancing blow.*
Phrases **catch it** (*informal*) to get into trouble: *You'll catch it when Mum finds out!* **catch on 1** to become fashionable. **2** to begin to understand. **catch out** to show that someone is lying: *They tried all sorts of tricks to catch her out, but she stuck to her story.* **catch up** to become level with or overtake.
Word Family **catch** *noun* (*plural* **catches**) **1** the act of catching. **2** anything which fastens or holds: *a safety catch.* **3** anything which is caught: *a good catch of fish.* **4** a complication or trick: *It's too good to be true – what's the catch?* **5** a wobbly note in a person's voice. **6** (*informal*) a good person to have a relationship with: *She's going to marry William – he's quite a catch!*; **catcher** *noun* a person or thing that catches; **catching** *adjective* (*informal*) infectious: *'I've got mumps.'– 'Is it catching?'*

catchment area *noun*
1 the drainage area of a river and its tributaries.
2 a geographical area served by a particular institution, such as a school.

catchphrase *noun*
a phrase often used by someone who is well known.

catch-22 *noun*
a situation that is impossible to resolve. [from the title of a book by Joseph Heller, 1961]

catchup ⇨ KETCHUP.

catchword *noun*
a word or phrase repeated to achieve effect, such as a slogan in an election.

catchy *adjective* (**catchier; catchiest**)
easily remembered: *a catchy tune.*

catechism (**kat**-a-kizm) *noun*
Christianity a book of instruction containing a summary of beliefs in the form of questions and answers.

categorical (kat-a-**gorr**-i-k'l) *adjective*
direct or unconditional: *His reply was a categorical 'No!'*
Word Family **categorically** *adverb*.

category (**kat**-a-gree) *noun* (*plural* **categories**)
a division or class of things.
Word Family **categorize, categorise** *verb* to put into a category or categories.
[Greek *kategoria* a statement]

cater (**kay**-ter) *verb*
to provide and serve food and drink, especially at private parties.
Phrase **cater for** to provide what is wanted by: *a radio station that caters mainly for under-25s.*
Word Family **caterer** *noun*; **catering** *noun*.

caterpillar (**kat**-a-pill-a) *noun*
1 the larva of a butterfly or moth.
2 (**Caterpillar**) (*trademark*) a tractor or other device which moves on an endless ribbed belt passing around its wheels.
[Old French *chatepelose* hairy cat]

caterwaul (**kat**-a-wawl) *verb*
to cry or howl like a cat.

catfish *noun* (*plural* **catfish** or **catfishes**)
any of a large group of fish, usually freshwater, with whiskers near the mouth and a ridged spine which can inflict painful wounds.

catgut *noun*
the dried twisted intestines of sheep or other animals, used to make strings for musical instruments, tennis rackets, etc.

catharsis (ka-**thar**-sis) *noun* (*plural* **catharses**)
the release or relief of strong feelings, e.g. by acting out an impulse in drama, art, etc.
Word Family **cathartic** *adjective*.
[Greek *katharsis* cleansing]

cathedral (ka-**thee**-dr'l) *noun*
Christianity the principal church in a diocese, containing the bishop's throne.
[Greek *kathedra* chair]

catherine-wheel *noun*
a firework which spins as it burns.

catheter (**kath**-i-ta) *noun*
Medicine a hollow tube inserted to drain fluids, especially urine, from the body.
[Greek *katheter* anything let down into]

cathode *noun*
a negative electrode. Compare ANODE.
[Greek *kata* down + *hodos* a way]

cathode-ray tube *noun*
a vacuum tube in which a beam of electrons produces a bright spot on a luminescent screen at the front of the tube. A television picture tube is a special type of cathode-ray tube.

catholic (**kath**-a-lik) *adjective*
1 liberal or wide-ranging: *His taste in music is catholic.*
2 (**Catholic**) *Christianity* of or relating to the Roman Catholic Church.
Word Family **Catholic** *noun* a member of the Roman Catholic Church;
Catholicism (ka-**thol**-a-sizm) *noun* the beliefs and practices of the Roman Catholic Church.
[Greek *katholikos* universal]

catkin *noun*
a spike of soft down-like flowers hanging from twigs, e.g. on a willow or birch.

cat litter ⇨ LITTER (definition 3).

catnap *noun*
a brief sleep.
• **catnap** *verb* (**catnaps; catnapping; catnapped**).

catnip *noun* also called **catmint**.
a variety of mint plant with strongly scented leaves.

cat-o'-nine-tails *noun* (*plural* **cat-o'-nine-tails**)
(*formerly*) a whip for flogging a person, usually consisting of nine knotted cords attached to a handle.

cat's cradle *noun*
a children's game played with a loop of string wound around the fingers.

Catseye *noun*
(*trademark*) a reflector marking the centre or boundaries of a road.

cat's eye *noun*
a gem of the quartz group.

cattery *noun* (*plural* **catteries**)
a place where cats are looked after, e.g. when their owners go on holiday.

cattle *plural noun*
cows and bulls.

cattle grid *noun*
a metal grid across a road, that animals will not cross.

catty *adjective* (**cattier; cattiest**)
(*informal*) spiteful: *a catty remark.*

catwalk *noun*
a narrow path or platform, e.g. one that fashion models walk along.

Caucasian (kaw-**kay-zh**'n) *noun*
any of a major race of people, including those of Europe, south-west Asia and northern Africa, with light to brown skin and fine, straight or wavy hair.
• **Caucasian** *adjective*.
[after *Caucasia*, Russia, where the race supposedly originated]

caucus (**kaw**-kus) *noun* (*plural* **caucuses**)
a small group within a political party, formed to influence policy.

caught (**kawt**) the past tense and past participle of **catch**.

cauldron (**kawl**-dr'n) *noun*
a large pot for cooking.
[Latin *calidarium* a hot bath]

cauliflower (**kol**-li-flower) *noun*
a large white vegetable with a compact head of many sections, each with a broad stalk.

cauliflower ear *noun*
a flattened or deformed ear, especially one caused by blows in boxing.

caulk (*rhymes with* walk) *verb*
to fill seams or joints, such as gaps between planks in a boat, to make them watertight, etc.

cause *noun*
1 anything which produces an effect, action or result: *A faulty wire was the cause of the fire.*
2 a reason: *You have no cause to complain.*
3 a principle or political movement: *devoted to the cause of votes for women.*

• **cause** *verb* to bring about: *What caused the explosion?*
[Latin *causa*]

cause célèbre (koze say-**leb**-ra) *noun* (*plural* **causes célèbres**) (koze say-**leb**-ra) a lawsuit which causes a lot of debate or interest.

causeway *noun*
a raised road or path, e.g. across wet or swampy ground.

caustic (kos-tik *or* kaw-stik) *adjective*
1 *Chemistry* (of an alkali) able to corrode organic matter.
2 sarcastic: *her caustic wit.*
Word Family **caustically** *adverb.*
[Greek *kaustikos* capable of burning]

cauterize, cauterise (kawt-a-rize) *verb*
to seal or destroy tissue by burning.

caution (kaw-sh'n) *noun*
1 the act of taking care, especially to avoid danger: *Drive with caution.*
2 an official warning: *The policeman let the boys off with a caution.*
Word Family **caution** *verb* to warn or advise; **cautionary** *adjective.*
[Latin *cautio* wariness]

cautious (kaw-shus) *adjective*
very careful or wary: *her cautious approach to the subject of a pay rise.*
Word Family **cautiously** *adverb;* **cautiousness** *noun.*

cavalcade (kavv-'l-kade) *noun*
a procession of horsemen, official cars, etc.

cavalier (kavv-a-leer) *noun*
(*formerly*) a knight.
• **cavalier** *adjective* arrogant or offhand.
[French, a horserider]

cavalry (kavv-'l-ree) *noun* (*plural* **cavalries**)
the branch of the army which originally fought on horseback. Compare INFANTRY.
Word Family **cavalryman** *noun* (*plural* **cavalrymen**).
[French *cavallerie*]

cave *noun*
an underground space in the earth's surface.
• **cave** *verb*
Phrase **cave in** 1 to collapse. 2 to submit or yield.
[Latin *cavum* a hollow]

caveat (kavv-i-at) *noun*
a warning.
[Latin, let a person beware]

caveman *noun* (*plural* **cavemen**)

a person who lived in a cave in prehistoric times.

cavern (kavv-'n) *noun*
a large cave.
Word Family **cavernous** *adjective* deep or hollow.

caviare (kavv-i-ah) *noun* also **caviar**
the tiny salted eggs of the sturgeon or other fish, considered a delicacy.

cavil (kavv-il) *verb* (**cavils; cavilling; cavilled**)
to quibble or make petty objections.
[Italian *cavilla* mockery]

cavity (kavv-i-tee) *noun* (*plural* **cavities**)
a hole or hollow in a solid object.

cavort (ka-vort) *verb*
to jump or dance around.

caw *noun*
the harsh cry of a crow, magpie, etc.
• **caw** *verb.*

cayenne *noun*
a hot red pepper.

cayman *noun*
any of a group of South American freshwater reptiles, related to the alligator.

CD *noun*
short form of **compact disc**.

CD-ROM (see-dee-**rom**) *noun*
a compact disc on which very large amounts of data can be stored for use by a computer.
[*compact disc read-only memory*]

cease *verb*
to stop or come to an end.
Word Family **ceaseless** *adjective* without end; **ceaselessly** *adverb.*
[Latin *cessare* to give way, to rest]

cease-fire *noun*
an end of hostilities, especially a truce.

cedar (seed-a) *noun*
any of a group of evergreen trees with short needle-like leaves, seeds in cones and hard red wood used for timber.
[Greek *kedros*]

cede (seed) *verb*
to give up or surrender something.
[Latin *cedere* to yield]

cedilla (si-**dill**-a) ⇨ ACCENT.
[Spanish, a little *z*]

ceilidh (**kay**-lee) *noun*
an informal evening of song, dance and story-telling.
[Gaelic, a visit]

ceiling (**see**-ling) *noun*
1 the inner upper surface of a room.

2 an upper limit: *a ceiling on local authority spending.*

celandine (**sel**-'n-dine) *noun*
a small plant with yellow flowers.
[Greek *khelidon* a swallow, as the celandine flower appears and departs with the swallows]

celebrate (**sel**-a-brate) *verb*
1 to do something to show that a special event has happened: *That's great news! Let's celebrate!*
2 to hold a ceremony: *The priest celebrated Mass.*
3 to praise: *Her beauty was celebrated in poetry.*
Word Family **celebrated** *adjective* famous; **celebration** (sel-a-**bray**-sh'n) *noun* 1 the act of celebrating: *Come and join the celebrations!* 2 anything that celebrates something: *The film is a celebration of his life;* **celebrant** (**sel**-a-br'nt) *noun* a person leading or taking part in a ceremony or celebration.
[Latin *celebrare* to make widely known]

celebrity (si-**leb**-ra-tee) *noun* (*plural* **celebrities**)
1 a well-known person.
2 fame: *enjoying his new-found celebrity.*
[Latin *celeber* famous]

celeriac (si-**lair**-i-ak) *noun*
a variety of celery with swollen turnip-like roots, used in cooking.

celerity (si-**lerr**-a-tee) *noun*
swiftness or speed.
[Latin *celer* swift]

celery (**sel** n-ree) *noun*
a vegetable with long pale green edible stalks.

celestial (si-**lest**-i-'l) *adjective*
heavenly or divine.
[Latin *caelestis* of the sky]

celibacy (**sel**-i-b'-see) *noun*
the state of remaining unmarried and not having sexual intercourse, especially because of religious vows.
Word Family **celibate** *adjective, noun.*
[Latin *caelebs* bachelor]

cell (sel) *noun*
1 a small room, usually for one person, e.g. in a prison or monastery.
2 *Biology* a unit of protoplasm, usually containing a nucleus. It is enclosed by a membrane in animals and by a cell wall in plants: *red blood cells.*
3 *Electricity* a single device for producing electricity by chemical action.

4 a small group or unit dependent on a larger organization: *A communist cell was established in every small town.*
[Latin *cella* storeroom]

cellar (**sel**-a) *noun*
1 an underground room, usually beneath a building and used to store wine, etc.
2 a stock of wine.

cello (**chel**-o) *noun*
short form of **violoncello** *Music* a large low-pitched stringed instrument, usually played with a bow by a seated player.
Word Family **cellist** (**chel**-ist) *noun* a person who plays the cello.

Cellophane (**sel**-o-fane) *noun*
(*trademark*) a transparent waterproof paper used for wrapping food, etc.

cellular (**sel**-yew-la) *adjective*
1 relating to or composed of cells.
2 having small holes that trap air for insulation: *a cellular blanket.*

cellular telephone *noun* also **cellphone**
a telephone which uses a network of transmitters, each serving a small area known as a cell.

cellulite (**sel**-yoo-lite) *noun*
fat just under the surface of the skin that looks rather lumpy.

celluloid (**sel**-yoo-loyd) *noun*
a hard elastic inflammable plastic which softens when heated.
[CELLULOSE + *-oid*]

cellulose (**sel**-yoo-loze) *noun*
Chemistry a complex substance consisting of long chains of glucose units forming strong fibres, found in cell walls of plants. It is used in making paper, plastics and explosives.

Celsius (**sel**-si-us) *adjective*
of or relating to a scale of temperature with 0°C set at the melting point of ice, and 100°C set at the boiling point of water. Compare FAHRENHEIT.
[after *Anders Celsius*, 1701-1744, a Swedish astronomer]

Celtic (**kel**-tik *or* **sel**-tik) *adjective*
of or relating to the languages or inhabitants of ancient Gaul and ancient Britain, or their descendants today.
[Latin *Celtae* the Celts]

cement (si-**ment**) *noun*
1 a powder that sets to a hard mass when mixed with water, used in building.

2 any substance which joins or fills, such as the natural material which binds rock particles together, or the adhesive substance used to fill teeth.
Word Family **cement** *verb* **1** to cover with cement. **2** to join firmly with or as if with cement.
[Latin *caementum* rubble]

cemetery (sem-a-tree) *noun* (*plural* **cemeteries**)
an area of land reserved for the burial of the dead.

> The origins of the word **cemetery** were not at first associated specifically with death. It comes from the Latin *coemeterium*, from the Greek *koimetrion*, which originally meant 'a dormitory, a place to sleep'. It was only later that Greek Christian writers used it of a burial ground. To call a burial ground 'a sleeping place' is an example of *euphemism*, the use of a more pleasant term to avoid something harsh.

cenotaph (sen-a-taf *or* sen-a-tahf) *noun*
a monument, especially a war memorial, in memory of a person or people whose bodies are buried elsewhere.
[Greek *kenos* empty + *taphos* tomb]

censer (sen-sa) *noun*
a container in which incense is burned for religious ceremonies.

> ! The words *censer*, *censor* and *censure* are similar in spelling and pronunciation but very different in meaning. *Censer* ends in *er* and means 'a container for incense'; *censor* ends in *or* and means 'a person who cuts out undesirable parts from books, films, etc.'; *censure* ends in *ure* and means 'blame'. Both *censor* and *censure* are also used as verbs.

censor (sen-sa) *noun*
an official appointed to examine books, newspapers, films, etc. and cut out any parts believed to be undesirable.
Word Family **censor** *verb* to perform the work of a censor; **censorship** *noun* the act or process of censoring.
[Latin, a magistrate]

> ! Do not confuse *censor* with CENSER.

censorious (sen-saw-ri-us) *adjective*
criticizing or having a tendency to criticize.
Word Family **censoriously** *adverb*; **censoriousness** *noun*.

censure (sen-sha) *noun*
a formal expression of blame or disapproval.
● **censure** *verb*.

> ! Do not confuse *censure* with CENSER.

census (sen-sus) *noun* (*plural* **censuses**)
an official count of the inhabitants of a country.
[Latin]

cent (sent) *noun*
a coin worth one hundredth of certain units of money, e.g. the dollar.
[Latin *centum* hundred]

centaur (sen-taw) *noun*
Greek mythology a creature with the head and upper body of a man, and the lower body and legs of a horse.

centenary (sen-**tee**-na-ree *or* sen-**tenn**-a-ree) *noun* (*plural* **centenaries**)
a 100th anniversary.

centigrade (sen-ti-grade) *adjective*
a former word for **Celsius**.

centilitre *noun* (*American* **centiliter**)
a unit of volume equal to one hundredth of a litre. *abbrev.* cl.
[*centi-* + LITRE]

centimetre *noun* (*American* **centimeter**)
a unit of length equal to one hundredth of a metre. *abbrev.* cm.
[*centi-* + METRE]

centipede (sen-ti-peed) *noun*
a small long thin creature with a segmented body and many pairs of legs.
[Latin *centum* hundred + *pedis* of a foot]

central (sen-tr'l) *adjective*
1 at or near the centre: *villages in central Africa*.
2 principal or chief: *the central aim of this new law*.
Word Family **centrally** *adverb*.

central business district *noun*
the area in the centre of a town or city where many shops and offices are concentrated.

central heating *noun*
a system of heating a building from one source by circulating steam, hot water or air through pipes.

centralize, centralise (sen-tra-lize) *verb*
to bring under central control: *The government decided to centralize the education system*.
Word Family **centralization** (sen-tra-lie-**zay**-sh'n) *noun*.

central locking *noun*
a system in a car which locks or unlocks all the doors at the same time.

central nervous system ⇨ NERVOUS SYSTEM.

central processing unit *noun*
the part of a computer which controls its operations.

central reservation *noun*
an area along the middle of a large road which separates traffic moving in opposite directions.

centre (sen-ta) *noun* (*American* **center**)
1 a middle point, especially of a circle or sphere: *She hit the target in the centre.*
Figurative He is always the centre of attention.
2 a principal place for something: *London is a major financial centre.*
3 (**Centre**) the politicians and their supporters in any political party who hold moderate views on most issues, as opposed to the left wing or right wing.
4 *Sport* a player in one of various positions across or down the centre of a field.
• **centre** *verb* to place in, at or towards the centre.
Phrase **centre on, centre around** to have as the main area of concern: *The debate centres on whether a ten-year-old can distinguish between right and wrong.*
[Greek *kentron* a sharp point]

centre of gravity *noun* (*plural* **centres of gravity**)
the point at which the weight of a body may be taken as acting. The body will balance if supported at this point.
⇨ WEIGHT *noun* (definition 2).

centrepiece *noun*
1 a decorative object or arrangement, especially one placed at the centre of a dining table.
2 a chief feature.

centrifugal (sen-tri-**few**-g'l *or* sen-**triff**-yew-g'l) *adjective*
moving or tending to move away from the centre.

centrifuge (**sen**-tri-fewj) *noun*
a machine which spins so that centrifugal force is created inside it, used to separate liquids from solids.

centripetal (sen-tri-**pee**-t'l *or* sen-**trip**-i-t'l) *adjective*
towards or moving towards the centre.

centurion (sen-**tyoor**-ri-on) *noun*
Ancient history an officer in the Roman army commanding a company of 100 foot soldiers.

century (**sen**-cha-ree) *noun* (*plural* **centuries**)
1 a period of 100 years.
2 any group or collection of 100, e.g. of runs in cricket.
[Latin *centum* hundred]

cephalopod (**sef**-a-la-pod) *noun*
any of a group of molluscs which have tentacles attached to their heads, e.g. the squid, octopus and cuttlefish.
[Greek *kephalé* head + *podos* of a foot]

ceramics (si-**ram**-iks) *plural noun*
1 (*used with singular verb*) the art of making pottery, etc. from moist clays which are shaped, then fired to dry and harden.
2 any articles made in this way.
Word Family **ceramic** *adjective*.
[Greek *keramikos* of pottery]

cereal (**seer** i-al) *noun*
1 any cultivated plant belonging to the grass family, producing an edible starchy seed.
2 a food made from such seed.
[after *Ceres*, the goddess of agriculture in Roman mythology]

> ! The words *cereal* and *serial* sound the same but have different spellings and meanings. A *cereal* is a plant or a breakfast food; a *serial* is a story presented in parts.

cerebral (**serr**-i-br'l) *adjective*
1 of or relating to the brain.
2 intellectual.

cerebral palsy *noun*
a form of paralysis usually due to brain injury at or during birth, causing difficulty in developing controlled movements.

ceremonial (serr-i-**mo**-nee-'l) *adjective*
relating to formal or ritual occasions, etc.
Word Family **ceremonial** *noun* formalities; **ceremonially** *adverb*.

ceremonious (serr-i-**mo**-nee-us) *adjective*
elaborately formal or polite.
Word Family **ceremoniously** *adverb*; **ceremoniousness** *noun*.

ceremony (**serr**-a-mo-nee) *noun*
1 the formal behaviour or set of acts performed on certain sacred or important occasions: *an initiation ceremony.* □ *a wedding ceremony.*
2 formal politeness.
[Latin *caerimonia* reverence]

cerise (s'-**rees** or s'-**reez**) noun
a bright cherry-red colour.
● **cerise** adjective.
[French, cherry]

certain (**sir**-t'n) adjective
1 completely sure or free from doubt: I am
certain he will come.
2 particular: They wouldn't tell me certain
things.
3 not easy to define: He has a certain
charm.
4 limited: I agree with you to a certain extent.
5 not named but assumed to be known:
Everyone knows a certain person is responsible
for the theft.
Word Family certainly adverb without
doubt; **certainly!** interjection of course!;
certainty noun (plural **certainties**) 1 the
state of being certain. 2 a person or thing
about which it is possible to be certain.
[Latin certus settled]

certificate (sir-**tif**-i-k't) noun
a document or printed statement, often
used as evidence for something: a birth
certificate.

certify (**sir**-ti-fie) verb (**certifies**;
certifying; **certified**)
1 to confirm that something is true or
genuine.
2 to officially declare a person insane.

certitude (**sir**-ti-tewd) noun
a sense of absolute conviction.

cervical (**sir**-vi-k'l or sir-**vie**-k'l) adjective
1 of or relating to the neck.
2 of or relating to the cervix of the uterus:
cervical cancer.

cervical screening noun
the routine and regular examination of
women to check for early signs of cancer
of the cervix.

cervical smear noun
the collection of a sample of cells from the
cervix of the uterus so that they can be
examined under a microscope for early
signs of cancer.

cervix (**sir**-viks) noun (plural **cervices**)
(**sir**-vi-seez)
1 Anatomy the opening of the uterus of
mammals which leads into the vagina.
2 Anatomy the neck.
[Latin, neck]

cessation (sess-**ay**-sh'n) noun
a ceasing or stopping.

cesspool (**sess**-pool) noun also called
cesspit.
a hole or pit into which drains empty.

cha-cha noun
a fast dance from South America.

chafe verb
1 to wear or make sore by rubbing: The
new shoes chafed his feet.
2 to become irritated or impatient.
[French chauffer to warm]

chaff[1] (chahf or chaff) noun
1 the husks of grains and grasses separated
from the seeds.
2 a finely chopped hay used as fodder.

chaff[2] verb
to tease or make fun of.

chaffinch noun (plural **chaffinches**)
a small European finch with a reddish-
brown breast.

chagrin (**shag**-rin or sha-**green**) noun
a feeling of annoyance or disappointment.
[French]

chain noun
1 a series of interlocked rings or links,
usually of metal.
2 any connected series: a mountain chain.
□ She owns a chain of motels.
3 Chemistry a number of similar atoms
joined together, particularly carbon atoms,
whose chains form the basis of all organic
compounds.
4 (formerly) a unit of length equal to
22 yards, about 20 m.
5 (**chains**) an apparatus put on vehicle
wheels to help them grip in snow and ice.
Phrase in chains kept as a prisoner.
Word Family chain verb to bind or fasten
with a chain.

chain gang noun
a group of convicts chained together.

chain letter noun
a letter sent to a number of people who are
all asked to send copies to more people.

chain mail noun
a flexible armour made of linked metal
rings.

chain reaction noun
1 Chemistry a reaction which produces
substances that take a further part in the
reaction, the rate of which rapidly
increases. Most gaseous explosions are
chain reactions.
2 any series of reactions caused by a single
event.

chainsaw noun
a portable saw consisting of a continuous
turning loop of chain with teeth set on it,
powered by a small motor.

chain-smoke *verb*
to smoke cigarettes, etc. continually.
Word Family **chain-smoker** *noun*.

chain store *noun*
any of a group of shops owned and
controlled by one company.

chair *noun*
1 a movable seat for one person, usually
with four legs and a support for the back.
2 a person who presides over business at a
meeting: *Please direct your questions to the
chair.*
3 the position of a professor in a university.
Phrase **take the chair** to preside over a
meeting.
Word Family **chair** *verb* to preside over a
meeting.

chair lift *noun*
a series of seats hanging from a moving
overhead cable, used to take people up
and down a mountain, etc.

chairman *noun* (*plural* **chairmen**)
1 a chairperson, especially a male one.
2 the chief executive of a company.
Word Family **chairmanship** *noun* the
position or period in office of a chairman.

chairperson *noun*
a person who presides over a meeting.

chairwoman *noun* (*plural* **chairwomen**)
a female chairperson.

chaise (shaze) *noun*
an open two-wheeled carriage with a
hood, pulled by a horse.
[French]

chaise longue (shaze long) *noun*
a chair with a long seat which serves as a
full-length leg rest.
[French]

chalcedony (kal-sed-a-nee) *noun*
Geology any of a group of minerals
composed of very fine quartz crystals.
[Greek *khalkedon*]

chalet (shall-ay) *noun*
a building, often wooden, with a wide
gently sloped overhanging roof, common
in Switzerland and other alpine regions.
[Swiss-French]

chalice (chall-iss) *noun*
1 *Christianity* a sacred vessel like a large
goblet, used in religious services to hold
Communion wine.
2 a poetic word for a drinking cup.
[Latin *calix* cup]

chalk (*rhymes with* walk) *noun*
1 *Geology* a soft white fine-grained
limestone, composed of minute fossils.

2 a piece of this substance, used for writing
or drawing.
• **chalk** *verb* to mark or write with chalk.
Phrases **chalk up** to score or record.
chalk up to to think of something as the
result of: *OK, so you've lost a lot of money,
but you'll just have to chalk it up to
experience.*
Word Family **chalky** *adjective* (**chalkier**;
chalkiest) having the colour or texture of
chalk; **chalkiness** *noun*.
[Latin *calx* lime]

challenge *noun*
1 an invitation to engage in a contest: *He
issued a challenge to his rival.*
2 a call or demand to explain, identify
oneself, etc.: *The sentry shouted a challenge
to the approaching group.*
3 a test of one's strength or ability: *This
work presents a real challenge.*
4 questioning and doubt: *their challenge to
the authority of the school.*
Word Family **challenge** *verb*;
challenging *adjective*.

challenged *adjective*
a more positive term for disabled or
handicapped: *visually challenged.*

> The use of **challenged** is part of the
> modern trend towards being more
> sensitive about language and thinking
> about how people feel about which
> words are applied to them. *Challenged* is
> usually preceded by an adverb
> indicating the nature of the challenge,
> e.g. *visually challenged, mentally
> challenged* and *physically challenged.*

challenger *noun*
a person or team playing against an official
champion, hoping to win the title.

chamber (chame-ber) *noun*
1 an old word for a room, especially a
bedroom.
2 a legislative, judicial or administrative
body: *The House of Commons is the lower
chamber of the British Parliament.*
3 a compartment or enclosed space: *the
chambers of the heart.*
4 the part of a rifle or revolver which takes
the cartridge.
5 (**chambers**) *Law* the rooms attached to
a courthouse where judges carry out legal
business which need not be done in court.
[Greek *kamara* a (vaulted) room]

chamberlain (chame-ber-lin) *noun*
a high official in the court of a monarch.

chambermaid *noun*
a woman employed to clean bedrooms in hotels, etc.

chamber music *noun*
any music composed for a small group of instruments, originally for performance in a private home or small concert hall.

chamber of commerce *noun*
an association of business people for the protection and promotion of commerce.

chamber pot *noun*
a portable bowl used in bedrooms instead of a toilet.

chameleon (ka-**mee**-li-an) *noun*
1 any of various slow-moving tree-dwelling lizards which are able to change colour to blend with their surroundings.
2 a person who is changeable or fickle.
[Greek *khamai* ground + *leon* lion]

chamois *noun* (*plural* **chamois**)
1 (**sham**-wah) an antelope found in the mountains of Europe and Asia.
2 (**sham**-ee) short form of **chamois leather** a soft leather used for cleaning, etc.

champ *verb*
to bite on or munch.
Phrase **champ at the bit** to show restless impatience.

champagne (sham-**pane**) *noun*
a sparkling white wine which is fermented in the bottle.
[made in *Champagne*, France]

champion *noun*
1 a person or thing that wins first prize or takes first place in a competition.
2 a person who supports or defends an important cause: *She is well known as a champion of free speech.*
Word Family **champion** *verb* to support or defend; **champion** *adjective* 1 being first or best of all competitors. 2 (*informal*) excellent.
[Latin *campio* a fighter on a battlefield]

championship *noun*
1 the position or honour of being a champion.
2 a competition to decide who will be champion.
3 defence or support of an idea.

chance (*rhymes with* dance) *noun*
1 the random or unexpected nature of events: *Their careful preparations left nothing to chance.*
2 a possibility: *There's a good chance he'll be at the party.*

3 an opportunity: *This is your chance to prove yourself.*
4 a risk: *I'm not taking any chances!*
Phrase **on the off chance** (*informal*) in case one might be lucky: *I didn't expect her to phone, but I waited in on the off chance.*
Word Family **chance** *verb* 1 to do something or happen by chance: *I chanced to see him the very next day.* 2 to attempt or risk: *In spite of my warning he said he would chance it;* **chance on** to find by accident; **chancy** *adjective* (**chancier; chanciest**) risky or uncertain.

chancel (**chahn**-s'l *or* **chan**-s'l) *noun*
the part of a church near the altar, set aside for the clergy and choir.

chancellor (**chahn**-s'l-a *or* **chan**-s'l-a) *noun*
1 a title for various high officials.
2 the honorary head of a university who has few official duties.
3 in some countries, e.g. Germany, the equivalent of prime minister.
Word Family **chancellorship** *noun.*

chandelier (shand-a-**leer**) *noun*
an ornamental support for two or more lights, which hangs from a ceiling.
[French *chandelle* candle]

chandler *noun*
1 (*formerly*) a person who made or sold candles, soap, etc.
2 a dealer in special types of goods, such as the rope, tackle, etc. for a ship.

change *verb*
1 to make or become different.
2 to exchange: *Will you change places with me?*
3 to put on different clothes.
4 to get on a different vehicle: *If you get the 8.40 train you have to change at Bristol.*
• **change** *noun*
1 the act of changing.
2 anything which is changed or different.
3 any money returned when the amount given is greater than necessary.
4 also **small change** any money in the form of coins as distinct from banknotes.
5 (*informal*) the menopause.
Word Family **changeable** *adjective* liable to change.

changeling *noun*
a child who is exchanged or substituted secretly for another, traditionally by fairies.

change of life ⇨ MENOPAUSE.

changeover *noun*
the changing of one system, position, etc. for another.

channel *noun*
1 a passage or stretch of water.
2 the deeper part of a waterway such as a river or harbour.
3 any passage through which something is carried or directed.
4 (*usually* **channels**) a system by which something is done: *You must make your request through the proper channels.*
5 the waveband used by a particular transmitter, television or radio station.
• **channel** *verb* (**channels; channelling; channelled**)
1 to form or cut a channel in.
2 to direct: *When she left, he channelled his energies into pig farming.*
[Latin *canalis* canal]

chant *noun*
1 the music to accompany the singing of psalms.
2 a monotonous singsong speaking voice.
• **chant** *verb*
1 to sing.
2 to speak in a singsong manner: *The crowd chanted 'we want jobs' for about an hour.*
[Latin *cantare* to sing]

Chanukkah ⇨ HANUKKAH.

chaos (**kay**-os) *noun*
total confusion or disorder.
Word Family **chaotic** (kay-**ott**-ik) *adjective*; **chaotically** *adverb*.
[Greek *khaos* a void or chasm]

chap¹ *verb* (**chaps; chapping; chapped**)
(of skin, hands, etc.) to become cracked, split or roughened as a result of cold or exposure.

chap² *noun*
(*informal*) a man.
[from *chapman*, an old word for a hawker or pedlar]

chapatti (cha-**pat**-ee) *noun*
a thin cooked pancake, in Indian cooking.
[Hindi]

chapel *noun*
1 a room or building, other than a church, used for worship.
2 a section of a large church or cathedral which has its own altar.
3 a service held in such a place.

chapel of rest *noun*
a place where a dead body lies before a funeral.

chaperone (**shap**-a-rone) *noun* also **chaperon**
an older person in charge of a young unmarried woman or unmarried couples.
Word Family **chaperone** *verb*.

chaplain (**chap**-lin) *noun*
Christianity a clergyman looking after the religious needs of an institution, such as a school, hospital or regiment.
Word Family **chaplaincy** *noun*.

chaps *plural noun*
American strong leather protective trousers with no seat, worn by cowboys, etc. when riding.

chapter *noun*
1 a section of a book.
2 a branch of a society.
3 *Religion* a meeting of monks or of the canons of a cathedral.
Phrase **chapter and verse** an exact reference or source of a piece of information.

char¹ *verb* (**chars; charring; charred**)
1 to reduce to black carbon because of incomplete burning.
2 to scorch.

char² *noun*
any of various fish related to the trout.

char³ *noun*
(*informal*) a charwoman.

charabanc (**sharr**-a-bang) *noun*
an open four-wheeled carriage with bench seats.
[French *char carriage* + *à bancs* with chairs]

character (**karr**-ik-ta) *noun*
1 the combination of qualities which distinguishes an individual, thing, or group: *It is not in his character to be dishonest.* □ *Their house is nice, but it lacks character.*
2 the quality of moral strength or integrity: *Some schools place great emphasis on building character.*
3 a person portrayed in a novel, play, film, etc.
4 (*informal*) a person, especially an odd person: *Our postman is a real character.*
5 a symbol or letter used in writing or printing: *Chinese characters.*
Word Family **characterless** *adjective*.
[Greek *kharakter* a seal or its impression]

characteristic (karr-ik-ta-**rist**-ik) *noun*
a distinguishing feature: *Being aggressive seems to be a characteristic of drunken drivers.*

Word Family **characteristic** *adjective*
typical: *With characteristic modesty, he gave
them all the credit;* **characteristically**
adverb.

characterize, characterise (karr-ik-ta-
rize) *verb*
1 to distinguish or mark: *His work is
characterized by attention to detail.*
2 to describe the qualities or
characteristics of.
Word Family **characterization (karr**-ik-
ta-rie-**zay**-sh'n) *noun* the dramatizing of
character: *Her last novel had an ingenious
plot but poor characterization.*

charade (sha-**rahd**) *noun*
1 something which is pointless or
deceptive.
2 (**charades**) a game in which certain
players mime a word or phrase which
others try to guess.

charcoal *noun*
1 black impure carbon which remains after
the incomplete burning of plant or animal
tissue. Being porous, it is often used for
filters, etc.
2 charred willow used for drawing: *a stick
of charcoal.*

charge (*rhymes with* large) *verb*
1 to ask as payment: *They charge very high
prices for all their meat.*
2 to record as a debt to be paid: *Please
charge it to my account.*
3 to attack by rushing forward: *The bull
charged him.*
4 to accuse formally: *He was charged with
assault.*
5 to command or instruct: *He charged me to
stay until help arrived.*
6 to fill or supply: *Her words were charged
with meaning.* □ *Please charge your glasses.*
7 to fill with electricity: *charging her car
battery.*
• **charge** *noun*
1 the price for a service: *There's no delivery
charge.*
2 the act of charging: *a cavalry charge.*
3 any person or thing in the care of
another: *The teacher and her charges
crowded into the museum.*
4 an official accusation: *arrested on a charge
of assault.*
5 an explosive.
6 ⇨ ELECTRIC CHARGE.
7 a strong emotion.
8 an order.
Phrases **in charge** in command: *Who's in
charge here?* **reverse the charges** to get

the person who receives a telephone call to
pay for it.
Word Family **chargeable** *adjective* **1** that
must be paid. **2** that can be officially acted
on: *a chargeable offence.*
[Latin *carricare* load]

charge card *noun*
a card issued by shops to enable customers
to obtain goods and pay later.

chargé d'affaires (shar-*zh*ay da-**fair**)
(*plural* **chargés d'affaires**)
Politics an official who replaces an
ambassador when he or she is away.
[French *chargé* entrusted + *d'affaires* with
affairs]

charger (char-ja) *noun*
1 a cavalry horse.
2 an apparatus used for charging batteries.

chargrill *verb*
to grill quickly at a high heat.

charily *adverb* ⇨ CHARY.

chariness *noun* ⇨ CHARY.

chariot *noun*
an open two-wheeled carriage pulled by
horses and formerly used in wars, racing,
etc.
Word Family **charioteer** *noun* the driver
of a chariot.

charisma (ka-**riz**-ma) *noun*
a special quality or power to attract people
and inspire their devotion.
Word Family **charismatic (karr**-iz-**mat**-
ik) *adjective* **1** having or showing charisma.
2 denoting a modern movement within the
Christian Church which emphasizes
spiritual gifts such as healing or speaking
with tongues.
[Greek, a divine gift]

charity (charr-i-tee) *noun* (*plural*
charities)
1 the helping of poor or underprivileged
people.
2 an organization or fund set up for this
purpose.
3 a loving kindness towards others.
Word Family **charitable** *adjective*
concerned with or showing charity;
charitably *adverb;* **charitableness** *noun.*
[Latin *caritas* dearness]

charity shop *noun*
a shop that sells mainly second-hand items
to raise money for a charity.

charlady *noun* (*plural* **charladies**)
⇨ CHARWOMAN.

charlatan (shar-la-t'n) *noun*
an impostor or fake.

charleston (**charl**-st'n) *noun*
a very lively dance that was popular in the
1920s.
[from *Charleston*, an American city where
the dance first began]

charlie *noun*
(*informal*) a fool.

charm *noun*
1 a magic formula or spell.
2 any object worn or carried because it is
believed to have magic powers.
3 a trinket worn on a bracelet.
4 the power or quality of attracting or
pleasing: *a man of great charm.*
Phrase **work like a charm** to work
successfully or perfectly.
Word Family **charm** *verb* 1 to act on
with magic. 2 to please or attract greatly;
charming *adjective* delightful;
charmingly *adverb*; **charmer** *noun*
(*informal*) a person who charms.

charnel house *noun*
(*formerly*) a place where the bodies or
bones of the dead were kept.

chart *noun*
1 a sheet or record showing special
information, variations, etc. in a diagram
or table: *a weather chart.*
2 *Geography, Nautical* a map showing sea-
depth and coastal outlines.
3 (**charts**) a list of the most popular songs
played on the radio, etc.
• **chart** *verb* to make a map or chart of.
[Latin *charta* a writing]

charter *noun*
1 any written or printed statement of
rights, permission, etc. granted by a ruler
or government.
2 the leasing or hiring of a vehicle,
especially an aeroplane or boat.
Word Family **charter** *verb* to hire or
lease; **chartered** *adjective* qualified as a
member of a professional organization: *a
chartered accountant.*

charter flight *noun*
a flight in a plane on which travel
companies have booked all the seats.

chartreuse (shah-**trerz**) *noun*
a pale green or yellow liqueur.
[first made at *La Grande Chartreuse*, a
French monastery]

charwoman *noun* (*plural* **charwomen**)
also called **charlady**.
a woman employed to do cleaning.

chary (**chair**-ee) *adjective* (**charier;
chariest**)
cautious or wary.
Word Family **charily** *adverb*; **chariness**
noun.

chase *verb*
to pursue, especially in order to chase or
overtake.
• **chase** *noun*
1 the act of chasing or hunting.
2 any private land on which animals to be
hunted are kept.
Phrase **give chase** to set out in pursuit.

chaser *noun*
(*informal*) a drink of alcohol taken after a
weaker or stronger drink.

chasm (**ka**-z'm) *noun*
1 a gorge or any deep opening in the
earth's surface.
2 a very great difference between people.
[Greek *khasma*]

chassis (**shass**-ee) *noun* (*plural* **chassis**)
(**shass**-eez)
the frame of a motor vehicle on which the
body, wheels and other fittings are
mounted.
[French]

chaste (chayst) *adjective*
1 not having sexual intercourse outside
marriage.
2 restrained and simple in style.
Word Family **chastity** (**chas**-ti-tee) *noun*
the quality of being chaste; **chastely**
adverb.
[Latin *castus* pure]

chasten (**chay**-s'n) *verb*
1 to have the effect of making someone
feel rather ashamed, less confident, etc.
2 an old word for **punish**.

chastise (chast-**ize**) *verb*
1 to criticize severely or reproach.
2 (*dated*) to punish, usually by beating.
Word Family **chastisement** *noun*.

chastity belt *noun*
a belt with a lock or device to prevent
sexual intercourse, which women in the
Middle Ages were sometimes forced to
wear while their husbands were away.

chat¹ *verb* (**chats; chatting; chatted**)
to talk casually or lightly.
Phrase **chat up** (*informal*) to talk
flirtingly or persuasively with.
• **chat** *noun* an informal conversation.

chat[2] *noun*
a European bird related to the thrush.

chateau (sha-toe) *noun* (*plural* **chateaux** (sha-toe *or* sha-toze) or **chateaus** (sha-toze))
a French castle or large country house.
[French]

chatline *noun*
a system which allows a lot of people to talk to each other on the telephone at the same time.

chat room *noun*
an area on the Internet where people can have a conversation or discussion.

chat show *noun*
a radio or television programme in which celebrities are interviewed informally.

chattel *noun*
(*usually* **chattels**) a personal possession, usually movable, as distinct from land and buildings.
[Old French *chatel* cattle]

chatter *verb*
1 to talk rapidly, especially in a very casual or silly manner.
2 to utter short inarticulate sounds: *Squirrels chattered in the trees.*
3 to click together rapidly: *His teeth chattered with cold.*
Word Family **chatter** *noun*; **chatterbox**, **chatterer** *noun* a person who is very talkative; **chatty** *adjective* (**chattier**; **chattiest**) informal or conversational; **chattily** *adverb*.

chattering classes *plural noun*
(*informal*) people who consider themselves articulate, well-informed and able to express views on social, political and topical issues.

chat-up line *noun*
something said in order to try to start a relationship with a person one is interested in as a boyfriend or girlfriend.

chauffeur (sho-fa) *noun*
a person employed to drive a car.
• **chauffeur** *verb* to act as a chauffeur for.
[French, stoker]

chauvinism (sho-va-nizm) *noun*
1 an extreme or unthinking enthusiasm for the military glory of one's country.
2 an excessive loyalty to or belief in the superiority of a cause: *male chauvinism.*
Word Family **chauvinist** *noun*; **chauvinistic** (sho-va-**nist**-ik) *adjective*; **chauvinistically** *adverb*.

The word **chauvinism** is now most commonly found describing the kind of disregard of women's rights held by some men. *Chauvinism* actually means 'an exaggerated belief in the superiority of any group to which one belongs'. In the case of *male chauvinism* the group is the male sex. *Chauvinism* originally meant 'extreme patriotism', particularly in a military context. It takes its name from Nicholas Chauvin, a French soldier in Napoleon's campaigns who was noted for his blind patriotism towards France and his excessive admiration for Napoleon's achievements.

cheap *adjective*
1 costing a relatively low amount: *Strawberries are cheap at the moment.*
2 not costing much and not of good quality: *If you want the dress to hang properly, don't use cheap material.*
3 unpleasant and mean: *That was a cheap trick!*
Word Family **cheaply** *adverb*; **cheapness** *noun*; **cheapskate** *noun* (*informal*) a person who is stingy.
[Old English *ceap* barter]

cheapen *verb*
1 to make cheap or cheaper.
2 to cause to be treated with contempt.

cheat *verb*
to act deceitfully or dishonestly to gain something.
• **cheat** *noun*
1 a person who cheats.
2 an act of cheating.

check *verb*
1 to investigate or establish the correctness of: *Add up these figures and then check the total.*
2 to stop or control: *He was going to say something, but checked himself.*
3 to be accurate: *Her story checks with the facts.*
4 *Chess* to directly threaten an opponent's king.
Phrases **check in** to arrive at a hotel, etc. and register. **check off** to mark as correct: *He checked off the listed items one by one.* **check out** 1 to pay the bill at a hotel, etc. and leave. 2 (*informal*) to visit or look at in order to inspect or find out about: *Let's go and check out that new coffee bar.*
• **check** *noun*
1 any method or device for examining accuracy, correctness, etc.: *New products undergo a number of checks.*

2 control: *You must keep your temper in check.*

3 a pattern consisting of squares, e.g. those on a chessboard.

4 *Chess* a situation in which a king is directly threatened by an opposing piece.

5 *American* a cheque.

6 *American* a tick showing that something is correct or has been selected.

7 *American* a bill in a restaurant, etc.

Word Family **check, checked** *adjective* having a pattern of small squares.

checkers *plural noun*
American draughts.

checking procedures *plural noun*
checks put in place during production to make sure everything works properly.

checkmate *noun*
1 short form is **mate** *Chess* the winning move, in which the opponent's king is prevented from making any move to escape a check.

2 any complete or total defeat.

Word Family **checkmate** *verb*.

[Persian *shah* the king + *mat* is dead]

checkout *noun*
the exit desk of a large store, usually a supermarket, where a customer's purchases are paid for.

checkpoint *noun*
a point where traffic or competitors are stopped for inspection, etc.

check-up *noun*
(*informal*) a thorough examination, especially a regular medical examination.

cheddar *noun*
a firm English cheese.

[originally made in *Cheddar* in Somerset]

cheek *noun*
1 *Anatomy* the side of the face below the eye.

2 *Anatomy* a buttock.

3 insolent or impudent behaviour.

Phrase **cheek by jowl** side by side.

Word Family **cheeky** *adjective*
(**cheekier; cheekiest**) impudent; **cheekily** *adverb*; **cheekiness** *noun*.

cheep *verb*
to make a faint chirping like a young bird.
• **cheep** *noun*.

cheer *verb*
1 to shout out encouragement or approval.

2 to fill with hope: *She was cheered by the good news.*

Phrase **cheer up** to make or become happier: *The party will cheer you up.*

Word Family **cheer** *noun* **1** a shout of approval, etc. **2** a happy feeling; **cheerful** *adjective* in good spirits; **cheerfully** *adverb*; **cheerfulness** *noun*; **cheerless** *adjective* miserable or mournful; **cheerlessly** *adverb*; **cheerlessness** *noun*.

cheerio *noun, interjection*
(*informal*) goodbye.

cheerleader *noun*
a member of a group of people who perform organized cheering for their team, university, etc.

cheers *interjection*
1 (as a toast) to your health! all the best!

2 (*informal*) thank you or goodbye.

cheery *adjective* (**cheerier; cheeriest**)
bright and cheerful.

Word Family **cheerily** *adverb*; **cheeriness** *noun*.

cheese (cheez) *noun*
any of various solid foods made from milk: *cream cheese.* □ *cottage cheese.*

Phrases **hard cheese** (*dated*) bad luck!

say cheese (*informal*) to smile for a photograph.

[Latin *caseus*]

cheesecake *noun*
a cake made using soft cheese, topped with fruit, toffee, etc.

cheesecloth *noun*
a loosely woven fabric, formerly used in cheese-making.

cheesed off *adjective*
1 (*informal*) bored.

2 (*informal*) angry or disgusted.

cheese straw *noun*
a long thin piece of pastry flavoured with cheese.

cheetah (chee-ta) *noun*
a long-legged mammal of the cat family, living in Africa and Asia. It is the fastest land animal.

[Sanskrit *chitra* spot]

chef (shef) *noun*
a cook, especially the head cook in a restaurant.

[French, chief]

chemical (kem-i-k'l) *adjective*
of or relating to the science or processes of chemistry.

Word Family **chemical** *noun* any substance used or produced in a chemical process; **chemically** *adverb*.

chemical engineering *noun*
the study and development of the applications of chemistry to industrial processes.

chemical etching *noun*
a method of producing electronic circuit boards by the controlled dissolving of copper.

chemical formula ⇨ FORMULA (definition 3).

chemical warfare *noun*
any warfare using chemical weapons other than explosives, especially poisonous gases, irritants, etc.

chemise (sh'-**meez**) *noun*
a woman's loose undergarment.

chemist (**kem**-ist) *noun*
1 a scientist who specializes in chemistry.
2 a pharmacist.
3 a pharmacy.

chemistry (**kem**-i-stree) *noun*
the study of the composition of substances and their effect upon each other.
[Greek *khemia* the (Egyptian) art of transmuting metals (alchemy)]

chemotherapy
(kee-mo-**therr**-a-pee) *noun*
the treatment of disease, especially cancer, using chemicals.

chenille (sh'-**neel**) *noun*
a fabric with a cut pile on both sides and velvety or woolly lines or ridges.
[French, hairy caterpillar]

cheque (chek) *noun* (*American* **check**)
a written order, usually on a printed form, directing a bank to pay a specific amount from a person's account.
Word Family **chequebook** *noun* a booklet containing a series of cheques.

cheque card *noun*
a stiff plastic card issued by banks as a guarantee of cheques written by their clients.

chequered *adjective*
1 having a pattern of squares.
2 varied or eventful.

chequers (**chek**-erz) *plural noun*
1 a pattern of squares or checks.
2 ⇨ CHINESE CHEQUERS.

cherish *verb*
1 to love or care for tenderly: *The old lady cherished her few possessions.*
2 to keep firmly in one's mind: *cherished memories.*
[French *cher* dear]

cheroot (sha-**root**) *noun*
a thin cigar with open ends.
[Tamil]

cherry *noun* (*plural* **cherries**)
1 a small round juicy red fruit with a small stone.
2 the wood of the tree on which it grows.
3 a bright purplish-red colour.
● **cherry** *adjective*.

cherub (**cherr**-ub) *noun* (*plural* **cherubs**)
1 (*plural* **cherubim** or **cherubs**) an angel, often pictured as a chubby-faced child with wings.
2 a well-behaved child.
Word Family **cherubic** (cher-**roo**-bik) *adjective*.

chess *noun*
a game played by two players on a square **chessboard** with 64 alternately light and dark squares. Each player has 16 **chessmen**: a king and queen, two bishops, two knights, two rooks and eight pawns; they are moved according to specific rules with the aim of checkmating the opponent's king.

chest *noun*
1 *Anatomy* the upper front part of the body, between the neck and the abdomen.
2 a box with a hinged or detachable lid, used for storing things.
Phrase **get something off one's chest** (*informal*) to confess or tell of a worry.
Word Family **chesty** *adjective* (**chestier; chestiest**) suffering from or showing a disease of the chest: *a chesty cough*; **chestiness** *noun*.

chestnut *noun*
1 a large edible nut growing on trees.
2 the tree on which this nut grows, or its wood.
3 a coppery-brown horse.
4 a coppery-brown colour.
5 also **old chestnut** (*informal*) an old joke.
[Greek *kastanea*]

chest of drawers *noun* (*plural* **chests of drawers**)
a piece of furniture with drawers, for storing clothes, etc.

chevron (**shev**-r'n) *noun*
a V-shaped stripe worn on the sleeve of a uniform to indicate non-commissioned rank.

chew *verb*
to crush or grind with the teeth.
Phrase **chew over** to consider or ponder.
Word Family **chew** *noun* 1 the act of chewing. 2 anything which is chewed or

for chewing, such as a sweet; **chewy**
adjective (**chewier; chewiest**) which can
be or needs to be chewed: *a chewy piece of
meat;* **chewiness** *noun.*

chewing gum *noun*
a sweet which can be chewed for a long
time without dissolving in the mouth.

chic (sheek *or* shik) *adjective*
elegant and stylish, especially in dress.
[French]

chick *noun*
1 a young bird, especially a young chicken.
2 (*informal*) a young woman. This term is
often considered offensive to women.

chicken *noun*
1 the common domestic fowl.
2 the meat of this bird.
3 (*informal*) a coward.
• **chicken** *verb*
Phrase **chicken out** (*informal*) to lose
one's nerve.

chicken feed *noun*
(*informal*) an insignificant amount of
money.

chickenpox *noun*
a highly contagious disease causing small
blisters, most common among children.

chickpea *noun*
a large yellow edible pea-like seed.

chickweed *noun*
a common weed with small white star-
shaped flowers.

chicory (chick-a-ree) *noun*
a herb whose leaves are used in salads and
whose root is used as a coffee substitute.
[Greek *kikhorion*]

chide *verb* (**chides, chiding; chided** *or*
chid; chided *or* **chidden**)
to scold or rebuke.

chief (cheef) *noun*
the head or ruler of a group.
Word Family **chief** *adjective* highest in
rank or importance: *our chief complaint.*
□ *the chief priest;* **chiefly** *adverb* to the
greatest degree or extent.

chief petty officer *noun*
Navy a non-commissioned officer ranking
between petty officer and warrant officer.

chieftain (cheef-t'n) *noun*
the leader of a clan or tribe.

chiffon (shiff-on) *noun*
a thin sheer fabric made from silk, nylon
or rayon.
[French]

chignon (sheen-yon) *noun*
a hairstyle in which long hair is arranged
in a roll at the back of the head.
[French, nape]

chihuahua (chi-wah-wah) *noun*
a very small dog with large pointed ears.
[originally from *Chihuahua*, Mexico]

chilblain *noun*
an inflamed swelling of the fingers, toes,
etc. caused by poor blood circulation in
cold weather.

child *noun* (*plural* **children**)
1 any young person.
2 a son or daughter.
Phrase **with child** (*dated*) pregnant.
Word Family **childless** *adjective.*

child abuse *noun*
treating a child badly, especially through
physical injury or sexual interference.

child benefit *noun*
money given to parents by the government
for each of their children.

childbirth *noun*
the act of giving birth to a child.

childhood *noun*
the state or time of being a child.
Phrase **second childhood** a state of
foolishness in old age.

childish *adjective*
1 like that of a child: *her childish voice.*
2 immature: *his childish behaviour.*
Word Family **childishly** *adverb;*
childishness *noun.*

childlike *adjective*
having the innocence, openness or
freshness of a child.

childminder *noun*
a person who is paid to look after children
while their parents are at work, etc.

childproof *adjective*
not able to be opened or used by a child:
childproof medicine bottles

children
the plural of **child**.

child's play *noun*
a very easy task.

chill *noun*
1 a sensation of cold: *There's a bit of a chill
in the air.*
Figurative News of the crash cast a chill
over the meeting.
2 a fever preceded by shivering.
• **chill** *verb* to make or become cold: *Chill
the wine before serving.*

Phrase chill out (*informal*) to relax or calm down.
• **chill** *adjective* cold enough to make one shiver.
Word Family chilling *adjective* frightening; **chillingly** *adverb*; **chilly** *adjective* (**chillier; chilliest**); **chilliness** *noun*.

chilli *noun* (*plural* **chillies**)
a hot spice made from the pod of a variety of pepper.

chime *noun*
1 a bell or device which creates a ringing musical sound: *a door chime*.
2 a tuned set of bells.
• **chime** *verb* to ring bells or to make the sound of bells.

chimera (kie-**meer**-a) *noun* also **chimaera**
an unreal or fanciful idea or image.
[after *Chimaera*, a monster in Greek mythology]

chimney (**chim**-nee) *noun*
1 an upright hollow structure which carries away smoke from a fire by creating a draught.
2 a glass tube for enclosing the flame of a lamp.
[Greek *kaminos* furnace]

chimney piece *noun*
a mantelpiece.

chimney stack *noun*
a group of chimneys built as one unit on a roof.

chimney sweep *noun*
a person employed to clean out chimneys.

chimpanzee *noun*
short form is **chimp** an African ape noted for its intelligence.
[Bantu]

chin *noun*
Anatomy the lower part of the face, below the mouth.
Phrase **keep one's chin up** to remain cheerful, especially under stress.

china *noun*
1 a type of pottery which is hard and non-porous, made by firing clay at high temperatures.
2 cups, plates, etc. made from this.

chinchilla *noun*
1 a small squirrel-like mammal found in the mountains of South America.
2 the fur of this animal.

Chinese chequers *plural noun*
(*used with singular verb*) a game played with pegs or marbles on a board with holes.

chink[1] *noun*
a small crack or opening.

chink[2] *verb*
to make a short sharp ringing or metallic sound.
• **chink** *noun*.

chinos (**chee**-noze) *plural noun*
trousers made from a very strong cotton.

chintz *noun*
a glazed cotton fabric with printed flowery designs, used for curtains and loose covers on furniture.
[Hindi *chint* stain]

chip *noun*
1 a small piece or slice, usually broken or cut from something larger: *wood chips*.
2 a mark caused by breaking off a small piece: *This cup has a chip in it*.
3 a long thin piece of fried potato.
4 ⇨ MICROCHIP.
5 a small disc or counter used in certain card or gambling games.
6 *Sport* a short high shot or kick.
Phrases **a chip off the old block** a person who is very like one or both parents. **a chip on one's shoulder** a grudge or resentment.
• **chip** *verb* (**chips; chipping; chipped**)
1 to remove a chip or chips from: *Be careful not to chip that plate*.
2 to hit or cut with short strokes.
Phrase **chip in** 1 to contribute: *We all chipped in to buy the present*. 2 to interrupt.

chipboard *noun*
a material made of sawdust, wood scraps or similar material pressed into sheets and used for boxes, furniture, etc.

chipmunk *noun*
a squirrel-like mammal with a striped back, found in North America.

chipolata *noun*
a thin sausage.
[Italian *cipollata* a dish of onions]

chippy *noun* (*plural* **chippies**) also **chippie**
1 (*informal*) a fish and chip shop.
2 (*informal*) a carpenter.

chiropody (ki-**rop**-a-dee) *noun*
the treatment of minor foot complaints, such as corns.
Word Family chiropodist *noun*.
[Greek *kheir* hand + *podos* of a foot]

chiropractic (kie-ro-prak-tik) *noun*
a method of treating disease by
manipulating segments of the spinal
column.
Word Family **chiropractor** *noun*.
[Greek *kheir* hand + *praktikos* practical]

chirp *verb* also called **chirrup**.
to make a short high-pitched sound like a
bird.
Word Family **chirp** *noun*; **chirpy**
adjective (**chirpier; chirpiest**) (*informal*)
lively or chatty; **chirpily** *adverb*.

chisel (chizz-'l) *noun*
a tool with a finely sharpened edge at one
end, used for cutting and shaping.
• **chisel** *verb* (**chisels; chiselling;
chiselled**) to use or cut with a chisel.
Word Family **chiselled** *adjective* **1** cut
with a chisel. **2** clear-cut or well-shaped.

chit[1] *noun*
a note, especially a bill or account.

chit[2] *noun*
Phrase **chit of a girl** a young girl or
woman.

chit-chat *noun*
any casual or light-hearted conversation.

chivalry (shivv-'l-ree) *noun*
1 polite or courteous behaviour.
2 *Medieval history* the knightly system of
virtue, honour, courage, duty, etc.
Word Family **chivalrous** *adjective*;
chivalrously *adverb*, **chivalrousness**
noun.
[Old French *chevalerie*, from *cheval* horse]

chive *noun*
a plant related to the onion, used to add
flavour in cooking.

chivvy *verb* (**chivvies; chivvying;
chivvied**) also **chivy**
(*informal*) to encourage or nag into doing
something.

chlorinate (klorr-i-nate) *verb*
to combine or treat with chlorine,
especially to disinfect water.
Word Family **chlorination** (klorr-i-nay-
sh'n) *noun*.

chlorine (klaw-reen) *noun*
a poisonous greenish-yellow gas with a
choking irritating smell, used as a bleach
and to purify water. ⇨ HALOGEN.
[Greek *khloros* green]

chlorofluorocarbon *noun*
short form is **CFC** one of a number of
chemical compounds released into the
atmosphere through the use of

refrigerators, aerosols, etc. and considered
to be harmful to the ozone layer.
[CHLOR(ine) + *o* + FLUOR(ine) + *o* +
CARBON]

chloroform (klorr-a-form) *noun*
a colourless liquid with a strong smell,
used as an anaesthetic and a solvent.

chlorophyll (klorr-a-fil) *noun*
Biology the green pigment, found in most
plants, which traps energy from sunlight
and makes photosynthesis possible.
[Greek *khloros* green + *phyllon* leaf]

chloroplast (klorr-a-plast) *noun*
Biology an organelle found in plant cells
which undergoes photosynthesis.
Chloroplasts contain the pigment
chlorophyll.

chock *noun*
1 a block of wood or other material used as
a wedge to prevent movement of a door,
furniture, etc.
2 *Nautical* a heavy fitting through which a
rope, etc. can be passed.

chock-a-block *adverb*
(*informal*) tightly packed or filled.

chock-full *adjective*
(*informal*) tightly packed or filled.

chocoholic *noun* also **chocaholic**
a person who is addicted to chocolate.
[CHOC(olate) + *-oholic*]

chocolate (chok-lit) *noun*
1 a sweet or flavouring made from cacao.
2 a dark brown colour.
Word Family **chocolate** *adjective*
[Aztec *chocolatl*]

choice (*rhymes with* voice) *noun*
1 the act of choosing: *The choice between the
two candidates was very difficult.*
2 anything which is chosen: *That was a
good choice.*
3 the power or right to choose: *freedom of
choice.*
4 a variety of things from which to choose:
a college offering a wide choice of subjects.
Word Family **choice** *adjective* **1** excellent
or fine. **2** carefully selected.

choir (kwire) *noun*
1 a group of singers, e.g. in a church.
2 the part of a church between the nave
and the altar, set aside for the choir.

choke *verb*
1 to stop or cause to stop breathing by
pressing on or blocking the throat: *This
collar is choking me!*
Figurative He choked back a sob.

2 to fill completely: *The garden is choked with weeds.*
• **choke** *noun*
1 a device which increases the proportion of fuel to air entering an internal-combustion engine.
2 the act or sound of choking.

cholera (**koll-**'r-a) *noun*
an often fatal bacterial disease causing severe vomiting and diarrhoea, spread by contaminated water.
[Greek *kholera*]

cholesterol (k'-**lest**-a-rol) *noun*
Biology a fatty substance found in some animal tissues, too much of which can damage one's heart.
[Greek *kholē* bile + *stereos* solid]

chomp *verb*
to munch noisily.

choose (chooz) *verb* (**chooses; choosing; chose; chosen**)
to decide on or take from a number of things.
Word Family **choosy** *adjective* (**choosier; choosiest**) fussy or difficult to please.

chop[1] *verb* (**chops; chopping; chopped**)
1 to cut with heavy strokes: *Chop the onions finely.*
2 *Sport* to hit the ball with a short downward stroke.
• **chop** *noun*
1 a cutting stroke or movement.
2 a small cut of lamb or pork containing a bone.
Phrase **get the chop** (*informal*) to be dismissed from a job.

chop[2] *verb* (**chops; chopping; chopped**)
Phrase **chop and change** to change repeatedly.

chopper *noun*
1 a person or thing that chops.
2 (*informal*) a helicopter.
3 (*informal*) a motorcycle with high handlebars.
4 (**choppers**) (*informal*) teeth.

choppy *adjective* (**choppier; choppiest**)
(of water, wind, etc.) forming short irregular waves or movements.
Word Family **choppiness** *noun*.

chops *plural noun*
(*informal*) the jaws.

chopsticks *plural noun*
a pair of fine sticks made of ivory, bamboo, etc. used to raise food to the mouth.
[Pidgin *chop* quick + STICKS]

chop suey (chop **soo**-ee) *noun*
a Chinese dish of chopped meat, rice and vegetables.
[Chinese, mixed bits]

choral (**kor**-al) *adjective*
of or sung by a choir or chorus.

chorale (kor-**rahl**) *noun*
Music a simple slow tune or hymn sung or played in harmony.

chord[1] (kord) *noun*
Maths a straight line joining two points on a curve.
[from CORD]

chord[2] *noun*
Music a group of three or more notes played together in harmony.
[from ACCORD]

> ! The words *chord* and *cord* sound the same but have different spellings and meanings. A *chord* is a straight line in maths or a group of notes in music; *cord* is strong thick string or ribbed fabric.

chore (chaw) *noun*
a small job considered to be boring, unpleasant, etc.

chorea (korr-**ee**-a) *noun* also called **St Vitus's dance**.
a disease in which there is uncontrolled involuntary movement of the limbs.
[Greek *khoreia* dance]

choreography (korr-i-**og**-ra-fee) *noun*
the art of composing, arranging or directing ballets and dance routines.
Word Family **choreographer** *noun*; **choreograph** (**korr**-i-o-grahf) *verb*.
[Greek *khoreia* dance + *graphein* to write]

chorister (**korr**-is-ta) *noun*
a singer in a choir.

chortle (**chaw**-t'l) *verb*
to chuckle and snort with glee.
• **chortle** *noun*.
[from CH(uck)LE + (sn)ORT, coined by Lewis Carroll in 1871]

chorus (**kaw**-rus) *noun* (*plural* **choruses**)
1 a song or part of a song which is sung by a number of singers.
2 a part of a song which is repeated at intervals.
3 *Theatre* a group of singers or dancers who perform together.
4 *Theatre* a performer or group of performers who comment on the action of a play.
• **chorus** *verb* to sing or speak in a chorus.
[Greek *khoros*]

chose the past tense of **choose**.

chosen the past participle of **choose**.

choux pastry (shoo **pay**-stri) *noun*
a light pastry made with an egg, used in
eclairs and profiteroles.
[French *chou* cabbage, round cream-filled
pastry].

chow mein (chow **mane**) *noun*
a Chinese dish of fried noodles, shredded
chicken and vegetables.
[Chinese, fried flower]

Christ *noun* also called **Jesus**.
a religious teacher, living in Israel about
2000 years ago, who preached universal
love; the central figure of Christian history
and devotion.
[Greek *khristos* anointed]

christen (**kriss**-'n) *verb*
1 to baptize.
2 to give a name to, especially at baptism.
3 (*informal*) to use for the first time: *Have
you christened that new skateboard yet?*
Word Family **christening** *noun*.
[Old English *cristnian* to make Christian]

Christendom (**kriss**-'n-d'm) *noun*
all Christian people or churches.

Christian (**kris**-ch'n) *adjective*
1 of or relating to Christ and the religion
based on his teachings.
2 kind or humane.
Word Family **Christian** *noun*;
Christianity (kris-ti-**ann**-i-tee) *noun* the
Christian religion or beliefs.

Christian name *noun*
a person's first name or names, as distinct
from his or her surname.

Christian Scientist *noun*
a member of a religious sect founded in
America in the 19th century by Mary
Baker Eddy, emphasizing the need for
pure goodness and believing that disease
can be cured by spiritual methods

Christmas (**kris**-mus) *noun* (*plural*
Christmases)
Christianity the annual festival celebrating
the birth of Christ.
Christmas Day the day of Christmas
celebrations, 25 December.
Christmas Eve the day and night before
Christmas Day.

chromatic (kro-**matt**-ik) *adjective*
of or relating to colour or colours.

chrome (krome) *noun*
something which is coated with
chromium.

chromium (**kro**-mee-um) *noun*
a hard metal used to make stainless steel
and for protective electroplating.
[Greek *khroma* colour, as lead chromates
are used in paint]

chromosome (**kro**-ma-soam) *noun*
Biology a thread-like body found in the
nuclei of most cells which carries the
genetic information needed to pass on
characteristics to the next generation.
[Greek *khroma* colour + *soma* body]

chronic (**kron**-ik) *adjective*
1 continuing or firmly established: *chronic
bronchitis*.
2 (*informal*) terrible.
Word Family **chronically** *adverb*.
[Greek *khronos* time]

chronic fatigue syndrome *noun* also
called **myalgic encephalomyelitis**.
Medicine a condition in which one feels
constantly tired and weak.

chronicle (**kron**-i-k'l) *noun*
a history or record of events in the order in
which they happened.
Word Family **chronicle** *verb*, **chronicler**
noun.
[Greek *khronika* annals]

chronological (kron-a-**loj**-i-k'l) *adjective*
arranged in the order of time.
Word Family **chronologically** *adverb*.

chronology (kr'-**noll**-i-jee) *noun* (*plural*
chronologies)
1 a record of the particular order of events
in time.
2 the science of establishing and fixing
historical dates.

chronometer (kr'-**nom**-i-ta) *noun*
a specially designed clock used in
navigation and other fields where precise
measurement of time is required.

chrysalis (**kriss**-a-lis) *noun* (*plural*
chrysalises) also called **chrysalid**.
the hard-shelled pupa of a butterfly or
moth.
[Greek *khrysallis* from *khrysos* gold]

chrysanthemum (kriz-**anth**-a-mum)
noun
any of a large group of plants with large
showy brightly-coloured flowers.
[Greek *khrysos* gold + *anthos* flower]

chub *noun*
a common freshwater fish related to the
carp.

chubby *adjective* (**chubbier; chubbiest**)
plump and rounded.
Word Family **chubbiness** *noun*.

chuck¹ *verb*
1 (*informal*) to throw.
2 (*informal*) to stop.
Phrases **chuck it down** (*informal*) to rain very heavily. **chuck under the chin** to pat or tap lightly under the chin.

chuck² *noun*
1 a cut of beef between the neck and the shoulder blade.
2 the part of a drill used to hold the bit.
3 a similar part of a lathe used to hold the object being turned.

chuckle *verb*
to laugh softly or to oneself.
• **chuckle** *noun*.

chuffed *adjective*
(*informal*) pleased or delighted.

chug *verb* (**chugs; chugging; chugged**)
1 to make a dull short repeated sound: *The boat's engine chugged away merrily.*
2 to move while making this sound: *A train chugged into sight.*
• **chug** *noun*.

chukka *noun* also **chukker**
any of the periods into which a polo match is divided.

chum *noun*
(*dated*) a close friend or companion.
Word Family **chummy** *adjective* (**chummier; chummiest**) very friendly; **chummily** *adverb*; **chumminess** *noun*.

chump *noun*
(*dated informal*) a silly person.

chump chop *noun*
a chop cut from the tail end of the loin.

chunk *noun*
a thick or large uneven piece.
Word Family **chunky** *adjective* (**chunkier; chunkiest**) 1 in a chunk or chunks. 2 thickset or stocky; **chunkiness** *noun*.

church *noun* (*plural* **churches**)
1 *Christianity* a building for public worship and services.
2 (**Church**) the whole community of believers or any branch within it: *the Presbyterian Church.*
• **church** *adjective* relating to religious or ecclesiastical matters.
[Greek *kyriakon* (house) of the Lord (*kyrios*)]

Church of England *noun* also called **Anglican Church**.
the national religion of England, with branches in other countries, which separated from the Roman Catholic Church in the 16th century, and which has both Catholic and Protestant characteristics.

church school *noun*
a school connected with the Church of England.

churchwarden *noun*
a person chosen by the people who go to a church to look after its property.

churchyard *noun*
the area next to a church, often used as a cemetery.

churlish *adjective*
1 bad-tempered.
2 rustic.
Word Family **churl** *noun* 1 a bad-tempered person. 2 an old word for a peasant; **churlishly** *adverb*; **churlishness** *noun*.

churn *noun*
1 a machine for agitating cream until butter is produced.
2 a large metal milk can.
• **churn** *verb* to stir or agitate violently, as when making butter.
Phrase **churn out** to produce in a routine way.

chute (shoot) *noun*
1 a sloping passage or channel for carrying things to a lower level.
2 (*informal*) a parachute.

chutney (chut-nee) *noun*
a thick spicy sauce made from mangoes and other fruit or vegetables.
[Hindi]

chutzpah (**huts**-pa) *noun*
great self-confidence and audacity.
[Yiddish]

ciabatta (ch'-**bah**-ta) *noun*
a flat Italian loaf of bread which is made using olive oil.

ciao (chow) *interjection*
(*informal*) an expression used as a greeting or a farewell.
[Italian]

cicada (si-**kah**-da) *noun*
an insect with long wings. The males produce a very long shrill noise after dark.
[Latin]

cicatrice (**sik**-a-treece) *noun*
also **cicatrix** (**sik**-a-triks) (*plural* **cicatrices**) (sik-a-**try**-seez)
the tissue forming over a wound and later becoming a scar.
[Latin *cicatrix*]

cider (**sigh**-da) *noun*
an alcoholic drink made from fermented apple juice.

cigar (si-**gar**) *noun*
a cylinder of rolled up tobacco leaves for smoking.
Phrase **close but no cigar** (*informal*) nearly correct or nearly successful.
[Spanish *cigarro*]

cigarette *noun*
a narrow cylinder of cut tobacco rolled in thin paper for smoking.
[French, little cigar]

cinch (sinch) *noun* (*plural* **cinches**)
(*informal*) anything which is easy or certain.

cinder (**sin**-da) *noun*
any burnt or partly burnt piece or particle.

cinema (**sin**-i-ma) *noun*
1 a public theatre in which films are shown on a screen.
2 the film industry.
Word Family **cinematic** (sin-i-**mat**-ik) *adjective*.
[Greek *kinema* motion]

cinematography (sin-i-ma-**tog**-ra-fee) *noun*
the art or process of making films.

cinnamon (**sin**-a-m'n) *noun*
1 a sweet spice made from the inner bark of some tropical trees, used in cooking and medicine.
2 a yellowish or reddish-brown colour.
[Greek *kinnamon*]

cipher (**sigh**-fer) *noun* also **cypher**
1 any method of secret writing, especially using codes or symbols.
2 any person or thing having no importance or influence.
3 the figure 0, representing nought.
[Arabic *sifr* empty]

circa (**sir**-ka) *preposition, adverb*
about or approximately.
[Latin]

circle (**sir**-k'l) *noun*
1 a closed round flat figure on which every point is always the same distance from the centre.
2 any object, arrangement, path, etc. in the shape of a circle or part of a circle.
3 a loosely connected group: *She has a strange circle of friends.*
Phrase **come full circle** to return to the original or first position.
• **circle** *verb*
1 to draw a circle around.
2 to move in or form a circle.
[Latin *circulus*]

circlet (**sir**-klit) *noun*
1 a small circle or ring.
2 a decorative band worn on the head, neck or arm.

circuit (**sir**-kit) *noun*
1 a circular line or path: *He ran five circuits of the track.*
2 *Electricity* any electrical network which has at least one closed path for the flow of current.
integrated circuit *Electronics* a complete circuit of many components etched on a minute silicon chip, and much smaller than a printed circuit.
printed circuit *Electronics* a circuit formed by printing or soldering it onto a surface instead of using wires.
Word Family **circuitry** *noun* any system of electrical circuits.

circuitous (sir-**kew**-it-us) *adjective*
indirect or roundabout: *circuitous reasoning.*
Word Family **circuitously** *adverb*; **circuitousness**, **circuity** *noun*.
[Latin *circuitus* a roundabout way]

circular (**sirk**-yoo-la) *adjective*
of, forming or moving in a circle.
Figurative a circular argument.
• **circular** *noun* a notice or letter which is sent to a number of people.
Word Family **circularity** (sirk-yoo-**larr**-i-tee) *noun*.

circular saw *noun*
a saw with a flat rotating disc, powered by electricity.

circulate (**sir**-kew-late) *verb*
1 to move in a circle or circuit.
2 to pass from place to place: *The rumour circulated rapidly in the small town.*
Word Family **circulatory** (sir-kew-**lay**-t'-ree) *adjective*.

circulation *noun*
1 the act of circulating: *The circulation of the news was banned by the government.*
2 a circuit or circular movement: *blood circulation.*
3 the number of copies of an issue of a newspaper or magazine which are distributed or sold.

circulatory system *noun*
the heart, blood vessels, lymph and lymphatic vessels, which transport substances around the body.

circumcise (**sir**-k'm-size) *verb*
to remove the foreskin of the penis, often as a religious rite, e.g. in Islam and Judaism.

Word Family circumcision (sir-k'm-**sizh**-'n) *noun* the act or ceremony of circumcising.
[*circum-* + Latin *caedere* to cut]

circumference (sir-**kum**-fr'nce) *noun*
1 the outer line of a circle.
2 the length of this line.

circumflex *Language* ⇨ ACCENT.

circumlocution
(sir-k'm-la-**kew**-sh'n) *noun*
1 a roundabout or too lengthy way of speaking.
2 anything said or written in this way.
[*circum-* + *locution* speaking]

circumnavigate (sir-k'm-**nav**-i-gate) *verb*
Nautical to sail around something, especially the world.
Word Family circumnavigation (sir-k'm-nav-i-**gay**-sh'n) *noun*.

circumscribe (sir-k'm-skribe) *verb*
1 to keep within firm limits.
2 to draw or form a line around.
[*circum-* + Latin *scribere* to write]

circumspect *adjective*
cautious and watchful.
Word Family circumspectly *adverb*; **circumspection** *noun*.
[Latin *circumspectus* a looking around]

circumstance (sir-k'm-stance) *noun*
a condition which accompanies or affects a particular event: *Don't judge him until you have found out all the circumstances.*

circumstantial (sir-k'm-**stan**-sh'l) *adjective*
containing full details or circumstances.
[*circum-* + Latin *stans, stantis* standing]

circumstantial evidence *noun*
Law any evidence which supplies reasonable but not definite grounds for believing in a fact.

circumvent (sir-k'm-**vent**) *verb*
to avoid or find a way round: *It was impossible to circumvent the rules.*
Word Family circumvention *noun*.
[*circum-* + Latin *ventus* come]

circus (sir-kus) *noun* (*plural* **circuses**)
1 a form of entertainment consisting of acrobats, clowns and sometimes trained animals, usually performed by a travelling group.
2 a place, formerly circular, where several streets converge: *Piccadilly Circus.*
3 *Ancient history* a circular place with seats on all sides, used for public sports, etc. in Rome.

> The word **circus** comes to English from Latin, in which it means 'a ring or circle'. It was used by the ancient Romans to refer to a circular arena in which public performances and contests were held, e.g. chariot races, athletic contests or gladiator fights. In English the word was originally used only to refer historically to the Roman *circus* but in the late 18th century it began to be used for a circular arena in Britain where variety entertainment took place, now mostly associated with clowns, acrobats or performing animals.

cirrhosis (si-**ro**-sis) *noun*
a very serious disease of the liver, sometimes due to drinking large amounts of alcohol.
[Greek *kirros* tawny + -OSIS]

cirrus (**sirr**-us) *noun* (*plural* **cirri**) (**sirr**-eye)
a high feathery cloud.
[Latin, ringlet]

cissy *noun* (*plural* **cissies**) ⇨ SISSY.

cistern (**sis**-t'n) *noun*
a container where liquid is stored, such as one holding water to flush a toilet.

citadel (**sitt**-a-del) *noun*
a fortress protecting or overlooking a city.
[Italian *citadella* little city]

cite (site) *verb*
1 to quote or refer to.
2 to commend for bravery.
3 to summon or call, especially to appear in a court of law.
Word Family citation (sigh-**tay**-sh'n) *noun*.
[Latin *citare* to call to witness]

citizen (**sitt**-i-z'n) *noun*
a person belonging to or living in a city or country, usually with certain rights and duties.
Word Family citizenship *noun* the status or rights of a citizen; **citizenry** *noun* any or all citizens.

citric acid (sit-rik **ass**-id) *noun*
an acid present in large quantities in lemons but found in most living cells.

citrus (**sit**-rus) *noun*
any of a group of evergreen trees including the lemon, orange, etc.
[Latin]

city (**sit**-ee) *noun* (*plural* **cities**)
1 any large or important town, often with a cathedral and usually the centre of a region.

2 its inhabitants.

3 (**the City**) the City of London, the square mile which contains the chief financial institutions of the UK.

city slicker *noun*
a smartly dressed businessman who arouses suspicions of sharp practice.

civet (**siv-it**) *noun* also **civet cat**
a small spotted African or Asian mammal of the cat family which has a strong musky smell.

civic (**siv-ik**) *adjective*
of or relating to a city or citizens.
[Latin *civis* citizen]

civil (**siv-v'l**) *adjective*
1 of or relating to citizens or citizenship: *civil law*.
2 of or relating to private citizens and community life as distinct from military or religious matters: *a civil marriage*.
3 polite: *You could at least try to be civil!*
Word Family civilly *adverb*; **civility** *noun* (*plural* **civilities**) 1 politeness. 2 a polite expression.

civil engineering *noun*
the design and construction of public works such as bridges, large buildings, roads, etc.

civilian (si **vil-y'n**) *noun*
a person who is not a member of the armed forces.

civilization, civilisation (siv-i lie-**zay**-sh'n) *noun*
1 a society of any period or place which is unified by language and has distinctive legal systems, customs, art styles and governing powers.
2 the process in a society which brings about such a unity.
3 an advanced stage of society and culture, embodied in a high level of art, science and government: *China achieved civilization thousands of years ago*.
Word Family civilize (**siv-i-lize**) *verb* to improve or educate.

civil rights *plural noun*
the natural rights of a citizen or individual in society, often established in the country's constitution.

civil service *noun*
(*usually* **Civil Service**) the staff employed by the central government in the various departments of state, excluding political, judicial and military personnel.
Word Family civil servant *noun* a person who works in the civil service.

civil war *noun*
any war between people of the same country.

civvies *plural noun*
(*informal*) ordinary clothes, not a uniform.

clack *verb*
to make a sharp, harsh, metallic sound.
• **clack** *noun*.

clad a past tense and past participle of **clothe**.

cladding *noun*
a protective layer of one material over another.

claim *verb*
1 to demand or state as a right: *No one claimed the money*.
Figurative *New problems are continually claiming his attention* (= requiring).
2 to say without proof: *She claimed that she'd seen a ghost*.
• **claim** *noun*
1 the assertion of a right: *a pay claim*.
2 a right to something: *She has a claim to the treasure*.
3 a statement which is not proved: *her claim that she saw a ghost*.
4 anything which is claimed, such as a piece of land for mining rights.

claimant *noun*
a person who makes a claim for state benefit or on an insurance policy.

clairvoyance (klair-**voy**-'nce) *noun* also called **second sight**.
the apparent ability to perceive objects or events which are outside the range of the senses.
Word Family clairvoyant *adjective, noun*.
[French *clair* clear + *voyant* seeing]

clam *noun*
a small edible sea animal in a shell.
• **clam** *verb* (**clams; clamming; clammed**)
Phrase clam up (*informal*) 1 to remain silent. 2 to stop talking.

clamber *verb*
to climb with effort or difficulty, especially using both hands and feet.

clammy *adjective* (**clammier; clammiest**)
cold and damp.
Word Family clammily *adverb*; **clamminess** *noun*.

clamour *noun* (*American* **clamor**)
a loud noise or outcry, especially of dissatisfaction or protest: *There is a general clamour for improved education*.

• **clamour** *verb*.
[Latin *clamor* a shout]

clamp *noun*
1 any of various devices for pressing, holding or fastening things together, usually with adjustable ends connected by a screw.
2 a wheel clamp.
• **clamp** *verb*
1 to fasten with or fix in a clamp.
Figurative A hand was clamped firmly over his mouth.
2 to immobilize a car by attaching a wheel clamp to it.
Phrase **clamp down** to become more strict: *The government is clamping down on the use of drugs.*
Word Family **clamper** *noun* a person who attaches wheel clamps to cars.

clan *noun*
1 *Anthropology* a social group descended in either the male or female line from a real or supposed common ancestor.
2 a large family or group of related families.
Word Family **clansman** *noun* (*plural* **clansmen**) a member of a clan, especially of Scottish Highlanders; **clanship** *noun*.

clandestine (klan-**dest**-in *or* klan-dest-ine) *adjective*
surreptitious or secretive, especially to deceive or conceal.
Word Family **clandestinely** *adverb*.
[Latin *clandestinus* secret]

clang *verb*
to make a loud resonant metallic sound: *The cell door clanged shut.*
• **clang** *noun*.

clanger *noun*
(*informal*) a stupid or embarrassing remark, mistake, etc.

clank *verb*
to make a hard dull metallic sound.
• **clank** *noun*.

clap¹ *verb* (**claps; clapping; clapped**)
1 to strike the hands together with a sharp sudden sound.
2 to slap or grasp: *A large hand clapped him on the shoulder.*
3 to put quickly: *She clapped her hand over her mouth.*
• **clap** *noun*
1 the act or sound of clapping, especially as an expression of approval, etc.
2 a loud sudden noise: *A clap of thunder frightened the horse.*

Word Family **clapper** *noun* a thing that makes a loud sound, such as the tongue of a bell.

clap² *noun*
(*informal*) any venereal disease, especially gonorrhoea.

clapped-out *adjective*
(*informal*) completely worn out.

clapperboard *noun*
Films a jointed board with a number on it, clapped at the beginning of each shot to help in identification.

claptrap *noun*
(*informal*) any pretentious or insincere language.

claret (**klarr**-et) *noun*
1 a dry red wine.
2 a deep purplish-red colour.
[Old French, light-coloured]

clarify (**klarr**-i-fie) *verb* (**clarifies; clarifying; clarified**)
1 to make clear: *Can you clarify the problem for me?*
2 to remove impurities by heating: *clarified butter.*
Word Family **clarification** (klarr-i-fi-**kay**-sh'n) *noun*.
[Latin *clarus* clear + *facere* to make]

clarinet *noun*
Music a wind instrument with a straight tube and a single-reed mouthpiece, played by means of fingerholes and keys.
Word Family **clarinettist** *noun* a person who plays the clarinet.

clarity (**klarr**-i-tee) *noun*
clearness.

clash *verb*
1 to collide or hit with a loud harsh sound: *The cymbals clashed dramatically.*
2 to disagree or conflict: *Our tastes in most things clash dreadfully.*
3 to coincide badly: *My French and biology classes clash on Monday mornings.*
• **clash** *noun* (*plural* **clashes**) the act or sound of clashing.

clasp (klahsp) *noun*
1 any of various devices with a catch, used to fasten or join two things together.
2 a hold or grasp: *a firm clasp of the hand.*
• **clasp** *verb*
1 to fasten with a clasp.
2 to hold or grasp tightly.

clasp knife *noun* (*plural* **clasp knives**)
a penknife.

class noun (plural **classes**)
1 any number of people or things seen as a division or group, based on type, quality, etc: *this class of insects.*
2 *Sociology* a group of people in a society who have similar occupations, incomes, and social and political attitudes.
⇨ MIDDLE CLASS; UPPER CLASS; WORKING CLASS.
3 *Education* a group of students taught together.
4 *Education* the meeting of students for a lesson.
5 (*informal*) a high quality in manner, dress, etc.: *That girl certainly has class.*
● **class** verb to arrange or rate according to type, quality, etc.
[Latin *classis* a social class]

classic adjective
1 of the highest class or quality: *a classic story.*
2 serving as a model or guide: *Here is a classic example of bad architecture.*
3 (of clothing) simple and elegant in style.
● **classic** noun
1 a person or thing considered to be of the highest standard or quality: *This novel is a modern classic.*
2 (**classics**) the languages, literature and history of ancient Greece and Rome, or the study of these.

classical adjective
1 of or characteristic of the art, literature or civilization of ancient Greece and Rome.
2 (of music) having a serious artistic intent and usually taking the form of a symphony, concerto, etc.
Word Family classically adverb.

classification (klass-i-fi-kay-sh'n) noun
1 the act of classifying.
2 a class or division.
3 *Biology* the ordering of animals and plants, based on similarities, into a series of groups which indicate evolutionary relationships.
Word Family classificatory adjective.

classified advertisement noun
a small advertisement printed in a magazine or newspaper, sent in by a person who wants to sell something, find work, etc.

classify (klass-i-fie) verb (**classifies; classifying; classified**)
1 to arrange or organize in classes.
2 to declare that a government or military document must be kept secret.
Word Family classifiable adjective.

classmate noun
a person in the same class in a school or college.

classroom noun
a room where a class of students meets to have a lesson.

classy (klah-see) adjective (**classier; classiest**)
(*informal*) elegant or stylish.

clatter verb
to make rapid harsh rattling sounds.
● **clatter** noun.

clause noun
1 *Grammar* a group of words that makes sense and normally contains a verb: *The sentence 'I don't understand why you said that' contains two clauses, 'I don't understand' and 'why you said that'.*
2 a separate part of a contract, treaty, etc.

claustrophobia (klos-tra-fo-bi-a) noun
an abnormal fear of being shut in.
Word Family claustrophobic adjective.
[Latin *claustrum* enclosure + PHOBIA]

clavichord (klav-i-kawd) noun
Music an early keyboard instrument, similar to a piano.
[Latin *clavis* key + *chorda* chord]

clavicle (klav-i-k'l) ⇨ COLLARBONE.

claw noun
1 a hard sharp nail, usually curved and pointed, on the end of the limb of an animal.
2 the jointed grasping part of a crab, etc.
3 any similar part or object.
● **claw** verb to scratch, tear or pull with or as if with the claws.

claw hammer noun
a hammer which has one end of the head curved and split for pulling out nails.

clay noun
a common earthy mineral which is soft when wet and hard when baked, used for making bricks, pottery, etc.

claymore noun
a large broadsword formerly used by Scottish Highlanders.

clay pigeon noun
a disc, usually made of baked clay, which is hurled into the air as a target for shotgun practice.

clean adjective
1 free from dirt or bacteria: *a clean cup.*
2 not yet used: *a clean piece of paper.*
3 not breaking rules: *a clean fight.*
4 not indecent or immoral: *Keep your jokes clean!*

5 elegant and simple: *the car's clean lines.*
• **clean** *verb* to make clean.
Phrases clean out 1 to make clean and tidy: *She cleaned out the cupboards.*
2 (*informal*) to take all the money of: *We played cards, and she cleaned me out!*
clean up 1 to tidy: *Please clean up your room.* 2 (*informal*) to make a lot of money: *He cleaned up at the casino.*
• **clean** *adverb* cleanly or completely: *Sorry – I clean forgot!*
Phrase come clean (*informal*) to make a full confession.
Word Family clean *noun* an act of cleaning; **cleanness** *noun*; **cleanly** *adverb*.

clean-bowl *verb*
Cricket to dismiss a batsman by bowling a ball which hits the stumps and dislodges the bails.

clean-cut *adjective*
1 having a clearly defined shape.
2 (of a person) clean and tidy in appearance.

cleaner *noun*
a person or thing that cleans.
Phrase take someone to the cleaners (*informal*) to defeat someone very severely, especially so that they lose a lot of money.

cleanliness (**klenn**-li-ness) *noun*
the state of being clean and neat.
Word Family cleanly *adjective* (**cleanlier; cleanliest**) (*formal*) careful to keep clean.

cleanse (klenz) *verb*
to make thoroughly clean or pure.
Word Family cleanser *noun*.

clean-shaven *adjective*
(of a man) having no hair on the chin or upper lip.

clear (*rhymes with* here) *adjective*
1 transparent or free from darkness, cloudiness, etc.: *clear water.*
2 distinct or plain: *He left clear instructions.*
3 free of obstruction: *a clear path.*
Figurative Tuesday's clear – I can do it then.
4 free from guilt: *a clear conscience.*
• **clear** *verb*
1 to make or become clear or clearer: *The sky cleared.*
2 to go over without touching: *The athlete cleared the high jump bar.*
3 to say that a person is not guilty: *He was cleared of murder.*
4 to organize official permission for: *I'll have to clear it with the headteacher.*

5 to be allowed to pass: *after they had cleared customs.*
6 to pay back: *Clear your debts.*
7 to get as profit: *We cleared £1000 this week.*
Phrases clear out (*informal*) to go away.
clear up 1 to become fine and sunny again. 2 to solve or make clear. 3 to tidy up: *Let's clear up this mess before Dad gets back.*
• **clear** *noun*
Phrase in the clear free from guilt or blame.
Word Family clear *adverb* distinctly or completely; **clearly** *adverb* 1 in a clear way. 2 without doubt: *There's clearly been a mix-up;* **clearness** *noun*.
[Latin *clarus* clear]

clearance *noun*
1 a clear space or distance between objects.
2 a clearing away: *slum clearance.*
3 official permission for something.

clear-cut *adjective*
distinctly defined.

clearing *noun*
a piece of land cleared of trees.

clearing house *noun*
an institution which settles debts and other transactions, e.g. between banks.

clearout *noun*
(*informal*) an act of tidying up and throwing away.

clear-sighted *adjective*
good at thinking clearly, especially about the future.

clearway *noun*
a road along which vehicles are not allowed to park.

cleat (kleet) *noun*
1 a piece of metal or wood around which a rope can be tied.
2 a piece of metal or wood fixed across a surface to give it strength.
3 a metal or rubber fitting for boot soles, to prevent slipping.

cleavage (**klee**-vij) *noun*
1 a division or split.
2 the separation between a woman's breasts.

cleave[1] *verb* (**cleaves; cleaving; cleaved, cleft** or **clove; cleaved, cleft** or **cloven**)
to split or separate, especially by cutting.
Word Family cleaver *noun* a heavy chopper used to divide large sections of meat, etc.

cleave² *verb*
a poetic word meaning 'to stick firmly'.

clef *noun*
Music a sign on the staff which indicates the name and pitch of the notes which follow it.
bass clef a sign on the fourth line of the staff which indicates that the note F is on this line.
treble clef a sign on the second line of the staff which indicates that the note G is on this line.
[French, key]

cleft¹ *noun*
a crack or split.

cleft² *adjective*
split or divided.
• **cleft** a past tense and past participle of **cleave¹**.

cleft palate *noun*
a condition in which a child is born with a longitudinal slit along the roof of the mouth, causing difficulty in speaking clearly.

clematis (klemm-a-tiss *or* klem-**ay**-tiss) *noun*
any of a group of climbing plants.
[Greek *klematis* of a vine-branch]

clemency (klemm-'n-see) *noun*
1 mercy or kindness.
2 pleasantness or mildness.
Word Family **clement** *adjective*.
[Latin *clemens* gentle]

clementine (klem-en-teen *or* klem-en-tine) *noun*
a small sweet orange citrus fruit.

clench *verb*
to close or clasp tightly: *He clenched his teeth in pain.*
• **clench** *noun*.

clerestory (kleer-stor-i) *noun* (*plural* **clerestories**)
Architecture the part of the wall of a church nave which is above the aisle roof and is furnished with windows.
[CLEAR + STOREY]

clergy (kler-jee) *noun*
(*usually used with plural verb*) *Christianity* all those who are trained and ordained as priests or ministers.
Word Family **clergyman** *noun* (*plural* **clergymen**); **clergywoman** *noun* (*plural* **clergywomen**).

cleric (klerr-ik) *noun*
a member of the clergy.

clerical (klerr-i-k'l) *adjective*
1 relating to clerks or office workers: *a clerical error.*
2 relating to the clergy: *a clerical collar.*

clerihew (klerr-i-hew) *noun*
a four-line comic verse with two rhyming couplets, the first line being the name of the person about whom the poem is written.
[after *Edmund Clerihew Bentley*, 1875-1956, an English writer]

clerk (klark) *noun*
1 a person employed to keep records of accounts or to deal with correspondence.
2 (*especially American*) a sales assistant or a hotel receptionist.

clever *adjective*
1 quick or intelligent: *a clever solution to the problem.*
2 skilful: *her clever hands.*
Word Family **cleverly** *adverb*; **cleverness** *noun*.

cliché (klee-shay) *noun*
an idea or saying which is considered to be overused or trite.

The word **cliché** has come into English from the French verb *clicher* (to stereotype), a reference to a method of making printing plates from a mould. Print that was *cliché* had been repeated over and over again in identical form from a single printing plate. In the same way a *cliché* in the language is a word or phrase that is repeated again and again. People use *clichés* without realizing and they are heard everywhere, particularly in public speeches, e.g. 'at this moment in time', 'unaccustomed as I am to public speaking' and 'ongoing situation'.

click *noun*
1 a short sharp snapping sound: *the click of a key in the lock.*
2 *Computers* the action or sound of pressing a mouse button
• **click** *verb*
1 to make a click or clicks: *The door clicked shut behind them.* □ *Click on the printer icon to print the document.*
2 (*informal*) to be a success.
3 (*informal*) to become clear suddenly: *It finally clicked that she had been lying all along.*

client (klie-'nt) *noun*
1 a person who pays for the help or services of a professional person or institution: *a lawyer's clients.*

2 *Computers* a computer in a network that gets information from a server.
[Latin *cliens*]

clientele (klee-on-**tel**) *noun*
all the clients of a particular person or institution.
[French]

cliff *noun*
a very steep slope of rock, especially on the coast.

cliffhanger *noun*
a story or event which is full of suspense or uncertainty: *His first novel was a real cliffhanger.*

climactic (klie-**mak**-tik) *adjective*
of or being a climax.

climate (**klie**-mit) *noun*
1 the weather conditions of a place or region during a year.
2 the general attitudes or feelings of a group of people: *The climate of opinion is against the government.*
Word Family **climatic** (klie-**matt**-ik) *adjective*; **climatically** *adverb*.
[Greek *klimatos* of a region]

climax (**klie**-maks) *noun* (*plural* **climaxes**)
the highest or most exciting point of anything: *The play reached its climax in the second act.*
● **climax** *verb*.
[Greek *klimax* a ladder or staircase]

climb (klime) *verb*
to move or go upwards: *The plane climbed steadily.*
Phrase **climb down 1** to go down or descend, especially with effort. **2** to withdraw or admit to being wrong: *The government has climbed down over its new taxation measures.*
Word Family **climb** *noun* **1** the act of climbing. **2** a place or height to be climbed; **climber** *noun* **1** a person who climbs. **2** a plant which grows by attaching itself to a support.

clime *noun*
an old word for a region.

clinch *verb*
1 to make something secure: *The signing of this document will clinch the deal.*
2 *Boxing* to hug an opponent in order to prevent blows being struck.
Word Family **clinch** *noun* **1** a struggle with an opponent. **2** (*informal*) an embrace; **clincher** *noun* (*informal*) something which is decisive.

cling *verb* (**clings; clinging; clung**)
to be attached or remain close: *The little girl clung to her mother.*

cling film *noun*
a thin transparent film used as a covering to keep food fresh or clean.

clinic *noun*
1 a specialized section of a hospital, usually treating outpatients.
2 any medical centre, especially one giving special treatment, such as X-rays, etc.
3 an occasion when a special treatment centre is open: *The clinic is held on a Friday.*
[Greek *klinikos* of a bed]

clinical *adjective*
1 of or relating to a clinic.
2 of or relating to the treatment or management of disease in a patient.
3 scientific and unemotional: *He has developed a clinical attitude towards death.*
Word Family **clinically** *adverb*.

clink¹ *verb*
to make a light ringing or metallic sound: *Her fork clinked against the glass dish.*
● **clink** *noun*.

clink² *noun*
(*informal*) a jail.
[from a prison in *Clink Street*, London]

clinker *noun*
the residue left in coke ovens, etc. after the burning process.

clip¹ *verb* (**clips; clipping; clipped**)
1 to cut or trim with or as if with scissors, etc.: *The hedge was clipped in the shape of a pheasant.*
2 to hit sharply or quickly: *The car clipped the edge of the fence.*
● **clip** *noun*
1 the act of clipping.
2 something which is clipped or cut, especially a short piece of film taken from a longer one: *a clip from the new Bond film.*
3 (*informal*) a short sharp hit: *His mum gave him a clip round the ear.*
4 (*dated informal*) speed.

clip² *noun*
1 any device for holding or gripping: *a paper clip.*
2 a metal container for the cartridges of a gun.
● **clip** *verb* (**clips; clipping; clipped**) to fasten with a clip.

clip art *noun*
Computers pictures or symbols which can be cut and pasted from software into one's own work on a computer.

clipboard *noun*
1 a piece of board with a clip on it, used to hold and support papers while writing away from a desk, etc.
2 *Computers* a place where text or pictures are kept between cutting and pasting.

clip-clop *verb* (**clip-clops; clip-clopping; clip-clopped**)
to move with a regular heavy sound: *a horse clip-clopping along the road.*

clipped (klipt) *adjective*
(of speech) having an unusually short sharp sound.

clipper *noun*
1 (*usually* **clippers**) any of various devices for clipping or cutting: *nail clippers.*
2 a fast sailing ship of the 19th century with tall masts.

clipping *noun*
anything which is clipped off or cut out.

clique (kleek) *noun*
a small group of people which snobbishly excludes others.
Word Family **cliquey** *adjective* (**cliquier; cliquiest**); **cliquish** *adjective*; **cliquishness** *noun*.

clitoris (klitt-a-ris) *noun*
Anatomy a small organ in the upper part of the female vulva, containing erectile tissue.
Word Family **clitoral** *adjective*.

cloak *noun*
1 a long loose piece of clothing without sleeves, usually fastened at the neck and worn over clothes.
2 something which covers or hides: *The soldiers marched under the cloak of darkness.*
• **cloak** *verb* to cover with or as if with a cloak.

cloak-and-dagger *adjective*
full of espionage, intrigue and secrecy.

cloakroom *noun*
a room for leaving coats, etc., sometimes with a basin or toilet.

clobber[1] *verb*
(*informal*) to hit heavily.

clobber[2] *noun*
(*informal*) clothing and personal possessions.

cloche (klosh) *noun*
1 a woman's small close-fitting round hat.
2 a glass or plastic covering to protect garden plants.
[French, bell]

clock *noun*
1 a mechanical or electrical instrument with moving hands for measuring and showing time.
2 (*informal*) a milometer.
Phrases **against the clock** in a race to finish before a certain time. **around the clock** all day and all night.
• **clock** *verb*
1 (*informal*) to achieve or measure the time of.
2 (*informal*) to see.
3 (*informal*) to hit.
Phrases **clock in** to register one's time of arrival. **clock out** to register one's time of departure.

clock-watch *verb*
to be very aware of the time while one is working because one is very keen to leave work.

clockwise *adverb, adjective*
in the same direction as the moving hands of a clock. Compare ANTICLOCKWISE.

clockwork *noun*
a mechanism which can be wound up with a key.
Phrase **like clockwork** smoothly, perfectly.

clod *noun*
1 a lump or mass, especially of earth or clay.
2 (*informal*) a stupid person.

clodhopper *noun*
(*informal*) a stupid or clumsy person.

clog[1] *noun*
a heavy shoe with a thick sole which is usually made of wood or cork.

clog[2] *verb* (**clogs; clogging; clogged**)
to block or become blocked: *The sink is clogged with dirt.*

cloister (kloy-sta) *noun*
1 a monastery or convent.
2 a roofed path joined to a church or other building and usually situated around an open courtyard.
Word Family **cloistered** *adjective*
1 secluded or sheltered: *living a cloistered life.* 2 having a covered path.
[Latin *claustrum* an enclosure]

clone *noun*
1 *Biology* a group of cells or organisms which are genetically identical, having all been produced from the same original cell, or any member of this group.
2 *Biology* a group of plants grown from parts of a single plant.

3 a person or thing that closely resembles another.
● **clone** *verb* to produce a clone of.
[Greek *klon* a twig]

clop *noun*
the light drumming sound made by a horse's hoofs on a hard surface.
● **clop** *verb* (**clops; clopping; clopped**).

close¹ (kloze) *verb*
1 to shut.
2 to stop: *We will close the meeting now.*
Phrases **close in** to approach and surround gradually. **close up** to come together.
● *noun* an end or conclusion: *at the close of day.*
[Latin *clausus* shut]

close² (kloze) *adjective, adverb*
1 near: *Don't go too close to the edge.*
2 not having much difference in time, skill, etc. between competitors: *The race was very close.*
3 careful and thorough: *upon close examination.*
4 strongly united: *a close group of friends.*
5 carefully protected: *a close secret.*
6 airless: *It's rather close in here.*
● *noun* the land around a cathedral or other building.
Word Family **closely** *adverb*; **closeness** *noun*.

closed book *noun*
1 (*informal*) a matter about which one knows very little.
2 (*informal*) a matter which is completely finished.

closed-circuit television *noun*
a system which transmits images to a limited number of television screens, used in crime prevention, etc.

closed shop *noun*
a factory or industry where all the workers must belong to a trade union. Compare OPEN SHOP.

close-knit *adjective*
strongly united.

close season *noun*
a period of time when a particular animal cannot legally be killed by hunters: *the close season for duck shooting.*

closet (klozz-it) *noun*
a room or cupboard for storing clothing, etc.
Phrase **come out of the closet** to say publicly that one is homosexual.
● **closet** *verb* to shut up in a private room for discussion, etc.
● **closet** *adjective* secret: *a closet Socialist.*

close-up (klose-up) *noun*
a close view of anything, especially a photograph taken at close range.

closure (klo-zher) *noun*
1 the act of closing: *the closure of the mines.*
2 *Parliament* the stopping of a debate, after which a vote is taken to decide the issue.

clot *noun*
1 a mass or lump: *a blood clot.*
2 (*informal*) a stupid person.
● **clot** *verb* (**clots; clotting; clotted**) to form into clots: *clotted cream.*

cloth *noun*
1 any fabric, usually made by weaving wool, cotton or other yarn and used to make clothes, curtains, etc.
2 a piece of cloth used for a particular purpose: *a tablecloth.*
3 (**the cloth**) the profession of the clergy.

clothe (klothe) *verb* (**clothes; clothing; clothed** or **clad**)
to dress or provide with clothes.
Figurative The city streets were clothed in mist.

clothes *plural noun*
all the items worn to cover the body.

clothes horse *noun*
a frame on which clothes are hung to dry them.

clothes line *noun*
a cord on which clothes are hung to dry them.

clothing (klo-thing) *noun*
clothes.

cloud *noun*
1 a dense mass of suspended water drops or ice crystals formed in the air by the condensation of water vapour.
2 any similar dark or moving mass: *a cloud of smoke.*
Phrases **on cloud nine** (*informal*) extremely happy. **under a cloud** under suspicion.
● **cloud** *verb* to make or become covered or shadowed with or as if with clouds: *Her eyes clouded with tears.*
Word Family **cloudy** *adjective* (**cloudier; cloudiest**) **1** full of clouds. **2** opaque or indistinct; **cloudiness** *noun*; **cloudless** *adjective*.

cloudburst *noun*
a sudden fall of very heavy rain.

cloud cuckoo land *noun*
an imaginary place where everything is perfect.

[from the name of a city in the play *Birds* by the Greek writer Aristophanes]

clout *noun*
1 (*informal*) a blow or knock, especially with the hand.
2 (*informal*) influence or power.
• **clout** *verb*.

clove[1] *noun*
a sweet hot spice made from the dried flower bud of a tropical tree and used in cooking.

clove[2] *noun*
any of the small rounded separate sections of a bulb: *a clove of garlic*.

clove[3] a past tense of **cleave**[1].

cloven a past participle of **cleave**[1].

cloven hoof *noun*
an animal's foot which is divided into two parts, e.g. that of a cow.

clover *noun*
a plant grown as food for cattle and sheep and also to add nitrogen to the soil.
Phrase **in clover** in great comfort or luxury.

cloverleaf *noun*
1 the leaf of a clover, which usually has three parts.
2 a major road junction with a pattern of ramps, underpasses, etc. resembling a four-leaved clover.

clown *noun*
1 a comic actor in a circus or pantomime.
2 any funny or clumsy person.
Word Family **clown** *verb* to perform as or like a clown; **clownery** *noun*; **clownish** *adjective*.

cloy *verb*
to make someone sickened or sated by an excess of something: *The romance of the movie began to cloy after two hours.*
Word Family **cloying** *adjective*.

club *noun*
1 a heavy stick, usually thicker at one end.
2 also **golf club** a stick with a shaped wooden or metal head, used in golf.
3 an organized group of people, sharing similar beliefs or interests and having regular meetings: *a chess club*.
4 a social meeting-place for its members, often with a bar, restaurant, and facilities for sports or games.
5 (*informal*) a nightclub.
6 *Cards* a black figure like a cloverleaf on a playing card.
7 *Cards* a playing card with this figure.
8 (**clubs**) *Cards* the suit with this figure.

Phrase **in the club** (*informal*) pregnant.
• **club** *verb* (**clubs; clubbing; clubbed**)
1 to hit with or as if with a club.
2 to join together for a particular purpose: *We all clubbed together to buy a boat.*
3 (*informal*) to go out to nightclubs.
Word Family **clubhouse** *noun* the buildings used by members of a club or association.

club car *noun*
(*especially American*) a railway carriage with comfortable seats and good facilities.

club foot *noun*
a deformed foot, usually with the sole turning inwards and the heel raised.
Word Family **club-footed** *adjective*.

cluck *verb*
to make a short cry like a brooding hen: *His mother clucked her disapproval.*
• **cluck** *noun*.

clue (kloo) *noun*
anything which gives a guide to the solution of a problem, mystery, question, etc.: *look for clues to the identity of the thief.*
Word Family **clueless** *adjective* (*informal*) stupid.

> A **clue** is something we usually associate with detective stories or with crossword puzzles. In origin it is another spelling of *clew*, an old word meaning 'a ball of thread'. The connection between this and help with a problem goes back to ancient Greece when Theseus took a ball of thread into the Minotaur's labyrinth with him, unravelling it as he went so that he could retrace his steps later.

clued-up *adjective*
(*informal*) knowing a lot about something.

clump *noun*
1 a cluster or mass of things together: *a clump of trees*.
2 a heavy dull noise or tread.
• **clump** *verb*.

clumsy (klum-zee) *adjective* (**clumsier; clumsiest**)
1 awkward and ungraceful: *a clumsy catch*.
2 not polished or elegant: *a clumsy apology*.
Word Family **clumsily** *adverb*; **clumsiness** *noun*.

clung the past tense and past participle of **cling**.

cluster noun
a number of things growing, grouped or moving together: *The guests stood in clusters at the gate.*
• **cluster** verb.

clutch[1] verb
to seize and hold tightly: *I clutched at her arm for reassurance.*
• **clutch** noun (plural **clutches**)
1 the act of clutching.
2 a device by which working parts of a machine may be easily engaged or disengaged while the machine is operating.
3 (**clutches**) power: *Bilbo fell into the clutches of the trolls.*

clutch[2] noun (plural **clutches**)
a number of things produced at one time, especially a hatch of eggs or chickens.

clutch bag noun
a handbag without handles or a strap, used by women when they go out in the evening.

clutter verb
to make untidy or confused: *The room was cluttered with old newspapers.*
• **clutter** noun.

coach noun (plural **coaches**)
1 a comfortable single-decker bus.
2 a railway carriage.
3 a large enclosed carriage drawn by horses.
4 a person employed to teach, train or prepare people for a particular purpose.
Word Family **coach** verb to train or prepare.

coaching inn noun
(*formerly*) an inn where coaches stopped to change horses.

coachman noun (plural **coachmen**)
a man employed to drive a coach drawn by horses.

coagulate (ko-**ag**-yoo-late) verb
to change from a liquid into a solid thickened state, such as a clot.
Word Family **coagulant** noun a substance which causes a liquid to coagulate; **coagulation** (ko-ag-yoo-**lay**-sh'n) noun.
[Latin *coagulum* rennet]

coal noun
a black burnable rock composed of layered deposits of carbon-bearing material derived from vegetable matter.
Phrases **coals to Newcastle** a superfluous act, like sending coal to where coal comes from. **haul over the coals** to scold.

coalesce (ko-a-**less**) verb
to join, grow or come together.
Word Family **coalescence** noun.
[Latin *coalescere* to grow together]

coalition (ko-a-**lish**-'n) noun
1 a union or joining together of several things.
2 a joining together of political parties with each retaining its own principles.

coalman noun (plural **coalmen**)
a man who delivers coal to people's houses.

coal scuttle noun
a bucket in which coal for a fire is carried or stored.

coal tar noun
a thick black liquid made by heating coal, used in making chemical products.

coarse (*rhymes with* horse) adjective
1 composed of large particles: *coarse sand.*
2 rough or harsh: *The coarse cloth scratched her skin.*
3 crude and vulgar: *a coarse joke.*
Word Family **coarsely** adverb; **coarseness** noun; **coarsen** verb.

coarse fishing noun
freshwater fishing with a hook and bait and not a fly. Compare FLY-FISHING.

coast noun
1 the area of land which borders the sea or any large area of water.
2 the seaside.
Phrase **the coast is clear** there is no danger.
• **coast** verb to move without effort: *The bicycle coasted down the hill.*
Word Family **coastal** adjective of or at a coast.
[Latin *costa* rib or flank]

coaster noun
1 a small mat or tray placed under a drinking glass to protect the table surface.
2 a ship taking cargo along the coast.
3 (*informal*) a roller coaster.

coastguard noun
an officer or group of officers whose job is to patrol a coast for smugglers, ships in trouble, etc.

coastline noun
the outline of a coast.

coat noun
1 a piece of clothing with long sleeves which fastens down the front, worn over other clothes.

2 any outer covering: *a dog's wiry coat.*
□ *a coat of paint.*
Word Family coat *verb* to provide with a
coat or cover; **coating** *noun* a layer.

coat hanger *noun*
a curved piece of plastic, wood or wire
used for hanging clothes up in a wardrobe,
etc.

coat of arms *noun* (*plural* **coats of arms**)
Heraldry a shield decorated with pictorial
designs and used by noble families, etc.

coat-tails *plural noun*
the long pieces which hang down from a
man's tailcoat.
Phrase on someone's coat-tails relying
on the help of another person's power or
influence.

coax (cokes) *verb*
to get something by flattery or patient
persuasion. *The dog had to be coaxed into
having a bath.*
Word Family coaxingly *adverb.*

coaxial cable (ko-ak-si-al **kay**-b'l) *noun*
Radio a cable with a pair of electrical
conductors, one inside the other, used to
carry high-frequency signals such as
television programmes.

cob *noun*
1 ⇨ CORNCOB.
2 a male swan.
3 a sturdy short-legged horse for riding.

cobalt (ko-bawlt) *noun*
a hard magnetic metal, similar to iron,
used in alloys. Its compounds are used in
glass and as dyes.

cobble¹ *verb*
1 to make or mend shoes.
2 to make or put together clumsily.
Word Family cobbler *noun* a person who
mends shoes.

cobble² *noun* also **cobblestone**
a rounded stone used for paving.
● **cobble** *verb* to pave with cobbles: *cobbled
streets.*

COBOL *noun*
Computers a computer programming
language mainly used in business.
[CO(mmon) B(usiness) O(riented)
L(anguage)]

cobra *noun*
any of a group of very poisonous snakes of
Africa and Asia noted for spreading their
neck-ribs to form a hood of skin when
disturbed.
[Latin *colubra* snake]

cobweb *noun*
a thin thread or threaded structure spun
by spiders to catch prey, usually insects.
Phrase blow away the cobwebs
(*informal*) to clear the mind with healthy
activity.
[Middle English *coppe* spider + WEB]

cocaine (ko-**kane**) *noun*
a bitter crystalline drug made from the
dried leaves of a tropical plant and used as
an anaesthetic and illegally for pleasure.
⇨ CRACK *noun* (definition 7).

coccyx (**kok**-siks) *noun* (*plural* **coccyxes**
or **coccyges** (**kok**-si-jeez))
Anatomy the small rough triangular bone
at the base of the spine.
[Greek *kokkyx* cuckoo, because the bone
was thought to resemble its bill]

cochineal (koch-i-**neel**) *noun*
a red dye obtained from an insect and
used as a food-colouring.
[Spanish *cochinilla* woodlouse]

cock¹ *noun*
1 a male adult bird, especially a domestic
fowl.
2 a device used to control the flow of a
liquid or gas, e.g. a valve.
3 the hammer of a gun.
4 a weathervane shaped like a rooster.
● **cock** *verb* to pull back and set the
hammer of a gun before firing.

cock² *verb*
to turn upwards or to the side in a jaunty
or defiant manner: *He cocked an eyebrow at
me mischievously.*

cockade *noun*
a knot of ribbons worn on a hat, usually as
part of a uniform.

cock-a-hoop *adjective*
extremely pleased.

cock and bull story *noun* (*plural* **cock
and bull stories**)
(*informal*) a ridiculous and very unlikely
story.

cockatoo (kok-a-**too**) *noun*
a large crested parrot, found in Australia
and New Guinea.

cockchafer *noun*
a large brown European beetle which flies
with a loud whirring noise.

cockcrow *noun*
an old word for **dawn**.

cockerel *noun*
a young domestic cock.

cock-eyed *adjective*
1 crooked or twisted to one side.

2 (*informal*) absurd or foolish.
3 having a squint.

cockfighting *noun*
the sport of making two cocks fight each other, illegal in Britain.

cockle *noun*
an edible bivalve mollusc with a ribbed shell.
Phrase **warm the cockles of the heart** to make one feel a glow of contentment.

cockney (kok-nee) *noun*
(*often* **Cockney**) a native of the East End of London, especially one who has a characteristic accent.

cockpit *noun*
the space for the pilot or crew controlling an aircraft or spacecraft.

cockroach *noun* (*plural* **cockroaches**)
a large insect with a dark oval flattened body, long legs and antennae.

cockscomb *noun*
1 ⇨ COMB *noun* (definition 4).
2 *also* **coxcomb** a tropical pot plant with a crest of tiny red, yellow or purple flowers.

cocksure (kok-shaw) *adjective*
overconfident: *a cocksure young man*.
Word Family **cocksureness** *noun*.

cocktail *noun*
1 a strong alcoholic drink made of one or more spirits and often sweetened.
2 a dish of seafood served as an appetizer: *a prawn cocktail*.
3 a mixture of fruit.
4 any mixture of very different factors: *a dangerous cocktail of political opinions*.

cocktail party *noun* (*plural* **cocktail parties**)
a formal party with drinks and a buffet, at which people do not dance.

cocktail stick *noun*
a pointed stick on which small pieces of cheese, sausage, etc. are served.

cocky *adjective* (**cockier; cockiest**)
(*informal*) arrogant or conceited.
Word Family **cockily** *adverb*; **cockiness** *noun*.

cocoa (ko-ko) *noun*
1 the crushed seeds of the cacao tree.
2 a drink made from this.

cocoa bean *noun*
the seed of the cacao tree.

cocoa butter *noun*
a mixture of semisolid oils derived from cocoa, used in the manufacture of chocolate.

coconut (ko-k'-nut) *noun*
1 the large seed of a palm tree, with a hard shell and a white fleshy edible lining, containing a milky liquid.
2 the white lining of this seed, often grated and used in cooking.
[Spanish *coco* grinning face, which the base of the shell resembles]

coconut ice *noun*
a sweet made from sugar and coconut.

coconut matting *noun*
a hard matting made from the stringy material on the shell of the coconut.

coconut shy *noun*
an entertainment at fairs, etc. in which coconuts are set up as targets to be thrown at, and awarded as prizes.

cocoon (k'-koon) *noun*
1 *Biology* a protective covering made by an insect for the pupa.
2 anything that makes one feel protected and comfortable.
• **cocoon** *verb*.

cod *noun* (*plural* **cod**)
a large edible fish.

coda (ko-da) *noun*
Music the section of music at the end of a movement.
[Italian, from Latin *cauda* tail]

coddle *verb*
1 to boil gently.
2 to pamper or indulge.

code *noun*
1 a set of letters, numbers, symbols, etc. used to communicate secretly: *British intelligence cracked the Germans' code*.
2 a set of numbers used before a personal telephone number, showing the area it is in.
3 a systematic collection of rules relating to a particular subject: *a code of behaviour*.
• **code** *verb*.

codeine (ko-deen) *noun*
a chemical made from opium and used in medicine to relieve pain.
[Greek *kodeia* poppyhead]

code name *noun*
a name given to a person, plan, etc. that only a few people know.
• **code-name** *verb*.

codger *noun*
(*informal*) an odd, usually old, person.

codicil (kodd-i-sil) *noun*
a supplement or added part, especially to a will.
[Latin *codicilli* a note]

codify (ko-di-fie) *verb* (**codifies;
codifying; codified**)
1 to arrange systematically.
2 to put into a code.
Word Family codification (ko-di-fi **kay**-
sh'n) *noun.*

cod liver oil *noun*
an oil which is obtained from the liver of
cod or sharks, and is used as a source of
vitamins A and D.

codpiece *noun*
a pouch attached to the crotch of tight-
fitting breeches, worn by men in the
Middle Ages.

codswallop (kodz-woll-'p) *noun*
(*informal*) any nonsense or rubbish.
[originally ginger beer, invented by *Hiram
Codd* of London in 1871; *wallop* meaning
poor beer]

co-od *adjective*
(*informal*) co-educational.

co-education (ko-ed-yoo-**kay**-sh'n) *noun*
the teaching of males and females
together.
Word Family co-educational *adjective.*

coefficient (ko-a-**fish**-'nt) *noun*
Maths a number or symbol placed in front
of, and multiplying, another quantity: *In*
$3a^2y$, $3a^2$ *is the coefficient of* y.

coelacanth (see-la-kanth) *noun*
a fish thought to have been extinct for 70
million years, until in 1938 a living
specimen was found.
[Greek *koilos* hollow + *akantha* spine]

coerce (ko-**erse**) *verb*
(*formal*) to force or compel.
Word Family coercion (ko-er-uh'n)
noun, coercive (ko-er-siv) *adjective.*
[Latin *coercere* to restrain]

coexist (ko-eg-**zist**) *verb*
to exist together.
Word Family coexistence *noun;*
coexistent *adjective.*

coffee *noun*
1 a brown powder made by grinding the
bean-like seeds of a tropical shrub.
2 a drink made from this.

coffee bar *noun*
a place serving coffee, tea, light meals,
cakes, etc.

coffee morning *noun*
a social occasion in the morning where
people meet informally, e.g. at a church
hall.

coffee table *noun*
a low table, used especially in a living
room.

coffee-table book *noun*
a large glossy book with many pictures.

coffer *noun*
1 a large strong box, especially for storing
money or valuables.
2 (**coffers**) the treasury or funds: *The
coffers of the Church were badly depleted.*
3 a decorative sunken panel in a ceiling,
etc.

coffin *noun*
a box into which a dead body is placed for
burial.
[Greek *kophinos* basket]

cog *noun*
1 a tooth or projection on a wheel or bar
which fits into and pushes against a
matching tooth or projection on another
wheel or bar.
2 an insignificant person in a large
organization.

cogent (ko-j'nt) *adjective*
having the power to convince or prove:
cogent arguments.
Word Family cogently *adverb;* cogency
noun.
[Latin *cogens* compelling]

cogitate (koj-i-tate) *verb*
(*formal*) to think hard or ponder.
Word Family cogitation (koj-i-tay-sh'n)
noun.
[Latin *cogitare* to consider thoroughly]

cognac (kon-yak) *noun*
a fine brandy.
[first made in *Cognac*, France]

cogwheel *noun*
a wheel with cogs, used to transmit or
receive motion.

cohabitation (ko-hab-i-tay-sh'n) *noun*
the act of living together and having a
sexual relationship outside marriage.
Word Family cohabit (ko-**hab**-it) *verb.*

cohere (ko-**heer**) *verb*
1 to stick together.
2 (of an argument) to agree or be
consistent.
Word Family coherence *noun;* coherent
adjective; coherently *adverb.*
[Latin *cohaerere* to stick together]

cohesion (ko-hee-*zh*'n) *noun*
the state of cohering.
Word Family cohesive *adjective.*

cohort *noun*
1 *Ancient history* a tenth part of a Roman legion.
2 a group or band, especially of warriors.

coif *noun*
a close-fitting cap or hood.

coiffeur (kwa-**fer**) *noun*
(*formal*) a hairdresser.
[French]

coil *noun*
1 a length of rope, wire, etc. wound into a continuous series of rings or spirals.
2 a single ring in such a series.
3 a contraceptive device fitted inside a woman's uterus.
4 *Electronics* a device for carrying an electric current.
• **coil** *verb*.

coin *noun*
a metal disc stamped to show its value as money.
• **coin** *verb*
1 to make coins.
2 to invent: *Who coined the word 'brunch'?*
Phrase **coin it in** (*informal*) to make a lot of money very easily.
Word Family **coinage** *noun*.

coincide (ko-in-**side**) *verb*
1 to occur at the same time or place.
2 (of ideas) to agree: *Her opinions usually coincide with mine.*

coincidence (ko-**in**-si-d'nce) *noun*
1 something which occurs at the same time as another thing by chance: *It was a complete coincidence that he should arrive just as we were talking about him.*
2 the act of coinciding.
Word Family **coincidental** (ko-in-si-**den**-t'l) *adjective* of or involving a coincidence; **coincidentally** *adverb*.
[*co-* + Latin *incidere* to happen]

coitus (**ko**-it-us *or* **koy**-it-us) *noun also* **coition** (ko-**ish**-'n)
(*formal*) the act of sexual intercourse.
[Latin *coire* to go together]

coke *noun*
1 a hard porous solid prepared by heating coal in the absence of air, used as fuel or in the production of iron and steel.
2 (*informal*) cocaine.

col *noun*
Geography a saddle between two higher parts of a mountain range, etc.
[French, neck]

cola *noun*
a non-alcoholic carbonated drink.

colander (**kull**-'n-da) *noun*
a bowl with a lot of small holes in it, used for draining off liquids from food.
[Latin *colare* to strain]

> **!** Do not confuse *colander* with CALENDAR.

cold *adjective*
1 lacking heat or having a low temperature: *cold toes.* □ *a cold morning.*
2 not friendly or not emotional: *his cold stare.*
3 (*informal*) unconscious: *The boxer knocked his rival cold with his first punch.*
Phrase **leave someone cold** to fail to excite someone.
• **cold** *noun*
1 an absence of heat or warmth.
2 *Medicine* an infectious disease causing fever, a sore throat and a blocked nose.
Phrase **out in the cold** neglected and left out.
Word Family **cold** *adverb* completely: *He stopped cold*; **coldly** *adverb* in a cold way: *She looked at him coldly*; **coldness** *noun*.

cold-blooded *adjective*
1 deliberately cruel: *a cold-blooded act.*
2 *Biology* having a body temperature which changes with the temperature of the environment. Fish and snakes are cold-blooded. Compare WARM-BLOODED.
Word Family **cold-bloodedly** *adverb*; **cold-bloodedness** *noun*.

cold comfort *noun*
little or no comfort or consolation.

cold cream *noun*
a thick cream-like substance used to clean or soften the skin.

cold frame *noun*
a wooden frame covered with glass in which young plants can be grown.

cold front *noun* ⇨ FRONT *noun*.

cold-hearted *adjective*
indifferent or unsympathetic.
Word Family **cold-heartedly** *adverb*; **cold-heartedness** *noun*.

cold snap *noun*
a sudden short period of very cold weather.

cold sore *noun*
a viral skin infection causing sores on or near the lips, especially during a cold.
⇨ HERPES.

cold storage *noun*
the storage of perishable foods, etc. in a refrigerated place.

Figurative They put the suggestion in cold *storage* (= a state of indefinite postponement).

cold turkey *noun*
(*informal*) the symptoms resulting from the sudden withdrawal of narcotic drugs.

cold war *noun*
a state of hostility between countries, which stops short of fighting.

coleslaw *noun*
a salad made from raw shredded cabbage with a creamy dressing.
[Dutch *kool* cabbage + *sla* salad]

coley *noun* (*plural* **coley** or **coleys**)
an edible fish of the cod family.

colic (**koll**-ik) *noun*
severe recurring spasms of pain in the abdomen due to partial or complete blockage of a hollow organ, such as the bowel.
Word Family **colicky** *adjective*.

collaborate (k'-**labb**-a-rate) *verb*
to work together: *The two departments collaborated on the project.*
Word Family **collaboration** (k'-labb a-ray-sh'n) *noun*; **collaborator** *noun* a person who collaborates.

> The words **collaborate** and **cooperate** both mean 'to work together' but cannot always be substituted for each other. In English there are many words which are almost synonyms but which are distinguished from each other by shades of meaning. *Collaborate* has a meaning which is derogatory - 'to cooperate with the enemy', e.g. during wartime when the collaboration involves an one's own country. It also has a positive meaning which is closer to *cooperate*, used when the collaboration involves an intellectual enterprise such as writing a book or opera or carrying out scientific research.

collage (**kol**-ahzh or k'-**lahzh**) *noun*
an art form in which various materials such as paper, cloth or string are stuck onto a surface.
[French, gluing]

collagen (**kol**-a-jen) *noun*
a protein found in connective tissue and bones.
[Greek *kolla* glue + *-gen*]

collapse *verb*
1 to fall down suddenly.
2 to fail suddenly: *The company collapsed.*
3 to fold up: *This bed collapses for storage.*

Word Family **collapsible** *adjective*; **collapse** *noun*.
[*col-* + Latin *lapsus* a fall]

collar *noun*
1 anything worn or tied around the neck: *a dog's collar.*
2 the part of a shirt, coat, etc. which surrounds the neck and is usually folded over.
3 a part of a harness, around the horse's shoulders, which enables a load to be pulled.
4 any of various devices encircling a pipe, shaft, rod, etc.
Phrase **hot under the collar** (*informal*) angry and upset.
• **collar** *verb* (*informal*) to seize by the collar or neck.
Figurative He collared me on the way to *work and asked me for a loan.*
Phrase **collar the market** to gain a monopoly.
[Latin *collum* neck]

collarbone *noun* also called **clavicle**.
Anatomy either of two long slender bones joining the chest to the shoulders.

collate (k'-**late**) *verb*
1 to arrange in the correct order: *This printer collates as it prints.*
2 (*formal*) to compare copies, accounts, etc. carefully in order to find any differences between them.
Word Family **collation** (k'-**lay**-sh'n) *noun* the act of collating.
[*col-* + Latin *latus* brought]

collateral (ko-**lat**-a-r'l) *adjective*
secondary or subordinate.
• **collateral** *noun* an asset, such as a car, given as a guarantee for the repayment of a loan.
[*col-* + Latin *lateris* of a side]

colleague (**koll**-eeg) *noun*
a fellow member of a company, profession, etc.
[Latin *conlega*]

collect[1] (k'-**lekt**) *verb*
1 to gather together or accumulate.
2 to accumulate a set of related objects over a period of time: *She collects matchboxes.*
3 to fetch: *The postman collects the letters twice a day.*
4 to gain control of: *I struggled to collect my thoughts.*
• **collect** *adjective, adverb* American to be paid for on delivery: *to send a parcel collect.*
Word Family **collection** (k'-**lek**-sh'n) *noun* 1 the act of collecting. 2 anything

which is collected, such as the money collected during a church service;
collected *adjective* self-possessed;
collectedly *adverb*; **collectedness** *noun*.
[Latin *collectus* gathered together]

collect² (**kol**-ekt) *noun*
Christianity a short set prayer in a traditional form, usually for a season of the year.

collectable *noun* also **collectible**
an object likely to be of interest to collectors.

collective *adjective*
1 combined or united: *a collective effort*.
2 forming a collection: *His publishers have produced a collective edition of his works*.
• **collective** *noun* ⇨ COMMUNE¹ (definition 2).
Word Family collectively *adverb*.

collective noun *noun*
Grammar a singular noun which refers to a group of things or people, such as *flock* or *crew*.

collectivism *noun*
any social or political system based on equal sharing of work, products, etc., such as socialism.
Word Family collectivize, collectivise *verb* to organize according to the principles of collectivism; **collectivist** *noun*, *adjective*.

collector *noun*
a person who collects: *a debt collector*.
□ *a stamp collector*.

college (**kol**-ij) *noun*
1 a place where one goes after leaving school for further education: *an agricultural college*.
2 a large school.
3 one part of the structure of certain universities: *Which Oxford college were you at?*
4 *American* an institution giving a general higher education.
5 an organized group of people with a common profession, interest or pursuit: *the Royal College of Surgeons*.
Word Family collegiate (k'-**lee**-jit) *adjective* of or relating to a college.
[Latin *collegium*]

collide (k'-**lide**) *verb*
to crash together or come into violent contact.
Word Family collision (k'-**lizh**-'n) *noun*.
[*col-* + Latin *laedere* to injure]

collie *noun*
a large long-haired sheepdog.

collier (**kol**-i-a) *noun*
1 a ship which carries coal.
2 a coal miner.
Word Family colliery (**kol**-i-a-ree) *noun* (*plural* **collieries**) a coal mine with its buildings and equipment.

colloid (**kol**-oyd) *noun*
Chemistry a suspension of very fine particles in a liquid. The particles are finer than a simple suspension, but larger than particles in a solution.
Word Family colloidal (k'-**loy**-d'l) *adjective*.
[Greek *kolla* glue + *-oid*]

colloquial (kol-o-**kwee**-al) *adjective*
belonging to casual conversation, as distinct from written or formal speech: *Our teacher told us not to use colloquial expressions in our essays*. Compare SLANG.
Word Family colloquially *adverb*;
colloquialism *noun* a colloquial expression.

collusion (k'-**loo**-*zh*'n) *noun*
a secret agreement between two or more people to defraud another.
Word Family collude *verb*.
[*col-* + Latin *ludere* to play]

collywobbles *plural noun*
(*informal*) a slight discomfort in the stomach, especially one due to nervousness.

cologne (k'-**lone**) *noun* ⇨ EAU DE COLOGNE.

colon¹ (**ko**-lon) *noun*
a punctuation mark (:), used before a quotation, list, statement, etc. introduced by the previous words: *Hannah sent invitations to the following people: Megan, Peter, Ali and Kate*. Compare SEMICOLON.

colon² *noun*
Anatomy the large thin-walled tube forming the lower part of the alimentary canal.
[Greek *kolon*]

colonel (**ker**-n'l) *noun*
Army a commissioned officer ranking between lieutenant colonel and brigadier.
[Latin *columna* a column]

colonial (k'-**lo**-nee-al) *noun*
a person who lives in a colony.
• **colonial** *adjective* of or relating to a colony or a colonist.

colonialism *noun* ⇨ IMPERIALISM.

colonize, colonise (**kol**-a-nize) *verb*
to make into a colony: *Australia was colonized by Great Britain*.

Word Family **colonization** (kol-a-nigh-zay-sh'n) *noun*.

colonnade (kol-a-nade) *noun*
a series of columns supporting a roof, a series of arches, etc.

colony (kol-a-nee) *noun* (*plural* **colonies**)
1 a country settled in and developed by another and remaining under its control. Compare PROTECTORATE.
2 the group of people living in such a settlement.
3 any group of people with similar interests, background, etc. who live together: *a nudist colony.* □ *a colony of Australians in London.*
Word Family **colonist** *noun* a person who lives in or first establishes a colony.
[Latin *colonus* a farmer, a colonist]

colophon (kol-a-fon) *noun*
any decorative initial or small drawing identifying a publishing firm and printed on its books.
[Greek *kolophon* the end]

coloration (kull-er-ay-sh'n) *noun* also **colouration**
arrangement of colours: *the insect's delicate coloration.*

colossal (k'-loss-'l) *adjective*
enormous.
[Greek *kolossos* a giant statue]

colossus (k'-loss-us) *noun* (*plural* **colossi** (k'-loss-eye) or **colossuses**)
anything of enormous size or importance
[from the bronze statue of Apollo at Rhodes, called the *Colossus*, whose legs straddled the entrance to the harbour]

colour (kull-a) *noun* (*American* **color**)
1 the sensation produced in the brain by light of different wavelengths hitting the eye.
2 red, yellow, blue, etc.: *What colour is her car?*
3 a person's complexion or skin pigmentation.
4 interest and excitement: *the colour of the local markets.*
5 (**colours**) an award, such as that given to leading players in a team.
6 (**colours**) any distinctive colour, symbol, flag, etc. of identification: *a jockey's colours.*
Phrases **off colour** unwell: *He seemed a little off colour.* **troop the colour** to carry the colours or flag of a regiment ceremoniously before the troops on parade. **true colours** real and less pleasant nature: *You wait – you'll see him in*

his true colours before long! **with flying colours** very successfully: *She passed her exams with flying colours.*
• **colour** *verb*
1 to add colour, e.g. by painting or dyeing.
2 to blush.
3 to influence: *His story was coloured by emotion.*
Word Family **coloured** *adjective* 1 having colour. 2 of or relating to a member of any non-white race of people. This term is often considered offensive; **colourful** *adjective* 1 full of colour. 2 interesting or picturesque; **colourfully** *adverb*; **colourfulness** *noun*; **colourless** *adjective* 1 having little or no colour. 2 uninteresting; **colourlessly** *adverb*; **colourlessness** *noun*.
[Latin *color*]

colour bar *noun*
any discrimination against members of a non-white race.

colour-blind *adjective*
unable to distinguish between colours.
Word Family **colour blindness** *noun*.

colour-code *verb*
to put different coloured marks on different items in order to show which set of things they belong to.

colour-fast *adjective*
(of fabrics) dyed with colours that will not run or fade when put in water.

colouring *noun*
1 a substance that gives food, drink, etc. added colour.
2 a person's complexion or skin pigmentation.

colt *noun*
a young male horse, especially one up to three years old.
Word Family **coltish** *adjective* young or inexperienced.

columbine *noun*
a garden plant whose flowers have five petals resembling a cluster of doves.
[Latin *columba* a dove]

column (kol-um) *noun*
1 an upright support, usually made of brick or stone.
2 anything with a similar shape, e.g. the vertical blocks of lines of type on a page: *This page has two columns.* □ *a thin column of smoke.*
3 a short magazine or newspaper article which appears regularly, usually written by the same person.

4 *Military* a formation of troops or vehicles following one after another.
[Latin *columna*]

columnist (**kol**-um-nist) *noun*
a person who writes a newspaper or magazine column.

coma (**ko**-ma) *noun*
a state of deep unconsciousness, usually due to injury or disease.
Word Family **comatose** *adjective* affected with or as if with coma.
[Greek *koma* deep sleep]

comb (kome) *noun*
1 an object of plastic, metal, etc. with teeth for smoothing or untangling hair, wool, etc.
2 any part or device with the shape or function of a comb.
3 an act of combing: *Give your hair a comb.*
4 short form of **cockscomb** *Biology* the fleshy growth on the head of a domestic fowl.
● **comb** *verb*
1 to arrange or untangle with a comb.
2 to search thoroughly: *Police combed the district for the missing child.*

combat (**kom**-bat) *noun*
1 a fight or battle.
2 any vigorous opposition or struggle.
● **combat** *verb* (**combats; combating** or **combatting; combated** or **combatted**)
to oppose or fight against.
Word Family **combatant** (**kom**-ba-t'nt) *noun* a person taking part in a fight or combat; **combatant** *adjective*.
[*com-* + Latin *battuere* to strike]

combat fatigue *noun* also called **shell shock.**
a mental disorder caused by extreme stress, especially among soldiers at war.

combative (**kom**-ba-tiv) *adjective*
eager to fight.

combination (kom-bi-**nay**-sh'n) *noun*
1 the act of combining.
2 anything formed by a number of things joining or combining: *Salmon and asparagus make a delicious combination.*
3 *Maths* a set of elements selected from a given larger set, regardless of their arrangement. Compare PERMUTATION (definition 2).
4 (**combinations**) (*formerly*) a one-piece undergarment which covered the whole body.

combination lock *noun*
a lock which can only be opened if its dial is turned through a certain sequence of positions which are shown by numbers or letters.

combine (kom-**bine**) *verb*
to join several things into one: *They all combined their talents to put on a show.*
● **combine** (**kom**-bine) *noun* a combination, especially of people or businesses joining together for commercial or political reasons, e.g. to fix prices.
[*com-* + Latin *bini* a pair]

combine harvester *noun*
a machine which reaps, threshes and winnows grain in one process.

combo *noun*
(*informal*) a small group of jazz musicians.

combustible (kom-**bust**-a-b'l) *adjective*
able to burn.
Word Family **combustibility** (kom-bus-ti-**bill**-i-tee) *noun*.

combustion (kom-**bus**-ch'n) *noun*
1 the act or process of burning.
2 *Chemistry* a chemical reaction in which a substance combines with oxygen to produce heat and light.
[Latin *combustus* burnt up]

come (kum) *verb* (**comes; coming; came; come**)
1 to approach or move towards: *Come and sit beside me.*
2 to arrive or reach: *They came to a deserted house.* □ *Hitler came to power in 1933.*
3 to occur or happen: *My birthday comes after yours.*
4 to change into a particular state: *The parcel came undone.*
5 (*informal*) to have an orgasm.
Phrases **come about** to happen. **come across 1** to find or meet with, especially by chance. **2** to be understood. **come along** to hurry. **come by** to acquire: *How did you come by that painting?* **come forward** to present oneself to give information or evidence. **come from 1** to be from: *They come from Bristol.* **2** to be produced by or in: *Honey comes from bees.* **come in for** to receive: *She came in for a lot of criticism in the press.* **come into** to inherit. **come in useful, come in handy** to be useful. **come of** to result from: *See what comes of lying!* **come off 1** to take place. **2** to succeed. **3** to become unfastened. **come on 1** to progress. **2** to appear onstage. **3** to hurry. **come on to** (*informal*) to show that one is sexually interested in: *That guy's coming on to you, Hannah!* **come out 1** to be published. **2** to become evident. **3** to get a particular place in a test, competition, etc.: *I came out on*

top. **4** to go on strike. **5** (*informal*) to say publicly that one is homosexual. **come out with** to tell or reveal: *He suddenly came out with the whole story.* **come over** to affect: *I'm sorry – I don't know what came over me!* **come round 1** to regain consciousness. **2** to change an opinion, etc. **come through** to survive: *She came through two bouts of pneumonia.* **come to 1** to total. **2** to regain consciousness. **come to pass** an old phrase meaning 'to happen'. **come up** to occur: *A new problem has come up.* **come up against** to be confronted with. **come upon** to find by chance: *We came upon a pile of old coins.* **come up with** to produce or propose. **come what may** whatever happens.

comeback *noun*
1 a return to a previous position of success.
2 (*informal*) a clever reply.

comedian (k'-meed-i-an) *noun*
1 a performer in a comedy or comic act.
2 any person who is or attempts to be funny.
Word Family **comedienne** (k' m'e'-i-en) *noun* a female comedian.

> The word **comedienne** is still commonly used for a comedian who is a female and it seems to be quite acceptable. However this is not true of all feminine forms of words. Some of these are considered sexist or patronizing and are best avoided, e.g. *authoress, poetess* and *sculptress. Author, poet* and *sculptor* are considered to be neutral terms rather than only masculine forms. This feature of language is still in a state of change and there are some inconsistencies, e.g. *hostess* and *waitress* are still commonly used without much objection.

comedown *noun*
1 a loss of a position of success.
2 a feeling of disappointment and anticlimax.

comedy (kom-a-dee) *noun* (*plural* **comedies**)
1 any form of entertainment which causes amusement or light-hearted enjoyment. Compare TRAGEDY (definition 1).
2 any funny event or series of events.
black comedy a comedy with a tragic, gruesome or pessimistic theme.
[Greek *komoidia*]

comely (kum-lee) *adjective* (**comelier; comeliest**)
(*dated*) pleasing or attractive.
Word Family **comeliness** *noun*.

come-on *noun*
(*informal*) any behaviour intended to make another person interested, usually in a sexual way.

comestible (kom-est-i-b'l) *noun*
(*usually* **comestibles**) food.

comet *noun*
a celestial body moving around the sun and containing a bright nucleus surrounded by a hazy cloud which extends into a tail.
[Greek *kometes* long-haired]

comeuppance *noun*
(*informal*) a deserved punishment.

comfort (kum-fut) *noun*
1 a state of pleasant freedom from suffering: *They live in great comfort.*
2 hope or consolation: *a few words of comfort.*
3 anything which causes comfort or relief: *Visits from old friends are a comfort to her.*
• comfort *verb* to cause to be less unhappy: *She comforted us in our grief.*
Word Family **comforting** *adjective*; **comfortingly** *adverb*; **comfortless** *adjective*.
[*com-* + Latin *fortis* strong]

comfortable (kumf-ta-b'l) *adjective*
1 giving comfort: *a comfortable old armchair.*
2 being in a state of comfort: *I'm comfortable here, thanks.*
Word Family **comfortably** *adverb*.

comforter (kum-f'-ter) *noun*
1 a person or thing that comforts.
2 (*formerly*) a thick woollen scarf or wrapper.

comfy (kum-fee) *adjective* (**comfier; comfiest**)
(*informal*) comfortable.

comic *adjective*
of or relating to comedy: *a comic actor.*
• comic *noun*
1 a magazine of stories, etc. told in comic strips.
2 a funny person or actor: *He is a natural comic.*

comical *adjective*
amusing or funny: *His comical expression made us all laugh.*
Word Family **comically** *adverb*.

comic relief ⇨ LIGHT RELIEF.

comic strip *noun* also called **cartoon**.
a series of drawings which tell a story or
joke.

comma *noun*
a punctuation mark (,), used to show
pauses in sentences, to separate items in
lists, to divide or enclose clauses, etc.: *He
played tennis, cricket, football and golf every
week.* □ *The local shop, which sells most
things, is closed on Wednesday afternoon.*

command *verb*
1 to order.
2 to have control over: *He commands a unit
of 50 men.*
3 to deserve to receive: *She commands great
respect.*
4 (*formal*) to dominate: *The hotel
commands a wonderful view of the valley.*
● **command** *noun*
1 an order given: *He ignored the commands
to stop.*
2 the possession of control or authority:
Who is in command here?
3 the ability to use something: *Her
command of the language is excellent.*
4 *Military* a force or clearly defined region
under the authority of an officer.
***Word Family* commanding** *adjective*
showing superior authority or strength.
[*com-* + Latin *mandare* to entrust]

commandant (komm-'n-dant) *noun*
the commanding officer of a military
establishment, such as a fortress or school.

commandeer (komm-'n-**deer**) *verb*
to take or seize something, especially for
official use: *The police commandeered a
private launch to continue the chase.*

commander (k'-**mahn**-da) *noun*
1 any person who leads or has command,
such as the chief commissioned officer of a
military unit.
2 *Navy* a commissioned officer ranking
between lieutenant commander and
captain.

commandment (k'-**mahnd**-m'nt) *noun*
Religion a divine law: *the story of Moses and
the Ten Commandments.*

commando (k'-**mahnd**-o) *noun*
a member of a special combined military
and naval force trained for swift
destructive raids or attacks.

command performance *noun*
the performance of a play or other
entertainment at the request of a monarch
or other high official.

commemorate (k'-**mem**-a-rate) *verb*
to honour the memory of something.
***Word Family* commemoration** (k'-
mem-a-**ray**-sh'n) *noun*; **commemorative**
adjective.
[*com-* + Latin *memorare* to mention]

commence *verb*
(*formal*) to start or begin.
***Word Family* commencement** *noun.*

commend *verb*
1 to praise or speak of as worthy, suitable,
etc.: *The young soldier was commended for his
bravery in action.*
2 (*formal*) to give to the care of: *He
commended his soul to the Lord.*
***Word Family* commendation** *noun* **1** an
official honour: *a commendation for bravery.*
2 any praise or approval; **commendable**
adjective being worthy of praise;
commendably *adverb*; **commendatory**
adjective giving praise or approval.
[*com-* + Latin *mandare* to entrust]

commensurate (k'-**men**-sha-rit) *adjective*
(*formal*) being of the same or equal value.
[*com-* + Latin *mensura* measurement]

comment *noun*
a note or remark made to explain, criticize,
etc.
● **comment** *verb.*

commentary (**komm**-'n-tree) *noun*
(*plural* **commentaries**)
1 a continuous sequence of written
comments or notes which explain or give
further information on a text.
2 a spoken description on radio or
television of an event while it is happening.
[Latin *commentari* to think over]

commentate *verb*
to act as a commentator.

commentator (**komm**-'n-tay-ta) *noun*
a person who gives a commentary: *a racing
commentator.*

commerce *noun*
1 any trade or business activity.
2 (*dated*) any exchange, especially between
people.
[*com-* + Latin *mercis* of merchandise]

commercial (k'-**mer**-sh'l) *adjective*
1 of or relating to commerce: *commercial
vehicles.*
2 made for sale or profit: *Her last book was
not a commercial success.*
3 financed or sponsored by advertisers:
commercial radio.
commercial farming farming in which
crops or animals are grown for sale.

Compare SUBSISTENCE FARMING under
SUBSISTENCE.
commercial practices systems used by
business.
• **commercial** *noun* an advertisement on
radio or television.
Word Family **commercialize,
commercialise** *verb* to turn something
into a business or money-making project;
commercialization *noun*.

commercial traveller *noun*
(*dated*) a sales representative.

commiserate (k'-miz-a-rate) *verb*
to express sorrow or pity: *They
commiserated with me about the accident.*
Word Family **commiseration** (k'-miz-a-
ray-sh'n) *noun*.
[*com-* + Latin *misereri* to pity]

commissar (kom-i-sar) *noun*
the head of a government department in
certain countries, especially Russia.

commission (k'-mish-'n) *noun*
1 any fee paid to an agent for services such
as buying or selling goods.
2 an order for a particular task, duty or
appointment: *Who got the commission to
build the bridge?*
3 a group of people officially appointed for
a particular duty: *a government commission
on women's rights.*
4 an appointment to a high rank in one of
the armed forces: *She finally received her
commission.*
5 (*formal*) the act of committing.
Phrase **out of commission** not
functioning.
• **commission** *verb*
1 to give a commission to.
2 to ask someone to produce: *The bishop
commissioned a portrait of himself.*

commissionaire (k'-mish-'n-**air**) *noun*
a doorkeeper in uniform, e.g. at a hotel.

commissioner (k'-mish-'n-er) *noun*
an appointed official, especially one in
charge of a department: *a police
commissioner.*

commit (k'-mit) *verb* (**commits;
committing; committed**)
1 to do or perform: *Dr Crippen committed
murder.*
2 to promise that a person or organization
will do something: *The Prime Minister has
now committed himself to reform the system.*
3 to send to an institution, especially a
mental hospital.
4 to give or put into the trust or charge of:
She committed the whole poem to memory.

Word Family **commitment** *noun* 1 a
promise to do something. 2 the state of
being committed: *We appreciate your loyalty
and commitment.* 3 also **committal**
(*formal*) the act of committing.
[Latin *committere* to entrust]

committee *noun*
a small group of people appointed to
represent a larger group.

commode *noun*
a low box-like stand into which a chamber
pot is fitted.

commodious (k'-mo-dee-us) *adjective*
(*formal*) spacious.

commodity (k'-mod-i-tee) *noun* (*plural*
commodities)
anything useful, especially an article of
trade: *the export of cotton, tea and other
commodities.*

commodore (komm-a-dor) *noun*
1 *Navy* a commissioned officer ranking
between captain and rear admiral.
2 the president of a yacht or boat club.

common *adjective*
1 usual or frequent: *a common event.*
2 ordinary: *common salt.* □ *the common man.*
3 shared by two or more people: *It is
common knowledge that she is a thief.*
□ *united for the common good.*
4 rough and socially inferior: *a rather
common girl.*
Phrase **common to** shared by: *analysing
the features common to both cases.*
• **common** *noun* a piece of land used by a
community for grazing animals, etc.
Phrase **in common** shared: *They don't
have much in common.*
Word Family **commonly** *adverb*.

common denominator *noun*
1 a quality shared by a group.
2 *Maths* ⇨ DENOMINATOR.

commoner *noun*
a person who is not a peer.

common fraction *noun* also called
proper fraction; vulgar fraction.
Maths a fraction less than 1, e.g. $\frac{1}{2}$ or $\frac{7}{10}$.

common law *noun*
Law the system of law based on old
customs or court decisions, as distinct
from laws made by an Act of Parliament.

Common Market *noun*
(*dated*) the European Union.

common-or-garden *adjective*
ordinary or uninteresting.

commonplace *adjective*
ordinary or dull.

common room *noun*
sitting room for students or staff in a school or college.

commons *plural noun*
1 (*formerly*) commoners, as a group.
2 (**the Commons**) the House of Commons.

common sense *noun*
practical sense or judgement: *She is very intelligent but lacks common sense.*

Commonwealth *noun*
1 also **British Commonwealth** an association of independent countries which were once ruled by Britain, with the Queen as its head.
2 a federation of states.
3 *History* a republic, especially England under Cromwell.

commotion (k'-mo-sh'n) *noun*
a noisy or violent disturbance.

communal (kom-yoo-n'l *or* k'-**mew**-n'l) *adjective*
being shared or for common use: *a communal bathroom.*
Word Family **communally** *adverb.*

commune¹ (kom-yoon) *noun*
1 a local community having a degree of self-government, but subject to central control.
2 also called **collective**. a group of people who share property and tasks, living together by their own rules and standards.
[Latin *communis* shared]

commune² (k'-**mewn**) *verb*
(*dated*) to talk together.

communicable (k'-**mew**-ni-k'-b'l) *adjective*
able to be passed on.

communicate (k'-**mew**-ni-kate) *verb*
1 to pass on or share information or feelings: *He finds it difficult to communicate with young people.*
2 (*formal*) to pass on: *diseases communicated by coughing.*
3 (of rooms) to join.
4 *Christianity* to administer or receive Communion.
Word Family **communicator** *noun* a person who communicates information; **communicant** *noun* a person who receives or is entitled to receive Communion; **communicative** *adjective* willing to communicate.
[Latin *communicare* to confer with]

communication *noun*
1 the act of communicating: *There is not much communication between the two families.*
2 something which is communicated: *She received an important communication.*
3 (**communications**) the means of travelling or sending messages, etc. between places: *a communications satellite.*

communion (k'-**mewn**-y'n) *noun*
1 a sharing or exchange of thoughts or feelings.
2 (**Communion**) short form of **Holy Communion** *Christianity* a ceremony at which people receive bread and wine from a priest, to remember Christ.

communiqué (k'-**mew**-ni-kay) *noun*
an official statement, especially one made by a government concerning special events.

communism (**kom**-yoo-nizm) *noun*
the belief in or practice of a social system based on the sharing of all work and property by the whole community. Compare CAPITALISM.
Word Family **communist** *noun, adjective.*

community (k'-**mew**-ni-tee) *noun* (*plural* **communities**)
1 any group living in one place or having common interests.
2 the general public: *Crime prevention is the responsibility of the whole community.*
3 (*formal*) a sharing: *a community of interests.*

community home *noun*
a school where young people who have committed a crime live.

community policing *noun*
the provision of police officers in an area who are either from the area or well known to the residents.

community service *noun*
unpaid work done to benefit the community in some way, sometimes undertaken under a court order by people who would otherwise have gone to prison.

commute (k'-**mewt**) *verb*
1 to travel regularly between home and work.
2 to alter or make less severe: *The prisoner's death sentence was commuted to life imprisonment.*
Word Family **commuter** *noun* a person who commutes between home and work.
[Latin *commutare* to alter]

compact¹ (kom-**pakt**) *adjective*
closely packed or fitted together.
• **compact** (kom-pakt) *noun* a container
for face powder.
Word Family **compact** (kom-**pakt**) *verb*
to join or pack firmly together; **compactly**
adverb; **compactness** *noun*.

compact² (**kom**-pakt) *noun*
a formal agreement or contract.

compact disc *noun*
short form is **CD** a flat thin circular piece
of plastic which can hold audio and visual
images for playback on an appropriate
machine (**compact disc player**).

companion (k'm-**pan**-y'n) *noun*
1 a person who accompanies or associates
with another: *a travelling companion.*
2 either of a pair of matching things: *Do
you have the companion to the first volume?*
Word Family **companionship** *noun*.
[com- + Latin *panis* bread, originally a
person who ate bread with another]

companionable (k'm-**pan**-y'n-a-b'l)
adjective
friendly: *a companionable silence.*

companionway *noun*
steps which go from one deck of a ship to
another.

company (**kum**-pa-nee) *noun* (*plural*
companies)
1 a business organization: *Microsoft and
other computer companies.*
2 being with another person or other
people: *Would you like some company?*
□ *I enjoy his company.*
3 an army unit consisting of three
platoons.
Phrases **keep someone company** to
spend time with someone. **part company**
to separate from someone.

company car *noun*
a car provided by a person's employer,
used for business or pleasure.

comparative (k'm-**parr**-a-tiv) *adjective*
1 *Grammar* ⇨ DEGREE (definition 6).
2 measured by a comparison which is
not clearly stated: *This was a time of
comparative peace in the Welsh borders.*
3 based on or involving comparison: *a
comparative study.*
• **comparative** *noun* a form of an
adjective or adverb which compares
quality or degree: *The comparative of 'good'
is 'better'.*
Word Family **comparatively** *adverb*.

compare (kom-**pair**) *verb*
1 to judge or note the similarities or
differences of: *Let's compare your answers
with mine.*
2 to represent as similar or like: *The press
compared him to Einstein.*
Phrases **cannot compare with** is not as
good as: *The film cannot compare with the
book.* **compare notes** (*informal*) to
exchange ideas, feelings, etc.: *They
compared notes on the party.*
• **compare** *noun*
Phrase **beyond compare, without
compare** without comparison or equal:
riches beyond compare.
Word Family **comparable** (**kom**-pra-
b'l) *adjective* able or suitable to be
compared.
[Latin *comparare* to match together]

> [!] Compare to and compare with are
> sometimes interchangeable, but
> *compare to* is generally used to say that
> one person or thing is like another, as in
> *The author compares the hills to a rolling
> sea*, and *compare with* is generally used
> to discuss similarities and differences,
> as in *Write an essay comparing life in
> Britain with life in Japan.*

comparison (k'm-**parr**-i-s'n) *noun*
1 the act of comparing.
2 likeness or similarity: *There is no
comparison between them.*

compartment *noun*
any of several separate parts or divisions
of a structure: *a luggage compartment in a
train.* □ *He keeps everything in separate
compartments in his brain.*
Word Family **compartmentalize,
compartmentalise** *verb* to put into
separate compartments;
compartmentalization *noun*.
[com- + Latin *partiri* to share]

compass (**kum**-pus) *noun* (*plural*
compasses)
1 an instrument used to find direction,
with a magnetized needle which points to
magnetic north.
2 also **pair of compasses** an instrument
for drawing circles, consisting of two rods,
one pointed and the other holding a
marker, hinged together at one end.
3 (*formal*) the range or limits of anything:
matters beyond the compass of this enquiry.
Word Family **compass** *verb* an old word
for **surround**.

compassion (k'm-**pash**-'n) *noun*
a strong feeling of understanding, pity or
sympathy for the sufferings of another
person.
Word Family **compassionate** *adjective*;
compassionately *adverb*.
[*com-* + Latin *passus* suffered]

compassion fatigue *noun*
an indifference towards the hardship of
those in need, caused by having been
exposed to a great many charitable
appeals.

compatible (k'm-**pat**-i-b'l) *adjective*
able to exist together in harmony: *Our
political ideas are not compatible.*
Word Family **compatibly** *adverb*;
compatibility (k'm-pat-i-**bill**-i-tee) *noun*.

compatriot (k'm-**pat**-ri-'t) *noun*
a person from the same country as oneself.

compel (k'm-**pell**) *verb* (**compels;
compelling; compelled**)
to force: *I felt compelled to tell him the truth.*
Word Family **compelling** *adjective*
forceful: *a compelling argument.*
[Latin *compellere*]

compendium *noun* (*plural*
compendiums or **compendia**)
a detailed or comprehensive summary.
[Latin, an abbreviating]

compensate (**kom**-pen-sate) *verb*
to make up for something: *No amount of
money could compensate for the damage to his
reputation.*
Word Family **compensatory** (kom-pen-
say-ta-ree *or* kom-**pen**-sa-tree) *adjective*.
[Latin *compensare* to counterbalance]

compensation (kom-pen-**say**-sh'n) *noun*
1 something which compensates for loss or
injury, especially a sum of money: *The
court awarded her £50 000 compensation.*
2 the act of compensating.

compère (**kom**-pair) *noun*
a person who introduces each item in a
radio or television programme, theatre
show, etc.
• **compère** *verb*.

compete (kom-**peet**) *verb*
to take part in a competition or contest:
*Small shops cannot compete with the
supermarkets.*
Word Family **competitor** (kom-**pet**-i-ta)
noun.
[*com-* + Latin *petere* to seek]

competent (**kom**-pi-t'nt) *adjective*
having the ability, power or qualifications

to do something: *He's not an expert rider,
but he's pretty competent.*
Word Family **competence, competency**
noun.

competition (kom-pa-**tish**-'n) *noun*
1 any activity in which people try to outdo
or defeat each other: *a wrestling
competition.*
2 the act of competing: *There was fierce
competition for the contract.*
3 the person or group that one opposes in
a competition: *The competition was poor.*
Word Family **competitive** (kom-**pet**-a-
tiv) *adjective* of or involving competition;
competitively *adverb*.

compile *verb*
to collect and put together a number of
things, especially to form a book, etc.: *The
index was compiled by a computer.*
Word Family **compilation** (kom-pi-**lay**-
sh'n) *noun*; **compiler** *noun*.
[Latin *compilare* to cram together hastily]

complacent (k'm-**play**-s'nt) *adjective*
self-satisfied or smug.
Word Family **complacently** *adverb*;
complacence, complacency *noun*.
[*com-* + Latin *placere* to please]

complain *verb*
to talk of or express dissatisfaction, pain,
etc.: *They have complained to the police
about the threats.*
Word Family **complainingly** *adverb*;
complainer *noun*.
[*com-* + Latin *plangere* to bewail]

complainant *noun*
Law a plaintiff.

complaint *noun*
1 an expression or statement of
discontent, pain, etc.
2 an illness: *Measles is usually quite a mild
complaint.*

complement (**kom**-pli-m'nt) *noun*
1 anything which completes or makes
something else whole: *Choose a wine that is
a good complement to fish.*
2 the full or total number or amount: *the
ship's complement.*
3 *Maths* the number of degrees that must
be added to an acute angle to make it a
right angle.
4 *Grammar* a word, phrase or clause that
adds to the meaning of another element of
a sentence.
Word Family **complement** (**kom**-pli-
ment) *verb*; **complementary** (kom-pli-
men-ta-ree) *adjective*.

> ⚠️ The words *complement* and *compliment* sound the same but have different spellings and meanings. *Complement* has two *e*'s and means 'something added'; *compliment* has an *i* in the middle and means 'an expression of praise'. There are many such pairs of words, called *homophones*, in English, e.g. *currant/current, elicit/illicit, fair/fare, gait/gate, hangar/hanger, key/quay, knead/need, leak/leek, muscle/mussel, pail/pale, pain/pane, principal/principle, stationary/stationery, waive/wave.*

complementary medicine *noun*
a form of medical treatment which uses techniques not generally accepted by conventional doctors, such as acupuncture and homeopathy.

complete (k'm-**pleet**) *adjective*
1 having all its parts: *Is this jigsaw complete?*
2 finished: *When will the work be complete?*
3 in every way: *He is a complete fool.*
Word Family **complete** *verb* 1 to make whole or perfect. 2 to finish or bring to an end; **completely** *adverb*; **completeness** *noun*.
[*com-* + Latin *pletus* filled up]

completion (k'm-**plee**-sh'n) *noun*
1 the act of making complete: *The completion of the bridge took five years.*
2 the state of being complete: *The project was nearing completion*

complex *adjective*
intricate or complicated: *a complex design.*
• **complex** *noun* (*plural* **complexes**)
1 anything made up of different connected parts: *a shopping complex.*
2 *Psychology* any confused mental state resulting from past and sometimes repressed experiences.
3 (*informal*) an overanxious attitude: *She has a complex about her weight.*
Word Family **complexity** *noun* (*plural* **complexities**).
[Latin *complexus* an embrace]

complexion (kom-**plek**-sh'n) *noun*
1 the natural appearance or colour, especially of the skin.
2 (*formal*) the nature of something: *The quarrel changed the complexion of their relationship.*

complicate (kom-pli-kate) *verb*
to make something difficult to do, understand, etc.
Word Family **complicated** *adjective*
1 difficult. 2 made up of many parts: *a*

complicated machine; **complication** (kom-pli-**kay**-sh'n) *noun* 1 a difficulty. 2 an illness in addition to an existing illness: *The patient developed complications and died.*
[*com-* + Latin *plicare* to fold]

complicity (k'm-**pliss**-i-tee) *noun*
(*formal*) the state of being a partner in wrongdoing: *The driver of the getaway van was charged with complicity in the robbery.*
[Late Latin *complicis* of a confederate]

compliment (kom-pli-m'nt) *noun*
1 an expression of praise or respect: *He paid his girlfriend a lovely compliment.*
2 (**compliments**) greetings or kind wishes: *Give my compliments to your mother.*
Word Family **compliment** (kom-pli-ment) *verb*; **complimentary** (kom-pli-**men**-ta-ree) *adjective* 1 expressing a compliment. 2 free of charge.

> ⚠️ Do not confuse *compliment* with COMPLEMENT.

compline (komp-lin) *noun*
Christianity evening service.
[Latin (*hora*) *completa* the final hour]

comply (kom-**ply**) *verb* (**complies; complying; complied**)
to do what is asked or demanded: *All competitors will comply with the rules.*
Word Family **compliant** *adjective* willing to comply; **compliantly** *adverb*; **compliance, compliancy** *noun*.

component (k'm-**po**-nent) *noun*
1 anything which forms part of a whole system, machine, design, etc: *An engine has many components.*
2 *Physics* the effect of a force in a particular direction. A force can be thought of as a combination of two or more components.
[*com-* + Latin *ponere* to put]

comport (k'm-**port**) *verb*
Phrase **comport oneself** (*formal*) to behave.
Word Family **comportment** *noun* behaviour.
[*com-* + Latin *portare* to carry]

compose (k'm-**poze**) *verb*
1 to make up or form: *The exam is composed of four sections.*
2 to put words, ideas, notes, etc. together in literary or musical form.
3 to control or make calm: *She tried to compose her thoughts.*
Word Family **composer** *noun* a person who composes music, etc.; **composed** *adjective* calm; **composedly** (k'm-**po**-zid-

lee) *adverb*; **composure** (kom-**po**-zher)
noun calmness or self-control.

composite (kom-pa-zit) *adjective*
1 made up of different parts.
2 (of a plant) having flowers with heads
made up of many small flowers: *The daisy
is a composite plant.*
3 (of a material) made by combining more
than one material to improve its
properties.
• **composite** *noun* something made up of
different parts, such as a composite
material or a composite plant.
Word Family **compositely** *adverb*;
compositeness *noun*.
[*com-* + Latin *positus* placed]

composition (kom-pa-**zish**-'n) *noun*
1 the act of composing: *The composition of
the symphony took three years.*
2 something which is composed: *It was his
last but greatest composition.*
3 the way something is composed: *studying
the composition of the earth's atmosphere.*
4 an essay.

compositor (kom-**pozz**-i-ta) *noun*
a person who typesets.

compos mentis (kom-pus **men**-tis)
adjective
having complete control of one's mental
powers.
[Latin]

compost (kom-posst) *noun*
a mixture of decaying plant matter put in
the soil to fertilize it.

compound¹ (kom-pound) *adjective*
made up of two or more parts, actions,
etc.: *'Blackberry' is a compound word.*
• **compound** *noun*
1 anything made up of combined parts.
2 *Chemistry* a pure substance in which
elements are chemically combined in a
definite ratio. Water (H_2O) is a compound
in which atoms of hydrogen and oxygen
are bound together in the ratio 2:1.
Compare ELEMENT (definition 1).
3 *Grammar* a word made up of two other
words, e.g. *handbag* or *brainwash*.
• **compound** (k'm-**pound**) *verb*
1 to put parts together to form a whole.
2 to make worse: *He compounded his crime
by lying about it.*

compound² (kom-pound) *noun*
an enclosed area with buildings, used as a
residence for workers, a prison during war,
etc.

compound interest *noun* ⇨ INTEREST
noun.

comprehend (kom-pri-**hend**) *verb*
1 to understand or know fully: *It was
difficult to comprehend the importance of what
had happened.*
2 (*formal*) to include.
[*com-* + Latin *prehendere* to take hold of]

comprehensible (kom-pri-**hen**-sa-b'l)
adjective
able to be comprehended.
Word Family **comprehensibly** *adverb*;
comprehensibility (kom-pri-hen-sa-
bill-i-tee) *noun.*

comprehension (kom-pri-**hen**-sh'n)
noun
the act or power of understanding: *Such
behaviour is totally beyond my
comprehension.*

comprehensive *adjective*
inclusive or detailed in content: *a
comprehensive report of the trial.*
Word Family **comprehensively** *adverb.*

comprehensive school *noun*
a secondary school for children of all
abilities.

compress (k'm-**press**) *verb*
to press closely together or force into a
smaller space: *tanks of compressed air.*
• **compress** (**kom**-press) *noun*
Medicine a soft pad of material held against
the body or a wound, especially to apply
pressure.
Word Family **compressor** *noun* anything
which compresses, such as a machine for
compressing gases; **compression** (kom-
presh-'n) *noun*; **compressive** *adjective.*
[*com-* + Latin *pressus* pressed]

compressive strength *noun*
the ability of a material to resist crushing.

comprise (k'm-**prize**) *verb*
to consist of: *The country comprises six
independent regions.*

> ⚠ Both *comprise* and *consist of* mean
> 'to be composed of', but note
> their usage. A whole *comprises* (or
> *consists of*) all its parts: *The company
> comprises* (or *consists of*) *ten separate
> divisions.* Note that the separate parts
> *make up* but do not *comprise* the whole.
> Note too that the use of *comprise*
> followed by *of* is incorrect.

compromise (kom-pra-mize) *verb*
1 to settle differences by each side giving
up something and receiving less than it
asked for: *The strike was settled when the*

management and the unions compromised on wage increases.
2 to accept less than the ideal: *You will have to learn to compromise.*
3 to expose to danger, suspicion, etc: *Do not compromise your position by acting foolishly.*
• **compromise** *noun*
1 a settlement by compromising.
2 an acceptance of less than the ideal.
[*com-* + Latin *promissus* promised]

compulsion (k'm-**pul**-sh'n) *noun*
1 the act of compelling or forcing: *There is no compulsion for you to come with us.*
2 a strong, often unreasonable, urge: *She felt a sudden compulsion to run away.*
[Latin *compulsus* forced]

compulsive (k'm-**pul**-siv) *adjective*
having an uncontrollable urge or desire: *a compulsive gambler.*
Word Family **compulsively** *adverb.*

compulsory (k'm-**pul**-sa-ree) *adjective*
forced or required: *English lessons are compulsory for all pupils.*
Word Family **compulsorily** *adverb*; **compulsoriness** *noun.*

compunction (k'm-**punk**-sh'n) *noun*
a feeling of regret or uneasiness caused by guilt or shame: *She felt no compunction in hitting the burglar.*
[*com-* + Latin *punctus* stung, troubled]

compute (k'm-**pewt**) *verb*
to find an answer by calculating mathematically.
Word Family **computation** (kom-pew-**tay**-sh'n) *noun* 1 the act of calculating.
2 the amount calculated.
[Latin *computare* to reckon up]

computer (k'm-**pew**-ta) *noun*
an electronic machine performing complicated calculations very rapidly and capable of storing and retrieving information.

computer-aided design *noun*
short form is **CAD** the use of computers to design on screen.

computer-aided manufacturing *noun*
short form is **CAM** the use of computers to control manufacturing processes. Industrial examples include electronic knitting machines and packaging cutters.

computer game *noun*
a game of skill played on a computer screen, the moves being made on a keyboard or by means of a joystick, mouse, etc.

computer graphics ⇨ GRAPHICS (definition 2).

computer-integrated manufacture *noun*
short form is **CIM** the automatic transfer of information between the head office and factory of a company.

computerize, computerise *verb*
to use computers to organize a system.
Word Family **computerization** *noun.*

computer-literate *adjective*
having the necessary knowledge to use computers.
Word Family **computer literacy** *noun.*

computer science *noun*
the study of computers.

computer virus ⇨ VIRUS (definition 3).

comrade (**kom**-rad *or* **kom**-rade) *noun*
1 a close or loyal friend.
2 a fellow member of a trade union or political party, especially a communist party.
Word Family **comradeship** *noun.*
[Spanish *camarada* room-mate]

con[1] *noun*
an argument or person against something. See PRO[1].
[short form of *contra-*]

con[2] *verb* (**cons; conning; conned**)
(*informal*) to trick or swindle.
Word Family **con** *noun.*
[short form of CONFIDENCE TRICK]

con[3] *verb* (**cons; conning; conned**)
(*dated*) to study or learn thoroughly.

con[4] *noun*
(*informal*) a convict.

concave *adjective*
shaped like the inside of a bowl. Compare CONVEX.
concave lens a lens which makes parallel light rays diverge.
concave mirror a mirror which makes parallel light rays converge.
[*con-* + Latin *cavus* hollow]

conceal (k'n-**seel**) *verb*
to keep from view or discovery: *The cupboard concealed a hole in the wall.*
Word Family **concealment** *noun.*
[*con-* + Latin *celare* to hide]

concede (k'n-**seed**) *verb*
1 to admit or allow an argument, claim, etc.: *Concede defeat or die!*
2 to give up to an opponent: *Germany was forced to concede a lot of territory.*
[*con-* + Latin *cedere* to yield]

conceit (k'n-**seet**) *noun*
1 a very high opinion of oneself or one's abilities.
2 *Literature* an exaggerated or elaborate metaphor, simile, etc.
Word Family **conceited** *adjective*; **conceitedly** *adverb*; **conceitedness** *noun*.

conceive (k'n-**seev**) *verb*
1 to form, hold or imagine an idea, opinion, etc.: *It is difficult to conceive of such wealth.*
2 to become pregnant.
Phrase **be conceived** (of a baby) to start to exist in the mother's uterus.
Word Family **conceivable** *adjective* able to be conceived or believed: *We tried in every conceivable way to get tickets for the concert;* **conceivably** *adverb*.

concentrate (**kon**-sen-trate) *verb*
1 to direct one's thoughts or actions towards something: *How can I concentrate with all this noise?*
2 to bring or come towards a central point: *He concentrated his troops in the mountainous areas.*
3 to make or become more intense, stronger, purer, etc.: *concentrated acid.*
• **concentrate** *noun* a concentrated form of a solid or liquid.
Word Family **concentration** (kon-sen-**tray**-sh'n) *noun* 1 the act of concentrating: *This work needs close concentration.* 2 the state of being concentrated. 3 the amount of a dissolved substance present in unit volume of solution.

concentration camp *noun*
a place where political prisoners, refugees, etc. are held, especially the Nazi camps of the Second World War.

concentric (k'n-**sen**-trik) *adjective*
(of two or more shapes) having a common centre: *concentric circles.*

concept (**kon**-sept) *noun*
an idea, especially one generalized from various instances: *modern concepts of right and wrong.*
concept screening the process of choosing ideas for production.
Word Family **conceptual** (k'n-**sep**-tew-'l) *adjective*; **conceptually** *adverb*; **conceptualize, conceptualise** *verb*.
[Latin *conceptus* perceived]

conception (k'n-**sep**-sh'n) *noun*
1 an idea or thought: *They had little conception of the importance of this moment in their lives.*
2 the act of thinking of an idea or plan.

3 the starting of a baby's existence in the mother's uterus.

concern (k'n-**sern**) *verb*
1 to be about: *more news concerning the Turkish earthquake.*
2 to be of interest or importance to: *It is a problem which concerns only the family.*
3 to worry or involve: *I'm fine – please don't concern yourself.*
• **concern** *noun*
1 anything which is of interest or importance: *Your money problems are no concern of mine.*
2 anxiety or worry: *The doctor said there was no immediate cause for concern.*
3 any business or enterprise: *The farm is a small fruit-growing concern.*
Word Family **concerning** *preposition* about.
[*con-* + Latin *cernere* to discern]

concert (**kon**-sert) *noun*
a public performance by musicians, singers, etc.
Phrase **in concert** 1 (*formal*) acting together. 2 playing at a public performance: *tickets to see Michael Jackson in concert.*
• **concert** (k'n-**sert**) *verb* to do together or in agreement.
Word Family **concerted** *adjective* planned or decided by agreement.

concertina (kon-sa-**tee**-na) *noun*
Music a small accordion, played by pressing buttons at each end.

concerto (k'n-**cher**-toe) *noun* (*plural* **concertos** or **concerti** (k'n-**cher**-tee))
Music a composition, usually in three movements, which has one or more parts for solo instruments.

concession (k'n-**sesh**-'n) *noun*
1 anything conceded or granted: *The company refused to make any concessions to the trade unions.*
2 the act of conceding.
3 a right or privilege granted by a government, institution, etc.: *student concessions for cheap travel.*
4 a person entitled to a special right or privilege: *Tickets £10 (Concessions £6).*

conch (konch) *noun* (*plural* **conches**)
the spiral shell of a marine mollusc.

conchie *noun*
(*informal*) a conscientious objector.

concierge (kon-see-**airzh**) *noun*
the doorkeeper or porter of a hotel, block of flats, etc.
[French]

conciliate (k'n-**sill**-ee-ate) *verb*
1 to gain goodwill, support or favour by friendly acts: *He tried to conciliate his wife by buying her flowers.*
2 (*formal*) to reconcile.
Word Family conciliator *noun*; **conciliatory** (k'n-**sill**-ee-a-tree) *adjective*; **conciliation** (k'n-sill-ee-**ay**-sh'n) *noun*.

concise (k'n-**sice**) *adjective*
giving a lot of clear information in few words: *her concise writing style.*
Word Family concisely *adverb*; **conciseness** *noun*.
[Latin *concisus* cut short]

conclave *noun*
1 a private or secret meeting.
2 *Roman Catholicism* a meeting of cardinals.
[*con-* + Latin *clavis* a key]

conclude *verb*
1 to bring or come to an end: *The meeting concluded with a short prayer.*
2 to agree formally: *to conclude a peace treaty.*
3 to reach an opinion: *I concluded that she must have been lying.*
[Latin *concludere*]

conclusion (k'n-**kloo**-zh'n) *noun*
1 the end or last part of something.
2 the act of agreeing formally.
3 a final result, decision or opinion.
Phrase **jump to conclusions** to make judgements too quickly.

conclusive (k'n-**kloo**-siv) *adjective*
final and leaving no doubt. *The fingerprints in the house were conclusive proof of his guilt.*
Word Family conclusively *adverb*; **conclusiveness** *noun*.
[*con-* + Latin *currere* to run]

concoct (k'n-**kokt**) *verb*
1 to make or create by preparing and mixing: *He's concocting some kind of soup.*
2 to invent: *I'll concoct an excuse for being late.*
Word Family concoction *noun* something which has been concocted.
[Latin *concoctus* thoroughly cooked]

concord (**kon**-kord) *noun*
agreement or harmony between people or things.
[*con-* + Latin *cordis* of the heart]

concordat (kon-**kor**-dat) *noun*
a formal pact or agreement, especially one between the Pope and a government concerning control of church affairs.

concourse *noun*
1 an open area where paths meet and people can assemble: *the airport concourse.*

2 (*formal*) a crowd of people.
[*con-* + Latin *cursus* a running]

concrete (**kon**-kreet) *noun*
a mixture of cement, sand, water and minerals which sets very hard and is used for building, etc. Compare MORTAR².
● **concrete** *adjective*
1 having physical existence: *Trees are concrete objects.*
2 specific or particular: *Give me a concrete example.*
● **concrete** *verb* to lay concrete.
Word Family concretion (k'n-**kree**-sh'n) *noun* a solid mass formed by matter accumulating over time; **concretely** *adverb*.
[Latin *concretus* condensed]

concrete noun *noun*
a noun relating to things you can touch, taste, hear or smell. Compare ABSTRACT NOUN.

concubine (**kon**-kew-bine) *noun*
a mistress or secondary wife, e.g. in some Eastern societies.
[*con-* + Latin *cumbere* to lie]

concur (k'n-**ker**) *verb* (**concurs; concurring; concurred**)
1 (*formal*) to agree: *Our political opinions usually concur.*
2 (*formal*) to occur at the same time.
Word Family concurrent (k'n-**kurr**-'nt) *adjective* 1 in agreement. 2 existing or occurring together. 3 *Maths* intersecting at one point; **concurrently** *adverb*; **concurrence** *noun*.
[*con-* + Latin *currere* to run]

concussion (k'n-**kush**-'n) *noun*
a temporary injury to the brain due to a sudden shock, such as a fall or blow, and causing headache, dizziness, blurred vision, etc.
Word Family concuss *verb*.
[Latin *concussus* shaken violently]

condemn (k'n-**dem**) *verb*
1 to express strong disapproval of: *The President condemned the terrorist acts.*
2 to make a judgement against: *The murderer was condemned to life imprisonment.*
3 to force to endure: *The accident condemned him to a wheelchair for many years.*
4 to officially declare unfit for use: *The old houses were condemned by the council.*
Word Family condemnation (kon-dem-**nay**-sh'n) *noun*; **condemnatory** (k'n-**dem**-na-tree) *adjective*.
[*con-* + Latin *damnare* to condemn]

condemned cell *noun*
(*formerly*) a prison cell for someone sentenced to be executed.

condense (k'n-**dense**) *verb*
1 to reduce in volume or make more dense.
2 (of a gas or vapour) to change or be changed into a liquid.
3 (of light) to focus upon an object.
Word Family **condensation** (kon-den-**say**-sh'n) *noun* 1 the act or process of condensing. 2 small drops of liquid formed on a cold surface.
[*con-* + Latin *densus* crowded]

condensed milk *noun*
a thick sweet milk sold in tins.

condenser ⇨ CAPACITOR.

condescend (kon-di-**send**) *verb*
1 to graciously accept a lower position, duty, etc.
2 to do something in an ungracious or patronizing manner: *They actually condescended to wash the dishes.*
Word Family **condescension** (kon-di-**sen**-sh'n) *noun*; **condescendingly** *adverb*.
[*con-* + Latin *descendere* to come down]

condiment *noun*
anything used to flavour or season food, such as spices, pickles, etc.
[Latin *condire* to pickle]

condition (k'n-**dish**-'n) *noun*
1 the particular state or circumstances of a person or thing: *The house is in a very neglected condition.*
2 something which another thing depends on or is limited by: *There are no conditions attached to the free offer.*
3 an illness: *My father has a slight heart condition.*
Phrases **on condition that** only if: *You can stay up late on condition that you don't make any noise.* **out of condition** not fit.
● **condition** *verb*
1 to limit or regulate.
2 to make fit, healthy, etc., e.g. by applying special liquids: *You should condition your hair after shampooing.*
3 *Psychology* to create responses to stimuli which would not normally produce such responses.
Word Family **conditioner** *noun* a thing that conditions, especially a liquid used on the hair after shampooing.
[Latin *condicio* an agreement]

conditional (k'n-**dish**-a-n'l) *adjective*
containing conditions or depending on certain other facts or events: *The job offer is conditional on my exam results.*

conditioning *noun*
Psychology a method of learning in which a response comes to be associated with a stimulus which would normally not produce that response. This result may be achieved through a system of reward and punishment.
Word Family **conditioned** *adjective* (of an action) learned as a result of conditioning.

condolence (k'n-**doe**-l'nce) *noun*
(*usually* **condolences**) a declaration of sympathy: *Please accept our condolences on your father's death.*
[*con-* + Latin *dolens* grieving]

condom *noun* also called **sheath**.
a covering made of thin rubber worn over the penis during sexual intercourse to prevent conception or infection.

condominium (kon-da-**min**-ee-um) *noun*
1 joint sovereignty.
2 a country under joint sovereignty.
3 also **condo** (*informal*) *American* an apartment block in which the apartments are individually owned and the common areas are jointly owned.

condone *verb*
to accept or forgive: *We cannot condone violence in any society.*
[Latin *condonare* to forgive]

condor *noun*
a very large American vulture.

conducive (k'n-**dew**-siv) *adjective*
Phrase **conducive to** helpful in producing.

conduct (**kon**-dukt) *noun*
1 a person's behaviour.
2 management or guidance: *the conduct of the war.*
● **conduct** (k'n-**dukt**) *verb*
1 to control, direct or manage: *to conduct a meeting.*
2 to direct the playing of music.
3 to guide or lead: *A security guard conducted us out of the building.*
4 to carry or transmit: *Electricity is conducted along wires.*
Phrase **conduct oneself** (*formal*) to behave: *They conducted themselves with great dignity.*
[*con-* + Latin *ductus* led]

conduction (k'n-**duk**-sh'n) *noun*
the carrying or transmitting of something
along or through a body, especially energy
such as heat and electricity. Compare
CONVECTION.

conductivity (kon-duk-**tiv**-i-tee) *noun*
Physics the ability of a substance to
conduct energy such as light, sound or
electric current.
Word Family **conductive** (k'n-**duk**-tiv)
adjective.

conductor *noun*
1 a person who conducts, directs or heads:
the conductor of an orchestra.
2 a person in charge of passengers,
collecting fares, etc. on public transport:
a bus conductor.
3 *Physics* a substance or object which will
allow a particular type of energy to flow
through it: *a lightning conductor*.
Word Family **conductress** *noun* (*plural*
conductresses) (*dated*) a female
conductor.

conduit (**kon**-dit *or* **kond**-yoo it) *noun*
1 a pipe or channel, such as a drain.
2 a protective tube covering electrical
wires.

cone *noun*
1 a solid or hollow body with a curved or
circular base which narrows to a point.
2 any object or device with this shape:
an ice-cream cone.
3 *Biology* a reproductive structure of seed-
bearing parts arranged spirally around the
centre, e.g. a pine cone.
4 also **traffic cone** a cone-shaped object
used to mark off areas of roads, e.g. to
indicate no-parking areas.
• **cone** *verb* also **cone off** to close by
putting traffic cones across: *The police have
coned off the road*.
Word Family **conic** (**kon**-ik), **conical**
adjective; **conically** *adverb*.
[Greek *konos* a pine cone]

confection (k'n-**fek**-sh'n) *noun*
(*formal*) a sweet or sweet-tasting dish.
[*con-* + Latin *factus* made]

confectioner (k'n-**fek**-sh'n-a) *noun*
a person who makes or sells sweets, cakes,
ice creams, etc.
Word Family **confectionery** *noun*
any or all sweets.

confederacy (k'n-**fed**-er-a-see) *noun*
(*plural* **confederacies**) also called
confederation (k'n-fed-er-**ay**-sh'n).
a group of people or nations joined for a
common cause.

confederate *adjective*
united or joined by agreement.
• **confederate** *noun*
1 an ally or accomplice: *a confederate in
crime*.
2 (*usually* **Confederate**) *American history*
a soldier fighting for the independence of
the eleven southern states which seceded
from the Union during the Civil War
(1861-1865).

confer (k'n-**fer**) *verb* (**confers**;
conferring; conferred)
1 to give or award: *A medal was conferred
upon him*.
2 to discuss or exchange opinions: *The
lawyers conferred for several minutes before
answering*.
Word Family **conferment** *noun*.
[*con-* + Latin *ferre* to bring]

conference *noun*
a meeting for discussion or exchange of
opinions: *He's attending a dental conference
in London*.

conference centre *noun*
a hotel or other large building with all the
facilities necessary for a large number of
people to meet for business discussions.

confess *verb*
to admit something: *She has confessed to the
crime*.
Word Family **confession** (k'n-**fesh**-'n)
noun 1 the act of confessing. 2 something
which is confessed; **confessor** *noun* a
person who makes or receives a
confession; **confessional** *noun* a small
stall in a church where priests hear
confessions.
[Latin *confessus* declared]

confetti *plural noun*
small pieces of coloured paper or foil
thrown into the air at weddings,
celebrations, etc.

> The word **confetti** is the plural of Latin
> *confetto* (a sweet), which came into the
> Italian language. The Italians had a
> custom of throwing sweets at carnivals
> and this is the origin of the British
> custom of throwing *confetti* at weddings.

confidant (**kon**-fi-dant, kon-fi-**dant** *or*
kon-fi-**dahnt**) *noun*
a person with whom secret or private
matters are discussed.
Word Family **confidante** *noun* a female
confidant.

confide (k'n-**fide**) *verb*
to trust with a secret: *She confided to me
that her husband has a criminal record*.

Phrases **confide in** to speak to about private matters. **confide to** (*dated*) to place in the care of.
[*con-* + Latin *fides* trust]

confidence (kon-fi-d'nce) *noun*
1 a firm trust: *I have full confidence in the surgeon.*
2 a sureness or trust in oneself: *The confidence of her violin playing was remarkable for a ten-year-old.*
3 a secret.
Phrase **in confidence** as a secret: *He mentioned it in strict confidence.*
Word Family **confident** *adjective* sure or certain; **confidently** *adverb*.

confidence trick *noun*
a fraud carried out by first gaining a person's confidence.
Word Family **confidence trickster** *noun*.

confidential (kon-fi-**den**-sh'l) *adjective*
1 secret or private: *confidential documents.*
2 entrusted with secret or private matters: *a confidential secretary.*
Word Family **confidentially** *adverb*; **confidentiality** (kon-fi-den-shee-**al**-i-tee) *noun*.

configuration (k'n-fig-yoo-**ray**-sh'n) *noun*
1 (*formal*) the arrangement of all the elements and details within a form.
2 *Astrology* ⇨ ASPECT (definition 3).

confine (k'n-**fine**) *verb*
1 to restrict or limit: *Please confine your remarks to the subject being discussed.*
2 to shut away: *Difficult prisoners are confined in a separate part of the prison.*
Word Family **confinement** *noun* 1 the act of confining. 2 the state of being imprisoned: *He was sentenced to solitary confinement.* 3 the period when a woman is in bed during childbirth; **confines** (kon-fines) *plural noun* (*formal*) limits or boundaries.
[*con-* + Latin *finis* boundary]

confirm (k'n-**firm**) *verb*
1 to show something to be true or correct: *There was no evidence to confirm his story.*
2 to approve formally or make valid: *a letter confirming her appointment to the post.*
3 *Christianity* to admit to full membership of the Church: *I will be confirmed next year.*
Word Family **confirmation** (kon-fer-**may**-sh'n) *noun* 1 the act of confirming. 2 something which confirms, such as proof or evidence. 3 *Christianity* a ceremony in which baptized people confirm their baptismal vows and are fully admitted to

the Church; **confirmatory** *adjective* serving to confirm.
[*con-* + Latin *firmare* to make firm]

confirmed *adjective*
firmly established in an idea or pattern of life: *My uncle is a confirmed bachelor.*

confiscate (**kon**-fi-skate) *verb*
to take or seize with authority: *The drugs and weapons were confiscated by customs officers.*
Word Family **confiscation** (kon-fi-**skay**-sh'n) *noun*.
[Latin *confiscare* to seize for the public treasury (*fiscus*)]

conflagration (kon-fla-**gray**-sh'n) *noun*
(*formal*) a huge destructive fire.
[*con-* + Latin *flagrare* to blaze]

conflict (**kon**-flikt) *noun*
1 a battle or struggle: *Two hundred soldiers died in the conflict.*
2 the opposition of two forces or things: *The conflict of ideas in the debate was very stimulating.*
• **conflict** (k'n-**flikt**) *verb* to be or come into opposition: *His modern ideas conflict with the head teacher's old-fashioned policies.*
Word Family **conflicting** *adjective* in opposition: *He received conflicting advice from the two doctors.*
[Latin *conflictus* dashed together]

confluence (**kon**-floo-ence) *noun*
1 the flowing together of two streams.
2 the place where they meet.
[*con-* + Latin *fluens* flowing]

conform (k'n-**form**) *verb*
to be or act in agreement or accordance, especially with rules, customs, etc.: *The architect's plan must conform to building regulations.*
Word Family **conformity** *noun* agreement or accordance; **conformist** *noun* a person who conforms.
[Latin *conformare* to shape]

confound *verb*
1 to confuse or bewilder completely.
2 to fail to distinguish between.
3 (*dated*) to defeat or overthrow.
4 (*dated*) used to express annoyance: *Confound the man!*
Word Family **confounded** *adjective* (*dated*) damned: *It's a confounded nuisance.*
[*con-* + Latin *fundere* to mix up, bewilder]

confront (k'n-**frunt**) *verb*
to be, come or bring face to face with: *The detective confronted the suspect with the stolen goods.*

Word Family confrontation (kon-frun-**tay**-sh'n) *noun* the act of confronting or opposing, especially in a hostile manner. [*con-* + Latin *frontis* of a face]

confuse (k'n-**fewz**) *verb*
1 to puzzle or bewilder: *Her complicated road directions always confuse me.*
2 to mistake one thing or person for another: *He confused me with my sister.*
3 to introduce disorder into: *Ignore this set of figures – they'll only confuse the issue.*
Word Family confusedly (k'n-**few**-zid-lee) *adverb* in a confused manner; **confusingly** *adverb* in a manner which is likely to cause confusion; **confusion** (k'n-**few**-zh'n) *noun* 1 the act of confusing.
2 the state of being confused: *There is a lot of confusion among the students about holiday dates.* 3 disorder: *The players were running about in total confusion.*
[Latin *confusus* mixed, jumbled]

confute *verb*
to prove to be wrong or incorrect.
Word Family confutation *noun*.
[Latin *confutare* to check]

congeal (k'n-**jeel**) *verb*
to change from a liquid to a jelly-like solid state, especially as a result of cooling.
[*con-* + Latin *gelare* to freeze]

congenial (k'n-**jee**-nee-'l) *adjective*
(*formal*) pleasant or agreeable.
Word Family congenially *adverb*.
[*con-* + GENIAL]

congenital (k'n-**jen**-it-'l) *adjective*
1 of or relating to any condition acquired at or before birth: *a congenital heart defect.*
2 (*informal*) deep-rooted: *He has a congenital dislike of insurance salesmen.*
Word Family congenitally *adverb*.
[*con-* + Latin *genitus* born]

conger (**kon**-ga) *noun* also **conger eel**
a large eel, found especially along rocky coastlines.
[Latin]

congested (k'n-**jest**-id) *adjective*
1 overcrowded or too full: *congested streets.*
2 *Medicine* (of an organ) containing too much fluid.
Word Family congestion *noun*.
[Latin *congestus* heaped up]

conglomerate (k'n-**glomm**-a-rit) *noun*
1 something composed of different or random things, such as a large company which incorporates many different sorts of businesses.

2 *Geology* a sedimentary rock formed of rounded pebbles deposited in or by water and cemented together.
Word Family conglomeration (k'n-glomm-a-**ray**-sh'n) *noun* a collection of different things.
[*con-* + Latin *glomeris* of a ball]

congratulate (k'n-**grat**-yoo-late) *verb*
to express pleasure at another's success or good fortune: *We congratulated her on her exam results.*
Word Family congratulation (k'n-grat-yoo-**lay**-sh'n) *noun*; **congratulatory** (k'n-**grat**-yoo-la-tree) *adjective*.
[*con-* + Latin *gratulari* to wish joy]

congregate (**kon**-gri-gate) *verb*
to come together in a group.
Word Family congregation (kon-gri-**gay**-sh'n) *noun* 1 the act of congregating.
2 a gathering or assembly, especially of people in a church.
[*con-* + Latin *gregis* of a flock]

congress *noun* (*plural* **congresses**)
1 a formal meeting of people with similar interests, for discussion of problems, etc.
2 (**Congress**) *Politics* the body of elected representatives in America, consisting of the Senate and the House of Representatives.
Word Family congressional (k'n-**gresh**-'n-'l) *adjective*.

congruent (**kon**-groo-ent) *adjective*
1 agreeing in nature or qualities.
2 identical in every aspect: *congruent triangles.*
Word Family congruence *noun*.
[Latin *congruens* running together]

conic *adjective* ⇨ CONE.

conical *adjective* ⇨ CONE.

conifer (**kon**-iff-a) *noun*
any of a group of evergreen trees which have cones, such as the pine or fir.
Word Family coniferous (k'-**nif**-er-us) *adjective*.

conjecture (k'n-**jek**-cher) *verb*
(*formal*) to guess or make a judgement without sufficient evidence.
Word Family conjecture *noun*; **conjectural** *adjective*.
[Latin *conjectus* deduced]

conjugal (**kon**-joo-g'l) *adjective*
(*formal*) relating to marriage.
[Latin *conjugis* of a wife]

conjugation (kon-joo-**gay**-sh'n) *noun*
Grammar the inflections of a verb which express its tense, number, person, etc., especially in a language such as Latin:

What conjugation is the verb 'salio'?
Compare DECLENSION (definition 1).
Word Family conjugate (kon-joo-gate)
verb **1** to list the inflections of a verb: *The
teacher asked me to conjugate the Latin verb
'amo'.* **2** (of a verb) to have different
inflections.

conjunction (k'n-**junk**-sh'n) *noun*
1 *Grammar* a word which joins parts of
sentences or clauses, e.g. *and* or *if*.
2 the act of joining or the state of being
joined: *The police worked in conjunction with
the health department to fight the epidemic.*
3 a simultaneous occurrence of events.
[Latin *conjunctus* yoked together]

conjunctivitis (k'n-junk-ti-**vie**-tis) *noun*
an infection of the membrane which lines
the eyelids and covers the front of the
eyeball.

conjure (**kun**-ja) *verb*
to summon or produce by or as if by
magic: *The magician conjured a rabbit from
his hat.*
Phrase conjure up to bring to mind: *The
music conjured up a vision of the sea.*
Word Family conjurer, conjuror *noun* a
magician.

conk *noun*
(*dated informal*) the nose.
● **conk** *verb*
Phrase conk out (*informal*) to stop
functioning.

conker *noun*
1 a horse chestnut.
2 (**conkers**) a children's game with
conkers threaded on string.

con man *noun* (*plural* **con men**)
(*informal*) a man who cheats people using
confidence tricks.

connect (k'-**nekt**) *verb*
1 to join or be joined: *First connect the two
longest pieces together.*
2 to join to a power supply: *Our phone isn't
connected yet.*
3 to associate or relate: *The two events are
not connected.*
4 (of a bus, train, etc.) to arrive in time for
passengers to get onto another: *I need a
train that connects with the 8.15 to Oxford.*
5 (*informal*) (of a punch) to hit
successfully.
[*con-* + Latin *nectere* to bind]

connection *noun* also **connexion**
1 a relationship.
2 something that joins.
3 a wire that joins parts of an electrical
circuit: *a loose connection.*

4 the act of joining: *Connection of the line
will take place on Monday.*
5 a bus, train, etc. which arrives in time to
meet another: *I missed my connection.*
6 (**connections**) friends or contacts: *She
only got the job because her family has
connections in the City.*
Phrases in connection with (*formal*)
concerning. **in this connection** (*formal*)
with regard to this.

conning tower *noun*
the superstructure of a submarine, which
serves as an observation tower as well as
an entrance.

connive (k'-**nive**) *verb*
to plot or conspire.
Phrase connive at, connive in to
encourage or allow wrongdoing by
pretending not to notice it.
Word Family connivance *noun.*
[Latin *connivere* to shut the eyes]

connoisseur (kon-na-**sir**) *noun*
a person who is experienced and
discriminating in a particular area of
knowledge.
[Old French, one who knows]

connotation (kon-o-**tay**-sh'n) *noun*
the idea that a word gives, as opposed to
its strict meaning: *The word 'snuggle' has
connotations of comfort and security.*

connote (k'-**note**) *verb*
(of a word, etc.) to suggest or imply.

> ⚠️ The words *connote* and *denote* have
> related but separate meanings:
> *connote* refers to all of the meanings
> suggested or implied by a word,
> whereas *denote* refers to the strict
> meaning of a word.

connubial (k'-**new**-bee-'l) *adjective*
of or relating to marriage.
[*con-* + Latin *nubere* to marry]

conquer (**kon**-ka) *verb*
to defeat or overcome, e.g. to gain control
of territory, etc.
Word Family conqueror *noun.*

conquest (**kon**-kwest) *noun*
1 the act of conquering: *The conquest of the
mountain region cost many lives.*
2 anything which is conquered: *Gaul was
one of Caesar's conquests.*

consanguinity (kon-san-**gwinn**-a-tee)
noun
a relationship by descent from a common
ancestor.
[*con-* + Latin *sanguis* blood]

conscience (kon-sh'nce) *noun*
a person's sense of right and wrong,
especially in relation to his or her own
actions and motives.
Phrases **in all conscience** (*formal*)
being completely fair and honest. **on one's
conscience** in one's mind causing guilty
feelings.
[*con-* + Latin *sciens* knowing]

> ! Do not confuse the noun
> *conscience*, meaning 'a sense of
> right and wrong', with the adjective
> *conscious*, meaning 'awake or aware'.

conscience-stricken *adjective*
feeling extremely guilty and sorry.

conscientious (kon-shi-**en**-shus) *adjective*
scrupulous or painstakingly careful: *She is
a conscientious worker.*
Word Family **conscientiously** *adverb*;
conscientiousness *noun*.

conscientious objector *noun*
a person who refuses to do military service
because of his or her religious or moral
beliefs.

conscious (**kon**-shus) *adjective*
1 awake: *She wanted to stay conscious during
her baby's birth.*
2 aware: *I was conscious of a faint smell of
burning.*
3 deliberate: *His action was a conscious
attempt to conceal the truth.*
Word Family **consciously** *adverb*;
consciousness *noun*.

> ! Do not confuse *conscious* with
> CONSCIENCE.

conscript (k'n-**skript**) *verb*
to call up or enlist recruits for compulsory
military service.
Word Family **conscript** (**kon**-skript)
noun a person who is conscripted,
conscription *noun*.
[*con-* + Latin *scriptus* written on a list,
enlisted]

consecrate (**kon**-si-krate) *verb*
to dedicate to a special or sacred
purpose: *The altar was consecrated to the
god Horus.*
Word Family **consecration** (kon-si-
kray-sh'n) *noun*.
[*con-* + Latin *sacer* sacred]

consecutive (k'n-**sek**-yoo-tiv) *adjective*
following without interruption: *She missed
school on four consecutive days.*
Word Family **consecutively** *adverb*.
[*con-* + Latin *secutus* followed]

> ! Both *consecutive* and *successive*
> refer to things following one
> another, but *consecutive* refers to an
> arranged or logical sequence
> (*consecutive pages*), whereas *successive*
> refers to any sequence (*successive
> attempts*).

consensus *noun* (*plural* **consensuses**)
a general agreement: *There was a consensus
of opinion at the meeting that the treasurer
should resign.*
[*con-* + Latin *sensus* a sentiment]

> ! Note the spelling of *consensus*: it
> has one *c* and three *s*'s, and not
> two *c*'s and two *s*'s.

consent (k'n-**sent**) *verb*
to agree, accept or give permission.
● **consent** *noun* any permission or
agreement. ⇨ AGE OF CONSENT.
[*con-* + Latin *sentire* to feel]

consenting adult *noun*
an adult who can decide legally to have
sex, especially homosexual sex, with
another adult.

consequence (**kon**-si-kw'nce) *noun*
1 an effect or result: *Lung cancer is a
possible consequence of smoking.*
2 importance or distinction: *He was a man
of some consequence in the business world.*
Phrases **in consequence** as a result.
take the consequences to accept what
happens as the result of one's actions.
Word Family **consequent** *adjective*
following as a result; **consequential** (kon-
si-**kwen**-sh'l) *adjective*.
[*con-* + Latin *sequens* following]

consequently *adverb*
as a result.

> ! Both *consequently* and *subsequently*
> mean 'afterwards', but *consequently*
> means 'as a result' (*His car broke down
> and consequently he missed the
> appointment*) whereas *subsequently*
> simply means 'later' (*The hero
> subsequently dies*).

conservation (kon-sa-**vay**-sh'n) *noun*
1 the act of preventing something from
being wasted or used up.
2 the preservation of natural
environments, especially by the wise use of
resources.
Phrase **conservation of energy** the law
that within a given system the total
quantity of energy is constant.
Word Family **conservationist** *noun*.

Conservation is an example of an existing word which has taken on a new, or rather a more specific, meaning. It used to mean the conserving of anything at all but it became, in the latter part of the 20th century, specifically associated with conserving the environment. Our belated concern for the environment has produced several such developments, e.g. *green* has come to be used for 'protective of the environment' and words that would otherwise have remained specialist have become household words, e.g. ecological, ozone layer, biodiversity, CFCs.

conservative (k'n-**ser**-va-tiv) *adjective*
1 (**Conservative**) *British politics* connected with the **Conservative Party**, one of the three major parties: *The Conservative candidate made a speech.*
2 opposed to any great or sudden change: *the conservative elements in the army.*
3 moderate in amount: *a conservative estimate.*
4 traditional in style: *a conservative suit.*
Word Family conservative *noun*
1 a supporter of conservative ideas.
2 (**Conservative**) a member of the Conservative Party; **conservatively** *adverb*; **conservatism** *noun* a cautious approach to new ideas or changes.

conservatoire (k'n-**ser**-va-twah) *noun* a special school for people to train as actors or musicians.

conservatory (k'n-**ser**-va-tree) *noun* (*plural* **conservatories**) a greenhouse attached to a house, where exotic plants can be grown.

conserve (k'n-**serve**) *verb* to keep something valuable, especially to prevent it being wasted or used up: *During the drought the public was urged to conserve water.*
● **conserve** (**kon**-serve) *noun* jam or a similar preserve.

consider (k'n-**sid**-a) *verb*
1 to think carefully in order to decide: *My dad's considering getting a new car.*
2 to think about: *You should consider how your parents will feel if you leave.*
3 to believe: *He considers himself a genius!*
4 to look carefully at.
Word Family considerable *adjective* great; **considerably** *adverb*; **considering** *adverb* (*informal*) taking everything into account.
[Latin *considerare* to look at carefully]

considerate (k'n-**sid**-a-rit) *adjective* thoughtful of other people's feelings and needs.
Word Family considerately *adverb*.

consideration (k'n-sid-a-**ray**-sh'n) *noun*
1 the act of considering: *After careful consideration we signed the lease.*
2 a factor taken into account: *One of my main considerations is how my family will cope with life abroad.*
3 respect and thoughtfulness: *She shows no consideration for others.*
4 (*formal*) any payment for a service, etc.: *He will do the job for a small consideration.*

consign (k'n-**sine**) *verb*
1 to hand over formally.
2 to forward and deliver goods.
Word Family consignment *noun* 1 the act of consigning. 2 anything which is consigned.
[Latin *consignare* to seal up]

consist (k'n-**sist**) *verb*
Phrase consist of to be made up of: *The mixture consists of three eggs, two cups of milk and a little sugar.*

> ❗ On the use of *consist of* and *comprise* ⇨ COMPRISE.

consistency *noun* (*plural* **consistencies**) also **consistence**
1 any agreement or correspondence between things: *There is a lack of consistency in her statements to the police.*
2 the density or texture of something: *Whip the eggs until they have a fluffy consistency.*
Word Family consistent *adjective*; **consistently** *adverb*.

consolation prize *noun* a prize given to the runner-up in a competition.

console[1] (k'n-**sole**) *verb* to give comfort to: *We tried to console her.*
Word Family consolation (kon-so-**lay**-sh'n) *noun* 1 the act of consoling.
2 something which consoles; **consolatory** (k'n-**soll**-a-tree) *adjective*.
[*con-* + Latin *solari* to comfort]

console[2] (**kon**-sole) *noun*
1 a flat panel with a set of controls in it.
2 also **games console** a machine for playing computer games on.

consolidate (k'n-**soll**-i-date) *verb*
1 to strengthen or make solid: *You must consolidate the gains you have already made.*
2 to merge: *The two companies decided to consolidate rather than compete.*

Word Family consolidation (k'n-soll-i-**day**-sh'n) *noun*.

consommé (k'n-**som**-ay) *noun*
a clear thin soup made from meat juices.

consonant (**kon**-sa-nant) *noun*
1 *Language* a sound pronounced with partial or complete blockage of the breath.
2 *Language* any of the letters of the alphabet expressing these sounds, being all those except *a, e, i, o, u* and sometimes *y*. Compare VOWEL.
• **consonant** *adjective* in agreement or accord: *His behaviour is not consonant with his beliefs*.
[*con-* + Latin *sonus* sound]

consort[1] (**kon**-sort) *noun*
a husband or wife, especially of a reigning monarch.
• **consort** (k'n-**sort**) *verb*
Phrase **consort with** to associate with.
[Latin *consors, consortis* sharing a common destiny]

consort[2] (**kon**-sort) *noun*
Music a harmonious group of instruments or voices.

consortium (k'n-**sor**-ti-um) *noun* (*plural* **consortia** or **consortiums**)
1 a temporary combination of banks or corporations to carry out some large-scale financial operation.
2 any partnership.
[Latin, partnership]

conspicuous (k'n-**spik**-yew-us) *adjective*
easily seen or standing out very clearly: *The brightly coloured dress made her conspicuous in the crowd*.
[Latin *conspicuus* in sight]

conspire (k'n-**spire**) *verb*
1 to plan secretly to do something wrong or illegal.
2 (*formal*) (of circumstances) to combine or act together: *Everything conspired to destroy their happiness*.
Word Family conspiracy (k'n-**spirr**-a-see) *noun* (*plural* **conspiracies**) a plot; **conspirator** (k'n-**spirr**-i-ta) *noun* a person who conspires; **conspiratorial** (k'n-spirr-a-**taw**-ree-ul) *adjective*.
[Latin *conspirare* to breathe together]

constable (**kun**-sta-b'l *or* **kon**-sta-b'l) *noun*
a police officer below the rank of sergeant.
Word Family constabulary (k'n-**stab**-yoo-la-ree) *noun* (*plural* **constabularies**) the police force of a city or district.
[Late Latin, head officer of the stable]

constant (**kon**-st'nt) *adjective*
1 not changing: *the constant din*.
2 regular: *their constant arguing*.
3 (*dated*) loyal or faithful: *a constant wife*.
• **constant** *noun*
1 a number, quantity or factor which does not change.
2 *Maths* a term in an algebraic equation which does not change its value.
Word Family constantly *adverb*; **constancy** *noun*.
[*con-* + Latin *stans, stantis* standing]

constellation (kon-sta-**lay**-sh'n) *noun*
1 *Astronomy* any pattern into which stars are grouped and according to which they are named, such as Orion or the Great Bear.
2 (*formal*) a group of related people or things.
[*con-* + Latin *stella* star]

consternation (kon-sta-**nay**-sh'n) *noun*
sudden dismay or confusion: *To his great consternation he saw a policeman on the doorstep*.
[Latin *consternare* to stampede]

constipation (kon-sti-**pay**-sh'n) *noun*
a difficulty in emptying the bowels.
Word Family constipated (**kon**-sti-pay-tid) *adjective*.
[*con-* + Latin *stipare* to press together]

constituency (k'n-**stit**-yew-'n-see) *noun* (*plural* **constituencies**)
1 an area of a country that elects one representative to Parliament: *Who is the MP for your constituency?*
2 all the voters in such an area.

constituent (k'n-**stit**-yew-'nt) *adjective*
forming a necessary part of a whole: *Oxygen and hydrogen are the constituent elements of water*.
• **constituent** *noun*
1 a necessary part of a whole.
2 a person living in a constituency, who is entitled to vote in an election.
[*con-* + Latin *statuere* to set up]

constitute (**kon**-sti-tewt) *verb*
1 to make up or form: *Seven days constitute a week*.
2 to establish formally.

constitution (kon-sti-**tew**-sh'n) *noun*
1 *Politics* the group of laws or principles on which the government of a country is based.
2 the act or process of constituting.
3 the way something is constituted.
4 strength or health: *He has the constitution of an ox*.

constitutional *noun*
(*dated*) a walk for the sake of one's health.
• **constitutional** *adjective* relating to a
constitution.
Word Family **constitutionally** *adverb*.

constrain *verb*
(*formal*) to compel by physical or moral
force.
Word Family **constrained** *adjective*
forced and unnatural; **constraint** *noun*
1 restriction. **2** compulsion. **3** a limitation.

constrict *verb*
to make narrower or tighter.
Word Family **constriction** *noun*;
constrictor *noun* a snake which kills by
tightening its body around its prey.
[*con-* + Latin *strictus* bound]

construct *verb*
to make or put together in a careful or
intricate way: *constructing a new bridge.*
□ *Think how to construct your essay.*
Word Family **construction** *noun* **1** the
act of constructing. **2** something which
has been constructed, such as a building.
3 *Grammar* the arrangement of words into
phrases or sentences. **4** (*formal*) meaning
or explanation.
[*con-* + Latin *structus* built]

constructive *adjective*
tending to construct or be helpful: *Our
teacher usually gives constructive criticism.*
Word Family **constructively** *adverb*;
constructiveness *noun*.

construe (k'n-**stroo**) *verb*
(*formal*) to interpret or explain.

consul (**kon**-s'l) *noun*
a government official sent to a foreign
country to look after people from his or
her own country. Compare AMBASSADOR.
Word Family **consular** *adjective*;
consulate *noun* the offices and official
home of a consul.
[Latin, one of the two highest magistrates
in the Republic]

consult *verb*
to seek advice from.
Word Family **consultation** *noun* **1** a
meeting in order to discuss something.
2 the act of consulting.

consultant *noun*
a person who gives expert or professional
advice, such as a surgeon, engineer, etc.

consulting room *noun*
a room in which a doctor gives advice to
patients.

consume (k'n-**syoom**) *verb*
1 to use or absorb all of something: *The
climb had consumed all his strength.*
2 to eat or drink.
3 (of a fire) to destroy.
Phrase **be consumed with** (of a person)
to be filled with: *He was consumed with
guilt.*

consumer (k'n-**syoo**-ma) *noun*
any person who buys goods or services.

consumer goods *plural noun*
goods bought for personal or domestic
use.

consumer rights *plural noun*
the legal rights and regulations which
protect people when they buy goods or
services.

consumer society *noun* (*plural*
consumer societies)
a society in which a lot of consumer goods
are made and bought.

consummate (**kon**-sa-mate) *verb*
1 to make complete or perfect.
2 to make a marriage complete by having
sex.
Word Family **consummation** *noun*;
consummate (k'n-**sum**-it) *adjective* very
great.
[*con-* + Latin *summus* highest]

consumption (k'n-**sump**-sh'n) *noun*
1 the act of consuming.
2 the amount that is consumed: *This car
has a very high petrol consumption.*
3 (*Medicine dated*) tuberculosis of the
lungs.
Word Family **consumptive** *adjective*.

contact *noun*
1 a touching: *Avoid any contact between the
wires.*
2 communication: *She remained in contact
with her father.*
3 a person or thing that provides
communication with or between others.
4 *Electricity* any device which completes or
breaks a circuit.
5 (*informal*) a contact lens.
• **contact** *verb* to put or bring into
contact.
[*con-* + Latin *tactus* touched]

contact lens *noun* (*plural* **contact lenses**)
a small thin curved disc of glass or plastic
with a central lens, worn directly on the
eyeball instead of wearing glasses.

contagious (k'n-**tay**-jus) *adjective*
1 (of a disease) able to be spread or passed
on easily, especially by direct contact.
2 (of a person) having a contagious
disease.

Word Family **contagiously** *adverb*; **contagiousness** *noun* the fact of being contagious; **contagion** (k'n-**tay**-j'n) *noun* the passing on of a disease, undesirable idea, etc. from one person or thing to another.
[Latin *contagio* a contact]

> ! Both *contagious* and *infectious* describe diseases that can be passed on, but *contagious* strictly refers to a disease that is caught by touching someone or something carrying germs of the disease.

contain (k'n-**tain**) *verb*
1 to have inside: *This box contains all her jewellery.*
2 to check or restrain: *She contained her emotions.*
Word Family **containment** *noun*
1 the act or policy of preventing the expansion of hostile powers, etc. 2 the prevention, in uranium processing, of release of unacceptable quantities of radioactive material beyond a controlled zone.
[Latin *continere* to hold together]

container *noun*
1 any object in which things are carried or stored: *Use a tin or another metal container.*
2 a very large metal box in which goods are transported on a ship, aircraft, etc.

contaminate (k'n-**tam**-i-nate) *verb*
to pollute or make impure: *Drinking contaminated water made them ill.*
Word Family **contamination** (k'n-tam i-**nay**-sh'n) *noun*; **contaminant** *noun* anything which contaminates.
[Latin *contaminare* to bring into contact]

contemplate (**kon**-tom-plate) *verb*
1 to look at thoughtfully: *She contemplated the painting.*
2 to think about: *I am contemplating leaving my job.*
Word Family **contemplation** (kon-tem-**play**-sh'n) *noun* 1 the act of contemplating. 2 religious or spiritual meditation; **contemplative** (k'n-**tem**-pla-tiv) *adjective* quiet and thoughtful.
[Latin *contemplari* to gaze on]

contemporaneous (k'n-tem-pa-**ray**-ni-us) *adjective*
occurring at the same time.

contemporary (k'n-**tem**-pa-ra-ree) *adjective*
1 living, existing or occurring in the same period.
2 modern: *contemporary furniture.*

• **contemporary** *noun* (*plural* **contemporaries**) a person living at the same time or having the same age as another.
[*con-* + Latin *temporis* of time]

contempt *noun*
1 a feeling of scorn or utter dislike.
2 also **contempt of court** *Law* the act of showing disrespect to a court, often by disobeying its commands.
Phrase **beneath contempt** completely worthless.

contemptible *adjective*
deserving contempt.
Word Family **contemptibly** *adverb*.

contemptuous (k'n-**temp**-tew-us) *adjective*
showing contempt.
Word Family **contemptuously** *adverb*.

contend *verb*
1 to struggle or strive.
2 to claim: *I still contend that I was right.*
Word Family **contender** *noun*.

content¹ (**kon**-tent) *noun*
1 (*usually* **contents**) anything which is contained in something: *They examined the contents of the parcel.*
2 the amount contained: *What is the content of butterfat in milk?*
3 (**contents**) a list of topics or chapters in a book.
[*con-* + Latin *tenus* held fast]

content² (k'n-**tent**) *adjective*
satisfied or happy: *I am content to wait.*
Word Family **content** *verb* to make happy; **contentedly** *adverb*; **contentment** *noun*.
[Latin *contentus* satisfied]

contention (k'n-**ten**-sh'n) *noun*
1 a dispute: *a matter of contention.*
2 a point of view.
Phrases **in contention** having a chance of success. **out of contention** no longer having a chance of success.
Word Family **contentious** *adjective* causing contention; **contentiously** *adverb*.

contest (**kon**-test) *noun*
a competition: *a contest of strength.*
• **contest** (k'n-**test**) *verb* to take part in a contest or argument.
Word Family **contestant** (k'n-**test**-'nt) *noun* a person who takes part in a contest.
[*con-* + Latin *testari* to testify]

context (**kon**-tekst) *noun*
1 the circumstances, facts, etc. which surround something.

2 the words or phrases which are connected with and accompany a particular word or passage.
Word Family **contextual** (kon-**tekst**-yew-'l) *adjective*.
[*con-* + Latin *textus* woven]

continent (**kon**-ti-nent) *noun*
a large unbroken land mass, e.g. Europe or Asia.
Word Family **continental** (kon-ti-**nen**-t'l) *adjective* relating to a continent.
[Latin (*terra*) *continens* continuous land]

continental breakfast *noun*
a light breakfast of rolls or croissants, jam, fruit juice and coffee or tea. Compare ENGLISH BREAKFAST.

contingency (k'n-**tin**-j'n-see) *noun* (*plural* **contingencies**)
1 the fact of being uncertain or dependent on chance.
2 an event which is uncertain or subject to chance.
[Latin *contingens* touching closely]

contingent (kon-**tin**-j'nt) *noun*
a group that is part of a larger one: *a contingent of troops*.

continual (k'n-**tin**-yew-'l) *adjective*
occurring repeatedly or only with short breaks.
Word Family **continually** *adverb*.

! The words *continual* and *continuous* have related but separate meanings: *continual* describes something which happens repeatedly or most of the time (*I was annoyed by the continual interruptions*), while *continuous* refers to something which has no break between its beginning and end (*the continuous roar of the waterfall*).

continue (k'n-**tin**-yoo) *verb*
1 to go onwards or further in a particular activity or state: *It continued to rain all day*.
2 to start again after a break: *We will continue the meeting after lunch*.
Word Family **continuation** (k'n-tin-yoo-ay-sh'n), **continuance** *noun*.

continuity (kon-ti-**new**-i-tee) *noun*
1 the state of being continuous or in a logical sequence.
2 *Film* the process of making sure that all parts of a movie are consistent, e.g. that the costumes are the same within a scene.

continuous (k'n-**tin**-yoo-us) *adjective*
occurring without a break: *a continuous roll of drums*.

Word Family **continuously** *adverb*; **continuousness** *noun*.
[Latin *continuus* holding together]

! Do not confuse *continuous* with CONTINUAL.

continuous assessment *noun*
the judging of a student by work produced over the period of a course, rather than by examinations.

continuum (k'n-**tin**-yoo-um) *noun* (*plural* **continua**)
1 a continuous range between two extremes: *In society the rich and the poor are at opposite ends of a continuum*.
2 *Maths* all rational and irrational numbers.

contort *verb*
to twist or bend out of the normal shape: *His father's face was contorted with rage*.
Word Family **contortion** *noun*.
[*con-* + Latin *tortus* twisted]

contortionist (k'n-**tor**-sh'n-ist) *noun*
an acrobat who bends his or her body into unusual or difficult shapes.

contour (**kon**-toor) *noun*
1 the outline of a figure or body.
2 also **contour line** *Geography* a line on a map joining points which are an equal height above sea level.

contraband *noun*
any articles forbidden to be brought into or taken out of a country.
[*contra-* + Italian *bando* ban]

contraception (kon-tra-**sep**-sh'n) *noun*
the methods or process of preventing a woman becoming pregnant.
Word Family **contraceptive** *noun* any device or drug used for contraception; **contraceptive** *adjective*.
[*contra-* + (con)CEPTION]

contract (**kon**-trakt) *noun*
a legal or formal agreement made between two or more people.
contract bridge ⇨ BRIDGE[2].
● **contract** (k'n-**trakt**) *verb*
1 to become smaller or shorter: *Metal contracts as it cools*.
2 to make smaller or shorter.
3 to settle by agreement.
4 (*formal*) to get or catch: *He contracted hepatitis*.
Word Family **contraction** (k'n-**trak**-sh'n) *noun* **1** the act of contracting. **2** a shortened form of a word which ends in the same letter as the word itself, as in *St* for *Saint*. Compare ABBREVIATION

(definition 2). **3** a shortening and joining of two or more words with an apostrophe replacing omitted letters, as in *he'd* for *he had*. **4** a strong tightening of the muscles of a woman's uterus during childbirth.
[*con-* + Latin *tractus* drawn, dragged]

contractor (kon-**trak**-ta) *noun*
a person who agrees to supply goods or services, especially for building jobs.

contradict (kon-tra-**dikt**) *verb*
1 to assert the opposite.
2 not to agree with: *Their stories contradict each other.*
Word Family **contradiction** (kon-tra-**dik**-sh'n) *noun*; **contradictory** (kon-tra-**dik**-ta-ree) *adjective*.
[*contra-* + Latin *dicere* to say]

contraflow *noun*
a temporary traffic-flow system in which there is two-way traffic on one carriageway of a motorway.

contralto (k'n-**trahl**-toe) *noun* ⇨ ALTO.
[Italian]

contraption (k'n-**trap**-sh'n) *noun*
an elaborate device or gadget.

contrary *adjective*
1 (**kon**-tra-ree) opposite or opposed: *Contrary to all advice she sold the house.*
2 (k'n-**trair**-ree) deliberately perverse or wilful.
• **contrary** (**kon**-tra-ree) *noun* (*plural* **contraries**) the opposite of something.
Phrases **on the contrary** in opposition to what has been stated. **to the contrary** with the opposite effect.
Word Family **contrarily** *adverb*.
[Latin *contrarius* opposite]

contrast (k'n-**trast**) *verb*
to compare by showing differences: *to contrast good with bad.*
• **contrast** (**kon**-trahst) *noun*
1 the act of contrasting.
2 an obvious difference, e.g. between colours in a photograph, etc.
[*contra-* + Latin *stare* to stand]

contravene (kon-tra-**veen**) *verb*
(*formal*) to come into conflict with: *Such behaviour contravenes the rules.*
Word Family **contravention** (kon-tra-**ven**-sh'n) *noun*.
[*contra-* + Latin *venire* to come]

contretemps (**kon**-tra-tom) *noun*
an annoying, embarrassing or unfortunately timed event.
[French, out of time (in music)]

contribute (k'n-**trib**-yoot) *verb*
1 to give, especially with others: *Have you contributed towards her birthday present?*
2 to help to cause or increase: *The mistake contributed to his embarrassment.*
Word Family **contribution** (kon-trib-**yoo**-sh'n) *noun* **1** the act of contributing.
2 something which is contributed or given; **contributor** *noun* a person or thing that contributes; **contributory** (k'n-**trib**-yoo-tree) *adjective*.
[*con-* + Latin *tribuere* to allot]

con trick *noun*
(*informal*) a confidence trick.

contrite (k'n-**trite** *or* kon-**trite**) *adjective*
(*formal*) sorry or repentant.
Word Family **contritely** *adverb*; **contrition** (k'n-**trish**-'n) *noun*.
[Latin *contritus* bruised]

contrivance (k'n-**try**-v'nce) *noun*
1 a mechanical device.
2 the act or manner of contriving.

contrive *verb*
to plan, plot or find a way of doing something.
Word Family **contrived** *adjective*
unnatural.

control (k'n-**trole**) *verb* (**controls**; **controlling**; **controlled**)
to have power over: *I cannot control my temper.*
• **control** *noun*
1 the power to command: *Who has control over the board?*
2 the act of controlling.
3 (**controls**) the device used to operate a machine, vehicle, etc.
4 the people who control something: *air traffic control.*
5 something used as a standard when a scientific experiment is carried out: *Use one group of plants as a control.*
control program a computer program which controls a process such as cutting fabric.
control technology computer programs or equipment used to control electronic devices.
Word Family **controller** *noun*; **controllable** *adjective*.

controversy (k'n-**trov**-er-see *or* kon-tra-ver-see) *noun* (*plural* **controversies**)
a prolonged argument or difference of opinion.
Word Family **controversial** (kon-tra-**ver**-sh'l) *adjective* causing controversy; **controversially** *adverb*.
[*contra-* + Latin *versus* turned]

contusion (k'n-**tew**-zh'n) *noun*
Medicine a bruise.
[*con-* + Latin *tusus* beaten]

conundrum (k'-**nun**-dr'm) *noun*
a puzzle, especially a riddle whose answer
is a pun.

conurbation (kon-er-**bay**-sh'n) *noun*
a very large urban area formed by two or
more towns growing towards and meeting
each other.
[*con-* + Latin *urbs* city]

convalescence (kon-va-**less**-'nce) *noun*
1 gradual recovery after an accident,
illness, operation, etc.
2 the time this takes.
Word Family **convalesce** *verb*;
convalescent *adjective*, *noun*.
[*con-* + Latin *valescere* to grow strong]

convection (k'n-**vek**-sh'n) *noun*
Physics a process by which heat energy is
transferred within a liquid or gas, due to
the lighter parts rising and the denser
parts sinking. Compare CONDUCTION.
Word Family **convectional** *adjective*.
[*con-* + Latin *vectus* carried]

convectional rain *noun*
rain formed when warm moist air rises,
cools and condenses into cloud.

convene *verb*
1 to assemble for a public meeting: *The
committee will convene on Friday.*
2 to call together: *We need to convene an
extra meeting of the council.*
[*con-* + Latin *venire* to come]

convenience (k'n-**vee**-nee-'nce) *noun*
1 the state of being convenient.
2 a thing which gives comfort or is useful:
a house with all modern conveniences.
3 (*formal*) the state of being suitable for
one's personal needs: *Please notify us at
your convenience.*
4 also **public convenience** a toilet.

convenience food *noun*
food requiring little preparation.

convenient (k'n-**vee**-nee-'nt) *adjective*
useful or suitable for a purpose: *I hope the
meeting place is convenient for you.*
Word Family **conveniently** *adverb*.

convent (**kon**-v'nt) *noun*
1 a community of nuns.
2 the buildings in which they live.
[Latin *conventus* assembly]

convention (k'n-**ven**-sh'n) *noun*
1 a formal meeting, especially one of
people from a particular profession.

2 any generally accepted rule or custom,
especially for social behaviour.
3 a formal agreement between countries.

conventional (k'n-**ven**-sha-n'l) *adjective*
1 based on tradition or generally accepted
rules.
2 (of a weapon) not nuclear.
Word Family **conventionally** *adverb*;
conventionalism *noun* a tendency to be
conventional.

convent school *noun*
a school run by nuns.

converge (k'n-**verj**) *verb*
(of two or more people or things) to come
together and meet at a common point:
The paths converged at the fountain.
□ *Light rays converge at a point of focus.*
Word Family **convergence** *noun*;
convergent *adjective*.
[*con-* + Latin *vergere* to turn]

conversant (k'n-**ver**-s'nt) *adjective*
Phrase **conversant with** (*formal*) having
knowledge of.

conversation (kon-va-**say**-sh'n) *noun*
an informal exchange of words.
Word Family **conversational** *adjective*.

converse¹ (k'n-**verse**) *verb*
to talk informally.
• **converse** (**kon**-verse) *noun* an old word
for **conversation**.
[Latin *conversari* to associate with]

converse² (**kon**-verse) *noun*
something which is the opposite of
another.
Word Family **converse** *adjective*;
conversely *adverb*.
[Latin *conversus* turned round]

conversion (k'n-**ver**-sh'n *or* k'n-**ver**-zh'n)
noun
1 a change: *the conversion of the barn into
flats.*
2 a religious change: *St Paul's conversion to
Christianity.*
3 (in rugby and American football) kicking
the ball over the goal to get points after a
try or touchdown.

convert (k'n-**vert**) *verb*
1 to change into a different form, etc.:
They converted the garage into a study.
2 to cause to change to another way of life,
belief, etc.
• **convert** (**kon**-vert) *noun* a person who
has been converted.

convertible *adjective*
capable of being converted.
• **convertible** *noun* a car with a roof that
can be folded back.

convex *adjective*
shaped like the outside of a bowl.
Compare CONCAVE.
  convex lens a lens which makes parallel
  light rays converge.
  convex mirror a mirror which makes
  parallel light rays diverge.
  [Latin *convexus* an arch]

convey (k'n-**vay**) *verb*
to carry or communicate.
Word Family **conveyor, conveyer** *noun*
a mechanical device for moving objects.

conveyance (k'n-**vay**-'nce) *noun*
1 the act of conveying.
2 anything which carries or conveys, such
as a vehicle.
Word Family **conveyancing** *noun Law*
the process of transferring land from one
owner to another.

convict (k'n-**vikt**) *verb*
Law to declare a person guilty of a crime,
especially after a trial.
Word Family **convict** (**kon**-vikt) *noun* a
person declared guilty of a crime,
especially if in prison.
[*con-* + Latin *victus* conquered]

conviction (k'n-**vik**-ch'n) *noun*
1 a strong belief or opinion.
2 the act of convicting.
3 the state of being convicted: *He has had
eight convictions for burglary.*

convince *verb*
to persuade by argument or evidence.
Word Family **convincing** *adjective*;
convincingly *adverb*.
[*con-* + Latin *vincere* to conquer]

convivial (k'n-**viv**-ee-al) *adjective*
friendly and sociable.
Word Family **conviviality** (k'n-viv-ee-
al-i-tee) *noun*.
[Latin *convivium* a banquet]

convocation (kon-va-**kay**-sh'n) *noun*
a meeting or assembly, especially one of
Anglican clergymen.
[*con-* + Latin *vocare* to summon]

convoluted (kon-va-**loot**-id) *adjective*
1 coiled or twisted.
2 complex: *a convoluted argument.*
Word Family **convolution** *noun*.
[*con-* + Latin *volutare* to roll about]

convolvulus (k'n-**vol**-vew-lus) *noun*
(*plural* **convolvuluses**) also called
bindweed.
any of a group of climbing plants with
bell-shaped flowers.

convoy *noun*
a formation of ships, vehicles, etc., often
travelling with a protecting escort.
• **convoy** *verb*.

convulsion (k'n-**vul**-sh'n) *noun*
1 *Medicine* ⇨ FIT[2] (definition 2).
2 any violent agitation, such as excessive
laughter.
Word Family **convulse** *verb* to shake or
contort violently; **convulsive** *adjective* like
or produced by a convulsion.

coo *verb* (**coos; cooing; cooed**)
to make a soft murmuring sound like a
pigeon.

> The word **coo** is the written down form
> of the sound made by a pigeon. Such
> words are called either *imitative* or
> *onomatopoeic*. There are many examples
> in English: *buzz, bang, growl, splash,
> plop, swish, hiss, hush, thud* are just a few.

cook (*rhymes with* book) *verb*
to prepare by heating, especially food.
Phrase **cook up** to invent: *He has cooked
up some scheme to make money.*
• **cook** *noun* a person who cooks,
especially one employed to do so.
Word Family **cookery** *noun* the art or
practice of cooking; **cooker** *noun* an
apparatus for heating or cooking.

cook-chill *adjective*
(of food) prepared by cooking and chilling
rapidly to be sold for reheating later.

cookie *noun*
1 (*especially American*) a sweet biscuit.
2 (*informal*) a person of a particular kind.
She's a tough cookie.
3 *Computers* a piece of data that makes an
Internet server able to identify which web
sites a client has used.

cool *adjective*
1 moderately cold.
2 not very enthusiastic: *We received a cool
welcome.*
3 calmly relaxed.
4 (*informal*) acceptable or pleasing.
5 (of colour) having rather blue tones.
• **cool** *noun*
Phrases **keep one's cool** to stay calm
and relaxed. **lose one's cool** to lose one's
self-control.
Word Family **cool** *verb* to make or
become cool; **coolly** *adverb*; **coolness**
noun the state of being cool; **cooler** *noun*
1 something which makes or keeps cool.
2 (*informal*) a jail.

coolant *noun*
a substance used to remove heat from a primary source such as a reactor core.
• **coolant** *adjective*.

coop *noun*
a cage or pen for hens, etc.
• **coop** *verb*
Phrase **coop up** to confine or shut in.

co-op *noun*
(*informal*) a cooperative.

cooper (**koop**-a) *noun*
a person who makes or repairs barrels, tubs, etc.
[Latin *cupa* cask]

cooperate (ko-**op**-a-rate) *verb* also
co-operate
to work together.
Word Family **cooperation** (ko-op-a-**ray**-sh'n) *noun*.
[*co-* + Latin *operari* to work]

cooperative (ko-**op**-ra-tiv) *adjective* also
co-operative
helpful or willing to cooperate.
• **cooperative** *noun* a group of people who cooperate in an activity or business by sharing work, goods, services, etc.
Word Family **cooperatively** *adverb*.

coordinate (ko-**or**-di-nate) *verb* also
co-ordinate
1 to bring or place parts in proper relation to each other.
2 to make people or things work together harmoniously: *Her job was to coordinate the various sections of the factory.*
• **coordinate** (ko-**or**-di-nit) *noun* Maths a number that can be used to determine the position of a point, by reference to a set of axes, etc.
Word Family **coordination** (ko-or-di-**nay**-sh'n) *noun*; **coordinator** *noun*.
[*co-* + Latin *ordinis* of an order]

coot (*rhymes with* hoot) *noun*
1 any of various swimming birds with short wings and tail.
2 (*informal*) a fool.

cop *noun*
(*informal*) a police officer.
Phrase **not much cop** (*informal*) not very good.
• **cop** *verb* (**cops**; **copping**; **copped**)
(*informal*) to receive.
Phrases **cop it** 1 (*informal*) to be in a lot of trouble. 2 (*informal*) to be killed. **cop out** (*informal*) to avoid taking responsibility for something.
Word Family **cop-out** *noun* (*informal*) an avoidance of responsibility.

cope[1] *verb*
to deal with something difficult.

cope[2] *noun*
a long loose sleeveless cloak worn by Christian priests during processions, etc.

copeck ⇨ KOPEK.

copier *noun* ⇨ COPY.

co-pilot *noun*
an assistant to the main pilot of a plane.

coping (**ko**-ping) *noun*
the protective top layer of a wall, designed to carry away water.

copious (**ko**-pee-us) *adjective*
plentiful or abundant.
Word Family **copiously** *adverb*; **copiousness** *noun*.
[Latin *copia* plenty]

cop-out *noun* ⇨ COP.

copper[1] *noun*
1 a soft metal which is a good conductor of heat and electricity, often used in alloys.
2 (**coppers**) coins of low value made from or containing copper.
3 a large container used in the past for boiling clothes.
4 a lustrous reddish-brown colour.
Word Family **copper** *adjective*.
[Latin (*aes*) *Cyprium* Cyprus ore = copper]

copper[2] *noun*
(*informal*) a police officer.

copperplate *noun*
an elaborate precise style of handwriting.

coppice *noun*
a small wood or large clump of bushes.

copra *noun*
the dried white flesh of the coconut, used to make coconut oil.

copse *noun*
a small group of trees.

copulation (kop-yoo-**lay**-sh'n) *noun*
(*formal*) sexual intercourse.
Word Family **copulate** (**kop**-yoo-late) *verb*.
[Latin *copula* a rope, link]

copy *noun* (*plural* **copies**)
1 a reproduction: *Please make a copy of this letter.*
2 any individual example of a particular book, newspaper, etc.
3 any material to be printed.
• **copy** *verb* (**copies**; **copying**; **copied**)
1 to make a copy of.
2 to imitate.
Word Family **copier** *noun* (*informal*) a photocopier.
[Latin *copia* plenty]

copybook *noun*
a book with printed examples of
handwriting for learners to copy.
Phrase **blot one's copybook** to ruin
one's reputation or past record.
• **copybook** *adjective* exactly according to
the rules.

copycat *noun*
(*informal*) a person who copies the actions
or words of another.

copycat crime *noun*
a crime committed that is very similar to
one recently committed by someone else.

copyright *noun*
the exclusive right to distribute or control
something original, such as the
publication of a book, the performance of
a play, etc.
• **copyright** *verb* to acquire a copyright
for.

copywriter *noun*
a person who writes text for
advertisements, etc.

coq au vin (kok o **van**) *noun*
a casserole of chicken in red wine.
[French, cock in wine]

coquette (kok-**et**) *noun*
a woman who flirts.
Word Family **coquetry** (**kok**-i-tree)
noun; **coquettish** (kok-et-ish) *adjective*;
coquettishly *adverb*.
[French]

coracle (**korr**-a-k'l) *noun*
a small oval rowing boat made of animal
skins or canvas stretched over a light
wooden frame, formerly used in Wales and
Ireland.

coral *noun*
1 a coloured substance formed from the
skeletons of tiny sea animals in tropical
waters and often forming reefs. It is used
in jewellery, ornaments, etc.
2 a pale reddish-yellow colour.

cor anglais (kor ong-glay) *noun* (*plural*
cors anglais) (kor ong-glay) also called
English horn.
Music a long thin double-reed wind
instrument with a lower pitch than an
oboe.
[French *cor* horn + *anglais* English]

corbel *noun*
Architecture a projection from a wall,
especially one to support a beam.

cord *noun*
1 a strong thick string made by weaving or
twisting several strands together.

2 a ribbed fabric, especially corduroy.
3 (**cords**) a pair of corduroy trousers.
[Latin *corda* string]

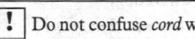 Do not confuse *cord* with CHORD.

cordial *adjective*
polite or friendly.
• **cordial** *noun* a liquid made into a drink
by adding water.
Word Family **cordially** *adverb* in a
cordial manner; **cordiality** (kor-di-**al**-i-
tee) *noun* a friendly politeness.
[Latin *cordialis* from the heart]

cordite *noun*
a smokeless explosive.

cordless *adjective*
(of an electrical device) having its own
internal source of electrical power, usually
a battery.

cordon *noun*
a line of troops, police, etc. guarding or
enclosing an area.
• **cordon** *verb*
Phrase **cordon off** to surround with
troops, police, etc.: *The army cordoned off
the site of the plane crash.*
[French, cord]

cordon bleu (kor-don **bler**) *adjective*
Cookery of the highest degree of
excellence.
[French, blue ribbon, being the ribbon
formerly worn by the highest order of
French knighthood]

corduroy (**kor**-da-roy *or* **kord**-ya-roy)
noun
a coarse thick-ribbed cotton fabric.

core *noun*
1 the central part of a fruit.
2 the essential part: *We must get to the core
of the problem.*
3 *Geology* the dense, partly molten, central
portion of the earth, beneath the mantle.
4 the central part of a nuclear reactor.
5 *Mining* a cylinder of rock cut out by a
drill and used for assays, etc.
Phrase **to the core** completely.
Word Family **core** *verb* to remove the
core from; **corer** *noun* a cylindrical knife
used for removing cores from fruit, etc.

co-respondent (ko-ri-**spon**-d'nt) *noun*
also **corespondent**
Law the person with whom someone in a
divorce case is said to have committed
adultery.

corgi *noun*
short form of **Welsh corgi** a breed of small short-legged dogs with erect ears.
[Welsh *cor-ci* dwarf dog]

coriander (korr-ee-**and**-er) *noun*
a herb whose leaves and seeds are used in cooking and medicine.
[Greek *koriannon*]

cork *noun*
1 the tough light bark of a variety of oak found in Mediterranean countries.
2 a small round piece of this material or of plastic, used as a stopper for a bottle.
Word Family **cork** *verb* to fit with a cork.

corkage (kor-kij) *noun*
a charge made by a restaurant for opening and serving bottles of wine supplied by the customers.

corker *noun*
(*dated informal*) an excellent person or thing.

corkscrew *noun*
a pointed spiral-shaped piece of metal for extracting the cork from a bottle.

corm *noun*
Biology the fleshy enlarged underground base of a plant's stem, which acts as an organ of vegetative reproduction.

cormorant (kor-ma-r'nt) *noun* also called **shag**.
a large diving seabird with a long neck and a pouch under the beak in which fish are held.
[Old French *corp* raven + *marenc* of the sea]

corn¹ *noun*
1 a general name for the seed of cereal plants, especially wheat.
2 (*especially American*) maize.

corn² *noun*
a hard area of skin, usually on the foot, caused by continual pressure or rubbing.

corn circle ⇨ CROP CIRCLE.

corncob *noun* also **cob**
the thick middle stem on which the kernels of maize grow.

corncrake *noun*
a bird with a loud rasping call.

cornea (kaw-nee-a) *noun*
the transparent membrane which covers the front of the eyeball.
[Latin *cornu* horn]

corned beef *noun*
beef preserved in salt.

cornelian (kor-**nee**-lee-an) ⇨ CARNELIAN.

corner *noun*
1 the point at which two edges, surfaces, etc. meet: *a street corner.*
2 a region: *Sightseers came from the four corners of the world.*
3 a difficult situation or position.
4 *Sport* a free shot taken from a corner of the field in hockey or soccer.
Phrases **cut corners** to take short cuts, especially in official procedure. **in someone's corner** supporting someone. **round the corner** very close.
• **corner** *verb*
1 to turn a corner, especially in a vehicle.
2 to force into a difficult or trapped situation: *The cat finally cornered the mouse.*

corner shop *noun*
a small shop selling a wide variety of goods.

cornerstone *noun*
1 a stone built into the corner of walls or foundations.
2 a basis or foundation: *They claimed democracy to be the cornerstone of their society.*

cornet *noun*
1 *Music* a brass wind instrument similar to a small trumpet.
2 a cone-shaped container for ice cream.

corn exchange *noun*
(*formerly*) a place where corn was traded.

cornflakes *plural noun*
a breakfast cereal made from maize.

cornflour *noun*
a flour made from finely ground maize, used to thicken sauces, etc.

cornflower *noun*
a small blue European flower.
[a wild variety grows among *corn*]

cornice (kor-niss) *noun*
1 *Architecture* a decorative moulding between a wall and the ceiling.
2 *Architecture* a part of the structure just above a column.

Cornish pasty *noun* (*plural* **Cornish pasties**)
an envelope of pastry containing baked meat, onion, potato and seasoning.

cornucopia (kor-new-**ko**-pee-a) *noun*
any unlimited supply.
[Latin *cornu* horn + *copiae* of plenty, after a magical horn in Greek mythology providing unlimited supplies of food, etc.]

corny *adjective* (**cornier; corniest**)
1 (*informal*) sickly sentimental.

2 (*informal*) old-fashioned.
3 (*informal*) weakly humorous.
Word Family **cornily** *adverb* in a corny way.

corolla (ka-**rol**-a) *noun*
the petals of a flower.
[Latin, little crown]

corollary (ka-**rol**-a-ree) *noun* (*plural* **corollaries**)
a natural consequence or result.

coronary (**korr**-en-ree) *adjective*
relating to the heart or the arteries which supply blood to it.

coronary thrombosis *noun* (*plural* **coronary thromboses**) also **coronary** (*plural* **coronaries**)
a sudden stopping of the blood going into the heart, resulting in a heart attack.

coronation (korr-a-**nay**-sh'n) *noun*
the ceremony of crowning a king or queen.

coroner (**korr**-a-na) *noun*
an official appointed by the government to make enquiries into any death that was not clearly due to natural causes.
[Middle English *corouner* officer of the crown]

coronet (korr-a-**net**) *noun*
1 a small crown worn by a member of a noble family.
2 a garland or ribbon worn by women as part of a headdress.

corporal[1] *adjective*
of or relating to the body.
[Latin *corporis* of the body]

corporal[2] *noun*
1 *Air force* a non-commissioned officer ranking between senior aircraftman and sergeant.
2 *Army* a non-commissioned officer ranking between lance corporal and sergeant.

corporal punishment *noun*
any physical punishment, especially caning or whipping.

corporate (**kor**-pa-rit) *adjective*
1 shared by all members of a group.
2 united.
3 relating to a large company.

corporation (kor-pa-**ray**-sh'n) *noun*
an association of people regarded in law as a single person, and formed to administer a city, public service, etc.

corporeal (kor-**paw**-ree-al) *adjective*
of or relating to physical matter.

corps (kor) *noun* (*plural* **corps**) (korz)
1 *Military* a wartime army unit consisting of several divisions.

2 any organized group: *the diplomatic corps*.
[French, body]

corpse *noun*
a dead body, usually of a human being.

corpulent (**kor**-pew-l'nt) *adjective*
fat or stout.
Word Family **corpulence** *noun*.

corpuscle (**kor**-pus-'l) *noun*
Biology a blood cell.
[Latin *corpusculum* little body]

corral (ka-**rahl**) *noun*
an enclosed area for horses, cattle, etc.
Word Family **corral** *verb* (**corrals; corralling; corralled**) to enclose in a corral.
[Spanish]

correct *adjective*
1 free from error.
2 in accordance with accepted standards: *correct behaviour*.
● **correct** *verb*
to make right or free of error: *My dad is always correcting my pronunciation*.
Word Family **correctly** *adverb*; **correctness** *noun* the state of being correct; **correction** *noun* 1 the act of correcting. 2 a mark or change made when correcting; **correctional**, **corrective** *adjective*; **corrective** *noun* something intended to correct.
[Latin *correctus* put straight]

correlate (**korr**-a-late) *verb*
to have or bring into a shared relationship.
Word Family **correlation** (korr-a-**lay**-sh'n) *noun* shared relationship.

correspond (korr-i-**spond**) *verb*
1 to be in agreement: *His actions do not correspond with his ideas*.
2 to communicate by writing letters.
3 to be similar to: *The British House of Commons corresponds to the Australian House of Representatives*.
Word Family **correspondent** *noun*
1 a person who communicates by letters.
2 a person employed by a newspaper, etc. to report regularly from another place or on a particular subject; **correspondingly** *adverb* in agreement.

correspondence (korr-i-**spon**-d'nce) *noun*
1 the fact of corresponding or agreeing.
2 the act of communicating by exchanging letters.
3 letters exchanged between people.

correspondence course *noun*
a course of study done at home, but in contact with a teacher by post.

corridor *noun*
1 a passage linking several rooms on one floor of a building.
2 any similar passage.
3 a narrow strip of air or land.

corrie *noun*
a hollow in the side of a hill or mountain, often containing a lake.
[Gaelic *coire* cauldron]

corrigenda (korr-i-**jen**-da) ⇨ ERRATA.

corroborate (ka-**rob**-a-rate) *verb*
to confirm or support evidence, stories, etc.
Word Family **corroboration** (ka-rob-a-**ray**-sh'n) *noun*; **corroborative** (ka-**rob**-a-ra-tiv) *adjective* providing confirmation.
[*cor-* + Latin *roboris* of strength]

corrode (ka-**rode**) *verb*
1 to destroy gradually by chemical action.
2 to eat away at: *Fear and guilt corroded his self-confidence.*
Word Family **corrosive** *adjective* capable of corroding.
[*cor-* + Latin *rodere* to gnaw]

corrosion (ka-**ro**-*zh*'n) *noun*
1 the act or process of corroding.
2 *Geography* the wearing away of rocks by salt and other chemicals in seawater. Compare ABRASION (definition 3); ATTRITION (definition 2).

corrugated iron *noun*
a sheet of iron or steel strengthened by parallel ridges or ripples and used on roofs, etc.

corrugation (korr-a-**gay**-sh'n) *noun*
a ridge or furrow, e.g. on the surface of a road.
[Latin *corrugatus* wrinkled]

corrupt (ka-**rupt**) *adjective*
1 dishonest, evil or no longer innocent.
2 *Computers* (of a program) unreliable.
Word Family **corrupt** *verb* to destroy the innocence, integrity or reliability of; **corruptly** *adverb*; **corruption** *noun*.
[Latin *corruptus* broken in pieces]

corsage (kor-**sah***zh*) *noun*
a very small bouquet of flowers to be pinned to a dress.
[French]

corsair *noun*
1 a North African pirate.
2 a fast ship used by such pirates.

corset *noun*
a stiffened but flexible piece of underwear, worn to shape or support the waist, abdomen or upper legs, especially by women.
Word Family **corsetry** (**kor**-sa-tree) *noun* 1 any or all corsets. 2 the process of making corsets.
[Old French, little body]

cortège (kor-**tayzh**) *noun*
1 a procession, especially at a funeral.
2 a group of attendants: *The king and his cortège arrived.*

cortex *noun* (*plural* **cortices**) (**kor**-ti-seez)
an outer layer, such as the bark of a tree.
[Latin, bark]

cortisone (**kor**-ti-zone) *noun*
a hormone secreted by the adrenal glands or made artificially, used especially in the reduction of inflammation.

corundum (k'-**run**-dum) *noun*
Geology a very hard mineral, used as a gem and as an abrasive.
[Tamil, ruby]

corvette *noun*
a small fast vessel used to escort convoys, etc.

cos *conjunction*
(*informal*) because.

cosecant (ko-**see**-kant) *noun*
Maths the reciprocal of sine. *abbrev.* cosec.

cosh *noun* (*plural* **coshes**)
a heavy, usually flexible, weapon.
Word Family **cosh** *verb* to hit with a cosh, especially on the head.

cosily *adverb* ⇨ COSY.

cosine (**ko**-sine) *noun*
Maths the ratio of the side adjacent to an angle in a right-angled triangle to the hypotenuse. *abbrev.* cosec.

cosiness *noun* ⇨ COSY.

cosmetic (koz-**met**-ik) *noun*
any product used to beautify or clean a part of the body, especially the face.
● **cosmetic** *adjective*
1 designed to add beauty to skin or hair.
2 superficial: *purely cosmetic changes to the law.*
Word Family **cosmetician** (koz-ma-**tish**-'n) *noun* an expert in the preparation or use of cosmetics.

> The word **cosmetic** is, surprisingly, related to *cosmos* in origin. *Cosmos* comes from the Greek *kosmos* (order) and *cosmetic* from *kosmeticos* (skilled in adornment). Connecting the two is a Greek verb, *kosmein*, meaning 'to put in order, to arrange, to adorn'.

cosmetic surgery *noun*
surgery performed in order to make a part of the body more attractive, e.g. to change the shape of the nose.

cosmic *adjective*
relating to the cosmos: *cosmic dust.*

cosmic rays *plural noun*
Astronomy the high-energy radiation which falls on the earth from outer space.

cosmology (koz-**moll**-a-jee) *noun*
the study of the nature, composition, origin and history of the universe.
Word Family **cosmological** (koz-ma-loj-i-k'l) *adjective;* **cosmologist** *noun.*

cosmonaut (**koz**-ma-nawt) *noun*
a Russian astronaut.
[COSMOS + Greek *nautes* sailor]

cosmopolitan (koz-ma-**pol**-i-t'n) *adjective*
1 of or relating to all parts of the world: *a very cosmopolitan crowd.*
2 being at home in all parts of the world and free from regional or national prejudices: *Travelling has given him a cosmopolitan outlook.*
Word Family **cosmopolitan** *noun* a person who is cosmopolitan; **cosmopolitanism** *noun.*
[COSMOS + Greek *polites* citizen]

cosmos *noun*
the whole universe, seen as an organized system.
[Greek *kosmos* order, the world]

Cossack *noun*
any of a people of southern Russia, famous as horsemen and dancers.

cosset *verb*
to pamper.

cossie *noun also* **cozzie**
(*informal*) a swimming costume.

cost *noun*
1 an amount given or required as payment: *The cost of building a house has increased.*
2 an amount needed or lost to get something: *The battle was won at the cost of many lives.*
3 (**costs**) *Law* the sum of money awarded by a court to pay lawyers' fees and other expenses.
● **cost** *verb* (**costs; costing; cost,** definition 3 **costed**)
1 to require the payment of: *The bike cost £100.*
Figurative His foolishness cost him his life.
2 (*informal*) to be expensive for: *If you want to know the secret, it'll cost you!*

3 to estimate the price of: *The carpenter costed the job.*

co-star *verb* (**co-stars; co-starring; co-starred**)
(of one actor or performer) to share equal status with another in a play, film, etc.
Word Family **co-star** *noun.*

cost-effective *adjective*
giving a good amount of profit in relation to the cost involved.

costermonger *noun*
short form is **coster** a person who sells fruit and vegetables from a stall or barrow.
[from old words *costard* a kind of apple + *monger* a trader]

costly *adjective* (**costlier; costliest**)
having a high cost or price: *a costly mistake.*
Word Family **costliness** *noun.*

cost of living *noun*
the cost of the necessities of life for a person or family, based on average prices of food, shelter, clothing, etc.

cost price *noun*
the amount paid by a manufacturer or merchant for something he intends to sell.

costume *noun*
1 the style of dress, etc. which is characteristic of or suitable for a particular time or place: *The actors all wore peasant costumes.*
2 ⇨ SWIMMING COSTUME.

costume drama *noun*
a film or television production in which historical costumes are worn.

costume jewellery *noun*
any decorative but inexpensive jewellery, such as paste or imitation gems.

cosy (**ko**-zee) *adjective* (**cosier; cosiest**)
warm and comfortable: *It's a cosy room in winter.*
● **cosy** *noun* (*plural* **cosies**) a padded cover for a teapot, etc. to keep it warm.
Word Family **cosily** *adverb,* **cosiness** *noun.*

cot *noun*
a small bed with enclosed sides, especially for a child.
[Hindi]

cotangent (ko-**tan**-j'nt) *noun*
Maths the reciprocal of tangent. *abbrev.* cot.

cot death *noun also called* **sudden infant death syndrome**.
the sudden unexplained death of a sleeping baby.

cote *noun*
a cage or shelter for birds or animals:
a dovecote.

coterie (kote-a-ree) *noun*
a close exclusive group of people.
[French]

cottage (kott-ij) *noun*
a small simple house, usually old and in
the country.
Word Family **cottagey** *adjective*.

cottage cheese *noun*
a soft white lumpy cheese made of milk
curd.

cottage hospital *noun*
a small local hospital in Britain.

cottage industry *noun* (*plural* **cottage
industries**)
any industry which can be done at home,
such as pottery, weaving, etc.

cottage pie ⇨ SHEPHERD'S PIE.

cotton *noun*
1 a tall plant grown for the soft white fibres
around its seeds which are used for
making cloth, etc.
2 a very fine thread spun from cotton
fibres: *a reel of blue cotton*.
3 a fabric made from cotton fibres.
• **cotton** *verb*
Phrase **cotton on** (*informal*) to notice or
realize: *No one has cottoned on to the mistake
yet*.
[from Arabic *kutn*]

cotton bud *noun*
a small stick with cotton wool on each
end, used for applying make-up, etc.

cotton candy *noun*
American candyfloss.

cotton gin *noun* also **gin**
a machine which separates the cotton
fibres from the seeds.

cotton wool *noun*
a fluffy mass of cotton fibres, used for
cleaning the skin, cuts, etc.

couch (kowch) *noun* (*plural* **couches**)
1 a sofa.
2 a flat bed with a headrest, used by
doctors for patients.
• **couch** *verb* to express or put into words:
Can you couch your question more simply?

couch grass (kooch grass or kowch
grass) *noun*
a tough coarse grass with long creeping
roots.

couch potato *noun* (*plural* **couch
potatoes**)
(*informal*) a person who spends a lot of
time watching television.

cougar (koo-ga) *noun*
American a puma.

cough (koff) *verb*
to eject air forcibly from the lungs with a
loud harsh sound.
Phrase **cough up** (*informal*) to produce:
Come on, cough up the money you owe me!
Word Family **cough** *noun* the act or
sound of coughing.

could (*rhymes with* good) *verb*
1 the past tense of **can**[1].
2 used instead of **can** as a polite form:
Could you help me?
3 might: *It could be true*.

couldn't *contraction*
a short form of **could not**: *We couldn't go*.

could've *contraction*
a short form of **could have**: *She could've
been killed!*

> **!** *Of* is sometimes incorrectly used
> instead of *'ve*: *You could've* [not
> *could of*] *told me earlier*.

coulomb (koo-lom) *noun*
the SI unit of electric charge. *abbrev.* C.
[after *C.A. Coulomb*, 1736-1806, a French
physicist]

council (kown-s'l) *noun*
a group of people appointed or elected to
meet regularly for discussion, making
decisions, etc.: *the city council*.
Word Family **councillor** *noun* a member
of a council.
[Latin *concilium* an assembly]

> **!** The words *council* and *counsel*
> sound the same but have different
> spellings and meanings. *Council* ends in
> *cil* and means 'a group of people
> meeting regularly'; *counsel* ends in *sel*
> and means 'advice' or 'a lawyer in
> court'.

council house *noun*
a house provided by the local council
which has a low rent.

council tax *noun*
a tax based on the value of people's
houses, charged to pay for local authority
services.

counsel (kown-s'l) *noun*
1 any advice or exchange of views.
2 *Law* a barrister or barristers,
representing a client in court.

Phrase keep one's own counsel to keep one's plans or views secret.
Word Family counsel verb (**counsels; counselling; counselled**).
[Latin *consilium* a consultation]

> ! Do not confuse *counsel* with
> COUNCIL.

counsellor (kown-s'l-a) noun
1 an adviser.
2 *American* a lawyer, especially a barrister.

count[1] verb
1 to say numbers in order.
2 to find the total number of: *They are counting the votes now.*
3 to include: *That's seven people for lunch, not counting the baby.*
4 to consider: *Count yourself lucky you weren't there!*
5 to be important or valuable: *Make everything you do count.*
Phrases count for to be worth: *Her advice counts for nothing.* **count in** (*informal*) to include: *A trip to London? Count me in!* **count on** to rely on or expect: *You can always count on Peter to eat all the cakes!* **count out** 1 to put down individually while counting: *I counted out the £20 notes.* 2 (*informal*) not to include.
● **count** noun
1 the act of counting.
2 the number arrived at by counting: *What was the final count?*
3 *Boxing* a referee's act of counting to ten.
4 a point for consideration: *I think you are wrong on several counts.*
5 *Law* any of the separate charges in an accusation: *You are charged with two counts of robbery.*

count[2] noun
a nobleman in certain European countries, such as France.
Word Family countess noun (*plural* **countesses**) 1 a female count. 2 the wife of a count.
[Latin *comitis* of a companion]

countdown noun
the final preparation for an event, especially firing a missile, launching a rocket, etc. The time of firing is taken as zero and the time (days, hours, minutes and seconds) is counted backwards to it.

countenance (kown-ti-nance) noun
a person's face or facial expression.
Phrase out of countenance disconcerted or embarrassed.
● **countenance** verb (*formal*) to support or approve.

counter[1] noun
1 a table or similar structure at which business is done in a shop, etc.
2 a small piece of wood, plastic or metal, used to keep scores in games.
Phrase under the counter secretly or dishonestly.

counter[2] adverb
in opposition or the opposite direction: *The result went counter to his hopes.*
● **counter** verb to meet or oppose in response: *The boxer countered his opponent's blow with a strong punch.*

counteract verb
to act against something and reduce its effectiveness.

counter-attack noun
an attack made in reply to another.
● **counter-attack** verb.

counterbalance verb
to weigh or act against with equal strength: *The company's reduced prices were counterbalanced by a general increase in sales.*
● **counterbalance** noun.

counterclockwise adjective, adverb
American anticlockwise.

counter-espionage noun also called **counter-intelligence**.
activity by one government or institution against the spies of another.

counterfeit (kown-ta-fit *or* kown-ta-feet) adjective
1 made in imitation or as a forgery: *counterfeit money.*
2 false or insincere.
Word Family counterfeit verb; **counterfeiter** noun.
[*contra*- + French *fait* made]

counterfoil ⇨ STUB (definition 2).

countermand (kown-ta-mahnd) verb
to cancel a command or instruction already given: *The captain's order was later countermanded by one from headquarters.*

counterpane noun
(*dated*) a bedspread or quilt.

counterpart noun
something which resembles or is the matching pair of another: *His job is unique and has no counterpart in any other profession.*

counterpoint noun
Music the playing of two or more melodies together, in harmony.

counterproductive adjective
having an opposite effect to what is wanted.

counter-revolution *noun*
a revolt against a government that was itself established by a previous revolution. *Word Family* **counter-revolutionary** *noun (plural* **counter-revolutionaries***).*

countertenor *noun*
Music the highest adult male singing voice.

counterweight (**kown**-ta-wate) *noun*
a weight which counterbalances another.

countess *noun* ⇨ COUNT².

countless *adjective*
being too many or unable to be counted.

countrified (**kun**-tri-fide) *adjective*
characteristic of country life, especially in not being sophisticated.

country (**kun**-tree) *noun (plural* **countries***)*
1 the defined area of land occupied by a particular nation and under one government: *the countries of Europe.*
2 all the people of a particular country: *The country responded to the President's call.*
3 any land outside cities or towns: *people who live in the country.*
4 any particular district or area: *This is very desolate country.*

country and western ⇨ COUNTRY MUSIC.

country club *noun*
a social club with sports facilities in a country area.

country cousin *noun*
an unsophisticated person who is unused to city life.

country dance *noun*
a traditional dance for groups of people.

country house *noun*
a large house in spacious grounds and rural surroundings (originally in distinction from the owner's town house in London).

countryman *noun (plural* **countrymen***)*
1 a person from the country and not the city.
2 a person from the same country as another.

country music *noun* also called **country and western**.
a form of popular music originally from the southern states of America, mostly featuring songs accompanied by guitar.

countryside *noun*
the land outside cities and towns, or a particular area in this: *The farm is set amongst densely wooded countryside.*

countrywoman *noun (plural* **countrywomen***)*
1 a woman from the country and not the city.
2 a woman from the same country as another.

county *noun (plural* **counties***)*
a geographical division of a kingdom for administrative and judicial purposes, but often having a historic basis.

county court *noun*
Law a local court which sits at intervals to deal with civil cases.

county town *noun*
the town where the administration of a county is based.

coup (koo) *noun (plural* **coups***)* (kooz)
1 an unexpected or clever victory.
2 ⇨ COUP D'ÉTAT.
[French, blow]

coup de grâce (koo de **grahs**) *noun (plural* **coups de grâce***)* (koo de **grahs**)
a deciding or finishing stroke.
[French, blow of grace]

coup d'état (koo day-**tah**) *noun (plural* **coups d'état***)* (koo day-**tah**)
Politics a sudden and often violent action or revolt, usually to overthrow a government.
[French, blow of state]

coupé (**koo**-pay) *noun* also **coupe** (coop)
an enclosed car with two doors.

couple (**kupp**-'l) *noun*
1 two things or people together: *a married couple.*
2 (*informal*) a small number: *I'll be with you in a couple of minutes.*
• **couple** *verb*
1 to join.
2 (of animals) to have sex.
[Latin *copula* a link]

couplet (**kup**-lit) *noun*
Poetry a pair of rhyming lines.

coupling (**kup**-ling) *noun* also **coupler**
any of various devices which connect parts or things.

coupon (**koo**-pon) *noun*
a detachable form or ticket used for entering competitions, entitling the holder to receive something in exchange, etc.
[French, a piece cut off]

courage (**kurr**-ij) *noun*
the ability to control fear when facing danger, pain or the unknown: *His family's support gave him courage to face his illness.*

Phrase **have the courage of one's convictions** to act according to one's beliefs.
Word Family **courageous** (ka-**ray**-jus) *adjective* having courage; **courageously** *adverb*.

courgette (koor-**zhet**) *noun*
a small edible marrow with a dark green skin and pale flesh.

> A **courgette** is known in America as a *zucchini* and is an example of the variation that occurs between the vocabularies of British and American English. *Courgette* comes from French and *zucchini* from Italian, but the differences between British and American English cannot always be put down to the words being borrowed from different foreign languages. Other examples include (British English first) *pavement/sidewalk*, *garden/yard*, (car) *boot/trunk*, *lift/elevator*, *handbag/purse*, *spring onion/scallion*, *aubergine/eggplant*.

courier (**koor**-ee-a) *noun*
1 a person or company appointed to carry messages or packages.
2 a person who accompanies tourists as a guide.
[Latin *currere* to run]

course (*rhymes with* horse) *noun*
1 the path or direction taken by anything: *The ship changed its course to avoid the storm.*
Figurative We will have to think of a new course of action.
2 the particular area on which a game, etc. is played: *a golf course.*
3 the normal order of movement or progress: *During the course of the discussion the truth became obvious.* □ *The storm ran its course.*
4 any of the separate parts of a meal. *I'll have soup for my first course.*
5 an organized series, especially of lessons: *We are taking a course of Italian lessons.*
6 *Building* a complete layer of bricks or stones in a wall.
Phrases **as a matter of course** as a natural right, consequence, etc.: *He will inherit the money as a matter of course.* **in due course** at the appropriate time: *Dinner will be ready in due course.* **of course** certainly: *Of course we will help you!*
• **course** *verb* (of liquid) to flow: *Tears of rage coursed down her face.*
Word Family **coursing** *noun* hunting with greyhounds.
[Latin *cursus* running, direction, flow]

coursebook *noun*
a book used regularly during a course of lessons.

coursework *noun*
work done during a course of study, especially work which counts towards a final mark or qualification.

court (kort) *noun*
1 a place where law cases are heard.
2 the judges or magistrates who sit in that place: *The court will retire to consider its verdict.*
3 *Sport* a level area marked with lines, for playing certain sports: *a tennis court.*
4 an open area surrounded by walls or buildings.
5 the official residence of a monarch.
6 the people who live or work there.
Phrases **hold court** to be at the centre of a group of admiring people. **out of court** unworthy of being considered. **pay court to** (*dated*) to seek the favour of.
• **court** *verb*
1 (*dated*) to seek the affections of.
2 to provoke: *Don't court trouble by answering back.*
[Latin *cohors* a courtyard, an escort]

court card *noun*
a playing card with a king, queen or jack on it.

courteous (**ker**-tee-us) *adjective*
polite and well-mannered.
Word Family **courteously** *adverb*; **courteousness** *noun*.

courtesan (**kor**-ti-zan) *noun*
a prostitute, especially one to men of wealth or high rank.

courtesy (**ker**-ti-see) *noun* (*plural* **courtesies**)
1 polite behaviour: *impressed by his courtesy.*
2 a polite act.

courtier (**kort**-ee-a) *noun*
a noble person entitled to attend a royal court.

courtly (**kort**-lee) *adjective* (**courtlier**; **courtliest**)
1 gracious or elegant: *a courtly bow.*
2 of or relating to the court of a monarch or ruler.
Word Family **courtliness** *noun*.

court martial (kort **mar**-sh'l) *noun* (*plural* **court martials** or **courts martial**)
1 the trial of a member of the armed forces by superior officers, for an offence against military law.
2 the officers brought together for such a trial.

Word Family **court-martial** *verb*
(**court-martials; court-martialling;
court-martialled**).

courtship *noun*
the act or time of courting.

court shoe *noun*
a woman's plain shoe with no laces or
buckles.

courtyard *noun*
an open area enclosed by buildings or
walls and usually paved, often at the front
of a large house or the back of an inn.

cousin (kuzz-'n) *noun*
1 also called **first cousin**. the child of
one's aunt or uncle.
2 a person or thing that is similar to
another.
first cousin once removed the child of
one's first cousin.
second cousin the child of one's parent's
first cousin.

couture ⇨ HAUTE COUTURE.

couturier (koo-**tew**-ree-ay) *noun*
a person who designs, makes or sells
fashionable clothes.

covalency (ko-**vay**-len-see) *noun*
1 *Chemistry* the phenomenon by which
two or more atoms share electrons, this
sharing process holding the component
atoms together in a single molecule.
2 *Chemistry* the number of electrons
available for sharing in this way: *Carbon
has a covalency of four.*

cove¹ *noun*
Geography a small bay or inlet.

cove² *noun*
(*dated informal*) a man.

coven (kuvv-'n) *noun*
a group or meeting of witches.

covenant (kuvv-a-nant) *noun*
a formal agreement or contract.

cover (kuvv-a) *verb*
1 to place something over or around
another thing: *She covered her head with a
scarf.*
2 to spread over: *Snow covered the lawn.*
3 to travel: *We've covered 30 miles today.*
4 to deal with: *This issue is covered in the
next chapter.*
5 to be enough for: *Will £100 cover the cost
of your trip?*
6 to report an event for a newspaper, radio
or television programme, etc.: *The
American election will be covered by our New
York political correspondent.*

7 to insure: *Are we covered against fire
damage?*
8 to protect or guard with a gun: *We
covered our captain while he ran up to the
building.*
9 *Sport* to watch closely: *I'll cover the centre
half.*
Phrases **be covered with** to be overcome
with: *She was covered with confusion.* **cover
for** 1 to take over the job of another
person temporarily. 2 to give an
explanation to defend another person:
Go on out – I'll cover for you with the boss.
cover up to prevent from being noticed.
● **cover** *noun*
1 anything which covers or provides
protection: *This book has a hard cover.*
2 shelter or protection: *The players ran for
cover as the rain started.*
3 insurance: *Have they got any cover for the
loss of the car?*
4 a means of hiding an illegal activity.
5 a place setting for one person in a
restaurant.
6 also **cover version** a recording of a song
made famous by another singer.
Phrase **break cover** to suddenly leave a
safe or sheltered place.
Word Family **covering** *noun* something
which covers.

coverage (kuvv-a-rij) *noun*
1 reporting in the media.
2 the extent to which something is
covered.

cover charge *noun*
a fixed additional charge made by a
restaurant, etc. for certain services.

covering letter *noun*
a letter which accompanies something and
explains or recommends it.

coverlet *noun*
(*dated*) a bedspread.

covert (kuvv-'t *or* ko-vert) *adjective*
disguised or secretive: *The guilty pair
exchanged covert glances.*
● **covert** (kuvv-'t) *noun* an area of thick
undergrowth which gives shelter to
animals, etc.

cover-up *noun*
an attempt to hide an unpleasant truth.

covet (kuvv-it) *verb*
to want something enviously or eagerly,
especially something belonging to
someone else.
Word Family **covetous** *adjective* full of
eager or envious desire; **covetously**
adverb; **covetousness** *noun*.

covey (kuvv-ee) *noun*
a flock of game birds, especially partridge.

cow[1] *noun*
1 an adult female bovine mammal raised on farms to give milk or beef.
2 the female of various mammals, especially the elephant, whale, etc. Compare BULL[1] (definition 2).
Phrase **till the cows come home** (*informal*) for a very long time.

cow[2] *verb*
to frighten or threaten into doing something: *The little boy was cowed into obedience by his father's violence.*

coward *noun*
a person who lacks courage.
Word Family **cowardly** *adjective, adverb*; **cowardice, cowardliness** *noun*.
[Latin *cauda* tail, referring to a dog with its tail between its legs]

cowboy *noun*
1 a man who works on a cattle ranch.
2 (*informal*) a person selling services which he or she is not qualified to offer, or which are carried out very poorly: *a cowboy builder.*

cower *verb*
to shrink or move away in fear.

cowl *noun*
1 a long loose robe with a hood, worn by monks.
2 the hood of a monk's robe.
3 any hood-shaped covering.
Word Family **cowling** *noun* the streamlined covering for an aircraft engine.

cowlick *noun*
a tuft of hair which hangs over the forehead.

cowpat *noun*
a piece of cow dung.

cowpox *noun*
a disease which is transmitted to human beings by cows and is similar to, but milder than, smallpox.

cowrie (kow-ree) *noun*
a shiny shell used formerly as money in Asia and Africa.

cowslip *noun*
a small plant with pale yellow scented flowers.

cox *noun* (*plural* **coxes**)
short form of **coxswain** (koks-'n) the person who steers a boat, especially in rowing.
• **cox** *verb* to act as a cox.

coxcomb (koks-kome) *noun*
1 an old word for a man who is excessively concerned about his appearance.
2 ⇨ COCKSCOMB (definition 2).

coy *adjective*
pretending to be shy or modest: *She looked up at him with a coy smile.*
Word Family **coyly** *adverb*; **coyness** *noun*.

coyote (koy-ote *or* koy-o-tee) *noun*
the prairie wolf of western North America.

coypu (koy-poo) *noun* also called **nutria**.
a beaver-like South American mammal.

cozzie ⇨ COSSIE.

crab *noun*
1 any of a group of crustaceans with a short flattened body and ten legs, the first two being pincers.
2 the flesh of this animal: *a crab sandwich.*
3 (**the Crab**) ⇨ CANCER (definition 2).
Phrase **catch a crab** to make a bad stroke with an oar.

crab apple *noun*
a small bitter variety of apple.

crabbed *adjective*
1 (of handwriting) difficult to read because the letters are too close together
2 bad-tempered.

crabby *adjective* (**crabbier; crabbiest**)
bad-tempered or irritable.

crack *verb*
1 to break without falling into pieces: *The cup cracked when I dropped it.*
2 to break open: *First crack an egg into a bowl.*
3 to make or cause to make a sharp sound: *She cracked the whip.*
4 (of a voice) to change sharply in pitch: *Her voice cracked with emotion.*
5 to hit hard: *I cracked my head on the door frame.*
6 to solve: *We finally cracked the mystery.*
Phrases **crack a joke** (*informal*) to tell a joke. **crack down on** to take severe measures against. **cracked up to be** (*informal*) said or believed to be: *He discovered that all-night parties weren't everything they were cracked up to be.* **crack on** (*informal*) to continue working. **crack up 1** (*informal*) to have a mental collapse.
2 (*informal*) to laugh a lot. **get cracking** (*informal*) to start an activity.
• **crack** *noun*
1 a line caused by breaking: *a crack in the cup.*
Figurative I opened the door just a crack.

2 a sudden sharp sound: *the crack of a pistol.*

3 a sudden change in pitch: *with a crack in her voice.*

4 a sudden hit: *a nasty crack on my head.*

5 (*informal*) an attempt: *Let me have a crack at it.*

6 (*informal*) a joke.

7 also **crack cocaine** a concentrated and highly addictive form of cocaine.

Phrases **crack of dawn** very early in the morning. **crack of the whip** (*informal*) a chance to do something.

crackbrained *adjective*
extremely stupid.

crackdown *noun*
a set of severe measures against a bad or illegal activity.

cracker *noun*
1 a roll of paper, often containing a gift or motto, which explodes harmlessly when the ends are pulled.
2 any firework which explodes.
3 a dry or savoury biscuit.
4 (*informal*) an excellent example of something.

crackers *adjective*
(*informal*) crazy.

cracking *adjective*
energetic or quick.

crackle *verb*
to make a series of small cracking sounds.
● **crackle** *noun*.

crackling *noun*
1 a series of small cracking sounds.
2 the crisp browned rind on roast pork.

crackpot *noun*
(*informal*) an eccentric or insane person.
● **crackpot** *adjective* eccentric or insane: *your crackpot schemes.*

cradle (**kray-d'l**) *noun*
1 a small bed for a baby, usually set on rockers.
2 the place where anything originates: *the cradle of freedom.*
3 any of various structures used as a support, such as the framework supporting a ship in dry dock.
● **cradle** *verb* to hold or protect as if in a cradle.

cradle-snatcher *noun*
a person who has a sexual relationship with someone who is much younger.
Word Family **cradle-snatch** *verb*.

craft *noun* (*plural* **crafts**)
1 a trade or art, especially one requiring skill with one's hands.
2 (**crafts**) things made with one's hands.
3 cunning or deceit.
4 (*plural* **craft**) a boat, aircraft or spaceship.
Word Family **craftsman** *noun* (*plural* **craftsmen**); **craftswoman** *noun* (*plural* **craftswomen**); **craftsmanship** *noun*.

crafty *adjective* (**craftier**; **craftiest**)
cunning or slyly deceitful.
Word Family **craftily** *adverb*; **craftiness** *noun*.

crag *noun*
a steep rugged rock.
Word Family **craggy** *adjective* (**craggier**; **craggiest**) rugged or rough.

cram *verb* (**crams**; **cramming**; **crammed**)
1 to overfill or squeeze into a space which is too small: *He crammed everything into a suitcase.*
2 to prepare for an examination by studying very hard.

cramp[1] *noun*
a sudden uncontrollable contraction of the muscles, especially in the arms and legs, usually accompanied by severe pain.

cramp[2] *verb*
to confine or restrain.
Phrase **cramp one's style** to hinder or restrict one's efforts.

crampon *noun*
a spiked metal plate worn on the shoe to prevent slipping when climbing on ice.

cranberry *noun* (*plural* **cranberries**)
a small red acid berry used in jams and sauces.

crane *noun*
1 a large wading bird with long legs.
2 any of various mechanical structures with a long arm for lifting heavy objects.
● **crane** *verb* to stretch out one's neck.

crane fly *noun* (*plural* **crane flies**) also called **daddy-long-legs**.
any of a group of slender insects with long fragile legs and two long wings.

cranium (**kray-ni-um**) *noun* (*plural* **craniums** or **crania**)
Anatomy the bony box of the skull enclosing the brain.
Word Family **cranial** *adjective* relating to the skull.
[Greek *kranion*]

crank *noun*
1 any of various devices for changing circular motion into motion up and down or backwards and forwards, etc. The simplest form consists of a bar projecting from, or at right angles to, a small wheel.
2 (*informal*) an eccentric person.
• **crank** *verb* to cause a shaft to move by using a crank.
Phrase **crank up** (*informal*) to increase the speed or intensity of.

crankshaft *noun*
the main shaft in an internal-combustion engine, which is made to turn by the up-and-down motion of the pistons.

cranky *adjective* (**crankier; crankiest**)
1 bad-tempered.
2 eccentric.

cranny *noun* (*plural* **crannies**)
a small crevice or opening.

crash *verb*
1 to come together and break or collapse noisily: *The cars crashed into each other.*
2 (of aircraft) to fall on to land or into the sea.
3 (of a business, a computer, etc.) to fail suddenly.
4 to move violently: *crashing about in the undergrowth.*
5 to make a sudden loud noise: *The thunder crashed.*
6 ⇒ GATECRASH.
Word Family **crash** *noun* (*plural* **crashes**) the act or sound of crashing; **crash** *adjective* (*informal*) intensive: *a crash course in scuba diving.*

crash helmet *noun*
a fibreglass or metal cap worn by motorcyclists, horseriders, racing drivers, etc. to protect the head in case of accident.

crash-landing *noun*
an emergency landing of an aircraft.
Word Family **crash-land** *verb.*

crass *adjective*
gross or stupid: *crass ignorance.*
Word Family **crassly** *adverb;* **crassness** *noun.*
[Latin *crassus* thick]

crate *noun*
a wooden box in which goods are packed for transport, storage, etc.
Word Family **crateful** *noun;* **crate** *verb.*

crater *noun*
a large hole, e.g. in the top of a volcano or resulting from an explosion.
[Greek *krater* mixing bowl]

cravat (kra-**vat**) *noun*
a man's scarf worn loosely folded round the neck.

crave *verb*
to desire intensely.
Word Family **craving** *noun.*

craven *adjective*
(*dated*) cowardly.

crawl *verb*
1 to move the body slowly along the ground, especially on one's hands and knees.
2 to move slowly: *The time crawled by.*
3 to be or feel as if covered with crawling things: *Her flesh crawled in horror.*
4 (*informal*) to behave in a way designed to win someone's favour: *He always crawls to the boss.*
• **crawl** *noun*
1 the act of crawling.
2 the fastest swimming style, in which there is an alternate overarm movement while the legs scissor-kick.
Word Family **crawler** *noun.*

crayfish *noun* (*plural* **crayfish** or **crayfishes**) also **crawfish**
a freshwater lobster.

crayon *noun*
a stick of coloured wax, chalk, etc. for writing or drawing.

craze *noun*
a popular fashion which does not last very long.

crazed *adjective*
wild or mad.

crazy (**kray**-zee) *adjective* (**crazier; craziest**)
insane.
Phrase **be crazy about** to be madly in love with. **like crazy** (*informal*) very fast or energetically.
Word Family **crazily** *adverb;* **craziness** *noun.*

crazy golf *noun*
a game like golf but played on a small area with obstacles that the players have to get the ball around.

crazy paving *noun*
ornamental paving composed of irregularly shaped slabs of various colours.

creak *verb*
to make or move with a squeaking or grating sound: *The door creaked eerily.*
Word Family **creak** *noun;* **creaky** *adjective* (**creakier; creakiest**).

cream *noun*
1 the fatty part of milk which rises to the top when the milk is left to stand.
2 any substance with the texture of cream, such as cosmetics, certain desserts, etc.
3 the best part of a group.
4 a yellowish-white colour.
● **cream** *verb*
1 to beat into a soft mixture.
2 (*informal*) to defeat.
Phrase **cream off** to take away the best part of a group.
Word Family **creamy** *adjective*
(**creamier; creamiest**) 1 like cream.
2 containing cream; **creaminess** *noun*.

cream cheese *noun*
a soft smooth cheese.

cream cracker *noun*
a dry savoury biscuit, often eaten with cheese.

creamery *noun* (*plural* **creameries**)
a place where butter and cheese are made.

cream soda *noun*
a fizzy drink with a vanilla flavour.

cream tea *noun*
a light meal of a pot of tea and scones with jam and cream.

crease *noun*
1 a line or mark produced in anything by folding or wrinkling.
2 *Cricket* any of three parallel lines drawn on the pitch near the stumps.
● **crease** *verb* to make a crease or creases in something.
Phrase **crease up** (*informal*) to burst out laughing.

create (kree-**ate**) *verb*
1 to produce or bring into existence:
According to the Bible, God created the world in seven days.
2 (*informal*) to make a fuss.
Word Family **creation** *noun* 1 the act of creating. 2 something which is created:
This dress is one of his latest creations.
3 (**Creation**) the world or universe, as created by God; **creative** *adjective* having or showing a talent for imaginative creation; **creatively** *adverb*; **creativity** (kree-ay-**tiv**-i-tee) *noun*; **creator** *noun*
1 a person or thing that creates. 2 (**the Creator**) God.

creative accounting *noun*
the use of loopholes or uncertainties in tax and financial legislation to make accounts seem misleadingly favourable.

creature (**kree**-cha) *noun*
any living thing, especially an animal other than a human being.
[Latin *creatura* something created]

creature comforts *plural noun*
the things that make life comfortable.

crèche (kresh *or* kraysh) *noun*
a nursery for young children run by an organization, e.g. by a company for its workers.

cred ⇨ STREET CRED.

credence (**kree**-d'nce) *noun*
(*formal*) belief or acceptance.

credentials (kri-**den**-sh'lz) *plural noun*
any letters or documents which prove the identity, honesty, etc. of a person.

credibility gap *noun*
the difference between what is said or promised and what is actually done, especially in politics.

credible *adjective*
able to be believed: *Her story is scarcely credible.*
Word Family **credibility** (kred-i-**bill**-i-tee) *noun*.

> [!] The words *credible* and *credulous* have related but separate meanings: *credible* describes something which can be believed, as in *a credible story*, while *credulous* describes someone who is liable to believe anything, as in *The more credulous members of the public fell for the hoax.*

credit *noun*
1 the ability to take goods away and pay for them later: *We bought the freezer on credit.*
2 belief in the truth of: *Don't give any credit to this theory.*
3 praise or acknowledgement: *She claimed credit for the company's achievement.*
4 a person or thing to be proud of: *You're a credit to your parents.*
5 the amount of money in one's favour in an account.
6 a record of such an amount entered in an account. Compare DEBIT.
7 (**credits**) the list of the people who took part in making a film or television programme.
8 *Education* a high pass in an examination.
9 *Education* a unit of work successfully completed in a particular course.
Phrases **in credit** having money in an account: *My bank account is in credit at the moment.* **to one's credit** 1 admirably: *To her credit, she never complained.* 2 already

achieved: *He has three award-winning films to his credit.*
Word Family credit *verb* **1** to believe.
2 to acknowledge or ascribe: *She was later credited with this invention.* **3** to add to an account; **creditable** (kred-it-a-b'l) *adjective* bringing honour or credit; **creditably** *adverb*.

credit card *noun*
a stiff plastic card entitling the holder to goods and services which are charged to his or her account and paid for later.

creditor *noun*
a person to whom money is owed.
Compare DEBTOR under DEBT.

creditworthy *adjective*
likely to pay back money that one owes.
Word Family creditworthiness *noun*.

credo (kree-doe *or* kray-doe) *noun*
a creed.
[Latin, I believe]

credulous (kred-yoo-lus) *adjective*
liable to believe anything, often without sufficient proof.
Word Family credulity (kred-**yoo**-li-tee) *noun*.

> ! Do not confuse *credulous* with CREDIBLE.

creed *noun*
1 a statement of the main beliefs of Christianity in a set form.
2 any system of beliefs, opinions, etc.

creek *noun*
1 a short arm of a river.
2 a narrow coastal inlet.
Phrase **up the creek** (*informal*) confused or in a difficult situation.

creel *noun*
a wicker basket, especially one used by anglers for carrying fish.

creep *verb* (**creeps; creeping; crept**)
1 to move or crawl close to the ground: *tiny creeping creatures.*
2 to move slowly, quietly or secretly: *It was after midnight, so she crept into the house.*
3 (of the skin) to feel as if covered with creeping things: *The sight of the snake made her flesh creep.*
4 (*informal*) to behave in a way designed to make someone like you.
• **creep** *noun* (*informal*) an unpleasant person.
Phrase **give someone the creeps** (*informal*) to make someone feel uneasy.
Word Family creeper *noun* a person or thing that creeps, especially a plant which

grows on or along a wall or other surface;
creepy *adjective* (**creepier; creepiest**)
(*informal*) horrible or frightening.

cremate (kre-mate) *verb*
to burn and reduce to ashes, especially a dead body.
Word Family cremation *noun* the act of cremating; **crematorium** (krem-a-taw-ree-um) *noun* a place where dead bodies are cremated.

crenellated (kren-i-lay-tid) *adjective*
provided with battlements.

Creole (kree-ole) *noun*
1 any person of European descent in the West Indies and South America.
2 any person descended from the original French or Spanish settlers of Louisiana in America.
3 a person of mixed descent who is native to these regions.
4 the languages spoken by these people.

creosote (kree-a-sote) *noun*
a dark oily liquid obtained by distilling tar and used for preserving wood.
[Greek *kreas* flesh + *soter* saviour, because of its antiseptic properties]

crêpe (krape) *noun*
1 a thin gauzy fabric with a crinkled surface, made from cotton or silk.
2 a hard wrinkled rubber.
3 a thin pancake.
[Old French *crespe* curled]

crêpe paper *noun*
a thin wrinkled paper.

crept the past tense and past participle of **creep**.

crescendo (kre-shen-doe) *noun*
a gradual increase in strength or loudness.
[Italian]

crescent (kress-'nt) *noun*
1 a curved shape or figure whose two ends each taper to a point.
2 something with this shape.
3 a curved street.
[Latin *crescens* increasing]

cress *noun*
any of various plants of the cabbage family, with sharp-tasting leaves.

crest *noun*
1 the highest part of something: *the crest of a hill.*
2 *Biology* a growth of hair or feathers on the top of an animal's head.
3 a distinguishing design, e.g. on a coat of arms, notepaper, etc.: *a family crest.*
Word Family crested *adjective*.

crestfallen *adjective*
dejected or disheartened.

cretin (**kret**-in) *noun*
(*informal*) a fool or stupid person.

Creutzfeldt-Jakob disease (kroits-felt **yak**-ob diz-eez) *noun*
short form is **CJD** a fatal disease involving degeneration of the nerve cells of the brain, causing dementia and lack of muscle coordination. A new variant of the disease is thought to be linked to bovine spongiform encephalopathy (BSE) in cattle.
[after *H. G. Creutzfeldt*, 1885-1964, and *A. Jakob*, 1884-1931, German neurologists]

crevasse (kre-**vass**) *noun*
a deep crack, especially in a glacier.
[French, crevice]

crevice (**krev**-iss) *noun*
a narrow crack or fissure.

crew¹ *noun*
1 all the people working on a ship or aircraft.
2 all these people except the officers: *The captain told the crew to calm the passengers down.*
3 a group of people who do a particular job together: *a camera crew.*
4 (*informal*) a group or mob.

crew² a past tense of **crow**.

crew cut *noun*
a very short haircut.

crew-necked *adjective*
(of a jumper or shirt) having a round neck without a collar. Compare POLO-NECK.

crib *noun*
1 a baby's cradle.
2 a rack or container in a stable, holding food for horses, cattle, etc.
3 a model of the scene at the birth of Jesus.
4 (*informal*) a book, etc. that one can copy illicitly to help in one's studies.
• **crib** *verb* (**cribs; cribbing; cribbed**) to copy illicitly.

cribbage (**krib**-ij) *noun*
a card game played by two to four people, in which the aim is to collect pairs, runs, etc.

crick *noun*
a sudden stiffness of the muscles of the neck and back, causing a sharp pain.
• **crick** *verb* to produce a crick in.

cricket¹ *noun*
a field game played between two teams of eleven players using bats and a ball.
Phrase **not cricket** (*informal*) not fair.
Word Family **cricketer** *noun*.

cricket² *noun*
an insect similar to a grasshopper.

crikey *interjection*
(*dated*) an expression of surprise.

crime *noun*
1 *Law* any act which is forbidden by law.
2 any foolish or wicked act.
Word Family **criminal** (**krim**-i-n'l) *noun* a person who is guilty or convicted of a crime; **criminal** *adjective* of, involving or guilty of a crime; **criminally** *adverb*.
[Latin *crimens* accusation, guilt]

criminalize, criminalise *verb*
1 to declare something to be against the law.
2 to cause someone to become a criminal.
Word Family **criminalization** (krim-i-n'l-eye-**zay**-sh'n) *noun*.

criminology (krim-i-**noll**-a-jee) *noun*
the study of crime and criminals.
Word Family **criminologist** *noun*.

crimp *verb*
to make wavy or curly.
• **crimp** *noun*.

Crimplene *noun*
(*trademark*) a type of fabric that does not crease easily.

crimson (**krim**-z'n) *noun*
a deep purplish-red colour.
Word Family **crimson** *verb* to become crimson, as when blushing; **crimson** *adjective*.

cringe (krinj) *verb*
1 to move back and down, e.g. in fear.
2 to behave in a way that shows one has no self-respect.
[Old English *cringan* to fall in battle]

crinkle *verb*
to wrinkle.
Word Family **crinkly** *adjective* (**crinklier; crinkliest**); **crinkle** *noun*.

crinoline (**krin**-a-leen *or* **krin**-a-lin) *noun*
1 any of various types of skirt flounced out with hoops or a bustle.
2 a coarse stiff horsehair fabric.
[Latin *crinis* hair + *linum* linen]

cripple *noun*
a person who cannot use one or more limbs, especially the legs.
Word Family **cripple** *verb* to disable.

crisis (**kry**-sis) noun (plural **crises**) (**kry**-seez)
a crucial time or turning point in any series of events: a political crisis.
[Greek krisis decision]

crisp adjective
1 firm but easily broken: a crisp piece of bacon.
2 fresh and invigorating: the crisp air.
3 brisk: her crisp manner.
• **crisp** noun also **potato crisp** a thin fried slice of potato: a bag of cheese and onion crisps.
• **crisp** verb to make or become crisp.
Word Family **crisply** adverb; **crispness** noun; **crispy** adjective (**crispier**; **crispiest**).
[Latin crispus curled]

crispbread noun
a brittle unsweetened type of biscuit made from rye or wheat and eaten instead of bread.

criss-cross adjective
crossed or having crossed markings.
• **criss-cross** verb.

criterion (kry-**teer**-ee-'n) noun (plural **criteria**)
a standard on which judgement can be based: deciding on the criteria for the selection of our candidate.
[Greek kriterion a standard or test]

> ! Note that criteria is the plural form of criterion and should not be used where the singular form is required, as in Value for money is the most important criterion.

critic noun
1 a person skilled in judging the merits of something: an art critic.
2 a person who points out faults or mistakes: He has always been a critic of this government.
[Greek kritikos capable of judging]

> ! Do not confuse critic with critique. Critique means 'a critical review', as in The magazine contains a critique of the new film.

critical adjective
1 tending to find fault: a critical attitude.
2 of serious or decisive importance: It was a critical period in his life.
3 relating to or involving criticism: a critical analysis.
4 Science denoting a constant value at which a substance undergoes an abrupt change: What is the critical temperature at which water changes to ice?

critical control points points in food production that must be carried out correctly to make the product safe.
Word Family **critically** adverb.

criticize, criticise (**krit**-i-size) verb
1 to find fault with: She's always criticizing the way I dress.
2 to make judgements as to merits and faults.
Word Family **criticism** (**krit**-i-sizm) noun 1 the act of criticizing. 2 a judgement: That is a valid criticism. 3 the detailed investigation or examination of literary works, etc.

critique (kri-**teek**) noun
a critical essay or review.
[French]

> ! Do not confuse critique with CRITIC.

croak verb
1 to make a low hoarse sound like a frog.
2 (informal) to die.
Word Family **croaky** adjective (**croakier**; **croakiest**); **croakily** adverb in a croaky way.

crochet (**kro**-shay) noun
a form of needlework using a needle with a hook at one end which is used to draw successive loops of yarn through preceding ones.
• **crochet** verb (**crochets**; **crocheting** (**kro**-shay-ing); **crocheted** (**kro**-shade)).
[French, a small hook]

crock¹ noun
an earthenware container or jar.

crock² noun
(informal) anything which is old or useless.

crockery noun
any earthenware or china objects such as dishes, etc.

> ! The word **crocodile** comes to English through Latin from Greek krokodilos (a lizard or crocodile). This in turn was derived from kroke (pebbles) and drilos (worm). Apparently the crocodile was so called because of its habit of basking on the sandbanks or river banks among the pebbles. Crocodile tears take their name from an ancient belief that crocodiles shed tears over their prey.

crocodile (**krok**-a-dile) noun
1 any of a group of large amphibious reptiles with tough armoured skin, found in tropical regions of Australia, Central

America, Africa and elsewhere and growing up to 5·4 m long.
2 leather made from the skin of this animal.
3 a line of people walking in pairs.

crocodile tears *plural noun*
false tears or sorrow.

crocus (**kro**-kus) *noun* (*plural* **crocuses** or **croci** (**kro**-kie *or* **kro**-kee))
a small plant with yellow, purple or white flowers growing from a bulb.
[Greek *krokos*]

croft *noun*
Scottish a small farm rented by a tenant farmer.
Word Family **crofter** *noun*.

croissant (**krwa**-son) *noun*
a flaky bread roll baked in a crescent shape.
[French, crescent]

crone *noun*
an ugly old woman.

crony (**kro**-nee) *noun* (*plural* **cronies**)
(*informal*) a close friend.

crook (*rhymes with* book) *noun*
1 a curved or hook-shaped stick: *a shepherd's crook.*
2 (*informal*) a criminal or dishonest person.
• **crook** *adjective* (*Australian informal*) ill.

crooked (**krook**-id) *adjective*
1 bent or twisted: *a crooked path.*
2 (*informal*) dishonest.
Word Family **crookedly** *adverb*; **crookedness** *noun*.

croon *verb*
to sing or hum softly: *She crooned the baby to sleep.*
Word Family **crooner** *noun* (*informal*) a popular singer of sentimental songs.
[Old German *kronen* to groan]

crop *noun*
1 a plant grown on a farm and used as food.
2 an amount harvested: *We had a good crop of apples this year.*
3 a number of people or things occurring at one time: *a crop of protests.*
4 a short haircut.
5 a short riding whip.
6 a pouch-like enlargement of the gullet in many birds, through which food passes and where digestion begins.
• **crop** *verb* (**crops; cropping; cropped**)
to cut off or cut short.
Phrase **crop up** to appear unexpectedly.

crop circle *noun* also called **corn circle**.
a circular flattened area in standing crops such as wheat, caused by unknown means but put down to various causes, such as weather conditions, alien spaceships or hoaxers.

cropper *noun*
Phrase **come a cropper** (*informal*)
1 to fall heavily. 2 to fail or collapse.

crop top *noun*
a woman's piece of clothing for the upper half of the body that shows her stomach.

croquet (**kro**-kay *or* **kro**-kee) *noun*
a game played on a lawn between teams of two or four players using mallets to hit balls through small hoops set in the ground.

croquette (kro-**ket**) *noun*
a ball of minced meat or mashed vegetables, usually coated in breadcrumbs and fried.
[French *croquer* to crunch]

crosier (**kro**-zee-a) *noun* also **crozier**
the staff carried by a bishop or abbot, shaped like a shepherd's crook.

cross *noun* (*plural* **crosses**)
1 a mark or sign made by one line intersecting another (+ or x).
2 a post with another piece of wood across it, on which people were executed in ancient times.
3 (**the Cross**) the cross used to execute Christ.
4 a cause of hardship: *Exams are a cross we all have to bear at some time!*
5 anything which is a combination of the qualities of two or more things: *She chose a colour that was a cross between blue and green.*
6 *Sport* a pass across the field in football, etc.
7 *Boxing* a diagonal punch.
Phrase **at cross purposes** (of two people) misunderstanding each other.
• **cross** *verb*
1 to go from one side to the other: *They crossed the road.*
2 to put a line or cross through: *We have crossed your name off the list.*
3 to meet and pass: *Our letters must have crossed in the post.*
4 to cross-breed.
5 to oppose or go against: *Do not cross him – he has a terrible temper.*
Phrases **cross oneself** *Christianity* to make the sign of the cross over one's chest.
cross the floor to join the other side in Parliament.

• **cross** *adjective* angry or annoyed.
Word Family **crossly** *adverb*; **crossness**
noun.

crossbar *noun*
1 the bar joining the two upright posts of a
goal.
2 the bar between the handlebars and the
seat on a bicycle.

cross benches *plural noun*
the seats in Parliament for people who are
not in the government or the opposition
party.

crossbones ⇨ SKULL AND CROSSBONES.

crossbow *noun*
a weapon consisting of a short strong bow
mounted at right angles to a thick bar with
a groove, along which a short arrow is
fired, used especially in the past.
Word Family **crossbowman** *noun* (*plural*
crossbowmen).

cross-breed *verb* (**cross-breeds**; **cross-
breeding**; **cross-bred**)
to produce a hybrid by mating two similar
but different types of organisms.
• **cross-breed** *noun*.

cross-check *verb*
to check the accuracy of something by
referring to another source.

cross-country *adjective*
not following the main roads: *a cross-
country run*.

cross-examine *verb*
to question a person in detail in order to
test the truth of answers already given,
especially in a court of law.
Word Family **cross-examination** *noun*;
cross-examiner *noun* a person who
cross-examines.

cross-eyed *adjective*
having a squint in which one eye turns
towards the other.

crossfire *noun*
1 *Military* the meeting of lines of fire from
two or more positions.
2 any violent meeting or exchange: *She got
caught in the crossfire of their argument*.

cross head *noun*
a word or phrase, usually in larger or
bolder font, inserted between paragraphs
in a newspaper to break up the text and
indicate the content of the next paragraph.

crossing *noun*
1 a place at which a road, etc. crosses
another or can be travelled across: *The cars
lined up at the railway crossing*.
2 a journey across the sea.

cross-legged *adjective, adverb*
having one leg placed across the other
when sitting.

crossly *adverb* ⇨ CROSS.

crossness *noun* ⇨ CROSS.

crosspatch *noun*
(*informal*) a cross or bad-tempered
person.

cross-question *verb*
to question a person in detail.

cross reference *noun*
a reference from one part of a book, etc. to
another, for extra information.

crossroads *noun* (*plural* **crossroads**)
1 a place where two or more roads cross
each other.
2 an important point in one's life or career.

cross section *noun*
1 a surface or piece made by cutting
crosswise through something.
2 a drawing or model of what something
would look like if it had been cut through
in this way.
3 a sample taken as a typical example: *The
poll was taken from a cross section of
secondary students*.

cross stitch *noun* (*plural* **cross stitches**)
an embroidery stitch resembling a small *x*.

crossword *noun* also **crossword puzzle**
a puzzle consisting of a rectangle divided
into squares, into which the answers to
numbered clues must be fitted
horizontally and vertically.

crotch *noun* (*plural* **crotches**) also called
crutch.
1 the place between the legs of the human
body.
2 any place which is forked.

crotchet *noun*
Music a note with a quarter of the time
value of a semibreve.
[French, a small hook]

crotchety (**krotch**-a-tee) *adjective*
(*informal*) cross or irritable.
Word Family **crotchetiness** *noun*.

crouch (*rhymes with* ouch) *verb*
to lower the body with the legs bent: *The
lion crouched in wait for its prey*.
• **crouch** *noun* (*plural* **crouches**).

croup (kroop) *noun*
an inflammation and swelling of the
larynx, especially in young children,
causing breathlessness and a high-pitched
cough.

croupier (**kroop**-ee-a *or* **kroop**-ee-ay)
noun
a person who collects and pays out money
at a gambling table.

crouton (**kroo**-ton) *noun*
a small cube of fried bread, served with
soups.
[French *croûte* crust]

crow (kro) *noun*
any of a family of birds with shiny black
feathers and a harsh voice.
Phrase **as the crow flies** in a straight
line: *The distance is 11 km as the crow flies,
but 15 km by road.*
● **crow** *verb* (**crows; crowing; crowed** *or*
crew; crowed)
1 to make the harsh loud cry of a crow or
rooster.
2 to boast or express glee.

crowbar *noun*
a long metal bar, used as a lever.

crowd (*rhymes with* loud) *noun*
1 a large unorganized group of people:
A crowd gathered around her.
2 (*informal*) a close set of friends: *I don't
see that crowd any more.*
● **crowd** *verb*
1 to come or pack together in a crowd: *The
fans crowded around the players.*
2 to push too close to: *Don't crowd him – he
needs air!*
Phrase **crowd out** to exclude by leaving
no space for.

crown *noun*
1 an ornamental headdress worn by a
monarch as a symbol of royal power.
2 (**the Crown**) the office or power of a
monarch.
3 a high award: *Which boxer will win the
crown tonight?*
4 anything in the shape of a crown.
5 the top or highest part of anything: *The
crown of his hat was dented.*
6 *Dentistry* the top of a tooth, or an
artificial replacement for it.
7 (*formerly*) an old British coin equal to 25
pence.
● **crown** *verb*
1 to give royal authority officially by
providing a crown.
2 to reward: *His efforts were crowned by
victory.*
3 to form the top of.
4 to complete: *To crown our misery, it started
raining.*
5 *Dentistry* to fit a crown on.
6 (*informal*) to hit on the head.
[Latin *corona* a garland]

Crown Court *noun*
(in England and Wales) a court which
hears serious criminal cases and cases
referred to it from a magistrates' court.

crown prince *noun*
the male heir of a monarch.

crown princess *noun* (*plural* **crown
princesses**)
1 the female heir of a monarch.
2 the wife of a crown prince.

crow's-feet *plural noun*
the wrinkles in the skin at the outer corner
of the eye.

crow's-nest *noun*
a box at the top of a mast of a sailing ship
for a lookout to watch from.

crozier ⇨ CROSIER.

crucial (**kroo**-sh'l) *adjective*
1 decisive or most important: *The crucial
moments of the game were just after half-time.*
2 (*informal*) excellent.

crucible (**kroo**-si-b'l) *noun*
a container in which substances are heated
or melted, usually made from a hard
substance such as porcelain.

crucifix (**kroo**-si-fiks) *noun* (*plural*
crucifixes)
Christianity a model of a cross carrying a
figure of Christ.
[Latin *crucifixus* fixed to a cross]

crucifixion (kroo-si-**fik**-sh'n) *noun*
1 the act of crucifying.
2 a picture or model of the putting to
death of Christ on the Cross.

crucify (**kroo**-si-fie) *verb* (**crucifies;
crucifying; crucified**)
1 to execute by nailing or tying the body to
a cross.
2 to treat severely or cruelly: *Her art
exhibition was crucified by the critics.*

crude *adjective*
1 natural, as distinct from refined or
manufactured: *crude sugar.* □ *crude oil.*
2 lacking refinement or elegance: *shocked
by his crude behaviour.*
Word Family **crudely** *adverb*; **crudity**
(**kroo**-di-tee), **crudeness** *noun*.
[Latin *crudus* raw, harsh]

cruel (**kroo**-'l) *adjective* (**crueller** *or*
crueler; cruellest *or* **cruelest**)
deliberately causing pain or suffering to
others.
Word Family **cruelty** *noun* (*plural*
cruelties) 1 the state of being cruel: *upset
by the cruelty of their remarks.* 2 a cruel act;
cruelly *adverb*.

cruelty-free *adjective*
(of cosmetics) made and developed without involving any cruelty to animals.

cruet (kroo-it) *noun*
1 a set of small containers for salt, pepper, vinegar, oil, etc.
2 any one of these containers.

cruise (krooz) *verb*
1 to sail or travel from place to place, usually for pleasure.
2 to travel at a moderate speed for efficiency or economy: *The jet cruised above the clouds.*
Word Family **cruise** *noun* a pleasure trip by boat; **cruiser** *noun* 1 a motor boat. 2 a medium-sized warship.

cruise missile *noun*
a type of guided nuclear missile that is directed by a computerized navigational system.

crumb (krum) *noun*
a tiny piece or flake, especially of food: *a few crumbs of cake on her plate.*
Word Family **crumbed** *adjective* coated with breadcrumbs.

crumble (krum b'l) *verb*
to break or fall into pieces: *She crumbled the earth between her fingers.*
● **crumble** *noun* a baked dessert consisting of fruit topped with a mixture of flour, fat and sugar.
Word Family **crumbly** *adjective* (**crumblier; crumbliest**) easily crumbled.

crumbs *interjection*
(*dated informal*) an expression of surprise or irritation.

crummy *adjective* (**crummier; crummiest**)
(*dated informal*) of very poor quality.

crumpet *noun*
1 a spongy bread-like food usually eaten toasted with butter, etc.
2 (*informal*) sexually attractive young women. This term is often considered offensive to women.

crumple *verb*
1 to crush into, or become full of, folds or wrinkles: *Be careful not to crumple your dress.*
2 to lose force completely.
● **crumple** *noun* an uneven fold or wrinkle.

crunch *verb*
to crush or grind noisily: *Their heavy boots crunched over the gravel.*
● **crunch** *noun* (*plural* **crunches**)

1 the act or sound of crunching.
2 (*informal*) a crisis: *The financial crunch will come when she changes her job.*

crusade (kroo-sade) *noun*
1 (**the Crusades**) *Medieval history* any of the military expeditions by Christians between the 11th and the 13th centuries to recapture the Holy Land (Palestine) from the Muslims.
2 any organized struggle or movement: *The government has begun a crusade against cigarette smoking.*
Word Family **crusade** *verb*; **crusader** *noun*.
[Spanish *Cruz* the Cross]

crush *verb*
1 to press or squeeze out of shape or into fine fragments: *Their car was crushed by a falling tree.*
2 to overpower or subdue completely: *Her spirit was crushed by the continual criticisms.*
● **crush** *noun* (*plural* **crushes**)
1 a large crowd pressed closely together: *a crush of excited spectators.*
2 (*informal*) an infatuation: *She has a crush on her new teacher.*
3 a drink made of crushed fruits with water added.

crust *noun*
1 the hard outer part of a loaf of bread or a pie.
2 a hard outer layer or surface.
3 *Geology* the outer layer of the earth, about 35 km thick in continental land masses, but much thinner under the oceans.
4 (*informal*) a living.
Word Family **crust** *verb* to form a crust; **crusty** *adjective* (**crustier; crustiest**)
1 of or having a crust 2 irritable; **crustily** *adverb*; **crustiness** *noun* irritability.
[Latin *crusta* rind]

crustacean (krus-tay sh'n) *noun*
any of a group of animals with a hard outer shell, including shrimps, crabs, etc.

crutch *noun* (*plural* **crutches**)
1 a stick, usually put under the armpit and used as an aid in walking.
2 something which supports.
3 the crotch.

crux *noun* (*plural* **cruxes** or **cruces** (**kroo**-seez))
the most basic or important point: *the crux of the matter.*
[Latin, cross]

cry *verb* (**cries; crying; cried**)
1 to utter a loud sound or call: *She cried out but I didn't hear.*
2 to produce tears from the eyes: *The baby began to cry.*
Phrase **cry off** (*informal*) to break a promise: *You can't cry off now.*
• **cry** *noun* (*plural* **cries**)
1 a loud sound or call: *No one heard her cry for help.*
2 a period of producing tears: *She had a good cry.*
3 a general or public demand.
Phrases **a far cry from** very different from. **in full cry** in eager pursuit.

crybaby *noun* (*plural* **crybabies**)
(*informal*) a person who cries too much about unimportant things.

crying shame *noun*
(*informal*) something which is shocking or very sad.

cryogenics *plural noun*
(*used with singular verb*) a branch of physics which studies phenomena at very low temperatures.
[Greek *kryos* frost + -*gen*]

cryonics *plural noun*
(*used with singular verb*) the deep-freezing of the body of someone who has died with the intention of reviving it in the future when science has progressed.

crypt (kript) *noun*
a cellar, especially one under a church that is used as a burial place.

cryptic (**krip**-tik) *adjective*
1 mysterious or secret: *a cryptic message.*
2 (of a crossword) having complex clues.
Word Family **cryptically** *adverb*.
[Greek *kryptos* hidden]

cryptogram *noun*
anything written in code.
Word Family **cryptographer** *noun*; **cryptography** *noun*.
[Greek *kryptos* hidden + *gramma* letter]

crystal (**kriss**-t'l) *noun*
1 a clear mineral or glass similar to quartz.
2 an object or objects made from high-quality glass, such as drinking glasses, etc.
3 a piece of a substance which has a regular geometrical form: *a sugar crystal*.
Word Family **crystalline** *adjective* like or containing crystals.
[Greek *krystallos* ice]

crystal ball *noun*
a glass ball in which fortune-tellers say they can see the future or distant events.

crystal-gazing *noun*
the practice of looking into a crystal ball to try and predict the future or see distant events.

crystallize, crystallise (**kris**-ta-lize) *verb*
1 to form into crystals: *The solution will crystallize as it cools.*
2 to become clear and definite: *A new and better plan crystallized in his mind.*
Word Family **crystallization** (kris-ta-lie-**zay**-sh'n) *noun*; **crystallized** *adjective* (of fruit, etc.) coated with sugar.

crystal set *noun*
the earliest form of radio, in which the electric current is controlled by a crystal in contact with a fine wire.

CS gas *noun*
a strong type of tear gas.

cub *noun*
1 the young of a carnivorous mammal: *a lion cub.*
2 a learner or apprentice: *a cub reporter.*
3 (**Cub**) also **Cub Scout** a boy belonging to a junior section of the Scout Association.

cubbyhole *noun*
a small enclosed space or hiding place.

cube (kewb) *noun*
1 a solid or hollow body with six square faces.
2 *Maths* the third power of a number: *The cube of 2, written 2^3, is $2 \times 2 \times 2 = 8$.*
• **cube** *verb*
1 to cut or make into cubes.
2 *Maths* to find the cube of.
Word Family **cubic** *adjective* 1 having the shape of a cube. 2 being a measurement of space found by multiplying length by width by height: *The volume of this tank is six cubic metres.*
[Greek *kybos*]

cubicle (**kew**-bi-k'l) *noun*
a small separate compartment.
[Latin *cubiculum* bedchamber]

cubism (**kew**-bizm) *noun*
an art style originating in the early 20th century, aiming to analyse the structure or form of objects by expressing them in geometrical shapes.
Word Family **cubist** *noun, adjective*.

cubit *noun*
an old measure equal to the length of the forearm, about 50 cm.
[Latin *cubitum* elbow]

cuboid (kew-boyd) *adjective*
having the shape of a cube.
• **cuboid** *noun* a shape like a box, with six rectangular faces at right angles to one another.

cuckold (kukk-old) *noun*
the husband of an unfaithful wife.
Word Family **cuckold** *verb* to make a cuckold of.
[Old French *cucu* cuckoo]

cuckoo (ku-koo) *noun*
a grey bird that lays its eggs in the nests of other birds.

cuckoo clock *noun*
a wall clock out of which a wooden bird pops to indicate the time with a call like a cuckoo.

cuckoo spit *noun*
the protective layer of froth exuded by the larvae of various kinds of plant-sucking insects.

cucumber (kew-kum-ba) *noun*
a long green-skinned fleshy fruit, used in salads, etc.
[Latin *cucumeris* of a cucumber]

cud *noun*
the partially digested food which a ruminant animal returns to the mouth to chew again.
Phrase **chew the cud** (*informal*) to think deeply about something.

cuddle *verb*
to hold close affectionately.
Word Family **cuddle** *noun*; **cuddlesome, cuddly** *adjective* (**cuddlier; cuddliest**).

cudgel (kuj-'l) *noun*
a short club used as a weapon.
Phrase **take up cudgels for** to argue strongly on behalf of.
• **cudgel** *verb* (**cudgels; cudgelling; cudgelled**) to beat or hit with a cudgel.
Phrase **cudgel one's brains** to think very hard.

cue¹ (kew) *noun*
1 *Theatre* a word or action which is the signal for another actor to present a particular line or action.
2 a hint or guiding suggestion: *If you're unsure of what to do, take your cue from me.*
• **cue** *verb* (**cues; cueing** or **cuing; cued**) to give a cue to or for: *The director will cue you.*

cue² *noun*
Billiards a long rod used to hit a ball.

Cue is an example of how words in English can have the same spelling but different meanings and origins. *Cue* in the sense of 'billiard stick' comes from the French *queue* (tail), from the Latin *cauda*. The actors' *cue* is thought to come from '*Q*', once used in theatre scripts to represent the Latin word *quando* (when). Etymologies are frequently uncertain and it has been suggested that the actors' *cue* also comes from the 'tail' origin, one actor taking over from the tail of the previous one.

cue ball *noun*
Billiards the ball that is hit with the cue, usually a white one.

cuff¹ *noun*
1 a fold or band at the bottom of trousers or a sleeve.
2 (**cuffs**) (*informal*) handcuffs.
Phrase **off the cuff** (*informal*) spontaneously or without preparation.

cuff² *verb*
to strike with the hand or fist.
• **cuff** *noun*.

cufflink *noun*
either of a pair of decorative fastenings for shirt cuffs, used in place of a button.

cuirass (kwi-rass) *noun* (*plural* **cuirasses**)
a piece of protective armour, especially for the breast and back.

cuisine (kwi-zeen) *noun*
a particular type of cooking: *This restaurant specializes in Italian cuisine.*
[French, kitchen]

cul-de-sac (kul-de-sak) *noun*
a road closed at one end and giving access to a group of houses.
[French *cul* bottom + *de sac* of the sack]

culinary (kull-in-ree) *adjective*
relating to the kitchen, food or cooking.
[Latin *culina* kitchen]

cull *verb*
1 to control the population of a wild animal by killing some: *culling the seals every year.*
2 (*formal*) to pick or select.
• **cull** *noun*.

culminate (kul-mi-nate) *verb*
to reach the highest point or climax: *The argument culminated in a fight.*
Word Family **culmination** (kul-mi-nay-sh'n) *noun*.
[Latin *culminis* of the top]

culottes (kew-**lots**) *plural noun*
short trousers cut with wide or flared legs so that they look like a skirt.

culpable (**kul**-pa-b'l) *adjective*
(*formal*) deserving blame or punishment.
Word Family **culpably** *adverb*;
culpability (kul-pa-**bill**-i-tee) *noun*.
[Latin *culpa* blame]

culprit *noun*
a person guilty of a fault or crime.

cult *noun*
1 a specific system of beliefs and ceremonies, usually directed towards an object or person believed to have magical or religious significance. Compare SECT.
2 (*informal*) any group of people who hold strong beliefs.
[Latin *cultus* worship]

cultivate (**kul**-ti-vate) *verb*
1 to prepare, improve and work land in order to raise crops, cattle, etc.
2 to promote the growth or development of anything: *He cultivates friends that he feels may be useful to him.*
Word Family **cultivated** *adjective* refined or well-educated: *a cultivated woman*;
cultivation (kul-ti-**vay**-sh'n) *noun*;
cultivator *noun* 1 a person who cultivates.
2 an implement for loosening soil, etc.
[Latin *cultus* tilled]

cultural (**kul**-cher-'l) *adjective*
relating to culture: *one of the cultural events of the year.*
Word Family **culturally** *adverb.*

culture (**kul**-cher) *noun*
1 the distinctive practices and beliefs of a society: *the culture of Ancient Rome.*
2 a development or improvement of the intellect or behaviour due to education, training or experience: *a man of culture.*
3 the growing of crops or the raising of animals.
4 *Biology* the growing of micro-organisms in or on an artificial medium.
• **culture** *verb* *Biology* to grow micro-organisms in or on a medium in a laboratory.
[Latin *cultura* a cultivating]

culvert *noun*
a drain to allow water to pass under a road.

cum *preposition*
combined with: *a bedroom cum studio.*
[Latin, with]

cumbersome (**kum**-ba-sum) *adjective*
clumsy or difficult to manage.

cumin (**kum**-in) *noun* also **cummin**
a small plant whose seeds are used in cooking and medicine.

cummerbund *noun*
a broad sash worn around the waist, especially on formal occasions.
[Hindi, waist-band]

cumquat ⇨ KUMQUAT.

cumulative (**kew**-mew-la-tiv) *adjective*
increasing by continuous additions.
Word Family **cumulatively** *adverb.*

cumulonimbus (kew-mew-lo-**nim**-bus) *noun* (*plural* **cumulonimbi**) (kew-mew-lo-**nim**-bye)
a large cumulus cloud bearing rain.

cumulus (**kew**-mew-lus) *noun* (*plural* **cumuli**) (**kew**-mew-lie *or* **kew**-mew-lee)
a cloud which extends upwards with a rounded top and a flat base.
[Latin, a heap]

cuneiform (**kew**-ni-form *or* kew-**nay**-i-form) *noun*
an early form of writing, consisting of wedge-shaped symbols inscribed on clay or stone.
[Latin *cuneus* wedge + FORM]

cunning *adjective*
cleverly shrewd in getting what one wants, often by deceit.
Word Family **cunning** *noun*; **cunningly** *adverb.*

cup *noun*
1 a small open container with a handle, usually for drinking.
2 anything shaped like a cup, such as the round tin set into each hole on a golf course.
3 an ornamental cup used as a prize.
4 a competition with a cup for its prize: *The America's Cup is a famous yacht race.*
5 any of various drinks, usually a mixture of wine, spirits or juices.
Phrases **in one's cups** (*dated*) drunk.
one's cup of tea (*informal*) to one's liking: *Modern art isn't really my cup of tea.*
• **cup** *verb* (**cups; cupping; cupped**) to form into the shape of a cup: *He cupped his hand over the match to keep it alight.*

cupboard (**kubb**-'d) *noun*
an enclosed series of shelves or drawers for storage, often built into a wall.
Phrase **cupboard love** affection that is put on in order to try to get something from someone.

cupcake *noun*
a small round iced cake.

Cupid (kew-pid) *noun*
Roman mythology the god of love, the son
of Venus.
[Latin *cupido* desire, passion]

cupidity (kew-**pid**-i-tee) *noun*
(*formal*) a greed for possessions or wealth.

cupola (kew-pa-la) *noun*
a small dome-shaped roof.
[Italian]

cur *noun*
1 a growling dog.
2 a despicable person.

curable (kew-ra-b'l) *adjective*
able to be cured.

curare (kew-**rah**-ree) *noun*
a powerful poison obtained from a South
American tree.

curate (kew-rit) *noun*
Christianity a newly ordained priest who
assists a parish priest.
Word Family curacy (kew-ra-see) *noun*
(*plural* **curacies**) the office or position of
a curate.

curative (kew-ra-tiv) *adjective*
of or causing a cure.

curator (kew-**ray**-ter) *noun*
a guardian or director of a museum,
library, etc.

curb *noun*
1 anything which restrains or controls.
2 a strap or chain attached to the ends of a
horse's bit and passing under the chin to
help control the horse.
3 *American* a kerb.
● **curb** *verb* to control or restrain with or
as if with a curb.
[Latin *curvare* to bend]

> ⚠ The words *curb* and *kerb* sound
> the same but have different
> spellings and meanings in British
> English. *Curb* means 'something which
> controls', as in *a curb on inflation*; *kerb*
> means 'the edge of a pavement', as in
> *He stepped off the kerb without looking*. In
> American English the spelling *curb* is
> used in both senses.

curd *noun*
1 (also **curds**) a soft solid substance
obtained by allowing milk to coagulate,
used as a food or in cheese.
2 any similar substance: *bean curd*.

curdle *verb*
to coagulate or change into curd.

Phrase **make someone's blood curdle**
to frighten someone very much.

cure *verb*
1 to restore to health.
2 to make a disease, etc. go away: *The walk
in the fresh air cured my headache*.
3 to preserve meat or fish by drying,
smoking or salting.
● **cure** *noun*
1 anything which cures.
2 a return to health.
[Latin *cura* care]

curfew *noun*
1 an official instruction that people shall
remain indoors after a certain time at
night, usually during a war or emergency.
2 *History* the ringing of a bell at a fixed
time, especially in medieval Europe, as a
signal to cover fires or to regulate the
movement of citizens.
3 the time at which this bell was rung.
[Old French *cuevrefeu* cover fire]

Curia (kew-ree-a) *noun*
1 the court of the Pope.
2 the departments in charge of
administration at the palace of the Pope.
[Latin, the senate house]

curio (kew-ree-oh) *noun*
any collectable object considered to be
interesting or unusual.
[short form of CURIOSITY]

curious (kew-ree-us) *adjective*
1 eager or interested to know and learn.
2 unusual, strange or interesting: *What a
curious bracelet!*
Word Family curiously *adverb*;
curiosity (kew-ree-**oss**-i-tee) *noun* (*plural*
curiosities) 1 the state of being curious,
2 something unusual or strange.
[Latin *curius* inquisitive]

curl *verb*
1 to form into a curve, ring or spiral.
2 to move or cause to move in a curve or
spiral.
● **curl** *noun*
1 a curved or coiled piece of hair.
2 anything in the shape of a curve, spiral or
coil.
Word Family curly *adjective* (**curlier**;
curliest).

curler ⇨ ROLLER (definition 4).

curlew *noun* (*plural* **curlew** or **curlews**)
any of various birds with a down-curved
beak, living on estuaries and moorland.

curling *noun*
a game played on ice between two teams of four players who slide heavy round stones to a target.

curmudgeon (ker-**muj**-'n) *noun*
an irritable or miserly old man.
Word Family **curmudgeonly** *adjective*.

currant *noun*
1 a small dark seedless raisin.
2 a small round acid berry growing on a shrub.

currency (**kurr**-en-see) *noun* (*plural* **currencies**)
1 any banknotes or coins accepted as a medium of exchange in financial transactions: *the single European currency.*
2 (*formal*) the state of being commonly accepted or used: *ideas which are beginning to gain currency.*

current *adjective*
belonging to or existing in the present time: *the current government policy.*
• **current** *noun*
1 a flow or stream of water, air, etc.: *A current of cold air rushed in as the door opened.* □ *A strong current flowed round the headland.*
2 a large body of water, air, etc. moving in a particular direction: *The California current flows south off the west coast of North America.*
3 ⇒ ELECTRIC CURRENT.
Word Family **currently** *adverb.*
[Latin *currens, currentis* running]

curriculum (ka-**rik**-yoo-lum) *noun* (*plural* **curricula** or **curriculums**)
1 the subjects or courses usually taught in a school, university, etc.
2 any organized course of study.
Word Family **curricular** *adjective*.

curriculum vitae (ka-**rik**-yoo-lum **vee**-tie or ka-**rik**-yoo-lum **vee**-tee) *noun* (*plural* **curricula vitae**)
short form is **CV** a summary of one's career up to the present time.

curry[1] *noun* (*plural* **curries**)
1 a combination of hot spices made into a powder, sauce or paste.
2 a dish of meat or vegetables flavoured with this mixture.
Word Family **curried** *adjective* cooked or flavoured with curry: *a plate of curried eggs.*
[Tamil]

curry[2] *verb* (**curries**; **currying**; **curried**)
to groom a horse with a curry-comb.

curry-comb *noun*
an object with serrated ridges for cleaning brushes or removing dried mud from a horse.

curse (kerse) *noun*
1 a call or appeal to supernatural powers to bring harm or evil to another person.
2 anything which produces harm or evil.
3 an obscene oath or blasphemy.
Word Family **curse** *verb*; **cursed** (**ker**-sid *or* kerst) *adjective*.

cursive (**ker**-siv) *adjective*
(of writing or print) flowing and joined.

cursor (**ker**-sa) *noun*
a movable symbol on a computer screen to identify a specific position, e.g. where the next character comes.

cursory (**ker**-sa-ree) *adjective*
hasty or superficial: *He gave the letter only a cursory glance.*
Word Family **cursorily** *adverb*; **cursoriness** *noun*.

curt *adjective*
brief or abrupt, especially in a rude manner.
Word Family **curtly** *adverb*; **curtness** *noun*.
[Latin *curtus* shortened]

curtail (ker-**tale**) *verb*
(*formal*) to reduce or cut short.
Word Family **curtailment** *noun*.

curtain (**ker**-tin) *noun*
1 a length of cloth hung at a window or door to shut out light or for decoration.
2 anything which screens or covers: *a curtain of mist.*
3 *Theatre* the screen separating the audience from the stage, usually opened at the beginning of each act and closed at the end.
4 (**curtains**) (*informal*) the end, especially death.

curtain call *noun*
Theatre the appearance of an actor or actors on the stage after a performance so that the audience can applaud. Compare ENCORE.

curtain-raiser *noun*
1 *Theatre* a short play preceding the principal play.
2 any preliminary or introductory event.

curtsy (**kert**-see) *noun* (*plural* **curtsies**) also **curtsey**
a gesture of respect made by a woman or girl by bending one knee behind the other and lowering the body slightly.

• **curtsy** *verb* (**curtsies; curtsying; curtsied**).
[from COURTESY]

curvaceous (ker-**vay**-shus) *adjective*
having a full or shapely figure.
Word Family **curvaceousness** *noun*.

curvature (**ker**-va-cher) *noun*
1 the state of being curved: *He suffers from curvature of the spine.*
2 the amount or degree to which something is curved.

curve *noun*
1 a line or form which bends continuously and has no angles or straight parts.
2 *Maths* the line, which may be a straight line, connecting all the points on a graph.
Word Family **curve** *verb*; **curvy** *adjective* (**curvier; curviest**) having curves.
[Latin *curvus* curved]

cushion (**kush**-'n) *noun*
1 a bag with a soft filling such as feathers or rubber, used for comfort when sitting, etc.
2 anything which provides soft support or absorbs shock: *A hovercraft travels on a cushion of air.*
• **cushion** *verb* to protect against or lessen the shock of something.

cushy (**kush**-ee) *adjective* (**cushier; cushiest**)
(*informal*) easy or comfortable: *a cushy job.*
Word Family **cushiness** *noun*.
[Hindi *khush* pleasant]

cusp *noun*
a pointed end especially where two curved lines meet, such as the point of a crescent moon, the ridge on a tooth, etc.
[Latin *cuspis* point]

cuss *verb*
(*informal*) to swear or curse.
• **cuss** *noun*
1 (*informal*) a curse.
2 (*informal*) an odd person.
Word Family **cussed** (**kuss**-id) *adjective* obstinate or difficult; **cussedness** *noun* obstinacy.

custard (**kus**-tid) *noun*
a sweet dish made from a thickened mixture of eggs, sugar and milk.

custody (**kus**-ta-dee) *noun*
the care or authorized keeping of a person or thing: *The little girl remained in her mother's custody.*
Word Family **custodian** (kus-**toe**-dee-an) *noun* a person who has custody or keeping of something; **custodianship**
noun; **custodial** *adjective* relating to custody: *a custodial sentence.*
[Latin *custodis* of a guardian]

custom *noun*
1 a usual or generally accepted action, practice or form of behaviour: *It is the custom in our house to have a late dinner.*
2 the regular customers of a shop, etc.

customary (**kust**-'m-ree) *adjective*
based on custom or accepted practice: *It is customary for all workers to wear a uniform.*
Word Family **customarily** *adverb*.

custom-built (kust-'m-**bilt**) *adjective* also called **custom-made**.
made to the specific order of the customer.

customer *noun*
1 a person who buys goods or services.
2 (*informal*) a person of a particular kind: *He's an odd customer.*

custom house *noun* also **customs house**
an office where customs duty was collected in the past.

customize, customise *verb*
to alter specially for a particular person.

customs *plural noun*
1 the government organization collecting taxes on objects brought into or out of a country.
2 also **customs duty** the tax paid on such goods.

cut *verb* (**cuts; cutting; cut**)
1 to penetrate or separate with something sharp: *I cut the apple into four pieces.*
2 to make using something sharp: *He cut a neat hole in the tarpaulin.*
3 to take out: *Cut the last line of this speech.*
4 to stop: *Quick – cut the engine!*
5 to reduce or shorten: *Manufacturers must cut their prices.* □ *She cut my hair*
6 to go directly: *We cut through the fields to save time.*
7 to cross: *Line A cuts line B at point C.*
8 to divide: *The dealer cut the pack of cards.*
9 to hurt: *I was cut by their remarks.*
10 *Sport* to hit the ball so that it spins or changes direction in its flight.
11 to make less pure: *powdered heroin cut with washing powder.*
12 (*informal*) to make a recording.
13 (*informal*) not to attend: *She's cut three lectures this week.*
Phrases **be cut out for, be cut out to be** (*informal*) to have the qualities necessary for or to be: *I'm afraid I'm not cut out to be a nurse.* **cut and dried** clear or settled. **cut and run** (*informal*) to escape from an awkward situation. **cut a tooth** (of a baby)

to have a tooth emerge through the gum.
cut in 1 to interrupt. **2** (of a machine) to
start to function. **3** to include someone.
cut it fine (*informal*) to give oneself very
little time to achieve what one needs to.
cut it out (*informal*) stop it. **cut off 1** to
intercept: *Try to cut him off at the crossroads.*
2 to disconnect: *Our phone has been cut off.*
3 to disinherit: *He was cut off without a*
penny. **cut out 1** to exclude. **2** (of a
machine) to stop functioning. **cut short**
to end abruptly. **cut someone dead**
(*informal*) to ignore someone. **cut**
someone up (*informal*) (of a driver) to
pull in front of someone too sharply. **cut**
up (*informal*) very upset: *He was really cut*
up about it.
• **cut** *noun*
1 the result of cutting, such as a mark,
wound, etc.
2 a piece cut off: *a cut of meat.*
3 a blow or stroke, especially one which
cuts.
4 a reduction: *a cut in the price of petrol.*
5 (*informal*) a share: *What's your cut of the*
profits?
6 a style in which something is cut: *the cut*
of his suit.
7 a part of a film, etc. which is taken out:
The producer wanted further cuts to be made.
8 *Sport* a stroke at the ball which causes it
to spin or change direction in its flight.
Phrases **a cut above** (*informal*) superior
to. **the cut and thrust** the normal rather
aggressive style in which an activity is
done: *part of the cut and thrust of politics.*

cutback *noun*
a reduction: *cutbacks in public expenditure.*

cute *adjective*
1 attractive or pleasing: *a cute little dog.*
2 (*informal*) clever or too clever: *Don't try*
to be cute with me, young man!
Word Family **cutely** *adverb*; **cuteness**
noun.

cuticle (**kew**-ti-k'l) *noun*
the skin that covers the base of the
fingernails and toenails.

cutlass (**kut**-l's) *noun* (*plural* **cutlasses**)
a short heavy sword with a curved blade.

cutlery (**kut**-la-ree) *noun*
knives, forks and spoons.
Word Family **cutler** *noun* a person who
makes or sells cutlery.

cutlet *noun*
a small piece of meat containing a bone.

cut-off *noun*
the limit or point at which something ends
or is completed.

cut-out *noun*
a figure or shape cut out of cardboard,
wood, etc.

cutter *noun*
Nautical a warship's small boat fitted with
sails and oars.

cut-throat *adjective*
ruthless or merciless: *cut-throat competition.*
• **cut-throat** *noun*
1 also **cut-throat razor** a razor with a
large open blade.
2 (*dated*) a ruthlessly violent person,
especially one considered capable of
murder.

cutting *noun*
1 anything which is cut off or out: *a*
newspaper cutting.
2 anything which is produced by cutting,
such as an excavation through a hill, etc.
when building a road or railway.
• **cutting** *adjective*
1 bitter: *the cutting wind.*
2 hurtful: *a cutting remark.*

cutting edge *noun*
the most advanced stage: *pioneering work at*
the cutting edge of laser technology.

cuttlefish *noun* (*plural* **cuttlefish** *or*
cuttlefishes)
a flat squid-like marine mollusc that
produces an inky substance when
attacked.

cyanide (**sigh**-a-nide) *noun*
an extremely strong poison.

cybercafé *noun*
a café providing customers with access to
the Internet.

cybernetics (sigh-ber-**net**-iks) *plural noun*
(*used with singular verb*) the study of
methods of communication and control
common to living things and machines.
[Greek *kybernetes* helmsman]

cyberpunk *noun*
(*informal*) a person who breaks into
computer systems illegally.

cyberspace *noun*
the place where information, etc. is
exchanged by computers.

cyborg *noun*
a person with bionic parts, giving
superhuman powers.

cyclamate (sik-la-mate *or* sigh-kla-mate)
noun
any of a group of artificial chemicals used
as low-calorie substitutes for sugar.

cyclamen (sik-la-m'n) *noun*
a small flowering plant, often grown
indoors.

cycle (sigh-k'l) *noun*
1 a series of events which are repeated in a
regular order: *the cycle of the seasons*.
2 any complete period or course: *a life
cycle*.
3 a series of poems or songs.
4 a bicycle.
• **cycle** *verb*
1 to ride a bicycle.
2 to move in cycles.
[Greek *kyklos* a circle]

cyclic (sigh-klik *or* sik-lik) *adjective*
of or recurring in cycles.

cyclist (sigh-klist) *noun*
a person who rides a bicycle or
motorcycle.

cyclone (sigh-klone) *noun*
1 ⇨ TROPICAL CYCLONE.
2 ⇨ LOW[1] *noun* (definition 2).
Word Family **cyclonic** (sigh-**klon**-ik)
adjective.

Cyclops (sigh-klops) *noun*
Greek mythology any of a race of giants
with one eye in the centre of the forehead.
[Greek *Kyklops* round-eyed]

cygnet (sig-nit) *noun*
the young of a swan.
[Greek *kyknos* a swan]

cylinder (sill-in-da) *noun*
1 a solid or hollow body having circular
equal ends and parallel sides.
2 something which has this shape.
3 the rotating part of a revolver containing
the cartridge chambers.
4 a chamber in an internal-combustion
engine within which a mixture of petrol
and air is compressed by the piston and
exploded by a spark from a spark plug.

Word Family **cylindrical** (sill-**in**-dri-k'l)
adjective.
[Greek *kylindein* to roll]

cylinder head *noun*
a heavy metal cover over the cylinders of
an internal-combustion engine, usually
forming part of the combustion space.

cymbals (sim-b'lz) *plural noun*
Music a percussion instrument consisting
of two slightly concave brass plates which
are either clashed against each other or hit
separately with a stick.
[Greek *kymbalon*]

cynical (sin-i-k'l) *adjective*
having no belief or trust in goodness,
honesty, sincerity, etc.
Word Family **cynic** *noun*; **cynically**
adverb; **cynicism** (sin-i-sizm) *noun*.
[Greek *kynikos* dog-like, churlish]

cypher ⇨ CIPHER.

cypress (sigh-pris) *noun* (*plural*
cypresses)
an evergreen tree with dark needle-like
leaves and hard wood.
[Greek *kyparissos*]

cyst (sist) *noun*
Medicine an abnormal closed sac
containing fluid.
Word Family **cystic** *adjective*.
[Greek *kystis* bladder]

cystic fibrosis *noun*
Medicine a very serious hereditary disease
affecting some of the body's glands.

cystitis *noun*
inflammation of the inner lining of the
bladder, causing discomfort and a
frequent need to urinate.

cytoplasm (sigh-toe-plazm) *noun*
Biology a jelly-like material which
surrounds the nucleus of a cell and
contains most of the cell's organelles.

czar (zar) ⇨ TSAR.

czarina (zar-ee-na) ⇨ TSARINA.

Dd

dab¹ *verb* (**dabs; dabbing; dabbed**)
to touch or apply lightly: *The girl dabbed make-up on her cheeks.*
● **dab** *noun*
1 the act of dabbing.
2 a small amount.

dab² *noun*
an edible marine flatfish related to the plaice.

dabble *verb*
1 to splash in a liquid, especially with the hands or feet.
2 to do as a hobby or casual interest: *She dabbles in pottery during her spare time.*
Word Family **dabbler** *noun.*

dabchick *noun*
a small grebe.

dab hand *noun*
(*informal*) an expert: *He is a dab hand at photography.*

dace *noun* (*plural* **dace**)
a small freshwater fish related to the chub.

dacha *noun*
a Russian country house provided by the state for those approved of by the authorities.
[Russian, payment]

dachshund (**daks**-hoond) *noun*
one of a breed of small short-legged dogs with long bodies.
[German *Dachs* badger + *Hund* dog]

dactyl (**dak**-til) *noun*
Poetry a group of syllables consisting of one stressed followed by two unstressed syllables or one long followed by two short syllables.
[Greek *daktylos* finger, which has three bones]

dad *noun*
(*informal*) a father.

daddy *noun* (*plural* **daddies**)
(*informal*) a father.

daddy-long-legs *noun* (*plural* **daddy-long-legs**) also called **cranefly**.
any of a group of insects with a tiny round body and very long slender legs. The larvae, called **leatherjackets**, are a garden pest.

dado (**day**-doe) *noun*
1 any panelling or other decoration at the base of the wall of a room.
2 a decorative border at picture-rail level on the wall of a room.

daffodil *noun*
an early spring plant of the narcissus family with reed-like leaves and bright yellow or creamy white trumpet-shaped flowers, growing from a bulb.
[from Greek *asphodelos* asphodel]

daft (dahft) *adjective*
foolish or mildly insane.

dagger *noun*
a short-bladed weapon, like a small sword.
Phrase **look daggers at** to cast angry or threatening glances at.

daguerreotype (da-**gerr**-o-type) *noun*
an early image-fixing process, related to photography, where a positive image becomes etched upon a sensitive metal plate.
[invented by *L. J. M. Daguerre*, 1789-1851]

dahlia (**dale**-ya) *noun*
an autumn garden plant with brightly coloured flowers, growing from a tuber.
[after *A. Dahl*, 1751-1789, a Swedish botanist]

Dáil Éireann (doyl **air**-an) *noun*
short form is **Dáil** the lower house of parliament in the Republic of Ireland.
[Irish *dáil* assembly + *Éireann* Irish]

daily *adjective*
of or occurring every day.
● **daily** *adverb* happening every day.
● **daily** *noun* (*plural* **dailies**)
1 (*informal*) a newspaper published every weekday.
2 (*dated informal*) a cleaning woman who comes every day.

dainty *adjective* (**daintier; daintiest**)
very delicate or neat.
Word Family **daintiness** *noun;* **daintily** *adverb.*

daiquiri (**die**-ki-ree) *noun*
a cocktail made from rum, lime juice and sugar.

dairy *noun* (*plural* **dairies**)
a place where milk is stored, processed or sold.
dairy cattle any cattle bred or kept to produce milk rather than meat.

dairy farm a farm producing milk or milk products.

dais (day-iss) *noun* (*plural* **daises**)
a raised platform, e.g. for a speaker.

daisy (day-zee) *noun* (*plural* **daisies**)
any of a group of plants with composite flowers, usually with a yellow centre.
[Middle English *dayseye* day's eye, because it opens in the morning]

daisy wheel *noun*
a component of some kinds of printer that carries the letter type to be printed and is shaped like a wheel with a different character at the end of each spoke.

dal ⇨ DHAL.

dale *noun*
a valley, especially in northern England.

> **Dale** is an example of a word that is common in several parts of Britain but not in Britain as a whole. Despite the fact that Britain is a small country geographically, there is quite a wide variation from area to area both in the pronunciation of words and in the words themselves. Many words which differ refer to geographical features, such as *dale* in Yorkshire and *glen* in Scotland, while others refer to everyday things, such as *butty* (sandwich) in the North of England.

dally *verb* (**dallies; dallying; dallied**)
1 to trifle with, as in a love affair.
2 to waste time.
Word Family **dalliance** *noun*.

Dalmatian *noun*
any of a breed of large short-haired white dogs with black spots.
[after *Dalmatia*, a region of Croatia]

dam[1] *noun*
a wall or other structure built to keep water back, e.g. across a river. Compare DYKE.
● **dam** (**dams; damming; dammed**)
verb to build a dam across a river, etc.

dam[2] *noun*
a female parent, especially of a mammal.
[shortening of DAME]

damage (dam-ij) *noun*
1 any injury which causes loss of usefulness or value.
2 (**damages**) *Law* a sum of money that is claimed because of a loss, e.g. when a contract has been broken.
3 (*informal*) the cost.
● **damage** *verb* to cause damage to.

Word Family **damagingly** *adverb*.
[Latin *damnum* damage]

damage limitation *noun*
action taken to try to limit or minimize the effects of some kind of damage, such as an error of judgement, a tactless remark, or an accident.

damask (dam-'sk) *noun*
a twilled cotton fibre or linen fabric.

dame *noun*
1 (**Dame**) a form of address for a woman of rank.
2 (*informal*) a woman.

damn (dam) *verb*
to curse or condemn.
Word Family **damn!, damnation!** *interjection;* **damnation** (dam-**nay**-sh'n) *noun* the state of being damned, especially to hell; **damnable** (dam-na-b'l) *adjective*
1 deserving to be damned: *a damnable offence.* 2 (*informal*) annoying or unpleasant; **damnably** *adverb;* **damned** *adjective* 1 condemned to hell: *a damned soul.* 2 (*informal*) very annoying: *What a damned cheek;* **damned** *adverb* (*informal*) extremely, very; **damning** *adjective* proving guilt.
[Latin *damnare* to condemn]

damp *adjective*
moist or slightly wet.
● **damp** *noun*
1 any moisture or moistness.
2 a poisonous or suffocating vapour or gas, especially in a mine.
● **damp** *verb*
1 to make damp.
2 to discourage or dull: *The disappointment damped our enthusiasm a bit.*
3 *Physics, Music* to reduce the amplitude of a vibrating string, wave, etc.
4 to reduce the energy of.
Word Family **damply** *adverb;* **dampness** *noun.*

dampen *verb*
1 to make damp.
2 to dull or depress: *The dark sky dampened our enthusiasm for a picnic.*
Word Family **dampener** *noun* something which dulls or depresses.

damper *noun*
1 a movable metal plate for regulating the flow of air into a fire in a stove or furnace.
2 a device in a keyboard instrument which deadens the vibration of the strings.
Phrase **put a damper on** to affect something so that people feel sad or disappointed.

damsel (**dam**-z'l) *noun*
an old word for a young unmarried
woman.

damson *noun*
a small purple plum.
[from *Damascene*, of *Damascus*]

dance *noun*
1 a series of steps and movements, usually
in time to music.
2 a piece of music for this.
3 a social function at which one dances.
● **dance** *verb*
1 to perform a dance.
2 to move quickly or nimbly.
Phrase **dance attendance on** to be
excessively polite or obliging to.
Word Family **dancer** *noun*; **dancing**
noun.

dandelion (**dan**-di-lie-on) *noun*
a small weed with deeply notched leaves
and bright yellow flowers which form a
ball of downy seeds.
[French *dent* tooth + *de lion* of lion,
because of the shape of the leaves]

dandle *verb*
to move a child up and down on one's
knees or in one's arms.

dandruff *noun* also called **scurf**.
small scales of dead skin on the scalp.

dandy *noun* (*plural* **dandies**)
a man who is excessively concerned with
his clothes and appearance.

danger (**dane**-ja) *noun*
1 a likelihood of harm or injury: *The
mountaineer enjoyed the element of danger
in the sport.*
2 something which may cause danger:
That hidden reef is a danger to shipping.
Word Family **dangerous** *adjective*;
dangerously *adverb*; **dangerousness**
noun.

dangle *verb*
to swing or hang loosely.

dank *adjective*
unpleasantly damp: *a dank cellar.*
Word Family **dankly** *adverb*; **dankness**
noun.

dapper *adjective*
(of a person) neat and smart.

dappled *adjective*
having spots of different colours.
Word Family **dapple** *verb* to mark with
spots of different colours.

dare *verb*
1 to be bold enough: *He dared to contradict
his parents.*

2 to challenge: *I dare you to do it.*
Phrase **dare say** *I dare say we will win*
(= suppose).
● **dare** *noun* a challenge.
Word Family **daren't** *contraction* a short
form of **dare not**; **daring** *adjective*;
daringly *adverb*.

daredevil *noun*
a reckless person.

dark *adjective*
1 with little or no light.
2 (of colours, surfaces, etc.) reflecting or
radiating little or no light.
3 not pale: *He has a dark complexion.*
Figurative She gave him a dark look
(= angry). □ *He brooded over dark thoughts*
(= sad or evil). □ *Sue tried to keep the news
dark* (= secret).
● **dark** *noun*
1 an absence of light: *children afraid of the
dark.*
2 nightfall: *Be home before dark.*
Phrase **in the dark** in ignorance or
without knowledge.
Word Family **darkness** *noun* 1 absence
of light 2 the state or quality of being
dark; **darkly** *adverb*; **darken** *verb* to make
or become dark or darker.

Dark Ages *plural noun*
a name given to the period about
A.D. 450-1000.

dark horse *noun*
a person of unknown capabilities.

darkroom *noun*
a lightproof room for developing and
printing films.

darling *noun*
a person or thing very much loved.
*Figurative He is the latest darling of the
social world* (= favourite).

darn¹ *verb*
to repair a hole in a garment by using
interlacing stitches.
Word Family **darn** *noun*; **darning** *noun*
anything which has been or needs to be
darned.

darn² *interjection*
(*informal*) a mild exclamation of irritation,
etc.
Word Family **darned** *adjective*, *adverb*
(*informal*) damned.

dart *noun*
1 a small sharp metal arrow with feathers
at one end.
2 (**darts**) a game in which each player
throws a series of darts at a numbered
target.

3 a sudden swift movement: *He made a dart for the door.*

4 a tapering tuck sewn in a garment to alter its shape.

• **dart** *verb* to move swiftly.

Darwinism *noun*
Biology the theory of evolution of separate species from a common origin. ⇨ NATURAL SELECTION.

[suggested by *Charles Darwin*, 1809-1882]

dash¹ *verb*
1 to rush: *He dashed across the road.*
2 to throw or strike violently: *The boat was dashed against the rocks during the storm.*
Figurative His hopes were dashed when she left him (= ruined, frustrated).
Phrase **dash off** *He dashed off an article for the school newspaper* (= wrote hurriedly).

• **dash** *noun* (*plural* **dashes**)
1 a sudden rush or violent movement: *The ambulance made a mercy dash to the hospital.*
2 a small quantity added to something: *He always has whisky with a dash of water.*
3 vigour: *an exciting performance which was full of dash.*
4 a punctuation mark ( ), used to separate off a group of words from the rest of the sentence, to introduce an explanatory statement, etc.: *She was clutching her most treasured possession – a picture of her two grandchildren.*
Phrase **cut a dash** to be very impressive in appearance, behaviour, etc.

dash² *interjection*
(*informal*) a mild exclamation of irritation.

dashboard *noun*
the instrument panel of a motor vehicle or aeroplane.

dashing *adjective*
showy, stylish or spirited.
Word Family **dashingly** *adverb.*

dastardly (dass-t'd-lee) *adjective*
(*dated*) mean and cowardly.

data (**day** ta) *noun*
facts or information.

> ! The word **data**, strictly speaking, is a plural noun, which has the singular form *datum*, derived directly from Latin, but the use of *datum* is rare in modern English. In fact, *data* is increasingly being treated as a singular noun which cannot be made plural, like *information*, as in *The data has been gathered from a variety of sources.*

database *noun*
Computers a store of computerized information which can be retrieved in a variety of ways.

data capture *noun*
Computers the conversion of information to machine-readable form.

data file *noun*
Computers an electronic means of storing information, such as the results of the census.

data handling *noun*
Computers working with and drawing conclusions from collections of information stored in a database.

data logging *noun*
using sensing technology, e.g. temperature sensors, to record and store information.

data processing *noun*
Computers a series of operations performed on data by a computer to retrieve or interpret information.

date¹ *noun*
1 a particular date or period of time.
2 day, month and year: *Please state your date of birth.*
3 the year inscribed: *What is the date on that coin?*
4 (*informal*) an appointment to meet someone: *She's got a date with Christopher tonight.*
5 (*informal*) the person with whom an appointment is made.
Phrases **out of date** old-fashioned or obsolete. **to date** *I have collected over 1000 stamps to date* (= until the present time).
• **date** *verb*
1 to assign a date to: *to date an ancient manuscript.*
2 to put or have a date on: *All letters should be dated correctly.*
3 to become out of date: *Most 19th-century scientific textbooks are badly dated by now.*
4 (*informal*) to go out with somebody.
Phrases **date from, date back to** *This church dates from Norman times* (– has existed since).

date² *noun*
a small oblong brown fruit of a palm, widely grown in Africa and the Middle East.

date line *noun*
1 a line at the start of a letter, newspaper article, etc. giving the date and place of origin.
2 (**Date Line**) the International Date Line.

date rape *noun*
rape which takes place during an arranged social meeting, carried out by someone the victim knows.

datum (day-t'm) *noun* (*plural* **data**)
(*technical*) a piece of information. ⇨ DATA.

daub (dawb) *verb*
to cover a surface with paint, mud, etc.
• **daub** *noun* a covering of sticky material,
such as clay: *a hut made of wattle and daub*.
Word Family **dauber** *noun* an unskilful
painter.

daughter (daw-ta) *noun*
1 a female child in relation to her parents.
2 a female person strongly influenced by
or involved with something: *the daughters
of the revolution*.
Word Family **daughterly** *adjective*.

daughter-in-law *noun* (*plural*
daughters-in-law)
the wife of one's son.

daunt (dawnt) *verb*
to discourage or lessen the enthusiasm of.
Word Family **dauntless** *adjective* not
easily discouraged; **dauntlessly** *adverb*.

dauphin (daw-fin *or* doe-fan) *noun*
History the title given to the eldest son of
the king of France, from the 14th century
to the 19th century.

davenport *noun*
1 a small ornamental writing desk.
2 *American* a large sofa.

davit *noun*
Nautical either of a pair of curved arms at
the side of a ship by which small boats, etc.
may be raised from or lowered into the
water by means of tackle.

Davy lamp *noun*
History a safety lamp used by coal-miners.
[invented by *Sir Humphry Davy*, 1778-
1829, a British chemist]

dawdle *verb*
to waste time or fall behind, e.g. when
walking.
Word Family **dawdler** *noun*.

dawn *noun*
1 the first appearance of daylight.
2 (*formal*) the beginning of something:
since the dawn of time.
• **dawn** *verb*
1 to begin to grow light.
2 to begin to develop or be perceived.

day *noun*
1 the period of light from dawn to dusk.
2 the 24-hour period from one midnight
to the next.
3 the period one is awake or active: *I've
had a hard day*.

4 *Astronomy* the time taken for the earth or
another planet to rotate once on its axis.
Compare SIDEREAL DAY; SOLAR DAY.
5 (*often* **days**) a particular period: *in days
gone by*.
Phrases **be early days** to be too soon to
be certain what will happen. **call it a day**
to finish or stop. **carry the day** to win.
day in, day out every day or indefinitely.
win the day to be most successful: *Our
team won the day in all sections*.

daybreak *noun*
the dawn.

daydream *noun*
an imaginative fantasy indulged in while
awake.
Word Family **daydream** (**daydreams**;
daydreaming; **daydreamed** or
daydreamt (**day**-dremt)) *verb*;
daydreamer *noun*.

daylight saving time *noun*
(*especially American*) summer time.

daze *verb*
to stun or bewilder.
Word Family **daze** *noun* a feeling of
bewilderment or confusion; **dazed**
adjective; **dazedly** (**day**-zid-lee) *adverb*.

dazzle *verb*
to overpower with or as if with intense
light.
Figurative Her beautiful face dazzled the
stranger (= excited admiration in).
Word Family **dazzling** *adjective*.

D-Day *noun*
6 June 1944, when Allied forces landed in
Europe.
[*D* is the military symbol for the day on
which an operation is planned to begin]

deacon *noun*
1 *Christianity* a member of the third order
of clergy, ranking beneath bishops and
priests and assisting them in their duties.
2 *Christianity* a lay person who assists in
worship and takes care of other lay
matters, in some Protestant churches.
[Greek *diakonos* servant]

deaconess *noun* (*plural* **deaconesses**)
Christianity a woman minister in certain
churches, especially concerned with work
for charity.

deactivate (dee-**ak**-ti-vate) *verb*
to make inactive or reduce the activity of.
Word Family **deactivation** (dee-ak-ti-
vay-sh'n) *noun*.

dead (ded) *adjective*
without life or no longer living: *The dead
leaves fell from the tree*.

Figurative Latin is a dead language (= no longer spoken). □ *There was a dead silence* (= complete, absolute). □ *She fell down in a dead faint* (= resembling death). □ (*informal*) *I'm really dead by the end of the week* (= exhausted).

dead weight something that is extremely heavy and difficult to carry: *The sleeping child was a dead weight in my arms.*

• **dead** *plural noun* people who are dead: *A memorial was erected to the dead of the Second World War.*

• **dead** *noun* the middle or quiet part: *in the dead of night.*

• **dead** *adverb*
1 completely: *You are dead wrong.*
2 abruptly: *He stopped dead in his tracks.*
3 directly: *The reef lay dead ahead.*
Word Family deaden *verb* to reduce or make dull: *He was given medicine to deaden the pain.*

dead beat *adjective*
(*informal*) exhausted: *I'm dead beat by Friday.*

dead-end *adjective*
1 (of a street) having one end closed.
2 (of a job) leading nowhere or having no future.
Word Family dead end *noun* 1 a dead-end street. 2 a point or condition from which no progress can be made.

dead heat *noun*
a competition or race in which two or more competitors have an equal score or finish together.

dead letter *noun*
1 a law which has not been abolished formally but is no longer observed.
2 a letter which cannot be delivered because it is wrongly addressed.

deadline *noun*
the time by which something must be done: *The deadline for entries is next Friday.*

deadlock *noun*
a situation from which further progress is impossible.
• **deadlock** *verb.*

deadly *adjective* (**deadlier; deadliest**)
1 causing or tending to cause death: *a deadly poison.*
2 aiming to destroy or defeat: *deadly enemies.*
3 like death: *a deadly paleness.*
• **deadly** *adverb*
1 in a manner suggesting death.
2 excessively: *deadly dull.*
Word Family deadliness *noun.*

deadly nightshade ⇨ BELLADONNA.

deadpan *adjective*
(of a face) lacking expression or reaction.

deaf (def) *adjective*
1 unable to hear or to hear well.
2 refusing to listen: *He turned a deaf ear to her pleas.*
• **deaf** *plural noun* people who are deaf.
Word Family deafness *noun.*

deafen (def-'n) *verb*
1 to make deaf.
2 to overwhelm with noise.
Word Family deafening *adjective;*
deafeningly *adverb.*

deaf mute *noun*
a person who is deaf and dumb. This term is often considered offensive.

deal¹ *verb* (**deals; dealing; dealt** (delt))
1 to be occupied with or manage: *Let us deal with this problem first.*
2 to do business with: *I always deal with that company.*
3 to distribute: *We dealt a hand of cards.*
4 to deliver: *The boxer dealt his opponent a heavy blow.*
• **deal** *noun*
1 an agreement or arrangement: *We made a deal not to say anything.*
2 the act or an instance of dealing.
Phrases **a good deal of** a large amount or quantity of. **a great deal of** much or most. **a raw deal** any unfair treatment.
Word Family dealer *noun* a trader or merchant; **dealings** *plural noun.*

deal² *noun*
softwood, usually pine, in boards or planks.

dean *noun*
1 a teacher or official in charge of students and the internal running of a college or a faculty of a university.
2 *Christianity* the chief member of the clergy of a cathedral, college church or part of a diocese.
Word Family deanery *noun* (*plural* **deaneries**) 1 the residence of a dean. 2 the office of a dean.

dear *adjective*
1 beloved or highly regarded: *a dear friend.*
2 a greeting in letters, etc.: *Dear Miss Williamson.*
3 expensive.
Word Family dear *noun, adverb;* **dearly** *adverb.*

dearth (derth) *noun*
a lack or scarcity.

death (deth) *noun*
1 the act of dying: *His death occurred last week.*
2 the state of being dead: *He drank himself to death.*
Figurative It was the death of all hope (= extinction). □ *a hero's death* (= manner of dying).
Phrases **do to death** 1 to kill. 2 to repeat until stale. **put to death** to execute. **sick to death** (*informal*) extremely annoyed or irritated.

death by misadventure ⇨ MISADVENTURE (definition 1).

death duty *noun* (*plural* **death duties**)
a tax paid when one inherits property.

deathly *adjective* (**deathlier; deathliest**)
like death.
• **deathly** *adverb*
1 in a manner resembling death.
2 extremely or utterly: *deathly afraid.*

death rate *noun*
the number of deaths in proportion to the total population at a given time, expressed per 1000 people. Compare BIRTH RATE.

deathtrap *noun*
a situation involving risk of death: *This intersection is a deathtrap.*

death-watch beetle *noun*
a small furniture beetle, the larvae of which seriously damage ancient timber. [from its mating call, like a ticking watch and made by knocking its head against the wood, once thought to herald death in the household]

deb *noun*
(*informal*) a debutante.

debacle (day-**bah**-k'l) *noun*
a sudden or overwhelming collapse or disaster.
[French *débâcler* to unfasten]

debar *verb* (**debars; debarring; debarred**)
1 to exclude: *He was debarred from the club.*
2 to prevent or prohibit: *He was debarred from driving after the accident.*
Word Family **debarment** *noun.*

debase *verb*
to lower in quality, rank or dignity.
Word Family **debasement** *noun*; **debaser** *noun.*

debate *noun*
1 a discussion, especially of a public question.
2 an organized contest in which opposing points of view are argued.
• **debate** *verb*
1 to discuss.
2 to consider: *I'm debating whether to sell my car or not.*
Word Family **debater** *noun*; **debatable** *adjective* open to question.

debauchery (di-**baw**-cha-ree) *noun*
an excessive indulgence in sensual pleasures.
Word Family **debauch** *verb*; **debauched** *adjective* corrupt.

debenture (di-**ben**-cher) *noun*
an interest-bearing loan or mortgage on the assets of a company.
[Latin *debens* owing]

debility (di-**bill**-i-tee) *noun* (*plural* **debilities**)
a general weakness or feebleness.
Word Family **debilitate** *verb*; **debilitating** *adjective*; **debilitation** (di-bill-i-**tay**-sh'n) *noun.*
[Latin *debilis* weak]

debit *noun*
a record of a debt entered in an account. Compare CREDIT (definition 6).
• **debit** *verb.*

debit card *noun*
a card by means of which the cost of a purchase is debited electronically from the holder's bank account.

debonair (**debb**-a-nair) *adjective*
urbane or pleasantly gracious.
[French *de bon* of good + *aire* disposition]

debriefing (dee-**bree**-fing) *noun*
the questioning of soldiers, astronauts, etc who have returned from a mission, in order to assess the success of the mission.
Word Family **debrief** *verb.*

debris (**deb**-ree *or* **day**-bree) *noun*
the remains of anything broken or destroyed: *The road was covered with debris after the accident.*
[French *ébriser* to break down]

debt (det) *noun*
anything which one person owes to another.
bad debt a debt unlikely to be paid.
Word Family **debtor** *noun* a person who owes money to another. Compare CREDITOR.
[Latin *debitum*]

debt counselling *noun*
professional advice provided for those who are unable to meet their financial commitments.

debug *verb* (**debugs; debugging; debugged**)
1 to discover and remove faults in a computer program, electronic device, etc.
2 (*informal*) to remove electronic listening devices from.

debunk *verb*
(*informal*) to expose exaggeration or falseness.

debut (**day-bew**) *noun*
1 a first public appearance on the stage, television, etc.
2 (*dated*) an introduction and entry into society: *The President's daughter made her debut last night.*
• **debut** *verb* to make a first appearance on or as something.
Word Family debutante (**deb-yoo-tahnt**) *noun* a young woman who makes her social debut.
[French *débuter* to make the first stroke in a game]

decade (**dek-ade**) *noun*
a period of ten years.

decadence (**dekk-a-d'nce**) *noun*
a process or condition of deterioration, especially in a moral or artistic sense: *The decadence of the 1890s showed itself in a taste for exotic and perverse pleasures.*
Word Family decadent *adjective* involved in or practising decadence; **decadently** *adverb*.
[*de-* + Latin *adere* to fall]

decaf (**dee-kaff**) *noun*
(*informal*) decaffeinated coffee.

decaffeinated (**dee-kaff-in-ay-tid**) *adjective*
(of coffee or tea) having had most of the caffeine removed.

decagon (**dekk-a-g'n**) *noun*
any closed plane figure with ten straight sides.
Word Family decagonal (**dek-agg-a-n'l**) *adjective*.
[*deca-* + Greek *gonia* corner]

decahedron (**dekk-a-hee-dr'n**) *noun*
(*plural* **decahedra** or **decahedrons**)
a solid or hollow body with ten plane faces.
Word Family decahedral *adjective*.
[*deca-* + Greek *hedra* base]

Decalogue (**dekk-a-log**) *noun*
the Ten Commandments.
[Greek *dekalogos*]

decamp *verb*
to leave suddenly or secretly: *The accountant decamped with the company funds.*
Word Family decampment *noun*.

decant (**di-kant**) *verb*
to pour a liquid, especially wine, from one container to another.

decanter *noun*
an ornamental flask or bottle for serving wines.

decapitate (**di-kapp-i-tate**) *verb*
to behead.
Word Family decapitation (**di-kapp-i-tay-sh'n**) *noun*.
[*de-* + Latin *caput* head]

decarbonize, decarbonise *verb*
to remove accumulated deposits of carbon from the combustion chamber of an internal-combustion engine.

decathlon (**di-kath-lon**) *noun*
a contest in which athletes compete for the highest total score in ten separate events.
[*deca-* + Greek *athlon* contest]

decay *verb*
1 to rot away or deteriorate: *The previous owners allowed the house to decay around them.* □ *The leaves slowly decayed on the lawn.*
2 *Physics* (of a nucleus) to disintegrate owing to the effect of radioactivity.
Word Family decay *noun*.
[Latin *de-* down *cadere* to fall]

decease (**di-seece**) *noun*
(*formal*) death: *On his uncle's decease he expects to become a wealthy man.*
[*de-* + Latin *cessus* gone]

deceased (**di-seest**) *adjective*
(*formal*) dead.
• **deceased** *noun* (*plural* **deceased**)
(*formal*) a person who has recently died: *the relations of the deceased.*

deceit (**di-seet**) *noun*
1 the act or practice of misleading someone by concealing or distorting the truth.
2 a trick or stratagem.
Word Family deceitful *adjective*; **deceitfully** *adverb*; **deceitfulness** *noun*.
[Latin *decipere* to cheat]

deceive (**di-seev**) *verb*
to mislead by concealing or distorting the truth.
Word Family deceiver *noun*.

decelerate (**dee-sell-a-rate**) *verb*
to decrease in velocity.

Word Family **deceleration** (dee-sell-a-**ray**-sh'n) ⇨ RETARDATION at RETARD; **decelerator** *noun* something which causes deceleration.

December (di-**sem**-ba) *noun*
the twelfth month of the year, after November.
[Latin *decem* ten, because December was the tenth month of the Roman calendar]

decent (**dee**-s'nt) *adjective*
1 conforming to accepted social standards in matters of taste or conduct.
2 respectable: *They come from a very decent family.*
3 fair, tolerable: *The workers demanded a decent living wage.*
4 kind: *It was decent of you to lend me your car.*
5 properly dressed: *Are you decent?*
Word Family **decency** *noun* (*plural* **decencies**) **1** the state or quality of being decent. **2** (**decencies**) the requirements of a decent way of life: *The corpse was buried so hastily that none of the decencies could be observed;* **decently** *adverb*.
[Latin *decens* seemly or proper]

decentralization, decentralisation
(dee-sen-tra-lie-**zay**-sh'n) *noun*
the distribution of administrative powers among local or regional authorities.
Word Family **decentralize** (dee-**sen**-tra-lies) *verb*.

deception (di-**sep**-sh'n) *noun*
1 the act of deceiving: *The impostor practised deception on his victims.*
2 the state of being deceived.
3 a trick or artifice: *His mean deceptions were finally exposed.*
Word Family **deceptive** *adjective* deceiving or misleading; **deceptively** *adverb*.

decibel (**dess**-i-bel) *noun*
a unit of sound intensity.

decide (di-**side**) *verb*
1 to make a choice: *She decided to continue despite her lawyer's advice.*
2 to settle a question or conflict: *The election will not be decided until all votes are counted.*
Word Family **decided** *adjective* definite or unquestionable: *There is a decided difference between them;* **decidedly** *adverb*; **decider** *noun*.
[Latin *decidere* to cut short to settle]

deciduous (di-**sid**-yew-us) *adjective*
Biology of or relating to an animal or plant which regularly sheds part of itself, such as skin, antlers, leaves, etc.
[Latin *decidere* to fall down]

decimal (**dess**-i-m'l) *noun*
a fraction in which the denominator is a power of ten. These fractions are usually written with a point, called the **decimal point**, as in 0.03 ($\frac{3}{100}$).
• **decimal** *adjective*
1 expressed or expressible as a decimal: *a decimal fraction.*
2 relating to or based on tens: *decimal currency.*
decimal notation the use of a decimal point or other marker, e.g. writing $\frac{3}{100}$ as 0.03. In some countries a comma is used instead, as in 0,03.
Word Family **decimally** *adverb*; **decimalize, decimalise** *verb* to express in decimals; **decimalization** (dess-i-m'l-eye-**zay**-sh'n) *noun*.
[Latin *decimus* tenth]

decimate (**dess**-i-mate) *verb*
to kill or destroy a large part of: *The massive air raids decimated the civilian population.*
Word Family **decimation** (dess-i-**may**-sh'n) *noun*.
[Latin *decimare* to kill every tenth man, as punishment in a disgraced army]

> **!** The original meaning of *decimate*, 'to kill every tenth man', has been almost completely replaced by the modern meaning, 'to kill or destroy a large part of' but some people still consider the modern meaning to be wrong.

decipher (di-**sigh**-fer) *verb*
1 to find the meaning of something indistinct or hard to understand: *The lawyer tried to decipher the faded writing of the will.*
2 to decode something written in cipher.
Word Family **decipherable** *adjective*.

decision (di-**sizh**-'n) *noun*
1 the act of deciding: *He was faced with a difficult decision.*
2 a judgement reached or given: *The government's decision on wage rises will be announced soon.*
3 a firmness or lack of hesitation: *act with decision.*

decisive (di-**sigh**-siv) *adjective*
1 giving a definite result or determining the course of something: *It was the decisive battle of the war.*

2 determined or resolute: *The sergeant gave his orders in a decisive tone of voice.*
Word Family decisively *adverb*; **decisiveness** *noun*.

deck *noun*
1 a horizontal floor or platform extending from one side of a ship to the other.
2 any similar platform or level: *the top deck of the bus.*
3 *American* a pack of cards.
4 *Audio* ⇨ TAPE DECK.
• **deck** *verb* to decorate or adorn: *They decked the streets with flags.*
Phrase deck out to clothe or attire.
Word Family decking *noun* any material, especially timber, used to make the deck of a ship, a platform in a garden, etc.

deckchair *noun*
a light folding chair, used outdoors, with the back and seat usually made of canvas.

declaim *verb*
to speak formally or rhetorically, especially in public; *The Church council declaimed against the decay of public morals.*
Word Family declamation (dek-la-may-sh'n) *noun*; **declamatory** (di-klamm-a-tree) *adjective*.
[Latin *declamare* to shout down]

declaration (dek-la-ray-sh'n) *noun*
1 the act of declaring.
2 something which is declared: *The American Declaration of Independence was written in 1776.*
Word Family declaratory (di-klarr-a-tree), **declarative** *adjective* serving to explain or make clear: *a declaratory statement.*

declare (di-klair) *verb*
1 to announce formally or officially: *The authorities declared a ban on all fires in the open.*
2 to assert forcefully: *She declared that she would never darken his door again.*
3 to make a statement of goods on which customs duties must be paid.
4 *Cricket* to close an innings voluntarily, before all ten wickets have fallen.
Word Family declarable *adjective*; **declared** *adjective* openly stated; **declaredly** (di-klair-id-lee) *adverb*.
[Latin *declarare* to announce with authority]

declassify *verb* (**declassifies**; **declassifying**; **declassified**)
to remove a document from a security classification.

declension (di-klen-sh'n) *noun*
1 *Grammar* the inflection of a noun, pronoun or adjective, to express its case, number or gender. Compare CONJUGATION.
2 a downward slope or movement: *the steep declension of the land near the sea.*

declination (dek-li-nay-sh'n) *noun*
1 *Astronomy* the angular distance of a planet or star north or south of the celestial equator.
2 a downward bend or slope.
3 the deviation of the needle of a compass from true north or south.

decline *verb*
1 (*formal*) to refuse politely: *He declined our offer of a loan.*
2 to slope or cause to slope downward: *This road declines steeply for the next two miles.*
3 to decrease: *Profits declined in the first six months of the year.*
4 to weaken: *As he grew older his health began to decline.*
5 *Grammar* to list the inflections of a noun, pronoun or adjective.
• **decline** *noun*
1 a falling or sinking: *a decline in prices.*
2 a downward slope or incline.
3 a decrease or weakening: *a decline in health.*
[Latin *declinare* to deviate]

declivity (di-klivv-i-tee) *noun* (*plural* **declivities**)
a steep downward slope.
[Latin *declivis* steep]

declutch *verb*
to disengage the clutch of a motor vehicle when changing gears.

decode (dee-kode) *verb*
to convert a code into the original message or form.
Word Family decoder *noun*.

décolleté (day-kol-tay) *adjective*
(of a dress) having a low neckline.
Word Family décolletage (day-kolt-ahzh) *noun* the neckline of a dress cut low in front.
[*de*- + Latin *collum* neck]

decommission *verb*
to dismantle a nuclear reactor which is no longer in use.

decompose (dee-k'm-poze) *verb*
1 to decay: *The corpse had begun to decompose by the time the police found it.*
2 to break down or separate into component parts or elements: *Some*

bacteria decompose nitrates to nitrogen and oxygen.
Word Family decomposition (dee-kom-pa-**zish**-'n) *noun*; **decomposable** *adjective*; **decomposer** *noun Biology* any organism, such as a fungus, which obtains energy by breaking down complex substances into simpler ones.

decompress (dee-k'm-**press**) *verb*
to relieve pressure.
Word Family decompression (dee-k'm-**presh**-'n) *noun*.

decompression chamber *noun*
a chamber in which divers, or pilots of unpressurized aircraft, are treated for decompression sickness.

decompression sickness *noun* also called **caisson disease; the bends**.
the appearance of nitrogen bubbles in the blood when external pressure changes too quickly, as when a diver ascends to the surface too rapidly.

decongestant (dee-k'n-**jest**-'nt) *noun*
a medicine which relieves nasal congestion.

decontaminate (dee-k'n-**tamm**-i-nate) *verb*
to neutralize or destroy the harmful effects of poisonous chemicals or radioactive substances.
Word Family decontamination (dee-k'n-tamm-i-**nay**-sh'n) *noun*.

decor (**day**-kor) *noun*
1 the style or scheme of decoration in a room, home, restaurant, etc.
2 *Theatre* the scenery or scenic decoration.
[French, from Latin *decor* grace, beauty]

decorate (**dekk**-a-rate) *verb*
1 to add to something to make it look more beautiful or pleasing: *They decorated the kitchen in vivid colours.* □ *a Christmas tree decorated with coloured lights.*
2 to confer honour on a person by awarding a medal, badge, etc.: *His father was decorated for bravery during the Second World War.*
Word Family decoration (dekk-a-**ray**-sh'n) *noun* 1 the act of decorating.
2 something which decorates or makes more beautiful. **decorator** *noun* a person who decorates houses, offices etc. as a profession; **decorative** (**dek**-ra-tiv) *adjective*; **decoratively** *adverb*; **decorativeness** *noun*.
[Latin *decorare* to adorn]

decorous (**dekk**-a-rus) *adjective*
conforming to accepted social standards of propriety or good taste: *Her decorous behaviour made her a welcome guest.*
Word Family decorously *adverb*; **decorousness** *noun*.

decorum (di-**kaw**-r'm) *noun*
propriety and good taste in conduct, dress, speech, etc.
[Latin, propriety, grace]

decoy (**dee**-koy) *noun*
1 a bird or model of a bird, used to lure game.
2 a person used to lure or entice another into a trap.
• **decoy** *verb* to lure or trap by using a decoy.
[Dutch *de kooi* the cage]

decrease (di-**kreece**) *verb*
to make or become less in size, quantity, intensity, etc.
• **decrease** (**dee**-kreece) *noun*
1 the process of decreasing: *Industrial accidents are on the decrease.*
2 the amount by which something is decreased: *a large decrease in industrial accidents.*
Word Family decreasing *adjective*; **decreasingly** *adverb*.
[Latin *decrescere* to grow less]

decree (di-**kree**) *noun*
1 an official pronouncement or edict: *The government decree announced an amnesty for all political prisoners.*
2 *Law* a court order or judgement.
• **decree** *verb* (**decrees; decreeing; decreed**) to issue a decree.
Figurative Fate decreed that she would never have children (= ordained).
[Latin *decretus* a decision]

decree absolute *noun* (*plural* **decrees absolute**)
Law a decree of divorce which makes it final.

decree nisi (di-kree **nigh**-sigh) *noun* (*plural* **decrees nisi**)
Law a decree of divorce which will be made final after six weeks unless cause is shown why it should not be made final.
[Latin *decretus* a decision + *nisi* unless]

decrepit (di-**krepp**-it) *adjective*
broken down by old age or ill health.
Word Family decrepitude *noun*.
[*de-* + Latin *crepare* to creak]

decretal *adjective*
of a decree.

decriminalize, decriminalise verb
to declare to be no longer a criminal
offence.
Word Family **decriminalization** (dee-
krimm-in-al-eye-**zay**-sh'n) *noun*.

decry *verb* (**decries; decrying; decried**)
to condemn or speak disparagingly of.

dedicate *verb*
1 to devote: *He dedicated himself to work.*
2 (of an author) to inscribe a book, poem,
etc. with a person's name as a sign of
affection, gratitude, respect, etc.
Word Family **dedication** (dedd-i-**kay**-
sh'n) *noun*; **dedicated** *adjective* wholly
devoted to something; **dedicatory**
adjective.
[Latin *dedicare* to devote to a purpose]

deduce (di-**dewce**) *verb*
to reach a conclusion by reasoning from
something known: *The detective deduced
from the size of the footprints that the intruder
was a child.*
Word Family **deducible** *adjective*.
[*de-* + Latin *ducere* to lead]

> [!] Do not confuse *deduce* with *deduct*.
> *Deduct* means 'to take away', as in
> *Deduct 48 from the total*. Note that
> *deduction*, however can mean 'the
> process of deducing' and 'the process of
> deducting'.

deduct *verb*
to take away from a total amount: *He
deducted the running costs of his car from his
taxable income.*
Word Family **deductible** *adjective*.

> [!] Do not confuse *deduct* with
> *deduce*.

deduction *noun*
1 the act or process of deducting.
2 something which is deducted: *a tax
deduction.*
3 a process of reasoning from a general law
to a particular instance.
4 a conclusion reached by this process.
Compare INDUCTION (definition 3).
Word Family **deductive** *adjective* arguing
or reasoning by deduction; **deductively**
adverb.

deed *noun*
1 an act or something done.
2 an exploit or feat: *The deeds of Richard the
Lion Heart were celebrated in song and
legend.*
3 *Law* a formal document which is proof
of an agreement between two or more
people, especially in the transfer of land.

deed poll *noun*
Law a deed declaring formally and
publicly a person's act or intentions,
especially in the case of changing one's
name.

deem *verb*
1 to think or to have an opinion: *The lawyer
deemed it against his client's interests to call
the witness.*
2 *Law* to assume as a fact.

deep *adjective*
1 far down or going far down: *Take a deep
breath.* □ *The water is only a few metres deep
at this point.*
2 extending far in width: *I pushed it to the
back of that deep shelf.*
3 low in pitch: *The Lord Mayor spoke in a
deep commanding voice.*
4 intense: *She has a deep mistrust of
politicians.*
5 far distant: *The radio telescope receives
signals from deep space.*
6 (*informal*) shrewd, cunning: *He appears
to be very open, but I was told he's a deep one.*
7 engrossed, occupied: *We discovered him
deep in thought.*
8 (*informal*) difficult, involved: *Nuclear
physics is too deep for me.*
Phrase **go off the deep end** (*informal*) to
become enraged.
• **deep** *noun* any deep place, especially in
the ocean: *Our ancestors believed in monsters
of the deep.*
Word Family **deep, deeply** *adverb*;
deepness *noun*; **deepen** *verb*.

deep freeze *noun*
a freezer.
Word Family **deep-freeze** *verb*.

deep-fry *verb* (**deep-fries; deep-frying;
deep-fried**)
to cook something by immersing it in hot
oil.

deer *noun* (*plural* **deer**)
any of various hoofed mammals, the males
of which have antlers, e.g. the red deer and
fallow deer.

deerstalker *noun*
a helmet-shaped cloth cap with ear flaps
and a peak at the back and the front.

def *adjective* (**deffer; deffest**)
(*informal*) excellent, great.
[possibly from black slang, definitive]

deface (di-**face**) *verb*
to damage or spoil something deliberately:
*Vandals had defaced the railway carriage by
slashing the seats.*
Word Family **defacement** *noun*.

de facto (day **fak**-toe) *adjective*
occurring or existing in fact, even if
not by right: *The rebels formed a de facto
government.* Compare DE JURE.
[Latin, from the fact]

defame (di-**fame**) *verb*
to destroy or attempt to destroy a person's
good name and reputation.
Word Family **defamation** (deff-a-
may-sh'n) *noun* the wrong of injuring a
person's good name without cause: *to sue
for defamation of character;* **defamatory**
(di-**famm**-a-tree) *adjective.*

default (di-**fawlt**) *noun*
a failure to perform a required act.
Phrases **by default** without having to
compete: *They won the game by default
when the opposing team didn't turn up.* **in
default of** in the absence of.
Word Family **default** *verb;* **defaulter**
noun.

defeat (di-**feet**) *verb*
1 to win a victory over: *The enemy forces
were defeated by superior numbers.*
2 to frustrate or thwart: *Repeated strikes
defeated the company's hopes of expanding
production.*
• **defeat** *noun*
1 the act of defeating: *His defeat of the World
Champion earned him renown in the boxing
world.*
2 a loss: *The football team suffered four
successive defeats.*

defeatist *noun*
a person who expects defeat or failure and
therefore considers that there is no point
in making an effort.
Word Family **defeatist** *adjective;*
defeatism *noun.*

defecate (**deff**-a-kate) *verb*
to expel faeces from the bowels.
Word Family **defecation** (deff-a-**kay**-
sh'n) *noun.*
[*de-* + Latin *faeces* dregs]

defect¹ (**dee**-fekt) *noun*
a fault or flaw: *The spluttering noise in the
stereo was caused by a defect in the amplifier.*
[Latin *defectus* failed]

defect² (di-**fekt**) *verb*
to abandon a cause or desert one's
country, especially for political reasons:
The spy attempted to defect to the East.
Word Family **defection** *noun;* **defector**
noun.
[Latin *defectus* deserted]

defective (di-**fek**-tiv) *adjective*
1 having a defect: *The police officer pointed
out that the car's brakes were defective.*
2 *Psychology* having less than normal
intelligence.
Word Family **defectively** *adverb;*
defectiveness *noun.*

defence (di-**fence**) *noun* (*American*
defense)
1 the act or process of defending: *The
defence of the outpost cost many lives.*
2 something that defends: *The city's
defences were weakened by continual artillery
fire.*
3 an argument or speech in justification of
something: *He put up an able defence of the
new traffic scheme.*
4 *Law* the pleading of a defendant in
answer to the charge against him or her.
5 *Law* the defendant together with his or
her legal counsel: *The defence rests its case,
Your Honour.*
Word Family **defenceless** *adjective;*
defencelessness *noun.*

defence mechanism *noun*
Psychology a process by which a person,
often unconsciously, protects himself or
herself from threatening or unpleasant
ideas or emotions.

defend *verb*
1 to protect from danger or attack: *to
defend one's honour.*
2 to uphold or support, especially a belief
or opinion: *The Minister defended the
Government's housing scheme.*
3 *Law* (of a barrister) to represent a
defendant in a court case.
Word Family **defendable** *adjective;*
defender *noun.*
[Latin *defendere* to protect]

defendant (di-**fend**-'nt) *noun*
Law a person against whom a charge or
suit is brought in a court. Compare
PLAINTIFF.

defensible (di-**fens**-i-b'l) *adjective*
capable of being defended: *a defensible
argument.*
Word Family **defensibly** *adverb;*
defensibility (di-fens-i-**bill**-it-ee) *noun.*

defensive *adjective*
serving to defend: *a defensive manoeuvre by
the army.* □ *Her attitude was defensive.*
Word Family **defensively** *adverb;*
defensiveness *noun.*

defer[1] (di-**fir**) *verb* (**defers; deferring; deferred**)
to delay or postpone intentionally: *The surgeon deferred the operation until the results of tests were checked.*
Word Family deferment, deferral *noun.*
[Latin *differre* to delay]

defer[2] *verb* (**defers; deferring; deferred**)
to give way or yield to the opinion or authority of another: *He refused to defer to his father when it came to politics.*
Word Family deference (**deff**-a-r'nce) *noun* courteous and polite respect: *He treats his parents with deference even when he disagrees with them;* **deferential** (deff-a-**ren**-sh'l) *adjective;* **deferentially** *adverb.*
[Latin *deferre* to grant]

defiance (di-**fie**-'nce) *noun*
the state of defying or refusing to recognize authority: *He expressed his defiance in wild behaviour.*
Word Family defiant *adjective;* **defiantly** *adverb.*

deficiency (di-**fish**-'n see) *noun* (*plural* **deficiencies**)
a lack or insufficiency: *A deficiency of iron in the body may cause anaemia.*
Word Family deficient *adjective.*
[Latin *deficiens*]

deficit (**deff**-i-sit) *noun*
Commerce the amount by which expenditure exceeds receipts.
[Latin, it fails]

defile[1] (di-**file**) *verb*
1 to make filthy or unclean: *Toxic chemicals had defiled the river.*
2 to corrupt or desecrate.
Word Family defilement *noun.*
[Middle English *defoul*]

defile[2] (dee-**file**) *noun*
a narrow pass or gorge between mountains.
[French *défiler* to go in file]

define (di-**fine**) *verb*
1 to state the exact meaning of: *Define that word.*
2 to describe the nature or properties of: *Define an elementary particle for me.*
3 to determine or state the limits or boundary of: *Please define the area you are describing.*
4 to make the outline or form show clearly: *The artist defined the shape by drawing a black line around it.*
Word Family definable *adjective.*
[*de-* + Latin *finis* a limit]

definite (**deff**-a-nit) *adjective*
1 clear or unambiguous: *She didn't give me a definite answer either way.*
2 sure, certain: *She was definite that she had seen that face before.*
Word Family definitely *adverb;* **definiteness** *noun.*

definite article ⇨ ARTICLE.

definition (deff i-**nish**-'n) *noun*
1 the act of defining.
2 the statement of the precise meaning of a word, phrase, term, etc.
3 *Physics* the clarity of an image formed by a mirror, lens or cathode-ray tube.
4 *Physics* the clarity of reproduction of sound.

definitive (di-**finn**-i-tiv) *adjective*
1 final or conclusive: *The Battle of Britain was a definitive victory in the Second World War.*
2 being the most authoritative or comprehensive: *a definitive history of the Middle Ages.*
Word Family definitively *adverb.*
[Latin *definitus* brought to a finish]

deflate *verb*
1 to release air or gas from a container such as a balloon, tyre, etc.
Figurative The scandal deflated his good name (= reduced).
2 *Economics* to produce deflation.

deflation (di-**flay**-sh'n) *noun*
1 the act of deflating.
2 *Economics* any measures taken to lower the prices of goods and services, such as the reduction of the amount of currency in circulation, or the effects of such measures. Compare INFLATION (definition 1).
Word Family deflationary *adjective.*
[*de-* + (in)FLATION]

deflect (di-**flekt**) *verb*
to turn aside: *The golf ball hit a tree and was deflected from its course.* □ *Jimmy is easily distracted or deflected from his purpose.*
Word Family deflection, deflexion *noun;* **deflective** *adjective* causing deflection.
[*de-* + Latin *flectere* to bend]

deflower (dee-**flower**) *verb*
to deprive of virginity.

defoliate (di-**fole**-ee-ate) *verb*
to strip plants of their leaves, especially by using a chemical spray.
Word Family defoliant *noun* a chemical that is used to strip plants of their leaves; **defoliation** (di-fole-ee-**ay**-sh'n) *noun.*
[*de-* + Latin *folium* leaf]

deforestation (dee-forr-i-**stay**-sh'n) *noun*
the removal of trees or forests.
Word Family **deforest** (dee-**forr**-ist)
verb.

deform (di-**form**) *verb*
to spoil or disfigure the natural shape or
appearance of: *His leg was deformed by a
large tumour.*
Word Family **deformation** (dee-form-
ay-sh'n) *noun*; **deformity** *noun* (*plural*
deformities) **1** the state of being
deformed **2** something which is
deformed.

defraud (di-**frawd**) *verb*
to cheat or swindle a person out of
property or a right.

defray (di-**fray**) *verb*
(*formal*) to pay: *The expenses of the
motorway are to be defrayed out of taxation.*
Word Family **defrayal, defrayment**
noun a payment of costs or expenses;
defrayable *adjective*.

defrock (dee-**frok**) *verb* also called
unfrock.
Religion to expel a priest from the
priesthood for an offence.

defrost (dee-**frost**) *verb*
1 to remove ice and frost from a
refrigerator.
2 to thaw out frozen food.

deft *adjective*
skilful or adroit: *Her deft hands swiftly
bandaged the wound.*
Word Family **deftly** *adverb*; **deftness**
noun.

defunct (di-**funkt**) *adjective*
having ceased to exist or function: *All
London's trolleybuses are now defunct.*
[Latin *defunctus* dead]

defuse (dee-**fewz**) *verb*
to remove the fuse of: *Experts were called in
to defuse the unexploded bomb.*
Figurative The diplomat tried to defuse the
tense political situation (= make safe or
calm).

defy (di-**fie**) *verb* (**defies; defying;
defied**)
to oppose actively or boldly, often in the
sense of a challenge: *The cornered man
defied the police to come and get him.*
Figurative The speed and ferocity of the
bushfire defied belief (= went beyond).

degenerate (di-**jenn**-a-rate) *verb*
1 to lose or decline in good qualities: *He
degenerated into a selfish playboy.* □ *His
health degenerated rapidly.*

2 *Biology* to change to a less complex,
specialized or active form: *In man, the
appendix has degenerated to the stage where it
serves no useful purpose.*
• **degenerate** (di-**jenn**-a-rit) *adjective*
degraded or corrupt: *a weak and degenerate
ruler who ignored the people's needs.*
• **degenerate** (di-**jenn**-a-rit) *noun* a
person who has degenerated: *He has
become a moral degenerate.*
Word Family **degenerately** *adverb*;
degeneracy *noun*; **degeneration** (di-
jenn-a-**ray**-sh'n) *noun* **1** the process of
degenerating. **2** the state of being
degenerate; **degenerative** *adjective*.
[*de-* + Latin *genus* a breed, a kind]

degrade (di-**grade**) *verb*
1 to lower in rank, status, quality or
degree.
2 to deprave, corrupt or disgrace: *I felt
degraded by my disgusting actions.*
3 *Geography* to wear down by erosion.
4 *Chemistry* (of complex compounds) to
break down into simpler compounds.
Word Family **degradation** (deg-ra-**day**-
sh'n) *noun* **1** the act of degrading. **2** the
state of being degraded.
[*de-* + Latin *gradus* a step]

degree (di-**gree**) *noun*
1 a step or level in a scale or process: *the
degree of proficiency reached by a student.*
□ *Aunt Emily came from a family of high
degree.*
2 *Maths* a unit of angular measurement,
one 360th of a full circle.
3 *Geography, Astronomy* a unit of latitude
or longitude.
4 *Physics, Chemistry* a unit in a temperature
scale.
5 *Education* a certificate given to show
that a student has completed all the
requirements in a course of study.
6 *Grammar* any of three forms taken by an
adjective or adverb to express comparison,
being **positive** (she is *tall*), **comparative**
(she is *taller* than her sister) or **superlative**
(she is the *tallest* in her class).
Phrase **the third degree** the use of
extreme methods, often torture, to obtain
information or a confession from a person.

dehumanize, dehumanise (dee-**hew**-
ma-nize) *verb*
to brutalize or take away the human
qualities of.
Word Family **dehumanization** (dee-
hew-ma-nigh-**zay**-sh'n) *noun*.

dehydrate (dee-**high**-drate) *verb*
to lose or remove water.

Word Family dehydration (dee-high-dray-sh'n) noun.
[Greek de- away + hydor water]

deify (dee-iff-eye or day-iff-eye) verb
(**deifies; deifying; deified**)
to make or worship as a god.
Word Family deification (dee-iff-i-kay-sh'n or day-iff-i-kay-sh'n) noun.

deign (dane) verb
to condescend: She would not deign to answer such a rude question.

deism (dee-izm or day-izm) noun
a belief in the existence of a god, based only upon reason or logic and denying all supernatural revelation. Compare THEISM.
Word Family deist noun; **deistic** adjective.
[Latin deus god]

deity (dee-a-tee or day-a-tee) noun (plural **deities**)
1 a god or goddess.
2 the divine nature of a god.
Phrase the Deity God.

déja vu (day-zha voo) noun
a feeling of familiarity when encountering a completely new scene or experience.
[French]

dejected (di-jek-tid) adjective
sad and depressed.
Word Family dejectedly adverb;
dejection noun; **deject** verb.
[de- + Latin jactus thrown]

de jure (day joo-ray) adjective
occurring or existing by right, even if not in fact: Though in exile, he was still the de jure president. Compare DE FACTO.
[Latin, by right]

dekko noun
(informal) a look: Let's have a dekko at the bike.
[Hindi]

delay (di-lay) verb
1 to put off until later: We must delay our departure until next week.
2 to make late: The flat tyre delayed us for several hours.
Word Family delay noun.

delectable (di-lek-ta-b'l) adjective
delightful or pleasing.
Word Family delectably adverb.

delectation (dee-lek-tay-sh'n) noun
(formal) delight or enjoyment.
[Latin delectare to attract]

delegate (dell-i-gate) verb
1 to appoint or send someone as a representative: When he could not go to the meeting he delegated Smith to go.
2 to give powers, duties, etc. to someone else: She delegated work to her assistant.
• **delegate** (dell-i-git) noun a person who acts for or represents another;
delegation (dell-i-gay-sh'n) noun
1 the act of delegating.
2 a group of delegates.
[de- + Latin legare to depute]

delete (di-leet) verb
to strike out or erase: Several scenes have been deleted from the film.
Word Family deletion noun 1 the act of deleting. 2 something deleted.
[Latin deletus wiped out]

deleterious (dell-i-tee-ri-us) adjective
harmful, especially to health.
[Greek deleterios poisonous]

deliberate (di-libb-a-rit) adjective
1 carefully considered and intended: a deliberate act of cruelty.
2 slow and cautious in action, etc.: The politician has a deliberate manner.
• **deliberate** (di-libb-a-rate) verb to think or talk about carefully: The jury deliberated before giving a verdict.
Word Family deliberately adverb;
deliberateness noun; **deliberation** (di-libb-a-ray-sh'n) noun 1 careful consideration. 2 slowness or caution in action, etc.; **deliberative** adjective involved in deliberation.
[de- + Latin libra scales]

delicacy (dell-ik-a-see) noun (plural **delicacies**)
1 a fineness of texture, quality, manner, etc.
2 weakness. The delicacy of the child's health leaves him prone to sickness.
3 the state of requiring careful or tactful treatment: a matter of some delicacy.
4 anything fine or pleasing, especially to the palate: Many people think caviar is a delicacy.

delicate (dell-i-kit) adjective
fine in texture, quality, manner, etc.
Figurative a delicate vase (= fragile).
□ a delicate situation (= requiring tact).
Word Family delicately adverb;
delicateness noun.
[Latin delicatus dainty]

delicatessen (dell-i-ka-tess-'n) noun
a shop selling cooked meats, cheeses and other foods, especially ones which have been imported.
[German Delikatesse delicacy]

delicious (di-**lish**-us) *adjective*
highly pleasing, especially in taste or smell:
a delicious meal.
Word Family deliciously *adverb*;
deliciousness *noun*.
[Latin *deliciae* enticements]

delight (di-**lite**) *noun*
1 any great pleasure or joy.
2 anything which gives pleasure.
Word Family delight *verb*; **delighted**
adjective; **delightedly** *adverb*; **delightful**
adjective highly pleasing; **delightfully**
adverb; **delightfulness** *noun*.

delimit (di-**limm**-it) *verb*
to fix or mark the limits of.
Word Family delimitation (di-limm-it-
ay-sh'n) *noun*.
[*de-* + Latin *limitis* of a boundary]

delineate (di-**lin**-ee-ate) *verb*
to describe or give an outline of: *He
delineated the plan.*
Word Family delineation (di-linn-ee-
ay-sh'n) *noun*.
[*de-* + Latin *linea* a line]

delinquent (di-**link**-w'nt) *noun*
a person who fails in his or her duty or is
guilty of misdeeds: *a juvenile delinquent.*
• **delinquent** *adjective* failing in a duty or
obligation.
Word Family delinquently *adverb*;
delinquency *noun* (*plural*
delinquencies).
[Latin *delinquens* being at fault]

delirious (di-**lirr**-ee-us) *adjective*
1 affected with delirium.
2 wildly excited or enthusiastic.
Word Family deliriously *adverb*.
[Latin *delirus* demented]

delirium (di-**lirr**-ee-um) *noun*
1 a disorder of the mind, usually
temporary, that causes visions, delusions
and irrational behaviour.
2 any wild emotion or excitement.

delirium tremens (di-lirr-ee-um tree-
menz) *noun*
short form is **DTs** a state of delirium and
shaking as a symptom of prolonged
alcoholism.
[Latin *tremens* trembling]

deliver (di-**livv**-a) *verb*
1 to give into the possession of someone
else: *to deliver a letter.*
2 to give birth to, or assist at a birth.
3 to direct, cast: *The bowler delivered the
ball to the batsman.*
4 to save: *They were delivered from the peril.*

5 to pronounce: *The jury delivered its
verdict.*
Word Family deliverance *noun* release
or rescue; **delivery** *noun* (*plural*
deliveries) 1 the act of delivering: *There
will be no mail delivery on Saturdays.* 2 the
act or manner of giving or sending forth:
The actor had very poor delivery.
□ *another good delivery from the bowler.*
[*de-* + Latin *liberare* to set free]

dell *noun*
a small valley.

delphinium (del-**finn**-ee-um) *noun*
a garden plant with spikes of blue flowers.

delta *noun*
1 the fourth letter of the Greek alphabet.
2 a deposit, usually fan-shaped, of large
amounts of silt at the mouth of a river,
which divides it into branches.
[from the triangular shape of the Greek
letter]

delude (di-**lood**) *verb*
to mislead or deceive.
Word Family deluded *adjective*.
[*de-* + Latin *ludere* to mock]

deluge (**del**-yooj) *noun*
a flood or downpour.
Figurative *At the press conference he faced
a deluge of questions* (= overwhelming
number).
• **deluge** *verb*.

delusion (di-**loo**-*zh*'n) *noun*
1 the act of deluding.
2 the fact of being deluded.
3 a false opinion: *He has delusions about his
own importance.*
4 a belief which is held even though there
is contradictory evidence, etc.
Word Family delusive (di-loo-siv),
delusory *adjective*.

> [!] Both *delusion* and *illusion* describe
> false or deceptive mental
> experiences. A *delusion* is an extreme
> belief which is persistently held, despite
> all evidence to the contrary (*a delusion
> that she was being held prisoner in the
> hospital*), whereas an *illusion* is simply
> an incorrect perception (*The shading
> gives an illusion of depth*).

de luxe (di **luks** *or* di **looks**) *adjective*
luxurious or of a high quality: *a de luxe
hotel.*
[French, of luxury]

delve *verb*
to search deeply: *In the investigation you
must delve into all the evidence.*

demagogue (**demm**-a-gog) *noun*
a leader who uses people's emotions and
prejudices for his or her own interests.
Word Family **demagoguery** (demm-a-
gogg-a-ree), **demagogy** *noun*;
demagogic (demm-a-**gogg**-ik).
[Greek *demos* people + *agogos* leader]

demand (di-**mahnd**) *verb*
1 to ask for strongly: *She demanded to see
the manager.*
2 to require: *This job demands skill.*
● **demand** *noun*
1 the act of demanding.
2 something which is demanded.
3 a requirement: *all the demands on my
time.*
4 the state of being required: *articles in
great demand.*
5 *Commerce* any specific need for goods or
services.
Word Family **demanding** *adjective*.
[*de-* + Latin *mandare* to order]

demarcation *noun*
1 the division of anything into separate
parts.
2 the fixing or marking of boundaries or
limits.
Word Family **demarcate** (dee-mar-
kate) *verb* to fix or mark the boundaries of.

demean (di-**meen**) *verb*
to lower in dignity: *Do not demean yourself
by falling for their tricks.*
Word Family **demeaning** *adjective*.

demeanour (di-**mee**-na) *noun*
(*formal*) a person's behaviour or manner.

demented (di-**men**-tid) *adjective*
1 suffering from dementia.
2 (*informal*) crazy, uncontrolled.
Word Family **dementedly** *adverb*.
[*de-* + Latin *mentis* of the mind]

dementia (di-**men**-sha) *noun*
Psychology a decrease of mental powers
characteristic of some mental disorders,
and often only temporary.

demerara (demm-a-**rair**-a) *noun*
unrefined brown sugar.
[after a town in Guyana]

demerit (dee-**merr**-it) *noun*
a fault.

demesne (di-**mane** *or* di-**meen**) *noun*
1 the possession of land as one's own.
2 the land and buildings possessed.

demigod *noun*
1 a being who is part god and part man.
2 a person worshipped as if he or she is a
god.

demijohn *noun*
a large narrow-necked bottle, usually
covered in cane.

demilitarize, demilitarise (dee-**mill**-it-
a-rize) *verb*
to remove all military equipment and
personnel from: *a demilitarized zone.*
Word Family **demilitarization** (dee-
mill-it-ar-eye-**zay**-sh'n) *noun*.

demise (di-**mize**) *noun*
(*formal*) death.

demo *noun*
(*informal*) a demonstration.

demobilize, demobilise (dee-**mo**-bill-
ize) *verb*
short form is **demob** to disband armed
forces.
Word Family **demobilization** (dee-mo-
bill-ize-**ay**-sh'n) *noun*.

democracy (di-**mok**-ra-see) *noun* (*plural*
democracies)
the government of a country by its
people, usually through a parliament of
representatives elected by them.
Word Family **democrat** (**demm**-a-krat)
noun; **democratic** (demm-a-**kratt**-ik)
adjective; **democratically** *adverb*.
[Greek *demos* people + *kratia* rule]

democratize, democratise (di-**mok**-ra-
tize) *verb*
to make or become democratic.
Word Family **democratization** (di-
mok-ra-tie-**zay**-sh'n) *noun*.

demographic time bomb *noun*
a predicted decrease in the number of
young people available for work following
an earlier drop in the birth rate.

demography (di-**mog**-ra-fee) *noun*
the study of the statistics of birth, illness
and death in communities.
Word Family **demographer** *noun*;
demographic (demm-a-**graff**-ik)
adjective.
[Greek *demos* people + *graphein* to write]

demolish (di-**moll**-ish) *verb*
to pull down or destroy: *The house was
demolished and flats erected.* □ *He demolished
the weak argument.*
Word Family **demolition** (demm-a-
lish-'n) *noun*.
[*de-* + Latin *moliri* to construct]

demon (**dee**-m'n) *noun*
1 an evil spirit or devil.
2 a person of great energy: *He is a demon
for work.*
Word Family **demoniacal** (dee-ma-
nigh-i-k'l), **demonic** (di-**monn**-ik),

demoniac (di-**mo**-nee-ak) *adjective;*
demonize, demonise *verb* to regard as
evil: *a politician demonized by the media;*
demonization (dee-ma-nigh-**zay**-sh'n)
noun.
[Greek *daimon* a god]

demonstrate (**dem**-'n-strate) *verb*
1 to prove by arguments, evidence, etc.
2 to exhibit or show: *She demonstrates great
ability.*
3 to show and explain: *He demonstrated the
new machine.*
4 to hold a public meeting or march: *Over
1000 people demonstrated in support of higher
wages.*
Word Family **demonstration** (dem-'n-
stray-sh'n) *noun* 1 a clear proof: *a
demonstration that the earth is round.* 2 an
exhibition or explanation by means
of examples, experiments, etc.: *a
demonstration of a new car.* 3 a show or
expression: *a demonstration of love.* 4 a
display of public feeling, e.g. a mass
meeting or march; **demonstrable**
(**dem**-'n-str'-b'l) *adjective* able to be
demonstrated; **demonstrably** *adverb;*
demonstrator *noun.*
[*de-* + Latin *monstrare* to show]

demonstrative (di-**mon**-stra-tiv) *adjective*
1 showing one's feelings or affections
openly.
2 serving to explain or prove.
Word Family **demonstratively** *adverb.*

demoralize, demoralise (di-**morr**-a-
lize) *verb*
to reduce the confidence or morale of: *She
was demoralized when she failed her driving
test.*
Word Family **demoralized** *adjective;*
demoralizing *adjective;* **demoralization**
(di-morr-a-lie-**zay**-sh'n) *noun.*

demo tape *noun*
an audio tape sent by a singer, band, etc.
to a recording studio as an example of
their work.

demote *verb*
to lower in rank.
Word Family **demotion** *noun.*

demur (di-**mur**) *verb* (**demurs;
demurring; demurred**)
to make objections or disagree.
Word Family **demur, demurral** *noun.*

demure (dim-**yoor**) *adjective*
1 affectedly modest.
2 quiet and serious.

Word Family **demurely** *adverb;*
demureness *noun.*

den *noun*
1 a place, such as a cave, where wild
animals live.
2 a quiet cosy room for personal use.
3 a place, abode: *a den of iniquity.*

denary system (**dee**-na-ree sis-t'm) *noun*
Maths the number system in common use,
writing numbers to base ten, e.g. twenty-
three as $2 \times 10 + 3$, i.e. 23. Compare
BINARY NUMBER SYSTEM.

denial (di-**nigh**-al) *noun*
the act of denying.

denier (**denn**-i-a) *noun*
a unit of weight used to measure the
fineness of silk, cotton, etc. and equal to
the weight in grams of 9000 m of yarn.
[French, a standard weight]

denigrate (**denn**-i-grate) *verb*
to attack the reputation of.
Word Family **denigration** (denn-i-**gray**-
sh'n) *noun.*
[*de-* + Latin *niger* black]

denim *noun*
1 a strong cotton fabric of twill weave,
used for trousers, etc.
2 (**denims**) jeans made of denim.
[French *de nimes* from Nîmes, France,
where it was first made]

denizen (**denn**-iz-'n) *noun*
a resident or inhabitant.

denominate (di-**nom**-in-ate) *verb*
to give a specific name to.

denomination (di-nom-i-**nay**-sh'n) *noun*
1 a religious movement or group sharing
common beliefs and identified by a
particular name.
2 a unit of a specified value in a system of
weights or currency: *In Britain the coin of
the lowest denomination is the penny.*
Word Family **denominational** *adjective*
relating to a religious group.

denominator (di-**nomm**-i-nay-ta) *noun*
Maths the part of the fraction below the
line, showing how many equal parts a
quantity is divided into, such as the 4 in $\frac{1}{4}$.
Two fractions which have the same
denominator, such as $\frac{1}{4}$ and $\frac{3}{4}$, are said to
have a **common denominator**. Compare
NUMERATOR.

denote *verb*
1 to indicate or be a sign of: *An asterisk
often denotes a footnote.*
2 to mean or designate: *What does this word
denote?*

Word Family denotation (dee-no-**tay**-sh'n) *noun*.

> ! Do not confuse *denote* with
> CONNOTE.

denouement (day-**noo**-mon) *noun*
the final unravelling of a plot or story.
[French *dénouer* to untie]

denounce *verb*
1 to speak or inform against: *He was denounced as a traitor.*
2 to express strong disapproval: *All banks denounced the government's policy on home loans.*
[Latin *denuntiare* to announce to warn]

dense *adjective*
1 thickly or closely packed together: *The airport was closed owing to dense fog.*
2 (*informal*) stupid.
Word Family densely *adverb*; **denseness** *noun*.
[Latin *densus* crowded]

density (**den**-sa-tee) *noun* (*plural* **densities**)
1 the state or quality of being dense.
2 *Physics* a measure of the concentration of mass in a substance. The numerical value for density is calculated by dividing the mass of a given amount of the substance by its volume.

dent *noun*
a hollow in a surface, usually due to a blow.
• **dent** *verb* to make a dent in.

dental *adjective*
of or relating to the teeth.

dental floss ⇨ FLOSS (definition 3).

dentine (**den**-teen) *noun*
a hard tissue found underneath the enamel of teeth.

dentist *noun*
a person medically qualified to care for people's teeth, including doing surgical operations and fitting false teeth.
Word Family dentistry *noun*.
[Latin *dens* tooth]

dentition *noun*
the type, number and arrangement of teeth in the mouth.

denture (**den**-cher) *noun*
a plate with one or more artificial teeth.

denude (di-**newd**) *verb*
to make bare or naked.
Word Family denudation (dee-new-**day**-sh'n) *noun*.
[*de-* + Latin *nudus* naked]

denunciation *noun*
the act of denouncing.

deny (di-**nigh**) *verb* (**denies; denying; denied**)
1 to declare as untrue: *He denied their charges of assault.*
2 to refuse to believe or acknowledge: *She denies the existence of a god.*
3 to refuse to grant: *They denied him the right to see a lawyer.*

deodorant (dee-o-da-r'nt) *noun*
any substance for masking smells.

deodorize, deodorise (dee-o-da-rize) *verb*
to remove smells.
Word Family deodorizer *noun*.

deoxyribonucleic acid (dee-oks-i-rye-bo-new-klee-ik **ass**-id) *noun*
short form is **DNA** *Biology* a complex molecule with the shape of a double-stranded helix which is found in most living organisms and carries hereditary information.

> The term **deoxyribonucleic acid** is hardly ever used, except occasionally by specialists in the field. Instead, the abbreviation *DNA* is used. This is just one example of the use of abbreviations in present-day English. Terms such as *BBC*, *VCR* and *VDU* are more common than their longer equivalents – British Broadcasting Corporation, video cassette recorder, and visual display unit. When the letters of the abbreviations form a word, which happens more and more these days, this is known as an acronym, e.g. *Apex* (Advance Purchase Excursion), and *BAFTA* (British Academy of Film and Television Arts).

depart *verb*
1 to leave.
2 to vary from the normal course: *He departed from the topic to talk about the coming exams.*
Word Family departed *adjective* (*formal*) dead.

department *noun*
any of the various sections into which something is divided: *The shoe department is on the first floor.* □ *Which government department is in charge of social welfare?*
Word Family departmental (dee-part-**men**-t'l) *adjective*; **departmentally** *adverb*.
[Latin *dispertire* to separate into parts]

department store *noun*
a large shop in which many kinds of goods are sold in different departments.

departure (di-**par**-cher) *noun*
the act of departing: *Time of departure is
7 p.m.* □ *This is a departure from the normal
routine.*

depend *verb*
1 to rely: *You may depend on him for support.*
2 to be determined by: *It all depends on the
weather.*
Word Family dependable *adjective* able
to be depended on; **dependably** *adverb*;
dependability (de-pend-a-**bill**-it-ee)
noun the state of being dependable;
dependent *adjective* depending on
something else; **dependence** *noun* the
state of being dependent; **dependant**
noun a person who depends on another for
aid or support.
[*de-* + Latin *pendere* to hang]

> ! Do not confuse the noun
> *dependant*, as in *I have no
> dependants to support,* with the adjective
> *dependent,* as in *They are dependent on
> their parents.*

dependency *noun* (*plural* **dependencies**)
1 the state of being dependent.
2 a small country ruled by another.

depersonalize, depersonalise (dee-
pers-'na-lize) *verb*
1 to make less personal: *The introduction of
computers depersonalized the company.*
2 *Psychology* to lose the feeling of the
reality of one's own personality or body.
Word Family depersonalization (dee-
pers-'na-lie-**zay**-sh'n) *noun.*

depict *verb*
to represent in words or a picture.
Word Family depiction *noun.*
[*de-* + Latin *pictus* painted]

depilatory (di-**pill**-a-tree) *adjective*
(of cosmetics) able to remove hair from
the body.
• **depilatory** *noun* (*plural* **depilatories**) a
depilatory substance.
Word Family depilate (**depp**-i-late) *verb.*
[*de-* + Latin *pilus* hair]

deplete (di-**pleet**) *verb*
to reduce or lessen until little remains: *The
stock was depleted by the increased demand.*
Word Family depletion *noun.*
[Latin *depletus* emptied out]

deplore (di-**plaw**) *verb*
to feel or express pity or disapproval.
Word Family deplorable *adjective*
worthy of regret or reproach: *The wretched
state of their house is deplorable;* **deplorably**
adverb.
[Latin *deplorare* to weep bitterly]

deploy (di-**ploy**) *verb*
to spread out troops, etc., especially in
strategic positions.
Word Family deployment *noun.*

depopulate (dee-**pop**-yoo-late) *verb*
to reduce the population of: *The country
has been depopulated by famine.*
Word Family depopulation (dee-pop-
yew-**lay**-sh'n) *noun.*

deport (di-**port**) *verb*
1 to expel from a country.
2 to conduct or behave: *He deported himself
with dignity in a trying situation.*
Word Family deportation (dee-paw-
tay-sh'n) *noun;* **deportee** *noun* (dee-paw-
tee) a person who is deported.
[*de-* + Latin *portare* to carry]

deportment *noun*
the manner of conducting oneself.

depose (di-**poze**) *verb*
to remove from office or from a position of
power: *The President was deposed by a
military coup.*

deposit (di-**pozz**-it) *verb*
1 to put or lay down: *Silt was deposited at
the mouth of the river.*
2 to put for safekeeping: *She deposited her
jewels in the bank's safe.*
3 to make a part payment.
• **deposit** *noun*
1 something which is deposited: *a chalky
deposit at the bottom of the bowl.*
2 a part payment, e.g. to prevent
something from being sold to someone
else.
3 a sum of money paid into a bank
account.
Word Family depositor *noun.*
[*de-* + Latin *positus* placed]

deposition (depp-a-**zish**-'n) *noun*
1 the act of deposing.
2 the act of depositing.
3 *Law* the written record of evidence given
under oath.

depository (di-**pozz**-i-tree) *noun* (*plural*
depositories)
(*formal*) a storehouse.

depot (**depp**-o) *noun*
1 a place where things are kept or stored: *a
bus depot.*
2 *American* a railway or bus station.

deprave (di-**prave**) *verb*
to corrupt or make bad.
Word Family depraved *adjective;*
depravity (di-**prav**-i-tee) *noun* (*plural*
depravities).
[Latin *depravare* to make crooked]

deprecate (**dep**-ri-kate) *verb*
to express disapproval of.
Word Family **deprecating** *adjective*;
deprecatingly *adverb*; **deprecation** (dep-ri-**kay**-sh'n) *noun*; **deprecatory** (dep-ri-**kay**-ta-ree) *adjective* 1 expressing disapproval. 2 apologetic.
[*de-* + Latin *precari* to pray]

depreciate (di-**pree**-shi-ate) *verb*
1 to lessen in value. Compare APPRECIATE (definition 3).
2 to disparage or belittle.
Word Family **depreciation** (di-pree-shi-ay-sh'n) *noun*; **depreciatory** *adjective*.
[*de-* + Latin *pretium* price]

depredation (dep-ri-**day**-sh'n) *noun*
the act of preying upon or plundering.
Word Family **depredator** (**dep**-ri-date-or) *noun*.
[*de-* + Latin *praedari* to plunder]

depress (di-**press**) *verb*
1 to sadden or lower the spirits of: *The thought of retiring depresses him.*
2 to lower or press down on: *To operate the machine depress this lever.*
3 to lower or lessen in value, price, etc.
Word Family **depressed** *adjective*;
depressing *adjective*; **depressingly** *adverb*; **depressive** *adjective*.
[Latin *depressus* weighed down]

depressant (di-**press** 'nt) *adjective*
1 serving to lower the rate of bodily processes.
2 tending to sadden or lower the spirits of.
• **depressant** *noun* ⇨ SEDATIVE.

depressed area *noun*
an area where there is widespread unemployment, low incomes and poor housing.

depression *noun*
1 the state of being depressed.
2 a sunken part or place.
3 *Weather* ⇨ LOW[1] *noun* (definition 2).
4 *Economics* a decline in business activity, usually accompanied by an increase in unemployment and a lowering of income.

deprive (di-**prive**) *verb*
to take away from or withhold something: *Her broken leg deprived her of her daily run.*
Word Family **deprived** *adjective*;
deprivation (dep-ri-**vay**-sh'n) *noun*.
[*de-* + Latin *privare* to rob]

deprogramme *verb* (*American* **deprogram**)
to free from brainwashing.

depth *noun*
1 the state of being deep.

2 the distance downwards, inwards or backwards: *The depth of the pool is 3 m.*
□ *What is the depth of this shelf?*
3 (*usually* **depths**) a deep or distant part: *to plumb the depths of the sea.*
4 (*usually* **depths**) an intense state or feeling: *We found him in the depths of despair.*
Figurative *The ship struck the reef in the depth of night* (= most intense part). □ *The picture has great depth of colour* (= richness). □ *Politics is definitely out of my depth* (= understanding, comprehension).

depth charge *noun*
a type of bomb designed to explode under water and used to destroy submarines.

deputation (dep-yoo-**tay**-sh'n) *noun*
a group appointed to represent others: *The employer talked with the deputation from a trade union.*

depute (di-**pute**) *verb*
1 to appoint as one's agent or deputy.
2 to assign a responsibility, task, etc. to a deputy.

deputize, deputise (dep yoo-**tize**) *verb*
1 to act as a deputy: *Can you deputize for the boss while he is away?*
2 to appoint as a deputy.

deputy (**dep**-yoo-tee) *noun* (*plural* **deputies**)
1 an appointed or elected assistant: *the deputy prime minister.*
2 a person appointed to act for another.

derail *verb*
to cause a railway vehicle to leave the track.
Word Family **derailment** *noun*.

derange *verb*
to throw into disorder or confusion: *His mind was deranged by his bereavement.*
Word Family **deranged** *adjective* disturbed or insane; **derangement** *noun*.

derby (**dar**-bee) *noun* (*plural* **derbies**)
1 an important race: *the Greyhound Derby.*
2 *American* a bowler hat.
local derby a match, especially soccer, between local teams.
[after *the Derby*, the premier flat race for horses]

derecognize, derecognise *verb*
to end recognition of: *The company has derecognized the union.*

derelict (**derr**-i-likt) *adjective*
abandoned or neglected: *a derelict old house.*
• **derelict** *noun* (*formal*) a neglected person, especially a vagrant.

Word Family **dereliction** (derr-i-**lik**-sh'n) *noun*.
[Latin *derelictus* forsaken]

deride (di-**ride**) *verb*
(*formal*) to mock or jeer in contempt: *The others derided his ignorant questions.*
[Latin *deridere* to laugh to scorn]

de rigueur (der ri-**ger**) *adjective*
necessary or required by tradition or social custom.
[French]

derision (di-**rizh**-'n) *noun*
the act of deriding or mocking: *His speech was greeted with derision by the crowd.*
Word Family **derisive** (di-**rye**-siv) *adjective* mocking; **derisively** *adverb*; **derisory** (di-**rye**-za-ree) *adjective* mocking or inviting derision.

derivation (derr-i-**vay**-sh'n) *noun*
1 the act or process of deriving.
2 the source or origin of anything: *That word has a Latin derivation.*
3 *Maths* the proof of a theorem.
4 *Grammar* the process by which new words are formed from existing root words by adding affixes: *'Understanding' and 'misunderstand' are formed from 'understand' by derivation.*
[Latin *derivare* to draw off]

derivative (di-**riv**-a-tiv) *adjective*
1 being derived from another source.
2 copied, not original: *This essay is obviously derivative.*
● **derivative** *noun*
1 anything which is derived, such as one chemical compound prepared from another: *Petrol is a derivative of crude oil.*
2 *Maths* the instantaneous rate of change of a function, with respect to the independent variable.

derive (di-**rive**) *verb*
1 to come or obtain from a source or origin: *Many English words derive from ancient Greek.*
2 (*formal*) to get, obtain: *He derives much pleasure from gardening.*

dermatitis (derm-a-**tie**-tis) *noun*
Medicine an inflammation or allergy of the skin.
[Greek *dermatos* of the skin + -*itis*]

dermatology (derm-a-**toll**-a-jee) *noun*
the study of the skin and its diseases.
Word Family **dermatologist** *noun*.

derogatory (di-**rogg**-a-tree) *adjective*
tending or intended to damage or discredit: *a derogatory name.*

Word Family **derogatorily** *adverb*; **derogate** (**derr**-a-gate) *verb* to damage or take away a good quality, etc.; **derogation** (derr-a-**gay**-sh'n) *noun*.

derrick *noun*
a stationary device for supporting or lifting, such as a ship's crane or the framed tower erected over oilwells.
[after *Derrick*, a famous hangman in London in the early 17th century]

derring-do *noun*
an old word meaning 'great courage or daring'.
[from *daring to do*]

derv *noun*
a diesel oil for large road vehicles.
[from D(iesel) E(ngined) R(oad) V(ehicle)]

dervish *noun* (*plural* **dervishes**)
a member of any of various Muslim mendicant orders devoted to poverty and chastity, some of whom achieve religious ecstasy through religious chants, whirling dances, etc.
[Persian *darvesh* poor]

desalination (dee-sall-i-**nay**-sh'n) *noun*
the process of removing salt from sea water, usually by distillation, to make it suitable for drinking or for use in farm irrigation.
Word Family **desalinate** *verb*.
[*de*- + Latin *salis* of salt]

descant (**dess**-kant) *noun*
Music an extra part in a song or melody, played or sung at a higher pitch.

descend (di-**send**) *verb*
1 to come or go down: *He descended the ladder carefully.* □ *The road descends steeply to the lake.*
2 to derive by birth: *He is descended from French ancestors.*
3 to lower oneself: *She would not descend to such nastiness.*
Phrase **descend on, descend upon** *The whole family descended on us last weekend* (= visited unexpectedly).
Word Family **descendant** *noun* a person who is descended from another.

descent (di-**sent**) *noun*
1 the act of descending: *Their descent from the snow-covered peak was dangerous.*
2 a slope: *The road follows a steep descent into the valley.*
3 the relationship or link between a person and his or her ancestors.

describe (di-**skribe**) *verb*
1 to give a picture or account of something in words: *Can you describe the man who attacked you?*
2 *Maths* to draw: *Describe a line between points A and B.*
[*de-* + Latin *scribere* to write]

description (di-**skrip**-sh'n) *noun*
1 a picture in words: *She was able to give a detailed description of the thief.*
2 sort, variety: *The vintage car rally was attended by old cars of every description.*
Word Family **descriptive** *adjective* relating to or using description: *descriptive poetry.*

descry (di-**skry**) *verb* (**descries; descrying; descried**)
to catch sight of something distant or difficult to see: *The lookout descried three enemy ships on the horizon.*

desecrate (**dess**-i-krate) *verb*
to misuse something sacred by treating it with disrespect.
Word Family **desecration** (dess-i-**kray**-sh'n) *noun;* **desecrator** *noun.*
[*de-* + Latin *sacer* sacred]

desegregate (dee-**seg**-ri-gate) *verb*
to end segregation of different races, sexes, etc.
Word Family **desegregation** (dee-seg-ri-**gay**-sh'n) *noun.*

deselect *verb*
1 not to readopt someone as a parliamentary candidate.
2 not to choose as part of a group, team etc. someone who was previously a member.

desensitize, desensitise (dec-**sen**-si-tize) *verb*
to make less sensitive.
Word Family **desensitization** (dee-sen-si-tize-**ay**-sh'n) *noun.*

desert[1] (**dezz**-ert) *noun*
a barren, often sandy, area of land having low rainfall.
Word Family **desertification** (dezz-ert-if-i-**kay**-sh'n) *noun* the act of converting fertile land into desert.
[Latin *desertus* forsaken]

desert[2] (di-**zert**) *verb*
to leave or abandon, especially without intending to return: *to desert the army.*
Word Family **deserted** *adjective;* **deserter** *noun;* **desertion** *noun* the act of deserting.

⚠️ Do not confuse *desert* and *dessert*. When *desert* means 'to leave or abandon' it sounds the same as *dessert*, which has two s's and means 'sweet food served at the end of a meal'.

deserts (di-**zerts**) *plural noun*
a deserved reward or punishment: *I hope that bad driver gets his just deserts.*

deserve (di-**zerv**) *verb*
to earn or have a right to: *He deserves to win because he tries so hard.*
Word Family **deservedly** (di-**zerv**-id-lee) *adverb* justly; **deserving** *adjective* worthy of help, reward, etc.: *Please give generously to this deserving charity;* **deservingly** *adverb.*
[Latin *deservire* to serve with devotion]

déshabillé (day-za-**bee**-yay) *adjective*
carelessly or only partly dressed.
[French *déshabiller* to undress]

desiccate *verb*
to dry thoroughly, especially in order to preserve.
Word Family **desiccation** (dess-i-**kay**-sh'n) *noun;* **desiccator** *noun* any of various devices used for drying foodstuffs or chemical substances.
[*de-* + Latin *siccus* dry]

desideratum (di-zidd-er-**ah**-t'm) *noun* (*plural* **desiderata**)
(*formal*) something which is lacking but desired.
[Latin]

design (di-**zine**) *verb*
1 to invent or plan, especially by preparing outlines or drawings: *Their house was designed by a young architect.*
2 (*dated*) to intend
● **design** *noun*
1 an outline or drawing from which something is made.
2 the art of designing: *a school of graphic design.*
3 the arrangement of lines, shapes and details which gives unity to a painting, structure, etc.
4 a plan or scheme.
Phrases **by design** *Police feel that the huge fire was lit by design* (= deliberately, on purpose). **have designs on** *I think the dog has designs on your meal* (= wants, intends to take).
Word Family **designing** *adjective* cunning or crafty; **designedly** (di-**zine**-id-lee) *adverb* on purpose.

designate (dezz-ig-nate) *verb*
1 to mark or point out clearly: *Voters should designate their preferences by ticks in the margin.*
2 to nominate or appoint to a position.
• **designate** (dezz-ig-nit) *adjective* appointed but not yet installed.
Word Family **designation** (dezz-ig-**nay**-sh'n) *noun* 1 the act of designating or appointing. 2 a name.
[Latin *designatus*]

designated driver *noun*
(*especially American*) a person appointed not to drink alcohol at a social occasion and to drive others home afterwards.

designated tolerances *plural noun*
detailed tolerance levels for a manufactured product.

design brief *noun*
a short statement indicating the outline of a problem prior to designing.

designer *noun*
a person who creates and produces designs: *a fashion designer.*
• **designer** *adjective*
1 bearing the label of a well-known designer: *designer jeans.*
2 fashionable: *designer stubble.*

designer drug *noun*
a synthetic addictive drug, deliberately designed so it can be manufactured legally although it has the same effects as some banned drugs.

design specification *noun*
a detailed design description.

desirable (di-zire-a-b'l) *adjective*
1 worthy to be desired: *It is not a very desirable area to live in.*
2 advisable: *I don't think that is a desirable idea.*
3 sexually attractive: *She's a very desirable woman.*
Word Family **desirability** (di-zire-a-**bill**-it-ee) *noun.*

desire (di-zire) *verb*
1 (*formal*) to hope strongly to have or obtain: *He desires success more than anything.*
2 (*formal*) to ask for or request: *The manager desires that all the staff should come to his office.*
• **desire** *noun* a strong hope or longing.
Word Family **desirous** *adjective* desiring.
[Latin *desiderare*]

desist (di-zist) *verb*
(*formal*) to cease or stop: *Please desist from making that dreadful noise!*
[*de-* + Latin *sistere* to stop]

desk *noun*
a table designed for use when reading or writing.

desktop *adjective*
(of a computer system or word-processing system) small enough to use at a desk.

desktop publishing *noun*
short form is **DTP** the combining of text, graphics and layout to produce printed material of a publishable standard by means of a desktop computer system.

desolate (dess-a-lit) *adjective*
lonely, bare or dismal: *It's a bleak and desolate part of the country.* □ *She lived a desolate friendless life.*
• **desolate** (dess-a-late) *verb* to make desolate: *The troops desolated much farmland in their raids.*
Word Family **desolately** *adverb*; **desolation** (dess-a-**lay**-sh'n) *noun* 1 the state of being wretched or lonely. 2 the act of making desolate; **desolateness** *noun* the state of being desolate.
[*de-* + Latin *solus* alone]

despair (dis-**pair**) *noun*
1 a complete loss of hope: *to weep in despair.*
2 something which causes a loss of hope: *She is the despair of her family.*
• **despair** *verb* to be filled with despair.
Word Family **despairing** *adjective*.

despatch ⇨ DISPATCH.

desperado (desp-a-**rah**-doe) *noun* (*plural* **desperadoes** or **desperados**)
a reckless or dangerous criminal.

desperate (desp-a-rit) *adjective*
1 being full of despair and ready to take any risk: *The bank clerk made a desperate attempt to tackle the thieves.*
2 dangerous, violent: *The police have issued a warning that three desperate criminals are in the area.*
3 extremely serious: *The drought has caused a desperate shortage of staple foods.*
Word Family **desperately** *adverb*; **desperateness** *noun* the state of being desperate; **desperation** (desp-a-**ray**-sh'n) *noun* extreme despair.
[*de-* + Latin *sperare* to hope]

despicable (di-**spikk**-a-b'l) *adjective*
deserving contempt or scorn: *His cruel treatment of that dog is quite despicable.*
Word Family **despicably** *adverb*.
[*de-* + Latin *spicere* to look]

despise (di-**spize**) *verb*
to feel scorn or contempt for: *I despise bigots.*

despite (di-**spite**) *preposition*
in spite of: *She continued despite our warning.*

despoil (di-**spoil**) *verb*
to rob or plunder.
Word Family despoliation (di-spole-ee-ay-sh'n) *noun.*

despondent *adjective*
unhappy or melancholy due to disappointment, etc.: *The players were despondent at losing the game.*
Word Family despondently *adverb*;
despondency *noun.*
[Latin *despondere* to lose courage]

despot (**dess**-pot) *noun*
a ruler with complete and oppressive power.
Word Family despotic (dess-**pott**-ik) *adjective*; **despotically** *adverb.*
[Greek *despotes* master]

despotism *noun* also called **autocracy**.
1 any unlimited power.
2 a government with complete power, authority and control.

des res (dez **rez**) *noun*
(*informal*) a desirable residence.

> The informal phrase **des res** pokes fun at the language of estate agents, who are known for exaggerating the advantages of the houses on their lists in order to attract customers. The jargon of several professions has spread into the general language.

dessert (di-**zert**) *noun*
any sweet food served as the last course of a meal.

> **!** Do not confuse *dessert* with *desert*:
> ⇒ DESERT².

dessertspoon *noun*
an oval spoon between a teaspoon and a tablespoon in size.
[French *desservir* to clear the table]

destination *noun*
the place or point to which someone or something is going: *Their destination was Sydney but they went via Asia.*

destine (**dest**-in) *verb*
to set apart for a particular use, future, etc.: *She was destined to die young.*

destiny (**dest**-i-nee) *noun* (*plural* **destinies**)
1 the inevitable fate or course of events which affect a person, considered to be beyond human control: *His final destiny was a lonely death.*
2 the power believed to determine these events: *Destiny has played us a cruel trick.*
[Latin *destinare* to determine beforehand]

destitute (**dest**-i-tewt) *adjective*
completely deprived of or without something.
Word Family destitution (des-ti-**tew**-sh'n) *noun.*

destroy (di-**stroy**) *verb*
1 to ruin or make useless: *The fire completely destroyed the building.*
2 to put an end to.
[*de*- + Latin *struere* to build]

destroyer *noun*
1 a person or thing that destroys.
2 a small fast warship.

destructible *adjective*
able to be destroyed.

destruction *noun*
1 the act of destroying: *The insects' destruction of the crops was complete.*
2 the state of being destroyed: *The destruction throughout the countryside was terrible.*
3 a cause or means of destroying: *Drinking was his final destruction.*

destructive *adjective*
tending or intended to destroy or hurt.
Word Family destructively *adverb*;
destructiveness *noun.*

desultory (**dezz**-ul-tree) *adjective*
disconnected or random: *The desultory chatter faded away as the teacher entered the room.*
Word Family desultorily *adverb*;
desultoriness *noun.*

detach (di-**tach**) *verb*
to separate or take apart: *Detach this coupon from the page by cutting along the dotted line.* □ *A small troop was detached to guard the town.*
Word Family detached *adjective*
1 separate or unattached. **2** not joined to another: *This is the only detached house in the street.* **3** objective, unconcerned: *He takes a surprisingly detached view of his own life*; **detachable** *adjective* able to be detached.

detachment *noun*
1 the state of being detached or unconcerned: *His air of detachment makes it difficult to talk to him.*
2 the act of detaching or separating.
3 something which is detached from a larger group, etc., such as a number of troops sent out for a particular task.

detail (**dee**-tale) *noun*
1 all the small particular parts which make up a whole: *The elaborate detail in the painting received close examination.* □ *Tell us all the details of the party.*
2 a small group chosen for a special task: *The young constable joined the traffic detail.*
● **detail** *verb*
1 to describe fully: *Let me detail my plans for tomorrow.*
2 to choose or appoint for a special task: *He was detailed to supervise the clean-up.*
Word Family **detailed** *adjective.*

detain (di-**tane**) *verb*
to keep back or confine: *Police detained three men for questioning.*
Word Family **detainment** *noun*; **detainee** (de-tay-**nee**) *noun* a person confined or imprisoned, especially by police.
[*de-* + Latin *tenere* to hold]

detect *verb*
to discover or notice: *Do I detect a smell of burning in the kitchen?*
Word Family **detectable** *adjective*; **detection** *noun* the act of detecting: *He has always been fascinated by methods of crime detection.*
[*de-* + Latin *tectus* covered]

detective *noun*
a member of the police force or a private organization who obtains information or evidence about crimes, criminals, etc.

detector *noun*
1 a person or thing that detects.
2 *Radio* a device which registers or records signals, currents, etc.

détente (day-**tont**) *noun*
an easing or relaxing of strained relationships between countries.
[French, a relaxation]

detention *noun*
1 the act of detaining.
2 the confining or keeping back of a person, often as a form of punishment.

detention centre *noun*
an institution where certain people, such as illegal immigrants, are detained for a short time.

deter (di-**ter**) *verb* (**deters; deterring; deterred**)
to discourage by creating fear, doubt, etc.: *Don't be deterred by his haughty manner.*
[*de-* + Latin *terrere* to frighten]

detergent (di-**ter**-j'nt) *noun*
any cleaning agent, especially a synthetic substance made from petroleum products.
● **detergent** *adjective* having the power to clean or purify.
[Latin *detergere* to wipe off]

deteriorate (di-**teer**-i-a-rate) *verb*
to become worse or of less value: *Their standard of living deteriorated.*
Word Family **deterioration** (di-teer-i-a-**ray**-sh'n) *noun.*
[Latin *deterior* worse]

determinant (di-**ter**-mi-nant) *noun* also **determinative**
anything which decides or determines: *Cost was the main determinant in their decision to drop the plan.*

determinate (di-**ter**-mi-nit) *adjective*
definite or fixed: *There is no determinate time limit for repaying our loan.*
Word Family **determinately** *adverb*; **determinateness** *noun.*

determine (di-**ter**-min) *verb*
1 to decide or establish: *Society determines a large part of our attitudes.*
2 to settle conclusively: *Three judges were appointed to determine the dispute.*
Word Family **determined** *adjective* firmly decided or resolved: *We could see that she was really determined to come*; **determinedly** *adverb*; **determinable** *adjective*; **determination** (di-ter-mi-**nay**-sh'n) *noun* 1 the quality of being firmly decided or determined: *determination to win.* 2 the act of determining or deciding; **determiner** *noun* a word such as *a, the, many* or *this* which comes before a noun or noun phrase.
[*de-* + Latin *terminare* to set a boundary to]

determinism (di-**ter**-mi-nizm) *noun*
Philosophy the belief that we are not free to act otherwise than we do since all our actions are determined by past events and our environment.
Word Family **determinist** *noun*; **determinist, deterministic** (di-ter-mi-**nist**-ik) *adjective.*

deterrent (di-**terr**-'nt) *noun*
anything which deters or restrains: *The sight of the sharks was a deterrent even to enthusiastic swimmers.*

Word Family **deterrent** *adjective*;
deterrence *noun*.

detest (di-**test**) *verb*
to hate or dislike strongly.
Word Family **detestable** *adjective*
deserving to be detested: *What a detestable
liar!*; **detestably** *adverb*; **detestation** (dee-
test-**ay**-sh'n) *noun*.

detonate (**det**-a-nate) *verb*
to explode or cause to explode violently.
Word Family **detonation** (det-a-**nay**-
sh'n) *noun*; **detonator** *noun* a small
explosive device used to make another
substance or object explode.
[*de-* + Latin *tonare* to thunder]

detour (**dee**-toor) *noun*
an alternative route.
• **detour** *verb* to make a detour.
[French, a way round]

detox (dee-**toks**) *noun*
(*informal*) detoxification.

detoxify *verb* (**detoxifies; detoxifying;
detoxified**)
1 to remove poisonous substances from.
2 to take no alcohol or drugs until the
bloodstream is cleared of all toxins.
Word Family **detoxification** (dee-toks-
if-i-**kay**-sh'n) *noun*.

detract (di-**trakt**) *verb*
to take away from the value or quality of
something: *His baldness rather detracts from
his good looks.*
Word Family **detraction** *noun*
1 belittlement or slander: *His criticism of
the artist's work seems to be based on personal
detraction.* 2 the act of detracting;
detractive *adjective*; **detractor** *noun*.
[Latin *detractus* dragged off]

detrimental (det-ri-**men**-t'l) *adjective*
harmful or damaging: *Smoking is
detrimental to your health.*
Word Family **detrimentally** *adverb*;
detriment (**det**-ri-ment) *noun* any harm
or damage.
[Latin *detrimentum* a rubbing off]

detritus (di-**try**-tus) *noun*
Geology any particles of rock or other
material which are worn or broken away
by weathering, erosion, etc.
[Latin, rubbed away]

de trop (der **tro**) *adjective*
unwelcome or in the way: *He felt himself to
be de trop at the party.*
[French, (one) too many]

deuce¹ (dewce) *noun*
1 the number two on playing cards or dice.
2 *Tennis* a stage in the game where scores
are equal and one player must win two
consecutive points to win the game.
[Old French *deus* two]

deuce² *noun*
(*informal*) bad luck or the devil.
Word Family **deuced** (**dew**-sid) *adjective*
(*informal*) annoying.
[from DEUCE¹, the throw of the dice which
is the least wanted]

devalue (dee-**val**-yoo) *verb* also **devaluate**
1 *Economics* to lower the value of the
currency of one country in relation to the
currencies of other countries or to gold,
thus making imports dearer and exports
cheaper.
2 to lower or reduce the value of anything.
Word Family **devaluation** (dee-vall-yoo-
ay-sh'n) *noun*.

devastate (**devv**-a-state) *verb*
to make desolate: *We were devastated by the
loss of the two cats.*
Word Family **devastated** *adjective*;
devastating *adjective*; **devastatingly**
adverb; **devastation** (devv-a-**stay**-sh'n)
noun.
[*de-* + Latin *vastare* to lay waste]

develop (di-**vell-up**) *verb*
1 to grow or cause to grow more fully or
completely: *Girls develop breasts at puberty.*
2 to expand: *You must develop your
knowledge.*
3 to create and advance: *The council has
developed a plan to block off traffic from the
city.*
4 *Photography* to treat exposed film, etc.
with chemicals to produce a visible image.
5 to build on or increase the value of land,
e.g. by providing electricity, sewerage, etc.
[French *développer* to unwrap]

developer *noun*
1 a person or organisation that develops
land.
2 *Photography* the chemical used to
develop film.

developing country *noun* (*plural*
developing countries)
a poor country with few industries,
hospitals, etc.

development *noun*
1 the act of developing: *Land development
in the outer suburbs has caused a rise in
prices.*
2 changes which lead to improvement or
growth in a country, region, area or
population. Development is a process
which can be economic (leading to

increased wealth), social (leading to improvements in people's lives), political (e.g. through greater democracy) or cultural (e.g. through improvements in the arts).
3 a new stage or event during growth or evolution: *Are there any developments in the industrial dispute?*
Word Family **developmental** *adjective.*

deviant *adjective*
different from what is usual or accepted.
• **deviant** *noun* a person or thing that is deviant.
Word Family **deviance, deviancy** *noun.*

deviate (dee-vee-ate) *verb*
1 to differ or turn aside from what is usual or accepted: *Let us deviate from the lecture for a moment and talk about exams.*
2 to differ from an established average.
[Latin *de-* off + *via* the way]

deviation (dee-vee-**ay**-sh'n) *noun*
1 the act of deviating.
2 a movement away from the acceptable route, established average, etc.
3 *Maths* the difference between any element in a set of observations and some standard value, often the mean.
standard deviation *Maths* a quantity that measures the spread of a set of values around the average.

device (di-**vice**) *noun*
anything which is invented or used for a particular purpose, especially a mechanical tool.
Figurative A metaphor is a literary device (= tool). □ *I have a device to make sure we are not seen* (= plan, scheme). □ *The kangaroo and the emu are devices on the Australian coat of arms* (= emblems, figures).
Phrase **leave to one's own devices** *Let's see how he does it if he is left to his own devices* (= allowed to do as he wishes).

devil (dev-'l) *noun*
1 (*sometimes* **Devil**) *Religion* the chief spirit of evil opposed to God.
2 (*sometimes* **Devil**) *Religion* any subordinate evil spirit opposed to God.
3 a very evil person.
4 (*informal*) an unlucky or unfortunate person: *Poor devil!*
5 a person of great energy, skill, etc.: *She's a devil at tennis.*
Phrases **give the devil his due** to be fair or just, even to the wicked. **play the devil with** to ruin or upset badly. **speak of the**

devil, talk of the devil here comes the person we were just speaking about.
• **devil** *verb* (**devils; devilling; devilled**)
Cooking to grill or prepare food with hot spices, such as mustard, etc.

devilish (dev-'l-ish) *adjective*
1 evil or like a devil.
2 (*informal*) great: *devilish skill.*
Word Family **devilish, devilishly** *adverb.*

devil-may-care *adjective*
careless or reckless: *He had a devil-may-care attitude to his work, which worried his parents.*

devilry *noun* (*plural* **devilries**) also **devilment**
mischievous or wicked behaviour.

devil's advocate *noun*
a person who tests an argument or policy by putting forward the criticisms likely to be made by its opponents.

devious (dee-vee-us) *adjective*
1 tricky, dishonest: *I think he makes his money in devious ways.*
2 not straight or direct: *We came by a devious route to avoid the traffic.*
Word Family **deviousness** *noun*; **deviously** *adverb.*

devise (di-**vize**) *verb*
1 to make or think out: *We have devised a perfect scheme for dividing the work.*
2 *Law* to bequeath.

devitalize, devitalise (dee-**vie**-ta-lize) *verb*
to make weak or lifeless.

devoid (di-**void**) *adjective*
empty or lacking.

devolve *verb*
to pass on or transfer: *During his absence the ambassador's duties devolved on his assistant.*
Word Family **devolution** (dee-va-**loo**-sh'n) *noun* the transfer of power.
[Latin *devolvere* to roll down]

Devonian (di-**voh**-nee-an) ⇨ PALAEOZOIC.

devoré (di-**vaw**-ray) *noun*
velvet with a pattern burnt into the pile.
[French, devoured]

devote (di-**vote**) *verb*
to give all one's time or attention to something: *He devotes his days to reading.*
Word Family **devoted** *adjective* very loving or affectionately attached: *She is devoted to her horses.*

devotee (devv-o-tee) *noun*
a fanatical or enthusiastic follower: *He is a devotee of football.*
[*de-* + Latin *votus* vowed]

devotion *noun*
1 a strong love or affection.
2 (*usually* **devotions**) prayers or worship: *The priest spent two hours at his devotions.*
Word Family **devotional** *adjective* used in devotions: *The church's library was filled with devotional literature.*

devour (di-vowr) *verb*
1 to eat or swallow greedily: *The lion devoured its kill.*
2 to destroy: *The fire devoured many acres of crops.*
3 to take in, absorb: *She devoured every detail of the story.*
4 to fill: *An overwhelming fear devoured her.*
Word Family **devouringly** *adverb*.
[*de-* + Latin *vorare* to swallow]

devout (di-vowt) *adjective*
devoted to one's religion: *The devout old man went to church daily.*
Figurative a devout tennis fan (= keen, devoted).
Word Family **devoutly** *adverb*; **devoutness** *noun*.

dew *noun*
drops of moisture accumulated on the ground during calm weather when the night air near the ground cools.

dewlap *noun*
the loose fold of skin under the throat of cattle or other animals.

dewy *adjective* (**dewier; dewiest**)
being moist with or as if with dew.

dewy-eyed *adjective*
naive or trusting.

dexterity (deks-terr-i-tee) *noun*
a manual or mental adroitness.
Word Family **dextrous** (deks-trus), **dexterous** *adjective*; **dextrousness** *noun*.
[Latin *dexter* on the right]

dextrose *noun*
a sugar, found in animal and plant tissues, which can be produced artificially from starch.

dhal (dahl) *noun* also **dal**
1 an edible pea-like seed used in Indian cooking.
2 a purée made with these or with lentils.
[Hindi]

dhansak (dun-sahk) *noun*
an Indian dish of meat or vegetables with lentils and spices.
[Gujarati]

dharma (dar-ma) *noun*
Hinduism duty, codes of conduct and the practice of religion itself.
[Sanskrit]

dhoti (doe-tee) *noun*
a garment worn by Hindu men.
[Hindi]

dhow (*rhymes with* cow) *noun*
a small Arab trading vessel with one sail, regularly crossing the Indian Ocean.
[Arabic]

diabetes (die-a-bee-teez) *noun*
a disease caused by a build-up of sugar in the blood, due to lack of insulin to metabolize it.
Word Family **diabetic** (die-a-bett-ik) *adjective, noun*.
[Greek *diabainein* to go through]

diabolical (die-a-boll-i-k'l) *adjective* also **diabolic**
devilish or extremely wicked.
Word Family **diabolically** *adverb*.
[Greek *diabolos* a slanderer]

diacritic (die-a-kritt-ik) *adjective* also **diacritical**
Language serving to distinguish: *A circumflex is a diacritic symbol.*
[Greek *diakritikos* distinguishing]

diadem (die-a-dem) *noun*
a crown or headband, worn usually by royalty.
[Greek *diadema* a headband]

diaeresis (die-err-i-sis) *noun* (*plural* **diaereses**) (die-err-i-seez) ⇨ ACCENT.
[Greek *diairesis* separation]

diagnosis (die-ag-no-sis) *noun* (*plural* **diagnoses**) (die-ag-no-seez)
1 *Medicine* the determination of the cause of a disease by studying the symptoms, signs and results of tests.
2 *Biology* a description which enables an organism to be identified.
Word Family **diagnose** (die-ag-noze) *verb* to make a diagnosis; **diagnostic** (die-ag-nos-tik) *adjective*; **diagnostician** (die-ag-nos-tish-'n) *noun*.
[Greek, a distinguishing]

diagonal (die-agg-a-n'l) *adjective*
1 having an oblique or slanted direction.
2 *Maths* connecting two non-adjacent vertices or edges.
• **diagonal** *noun* a diagonal line or plane.
Word Family **diagonally** *adverb*.
[*dia-* + Greek *gonia* a corner]

diagram 274 **diastole**

diagram (die-a-gram) *noun*
a simplified drawing which explains,
represents or describes.
Word Family diagrammatic (die-a-gra-
matt-ik) *adjective*; **diagrammatically**
adverb.
[*dia-* + Greek *gramma* something written]

dial (*rhymes with* pile) *noun*
the front part or face of a clock, telephone,
gauge, or other instrument.
• **dial** *verb* (**dials; dialling; dialled**) to
use a telephone dial to ring a number.

dialect *noun*
the language, usually spoken, of a certain
class or region, as a variant form of the
established language of the whole country.
Word Family dialectal (die-a-**lek**-t'l)
adjective.

dialectic *noun*
(*often* **dialectics**) the art or process of
logical argument to establish or discover a
truth, etc.
Word Family dialectical *adjective*.
[Greek *dialektos* conversation]

dialogue (die-a-log) *noun* (*American*
dialog)
1 a conversation, either spoken or written,
between two or more people.
2 any exchange of thoughts or ideas.
3 the spoken text of a play or film.
[Greek *dialogos* conversation]

dialysis (die-**al**-i-sis) *noun* (*plural*
dialyses) (die-**al**-i-seez)
1 *Physics* the separation of colloidal
particles from dissolved substances in
a solution by diffusion through a
membrane.
2 a treatment used in kidney disease
in which blood is purified using this
technique by means of a kidney machine.
Word Family dialyse (**die**-a-lize) *verb*.
[Greek, a separating]

diamanté (die-a-**mon**-tay) *noun*
a fabric made to glitter by covering it with
shiny particles.
[French *diamant* diamond]

diameter (die-**amm**-i-ter) *noun*
1 *Maths* a chord passing through the
centre of a circle.
2 *Maths* the length of this line.
[*dia-* + Greek *metron* a measure]

diametric (die-a-**met**-rik) *adjective* also
diametrical
1 relating to a diameter.
2 absolute or direct: *Good and bad are
diametric opposites.*
Word Family diametrically *adverb*.

diamond (**die**-a-m'nd) *noun*
1 a natural crystalline form of carbon
which is colourless when pure. It is the
hardest known substance and is used for
cutting-tools and drill tips and as a gem.
2 a plane figure having four equal sides,
with diagonals which are vertical and
horizontal.
3 *Cards* a red figure like a diamond on a
playing card.
4 *Cards* a playing card with this figure.
5 (**diamonds**) *Cards* the suit with this
figure.
6 *Baseball* the distance or area between the
four bases.
• **diamond** *adjective*
1 of, made of or shaped like a diamond.
2 indicating the 60th (sometimes the 75th)
anniversary of an event, e.g. a wedding
anniversary.
[Greek *adamantis* of adamant]

diaper (**die**-per) *noun*
American a nappy.
[Greek *diaspros* pure white]

diaphanous (die-**aff**-a-nus) *adjective*
transparent: *Chiffon is a diaphanous fabric.*
[*dia-* + Greek *phainein* to show]

diaphragm (**die**-a-fram) *noun*
1 *Anatomy* any membrane which separates
and divides, particularly the muscular wall
separating the chest from the abdomen in
mammals.
2 *Photography* an adjustable hole in a
camera, controlling the amount of light
which passes through the lens on to the
film.
3 also called **cap**. a contraceptive device
which fits over the woman's cervix.
[*dia-* + Greek *phragma* a fence]

diarrhoea (die-a-**ree**-a) *noun*
Medicine an intestinal disorder which
causes the faeces to be fluid and their
passage frequent.
[Greek *diarrhoia* a flowing through]

diary (**die**-a-ree) *noun* (*plural* **diaries**)
1 a book in which one records experiences,
feelings, thoughts, etc. day by day.
2 a book in which a record of one's
appointments, etc. is kept.
Word Family diarist *noun* a person who
keeps a diary.
[Latin *diarius* daily]

diastole (die-**ast**-a-lee) *noun*
Biology the rhythmical relaxation phase of
the heartbeat. Compare SYSTOLE.
Word Family diastolic (die-a-**stoll**-ik)
adjective.
[Greek *diastolé* expansion]

diatribe (die-a-tribe) *noun*
a bitter attack or criticism.
[*dia-* + Greek *tribein* to rub]

diazepam (die-**azz**-i-pam) *noun*
Medicine a drug used as a sedative.

dibble *noun* also **dibber**
a short pointed tool used to make holes in
the ground for planting seeds, etc.

dice *plural noun* (*singular* **dice** or **die**)
1 small cubes of plastic, wood, etc.
which have each side marked with dots
representing the numbers one to six, used
in some games.
2 (*used with singular verb*) any game,
especially a gambling game, in which these
objects are thrown on to a flat surface.
3 any small cubes: *Cut the meat into dice.*
Phrase **load the dice 1** to make dice
heavier on one side so that they will
often land in a certain way. **2** to place
someone in a particularly favourable or
unfavourable position.
• **dice** *verb*
1 to cut into small pieces.
2 to play with dice.

dicey (die-see) *adjective* (**dicier; diciest**)
(*informal*) risky or dangerous.

dichlorodiphenyltrichloroethane (die-
klaw-ro-die-fen-'l-try-klaw-ro-**ee**-thane)
noun
short form is **DDT** a white powder used
as an insecticide.

dichotomy (die-**kott**-a-mee) *noun* (*plural*
dichotomies)
a division into two contradictory parts.
[Greek *dikho-* apart + *tomé* division]

dicky¹ *noun* (*plural* **dickies**)
(*informal*) a false shirt front.

dicky² *adjective* (**dickier; dickiest**)
(*informal*) shaky or unsound: *a dicky heart.*

dicta
a plural of **dictum**.

Dictaphone *noun*
(*trademark*) a machine similar to a tape
recorder, used to record and replay
dictation.

dictate (dik-tate) *verb*
1 to say or speak something to be written
or recorded by another person.
2 to command or order.
• **dictate** (dik-tate) *noun*
an authoritative order.
Word Family **dictation** (dik-**tay**-sh'n)
noun.
[Latin *dictare* to say repeatedly]

dictator *noun*
a ruler with unlimited power, especially
one who has taken control by force.
Word Family **dictatorship** *noun.*
[Latin]

dictatorial (dik-ta-taw-ree-al) *adjective*
1 of or relating to a dictator.
2 domineering: *The manager's dictatorial
behaviour made him unpopular.*
Word Family **dictatorially** *adverb.*

diction (dik-sh'n) *noun*
1 a style of speaking or writing.
2 the degree of distinctness or clarity in
speech.
[Latin *dictio* speaking]

dictionary (dik-sh'n-ree) *noun* (*plural*
dictionaries)
a book listing words of a language in
alphabetical order with their meanings,
pronunciation, use and derivation.

dictum *noun* (*plural* **dicta** or **dictums**)
1 formal statement of opinion.
2 a popular saying.
[Latin]

did the past tense of **do**.

didactic (die-**dak**-tik) *adjective*
intended to teach or instruct.
Word Family **didacticism** (die-**dak**-ti-
sizm) *noun*; **didactically** *adverb.*
[Greek *didaskein* to teach]

diddle *verb*
(*informal*) to cheat or swindle.

didn't *contraction*
a short form of **did not**: *I didn't see her.*

die¹ *verb* (**dies; dying; died**)
1 to stop living, when all vital functions
cease.
2 to cease to exist: *That law died in the 19th
century!*
Figurative The engine died and the car drew
to a standstill (= stopped). □ *The chatter died
away as the door was thrown open* (= faded).
3 (*informal*) to desire greatly: *I am dying for
an ice cream.*
Phrases **die down** to subside: *The noise
died down gradually.* **die out** to disappear.

die² *noun*
1 a tool used to shape a material, e.g. by
forging or extrusion.
2 *Metallurgy* a hole in a block through
which wire can be drawn.
3 *Metallurgy* a hole lined with teeth for
cutting a thread on bolts, screws, etc.
4 a singular of **dice**.
Phrase **the die is cast** the decision or
situation cannot be changed.

diehard *noun*
a person who stubbornly resists change.

diesel (**dee**-z'l) *noun*
any vehicle powered by a diesel engine.

diesel engine *noun*
an internal-combustion engine in which
the mixture of fuel and air is ignited by the
heat produced when it is compressed in
the cylinders.
[invented by *R. Diesel*, 1858-1913, a
German engineer]

diesel oil *noun*
an oily liquid extracted after petrol and
kerosene have been distilled from crude
oil, used as fuel in diesel engines.

diet¹ (**die**-et) *noun*
1 the usual food which one eats.
2 a restricted selection of food to regulate
weight, cure disease, etc.
• **diet** *verb* to eat restricted foods,
especially to regulate weight.
Word Family **dietary** (**die**-a-tree)
adjective; **dieter** *noun*; **dietitian** (die-a-
tish-'n) *noun* also **dietician** a person
trained to plan balanced diets.
[Greek *diaita* a way of life]

diet² *noun*
a formal congress of the states of an
empire, etc. to discuss or carry out its
business.

dietary fibre ⇨ FIBRE (definition 3).

dietetics (die-a-**tett**-iks) *plural noun*
(*used with singular verb*) the study of the
composition of foods and the control of
the diet.
Word Family **dietetic** *adjective*.

differ *verb*
1 to be unlike.
2 to have different or opposing opinions,
beliefs, etc.

difference *noun*
1 the state of being different.
2 a point which differs: *I can see no
difference between the two.*
3 an argument.
4 *Maths* the amount by which one number
is greater or less than another.
5 *Maths* the amount remaining when one
quantity is subtracted from another.

different *adjective*
1 not alike.
2 separate: *We rang on three different
occasions.*
3 unusual: *Let's do something different today.*
Word Family **differently** *adverb*.

| ! | *Different* may be followed by *from, to,* or *than,* but *different from,* as in *Your jacket is different from mine,* is the form considered correct by most people in British English. |

differential (diff-a-**ren**-sh'l) *noun*
Engineering a gear mechanism which
drives two shafts, such as the axles in a
motor vehicle, allowing them to rotate at
different speeds.
• **differential** *adjective* of or expressing a
difference.

differentiate (diff-a-**ren**-shi-ate) *verb*
to notice or indicate differences between.
Word Family **differentiation** (diff-a-
ren-shi-**ay**-sh'n) *noun*.

differently abled *adjective*
a politically correct term for 'disabled' or
'handicapped', on the grounds that it
suggests a more positive way of looking at
things.

difficult *adjective*
1 hard to do or accomplish.
2 (*informal*) being hard to please or get
along with.
Word Family **difficulty** *noun* (*plural*
difficulties) 1 the fact of being difficult.
2 trouble or hardship: *I had great difficulty
understanding his mumbled words.* □ *the
company's financial difficulties.* 3 anything
which is difficult: *They succeeded in
overcoming the difficulties.*
[Latin *difficultas* a difficulty]

diffidence (**diff**-i-d'nce) *noun*
a lack of self-confidence.
Word Family **diffident** *adjective*;
diffidently *adverb*.
[Latin *diffidens* mistrusting]

diffraction (de-**frak**-sh'n) *noun*
Physics the bending of waves, e.g. of light,
around the edge of an object. When light
rays pass through a narrow gap they bend
outwards so that the light spreads out.
Word Family **diffract** *verb*; **diffractive**
adjective.
[Latin *diffractus* broken in pieces]

diffuse (dif-**yooz**) *verb*
to spread out or scatter.
• **diffuse** (dif-**yooce**) *adjective* spread out
or scattered.
Figurative The diffuse prose was difficult to
read (= very long).
Word Family **diffuser** *noun* something
which diffuses or causes diffusion, such as
glass placed over the lens of a camera to
soften or enlarge the picture; **diffusible**
adjective.
[Latin *diffusus* spread out]

diffusion (dif-**yoo**-*zh*'n) *noun*
1 the act of diffusing.
2 *Physics* the mixing of molecules of different gases.
3 *Physics* the scattering and criss-crossing of light rays produced by reflection from a rough surface or passage through frosted glass, fog, etc.

dig *verb* (**digs; digging; dug**)
1 to break up, remove or turn over soil, etc. with a spade or similar tool.
2 to make a hole with or as if with a spade. *Figurative He dug his hands into his pockets and walked off* (= thrust, pushed). □ *She dug around for a suitable answer* (= searched).
3 (*dated*) to understand or appreciate.
4 to poke.
Phrases **dig one's heels in** ⇨ HEEL¹. **dig up, dig out** to find: *Where did you dig up that old hat?*
● **dig** *noun*
1 a poke: *a dig in the ribs.*
2 (**digs**) any rented accommodation for students, etc.
3 an archaeological excavation.

digest (die-**jest**) *verb*
to break up food in the alimentary canal so that it can be absorbed into the body.
Figurative The judge had to digest many facts before making a decision (= take in, absorb).
● **digest** (**die**-jest) *noun*
1 a shortened version of a book, report, etc.
2 a collection of such works.
Word Family **digestion** *noun* the function or process of digesting food; **digestible** *adjective* able to be digested; **digestibility** (die-jest-i-**bill**-it-ee) *noun*; **digestive** *adjective*.
[Latin *digestus* distributed]

digger *noun*
1 a person or thing that digs.
2 (**Digger**) (*informal*) a soldier from Australia or New Zealand.

diggings *plural noun*
a place where digging is carried out, such as a mine.

digit (**dij**-it) *noun*
1 a finger or toe.
2 any of the figures, 0–9, in the Arabic system.
Word Family **digital** (**dij**-i-t'l) *adjective* **1** storing information in the form of numbers: *a digital recording.* **2** having or resembling a digit or digits; **digitally** *adverb*.
[Latin *digitus* finger or toe]

digital audio tape *noun*
short form is **DAT** magnetic tape used for digital recordings.

digital camera *noun*
a camera which records photographs in electronic form so that they can be transferred to a computer.

digital videodisc *noun*
short form is **DVD** a high-quality compact disc which can store large amounts of video and audio information.

digital watch *noun* (*plural* **digital watches**) also **digital clock**
a watch or clock on which the time is indicated directly by numbers rather than by a dial and pointers. Compare ANALOGUE WATCH.

digitize, digitise *verb*
to convert information into numbers for storing in a computer.

dignify *verb* (**dignifies; dignifying; dignified**)
to confer honour or dignity upon.
Word Family **dignified** *adjective* full of dignity.

dignitary (**dig**-na-tree) *noun* (*plural* **dignitaries**)
a person of high rank.

dignity *noun*
1 a bearing or character which commands respect: *The former champion accepted his defeat with great dignity.*
2 a high rank or office.
Phrase **stand on one's dignity** to insist that people treat one with the proper respect.
[Latin *dignitas* worthiness]

digress (die-**gress**) *verb*
to deviate from the main line or purpose
Word Family **digression** (die-**gresh**-'n) *noun*; **digressive** *adjective* tending to digress.
[Latin *digressus* having moved away]

dike ⇨ DYKE.

dilapidated (di-**lapp**-i-day-tid) *adjective*
fallen into ruin or disrepair: *It would be expensive to restore such a dilapidated old house.*
Word Family **dilapidation** *noun* (de-lapp-i-**day**-sh'n).
[*di-* + Latin *lapides* stones]

dilate (die-**late**) *verb*
to make or become larger or wider.
Word Family **dilation** (die-**lay**-sh'n), **dilatation** (die-la-**tay**-sh'n) *noun* **1** the act of dilating. **2** a dilated part; **dilator** *noun*

something which dilates, e.g. a muscle, drug, etc.
[*di-* + Latin *latus* wide]

dilatory (**dill**-a-tree) *adjective*
1 slow to act, decide, etc.
2 intended to delay.
Word Family **dilatorily** *adverb*; **dilatoriness** *noun*.
[Latin *dilatus* postponed]

dilemma *noun*
a situation requiring a choice between difficult or undesirable alternatives.
[*di-* + Greek *lemma* an assumption]

dilettante (dill-i-**tan**-tee) *noun* (*plural* **dilettanti** or **dilettantes**)
a person who concerns or amuses himself or herself with culture and the arts in a casual or amateur manner.
Word Family **dilettantism** *noun*.
[Italian]

diligent (**dill**-i-j'nt) *adjective*
careful and earnest in one's work.
Word Family **diligence** *noun*.
[Latin *diligens* conscientious]

dill *noun*
a small plant, the seeds and leaves of which are used in medicine, cooking and pickling foods.

dillydally *verb* (**dillydallies; dillydallying; dillydallied**)
to waste time, especially by being undecided.

dilute (die-**loot**) *verb*
to make weaker or thinner, by adding water, etc.
Word Family **dilute** *adjective* reduced or weakened; **diluent** (**dill**-yoo-'nt) *adjective* serving to dilute.
[Latin *dilutus* washed apart]

dilution (die-**loo**-sh'n) *noun*
1 the act of diluting.
2 *Chemistry* the amount of solvent in which a unit quantity of solute is dissolved.

dim *adjective* (**dimmer; dimmest**)
1 faint or unclear, due to a lack of light, colour, etc.
2 clouded: *Her eyes were dim with tears.*
3 adverse: *Our mother takes a dim view of our jokes.*
4 (*informal*) stupid: *He is quite dim when it comes to physics.*
• **dim** *verb* (**dims; dimming; dimmed**)
to make dim: *We dimmed the lights.*
Word Family **dimly** *adverb*; **dimness** *noun*.

dime *noun*
American a ten-cent coin.

dimension (di-**men**-sh'n) *noun*
(*usually* **dimensions**) the size of anything, especially the length, width or height.
Word Family **dimensional** *adjective* having the specified number of dimensions: *three-dimensional*.
[Latin *dimensio* a measuring]

diminish *verb*
to make or become smaller: *Drought diminished the country's food supplies.*
Word Family **diminution** (dimm-i-**new**-sh'n) *noun* the process of diminishing.

diminishing returns *noun*
Economics a theory stating that there comes a point where further increases in tax, investment, effort, etc. become less and less profitable or effective.

diminutive (dim-**in**-yoo-tiv) *adjective*
1 very small.
2 *Grammar* (of a suffix) indicating smallness, affection, etc., as in *piglet*.
• **diminutive** *noun* a short form of a name.
Word Family **diminutively** *adverb*; **diminutiveness** *noun*.
[Latin *diminutus* diminished]

dimity (**dimm**-i-tee) *noun*
a thin cotton fabric woven with a stripe or check in a heavier yarn.
[*di-* + Greek *mitos* a thread]

dimmer *noun*
a person or thing that dims, especially a switch for dimming lights.

dimple *noun*
a small hollow or fold, especially on the cheek.
• **dimple** *verb* to make or produce dimples: *Her face dimpled as she laughed.*

dim sum *noun*
small pieces of meat or vegetables wrapped in pastry and steamed or fried.
[Cantonese]

din *noun*
a loud noise.

dinar (**dee**-nar) *noun*
the basic unit of money in the states of Yugoslavia and certain other countries.
[Arabic]

dine *verb*
to eat a meal, especially the main meal of the day.
Word Family **diner** *noun* 1 a person who dines. 2 *Railways* ⇨ DINING CAR.
3 *American* a roadside snack bar.

dinette (die-**net**) *noun*
a small room or part of a room set aside
for eating.

ding-dong *adjective*
(*informal*) vigorous: *The argument turned
into a ding-dong fight.*

dinghy (**ding**-gee) *noun* (*plural* **dinghies**)
a small boat which may be rowed or sailed.
[Hindi]

dingle *noun*
an old word for a small deep wooded
valley.

dingo *noun* (*plural* **dingoes** or **dingos**)
a wild dog of Australia, about 50 cm high
and usually sandy-coloured.
[Aboriginal]

dingy (**din**-jee) *adjective* (**dingier**;
dingiest)
dark, dull or shabby: *a dingy room lit only
by candles.*
Word Family **dinginess** *noun.*

dining car *noun* also called **diner**
Railways a carriage in which meals or
snacks are served.

dinner *noun*
1 the main meal of the day, eaten at
midday or in the evening.
2 a formal meal.

dinner jacket *noun*
a jacket, usually black, worn with a bow tie
on formal occasions, especially at night.

dinosaur (**die**-na-sawr) *noun*
a long-extinct reptile of the Mesozoic era,
the largest land animal ever known.
[Greek *deinos* terrible + *sauros* lizard]

dint *noun*
a dent.
Phrase **by dint of** *She won by dint of her
great enthusiasm* (= by the force or power
of).
● **dint** *verb* to make a dent in.

diocese (**die**-a-siss) *noun* also called **see**
Christianity a district under the religious
control of one bishop or archbishop.
Word Family **diocesan** (die-**oss**-i-san)
adjective, noun.
[Latin *diocesis* district]

diode (**die**-ode) *noun*
Electricity a valve with two electrodes, used
for converting alternating current into
direct current.
[*di*- + Greek *hodos* a way]

Dionysus (die-a-**nice**-us) *noun*
Greek mythology the god of wine and
fertility.
Word Family **Dionysiac** (die-a-**nizz**-

ee-ak), **Dionysian** (die-a-**nizz**-ee-an)
adjective.

diorama *noun*
a miniature three-dimensional scene with
modelled, painted figures and a painted
background.
[*dia*- + Greek *horama* a sight]

dioxide (die-**ok**-side) *noun*
Chemistry an oxide with two atoms of
oxygen per molecule.

dioxin *noun*
a toxic chemical which occurs as a by-
product of some manufacturing processes.

dip *verb* (**dips**; **dipping**; **dipped**)
1 to put or lower briefly into something,
especially a liquid: *Dip the fish in batter
before cooking.*
2 to scoop or lift: *They dipped water out of
the boat with a bucket.*
3 to become slightly involved: *I have only
dipped into the subject.*
4 to immerse sheep, etc. in a solution to
destroy bacteria, parasites, etc.
5 to drop or direct downwards: *He dipped
his car's lights as he approached the hill.*
● **dip** *noun*
1 anything into which something is
dipped: *a sheep dip.* □ *a savoury dip for
biscuits.*
2 a plunge or brief immersion: *Let's have a
dip in the sea before lunch.*
3 a downward slope or movement: *There is
a slight dip in the road ahead.*
4 *Geology* the angle which a stratum makes
with a horizontal plane.

diphtheria (dip-**theer**-i-a *or* diff-**theer**-
i-a) *noun*
an infectious bacterial disease causing
inflammation or blockage of the throat,
usually in children.
[Greek *diphthera* a membrane]

diphthong (**diff**-thong) *noun*
Language one sound made up of two vowel
sounds, as *ou* in *loud* (la ood)
[*di*- + Greek *phthongos* sound]

diploma (di-**plo**-ma) *noun*
Education a certificate awarded when a
student has satisfactorily completed a
particular course of study.
[Greek *diploma* folded letter (of
recommendation)]

diplomacy (di-**plo**-ma-see) *noun*
1 the art of maintaining relationships and
agreements between countries.
2 any tact or skill in dealing with people: *It
will take some diplomacy to break the news.*

Word Family **diplomat** (**dip**-la-mat)
noun a person employed or skilled in
diplomacy.
[Greek *diploma* folded letter (of
recommendation)]

diplomatic (dip-la-**matt**-ik) *adjective*
1 of or engaged in diplomacy: *a member of
the diplomatic service.*
2 tactful.
Word Family **diplomatically** *adverb.*

diplomatic immunity *noun*
the immunity of diplomatic officials from
the laws of the country in which they are
working.

dipper[1] *noun*
a bird resembling a large wren.

dipper[2] *noun*
anything used for dipping, such as a ladle.

dipsomaniac (dip-so-**may**-nee-ak) *noun*
an alcoholic.
Word Family **dipsomania** *noun.*
[Greek *dipsa* thirst + MANIAC]

dipstick *noun*
1 a rod used for measuring the amount of
liquid in a container.
2 (*informal*) an idiot.

diptych (**dip**-tik) *noun*
a pair of paintings on two panels, which
are often hinged together. Compare
TRIPTYCH.
[Greek *diptykos* double-folded]

dire *adjective*
disastrous or terrible: *The snow had a dire
effect on their crops.*

direct *verb*
1 to guide or control: *Who directed the
company while the chairman was away?*
2 to show the way: *Can you direct me to the
post office?*
3 to order: *Who directed you to say that?*
4 to turn: *Try to direct your efforts towards
something useful.*
5 to organize and supervise the actors and
actual performance of a play or film.
• **direct** *adjective*
1 straight or uninterrupted: *a direct line.*
2 frank: *a direct question.*
3 immediate, in an unbroken line: *a direct
descendant of Queen Victoria.*
4 exact or absolute: *That is the direct
opposite of what you said earlier.*
Word Family **directness** *noun;* **directly**
adverb.

direct current ⇨ ELECTRIC CURRENT.

direct debit *noun*
an arrangement with a bank in which
money is transferred from a person's
account to a company's account at regular
intervals.

directed number *noun*
Maths a number which has a plus or minus
sign to distinguish between direction as
well as magnitude: *+4 and –3 are directed
numbers.*

direction *noun*
1 the act of directing: *He acted under the
direction of his boss.*
2 the point or position towards which
something faces or moves: *He drove off in
the direction of the city.*
3 (*often* **directions**) guidance: *Can you
give me directions to the zoo?*
Word Family **directional** *adjective*
relating to direction in space;
directionless *adjective.*

direction-finder *noun*
Radio a device similar to an aerial,
attached to a receiver, used to establish the
direction from which radio waves are sent.

directive *noun*
any detailed instruction or command: *The
staff received directives on what to wear.*

direct object *noun*
Grammar the person or thing directly
affected by the action of a verb: *In the
sentence 'The dog wagged its tail', 'its tail' is
the direct object.*

director *noun*
1 a person who controls the affairs of a
business company.
2 the person who directs actors and the
artistic performance of a play or film.
Compare PRODUCER.
Word Family **directorship** *noun;*
directorial (dirr-ek-**taw**-ri-al) *adjective.*

directorate *noun*
1 the position or office of a director.
2 a board of directors.

director-general *noun* (*plural* **directors-
general**)
the person in charge of a large
organization: *the director-general of the
BBC.*

directory *noun* (*plural* **directories**)
a book with an alphabetical list of names
or subjects: *a street directory.*

direct speech *noun*
the exact words used by a speaker, usually placed inside speech marks: *'Where are you going?' asked Jack*. Compare INDIRECT SPEECH.

dirge (derj) *noun*
a sad slow song of lament.

dirigible (**dirr**-ij-a-b'l) *adjective*
able to be controlled or steered.
• **dirigible** *noun* an airship which may be controlled, directed or steered.

dirk *noun*
a dagger, especially one formerly used by Scottish Highlanders.

dirndl (**dern**-d'l) *noun*
a colourful dress with a close-fitting top and a full skirt, worn by girls in the Austrian mountains.
[Austro-German, little girl]

dirt *noun*
1 any unclean matter or substance: *Please clean that dirt off your clothes.*
2 any earth or soil.

dirt cheap *adjective*
(*informal*) very inexpensive.

dirty *adjective* (**dirtier; dirtiest**)
covered with dirt: *I must clean these dirty windows.*
Figurative The footballer was suspended for dirty play (= unfair). □ *The book was banned for a while because of its dirty language* (= indecent). □ *dirty weather* (= rough, stormy).
• **dirty** *verb* (**dirties; dirtying; dirtied**) to make dirty.
Word Family **dirtily** *adverb*, **dirtiness** *noun*.

dis (diss) *verb* (**disses; dissing; dissed**) also **diss**
(*informal, especially American*) to insult or treat with disrespect: *She dissed her ex-boyfriend to all her friends.*

disability (diss-a-**bill**-i-tee) *noun* (*plural* **disabilities**)
a lack or loss of faculty or power: *She obviously has a serious reading disability.*

disable (diss-**ay**-b'l) *verb*
to take away or destroy the ability or power of: *The yacht was disabled during the storm.*
Word Family **disabled** *adjective* having a physical or mental disability: *a disabled soldier;* **disablement** *noun*.

disabuse (diss-a-**bewz**) *verb*
to free from error or misunderstanding.

disadvantage (diss-ad-**vahn**-tij) *noun*
an unfavourable or harmful condition, circumstance, etc.: *The lecturer's soft voice put him at a disadvantage in the large hall.*
Word Family **disadvantage** *verb*;
disadvantaged *adjective* placed in unfavourable or poor circumstances: *disadvantaged children;* **disadvantageous** (diss-ad-van-**tay**-jus) *adjective* unfavourable.

disaffected *adjective*
having become discontented or disloyal.
Word Family **disaffection** *noun*.

disagree (diss-a-**gree**) *verb* (**disagrees; disagreeing; disagreed**)
to have a different opinion or view: *I must disagree with what you said.*
Phrase **disagree with** *Rich food disagrees with my stomach* (= upsets).
Word Family **disagreement** *noun* 1 the act of disagreeing. 2 an argument.

disagreeable *adjective*
unpleasant or offensive.
Word Family **disagreeably** *adverb*.

disallow *verb*
to refuse to allow or accept.
Word Family **disallowance** *noun*

disappear *verb*
to go out of sight: *My gloves have disappeared from the sideboard.*
Word Family **disappearance** *noun*.

disappoint *verb*
1 to fail to be equal to what is expected or hoped for: *The film disappointed me.*
2 to make unhappy: *We were disappointed that you couldn't come.*
Word Family **disappointing** *adjective* causing disappointment: *a very disappointing piece of work;*
disappointingly *adverb*; **disappointment** *noun* 1 the state of being disappointed: *Our disappointment at the result was enormous.*
2 anything which disappoints: *His exam results were a disappointment.*

disapprobation (diss-ap-ro-**bay**-sh'n) *noun*
(*formal*) disapproval.

disapprove (diss-a-**proov**) *verb*
to have or show an unfavourable opinion: *The family disapproves of his new group of friends.*
Word Family **disapproval** *noun* the act or a feeling of disapproving;
disapproving *adjective*; **disapprovingly** *adverb*.

disarm *verb*
1 to take away weapons or the means of attack: *Police disarmed the two men.*
2 to overcome the suspicions, hostility, etc. of: *Her frankness disarmed the reporters.*
Word Family **disarming** *adjective* tending to charm or win over: *his disarming smile*; **disarmingly** *adverb.*

disarmament *noun*
the limiting of the number of military forces and equipment.

disarrange *verb*
to disturb the order or arrangement of: *The strong wind had disarranged her hair.*
Word Family **disarrangement** *noun.*

disarray *noun*
a confusion or lack of order.
Word Family **disarray** *verb.*

disassembly *noun*
taking a product apart to see how it is made.

disassociate (diss-a-**so**-see-ate) *verb*
to dissociate.

disaster (di-**zah**-sta) *noun*
a very unfortunate accident or event.
Word Family **disastrous** *adjective* causing ruin or disaster; **disastrously** *adverb.*
[*dis-* + Italian *astro* a lucky star]

disavow *verb*
to deny or reject responsibility, etc. for.
Word Family **disavowal** *noun.*

disband *verb*
(of a group) to break up or separate: *The gang disbanded as soon as they had the money.*

disbelief (diss-be-**leef**) *noun*
a refusal or inability to believe.
Word Family **disbelieve** *verb.*

disburden *verb*
to relieve of or remove a burden.

disburse *verb*
to pay out.
Word Family **disbursement** *noun*
1 the act of paying out: *The disbursement of committee funds must be controlled.* **2** the money paid: *This month's miscellaneous disbursements total £247.*
[*dis-* + Medieval Latin *bursa* purse]

disc *noun* (*American* **disk**)
1 any flat round object or part, such as a coin or the rings of cartilage in the vertebral column.
2 a record or compact disc.
3 *Computers* ⇨ DISK (definition 1).
[Greek *diskos*]

Disc is an example of a word with alternative spellings. In English, spelling is usually standardized, but this is not always the case. In the case of *disc* and *disk*, *disc* is the usual British form and *disk* the American form. When applied to computers, however, *disk* is the more common spelling, as in *floppy disk*, but *disc* is also found, as in *compact disc read-only memory* (CD-ROM).

discard (diss-**kard**) *verb*
to put or throw away: *Discard all bruised or damaged fruit before cooking.*
● **discard** (**diss**-kard) *noun*
1 the act of discarding.
2 anything which is discarded.

disc brake *noun*
a type of brake consisting of a flat metal disc which is gripped by pads, used in motor vehicles and the undercarriages of aircraft.

discern (diss-**ern**) *verb*
1 to see or recognize clearly: *Our mother discerned from our silence that we were angry.*
2 to discriminate or judge between.
Word Family **discerning** *adjective* perceptive or discriminating: *a discerning knowledge of wine*; **discerningly** *adverb*; **discernment** *noun*; **discernible** *adjective* able to be seen or recognized; **discernibly** *adverb.*
[*dis-* + Latin *cernere* to separate]

discharge (diss-**charj**) *verb*
1 to relieve of a load, duty, etc.: *The injured soldier was discharged from all combat duties.*
2 to send out or away: *to be discharged from hospital.*
3 to pay: *The company has now discharged all its debts.*
4 to release: *The factory discharges its waste into the sea.*
5 to dismiss: *The driver was discharged for stealing.*
6 *Electronics* to remove or reduce an electric charge.
● **discharge** (**diss**-charj) *noun*
1 the act of discharging.
2 a person or thing that is discharged.

disciple (di-**sigh**-p'l) *noun*
a follower, companion or student: *the disciples of Christ.*
Word Family **discipleship** *noun.*
[Latin *discipulus* a learner]

discipline (**diss**-a-plin) *noun*
1 the establishing of correct order and behaviour with rules, training, etc.: *There* not enough discipline in this class.

2 the methods used to establish correct order, such as rules, instruction, punishment, etc.: *More discipline will be used in future.*

3 a branch or subject of learning, etc.: *The science disciplines are not taught at this college.*

• **discipline** *verb* to use discipline on.
Word Family discipline (**diss**-a-plin-ree) *adjective* of or promoting discipline; **disciplinarian** (diss-a-plin-**air**-i-an) *noun* a person who uses or encourages firm discipline.
[Latin *disciplina* training]

disc jockey *noun*
a person who introduces and plays pop records on radio programmes or at a nightclub.

disclaim *verb*
to deny connection or a claim to: *He has disclaimed the inheritance for personal reasons.*
Word Family disclaimer *noun* a statement which disclaims.

disclose (diss-**kloze**) *verb*
to allow to be seen or known. *The solicitor disclosed the contents of the will after the funeral.*
Word Family disclosure (diss-**klo**-zha) *noun.*

disco *noun*
1 a dance or party with a disc jockey, recorded pop music and often special lighting effects.
2 a club where such a dance is held.
3 the equipment and operator that provide the music for such a dance.
[discotheque]

discolour *verb* (*American* **discolor**)
to change or spoil the colour of: *Her dress was discoloured by stains.*
Word Family discoloration (diss-kull-a-**ray**-sh'n) *noun.*

discomfit (diss-**kum**-fit) *verb*
to frustrate, defeat or humiliate.
Word Family discomfiture (diss-**kum**-fi-cher) *noun.*

discomfort (diss-**kum**-f't) *noun*
a lack of comfort or peace: *The crowded bus caused them great discomfort.*

discompose *verb*
to disturb the calmness of: *The shouting audience discomposed the actors.*
Word Family discomposure (diss-kom-**po**-zha) *noun* the state of being discomposed.

disconcert (diss-kon-**sert**) *verb*
to upset or perturb: *She was disconcerted by the family's silent stares.*
Word Family disconcerted *adjective*; **disconcerting** *adjective*; **disconcertingly** *adverb.*

disconnect *verb*
to take apart or detach: *The electricity was disconnected because we did not pay the bill.*
Word Family disconnected *adjective*
1 not connected. 2 having unrelated parts: *The disconnected film was very difficult to follow;* **disconnection** *noun.*

disconsolate (diss-kon-sa-lit) *adjective*
unhappy and unable to be comforted.
Word Family disconsolately *adverb*; **disconsolation** (diss-kon-sa-**lay**-sh'n) *noun.*

discontent *noun* also **discontentment**
a lack of contentment or satisfaction.
Word Family discontented *adjective*; **discontentedly** *adverb.*

discontinue (diss-kon-**tin**-yoo) *verb*
to end or cause to end.
Word Family discontinuation (diss-kon-tin-yoo-**ay**-sh'n) *noun.*

discontinuous (diss-kon-**tin**-yoo-us) *adjective*
interrupted or not continuous.
Word Family discontinuously *adverb*; **discontinuity** (diss-kon-ti-**new**-it-ee) *noun.*

discord (**diss**-kawd) *noun*
1 a disagreement or difference of opinion.
2 any arguments or fighting caused by this.
3 lack of harmony: *The audience flinched at the discord in the symphony.*
Word Family discordant (diss-**kawd**-'nt) *adjective* lacking agreement or harmony: *Their discordant political opinions lead to many arguments;* **discordantly** *adverb*; **discordance** *noun.*
[*dis* + Latin *cordis* of the heart]

discotheque (**diss**-ko-tek) *noun*
a place for dancing, usually to recorded music.
[French, record library]

discount (**diss**-count) *noun*
a reduction in price: *A discount is available for cash purchases.*
• **discount** (diss-**count**) *verb*
1 to reduce the price of something, often by a set amount or percentage.
2 to ignore or refuse to believe: *You should not discount all the rumours that you hear.*
Word Family discounter *noun.*

discourage (diss-**kurr**-ij) *verb*
to take away the hope or confidence of:
Don't be discouraged by their criticisms.
Word Family **discouraging** *adjective*;
discouragingly *adverb*; **discouragement**
noun.

discourse (**diss**-korse) *noun*
a lecture, speech or discussion, especially a
formal one.
• **discourse** (diss-**korse**) *verb* to talk or
discuss.
[Latin *discursus* a running to and fro]

discourteous (diss-**ker**-ti-us) *adjective*
not polite.
Word Family **discourtesy** *noun* (*plural*
discourtesies).

discover *verb*
1 to find out or realize something not
known before.
2 to find: *I have discovered a new cake shop.*
Word Family **discovery** *noun* (*plural*
discoveries) 1 the act of discovering.
2 anything which is discovered;
discoverer *noun* a person who has
discovered something.

discredit *verb*
to destroy confidence in: *The author's
theory was discredited by leading economists.*
Word Family **discredit** *noun*;
discreditable *adjective* causing discredit
or disgrace: *His discreditable behaviour
angered his family*; **discreditably** *adverb.*

discreet *adjective*
tactful and careful to avoid mistakes,
embarrassment, etc.
Word Family **discreetly** *adverb*;
discreetness *noun.*
[Latin *discretus* discerned]

> **!** The words *discreet* and *discrete*
> sound the same but have different
> spellings and meanings. *Discreet* means
> 'tactful', as in *a discreet reminder*; *discrete*
> is a less common word meaning
> 'separate'.

discrepancy (diss-**krepp**-'n-see) *noun*
(*plural* **discrepancies**)
a lack of consistency or agreement.
Word Family **discrepant** *adjective.*
[Latin *discrepans* out of tune]

discrete *adjective*
1 separate.
2 having many or separate parts.
Word Family **discretely** *adverb*;
discreteness *noun.*
[Latin *discretus* separated]

> **!** Do not confuse *discrete* with
> DISCREET.

discretion (diss-**kresh**-'n) *noun*
1 the quality of being discreet: *We would
appreciate your discretion in this matter.*
2 the freedom to act or decide for oneself.
Phrase **at one's discretion** *You may
decide the price at your discretion* (= as you
wish).
Word Family **discretionary** *adjective.*

discriminate (diss-**krimm**-i-nate) *verb*
to notice, indicate or treat with a
difference: *That company discriminates
against its female employees.*
Word Family **discriminating** *adjective*
showing good taste or judgement;
discrimination *noun* (diss-krimm-i-
nay-sh'n) 1 the act of discriminating.
2 good judgement; **discriminatory**,
discriminative *adjective* indicating
differences.
[Latin *discriminis* of a dividing line]

discursive (diss-**ker**-siv) *adjective*
1 passing irregularly from one point or
subject to another.
2 based on reasoning: *a discursive
argument.*
[Latin *discursus* a running to and fro]

discus (**disk**-us) *noun* (*plural* **discuses**)
1 *Athletics* a disc-shaped wooden plate
thrown in competitions.
2 *Athletics* the contest in which it is
thrown.
[Greek]

discuss (diss-**kuss**) *verb*
1 to speak about together and exchange
opinions: *We must discuss the idea in detail.*
2 to argue for and against: *Discuss this
question in an essay.*
Word Family **discussion** (diss-**kush**-'n)
noun a talk to exchange opinions or views.

disdain *verb*
to regard or treat with scorn: *He disdained
their offer of help.*
Word Family **disdain** *noun*; **disdainful**
adjective; **disdainfully** *adverb.*
[*dis-* + Latin *dignus* worthy]

disease (diz-**eez**) *noun*
an unhealthy state of all or part of a body.
Word Family **diseased** *adjective* affected
by disease.
[*dis-* + French *aise* ease]

disembark (diss-em-**bark**) *verb*
to go or put ashore from a ship or aircraft.
Word Family **disembarkation** (diss-em-
bar-**kay**-sh'n) *noun.*

disembodied *adjective*
separated from the body.

disembowel *verb* (**disembowels;
disembowelling; disembowelled**)
to remove the bowels or intestines.

disempower *verb*
to deprive of power.

disenchant (diss-en-**chahnt**) *verb*
to cause to lose illusions or beliefs: *The
country family soon became disenchanted
with city life.*
Word Family **disenchantment** *noun.*

disencumber *verb*
to free from a burden or hindrance.

disenfranchise (diss-en-**fran**-chize) *verb*
also **disfranchise**
to take away a person's rights of
citizenship, especially the right to vote.
Word Family **disenfranchisement**
noun.

disengage *verb*
1 to release or unfasten.
2 to stop fighting: *The troops disengaged and
returned to camp.*
Word Family **disengagement** *noun.*

disentangle *verb*
to clear or make free of tangles: *It was
difficult to disentangle sense from nonsense in
the poem.*
Word Family **disentanglement** *noun.*

disfavour *noun* (*American* **disfavor**)
disapproval.

disfigure (diss-**fig**-a) *verb*
to spoil the appearance, shape or effect of.
Word Family **disfigurement** *noun.*

disgorge (diss-**gorj**) *verb*
to emit or eject, as if from the throat:
*The train disgorged its passengers onto the
platform*

disgrace *noun*
1 a loss of favour, approval or respect:
*You are in disgrace with the whole family for
telling such a lie.*
2 anything which causes disgrace or
reproach: *This untidy room is an absolute
disgrace!*
Word Family **disgrace** *verb*; **disgraceful**
adjective bringing disgrace; **disgracefully**
adverb.

disgruntled *adjective*
displeased or in a bad mood.

disguise (diss-**gize**) *verb*
to change the appearance of something in
order to conceal its identity, true nature,
etc.
Word Family **disguise** *noun.*

disgust *noun*
a strong feeling of dislike.

• **disgust** *verb* to cause disgust in.
Word Family **disgusted** *adjective*;
disgustedly *adverb*; **disgusting** *adjective*
causing disgust; **disgustingly** *adverb* to a
disgusting degree.
[*dis-* + Latin *gustare* to taste]

dish *noun* (*plural* **dishes**)
1 a shallow flat-bottomed vessel from
which food may be served or eaten.
2 anything shaped like this.
3 a particular kind or preparation of food:
*My favourite dish is roast chicken with
vegetables.*
4 (*informal*) an attractive person.
5 a satellite dish.
• **dish** *verb*
Phrases **dish out, dish up** to serve or
distribute.
Word Family **dished** *adjective* concave.

disharmony (diss-**har**-ma-nee) *noun*
a lack of harmony.
Word Family **disharmonious** (diss-har-
mo-nee-us) *adjective.*

dishearten (diss-**har**-t'n) *verb*
to discourage: *He was disheartened by the
slow progress of his work.*
Word Family **disheartening** *adjective*;
dishearteningly *adverb.*

dishevelled (di-**shev**-'ld) *adjective*
(of the clothes or hair) untidy, unkempt or
disarranged.
Word Family **dishevel** *verb* (**dishevels;
dishevelling; dishevelled**) *verb.*
[*dis-* + Old French *chevel* hair]

dishonest (diss-**onn** ist) *adjective*
not honest.
Word Family **dishonestly** *adverb*;
dishonesty *noun.*

dishonour (diss-**onn** a) *noun* (*American*
dishonor)
1 a loss of honour or reputation: *His
actions brought dishonour upon his family.*
2 a person or thing that causes dishonour:
He was a dishonour to his battalion.
• **dishonour** *verb*
1 to bring dishonour on or to.
2 *Commerce* to refuse to honour a cheque,
bank draft, etc.
Word Family **dishonourable** *adjective*;
dishonourably *adverb.*

dishy *adjective* (**dishier; dishiest**)
(*informal*) very attractive.

disillusion (diss-a-**loo**-*zh*'n) *verb*
to disenchant or make aware of unpleasant
realities.
Word Family **disillusionment** *noun.*

disincentive (diss-in-**sen**-tiv) *noun*
something which discourages effort, such
as low wages.

disincline (diss-in-**kline**) *verb*
to make or be reluctant: *I felt disinclined to
argue with him over such a small matter.*
Word Family **disinclination** (diss-in-
kla-**nay**-sh'n) *noun*.

disinfect *verb*
to destroy all the bacteria in or on
something.
Word Family **disinfectant** *noun* any
chemical which destroys bacteria;
disinfection *noun*.

disinformation *noun*
deliberately misleading information.

disingenuous (diss-in-**jen**-yew-us)
pretending to be less artful, or more
candid, than one is.
Word Family **disingenuously** *adverb*.

disinherit (diss-in-**herr**-it) *verb*
to exclude an heir from an inheritance.

disintegrate (diss-**in**-ti-grate) *verb*
1 to break into fragments.
2 to lose unity or cohesion.
Word Family **disintegration** (diss-in-ti-
gray-sh'n) *noun* 1 the act or process of
disintegrating: *Beneath the glacier the rocks
underwent a slow disintegration.* 2 the state
of being disintegrated.

disinter (diss-in-**ter**) *verb* (**disinters;
disinterring; disinterred**)
to dig up something buried, especially a
corpse: *The body was disinterred for
examination by the coroner.*
Word Family **disinterment** *noun*.

disinterested *adjective*
unaffected by personal interest,
involvement or advantage: *a disinterested
judge.*
Word Family **disinterestedly** *adverb*;
disinterestedness *noun*; **disinterest**
noun a lack of interest or concern.

> ⚠ Both *disinterested* and *uninterested*
> refer to a lack of interest, but
> *disinterested* describes impartiality or
> absence of selfishness, whereas
> *uninterested* suggests merely indifference
> or lack of sympathy.

disjointed *adjective*
disconnected or incoherent.
Word Family **disjointedly** *adverb*;
disjointedness *noun*.

disjunctive *adjective*
serving to disconnect or separate.
[*dis-* + Latin *junctus* joined]

disk *noun*
1 also **disc** *Computers* a thin cicular
magnetic plate used for storing data or
programs. ⇨ FLOPPY DISK; HARD DISK.
2 *American* a disc.

> On the spellings *disc* and *disk* ⇨ DISC.

disk drive *noun*
the part of a computer which allows
it to read information from and store
information on a disk.

diskette *noun*
Computers a floppy disk.

dislike *verb*
to have no liking for.
Word Family **dislike** *noun*; **dislikable,
dislikeable** *adjective*.

dislocate (**diss**-la-kate) *verb*
to put something out of the proper place
or position, e.g. two bones forming a joint.
Word Family **dislocation** (diss-la-**kay**-
sh'n) *noun* 1 the act of dislocating. 2 the
state of being dislocated. 3 *Geography* a
fault.

dislodge *verb*
to move or force out of place or position.
Word Family **dislodgement** *noun*.

disloyal *adjective*
not loyal.
Word Family **disloyally** *adverb*;
disloyalty *noun*.

dismal (**diz**-m'l) *adjective*
gloomy or melancholy: *What dismal
weather!*
Word Family **dismally** *adverb*.
[Latin *dies mali* unlucky days]

dismantle *verb*
1 to take to pieces: *We had to dismantle the
engine to inspect the crankshaft bearings.*
2 to strip of fittings, apparatus, etc.: *The
old warship was dismantled as part of its
conversion to a transport vessel.*
[*dis-* + MANTLE]

dismay *noun*
a feeling of fear or hopelessness.
• **dismay** *verb* to fill with dismay.

dismember *verb*
to tear or cut the limbs from.
*Figurative The conquering powers
dismembered the defeated country* (= divided
into parts).
Word Family **dismemberment** *noun*.

dismiss *verb*
1 to send away or allow to leave: *to dismiss
a class.*

2 to remove: *He was dismissed from the police force for taking bribes.*
3 to reject: *He dismissed the idea as a complete waste of time.*
4 *Cricket* to get out: *The fast bowler dismissed the batsman for five runs.*
Word Family dismissal *noun* 1 the act of dismissing. 2 the state of being dismissed. 3 a spoken or written order of discharge; **dismissive** *adjective* expressing contempt or dismissal; **dismissively** *adverb.*
[*dis-* + Latin *missus* sent]

dismount *verb*
1 to get down from a horse, bicycle, etc.: *She dismounted to open the gate.*
2 to remove: *The gun was dismounted from the guncarriage.*
3 to knock off a horse: *The knight was dismounted by a powerful blow of the lance.*

disobey (diss-o-**bay**) *verb*
to fail or refuse to obey.
Word Family disobedient (diss-a-bee-di-ent) *adjective;* **disobediently** *adverb;* **disobedience** *noun.*

disoblige *verb*
to fail or refuse to oblige.
Word Family disobliging *adjective.*

disorder *noun*
1 a lack of order or arrangement.
2 an ailment: *He suffered for years from a variety of stomach disorders.*
3 a riot: *Troops were finally called in to put down the disorders in the capital.*
Word Family disorder *verb;* **disorderly** *adverb;* **disorderliness** *noun.*

disorganize, disorganise *verb*
to upset the organization of: *The heavy snowfall disorganized public transport services.*
Word Family disorganized *adjective* lacking organization: *His work is completely disorganized;* **disorganization** (diss-or-gan-eye-**zay**-sh'n) *noun.*

disorientate (diss-**aw**-ri-en-tate) *verb* also **disorient** (diss-**aw**-ri-ent)
to confuse, especially about direction.
Word Family disorientated *adjective;* **disorientation** (diss-awr-i-en-**tay**-sh'n) *noun.*

disown *verb*
to refuse to acknowledge as one's own: *After his wild pranks at college the family disowned him completely.*

disparage (diss-**parr**-ij) *verb*
to belittle or treat slightingly: *The modest girl disparaged her own abilities.*

Word Family disparaging *adjective;* **disparagingly** *adverb;* **disparagement** *noun.*

disparate (diss-pa-rit) *adjective*
basically unlike or different.
Word Family disparity (diss-**parr**-a-tee) *noun* (*plural* **disparities**) a lack of equality or similarity.
[Latin *dispar* unequal]

dispassionate (diss-**pash**-a-nit) *adjective*
free from emotion or bias.
Word Family dispassionately *adverb.*

dispatch *verb* also **despatch**
1 to send off: *Dispatch this urgent telegram immediately.*
2 to kill: *The gladiator dispatched his opponent.*
3 to transact or finish: *Their business was quickly dispatched.*
● **dispatch** *noun* (*plural* **dispatches**)
1 the act of dispatching: *Please speed up the mail dispatch.*
2 efficiency or promptness: *He completed the task with dispatch, and was back for more work.*
3 a service or a means by which messages or goods are sent speedily: *He sent the urgent message by special dispatch.*
4 a story sent in by a media reporter.
5 an official communication carried by special messenger, e.g. between officers of an army.
[Italian *dispacciare* to hasten]

dispel (diss-**pel**) *verb* (**dispels; dispelling; dispelled**)
to drive off or scatter: *The clear sky dispelled all fears of rain.*
[Latin *dispellere* to drive apart]

dispense *verb*
1 to deal out or distribute: *He dispensed money to the poor.*
2 to mix, prepare and give out medicines, etc., e.g. on prescription.
Phrase **dispense with** to do without or do away with.
Word Family dispensation (diss-pen-**say**-sh'n) *noun* 1 the act of dispensing: *Law courts supervise the dispensation of justice.* 2 something dispensed: *money and other charitable dispensations.* 3 a management or system. 4 *Roman Catholicism* the removal or relaxation of a law, penalty, etc.; **dispensable** *adjective* able to be done without; **dispensary** *noun* (*plural* **dispensaries**) a place where something such as medicine is dispensed; **dispenser** *noun* a machine or device which dispenses: *a cash dispenser.*
[Latin *dispensare* to pay out]

disperse *verb*
1 to scatter: *The demonstrators dispersed when the police charged the crowd.*
2 to drive away: *The sun dispersed the morning mists.*
3 to spread: *Knowledge of how to use iron took a long time to disperse throughout Europe.*
[*di-* + Latin *spargere* to scatter]

dispersion (diss-**per**-sh'n) *noun* also **dispersal**
1 the act of dispersing.
2 the state of being dispersed.

dispirited *adjective*
depressed or disheartened.
Word Family **dispiritedly** *adverb*; **dispiritedness** *noun*; **dispiriting** *adjective*; **dispiritingly** *adverb*; **dispirit** *verb*.

displace *verb*
1 to put out of its usual place: *He had displaced his shoulder bone.*
Figurative After the scandal about police corruption several senior police officers were displaced from positions of high authority (= removed).
2 to take the place of: *Bob has displaced Rick in Ellen's affections.*

displaced person *noun* (*plural* **displaced persons**)
a person forced to leave his or her own country, such as a refugee.

displacement *noun*
1 the act of displacing.
2 the state of being displaced.
3 the weight of water displaced by a ship: *a liner of 25 000 tonnes' displacement.*

displacement reaction *noun*
Chemistry a chemical reaction in which one atom, ion or molecule replaces another.

display *verb*
to show: *to display fear.* □ *to display goods in a shop window.*
● **display** *noun*.
[*dis-* + Latin *plicare* to fold]

displease *verb*
to offend or cause dissatisfaction.
Word Family **displeased** *adjective*; **displeasing** *adjective*; **displeasure** (dis-**plezh**-a) *noun*.

disport *verb*
Phrase **disport oneself** to divert or amuse oneself.

disposal *noun*
the act of disposing: *rubbish disposal.*
Phrase **at one's disposal** under one's control or direction.

dispose (diss-**poze**) *verb*
1 to make willing: *The high salary disposed her to accept the job.*
2 to make susceptible: *His weak constitution disposes him to illness.*
3 to put in a certain order or arrangement: *The troops were disposed in ranks.*
Phrase **dispose of** to get rid of or part with.
Word Family **disposable** *adjective* able to be disposed of.
[Latin *dispositum* distributed]

disposition (diss-pa-**zish**-'n) *noun*
1 a person's natural way of acting or thinking: *He has a cheerful disposition.*
2 a tendency or inclination: *He has a disposition to argue when drunk.*
3 the act of putting in order or position: *The general supervised the disposition of his troops on the battlefield.*

dispossess (diss-pa-**zess**) *verb*
to deprive of possession: *The settlers dispossessed the original inhabitants of their land.* □ *Rage dispossessed him of his senses.*
Word Family **dispossession** (diss-pa-**zesh**-'n) *noun*.

disproportionate (diss-pra-**por**-sh'n-ate) *adjective* also **disproportional**
lacking in proportion.
Word Family **disproportion** *noun*; **disproportionately** *adverb*.

disprove (diss-**proov**) *verb*
to prove to be false or wrong.

dispute *verb*
1 to argue, quarrel or debate.
2 to question the truth or validity of: *He disputed her account of the incident.*
Word Family **dispute** *noun*; **disputable** *adjective*; **disputant** *noun* a person who disputes; **disputation** (diss-pew-**tay**-sh'n) *noun* the act of disputing.
[Latin *disputare* to discuss]

disqualify (diss-**kwoll**-i-fie) *verb* (**disqualifies; disqualifying; disqualified**)
1 to make unsuitable for or unable to do something: *His poor eyesight disqualified him from military service.*
2 to deprive of the right to compete in a contest.
Word Family **disqualification** (diss-kwoll-i-fi-**kay**-sh'n) *noun*.

disquiet *verb*
to make anxious or uneasy.
Word Family **disquiet, disquietude** *noun*; **disquieting** *adjective* causing disquiet.

disregard *verb*
to pay no attention to.
Word Family **disregard** *noun* a lack of attention or regard.

disrepair *noun*
the state of needing repair.

disreputable (diss-**rep**-yew-ta-b'l) *adjective*
1 having a bad reputation: *He haunts disreputable nightclubs.*
2 not respectable in appearance: *She wore a disreputable old coat.*
Word Family **disreputably** *adverb*; **disrepute** (diss-ri-**pewt**) *noun* the condition of being disreputable.

disrespect *noun*
a lack of respect.
Word Family **disrespectful** *adjective*; **disrespectfully** *adverb*.

disrobe *verb*
to undress: *The bishop disrobed after the coronation ceremony.*

disrupt *verb*
to break up or throw into confusion: *The hecklers succeeded in disrupting the meeting.*
Word Family **disruptive** *adjective* tending to disrupt; **disruption** (diss-**rup**-sh'n) *noun*.
[*dis-* + Latin *ruptus* broken]

diss ⇨ DIS.

dissatisfy *verb* (**dissatisfies; dissatisfying; dissatisfied**)
to make discontented or fail to satisfy; *He was dissatisfied with his salary.*
Word Family **dissatisfaction** (diss-sat-iss-**fak**-sh'n) *noun*.

dissect (die-**sekt**) *verb*
to cut an organism apart to examine its structure.
Figurative The barrister dissected the evidence (= examined carefully).
Word Family **dissection** *noun* 1 the act of dissecting. 2 the state of being dissected. 3 something which has been dissected.
[Latin *dissectus* cut up]

dissemble *verb*
1 to disguise or hide one's real feelings, thoughts, etc.: *She dissembled her rage with a sweet smile.*
2 to feign or pretend: *The bored party guest dissembled gaiety.*

Word Family **dissembler** *noun*.
[*dis-* + Latin *simulare* to imitate]

disseminate *verb*
to scatter or spread widely: *The news was quickly disseminated by radio.*
Word Family **dissemination** (de-semm-i-**nay**-sh'n) *noun*.
[*dis-* + Latin *seminare* to sow]

dissension (diss-**en**-sh'n) *noun*
angry quarrelling or disagreement.

dissent *verb*
1 to differ in opinion: *One jury member dissented from the opinion of his fellow jurors.*
2 *Religion* to refuse to conform to the rules or beliefs of an established church.
Word Family **dissent** *noun*; **dissentient** (diss-**en**-sh'nt) *adjective* differing from the general opinion; **dissenter** *noun*.
[*dis-* + Latin *sentiri* to feel]

dissertation (diss-a-**tay**-sh'n) *noun*
1 a long essay or thesis.
2 a formal speech.

disservice *noun*
any harmful or unhelpful action: *to do someone a disservice.*

dissidence (**diss**-i-d'nce) *noun*
any disagreement.
Word Family **dissident** *adjective* differing; **dissident** *noun* a person who disagrees.
[Latin *dissidere* to sit apart]

dissimilar *adjective*
unlike or different.
Word Family **dissimilarity** (di-simm-i-**larr**-i-tee) *noun* (*plural* **dissimilarities**); **dissimilarly** *adverb*.

dissimulate (di-**sim**-yoo-late) *verb*
to disguise or hide under a pretence.
Word Family **dissimulation** (de-sim-yoo-**lay**-sh'n) *noun*; **dissimulator** *noun*.

dissipate (**diss**-i-pate) *verb*
1 to disperse: *I tried to dissipate the child's fear of the dark.*
2 to waste foolishly or fritter away: *He dissipated his energies in a frantic attempt to do everything at once.*
Word Family **dissipated** *adjective*; **dissipation** (diss-i-**pay**-sh'n) *noun* 1 the act of dissipating. 2 a dissolute way of life.
[Latin *dissipare* to scatter]

dissociate (di-**so**-see-ate) *verb* also **disassociate**
to separate from or not associate with: *We don't agree with you and dissociate ourselves from your comments.*

Word Family **dissociation** (di-so-see-ay-sh'n) *noun* **1** the act of dissociating. **2** the state of being dissociated.

dissoluble (di-**sol**-yew-b'l) *adjective*
capable of being dissolved.
Word Family **dissolubility** (di-sol-yew-**bill**-it-ee) *noun*.

dissolute (**diss**-a-loot) *adjective*
debauched or sexually unrestrained.
Word Family **dissoluteness** *noun*;
dissolutely *adverb*.
[Latin *dissolutus* lax]

dissolve (di-**zolv**) *verb*
1 *Chemistry* to enter into solution.
2 to bring to or come to an end: *to dissolve a marriage.* □ *to dissolve parliament.*
Figurative The figure dissolved into the mist (= disappeared gradually).
Phrase **dissolve into tears** to be overcome by emotion and begin to cry.
Word Family **dissolution** (diss-a-**loo**-sh'n) *noun* **1** the act of dissolving: *The election defeat caused the dissolution of parliament.* **2** the state of being dissolved: *Parliament was soon in dissolution.*
[Latin *dissolvere* to unloose]

dissonance (**diss**-a-nance) *noun*
a discord or disagreement, especially of sounds.
Word Family **dissonant** *adjective*;
dissonantly *adverb*.
[*dis-* + Latin *sonus* sound]

dissuade (diss-**wade**) *verb*
to persuade against doing something: *The policeman finally dissuaded the young man from jumping off the roof.*
Word Family **dissuasion** (diss-**way**-zh'n) *noun*.
[*dis-* + Latin *suadere* to persuade]

distaff (**diss**-tahf) *noun*
a part of a spinning wheel which holds the cotton or other raw material to be spun.

distaff side *noun*
the female branch of a family.

distal *adjective*
Anatomy being situated away from the point of origin or attachment: *Toenails are at the distal ends of toes.* Compare PROXIMAL.

distance *noun*
1 the extent of space or time between two points or things: *The distance from here to Bristol is about 500 km.* □ *a distance of 50 years.*
2 a long way away: *The dirty city looked quite pleasant from a distance.*

Phrase **keep one's distance** to avoid familiarity.
● **distance** *verb* to put at a distance: *Try to distance yourself from your present troubles and look at them objectively.*

distance learning *noun*
a method of studying by correspondence, broadcasts and the Internet.

distant *adjective*
1 situated at a considerable distance: *The sun is distant from the earth.*
2 away: *We were headed for a village 3 km distant.*
3 not close: *A second cousin is a distant relative.*
4 reserved, not friendly: *My ex-girlfriend greeted me with a distant nod.*
Word Family **distantly** *adverb*.
[Latin *distans distantis* standing apart]

distaste *noun*
a dislike or aversion.
Word Family **distasteful** *adjective*;
distastefully *adverb*; **distastefulness** *noun*.

distemper[1] *noun*
an infectious viral disease in young dogs, which is often fatal.

distemper[2] *noun*
a type of paint in which powdered colours are mixed with gluey or starchy substances, used in interior decoration, etc.

distend (diss-**tend**) *verb*
to expand or swell: *Their bellies were distended by overeating.*
Word Family **distended** *adjective*;
distension *noun*.
[*dis-* + Latin *tendere* to stretch]

distil (diss-**til**) *verb* (**distils; distilling; distilled**)
1 to subject to distillation: *to distil water.*
2 to extract by means of distillation: *Petrol is distilled from crude oil.*
Figurative The jury must distil the truth from this mass of conflicting evidence (= extract).
[Latin *destillare* to drip down]

distillation (diss-ti-**lay**-sh'n) *noun*
Chemistry a process for purifying liquids, by which solid impurities are separated by boiling off the liquid and then cooling it in a separate condensing chamber. A mixture of liquids with different boiling points is separated out by **fractional distillation**.
Word Family **distillate** *noun* (**diss**-ti-late) **1** a distilled liquid. **2** diesel fuel, one of the fractions distilled from crude oil.

distillery *noun* (*plural* **distilleries**)
a place where alcoholic spirits are made.
Word Family **distiller** *noun* a person or
thing that distils.

distinct *adjective*
1 plain: *Outlines become more distinct when I
wear my glasses.*
2 definite: *She has recently shown a distinct
improvement in her work.*
3 different or separate: *Bats and birds
belong to two distinct species.* □ *You must keep
the two ideas distinct in your mind.*
Word Family **distinctly** *adverb*;
distinctness *noun*.
[Latin *distinctus* separated]

distinction *noun*
1 the act of distinguishing: *He makes no
distinction between rich and poor.*
2 a difference: *What is the distinction
between the two words?*
3 special favour or attention: *The prince
treated me with distinction all evening.*
4 renown: *Charles Dickens is a writer of
distinction.*
5 the highest honour awarded in an
examination at a university, etc.: *She got a
distinction in History.*
Word Family **distinctive** *adjective*
characteristic; **distinctively** *adverb*;
distinctiveness *noun*.

distinguish (diss-**ting**-gwish) *verb*
1 to recognize as being distinct or
different: *Fool's gold, which is really iron
pyrites, is difficult to distinguish from real
gold.*
2 to see or hear plainly: *From our seats at
the back of the theatre it was hard to
distinguish what the actors were saying.*
3 to make different or set apart: *The ability
to use language symbols distinguishes human
beings from animals.*
4 to make famous: *He distinguished himself
in the field of medical research.*
Word Family **distinguishable** *adjective*.
[Latin *distinguere* to separate]

distinguished *adjective*
1 famous or eminent.
2 having the appearance of an important
person: *Her distinguished air caused people to
treat her with great respect.*

distort *verb*
to pull or twist out of its usual shape: *Her
face was distorted with pain.*
Figurative His account distorted the truth
(= misrepresented).
Word Family **distorted** *adjective*;
distortion *noun* 1 the act of distorting.

2 the state of being distorted. 3 something
which is distorted.
[*dis-* + Latin *tortus* twisted]

distract *verb*
to divert the attention of: *The radio distracts
me from my work.*
Word Family **distracted** *adjective*
confused or greatly troubled in the mind;
distractedly *adverb*; **distracting**
adjective; **distraction** *noun* 1 the act of
distracting. 2 the state of being distracted:
*You'll drive her to distraction with your
behaviour.* 3 something which distracts:
The radio is a constant distraction.
[*dis-* + Latin *tractus* dragged]

distrain *verb*
Law to seize goods in payment of a debt.
Word Family **distraint** *noun* the seizure
of goods in order to obtain payment of a
debt.

distraught (diss-**trawt**) *adjective*
deeply upset or troubled in mind: *The
distraught woman kept tearing at her hair.*

distress *noun*
1 any acute or extreme suffering or
trouble: *His mother's death had caused him
great distress.*
2 serious difficulties or danger: *We picked
up the radio signals of a ship in distress.*
• **distress** *verb* to cause distress to.
Word Family **distressing** *adjective*;
distressingly *adverb*; **distressful** *adjective*
1 causing distress. 2 full of distress.

distribute (diss-**trib**-yoot) *verb*
1 to divide and share out: *The dying man
distributed all his goods among his children.*
2 to spread out: *The explosion distributed
wreckage over a wide area.*
3 to sort out or classify: *The results were
distributed into three main categories.*
Word Family **distribution** (diss-tri-bew
sh'n) *noun* 1 the act of distributing: *The
distribution of presents took a long time.*
2 the manner of being distributed. *We
studied the distribution of plants in the area.*
3 *Maths* the frequency of sets of values
in observations; **distributional,
distributive** *adjective*; **distributor** *noun*
1 a person or thing that distributes. 2 a
device in a petrol engine which directs the
surge of electricity from the coil to each
spark plug in the correct sequence.
[*dis-* + Latin *tribuere* to allot]

district *noun*
a region, especially one marked off for
administrative purposes, etc.

district nurse *noun*
a nurse who visits patients in their homes.

distrust *noun*
a lack of trust or confidence.
Word Family distrust *verb*; **distrustful** *adjective*; **distrustfully** *adverb*.

disturb *verb*
1 to break or destroy the peace, quiet or rest of: *The noise of fighting dogs disturbed the night.*
2 to put out of order, interfere with: *Who has disturbed the papers on my desk?*
3 to trouble: *He was deeply disturbed by news of his father's illness.*
4 to interrupt: *They came home early and disturbed an intruder in the house.*
Word Family disturbance *noun* 1 the act of disturbing. 2 the state of being disturbed. 3 anything which disturbs; **disturbing** *adjective*; **disturbingly** *adverb*.
[*dis-* + Latin *turba* an uproar]

disunity (diss-**yew**-ni-tee) *noun*
a lack of unity: *If there is disunity in the ranks, we shall fail.*
Word Family disunion *noun*; **disunite** (diss-yoo-**nite**) *verb*.

disuse (diss-**yooce**) *noun*
a lack of use or the state of not being used: *The door latch was rusted from disuse.*
• **disuse** (diss-**yooz**) *verb*.

ditch *noun* (*plural* **ditches**)
a long narrow trench dug in the earth.
• **ditch** *verb*
1 to land an aircraft in the sea in an emergency.
2 (*informal*) to get rid of: *The criminal ditched the stolen car.*

dither (**dith**-a) *verb*
to fuss about in a confused or indecisive way.
• **dither** *noun*.

ditto *noun*
a word or mark used in lists, etc. to indicate repetition of the same word or words.
• **ditto** *adverb* likewise.

> The word **ditto** comes to English from Italian, being a dialect form of *detto* (said). This, in turn, comes from Latin *dictus* (said), from *dicere* (to say) and was originally used in Italian to avoid repeating the month in dates. In English, *ditto* is used to avoid repetition of the details in lists and often appears as the symbol ".

ditty *noun* (*plural* **ditties**)
a short song.

diuretic (die-ya-**rett**-ik) *noun*
a drug which increases the amount of liquid urinated.
[*di-* + Greek *ouresis* urination]

diurnal (die-**er**-n'l) *adjective*
1 lasting one day.
2 of or belonging to the daytime: *A diurnal animal is awake during the day and sleeps at night.* Compare NOCTURNAL.
[Latin *diurnus* by day]

diva (**dee**-va) *noun*
a female opera singer ⇨ PRIMA DONNA.
[Italian, goddess]

Divali ⇨ DIWALI.

divan (di-**van**) *noun*
a low bed-like seat with no back or sides.
[Arabic *diwan* a bench, a court]

dive *verb*
1 to plunge head first, often from a height, into the water.
2 to go deeply under water: *She dives for pearls.*
Figurative *Share prices dived on the Stock Exchange* (= dropped sharply). □ *He dived into the bushes to avoid the car* (= leapt).
□ *He dived into his pocket and pulled out some money* (= reached quickly).
• **dive** *noun*
1 the act of diving.
2 (*informal*) a cheap disreputable place.
Word Family diver *noun* 1 a person or thing that dives e.g. a naval frogman.
2 any of a family of large birds that can swim under water.

dive-bomber *noun*
a military aeroplane which drops bombs while diving steeply towards its target.
Word Family dive-bomb *verb*.

diverge (die-**verj**) *verb*
to move apart or branch off in different directions: *The road and railway line diverge at the foot of the hill.* □ *Light rays diverge when they pass through a concave lens.*
Figurative *My brother-in-law and I diverge on many issues* (= disagree). □ *Let me diverge for a moment from my theme to tell a little story* (= digress).
Word Family divergent *adjective*; **divergence** *noun*.
[*di-* + Latin *vergere* to turn]

divers (**die**-verz) *adjective*
an old word meaning 'several' or 'various'.

diverse (die-**verse** *or* **die**-verse) *adjective*
of different kinds, forms, etc.: *The people at the meeting had very diverse backgrounds.*
Word Family diversity (die-**verse**-it-tee) *noun*; **diversely** *adverb*.
[Latin *diversus* different separate]

diversify (die-**verse**-i-fie) *verb*
(**diversifies; diversifying; diversified**)
to give variety or diversity to: *During her
medical course she had little time to diversify
her interests.* □ *The company chairman urged
the board to diversify investments.*
Word Family **diversification** (die-verse-
if-i-**kay**-sh'n) *noun.*

diversion (die-**ver**-*zh*'n) *noun*
1 the act of turning aside.
2 a detour.
3 an amusement or hobby: *For most people
chess is a diversion rather than a serious
study.*
4 *Military* a manoeuvre to draw the
enemy's attention away from the main
point of an attack.
Word Family **diversionary** *adjective.*

divert (die-**vert**) *verb*
1 to turn or cause to turn in another
direction: *to divert traffic.*
2 to turn from serious thought or activity,
especially by amusement.
Word Family **diverting** *adjective.*

divest (die-**vest**) *verb*
to strip or deprive of: *The new law divests
landowners of some of their privileges.*
[*di-* + Latin *vestire* to clothe]

divide *verb*
1 to separate into parts: *We divided the loot
into equal shares.*
Figurative Opinions divided over the issue
(– went different ways, were no longer
united)
2 *Maths* to calculate how many times one
number contains another: *Twelve divided
by four equals three.*
3 *Parliament* to vote on a question by
separating into two groups, for *and* against
the issue.
• **divide** *noun*
1 *Geography* a range of mountains
separating rivers flowing towards opposite
sides of a continent.
2 *Geography* a watershed.
Word Family **divider** *noun.*

dividend (**divv**-i-dend) *noun*
1 a share of something which has
been divided, such as money paid to
shareholders from a company's profits.
2 *Maths* ⇨ DIVISION (definition **6**).

divine (div-**vine**) *adjective*
1 of or relating to God or a god.
2 sacred.
3 (*informal*) wonderful or excellent: *She
said my dress was divine.*
• **divine** *noun Christianity* a theologian.

• **divine** *verb* to learn or discover by
intuition, inspiration or magic.
Word Family **divinely** *adverb;*
divination (divv-i-**nay**-sh'n) *noun* the
foretelling of events; **diviner** *noun.*

diving *noun*
the sport in which a person dives into the
water from a board, set at various heights,
often performing prescribed movements
while in the air.

divining rod ⇨ WATER DIVINER.

divinity (div-**vin**-i-tee) *noun* (*plural*
divinities)
1 the quality of being divine.
2 a divine being; a god.
3 the formal study of religion or scriptures.

divisible (div-**viz**-i-b'l) *adjective*
able to be divided: *21 is exactly divisible by 3.*
Word Family **divisibility** (div-izz-i-**bill**-
it-ee) *noun.*

division *noun*
1 the act of dividing.
2 the state of being divided: *The division of
opinions became obvious during the debate.*
3 any of the parts into which something is
divided: *He was sent to the spare parts
division of the factory.*
4 *Biology* one of the large groups used in
the classification of plants.
5 *Military* a tactical army unit consisting of
three or more brigades.
6 *Maths* the operation of dividing one
number (the **dividend**) by another (the
divisor) to obtain the quotient.
Word Family **divisional** *adjective.*

divisive (di-**vie**-siv) *adjective*
creating division or dissension.
Word Family **divisively** *adverb;*
divisiveness *noun.*

divisor (div-**vie**-zer) *noun*
Maths ⇨ DIVISION (definition **6**).

divorce (div-**vorse**) *noun*
1 *Law* the ending of a marriage by a court
decree.
2 any complete separation.
Word Family **divorce** *verb;* **divorcee**
(de-vor-**see**) *noun* a divorced person.
[Latin *divortium* separation]

divot (div-'t) *noun*
Sport a piece of turf cut out by the edge of
a club or bat as the player hits the ball.

divulge (die-**vulj**) *verb*
to disclose or reveal a secret, etc.: *The
official refused to divulge the information to
the press.*
Word Family **divulgence** *noun.*
[Latin *divulgare* to make publicly known]

divvy *noun* (*plural* **divvies**)
(*informal*) a stupid or inept person.

Diwali (di-**wah**-lee) *noun* also **Divali**
a festival of lights widely celebrated by
Sikhs and Hindus. For many Hindus it
marks the new year.
[Hindi]

dizzy *adjective* (**dizzier; dizziest**)
having or causing a sensation of spinning.
Figurative He was dizzy with success
(= overcome).
Word Family **dizziness** *noun*; **dizzily**
adverb.

djinn (jin) ⇨ JINN.

DNA *noun*
short form of **deoxyribonucleic acid**.

DNA fingerprinting ⇨ GENETIC
FINGERPRINTING.

do (doo) *verb*
(**I do; we, you, they do; he, she, it does;
doing; did; done;** *old forms:* thou **doest**
or **dost;** he, she, it **doeth** or **doth**)
1 to perform an action: *She still hasn't done
her homework.*
2 to attend to: *Who'll do the dusting?*
□ *Have you done your teeth?* □ *Mrs Jones is
doing the flowers for the wedding.*
3 used in questions: *Did you kill her?*
4 used in negatives: *I did not know her.*
5 used to emphasize a verb: *Do stop talking
nonsense.*
6 used as a substitute for a verb that has
already been used: *She looks even younger
now than she did* (= looked before).
7 to cause: *His attitude can do harm.*
8 to render: *The critics did justice to the play.*
9 to travel at: *The car will do 100 miles per
hour.*
10 to cover: *We did half the journey today.*
11 to make: *We are doing a film on camels.*
12 to study: *My sister does French at school.*
13 to cook: *The roast will be done soon.*
14 to solve: *Can you do this crossword?*
15 to be enough: *Will two sugars do?*
16 to work at: *What will you do when you
leave school?*
17 to manage: *How are you doing?*
18 (*informal*) to spoil or ruin: *You've really
done it this time.*
Phrases **could do with** *The house could do
with a coat of paint* (= needs, would benefit
from). **done for** (*informal*) dead or
doomed. **do or die** to make a great effort.
do out of (*informal*) *She was done out of the
job* (= cheated out of). **do up** *This house
needs doing up* (= renovating decorating).
● **do** *noun* (*plural* **dos** or **do's**)

1 something which should be done: *the
do's and don't's of social behaviour.*
2 (*informal*) a party or celebration.

dobbin *noun*
a horse, especially a patient plodding farm
horse.

docile (**doe**-sile) *adjective*
easily managed or led: *The wild colt was
broken and made docile.*
Word Family **docilely** *adverb*; **docility**
(doe-**sill**-i-tee) *noun*.
[Latin *docilis* easily taught]

dock¹ *noun*
1 a wharf.
2 a harbour with equipment for loading,
unloading or repairing ships.
● **dock** *verb*
1 to come or bring into a dock.
2 to lock spacecraft together while in orbit.
Word Family **dockage** *noun* the charge
for using a dock; **docker** *noun* a person
employed to work on the docks loading
and unloading ships etc.

dock² *noun*
the solid part of an animal's tail, as distinct
from the hair.
● **dock** *verb*
1 to cut off part of an animal's tail.
2 to deduct from: *to dock someone's
allowance.*

dock³ *noun*
Law the enclosure in a courtroom where
the accused person stands.
[Flemish *dok* a cage]

dock⁴ *noun*
a weed with green flowers and leaves that
may be used to relieve nettle stings.

docket *noun*
1 a label on a package listing contents, etc.
2 a receipt, especially for customs duties.

dockyard *noun*
a harbour where ships are built and
repaired.

Doc Martens *plural noun*
(*trademark*) a brand of sturdy high lace-up
boots with thick lightweight soles.

doctor *noun*
1 a person allowed by law to practise
medicine, or some branch of it.
2 a person who has received the highest
university degree, usually after several
years of research or study beyond a
bachelor's degree.
3 (**Doctor**) a title of respect for such
persons.
● **doctor** *verb*
1 to treat with medicines.

2 (*informal*) to tamper with or alter.
Word Family doctoral *adjective*;
doctorate *noun* the degree received by a doctor.
[Latin *teacher*]

doctrinaire *adjective*
1 dogmatic: *He shouts his views in a doctrinaire manner.*
2 theoretical: *doctrinaire socialism.*

doctrine (dok-trin) *noun*
a particular principle, belief or theory: *a religious doctrine.*
Word Family doctrinal (dok-**try**-n'l) *adjective*; **doctrinally** *adverb.*

docudrama (dok-yoo-dra-ma) *noun*
a film combining elements of drama and documentary.

document (dok-yoo-m'nt) *noun*
a written piece of information, evidence, etc.: *When you apply for a passport you must supply certain documents, such as a birth certificate.*
• **document** (dok-yoo-ment) *verb* to supply with or support by documents.
Word Family documentary (dok-yoo-**men**-tree) *noun* (*plural* **documentaries**)
a non-fiction film; **documentary** *adjective*; **documentation** (dok-yoo-men-**tay**-sh'n) *noun.*
[Latin *documentum* a lesson or example]

docusoap (dok-yoo-sope) *noun*
a television documentary following a group of people over a period of time.

dodder *verb*
to shake or totter.
Word Family doddery, doddering *adjective*; **dodderer** *noun.*

dodecahedron (doh-dek-a-hee-dr'n or doh-dek-a-hed-r'n) *noun* (*plural* **dodecahedrons** or **dodecahedra**)
a solid or hollow body with twelve pentagonal faces.
Word Family dodecahedral *adjective.*
[*dodeca-* + Greek *hedra* a base]

dodge *verb*
to move aside or change position suddenly, especially so as to avoid something: *Paul dodged when he saw the car coming towards him.*
Figurative The Mayor had no trouble in dodging the reporters' questions (= evading).
• **dodge** *noun*
1 the act of dodging.
2 (*informal*) a trick.
Word Family dodger *noun* (*informal*) a sly or tricky person.

dodgeball *noun*
(*especially American*) a game in which players try to hit each other with a large ball.

dodgem (doj-'m) *noun*
a small low-powered electric car driven in special rinks at amusement parks, etc.

dodgy *adjective* (**dodgier; dodgiest**)
(*informal*) risky or unsound.

dodo (doe-doe) *noun*
a large extinct flightless bird of Mauritius.
[Portuguese *doudo* silly]

doe *noun*
a female deer, rabbit, etc. Compare BUCK[1].

doer (doo-a) *noun*
a person of action.

does (duzz) the third person singular present tense of **do**.

doeskin (doe-skin) *noun*
1 a leather made from the skin of a doe.
2 a woollen fabric in a twill weave.

doesn't *contraction*
a short form of **does not**: *He doesn't like football.*

doest (doo-ist) an old form of the second person singular present tense of **do**.

doeth (doo-ith) an old form of the third person singular present tense of **do**.

doff *verb*
to take off: *He doffed his hat.*
[from *do off*]

dog *noun*
1 any of various breeds of four-legged flesh-eating mammals, either wild, such as the dingo, or domesticated, such as the poodle.
2 the male of this animal.
3 (*informal*) a despicable man.
4 (*dated*) a fellow: *a gay dog.*
5 (**dogs**) greyhound racing: *to have a bet on the dogs.*
Phrases dog in the manger a person who keeps something of no particular use to himself or herself so that others cannot use it. **go to the dogs** (*informal*) to go to ruin. **lead a dog's life** to have a harassed or unhappy existence. **let sleeping dogs lie** to leave a situation as it is.
• **dog** *verb* (**dogs; dogging; dogged**) to chase relentlessly.
Word Family doggish *adjective*; **doggishly** *adverb.*

dog collar *noun*
(*informal*) the reversed collar worn by members of the clergy.

dog days *plural noun*
the hottest days of the year, particularly
from early July to mid-August in the
Northern Hemisphere.
[thought by the Romans to coincide with
the period when the Dog Star rose with
the sun]

dog-ear *noun*
a creased corner of a page which has been
folded over like a dog's ear.
Word Family **dog-eared** *adjective.*

dogfight *noun*
a fierce fight between aircraft at close
range.

dogged (dogg-id) *adjective*
obstinate.
Word Family **doggedly** *adverb*;
doggedness *noun.*

doggerel *noun*
any poorly written verse with faulty rhyme
and rhythm.

doggo *adverb*
Phrase **lie doggo** to hide or remain in
concealment.

doggy *adjective* (**doggier; doggiest**)
of or resembling a dog.

dogma *noun*
any established opinion or system of
principles or beliefs, such as those laid
down by a church.
Word Family **dogmatic** (dog-**matt**-ik)
adjective stating opinions in a positive or
overbearing manner; **dogmatically**
adverb; **dogmatist** *noun* a dogmatic
person; **dogmatism** *noun*; **dogmatize,
dogmatise** *verb.*

dog-paddle *noun*
a simple swimming stroke in which the
swimmer paddles his or her arms and legs
below the surface of the water.

dogsbody *noun* (*plural* **dogsbodies**)
(*informal*) a drudge.

dog's breakfast *noun*
(*informal*) a mess.

dog-tired *adjective*
extremely tired.

dogwatch *noun* (*plural* **dogwatches**)
Nautical either of the two short, two-hour
watches (4–6 p.m. and 6–8 p.m.).

doh *noun*
Music the spoken name for the first note in
the scale. The notes in ascending order
are: **doh, ray, me, fah, soh, lah, te, doh.**

doily *noun* (*plural* **doilies**)
a small decorative napkin made of paper,
lace, etc. placed under objects on a shelf,
table, etc.

doing (doo-ing) *noun*
an action for which one is responsible: *It is
your doing that we're late.*

doldrums (doll-dr'mz) *plural noun*
1 a time of inactivity, low spirits, etc.
2 *Geography* the equatorial region where
both calm and very turbulent weather is
common.

dole *noun*
(*informal*) the money paid by a
government to unemployed people who
cannot find a suitable job.
Phrase **on the dole** receiving
unemployment payment.
• **dole** *verb*
Phrase **dole out** to distribute, especially
in small portions.

doleful *adjective*
sad or full of grief: *The funeral was a doleful
affair.*
Word Family **dolefully** *adverb*;
dolefulness *noun.*
[from *dole* an old word for grief]

doll *noun*
1 a toy which resembles a person.
2 (*informal*) an attractive young woman.
• **doll** *verb*
Phrase **doll up** (*informal*) to dress
smartly or showily.

dollar *noun*
the basic unit of money in America,
Australia and certain other countries.
[German *Thaler* a silver coin]

dollop *noun*
(*informal*) a lump or mass, especially of
food: *a large dollop of mashed potato.*

dolly *noun* (*plural* **dollies**)
1 a child's name for a doll.
2 a low platform on wheels which is used
to move heavy equipment, such as
cameras around a studio, etc.
Word Family **dolly** *verb* (**dollies;
dollying; dollied**) (of a camera) to be
moved around on a dolly.

dolma (doll-ma) *noun* (*plural* **dolmas** or
dolmades (dol-**ma**-dez))
a Greek dish of meat and rice enclosed in
vine leaves.
[Modern Greek *ntolmas*]

dolmen *noun*
Archaeology a structure consisting of two
or more large upright stones capped by a
horizontal stone.

dolomite *noun*
1 a very common mineral, calcium magnesium carbonate.
2 any rock consisting mainly of this mineral.
[after *D.G. de Dolomieu*, 1750-1801, a French geologist]

dolorous *adjective*
a poetic word meaning 'sad, mournful'.
Word Family **dolour** *noun* grief, sorrow; **dolorously** *adverb*.
[Latin *dolor* grief]

dolphin (**doll**-fin) *noun*
any of a group of large, highly intelligent marine mammals with a long snout, similar to whales and porpoises.

dolphinarium *noun* (*plural* **dolphinariums** or **dolphinaria**)
an aquarium for dolphins.

dolt *noun*
a stupid person.
Word Family **doltish** *adjective*; **doltishly** *adverb*; **doltishness** *noun*.

dom *noun*
(*often* **Dom**) *Christianity* a title for a monk in certain religious orders.

domain *noun*
1 a territory under rule or control.
2 an area of action or interest: *The book belongs to the domain of philosophy rather than that of practical politics.*
3 *Maths* the set of possible values for the independent variable of a function.

domain name *noun*
a series of words or characters that is used to access a particular web site on the Internet.

dome *noun*
a hemispherical roof.
Word Family **domed** *adjective*.

domestic *adjective*
1 of or relating to the home or family: *The quarrel was purely a domestic affair.*
2 tame: *domestic animals.*
3 relating to business within a country: *domestic air transport.*
domestic service employment as a household servant.
domestic system the manufacture of goods in the worker's own home.
• **domestic** *noun* a person employed to do household chores.
Word Family **domestically** *adverb*; **domesticate** *verb*; **domestication** (da-mess-ti-**kay**-sh'n) *noun* the act of domesticating; **domesticity** (domm-ess-**tiss**-i-tee) *noun* the state of being domesticated.
[Latin *domus* a home]

domicile (**domm**-i-sile) *noun*
a home or established place of residence.
Word Family **domicile** *verb*; **domiciliary** (domm-i-**sill**-i-a-ree) *adjective*.

dominant *adjective*
1 having the most influence, power or control: *In our house my father is the dominant person.*
2 main, major: *The dominant peak in the range is Mont Blanc.*
3 *Biology* of or relating to a hereditary character which shows itself even though the gene for it is inherited from only one parent. Compare RECESSIVE.
Word Family **dominance** *noun*.
[Latin *dominus* lord]

dominate *verb*
1 to rule over or control.
2 to tower over: *The mountain dominates the village.*
Word Family **domination** (domm-i-**nay**-sh'n) *noun*.

domineering *adjective*
tyrannical or arrogant.
Word Family **domineeringly** *adverb*; **domineer** *verb*.

dominie (**domm**-in-ee) *noun*
Scottish a schoolmaster.
[Latin *domine* O sir!]

dominion (d'-**min**-y'n) *noun*
1 the power or right to govern or control.
2 an area that is governed.
3 a self-governing country of the British Commonwealth.

domino *noun* (*plural* **dominoes**)
1 (**dominoes**) (*used with singular verb*) a game played with small flat oblong pieces whose faces are divided into two, each half being blank or marked with one to six spots.
2 one of these pieces.

domino theory *noun*
a theory which suggests that political change in one country tends to precipitate similar change in neighbouring countries, resulting in a chain reaction like a falling row of dominoes.

don[1] *noun*
1 a Spanish nobleman.
2 a college tutor or fellow, especially at Oxford or Cambridge.
[Spanish]

don² *verb* (**dons; donning; donned**)
to put on clothes, etc.
[from *do on*]

donate (doe-**nate**) *verb*
to give as a gift: *He donated £50 to the appeal.*
Word Family **donation** (doe-**nay**-sh'n) *noun* **1** the act of donating. **2** something which is donated; **donator** *noun*.
[Latin *donare* to give]

done the past participle of **do**.

doner kebab (donn-a ki-**bab**) *noun*
a Turkish dish consisting of lamb roasted on a spit and cut into thin slices, often served in pitta bread.

Don Juan (don jew-'n *or* don **wahn**) *noun*
a womanizer.
[after such a character in an old Spanish legend]

donkey *noun*
1 a long-eared mammal related to the horse and valued as a pack animal because of its sure-footedness and endurance.
2 (*informal*) a silly person.

donkey's years *plural noun*
(*informal*) a long time.

donnish *adjective*
(*informal*) stuffy or pedantic.

donor (doe-ner) *noun*
a person who donates something: *a blood donor.*

donor card *noun*
a card which people carry to indicate their desire to donate their organs in the event of their death.

don't (dohnt) *contraction*
a short form of **do not**: *Don't talk to strangers.*

doodle *verb*
to draw or scribble idly.
Word Family **doodle** *noun*; **doodler** *noun*.

doodlebug *noun* also called **flying bomb**.
a nickname for the German pilotless bomber, launched against the London area in 1944.

doom *noun*
an unhappy or terrible fate: *The general sent the soldiers to their doom.*
• **doom** *verb* to condemn to ruin or destruction: *Because of lack of finance the project was doomed from the start.*

doomsday *noun*
Religion the day of Judgement, at the end of the world.

door *noun*
1 a movable barrier which opens or closes the entrance to a room, etc.
2 the entrance itself.
3 any means of access: *the door to success.*
Phrases **next door to** in the next house, room, etc. **out of doors** in the open air.

doorstep *verb* (**doorsteps; doorstepping; doorstepped**)
to go from door to door, either trying to sell things or to canvass.

dope *noun*
1 (*informal*) any illegal drug.
2 (*informal*) a stimulating drug given illegally to racehorses, etc. so as to improve their performance.
3 (*informal*) a stupid person.
4 (*informal*) information: *Give us the dope on the secret meeting.*
• **dope** *verb* (*informal*) to administer drugs to.
Word Family **dopey** *adjective* (**dopier; dopiest**) (*informal*) stupid.
[Dutch *doop* a sauce]

doppelgänger (dop-p'l-geng-a) *noun*
a ghostly double of a living person.
[German, double-goer]

dork *noun*
(*informal*) a stupid or contemptible person.

dormant *adjective*
1 in a state resembling sleep.
2 non-active, e.g. during hibernation.
3 (of a volcano) not active but still capable of erupting. Compare ACTIVE (definition 4); EXTINCT (definition 2).
Word Family **dormancy** *noun*.
[Latin *dormire* to sleep]

dormer *noun*
an upright window built out from a sloping roof.

dormitory (dor-ma-tree) *noun* (*plural* **dormitories**)
a large room in an institution, such as a boarding school, where several people sleep.

dormouse *noun* (*plural* **dormice**)
a mouse-like mammal, living in trees and feeding on acorns and nuts; it sleeps for six months of the year.

dorsal *adjective*
Biology relating to the back of an organ or organism.
[Latin *dorsum* back]

dory *noun* (*plural* **dories**) also called **John Dory**.
an edible yellow marine fish.
[French *doré* gilded]

dose *noun*
1 the amount of medicine to be taken at one time: *The dose is written on the bottle.*
2 any portion or quantity.
Word Family **dose** *verb*; **dosage** *noun*
1 the giving of medicine in doses. 2 the amount given.
[Greek *dosis* a gift]

dosh *noun*
(*informal*) money.

doss *verb*
(*informal*) to sleep, especially in a cheap lodging house or temporary place.
Phrase **doss around** (*informal*) to spend time doing nothing very much.
● **doss** *noun* (*plural* **dosses**) (*informal*) a temporary sleeping place.

dosshouse *noun*
(*informal*) a place providing cheap lodging.

dossier (**doss**-i-a) *noun*
a collection of documents containing special information on some person or subject.

dost (dust) an old form of the second person singular present tense of **do**.

dot[1] *noun*
a small spot or point, such as a full stop.
Phrases **in the year dot** (*informal*) long ago. **on the dot** (*informal*) punctually.
● **dot** *verb* (**dots**; **dotting**; **dotted**) 1 to mark with or as if with dots. 2 to place like dots.

dot[2] *noun*
an old word for a dowry.

dotage (**doe**-tij) *noun*
a feebleness of mind, especially resulting from old age: *He has been in his dotage since he was 60.*

dotard (**dote**-ard) *noun*
an old feeble-minded person.

dot com *noun* also **dot com company**
a commercial organization with an Internet address ending in '.com'.

dote *verb*
1 to lavish excessive love or affection on: *She really dotes on that child.*
2 an old word meaning 'to be senile'.
Word Family **doting** *adjective*; **dotingly** *adverb*.

doth an old form of the third person singular present tense of **do**.

dot matrix *noun* (*plural* **dot matrices** or **dot matrixes**)
a device bearing patterns of dots, used to print words or letters.

dotty *adjective* (**dottier**; **dottiest**)
(*informal*) crazy or eccentric.

double (**dub**-'l) *adjective*
1 twice as big: *a double whisky.*
2 having two parts, etc.: *The expression 'like a bomb' has a double meaning.*
3 *Music* (of an instrument) producing tones one octave lower than the notes indicated on a score: *a double bassoon.*
● **double** *noun*
1 a twofold size or amount: *Twelve is the double of six.*
2 a substitute: *The actor used a double for the dangerous stunts.*
3 a duplicate: *He is the exact double of his twin.*
4 a sudden backward turn or bend: *He made a quick double to escape his pursuer.*
5 a bet in which the winners of two races must be chosen.
6 (**doubles**) a game in which there are two players on each side.
Phrase **at the double** quickly.
● **double** *verb*
1 to make or become twice as great: *to double a bet.* □ *They doubled their money by investing in stocks.*
2 to bend or fold with one part on another.
3 to serve in two capacities, e.g. as a person who plays two instruments in a band.
4 to act as a double in a film, etc.
Phrases **double back** to turn back on a course. **double up** 1 to duplicate an item, etc., especially inadvertently. 2 to curl up the body in pain or laughter.
[Latin *duplus* twofold]

double agent *noun*
a spy working simultaneously for two opposing governments or organizations.

double bass *noun* (*plural* **double basses**)
Music a very large low-pitched stringed instrument played with a bow.

double-breasted *adjective*
(of a coat) having overlapping flaps at the front and two rows of buttons. Compare SINGLE-BREASTED.

double-click *verb*
Computers to press a mouse button twice in rapid succession, e.g. in order to open a file or start a program.

double-cross *verb*
(*informal*) to betray.
Word Family **double-cross** *noun*;
double-crosser *noun*.

double-dealing *noun*
deceitfulness.
Word Family **double-dealing** *adjective*;
double-dealer *noun*.

double-decker *adjective*
having two tiers or layers: *a double-decker bus*.
• **double-decker** *noun*
a bus with two tiers.

double-edged *adjective*
1 having two cutting edges.
2 having two effects or meanings: *Her praise was double-edged.*

double entendre (dub-'l on-**ton**-dra) *noun*
a word or phrase with a second or hidden meaning.
[French *double* double + *entendre* to hear]

double glazing *noun*
windows with two thicknesses of glass, designed to prevent draughts and shut out noise.

double-jointed *adjective*
having very flexible joints which allow free or unusual movement.

double negative *noun*
Grammar the use of two negative forms, often for emphasis, which effectively cancel each other out: *'I didn't say nothing' is a double negative.*

double-park *verb*
to park parallel to another parked car.

double standard *noun*
a moral or social principle which one person or group expects another to follow, without doing so themselves.

double star ⇨ BINARY STAR.

doublet (**dub**-lit) *noun*
1 a close-fitting upper garment worn by men from the 15th to the 17th century.
2 a pair of similar things.
3 one of a pair of similar things.

double take *noun*
a surprised second look at something not understood or seen clearly at first.

doubletalk *noun*
any ambiguous talk.

double time *noun*
the payment of double wages to employees who work extra hours, e.g. on a public holiday.

double whammy *noun* (*plural* **double whammies**)
(*informal*) an exceptionally severe mishap or stroke of bad luck.

doubloon (dub-**loon**) *noun*
(*formerly*) a Spanish gold coin, no longer used.

doubly (**dub**-lee) *adverb*
1 twice as much or many.
2 in two ways.

doubt (*rhymes with* out) *noun*
a feeling of uncertainty, disbelief or distrust: *There is no doubt that you were wrong.*
• **doubt** *verb* to feel uncertain or hesitant about: *I doubt whether we will get there before 7 p.m.*
Word Family **doubter** *noun*; **doubtingly** *adverb*; **doubtless, doubtlessly** *adverb* without a doubt.
[Latin *dubitare* to hesitate]

doubtful *adjective*
1 having doubts: *She seemed doubtful about being able to come.*
2 causing doubt.
Word Family **doubtfully** *adverb*;
doubtfulness *noun*.

douche (doosh) *noun*
1 a jet of liquid applied to the body, especially to the vagina, for hygiene or as a means of contraception.
2 an instrument used to apply it.
Word Family **douche** *verb*.
[French, shower]

dough (doe) *noun*
1 a thick paste of flour and milk or water, used to make bread, cakes, etc.
2 (*informal*) money.
Word Family **doughy** *adjective*
(**doughier; doughiest**).

doughnut *noun*
a round or ring-shaped sweet cake, usually deep-fried.

doughnutting *noun*
the clustering of people round a central figure, as politicians round a speaker in parliament, to give an impression that there are a great many present.

doughty (**dow**-tee) *adjective* (**doughtier; doughtiest**)
an old word meaning 'brave' or 'bold'.

dour (**doo**-er) *adjective*
sullen or gloomy.
[Latin *durus* hard]

douse (*rhymes with* mouse) *verb also*
dowse
to throw water on, such as on a fire to
extinguish it.
Figurative Last one to bed douses the lights
(= puts out, extinguishes).

dove (duv) *noun*
1 a bird resembling a pigeon.
2 a person favouring mild action, such as
peace or friendship with another country.
Compare HAWK[1] (definition 2).
Word Family **dovish** *adjective.*

dovetail *noun*
a joint made by cutting one or more
wedge-shaped holes in the end of one
piece of timber, etc., into which the
matching end of another piece is
interlocked.
Word Family **dovetail** *verb.*

dowager (dow-ij-a) *noun*
1 a woman who has inherited a title or
property from her deceased husband.
2 any dignified elderly lady.

dowdy *adjective* (**dowdier; dowdiest**)
shabbily or unfashionably dressed.
Word Family **dowdiness** *noun;* **dowdily**
adverb.

dowel (*rhymes with* towel) *noun*
a narrow cylindrical piece of wood or
metal fitted into matching holes in two
surfaces, to join them.

down[1] *adverb, preposition, adjective*
from a higher to a lower position, level,
degree, etc.: *She came down the stairs very
slowly.* ☐ *Slow down at intersections.* ☐ *the
down escalator.* ☐ *The back tyre was down*
(= flat). ☐ *She was knocked down by the
galloping horse* (= to the ground). ☐ *Boil the
syrup down until it thickens* (= to a smaller
volume). ☐ *The house was passed down from
their ancestors* (= by way of inheritance).
☐ *She is kept down by her husband* (= in
submission). ☐ *I felt rather down the day
after the accident* (= unhappy, depressed).
☐ *I will put down £5 and pay the rest next
week* (= as a deposit). ☐ *New Zealand is
down by 42 runs this innings* (= losing by).
☐ *Take down my address* (= in writing). ☐ *It
was hard to settle down to study* (= in place,
in preparation).
Phrases **be down to earth** ⇨ EARTH.
down and out *The street was full of down
and out derelicts* (= penniless, jobless).
down on *This town is down on tourists*
(= severe or critical towards). **down with**
1 *Down with homework!* (= let's get rid of).
2 *He is down with measles* (= sick in bed
with). **send down** ⇨ SEND.

● **down** *noun*
1 (*informal*) a reversal or descent: *the ups
and downs of life.*
2 a feeling of dislike or hostility: *She has a
down on us at the moment.*
● **down** *verb*
(*informal*) to put or throw down: *The
workers downed tools and went on strike.*
Figurative Down your coffee and let's go
(= drink).

down[2] *noun*
1 the first soft fluffy feathers on some
birds.
2 any soft furry growth.

down[3] *noun*
(*usually* **downs**) any open rolling country.

downbeat *adjective*
(*informal*) casual, unemphatic or gloomy.

downcast *adjective*
1 looking downwards: *Her downcast eyes
avoided the dreadful sight.*
2 sad or depressed.

downer *noun*
1 (*informal*) something depressing or
discouraging.
2 (*informal*) a drug which counteracts
stimulation. Compare UPPER[2].

downfall *noun*
1 a destruction or ruin: *His love of
adventure caused his downfall.*
2 anything which causes destruction or
ruin: *Gambling was his downfall.*

downgrade *verb*
to reduce in status, salary, etc.

downhearted *adjective*
discouraged or dejected.

downhill *adverb, adjective*
in a downward direction.
Phrase **go downhill** *He went downhill very
rapidly after the second heart attack* (= got
worse).

download *verb*
to transfer data from one computer system
to another: *I downloaded the game from the
Internet.*
● **download** *noun.*

downmarket *adjective*
inferior in quality or style.

down payment *noun*
the first payment of a series, usually made
before delivery of the goods.

downpipe *noun*
a pipe down the side of a building which
carries water away from the guttering.

downpour *noun*
a heavy shower of rain.

downright *adjective*
1 complete: *a downright fool.*
2 honest or candid: *downright sincerity.*
• **downright** *adverb* completely: *He was downright rude.*

downriver *adjective, adverb*
at or to a place nearer the mouth of a river.

downside *noun*
the negative or disadvantageous side of something.

downsize *verb*
to reduce in number or size: *downsize a workforce.*

Down's syndrome *noun*
a condition caused by abnormal chromosomes, resulting in reduced mental powers, slanted eyes and short broad hands.

downstage *adverb, adjective*
Theatre at or towards the front of the stage: *The actors stood downstage from the chorus.*

downstairs *adverb*
to, at or on a lower floor: *I told them to wait downstairs.*
Word Family **downstairs** *adjective*; **downstairs** *noun.*

downstream *adverb, adjective*
in the direction of the moving stream or current: *The canoe was carried rapidly downstream.*

downswing *noun*
a swinging downwards.
Figurative How can we stop a downswing in the economy? (= decline).

down time *noun*
a period of time when work is not in progress, e.g. because of failure of equipment.

downtown *adverb, adjective*
American in or to the main business section of a city: *We went downtown for dinner.*

downtrodden *adjective*
oppressed or badly treated.

downturn *noun*
a decline.

down under *noun*
(*informal*) Australia and New Zealand.
Word Family **down under** *adverb.*

downward *adjective*
moving or directed down.
Word Family **downwards, downward** *adverb* towards a lower place or level.

downwind *adverb, adjective*
in the direction in which the wind is blowing.

downy *adjective* (**downier; downiest**)
covered in down (soft feathers).

dowry *noun* (*plural* **dowries**)
any property or money a bride brings to her husband at marriage, usually provided by her father.

dowse[1] ⇨ DOUSE.

dowse[2] (*rhymes with* cows) *verb*
to search for water, etc. with a divining rod.
Word Family **dowser** *noun* a water diviner.

doyen *noun*
the eldest or leading member of a group.
Word Family **doyenne** (doy-**en**) *noun* a female doyen.
[French dean]

doze *verb*
to sleep lightly or briefly: *He dozed by the fire for a few minutes.*
Word Family **doze** *noun*; **dozy** *adjective* (**dozier; doziest**) 1 drowsy. 2 (*informal*) slow or stupid.

dozen (**duz**-en) *noun*
any group of twelve things.
[French *douze* twelve]

drab *adjective* (**drabber; drabbest**)
1 (*informal*) dull, boring: *What a drab, humourless discussion.*
2 having a dull brown or greyish colour: *The drab uniforms of the soldiers blended wit*▮ *the colourless buildings.*

drachm (dram) *noun*
an old unit of mass equal to about 3·89 g.

drachma (**drak**-ma) *noun* (*plural* **drachmas** or **drachmae** (**drak**-mee))
the basic unit of money in modern and ancient Greece.

draconian *adjective*
harsh or severe: *draconian punishment.*

Draconian is derived from Draco, an Athenian statesman who in 621 B.C. was responsible for drawing up a new set of laws. They were supposedly drawn up to get rid of inconsistencies in the old laws which were causing discontent. However, the people were even less happy with the new laws which were so harsh that the most minor offence could be punished by death. Thus, Draco's name came to be associated with exceptional harshness.

draft *noun*
1 a first or preliminary version of a speech or document.
2 a written order for payment of money, especially from a bank.
3 a detachment or contingent selected for a particular purpose.
Phrase **the draft** (*especially American*) conscription.
• **draft** *verb*
1 to make a draft or outline of: *His advisers drafted the main points of his speech.*
2 *American* to conscript.

drag *verb* (**drags; dragging; dragged**)
1 to pull along with effort or difficulty: *They dragged the table over to the window.*
Figurative Her first week in hospital dragged (= passed slowly). □ *He dragged thoughtfully on his pipe* (= puffed heavily). □ *Your skirt is dragging along behind you* (= trailing).
2 to search with nets, etc.: *Police dragged the river for the stolen car.*
3 (*informal*) a puff of a cigarette, etc.
Phrase **drag one's feet** to move or act slowly.
• **drag** *noun*
1 anything which is dragged, such as a fishing net.
2 anything which slows down progress or movement, especially the force of a current of water or air against a moving body.
3 (*informal*) a very boring person or thing.
4 female clothing when worn by a male.
5 a car acceleration race.

dragnet *noun*
1 a net dragged through water to catch fish, etc.
2 any intricate system for catching or trapping, such as is used by the police force.

dragoman *noun* (*plural* **dragomans** or **dragomen**) an interpreter or guide in Middle Eastern countries such as Turkey. [Arabic *targuman* interpreter]

dragon (drag-'n) *noun*
1 *Mythology* a monster, usually pictured as a huge winged fire-breathing reptile with claws and scaly skin.
2 (*informal*) a strict or overbearing person, especially a woman.
3 any of various tree-dwelling or running lizards.
[Greek *drakon* serpent]

dragonfly *noun* (*plural* **dragonflies**)
any of a group of large harmless insects often with slender, brightly coloured bodies and wings.

dragoon (dra-**goon**) *noun*
1 (*formerly*) a cavalry soldier trained to fight on foot.
2 a member of certain former cavalry regiments, now part of the Royal Armoured Corps.
• **dragoon** *verb*
to force, often by violent or oppressive means: *The whole town was dragooned into feeding and serving the invading army.*
[after their carbines, once called *dragons*]

drag queen *noun*
a man, especially a performer, who dresses as a woman in an exaggerated or theatrical style.

dragster *noun*
a low car built to race at full speed over very short distances.

drain *verb*
to remove or empty slowly, especially liquids: *The swamp areas were drained to reduce the risk of malaria.*
Figurative The country's fuel reserves were drained during the petrol strike (= used up). □ *He drained his glass and stood up to leave* (= emptied).
• **drain** *noun*
1 any pipe, channel or other device which carries water, etc., especially away from a building.
2 anything which causes loss or expense: *His long stay in the nursing-home was a drain on the family's savings.*
Phrase **down the drain** *Buying all those clothes is just money down the drain* (= wasted).
Word family **drainage** *noun* 1 the act of draining. 2 a system of drains. 3 anything which is drained or carried away, such as sewage.

drainage basin *noun* also called **river basin**.
the area which is drained by a river and its tributaries.

drake *noun*
a male duck.

dram *noun*
1 an obsolete unit of mass equal to about 1·77 g.
2 a small quantity of anything, especially alcohol.

drama (**drah**-ma) *noun*
1 a play or other literary composition, especially one in which there is conflict or tragedy.
2 the art of composing and presenting such works, especially for the theatre.
3 an event which is exciting or interesting: *The drama of the election held everybody's attention.*
[Greek, a deed, a (tragic) play]

dramatic (dra-**matt**-ik) *adjective*
1 of or relating to drama or the theatre: *He is doing a course in dramatic production.*
2 lively, forceful or exciting: *The commentator gave a dramatic description of the match.*
Word Family **dramatics** *plural noun*
1 any dramatic productions: *amateur dramatics.* 2 any exaggerated behaviour; **dramatically** *adverb.*

dramatis personae (**dram**-a-tis per-**so**-nigh) *noun*
Theatre a list of the characters in a play.
[Latin]

dramatist (**dram**-a-tist) *noun*
a person who writes plays.

dramatize, dramatise *verb*
1 to put a story, etc. into the form of a play.
2 to express in a dramatic way: *He dramatized his account of the meeting.*
Word Family **dramatization** (dram-a-tie-**zay**-sh'n) *noun.*

drank the past tense of **drink**.

drape *verb*
to hang or adjust loosely in folds: *She draped a blanket around her shoulders to keep warm.*
Figurative He draped his legs over the arm of the chair (= placed casually).

draper *noun*
a person who sells textiles and clothes to the public.
Word Family **drapery** *noun* (*plural* **draperies**) 1 any textiles or fabric, especially when used as curtains or covers.
2 a draper's shop.

drastic *adjective*
extremely strong or violent: *The rain had a drastic effect on the crops.*
Word Family **drastically** *adverb.*

drat *interjection*
curse or damn: *Drat this terrible weather.*

draught (*rhymes with* raft) *noun* (*American* **draft**)
1 a flow of air through an enclosed space: *Close the door to keep out the draught.*
2 a drink: *He drank a long draught of water.*

3 *Nautical* the depth of water a vessel needs in order to float.
4 a haul of fish.
• **draught** *adjective*
1 (of animals) used for pulling loads: *a draught horse.*
2 (of drinking liquids) being drawn straight from the container without being bottled: *draught beer.*
Word Family **draughty** *adjective* (**draughtier; draughtiest**) having draughts: *What a draughty old house!*

draughts (*rhymes with* rafts) *plural noun* (*American* **checkers**)
(*used with singular verb*) a game for two players, each with twelve pieces which are moved diagonally on a board of 64 alternately coloured squares.

draughtsman *noun* (*plural* **draughtsmen**)
1 a person who draws architectural plans, etc.
2 any of the 24 pieces or discs used in draughts.
Word Family **draughtsmanship** *noun.*

draw *verb* (**draws; drawing; drew; drawn**)
1 to make a picture or outline with pen, pencils, etc.: *She drew a quick map of the area.*
2 to describe in words: *The characters in the play are not well drawn.*
3 to pull: *Draw your chair closer to the fire.*
Figurative She drew a deep breath before diving under the water (= took in). □ *As Christmas draws nearer the city becomes crowded* (= moves, comes). □ *The visiting ballet company drew large audiences* (= attracted). □ *I can only draw one conclusion from your behaviour* (= make, arrive at).
4 to pick or choose at random: *Let us draw lots to decide who goes first.*
5 to end a competition or game with no outright winner.
6 *Commerce* to prepare a cheque or bill of exchange, etc. The person ordering payment is called the **drawer** and the person from whom payment is required is called the **drawee**. The person to whom the payment is made is called the payee, who may or may not be the drawer.
Phrases **draw on, draw upon** *The stranded hikers had to draw on their emergency food supplies* (= make use of).
draw out 1 *Let's not draw out this boring discussion any longer* (= extend, lengthen).
2 *The shy guest was drawn out by their friendliness* (= encouraged to talk). **draw**

the line at ⇨ LINE¹. **draw up 1** *The car
drew up at the kerb* (= stopped). **2** *The
battalion was drawn up for battle*
(= arranged in formation). **3** *The two
governments will draw up a trade agreement*
(= prepare).
● **draw** *noun*
1 the act of drawing: *a lottery draw.*
2 the state of being drawn: *The game ended
in a draw.*
3 anything which draws or attracts: *This
new actress is bound to be a great draw.*

drawback *noun*
a disadvantage.

drawbridge *noun*
a bridge which may be raised and lowered.

drawer *noun*
1 (dror) a sliding storage compartment in
a piece of furniture.
2 (**drawers**) (*dated*) underpants.
3 (**draw-er**) a person who draws anything,
e.g. a person who draws a cheque.

drawing *noun*
any picture or composition made up of
lines and shades, usually of a single colour,
using a pen, pencil, brush, etc.

drawing pin *noun*
a short tack with a broad head designed to
be pushed in with the thumb.

drawing room *noun*
a room in a house used for receiving
guests, etc.
[from *withdrawing room*]

drawing software *noun*
computer programs that help one to draw
on screen.

drawl *verb*
to speak so that the vowel sounds are
much longer and slower than usual.
● **drawl** *noun.*

drawn *adjective*
1 haggard or lined: *Her face was drawn with
anxiety.*
2 pulled together: *drawn curtains.*
● **drawn** *verb* the past participle of **draw.**

drawstring *noun*
a cord or string, the end or ends of which
are pulled to close a bag, etc.

dray *noun*
a cart pulled by horses and used to carry
heavy loads.

dread (dred) *verb*
to have great fear or apprehension of:
He dreads driving in heavy traffic.
Word Family **dread** *noun, adjective;*
dreaded *adjective.*

dreadful *adjective*
1 causing dread or horror: *The details of the
dreadful accident were withheld.*
2 unpleasant or bad.: *What a dreadful day!*
Word Family **dreadfully** *adverb;*
dreadfulness *noun.*

dreadlocks *plural noun*
a Rastafarian hairstyle in which the hair is
twisted into tight braids or tightly curled
strands.

dreadnought (**dred**-nawt) *noun*
an old type of battleship built before the
First World War.

dream *noun*
1 a sequence of images occurring in the
mind during sleep.
2 any imagined vision, hope or fancy: *a
dream of future peace.*
3 anything which is beautiful or pleasing.
● **dream** *verb* (**dreams; dreaming;
dreamt** (dremt) or **dreamed**) to have a
dream.
Figurative Stop dreaming and concentrate
on your work (= daydreaming). □ *I never
dreamt we would win* (= imagined).
Phrase **dream up** *What mad idea will you
dream up next?* (= invent).
Word Family **dreamer** *noun;* **dreamless**
adjective; **dreamlike** *adjective;* **dreamy**
adjective (**dreamier; dreamiest**) vague,
unreal or dreamlike; **dreamily** *adverb.*

dreary *adjective* (**drearier; dreariest**)
dull or gloomy: *miles of dreary suburbs.*
Word Family **dreariness** *noun;* **drearily**
adverb; **drear** *adjective* a poetic word for
dreary.

dredge¹ *noun*
any of various machines using scoops or
suction pumps to draw up silt or other
materials from the bed of a river, etc.
Word Family **dredge** *verb* **1** to use a
dredge. **2** to explore or remove with or as
if with a dredge; **dredger** *noun* a boat
equipped with a dredge.

dredge² *verb*
to sprinkle or scatter: *Dredge the cutlets with
flour before frying.*
Word Family **dredger** *noun* an
implement used for sprinkling.

dregs *plural noun*
1 the sediment of wine or other liquids.
2 the most worthless or inferior parts of
anything: *He treats us like the dregs of
humanity.*

drench *verb*
1 to soak or wet completely: *We were
drenched in the storm.*

2 to give medicine to an animal.
Word Family drench *noun*.

dress *noun* (*plural* **dresses**)
1 a piece of female clothing consisting of a
skirt and a top in one piece.
2 any clothing.
3 formal clothing.
● **dress** *verb*
1 to put on clothes.
2 to put on formal clothes.
3 to treat: *The nurse dressed and bandaged
his cuts* (= treated).
4 to decorate: *The shop windows were
dressed for the Christmas sale.*
Phrases dress down *He was severely
dressed down for cheating* (= scolded). **dress
up 1** *Let's dress up as pirates* (= put on the
costume of). **2** *Do I need to dress up for
dinner?* (= wear formal clothes).

dressage (dress-ahj) *noun*
1 the art of training a horse in obedience,
etc.
2 a competition based on these skills.

dress circle *noun*
the curving section of seats upstairs in a
theatre.

dresser *noun*
1 a piece of kitchen furniture with open
shelves at the top, drawers for cutlery and
cupboards at the bottom.
2 *American* a dressing table.
3 a person who looks after and arranges
the clothes of an actor or actress in a
theatre's dressing room.

dressing *noun*
1 a sauce for food: *salad dressing.*
2 a medicated cloth for covering and
protecting a wound.
3 anything used to treat or prepare soil,
such as fertilizer, compost, etc.

dressing gown *noun*
a loose coat, usually tied with a sash and
worn over nightclothes.

dressing room *noun*
a room set aside for a person to dress in,
e.g. one backstage in a theatre.

dressing table *noun*
a bedroom table with drawers and usually
a mirror on top, used when dressing.

dress rehearsal ⇨ REHEARSAL.

drew the past tense of **draw**.

dribble *verb*
1 to flow or allow to flow in slow small
drops: *Blood dribbled from the cut on her
knee.*

2 *Sport* to propel the ball with a series of
short kicks, pushes or bounces.
● **dribble** *noun*.

driblet *noun*
a very small amount of anything.

dribs and drabs *plural noun*
(*informal*) any small irregular amounts: *He
paid his rent in dribs and drabs.*

drier ⇨ DRYER.

drift *verb*
to be carried or moved along without
particular direction: *The boat drifted on the
calm sea after the engine broke down.*
*Figurative He has drifted about the country
all his life* (= wandered aimlessly).
● **drift** *noun*
1 a drifting or carrying movement: *the drift
of the tides.*
*Figurative The drift of world events seemed
to be towards peace* (= trend, movement).
□ *What was the main drift of his argument?*
(= aim, meaning).
2 *Geography* any deposit on the earth
transported by wind, a glacier or water.
3 *Geography* a broad shallow current in the
sea or a lake.
4 *South African* a ford.

drifter *noun*
a person who drifts without aim or
purpose.

driftwood *noun*
any wood found floating in the sea or
deposited on the beach.

drill[1] *noun*
1 any of various tools for boring holes.
2 any strict method of exercise and
training, e.g. for soldiers.
*Figurative What is the drill for insuring my
car?* (= procedure).
● **drill** *verb*
1 to make holes with a drill.
2 to train and instruct by strict methods.

drill[2] *noun*
1 a small furrow in the soil, in which seeds
are planted.
2 a machine which plants seeds in rows
and covers them with soil.
● **drill** *verb*.

drill[3] *noun*
a strong cotton fabric used to make
uniforms, sails, etc.

drily *adverb* also **dryly**
in a dry manner.

drink verb (drinks; drinking; drank; drunk)
1 to take in or swallow liquid: *Drink your tea while it's still hot.*
2 to consume alcohol: *I don't think that they drink at all.*
Figurative We eagerly drank in every word of his story (= took, absorbed).
• **drink** noun
1 any liquid for drinking: *I need a drink of water.*
2 an alcoholic drink: *Let's have a drink before dinner.*
3 (informal) the sea.
Word Family **drinkable** adjective fit for drinking; **drinker** noun.

drink-driving noun
driving while under the influence of alcohol.

drip verb (drips; dripping; dripped)
to fall or allow to fall in drops: *Water was dripping noisily from the leaking tap.*
• **drip** noun
1 the act of dripping.
2 the liquid which drips or the noise it makes.
3 *Surgery* a device for intravenous feeding.
4 (informal) an insipid or foolish person.
Word Family **drippy** adjective (**drippier; drippiest**) (informal) insipid or foolish.

drip-dry adjective
(of fabric) drying without creases.

dripping noun
the fat obtained while cooking meat, which can be reused.

drive verb (drives; driving; drove; driven (driv-'n))
1 to operate, control or guide a motor vehicle, machine, etc.: *Can you drive a car yet?*
2 to guide or cause to move: *Drive the cows into the next paddock.* □ *The engine was driven by steam.*
Figurative She drives me mad with her chatter (= sends, makes). □ *The snow drove against the house* (= dashed). □ *What are your questions driving at?* (= aiming).
3 to hit a golf ball hard.
• **drive** noun
1 the act of driving or being driven: *Let's go for a drive in the country.*
2 also **driveway** a private road or path leading to a house, etc.
3 a source of motivation: *the sex drive.*
4 energy or vigour: *She shows ambitious drive at work.*

5 an organized attempt or effort: *We are planning a drive to raise money for a new library.*
6 a means of mechanical power: *a chain drive.*
7 a means of applying power: *four-wheel drive.*
Word Family **driver** noun; **driving** adjective.

drive-by adjective
(especially American) (of a shooting) carried out from a moving vehicle.

drive-in adjective
relating to an establishment designed for customers to be served or attended in their cars: *a drive-in bank.*
• **drive-in** noun.

drivel (driv-'l) verb (drivels; drivelling; drivelled)
1 to talk or act foolishly.
2 (dated) to dribble or drool.
• **drivel** noun.

driveshaft noun
a spinning shaft which transmits power from the gearbox to the differential of a motor vehicle.

drive-through adjective
(especially American) relating to a restaurant designed for customers to be served without leaving their vehicles.

driveway noun
a private road or path leading to a house, etc

driving range noun
a place where golfers may practise driving.

drizzle verb
to rain in light small drops.
Word Family **drizzle** noun; **drizzly** adjective.

droll adjective
strangely comical or amusing. *What a droll remark!*
Word Family **drollery** noun; **drollness** noun; **drolly** adverb.

dromedary (drom-a-dree) noun (plural dromedaries)
a camel with one hump.

drone¹ verb
to make a dull continuous sound: *The voice of the lecturer droned on in the half-filled hall.*
• **drone** noun
1 a dull continuous sound or voice.
2 a boring person or dull speaker.

drone² *noun*
1 a male bee which develops from an unfertilized egg, does not produce honey and dies or is killed soon after mating.
2 a lazy person.

drool *verb*
to dribble saliva.
Phrase **drool over** (*informal*) to regard with greedy desire.

droop *verb*
to hang or bend down loosely: *Her head drooped wearily over her books.*
Figurative His spirits drooped after several hours of waiting for rescue (= fell, sank).
Word Family **droopy** *adjective* (**droopier; droopiest**).

drop *verb* (**drops; dropping; dropped**)
1 to fall: *Beads of water were still dropping from the branches.* □ *He has dropped into the habit of arriving late.*
2 to cause or allow to fall: *Drop that gun or you're a dead man!*
3 to make or become lower: *I've dropped the hem another couple of inches.*
Figurative Please drop me at the corner (= let out). □ *She was dropped from the team because of injury* (= left out). □ *I dropped maths at the beginning of the year* (= stopped studying). □ *Drop me a note to say you arrived safely* (= send). □ *Stop arguing and we'll drop the whole subject* (= end).
Phrases **drop in** to make a visit. **drop off**
1 *Don't drop off in front of the fire* (= fall asleep). 2 *Sales dropped off after Christmas* (= decreased). **drop out** to withdraw or disappear.
• **drop** *noun*
1 the act of dropping: *a drop in prices.*
2 the amount by which something drops: *a cliff with a 500 m drop.*
3 a very small quantity or amount, especially a small sphere of liquid.
4 a lozenge: *Have one of my cough drops.*
Phrase **at the drop of a hat** without hesitation.

drop-dead *adverb*
(*informal*) strikingly: *drop-dead gorgeous.*

drop kick *noun*
Football a kick in rugby in which the ball is dropped at an angle and kicked as it leaves the ground.
Word Family **drop-kick** *verb*.

droplet *noun*
a small drop.

dropout *noun*
a person who rejects or withdraws from an established institution or normal society.

dropper *noun*
a device consisting of a tube with a rubber bulb at one end, for releasing a liquid in drops.

droppings *plural noun*
the dung of animals.

drop scone *noun*
a small thick pancake cooked on a griddle.

dropsy ⇨ OEDEMA.

dross *noun*
1 a scum of oxide and other impurities on the surface of molten metal.
2 any waste matter.

drought (*rhymes with* out) *noun*
a long period of weather without rain.

drove¹ the past tense of **drive**.

drove² *noun*
1 a group of sheep, cattle, etc. in one herd.
2 (*usually* **droves**) a large crowd of people: *Spectators turned up in droves.*
Word Family **drover** *noun*.

drown *verb*
to die or cause to die by suffocating in water or other liquid.
Figurative The roars of the crowd drowned his voice (= overwhelmed, muffled).

drowse (*rhymes with* cows) *verb*
to be half asleep: *He spent the afternoon drowsing by the fire.*
Word Family **drowse** *noun*; **drowsy** *adjective* (**drowsier; drowsiest**) tired or half asleep; **drowsily** *adverb*; **drowsiness** *noun*.

drub *verb* (**drubs; drubbing; drubbed**)
to beat severely.
Word Family **drubbing** *noun*.

drudge *noun*
a person who works at a dreary or uninteresting task.
Word Family **drudge** *verb*; **drudgery** *noun* any hard or uninteresting work.

drug *noun*
1 any chemical substance used to treat disease.
2 any addictive substance, such as certain narcotics.
• **drug** *verb* (**drugs; drugging; drugged**)
to administer a drug to.
Figurative She was still drugged with sleep as she stumbled to the shower (= stupefied).

druggist *noun*
American a pharmacist.

drugstore *noun*
American a shop selling general goods and sometimes prescription medicines.

Druid (**droo**-id) *noun*
a priest of an ancient Celtic religion.

drum *noun*
1 *Music* any of various percussion instruments consisting of a tightly stretched skin or membrane on a round frame, which is struck with sticks or the hands.
2 a large spool wound with cable, wire or heavy rope.
3 a cylindrical container: *a petrol drum.*
Phrase **beat the drum for** to proclaim or praise.
• **drum** *verb* (**drums; drumming; drummed**) to thump or tap rhythmically on, or as if on, a drum.
Figurative The army *certainly drums discipline into its recruits* (= forces by repetition).
Phrases **drum out** to expel or dismiss in disgrace. **drum up** *He's trying to drum up support for his ideas* (= obtain).
Word Family **drummer** *noun* a person who plays a drum.

drumstick *noun*
1 a stick used for beating a drum.
2 the lower part of the leg of a chicken, duck or turkey.

drunk *adjective*
intoxicated or overcome with alcohol.
• **drunk** *noun* a person who is often drunk.
• **drunk** *verb* the past participle of **drink**.

drunkard (**drunk**-'d) *noun*
a person who is often drunk.

drunken *adjective*
of or showing the effects of drinking alcohol: *His drunken behaviour embarrassed all the guests.*
Word Family **drunkenly** *adverb*; **drunkenness** *noun* the state of being drunk.

dry *adjective* (**drier; driest**)
1 not wet or producing liquid: *Wood must be dry or it will not burn properly.*
2 unbuttered: *a boiled egg and a piece of dry toast.*
3 uninteresting: *They found the speech rather dry and boring.*
4 plain: *His short talk gave only the dry facts.*
5 without alcohol: *We found that the party was dry.*
6 tersely expressed, ironically matter-of-fact: *a dry sense of humour.*
7 (of wines, biscuits, etc.) not sweet.
• **dry** *verb* (**dries; drying; dried**) to make or become free of moisture: *Please dry the plates thoroughly before you put them away.*

Phrases **dry out 1** to make or become free of moisture. 2 (*informal*) to undergo or cause to undergo treatment for alcoholism. **dry up 1** *The stream dries up in summer* (= becomes completely dry).
2 *She dried up as she stood nervously on the stage* (= forgot her lines). 3 (*informal*) *Please dry up, I can't concentrate with all that chatter* (= be quiet).

dryad *noun*
Greek mythology a nymph of the woods.
[Greek *dryados* of a tree]

dry-cleaning *noun*
the process of cleaning clothes with chemical solvents, etc.
Word Family **dry-clean** *verb*; **dry-cleaner** *noun.*

dry dock *noun*
a dock from which the water may be removed to allow a ship to be painted and repaired.

dryer *noun* also **drier**
1 anything which dries: *a hand dryer.*
2 a substance added to paints, varnishes, etc., to make them dry more quickly.

dry fry *verb* (**dry-fries; dry-frying; dry-fried**)
to fry without any added fat.

dry goods *plural noun*
1 any non-liquid goods, such as corn.
2 *American* textiles, as opposed to groceries and hardware.

dry ice *noun*
frozen carbon dioxide, which is useful as a refrigerant because it evaporates directly from solid ice into a gas. ⇨ SUBLIME.

dryly ⇨ DRILY.

dryness *noun*
the state of being dry.

dry rot *noun*
a decay caused by fungi in dry seasoned timber which has not been kept properly ventilated.

dry run *noun* also **dummy run**
(*informal*) a try-out or rehearsal.
[formerly it referred to American army manoeuvres in which blank cartridges were fired]

DTs ⇨ DELIRIUM TREMENS.

dual (**dew-**'l) *adjective*
1 having two parts: *This car has dual controls.*
2 relating to two.
[Latin *duo* two]

> ! The words *dual* and *duel* sound the same but have different spellings and meanings. *Dual* with an *a* is an adjective meaning 'having two parts', as in *dual carriageway*; *duel* with an *e* is a noun meaning 'a combat', as in *He challenged his rival to a duel.*

dual carriageway *noun*
a main road divided into two separate one-way roads, but not qualifying as a motorway.

dualism (dew-a-lizm) *noun* also **duality** (dew-**al**-i-tee)
the state of having two parts.
Word Family **dualistic** (dew-a-**list**-ik) *adjective*; **dualist** *noun*.

dub¹ *verb* (**dubs; dubbing; dubbed**)
1 to strike lightly on the head or shoulder when conferring a knighthood.
2 to dress the surface of wood or leather.

dub² *verb* (**dubs; dubbing; dubbed**)
Film to change or add to the soundtrack of a film, e.g. by replacing the original dialogue with one in a different language.
• **dub** *noun* a type of reggae which involves remixing samples from other recordings.

dubbin *noun*
a mixture of oil and tallow used to soften and waterproof leather.

dubious (dew-bi-us) *adjective*
1 doubtful or uncertain.
2 open to question or suspicion: *The motives for his generosity are rather dubious.*
Word Family **dubiousness, dubiety** (dew-**by**-a-tee) *noun*; **dubiously** *adverb*.
[Latin *dubium* doubt]

ducal (**dew**-k'l) *adjective*
of or relating to a duke.

ducat (**duk**-'t) *noun*
an old European gold coin.

duchess (**dutch**-iss) *noun* (*plural* **duchesses**)
1 a female duke.
2 the wife of a duke.

duchy (**dutch**-ee) *noun* (*plural* **duchies**)
the land ruled by a duke or duchess.

duck¹ *noun*
any of various wild or domesticated waterbirds with a broad flat bill, short legs and webbed feet.

duck² *verb*
1 to stoop or move aside quickly: *He ducked his head as the ball hurtled past.*
2 (*informal*) to avoid: *She tries to duck responsibility.*

3 to plunge or be plunged quickly under water.
Word Family **duck** *noun*.

duck³ *noun*
Cricket a batsman's score of zero.

duck⁴ *noun*
a heavy plain fabric used for tents, bags, etc.

duck-billed platypus ⇨ PLATYPUS.

duckboard *noun*
one section of a wooden pathway laid over a swamp or heavy mud.

duckling *noun*
a young duck.

duct *noun*
any tube through which gases or liquids are conveyed, such as the tubes through which the secretions of certain glands flow in the bodies of animals.
Word Family **ducting** *noun*.
[Latin *ductus* conveyed]

ductile *adjective*
1 able to be drawn out into thin wires. Compare MALLEABLE (definition 1).
2 able to be shaped or moulded.
3 easily influenced: *It was easy to persuade such a ductile audience.*
Word Family **ductility** (duk-**till**-a-tee) *noun*.

dud *noun*
1 (*informal*) a person or thing that is a failure, such as a bomb which fails to explode.
2 (*informal*) anything which is fake or useless, such as a counterfeit coin.

dude (dood) *noun*
1 (*American informal*) a man.
2 a fop.

dude ranch *noun* (*plural* **dude ranches**)
American a farm operated as a holiday resort for tourists.

dudgeon (**dud**-jen) *noun*
a feeling of anger or hurt pride.

duds *plural noun*
(*informal*) clothes or belongings.

due (dew) *adjective*
1 owing or expected: *The rent is due next Wednesday.*
2 proper or adequate: *You must take due care when driving on wet roads.*
Phrase **due to** *His stutter is due to extreme shyness* (= caused by).
• **due** *noun*
1 any thing which is owed or deserved: *Success is his due for so much hard work.*
2 (**dues**) a membership fee or payment.

• due *adverb*
(of direction) directly or exactly: *We sailed due east towards the islands.*

> ⚠ *Due to* means 'caused by' and refers back to a noun, not a clause: *The cancellation of the match was due to rain.* It is often used instead of *owing to* with the meaning 'because of', as in *The match was cancelled due to rain,* but this is thought by many people to be wrong.

due diligence *noun*
steps taken by manufacturers to ensure that a product is well made.

duel (**dew**-el) *noun*
1 a pre-arranged combat between two people, fought under fixed conditions with deadly weapons, to avenge an insult, etc.
2 any contest between two people, groups, etc.
Word Family **duel** (**duels; duelling; duelled**) *verb*; **dueller, duellist** *noun.*

> ⚠ Do not confuse *duel* with DUAL.

duenna (doo-**enn**-a) *noun*
a woman acting as an escort or chaperone to a young woman, especially in Spain or Portugal.
[Spanish *dueña*]

duet (dew-**et**) *noun*
a piece of music to be sung or played by two people.

duffel *noun* also **duffle**
a coarse woollen fabric with a thick nap on both sides.
[after *Duffel,* a Dutch town]

duffel bag *noun*
a cylindrical canvas bag for carrying light personal articles.

duffel coat *noun*
a heavy woollen coat with a hood, usually knee-length and fastened with toggles.

duffer *noun*
(*informal*) a person who is slow to learn.

dug[1] the past tense and past participle of **dig**.

dug[2] *noun*
the udder or nipple of a female animal.

dugong (doo-**gong**) *noun* also called **sea cow**.
a large herbivorous aquatic mammal which lives in tropical waters and has a whale-like body, flipper-like limbs and a flat rounded tail.
[Malay]

dugout *noun*
1 a canoe made by hollowing out a log.
2 a shelter dug in the ground for protection, e.g. in a trench during the First World War.

duke *noun*
1 the ruling prince of a small state.
2 a nobleman of the highest rank after a prince.
Word Family **dukedom** *noun* 1 a duchy
2 the rank or office of a duke.
[Latin *dux* leader]

dulcet (**dul**-sit) *adjective*
(of sounds) pleasing or soothing.

dulcimer (**dull**-sim-a) *noun*
Music an old instrument, still used in traditional music, in which strings stretched over a sounding board are struck with hammers.

dull *adjective*
not bright, sharp or clear: *The dull light made it difficult to read.*
Figurative He was a *dull* student and could not understand maths (= unintelligent, slow). □ *She put aside the* dull *book and went to play outside* (= uninteresting).
• dull *verb* to make or become dull.
Word Family **dully** *adverb*; **dullness** *noun.*

dullard *noun*
(*formal*) a dull or stupid person.

duly (**dew**-lee) *adverb*
1 at the appropriate time.
2 in the appropriate manner.

dumb (dum) *adjective*
1 not able to speak.
2 (*informal*) lacking intelligence.
• dumb *verb*
Phrase **dumb down** (*informal*) to make something simpler or more exciting so that it can be understood or appreciated by more people.
Word Family **dumbness** *noun*; **dumbly** *adverb.*

dumb-bell *noun*
an apparatus similar to a barbell, but smaller and used in one hand.

dumbfound *verb*
to amaze or surprise greatly.

dumbstruck *adjective*
unable to speak because of shock.

dumb waiter *noun*
1 *American* a small box-like lift used to carry food or other goods between the floors of a building.

2 a stand, often on wheels, with shelves for serving food at table.

dumdum *noun*
a hollow-nosed bullet which flattens out on impact, inflicting a severe wound.
[after *Dum Dum*, India, a former military and ammunitions centre]

dummy *noun* (*plural* **dummies**)
1 a model or imitation of something used for display, etc., such as a sample of a book to be printed.
2 a rubber teat given to a baby to suck.
3 (*informal*) a stupid person.
• **dummy** *adjective* imitation or substitute.

dummy run ⇨ DRY RUN.

dump¹ *verb*
1 to throw down or unload heavily.
Figurative The campers dumped their rubbish at the tip (= left, disposed of).
□ *The bankrupt man was dumped by his former friends* (= rejected).
2 *Commerce* to sell some commodity in large quantities at a low price, often in a foreign country.
• **dump** *noun*
1 any place where things are dumped or discarded: *a rubbish dump*.
2 a pile of discarded or dumped things.
3 a storage place or depot, especially for military supplies.
4 (*informal*) any place which is unattractive or uncared for.

dump² *noun*
Phrase **in the dumps** (*informal*)
depressed, gloomy: *He's been in the dumps all day for no apparent reason.*

dumpling *noun*
a small ball of savoury or sweet dough, cooked in soups, stews, etc.

dumpy *adjective* (**dumpier; dumpiest**)
short and plump.

dun¹ *noun*
1 a muddy greyish-brown colour.
2 a horse of this colour.

dun² *verb* (**duns; dunning; dunned**)
to make constant or repeated demands especially for the payment of debts, etc.
• **dun** *noun*
1 a person who duns.
2 a demand for payment.

dunce *noun*
an unintelligent person.

dune (*rhymes with* tune) *noun*
short form of **sand dune** a mound or ridge of sand built up by the wind.

dung *noun*
any animal manure.

dungarees *plural noun*
trousers or overalls made from a coarse cotton fabric.
[Hindi]

dungeon (**dun**-jen) *noun*
a dark cell or room, especially one which is underground.

dunghill *noun*
a pile of dung.

dunk *verb*
to dip something briefly into a liquid, e.g. biscuits into tea.

duo *noun*
any group of two people or things.
[Greek and Latin, two]

duodenum (dew-o-**deen**-'m) *noun*
Anatomy the C-shaped first part of the small intestine, receiving bile from the gall bladder and digestive juices from the pancreas.
Word Family **duodenal** *adjective*.
[Latin *duodecim* twelve, because it was considered to be twelve finger breadths long]

dupe *verb*
to deceive or trick.
• **dupe** *noun* a person who has been deceived or tricked.

duplex (**dew**-pleks) *adjective*
1 double.
2 having two identical parts which are used together: *a duplex chain*.

duplicate (**dew**-pli-kit) *adjective*
1 being exactly like or copied from another thing: *Use the scanner to make a duplicate copy of this letter.*
2 having two identical parts.
• **duplicate** *noun* anything which is identical to something else, especially an exact copy or imitation.
Word Family **duplicate** (**dew**-pli-kate) *verb*; **duplication** (dew-pli-**kay**-sh'n) *noun*.
[Latin *duplex, duplicis* double]

duplicator (**dew**-pli-kay-ta) *noun*
a machine which makes copies of printed matter, e.g. from a stencil.

duplicity (dew-**pliss**-i-tee) *noun*
deceitfulness or hypocrisy.

durable (**dew**-ra-b'l) *adjective*
not easily worn out.
Word Family **durability** (dew-ra-**bill**-it-ee) *noun*; **durably** *adverb*.
[Latin *durus* hard]

duration (dew-**ray**-sh'n) *noun*
the length of time for which something exists or continues.

duress (dew-**ress**) *noun*
the use of force to achieve something, especially illegally: *The witness claimed his evidence was given under duress.*

during (**dew**-ring) *preposition*
within the time of: *He was very unhappy during his childhood.*

durst *verb*
an old word meaning 'dared'.

durum wheat (**dew**-r'm weet) *noun*
a type of hard wheat used to make pasta.

dusk *noun*
the period of half-light in the early part of the evening.

dusky *adjective* (**duskier; duskiest**)
dark, especially in a shadowy or dim way.
Word Family **duskiness** *noun*; **duskily** *adverb*.

dust *noun*
a fine powder, e.g. of earth.
Phrase **bite the dust** (*informal*) to be killed or wounded.
• **dust** *verb*
1 to remove dust from something.
2 to sprinkle with a powdered substance.

dustbin *noun*
a container for domestic refuse.

dust bowl *noun*
an artificial desert created by growing too many crops, causing impoverished topsoil to be blown away in dust storms after drought.

dustcoat *noun*
a light loose-fitting coat worn over clothes for protection, e.g. in a laboratory.

duster *noun*
a cloth for removing dust.

dust jacket *noun*
a printed paper cover or wrapper put around a hardback book.

dustman *noun* (*plural* **dustmen**)
a refuse collector.

dust-up *noun*
(*informal*) a fight or commotion.

dusty *adjective* (**dustier; dustiest**)
covered with dust.

duty (**dew**-tee) *noun* (*plural* **duties**)
1 what a person is obliged, or feels obliged, to do: *What are my duties as host of the party?*
2 a moral obligation: *You have a duty to look after your parents.*

3 any of various government taxes: *a customs duty.*
Phrases **off duty** not at work. **on duty** at work.
Word Family **dutiful** *adjective* performing the necessary duties; **dutifully** *adverb*; **dutiable** *adjective* subject to a tax or duty.

duty-free *adjective*
free of customs duty.

duvet (**doo**-vay) *noun*
a thick downy quilt used on a bed as a substitute for blankets.
[French, down]

dwarf (dwawf) *noun* (*plural* **dwarfs** or **dwarves**)
1 *Folklore* a very small human-like being, often having magical powers.
2 anything, such as an animal or plant, which is much smaller or shorter than the average.
• **dwarf** *verb* to cause to appear very small: *The factory was dwarfed by the multi-storey buildings on either side of it.*
Word Family **dwarfish** *adjective* very small like a dwarf.

dweeb *noun*
(*informal*) a stupid or ineffectual person.

dwell *verb* (**dwells; dwelling; dwelt** or **dwelled**)
1 (*formal*) to live as a resident.
2 to continue or remain: *Let's not dwell on such an unpleasant topic.*
Word Family **dweller** *noun*.

dwelling *noun*
(*formal*) a house or home.

dwindle *verb*
to make or become smaller and smaller.

dye *noun*
any substance used to colour material.
• **dye** *verb* (**dyes; dyeing; dyed**) to colour with or as if with a dye.
Word Family **dyer** *noun*.

dyed-in-the-wool *adjective*
complete, through and through.

dyestuff *noun*
any substance producing, or used as, a dye.

dying the present participle of **die**[1].

dyke (dike) *noun* also **dike**
1 a ridge or wall built along a river or the sea to stop the water rising on to the land. Compare DAM[1].
2 *Geology* the solidified rock found in vertical cracks between other rocks.

• **dyke** *verb* to enclose or protect with a dyke.

dynamic (die-**namm**-ik) *adjective*
relating to motion, force or energy.
Figurative She succeeds because of her dynamic personality (= forceful, vigorous).
Word Family **dynamics** *plural noun*
1 *Physics* (*used with singular verb*) the study of the motion of bodies or particles. **2** the forces at work in something: *the dynamics of mental illness;* **dynamically** *adverb;*
dynamism (**die**-na-mizm) *noun*.
[Greek *dynamis* power]

dynamite (**die**-na-mite) *noun*
1 a high explosive made by absorbing nitroglycerine in some suitable substance.
2 (*informal*) a person or thing seen as dangerous or troublesome.

dynamo (**die**-na-mo) *noun*
1 *Electricity* a generator used to produce direct current. Compare ALTERNATOR.
2 (*informal*) a very energetic person.

dynamometer (die-na-**momm**-it-a) *noun*
a device which measures power, especially of an engine.

dynasty (**din**-a-stee) *noun* (*plural* **dynasties**)
a series of monarchs belonging to the same family: *The Habsburg dynasty in Austria ruled from the 13th to the early 20th century.*
Word Family **dynastic** (din-**ast**-ik) *adjective;* **dynast** *noun* a ruler, especially a hereditary one.
[Greek *dynastes* a ruler]

dysentery (**diss**-'n-tree) *noun*
an infection of the bowel causing fever, abdominal pain and diarrhoea, usually spread by contaminated food and water.
[Greek *dys-* bad + *entera* bowels]

dysfunction (diss-**funk**-sh'n) *noun*
Medicine the poor functioning of an organ.

dysfunctional *adjective*
unable to function normally: *a dysfunctional family.*

dyslexia (diss-**lek**-si-a) *noun*
an extreme difficulty in learning to read and spell.
Word Family **dyslexic, dyslectic** *adjective.*
[Greek *dys-* bad + *lexis* speech]

dyspepsia (diss-**pep**-si-a) *noun*
indigestion.
Word Family **dyspeptic** *adjective*
1 suffering from indigestion. **2** gloomy or pessimistic.
[Greek *dys-* bad + *peptikos* able to digest]

Ee

each *adjective, pronoun, adverb*
every one considered individually: (as an
adjective) *Each story had an interesting plot.*
□ (as a pronoun) *Each went his own way.*
□ (as an adverb) *Apples cost 30 pence each.*

> ❗ Note that when *each* is the subject
> of a sentence it is used with a
> singular verb, e.g. *Each girl has a bicycle.*
> □ *Each of them has a bicycle.*

each other *pronoun*
the other one, or the other ones· *We all
looked at each other guiltily.*

each way *adverb*
(of a bet) paying whether the racehorse or
greyhound finishes first, second or third.

eager *adjective*
keen or showing desire: *He is eager to win
the race.*
Word Family eagerly *adverb;* **eagerness**
noun.

eager beaver *noun*
(*informal*) an extremely enthusiastic
person.

eagle *noun*
1 a large strong bird of prey with a huge
hooked beak.
2 *Golf* a score of two strokes less than par
for a hole. Compare BIRDIE.
Word Family eaglet *noun* a young eagle.

ear¹ *noun*
1 *Anatomy* the external organ of hearing
2 a perception of the difference between
sounds: *She has a good ear for music.*
3 willingness to listen: *She found he had a
sympathetic ear.*
Phrases be all ears (*informal*) to listen
eagerly. **bend someone's ear** (*informal*)
to talk to someone at length about one's
problems. **have an ear to the ground,
keep an ear to the ground** to be well-
informed. **play it by ear** to see how things
go and improvise measures accordingly.
prick up one's ears 1 to raise the ears:
The dog pricked up its ears. **2** to listen
attentively: *She pricked up her ears when she*

heard them mention her name. **up to one's
ears in** (*informal*) deeply involved in or
very busy with. **wet behind the ears**
immature or naive.

ear² *noun*
the part of a cereal plant containing the
seeds or flowers.

eardrum *noun*
Anatomy a taut membrane in the ear which
vibrates as soundwaves enter it, passing
these vibrations to the inner ear.

earful *noun*
(*informal*) a strong expression of anger:
*My brother gave me an earful when he saw
what I had done.*

earl (erl) *noun*
a nobleman ranking between a marquis
and a viscount.
Word Family earldom *noun* the rank or
title of an earl.

Earl Grey *noun*
a type of tea.
[after the second *Earl Grey*, 1764-1845,
who brought it to England from China]

early (er-lee) *adverb, adjective* (**earlier;
earliest**)
1 in the first part of a particular division of
time: *early in the morning.*
2 prior to the usual or arranged time: *We
took an early lunch.*
3 far back in time: *early British history.*
Word Family earliness *noun.*

earmark *verb*
to set aside for a special purpose. *We had
earmarked the money for our holiday.*
[from the practice of marking the ear of an
animal for identification]

earmuffs *plural noun*
ear coverings connected by a strip of
plastic worn over the head.

earn (ern) *verb*
to gain as a result of one's labour, etc.: *He
earns £150 a week.* □ *She earned a
reputation as a good doctor.*
Word Family earner *noun.*

earnest (er-nest) *adjective*
serious or zealous: *an earnest young man.*
● **earnest** *noun*
Phrase in earnest serious: *I think he is in
earnest.*
Word Family earnestness *noun;*
earnestly *adverb.*

earnings (er-ningz) *plural noun*
any money earned.

earphone *noun*
a device worn on or in the ear to assist in hearing sound from a radio, telephone, etc.

earpiece *noun*
any part of a machine that is held to or put into the ear.

ear-piercing *adjective*
(of a sound) extremely high and loud.
● **ear-piercing** *noun* the making of holes in the ear so that studs or earrings can be worn.

earplug *noun*
a soft mass of wax, cotton wool, etc. inserted into the ear to block out noise or water.

earring *noun*
any ring or ornament for the ear.

earshot *noun*
the reach or range of hearing.

earth (erth) *noun*
1 (*often* **Earth**) *Astronomy* the planet in the solar system on which we live.
2 the dry land, especially the soil.
3 *Electricity* an electrical connection to the ground, for safety.
4 the hole or shelter of a burrowing animal.
Phrases **be down to earth** to be practical. **come down to earth** to return to reality. **cost the earth** (*informal*) to be extremely expensive. **run someone to earth** to track someone down.
● **earth** *verb Electricity* to connect electrical devices to the ground, for safety.

earthen (**er**-th'n *or* **er**-*th*'n) *adjective*
made of earth or baked clay.

earthenware *noun*
1 a type of pottery which is fired at low temperatures, so that it is porous and not very strong.
2 cups, plates, etc. made from this.

earthling *noun*
a human inhabitant of the Earth.

earthly (**erth**-lee) *adjective*
of or inhabiting the earth.
Phrases **no earthly** (*informal*) no possible: *This machine is of no earthly use.* **not have an earthly** (*informal*) to have no idea, chance, etc. at all.

earthquake (**erth**-kwake) *noun*
a movement in the earth's crust, caused by a build-up of pressure which sends out a series of three distinct sets of shockwaves.

earthwork *noun*
a large bank of earth thrown up by soldiers as a defence.

earthworm *noun*
any of various kinds of segmented worms whose activity helps to fertilize and drain the soil.

earthy (**erth**-ee) *adjective* (**earthier; earthiest**)
1 of or relating to the earth.
2 hearty, coarse or lacking refinement.

ear trumpet *noun*
a large tube with a wide end, formerly used to help people hear.

earwig *noun*
any of a group of insects with pincers on the tail end of the abdomen.
● **earwig** *verb* (**earwigs; earwigging; earwigged**) (*informal*) to eavesdrop.

ease (eez) *noun*
freedom from pain, worry or difficulty: *She accomplished her goal with ease.* □ *His wealth allowed him to live a life of ease.*
Phrase **at ease, stand at ease** (used as a command) stand with the feet apart and the hands clasped behind the back.
● **ease** *verb*
1 to free from pain, worry or difficulty.
2 (of pain, difficulty, etc.) to become less.
3 to move slowly and carefully.

easel (**eez**-'l) *noun*
an upright frame-like structure used to hold a painter's canvas, a blackboard, etc.

> The word **easel** has its origin in the Dutch *ezel* (a donkey), which is related to the German *Esel* and the English *ass*. Just as the owner loads a burden on a donkey so does an artist load a painting on an *easel*.

easily *adverb*
1 with ease: *I can easily find out.*
2 without question: *This is easily the best method.*

east *noun*
1 the direction of the sun at sunrise.
2 the cardinal point of the compass at 90° to the right of north and opposite west.
3 (**the East**) the countries of Asia.
4 (**the East**) (*formerly*) the countries of Europe and Asia with communist governments, such as the former Soviet Union.
Word Family **east** *adjective, adverb.*

Easter *noun*
Christianity a festival to commemorate the resurrection of Christ.

easterly *adjective*
(of a direction, course, etc.) from or towards the east: *We set off on an easterly course.*
• **easterly** *noun* (*plural* **easterlies**)
a wind coming from the east.
• **easterly** *adverb*.

eastern *adjective*
(of a place) situated in the east: *the eastern states of America.*
Word Family easternmost *adjective* furthest east.

Eastern Orthodox Church
⇨ ORTHODOX CHURCH.

eastward (eest-w'd) *adjective*
towards the east.
Word Family eastwards, eastward *adverb*.

easy (ee-zee) *adjective* (**easier; easiest**)
1 not difficult: *an easy exam.*
2 free from pain, worry or difficulty: *What an easy life he leads!*
3 relaxed: *with an easy grin.*
Phrases **be easy** (*informal*) not to mind which choice is made: *'Cinema or theatre?' – 'I'm easy.'* **go easy on** (*informal*) not to criticize too harshly. **take it easy, take things easy** not to make a lot of effort.
Word Family easiness *noun*.

easy chair *noun*
a comfortable chair, usually an armchair.

easy-going *adjective*
relaxed or unconcerned.

easy street *noun*
Phrase **on easy street** (*informal*) financially very comfortable.

eat *verb* (**eats; eating; ate; eaten**)
1 to chew and swallow food.
2 to have a meal: *We will eat at 8 p.m.*
3 to destroy or damage, especially gradually: *The acid ate into the metal.*
4 (*informal*) to make nervous or irritable.
Word Family eater *noun*.

eating disorder *noun*
a medical condition in which people's eating patterns are not normal, e.g. anorexia (when people undereat) or bulimia (when they overeat and deliberately vomit).

eau de cologne (o d' ka-**lone**) *noun*
short form is **cologne** a perfume diluted with alcohol which dries and cools the skin.
[French, water of *Cologne*, where it was first made]

eaves *plural noun*
the lower edge of a roof which overhangs the walls.

eavesdrop *verb* (**eavesdrops; eavesdropping; eavesdropped**)
to listen secretly to a conversation.
Word Family eavesdropper *noun*.
[from 'to be on the *eavesdrop*', the place on which water dropped from the eaves]

ebb *noun*
1 the return of the tide towards the sea.
2 a point of decline: *His business was at a low ebb.*
• **ebb** *verb*.

ebony (**ebb**-a-nee) *noun*
a very hard black wood obtained from a tropical tree.
[Greek *ebenos*]

ebullient (ib-**bul**-y'nt *or* ib-**bul**-y'nt) *adjective*
full of excitement or enthusiasm.
Word Family ebullience *noun*; **ebulliently** *adverb*.
[Latin *ebulliens* bubbling]

eccentric (ek-**sen**-trik) *adjective*
1 different, peculiar or irregular: *an eccentric person who collects old shoes.*
2 *Maths* not having the same centre.
3 *Maths* being off-centre.
4 (of a planet's orbit, etc.) deviating from a circular form.
Word Family eccentric *noun* a person who is different or peculiar; **eccentrically** *adverb*; **eccentricity** (ek-sen-**triss**-i-tee) *noun* (*plural* **eccentricities**).
[Greek *ek* out + *kentron* centre]

ecclesiastic (ik-**klee**-zee-ass-tik) *noun*
(*formal*) a priest.
Word Family ecclesiastical, ecclesiastic *adjective* of or relating to the Christian Church; **ecclesiastically** *adverb*.
[Greek *ekklesia* assembly, church]

echelon (**esh**-a-lon) *noun*
1 a particular group or grade of people within a system: *the higher echelons of industry.*
2 an arrowhead formation of infantry, aircraft or warships to give maximum firepower in all directions.
[French *échelon* rung of a ladder]

echo (**ek**-o) *noun* (*plural* **echoes**)
1 a repetition of sound produced by soundwaves reflecting off a surface.
2 any repetition or imitation.
Word Family echo *verb* (**echoes; echoing; echoed**); **echoless** *adjective*.
[Greek *ekho*]

eclair (**ay**-klair *or* i-**klair**) *noun*
a light finger-shaped cake with a cream or custard filling and coated with icing.
[French *éclair* lightning, because it is eaten in a flash]

eclectic (ik-**klek**-tik) *adjective*
using or derived from many different sources.
Word Family **eclectic** *noun*; **eclectically** *adverb*; **eclecticism** (ik-**klek**-ti-sizm) *noun*.
[Greek *eklektikos* picking out]

eclipse (ik-**klips**) *noun*
1 *Astronomy* the passing of one planet or satellite, especially the sun, moon or earth, in front of another.
2 any overshadowing or loss of brilliance.
• **eclipse** *verb*
1 to cause an eclipse.
2 to surpass or overshadow.
[Greek *ekleipsis* a failing to appear]

eco-friendly *adjective*
not harming or endangering the environment.

ecology (ee-**koll**-a-jee *or* ek-**oll**-a-jee) *noun*
a branch of biology involving the study of the interactions of animals and plants with each other and their environment.
Word Family **ecologist** *noun*; **ecological** (ee-ka-**loj**-i-k'l) *adjective*; **ecologically** *adverb*.
[Greek *oikos* household + -*logy*]

e-commerce *noun*
business done using electronic data transfer, especially over the Internet.
[*e-* + COMMERCE]

economic (ee-ka-**nom**-ik *or* ek-a-**nom**-ik) *adjective*
1 of or relating to the economy or to economics.
2 economical.

economical (ee-ka-**nom**-i-k'l *or* ek-a-**nom**-i-k'l) *adjective*
careful with money or resources and avoiding unnecessary expense or waste.
Word Family **economically** *adverb*.

economics (ee-ka-**nom**-iks *or* ek-a-**nom**-iks) *plural noun*
1 (*used with singular verb*) the study of the production and distribution of goods, services and wealth.
2 the financial aspects: *The economics of this project are not sound.*
Word Family **economist** (ee-**kon**-a-mist *or* ek-**kon**-a-mist) *noun*.

[Greek *oikonomia* household management]

economize, economise (ee-**kon**-a-mize *or* ek-**on**-a-mize) *verb*
to manage one's resources well and avoid unnecessary expense or waste.

economy (ee-**kon**-a-mee *or* ek-**on**-a-mee) *noun* (*plural* **economies**)
1 the system for the management of the money, property and goods of a country or region: *the strong economies of western Europe.*
2 careful management of money or resources: *With a little economy, our supply should last all winter.*
3 also **economy class** the cheapest class of air or rail travel.
• **economy** *adjective* giving the best value for money: *an enormous economy pack of washing powder.*

ecosphere *noun*
the parts of the universe where living organisms can exist.

ecosystem (ee-ko-sis-t'm *or* ek-o-sis-t'm) *noun*
a community of animals and plants together with the environment in which they live. Each part of the ecosystem both supports and depends on the other parts.

ecstasy (**ek**-sta-see) *noun* (*plural* **ecstasies**)
1 an extreme state of emotion, especially delight.
2 a delighted mood.
3 a mystical spiritual trance or frenzy.
4 (**Ecstasy**) an illegal hallucinogenic designer drug.
Word Family **ecstatic** (ek-**stat**-ik) *adjective*; **ecstatically** *adverb*.
[Greek *ekstasis* standing aside, a trance]

| ! | Note the spelling of *ecstasy*: it has an *s* before the final *y*. |

ectoplasm *noun*
a thick bright substance that is said to come from a medium during a trance.

ecu (**ay**-kew) *noun*
(*formerly*) a unit of money in the European Union, replaced by the euro.
[acronym of European Currency Unit]

ecumenical (ek-yoo-**men**-i-k'l) *adjective*
Religion of or relating to the whole Christian Church, or to the movement within the Christian Church towards cooperation and eventual unity.
Word Family **ecumenism** (ik-**yoo**-men-izm) *noun*.

eczema (eks-i-ma) *noun*
an inflammation of the skin causing an itchy, flaky or inflamed surface.

eddy *noun* (*plural* **eddies**)
a circular or whirling current.
● **eddy** *verb* (**eddies; eddying; eddied**).

edelweiss (aid-'l-vice) *noun*
an Alpine plant with white flowers.
[German *edel* noble + *weiss* white]

Eden *noun*
1 *Biblical* the garden which was the first home of Adam and Eve.
2 a delightful place or condition of innocence and purity.

edge (ej) *noun*
1 a border or line where one thing ends or meets another: *the edge of a cliff.* □ *the edge of a coin.*
2 the thin sharp side of a blade, etc.
3 an advantage: *Because of his experience he has an edge over the other applicants.*
Phrases **on edge** nervous and uncomfortable: *She felt on edge because the plane was late.* **take the edge off** to reduce the severity of: *That snack took the edge off my hunger.*
● **edge** *verb*
1 to provide with an edge.
2 to move gradually or cautiously: *He edged his way up the face of the cliff.*

edgeways *adverb* also **edgewise**
with an edge forwards.

edgy (ej-ee) *adjective* (**edgier; edgiest**)
irritable or nervous.
Word Family **edgily** *adverb*; **edginess** *noun.*

edible (ed-i-b'l) *adjective*
fit to be eaten.
Word Family **edibility** (ed-i-bill-i-tee) *noun.*
[Latin *edere* to eat]

edict (ee-dikt) *noun*
an official command.

edifice (ed-i-fiss) *noun*
a large or imposing building.
[Latin *aedis* a house + *facere* to make]

edify (ed-i-fie) *verb* (**edifies; edifying; edified**)
to instruct, especially for personal or moral improvement.
Word Family **edification** (ed-i-fi-kay-sh'n) *noun.*

edit *verb*
1 to put together material, often from a lot of sources, to make a book, film, etc.

2 to correct and prepare a manuscript for printing.
3 to be the person in charge of a newspaper, etc.
[Latin *editus* put forth]

edition (i-dish-'n) *noun*
any of the copies of a book, newspaper, etc. printed at one time.

editor *noun*
1 a person who edits books, films, etc.
2 a person responsible for the content of all or a part of a newspaper, magazine, etc.: *She is the fashion editor of a national paper.*

editorial *noun* also called **leader; leading article.**
an article in a newspaper, etc. expressing the opinion of the newspaper on current issues.
● **editorial** *adjective* of or relating to editing or an editor.

educate (ed-yoo-kate) *verb*
to instruct or develop, especially through formal teaching or training.
Word Family **educated** *adjective* 1 having undergone education. 2 showing culture and learning; **educable** *adjective* able to be educated.

educated guess *noun* (*plural* **educated guesses**)
a guess based on knowledge: *I didn't know the answer, but I took an educated guess and it turned out to be right.*

education (ed-yoo-kay-sh'n) *noun*
1 the act or process of educating: *Education is free in some countries.*
2 the teaching profession: *My mother was in education.*
Word Family **educational** *adjective*; **educationist, educationalist** *noun* an expert in the theory or method of education, **educator** *noun* (*formal*) a teacher.
[Latin *educare* to train]

eek *interjection* (*informal*) used to express surprise or slight alarm.

eel *noun*
any of a large group of snake-like edible fish which migrate from rivers to the Sargasso Sea to breed.

e'en (een) *adverb*
a poetic word for **even.**

e'er (air) *adverb*
a poetic word for **ever.**

eerie (eer-ee) *adjective* (**eerier; eeriest**)
strange or weird.

Word Family eerily adverb; **eeriness** noun.

efface (if-**face**) verb
(formal) to wipe out or destroy.
Word Family effacement noun.

effect (if-**fekt**) noun
1 a direct result: What is the effect of sunlight on this fabric?
2 the power to produce results: Our arguments had no effect.
3 the state of being in operation: His plan was put into effect.
4 a technique or device used to create an impression, e.g. in the theatre: special effects.
5 (**effects**) (formal) any goods or movable objects: He only has a few personal effects.
Phrases for effect in order to create a particular impression on other people. **in effect** in reality. **take effect** to begin to operate. **to this effect, to that effect** with this or that meaning or result: Yes, I recall she did say something to that effect.
• **effect** verb (formal) to bring about, achieve or cause to happen.
[Latin effectus made or brought about]

> [!] Do not confuse effect with AFFECT.

effective (if-**fek**-tiv) adjective
1 producing the intended effect: Advertising is an effective way of increasing sales.
2 actual: This moment was the effective end of their relationship.
3 in operation: The pay rise is effective from last month.
Word Family effectively adverb; **effectiveness** noun.

> [!] The words effective and efficient have related but separate meanings. Effective means 'producing the intended effect', whereas efficient means 'working well with minimum waste of effort': This method of keeping your accounts may be effective but it is not efficient (= it may produce the results you want, but it is not the best or quickest way).

effeminate (if-**fem**-i-nit) adjective
(of a man) having excessively feminine qualities.
Word Family effeminately adverb; **effeminacy** noun.

effervesce (eff-a-**vess**) verb
1 to give off small bubbles of gas.

2 to be lively or vivacious.
Word Family effervescence noun; **effervescent** adjective.
[Latin effervescere to begin to boil over]

effete (ef-**feet**) adjective
exhausted, feeble or lacking energy.
[Latin effetus worn out by child-bearing]

efficacious (eff-i-**kay**-shus) adjective
effective, especially as a method or remedy.
Word Family efficacy (**eff**-ik-a-see) noun.

efficient (if-**fish**-'nt) adjective
1 working well and able to obtain the desired results: an efficient secretary.
2 (of machinery, etc.) producing the desired result with minimum waste or expenditure of energy.
Word Family efficiency noun; **efficiently** adverb.

> [!] Do not confuse efficient with EFFECTIVE.

effigy (**eff**-i-jee) noun (plural **effigies**)
an image or sculptured likeness of a person.

> The word **effigy** is derived from the Latin noun effigies (a likeness or representation), from the Latin verb effingere (to form or portray). Effigy was originally borrowed into English as effigies, and Shakespeare used this form. Later this was mistakenly thought to be a plural form and effigy came into being.

effluence (ef-loo-'nce) noun
1 an outward flow.
2 any substance which flows out.

> [!] Do not confuse effluence with AFFLUENCE.

effluent (ef-loo-ent) noun
any waste liquid flowing out of a sewage farm, chemical works, etc.
[Latin effluens flowing out]

effluvium (ef-**loo**-vee-um) noun (plural **effluvia**)
a foul-smelling vapour.

effort noun
1 a use of physical or mental energy: Come on, make more effort!
2 a struggle or attempt: All our efforts were in vain.
3 Physics a force acting on something.
Word Family effortless adjective done without, or as if without, effort; **effortlessly** adverb; **effortlessness** noun.

effrontery (if-**frunt**-a-ree) *noun*
a shameless or impudent boldness.

effusion (if-**few**-*zh*'n) *noun*
1 an unreserved expression of feelings, etc.
2 the act of pouring forth.

effusive *adjective*
unreserved or freely showing one's
feelings.
Word Family **effusively** *adverb*;
effusiveness *noun*.
[Latin *effusus* poured out]

egalitarian (ig-al-i-**tair**-ee-an) *adjective*
of or favouring equality for all people.
Word Family **egalitarian** *noun* a person
who favours equality; **egalitarianism**
noun.
[French *égalité* equality]

egg¹ *noun*
1 the roundish object formed during the
development of a bird or reptile and
consisting of a shell which contains a yolk
surrounded by a clear fluid substance. If
fertilized the egg may develop into a new
organism.
2 an infertile egg of the domestic hen,
eaten raw or cooked.
3 *Biology* a female reproductive cell.
4 (*dated informal*) a person of the stated
kind: *He's a bad egg.*
Phrases **as sure as eggs** (*informal*) safely
predictable. **have egg on one's face** to be
made to look foolish **put all one's eggs
in one basket** to risk everything in one
attempt.

egg² *verb*
Phrase **egg someone on** (*informal*) to
urge or encourage someone.

egghead *noun*
(*informal*) a highly educated person.

egg-nog *noun*
a drink made from milk, eggs and spices,
usually with wine or spirits.

egg white *noun* also called **albumen**.
the clear outer fluid substance in an egg,
which becomes firm and white when
cooked.

ego (**ee**-go or **egg**-o) *noun*
1 self-esteem: *Their criticisms bruised her
ego.*
2 *Psychology* the part of a person which is
able to think, feel, act and distinguish itself
from all other people or objects. The ego is
the conscious part of the personality.
Compare ID.
[Latin, I]

egocentric (ee-go-**sen**-trik or egg-o-**sen**-
trik) *adjective*
concerned mostly with one's own interests
and considering everything in relation to
oneself.
Word Family **egocentricity** (ee-go-sen-
triss-i-tee or egg-o-sen-**triss**-i-tee) *noun*.

egoist (**ee**-go-ist or **egg**-o-ist) *noun*
a self-interested or conceited person.
Word Family **egoistic** (ee-go-**iss**-tik or
egg-o-**iss**-tik) *adjective*; **egoism** *noun*.

egotist (**ee**-ga-tist or **egg**-a-tist) *noun*
1 an offensively selfish person.
2 a person who talks far too much about
himself or herself.
Word Family **egotistic** (ee-ga-**tist**-ik or
egg-a-**tist**-ik), **egotistical** *adjective*;
egotism *noun*.

ego trip *noun*
activity which makes one feel very
important: *Being in the first team is a real
ego trip for him!*

Eid (eed) *noun* also called **Id**.
a Muslim feast for thanking Allah and
celebrating a happy occasion, e.g. the end
of Ramadan or the hajj.
[Arabic]

eiderdown (**eye**-der-down) *noun*
a quilt or bedspread.
[from *eider*, a species of duck, the soft
breast feathers of which were originally
used to fill bedspreads]

eight (ate) *noun*
1 a cardinal number, the symbol 8 in
Arabic numerals, VIII in Roman
numerals.
2 *Rowing* the crew of a light narrow racing
boat, consisting of a cox and eight rowers.
Phrase **have one over the eight**
(*informal*) to become slightly drunk
Word Family **eight** *adjective*; **eighth**
noun, adjective

eighteen (ay-**teen**) *noun*
a cardinal number, the symbol 18 in
Arabic numerals, XVIII in Roman
numerals.
Word Family **eighteen** *adjective*;
eighteenth *noun, adjective*.

eighth note ⇨ QUAVER (definition 2).

eighty (**ay**-tee) *noun* (*plural* **eighties**)
1 a cardinal number, the symbol 80 in
Arabic numerals, LXXX in Roman
numerals.
2 (**eighties**) the numbers 80 to 89 in a
series, such as the years in a century.
Word Family **eighty** *adjective*; **eightieth**
noun, adjective.

eisteddfod (eye-**sted**-f'd) *noun*
(*plural* **eisteddfods** or **eisteddfodau**
(eye-sted-**fod**-eye)) a festival for musical
competitions.
[Welsh, session]

either (**eye**-*th*a *or* **ee**-*th*a) *adjective,
pronoun, conjunction, adverb*
1 one or the other of two things: (as an
adjective) *I do not like either colour very
much.* □ (as a pronoun) *I have two pens, so
take either.* □ (as a conjunction) *Either
phone or write a letter.* □ (as an adverb) *He
must be either blind or stupid.*
2 both one and the other: *There were guards
on either side of the President.*

> ⚠ In formal English, *either . . . or*
> should be followed by a singular
> verb (*Either James or Sarah is responsible
> for this*) unless at least one of the
> alternatives referred to is plural (*Either
> coins or notes are acceptable*).

ejaculation (i-jak-yoo-**lay**-sh'n) *noun*
1 (*formal*) a sudden exclamation.
2 the discharge of semen from the penis.
Word Family ejaculate (i-**jak**-yoo-late)
verb; **ejaculatory** *adjective*.
[Latin *ejaculari* to shoot forth]

eject (i-**jekt**) *verb*
to force out or cause to be removed: *Police
were called to eject the demonstrators from the
building.*
Word Family ejection *noun*; **ejector**
noun a person or device that ejects.
[Latin *ejectus* cast out]

eke *verb*
Phrases eke out a living to manage to
make enough money to survive on. **eke
something out** to try to make something
last: *Can we eke out our supplies till winter?*

elaborate (e-**lab**-a-rit) *adjective*
carefully detailed and exact: *an elaborate
design.*
● **elaborate** (e-**lab**-a-rate) *verb* to work
out or describe in detail: *She spent some
time elaborating her plan.*
Phrase elaborate on to give further
details about: *He refused to elaborate on his
remark.*
Word Family elaborately *adverb*;
elaborateness *noun* the quality of being
elaborate; **elaboration** (e-lab-a-**ray**-sh'n)
noun.
[Latin *elaborare* to use every effort]

élan (ay-**lan**) *noun*
enthusiasm or liveliness: *He approaches life
with great élan.*
[French *élancer* to hurl or rush forward]

eland (**ee**-land) *noun*
an ox-like African antelope with short
twisted horns.
[Dutch, elk]

elapse *verb*
(of time) to pass.
[Latin *elapsus* slipped away]

elastic (i-**lass**-tik) *adjective*
1 able to recover its shape after being
pulled, pressed, etc.
2 flexible: *Our schedule for the trip is quite
elastic.*
● **elastic** *noun* any material which returns
to its original shape after being pulled,
pressed, etc.
Word Family elasticity (ill-ass-**tiss**-i-
tee) *noun*.

elastic band ⇨ RUBBER BAND.

Elastoplast *noun*
(*trademark*) a covering for a wound on an
adhesive tape backing.

elated (i-**lay**-t'd) *adjective*
filled with pleasure and excitement: *She
seemed positively elated by the news.*
Word Family elatedly *adverb*; **elation,
elatedness** *noun*.
[Latin *elatus* raised, carried away]

elbow (**el**-bo) *noun*
1 *Anatomy* the joint in the middle of the
arm.
2 anything which is bent or shaped like an
elbow, such as a joint in a pipe.
Phrase give someone the elbow
(*informal*) to stop having a relationship
with someone.
● **elbow** *verb* to push or nudge with the
elbow: *We elbowed our way through the
crowd.*

elbow grease *noun*
(*informal*) any hard work or effort.

elbow room *noun*
(*informal*) enough room to move freely.

elder[1] *adjective*
(of a person, especially a relation) older:
This is my elder brother, Tom.
● **elder** *noun*
1 a person with influence or authority in a
group: *The tribal elders held a council.*
2 a person who is older: *She is my elder by
four years.*
3 *Christianity* a member of the early
Church with spiritual authority.
4 *Christianity* a lay official in some
Protestant sects.

> ! The adjective *elder* describes an older person (*my elder brother*) but cannot be used in place of *older* when comparing the ages of two people (*Kate is older than Yasmin*). ⇨ OLD.

elder² *noun*
any of a group of shrubs and trees with white scented flowers and black or red berries.

elderly *adjective*
rather old.

elder statesman *noun* (*plural* **elder statesmen**)
a person in politics or public life who is greatly respected.

eldest *adjective*
(of a person, especially a relation) oldest: *My eldest sister is overseas.*
• **eldest** *noun* the oldest: *Which of you three is the eldest?*

> ! On the use of *eldest* or *oldest* ⇨ OLD.

El Dorado (el-dor-**ah**-doe) *noun* also **eldorado**
any place where fortunes can be made quickly.
[Spanish *El Dorado* the Gilded One, the name given by the Conquistadores to the ruler of the legendary golden city they hoped to find north of the Amazon]

elect *verb*
to choose, especially by voting.
• **elect** *adjective*
1 chosen or selected.
2 (*used after a noun*) chosen for an office or position but not yet installed: *She is the ambassador elect.*
[Latin *electus* picked out]

election *noun*
1 the selection by voting of one or more people for position or office.
2 (*formal*) the act of choosing something.
by-election a political election held in one local area to choose its representative for parliament.
general election in the United Kingdom, the election of the whole of the House of Commons.

electioneer (ill-ek-sh'-**neer**) *verb*
to work for the election of a particular candidate or party.

elective *adjective*
1 relating to or appointed by election.
2 (of medical treatment) chosen by the patient, and not urgent.

elector *noun*
1 a person who is entitled to vote.
2 (**Elector**) *History* a prince entitled to participate in the choice of a Holy Roman Emperor.
Word Family **electoral** *adjective* relating to electors or political elections.

electoral roll *noun* also called **electoral register**.
a list of all the people who are entitled to vote.

electorate (i-**lek**-ta-rit) *noun*
all the people living in an area who are entitled to vote.

electric *adjective*
1 involving or producing electricity: *an electric current.*
2 thrilling or exciting: *There was an electric atmosphere during the competition.*
Word Family **electrical** *adjective* involving or producing electricity; **electrically** *adverb*.

electrical engineering *noun*
the branch of applied science which is concerned with electric power, especially with the design and construction of electrical machinery, power lines and electronic equipment.

electric chair *noun*
a device which uses electricity to execute a convicted criminal.

electric charge *noun*
short form is **charge** *Electricity* a quantity of energy, which may be positive or negative. Bodies with the same electric charge repel each other and bodies with the opposite electric charge attract each other.

electric current *noun*
short form is **current** *Electricity* the rate of transfer of an electric charge.
alternating current an electric current which regularly changes in magnitude and direction, so that the average flow over a period is zero.
direct current an electric current which does not change direction, although its magnitude may vary.

electric eye *noun*
(*informal*) a photoelectric cell.

electric field *noun*
an area of space inside which a positive electric charge will experience a force in the direction of the field.

electric guitar *noun*
a guitar with a device which transmits the sounds through an amplifier to a loudspeaker.

electrician (ill-ek-**trish**-'n) *noun*
a person trained in the installation, repair and maintenance of electrical equipment.

electricity (ill-ek-**triss**-i-tee) *noun*
1 the energy released by the movement of charged particles, such as electrons.
2 the supply of electric power to a building, etc.
3 a feeling of great excitement.

electric storm *noun*
a thunderstorm with lightning.

electrify (ill-ek-tri-fie) *verb* (**electrifies; electrifying; electrified**)
1 to convert to operating by electricity: *The railway line was electrified in 1999.*
2 to thrill, shock or excite: *The audience was electrified by the music.*
Word Family **electrification** (ill-ek-tri-fi-**kay**-sh'n) *noun*; **electrifying** *adjective*.

electrocardiogram
(ill-ek-tro-**kar**-dee-o-gram) *noun*
short form is **ECG** a representation of the heartbeat made by recording the flow of electric currents in the heart muscle.
[*electro-* + Greek *kardia* heart + *gramma* something written]

electroconvulsive therapy *noun*
Medicine the application of electric shocks to the brain as a method of treating depression, etc.

electrocute (i-**lek**-tra-kewt) *verb*
to kill with an electric shock.
Word Family **electrocution** (ill-ek-tra-**kew**-sh'n) *noun*.

electrode *noun*
Electricity a conductor by which electrons enter, leave or are controlled within an electrical device.
[*electro-* + Greek *hodos* a way]

electroencephalogram
(i-lek-tro-en-**seff**-a-lo-gram) *noun*
short form is **EEG** the recording of the electrical activity of the brain.
[*electro-* + Greek *enkephalos* brain + *gramma* something written]

electrolysis (ill-ek-**troll**-a-sis) *noun*
Chemistry a process in which a chemical reaction occurs as a result of an electric current being passed through an electrolyte. Decomposition of compounds can be achieved by electrolysis.
[*electro-* + Greek *lysis* a loosening]

electrolyte (i-**lek**-tra-lite) *noun*
Chemistry a compound which, in solution or when molten, forms ions which conduct electricity.

electromagnet *noun*
a device consisting of a coil of wire around a soft iron core which becomes a magnet when electricity flows through the coil.
Word Family **electromagnetic** *adjective*
⇨ MAGNETIC (definition 1);
electromagnetism *noun* the magnetism caused by a moving electric charge.

electromagnetic radiation *noun*
Physics a form of radiation consisting of **electromagnetic waves** which consist of an electric field and a magnetic field at right angles to each other: *Heat, light, X-rays and radio waves are all forms of electromagnetic radiation.*

electromagnetic spectrum *noun*
the range of electromagnetic radiation, from the short wavelengths and high energy of X-rays, gamma rays, etc. to the long wavelengths and low energy of infrared, radio waves, etc.

electromotive force *noun*
short form is **emf** *Electricity* the amount of energy, measured in volts, required to produce a flow of electricity.

electron *noun*
Physics the stable negatively charged elementary particle which orbits atomic nuclei and forms the basis of electricity.
[from ELECTR(ic) + (i)ON]

electronic (ill-ek-**tron**-ik) *adjective*
1 using microchips, transistors, etc. which affect electric current as it passes through: *electronic equipment.* □ *electronic music.*
2 using a computer network: *the increase in electronic shopping.*
3 of or relating to electrons.
Word Family **electronically** *adverb*.

electronic mail *noun*
(*formal*) email.

electronic publishing *noun*
the publication of material in machine-readable form, so that it can be directly processed by computer, rather than in printed form on paper.

electronics (ill-ek-**tron**-iks) *plural noun*
1 (*used with singular verb*) *Physics* the study of the flow of electricity in a gas, semiconductor, etc., and of devices and systems to control and utilize it.
2 devices which use microchips, transistors, etc.

electronic tagging *noun*
a system whereby a person agrees to wear an electronic device so that the police can keep track of his or her activities.

electroplate *verb*
to coat with a thin film of metal by electrolysis.
Word Family **electroplating** *noun*.

electrostatic (ill-ek-tro-**stat**-ik) *adjective*
Physics of or relating to stationary electric charges, and not electric currents.

elegant *adjective*
tasteful and refined, especially in dress or manner: *She wore a simple but elegant dress.*
Word Family **elegantly** *adverb*; **elegance** *noun*.
[Latin *elegans* discriminating]

elegiac (ell-a-**jie**-ak) *adjective*
of or suited to an elegy.

elegy (**ell**-a-jee) *noun* (*plural* **elegies**)
a sad song or poem in memory of a dead person.
[Greek *elegos* a song of mourning]

element (**ell**-a-m'nt) *noun*
1 *Chemistry* a substance made up of atoms all of which have the same number of protons. Compare COMPOUND[1] *noun* (definition 2).
2 a basic and necessary part or feature of a whole: *Which elements of his character stand out in your memory?*
3 a small amount: *There is an element of truth in what she says.*
4 (**the elements**) the basic principles or beginnings of a subject: *the elements of grammar.*
5 (**the elements**) the forces of nature, weather, etc.: *The abandoned house had been exposed to the elements for years.*
6 a preferred or more suitable environment: *She is in her element at parties.*
7 *Electricity* a wire conductor in an electrical appliance, etc. which opposes the electric current and changes it into heat.
8 any of the four substances, air, earth, water and fire, which ancient philosophers believed combined to form the universe.
Word Family **elemental** (ell-a-**men**-t'l) *adjective*; **elementally** *adverb*.
[Latin *elementum*]

elementary (ell-a-**men**-tree) *adjective*
basic, simple or undeveloped: *an elementary mistake.*

elementary particle *noun* also called **fundamental particle**.
Physics any of the basic units from which all matter is composed, e.g. the electron, proton, neutron or positron.

elementary school *noun*
American a primary school.

elephant *noun* (*plural* **elephant** or **elephants**)
a member of either of two species of very large plant-eating mammals of Africa and Asia, with thick leathery skins, long trunks and curved tusks. The African elephant has larger fan-shaped ears.
Word Family **elephantine** (ell-a-**fan**-tine) *adjective* of or like an elephant.

elevate (**ell**-a-vate) *verb*
(*formal*) to lift up or raise: *The teacher's presence in the room elevated our discussions.*
[Latin *elevare* to lift up]

elevation *noun*
1 the height of anything, especially above the ground or sea level.
2 (*formal*) the act of elevating: *His elevation to the position of manager came as a surprise.*
3 *Architecture* a drawing of one side of a building.
4 also called **altitude**. *Astronomy* an angle made above the horizon or horizontal plane, e.g. by a star or planet.

elevator (**ell**-a-vay-ta) *noun*
1 (*especially American*) a lift.
2 a person or thing that lifts.

eleven *noun*
1 a cardinal number, the symbol 11 in Arabic numerals, XI in Roman numerals.
2 the eleven players in a cricket, soccer, etc. team.
Word Family **eleven** *adjective*, **eleventh** *noun*, *adjective*.

eleven-plus *noun*
an examination taken at the age of eleven or twelve, especially in the past, to decide the type of state secondary school best suited to the pupil.

elevenses *noun*
(*dated informal*) a morning snack eaten at about 11 a.m.

eleventh hour *noun*
the very last moment when something can possibly be done: *The rescue team arrived at the eleventh hour.*

elf *noun* (*plural* **elves**)
Folklore a small, often mischievous, fairy.
Word Family **elfin, elfish, elvish** *adjective* of or like an elf.

elicit (il-**liss**-it) *verb*
(*formal*) to bring or cause to come out:
*The book fails to elicit the truth about his
death.*

elide *verb*
to leave out a sound, such as a vowel or
syllable, when pronouncing a word, e.g.
the *a* in *we're* (we are).
Word Family **elision** (ee-**lizh**-'n) *noun.*
[Latin *elidere* to knock out]

eligible (**ell**-i-j'-b'l) *adjective*
1 suitable or having the right
qualifications.
2 making a good future marriage partner:
an eligible bachelor.
Word Family **eligibly** *adverb;* **eligibility**
(ell-ij-a-**bill**-a-tee) *noun.*
[Latin *eligere* to pick out]

eliminate (il-**lim**-i-nate) *verb*
to remove or get rid of: *We have eliminated
several more names from the list.*
Word Family **elimination** (il-lim-i-**nay**-
sh'n) *noun.*
[Latin *eliminare* to throw outside]

élite (ay-**leet**) *noun*
a superior few people within a group or
society.
[French *élit* chosen]

elixir (ee-**lik**-sa) *noun*
a potion or remedy believed to prolong life
or cure anything: *the elixir of eternal youth.*
[Arabic *al-iksir* the philosopher's stone of
alchemy]

elk *noun* (*plural* **elk** or **elks**)
the largest existing deer of Europe, Asia
and North America.

ell *noun*
an old measure equal to about 45 inches,
about 1·1 m.

ellipse *noun*
a regular oval shape formed when a cone is
cut by a plane which is not parallel to, and
does not pass through, the base of the
cone.

ellipsis (el-**lip**-siss) *noun* (*plural* **ellipses**)
(el-**lip**-seez)
1 *Grammar* the leaving out of a word or
words in a sentence, which would make it
more complete or correct, as in *While (I
was) waiting for the train I read a magazine.*
2 *Grammar* a mark, such as – or . . ., used
to indicate this.
[Greek *elleipsis* a falling short]

elliptic *adjective* also **elliptical**
1 having the shape of an ellipse.
2 of or relating to ellipsis.
Word Family **elliptically** *adverb.*

elm *noun*
any of a group of very tall deciduous trees
used for timber.

elocution (ell-o-**kew**-sh'n) *noun*
the art or study of speaking clearly or well
in public.
Word Family **elocutionary** *adjective.*
[Latin *elocutio* oratorical delivery]

elongate (ee-long-gate) *verb*
to make or become longer.
Word Family **elongation** (ee-long-**gay**-
sh'n) *noun.*

elope *verb*
to run away with a lover, especially in
order to get married without parental
permission.
Word Family **elopement** *noun.*

eloquent (**ell**-a-kw'nt) *adjective*
1 skilful, fluent and expressive in speech.
2 (*formal*) expressing something strongly.
Word Family **eloquently** *adverb;*
eloquence *noun.*
[Latin *eloquens* speaking out]

else *adverb*
1 other than or as well: *Do you want
anything else to eat?*
2 otherwise: *We must leave now else we'll be
late.*
Phrase **or else** (*informal*) or there will be
trouble: *Do as I say – or else!*

elsewhere *adverb*
in or to another place: *That restaurant was
packed, so we had to go elsewhere.*

elucidate (il-**loo**-si-date) *verb*
(*formal*) to make clear or distinct: *Will you
elucidate the main points of the plan?*
Word Family **elucidation** (il-loo-si-**day**-
sh'n) *noun.*
[Latin *e-* perfectly + *lucidus* clear, from
lucis of light]

elude *verb*
to escape from or avoid cleverly: *The
robbers had eluded police for three weeks.*
Word Family **elusion** *noun.*
[Latin *eludere* to outmanoeuvre]

elusive *adjective*
difficult to catch, recall, etc.
Word Family **elusiveness** *noun.*

elves
the plural of **elf**.

elvish *adjective* ⇨ ELF.

emaciated (im-**may**-see-ate-id) *adjective*
extremely thin: *the prisoners' emaciated
bodies.*
Word Family **emaciation** (im-may-see-
ay-sh'n) *noun.*
[Latin *e-* very + *macies* thinness]

email *noun*
1 a system for sending and receiving messages using a computer network, usually the Internet.
2 a message or messages sent or received in this way.
Word Family **email** *verb*; **emailer** *noun*.
[e- + MAIL]

emanate (em-a-nate) *verb*
(*formal*) to come or be produced from: *His fear of water emanated from an accident when he was young.*
Word Family **emanation** (em-a-**nay**-sh'n).
[Latin *emanare* to flow out]

emancipate (im-**man**-si-pate) *verb*
to set free from any restraint, especially slavery.
Word Family **emancipation** (im-man-si-**pay**-sh'n) *noun* the act of setting free: *fighting for the emancipation of women.*

The word **emancipate** comes from Latin *emancipare*, a verb used in ancient Rome to refer to the freeing of a son from the legal authority of his father. The word is related to the Latin noun *mancipium* (ownership), and *emancipate* was first used in English to mean 'to free people from slavery'. It then came to mean 'to free people, e.g. women, from social or legal restrictions'.

emasculate (im-**mass**-kew-late) *verb*
1 to take away the strength of: *a decision which effectively emasculated the new law.*
2 to take away the masculinity of: *He was emasculated by 40 years spent with his overbearing mother.*
3 to castrate.
Word Family **emasculation** (im-mass-kew-**lay**-sh'n) *noun.*
[Latin *e* on + *masculus* male]

embalm (em-**bahm**) *verb*
to preserve a dead body by treating it with chemicals.
Word Family **embalmer** *noun.*

embankment *noun*
any raised wall or mound used to support a road, hold back water, etc.

embargo *noun* (*plural* **embargoes**)
an official order which stops or restricts trade, movement of ships, etc.: *an oil embargo.*
[Spanish *embargar* to restrain]

embark *verb*
to get on a ship or aircraft.
Phrase **embark on, embark upon** to start.
Word Family **embarkation** *noun.*

embarrass *verb*
1 to cause to feel uncomfortable or self-conscious: *She was embarrassed by her mother's behaviour.*
2 to cause to have money problems: *financially embarrassed.*
Word Family **embarrassing** *adjective*; **embarrassingly** *adverb*; **embarrassed** *adjective*; **embarrassedly** *adverb* in an embarrassed way; **embarrassment** *noun*
1 the state of being embarrassed: *We noticed their slight embarrassment.*
2 anything which causes one to be embarrassed: *His lack of tact has always been an embarrassment to us.*

> ! Note the spelling of *embarrass*: it has two *r*'s and two *s*'s.

embassy (em-ba-see) *noun* (*plural* **embassies**)
1 the offices and official home of an ambassador.
2 an ambassador and his or her staff.

embattled *adjective*
surrounded by enemies, trouble, etc.: *The embattled President struggled to express himself.*

embed *verb* (**embeds; embedding, embedded**)
to sink or fix firmly into a substance: *The boulders were completely embedded in the soil.*

embellish *verb*
to add details or decoration to: *Tell the story simply, without embellishing the facts.*
Word Family **embellishment** *noun* 1 the act of embellishing. 2 any added details or decoration.
[em- + Latin *bellus* handsome]

ember *noun*
(*often* **embers**) a burning piece of wood, ash, etc., especially in the remains of a fire.

embezzle *verb*
to steal money placed in one's care: *The bank clerk had embezzled £10 000.*
Word Family **embezzlement** *noun*; **embezzler** *noun* a person who embezzles.

embitter *verb*
to make a person feel bitter.
Word Family **embitterment** *noun.*

emblazon (em-**blay**-z'n) *verb*
to decorate richly, especially with heraldic inscriptions and devices.

emblem (em-bl'm) *noun*
a distinctive object or design which represents or symbolizes something: *A dove is the emblem of peace.*

embody verb (**embodies; embodying; embodied**)
1 to represent or give a form to: *She embodies both beauty and nobility.*
2 to include.
Word Family embodiment noun anything which embodies something.

embolden verb
(*formal*) to encourage or make bold.

embolism (**em**-ba-lizm) noun
Medicine the blocking of a blood vessel by material, e.g. tissue fragments, which is carried in the blood and lodges in a vein or artery.

emboss verb
to carve, mould or stamp a design so that it stands out on a surface.

embrace verb
1 to hug or take closely in one's arms.
2 (*formal*) to include: *The speech embraced many interesting issues.*
3 (*formal*) to accept or receive willingly.
• **embrace** noun.
[em- + Latin *bracchium* arm]

embrocation (em-bra-**kay**-sh'n) noun
an ointment or lotion rubbed on the body to relieve pain or stiffness.
[Greek *embrokhé* lotion]

embroider verb
to sew with decorative stitches.
Figurative I decided to embroider the story a little.
Word Family embroiderer noun; **embroidery** noun 1 the art of embroidering. 2 anything which is embroidered: *The cuffs on her shirt were edged with embroidery.*

embroil verb
to involve in something that it is difficult to get out of: *I'm afraid we got embroiled in an argument.*

embryo (**em**-bri-o) noun
Biology an organism in the early stages of development from a fertilized egg.
Phrase **in embryo** in the early stages: *Our plans are still in embryo.*
Word Family embryonic (em-bri-**on**-ik) adjective 1 undeveloped like an embryo.
2 of an embryo.
[Greek *embryon*]

emend (im-**mend**) verb
to remove errors from a manuscript or text.
Word Family emendation (ee-men-**day**-sh'n) noun.

> [!] Do not confuse *emend* with AMEND.

emerald noun
1 a rare bright green variety of beryl, used as a gem.
2 a strong bright green colour.
• **emerald** adjective.
[Greek *smaragdos*]

emerge (im-**merj**) verb
1 to appear or come into sight, especially after being hidden: *The sun emerged again from behind the clouds.*
2 to become known: *Some new facts have now emerged.*
3 to come through a difficult time: *We emerged from the bankruptcy stronger than we had been before.*
Word Family emergence noun.
[Latin *emergere* to rise from the waters]

emergency (im-**mer**-j'n-see) noun (plural **emergencies**)
a sudden serious event for which immediate action is necessary: *In an emergency, ring me on this number.*
• **emergency** adjective designed or useful as a standby or substitute in case of need: *emergency brakes.*

emergent (im-**mer**-j'nt) adjective also **emerging**
coming into view or independent existence, often unexpectedly: *This country must now be seen as an emergent nuclear power.*

emeritus (ee-**merr**-i-tus) adjective
(of a professor, etc.) retired but keeping an honorary title because of outstanding service.
[Latin, having served his time (in the army)]

emery (**em**-a-ree) noun
a very hard mineral substance used for grinding and polishing.

emery board noun
a strip of card or wood coated with emery and used to file fingernails.

emetic (im-**met**-ik) noun
a substance used to cause vomiting.
[Greek *emetiké*]

emigrate (**em**-i-grate) verb
to go from one's own country to live in another. Compare IMMIGRATE.
Word Family emigration (em-i-**gray**-sh'n) noun the act of emigrating; **emigrant** noun a person who emigrates.
[Latin *emigrare* to move out]

émigré (**em**-i-gray) noun
a person who emigrates to escape political persecution.
[French]

eminent *adjective*
1 having high rank, distinction or reputation: *an eminent professor.*
2 (*formal*) remarkable.
Word Family **eminence** *noun* 1 a position of high rank or distinction: *He was pleased that a woman of her eminence would agree to represent him.* 2 (**Eminence**) *Roman Catholicism* a title of respect for a cardinal; **eminently** *adverb.*
[Latin *eminens* standing out, lofty]

emir (em-**eer**) *noun* also **amir**
a governor, prince, nobleman, chief or high official of a Muslim state.
[Arabic *amir* ruler]

emissary (**em**-i-sa-ree) *noun* (*plural* **emissaries**)
a person sent as a diplomatic representative on a special mission, envoy.

emit (im-**mit** *or* ee-**mit**) *verb* (**emits; emitting; emitted**)
1 to give out: *The soil is still emitting radiation.*
2 to utter: *She suddenly emitted a shriek of horror.*
Word Family **emission** (im-**mish**-'n *or* ee-**mish**-'n) *noun* 1 the act of emitting. 2 anything which is emitted.
[Latin *emittere* to send forth]

emollient *adjective*
having the power to soothe or soften: *an emollient face lotion.*
● **emollient** *noun.*
[Latin *emolliens* making soft]

emolument (im-**mol**-yoo-m'nt) *noun* (*formal*) any profit from employment, such as a fee, salary, etc.
[Latin *emolumentum* gain, profit]

emotion (im-**mo**-sh'n) *noun*
any strong sensation, such as fear, joy, sorrow, etc.: *Her voice expressed her intense emotion.*
Word Family **emotional** *adjective* 1 of or caused by emotion: *She gets very emotional about animals;* **emotionally** *adverb;* **emotive** *adjective* stirring up emotion: *an emotive assertion;* **emotively** *adverb;* **emotionalism** *noun* the tendency to display excessive emotion.

> **!** The words *emotional* and *emotive* have related but separate meanings: *emotional* means 'of or caused by emotion', whereas *emotive* means 'stirring up emotion'. An *emotional speech* is given by a speaker affected by emotion, whereas an *emotive speech* is given by a speaker trying to arouse emotion in the audience.

empathy (**em**-pa-thee) *noun*
an ability to see into another person's mind and heart and so reach a full and sympathetic understanding of his or her thoughts, feelings or experience.
Word Family **empathize, empathise** *verb.*
[a translation into Greek form of German *Einfühlung* in-feeling]

emperor *noun*
the male ruler of an empire.
[Latin *imperator*]

emphasis (**em**-fa-sis) *noun* (*plural* **emphases**) (**em**-fa-seez)
a stress on or importance attached to something: *Teachers are putting more emphasis on spelling now.*
Word Family **emphasize, emphasise** *verb* to put emphasis upon: *I can't emphasize this point too strongly;* **emphatic** (em-**fat**-ik) *adjective* full of force and emphasis: *Her emphatic answer startled the reporter;* **emphatically** *adverb.*
[Greek]

emphysema (em-fi-**see**-ma) *noun* *Medicine* an abnormal air-filled enlargement of especially the lungs, causing difficult breathing and increased susceptibility to infection.
[Greek, a stomach inflation]

empire *noun*
1 a group of countries ruled by a single person or government.
2 any supreme government or control.
[Latin *imperium*]

empirical (em-**pirr**-i-k'l) *adjective* also **empiric**
based on or guided by experience, experiment or observation, as distinct from theory.
Word Family **empirically** *adverb.*
[Greek *empeirikos* experienced]

empiricism (em-**pirr**-a-sizm) *noun* *Philosophy* the belief that experience is the basis of all knowledge.
Word Family **empiricist** *noun, adjective.*

emplacement *noun*
a prepared position or place, especially for a heavy gun.

employ *verb*
1 to give work to or use the services of: *The company employs 1300 workers.*
2 to use: *He had to employ all his cunning to get the information.*
Word Family **employment** *noun* 1 the state of being employed: *Are you in employment at the moment?* 2 the act of

employing: *This company encourages the employment of school leavers*; **employer** *noun*; **employee** *noun* a person in paid employment.

emporium (em-**paw**-ree-um) *noun* (*plural* **emporia** (em-**paw**-ree-a) or **emporiums**)
(*formal*) a large shop selling a variety of goods.
[Greek *emporion* a trading place]

empower *verb*
(*formal*) to give power or authority to: *The police are empowered to arrest any violent demonstrators.*
Word Family empowerment *noun*.

empress *noun* (*plural* **empresses**)
1 a female ruler of an empire.
2 the wife of an emperor.

empty *adjective* (**emptier; emptiest**)
1 having nothing inside: *an empty glass.*
2 false or meaningless: *empty praise.*
Phrase **be empty of** (*formal*) not to have any of something: *Her life seemed empty of meaning.*
• **empty** *verb* (**empties; emptying; emptied**)
1 to make or become empty: *I emptied the bucket.*
2 to remove from a container to another place: *I emptied the contents of the drawers onto the carpet.*
3 to discharge: *This river empties into the sea.*
Word Family emptily *adverb*; **emptiness** *noun*; **empty** *noun* (*plural* **empties**) something which is empty.

empty-handed *adjective*
not having obtained the things one wanted.

empty-headed *adjective*
(*informal*) foolish.

emu (**ee**-mew) *noun*
a large flightless Australian bird.

emulate (**em**-yoo-late) *verb*
to try to equal or do better than: *She tried desperately to emulate her mother's achievements.*
Word Family emulation (em-yoo-**lay**-sh'n) *noun*.
[Latin *aemulari*]

emulsion (im-**mul**-sh'n) *noun*
1 a fine milky suspension of one liquid in another, such as oil in water.
2 also **emulsion paint** a type of paint for walls, etc. that is not shiny.
3 *Photography* a fine light-sensitive coating on a film, etc.

enable (en-**ay**-b'l) *verb*
to make able or possible: *The fine weather enabled us to spend a lot of time outside.*

enact *verb*
1 to act out: *a scene enacted in many homes up and down the land.*
2 to make into a law or act.
Word Family enactment *noun*.

enamel *noun*
1 any of various mineral substances, similar in composition to glass, used to decorate metal, ceramic and glass surfaces.
2 the very hard creamy-white shiny coating on the outside of teeth.
3 an artistic work using enamel substances: *an exhibition of pottery and enamels.*
• **enamel** *verb* (**enamels; enamelling; enamelled**) to coat or decorate with enamel.

enamour (en-**am**-a) *verb*
Phrase **be enamoured of** to be delighted, charmed or in love with.
[*en-* + French *amour* love]

en bloc (on **blok**) *adverb*
as a whole.
[French]

encamp *verb*
to settle in a camp.
Word Family encampment *noun*.

encapsulate (en-**kaps**-yoo-late) *verb*
1 to enclose in a small space.
2 to express in a concise form: *He encapsulated his advice in a single word: Don't.*
Word Family encapsulation (en-kaps-yoo-**lay**-sh'n) *noun*.

encase *verb*
to cover or surround with or as if with a case.

encephalitis (en-keff-a-**lie**-tis *or* en-seff-a-**lie**-tis) *noun*
inflammation of the brain.
[Greek *enkephalos* brain + *-itis*]

enchant *verb*
1 to charm or delight: *We were all enchanted by the tiny puppets.*
2 to use magic or spells on: *The witch enchanted the prince and turned him into a toad.*
Word Family enchantment *noun* 1 the state of being enchanted. 2 anything which enchants; **enchanting** *adjective*; **enchantingly** *adverb*; **enchanter** *noun* a person who enchants.

enchilada (en-chill-**ah**-da) *noun*
a thin pancake filled with meat or cheese,
covered with a hot sauce. ⇨ TORTILLA.
[Latin American Spanish, flavoured with
chilli]

encircle (en-**sir**-k'l) *verb*
to surround or form a circle round: *The
field was encircled with oak trees.*

enclave (en-klave) *noun*
1 a territory or district completely
surrounded by foreign land.
2 a district, e.g. in a city, inhabited by a
minority group.
[French *enclaver* to shut in]

enclose *verb*
1 to put or shut in completely: *The garden
was enclosed by a high brick wall.*
2 to send with a letter or parcel: *I enclose a
cheque for £20.*

enclosure (en-**klo**-*zh*er) *noun*
1 a place which is enclosed: *The horses were
kept in an enclosure during the sale.*
2 something put in with a letter or parcel.
3 the act of enclosing.
4 *History* the act of fencing common land
in order to make it private property, widely
practised in Britain in the 18th and 19th
centuries.

encode *verb*
to put into code.

encompass (en-**kum**-pis) *verb*
1 (*formal*) to surround.
2 to include as part of a wide subject area:
*The new act encompasses all previous
national and local traffic regulations.*

encore (on-kor) *noun*
Theatre an extra performance given in
response to applause or calls by an
audience after the main performance has
finished. Compare CURTAIN CALL.
• **encore** *interjection* a call for an extra
performance.
[French, again]

encounter *verb*
to meet or be faced with: *We encountered
some language difficulties in Germany.*
• **encounter** *noun* a meeting, especially
with something difficult or unexpected.

encourage (en-**kurr**-ij) *verb*
to give hope or confidence to: *The team
was encouraged by the shouts and applause.*
Word Family encouragement *noun*
1 the act of encouraging: *She needs a little
more encouragement.* **2** anything which
encourages: *Your interest in the project is a
great encouragement to us;* **encouragingly**
adverb.

encroach *verb*
***Phrase* encroach on, encroach upon** to
intrude on or go beyond the set limits of: *I
hope that we are not encroaching on your free
time.*
Word Family encroachment *noun.*

encrust *verb* also **incrust**
to cover with or form a crust: *The purse was
encrusted with beads.*
Word Family encrustation *noun.*

encrypt *verb*
to put into code.
Word Family encryption *noun.*

encumber *verb*
(*formal*) to burden or overcome: *The
company is encumbered with many debts.*
Word Family encumbrance *noun*
anything which burdens or hinders: *My
grandmother began to feel she was an
encumbrance to the family.*

encyclical (en-**sigh**-kli-k'l *or* en-**sik**-li-k'l)
noun
Roman Catholicism a letter written by the
Pope for wide distribution.

encyclopedia (en-sigh-kla-**pee**-dee-a)
noun also **encyclopaedia**
a book or set of books giving information
about every branch of a subject or about
many subjects, usually arranged in
alphabetical order.
Word Family encyclopedic *adjective*
knowing about or dealing with a wide
variety of subjects.
[Greek *enkyklios* general + *paideia*
education]

> The spelling **encyclopedia** came to
> Britain from America and is
> increasingly replacing the spelling
> *encyclopaedia*, partly because of a
> commercial influence – American
> books being sold in Britain and vice
> versa. This change from *ae* to *e* is also
> happening in other areas of
> international interest, especially
> medicine.

end *noun*
1 the last or concluding part: *What
happened at the end of the film?*
2 the farthest part: *You hold the other end of
the rope.*
3 the part of a sports field, etc. which is
defended by a particular team or player:
the fans at the Everton end.
4 a small part left over: *an ashtray full of
cigarette ends.*
5 an aim or purpose: *Does the end justify the
means?*

6 death: *He met an unfortunate end in a boating accident.*
Phrases **at a loose end** without anything to do. **at the end of the day** when everything has been considered. **be the end** (*informal*) to be unbearable: *Honestly, how could you forget? You really are the end!* **end to end** with the ends touching. **in the end** finally. **keep one's end up** (*informal*) to do quite well in a difficult situation. **make ends meet** to make enough money to live on. **no end of** (*informal*) a lot of. **on end 1** upright: *His hair stood on end.* **2** continuously: *She chattered for hours on end.*
• **end** *verb* to come or bring to an end: *The meeting ended early.*
Phrases **end in** to result in: *Their gamble ended in disaster.* **end it all** (*informal*) to commit suicide. **end up** to be in a particular place or state which one had not intended to be in: *I ended up helping my parents all day.*
Word Family **ending** *noun* the last or concluding part.

endanger (en-**dane**-jer) *verb*
to expose to danger: *You will endanger your health if you work so hard.*

endangered species *noun* (*plural* **endangered species**)
a species of plant or animal that is in danger of extinction, e.g. from destruction by people or from the loss of its natural environment.

endear *verb*
Phrase **endear someone to** to make someone loved by: *Her simple happiness endeared her to all of us.*
Word Family **endearment** *noun* a gesture or expression of affection, such as fond words; **endearingly** *adverb*.

endeavour (en-**dev**-a) *verb* (*American* **endeavor**)
to make an effort: *We must endeavour to work harder.*
• **endeavour** *noun* an effort or attempt. [French *se mettre en devoir* to do one's utmost]

endemic (en-**dem**-ik) *adjective*
(of a disease, etc.) characteristic of or widespread among a particular group of people.

endive *noun*
a herb with pale crinkly leaves, used in salads.

endless *adjective*
continuous or without an end: *Life seemed to be one endless round of parties.*

Word Family **endlessly** *adverb*; **endlessness** *noun*.

endorse *verb*
1 to give approval or support to: *I would like to endorse everything that my colleague has just said.*
2 to write something on a document, such as comments or a signature: *The court endorsed her driving licence with the speeding offence.*
Word Family **endorsement** *noun*.
[*en-* + Latin *dorsum* back]

endothermic *adjective*
denoting a chemical reaction during which energy is taken in from the surroundings and converted into chemical energy.
Compare EXOTHERMIC.

endow *verb*
to give or provide a fund or income.
Phrase **be endowed with** to have the gift of: *She is endowed with great musical talent.*

endowment *noun*
1 the act of endowing.
2 (*usually* **endowments**) a natural gift or talent.

endowment policy *noun* (*plural* **endowment policies**)
a type of insurance policy in which one pays regular sums over a long period and receives a lump sum at the end of it, or one's family receives money in the event of one's death.

end product *noun*
the final product or result of anything.

endurance (end-**yoor**-'nce) *noun*
the ability or power to endure: *The cross-country hike was a test of their endurance.*

endure (end-**yoor**) *verb*
1 to suffer, bear or put up with: *It is difficult to endure this pain.*
2 (*formal*) to continue to exist: *His fame endured long after his death.*
Word Family **endurable** *adjective* able to be endured; **enduring** *adjective* **1** long-lasting. **2** patient.

end-user *noun*
a person who uses a product: *A designer must always remember the end-user.*

endways *adverb* also **endwise**
1 with the end forwards.
2 with the ends touching.

enema (**en**-em-a) *noun*
Medicine the placing of a fluid in the rectum to encourage the expulsion of faeces.
[Greek, an injection]

enemy (en-a-mee) *noun* (*plural* **enemies**)
a person, group or thing that is hostile,
aggressive or violently opposed to another:
The two men were bitter enemies.
• **enemy** *adjective* hostile or representing
the enemy: *the enemy guns.*

energetic (en-a-jet-ik) *adjective*
active or full of energy: *How can you be so
energetic so early in the morning?*
Word Family energetically *adverb.*

energy (en-a-jee) *noun* (*plural* **energies**)
1 the physical ability, force or power to act,
work, etc.: *Don't waste your energy moving
the furniture around.*
2 power that can be used to do work with
machines, etc.: *trying to harness the sun's
energy.* □ *available energy sources.*
Word Family energize, energise *verb* to
fill with energy.
[*en-* + Greek *ergon* work]

energy crisis *noun* (*plural* **energy crises**)
a crisis caused by a world shortage of
easily obtainable energy sources.

enfant terrible (on-fon terr-eeb-'l) *noun*
(*plural* **enfants terribles**) (on-fon terr-
eeb-'l)
a person who is known for
unconventional, indiscreet or
embarrassing behaviour.
[French *enfant* child + *terrible* terrible]

enfeeble *verb*
(*formal*) to make weak or feeble.
Word Family enfeeblement *noun.*

enfold *verb*
to wrap around or embrace: *She enfolded
the child in her arms.*

enforce *verb*
to compel obedience to: *Policemen enforce
the law.*
Word Family enforcement *noun* the act
of enforcing; **enforceable** *adjective.*

enfranchise (en-fran-chize) *verb*
to give political or civil rights to, e.g. the
right to vote.
Word Family enfranchisement *noun.*

engage (en-gayj) *verb*
1 to obtain the attention, aid, services, etc.
of: *They engaged a guide to lead them over the
mountains.*
2 to begin to fight: *The armies engaged at
dawn.*
3 (*formal*) to agree to employ: *Her ladyship
engaged a new butler today.*
4 to make two pieces of machinery lock or
move together.
5 (of two pieces of machinery) to lock
together.

Phrase **engage in 1** to take part in:
*Employees of this firm must not engage in any
other work.* **2** to make someone join: *They
engaged the man in conversation while their
accomplice stole his car.*

engaged *adjective*
1 in a relationship that will lead to
marriage: *My son is engaged to a very nice
girl.*
2 busy.
3 (of a toilet or telephone line) already
being used.

engagement (en-gayj-m'nt) *noun*
1 a promise or agreement, especially to
marry: *an engagement ring.*
2 an appointment or arrangement: *a
business engagement.*
3 the act of engaging.

engaging (en-gay-jing) *adjective*
charming, attractive or interesting: *an
engaging smile.*
Word Family engagingly *adverb*;
engagingness *noun.*

engender (en-jen-da) *verb*
(*formal*) to cause or produce: *Racial
prejudice engenders bitterness and often
violence.*

engine (en-jin) *noun*
1 any device which produces mechanical
energy from other forms of energy: *an
internal-combustion engine.*
2 a machine that pulls a railway train.
[Latin *ingenium* genius, an invention]

engineer (en-ja-neer) *noun*
a person trained or skilled in designing,
constructing or maintaining machinery,
bridges, chemical plants, etc.
• **engineer** *verb*
1 to make as an engineer: *a beautifully
engineered car.*
2 to contrive cleverly: *He engineered his own
election to the council.*
Word Family engineering *noun.*

English breakfast *noun*
a breakfast of bacon, eggs, etc., toast, and
tea or coffee. Compare CONTINENTAL
BREAKFAST.

English horn ⇨ COR ANGLAIS.

engorge (en-gorj) *verb*
Medicine to become filled with blood.
Word Family engorgement *noun.*

engrave *verb*
to cut marks, such as letters or designs,
into a hard surface.
Figurative The incident was engraved upon
his memory.

Word Family engraver *noun*; **engraving**
noun **1** a design produced by cutting into a
hard surface. **2** a print produced from an
engraved plate.

engross *verb*
to take and hold all the attention or time
of: *He was completely engrossed in the novel.*
Word Family engrossing *adjective*.
[French *en gros* wholesale]

engulf *verb*
to swallow or surround completely: *The
house was soon engulfed by the flames.*

enhance *verb*
to make more valuable or attractive: *Your
meal will be greatly enhanced by their
delicious wines.*
Word Family enhancement *noun*.

enigma (in-**nig**-ma) *noun*
anything which puzzles or is difficult to
explain: *Her different moods were an enigma
to us.*
Word Family enigmatic (en-nig-**mat**-ik)
adjective; **enigmatically** *adverb*.
[Greek *ainigma* riddle]

enjoin *verb*
to urge or command.

enjoy *verb*
1 to find delight in: *I really enjoyed the
party.*
2 (*formal*) to have: *The children all enjoy
good health.*
Word Family enjoyable *adjective* giving
pleasure or joy: *an enjoyable holiday*;
enjoyably *adverb*; **enjoyment** *noun*.

enlarge *verb*
to make larger.
Phrase enlarge on, enlarge upon to
give more detail about: *We asked the
speaker to enlarge on several of the points
mentioned.*

enlargement *noun*
1 the act of enlarging.
2 something, especially a photograph,
which has been enlarged.

enlighten *verb*
to give knowledge or understanding to.
Word Family enlightened *adjective* well-
informed and free from prejudice,
ignorance, etc.: *living in an enlightened age*;
enlightenment *noun* **1** the act of
enlightening. **2** the state of being
enlightened.

enlist *verb*
1 (*formal*) to request and obtain: *They
enlisted our help in moving the furniture.*
2 to join one of the armed services.
Word Family enlistment *noun*.

enliven (en-**lie**-v'n) *verb*
to make more lively: *our efforts to enliven the
party.*

en masse (on **mass**) *adverb*
all together: *The family arrived en masse for
the barbecue.*
[French]

enmesh *verb*
to catch or tangle up, as if in a net.

enmity (**en**-ma-tee) *noun* (*plural*
enmities)
a hatred, hostility or violent opposition:
*Their trade policies aroused the enmity of the
neighbouring countries.*

ennoble (in-**no**-b'l) *verb*
to make noble or dignified.
Word Family ennoblement *noun*.

ennui (on-**wee**) *noun*
a listless boredom or lack of interest.
[French]

enormity *noun*
1 hugeness: *The enormity of the task
overwhelmed us.*
2 the quality of being outrageous: *the
enormity of her crime.*

enormous (in-**nor**-mus) *adjective*
very large.
Word Family enormously *adverb*;
enormousness *noun*.

enough (in-**nuf**) *adjective*, *adverb*
1 as much or as many as is needed: (as an
adjective) *Do you have enough money?* □ (as
an adverb) *This meat is not cooked enough.*
2 rather: *That took you long enough!*
□ *Oddly enough, he didn't mention it at all.*
● **enough** *noun* a sufficient or necessary
amount: *Have you got enough to pay for the
tickets?*

enquire (en-**kwire**) *verb* also **inquire**
to ask: *She enquired about my health.*
Phrase enquire into to investigate.
Word Family enquirer *noun*.

enquiry *noun* (*plural* **enquiries**) also
inquiry (*plural* **inquiries**)
1 a question.
2 an investigation.

enrage *verb*
to make very angry.

enrapture (en-**rap**-cher) *verb*
to fill with great delight or rapture.

enrich *verb*
1 to improve or make richer: *The soil was
enriched with compost.*

2 *Chemistry* to increase the amount of a particular isotope in a mixture of the isotopes of an element: *enriched uranium*.
Word Family enrichment *noun*.

enrol (en-**role**) *verb* (**enrols; enrolling; enrolled**)
to enter one's name or have it entered on a list or register for membership, etc.
Word Family enrolment *noun*.

en route (on **root**) *adverb*
on the way: *We will stop and buy food en route.*
[French]

ensconce (en-**skonce**) *verb*
Phrases be ensconced to be settled in comfort. **ensconce oneself** to settle or establish oneself in comfort: *She ensconced herself by the fire with a book.*

ensemble (on-**som**-b'l) *noun*
1 all the parts of a whole, seen or considered together.
2 any small group of musicians.
3 a matching outfit.
[French, together]

enshrine *verb*
to cherish or keep as if in a shrine.

enshroud *verb*
to shroud or cover.

ensign (en-**sine**) *noun*
1 a flag, especially of a country or particular group.
2 (*formerly*) the lowest commissioned officer in the British infantry.
3 the lowest ranking commissioned officer in the American navy.
blue ensign the flag of customs and other government departments.
red ensign the flag of the merchant navy.
white ensign the flag of the Royal Navy and the Royal Yacht Squadron.

enslave *verb*
to dominate or make a slave of.
Word Family enslavement *noun*.

ensnare *verb*
to catch in or as if in a snare or trap.
Word Family ensnarement *noun*.

ensue *verb*
to happen afterwards, especially as a result: *A fight ensued.*

en suite (on **sweet**) *noun*
a bathroom which is joined to a bedroom.
● **en suite** *adjective*
1 (of a bedroom) having a connected bathroom.

2 (of a bathroom) joined to a bedroom.
[French, in sequence]

ensure (en-**shor**) *verb*
to make sure or certain: *We must ensure that the dogs do not escape.*

> ⚠ Do not confuse *ensure* with *insure*. *Insure* means 'to guarantee against risk or harm', as in *You should insure your property against fire*.

entail *verb*
1 to involve as a necessary part of a process: *This project will entail a lot of extra reading.*
2 *Law* to limit an inheritance to a fixed line of heirs who may neither sell it nor give it away.

entangle *verb*
to make or become caught up or tangled.
Word Family entanglement *noun*.

entente (on-**tont**) *noun* also **entente cordiale** (on-tont kor-dee-**ahl**)
a friendly understanding or agreement, especially between governments.
[French]

enter *verb*
1 to come or go into: *We entered the theatre by the side door.*
2 to compete in: *Are you going to enter the race?*
3 to put in: *First the computer asks you to enter your password.*
Phrase enter into to become involved in.
[Latin *intrare* to go in]

enterprise *noun*
1 any attempted project, task, etc.: *He wanted us to join him in his new enterprise.*
2 an organized business or company: *They manage a small mail-order enterprise.*
3 energetic resourcefulness and spirit.

enterprising *adjective*
bold, resourceful and energetic: *an enterprising plan.*
Word Family enterprisingly *adverb*.

entertain *verb*
1 to keep amused, interested or attentive: *A magician entertained the children before the concert.*
2 to admit or receive guests: *She enjoys entertaining.*
3 (*formal*) to consider as a possibility: *I cannot entertain such an outrageous idea.*
Word Family entertaining *adjective*; **entertainingly** *adverb*; **entertainer** *noun* a person who entertains, especially a professional performer; **entertainment** *noun* **1** the act of entertaining. **2** anything

which entertains, such as a public performance.

enthral (en-**thrawl**) *verb* (**enthrals; enthralling; enthralled**) (*American* **enthrall**)
to hold the fascinated attention of: *Our grandfather enthralled us with his ghost stories.*

enthrone *verb*
to place on or as if on a throne.
Word Family **enthronement** *noun*.

enthusiasm (en-**thew**-zee-azm) *noun*
a strong interest, eagerness or delight: *The audience showed their enthusiasm by thunderous applause.*
Word Family **enthusiast** *noun* a person who has great enthusiasm for a particular activity, etc.: *a skiing enthusiast*;
enthusiastic (en-thew-zee-**ast**-ik) *adjective* full of enthusiasm;
enthusiastically *adverb*; **enthuse** *verb* to be or make enthusiastic.
[Greek *enthousiasmos* possessed by a god]

entice *verb*
to attract or tempt with promises, bait, etc.: *We tried to entice the cat down from the tree with a saucer of milk.*
Word Family **enticement** *noun* **1** the act of enticing. **2** something used to entice;
enticing *adjective*; **enticingly** *adverb*.

entire *adjective*
whole and undivided: *Her entire wealth was donated to a Lost Dogs' Home.*
Word Family **entirety** (en-**tire**-a-tee) *noun* the wholeness or completeness of anything: *The evidence must be presented in its entirety*; **entirely** *adverb* completely or exclusively.

entitle *verb*
1 to give a name or title to, e.g. a book. **2** to allow or give a right to: *You are entitled to your own opinion.*
Word Family **entitlement** *noun*.

entity (en-ti-tee) *noun* (*plural* **entities**)
anything which has a real independent existence.

entomb (en-**toom**) *verb*
to bury in or as if in a tomb.
Word Family **entombment** *noun*.

entomology (en-ta-**moll**-a-jee) *noun*
the study of insects.
Word Family **entomologist** *noun*;
entomological (en-ta-m'-**loj**-i-k'l) *adjective*.
[Greek *entoma* insects + -*logy*]

entourage (**on**-too-rah*zh*) *noun*
a group of attendants or followers: *The President arrived with his usual entourage of bodyguards.*
[French *entourer* to surround]

entrails (**en**-trales) *plural noun*
the intestines or inner parts.

entrance[1] (**en**-tr'nce) *noun*
1 any place by which one enters.
2 the act of entering: *Her entrance was greeted with wild applause.*
3 the right or permission to enter: *The management has the right to refuse entrance.*

entrance[2] (in-**trance**) *verb*
to fill with wonder and delight: *We were entranced by the delicate music.*
Word Family **entrancement** *noun*;
entrancing *adjective*; **entrancingly** *adverb*.

entrant (en-tr'nt) *noun*
a person who officially enters a competition or organization.

entrap *verb* (**entraps; entrapping; entrapped**)
to trick or catch in or as if in a trap.
Word Family **entrapment** *noun*.

entreat *verb*
(*formal*) to ask or request earnestly: *They entreated her not to go out after dark.*
Word Family **entreaty** *noun* (*plural* **entreaties**) an earnest request.

entrée (**on**-tray) *noun*
1 the main dish of a meal.
2 a small meat dish served before the main course of a meal.
3 the right or privilege to enter.
[French *entrer* to enter]

entrench *verb*
1 to establish or settle firmly: *He is completely entrenched in his beliefs and will not change.*
2 *Military* to defend or consolidate a position by digging trenches.
Word Family **entrenchment** *noun*
1 *Military* any defensive fortification consisting of trenches. **2** the act of entrenching or the state of being entrenched.

entrepreneur (on-tra-pr'-**ner**) *noun*
a person who undertakes and controls a business venture, especially one in which risk is involved.
Word Family **entrepreneurial** *adjective*.
[French *entre* between + *preneur* taker]

entrust *verb*
to give for safe keeping: *He entrusted the documents to his lawyer.*
Word Family **entrustment** *noun*.

ntry noun (plural **entries**)
1 the act of entering: *Their entry into the house was not noticed.*
2 any place by which one enters: *The entry to the stables was in the yard.*
3 anything which is written or recorded: *the captain's entries in the log.*
4 a person or thing entered in a competition: *We have a late entry in the next race.* □ an entry form.

ntwine verb
to twine or curl around, together, etc.

-number noun
a number preceded by the letter E that is used in lists of food ingredients to represent a particular food additive.
[E for European; the numbers being part of the European Union's food regulations]

numerate (in-**new**-ma-rate) verb
(*formal*) to name or list one by one.
Word Family **enumeration** (in-new-ma-**ray**-sh'n) *noun* the act of enumerating.

nunciate (in-**nun**-si-ate) verb
1 to pronounce: *She enunciates all her words with great care.*
2 (*formal*) to state or declare.
Word Family **enunciation** (in-nun-si-**ay**-sh'n) *noun*.

nvelop (in-**vell**-'p) verb
to wrap up or cover completely: *The mountains were enveloped in cloud.*
Word Family **envelopment** noun.

> ! Do not confuse *envelop* with *envelope*. The verb *envelop* does not have an *e* at the end, unlike the noun *envelope*, which rhymes with *hope*.

nvelope (**en**-va-lope *or* **on**-va-lope) noun
a cover, especially the flat folded sheet of paper used to enclose letters, etc.
[French *enveloper* to wrap up]

> ! Do not confuse *envelope* with ENVELOP.

nviable (**en**-vee-a-b'l) adjective
desirable or worthy to be envied: *The President's job is not an enviable one.*

nvious (**en**-vee-us) adjective
full of envy: *He felt proud when he saw the envious glances at his car.*
Word Family **enviously** adverb; **enviousness** noun.

nvironment (en-**vie**-r'n-m'nt) noun
1 the surrounding influences, physical conditions or circumstances of anything: *The home environment of a child has an important effect on its attitudes in later life.*

2 (**the environment**) the natural surroundings in which people, animals and plants live: *Choose products which are not harmful to the environment.*
Word Family **environmental** (en-vie-r'n-**men**-t'l) *adjective*; **environmentally** *adverb*; **environmentalist** *noun* a person concerned with the problems of the environment, especially the effects of pollution.

environmentally friendly adjective
not harmful to the natural world.

environs (en-**vie**-r'nz) plural noun
(*formal*) the surrounding districts or suburbs of a city, town, etc.
[French, surroundings]

envisage (en-**viz**-ij) verb
to see or picture in the mind: *I didn't envisage that there would be such a crowd here.*

envoy (**en**-voy) noun
an official representative, especially a diplomat sent to another country.
[French *envoyé* sent]

envy (**en**-vee) noun
a feeling of discontent or resentment aroused by seeing another person's good fortune, superiority, etc., usually accompanied by a desire to possess the advantages of the other person.
Phrase **be the envy of** to be something which causes envy in: *Their swimming pool is the envy of the neighbourhood.*
• **envy** verb (**envies**; **envying**; **envied**) to regard with envy: *It is difficult not to envy his success.*
Word Family **envyingly** adverb.

enzyme (**en**-zime) noun
a substance, usually a protein, which can cause changes in plants or animals, although it is not changed itself.
[*en-* + Greek *zymé* yeast]

eon ⇨ AEON.

epaulette (ep-a-let) noun (*American* **epaulet**)
a buttoned shoulder flap on military uniforms.
[French *épaule* shoulder]

épée (**ay**-pay *or* **ep**-ay) noun
a stiff steel fencing sword.
[French]

ephemeral (i-**fem**-a-r'l) adjective
lasting only a short time.
Word Family **ephemera** plural noun items or interests which last only a short time; **ephemerally** adverb.
[*epi-* + Greek *hemera* day]

epic *noun*
1 a long story of heroic events and actions, often in a noble style.
2 any great or dramatic event likened to an epic.
• **epic** *adjective*
1 of or characteristic of an epic.
2 grand or heroic.
[Greek *epikos*]

epicentre (ep-i-sen-ta) *noun* (*American* **epicenter**)
a point on the surface of the earth directly above the point of origin of an earthquake or impact of a bomb.

epicure (ep-ik-yoor) *noun*
a person who appreciates or cultivates fine taste in wine, food, the arts, etc.
Word Family **epicurean** (ep-i-**kew**-ree-an) *adjective* of or fit for an epicure;
epicurean *noun*.
[after *Epicurus*, a Greek philosopher in the fourth century B.C. who taught that the highest good in life is happiness]

epidemic (ep-i-**dem**-ik) *noun*
the occurrence of a disease in one area that for a short time affects many individuals in that area. Compare PANDEMIC.
• **epidemic** *adjective*.
[*epi-* + Greek *demos* people]

epidermis (ep-i-**der**-mis) *noun*
Biology the skin or outside layer of cells in animals or plants.
[Greek, the outer skin]

epiglottis (ep-i-**glot**-iss) *noun* (*plural* **epiglottises**)
Anatomy a movable ridge of cartilage at the back of the throat, which prevents food entering the windpipe during swallowing.
[*epi-* + Greek *glotta* tongue]

epigram *noun*
1 a short poem with one theme and usually a witty or satirical ending.
2 any concise witty statement.
Word Family **epigrammatic** (ep-i-gra-**mat**-ik) *adjective*; **epigrammatically** *adverb*.
[Greek *epigramma* an inscription]

epigraph (**ep**-i-graf *or* **ep**-i-grahf) *noun*
a brief inscription or quotation, e.g. on a statue or at the beginning of a book, poem, etc.

epilepsy (**ep**-i-lep-see) *noun*
a nervous disease, sometimes due to brain damage and causing fits.
Word Family **epileptic** (ep-i-**lep**-tik) *noun* a person who suffers from epilepsy; **epileptic** *adjective*.
[Greek *epilepsia* an attack]

epilogue (**ep**-i-log) *noun*
the closing part or speech of a play, book, etc. Compare PROLOGUE (definition 1).
[Greek *epilogos* conclusion]

Epiphany (ip-**iff**-a-nee) *noun*
Christianity a festival celebrated on 6 January, to commemorate the showing of the infant Christ to the Magi.
[Greek *epiphaneia* manifestation]

episcopal (ip-**iss**-ka-p'l) *adjective*
1 of or relating to a bishop.
2 (of a Church) governed by bishops: *the protestant Episcopal Church in America*.
Word Family **episcopalian** (ip-iss-ka-**pay**-lee-an) *noun* a person who supports episcopal church government;
episcopalian *adjective*.
[Greek *episkopos* overseer]

episode (**ep**-i-sode) *noun*
1 an incident or event in a larger series or course of events.
2 one complete section of a radio or television serial.
Word Family **episodic** (ep-i-**sod**-ik) *adjective*; **episodically** *adverb*.
[Greek *epeisodios* an interlude]

epistle (ip-**iss**-'l) *noun*
a letter, especially any of the apostles' letters in the New Testament.
[Greek *epistolé* letter]

epitaph (**ep**-i-tahf) *noun*
a short inscription on a tomb.
[Greek *epitaphios* over the grave, a funeral oration]

epithet (**ep**-i-thet) *noun*
a word or name, especially one used to describe a particular characteristic of a person, as in Ethelred *the Unready*.
[Greek *epithetos* added]

epitome (ip-**it**-a-mee) *noun*
1 any person or thing that is typical or characteristic of some quality, etc.: *He is the epitome of generosity*.
2 a summary.
Word Family **epitomize, epitomise** *ve* to be very typical or characteristic of.
[Greek, incision, abridgement]

epoch (**ee**-pok) *noun*
a particular period of time, especially one seen as a new or significant beginning.
Word Family **epoch-making** *adjective* opening a new era of time or progress: *It was an epoch-making discovery for medical science*.

The word **epoch** is frequently used in modern English to mean a historical period or a long period of time marked by a particular characteristic: *the Tudor epoch.* □ *the epoch of steam.* This has occurred partly through confusion with 'era', but *epoch* was originally restricted to 'a point marking the beginning of a new period of time' rather than the period of time itself. Now both meanings are found. It comes through Latin from Greek *epokhé* (a pause or stoppage).

eponymous (ip-**on**-im-us) *adjective*
(of a person) giving the name to a place, work, invention, etc.: *David Copperfield, the eponymous hero of Dickens's novel.*
Word Family eponym (**ep**-a-nim) *noun.*
[*epi-* + Greek *onyma* name]

epoxy (ee-**pok**-see) *noun* (*plural* **epoxies**)
also **epoxy resin**
Chemistry any of a wide variety of synthetic organic compounds which contain oxygen and are used in plastics, surface coatings and adhesives.

epsilon (ep-**sigh**-lon) *noun*
the fifth letter of the Greek alphabet, representing short *e*.

equable (**ek**-wa-b'l) *adjective*
(of climate, mood, etc.) steady, even or regular.
Word Family equably *adverb*;
equability (ek-wa-**bill**-i-tee) *noun.*

equal (**eek**-w'l) *adjective*
having the same size, amount, degree, value, etc.: *We received equal shares of the money.*
Phrase equal to capable of coping with: *I do not feel equal to the occasion.*
• **equal** *verb* (**equals; equalling; equalled**) to be or do something equal to: *Ten plus three equals thirteen.* □ *I doubt if you will equal her record.*
• **equal** *noun* a person or thing which is equal to another.
Word Family equally *adverb*; **equality** (ik-**woll**-i-tee) *noun.*
[Latin *aequus* even]

equalize, equalise (**eek**-wa-lize) *verb*
to make equal: *The air pressure is then equalized in both chambers.*
Word Family equalization (eek-wa-lie-**zay**-sh'n) *noun*; **equalizer** *noun*
something which equalizes.

equals sign *noun*
Maths the sign =, meaning 'is equal to'.

equanimity (ek-wa-**nim**-i-tee) *noun*
a calmness of mood or temper.
[*equi-* + Latin *animus* mind]

equate (ik-**wate**) *verb*
to see or represent one thing as equal to another.

equation (ik-**way**-*zh*'n) *noun*
1 *Maths* a formula stating that two expressions have equal value.
2 the act of making or representing as equal.

equator (ik-**way**-ta) *noun*
an imaginary line around the earth's surface lying midway between the North and South Poles at 0° latitude.
Word Family equatorial (ek-wa-**taw**-ree-'l) *adjective* of, near or characteristic of the equator.
[Latin *circulus aequator diei et noctis* circle equalizing day and night]

equerry (**ek**-wa-ree) *noun* (*plural* **equerries**)
1 an officer who attends a member of the British royal family or their representatives in other countries.
2 a person who looks after the horses of a royal household, etc.

equestrian (ik-**west**-ree-an) *noun*
a horse rider.
• **equestrian** *adjective* of or relating to horse riding: *an equestrian event.*
Word Family equestrianism *noun.*
[Latin *equester* from *equus* horse]

equidistant (eek-wi-**dist**-ant) *adjective*
(of two or more things) at an equal distance.

equilateral (eek-wi-**lat**-a-r'l) *adjective*
having sides equal in length.

equilibrium (eek-wi-**lib**-ree-um) *noun* (*plural* **equilibria**)
a state of equal balance or rest between opposing forces.
[*equi-* + Latin *libra* balance]

equine (**ek**-wine) *adjective*
of or resembling a horse.

equinox (**eek**-wi-noks) *noun* (*plural* **equinoxes**)
the time when the sun crosses the equator, making day and night all over the earth of equal length, occurring on about 21 March (the **vernal equinox**) and 22 September (the **autumnal equinox**).
[*equi-* + Latin *nox* night]

equip (i-kwip) *verb* (**equips; equipping; equipped**)
to provide or fit with what is needed for a particular purpose: *The climbers were not properly equipped for their expedition.*

equipment (i-**kwip**-m'nt) *noun*
1 the things which are needed or used for a particular purpose or task: *Their shop sells all kinds of sporting equipment.*
2 the act of equipping.

equitable (ek-wit-a-b'l) *adjective*
(*formal*) fair and just.
Word Family **equitably** *adverb.*

equitation (ek-wi-**tay**-sh'n) *noun*
(*formal*) horsemanship.
[Latin *equus* horse]

equity (**ek**-wi-tee) *noun*
1 (*formal*) the quality of being fair or impartial.
2 *Finance* the total owned by a person or company when all of their debts have been paid off.
[Latin *aequitas* fairness, justice]

equivalent (ik-**kwiv**-a-l'nt) *adjective*
equal or nearly equal in value, effect, amount, etc.
• **equivalent** *noun* a person or thing that matches another: *What is the American equivalent of a cream tea?*
Word Family **equivalently** *adverb*; **equivalence, equivalency** *noun.*
[*equi-* + Latin *valens* strong]

equivocal (ik-**kwiv**-a-k'l) *adjective*
ambiguous or unclear.

equivocate (ik-**kwiv**-a-kate) *verb*
to mislead or evade by using ambiguous language.
Word Family **equivocation** (ik-kwiv-a-**kay**-sh'n) *noun.*
[*equi-* + Latin *vocis* of a voice]

era (**eer**-a) *noun*
1 a period of time counted from a particular fixed point in the past: *the Christian era.*
2 a period of time marked by distinctive events or features: *an era of progress.*

eradicate (i-**rad**-i-kate) *verb*
to uproot or get rid of completely: *We have succeeded in eradicating smallpox from this country.*
Word Family **eradication** (i-rad-i-**kay**-sh'n) *noun.*
[Latin *e-* away + *radicis* of a root]

erase (i-**raze**) *verb*
to rub out or clean off.

Word Family **eraser** *noun* anything which erases, especially a rubber.
[Latin *erasus* scratched out]

ere (air) *preposition, conjunction*
an old word for **before.**

erect (i-**rekt**) *adjective*
upright or on end.
• **erect** *verb*
1 to build, construct or establish: *A monument was erected in his honour.*
2 to raise into an upright position.
Word Family **erectly** *adverb*; **erectness** *noun.*

erection *noun*
1 the act of erecting.
2 anything which has been erected, such a a building.
3 the expanding and hardening of the penis or clitoris when it fills with blood due to sexual stimulation.

ergo *conjunction, adverb*
an old word meaning 'therefore'.
[Latin]

ergonomics (er-go-**nom**-iks) *plural noun*
(*used with singular verb*) the study of the physical relationship between people and their working environment.

ermine (**er**-min) *noun* (*plural* **ermine** or **ermines**)
1 a mammal of the weasel family with a black-tipped tail and brown fur which turns white in winter. It is called a **stoat** while it has its brown coat.
2 the valuable white fur of this animal.

erode (i-**rode**) *verb*
to wear or eat away: *The soil was eroded by wind.* □ *The value of her savings was eroded by inflation.*
Word Family **erosive** *adjective* causing erosion.
[Latin *e-* away + *rodere* to gnaw]

erogenous (i-**roj**-i-nus) *adjective*
arousing or tending to arouse sexual excitement.
[Greek *eros* love + *-gen*]

erosion (i-**ro**-*zh*'n) *noun*
the act or process of eroding, especially th wearing away of the land surface by sun, wind, water, frost or ice.

erotic (i-**rot**-ik) *adjective*
1 of or relating to sexual love: *erotic poems.*
2 arousing sexual desire: *a very erotic performance by the striptease dancer.*
Word Family **erotica** (i-**rot**-i-ka) *plural noun* (*used with singular or plural verb*) any art or literature based on, or attempting to

stimulate, sexual love or desire; **erotically**
adverb; **eroticism** (i-**rot**-i-sizm) *noun*.
[after *Eros*, the god of love in Greek
mythology]

err (er) *verb*
to make mistakes or go astray.
Phrase **err on the side of** to show too
much of a quality in order to be safe: *I
decided to err on the side of caution and not
ask after his wife.*
[Latin *errare* to stray]

errand *noun*
a short trip for a particular task or
purpose: *My mum asked me to run a few
errands for her.*

errant *adjective*
1 straying or misbehaving: *her errant
husband.*
2 wandering or travelling. ⇨ KNIGHT
ERRANT.

errata (e-**rah**-ta) *plural noun*
(*singular* **erratum**) also **corrigenda**
any printing or writing errors, often noted
in a list added to a book after it has been
printed.

erratic (i-**rat**-ik) *adjective*
lacking a fixed or certain course or
pattern: *erratic winds.* □ *erratic behaviour.*
Word Family **erratically** *adverb*.

erroneous (i-**ro**-nee-us) *adjective*
(*formal*) containing errors or mistakes.
Word Family **erroneously** *adverb*.
[Latin *erroneus* straying]

error *noun*
a mistake.
Phrase **in error** mistaken.
[Latin, a wandering about]

ersatz (**air**-sats) *adjective*
being an imitation, usually inferior.
[German *Ersatz* replacement]

erstwhile *adjective*
former, previous.
[from *erst*, an old word for earliest +
WHILE]

erudite (**er**-oo-dite) *adjective*
having or showing great learning.
Word Family **eruditely** *adverb*;
erudition (er-oo-**dish**-'n) *noun*.

erupt *verb*
1 (of a volcano) to send out lava, etc.
2 to burst or force out violently: *Rioting
erupted in the city centre.*
3 to break out: *Her skin erupted into a rash.*
Word Family **eruption** *noun*.

escalate (**esk**-a-late) *verb*
to increase, intensify or enlarge by stages:
The war was escalated on several fronts.
Word Family **escalation** (esk-a-**lay**-sh'n)
noun.

escalator (**esk**-a-lay-ter) *noun*
a moving mechanical stairway which
consists of an endless belt.

escalope (**esk**-a-lop) *noun*
a very thin slice of meat, especially veal.
[French]

escapade (**esk**-a-pade) *noun*
a reckless or wild adventure.

escape *verb*
1 to get free from capture, confinement,
pursuit, etc.: *The rabbit escaped from its
hutch.*
2 to avoid: *They were lucky to escape injury
in the accident.*
3 to fail to be noticed by: *The mistake had
escaped his attention.*
● **escape** *noun*
1 the act of escaping: *His escape from prison
was organized by the rest of the gang.*
2 any means of escaping: *a fire escape.*
□ *She sees films as an escape from everyday
life.*
Word Family **escapee** (es-kay-**pee**) *noun*
a person who has escaped from captivity.

escapism (es-**kay**-pizm) *noun*
the tendency to avoid unpleasant reality by
entertaining or absorbing the mind in
other matters.
Word Family **escapist** *noun, adjective*.

escarpment *noun*
a long steep ridge of rock.

eschew (es-**choo**) *verb*
(*formal*) to avoid or keep away from.
Word Family **eschewal** *noun*.

escort (**es**-kort) *noun*
a person or group that travels with or
accompanies another.
● **escort** (es-**kort**) *verb* to go with as an
escort or to offer protection.

escudo (es-**kew**-doh *or* es-**koo**-doh) *noun*
the basic unit of money in Portugal and
Cape Verde.

escutcheon (es-**kuch**-'n) *noun*
Heraldry the shield in a coat of arms,
usually divided into segments.

esoteric (ess-o-**terr**-ik) *adjective*
made for or understood by only a small
select group.
Word Family **esoterically** *adverb*.
[Greek *esoterikos* inner]

espadrille (es-pa-drill) *noun*
a sandal with a canvas upper and a rope sole, often tied round the ankle or leg with laces.
[French]

espalier (es-**pall**-ya) *noun*
a tree or shrub trained to climb a trellis or other framework.
Word Family **espalier** *verb*.
[Italian *spalliera* a support]

especial (es-**pesh**-'l) *adjective*
special or particular.
Word Family **especially** *adverb* in particular: *I didn't especially like him.* □ *He made the costume especially for the show.*

Esperanto (es-pa-**ran**-toh) *noun*
a language invented in 1877 by Dr L. Zamenhof, a Polish scholar, using common words from the major European languages and intended for international use.
[Spanish *esperanza* hope, Zamenhof's pen-name]

espionage (es-pee-a-nah*zh*) *noun*
the act of spying, especially on foreign governments.
[French]

esplanade (es-pla-nahd *or* es-pla-nayd) *noun*
a public path or road, usually by the sea.
[Spanish]

espouse (es-**powz**) *verb*
(*formal*) to take up the cause or ideas of: *The government has espoused the conservation movement.*
Word Family **espousal** *noun* support or advocacy.

espresso *noun*
a strong coffee made by forcing steam under pressure through ground coffee beans.
[Italian, pressed out]

esprit de corps (es-pree de **kor**) *noun*
a feeling of loyalty and enthusiasm uniting members of a group.
[French, the corps spirit]

espy *verb* (**espies; espying; espied**)
a poetic word meaning 'to catch sight of'.

esquire (es-**kwire**) *noun*
1 (**Esquire**) a polite title for a man, used when addressing a letter, etc.
2 ⇨ SQUIRE (definition 2).
[Latin *scutarius* shield-bearer]

essay (**ess**-ay) *noun*
1 a short piece of writing.
2 (*formal*) an attempt.

Word Family **essay** (ess-**ay**) *verb* to attempt or put to the test; **essayist** *noun* a person who writes essays.
[French *essai* attempt]

essence *noun*
1 the property of a thing which gives it its identity: *Her painting tries to capture the essence of childhood.*
2 also called **extract**. a concentrated form of any substance: *vanilla essence.*
Phrases **in essence** basically. **of the essence** extremely important: *Hurry! Time is of the essence!*

essential (iss-**en**-sh'l) *adjective*
1 absolutely necessary: *It is essential to read the questions carefully.*
2 relating to the essence or most fundamental part.
Word Family **essential** *noun* something which is extremely important; **essentially** *adverb*.

essential oil *noun*
an oil derived from a plant which evaporates quickly, used in aromatherapy.

establish *verb*
1 to set up or create: *The company was established in 1999.*
2 to make accepted: *He had established himself as their leader.*
3 to find out or prove: *Police have not yet established the reasons for the attack.*
Word Family **established** *adjective* (of a Church or religion) officially recognized, and often supported, by the government of a country.
[Latin *stabilis* stable]

establishment *noun*
1 the act of establishing: *the delay in the establishment of the new law.*
2 a household.
3 any established and organized group, business or institution.
4 (**the Establishment**) an established group having power and status in a community, often considered to be conservative or reactionary.

estate *noun*
1 a large piece of private land, especially in the country.
2 an area of land developed for housing.
3 *Law* a person's possessions, especially those left by a dead person.
4 (*formal*) a person's circumstances or condition in life or society: *the holy estate of matrimony.*
5 (*informal*) an estate car.

estate agent *noun*
a person who buys and sells houses or land on behalf of other people.
Word Family **estate agency** *noun* (*plural* **estate agencies**) the business or premises of an estate agent.

estate car *noun*
a car with a long body and space behind the rear seats for luggage.

esteem *verb*
1 (*formal*) to regard with great respect or favour: *a greatly esteemed leader.*
2 (*dated*) to consider to be.
• **esteem** *noun* respect or a favourable opinion.

estimable (est-im-a-b'l) *adjective*
(*formal*) worthy of esteem or respect.
Word Family **estimably** *adverb.*

estimate (est-i-mayt) *verb*
to judge or calculate approximately: *I estimate the cost to be about £200.*
• **estimate** (est-i-m't) *noun* an approximate opinion, judgement or calculation· *I got estimates from three builders.*
Word Family **estimation** (est-i-may-sh'n) *noun* 1 the act of estimating. 2 a judgement or opinion: *In your estimation, what are the chances of success?*; **estimator** *noun.*
[Latin *aestimare* to judge the price or worth of]

estrange *verb*
to turn away or lose the affections, loyalty, etc. of.
Word Family **estranged** *adjective* no longer in a relationship with: *a letter from his estranged wife*; **estrangement** *noun.*

estuary (es-tew-a-ree) *noun* (*plural* **estuaries**)
the wide mouth of a river, where its current meets and is affected by the sea's tides.
[Latin *aestus* tide]

et cetera (et set-er-a) *adverb* also **etcetera**
and other similar things as well: *I packed my sunglasses, swimsuit, etc. abbrev.* etc.
[Latin *et* and + *cetera* the rest]

etch *verb*
to engrave a picture on a metal plate by scratching the design through a layer of wax and then letting acid eat into the exposed metal.
Figurative His face was etched in her memory.

Word Family **etching** *noun* a print produced from a picture etched on a metal plate.

eternal (i-ter-n'l) *adjective*
lasting for ever, with no beginning or end.
Figurative Please stop this eternal quarrelling!
Word Family **eternally** *adverb.*

eternal triangle *noun*
the situation which occurs when one person in a relationship takes a second lover, seen as an ageless or continual event.

eternity (i-ter-na-tee) *noun* (*plural* **eternities**)
an endless time without beginning or end, especially as distinct from mortal life.
Figurative It took an eternity for the doctor to arrive.

ethane (ee-thane) *noun*
Chemistry a colourless odourless hydrocarbon gas.

ether (ee-tha) *noun*
1 a volatile liquid used as an anaesthetic and as a solvent.
2 also **aether** a poetic word for the heavens or upper regions of space.
3 also **aether** a substance which was believed by 19th-century scientists to fill all space and transmit light, heat, etc.
[Greek *aither* upper air]

ethereal (ee-theer-ee-al) *adjective* also **etherial**
1 of the heavens or pure upper regions of space.
2 light and delicate.
Word Family **ethereally** *adverb.*

ethic *noun*
a principle or rule of right conduct.
Word Family **ethical** *adjective* 1 in agreement with accepted principles or rules for right conduct: *Was her doctor's behaviour ethical?* 2 of or relating to ethics; **ethically** *adverb.*

ethics *plural noun*
1 a system of rules or principles for behaviour within a group or society, according to which actions are judged.
2 (*used with singular verb*) any science or study of morals and moral standards, especially as a branch of philosophy or law.
3 the rightness or moral quality of an action, etc.

ethnic *adjective*
1 of or relating to a particular population having a common language or common racial or cultural origins.

2 rather colourful and unusual to Western peoples: *He likes drums and ethnic music.*
Word Family ethnically *adverb.*
[Greek *ethnos* nation]

ethnic cleansing *noun*
the removal from an area of an ethnic group or groups, either by means of extermination or forced migration, by another militarily superior group.

ethnic minority *noun* (*plural* **ethnic minorities**)
a group of people who are not of the same racial origin as the main group of people in a country.

ethos (ee-thos) *noun*
the fundamental and distinctive character or spirit of a social group, culture, etc.
[Greek, nature, habits]

etiology ⇨ AETIOLOGY.

etiquette (et-i-ket) *noun*
the rules of conduct for a particular group or social situation.
[French]

etymology (et-i-**moll**-a-jee) *noun* (*plural* **etymologies**)
1 the study of the origin, history and changes of form in a word or words.
2 an account of the history of a particular word.
Word Family etymologist *noun*;
etymological (et-i-ma-**loj**-i-k'l) *adjective*;
etymologically *adverb.*
[Greek *etymon* the true meaning + *-logy*]

eucalyptus (yoo-ka-**lip**-tus) *noun* (*plural* **eucalyptuses** or **eucalypti** (yoo-ka-**lip**-tie))
a tall Australian tree whose leaves produce a strong-smelling oil used in medicine.
[Greek *eu* well + *kalyptos* covered (of the bud)]

Eucharist (**yoo**-ka-rist) *noun*
1 *Christianity* a service which celebrates the Last Supper.
2 *Christianity* the consecrated bread and wine used in this sacrament.
Word Family Eucharistic (yoo-ka-**rist**-ik) *adjective.*
[Greek *eukharistos* grateful]

eugenics (yoo-**jen**-iks) *plural noun*
(*used with singular verb*) the science of improving the qualities of offspring, e.g. by careful selection of parents, control of genes, etc.
Word Family eugenic *adjective*;
eugenicist (yoo-**jen**-a-sist) *noun* a person who advocates eugenics.
[Greek *eu* good + *-gen*]

eulogy (yoo-la-jee) *noun* (*plural* **eulogies**)
also called **panegyric**.
a speech or piece of writing in praise of a person.
Word Family eulogistic (yoo-la-**jist**-ik) *adjective*; **eulogistically** *adverb*; **eulogize, eulogise** *verb* to praise highly; **eulogist** *noun.*
[Greek *eu* good + *-logy*]

eunuch (**yoo**-nuk) *noun*
a castrated man, especially one formerly used as a harem attendant by Eastern rulers.
[Greek *eunouchos* chamber attendant]

euphemism (**yoo**-fa-mizm) *noun*
1 the use of a mild or indirect expression instead of one considered likely to offend or upset.
2 any expression substituted in this way: *'To pass away' is a euphemism for 'to die'.*
Word Family euphemistic (yoo-fa-**mis**-tik) *adjective*; **euphemistically** *adverb.*
[Greek *eu* good + *phemé* speaking]

euphonious (yoo-**foe**-nee-us) *adjective*
pleasant-sounding.
Word Family euphoniously *adverb*;
euphony (**yoo**-fa-nee) *noun.*
[Greek *eu* good + *phoné* sound]

euphonium (yoo-**foe**-nee-um) *noun*
Music a brass wind instrument similar to the tuba.

euphoria (yoo-**faw**-ree-a) *noun*
a feeling of elation or happiness, especially one based on illusion.
Word Family euphoric (yoo-**forr**-ik) *adjective*; **euphorically** *adverb.*
[Greek *eu* good + *phoros* bearing]

eureka (yoo-**ree**-ka) *interjection*
an exclamation of triumph at a discovery.
[Greek *heureka* I have found it, attributed to Archimedes when he conceived his Principle, about 260 B.C.]

eurhythmics *plural noun*
(*used with singular verb*) a system of developing grace and rhythm through movements of the body made in response to music.
[Greek *eu* good + *rhythmos* rhythm]

euro (**yoor**-oh) *noun*
1 the system of having one currency in the European Union: *Another country has joined the euro.*
2 the basic unit of money in this system: *We paid in euros.*

Eurodollar (**yoor**-oh-doll-er) *noun*
an American dollar deposited in banks in Europe because it is a freely convertible

currency not subject to national legal restrictions.

Euro-MP (yoor-oh em **pee**) *noun*
a member of the European Parliament.

European Economic Community *noun*
the European Union.

European Parliament *noun*
a parliament elected by the people who live in the countries of the European Union.

European Union *noun* also called **European Community**.
an economic and political association of European countries.

Euro-sceptic *noun*
a person who does not like the European Union.

Eurostar *noun*
(trademark) a high-speed train that travels between London and other major European cities, e.g. Paris.

Eustachian tube (yoo-**stay**-sh'n tewb) *noun*
Anatomy either of two fine tubes connecting the inner ears to the back of the nose and throat, balancing the air pressure inside and outside the eardrum.
[after *B. Eustachio*, about 1520-1574, an Italian anatomist]

euthanasia (yoo tha-**nay**-zee-a) *noun*
the causing of death painlessly, or by withholding treatment, especially when a person is suffering from an incurable disease.
[Greek *eu* good + *thanatos* death]

evacuate (iv-**ak**-yoo-ate) *verb*
1 to remove to a safe place: *Hundreds of families were evacuated from the flooded town.*
2 to take all the people out of: *The army evacuated the village.*
3 (*formal*) to empty.
Word Family **evacuation** (iv-ak-yoo-**ay**-sh'n) *noun*; **evacuee** (iv-ak-yoo-ee) *noun* a person who is evacuated.

evade *verb*
to escape or avoid cleverly.

evaluate (iv-**al**-yoo-ate) *verb*
1 to estimate the amount, quantity or value of.
2 to consider the quality or success of: *They were asked to evaluate the design.*
Word Family **evaluation** (iv-al-yoo-**ay**-sh'n) *noun*.

evanescent (ev-a-**ness**-'nt) *adjective*
passing away or vanishing.
[Latin *evanescere* to vanish]

evangelical (ee-van-**jell**-i-k'l) *adjective*
1 *Christianity* of or relating to the Gospel.
2 *Christianity* denoting a group or Church which places particular emphasis on the Bible as sole authority in matters of faith and conduct.
3 extremely enthusiastic about communicating ideas: *her evangelical fervour.*
● **evangelical** *noun*.

evangelist (iv-**an**-ja-list) *noun*
1 *Christianity* any of the authors of the four Gospels in the New Testament.
2 *Christianity* a preacher of the Gospel.
3 any preacher who stresses the necessity for conversion before salvation.
4 a person who is very keen to communicate ideas about something.
Word Family **evangelistic** (iv-an-ja-**list**-ik) *adjective*; **evangelism** *noun*; **evangelize, evangelise** *verb*.
[Greek *eu* good + *angelia* news]

evaporate (iv-**ap**-a-rate) *verb*
to change from liquid into vapour as a result of heat.
Figurative Her hopes suddenly evaporated.
Word Family **evaporation** (iv-ap-a-**ray**-sh'n) *noun*.

evaporated milk *noun*
a thick sweet milk sold in tins.

evasion (iv-**ay**-zh'n) *noun*
1 the act of evading: *He was arrested for income tax evasion.*
2 an example of evading: *an interview full of evasions and half-truths.*
Word Family **evasive** (iv-ay-siv) *adjective* characterized by evasion; **evasively** *adverb*; **evasiveness** *noun*.

eve *noun*
the day or evening before an important day or event: *Christmas Eve.*

even (ee-v'n) *adjective*
1 having no change in level, quality, amount, etc.: *The cricket pitch is not as even as it should be.*
2 calm and steady: *He has an even temper.*
3 equal: *The scores were even at half-time.*
4 *Maths* (of a number) having no remainder when divided by two, e.g. 2, 4, 6, etc. Compare ODD (definition 2).
Phrases **get even with** to take revenge on.
● **even** *verb* to make or become even.
● **even** *adverb*
1 used to show that something is unexpected: *She wasn't rude to us – she even gave us a drink!*

2 used to show that something is stronger, greater, etc.: *I thought our car was big, but theirs is even bigger.*
3 indeed: *He was surprised, amazed even.*
Phrases **break even** not to make a profit or loss: *This financial year the company broke even for the first time.* **even as** at the same time as. **even if** it does not matter if. **even so** anyway. **even though** in spite of the fact that: *I went to the party even though I didn't feel well.*
Word Family **evenly** *adverb*; **evenness** *noun*.

even-handed *adjective*
just and fair: *her even-handed treatment of all the children.*

evening (eev-ning) *noun*
the part of the day between sunset and nightfall.

evening class *noun* (*plural* **evening classes**)
a lesson for adults in the evening, held at a school, college, etc.

evening dress *noun*
the clothes worn on formal occasions in the evening.

evening star *noun*
a planet seen in the west after sunset, especially Venus.

even money *noun*
a winning payment which is the same amount as the money placed on the bet.

evens *plural noun*
an equal probability, e.g. of winning or losing.

evensong *noun*
Christianity an Anglican service held in the evening.

event (i-**vent**) *noun*
1 anything which happens or takes place, especially something important.
2 *Sport* any of the separate competitions in a programme: *The long jump is the third event after lunch.*
3 *Maths* the outcome of a trial in probability.
Phrases **at all events, in any event** whatever happens. **in the event** on the actual occasion. **in the event of** if it happens that.
Word Family **eventful** *adjective* full of events or incidents, especially exciting ones; **eventfully** *adverb*; **eventfulness** *noun*.
[Latin *eventus* consequence, event]

eventide *noun*
a poetic word for **evening**.

eventual (i-ven-tew-'l) *adjective*
happening finally or in the end: *What was the eventual outcome of their argument?*
Word Family **eventually** *adverb*; **eventuality** (i-ven-tew-**al**-i-tee) *noun* (*plural* **eventualities**).

ever *adverb*
1 at any time: *Have you ever seen such a violent storm?* □ *I hardly ever go to the cinema.*
2 always: *The universe will last for ever.* □ *They lived happily ever after.*
3 used after *what, how, where,* etc. to add emphasis: *What ever did she mean?*
Phrase **ever so, ever such** (*informal*) very: *They were ever so pleased!* □ *We had ever such a good time.*

> [!] In writing, when *ever* is used to add emphasis to the question words *what, how, where, when,* etc., there is usually a space between the two words: *What ever did he say to that?* □ *How ever did they find out?* When written as one word, *whatever, however,* etc. usually mean 'it does not matter what', 'it does not matter how', etc.: *Whatever her parents say, she's going to marry him.* □ *Do it however you like.*

evergreen *noun*
a tree or plant which has leaves throughout the year.
• **evergreen** *adjective*.

everlasting *adjective*
continuing for ever.
Word Family **everlastingly** *adverb*; **everlastingness** *noun*.

evermore *adverb*
a poetic word meaning 'for ever'.

every (ev-ree) *adjective*
1 used to refer to all separate members of a group: *Every girl in that family has red hair.*
2 the greatest possible degree of: *We wish you every happiness in your new home.*
Phrases **every bit as** exactly as: *The day was every bit as cold as they predicted.* **every now and again, every so often** occasionally. **every other** every second: *She comes to clean the house every other week.*

everybody *pronoun*
every person.

everyday *adjective*
1 suitable for ordinary occasions: *her everyday clothes.*
2 usual or routine: *His everyday business worries vanished during the holiday.*

everyone *pronoun*
every person.

everything *pronoun*
1 all things: *This bag will hold everything.*
2 the most important thing: *Her family is everything to her.*

everywhere *adverb*
in, at or to all places.

evict (i-**vikt**) *verb*
to expel a tenant.
Word Family eviction *noun*.

evidence (**ev**-i-d'nce) *noun*
1 anything which provides a basis for belief: *I don't think you have any evidence for that statement.* □ *There was little evidence of suffering in her face.*
2 *Law* the statements, documents or objects presented in a court to prove disputed facts.
Phrase in evidence very clear to see: *Her talent was very much in evidence during the play.*
Word Family evidence *verb* to show clearly; **evidential** (ev-i-**den**-sh'l) *adjective* serving as or based on evidence.
[Latin *evidens* plain to see]

evident *adjective*
clearly seen or understood: *It was evident that she was not amused.*
Word Family evidently *adverb*.

evil (**ee**-vil) *adjective*
1 morally bad: *evil deeds.*
2 causing injury, damage, etc.: *Smoking is an evil habit.*
3 (*informal*) very unpleasant: *an evil smell.*
• **evil** *noun* anything which is evil or causes harm, suffering, etc.: *the evils of war.*
Word Family evilly *adverb*; **evilness** *noun*

evil eye *noun*
a stare believed to have the power to cause bad luck, injury, etc.

evil-minded *adjective*
full of malice or evil intentions

evince *verb*
(*formal*) to indicate or show clearly.

eviscerate (i-**viss**-a-rate) *verb*
to remove the intestines or bowels of.
Word Family evisceration (i-viss-a-**ray**-sh'n) *noun*.
[Latin *e-* out + *viscera* the internal organs]

evocative (i-**vok**-a-tiv) *adjective*
having the power to evoke a response: *a haunting, evocative piece of music.*
Word Family evocation (ee-vo-**kay**-sh'n or ev-o-**kay**-sh'n) *noun* the act of evoking

or summoning; **evocatively** *adverb*; **evocativeness** *noun*.
[Latin *e-* out + *vocare* to call]

evoke (i-**voke**) *verb*
to call up or produce: *The song evoked memories of her childhood.*

evolution (ee-va-**loo**-sh'n or ev-a-**loo**-sh'n) *noun*
1 any gradual process of growth or development: *the evolution of the computer from the 1930s to the present day.*
2 *Biology* the slow continuous process of change in the characteristics of organisms from one generation to the next.
⇨ DARWINISM; NATURAL SELECTION.
Word Family evolutionary *adjective*; **evolutionist** *noun* a person who believes in biological evolution.
[Latin *evolutus* unrolled]

evolve *verb*
1 to grow or develop gradually.
2 *Biology* to develop by the processes of evolution.

ewe (yoo) *noun*
a female sheep.

ewer (**yoo**-a) *noun*
a large jug with a wide spout, especially one holding water for washing.

ex *noun* (*plural* **exes**)
(*informal*) a former husband, wife or partner: *The kids are with my ex.*

exacerbate (eg-**zass**-a-bate) *verb*
to intensify or make worse: *Tension between the countries was exacerbated by this incident.*
Word Family exacerbation (eg-zass-a-**bay**-sh'n) *noun*.
[*ex-* + Latin *acerbus* bitter]

exact (eg-**zakt**) *adjective*
precisely correct or accurate: *What is the exact time?*
• **exact** *verb* to demand or require using threats, force or other pressure. *The king exacted tributes from the local people.*
Word Family exacting *adjective* having strict demands or requirements: *an exacting job;* **exactly** *adverb* 1 in an exact manner: *It is important to measure the ingredients exactly.* 2 completely: *I suggest you do exactly as he says;* **exactness**, **exactitude** (eg-**zak**-ti-tewd) *noun* the quality of being exact; **exactingly** *adverb*; **exactingness** *noun*.
[Latin *exactus* exacted, exact]

exaggerate (eg-**zaj**-a-rate) *verb*
to represent something beyond its true limits, value or size: *Fishermen sometimes exaggerate the size of their catch.*

***Word Family* exaggeration** (eg-zaj-a-ray-sh'n) *noun* **1** the act of exaggerating. **2** a statement which exaggerates: *I think her description of the argument was an exaggeration;* **exaggerator** *noun*.
[*ex-* + Latin *aggerare* to heap up]

exalt (eg-**zawlt**) *verb*
1 to lift or raise in rank, quality, honour, etc.
2 to praise highly.
***Word Family* exaltation** (eg-zawl-**tay**-sh'n) *noun* **1** the act of exalting. **2** rapture or excitement, often unnatural.
[*ex-* + Latin *altus* high]

exam *noun*
(*informal*) an examination.

examine (eg-**zam**-in) *verb*
1 to inspect or test carefully: *She examined the food suspiciously.*
2 to test the knowledge, qualifications, etc. of a person by questions or exercises.
***Word Family* examination** (eg-zam-in-ay-sh'n) *noun* **1** the act of examining. **2** a written or oral test of a person's understanding and knowledge of a subject; **examinee** (eg-zam-in-**ee**) *noun* a person who is examined; **examiner** *noun* a person who examines.
[Latin *examinare* to weigh, test]

example (eg-**zahm**-p'l) *noun*
1 something which is seen to represent the qualities of other things in its group or kind: *This house is a good example of Victorian architecture.*
2 something to be learnt from: *I hope her mistakes will be an example to you.*
3 something used to illustrate a general principle or set of rules: *Follow the examples on the opposite page.*
***Phrase* for example** as an illustration: *Several people wanted the job – Nasim, for example.* *abbrev.* e.g.
[Latin *exemplum* a sample]

exasperate (eg-**zah**-spa-rate) *verb*
to irritate or provoke intensely: *What an exasperating little man!*
***Word Family* exasperatedly** *adverb*; **exasperatingly** *adverb* in a manner which exasperates; **exasperation** (eg-zah-spa-ray-sh'n) *noun*.
[*ex-* + Latin *asper* rough]

excavate (**eks**-ka-vate) *verb*
1 to make a hole in.
2 to uncover by digging: *Several ancient bowls were excavated at the building site.*
***Word Family* excavation** (eks-ka-**vay**-sh'n) *noun* **1** the act of excavating. **2** a hole or site being excavated: *an archaeological*

excavation; **excavator** *noun* a person or thing that excavates.
[*ex-* + Latin *cavus* hollow]

exceed (ek-**seed**) *verb*
to go beyond the fixed or expected limits of: *The success of the party far exceeded our hopes.*
***Word Family* exceeding** *adjective* an old word for great or extreme; **exceedingly** *adverb* extremely.
[Latin *excedere* to go beyond]

excel (ek-**sel**) *verb* (**excels; excelling; excelled**)
to be unusually talented or better than others: *She excels in all the science subjects.*
***Phrase* excel oneself** to do extremely well at something.

excellence (**ek**-sa-l'nce) *noun*
the quality of being excellent.
[Latin *excellens* surpassing]

Excellency *noun* (*plural* **Excellencies**)
a form of address used to or about certain officials, such as governors, ambassadors, etc: *Here are the documents, Your Excellency.*

excellent (**ek**-sa-l'nt) *adjective*
having unusual and superior merit: *an excellent wine.* □ *Your work is excellent, Nicole.*
***Word Family* excellently** *adverb*.

except (ek-**sept**) *preposition*
with the exception of: *I like all card games except bridge.*
• **except** *conjunction* with the exception: *They look very alike, except he has shorter hair than his brother.*
• **except** *verb* to leave out.
[Latin *exceptus* removed]

> ⚠ Do not confuse *except* with ACCEPT.

exception (ek-**sep**-sh'n) *noun*
1 the act of leaving out or excluding.
2 something which is left out of or does not conform to a general rule, etc.
3 an opposition or objection: *We all took exception to her unfair criticism.*
***Word Family* exceptionable** *adjective* likely to cause objection; **exceptional** *adjective* unusual or extraordinary; **exceptionally** *adverb*.

excerpt (**ek**-serpt) *noun*
an extract from a book, speech, etc.
[Latin *excerptus* picked out]

excess (ek-**sess**) *noun* (*plural* **excesses**)
1 an extreme or unrestrained quantity, degree, extent, etc.: *She showed an excess of enthusiasm.*

2 an amount which is left over or greater than is necessary or wanted: *The farm produced an excess of dairy products last year.*
3 the condition or fact of exceeding what is usual, necessary or approved: *Avoid excess in all things.*
Phrase in excess of more than.
● **excess** *adjective* more than is usual, necessary or approved: *Wipe off any excess liquid with a cloth.*

> ⚠ Do not confuse *excess* with ACCESS.

excessive *adjective*
extreme or beyond the usual limit: *Even my parents think we get an excessive amount of homework.*
Word Family excessively *adverb*; **excessiveness** *noun.*

exchange *verb*
to give or receive one thing in return for another: *We all exchanged gifts on Christmas Day.*
● **exchange** *noun*
1 the act of exchanging: *The store agreed to do an exchange for me.*
2 a short angry argument or fight.
3 a place for buying, selling or exchanging goods, shares, etc.: *a stock exchange.*
4 ➪ TELEPHONE EXCHANGE.
5 the changing of money from the currency of one country to the currency of another, e.g. changing pounds sterling to dollars.
Word Family exchangeable *adjective* able to be exchanged or returned.

exchange rate ➪ RATE OF EXCHANGE.

exchequer (eks-**chek**-ă) *noun*
(*sometimes* **Exchequer**) the treasury of a country, state or organization.

> **Exchequer** is one of many words that came into English from French during the Norman Conquest of England. It came from Old French *eschequier* (a chessboard). The word takes its modern meaning from the fact that the people who collected and managed the royal revenue in Norman times used a table with a chequered cloth on it, counters being placed on the squares of the cloth as a primitive aid to calculation.

excise[1] (**ek**-size) *noun*
a tax on the production, sale, etc. of certain goods, such as tobacco.

excise[2] (ek-**size**) *verb*
to cut out or off: *The censor excised several passages from the book.*
Word Family excision (ek-**sizh**-'n) *noun.*

excitable (ek-**site**-a-b'l) *adjective*
easily excited.
Word Family excitably *adverb*; **excitableness, excitability** (ek-site-a-**bill**-i-tee) *noun.*

excite (ek-**site**) *verb*
1 to cause a strong feeling of enthusiasm and interest in: *The children were excited about their trip to the zoo.*
2 to arouse: *The odd question excited her suspicions.*
3 *Physics* to add energy to a nucleus, atom or molecule.
Word Family excitement *noun* **1** the state of being excited: *There was great excitement in the crowd.* **2** an exciting event; **excited** *adjective*; **excitedly** *adverb*; **exciting** *adjective*; **excitingly** *adverb.*

exclaim (eks-**klame**) *verb*
to speak out suddenly and loudly.
Word Family exclamation (eks-kla-**may**-sh'n) *noun* **1** a cry or other loud expression. **2** *Grammar* an interjection; **exclamatory** (eks-**klam**-a-tree) *adjective* using or expressing an exclamation.

exclamation mark *noun*
a punctuation mark (!), used to indicate strong emphasis: *Look out!*

exclude (eks-**klood**) *verb*
1 to leave out: *I haven't excluded that possibility entirely.*
2 not to give entry, rights, etc. to: *She was excluded from membership.*
3 to prevent from attending school: *He was excluded for three months.* Compare EXPEL (definition 2).
Word Family exclusion (eks-**kloo**-zh'n) *noun* the act of excluding.

exclusive (eks-**kloo**-siv) *adjective*
1 belonging to a single individual, group, source, etc.: *We have exclusive rights to the book.* □ *an exclusive interview.*
2 expensive and fashionable: *He belongs to an exclusive golf club.*
3 incompatible: *mutually exclusive ideas.*
Phrase exclusive of not including: *This is the price, exclusive of delivery costs.*
Word Family exclusively *adverb*; **exclusiveness** *noun.*

excommunicate (eks-k'-**mew**-ni-kate) *verb*
Religion to officially cut off from membership of a church.
Word Family excommunication (eks-k'-mew-ni-**kay**-sh'n) *noun.*

ex-con noun
(*informal*) a person who was formerly a convict.

excrement (**eks**-kra-m'nt) noun
faeces.
Word Family **excremental** (eks-kra-**men**-t'l) *adjective*.

excrescence (eks-**kress**-'nce) noun
any additional growth or outgrowth, especially an abnormal one.

excrete (eks-**kreet**) verb
to discharge or expel from a body, especially harmful or waste matter.
Word Family **excreta** *plural noun* any matter excreted from a body; **excretion** *noun* 1 the act of excreting. 2 anything which is excreted.
[Latin *excretus* sifted out]

excruciating (ek-**skroo**-shee-ayt-ing) *adjective*
1 (of pain) very intense.
2 very embarrassing or tedious.
Word Family **excruciatingly** *adverb*.
[Latin *excruciare* to torture]

exculpate (**eks**-kul-pate) verb
(*formal*) to free from blame or guilt.
[*ex-* + Latin *culpa* blame]

excursion (eks-**ker**-sh'n) noun
1 a short trip or outing.
2 a deviation or digression.
[Latin *excursio* a running out]

excuse (eks-**kewz**) verb
1 to forgive or overlook a fault, etc.: *Please excuse me for being so late.*
2 to justify: *His unhappiness does not excuse his rudeness.*
3 to release from a duty: *Can I be excused from assembly today?*
Phrases **be excused** (*informal*) to go to the toilet: *The little boy asked if he could be excused.* **excuse oneself** to say politely that one is leaving.
● **excuse** (eks-**kewce**) noun a reason given to explain or defend a fault, etc.
Phrase **an excuse for** (*informal*) a very poor example of.
Word Family **excusable** *adjective* worthy of being excused.

excuse-me noun
(*informal*) a dance in which people can interrupt each other and change partners.

ex-directory adjective
(of a person or a telephone number) not listed in the telephone directory.

exeat (**ek**-see-at) noun
permission to leave, especially for a brief absence from school.
[Latin, let him or her go out]

execrable (**ek**-sik-ra-b'l) *adjective*
very bad or detestable.
Word Family **execrably** *adverb*.

execrate (**ek**-si-krate) verb
(*formal*) to denounce violently or curse.
[*ex-* + Latin *sacra* the sacred rites]

execute (**ek**-si-kewt) verb
1 to put to death as legal punishment: *Sir Walter Raleigh was executed.*
2 (*formal*) to do, accomplish or perform: *The diver executed a perfect somersault.*
3 *Law* to carry out the terms of a will, etc.
4 *Computers* to run a program.
Word Family **execution** (ek-si-**kew**-sh'n) *noun* 1 the putting to death of a convicted criminal. 2 the carrying out of a task: *He was praised for his prompt execution of the command;* **executioner** *noun* a public official appointed to perform the punishment of execution.
[Latin *exsecutio* a following-up]

executive (eg-**zek**-yoo-tiv) *adjective*
1 having authority or power to decide, direct or administer: *The company has promoted him to an executive position.*
2 of, for or suitable for people in positions of authority: *the executive washroom.*
● **executive** noun
1 a person with administrative power, e.g. in a company.
2 the part of an organization which puts policies into effect, such as the Cabinet in a government.

executor (eg-**zek**-yoo-ta) noun
Law a person appointed to carry out the instructions in a will.
Word Family **executrix** (eg-**zek**-yoo-triks) *noun* (*plural* **executrices** (eg-zek-yoo-**try**-seez) or **executrixes**) a female executor.

exemplary (eg-**zem**-pla-ree) *adjective*
1 serving as a model or example worthy of imitation.
2 (of a punishment) serving as a warning.

exemplify (eg-**zem**-pli-fie) verb
(**exemplifies; exemplifying; exemplified**)
1 to illustrate by using examples.
2 to be an example of.
Word Family **exemplification** (eg-zem-pli-fi-**kay**-sh'n) *noun*.

exempt (eg-**zempt**) verb
to free or release from a duty, obligation, etc.: *He was exempted from military service because of his religious beliefs.*
Word Family **exempt** *adjective;* **exemption** *noun*.
[Latin *exemptus* removed]

exercise (ek-sa-size) *noun*
1 any activity performed as a means of training, physical conditioning, etc.: *She does some stretching exercises every morning.*
2 any lesson, problem, etc. designed to train some particular function or skill: *maths exercises.*
3 a putting into action or effect: *In the exercise of his duties a judge must always be impartial.*
• **exercise** *verb*
1 to put through practice or exercises in order to train, improve, etc.: *She exercised the horse for several hours before the competition.*
2 to put into effect: *I must exercise my powers as chairman and close the meeting.*
3 (*formal*) to confuse and concern: *The problem exercised his mind greatly.*
[Latin *exercere* to train or practise]

exercise bike *noun*
a stationary piece of machinery with pedals, used indoors as a form of exercise.

exert (eg-zert) *verb*
to apply or put into force: *The community exerted pressure on the local council.*
Phrase **exert oneself** to make an effort.
Word Family **exertion** *noun* any vigorous effort or action.
[Latin *exsertus* put forth]

exeunt (ek-see-unt *or* ek-say-unt) *verb*
(used as a stage direction) they go out.

exfoliate (eks-fole-ee-ate) *verb*
1 to fall from a surface in thin flakes.
2 to scrub the skin in order to remove any dead cells.
Word Family **exfoliation** (eks-fole-ee-ay-sh'n) *noun* the process of exfoliating; **exfoliant, exfoliator** *noun* something which exfoliates.

ex gratia (eks gray-shee-a) *adverb, adjective*
as a special favour, although there is no legal obligation: *The travel company did not accept any responsibility, but gave us an ex gratia payment.*
[Latin, from favour]

exhale (eks-hale) *verb*
to breathe out or give off.
Word Family **exhalation** (eks-sa-lay-sh'n) *noun* 1 the act of exhaling.
2 something which is exhaled.

exhaust (eg-zawst) *verb*
1 to tire out: *I'm completely exhausted!*
2 to use up or drain completely: *They soon exhausted the supply of biscuits.*

Figurative We had exhausted the topic of our holiday and began to talk about other things.
• **exhaust** *noun*
1 the hot gases which are discharged from an internal-combustion engine.
2 also **exhaust pipe** the pipe or other outlet through which the hot gases are discharged.
Word Family **exhaustion** *noun* the act of exhausting or the state of being exhausted: *I was taken to hospital suffering from exhaustion;* **exhaustive** *adjective* extremely thorough: *an exhaustive enquiry into the murder;* **exhaustively** *adverb;* **exhaustiveness** *noun;* **exhaustible** *adjective* able to be exhausted.
[Latin *exhaustus* drained dry]

exhibit (eg-zibb-it) *verb*
to show or display: *an artist who has exhibited his work all over the world.*
• **exhibit** *noun* any object or collection of objects which are exhibited.
Word Family **exhibitor** *noun* a person who exhibits.

exhibition (ek-si-bish-'n) *noun*
1 a public show or display: *an art exhibition.*
2 a scholarship.
Phrase **make an exhibition of oneself** to act in a foolish or ridiculous way.
[Latin *exhibitus* produced in public]

exhibitionist (ek-si-bish-'n-ist) *noun*
a person who behaves in a way designed to attract attention.
Word Family **exhibitionistic** (ek-si-bish-'n-ist-ik) *adjective;* **exhibitionism** *noun.*

exhilarate (eg-zill-a-rate) *verb*
to make lively or cheerful: *We were all exhilarated by the sea air.*
Word Family **exhilaratingly** *adverb;* **exhilaration** (eg-zill-a-ray-sh'n) *noun.*
[*ex-* + Latin *hilaris* cheerful]

exhort (eg-zort) *verb*
to urge or request earnestly.
Word Family **exhortation** (eg-zor-tay-sh'n) *noun* 1 the act of exhorting. 2 any sincere request or persuasion.

exhume (eks-yoom) *verb*
to disinter a dead body for examination.
Word Family **exhumation** (eks-yoo-may-sh'n) *noun.*
[*ex-* + Latin *humus* ground]

exile *noun*
1 a long absence from one's home or country, often imposed as a punishment.

2 a person separated from his or her home or country in this way.
- **exile** *verb*.

[*ex-* + Latin *solum* soil, country]

exist (eg-**zist**) *verb*
1 to have life or reality: *Does God exist?*
2 to be found: *This species exists only in the mountainous regions of South America.*
[Latin *exsistere* to come forth]

existence (eg-**zist**-'nce) *noun*
1 the state or fact of existing or being: *I don't believe in the existence of ghosts.*
2 a way of being or living: *He lives the lonely existence of a friendless old man.*
Word Family **existent** *adjective* having existence or reality.

existentialism (eg-zi-**sten**-sha-lizm) *noun*
Philosophy any of various systems of thought emphasizing the loneliness of the individual, and his or her freedom and sole responsibility in making personal choices.
Word Family **existentialist** *noun*;
existential, existentialist *adjective*.

exit *noun*
1 a way out: *The exit was blocked.*
2 a departure or going out, such as an actor's departure from the stage: *She made a hasty exit.*
3 a place on a motorway where vehicles can leave by a slip road.
- **exit** *verb*
1 to go out.
2 *Computers* to leave a program.
[Latin, he or she goes out]

Exocet *noun*
(*trademark*) a kind of rocket-propelled short-range guided missile.

exodus (**ek**-sa-dus) *noun* (*plural* **exoduses**)
1 the departure of a large number of people.
2 (**Exodus**) the departure of the Israelites from Egypt, as recounted in the second book of the Old Testament.
[Greek, a going out]

exonerate (eg-**zon**-a-rate) *verb*
to set free from blame or responsibility.
Word Family **exoneration** (eg-zon-a-**ray**-sh'n) *noun*.
[*ex-* + Latin *onere* from a burden]

exorbitant (eg-**zor**-bi-t'nt) *adjective*
(of a price or amount demanded) much too great: *They're asking £100? That really is exorbitant!*
Word Family **exorbitantly** *adverb*.
[*ex-* + Latin *orbita* a rut]

exorcize, exorcise (**ek**-sor-size) *verb*
to drive out an evil spirit by religious ceremonies.
Word Family **exorcism** (**ek**-sor-sizm) *noun* the act of exorcizing; **exorcist** *noun* a person who exorcizes.
[*ex-* + Greek *orkizein* to give the oath to]

exothermic *adjective*
denoting a chemical reaction during which chemical energy is converted to heat energy and given off to the surroundings. Compare ENDOTHERMIC.

exotic (eg-**zot**-ik) *adjective*
1 foreign or introduced from another country: *a basket of exotic fruits.*
2 strikingly different or fascinating.
Word Family **exotically** *adverb*;
exoticism (eg-**zot**-iss-izm) *noun* the quality of being exotic.
[Greek *exotikos* foreign]

expand *verb*
1 to make or become larger: *The company had to expand to cope with all the work.*
2 to express in a more detailed way: *We asked her to expand on her ideas.*
3 to become more friendly and talkative.
[Latin *expandere* to spread out]

expanse *noun*
a large or widespread area.

expansion (eks-**pan**-sh'n) *noun*
1 the act of expanding or enlarging.
2 any expanded or enlarged part.

expansive *adjective*
1 having a wide range or extent.
2 relaxed and open: *Her expansive manner makes all guests feel welcome.*
Word Family **expansively** *adverb*;
expansiveness *noun*.

expatiate (eks-**pay**-shee-ate) *verb*
to speak or write more fully.
[*ex-* + Latin *spatiari* to walk]

expatriate (eks-**pat**-ree-it *or* eks-**pay**-tree-it) *noun*
a person living outside his or her native country.
[*ex-* + Latin *patria* native land]

expect *verb*
1 to believe that a particular thing will take place: *We expect him to arrive before lunch.*
2 to suppose or presume: *I expect you are right.*
Phrases **be expecting** (*informal*) (of a woman) to be pregnant. **expect something of** to believe that someone will be or do something: *I'm very upset at my son's behaviour: I expected more of him.*
[Latin *exspectare* to wait]

expectancy noun (plural **expectancies**)
1 hope.
2 a future probability: *The life expectancy of men is now about 75.*

expectant adjective
1 hopeful: *There was an expectant silence.*
2 (of a woman) pregnant.
Word Family **expectantly** adverb.

expectation noun
1 the act or state of expecting: *We waited eagerly in expectation of a delicious dinner.*
2 something which is expected: *The concert did not live up to our expectations.*

expectorate (eks-**pek**-ta-rate) verb
to cough or spit in order to remove matter from the lungs or throat.
Word Family **expectoration** (eks-pek-ta-**ray**-sh'n) noun; **expectorant** noun a medicine which causes a person to expectorate.
[Latin *ex pectore* from the chest]

expedient (eks-**pee**-di-'nt) adjective
1 serving one's interest or advantage, although not necessarily right: *I knew who was to blame, but it was expedient to keep quiet about it.*
2 suitable or advisable under the circumstances.
Word Family **expedient** noun anything which is expedient; **expediently** adverb; **expediency, expedience** noun the quality of being expedient.
[Latin *expediens* being advantageous]

expedite (eks-pa-dite) verb
(*formal*) to hasten the progress of.
Word Family **expeditious** (eks-pa-**dish**-us) adjective quick or prompt; **expeditiously** adverb.
[Latin *expedire* to extricate]

expedition (eks-pa-**dish**-'n) noun
1 a trip made for a special purpose, such as to explore.
2 the people on such a trip.
3 (*formal*) a promptness in accomplishing something.
Word Family **expeditionary** adjective relating to an expedition.

expel verb (**expels; expelling; expelled**)
1 to force or drive out.
2 to force to leave a school permanently: *John was expelled for smoking.* Compare EXCLUDE (definition 3).

expend verb
to use up or spend.
[Latin *expendere* to weigh out]

expendable adjective
1 capable of being expended.
2 able to be sacrificed to achieve an aim.

expenditure (eks-**pen**-di-cher) noun
1 the act of expending.
2 the amount of money spent: *an increase in public expenditure.*

expense noun
1 the cost involved in doing something.
2 (*often* **expenses**) the money spent, needed or provided for a particular purpose: *travelling expenses.*
Phrases **at someone's expense** 1 paid for by someone. 2 having the effect of making someone look bad or stupid: *We decided to play a joke at his expense.* **at the expense of** at the cost of: *I won, but at the expense of our friendship.*

expense account noun
a list of expenses incurred by an employee, e.g. hotel bills when travelling, that are paid by an employer as well as the usual salary or claimed as a tax deduction.

expensive adjective
costing a lot.
Word Family **expensively** adverb; **expensiveness** noun.

experience (eks-**peer**-i-'nce) noun
1 any event or circumstance which one has lived through, encountered or observed.
2 any skill or knowledge gained in such circumstances.
● **experience** verb to have, feel or suffer an experience: *She had never experienced rejection before.*

experiment (eks-**perr**-i-m'nt) noun
a test to show a known truth, examine a hypothesis or discover something unknown.
Word Family **experiment** verb 1 to perform an experiment. 2 to try something new: *teenagers experimenting with drugs;* **experimental** (eks-perr-i-**men**-t'l) adjective; **experimentally** adverb; **experimentation** (eks-perr-i-men-**tay**-sh'n) noun the process of making experiments; **experimenter** noun a person who experiments.
[Latin *experimentum* proof from experience]

expert noun
a person who has special knowledge.
Word Family **expert** adjective; **expertly** adverb; **expertness** noun skill: *marvelling at the expertness of their fingers;* **expertise** (eks-per-**teez**) noun the skill or knowledge of an expert: *her expertise in business.*

expert system noun
Computers a computer system designed to be able to make decisions: *Doctors are*

beginning to use expert systems to help in their diagnoses.

expiate (eks-pee-ate) *verb*
to make amends for.
***Word Family* expiation** (eks-pee-**ay**-sh'n) *noun.*
[Latin *expiare* to purify]

expire *verb*
1 to come to an end: *The contract expired last week.*
2 (*formal*) to die.
3 (*formal*) to breathe out.
***Word Family* expiry** (eks-**pie**-ree), **expiration** (eks-pi-**ray**-sh'n) *noun.*
[*ex-* + Latin *spirare* to breathe]

explain *verb*
to make clear and understandable: *Our teacher explained the meaning of the poem.*
***Phrase* explain away** to make appear unimportant: *She tried to explain her rudeness away by saying she had been exhausted.*
***Word Family* explanation** (eks-pla-**nay**-sh'n) *noun* 1 an act of explaining. 2 a reason: *What was his explanation?*; **explanatory** (eks-**plan**-a-tree) *adjective* serving to explain: *Read the explanatory notes below.*
[Latin *explanare* to make level or plain]

expletive (eks-**plee**-tiv) *noun*
a swear word.

explicable *adjective*
able to be explained.

explicit (eks-**pliss**-it) *adjective*
clearly and precisely expressed.
***Word Family* explicitly** *adverb;* **explicitness** *noun.*

explode *verb*
1 to burst violently: *The gas main exploded.* □ *The police exploded the bomb safely.*
***Figurative* ‘Get out!’ he exploded.**
2 to show to be wrong: *Further experiments exploded their early theories.*
***Word Family* exploded** *adjective* (of a drawing) showing all the parts of a machine, etc. separately but in their correct relationship to each other, so that one can see how they fit together: *an exploded view of the engine.*

exploit (eks-**ployt**) *verb*
to use for profit or personal gain: *It would be unfair of you to exploit this information.*
• **exploit** (eks-ployt) *noun* a notable act.
***Word Family* exploitation** (eks-ploy-**tay**-sh'n) *noun* the act of exploiting: *Paying young people such low wages is sheer exploitation;* **exploiter** *noun;* **exploitative**

(eks-**ploy**-ta-tiv) *adjective* serving to exploit; **exploitable** *adjective.*

explore *verb*
1 to travel for the purpose of discovery.
2 to examine closely: *We explored all the possibilities before reaching a decision.*
***Word Family* explorer** *noun* a person who explores; **exploration** (eks-pla-**ray**-sh'n) *noun;* **exploratory** (eks-**plorr**-a-tree) *adjective.*
[Latin *explorare* to investigate]

explosion (eks-**plo**-zh'n) *noun*
1 a violent and rapid release of energy.
2 the loud sound accompanying this.
3 a sudden outburst, increase, etc.: *a population explosion.*

explosive (eks-**plo**-siv) *adjective*
1 of or relating to an explosion: *the explosive force of the bomb.*
2 tending to create strong feelings: *an explosive issue.*
• **explosive** *noun* a substance capable of exploding.
***Word Family* explosively** *adverb.*

exponent *noun*
1 a person who explains, supports or exemplifies something.
2 also called **index; power**. *Maths* a symbol placed above and to the right of a number, indicating the number of times it is to be multiplied by itself, e.g. the 3 in 4^3, which means $4 \times 4 \times 4$.
[Latin *exponens* displaying]

exponential (eks-pa-**nen**-sh'l) *adjective*
increasing more and more rapidly.
***Word Family* exponentially** *adverb.*

export *verb*
to send goods or services to another country. Compare IMPORT (definition 1).
• **export** *noun*
1 the act of exporting.
2 anything which is exported: *List the main exports of Brazil.*
***Word Family* exporter** *noun* a person or company that exports; **exportation** *noun;* **exportable** *adjective* able to be exported.
[Latin *exportare* to convey out]

expose *verb*
1 to uncover and reveal: *a Tudor house with exposed beams.*
2 to make public the faults, etc. of: *He threatened to expose her in the Sunday papers.*
3 *Photography* to subject a film, etc. to the action of light.
***Phrase* expose oneself** (of a man) to show one's genitals in order to shock.

exposé (eks-**po**-zay) *noun*
a public statement, especially of something
shocking.
[French]

exposition (eks-pa-**zish**-'n) *noun*
1 a detailed explanation.
2 a public exhibition.
[French, exhibition]

expostulate (eks-**poss**-tew-late) *verb*
to protest in an agitated way.
Word Family **expostulation** (eks-poss-
tew-**lay**-sh'n) *noun.*

exposure (eks-**po**-zher) *noun*
1 the act of exposing, especially to
something harmful: *the dangers of exposure
to nuclear radiation.*
2 the effects of being exposed, especially to
the weather: *The climbers were suffering from
exposure.*
3 a position in relation to direction or
weather: *The house has a northern exposure.*
4 *Photography* the length of time a film,
etc. is exposed to light.

expound *verb*
(*formal*) to state in detail.

express *verb*
1 to show or reveal, usually by putting into
words: *He has difficulty in expressing his
feelings.*
2 *Maths* to represent: *Express this fraction
as a decimal.*
3 to send fast or by special delivery.
4 (*formal*) to press out: *Mothers who express
their milk.*
• **express** *adjective*
1 definite or explicit: *The money is set aside
for an express purpose.*
2 fast: *an express train.*
• **express** *noun*
1 also **express train** a very fast train.
2 a speedy system of sending money,
parcels, etc.
Word Family **express** *adverb* fast: *Send
the parcel express;* **expressly** *adverb*
explicitly: *Your father expressly told you to be
back by midnight;* **expressible** *adjective*
able to be put into words.
[Latin *expressus* pressed out]

expression (eks-**presh**-'n) *noun*
1 the act of expressing: *He gave her a ring
as an expression of his love.*
2 an indication of feeling on the face, in
the voice, etc.: *Her sad expression told us
something was wrong.*
3 a word or group of words: *Find two
expressions in the passage that indicate how
the author felt about his wife.*

4 *Maths* a symbol, or collection of
symbols, used to represent a quantity.
Word Family **expressionless** *adjective*;
expressionlessness *noun.*

expressionism (eks-**presh**-'n-izm) *noun*
a style of painting using simple
exaggeration and distortions of line and
colour with the intention of achieving
great emotional impact.
Word Family **expressionist** *adjective,
noun.*

expressive *adjective*
full of expression or feeling: *The mime
artist had an expressive face.*
Word Family **expressively** *adverb*;
expressiveness *noun.*

expressway *noun*
(*especially American*) a motorway in or near
a city.

expropriate (eks-**pro**-pree-ate) *verb*
to take or acquire from another, e.g. for
public use: *The police expropriated his house
during the flood and used it as a soup kitchen.*
Word Family **expropriation** (eks-pro-
pree-**ay**-sh'n) *noun.*
[*ex*- + Latin *proprium* property]

expulsion (eks-**pul**-sh'n) *noun*
the act of expelling: *After his expulsion from
school, John joined the Navy.*

expulsive *adjective*
tending to expel: *the expulsive force of the
rocket.*

expunge (eks-**punj**) *verb*
to rub out or erase completely.

expurgate (**eks**-pa-gate) *verb*
to amend by removing offensive parts, e.g.
obscene passages in a book.
Word Family **expurgation** (eks-pa-**gay**-
sh'n) *noun.*
[*ex*- + Latin *purgare* to cleanse]

exquisite (eks-**kwiz**-it *or*
eks-kwiz-it) *adjective*
1 having great beauty or excellence.
2 intense: *exquisite pleasure.*
Word Family **exquisitely** *adverb*;
exquisiteness *noun.*
[Latin *exquisitus* sought out]

extant *adjective*
(*formal*) still existing.

extemporary (eks-**tem**-pa-ra-ree)
adjective also **extemporaneous** (eks-tem-
pa-**ray**-nee-us)
impromptu or without preparation: *an
extemporary speech.*
Word Family **extempore** (eks-**tem**-pa-
ree) *adjective, adverb*; **extemporize,**

extemporise *verb* to do something impromptu; **extemporarily, extemporaneously** *adverb*.
[Latin *ex tempore* on the spur of the moment]

extend *verb*
1 to spread or stretch out: *The hills seemed to extend for ever.*
2 to offer: *The local villagers extended their hospitality to the refugees.*
Phrase **extend to** to apply to.

extended family *noun* (*plural* **extended families**)
a family unit comprising not only a couple and their children but other relatives such as grandparents. Compare NUCLEAR FAMILY.

extension (eks-**ten**-sh'n) *noun*
1 the act of extending or the state of being extended.
2 an additional part or facility: *We built an extension onto the house.* □ *Our telephone has an extension upstairs.*
3 also **extension lead** a length of electrical cable used to connect a piece of equipment to a power supply a long distance away.
[*ex-* + Latin *tensus* stretched]

extensive *adjective*
large or widespread: *An extensive search was made for the missing child.*
Word Family **extensively** *adverb*.

extensive farming *noun*
farming over a wide area, often with low inputs. Compare INTENSIVE FARMING.

extent *noun*
1 the range or scope of anything: *The extent of his power is limited by the government.* □ *I agree with her to a certain extent.*
2 an area of something.

extenuating (eks-**ten**-yoo-ate-ing) *adjective*
making a fault, crime, etc. appear less serious, e.g. by being an understandable reason for it: *To be fair to these men, there were extenuating circumstances.*
[Latin *extenuatus* made thin]

exterior (eks-**teer**-ee-a) *adjective*
outside: *exterior decoration.* □ *exterior influences.*
• **exterior** *noun* the outer surface or view: *The exterior of the house is in bad repair.*
[Latin, outer]

exterminate (eks-**term**-i-nate) *verb*
to destroy completely: *Australian farmers need to exterminate many thousands of rabbits.*

Word Family **extermination** (eks-term-i-**nay**-sh'n) *noun* the act of exterminating; **exterminator** *noun*.
[Latin *exterminare* to expel outside the boundaries]

external *adjective*
of or relating to the outside or outer part: *The car's external appearance is good.* □ *The government has been subject to external pressures.* □ *External students study by correspondence.*
Word Family **externals** *plural noun* any non-essential or superficial aspects, circumstances, etc.; **externally** *adverb*; **externalize, externalise** *verb* to make or treat as external.

extinct *adjective*
1 no longer in existence: *Dinosaurs are now extinct.*
2 (of a volcano) no longer capable of erupting. Compare ACTIVE (definition 4); DORMANT (definition 3).
Word Family **extinction** *noun*.

extinguish (eks-**ting**-gwish) *verb*
to put out or bring to an end: *We extinguished the fire.* □ *All hope was extinguished when the crashed plane was found.*

extinguisher ⇨ FIRE EXTINGUISHER.

extirpate (eks-**ter**-pate) *verb*
(*formal*) to destroy completely.
Word Family **extirpation** (eks-ter-**pay**-sh'n) *noun*.
[Latin *ex stirpe* by the root]

extol (eks-**tole**) *verb* (**extols; extolling; extolled**)
to praise highly: *She extolled the virtues of hard work.*
[Latin *extollere* to lift up]

extort *verb*
to obtain money, information, etc. by the use of threats or violence.
Word Family **extortion** *noun* the act of extorting; **extortionist** *noun*; **extortionate** *adjective*.
[Latin *extortus* twisted out]

extra *adjective, adverb*
1 more than is usual or necessary: *My parents gave me some extra pocket money.*
2 in addition: *The bill came to £25, and service was extra.*
• **extra** *noun*
1 anything which is additional.
2 a special edition of a newspaper.
3 *Films* a person hired for a very small part, such as being a member of a large crowd.

4 *Cricket* any run gained by the batting side other than by hitting the ball, e.g. by a wide, bye, etc.

extract (eks-**trakt**) *verb*
1 to get out with difficulty or by force: *The dentist extracted my tooth.* □ *The police finally managed to extract the information from him.*
2 to obtain or derive: *The oil is extracted from the rock.*
● **extract** (**eks**-trakt) *noun*
1 a passage taken from a book, etc.
2 ⇨ ESSENCE (definition 2).
Word Family **extractor** *noun* a person or thing that extracts.
[Latin *extractus* pulled out]

extraction (eks-**trak**-sh'n) *noun*
1 the act of extracting.
2 descent: *They are of Russian extraction.*
3 *Chemistry* the separation of a part from a mixture usually by using a solvent which selectively dissolves the required part.

extra-curricular (eks-tra-kurr-**ik**-yoo-la) *adjective*
outside the usual curriculum.

extradite (**eks**-tra-dite) *verb*
to hand over a criminal to another country or authority.
Word Family **extradition** (eks-tra-**dish**-'n) *noun.*

> The word **extradite** is an example of a back-formation. This refers to a word, usually a verb, which is formed by removing a suffix from an existing word. *Extradite* comes from *extradition*, borrowed into English from French. Other examples of back-formations include *donate* from *donation*, *burgle* from *burglary*, *enthuse* from *enthusiasm*, *reminisce* from *reminiscence*.

extramarital *adjective*
(of a sexual relationship) happening outside marriage.

extramural (eks-tra-**mew**-r'l) *adjective*
(of university studies) for non-resident students.
[Latin *extra muros* outside the walls]

extraneous (eks-**tray**-nee-us) *adjective*
not relevant or essential.
Word Family **extraneously** *adverb*; **extraneousness** *noun.*

extraordinary (eks-**tror**-d'n-ree) *adjective*
1 unusual or remarkable.
2 (of a meeting) specially organized.
Word Family **extraordinarily** *adverb.*

extrapolate (eks-**trap**-pa-late) *verb*
to estimate an unknown quantity by projecting from the basis of what is already known.
Word Family **extrapolation** (eks-trap-a-**lay**-sh'n) *noun.*
[*extra-* + (inter)POLATE]

extrasensory perception *noun*
any knowledge or experience gained without the use of normal senses, e.g. by clairvoyance.

extraterrestrial (eks-tra-terr-**est**-ree-al) *adjective*
from outside the earth: *extraterrestrial beings.*
● **extraterrestrial** *noun.*

extravagant (eks-**trav**-a-g'nt) *adjective*
1 wasteful, especially with money.
2 exceeding reasonable limits: *extravagant praise.*
Word Family **extravagantly** *adverb*; **extravagance** *noun* **1** wastefulness. **2** an item on which money has been wasted: *I agree, an electric toothbrush is a bit of an extravagance.*
[*extra-* + Latin *vagans* straying]

extravaganza (eks-trav-a-**gan**-za) *noun*
an elaborate spectacular entertainment.
[Italian]

extreme *adjective*
1 of the highest degree: *They are in extreme danger.*
2 going beyond the usual limits: *an extreme fashion.*
3 outermost: *at the extreme edge of the known universe.*
● **extreme** *noun*
1 the highest degree of something.
2 the furthest limit: *She seems to veer from one extreme to the other.*
Phrase **in the extreme** very.
Word Family **extremely** *adverb* very.
[Latin *extremus* outermost]

extreme unction ⇨ UNCTION.

extremist (eks-**tree**-mist) *noun*
a person who holds extreme political opinions: *a right-wing extremist.*
Word Family **extremism** *noun.*

extremity (eks-**trem**-i-tee) *noun* (*plural* **extremities**)
1 the extreme part or end of anything.
2 (**extremities**) the ends of the limbs.
3 an extreme degree of something.

extricate (**eks**-tri-kate) *verb*
to free from difficulty or entanglement: *I finally managed to extricate myself from her embrace.*

Word Family **extrication** (eks-tri-**kay**-sh'n) *noun*.
[*ex-* + Latin *tricae* hindrances]

extrovert *noun*
1 a cheerful outgoing person.
2 *Psychology* a person interested chiefly in other people and the world around him or her rather than his or her own thoughts and feelings. Compare INTROVERT (definition 2).
[*extra-* + Latin *vertere* to turn]

extrude *verb*
to force or push out.
Word Family **extrusion** (eks-**troo**-*zh*'n) *noun*.
[*ex-* + Latin *trudere* to push]

exuberant (eg-**zoo**-ba-r'nt) *adjective*
extremely lively and vigorous.
Word Family **exuberance** *noun*;
exuberantly *adverb*.
[*ex-* + Latin *uberans* fruitful]

exude (egz-**yood**) *verb*
1 to ooze.
2 to display: *He positively exudes confidence.*
[Latin *exudare* to sweat out]

exult (eg-**zult**) *verb*
to rejoice greatly.
Word Family **exultant** *adjective*;
exultantly *adverb*; **exultation** (eg-zul-**tay**-sh'n) *noun*.
[*ex-* + Latin *saltare* to leap]

eye *noun*
1 *Anatomy* the organ of sight.
2 something which has the shape, function, etc. of an eye: *the eye of a needle.* □ *an electronic eye.*
3 *Weather* the small central area of a tropical cyclone where the wind is calm.
Phrases **an eye for an eye** retaliation against somebody in a similar degree or in a similar way. **clap eyes on** (*informal*) to see. **get one's eye in, keep one's eye in** (in ball games, darts, etc.) to get or keep the ability to throw or hit accurately. **give someone the eye** (*informal*) to make it clear that one is sexually interested in someone. **have an eye for** to have an ability to identify or assess: *She has an excellent eye for detail.* **have one's eye on, keep one's eye on** to observe closely: *I've got my eye on you boys!* **in the eyes of** in the opinion of: *In the eyes of the law he is guilty.* **keep one's eyes peeled** (*informal*) to keep watch carefully. **make eyes at** to indicate sexual interest in by one's expression. **one in the eye for** an annoyance or setback for. **see eye to eye** to agree. **turn a blind eye to** to pretend

not to notice. **with an eye to** with the intention of achieving. **with one's eyes open** aware of the possible risks.
● **eye** *verb* (**eyes; eyeing** or **eying; eyed**) to observe or watch closely: *We eyed the dog nervously.*

eyeball *noun*
the soft part of the eye, protected by the eye socket.
● **eyeball** *verb* to look straight at.

eyebath *noun*
a small cup for applying liquids to the eye.

eyebrow *noun*
Anatomy a strip of hair on the forehead just above the eye.
Phrase **raise one's eyebrows, raise an eyebrow** to indicate disapproval or surprise.

eye-catching *adjective*
very striking in appearance.

eyelash *noun* (*plural* **eyelashes**)
any or all of the hairs forming a fringe at the edge of each eyelid.

eyelet *noun*
1 a small hole with a trimmed edge, e.g. in a shoe for the lace.
2 a small metal ring used to reinforce such a hole.

eyelid *noun*
Anatomy a fold of skin which closes to protect the eye and spread lubricating fluid over it.

eyeliner *noun*
a dark cosmetic substance applied along the edges of the eyelids to accentuate the shape of the eye.

eye-opener *noun*
(*informal*) something which causes great surprise.

eyepatch *noun* (*plural* **eyepatches**)
a covering worn over the eye to protect it.

eyepiece *noun*
the lens or group of lenses in an optical instrument, such as a telescope, closest to the viewer's eye.

eyeshadow *noun*
a coloured cosmetic substance applied to the eyelids to make the eyes look more attractive.

eyesight *noun*
the power to see.

eye socket *noun*
Anatomy either of two holes in the front of the skull in which the eyes are located.

eyesore *noun*
something which is offensive to look at.

eye tooth *noun* (*plural* **eye teeth**)
an upper canine tooth.
Phrase **give one's eye teeth for** to be
willing to give up a great deal for.

eyewitness *noun* (*plural* **eyewitnesses**)
a person who has seen an event and can
give evidence about it.

eyrie (**eer**-ee) *noun*
an eagle's nest, usually built on a
mountain or cliff.

Ff

fa ⇨ FAH.

Fabian *adjective*
1 achieving socialist aims by gradual evolution, not revolution.
2 cautious or avoiding pitched battles.
[after *Fabius Cunctator*, a Roman general who checked Hannibal by avoiding pitched battles]

fable *noun*
1 a short story with a moral, often about supernatural people or animals.
2 a legend or myth.
Word Family **fabled** *adjective* 1 famous. 2 mythical.
[Latin *fabula* a story]

fabric *noun*
1 a thin solid substance made by weaving, knitting or felting fibres and used to make clothes, curtains, etc.
2 a framework or structure.
Figurative Apathy is undermining the fabric of our society.
[Latin *fabrica* skilled work]

fabricate *verb*
1 to make up or invent: *The gang had carefully fabricated their alibi.*
2 to assemble ready-made sections of something.
Word Family **fabrication** *noun* 1 the act of fabricating. 2 something which is fabricated, such as a lie; **fabricator** *noun*.

fabulous (**fab**-yoo-lus) *adjective*
1 (*informal*) wonderful or very good: *What a fabulous dress!*
2 of or occurring in fable: *Dragons are fabulous beasts.*
Word Family **fabulously** *adverb*; **fabulousness** *noun*.

facade (fa-**sahd**) *noun*
1 the outside front of a building.
2 a false or deceptive exterior: *Behind her tough facade hides a frightened little girl.*
[French]

face *noun*
1 the front part of the head from the forehead to the chin.
2 an expression: *He had a sad face.*
3 a surface, especially of a solid shape.
4 the side of a mountain or cliff.
Phrases **in the face of** 1 when confronted with: *What could he do in the face of all these difficulties?* 2 in spite of : *She succeeded in the face of continual opposition.* **keep a straight face** to show no emotion or amusement. **lose face** to lose standing or reputation: *I'll lose face if I back down now.* **make faces** to grimace. **on the face of it** judging by the appearance.
● **face** *verb*
1 to look or turn the face towards: *Face me when you are speaking to me.* □ *The windows face the sea.*
2 to be opposite: *the illustration facing page 3.*
3 to meet or confront: *He strode out of the house to face the waiting reporters.*
4 to cover with a layer of another material: *The builder faced the brick wall with stone blocks.*
Phrase **face up to** to acknowledge: *We have to face up to the fact that he will never walk again.*
[Latin *facies*]

faceless *adjective*
remote or anonymous: *faceless civil servants.*

facelift *noun*
the use of plastic surgery to remove wrinkles, scars, etc. from the face.
Figurative The old building got a facelift when the painters moved in (= improved appearance).

face pack *noun*
a liquid or paste for cleaning the skin, left to set on the face and then washed off.

facet (**fass**-it) *noun*
1 an aspect: *There are many facets to a business like publishing.*
2 one of the sides of a cut gem.
3 *Biology* the cornea of one element of a compound eye, as found in some insects.

facetious (fa-**see**-shus) *adjective*
of an ill-timed or silly attempt to be amusing: *No one appreciates facetious remarks during a serious discussion.*

face value *noun*
1 *Commerce* the value stated on a document, a company's shares, etc.
2 the direct or apparent meaning of something: *I took what you said at face value.*

facia ⇨ FASCIA.

facial (**fay**-sh'l) *noun*
a treatment of the face involving careful cleaning, toning, massage and applying new make-up.
• **facial** *adjective* of or for the face: *facial acne.* ◻ *facial cream.*
Word Family **facially** *adverb.*

facile (**fas**-ile) *adjective*
done or produced with ease or too little thought or care.
[Latin *facilis* easy]

facilitate (fa-**sil**-i-tate) *verb*
to make easier or assist: *A computer would facilitate the process.*
Word Family **facilitation** (fa-sil-i-**tay**-sh'n) *noun.*

facility (fa-**sil**-i-tee) *noun* (*plural* **facilities**)
1 something that makes it easy to do things: *excellent leisure facilities.*
2 an ease or readiness in doing something: *His facility at knitting surprised everyone.*

facing (**fay**-sing) *noun*
a piece of material applied to an outer edge or layer of something.

facsimile (fak-**sim**-i-lee) *noun*
an exact reproduction.
[Latin *fac* make + *simile* like]

fact *noun*
1 something that has really occurred or actually exists.
2 something known to be true or accepted as true: *No one can deny the fact that fire burns.*
Phrase **in fact, in point of fact** really, indeed.
[Latin *factus* done]

faction[1] (**fak**-sh'n) *noun*
a small discontented group within a larger one.
Word Family **factional** *adjective* of or relating to a faction; **factionalism** *noun.*
[Latin *factions* of a (political) party]

faction[2] *noun*
the dramatization of a real event or situation to make a television programme or a story.
[FAC(t) + (fic)TION]

factitious (fak-**tish**-us) *adjective*
artificial or false: *Advertising often creates a factitious demand for one particular brand of goods.*
[Latin *facticius* artificial]

factor *noun*
1 a thing that helps to bring about a result: *Hard work was one factor in his success.*

2 *Maths* an integer that divides exactly into another integer: *3 is a factor of 6.*
3 *Biology* a gene or a genetic unit of heredity.
4 a person who buys, sells or acts as an agent for another.
Word Family **factorize, factorise** *verb* *Maths* to break up into factors; **factorization** *noun.*

factor VIII *noun* also **factor eight**
one of the proteins which form the clotting agent in blood and which is missing in the blood of haemophiliacs.

factory (**fak**-ta-ree) *noun* (*plural* **factories**)
a building or group of buildings where something is manufactured or assembled.

factory ship *noun*
a fishing ship which processes and freezes its catch while still at sea.

factotum (fak-**toe**-t'm) *noun* (*plural* **factotums**)
a person who does all kinds of work.
[Latin *fac* do + *totum* all]

factual *adjective*
based on facts.
Word Family **factually** *adverb.*

faculty (**fak**-'l-tee) *noun* (*plural* **faculties**)
1 a power of the mind or body: *the faculty of reason.* ◻ *the faculties of sight and hearing.*
2 an ability or aptitude for something: *Small children have an uncanny faculty for getting into trouble.*
3 a section of a university or college studying related subjects.
4 the teaching staff of such a section.
[Latin *facultas* ability]

fad *noun*
a temporary enthusiasm.
Word Family **faddish** *adjective.*

faddy *adjective* (**faddier, faddiest**)
fussy about food.
Word Family **faddiness** *noun.*

fade *verb*
1 to lose or cause to lose brightness or colour: *This material has faded with the years.* ◻ *Sunlight has faded this material.*
2 to disappear gradually: *His smile faded.*
3 *Film* to change the clarity of a picture slowly by increasing it (**fade in**) or decreasing it (**fade out**).

faeces (**fee**-seez) *plural noun* (American **feces**)
Biology the solid waste material remaining after digestion, expelled from the lower end of the alimentary canal.

Word Family **faecal** (**feek-**'l) *adjective*.
[Latin, dregs]

fag *noun*
1 (*informal*) a cigarette.
2 (*informal*) anything causing weariness:
Going shopping is a real fag.
3 (in certain public schools) a junior pupil
required to perform certain services for a
senior.

faggot *noun*
1 a kind of meatball made with liver.
2 a bundle of sticks, twigs, etc. bound
together and used for fuel.

fah *noun* also **fa**
Music a note in the scale. ⇨ DOH.

Fahrenheit (**farr-**en-hite) *adjective*
of or relating to a scale of temperature
with the melting point of ice (0°C) set at
32°F and the boiling point of water
(100°C) set at 212°F. Compare CELSIUS.
[after *Gabriel Fahrenheit*, 1686-1736, a
German physicist]

fail *verb*
1 to be unsuccessful: *He failed to make his
meaning clear.*
2 not to give a pass mark to: *The driving
instructor failed me.*
3 to go out of business: *The bank failed.*
4 to lose strength or cease to function: *His
health has been failing for years.* □ *He ran into
the back of a van when his brakes failed.*
5 to omit or neglect: *He failed to keep his
promise.*
6 to let down: *She felt that her family had
failed her.*
• **fail** *noun* a mark awarded to an
examinee which is below the pass mark.
Phrase **without fail** for certain.
Word Family **failure** *noun*.

failing *noun*
a weakness or shortcoming: *We all have our
little failings.*
• **failing** *preposition* in the absence of:
Failing payment, we will be forced to sue.

fail-safe *adjective*
1 relating to a supplementary device which
automatically comes into action if the
main mechanism fails, e.g. in a lift.
2 not likely or not able to fail.

fain *adverb*
an old word meaning 'gladly' or 'willingly'.

faint *adjective*
1 weak or indistinct: *a faint light glimmering
in the distance.* □ *a faint hope.*
2 liable to lose consciousness: *For days
after the accident she felt faint and weak.*

• **faint** *noun* a sudden loss of
consciousness.
• **faint** *verb* to lose consciousness
temporarily.
Word Family **faintly** *adverb*; **faintness**
noun.

faint-hearted *adjective*
lacking courage or conviction.
Word Family **faint-heartedly** *adverb*;
faint-heartedness *noun*.

fair[1] *adjective*
1 honest or in accordance with the rules: *a
fair trial.* □ *a fair fight.*
2 average or moderately good: *She has a
fair knowledge of German.*
3 light in complexion or colouring.
4 without rain: *fair weather.*
5 an old word meaning **beautiful**: *a fair
maiden.*
• **fair** *adverb* in a fair manner: *She doesn't
play fair!*
Phrase **fair and square** *I hit him fair and
square on the jaw* (= directly, straight).
Word Family **fairly** *adverb* 1 in a fair
manner: *Treat other people fairly.* 2 quite:
I was fairly tired; **fairness** *noun*.

fair[2] *noun*
1 an amusement show.
2 a place at which goods are exhibited,
bought and sold.

Fair Isle *noun*
a complex multicoloured pattern knitted
into a piece of clothing.
[first made on *Fair Isle*, Scotland]

fairway *noun*
Golf the cleared ground on a golf links,
between the tee and the green.

fairy *noun* (*plural* **fairies**)
Folklore a small supernatural being with
magical powers.

fairy lights *plural noun*
small coloured lights used for decoration.

fairy tale *noun*
a story about fairies or magical events.

fait accompli (fate a-kom-**plee**) *noun*
a thing which is already done.
[French, fact accomplished]

faith *noun*
1 trust or confidence.
2 belief in a religion.
3 a religion or religious movement.
Phrase **in good faith** *He made the offer in
good faith* (= sincerely, honestly).

faithful *adjective*
1 loyal: *a faithful servant.*
2 accurate or truthful: *a faithful description.*

Word Family **faithfully** *adverb*;
faithfulness *noun*; **faithless** *adjective*
1 not faithful. 2 not trustworthy.

faith healer *noun*
a person attempting to cure illness, etc.
through religious faith.
Word Family **faith healing** *noun*.

fake *adjective*
not genuine.
• **fake** *noun* somebody who or something
which is not genuine.
• **fake** *verb* to reproduce or imitate in
order to deceive: *He faked a headache.*
Word Family **faker** *noun*; **fakery** *noun*
false or deceptive actions.

fakir (**fay**-keer *or* **fak**-eer) *noun*
a Muslim devoted to poverty and chastity.
[Arabic *faqir* poor man]

falafel (fa-**laf**-al *or* fa-**lah**-fal) *noun* also
felafel
a snack common in Middle Eastern
cooking, consisting of balls made out of
chickpeas and spices and fried.
[Arabic]

falcon *noun*
a bird of prey with long wings, often used
to hunt other birds or game.
Word Family **falconer** *noun* a person
who hunts with or trains falcons; **falconry**
noun.

fall (fawl) *verb* (**falls**; **falling**; **fell**; **fallen**)
1 to move downwards: *A leaf fell from the
tree.* □ *Prices fell.*
2 to hang down: *Her hair fell softly about her
shoulders.*
3 to show dejection: *His face fell when he
heard the news.*
4 to be killed: *Many men fell in the war.*
5 to collapse: *She stumbled and fell.*
6 to be defeated or captured: *The city fell
after much fighting.*
7 to land: *The book fell on my head.*
8 to become less: *The wind has fallen.*
9 to occur: *My birthday always falls in the
summer holidays.*
10 to become: *She fell asleep.*
Phrases **fall back** to retreat. **fall back on**
to have recourse to. **fall for** 1 to be
deceived by. 2 to fall in love with. **fall foul
of** to come into conflict with. **fall in** to
take one's proper place in a formation or
group. **fall on, fall upon** to rush suddenly
at or attack. **fall out** 1 to leave the ranks or
a formation. 2 to quarrel. 3 to happen or
result. **fall through** to come to nothing.
fall to to be the duty of: *It fell to me to
introduce them.*
• **fall** *noun*

1 the act or an instance of falling: *She had
a bad fall.*
2 something which has fallen: *a light fall of
snow.*
3 a waterfall.
4 *American* the autumn.
Phrase **be riding for a fall** to be heading
for trouble.

fallacy (**fal**-a-see) *noun* (*plural* **fallacies**)
1 a mistaken or false belief or opinion.
2 *Logic* an error in reasoning.
Word Family **fallacious** (fa-**lay**-shus)
adjective; **fallaciously** *adverb*;
fallaciousness *noun*.
[Latin *fallax, fallacis* deceiving]

fall guy *noun*
(*informal*) a person who is left to take the
blame or punishment.

fallible (**fal**-a-b'l) *adjective*
liable to be mistaken.
Word Family **fallibility** (fal-a-**bil**-i-tee)
noun.

falling star ⇨ METEOR.

Fallopian tube (fal-o-**pee**-an **tube**) *noun*
Anatomy the tube through which the ovum
moves from an ovary to the uterus.

fallout *noun*
1 *Physics* a radioactive substance on the
earth's surface or in the atmosphere,
resulting from nuclear explosions.
2 the incidental results or by-products of
an experiment or event.

fallow[1] (**fal**-o) *adjective*
left uncultivated: *fallow land.*

fallow[2] *noun*
a light yellow or brown colour.
• **fallow** *adjective* of this colour: *a fallow
deer.*

false (fawls) *adjective*
1 not true or correct: *a false statement.*
2 not genuine: *false teeth.*
3 not faithful or loyal: *a false friend.*
Word Family **falsely** *adverb*; **falseness**
noun the quality of being false; **falsity**
noun (*plural* **falsities**) 1 falseness.
2 something which is false.
[Latin *falsus* mistaken, untrue]

falsehood *noun*
a lie.

false memory *noun*
a supposed memory of early childhood
events, especially child abuse, which
comes to light only under psychotherapy
by means of psychoanalysis.

false pretences *plural noun*
misrepresentation of one's circumstances,
identity, etc.

false rib ⇨ FLOATING RIB.

falsetto (fawl-**set**-o) *noun* (*plural*
falsettos)
an unusually high-pitched man's voice.

falsify (**fawl**-si-fie) *verb* (**falsifies;
falsifying; falsified**)
to make false: *He managed to falsify the
evidence by lying.*
Word Family **falsification** (fawl-si-fi-
kay-sh'n) *noun*.

falsity ⇨ FALSE.

falter (**fawl**-ter) *verb*
to hesitate or waver: *The line of troops
faltered.*
Word Family **falteringly** *adverb*.

fame *noun*
the condition of being widely known or
esteemed.
[Latin *fama* reputation]

familiar (fa-**mil**-ya) *adjective*
1 well known: *a familiar face.*
2 having a thorough knowledge: *Are you
familiar with radio technology?*
3 intimate or close: *on familiar terms.*
4 too intimate or presumptuous: *Don't be
so familiar with your teacher.*
• **familiar** *noun* also called **familiar
spirit**. a demon supposed to attend a
witch at her call.
Word Family **familiarly** *adverb*;
familiarity (fa-mil-i-**ar**-i-tee) *noun*;
familiarize (fa-**mil**-ya-rize), **familiarise**
verb to make or become familiar:
Familiarize yourself with the controls;
familiarization (fa-mil-ya-rye-**zay**-sh'n)
noun.
[Latin *familiaris* of the household]

family *noun* (*plural* **families**)
1 a group consisting of parents and their
children. ⇨ NUCLEAR FAMILY.
2 all persons descended from the same
ancestors, such as parents, children, aunts,
uncles, cousins, etc. ⇨ EXTENDED FAMILY.
3 *Biology* the group below order in the
classification of animals and plants.
Word Family **familial** (fa-**mil**-yal)
adjective.

family planning *noun*
the regulating of the number and the
timing of children born into a family,
especially with contraception.

family tree *noun*
a chart showing the descent and
relationship of members of a family.

famine (**fam**-in) *noun*
a widespread and serious shortage of food.
[French *faim* hunger]

famished *adjective*
(*informal*) extremely hungry.

famous (**fay**-mus) *adjective*
being celebrated or known by many
people.
Word Family **famously** *adverb* **1** in a
famous way. **2** (*informal*) excellently.

fan¹ *noun*
a device, operated by hand or
mechanically, for creating a current of air.
• **fan** *verb* (**fans; fanning; fanned**)
to send a current of air onto.
Figurative *to fan the flames of discontent*
(= increase).
Phrase **fan out** to spread out like a fan:
The searchers fanned out across the field.

fan² *noun*
an enthusiastic follower or devotee: *a
football fan.*
[shortening of *fanatic*]

fanatic (fa-**nat**-ik) *noun*
a person with an excessive enthusiasm for
something: *a film fanatic.*
Word Family **fanatic, fanatical**
adjective; **fanatically** *adverb*; **fanaticism**
(fa-**nat**-i-sizm) *noun*.
[Latin *fanaticus* inspired by a god,
frenzied]

fancy *verb* (**fancies; fancying; fancied**)
1 to imagine: *Fancy living with him all your
life.*
2 to have a liking or preference for: *What
do you fancy for dinner tonight?*
3 to find attractive: *I can't believe you fancy
him.*
• **fancy** *noun* (*plural* **fancies**)
1 a fondness or liking.
2 imagination: *a mixture of fact and fancy.*
3 something imagined.
• **fancy** *adjective* (**fancier; fanciest**) not
plain or ordinary: *a fancy hat.*
Word Family **fancier** *noun* a person with
a special interest or enthusiasm; **fanciful**
adjective in one's imagination; **fancifully**
adverb; **fancy-free** *adjective* not in love.
[shortening of FANTASY]

fancy dress *noun*
clothes worn by a person to represent a
costume of another time, a famous
character, an animal, etc.

fanfare *noun*
a loud elaborate musical introduction
played on trumpets, etc.

fang *noun*
a long pointed tooth.

fanlight *noun*
a window above a door.

fantail *noun*
a bird with a fan-like tail, especially a domestic pigeon.

fantasia (fan-tay-zi-a) *noun*
a piece of music, literature, etc. that follows no set rules.

fantastic (fan-**tas**-tik) *adjective*
1 (*informal*) wonderful: *What a fantastic party.*
2 unlikely or hard to believe: *a fantastic plan to take over the world.*
3 having the characteristics of fantasy: *fantastic sea creatures.*
Word Family fantastically *adverb.*

> The word **fantastic** is now commonly used to express one's appreciation or approval of something extremely good or impressive. This meaning has developed from the original meaning of 'imaginary, unreal, of the kind of thing found in fantasy', the connection being that some things are so impressive as to be almost unbelievable or unreal.

fantasy (**fan**-ta-see) *noun* (*plural* **fantasies**)
1 a wild or extravagant imagination.
2 a product of this, such as a daydream.
3 fiction that contains adventure and imaginary situations.
Word Family fantasize, fantasise *verb* to daydream.

fanzine (fan-zeen) *noun*
a magazine produced for fans of a particular interest or hobby: *a pop music fanzine.*
[FAN² + (maga)ZINE]

far *adverb* (**further** or **farther**; **furthest** or **farthest**)
1 to, from, or at a considerable distance: *How far did you go?* □ *She can see far into the future.*
2 to a considerable degree: *He's far better now that he has moved to another school.*
Phrases **as far as** to the extent that: *As far as I know, she still lives there.* **by far** very much. **far and away** very much. **far be it from me** I would not hope or dare to: *Far be it from me to criticize your work.* **so far** 1 up till now. 2 to a limited extent.
● **far** *adjective* (**further** or **farther**; **furthest** or **farthest**)
1 distant: *a far country.*
2 more distant: *the far corner of the room.*

farce *noun*
1 a play intended merely to amuse, usually emphasizing situation rather than character, and often containing an improbable plot and slapstick humour.
2 an absurd or futile situation or set of events: *The Peace Conference was a farce because it solved nothing.*
Word Family farcical (**far**-si-k'l) *adjective*; **farcically** *adverb.*

fare *noun*
1 a fee a passenger is charged for the use of transport.
2 food provided, especially in a restaurant: *good country fare.*
● **fare** *verb*
1 to manage: *How did you fare in your interview?*
2 an old word meaning **go**.

Far East *noun*
the countries of eastern and south-eastern Asia, such as China and Japan.

farewell (fair-**well**) *interjection*
goodbye.
● **farewell** *noun* a leave-taking.

far-fetched *adjective*
improbable or only remotely connected: *He has a habit of making far-fetched comparisons.*

farinaceous (fa-rin-ay-shus) *adjective*
containing flour, meal or starch.
[Latin *farina* flour]

farm *noun*
an area of land used to raise crops or animals.
● **farm** *verb* to use land for growing crops, raising animals, etc.
Phrase **farm out** to give or send out to others: *They have farmed out that side of the business to subcontractors.*
Word Family farmer *noun*; **farming** *noun.*

far out *adjective*
unconventional.

farrago (fa-**rah**-go) *noun* (*plural* **farragos**)
a confused mixture.
[Latin, mixed fodder]

farrier *noun*
a blacksmith who shoes horses.
[Latin *ferrum* iron]

farrow *noun*
a litter of pigs.

farther
a comparative of **far**.

> ! Both *farther* and *further* can be used of distances, as in *My house is farther/further from the station*, but only *further* can be used to mean 'additional', as in *Have you anything further to say?*

farthest

a superlative of **far**.

farthing (far-*thing*) *noun*
(*formerly*) an old British coin equal to about one-tenth of a current penny.
[Old English *feortha* fourth]

fascia (fay-sha) *noun* (*plural* **fascias**) also **facia**
1 the dashboard of a motor vehicle.
2 a nameplate over the front of a shop.
3 (**fash**-a) (*plural* **fasciae**) (**fash**-i-ee) *Anatomy* the layers of fibrous connective tissue beneath the skin, enclosing or connecting muscles or internal organs.
Word Family **fascial** *adjective*.

fascinate (fas-i-nate) *verb*
to attract irresistibly or hold spellbound: *The audience was fascinated by the speaker.*
Word Family **fascination** (fas-i-**nay**-sh'n) *noun*; **fascinating** *adjective*; **fascinatingly** *adverb*.
[Latin *fascinare* to cast a spell on]

fascism (**fash**-izm) *noun*
a form of extreme right-wing dictatorship in which the government controls all the affairs of a country, including industry and finance, and restricts individual liberties. It is characterized by an aggressive nationalism.
Word Family **fascist** *noun*, *adjective*.
[from *fasces*, the ancient Roman symbol of state power, first adopted by the Italian dictatorship, as its emblem, in 1922]

fashion (**fash**-'n) *noun*
1 a style or custom, e.g. of dress, manners, etc., which is considered the most admirable or worthy of imitation at a certain time.
2 a way or manner of doing something: *He works in a businesslike fashion.*
Phrase **after a fashion** *Because of his rush he only finished the job after a fashion* (= in a way, but not well).
Word Family **fashion** *verb* to form or mould; **fashionable** *adjective* conforming to fashion; **fashionably** *adverb*.

fast¹ *adjective*
1 swift or quick: *a fast horse.*

2 ahead of the correct time: *That clock is fast.*
3 firmly fixed: *The post is fast in the ground.*
□ *Fast colours will not run when the garment is washed.*
4 close: *fast friends.*
• **fast** *adverb*
1 quickly: *Don't speak so fast.*
2 firmly, securely or tightly: *Hold fast to the rail.* □ *She was fast asleep.*
Word Family **fastness** *noun* (*plural* **fastnesses**) 1 a remote hideout: *The bandits fled to their mountain fastness.* 2 the state of being fixed or firm.

fast² *noun*
a time of eating little or no food, e.g. as a religious duty or in protest.
• **fast** *verb*.

fasten (fah-s'n) *verb*
to fix safely or join together: *He fastened his seat belt before starting the car.*
Phrase **fasten on, fasten upon** to seize or lay hold of.
Word Family **fastening** *noun*; **fastener** *noun*.

fast food *noun*
food such as hamburgers, hot dogs etc. that can be prepared and served quickly.

fastidious (fass-**tid**-i-us) *adjective*
fussy or difficult to please.
Word Family **fastidiously** *adverb*; **fastidiousness** *noun*.
[Latin *fastidium* distaste]

fast track *noun*
a quick way of getting through a system.
Word Family **fast-track** *verb*.

fat *noun*
1 the greasy white or yellow substance in animal bodies, forming a store of food and providing insulation.
2 a substance made from animal fat or from plants, used for cooking, e.g. butter or margarine.
• **fat** *adjective* (**fatter; fattest**)
1 plump.
2 (*informal*) large or abundant: *a fat profit.*
Word Family **fatness** *noun*.

fatal (fay-t'l) *adjective*
1 causing death: *a fatal blow to the head.*
2 decisive or fateful: *The fatal day finally arrived.*
Word Family **fatally** *adverb*.
[Latin *fatalis* preordained, deadly]

> ! Do not confuse *fatal* with *fateful*.
> Only *fatal* can be used to mean
> 'causing death', as in *a fatal accident*. If
> an event, action or decision is *fateful*, it
> has an important, often bad, effect on
> future events: *the fateful decision to stray
> from the path*.

fatalism (fay-ta-lizm) *noun*
a tendency to accept everything as
inevitable or unchangeable.
Word Family **fatalist** *noun*; **fatalistic**
(fay-ta-**list**-ik) *adjective*; **fatalistically**
adverb.

fatality (fa-tal-i-tee) *noun* (*plural*
fatalities)
1 a disaster resulting in death.
2 a person killed in a disaster or accident.
3 the condition of being subject to fate: *He
believed in the fatality of human life.*

fate *noun*
1 the power that predetermines events:
The Greeks believed fate ruled human life.
2 the final condition of a person or thing:
concern for the fate of the missing yachtsman.
Word Family **fated** *adjective* destined.

fateful *adjective*
decisively important, having disastrous
consequences: *the fateful decision to stray
from the path*.

> ! Do not confuse *fateful* with FATAL.

father (fah-tha) *noun*
1 a male parent.
2 a man who starts or establishes
something: *the father of science*.
3 (**Father**) *Christianity* a name for God.
4 (**Father**) *Christianity* a title for a priest
or abbot.
Word Family **father** *verb*; **fatherhood**
noun; **fatherly** *adjective*.

Father Christmas *noun*
the legendary person bringing presents to
children at Christmas.

father-in-law *noun* (*plural* **fathers-in-
law**)
one's husband's or wife's father.

fatherland *noun*
the land of one's birth.

fathom (fath-um) *noun*
a unit used for measuring the depth of
water, equal to about 1·83 m, or 6 feet.
● **fathom** *verb*
1 to understand or work out.
2 to the depth of.
Word Family **fathomable** *adjective*;
fathomless *adjective*.

fatigue (fa-teeg) *noun*
1 the state of being very tired, especially
owing to vigorous activity.
2 *Metallurgy* the weaknesses caused in a
material by repeated stresses, vibrations,
etc.
3 (**fatigues**) non-military tasks, such as
digging ditches, assigned to soldiers in
training, sometimes as a punishment.
4 (**fatigues**) the work clothes worn by
soldiers doing manual work.
Word Family **fatigue** *verb* (**fatigues**;
fatiguing; **fatigued**) to tire.
[Latin *fatigare* to weary]

fatness ⇨ FAT.

fatten *verb*
to make fat or fatter.

fatty *adjective* (**fattier**; **fattiest**)
containing plenty of fat.
Word Family **fattiness** *noun*.

fatty acid *noun*
Chemistry an organic acid, such as acetic
acid. Fatty acids with large molecules form
essential parts of soaps, fats and oils.

fatuous (fat-yew-us) *adjective*
stupid or foolish.
Word Family **fatuously** *adverb*;
fatuousness *noun*.
[Latin *fatuus* gaping]

fatwa (fat-wah) *noun*
Islam a ruling on a point of law.

faucet (faw-set) *noun*
(*especially American*) a tap.

fault (fawlt) *noun*
1 a thing which makes a person or thing
imperfect.
2 the responsibility or cause of blame for
wrongdoing: *Whose fault is it that you
missed the train?*
3 *Tennis* a breaking of the rules when
serving. A **foot fault** is when a player steps
over the baseline while serving
4 *Geography* a break in a rock formation
caused by movement of the earth's crust.
Phrase **find fault** to criticize.
Word Family **fault** *verb*; **faulty** *adjective*
(**faultier**; **faultiest**); **faultily** *adverb*;
faultiness *noun*.

fauna (faw-na) *noun*
Biology all the animals of a certain area or
period. Compare FLORA.
[after *Fauna*, Roman goddess of the earth]

faux pas (foe pah) *noun* (*plural* **faux pas**)
(foe **pah**)
an indiscreet remark or action, especially a
social blunder.
[French, false step]

favour noun (*American* **favor**)
1 a helpful or considerate act: *Would you do me a favour and lend me some money?*
2 a friendly attitude or condition: *It did not take him long to win her favour.* □ *His superiors viewed his request with favour.*
Phrases **curry favour** to seek or gain approval by flattery, etc. **find favour** to gain acceptance or approval. **in favour** having approval. **in favour of** 1 in support of: *We were all in favour of accepting the offer.* 2 to the advantage of: *The new method worked in favour of everyone.* 3 to be replaced by: *He swapped his bike in favour of a new one.* **out of favour** not having approval.
● **favour** verb
1 to like or support: *Fortune favoured us.*
2 to oblige: *She favoured me with a sweet smile.*
3 to treat gently or spare: *The dog favoured his sore paw.*
Word Family **favourable** adjective helpful or approving; **favourably** adverb.
[Latin *favor*]

favourite adjective (*American* **favorite**)
liked above all others: *My favourite animal is the elephant.*
● **favourite** noun
1 a person or thing liked above all others.
2 *Sport* a competitor expected to win.
Word Family **favouritism** noun the unfair liking or support of one person or group.

fawn[1] noun
1 a young deer.
2 a light yellowish-brown colour.
Word Family **fawn** adjective.

fawn[2] verb
1 (of people) to try to win someone's favour by flattery, etc.
2 (of dogs) to show pleasure and affection by tail-wagging, licking, etc.
Word Family **fawning** adjective; **fawningly** adverb.

fax noun (*plural* **faxes**)
1 also called **fax machine**. a machine which scans pieces of written information electronically and transfers the information to a receiving machine by means of a telephone line.
2 a copy of a document, map, picture, etc. produced in this way.
● **fax** verb.
[shortening of FACSIMILE]

faze verb
(*informal*) to disconcert: *She was fazed by all the photographers.*

fealty (feel-tee) noun
loyalty, especially the sworn loyalty of a medieval vassal to a lord.

fear noun
1 a troubled feeling caused by awareness or expectation of danger or some frightening event.
2 an old word meaning 'awe and reverence': *the fear of God.*
Phrase **no fear!** certainly not!
● **fear** verb
1 to feel fear.
2 to suspect: *I fear that she misunderstood me.*
Word Family **fearful** adjective 1 having or causing fear. 2 (*informal*) great; **fearfully** adverb; **fearsome** adjective causing fear.
[Old English *faer* danger, sudden calamity]

feasibility study noun (*plural* **feasibility studies**)
a study undertaken to determine whether something can be done or whether a problem can be solved.

feasible (fee-zi-b'l) adjective
capable of being done or put into effect: *The plan wasn't feasible.*
Word Family **feasibly** adverb; **feasibility** (fee-zi-**bil**-i-tee) noun.

feast noun
1 a large elaborate meal.
2 a thing that gives pleasure: *The concert was a musical feast.*
3 a religious festival.
● **feast** verb.
[Latin *festus* full of rejoicing]

feat noun
a remarkable achievement.

feather (fe-*th*a) noun
1 a light fluffy structure with a hollow shaft that grows from a bird's skin.
2 a similar synthetic object, e.g. on a dart, arrow, etc.
Phrase **a feather in one's cap** an achievement to be proud of.
Word Family **feathered, feathery** adjective.

featherweight (fe-*th*a-wate) noun
a weight division in boxing, not exceeding 57 kg (9 stone).

feature (fee-cha) noun
1 a distinguishing aspect or part: *The room had some interesting features.*
2 a part of the face.
3 a special descriptive article or interview in a newspaper, magazine, etc.

4 also called **feature film**. a film which is the main one shown in a cinema programme.
● **feature** *verb*
1 to make a feature of.
2 to present.

febrile *adjective*
having a fever.

February *noun* (*plural* **Februaries**)
the second month of the year, after January and before March.

> **February** is, etymologically, the month of purification, although nowadays it is often thought of as the month of romance because St Valentine's Day is on 14 February. The name came into English by way of Old French *feverier* from Latin *februarius*. This in turn came from *februa*, a purification festival held on 15 February.

feckless *adjective*
1 feeble or ineffective.
2 worthless or irresponsible.
Word Family **fecklessly** *adverb*;
fecklessness *noun*.
[Scots *feck* worth + *-less*]

fecund (fek-und *or* fee-kund) *adjective*
very fertile.
Word Family **fecundity** (fi-**kun**-di-tee)
noun.
[Latin *fecundus* fruitful]

fed *verb*
the past tense and past participle of **feed**.
Phrase **fed up** out of patience, disgusted.

federal *adjective*
of the joining of states or countries under one central government, as distinct from each state's separate government.
Word Family **federalist** *noun* a supporter of federal government; **federalism** *noun*.
[Latin *foederis* of a league]

federation *noun*
a group of states or organizations.

fee *noun*
1 a charge or payment, e.g. for a professional service.
2 *Medieval history* the land rented by a nobleman to a vassal in return for personal and military service.

feeble *adjective*
weak or ineffective.
Word Family **feebleness** *noun*; **feebly** *adverb*.

feeble-minded *adjective*
stupid.
Word Family **feeble-mindedness** *noun*.

feed *verb* (**feeds**; **feeding**; **fed**)
1 to give food to.
2 to keep supplied: *We fed the material into the machine.*
● **feed** *noun* food, especially for livestock.

feedback *noun*
1 information that helps to calculate the results or success of something.
2 the return of part of the output of a device into the input, e.g. an amplifier. Feedback causes the intense howling sometimes heard in public address systems.

feel *verb* (**feels**; **feeling**; **felt**)
1 to perceive through the sense of touch.
2 to examine by touching: *In the dark we felt our way down the stairs.*
3 to have a particular sensation: *His skin felt smooth.*
4 to be conscious of or affected by: *He felt ashamed.* □ *We felt it was time to leave.*
Phrases **feel for** to have sympathy for.
feel like to want: *I feel like a bath.* □ *Do you feel like some chips?* **feel like oneself** to be in one's normal state of health, spirits, etc.
feel up to to seem to oneself to be capable of or ready to do something.

feeler *noun*
1 an organ of touch in insects, such as an antenna.
2 an action or remark intended to discover someone's thoughts or intentions: *to put out feelers.*

feeling *noun*
1 an awareness or sensation: *I have a feeling this plan will not work.* □ *a feeling of joy.*
2 (**feelings**) the emotional part of a person, as distinct from the intellect: *His feelings were hurt.*
3 the sense of touch.
4 sympathy or sensitivity: *She has no feeling for her husband.*

feet
the plural of **foot**.

feign (fane) *verb*
to pretend or invent in order to deceive: *She feigned a headache so as to miss the party.*

feint (faint) *noun*
a pretended attack, e.g. in boxing or fencing.
● **feint** *verb*.

felafel ⇨ FALAFEL.

feldspar *noun* also **felspar**
an alkaline aluminium silicate mineral. Feldspar is an important part of igneous rocks such as granite.
[German *Feld* field + SPAR[3]]

felicitations (fi-lis-i-**tay**-sh'nz) *plural noun*
congratulations.

felicity (fi-**lis**-i-tee) *noun* (*plural* **felicities**)
1 great happiness.
2 an aptness of manner or style.
3 an instance of this.
Word Family **felicitous** *adjective* apt.

feline (**fee**-line) *adjective*
of or like a cat.
[Latin *feles* a cat]

fell[1] the past tense of **fall**.

fell[2] *verb*
to cut or knock down, especially trees.

fell[3] *noun*
an area of high moorland.

fellow *noun*
1 (*informal*) a man or boy.
2 a comrade, associate or peer.
3 a member of an academic or professional
society.
4 also called **research fellow**. *Education* a
postgraduate research student in a
university who receives money from an
established fund.
5 a member of the governing body of a
college.
• **fellow** *adjective* sharing something, e.g. a
job: *fellow students*.
Word Family **fellowship** *noun*
1 companionship. 2 the position held by a
fellow at a university.

felony (**fel**-a-nee) *noun* (*plural* **felonies**)
Law a serious crime, such as murder.
Word Family **felon** *noun* a person who
has committed a felony; **felonious**
(fe-**lo**-nee-us) *adjective*.

felspar ⇨ FELDSPAR.

felt[1] the past tense and past participle of
feel.

felt[2] *noun*
a matted fabric of wool, fur or hair.

female *noun*
1 a person of the sex which conceives and
has children; a woman or girl.
2 an animal of this sex.
3 *Biology* a flower which has only fruiting
organs (the style and the ovary).
• **female** *adjective* 1 of or characteristic of
a female. 2 designed for a corresponding
part to fit into it: *a female socket*.

feminine (**fem**-i-nin) *adjective*
1 of or relating to the female sex.
2 having the qualities said to be
appropriate to females.

3 *Grammar* ⇨ GENDER (definition 1).
Word Family **femininity** (fem-i-**nin**-i-
tee) *noun*.

feminism (**fem**-i-nizm) *noun*
the principle or practice of equal rights for
women.
Word Family **feminist** *noun*, *adjective*.

femme fatale (fam fa-**tahl**) *noun* (*plural*
femmes fatales) (fam fa-**tahl**)
a dangerously attractive woman.
[French, fatal woman]

femur (**fee**-ma) *noun* (*plural* **femurs** or
femora (**fem**-a-ra))
Anatomy the long bone of the thigh or
upper hindlimb in animals, joining the hip
to the knee.
Word Family **femoral** (**fem**-a-r'l)
adjective.
[Latin, the thigh]

fen *noun*
an area of low marshy land.

fence *noun*
1 a barrier or boundary of wire, wood etc.
around an area.
2 a hedge or other obstacle to be jumped
in a steeplechase or showjumping
competition.
3 (*informal*) a person who receives and
disposes of stolen goods.
Phrase **sit on the fence** to remain
neutral.
• **fence** *verb*
1 to build or put a fence around.
2 to take part in the sport of fencing.
3 to avoid direct questions, arguments, etc.
4 (*informal*) to receive and dispose of
stolen goods.
Word Family **fencer** *noun*.
[shortening of *defence*]

fencing *noun*
1 the sport of fighting with long slender
swords.
2 material used for fences.

fend *verb*
to repel or resist: *He fended off the blows
with his arms*.
Phrase **fend for oneself** to protect or
provide for oneself.

fender *noun*
1 a metal surround on a fireplace to
prevent coal or logs rolling out of a fire.
2 *American* a mudguard or wing of a
vehicle.
3 the roping or other material hung over a
ship's side when docking.

fennel *noun*
a tall herb with yellow flowers, used in cooking and medicine.

feral (ferr-'l or fear-'l) *adjective*
(of an animal or plant) wild.
[Latin *ferus* wild]

ferment (fer-ment) *verb*
to convert sugar to carbon dioxide and alcohol, usually with yeast or bacteria carrying out the necessary chemical reactions.
• **ferment** (fer-ment) *noun* a state of excitement or agitation.
Word Family **fermentation** (fer-men-tay-sh'n) *noun*.
[Latin *fermentum* yeast]

fern *noun* (*plural* **fern** or **ferns**)
a plant with large feather-like leaves and no flowers usually growing in damp areas and reproducing by spores.

ferocious (fe-ro-shus) *adjective*
extremely savage or cruel.
Word Family **ferociously** *adverb*; **ferocity** (fe-ros-i-tee), **ferociousness** *noun*.
[Latin *ferox, ferocis* fierce]

ferret *noun*
a domesticated polecat trained to drive rabbits and rats from their holes.
• **ferret** *verb* (**ferrets; ferreting; ferreted**)
1 to hunt with a ferret.
2 to search out.
[Latin *fur* thief]

ferric *adjective*
Chemistry of or relating to compounds of iron in which iron has a valency of three.
[Latin *ferrum* iron]

ferromagnetic ⇨ MAGNETIC (definition 1).

ferrous *adjective*
1 *Chemistry* of or relating to compounds of iron in which iron has a valency of two.
2 (of metal) containing iron.

ferrule (ferr-ool or ferr-ul) *noun* also **ferrel**
a ring or cap fitted over the end of something, e.g. on the end of an umbrella.

ferry *noun* (*plural* **ferries**)
a boat used to carry passengers, vehicles, etc. across a short stretch of water.
• **ferry** *verb* (**ferries; ferrying; ferried**)
to transport from one place to another, especially on a ferry.

fertile *adjective*
1 *Biology* capable of sexual reproduction.
2 *Biology* capable of developing: *a fertile seed.*

3 highly productive: *fertile soil.* □ *a fertile imagination.*
Word Family **fertility** (fer-til-i-tee) *noun*.
[Latin *fertilis* able to bear]

fertilize, fertilise *verb*
1 *Biology* to unite male and female reproductive cells.
2 to add substances to the soil to increase growth.
Word Family **fertilizer** *noun* a substance used to fertilize soil; **fertilization** *noun*.

fervent *adjective*
warm or enthusiastic: *a fervent admirer.*
Word Family **fervently** *adverb*.
[Latin *fervens* boiling]

fervid *adjective*
spirited or passionate: *a fervid defence of his actions.*
Word Family **fervidly** *adverb*.

fervour *noun* (*American* **fervor**)
enthusiasm or passion.

fester *verb*
1 to produce pus, as in a wound.
2 to irritate or rankle.

festival *noun*
1 a day or period of celebration.
2 a series of events, especially held annually: *a beer festival.* □ *a film festival.*

festive *adjective*
1 of or relating to a feast or festival.
2 joyous.

festivity (fess-tiv-i-tee) *noun* (*plural* **festivities**)
1 the gaiety characteristic of a festival.
2 (**festivities**) joyous celebrations: *wedding festivities.*

festoon *noun*
1 a chain of ribbons, flowers, etc. hung decoratively between two points.
2 a sculptured form of a decorative chain.
• **festoon** *verb*.

feta *noun* also **fetta; feta cheese**
a white Greek cheese made from goat's or sheep's milk.

fetal ⇨ FETUS.

fetch *verb*
1 to go for and bring back: *She went to fetch a policeman.*
2 to sell for: *The chair fetched a good price at the auction.*
• **fetch** *noun* the furthest distance over the sea that winds can blow.

fetching *adjective*
attractive or charming.
Word Family **fetchingly** *adverb*.

fête (fate) *noun*
a small fair, usually held to raise money for an institution or charity.
• **fête** *verb* to honour or celebrate by entertaining.
[French, feast]

fetid (fet-id *or* feet-id) *adjective* also **foetid**
having a foul smell.
[Latin *fetidus*]

fetish (fet-ish) *noun* (*plural* **fetishes**)
1 an excessive devotion to or obsession with anything.
2 an object worshipped because it is believed that powerful spirits live in it.
Word Family fetishistic (fet-ish-**ist**-ik) *adjective*; **fetishism** *noun*.

fetlock *noun*
Anatomy the part of a horse's leg just above the hoof, often with a tuft of hair on it.

fetta ⇨ FETA.

fetter *noun*
1 a chain placed around a prisoner's ankles to prevent movement or escape.
2 anything that restricts or hinders.
• **fetter** *verb*.

fettle *noun*
Phrase **in fine fettle** in good health or spirits.

fetus (fee-tus) *noun* (*plural* **fetuses**) also **foetus**
Biology the unborn offspring of a person or animal.
Word Family fetal *adjective*.

feud (fewd) *noun*
a long-standing bitter quarrel, especially between families.
• **feud** *verb*.

feudalism (few-da-lizm) *noun*
Medieval history the system of social and political organization common from the 9th century to the 15th century, in which land was held by a vassal in return for homage and service to the lord.
Word Family feudal *adjective*.

fever (fee-va) *noun*
1 an increased body temperature due to disease.
2 a state of excitement: *The fans were in a fever of anticipation.*
Word Family fevered *adjective* affected by fever; **feverish** *adjective* of, like or having a fever; **feverishly** *adverb*; **feverishness** *noun*.
[Latin *febris*]

few *adjective*
not many: *Few people came.*

• **few** *noun* a small number: *His books are read by the few who share his ideas.*
Phrases **a good few**, **quite a few** a fairly large number. **few and far between** sparse or rare.

> ⚠ Do not confuse *fewer* with *less*. *Fewer* is used with plural nouns referring to things which can be counted (*I saw fewer people in town today*), whereas *less* is used with singular nouns referring to things which cannot be counted (*This recipe uses less sugar*).

fey (fay) *adjective*
strange or unworldly.

fez *noun* (*plural* **fezzes**)
a conical stiff cap with a flat top and a long tassel, formerly the national headdress of Turkey.
[after *Fez*, a town in Morocco]

fiancé (fee-**on**-say) *noun*
a man who is engaged to be married.
[French]

fiancée (fee-**on**-say) *noun*
a woman who is engaged to be married.
[French]

fiasco (fee-**ass**-ko) *noun* (*plural* **fiascos**)
a complete or disastrous failure.

> The word **fiasco** comes, surprisingly, from the Italian word for 'a bottle'. It was used in the English sense in Italian theatrical slang in *far fiasco* meaning 'to fail completely as a performance'. The connection between 'utter failure' and 'a bottle' has never been explained.

fib *noun*
a harmless or trivial lie.
Word Family fib *verb* (**fibs**; **fibbing**; **fibbed**) to tell a fib; **fibber** *noun* a person who tells a fib.

fibre (fie-ba) *noun* (*American* **fiber**)
1 a thread or thread-like piece.
2 a material made from threads.
3 also called **dietary fibre**. the indigestible parts of foods of plant origin, which add roughage to the diet.
4 strength of character: *a person with great moral fibre.*
Word Family fibrous *adjective*.
[Latin *fibra*]

fibreglass *noun*
a material made from fine glass fibres which are woven and saturated with resins, used for the bodies of cars, small boats, etc.

fibroid (fie-broyd) *adjective*
resembling or composed of fibre or fibrous tissue.

• **fibroid** *noun* a fibroid tumour of the womb.
[FIBR(e) + *-oid*]

fibrosis (fie-**bro**-sis) *noun*
the production of fibrous tissues, as in the healing of a wound.
[FIBR(e) + *-osis*]

fibrositis (fie-bro-**sigh**-tis) *noun*
a mild inflammation in fibrous or muscular tissue, causing pain and difficulty in movement.
[Latin *fibrosus* fibrous + *-itis*]

fibula (**fib**-yoo-la) *noun* (*plural* **fibulae** (**fib**-yoo-lee) or **fibulas**)
Anatomy the thinner of the two long bones of the lower leg or hind limb.
Word Family **fibular** *adjective*.
[Latin, a fastener]

fickle *adjective*
inconstant in feelings or intentions.
Word Family **fickleness** *noun*.

fiction (**fik**-sh'n) *noun*
1 novels, short stories or other imaginative prose writings.
2 something imagined or invented: *The judge said the whole case was fiction.*
[Latin *fictio, fictionis* a forming, feigning]

fictional *adjective*
belonging to or having the nature of fiction.
Word Family **fictionally** *adverb*

> ⚠ The words *fictional* and *fictitious* have related but separate meanings: *fictional* means 'belonging to fiction, imaginary', whereas *fictitious* means 'invented or false'.

fictitious (fik-**tish**-us) *adjective*
1 false or untrue: *The newspaper story was distorted and perhaps even fictitious.*
2 imaginatively created or invented: *The novelist claimed that all his characters were fictitious.*
Word Family **fictitiously** *adverb*.

> ⚠ Do not confuse *fictitious* with FICTIONAL.

fiddle *noun*
1 *Music* (*informal*) a violin.
2 (*informal*) an underhand or illegal enterprise.
Phrases **fit as a fiddle** very healthy. **play second fiddle** to take second place: *She dislikes playing second fiddle to her husband.*
• **fiddle** *verb*
1 (*informal*) to move the hands restlessly or aimlessly.

2 (*informal*) to distort or falsify dishonestly: *The clerk fiddled the accounts.*
Word Family **fiddler** *noun* (*informal*).

fiddlesticks *interjection*
(*informal*) nonsense.

fiddly *adjective* (**fiddlier; fiddliest**)
(*informal*) intricate and difficult: *fiddly little buttons.*

fidelity (fi-**del**-i-tee) *noun*
1 loyalty: *The king rewarded his old servant for his fidelity.*
2 exactness or accuracy: *the fidelity of sound produced by a radio.*
[Latin *fides* trust]

fidget (**fij**-it) *verb*
to move restlessly or impatiently: *The children began to fidget during the long church service.*
Word Family **fidget** *noun* a person who fidgets; **fidgety** *adjective*.

fie (*rhymes with* die) *interjection*
an old word used as an exclamation of shock or disgust.

fief (feef) *noun*
Medieval history a fee.

field (feeld) *noun*
1 an open cleared area of land used for farming, etc.
2 an area of land containing natural resources: *a coalfield.*
3 a place where a particular event or activity takes place: *a field of battle.*
4 an area: *It lay outside my field of vision.*
□ *He works in the field of science.*
5 *Sport* the arrangement of players in a side: *a defensive field.*
6 *Horseracing* all the horses in a race.
7 *Physics* the space in which a force exerts its influence.
Phrase **in the field** doing fieldwork.
• **field** *verb*
1 *Sport* to stop or catch the ball, and return it from a position on the field.
2 *Sport* to put a team into the field.
3 to fend off by verbal agility: *The politician fielded the reporter's probing questions.*
• **field** *adjective*
1 carried out away from an office or laboratory.
2 able to be moved easily from one position to another: *field artillery.*
Word Family **fielder** *noun*.

field day *noun*
1 an enjoyable or successful time.
2 *Military* a day for training exercises, manoeuvres, etc.

field events *plural noun*
athletic events which are not races, e.g.
throwing and jumping.

field glasses ⇨ BINOCULARS.

field marshal *noun*
Army a commissioned officer of the
highest rank.

field sports *plural noun*
outdoor sports, especially hunting,
shooting and fishing.

fieldwork *noun*
work, such as the collection of data,
carried out in a natural setting.

fiend (feend) *noun*
1 a devil or evil spirit.
2 a cruel or wicked person.
3 (*informal*) an addict: *a golf fiend.*
Word Family **fiendish** *adjective* 1 cruel.
2 very difficult; **fiendishly** *adverb*.

fierce *adjective*
1 hostile, threatening or aggressive: *a fierce
dog.*
2 intense, severe: *fierce competition.*
Word Family **fiercely** *adverb*; **fierceness**
noun.

fiery (**fire**-ee) *adjective* (**fierier; fieriest**)
1 of or like fire.
2 passionate or intense: *a fiery temper.*

fiesta (fee-**es**-ta) *noun*
a festival.
[Spanish]

fife *noun*
Music a high-pitched flute used in military
bands.
Word Family **fifer** *noun*.

fifteen *noun*
a cardinal number, the symbol 15 in
Arabic numerals, XV in Roman numerals.
Word Family **fifteen** *adjective*; **fifteenth**
adjective, noun.

fifth ⇨ FIVE.

fifth column *noun*
a group of traitors.
[in the Spanish Civil War, 1936, Madrid
was attacked by four columns of fascist
troops, while a *fifth column* of fascists
within the city assisted them]

fifty *noun* (*plural* **fifties**)
1 a cardinal number, the symbol 50 in
Arabic numerals, L in Roman numerals.
2 (**fifties**) the numbers 50 to 59 in a
series, such as the years within a century.
Word Family **fifty** *adjective*; **fiftieth**
adjective, noun.

fifty-fifty *adjective, adverb*
1 in two equal portions.
2 having equal chances.

fig *noun*
a soft dark-skinned fruit containing many
seeds, eaten fresh, preserved or dried.

fight *noun*
1 a struggle, quarrel or contest.
2 the ability or desire to fight: *After ten
years in prison there was no fight left in him.*
• **fight** *verb* (**fights; fighting; fought**)
1 to take part in a battle or physical
contest.
2 to take part in a campaign: *fighting for
justice.*
3 to quarrel.
4 to struggle: *She had to fight to make herself
heard.* □ *fighting for breath.*
Phrase **fighting fit** very fit or healthy.
Word Family **fighter** *noun*.

figment *noun*
something imagined.

figurative (**fig**-a-ra-tiv) *adjective*
1 involving a metaphor or figure of speech
to create a particular impression or mood.
2 *Art* representing a figure: *a figurative
painting.*
Word Family **figuratively** *adverb*;
figurativeness *noun*.

figure (**fig**-a) *noun*
1 a symbol for a number.
2 a form or shape: *geometrical figures.* □ *a
girl's slim figure.*
3 an amount or sum.
4 (**figures**) calculations, arithmetic.
5 a person or character: *a famous literary
figure.*
6 a diagram.
7 a movement, especially in skating.
Phrase **cut a fine figure** to create a fine
appearance.
• **figure** *verb*
1 to appear conspicuously: *His name figures
quite often in historical documents of that
time.*
2 (*especially American informal*) to think.
3 (*especially American informal*) to be as
one expected: *That figures!*
Phrase **figure out** *It was very difficult to
figure out what he meant* (= understand,
work out).
[Latin *figura* shape]

figurehead *noun*
1 *Nautical* a carved model of a woman or
mermaid decorating the bow of a sailing
ship.
2 a person in a high position but having no
real power.

figure of speech noun (plural **figures of speech**)
an expression, such as a simile or metaphor, in which words are not used in their usual sense.

figurine (fig-a-reen or fig-yor-een) noun
a small sculptured or carved figure.

filagree ⇨ FILIGREE.

filament (fil-a-ment) noun
1 a very fine thread or thread-like part, such as the wire in a light bulb which heats as electricity passes through it.
2 Biology the stalk of a stamen, supporting the anther.
[Latin filum a thread]

filch verb
(informal) to pilfer.

file¹ noun
1 a group of papers or records kept in order.
2 a container in which papers are kept.
3 Computers a collection of related data under a specific name.
Phrase **on file** on record in a file.
• **file** verb
1 to put papers, documents, records, etc. in order, for easy access.
2 Law to begin a lawsuit by bringing it before a court.
3 (of a reporter) to send in a story to a newspaper.

file² noun
a flat or rounded steel tool, with fine ridges or teeth, for smoothing metal or wood.
• **file** verb.

file³ noun
a row or line of people or things placed one behind the other.
• **file** verb to march or walk one behind the other: The students filed out.

filial (fil-i-ul) adjective
relating to or expected of a son or daughter.
Word Family **filially** adverb.
[Latin filius son]

filibuster (fil-i-bus-ta) verb
to obstruct business in parliament by making long speeches or using other delaying tactics.
Word Family **filibuster** noun;
filibusterer noun.
[Spanish filibustero a pirate]

filigree (fil-i-gree) noun also **filagree**
delicate ornamental work of metallic thread, especially of gold or silver, woven into a lace-like design.
Word Family **filigreed** adjective.

filings (fie-lingz) plural noun
the small particles removed by a file.

fill verb
1 to make or become full: Let me fill your glass. □ The dam filled during the wet season.
2 to occupy: Has the position been filled?
3 to take up time: She filled her spare moments by reading.
4 to satisfy: The book fills a need.
Phrases **fill in** 1 It took an hour to fill in the forms (= complete). 2 What's the best way to fill in time? (= occupy). 3 She filled in for me when I was sick (= stood in). **fill out** 1 He didn't begin to fill out till he was over forty (= put on weight). 2 Please fill out this form (= complete).
• **fill** noun a full supply or quantity: We let the thirsty horses drink their fill.
Word Family **filler** noun a person or thing that fills, such as putty used to fill cracks; **filling** noun anything that fills, such as amalgam used to fill a tooth;
filling adjective causing a feeling of being full.

fillet noun
1 a boneless section of meat or fish
2 a cut of tender meat, usually from the loin.
• **fillet** verb (**fillets; filleting; filleted**)
1 to take the bones out of fish.
2 to cut into fillets.

filling station noun
a service station for selling fuel, oil, etc. to motorists.

fillip noun
a boost: The newspaper article gave the fund drive a fillip.

filly noun (plural **fillies**)
a female horse or pony up to four years old.

film noun
1 Photography a strip of cellulose ester, coated with a light-sensitive emulsion which will record a series of separate images when exposed in a camera.
2 a series of filmed images projected consecutively at high speed to show a story or sequence of events.
3 a very thin skin, membrane or coating: a film of oil on the water.
• **film** verb
1 to make into a film, to record.
2 to cover with or as if with a film: His eyes filmed with tears.

filmy adjective (**filmier; filmiest**)
very thin, transparent: a filmy nightdress.

filo (**fee**-lo) *noun* also **phyllo**
a kind of very flaky pastry used in sheets in Middle Eastern cooking.
[Modern Greek *phyllon*]

Filofax (**fie**-lo-fax) *noun* (*plural* **Filofaxes**)
(*trademark*) a loose-leaf personal organizer.

> **Filofax** is a trademark and should always be spelt with a capital letter. The non-trademark name for a product is its *generic* name – in the case of Filofax it is 'personal organizer'. In the same way, *Biro*, *Hoover* and *Xerox* are trademarks and *ballpoint pen*, *vacuum cleaner* and *photocopier* are generic names.

filter *noun*
a substance or device which prevents certain materials passing through it while allowing the passage of others, such as porous paper to separate sand from water, or a screen on a camera lens to control the colours reaching the film.
• **filter** *verb*
1 to remove or separate by a filter.
2 to pass through or as if through a filter: *The new ideas finally filtered through into people's minds.*
Word Family **filtration** *noun* the act or process of filtering; **filtrate** *noun* a liquid that has passed through a filter.

filth *noun*
1 dirt.
2 something obscene or disgusting.
Word Family **filthy** *adjective* (**filthier**; **filthiest**); **filthily** *adverb*; **filthiness** *noun*.

fin *noun*
1 an external thin structure on an aquatic animal, used to guide or propel it.
2 a fin-shaped structure on an aircraft, submarine, etc. which has a stabilizing or guiding function.
3 a fin-like projection on a radiator, the cylinders of an air-cooled internal combustion engine, etc., used to dissipate heat.

final (**fie**-n'l) *adjective*
1 coming at the end: *The final preparations have been completed.*
2 decisive: *My answer is final.*
• **final** *noun*
1 a contest coming at the end of a series.
2 (**finals**) a series of examinations at the end of a course at university.
Word Family **finally** *adverb*; **finality** (fie-**nal**-i-tee) *noun* the state of being final; **finalist** *noun* a person qualified to take part in a final.
[Latin *finis* limit, end]

finale (fin-**ah**-lee *or* fin-**ah**-lay) *noun*
the last or concluding part of anything, such as the last movement of a piece of music or the last act of a play, ballet or opera.

finalize, finalise *verb*
to put into final form: *finalizing the wedding plans.*

finance (**fie**-nance *or* fie-**nance**) *noun*
1 money or funds: *The finances of the club are running low.*
2 the management of money: *She is an expert in finance.*
• **finance** *verb* to provide money for.
Word Family **financial** *adjective* of or relating to finance: *my financial adviser*; **financially** *adverb*.

financial year *noun*
a specified period of twelve months, used by governments and businesses when accounting for money received and paid.

financier (fie-**nan**-si-a) *noun*
a person skilled or engaged in borrowing and lending money, especially on a large scale.

finch *noun* (*plural* **finches**)
a small bird such as a chaffinch, goldfinch or bullfinch, which has a strong beak for crushing seeds.

find *verb* (**finds**; **finding**; **found**)
1 to meet with by chance: *I found a pound coin.*
2 to obtain by search or effort: *I found the answer.*
3 to discover by experience: *She found that she worked better at night.*
4 to declare or pronounce: *They found him guilty of murder.*
5 to reach: *The arrow found its mark.*
6 to manage to arrange: *I couldn't find the time.*
Phrase **find someone out** *Most criminals assume they won't be found out* (= detected).
• **find** *noun* something found, especially something valuable.
Word Family **finder** *noun*.

finding *noun*
1 *Law* the decision of a court on a question of fact at the end of a court case.
2 (**findings**) *American* pins and clasps used in jewellery making.

fine[1] *adjective*
1 of very high quality: *a fine building.* □ *fine gold.*
2 thin, slender: *a fine thread.*
3 sunny, bright: *a fine day.*
4 delicate: *fine needlework.*

5 subtle, difficult to grasp: *a fine distinction.*
6 composed of minute particles: *a fine dust.*
Word Family fine adverb well; **finely** adverb; **fineness** noun.

fine² noun
a sum of money paid as punishment for breaking a law or rule.
• **fine** verb.

fine art noun also **fine arts**
art which is considered the highest expression of beauty, such as painting, music, architecture, poetry, etc.

finery (fie-na-ree) noun
richly elegant clothes.

finesse (fin-ess) noun
skill or delicacy in doing something: *The ambassador conducted negotiations with great finesse.*
[French, fineness]

finger noun
1 *Anatomy* each of the five members of the hand, especially one other than the thumb.
2 a finger-like piece, part or measure: *the finger of a glove.* □ *a finger of toast.* □ *a finger of gin.*
Phrases **burn one's fingers, get one's fingers burnt** to try to do something and get hurt in some way: *He burnt his fingers in a business deal.* **have a finger in every pie, have a finger in many pies** to be involved in many enterprises. **keep one's fingers crossed** to hope for good luck. **lay a finger on** to harm or touch. **put one's finger on** to identify or locate: *I couldn't quite put my finger on what was bothering me.* **twist round one's little finger** to manipulate or dominate.
• **finger** verb to touch or handle with the fingers.

fingerboard noun
Music the wooden part of a stringed instrument, against which the strings are pressed to vary the pitch of a note.

finger bowl noun
a small bowl to hold water for rinsing the fingers at a meal.

fingernail noun
the horny growth at the end of a finger.

fingerprint noun
the pattern formed by the tiny ridges on the tips of the fingers.
• **fingerprint** verb to record a person's fingerprints with ink, for purposes of identification.

finicky (fin-i-kee) adjective also **finicking**
fussy or too particular.

finis (fin-is) noun
the end.
[Latin]

finish verb
1 to bring or come to an end: *I shall finish the job by tomorrow.*
2 to complete the last stage of a race.
3 to put a final coating or surface on.
Phrase **finish off** 1 to consume completely. 2 (*informal*) to kill.
• **finish** noun (*plural* **finishes**)
1 the end or conclusion.
2 a surface or coating: *a shiny finish.*

finite (fie-nite) adjective
having limits or bounds: *Some scientists think the universe is finite.*
Word Family finitely adverb; **finiteness** noun.
[Latin *finitus* bounded]

finnan noun also called **finnan haddock**.
a large split haddock smoked over a peat fire.
[after *Findon*, a Scottish fishing village]

fiord ⇨ FJORD.

fir noun
an evergreen northern hemisphere tree with erect cones and short needle-like leaves.

fire noun
1 the flame, heat and light produced by burning
2 a body of burning material
3 energy, intensity: *a speech full of fire.*
4 the discharge of firearms or artillery.
Phrases **catch fire** to burst into flames. **hang fire** to delay. **on fire** burning. **open fire** to start shooting. **play with fire** to take chances with something dangerous. **under fire** 1 being shot at. 2 under criticism or verbal attack.
• **fire** verb
1 to discharge firearms, artillery, etc.
2 to direct questions at someone.
3 (*informal*) to dismiss from a job.
4 to harden pottery or bricks in a kiln by heating it slowly to a high temperature.
5 (of an engine) to start.
6 to set on fire.
7 to inspire: *fired with the idea of running away.*
Phrase **fire away** (*informal*) to begin speaking.

firearm noun
a rifle, revolver or light machine gun.

fireball *noun*
a brightly burning sphere, such as a
meteor.

firebrand *noun*
a person who excites or inspires passions,
trouble, etc.

firebreak *noun*
a strip of land which is cleared to stop the
spread of a fire.

firebrick *noun*
a brick made of a special heat-resistant
clay, used in chimneys, etc.

fire brigade *noun*
an organized group of firefighters, usually
belonging to a particular district and
wearing a uniform.

firecracker *noun*
(*especially American*) a firework which
explodes.

firedamp *noun*
the methane gas found in coal mines,
potentially explosive in air.

firedog *noun* also called **andiron**.
either of a pair of iron supports holding
logs in a fireplace.

fire drill *noun*
a practice in the use of firefighting
equipment or methods of escape in case of
fire.

fire engine *noun*
a motor vehicle equipped for fighting fires
with hoses, pumps, etc.

fire escape *noun*
an exit from a building for use in case of
fire, such as an outside staircase.

fire extinguisher *noun*
a portable appliance which contains liquid
or foam, used to put out fires.

firefighter *noun*
a person who fights fires.

firefly *noun* (*plural* **fireflies**)
a soft-bodied nocturnal beetle which can
produce light.

fireguard *noun* also called **fire screen**.
a metal screen placed in front of a fire for
protection.

fire irons *plural noun*
tools for arranging a fire, especially tongs,
a poker, etc.

firelighter *noun*
a block of a highly flammable substance,
used to start fires.

fireman *noun* (*plural* **firemen**)
1 a man skilled or trained in preventing or
fighting fires.

2 also called **stoker**. a person who tends
the fire in a steam engine.

fireplace *noun*
the part of a chimney opening into a room,
in which fires are lit.

firepower *noun*
the amount of fire delivered by a weapon
or military unit.

fireproof *adjective*
designed or constructed so as to resist fire.
Word Family **fireproof** *verb*.

fire screen ⇨ FIREGUARD.

fire station *noun*
a building used by a fire brigade for
storing equipment, etc.

fire trap *noun*
a building which is especially dangerous in
the event of fire.

firewall *noun*
a wall designed to resist fire and stop it
spreading, e.g. between the engine
compartment and the rest of an aircraft.

firework *noun*
1 an explosive device used to produce a
bright light or a loud noise, often for a
display or as a signal at night.
2 (**fireworks**) an outburst of bad temper,
violence, etc.

firing line *noun*
the point at which troops are close enough
to the enemy positions to fire on them.
Phrase **in the firing line** subjected by
one's position or situation to blame, verbal
attack, etc.

firing squad *noun*
a group of soldiers appointed to shoot a
condemned person.

firm[1] *adjective*
1 solid, secure: *firm ground*.
2 steady, strong: *a firm handshake*.
3 lasting: *firm friends*.
4 fixed, definite: *a firm answer*.
5 determined: *You have to be firm with him*.
Word Family **firm** *verb* to make or
become firm; **firmly, firm** *adverb*;
firmness *noun*.

firm[2] *noun*
a business organization, such as a
company or partnership.
[Italian *firma* a signature]

firmament *noun*
a poetic word for the sky.
[Latin *firmamentum* a support]

first *adjective, adverb*
1 being number one in a series.

2 before all others in time, importance, etc.

• **first** *noun*
1 (*informal*) a thing which is first in time, importance, etc.: *This model is an exciting first in car design.*
2 first-class honours in a university exam.
Word Family **firstly** *adverb*.

first aid *noun*
emergency assistance given to a sick or injured person after an accident, etc.

firstborn *noun*
someone's eldest child.

first class *noun*
the most expensive and comfortable passenger accommodation on a train, aeroplane, etc.
Word Family **first-class** *adjective* 1 being the highest grade possible in passing an examination. 2 of the highest or best quality: *a first-class restaurant.* 3 of or relating to the first class: *a first-class carriage.*

first cousin ⇨ COUSIN.

first-day cover *noun*
an envelope on which a newly issued postage stamp is stuck.

first-hand *adjective*
direct from the original source: *We receive first-hand racing information from the jockeys.*

first lady *noun* (*plural* **first ladies**)
the wife of the American President or a head of state.

firstly ⇨ FIRST.

first night *noun*
the first performance of a play, opera, etc.

first person ⇨ PERSON (definition 3).

first principles *plural noun*
the fundamental principles from which a law, concept, etc. is derived.

first-rate *adjective*
excellent.

firth *noun*
a long narrow inlet of the sea.

fiscal *adjective*
of or relating to finance, especially government finance: *fiscal policy.*
[Latin *fiscus* a purse]

fish *noun* (*plural* **fish** or **fishes**)
a cold-blooded aquatic animal having a spine and gills and usually with fins and scales on its body.
Phrases **a fish out of water** a person who is ill at ease or uncomfortable in new or strange surroundings. **other fish to fry** other more important matters or business to be dealt with.

• **fish** *verb*
1 to catch or attempt to catch fish.
2 to search for or remove: *He fished a handkerchief out of his back pocket.*
3 to seek by indirect methods: *to fish for compliments.*
Word Family **fishing** *noun* the art or practice of catching fish; **fisherman** *noun* (*plural* **fishermen**) a person who fishes.

fish cake *noun*
a patty made from fish and potato, cooked in breadcrumbs.

fishery *noun* (*plural* **fisheries**)
1 a place where fish are bred, hatched and reared.
2 the occupation or industry of catching fish.

fisheye *noun*
Photography an extremely curved lens with a viewing angle of up to 180°.

fishmonger (**fish**-mung-ga) *noun*
a person who sells fish.

fishplate *noun*
a thin rectangular plate, usually steel, for joining railway lines, stanchions, etc.

fishwife *noun* (*plural* **fishwives**)
1 a coarse or abusive woman.
2 an old word meaning 'a woman who sells fish'.

fishy *adjective* (**fishier; fishiest**)
1 of or like fish.
2 (*informal*) causing doubt or suspicion: *There is something fishy about him.*

fissile *adjective*
1 *Physics* capable of undergoing nuclear fission by any process.
2 able to be split or divided.
[Latin *fissilis* easily split]

fission (**fish**-'n) *noun*
1 the act of splitting or dividing into parts, such as the biological reproduction of an organism by dividing into several parts, each of which forms a new organism.
2 ⇨ NUCLEAR FISSION.

fissure (**fish**-a) *noun*
a narrow opening formed by cleavage or the separation of parts.

fist *noun*
a tightly closed hand.
Word Family **fistful** *noun* a handful.

fisticuffs *plural noun*
fighting with the fists.

fistula (fist-yoo-la) *noun* (*plural* **fistulas** or
fistulae (fist-yoo-lee))
a body passage formed by disease or by
surgery, linking a hollow space or abscess
to the surface of the skin.
Word Family **fistular** *adjective*.
[Latin, a tube]

fit[1] *verb* (**fits; fitting; fitted**)
1 to be or make the right shape or size for:
These shoes do not fit properly. □ *The
salesman fitted the jacket.*
2 to put carefully into place: *The mechanic
fitted new wheels on the car.*
3 to be or make suitable or appropriate to:
The punishment must be made to fit the crime.
□ *She has few qualities which fit her for
leadership.*
Phrases **fit in 1** to have room for. **2** to
adapt to. **fit out, fit up** to equip.
● **fit** *adjective* (**fitter; fittest**)
1 suitable or right: *That burnt toast is not fit
to be eaten.*
2 being in good health or physical
condition: *She is still not quite fit after her
long illness.*
● **fit** *noun* the manner in which something
fits: *The fit of that coat is perfect.*
Word Family **fitness** *noun*.

fit[2] *noun*
1 a sudden violent burst or outburst: *In a
fit of rage she threw the plate against the wall.*
2 also called **convulsion**. *Medicine* an
uncontrollable repeated contraction of the
muscles, leading to a loss of
consciousness.
Phrase **in fits and starts, by fits and
starts** in intermittent bursts: *We got the
decorating done in fits and starts.*
Word Family **fitful** *adjective* irregular or
intermittent; **fitfully** *adverb*; **fitfulness**
noun.
[Old English *fytt* a struggle]

fitter *noun*
a person whose work is to fit things,
especially in the assembly of mechanical
parts or machines.

fitting *noun*
1 (*usually* **fittings**) a device or equipment
provided for something, such as
furnishings or fixtures in a house.
2 the act of fitting, especially the trying on
and adjusting of clothes for size.
3 a size: *The shoes come in several width
fittings.*
Word Family **fitting** *adjective* appropriate
or suitable; **fittingly** *adverb*; **fittingness**
noun.

five *noun*
a cardinal number, the symbol 5 in Arabic
numerals, V in Roman numerals.
Word Family **five** *adjective*; **fifth** *noun*,
adjective.

fiver *noun*
(*informal*) a five-pound note.

fives *plural noun*
a game similar to squash but in which a
hard ball is played with the gloved hand.
[possibly from *bunch of fives*, the fingers of
the hand]

fix *verb*
1 to make or hold secure: *The post was fixed
into the ground.*
2 to repair or put in good condition: *Can
you fix this broken light?*
3 to make permanent and unchanging: *He
fixed the colour with a chemical spray.*
4 to direct: *We fixed our attention on the
speaker.*
5 to settle: *Have they fixed a date for the party?*
6 (*informal*) to arrange dishonestly: *The
fight was fixed.*
7 (*especially American informal*) to prepare:
I'll fix us something to eat.
Phrase **fix on, fix upon** *We have not yet
fixed on a place to go for our holiday*
(= decided on, chosen).
● **fix** *noun* (*plural* **fixes**)
1 (*informal*) a difficult or awkward
situation.
2 the finding of one's position or bearings
by observation, calculation, etc.
3 (*informal*) an injection of a hard drug
such as heroin.
Word Family **fixedly** (fik-sid-lee) *adverb*;
fixer *noun*.

fixation *noun*
Psychology a persistent attachment to a
person, object or type of behaviour,
usually formed at an early stage in
psychological development and leading to
an inability to form normal relationships.
Word Family **fixate** *verb*.

fixative (fik-sa-tiv) *noun*
a substance which fixes, hardens or
preserves.

fixed star *noun*
Astronomy a star in a constellation which,
being so remote, appears not to move in
relation to its companion stars.

fixity (fik-si-tee) *noun*
the state of being fixed or permanent.

fixture (fiks-cha) *noun*
1 (*usually* **fixtures**) an object which is fixed into position, such as the lights in a house.
2 (*informal*) a person who has been in a particular place for a long time.
3 a sporting event arranged for a particular date.

fizz *verb*
to hiss or bubble vigorously.
Word Family **fizz** *noun* (*plural* **fizzes**); **fizzy** *adjective* (**fizzier; fizziest**); **fizzily** *adverb*; **fizziness** *noun*.

fizzle *verb*
to splutter weakly.
Phrase **fizzle out** *The party fizzled out after the music stopped* (= ended feebly or in failure).
Word Family **fizzle** *noun*.

fjord (fee-**ord**) *noun* also **fiord**
a long deep narrow inlet of the sea with steep sides, originally deepened by the action of glaciers. Compare RIA.
[Norwegian]

flabbergast (**flab**-a-gahst) *verb*
(*informal*) to shock or astonish extremely.

flabby *adjective* (**flabbier; flabbiest**)
hanging loosely and limply.
Word Family **flab** *noun*; **flabbily** *adverb*; **flabbiness** *noun*.

flaccid (**flas**-id *or* **flak** sid) *adjective*
flabby or drooping: *His flaccid muscles indicated a lack of exercise.*
Word Family **flaccidity** (fla sid-i-tee *or* flak sid i tee) *noun*; **flaccidly** *adverb*
[Latin *flaccidus* flabby]

flack ⇨ FLAK.

flag[1] *noun*
a square or oblong cloth with a distinctive pattern, usually coloured, indicating nationality, ownership, a club or a signal; usually attached by one edge to a cord, stick or post.
• **flag** *verb* (**flags; flagging; flagged**)
to mark or signal.
Phrase **flag down** to wave or signal a person to stop.

flag[2] *verb* (**flags; flagging; flagged**)
to weaken or lose strength: *Our enthusiasm flagged as we realized the hard work ahead.*

flag[3] *noun* also called **flagstone**.
a flat rectangular piece of stone used for making paths.

flagellate (**flaj**-a-late) *verb*
to whip or flog.

Word Family **flagellation** (flaj-a-**lay**-sh'n) *noun*.

flagellum (fla-**jell**-um) *noun* (*plural* **flagella**)
Biology a long hair-like appendage serving as an organ of locomotion on bacteria, etc.
Word Family **flagellate** *adjective* having flagella.
[Latin, a whip]

flagon *noun*
a large bottle or container for wine or liquor.

flagrant (**flay**-gr'nt) *adjective*
being shamefully or deliberately obvious: *His flagrant disobedience made the teachers very angry.*
Word Family **flagrantly** *adverb*; **flagrancy** *noun*.
[Latin *flagrans* blazing]

> ⚠ Do not confuse *flagrant* with BLATANT.

flagship *noun*
1 a ship carrying the admiral of a fleet.
2 a company's best or most important thing: *a flagship store.*

flagstone ⇨ FLAG[3].

flail *noun*
a tool with a long handle and a freely moving bar at the end, used to thresh grain.
• **flail** *verb* to thrash about: *The swimmer's arms flailed wildly as the wave swept over him.*

flair *noun*
a natural ability or talent
[Old French *flairer* to smell out]

flak *noun* also **flack**
1 anti-aircraft fire.
2 severe criticism.
[from German, FL(ieger)A(bwehr) K(anone), anti-aircraft gun]

flake *noun*
a small light piece of anything, especially one detached from a larger mass: *a flake of skin.* □ *a snowflake.*
• **flake** *verb* to peel, separate or fall in flakes.
Phrase **flake out** *The athlete flaked out after completing the race* (= collapsed, fainted).
Word Family **flaky** *adjective* (**flakier; flakiest**); **flakily** *adverb*; **flakiness** *noun*.

flamboyant (flam-**boy**-ant) *adjective*
bold, elaborate or showy, especially in an exaggerated way: *to wear flamboyant clothing.*

Word Family **flamboyantly** *adverb*;
flamboyance, flamboyancy *noun*.
[French, flaming]

flame *noun*
1 a sheet or tongue of fire.
2 a reddish-orange colour.
3 (*Computers informal*) a rude message
sent by email.
Phrase **old flame** an ex-boyfriend or ex-
girlfriend.
• **flame** *verb*
1 to burn or glow with flames.
2 to become red with embarrassment.
3 (*Computers informal*) to send a rude
message to.

flamenco (fla-**menk**-o) *noun*
a lively style of guitar music and dancing
characteristic of the gypsies of southern
Spain.

flamingo (fla-**ming**-go) *noun* (*plural*
flamingos or **flamingoes**)
a long-legged tropical wading bird with a
long neck and pink or red feathers.
[Latin *flamma* a flame]

flammable *adjective*
easily burnt.
Word Family **flammability** *noun*.

> ⚠ Both *flammable* and *inflammable*
> mean 'easily burnt'. People started
> using *flammable* because *inflammable*
> sounded as if it meant 'not flammable'.

flan *noun*
a round open pastry shell containing a
sweet or savoury filling: *a cheese flan.*

flange *noun*
a projecting rim by which objects are
joined or kept in place.

flank *noun*
1 the fleshy part of the side of animals,
including people.
2 a cut of meat from the flank of an animal.
3 the side of anything: *The left flank of the
army opened fire first.*
• **flank** *verb* to be situated at the flank or
side of, especially to provide protection:
the pop star, flanked by bodyguards.

flannel *noun*
1 a warm soft woollen fabric.
2 (**flannels**) clothes made of flannel,
especially cricket trousers.
3 a cloth for washing one's face or body.
4 (*informal*) nonsense or insincere talk:
*She gave me some flannel about the machine
being broken.*
• **flannel** *verb* (**flannels; flannelling;
flannelled**) (*informal*) to talk nonsense or
talk insincerely.

> **Flannel** is thought to be one of the few
> words that have come into English from
> Welsh. It appears to be a form of
> Middle English *flanen* (sackcloth),
> which was borrowed from Welsh
> *gwlanen* (woollen cloth) from *gwlan*
> (wool). The reason for using *flannel* to
> mean 'nonsense' or 'insincere talk' is
> uncertain.

flannelette (flan-a-**let**) *noun*
a soft cotton fabric made to imitate
flannel.

flap *noun*
1 a loose, partly joined piece: *an envelope
flap.*
2 a swinging or waving movement.
3 (*informal*) a fuss or panic.
4 ⇨ AIR BRAKE.
• **flap** *verb* (**flaps; flapping; flapped**)
1 to move vigorously up and down.
2 to swing or wave loosely: *The flag flapped
in the breeze.*
3 (*informal*) to panic or make a fuss.

flapjack *noun*
1 a biscuit made from oats, butter and
syrup.
2 *American* a thick pancake.

flapper *noun*
(*informal*) a defiantly unconventional
young woman in the 1920s.

flare *verb*
1 to burst into a bright strong flame: *The
match flared in the darkness.*
*Figurative Tempers flared during the long
and exhausting debate* (= erupted, burst
fiercely).
2 to spread or curve outwards: *Her skirt
flared from the waist.*
3 to dilate: *The horse flared its nostrils.*
Phrase **flare up** to become more intense,
violent, etc.
• **flare** *noun*
1 a flaring or blazing flame.
2 a device which gives a brilliant white or
coloured light, used as a distress signal at
sea, etc.
3 a spreading or curving outwards.
4 (**flares**) flared trousers

flash *noun* (*plural* **flashes**)
1 a sudden burst of light, fire, colour, etc.:
a flash of lightning.
2 *Photography* a device attached to a
camera to provide a brief source of
artificial light for a photograph.
3 a brief burst: *a flash of inspiration.*
4 an emblem of a military unit, usually
worn on the sleeve.

Phrases **flash in the pan** *His clever solution to the problem was a flash in the pan* (= brilliant but short-lived effort). **in a flash** *This detergent will clean your windows in a flash* (= instantly, at once).

• **flash** *verb*
1 to give off or send a flash.
Figurative Her eyes flashed with rage.
2 to go suddenly and quickly: *An idea flashed through his mind.*
3 (*informal*) to display ostentatiously: *He flashed his money about to impress people.*
4 to show quickly: *She flashed her new wedding ring at us.*
• **flash** *adjective* (*informal*) showy or vulgar: *a flash suit.*

flashback *noun*
a return to events or actions which occurred in the past, such as the showing of parts of a story out of sequence in a film or novel.

flash flood *noun*
a sudden flood, such as water rushing down a mountain valley after heavy rain.

flashing *noun*
Building a protective strip of metal used to cover corners or joints, e.g. where a roof meets a wall.

flashlight *noun*
a torch or other light with a very bright strong beam.

flashpoint *noun*
1 *Chemistry* the lowest temperature at which a substance gives off sufficient vapour to produce a flash in the presence of a small flame.
2 an uncontrollable level of violence or anger.

flashy *adjective* (**flashier; flashiest**)
showy or vulgar: *a flashy new car.*

flask *noun*
a small flat bottle for liquids.

flat¹ *adjective* (**flatter; flattest**)
1 level and smooth: *The flat desert country stretched unendingly to the horizon.*
2 not deep or high: *flat shoes.*
3 fixed or absolute: *There is a flat rate for the hire of all cars.* □ *His flat refusal did not surprise us.*
4 *Music* being lowered in pitch by a semitone. Compare SHARP *adjective* (definition 2).
5 deflated: *a flat tyre.*
6 without bubbles: *This lemonade is flat.*
7 monotonous, uninteresting: *a rather flat voice.*
8 having no charge: *a flat battery.*

• **flat** *noun*
1 a flat surface or part.
2 (*informal*) a flat tyre.
3 (**flats**) low-lying land, especially near water.
4 *Music* a flat note.
5 *Music* the sign (♭) indicating a flat.
• **flat** *adverb*
1 in a flat position: *He laid the paper flat on the table.*
2 exactly or absolutely: *Be here in 20 minutes flat.*
Phrases **fall flat** to fail. **flat out** as fast as possible.
Word Family **flatness** *noun*; **flatly** *adverb*.

flat² *noun*
one or more rooms rented to live in, usually with a kitchen and bathroom.

flatfish *noun* (*plural* **flatfish** or **flatfishes**)
a fish such as the flounder, which swims on its side and has a flattened body and both eyes on one side of its head.

flat-footed *adjective*
1 having the arch of the foot flattened so that most of the sole rests on the ground when standing.
2 (*informal*) clumsy or awkward.

flat iron *noun*
(*formerly*) an iron that is heated on a stove or fire.

flatmate *noun*
someone who shares a flat.

flat race *noun*
a horse race run on a level course with no obstacles.

flatten *verb*
to make or become flat.

flatter *verb*
1 to praise extremely, especially in order to please or win favour.
2 to please or make grateful: *The young mother was flattered by our attention to her baby.*
3 to show or portray favourably: *This photo really flatters you.*
Phrase **flatter oneself** *Do not flatter yourself that you will win the prize* (= wrongly believe).
Word Family **flattering** *adjective*; **flatterer** *noun* a person who flatters; **flattery** *noun*.

flatulent (**flat**-yoo-lent) *adjective*
having excess gas in the stomach or intestines, causing a bloated feeling.
Word Family **flatulence, flatulency** *noun*; **flatulently** *adverb*.
[Latin *flatus* blowing]

flaunt (flawnt) *verb*
to display boldly or ostentatiously.

> ❗ Do not confuse *flaunt* with *flout*.
> *Flout* means 'to treat with
> contempt', as in *He flouted the rules*.
> *Flaunt* means 'to display boldly or
> ostentatiously': *to flaunt one's wealth*.

flautist (**flaw**-tist) *noun*
a person who plays the flute.

flavour (**flay**-va) *noun* (*American* **flavor**)
1 a distinctive taste.
2 a characteristic quality: *The theme park
has an American flavour*.
Phrase **flavour of the month** a person
or thing that is popular or fashionable at a
given time.
• **flavour** *verb* to give flavour to: *The stew
was flavoured with fresh herbs*.
*Figurative He flavoured his story with
many romantic details* (= added colour to).
Word Family **flavoursome** *adjective* full
of flavour.

flavouring *noun*
a substance used to add flavour.

flaw *noun*
1 a thing which lessens the value or beauty
of a thing or a person: *Laziness is the only
flaw in her character*.
2 a crack or break: *The antique cup had a
small flaw in the handle*.
Word Family **flaw** *verb* to spoil or mar;
flawless *adjective*; **flawlessly** *adverb*;
flawlessness *noun*.

flax *noun*
1 an annual plant with narrow leaves and
blue flowers, cultivated for its seeds
(linseed) and fine fibre.
2 a fibre made from flax and used to make
linen yarn.

flaxen *adjective*
1 of or made of flax.
2 a poetic word meaning 'pale yellow like
flax': *flaxen hair*.

flay *verb*
1 to strip the skin off.
2 to whip.
3 to criticize harshly.

flea *noun*
a small wingless leaping insect which sucks
blood and is parasitic on mammals and
birds.
Phrase **a flea in one's ear** a sharp
rebuke.

flea market *noun*
a market, especially one in the open air,
where second-hand articles are sold.

fleck *noun*
a small spot or mark of colour or light.
Word Family **flecked** *adjective* marked
with flecks or spots.

fledged *adjective*
having feathers and able to fly.

fledgling *noun* also **fledgeling**
1 a young bird just able to fly.
2 a young or inexperienced person or
thing: *a fledgling democracy*.

flee *verb* (**flees**; **fleeing**; **fled**)
to run away from danger, pursuers, etc.:
The villagers fled as the troops invaded.

fleece *noun*
1 the wool of a sheep, especially the wool
shorn at one time.
2 a fabric with a soft pile, used for lining
clothing to give it extra warmth.
3 a piece of clothing made from fleece,
especially a sweatshirt or jacket.
• **fleece** *verb* (*informal*) to swindle:
Investors were fleeced by the company.
Word Family **fleecy** *adjective* (**fleecier**;
fleeciest) being lined with or made of
fleece.

fleet¹ *noun*
1 a large group of ships or other vehicles
travelling together or organized by one
company.
2 *Navy* the largest organized unit of ships
or warships under one officer.

fleet² *adjective*
swift or fast.
Word Family **fleetness** *noun*; **fleetly**
adverb.

fleeting *adjective*
passing or moving swiftly: *a fleeting glance*.
Word Family **fleetingly** *adverb*.

flesh *noun*
1 the soft part of an animal body, fruit or
vegetable, excluding the skin, etc.
2 the physical body or nature of a person,
as distinct from the soul or spirit.
3 the surface of the body: *His flesh was pale*.
Phrase **in the flesh** *You will soon be able to
see this famous international star in the flesh*
(= in person).
• **flesh** *verb*
Phrase **flesh out** to add substance to: *She
fleshed out the story with some more details*.

fleshly *adjective*
of or relating to flesh or the body,
especially as distinct from the spirit.

fleshpots *plural noun*
places devoted to luxury or enjoyment.

fleshy *adjective* (**fleshier; fleshiest**)
plump or soft, like flesh.
***Word Family* fleshiness** *noun*.

fleur-de-lis (fler-de-lee) *noun* (*plural*
fleurs-de lis) (fler-de-lee) also **fleur-de-lys**
an emblem with three petals or leaves
gathered at the base, which was used as
the armorial bearings of the French
monarchy.
[French *fleur* flower + *de lys* of lily]

flew the past tense of **fly**[1].

flex[1] *verb*
to bend or stretch something springy, such
as a muscle.

flex[2] *noun* (*plural* **flexes**)
a length of insulated electric cable.

flexible *adjective*
1 able to be bent easily.
2 adaptable: *The arrangements are quite
flexible.*
***Word Family* flexibly** *adverb*; **flexibility**
noun.
[Latin *flexibilis* pliant, tractable]

flexitime *noun* (*American* **flextime**)
the policy of allowing employees to vary
their time of arrival and departure as long
as they work for the usual number of hours
in a week.

flibbertigibbet (flib-a-tee-jib-et) *noun*
a silly or flighty person.

flick *noun*
1 a quick light movement.
2 a movement of one's finger against one's
thumb.
3 (*informal*) a film at the cinema.
4 (**the flicks**) (*informal*) the cinema.
• **flick** *verb*
1 to make a quick light movement.
2 to send by a flick of the fingers: *She
flicked a pea at him.*
3 to look quickly: *flicking through the TV
channels.*

flicker *verb*
to burn, shine or move briefly and
unsteadily: *The dying fire flickered gently.*
• **flicker** *noun*
1 a brief unsteady movement or light:
*There was a flicker of light from the bulb
before it burnt out.*
2 a brief feeling: *a flicker of hope.*
[Old English *flicorian* to move the wings]

flick knife *noun* (*plural* **flick knives**)
a knife with a spring-loaded retractable
blade which is released when a switch is
pressed.

flier ⇨ FLYER.

flight *noun*
1 the act or manner of flying.
2 a journey made by air: *a flight across the
Atlantic.*
3 a number of things flying together: *A
flight of seagulls swooped down to the water.*
4 an unbroken row of stairs.
***Phrases* flight of fancy** a soaring of the
imagination. **take flight** to flee or run
away.

flight deck *noun*
1 the part of an aeroplane where the
controls are situated.
2 ⇨ AIRCRAFT CARRIER.

flightless *adjective*
not able to fly.

flight lieutenant *noun*
Air force a commissioned officer ranking
between flying officer and squadron
leader.

flight sergeant *noun*
Air force a non-commissioned officer
ranking between sergeant and warrant
officer.

flighty *adjective* (**flightier; flightiest**)
silly, frivolous or fickle.

flimsy *adjective* (**flimsier; flimsiest**)
weak and easily damaged or destroyed.
***Word Family* flimsiness** *noun*.

flinch *verb*
to move back or away from, as in fear,
repulsion, etc.
***Word Family* flinch** *noun* (*plural*
flinches).

fling *verb* (**flings; flinging; flung**)
to throw violently: *He flung the door open.*
***Phrase* fling oneself into** to get
enthusiastically involved in.
• **fling** *noun*
1 a spree.
2 a relationship or love affair that only lasts
a short time.

flint *noun*
1 a very hard brittle form of silica which
produces a spark when struck with steel.
2 the alloy which produces a spark in
cigarette lighters.

flintlock *noun*
a musket fired by lighting the gunpowder
with a spark from a flint.

flinty *adjective* (**flintier; flintiest**)
1 of or resembling flint.
2 hard, cruel: *a flinty stare.*

flip *verb* (**flips; flipping; flipped**)
1 to move or throw with a snapping or jerking movement: *to flip a coin into the air.*
2 (*informal*) to become angry or upset.
3 (*informal*) to go mad.
• **flip** *noun* a quick abrupt movement: *a flip of the wrist.*

flip-flop *noun*
1 a type of beach sandal with a thong that fits between the toes.
2 an electronic device which has alternate states, such as on or off.

flippant *adjective*
not suitably or sufficiently serious.
Word Family flippancy *noun*; **flippantly** *adverb.*

flipper *noun*
1 *Anatomy* a broad flat limb on certain aquatic animals, such as whales and seals, used for swimming, guidance, etc.
2 a rubber object shaped like an animal flipper attached to the feet to aid swimming.

flip side *noun*
(*informal*) the side of a record carrying a less important song.

flirt *verb*
1 to behave in a light-hearted amorous manner.
2 to treat or consider light-heartedly: *We have been flirting with the idea of buying a new car.*
3 to risk: *flirting with death.*
Word Family flirt *noun* a person who flirts; **flirtation** *noun* 1 the act of flirting. 2 a light-hearted love affair; **flirtatious** *adjective* given to flirtation; **flirtatiously** *adverb*; **flirtatiousness** *noun.*

flit *verb* (**flits; flitting; flitted**)
to move lightly and quickly: *She saw a shadow flit behind the tree.*

flitter *verb*
to flutter.

float *verb*
1 to rest on, move or be held up in air, liquid, etc.: *She floated on her back in the pool.*
2 to drift: *She floated through the day in happy contentment.*
3 *Commerce* to sell shares to the public so that a company may gain listing on a stock exchange.
4 *Commerce* to remove restrictions on the value of a currency in the world market so that it may find its own natural level.
• **float** *noun*

1 a thing which floats or provides support for floating, such as the quill and cork device on a fishing line, or the floating device in a cistern or carburettor which regulates the level or supply of liquid.
2 a low cart or platform on wheels, drawn in processions.
3 ⇨ MILK FLOAT.
4 a small reserve of cash to provide a shop or stall with the means of giving change on the first sales.

floatation ⇨ FLOTATION.

floating rib *noun* also called **false rib**.
Anatomy any of the lower two pairs of ribs, so called because they are not joined to the sternum.

flocculant (flok-yoo-l'nt) *noun*
a substance added to solutions to cause the clotting of fine particles into larger lumps.
Word Family flocculation (flok-yoo-**lay**-sh'n) *noun.*

flock[1] *noun*
1 a group of birds, sheep or goats.
2 a crowd of people.
• **flock** *verb* to go or gather in a flock.

flock[2] *noun*
1 wool refuse, rags, etc. cut in small pieces and used to stuff furniture, mattresses, etc.
2 a tuft of wool, hair or other substance.
[Latin *floccus*]

floe *noun*
a small mass of floating ice.
[Norwegian *flo* a layer]

flog *verb* (**flogs; flogging; flogged**)
1 to strike or beat with a whip, stick, etc.
2 (*informal*) to sell.
Word Family flogging *noun* a punishment by whipping or beating.

flood (flud) *noun*
1 an overflowing of water, especially onto land which is usually dry.
2 a large flow or stream: *A flood of congratulations greeted the winners.*
3 a floodlight.
• **flood** *verb*
1 to rise or overflow in a flood.
2 to occur in great quantities: *Entries flooded in for the competition.*

floodlight *noun*
a light with a strong broad beam, used in a theatre or outdoors.
• **floodlight** *verb* (**floodlights; floodlighting; floodlit**).

flood plain *noun*
the flat land beside a river which is covered by water when the river floods.

floor *noun*
1 the lower horizontal surface of a room or other structure.
2 the main part of a hall, etc.: *the floor of the stock exchange.*
3 a storey of a building.
4 the bottom of something: *on the sea floor.*
Phrases **have the floor, take the floor**
When he has the floor nobody is allowed to interrupt (= is speaking). **wipe the floor with** *The champion wiped the floor with his opponent* (= defeated completely).
• **floor** *verb*
1 (*informal*) to defeat or knock down.
2 (*informal*) to stun or confound: *I was quite floored by her sudden change of mood.*
Word Family **flooring** *noun* 1 a floor or floors. 2 the materials used to make a floor.

floor show *noun*
a form of entertainment consisting of songs, dances or a comedy act, usually in a nightclub.

floozy (**floo**-zee) *noun* also **floozie** (*plural* **floozies**)
(*informal*) a promiscuous or vulgar woman.

flop *verb* (**flops; flopping; flopped**)
1 to fall, drop or collapse suddenly.
2 (*informal*) to fail.
Word Family **flop** *noun* (*informal*) a failure; **floppy** *adjective* (**floppier; floppiest**) tending to droop or flop; **floppiness** *noun*; **floppily** *adverb*.

floppy disk *noun*
short form is **floppy** a flexible computer disk, usually in a rigid case, which is used to store or transfer data.

flora *noun*
Biology all the plants of a certain area or period. Compare FAUNA.
[Latin *Flora* goddess of flowers]

floral *adjective*
of or relating to flowers.
[Latin *floris* of a flower]

floret *noun*
1 a small individual flower of a composite flower head.
2 a small stem of cauliflower or broccoli.

floribunda *noun*
a plant which produces dense clusters of flowers: *a floribunda rose.*

floriculture *noun*
the production and cultivation of flowers and other decorative plants.
Word Family **floricultural** *adjective*; **floriculturist** *noun*.

florid (*rhymes with* horrid) *adjective*
1 flushed or highly coloured: *a healthy florid complexion.*
2 highly decorated or elaborate: *His florid prose was difficult to read and understand.*
[Latin *floridus* flower]

florin (**florr**-in) *noun*
(*formerly*) an old British coin equal to ten pence.

florist (**florr**-ist) *noun*
a person who sells flowers, indoor plants, etc.

floss *noun* (*plural* **flosses**)
1 a fine silk fibre used for decoration in embroidery.
2 a silky thread-like substance.
3 also called **dental floss**. soft thread used to clean between one's teeth.
• **floss** *verb* to use floss on one's teeth.

flotation (flo-**tay**-sh'n) *noun* also **floatation**
1 the act of floating or causing to float.
2 *Geology* a process for separating different materials in an ore by suspending them in a liquid.

flotilla (fla-**til**-a) *noun*
a small fleet, or a division of a fleet.
[Spanish]

flotsam *noun*
wreckage or rubbish floating on the sea. Compare FLOTSAM.

flounce[1] *verb*
to move or go with quick impatient movements: *She flounced furiously out of the room, slamming the door behind her.*
• **flounce** *noun*.

flounce[2] *noun*
a strip of gathered material attached by one edge to a skirt, etc. for decoration.

flounder[1] *verb*
to struggle helplessly or clumsily
Figurative *He floundered through his speech and sat down with relief.*

flounder[2] *noun*
a flatfish with a large mouth and both eyes usually occurring on the left side of the head.

flour *noun*
a finely ground substance made from wheat or another grain, used in cooking.
Word Family **floury** *adjective* like or covered with flour.

flourish (**flurr**-ish) *verb*
1 to grow or be well, healthy, active, etc.: *Business flourished under the new management.*

2 to wave or display enthusiastically: *She rushed in, flourishing her first pay cheque.*
● **flourish** *noun* (*plural* **flourishes**)
1 an enthusiastic wave or display.
2 a decorative curve in handwriting.
3 *Music* a fanfare.
[Latin *florere* to bloom]

flout (*rhymes with* out) *verb*
to ignore or treat with contempt: *Despite the school's stern warnings, he continues to flout the rules.*

> ! Do not confuse *flout* with FLAUNT.

flow (flo) *verb*
1 (of liquid) to move smoothly: *Water flowed from the roof down the walls.*
2 to hang loosely: *Her hair flowed down her back.*
3 to proceed smoothly: *The meeting was flowing along nicely until she interrupted.*
● **flow** *noun*
1 a continuous flowing or pouring movement.
2 the quantity or volume which flows.

flow chart *noun* also called **flow diagram**.
a diagram showing a logical step-by-step sequence of events in a process, activity, story, etc.

flower *noun*
1 *Biology* the part of a seed plant containing the reproductive organs.
2 a plant grown or considered for its decorative flowers.
3 the best or finest part or example of anything: *He died tragically in the flower of his youth.*
● **flower** *verb* to produce flowers.
Figurative His talent flowered under the encouragement of his teacher (= developed fully).

flower bed *noun*
a patch of ground where flowering plants are grown in a garden, park, etc.

floweret *noun*
a floret.

flower head *noun*
a flower consisting of a dense cluster of small individual flowers.

flowery *adjective*
1 like or full of flowers: *a flowery shirt.*
2 highly decorative or elaborate: *flowery language.*

flown the past participle of **fly**[1].

flu *noun*
influenza.

> The word **flu** is a common shortening of *influenza* which came into English from Italian, where it meant not only 'influence' but was also the name given to an outbreak of a specific disease. A disease known as *influenza di catarro* (catarrh) broke out in Italy in 1743 and spread throughout Europe, including Britain (where it was known simply as *influenza*).

fluctuate (**flukt**-yoo-ate) *verb*
to vary in a wave-like or irregular way: *Her moods fluctuate between extreme happiness and deep depression.*
Word Family **fluctuation** (flukt-yoo-**ay**-sh'n) *noun*.
[Latin *fluctuare* to move like the waves]

flue (floo) *noun*
1 a passage for smoke in a chimney.
2 a pipe or tube, e.g. on an oven or furnace, through which smoke and hot gases are drawn off.

fluent (**floo**-ent) *adjective*
1 able to express oneself clearly and easily: *Her fluent Italian surprised the other tourists.*
2 flowing smoothly and gracefully: *the fluent curves of the dome-shaped building.*
Word Family **fluency** *noun*; **fluently** *adverb*.
[Latin *fluens* flowing]

fluff *noun*
1 a light downy substance.
2 (*informal*) a mistake.
● **fluff** *verb*
1 to make or become puffed out.
2 (*informal*) to do clumsily or unsuccessfully: *She fluffed her lines in the play.*
Word Family **fluffy** *adjective* (**fluffier**; **fluffiest**) like or covered with fluff; **fluffiness** *noun*.

fluid (**floo**-id) *noun*
a substance, a liquid or gas, which flows.
● **fluid** *adjective*
1 of or consisting of fluid.
2 able to flow.
3 flowing and smooth: *his fluid movements.*
Word Family **fluidity** (floo-**id**-i-tee) *noun*; **fluidly** *adverb*.

fluid ounce *noun*
a unit of volume for liquids, equal to one-twentieth of a pint (about 28·4 ml).

fluke[1] *noun*
a stroke of good luck.
Word Family **fluke** *verb* to win or gain by a fluke; **fluky, flukey** *adjective* obtained by chance or a fluke: *a fluky shot.*

fluke² noun
a parasitic flatworm with one or more
suckers.

flume noun
1 an artificial water channel for industrial
use or for carrying logs.
2 a water slide into a swimming pool.
[Latin *flumen* a river]

flummery noun (*plural* **flummeries**)
a light fluffy dessert made of milk, eggs,
sugar, flour, etc.
[Welsh]

flummox verb
(*informal*) to bewilder or confuse.

flung the past tense and past participle of
fling.

flunkey noun also **flunky** (*plural* **flunkies**)
a male servant.

fluorescence (flor-**ess**-ence) noun
1 the property, possessed by certain
substances, of absorbing radiation of a
particular wavelength and giving it off as
light.
2 the light produced by fluorescence.
Word Family **fluorescent** *adjective*
having the property of fluorescence, as
certain electric lights; **fluoresce** *verb*.

fluoridate verb
to add small traces of a fluoride to
something, especially a water supply, to
strengthen tooth enamel.
Word Family **fluoridation** noun.

fluoride (**floor**-ide) noun
a chemical compound containing fluorine.

fluorine (**floor**-een) noun
a yellow, highly reactive gas. Its organic
compounds are widely used in industry,
especially in plastics and as refrigerants.
⇨ HALOGEN.

flurry noun (*plural* **flurries**)
1 a sudden whirling movement: *a flurry of
snow*.
2 a confused hurry: *in a flurry of excitement*.
● **flurry** verb (**flurries**; **flurrying**;
flurried) to swirl.

flush¹ verb
1 to make or become red: *The child's face
was flushed with joy and excitement*.
2 to elate, excite: *flushed with success*.
3 to flood with water for cleaning
purposes.
4 *Hunting* to cause game to burst from
hiding.
● **flush** noun (*plural* **flushes**)
1 a red or rosy glow of colour.
2 an act of flushing.
3 freshness: *the flush of youth*.

flush² adjective
1 even or level: *This picture is not quite flush
with the top of the door*.
2 (*informal*) having plenty of money.

flush³ noun (*plural* **flushes**)
Cards a hand all of one suit.

fluster verb
to make confused, excited or nervous.
● **fluster** noun a nervous or confused state.

flute noun
1 *Music* a wind instrument consisting of a
long silver tube with keys or fingerholes,
held by the player who blows air across the
mouthpiece.
2 *Architecture* a long rounded furrow or
channel, e.g. on a column.
● **flute** verb
1 to play or make sounds like a flute.
2 to form flutes or furrows in a surface.
Word Family **fluted** *adjective*; **fluting**
noun.

flutter verb
to wave or move quickly and lightly: *The
flag fluttered in the breeze*.
● **flutter** noun
1 a light quick movement.
2 a nervous or excited state.
3 (*informal*) a bet.

fluvial (**floo**-vi-al) adjective
of or produced by a river: *fluvial deposits*.
[Latin *fluvius* a river]

flux noun (*plural* **fluxes**)
1 a flowing or continuous movement or
change.
2 *Physics* a flow of matter or energy.
3 *Physics* the rate of a flow of matter or
energy.
4 *Metallurgy* a substance used to assist the
joining or fusion of two metals.
[Latin *fluxus* flowing]

fly¹ verb (**flies**; **flying**; **flew**; **flown**)
1 to move or cause to move through the
air: *The seagull flew high above the water*.
2 to move quickly: *The door flew open*. □
Doesn't time fly!
3 (*informal*) to leave quickly: *The gang will
probably try to fly the country*.
● **fly** noun (*plural* **flies**)
1 also **flies** the front fastener of a pair of
trousers, usually consisting of buttons or a
zip covered with a flap of cloth.
2 a flap of cloth forming the door of a tent.
3 (**the flies**) *Theatre* the space above the
stage, used for storing scenery, etc.

fly² noun (*plural* **flies**)
1 a two-winged insect in which the hind
legs are modified to aid balance.

2 a similar but unrelated winged insect, such as the firefly.
Phrases **a fly in the ointment** *His bad temper was rather a fly in the ointment* (= spoiling element). **there are no flies on** *There are no flies on that shrewd young man* (= is nothing naive or incautious about).

flyblown *adjective*
dirty because of contamination by flies.

fly-by-night *adjective*
untrustworthy, avoiding responsibilities, debts, etc.: *a fly-by-night ticket agency.*

flycatcher *noun*
a small bird which perches upright on vantage points and swoops on passing insects.

flyer *noun also* **flier**
1 a person or thing that flies, such as a pilot.
2 a leaflet or small poster.

fly-fishing *noun*
fishing with artificial flies as bait. Compare COARSE FISHING.

flying boat *noun*
an aeroplane designed to take off and land on water.

flying bomb ⇨ DOODLEBUG.

flying buttress *noun* (*plural* **flying buttresses**)
Architecture an arched support for a wall which stands separately but is attached by one or more bars or structures. Compare BUTTRESS.

flying doctor *noun*
Australian a doctor using air transport to reach patients in otherwise inaccessible bush or inland areas.

flying fish *noun* (*plural* **flying fish** or **flying fishes**)
a fish with an enlarged wing-like pectoral fin enabling it to glide through the air.

flying fox *noun* (*plural* **flying foxes**)
a large tropical fruit-eating bat with a head resembling that of a fox.

flying officer *noun*
Air force a commissioned officer ranking between pilot officer and flight lieutenant.

flying saucer *noun*
a disc-shaped object in the sky, thought to be an alien spacecraft.

flying squad *noun*
a police squad available for special assignments in any part of the country.

flying trapeze ⇨ TRAPEZE (definition 1).

flyleaf *noun* (*plural* **flyleaves**)
a blank page at the beginning or end of a book.

flyover *noun*
a bridge which carries one road over another at an intersection.

flypaper *noun*
a strip of paper treated with sticky poison for catching flies.

flyweight *noun*
a weight division in boxing, not exceeding 51 kg (8 stone).

flywheel *noun*
a heavy wheel which, because of its momentum, tends to smooth out rapid variations in speed, as in motor vehicle engines, machinery, etc.

foal *noun*
the young of a horse or ass.
● **foal** *verb* to produce a foal.

foam *noun*
1 a collection of tiny bubbles of gas or liquid formed on a surface.
2 a light spongy material used for insulation in packaging, etc.
Word Family **foam** *verb*; **foamy** *adjective*; **foaminess** *noun.*

fob[1] *noun*
1 a chain, ribbon, etc. attached to a watch and worn hanging from the pocket.
2 the tab of a key ring.

fob[2] *verb* (**fobs**; **fobbing**; **fobbed**)
Phrase **fob off** to get rid of, especially in a cunning way.

focal (fo-kal) *adjective*
relating to a focus.

focal point *noun*
1 the main point of interest, activity, etc.
2 *Physics* a focus.

fo'c'sle ⇨ FORECASTLE.

focus (fo-kus) *noun* (*plural* **focuses** or **foci** (fo-sigh))
1 the position or adjustment of an object or optical device needed to produce a clearly defined image: *My camera is not in focus.*
2 *Physics* the point at which converging rays, such as light, meet.
3 *Physics* the point from which diverging rays, such as light, appear to come.
4 a central point of attention, attraction, etc.
5 *Maths* a fixed point.
6 *Geology* the point beneath the earth's crust where an earthquake starts.

• **focus** *verb* (**focuses** or **focusses;**
focusing or **focussing; focused** or
focussed)
1 to bring into focus.
2 to concentrate: *Just focus on getting better.*
[Latin, *fireplace, hearth*]

fodder *noun*
1 food given to livestock, such as hay.
2 people considered as being consumed or
used up in a particular process or activity:
factory fodder.

foe *noun*
an enemy or opponent.

foetid ⇨ FETID.

foetus ⇨ FETUS.

fog *noun*
1 a dense mass of water droplets
suspended in the air.
2 *Photography* the darkening of a negative
or print due to light or chemicals.
• **fog** *verb* (**fogs; fogging; fogged**) to
make or become cloudy.
Word Family **foggy** *adjective* (**foggier;**
foggiest), **fogginess** *noun.*

fogey (**foe**-gee) *noun* also **fogy** (*plural*
fogies)
a person with extremely old-fashioned
ideas.

foghorn *noun*
Nautical a horn used by a ship in fog to
warn other ships that it is nearby.

foible *noun*
a slight peculiarity or defect of character.

foie gras ⇨ PATE DE FOIE GRAS.

foil[1] *verb*
to prevent from being successful: *The
attempted robbery was foiled by the quick
action of the clerk.*

foil[2] *noun*
1 a fine paper-like sheet of metal.
aluminium foil.
2 something which improves or
distinguishes the characteristics of
something else by contrast: *The green
leaves provided an attractive foil for the red
roses.*
3 *Architecture* a leaf-shaped decorative
division, especially around church
windows.

foil[3] *noun*
a steel sword used in fencing, having a
blade with a rounded button on its point.

foist *verb*
to impose something on a person by deceit
or trickery.

fold[1] *verb*
1 to bend or cause to bend over on itself:
He folded up the newspaper. □ *She folded her
arms.*
2 to wrap in one's arms.
3 *Cooking* to mix ingredients by slowly and
gently turning one part over another: *Fold
in the flour.*
4 (*informal*) to collapse or fail: *The youth
club folded after a few months.*
• **fold** *noun*
1 the act or an instance of folding.
2 the junction of two folded parts.
3 *Geology* a bend in layers of rock caused
by movement in the earth's crust. **Fold
mountains** are formed by immense
pressures in the earth's crust.

fold[2] *noun*
an enclosed area for sheep.
Phrase **return to the fold** to return to
one's family or other group that one has
deserted.

folder *noun*
1 a folded piece of cardboard, plastic, etc.
to hold loose papers.
2 *Computers* a group of related files.

foliage (**foe**-lee-ij) *noun*
leaves, especially all the leaves on a tree or
plant.
[Latin *folium* leaf]

folic acid *noun*
one of the substances in the vitamin B
group, used in treating some types of
anaemia.

folio (**foe**-lee-o) *noun*
1 *Printing* a sheet of paper folded once.
2 *Printing* a page number.
3 a book made up of sheets of paper folded
once.

folk (foke) *plural noun*
1 (*sometimes* **folks**) (*informal*) people.
2 also called **folk music**. traditional music
handed down through many generations
of people.
Phrase **one's folks** one's parents.
• **folk** *adjective* relating to ordinary people
or their customs: *a folk hero.*

folk dance *noun*
a traditional dance of a particular country
or region.

folklore *noun*
the traditional customs, legends and
beliefs of the people of a particular
country or region.

folk song noun
1 a traditional song handed down through many generations of people in a particular country or region.
2 a song with a similar style of music.

follicle noun
Biology a very small sac or gland.

follow verb
1 to come or go behind.
2 to go along: *Follow this path.*
3 to obey: *They followed the teacher's instructions.*
4 to come as a result of: *This conclusion follows from the evidence.*
5 to understand: *I didn't quite follow you.*
6 to watch the progress of: *We followed her career with interest.*
7 to imitate: *Follow my example.*
8 to support: *She follows Manchester United.*
Phrases **follow on** *Cricket* to be obliged to bat again immediately, having failed to obtain half of the other team's score in the first innings. **follow through** to continue the swing of a racket or bat after the ball has been hit. **follow up** to pursue to a conclusion.
Word Family **follower** noun a person who follows, especially one who imitates or admires another.

following adjective
about to be mentioned: *Will the following people stand up?*
• **following** noun a group of supporters: *The band has a loyal following.*

folly noun (plural **follies**)
1 foolishness or a foolish act.
2 a building that has no purpose.
[French *folie* madness]

foment (foe-ment) verb
to promote the development of trouble or rebellion.

fond adjective
1 liking or loving: *She has always been fond of children.*
2 cherished: *fond memories of their honeymoon.*
3 foolish or unlikely: *She had fond hopes of her parents getting back together.*
Word Family **fondly** adverb; **fondness** noun.

fondant noun
a thick sugary paste used in icing and sweets.

fondle verb
to handle or stroke with affection.

fondue (fon-doo or fond-yoo) noun
a dish cooked in a special pot at the table, such as a mixture of cheese, wine and spices into which cubes of bread are dipped.
[French *fondre* to melt]

font[1] noun
Christianity a basin, usually stone, which holds water for baptism in a church.

font[2] noun also **fount**
Printing, Computers a complete range of type characters in one size and face.

food noun
something that people, animals or plants take in or absorb to keep them alive and healthy.
Phrase **food for thought** something that makes one think.

food chain noun
Biology a chain of organisms in which energy is passed from one organism to the one that eats it: *Grass is eaten by cows, which are eaten by people, further along the food chain.*

food processor noun
an electric kitchen appliance with various attachments for mixing, blending, chopping, grating and kneading.

food safety noun
the process of making food safe to eat.

foodstuff noun
a substance suitable for use as food.

food technology noun
the study of how food products are designed and made.

fool[1] noun
1 a person who lacks sense and judgement: *He was a fool to believe their lies.*
2 a person who is an object of ridicule, disrespect, etc.: *They made a fool of you.*
3 (*formerly*) a jester kept by kings, etc. to entertain at court.
• **fool** verb
1 to trick or deceive.
2 to joke or play: *Stop fooling about and do some work.*

> The word **fool** came into English from Old French *fol* (a mad or stupid person). It in turn came from the Latin word *follis*, which originally meant 'bellows' or 'windbag' and then came to mean someone who uttered only wind, 'an idiot' in other words. Formerly, royal households kept a *fool* (who often wore a cap with bells on it) to entertain them with his foolish actions and remarks. Many of Shakespeare's plays have *fools* in them and although they seem to be talking nonsense the meaning of what they say is often quite deep.

fool² *noun*
a dessert made from fruit and cream whipped together: *gooseberry fool*.

foolhardy *adjective* (**foolhardier; foolhardiest**)
unwisely bold or rash.
Word Family **foolhardiness** *noun*; **foolhardily** *adverb*.

foolish *adjective*
lacking sense or wisdom.
Word Family **foolishly** *adverb*; **foolishness** *noun*.

foolproof *adjective*
of a kind that no one can mistake or misuse: *a foolproof plan*.

foolscap *noun*
a traditional size of paper about 330 mm x 210 mm.

fool's gold *noun*
a yellow mineral, especially pyrite, that looks like gold.

foot *noun* (*plural* **feet**)
1 *Anatomy* the lower end of the leg below the ankle.
2 something which has the position or function of a foot.
3 the lower end, bottom: *the foot of the hill*.
4 a unit of length equal to 12 inches or about 30 cm. *abbrev.* ft.
5 *Poetry* the basic unit of division in scansion, each with two or three syllables.
Phrases **fall on one's feet, land on one's feet** to be lucky or successful. **find one's feet** to become independent of the help of others. **get cold feet, have cold feet** to lose one's nerve or confidence. **my foot!** nonsense! **put one's foot down** to be strict or firm. **put one's foot in it** to make an embarrassing blunder. **stand on one's own two feet** to be self-sufficient. **sweep off one's feet 1** to knock over: *The wave swept her off her feet.* **2** to impress or overwhelm.
● **foot** *verb*
1 (*informal*) to pay: *He footed the bill.*
2 to walk: *We footed it to the shop.*

footage *noun*
1 *Film* a length of film.
2 length in feet.

foot-and-mouth disease *noun*
an infectious viral disease of cattle and similar animals, causing puffy growths around the feet and mouth.

football *noun*
1 a leather ball inflated by means of a rubber bladder.

2 a field game played with a football, such as rugby, soccer or American football.
Word Family **footballer** *noun*.

football pools ⇨ POOL² (definition 4).

footfall *noun*
a footstep.

foot fault ⇨ FAULT (definition 3).

foothill *noun*
a hill at the base of a mountain range.

foothold *noun*
1 a place giving support for the foot in climbing, etc.
2 a secure position from which one may advance, succeed or make progress.

footing *noun*
1 a secure position of or for the feet.
2 a basis: *Let's put the interview on a more relaxed footing.*

footlights *plural noun*
Theatre a row of lights set at the edge of the stage.

footloose *adjective*
free of responsibilities and able to travel about.

footman *noun* (*plural* **footmen**)
a male servant employed to wait at table, attend the door, etc.

footnote *noun*
an explanation or note printed in smaller type at the bottom of a page in a book.

footpad *noun*
(*formerly*) a highwayman on foot.

footpath *noun*
a path for people to walk on.

footprint *noun*
a mark left by someone's foot or shoe.

foot rot *noun*
an infection of the feet of sheep due to constantly wet ground, causing inflammation and decay of the toes which leads to lameness.

footstep *noun*
a tread of a foot or the sound it produces.
Phrase **follow in someone's footsteps** to continue or imitate the progress of another.

footwork *noun*
the manner in which the feet are moved, e.g. in boxing.

fop *noun*
a man who is very concerned with his clothes and appearance.
Word Family **foppish** *adjective*.

for *preposition*

1 with the purpose or intention of: *These apples are for cooking.*

2 to go to: *She left for the city.*

3 directed to: *a letter for me.*

4 because of: *shouting for joy.*

5 in favour of, in support of: *We voted for the motion.*

6 during the time or distance of: *walking for hours.*

7 at the price of: *a book for £10.*

8 in honour of: *a medal for his bravery.*

9 instead of: *using leaves for plates.*

10 to be used by: *a book for children.*

11 on behalf of: *He signed the card for all of us.*

12 in spite of: *For all her talking, she's quite shy.*

13 considering the usual nature of: *She's tall for a girl.*

• **for** *conjunction* since or because: *I cannot go, for I am ill.*

forage (*rhymes with* porridge) *verb*
to hunt or search, especially for food.

• **forage** *noun* fodder, especially for horses and cattle.

foray (**forr**-ay) *noun*
a plundering raid.
Figurative He made a brief foray into another sort of work (= entry, attempt).

forbear[1] *verb* (**forbears; forbearing; forbore; forborne**)
to refrain from.
Word Family **forbearance** *noun*.

forbear[2] ⇨ FOREBEAR.

forbid *verb* (**forbids; forbidding; forbade** or **forbad; forbidden**)

1 to command not to do: *I forbid you to go out.*

2 not to allow: *Smoking was forbidden.*

forbidding *adjective*
disagreeable, frightening or off-putting: *a forbidding task.*

force *noun*

1 the strength of something: *the force of the wind.*

2 *Physics* the vector quantity equal to the mass of a body multiplied by its acceleration.

3 *Physics* a push or a pull which can cause an object to speed up, slow down, change direction or change shape.

4 an organized body of people: *a police force.*

5 violence, or the threat of violence: *They used force to enter the building.*

Phrase **in force 1** *They attacked in force* (= in full strength). **2** *The new law is now in force* (= operative, effective).

• **force** *verb*

1 to make or cause to do something, often using effort or strength.

2 to produce or do with effort: *She felt like crying but forced a smile.*

3 to break open: *We forced the lock.*

Word Family **forced** *adjective* not genuine; **forceful** *adjective* powerful or vigorous; **forcefully** *adverb*; **forcefulness** *noun*.

[Latin *fortis* strong]

forcemeat *noun*
a stuffing for meat, usually consisting of minced meat, breadcrumbs, etc.

forceps *plural noun* also called **pair of forceps**.
Medicine a pair of tongs for holding tissues or objects, e.g. during an operation, or used to help deliver a baby.

forcible (**fors**-i-b'l) *adjective*
using force.
Word Family **forcibly** *adverb*.

ford *noun*
a shallow part of a river where people may cross on foot or in vehicles.
Word Family **ford** *verb*.

fore *adjective*
located at or towards the front.

• **fore** *adverb Nautical* at or towards the bow. Compare AFT.

• **fore** *noun*
Phrase **to the fore** in or to a conspicuous position.

• **fore** *interjection*
Golf a cry used to warn other players that a ball has been hit nearby.

forearm *noun*
Anatomy the lower part of the arm.

forebear *noun* also **forbear**
an ancestor.

forebode *verb*
an old word meaning 'to predict, especially something ominous'.
Word Family **foreboding** *noun* a premonition; **forebodingly** *adverb*.

forecast *verb* (**forecasts; forecasting; forecast** or **forecasted**)
to predict.
Word Family **forecast** *noun*; **forecaster** *noun* a person who forecasts.

forecastle (**foke**-s'l) *noun* also **fo'c'sle**
the part of a ship near the bow, where the crew live.

foreclose *verb*
Law to take over or remove property on which mortgage payments have not been paid.
Word Family **foreclosure** *noun*.

forecourt *noun*
1 an enclosed court in front of a large building.
2 the front part of a garage, where petrol is sold.

forefather *noun*
an ancestor.

forefinger *noun*
Anatomy the first finger, next to the thumb.

forefront *noun*
the front place or position.

foregather, forgather *verb*
(*formal*) to gather together.

forego *verb* (**foregoes; foregoing; forewent; foregone**) ⇨ FORGO.

> ⚠ Both *forgo* and *forego* can be used to mean 'to do without', as in *We had to forgo/forego our pay rise.* Note that *foregone*, however, is the only possible spelling in the phrase *foregone conclusion*, because it comes from an old verb *forego*, meaning 'to go before'.

foregone conclusion *noun*
an inevitable result or conclusion.

foreground *noun*
the part of a picture or view nearest the observer's eye.

forehand *noun*
Tennis a stroke made with the palm of the hand facing forward. Compare BACKHAND.

forehead (**forr**-id *or* **for**-hed) *noun*
Anatomy the area at the top and front of the face, above the eyes and below the hairline.

foreign (**forr**-in) *adjective*
1 relating to or from a country other than one's own: *a foreign language*.
2 not belonging to the place where it is found: *foreign matter in the eye*.
3 unfamiliar or strange.
Word Family **foreigner** *noun* a person from another country.
[Latin *foras* out of doors, abroad]

foreign correspondent *noun*
a person who sends news from abroad to a newspaper, broadcasting organization, etc.

Foreign Secretary *noun* (*plural* **Foreign Secretaries**) also called **Foreign Minister**.
the senior government minister in charge of foreign affairs.

foreknowledge (**for**-nol-ij) *noun*
knowledge of something before it happens.

foreland *noun*
a cape or headland.

forelock *noun*
the part of the hair that grows or hangs from the top of the forehead.

foreman *noun* (*plural* **foremen**)
1 a person in charge of a group of workers.
2 the spokesman for a jury.

foremost *adjective*
first in position, rank, etc.

forename *noun*
a first name.

forensic (fo-**ren**-zik) *adjective*
of or employed in legal proceedings, especially in relation to crime investigation: *forensic tests*.
[Latin *forensis* of the forum]

forerunner *noun*
a person who or situation which introduces or does something first: *Medieval guilds were the forerunners of trade unions.*

foresail (**for**-sail *or* **for**-s'l) *noun*
Nautical the principal sail hoisted in front of the main mast.

foresee *verb* (**foresees; foreseeing; foresaw; foreseen**)
to see or know beforehand.
Word Family **foreseeable** *adjective*.

foreshadow *verb*
to suggest or indicate beforehand.

foreshore *noun*
the beach or section of the shore between the high- and low-water marks.

foreshorten *verb*
1 to reduce the length of part or all of a represented object, so that it appears to the viewer to be in correct perspective.
2 to cut short or reduce.

foresight *noun*
the act or ability of foreseeing.

foreskin *noun* also called **prepuce**.
Anatomy a fold of skin which covers the tip of the penis.

forest (**forr**-ist) *noun*
1 a large area of land covered with trees.

2 a thick cluster of objects: *a forest of sails in the harbour.*

forestall (for-**stawl**) *verb*
to prevent or deal with beforehand.

forestry (**forr**-a-stree) *noun*
the study of planting and maintaining forests.
***Word Family* forester** *noun* a person skilled or trained in forestry.

foretell *verb* (**foretells; foretelling; foretold**)
to predict or prophesy.

forethought (**for**-thawt) *noun*
prudent and careful planning for the future.

forever *adverb*
1 also **for ever** for all time: *Will you love me forever?*
2 continually, persistently: *They are forever quarrelling.*

> [!] Both *forever* and *for ever* can be used to mean 'for all time', but only *forever* can be used to mean 'continually'.

forewarn (for-**wawn**) *verb*
to warn in advance: *We had been forewarned about the delays.*

forewent ⇨ FORGO.

foreword (**for**-werd) *noun*
an introduction in a book, usually written by someone other than the author.
Compare PREFACE.

forfeit (**for**-fit) *noun*
a penalty or fine, especially something given up or lost as punishment.
***Word Family* forfeit** *verb* to lose as a forfeit; **forfeiture** *noun* the act of forfeiting.

forgather ⇨ FOREGATHER.

forge[1] (forj) *noun*
1 the place in which a smith, especially a blacksmith, works.
2 a furnace, etc. in which metal is heated before shaping.
● **forge** *verb*
1 to work heated metal by hammering or pressing it into shape.
2 to form: *The countries forged a strong link.*
3 to make or reproduce for fraudulent purposes: *a forged ten-pound note.*
***Word Family* forger** *noun.*

forge[2] *verb*
to advance gradually and steadily: *forging ahead with plans for a new sports hall.*

forgery (**for**-ja-ree) *noun* (*plural* **forgeries**)
1 the producing of an imitation in order to deceive or pass it off as genuine.
2 anything made in this way.

forget *verb* (**forgets; forgetting; forgot; forgotten**)
1 to fail to remember.
2 to stop thinking about: *I can't forget my strange dream.*
***Phrase* forget oneself** to lose one's reserve or self-restraint.
***Word Family* forgetful** *adjective* tending to forget; **forgetfully** *adverb*; **forgetfulness** *noun*; **forgettable** *adjective* able to be forgotten.

forget-me-not *noun*
a small plant with blue flowers, considered to be a symbol of friendship and constancy.

> The **forget-me-not** takes its name from a legend. The story is that a German knight was picking some of the small blue flowers on a river bank for his sweetheart when he slipped and fell in the river and drowned. As he was swept away he called to his sweetheart 'Vergissmeinnicht', which means 'Forget me not'.

forgive *verb* (**forgives; forgiving; forgave; forgiven**)
1 to cease to resent: *to forgive one's enemies.*
2 to give pardon for a fault, etc.
***Word Family* forgiveness** *noun*; **forgivable** *adjective* able to be forgiven; **forgivably** *adverb*; **forgiving** *adjective* tending to forgive; **forgivingly** *adverb*.

forgo *verb* (**forgoes; forgoing; forwent; forgone**) also **forego**
to abstain from or do without: *Students usually forgo many social activities during their exams.*

> [!] For the spellings *forego* and *forgo* ⇨ FOREGO.

fork *noun*
1 an instrument with two or more prongs, for eating, gardening, etc.
2 a part or place where something divides into branches: *a fork in the road.*
3 either of the branches into which something divides: *Take the left fork.*
● **fork** *verb*
1 to divide into branches.
2 to lift, toss, pierce, etc. with a fork.
***Phrase* fork out** *He had to fork out the whole £50* (= give, hand over).

forklift truck *noun*
a vehicle with two movable horizontal arms at the front for lifting and carrying goods in factories, warehouses, etc.

forlorn *adjective*
1 sad or pitiful: *Her forlorn face told of her suffering.*
2 with little or no expectation of being fulfilled: *forlorn hopes.*
Word Family forlornly *adverb*; **forlornness** *noun*.

form *noun*
1 shape or structure: *the human form.*
2 the particular state, character or appearance of something: *water in the form of steam.*
3 a kind or variety: *a new form of plant life.*
4 condition or fitness: *She's in good form at the moment.*
5 a printed piece of paper with spaces which are to be filled in with appropriate information.
6 a class, especially in a secondary school.
7 a long bench.
8 a mould for concrete.
• **form** *verb*
1 to shape: *He formed the clay into a ball.*
2 to be an element of: *The walls form a square courtyard.*
3 to have as its parts: *The class is formed of 24 students.*
4 to devise: *I have formed a plan for our escape.*
5 to develop: *It's easy to form bad habits.*
6 to arrange, organize: *Let's form a committee.*

formal *adjective*
1 following accepted conventions, forms, etc.: *Please make a formal application in writing.*
2 stiff, not relaxed: *a formal manner.*
3 relating to form rather than content: *He made a formal analysis of the piece of music.*
Word Family formally *adverb*.

formaldehyde (for-**mal**-da-hide) *noun*
a gas (formula HCHO) which has a very irritating smell. It is soluble in water and is used in making plastics and dyes, and in the textile industry.

formality *noun* (*plural* **formalities**)
1 the following of accepted conventions.
2 an established procedure or order.

formalize, formalise *verb*
to give a legal or official form to: *to formalize a relationship by getting married.*
Word Family formalization *noun*.

format *noun*
1 the plan, style or layout of something: *the format of a new television series.*
2 *Computers* the way in which data is displayed or stored.
• **format** *verb* (**formats; formatting; formatted**) *Computers* to put into a format: *to format a disk.*

formation *noun*
1 the process of forming: *the formation of a committee to tackle the problem.*
2 the manner in which something is formed or arranged: *The aircraft flew in close formation over the city.*
3 something which is formed: *a rock formation.*
[Latin *formare* to mould]

formative (**for**-ma-tiv) *adjective*
1 having the power to form or shape: *My first head teacher was a formative influence on my life.*
2 of or relating to formation or development: *the formative years.*

former¹ *adjective*
1 coming before in time, place or order: *a former president.*
2 being the first mentioned of two: *The tiger resembles the leopard, but the former has stripes instead of spots.* Compare LATTER (definition 1).

former² *noun*
a tool used repeatedly to bend a piece of material into a given shape.

formerly *adverb*
in time past: *A convent was formerly called a nunnery.*

Formica (for-**my**-ka) *noun*
(*trademark*) a hard, usually heat-resistant plastic used to cover tables, doors, etc.

formic acid *noun*
a colourless irritant fluid found in ants and nettles, and synthesized for use in the production of textiles and in other industries.
[Latin *formica* ant]

formidable (**for**-mid-a-b'l *or* for-**mid**-a-b'l) *adjective*
1 causing fear and apprehension: *The head teacher had a formidable appearance, but in fact he was a very gentle man.*
2 difficult or requiring great effort to overcome: *Cleaning up the city was a formidable task.*
Word Family formidably *adverb*.
[Latin *formido* a fear]

formula (*form*-yoo-la) *noun* (*plural* **formulas**)

1 an established procedure for doing something, such as a set wording for a ceremony, etc.

2 (*plural* **formulae**) (*form*-yoo-lee) *Maths* a general statement of the relationship between two or more quantities: *d = 2r is a formula stating that the diameter of a circle, d, is always twice the radius, r.*

3 (*plural* **formulae**) (*form*-yoo-lee) also called **chemical formula**. *Chemistry* the representation of atoms in a radical or molecule by the use of symbols for each atom: *The formula for water, H_2O, shows that a molecule of water is composed of two atoms of hydrogen (H) and one atom of oxygen (O).*

4 a liquid food or preparation, e.g. for a baby.

5 *Car racing* any of the classes into which competing cars are divided: *Formula One.*
[Latin]

formulate (*form*-yoo-late) *verb*
1 to express in a systematic or precise way.
2 to state as a formula.
Word Family **formulation** (form-yoo-*lay*-sh'n) *noun*.

fornication (for-ni-*kay*-sh'n) *noun* (*formal*) sexual intercourse between a man and woman who are not married to each other.
Word Family **fornicate** (*for*-ni-kayt) *verb*.
[Latin *fornicis* of a brothel]

forsake *verb* (**forsakes; forsaking; forsook; forsaken**)
to desert, abandon or give up.
Word Family **forsakenly** *adverb*.

forsooth (for-*sooth*) *adverb*
an old word meaning 'indeed' or 'in truth'.

forswear (for-*swair*) *verb* (**forswears; forswearing; forswore; forsworn**)
to swear to give up completely: *After the accident she forswore driving.*

fort *noun*
a strengthened building for defence, such as a castle.
Phrase **hold the fort** to manage or look after affairs during someone's absence.
[Latin *fortis* strong]

forte¹ (*for*-tay) *noun*
something in which a person excels.
[French, strong]

forte² *adverb*
Music loudly.
[Italian]

forth *adverb*
an old word meaning 'out' or 'forward': *from that day forth.* □ *They set forth on their journey.*

forthcoming *adjective*
1 approaching in time: *the forthcoming royal visit.*
2 available when required: *We were ready to start building, but finance was not forthcoming.*
3 helpful with information, etc.: *The secretary was quite rude and not at all forthcoming.*

forthright *adjective*
outspoken or straightforward.
Word Family **forthright** *adverb*; **forthrightness** *noun*.

forthwith *adverb*
immediately.

fortieth ⇨ FORTY.

fortification *noun*
1 the act of fortifying.
2 a building or structure designed to protect a place against attack.

fortify (*for*-ti-fie) *verb* (**fortifies; fortifying; fortified**)
1 to strengthen: *They fortified the castle with a moat.*
2 to encourage: *He fortified himself with a strong drink.*
3 to strengthen wine by adding alcohol.

fortissimo (for-*tiss*-i-mo) *adverb*
Music very loudly.
[Italian]

fortitude (*for*-ti-tewd) *noun*
patient courage or strength.

fortnight *noun*
a period of two weeks.
Word Family **fortnightly** *adjective*, *adverb* once every fortnight.
[from FOURT(een) + NIGHT(s)]

Fortran *noun*
Computers a language mainly used in science applications.
[FOR(mula) TRAN(slation)]

fortress *noun* (*plural* **fortresses**)
a castle or a town that has been strengthened to make it harder to attack.

fortuitous (for-*tew*-i-tus) *adjective*
happening by accident or chance.
Word Family **fortuitously** *adverb*; **fortuitousness** *noun*.
[Latin *forte* by chance]

fortunate (*for*-tew-nit) *adjective*
1 lucky.
2 favourable.
Word Family **fortunately** *adverb*.

fortune *noun*
1 chance or luck regarded as a cause of events and changes in one's life: *How long will our good fortune last?*
2 wealth or riches: *The farmer made a fortune when oil was discovered on his property.*
Phrase **tell someone's fortune** to predict future events in a person's life.

fortune cookie *noun*
American a biscuit containing a piece of paper on which is printed a prediction of future events.

fortune-hunter *noun*
a person who seeks a fortune, especially through marriage.

fortune-teller *noun*
a person who professes to see future events related to another person, e.g. by palmistry.

forty *noun* (*plural* **forties**)
1 a cardinal number, the symbol 40 in Arabic numerals, XL in Roman numerals.
2 (**forties**) the numbers 40 to 49 in a series, such as the years within a century.
Word Family **forty** *adjective*; **fortieth** *noun, adjective*.

forum *noun*
1 (*plural* **forums**) an assembly for discussion, usually public.
2 (*plural* **fora**) *Ancient history* the public square in a Roman town, used for business and meetings.

forward (**for**-w'd) *adjective*
1 near or moving towards the front: *We took up a forward position on the battlefield.*
2 of or for the future: *forward planning.*
3 bold or presumptuous: *a forward young lady.*
● **forward** *adverb* also **forwards**
1 towards the front: *Forward march!*
2 in the usual order: *counting forward.*
3 towards the future: *We've got to look forward now.*
● **forward** *noun Sport* a player in an attacking position.
● **forward** *verb* to send on: *He forwarded the mail to my new address.*
Word Family **forwardly** *adverb*; **forwardness** *noun*.

forwent the past tense of **forgo**.

fossil *noun*
1 *Geology* the remains, impression or trace of any living thing preserved in or as a rock.
2 an old-fashioned person or thing.

Word Family **fossilize, fossilise** *verb*; **fossilization** *noun*.
[Latin *fossilis* dug up]

fossil fuel *noun*
a fuel formed from something living in the past, such as coal or oil.

foster *verb*
1 to encourage or promote the growth or development of: *to foster good relations with one's neighbours.*
2 to bring up a child who is not one's own son or daughter without legal adoption.

foster-child *noun* (*plural* **foster-children**)
a child brought up by someone other than his or her own parents.

foster home *noun*
the home where a foster-child lives.

foster-parent *noun*
someone who takes the place of a parent in bringing up a child.

fought the past tense and past participle of **fight**.

foul (fowl) *adjective*
1 offensive to the senses, e.g. tasting or smelling bad.
2 wicked or obscene: *foul language.*
3 stormy or disagreeable: *foul weather.*
4 *Sport* relating to a foul.
Phrase **foul play** *The police suspect foul play* (= violent crime or murder).
● **foul** *noun Sport* a breaking of the rules in a sport or game.
● **foul** *adverb* in a foul manner.
● **foul** *verb*
1 to make or become foul or dirty.
2 to entangle or become entangled: *The rope has fouled in the pulley.*
3 *Sport* to commit a foul against.
Word Family **foully** *adverb*; **foulness** *noun* the state or quality of being foul.

found[1] the past tense and past participle of **find**.

found[2] *verb*
1 to set up or establish: *to found a kingdom in a new land.*
2 to base: *a story founded on fact.*

found[3] *verb*
to melt metal or glass for moulding and casting.

foundation *noun*
1 the act of founding: *after the foundation of the colony.*
2 anything on which something rests or is based: *the foundations of a building.* □ *The foundation of democracy is the free vote.*

3 an institution supported by donations or a legacy: *a foundation for cancer research.*
4 *Beauty* a cream or liquid, often in the form of a cake or stick, used as a base for other make-up.

foundation garment *noun*
a piece of women's underwear worn to shape or support the body, such as a bra or a corset.

founder[1] *noun*
someone who founds something, e.g. a company or institution.

founder[2] *verb*
1 (of ships) to fill with water and sink.
2 (of plans) to come to nothing.
3 (of horses) to go lame.

foundling *noun*
a child abandoned by his or her parents.

foundry *noun* (*plural* **foundries**)
a factory where metal is moulded and cast.

fount[1] *noun*
a poetic word for a fountain or spring.

fount[2] ⇨ FONT[2].

fountain (**fown**-t'n) *noun*
1 a spring of water, especially an artificially constructed jet of water.
2 a structure for discharging a jet or jets of water.
[Latin *fontis* of a spring]

fountainhead *noun*
a primary source.

fountain pen *noun*
a pen containing a reservoir of ink which flows down the nib on contact with paper.

four (for) *noun*
1 a cardinal number, the symbol 4 in Arabic numerals, IV in Roman numerals.
2 *Cricket* a score of four runs, obtained when a batsman hits the ball to the boundary.
3 *Rowing* a racing boat for a cox and four rowers each with one oar.
4 *Rowing* the crew of such a boat.
Phrase **on all fours** on hands and knees.
Word Family **four** *adjective*; **fourth** *adjective, noun*; **fourthly** *adverb*.

four-poster *noun* also called **four-poster bed.**
a bed with a post at each corner to support a canopy or curtain above it.

fourscore *adjective*
an old word meaning 'four times twenty', 'eighty'.

four-stroke *adjective*
of or relating to an internal-combustion engine in which the fuel is taken into the cylinder, compressed, burnt and released into the exhaust in four successive strokes of the piston. Compare TWO-STROKE.

fourteen *noun*
a cardinal number, the symbol 14 in Arabic numerals, XIV in Roman numerals.
Word Family **fourteen** *adjective*; **fourteenth** *noun, adjective*.

fourth dimension *noun*
Physics time.

fowl *noun* (*plural* **fowl** or **fowls**)
a bird, especially one bred or kept for its flesh and eggs, such as the hen.

fox *noun* (*plural* **foxes**)
1 a small dog-like mammal with reddish-brown fur, a pointed muzzle, upright ears and a bushy tail.
2 (*informal*) a crafty person.
● **fox** *verb* (*informal*) to deceive or trick.

foxglove *noun*
a plant with many trumpet-shaped white or purple flowers on one long stem. The leaves of the foxglove are used to produce a heart stimulant.

foxhound *noun*
a hound bred for fox-hunting.

fox-hunting *noun*
the sport of hunting a fox, using dogs and horses.

fox terrier *noun*
a small wire-haired or smooth-haired dog, once used to dig out foxes.

foxtrot *noun*
a ballroom dance for two people consisting of varied groups of quick or slow short steps.
Word Family **foxtrot** *verb* (**foxtrots; foxtrotting; foxtrotted**).

foxy *adjective* (**foxier; foxiest**)
1 resembling a fox.
2 (*informal*) crafty, cunning.
3 (*American informal*) physically attractive.
Word Family **foxiness** *noun*.

foyer (**foy**-ay) *noun*
an entrance hall, especially in a theatre, hotel or large building.
[French, hearth, home]

fracas (**frak**-ah) *noun* (*plural* **fracas**) (**frak**-ahz)
a noisy disturbance or fight.
[French]

fraction (frak-sh'n) *noun*
1 *Maths* a quantity that is not a whole number, often represented by figures above and below a line, e.g. $\frac{3}{4}$ or $\frac{7}{8}$.
2 a part, especially a small part, of something: *Only a fraction of the members attended the meeting.*
Word Family **fractional** *adjective*; **fractionally** *adverb*.
[Latin *fractus* broken]

fractional distillation ➪ DISTILLATION.

fractious (frak-shus) *adjective*
irritable or bad-tempered.
Word Family **fractiously** *adverb*; **fractiousness** *noun*.

fracture (frak-cha) *noun*
a break or crack, especially in a bone.
• **fracture** *verb*.

fragile (fraj-ile) *adjective*
easily broken or damaged.
Word Family **fragility** (fra-**jil**-i-tee) *noun*.

fragment (frag-m'nt) *noun*
1 a part broken off.
2 an incomplete part: *He overheard fragments of the conversation.*
Word Family **fragment** (frag-**ment**) *verb* to break into fragments; **fragmentary** *adjective*; **fragmentation** *noun* the act or process of fragmenting.

fragrance (fray-gr'nce) *noun*
1 a pleasant smell.
2 a perfume.

fragrant (fray-gr'nt) *adjective*
having a pleasant smell.
Word Family **fragrantly** *adverb*.

frail *adjective*
1 delicate in health: *a frail child.*
2 easily broken: *a frail boat.*
[Latin *fragilis* fragile]

frailty *noun*
weakness.

frame *noun*
1 an enclosing border for a picture, etc.
2 a structure composed of parts joined together: *a bicycle frame.*
3 (**frames**) the part of a pair of glasses which holds the lenses.
4 a small picture on a strip of film.
5 *Snooker* the wooden triangle in which the balls are set at the start of a game.
6 *Snooker* the time it takes to play all the balls into the pockets.
Phrase **frame of mind** a state of mind, a mood.
• **frame** *verb*
1 to provide with a frame.

2 to arrange or give shape to: *He framed the question carefully.*
3 (*informal*) to incriminate with falsely arranged evidence.

frame-up *noun*
(*informal*) a conspiracy to incriminate a person falsely, or to bring about a fraudulent outcome to a contest, etc.

framework *noun*
a structure composed of parts joined together.

franc (frank) *noun*
the basic unit of money in Belgium, France, Switzerland and certain other countries.

franchise (fran-chize) *noun*
a right or privilege, such as the right to vote or the permission given by a manufacturer for a retailer to sell particular goods.

frangipani (fran-ji-**pan**-i) *noun* (*plural* **frangipanis**)
a tree with fragrant, slightly waxy flowers from which perfume is made.

frank[1] *adjective*
open in thought or speech: *a frank answer.*
Word Family **frankly** *adverb*; **frankness** *noun*.

frank[2] *verb*
to mark a letter with an official stamp to show that the postage has been paid.

frankfurter *noun*
a smoked sausage.
[from *Frankfurt-um-Main*, Germany]

frankincense (frank-in-sense) *noun*
a pleasant-smelling gum resin.

frantic *adjective*
nearly mad with grief, excitement, pain, etc.
Word Family **frantically** *adverb*.
[Greek *phrenetikos* having inflammation of the brain]

fraternal (fra-ter-n'l) *adjective*
of or like a brother or brothers: *fraternal feelings.* □ *I gave him a fraternal hug.*
fraternal twins ➪ TWIN *noun*.
Word Family **fraternally** *adverb*.

The word **fraternal** means 'brotherly' but there is no word *frater* in English. There is a range of words in English where an adjective has come from one language and the corresponding noun from another. *Fraternal* has come from Latin *frater* (brother); *brother* has come from Old English *brothor* and is very like the German *Bruder* and the Dutch *broeder*.

fraternity (fra-**tern**-i-tee) *noun* (*plural* **fraternities**)
1 a group of people who share an interest or purpose: *the medical fraternity.*
2 *American* a society of male students. Compare SORORITY.

fraternize, fraternise (**frat**-ern-ize) *verb*
to associate with others in a friendly way.
Word Family **fraternization** (frat-ern-eye-**zay**-sh'n) *noun.*

fratricide (**frat**-ri-side) *noun*
1 *Law* the crime of killing one's brother or sister.
2 *Law* a person who does this.
[Latin *frater* brother + *caedere* to kill]

Frau (*rhymes with* cow) *noun* (*plural* **Frauen**) (**frow**-en)
the title for a married German woman.

fraud (frawd) *noun*
1 the act of deliberately deceiving another person, especially for unlawful gain.
2 a person who is not what he or she pretends to be.
Word Family **fraudulent** (**fraw**-dew-l'nt) *adjective* deceiving, dishonest; **fraudulently** *adverb*; **fraudulence** *noun.*
[Latin *fraudis* of deception]

fraught (frawt) *adjective*
involving or accompanied by something undesirable: *an undertaking fraught with danger.*

Fräulein (**fraw**-line *or* **froy**-line) *noun*
the title for an unmarried German woman.

fray¹ *verb*
1 (of cloth) to become worn, so that there are loose threads.
2 (of a person's temper) to become strained: *Tempers became frayed at the club.*

fray² *noun*
(**the fray**) a noisy dispute or fight.

frazzled *adjective*
1 exhausted.
2 burnt and shrivelled.

freak *noun*
1 also called **freak of nature**. a very unusual person or animal: *The calf with five legs was a freak.*
2 an unusual event: *By some freak, the car stayed on the road after it skidded.*
3 (*informal*) someone who is very keen on a particular thing: *a gym freak.*
• **freak** *verb*
Phrase **freak out** to react in an extreme way, or make someone react in an extreme way: *The film freaked her out.*
Word Family **freakish** *adjective.*

freckle *noun*
a small brown mark or spot on the skin.
Word Family **freckly** *adjective.*

free *adjective* (**freer; freest**)
1 not restrained by authority or external forces: *a free citizen.* □ *free choice.*
2 without payment or charge: *a free ride.*
3 unoccupied.
4 not attached.
5 generous, ready: *very free with his advice.*
Phrases **free and easy** casual or relaxed.
free of, free from without: *Your teeth are free of decay.*
• **free** *verb* (**frees; freeing; freed**) to set or make free.
Word Family **free, freely** *adverb.*

freebooter *noun*
a buccaneer or pirate.

Free Church *noun*
a Nonconformist denomination of the Christian Church.

freedom *noun*
the state or condition of being free: *fighting for freedom.* □ *freedom of speech.* □ *The tight clothes allowed her little freedom of movement.*

free enterprise *noun*
commerce or private business in which competition may occur with a minimum of government control.

free fall *noun*
movement caused by the force of gravity only, such as before the parachute opens in a parachute descent.

free-for-all *noun*
a dispute or contest which is open to everyone.

freehand *adjective, adverb*
done by hand without the aid of instruments or measurement: *a freehand sketch.*

freehold *noun*
Law a house or land which is owned, not rented, or the ownership of such property. Compare LEASEHOLD.
Word Family **freeholder** *noun* an owner of freehold property.

free house *noun*
a public house free to sell any brand of beer. Compare TIED HOUSE.

freelance (**free**-lahnce) *noun*
1 a person, e.g. a journalist or artist, who sells work to employers rather than working on a full-time basis for a salary.
2 *Medieval history* a wandering knight.
Word Family **freelance** *verb* to work as a freelance; **freelance** *adjective.*

freely *adverb* ⇨ FREE.

Freemason *noun*
a member of a secret order which promotes mutual assistance and brotherly love among its members.

free port *noun*
a port without taxes, open to all traders.

freepost *noun*
a postal service by which the charge for posting is borne by the organization or firm to which the communication is sent and not by the sender.

free-range egg *noun*
an egg laid by a free-range hen.

free-range hen *noun*
a hen free to range for food. Compare BATTERY HEN.

freesia (**free-***zh*a) *noun*
a plant with fragrant white or yellow flowers growing from a corm.
[after *F. H. T. Freese*, 1795-1876, a German physician]

freestyle *noun*
Swimming a race in which competitors may use any style of swimming.

freethinker *noun*
a person who remains independent of or unaffected by tradition, authority, etc.

free trade *noun*
international trade unrestricted by taxes, quotas or other forms of protection by government regulations.

free verse ⇨ VERSE.

freeway *noun*
American a motorway.

freewheel *verb*
to coast on a bicycle without pedalling.

free will *noun*
1 the power to choose or decide freely.
2 *Philosophy* the doctrine that people are free to work out their own destiny.

freeze *verb* (**freezes; freezing; froze; frozen**)
1 to change into ice or a solid.
2 to become blocked or ineffective due to frost, ice, etc.: *The pipes froze.*
3 to be very cold: *You will freeze without a coat.*
4 to be unable to move: *She froze with horror.*
5 to fix: *The government froze wages for six weeks.*
● **freeze** *noun*
1 an act of freezing.
2 (*informal*) a period of intensely cold weather.

freeze-dry *verb* (**freeze-dries; freeze-drying; freeze-dried**)
to dry food or chemicals while frozen to prepare them for longer periods of storage.

freezer *noun*
a refrigerator or part of a refrigerator where food is kept frozen.

freezing point *noun*
the constant temperature, at a given pressure, at which a liquid freezes.

freight (**frate**) *noun*
1 goods which are transported as cargo.
2 the carrying of goods or cargo by land, sea or air.
3 the charge for carrying freight.
Word Family **freight** *verb* to carry or send by freight; **freighter** *noun* a ship or aircraft which carries freight.

French bean *noun*
the green pod of a tall climbing plant, eaten as a vegetable.

French chalk *noun*
powdered talc used in dry-cleaning, soap manufacture, toilet products, etc.

French horn *noun*
Music a brass wind instrument consisting of a long coiled tube ending in a flared bell.

French seam *noun*
Needlework a seam sewn on both sides of the material.

French window *noun*
one of a pair of glass doors which open outwards.

frenetic (fra-**net**-ik) *adjective*
frantic or highly excited.
Word Family **frenetically** *adverb*.

frenzy *noun* (*plural* **frenzies**)
an extreme excitement, agitation or activity.
Word Family **frenzied** *adjective* highly excited or maddened.
[Greek *phrenitis* inflammation of the brain]

Freon (**free**-on) *noun*
(*trademark*) *Chemistry* any of a group of fluorocarbon monomers used as refrigerants and solvents.

frequency (**free**-kw'n-see) *noun* (*plural* **frequencies**)
1 the number of times something occurs, especially in a particular interval of time, space, etc.
2 the state or fact of being frequent: *The frequency of her visits became tedious.*

3 *Music, Physics* the number of oscillations per second of a wave or wave-like phenomenon, including sound, light, etc. [Latin *frequens* crowded, repeated]

frequency modulation *noun*
a method used in very high frequency (VHF) broadcasting in which the frequency of the transmitted wave is varied. Compare AMPLITUDE MODULATION.

frequent (**free**-kw'nt) *adjective*
1 occurring often or at short intervals: *She has frequent attacks of asthma.*
2 regular, constant: *He is a frequent visitor at their house.*
● **frequent** (free-**kwent**) *verb* to go often to a place: *As a collector he frequents second-hand bookshops.*
Word Family **frequently** *adverb*.

fresco *noun* (*plural* **frescoes** or **frescos**)
a painting done with water-based paint on a plastered wall, usually when it is still damp.
[Italian, fresh]

fresh *adjective*
1 recently made, obtained, arrived, etc.: *They get fresh milk and eggs from the farm.* □ *a young doctor fresh from medical school.*
2 full of energy or brightness: *I feel quite fresh after that sleep.*
3 not salt: *fresh water.*
4 bright: *fresh colours.*
5 cool: *fresh autumn days.*
6 healthy: *a fresh complexion.*
7 cheeky: *Don't get fresh with me, young lady.*
Word Family **freshly** *adverb*; **freshness** *noun*.

freshen *verb*
1 to make or become fresh.
2 (of a wind) to increase in strength or become cold.
Phrase **freshen up 1** to wash and change one's clothes, etc. **2** to make fresher.

fresher *noun* also called **freshman**.
(*informal*) a first-year student at a college or university.

freshwater *adjective*
of, consisting of or living in fresh water: *a freshwater fish.*

fret¹ *verb* (**frets; fretting; fretted**)
to worry or be anxious, unhappy or irritable: *She's fretting about the keys she lost.*
Word Family **fretful** *adjective* irritable or given to fretting; **fretfully** *adverb*; **fretfulness** *noun*.

fret² *noun*
an ornamental band or design consisting of repeated geometrical lines or figures.
Word Family **fretwork** *noun*; **fretted** *adjective* decorated with frets.

fret³ *noun*
Music a wooden or metal ridge set across the fingerboard of a stringed instrument.
Word Family **fretted** *adjective* having frets.

fretsaw *noun*
a saw with a long fine blade set in a frame, used for cutting ornamental work in wood.

Freudian slip (froy-dee-an slip) *noun*
a slip of the tongue which may reveal a person's unconscious feelings.
[after *Sigmund Freud*, 1856-1939, an Austrian psychoanalyst]

friable (**fry**-a-b'l) *adjective*
crumbly or easily crumbled: *Sandstone is often friable.*
Word Family **friableness, friability** (fry-a-**bil**-i-tee) *noun*.

friar (**fry**-a) *noun*
Roman Catholicism a brother of certain religious orders, especially those orders which work among the people and not in a monastery, and which formerly lived by begging.
Word Family **friary** *noun* (*plural* **friaries**) a community of friars.
[Latin *frater* brother]

fricassée *noun*
a dish of veal or chicken cut up and cooked in a white sauce.
[French]

friction *noun*
1 the rubbing of one object or surface against another.
2 *Physics* the forces which tend to prevent the movement of one surface over another resulting from the nature of the two surfaces.
3 conflict: *Her actions caused much friction in the family.*
Word Family **frictional** *adjective* relating to or produced by friction; **frictionally** *adverb*; **frictionless** *adjective*.
[Latin *frictus* rubbed]

Friday *noun*
the sixth day of the week, after Thursday and before Saturday.

fridge *noun*
a refrigerator.

friend (frend) *noun*
a person whom one knows and likes well.

friendly *adjective* (**friendlier; friendliest**)
1 like a friend.
2 pleasant.
3 on one's side in a war.
Word Family **friendliness** *noun*;
friendship *noun*; **friendless** *adjective*.

friendly fire *noun*
accidental assault or attack by one's own
side: *soldiers killed by friendly fire*.

friendly society *noun* (*plural* **friendly
societies**)
a society in which voluntary subscriptions
from the members are used to provide
them with assistance in case of illness, etc.

Friesian (**free-***zh*'n) *noun*
any of a breed of black-and-white dairy
cattle which originated in Friesland in the
Netherlands.

frieze (freeze) *noun*
a decorative strip or band on a wall.

frigate (**frig-**it) *noun*
1 a small destroyer used to escort other
ships.
2 a medium-sized warship used from the
17th century to the 19th century.

frigate bird *noun*
a tropical seabird with long wings, able to
fly long distances.

fright *noun*
1 sudden intense fear, usually as a reaction
to something threatening: *The huge shadow
on the wall gave him an awful fright*.
2 a strange or grotesque sight: *You look a
fright in that old coat*.

frighten *verb*
to terrify or fill with fear.
Word Family **frightened** *adjective*;
frightening *adjective*; **frighteningly**
adverb.

frightful *adjective*
1 shocking, revolting or causing fright.
2 (*informal*) bad or unpleasant.
Word Family **frightfully** *adverb*;
frightfulness *noun*.

frigid (**frij-**id) *adjective*
1 intensely cold.
2 unfriendly, cold.
3 sexually unresponsive.
Word Family **frigidly** *adverb*; **frigidity**
(fri-**jid-**i-tee), **frigidness** *noun*.
[Latin *frigus* cold]

frill *noun*
1 an ornamental strip or border, usually
gathered, used for trimming, etc.: *a hem
with frills*.

2 something unnecessary or merely
ornamental: *a cheap flight with no frills*.
Word Family **frilly** *adjective*.

fringe *noun*
1 an ornamental border with hanging
threads, especially on a carpet, tablecloth,
etc.
2 the hair falling over the forehead.
3 the edge of something: *a cottage on the
fringe of the forest*.
Word Family **fringed** *adjective*.

fringe benefit *noun*
a benefit received by an employee in
addition to wages or salary, such as a
pension, the use of a car, etc.

frippery *noun* (*plural* **fripperies**)
unnecessary decoration or display, as in
one's manner of dress.

Frisbee (**friz-**bee) *noun*
(*trademark*) a light plastic disc thrown with
a spinning motion as a game.

frisk *verb*
1 to search a person for concealed
weapons or drugs by running the hands
rapidly over the clothes.
2 to move about with quick eager playful
movements: *The dogs frisked all over the
picnic area*.
Word Family **frisk** *noun*; **frisky** *adjective*
(**friskier; friskiest**) lively or playful;
friskily *adverb*; **friskiness** *noun*.

fritter[1] *verb*
to waste or squander little by little: *He
frittered away his money on gambling*.

fritter[2] *noun*
a piece of food, such as a slice of meat or
fruit, coated in a batter and deep-fried.
[Latin *frictus* fried]

frivolous (**friv-**a-lus) *adjective*
1 of little importance: *The chairman
dismissed the motion as frivolous*.
2 silly, not sensible: *a frivolous person*.
Word Family **frivolously** *adverb*;
frivolousness *noun*, **frivolity** (fri-**vol-**i-
tee) *noun* the state or quality of being
frivolous.
[Latin *frivolus* trifling]

frizz *verb*
(of hair) to form into small tight waves or
curls.
Word Family **frizz** *noun* tightly curled
hair; **frizzy** *adjective* (**frizzier; frizziest**)
consisting of tight curls; **frizziness** *noun*.

fro ⇨ TO.

frock *noun*
a woman's or girl's dress: *a cotton frock*.

frock coat *noun*
(*formerly*) a coat worn by men, close-fitting to the waist and flaring out to the knees, now worn sometimes for weddings.

frog[1] *noun*
a web-footed amphibious animal without a tail, which moves by jumping.
Phrase **have a frog in the throat** to be hoarse.

frog[2] *noun*
a decorative fastener, consisting of a button passed through a long narrow loop.

frog[3] *noun*
a horny growth in the underside of a horse's hoof.

frogman *noun* (*plural* **frogmen**)
a person trained and equipped for underwater work, such as reconnaissance, demolition, etc.

frogmarch *verb*
to push or carry someone with his or her arms held behind the back.

frolic *verb* (**frolics; frolicking; frolicked**)
to play merrily and joyfully.
Word Family **frolic** *noun* playful fun or merriment; **frolicsome** *adjective* playful or full of fun.

from *preposition*
a word used to indicate the following:
1 a starting point in space, time or order: *driving from Oxford to Cambridge.* □ *He came from eighth place to win.*
2 removal or absence: *She is away from school today.*
3 release: *freedom from hunger.*
4 difference: *I can't tell one twin from the other.*
5 source or origin: *a letter from his uncle.*
6 reason or cause: *His mother suffered from bad eyesight.*

fromage frais (fro-ma*zh* fray) *noun*
1 a smooth white cheese made from curds.
2 a low-fat dessert made from this with fruit etc. added.
[French, fresh cheese]

frond *noun*
Biology the large feather-like leaf of a fern.

front (frunt) *noun*
1 the foremost or most important side, surface or part: *The entrance is at the front of the building.* □ *The title is at the front of the book.*
2 a place or position directly before anything.
3 *Military* the line or area between opposing armies when fighting is taking place.

4 a group of people joined together for a particular purpose, usually political: *the National Front.*
5 *Weather* a boundary between two air masses of different density.
6 an appearance or bearing: *He put on a bold front to cover up his shyness.*
7 a cover: *The import business was a front for the spy ring.*

cold front *Weather* a front in which advancing cold air near the ground wedges under and displaces warmer air.

occluded front *Weather* a situation in which a cold front overtakes a warm front, forcing the warm air up to a higher level.

warm front *Weather* a front in which advancing warm air near the ground rises over colder air.

● **front** *verb*
1 to face in the direction of: *Their house fronts the ocean.*
2 to be at the front of: *fronting an organization.*
3 to present: *fronting the TV news.*
4 to serve as a front for.
Word Family **front** *adjective* of or situated at the front; **frontal** *adjective* **1** of or to the front. **2** relating to the forehead.
[Latin *frontis* of the forehead]

frontage (**frun**-tij) *noun*
1 the front of a building or block of land.
2 the land or position adjacent to a street, river, etc.

frontbencher *noun*
Parliament a member who is a minister or an Opposition spokesman, and who sits at the front of the chamber. Compare BACK-BENCHER.

frontier (frun-**teer**) *noun*
1 a border or region which forms a dividing line, as between settled and unsettled areas.
2 an area that has not been fully explored: *Cancer research is one of the frontiers of medical science.*
Word Family **frontiersman, frontierswoman** *noun* a person who lives on a frontier.

frontispiece (**frun**-tis-peece) *noun*
an illustration facing the title page of a book.

frost *noun*
minute particles of frozen moisture formed when the air in contact with the ground is below freezing point. Compare HOAR FROST; RIME[2].
Word Family **frost** *verb* **1** to freeze. **2** to cover with frost or frosting.

frostbite noun
Medicine a freezing of tissues due to extreme cold, causing pale firm skin, usually on the toes, fingers or face, and in extreme cases resulting in gangrene.
Word Family **frostbitten** *adjective*.

frosting noun
1 *American* icing.
2 a roughened or speckled surface on glass or metal.

frosty adjective (**frostier; frostiest**)
1 cold enough for frost to form: *a frosty morning*.
2 covered with frost: *frosty grass*.
3 hostile, unfriendly: *There was a frosty silence between them*.
Word Family **frostily** *adverb*; **frostiness** *noun*.

froth noun
a mass of small bubbles or foam.
• **froth** *verb*
1 to give out froth: *to froth at the mouth*.
2 to cover with froth or foam.
Word Family **frothy** *adjective* (**frothier; frothiest**); **frothily** *adverb*; **frothiness** *noun*.

frown verb
to draw the brows together expressing displeasure, thoughtfulness, etc.
Phrase **frown on, frown upon** to disapprove of.
Word Family **frown** *noun*; **frowningly** *adverb*.

frowzy (frow-zee) adjective (**frowzier; frowziest**) also **frowsy** (frowsier; frowsiest)
untidy and dirty.
Word Family **frowzily** *adverb*; **frowziness** *noun*.

froze the past tense of **freeze**.

frozen adjective
1 made into or covered with ice: *a frozen lake*.
2 preserved by freezing: *frozen peas*.
• **frozen** the past participle of **freeze**.

fructify (fruk-ti-fie) verb (**fructifies; fructifying; fructified**)
to bear fruit.
Word Family **fructification** (fruk-ti-fi-kay-sh'n) *noun*.

fructose (fruk-tose) noun also called **fruit sugar**.
the sugar (formula $C_6H_{12}O_6$), found in overripe fruit, flower nectar and honey.

frugal (froo-g'l) adjective
careful or economical.

Word Family **frugally** *adverb*; **frugality** (froo-**gal**-i-tee), **frugalness** *noun*.

fruit (rhymes with hoot) noun
1 the edible part of a plant developed from a flower, such as an apple, etc.
2 *Biology* the fertilized and developed ovary of a plant.
3 a product or result: *the fruit of many years of hard work*.
Word Family **fruit** *verb* to bear fruit; **fruitful** *adjective* 1 bearing fruit abundantly. 2 useful or productive; **fruitless** *adjective*; **fruitlessly** *adverb*; **fruitlessness** *noun*.
[Latin *fructus* the produce, profit]

fruit fly noun (plural **fruit flies**)
a small fly, the larvae of which cause damage to fruit.

fruition (froo-ish-'n) noun
the final achievement of a desired result: *It will still be some time before the plan comes to fruition*.
[Latin *frui* to enjoy]

fruit machine noun
a coin-operated gambling machine in which a lever spins drums bearing symbols, such as fruit, and dividends are paid for certain combinations of these when they come to rest.

fruit sugar ⇨ FRUCTOSE.

fruity adjective (**fruitier; fruitiest**)
1 having the taste or smell of fruit.
2 rich: *His fruity voice filled the hall*.

frump noun
a woman who is dressed in old-fashioned or unattractive clothes.
Word Family **frumpish, frumpy** *adjective*; **frumpishly, frumpily** *adverb*; **frumpishness, frumpiness** *noun*.

frustrate verb
to disappoint or thwart one's hopes, plans, etc.
Word Family **frustration** *noun*.
[Latin *frustra* in vain]

fry¹ verb (**fries; frying; fried**)
to cook in hot fat or oil.

fry² plural noun
1 newly hatched fishes.
2 young or small animals.

FTSE index (**fut**-si in-deks) noun also called **FT index**.
an index produced by a newspaper, the *Financial Times*, based on an average of 100 sets of shares, giving an indication of the daily movements of the stock market.

fuchsia (*few*-sha) *noun*
a garden shrub with drooping trumpet-shaped, usually red or purple flowers. [after *L. Fuchs*, 1501-1566, a German botanist]

fuddled *adjective*
confused or muddled.

fuddy-duddy *noun* (*plural* **fuddy-duddies**)
(*informal*) a prim, old-fashioned or boring person.

fudge *noun*
a soft sweet made by boiling milk, sugar and butter.
• **fudge** *verb* to make vague or unclear, especially to hide something: *They have fudged the issue.*

fuel (*few*-'l) *noun*
a substance used for producing heat and energy.
Word Family **fuel** *verb* (**fuels; fuelling; fuelled**) to provide with fuel.

fuel injection *noun*
a method of spraying fuel directly into the manifold of an engine instead of using a carburettor.

fug *noun*
(*informal*) a smoke-filled or stifling atmosphere.

fugitive (*few*-ji-tiv) *noun*
a person who flees or runs away. [Latin *fugere* to flee]

fugue (fewg) *noun*
Music a contrapuntal composition for several parts, each of which imitates the previous one. [Latin *fuga* flight]

fulcrum ➭ LEVER.

fulfil (ful-*fill*) *verb* (*American* **fulfill**) (**fulfils; fulfilling; fulfilled**)
1 to satisfy: *His desire for fame was fulfilled by the success of his first novel.*
2 to carry out: *to fulfil a promise.*
Word Family **fulfilment** *noun*.

full *adjective*
1 having or containing as much as possible.
2 rich, strong: *His full voice drowned out the piano.*
3 having wide loose folds: *a full skirt.*
4 complete: *the full story.*
5 busy, active: *a full life.*
Phrases **full of** *She's so full of the wedding plans she hardly knows what's going on around her* (= absorbed in). **full of oneself**

She is rather bossy and full of herself (= conceited).
• **full** *adverb*
1 completely.
2 directly: *The ball hit him full in the face.*
• **full** *noun*
Phrase **in full** completely.
Word Family **fully** *adverb* to a complete or full degree; **fullness, fulness** *noun*.

fullback *noun*
Football the player who defends his or her team's goal.

full-blooded *adjective*
vigorous and healthy.

full-blown *adjective*
completely developed: *There was one full-blown rose on the bush.* □ *The discussion turned into a full-blown argument.*

full board *noun*
an arrangement at a hotel, etc. in which one gets a room, breakfast, lunch and dinner. Compare HALF BOARD.

full-bodied *adjective*
having all possible strength, flavour, etc.

full house *noun*
1 a theatre with all the seats sold for a performance.
2 *Cards* a hand in poker consisting of three of a kind and a pair, such as three kings and two tens.

full moon *noun*
the moon when a complete circle can be seen.

full nelson ➭ NELSON.

fullness ➭ FULL.

full stop *noun*
a punctuation mark (.) used at the end of a sentence or in an abbreviation.

full-time *adjective*
taking all of one's time or normal working hours.

fully ➭ FULL.

fulmar *noun*
a grey and white seabird often seen following trawlers in northern waters.

fulminate (*ful*-mi-nate) *verb*
to make loud or violent denunciations: *He was fulminating against the government.*
Word Family **fulmination** (ful-mi-*nay*-sh'n) *noun*.
[Latin *fulminare* to hurl thunderbolts]

fulness ➭ FULL.

fulsome (*ful*-s'm) *adjective*
excessive in an insincere way.

Word Family **fulsomely** *adverb*;
fulsomeness *noun*.

fumble *verb*
to feel, grope about or handle clumsily: *He fumbled at his shirt button.* □ *She fumbled the catch.*
Word Family **fumble** *noun*; **fumbler** *noun* a person who fumbles.

fume *noun*
a strong-smelling smoke, gas, etc.
• **fume** *verb* to give off fumes.
Figurative He fumed with indignation (= burnt, raged).
[Latin *fumus* smoke]

fumigate (few-mi-gate) *verb*
to use smoke and fumes to disinfect.
Word Family **fumigation** (few-mi-**gay**-sh'n) *noun*.

fun *noun*
playfulness or amusing enjoyment.
Phrase **make fun of, poke fun at** *You should not make fun of that poor old man* (= ridicule).
• **fun** *adjective* (*informal*) amusing, enjoyable: *a fun time.* □ *a fun person.*

> **Fun** is one of several words in modern English which have begun to be used as a different part of speech. Until recently *fun* was used as a noun but the adjective is becoming increasingly common in informal situations. New words formed in this way are often verbs, e.g. the verb formed from the noun *party*, as in *They had been partying all night.*

function (funk-sh'n) *noun*
1 the special purpose or working use of anything: *Your function as captain is to lead and inspire the team.* □ *An important function of Blackpool is as a holiday resort.*
2 a formal ceremony or gathering: *The hall is available for private functions.*
• **function** *verb* to perform or carry out one's normal work or function.
Word Family **functional** *adjective* 1 of or designed for a particular function. 2 in working order; **functionally** *adverb*.
[Latin *functio* a performance (of duty, etc.)]

functionary *noun* (*plural* **functionaries**)
an official.

fund *noun*
1 a supply or stock of something, especially money: *He has an unlimited fund of jokes.*
2 (**funds**) available money: *What funds do you have for the holiday?*

• **fund** *verb* to find money or funds for: *How was the school hall funded?*
[Latin *fundus* a piece of land]

fundamental *adjective*
1 being a basis or starting point of something complex: *This course will give you a fundamental knowledge of the language.*
2 affecting or having to do with the basis of something: *We need fundamental changes before the organization will make a profit.*
Word Family **fundamentally** *adverb*.
[Latin *fundamentum* a foundation]

fundamental particle ⇨ ELEMENTARY PARTICLE.

funeral (few-na-r'l) *noun*
1 a ceremony for the burial or cremation of a dead person.
2 a funeral procession.
Word Family **funereal** (few-**neer**-i-al) *adjective* 1 of or relating to a funeral.
2 gloomy or mournful.
[Latin *funeris* of a burial]

fungicide (funj-i-side *or* fung-gi-side) *noun*
a substance that kills fungi.

fungus *noun* (*plural* **fungi** (**fung**-guy *or* funj-eye) *or* **funguses**)
a simple plant, such as a mould, mushroom or toadstool, which lacks chlorophyll.
Word Family **fungal, fungous** *adjective* of or relating to a fungus; **fungoid** *adjective* of or growing like a fungus.
[Latin, mushroom]

funicular railway (few-**nik**-yoo-la *or* fa-**nik**-yoo-la) *noun*
a railway system of cable-linked trains for steep slopes.
[Latin *funiculus* a cord]

funk *noun*
(*informal*) a state of terror or extreme nervousness.

funnel *noun*
1 a tube with a wide mouth narrowing to a thin outlet, often used to pour liquid into bottles.
2 the metal chimney on ships and steam engines.
• **funnel** *verb* (**funnels; funnelling; funnelled**) to converge to or into a particular place, etc.: *The police funnelled the angry crowd into a blind alley.*

funny *adjective* (**funnier; funniest**)
1 causing laughter and amusement.
2 strange or peculiar.

Word Family **funnily** *adverb*; **funniness** *noun*.

funny bone *noun*
(*informal*) *Anatomy* a ridge on the humerus near the elbow over which a nerve passes.

fun run *noun*
(*informal*) a run in which participants run for entertainment or to raise funds for charity rather than competitively.

fur *noun*
1 the soft thick hair of some animals, such as the beaver or rabbit.
2 a piece of clothing made of treated animal fur.
3 a soft coating on a surface, especially on the tongue.
Word Family **furry** *adjective* (**furrier**; **furriest**) covered with or resembling fur; **furriness** *noun*.

furbish *verb*
to polish or make as if new.

furious (fyor-i-us) *adjective*
1 extremely or violently angry.
2 intense, uncontrolled: *Furious waves lashed the beach.*
Word Family **furiously** *adverb*.
[Latin *furiosus* frantic]

furl *verb*
to roll up tightly.

furlong *noun*
a unit of length equal to one-eighth of a mile, about 201 m.
[Old English *furh* furrow + *long* long, the length of a furrow in a common field]

furlough (**fir**-lo) *noun*
Military a holiday or leave of absence.

furnace (**fir**-niss) *noun*
a structure containing a fire of intense heat, used for generating steam, melting ore, etc.

furnish *verb*
to supply or equip, especially with appliances, furniture, etc.

furnishings *plural noun*
the furniture and other items, e.g. carpets and curtains, used in a house or room.

furniture (**fir**-nich-er) *noun*
movable objects for use in buildings, such as chairs or tables.

furore (**few**-ror *or* few-**ror**-i) *noun*
1 a general uproar or disorder.
2 an outburst of enthusiasm, anger or excitement.
[Italian, raging]

furrier (**furr**-i-a) *noun*
a person who treats, prepares, buys or sells furs.

furriness ⇨ FUR.

furrow *noun*
1 a narrow trench made in the ground, especially by a plough.
2 anything which resembles a furrow: *the furrows of his brow.*
Word Family **furrow** *verb*.

furry ⇨ FUR.

further (**fir**-ther) *adverb*, *adjective*
1 a comparative of **far**.
2 in addition or more: *This theatre will be closed until further notice.*
3 furthermore.
• **further** *verb* to promote or help move forward: *He furthered the cause of social reform with progressive legislation.*
Word Family **furtherance** *noun* the act of furthering.

> ⚠ On the use of *farther* and *further* ⇨ FARTHER.

further education *noun*
education at a college. Compare HIGHER EDUCATION.

furthermore *adverb*
also, besides: *It's too cold to go out, and furthermore, it's going to rain.*

furthest
a superlative of **far**.

furtive (**fir**-tiv) *adjective*
secretive or sly.
Word Family **furtively** *adverb*; **furtiveness** *noun*.
[Latin *furtivus* stolen]

fury (fyor-ee) *noun*
a state of violent excitement or anger.
[Latin *Furia* a spirit of madness]

furze *noun*
gorse.

fuse¹ (fewz) *noun*
1 a device which protects electric circuits by melting when the current exceeds a specified limit.
2 any of various devices, such as a cord soaked in a combustible substance, used to ignite explosives.
• **fuse** *verb* (of an electric circuit) to burn out.

fuse² *verb*
1 to combine or join by melting together.
2 to melt or become liquid.
Word Family **fusible** *adjective* able to be melted.
[Latin *fusus* poured]

fuselage (fewz-a-lah*zh*) *noun*
the body of an aircraft.
[French *fuselé* spindle-shaped]

fusilier (fewz-a-**leer**) *noun*
(*formerly*) a soldier armed with a musket
or flintlock.
[French *fusil* gun]

fusillade (fewz-i-lade *or* fewz-i-lahd) *noun*
a simultaneous or continuous discharge of
firearms.

fusion (few-*zh*'n) *noun*
1 the act of fusing, melting or joining.
2 the state of being fused or melted.
3 ⇨ NUCLEAR FUSION.

fuss *noun*
an unnecessary display of excitement or
anxiety.
Word Family fuss *verb*.

fusspot *noun*
(*informal*) a person who is always making a
fuss.

fussy *adjective* (**fussier; fussiest**)
1 too concerned or particular about
details, etc.
2 full of elaborate or unnecessary detail: *a
fussy dress with flowers, ribbons and false
buttons.*
Word Family fussily *adverb*; **fussiness**
noun.

fustian *noun*
a coarse strong cotton fabric.

fusty *adjective* (**fustier; fustiest**)
1 mouldy or stale.
2 old fashioned or extremely conservative.
Word Family fustiness *noun*.

futile (**few**-tile) *adjective*
having no use, effect or result: *Her efforts to
clean the house were made futile by the
children running in and out.*
Word Family futilely *adverb*; **futility**
(few-**til**-i-tee) *noun*.
[Latin *futilis* leaky]

futon (**foo**-ton) *noun*
a padded quilt laid on the floor or on a
mattress or light frame, for sleeping on.
[Japanese]

future (**few**-cher) *noun*
1 the time or events still to come.
2 a chance of success: *There doesn't seem to
be any future in their relationship.*
• **future** *adjective*
1 of or occurring at a later time than the
present: *What are your future plans?*
2 *Grammar* (of a verb form) used when
referring to something that will happen in
the future.
[Latin *futurus* about to be]

futuristic *adjective*
relating to things that are likely to happen
or be produced in the future.

fuzz¹ *noun*
a fluffy frizzy substance, especially hair.

fuzz² *noun*
(*informal*) the police.

fuzzy *adjective* (**fuzzier; fuzziest**)
1 covered with or resembling fuzz.
2 unclear or blurred.
Word Family fuzzily *adverb*; **fuzziness**
noun.

Gg

gab verb (**gabs; gabbing; gabbed**)
(informal) to talk idly or too much.

gabble verb
to speak so rapidly that one cannot be
understood.
Word Family gabble noun; **gabbler** noun
a person who gabbles.

gaberdine (gab-a-**deen**) noun also
gabardine
a strong fabric usually made from wool,
cotton or viscose, often used for raincoats.
[Old French *gallevardine* pilgrim's robe]

gable (rhymes with table) noun
any triangular section of an outside wall
between sloping roofs.
Word Family gabled adjective.

gad verb (**gads; gadding; gadded**)
Phrase **gad about** (informal) to travel or
move about restlessly or excitedly.
Word Family gadabout noun.

gadfly noun (plural **gadflies**)
1 any of various kinds of fly which bite
cattle and horses.
2 (informal) a person who provokes or
irritates another person.

gadget (gaj-et) noun
any small device or tool, usually a
mechanical one.
Word Family gadgetry noun gadgets.

Gaelic (gay-lik) adjective
of or relating to the inhabitants of
Scotland and Ireland, and their languages.

gaff¹ noun
1 a strong hook with a long handle, used
for landing large fish.
2 *Nautical* a spar on the top of a sail.

gaff² noun
Phrase **blow the gaff** (informal) to let out
a secret.

gaffe (gaf) noun also **gaff**
a blunder, e.g. an indiscreet act or remark.

gaffer noun
1 (informal) an old man.
2 (informal) a boss.

3 a chief lighting man in the film industry.
[short form of *godfather*]

gag¹ noun
anything placed in or over the mouth to
prevent speech, sound, etc.
• **gag** verb (**gags; gagging; gagged**)
1 to stop from speaking.
2 to choke.

gag² noun
a joke, especially an impromptu joke made
on stage.

gaga (gah-gah) adjective
(informal) senile or childishly foolish.
[French, mad]

gaggle noun
1 a flock of geese.
2 any noisy group.

gaiety (gay-a-tee) noun
the state of being happy and joyful.

gaily adverb ⇨ GAY.

gain verb
1 to obtain something wanted or needed:
You will gain a slight advantage if you do this.
2 to increase: *I have gained two kilos in
weight.*
3 (of a clock) to get ahead of the correct
time: *My watch has gained five minutes.*
4 (formal) to reach or arrive at: *We gained
the summit of the mountain.*
Phrase **gain on, gain upon** to get closer
to something or someone being pursued.
• **gain** noun an increase, especially of
money, possessions, etc.

gainful adjective
profitable.
Word Family gainfully adverb.

gainsay verb (**gainsays; gainsaying;
gainsaid**)
(formal) to deny.

gait noun
a manner of moving, especially walking: *a
shuffling gait.*

gaiter (gay-ta) noun
a covering for the lower leg or ankle, made
of cloth, leather, etc.

gala (gah-la) adjective
festive or marked by celebration: *a gala
occasion.*
• **gala** noun
1 a festival or a celebration.
2 a special sports meeting.
[Old French *gale* pleasure]

galaxy (gal-ak-see) noun (plural **galaxies**)
1 *Astronomy* any of the millions of
enormous, regularly shaped collections of
stars, dust and gas.

2 (the Galaxy) the Milky Way.
3 a glittering collection of people: *A galaxy of famous film stars attended the concert.*
Word Family galactic (ga-**lak**-tik) *adjective*
[Greek *galaktos* of milk]

gale *noun*
1 a strong wind of at least 39 miles (63 km) per hour.
2 (*informal*) a noisy outburst: *gales of laughter.*

gall¹ (gawl) *noun*
1 impudence: *He had the gall to ask for another loan.*
2 bitterness.

gall² *noun*
a sore spot on the skin, especially of horses, caused by rubbing, etc.
• **gall** *verb*
1 to irritate.
2 to rub or chafe.
Word Family galling *adjective*; **gallingly** *adverb*.

gall³ *noun*
an abnormal external growth on plants.

gallant (**gal**-ant) *adjective*
1 brave or courageous: *a knight's gallant deeds.*
2 (**gal**-ant *or* ga-**lant**) courteous and attentive to women: *He was very gallant at the ball.*
• **gallant** (**gal**-ant *or* ga-**lant**) *noun* a fashionable or dashing man, especially one who is very attentive to women.
Word Family gallantry *noun* chivalrous or heroic behaviour; **gallantries** *plural noun* polite acts; **gallantly** *adverb*; **gallantness** *noun* the quality of being courteous.

gall bladder (**gawl** blad-a) *noun*
Anatomy a small bag underneath the liver, which stores bile and releases it into the duodenum to aid fat digestion.

galleon *noun*
a very large sailing ship, used between the 15th and 18th centuries.

gallery (**gal**-a-ree) *noun* (*plural* **galleries**)
1 a room for displaying works of art.
2 a raised enclosed passage.
3 also called **balcony**. a structure projecting from the inside walls of a building, e.g. in a theatre, and containing seats.
4 a long narrow room: *a shooting gallery.*
Phrase **play to the gallery** to act in a way calculated to be popular with the majority of people.

galley *noun*
1 a ship's kitchen.
2 an early seagoing vessel propelled by oars, or oars and sails.

Gallic *adjective*
of France or its inhabitants.

gallivant (**gal**-i-vant) *verb*
(*informal*) to move or go about in a frivolous manner or in search of pleasure.

gallon *noun*
a unit of volume for liquids equal to 8 pints, or about 4·55 litre. In America it is equal to about 3·79 litre. *abbrev.* gal.

gallop *noun*
1 the fastest gait of a horse.
2 a ride at this speed: *We had a good gallop.*
Word Family gallop *verb* **1** to ride or run at a gallop. **2** to rush.

gallows (**gal**-oze) *plural noun*
(*used with singular or plural verb*) a wooden frame with two upright posts and a crosspiece, used to hang a person.

gallstone (**gawl**-stone) *noun*
Medicine a small stony mass often formed in the gall bladder or the bile passages.

Gallup poll *noun*
(*trademark*) a public opinion poll, often used to predict election results.
[after *G. H. Gallup*, 1901-1984, an American statistician]

galore (ga-**lor**) *adverb*
in large amounts: *We seem to have parties galore next month.*

galoshes *plural noun*
a pair of waterproof covers worn over ordinary shoes for protection.

galumph (gal-**umf**) *verb*
to move in a heavy clumsy way.
[from GAL(lop) + (tri)UMPH, coined by Lewis Carroll in 1871]

galvanize, galvanise (**gal**-va-nize) *verb*
1 to stimulate into action: *The workers were galvanized into action by the whistle.*
2 *Metallurgy* to coat a material, especially iron, by dipping it into molten zinc.
Word Family galvanization (gal-va-nigh-**zay**-sh'n) *noun*.

gambit *noun*
any action by which one hopes to gain an advantage.
[Italian *gambetto* a tripping-up]

gamble *verb*
to take a risk, usually involving the loss of something valuable on the outcome of a chance.

Word Family **gamble** *noun*; **gambler**
noun a person who gambles.
[Middle English *gamen* to play]

gambol *verb* (**gambols**; **gambolling**;
gambolled)
to skip or spring about in play.

game¹ *noun*
1 a form of sport or amusement, especially
one with rules: *chess and other board games*.
2 a single period of playing a sport or
amusement: *I won the first three games*.
3 (**games**) a period of sports training in a
school.
4 (**games** or **Games**) an athletic contest:
the Highland Games.
5 (*informal*) a profession or pursuit: *She's
in the advertising game*.
6 (*informal*) a scheme or plan: *I'm wise to
your little game!*
7 any wild animals hunted for sport or
food.
8 the flesh of such animals.
Phrases **fair game** any target thought fit
for attack, criticism, etc. **off one's game**
(*informal*) not playing to one's usual
standard. **on the game** (*informal*) working
as a prostitute. **play the game** to act
fairly. **the game is up** (*informal*)
someone's plot or trick is revealed and
cannot continue.
● **game** *adjective*
1 of or relating to animals hunted for sport
or food: *shooting game birds*.
2 (*informal*) willing or having the spirit for
something: *Ask Jack – he's game for
anything!*
Word Family **gamely** *adverb* bravely;
gameness *noun* braveness or willingness.

game² *adjective*
(*dated*) (of a leg) lame.

gamecock *noun* also called **gamefowl**.
a cock trained for fighting.

gamekeeper *noun*
a person employed on an estate to look
after game, prevent poaching, etc.

game plan *noun*
a strategy.

games console ⇨ CONSOLE²
(definition 2).

game show *noun*
a television show in which people try to
win prizes.

gamesmanship *noun*
the strategy of winning a contest by using
every possible interpretation of the rules,
although never actually cheating.

gamete (**gam**-eet) *noun*
a male or female sex cell found in an
animal or plant that reproduces sexually.

gamey ⇨ GAMY.

gaming *noun*
playing card games, etc. for money: *They
spent all night at the gaming tables in the
casino*.

gamma *noun*
the third letter of the Greek alphabet.

gamma ray *noun*
Physics a form of electromagnetic radiation
similar to, but of shorter wavelength than,
X-rays.

gammon *noun*
the quick-cured hind leg of a bacon pig,
boiled or grilled as rashers. Compare
HAM¹.

gammy *adjective* (**gammier**; **gammiest**)
(*informal*) (of a leg) lame.

gamp *noun*
(*dated informal*) an umbrella.
[after *Sairey Gamp* in Dickens's *Martin
Chuzzlewit*]

gamut (**gam**-ut) *noun*
the entire range: *Her face expressed the full
gamut of emotions*.

gamy *adjective* (**gamier**; **gamiest**) also
gamey
(of meat) having the strong flavour
characteristic of game.

gander *noun*
1 a male goose.
2 (*informal*) a look or glance.

gang *noun*
a group of people working together or
associating for a particular purpose: *a road
gang*. □ *a gang of criminals*.
● **gang** *verb*
Phrases **gang together** to form as a
gang: *Groups of residents ganged together to
fight the developers*. **gang up on** to join
together against.

gangling *adjective* also **gangly** (**ganglier**;
gangliest)
awkwardly tall and spindly.

gangplank *noun*
Nautical a plank used as a temporary
bridge between a ship and the shore or
another ship.

gangrene (**gang**-green) *noun*
the death of tissue, usually in the limbs,
due to a lack of blood.
Word Family **gangrenous** (**gang**-grin-
us) *adjective*.
[Greek *gangraina* an eating sore]

gangster *noun*
a member of a gang of criminals.

gangway *noun*
1 a passage between seats, e.g. in a theatre.
2 *Nautical* a railed bridge temporarily
linking ship and dockside.
• **gangway** *interjection* clear the way!

gannet *noun*
a white goose-sized seabird with black-
tipped wings, which plunges on fish from a
height.

gantry *noun* (*plural* **gantries**)
an overhead framework which supports a
load, such as a mobile crane or railway
signals.

gaol ⇨ JAIL.

gap *noun*
an unfilled space: *peeping through a gap in
the hedge*.
Figurative a wide gap between their views.

gape *verb*
1 to be or become wide open: *His flesh
gaped where the knife had gone in*.
2 to stare in amazement, especially with
the mouth open: *She just gaped at me
blankly*.
Word Family **gape** *noun*; **gaping**
adjective; **gapingly** *adverb*.

garage (**garr**-ahj) *noun*
1 a building where motor vehicles are
housed or repaired.
2 a service station.
[French *garer* to put in shelter]

garage sale *noun*
a sale of used and unwanted household
goods held in a garage, e.g. by people
leaving the district.

garam masala (gar-am ma-**sahl**-a) *noun*
a mixture of ground spices used in Indian
cookery.
[Hindi *garam* hot + *masala* spice]

garb *noun*
clothes: *clerical garb*.
• **garb** *verb* to clothe.

garbage (**gar**-bij) *noun*
any rubbish, especially household refuse.

garble *verb*
to say or report something in a hasty or
distorted way, so that it cannot be
understood.

garden *noun*
1 any piece of ground used for growing
flowers, fruit or vegetables.
2 (*usually* **gardens**) ornamental grounds
used as a public park.

Phrase **lead someone up the garden
path** to mislead someone purposely.
Word Family **garden** *verb*; **gardener**
noun a person who tends a garden;
gardening *noun*.

gardenia (gar-**deen**-ya) *noun*
a hothouse plant with large fragrant white
or yellow flowers.
[after *A. Garden*, 1730-1791, an American
botanist]

gargantuan (gar-**gan**-tew-an) *adjective*
gigantic.
[after *Gargantua*, a greedy giant king in a
16th-century satire by Rabelais]

gargle *verb*
to keep a liquid in the back of the mouth
while blowing a stream of air through it
from the lungs.
• **gargle** *noun*.
[Latin *gurgulio* gullet]

gargoyle (**gar**-goil) *noun*
a decorative rainwater spout on the side
of a building, often in the shape of a
grotesque animal or human.

garish (**gair**-ish) *adjective*
excessively coloured or ornamented.
Word Family **garishly** *adverb*;
garishness *noun*.

garland *noun*
a wreath or ring of flowers used for
decoration or as a token of honour.
• **garland** *verb* to decorate with garlands.

garlic *noun*
the strong-flavoured bulb of a lily-like
plant, used in salads and cooking.
Word Family **garlicky** *adjective*.

garment *noun*
an article of clothing.

garner *verb*
to gather in or store up.

garnet *noun*
Geology a hard crystalline mineral of many
colours, used as a gem in its dark red
form.

garnish *verb*
to decorate.
• **garnish** *noun* anything added for
decoration, especially to food.

garret *noun*
an attic room.

garrison *noun*
1 a group of soldiers stationed in a
building or town.
2 the fort or building where the soldiers
are based.
• **garrison** *verb*.

garrotte (ga-**rot**) *noun* also **garotte**
an instrument used for strangling or
throttling, especially a length of wire.
• **garrotte** *verb*.
[Spanish *garrote* a stick used for twisting a
cord tight]

garrulous (**garr**-a-lus *or* **garr**-yoo-lus)
adjective
very talkative.
Word Family **garrulously** *adverb*;
garrulousness *noun*.

garter *noun*
a band of elastic worn around the leg to
keep a sock or stocking in place.

gas *noun* (*plural* **gases** *or* **gasses**)
1 *Physics* an air-like substance, often
invisible, which has no definite volume
and completely fills any container in which
it may be kept. Compare LIQUID *noun*;
SOLID *noun*.
2 any of various gases or mixtures of gases
used as fuel, etc.: *natural gas*.
3 *Medicine* a mixture of such substances
used as an anaesthetic.
4 *American* petrol.
Phrase **be a gas** (*dated informal*) to give
great pleasure or delight.
• **gas** *verb* (**gases**; **gassing**; **gassed**)
1 to overcome or suffocate with gas.
2 (*informal*) to talk idly or boastfully.
Word Family **gaseous** (**gass**-ee-us *or*
gay-see-us) *adjective* of or like gas; **gassy**
adjective (**gassier**; **gassiest**) full of gas.

gasbag *noun*
(*informal*) a talkative person.

gash *noun* (*plural* **gashes**)
a long deep wound, especially in the flesh.
• **gash** *verb*.

gasket *noun*
any material used to seal joints and
prevent gas escaping.

gas man *noun* (*plural* **gas men**)
an official working for a company selling
gas who comes to people's houses to read
the gas meter.

gas mantle ⇨ MANTLE (definition 4).

gas mask *noun* also called **respirator**
a face mask which filters air through
certain chemicals before it is inhaled, in
order to prevent poisoning or irritation by
gases.

gas meter *noun*
an instrument for measuring the amount
of gas used in a building.

gasoline (gass-a-**leen**) *noun* also **gasolene**
American petrol.

gasometer (gass-**om**-it-a) *noun*
a large cylindrical tank for storing gas.

gasp (gahsp) *verb*
1 to take in a breath very quickly, e.g.
because one is shocked.
2 to struggle for breath with the mouth
open.
• **gasp** *noun*
Phrase **the last gasp** the point of death
or final decision.

gas-permeable *adjective*
(of a contact lens) able to let oxygen into
the eye.

gas ring *noun*
a metal ring pierced with holes, through
which gas is supplied for cooking.

gassy *adjective* ⇨ GAS.

gastric *adjective*
Anatomy of or relating to the stomach.

gastro-enteritis
(gas-tro-en-ter-**eye**-tis) *noun*
an inflammation of the stomach and
intestines, dangerous in young children.

gastronomy (gas-**tron**-a-mee) *noun*
the art and knowledge of food and eating.
Word Family **gastronomic** (gas-tra-
nom-ik) *adjective*; **gastronomically**
adverb.
[*gastro-* + Greek *nomos* an arrangement]

gastropod *noun*
any of a group of molluscs, including
snails, that have an external coiled shell
and a muscular foot on which they slide
about.
[*gastro-* + Greek *podos* of a foot]

gate *noun*
1 a movable barrier, usually on hinges,
which opens and closes an entrance in a
fence, etc.
2 any device or structure which regulates
passage or provides entrance.
3 the total amount of money paid by
spectators for admission to a public
exhibition, sporting match, etc.

gateau (ga-**toe**) *noun* (*plural* **gateaus** (ga-
toze) *or* **gateaux** (ga-**toe** *or* ga-**toze**))
a large cake, often filled and decorated
with cream and icing.

gatecrash *verb*
to attend a party or other gathering
without having been invited.
Word Family **gatecrasher** *noun*.

gatepost *noun*
either of the two fence posts between
which a gate is hung.

gateway *noun*
1 a space or structure within which a gate is situated.
2 (*informal*) an entrance: *Hawaii – the gateway to the Pacific.*

gather *verb*
1 to pick up or bring together: *He gathered up the papers he had dropped.*
Figurative I tried to gather my thoughts.
2 to draw together in folds: *Her skirt was gathered at the waist.*
3 to increase in: *The car gathered speed.*
4 to conclude or understand: *I gather you are not very enthusiastic.*
• **gather** *noun* a drawing together, especially of folds in fabric.
Word Family **gathering** *noun* a group of people assembled together.

gauche (gohsh) *adjective*
awkward or tactless.
Word Family **gauchely** *adverb*;
gaucheness *noun*.
[French, left, left hand]

gaucho (gow-cho) *noun*
a South American cowboy of mixed Spanish and Indian parentage.

gaudy (gaw-dee) *adjective* (**gaudier; gaudiest**)
vulgarly bright or showy.
Word Family **gaudiness** *noun*; **gaudily** *adverb*.

gauge (gayj) *noun*
1 an instrument for measuring something, such as pressure, temperature, etc.
2 a scale or standard of measure: *Team-building exercises are a good gauge of a person's character.*
3 the thickness or diameter of something.
4 *Railways* the distance between the rails.
• **gauge** *verb* to measure or estimate: *It was not difficult to gauge his motives.*

gaunt (gawnt) *adjective*
thin or haggard.
Word Family **gauntness** *noun*.

gauntlet[1] (gawnt-let) *noun*
1 a mailed or armoured glove.
2 a strong glove with a wide cuff reaching to the elbow.
Phrases **pick up the gauntlet, take up the gauntlet** to accept a challenge. **throw down the gauntlet** to issue a challenge.
[Old French *gant* glove]

gauntlet[2] *noun*
Phrase **run the gauntlet** 1 (*formerly*) (of a soldier) to be forced to run between two rows of men who hit the passing victim

with sticks, as a punishment. 2 to expose oneself to extreme danger, criticism, etc.
[Swedish *gata* lane + *lopp* a running course]

gauze (gawz) *noun*
1 any thin transparent woven fabric.
2 any similar open material consisting of crossed lines, such as wire.

gave the past tense of **give**.

gavel (gavv-'l) *noun*
a small hammer used to signal for silence in court, at a meeting, etc.

gavotte (ga-vot) *noun*
a lively French dance, popular in the past.
[French]

gawk *verb*
to stare stupidly or rudely.
Word Family **gawker** *noun*.

gawky *adjective* (**gawkier; gawkiest**)
awkward or clumsy.
Word Family **gawkily** *adverb*; **gawkiness** *noun*.

gay *adjective*
1 homosexual.
2 (*dated*) happy and full of joy.
• **gay** *noun* a homosexual person, especially a man.
Word Family **gaily** *adverb* in a joyful manner; **gayness** *noun* the state of being homosexual.

gaze *verb*
to look with fixed attention, curiosity, etc.
• **gaze** *noun*.

gazebo (ga-zee-bo) *noun*
a structure that has a wide view, e.g. a glass pavilion in a garden.

gazelle (ga-zel) *noun*
a small African or Asian antelope.
[Arabic]

gazette (ga-zet) *noun*
1 an official or government publication.
2 a title for certain newspapers.
[Italian *gazeta* a Venetian coin, the price of a gazette]

gazetteer (gaz-a-teer) *noun*
a geographical dictionary.

gazpacho (gas-pach-o) *noun*
a cold soup made from salad vegetables.
[Spanish]

gazump (ga-zump) *verb*
(*informal*) to outbid the original buyer of a property after his or her offer has been accepted by the vendor.

g'day *interjection*
Australian an expression used on meeting someone.

gear *noun*
1 a mechanism for transmitting or changing movement, e.g. by cogwheels: *She put the car into second gear.*
2 any tools or apparatus for a particular purpose: *He packed his fishing gear into the car.*
3 (*informal*) any clothes.
4 (*informal*) illegal drugs.
Phrase in gear having the gear of a motor vehicle engaged.
• **gear** *verb* to adjust or adapt: *Our schools are now geared up to teach English for an hour a day.*

gearbox *noun* (*plural* **gearboxes**)
the case within which the gears of a motor vehicle are enclosed.

gear lever *noun* also called **gearstick**.
a rod used to change the gears in a motor vehicle.

gecko *noun* (*plural* **geckos** or **geckoes**)
a small nocturnal lizard.
[Malay]

gee (jee) *verb*
Phrases gee someone up (*informal*) to encourage someone to make more effort.
gee up! (said to a horse) go faster!

geek *noun*
1 (*informal*) a stupid or annoying person.
2 (*informal*) a person who is obsessed with electronic equipment, especially computers.
Word Family geeky *adjective* (**geekier**; **geekiest**).

geese
the plural of **goose**.

geezer *noun*
(*informal*) a man.
[from *guiser*, an old word for a person who wears a disguise]

Geiger counter (**gie**-ga count-er) *noun*
a portable instrument used for detecting and measuring radioactivity.
[after *H. Geiger*, 1882-1945, a German physicist]

geisha (**gay**-sha) *noun* (*plural* **geisha** or **geishas**)
a Japanese girl trained to entertain with dancing, conversation, etc.
[Japanese, entertainer]

gel¹ (jel) *noun*
a jelly-like substance, e.g. a cosmetic preparation used to set hair.

• **gel** *verb* (**gels**; **gelling**; **gelled**) to form or become a gel.
[short form of *gelatin*]

gel² *verb* ⇨ JELL.

gelatin (**jell**-a-tin) *noun* also **gelatine** (**jell**-a-teen)
1 a complex protein derived from animal tissue, soluble in water and setting into a jelly. It is used in foods, photography and medicine.
2 a type of explosive.
Word Family gelatinous (jel-**at**-in-us) *adjective* of or like jelly.
[Latin *gelatus* frozen]

geld (geld) *verb*
to castrate an animal, especially a horse.
Word Family gelding *noun* a castrated animal, especially a horse.

gelignite (**jell**-ig-nite) *noun*
an explosive containing nitroglycerine, used for blasting.
[GEL(atin) + Latin *ignis* fire]

gem (jem) *noun*
1 also **gemstone** a precious or semi-precious stone, cut and polished in order to show off its beauty.
2 anything which is highly valued for its worth or beauty: *This poem is a literary gem.*

Gemini (**jem**-in-eye) *noun*
Astrology a group of stars, the third sign of the Zodiac; the sign of the Twins.

gen (jen) *noun*
(*informal*) the general or correct information about something.
• **gen** *verb* (**gens**; **genning**; **genned**)
Phrase gen up on (*informal*) to find out more facts about.
[from GEN(eral information)]

gendarme (**zhon**-darm) *noun*
a member of the armed military police force in certain European countries, such as France.
Word Family gendarmerie (zhon-**dar**-ma-ree) *noun* a force of gendarmes.
[French *gens* men + *d'armes* bearing arms]

gender (**jen**-da) *noun*
1 *Grammar* any of the classifications given to nouns or pronouns usually according to the sex of the person or thing described, i.e. **masculine** (he); **feminine** (she) or **neuter** (it).
2 (*informal*) the sex of a person or animal.

gene (jeen) *noun*
Biology the unit of inheritance. Genes are composed of lengths of DNA holding the genetic codes for an individual's characteristics.

genealogy (jeen-ee-**al**-a-jee) noun (plural **genealogies**)
a family tree or the record of a person's ancestors and relatives.
Word Family **genealogical** (jee-nee-a-**loj**-i-k'l) adjective; **genealogist** (jeen-ee-**al**-a-jist) noun.
[Greek *genea* race + *-logy*]

genera (jen-er-a)
the plural of **genus**.

general (jen-a-r'l) adjective
1 of, affecting or including all or most people or things: *a general election.* □ *the general public.*
2 vague or not detailed: *Just give me a general idea of what the work involves.*
3 (used after a job title) having superior or chief rank: *the director general of the BBC.*
• **general** noun Army a commissioned officer ranking between lieutenant general and field marshal.
Phrase **in general 1** as a whole, not specific: *We spoke about things in general.*
2 usually: *In general, summer is a warm season.*

general anaesthetic noun
an anaesthetic that affects the whole body, so that the patient loses consciousness.
Compare LOCAL ANAESTHETIC.

general election ⇨ ELECTION.

generalissimo (jen-a-r'l-**iss**-i-mo) noun
a title for the supreme commander of the armed forces in certain countries.

generality (jen-a-**ral**-i-tee) noun (plural **generalities**)
1 a vague or general statement.
2 a general principle.

generalize, generalise (jen-er-a-lize) verb
1 to draw a general conclusion from one or more particular cases.
2 to make a vague or sweeping statement.
Word Family **generalization** (jen-er-a-lie-**zay**-sh'n) noun.

generally adverb
1 usually: *I am generally home by 7 p.m.*
2 in a general or vague way: *Generally speaking I don't like small dogs.*
3 by most people: *My plan was generally approved.*

general practitioner noun
short form is **GP** a doctor who deals with the general health of a community and not with specialized areas of medicine.

general staff noun
(used with singular or plural verb) a group of officers assisting a commander in planning military operations.

general strike noun
an occasion when workers in a lot of different industries all strike at the same time.

generate (jen-a-rate) verb
to produce or cause: *ideas generated at the meeting.* □ *Friction generates heat.*

generation (jen-a-**ray**-sh'n) noun
1 each successive stage in a family descent: *Three generations of the family were present – father, son and grandson.*
2 the average time between any two such stages, usually considered as being about 30 years among human beings.
3 any group of people born at about the same time: *They had become known as the pop generation.*
4 the act of generating or producing: *the generation of electricity.*

generation gap noun
the difference in ideas and attitudes between older people and young people that leads to lack of understanding.

generator (jen-a-ray-ter) noun
a device which converts one form of energy into another, especially a machine which produces electrical energy from mechanical energy.

generic (ji-**nerr**-ik) adjective
of or common to a whole genus or group: *Hoover has become a generic name for vacuum cleaners.*
Word Family **generically** adverb.
[Latin *generis* of a kind]

generous (jen-a-rus) adjective
1 ready to give freely.
2 plentiful or large: *generous slices of cake.*
Word Family **generously** adverb; **generosity** (jen-a-**ross**-i-tee) noun the quality of being generous or unselfish.
[Latin *generosus* of noble birth]

genesis (jen-a-sis) noun (plural **geneses**) (jen-a-seez)
a beginning or creation.
[Greek]

gene therapy noun
Biology the repair of imperfect cells by putting healthy genes into them.

genetic (ji-**net**-ik) adjective
1 of or relating to genes or genetics.
2 of or relating to genesis or creation.
Word Family **genetically** adverb **1** in a way that relates to genes: *genetically*

imperfect. **2** using technology concerned with genes: *genetically modified foods*.

genetic counselling *noun*
professional advice given to potential parents with regard to the possible transmission of genetic abnormalities in any children born to them.

genetic engineering *noun*
the artificial change or manipulation of the genetic constitution, or DNA, of living things.

genetic fingerprinting *noun* also called **genetic profiling; DNA fingerprinting**. the identification of a person's DNA pattern obtained by analysing samples of blood, saliva or semen and used, for example, in forensic medicine to identify criminals.

genetic modification *noun*
the alteration of the genetic make-up of living things using technological methods, e.g. by transferring genes from other organisms, for purposes such as the improvement of crop yield or people's health.

genetics (ji-**net**-iks) *plural noun* (*used with singular verb*) the study of heredity and the differences between living things due to inheriting certain characteristics.
Word Family geneticist (ji-**net**-a-sist) *noun*.
[Greek *gennetikos* productive]

genial (**jeen**-ee-'l) *adjective*
mildly pleasant, kind or favourable: *My uncle's genial manner*.
Word Family genially *adverb*; **geniality** (jeen-ee-**al**-i-tee) *noun*.
[Latin *genialis* productive]

genie (**jee**-nee) *noun* (*plural* **genii** (**jee**-nee-eye) or **genies**)
Folklore a spirit or demon, especially one changing into many different forms.
[Arabic *jinni*]

genitals (**jen**-i-t'ls) *plural noun* also **genitalia** (jen-i-**tay**-lee-a)
Anatomy the organs of reproduction, i.e. the penis, testes and associated parts in the male and the ovaries, uterus, vagina and associated parts in the female.
Word Family genital *adjective*.

genitive case (**jen**-it-iv case) *noun*
a grammatical case expressing a relationship of possession or source.

genius (**jee**-nee-us) *noun* (*plural* **geniuses**)
1 an exceptionally high intelligence or creative ability.
2 a person with this talent or ability.
3 any natural ability or talent: *He has a genius for getting into trouble*.
[Latin, a natural taste]

genocide (**jen**-o-side) *noun*
a systematic attempt to destroy a racial group or nation.
Word Family genocidal (jen-o-**side**-al) *adjective*.
[Greek *genos* race + Latin *caedere* to kill]

genome (**jee**-nohm) *noun*
Biology the whole set of genetic materials of a person, animal or plant.

genre (**zhon**-ra) *noun*
a style, variety or category, especially in art, film, literature, etc.: *the science fiction genre*.
[French]

gent (jent) *noun*
(*informal*) a gentleman.

genteel (jen-**teel**) *adjective*
over-refined in manners, speech or outlook.
Word Family genteelly *adverb*; **gentility** (jen-**till**-i-tee) *noun*.

gentile (**jen**-tile) *noun*
(*often* **Gentile**) any person who is not Jewish, especially a Christian.
[Late Latin *gentilis* foreign]

gentle *adjective*
1 soft or kind: *Her gentle words soothed his anger*. □ *a gentle breeze*.
2 not steep: *gentle slopes*.
Word Family gently *adverb*; **gentleness** *noun*.

gentleman *noun* (*plural* **gentlemen**)
1 a well-bred educated man with socially correct manners.
2 (used as a polite form of address) any man.
Word Family gentlemanly *adjective*.

gentleman's agreement *noun*
an agreement guaranteed by trust and honour rather than by legal means.

gentleman's gentleman *noun* (*plural* **gentleman's gentlemen**) ⇨ VALET (definition 1).

gentlewoman *noun* (*plural* **gentlewomen**)
an old word for a woman of high social class.

gentrification *noun*
the renovation and upgrading of property or of an area.
Word Family **gentrify** *verb* (**gentrifies; gentrifying; gentrified**).

gentry (**Jen**-tree) *plural noun*
the well-born or privileged people in a society.

gents *noun*
a public toilet for men.

genuflect (**jen**-yoo-flekt) *verb*
to kneel or bend the knee or knees, especially as an act of worship.
Word Family **genuflection, genuflexion** (jen-yoo-**flek**-sh'n) *noun*.
[Latin *genu* knee + *flectere* bend]

genuine (**jen**-yoo-in) *adjective*
1 real or true: *genuine fear.* □ *a genuine antique.*
2 sincere: *She comes across as a very genuine person.*
Word Family **genuinely** *adverb*; **genuineness** *noun*.

genus (**jee**-nus) *noun* (*plural* **genera**) (**jen**-er-a)
Biology the group below family, used in the classification of animals or plants.
[Latin, a stock, category]

geochemistry (jee-o-**kem**-i-stree) *noun*
the study of the chemical composition of the earth's crust, and the changes taking place within it.
Word Family **geochemist** *noun*; **geochemically** *adverb*.

geodesy (jee-**odd**-a-see) *noun* also called **geodetics** (jee-o-**dett**-iks).
the science of surveying large areas of the earth, allowing for its curvature.
[*geo-* + Greek *daisia* division]

geography (jee-**og**-ra-fee) *noun*
1 the study of the earth's surface, including its physical features, climates, soils, population distribution, etc.
2 the physical features of a particular area
Word Family **geographer** *noun* a person who studies geography; **geographic** (jee-o-**graf**-ik), **geographical** *adjective*; **geographically** *adverb*.
[*geo-* + Greek *graphein* to write]

geology (jee-**oll**-a-jee) *noun*
1 the study of the earth, its origin, structure, composition and history.
2 the features of a region in relation to geology: *the geology of the local area.*
Word Family **geological** (jee-o-**loj**-i-k'l) *adjective*; **geologically** *adverb*; **geologist** (jee-**oll**-a-jist) *noun*.
[*geo-* + *-logy*]

geometric (jee-o-**mett**-rik) *adjective* also **geometrical**
1 of or relating to geometry.
2 using or resembling the lines and shapes characteristic of geometry: *geometric patterns.*
Word Family **geometrically** *adverb*.

geometry (jee-**om**-a-tree) *noun*
a branch of maths studying the properties of figures in space.
Word Family **geometrician** (jee-om-a-**trish**-'n) *noun*.
[*geo-* + Greek *metron* a measure]

geophysics (jee-o-**fizz**-iks) *plural noun*
(*used with singular verb*) the study of the physical processes related to the earth's structure, e.g. gravitation, tides, earthquakes and the earth's magnetism.
Word Family **geophysicist** *noun*; **geophysical** *adjective*.

Geordie (**jor**-di) *noun*
(*informal*) a native of Tyneside.
[from the nickname for *George*]

Georgian (**jor**-j'n) *adjective*
relating to a style of architecture which was popular in Britain between the reigns of George I and George IV (1714-1830).

geotextile (jee-o-**teks**-ile) *noun*
a textile product which is designed for use in the ground.

geothermal (jee-o-**ther**-m'l) *adjective*
of or relating to the internal heat of the earth.

geranium (jer-**ray**-nee-um) *noun*
a plant with red, pink or white flowers.
[Greek *geranos* a crane, because the fruit of the plant was thought to resemble a crane's bill]

gerbil (**jer**-bil) *noun*
a small rodent with a long tail, often kept as a pet.

geriatrics (jerr-ee-**at**-riks) *plural noun*
(*used with singular verb*) the branch of medicine concerned with the care of old people.
Word Family **geriatric** *adjective* of or relating to the care of old people; **geriatric** *noun* an old person; **geriatrician** (jerr-ee-a-**trish**-'n) *noun* a doctor specializing in the care of the old.
[Greek *geras* old age + *iatros* physician]

germ (jerm) *noun*
1 any micro-organism which may cause disease.
2 anything which serves as a basis or beginning of growth, development, etc.:

The germ of an escape plan formed in her mind.

[Latin *germen* a bud]

germane (jer-**mane**) *adjective*

relevant.

[Latin *germanus* of the same parents]

German measles *plural noun* also called **rubella**.

(*used with singular verb*) a mild infectious disease, usually in children, causing red spots. If contracted in early pregnancy it may damage the unborn child.

German shepherd *noun* also called **Alsatian**.

a breed of large strong smooth-haired dogs, often used as police dogs.

German silver ⇨ NICKEL SILVER.

germinate (jer-mi-nate) *verb*

to develop and grow, as a plant from a seed.

Word Family germination (jer-mi-**nay**-sh'n) *noun*.

germ warfare *noun*

the use of weapons which release bacteria, viruses, etc. to destroy life.

gerrymander (jerr-ee-man-da) *verb*

Politics to arrange the boundaries of electorates to the advantage of a particular party or candidate.

Word Family gerrymandering *noun*.

[from E. Gerry, a governor of Massachusetts who created new boundaries there in 1812 + (sala)MANDER, which animal the rearranged map was considered to resemble]

gerund (jerr-und) *noun*

Grammar a noun formed from a verb, e.g. *smoking, reading,* etc.

Gestapo (ges-**tah**-po) *noun*

the secret police in Germany from 1933-1945, working to ensure obedience to the Nazi government.

[German GE(heime) STA(ats) PO(lizei) secret state police]

gestation (jes-**tay**-sh'n) *noun*

Biology the act or period of carrying a developing embryo in the uterus.

Word Family gestate (jes-**tate**) *verb*.

[Latin *gestatus* carried]

gesticulate (jes-**tik**-yoo-late) *verb*

to make gestures, especially for emphasis or explanation.

Word Family gesticulation (jes-tik-yoo-**lay**-sh'n) *noun*.

gesture (jes-cher) *noun*

1 a movement of the body or limbs, made to express or emphasize an idea, emotion, etc.

2 an action done to indicate one's feelings or intentions: *She told him as a gesture of her friendship.*

• **gesture** *verb*.

get *verb* (**gets**; **getting**; **got**)

1 to receive: *He got your email today.* □ *We all got a terrible fright!*

2 to succeed in obtaining: *My sister got three A levels.* □ *Did the police get the burglar?*

3 to fetch: *Can you get the paper for me?*

4 to catch an illness: *I don't want to get flu.*

5 to catch a public transport vehicle: *My mum gets the train to work.*

6 to move into a stated position or condition: *Get out of my room!* □ *When did you get online?* □ *We couldn't get the goat through the gate.*

7 to become: *I got soaked!* □ *This cheese is getting rather old.*

8 to put into a stated position or condition: *She was getting ready to go out.* □ *I got the last question wrong.* □ *We finally got them to open the door.*

9 to hear or understand: *You just don't get it, do you?*

10 (*informal*) to annoy: *It gets me that he never told us.*

11 (*informal*) to punish: *I'll get you for this!*

12 (*informal*) to confuse: *That's a tricky question – you've got me there!*

Phrases **be getting on** (*informal*) to be quite old. **get across** to make understood. **get along** 1 to manage. 2 to make progress. 3 to be friendly with someone. **get around, get about** 1 to move around. 2 to circulate: *The rumour got around.* **get at** 1 to reach: *That shelf is difficult to get at.* 2 to suggest in an indirect way: *Exactly what are you getting at?* 3 (*informal*) to influence unfairly, e.g. with money: *Some of the jury had been got at.* 4 (*informal*) to criticize, especially indirectly: *I felt he was getting at me.* **get away** to escape. **get away with** to escape punishment for. **get back at** (*informal*) to get revenge on. **get back to someone** to contact someone again later: *I'll have to get back to you on that.* **get by** to manage: *How will we get by without a car?* **get down to** to begin to concentrate on. **get off** to escape the consequences of one's actions. **get off with** (*informal*) to start a sexual relationship with. **get on** 1 to make progress. 2 to manage or succeed. 3 to be friendly with someone. **get out of** to manage to avoid: *I got out of the washing-up by saying I had loads of homework.* **get over** to recover from: *It took her years to get over the accident.* **get round 1** to overcome. **2** to humour someone into being nice, lenient, etc. **get round to, get around to** to arrive at the point of: *We finally got round to discussing tactics.* **get through 1** to use up: *The kids got through seven packets of biscuits last week!* **2** to succeed in talking to someone on the telephone. **get through to someone** (*informal*) to make someone understand. **get to** (*informal*) to annoy. **get up 1** to rise, especially from bed. **2** (of the sea or the wind) to increase in power.

getaway *noun*
an escape, especially after a crime.

get-together *noun*
an informal gathering or party.

get-up *noun*
(*informal*) an outfit or costume.

geyser *noun*
1 (**gie**-za or **gee**-za) a spring which sends up jets of hot water and steam.
2 (**gee**-za) a gas device which heats but does not store water.
[Icelandic *geysir* a hot spring]

ghastly (**gahst**-lee) *adjective* (**ghastlier; ghastliest**)
1 dreadful or terrifying.
2 (*informal*) extremely unpleasant: *What a ghastly smell!*
3 extremely pale.
Word Family **ghastliness** *noun*.

ghee (gee) *noun*
a special melted butter used in Indian cooking.

gherkin (**ger**-kin) *noun*
a small cucumber, usually pickled.

ghetto (**get**-toh) *noun* (*plural* **ghettos** or **ghettoes**)
an area in a city where a minority group lives separately from other groups in the community.
[Italian]

ghetto blaster *noun*
(*informal*) a large portable radio or cassette or CD player.

ghost *noun*
1 the spirit or semblance of a dead person, believed to visit or haunt living people.
2 a trace: *the ghost of a smile.*
Phrase **give up the ghost** (*informal*) to die.

• **ghost** *verb* also **ghostwrite** to act as a ghostwriter.
Word Family **ghostly** *adjective* (**ghostlier; ghostliest**); **ghostliness** *noun.*

ghost town *noun*
a town in which very few people now live.

ghostwriter *noun*
a person who writes a work which will be attributed to another person, who commissioned it.

ghoul (gool) *noun*
1 an evil spirit believed, in some Eastern countries, to eat human bodies or rob graves.
2 a person who enjoys revolting or horrible things.
Word Family **ghoulish** *adjective*; **ghoulishly** *adverb*; **ghoulishness** *noun.*
[Arabic]

ghyll ⇨ GILL[3].

giant (**jie**-ant) *noun*
a person or thing of unusually large size, importance, etc.
Word Family **giant** *adjective*; **giantess** *noun* (*plural* **giantesses**) a female giant.

giant panda ⇨ PANDA.

gibberish (**jib**-a-rish) *noun*
any rapid or unintelligible talk.

gibbet (**jib**-it) *noun*
an upright post with a crosspiece, used to hang a person.

gibbon (**gib**-'n) *noun*
a small long-armed ape, living in the forests of tropical Asia.

gibe ⇨ JIBE[1].

giblets (**jib**-l'ts) *plural noun*
the heart, neck and gizzard of a fowl, usually removed from the bird and cooked separately.

giddy (**gid**-ee) *adjective* (**giddier; giddiest**)
1 having a light-headed spinning sensation.
2 frivolous or flighty: *a giddy girl.*
Word Family **giddily** *adverb*; **giddiness** *noun.*

gift *noun*
1 a present.
2 a special ability: *She has a gift for languages.*
Phrase **gift of the gab** a talent for talking easily or well.
Word Family **gifted** *adjective* having a special ability or talent.

gift-horse *noun*
Phrase **look a gift-horse in the mouth**
to accept a gift or favour ungraciously.

> The phrase **look a gift-horse in the mouth** literally refers to a way of assessing a horse's age by opening its mouth and examining its teeth. It was obviously impolite to do this when given a horse as a gift because one would be seen to be checking up on its age in order to assess its value.

gift-wrapped *adjective*
wrapped in decorative paper and ribbon.

gig¹ *noun*
1 an open two-wheeled carriage pulled by one horse.
2 (*informal*) an engagement, especially for a band or pop group, for one performance only.

gig² *noun*
(*informal*) a gigabyte.

gigabyte (**gig**-a-bite) *noun*
Computers a unit of computer data or storage space equal to 1024 megabytes.
abbrev. Gb; GB.

gigantic (jie-**gan**-tik) *adjective*
extremely large.
Word Family **gigantically** *adverb.*

giggle *verb*
to laugh in a silly or nervous manner.
Word Family **giggle** *noun*; **giggly** *adjective* (**gigglier; giggliest**).

gigolo (**jig**-a-lo) *noun*
a young man who is employed as a dancing partner or escort, or is kept as a lover, by an older woman.
[French]

gild *verb* (**gilds; gilding; gilded** or **gilt**) to cover with a fine layer of gold or golden colour.
Phrase **gild the lily** to spoil beauty by overdecorating.
Word Family **gilding** *noun* **1** a golden surface or coating. **2** any fine but deceptive appearance.

gilet (**zhee**-lay) *noun*
a padded jacket with no sleeves.

gill¹ (gill) *noun*
1 *Biology* an external organ in fish and other aquatic animals, used for gas exchange in respiration.
2 one of the thin vertical plates on the underside of the cap of a mushroom, etc.
Phrase **green about the gills** (*informal*) sickly in appearance.

gill² (jill) *noun*
a unit for measuring liquids, equal to a quarter of a pint.

gill³ (gill) *noun* also **ghyll**
a deep wooded glen or a mountain torrent, especially in the Lake District.

gillie (**gill**-ee) *noun*
Scottish a guide and attendant employed by anglers and deerstalkers.
[Gaelic *gille* lad]

gilt *noun*
a thin layer of gold or similar material.
• **gilt** *verb* a past tense and past participle of **gild**.
• **gilt** *adjective* golden.

gilt-edged *adjective*
1 having the edges gilded.
2 of the highest quality, especially of stocks which are considered extremely safe as an investment.

gimlet *noun*
a small tool with a pointed spiral end for drilling holes.
Figurative his gimlet eyes (= very penetrating).

gimme *contraction*
(*informal*) a short form of **give me**.

gimmick *noun*
a new or tricky method or device, especially one intended to boost sales.
Word Family **gimmicky** *adjective.*

gin¹ (jin) *noun*
a strong alcoholic drink made from rye or other grain and flavoured with juniper berries.

gin² *noun*
1 ⇨ COTTON GIN.
2 a trap or snare for animals.
[Old French *engin* engine]

ginger (**jin**-ja) *noun*
1 the strong-smelling root of a tropical plant, used in cooking and medicine.
2 a sandy-red colour.
Word Family **gingery** *adjective* like ginger: *a gingery smell*; **ginger** *adjective* (of hair) sandy-red.

ginger ale *noun* also called **ginger beer**.
a fizzy drink, sometimes alcoholic, with a ginger flavour.

gingerbread *noun*
a treacle or honey cake flavoured with ginger.

ginger group *noun*
a group of people working within a larger group or association to introduce changes or a modern outlook.

gingerly (**jin**-ja-lee) *adverb, adjective*
with extreme caution or care.

ginger nut *noun*
a hard biscuit flavoured with ginger.

gingham (**ging**-um) *noun*
a cotton fabric with a coloured check
pattern.

gingivitis (jin-ji-**vie**-tis) *noun*
Medicine an infection of the gums.
[Latin *gingiva* gum + *-itis*]

gin rummy *noun*
a card game similar to rummy.

ginseng (**jin**-seng) *noun*
a medicinal plant with an aromatic root.
[Chinese]

gipsy ⇨ GYPSY.

giraffe (ji-**rahf**) *noun*
an extremely tall spotted mammal which
has a long neck and feeds on leaves in
open forests in Africa.

gird *verb* (**girds; girding; girt** or **girded**)
1 to encircle with or as if with a belt, band,
etc.
2 to prepare for action

girder *noun*
a large, usually horizontal, beam
supporting a structure

girdle *noun*
1 a belt or cord worn around the waist.
2 any belt or band, such as a ring of bark
cut from a tree trunk.
3 an elasticated corset.
• **girdle** *verb* to encircle or enclose.

girl *noun*
a female child.
Word Family girlish *adjective*; **girlishly**
adverb; **girlhood** *noun*.

girlfriend *noun*
a person's chosen female companion,
especially in a romantic or sexual sense.

giro (**jie**-ro) *noun*
1 a cheap method of transferring money
directly from one account to another
through a post office or bank.
2 a cheque paid by this method, especially
a social security cheque.
[Italian, circulation]

girt a past tense and past participle of **gird**.

girth *noun*
1 the measurement around something.
2 a band passed under a horse's belly to
hold a saddle or pack in place.

gist (jist) *noun*
the essential part of something: *What
exactly is the gist of your argument?*

gite (zheet) *noun*
a furnished holiday home in France.

give *verb* (**gives; giving; gave; given**)
1 to provide or hand over, especially
without expecting payment, etc. in return:
She gave the beggar some coins. □ *What did
you give them for Christmas?*
2 to allow to have: *I'll give you just one more
chance!*
3 to supply with: *Whatever gave you that
idea?*
4 to produce: *He gave a little sigh.*
5 to cause to happen: *The Prime Minister is
giving a press conference later today.*
6 to bend under pressure: *Watch out! That
branch you're on is beginning to give!*
7 (*informal*) to acknowledge the truth of:
*She's a brave opponent, I'll give you that, but
she has no chance.*
8 *Sport* to judge to be: *The referee gave him
offside.*
9 (used in offering toasts at formal
occasions) to call for acknowledgement to
be given to: *Ladies and gentlemen, I give you
the new world champion.*
Phrases be given to to be in the habit of:
He is given to lying. **give away 1** to reveal
information about someone: *Her smile gave
her away.* **2** to present the bride to the
bridegroom at a wedding. **give in** to
acknowledge defeat: *I give in, what's the
answer?* **give off** to send out: *The milk was
giving off a bad smell.* **give onto** to have a
view of. **give or take** approximately: *He
must be 70, give or take a year.* **give out 1** to
be completely used up. **2** to stop
functioning completely. **give over 1** to
devote completely: *The day was given over
to celebrating.* **2** (*informal*) to stop. **give up
1** to surrender: *You must give yourself up.*
2 to stop: *Mum is trying to give up smoking.*
give way to yield, especially in traffic.
• **give** *noun* the quality of being able to
bend or stretch.
Phrase give and take willingness to
make compromises.

gizmo (**giz**-moh) *noun* also **gismo**
(*informal*) a gadget.

gizzard *noun*
a muscular organ in certain animals, such
as birds, which grinds and digests food.

glacé (**gla**-say) *adjective*
(of fruit) coated with sugar.
[French, iced]

glacier (**glay**-see-a *or* **gla**-see-a) *noun*
a large mass of moving ice, formed from
compacted snow.

Word Family glacial (glay-sh'l) *adjective*
1 relating to or associated with the action of ice or glaciers. **2** extremely cold or unfriendly: *a glacial stare;* **glaciation** (glay-see-**ay**-sh'n) *noun* the action of covering with ice.
[French *glace* ice]

glad *adjective* (**gladder; gladdest**)
pleased or happy.
Word Family gladly *adverb;* **gladness** *noun;* **gladden** *verb* to make or become glad.

glade *noun*
an open space in a forest.

gladiator (glad-ee-ay-ta) *noun*
Ancient history a person trained to perform public fights in Roman arenas.
Word Family gladiatorial (glad-ee-a-**taw**-ree-'l) *adjective.*
[Latin *gladius* sword]

gladiolus (glad-ee-ole-us) *noun*
(*plural* **gladioli**) (glad-ee-**ole**-eye)
a garden plant with reed-like leaves and brightly coloured flowers on a long stem.
[Latin *gladius* sword]

Gladstone bag *noun*
a light travelling case consisting of two compartments hinged together at the centre.
[after *W. E. Gladstone,* 1809-1898, a British statesman]

glamour (glam-a) *noun* (*American* **glamor**)
an attractive charm or fascinating quality.
Word Family glamorous *adjective;* **glamorously** *adverb;* **glamorize,** **glamorise** *verb* to make glamorous or attractive.

glance *verb*
1 to look briefly.
2 to be deflected off an object: *The bullet glanced off the tree and struck the wall.*
Word Family glance *noun.*

gland *noun*
Anatomy a group of cells which produce a substance necessary for the body to function, such as the salivary glands.
Word Family glandular (glan-dew-la) *adjective.*
[Latin *glandis* of an acorn]

glandular fever *noun*
an infectious viral disease causing fever and swollen lymph glands.

glare *noun*
1 an angry or fixed look.
2 a bright intense light.
Word Family glare *verb;* **glaring** *adjective* **1** dazzlingly bright. **2** very

conspicuous; **glaringly** *adverb;* **glary** *adjective.*

glasnost (glaz-nost) *noun*
a policy of openness with regard to government and public affairs.
[Russian]

glass *noun* (*plural* **glasses**)
1 a transparent brittle substance composed of silicates of various metals, especially sodium and calcium.
2 also **glassware** objects made of glass: *a collection of Roman glass.*
3 a container for drinking from: *a wine glass.*
4 an old word for a mirror.

glass-blowing *noun*
the art of shaping glass by heating it and then blowing into it while it is liquid.
Word Family glass-blower *noun.*

glasses *plural noun* also called **spectacles.**
a pair of lenses in a frame which rests on the nose and ears, worn to improve eyesight.

glass fibre *noun*
a flame-resistant plastic or fabric made from very thin fibres of glass.

glasshouse *noun*
1 a greenhouse.
2 (*Military informal*) a place where people are locked up.

glassy *adjective* (**glassier; glassiest**)
1 of or having the texture, appearance, etc. of glass.
2 expressionless: *a glassy stare.*
Word Family glassily *adverb;* **glassiness** *noun.*

glaucoma (glaw-ko-ma) *noun*
Medicine an increased pressure by the fluid in the eyeball, which may lead to blindness if not treated.
[Greek *glaukos* bluish-green + *-oma* a tumour]

glaze *noun*
1 a smooth glossy surface or coating: *the glaze on an iced bun.*
2 any substance which produces such a surface: *a pottery glaze.*
• **glaze** *verb*
1 to fit or cover with glass.
2 to cover with glaze.
Word Family glazier (glay-zee-a) *noun* a person who fits windows, etc. with glass.

gleam *noun*
1 a brief flash of light or a subdued glow of light.
2 a brief showing of a feeling.
• **gleam** *verb.*

glean *verb*
to gather or collect.

glee *noun*
1 lively joy or amusement.
2 an unaccompanied part song for three or more voices.
Word Family **gleeful** *adjective* merry or joyful; **gleefully** *adverb*.

glen *noun*
Scottish a small narrow valley.

glib *adjective*
easy and fluent, but often superficial or insincere.
Word Family **glibly** *adverb*; **glibness** *noun*.
[Dutch *glibberig* slippery]

glide *verb*
1 to move smoothly or effortlessly: *The ghost glided out of the room.*
2 (of a bird, aeroplane, etc.) to fly in the air by using air currents or already acquired momentum.
Word Family **glide** *noun* a gliding movement, as in a dance; **glider** *noun* 1 an aeroplane without an engine which is kept aloft by the action of air currents. 2 a person or thing that glides; **glidingly** *adverb*.

glimmer *noun*
1 a faint wavering light: *a glimmer of moonlight through the trees.*
2 a faint sign: *The news brought no glimmer of hope.*
Word Family **glimmer** *verb*; **glimmeringly** *adverb*.

glimpse *noun*
a brief view or look: *People waited for hours to catch a glimpse of the film star.*
• **glimpse** *verb*.
[Middle English *glimsen* to shine faintly]

glint *noun*
a quick bright flash of light, especially off a reflecting surface such as metal.
• **glint** *verb*.

glisten (gliss-'n) *verb*
to shine or sparkle, e.g. as a wet or highly polished surface does.
• **glisten** *noun*.

glitch *noun* (*plural* **glitches**)
(*informal*) a hitch or setback.

glitter *verb*
to sparkle with reflected light.
• **glitter** *noun*.
Word Family **glittery** *adjective*; **glittering** *adjective* glamorous: *her glittering rise to stardom.*

glitzy (glit-si) *adjective* (**glitzier; glitziest**)
(*informal*) showy, flashy.
[perhaps a blend of *glitter* and *ritzy*]

gloaming *noun*
(**the gloaming**) an old word for twilight or dusk.

gloat (*rhymes with* boat) *verb*
to think about or gaze on with pleasure or malicious delight: *He was obviously gloating over his opponent's hopeless position.*
Word Family **gloatingly** *adverb*; **gloater** *noun*.

global warming *noun*
a long-term gradual increase in climatic temperatures caused by the greenhouse effect.

globe *noun*
1 a sphere or spherical object.
2 a sphere with a map of the earth on it.
3 (**the globe**) the earth: *The Bible is translated into many languages of the globe.*
Word Family **global** (glo-b'l) *adjective* 1 of or relating to a globe. 2 relating to the whole world. 3 relating to the whole of something; **globalization, globalisation** (glo-b'l-ize-ay-sh'n) *noun* the process by which people, countries and economies are becoming increasingly interconnected with others around the world; **globally** *adverb*.
[Latin *globus*]

globe artichoke *noun*
a plant with an edible flower head consisting of many small fleshy leaves.

globetrotter *noun*
(*informal*) a person who travels widely.

globule (glob-yool) *noun*
a drop of liquid.
Word Family **globular** *adjective* 1 composed of globules. 2 globe-shaped.

glockenspiel (glok-en-shpeel) *noun*
Music a percussion instrument of tuned metal bars played with small hammers.
[German *Glocke* bell + *spielen* to play]

gloom *noun*
1 darkness, dimness or deep shadow.
2 a state of depression or hopelessness.
Word Family **gloomy** *adjective* (**gloomier; gloomiest**); **gloomily** *adverb*; **gloominess** *noun*.

glorify (glaw-ri-fie) *verb* (**glorifies; glorifying; glorified**)
to praise, honour or make glorious.
Word Family **glorified** *adjective* 1 made glorious. 2 (*informal*) given more importance than is due: *He calls himself a clerical assistant, but he's just a glorified tea*

boy; **glorification** (glaw-ri-fi-**kay**-sh'n) *noun*.

glory *noun* (*plural* **glories**)
1 high praise, honour or renown: *Our team basked in the glory of winning the big match.*
2 an object of pride: *a stately home which is one of the glories of colonial architecture.*
3 magnificence or radiant beauty: *a painting showing Christ in all his glory.*
• **glory** *verb* (**glories; glorying; gloried**)
1 to rejoice triumphantly.
2 to exult arrogantly or boastfully: *Students glory in their ability to embarrass a teacher.*
Word Family glorious *adjective* 1 having or bringing glory. 2 magnificent; **gloriously** *adverb*; **gloriousness** *noun*.
[Latin *gloria*]

glory hole *noun*
(*dated informal*) a very untidy room used for storage.

gloss¹ *noun* (*plural* **glosses**)
a surface shine or lustre.
Figurative *Don't be taken in by his gloss of respectability.*
• **gloss** *verb* to put a gloss on.
Phrase gloss over to cover up or disguise: *At the interview he tried to gloss over his lack of qualifications.*
Word Family glossy *adjective* (**glossier; glossiest**); **glossy** *noun* (*plural* **glossies**) an expensive magazine printed on glossy paper; **glossily** *adverb*; **glossiness** *noun*.

gloss² *noun* (*plural* **glosses**)
a note written in the margin or between the lines of a text, explaining a difficult passage.
• **gloss** *verb* to insert glosses in a text.

glossary (**gloss**-a-ree) *noun* (*plural* **glossaries**)
a list of technical terms or dialect words, usually at the end of a book, with explanations or definitions.
[Greek *glossa* a tongue, a foreign word]

glove (gluv) *noun*
a fitted covering for the hand, with a separate part for each finger.
Word Family gloved *adjective*; **glover** *noun* a person who makes gloves.

glove compartment *noun* also called **glovebox** (*plural* **gloveboxes**).
a small compartment in the dashboard of a car in which small articles, maps, etc. are kept.

glow (*rhymes with* slow) *verb*
to give off light and heat without flame: *The embers glowed in the hearth.*

Figurative *The cold wind makes your cheeks glow* (= be red and shining).
• **glow** *noun* a steady radiance.
Word Family glowing *adjective* 1 intense and brilliant: *glowing colours.*
2 enthusiastic: *She came home with a glowing report from her teacher,* **glowingly** *adverb*.

glower (*rhymes with* flower) *verb*
to stare sullenly or angrily.
Word Family glower *noun*; **glowering** *adjective*; **gloweringly** *adverb*.

glow-worm *noun*
a type of beetle whose females glow in the dark to attract the male.

glucose (**gloo**-koze) *noun*
a simple sugar, found in animals and plants and used as a source of energy in respiration.
[Greek *glykys* sweet]

glue (gloo) *noun*
a substance used to stick things together.
• **glue** *verb* to stick or adhere firmly.
Figurative *They were glued to the television all evening.*
Word Family gluey *adjective* like or covered with glue.

glue-sniffing *noun*
the breathing in of fumes from glue or a similar substance in order to change one's mental state.

glug *verb* (**glugs; glugging; glugged**)
(*informal*) to pour or drink making a gurgling sound.
• **glug** *noun*.

glum *adjective* (**glummer; glummest**)
downcast or dejected.
Word Family glumly *adverb*; **glumness** *noun*.

glut *noun*
an excess: *A glut of tomatoes brought the price down sharply.*

gluten (**gloo**-t'n) *noun*
a tough rubbery substance which remains in flour when the starch is taken out.

glutinous (**gloo**-tin-us) *adjective*
thick and sticky.
[Latin *glutinis* of glue]

glutton *noun*
1 a person who eats to excess.
2 a person with a great capacity or tendency to take, etc.: *a glutton for punishment.*
Word Family gluttonous *adjective*; **gluttonously** *adverb*; **gluttony** *noun* the habit or practice of eating to excess.
[from Latin]

gnarled (narld) *adjective*
knotty, twisted and rough: *a gnarled old tree*.

gnash (nash) *verb*
to grind the teeth together, especially in pain or rage.
• **gnash** *noun* (*plural* **gnashes**).

gnat (nat) *noun* also called **midge**.
any of a group of small biting flies related to the mosquito.

gnaw (naw) *verb*
1 to chew or bite on something persistently.
2 to trouble: *The crime gnawed his conscience*.
Word Family **gnawingly** *adverb*
persistently.

gnome (nome) *noun*
1 *Folklore* a small dwarf-like old man, believed to live in underground caves in order to guard the precious metals.
2 a garden ornament in the form of an old man.
Word Family **gnomish** *adjective*.

gnu (noo *or* new) *noun* also called **wildebeest**.
a large antelope with a head like an ox.

go *verb* (**goes; going; went; gone**)
1 to move: *The car is going too fast*.
2 to leave: *I'm afraid I have to go now*.
3 to travel in order to do an activity: *They've gone fishing*.
4 to become: *Her aunt went mad.* □ *The leaves were going brown*.
5 to become weak: *My voice is going*.
6 (of time) to pass: *Ten minutes went by*.
7 to stop existing: *Their civilization has long gone*.
8 to start doing something: *Let's go!*
9 (of a machine) to function: *My watch won't go*.
10 to progress: *The party's going well!*
11 to make a particular sound or movement: *The cow suddenly went 'moo'*.
12 to reach: *That alley goes to the shops*.
13 to be put: *Where does this pan go?*
14 to be said or sung: *I can't remember how the tune goes*.
15 to be accepted: *Whatever she says goes*.
16 to be sold: *Their house went for £100 000*.
17 (of a number) to divide: *Two goes into ten five times*.
18 to match: *Orange doesn't really go with purple*.
Phrases **be going to** 1 to have the intention of: *He's going to swim the Channel*. 2 to be certain to or expected to: *It's going to rain*. **go about** (of a ship) to turn around. **go along with** to agree with: *He refused to go along with my plan*. **go back on** to fail to keep: *You can't go back on your promise*. **go by, go under** to be known by: *Now that he's out of prison, he goes by the name of Standish*. **go down** 1 to be defeated: *Their team went down in the finals*. 2 to be remembered: *The battle went down in history*. 3 to fall ill: *She has gone down with tonsillitis*. 4 (*informal*) to go to prison. **go for** 1 to choose: *He goes for girls with dark hair*. 2 to attempt to get: *I decided to go for that job*. 3 to apply to: *You're lazy – and that goes for you, too!* 4 to attack: *The dog suddenly went for me*. **go in for** 1 to enter a competition. 2 to have an interest in: *Do you go in for old movies?* **go into** to investigate: *I didn't go into the details*. **go it alone** (*informal*) to do something by oneself. **go off** 1 to explode: *The fireworks went off suddenly*. 2 (of an alarm) to begin to make a noise. 3 (of food) to go bad. 4 (*informal*) to stop liking: *I've gone off coffee lately*. **go on** 1 to continue. 2 to talk continually: *He went on about his children*. **go on!** an expression of disbelief. **go out** to have a romantic relationship with someone. **go over** 1 to check: *We went over the small print in the contract*. 2 to be received: *Her speech went over very well*. **go through** 1 to endure: *He will go through any trials for his beliefs*. 2 to use up: *She goes through money like a house on fire!* **go through with** to persevere with: *He threatened to leave her, but he couldn't go through with it*. **go up** to explode or catch fire. **go with** to give one's agreement to. **go without** to manage or suffer without something wanted or needed.
• **go** *noun* (*plural* **goes**)
1 a try or attempt: *She wants to have a go at learning German*.
2 a turn in a game or series: *It's your go*.
3 a success: *They failed to make a go of it*.
4 spirit or energy.
5 bustling activity: *It's all go here!*
Phrases **from the word go** from the beginning. **on the go** very busy and active.

goad *noun*
a pointed stick used to drive cattle, etc.
• **goad** *verb* to prod or drive with a goad.
Figurative His wife's constant nagging goaded him to a fury.

go-ahead *noun*
(**the go-ahead**) (*informal*) permission to proceed.
• **go-ahead** *adjective* (*informal*)
enterprising and ambitious.

goal *noun*
1 *Sport* any of various structures or areas in field games through or over which a ball must be directed for a player to score.
2 *Sport* a point scored: *We got three goals*.
3 an aim or purpose towards which effort is directed: *My goal in life is to have a big house in the country*.
Word Family goalless *adjective* without goals: *a goalless draw*.

goalkeeper *noun*
Sport a player whose task is to stop the ball from entering the goal area.
Word Family goalie *noun* (*informal*) a goalkeeper.

goal kick *noun*
Sport a kick by the defending side from its own goal area.

goalmouth *noun*
Sport the area in front of the goal.

goalpost *noun*
Sport either of the two posts that are joined by a crossbar to form a goal in certain sports.
Phrase move the goalposts to change the rules suddenly and without warning.

goat *noun*
1 any of a group of wild or domesticated mammals with horns, shaggy hair and a beard, which eat shrubs, etc. and are valued for their meat and milk.
2 (*informal*) a man who is lecherous.
3 (*informal*) a stupid person.
Phrases act the goat to play around in a silly way. **get someone's goat** to annoy or irritate someone.
Word Family goatherd *noun* a person who looks after goats.

goatee (go-tee) *noun*
a small beard trimmed to a point below the chin, like a goat's beard.

gob¹ *noun*
a lump or mass.
[Old French *gobe* a mouthful]

gob² *noun*
(*informal*) the mouth.

gobbet *noun*
a piece or hunk: *a gobbet of food*.

gobble¹ *verb*
to eat and swallow rapidly.

gobble² *verb*
to make the throaty sound of a turkey.

gobbledegook (gobb-'l-dee-gook) *noun*
also **gobbledygook**
(*informal*) confusing, pompous and roundabout language.

go-between *noun*
a person who carries messages, proposals, etc. between two people or groups.

goblet *noun*
a large-bowled drinking vessel with a stem and a base but no handles.

goblin *noun*
Folklore a mischievous ugly elf.

gobsmacked *adjective*
(*informal*) completely astonished.
[*gob*, mouth]

gobstopper *noun*
a large round sweet for sucking.

go-cart ⇨ GO-KART.

god *noun*
1 (**God**) *Judaism, Christianity, Islam* the one Supreme Being, creator and ruler of the universe.
2 a worshipped being who is thought to have power over human affairs: *In Greek mythology Eros is the god of love.*
3 the image of a god or an idol.
4 a person viewed as or worshipped like a god.
5 (**the gods**) the highest gallery seats in a theatre.
Word Family godlike *adjective*; **godless** *adjective* 1 not believing in God. 2 evil or wicked; **godly** *adjective* (**godlier; godliest**) pious; **godliness** *noun*.

godchild *noun* (*plural* **godchildren**)
Christianity a child for whom an adult takes spiritual responsibility at its baptism.

goddess *noun* (*plural* **goddesses**)
1 a female being who is worshipped.
2 a woman who is adored for her beauty.

godfather *noun*
1 a male godparent.
2 the head of a criminal organization, especially an American Mafia one.

godforsaken *adjective*
(of a place) desolate and unappealing.

godhead *noun*
(*often* **Godhead**) *Religion* a god or the actual nature of a god.

godmother *noun*
a female godparent.

godparent *noun*
Christianity a person who takes spiritual responsibility for a child at its baptism.

godsend *noun*
an unexpected piece of good fortune.

Godspeed *interjection*
(*dated*) have a safe and successful journey!

goer (go-er) *noun*
a person or thing that goes.

gofer (go-fer) *noun* also **gopher**
(*informal*) a person who runs errands.

go-getter *noun*
(*informal*) a forceful and energetic person
who is successful in getting what he or she
wants.

goggle *verb*
to stare with widely opened eyes: *She
goggled at the picture.*
• **goggles** *plural noun* a protective eye
mask, as worn by skin-divers etc.

go-go dancing *noun*
a fast dance with sexual movements,
performed e.g. by girls in nightclubs.

going (go-ing) *noun*
the condition of something: *That path is
rough going.*
• **going** *adjective*
1 obtainable: *Is there any cake going?*
2 current: *I bought it for less than the going
rate.*

going concern *noun*
a profitable business.

going-over *noun*
1 an inspection: *I gave the car a thorough
going-over.*
2 (*informal*) a beating: *The informer got a
going-over from the gangsters.*

goings-on *plural noun*
actions or events, especially ones
disapproved of.

goitre (goy-ter) *noun*
an enlarged thyroid gland, causing
swelling of the neck.
[Latin *guttur* the throat]

go-kart *noun* also **go-cart**
a low flat vehicle with wheels and an
engine, used for sport.

gold *noun*
1 a soft yellow metal, used in decoration
and jewellery.
2 a deep yellowish-brown colour.
3 objects made of gold.
4 money or wealth.
5 a gold medal.
Word Family **golden** *adjective* **1** also **gold**
gold in colour: *golden hair.* **2** also **gold**
made of gold: *a golden chalice.* **3** (of an
opportunity) ideal or excellent. **4** (of a
period of history) very settled and
prosperous.

gold-digger *noun*
1 a person who digs for gold.

2 (*informal*) a person, especially a woman,
who forms relationships only in order to
acquire money or profit.

golden handshake *noun*
(*informal*) a sum of money given to an
employee on leaving a company,
sometimes as compensation for being
made redundant.

golden jubilee *noun*
the 50th anniversary of an important
event.

golden ratio *noun*
the ratio (g) such that $g : 1 = (g + 1) : g$,
which has a value of $\frac{1}{2}(1 + \sqrt{5})$. It has
many applications in art, architecture, etc.

golden rule *noun*
any basic or important rule.

golden syrup *noun*
a thick sweet liquid made from sugar cane.

golden wedding *noun*
the 50th anniversary of a wedding.

goldfish *noun* (*plural* **goldfish** or
goldfishes)
any of several small varieties of carp,
usually golden in colour and kept in an
aquarium.

gold leaf *noun*
gold that has been hammered into very
thin sheets, used to gild things.

gold medal *noun*
a medal made of gold or gold in colour
awarded to the winner of a race or
competition.

gold mine *noun*
1 a place where gold is obtained from the
ground.
2 a plentiful source of money or something
else that is greatly desired.

gold plate
tableware, etc. made of gold or thinly
veneered with gold leaf.
Word Family **gold-plate** *verb* to cover
with a thin layer of gold.

gold reserve *noun*
the gold held by a central authority to
maintain the value of paper money.

gold rush *noun* (*plural* **gold rushes**)
a mass movement of people to an area
where gold has been discovered.

goldsmith *noun*
a person who makes articles of gold.

gold standard *noun*
a monetary system in which the currency
unit is based on gold of a fixed weight.

golf *noun*

an outdoor game in which a player attempts to hit a small ball into a series of holes with special clubs, using as few strokes as possible.

Word Family **golf** *verb*; **golfer** *noun*.

golf club *noun* ⇨ CLUB (definition 2).

golf course *noun*

the ground over which golf is played. A sandy seaside course is also called a **golf links**.

golliwog *noun* also **golly** (*plural* **gollies**) (*informal*) a soft floppy doll with a black face.

golly *interjection*

(*dated*) an exclamation of surprise or pleasure.

gonad (go-nad) *noun*

Anatomy a sex gland, such as the testis in the male or the ovary in the female.

[Greek *goné* seed]

gondola (gon-da-la) *noun*

1 a narrow boat with high pointed ends, which is propelled from the stern with an oar, used on canals in Venice.

2 the passenger compartment on a ski lift, or hanging from an airship or balloon.

Word Family **gondolier** (gon-da-**leer**) *noun* a person who propels a gondola with an oar.

[Italian]

gone (gon) *adjective*

Phrase **far gone** dying or almost exhausted.

• **gone** *verb* the past participle of **go**.

Word Family **goner** *noun* (*informal*) a person or thing that is dead, ruined or past help.

gong *noun*

1 a large metal disc which is hit with a hammer, used to summon people to a meal, etc.

2 (*informal*) a medal.

[Malay]

gonorrhoea (gon-na-ree-a) *noun*

(*American* **gonorrhea**)

a venereal disease causing a thick creamy discharge from the sexual organs and pain on passing urine.

[Greek *gonos* semen + *rhoia* a flow]

goo *noun*

(*informal*) a thick sticky substance.

Word Family **gooey** *adjective*.

good *adjective* (**better**; **best**)

1 favourable or desirable: *Can you recommend a good restaurant?*

2 satisfying: *We had a good time.*

3 in an adequate condition: *His work is not good enough.*

4 skilful: *She's good at maths.*

5 morally right or kind: *good deeds.*

6 well-behaved: *Be good!*

7 thorough: *Go on, have a good cry.*

8 used in greetings: *Good morning, Mr Hussein.*

Phrases **as good as** very nearly: *It's as good as done.* **good and** (*informal*) completely: *I'll do it when I'm good and ready.* **make good 1** to be successful: *Since she went into films she has made good.* **2** to repair or pay for: *I offered to make good the damage.* **very good** (*dated*) certainly: '*Very good, sir,' said the butler.*

• **good** *noun*

1 something which is good, beneficial, profitable, etc.: *That attitude will do more harm than good.* □ *You should have a holiday for your own good.*

2 (**goods**) articles of trade, especially those which are transportable: *imported goods.*

3 possessions: *He left her all his worldly goods.*

Phrases **be no good, not be any good** not to be satisfactory. **be up to no good** to be doing something mischievous or wrong. **for good, for good and all** permanently: *I heard that she'd given up teaching for good.* **good for you!** well done!

• **good** *interjection* an expression of satisfaction or approval.

> [!] Note that *good* is not an adverb: if something is done in a good way it is done *well*, as in *The team played well today.*

goodbye *interjection*

an expression used when parting.

• **goodbye** *noun.*

[short form of *God be with ye*]

good faith *noun*

Phrase **in good faith** having, showing or expecting the qualities of honesty or sincerity.

good-for-nothing *adjective*

worthless.

• **good-for-nothing** *noun.*

Good Friday *noun*

Christianity the Friday before Easter, a holiday in memory of the crucifixion of Christ.

good-hearted *adjective*

kind.

good-humoured *adjective*

pleasant and cheerful.

Word Family **good-humouredly** *adverb.*

goodie noun ⇨ GOODY.

goodish adjective
fairly good or fairly big.

good-looking adjective
having an attractive face.

goodly adjective (**goodlier; goodliest**)
an old word for large or pleasant.

good-natured adjective
having a pleasant disposition.
Word Family **good-naturedly** adverb;
good-naturedness noun.

goodness noun
the quality of being good.
• **goodness** interjection an exclamation of
surprise or other emotion.

goodnight interjection
an expression used when parting at night.

good-oh interjection
(dated informal) an exclamation of
approval or satisfaction.

good Samaritan ⇨ SAMARITAN.

goodwill noun
1 a friendly disposition or cheerful
attitude.
2 the good reputation and friendly
relations with customers of a well-
established business: *The goodwill will be
sold with the business.*

goody noun (plural **goodies**) also **goodie**
1 (usually **goodies**) any nice things,
especially food.
2 a good person, especially the hero of a
film.
• **goody** interjection an exclamation of
delight.

goody-goody noun (plural **goody
goodies**)
a person who is keen to appear virtuous.
• **goody-goody** adjective.

gooey adjective ⇨ GOO.

goof noun
1 (informal) a mistake.
2 (informal) any foolish or stupid person.
• **goof** verb (informal) to blunder or
bungle.
Phrase **goof off** (informal) to try to avoid
work.
Word Family **goofy** adjective (**goofier;
goofiest**); **goofily** adverb; **goofiness** noun.

googly noun (plural **googlies**)
Cricket a ball spun with a wrist action
which turns it in the opposite direction to
that expected by the batsman.

goon noun
1 (informal) any stupid or awkward
person.

2 *American* a hired thug.
[after the hairy monster on a desert island
where Popeye the Sailor was stranded]

goose noun (plural **geese**)
1 any of various wild or domesticated web-
footed birds, larger than ducks, kept on
farms to be fattened for eating.
2 (informal) a silly or foolish person.
Phrases **cook one's goose** to spoil one's
chances, plans, etc. **wild goose chase** any
pointless pursuit.

gooseberry (**guz**-b'-ree) noun (plural
gooseberries)
1 a round green acid edible berry, growing
on a prickly bush.
2 (informal) a person who feels awkward
in the presence of two other people,
especially two who are romantically
interested in each other.

goose pimples plural noun also called
gooseflesh.
a bumpy skin due to cold or fear, when the
muscle fibres at the base of the hairs
contract.

goose step noun
a way of marching without bending the
knees, kicking each leg forward stiffly and
sharply.

gopher (go-fer) noun
1 any of various North American
burrowing animals, including ground
squirrels.
2 ⇨ GOFER.
[French *gaufre* a honeycomb (of burrows)]

Gordian knot noun
Phrase **cut the Gordian knot** to solve a
difficulty in an unorthodox or forceful
way.

> The expression **Gordian knot** refers to
> something very difficult to carry out.
> Gordius, a peasant who became King
> of Phrygia, fastened the yoke of his
> wagon to a beam with a rope in such a
> way that no one could untie the knot.
> The story was that whoever could undo
> it would reign over the whole of the
> East. Alexander the Great cut the knot
> in two with his sword instead of trying
> to untie it, so giving rise to the phrase
> *cut the Gordian knot*, meaning 'to solve a
> difficulty by force or by an unusual
> method'.

gore¹ noun
any clotted blood from a cut or wound.
Word Family **gory** adjective (**gorier;
goriest**) 1 bloody. 2 (informal)
unpleasant: *go into all the gory details.*

gore² *verb*
to wound or pierce, e.g. with a horn: *The matador was gored to death by the bull.*

gorge (gorj) *noun*
a narrow steep-sided river valley.
Phrase **make someone's gorge rise** to give someone a feeling of disgust or repulsion.
Word Family **gorge** *verb* to stuff with food or eat greedily; **gorger** *noun.*

gorgeous (gor-jus) *adjective*
1 splendid in appearance or colouring.
2 (*informal*) very good or enjoyable.
Word Family **gorgeously** *adverb;* **gorgeousness** *noun.*

gorgon (gor-g'n) *noun*
a terrifying or ugly woman.
[after the *Gorgons,* three sisters in Greek mythology who had snakes instead of hair, and who turned those who looked at them to stone]

gorilla *noun*
1 a very large ape found in the tropical forests of Africa.
2 (*informal*) a heavily built violent-looking man.

gormless *adjective*
(*informal*) stupid.
Word Family **gormlessly** *adverb.*

gorse (*rhymes with* horse) *noun* also called **furze.**
a wild prickly evergreen shrub with yellow flowers during most of the year.

gory *adjective* ⇨ GORE¹.

gosh *interjection*
(*dated*) an exclamation of surprise.

goshawk (goss-hawk) *noun*
a powerful hawk, sometimes trained for hunting.
[*gos-* for *goose*]

gosling *noun*
a young goose.

go-slow *noun*
the deliberate slowing down of work or production by workers, as a threat or protest to employers.

gospel *noun*
1 (**Gospel**) the account of the life of Christ told in the first four books of the New Testament.
2 any one of these books.
3 something which is accepted as unquestionably true: *You can take what he says as gospel.*
4 also **gospel music** an enthusiastic style of singing religious songs.
[Old English *god* good + *spell* news]

gossamer (goss-a-ma) *noun*
1 a thread or web of the fine silky substance made by spiders.
2 an extremely delicate variety of gauze.
• **gossamer** *adjective* light and fine as gossamer.

gossip *noun*
1 idle talk, especially about other people's private lives.
2 a person who talks idly or lets out secrets.
Word Family **gossip** *verb;* **gossipy** *adjective.*

gossip column *noun*
a column in some newspapers dealing with the social and private activities of famous people.
Word Family **gossip columnist** *noun.*

got the past tense and past participle of **get.**
Phrases **have got** have: *I have got a cold.* **have got to** have to or must: *I have got to be home by midnight.*

gotcha *interjection*
(*informal*) I have got you, I have caught you out.

Gothic *adjective*
1 relating to the style of art and architecture of medieval Europe, in which pointed arches, tall pillars, etc. expressed a strong sense of upward movement.
2 (of literature, etc.) concerned with horror or grotesque mystery.

gotten *American* a past participle of **get.**

> **!** The past participle *gotten* is widely used instead of *got* in American English. In British English *gotten* is only used in the adjective *ill-gotten,* meaning 'obtained dishonestly'.

gouge (gowj) *noun*
a chisel with a curved blade for cutting grooves.
• **gouge** *verb* to scoop out with or as if with a gouge: *They gouged his eyes out with their thumbs.*

goulash (goo-lash) *noun* (*plural* **goulashes**)
a stew of meat and onions flavoured with paprika.
[Hungarian *gulyás-hús* shepherd's meat]

gourd (goord) *noun*
1 a climbing plant which produces large hard-skinned fruit.
2 a dried shell of such fruit, used as a bowl, cup, etc.

gourmand (**goor**-mand) *noun*
a person who is too fond of good food.
[Middle English from Old French]

gourmet (**goor**-may) *noun*
a person who displays a fine knowledge of
food and drink.
[French, wine-taster]

gout (*rhymes with* out) *noun*
1 a disease that causes painful
inflammation of the joints, especially in
the big toe.
2 a poetic word for a drop or clot,
especially of blood.
Word Family **gouty** *adjective*.

govern (**guv**-'n) *verb*
1 to rule with authority: *The country is
governed by three army officers.*
2 to control: *You must learn to govern your
temper.*
3 *Grammar* to require a noun or pronoun
to be in a particular case, or a verb to be in
a certain mood: *In the sentence 'We left
them', the verb 'left' governs the objective case
of the pronoun, so 'them' is used instead of
'they'.*
Word Family **governance** *noun*.
[Latin *gubernare* to steer]

governess (**guv**-a-ness) *noun* (*plural
governesses*)
a female teacher employed in a private
household.

government (**guv**-'n-m'nt) *noun*
1 (*used with singular or plural verb*) the
group of officials elected or appointed to
control and organize a country.
2 the control or organization of a country.
Word Family **governmental** (guv-'n-
ment-'l) *adjective*.

governor (**guv**-'n-a) *noun*
1 any person who governs or controls,
such as the official in charge of a country,
state, prison, etc.
2 the representative of a monarch in a
dependent territory: *the Governor of
Jamaica.*
3 (*informal*) a form of respectful address:
Excuse me, governor.
4 anything which controls or regulates,
such as a device which limits engine
speeds.
Word Family **governorship** *noun*.

gown *noun*
1 a dress, especially a long or formal one.
2 a long loose cloak with wide sleeves,
worn as a sign of rank in some professions:
an academic gown.

grab *verb* (**grabs; grabbing; grabbed**)
1 to seize, especially roughly or hastily: *The
little girl grabbed a handful of chocolates.*
2 (*informal*) to impress: *How does the news
grab you?*
• **grab** *noun.*

grace *noun*
1 an elegance or beauty of form,
movement, expression, etc.: *the ballet
dancer's grace.*
Figurative At least he had the grace to
apologize.
2 any favour or mercy.
3 a short prayer said before or after a meal.
4 *Christianity* the freely given and
unmerited favour of God's love for
humanity.
Phrases **Her Grace, His Grace, Your
Grace** a form of address used to a
duchess, a duke or an archbishop. **put on
airs and graces** to behave in an affected
way intended to impress other people.
with bad grace grudgingly. **with good
grace** willingly.
• **grace** *verb* to confer honour upon: *Are
you going to grace the occasion with your
presence?*
Word Family **graceful** *adjective*;
gracefully *adverb*; **gracefulness** *noun*;
graceless *adjective*.
[Latin *gratia* a pleasingness]

gracious (**gray**-shus) *adjective*
kind or courteous: *The Queen greeted us
with a gracious smile.*
• **gracious** *interjection* an exclamation of
surprise.
Word Family **graciously** *adverb*;
graciousness *noun*.

gradation (gra-**day**-sh'n) *noun*
the state or process of change taking place
by degrees or stages: *the almost
imperceptible gradation of colours in a
rainbow.*

grade *noun*
1 a step or stage in rank, quality, value or
skill: *a high grade of uranium.*
2 a mark given to a student: *a C grade.*
3 *American* a set of pupils in a school: *I'm
in the second grade.*
Phrase **make the grade** to achieve a
desired standard.
• **grade** *verb* to arrange in grades or
classes: *Eggs are graded by size.*
[Latin *gradus* a step]

grade school *noun*
(*American dated*) a primary school.

gradient (gray-di-'nt) *noun*
the steepness of a slope expressed as
height risen per unit of horizontal distance
covered: *A road which rises 100 m while
covering 1000 m on the map has a gradient of
1 in 10.*

gradual (grad-yew-'l) *adjective*
taking place by degrees: *Over the years there
has been a gradual change in moral attitudes.*
Word Family gradually *adverb*;
gradualness *noun*.

graduate (grad-yoo-it) *noun*
a person who has received a diploma or
degree, at the end of a course of study,
from a college or university. Compare
POSTGRADUATE.
• **graduate** (grad-yoo-ate) *verb*
1 to receive an academic degree: *He
graduated in law.*
2 to mark with degrees for measuring: *a
ruler graduated in centimetres.*
Word Family graduation (grad-yoo-ay-
sh'n) *noun*.

graffiti (gra-fee-ti) *plural noun (singular
graffito)*
any unauthorized drawings or inscriptions
on a wall, etc.
[Italian *graffio* a scratch]

graft¹ (grahft) *noun*
1 any shoot or bud united with a living
plant to form a new growth.
2 an operation to replace diseased or
damaged tissue with tissue from another
part of the body, or with artificial material:
She had to have a skin graft.
3 the tissue used in such an operation.
• **graft** *verb*.

graft² *noun*
1 (*informal*) the unscrupulous use of one's
position to gain profit or advantage.
2 (*informal*) anything gained by such
means.
3 (*informal*) hard work.
Word Family graft *verb*; **grafter** *noun*.

Grail *noun* also **Holy Grail**
Medieval mythology the chalice used by
Christ at the Last Supper, especially as
sought by King Arthur's knights.

grain *noun*
1 any or all cereal plants.
2 the seeds of these plants: *The silo was full
of grain.*
3 a single seed of these plants: *a grain of
wheat.*
4 any small hard particle: *a grain of sand.*
5 the smallest amount of something: *He
hasn't a grain of sense in his head.*

6 the smallest unit of mass in the troy and
avoirdupois systems.
7 the lines and patterns made by fibres in
wood, fabric, etc., or by strata in a mineral
substance.
Phrases **go against the grain** to be
contrary to one's natural inclinations. **take
something with a grain of salt** not to
believe every word of something.
Word Family grainy *adjective* (**grainier;
grainiest**) 1 of, like or composed of
grains. 2 (of wood) having a prominent
grain.

gram *noun* also **gramme**
a metric unit of mass equal to one
thousandth of a kilogram. *abbrev.* g.

grammar (gramm-a) *noun*
1 the science or study of words and their
relationships in a language.
2 a book about grammar.
Word Family grammatical (gra-mat-i-
k'l) *adjective* 1 of or relating to grammar.
2 following the rules of grammar: *She
speaks grammatical English*;
grammatically *adverb*;
grammaticalness *noun*; **grammarian**
(gra-**mair**-ee-'n) *noun* an expert in
grammar.

grammar school *noun*
1 a secondary school, usually with
selective entry.
2 *History* an old-established school
founded primarily to teach Latin.

gramophone (gram-a-fone) *noun*
(*dated*) a record player.

grampus *noun* (*plural* **grampuses**)
1 a large dolphin-like marine mammal.
2 a blustering, snorting person.

gran *noun*
(*informal*) one's grandmother.

granary (gran-a-ree) *noun* (*plural
granaries*)
a building for storing grain.

grand *adjective*
1 magnificent or splendid: *a grand display.*
2 noble or proud: *the grand ladies of the
court.*
3 the main or most important: *the grand
staircase*. □ *the Grand Canal in Venice.*
4 (*informal*) excellent: *That's grand, thanks.*
5 (of family relationships) being one
generation removed from the relationship
named: *a grandmother.*
6 *Law* (of a crime) serious.
• **grand** *noun* (*plural* **grands**)
1 (*plural* **grand**) (*informal*) one thousand
pounds or dollars.

2 a grand piano.
Word Family grandly *adverb*;
grandness *noun*.
[Latin *grandis* full-grown]

grandad *noun* also **granddad**
1 (*informal*) one's grandfather.
2 a style of shirt having an upright collar
fastened with buttons.

grandchild *noun* (*plural* **grandchildren**)
a child of one's son or daughter.
Word Family granddaughter *noun*;
grandson *noun*.

grandee *noun*
a Spanish nobleman.
[from Spanish]

grandeur (**grand**-yer) *noun*
greatness or magnificence: *the grandeur of
the Alps*.
[French]

grandfather ⇨ GRANDPARENT.

grandfather clock *noun*
a large clock operated by a pendulum, in a
tall wooden case.

grandiloquence (gran-**dill**-a-kw'nce)
noun
a pompous or long-winded way of
speaking.
Word Family grandiloquent *adjective*;
grandiloquently *adverb*.
[Latin *grandis* grand + *loquens* speaking]

grandiose (**grand**-ee-oze) *adjective*
large and impressive, but too grand or
pompous.
Word Family grandiosely *adverb*;
grandioseness *noun*.

grand jury *noun* (*plural* **grand juries**)
in America, a group of people called to
decide whether there is sufficient evidence
to try someone charged with a crime.

grandly *adverb* ⇨ GRAND.

grandma *noun*
(*informal*) one's grandmother.

grandmama *noun*
(*dated informal*) one's grandmother.

grand master *noun*
a highly expert player and winner of
international competitions in games such
as chess or bridge.

grandmother ⇨ GRANDPARENT.

grandness *noun* ⇨ GRAND.

grand opera *noun*
an opera on a serious subject in which all
parts are sung and there is no spoken
dialogue.

grandpa *noun*
(*informal*) one's grandfather.

grandpapa *noun*
(*dated informal*) one's grandfather.

grandparent *noun*
a parent of one's parent.
Word Family grandmother *noun*;
grandfather *noun*.

grand piano ⇨ PIANO¹.

Grand Prix (gron **pree**) *noun* (*plural*
Grands Prix) (gron **pree**)
any of various major races for cars or
motorcycles.
[French *grand* big + *prix* prize]

grand slam *noun*
1 the achievement of winning all of a set of
sports competitions.
2 ⇨ SLAM².

grandson ⇨ GRANDCHILD.

grandstand *noun*
a raised, often sloping, structure with seats
for watching sporting events, etc.

grand total *noun*
the final amount after all the calculations
have been made.

grange (*rhymes with* strange) *noun*
1 a country house with its various farm
buildings.
2 *Medieval history* a barn.

granite (**gran**-it) *noun*
Geology a hard coarse-grained rock, used
as a building material.
[Italian *granito* grained]

granny *noun* (*plural* **grannies**) also
grannie
(*informal*) one's grandmother.

granny flat *noun*
a self-contained flat within a family home
for an elderly relative.

granny knot *noun*
a knot similar to a reef knot, but capable of
slipping.

grant *verb*
1 to give as a favour or privilege or in
response to a request: *The King granted
him his wish.*
2 to admit or acknowledge: *I grant that
point.*
Phrase take for granted 1 to assume: *I
took it for granted you'd be home on time.*
2 to accept without appreciating: *He takes
his wife's hard work for granted.*
● **grant** *noun* something which is granted,
especially money or land: *The museum
relies on a government grant.*

granulated (gran-yoo-late-id) *adjective*
(of white sugar) in the form of granules.

granule (gran-yool) *noun*
a small particle.
Word Family **granular** *adjective*.

grape *noun*
1 a small round green or purple fruit, growing in clusters on vines. Grapes can be eaten fresh, dried (as currants or raisins), or made into wine.
2 a dark purplish-red colour.
• **grape** *adjective*.

grapefruit *noun*
a large round yellow citrus fruit with a thick skin and a juicy acid centre.

grapeshot *noun*
a cluster of small iron balls, formerly used as ammunition in cannons.

grapevine *noun*
1 any vine which bears grapes.
2 (*informal*) any means by which rumours or secrets are passed on, e.g. by word of mouth.

graph (graf *or* grahf) *noun*
a diagram produced by plotting, often on squared paper, the relationship between two variables along a horizontal and vertical line (axis) respectively.

graphic (graf-ik) *adjective*
1 of or relating to writing, drawing or painting: *graphic techniques*.
2 vivid or life-like: *a graphic account of the battle*.
• **graphic** *noun* Computers a drawing, graph, etc. on a screen or stored as data.
Word Family **graphics** *plural noun*
1 (*used with singular verb*) the art of drawing, especially of making geometrical drawings in engineering and architecture.
2 also **computer graphics** images formed or manipulated on a computer; **graphically** *adverb*.

graphic design *noun*
the skill of putting together pictures and text in magazines, etc.
Word Family **graphic designer** *noun*.

graphics tablet *noun*
a device connected to a computer which enables the user to create pictures on the screen by means of a stylus.

graphite (graf-ite) *noun*
a soft black form of carbon, used in pencils and as a lubricant.

graphology (gra-foll-a-jee) *noun*
the study of handwriting, usually to analyse the writer's personality, etc.

graph paper *noun*
a piece of paper printed with small regular squares, used for drawing graphs and diagrams.

grapple *verb*
to struggle or wrestle: *She grappled with the problem*.

grappling hook *noun* also called **grapnel**, **grappling iron**.
any of various implements for hooking, grasping or holding, especially a small anchor with several hooks at the end.

grasp *verb*
1 to seize firmly, especially with the hands or arms.
2 to understand: *He tried hard to grasp the argument*.
Phrase **grasp at** to try to seize: *I grasped at the rope as it swung near*.
• **grasp** *noun*
1 a firm hold or grip.
2 understanding: *She has a thorough grasp of the problem*.
Word Family **grasping** *adjective* greedy.

grass *noun* (*plural* **grasses**)
1 any of a large group of plants with narrow leaves and jointed stems.
2 any ground, especially lawn or pasture, covered with such plants.
3 (*informal*) cannabis.
4 (*informal*) a person who gives information to the police.
Phrase **be put out to grass** to be retired from active service.
• **grass** *verb* to cover with grass.
Phrase **grass on** (*informal*) to give information about someone or something to the police.
Word Family **grassy** *adjective* (**grassier**; **grassiest**).

grasshopper *noun*
any of a group of herbivorous insects, including locusts, with hind legs adapted for jumping.

grassland *noun*
an area where only grass grows, usually because of low rainfall.

grass roots *adjective*
(*informal*) emerging spontaneously from the people: *There was a great deal of grass roots opposition to the government's proposals*.

grass snake *noun*
a harmless brown ringed snake.

grass widow *noun*
a woman whose husband is away temporarily, e.g. on a business trip.

grate¹ *noun* also **grating**
any of various metal frameworks of
crossed or parallel bars, e.g. one used to
hold fuel in a fireplace.

grate² *verb*
1 to shred or to reduce to small particles,
usually by rubbing against a rough
surface: *Grate the cheese into the pan.*
2 to make or cause to make a harsh
rasping sound: *The knife grated on the stone.*
3 to have an irritating effect: *His bad
manners grated on all of us.*
Word Family gratingly *adverb*.

grateful *adjective*
feeling or expressing thanks: *I'm grateful
for your help.*
Word Family gratefully *adverb*;
gratefulness *noun*.

grater *noun*
a kitchen utensil for shredding vegetables,
cheese, etc.

gratify (grat-i-fie) *verb* (**gratifies;
gratifying; gratified**)
to give pleasure to or satisfy.
Word Family gratifying *adjective*;
gratifyingly *adverb*; **gratification** (grat-
if-i-**kay**-sh'n) *noun*.

gratis (**grah**-tiss *or* **grat**-iss) *adverb*,
adjective
for nothing; free.
[Latin, out of kindness]

gratitude (**grat**-i-tewd) *noun*
the state of being grateful: *She found it hard
to express her gratitude.*
[Latin *gratus* pleasing]

gratuitous (gra-**tew**-i-tus) *adjective*
1 unnecessary: *The film was full of
gratuitous violence.*
2 free of charge.
Word Family gratuitously *adverb*,
gratuitousness *noun*.
[Latin *gratuitus* done as a favour]

gratuity (gra-**tew**-i-tee) *noun* (*plural*
gratuities)
something given freely, especially a gift of
money, such as a tip.

grave¹ (grayv) *noun*
1 the burial place of a corpse, especially a
hole dug in the ground.
2 (**the grave**) death.
Phrases have one foot in the grave to
be old, very ill or near to death. **turn in
one's grave** to be horrified: *Modern dances
would make grandad turn in his grave.*

grave² (grayv) *adjective*
serious or requiring careful consideration:
*A grave situation has developed in the Middle
East.* □ *a grave illness.*
Word Family gravely *adverb*.
[Latin *gravis* heavy]

grave³ (grahv) *noun Language* ⇨ ACCENT.

gravel (**grav** 'l) *noun*
Geology any stones larger than coarse sand
and finer than pebbles.
Word Family gravel *verb* (**gravels;
gravelling; gravelled**) to cover with
gravel; **gravelly** *adjective* 1 of, like or
containing gravel. 2 (of a voice) harsh or
hoarse.

graven image *noun*
an idol in the form of a carved figure.

gravestone *noun*
a stone, usually engraved or ornamental,
placed at the head of a grave.

graveyard *noun*
a cemetery, often surrounding a church.

gravitate (**grav**-i-tate) *verb*
to move or have a natural attraction
towards: *The children gravitated towards the
Christmas tree.*

gravitation (grav-i-**tay**-sh'n) *noun*
1 *Physics* the force of attraction between all
particles or bodies or the acceleration of
one towards another.
2 *Physics* the process caused by this force.
3 a natural tendency or attraction towards
something.
Word Family gravitational *adjective*.

gravity (**grav**-i-tee) *noun*
1 *Physics* the force existing between any
two bodies because of their mass, such
as the force between the earth and an
object on its surface. ⇨ WEIGHT *noun*
(definition 2).
2 seriousness: *unaware of the gravity of her
crime.*
[Latin *gravitas* weight, dignity]

gravy (**gray**-vee) *noun* (*plural* **gravies**)
a sauce, usually seasoned and thickened,
made from the juices produced while
cooking meat.

gravy boat *noun*
a long low jug used for serving gravy.

gravy train *noun*
(*informal*) a source of easy profit.

graze¹ *verb*
1 (of cattle, sheep, etc.) to eat grass.
2 to keep cattle or sheep.
3 (*informal*) to eat snacks frequently rather
than eating meals.

4 (*informal*) to change rapidly between television channels.
Word Family **grazing** *noun* land on which grass is grown for sheep and cattle to graze: *rough grazing*.

graze² *verb*
to touch or scrape lightly in passing.
• **graze** *noun* a slight scrape or abrasion.

grease (greece) *noun*
1 animal fat, especially when melted.
2 any soft oily or fatty substance.
• **grease** *verb* to put grease on or in.
Word Family **greasy** *adjective* (**greasier; greasiest**); **greasily** *adverb*; **greasiness** *noun*.

grease gun *noun*
any of various devices for forcing grease into mechanical parts.

grease monkey *noun*
(*informal*) a mechanic.

greasepaint *noun*
any make-up used by actors or performers, formerly a mixture of lard or fat with colouring.

great (grate) *adjective*
1 large or considerable: *There was a great rumble of thunder.* □ *She was in great pain.*
2 important or remarkable: *He is one of the great jazz musicians of this century.*
3 (*informal*) very good: *It was a great party.*
4 (of family relationships) being one generation removed from the named relationship: *a great-grandmother.*
Word Family **great** *noun* a significant or important person; **greatly** *adverb*; **greatness** *noun*.

greatcoat *noun*
a long heavy overcoat.

Great Dane *noun*
any of a breed of tall strong smooth-haired dogs, originally used to hunt wild boar.

grebe (greeb) *noun*
any of various short-winged almost tailless diving birds.

Grecian (**gree**-sh'n) *adjective*
of or relating to ancient Greece.

greed *noun*
an extreme desire for more than is needed or deserved, especially of food or wealth.
Word Family **greedy** *adjective* (**greedier; greediest**) very eager for large quantities of anything; **greedily** *adverb*; **greediness** *noun*.

green *noun*
1 a primary colour like that of growing grass; the colour between yellow and blue in the spectrum.

2 a grassy lawn or area, such as a **putting green** which surrounds each hole on a golf course.
3 (**greens**) any green or leafy vegetable.
• **green** *adjective*
1 having the colour green.
2 covered with grass or leaves: *green fields*.
3 consisting of green or leafy vegetables: *a green salad*.
4 relating to the conservation of the environment: *green issues*.
5 supporting the conservation of the environment: *the Green Party*.
6 unripe.
7 inexperienced.
8 sickly-looking: *She went rather green when the plane took off.*
Phrase **be green, go green** to be or become envious of someone.
Word Family **greenish** *adjective*; **green** *verb* to make or become green; **greenness** *noun*.

> **Green** is the colour of growing plants so it is not surprising that it has come to mean 'caring about the natural world around us'. It became very popular at a time when more and more people were beginning to be concerned about the destruction of the environment and it had the advantage of being a much simpler word than 'environmental' or 'ecological'. Its popularity was influenced by the German *grün* (green), since Germany was the first country to associate the colour with ecological issues.

greenback *noun*
(*American informal*) a dollar.

green belt *noun*
an area around a city where building is not allowed.

green card *noun*
1 an international certificate of motor insurance for UK drivers.
2 in America, a document allowing a foreigner to stay permanently.

greenery *noun*
any green foliage or plants.

green-eyed monster *noun*
(*informal*) jealousy.

greenfield site *noun*
a site for housing, industry, etc. which has never been built on before.

green fingers *plural noun*
(*informal*) a skill in gardening and growing plants.

greenfly noun (*plural* **greenfly** or **greenflies**)
a green aphid.

greengage noun
a sweet green fruit like a small plum.

greengrocer noun
a person selling fresh fruit and vegetables.

greenhorn noun
(*informal*) an inexperienced person.

greenhouse noun
a sheltered glass building for growing plants.

greenhouse effect noun
the increased warming of the earth caused by the atmosphere acting like the glass of a greenhouse, as pollutants build up in it.

greenhouse gas noun (*plural* **greenhouse gases**)
a gas which contributes to the greenhouse effect, e.g. carbon dioxide.

greenish ⇨ GREEN.

green light noun
(*informal*) permission or the opportunity to proceed with a project.
[from the railway signal light]

greenness noun ⇨ GREEN.

green room noun
a backstage room in a theatre or TV studio where performers can relax.

greenstick fracture noun
Medicine a fracture of a bone in which only one side is broken, mainly occurring in children.

greensward ⇨ SWARD.

Greenwich Mean Time (gren-ich **meen** time) noun
the time at Greenwich, used internationally as a standard reference.
[former London site of the Royal Observatory]

Greenwich meridian (gren-ich ma-**rid**-ee-an) noun
the line of longitude 0° through Greenwich in London, from which other measures of longitude are taken.

greenwood noun
an old word for a forest.

greet verb
to meet and welcome.
Word Family **greeting** noun any word or gesture of goodwill or welcome.

gregarious (gri-**gair**-ee-us) adjective
1 tending to live or form in groups.
2 sociable, friendly.

Word Family **gregariously** adverb; **gregariousness** noun.
[Latin *gregis* of a flock]

Gregorian calendar noun
the calendar in everyday use, having 365 days per year and 366 days in a leap year.
[established by *Pope Gregory XIII*, 1582]

gremlin noun
an imaginary gnome-like creature which people often blame for engine and other mechanical troubles.

grenade (gren-**ade**) noun
a small bomb thrown by hand or fired from a rifle.
[Spanish *granada* a pomegranate]

grenadier (gren-a-**deer**) noun
1 a member of the Grenadier Guards.
2 (*formerly*) a soldier who used grenades.

grew (groo) the past tense of **grow**.

grey (gray) noun (*American* **gray**)
1 a colour between black and white.
2 anything of this colour, especially a horse.
Word Family **grey** adjective; **grey** verb to make or become grey; **greyish** adjective; **greyness** noun.

grey area noun
an issue which is not clearly defined.

greyhen ⇨ BLACKCOCK.

greyhound noun
any of a breed of slender long-legged smooth-haired dogs, noted for their speed.

grey matter noun
1 *Anatomy* the parts of the central nervous system composed of nerve cells.
2 (*informal*) brain or intelligence.

grid noun
1 a framework of parallel or crossed bars.
2 a network of regular vertical and horizontal lines on a map, used for reference.
3 a network of cables connecting power stations.
4 *Car racing* the starting place where cars line up before a race.

griddle noun
a flat iron plate for baking or toasting cakes, biscuits, etc.

gridiron (**grid**-eye-’n) noun
1 a grill.
2 *American* a form of football played between two teams of eleven players who try to score by running with or passing the ball to the opponents’ goal line.

3 *American* the field, which is marked with white parallel lines at equal intervals, on which this game is played.

gridlock *noun*
a serious traffic jam across a network of streets.

grief (greef) *noun*
1 a deep or intense sorrow.
2 anything which causes sorrow or distress.
Phrases **come to grief** to fail or meet with disaster. **good grief!** an exclamation of surprise.
Word Family **grieve** *verb* to cause or feel grief.
[Latin *gravis* heavy]

grievance (gree-v'nce) *noun*
a real or imaginary cause for complaint.

grievous (gree-vus) *adjective*
severe or terrible: *He was charged with grievous bodily harm.*
Word Family **grievously** *adverb*.

griffin *noun* also **griffon**; **gryphon**
Greek mythology a creature with the head and wings of an eagle and the body of a lion.
[Greek *grypos* hook-nosed]

grill *noun*
1 a device on a cooker that radiates heat downward to cook food.
2 a metal utensil with parallel bars on which meat, etc. is cooked by direct heat.
3 any food cooked on or under a grill: *a mixed grill*.
4 a restaurant that serves grilled food.
● **grill** *verb*
1 to cook food on or under a grill.
2 (*informal*) to question persistently.

grille (gril) *noun*
a metal screen or lattice, often decorative, e.g. for a gate or the front of a vehicle.

grim *adjective* (**grimmer**; **grimmest**)
1 severe or merciless: *his grim expression*.
2 stern or harsh in appearance: *He approached the grim castle with fear.*
3 (*informal*) unpleasant.
Word Family **grimly** *adverb*; **grimness** *noun*.

grimace *verb*
to twist or distort the face, expressing pain, annoyance, etc.
● **grimace** *noun*.
[Spanish *grimazo* a caricature]

grime *noun*
any dirt, especially as a thick layer or ingrained into a surface.

Word Family **grime** *verb*; **grimy** *adjective* (**grimier**; **grimiest**); **griminess** *noun*.

grin *verb* (**grins**; **grinning**; **grinned**)
1 to smile widely in a relaxed, friendly or amused way.
2 to draw back the lips and show the teeth, in anger, pain, etc.
● **grin** *noun*.

grind (*rhymes with* kind) *verb* (**grinds**; **grinding**; **ground**)
1 to rub or crush a substance so as to reduce it to a powder.
2 to rub hard, especially in order to produce a smooth or sharp surface.
3 to work or produce by turning a handle: *The old man was grinding out a tune on a barrel organ.*
4 (*informal*) to work or study very hard or with great effort.
● **grind** *noun*
1 the act or noise of grinding.
2 (*informal*) any hard or monotonous work.
Word Family **grinder** *noun* a person or thing that grinds.

grindstone *noun*
a large coarse stone, shaped like a wheel and turned to grind, polish or sharpen tools.

gringo *noun*
(*informal*) (in Central and South America) a foreigner, especially a North American.
[Spanish, gibberish]

grip *verb* (**grips**; **gripping**; **gripped**)
1 to take or hold firmly.
2 to fascinate: *The audience was gripped by the dramatic scene.*
● **grip** *noun*
1 the act or power of gripping: *His grip on the branch loosened and he fell out of the tree.*
2 understanding.
3 a part of a handle intended to be gripped.
4 a hairgrip.
5 a light travelling bag.
Phrase **come to grips with, get to grips with** to deal with decisively or energetically.
Word Family **gripping** *adjective* very exciting; **grippingly** *adverb*.

gripe *noun*
1 (**gripes**) any sharp or violent pains in the abdomen.
2 (*informal*) a complaint or grumble.
● **gripe** *verb* (*informal*) to grumble or complain persistently.

grisly (griz-lee) *adjective* (**grislier;
grisliest**)
causing fear or horror.

grist *noun*
any grain to be ground or already ground.
***Phrase* grist to one's mill** something
which may be useful or advantageous.

gristle (griss-'l) *noun*
any cartilage present in meat.
***Word Family* gristly** *adjective* (**gristlier;
gristliest**) of or containing gristle.

grit *noun*
1 any small hard particles of stone, etc.
2 strength or courage.
• **grit** *verb* (**grits; gritting; gritted**) to
clench or grind: *She gritted her teeth.*
***Word Family* gritty** *adjective* (**grittier;
grittiest**); **grittily** *adverb*; **grittiness**
noun.

grizzle *verb*
(*informal*) to whine or complain.
***Word Family* grizzle** *noun*; **grizzler**
noun a person who grizzles.

grizzled (grizz-'ld) *adjective*
(of hair, etc.) grey.
[French *gris* grey]

grizzly bear ⇨ BEAR[2].

groan *verb*
1 to make a long low deep sound: *We all
groaned in despair at the thought of more
work.*
2 to be laden: *The table groaned under the
mountain of food.*
• **groan** *noun*.

groat *noun*
(*formerly*) an old English coin worth about
1·7 pence.

grocer (gro-ser) *noun*
a person selling general foods or
household goods.
***Word Family* grocery** *noun* (*plural*
groceries) 1 a grocer's shop.
2 (**groceries**) any articles bought from a
grocer, such as tea, sugar, cereals, etc.

grog *noun*
rum mixed with water.

groggy *adjective* (**groggier; groggiest**)
dazed and unsteady: *She got out of bed still
groggy with sleep.*
***Word Family* groggily** *adverb*;
grogginess *noun*.

groin *noun*
Anatomy the area at the base of the trunk
where the thighs join the body and where
the genitals are situated.

grommet *noun*
Medicine a tiny device put into the
eardrum to remove fluid and improve
hearing.

groom *noun*
1 short form of **bridegroom** a man who is
about to be or is newly married.
2 a person who cares for horses.
• **groom** *verb*
1 to brush and clean a horse.
2 to make neat and tidy: *Her hair is always
beautifully groomed.*
3 to prepare carefully: *She was groomed
from childhood to be a politician.*

groove *noun*
a long narrow channel in a hard material.
***Word Family* groovy** *adjective*
(**groovier; grooviest**) (*dated
informal*) very enjoyable or exciting.

grope *verb*
to feel or search uncertainly: *I groped for
the light switch in the dark.*
***Figurative* I** was groping for his name all
through our conversation.
***Word Family* groping** *adjective*;
gropingly *adverb*.

gross (groce) *adjective*
1 unattractively large.
2 coarse or vulgar.
3 (*informal*) revolting.
4 being the total amount without
deductions: *What is your gross salary?*
Compare NET[2] *adjective*.
5 (*formal*) extremely bad: *The doctor was
found guilty of gross negligence.*
• **gross** *noun* (*plural* **grosses**)
1 (*plural* **gross**) any group of twelve dozen
or 144.
2 a total profit or income.
• **gross** *verb* to earn a total of.
***Word Family* grossly** *adverb*; **grossness**
noun.

gross domestic product *noun*
the value of all the goods and services
produced within a country, used as a
measure of the country's wealth. Compare
GROSS NATIONAL PRODUCT.

gross national product *noun*
the value of all the goods and services
produced by a country, plus any income
earned from abroad and minus any money
paid overseas, used as a measure of the
country's wealth. Compare GROSS
DOMESTIC PRODUCT.

grotesque (gro-**tesk**) *adjective*
odd or unnatural in shape, appearance, etc.: *The grotesque statue frightened the children.*
Word Family **grotesquely** *adverb*; **grotesqueness** *noun*.
[Italian *grottesca* like an excavation, because art works dug up by archaeologists were considered bizarre]

grotto *noun* (*plural* **grottoes** or **grottos**)
a cave or cave-like area, especially a picturesque one.
[from Italian]

grotty *adjective* (**grottier**; **grottiest**)
(*informal*) dirty or unpleasant.
Word Family **grottiness** *noun*.
[short form of *grotesque*]

grouch (*rhymes with* crouch) *verb*
to complain or grumble.
Word Family **grouch** *noun* (*plural* **grouches**) **1** a complaint. **2** a person who complains or grumbles; **grouchy** *adjective* (**grouchier**; **grouchiest**); **grouchily** *adverb*; **grouchiness** *noun*.

ground¹ *noun*
1 the solid surface of the earth: *She fell to the ground unconscious.*
2 soil or earth: *The crops could not survive on the stony ground.*
3 an area used for a particular purpose: *a cricket ground.* □ *the hospital grounds.*
4 the position held by a person or group: *The demonstrators stood their ground and refused to move on.*
5 (**grounds**) a basis or reason: *What are the grounds for the divorce?*
Phrases **break new ground** to develop ideas, etc. that are very new and different. **gain ground 1** (of an idea) to become more accepted. **2** to get closer to something one is chasing. **go to ground** to retreat to a safe hiding place. **lose ground** to lose one's advantageous position. **on the ground** in the place of action, and not at a distance. **stand one's ground** to remain firm.
● **ground** *verb*
1 to prevent from flying.
2 (*informal*) to prevent from going out with friends as a punishment: *My mum grounded me for a whole month!*
3 to put on the ground or touch the ground with.
Phrase **be grounded in** to have a good basic knowledge of: *All our pupils are well grounded in science subjects.*

ground² *adjective*
consisting of fine dust-like particles as the result of grinding: *ground pepper.*
● **ground** *verb* the past tense and past participle of **grind**.
Word Family **grounds** *plural noun* sediment consisting of something which has been ground: *coffee grounds.*

groundbait *noun*
bait that is thrown into the water while fishing.

ground-breaking *adjective*
pioneering.

ground crew *noun*
the mechanics and other non-flying people working at an airfield.

ground floor *noun*
the floor at ground level in a building.

ground glass *noun*
1 a non-transparent type of glass.
2 glass in the form of powder.

grounding *noun*
any basic training or knowledge.

groundless *adjective*
having no basis or reason.
Word Family **groundlessly** *adverb*; **groundlessness** *noun*.

groundling *noun*
History a person who stood in the cheapest part of a theatre to watch the performance.

groundnut *noun*
a peanut.

ground rent *noun*
the rent paid to a landowner for the lease of the land on which a building is sited.

groundsheet *noun*
a waterproof sheet spread on the ground for protection from moisture, etc.

groundsman *noun* (*plural* **groundsmen**)
a person in charge of the care and maintenance of a sports field, etc.

ground speed *noun*
the speed of an aircraft relative to the ground directly underneath it. Compare AIR SPEED.

groundstroke *noun*
Sport a stroke made after the ball has bounced.

groundswell *noun*
the smooth massive waves resulting from a distant or past severe storm.

groundwater *noun*
water which lies underground in pores or spaces in the rocks, below the water table.

groundwork *noun*
the basis or foundation of anything.

ground zero *noun*
the point on the surface of the earth that is immediately above or below a nuclear bomb blast.

group (groop) *noun*
1 a number of people or things considered together, usually having related or similar characteristics.
2 *Medicine* a blood group.
3 *Chemistry* a vertical column in the periodic table containing elements with similar properties.
4 *Military* a tactical unit of an air force, consisting of several squadrons, a headquarters, etc.
5 *Maths* a set of elements subject to certain laws of operation.
• **group** *verb* to form into a group or groups.
Word Family **grouping** *noun* an arrangement of people or things to form a group.

group captain *noun*
Air force a commissioned officer ranking between wing commander and air commodore.

groupie (groop-ee) *noun*
(*informal*) a very keen fan of a celebrity or pop group who follows them on tour.

group therapy *noun*
the formation of groups of people with similar problems, e.g. alcoholism, to exchange ideas on their difficulties and successes.

grouse¹ (*rhymes with* house) *noun* (*plural* **grouse**)
any of various plump birds with feathered feet, shot for game.

grouse² *verb*
(*informal*) to grumble or complain.
• **grouse** *noun*.

grout (*rhymes with* out) *verb*
Building to fill or cover joints between tiles, bricks or stones with a thin mortar, often waterproof.
• **grout** *noun*.

grove *noun*
a small group of trees.

grovel (grov-'l) *verb* (**grovels; grovelling; grovelled**)
1 to act in an excessively humble or undignified way.
2 to throw oneself or lie on the ground, especially in fear, humility, etc.

Word Family **groveller** *noun*; **grovelling** *adjective*; **grovellingly** *adverb*.

grow (gro) *verb* (**grows; growing; grew; grown**)
1 to become larger in size, amount, etc.: *We grow quite rapidly during adolescence.* □ *Our fears grew as night fell.*
2 to develop: *Oak trees grow from acorns.*
3 to become: *The thunder grew louder.*
4 to produce by growing: *My dad's grown a beard.*
Phrases **grow on** to become more attractive to: *It's an odd colour, but it grows on you after a while.* **grow out of 1** to become too big for: *She's grown out of that jumper.* 2 to result from: *Their friendship grew out of their mutual loneliness.* **grow up** to become an adult.
Word Family **grower** *noun* 1 a person who grows things: *a fruit grower.*
2 anything which grows in a particular way: *That rose is a vigorous grower.*

growl (growl) *verb*
1 (of a dog, etc.) to make a deep and threatening rumbling sound.
2 to say something in a low rough voice.
Word Family **growl** *noun*; **growling** *noun, adjective*; **growlingly** *adverb*.

grown-up *adjective*
adult.
• **grown-up** *noun* (*informal*) an adult.

growth *noun*
1 the act or process of growing: *We did a survey on population growth.*
2 something which has grown.
3 *Medicine* a tumour.

growth industry *noun* (*plural* **growth industries**)
an industry which is growing particularly fast.

groyne *noun*
a stone or timber barrier built out from the seashore to check the movement of sand by longshore drift.

grub *noun*
1 a worm-like larva of certain insects.
2 (*informal*) food.
• **grub** *verb* (**grubs; grubbing; grubbed**)
1 to turn over the soil.
2 to dig up by the roots.

grubby *adjective* (**grubbier; grubbiest**)
dirty or unkempt.
Word Family **grubbily** *adverb*; **grubbiness** *noun*.

grudge *noun*
a deep feeling of resentment, envy, etc.

Word Family **grudge** *verb* **1** to feel a grudge because of another's wealth, good fortune, etc. **2** to give or allow unwillingly; **grudgingly** *adverb*.

gruel (groo-'l) *noun*
a thin cereal made by boiling oatmeal in water or milk.

gruelling *adjective*
exhausting or severe.

gruesome (groo-sum) *adjective*
causing horror or disgust.

gruff *adjective*
rough or harsh: *a gruff voice*.
Word Family **gruffly** *adverb*; **gruffness** *noun*.

grumble *verb*
to complain discontentedly.
Word Family **grumble** *noun*; **grumbler** *noun* a person who grumbles; **grumbling** *adjective*; **grumblingly** *adverb*.

grumpy *adjective* (**grumpier; grumpiest**)
bad-tempered or surly.
Word Family **grumpily** *adverb*; **grumpiness** *noun*.

grunge *noun*
1 dirt, grime.
2 also **grunge rock** a style of rock music which has a harsh guitar sound.
3 a fashion style in which people wear torn clothes and dress untidily.
Word Family **grungy** *adjective* (**grungier; grungiest**).

grunt *verb*
to make a low harsh sound like a pig.
• **grunt** *noun*.

gryphon ⇨ GRIFFIN.

G-string *noun*
a strip of cloth between the legs secured by a string round the waist.

G-suit *noun*
an inflatable suit worn by fighter pilots to prevent blackouts at high speed.

guacamole (gwak-a-**mole**-ay) *noun*
a dish made of crushed avocados.
[Latin American Spanish]

guano (**gwah**-no) *noun*
the droppings of seabirds, or a synthetic product of similar composition, used as manure and in chemical fertilizers.

guarantee (garr-en-**tee**) *noun*
1 a formal or official promise that something is made or will be done to specified standards.
2 an assurance: *Money is no guarantee of happiness*.

3 *Law* a written promise to be responsible for someone else's debts if the person does not pay them himself or herself.
• **guarantee** *verb*.

guarantor (garr-en-**tor**) *noun*
a person who makes or gives a guarantee.

guard (gard) *verb*
to watch over in order to keep safe or under one's control.
Phrase **guard against** to take precautions against: *Take a lot of vitamin C to guard against a cold*.
• **guard** *noun*
1 a person who guards: *the guard on a train*.
2 a group of people who guard: *The President had a guard of honour*.
3 the act of guarding: *The prisoner was kept under close guard*.
4 a piece of equipment designed to give some form of physical protection, e.g. shinguards, fireguards and mudguards.
5 anything which offers protection: *An insurance policy provides a guard against loss*.
Word Family **guarded** *adjective* cautious; **guardedly** *adverb*.

guardian (**gar**-dee-an) *noun*
1 a person who guards or protects.
2 *Law* a person who has the right and duty to protect another person.
Word Family **guardianship** *noun*.

guardroom *noun*
a building housing military police on duty and their prisoners.

guava (**gwah**-va) *noun*
a tropical American tree, the fruit of which is used to make jam, jelly, etc.

gudgeon (**guj**-'n) *noun*
any of a group of small fish much used for bait.
[Greek *kobios*]

guerrilla (ger-**ill**-a) *noun* also **guerilla**
a member of an independent military force, often revolutionary, which makes surprise attacks on enemy positions, supplies, etc.
[Spanish, little war]

guess (gess) *verb*
1 to give an answer or opinion based on uncertain knowledge.
2 to find or give the correct answer: *I guessed what he had in mind*.
3 (*informal*) to suppose: *'Are you going to tell her?'* – *'I guess so.'*

Word Family guess *noun* (*plural* guesses); guesswork *noun* something based on guessing.

guesstimate (gess-ti-m't) *noun* (*informal*) an estimate based chiefly on guessing.

guest (gest) *noun*
1 a person who receives hospitality, entertainment, etc. from another.
2 a person who pays for board, lodging, etc.: *a hotel guest.*
Phrases be my guest (*informal*) please do it, take it, etc. guest of honour the most important guest at a social event.

guesthouse (gest-house) *noun* a house which gives temporary accommodation to paying guests, e.g. during holidays, etc.

guff *noun* (*informal*) nonsense.

guffaw *noun* a noisy coarse laugh.
• guffaw *verb.*

guide (*rhymes with* wide) *verb*
1 to show the way to: *We guided them to the exit.*
2 to direct a person's actions: *Be guided by your instincts.*
• guide *noun*
1 a person who guides, especially one employed to guide tourists, etc.
2 also guidebook a book with useful advice or information, e.g. for visitors or travellers.
3 (Guide) a member of the Guide Association, an organization for girls which emphasizes self-reliance and proficiency in a wide range of activities.
Word Family guidance *noun* 1 the act of guiding. 2 advice or instruction.

guided missile *noun* a missile whose direction is controlled throughout its flight. Compare BALLISTIC MISSILE.

guide dog *noun* a dog of a suitable breed, such as a Labrador, specially trained to lead a blind person.

guideline *noun* an informal rule or piece of advice about how to do something.

guild (gild) *noun* a group of people, such as weavers, belonging to the same trade and joined together for mutual protection.

guilder *noun* the basic unit of money in the Netherlands.

guile (gile) *noun* deceit or cunning.
Word Family guileless *adjective* sincere and honest; guilelessly *adverb.*

guillemot (gil-ee-mot) *noun* a diving bird of the auk family. [French]

guillotine (gill-o-teen) *noun*
1 a machine consisting of a heavy blade which falls between two grooved posts, used to behead a person.
2 a device with a long blade for trimming paper.
3 a timetable imposed to limit discussion of a bill and hasten it through Parliament.
• guillotine *verb.*
[after *J. I. Guillotin*, 1738-1814, a French doctor who recommended its use]

guilt (gilt) *noun*
1 the condition of being responsible for a wrongdoing.
2 a feeling of shame or shame for a wrongdoing, etc.

guilty (gil-tee) *adjective* (guiltier; guiltiest)
1 having done wrong: *We all knew he was guilty.*
2 feeling or showing guilt: *She had a guilty conscience after she lied to her mother.*
Word Family guiltily *adverb*; guiltiness *noun.*

guinea (ginn-ee) *noun* (*formerly*) a sum of money equal to £1·05.

guineafowl (ginn-ee-fowl) *noun* (*plural* guineafowl) a dark grey bird with white spots, valued for its flesh and eggs. The female is called a guinea hen.
[first bred on the *Guinea* coast, Africa]

guinea pig (ginn-ee pig) *noun*
1 a short-eared short-tailed rodent, kept as a pet and used in laboratory experiments, originally bred by the Indians of the Andes for its flesh.
2 (*informal*) a person used as the subject of an experiment.

guise (gize) *noun* an external appearance, especially an assumed appearance.

guitar (gi-tar) *noun* *Music* any of a family of fretted instruments, usually with six strings, which are plucked with the fingers or a plectrum.
Word Family guitarist *noun.*

gulch noun (plural **gulches**)
American a narrow deep ravine.

gulf noun
1 a large bay which extends far into the land area.
2 a wide gap or distance: *The gulf between them widened over the years.*
3 a chasm.

gull[1] noun
short form of **seagull** any of a family of long-winged seabirds with webbed feet, often white with grey wings.

gull[2] verb
to cheat or deceive.

gullet noun
Anatomy the oesophagus.

gullible adjective
easily cheated or deceived.
Word Family **gullibly** adverb; **gullibility** (gull-i-**bill**-i-tee) noun.

gully noun (plural **gullies**) also **gulley**
1 Geography a long narrow channel cut by water or due to soil erosion.
2 Cricket a fielding position between slips and point, or a player in this position.

gulp verb
1 to swallow in large amounts.
2 to make a swallowing movement, e.g. because one is very surprised.
• **gulp** noun.

gum[1] noun
1 any of a group of water-soluble complex substances derived from plants and used as glues, in medicine, in food and in industrial substances.
2 (informal) chewing gum or bubblegum.
3 a hard gelatinous sweet.
Word Family **gum** verb (**gums; gumming; gummed**) to fill, cover or stick together with or as if with gum; **gummy** adjective (**gummier; gummiest**).

gum[2] noun
Anatomy the firm flesh in which the teeth are set.

gum[3] noun
Phrase **by gum!** an expression used to emphasize something.

gumboot noun
(dated) a wellington.

gumption (**gump**-sh'n) noun
(informal) initiative and common sense.

gumshield noun
a pad or plate worn by sports players to protect their teeth.

gum tree noun
a eucalyptus.
Phrase **up a gum tree** (informal) in a serious predicament.

gun noun
any weapon or device which has a tube or barrel through which a bullet, shell or substance is discharged.
Phrases **go great guns** to make very good progress. **jump the gun** to start prematurely. **stick to one's guns** to insist on one's ideas, rights, etc.
• **gun** verb (**guns; gunning; gunned**) to hunt or shoot with a gun.

gunboat noun
a boat with light guns, used for patrols, etc.

gun carriage (**gun** car-ij) noun
the wheeled structure on which an artillery gun is mounted.

guncotton noun
a powerful explosive.

gun dog noun
a dog, such as a spaniel, pointer or setter, trained to find or fetch game birds.

gunfire noun
the repeated firing of a gun or guns.

gunge noun
(informal) a sticky messy substance.

gung-ho adjective
excessively enthusiastic.
[Chinese *kung* to work + *ho* together; adopted as a motto by some American troops in the Second World War]

gunk noun
(informal) an unpleasantly messy substance.

gunman noun (plural **gunmen**)
a man who uses a gun to commit a crime or a terrorist act.

gunmetal noun
a dark grey alloy of copper, tin and zinc, used for belt buckles, etc.

gunnel ⇨ GUNWALE.

gunner noun
1 a private in an artillery unit.
2 (informal) any member of an artillery unit.
3 the officer in charge of a ship's guns.

gunpoint noun
Phrase **at gunpoint** in the act of threatening someone or being threatened with a gun.

gunpowder *noun*
a mixture of potassium nitrate, powdered charcoal and sulphur, used as an explosive.

gunrunning *noun*
the smuggling of guns between countries.
Word Family gunrunner *noun*.

gunshot *noun*
1 the range of a gun.
2 the firing or discharge of a gun.
3 the bullet fired from a gun.

gunsmith *noun*
a person who makes or repairs firearms.

gunwale (gun-n'l) *noun* also **gunnel**
Nautical the upper edge around the hull of a small boat or, formerly, a warship.

guppy *noun* (*plural* **guppies**)
a small West Indian fish, often kept in home aquariums.

gurdwara (gerd-**wah**-ra) *noun*
a Sikh place of worship.
[Punjabi *gurduara* doorway to the guru]

gurgle *verb*
to make a bubbling sound, such as that made by flowing water.
• **gurgle** *noun*.

guru (goo-roo) *noun*
1 *Hinduism* a spiritual teacher.
2 *Sikhism* the title of each of the first ten teachers of the Sikh religion.
3 a respected teacher: *My manager called in a computer guru.*
[Hindi]

Guru Granth Sahib (goo-roo grunt sa-ib) *noun*
the sacred collection of Sikh scriptures.
[Punjabi]

gush *verb*
1 to flow suddenly and with force.
2 to display emotion or enthusiasm extravagantly.
Word Family gush *noun* (*plural* **gushes**); **gushy** *adjective* (**gushier**; **gushiest**); **gushing** *adjective*; **gusher** *noun*.

gusset *noun*
a flat insert, usually triangular, to connect and reinforce the parts of something, such as the crotch of a piece of underwear.

gust *noun*
a sudden rush or burst.
Word Family gust *verb*; **gusty** *adjective* (**gustier**; **gustiest**); **gustily** *adverb*; **gustiness** *noun*.

gusto *noun*
a vigorous enjoyment.
[Italian, taste, relish]

gut *noun*
1 ⇨ INTESTINE.

2 (**guts**) the entrails.
3 (**guts**) (*informal*) courage or endurance: *It takes guts to sail around the world alone.*
4 a fibre made from the intestines of some animals, used for violin strings, tennis rackets, etc.
• **gut** *verb* (**guts**; **gutting**; **gutted**)
1 to take out the entrails of.
2 to destroy the interior of: *The house was gutted by fire.*

gutted *adjective*
(*informal*) very upset.

gutter *noun*
1 a channel for carrying fluids away.
2 any low-class, wretched or degrading surroundings: *She rose from the gutter to stardom.*

guttering *noun*
the gutters of a building.

guttersnipe *noun*
a street urchin.

guttural (gut-a-r'l) *adjective*
(of a sound or voice) throaty or harsh.
Word Family gutturally *adverb*.

guy[1] (*rhymes with* high) *noun*
1 (*informal*) a man.
2 a figure representing Guy Fawkes, burnt on 5 November.

guy[2] *noun*
a rope or device used to steady, guide or fix something firmly in place.
• **guy** *verb*.

guzzle *verb*
to eat or drink greedily.
Word Family guzzler *noun*.

gybe (jibe) *verb* also **jibe**
Nautical to turn a boat, when sailing before the wind, so that the boom swings across from one side to the other.
• **gybe** *noun*.

gym (jim) *noun*
1 (*informal*) a gymnasium.
2 (*informal*) gymnastics.

gymkhana (jim-**kah**-na) *noun*
a horse-riding competition consisting of various events.

> The word **gymkhana** was brought to Britain from India and is derived from Hindi *gendkhana* (ball-house or racket court). *Gymkhana* in Britain at first referred to a sports ground, the meaning perhaps being affected by confusion with *gymnasium*; the horse-riding sense developed after the First World War.

gymnasium (jim-**nay**-zee-um) *noun*
(*plural* **gymnasiums** or **gymnasia**)
a room fitted with equipment for physical
training and gymnastics.
[Greek *gymnazein* to exercise]

gymnastics (jim-**nas**-tiks) *plural noun*
1 any exercises which develop agility,
suppleness and strength.
2 (*used with singular verb*) the principles of
such exercises.
Word Family **gymnastic** *adjective*;
gymnast (**jim**-nast) *noun* a person trained
or skilled in gymnastics.

gymslip *noun*
a sleeveless dress worn by schoolgirls,
especially in former times.

gynaecology (gie-na-**koll**-a-jee) *noun*
the study of the female reproductive
system and its diseases.
Word Family **gynaecological** (gie-na-
ka-**loj**-i-k'l) *adjective*; **gynaecologist** *noun*.
[Greek *gynaikos* of a woman + *-logy*]

gypsum (**jip**-sum) *noun*
a soft mineral used for plaster of Paris and
as a fertilizer.

gypsy (**jip**-see) *noun* (*plural* **gypsies**) also
gipsy
a member of a travelling people who speak
Romany, a language related to Hindi.
• **gypsy** *adjective* of or relating to gypsies:
a gypsy caravan.
[a short form of *Egyptian*, because they
were believed to come from Egypt]

gyrate (jie-**rate**) *verb*
to revolve or move in a circle.
Word Family **gyration** *noun* a turning or
circular movement.

gyroscope (**jie**-ra-skope) *noun*
a device consisting of a rotating wheel
which resists any movement when
spinning, used as the basis of stabilizers in
ships, compasses, etc.
[Greek *gyros* ring + *skopein* to look at]

Hh

ha *interjection* also **hah**
an exclamation of triumph, suspicion, surprise, etc.

habeas corpus (hay-bee-ass **kor**-pus) *noun*
Law an order that an imprisoned person must be brought before a court for trial, as a protection against illegal imprisonment.
[Latin, *you shall produce the body*]

haberdasher (**hab**-a-dash-a) *noun*
1 a person who sells items such as ribbons, thread, needles, etc.
2 *American* a person who sells men's hats, shirts, socks, etc.
Word Family **haberdashery** *noun* (*plural* **haberdasheries**) 1 the goods sold by a haberdasher. 2 the shop in which such goods are sold.

habit *noun*
1 a regular practice or usage.
2 the clothing worn by members of a religious order: *a monk's habit.*
3 an old word meaning clothing.
Word Family **habitual** (ha-**bit**-yew-'l) *adjective*; **habitually** *adverb*.

habitable (**hab**-it-a-b'l) *adjective*
fit to be lived in: *a house in habitable condition.*
Word Family **habitability** (hab-it-a-**bill**-i-tee) *noun*.

habitat (**hab** i-tat) *noun*
the particular environment where a plant or animal is usually found, e.g. in the sea, in alpine areas, etc.

habitation (hab-i-**tay**-sh'n) *noun*
1 (*formal*) a home.
2 the act of inhabiting: *slums unfit for human habitation.*

habituate (ha-**bit**-yoo-ate) *verb*
to accustom: *Nurses are habituated to the sight of blood.*

hacienda (hass-ee-**en**-da) *noun*
Spanish-American a large estate.
[Spanish]

hack[1] *verb*
1 to cut roughly or clumsily: *She hacked away at the tree trunk.*
2 to cough spasmodically with a dry throat.
3 to gain unauthorized access to a computer system.
Phrase **hack it** (*informal*) to cope.
● **hack** *noun*
1 any cut or gash.
2 a short dry cough.

hack[2] *noun*
1 a horse used for general riding.
2 any old worn-out horse.
3 a ride on a horse.
4 a person employed to do dull and arduous literary work.
Word Family **hack** *verb* to ride a horse for pleasure.
[shortening of *hackney*]

hacker *noun*
a person who illegally gains access to a computer program.

hackles *plural noun*
the hairs on the back of an animal's neck.
Phrase **make someone's hackles rise** to make someone very angry.

hackney *noun*
1 one of a breed of horses for ordinary riding or for pulling carriages.
2 a horse-drawn cab kept for hire.

hackneyed (**hak** nid) *adjective*
stale or trite, as a result of too frequent use: *a hackneyed phrase.*

hacksaw *noun*
a saw with a narrow blade set in a frame, used for cutting metal, etc.

had the past tense and past participle of **have.**

haddock (**had**-'k) *noun*
any of a group of edible fish related to the cod and found in the North Atlantic, often eaten smoked. ⇨ FINNAN.

Hades (**hay** deez) *noun*
Mythology the underworld, where the spirits of the dead go.
[after *Hades*, the god of the underworld in Greek mythology]

hadn't *contraction*
a short form of **had not**: *She hadn't forgotten.*

haematite (**hee**-ma-tite) *noun* (*American* **hematite**)
Geology a common mineral, the principal source of iron.
[Greek *haimatites* blood-like]

haematology (hee-ma-**tol**-a-jee) *noun*
(*American* **hematology**)
Medicine the study of the nature, function and diseases of the blood.
Word Family **haematologist** *noun*.
[Greek *haimatos* of blood + -*logy*]

haemoglobin (hee-ma-**glo**-bin) *noun*
(*American* **hemoglobin**)
Biology a red pigment found in the red blood cells of vertebrates, which transports oxygen around the body.

haemophilia (hee-ma-**fill**-ee-a) *noun*
(*American* **hemophilia**)
a hereditary disease in which blood clots poorly, causing small injuries to bleed excessively.
Word Family **haemophiliac** *noun* a person with haemophilia.
[Greek *haima* blood + *philein* to love]

haemorrhage (**hem**-a-rij) *noun*
(*American* **hemorrhage**)
a loss of blood, especially internally.
• **haemorrhage** *verb*.
[from Greek]

haemorrhoids (**hem**-a-roidz) *plural noun*
(*American* **hemorrhoids**) also called **piles**.
a painful expanded mass of veins in the anus.

haft (*rhymes with* raft) *noun*
the handle of a knife, dagger, or sword.

hag *noun*
1 an ugly old woman.
2 a witch.

haggard (**hag**-'rd) *adjective*
looking worn-out or exhausted.
Word Family **haggardly** *adverb*; **haggardness** *noun*.

haggis *noun* (*plural* **haggis**)
Scottish a food like a large sausage, made of the offal of a sheep, minced with oatmeal, suet, flavourings, etc. and boiled in a bag made from the sheep's stomach.

haggle *verb*
to argue or dispute in a petty way, especially over a price.
Word Family **haggler** *noun*.

hagiography (hag-ee-**og**-ra-fee) *noun*
the biography of saints.
[Greek *hagios* holy + *graphein* to write]

hag-ridden *adjective*
tormented or distressed.

hah ⇨ HA.

ha-ha *noun*
a fence sunk in a ditch so that it does not spoil the view from a house.
[French]

haiku (**high**-koo) *noun* (*plural* **haiku** or **haikus**)
a Japanese verse form in three lines of five, seven and five syllables respectively.
[Japanese, shortening of *haikai no ku*, light verse]

hail[1] *verb*
1 to greet or welcome.
2 to acclaim enthusiastically: *The critics hailed her latest play as a triumph*.
Phrase **hail a taxi** to signal to a taxi to stop. **hail from** to have one's origins in.
• **hail** *noun* a shout to attract attention.
• **hail** *interjection* an old exclamation of greeting or welcome.

hail[2] *noun*
1 frozen raindrops which fall from the sky in a shower.
2 a shower of things: *The gangster died in a hail of bullets*.
• **hail** *verb* to fall as hail.
Word Family **hailstone** *noun* a pellet of hail; **hailstorm** *noun*.

hail-fellow-well-met *adjective*
very familiar or effusively friendly: *I can't stand his hail-fellow-well-met heartiness*.

Hail Mary *noun*
a prayer to the Virgin Mary.

hair *noun*
1 *Anatomy* any of the fine thread-like structures which grow from the skin of most animals.
2 a growth of such threads, forming the natural covering of the human head, etc.
3 any fabric made from the fur of an animal: *a camel-hair coat*.
Phrases **hair of the dog** (*informal*) an alcoholic drink taken when one feels bad due to drinking previously. **hair's breadth** an extremely short distance. **let one's hair down** (*informal*) to behave in a relaxed or uninhibited way. **split hairs** to make unimportant or petty distinctions. **without turning a hair** (*informal*) remaining calm or untroubled.

hairband *noun*
a strip of cloth or plastic used to keep a woman's hair in place.

hairbrush *noun* (*plural* **hairbrushes**)
a brush used to keep one's hair tidy.

haircut *noun*
1 the act of cutting hair.
2 the style in which hair is cut.

hairdo *noun*
(*informal*) a hairstyle.

hairdressing *noun*
the art of cutting, styling, colouring and caring for the hair.
Word Family **hairdresser** *noun* a person who is trained or skilled in hairdressing.

hairdryer *noun* also **hairdrier**
a machine for blowing air onto the hair to dry it.

hairiness ⇨ HAIRY.

hairline *noun*
1 the junction between the edge of the hair and the skin, especially at the forehead.
2 a very thin line.

hairpiece *noun*
a mass of real or artificial hair attached to a base, worn on the head to cover a bald patch or to add to a hairstyle.

hairpin *noun*
a loop of thin metal squeezed together, used to hold the hair in place.

hairpin bend *noun*
a U-shaped bend in a road.

hair-raising *adjective*
terrifying.

hair shirt *noun*
a shirt of rough material, worn as a penance.

hairslide *noun*
a clip pushed into a woman's hair to keep it in position.

hair-splitting *noun*
the act of making petty or unnecessary distinctions.

hairspring *noun*
a fine coiled spring in a watch or clock, which helps to regulate the beats.

hairstyle *noun*
the way in which the hair is arranged.
Word Family **hairstylist** *noun*.

hair trigger *noun*
a trigger which is operated by a very slight pressure.

hairy *adjective* (**hairier; hairiest**)
1 covered with or resembling hair.
2 (*informal*) dangerous or hair-raising.
Word Family **hairiness** *noun*.

hajj (haj) *noun* also **haj**
a pilgrimage to Mecca, which each Muslim must try to undertake at least once in a lifetime.
Word Family **hajji** (**haj**-ee) *noun* a male Muslim who has been on a pilgrimage to Mecca; **hajjah** (**haj**-a) *noun* a female Muslim who has been on a pilgrimage to Mecca.

hake *noun*
any of a group of marine fish related to the cod.

halal (hal-**ahl**) *noun*
meat from animals that have been slaughtered in accordance with Islamic law.
[Arabic, lawful]

halberd *noun* also **halbert**
a medieval spear with an axe-like blade.
Word Family **halberdier** (hal-ba-**deer**) *noun* a soldier armed with a halberd.

halcyon (**hal**-see-an) *adjective*
calm or peaceful.
[Greek *halkyon* kingfisher, in mythology a bird believed to have the power to calm the winter seas while hatching its eggs in a floating nest]

hale *adjective*
in good health.

half (hahf) *noun* (*plural* **halves**)
1 either of two equal parts into which something is divided.
2 (*informal*) half a pint of beer
3 (*informal*) a half-price ticket.
Phrases **go halves** to share something equally. **not do things by halves** to do things in a very thorough way. **too clever by half** excessively clever.
● **half** *adjective*
1 being either of two equal parts of something: *I only want a half bottle of wine.*
2 incomplete: *a half truth.*
● **half** *adverb* to the extent of half or approximately half: *The sink is half full of dishes.*
Phrases **half past** thirty minutes after the hour mentioned: *It's half past two.* **not half**
1 (*informal*) extremely: *I didn't half feel a fool!* 2 (*informal*) not at all: *That pizza wasn't half bad!* **not half as** not nearly as: *The exam wasn't half as bad as last year's.*

half a crown ⇨ HALF-CROWN.

halfback *noun*
Football a player in a position halfway between the centre players and the fullbacks.

half-baked *adjective*
(*informal*) incomplete or immature: *half-baked ideas.*

half board *noun*
an arrangement at a hotel, etc. in which one gets a room, breakfast and dinner, but not lunch. Compare FULL BOARD.

half-breed *noun* also **half-caste**
an offensive term for a person who has parents of different races.

half-brother *noun*
a male who has only one parent in common with someone else.

half-cock *noun*
a safe position of the firing mechanism of a rifle or revolver, between fired and fully cocked.
Phrase **go off at half-cock** (*informal*) to act prematurely and unsuccessfully.

half-crown *noun* also **half a crown**
(*formerly*) an old British coin equal to 12·5 pence.

half-cut *adjective*
(*informal*) drunk.

half-hearted *adjective*
having or displaying little enthusiasm or interest.
Word Family **half-heartedly** *adverb*; **half-heartedness** *noun*.

half holiday *noun*
half of a day given as a holiday from school.

half-life *noun*
Physics the time taken for the radioactivity of a particular substance to decay to half its original value.

half-mast *adverb*
(of a flag) flown halfway down the pole, as a signal of mourning, distress, etc.

half measures *plural noun*
actions taken which do not deal with a problem adequately.

half-nelson ⇨ NELSON.

half note *noun*
American a minim.

halfpenny (**hape**-nee) *noun* (*plural* **halfpennies**) also **ha'penny** (*plural* **ha'pennies**)
(*formerly*) an old British coin equal to half a penny.
Word Family **halfpenny** *adjective* of little value.

half-rhyme *noun*
a word that almost rhymes with another: *'Polish' is a half-rhyme for 'relish'*.

half-sister *noun*
a female who has only one parent in common with someone else.

half-term *noun*
a holiday halfway through a school term.

half-timbered *adjective*
having walls with a timber frame filled with plaster or bricks.

half-time *noun*
the interval midway through a game.

half-volley *noun*
a hitting or kicking of a ball immediately after it bounces.

halfway *adjective*
at or to a point midway between two things, places, etc.
• **halfway** *adverb* to or at half the distance.
Phrase **meet someone halfway** to compromise.

halfway house *noun*
a place where former prisoners, drug addicts, etc. can stay and receive support for a time after their release from an institution.

halfwit *noun*
a feeble-minded or foolish person.
Word Family **half-witted** *adjective*; **half-wittedly** *adverb*; **half-wittedness** *noun*.

halibut *noun*
any of a group of large edible flatfish.

halitosis (hal-i-**toe**-sis) *noun*
unpleasant-smelling breath.
[Latin *halitus* breath + *-osis*]

hall (hawl) *noun*
1 the entrance room of a building.
2 a passage or corridor in a building.
3 a large building or room, used especially for public meetings, entertainment, etc.
4 a large country house, especially one belonging to the chief landowner in the district.
5 also **hall of residence** at a university, a building with a lot of rooms for students to live in.

hallelujah (hal-i-**loo**-ya) *noun* also called **alleluia**.
Judaism, Christianity a song or exclamation of praise to God.
[Hebrew *halleluyah* praise Jehovah]

hallmark (**hawl**-mark) *noun*
1 a mark placed on an article to indicate quality, purity, etc.
2 a distinguishing sign: *He has all the hallmarks of a real star.*

hallo ⇨ HELLO.

halloo *interjection*
a cry used to encourage hounds during a hunt, to attract attention, etc.

hallow *verb*
to make or honour as holy.
Word Family **hallowed** *adjective*.

Halloween (hal-o-**een**) *noun* also **Hallowe'en**
an annual festival celebrated on 31 October, the eve of All Saints' Day.

Halloween occurs on the eve of All Saints' Day, a Christian festival celebrated on 1 November in honour of all the saints. *Hallow* comes from Old English *halig* (holy); 31 October, however, when Halloween takes place, was a Celtic pagan festival to mark the last day of the year. Many of the beliefs and traditions now associated with Halloween had their origins in the Celtic festival, e.g. the belief that witches and warlocks travel around on that night.

hallucination (ha-loo-si-**nay**-sh'n) *noun*
the experience of seeing or hearing things that seem to be real, but do not actually exist.
Word Family hallucinate (ha-**loo**-si-nate) *verb* to experience hallucinations; **hallucinatory** (ha-**loo**-sin-ay-tree) *adjective*.

hallucinogenic (ha-loo-sin-a-**jen**-ik) *adjective*
producing hallucinations.
Word Family hallucinogen (ha-**loo**-sin-a-jen) *noun* a drug which produces hallucinations.

halo (**hay**-lo) *noun* (*plural* **haloes** or **halos**)
a brightness or circle of light around the head of a religious image or figure.
[Greek *halos* the sun's disc]

halogen (**hal**-a-j'n) *noun*
Chemistry any of the univalent reactive non-metal elements (fluorine, chlorine, bromine, iodine and astatine), which form group VIII in the periodic table.
[Greek *halos* or salt + *-gen*]

halt (hawlt) *verb*
to make a temporary stop.
• **halt** *noun*.

halter (**hawl**-ta) *noun*
a device made of rope or straps, fitted around the head of a horse, cow, etc. for tying or leading it.
• **halter** *verb* to fit or restrain with a halter.

halter neck *noun*
a style of neckline in clothing in which the top part is fastened behind the neck, leaving the back and shoulders bare.

halting (**hawlt**-ing) *adjective*
hesitating or wavering: *halting speech*.
Word Family haltingly *adverb*.

halva (**hal**-va) *noun* also **halvah**
a Middle Eastern sweet made from sesame seeds, honey and nuts.
[Yiddish from Arabic *halwa*]

halve (hahv) *verb*
1 to divide into halves: *We halved the cake.*
2 to reduce by half: *Express trains have halved the time the journey takes.*

halves
the plural of **half**.

halyard (**hal**-y'd) *noun*
Nautical a wire or rope used to hoist or lower a sail.

ham[1] *noun*
1 the slow-cured hind leg of a bacon pig, bought ready cooked and usually eaten cold. Compare GAMMON.
2 (**hams**) the back of the thighs, or the thigh and buttocks.

ham[2] *noun*
1 an actor who exaggerates his or her role.
2 also **radio ham** (*informal*) an amateur radio operator.
• **ham** *verb* (**hams; hamming; hammed**)
Phrase **ham it up** (*informal*) to exaggerate or overact.

hamburger *noun* also called **beefburger; burger**.
a flat round cake of seasoned minced meat, usually served in a round bread roll.

ham-fisted *adjective*
(*informal*) clumsy: *He made a ham-fisted attempt at an apology.*

hamlet *noun*
a small village.

hammer *noun*
1 a tool with a handle and a heavy metal head for driving in nails, etc.
2 anything with the shape or function of a hammer, such as the padded lever which strikes the strings in a piano or the part of a gun which strikes the percussion cap and causes it to explode.
3 *Athletics* a metal ball attached to a flexible handle, which is thrown in contests.
Phrases **come under the hammer, go under the hammer** to be sold by auction. **hammer and tongs** (*informal*) with great noise, energy or violence: *We could hear the neighbours going at it hammer and tongs.*
• **hammer** *verb*
1 to strike with or as if with a hammer.
2 (*informal*) to defeat thoroughly.
Phrases **hammer away** to work hard and persistently. **hammer something into** to try to make someone learn or understand something by stating it forcefully. **hammer something out 1** to

work out the details of a deal using a lot of effort. **2** to play a tune in an amateurish way.

hammerhead shark *noun*
a type of shark with a head that resembles a double-headed hammer.

hammerlock *noun*
a wrestling hold in which the opponent's arm is twisted and pushed behind his back.

hammer toe *noun*
a deformed toe which points downwards permanently.

hammock *noun*
a sheet of canvas or netting suspended by cords at each end, serving as a sailor's bed, etc.

hammy *adjective* (**hammier; hammiest**)
(of a performance) very exaggerated.
Word Family hamminess *noun*.

hamper[1] *verb*
to obstruct or impede.

hamper[2] *noun*
a large basket, usually with a lid.

hamster *noun*
a small short-tailed rodent which stores its food in its cheek pouches.

hamstring *noun*
1 any of the tendons at the back of the knee.
2 the large sinew at the back of the hock in a quadruped.
• **hamstring** *verb* (**hamstrings; hamstringing; hamstrung**)
1 to cripple by cutting the hamstring.
2 to obstruct severely.

hand *noun*
1 *Anatomy* the part of the arm beyond the wrist, used for holding, grasping, etc.
2 something with the shape, position or function of a hand: *the hands of a clock.*
3 a worker or helper employed in a particular situation: *a factory hand.*
4 (**someone's hands**) someone's control or responsibility: *The matter is out of my hands.*
5 (**a hand**) an active part in an event: *Do you think he had a hand in the robbery?*
6 (**a hand**) help: *Give me a hand, will you!*
7 a round of applause: *Give the actors a big hand.*
8 a style of handwriting.
9 *Cards* all the cards held by a player.
10 *Cards* any part of a game in which these cards are played.
11 a unit used to measure the height of horses, equal to 10·2 cm (about 4 inches).

Phrases **at hand** close in time or space: *The end of the world is at hand.* **be an old hand** to be very experienced. **by hand** by a person. **change hands** to pass from one owner to another. **force someone's hand** to compel someone to act before he or she is ready to. **get the upper hand, have the upper hand** to win or hold an advantage. **hand in glove with** in close cooperation with. **hand over fist** (of making or spending money) very quickly. **hand to mouth** at the most basic level of existence. **hands down** easily: *They won the game hands down.* **hands off!** do not touch or interfere. **in hand 1** in progress: *Concentrate on the work in hand.* **2** under control: *Don't worry – the situation is in hand.* **keep one's hand in** to practise so as to remain skilful. **on every hand** a poetic phrase meaning 'all around'. **on the one hand, on the other hand** used to introduce different points relevant to a discussion: *I know the new job isn't very well-paid. On the other hand, it is very interesting.* **out of hand 1** out of control: *The situation was getting out of hand.* **2** without proper consideration: *She dismissed the matter out of hand.* **play into someone's hands** to act in such a way as to give someone the advantage. **show one's hand** to reveal one's intentions. **take a hand** to have an influence over a situation. **to hand** easily available: *Keep the letter to hand – we may need it.* **try one's hand at** to attempt to do something, especially something which one has not done before. **turn one's hand to** to be able to do or willing to try: *I'm a boatbuilder, but I'll turn my hand to any kind of woodwork.* **wash one's hands of** to disclaim all responsibility for. **wring one's hands** to clasp, squeeze or twist one's hands together in despair, grief, etc.
• **hand** *verb* to give or pass with the hands: *Hand me that spade, will you?*
Phrases **hand down 1** to pass on: *a story handed down through the generations.* **2** to announce officially: *The court handed down its decision.* **hand out** to distribute. **hand over** to pass on to someone else. **have to hand it to someone** to have to admit that someone has done very well.

handbag *noun*
a bag for carrying small articles such as a handkerchief, money, keys, etc., mainly used by women.

handbill *noun*
a small printed paper or advertisement given out by hand.

handbook *noun*
a reference book on a subject.

handbrake *noun*
a brake in a motor vehicle that is operated by hand.

handcuffs *plural noun*
a pair of metal rings joined by a chain to lock around a prisoner's wrists.
Word Family **handcuff** *verb*.

handful *noun*
1 as much as can be held in the hand.
2 a small number: *Only a handful of residents attended the meeting.*
3 (*informal*) a person or thing that is difficult to control.

handicap *noun*
1 any physical or mental disability which prevents or restricts normal achievement.
2 *Sport* a disadvantage or advantage placed on competitors of different standards in a race or match, to try to equalize their chances of winning.
• **handicap** *verb* (**handicaps; handicapping; handicapped**)
1 to be a handicap to.
2 to impose a handicap on.

handicraft *noun*
1 the art of making things with the hands.
2 any article made with the hands.

handily ⇨ HANDY.

handiness ⇨ HANDY.

hand-in-glove *adjective, adverb*
in close collaboration.

handiwork *noun*
1 any work done with the hands.
2 something that one has done: *This disaster was all your handiwork.*

handkerchief (hank-a-cheef) *noun*
(*plural* **handkerchiefs** or **handkerchieves**)
a small square piece of cloth for wiping the nose or face.

handle *noun*
1 the part of an object or device by which it is held.
2 (*informal*) a name or title.
Phrase **fly off the handle** (*informal*) to become very angry suddenly.
• **handle** *verb*
1 to feel or touch with the hands.
2 to cope with: *She handled the difficult situation very well.*
3 to deal with: *We only handle antiques in this shop.*
Word Family **handler** *noun*.

handlebar *noun*
(*often* **handlebars**) a bar at the front of a bicycle, motorcycle, etc., used for steering.

handmaid *noun* also **handmaiden**
an old word for a female servant.

hand-me-down *noun*
something, especially clothing, which is handed down from one person to another.

handout *noun*
1 anything which is given away to someone in need.
2 a prepared statement given to the press for publication.

handover *noun*
the passing of something to another person or group of people: *The handover of power went off peacefully.*

hand-pick *verb*
to choose carefully: *She decided to hand-pick her best workers for this job.*

handrail *noun*
a light bar along the edge of stairs or steps, used as a support.

handset *noun*
the part of a telephone held in the hand, containing both the transmitter and receiver.

hands-free *adjective*
designed to be operated without using the hands.

handshake *noun*
the grasping of hands by two people as a sign of greeting, agreement, etc ⇨ GOLDEN HANDSHAKE.

handsome (han-s'm) *adjective*
1 attractive or pleasing in appearance.
2 considerable. *We expect a handsome return on our investment.*
3 (*formal*) having value and quality: *She gave them a most handsome wedding present.*
Word Family **handsomely** *adverb*; **handsomeness** *noun*.

hands-on *adjective*
having personal, especially practical, involvement: *We like graduates who already have some hands-on experience of the job.*

handspring *noun*
a somersault in which the body turns in the air while supported with one or both hands.

handstand *noun*
the balancing of the body upside-down in a vertical position, using the hands as a base.

hand-to-hand *adjective*
at very close quarters: *hand-to-hand combat.*

hand-to-mouth *adjective, adverb*
having little or no resources: *That year our family lived hand-to-mouth.*

handwriting *noun*
1 any writing done by hand.
2 a particular or individual style of writing: *She has neat handwriting.*

handy *adjective* (**handier; handiest**)
1 nearby or easily reached: *Keep your weapons handy.*
2 useful: *This is a very handy screwdriver.*
3 skilful.
Phrase **come in handy** (*informal*) to be useful.
Word Family **handily** *adverb*; **handiness** *noun.*

handyman *noun* (*plural* **handymen**)
a person who is skilled at doing repairs, decorating, etc. around a building.

hang *verb* (**hangs; hanging; hung,** definition **4 hanged**)
1 to suspend or be suspended from above: *Let me hang your coat up.* □ *The branches hung down over the path.*
2 to attach: *It took hours to hang the wallpaper.*
3 to remain: *A stale smell hung in the air.*
4 to suspend a person by the neck until dead.
5 to suspend (meat) on a hook until dry or tender: *Hang the grouse for a week before cooking it.*
Phrases **hang about, hang around** to pass time without aim or purpose. **hang back** to hesitate: *She tends to hang back when someone asks for her opinion.* **hang on**
1 to keep a tight hold.
2 not to give up: *Hang on! The ambulance is coming.*
3 (*informal*) to wait briefly: *Hang on – just coming!*
4 to depend on: *It all hangs on what her father says.*
5 to concentrate on: *The children hung on his every word.* **hang one's head** to show that one is ashamed, especially by dejectedly drooping one's head. **hang out** (*informal*) to spend time relaxing: *At the weekends, we all hang out in the local coffee bar.* **hang up** to end a telephone conversation by replacing the receiver. **let it all hang out** (*informal*) to be very relaxed and no longer mind what other people think.
• **hang** *noun* the way in which something hangs: *She adjusted the hang of her skirt.*
Phrase **get the hang of** (*informal*) to understand the correct or particular way of doing, using, etc.: *I can't get the hang of this machine.*
• **hang** *interjection* **hang it all** (*dated*) an expression of annoyance.

> ! *Hung* is the past tense and past participle of *hang* in most senses of the verb, but *hanged* is used when a person is killed by being suspended from a rope around the neck: *She hanged herself.* □ *He was hanged for murder.*

hangar (**hang**-a) *noun*
a building in which aircraft are kept.

hangdog *adjective*
ashamed or furtive: *a hangdog expression.*

hanger *noun*
any device on which things may be hung: *a coat hanger.*

hanger-on *noun* (*plural* **hangers-on**)
(*informal*) a person who attaches himself or herself to another in a parasitic way.

hang-glider *noun*
Sport a large kite-like apparatus used for gliding through the air from a hilltop, etc.
Word Family **hang-gliding** *noun.*

hanging *noun*
1 an execution performed by hanging a person by the neck.
2 a piece of material hung from a wall, a bedpost, etc.

hangman *noun* (*plural* **hangmen**)
1 a person appointed to hang people condemned to death.
2 a children's game in which the letters of a word must be guessed before a hanged person is drawn.

hangnail *noun*
torn skin at the base of a fingernail.

hangover *noun*
1 the unpleasant after-effects of drinking too much alcohol.
2 something remaining or left over from an earlier time.

hang-up *noun*
(*informal*) an obsession or emotional difficulty, especially one which stops a person from behaving in a relaxed and natural way.

hank *noun*
a skein, coil or loop: *a hank of hair.*

hanker *verb*
Phrase **hanker after, hanker for, hanker to do something** to have a restless desire for something: *She found that years later she still hankered after the excitement of circus life.*
Word Family **hankering** *noun.*

hanky noun (plural **hankies**) also **hankie** (informal) a handkerchief.

hanky-panky noun
(informal) any mischievous or tricky activity.

Hanover (**han**-o-ver) noun
the royal family in Britain from 1714 to 1837.

Hansard noun
the official published reports of debates in the British, Canadian, Australian or New Zealand parliaments.
[after *L. Hansard* and his descendants, who printed and published them in Britain from 1774]

hansom (**han**-s'm) noun also **hansom cab**
a two-wheeled covered carriage for two passengers, pulled by a horse and with an elevated seat at the rear for the driver.
[after *J. A. Hansom*, 1803-1882, a British architect who patented it]

Hanukkah (**han**-uk-a) noun also **Chanukkah**
a Jewish festival of lights, lasting eight days, which commemorates the renewing of the Temple in Jerusalem.
[Hebrew]

ha'penny ⇨ HALFPENNY.

haphazard (hap-**hazz**-'d) adjective
random or occurring merely by chance.
Word Family **haphazardly** adverb; **haphazardness** noun.

hapless adjective
unfortunate or unlucky.
Word Family **haplessly** adverb.

haply adverb
an old word meaning 'perhaps or by chance'.

happen verb
1 to be or become an event: *The burglary happened while we were on holiday.*
2 to be or do by chance: *I happened to meet her in the street.*
Phrase **as it happens** actually.
Word Family **happening** noun 1 an event. 2 (informal) an improvised entertainment, usually intended to startle any observers.

happy adjective (**happier**; **happiest**)
1 feeling or showing contentment or pleasure: *She is happy in the new job.*
2 willing: *always happy to help.*
3 lucky: *a happy chance.*
4 (informal) having an excessive liking for: *The new sheriff is trigger-happy.*

Word Family **happily** adverb; **happiness** noun.

happy-go-lucky adjective
carefree or trusting to luck.

happy hour noun
a period of time in a bar, such as early evening, when drinks are sold at a cheaper price.

hara-kiri (harr-a-**kirr**-ee) noun
a traditional form of suicide in Japan by cutting open the abdomen, especially used by the upper class or officials who have been disgraced.
[Japanese, belly cut]

harangue (ha-**rang**) noun
a passionate vehement speech.
● **harangue** verb.

harass (**harr**-ass or ha-**rass**) verb
to pester or torment.
Word Family **harassingly** adverb; **harassment** noun.
[Old French *harer* to set a dog on]

> ❗ Note that there is only one *r* in **harass**.

harbinger (**har**-bin-ja) noun
a person or thing that announces or comes before a future event.

> The word **harbinger** comes from the Old French *herberge* (lodging); English borrowed it as *herbegere*, the *n* being added later on. The meaning developed from 'lodging' to the word for someone sent on ahead to arrange lodging for an army or royal party. From this it is a short step to the modern meaning.

harbour (**har**-ba) noun (American **harbor**)
a sheltered area of water deep enough for ships to anchor in.
● **harbour** verb
1 to give shelter to. *It is illegal to harbour an escaped criminal.*
2 to keep secretly in the mind: *She is not a person to harbour a grudge.*
3 to take shelter in a harbour.

hard adjective
1 firm, solid or not easily cut: *The ground was as hard as iron.*
2 requiring considerable effort or endurance: *hard work.*
3 difficult: *The questions are too hard for me.* □ *Their family has had a very hard life.*
4 not kind: *You're too hard on the children sometimes.* □ *I'm really sorry – no hard feelings, I hope?*
Figurative It was a hard winter.

5 based on provable fact: *We haven't got any hard evidence against them.*
6 (of water) having mineral salts which prevent the lathering of soap.
7 (of the sounds *c* and *g*) pronounced sharply, as in *cattle* and *game.*
Phrases **hard and fast** firmly fixed: *a hard and fast rule.* **hard of hearing** partly deaf. **hard up** (*informal*) short of money.
• **hard** *adverb*
1 using a lot of energy and effort: *Don't work too hard!*
2 heavily or strongly: *It was raining hard.*
3 solid: *The concrete had set hard.*
Phrases **be hard put** to find it very difficult: *She was hard put to explain the money under her bed.* **hard by** an old word meaning 'close to'. **hard done by** treated unfairly.
Word Family **hardness** *noun* the state or quality of being hard.

hardback *noun*
a book bound with a stiff cover. Compare PAPERBACK.

hardbitten *adjective*
tough and cynical: *By now she was a seasoned, hardbitten political campaigner.*

hardboard *noun*
a building material made of wood fibres pressed into sheets.

hard cash *noun*
actual coins and notes, and not cheques, credit cards, etc.

hard coal ⇨ ANTHRACITE.

hard copy *noun*
Computers any printed output from a computer.

hard core *noun*
1 a resistant central part of something: *The hard core of the movement refused to compromise on any issue.*
2 very explicit pornography.
3 rubble used in building.
Word Family **hard-core** *adjective* 1 deep-rooted or absolute. 2 (of pornography) very explicit.

hard court *noun*
a tennis court of asphalt, clay or any surface except grass.

hard disk *noun* also called **hard drive**.
the main disk in a computer, which stores very large amounts of information.

hard drug *noun*
any drug, such as heroin, considered to cause addiction. Compare SOFT DRUG.

harden *verb*
to make or become hard.
Word Family **hardened** *adjective*.

hard-headed *adjective*
shrewd or practical, especially in business matters.
Word Family **hard-headedness** *noun*.

hard-hearted *adjective*
unfeeling or unsympathetic.
Word Family **hard-heartedly** *adverb*; **hard-heartedness** *noun*.

hardily ⇨ HARDY.

hardiness ⇨ HARDY.

hard labour *noun*
the heavy manual labour formerly imposed on prisoners sentenced for serious crimes.

hard line *noun*
a very determined viewpoint that will not be changed by persuasion.
Word Family **hardliner** *noun*.

hard liquor *noun*
strong alcoholic drink.

hardly *adverb*
1 barely or not quite: *There is hardly any water left.*
2 almost not: *He hardly ever visits his grandmother.*
3 not at all: *Your failure to win the prize is hardly my fault!*
4 an old word meaning 'severely or harshly'.

hardness ⇨ HARD.

hard-pressed *adjective*
in a stressed and difficult state: *We'll be hard-pressed to get this all done by Tuesday!*

hard sell *noun*
the use of aggressive and insistent sales techniques. Compare SOFT SELL.

hardship *noun*
1 a state of suffering, trial or severe need.
2 something which causes such suffering.

hard shoulder *noun*
an additional lane provided on motorways for parking in the event of a breakdown or other emergency.

hardware *noun*
1 *Computers* the machinery and cables, etc. of a computer. Compare SOFTWARE.
2 articles such as cutlery, tools, building and gardening supplies, etc.
3 (*informal*) a weapon or weapons, especially a gun.

hardwood *noun*
the compact wood from flowering deciduous trees, such as oak or mahogany. Compare SOFTWOOD.

hardy *adjective* (**hardier; hardiest**)
strong, durable or capable of resisting exposure, hardship, etc.: *a hardy breed of cattle*.
Word Family **hardily** *adverb;* **hardiness** *noun* strength, toughness or ability to endure.

hare *noun*
a mammal related to the rabbit but with longer ears and stronger hind legs.
Phrase **run with the hare and hunt with the hounds** to give support to both sides in a quarrel.
• **hare** *verb* to run or move very fast.

harebell *noun*
the Scottish bluebell.

hare-brained *adjective*
reckless or rash.

harelip *noun*
a deformed upper lip which has a vertical slit or slits in it.

harem (**hair**-em *or* hah-**reem**) *noun*
1 the women of a Muslim household, including wives, female relatives, concubines, etc. who live in a separate part of the house.
2 the part of a Muslim household where the women live.
[Arabic *harim* forbidden]

haricot bean (harr-i-ko **been**) *noun*
a kidney bean (**haricot blanc**) or French bean (**haricot vert**).
[French]

hark *verb*
an old word meaning 'to listen'.
Phrase **hark back** to refer back to an earlier subject.

harken → HEARKEN.

harlequin (**harl**-i-kwin) *adjective*
having bright or varied colours
[after *Harlequin*, a traditional pantomime character who wears a mask and a brightly coloured costume with a diamond pattern]

harlot *noun*
an old word for a prostitute.
Word Family **harlotry** *noun* the practice of prostitution.

harm *noun*
damage: *It won't do you any harm to wait a little longer*.
• **harm** *verb* to damage or hurt.

Word Family **harmful** *adjective* causing or likely to cause harm; **harmfully** *adverb;* **harmless** *adjective* not having the power or tendency to harm; **harmlessly** *adverb;* **harmlessness** *noun*.

harmonic (har-**mon**-ik) *noun* also called **overtone**.
Music any of the series of almost inaudible tones above the note played e.g. on a violin string.
Word Family **harmonic** *adjective* **1** full of harmony. **2** relating to harmony or harmonics as distinct from rhythm or melody; **harmonics** *plural noun* (*used with singular verb*) the science or study of musical sounds.

harmonica (har-**mon**-ik-a) *noun* also called **mouth organ**.
Music a small rectangular wind instrument with metal reeds which produce notes when blown into or sucked.

harmonious (har-**mo**-nee-us) *adjective*
1 tuneful.
2 showing agreement in ideas, actions, etc.: *a harmonious relationship*.
Word Family **harmoniously** *adverb;* **harmoniousness** *noun*.

harmonium (har-**mo**-nee-um) *noun*
Music a small reed organ in which air is pumped out through the reeds.

harmonize, harmonise *verb*
1 to bring into harmony.
2 *Music* to play or sing in harmony.
3 *Music* to add notes in harmony with a main melody.
Word Family **harmonization** *noun*.
[Greek *harmonia* a fitting together]

harmony (**har**-ma-nee) *noun* (*plural* **harmonies**)
1 *Music* the blending of different notes to make chords.
2 *Music* the science of the structure or combination of chords.
3 a state of agreement or pleasing arrangement: *They live in perfect harmony*.

harness (**har**-niss) *noun* (*plural* **harnesses**)
1 the straps and fittings by which a horse or other animal pulls a vehicle.
2 any arrangement of straps, etc. by which something is attached or raised.
3 an old word for armour.
Phrase **in harness** at one's regular work.
• **harness** *verb*
1 to put a harness on.
2 to make use of: *harnessing the energy of the wind and waves*.

harp *noun*
Music a large instrument with strings set in a triangular frame and plucked with the fingers.
• **harp** *verb*
Phrase **harp on** to speak about or insist on tediously.
Word Family **harpist, harper** *noun* a person who plays a harp.

harpoon *noun*
a spear attached to a line, thrown by hand or shot from a gun, used for catching whales or fish.
• **harpoon** *verb*.

harpsichord (**harp**-si-kord) *noun*
Music a keyboard instrument in which the strings are sounded by a plucking mechanism.
Word Family **harpsichordist** *noun*.

harpy *noun* (*plural* **harpies**)
Greek mythology a cruel creature with the head of a woman and the body of a bird.

harridan (**harr**-i-d'n) *noun*
a vicious old woman.

harrow *noun*
a heavy frame set with spikes or discs, used to level soil, cover seed, break clods, etc.
• **harrow** *verb* to break or level soil with a harrow.
Word Family **harrowing** *adjective* extremely distressing or disturbing; **harrowingly** *adverb*.

harry *verb* (**harries; harrying; harried**)
to harass or torment by repeated attacks, demands, etc.

harsh *adjective*
1 disagreeable, rough or jarring to the senses: *a harsh wind.*
2 cruel or severe: *The prisoners complained of harsh treatment.*
Word Family **harshly** *adverb*; **harshness** *noun*.

hart *noun*
a stag.

harum-scarum (hair-'m-**skair**-'m) *adjective*
reckless or wild.

harvest (**har**-vist) *noun*
1 the gathering of a crop or crops.
2 the crop, especially grain, which is gathered.
3 the season when crops are gathered.
• **harvest** *verb* to gather or collect, especially a crop.
Word Family **harvester** *noun* a person or machine that harvests crops.

harvest festival *noun*
a thanksgiving service after the harvest, when churches are decorated with corn, fruit, flowers, etc.

harvest home *noun*
a special ceremony held at the end of harvesting.

has the third person singular present tense of **have**.

has-been *noun*
a person or thing that is no longer successful, popular, useful, etc.

hash[1] *noun* (*plural* **hashes**)
1 a dish of small pieces of meat cooked or reheated with vegetables.
2 a jumble or muddle.
Phrase **make a hash of** to ruin or make a mess of something.
[French *hache* an axe]

hash[2] *noun*
(*informal*) hashish.

hash[3] *noun*
the symbol #.

hashish *noun*
cannabis.
[Arabic, dried herb]

hasn't *contraction*
a short form of **has not**: *It hasn't rained for days.*

hasp *noun*
a fastener for a door, etc., consisting of a metal plate which fits over a U-shaped staple and is secured by a padlock or pin.

hassle *verb*
(*informal*) to harass or trouble.
• **hassle** *noun*.

hassock (**hass**-uk) *noun*
1 a thick cushion for kneeling.
2 a tuft or clump of thick grass.

hast the old form of the second person singular present tense of **have**.

haste (*rhymes with* paste) *noun*
speed or hurry in actions.
Word Family **hasten** (**hay**-s'n) *verb* to move or act with speed; **hasty** *adjective* (**hastier; hastiest**) 1 moving, made or performed with haste. 2 irritable or easily angered; **hastily** *adverb*; **hastiness** *noun*.

hat *noun*
any shaped covering for the head, worn for decoration or protection.
Phrases **pass the hat round** to collect contributions for something. **take one's hat off to** to feel admiration for. **talk through one's hat** (*informal*) to talk

nonsense. **throw one's hat into the ring** to say that one will respond to a challenge from someone. **under one's hat** secret: *Keep this information under your hat.*

hatch¹ *verb*
1 to produce offspring from eggs.
2 to break out of an egg.
3 (of an egg) to break open so that a young animal can come out.
4 to devise: *They hatched a scheme to defraud the bank.*
Word Family hatchery *noun* (*plural* **hatcheries**) a place for hatching eggs.

hatch² *noun* (*plural* **hatches**)
1 an opening in a floor, wall, ceiling, etc.
2 a cover for such an opening.
Word Family hatchway *noun* the opening of a hatch or trapdoor, especially in a ship's deck.

hatchback *noun*
a car with a sloping rear door which opens upwards.

hatchet *noun*
a short-handled axe.
Phrase bury the hatchet to make peace after a quarrel or disagreement.

hatchet job *noun*
(*informal*) a severe attack in words.

hatchet man *noun* (*plural* **hatchet men**)
(*informal*) a person hired or instructed to carry out unpleasant tasks such as sacking people.

hatchling *noun*
an animal or bird that has just been hatched.

hate *verb*
to have a passionate or strong dislike for someone or something.
• **hate** *noun*
1 a feeling of strong or passionate dislike.
2 something which is hated.

hateful *adjective*
detestable or provoking hate.
Word Family hatefully *adverb*;
hatefulness *noun*.

hath the old form of the third person singular present tense of **have**.

hatha yoga (hu-ta **yo**-ga *or* ha-tha **yo**-ga)
⇨ YOGA.

hatred (**hay**-trid) *noun*
a hate or passionate dislike.

hatstand *noun*
a tall piece of furniture for hanging hats on.

hatter *noun*
a person who makes or sells hats.
Phrase mad as a hatter mad or eccentric.

hat-trick *noun*
1 *Cricket* the achievement of a bowler taking three wickets within three successive balls.
2 any similar achievement of three wins or successes in a row.

haughty (*rhymes with* naughty) *adjective*
(**haughtier**; **haughtiest**)
rudely or excessively proud.
Word Family haughtily *adverb*;
haughtiness *noun*.

haul *verb*
1 to pull or drag, usually with considerable effort.
2 to transport goods, especially in a road vehicle.
• **haul** *noun*
1 the act of hauling or pulling.
2 a quantity caught, stolen, etc.: *a heavy haul of fish in the net.*
3 a distance that must be travelled: *It's a long haul to the next large town.*
Word Family haulage *noun* 1 the act of hauling or transporting. 2 the cost of hauling, transport, etc.; **haulier** *noun* a person or business concerned with haulage.

haunch *noun* (*plural* **haunches**)
1 the upper thigh and buttock: *Our guide was squatting on his haunches waiting for us.*
2 the hindquarter of an animal.

haunt *verb*
1 to visit or appear repeatedly as a ghost or spirit: *The spirit of the murdered prince haunts the castle.*
2 to worry or disturb: *She was haunted by her memories.*
• **haunt** *noun* a place which is frequently visited: *the haunts of his student days.*
Word Family haunting *adjective*
evocative: *haunting music.*

hautboy (**hote**-boy) *noun*
an old word for an oboe.
[French *haut* high + *bois* wood]

haute couture (ote koot-**yoor**) *noun* also **couture**
the most fashionable or elegant clothes, made by the leading fashion designers.
[French, high fashion]

have (hav) *verb*
(I **have**; he, she, it **has**; we, you, they **have**; **having**; **had**; *old forms* thou **hast**; he, she, it **hath**)

1 also **have got** to possess or hold: *I have a surprise for you.* □ *Have you got the key?*
2 to be made up of: *A pack has 52 cards in it.*
3 to experience or feel: *She had measles last year.* □ *I have a few doubts about this.*
4 to receive: *I've had some good news.*
5 to engage in an action or activity: *Have a look at this!* □ *I had a good swim this morning.*
6 to eat, drink, or smoke: *We had a coffee after lunch.*
7 to allow: *I'm not having any more of that behaviour!*
8 to cause to be done: *My parents are having the house painted.*
9 to give birth to: *The cat's had kittens!*
10 used with past participles to express completed actions: *He has finished his meal.* □ *I had found the map by the time she left.* □ *She will have told them by now.*
Phrases **be had** (*informal*) to be cheated or deceived: *When I opened the envelope I realized I'd been had.* **had better** should: *I'd better post this letter now.* **have had it** 1 to be beyond hope or repair: *We can't use his car because it has really had it.* 2 to have lost patience with a situation: *That's it! I've had it. I'm going home.* **have it in for** (*informal*) to hold a grudge against. **have it out** (*informal*) to come to a settlement with someone by frank discussion or conflict. **have someone on** (*informal*) to tease someone, usually as a joke: *No! You're having me on!* **have to, have got to** must: *She has to be at work by eight a.m.* **have someone up** (*informal*) to bring someone before a court: *He was had up for careless driving.*
Word Family **haven't** *contraction* a short form of **have not**.

haven (hay-v'n) *noun*
a place of shelter or safety, such as a harbour or safety for ships.

haver (hay-ver) *verb*
1 to vacillate.
2 *Scottish* to talk nonsense.

haversack (hav-a-sak) *noun*
any of various light packs carried on the back, especially by hikers or soldiers.
[German *Hafersack* oats-sack]

havoc (hav-uk) *noun*
destruction, damage or chaos.
Phrase **play havoc with** to destroy or ruin.

hawk¹ *noun*
1 a general term for birds of prey which hunt during the day, including falcons and buzzards.
2 a person who is aggressive or militant. Compare DOVE.
• **hawk** *verb* to hunt with trained hawks.
Word Family **hawkish** *adjective* fierce; **hawkishly** *adverb*; **hawkishness** *noun*; **hawker** *noun* a person who hunts with hawks.

hawk² *verb*
to offer goods for sale by going from house to house.
Word Family **hawker** *noun* a person who hawks goods.

hawk³ *verb*
to cough or spit noisily.

hawk-eyed *adjective*
having keen or sharp eyesight.

hawser *noun*
Nautical a thick rope or cable.

hawthorn *noun* also called **may**.
a thorny shrub or tree with white or pink blossom and red berries (called **haws**), often used to form hedges.

hay *noun*
any cut grass which is dried and used as fodder. Compare STRAW (definition 1).

haycock *noun*
a small pile of hay left in a field to dry.

hay fever *noun*
Medicine an allergy due to sensitivity to certain pollens, causing frequent sneezing, blocked nasal passages and redness and watering of the eyes.

haystack *noun* also called **hayrick**.
a large pile of hay stored in the open air, sometimes with a cover.

haywire *adjective*
(*informal*) out of control: *The machine suddenly went haywire.*

hazard (hazz-'d) *noun*
1 a risk or source of danger.
2 *Golf* an obstacle such as a bunker, water, rough grass, etc.
• **hazard** *verb* to risk or venture, especially when the result is in doubt: *I decided to hazard a guess at her age.*
Word Family **hazardous** *adjective* dangerous or risky; **hazardously** *adverb*; **hazardousness** *noun*.
[Arabic *az-zahr* the die]

hazard lights *plural noun*
flashing lights on a vehicle, warning other drivers that it is moving very slowly or has stopped.

haze *noun*
1 a suspension of fine dust, smoke or vapour particles in the air, which reduces visibility.
2 a confused state: *in an alcoholic haze.*
Word Family hazy *adjective* (**hazier; haziest**) 1 misty. 2 dim or vague; **haziness** *noun.*

hazel (**hayz-'l**) *noun*
1 a small evergreen tree or shrub which produces edible nuts (**hazelnuts**).
2 a light yellowish-brown colour.
• **hazel** *adjective.*

H-bomb ⇨ HYDROGEN BOMB.

he *pronoun* (*plural* **they**)
1 the third person singular nominative pronoun, used to indicate a male: *He ate the cake.* ⇨ HIM; HIS; SHE.
2 used to represent any person whose sex is not specified: *He who hesitates is lost.*
3 used as a noun: *Is the cat a he?*
4 used in combination to indicate a male: *a he-goat.*

> **He, his,** etc. were considered until relatively recently to be perfectly acceptable to describe someone whose sex was unknown, as in *Each pupil should have his own book.* Nowadays people try to avoid this apparent masculine bias. To avoid using the clumsy *he or she* or *he/she* it is sometimes possible to put the whole phrase in the plural using *they, their,* etc., as in *The pupils brought their own books.*

head (**hed**) *noun*
1 *Anatomy* the part of the body above the neck, containing the brain, eyes, etc.
2 something which has the shape, position or function of a head: *a head of cabbage.* ⬜ *the head of a nail.*
3 the height of a head: *He's now a head taller than his father.*
4 the front: *At last we reached the head of the queue.*
5 the source of a river, etc.: *the head of the Nile.*
6 the leader, commander or chief executive of a nation, institution, company, etc.
7 a head teacher.

8 an individual person or animal: *The cost of the meal was £30 a head.* ⬜ *The farmer sold 50 head of cattle.*
9 *Audio* a small magnetic device which records sound in a tape recorder.
10 the foam on a liquid which has just been poured, especially beer.
11 (**heads**) the side of a coin bearing the image of a head.
Phrases **be on one's own head** to be one's own responsibility. **bite someone's head off** to respond angrily: *She bit my head off when I gave her some advice.* **come to a head** to come to a crisis point. **give someone his** or **her head** to allow someone to act completely as he or she wants to. **go to one's head 1** to make one slightly drunk. **2** (of success) to make someone conceited. **a head for 1** a skill at: *I haven't got much of a head for figures.* **2** an ability to endure: *He has no head for heights.* **(with one's) head in the clouds** extremely impractical, not understanding the real world. **head over heels 1** somersaulting: *She tumbled head over heels down the stairs.* **2** very much in love. **heads or tails** a call made before tossing a coin to guess which side up it will fall. **heads will roll** people who are responsible will have to leave their jobs. **keep one's head** to remain calm. **laugh one's head off** to laugh loudly or excessively. **lose one's head** to panic. **make head or tail of** to understand any of: *I can't make head or tail of this letter.* **off one's head, out of one's head** (*informal*) mad. **off the top of one's head** without thinking carefully. **over one's head 1** to a higher authority. **2** beyond one's understanding: *I'm afraid that book is way over my head.* **turn someone's head** to make someone vain: *Don't let their flattery turn your head.*
• **head** *verb*
1 to lead or be in front of.
2 to give a heading to.
3 to go in the direction of: *We headed home.*
4 *Soccer* to propel or direct the ball with the head.
Phrase **head off** to intercept: *Head those sheep off before they reach the gate.*
• **head** *adjective* having a position of leadership or authority.

headache (**hed**-ake) *noun*
a pain in the head.
Figurative *Her continual complaints are a real headache to the police.*
Word Family headachy *adjective.*

headboard *noun*
a panel at the head of a bed.

headbutt *verb*
to attack by banging one's head into someone else's.

head case *noun*
(*informal*) a mentally ill person.

headdress *noun* (*plural* **headdresses**)
a covering or decoration for the head worn on ceremonial occasions.

header *noun*
1 (*informal*) a head-first dive or fall.
2 a hit of a ball with the head.

head first *adverb*
with the head first: *He plunged head first into the icy water.*
Figurative She always goes head first into new adventures.

headgear *noun*
things worn on the head.

headhunting *noun*
1 the practice among some tribes of cutting off the heads of enemies and keeping them as trophies or charms.
2 the practice of approaching someone and offering a job with another organization.
Word Family **headhunt** *verb*; **head-hunter** *noun.*

heading *noun*
a group of words printed above an article, a page of a book, etc. to indicate what follows.

headland *noun* also called **promontory**.
a piece of land which juts out into the sea.

headlight *noun* also **headlamp**
any of the large lights at the front of a motor vehicle.

headline *noun*
1 *Newspapers* the title of an article printed in large bold type.
2 (**the headlines**) a broadcast summary of news.

headlong *adjective, adverb*
head first.

headman *noun* (*plural* **headmen**)
the chief of a tribe.

headmaster *noun*
a male head teacher.

headmistress *noun* (*plural* **headmistresses**)
a female head teacher.

head-on *adjective, adverb*
with the front parts meeting first: *a head-on collision.*

headphones *plural noun* also called **headset**.
a pair of small speakers, one for each ear, mounted on a band which can be connected to a radio, etc.

headpiece *noun*
any covering for the head, especially a helmet.

headquarters *plural noun*
(*used with plural or singular verb*) the central office or building of an organization.

headrest *noun*
a support for the head on top of the back of a chair.

headroom *noun*
the amount of space above or around a head or the top of something: *There wasn't much headroom in the cabin.* □ *Is there enough headroom for the bus to pass under the bridge?*

headship *noun*
the position or period of being a leader, head teacher, etc.

headstand *noun*
the act of balancing the body upright, using either the head or the arms as a support.

headstone *noun*
a gravestone.

headstrong *adjective*
obstinate or determined, especially about having one's own way.

head teacher *noun*
a teacher in charge of a school.

headwaters *plural noun*
the upper tributaries of a river.

headway *noun*
any progress: *The police have made little headway in the investigation.*

headwind (hed-winned) *noun*
a wind blowing in the opposite direction to that in which a vehicle is travelling, thus decreasing its speed. Compare TAILWIND.

heady *adjective* (**headier; headiest**)
having an intoxicating effect.

heal *verb*
to make or become healthy or free of disease.
Word Family **healing** *adjective* able to heal; **healer** *noun.*

health (helth) *noun*
1 a normal functioning of the body and mind.
2 a person's mental or physical state: *His health is no longer good.*

Phrases **drink someone's health** to drink a toast to someone. **in rude health** extremely healthy.
Word Family **healthy** *adjective* (**healthier; healthiest**) **1** in good health: *a healthy baby*. **2** good for the health: *a healthy climate*. **3** characteristic of health: *a healthy glow in her cheeks*. **4** very satisfactory in amount: *a healthy number of orders*; **healthily** *adverb*; **healthiness** *noun*; **healthful** *adjective*.

health farm *noun*
a place where people go to improve health through exercise, good diet, etc.

health food *noun*
food considered of benefit to health, such as organically grown vegetables or food produced without chemical additives.

health visitor *noun*
a person whose job is to visit new mothers, very sick people, etc. in their own homes and advise them on health matters.

health warning *noun*
a warning printed on certain products, such as cigarettes, indicating that they might cause damage to the health of the user.

heap *noun*
1 a pile.
2 (*often* **heaps**) a lot: *We've got heaps of time before the plane leaves.*
3 (*informal*) something very old or in bad condition, such as an old car.
• **heap** *verb* to pile up or put in a heap: *She heaped the chips onto my plate.*
Figurative Insults were heaped on the head of the unfortunate official.

hear *verb* (**hears; hearing; heard** (herd))
1 to become aware of through the ears.
2 to be told: *I hear you're getting married.*
3 (*of a judge, etc.*) to listen officially to: *Judge Jefferies will hear this case in Court 7.*
Phrases **hear from** to get a letter, email, etc. from: *Have you heard from your brother recently?* **hear, hear!** a public expression of agreement with something said. **hear someone out** to listen to everything that someone wants to say. **not hear of** to refuse to allow: *She would not hear of us paying for dinner.*
Word Family **hearer** *noun*.

hearing *noun*
1 the power or faculty by which sound is perceived: *The old man's hearing is not good.*
2 the range within which something can be heard: *We called for help, but no one was within hearing.*
3 the opportunity of being heard: *Please give us a hearing.*
4 a trial in court.

hearing aid *noun*
a small device worn in the ear to help a person to hear.

hearken (**hark-'n**) *verb* also **harken**
an old word meaning 'to listen'.

hearsay *noun*
any rumour or gossip.

hearse (*rhymes with* purse) *noun*
any vehicle for carrying a corpse to the place of burial or cremation.

heart (hart) *noun*
1 *Anatomy* the muscular pump within the chest which circulates the blood.
2 one's emotions, affections or capacity for love, as distinct from the intellect: *He has a kind heart.*
3 courage or enthusiasm: *They have no heart for fighting.*
4 the centre or most important part of anything: *Now we're getting to the heart of the matter.*
5 a figure in the shape of a heart.
6 *Cards* a playing card with a red figure like a heart on it.
7 (**hearts**) *Cards* the suit with this figure.
Phrases **after one's own heart** sharing one's tastes: *When it comes to wines, he is a man after my own heart.* **by heart** from memory: *You must learn these rules by heart.* **close to one's heart** important to one: *Women's rights is an issue that is very close to her heart.* **have a heart** to be sympathetic or kind. **have one's heart in one's mouth** to be afraid. **have something at heart** to be most concerned about something: *I know he has your best interests at heart.* **in one's heart of hearts** deep inside one: *In my heart of hearts I knew he was right.* **lose one's heart to** to fall in love with. **set one's heart at rest** to relax or remove anxiety. **take to heart** to take very seriously: *Don't take their jokes so much to heart.* **wear one's heart on one's sleeve** to display one's feelings too openly.

heartache (**hart-**ake) *noun*
a painful sorrow or unhappiness.

heart attack *noun*
a deficiency in blood supplied to the heart muscle due to a blockage in an artery, leading to reduced efficiency of blood pumping.

heartbroken *adjective*
overcome with grief, misery, etc.

Word Family heartbrokenly *adverb*;
heartbreak *noun* an overwhelming
sorrow or grief; **heartbreaking** *adjective*;
heartbreakingly *adverb*.

heartburn *noun*
a burning sensation in the chest due to
excess acid in the stomach.

hearten *verb*
to cheer up or encourage.
Word Family heartening *adjective*;
hearteningly *adverb*.

heart failure *noun*
any failure or faulty functioning of the
heart pump.

heartfelt *adjective*
deeply felt or sincere.

hearth (harth) *noun*
the floor of a fireplace and the area around
it.

heartily ⇨ HEARTY.

heartiness ⇨ HEARTY.

heartless *adjective*
cruel or without mercy.
Word Family heartlessly *adverb*;
heartlessness *noun*.

heart murmur *noun*
a sound caused by an irregular flow of
blood in the heart.

heart-rending *adjective*
causing or expressing great grief.

heartstrings *plural noun*
one's deepest or strongest feelings.

heart-throb *noun*
(*informal*) a person with whom one is
infatuated.

heart-to-heart *adjective*
frank or sincere.
• **heart-to-heart** *noun* a serious
conversation about very personal matters.

hearty (har-tee) *adjective* (**heartier;
heartiest**)
1 enthusiastic, friendly or sincere.
2 strong and healthy.
3 (of food) substantial, satisfying.
Word Family heartily *adverb*;
heartiness *noun*.

heat *noun*
1 the condition or sensation of being hot:
The heat of a tropical summer is very tiring.
Figurative In the heat of the argument
many insults were exchanged.
2 a source of heat: *Turn the heat up under
the carrots.*
3 (**the heat**) (*informal*) intense pressure:
After this scandal, the heat was really on.

4 a single division in a competition, the
winner of which takes part in further or
final rounds.
5 *Physics* a form of energy, causing or
caused by the vibrations of the molecules
of a substance.
Phrase on heat *Biology* (of a female
mammal) willing to receive the male
sexually.
Word Family heat *verb* to make or
become hot; **heater** *noun* any device for
heating, such as a radiator; **heated**
adjective vehement: *a heated argument.*
heatedly *adverb* vehemently.

heath *noun*
1 an area of flat land covered with low
shrubby vegetation.
2 any of various low evergreen shrubs,
some of which are also called heathers.

heathen (hee-*th*'n) *noun*
1 a person who does not worship the God
of the established religions.
2 any irreligious or barbaric person.
Word Family heathenish *adjective*;
heathenism *noun*.

heather (he*th*-a) *noun*
a type of low evergreen autumn-flowering
shrub, usually growing on moors.

Heath Robinson *adjective*
(of a machine) ingenious but complicated
and impractical.
[after *W. Heath Robinson*, 1872-1944, an
artist]

heatstroke *noun*
a fever or collapse due to exposure to
excessive heat and dehydration.

heatwave *noun*
a period of unusually hot weather.

heave (*rhymes with* sleeve) *verb* (**heaves;
heaving; heaved** or *Nautical* **hove**)
1 to raise, lift or throw with an effort.
2 to rise and fall: *His chest heaved with pain.*
3 to utter a sigh: *She heaved a sigh of relief
as the last guest departed.*
Phrases heave in sight to appear. **heave
to** *Nautical* to stop the forward movement
of a ship, especially by heading into the
wind.
• **heave** *noun*.

heaven (*rhymes with* seven) *noun*
1 the place where gods, angels and other
supernatural beings live.
2 (*often* **Heaven**) the place or state in
which souls will be united with God after
death, often considered as a reward for the
righteous or faithful. Compare HELL
(definition 2).

3 any place or condition of extreme bliss or happiness.
4 (**the heavens**) the sky.
Phrases **move heaven and earth to do something** to try extremely hard to to something. **seventh heaven** a state of extreme happiness.
Word Family **heavenly** *adjective* 1 of or belonging to heaven or the heavens.
2 excellent, pleasing or beautiful;
heavens! *interjection* an exclamation of surprise; **heavenward** *adjective, adverb* towards heaven or the sky.

eaven-sent *adjective*
provided by a miracle or extreme good fortune.

eavy (**hev**-ee) *adjective* (**heavier; heaviest**)
1 having great weight or force: *a heavy suitcase.* □ *heavy rain.*
2 great in amount: *He had to pay a heavy fine.*
3 requiring a lot of effort: *heavy work.*
4 full of gloom: *She packed her bags with a heavy heart.*
5 (of food) hard to digest.
6 serious and difficult to cope with: *Our conversation got a bit heavy in the early hours of the morning.*
• **heavy** *noun* (*plural* **heavies**)
1 (*informal*) a person of great influence or importance.
2 (*informal*) a thug or tough person.
Word Family **heaviness** *noun;* **heavily** *adverb.*

eavy-duty *adjective*
designed for strength and durability.

eavy-handed *adjective*
harsh and lacking delicacy or subtlety.
Word Family **heavy-handedly** *adverb;* **heavy-handedness** *noun.*

eavy industry *noun*
the making of large items, e.g. vehicles and machinery, and the producing of raw materials. Compare LIGHT INDUSTRY.

eavy metal *noun*
a style of loud energetic rock music with a strong beat.

eavyweight (**hev**-ee-wate) *noun*
1 the heaviest weight division in boxing, about 80 kg or 12½ stone.
2 (*informal*) a person of great influence or importance.

ebrew (**hee**-broo) *noun*
the ancient Jewish language used in the Old Testament and now the official language of Israel.

Word Family **Hebrew, Hebraic** (hee-**bray**-ik) *adjective.*

heck *interjection*
an expression of annoyance.

heckle *verb*
to disturb or harass with persistent questions, interruptions, etc.
Word Family **heckler** *noun* a person who heckles.

hectare (**hek**-tar) *noun*
a metric unit of area used in land measurement, equal to 10 000 m^2 or about 2·5 acres.

hectic *adjective*
full of energetic activity, haste, confusion, etc.
Word Family **hectically** *adverb.*

> The word **hectic** originally had nothing to do with the busy activity with which we associate it today. It meant 'suffering from a fever of the kind found in tuberculosis' and then went on also to mean 'fevered or red' as in 'a hectic colour on her cheeks'. In the 20th century it came to mean the kind of rushing activity that causes this fevered look.

hector (**hek**-ta) *verb*
to treat in a bullying, domineering way.
[after *Hector* of Troy in Homer's 'Iliad']

he'd *contraction*
a short form of **he had** or **he would**: *He said he'd never been to Rome.* □ *He'd love to go to Florida.*

hedge (hej) *noun*
1 a row of similar shrubs, usually cut evenly and grown close together to form a boundary or barrier.
2 any method of protection against loss: *We bought the shares as a hedge against inflation.*
• **hedge** *verb*
1 to surround or enclose with a hedge.
2 to avoid direct commitment by evasive answers to questions, etc.
3 to protect oneself against loss.
Phrase **hedge in** to restrict: *He felt hedged in by rules and regulations.*

hedgehog *noun*
a small nocturnal mammal, related to shrews and moles, which has a protective coat of long spines.

hedgerow *noun*
a hedge bordering a field.

hedonism (heed-'n-izm) *noun*
Philosophy the belief that happiness or pleasure is the chief or proper aim in life.
Word Family **hedonistic** (heed-'n-**ist**-ik) *adjective*; **hedonistically** *adverb*; **hedonist** *noun*.
[Greek *hedoné* pleasure]

heebie-jeebies *plural noun*
(*informal*) a state of nervousness.

heed *verb*
(*formal*) to listen or pay attention to.
Word Family **heed** *noun* attention; **heedful** *adjective* attentive; **heedless** *adjective*.

heel¹ *noun*
1 *Anatomy* the rear part of the foot below the ankle.
2 the part of a shoe, sock, etc. covering the heel.
3 something with the shape, position or function of a heel: *the heel of a golf club*.
4 (*dated*) an untrustworthy or contemptible person, especially a man.
Phrases **at one's heels, on one's heels** close behind one. **come to heel** 1 (of a dog) to come and stay at heel. 2 to submit to authority. **cool one's heels, kick one's heels** to wait or be kept waiting. **dig one's heels in** to maintain one's position obstinately. **down at heel** shabby or untidy. **hard on the heels of** very close behind. **kick up one's heels** to have fun. **show a clean pair of heels to** to outdistance and beat. **take to one's heels** to run away.
• **heel** *verb*
1 to put a heel or heels on: *I must have my shoes heeled.*
2 to follow close behind: *'Heel, Spot!' shouted the dog's owner.*

heel² *verb*
Nautical (of a ship) to lean or cause to lean to one side.

hefty *adjective* (**heftier**; **heftiest**)
1 heavy and strong.
2 large in amount: *a hefty tax.*
Word Family **heftiness** *noun*.

hegemony (hig-**em**-a-nee) *noun*
a leadership or powerful influence, especially of one state or country over others.
[Greek]

heifer (**heff**-a) *noun*
a cow under three years of age which has not yet had a calf.

height (hite) *noun*
1 the distance from the bottom or a given level to the top of something.
2 a high level, place or part.
3 the highest level or degree: *She thinks her clothes are the height of fashion.*
Word Family **heighten** *verb* to increase in height or intensity.

heinous (**hee**-nus *or* **hay**-nus) *adjective*
(*formal*) hateful or vile: *a heinous crime.*
Word Family **heinously** *adverb*; **heinousness** *noun*.

heir (air) *noun*
1 a person who inherits, or will later inherit, money, property, a title, etc.
2 a person, group or society to which something such as tradition, ideas, etc. is passed on.

heir apparent *noun* (*plural* **heirs apparent**)
a person who has an unquestionable right to succeed to a throne or title.

heiress *noun* (*plural* **heiresses**)
a female who inherits, or will later inherit, money, property, a title, etc.

heirloom (**air**-loom) *noun*
any family possession passed down from generation to generation.

heir presumptive *noun* (*plural* **heirs presumptive**)
a person who will succeed to a throne or title unless someone with a higher claim is born.

heist (highst) *noun*
(*informal*) a robbery.

held the past tense and past participle of **hold**.

helical (**hell**-i-k'l) *adjective*
of or shaped like a helix.

helices
the plural of **helix**.

helicopter *noun*
an aircraft which takes off vertically and which is supported and moved forward by a rotor.
[Greek *heliko* helix + *pteron* wing]

heliograph (**hee**-lee-o-graf) *noun*
a device for signalling by using a movable mirror to reflect sunlight in flashes.
• **heliograph** *verb*.
[*helio*- + Greek *graphein* to write]

heliport *noun*
a landing place for helicopters, often on the roof of a building.

helium (hee-lee-um) *noun*
a colourless inert gas much lighter than air, traces of which are found in the earth's atmosphere and in natural gas.
[Greek *helios* sun]

helix (hee-lix) *noun* (*plural* **helices**) (hee-li-seez *or* hell-i-seez)
a spiral or coil, such as a corkscrew.
[Greek]

hell *noun*
1 the place where the dead, evil spirits and devils live.
2 (*often* **Hell**) the place or state in which souls will be separated from God after death, often considered as a punishment for the wicked. Compare HEAVEN (definition 2).
3 any place or condition of misery or unpleasantness.
Phrases **come hell or high water** (*informal*) in spite of any problems involved. **for the hell of it** (*informal*) for fun or no particular reason. **hell for leather** at top speed. **play hell with** (*informal*) to cause a lot of trouble with: *This cold weather plays hell with his rheumatism.* **there will be hell to pay** there will be a lot of trouble.

he'll *contraction*
a short form of **he will**: *He'll be here shortly.*

hell-bent *adjective*
recklessly determined.

hellcat *noun*
a nasty violent woman.

Hellenic (hil-en-ik) *adjective*
1 of the modern Greeks.
2 of the ancient Greeks, and their language and culture before the time of Alexander the Great, about 330 B.C.

hellhole *noun*
a terrible place, especially a dark one.

hellish *adjective*
(*informal*) extremely unpleasant or difficult.
Word Family **hellishness** *noun*; **hellishly** *adverb*.

hello *interjection* also **hallo; hullo**
a cry of greeting or to attract attention.

helm *noun*
1 a tiller or wheel connected to a rudder for steering a boat.
2 any position of leadership or control.
Word Family **helmsman** *noun* (*plural* **helmsmen**).

helmet *noun*
any of various protective coverings for the head.

help *verb*
to make something easier, better or less painful for a person or thing: *Can I help to carry your bags?* □ *This medicine helps me to sleep.*
Phrases **cannot help, could not help** cannot or could not stop oneself from: *She couldn't help smiling at the thought of it.* **cannot help oneself, could not help oneself** cannot or could not stop oneself from doing something: *I'm afraid I just couldn't help myself – I fell about laughing!* **help oneself to** to take.
• **help** *noun*
1 the act of helping or relieving: *I need your help.*
2 any person or thing that helps: *Your suggestions have been a great help to us.*
Phrase **there is no help for it** there is no way of changing the situation.
Word Family **helper** *noun*.

helpful *adjective*
useful or giving help.
Word Family **helpfully** *adverb*; **helpfulness** *noun*.

helping *noun*
a quantity of food served to a person at one time.

helpless *adjective*
1 unable to protect oneself: *He felt utterly abandoned and helpless.*
2 not able to be controlled: *helpless laughter.*
Word Family **helplessly** *adverb*; **helplessness** *noun*.

helpline *noun*
a telephone service for people who need advice about something: *Phone the manufacturer's helpline about that dish.*

helpmate *noun*
a helpful friend or companion.

helter-skelter *adverb*
in great haste or disorder.
• **helter-skelter** *noun* a very tall spiral slide at a fairground.

hem *noun*
the edge of a piece of clothing or cloth which has been turned under and sewn down.
• **hem** *verb* (**hems; hemming; hemmed**)
to fold back and sew down the edge of fabric, etc.
Phrase **hem in** to surround: *We were hemmed in on all sides by shouting spectators.*

he-man *noun* (*plural* **he-men**)
a strong or aggressively masculine man.

hemisphere (**hem**-i-sfeer) *noun*
a half of a sphere, such as the northern
hemisphere and the southern hemisphere,
which are the halves of the earth north and
south of the equator.

hemline *noun*
the length of a dress or skirt.

hemlock *noun*
a poisonous plant with purple spotted
stems and small white flowers, used as a
sedative.

hemp *noun*
1 a tall herb, originally from Asia, but now
widely cultivated.
2 the stem fibres of this plant, used to
make rope, etc.
3 cannabis.

hen *noun*
a female bird, especially a female adult
chicken.

henbane *noun*
a poisonous plant with an unpleasant
smell.

hence *adverb*
1 for this reason.
2 from this time.
Word Family **henceforth,
henceforward** *adverb* from now on.

henchman *noun* (*plural* **henchmen**)
a follower or supporter, especially of a
criminal, etc.

henna *noun*
a shrub from North Africa and Asia, the
leaves of which contain a reddish-orange
dye, used in cosmetics.

hen night *noun*
a social gathering for women only, held
shortly before the wedding of one member
of the group. Compare STAG NIGHT.

henpecked *adjective*
dominated or nagged by a woman.

hepatitis (hep-a-**tie**-tis) *noun*
an infectious viral inflammation of the
liver, causing fever and jaundice, usually in
young adults.
[Greek *hepatos* of liver + *-itis*]

heptagon (**hep**-ta-gon) *noun*
any closed plane figure with seven straight
sides.
[Greek *hepta* seven + *gonia* corner]

her *pronoun* (*plural* **them**)
the objective form of **she**: *I saw her earlier.*
□ *Give the cake to her.*

• **her** *possessive adjective* belonging to her:
This is her car.

herald *noun*
a messenger.
*Figurative The swallows are a herald of
summer.*
• **herald** *verb* to proclaim or usher in: *The
new government heralded an era of reform.*

heraldry (**herr**-'l-dree) *noun*
1 the art or science of tracing and
recording the histories of families, their
coats of arms, etc.
2 any symbols or devices related to this
process, such as coats of arms, etc.
Word Family **heraldic** (her-**ald**-ik)
adjective.

herb *noun*
a flowering plant with a non-woody stem
above the ground that is used in medicine,
cooking, etc.
Word Family **herbal** *adjective* of or
consisting of herbs: *a herbal remedy*;
herbalist *noun* a person who uses herbs to
treat diseases.
[Latin *herba* grass]

herbaceous border (her-bay-shus **bor**-
der) *noun*
a long flower bed or series of flower beds.

herbicide (**herb**-i-side) *noun*
a poisonous substance used to kill
unwanted plants.

herbivorous (her-**biv**-er-us) *adjective*
of or relating to an organism which eats
plants.
Word Family **herbivore** (**her**-bi-vor)
noun.
[Latin *herba* grass + *vorare* to devour]

herculean (her-kew-lee-an) *adjective*
having or requiring great strength.
[after *Hercules*, a hero in Greek and
Roman mythology who was celebrated for
his strength]

herd *noun*
1 a group of animals, especially cattle.
2 a large group of people.
• **herd** *verb*
1 to unite or assemble as a group.
2 to look after or drive a group of cattle,
sheep, etc.
Word Family **herdsman** *noun* (*plural*
herdsmen), **herder** the keeper of a herd
of cattle, sheep, etc.

here *adverb*
1 at, to or in this place: *Put it down just
here.* □ *Come here!*
2 at this point: *Here I would like to expand
my argument.*

Phrases **here and there** in or to various places. **here's to** used to introduce a toast to someone. **neither here nor there** irrelevant or unimportant.

• **here** *noun*
Phrase **the here and now** this world or life.

hereabouts *adverb* also **hereabout**
in this general area.

hereafter *adverb*
1 (*formal*) after this in time, order, etc.
2 in the afterlife.
• **hereafter** *noun* the afterlife.

hereby *adverb*
(*formal*) by this means.

hereditary (h'-**red**-i-tree) *adjective*
derived or inherited from one's parents or ancestors: *a hereditary disease.* □ *a hereditary title.*
Word Family **heredity** *noun* 1 the transmitting of characteristics from parents to offspring through the genes.
2 the characteristics transmitted.
[Latin *heredis* of an heir]

herein *adverb*
(*formal*) in or into this place.

hereinafter *adverb*
(*formal*) afterwards in this document, etc.

hereof *adverb*
(*formal*) of or about this.

here's *contraction*
a short form of **here is**: *Here's the bus.*

heresy (**herr**-a-see) *noun* (*plural* **heresies**)
1 any belief or teaching which opposes an established doctrine, especially that of a church or religion.
2 the holding of such opinions.
Word Family **heretic** *noun* a person who holds such opinions; **heretical** (h'-**ret**-i-k'l) *adjective* expressing heresy; **heretically** *adverb*.
[Greek *hairesis* choice, a sect]

hereto *adverb*
(*formal*) to this place, thing, etc.

heretofore *adverb*
(*formal*) before this time.

hereupon *adverb*
(*formal*) upon this.

herewith *adverb*
(*formal*) together with this.

heritage (**herr**-i-tij) *noun*
1 a position, possession or privilege which is inherited.

2 the sum of things, such as historical sites, architectural features or natural environment, handed down from generation to generation in a country or area.

heritage trail *noun*
a walk or tour round sites of local interest.

hermaphrodite (her-**maf**-ra-dite) *noun*
Biology an animal or plant with both male and female reproductive organs.
Word Family **hermaphroditic** (her-maf-ra-**dit**-ik) *adjective*.
[after *Hermaphrodites*, the son of Hermes and Aphrodite in Greek mythology, who became united in one body with a nymph]

hermetic (her-**met**-ik) *adjective*
airtight.
Word Family **hermetically** *adverb*.

hermit *noun*
a person who lives in seclusion, often for religious reasons.
Word Family **hermitage** (**her**-mit-ij) *noun* a place of retreat or seclusion.
[Greek *eremites* of the desert]

hermit crab *noun*
a type of crab which lives inside the cast-off shell of a mollusc for protection.

hernia (**her**-nee-a) *noun* also called **rupture**.
Medicine the protruding of an organ, such as the intestine, through the wall of its surrounding tissue.

hero (**heer**-o) *noun* (*plural* **heroes**)
1 a person who displays courage or noble qualities.
2 the main male character in a story, play, etc.
Word Family **heroic** (hi-**ro**-ik) *adjective*
1 brave, courageous or noble: *a heroic rescue.* 2 adapted from or characteristic of classical epic poetry; *heroic couplets*; **heroically** *adverb*; **heroics** *plural noun* melodramatic behaviour or language.
[Greek *heros*]

heroin (**herr**-o-in) *noun*
a drug made from morphine, originally used as a sedative but now also used as a highly addictive hallucinatory drug.

heroine (**herr**-o-in) *noun*
1 a woman who displays courage or noble qualities.
2 the main female character in a story, play, etc.

heroism (**herr**-o-izm) *noun*
1 noble or heroic actions.
2 the qualities of a hero or heroine.

heron *noun*
a wading bird with long legs, neck and beak.

hero-worship *verb* (**hero-worships; hero-worshipping; hero-worshipped**)
to have an extreme admiration for another person.
Word Family **hero-worship** *noun*; **hero-worshipper** *noun*.

herpes (**her**-peez) *noun*
a viral disease which produces cold sores around the nose, mouth or genitals.
[Greek, a creeping infection]

Herr (hair) *noun* (*plural* **Herren**) (**herr-en**)
the title for a German man.

herring *noun*
a coldwater fish which occurs in enormous shoals off Atlantic shores.

herringbone *noun*
a pattern consisting of rows of slanted parallel lines, with the direction of the slant alternating from row to row, used in textiles, embroidery, etc.

hers *possessive pronoun* (*plural* **theirs**)
belonging to her: *That bike is hers*.

> [!] Note that there is no apostrophe in *hers*.

herself *pronoun*
1 the reflexive form of **she**: *She bought herself a bar of chocolate as a treat.*
2 the emphatic form of **she**: *The princess herself wrote this letter.*
3 having her normal or usual personality: *For weeks after the accident she was not herself.*

hertz (hurts) *noun* (*plural* **hertz**)
the SI unit of frequency, equal to one cycle per second. *abbrev.* Hz.
[after *Heinrich Hertz*, 1857-1894, a German physicist]

he's *contraction*
a short form of **he is** or **he has**: *He's taller than his brother.* □ *He's got a new watch.*

hesitate (**hez**-i-tate) *verb*
to show uncertainty or unwillingness.
Word Family **hesitation** (hez-i-**tay**-sh'n) *noun*; **hesitant** *adjective* slow due to uncertainty; **hesitantly** *adverb*; **hesitance, hesitancy** *noun*.
[Latin *haesitare* to stick fast, stammer]

hessian (**hess**-ee-an) *noun* also called **burlap**.
a strong coarse fabric made from jute, used for sacks, etc.

heterodox (**het**-a-ro-doks) *adjective*
not agreeing with established or accepted beliefs, especially religious doctrine.
Word Family **heterodoxy** *noun*.
[*hetero-* + Greek *doxa* opinion]

heterogeneous (het-a-ro-**jee**-nee-us) *adjective*
composed of many different parts.
[*hetero-* + *-gen*]

heterosexual (het-a-ro-**seks**-yew-'l) *adjective*
being sexually attracted to members of the opposite sex. Compare HOMOSEXUAL.
Word Family **heterosexual** *noun* a heterosexual person; **heterosexuality** (het-a-ro-seks-yoo-**al**-i-tee) *noun*.

het-up *adjective*
(*informal*) anxious or worried.
[from *heated*]

hew *verb* (**hews; hewing; hewed; hewed** or **hewn**)
to cut with a strong chopping action.
Word Family **hewer** *noun*.

hex *verb*
to bewitch or cast a spell on.
• **hex** *noun* (*plural* **hexes**) a spell.

hexagon *noun*
any closed plane figure with six straight sides.
Word Family **hexagonal** (heks-**ag**-a-n'l) *adjective*.
[*hexa-* + Greek *gonia* corner]

hexameter (heks-**am**-it-a) *noun*
Poetry a line with six metrical feet, for example *Down in a deep dark hole sat an old cow munching a beanstalk.*

hey *interjection*
an exclamation of surprise, pleasure, etc., or used to attract attention.

heyday *noun*
the period of greatest prosperity, power, etc.

hey presto *interjection*
an exclamation used at the end of some feat, trick or accomplishment.

hi *interjection*
(*informal*) an exclamation used as a greeting.

hiatus (high-**ayt**-us) *noun* (*plural* **hiatuses**)
a gap or interruption.
[Latin]

hibernate (**high**-ber-nate) *verb*
Biology to spend winter in a resting or inactive state.

Word Family **hibernation** (high-ber-nay-sh'n) *noun*.

hibiscus (hib-**isk**-us) *noun*
a tropical shrub with brightly coloured flowers.
[Greek *hibiskos* marshmallow]

hiccup (**hik**-up) *noun* also **hiccough**
1 the short characteristic sound produced when the larynx closes involuntarily after a contraction of the diaphragm.
2 (*informal*) a minor setback, a snag.
• **hiccup** *verb* (**hiccups; hiccupping; hiccupped**).

hick *noun*
(*informal*) an unsophisticated person, especially one from the country.

hickory (**hik**-a-ree) *noun*
any of a group of deciduous American trees, some varieties of which bear nuts such as the pecan, and others produce a high-quality wood.

hide[1] *verb* (**hides; hiding; hid; hidden**)
to prevent from being seen or discovered: *He hid his true feelings.*
• **hide** *noun* a place from which one can watch wildlife secretly.

hide[2] *noun*
the skin of an animal, such as a calf.
Phrase **neither hide nor hair of** no sign or clue of.

hide-and-seek *noun*
a children's game in which one person looks for all the other players, who hide.

hidebound *adjective*
rigidly conventional in one's ideas.

hideous (**hid**-ee-us) *adjective*
ugly or repulsive.
Word Family **hideously** *adverb*;
hideousness *noun*.

hideout *noun*
a hiding place.

hiding *noun*
(*informal*) a flogging or thrashing.
Phrase **be on a hiding to nothing** to be very unlikely to make any progress.

hie (high) *verb* (**hies; hieing** or **hying; hied**)
an old word meaning 'to hasten'.

hierarchy (**hire**-ar-kee) *noun* (*plural* **hierarchies**)
a body of persons or things arranged or organized according to rank, authority or importance: *The Prime Minister is at the top of the government hierarchy.*
Word Family **hierarchical** (hire-**ark**-i-k'l) *adjective* of or belonging to a hierarchy.

The word **hierarchy** comes from the Greek *hierarkhēs* (a chief priest). At first *hierarchy* referred to the medieval categorization of angels into cherubs, seraphs, etc. and then, keeping its religious connections, it was applied to the grades of clergy in the 17th century. After that it developed into any kind of graded system.

hieroglyph (**high**-ra-glif) *noun*
a picture, symbol, etc. used to represent a word or sound, as in the ancient Egyptian system of writing.
Word Family **hieroglyphic** (high-ra-gliff-ik) *adjective*; **hieroglyphics** *plural noun* 1 (*used with singular verb*) a system of writing using hieroglyphs. 2 (*informal*) indecipherable or illegible handwriting.
[Greek *hieros* sacred + *glyphé* a carving]

hi-fi *noun*
1 short form of **high fidelity** the ability to reproduce sounds accurately using mechanical and electronic means: *hi-fi equipment.*
2 a system for producing these sounds: *He's got an expensive hi-fi.*

higgledy-piggledy *adverb, adjective*
(*informal*) in a disorganized or confused manner.

high (*rhymes with* my) *adjective*
1 tall or elevated: *a high building.*
2 of great size, quantity or degree: *She's got a very high temperature.*
3 of great status or importance: *He was promoted to a high rank.*
4 shrill or sharp in tone, sound, etc.: *a high voice.*
5 (of ideas, etc.) showing good moral qualities: *He has high political ideals.*
6 (of food) beginning to go bad.
7 (*informal*) being stimulated by a drug such as cannabis
Phrase **high and mighty** (*informal*) arrogant or haughty.
• **high** *adverb* in or to a high position, degree, etc.: *The plane flew high overhead.* □ *Aim high and you will succeed.*
Phrases **high and dry** stranded or abandoned. **high and low** everywhere: *We searched high and low.*
• **high** *noun*
1 a high level: *Prices reached an all-time high.*
2 (*informal*) a state of great pleasure and excitement.
3 also called **anticyclone**. *Weather* an area of calm winds and high pressure from which winds blow clockwise in the

northern hemisphere and anticlockwise in the southern hemisphere. Compare LOW[1] *noun* (definition 2).
Word Family **highly** *adverb*.

highbrow *adjective*
(*informal*) intellectual.
• **highbrow** *noun*.

high chair *noun*
a tall enclosed chair for babies to sit in while eating or being fed.

High Church *adjective* also called **Anglo-Catholic**.
belonging to a section of the Church of England which stresses the importance of Catholic ritual, sacraments and the confessional. Compare LOW CHURCH.

high commissioner *noun*
the chief representative of a British Commonwealth country in the country of another member.

higher education *noun*
post-secondary and especially university education. Compare FURTHER EDUCATION.

high explosive *noun*
a powerful fast-acting explosive.

high fidelity ⇨ HI-FI (definition 1).

high five *noun*
a gesture in which two people slap their palms together high above their heads in triumph or greeting.

high-flier *noun*
(*informal*) an ambitious person likely to reach the top of a profession.

high-flown *adjective*
(of language) extravagant or pretentious.

high frequency *noun*
a radio frequency in the range 3–30 megahertz.

high-handed *adjective*
arrogant or overbearing.
Word Family **high-handedly** *adverb*; **high-handedness** *noun*.

high jump *noun*
Athletics the athletics event of jumping over a high bar.
Phrase **be for the high jump** (*informal*) to be going to be severely told off.

highland *noun* also **highlands**
an area of hills or mountains.
Word Family **highlander** *noun* a person from the highlands.

Highland fling *noun*
a Scottish Highland dance to the bagpipes.

Highland Games *plural noun*
an annual meeting of Scottish Highlanders for sports contests, e.g. tossing the caber, and also for dancing and music.

high-level *adjective*
involving or carried out by persons of high position or rank: *high-level talks*.

high life *noun* also **high living**
luxurious living, as practised by the wealthy.

highlight *noun*
1 an outstanding event, detail, etc.
2 a lighter area put into the hair by bleaching or dyeing.
3 *Art* any of the most intensely lit details in a painting or photograph.
• **highlight** *verb* to emphasize or make prominent.

highlighter *noun*
a fluorescent pen used to make parts of a text stand out clearly.

highly ⇨ HIGH.

highly strung *adjective*
acutely tense, nervous or sensitive.

high-minded *adjective*
characterized by morally lofty ideals or conduct.

highness *noun*
1 the state of being high.
2 (**Highness**) (*plural* **Highnesses**) a form of address used to members of royalty.

high-octane *adjective*
(of petrol) having a high octane number and therefore very efficient.

high-pitched *adjective*
1 (of a sound) having a high pitch.
2 (of a discussion, etc.) intensely emotional.
3 (of a roof) having a steep slope.

high-powered *adjective*
(*informal*) very forceful and dynamic.

high-rise *adjective*
multistorey.

high road *noun*
1 a highway.
2 a direct or easy way: *the high road to success*.

high school *noun*
a secondary school.

high seas *plural noun*
the area of sea outside the boundary claimed by any country as territorial waters.

high season *noun*
the busiest time of the holiday period, and usually the most expensive. Compare LOW SEASON.

high-spirited *adjective*
bold, excitable or vivacious.

high spot *noun*
an outstanding feature in a programme, etc.

high street *noun*
the most important street in a town, often with a lot of shops in it.

high tea *noun*
a late tea or early supper, often including a cooked dish.

high-tech *adjective* also **hi-tech**
short for **high-technology** using or needing any form of sophisticated industrial process, particularly one of an electronic nature.

high-tension *adjective*
Electricity of or relating to electric cables, etc. carrying a high voltage.

high tide ⇨ TIDE *noun* (definition 1).

high time *noun*
the time just before it is too late: *It's high time you were in bed, young lady!*

high treason ⇨ TREASON.

high-water mark *noun*
the level along the shore reached by the sea at high tide.

highway *noun*
1 (*especially American*) any public road.
2 the easiest or best route.

highwayman *noun* (*plural* **highwaymen**)
(*formerly*) a robber on a highway, especially one on horseback.

hijab (hij-ab) *noun*
a headscarf or modest dress worn by Muslim women, as required by their religion.
[Arabic, curtain]

hijack (high-jak) *verb*
to steal or take over a travelling vehicle by force, for political or other reasons.
Word Family **hijack, hijacking** *noun*;
hijacker *noun* a person who hijacks.

hike *verb*
1 to walk long distances through the country.
2 to increase a price sharply.
Phrase **hike up** (*informal*) to lift up.
Word Family **hike** *noun*; **hiker** *noun* a person who hikes.

hilarious (hill-air-ee-us) *adjective*
extremely funny or merry.
Word Family **hilariously** *adverb*;
hilarity (hill-arr-i-tee) *noun*.
[Greek *hilaros* cheerful]

hill *noun*
1 a raised rounded area of land.
2 a pile or mound: *an anthill*.
Phrase **over the hill** (*informal*) no longer energetic, capable, etc.
Word Family **hilly** *adjective* (**hillier; hilliest**) having many hills.

hillbilly *noun* (*plural* **hillbillies**)
an unsophisticated person from the country, especially one from a mountainous area.

hillock *noun*
a small hill.
Word Family **hillocky** *adjective*.

hill station *noun*
in India, a town low in a mountainous area which has a pleasant climate in the hottest season.

hilt *noun*
the handle of a sword, dagger, etc.
Phrase **to the hilt** fully, completely.

him *pronoun* (*plural* **them**)
the objective form of **he**: *I hit him.* □ *Give the cake to him.*

himself *pronoun*
1 the reflexive form of **he**: *He looked at himself in the mirror.*
2 the emphatic form of **he**: *The head teacher himself will chair the meeting.*
3 having his normal or usual personality: *For weeks after the accident he was not himself.*

hind¹ (*rhymes with* find) *adjective*
being at the back: *the hind legs.*

hind² *noun*
a female deer, especially a red deer more than three years old.

hinder (hin-da) *verb*
to prevent or hamper.

hindmost *adjective*
furthest back.

hindquarters (hined-kwor-taz) *plural noun*
the back part and back legs of an animal.

hindrance (hin-dr'nce) *noun*
1 something which obstructs or hinders.
2 the act of hindering.

hindsight (hined-sight) *noun*
any insight into an event after it has occurred.

Hinduism (**hin**-doo-izm) *noun* also called
Sanatan Dharma.
a religious, philosophical and cultural
system widespread in India, having many
gods and goddesses but regarding them as
different forms of one supreme source of
life.
Word Family Hindu *noun, adjective.*

hinge (hinj) *noun*
the movable joint on which a door, gate or
lid swings.
• **hinge** *verb* to attach by or fit with a
hinge.
Phrase **hinge on** to depend on: *It all
hinges on your decision.*

hinny *noun* (*plural* **hinnies**)
the offspring of a female donkey and a
stallion. Compare MULE (definition 1).

hint *noun*
1 a subtle or slight suggestion.
2 a helpful suggestion: *a page of gardening
hints.*
3 a small amount: *There was a hint of envy
in her voice.*
• **hint** *verb.*

hinterland *noun*
1 the remote areas of a country.
2 the land surrounding and served by a
port or city.
[German]

hip¹ *noun*
Anatomy the projecting part on each side
of the body between the waist and thighs.

hip² *noun*
the ripe fruit of a rose.

hip³ *interjection*
Phrase **hip, hip, hurrah!, hip, hip,
hooray!** used as a cheer.

hip⁴ *adjective* (**hipper; hippest**)
(*informal*) up-to-date with current
fashions or trends.

hip flask *noun*
a small flask intended for carrying in a
pocket and usually for filling with a strong
alcoholic drink.

hip hop *noun*
1 a pop culture movement featuring rap,
break-dancing, strong beat dance music
and graffiti.
2 the dance music associated with this
culture.
[*hip*, cool; *hop*, dance]

hippo *noun*
(*informal*) a hippopotamus.

hippodrome (**hip**-a-drome) *noun*
Ancient history an arena for horse races,
etc.
[Greek *hippos* horse + *drommos*
racecourse]

hippopotamus (hip-a-**pot**-a-mus) *noun*
(*plural* **hippopotamuses** or
hippopotami (hip-a-**pot**-a-my))
a heavy thick-skinned semi-aquatic
African mammal with a broad head and
muzzle.
[Greek *hippopotamos* a river-horse]

hippy *noun* (*plural* **hippies**) also **hippie**
a person who rejects conventional social
standards in favour of universal love and
fellowship.

hipster *adjective*
(of trousers, skirts, etc.) hanging from the
hips rather than the waist.

hire *verb*
to obtain the services of someone, or the
temporary use of something, in return for
payment: *We hired a boat for the afternoon.*
Phrase **hire out** to permit the temporary
use or services of, for payment.
• **hire** *noun*
1 the price asked or paid in exchange for
hiring.
2 the act of hiring.

hireling *noun*
a person whose services may be hired,
often someone despised for this reason.

hire purchase *noun*
a system of buying by which a person pays
a specified number of instalments and has
the use of the object after the first
payment.

hirsute (**her**-syoot) *adjective*
hairy.
[from Latin]

his *possessive adjective* (*plural* **their**)
belonging to him: *Is that his car?*
• **his** *possessive pronoun* (*plural* **their**)
belonging to him: *I think this is his.*

hiss *verb*
1 to make a sharp prolonged *s* sound.
2 to express disapproval or dislike by
making this sound.
• **hiss** *noun* (*plural* **hisses**).

hist *interjection*
a word used to attract attention, etc.

histogram (**hist**-o-gram) *noun*
Maths a statistical diagram of rectangles in
which the area of each rectangle represents
frequency. Compare BAR CHART.

historian (hiss-taw-ree-un) *noun*
a person who writes history or is an expert
in history.
[Greek *historia* a finding out]

historic (hiss-**torr**-ik) *adjective*
memorable or sure of a place in history:
Their wedding was a historic occasion.

historical (hiss-**torr**-i-k'l) *adjective*
1 relating to history, especially as distinct
from legend.
2 concerned or dealing with history.
Word Family **historically** *adverb*.

history (hiss-tree) *noun*
1 the past, or the study of the past.
2 (*plural* **histories**) a systematic and
chronological record of past events
relating to a particular period, country,
etc.: *I'm writing a history of sailing.*

> The word **history** was originally not
> connected specifically with the past. Its
> origins lie in the Greek *histor* (a learned
> man or judge), giving Latin *historia*
> (enquiry or knowledge obtained by
> enquiry). This then developed into a
> written account of one's enquiries, a
> narrative. In English it first meant a
> fictional narrative as well as a factual
> account of the past.

histrionic (hiss-tree-**on**-ik) *adjective*
theatrical or overdone.
Word Family **histrionics** *plural noun* any
exaggerated or dramatic behaviour;
histrionically *adverb*.
[Latin *histrionis* of an actor]

hit *verb* (**hits; hitting; hit**)
1 to strike: *I hit the ball over the fence.* □ *The
car hit a tree.*
2 to severely affect: *Every farmer in the
district was hit by the drought.*
3 to move or drive by hitting: *She hit the
ball over 100 metres.*
4 to score by doing this: *The batsman hit
another six.*
5 (*informal*) to reach: *When do you think
we'll hit a road?*
Phrases **hit it off** (*informal*) to establish a
friendly relationship: *The children hit it off
immediately.* **hit on** (*informal*) to show that
one is sexually interested in. **hit on, hit
upon** (*informal*) to discover: *I have just hit on the
perfect solution.*
● **hit** *noun*
1 an impact or blow.
2 anything which is very successful or
popular: *Their new song is sure to be a hit.*
3 *Computers* an answer to a search
performed on a computer: *I got 47 hits
when I put 'snowboard' in.*

4 (*informal*) an injection of a hard drug.
Word Family **hitter** *noun*.

hit-and-miss *adjective* also **hit-or-miss**
random: *I did my best to remember them all,
but it was a bit hit-and-miss.*

hit-and-run *adjective*
(of a motorist) failing to stop after having
an accident.

hitch *verb*
1 to fasten or tie: *He hitched the horsebox to
the car.*
2 to pull up quickly or jerkily: *She hitched
up her tights.*
3 (*informal*) to hitch-hike.
Phrase **get hitched** (*informal*) to get
married.
● **hitch** *noun* (*plural* **hitches**)
1 any difficulty or obstruction: *There has
been a slight hitch in our plans.*
2 a sudden lifting or pulling.
3 *Nautical* any of various ways of fastening
one rope to another or round a bollard,
etc.

hitch-hike *verb*
to travel by getting free rides in passing
vehicles.
Word Family **hitch-hiker** *noun*.

hi-tech ⇨ HIGH-TECH.

hither (**hith**-a) *adverb*
an old word meaning 'to or towards this
place'.
Phrase **hither and thither** in different
directions.

hitherto *adverb*
until now.

hit list *noun*
(*informal*) a list of people or things to be
destroyed or got rid of

hit man *noun* (*plural* **hit men**)
a person hired to carry out unpleasant
tasks such as destroying or getting rid of
people or things.

hit parade *noun*
(*dated*) a weekly list of the highest-selling
songs in popular music.

hitter ⇨ HIT.

hive (*rhymes with* five) *noun*
1 a beehive.
2 a colony of bees living in this structure.
Phrase **hive of activity** a very busy or
active place: *The sewing room was a hive of
activity.*
● **hive** *verb* to put or store in a hive.
Phrase **hive off** to separate one part from
a larger organization.

hives *plural noun* also called **nettlerash**; **urticaria**.
a skin condition, usually a form of allergy, which causes small red itchy spots.

HIV-positive *adjective*
having had a test for the virus that causes Aids which shows that it is present.

hiya *interjection*
(*informal*) used as a greeting.

hoard (hord) *noun*
a hidden store or fund.
Word Family **hoard** *verb* to save and store up; **hoarder** *noun*.
[Middle English *hord* treasure]

> [!] The words *hoard* and *horde* sound the same but have different spellings and meanings. *Hoard* means 'a hidden store' or 'to save and store up', as in *a hoard of treasure*; *horde* means 'a large group of people or animals', as in *hordes of sightseers*.

hoarding *noun*
1 a temporary fence, such as one enclosing a construction site.
2 also called **billboard**. a board for advertisements or posters.

hoar frost *noun*
the ice crystals which form on the ground instead of dew when the temperature is below freezing. Compare FROST; RIME[2].

hoarse (horse) *adjective*
having a rough or croaking sound: *a hoarse cry*.
Word Family **hoarsely** *adverb*; **hoarsen** *verb*; **hoarseness** *noun*.

hoary *adjective* (**hoarier**; **hoariest**)
1 greyish-white in colour.
2 trite.

hoax (*rhymes with* cokes) *noun* (*plural* **hoaxes**)
a mischievous trick or something intended to deceive.
Word Family **hoax** *verb*; **hoaxer** *noun*.

hob *noun*
1 the flat top part of a cooker with hotplates or burners.
2 a shelf close to a fire for heating kettles, etc. or keeping them hot.

hobble *verb*
1 to walk with pain or difficulty.
2 to tie the legs of a horse to restrict its movement.

hobbledehoy *noun*
an old word meaning 'an awkward or clumsy youth'.

hobby *noun* (*plural* **hobbies**)
any activity which is done in one's spare time for personal enjoyment.

hobby horse *noun*
1 a stick with a horse's head and sometimes with wheels on the other end, for children to ride.
2 a favourite or obsessive interest: *Women's rights is one of her hobby horses*.

hobgoblin *noun*
Folklore a mischievous goblin.

hobnail *noun*
a large nail with a wide head, used in the base of heavy shoes.

hobnob *verb* (**hobnobs**; **hobnobbing**; **hobnobbed**)
(*informal*) to meet or associate in a friendly way, especially with one's social superiors.

hobo *noun* (*plural* **hoboes** or **hobos**)
(*American*) a tramp.

Hobson's choice *noun*
an apparent choice which in fact does not exist.
[*Thomas Hobson* was a 17th-century hirer of horses who always made the customer take the one nearest the door]

hock[1] *noun*
the joint above the fetlock in the lower part of the leg of a horse or other animal.

hock[2] *noun*
a dry white wine from the Rhine valley.
[after *Hochheim* in the Rhineland]

hock[3] *verb*
(*informal*) to pawn.
● **hock** *noun*
Phrase **in hock** pawned.

hockey *noun*
a game for two teams of eleven players who use long-handled sticks with curved ends to try to hit the ball into the opponents' goal.

hocus-pocus *noun*
1 an exclamation used in conjuring as a spell.
2 any complex talk intended to conceal the simplicity of something.

hod *noun*
1 a light trough-shaped container on a long handle, for carrying bricks or mortar.
2 a coal scuttle.

hoe *noun*
any of various long-handled tools with prongs or a flat iron blade for loosening soil, etc.

Word Family **hoe** *verb* (**hoes; hoeing; hoed**); **hoer** *noun.*

hog *noun*
1 a pig, especially a castrated male.
2 a greedy or dirty person.
Phrase **go the whole hog** to do something thoroughly and completely.
• **hog** *verb* (**hogs; hogging; hogged**) (*informal*) to take more than one's share of.

hogmanay (hog-ma-**nay**) *noun*
Scottish New Year's Eve.

hogshead *noun*
1 an old unit of volume for alcoholic drinks, usually equal to 52·5 gallons or about 240 l.
2 a large cask of this volume.

hogwash (hog-wosh) *noun*
(*informal*) nonsense.

hoi polloi (hoy pa-**loy**) *noun*
the common people.
[Greek, the many]

hoist (*rhymes with* moist) *verb*
to lift or raise, especially by using a mechanical device.
• **hoist** *noun* any of various lifting devices using a pulley or a hydraulic system.

hoity-toity *adjective*
haughty.

hokum *noun*
(*informal*) nonsense.

hold[1] *verb* (**holds; holding; held**)
1 to have and keep, especially in the hands: *She was holding a wooden box.* □ *That chair won't hold you.*
2 to contain or be filled with: *This jug holds one litre.*
3 not to use: *We held our breath.*
4 to remain in place: *They battered at the door, but it held.*
5 to occupy or possess: *He has held the office of President for three years.*
6 to continue: *The captain told me to hold my course.* □ *Our luck held.*
7 to be valid or have force: *What I said then still holds.*
8 to detain: *Try to hold them here until the police arrive.*
9 to make happen: *Where is the meeting being held?*
10 to have (an opinion): *The judge held that the contract was invalid.*
Phrases **hold back** to hesitate. **hold forth** to talk at length. **hold good, hold true** to be valid. **hold hard!** (*dated*) wait! **hold it!** wait! **hold on 1** to wait. **2** to continue despite difficulties. **hold one's own** to put up a good resistance: *I thought our team held their own.* **hold out** to last: *Will our supplies hold out?* **hold out for** to continue demanding: *We held out for a higher price.* **hold out on** to refuse to give to: *Come on, you're holding out on us – what else did she say?* **hold up 1** to delay: *What held up the train?* **2** to rob with the threat of violence: *They held up the stagecoach.* **not hold with** (*informal*) to disapprove of: *My parents don't hold with loud music.*
• **hold** *noun*
1 the act of holding or gripping: *His hold on the rope loosened and he fell.*
2 something to hold a thing by.
3 a strong influence or power: *The union has a hold on most workers in the trade.*
Phrases **on hold 1** waiting for a telephone line to be connected. **2** not being acted upon at the moment. **take hold** (of a drug, etc.) to begin to work.
Word Family **holder** *noun* a person or thing that holds.

hold[2] *noun*
the inner part of a ship or aircraft, where goods are carried.

holdall (holed-awl) *noun*
a light bag or case.

holdings *plural noun*
property owned, especially stocks and shares.

hold-up *noun*
1 something that causes a delay.
2 a violent robbery.

hole *noun*
1 an opening or hollow in something solid.
2 a fault: *Your argument is full of holes.*
3 (*informal*) a dirty or depressing place.
4 an awkward situation: *His gambling has got him into a financial hole.*
5 *Golf* a small tin-lined hole in the ground, into which the ball must be hit.
6 *Golf* the distance between a tee and the green.
• **hole** *verb*
1 to make a hole or holes in.
2 *Golf* to hit into a hole.
Phrase **hole up** (*informal*) to hide: *The guerrillas were holed up in the mountains.*

hole-and-corner *adjective*
secret or underhand.

Holi (ho-lee) *noun*
a Hindu festival celebrated in the spring in honour of Krishna.
[Hindi]

holiday (holl-i-day) *noun*
1 also called **vacation**. a period of rest from work, school, etc., usually a specified number of weeks in a year.
2 any day on which work or business stops, especially in honour of a person or past event.
• **holiday** *verb*.
[HOLY + DAY]

holiday camp *noun*
a specially built village for people, especially families, to spend their holiday in.

holidaymaker *noun*
a tourist.

holier-than-thou *adjective*
smug or self-righteous.

holiness (ho-lee-ness) *noun*
1 the state of being holy.
2 (**His/Your Holiness**) a title of respect for the Pope.

holler *verb*
(*informal*) to shout loudly.
• **holler** *noun*.

hollow (holl-o) *adjective*
1 not solid or filled: *My Easter egg was hollow.*
2 sunken: *His hollow cheeks told me he was ill.*
3 dull and echoing: *a hollow thud.*
4 worthless: *It was a hollow victory.*
5 insincere.
• **hollow** *noun*
1 an empty space or gap.
2 a small valley: *a leafy hollow near the river.*
Word Family hollow *verb* to make or become hollow; **hollowness** *noun*; **hollowly** *adverb*.

holly *noun*
an evergreen shrub with red berries and sharp pointed shiny leaves, often used as a Christmas decoration.

hollyhock *noun*
a tall plant with spikes of many large brightly coloured flowers.

holocaust (holl-a-kawst) *noun*
any great destruction or loss of life.
[Greek *holokaustos* burnt whole]

hologram (holl-a-gram) *noun*
a three-dimensional image created using light from a laser instead of a lens.
Word Family holographic (holl-a-**graf**-ik) *adjective*; **holographically** *adverb*.

holster *noun*
a leather case for a pistol, attached to a belt or saddle.

holt (*rhymes with* bolt) *noun*
the lair of certain animals, especially the otter and badger.

holy *adjective* (**holier; holiest**)
1 sacred: *a holy day.*
2 pious: *a holy person.*

Holy Communion ⇨ COMMUNION (definition 2).

Holy Spirit *noun* also called **Holy Ghost**. *Christianity* the third person of the Trinity.

Holy Week *noun*
the week before Easter, when Christians recall the last week of Jesus' life on earth.

homage (hom-ij) *noun*
an act or expression of respect or honour.

homburg *noun*
a man's felt hat.
[from the German spa where it became fashionable]

home *noun*
1 the place where one lives, belongs or was born: *He left home at 19 to see the world.*
□ *Australia is the home of the kangaroo.*
2 a house, flat, etc.: *The council is building 3000 new homes.*
3 an institution which provides care and services: *a home for the elderly.*
4 a place or region used as headquarters or a base for activities, etc.
5 *Baseball* the base at which the batter stands, and the last to be touched when completing a run around the diamond.
Phrase **at home** 1 comfortable: *I felt very much at home there.* 2 (*formal*) receiving visitors.
• **home** *adjective* connected with one's home or country: *the Home Secretary.*
□ *the home team.*
• **home** *adverb*
1 in or to one's home or country: *Please come straight home after the party.*
2 to the point aimed at: *He drove the last nail home with a sigh of relief.*
Phrase **bring home to someone** to make someone understand.
• **home** *verb* (of an animal) to go home.
Phrase **home in on** to direct or be directed towards a target or destination: *The aeroplane homed in on the radar beam.*
Word Family **homeless** *adjective*; **homelessness** *noun*.

home economics *plural noun*
(*used with singular verb*) the skills of cooking and managing a household, taught as a school subject.

Home Front *noun*
the part played in the war effort by the people of Britain during the First and Second World Wars.

Home Guard *noun*
an army of citizens organized to defend Britain against invasion during the Second World War.

home help *noun*
a person employed to clean someone's home, who helps elderly or ill people with their housework.

homeland *noun*
one's native land.

homely *adjective* (**homelier; homeliest**)
1 simple and plain: *homely food.*
2 *American* not attractive: *a homely girl.*

homeopathy (ho-mee-**op**-a-thee) *noun*
also **homoeopathy**
a type of alternative medicine which treats illnesses using tiny amounts of plant, animal and mineral extracts.
Word Family **homeopath** (**home**-ee-o-path) *noun*; **homeopathic** (ho-mee-o-**path**-ik) *adjective*; **homeopathically** *adverb*.
[Greek *homoios* similar + *pathos* suffering]

home page *noun*
Computers the first page that comes up on a computer when it is connected to the Internet.

home rule *noun*
1 the right of internal self-government granted to a region of a state.
2 (**Home Rule**) *History* this right for Ireland.

home run *noun* also called **homer**.
Baseball a non-stop run around all the bases, made by a batter who has hit the ball a long distance.

homesick *adjective*
depressed because of a longing for home.
Word Family **homesickness** *noun*

homespun *adjective*
1 spun or made at home.
2 simple and unrefined: *her homespun philosophy of life.*

homestead (**home**-sted) *noun*
the house and outbuildings on a farm or property.
Word Family **homesteader** *noun.*

home straight *noun* also **home stretch**
the straight part of a racetrack leading to the finishing line.

home truth *noun*
a statement of fact about a person, told in the knowledge that it will be painful or difficult to accept.

homeward *adjective*
towards home.
Word Family **homewards, homeward** *adverb.*

homework *noun*
a school task for a student to do at home.
Phrase **do one's homework** to carry out proper research into something.

homeworker *noun*
a person who does a job from home.

homey *adjective* (**homier; homiest**) also **homy**
cosy, like one's home.

homicide (**hom**-i-side) *noun*
the crime of killing a person.
Word Family **homicidal** (hom-i-**sigh**-d'l) *adjective* of homicide, or having a tendency towards homicide; **homicidally** *adverb.*
[Latin *homo* man + *caedere* to kill]

homily (**hom**-i-lee) *noun* (*plural* **homilies**)
a sermon, or any moralizing talk.
[Greek *homilia* a communion]

homing pigeon *noun*
a pigeon trained to fly home from wherever it is released, especially in competitions.

homoeopathy ⇨ HOMEOPATHY.

homogeneous (ho-mo-**jee**-nee-us) *adjective*
composed of parts of the same kind.
Word Family **homogeneously** *adverb*; **homogeneity** (ho-mo-ji-nee-a-tee) *noun.*
[*homo-* + *-gen*]

homogenized, homogenised (ha-**moj**-a-nixed) *adjective*
(of milk) thoroughly treated so that the milk and cream do not separate.
Word Family **homogenization** (ha-moj-a-nye-**zay**-sh'n) *noun.*

homograph (**hom**-a-graf) *noun*
a word having the same spelling as another but a different meaning or sound, e.g. *lead* (= metal) and *lead* (= guide).
[*homo-* + Greek *graphos* writing]

homonym (**hom**-a-nim) *noun*
a word having the same sound and spelling as another, but a different meaning, e.g. *peer* (= lord) and *peer* (= look).
[*homo-* + Greek *onyma* name]

homophobia (ho-mo-**fobe**-ee-a) *noun*
dislike or fear of homosexual people or
homosexuality.
Word Family **homophobic** *adjective*.

homophone (**hom**-a-fone) *noun*
a word having the same sound as another
but a different meaning or spelling, e.g.
sail and *sale*.
[*homo*- + Greek *phone* sound]

Homo sapiens (ho-mo **sap**-ee-enz) *noun*
the species to which modern human
beings belong.
[Latin, wise man]

homosexual (ho-mo-**seks**-yew-'l)
adjective
sexually attracted to members of one's
own sex. Compare HETEROSEXUAL.
Word Family **homosexual** *noun* a
homosexual person; **homosexuality** (ho-
mo-seks-yoo-**al**-i-tee) *noun*.

homy ⇨ HOMEY.

honcho (**hon**-cho) *noun*
(*informal*) a boss or leader.
[Japanese *hancha* group leader]

hone *verb*
to make sharper or more efficient.

honest (**onn**-ist) *adjective*
truthful or free from deceit or pretence.
Word Family **honesty** *noun*; **honestly**
adverb.
[Latin *honestus* honourable]

honey (*rhymes with* funny) *noun*
1 a thick sweet liquid produced by bees
from nectar for food.
2 any sweet person, thing or quality.

honeycomb (**hun**-ee-kome) *noun*
a structure of wax made by bees,
containing rows of cells in which honey
and pollen are stored and eggs and larvae
develop.
• **honeycomb** *verb* to pierce with many
holes: *a hill honeycombed with caves*.

honeyed (**hun**-id) *adjective* also **honied**
containing or full of honey.

honeymoon *noun*
1 the holiday taken by a newly married
couple.
2 any early harmonious period in a
relationship, union, etc.

honeysuckle *noun*
any of various climbing shrubs with
fragrant trumpet-shaped yellow or pink
flowers.

honk *noun*
a harsh deep sound, such as the cry of a
goose, the horn of a car, etc.
• **honk** *verb*.

honky-tonk *noun*
1 an early form of ragtime piano music,
characterized by tinny echoing notes.
2 *American* a cheap dance hall or
nightclub.

honorary (**on**-a-ra-ree) *adjective*
given or received as an honour, without
the usual duties, payment, etc.: *He
remained honorary chairman despite his
retirement.*

honorific (on-a-**riff**-ik) *noun*
any title or term of respect, such as Sir,
Doctor, Your Majesty, etc.

honour (**on**-a) *noun* (*American* **honor**)
1 great respect, or an expression or display
of respect: *She was received with honour in
her home town.*
2 anything which brings respect or credit:
He's an honour to the school.
3 a good or noble character: *a man of
honour.*
4 (*dated*) a woman's chastity.
5 a privilege: *It is an honour to serve you.*
6 a title or decoration awarded by a
monarch or government.
7 *Education* a high grade in passing an
examination.
8 (**honours**) *Education* a course or degree
in which high achievement is necessary to
graduate: *an honours degree in Law.*
Phrases **do the honours** to act as the
host: *Will you do the honours and carve the
meat up?* **on one's honour, upon one's
honour** bound by a promise or sense of
responsibility.
• **honour** *verb*
1 to show respect or honour for.
2 to fulfil or pay: *The bank refused to honour
his cheque.*
[from Latin]

honourable (**on**-er-a-b'l) *adjective*
(*American* **honorable**)
1 having high principles: *an honourable
man.*
2 based on the principles of honour: *an
honourable agreement.*
3 worthy of honour.
4 (**Honourable**) a title given to certain
important people.
Word Family **honourably** *adverb*;
honourableness *noun*.

hooch *noun*
(*informal*) alcoholic drink.

hood (hud) *noun*
1 a soft loose covering for the head and
neck.

2 something which has the shape, position or function of a hood, such as the canvas roof of a car.

3 (*informal*) a hoodlum.

4 *American* the bonnet of a car.

Word Family **hooded** *adjective* covered with or as if with a hood.

hoodlum (**hood**-l'm) *noun*
a gangster or violent destructive youth.

hoodoo (**hoo**-doo) *noun*
1 bad luck.
2 voodoo.

hoodwink (**hud**-wink) *verb*
to deceive or trick.

hooey (**hoo**-ee) *noun*
(*informal*) nonsense.

hoof *noun* (*plural* **hoofs** or **hooves**)
the hard covering encasing the foot of some animals, such as the ox and horse.
Phrase **on the hoof** 1 (of livestock) still alive. 2 (*informal*) without any preparation.
Word Family **hoofed** *adjective* having hoofs.

hoo-ha *noun*
(*informal*) a fuss.

hook (**huk**) *noun*
1 any of various curved or angular devices for pulling or grasping: *a fishhook*.
2 something which has the shape or function of a hook, such as a sharply curved part or angle.
3 also called **pull**. *Sport* a stroke in which the ball curves away behind or to the side of the player. Compare SLICE *noun* (definition 4).
4 *Boxing* a short swinging blow made with the arm bent.
Phrases **by hook or by crook** by any means, however desperate. **hook, line and sinker** completely. **off the hook** 1 (*informal*) freed from blame, a difficulty, etc. 2 (of a telephone) with the receiver off its rest. **sling one's hook** (*informal*) to leave.
Word Family **hook** *verb*; **hooked** *adjective*
1 having or resembling a hook.
2 (*informal*) addicted.

hookah (**huk**-ah) *noun* also called **water pipe**.
an Oriental tobacco pipe with a long tube which passes through a container of water to cool the smoke.
[Arabic, jar]

hook and eye *noun*
a fastener for clothes consisting of a small hook which catches onto a loop of thread or wire.

hooker *noun*
1 *Rugby* a player whose task is to hook the ball from the scrum.
2 (*informal*) a prostitute.

hookey *noun* also **hooky**
Phrase **play hookey** (*informal*, *especially American*) to stay away from school without permission.

hook-up *noun*
a connection or joining, e.g. between several radio or television stations to broadcast a special programme.

hooligan (**hoo**-li-g'n) *noun*
a young ruffian.
Word Family **hooliganism** *noun*.

hoop *noun*
a circular band or ring, sometimes used to support or strengthen something.
Word Family **hoop** *verb* to fasten or encircle with a hoop.

hoopla *noun*
a game in which small hoops are thrown in an attempt to encircle objects offered as prizes.

hooray ⇨ HURRAH.

Hooray Henry *noun* (*plural* **Hooray Henrys** or **Hooray Henries**)
(*informal*) a young upper-class male with a loud hearty voice, thought typical of his class. Compare SLOANE.

hoot *verb*
1 to make a hollow sound like the cry of an owl.
2 to express disapproval or derision by making such a sound.
3 to sound a horn.
● **hoot** *noun*
1 the act or sound of hooting.
2 (*informal*) an amusing or funny thing.
Phrase **not care a hoot, not give a hoot** (*informal*) not to care at all.
Word Family **hooter** *noun* 1 something which hoots, such as a horn. 2 (*informal*) a nose.

Hoover *noun*
(*trademark*) a vacuum cleaner.
● **hoover** *verb* to use a vacuum cleaner on.

hooves
a plural of **hoof**.

hop[1] *verb* (**hops; hopping; hopped**)
1 (of a person) to jump on one foot.

2 (of an animal) to jump on all feet. **3** to move quickly: *I hopped onto a bus.*
Phrase **hop it!** (*informal*) go away!
• **hop** *noun*
1 a light springy jump, especially on one foot.
2 a short trip.
3 (*informal*) a dance.
Phrase **on the hop 1** (*informal*) unprepared. **2** (*informal*) moving and busy.

hop² *noun*
a twining plant whose dried ripe flowers are used in brewing, medicine, etc.

hope *verb*
to wish for or look forward to something in the future: *I hope he comes to the party.*
Phrase **hope against hope** to hope even though there is almost no chance of one's hope being fulfilled.
• **hope** *noun*
1 a wish that what is anticipated or expected will occur.
2 a reason for confidence, hope or expectation: *There isn't much hope that the little boy will be found.*
3 a person or thing in which one places confidence.
Word Family **hopeful** *adjective* full of hope or expectation; **hopefully** *adverb* **1** in a hopeful way: *He looked at us hopefully.* **2** it is to be hoped that: *Hopefully she won't even notice*; **hopefulness** *noun*; **hopeless** *adjective* **1** allowing no hope. **2** impossible; **hopelessness** *noun*.

> ⚠ The use of *hopefully* to mean 'it is to be hoped that' is thought by some people to be wrong, even though it is now extremely common.

hopper *noun*
a funnel-shaped device in which materials, such as grain, are stored and then released through the bottom.

hopping mad *adjective*
(*informal*) very angry.

hopscotch *noun*
a children's game in which each player tosses an object into a pattern of squares drawn on the ground, then hops along the pattern to retrieve it.

horde *noun*
a large group of people, animals or insects.

> ⚠ Do not confuse *horde* with HOARD.

horizon (ha-**rye**-z'n) *noun*
1 the apparent boundary of the sea or flat land with the sky.
2 a limit or range, e.g. of experience.
Phrase **on the horizon** anticipated in the future.
[Greek *horizon* (*kyklos*) limiting circle]

horizontal (horr-i-**zont**-'l) *adjective*
parallel to the horizon. Compare VERTICAL.
Word Family **horizontal** *noun* a horizontal line, plane or position; **horizontally** *adverb*.

hormone *noun*
Biology an organic substance produced in one part of an organism and transported to another part where it controls various metabolic functions.
Word Family **hormonal** (hor-**mo**-n'l) *adjective*.
[Greek *hormon* setting in motion]

hormone replacement therapy *noun*
short form is **HRT** a treatment which boosts levels of oestrogen to relieve some of the symptoms of the menopause.

horn *noun*
1 a hollow growth on the head of certain animals, consisting of a tough fibrous layer over a permanent bony core. Compare ANTLER.
2 a projection on an animal's head: *a snail's horns.*
3 a drinking container made of horn.
4 *Music* a coiled brass wind instrument in which the sound produced is controlled by the player's lips.
5 a warning device that makes a loud noise: *The driver sounded his horn.*
Phrases **on the horns of a dilemma** having to make an extremely difficult choice. **pull in one's horns** to do or spend less.
Word Family **horned** *adjective* having horns; **hornless** *adjective*; **horny** *adjective* (**hornier; horniest**) **1** hard and rough like a horn. **2** (*informal*) sexually aroused; **horniness** *noun*.

hornbill *noun*
any of various tropical birds with a very large bill.

hornet *noun*
a very large wasp with an extremely painful sting.
Phrase **a hornet's nest** a lot of indignation and noisy opposition.

hornpipe *noun*
1 a lively dance for one person, originally performed by sailors.
2 the music for such a dance.

horology (hor-**oll**-a-jee) *noun*
the science of measuring time, making clocks, etc.
[Greek *hora* hour + *-logy*]

horoscope (**horr**-a-skope) *noun*
Astrology an analysis of the position of the stars at a particular place and time, e.g. at a person's birth, in order to predict future events and analyse character.
[Greek *horoskopos* one who observes the hour of a birth]

horrendous (ha-**rend**-us) *adjective*
dreadful or horrible.
Word Family **horrendously** *adverb*.
[from Latin]

horrible (**horr**-i-b'l) *adjective*
1 causing horror.
2 (*informal*) extremely unpleasant or offensive.
Word Family **horribly** *adverb*.

horrid *adjective*
extremely unpleasant.
Word Family **horridly** *adverb*.
[Latin *horridus* shaggy, uncouth]

horrific (ha-**riff**-ik) *adjective*
causing horror.

horror (**horr** a) *noun*
1 an intense feeling of repugnance and fear.
2 something which causes dislike or horror.
3 (*informal*) a naughty child.
Word Family **horrify** (**horr**-i-fie) *verb*
(**horrifies; horrifying; horrified**).
[Latin]

hors d'oeuvre (or **derv**) *noun* (*plural* **hors d'oeuvres**)
any of a variety of appetizers such as olives, curried eggs, etc., served before the main meal.
[French, apart from the main work]

horse *noun*
1 a hoofed mammal with a long mane and tail, used for riding on and pulling carts, etc.
2 a male horse as distinct from the female (called a mare).
3 a device or frame on which one sits, exercises, etc. or on which something is supported: *a vaulting horse*. □ *a clothes horse*.
Phrases **back the wrong horse** to support what turns out to be an unsuccessful cause, especially in politics.
flog a dead horse to waste one's time on a hopeless cause. **from the horse's mouth** from an authoritative source. **get**

on one's high horse to act haughtily.
hold one's horses to restrain oneself.
⇨ DARK HORSE; WHITE HORSES.
• **horse** *verb*
Phrases **horse about, horse around** to act or play roughly or boisterously.
Word Family **horsy, horsey** *adjective*
1 horse-like in appearance or manner.
2 concerned with or devoted to horses.

horseback *adjective, adverb*
mounted on a horse.

horsebox *noun* (*plural* **horseboxes**)
a closed van which can be hitched on to a motor vehicle for transporting a horse to a hunt, racecourse, etc.

horse chestnut *noun*
1 a large tree with white flowers in May.
2 the bitter brown nut from this tree, eaten by cattle, etc. (but not by horses), and used as a conker.

horsefly *noun* (*plural* **horseflies**)
a large fly which bites horses and other animals and sucks their blood.

horsehair *noun*
the coarse hair taken from a horse's tail or mane, used to stuff mattresses, etc.

horseman *noun* (*plural* **horsemen**)
a male rider of horses.

horsemanship *noun*
the skill of caring for and riding horses.

horseplay *noun*
any noisy or rough play.

horsepower *noun*
a unit of power, equal to about 746 watts.
abbrev hp.

horseradish *noun*
a white root with an extremely strong smell and taste, used in sauces, etc.

horse sense *noun*
(*informal*) common sense.

horseshoe *noun*
1 a U-shaped piece of iron, nailed to the bottom of a horse's hoof to protect it.
2 something of this shape, often regarded as a symbol of good luck.

horse-trading *noun*
(*informal*) hard bargaining.

horsewhip *noun*
a long whip used in driving horse-drawn vehicles.
• **horsewhip** *verb* (**horsewhips; horsewhipping; horsewhipped**) to lash a person with a horsewhip.

horsewoman *noun* (*plural* **horsewomen**)
a female rider of horses.

horsey, horsy ⇨ HORSE.

horticulture (hor-ti-kul-cher) *noun*
the science or study of cultivating and
maintaining garden plants.
Word Family horticultural (hor-ti-kul-cha-r'l) *adjective*; **horticulturist** *noun*.
[Latin *hortus* garden + CULTURE]

hosanna (ho-**zan**-a) *noun* also **hosannah**
a cry of praise to God.
[Hebrew *hoshi' ahnna* save, pray]

hose (hoze) *noun*
1 also **hosepipe** a flexible tube for
carrying or spraying water, etc.
2 hosiery.
● **hose** *verb* to spray or wet with water, etc.
from a hose.

hosiery (ho-zha-ree) *noun*
socks, stockings and other items for the
feet or legs.
Word Family hosier *noun* a person who
makes or sells hosiery.

hospice (hoss-piss) *noun*
1 a nursing home for patients in the later
stages of terminal illnesses such as cancer.
2 a house for travellers, etc., especially one
kept by a religious order.

hospitable (hoss-**pit**-a-b'l) *adjective*
giving a warm welcome to guests or
strangers.
Word Family hospitably *adverb*;
hospitality (hoss-pi-**tal**-i-tee) *noun*.
[Latin *hospes* a host, a guest]

hospital (hoss-pit-'l) *noun*
a place where sick or injured people are
given medical treatment.
Word Family hospitalize, hospitalise
verb to place in a hospital for treatment;
hospitalization (hoss-pit-'l-eye-**zay**-sh'n) *noun*.
[Latin *hospitalis* relating to guests]

host¹ (*rhymes with* most) *noun*
1 a person who entertains guests.
2 the presenter of a radio or TV broadcast.
3 *Biology* an organism on or in which a
parasite lives.
Word Family host *verb* to act as a host.

host² *noun*
1 a large group of people or things: *a host
of angels*.
2 an old word for an army.

host³ *noun*
(**the Host**) *Christianity* the consecrated
bread used for Communion.
[Latin *hostia* a victim]

hostage (hoss-tij) *noun*
a person held or given as a pledge that
certain actions will be performed.
[Latin *obses*]

hostel (hoss-t'l) *noun*
a supervised house which gives
accommodation at low rents, e.g. for
students, nurses, etc.
[Old French]

hosteller *noun*
a person who stays in youth hostels.

hostelry *noun* (*plural* **hostelries**)
an inn.

hostess *noun* (*plural* **hostesses**)
1 a woman who entertains guests.
2 a woman who works entertaining male
customers in a bar, etc.

hostile (hoss-tile) *adjective*
1 unfriendly or showing a desire to fight.
2 of or relating to an enemy: *hostile
territory*.
Word Family hostilely *adverb*; **hostility**
(hoss-**till**-i-tee) *noun* 1 the state of being
hostile. 2 (**hostilities**) open warfare.
[from Latin]

hostler ⇨ OSTLER.

hot *adjective* (**hotter; hottest**)
1 having or producing a high temperature.
2 very spicy: *a hot curry*.
3 passionate or intense: *her hot temper*.
4 (of news) fresh.
5 controversial: *a hot political issue*.
6 (*informal*) skilled: *He's not too hot at
maths*.
7 (*informal*) (of goods) stolen.
8 radioactive, especially to a degree
injurious to health.
***Phrases* hot on** (*informal*) very strict
concerning: *Mr Grimes is pretty hot on
discipline*. **hot on the trail of** close to
catching or finding. **hot under the
collar** (*informal*) angry. **not so hot**
(*informal*) disappointing.
Word Family hotly *adverb*; **hotness**
noun; **hottish** *adjective*.

hot air *noun*
(*informal*) any empty or pretentious talk or
writing.

hotbed *noun*
a place favouring rapid growth, especially
of something bad: *a hotbed of vice*.

hot-blooded *adjective*
passionate or excitable.

hot chocolate *noun*
a drink made from hot milk or water and
powdered chocolate.

hotchpotch *noun*
a jumble.

hot cross bun *noun*
a bun with a cross on its top, traditionally eaten on Good Friday.

hot dog *noun*
a hot frankfurter or other sausage served in a long bread roll.

hotel *noun*
a building providing accommodation for paying guests.
Word Family **hotelier** (ho-**tel**-ee-ay) *noun* a person who runs a hotel.

hot flush *noun* (*plural* **hot flushes**)
a period of time when one feels suddenly unnaturally hot, associated especially with women going through the menopause.

hotfoot *adverb*
in great haste: *She arrived hotfoot from the scene of the accident.*
• **hotfoot** *verb*
Phrase **hotfoot it** to hurry.

hot-headed *adjective*
impetuous or rash.
Word Family **hothead** *noun*; **hot-headedly** *adverb*; **hot-headedness** *noun*.

hothouse *noun*
a greenhouse maintained at a high temperature.

hotline *noun*
a direct telephone link open for instant contact between the heads of major governments in case of an emergency.

hotly ⇨ HOT.

hotness ⇨ HOT.

hot pants *plural noun*
extremely tight shorts, worn by women.

hotplate *noun*
a heated metal plate, usually on a stove, on which food is cooked or heated.

hotpot *noun*
meat and vegetables cooked in a casserole.

hot potato *noun* (*plural* **hot potatoes**)
(*informal*) a troublesome subject or situation which no one wants to deal with.

hot rod *noun*
an old car which has been modified to increase its speed.
Word Family **hot-rod** *verb* (**hot-rods; hot-rodding; hot-rodded**).

hot seat *noun*
(*informal*) a position involving difficulties or danger.

hotshot *noun*
(*informal*) a very skilled or succesful person.

hot spot *noun*
an area of potential violence; a trouble spot.

hottish ⇨ HOT.

hot-water bottle *noun*
a flat rubber bag into which hot water is put, for warming a bed, etc.

hot-wire *verb*
(*informal*) to start a vehicle using the wires leading to the engine, rather than a key.

Houdini *noun*
a person who escapes easily.
[after *Harry Houdini*, 1874-1926, an American magician (real name Ehrich Weiss)]

hommos ⇨ HUMMUS.

hound (*rhymes with* round) *noun*
1 a dog, especially one trained to hunt by following a scent.
2 (*informal*) an addict or enthusiast.
• **hound** *verb* to pursue or harass relentlessly: *The landlord has been hounding us for the rent.*

houndstooth *noun*
a pattern of contrasting jagged checks.

hour (our) *noun*
1 a unit of time equal to 60 minutes, one 24th part of a day.
2 (**hours**) the usual or specific time for something: *during office hours.*
3 a point in time: *You can't phone them at this hour!*
Word Family **hourly** *adjective, adverb* done or occurring every hour.
[Greek and Latin]

hourglass *noun* (*plural* **hourglasses**)
an instrument for measuring time, consisting of two glass bulbs joined by a narrow passage through which sand runs from one bulb to the other in a set time.

house *noun*
1 a building or part of a building where people live.
2 a household: *Shh! You'll wake the whole house!*
3 a building or establishment for a particular purpose: *the reptile house at the zoo.* □ *a house of worship.* □ *a publishing house.*
4 a family considered as a line of descent: *the house of Stuart.*

5 *Education* a section of a school which contains some students from every age group, for sport, debates, etc.
6 a legislative or advisory group: *the House of Commons.*
7 a theatre.
8 the audience in a theatre, debate, etc.
9 *Astrology* ⇨ ZODIAC.
Phrases **bring the house down** to be very enthusiastically received. **get on like a house on fire** (*informal*) to have, or begin to have, an extremely good relationship. **keep house** to manage household affairs. **on the house** free: *The landlord offered everyone a drink on the house.* **round the houses** from one place to another.
• **house** *adjective*
1 (of hospital staff) resident: *a house surgeon.*
2 (of wine) sold in a restaurant and not under a brand name.
• **house** (*rhymes with* cows) *verb*
1 to put in a house.
2 to contain or shelter.

house arrest *noun*
the keeping of an arrested person in his or her own home.

houseboat *noun*
a boat permanently moored in a river or lake and fitted with living accommodation.

housebound *adjective*
unable to leave one's home.

housebreaker *noun*
a person who breaks into and enters a house for a criminal purpose.
Word Family **housebreaking** *noun.*

housefly *noun* (*plural* **houseflies**)
a common fly which breeds in dung and refuse.

household *noun*
all the people of a house or home.
Word Family **householder** *noun* the owner or tenant of a house.

household name *noun* also **household word**
a well-known name, thing, or phrase.

house husband *noun*
a man who looks after the day-to-day running of a household, often while his wife goes out to work.

housekeeper *noun*
a person who directs and manages a household.

Word Family **housekeeping** *noun* 1 the duties of a housekeeper. 2 the money used for managing a household.

housemaid *noun*
a female household servant.

house martin *noun*
a member of the swallow family which builds nests in the eaves of houses.

housemaster *noun*
a male teacher in charge of a group of children at a boarding school.

housemistress *noun* (*plural* **housemistresses**)
a female teacher in charge of a group of children at a boarding school.

House of Commons *noun*
the lower house of the British parliament, consisting wholly of elected members.

house officer *noun* also **houseman** (*plural* **housemen**)
a junior doctor training in a hospital.

House of Lords *noun*
the upper house of the British parliament, consisting of hereditary and life peers and senior bishops.

House of Representatives *noun*
the lower house of some parliaments, e.g. Congress in the United States.

houseroom *noun*
Phrase **not give something houseroom** not to be prepared even to consider owning something.

house-trained *adjective*
(of a pet) trained not to excrete inside the house.

house-warming *noun*
a party to celebrate one's moving into a new home.

housewife *noun* (*plural* **housewives**)
a woman, especially a married woman, who is in charge of a household.
Word Family **housewifely** *adjective.*

housework *noun*
the work of cleaning, cooking, etc. for a household.

housey-housey *noun* also **housie-housie**
an old word for **bingo**.

housing (**how**-zing) *noun*
1 houses or accommodation.
2 the providing of houses: *This office is responsible for student housing.*
3 a framework or covering which supports or protects parts of a machine.

hove *Nautical* a past tense and past participle of **heave**.

hovel (hovv-'l) *noun*
a small house in poor condition.

hover (hovv-a) *verb*
1 to fly or remain in the air as if suspended.
2 to linger or wait close by.
3 to waver: *He hovered between life and death.*

hovercraft *noun* (*plural* **hovercraft**)
a vehicle designed to travel over a surface, usually water, supported on a cushion of air.

how *adverb*
1 by what means or in what manner: *How did you do it?*
2 in what state or condition: *How are you?*
3 to what extent, amount, etc.: *How often do you see her?*
4 at what rate or price: *How much is it?*
5 for what reason: *How is it that you are late?*
Phrases **and how!** (*informal*) used to stress agreement with the previous remark. **how about?** 1 used to make a suggestion: *How about a nap?* 2 what is to be done concerning?: *How about your sister – shall we invite her along?* **how come?** (*informal*) why?
● **how** *conjunction*
1 in what way or manner: *Tell us how to do it.*
2 of the state or condition in which: *I wonder how this hat looks.*
3 concerning degree or amount: *Does it really matter how late we are?*
Phrase **how do you do?** a formal greeting when meeting someone for the first time.

howdah (*rhymes with* powder) *noun*
a seat, usually with a railing and canopy, placed on the back of an elephant.
[Arabic]

however *adverb*
1 no matter how: *Buy the dress however much it costs.*
2 by whatever manner: *Do it however you like.*
3 nevertheless: *I don't like him. However, I'll invite him, since he's your brother.*

> ! On *how ever* and *however* ⇨ EVER.

howitzer *noun*
a cannon which fires shells high into the air, to hit targets which cannot be reached directly.

howl *verb*
to utter a loud long mournful cry, like that of a dog or wolf.
Word Family **howl** *noun*; **howling** *adjective* (*informal*) enormous.

howler *noun*
(*informal*) a ridiculous mistake.

how's *contraction*
a short form of **how is**: *How's your work going?*

hub *noun*
the central part of a wheel, fan, etc.

hubbub *noun*
a confused noise or uproar.

> The word **hubbub** is probably Celtic in origin, having come from Irish Gaelic *hooboobbes*, which in turn is probably related to an Old Irish battle-cry *abu*. Originally in English *hubbub* meant 'a noisy battle-cry' before it acquired its present meaning. It is also thought to be related to the Scots Gaelic *ub, ub,* an exclamation of contempt.

hubby *noun* (*plural* **hubbies**)
(*informal*) a husband.

hubcap *noun*
a cover for the hub of a wheel.

hubris (hew-bris) *noun*
arrogant pride inviting disaster.
[Greek]

huckleberry *noun* (*plural* **huckleberries**)
an American shrub with small dark blue edible berries.

huddle *verb*
1 to crowd together.
2 to curl or hunch oneself up.
Word Family **huddle** *noun* 1 a confused jumble. 2 a private conference.

hue *noun*
(*formal*) a colour: *autumn leaves of every imaginable hue.*

hue and cry *noun*
a loud outcry of protest or pursuit.

huff *noun*
a fit of petulance: *My sister went off in a huff.*
● **huff** *verb*
Phrase **huff and puff** to blow repeatedly.
Word Family **huffy** *adjective* (**huffier**; **huffiest**) easily angered or offended; **huffily** *adverb*; **huffiness** *noun*.

hug *verb* (**hugs**; **hugging**; **hugged**)
1 to clasp tightly in the arms, especially in affection.

2 to keep close to: *The little boat hugged the shore for shelter.*
Word Family **hug** *noun*; **huggable** *adjective* making one inclined to hug.

huge (hewj) *adjective*
extremely large.
Word Family **hugely** *adverb*; **hugeness** *noun.*

hugger-mugger *noun*
1 a muddle or confusion.
2 an old word meaning secrecy.

huh *interjection*
1 an exclamation of surprise, disbelief, or scorn.
2 used as a question to ask for agreement.

hula (hoo-la) *noun* also **hula-hula**
a Hawaiian dance in which intricate hand and arm movements tell a story.
[Hawaiian]

hula hoop *noun*
a hoop moved around the body by swinging the hips.

hula skirt *noun*
a skirt made of grass blades attached to a waistband, as worn by hula dancers.

hulk *noun*
1 the body or wreck of an old boat, originally used as a prison, etc.
2 a person or thing that is bulky or unwieldy.
Word Family **hulking** *adjective* (*informal*) heavy and clumsy.

hull¹ *noun*
the body of a boat or the fuselage of a rocket, etc.

hull² *noun*
1 the shell or outer covering of a seed or fruit.
2 the small leaves at the top of a strawberry or similar fruit, detached before eating.
• **hull** *verb* to shell peas, peanuts, etc.

hullabaloo (hull-a-ba-loo) *noun*
(*informal*) an uproar.

hullo ⇨ HELLO.

hum *verb* (**hums; humming; hummed**)
1 to make a continuous droning sound.
2 to sing with the lips closed.
3 (*informal*) to be full of activity.
Phrase **hum and haw** to waver between one decision and another.
• **hum** *noun.*

human (hew-m'n) *adjective*
1 relating to or characteristic of people, as opposed to animals.
2 kind and pleasant: *She can be quite human at times!*

Word Family **human** *noun* a human being; **humanly** *adverb* as regards human beings: *It just wasn't humanly possible to finish all that homework in one evening.*
[from Latin]

human being *noun* also **human**
a person, not an animal.

humane (hew-mane) *adjective*
feeling or showing tenderness or kindness for those suffering or in distress.
Word Family **humanely** *adverb*; **humaneness** *noun.*
[from Latin]

human geography *noun*
the geography of human features, patterns, and processes. Compare PHYSICAL GEOGRAPHY.

human immunodeficiency virus *noun*
short form is **HIV** a virus whose presence in the body can lead to the development of Aids.

humanism (hew-ma-nizm) *noun*
a concern with human ideals or interests rather than abstract or theoretical subjects.
Word Family **humanist** *noun.*

humanitarian (hew-man-i-tair-ee-an) *adjective*
concerned with the needs and welfare of mankind in general.
Word Family **humanitarian** *noun*; **humanitarianism** *noun.*

humanity (hew-man-i-tee) *noun*
1 the human race.
2 the quality of being humane: *Show humanity to others.*
3 the state of being human.
4 (**the humanities**) also called **the arts**.
the study of subjects such as classical literature, history or philosophy, as distinct from the sciences.

humanize, humanise (hew-ma-nize) *verb*
to make or become human or humane.
Word Family **humanization** (hew-ma-nye-zay-sh'n) *noun.*

humankind *noun*
all people.

humanly ⇨ HUMAN.

human nature *noun*
the qualities or characteristics inherent in all human beings.

humanoid (hew-man-oid) *noun*
a creature or machine that looks similar to a human being.
• **humanoid** *adjective.*

human shield *noun*
a person or group of people, especially from the enemy's side, placed at a site likely to be attacked in order to discourage attack.

humble *adjective*
1 modest and aware of one's failings, etc. **2** low in rank or importance: *She was of humble birth.*
Phrase **eat humble pie** to be humiliated or made to apologize humbly.
Word Family **humble** *verb* **1** to humiliate. **2** to lower in rank or importance; **humbleness** *noun*; **humbly** *adverb*; **humility** (hew-**mill**-i-tee) *noun* the quality of being humble.
[Middle English *umbles* the edible organs of an animal, eaten by the poor]

humbug *noun*
1 insincerity.
2 nonsense.
3 a hard peppermint sweet, usually striped.

humdinger *noun*
(*informal*) something which is remarkable or extraordinary.

humdrum *adjective*
dull and unexciting.

humerus (hew-ma-rus) *noun* (*plural* **humeri**) (hew-ma-rye)
Anatomy the long bone of the upper arm or forelimb.

humid (hew-mid) *adjective*
containing a large amount of vapour or water.
Word Family **humidly** *adverb*, **humidity** (hew-**mid**-i-tee) *noun* the state of being humid.
[from Latin]

humiliate (hew-**mill**-ee-ate) *verb*
to lower the pride, position or dignity of.
Word Family **humiliation** (hew-mill-ee-ay-sh'n) *noun* **1** the act of humiliating. **2** anything which humiliates.

humility ⇨ HUMBLE.

hummingbird *noun*
a brightly coloured fast-moving bird, whose narrow wings hum during flight.

hummock *noun*
a hillock.

hummus (hoo-mus *or* hu-mus) *noun* also **hoummos; humous**
a spread or dip made from puréed chick peas and tahini.
[Turkish *humus*]

humorist (hew-ma-rist) *noun*
a person who uses humour, especially a performer or writer of comedy.

humorous (hew-ma-rus) *adjective*
causing laughter or amusement.
Word Family **humorously** *adverb*; **humorousness** *noun*.

> ⚠ Note the spelling of *humorous*: it does not have a *u* before the *r*, unlike the noun *humour*.

humour (hew-ma) *noun* (*American* **humor**)
1 the quality of being funny: *I could not see the humour in the situation.*
2 a mood or state of mind: *good humour.*
• **humour** *verb* to indulge or satisfy the wishes, mood, etc. of another.
Word Family **humourless** *adjective*; **humourlessness** *noun*.

hump *noun*
a rounded mass or bump, e.g. that on the back of a camel.
Phrase **get the hump** (*informal*) to become annoyed.
• **hump** *verb* (*informal*) to carry.

humph *interjection*
an exclamation of doubt or dissatisfaction.

humus (hew-mus) *noun*
decaying vegetable matter in soil which makes it more fertile.

hunch *verb*
to bend or draw up in a hump: *She sat hunched over the heater to get warm.*
• **hunch** *noun* (*plural* **hunches**)
1 a hump.
2 a feeling or suspicion about something.

hunchbacked *adjective* also **humpbacked**
having severe curvature of the spine which causes a hump on the back.
Word Family **hunchback** *noun* a word for a hunchbacked person, now usually considered offensive.

hundred *noun* (*plural* **hundreds** *or* **hundred**)
a cardinal number, the symbol 100 in Arabic numerals, C in Roman numerals.
Word Family **hundred** *adjective*; **hundredth** *noun*, *adjective*.

hundreds and thousands *plural noun*
tiny colourful strands of sugar, used e.g. to decorate cakes.

hundredweight *noun*
a unit of mass equal to 112 pounds in the avoirdupois system or about 50·8 kg.
abbrev. cwt.

hung a past tense and past participle of **hang**.

> [!] On the use of *hanged* and *hung*
> ⇨ HANG.

hunger *noun*
1 the need or desire for food.
2 any strong need or desire: *She has a hunger for knowledge.*
Word Family **hunger** *verb*; **hungry** *adjective* (**hungrier; hungriest**) feeling or showing hunger; **hungrily** *adverb*; **hungriness** *noun*.

hunger strike *noun*
a persistent refusal to eat, usually as a protest against imprisonment, etc.

hung jury *noun* (*plural* **hung juries**)
a jury that fails to reach a verdict.

hung-over *adjective*
suffering from a hangover.

hung parliament *noun*
a parliament in which no party has an overall majority.

hunk *noun*
1 a large piece: *a hunk of bread.*
2 (*informal*) a sexually attractive man.
Word Family **hunky** *adjective* (**hunkier; hunkiest**).

hunky-dory *adjective*
(*informal*) very good or satisfactory.

hunt *verb*
1 to chase wild animals in order to catch or kill them, often as a sport.
2 to search or look for.
• **hunt** *noun*
1 the act of searching or hunting.
2 an organized group of people meeting to hunt together.
Word Family **hunter** *noun* 1 a person who hunts or searches. 2 a horse used or bred for hunting; **hunting** *noun* the activity of chasing wild animals; **huntsman** *noun* (*plural* **huntsmen**) 1 a person who supervises the hounds at a hunt. 2 a person who hunts; **huntress** *noun* (*plural* **huntresses**) a poetic word for a woman who hunts.

hurdle *noun*
1 any of a series of barriers set across a racetrack to be jumped by competitors.
2 (**hurdles**) a race in which these barriers must be jumped.
3 any obstacle or difficult problem to be overcome.
4 a framework used as a temporary fence.
Word Family **hurdle** *verb*; **hurdler** *noun*.

hurdy-gurdy *noun* (*plural* **hurdy-gurdies**)

a barrel organ or similar musical instrument played by turning a handle.

hurl *verb*
to throw with great force or violence: *The demonstrators hurled bricks through windows.*

hurling *noun* also called **hurley**
Irish hockey, in which teams of 15 people play with wide-bladed sticks.

hurly-burly *noun*
a noisy commotion or uproar.

hurrah *interjection* also **hurray; hooray**
a cry of approval, joy, encouragement, etc.

hurricane (**hurr**-i-k'n) *noun*
1 *Weather* a strong wind of at least 120 km per hour.
2 ⇨ TROPICAL CYCLONE.
[from Spanish from Carib]

hurricane lamp *noun*
a paraffin lamp with a wick which is protected by glass.

hurry *verb* (**hurries; hurrying; hurried**)
to do or cause to do quickly: *We hurried to the station.* □ *His boss hurried him into a decision.*
Word Family **hurry** *noun* (*plural* **hurries**); **hurried** *adjective*; **hurriedly** *adverb*.

hurt *verb* (**hurts; hurting; hurt**)
1 to cause bodily injury or pain: *The dog won't hurt you.*
2 (of a part of the body) to be painful: *My leg hurts.*
3 to have a bad effect on: *It won't hurt you to help for once.*
4 to upset: *I was very hurt by his coldness.*
Word Family **hurt** *noun*; **hurtful** *adjective* causing hurt or harm; **hurtfully** *adverb*; **hurtfulness** *noun*.

hurtle *verb*
to move or rush noisily or violently.

husband *noun*
the male partner in a marriage.
• **husband** *verb* to manage or use, especially in an economical way: *Our nation must husband its resources.*

husbandry *noun*
1 the business of farming and agriculture.
2 any careful or economical management.

hush *verb*
to make or become silent.
Phrase **hush up** to keep secret: *We must hush up this scandal.*
Word Family **hush** *noun* (*plural* **hushes**) a silence or stillness; **hush!** *interjection* be quiet!

hush-hush *adjective*
(*informal*) strictly confidential.

hush money *noun*
a bribe to keep silent about something.

husk *noun*
the dry outer covering of a fruit or seed,
especially of an ear of wheat.
• **husk** *verb* to remove the husk from.

husky[1] *adjective* (**huskier; huskiest**)
1 having a dry hoarse or whispering
sound.
2 strongly or heavily built.
Word Family **huskily** *adverb*; **huskiness**
noun.

husky[2] *noun* (*plural* **huskies**)
any of a breed of large sturdy dogs, often
used to pull sledges across snow.

hussar (hu-**zah**) *noun*
a soldier in one of the light cavalry
regiments of some European countries,
originally Hungary, noted for their
colourful uniforms.

hussy (*rhymes with* fussy) *noun* (*plural*
hussies)
(*dated*) a badly behaved or worthless
female.
[Middle English *huswif* housewife]

hustings *plural noun*
the campaigns, speeches, etc. which take
place before a political election.
[from *hustings*, an old word for the
platforms from which candidates spoke]

hustle (huss-'l) *verb*
1 to push or jostle roughly.
2 (*informal*) to earn money in questionable
or illegal ways.
Word Family **hustle** *noun*; **hustler** *noun*
a person who hustles.

hut *noun*
a simple house, usually with only one
room.

hutch *noun* (*plural* **hutches**)
a box or cage with wire mesh on one side,
in which rabbits, etc. are kept.

hyacinth (high-a-sinth) *noun*
a small garden plant growing from a bulb,
with spikes of bell-shaped flowers.
[Greek *Hyakinthos* a boy loved by Apollo]

hyaena ⇨ HYENA.

hybrid (**high**-brid) *noun*
1 *Biology* any organism resulting from
parents of different species, for example, a
mule.
2 anything which has mixed origins or is
composed of mixed parts.
[from Latin]

hydra (**high**-dra) *noun*
Biology a microscopic freshwater animal.
[from the *Hydra* in Greek mythology, a
snake whose heads grew again
immediately if they were cut off]

hydrangea (high-**drane**-ja) *noun*
a garden shrub with large showy clusters
of flowers.

hydrant *noun*
an upright pipe connected to a water main
and to which a hose can be attached.

hydraulic (high-**droll**-ik) *adjective*
operated by or using a liquid.
Word Family **hydraulically** *adverb*;
hydraulics *plural noun* (*used with singular
verb*) the study of the motion of liquids
and its application in engineering.
[*hydro-* + Greek *aulos* pipe]

hydraulic pressure *noun*
Geology the force of waves compressing air
in cracks in rocks.

hydro (**high**-dro) *noun*
a spa hotel providing medical treatment
with mineral waters.

hydrochloric acid (high-dra-klorr-ik **ass**-
id) *noun*
Chemistry a colourless corrosive acid used
in many chemical and industrial processes.

hydroelectric *adjective*
of or relating to electricity produced by the
energy of flowing water, e.g. from a dam.
Word Family **hydroelectricity** *noun*.

hydrofoil (**high**-dra-foil) *noun*
a boat with ski-like fixtures which support
the hull above the water when the boat has
reached sufficient speed.

hydrogen (**high**-dra-j'n) *noun*
a colourless odourless inflammable gas
which is the lightest and simplest of all
known elements.
[*hydro-* + *gen*]

hydrogen bomb *noun*
short form is **H-bomb** ⇨ NUCLEAR WEAPON
(definition 2).

hydrophobia (high-dra-**fo**-bee-a) *noun*
an abnormal fear of water, as in rabies.
Word Family **hydrophobic** *adjective*.
[*hydro-* + Greek *phobia* fear]

hydroplane (**high**-dra-plane) *noun*
1 a seaplane.
2 a light fast boat designed to skim along
the surface of the water.

hydroponics *plural noun*
(*used with singular verb*) the growing of
plants without soil, on wet sand, peat,
water, etc.

Word Family **hydroponic** *adjective*; **hydroponically** *adverb*.
[*hydro-* + Greek *ponos* work]

hyena (high-**ee**-na) *noun* also **hyaena**
an African and Asian mammal of the dog family with powerful jaws and short hind legs.

hygiene (**high**-jeen) *noun*
1 the study of ways to preserve health.
2 the practice of keeping clean: *the importance of personal hygiene.*
Word Family **hygienist** (high-**jeen**-ist) *noun*.
[Greek *hygieiné* of health]

> ! Note that the spelling of *hygiene* follows the rule 'i before e'.

hygienic (high-**jee**-nik *or* high-**jenn**-ik) *adjective*
clean and healthy.
Word Family **hygienically** *adverb*.

hying
a present participle of **hie**.

hymen (**high**-m'n) *noun*
Anatomy a fold of membrane which partly covers the entrance to the vagina in virgins.
[Greek, thin skin]

hymn (him) *noun*
a song of praise, especially one dedicated to a god.
Word Family **hymnal** (**him**-n'l) *noun* a book containing hymns.
[from Greek]

hype *noun*
(*informal*) the publicity and fuss that surrounds an event.
• **hype** *verb*.

hyped up *adjective*
(*informal*) tense and excited.

hyperactive (high-per-**ak**-tiv) *adjective*
also **hyper** (*informal*)
uncontrollably overactive.
Word Family **hyperactivity** (high-per-ak-**tiv**-i-tee) *noun*.

hyperbola (high-**per**-ba-la) *noun* (*plural* **hyperbolas** or **hyperbolae**)
Maths a plane regular curve formed when a cone is cut by a plane which makes a greater angle with the base than the side does.

hyperbole (high-**per**-ba-lee) *noun*
a deliberate exaggeration used for effect only.
[*hyper-* + Greek *bolé* a throw]

hyperbolic (high-per-**boll**-ik) *adjective*
1 of or relating to a hyperbola.
2 of or relating to a hyperbole.

hypercritical (high-per-**krit**-i-k'l) *adjective*
excessively critical.
Word Family **hypercritically** *adverb*.

hyperlink *noun*
Computers a connection made quickly between pages on a computer screen by clicking on a highlighted place.

hypermarket (**high**-per-mark-it) *noun*
a very large supermarket, often situated on the outskirts of a town.

hypersensitive (high-per-**sen**-sa-tiv) *adjective*
excessively sensitive.
Word Family **hypersensitivity** (high-per-sen-sa-**tiv**-i-tee) *noun*.

hyperspace *noun*
in science-fiction stories, a dimension in which one can travel faster than the speed of light.

hypertension (high-per-**ten**-sh'n) *noun*
abnormally high blood pressure.

hypertext *noun*
Computers a system which allows hyperlinks to be created and used.

hyphen (**high**-f'n) *noun*
a punctuation mark (-), used to join words or parts of words, as in *old-fashioned.*
Word Family **hyphenate** *verb* to join words with a hyphen; **hyphenation** (high-f'n-**ay**-sh'n) *noun*.
[Greek, together]

hypnosis (hip-**no**-sis) *noun*
an artificially produced sleep-like state, in which sensations like pain are reduced and the patient becomes more relaxed, with increased susceptibility to suggestion.
Word Family **hypnotism** (**hip**-na-tizm) *noun* the act or practice of causing hypnosis; **hypnotist** *noun*; **hypnotize**, **hypnotise** *verb*; **hypnotic** (hip-**not**-ik) *adjective*; **hypnotically** *adverb*.
[Greek *hypnos* sleep]

hypnotherapy *noun*
the use of hypnosis to cure people of anxiety, a bad habit, etc.
Word Family **hypnotherapist** *noun*.

hypo-allergenic *adjective*
not likely to cause an allergic reaction: *a hypo-allergenic face cream.*

hypochondriac (high-po-**kon**-dree-ak) *noun*
a person who is abnormally concerned about his or her health, especially one who exaggerates minor symptoms, etc.
Word Family **hypochondria** *noun*.

[Greek *hypokhondria* the part of the belly where melancholy was thought to originate]

hypocrisy (hip-**ok**-ra-see) *noun* (*plural* **hypocrisies**)
the pretence of having certain qualities, beliefs or feelings, especially admirable or virtuous ones.
Word Family **hypocrite** (**hip**-a-krit) *noun* a person who practises hypocrisy, especially one pretending to be virtuous; **hypocritical** (hip-a-**krit**-i-k'l) *adjective*; **hypocritically** *adverb*.
[Greek *hypokrisis* pretence]

hypodermic (high-pa-**der**-mik) *noun*
a needle used to introduce liquid medicines under the skin.
[Greek *hypo* under + *derma* skin]

hypotenuse (high-**pot**-in-yooz) *noun*
the longest side, opposite the right angle, of a right-angled triangle.
[Greek *hypoteinein* to stretch under]

hypothermia (high-po-**ther**-mee-a) *noun*
the condition in which the temperature of the body is below normal, often dangerously so.
[Greek *hypo* under + *therme* heat]

hypothesis (high-**poth**-i-sis) *noun* (*plural* **hypotheses**) (high-**poth**-i-seez)
a suggestion or statement offered as an explanation or starting point for reasoning, etc.

Word Family **hypothesize, hypothesise** *verb* to form a hypothesis.
[Greek *hypo* under + *thesis* a placing]

hypothetical (high-pa-**thet**-i-k'l) *adjective*
assumed or supposed.
Word Family **hypothetically** *adverb*.

hysterectomy (hist-a-**rek**-ta-mee) *noun* (*plural* **hysterectomies**)
Medicine an operation to remove the uterus.
[Greek *hustera* womb + *ektomé* a cutting out]

hysteria (hiss-**teer**-ec-a) *noun*
1 an uncontrollable outburst of extreme emotion, excitement, etc.
2 *Psychology* a form of neurosis in which a person shows symptoms of illness to obtain relief from stress.
Word Family **hysterical** (hiss-**terr**-i-k'l) *adjective* 1 showing or suffering from hysteria. 2 (*informal*) very funny; **hysterically** *adverb*; **hysterics** (hiss-**terr**-iks) *plural noun* a hysterical outburst.

> The word **hysteria** is derived from the Greek *husterikos* (of the uterus), which in turn is derived from *hustera* (the uterus). Hysteria was coined in the 19th century when it was wrongly thought that this neurotic condition originated in a disorder of the uterus and was restricted to women.

Ii

I *pronoun* (*plural* **we**)
the first person singular nominative
pronoun: *I have a new book.* ⇨ ME¹; MINE;
MY.

> ❗ On *between you and I* and *between
> you and me* ⇨ ME¹.

ibex (**eye**-beks) *noun* (*plural* **ibexes**)
a wild goat with long curved horns, found
in the mountains of Europe and Asia.

ibis (**eye**-bis) *noun* (*plural* **ibises**)
a large wading bird with a long curved bill.

ibuprofen (eye-bew-**pro**-f'n) *noun*
a drug used to relieve pain and
inflammation.

ice *noun*
1 *Physics* a form of water in its solid state,
below 0°C.
2 any substance resembling ice, such as ice
cream.
Phrases **break the ice** to make the
atmosphere relaxed: *It took some time to
break the ice at the party.* **cut no ice** to have
no effect or influence: *Flattering speech cuts
no ice with him.* **on ice** waiting or in
reserve. **on thin ice** in a risky or uncertain
position.
● **ice** *verb*
1 to freeze or make very cold.
2 to cover or become covered with ice.
3 to coat a cake, etc. with icing.

ice age *noun*
Geology any of several periods of time
during which ice sheets covered large areas
of the earth.

iceberg *noun*
a large mass of ice floating at sea having
broken from a glacier or an ice cap, and of
which only one-ninth is visible.
[Old Dutch *ijs* ice + *berg* mountain]

iceberg lettuce *noun*
a type of lettuce with crisp pale green
leaves.

icebox *noun* (*plural* **iceboxes**)
1 a box or compartment holding ice to
keep food cool.
2 an old American word for a refrigerator.

ice-breaker *noun*
1 a ship with a reinforced hull used for
clearing or channelling through ice.
2 a person or thing that helps to relax the
atmosphere.

ice cap *noun*
a covering of ice over an area, sometimes
vast, and sloping in all directions from the
centre.

ice cream *noun*
a sweet frozen food made from cream,
flavouring, eggs, sugar, etc.

iced tea *noun* also **ice tea**
a drink of chilled sweetened tea.

icefloe *noun*
a sheet of floating ice. A large icefloe is
called an **ice field**.

ice hockey *noun*
a strenuous form of hockey played on ice
by teams of six skaters (with ten reserves)
who try to strike a rubber disc (puck) into
the goal.

ice lolly *noun* (*plural* **ice lollies**)
short form is **lolly** a piece of water ice or
ice cream on a stick.

ice rink ⇨ RINK (definition 1).

ichthyology (ik-thi-**oll**-a-jee) *noun*
the study of fish.
[Greek *ikhthys* fish + -*logy*]

icicle (*rhymes with* bicycle) *noun*
a pointed hanging stick of ice formed by
the freezing of dripping water.

icier ⇨ ICY.

icing *noun*
a soft sugary coating used to decorate
cakes.

icing sugar *noun*
very fine sugar used to make icing.

icon (**eye**-kon) *noun*
1 also **ikon** an image, symbol or picture,
usually of a sacred or religious subject,
used as an aid to devotion, especially in
Christian Orthodox tradition.
2 a person who is respected as a symbol of
something: *a fashion icon.*
3 *Computers* a picture or symbol in a
graphic display on a VDU screen,
especially one that represents a particular
facility available to users.
[Greek *eikon* an image]

iconoclast (eye-**konn**-a-klast) *noun*
1 a person who destroys sacred or religious images.
2 a person attacking established or popular beliefs.
Word Family **iconoclasm** *noun*;
iconoclastic (eye-konn-a-**klast**-ik) *adjective*.
[Greek *eikon* image + *klastos* shattered]

icy *adjective* (**icier**; **iciest**)
1 of, like or covered with ice.
2 very cold: *an icy wind*.
3 very unfriendly: *an icy welcome for being late*.
Word Family **icily** *adverb*; **iciness** *noun*.

id *noun*
Psychology the unconscious part of the personality, which is the source of instinctive energy and has no contact with the outside world. Compare EGO (definition 2).
[Latin, it]

Id (eed) ⇨ EID.

I'd *contraction*
a short form of **I would**, **I should** or **I had**: *I'd rather go to the cinema*.

idea (eye-**deer**) *noun*
1 something conceived as a result of thought: *Have you any idea of how to do the job?*
2 a belief or opinion: *He has some very unusual political ideas.*
3 a plan: *Do you have any particular ideas for redecorating the house?*
4 (*informal*) meaning or significance: *What's the idea of bursting in without knocking?*

ideal (eye-**deel**) *adjective*
1 best, perfect or most suitable: *an ideal place for a picnic*.
2 existing only in the mind or imagination.
■ **ideal** *noun*
1 an example, idea, aim, etc. of the highest or most perfect standard: *She is my ideal of womanhood.* ▢ *His ideals do not allow him to lie.*
2 something which exists only in the mind or imagination.
Word Family **ideally** *adverb* 1 perfectly.
2 in theory.

idealism (eye-**deel**-izm) *noun*
1 the pursuit of what one considers to be ideal.
2 the seeing of things as ideals.
Word Family **idealist** *noun* 1 a person who holds or pursues ideals. 2 a person whose ideals are unrealistic or impractical;

idealistic (eye-deel-**ist**-ik) *adjective*;
idealistically *adverb*.

idealize, idealise (eye-**deel**-ize) *verb*
to regard or hold up as an ideal: *She idealizes her clever brother*.
Word Family **idealization** (eye-deel-eye-**zay**-sh'n) *noun*.

idée fixe (ee-day **feeks**) *noun* (*plural* **idées fixes**) (ee-day **feeks**)
an obsession.
[French, fixed idea]

identical (eye-**den**-ti-k'l) *adjective*
exactly equal or the same.
identical twins ⇨ TWIN *noun*.
Word Family **identically** *adverb*.

identify (eye-**den**-ti-fie) *verb* (**identifies**; **identifying**; **identified**)
1 to establish as being a particular person, thing or quality: *He identified the ring as his mother's*.
2 to represent or treat as the same: *He identifies his aims with those of the party*.
Word Family **identification** (eye-den-ti-fi-**kay**-sh'n) *noun* 1 the act of identifying.
2 something which proves the identity of a person; **identifiable** *adjective*.

Identikit (eye-**den**-ti-kit) *noun*
(*trademark*) a system of drawings used by the police for identifying criminals, made by sorting through drawings of parts of the face until a likeness is made.

identity (eye-**den**-ti-tee) *noun* (*plural* **identities**)
1 the fact of being what or who one is: *Show us your passport to prove your identity*.
2 exact sameness or likeness.
3 *Maths* an equation which is true for all values of its variables.
[Latin *idem* the same]

identity parade *noun*
a presentation at which witnesses are asked by the police to identify a suspect from among a group of people of similar appearance.

ideology (eye-dee-**oll**-a-jee) *noun* (*plural* **ideologies**)
the organized system of beliefs or way of thinking of a person or group: *fascist, communist and democratic ideologies*.
Word Family **ideologist** *noun*;
ideological (eye-dee-a-**loj**-i-k'l) *adjective*;
ideologically *adverb*.

ides (*rhymes with* rides) *plural noun*
Ancient history the Roman name given to the 15th days of March, May, July and October, and to the 13th days of the other months.

idiocy (id-i-a-see) *noun* (*plural* **idiocies**)
1 the fact or state of being an idiot.
2 any stupid or senseless behaviour.

idiom (id-i-um) *noun*
1 a phrase or expression whose meaning is not to be taken literally, for example *over the moon*, meaning 'extremely happy'.
2 the language or form of expression peculiar to one individual or group.
Word Family **idiomatic** (id-i-a-**mat**-ik) *adjective* 1 of or expressing an idiom.
2 (of language) informal; **idiomatically** *adverb*.
[Greek *idioma* a peculiarity]

idiosyncrasy (id-i-o-**sink**-ra-see) *noun* (*plural* **idiosyncrasies**)
any behaviour or character which is peculiar to one individual or group.
Word Family **idiosyncratic** (id-i-o-sin-**kratt**-ik) *adjective*; **idiosyncratically** *adverb*.
[Greek *idios* own, personal + *sygkresia* mixture]

idiot *noun*
1 (*informal*) a hopelessly foolish or senseless person.
2 an old word for a person with subnormal intellectual development who is considered unable to be educated.
Word Family **idiotic** (id-i-**ott**-ik) *adjective*; **idiotically** *adverb*.
[Greek *idiotes* a private person, non-official, ignoramus]

idle (eye-d'l) *adjective*
1 not busy, working or in use: *The machine had been idle since the workers went on strike.*
2 useless, worthless: *Ignore their idle gossip.*
3 weak, groundless: *an idle threat.*
● **idle** *verb*
1 to move or pass time in an idle manner.
2 (of machinery, engines, etc.) to move or turn at minimum speed.
Word Family **idleness** *noun*; **idly** *adverb*; **idler** *noun* a lazy person.

idol (eye-d'l) *noun*
1 a statue, picture, or image representing a deity and used as an object of worship.
2 any person who is blindly adored: *a film idol.*
[Greek *eidolon* an image]

idolater (eye-**doll**-a-ter) *noun*
a person worshipping an idol or idols.

idolatry (eye-**doll**-a-tree) *noun*
1 the worship of idols.
2 any blind devotion or adoration.
Word Family **idolatrous** *adjective*.
[Greek *eidolon* an image + *latreia* worship]

idolize, idolise (eye-da-lize) *verb*
to worship or admire blindly.
Word Family **idolization** (eye-da-lie-zay-sh'n) *noun*.

idyll (id-il) *noun*
a short poem or piece of descriptive music concerned with romanticized rural life.
Word Family **idyllic** (id-**ill**-ik) *adjective*
1 relating to an idyll. 2 naturally simple or charming.
[Greek *eidyllion*]

if *conjunction*
1 used to express a condition: *You may stay up late if you are good.*
2 used to ask an indirect question: *Tell me if you are tired.*
3 used instead of *when*: *If you add two and two, you get four.*
Phrases **as if** used to suggest that the opposite is true: *It isn't as if you are very busy.* **if only** used to introduce an unfulfilled wish: *If only it would stop raining!* **ifs and buts** *Give me a straight answer, not a lot of ifs and buts* (= doubts and qualifications). **if you ask me** *If you ask me Bill is crazy* (= I think).

iffy (if-i) *adjective* (**iffier; iffiest**)
(*informal*) dubious or uncertain: *His background is a bit iffy.*

igloo *noun*
a small dome-shaped house made of snow blocks.

igneous (ig-ni-us) *adjective*
Geology relating to rocks formed from molten material which cooled and solidified either deep below the earth's surface, such as granite, or on the surface, such as basalt.
[Latin *igneus* fiery or burning]

ignite *verb*
to catch or set on fire.

ignition (ig-**nish**-'n) *noun*
1 the act of igniting.
2 the system for producing the correctly timed sequence of electric sparks which ignite the fuel in an engine.
3 the burning of the fuel in an engine.
[Latin *ignis* fire]

ignoble *adjective*
(*formal*) below the commonly accepted standards of worthiness, honour or excellence: *an ignoble act.*
Word Family **ignobly** *adverb*; **ignobility** (ig-no-**bill**-i-tee) *noun*.
[Latin *ignobilis* insignificant]

ignominious (ig-na-**minn**-i-us) *adjective*
marked by or deserving humiliation and disgrace: *an ignominious defeat.*

Word Family ignominiously *adverb*;
ignominy (ig-na-**minn**-ee) *noun* disgrace
or humiliation.
[Latin *ignominia* disgrace]

ignoramus (ig-na-**ray**-mus) *noun*
(*plural* **ignoramuses**)
an ignorant person.
[Latin, we do not know]

ignorant (**ig**-na-r'nt) *adjective*
1 having little or no knowledge: *I'm quite
ignorant about art.*
2 (*informal*) uninformed: *What an ignorant
question!*
Word Family ignorantly *adverb*;
ignorance *noun*.

ignore *verb*
to fail or refuse to notice, pay attention,
etc.

iguana (ig-**wah**-na) *noun*
any of a group of tropical lizards growing
up to about 1·8 m long and found mainly
in South America.
[Spanish from Carib]

ikebana (ikk-i-**bah**-na) *noun*
the Japanese art of flower arrangement.
[Japanese, living plant]

ikon ⇨ ICON.

ileum (**ill**-i-um) *noun* (*plural* **ilea**) (**ill**-i-a)
Anatomy a portion of the small intestine,
which absorbs digested food.
Word Family ileac (**ill**-i-ak) *adjective*.

ilk *noun*
a type or kind: *People of his ilk are never
happy.*

ill *adjective*
1 not well or healthy.
2 not good or favourable: *The family has
suffered much ill luck.*
Phrase ill at once uncomfortable or
uneasy.
• **ill** *noun*
1 any evil or immorality.
2 any harm or disaster.
• **ill** *adverb*
1 (*formal*) badly.
2 scarcely: *We can ill afford to lose another
member.*

I'll *contraction*
a short form of **I will** or **I shall**: *I'll try
again later.*

ill-advised *adjective*
not sensible or prudent.

ill-bred *adjective*
not polite or well-mannered.
Word Family ill breeding *noun*.

illegal (il-**lee**-g'l) *adjective*
not allowed by law.
Word Family illegally *adverb*; **illegality**
(ill-i-**gal**-i-tee) *noun* (*plural* **illegalities**).

illegible (il-**lej**-i-b'l) *adjective*
not able to be read or deciphered clearly.
Word Family illegibly *adverb*;
illegibility (il-lej-i-**bill**-i-tee) *noun*.

illegitimate (ill-i-**jitt**-i-mit) *adjective*
1 not legal.
Figurative *We declared that his argument
was illegitimate* (= not valid or logical).
2 born of parents who were not married.
Compare LEGITIMATE (definition 3).
Word Family illegitimately *adverb*;
illegitimacy *noun*.

ill fame *noun*
(*dated*) a bad or immoral reputation.

ill-fated *adjective*
doomed or destined for disaster.

ill-favoured *adjective*
not attractive or pleasing in appearance.

ill-founded *adjective*
based on false facts or reasoning: *an ill-
founded rumour.*

ill-gotten *adjective*
obtained dishonestly: *ill-gotten gains.*

ill humour *noun*
an unpleasant mood: *His ill humour spoilt
the dinner party.*

illiberal *adjective*
narrow-minded or intolerant.

illicit (il-**liss**-it) *adjective*
not legal or permitted.
Word Family illicitly *adverb*; **illicitness**
noun.

illiterate (il-**litt**-a-rit) *adjective*
1 not able to read and write.
2 ignorant in a particular subject: *They are
politically illiterate.* Compare INNUMERATE.
• **illiterate** *noun* a person who is illiterate.
Word Family illiteracy *noun*.

ill-mannered *adjective*
(*formal*) bad-mannered or rude.

illness *noun* (*plural* **illnesses**)
1 the state or time of being in bad health.
2 an ailment or disease.

illogical (il-**loj**-i-k'l) *adjective*
not logical or reasonable.
Word Family illogically *adverb*;
illogicality (il-loj-i-**kal**-i-tee) *noun* (*plural*
illogicalities).

ill-starred *adjective*
unlucky or ill-fated.

ill-timed *adjective*
done or occurring at a bad or
inappropriate time.

ill-treat *verb*
to treat badly.
Word Family ill-treatment *noun*.

illuminate (il-**yoo**-mi-nate *or* ill-**oo**-mi-nate) *verb*
1 also **illumine** (il-**yoo**-min *or* ill-**oo**-min) to give light to.
Figurative Can you illuminate this discussion for me? (= make clear).
2 to decorate a book, page, etc., especially with flourishes on the letters, bright colours, etc.
Word Family illuminating *adjective*;
illumination (il-yoo-min-**ay**-sh'n *or* ill-oo-min-**ay**-sh'n) *noun*; **illuminator** *noun*.
[*il-* + Latin *luminis* of light]

illusion (il-**yoo**-*zh*'n *or* ill-**oo**-*zh*'n) *noun*
1 a false or deceptive appearance, belief, etc.
2 the perceiving of something wrongly or in a way which does not actually exist:
Heavy fog created the illusion that it was night-time.
Word Family illusional *adjective*.
[Latin *illudere* to mock]

> ! Do not confuse *illusion* with
> DELUSION.

illusionist (il-**yoo**-*zh*'n-ist *or* ill-**oo**-*zh*'n-ist) *noun*
a conjuror using mirrors or other devices to produce special effects.

illusory (il-**yoo**-za-ree *or* ill-**oo**-za-ree) *adjective* also **illusive**
1 causing deception or illusion.
2 unreal.
Word Family illusorily *adverb*;
illusoriness *noun*.

illustrate (**ill**-a-strate) *verb*
1 to provide a book or other publication with drawings, diagrams, etc. related to the text.
2 to make clear or explain, as with examples, etc.
Word Family illustrative *adjective*
serving to illustrate or explain; **illustrator** *noun* an artist who illustrates books, etc.
[*il-* + Latin *lustrare* to light]

illustration (ill-a-**stray**-sh'n) *noun*
1 the act of illustrating or explaining.
2 a reproduction of a drawing, photograph, etc. in a book or other publication.

3 anything which explains or demonstrates: *She quoted the words of several modern scientists as an illustration of her argument.*

illustrious (il-**lust**-ri-us) *adjective*
famous or celebrated.
Word Family illustriously *adverb*;
illustriousness *noun*.

ill will *noun*
unfriendliness or hostility.

I'm *contraction*
a short form of **I am**: *I'm not afraid of him.*

image (**imm**-ij) *noun*
1 a representation or likeness of something: *Despite her long absence her image remains in my memory.*
Figurative She is the image of her mother (= exact copy or likeness).
2 the way a person appears to himself or herself or to others: *The Prime Minister's public image has deteriorated.*
3 *Physics* an optical reproduction or duplicate of something, especially one formed by a lens or mirror.
4 a description of something in speech or writing to suggest a certain picture or idea of that thing: *In describing him she used the image of a dog in the manger.*
● **image** *verb* to imagine, reproduce or represent.
[from Latin]

image board *noun*
a collage creating the style of the market being designed for.

imagery (**imm**-ij-ree) *noun*
1 any mental pictures or images.
2 the creation or use of images in speech or writing to produce a vivid sensory picture.
3 a pattern of images used.

imaginary (im-**maj**-in-ree) *adjective*
having existence only in the imagination:
Your fears are purely imaginary.

imagination (im-maj-in-**ay**-sh'n) *noun*
the ability to form an image or concept of something that is not present or is not in one's experience.

imaginative (im-**maj**-in-a-tiv) *adjective*
of or coming from the imagination, especially in a creative or unusual way.
Word Family imaginatively *adverb*;
imaginativeness *noun*.

imagine (im-**maj**-in) *verb*
1 to use one's imagination.
2 to suppose: *I imagine that you're right.*

3 to guess: *It was hard to imagine what would happen.*
Word Family imaginable *adjective.*

imago (im-**ay**-go) *noun* (*plural* **imagos** or **imagines** (im-**ay**-jin-eez))
Biology an adult insect.
[Latin]

imam (im-**ahm**) *noun*
Islam the leader of communal prayer in Muslim worship.
[Arabic]

imbalance *noun*
a lack of proportion or equality.

imbecile (im-bi-seel) *noun*
1 (*informal*) any stupid person.
2 an old word for a person of very low intelligence.
Word Family imbecile, imbecilic (im-bi-**sill**-ik) *adjective;* **imbecility** (im-bi-**sill**-i-tee) *noun* (*plural* **imbecilities**).
[Latin *imbecillus* feeble]

imbibe *verb*
(*formal*) to drink.
[*im-* + Latin *bibere* to drink]

imbroglio (im-**brole**-ec-o) *noun*
a complicated disagreement.
[Italian *imbrogliare* to confuse]

imbue (im-**bew**) *verb* (**imbues; imbuing; imbued**)
(*formal*) to fill with a quality or feeling: *His poems are imbued with a spirit of joy.*

imitate (**imm**-i-tate) *verb*
to follow the style or pattern set by another.
Word Family imitator *noun* a person, especially an actor, who imitates; **imitative** (**imm**-it-a-tiv) *adjective.*

imitation (imm-i-**tay**-sh'n) *noun*
1 the act of imitating: *His imitation of her gestures was perfect.*
2 a copy or reproduction: *These jewels are imitations.*
[from Latin]

immaculate (im-**mak**-yoo-lit) *adjective*
1 having no blemish, fault or impurity
2 perfectly clean or spotless.
Word Family immaculately *adverb;* **immaculateness** *noun.*
[*im-* + Latin *macula* a spot]

immaculate conception *noun*
Roman Catholicism the teaching that from the moment the Virgin Mary was conceived she was without sin.

immaterial (imm-a-**teer**-i-ul) *adjective*
1 unimportant or irrelevant: *Cost is immaterial if you want good quality.*
2 having no physical form: *Angels are immaterial beings.*
Word Family immaterially *adverb;* **immateriality** (imm-a-teer-i-**al**-i-tee) *noun.*

immature (imm-at-**yoor** *or* imm-a-**choor**) *adjective*
not mature or developed.
Word Family immaturely *adverb;* **immaturity** *noun.*

immeasurable *adjective*
too large or extreme to be able to be measured.
Word Family immeasurably *adverb.*

immediate (im-**mee**-di-it) *adjective*
1 done or occurring without delay.
2 nearest or closest: *my immediate circle of friends.*
3 relating to the present time: *We have no immediate plans for the house.*
Word Family immediately *adverb*
1 at once: *I'll do it immediately.* 2 closely or directly; **immediately** *conjunction* as soon as: *The President left immediately he finished speaking;* **immediacy** *noun.*

immemorial (imm-a-**maw**-ri-ul) *adjective*
not within human memory or recorded knowledge: *This temple dates from time immemorial.*
Word Family immemorially *adverb.*
[*im-* + Latin *memoria* memory]

immense *adjective*
very large or great: *his immense shoulders.* □ *immense good luck.* □ *immense pleasure.*
Word Family immensely *adverb;* **immensity** *noun.*
[*im-* + Latin *mensus* measured]

immerse (im-**merse**) *verb*
to put in or under a liquid.
Figurative *He is completely immersed in writing his new book* (= involved, absorbed).
[*im-* + Latin *mersus* dipped]

immersion (im-**mer**-sh'n) *noun*
1 the act of immersing.
2 *Astronomy* the disappearance of a planet or star during an eclipse, etc.

immersion heater *noun*
a hot-water system with an electric element inside the tank.

immigrate (**imm**-i-grate) *verb*
to enter and settle in a country or region in which one was not born. Compare
EMIGRATE.
Word Family immigration (imm-i-**gray**-sh'n) *noun;* **immigrant** *noun* a person who immigrates.

imminent (**imm**-i-n'nt) *adjective*
about to occur at any moment.
Word Family **imminently** *adverb*;
imminence *noun*.
[Latin *imminere* to threaten]

immiscible (im-**miss**-i-b'l) *adjective*
not able to be mixed or combined.

immobile (im-**mo**-bile) *adjective*
not moving or mobile.
Word Family **immobility** (imm-a-**bill**-i-tee) *noun*.

immobilize, immobilise (im-**mo**-bil-ize)
verb
to make incapable of movement.
Word Family **immobilizer** *noun*;
immobilization (im-mo-bil-eye-**zay**-sh'n) *noun*.

immoderate (im-**modd**-a-rit) *adjective*
extreme or unreasonable.
Word Family **immoderately** *adverb*;
immoderation (imm-odd-a-**ray**-sh'n) *noun*.

immodest *adjective*
without shame or modesty.
Word Family **immodestly** *adverb*;
immodesty *noun*.

immoral (im-**morr**-'l) *adjective*
not moral or not in accord with accepted
moral standards.
Word Family **immorally** *adverb*;
immorality (imm-a-**rall**-i-tee) *noun*.

> ⚠ Do not confuse *immoral* with
> AMORAL.

immortal (im-**mor**-t'l) *adjective*
1 not subject to death or destruction:
immortal gods.
2 everlasting: *immortal fame*.
● **immortal** *noun* an immortal person or
thing.
Word Family **immortally** *adverb*;
immortality (imm-or-**tal**-i-tee) *noun*;
immortalize, immortalise *verb*.

immovable (im-**moo**-va-b'l) *adjective* also
immoveable
not able to be moved or changed.
Word Family **immovably** *adverb*.

immune (im-**yoon**) *adjective*
1 protected or safe, e.g. from a disease.
2 *Biology* producing antibodies which kill
germs in the body: *the immune system*.
Word Family **immunity** *noun* (*plural*
immunities) 1 the state of being
immune. 2 special exemption;
immunize, immunise (**im**-yoo-nize)
verb to make immune, especially by
inoculation or vaccination;

immunization (im-yoo-nigh-**zay**-sh'n)
noun.
[Latin *immunis* exempt from public
service]

immunology (im-yoo-**noll**-a-jee) *noun*
the study of immunity from disease and
methods of producing it.
Word Family **immunologist** *noun*.

immure (imm-**yoor**) *verb*
to enclose or shut in, usually within walls.
[*im-* + Latin *murus* a wall]

immutable (im-**mew**-ta-b'l) *adjective*
not changing or able to be changed.
Word Family **immutably** *adverb*;
immutability (im-mewt-a-**bill**-i-tee)
noun.

imp *noun*
1 a small mischievous magical creature in
fairy tales.
2 a mischievous or naughty child.

impact (im-pakt) *noun*
1 the striking or contact of one thing
against another: *The impact of the blow
knocked him over.*
2 an effect: *The news had little impact on us.*
● **impact** (im-**pakt**) *verb* to have an
impact or effect: *The new regulations will
impact on the poor.*
Word Family **impacted** (im-**pak**-tid)
adjective 1 pressed or forced closely
together. 2 (of a tooth) not able to grow
out naturally.
[Latin *impactus* thrust against]

impair *verb*
to spoil or make worse.
Word Family **impairment** *noun*.

impala (im-**pah**-la) *noun* (*plural* **impala**)
a large African antelope.

impale *verb*
to pierce through or fix on a sharp pointed
object.

impalpable (im-**pal**-pa-b'l) *adjective*
not able to be touched or felt.
*Figurative The painting had an impalpable
beauty* (= not easy to understand or
explain).
Word Family **impalpably** *adverb*;
impalpability (im-pal-pa-**bill**-i-tee)
noun.

impart *verb*
1 (*formal*) to tell: *The head teacher imparted
the latest news to the parents.*
2 to give: *Candlelight imparted a cosy glow to
the room.*

impartial (im-**par**-sh'l) *adjective*
free from bias, prejudice or favouritism.

Word Family **impartially** *adverb*;
impartiality (im-par-shi-**al**-i-tee) *noun*.

impassable (im-**pah**-sa-b'l) *adjective*
not able to be travelled or passed along.
Word Family **impassability** (im-pah-sa-**bill**-i-tee) *noun*.

impasse (**am**-pass) *noun*
a situation which allows no escape or
solution.
[French]

impassioned (im-**pash**-'nd) *adjective*
full of feeling or passion.
Word Family **impassion** *verb*.

impassive *adjective*
not feeling or expressing emotion: *Her
impassive reaction to the news was very
surprising.*
Word Family **impassively** *adverb*;
impassivity (im-pa-**sivv**-i-tee) *noun*.

impatient (im-**pay**-sh'nt) *adjective*
eager for relief, change or progress:
impatient because of the delay.
Word Family **impatiently** *adverb*;
impatience *noun*.

impeach *verb*
1 *Law* to accuse a government official of a
crime against the public.
2 to attack or bring a charge against.
Word Family **impeachment** *noun*;
impeachable *adjective* making one likely
to be impeached.

impeccable (im-**pekk**-a-b'l) *adjective*
faultless.
Word Family **impeccably** *adverb*;
impeccability (im-pekk-a-**bill**-i-tee)
noun.
[*im-* + Latin *peccare* to sin]

impecunious (im-pi-**kew**-ni-us) *adjective*
(*formal*) having little or no money.
Word Family **impecuniousness** *noun*.
[*im-* + Latin *pecunia* money]

impedance (im-**pee**-d'nce) *noun*
Electricity the total resistance presented by
a circuit to an alternating current.

impede (im-**peed**) *verb*
to obstruct.
[Latin *impedire* from *pes, pedis* a foot]

impediment (im-**pedd**-i-m'nt) *noun*
1 an obstacle or obstruction.
2 a defect, especially of speech.

impel (im-**pel**) *verb* (**impels; impelling;
impelled**)
1 to urge to action.
2 to cause to move.
[Latin *impellere* to push against]

impending *adjective*
about to happen or come: *The town
prepared for the impending flood.*
[Latin *impendere* to hang over]

impenetrable (im-**pen**-it-ra-b'l) *adjective*
not able to be penetrated or entered.
*Figurative The crime remained an
impenetrable mystery* (= incomprehensible).
Word Family **impenetrability** (im-pen-it-ra-**bill**-i-tee) *noun*.

impenitent (im-**pen**-i-t'nt) *adjective*
not repenting.

imperative (im-**perr**-a-tiv) *adjective*
1 essential or compulsory: *It is imperative
that we get there on time.*
2 commanding or requiring obedience:
*His imperative gesture made us leave without
further ado.*
3 *Grammar* in the imperative mood.
• **imperative** *noun*
1 something that is imperative.
2 *Grammar* the imperative mood.
⇨ MOOD².
[Latin *imperare* to command]

imperceptible (im-pa-**sept**-i-b'l) *adjective*
almost unable to be seen or perceived:
*Through the heavy beard his smile was
imperceptible.*
Word Family **imperceptibly** *adverb*.

imperfect (im-**per**-fikt) *adjective*
not perfect or complete.
Word Family **imperfectly** *adverb*;
imperfection (im-pa-**fek**-sh'n) *noun*
1 the state of being imperfect. 2 a fault or
flaw.

imperial (im-**peer**-i-ul) *adjective*
1 of or characteristic of an empire or its
ruler.
2 (of weights and measures) standardized
by British law: *an imperial gallon.*

imperialism (im-**peer**-i-a-llzm) *noun* also
called **colonialism**.
the dominance of one country over
another, either by direct rule or by
economic or military influence.
Word Family **imperialist** *noun*;
imperialist, imperialistic (im-peer-i-a-**list**-ik) *adjective*.
[Latin *imperium* command, sovereignty]

imperil (im-**per**-il) *verb* (**imperils;
imperilling; imperilled**)
to put in danger.

imperious (im-**peer**-i-us) *adjective*
arrogant or domineering.
Word Family **imperiously** *adverb*;
imperiousness *noun*.

imperishable *adjective*
not able to perish or be destroyed.

impermeable (im-**per**-mi-a-b'l) *adjective*
not able to be passed through: *Water cannot pass through impermeable rocks.*
Compare PERMEABLE.
Word Family **impermeability** (im-per-mi-a-**bill**-i-tee) *noun.*

impersonal (im-**per**-sa-n'l) *adjective*
1 not influenced by or expressing personal feelings: *Doctors cultivate an impersonal attitude towards patients.*
2 *Grammar* not referring to a particular person or thing. For example, in the sentence *It seems you are right,* 'it' is an impersonal pronoun.
Word Family **impersonally** *adverb.*

impersonate (im-**per**-sa-nate) *verb*
to imitate or act the part of.
Word Family **impersonator** *noun* a person, especially an actor, who impersonates others; **impersonation** (im-per-sa-**nay**-sh'n) *noun.*

impertinent (im-**per**-ti-nant) *adjective*
1 rude or presumptuous.
2 (*formal*) not relevant or appropriate.
Word Family **impertinently** *adverb;* **impertinence** *noun* 1 the state of being impertinent. 2 any cheeky or impudent behaviour.

imperturbable (im-pa-**ter**-ba-b'l) *adjective*
not easily agitated or excited.
Word Family **imperturbably** *adverb;* **imperturbability** (im-pa-ter-ba-**bill**-i-tee) *noun.*

impervious (im-**per**-vi-us) *adjective*
not allowing the passage of fluids, etc.
impervious rock.
Phrase **impervious to** *She is impervious to criticism from anybody* (= unaffected by).
Word Family **imperviousness** *noun;* **imperviously** *adverb.*

impetigo (im-pi-**tie**-go) *noun*
an infectious condition of the skin which causes pustules, usually on the face, especially in children.
[Latin *impetere* to attack]

impetuous (im-**pet**-yew-us) *adjective*
hasty or rash.
Word Family **impetuously** *adverb;* **impetuosity** (im-pet-yoo-**oss**-i-tee), **impetuousness** *noun.*

impetus (**imp**-i-tus) *noun* (*plural* **impetuses**)
1 the energy or force of something which is moving.

2 a stimulus or impulse: *Success provided a new impetus to work harder.*
[Latin, an attack]

impiety (im-**pie**-a-tee) *noun* (*plural* **impieties**)
a lack of respect or reverence.

impinge (im-**pinj**) *verb*
1 to have an effect or impact on.
2 to break in or interrupt: *The harsh voice impinged on the restful silence.*
[Latin *impingere* to thrust against]

impious (**im**-pi-us) *adjective*
without respect or reverence.
Word Family **impiously** *adverb;* **impiousness** *noun.*

impish *adjective*
mischievous or playfully naughty.
Word Family **impishly** *adverb;* **impishness** *noun.*

implacable (im-**plakk**-a-b'l) *adjective*
not able to be appeased or pacified: *an implacable enemy.*
Word Family **implacably** *adverb;* **implacability** (im-plakk-a-**bill**-i-tee) *noun.*

implant (im-**plahnt**) *verb*
to plant or fix in: *The image was firmly implanted in her mind.*
• **implant** (**im**-plahnt) *noun* any substance put into a body, such as a grafted tissue, a drug, radioactive substances, etc.
Word Family **implantation** (im-plahn-**tay**-sh'n) *noun.*

implausible (im-**plaw**-za-b'l) *adjective*
not appearing likely to be true.
Word Family **implausibly** *adverb;* **implausibility** (im-plawz-a-**bill**-i-tee) *noun.*

implement (**im**-pli-m'nt) *noun*
any tool.
• **implement** (**im**-pli-ment) *verb* to put into use or effect: *The new road rules will be strictly implemented.*
Word Family **implementation** (im-pli-men-**tay**-sh'n) *noun.*
[Latin *implere* to fill up]

implicate (**im**-pli-kate) *verb*
to involve in or with something: *He is implicated in the crime because he knew of it beforehand.* □ *The evidence implicates him.*
[from Latin]

implication (im-pli-**kay**-sh'n) *noun*
1 the state of being implicated: *Her implication in the crime was proved beyond doubt.*

2 anything which is implied or suggested: *The serious implications of his words only struck us later.*

implicit (im-**pliss**-it) *adjective*
1 being implied or suggested but not actually expressed: *our parents' implicit disapproval.*
2 absolute or unquestioning: *an implicit belief in all she was taught.*
Word Family implicitly *adverb*; **implicitness** *noun.*
[Latin *implicitus* involved]

implore *verb*
to ask earnestly or urgently.
Word Family imploring *adjective*; **imploringly** *adverb.*
[*im-* + Latin *plorare* to weep]

implosion (im-**plo**-*zh*'n) *noun*
a bursting inwards.
Word Family implode *verb.*
[*im-* + (ex)PLOSION]

imply (im-**ply**) *verb* (**implies; implying; implied**)
1 to suggest in a subtle or indirect way: *Her tone of voice implied that she was very busy.*
2 to require or involve logically or necessarily: *Movement implies energy.*

> ⚠️ Do not confuse *imply* with *infer*. *Infer* means 'to deduce or conclude from information available', as in *I infer from your remark that you have not read the article.* The use of *infer* in the same way as *imply* to mean 'to suggest or hint' has become so common that some dictionaries now give 'to imply' as an additional sense of *infer*, but many people still consider this to be wrong.

impolite *adjective*
not polite.
Word Family impolitely *adverb*; **impoliteness** *noun.*

imponderable (im-**pond**-er-a-b'l) *adjective*
not able to be weighed or estimated.
● **imponderable** *noun* something which cannot be weighed or estimated.
Word Family imponderably *adverb.*
[*im-* + Latin *ponderis* of a weight]

import (im-**port**) *verb*
1 to bring in goods or services from an outside source, especially a foreign country. Compare EXPORT.
2 *Computers* to transfer data into a file.
3 an old word meaning 'to mean or signify'.
● **import** (im-port) *noun*

1 anything which is imported or brought in from outside.
2 (*formal*) the meaning: *What was the import of his visit?*
3 (*formal*) importance: *It was a message of some import for all of us.*
Word Family importation (im-por-**tay**-sh'n) *noun* **1** the act of importing, especially foreign goods. **2** something that is imported; **importer** *noun.*
[*im-* + Latin *portare* to carry]

important (im-**port**-'nt) *adjective*
1 of great meaning, significance, value, etc.: *an important role in the play.*
2 having great power or influence: *an important person.*
Word Family importance *noun*; **importantly** *adverb.*

importunate (im-**port**-yoo-nit) *adjective* (*formal*) urgent or persistent.
Word Family importunately *adverb*; **importunity** (im-por-**tew**-ni-tee) *noun.*

importune (im-**port**-yoon) *verb* (*formal*) to beg or press for urgently.
[Latin *importunus* inconvenient]

impose (im-**poze**) *verb*
1 to establish or place from, or as if from, a position of authority: *The judge imposed a heavy fine on the vandals.*
2 to make demands, take advantage of: *I'm sorry to impose on you like this.*
[Latin *impositus* placed upon]

imposing *adjective*
impressive.

imposition (im-pa-**zish**-'n) *noun*
1 the act of laying or placing on.
2 anything which is imposed, such as a burden, punishment, etc.
3 an act of taking advantage of.

impossible *adjective*
1 not possible.
2 not able to be tolerated: *What an impossible person!*
Word Family impossibly *adverb*; **impossibility** (im-poss-i-**bill**-i-tee) *noun* (*plural* **impossibilities**).

impost (im-post) *noun*
a tax or duty, especially customs duty.

impostor (im-**poss**-ta) *noun* also **imposter**
a person who deceives or commits a fraud, especially under an assumed name.
Word Family imposture *noun* **1** the act or practice of deceiving. **2** a deception.

impotent (im-pa-t'nt) *adjective*
1 having no strength, power or effect.

2 (of a man) unable to develop an erection in response to sexual stimuli.
Word Family **impotently** *adverb*;
impotence, impotency *noun*.

impound (im-**pound**) *verb*
to seize legally: *The stolen goods were impounded by the police.*

impoverish (im-**povv**-a-rish) *verb*
to make poor: *The family was impoverished by years of medical costs.*
Figurative Language is impoverished by misuse (= made poor in quality).
Word Family **impoverishment** *noun*.

impracticable (im-**prak**-tik-a-b'l) *adjective*
not practicable or possible.
Word Family **impracticability** (im-prak-tik-a-**bill**-i-tee) *noun*.

impractical (im-**prak**-ti-k'l) *adjective*
not practical, unrealistic.

imprecation (im-pri-**kay**-sh'n) *noun* (*formal*) a curse.
Word Family **imprecatory** (**im**-pri-kate-a-ree) *adjective*.
[Latin *imprecari* to invoke a curse]

impregnable (im-**preg**-na-b'l) *adjective*
not able to be taken or overcome: *The strong walls of the fort made it impregnable.*
Word Family **impregnably** *adverb*;
impregnability (im-preg-na-**bill**-i-tee) *noun*.
[from Old French]

impregnate (**im**-preg-nate) *verb*
1 to fill throughout: *The water was impregnated with salt.*
2 to fertilize or make pregnant.
Word Family **impregnation** (im-preg-**nay**-sh'n) *noun*.
[from Latin]

impresario (im-pri-**sah**-ri-o) *noun*
a producer or manager of theatrical or musical entertainments.
[Italian *impresa* enterprise]

impress¹ (im-**press**) *verb*
1 to affect or influence the opinion of, especially favourably: *We were all impressed by the excellent food at the hotel.*
2 to press or stamp.
Phrase **impress something on** to cause to understand the importance of: *You must impress the urgency of the situation on her.*
● **impress** (**im**-press) *noun* a mark made by pressing or stamping.

impress² (im-**press**) *verb*
History to take forcibly for public use or service: *Civilians were impressed into the armed forces when war broke out.*

impression (im-**presh**-'n) *noun*
1 an effect or influence on the mind or feelings: *His rudeness creates a bad impression.* □ *I get the impression you don't like him.*
2 an imitation: *He does impressions of famous people as a stage act.*
3 a mark or shape made by pressing, stamping, etc.: *The dentist made an impression of her front teeth.*

impressionable (im-**presh**-'na-b'l) *adjective*
easily impressed or influenced.

Impressionism (im-**presh**-'n-izm) *noun*
a style of painting, music or literature aimed at suggesting mood or immediate feelings about a subject, rather than close surface detail or analysis.
Word Family **impressionist** *noun*
1 (**Impressionist**) a person using the style of impressionism. **2** a person who imitates people.

impressionistic *adjective*
giving an approximate idea of what something is like, based on ideas rather than facts.

impressive *adjective*
having a strong or awesome effect or impression.
Word Family **impressively** *adverb*;
impressiveness *noun*.

imprimatur (im-pri-**may**-ta) *noun*
official permission or approval to do something, such as to publish a book.
[Latin, let it be printed]

imprint (**im**-print) *noun*
a mark made by pressing or stamping.
Figurative His unhappy childhood left a powerful imprint on his character (= effect, impression).
● **imprint** (im-**print**) *verb* to print, stamp or impress.

imprison *verb*
to put in prison.
Word Family **imprisonment** *noun*.

improbable (im-**prob**-a-b'l) *adjective*
not probable or likely.
Word Family **improbably** *adverb*.

impromptu (im-**promp**-tew) *adjective, adverb*
done or made without any preparation, practice, etc.
[Latin *in promptu* in readiness]

improper (im-**prop**-a) *adjective*
not suitable or correct, especially according to moral conventions.
Word Family **improperly** *adverb*.

improper fraction *noun*
a fraction greater than 1, e.g. $\frac{6}{5}$. Compare
COMMON FRACTION.

impropriety (im-pra-**pry**-a-tee) *noun*
(*plural* **improprieties**)
1 the state of being improper or
unsuitable.
2 any improper action, etc.

improve (im-**proov**) *verb*
to make or become better: *I'm going to
improve my spelling.* □ *Your French accent is
improving!*

improvement *noun*
1 the act of improving.
2 any thing which improves or adds to the
beauty, value, etc. of another thing: *Bright
colours made a great improvement to the old
house.*

improvident (im-**provv**-i-d'nt) *adjective*
1 not cautious or prudent.
2 not providing for the future.
Word Family improvidently *adverb*;
improvidence *noun*.

improvise (im-pra-**vize**) *verb*
to do or create something without
preparation, sufficient materials, etc.
Word Family improvisation (im-pra-
vize-**ay**-sh'n) *noun* **1** the act of
improvising. **2** anything which is
improvised; **improviser** *noun*.
[Latin *improvisus* unexpected]

imprudent (im-**proo**-d'nt) *adjective*
not prudent or discreet.
Word Family imprudently *adverb*;
imprudence *noun*.

impudent (im-**pew**-d'nt) *adjective*
boldly rude or disrespectful.
Word Family impudently *adverb*;
impudence *noun*.
[from Latin]

impugn (im-**pewn**) *verb*
to challenge or call into doubt or question.
[*im-* + Latin *pugnare* to fight]

impulse (im-**pulse**) *noun*
1 a sudden urge or desire: *He felt a great
impulse to dance on the sand.*
2 a stimulating force or effect.
3 *Biology* a signal that transmits
information through nerves resulting in
bodily action.
4 *Physics* the product of a force and the
time for which it acts on a body.
[Latin *impulsus* pressure, incitement]

impulsion (im-**pul**-sh'n) *noun*
1 the act of impelling or driving forward.
2 a force or impulse.

impulsive (im-**pul**-siv) *adjective*
1 rash or hasty: *an impulsive spender.*
2 done on an impulse: *She gave an
impulsive smile.*
Word Family impulsively *adverb*;
impulsiveness *noun*.

impunity (im-**pew**-ni-tee) *noun*
a freedom from punishment or from the
consequences of one's actions.

impure (im-**pure**) *adjective*
not pure.
Word Family impurity *noun* (*plural*
impurities).

impute (im-**pewt**) *verb*
(*formal*) to attribute to or blame with.
Word Family imputation (im-pew-**tay**-
sh'n) *noun*.
[Latin *imputare* to debit or credit]

in *preposition*
a word used to indicate the following:
1 place: *a house in the country.*
2 time: *six in the morning.*
3 direction: *walk in a straight line.*
4 situation, condition: *They're in love.* □ *She
is in a rage.*
5 inclusion: *six children in the family.*
6 manner, method: *She talks in a posh way.*
□ *He paints in oil colours.*
7 form, shape: *Stand in a line.* □ *Her hair
hung in pigtails.*
8 activity: *She's in advertising.*
Phrases **in for** about to experience: *We
are in for rain.* **in on** aware of, involved in:
Who else is in on the joke? **in that** because.
● **in** *adjective, adverb*
1 special uses with many common verbs to
produce specific meanings: *come in* (= to
enter). □ *fill in* (= to complete, to
substitute). □ *give in* (= to surrender).
□ *step in* (= to intervene).
2 special uses with the verb 'to be': *She'll
be in late* (= back, at home). □ *She's in with
the boss* (= in a favoured position). □ *When
are raspberries in?* (= in season, available).
□ *Which team is in at the moment?*
(= batting).
3 most fashionable or up-to-date: *Are long
skirts in this winter?*
● **in** *noun*
Phrase **ins and outs** the details or
intricacies.
[Latin]

inability (inn-a-**bill**-i-tee) *noun*
a lack of power or capacity.

in absentia (in ab-**sen**-ti-a) *adverb*
(*formal*) in or during one's absence.
[Latin]

inaccessible (in-ak-**sess**-i-b'l)
adjective
not accessible or reachable.
Word Family **inaccessibly** *adverb*;
inaccessibility (in-ak-sess-i-**bill**-i-tee)
noun.

inaccurate (in-**ak**-yoo-rit) *adjective*
not accurate.
Word Family **inaccurately** *adverb*;
inaccuracy *noun* (*plural* **inaccuracies**).

inactive (in-**ak**-tiv) *adjective*
not active or working.
Word Family **inactively** *adverb*;
inactivity (in-ak-**tivv**-i-tee), **inaction**
noun.

inadequate (in-**add**-i-kwit) *adjective*
not adequate or enough.
Word Family **inadequately** *adverb*;
inadequacy *noun* (*plural* **inadequacies**).

inadmissible (in-ad-**miss**-i-b'l) *adjective*
not admissible.
Word Family **inadmissibly** *adverb*;
inadmissibility (in-ad-miss-i-**bill**-i-tee)
noun.

inadvertent (in-ad-**ver**-t'nt) *adjective*
not intended or deliberate: *Her hurtful
remark had been quite inadvertent.*
Word Family **inadvertently** *adverb*;
inadvertence, inadvertency *noun*.
[*in-*² + Latin *advertens* paying attention]

inalienable (in-**ay**-li-en-a-b'l) *adjective*
not able to be taken away: *Every citizen has
an inalienable right to life.*

inane *adjective*
silly or senseless.
Word Family **inanely** *adverb*; **inanity**
(in-**ann**-i-tee) *noun* (*plural* **inanities**).
[Latin *inanis* empty, vain]

inanimate (in-**an**-i-mit) *adjective*
not having life: *Chairs are inanimate objects.*

inapplicable (inn-a-**plik**-a-b'l) *adjective*
not applicable: *Your theory is inapplicable to
the present situation.*

inappropriate (in-a-**pro**-pree-it) *adjective*
not appropriate or suitable.
Word Family **inappropriately** *adverb*;
inappropriateness *noun*.

inapt *adjective*
1 unskilful.
2 not apt or appropriate.
Word Family **inaptly** *adverb*; **inaptitude**
noun a lack of skill or talent.

inarticulate (in-ar-**tik**-yoo-lit) *adjective*
1 not able to speak or express oneself
clearly: *She was made inarticulate by
indignation.*

2 not using human speech: *the inarticulate
cries of animals.*
Word Family **inarticulately** *adverb*;
inarticulateness *noun*.

inasmuch *adverb*
Phrase **inasmuch as** since or because.

inattentive *adjective*
not attentive.
Word Family **inattention,
inattentiveness** *noun*.

inaudible (in-**awd**-i-b'l) *adjective*
not able to be heard.
Word Family **inaudibly** *adverb*.

inauguration (in-aw-gyoo-**ray**-sh'n) *noun*
1 a formal or official introduction,
opening, etc., such as the installing of an
official in office.
2 any important beginning.
Word Family **inaugurate** (in-**aw**-gyoo-
rate) *verb*; **inaugural** *adjective* of or for an
inauguration.
[from Latin]

inauspicious (in-aw-**spish**-us) *adjective*
not favourable or auspicious.
Word Family **inauspiciously** *adverb*.

inboard *adjective, adverb*
within the hull of a boat: *an inboard motor.*

inborn *adjective*
natural or possessed from birth: *He has an
inborn artistic ability.*

inbred *adjective*
1 inborn.
2 relating to or resulting from inbreeding.

inbreeding *noun*
Biology the mating of closely related
individuals, which often discloses genetic
weaknesses.

incalculable (in-**kal**-kew-la-b'l) *adjective*
1 not able to be calculated.
2 uncertain or unpredictable.
Word Family **incalculably** *adverb*.

in camera *adverb*
Law in private.
[Latin, in the chamber]

incandescent (in-kan-**dess**-'nt) *adjective*
giving out light as a result of being heated.
Word Family **incandescence** *noun*;
incandesce *verb*.
[Latin *incandescens* becoming white]

incantation (in-kan-**tay**-sh'n) *noun*
1 a spell.
2 the chanting of a spell.
Word Family **incantatory** *adjective*.
[from Latin]

incapable (in-**kay**-pa-b'l) *adjective*
not capable: *He is incapable of talking quietly.*
Word Family incapability (in-kay-pa-**bill**-i-tee) *noun.*

incapacitate (in-ka-**pass**-i-tate) *verb*
to take away the strength, power or ability of: *The car accident incapacitated him for many weeks.*

incapacity (in-ka-**pass**-i-tee) *noun*
a lack of ability or capability.

incarcerate (in-**kar**-sa-rate) *verb*
to shut in or confine.
Word Family incarceration (in-kar-sa-**ray**-sh'n) *noun.*
[*in-*[1] + Latin *carcer* prison]

incarnate (in-**kar**-nit) *adjective*
1 having a body or human form: *a goddess incarnate.*
2 being the personification of: *That man is wisdom incarnate.*
Word Family incarnate (in-**kar**-nate) *verb;* **incarnation** (in-kar-**nay**-sh'n) *noun*
1 the act of becoming incarnate. **2** a person or thing seen as representing a special quality, etc. **3** (**the Incarnation**) *Christianity* the doctrine that God took human form in Christ.
[*in-*[1] + Latin *carnis* of flesh]

incendiary (in-**send**-ya-ree) *adjective*
relating to the starting of fires.
Figurative The union leader's incendiary speech inspired the workers (= provocative).
• **incendiary** *noun* (*plural* **incendiaries**)
a person or thing which starts fires.
[from Latin]

incense[1] (in-**sense**) *noun*
a gum or other substance which gives a pleasant smell when burnt, often used in religious ceremonies.

incense[2] (in-**sense**) *verb*
to enrage.
[Latin *incensus* kindled]

incentive (in-**sen**-tiv) *noun*
something which encourages a person to do something: *The promise of a holiday was an incentive for her to pass her exams.*
[Latin *incentivus* striking up a tune]

inception (in-**sep**-sh'n) *noun*
(*formal*) a beginning.
[from Latin]

incessant (in-**sess**-'nt) *adjective*
unceasing.
Word Family incessantly *adverb.*

incest (in-sest) *noun*
the act of sexual intercourse between a male and a female who are so closely related that any relationship between them is forbidden by law.
Word Family incestuous (in-**sest**-yoo-us) *adjective;* **incestuously** *adverb;* **incestuousness** *noun.*
[Latin *incestus* unchaste]

inch *noun* (*plural* **inches**)
1 a unit of length equal to one-twelfth of a foot or about 2.54 cm. *abbrev.* in.
2 a very small distance or margin: *He escaped death by inches.*
Phrase **every inch** in every respect: *The young ruler looked every inch a king in his ceremonial robes.*
• **inch** *verb* to move by inches or very small degrees.

inchoate (in-**ko**-ate) *adjective*
just begun, half-formed or undeveloped: *a vague inchoate idea.*
[from Latin]

incidence (in-si-d'nce) *noun*
1 the extent or frequency with which something occurs: *the incidence of road accidents.*
2 *Physics* the act or the manner of falling upon a surface: *Notice the angle of incidence of the light falling on this screen.*
3 *Maths* the partial overlapping of two figures, or a figure and a line.
[Latin *incidens* falling upon, happening]

incident (in-si-d'nt) *noun*
1 an event, especially one of less importance than others.
2 a serious or unpleasant event, such as a fight.

incidental (in-si-**den**-t'l) *adjective*
1 accompanying but not forming a necessary or important part of: *incidental music,* □ *incidental expenses.*
2 occurring with or as a natural result of: *scratches and bruises incidental to the profession of a lady wrestler.*
Word Family incidentally *adverb;* **incidentals** *plural noun* any minor expenses.

> ⚠ Do not confuse *incidental* with ACCIDENTAL.

incinerate (in-**sin**-a-rate) *verb*
to consume by burning.
Word Family incineration (in-sin-a-**ray**-sh'n) *noun;* **incinerator** *noun* an enclosed chamber for burning rubbish.
[*in-*[1] + Latin *cineris* of ashes]

incipient (in-**sip**-i-ent) *adjective*
in an early stage.
[Latin *incipiens* beginning]

incision (in-**sizh**-'n) *noun*
1 a cut or gash made with a sharp
instrument.
2 the act of making such a cut.
Word Family **incise** (in-**size**) *verb*.
[from Latin]

incisive (in-**sigh**-siv) *adjective*
penetrating or keen: *Her incisive comments
on the play summed it up in a nutshell.*
Word Family **incisively** *adverb*;
incisiveness *noun*.

incisor (in-**sigh**-zor) *noun*
Anatomy any of the sharp flat teeth at the
front of the jaw, for cutting and biting
food.

incite (in-**site**) *verb*
to stir up or provoke to action.
Word Family **incitement** *noun* 1 the act
of inciting: *They are charged with the
incitement of a riot.* 2 something which
incites: *Your words acted as an incitement to
the mob;* **inciter** *noun*.
[Latin *incitare* to urge on]

incivility *noun*
(*formal*) rudeness.

inclement (in-**klem**-'nt) *adjective*
(of the weather) stormy or harsh.
Word Family **inclemency** *noun*.

incline (in-**kline**) *verb*
1 to deviate from the vertical or horizontal.
*Figurative He inclined his head in silent
agreement* (= bent or bowed).
2 to have or cause a tendency: *I'm inclined
to be lazy.* □ *Your letter inclined her to think
you were in trouble.*
• **incline** (in-kline) *noun* a slope.
Word Family **inclination** (in-kli-**nay**-
sh'n) *noun* 1 a slope or slant. 2 the degree
of slope or slant. 3 a tendency or liking: *an
inclination to talk too much.*
[*in-*[1] + Latin *clinare* to bend]

include *verb*
to contain or consider as part of a group or
whole: *Don't forget to include her on the
invitation list.*
Word Family **inclusion** (in-**kloo**-*zh*'n)
noun; **inclusive** *adjective* 1 taking
everything into account: *Our charges are
inclusive of tips.* 2 including the limits
specified: *from 16 to 22 inclusive.* 3 (of
language) non-sexist; **inclusively** *adverb*;
inclusiveness *noun*.
[*in-*[1] + Latin *claudere* to shut]

incognito (in-kog-**nee**-toe) *adverb,
adjective*
with one's name, identity, etc. concealed:
travelling incognito.
[Italian, unknown]

incoherent (in-ko-**heer**-'nt) *adjective*
1 not connected or ordered: *Rewrite this
incoherent sentence.*
2 unable to express oneself clearly: *He was
incoherent with fury.*
Word Family **incoherently** *adverb*;
incoherence *noun*.

incombustible *adjective*
not easily set on fire.

income (in-kum) *noun*
the total of payments received, usually in a
year, from salary or wages, investments,
rents, business operations, etc.

income support *noun*
a social security payment for the
unemployed or people on low incomes.

income tax *noun*
a percentage of one's income that has to be
paid to the government.

incoming *adjective*
1 coming in: *the incoming tide.*
2 about to take office: *the incoming
President.*

incommensurate (in-ka-**men**-sha-rit)
adjective also **incommensurable**
disproportionate or not comparable: *His
notions of his own importance are
incommensurate with his abilities.*
Word Family **incommensurability** (in-
ka-men-sher-a-**bill**-i-tee) *noun*.

incommunicado (in-ka-mew-ni-**kah**-do)
adjective
without the means or right of
communicating with others, especially as a
prisoner.
[Spanish]

> The word **incommunicado** is
> sometimes used humorously in English
> to describe people who are not to
> be disturbed, e.g. in meetings or
> on holiday, as well as people who
> do not have access to means of
> communication, such as prisoners.
> Derived from Spanish, it means
> 'deprived of communication' and
> ultimately goes back to the Latin verb
> *communicare* (to share).

incomparable (in-**kom**-per-a-b'l)
adjective
1 not able to be equalled: *incomparable
beauty.*

2 not capable of comparison: *They are as incomparable as cheese and chalk.*
Word Family incomparably *adverb*; **incomparability** (in-kom-per-a-**bill**-i-tee) *noun*.

incompatible (in-kom-**pat**-i-b'l) *adjective*
1 unable to exist in harmony.
2 not consistent with; logically opposed to.
Word Family incompatibly *adverb*; **incompatibility** (in-kom-pat-i-**bill**-i-tee) *noun*.

incompetent (in-**kom**-pi-t'nt) *adjective*
not competent.
• **incompetent** *noun* a person who is incompetent.
Word Family incompetently *adverb*; **incompetence** *noun*.

incomplete *adjective*
not complete or finished.

incomprehensible (in-kom-pri-**hen**-si-b'l) *adjective*
not able to be understood.

inconceivable (in-kon-**see**-va-b'l) *adjective*
not able to be imagined.
Word Family inconceivably *adverb*.

inconclusive (in-kon-**kloo**-siv) *adjective*
1 not decisive or convincing: *an inconclusive argument.*
2 not bringing a definite result: *inconclusive experiments.*
Word Family inconclusively *adverb*; **inconclusiveness** *noun*.

incongruent (in-**kong**-grew-'nt) *adjective*
not congruent
Word Family incongruently *adverb*; **incongruence** *noun*.

incongruous (in-**kong**-grew-us) *adjective*
out of place or inappropriate: *The bathroom seemed an incongruous place for a writing desk.*
Word Family incongruously *adverb*; **incongruity** (in-kong-**grew**-i-tee) *noun* (*plural* **incongruities**) 1 the quality of being incongruous. 2 something incongruous.

inconnu (**ahn**-kon-oo) *noun*
an unknown person or thing.
[French, unknown]

inconsequent (in-**kon**-si-kw'nt) *adjective*
not consistent with or following logically from what has gone before: *an inconsequent remark.*
Word Family inconsequently *adverb*; **inconsequence** *noun*.

inconsequential (in-kon-si-**kwen**-sh'l) *adjective*
1 not consistent or logical.
2 of little or no importance.
Word Family inconsequentially *adverb*.

inconsiderable (in-kon-**sid**-er-a-b'l) *adjective*
1 small in value, amount, size, etc.
2 unworthy of notice.

inconsiderate (in-kon-**sid**-a-rit) *adjective*
lacking regard for the feelings of others.
Word Family inconsiderately *adverb*; **inconsiderateness** *noun*.

inconsistent (in-kon-**sist**-'nt) *adjective*
1 self-contradictory or lacking agreement between the parts: *Her account of the accident was inconsistent.*
2 not in harmony: *What he practises is inconsistent with what he preaches.*
3 changeable: *He's so inconsistent you never know what he'll do next.*
Word Family inconsistently *adverb*; **inconsistency** *noun* (*plural* **inconsistencies**) 1 the quality of being inconsistent. 2 something inconsistent.

inconsolable (in-kon-**sole**-a-b'l) *adjective*
not capable of being consoled, very sad

inconspicuous (in-kon-**spik**-yew-us) *adjective*
not conspicuous.
Word Family inconspicuously *adverb*; **inconspicuousness** *noun*.

inconstant (in-**kon**-st'nt) *adjective*
(*formal*) not constant: *inconstant winds.*
Word Family inconstancy *noun* (*plural* **inconstancies**).

incontestable (in-kon-**test**-a-b'l) *adjective*
beyond dispute.
Word Family incontestably *adverb*.

incontinent (in-**kon**-tin-ent) *adjective*
lacking self-control or self-restraint, e.g. being unable to control one's urination.
Word Family incontinence *noun*; **incontinently** *adverb*.

incontrovertible (in-kon-tra-**vert**-a-b'l) *adjective*
not able to be disputed.
Word Family incontrovertibly *adverb*.

inconvenient (in-kon-**vee**-ni-ent) *adjective*
not convenient, troublesome.
Word Family inconveniently *adverb*; **inconvenience** *noun* 1 the fact of being inconvenient. 2 something inconvenient; **inconvenience** *verb* to cause trouble, difficulty, etc. to.

incorporate (in-**kor**-pa-rate) *verb*
1 to take in or include as part of a whole:
*He incorporated my suggestion into his final
draft.*
2 to register a business as a company.
Word Family **incorporation** (in-kor-pa-
ray-sh'n) *noun.*

incorporeal (in-kor-**paw**-ri-ul) *adjective*
having no physical or bodily form.

incorrect (in-ka-**rekt**) *adjective*
not correct: *an incorrect answer.* □ *incorrect
behaviour.*
Word Family **incorrectly** *adverb;*
incorrectness *noun.*

incorrigible (in-**korr**-ij-a-b'l) *adjective*
incapable of reform or change: *an
incorrigible criminal.* □ *incorrigible habits.*
Word Family **incorrigibly** *adverb.*
[*in-²* + Latin *corrigere* to put straight]

incorruptible (in-ka-**rup**-ta-b'l) *adjective*
1 not capable of being corrupted.
2 not capable of physical decay.
Word Family **incorruptibly** *adverb;*
incorruptibility (in-ka-rup-ta-**bill**-i-tee)
noun.

increase (in-**kreece**) *verb*
to make or become greater or larger.
• **increase** (in-**kreece**) *noun*
1 a growing or becoming greater.
2 the amount of growth or addition.
Word Family **increasingly** *adverb* more
and more.
[*in-¹* + Latin *crescere* to grow]

incredible (in-**kred**-a-b'l) *adjective*
unbelievable: *an incredible act of rudeness.*
Word Family **incredibly** *adverb;*
incredibility (in-kred-a-**bill**-i-tee) *noun.*

> [!] The words *incredible* and
> *incredulous* have related but
> separate meanings: *incredible* describes
> something which cannot be believed, as
> in *an incredible story*, while *incredulous*
> describes someone who cannot believe
> something, as in *The teacher was
> incredulous when she heard the boy's
> excuse for being late.*

incredulous (in-**kred**-yoo-lus) *adjective*
disbelieving: *She dismissed my excuse with
an incredulous sneer.*
Word Family **incredulously** *adverb;*
incredulity (in-krid-**yoo**-la-tee) *noun.*

> [!] Do not confuse *incredulous* with
> INCREDIBLE.

increment (**in**-kri-m'nt) *noun*
1 an increase or gain: *His salary is subject to
annual increments.*

2 *Maths* a small change in a variable.
Word Family **incremental** (in-kri-
men-t'l) *adjective.*
[from Latin]

incriminate (in-**krim**-i-nate) *verb*
to involve or implicate in an accusation of
wrongdoing.
Word Family **incrimination** (in-krim-
in-**ay**-sh'n) *noun.*
[*in-¹* + Latin *criminis* of an accusation]

incrust ⇨ ENCRUST.

incubate (**in**-kew-bate) *verb*
to keep something at an even and
favourable temperature, as when hatching
eggs, keeping premature babies warm or
growing bacterial cultures.
Word Family **incubator** *noun* an
apparatus which regulates temperature in
an enclosed space; **incubatory** *adjective;*
incubation (in-kew-**bay**-sh'n) *noun.*
[*in-¹,* + Latin *cubare* to lie]

inculcate (**in**-kulk-ate) *verb*
to instil in the mind, especially by
repetition or persistent urging.
Word Family **inculcation** (in-kulk-**ay**-
sh'n) *noun.*
[Latin *inculcare* to tread in]

incumbent (in-**kum**-b'nt) *adjective*
(of an official or a government) currently
in office.
Phrase **incumbent on, incumbent
upon** resting upon one as a duty: *It is
incumbent upon you to warn the children of
the dangers of smoking.*
• **incumbent** *noun* a person holding an
office.
Word Family **incumbency** *noun* (*plural*
incumbencies) the period of holding an
office.
[*in-¹* + Latin *cumbens* lying]

incur (in-**ker**) *verb* (**incurs; incurring;
incurred**)
1 to become subject to: *to incur a fine.*
2 to bring upon oneself: *to incur great
expense.*
[Latin *incurrere* to run into]

incurable (in-**kew**-ra-b'l) *adjective*
not capable of being cured: *an incurable
disease.*
Word Family **incurably** *adverb;*
incurability (in-kew-ra-**bill**-i-tee) *noun.*

incursion (in-**ker**-sh'n) *noun*
(*formal*) a sudden attack or invasion.
Figurative Buying a car made a
considerable incursion into my savings
(= inroad).
[from Latin]

indebted (in-**dett**-id) *adjective*
1 owing money.
2 under an obligation.
Word Family **indebtedness** *noun*.

indecent (in-**dee**-s'nt) *adjective*
1 offensive to good taste.
2 (*informal*) unseemly: *He left the room in indecent haste.*
Word Family **indecently** *adverb*;
indecency *noun*.

indecent assault *noun*
a sexual attack that does not involve rape.

indecent exposure *noun*
the crime of showing one's sexual organs in a public place.

indecipherable (in-di-**sigh**-fer-a-b'l)
adjective
not capable of being deciphered.

indecision (in-di-**sizh**-'n) *noun*
the state of being unable to decide.
Word Family **indecisive** (in-di-**sigh**-siv)
adjective; **indecisively** *adverb*;
indecisiveness *noun*.

indecorous (in-**deck**-er-us) *adjective*
(*formal*) not decorous or tasteful.
Word Family **indecorously** *adverb*;
indecorum (in-di-**kaw**-rum) *noun*
indecorous behaviour.

indeed *adverb*
truly or in fact: *Were you pleased with your pay rise?' 'I was indeed!'*

indefatigable (in-di-**fat**-ig-a-b'l)
adjective
untiring or incapable of being tired out.
Word Family **indefatigably** *adverb*.
[*in-*[2] + Latin *defatigare* to wear out]

indefensible (in-di-**fen**-sa-b'l) *adjective*
not capable of being defended: *an indefensible error.* □ *an indefensible island.*

indefinable (in-di-**fine**-a-b'l) *adjective*
not capable of being defined: *an indefinable longing.*
Word Family **indefinably** *adverb*.

indefinite (in-**def**-in-it) *adjective*
1 not definite.
2 unlimited: *an indefinite amount of time.*
Word Family **indefinitely** *adverb*
without limits.

indefinite article → ARTICLE.

indelible (in-**dell**-i-b'l) *adjective*
incapable of being rubbed out or removed.
Word Family **indelibly** *adverb*;
indelibility (in-dell-i-**bill**-i-tee) *noun*.
[*in-*[2] + Latin *delere* to erase]

indelicate (in-**dell**-i-kit) *adjective*
lacking refinement or good taste: *an indelicate remark.*

indemnify (in-**dem**-ni-fie) *verb*
(**indemnifies; indemnifying; indemnified**)
1 to insure or protect against possible loss or damage.
2 to compensate for damage incurred.
Word Family **indemnification** (in-dem-ni-fi-**kay**-sh'n) *noun* 1 the process of indemnifying. 2 compensation.

indemnity (in-**dem**-ni-tee) *noun* (*plural* **indemnities**)
1 a protection or security against damage or loss.
2 compensation for damage or loss incurred.
3 *Law* a legal exemption from penalties incurred.
[Latin *indemnis* unharmed]

indent (in-**dent**) *verb*
1 to set a line or group of lines in from the margin when writing or printing.
2 to form deep notches or recesses in an edge or surface: *a coastline indented by the sea.*
Word Family **indentation** (in-den-**tay**-sh'n) *noun*.
[*in-*[1] + Latin *dentatus* toothed]

indenture (in-**den**-cher) *noun*
(*usually* **indentures**) an agreement made between two or more people, especially one between an apprentice and his or her employer.
● **indenture** *verb*.

independent (in-di-**pen**-d'nt) *adjective*
not dependent on, influenced by or controlled by others: *The colony fought to become independent of foreign control.* □ *Let me make an independent choice.*
Figurative Everyone made independent transport arrangements (= separate).
● **independent** *noun* a person or thing that is independent, especially a person who does not belong to any political party.
Word Family **independently** *adverb*;
independence *noun*.

independent means *plural noun*
an income derived by means other than earning a salary, etc.

in-depth *adjective*
detailed, thorough: *in-depth investigations.*

indescribable (in-di-**skribe**-a-b'l)
adjective
not able to be described.
Word Family **indescribably** *adverb*.

indestructible (in-di-**struck**-ta-b'l)
adjective
not capable of being destroyed.
Word Family **indestructibly** *adverb*;
indestructibility (in-di-struck-ta-**bill**-i-tee) *noun*.

indeterminable (in-di-**ter**-min-a-b'l)
adjective
not able to be ascertained or decided: *With
no clues, the killer's identity is indeterminable.*

indeterminate (in-di-**ter**-min-it) *adjective*
not fixed or definite.
Word Family **indeterminacy** *noun.*

index *noun* (*plural* **indexes** or **indices**)
1 a list of names, subjects, references, etc.
in alphabetical order, e.g. at the end of a
book.
2 anything that serves to indicate: *Alertness
is an index of intelligence.*
3 (*plural* **indices**) *Maths* ⇨ EXPONENT
(definition 1).
4 a chart or table of relative levels of
wages, prices, etc.
• **index** *verb*
1 to provide with or enter into an
alphabetical list.
2 to adjust wages, etc. to increases in the
cost of living.
Word Family **indexation** (in-dek-**say**-sh'n) *noun.*
[Latin, forefinger, sign]

index finger *noun*
the forefinger.

index-linked *adjective*
(of pensions etc.) directly linked to
changes in the cost-of-living index, the
government's official assessment of how
much ordinary household costs change.

Indian file ⇨ SINGLE FILE.

Indian ink *noun*
a black ink, originally from China and
Japan.

Indian summer *noun*
1 a period of fine warm summery weather
occurring in autumn.
2 a renewal of youthful spirits or health in
later life.

> The phrase **Indian summer** does not
> have anything to do with India. The
> term came to Britain from America
> where it has its origin in the fact that
> such spells of fine weather were more
> common in those parts of the country
> occupied by Native Americans than
> they were in the eastern regions
> occupied by the white population.

indiarubber ⇨ RUBBER[1] (definition 1).

indicate (**in**-di-kate) *verb*
1 to show or point out: *The signpost
indicates the way to town.*
2 to express in a general way: *He indicated
his intention of resigning.*
Word Family **indication** (in-di-**kay**-sh'n) *noun* 1 the act of indicating.
2 something which indicates.

indicative (in-**dick**-a-tiv) *adjective*
1 giving indications of: *That remark is
indicative of his whole attitude.*
2 *Grammar* in the indicative mood.
⇨ MOOD[2].
• **indicative** *noun* the indicative mood.

indicator (**in**-di-kay-ta) *noun*
1 a person or thing that shows or gives
information, such as a flashing light used
to indicate that a car is turning.
2 *Chemistry* a substance which, by a
distinct colour change, shows that a
chemical reaction is complete, or shows
the acidity or alkalinity (pH) of a solution.

indices (**in**-di-seez)
a plural of **index**.

indict (in-**dite**) *verb*
to accuse, as a means of bringing a person
to trial before a jury.
Word Family **indictable** *adjective* making
one liable to be indicted; **indictment** *noun*
a formal accusation.
[in^{-1} + Latin *dictare* to put in writing]

indie *adjective*
(*informal*) denoting an independent
record label, or a band signed to such a
company and considered more creative
than commercial.
• **indie** *noun*
an indie record label or band.

indifferent *adjective*
1 having no interest in or care for: *She's
indifferent to my suffering.*
2 mediocre or commonplace: *an indifferent
performance of the opera.*
Word Family **indifferently** *adverb*;
indifference *noun* 1 lack of interest or
concern. 2 mediocre quality.

indigenous (in-**dij**-i-nus) *adjective*
originating in or being native to a
particular place: *Tigers are indigenous to
India.*

indigent (**in**-di-j'nt) *adjective*
(*formal*) poor.
Word Family **indigence** *noun* poverty.

indigestion (in-di-**jes**-ch'n) *noun* also
called **dyspepsia**.
1 difficulty in digesting food properly.
2 any pain or discomfort from this.
Word Family **indigestible** *adjective* not
able to be digested.

indignant (in-**dig**-nant) *adjective*
angry at something unjust, unworthy or
ungrateful.
Word Family **indignantly** *adverb*;
indignation (in-dig-**nay**-sh'n) *noun*.

indignity (in-**dig**-ni-tee) *noun* (*plural*
indignities)
an act which humiliates or injures self-
respect: *the indignities suffered by prisoners of
war*.

indigo (**in**-dig-o) *noun*
1 a dark blue to purplish-blue colour.
2 the colour between blue and violet in the
spectrum.
3 an important blue dye, formerly
extracted from plants but now made
artificially.
● **indigo** *adjective*.

indirect *adjective*
not direct: *Her indirect reply suggested she
was hiding something.* □ *Taxes on goods and
services are indirect taxes.*
Word Family **indirectly** *adverb*;
indirectness *noun*.

indirect object *noun*
Grammar the person or thing indirectly
affected by the action of a verb. For
example, in the sentence *She gave him the
book*, 'him' is the indirect object.

indirect speech *noun* also called
reported speech.
Grammar the reporting of what someone
has said without using the exact words, for
example *He said that he had lost his key*.
Compare DIRECT SPEECH.

indiscernible (in-di-**ser**-na-b'l) *adjective*
not discernible or distinguishable.
Word Family **indiscernibly** *adverb*.

indiscipline *noun*
lack of discipline.

indiscreet *adjective*
not discreet.
Word Family **indiscreetly** *adverb*;
indiscretion (in-di-**skresh**-'n) *noun* **1** the
quality of being indiscreet. **2** an indiscreet
act or remark.

indiscriminate (in-dis-**krimm**-i-nit)
adjective
making no distinctions: *He's an
indiscriminate admirer of all music.* □ *The
troops dealt out indiscriminate slaughter.*

Word Family **indiscriminately** *adverb*;
indiscriminateness *noun*.

indispensable *adjective*
absolutely essential: *Oxygen is indispensable
to human life.*
Word Family **indispensably** *adverb*;
indispensability *noun*.

indisposed *adjective*
1 sick or ill, usually only to a slight degree.
2 disinclined or unwilling.
Word Family **indisposition** (in-disp-a-
zish-'n) *noun*.

indisputable (in-dis-**pew**-ta-b'l) *adjective*
beyond doubt or question.
Word Family **indisputably** *adverb*;
indisputability (in-dis-pew-ta-**bill**-i-tee)
noun.

indistinct *adjective*
not distinct or clear.
Word Family **indistinctly** *adverb*;
indistinctness *noun*.

indistinguishable (in-dis-**ting**-gwish-a-
b'l) *adjective*
not capable of being distinguished or
discerned.
Word Family **indistinguishably** *adverb*.

individual (in-di-**vid**-yew'l) *adjective*
1 of, for or existing as a single or separate
person or thing: *an individual portion of
cheese.* □ *individual members of a group*.
2 distinctive: *The author has a very
individual style.*
● **individual** *noun*
1 a single person or thing.
2 *Biology* a living thing capable of
independent existence.
3 *Biology* a single member of a colony.
Word Family **individually** *adverb*;
individualize, individualise *verb* **1** to
make or become individual. **2** to select for
special attention, **individualization** (in-
di-vid-yew-'l-eye-**zay**-sh'n) *noun*.
[Latin *individuus* indivisible]

individualist (in-di-**vid**-yew'l-ist) *noun*
1 a person of independent thought and
action.
2 a person who believes that personal
interests are more important than those of
society as a whole.
Word Family **individualism** *noun*;
individualistic (in-di-vid-yew-'l-**ist**-ik)
adjective.

individuality (in-di-vid-yoo-**all**-i-tee) *noun*
1 the particular characteristics which
distinguish a person from others and mark
him or her out as an individual.

2 the state of having separate independent existence.

indivisible (in-di-**vizz**-i-b'l) *adjective* not able to be divided.
Word Family **indivisibly** *adverb*; **indivisibility** (in-di-vizz-i-**bill**-i-tee) *noun*.

indoctrinate *verb*
1 to make someone accept a system of thought uncritically.
2 to instruct in a body of doctrine.
Word Family **indoctrination** (in-dock-trin-**ay**-sh'n) *noun*.

indolent (**in**-da-l'nt) *adjective*
(*formal*) lazy or idle.
Word Family **indolently** *adverb*; **indolence** *noun*.

indomitable (in-**domm**-it-a-b'l) *adjective* not capable of being subdued or conquered.
Word Family **indomitably** *adverb*.
[*in-²* + Latin *domitare* to tame]

indoor *adjective*
occurring, used, etc. inside a house or building: *indoor plants*.
Word Family **indoors** *adverb*.

indubitable (in-**dew**-bit-a-b'l) *adjective* certain or beyond doubt.
Word Family **indubitably** *adverb*.
[*in-²* + Latin *dubium* doubt]

induce (in-**dewce**) *verb*
1 to persuade or influence: *She induced me to stay another hour.*
2 to produce or cause: *Alcohol at lunchtime induces afternoon drowsiness.*
3 *Physics* to produce by induction.
4 *Medicine* to cause a woman to have a baby or an abortion, usually by using drugs.
Word Family **inducement** *noun* 1 the act of inducing. 2 an incentive.
[*in-²* + Latin *ducere* to lead]

induct *verb*
1 to install formally in office.
2 *American* to conscript into military service.

induction (in-**duck**-sh'n) *noun*
1 *Physics* the process by which a body, having electrical or magnetic properties, can produce similar properties on a nearby body without direct contact.
2 a process of inferring or aiming at a general law from observation of particular instances.
3 a conclusion reached by this process. Compare DEDUCTION (definition 4).

4 the act or ceremony of installing a person into an office.
Word Family **inductance** *noun* the ability of a circuit to produce induction; **inductive** *adjective*.

indulge (in-**dulj**) *verb*
1 to satisfy or yield to simple desires: *She likes to indulge her taste for cigars.* □ *He always indulges his children's wishes.*
2 (*informal*) to drink alcohol.
Word Family **indulgent** *adjective* inclined to indulge the wishes of others; **indulgently** *adverb*; **indulgence** *noun*
1 the habit or process of indulging: *Too much indulgence in wine made her ill.*
2 something indulged in: *Wine wasn't her only indulgence!* 3 any favourable treatment or privilege: *We'll grant you an indulgence of ten days to pay the debt.*
4 *Roman Catholicism* a statement from the Roman Catholic Church releasing a person from a penalty imposed for having sinned.
[from Latin]

industrial action *noun*
a strike, go-slow or sit-in.

industry (**in**-dus-tree) *noun* (*plural* **industries**)
1 any production or manufacturing business.
2 a branch of such a business: *the coal industry.*
3 hard work or diligence: *His quick success was due to his industry.*
Word Family **industrial** (in-**dust**-ri-al) *adjective;* **industrially** *adverb;* **industrialize, industrialise** *verb* to introduce industries on a large scale; **industrialization** (in-dust-ri-a-lie-**zay**-sh'n) *noun;* **industrialist** *noun* a person who owns or runs an industry; **industrious** *adjective* being conscientious or hard-working; **industriously** *adverb;* **industriousness** *noun.*
[Latin *industria* diligence]

inebriate (in-**ee**-bri-ate) *verb*
to intoxicate or make drunk.
● **inebriate** (in-**ee**-bri-it) *adjective* drunk or intoxicated.
Word Family **inebriation** (in-ee-bri-**ay**-sh'n) *noun.*
[from Latin]

inedible (in-**edd**-i-b'l) *adjective* not fit to be eaten.
Word Family **inedibility** (in-edd-i-**bill**-i-tee) *noun.*

ineffable (in-**eff**-a-b'l) *adjective*
1 (*formal*) beyond expression: *I have an ineffable contempt for laziness.*
2 (*formal*) that must not be spoken: *the ineffable name of the Lord.*
Word Family ineffably *adverb.*
[*in-²* + Latin *effari* to speak out]

ineffective (in-i-**fck**-tiv) *adjective*
not effective.
Word Family ineffectively *adverb*;
ineffectiveness *noun.*

ineffectual (in-i-**fek**-tyoo-'l) *adjective*
1 vain or futile: *ineffectual attempts.*
2 not producing the intended result.
Word Family ineffectually *adverb.*

inefficient (in-i-**fish**-'nt) *adjective*
not efficient.
Word Family inefficiently *adverb*;
inefficiency *noun* (*plural* **inefficiencies**).

inelegant (in-**ell**-i-g'nt) *adjective*
not elegant or graceful.
Word Family inelegantly *adverb.*

ineligible (in-**ell**-i-ja b'l) *adjective*
not eligible or qualified.
Word Family ineligibly *adverb*;
ineligibility (in-ell-i-ja-**bill**-i-tee) *noun.*

inept (in-**ept**) *adjective*
1 not suitable or appropriate.
2 awkward or foolish.
Word Family ineptly *adverb*; **ineptitude**
noun 1 the quality of being inept. 2 an
inept remark, act, etc.; **ineptness** *noun.*
[*in-²* + Latin *aptus* fitting]

inequality (in-i-**kwoll**-a-tee) *noun* (*plural*
inequalities)
1 the state of being unequal: *social
inequality.*
2 an instance of this.
3 *Maths* a statement that the value of one
expression is greater or less than another,
e.g. $x^2 > x + 1$.

inequitable (in-**ek**-wit-a-b'l) *adjective*
not equitable.
Word Family inequitably *adverb*;
inequity *noun* (*plural* **inequities**).

ineradicable (in-i-**rad**-ik-a-b'l) *adjective*
not eradicable.
Word Family ineradicably *adverb.*

inert (in-**ert**) *adjective*
1 sluggish or inactive.
2 *Chemistry* being very difficult to change
by chemical reaction.
Word Family inertly *adverb*; **inertness**
noun.
[Latin *iners* unskilled, idle]

inertia (in-**er**-sha) *noun*
1 *Physics* the tendency for the velocity of a
body to remain constant unless acted on
by a force. For example, the forward
movement of people in a car when it stops
suddenly is due to inertia.
2 a state of inactivity or sluggishness.

inertia selling *noun*
delivering goods which have not been
ordered or are not up to advertised quality
in the hope that a householder will not
bother to protest or to return them.

inescapable (in-is-**kape**-a-b'l) *adjective*
not able to be escaped or avoided.
Word Family inescapably *adverb.*

inessential (in-i-**sen**-sh'l) *adjective*
not essential or necessary.

inestimable (in-**est**-i-ma-b'l) *adjective*
not able to be estimated, especially of
great value.
Word Family inestimably *adverb.*

inevitable (in-**evv**-i-ta-b'l) *adjective*
not able to be avoided or prevented.
Word Family inevitably *adverb*;
inevitability (in-evv-it-a-**bill**-i-tee) *noun*
(*plural* **inevitabilities**).
[*in-²* + Latin *evitare* to escape]

inexact *adjective*
not exact or accurate.
Word Family inexactly *adverb*;
inexactness *noun.*

inexcusable (in-iks-**kew**-za-b'l) *adjective*
not excusable.
Word Family inexcusably *adverb.*

inexhaustible (in-eg-**zaw**-sti-b'l) *adjective*
(of a supply) not exhaustible.
Word Family inexhaustibly *adverb.*

inexorable (in-**eks**-er-o b'l) *adjective*
not able to be changed or made to yield.
Word Family inexorably *adverb.*
[*in-²* + Latin *exorare* to gain by entreaty]

inexpensive (in-eks-**pen**-siv) *adjective*
not expensive.
Word Family inexpensively *adverb*;
inexpensiveness *noun.*

inexperienced (in-eks-**peer**-i-enst)
adjective
lacking experience.
Word Family inexperience *noun.*

inexpert *adjective*
unskilled.
Word Family inexpertly *adverb.*

inexplicable (in-iks-**plik**-a-b'l) *adjective*
not able to be explained.
Word Family inexplicably *adverb.*

inexpressible (in-iks-**press**-a-b'l)
adjective
not able to be expressed or represented in
words.
Word Family **inexpressibly** *adverb*.

inexpressive (in-iks-**press**-iv) *adjective*
not expressive.
Word Family **inexpressively** *adverb*;
inexpressiveness *noun*.

in extremis (in eks-**tree**-mis) *adverb*
(*formal*) in great distress or near to death.
[Latin]

inextricable (in-iks-**trik**-a-b'l) *adjective*
1 impossible to extricate oneself from: *an
inextricable maze.*
2 too intricate or complicated to untangle:
an inextricable problem.
Word Family **inextricably** *adverb*.

infallible *adjective*
1 not capable of being wrong: *I am not
infallible.*
2 not liable to fail: *Is there an infallible
remedy for a cold?*
Word Family **infallibility** (in-fal-i-**bill**-i-
tee) *noun*.

infamous (**in**-fa-mus) *adjective*
1 having an extremely bad reputation.
2 shocking or detestable: *infamous
behaviour.*
Word Family **infamously** *adverb*.

infamy (**in**-fa-mee) *noun* (*plural* **infamies**)
1 the state or quality of being infamous.
2 an infamous act.
[*in-*[2] + Latin *fama* good repute]

infant (**in**-f'nt) *noun*
1 a baby or very young child.
2 *Law* any person who is too young to have
legal rights.
3 anything in the early stages of
development or progress.
Word Family **infant** *adjective*; **infantile**
adjective 1 of or occurring among infants.
2 babyish; **infancy** *noun*.
[Latin *infans* not speaking]

infanticide (in-**fan**-ti-side) *noun*
1 the crime of killing a newly born child.
2 a person who does this.
[INFANT + Latin *caedere* to kill]

infantile paralysis *noun*
an old word for polio.

infantry (**in**-f'n-tree) *noun*
the branch of an army consisting of
soldiers on foot. Compare CAVALRY.
Word Family **infantryman** *noun* (*plural*
infantrymen).
[Italian *infante* a page or foot soldier]

infatuate (in-**fat**-yoo-ate) *verb*
to inspire with foolish or unreasoning
passion.
Word Family **infatuation** (in-fat-yoo-
ay-sh'n) *noun*.
[Latin *infatuatus* made foolish]

infect (in-**fekt**) *verb*
1 to contaminate with disease organisms.
2 to transmit a disease to another.
3 to be transferred to: *His unhappy mood
infected us.*
4 *Computers* to affect with a virus.
[Latin *infectus* stained, tainted]

infection (in-**fek**-sh'n) *noun*
1 the act of infecting: *There is a danger of
infection.*
2 the state of being infected: *I've got an ear
infection.*
3 something, such as a germ, which
infects.

infectious *adjective*
1 communicated by infection: *infectious
diseases.*
2 liable to produce infection: *Are you still
infectious?*
3 tending to produce similar responses in
others: *infectious laughter.*
Word Family **infectiousness** *noun*.

> [!] Do not confuse *infectious* with
> CONTAGIOUS.

infer (in-**fer**) *verb* (**infers; inferring;
inferred**)
to conclude by reasoning: *From his sceptical
remarks I infer that he does not believe the
report.*
[from Latin]

> [!] Do not confuse *infer* with IMPLY.

inference (**in**-fa-r'nce) *noun*
1 the process of inferring.
2 something which is inferred.
Word Family **inferential** (in-fa-**ren**-sh'l)
adjective.

inferior (in-**feer**-i-a) *adjective*
1 poor in quality: *an inferior product.*
2 low or lower in order, degree, rank, etc.:
*Among the primates the baboon is inferior to
the orang-utan.*
3 situated under or beneath: *The two in
CO_2 is an inferior number.*
• **inferior** *noun* a person or thing that is
inferior.
Word Family **inferiority** (in-feer-i-**orr**-i-
tee) *noun*.
[Latin, lower]

inferiority complex noun (plural
inferiority complexes)
Psychology a group of suppressed emotions
arising from intense feelings of inferiority,
sometimes leading to aggressive behaviour
which is intended to conceal such feelings.

infernal (in-**fer**-n'l) adjective
1 of or relating to hell.
2 (informal) abominable: an infernal
commotion.
Word Family infernally adverb.
[Latin infernus that which lies beneath]

inferno (in-**fer**-no) noun
1 a large fire that is out of control: a raging
inferno.
2 (**Inferno**) hell.
[Italian]

infertile (in-**fer**-tile) adjective
not fertile.
Word Family infertility (in-fer-**till**-i-tee)
noun.

infest verb
to overrun in large numbers to a harmful
or unpleasant degree: Locusts infested the
area.
Word Family infestation (in-fes-**tay**-
sh'n) noun 1 the act of infesting. 2 the
state of being infested.
[Latin infestus hostile]

infidel (in-**fi**-del) noun
1 History a person who does not believe in
the religion of the speaker; used especially
by Christians about Muslims.
2 a literary word for a person who does not
believe in any religion.
[in-² + Latin fidelis faithful]

infidelity (in-fi-**dell**-i-tee) noun (plural
infidelities)
the action or a state of unfaithfulness,
especially adultery.

infield noun
Sport an inner part of the field, such as the
area near the wickets in cricket.
Word Family infielder noun a player in
the infield.

infighting noun
a struggle between members of the same
group or organization, e.g. for leadership
of a political party or other institution.
Word Family infighter noun.

infiltrate (in-**fill**-trate) verb
to filter into or through.
Figurative The spy infiltrated the enemy's
headquarters (= entered secretly).
Word Family infiltrator noun;
infiltration (in-fill-**tray**-sh'n) noun 1 the
act of infiltrating. 2 something which has

infiltrated. 3 Geography the movement of
water into the soil.

infinite (**in**-fi-nit) adjective
having no boundaries or limits in time,
space, etc.
Word Family infinitely adverb.
[in-² + Latin finitus defined]

infinitesimal (in-fin-i-**tess**-i-m'l) adjective
immeasurably small.

infinitive (in-**finn**-a-tiv) noun
Grammar the form of a verb which has no
tense, number or person, for example, to
buy, to look, to go.

infinity (in-**fin**-a-tee) noun
1 the state or quality of being infinite.
2 an indefinitely great amount or number.

infirm (in-**firm**) adjective
1 feeble in body or mind, especially from
old age.
2 an old word meaning 'irresolute'.
Word Family infirmity noun (plural
infirmities) a physical or moral
weakness.
[from Latin]

infirmary (in-**firm**-a-ree) noun (plural
infirmaries)
a hospital or place where sick people are
cared for.

inflame (in-**flame**) verb
1 to set on fire.
2 to arouse strong feelings in: His speech
was meant to inflame the people against their
leader.
3 to produce heat, redness or swelling in.
Word Family inflammatory adjective
tending to inflame.

inflammable adjective
easily set on fire.
Word Family inflammability noun.

> ❗ On the words inflammable and
> flammable ⇒ FLAMMABLE.

inflammation (in-fla-**may**-sh'n) noun
1 the act of inflaming.
2 the state of being inflamed.
3 a response by living tissue to injury or
infection, characterized by swelling,
redness, heat and pain.

inflate (in-**flate**) verb
1 to fill or expand with a gas.
2 to puff up with pride, satisfaction, etc.
3 Economics to produce inflation.
Word Family inflatable adjective.

inflation (in-**flay**-sh'n) noun
1 Economics a general rise in prices and fall
in the value of money which may have
various causes, e.g. increases in the cost

of imported raw materials, higher wages unmatched by higher productivity, or an increase in the amount of currency in circulation. Compare DEFLATION (definition 2).
2 the act of inflating: *The inflation of the balloons was aided by a bicycle pump.*
3 the state of being inflated.
Word Family **inflationary** *adjective* causing inflation in the economy.
[Latin *inflatus* blown into]

inflection (in-**flek**-sh'n) *noun* also **inflexion**
1 *Grammar* the change made in the form of a word to show its tense, number, case, gender, etc.: *The most common inflections in English are the suffix '-ed', which shows the past tense of regular verbs, and the suffix '-s', which shows the plural of regular nouns.*
⇨ CONJUGATION; DECLENSION (definition 1).
2 a bend or angle.
3 a slight change in modulation or pitch: *An inflection of the voice, or a raised eyebrow, can convey a great deal.*
Word Family **inflect** *verb*; **inflectional** *adjective*.
[Latin *inflexio* a bending]

inflexible (in-**fleks**-a-b'l) *adjective* not flexible: *an inflexible attitude.*
Word Family **inflexibly** *adverb*; **inflexibility** (in-fleks-a-**bill**-i-tee) *noun.*

inflict (in-**flikt**) *verb* to impose anything unwelcome, such as punishment.
Word Family **infliction** *noun* **1** the act of inflicting. **2** something inflicted.
[Latin *inflictus* struck against]

in-flight *adjective* provided on an aeroplane during a flight: *in-flight entertainment.*

inflorescence (in-flaw-**ress**-'nce) *noun*
1 *Biology* the arrangement of flowers on a stem.
2 *Biology* the flowering parts of a plant.
[Latin *inflorescens* coming into flower]

inflow (in-flo) *noun* a flowing in or arriving.

influence (in-floo-ence) *noun*
1 the power of people or things to produce effects on others, especially by invisible or indirect means: *Monet had a massive influence on this circle of painters.*
2 a person or thing possessing such power: *His sister is a good influence on him.*
3 power resulting from social position, wealth, etc.

Phrase **under the influence** (*informal*) affected by drinking alcohol.
Word Family **influence** *verb*; **influential** (in-floo-**en**-sh'l) *adjective*; **influentially** *adverb.*
[Latin *influens* flowing in]

influenza (in-floo-**en**-za) *noun* short form is **flu** an infectious viral disease causing symptoms such as aching muscles, fever, sneezing and sore eyes.
[Italian]

influx (in-fluks) *noun* (*plural* **influxes**) a flowing in: *This year there has been a large influx of tourists.*

inform (in-**form**) *verb*
1 to tell or give information.
2 (*formal*) to pervade: *The discussions were informed by a spirit of cooperation.*
Word Family **informed** *adjective* having information or knowledge: *informed users of this technology.*

informal (in-**for**-m'l) *adjective*
1 without ceremony or formality.
2 (of speech or writing) characteristic of ordinary conversation, as distinct from formal grammar or construction.
Word Family **informally** *adverb*; **informality** (in-fa-**mall**-i-tee) *noun.*

information (in-fa-**may**-sh'n) *noun*
1 knowledge communicated or received: *I got a lot of useful information out of her.*
2 the act of informing.
3 *Law* a formal charge made in a court.
Word Family **informative** (in-**for**-ma-tiv) *adjective* giving information.

information and communications technology *noun* technology relating to the use of computers for the communication of information.

information superhighway *noun* a far-ranging electronic network such as the Internet.

information technology *noun* technology relating to the gathering, recording and retrieval of information, especially when this is done electronically.

informer *noun*
1 also **informant** a person who gives incriminating information.
2 a person who gives information.

infotainment (in-fo-**tain**-ment) *noun* in television, the practice of presenting

serious or instructive programmes in an entertaining way.
[INFO(rmation) + (enter)TAINMENT]

infraction (in-**frak**-sh'n) *noun*
a breach or violation: *an infraction of the rules.*
[Latin *infractus* broken into]

infra dig *adjective*
(*informal*) beneath one's dignity.
[short form of Latin *infra dignitatem*]

infrared ⇨ LIGHT[1] *noun* (definition **3**).
[Latin *infra* below + RED]

infrastructure (**in**-fra-struk-cher) *noun*
the basic or supporting organization, services, facilities, etc. of an institution or a community.
Figurative The local council provided electricity, a bus service and other infrastructure for the new housing estate (= community services).
[Latin *infra* below + STRUCTURE]

infrequent *adjective*
not occurring often.
Word Family **infrequently** *adverb*;
infrequency *noun.*

infringe (in-**frinj**) *verb*
1 to break or ignore a rule, etc.
2 to trespass or encroach: *The neighbours infringed on our privacy.*
Word Family **infringement** *noun.*
[from Latin]

infuriate (in-**few**-ree-ate) *verb*
to make furious.
Word Family **infuriating** *adjective*;
infuriatingly *adverb.*

infuse (in-**fewz**) *verb*
1 to fill or inspire with: *His speech infused the pilots with courage.*
2 to steep or soak a substance in a liquid to extract its soluble parts.
[Latin *infusus* poured in]

infusion (in-**few**-*zh*'n) *noun*
1 the act of infusing.
2 something which is infused.
3 a liquid extract obtained by soaking a substance in a liquid: *Tea is an infusion of tea leaves in hot water.*

ingenious (in-**jee**-ni-us) *adjective*
1 (of things, actions, etc.) cleverly or skilfully made.
2 (of a person) inventive.
Word Family **ingeniously** *adverb*;
ingeniousness *noun.*
[Latin *ingenium* genius]

> ❗ Do not confuse *ingenious* with *ingenuous*. Ingenious means 'cleverly or skilfully made', as in *an ingenious device that folds away to a quarter of its size*. Ingenuous means 'innocent', as in *The girl captivated the audience with her ingenuous smile.*

ingénue (an-*zh*ay-**new**) *noun*
a simple innocent young woman, especially as represented on the stage.
[French]

ingenuity (in-ji-**new**-i-tee) *noun*
the quality of being ingenious.

ingenuous (in-**jen**-yew-us) *adjective*
(*formal*) innocent and without reserve or sophistication.
Word Family **ingenuously** *adverb*;
ingenuousness *noun.*
[Latin *ingenuus* freeborn, frank]

> ❗ Do not confuse *ingenuous* with INGENIOUS.

ingest (in-**jest**) *verb*
Biology to take food into an organism.
Word Family **ingestion** (in-**jes**-ch'n) *noun.*
[Latin *ingestus* carried in]

inglenook *noun*
a chimney corner or fireside corner.

inglorious *adjective*
dishonourable or shameful: *The beaten troops made an inglorious retreat.*
Word Family **ingloriously** *adverb.*

ingot *noun*
a mass of cast metal, especially gold or silver, prepared for later working.
[*in-*[1] + Old English *goten* poured]

ingrain *verb*
to fix firmly.
Word Family **ingrained** *adjective*

ingrate (**in**-grate) *noun*
an old word meaning 'an ungrateful person'.
[*in-*[2] + Latin *gratus* pleasant]

ingratiate (in-**gray**-shee-ate) *verb*
to establish oneself deliberately in the favour of another person: *He ingratiated himself with his boss by always agreeing with him.*
Word Family **ingratiating** *adjective*;
ingratiatingly *adverb.*
[*in-*[1] + Latin *gratia* favour]

ingratitude *noun*
the state of being ungrateful.

ingredient (in-**gree**-di-ent) *noun*
one of the parts of a mixture: *the ingredients of a cake.*
[Latin *ingrediens* entering]

ingress (**in**-gress) *noun* (*plural* **ingresses**)
1 (*formal*) a right to enter.
2 (*formal*) a going in.

in-group *noun*
a group of people with a strong feeling of belonging together and a tendency to exclude others.

inhabit (in-**hab**-it) *verb*
to live or dwell in.
Word Family **inhabitable** *adjective*; **inhabitant** *noun* a permanent resident.
[from Latin]

inhale (in-**hale**) *verb*
to draw in by breathing.
Word Family **inhalation** (in-ha-**lay**-sh'n) *noun* the act of inhaling; **inhalant** *noun* a substance inhaled for medicinal effect; **inhaler** *noun* a device to supply medication into the breathing passages.

inherent (in-**herr**-'nt) *adjective*
existing in something as a permanent and inseparable element, quality or attribute.
Word Family **inherently** *adverb*.
[Latin *inhaerere* to stick to]

> ! Do not confuse *inherent* with *innate*. *Inherent* means 'existing in something as a permanent and inseparable quality', as in *inequalities inherent in the present economic system*. *Innate* means 'inborn', as in *He has an innate talent for football*.

inherit (in-**herr**-it) *verb*
1 to receive property, a title, etc. upon the death of another person.
2 to receive genetic characters from one's ancestors.
Word Family **inheritor** *noun*.
[Latin *inhereditare* to appoint an heir]

inheritance (in-**herr**-i-t'nss) *noun*
1 the act of inheriting.
2 anything which is inherited.
3 *Law* the property which is received by an heir from a person who has died. Compare LEGACY (definition 1).

inhibit (in-**hib**-it) *verb*
1 to restrain, hinder or repress.
2 *Chemistry* to reduce the rate of a chemical reaction or stop it completely.
Word Family **inhibition** (in-hi-**bish**-'n) *noun*; **inhibitor** *noun* a substance which inhibits a chemical reaction; **inhibitory** *adjective* tending to inhibit.
[from Latin]

> ! The words *inhibit* and *prohibit* have related but separate meanings: *inhibit* means 'to hinder or repress' (*laws which inhibit the development of new products*), while *prohibit* means 'to forbid' (*laws which prohibit the employment of children*).

inhospitable (in-hos-**pit**-a-b'l) *adjective*
not hospitable or welcoming.
Word Family **inhospitably** *adverb*.

inhuman *adjective*
1 lacking in natural human feeling or sympathy for others.
2 not human.
Word Family **inhumanly** *adverb*.

inhumane *adjective*
not humane or compassionate.
Word Family **inhumanely** *adverb*.

inhumanity (in-hew-**man**-i-tee) *noun* (*plural* **inhumanities**)
1 the state or quality of being inhuman or inhumane.
2 an inhuman or inhumane act.

inimical (in-**imm**-i-k'l) *adjective*
1 (*formal*) adverse in tendency or effect.
2 (*formal*) unfriendly or hostile.
Word Family **inimically** *adverb*.
[*in-²* + Latin *amicus* a friend]

inimitable (in-**imm**-it-a-b'l) *adjective*
not able to be imitated.
Word Family **inimitably** *adverb*.

iniquity (in-**ik**-wa-tee) *noun* (*plural* **iniquities**)
1 a wicked or unjust act.
2 wickedness.
Word Family **iniquitous** *adjective*.
[from Latin]

initial (in-**ish**-'l) *adjective*
occurring at the beginning.
● **initial** *noun* the first letter of a name, word, etc.
● **initial** *verb* (**initials**; **initialling**; **initialled**) to mark or sign with one's own initials.
Word Family **initially** *adverb*.

initiate (in-**ish**-i-ate) *verb*
1 to begin or originate.
2 to introduce a person to a new activity, interest, etc.
3 to admit to membership, etc. with formal rituals or ordeals.
● **initiate** (in-**ish**-i-it) *noun* a person who has been initiated.
Word Family **initiation** (in-ish-i-**ay**-sh'n) *noun*; **initiator** *noun*.
[Latin *initium* a going in]

initiative (in-**ish**-a-tiv) *noun*
1 a ready ability or boldness in beginning or taking on new projects, etc.
2 an introductory act or step: *He took the initiative and began the conversation.*

inject (in-**jekt**) *verb*
1 to introduce fluid into the body, a cavity, etc.
2 to introduce something new: *He tried to inject some humour into the dull meeting.*
Word Family injection *noun*.
[Latin *injectus* thrown in]

injection moulding *noun*
the process of squeezing heated soft material through a nozzle into a mould.

injudicious (in-joo-**dish**-us) *adjective*
not sensible or discreet.
Word Family injudiciously *adverb*;
injudiciousness *noun*.

injunction (in-**junk**-sh'n) *noun*
Law a court order requiring or restricting a particular action.
[Latin *injunctus* enjoined]

injure (in-jer) *verb*
1 to do or cause harm to.
2 to do wrong or injustice to.
Word Family injury *noun* (*plural* **injuries**); **injurious** (in-**joor**-i-us) *adjective*; **injuriously** *adverb*.
[Latin *injuria* a wrong]

injury time *noun* also called **stoppage time**.
Sport extra time played at the end of a match to make up for the time lost because of injuries.

injustice (in-**just**-is) *noun*
1 a lack of justice.
2 an instance of this: *Such a severe fine was an injustice.*

ink *noun*
1 any of various strongly coloured liquids used for writing and printing.
2 a dark protective fluid ejected by the squid and related molluscs.

ink-jet printer *noun*
a printer which forms characters by means of tiny jets of ink.

inkling *noun*
1 a hint or suggestion: *The faint bark gave me an inkling of the puppy's whereabouts.*
2 a vague idea or notion: *I had no inkling that she was so ill.*
[Middle English *inkle* to speak in an undertone]

inkwell *noun*
a container for ink, usually set into a desk.

inky *adjective* (**inkier; inkiest**)
1 dark or murky: *inky shadows.*
2 resembling or stained with ink: *inky fingers.*

inland *adjective*
1 situated in the middle parts of a land mass: *an inland sea.*
2 occurring within the borders of a country.
Word Family inland *adverb*, *noun*.

inland revenue *noun*
1 government revenue from personal and corporation taxes, etc., but excluding customs and excise dues.
2 (**the Inland Revenue**) the department which collects these taxes.

in-law *noun*
a relative by marriage.

inlay (in-**lay**) *verb* (**inlays; inlaying; inlaid**)
to set something into a surface to form a design.
• **inlay** (in-**lay**) *noun*
1 a layer of material set into a surface.
2 *Dentistry* a filling which is fitted and fastened as one large piece.

inlet *noun*
1 a small narrow bay.
2 an entrance.
3 *Sewing* something put in or inserted.

in-line skate *noun*
a type of roller skate with a single row of wheels down the middle of the sole.

inmate *noun*
a person confined to a hospital, jail, etc.

in memoriam (in mim-**aw**-ri-um)
preposition
in memory of someone who has died.
[Latin]

inmost *adjective*
innermost.

inn *noun*
an old word meaning 'a small hotel' or 'a public house'.
[Old English, a dwelling]

innards (**in**-erds) *plural noun*
(*informal*) the internal parts of anything, especially the body.
[alteration of *inwards*]

innate (in-**ate**) *adjective*
1 inborn in one's nature: *an innate love of painting.*
2 *Philosophy* of or coming from the mind, as distinct from experience.
Word Family innately *adverb*.
[Latin *innatus* born]

> ! Do not confuse *innate* with
> INHERENT.

inner *adjective*
located or occurring further in: *an inner room.*
Figurative He never revealed his inner life to others (= private, secret).

inner city *noun* (*plural* **inner cities**)
the area of a city surrounding and close to the centre: *inner city deprivation.*

innermost *adjective*
farthest within.
Figurative one's innermost secrets (= most intimate).

innings *noun* (*plural* **innings**)
1 *Cricket* the period in which a player or team is batting.
2 a turn or period at some activity.

innkeeper *noun*
an old word for a person who runs an inn.

innocent (**inn**-a-s'nt) *adjective*
1 pure or free from evil and sin: *an innocent child.*
2 *Law* not guilty: *The jury found the prisoner innocent.*
3 simple, guileless: *She was innocent enough to believe the story.*
• **innocent** *noun* any naive or pure person.
Word Family **innocently** *adverb*; **innocence** *noun*.
[Latin *innocens* harmless]

innocuous (in-**ok**-yew-us) *adjective*
harmless.
Word Family **innocuously** *adverb*.

innovation (in-a-**vay**-sh'n) *noun*
1 the introduction of new things or methods.
2 something new or different which is introduced.
Word Family **innovator** (**in**-a-vay-ter) *noun* a person who brings or makes changes; **innovate** *verb*; **innovative**, **innovatory** *adjective*.
[Latin *innovare* to renew, start again]

innuendo (in-yoo-**en**-do) *noun* (*plural* **innuendoes** or **innuendos**)
an indirect comment, such as a hint or implication, usually unfavourable.
[Latin, by nodding at, hinting]

innumerable (in-**new**-mer-a-b'l) *adjective*
very numerous.
Word Family **innumerably** *adverb*.

innumerate (in-**yoom**-er-ut) *adjective*
not able to deal with maths and numbers properly. Compare ILLITERATE.

inoculate (in-**ok**-yoo-late) *verb*
to induce a mild form of a disease so as to produce immunity, by introducing a virus or bacteria into the body.
Word Family **inoculation** (in-ok-yoo-**lay**-sh'n) *noun* 1 the act of inoculating 2 the substance inoculated.

> The word **inoculate** has a distant connection with 'eye'. *Oculus* was the Latin word for 'eye' but it came to mean 'the bud of a plant' because this resembled an eye; the verb *inoculare* was coined to mean 'to graft on a bud'. The modern English meaning was based on the idea of grafting or implanting a virus into a body and was first used with reference to smallpox.

inoffensive (in-a-**fen**-siv) *adjective*
not offensive or objectionable.
Word Family **inoffensively** *adverb*; **inoffensiveness** *noun*.

inoperable (in-**op**-er-a-b'l) *adjective*
Medicine incapable of being cured or removed by surgical operation: *an inoperable brain tumour.*

inoperative (in-**op**-ra-tiv) *adjective*
not in operation: *This regulation proved impossible to enforce and is now inoperative.*

inopportune (in-**op**-a-tune) *adjective*
ill-timed: *You have chosen an inopportune moment for your request.*
Word Family **inopportunely** *adverb*.

inordinate (in-**or**-di-nit) *adjective*
excessive or unrestrained.
Word Family **inordinately** *adverb*.
[Latin *inordinatus* disordered]

inorganic *adjective*
1 (of a substance) not derived from living things.
2 *Chemistry* of or relating to a class of compounds which do not contain carbon. Compare ORGANIC (definition 5).

inpatient ⇨ PATIENT *noun*.

input (**in**-p*u*t) *noun*
something which is put in or inserted, such as the power fed into a electrical device or the information fed into a computer.
• **input** *verb* (**inputs**; **inputting**; **input** or **inputted**) to enter data into a computer.

inquest (**in**-kwest) *noun*
Law an official enquiry, especially one to determine how a person died.
[Old French]

inquire ⇨ ENQUIRE.

inquiry ⇨ ENQUIRE.

inquisition (in-kwi-**zish**-'n) *noun*
1 an investigation, especially a legal or official one.
2 any severe or harsh interrogation of a person.
3 (**Inquisition**) *History* a Roman Catholic tribunal which imposed severe penalties for heresy, especially the Spanish Inquisition.
Word Family **inquisitor** (in-**kwizz**-i-ter) *noun* a person who conducts or makes an inquisition; **inquisitorial** (in-kwizz-i-**taw**-ri-ul) *adjective*.

inquisitive (in-**kwizz**-a-tiv) *adjective*
1 fond of inquiring into other people's affairs.
2 eager to learn: *He has an inquisitive mind.*
Word Family **inquisitively** *adverb*; **inquisitiveness** *noun*.

inroads (**in**-roads) *plural noun*
an intrusion: *His continual questions are making inroads on my patience.*

inrush (**in**-rush) *noun* (*plural* **inrushes**)
a rushing in of something: *a sudden inrush of the tide.*

insane (in-**sane**) *adjective*
1 having a severe mental illness, especially one needing permanent nursing care in an institution.
2 extremely senseless or foolish: *insane schemes.*
Word Family **insanely** *adverb*; **insanity** (in-**sann**-i-tee) *noun*.
[*in*-² + Latin *sanus* healthy]

insanitary (in-**san**-i-tree) *adjective*
not sanitary or clean.

insatiable (in-**say**-sha-b'l) *adjective*
incapable of being satisfied: *an insatiable thirst.*
Word Family **insatiably** *adverb*; **insatiability** (in-say-sha-**bill**-i-tee) *noun*.

inscribe (in-**skribe**) *verb*
1 to write a dedication in a book.
2 to engrave.
3 *Maths* to draw a figure within another so that the inner figure touches the boundary of the outer at as many points as possible.
Word Family **inscription** (in-**skrip**-sh'n) *noun*.
[*in*-¹ + Latin *scribere* to write]

inscrutable (in-**skroo**-ta-b'l) *adjective*
not able to be penetrated or understood.
Word Family **inscrutably** *adverb*; **inscrutability** (in-skroo-ta-**bill**-i-tee) *noun*.
[*in*-² + Latin *scrutari* to search into]

insect (**in**-sekt) *noun*
an arthropod, the adult having six legs, sometimes wings, and a body divided into three parts (a head, a thorax and an abdomen), such as an ant or a beetle.
[*in*-¹ + Latin *sectus* cut]

insecticide (in-**sek**-ti-side) *noun*
any substance which is used to kill insects.

insectivorous (in-sek-**tivv**-a-rus) *adjective*
of or relating to an organism which eats insects.
Word Family **insectivore** (in-**sek**-ti-vor) *noun* an animal or plant which eats insects.
[*in*-¹ + Latin *vorare* to devour]

insecure (in-si-**kew**-er) *adjective*
1 anxious, uncertain, or lacking self-confidence.
2 unsafe or liable to give way, fall, etc.
Word Family **insecurely** *adverb*; **insecurity** (in-si-**kew**-ra-tee) *noun* (*plural* **insecurities**).

inseminate (in-**semm**-i-nate) *verb*
to introduce semen into the uterus of a female to cause fertilization.
Word Family **insemination** (in-semm-i-**nay**-sh'n) *noun*.
[Latin *inseminatus* sown, planted in]

insensate (in-**sen**-sate) *adjective*
not capable of feeling or sensation: *insensate rocks and stones.*
[*in*-² + Latin *sensus* sense]

insensible (in-**sen**-sa-b'l) *adjective*
1 deprived of consciousness: *He was insensible for hours after the blow on the head.*
2 incapable of feeling or perceiving: *He is insensible of ridicule.*
3 imperceptible: *The colour changed by insensible degrees.*
Word Family **insensibly** *adverb*; **insensibility** (in-sen-si-**bill**-i-tee) *noun*.

insensitive (in-**sen**-si-tiv) *adjective*
not sensitive.
Word Family **insensitively** *adverb*; **insensitivity** (in-sen-si-**tivv**-i-tee), **insensitiveness** *noun*.

inseparable (in-**sep**-er-a-b'l) *adjective*
not able to be separated or kept apart.
Word Family **inseparably** *adverb*.

insert (in-**sert**) *verb*
to put in: *to insert a key in a lock.* □ *to insert a notice in the paper.*
● **insert** (**in**-sert) *noun* something inserted or to be inserted.
Word Family **insertion** *noun* 1 the act of inserting. 2 something inserted.
[from Latin]

inset (**in**-set) *noun*
something set in or inserted: *a table-top with a marble inset.*
• **inset** (**in**-set) *verb* (**insets; insetting; inset**).

inshore *adjective, adverb*
(at sea) close to or towards the land.

inside *noun*
1 the inner part: *the inside of a suitcase.*
2 an inner side or surface: *the inside of the hand.*
3 (usually **insides**) (*informal*) the inner parts of a body or machine.
Phrases **inside out 1** with the inner side reversed to become the outer side: *My jumper was inside out.* **2** thoroughly: *She knows her job inside out.* **on the inside** being in a position of confidence, influence or special knowledge.
• **inside** *adjective*
1 inner or on the inside: *The story was continued on the inside pages of the paper.*
2 (*informal*) acting or originating from within a company, etc.: *The robbery was an inside job.* □ *inside information.*
• **inside** *preposition* within: *She stood inside the fence.*
• **inside** *adverb*
1 in or into the inner part: *Please come inside.*
2 on the inner side: *This jacket is purple inside.*
Phrase **inside of** (*informal*) *We can't supply the goods inside of a week* (= in less than).
Word Family **insider** *noun* 1 a member of a particular group, club, etc. 2 a person close to a source of knowledge or information.

insider dealing *noun*
the illegal use of confidential information in share dealing on the stock market.

insidious (in-**sidd**-i-us) *adjective*
1 sly or treacherous.
2 doing harm subtly or secretly: *Cancer is an insidious disease because it is often extremely advanced before it can be diagnosed.*
Word Family **insidiously** *adverb*; **insidiousness** *noun.*
[Latin *insidiosus* cunning, artful]

insight (**in**-site) *noun*
1 an understanding gained or given: *The film gave us an insight into the lives of primitive peoples.*
2 the power of having such understanding: *He was a man of great insight.*
Word Family **insightful** *adjective.*

insignia (in-**sig**-ni-a) *noun* (*plural* **insignia**)
the distinguishing marks or badges of office or honour.
[Latin *insignis* distinguished or marked]

insignificant (in-sig-**niff**-i-k'nt) *adjective*
unimportant or not significant.
Word Family **insignificantly** *adverb*; **insignificance** *noun.*

insincere (in-sin-**seer**) *adjective*
not sincere or genuine.
Word Family **insincerely** *adverb*; **insincerity** (in-sin-**serr**-i-tee) *noun.*

insinuate (in-**sin**-yoo-ate) *verb*
1 to suggest indirectly, usually something which is unpleasant.
2 to introduce slyly and gradually: *He insinuated himself into his employer's confidence.*
Word Family **insinuating** *adjective*; **insinuatingly** *adverb*; **insinuation** (in-sin-yoo-**ay**-sh'n) *noun.*
[Latin *insinuare* to wind one's way into]

insipid (in-**sip**-id) *adjective*
flavourless or uninteresting.
Word Family **insipidly** *adverb*; **insipidity** (in-si-**pid**-i-tee) *noun.*
[Latin *insipidus* tasteless]

insist *verb*
to maintain firmly a demand, statement, course of action, position, etc.: *She insisted on seeing my boss.*
Word Family **insistent** *adjective*
1 persistent. 2 compelling attention: *the dog's insistent barking;* **insistently** *adverb*; **insistence** *noun* 1 the act of insisting. 2 also **insistency** the quality of being insistent.
[Latin *insistere* to stand one's ground]

in situ (in **sit**-yew) *adverb*
in position.
[Latin]

insole *noun*
the inner sole of a shoe or boot, sometimes detachable.

insolent (**in**-sa-l'nt) *adjective*
insulting or disrespectful.
Word Family **insolently** *adverb*; **insolence** *noun.*
[Latin *insolens* arrogant]

insoluble (in-**sol**-yoo-b'l) *adjective*
1 incapable of being solved or explained.
2 unable to be dissolved in a particular solvent, usually water.
Word Family **insolubly** *adverb*; **insolubility** (in-sol-yoo-**bill**-i-tee) *noun.*

insolvent (in-sol-v'nt) *adjective*
(*formal*) unable to pay one's debts.
• **insolvent** *noun* a person who is
insolvent.
Word Family **insolvency** *noun*.

insomnia (in-som-ni-a) *noun*
an inability to sleep, often owing to anxiety
or depression.
Word Family **insomniac** (in-som-ni-ak)
noun a person suffering from insomnia.
[*in-²* + Latin *somnus* sleep]

insouciant (in-soo-sy'nt) *adjective*
(*formal*) indifferent or unconcerned about
consequences, public opinion, etc.
Word Family **insouciance** *noun*.
[French, from *souci* care]

inspect (in-spekt) *verb*
to look at carefully or officially: *to inspect
the troops.*
Word Family **inspection** *noun*;
inspector *noun* **1** an official appointed to
inspect. **2** a police officer ranking between
a sergeant and a chief inspector;
inspectorate *noun* **1** the office of an
inspector. **2** a group of inspectors. **3** the
district under an inspector.
[Latin *inspectus* looked into]

inspiration (in-spa-ray-sh'n) *noun*
1 the arousing of feelings, ideas, impulses,
etc., especially those that lead to creative
activity.
2 anything which arouses such activity:
*My wife has been my inspiration in all I
have done.*
Figurative Your idea of leaving before the
weekend rush was an inspiration (= a very
good idea).
3 (*formal*) the act of inhaling.
Word Family **inspirational** *adjective*.
[Latin *inspirare* to breathe into]

inspire (in-spire) *verb*
1 to uplift the mind or spirit: *The beauty of
nature inspired Wordsworth to write many
poems.*
2 to create a particular emotion in
someone: *His calm manner inspired me with
confidence.*
3 (*formal*) to inhale.
Word Family **inspiring** *adjective*.

instability (in-sta-bill-i-tee) *noun* (*plural*
instabilities)
a lack of stability, especially of character.

install (in-stawl) *verb*
1 to place or fix in position for use.
2 to establish in office.
Figurative He installed himself in the
comfortable armchair by the fire (= settled).

installation (in-sta-lay-sh'n) *noun*
1 the act of installing.
2 something which is installed or
established, such as a permanent military
base, a group of machines, etc.
3 an exhibit in an art gallery.

instalment (in-stawl-m'nt) *noun*
(*American* **installment**)
1 one of a series of cash payments paid, by
a buyer to a seller, for goods or services.
2 a single part of something which is
supplied or issued over a period of time:
Tune in to the next instalment of our serial.

instance (in-st'nss) *noun*
1 an example intended to prove or
illustrate a point, argument or general
truth: *Give us an instance of his cruelty.*
2 a particular case: *In this instance he was
right.*
Phrases **at the instance of** (*formal*) at
the request of. **for instance** as an
example.
• **instance** *verb* to give as an example.

instant (in-st'nt) *adjective*
1 immediate: *The troops are in a state of
instant readiness for battle.*
2 (of food) designed to be quickly
prepared, e.g. by simply adding water: *Do
you like instant coffee?*
• **instant** *noun*
1 a specific point of time: *Come home this
instant!*
2 a short space of time: *The bystanders
had gathered within an instant of the crash
occurring.*
Word Family **instantly** *adverb*.

instantaneous (in-st'n-tay-nee-us)
adjective
happening or done immediately.
Word Family **instantaneously** *adverb*;
instantaneousness *noun*.

instead (in-sted) *adverb*
in place of something: *There was no fish, so
we are having meat instead.*

instep *noun*
1 *Anatomy* the arched upper surface of the
human foot, between the ankle and the
toes.
2 the part of a shoe or sock covering the
instep.

instigate *verb*
to bring about, especially by provoking.
Word Family **instigator** *noun*;
instigation (in-stig-ay-sh'n) *noun*.
[Latin *instigare* to goad on]

instil (in-**stil**) *verb* (**instils; instilling; instilled**)(*American* **instill**)
to introduce gradually or by degrees: *Parents must instil good behaviour into their children from the start.*
Word Family **instillation** (in-sti-**lay**-sh'n) *noun*.
[Latin *instillare* to pour in drop by drop]

instinct (**in**-stinkt) *noun*
1 *Psychology, Sociology* the unlearned responses or tendencies of people and animals.
2 a natural aptitude or talent.
Word Family **instinctive** (in-**stink**-tiv), **instinctual** (in-**stink**-tyew'l) *adjective* of or resulting from an instinct; **instinctively** *adverb*.
[Latin *instinctus* instigated]

institute (**in**-sti-tewt) *noun*
1 an organization founded to promote some cause, such as education.
2 the buildings used by such an organization.
• **institute** *verb*
1 to establish or set up: *to institute a new law.*
2 to start: *to institute legal proceedings.*
[Latin *institutus* set up or established]

institution (in-sti-**tew**-sh'n) *noun*
1 an organization such as a hospital or university, established for a particular purpose.
2 the building or buildings used for this purpose.
3 any person who has become well-known because of long service: *Our postman had been doing the same round for so long he had become a local institution.*
4 something, such as a law or pattern of behaviour, which has become a recognized and accepted part of a culture, etc.
5 the act of instituting.
Word Family **institutional** *adjective*
1 of or relating to an institution. 2 being characterized by uniformity and dullness; **institutionally** *adverb*; **institutionalize, institutionalise** *verb* 1 to make into an institution. 2 to confine a person in an institution; **institutionalized** *adjective* having lived so long in an institution that it is very difficult to adjust to living outside one; **institutionalization** (in-sti-tew-sh'n-'l-eye-**zay**-sh'n) *noun*.

instruct (in-**strukt**) *verb*
1 to give orders or directions to: *The doctor has instructed me to stay in bed.*
2 to teach.

Word Family **instructor** *noun* someone who instructs: *a ski instructor;* **instructive** *adjective* informative or serving to instruct; **instructively** *adverb*; **instructiveness** *noun*.
[Latin *instructus* built on, equipped]

instruction (in-**struk**-sh'n) *noun*
1 (*usually* **instructions**) any orders or directions: *Follow the instructions on the packet carefully.*
2 (*formal*) teaching: *driving instruction.*
Word Family **instructional** *adjective*.

instrument (**in**-stra-m'nt) *noun*
1 a device or object for a particular purpose: *surgical instruments.*
2 a device for producing musical sounds: *The bassoon is a woodwind instrument.*
3 any person or thing used for a purpose: *She felt she was an instrument of God's will.*
4 *Law* a formal legal document.
• **instrument** (**in**-stra-ment) *verb* to arrange a piece of music for instruments, especially for an orchestra.
Word Family **instrumentation** (in-stra-men-**tay**-sh'n) *noun*.
[Latin *instrumentum* equipment]

instrumental (in-stra-**men**-t'l) *adjective*
1 serving as a means: *My friend was instrumental in getting me this job.*
2 of or for musical instruments: *instrumental music.*
• **instrumental** *noun* a piece of music, usually popular, performed without vocal accompaniment.
Word Family **instrumentally** *adverb*; **instrumentalist** *noun* a person who plays a musical instrument, especially in popular music.

instrumentality (in-stra-men-**tal**-i-tee) *noun*
the agency or means by which something is done: *He got the job through the instrumentality of his father-in-law.*

insubordinate (in-sa-**bor**-di-nit) *adjective* disobedient or rebellious.
Word Family **insubordinately** *adverb*; **insubordination** (in-sa-bor-di-**nay**-sh'n) *noun*.

insubstantial (in-sub-**stan**-sh'l) *adjective*
1 not strong or substantial: *Her brief explanation was very insubstantial.*
2 imaginary or not real: *He is full of insubstantial fears about being alone.*

insufferable (in-**suff**-er-a-b'l) *adjective* (*formal*) intolerable or unbearable.
Word Family **insufferably** *adverb*; **insufferableness** *noun*.

insufficient (in-sa-**fish**-'nt) *adjective*
not sufficient or enough: *His earnings were insufficient to keep pace with his extravagant tastes.*
Word Family **insufficiently** *adverb*; **insufficiency** *noun* a lack.

insular (**in**-syoo-la) *adjective*
1 narrow-minded: *their absurdly insular prejudices.*
2 of or relating to an island.
Word Family **insularity** (in-syoo-**larr**-i-tee) *noun*.
[Latin *insula* an island]

insulate (**in**-syoo-late) *verb*
1 to cover with non-conducting material.
2 to protect from something unpleasant.
Word Family **insulation** (in-syoo-**lay**-sh'n) *noun* 1 any material used for insulating. 2 the act of insulating; **insulator** *noun* anything which insulates, especially against electricity.

insulin (**in**-syoo-lin) *noun*
Biology a hormone secreted in the pancreas, controlling the amount of glucose in the blood, used to treat diabetes.

> **Insulin** was first discovered by the Canadian physiologists Banting and Best in 1921. It is so called because *insulin* is produced in the islets of Langerhans, groups of cells in the pancreas, and *insula* is the Latin for 'island or islet'.

insult (in-**sult**) *verb*
to speak to or treat in a contemptuous or insolent way.
● **insult** (**in**-sult) *noun* an offensive remark or act.
Word Family **insulting** *adjective*; **insultingly** *adverb*.
[Latin *insultare* leap on or at]

insuperable (in-**soo**-p'ra-b'l) *adjective*
not capable of being overcome or surmounted.
Word Family **insuperably** *adverb*.

insupportable (in-sa-**por**-ta-b'l) *adjective*
unendurable or insufferable.

insurance (in-**shore**-ence) *noun*
1 a contract under which a person or company agrees to pay for any loss or damage to a person or to property provided the owner makes regular payments, called **premiums**: *We took out an insurance policy.*
2 the payment made to or by a company issuing an insurance.

3 the business of providing insurance: *Her dad's in insurance.*
4 any safeguard against risk or harm: *Most people keep their money in a bank as an insurance against burglary.*

insure (in-**shor**) *verb*
to guarantee against risk or harm, as with insurance.
Word Family **insurable** *adjective*; **insured** *noun* a person protected by insurance; **insurer** *noun* a person or company issuing insurance.

> [!] Do not confuse *insure* with ENSURE.

insurgency (in-**sir**-j'n-see) *noun* (*plural* **insurgencies**)
a revolt against a government.
Word Family **insurgent** *noun* a member of an insurgency; **insurgent** *adjective* rebellious.
[Latin *insurgens* rising]

insurmountable (in-sir-**mount**-a-b'l) *adjective*
not able to be overcome or surmounted.
Word Family **insurmountably** *adverb*.

insurrection (ins-a-**rek**-sh'n) *noun*
a revolt against an established government, especially an organized effort to seize political power.
Word Family **insurrectionary** *adjective*.
[Latin *insurrectus* risen]

insusceptible (in-sa-**sep**-ta-b'l) *adjective*
not liable to be influenced or affected by: *He is insusceptible to argument.*
Word Family **insusceptibility** (in-sa-sep-ta-**bill**-i-tee) *noun*.

intact (in-**takt**) *adjective*
remaining whole, unchanged or undamaged.
Word Family **intactness** *noun*.
[Latin *intactus* untouched]

intaglio (in-**tah**-li-o) *noun*
1 the art of engraving designs into a surface, especially on gems.
2 a method of printing from plates or cylinders on which the image has been etched below the surface.
[Italian *intagliare* to engrave]

intake *noun*
1 the act of taking in.
2 anything which is taken in: *a huge intake of students.*
3 the opening through which a fluid is taken into a container, pipe, etc.

intangible (in-**tan**-ji-b'l) *adjective*
1 incapable of being touched.

2 vague or indefinable: *He has intangible fears about his future.*
Word Family intangibly *adverb*; **intangibility** (in-tan-ji-**bill**-i-tee) *noun*.

integer (**in**-ti-jer) *noun*
Maths any posititive or negative whole number, e.g. −2, −1, 0, 1, 2, etc.
[Latin, intact]

integral (**in**-ti-grul) *adjective*
1 being an indispensable part of a whole: *Arms and legs are integral parts of the body.*
2 of or relating to integers.
Word Family integrally *adverb*.

integrate (**in**-ti-grate) *verb*
1 to combine parts into a whole: *The welfare plan integrated all the existing agencies into one comprehensive service.*
2 to absorb into a culture or society: *Some of the newcomers were more quickly integrated into the community than others.* Compare SEGREGATE.

integrated circuit ⇨ CIRCUIT.

integration (in-ti-**gray**-sh'n) *noun*
1 the bringing or fitting together of parts into a whole.
2 the policy or process of making public facilities, such as schools and transport, available to people of all races.

integrity (in-**teg**-ri-tee) *noun*
1 the quality of being honest and upright in character.
2 (*formal*) the state or condition of being complete: *The scholar had restored the text of the manuscript to its original integrity.*

intellect (**in**-ta-lekt) *noun*
1 the capacity of the mind to reason and grasp ideas, as distinct from feeling and will.
2 a person of good understanding or reasoning powers.
[from Latin]

> [!] Both *intellect* and *intelligence* refer to the capacity to know, reason and understand. *Intelligence* is the more general term, suggesting a natural ability to think and adapt, whereas *intellect* refers to a developed capacity to reason and test ideas.

intellectual (in-ta-**lek**-tyoo-al) *adjective*
1 of or relating to the intellect: *the intellectual powers.*
2 possessing or showing intellect: *He's a very intellectual author.*
• **intellectual** *noun* any person who enjoys intellectual pursuits or whose work requires a developed intellect.

Word Family intellectually *adverb*; **intellectualize, intellectualise** *verb* to treat in intellectual terms.

intelligence (in-**tell**-i-j'nce) *noun*
1 the ability to understand, reason and learn to adapt to new situations.
2 news or information, especially about important events.
3 *Military* the branch of an army which collects and analyses information about foreign armed forces and their equipment, etc.
Word Family intelligent *adjective*
1 having or showing intelligence. 2 (of a device or computer) able to adjust its behaviour to cope with circumstances; **intelligently** *adverb*.
[from Latin]

> [!] On the difference between *intelligence* and *intellect* ⇨ INTELLECT.

intelligence quotient *noun*
short form is **IQ** an indicator of a person's intelligence as measured by an intelligence test, and in relation to others of the same age. The IQ is mental age divided by real age, multiplied by 100. For the purpose of intelligence testing a person's 'real age' is frozen at 15. Thus the average IQ at any age up to 15 is 100, and the IQ of an eight-year-old with a mental age of ten is 125.

intelligence test *noun*
a method of measuring intelligence by using tasks and problems.

intelligentsia (in-tell-i-**jent**-si-a) *noun*
the intellectual class of society.
[Russian]

intelligible (in-**tell**-ij-a-b'l) *adjective*
capable of being understood.
Word Family intelligibly *adverb*; **intelligibility** (in-tell-ij-a-**bill**-i-tee) *noun*.

intemperate (in-**tem**-pa-rit) *adjective*
lacking moderation, e.g. in speech or in the consumption of alcohol.
Word Family intemperately *adverb*; **intemperance** *noun*.

intend *verb*
to plan or have as a purpose: *He intends to quit.* □ *a room intended for study.*
Word Family intended *noun* (*informal*) one's prospective husband or wife.
[Latin *intendere* to stretch (e.g. a bow), to aim]

intense (in-**tense**) *adjective*
1 very great or strong: *blinded by the intense light.* □ *intense happiness.*

2 hard: *He has devoted years of intense study to the problem.*
3 characterized by strong feelings: *an intense young man.*
Word Family intensely *adverb*; **intensify** *verb* (**intensifies**; **intensifying**; **intensified**) to make or become intense or more intense; **intensification** (in-ten-sif-i-**kay**-sh'n) *noun*.

intensity (in-**ten**-si-tee) *noun*
the quality of being intense.

intensive (in-**ten**-siv) *adjective*
1 concentrated: *an intensive course in economics.*
2 designed to produce maximum results.
3 *Grammar* giving force or emphasis: *'Certainly' is an intensive adverb.*
Word Family intensively *adverb*; **intensiveness** *noun*.

intensive care *noun*
closely monitored care of acutely ill patients in a special hospital unit.

intensive farming *noun*
farming in a small area, growing large amounts of food with high inputs.
Compare EXTENSIVE FARMING.

Intent¹ (in-**tent**) *noun*
any purpose or intention.
Phrase to all intents and purposes in almost every way.

intent² (in-**tent**) *adjective*
firmly fixed or concentrated.
Word Family intently *adverb*; **intentness** *noun*.
[Latin *intentus* stretched, aimed]

intention (in-**ten**-sh'n) *noun*
1 any plan of action, design, or purpose.
2 any goal or objective.
Word Family intentional *adjective* intended or deliberate; **intentionally** *adverb*.

inter (in-**ter**) *verb* (**inters**; **interring**; **interred**)
(*formal*) to place a corpse in a grave or tomb.
[*in-¹* + Latin *terra* earth]

interaction (in-ta-**rak**-sh'n) *noun*
the process of two things acting on each other.
Word Family interact *verb*; **interactive** *adjective* **1** (of two people or things) communicating with each other. **2** (of an electronic device) allowing direct communication between the user and the device: *an interactive computer game.*

inter alia (in-ter **ay**-lee-a) *adverb*
(*formal*) among other things.
[Latin]

interbreed *verb* (**interbreeds**; **interbreeding**; **interbred**)
to breed with an animal of a different species.

intercede (in-ta-**seed**) *verb*
to intervene on behalf of another person or group.
[Latin *intercedere* to come between]

intercept (in-ta-**sept**) *verb*
1 to stop or interrupt the progress of.
2 *Maths* to cut off by intersecting at two points.
● **intercept** (**in**-ta-sept) *noun*
Maths the point of intersection.
Word Family interception *noun*; **interceptor** *noun*.
[*inter-* + Latin *captus* seized]

intercession (in-ta-**sesh**-'n) *noun*
1 the act of interceding.
2 *Christianity* a prayer on behalf of someone else.
Word Family intercessory *adjective* making intercession.

interchange (in-ta-**chaynj**) *verb*
1 to change places or put in the place of each other.
2 to exchange.
3 to alternate: *an occasion when tears interchanged with smiles.*
● **interchange** (**in**-ta-chaynj) *noun*.
Word Family interchangeable *adjective*; **interchangeably** *adverb*.

intercom *noun*
short form of **intercommunication** a system of communication between rooms in a building, aircraft, etc., using telephones, microphones, etc.

interconnect *verb*
to connect or be connected one with the other.
Word Family interconnection *noun*.

intercontinental (in-ta-kon-ti-**nen**-t'l) *adjective*
1 between continents: *intercontinental shipping.*
2 able to reach from one continent to another: *an intercontinental ballistic missile.*

intercostal *adjective*
Anatomy of or relating to the muscles or spaces between the ribs.
[*inter-* + Latin *costa* rib]

intercourse *noun*
1 a communication or exchange of ideas, feelings, etc.: *social intercourse.*
2 ⇨ SEXUAL INTERCOURSE.

interdenominational (in-ta-din-omm-i-**nay**-sh'n-'l) *adjective*
of or common to two or more religious movements.

interdependent (in-ta-dip-**end**-'nt) *adjective*
being dependent on each other.
Word Family interdependence, interdependency *noun*.

interdict (**in**-ta-dikt) *noun*
Roman Catholicism a punishment by which a person remains a member of the Church, but is prohibited from taking part in certain religious acts.
• **interdict** (in-ta-**dikt**) *verb* to forbid or prohibit.
Word Family interdiction (in-ta-**dik**-sh'n) *noun*.
[Latin *interdictus* forbidden]

interest (**in**-ta-rest) *noun*
1 a feeling of curiosity, fascination, etc.: *She is beginning to show an interest in art.*
2 the cause of such a feeling: *This brochure should be of interest to you.*
3 importance: *Material possessions are of little interest to her.*
4 (*often* **interests**) well-being, profit or advantage: *Your parents have your interests at heart when they send you to school.*
5 a share or involvement, especially in property, business, etc.: *He has a controlling interest in the company.*
6 *Commerce* a payment for the use of money or credit, usually calculated as a percentage of the amount used or owed.
accrued interest *Commerce* interest calculated up to a certain date within the period of a loan.
compound interest *Commerce* interest calculated on the original amount of a loan together with the interest accumulated over a period.
simple interest *Commerce* interest calculated on the original amount of a loan only.
• **interest** *verb*
1 to arouse the curiosity of: *The old house interested the architect.*
2 to concern or involve: *We tried to interest him in buying a farm.*
Word Family interested *adjective* showing interest; **interestedly** *adverb*; **interesting** *adjective* arousing interest; **interestingly** *adverb*.
[Latin, it is of importance to]

interest-free *adjective, adverb*
having no interest charged: *an interest-free loan.*

interface *noun*
1 a surface forming a common boundary between two bodies.
2 the link between a computer and its user, or between two computer systems.

interfere (in-ta-**feer**) *verb*
1 to intrude in the affairs of others.
2 to hinder or impede: *He allowed his personal life to interfere with his work.*
3 *Physics, Radio* to cause interference.
Word Family interfering *adjective*; **interferingly** *adverb*; **interferer** *noun*.
[Old French *s'entreferir* to strike each other]

interference (in-ta-**feer**-'nce) *noun*
1 the act or fact of interfering.
2 *Physics* the meeting and combination of waves, the effect varying with the phase, amplitude and frequency of the waves.
3 *Radio* the receiving of radio signals with similar frequencies from more than one source.

intergalactic (in-ta-ga-**lak**-tik) *adjective*
Astronomy of or between galaxies.

interim (**in**-ta-rim) *adjective*
1 of or relating to an intervening period of time.
2 temporary: *An interim treaty was made while peace negotiations continued.*
• **interim** *noun* an intervening period of time.
[Latin, meanwhile]

interior (in-**tee**-ri-a) *adjective*
1 being inside: *an interior door.*
2 inland.
3 relating to the internal affairs of a country.
Word Family interior *noun*.
[Latin, inner]

interior decorator *noun*
a person who plans and carries out or supervises the decoration and furnishing of the inside of a building.

interior designer *noun*
a person trained to design and coordinate the inside form and appearance of a building.

interject (in-ta-**jekt**) *verb*
to break in with a comment while someone else is speaking.

interjection (in-ta-**jek**-sh'n) *noun*
1 the act of interjecting.
2 *Grammar* a word or phrase used to express surprise or anger, to attract attention, etc., e.g. *ouch!* or *Wow!*
[*inter-* + Latin *jactus* thrown]

interlace *verb*
to cross each other as if woven together.

interleave *verb*
to insert or provide blank pages in a book, e.g. for protecting illustrations, making notes, etc.

interlock (in-ta-**lok**) *verb*
to unite or join closely.
● **interlock** (**in**-ta-lok) *noun* a smooth knitted fabric, usually made from cotton and used for underwear.

interlocutor (in-ta-**lok**-yoo-ter) *noun*
a person taking part in a conversation or dialogue.
Word Family **interlocutory** *adjective*; **interlocution** (in-ta-lo-**kew**-sh'n) *noun* a conversation.
[*inter-* + Latin *locutus* spoken]

interloper *noun*
a person who intrudes or interferes.
Word Family **interlope** *verb*.

interlude (**in**-ta-lood) *noun*
1 an intervening episode, period, space, etc.
2 *Theatre* a short comedy placed between two plays, developed during the Renaissance.
[*inter-* + Latin *ludus* a game]

intermarry *verb* (**intermarries**; **intermarrying**; **intermarried**)
1 to marry someone who is not a member of one's own group or race.
2 (of families) to become connected by marriage.
3 to marry within one's family, tribe or clan.
Word Family **intermarriage** *noun*.

intermediary (in-ta-**meed**-i-a-ree) *noun*
(*plural* **intermediaries**)
a mediator or agent.
● **intermediary** *adjective*
1 being between.
2 acting as a mediator.

intermediate (in-ta-**mee**-di-it) *adjective*
situated or occurring between things in time, space, etc.: *Several intermediate products were formed during the chemical reaction.*

interment (in-**ter**-m'nt) *noun*
(*formal*) a burial.

interminable (in-**ter**-min-a-b'l) *adjective*
having no apparent end.
Word Family **interminably** *adverb*.

intermingle *verb*
to mix together: *Police intermingled with the crowd.*

intermission (in-ta-**mish**-'n) *noun*
1 a pause: *The rain poured down all day without intermission.*
2 *Theatre* an interval.

intermittent (in-ta-**mitt**-'nt) *adjective*
stopping and starting at intervals.
Word Family **intermittently** *adverb*.
[Latin *intermittens* leaving gaps]

intern (in-**tern**) *verb*
to confine to a country or place, especially during wartime.
● **intern** (**in**-tern) *noun* (*especially American*) a person training for a job, especially a trainee doctor in a hospital.

internal (in-**tern**-'l) *adjective*
1 of or relating to the inside or inner part of something.
2 of or relating to the domestic affairs of a country.
Word Family **internally** *adverb*.
[from Latin]

internal-combustion engine *noun*
an engine with one or more cylinders in which the process of combustion takes place within the cylinder.

internal rhyme *noun*
the positioning of rhyming words or sounds within a line of poetry. For example, the 'oh' sound which occurs four times in *Though the threat of snow was growing slowly* is an internal rhyme.

international (in-ta-**nash**-'n-'l) *adjective*
1 of or relating to more than one nation or nationality: *an international peacekeeping force.*
2 between or among nations: *an international trade agreement.*
Word Family **internationally** *adverb*; **internationalize, internationalise** *verb* to make international.

International Date Line *noun*
an imaginary North-South line through the Pacific at or near 180° longitude where the date changes by one day when it is crossed.

internationalism *noun*
the policy of countries working together for their common good. Compare NATIONALISM (definition 2).
Word Family **internationalist** *noun*.

internecine (in-ta-**nee**-sine) *adjective*
1 mutually destructive.
2 characterized by great slaughter: *an internecine war.*
[Latin *internecio* a massacre]

internee *noun*
a person who is interned.

Internet *noun*
short form is **Net** an international network of computers linked by telephone lines, enabling users to share and exchange information.

internment *noun*
confinement, imprisonment.

interpenetrate (in-ta-**pen**-i-trate) *verb*
1 to penetrate thoroughly.
2 to penetrate each other.
Word Family **interpenetration** (in-ta-pen-i-**tray**-sh'n) *noun*.

interplay *noun*
the effect of two or more things on each other.

Interpol *noun*
the International Criminal Police Organization, through which the police of member states help each other in dealing with crime. It is based in France.

interpolate (in-**ter**-pa-late) *verb*
1 to insert or introduce something between parts already there.
2 *Maths* to estimate an unknown quantity within the limits of what is known.
Word Family **interpolation** (in-ter-pa-**lay**-sh'n) *noun*.

interpose *verb*
1 to place between.
2 to interject a question or remark during a speech or conversation.
3 to mediate: *I interposed in their quarrel.*
Word Family **interposition** (in-ta-po-**zish**-'n) *noun* 1 the act of interposing.
2 something which is interposed.

interpret (in-**ter**-prit) *verb*
1 to show, clarify or explain the meaning of: *We interpreted his reply as an apology.*
2 to translate: *As she did not understand English, I had to interpret for her.*
Word Family **interpretation** (in-ter-pri-**tay**-sh'n) *noun*; **interpreter** *noun*.
[Latin *interpretari* to act as broker, to explain]

interracial (in-ta-**ray**-sh'l) *adjective*
1 existing between races or between members of different races.
2 of or for people of different races.

interregnum (in-ta-**reg**-num) *noun* (*plural* **interregnums** or **interregna**)
a time when a country has no official leader or government, such as the time between the death of a monarch and the beginning of the successor's rule.
[*inter-* + Latin *regnum* reign]

interrelate (in-ta-ri-**late**) *verb*
1 (of two or more things) to be connected and affect each other.
2 to bring two or more things into a relationship.
Word Family **interrelationship** *noun*.

interrogate (in-**terr**-a-gate) *verb*
1 to examine by close questioning, especially in a formal way.
2 to obtain data from (a database, etc.).
Word Family **interrogation** (in-terr-a-**gay**-sh'n) *noun*; **interrogator** *noun*.
[*inter-* + Latin *rogare* to ask]

interrogation mark ⇨ QUESTION MARK.

interrogative (in-ta-**rogg**-a-tiv) *adjective*
1 of the nature of a question.
2 *Grammar* (of a word, etc.) forming a question.
● **interrogative** *noun Grammar* an interrogative word.
Word Family **interrogatively** *adverb*; **interrogatory** *adjective* relating to, expressing or implying a question.

interrupt (in-ta-**rupt**) *verb*
1 to break the continuity of: *They interrupted their journey to stay with relatives for a week.*
2 to hinder or stop by breaking in on: *His speech was interrupted by many shouts.*
Word Family **interruption** *noun*.
[*inter-* + Latin *ruptus* broken]

intersect (in-ta-**sekt**) *verb*
1 to cut across or pass through: *The roads intersect at the bottom of a hill.*
2 *Maths* to have one or more points in common.
Word Family **intersection** *noun* 1 the place where two or more things intersect.
2 the act of intersecting.
[*inter-* + Latin *sectus* cut]

intersperse (in-ta-**sperse**) *verb*
to scatter or distribute irregularly among other things.
Word Family **interspersion** (in-ta-**sper**-sh'n) *noun*.
[*inter-* + Latin *sparsus* scattered]

interstellar *adjective*
between the stars.

interstice (in-**ter**-stis) *noun*
(*formal*) a small space between things or parts.
Word Family **interstitial** (in-ta-**stish**-'l) *adjective* pertaining to, situated in or forming an interstice; **interstitially** *adverb*.
[*inter-* + Latin *status* put]

intertwine *verb*
to twine together.

interval *noun*
1 an intervening space or period of time.
2 *Music* the difference in pitch between two notes.
3 also **intermission** *Theatre* the time between two acts of a play, two films, etc., when the audience leave their seats for refreshments.
[Latin *intervallum* the space between the ramparts]

intervene (in-ta-veen) *verb*
1 to step in, in order to solve, settle, correct, etc.: *The Prime Minister intervened in the dispute.*
2 to come between in time, place, etc.: *Nothing intervened and we were able to take our holiday as planned.*
Word Family intervening *adjective*; **intervention** (in-ta-ven-sh'n) *noun*.
[inter- + Latin *venire* to come]

interview *noun*
a formal meeting at which one or more people are asked questions about their work, lives, recent activities, etc.: *a job interview.* □ *Did you see the interview with Prince William on TV last night?*
Word Family interview *verb*; **interviewer** *noun* a person who asks the questions at an interview.

interweave *verb* (**interweaves**; **interweaving**; **interwove**; **interwoven**)
to weave together.

intestate (in-test-ate) *adjective*
Law having left no valid will. Compare TESTATE.

intestine (in-test-in) *noun* also called **bowel**; **gut**.
Anatomy the lower part of the food canal below the stomach, part of the alimentary canal.
large intestine the lower part of the bowels, including the colon and rectum.
small intestine the part of the intestine between the stomach and the large intestine.
Word Family intestinal (in-test-in-al) *adjective*.
[Latin *intestinus* internal]

intifada (in-ti-fah-da) *noun*
(in the Middle East) an uprising.
[Arabic *intifada* shake, shudder]

intimate¹ (in-ti-mit) *adjective*
1 closely acquainted: *an intimate friend.*
2 small and private: *an intimate dinner party.*

3 personal: *She refused to tell us all the intimate details.*
4 thorough: *He has an intimate knowledge of Dutch.*
Word Family intimately *adverb*; **intimacy** *noun* (*plural* **intimacies**).
[Latin *intimus* innermost]

intimate² (in-ti-mate) *verb*
to imply subtly.
Word Family intimation (in-ti-may-sh'n) *noun*.

intimidate (in-timm-i-date) *verb*
to frighten, especially in order to force someone to do something.
Word Family intimidated *adjective*; **intimidating** *adjective*; **intimidation** (in-timm-i-day-sh'n) *noun*.
[Latin *intimidare* to make timid]

into *preposition*
a word used to indicate the following:
1 motion or direction towards the inside: *We went into the shop.* □ *I helped him into the car.*
2 a change of condition or a result: *The rain changed into snow.* □ *She burst into tears.*
3 an entry or introduction: *They entered into an agreement.* □ *to go into politics.*
4 extent in time, space, etc.: *It rained well into the night.*
5 division: *Two into six goes three.*
Phrase be into (*informal*) to be deeply involved or interested in.

intolerable (in-toll-er-a-b'l) *adjective*
unbearable.
Word Family intolerably *adverb*.

intolerant (in-toll-a-r'nt) *adjective*
not tolerant.
Word Family intolerantly *adverb*; **intolerance** *noun*.

intonation (in-ta-nay-sh'n) *noun*
1 the rise and fall of the voice in speaking.
2 *Music* the manner of producing notes, especially in relation to accuracy of pitch.

intone *verb*
to speak with drawn-out vowel sounds and in a monotone, as when or as if reciting a prayer or chanting a psalm.

in toto *adverb*
(*formal*) wholly or absolutely.
[Latin]

intoxicate (in-tok-si-kate) *verb*
to cause to lose self-control, especially as the result of taking alcohol, drugs, etc.
Figurative *The team was intoxicated by success* (= wildly excited, elated).

Word Family intoxicant *noun*;
intoxication (in-tok-si-**kay**-sh'n) *noun*
drunkenness.

> The word **intoxicate** is etymologically
> connected with poison rather than
> alcohol as it comes from Latin
> *intoxicare*, 'to poison'. *Toxon* was the
> Greek word for 'a bow' and *toxicon
> pharmakon* referred literally to poison
> used in archery – on the tips of arrows.
> This became simply *toxicon* and went
> into Latin as *toxicum*.

intractable (in-**trak**-ti-b'l) *adjective*
stubborn or difficult to manage.
Word Family intractably *adverb*;
intractability (in-trak-ti-**bill**-i-tee),
intractableness *noun*.
[*in-*[2] + Latin *tractare* to handle]

intramural (in-tra-**mew**-r'l) *adjective*
existing within the bounds of an
institution, especially a university or
school.
[*intra-* + Latin *murus* a wall]

Intranet *noun*
Computers a network of computers within
an organization, e.g. a school or company,
enabling users to share and exchange
information.

intransigent (in-**tran**-si-j'nt) *adjective*
uncompromising.
● **intransigent** *noun* a person who is
uncompromising.
Word Family intransigently *adverb*;
intransigence, intransigency *noun*.
[*in-*[2] + Latin *transigens* transacting]

intransitive (in-**tran**-zi-tiv) *adjective*
Grammar (of a verb) not needing a direct
object to complete its meaning, e.g.
'walked' in *The boy walked slowly to buy a
book.* Compare TRANSITIVE.
Word Family intransitively *adverb*.

intravenous (in-tra-**vee**-nus) *adjective*
within a vein: *The nurse hooked up an
intravenous drip.*
Word Family intravenously *adverb*.
[*intra-* + Latin *vena* a vein]

intrepid (in-**trep**-id) *adjective*
fearless or bold.
Word Family intrepidly *adverb*;
intrepidity (in-trep-**id**-i-tee) *noun*.
[*in-*[2] + Latin *trepidus* alarmed]

intricate (**in**-tra-kit) *adjective*
1 having many interrelating parts or
elements: *an intricate machine.*
2 difficult to untangle: *an intricate knot.*

Word Family intricately *adverb*;
intricacy (**in**-tri-ka-see) *noun* (*plural*
intricacies).
[Latin *intricatus* entangled]

intrigue (in-**treeg**) *verb*
1 to arouse the interest or curiosity of,
especially by puzzling.
2 (*formal*) to make and carry out secret
plans: *The anarchists intrigued to overthrow
the government.*
● **intrigue** (**in**-treeg or in-**treeg**) *noun*
1 an underhand plot.
2 the use of such plots.
[Latin *intricare* to entangle]

intrinsic (in-**trin**-sik) *adjective*
(*formal*) belonging to a thing by its very
nature.
Word Family intrinsically *adverb*.
[Latin *intrinsecus* inwardly]

introduce *verb*
1 to make someone acquainted with:
*I would like to introduce you to a friend
of mine.*
2 to use or bring to notice first: *Who
introduced the fashion for miniskirts?*
3 to present for discussion: *He introduced a
bill in Parliament.*
4 to give first knowledge of: *This term the
class will be introduced to calculus.*
5 to institute: *The Prime Minister introduced
sweeping changes.*
6 to insert, put: *An amendment was
introduced into the bill.*
7 to preface: *He introduced his remarks with
a brief summary.*
Word Family introduction *noun* 1 the
act of introducing. 2 something which
introduces or is introduced; **introductory**
adjective forming an introduction.
[Latin *intro-* inwards + *ducere* to lead]

introspection (in-tra-**spek**-sh'n) *noun*
the examination of one's own thoughts,
sensations, etc.
Word Family introspective *adjective*;
introspectively *adverb*.
[Latin *intro-* inwards + *specere* to look]

introvert (**in**-tra-vert) *noun*
1 a shy reserved person.
2 *Psychology* a person interested chiefly in
his or her own thoughts and feelings rather
than in external things. Compare
EXTROVERT (definition 2).
● **introvert** (in-tra-**vert**) *verb* to turn
inwards.
[Latin *intro-* inwards + *vertere* to turn]

intrude *verb*
to thrust or force in, especially where one
is unwelcome.

Word Family **intruder** *noun;* **intrusive** *adjective* tending to intrude; **intrusively** *adverb;* **intrusiveness** *noun.*
[*in-*[1] + Latin *trudere* to thrust]

intrusion (in-troo-*zh*'n) *noun*
1 the act of intruding.
2 something which intrudes.

intuition (in-tew-**ish**-'n) *noun*
1 an understanding or insight arrived at without conscious reasoning.
2 the ability to perceive in this way.
Word Family **intuitive** (in-**tew**-a-tiv) *adjective;* **intuitively** *adverb.*
[Latin *intueri* to inspect]

inundate (**in**-un-date) *verb*
to overwhelm or cover with or as if with a flood: *We were inundated with applications.*
Word Family **inundation** (in un-**day**-sh'n) *noun.*
[*in-*[1] + Latin *unda* a wave]

inure (in-**yoor**) *verb*
(*formal*) to accustom to something unpleasant.

invade *verb*
1 to enter as an enemy, or in attack.
Figurative The dampness from the cellar invaded the living room (= moved into).
2 to violate or interfere with: *Do not invade his privacy.*
Word Family **invader** *noun;* **invasion** (in-**vay**-*zh*'n) *noun;* **invasive** *adjective.*
[Latin *invadere* to come in]

invalid[1] (**in**-va-lid) *noun*
a person who is sick or disabled for a long period of time.
● **invalid** *verb.*
Phrase **be invalided out of** to leave one of the armed forces because of illness or injury.
Word Family **invalidism** *noun* prolonged ill health; **invalidity** (in-va-**lid**-i-tee) *noun.*
[Latin *invalidus* weak]

invalid[2] (in-**vall**-id) *adjective*
not valid.
Word Family **invalidly** *adverb;* **invalidate** *verb* to make invalid; **invalidation** (in-vall-i-**day**-sh'n) *noun;* **invalidity** (in-va-**lid**-i-tee) *noun.*

invaluable *adjective*
extremely useful.
Word Family **invaluably** *adverb.*

invariable (in-**vair**-i-a-b'l) *adjective*
not subject to variation.
Word Family **invariably** *adverb.*

invasion ⇨ INVADE.

invective (in-**vek**-tiv) *noun*
(*formal*) violent accusation or abuse.
[Latin *invectus* attacked]

inveigh (in-**vay**) *verb*
Phrase **inveigh against** (*formal*) to protest or attack vehemently in words.
[Latin *invehere* to attack]

inveigle (in-**vay**-g'l) *verb*
Phrase **inveigle someone into** to persuade someone to do something by flattery, trickery, etc.
[Old French *aveugler* to blind]

invent *verb*
to conceive of or devise first: *Who invented the telephone?*
Figurative He invented a clever excuse (= made up, thought of).
Word Family **invention** (in-**ven**-sh'n) *noun* 1 the act or process of inventing: *When was the invention of the telephone?*
2 something which has been invented or made: *His machine was hailed as the best invention of its type;* **inventor** *noun;* **inventive** *adjective* 1 skilful at inventing.
2 of or relating to invention; **inventively** *adverb;* **inventiveness** *noun.*
[Latin *inventus* discovered]

inventory (**in**-ven-tree) *noun* (*plural* **inventories**)
a list of articles with the description and quantity of each.
● **inventory** *verb* (**inventories; inventorying; inventoried**) to make an inventory of.

inverse (in-**verse**) *adjective*
(*formal*) being reversed in order, opposite in nature, etc.: *4321 is the inverse order of 1234.*
● **inverse** *noun* the reverse or opposite.
Word Family **inversely** *adverb.*

inverse proportion *noun* also **inverse ratio**
a ratio in which one quantity increases in proportion as the other decreases.

invert *verb*
1 to turn upside down or inside out.
2 to reverse the position, order or condition of.
Word Family **inversion** (in-**ver**-*zh*'n) *noun* 1 the act of inverting. 2 the state of being inverted.
[*in-*[1] + Latin *vertere* to turn]

invertebrate (in-**ver**-ti-brit) *noun*
any animal without a backbone, e.g. an insect or worm. Compare VERTEBRATE.

inverted commas ⇨ SPEECH MARKS.

invest *verb*
1 to use something, especially money, in order to gain profit.
Figurative Her parents have invested a lot of money in furniture for the new house (= spent).
2 to provide or endow: *A president is invested with great power.*
Word Family **investor** *noun* a person or group that invests.
[Old French *investir* to clothe]

investigate (in-**vest**-i-gate) *verb*
to examine or search into thoroughly, especially to discover facts, causes, etc.: *The police are investigating the murder.*
Word Family **investigation** (in-vest-i-**gay**-sh'n) *noun*; **investigative** (in-**vest**-ig-a-tive), **investigatory** *adjective*; **investigator** *noun* a person who investigates crimes, etc.
[Latin *investigare* to follow the trail]

investiture (in-**vest**-i-cher) *noun*
the act or ceremony of bestowing official authority or position on a person.

investment *noun*
1 the act of investing.
2 anything, especially money, which is invested: *They felt that buying the house was an investment for the future.*

inveterate (in-**vet**-a-rit) *adjective*
being firmly established in a habit or practice: *an inveterate smoker.*
[Latin *inveteratus*]

invidious (in-**vid**-i-us) *adjective*
likely to cause offence, dislike or resentment: *She tends to make invidious comparisons between the students.*
[Latin *invidiosus* envious]

invigilate (in-**vij**-a-late) *verb*
to keep watch, especially over students in an exam.
Word Family **invigilator** *noun.*

invigorate (in-**vigg**-a-rate) *verb*
to fill with vigour or energy.
Word Family **invigorating** *adjective*; **invigoratingly** *adverb.*

invincible (in-**vin**-sa-b'l) *adjective*
not able to be defeated or conquered.
Word Family **invincibly** *adverb*; **invincibility** (in-vin-sa-**bill**-i-tee) *noun.*
[*in-²* + Latin *vincere* to conquer]

inviolable (in-**vie**-a-la-b'l) *adjective*
(*formal*) not to be violated or harmed.
Word Family **inviolability** (in-vie-a-la-**bill**-i-tee) *noun*; **inviolably** *adverb.*

inviolate (in-**vie**-a-lit) *adjective*
(*formal*) kept sacred or unharmed.

invisible (in-**vizz**-i-b'l) *adjective*
not visible.
Word Family **invisibly** *adverb*; **invisibility** (in-vizz-i-**bill**-i-tee) *noun.*

invisible exports *plural noun*
Commerce services to customers abroad, such as banking, insurance and shipping, which earn foreign currency in the same way as exported goods.

invisible imports *plural noun*
Commerce services provided from abroad, such as banking, insurance and shipping.

invisible ink *noun*
an ink which remains invisible until the paper's surface is heated or treated in a particular way.

invitation (in-vi-**tay**-sh'n) *noun*
a written or spoken request for a person to come, take part, etc.
Figurative The deserted house was an open invitation to vandals (= attraction, encouragement).
[from Latin]

invite (in-**vite**) *verb*
1 to request, especially in a formal way.
2 (*formal*) to tend to encourage or produce: *Carelessness invites accidents.*
● **invite** (**in**-vite) *noun* (*informal*) an invitation.
Word Family **inviting** *adjective*; **invitingly** *adverb.*

in vitro fertilization (in-**vee**-troh fer-til-ize-**ay**-sh'n) *noun*
short form is **IVF** an infertility treatment involving the fertilization outside the body of eggs from a woman's ovary and their re-implantation into her womb.

invoice (**in**-voice) *noun*
a list of goods or a detailed bill sent to a purchaser.
● **invoice** *verb.*

invoke (in-**voke**) *verb*
to appeal or call for earnestly, especially to a god.
Word Family **invocation** (in-vo-**kay**-sh'n) *noun.*
[*in-¹* + Latin *vocare* to call]

involuntary (in-**voll**-un-tree) *adjective*
being done or occurring without conscious control or choice: *She gave an involuntary cry of surprise.*
Word Family **involuntarily** *adverb.*

involve (in-**volv**) *verb*
1 to have or include as a part or element: *This job will involve a lot of travelling.*
2 to draw into or get into a complicated or difficult situation: *She became involved in the argument without meaning to.*
Figurative She is very involved in social work (= engrossed, absorbed).
Phrase **be involved with** to be having a relationship with: *He is involved with a French girl.*
Word Family **involvement** *noun.*
[*in-*[1] + Latin *volvere* to roll]

invulnerable (in-**vul**-ner-a-b'l) *adjective*
not able to be hurt or damaged: *He seemed to think he was invulnerable.*
Word Family **invulnerability** (in-vul-ner-a-**bill**-i-tee) *noun.*

inward (**in**-wud) *adjective*
relating to or situated inside: *The plane began its inward curve from the sea towards the airport.*
Figurative He found an inward peace from yoga (= mental, spiritual).
Word Family **inwards, inward** *adverb*
1 towards the inside or centre: *The bedroom windows face inwards to the courtyard.*
2 towards the mind or self: *You must look inwards for the cause of your unhappiness;*
inwardly *adverb;* **inwardness** *noun.*

in-your-face *adjective*
(*informal*) direct and confrontational.

iodine (**eye**-a-deen) *noun*
a greyish-black solid non-metal widely used as an antiseptic and in photography. It is essential in the diet. ⇨ HALOGEN.
[Greek *iodes* like a violet]

ion (rhymes with lion) *noun*
Chemistry an atom or group of atoms which has become electrically charged by losing one or more electrons (a **positive ion**) or gaining one or more electrons (a **negative ion**).
Word Family **ionic** (eye-**on**-ik) *adjective;*
ionization (eye-on-eye-**zay**-sh'n) *noun* the formation of ions; **ionize, ionise** *verb;*
ionizer *noun* a device which improves the air quality in a room by producing ions.
[Greek, going]

ionosphere (eye-**on**-a-sfeer) *noun*
the outer layers of the earth's atmosphere where the density is so reduced that electrically charged particles can exist.

iota (eye-**oh**-ta) *noun*
a very small quantity.

[from *iota*, the ninth and smallest letter of the Greek alphabet, equal to the English letter *i*]

ipso facto *adverb*
(*formal*) by that very fact: *He is leader of the ruling political party and, ipso facto, Prime Minister.*
[Latin]

irascible (irr-**ass**-i-b'l) *adjective*
irritable or easily angered.
Word Family **irascibly** *adverb;*
irascibility (irr-ass-i-**bill**-i-tee) *noun.*
[Latin *irasci* to grow angry]

irate (eye-**rate**) *adjective*
full of rage or a sense of outrage.

ire *noun*
anger or rage.
[Latin *ira*]

iridescent (irr-i-**dess**-'nt) *adjective*
having or showing rainbow colours.
Word Family **iridescently** *adverb;*
iridescence *noun.*
[Greek *iridos* of a rainbow]

iris (**eye**-ris) *noun* (*plural* **irises**)
1 *Anatomy* the coloured circular part at the front of the eye, capable of contracting or expanding.
2 any of a group of plants with sword-shaped leaves and flowers of striking colours.
[Greek, rainbow]

irk *verb*
(*formal*) to annoy or weary: *It irked him to wait for so long at the airport.*
Word Family **irksome** *adjective.*

iron (**eye**-on) *noun*
1 a magnetic metal which rusts readily in moist air. It is widely used in tools and machines and is essential to form blood.
2 a metal appliance with a smooth flat bottom, usually heated by an electric element and used for pressing clothes, etc.
3 something made of or as if of iron: *a fire iron.* ⇨ *hearts of iron.*
4 *Golf* any iron-headed club, used mainly for short or high strokes and each numbered according to the angle of the head to the handle. Compare WOOD (definition 4).
5 (**irons**) the shackles of a prisoner.
Phrases **have other irons in the fire** to have more than one option available to one. **strike while the iron is hot** to seize or make the most of a good opportunity.
• **iron** *verb* to press or smooth with an iron.

Phrase **iron out** to settle, work out: *Let us try to iron out our differences.*
Word Family **ironing** *noun* **1** the process of using an iron to press clothes, etc. **2** any clothes, linen, etc. which need to be ironed.

Iron Age *noun*
a period in history following the Bronze Age, during which weapons and tools were first made of iron.

Iron Curtain *noun*
Politics the imaginary barrier formed by the borders of Russia and the Communist countries supporting it, separating them from the rest of Europe before 1989.

ironic (eye-**ron**-ik) *adjective* also **ironical**
1 of or containing irony: *an ironic smile.*
2 tending to use irony: *an ironic person.*
Word Family **ironically** *adverb.*

iron lung *noun*
a chamber for paralysed patients which encloses the chest and, by changing the pressure inside the chamber, causes movement of the chest wall, so breathing for the patient.

ironmonger *noun*
a person who sells domestic metal goods, such as saucepans and nails.
Word Family **ironmongery** *noun* (*plural* **ironmongeries**).

iron pyrites ⇨ PYRITES.

iron rations *plural noun*
any food or other rations kept for an emergency.

ironwork *noun*
any objects or parts made of iron, such as decorative railings, etc.

irony (**eye**-ra-nee) *noun* (*plural* **ironies**)
1 a mockingly humorous use of words in which the intended meaning is the opposite of what is actually said.
2 a situation which seems to mock reasonable hopes: *By an irony of fate he died just before he was going to alter his will in my favour.*
[Greek *eironeia* understatement or pretended ignorance]

irradiate (irr-**ay**-dee-ate) *verb*
1 to brighten or illuminate.
2 *Physics* to expose to radiation or particles of any kind.
3 to treat (food) with small doses of radiation to slow down the rotting process.
Word Family **irradiation** (irr-ay-dee-**ay**-sh'n) *noun.*

irrational (irr-**ash**-a-n'l) *adjective*
1 not having the ability to reason.
2 not based on logic or reason: *an irrational argument.*
3 *Maths* relating to a number which cannot be expressed as a ratio of two integers, e.g. √2. Compare RATIONAL (definition **3**).
Word Family **irrationally** *adverb*; **irrationality** (irr-ash-a-**nall**-i-tee) *noun.*

irreconcilable (irr-ek-on-**sile**-a-b'l) *adjective*
not able to be reconciled.
Word Family **irreconcilably** *adverb.*

irredeemable (irr-i-**deem**-a-b'l) *adjective*
not able to be restored or redeemed.
Word Family **irredeemably** *adverb.*

irrefutable (irr-i-**few**-ta-b'l) *adjective*
not able to be proved false.
Word Family **irrefutably** *adverb*; **irrefutability** (irr-i-few-ta-**bill**-i-tee) *noun.*

irregular (irr-**eg**-yoo-la) *adjective*
1 not regular: *an irregular road surface.*
☐ *Shift workers keep very irregular hours.*
2 *Grammar* of a verb whose changes of form for each tense do not follow general rules. For example, *bring* is an irregular verb. Compare REGULAR (definition **4**).
3 not permanent: *Irregular troops were called in to join the offensive.*
Word Family **irregularly** *adverb*; **irregularity** (irr-eg-yoo-**larr**-i-tee) *noun* (*plural* **irregularities**).

irrelevant (irr-**ell**-a-v'nt) *adjective*
not relevant.
Word Family **irrelevantly** *adverb*; **irrelevance** *noun.*

irreligious (irr-i-**lij**-us) *adjective*
not religious.

irremediable (irr-i-**mee**-di-a-b'l) *adjective*
not able to be remedied or repaired.

irreparable (irr-**ep**-'ra-b'l) *adjective*
not able to be repaired or made better.
Word Family **irreparably** *adverb.*

irreplaceable (irr-i-**place**-a-b'l) *adjective*
not able to be replaced.

irrepressible (irr-i-**press**-a-b'l) *adjective*
not able to be controlled or held back: *an irrepressible giggle.*
Word Family **irrepressibly** *adverb.*

irreproachable (irr-i-**proach**-a-b'l) *adjective*
free from blame or fault.
Word Family **irreproachably** *adverb.*

irresistible (irr-i-**zist**-a-b'l) *adjective*
not able to be resisted: *irresistible charm.*
Word Family **irresistibly** *adverb.*

irresolute (irr-**ezz**-a-loot) *adjective*
hesitant or lacking in resolve.
Word Family **irresolutely** *adverb;*
irresolution (irr-ezz-a-loo-sh'n) *noun.*

irrespective (irr-i-**spek**-tiv) *adjective*
not considering or taking into account:
*Irrespective of our parents' wishes we stayed
up very late.*

irresponsible (irr-i-**spon**-sa-b'l) *adjective*
not responsible.
Word Family **irresponsibly** *adverb;*
irresponsibility (irr-i-spon-sa-**bill**-i-tee)
noun.

irretrievable (irr-i-**treev**-a-b'l) *adjective*
not able to be retrieved or recovered.
Word Family **irretrievably** *adverb.*

irreverent (irr-**ev**-a-r'nt) *adjective*
not reverent or respectful.
Word Family **irreverently** *adverb;*
irreverence *noun.*

irreversible (irr-i-**vers**-a-b'l) *adjective*
not able to be reversed or changed.
Word Family **irreversibly** *adverb.*

irrevocable (irr-**ev**-a-ka-b'l) *adjective*
not able to be revoked or changed.
Word Family **irrevocably** *adverb.*

irrigate *verb*
1 to supply land with water by means of
artificial channels through the fields, etc.
2 *Medicine* to rinse or wash with a flow of
liquid over a wound, etc.
Word Family **irrigation** (irr-i-**gay**-sh'n)
noun.
[*ir*- + Latin *rigare* to wet]

irritable (**irr**-it-a-b'l) *adjective*
1 being easily made impatient, angry or
irritated.
2 *Biology* (of an organism) able to react to
a stimulus.
Word Family **irritably** *adverb;*
irritability (irr-it-a-**bill**-i-tee) *noun.*

irritable bowel syndrome *noun*
a condition involving diarrhoea,
constipation and abdominal pain.

irritant (**irr**-i-t'nt) *noun*
anything which irritates: *Her methodical
tidiness was a great irritant to him.*

irritate (**irr**-i-tate) *verb*
1 to cause impatience or anger.
2 to cause discomfort such as itching or
rubbing: *The new shampoo irritated her
scalp.*

3 *Biology* to stimulate an organism to some
action or function.
Word Family **irritating** *adjective;*
irritatingly *adverb;* **irritation** (irr-i-**tay**-
sh'n) *noun.*
[from Latin]

irruption (irr-**up**-sh'n) *noun*
(*formal*) a sudden bursting in or invasion.
[*ir*- + Latin *ruptus* burst apart]

is the third person singular present tense of
be.

Islam (**iz**-lahm) *noun*
1 the Muslim religion, based on belief in
one supreme God (Allah). Peace is
attained through willing obedience to
Allah's divine guidance.
2 all Muslim believers or their civilization.
Word Family **Islamic** (iz-**lah**-mik)
adjective.
[Arabic *islam* resignation or submission to
the will of God]

island (**eye**-lund) *noun*
1 a smallish piece of land completely
surrounded by water.
2 something which has the shape, etc. of
an island: *a traffic island.*
Word Family **islander** *noun* a native or
inhabitant of an island.

isle (ile) *noun*
a poetic word for an island, especially a
small one.

islet (**eye**-lit) *noun*
a poetic word for a small island.

ism (izm) *noun*
(*informal*) a distinctive theory or doctrine.

isn't *contraction*
a short form of **is not**: *Lunch isn't ready
yet.*

isobar (**eye**-so-bar) *noun*
a line on a map joining places of equal air
pressure.
[*iso*- + Greek *baros* weight]

isohyet (eye-so-**high**-it) *noun*
a line on a map joining places of equal
rainfall.
[*iso*- + Greek *hyetos* rain]

isolate (**eye**-so-late) *verb*
to separate or put apart from others.
Word Family **isolated** *adjective;*
isolation (eye-so-**lay**-sh'n) *noun.*
[from Italian from Latin *insula* island]

isometric (eye-so-**met**-rik) *adjective*
of or having equal measurements.
isometric drawing a system of drawing
three-dimensional objects.

Word Family isometrics *plural noun*
(*used with singular verb*) any physical
exercises for strengthening muscles by
tensing one set of muscles at a time;
isometrically *adverb*; **isometry** (eye-
somm-a-tree) *noun* an equality of
measurement.
[*iso-* + Greek *metron* measure]

isomorphic (eye-so-**mor**-fik) *adjective*
of or having the same shape.
[*iso-* + Greek *morphé* a shape]

isosceles (eye-**soss**-a-leez) *adjective*
(of a triangle) having two sides equal.
[*iso-* + Greek *skelos* a leg]

isotherm (eye-so-therm) *noun*
a line on a map joining places of equal
temperature.
Word Family isothermal (eye-so-
therm-'l) *adjective*; **isothermally** *adverb*.
[*iso-* + Greek *thermé* heat]

isotope (eye-so-tope) *noun*
Chemistry an atom which has a different
number of neutrons from other atoms of
the same element. The isotopes of an
element have identical chemical properties
and vary only in those physical properties
which are affected by the mass of the
atom, such as density.
[*iso-* + Greek *topos* place (in the periodic
table)]

issue (ish-oo *or* iss-yoo) *noun*
1 a matter to be discussed, decided or
given attention: *Let's consider the political
issues.*
2 the act of giving out, delivering or
distributing: *The issue of new banknotes will
begin in two weeks.*
3 anything produced, given out or
distributed, especially at one time: *This is
the first issue of the evening paper.*
4 (*formal*) the act of going or flowing out:
the issue of blood from a wound.
5 (*formal*) anything which comes or flows
out.
6 *Law* children of one's own: *The old man
died without issue.*
Phrase take issue to disagree or argue:
I must take issue with you on that point.
● **issue** *verb*
1 to put out, deliver or distribute: *A gale
warning has been issued.*
2 to discharge or cause to flow out.
3 to proceed or come as a result: *A deep
friendship issued from their first meeting.*

isthmus (iss-muss) *noun* (*plural*
isthmuses)
a narrow strip of land joining two larger
areas of land.
[Greek *isthmos* narrow passage, neck]

it *pronoun*
1 (*plural* **they**) the third person singular
nominative pronoun, used when gender is
not indicated: *That's a nice car. Is it yours?*
2 (*plural* **them**) the third person singular
objective pronoun, used when gender is
not indicated: *I ate it all.* ⇨ ITS.
3 used to refer to a group of words which
follows: *It is easier if you read the instructions
first.*
4 used to indicate the general situation or
something which will be understood from
the context: *How was it in Edinburgh?* □ *It is
7.00 a.m.*

italic (it-**all**-ik) *noun*
(*usually* **italics**) a style of printing with
sloping characters, used for emphasis, etc.:
This is italic. Compare ROMAN.
Word Family italicize, italicise *verb* to
print in italics.
[as first used in *Italy*]

itch *noun* (*plural* **itches**)
a feeling of irritation on the skin causing a
desire or need to scratch.
● **itch** *verb*
1 to be a place of irritation: *My back itches.*
2 to experience an itch: *He was itching all
over.*
Phrase be itching to do something
(*informal*) to be impatient to do
something.
Word Family itchy *adjective* (**itchier**;
itchiest) having an itch.

it'd *contraction*
1 a short form of **it would**: *It'd be better if
you went home.*
2 a short form of **it had**: *She said it'd been
raining earlier.*

item (eye-t'm) *noun*
a single or separate thing in a list or series:
There are some valuable items for sale. □ *an
important news item.*
Word Family itemize, itemise *verb* to
give or state every item of.
[Latin, also]

iterate (it-a-rate) *verb*
(*formal*) to repeat.
[Latin *iterum* a second time]

itinerant (it-**in**-a-r'nt) *adjective*
(*formal*) travelling from place to place.
● **itinerant** *noun* (*formal*) a person who
travels from place to place.
[Latin *itineris* of a journey]

itinerary (eye-**tin**-a-rar-ee) *noun* (*plural*
itineraries)
the route or plan of a journey.

it'll *contraction*
a short form of **it will**: *It'll never be the same again.*

its *possessive adjective* (*plural* **their**)
belonging to it: *Has the house got its own garden?*
• **its** *possessive pronoun* (*plural* **theirs**)
belonging to it.

> ! Note that there is no apostrophe in the possessive adjective and pronoun *its*, meaning 'belonging to it', as in *The dog wagged its tail.* Do not confuse *its* with the contraction *it's*, meaning 'it is', as in *It's too late* or 'it has', as in *It's been cold today.*

it's *contraction*
1 a short form of **it is**: *It's cold outside.*
2 a short form of **it has**: *It's been cold today.*

> ! Do not confuse *it's* with ITS.

itself *pronoun*
1 the reflexive form of **it**: *This machine switches itself off.*

2 the emphatic form of **it**: *The journey is difficult, though the distance itself is not very great.*
3 its normal or usual self: *The dog was not itself while its owners were away.*

I've *contraction*
a short form of **I have**: *I've brought you a present.*

ivory (**eye**-va-ree) *noun* (*plural* **ivories**)
1 the hard whitish substance forming the tusks of elephants.
2 any similar substance.
3 a creamy-white colour.
• **ivory** *adjective*.
[Latin *eboris* of ivory]

ivory tower *noun*
an attitude of remoteness, withdrawal or aloofness, especially in relation to everyday life.

ivy (**eye**-vee) *noun* (*plural* **ivies**)
1 an evergreen climbing plant with dark shiny leaves, often used as an ornamental covering for walls, etc.
2 any of various climbing plants.

Jj

jab *verb* (**jabs**; **jabbing**; **jabbed**)
to push sharply, as with the end or point of something.
• **jab** *noun*
1 a sharp prod with something.
2 (*informal*) an injection.

jabber *verb*
to chatter or talk nonsense.

jacaranda (jak-a-**ran**-da) *noun*
any group of tropical trees with bluish-purple flowers.

jack *noun*
1 any of various mechanical devices for raising heavy objects, e.g. that used to support a car while changing a tyre.
2 also called **knave**. *Cards* a playing card with a picture of a prince, usually ranking just below a queen.
3 (**jacks**) *Games* a children's game in which each player tosses and catches five small objects, or the objects used in this game.
4 *Electricity* a socket which accepts a plug at one end and attaches to circuitry at the other.
5 ⇨ BOWLS.
Phrases **every man jack** (*informal*) everyone. **jack of all trades** a person who is able to do many different types of work.
• **jack** *verb*
Phrases **jack in** (*informal*) to stop doing. **jack up** to raise or increase.

jackal *noun*
a wild dog of Africa and Asia, hunting in packs and feeding on carrion.

jackanapes *noun*
an old word meaning 'a conceited man'.

jackass *noun* (*plural* **jackasses**)
1 a male ass.
2 a very stupid person.

jackboot *noun*
1 *History* a long cavalry boot coming up to the thigh.

2 this as a symbol of oppression, dictatorship and especially military government.

jackdaw *noun*
a shiny black bird related to the crow, with a reputation for stealing bright objects.

jacket *noun*
1 a short coat reaching to the waist or hips.
2 any outer coat or covering around something, as for protection, etc.: *a book jacket*. □ *potatoes cooked in their jackets*.

jack-in-the-box *noun* (*plural* **jack-in-the-boxes**)
a toy with a figure on a spring which jumps out of a box when the lid is opened.

jackknife (**jak**-nife) *noun* (*plural* **jackknives**)
a large clasp knife.
• **jackknife** *verb* to fold or bend double like a jackknife.

jackpot *noun*
1 the largest prize in a competition.
2 any accumulated sum or fund, e.g. the stakes in a gambling game.
Phrase **hit the jackpot** (*informal*) to be very successful or lucky.

Jacobean (jak-a-**bee**-an) *adjective*
(of architecture, furniture, etc.) in the styles favoured in the first half of the 17th century.
[after *Jacobus* the Latin form of *James*, i.e. James I]

Jacobite (**jak**-a-bite) *noun*
History a Tory who, after the Revolution of 1688, still campaigned for the restoration of the exiled Stuarts.
[after *Jacobus* the Latin form of *James*, i.e. James II and James the Old Pretender]

Jacuzzi (ja-**koo**-zee) *noun*
(*trademark*) a type of bath or small pool containing a device which swirls the water around.

jade *noun*
1 either of two types of hard, usually green, fine-grained minerals, used as an ornamental stone or in jewellery.
2 a light bluish-green colour.

jaded *adjective*
tired or worn-out.

jag *noun*
(*informal*) a spree, especially a drinking spree.

jagged (**jagg**-id) *adjective*
sharp and ragged: *the jagged edges of broken glass*.

jaguar (jag-yoo-a) *noun*
a large flesh-eating mammal of the cat family which has a tawny coat with black patches, found in the forests of tropical America.

jail *noun* also **gaol**
a prison.
Word Family jail *verb*; jailer *noun*.

Jainism (jane-izm) *noun*
an ancient Indian religion which does not recognize a Supreme Being and whose first principle is harmlessness in thought and action towards all life. ⇨ AHIMSA.
Word Family Jainist *noun*, *adjective*.

jalopy (ja-lop-ee) *noun* (*plural* **jalopies**)
(*informal*) a decrepit old car.

jam¹ *verb* (**jams**; **jamming**; **jammed**)
1 to squeeze into a very tight position: *She jammed everything into her handbag.*
2 to become or make unable to move: *The window was jammed.*
3 to block: *The street was jammed with traffic.*
4 to apply suddenly or violently: *I jammed on the brakes.*
5 *Radio* to send out signals intended to interfere with other signals of the same frequency.
6 *Music* to improvise with others.
• **jam** *noun*
1 the state of being jammed or blocked: *a traffic jam.*
2 (*informal*) a difficult situation.

jam² *noun*
a spread made by boiling fruit with sugar until it thickens and sets.
Word Family jammy *adjective* (**jammier**; **jammiest**) **1** like jam or covered with jam. **2** (*informal*) lucky.

jamb (jam) *noun*
the upright frame of a door or window.
[French *jambe* leg]

jamboree *noun*
a large rally or gathering.

jam-packed *adjective*
(*informal*) extremely crowded.

jam session *noun*
Music an informal gathering of musicians for an impromptu performance.

jangle *verb*
to make or cause to make a harsh or discordant sound
Word Family jangle *noun*; jangly *adjective*.

janitor *noun*
a caretaker.

January *noun* (*plural* **Januaries**)
the first month of the year, before February.

> **January** is called after *Janus*, the Roman god whose head had two faces, one facing towards the front and the new year and the other towards the back and the previous year. He was also the god of doors, gates and beginnings, *janus* being the Latin for 'an archway'.

jape *noun*
an old word for a practical joke.

jar¹ *noun*
a wide-mouthed, usually cylindrical, glass or pottery container, often with an airtight lid.

jar² *verb* (**jars**; **jarring**; **jarred**)
1 to cause a jolt, shock or sudden movement to: *He was jarred by the fall.*
2 to have an unpleasant or irritating effect on: *Her laugh jarred on my nerves.*
• **jar** *noun* a shock or jolt.

jardinière (jar-din-yair) *noun*
an ornamental pot or container for plants.
[French, female gardener]

jargon *noun*
the language of a certain class or profession, usually little understood by others: *The article was full of computer jargon.*

jasmine (jaz-min) *noun*
a small shrub or climbing plant with fragrant, white, yellow or pink flowers.
[from Persian]

jasper *noun*
Geology a reddish opaque stone, used in ornaments.

jaundice (jawn-dis) *noun*
Medicine a yellow discoloration of the skin due to a build up of bile in the blood and tissues.
Word Family jaundiced *adjective*
1 having jaundice. **2** having embittered or distorted views, ideas, etc.
[French *jaune* yellow]

jaunt (jawnt) *noun*
a short journey, especially one taken for pleasure.
• **jaunt** *verb*.

jaunty (jawn-tee) *adjective* (**jauntier**; **jauntiest**)
having a sprightly or self-assured air.
Word Family jauntily *adverb*; jauntiness *noun*.

javelin (jav-lin) *noun*
1 a light spear, especially one thrown in competitions.
2 the athletics competition in which this is thrown.

jaw *noun*
1 *Anatomy* either of two bones of the head in which the teeth are set.
2 (**jaws**) something which has the shape or function of the jaws, such as parts in a machine which grasp or hold things.
• **jaw** *verb* (*informal*) to talk or gossip.

jay *noun*
any of various colourful noisy birds related to the crow.

jaywalk *verb*
to cross a road carelessly, ignoring traffic lights or pedestrian crossing signals.
Word Family **jaywalker** *noun*.

jazz *noun*
Music a style of music developed by black Americans, with a lot of improvising and syncopated rhythms.
• **jazz** *verb*
Phrase **jazz up** (*informal*) to make bright or lively.
Word Family **jazzy** *adjective* (**jazzier; jazziest**) (*informal*) very bright or showy.

jealous (jell-us) *adjective*
1 resentful or suspicious of a rival or of another's success, advantage, etc.: *Her jealous husband watches every move she makes.*
2 careful to protect or guard.
Word Family **jealously** *adverb*; **jealousy** *noun* (*plural* **jealousies**).
[Greek *zelos* zeal]

jeans *plural noun*
a pair of denim trousers.

Jeep *noun*
(*trademark*) a small military vehicle used for communication and liaison purposes.
[from G(eneral) P(urpose vehicle)]

jeer *verb*
to make rude remarks at: *The crowd jeered him.*
Word Family **jeer** *noun*; **jeering** *adjective*; **jeeringly** *adverb*.

jehad ⇨ JIHAD.

Jehovah (j'-ho-va) *noun*
Judaism, Christianity a name for God used in the Old Testament.

Jekyll and Hyde *noun*
a person who has two very different sides to his or her character.

[after a character in R. L. Stevenson's *The Strange Case of Dr Jekyll and Mr Hyde*, 1886]

jell *verb* also **gel**
1 to set or form a jelly.
2 to take definite shape: *After a lot of discussion their plan began to jell.*

jelly *noun* (*plural* **jellies**)
1 a soft but firm food made with gelatine or by boiling a liquid containing sugar until it sets.
2 anything with the consistency of jelly.
Word Family **jellied** *adjective* set in a jelly: *jellied eels.*

jellyfish *noun* (*plural* **jellyfish** or **jellyfishes**)
any soft jelly-like marine organism, usually with an umbrella-like body and long tentacles.

jemmy *noun* (*plural* **jemmies**)
a short crowbar.
• **jemmy** *verb* (**jemmies; jemmying; jemmied**) (*informal*) to force open with a jemmy.

jenny ⇨ SPINNING JENNY.

jeopardize, jeopardise (jep-a-dize) *verb*
to risk or endanger.
Word Family **jeopardy** (jep-a-dee) *noun* danger or peril.

jerk *noun*
1 a quick sharp or violent movement.
2 (*informal*) an ignorant or disagreeable person.
Word Family **jerk** *verb* to move or make move with a jerk or jerks; **jerky** *adjective* (**jerkier; jerkiest**) consisting of jerks; **jerkily** *adverb*; **jerkiness** *noun*.

jerkin *noun*
a short sleeveless jacket.

jerry-built *adjective*
badly or cheaply built.

jerrycan *noun* also **jerrican**
a flat-sided closed container for carrying liquids such as water or petrol.

jersey (jer-zee) *noun*
1 a knitted woollen pullover.
2 a general term for knitted fabrics.
[after *Jersey* in the Channel Islands, where knitting was an important industry]

Jerusalem artichoke *noun*
a type of sunflower with an edible underground stem.

jess *noun* (*plural* **jesses**)
a short strap fastened around the leg of a hawk and attached to a leash.

jest *verb*
to speak jokingly or playfully.
Word Family jest *noun* a joke; **jester**
noun a person who jokes, especially a
professional clown at a medieval court;
jesting *adjective*; **jestingly** *adverb*.

Jesuit (jez-yoo-it) *noun*
Roman Catholicism a member of the
religious order called the **Society of
Jesus**, founded by Ignatius Loyola in the
16th century.

Jesus ⇨ CHRIST.

jet¹ *noun*
1 an aeroplane which is operated by jet
propulsion.
2 a strong continuous stream of liquid or
gas forced out under pressure.
3 a spout or device which emits such a
stream: *a gas jet*.
• **jet** *verb* (**jets; jetting; jetted**)
1 to emit a jet of liquid or gas.
2 to travel by jet.

jet² *noun*
1 *Geology* a hard black coal which can
be highly polished for use in jewellery,
carving, etc.
2 also **jet black** a deep black colour.

jet lag *noun*
great tiredness and other symptoms
experienced by a person on a flight that
travels through time zones.
Word Family jet-lagged *adjective*.

jetsam *noun*
any articles thrown from a ship to lighten
it, found afloat or on the beach. Compare
FLOTSAM.

jet set *noun*
a rich social group, especially one which
meets in fashionable parts of the world.

Jet ski *noun*
(*trademark*) a machine rather like a
motorcycle that skims across water.
Word Family jet-ski *verb*; **jet-skier**
noun.

jettison *verb*
to discharge or throw overboard.

jetty *noun* (*plural* **jetties**)
a small pier.

Jew *noun*
a person whose religion is Judaism. The
term is also used to show ethnic origin
without reference to religious observance.
Word Family Jewish *adjective*; **Jewry**
(joo-ree) *noun* the Jewish people.

jewel *noun*
1 a precious stone, e.g. a diamond.

2 an ornament containing precious stones.
3 (*informal*) a valued person or possession.
Word Family jewelled *adjective* adorned
with jewels; **jeweller** *noun* a person who
makes or deals in jewels or jewellery.

jewellery *noun* (*American* **jewelry**)
decorations for the body containing
jewels, precious metals, etc., e.g. necklaces
and bracelets.

Jew's harp *noun*
a simple musical instrument, one end
of which is held in the mouth while the
fingers pluck the flexible metal tongue.

jib¹ *noun*
1 *Nautical* a small foresail.
2 the projecting arm of a crane.

jib² *verb* (**jibs; jibbed; jibbing**)
to show reluctance or unwillingness.

jibe¹ *verb* also **gibe**
to make rude remarks.
• **jibe** *noun*.

jibe² ⇨ GYBE.

jiffy *noun*
(*informal*) a very short time.

jig *noun*
a fast bouncing or irregular dance, or
the music for such a dance.
• **jig** *verb* (**jigs; jigging; jigged**)
1 to dance a jig.
2 to move in a quick or jerky manner,
especially up and down.

jiggle *verb*
to move up and down or to and fro with
quick short jerks.
• **jiggle** *noun*.

jigsaw *noun*
1 a puzzle in which flat irregularly shaped
pieces are fitted together to form a picture.
2 a saw with a narrow vertical blade, used
for cutting curves, etc.

jihad (ji-had) *noun* also **jehad**
1 *Islam* a personal individual struggle
against evil in the way of Allah.
2 *Islam* a collective defence of the Muslim
community.
[Arabic]

jilt *verb*
to reject or cast aside a lover one has
encouraged.

jingle *noun*
1 a tinkling sound, such as that made by a
bunch of keys.
2 a short verse or line used to attract
attention and be memorable, often based
on alliteration or rhyme and set to music,
e.g. for television advertisements.

Word Family **jingle** *verb* to make or cause to make a tinkling or clinking sound; **jingly** *adjective*.

jingoism (**jing**-go-izm) *noun*
an aggressive nationalism.
Word Family **jingoist** *noun*.

jinks *plural noun*
Phrase **high jinks** (*informal*) any pranks or boisterous merrymaking.

jinn *noun* (*plural* **jinn** or **jinns**) also **djinn**
a genie.
[Arabic]

jinx *noun* (*plural* **jinxes**)
a person or thing believed to bring bad luck.
Word Family **jinxed** *adjective* pursued by bad luck.

jitterbug *noun*
an energetic dance popular in the 1940s.

jitters *plural noun*
(*informal*) nervousness.
Word Family **jittery** *adjective* extremely nervous.

jiu-jitsu ⇨ JU-JITSU.

jive *noun*
a dance to jazz or other lively music, popular in the 1940s and 1950s.
• **jive** *verb*.

job *noun*
1 any work or task, especially when done for a fee or wage.
2 the result of a person's work: *She did a good job of fixing the car.*
3 (*informal*) a procedure: *a nose job.*
4 (*informal*) a robbery or other criminal act.
Phrases **a good job** (*informal*) fortunate: *The banks were closed so it's a good job you lent me some cash.* **jobs for the boys** positions granted to one's friends, political supporters, etc. **just the job** (*informal*) exactly what is needed. **make the best of a bad job** to do what one can even though the situation is unsatisfactory.
Word Family **jobbing** *adjective* employed to do individual jobs for people; **jobless** *adjective*; **joblessness** *noun*.

jobber *noun*
a dealer in stocks and shares who does business only with stockbrokers and not with the public.

jobcentre *noun*
in Britain, a government office that helps people to find jobs.

job lot *noun*
a miscellaneous collection of goods sold together.

job-share *verb*
to do part of a paid job: *This position would suit a working mother who wants to job-share.*
• **job-share** *noun*.

jobsworth (**jobz**-werth) *noun*
(*informal*) an employee or official who sticks rigidly to petty rules, no matter what the circumstances.
[short for 'it's more than my *job's worth*']

jockey *noun*
a person who rides racehorses, especially as a profession.
• **jockey** *verb*
to manoeuvre: *All the managers were jockeying for promotion.*

jockstrap *noun*
a close-fitting support for the male genitals.

jocose (jo-**kose**) *adjective*
playfully humorous.
Word Family **jocosely** *adverb*; **jocosity** (jo-**koss**-i-tee) *noun*.
[Latin *jocosus* full of jest]

jocular (**jok**-yoo-la) *adjective*
joking or humorous.
Word Family **jocularly** *adverb*; **jocularity** (jok-yoo-**lar**-ri-tee) *noun*.
[Latin *jocularis* laughable]

jocund (**jok**-und) *adjective*
(*formal*) cheerful or merry.
Word Family **jocundly** *adverb*; **jocundity** (jok-**un**-da-tee) *noun*.
[Latin *jucundus* pleasing]

jodhpurs (**jod**-perz) *plural noun*
a pair of trousers which are loose to the knees and then close-fitting to the ankle, worn when riding horses.
[after the Indian city of *Jodhpur*]

jog *verb* (jogs; jogging; jogged)
1 to run at a slow steady pace.
2 to shake with a push or nudge.
Figurative *This should jog your memory.*
Word Family **jog** *noun*; **jogger** *noun* a person who jogs.

joggle *verb*
to shake slightly.
• **joggle** *noun*.

john *noun*
1 (*informal, especially American*) a toilet.
2 (*informal*) the client of a prostitute.

John Bull *noun*
a person who is typically English.

[probably from *The History of John Bull*, a satire by John Arbuthnot published in 1712]

John Dory ⇨ DORY.

johnny-come-lately *noun*
(*informal*) a newcomer.

joie de vivre (*zh*wa de **veev**-ra) *noun*
a lively and spirited attitude to life.
[French, joy of living]

join *verb*
1 to bring, come or put together.
2 to become a member of: *We decided to join the club.*
3 to meet with: *We're over there – do come and join us.*
Phrases **join in** to take part in: *Come and join in the celebrations!* **join up** to enlist in the armed forces.
● **join** *noun* a place where something joins.

joiner *noun*
a carpenter who specializes in jointing timber together, as in doors and window frames.
Word Family **joinery** *noun* the work done or produced by a joiner.

joint *noun*
1 a place where two or more parts or objects join: *arthritis in her knee joints.*
2 a cut of meat, especially one for roasting.
3 (*informal*) also called **reefer**. a cigarette containing cannabis, usually mixed with tobacco.
4 (*informal*) a club, bistro, etc., usually a disreputable one.
● **joint** *adjective* shared by or common to two or more: *The President and the Prime Minister issued a joint statement.*
Word Family **joint** *verb* 1 to unite with a joint or joints. 2 to divide into separate pieces, especially by cutting at the joints.
jointly *adverb.*

joist *noun*
a horizontal wooden or metal beam, used as a support for a floor or ceiling.

jojoba (ho-**hoh**-ba) *noun*
a shrub of the box family whose seeds give an oil that is used as a lubricant and in cosmetics.
[Mexican Spanish]

joke *noun*
1 something which is said or done to cause laughter or amusement.
2 (*informal*) a person or thing that is amusing or ridiculous.
Word Family **joke** *verb*; **joking** *adjective*; **jokingly** *adverb.*
[Latin]

joker *noun*
1 a person who plays jokes.
2 *Cards* an extra playing card in a pack, used as the highest card or with its value chosen by the player.
3 (*informal*) a foolish person.
Phrase **the joker in the pack** someone or something whose behaviour cannot be predicted.

jolly *adjective* (**jollier; jolliest**)
(*dated*) cheerful, amusing or pleasant.
● **jolly** *verb* (**jollies; jollying; jollied**)
Phrase **jolly someone along** to encourage someone to be cheerful.
● **jolly** *adverb* (*dated informal*) very: *Jolly good!*
Word Family **jolliness, jollity** (joll-a-tee) *noun* 1 lively and cheerful activity. 2 being jolly; **jollily** *adverb*; **jollification** *noun* merrymaking.

jolt *verb*
to move or shake jerkily or roughly: *The cart jolted over the bumpy track.*
● **jolt** *noun*

josh *verb*
(*informal*) to tease.

joss stick *noun*
a stick of incense used in worship by the Chinese.

jostle (joss-'l) *verb*
(of a person) to push or knock against roughly: *The crowd jostled him.*

jot *verb* (**jots; jotted; jotting**)
to write down briefly or quickly.
Word Family **jot** *noun* a small amount; **jotting** *noun* a brief note; **jotter** *noun* a small paper pad for making notes.

joule (jool) *noun*
Physics the SI unit of work and energy. abbrev. **J**.
[after *J. P. Joule*, 1818-1889, a British physicist]

journal (**jer**-n'l) *noun*
1 a daily record or diary, e.g. of financial transactions.
2 a periodical or magazine: *academic journals.*
[Latin *diurnus* by day]

journalism (**jern**-a-lizm) *noun*
the work of writing, editing or publishing newspapers, magazines, etc.
Word Family **journalist** *noun*;
journalistic (jern-'l-**ist**-ik) *adjective.*

journey (**jer**-nee) *noun*
1 a trip, especially by land.
2 the distance travelled in a certain time: *The mine is a day's journey from here.*
● **journey** *verb.*

joust (jowst) *noun*
Medieval history a competition between knights, on horseback and armed with lances.
• **joust** *verb*.

jovial *adjective*
merry and friendly or pleasant.
Word Family **jovially** *adverb*; **joviality** (jo-vee-**al**-i-tee) *noun*.

jowl (*rhymes with* foul) *noun*
the lower part of the cheek, especially when fleshy and sagging.

joy *noun*
1 a feeling or state of happiness or great pleasure.
2 anything which causes such a feeling.
Word Family **joyful, joyous** *adjective* full of joy or pleasure; **joyfully, joyously** *adverb*; **joyless** *adjective* dismal.

joyride *noun*
1 (*informal*) a fast drive in a stolen vehicle.
2 (*informal*) a pleasure ride.
Word Family **joyrider** *noun*; **joyriding** *noun*.

joystick *noun*
1 (*informal*) the pilot's control stick in an aircraft.
2 (*informal*) a handle for controlling how images move on a computer screen.

jubilant (**joob**-i-l'nt) *adjective*
expressing joy or exultation.
Word Family **jubilation** (joo-bi-**lay**-sh'n) *noun* great joy and excitement; **jubilantly** *adverb*.
[Latin *jubilans* shouting for joy]

jubilee (joo-bi-lee) *noun*
an anniversary or celebration.
[Hebrew *yobal* ram's horn (blown in a jubilee year)]

Judaism (joo-day-izm) *noun*
the religion of the Jews, deriving its authority and principles from the Old Testament, based on a belief in one supreme God.
Word Family **Judaic** (joo-**day**-ik) *adjective*.

judder *verb*
to shake heavily: *The truck juddered to a halt.*
• **judder** *noun*.

judge (juj) *noun*
1 a public officer appointed to settle disputes and administer legal justice.
2 a person appointed to decide in a competition or dispute.
3 a person qualified to give an opinion: *She is a good judge of horses.*

• **judge** *verb*
1 to hear and decide a case in a court of law.
2 to decide officially about: *He's judging at the dog show this year.*
3 to form or hold an opinion: *I can't really judge without knowing all the facts.*
[from Latin *jus* law + *dicere* to say]

judgement, judgment (**juj**-m'nt) *noun*
1 the ability to judge wisely.
2 an opinion or estimation.
3 the decision of a judge concerning the matter in dispute.

judicature (**joo**-dik-a-cher) *noun*
1 *Law* the administration of justice.
2 *Law* the system of courts and their judges.

judicial (joo-**dish**-'l) *adjective*
relating to a judge or justice.
Word Family **judicially** *adverb*.

judiciary (joo-**dish**-a-ree) *noun* (*plural* **judiciaries**)
1 the branch of government dealing with justice.
2 *Law* the system of courts and judges in a country.

judicious (joo-**dish**-us) *adjective*
sensible or discreet.
Word Family **judiciously** *adverb*; **judiciousness** *noun*.

judo (**joo**-doe) *noun*
a method of self-defence based on ju-jitsu, often used as a form of physical training.
[Japanese *ju* gentle + *do* way of life]

jug *noun*
1 a container with a spout and a handle, for holding or serving liquids.
2 an old word for a prison.
• **jug** *verb* (**jugs; jugging; jugged**)
to stew meat, especially hare or rabbit, in a casserole.

juggernaut (**jug**-a-nawt) *noun*
1 a huge lorry.
2 any large destructive force, especially one which attracts worship.
[after *Jagannath*, lord of the world, an enormous idol of the Hindu deity Krishna]

juggle *verb*
1 to toss and catch several objects in the air in a sequence, in order to keep them in continuous motion.
Figurative *I'll have to juggle the dates in my diary to fit you in.*
2 to alter dishonestly: *The boss was sent to prison for juggling the accounts.*

Word Family **juggler** *noun* a person who juggles, especially an entertainer.

jugular vein (jug-yoo-la **vane**) *noun* also **jugular**
the main vein of the neck.
[Latin *jugulum* the throat]

juice (*rhymes with* loose) *noun*
1 the liquid part of vegetables, fruit or meat.
2 the fluid in the organs of the body: *The gastric juices aid digestion.*
3 (*informal*) petrol, fuel or electric power.
Word Family **juicy** *adjective* (**juicier; juiciest**) 1 full of juice. 2 (*informal*) (of gossip) interesting; **juicily** *adverb*; **juiciness** *noun*.

ju-jitsu (joo-**jit**-soo) *noun* also **jiu-jitsu**
a Japanese method of self-defence without weapons, in which set techniques of balancing and leverage are used to overcome the opponent's strength, and from which karate and judo are derived.

jukebox *noun* (*plural* **jukeboxes**)
a machine in a café or pub that plays one of a selection of records when a coin is put in.

julep (**joo**-lep) *noun*
a sweet drink, especially one in which medicine is taken.

July (joo-**lie**) *noun*
the seventh month of the year, after June and before August.
[after the Roman statesman *Julius Caesar*, who was born in this month]

jumble *noun*
1 a state of confusion.
2 an assortment of articles of little value.
● **jumble** *verb* to confuse.

jumble sale *noun*
a sale of cheap assorted articles, often to aid charity.

jumbo *noun*
1 an affectionate name for an elephant.
2 also **jumbo jet** a very large aircraft.

jump *verb*
1 to move off the ground or some other surface by a sudden muscular effort of the legs: *The frog suddenly jumped.*
2 to go over by jumping: *Her horse jumped the wall.*
3 to move quickly: *We jumped into a taxi.*
4 to make a sudden surprised movement: *A bell suddenly rang and they all jumped.*
5 to increase sharply: *Her rent jumped from £50 a week to £80.*
6 (*informal*) to attack physically, taking the victim by surprise.

Phrases **jump at** to accept with enthusiasm: *He jumped at the chance to show his skills.* **jump on** (*informal*) to scold or reprimand. **jump the lights** to go through red traffic lights illegally. **jump to it!** (*informal*) hurry up!
Word Family **jump** *noun*; **jumpy** *adjective* (**jumpier; jumpiest**) nervous; **jumpily** *adverb*; **jumpiness** *noun*.

jumped-up *adjective*
(*informal*) conceited.

jumper[1] *noun*
a person or thing that jumps.

jumper[2] *noun* also called **pullover**; **sweater**.
a knitted piece of clothing worn on the upper part of the body for warmth.

jump jet *noun*
a plane that takes off vertically straight into the air.

jump lead *noun* also **jump leads** *plural noun*
a pair of wires for connecting a car battery to the engine of another car to restart it.

jump-off *noun*
Showjumping a final round to decide the winner of a competition.

jump-start *verb*
to start a car using a jump lead.
● **jump-start** *noun*.

jumpsuit *noun*
a piece of clothing consisting of trousers and a top in one piece, usually with long sleeves.

jumpy ⇨ JUMP.

junction (**junk**-sh'n) *noun*
1 a place where several things, such as roads, join or meet.
2 the act of joining.
3 the state of being joined.
[Latin *junctus* yoked]

junction box *noun* (*plural* **junction boxes**)
a box in which several electric circuits are connected.

juncture (**junk**-cher) *noun*
1 a point of time, especially a turning point or crisis.
2 a joint.

June *noun*
the sixth month of the year, after May and before July.
[after the Roman goddess *Juno*]

jungle *noun*
1 a dense tropical rainforest.
2 any wild or overgrown land.
[Hindi, from Sanskrit *jangala* dry]

junior *adjective*
1 younger.
2 lower in rank, etc.: *a junior member of staff*.
3 (**Junior**) used by the son when father and son have the same name.
● **junior** *noun*
1 a person who is younger than another: *She is my junior by three years.*
2 a person of lower rank.
[Latin, younger]

junior school *noun*
a primary school, especially one forming part of a larger school.

juniper (joo-nip-er) *noun*
an evergreen shrub producing purple berries which are used in cooking, medicine and making gin.

junk¹ *noun*
1 any discarded or worthless objects.
2 (*informal*) heroin.
● **junk** *verb* (*informal*) to throw away.

junk² *noun*
a Chinese flat-bottomed ship with a high stern and sails.

junket *noun*
1 a sweet thick food made by curdling milk with rennet.
2 (*informal*) an expensive trip, especially one that is paid for using public money.

junk food *noun*
food with little nutritional value.

junkie (junk-ee) *noun* also **junky** (*plural* **junkies**)
(*informal*) a drug addict.

junk mail *noun*
unsolicited mail of an unimportant nature, usually advertising circulars.

junta (jun-ta *or* hoon-ta) *noun*
a political group, usually of military officers, which has gained its power by force, e.g. after a revolution.

Jupiter (joo-pit-er) *noun*
Astronomy the largest planet in the solar system, the one fifth from the sun.
[after the chief Roman god *Jupiter*]

juridical (joo-rid-i-k'l) *adjective*
of or relating to the administration of justice.

jurisdiction (joor-is-dik-sh'n) *noun*
1 power or authority: *Your boss has no jurisdiction over your personal life.*
2 the range or area of control or authority: *Such matters are not in our jurisdiction.*

jurist (joor-ist) *noun*
a person who practises or is skilled in law.

juror (joor-a) *noun*
a member of a jury.

jury (joor-ee) *noun* (*plural* **juries**)
1 a group of people summoned to hear a legal case in court and give a verdict.
2 a group of people chosen to judge a competition, etc.
Phrase **the jury is out** no decision has yet been reached.
[Latin *juratus* having taken an oath]

just *adjective*
1 fair or impartial: *a just decision.*
2 morally proper or reasonable: *I do not want vengeance, only what is just.*
● **just** *adverb*
1 not long ago: *They have just left.*
2 by a small amount: *We just won.*
3 only: *She is just a child.*
4 exactly: *That is just the point.*
Word Family **justly** *adverb* 1 honestly or fairly. 2 accurately; **justness** *noun*.
[Latin]

justice (just-iss) *noun*
1 the quality of being just or fair.
2 the principle of fair treatment or conduct.
3 the administration of the law.
4 (**Justice of the Peace**) a judge or magistrate.
Phrase **do oneself justice** to do as well as one is capable of doing: *I'm afraid you didn't do yourself justice in your English exam.*

justify (just-i-fie) *verb* (**justifies; justifying; justified**)
to show or prove something to be just or right: *Can you justify your accusation?*
Word Family **justification** (just-if-i-kay-sh'n) *noun*; **justifiable** (just-i-fie-a-b'l) *adjective* able to be justified or defended; **justifiably** *adverb*.

jut *verb* (**juts; jutting; jutted**)
to stick out or protrude.

jute *noun*
a strong fibre made from an Asian plant, used to make rope, sacks, etc.
[Sanskrit *juta* braid of hair]

juvenile (joov-a-nile) *adjective*
1 of or for young people: *a juvenile court.*
2 childish or immature: *juvenile behaviour.*
Word Family **juvenile** *noun* a child or young person; **juvenilely** *adverb*.
[Latin]

juxtapose (juk-sta-poze) *verb*
to place next to or side by side.
Word Family **juxtaposition** (juk-sta-po-zish-'n) *noun*.
[Latin *juxta* nearby + *positus* placed]

Kk

kaftan *noun* also **caftan**
a long loose piece of clothing with wide
sleeves.

Kaiser (*rhymes with* wiser) *noun*
History an emperor in Austria (1804-
1918) or Germany (1871-1918).
[after *Caesar* Octavianus Augustus, the
first Roman Emperor]

kale *noun*
a variety of cabbage, the leaves of which do
not form a head.

kaleidoscope (ka-**lie**-da-skope) *noun*
a tube lined with mirrors, containing loose
pieces of coloured glass which are
reflected as changing symmetrical patterns
when the tube is rotated.
Word Family **kaleidoscopic** (ka-lie-da-
skop-ik) *adjective* **1** relating to a
kaleidoscope. **2** very intricate or complex.
[Greek *kalos* beautiful + *eidos* image +
skopein to look at]

kamikaze (kam-i-**kah**-zi) *noun*
any member of a Japanese air-force corps
in the Second World War who crashed
their aircraft into enemy targets.
[Japanese, divine wind]

kangaroo *noun*
an Australian grazing marsupial growing
up to about 2 m high, with powerful hind
legs for leaping and a heavy tail.
[Aboriginal]

kangaroo court *noun*
(*informal*) a court or trial conducted
without regard for legal procedure.

kapok (**kay**-pok) *noun*
the soft silky fibre surrounding the seeds
of a tropical tree, used for stuffing pillows.
[Malay]

kaput (ka-**put**) *adjective*
(*informal*) broken.

karaoke (kar-i-o-ki) *noun*
an entertainment in bars or nightclubs in
which people take it in turns to sing along
with a pre-recorded backing track of a
popular song.
[Japanese, empty orchestra]

karate (ka-**rah**-tee) *noun*
a method of self-defence developed
in Japan, in which the hands, elbows,
feet and knees are the only weapons
used.
[Japanese, empty hand]

karma *noun*
Buddhism, Hinduism the effect of a
person's deeds during life on his or her
status or position in a later incarnation.
[Sanskrit, action, fate]

kart *noun*
a wheeled frame fitted with a small engine,
in which young people compete at high
speeds.
Word Family **karting** *noun* racing in
karts.

kayak (**kie**-ak) *noun*
1 an Eskimo hunting boat.
2 a lightweight canoe with a small opening
for the occupant.

kebab (ki-**bab**) *noun*
1 ⇨ SHISH KEBAB.
2 any of various dishes containing grilled
or roasted meat, e.g. a doner kebab.

kedgeree (**kej**-a-ree) *noun*
a dish of flaked fish, egg and rice.
[Hindi]

keel *noun*
1 the lowest supporting structure of a
boat, running lengthwise along the
bottom.
2 a fixed or movable wooden board or
metal plate in a sailing-boat's bottom
which reduces leeway.
Phrase **on an even keel** in a steady or
balanced manner.
• **keel** *verb*
Phrase **keel over** (*informal*) to collapse
suddenly.

keelhaul *verb*
History to drag a man by ropes under a
ship's keel as a form of punishment.

keen *adjective*
1 enthusiastic: *a keen football player.*
2 sharp: *a keen blade.* □ *a keen wind.*
Phrase **be keen on** to be attracted to or
interested in: *I'm not too keen on cats.*
Word Family **keenly** *adverb*; **keenness**
noun.

keep *verb* (**keeps**; **keeping**; **kept**)
1 to have or continue to have possession
of: *I kept the ring for years.*
2 to look after: *My dad keeps pigeons.*
3 to continue being or doing something:
You should keep doing the exercises. □ *He kept
dreaming about the accident.*

4 (of food or drink) to stay fresh.
5 to be faithful to: *She never keeps her promises.*
6 to make entries in: *I've always kept a diary.*
7 to make late: *But I mustn't keep you – I'm sure you're busy.*
Phrases **keep back** to withhold. **keep from** to stop oneself doing something: *We could hardly keep from laughing.* **keep in with** to make an effort to remain on friendly terms with. **keep on** to continue doing. **keep on about** to talk constantly about. **keep on at** to irritate by constantly asking for something. **keep something from** to ensure that something remains secret from. **keep something up** to continue doing something. **keep to 1** to stay on: *Keep to the path.* **2** to obey: *You must keep to our agreement.* **keep to oneself** to stay alone or aloof from others. **keep up with** to remain at the same pace as. **keep up with the Joneses** to strive to maintain a standard of living at least as high as one's neighbours, often for snobbish reasons.
● **keep** *noun*
1 the things necessary for daily life, such as food, heating, etc.: *I insist on paying for my keep.*
2 the strongest building or central tower of a castle.
Phrase **for keeps** (*informal*) for ever.

keeper *noun*
any person who guards or defends: *a keeper at the zoo.* □ *The goalkeeper saved the ball.*

keep-fit *noun*
the activity of doing exercises in order to stay fit and healthy: *a keep-fit class.*

keeping *noun*
Phrases **in keeping with, out of keeping with** in, or not in, harmony or agreement with. **in someone's keeping** in the care of someone: *I'm leaving my papers in your keeping.*

keepsake *noun*
anything given or kept in memory of a particular person or event.

keg *noun*
a small barrel.

kelp *noun*
any of a group of very large brown seaweeds.

kelvin *noun*
the base SI unit of temperature, equal to 1° Celsius. *abbrev.* K.

Kelvin *adjective*
of or relating to a scale of temperature which starts at absolute zero (–273·15°C), so 0°C = 273·15 K.
[after *Lord Kelvin*, 1824-1907, a British physicist and mathematician]

ken *noun*
Phrase **beyond one's ken** outside one's range of sight, knowledge, etc.
● **ken** *verb* to know.
[Scottish; to know]

kendo (**ken**-doe) *noun*
a Japanese form of fencing using wood staves.

kennel *noun*
1 a house for a dog.
2 (**kennels**) (*used with singular or plural verb*) a place where dogs are kept or bred.
● **kennel** *verb* (**kennels; kennelling; kennelled**) to put or keep in a kennel.

kenning *noun*
a compound expression used in Old English and Old Norse poetry to refer to something without using its name, e.g. *mousecatcher* for *cat*.
[Old Norse *kenna* to know]

kept the past tense and past participle of **keep.**

kerb *noun* (*American* **curb**)
the raised stone or concrete edge between a footpath and a road.

> **!** Do not confuse *kerb* with CURB.

kerb-crawl *verb*
to drive slowly trying to pick up a prostitute.
Word Family **kerb-crawler** *noun.*

kerchief (**ker**-chif) *noun*
a scarf or piece of cloth, worn on the head or around the neck.

kernel (**ker**-n'l) *noun*
1 the softer, usually edible, part contained in the shell of a nut or the stone of a fruit.
2 the entire contents of a seed or grain within its coating.
3 the central or important part of something.

kerosene (**kerr**-a-seen) *noun* also **kerosine**
paraffin.
[Greek *keros* wax]

kestrel *noun*
a small falcon which hovers in the air over an animal which it is about to catch.

ketch *noun* (*plural* **ketches**)
a small two-masted yacht.

ketchup *noun* also **catchup**
a spicy tomato sauce.

The word **ketchup** is Chinese in
origin. *Koechiap* meant 'fish brine' in
the Amoy dialect of south-eastern
China, *koe* meaning 'seafood' and *chiap*
'sauce'. Originally spelt *catchup*, it came
into English probably via Malay *kichap*
in the late 17th century, later becoming
catsup and then *ketchup*. The spelling
catsup is still found in America.

kettle *noun*
a container with a spout and a lid, in
which water is boiled.
Phrase **kettle of fish** (*informal*) an issue
or a situation.

kettledrum *noun*
a large bowl-shaped drum.

key¹ (kee) *noun*
1 a metal device which is cut or shaped to
fit into and turn the mechanism of a lock,
wind a clock, etc.
2 a button or lever pressed to work
something, such as a piano, computer, etc.
3 an explanation of symbols,
abbreviations, etc., on a map.
4 an answer or a means of understanding
something: *I think that is the key to her
personality.*
5 *Music* a scale of notes related to each
other and to one basic note (the tonic,
keynote or doh).
• **key** *adjective* extremely important or
most important: *She holds a key position in
the government.*
• **key** *verb* also **key in** to enter into a
computer using the keyboard: *I'll key the
new data in tonight.*
Word Family **keyed-up** *adjective* highly
tense or excited.

key² *noun*
an island or reef: *the Florida Keys.*

keyboard *noun*
1 a group or line of keys to be pressed, e.g.
on a piano or computer.
2 an electronic musical instrument.

keyhole *noun*
a hole in a lock into which the key is put.

keyhole surgery *noun*
a kind of surgery carried out through a
very small incision using fibre-optic tubes
and therefore causing much less
discomfort and trauma to patients.

keynote *noun*
1 the main theme.
2 *Music* the lowest or tonic note, on which
a musical scale is based.

• **keynote** *adjective* (of a speech)
expressing the main theme of someone's
thinking or policies.

keypad *noun*
a small panel with buttons for operating an
electric calculator, television, etc.

key ring *noun*
a ring for holding keys together.

key signature *noun*
Music a combination of sharps or flats
shown at the left-hand side of the staff to
indicate the key.

key stage *noun*
any of the four stages of the national
curriculum.

keystone *noun*
the middle stone of an arch, which holds it
together.

keystroke *noun*
a single instance of pressing a key on a
computer keyboard.

khaki (**kah**-kee) *noun*
1 a dull yellowish-brown colour.
2 a strong cotton or wool fabric of this
colour, used for uniforms, etc.
• **khaki** *adjective.*
[Urdu, dust-coloured]

Khalsa (**kull**-sa) *noun*
the Sikh community.
[Urdu from Arabic, pure]

khazi *noun* (*plural* **khazies**)
(*dated informal*) a toilet.

kibbutz (ki-**buts**) *noun* (*plural* **kibbutzim**)
a communal farming settlement in Israel.
Word Family **kibbutznik** *noun* a person
living and working on a kibbutz.
[Hebrew, gathering]

kick *verb*
1 to strike with the foot: *He kicked the ball.*
2 to score by a kick.
3 to recoil, as a gun does after firing.
4 (*informal*) to stop a bad habit.
Phrases **kick about**, **kick around**
(*informal*) 1 to discuss and consider: *We
kicked a few ideas around.* 2 to remain
unused and neglected: *There's a screwdriver
kicking about somewhere.* 3 (of a person) to
drift from one place to another. **kick in** to
begin to be active. **kick off** to start a game
of football. **kick out** (*informal*) to get rid
of or dismiss. **kick someone upstairs**
(*informal*) to promote an unsuccessful
person to a position where he or she will
do less harm. **kick up** to cause (trouble).
• **kick** *noun*
1 the act of kicking.

2 (*informal*) a pleasant or stimulating sensation: *This home-made wine really has a kick in it.*
Phrase **for kicks** (*informal*) for a thrill.

kickback *noun*
(*informal*) any money paid to a person in exchange for a favour, especially as a bribe.

kick-off *noun*
a kick that starts a football match.

kick-start *verb*
to start using a sudden push down on a pedal: *She kick-started her motorbike.*
● **kick-start** *noun*.

kid¹ *noun*
1 a young goat.
2 a leather made from the skin of a young goat.
3 (*informal*) a child or young person.

kid² *verb* (**kids; kidding; kidded**)
to tease.

kid gloves *plural noun*
gloves made of kid leather.
Phrase **handle someone with kid gloves** to treat someone very gently or tactfully.

kidnap *verb* (**kidnaps; kidnapping; kidnapped**)
to take away a person illegally by force, usually with a demand for money in exchange for his or her release. Compare ABDUCT.
Word Family **kidnapper** *noun*.

kidney (**kid**-nee) *noun*
Anatomy either of two organs in the abdomen which remove waste products from the blood and excrete urine.

kidney bean *noun*
the dwarf French bean or haricot bean.

kidney dish *noun* (*plural* **kidney dishes**)
a kidney-shaped container used in medicine.

kidney machine *noun*
a machine that performs the function of the kidneys for people whose kidneys do not work.

kidney stone *noun*
a hard mass that forms in the kidneys.

kill *verb*
1 to deprive of life: *Smoking can kill.*
2 to deprive of life deliberately: *He killed the snake with an axe.*
3 to damage or destroy: *My new shoes are killing me!*
4 to pass time: *We had an hour to kill before the plane left.*

Word Family **kill** *noun* **1** the act of killing. **2** something which is killed; **killer** *noun*.

killer whale *noun*
a large toothed black and white whale that lives in groups.

killing *noun*
the act of deliberately depriving a person, etc. of life.
Phrase **make a killing** (*informal*) to get or win a very large amount of money.

killjoy *noun*
a person who deliberately spoils the enjoyment of others.

kiln *noun*
an oven for drying or baking bricks, lime and pottery.

kilobyte (**kill**-o-bite) *noun*
Computers a unit of computer data or storage space equal to 1024 bytes. *abbrev.* Kb; KB.

kilocalorie (**kill**-o-kall-a-ree) *noun*
a unit of energy equivalent to 1000 calories.

kilogram (**kill**-o-gram) *noun* also **kilo** (**kee**-lo); **kilogramme**
the base SI unit of mass, equal to 1000 g or about 2·2 lb. *abbrev.* kg.

kilometre (**kill**-a-meet-a *or* kill-**om**-it-a) *noun* (*American* **kilometer**)
a unit of length equal to 1000 m or about 0·62 mile. *abbrev.* km.

kiloton (**kill**-o-tun) *noun*
a unit for measuring the explosive force of a nuclear weapon by comparing it to the mass of trinitrotoluene (TNT) which would produce the same explosion. A 20-kiloton atomic bomb would have the same explosive force as 20 000 metric tons of TNT. Compare MEGATON.

kilowatt (**kill**-o-wot) *noun*
1000 watts. *abbrev.* kW.

kilt *noun*
a short skirt, usually of tartan wool, pleated with broad vertical folds, worn by Scottish Highlanders.

kimono (ki-**mo**-no) *noun*
1 a woman's long robe with wide sleeves, fastened with a sash, worn in Japan.
2 a loose dressing gown.

kin *plural noun*
a person's relatives.
Word Family **kinless** *adjective*.

kind¹ *adjective*
considerate, friendly or generous.

Word Family kindly adjective (**kindlier; kindliest**) (dated) kind: her kindly smile; **kindly** adverb 1 in a kind way. 2 please: Kindly move along the carriage; **kindness** noun 1 the quality of being kind. 2 (plural **kindnesses**) a kind act.

kind² noun
a class or category of similar or related things: What kind of jam is this?
Phrases in kind 1 in the same way: We took revenge in kind. 2 in goods rather than money. **kind of** (informal) rather: I was kind of glad.

kindergarten (kin-da-gar-t'n) noun also called **nursery school**.
a school for children under the age of five.
[German Kinder children + Garten garden]

kind-hearted adjective
kind, sympathetic.
Word Family kind-heartedly adverb; **kind-heartedness** noun.

kindle (kin-d'l) verb
1 to start and stimulate a flame in such a manner as to develop larger flames.
2 to excite or rouse: The idea kindled her enthusiasm.

kindling (kin-dling) noun
any material, usually small pieces of wood, used to start a fire.

kindred (kin-drid) plural noun also **kinsfolk**
a person's living relatives.
• **kindred** adjective
having similar or related qualities, views, etc.

kinetic (kin-et-ik) adjective
of or relating to motion.
[Greek kinetikos moving]

kinetic energy noun
Physics the energy a body possesses because it is moving. Compare POTENTIAL ENERGY.

king noun
1 a male ruler of a country, usually inheriting his position.
2 a person or thing having great power or control: The lion is considered the king of beasts.
3 Cards a playing card with a picture of a king, usually ranking just below an ace.
4 Chess the most important piece, which can move only one square at a time in any direction except when castling.
Word Family kingly adjective (**kinglier; kingliest**); **kingliness** noun.

kingdom (king-dum) noun
1 a territory ruled by a king or queen.
2 the province or sphere of a particular thing or activity: the plant and animal kingdoms.

kingfisher noun
a brightly coloured bird which catches fish or insects.

kingpin noun
(informal) the most important person in a group, organization, etc.

King's Bench ⇨ QUEEN'S BENCH.

King's Counsel ⇨ QUEEN'S COUNSEL.

King's English ⇨ QUEEN'S ENGLISH.

King's evidence ⇨ QUEEN'S EVIDENCE.

kingship noun
the office or dignity of a king.

king-sized adjective also **king-size**
larger than the usual size: a king-sized double bed.

kink noun
1 a short twist or curl.
2 a slight oddity or fault.
• **kink** verb to form twists or curls in.

kinky adjective (**kinkier; kinkiest**)
1 having kinks or twists.
2 (informal) eccentric or having bizarre tastes, especially in sexual behaviour.
Word Family kinkiness noun.

kinsfolk ⇨ KINDRED.

kinship noun
1 relationship by blood.
2 any relationship or resemblance.
Word Family kinsman (plural **kinsmen**), **kinswoman** (plural **kinswomen**) noun a male or female blood relative.

kiosk (kee-osk) noun
a booth selling cigarettes, newspapers, snacks, etc.
[Turkish kiushk a pavilion]

kip verb (**kips; kipping; kipped**)
(informal) to sleep.
• **kip** noun.

kipper noun
a salted and smoked herring.

kirk (rhymes with work) noun
Scottish a church.

kirtle noun
an old word for a skirt or dress.

kismet (kiz-met) noun
a person's fate or destiny.
[Arabic]

kiss verb
to touch or caress with the lips.

Figurative The breeze kissed the trees.
• **kiss** *noun* (*plural* **kisses**).

kiss curl *noun*
a small curl of hair, especially on the forehead.

kisser *noun*
1 a person who kisses.
2 (*informal*) the mouth.

kiss of life *noun*
mouth-to-mouth resuscitation.

kissogram (**kiss-a-gram**) *noun*
1 a greeting delivered by a person hired for this purpose, usually one wearing a costume.
2 the person delivering such a greeting.

kit *noun*
a collection of tools, supplies, etc. for a particular purpose: *a first-aid kit.* □ *a modelling kit.*
• **kit** *verb* (**kits; kitting; kitted**)
Phrase **kit out** to equip with everything needed for an activity.

kitbag *noun*
a long leather or canvas bag in which kit or other belongings are carried.

kitchen (**kit**-ch'n) *noun*
a room equipped for preparing and cooking food.

kitchen garden *noun*
a garden where fruit and vegetables are grown for one's own use.

kite *noun*
1 a light frame covered with fabric or paper, flown in the wind at the end of a string.
2 a large hawk with long pointed wings.
3 *Geometry* a quadrilateral with two pairs of equal adjacent sides and diagonals that cross at right angles.
Phrase **as high as a kite** (*informal*) completely unable to function because of drink or drugs.

kith and kin *plural noun*
a person's friends and relatives.

kitsch (**kitch**) *noun*
any art, literature, etc. which is considered to be pretentious or in bad taste.
Word Family **kitsch, kitschy** *adjective.*
[German]

kitten *noun*
the young of a domestic cat or certain other animals.
Phrase **have kittens** (*informal*) to be very agitated.
Word Family **kittenish** *adjective* playful.

kitty *noun* (*plural* **kitties**)
a fund or collection of money, especially one shared or contributed to by several people.

kiwi (**kee-wee**) *noun*
1 any of a group of flightless New Zealand birds. The kiwi is the national emblem of New Zealand.
2 (*informal*) a person from New Zealand.
[Maori]

Klaxon *noun*
(*trademark*) a loud funnel-shaped horn or hooter, formerly used on cars.

kleptomania (**klep-ta-may-nee-a**) *noun*
an uncontrollable desire to steal.
Word Family **kleptomaniac** *noun*, *adjective*.
[Greek *kleptes* thief + MANIA]

klick *noun*
(*informal*) a kilometre.

klutz *noun* (*plural* **klutzes**)
(*informal*) a stupid or clumsy person.

knack (**nak**) *noun*
the ability to do something well and easily.

knackered (**nak**-erd) *adjective*
(*informal*) completely exhausted.

knacker's yard *noun*
a place where old horses are slaughtered.

knapsack (**nap**-sak) *noun*
a light canvas or leather case, carried on the back for holding provisions, etc. when travelling.

knave (**nave**) *noun*
1 an old word for a dishonest or mischievous person.
2 *Cards* ⇨ JACK.
Word Family **knavery** *noun*; **knavish** *adjective*; **knavishly** *adverb*.

knead (**need**) *verb*
to press and mould with the hands, especially dough.

knee (**nee**) *noun*
1 *Anatomy* the joint between the thigh and the lower part of the leg.
2 the part of an article of clothing that covers a knee.
3 something which has the shape of a knee.
• **knee** *verb* (**knees; kneeing; kneed**) to strike or touch with the knee.

kneecap *noun*
Anatomy a movable curved piece of bone at the front of the knee.
• **kneecap** *verb* (**kneecaps; kneecapping; kneecapped**) to shoot in the leg as punishment.

knee-deep *adjective*
1 up to the knees in.
2 very much involved in.
3 (of liquid) of a depth that reaches the knees.

knee-jerk *adjective*
(of an action or feeling) instinctive and without thought: *Her father's knee-jerk reaction was to ban her friends from the house.*

kneel (neel) *verb* (**kneels; kneeling; knelt** or (*especially American*) **kneeled**)
to rest on or fall to the knees.

knees-up *noun*
(*informal*) a loud and cheerful party.

knell (nel) *noun*
the sound of a bell announcing a death or funeral.

knew (new) the past tense of **know**.

knickerbockers (**nik**-a-bok-ers) *plural noun*
a pair of short trousers drawn or gathered in at the knee.

knickers *plural noun*
any female underpants.
Phrase **get one's knickers in a twist** (*informal*) to become very agitated.

knick-knack (**nik**-nak) *noun* also **nick-nack**
any small decorative article of little value.

knife (nife) *noun* (*plural* **knives**)
a tool with a sharp blade set in a handle, used for cutting.
Phrase **go under the knife** (*informal*) to have an operation.
• **knife** *verb* to cut or stab with a knife.

knight (nite) *noun*
1 *Medieval history* a nobleman given military rank and honour by the king, usually after service as a page and then as a squire.
2 a man honoured by a monarch for merit or service to his country.
3 *Chess* a piece, usually in the shape of a horse's head, which is the only piece that can pass over another.
Word Family **knight** *verb* to dub or create a knight; **knightly** *adjective*; **knighthood** *noun* the rank of a knight.

knight errant *noun* (*plural* **knights errant**)
Medieval history a knight who travelled in search of fame and adventure.
[Old French *errant* roaming]

knit (nit) *verb* (**knits; knitting; knitted** or **knit**)
1 to interlock loops of yarn, especially wool, using needles or a machine, to make clothing, etc.
2 to join or unite: *The broken bones will soon knit together.*
Phrase **knit the brow** to frown.
Word Family **knits** *plural noun* knitted garments; **knitting** *noun* a piece of knitted work.

knitting machine *noun*
a machine used to produce knitting automatically.

knob (nob) *noun*
1 any rounded projection, such as a handle for a door, etc.
2 a small lump: *a knob of butter.*
Word Family **knobbly** *adjective* (**knobblier; knobbliest**).

knock (nok) *verb*
1 to strike a blow with the fist or knuckles: *I knocked on the door.*
2 to hit: *I knocked my knee on the desk.* □ *The dog knocked my bike over.*
3 to make by hitting: *We knocked a hole in the wall.*
4 (*informal*) to criticize.
5 (of a car engine, etc.) to make a thumping noise as a result of faulty combustion.
Phrases **knock about** (*informal*) 1 to wander or lead an aimless existence. 2 to be unused: *There's a stapler knocking about somewhere.* **knock back** (*informal*) 1 to consume. 2 to surprise very much. **knock down** 1 to sell at auction. 2 to reduce the price of. **knock it off** (*informal*) stop it. **knock off** (*informal*) 1 to stop an activity, especially work. 2 to steal. 3 to kill. 4 to compose an article, etc. hurriedly. 5 to deduct money, etc. **knock on** (*informal*) to become old. **knock out** 1 to hit or strike someone so that he or she loses consciousness. 2 (*informal*) to impress very much. 3 to make unable to continue competing: *She got knocked out in the third round.* **knock up** 1 also **knock together** to make hastily: *I quickly knocked up a bird table.* 2 (*informal*) to score. 3 (*informal*) *Sport* to practise using rackets before a match begins.
Word Family **knock** *noun* the act or sound of knocking.

knockabout *adjective*
(of comedy) slapstick.

knocker *noun*
1 a person or thing that knocks, such as a hinged bar attached to a door.
2 (*informal*) a critical person.

knock-kneed (nok-**need**) *adjective*
having legs that bend inwards, causing the knees to hit each other in walking.

knock-on effect (nok-on if-ekt) *noun*
an effect characterized by a series of events, each one caused by the preceding one.

knockout *noun*
1 the act of knocking a person unconscious.
2 (*informal*) a person or thing that is greatly attractive or successful.
3 a competition in which some competitors are eliminated at each round until only the winner is left.

knoll (nole) *noun*
a small round hill.

knot (not) *noun*
1 a fastening made by passing the free end of a piece of string, rope, etc. through a loop in it and pulling tight.
2 a group or cluster: *A small knot of people stood at the gate.*
3 a hard lump, e.g. of wood where a branch joins or once joined the trunk of a tree.
4 a unit of speed equal to one nautical mile per hour, used in air and sea navigation, equal to 0·514 m per second, or about 1·12 miles per hour.
Phrases **tie someone up in knots** (*informal*) to confuse someone badly. **tie the knot** (*informal*) to get married.
Word Family **knot** *verb* (**knots; knotting; knotted**); **knotty** *adjective* (**knottier; knottiest**).

know (no) *verb* (**knows; knowing; knew; known**)
1 to understand: *I know what you mean.*
2 to be sure: *I know I'm right.*
3 to be acquainted with: *Do you know Ahmed Sabry?*
4 to recognize: *I'd know that walk anywhere.*
• **know** *noun*
Phrase **in the know** having secret or inside information.
Word Family **knowing** *adjective* suggestive of secret knowledge: *'I expect he will,' she said with a knowing smile;* **knowingly** *adverb* 1 shrewdly.
2 intentionally.

know-all *noun* also **know-it-all**
(*informal*) a person who claims or appears to know everything.

know-how *noun*
the ability or skill to do something.

knowledge (noll-ij) *noun*
1 an acquaintance with or understanding of facts, actions, ideas, etc.: *Her knowledge of music is excellent.* □ *The workers had no knowledge of luxury.*
2 everything which is known: *This mystery is beyond human knowledge.*
Word Family **knowledgeable, knowledgeably** *adjective* possessing knowledge; **knowledgeably** *adverb*.

known (*rhymes with* bone) the past participle of **know**.

knuckle (nukk-'l) *noun*
1 the joint of a finger, especially the joint where the base of a finger meets the hand.
2 a cut of meat containing the knee of an animal.
Phrase **near the knuckle** (*informal*) very close to being offensive.
• **knuckle** *verb*
Phrases **knuckle down** I must knuckle down and finish that history essay. **knuckle under** to yield or submit.

knuckleduster *noun*
a series of metal rings joined to fit over knuckles of the fist, used as a weapon.

koala (ko-**ah**-la) *noun*
a tailless Australian marsupial with grey fur, a flat black nose and strong claws, living in and feeding on eucalyptuses. [Aboriginal]

koi (coy) *noun* (*plural* **koi**)
a large carp. [Japanese]

kookaburra (**kuk**-a-burr-a) *noun*
a brown and white Australian bird with an unusual laughing cry. [Aboriginal]

kopek *noun* also **copeck; kopeck**
a coin worth one hundredth of a rouble.

Koran (kaw-**rahn** or k'-**rahn**) *noun* also **Qur'an; Quran**
the Muslim holy book of Allah's final revelation to the Prophet Muhammad; the sacred scriptures of Islam.
Word Family **Koranic** (kor-an-ik) *adjective*.
[Arabic *qur'an* reading, recitation]

korma *noun*
an Indian dish of meat or vegetables braised in water, stock or yoghurt. [Hindi, braised meat]

kosher (ko-sha) *adjective*
1 (of food, etc.) prepared according to Jewish rules and rituals.
2 (*informal*) legal or above board. [Hebrew *kasher* fit, proper, lawful]

kowtow *verb*
to behave in a servile way.

> The word **kowtow** in English means 'to behave in a servile or too humble a way towards people in important positions'. It has come into English from Chinese where *k'o t'ou* meant 'to strike the forehead on the ground' – as a sign of respect to the emperor or someone important – *k'o* meaning 'to strike' and *t'ou* meaning 'head'.

kraal (krahl) *noun*
1 *South African* an enclosed area for cattle; a corral.
2 *South African* a village of huts surrounded by a stockade. [Afrikaans]

krona (kroh-na) *noun* (*plural* **kronor**) (**kroh**-na)
the basic unit of money in Sweden and Iceland.

krone (kroh-na) *noun* (*plural* **kroner**) (**kroh**-na)
the basic unit of money in Denmark and Norway.

krugerrand *noun*
a South African gold coin.

krypton (**krip**-tonn) *noun*
a colourless inert gas found in the earth's atmosphere, used in electric light bulbs. [Greek *kryptos* hidden]

kudos (**kew**-doss) *noun*
personal fame or glory. [Greek]

kudu (**koo**-doo) *noun*
a large African antelope. [Bantu]

kumquat (**kum**-kwot) *noun* also **cumquat**
a small orange citrus fruit with a sweet skin and acid flesh. [Chinese]

kung fu *noun*
the Chinese form of karate.

L1

la ⇨ LAH.

lab *noun*
(*informal*) a laboratory.

label (*rhymes with* table) *noun*
1 a piece of paper or other material attached to an object or person for identification.
2 (*informal*) a word or phrase used to describe a person or group.
3 a company that produces clothing or recorded music.
Word Family **label** *verb* (**labels; labelling; labelled**) to mark with a label.

laboratory (la-**borr**-a-tree) *noun* (*plural* **laboratories**)
a room or building fitted with apparatus for scientific experiments.
[Latin *laboratorium* workshop]

laborious (la-**baw**-ree-us) *adjective*
1 requiring effort or hard work.
2 showing too much evidence of effort.
Word Family **laboriously** *adverb*; **laboriousness** *noun*.

labour (**lay**-ba) *noun* (*American* **labor**)
1 any work or task involving effort.
2 workers considered together as a group: *the strength of organized labour.*
3 (**Labour**) short form of **Labour Party** *British politics* one of the three major parties: *Labour won the by-election.*
4 the effort involved in childbirth.
Phrase **in labour** giving birth: *She was in labour for four hours.*
● **labour** *verb*
1 to toil or strive.
2 to work or move with difficulty.
Phrase **labour under** to be the victim of a mistaken idea: *I was labouring under the impression that she was a qualified doctor.*
Word Family **Labour** *adjective* connected with the Labour Party; **labourer** *noun* a worker whose job requires strength rather than skill; **laboured** *adjective* done with unnatural difficulty.
[Latin *labor* toil, distress]

labour exchange *noun*
(*dated*) a jobcentre.

Labrador (**lab**-ra-dor) *noun*
one of a breed of large smooth-haired dogs, often used as retrievers.
[from *Labrador*, an area of Canada]

laburnum (la-**bern**-'m) *noun*
a tree with small yellow flowers and poisonous seeds.

labyrinth (**lab**-a-rinth) *noun*
1 a complicated network of passages or paths.
2 any confusing entanglement of things or events.
Word Family **labyrinthine** (lab-a-**rinth**-ine) *adjective*.
[from Greek]

lace *noun*
1 a fine net-like fabric of interwoven threads.
2 a cord for fastening or tightening shoes, clothing, etc.
● **lace** *verb* to tie together with laces: *Lace up your shoes.*
Phrase **lace with** to add a small amount to: *The pudding was laced with rum.*
Word Family **lacy** *adjective* (**lacier; laciest**).

laceration (lass-a-**ray**-sh'n) *noun*
a deep tear or cut in the skin.
[from Latin]

lachrymose (**lak**-ri-mose) *adjective*
tearful.

lack *noun*
an absence or shortage of something: *The drought caused a widespread lack of food.*
● **lack** *verb* to be without or in need of: *He lacks the necessary skill for the job.*
[Middle English *lak* deficiency]

lackadaisical (lak-a-**day**-zi-k'l) *adjective*
careless or slapdash.
Word Family **lackadaisically** *adverb*.
[from *lackaday* an old word meaning 'alas the day']

lackey *noun*
any servant, or a person who is treated as one, often regarded with contempt.
[from Arabic]

lacklustre (**lak**-lust-a) *adjective* (*American* **lackluster**)
dull or lacking in vitality: *the actor's lacklustre performance.*

laconic (la-**kon**-ik) *adjective*
very brief or concise in speech or style.
Word Family **laconically** *adverb*.

[Greek *Lakonikos* Spartan (as the Spartans never wasted words)]

lacquer (lak-a) *noun*
a protective, usually transparent, coating made from a resin or artificial substance and capable of taking a high polish.
• **lacquer** *verb* to coat with lacquer.

lacrosse (la-kross) *noun*
a field game for two teams of 12 in which the ball is moved around by means of long sticks with nets on the end.
[French (le jeu de) *la crosse* (the game of) the hooked stick]

lactate *verb*
Biology to secrete milk in the mammary glands.
Word Family **lactation** *noun*.
[Latin *lactis* of milk]

lactose *noun*
the sugar present in milk, used as a food and in medicine.

lacy ⇨ LACE.

lad *noun*
1 (*informal*) a boy.
2 (*informal*) a high-spirited young man.
3 (**the lads**) (*informal*) one's group of male friends.

ladder *noun*
1 a device with steps set into a frame, for climbing up and down.
Figurative her efforts to get up the promotion ladder.
2 also called **run**. a line of stitches which have come undone, e.g. in a pair of tights.
• **ladder** *verb* to cause a ladder in tights, etc.

laddie *noun*
Scottish a boy.

laden (lay-d'n) *adjective*
loaded: *The trees were laden with fruit.*

la-di-da *adjective* also **lah-di-dah**
(*informal*) pretentious in speech or actions.

ladies *noun*
1 the plural of **lady**.
2 also **ladies' room** a toilet for women in a public place.

ladies' fingers ⇨ OKRA.

lading (lay-ding) *noun*
freight or cargo.

ladle (lay-d'l) *noun*
a large deep spoon with a long handle, normally used for serving liquids such as soup.
• **ladle** *verb* to use a ladle.

lady (lay-dee) *noun* (*plural* **ladies**)
1 a woman: *Move over, Charlie, you're in the lady's way.* □ *a lady doctor.*
2 a woman with socially correct manners.
3 (**Lady**) a form of address for a countess, baroness, etc.: *Good morning, Lady Fothergill.*
[Old English *hlaefdige* loaf-kneader]

ladybird *noun*
a type of beetle, often red or orange with black spots.

Lady chapel *noun*
a chapel dedicated to the Virgin Mary.

lady-in-waiting *noun* (*plural* **ladies-in-waiting**)
a woman who attends a queen or princess.

ladykiller *noun*
(*informal*) a man who is supposed to be very attractive to women.

ladylike *adjective*
like or befitting a lady.

ladyship *noun*
(**Your Ladyship, Her Ladyship**) a way of talking to or about a titled woman: *Her Ladyship is not at home.*

lag[1] *verb* (**lags; lagging; lagged**)
to linger or loiter and so fall behind.
• **lag** *noun* ⇨ TIME LAG.

lag[2] *verb* (**lags; lagging; lagged**)
to insulate pipes to help to retain heat, prevent freezing, etc.
Word Family **lagging** *noun* any material used to insulate pipes, etc.

lag[3] *noun*
(*informal*) a convict.

lager (lah-ga) *noun*
a beer containing a small amount of hops, made and stored at low temperatures.
[German, a store]

lager lout *noun*
(*informal*) a young person who behaves badly towards others because of drinking too much.

laggard *noun*
a person who lags or falls behind.

lagoon (la-goon) *noun*
an area of salt water partly or completely separated from the sea by a sandbank, atoll or coral reef.
[Italian *laguna*]

lah *noun* also **la**
Music a note in the scale. ⇨ DOH.

laid the past tense and past participle of **lay**[1].

laid-back *adjective*
(*informal*) extremely relaxed or calm.

lain the past participle of **lie²**.

lair *noun*
the den or resting place of a wild animal.

laird *noun*
a landowner in Scotland.
[Scottish, lord]

laissez faire (lay-say **fair**) *noun*
the policy of not interfering with others,
especially in economic matters.
[French *laissez* leave + *faire* to do]

laity (**lay**-it-ee) *noun*
any people outside a particular profession,
especially those outside the clergy.
[Greek *laos* people]

lake *noun*
1 a large area of water surrounded by land.
2 any large area of liquid or similar
substance.
[Latin *lacus* a basin]

lam *verb* (**lams; lamming; lammed**)
Phrase **lam into** (*informal*) to hit
repeatedly.

lama (**lah**-ma) *noun*
Buddhism a priest or monk.
[Tibetan]

lamb (lam) *noun*
1 a young sheep.
2 the flesh of a lamb used as food.
3 a mild inoffensive person.
● **lamb** *verb* to give birth to lambs.

lambada (lam-**bah**-da) *noun*
an erotic dance of Brazilian origin in
which couples hold each other closely and
gyrate their hips rhythmically.
[Portuguese, the snapping of a whip]

lambaste (lam-**bayst**) *verb* also **lambast**
(lam-**bast**)
(*informal*) to scold severely.

lame *adjective*
1 crippled in a leg.
2 (of an excuse, etc.) imperfect or weak.
Word Family **lame** *verb* to make lame;
lameness *noun*; **lamely** *adverb*.

lamé (**lah**-may) *noun*
a fabric with silver or gold threads woven
into it.
[French]

lame duck *noun*
1 an ineffective person.
2 *American* an elected official who is near
the end of his or her time in office.

lament (la-**ment**) *verb*
to feel or express sorrow or regret for.
● **lament** *noun* also **lamentation** (lam-'n-
tay-sh'n)

1 an expression of grief or regret.
2 a formal expression of mourning in verse
or song.
Word Family **lamentable** (**lam**-'n-ta-
b'l) *adjective* regrettable; **lamentably**
adverb.
[Latin *lamentari* to weep or wail]

laminate (**lam**-in-ayt) *verb*
1 to make using a lot of thin layers.
2 to cover with a thin layer of metal or
plastic.
Word Family **lamination** (lam-in-**ay**-
sh'n) *noun*.

lamp *noun*
any of various lights using oil, gas or
electricity.

lampoon (lam-**poon**) *noun*
a satire based on a vicious or critical attack
on a person, institution, etc.
Word Family **lampoon** *verb* to attack in a
lampoon; **lampoonery** *noun* the art or act
of lampooning.

lamprey (**lam**-pree) *noun*
any of a group of eel-like aquatic animals.

Lancaster (**lank**-a-ster) *noun*
the royal house in England from 1399 to
1461.

lance (*rhymes with* dance) *verb*
to cut open with a scalpel or knife: *The
doctor lanced the abscess.*
● **lance** *noun* a long spear formerly used
by soldiers on horseback.
Word Family **lancer** *noun* a soldier of a
cavalry regiment formerly armed with
lances.
[Greek *lonkhē*]

lance corporal *noun*
Army a non-commissioned officer ranking
between private and corporal.

lancet (**lahn**-sit) *noun*
Medicine a small sharp knife for lancing
abscesses, etc.

land *noun*
1 the part of the earth's surface not
covered by water: *Will you travel by land or
sea?*
2 an area of ground: *The land in this part of
the country is very fertile.*
3 a country: *foreign lands.*
Phrase **see how the land lies** to
investigate a situation, etc.
● **land** *verb*
1 to come to land or shore: *The aircraft
landed safely.*
2 to come to rest or arrive in a place or
position: *The space capsule landed in the
ocean.*

3 to bring a fish out of the water, with a hook, net, etc.
4 (*informal*) to succeed in getting: *She landed a good job.*
5 (*informal*) to succeed in hitting with: *I landed him a blow on the head.*
Phrases **land someone in** (*informal*) to cause someone to be in: *The incident landed him in terrible trouble.* **land someone with** (*informal*) to cause someone to have to do something. **land up** to reach: *We landed up on the wrong side of the river.*
Word Family **landed** *adjective* owning or consisting of land.

landau (lan-daw) *noun*
a carriage with two seats facing each other, each covered by a hood.
[after the Bavarian town where first made]

landfall *noun*
an arrival at land, especially from a ship.

landfill site *noun*
a place where waste material is disposed of by burying it under layers of earth.

landform *noun*
any geographical feature, such as a mountain, valley, etc.

land girl *noun*
during the Second World War in Britain, a woman who worked on a farm.

landing *noun*
1 the act of landing: *The plane's landing was delayed owing to bad weather.*
2 the place where people or goods are landed: *The landing was crowded with onlookers when the ship docked.*
3 the open area at the top of a staircase or between two flights of stairs.

landing craft *noun*
a low flat-bottomed boat for landing troops, equipment, etc.

landing gear ⇨ UNDERCARRIAGE (definition 1).

landlady *noun* (*plural* **landladies**)
1 a woman who rents out rooms, houses, or land to tenants.
2 a woman who runs a public house.

landlocked *adjective*
almost or entirely surrounded by land.

landlord *noun*
1 a person, especially a man, who rents out land, houses or rooms to tenants.
2 a man who runs a public house.

landlubber *noun*
Nautical (*informal*) a person who knows little about boats or the sea.

landmark *noun*
1 an object that is easily seen and serves as a guide to travellers.
2 an event marking an important stage of development: *The discovery of gold was a landmark in the history of Australia.*

landmine *noun*
an explosive device placed in a concealed position on land.

landscape *noun*
1 the appearance of countryside or inland scenery.
2 a painting, etc. of such scenery.
3 a format where the top of the page is longer than the sides. Compare PORTRAIT.
• **landscape** *verb* to do landscape gardening.

landscape gardening *noun*
the art of providing gardens with trees, water features, etc. to produce attractive views of seemingly natural landscape.
Word Family **landscape gardener** *noun*.

landslide *noun* also **landslip**
1 a mass of soil and rocks which slides down a hillside.
2 an overwhelming victory.

lane *noun*
1 a narrow road or alley.
2 a strip marked with lines on each side, for separating lines of traffic, runners, etc.

language (lang-gwij) *noun*
1 the particular form of sounds or words used by a nation or group.
2 the use of sounds or words to express thoughts or feelings to others. *He always uses very emotional language.*
3 any method of communication: *the language of animals.*
4 the science or study of sounds and words.

language laboratory *noun* (*plural* **language laboratories**)
a place where languages are taught by means of computers, tape-recordings, etc.
[Latin *lingua* tongue]

languid (lang-gwid) *adjective*
1 having or showing no interest.
2 slow-moving from weakness or tiredness.
Word Family **languidly** *adverb*; **languidness** *noun*.
[from Latin]

languish (lang-gwish) *verb*
to become weak or feeble.

languor (lang-ger) *noun*
1 weakness or lack of energy.
2 a heavy stillness of the air.

Word Family **languorous** *adjective;*
languorously *adverb.*

lank *adjective*
1 (of a person) tall and lean.
2 (of hair) straight and limp or flat.
Word Family **lanky** *adjective* (**lankier;
lankiest**) (of a person) ungracefully tall
and thin; **lankiness** *noun.*

lanolin (**lan**-a-lin) *noun*
a waxy material used in ointments and
cosmetics.
[Latin *lana* wool + *oleum* oil]

lantern *noun*
1 a glass case with a metal frame
protecting a light.
2 *Architecture* an open part at the top of a
tower or dome.
3 *Architecture* a raised part of a roof
designed to let in light.

> The words *lantern* and *lamp* are both
> derived from the Greek noun *lampter*,
> which originally meant 'a bunch of
> burning sticks', later 'a torch' and then
> 'a lamp'. In Latin this became *lanterna*
> and English acquired *lantern* from this
> via Old French *lanterne*. Until the 19th
> century the spelling *lanthorn* was
> popular because the translucent covers
> of *lanterns* were often made of horn.

lanyard (**lan**-y'd) *noun* also **laniard**
1 *Nautical* a rope.
2 *Nautical* a cord worn round the neck or
shoulder to carry a whistle or knife.

lap¹ *noun*
the front of the body from the waist to the
knees when sitting: *She held the baby in her
lap.*
Phrases **in the lap of luxury** in
luxurious circumstances. **in the lap of the
gods** uncertain: *Your fate is in the lap of the
gods.*

lap² *noun*
1 *Sport* a single circuit around a racetrack.
2 one section of a journey.
● **lap** *verb* (**laps; lapping; lapped**) to
overtake by a lap in a race.

lap³ *verb* (**laps; lapping; lapped**)
1 to take up liquid with the tongue: *My cat
was lapping up the spilt milk.*
2 to move lightly against something: *We
heard the water gently lapping against the side
of the boat.*
Phrase **lap up** to accept eagerly: *She
lapped up all their compliments.*
Word Family **lap** *noun* the act or sound
of lapping.

lap dog *noun*
any small dog kept as a pet.

lapel (la-**pel**) *noun*
the part of a coat forming an extension of
the collar and folded over, reaching down
to where the fastening begins.

lapis lazuli (lap-iss **laz**-yoo-lie) *noun*
a rare deep-blue semi-precious stone used
mainly in jewellery.
[Latin, stone of azure]

lapsang souchong (lap-sang **soo**-shong)
noun
a type of tea.

lapse *noun*
1 a slight slip or failure: *He suffered a brief
lapse of memory.*
2 a gradual falling or slipping: *a lapse into
bad habits.*
● **lapse** *verb*
1 to slide or slip slowly: *She lapsed into
unconsciousness.*
2 to become void or ineffective: *Your visa
has lapsed.*
[Latin *lapsus* glided]

laptop *noun*
a portable computer.

lapwing *noun* also called **peewit.**
a large crested plover with a shrill cry.

larboard *noun*
Nautical an old word for the left side of a
boat or ship. ⇨ PORT².

larceny (**lar**-sa-nee) *noun* (*plural*
larcenies)
Law the stealing of another person's
possessions.

larch *noun* (*plural* **larches**)
a deciduous tree with cones, short needle-
like leaves and durable wood.
[from Latin]

lard *noun*
the fat from a pig, prepared for use in
cooking.
● **lard** *verb* to apply lard or grease to.
Phrase **lard something with** to add
non-essential features to something.
[from Latin]

larder *noun*
a cool ventilated room for storing foods.

large *adjective*
of more than ordinary size or amount.
Phrase **at large** not yet caught again after
escape: *The men are still at large.*
Word Family **largely** *adverb* mostly or to
a great extent; **largish** *adjective* rather
large; **largeness** *noun.*
[Latin *largus* abounding]

large intestine ⇨ INTESTINE.

largesse (lar-**jess**) *noun* also **largess**
1 the generous giving of gifts.
2 gifts which have been given generously.
[French]

lariat (**larr**-ee-ut) *noun*
a rope used as a lasso.
[Spanish *la reata* the rope]

lark¹ *noun*
any of various birds which sing in flight,
especially the skylark.
Phrase **be up with the lark** to get up
very early.

lark² *noun*
(*informal*) an amusing prank or frolic.
• **lark** *verb* to have fun or play pranks.

larkspur *noun*
a plant with spur-shaped flowers.

larva *noun* (*plural* **larvae**) (**lar**-vee)
Biology a self-sustaining pre-adult stage in
the life history of many animals and
differing from the mature adult in form.
Word Family **larval** *adjective*.
[Latin, a ghost, a mask]

laryngitis (larr-in-**jite**-iss) *noun*
an inflammation of the larynx causing
hoarseness and loss of voice.
[LARYNX + *-itis*]

larynx (**larr**-inks) *noun* (*plural* **larynges**
(la-**rin**-jeez) or **larynxes**) also called
voice box.
Anatomy the movable box of cartilage in
the neck, through which air passes from
the nose to the lungs, and in which the
sounds of speech are produced by the
vocal cords.
[Greek]

lasagne (la-**zan**-ya *or* la-**san**-va) *noun*
1 pasta in the form of broad flat sheets.
2 a baked dish consisting of layers of this
pasta, minced meat or vegetables,
tomatoes and cheese.
[Italian]

lascivious (la-**siv**-ee-us) *adjective*
feeling or expressing lust: *a lascivious leer*.
Word Family **lasciviously** *adverb*;
lasciviousness *noun*.
[Latin *lascivus* playful, impudent]

laser (**lay**-za) *noun*
an electronic device for producing
extremely powerful narrow beams of light,
used in drilling steel, medicine,
communications, etc.
[from L(ight) A(mplification) by
S(timulated) E(mission) of R(adiation)]

laser printer *noun*
a printer that uses a laser, attached to a
computer.

lash *verb*
1 to strike with a whip.
2 to beat or strike violently: *The rain lashed
the windows.*
3 to tie securely with rope, etc.
Phrase **lash out** 1 to kick or hit
violently: *The horse lashed out with its hind
legs.* 2 to attack with words: *The next
speaker lashed out at the government.* 3 to
spend money freely: *Tonight we'll really lash
out and go to the theatre.*
• **lash** *noun* (*plural* **lashes**)
1 the flexible part of a whip.
2 a blow with a whip, etc.: *The prisoner was
sentenced to 16 lashes.*
3 an eyelash.

lashing *noun*
1 a whipping or beating.
2 (**lashings**) (*informal*) large quantities:
apple pie and lashings of cream.

lass *noun* (*plural* **lasses**)
a girl or young woman.

lassie *noun*
Scottish a girl.

lassitude (**lass**-i-tewd) *noun*
tiredness.

lasso (lass-**oo**) *noun* (*plural* **lassos** or
lassoes)
a long rope with an adjustable noose at
one end, used to catch cattle, horses, etc.
• **lasso** *verb* (**lassoes**; **lassoing**; **lassoed**)
to catch with a lasso.
[Spanish *lazo* noose]

last¹ *adjective, adverb*
1 coming after all the others in time or
order: *My name was the last one on the list.*
□ *His horse finished last.*
2 final: *That's the last time I tell him a secret!*
3 coming immediately before the present:
I saw her only last week.
4 the least likely: *That's the last thing I
thought she'd do.*
• **last** *noun* anything which is at the end:
We have finished the last of the coffee.
Phrases **at last, at long last** after much
delay. **to the last** until the end.
Word Family **lastly** *adverb* finally.

last² *verb*
1 to continue: *The programme only lasted
half an hour.*
2 to be in an adequate condition: *Your
shoes won't last five minutes on those rocks!*
3 to be enough for: *The food will only last
another day.*

Word Family **lasting** *adjective* remaining in existence for a long time.

last³ *noun*
a model of the human foot used in making shoes.

last-ditch *adjective*
final and desperate: *a last-ditch attempt to prevent war.*

last post *noun*
Military the bugle call signalling soldiers to retire for the night, also used at military funerals and commemoration services. Compare REVEILLE.

Last Supper *noun*
Christianity the supper taken by Christ and his disciples on the eve of his Crucifixion.

latch *noun* (*plural* **latches**)
a simple fastening on a door, consisting of a bar which falls into a slot.
• **latch** *verb* to fasten with a latch.
Phrase **latch on** (*informal*) **1** to attach oneself. **2** to understand or comprehend.

latchkey *noun*
the key of the front door.

latchkey child *noun* (*plural* **latchkey children**)
a child who regularly lets himself or herself in after school because his or her parents are not at home.

late *adjective, adverb*
1 further on than the proper, usual or appointed time: *The train was late.*
2 being or occurring towards the end: *The sky had cleared by the late afternoon.*
3 (**the late, one's late**) (of a person) recently dead: *I knew her late husband quite well.*
Phrase **late of** (*formal*) until recently working or living at.
• **late** *noun*
Phrase **of late** recently.
Word Family **latest** *adjective* most recent: *the latest fashion*; **lately** *adverb* recently; **lateness** *noun*.

latecomer (late-kum-a) *noun*
a person who arrives late.

latent (lay-t'nt) *adjective*
(of a quality) present but not apparent or active: *a latent homosexual.*
Word Family **latency** *noun*.
[Latin *latens* lying hidden]

lateral (lat-a-r'l) *adjective*
of or relating to the side.
Word Family **laterally** *adverb*.
[Latin *lateris* of a side]

lateral thinking *noun*
a creative approach to problems which uses inventiveness and humour.

latex (**lay**-teks) *noun*
Biology a milky liquid which comes out of cut surfaces of some flowering plants, used in making rubber.
[Latin, liquid]

lath (lahth) *noun*
Building a narrow strip of wood used to support plaster on a wall or the tiles, etc. on a roof.

lathe (layth) *noun*
a machine which holds and turns pieces of wood, metal or other material, so that they are rotated against another tool for cutting or shaping.

lather (*rhymes with* father) *noun*
any foam or froth.
• **lather** *verb*
1 to form a lather: *Soap does not lather well in hard water.*
2 to make a lather on: *He lathered his chin before shaving.*

Latin *noun*
1 the language of the ancient Romans.
2 a member of any of the peoples whose languages are derived from Latin: *The Italians, French and Spanish are all Latins.*

Latin America *noun*
the countries of Central and South America in which Spanish or Portuguese is spoken.
Word Family **Latin American** *adjective*.

latitude (lat-i-tewd) *noun*
1 any distance north or south of the equator, measured in degrees. Compare LONGITUDE (definition 1).
2 also called **line of latitude**. an imaginary line around the world parallel with the equator.
3 freedom of action, opinion, etc.: *He's had a rough time recently, so let's allow him some latitude.*
[Latin *latitudo* breadth]

latrine (la-**treen**) *noun*
1 a pit or trench used as an outdoor toilet.
2 a toilet in a barracks, factory, etc.
[Latin *latrina* a bath]

latter *adjective*
1 being the second mentioned of two: *The tiger resembles the leopard, but the latter has spots instead of stripes.* Compare FORMER¹ (definition 2).
2 belonging to or coming near the end of something: *In the latter days of his life he became quite senile.*

Word Family **latterly** *adverb* **1** lately. **2** of the latter part of a period of time.

> ⚠️ *Latter* should only be used for the second of two things. If there are more than two things do not use *latter*: *Of beef and lamb, I prefer the latter.* □ *Of beef, lamb and pork, I prefer the last.*

latter-day *adjective*
modern: *a latter-day saint.*

lattice (lat-iss) *noun*
a structure of crossed strips, usually in a diamond pattern, used as a screen, etc.

lattice window *noun*
a window with small diamond-shaped panes separated by lead strips.

laud *verb*
an old word meaning 'to praise'.
Word Family **laudable** *adjective* deserving praise; **laudably** *adverb*; **laudatory** *adjective* expressing or showing praise.
[Latin *laudare* to praise]

laudanum (lawd-a-n'm) *noun*
a solution of opium in alcohol, used in medicine.

laugh (lahf) *verb*
to make sounds and facial movements expressing joy, amusement, derision, etc.
Phrases **laugh at** to make fun of. **laugh off** to make something seem unimportant by treating it lightly.
• **laugh** *noun*
1 the sound of laughing.
2 the act of laughing: *We all had a good laugh.*
Phrase **have the last laugh** to triumph or succeed after seeming at a disadvantage.
Word Family **laughter** *noun* **1** the action of laughing: *He was helpless with laughter.* **2** the sound of laughing; **laughable** *adjective* so bad as to cause laughter: *The scheme was completely laughable*; **laughably** *adverb*; **laughingly** *adverb* in a light joking way.

laughing gas *noun*
the gas nitrous oxide, which may produce an exhilarating effect when inhaled, used as an anaesthetic in dentistry, etc.

laughing stock *noun*
an object of general ridicule.

launch¹ (lawnch) *verb*
1 to put into the water: *They launched the canoes.*
2 to propel into the air: *The missiles are launched from tanks.*

3 to start: *The publisher launched an advertising campaign to promote the new book.*
Phrase **launch out** to start afresh: *He is going to launch out on a completely new career.*
• **launch** *noun* (*plural* **launches**).

launch² *noun* (*plural* **launches**)
a large sturdy open boat, usually with an engine.

launch pad *noun* also **launching pad**
the structure from which a rocket is launched.

launder (lawn-der) *verb*
1 to wash and iron clothes.
2 (*informal*) to transfer money in order to cover up where it came from.
Word Family **launderer** *noun* a person who launders; **laundress** *noun* (*plural* **laundresses**) a woman who washes clothes.
[Latin *lavanda* things to be washed]

launderette *noun* also **laundrette**
a coin-operated self-service laundry.

laundry (lawn-dree) *noun* (*plural* **laundries**)
1 a place where articles are washed.
2 any articles of clothing, etc. to be washed.

laurel (lorr-el) *noun*
an evergreen shrub with shiny leaves, used by the ancient Greeks and Romans to make victory wreaths.
Phrases **look to one's laurels** to be careful to keep a good position against competition from others. **rest on one's laurels** to be content with what one has already achieved.
[Latin *laurus*]

lava (lah-va) *noun*
Geology molten rock which flows onto the surface of the earth from an erupting volcano. Compare MAGMA.
[Italian, a stream]

lavatory (lav-a-tree) *noun* (*plural* **lavatories**)
a toilet.

> The word **lavatory** originally meant 'a place or vessel for washing in', being derived from the Latin *lavare* (to wash); it took on its present meaning in the 19th century. The word *toilet* was considered vulgar in the 1950s and *lavatory* was thus preferable. Nowadays *toilet* is the more usual word although there are several alternatives, some of them euphemisms, such as *loo*, *WC*, *ladies*, *gents* and *powder room*.

lavender (lav-in-da) *noun*
1 a pale violet colour.
2 a shrub with spikes of fragrant pale purple flowers.
3 the dried flowers or the perfume made from the oil from this plant.
• **lavender** *adjective*.

lavish (lav-ish) *verb*
to give abundantly or generously: *Everyone lavished attention on the sick child.*
Word Family lavish *adjective* abundant; **lavishly** *adverb*; **lavishness** *noun*.
[Old French *lavasse* a downpour of rain]

law *noun*
1 the body of official rules of a country which must be obeyed, or any one of these rules.
2 the profession which deals with these rules and their application: *to practise law.*
3 a statement about science or nature that seems to be true from our present knowledge: *Newton's first law of motion.*
4 something that has undisputed authority: *My father's word was law.*
5 (**the law**) (*informal*) the police force.
Phrase **lay down the law** to state one's opinions or wishes authoritatively.
Word Family lawful *adjective* allowed by law; **lawfully** *adverb*; **lawfulness** *noun*; **lawless** *adjective* 1 regardless of law.
2 unrestrained; **lawlessly** *adverb*; **lawlessness** *noun*.

law-abiding *adjective*
obeying the law.

law court *noun*
the room or building in which law cases are heard.

lawn *noun*
an area of neatly cut grass, e.g. in a private garden.

lawsuit *noun*
Law a proceeding in a court of law.

lawyer (loy-a) *noun*
Law a member of the legal profession.
Compare BARRISTER; SOLICITOR.

lax *adjective*
1 not strict or severe: *lax morals.* □ *lax discipline.*
2 (of muscles) loose.
Word Family laxly *adverb*; **laxity**, **laxness** *noun*.
[Latin *laxus* loose, slack]

laxative *noun*
any substance causing emptying of the bowels.

lay¹ *verb* (**lays; laying; laid**)
1 to put, place or set: *I laid the book on the table.* □ *She lays great emphasis on neatness.*
2 to prepare or arrange: *We laid careful plans.* □ *Please lay the table for dinner.*
3 (of an animal) to produce: *a hen that lays six eggs a day.*
4 to cause to settle or be inactive: *I sprinkled the path with water to lay the dust.*
5 to wager: *I'll lay five to one I can beat you home.*
Phrases **lay about** to hit out at violently.
lay down to state formally. **lay in** to build up a store of: *They began to lay in fuel for the winter.* **lay off** 1 to stop employing: *The company will have to lay off a thousand workers.* 2 (*informal*) to stop teasing or nagging someone. **lay on** to supply: *Their parents had laid on a fantastic meal for all of us.* **lay out** 1 to spread out fully: *We laid the canvas out on the dining table.* 2 to arrange: *This is how we're going to lay out the garden.*
3 to arrange a corpse ready to be buried. 4 (*informal*) to spend. **lay someone low** to cause someone to be inactive. **lay someone open to** to cause someone to be vulnerable to: *The admission that he had tried drugs immediately laid him open to attack from all sides.* **lay up** 1 to store up.
2 to cause to be inactive: *My mum's been laid up for weeks with back pain.*
• **lay** *noun* the way or position in which something is laid or lies: *the lay of the land.*

> **!** Do not confuse the verb *lay* with *lie*. The main sense of *lay* is 'to put something somewhere', and it must have an object: *Lay the dress on the bed.* The main sense of *lie* is 'to rest flat somewhere', and it has no object: *The dress was lying on the bed.* Confusion may arise because the past tense of *lie* is **lay**: *We lay in the sun all day.* The past tense of *lay* is **laid**: *I laid the table for dinner.*

lay² the past tense of **lie²**.

lay³ *adjective*
of or relating to the laity, as distinct from the clergy or the members of a profession: *a lay preacher.*

lay⁴ *noun*
an old word for a short song or poem.

layabout *noun*
a lazy person.

lay-by *noun*
a space at the side of a road where vehicles can stop temporarily without obstructing traffic.

layer *noun*
1 a single thickness or level.
2 (of hens, etc.) one that lays eggs.
• **layer** *verb* to spread or arrange in layers.

layette (lay-et) *noun*
a complete outfit of clothing for a newborn child.
[French, box or drawer]

layman *noun* (*plural* **laymen**) also **layperson** (*plural* **laypeople**)
1 a member of a church who is not a priest.
2 (*informal*) a non-expert.

layout *noun*
an arrangement or plan, e.g. of text on a page: *a diagram showing the layout of the ground floor.*

lazy (lay-zee) *adjective* (**lazier**; **laziest**)
unwilling to work or be active.
Figurative a lazy stream gurgling by.
Word Family **lazily** *adverb*; **laziness** *noun*; **laze** *verb* to be lazy or idle; **laze** *noun*.

lea (lee) *noun*
an old word for a meadow.

leach *verb*
Geology to remove soluble constituents, e.g. minerals, from soil, ashes, etc. by the percolating action of water.

lead¹ (leed) *verb* (**leads**; **leading**; **led**)
1 to take or guide: *The estate agent led us through the house.*
2 to direct or command: *Scott led an expedition to the Antarctic.*
3 to be ahead: *My horse led for most of the race.*
4 to have as an existence: *I'm afraid I lead rather a dull life.*
5 to start a card game with: *Frank led with the king of hearts.*
Phrases **lead someone on** to encourage someone to think that one is attracted to him or her when one is not. **lead to** to result in: *The incident led to him losing his job.*
• **lead** *noun*
1 the first place: *England soon took the lead.*
2 the extent to which something is ahead: *He had a lead of 100 m over his nearest rival.*
3 *Theatre* the main role in a play, or the actor playing it.
4 a clue: *At present there are no leads to the murderer's identity.*
5 ⇨ LEASH.
6 an electric wire: *Which lead goes to the computer?*

lead² (led) *noun*
1 a heavy soft metal widely used in alloys.
2 a long thin piece of graphite used in pencils.
Phrase **swing the lead** (*informal*) to try to avoid work.
Word Family **leaded** *adjective* (of petrol) containing lead; **leaden** *adjective* 1 having the colour or appearance of lead. 2 being as heavy or dull as lead. 3 (*dated*) made of lead; **leadenly** *adverb*.

leader (lee-da) *noun*
1 a person or thing that leads: *the leader of an expedition.*
2 *Newspapers* ⇨ EDITORIAL.
3 the first violin in an orchestra.
Word Family **leaderless** *adjective*.

leadership *noun*
1 the position, function, or guidance of a leader.
2 the ability to lead.

lead-in (leed-in) *noun*
an introduction to a speech, newspaper article, etc.

leading (lee-ding) *adjective*
chief or most important: *a leading expert in this field.*

leading article ⇨ EDITORIAL.

leading edge *noun*
1 the foremost edge of a moving object, such as an aircraft's wing or propeller blade.
2 the forefront of progress or development, especially in technology.

leading question *noun*
a question so worded that it suggests the desired answer.

leading rating *noun*
Navy a rank above able rating and below petty officer.

lead story (leed stor-ee) *noun* (*plural* **lead stories**)
the main news article on the front page of a newspaper.

leaf *noun* (*plural* **leaves**)
1 a flat structure, usually green, found on the stem of plants.
2 a single sheet of paper, especially in a book.
3 an extra panel to make a table larger, often hinged or sliding.
4 *Metallurgy* a very thin metal sheet: *gold leaf.*
Phrases **take a leaf out of someone's book** to follow someone's example. **turn**

over a new leaf to make a new and better start.
• **leaf** *verb* to put forth leaves.
Phrase **leaf through** to turn the pages of a book quickly.
Word Family **leafy** *adjective* (**leafier; leafiest**) covered with leaves; **leafiness** *noun*; **leafless** *adjective*.

leaflet *noun*
1 a flat or folded sheet of printed matter, usually giving information or advice.
2 a small leaf or leaf-like part.

league[1] (leeg) *noun*
1 an agreement made between people, groups or nations, for their mutual benefit, or the parties to such an agreement.
2 a group of sporting clubs which arranges matches between its member teams.
3 a standard of excellence: *He's just not in the same league as his brother.*
Phrase **in league with** allied with.
• **league** *verb* to form into or become a league.

league[2] (leeg) *noun*
an old unit of length equal to about three miles.

leak *verb*
1 (of a container) to let liquid or gas wrongly enter or escape.
2 (of a liquid or gas) to enter or escape.
3 to disclose information: *Someone leaked the story to the Sunday papers.*
• **leak** *noun*
1 any hole, etc. through which liquid or gas may wrongly enter or escape: *Did you find the leak?*
2 an act or instance of leaking.
Phrase **have a leak, take a leak** (*informal*) to urinate.
Word Family **leaky** *adjective* (**leakier; leakiest**); **leakiness** *noun*.

leakage (lee-kij) *noun*
1 the act or process of leaking.
2 something which leaks in or out.

lean[1] *verb* (**leans; leaning; leant** (lent) or **leaned**)
1 to bend from a vertical position or in a particular direction: *The waiter leaned over the table.* □ *Lean out of the window.*
2 to rest against or on for support: *We leaned against the fence.*
Phrases **lean on 1** to depend on.
2 (*informal*) to put strong pressure on.
lean towards to have a tendency towards.
Word Family **lean** *noun* an amount of bending from a vertical position; **leaning** *noun* a tendency towards: *I detect a certain leaning towards socialism in him.*

lean[2] *adjective*
1 thin, especially in a healthy way.
2 (of meat) containing little fat.
3 giving little comfort or reward: *the lean years after the war.*
Word Family **leanness** *noun*.

lean-to *noun*
a small building which is supported by the wall of a larger building.

leap *verb* (**leaps; leaping; leapt** (lept) or **leaped**)
to spring or jump.
Phrase **leap at** to accept eagerly.
• **leap** *noun* a jumping movement.
Phrases **a leap in the dark** an action the consequences of which cannot be foreseen. **by leaps and bounds** making extremely rapid progress.

leapfrog *noun*
a game in which one person jumps across another who is bent over.
• **leapfrog** *verb* (**leapfrogs; leapfrogging; leapfrogged**).

leap year ⇨ YEAR.

learn (lern) *verb* (**learns; learning; learnt** or **learned**)
1 to gain knowledge or skill from instruction or practice.
2 to be told: *I was sorry to learn of your illness.*
Word Family **learner** *noun* a person who is learning.

> [!] Do not confuse *learn* with *teach*: *learn* means 'to gain knowledge', as in *I'm learning to play the flute*, while *teach* means 'to give someone knowledge', as in *She's teaching me to play the flute.*

learned (ler-nid) *adjective*
having or requiring much knowledge.
Word Family **learnedly** *adverb*; **learnedness** *noun*.

learning (lern-ing) *noun*
the knowledge acquired by scholarly study.

learning curve *noun*
a person's speed of learning about a job, life, etc.: *It's a complicated piece of software requiring a steep learning curve from its young users.*

learning difficulties *plural noun*
difficulty in learning, especially when caused by a mental or psychological disorder.

learnt (lernt) a past tense and past participle of **learn**.

lease *noun*
a contract which allows a person to use or occupy property in return for rent.
Phrase **a new lease of life** a renewed enjoyment of life.
• **lease** *verb* to grant or take possession of by lease.

leasehold (**leese**-hold) *noun*
Law a right to use, for a specified period, land or property which one does not own. Compare FREEHOLD.
Word Family **leaseholder** *noun*.

leash *noun* (*plural* **leashes**) also called **lead**.
a strap or thong for restraining animals.

least *noun*
the smallest amount, quantity, degree, etc.: *He was not in the least embarrassed.*
Phrase **at least 1** at the lowest estimate: *He writes at least twice as fast as I do.*
2 even if nothing else: *At least you could say you're sorry.*
• **least** *adverb* a superlative form of **little**.
Phrase **not least** in particular: *He offended many people, not least the Queen Mother.*

leastways *adverb* also **leastwise**
(*informal*) at least.

leather (**leth**-a) *noun*
the tanned and prepared skin of animals.
Word Family **leathery** *adjective* like leather; **leatheriness** *noun*.

leatherjacket ⇨ DADDY-LONG-LEGS.

leave[1] *verb* (**leaves; leaving; left**)
1 to go out or away from: *We left the country and returned to the city.*
2 to cause or allow to remain: *Leave your bags on the hall table.* □ *Did you leave the radiator turned on?*
3 to have as a remainder: *Four from six leaves two.*
4 to give to after death: *My uncle left me a fortune in his will.*
5 to have as a surviving family member after death: *He leaves a wife and two children.*
Phrases **leave go** (*informal*) to stop holding. **leave off** (*informal*) to stop or discontinue. **leave out** to omit.
Word Family **leaver** *noun* a person who leaves.

leave[2] *noun*
1 also **leave of absence** permission to be absent from duty, or the period of such absence.
2 (*formal*) permission.
Phrase **take one's leave** to say goodbye.

leaves
the plural of **leaf**.

lechery (**letch**-a-ree) *noun*
an unpleasant feeling or display of sexual interest.
Word Family **lecherous** *adjective* disposed to or characterized by lechery; **lecherously** *adverb*; **lecherousness** *noun*; **lecher** *noun* a man disposed to lechery.

lecithin (**less**-a-thin *or* **lek**-a-thin) *noun*
Biology a nitrogenous fatty substance found in the nerve tissues, the yolk of eggs, etc., and prepared as a health food.
[Greek *lekithos* egg yolk]

lectern *noun*
a tall sloping desk from which lessons are read in a church, lecture-hall, etc.

lecture (**lek**-cher) *noun*
1 a formal talk given to teach or inform a group.
2 a long boring warning or scolding: *Dad gave me a lecture when I came home late.*
• **lecture** *verb*.
[Latin *lector* a reader]

lecturer (**lek**-cha-ra) *noun*
a person who gives lectures, especially at a university or college.
Word Family **lectureship** *noun* the position of a lecturer.

led the past tense and past participle of **lead**[1].

ledge (lej) *noun*
a narrow shelf: *a window ledge.* □ *a rocky ledge halfway down the cliff face.*

ledger (**lej**-a) *noun*
a set of bookkeeping accounts.

lee *noun*
1 *Nautical* the sheltered side which is not receiving the wind
2 *Nautical* the direction towards which the wind is blowing.

leech *noun* (*plural* **leeches**)
1 a small blood-sucking worm, living in water-holes or very damp places.
2 (*informal*) a parasitic person.

leek *noun*
a vegetable related to the onion, with a white cylindrical bulb and broad flat leaves.

leer *noun*
a look or roll of the eyes expressing slyness, malice, lust, etc.
Word Family **leer** *verb*; **leering** *adjective*; **leeringly** *adverb*.

leery *adjective* (**leerier; leeriest**)
(*informal*) wary or suspicious.

lees *plural noun*
the sediment of wine or other liquids.

leeward (lee-w'd *or* loo-'d) *adjective*,
adverb
Nautical of, on or towards the lee.
Compare WINDWARD.
• **leeward** *noun*.

leeway *noun*
1 extra time, etc. giving scope for
manoeuvre or a margin for error.
2 *Nautical* the drift of a ship or aircraft to
leeward.

left¹ *adjective*
1 of or relating to the side of a person or
thing which is towards the west when the
subject is facing north.
2 *Politics* of or relating to the left wing.
• **left** *noun*
1 (**the left**) anything on or towards the left
side.
2 (**the Left**) *Politics* all individuals and
groups with a socialist outlook.
3 a hit given with the left fist.
• **left** *adverb* on or to the left side: *Move left
a bit.*

left² the past tense and past participle of
leave¹.

left-handed *adjective*
1 preferring to use the left hand.
2 being done with or adapted to the left
hand.
Word Family **left-handedly** *adverb*; **left-
handedness** *noun*; **left-hander** *noun*.

leftist *noun*
Politics a person who holds or sympathizes
with the views of the left wing.
• **leftist** *adjective*.

leftover *noun*
(*often* **leftovers**) any food remaining after
a meal, especially when used for another
meal.

left-wing *adjective*
Politics radical, socialist, etc.: *Despite his
conservative background, David adopted left-
wing views at university.*
• **left wing** *noun* the most radical section
of a political party or group, usually
meaning (in a parliamentary democracy)
extremists in socialist parties and
moderates in conservative parties.
Word Family **left-winger** *noun*.
[from a European tradition that radical
members of a legislative assembly sit on
the President's left]

leg *noun*
1 *Anatomy* the part of the body between
the hip and the foot, bearing the weight of
the body.
2 anything shaped or used like a leg: *a
chair leg.*
3 the part of a piece of clothing covering
the leg.
4 any of the distinct parts of a course, race,
etc.: *We covered the last leg of our trip very
quickly.*
5 *Cricket* the part of the field lying to the
left of and behind a right-handed
batsman. Compare OFF *adjective*.
Phrases **not have a leg to stand on** not
to have a sound or logical basis for an
argument, etc. **on one's last legs** on the
verge of collapse or death. **pull
someone's leg** (*informal*) to make fun of
someone.
• **leg** *verb* (**legs; legging; legged**)
Phrase **leg it** (*informal*) 1 to walk. 2 to
run away.

legacy (leg-a-see) *noun* (*plural* **legacies**)
1 *Law* a gift of personal property made by
will to any person. Compare INHERITANCE
(definition 3).
2 anything handed down from ancestors
or predecessors.
[Latin *legare* to bequeath]

legal (lee-g'l) *adjective*
1 of or relating to law: *a legal document.*
2 lawful: *Copying someone else's signature on
a cheque isn't legal.*
Word Family **legally** *adverb*; **legalistic**
(lee-g'l-**ist**-ik) *adjective* showing over-strict
adherence to laws or rules.
[Latin *legis* of law]

legal aid *noun*
help towards legal costs, paid from
government funds to those who can show
need.

legality (lig-al-i-tee) *noun*
the state of being allowed by law.

legalize, legalise *verb*
to make legal.
Word Family **legalization** *noun*.

legal tender *noun*
banknotes and coins that must be
accepted when offered as payment for a
debt.

legate (leg-'t) *noun*
Roman Catholicism an official
representative of the Pope.

legation (lig-**ay**-sh'n) *noun*
1 *Politics* a group of diplomatic representatives led by an official below the rank of ambassador.
2 the offices or official home of a legate or a legation.

leg before wicket *adjective* also **leg before**
Cricket (of a batsman) used to describe a way of getting out in which the batsman's body intercepts a fairly bowled ball which would otherwise have hit the wicket.

legend (**lej**-'nd) *noun*
1 a traditional tale about a person or country, often regarded locally as history, but which may or may not be true.
2 an extremely famous person.
3 a written explanation of the symbols used in a map, diagram, etc., or an inscription on a coin, etc.
Word Family **legendary** *adjective*.
[Latin *legenda* things to be read]

legerdemain (lej-a-di-**mayn**) *noun*
↪ SLEIGHT OF HAND.

leggings *plural noun*
1 a tight-fitting piece of clothing for the legs.
2 protective trousers, worn over ordinary ones.

leggy *adjective* (**leggier; leggiest**)
having long legs.

legible (**lej**-a-b'l) *adjective*
able to be read easily.
Word Family **legibility** (lej-a-**bill**-i-tee) *noun*; **legibly** *adverb*.
[Latin *legere* to read]

legion (**lee**-j'n) *noun*
1 any of various **military** organizations or units: *the Foreign Legion*.
2 a vast multitude: *Her problems are legion*.
3 *Ancient history* a division of the Roman army, consisting of at least 3000 men.
Word Family **legionary, legionnaire** (lee-j'n-**air**) *noun* a member of a legion; **legionary** *adjective*.
[Latin *legere* to choose]

legislate (**lej**-i-slate) *verb*
to make or enact laws.
Word Family **legislative** (**lej**-i-sla-tiv) *adjective* 1 having the power or function to make laws: *a legislative assembly*. 2 of or produced by laws; **legislation** (lej-i-**slay**-sh'n) *noun* 1 the act of making laws. 2 a law or group of laws; **legislator** *noun*.

legislature (**lej**-i-slay-cher) *noun*
any organization which makes laws, such as a parliament.

legitimate (lij-**it**-a-mit) *adjective*
1 according to the law or established standards, etc.: *a legitimate business*.
2 logical and valid: *That is not a legitimate argument*.
3 born of parents who are legally married. Compare ILLEGITIMATE (definition 2).
Word Family **legitimately** *adverb*; **legitimacy, legitimateness** *noun*; **legitimize, legitimise** *verb* to make legal or legitimate.
[Latin *legitimare* to make lawful]

legless *adjective*
1 having no legs.
2 (*informal*) extremely drunk.

legume (**leg**-yoom) *noun*
any of a group of plants in which the fruit is a pod, such as the pea.
[Latin *legumen* a plant with pods, from *legere* to pick (pods)]

leg-up *noun*
an act of helping someone to get up onto something, e.g. by making one's hands into a firm base for a foot.

logwork *noun*
the necessary hard work involved in making a scheme work.

lei (lay) *noun*
a garland of flowers for the neck or head.
[Hawaiian]

leisure (*rhymes with* treasure) *noun*
the time free of work or duties.
Phrases **at leisure** 1 without activities organized for one. 2 without hurrying.
at one's leisure when one has some spare time.
Word Family **leisurely** *adjective, adverb* without haste; **leisureliness** *noun*.

leisure centre *noun*
a building where the public can swim or do other sports on payment of a charge.

lemming *noun*
a mouse-like mammal of Arctic regions, reputed to hurl itself off cliffs during periodic mass migrations.

lemon *noun*
1 a yellow citrus fruit with a bitter taste.
2 a pale yellow colour.
Word Family **lemony** *adjective*.
[Arabic *lima*]

lemonade *noun*
a drink containing lemon juice or flavoured with lemon, often carbonated.

lemon curd *noun*
a spread made of butter, eggs, sugar and lemons.

lemur (lee-ma) *noun*
a small nocturnal tree-dwelling mammal with a long furry tail, found in the forests of Madagascar and nearby islands.
[Latin *lemures* ghosts, from its appearance and nocturnal habits]

lend *verb* (**lends; lending; lent**)
1 to give something with the understanding that it will be returned: *Can you lend me £10?*
2 *Commerce* to permit the temporary use of money, etc. in return for payment: *The banks lend money at high interest rates.*
3 to add: *Dark clouds lent a threatening appearance to the sky.*
Word Family lender *noun*.

> ! Do not confuse *lend* with BORROW.

length *noun*
1 the distance from end to end: *What is the length of this room?*
2 the amount of time something lasts: *We were surprised by the length of the film.*
3 the quality of being long.
4 a piece of something thin: *a length of cable.*
5 *Sport* the body-length of a horse, boat, etc., used to judge the distance between competitors in a race.
Phrases **at length 1** in detail. **2** after some time. **go to any lengths** to do whatever is necessary.
Word Family lengthen *verb* to make or become longer; **lengthwise, lengthways** *adverb* in the direction of the length; **lengthy** *adjective* (**lengthier; lengthiest**) very long; **lengthiness** *noun*.

lenient (lee-nee-ent) *adjective*
mild, merciful or gentle.
Word Family leniently *adverb*; **leniency, lenience** *noun*.
[Latin *leniens* softening]

lens (lenz) *noun* (*plural* **lenses**)
1 any device, especially a curved piece of glass, which causes a beam of rays, such as light or an electron beam, to converge or diverge on passing through it.
2 (*informal*) a contact lens.
[Latin, a lentil]

lent the past tense and past participle of **lend**.

Lent *noun*
Christianity a fast of 40 days in preparation for Easter, in memory of Christ's fast in the wilderness.
Word Family Lenten *adjective*.

> The word **Lent** is etymologically connected with *length*. The Saxons called March *lencten monath*, because it was the month when days began to lengthen. In Middle English *Lenten*, later *Lente*, meant 'spring', the season when days lengthen; the religious festival is called *Lent* because it takes place in spring.

lentil *noun*
the edible bean-like seed of a pod-bearing plant.

lento *adverb*
Music slowly.
[Italian]

Leo (lee-o) *noun*
Astrology a group of stars, the fifth sign of the Zodiac; the sign of the Lion.
[Latin, lion]

leonine *adjective*
of or like a lion.

leopard (lep-erd) *noun*
a large flesh-eating Asian and African mammal of the cat family, usually having a tawny coat, with dark blotches.
Word Family leopardess *noun* (*plural* **leopardesses**) a female leopard.
[Latin *leo* lion + *pardus* panther]

leotard (lee-o-tard) *noun*
a close-fitting piece of clothing that covers the body to the top of the legs, worn by dancers, gymnasts, etc. performing physical exercises.
[after *J. Léotard*, 1842-1870, a French trapeze artist]

leper (lep-a) *noun*
a person who suffers from leprosy.
[Greek *lepros* scaly]

leprechaun (lep-ri-kawn) *noun*
in Ireland, an elfin cobbler supposed to possess a crock of gold.
[Irish, small body]

leprosy (lep-ra-see) *noun*
an infectious bacterial disease causing changes in the skin and nerves leading, if untreated, to extensive deformities.
Word Family leprous *adjective*.

lesbian *noun*
a female homosexual.
Word Family lesbianism *noun*.
[after *Lesbos*, the Greek island home of Sappho, the ancient poet of lesbian love]

lesion (lee-*zh*'n) *noun*
Medicine an injury or wound, especially a
scarring of internal tissue.
[Latin *laesionis* of an injury]

less *adjective*
not as much in size, amount or degree: *You
should eat less fat if you want to lose weight.*
• **less** *preposition* minus: *Seven less two is
five.*
Word Family less *adverb*; **lessen** *verb* to
make or become less.

> **!** Do not confuse *less* with FEWER.

lessee (less-**ee**) *noun*
Law a person to whom a lease is granted.

lesser *adjective*
smaller.

lesson *noun*
1 a period of time in which a pupil or
group of pupils is taught one particular
subject: *a maths lesson.*
2 something from which one learns or
should learn: *Let that be a lesson to you.*
3 *Christianity* a passage from the Bible
read aloud during a religious service.

lessor (less-**or**) *noun*
Law a person who grants a lease.

lest *conjunction*
1 so that it is impossible that: *lest we forget.*
2 because of the possibility that: *She was
frightened lest the vandals should return.*

let[1] *verb* (**lets**; **letting**; **let**)
1 to allow or permit: *Please let me come with
you!*
2 to rent or hire: *The sign said 'Rooms to let'.*
3 to make or cause to: *Do let us know your
decision.*
4 an auxiliary verb indicating intention or
suggestion: *Let's go.* □ *Let us pray.*
Phrases let alone not to mention: *I'm too
tired to walk, let alone run.* **let down 1** to
lower: *Will you let down the blinds?* **2** to fail
to do what someone expected: *I'm afraid
you have let us down badly.* **let fly** to attack.
let go to stop holding. **let off 1** to excuse: *I
will let you off without punishment this time.*
2 to cause to explode: *The boys let off a
firework in the playground.* **let on** (*informal*)
to tell: *Please don't let on to Mum about this.*
let oneself in for (*informal*) to cause
oneself to become involved in: *Oh no –
what have I let myself in for?* **let out 1** to
utter: *He let out a cry of rage.* **2** to make
larger: *Can you let out this dress at the seams?*
let up (*informal*) to lessen in intensity: *The
rain didn't let up for several days.* **let well**

alone (*informal*) to leave things as they
are.
Word Family let's *contraction* a short
form of **let us**: *Let's go now.*

let[2] *noun*
1 *Tennis* a service which must be repeated
because the ball has touched the net in
passing.
2 an old word for an obstacle or
obstruction: *without let or hindrance.*

let-down *noun*
a disappointment or failure.

lethal (lee-th'l) *adjective*
able to cause death.
Word Family lethally *adverb*.
[Latin *letum* death]

lethargic (le-**thar**-jik) *adjective*
being sluggishly lazy or inactive.
Word Family lethargically *adverb*;
lethargy (leth-a-jee) *noun.*
[Greek *lethargos* forgetful]

letter *noun*
1 a written symbol or mark for a speech
sound: *What letter comes after 'T' in the
alphabet?*
2 a written or printed message to a person
or group: *I wrote a letter to my cousin.*
3 the actual or exact words, as distinct
from the general meaning: *You must obey
these instructions to the letter.*
4 (**letters**) literature as a profession or a
culture: *a man of letters.*
Word Family letter *verb* to write on with
letters; **lettering** *noun* 1 the act of writing
with letters. 2 the letters used; **lettered**
adjective educated or cultured.
[Latin *littera* a letter of the alphabet]

letter box *noun* (*plural* **letter boxes**)
1 a fixed metal container in which letters
are put to be collected and delivered.
2 a box or opening at a house where letters
are delivered.

letterhead *noun*
a printed heading on writing paper giving
the name, address, etc. of the sender.

lettuce (let-iss) *noun*
a large vegetable, usually green, with many
leaves forming a loose head, used in
salads.
[Latin *lactuca*]

let-up *noun*
(*informal*) a relieving pause.

leukaemia (loo-**kee**-mee-a) *noun*
a sometimes fatal cancerous disease
causing excess production of white blood
cells.
[Greek *leukos* white + *haima* blood]

levee (lev-ay) *noun*
a formal assembly of guests, usually at a palace.
[French *levé* rising, as originally held when the king rose from bed]

level *noun*
1 a position, especially in relation to others: *orders from someone at the highest level of authority.*
2 a horizontal line or position: *We're parked in the multi-storey car park, on the second level.*
3 an instrument to check or indicate the horizontal.
Phrase **on the level** (*informal*) honest or genuine.
• **level** *adjective*
1 having a flat smooth surface.
2 calm: *a level voice.*
3 at the same height as something else.
4 equal: *And the two teams are level at half-time.*
5 horizontal.
Phrase **do one's level best** to do the most that one can.
• **level** *verb* (**levels; levelling; levelled**)
1 to make or become level or equal: *We levelled the ground before starting the wall.*
2 to aim or point: *The hijacker levelled a gun at the hostage.*
Phrase **level with** (*informal*) to be totally honest with.
Word Family **leveller** *noun* a person or thing that levels or makes even; **levelly** *adverb*; **levelness** *noun*.

level crossing *noun*
a place where a road crosses a railway line.

level-headed *adjective*
sensible or calm.
Word Family **level-headedly** *adverb*; **level-headedness** *noun*.

lever (lee-va) *noun*
1 any device consisting of a rigid bar pivoted on a fixed point, called the **fulcrum**, and used to raise or move a weight.
2 a handle used to operate a mechanism: *a gear lever.*
• **lever** *verb* to move with or apply a lever.
Word Family **leverage** (lee-va-rij) *noun*
1 the power or movement provided by a lever. 2 the power to influence.
[French, to raise]

leveret (lev-a-rit) *noun*
a young hare.
[Latin *leporis* of a hare]

leviathan (lev-eye-a-th'n) *noun*
anything which is very large, especially in the sea.
[after *Leviathan*, an unidentifiable sea-monster mentioned in the Old Testament]

levitation (lev-i-tay-sh'n) *noun*
the act of rising into the air without physical support.
Word Family **levitate** (lev-i-tayt) *verb*.
[Latin *levis* light]

levity (lev-i-tee) *noun*
light-heartedness or frivolity.

levy (lev-ee) *verb* (**levies; levying; levied**)
1 to impose or collect, with the use of authority or force: *A new tax was levied on alcohol.*
2 to conscript an army.
• **levy** *noun* (*plural* **levies**)
1 a raising or collecting, as of taxes.
2 something which is raised or collected.
[French *lever* to raise]

lewd *adjective*
obscene or arousing lust.
Word Family **lewdly** *adverb*; **lewdness** *noun*.

liability (lie-a-bill-i-tee) *noun* (*plural* **liabilities**)
1 an obligation, especially a financial debt: *When he became unemployed, he could not meet all his liabilities.*
2 a handicap or disadvantage: *Long skirts are a liability in wet weather.*
3 the state of being liable or under an obligation: *The company denied liability for the accident.*

liable (lie-a-b'l) *adjective*
legally responsible.
Phrase **liable to 1** likely to experience: *The coast is liable to storms in winter.* **2** likely to: *We are all liable to exaggerate from time to time.*

liaison (lee-ay-z'n) *noun*
a contact, connection or communication between people, groups, organizations, etc.
Word Family **liaise** *verb* to maintain contact with.
[French]

> ! Note the spelling of *liaison*: it has an *i* before and after the *a*.

liar *noun*
a person who tells lies.

Lib Dem *noun*
(*informal*) British *politics* a Liberal Democrat.

libel (**lie**-b'l) *noun*
Law a false and damaging written or printed statement against another person. Compare SLANDER.
Word Family **libel** *verb* (**libels; libelling; libelled**); **libellous** *adjective*; **libellously** *adverb*; **libeller** *noun*.

liberal (**lib**-a-r'l) *adjective*
1 favouring progress, reform and individual freedom in social or political matters.
2 (**Liberal**) *British politics* connected with the **Liberal Party**, a former party which became part of the Liberal Democrats.
3 generous or free in giving: *She is very liberal with her praise of others.*
4 not very exact: *The play is a liberal translation of an ancient epic poem.*
• **liberal** *noun*
1 a person with liberal or tolerant views, especially in politics.
2 (**Liberal**) a member of the Liberal Party.
Word Family **liberally** *adverb* freely or generously; **liberality** (lib-a-**ral**-i-tee), **liberalness** *noun*; **liberalism** *noun* any liberal principles, especially in a political or religious movement.
[Latin *liberalis* pertaining to a free man]

Liberal Democrat *noun*
British politics a member of the **Liberal Democrats**, one of the three largest parties.
• **Liberal Democrat** *adjective*.

liberate (**lib**-a-rate) *verb*
to set free.
Word Family **liberation** (lib-a-**ray**-sh'n) *noun* freeing; **liberator** *noun* a person who liberates.
[Latin *liber* free]

libertine (**lib**-a-teen) *noun*
a person considered to be immoral or lacking restraint.
[Latin *libertinus* a freedman]

liberty (**lib**-a-tee) *noun* (*plural* **liberties**)
1 the state of being neither confined nor controlled: *He gained his liberty after 37 years in prison.*
2 the power or right to do as one chooses.
3 a privilege: *Officers were granted certain liberties denied to the other soldiers.*
4 (*informal*) a cheeky act.
Phrase **at liberty** 1 allowed: *On days two and three of your holiday, you are at liberty to do as you wish.* 2 having escaped from captivity: *The prisoners were at liberty for several days.*

libidinous (lib-**id**-i-nus) *adjective*
full of lust or desires.
Word Family **libidinously** *adverb*; **libidinousness** *noun*.

libido (li-**bee**-doe) *noun*
sexual instinct.
[Latin, desire, caprice]

Libra (**lee**-bra) *noun*
Astrology a group of stars, the seventh sign of the Zodiac; the sign of the Scales.
[Latin, a pair of scales]

librarian (lie-**brair**-ee-an) *noun*
a person in charge of or helping in a library.
Word Family **librarianship** *noun*.

library (**lie**-bra-ree) *noun* (*plural* **libraries**)
1 a room or building where a collection of books is kept for people to read or borrow.
2 any collection of books: *He has a vast library of science fiction.*
[Latin *libraria* bookseller's shop, from *liber* book]

libretto *noun* (*plural* **libretti** or **librettos**)
the words or text of an opera.
Word Family **librettist** *noun* a person who writes libretti.
[Italian]

lice
the plural of **louse**.

licence (**lie**-s'nse) *noun* (*American* **license**)
1 permission to do something, especially formal or official permission.
2 a document showing this permission: *a driving licence.*
3 a deliberate avoidance of usual rules, etc. to achieve a particular effect: *poetic licence.*
4 unrestrained freedom: *The teacher allowed his students too much licence.*
Word Family **license** *verb* to give permission or a licence to; **licensee** (lie-s'n-**see**) *noun* a person to whom a licence is given, especially one to sell alcohol.
[Latin *licentia* freedom, from *licet* it is permitted]

> ⚠ Do not confuse the noun *licence*, as in *a television licence*, with the verb *license*, as in *a licensed restaurant*. The noun ends in *ce* and the verb ends in *se* (like *practice/practise* and *advice/advise*). In American English both the noun and the verb are spelt *license*.

licentious (lie-**sen**-shus) *adjective*
sexually unrestrained.
Word Family **licentiously** *adverb*; **licentiousness** *noun*.
[Latin *licentia* freedom abused, lawlessness]

lichen (lie-k'n *or* litch-'n) *noun*
Biology a plant formed by an association of a fungus and an alga, often appearing as a light green growth on tree trunks, rocks, etc.
[Greek *leikhen*]

lick *verb*
1 to pass the tongue over: *The dog licked the plate clean.*
2 to move lightly over: *The flames licked the side of the house.*
3 (*informal*) to defeat thoroughly.
Word Family lick *noun* 1 a stroke of the tongue. 2 a light touch; **licking** *noun* (*informal*) a thrashing or defeat.

lickety-split *adverb*
(*informal*) at full speed.

licorice ⇨ LIQUORICE.

lid *noun*
1 any movable cover for an opening or an open vessel, either detachable or hinged.
2 an eyelid.
Phrase **flip one's lid** (*informal*) to lose one's temper, sanity, etc.
Word Family lidded *adjective*.

lido (lee-do) *noun*
a public open-air swimming pool or bathing beach.
[*Lido,* a bathing beach near Venice]

lie¹ *noun*
a statement known not to be true by the person who makes it.
Phrase **give the lie to** to show to be untrue.
• lie *verb* (lies; lying; lied) to make untrue statements.

lie² *verb* (lies; lying; lay; lain)
1 to recline or rest flat on something: *The book lay on the table.* □ *You can't lie in bed all day.*
2 to be or remain: *The money lay in the bank for ten years.* □ *Your whole future lies ahead of you.*
Phrases **lie in** to remain in bed in the morning. **lie low** to hide: *The bandits lay low until the spring.* **take something lying down** to accept something without protest.
• lie *noun*
1 the position or direction in which something lies: *the lie of the land.*
2 the place or den where a creature lurks.

> ! Do not confuse *lie* with *lay.* ⇨ LAY¹.

lie detector *noun*
a device to measure pulse and breathing rates, which are thought to increase when a person is lying.

lief (leef) *adverb*
an old word meaning 'gladly or willingly'.

liege (leej) *noun*
a person who owed or received homage or service in feudal times.

lie-in *noun*
a longer time than usual of lying in bed in the morning.

lieu (loo) *noun*
Phrase **in lieu of** instead of: *I gave him my bicycle in lieu of cash.*
[French *au lieu de* in place of]

lieutenant (lef-ten-ent) *noun*
1 *Army* a commissioned officer ranking between second lieutenant and captain.
2 *Navy* a commissioned officer ranking between sub lieutenant and lieutenant commander.
3 a deputy or substitute.
Word Family lieutenancy *noun* (*plural* **lieutenancies**) the office of a lieutenant.
[French *lieu* place + *tenant* holding]

lieutenant colonel *noun*
Army a commissioned officer ranking between major and colonel.

lieutenant commander *noun*
Navy a commissioned officer ranking between lieutenant and commander.

lieutenant general *noun*
Army a commissioned officer ranking between major general and general.

life *noun* (*plural* **lives**)
1 the condition of growth and reproduction that distinguishes plants and animals from earth, stones, etc.
2 an individual's existence: *Two thousand lives were lost in the earthquake.*
3 a biography: *She wrote a life of Rasputin.*
4 a period of effectiveness or usefulness.
5 bustle and activity: *There doesn't seem to be much life in this town.*
6 short form of **life imprisonment** the maximum term of imprisonment.
Phrases **for the life of me** (*informal*) no matter how hard I try: *I can't for the life of me remember her name.* **not on your life** (*informal*) certainly not; never. **take one's life in one's hands** to risk death.

life assurance ⇨ LIFE INSURANCE.

lifebelt *noun*
a small buoyant belt worn to keep a person afloat in the water.

lifeblood (life-blud) *noun*
something which is necessary to maintain life: *Exports are this country's lifeblood.*

lifeboat *noun*
1 a boat based on the coast and equipped to rescue people or vessels in trouble at sea.
2 a boat carried on a ship's deck for use in a shipwreck.

lifebuoy (life-boy) *noun*
a ring or other object made of buoyant material to assist a person to remain afloat.

life cycle *noun*
Biology the whole span of life of an organism through its various changes of form, e.g. egg, larva, chrysalis and imago in the butterfly.

life expectancy *noun* (*plural* **life expectancies**)
the average number of years that people are expected to live. Life expectancy varies according to health, living conditions, etc.; it is usually greater for women than for men.

lifeguard *noun*
a person who rescues swimmers in danger of drowning and gives first aid.

life imprisonment ⇨ LIFE (definition 6).

life insurance *noun* also **life assurance**
an insurance providing payment of a specified sum of money when the person who is insured reaches a certain age or dies.

life jacket *noun*
a sleeveless buoyant jacket worn to keep a person afloat in the water.

lifeless *adjective*
1 no longer alive, or seeming to be no longer alive: *They carried his lifeless body away.*
2 having no living things: *The moon is lifeless.*
3 dull and spiritless.
Word Family **lifelessly** *adverb*; **lifelessness** *noun*.

lifelike *adjective*
resembling real life: *a lifelike portrait.*

lifeline *noun*
1 a rope connecting people to each other or to an object, used in a dangerous situation such as mountain climbing or deep-sea diving.
2 a person or thing that helps one to escape from an unpleasant situation.

lifelong *adjective*
lasting or continuing through the period of a lifetime: *a lifelong friendship.*

life peer *noun*
a peer whose title is not hereditary.

life preserver *noun*
1 a lifebelt or a jacket to keep a person afloat in the water.
2 a stick with a heavy knob at the end.

lifer *noun*
(*informal*) someone serving a life sentence of imprisonment.

lifesaver *noun*
(*informal*) a person or thing that saves one from an unpleasant situation.

life sciences *plural noun*
the branches of science which deal with the structure and behaviour of living organisms, including biology and botany.

lifespan *noun*
the usual or expected period between birth and death.

lifestyle *noun*
a person's typical way of life: *an affluent lifestyle.*

lifetime *noun*
the length of a person's life: *We had seen nothing like it in our lifetime.*

lift *verb*
1 to raise something to a higher position: *I couldn't lift the box onto the table.*
2 to raise or improve: *Our spirits lifted when we saw the bus coming.*
3 (of fog) to clear: *The mist should lift soon.*
4 to remove formally: *The ban on radios in school has been lifted.*
Phrase **lift off** (of an aircraft) to leave the ground.
• **lift** *noun*
1 the act of lifting: *Give it another lift from your end.*
2 a box-like device for moving people or goods vertically between different levels, as in a large store.
3 a free ride in a vehicle. *We hitched a lift into town.*
4 a feeling of well-being: *Their approval gave me a real lift.*
5 any upward force, especially that produced by air passing around an aircraft's wings.
Word Family **lifter** *noun*.

lift-off *noun* also called **blast-off**.
the moment at which a rocket leaves its launching pad.

ligament (lig-a-m'nt) *noun*
Anatomy any sheet or band of tough fibrous tissue connecting parts of the body such as bone joints.
[Latin *ligare* to bind]

ligature (lig-a-cher) *noun*
a thread used for tying blood vessels.

light¹ (lite) *noun*
1 the medium which makes things visible, such as the radiance from the sun.
2 any of various objects or devices for making things visible: *an electric light.*
3 *Physics* the form of electromagnetic radiation with a frequency of about 10^{12} Hz, to which the human eye is sensitive. Photographic materials may be sensitive to the frequencies immediately above the visible range (**ultraviolet**), or below it (**infrared**).
4 an object producing a flame: *He gave me a light for my cigar.*
5 a brightness in someone's eyes.
6 the way one looks at something mentally: *When I heard this I began to see things in a new light.*
7 (**lights**) traffic lights: *The lights changed when I was halfway across.*
Phrases **come to light** to be revealed: *New information has come to light.* **in the light of** because of: *In the light of your previous good behaviour, we shall let you off.* **see the light** to realize the truth. **throw light on** to help to solve: *Perhaps you can throw light on this mystery.*
• **light** *adjective*
1 well supplied with light: *The room is very light with the blinds up.*
2 pale: *a light green dress.*
• **light** *verb* (**lights; lighting; lit** or **lighted**)
1 to give light to: *The fire lit the whole room.* □ *The moon will light your way.*
2 to set burning: *I lit the fire.*
Phrase **light up 1** to become lighter or brighter: *His face lit up in a huge grin.* **2** to light a cigarette, pipe, etc.
Word Family **lightness** *noun.*

light² *adjective*
1 not heavy; having little weight.
2 not heavy or strong in force or intensity: *A light rain fell.*
3 not very serious, difficult or tiring: *Here is some light reading for the trip.*
4 nimble: *He is very light on his feet.*
5 (of sleep or a sleeper) easily disturbed.
6 (of food) small in amount and easy to digest.
7 (of soil) easy to break up.
8 (of the head) dizzy.
Phrase **make light of** to treat or consider as of little importance.
• **light** *adverb*
Phrase **travel light** to travel with a minimum of luggage.

Word Family **lightly** *adverb*; **lightness** *noun.*

light³ *verb* (**lights; lighting; lighted** or **lit**)
Phrase **light on, light upon** to come across by chance or accident: *He lit upon a clue.*

light-emitting diode *noun*
short form is **LED** a semiconductor used in electronic circuits which glows, e.g. to indicate that a piece of equipment is switched on.

lighten¹ *verb*
to make or become less dark.

lighten² *verb*
to make or become less heavy.

lighter¹ *noun*
a mechanical device for lighting cigarettes, cigars, etc.

lighter² *noun*
a barge.

light-fingered *adjective*
skilful at thieving or picking pockets.

light-headed *adjective*
dizzy: *We felt light-headed after the roller-coaster ride.*
Word Family **light-headedly** *adverb*; **light-headedness** *noun.*

light-hearted *adjective*
cheerful or carefree.
Word Family **light-heartedly** *adverb*; **light-heartedness** *noun.*

lighthouse *noun*
a tower on the coast that has a strong light to guide ships, etc.

light industry *noun*
the making of small goods, e.g. electrical items or kitchen utensils. Compare HEAVY INDUSTRY.

lighting *noun*
a style or an arrangement of lights.

lightness ⇨ LIGHT¹; LIGHT².

lightning *noun*
a brilliant flash of light in the sky caused by the discharge of natural electricity.
• **lightning** *adjective* extremely fast.

> **!** Note the spelling of *lightning*: there is no *e* between the *t* and the *n*. The word *lightening* is the present participle of the verb *lighten*.

lightning conductor *noun*
a metal rod or wire attached to a building, to protect it from lightning damage by earthing it.

light pen *noun*
a device which transmits information into a computer, e.g. from a bar code.

light relief noun also called **comic relief**.
Theatre an amusing or light-hearted
interlude during a serious play, to reduce
the tension.

lightship noun
a ship with bright lights, anchored in one
place to help guide other vessels.

lightweight adjective
1 having little weight.
2 of little importance.
• **lightweight** noun
1 a weight division in boxing, equal to
about 60 kg.
2 (*informal*) a person of little influence or
importance.

light year noun
Astronomy a unit of length equal to about
$9·46×10^{12}$ km (or nearly six million
million miles), being the distance that light
travels in one year.

like[1] preposition
1 in the same way as: *He acts like a baby*.
2 similar to: *She is very like her mother*.
3 typical of: *It would be just like her to do
that*.
4 used to introduce emphasis, etc.: *It
rained like anything*.
Phrase **feel like** to want or need: *Right
now I feel like a good meal*.
• **like** noun a match or equal: *I've never
heard the like!*
Phrase **and the like** and similar things:
*The room was full of tables, chairs and the
like*.
• **like** adjective similar in form or
character: *The two machines perform like
functions*.

like[2] verb
to enjoy or find agreeable: *I don't like
bananas*.
Phrases **I like that!** (*informal*) that is
very annoying! **should like, would like** to
want: *I'd like a coffee, please*. □ *Would you
like to come with us?*
Word Family like noun a preference or
something of which one is fond; **likable,
likeable** (**like-a-b'l**) adjective easily liked.

likely adjective (**likelier; likeliest**)
1 probable: *It is likely that it will rain this
evening*.
2 suitable or promising: *This is a likely spot
for catching fish*.
• **likely** adverb probably: *I shall very likely
be there*.
Word Family likelihood, likeliness
noun probability.

liken (**lie-k'n**) verb
Phrase **liken someone to, liken
something to** to compare someone or
something to: *He likened his house to a
palace*.

likeness noun (*plural* **likenesses**)
1 a resemblance.
2 an old word for a portrait.

likewise adverb
in the same way.

liking (**like-ing**) noun
a feeling of attraction or a preference.

lilac (**lie-l'k**) noun
1 a light purple colour.
2 a garden shrub with spikes of fragrant
purple or white flowers.
• **lilac** adjective.

> The word **lilac** comes from the
> Sanskrit word *nila* meaning 'dark blue',
> as does the name of the River Nile. This
> passed into Persian as *nil* and the
> adjective *nilak*, became *lilak*. English
> actually acquired the word *lilac* from
> Spanish via French and Arabic. The
> shrub of this name is so called from the
> colour of the flowers.

Lilliputian (**lill-i-pew-sh'n**) adjective
very small.
[after the tiny inhabitants of *Lilliput* in
Jonathan Swift's 'Gulliver's Travels']

lilt noun
a pleasant rhythmic change in pitch in a
voice, tune, etc.: *He speaks with an Irish lilt*.

lily (**lill-ee**) noun (*plural* **lilies**)
any of a group of plants with large sweet-
smelling trumpet-shaped flowers.
[from Latin]

lily-livered adjective
an old word meaning 'cowardly'.

limb (**lim**) noun
1 a leg, arm or wing of an animal.
2 any part which projects or extends, such
as the branch of a tree.
Phrase **out on a limb** isolated in an
awkward situation from which there is no
going back.

limber (**lim-ba**) adjective
supple or lithe.
• **limber** verb
Phrase **limber up** to do exercises, etc. in
order to warm up for more strenuous
activity.

limbo[1] noun
1 *Christianity* the place on the edge of hell,
formerly designated as suitable for the

souls of the just who lived before Christ, and for those of unbaptized infants.
2 a state of uncertainty.
[Latin *limbus* border or edge]

limbo² *noun*
a West Indian dance involving bending backwards to go under a horizontal bar.

lime¹ *noun*
a white powder, calcium oxide, used in cements, as a fertilizer in soil, etc.

lime² *noun*
1 a green citrus fruit, similar to a lemon but smaller and more bitter.
2 a bright light green colour.
[Arabic]

limeade *noun*
a drink containing lime juice or flavoured with lime, often carbonated.

limelight *noun*
1 the glare of publicity: *The band will do anything to stay in the limelight.*
2 the brilliant white light used in stage lighting.

limerick (**lim**-a-rik) *noun*
a five-line nonsense verse with strict rules of metre and rhyme, as in:
There was a young man of Bengal
Who went to a fancy-dress ball,
   He went, just for fun,
   Dressed up as a bun,
And a dog ate him up in the hall.
[from an Irish chorus, 'Will you come up to *Limerick*?']

limestone *noun*
Geology a sedimentary rock composed of calcium carbonate, often formed from the shells and skeletons of tiny organisms.

Limey (**lie**-mee) *noun*
(*American informal*) an Englishman.
[from the former use of *limes* on British ships to prevent scurvy]

limit *noun*
1 the furthest point that is possible or allowable: *There is a limit to what we can spend.* □ *What's the speed limit?*
2 a boundary.
***Phrases* be the limit** (*informal*) to be intolerable: *Honestly – she really is the limit sometimes!* **off limits** forbidden to military personnel except on official business.
• **limit** *verb* to restrict by imposing a limit: *I'll have to limit you to three chocolates each.*
***Word Family* limitation** *noun* 1 the act of limiting. 2 a restriction or shortcoming; **limitless** *adjective*; **limitlessness** *noun*.
[Latin *limitis* of a frontier]

limited (**lim**-it-id) *adjective*
confined or restricted: *I feel very limited having to live in a tent.*
***Word Family* limitedness** *noun*.

limo (**lim**-o) *noun*
(*informal*) a limousine.

limousine (**lim**-a-zeen) *noun*
any large luxurious car, especially if driven by a chauffeur.

The word **limousine** owes its origin to a kind of cloak. It was thought that the roof of this car, built at the beginning of the 20th century, resembled an unusual type of cloak worn by the inhabitants of *Limousin*, a former province in France. Nowadays *limousine* is used for any luxurious car, especially one with a glass partition separating driver and passenger.

limp¹ *verb*
to walk lamely or unevenly: *The dog limped across the road.*
• **limp** *noun* a lame walk.

limp² *adjective*
1 not stiff or firm.
2 lacking energy and enthusiasm.
***Word Family* limply** *adverb*; **limpness** *noun*.

limpet *noun*
any of a group of marine snails with a flat conical shell which is open underneath.

limpid *adjective*
clear or transparent.
***Word Family* limpidly** *adverb*; **limpidity** (**lim**-pid-i-tee) *noun*.
[from Latin]

linchpin *noun* also **lynchpin**
1 a metal peg in an axle which keeps a wheel in its place.
2 a person or thing that is essential to success.

linctus (**link**-tuss) *noun*
thick liquid medicine, used especially to cure a bad cough.

line¹ *noun*
1 a long narrow mark made on a surface: *He drew a line right across the page.*
2 a row: *a line of trees.*
3 a single row of words in poetry.
4 a length of cord, wire, rope, etc.: *a telephone line.* □ *a clothes line.*
5 the place where a race starts or finishes.
6 a railway track.
7 *Military* a connected set of defences: *behind enemy lines.*
8 (**the Line**) the equator.

9 (**lines**) an outline: *the elegant lines of the Porsche.*

10 a direction: *the bird's line of flight.* □ *We seem to be thinking along the same lines.*

11 an accepted set of ideas: *politicians who refuse to follow the party line.*

12 an area of activity or business: *What line are you in?*

13 a particular type of goods for sale: *This is one of our most popular lines.*

14 *Commerce* a company providing passenger transport: *a shipping line.*

15 (*informal*) a short letter: *I'll drop you a line when I arrive.*

Phrases **be in line for** to be likely to get. **be on the line** to be at risk: *Your job is on the line.* **be out of line** (*informal*) to be behaving in an unacceptable way. **bring someone into line** to make someone conform. **draw the line at** to protest at and refuse to do: *I draw the line at washing up as well as cooking.* **hard lines!** (*dated*) bad luck! **lay it on the line** to explain something very bluntly. **line of latitude** ⇨ LATITUDE (definition 2). **line of longitude** ⇨ LONGITUDE (definition 2). **read between the lines** to discover the real meaning in what a person writes or says.

• **line** *verb*

1 to mark or trace with lines.

2 to form a row along: *Hundreds of people lined the streets.*

Phrase **line up 1** to form or take position in a row. **2** to arrange or organize: *What have you got lined up for us tonight?*

[Latin *linea* a linen thread]

line² *verb*

to cover the inner side of something: *The coat was lined with fur.*

lineage (**lin**-ee-ij) *noun*

ancestry or descent: *a man of noble lineage.*

lineament (**lin**-ee-a-m'nt) *noun*

a distinctive feature or characteristic.

linear (**lin**-ee-a) *adjective*

1 relating to lines or length: *a metre is a linear measure.*

2 arranged in a line: *a linear sequence.*

line dancing *noun*

a type of country dancing in which the people taking part all line up and do the same movements together.

linen (**lin**-in) *noun*

1 a yarn or fabric made from flax.

2 clothes or other articles, such as sheets, made from linen or similar fabric.

Phrase **wash one's dirty linen in public** to let everyone know one's discreditable secrets.

liner (**line**-a) *noun*

a large passenger ship.

linesman *noun* (*plural* **linesmen**)

Sports an official who stands at the outer edge of a playing area and helps the referee to make certain decisions.

line-up *noun*

an arrangement of people or things in a line, for inspection, participation in a game, etc.

linger (**ling**-ga) *verb*

1 to remain or be unwilling to leave: *He lingered in the street long after she had gone.*

2 to continue only weakly: *The old man's hope lingered on for a few more days.*

Word Family **lingering** *adjective* long, protracted; **lingeringly** *adverb.*

lingerie (**lon**-zha-ree) *noun*

women's underwear.

[French, linen goods]

lingo (**ling**-go) *noun* (*plural* **lingos** or **lingoes**)

(*informal*) a language, especially one which you don't understand: *I would like to visit France but I don't speak the lingo.*

[from LINGUA FRANCA]

lingua franca (ling-gwa **frank**-a)

any language, such as pidgin English, known by and used between people of different nations as a general medium of communication.

[Italian, Frankish language]

linguist (**ling**-gwist) *noun*

a person who studies or speaks foreign languages.

linguistics (ling **gwis**-tiks) *plural noun*

(*used with singular verb*) the science and study of language.

Word Family **linguistic** *adjective* relating to language.

liniment (**lin**-a-m'nt) *noun*

any liquid, usually an oil, used to rub into the skin for sprains, etc.

[Latin *linere* to anoint]

lining (**lie**-ning) *noun*

a layer of material on the inside of something: *The coat's lining was made of silk.*

link *noun*

1 a loop or ring forming part of a chain.

2 anything which forms part of a connected series: *You've discovered the weak link in his argument.*

3 any bond or connection: *the link between music and art.*
Word Family link *verb* to join; **linkage** (**link**-ij) *noun* the action of linking; **link-up** *noun* a connection.

links ⇨ GOLF COURSE.

linnet *noun*
a small finch with a red forehead.
[Latin *linum* flax]

linoleum (lin-o-lee-um) *noun*
short form is **lino** a smooth strong floor covering made of canvas treated with cork, oil and colouring.
[Latin *linum* flax + *oleum* oil]

linseed (**lin**-seed) *noun*
the seed of flax, from which oil is obtained.

lint *noun*
1 a soft material made from linen, used for covering wounds, etc.
2 any bits of thread or fluff.

lintel *noun*
a horizontal support over a door or window.

lion *noun*
a large flesh-eating Asian and African mammal of the cat family, the male having a shaggy mane around its neck and shoulders.
Phrase the lion's share the largest portion: *John always grabs the lion's share of the cake.*
Word Family lioness *noun* (*plural* **lionesses**) a female lion; **lionize, lionise** *verb* to treat as a celebrity.
[Greek *leon*]

lion-hearted *adjective*
brave or fearless.

lip *noun*
1 *Anatomy* either of the two fleshy parts forming the front of the mouth.
2 something which has the shape or function of a lip: *the lip of a milk jug.*
3 (*informal*) impudence: *That's enough of your lip, young man!*
stiff upper lip a strong and determined attitude.
Phrases bite one's lip not to react as one wants to. **curl one's lip** to sneer. **pay lip service to** to express support for insincerely.

liposuction (**lip**-oh-suck-sh'n *or* **lie**-po-suck-sh'n) *noun*
a type of cosmetic surgery involving the removal of fat from under the skin of areas such as the thighs, stomach, etc. using a suction device through an incision.

lip-read (**lip**-reed) *verb* (**lip-reads; lip-reading; lip-read** (**lip**-red))
to understand speech by watching the lip movements of the speaker.
Word Family lip-reader *noun.*

lipsalve *noun*
a waxy substance put on the lips to keep them moist.

lipstick *noun*
a stick of waxy or paste-like lip colouring.

liquefied petroleum gas *noun*
short form is **LPG** a mixture of gaseous products of petroleum refining, mainly propane and butane, stored under pressure and used as a fuel, e.g. Calor gas.

liquefy (**lik**-wi-fie) *verb* (**liquefies; liquefying; liquefied**) also **liquify**
to make or become liquid.
Word Family liquefaction (lik-wi-**fak**-sh'n) *noun*; **liquefier** *noun.*

liqueur (lik-**yoor**) *noun*
a strong sweet alcoholic drink, usually drunk from a small glass after meals.

liquid (**lik**-wid) *noun*
Physics a water-like substance with a definite volume but taking the shape of the space in which it is kept. Compare GAS *noun* (definition 1); SOLID *noun.*
• **liquid** *adjective*
1 of or in the form of a liquid: *liquid food.*
2 (of sound or movement) flowing: *The dancer's movements were liquid and graceful.*
3 *Commerce* able to be easily exchanged for cash: *liquid assets.*
Word Family liquidly *adverb*; **liquidness** *noun*; **liquidize, liquidise** *verb.*

liquidate (**lik**-wi-date) *verb*
1 to pay or settle a debt.
2 to conclude the dealings of a business by using the assets to pay the debts.
3 (*informal*) to murder.
Word Family liquidation (lik-wi-**day**-sh'n) *noun*; **liquidator** *noun* a person appointed to conclude the dealings of a company.
[Latin *liquidus* fluid]

liquidity (lik-**wid**-i-tee) *noun*
the state of having cash or assets which can be easily exchanged for cash.

liquid paraffin ⇨ PARAFFIN.

liquor (**lik**-er) *noun*
any alcoholic drink, especially one made by distillation rather than fermentation.

liquorice (lik-a-riss *or* lik-a-rish) *noun* also **licorice**
a plant found in Europe and Asia, whose dried root is used to make sweets or flavouring.
[Greek *glykys* sweet + *rhiza* root]

lira (leer-a) *noun* (*plural* **lire** (leer-a *or* leer-ay)
the basic unit of money in Italy.
[Latin *libra* pound]

lisp *noun*
a speech defect in which 's' and 'z' are pronounced as 'th'.
• **lisp** *verb*.

lissom *adjective* also **lissome**
supple or graceful.
Word Family **lissomness** *noun*.
[alteration of *lithesome*]

list¹ *noun*
a number of things, such as names or numbers, set down or stated one after the other: *I made a list of things to buy.*
• **list** *verb* to make or put on a list.

list² *verb*
(of a structure) to lean over to one side.
• **list** *noun*.

listed building *noun*
a building protected by law from demolition or extensive alteration.

listen (liss-'n) *verb*
to pay attention to sound: *We were listening to the radio.*
Phrase **listen in 1** to eavesdrop. **2** to listen to a broadcast.
Word Family **listener** *noun* a person who listens, especially to radio.

listless *adjective*
having no energy or interest: *a listless reply.*
Word Family **listlessly** *adverb*; **listlessness** *noun*.

lit¹ a past tense and past participle of **light¹**.

lit² a past tense and past participle of **light¹**.

litany (lit-a-nee) *noun* (*plural* **litanies**)
Christianity a form of prayer consisting of a series of petitions said by the clergy, to which the congregation repeats a set response.
[Greek *litaneia* prayer]

litchi ⇨ LYCHEE.

literal (lit-a-r'l) *adjective*
corresponding exactly to the original, without any additional implications such as metaphorical ones: *a literal interpretation of the Bible that believes the world was created in six days.*

Word Family **literally** *adverb*; **literalness** *noun*.
[Latin *littera* letter of the alphabet]

literary (lit-er-a-ree) *adjective*
1 relating to books or literature: *literary criticism.*
2 having a knowledge of or fondness for literature.

literate (lit-er-it) *adjective*
able to read and write.
Word Family **literacy** (lit-er-a-see) *noun*.

literature (lit-er-a-cher) *noun*
1 poetry, fiction, essays, etc. as distinct from factual or journalistic writing.
2 any printed material on a particular subject: *travel literature.*

lithe (lithe) *adjective*
able to move or bend with ease.
Word Family **lithely** *adverb*; **litheness** *noun*.

lithium (lith-ee-um) *noun*
a metal, the lightest known solid, used in alloys to make glass and ceramics.
[Greek *litheios* of stone]

lithograph (lith-o-graf) *noun*
a print, especially a picture, produced by drawing on a flat, specially prepared stone or metal surface from which ink impressions are taken.
[Greek *lithos* stone + *graphein* to write]

litigate (lit-i-gate) *verb*
Law to conduct a dispute before a court of law.
Word Family **litigation** (lit-i-gay-sh'n) *noun*; **litigant** *noun* a person taking part in a law case; **litigious** (lit-ij-uss) *adjective* of, relating to or excessively fond of legal disputes.
[Latin *litigare* to go to law]

litmus *noun*
Chemistry a soluble substance which turns red in acids and blue in alkalis.

litre (lee-ta) *noun* (*American* **liter**)
a unit of volume for liquids equal to 1000 cubic centimetres, or about 1·75 pints. *abbrev.* l.
[Greek *litra* a unit of Sicilian currency]

litter *noun*
1 any rubbish or untidy mess, especially when left in a public place.
2 a number of offspring produced at one birth: *a litter of puppies.*
3 also **cat litter** a chemically treated substance on which cats can be trained to urinate and defecate.

4 a vehicle consisting of a couch mounted on a frame, often with a canopy, carried on poles by men or animals.
Word Family **litter** *verb* to scatter objects or rubbish untidily.

> The word **litter** is originally derived from Latin *lectus* (a bed), as is *lit*, the French word for 'bed'. *Litter* came to mean 'a portable bed', that is, 'a stretcher', although this use is now archaic. The modern meaning of 'rubbish' came from the fact that straw used to be spread over the floor to provide bedding.

litterbug *noun*
(*informal*) a person who litters public places.

little *adjective* (**littler; littlest**)
1 small: *a gorgeous little dog.*
2 short: *She should be here in a little while.*
3 (of a person) young: *We lived in the country when I was little.*
• **little** *adverb* (**less; least**)
1 not much.
2 (*formal*) not at all: *Little did we know that the train had left early.*
• **little** *noun*
1 a small amount: *May I have a little of your cake?*
2 a short time: *The sun rose a little after 5 a.m.*
Phrases **little by little** gradually. **make little of** not to be able to understand: *Her teacher could make little of the essay.* **think little of** to treat or regard as unimportant.
Word Family **littleness** *noun*.

liturgy (lit-a-jee) *noun* (*plural* **liturgies**)
Christianity the ritual of public worship.
Word Family **liturgical** (lit-**urj**-i-k'l) *adjective*.
[Greek *leitourgia* public duty, the priesthood]

live¹ (liv) *verb*
1 to have life: *How long do dogs usually live?*
2 to supply oneself with what is necessary to exist: *The survivors lived on berries and grasses.*
3 to spend one's life: *She now lives quietly in retirement.*
4 (*informal*) to have full experience of life: *You haven't lived until you have travelled the world!*
5 to have one's home: *I live in a small town.*
6 to remain: *That sight will live in my memory.*
Phrases **live down** to cause to be forgotten: *How can I live down such a terrible failure?* **live it up** (*informal*) to have a wild and exciting time: *They lived it up for three years until the money ran out.* **live up to** to act according to.

live² (*rhymes with* hive) *adjective*
1 living or having life: *transporting live animals.*
2 (of a bullet, etc.) unexploded.
3 (of a wire, etc.) electrically charged.
4 (of coals) burning.
5 (of a performance) not previously filmed or recorded: *a live concert.*
6 of current interest: *The election is no longer a live issue.*
• **live** *adverb* (of a radio or television programme) at the time of its happening.

livelihood *noun*
the means of earning the money to live.

livelong (liv-long) *adjective*
a poetic word meaning 'whole or complete'.
[LIEF + LONG]

lively (lyve-lee) *adjective* (**livelier; liveliest**)
full of energy or spirit: *a very lively song.*
Phrase **look lively!** (*informal*) move faster! **liveliness** *noun*.

liven (lie-ven) *verb*
Phrase **liven up** to make or become more lively, cheerful, etc.

liver (liv-a) *noun*
1 *Anatomy* the large organ in the abdomen which produces bile, removes wastes from the blood and controls the use of digested food.
2 an animal's liver eaten as food: *I don't like liver.*

liver spot *noun*
a small brown spot on the skin, found especially on the skin of elderly people.

livery (liv-a-ree) *noun* (*plural* **liveries**)
1 the distinctive clothes, emblems or uniform worn by a particular group, e.g. those formerly worn by the servants of a feudal noble's house.
2 the care and feeding of horses for money.
Phrase **at livery** (of a horse) kept and fed for the owner in return for payment.
Word Family **liveried** *adjective* wearing livery.
[Old French *livrée* a gift of clothes from a master to a servant]

livery stable *noun* also **livery yard**
a place where horses are looked after and hired out for money.

lives
the plural of **life**.

livestock (**lyve**-stok) *noun*
short form is **stock** all the horses, cattle, sheep, etc. kept on a farm.

live wire *noun*
(*informal*) an energetic or vivacious person.

livid (**liv**-id) *adjective*
1 (*informal*) very angry.
2 having a discoloured or bluish area, such as a bruise.
[Latin *lividus* leaden in colour, spiteful]

living (**liv**-ing) *adjective*
1 having life: *a living being.*
2 of or used for living: *a living allowance was provided for many students.*
• **living** *noun*
1 a livelihood: *How do you earn your living?*
2 a position as a vicar with money or property attached.

living room *noun* also called **lounge; sitting room.**
a room in a house used by members of a family for relaxing, entertaining, etc.

lizard (**liz**-'d) *noun*
any of various small to medium-sized reptiles, usually having four legs, slender bodies and long tails.

llama (**lah**-ma) *noun*
a camel-like South American mammal, valued for its thick fleecy wool and its use as a pack animal.
[Spanish]

lo *interjection*
an old word meaning 'look'.

load (*rhymes with* road) *noun*
1 an object, weight or quantity which is carried or supported.
2 a responsibility or burden: *Looking after five young children puts a big load on you.*
3 the resistance overcome by an engine.
4 *Electricity* the power demand made upon an electrical device.
5 (**a load of, loads of**) a lot of: *There'll be loads of food at the party.*
6 *Geography* the material carried along by a river.
Phrase **get a load of** (*informal*) to listen to or look at.
• **load** *verb*
1 to put a load or weight on: *The men loaded the truck with crates of fruit.*
2 to fill with ammunition: *The soldiers all loaded their guns.*
Word Family loading *noun* the act of a person or thing that loads; **loader** *noun.*

loaded *adjective*
1 carrying a load.

2 (*informal*) very rich.
3 (of a question, argument, etc.) biased: *You can't expect me to answer such a loaded question.*

loaf[1] *noun* (*plural* **loaves**)
1 a shaped baked mass of bread.
2 any shaped block or mass of food: *a loaf of sugar.*
Phrase **use one's loaf** (*informal*) to use one's common sense.

loaf[2] *verb*
to be lazy or idle.
Word Family loafer *noun* 1 a lazy or idle person. 2 (**Loafer**) (*trademark*) a flat leather shoe.

loam (*rhymes with* home) *noun*
a type of soil containing clay, sand and organic matter, usually very fertile.
Word Family loamy *adjective* (**loamier; loamiest**).

loan (lone) *noun*
1 the act of lending.
2 anything which is lent, especially a sum of money at a fixed rate of interest.

loan shark *noun*
(*informal*) a person who lends money at an extremely high rate of interest, often to people who cannot get a loan elsewhere.

loath (*rhymes with* oath) *adjective* also **loth**
unwilling or reluctant.
• **loath** *adverb*
Phrase **nothing loath** very willingly.
[Old English *lath* hateful]

loathe (loath) *verb*
to feel intense hatred and disgust for.
Word Family loathing *noun* an intense hatred and disgust; **loathingly** *adverb*; **loathsome** *adjective* hateful and disgusting; **loathsomeness** *noun.*

loaves
the plural of **loaf**[1].

lob *noun*
Sport the slow rising curved flight of a ball hit high in the air.
Word Family lob *verb* (**lobs; lobbing; lobbed**).

lobby *noun* (*plural* **lobbies**)
1 an entrance hall in a building.
2 a group of people who try to influence or persuade a law-making body: *the environmentalists' lobby.*
Word Family lobby *verb* (**lobbies; lobbying; lobbied**) to try to influence or gain advantage from a law-making body; **lobbyist** *noun.*

lobe *noun*
a rounded part or division, such as the fleshy lower part of the ear.
[Greek *lobos* a pod]

lobotomy (lo-**bot**-a-mee) *noun* (*plural* **lobotomies**)
Medicine an operation cutting into or across a lobe of the brain to alter brain function.
[LOBE + Greek *tomé* a cutting]

lobster *noun*
any of a group of large edible marine crustaceans, usually having two large pincers.
[Latin *locusta* a locust, a crustacean]

local (**lo**-k'l) *adjective*
relating to a particular place or part: *the local inhabitants.* □ *a local infection.*
• **local** *noun*
1 any person who is local.
2 (*informal*) a pub close to one's home.
Word Family **locally** *adverb* in or relating to a particular place.
[Latin *locus* a place]

local anaesthetic *noun*
an anaesthetic that affects only a limited area of the body. Compare GENERAL ANAESTHETIC.

local authority *noun* (*plural* **local authorities**)
the locally elected council which administers the affairs of a county, district, borough, etc.

local colour *noun*
the distinctive interest or feeling of a place or period of time.

locale (lo-**kahl**) *noun*
a particular place or setting, especially in relation to certain events.

local government *noun*
the system of using local authorities, partly financed by a local levy, to administer such powers as may be delegated to them by the central government.

locality (lo-**kall**-i-tee) *noun* (*plural* **localities**)
a place or district.

localize, localise *verb*
1 to limit to a particular place: *This seems to be just a localized problem.*
2 to make local in character.
Word Family **localization** (lo-ka-lie-zay-sh'n) *noun.*

locate (lo-**kate**) *verb*
to find or establish the position of: *We located the holes in the roof.*

Phrase **be located** to be in a particular place: *The X-ray department is located in the west wing.*

location (lo-**kay**-sh'n) *noun*
a place, especially one which is or will be settled, used, etc.: *This is the perfect location for a house.*
Phrase **on location** not in a film studio: *The scenes were filmed on location in Hawaii.*

loch (lok *or* lokh) *noun* also in Ireland **lough**
Scottish a long stretch of water which can either be a lake or an inlet of the sea.

loci
the plural of **locus**.

lock[1] *noun*
1 any of various mechanical fastening devices which can be operated by a key.
2 any of various devices which prevent or limit movement, etc.: *a gear lock.*
3 any of various holds or grips in wrestling, etc., especially one which limits the movement of the opponent.
4 *Nautical* an enclosed section of a river or canal with gates at each end, in which boats are raised or lowered from one level to another by altering the depth of the water.
Phrase **lock stock and barrel** completely.
• **lock** *verb*
1 to fasten or become fastened by means of a lock: *I locked the front door.*
2 to make or become securely fixed: *She panicked and locked her arms around her rescuer's neck.*
Phrases **lock away, lock up** to keep, imprison, etc. in a place fastened by a lock: *She locked up her jewels in the safe.*

lock[2] *noun*
1 a bunch or curl of hair.
2 (**locks**) the hair.

locker *noun*
a small cupboard or compartment with a lock, used for storing possessions.

locket (**lok**-it) *noun*
a small case to hold a portrait or other keepsake, usually made of gold or silver and worn on a chain around the neck.

lockjaw *noun*
a symptom of tetanus in which the jaw muscles tighten and prevent the mouth from being opened.

lockout *noun*
the refusal by an employer to let work continue, unless the employees work according to his or her terms.

locksmith *noun*
a person who makes or mends locks.

lock-up *noun*
(*informal*) a jail.

locomotion (lo-ko-mo-sh'n) *noun*
the act or power of moving from place to
place.
[Latin *loco* in place + *motio* a moving]

locomotive (lo-ko-**mo**-tiv) *noun*
a railway engine.

locum (lo-kum) *noun*
a doctor, clergyman, etc. who temporarily
takes over the work of another.
[shortening of Latin *locum tenens* one
holding the place]

locus (lo-kus) *noun* (*plural* **loci**) (**lo**-sigh *or*
lo-kie *or* **lo**-kee)
1 (*formal*) a place or position.
2 *Maths* the path traced by a point moving
according to a set rule.
[Latin]

locust (lo-kust) *noun*
any of various large grasshoppers which
migrate in vast swarms, eating all the
vegetation in their path.
[Latin *locusta*]

lode ⇨ VEIN (definition 3).

lodge *noun*
1 a house used for holidays or temporary
accommodation.
2 a small house, especially in a park or the
grounds of a larger house: *the gatekeeper's
lodge.*
3 a branch of certain societies or
associations, or its members.
● **lodge** *verb*
1 to live, especially in a rented room or
house.
2 to supply with a room or rooms,
especially temporarily: *The flood victims
were lodged in the school hall.*
3 to become stuck. *The bullet was lodged in
his leg.*
4 to place formally with an official body:
*We have lodged a complaint with the local
authority.*
Word Family lodger *noun* a person who
rents a room or rooms in another's house;
lodging *noun* (*usually* **lodgings**) a room
or rooms for living, especially if rented.

loft *noun*
1 the space between the ceiling of a room
and the roof above it.
2 the upper storey of an outbuilding such
as a stable.
3 a raised gallery in a church or hall.

4 *Sport* the high curving flight of a ball,
especially in golf.
● **loft** *verb* to hit a ball in a high arc.

lofty *adjective* (**loftier; loftiest**)
1 having great height.
2 noble: *lofty sentiments.*
3 proud and haughty: *Her lofty manner
annoyed me.*
Word Family loftily *adverb*; **loftiness**
noun.

log *noun*
1 a length of wood cut from the trunk or
branch of a tree.
2 short form of **logbook** any record of
progress, details, etc., especially on a ship.
3 (*informal*) a logarithm.
● **log** *verb* (**logs; logging; logged**)
1 to record in a log.
2 to cut down trees or cut them into logs.
Phrases **log in**, **log on** to begin a session
on a computer by performing the relevant
set of operations. **log off**, **log out** to end a
session on a computer.
Word Family logging *noun* the act or
business of cutting down trees for timber;
logger *noun.*

loganberry (lo-gan-**berr**-ee) *noun* (*plural*
loganberries)
a large edible dark red berry.
[first grown in America by *J. H. Logan*,
1841-1928]

logarithm (log-a-rithm) *noun*
short form is **log** *Maths* the exponent
indicating the power to which it is
necessary to raise a given number, called
the **base**, to produce another number.
In $y = bx$, x is the logarithm of y to the
base b and is written $x = logby$; the
antilogarithm of x is y.
Word Family logarithmic (log-a-**rith**-
mik), **logarithmical** *adjective.*
[Greek *logos* ratio + *arithmos* number]

loggerhead *noun*
Phrase **at loggerheads** in strong
disagreement: *The children have been at
loggerheads all afternoon.*

logic (loj-ik) *noun*
1 the art or science of reasoning.
2 a convincing reason or argument: *I
cannot see any logic in this decision.*
Word Family logical *adjective* 1 based on
the principles of logic: *a logical argument.*
2 able to reason soundly: *She has a very
logical mind;* **logically** *adverb*; **logicality**
(loj-ee-**kall**-i-tee), **logicalness** *noun*;
logician (loj-**ish**-'n) *noun* a person skilled
in logic.
[Greek *logiké* (*tekhné*) the reasoning (art)]

logistics (lo-**jis**-tiks) *plural noun*
1 (*used with singular verb*) the branch of military science concerned with the transport, quartering and supply of troops.
2 the detailed organization of some business or other operation.
Word Family **logistic, logistical** *adjective*; **logistically** *adverb*.
[French *logis* lodgings]

logjam *noun*
1 a mass of logs blocking a river.
2 a deadlock.

logo (lo-go) *noun*
a symbol used to represent and identify a particular company, product, etc.

loin *noun*
1 (*often* **loins**) the lower part of the body of a person or four-legged animal, between the ribs and the hips.
2 a cut of meat from this part of an animal.
Phrase **gird one's loins** to prepare for action.

loincloth *noun*
a strip of cloth worn around the loins.

loiter *verb*
1 to stand about aimlessly.
2 to move or proceed slowly.
Word Family **loiterer** *noun*.

loll *verb*
to rest or droop loosely or limply: *His head lolled sideways as he fell asleep in the chair.*

lollipop *noun*
a hard brittle sweet on a stick.

lollipop lady *noun* (*plural* **lollipop ladies**)
(*informal*) a woman employed to help children cross a road near their school.
Word Family **lollipop man** *noun* (*plural* **lollipop men**).

lollop *verb*
to move with heavy ungainly leaps.

lolly *noun* (*plural* **lollies**)
1 a lollipop.
2 ⇨ ICE LOLLY.
3 (*informal*) money.

lone *adjective*
alone or solitary.
Word Family **loner** *noun* a person who does not seek the company of others.

lonely *adjective* (**lonelier; loneliest**)
1 feeling sad or depressed because one is alone: *Were you lonely while we were on holiday?*
2 remote or isolated: *a lonely house in the middle of the moors.*

Word Family **loneliness** *noun*;
lonesome *adjective* lonely.

lonely hearts *plural noun*
people who try to make new relationships through advertising in a newspaper.
• **lonely hearts** *adjective*.

lone wolf *noun* (*plural* **lone wolves**)
a person who prefers to be or act alone.

long¹ *adjective*
1 having great or considerable size or distance from end to end: *a long walk.*
□ *a long time.*
2 of a specified size or distance: *The room is about 10 metres long.*
3 representing little likelihood of winning: *long odds.*
• **long** *adverb*
1 for a long time.
2 for a time or period: *How long did he stay?*
3 for the whole extent of: *We stood all day long in the queue to buy tickets.*
4 at a distant time: *It happened long before I was born.*
Phrases **as long as, so long as** on condition that: *You can come as long as you are very quiet.* **so long** (*informal*) goodbye.
• **long** *noun* a long time: *The job will not take long if we work hard.*
Phrases **before long** soon: *You'll be a teenager before long.* **the long and the short of** the basic or essential part of.

long² *verb*
to wish for strongly: *She longed for the end of winter.*
Word Family **longing** *noun* a strong wish or craving; **longingly** *adverb*.

longboat *noun*
the longest and strongest of the small boats that were carried by a sailing ship.

longbow *noun*
a large medieval bow, drawn by hand to fire long feathered arrows.

longevity (lon-**jev**-i-tee) *noun*
long life.
[Latin *longus* long + *aevum* age]

long face *noun*
an unhappy expression: *Why the long face, Ayesha?*

longhand *noun*
ordinary handwriting in which the words are written out in full. Compare SHORTHAND.

longitude (**long**-gi-tewd) *noun*
1 any distance east or west of the Greenwich meridian, measured in

degrees. Compare LATITUDE (definition 1).
2 also called **line of longitude**. an
imaginary line around the world passing
through the North and South Poles.
Word Family longitudinal (long-gi-
tewd-i-n'l) *adjective* **1** relating to longitude
or length. **2** running lengthwise;
longitudinally *adverb*.
[Latin *longitudo* length]

> [!] Note the spelling of *longitude*: it
> only has one *t* in it. It is
> pronounced **long**-gi-tewd and not
> **long**-ti-tewd.

long johns *plural noun*
(*informal*) a pair of long underpants.

long jump *noun*
Athletics the athletics event of jumping as
far forward as one can after a run-up.

long-playing *adjective*
(of a gramophone record) revolving $33\frac{1}{3}$
times per minute and usually containing
several tracks on each side.

long-range *adjective*
1 extending into the future: *the long-range
weather forecast*.
2 designed for a great distance.

longship *noun*
a long Viking warship with oars and a sail.

longshore drift *noun*
the movement of sand and pebbles carried
by waves along a beach.

long shot *noun*
a hopeful attempt considered unlikely to
succeed.

long-sighted *adjective*
able to see distant objects clearly.
Word Family long-sightedness *noun*.

long-standing *adjective*
having continued for a long time: *a long-
standing disagreement*.

long-suffering *adjective*
patient or uncomplaining in trouble.

long-term *adjective*
involving a long period of time.

long ton ⇨ TON (definition 1).

long wave *noun*
a radio wave having a wavelength above
1 km and a frequency below 300 kHz.
Compare MEDIUM WAVE; SHORT WAVE.

long-winded (long-**win**-did) *adjective*
tediously long: *a long-winded speech*.
Word Family long-windedness *noun*.

loo *noun*
(*informal*) a toilet.

The word **loo** is of uncertain origin. A
popular theory for which there is no
real evidence is that it comes from *gardy
loo*, a form of French *gardez l'eau*
(beware of the water), a call uttered
when people were throwing waste or
dirty water from the top storeys of
Edinburgh houses in the 18th century.
However, because *loo* did not appear
until the early part of the 20th century,
it seems more likely that it is derived
from *lieux d'aisance*, French for 'places
of ease' and thus 'lavatory' and that it
was British soldiers' slang in France
during the First World War.

look (luk) *verb*
1 to direct one's eyes: *Look at this beautiful
flower!*
2 to provide a view: *The back rooms all look
onto the river.*
3 to give the impression of being: *You look
very pleased with yourself!*
Phrases look after to attend to the
needs, wants, etc. of. **look down on** to
regard with contempt: *She looks down on us
because we are poor*. **look for** to try to find.
look forward to to wait for eagerly. **look
into** to investigate: *The police are looking
into the complaints*. **look lively, look sharp**
(*informal*) hurry up! **look out** to be
careful. **look to do something** to plan or
expect to do something. **look to someone**
to rely on someone. **look up 1** to try to
find: *Look it up in the dictionary.*
2 (*informal*) to visit: *Do look up my family if
you're going to London.* **3** (*informal*) to
improve: *Things have looked up since the
new manager arrived*. **look up to** to admire.
● **look** *noun*
1 the act of looking: *Let me have a look.*
2 the way of looking or appearing: *He has
the look of a hunted man.* □ *I don't like the
look of the place.*
3 (**looks**) a person's appearance.

lookalike *noun*
(*informal*) a person or thing that resembles
another closely.

look-in *noun*
(*informal*) a chance to take part: *There were
so many people waiting that we didn't get a
look-in.*

looking glass *noun* (*plural* **looking
glasses**)
an old word for a mirror.

lookout *noun*
1 a person who keeps watch.
2 a place, usually elevated, from which one
may observe or keep watch.

Phrase **be one's lookout** (*informal*) to be one's own matter for concern, and not anyone else's. **be on the lookout for** to be continuing to search for.

loom[1] *noun*
a machine for weaving yarn into fabric.

loom[2] *verb*
to appear in a huge distorted or indistinct form: *A monstrous shape loomed in the shadows.*

loony *adjective* (**loonier; looniest**)
(*informal*) crazy or foolish.
• **loony** *noun* (*plural* **loonies**).

loop *noun*
1 a curve doubling over itself so as to leave an opening in the middle of a closed shape.
2 something which has this shape.
• **loop** *verb*
1 to make or form into a loop.
2 to fasten or encircle with or as if with a loop.

loophole (**loop**-hole) *noun*
1 anything which provides a means of evasion: *Her lawyer found a loophole in the law and so she had to be released.*
2 a narrow vertical opening in a wall, especially in a fort or castle.

loopy *adjective* (**loopier; loopiest**)
(*informal*) crazy or foolish.

loose *adjective*
1 free from fastening or restraint: *The horse broke loose.*
2 not tight or firm: *I had a loose hold on the rope.*
3 not packed: *We bought loose potatoes at the farm.*
4 (*dated*) showing low moral standards: *a loose woman.*
Phrase **hang loose, stay loose** (*informal*) to remain relaxed and not get upset.
• **loose** *verb*
Phrase **on the loose** having escaped: *The murderer is still on the loose.*
Word Family **loose, loosen** *verb* to make or become loose or looser; **loosely** *adverb*; **looseness** *noun*.

> ❗ Do not confuse *loose* with *lose*. *Loose* has two *o*'s and is mainly used as an adjective, meaning 'not fastened' or 'not tight'; *lose* has one *o* and is mainly used as a verb, meaning 'to part with and be unable to find'.

loose box *noun* (*plural* **loose boxes**)
a stall for a horse, wide enough for it to move about in.

loose cannon *noun*
a person who is not under control and may cause trouble for others.

loose-leaf *adjective*
(of a book or folder) having a cover to or from which pages may be easily added or removed.

loot *noun*
goods obtained illegally, e.g. as by thieves, soldiers in time of war, etc.
• **loot** *verb* to pillage or plunder.
[Hindi]

lop *verb* (**lops; lopping; lopped**)
to cut off, e.g. the branches from a tree.

lope *verb*
to run with long bounding strides.
• **lope** *noun*.
[Icelandic *hlaupa* to leap]

lop-eared *adjective*
(of an animal) having long floppy ears.

lopsided *adjective*
having one side lower or smaller than the other.
Word Family **lopsidedly** *adverb*; **lopsidedness** *noun*.

loquacious (lo-**kway**-shus) *adjective*
very talkative.
Word Family **loquaciously** *adverb*; **loquaciousness, loquacity** (lo-**kwass**-i-tee) *noun*.
[Latin *loqui* to speak]

lord *noun*
1 any peer.
2 a person who has authority over others: *a feudal lord.*
3 (**Lord**) a form of address for a lord: *May I introduce you to Lord Archer?* □ *Thank you, My Lord.*
4 (**the Lords**) the House of Lords.
5 (**Lord**) *Religion* a name for God or Christ.
Phrase **live like a lord** to live in luxury.
• **lord** *verb*
Phrase **lord it over** to act in a domineering or arrogant manner towards.
Word Family **lordly** *adjective* (**lordlier; lordliest**) 1 suitable for a lord. 2 arrogant or haughty.
[Old English *hlaford* the keeper of the bread]

Lord Chancellor *noun*
the head of the legal profession, Leader of the House of Lords and a Cabinet Minister; as a political appointment the Lord Chancellor loses office on a change of government.

Lord Chief Justice *noun*
the senior permanent member of the judiciary, ranking next to the Lord Chancellor.

Lord Lieutenant (lord lef-**ten**-ent) *noun*
the monarch's representative in a county.

Lord Mayor ⇨ MAYOR.

lordship *noun*
(**Your Lordship, His Lordship**) a way of talking to or about a judge of the High Court or a holder of the title Lord: *Your Lordship is very kind.*

Lord's Supper *noun*
the Eucharist in some Christian Churches, especially Nonconformist Churches.

lore *noun*
any accumulated knowledge about a subject, especially of a traditional or popular nature: *the lore of herbalists.*

lorgnette (lorn-**yet**) *noun*
a pair of glasses held to the eyes by an ornamental handle.
[French *lorgner* to squint]

lorry *noun* (*plural* **lorries**)
a long motor vehicle used for carrying heavy loads.

lose (looz) *verb* (**loses; losing; lost**)
1 to part with, by chance or carelessness, and be unable to find: *She's lost her purse.* *Figurative He suddenly lost control and hit her.*
2 not to have any longer because of death: *She lost her husband recently.*
3 to get rid of: *I've lost a lot of weight.*
4 (of a clock) to get behind the correct time: *My watch has lost two minutes today.*
5 to fail to win: *We lost the match six-two.*
6 to fail to take when available: *Hurry, or you'll lose your chance!*
Phrase **lose it** (*informal*) to lose one's temper. **lose out** not to benefit.
Word Family **loser** *noun* 1 a person or thing that loses. 2 (*informal*) a person who will inevitably fail.

> ❗ Do not confuse *lose* with LOOSE.

loss *noun* (*plural* **losses**)
1 the act or an instance of losing: *The team suffered a decisive loss.*
2 a person or thing that is lost: *The money is a loss I cannot afford.*
3 the number or amount lost, such as casualties in a war, etc.: *Our losses were very heavy.*
Phrases **be at a loss** to be puzzled or uncertain. **cut one's losses** to decide to accept what one has already lost and move forward with a plan, etc.

loss-leader *noun*
a line of goods sold at a loss in a shop to attract custom for other goods.

lost cause *noun*
a person or thing that will inevitably fail.

lot *noun*
1 (**a lot** or **lots**) a large number or amount: *Lots of my friends have mobile phones.*
2 (**the lot**) all of something: *That's a good price – I'll take the lot.*
3 a number of things of the same kind: *The last lot of questions was pretty difficult.*
4 an article or group of articles for sale at an auction: *Lot 99 is an antique writing desk.*
5 any of a set of objects used to make a choice between people or things.
6 a person's fortune in life.
7 *Film* a site used for making films.
8 (*informal*) a person of a specified type: *Watch out – he's a bad lot.*
Phrase **throw in one's lot with** to support.

loth ⇨ LOATH.

lotion (lo-sh'n) *noun*
a mixture of an insoluble substance in a liquid, applied to the skin without rubbing.
[Old French, washing]

lottery *noun* (*plural* **lotteries**)
a form of gambling where many numbered tickets are sold, some of which entitle their owners to prizes.

lotto *noun*
a game for children that is similar to bingo.
[Italian]

lotus (lo-tus) *noun*
1 a type of waterlily, common in Egyptian and Hindu decorative art.
2 *Greek mythology* a plant whose fruit was believed to induce a dreamy state of forgetfulness.
[from Greek]

loud *adjective*
1 having or producing a high volume and intensity of sound.
2 having very bright colours.
● **loud** *adverb* loudly.
Phrase **out loud** in a way that can be heard.
Word Family **loudly** *adverb*; **loudness** *noun*.

loudhailer *noun*
a megaphone.

loudmouth *noun*

(*informal*) a person who talks too much, especially in a way that offends other people.

loudspeaker *noun*

short form is **speaker** *Audio* any of various devices for converting electronic signals into audible sound, as in a public-address system, radio, etc.

lough ⇨ LOCH.

lounge *verb*

to stand, sit, lie or move in a lazy relaxed manner.
• **lounge** *noun*
1 a living room.
2 a room in a hotel, airport, etc. where people can relax comfortably.

lounge suit *noun*

a man's suit for wearing during the day, to work, etc.

louse (*rhymes with* mouse) *noun* (*plural* **lice**)

1 a small wingless insect which may be parasitic on human beings.
2 (*informal*) a despicable person.
• **louse** *verb*
Phrase **louse up** (*informal*) to bungle or ruin.

lousy (*rhymes with* drowsy) *adjective* (**lousier; lousiest**)

1 (*informal*) very poor or bad: *What lousy weather!* □ *I feel lousy.*
2 infested with lice.

lout *noun*

a clumsy stupid ill-mannered person, especially a man.
Word Family **loutish** *adjective*.

louvre (loo-va) *noun*

a screen of sloping timber slats in a door or shutter to shut out light but permit ventilation.

love (luv) *verb*

1 to have a deep-seated affection for.
2 (*informal*) to have a liking or enthusiasm for: *I love ice cream.*
• **love** *noun*
1 a strong passion or deep-seated affection.
2 (*informal*) a liking or enthusiasm.
3 a person or thing that is loved.
4 *Tennis* a score of nil. A **love game** is a game in which one player does not score.
Phrases **for love** without payment. **for the love of** for the sake of. **in love** feeling deep affection. **make love 1** to have sexual intercourse. **2** (*dated*) to woo. **there's no**

love lost between there is dislike between.
Word Family **loveless** *adjective*; **lovelessness** *noun*; **lovable, loveable** *adjective* making one feel affection.

love affair ⇨ AFFAIR.

lovebird *noun*

any of various small African parrots, each pair keeping very close to each other when perching.

love child *noun* (*plural* **love children**)

an illegitimate child.

lovelorn *adjective*

a poetic word meaning 'forlorn because of love'.

lovely (luv-lee) *adjective* (**lovelier; loveliest**)

charming, delightful or beautiful.
Word Family **loveliness** *noun*.

love match *noun* (*plural* **love matches**)

a marriage based on love rather than on social or financial considerations.

lover (luv-a) *noun*

1 a person who is having a sexual relationship with someone, especially outside marriage.
2 a person who likes something: *a lover of modern art.*

lovesick *adjective*

feeling weak or unhappy because of love.
Word Family **lovesickness** *noun*.

lovey-dovey *adjective*

(*informal*) behaving in a very affectionate way.

loving *adjective*

showing or feeling love: *loving glances.* □ *loving friends.*
Word Family **lovingly** *adverb*; **lovingness** *noun*.

low¹ (lo) *adjective*

1 not tall or high: *a low shelf.*
2 of small magnitude, quantity, degree, etc.: *a low number.* □ *Our stock of food is very low.*
3 of little status or importance: *a person of low birth.*
4 not shrill, sharp or loud: *a low murmur.*
5 having a relatively simple structure: *A fungus is an example of a lower plant.*
6 (of methods, intentions, etc.) dishonest or contemptible: *What a low trick!*
7 (*informal*) tired or depressed: *I think she's feeling a bit low.*
• **low** *adverb* in, at or to a low position, point, price, etc.: *Aim low.* □ *The bell rang low and clear across the valley.*

• low *noun*
1 a low level: *Morale has reached an all-time low among the troops.*
2 also called **cyclone; depression**. *Weather* an area of low pressure into which strong winds blow anticlockwise in the northern hemisphere and clockwise in the southern hemisphere, bringing unsettled weather and rain. Compare HIGH *noun* (definition 3).
Word Family **lowness** *noun*.

low² *verb*
to make the hollow bellowing sound of cattle.
• low *noun*.

lowbrow (lo-brow) *adjective*
(*informal*) of low intellectual taste or standard.
• lowbrow *noun*.

Low Church *adjective*
belonging to a section of the Church of England which frowns on elaborate ritual and believes in salvation by faith (not sacraments). Compare HIGH CHURCH.

low-down (lo-down) *noun*
(*informal*) all the facts: *give me the low-down of what happened at the meeting.*
• low-down *adjective* (*informal*)
dishonourable or mean.

lower (lo-a) *verb*
to let or bring down: *Lower the blinds.*
□ *Lower your voice, please.*
Phrase **lower oneself** to lose one's dignity by doing something.

lower case *noun*
Printing small letters, e.g. u, b, c. Compare UPPER CASE.

lower house *noun* also **lower chamber**
the larger of two houses in a parliament, in the UK the House of Commons. Compare UPPER HOUSE.

low frequency *noun*
a radio frequency in the range 30–300 kilohertz.

low-key *adjective*
restrained or understated: *the awards ceremony was a very low-key affair.*

lowland *noun* also **lowlands**
an area of low flat land.

lowlife *noun* (*plural* **lowlifes**)
(*informal*) an unpleasant or criminal person.

lowly (lo-lee) *adjective* (**lowlier; lowliest**)
1 humble: *a lowly farmhouse.*
2 low in rank or position.

lowness ⇨ LOW¹.

low season *noun*
the quietest time of the holiday period, and usually the cheapest. Compare HIGH SEASON.

low-spirited *adjective*
sad.

low-tension (lo-ten sh'n) *adjective*
Electricity of or relating to electric cables, etc. carrying a low voltage.

low tide ⇨ TIDE *noun* (definition 1).

loyal *adjective*
showing continued attachment: *She is very loyal to her family.*
Word Family **loyally** *adverb*; **loyalty** *noun* (*plural* **loyalties**) the state or quality of being loyal.

loyalist *noun*
a person who is loyal, especially a supporter of a monarch or government.

lozenge (lozz-'nj) *noun*
1 a sweet tablet sucked to relieve a sore throat or cold.
2 a diamond-shaped figure.

lubricate (loo-bri-kate) *verb*
to apply oil or an oily substance to, in order to reduce friction, etc.
Word Family **lubrication** (loo-bri-kay-sh'n) *noun*; **lubricant** *noun* a substance which lubricates.
[Latin *lubricare* to make slippery]

lucerne (loo-sern) *noun* also called **alfalfa**.
a cereal plant used as fodder.
[French]

lucid (loo-sid) *adjective*
1 clear or easily understood: *a lucid explanation of the problem.*
2 rational or mentally sound: *Although he is senile he still has lucid moments.*
Word Family **lucidity** (loo-sid-i-tee), **lucidness** *noun*; **lucidly** *adverb*.
[Latin *lucidus* shining bright]

Lucifer (loo-sif-a) *noun*
an angel who led the revolt in heaven and was cast into hell; identified with Satan.
[Latin *lucis* of light + *ferre* to bear (= morning star)]

luck *noun*
1 the power that brings success or failure: *Luck was on our side.*
2 an advantage or success due to chance: *I wished them luck.* □ *That was a stroke of luck.*
Phrases **down on one's luck** going through an unlucky period. **push one's**

luck to rely too much on luck. **worse luck!** (*informal*) unfortunately: *I shan't be there, worse luck!*
• **luck** *verb*
Phrase **luck out** (*informal*) to have success due to luck.

lucky *adjective* (**luckier; luckiest**) having, bringing or resulting in good luck.
Word Family **luckily** *adverb*; **luckiness** *noun*.

lucky dip *noun* a barrel at fairs, etc. containing articles of varying value, into which a person dips for a prize.

lucrative (loo-kra-tiv) *adjective* profitable.
Word Family **lucratively** *adverb*; **lucrativeness** *noun*.
[Latin *lucrum* gain]

ludicrous (lood-i-krus) *adjective* absurdly funny.
Word Family **ludicrously** *adverb*; **ludicrousness** *noun*.
[Latin *ludicrum* a stage play]

ludo (loo-doe) *noun* a children's board game for two to four people using counters and dice.
[Latin, I play]

lug *verb* (**lugs; lugging; lugged**) to pull or drag with great effort.

luggage (lug-ij) *noun* any bags or suitcases taken on a journey.

lugger *noun* an old sailing vessel with square sails.

lughole *noun* (*informal*) an ear.

lugubrious (loo-goo-bri-us) *adjective* mournful or dismal.
Word Family **lugubriously** *adverb*; **lugubriousness** *noun*.
[Latin *lugubris* mourning]

lukewarm *adjective*
1 moderately warm.
2 unenthusiastic: *Our idea received a lukewarm reaction.*

lull *verb* to soothe or quieten: *Its mother's singing finally lulled the baby off to sleep.* □ *His explanation lulled my suspicions for a few days.*
• **lull** *noun* a brief calm.

lullaby (lull-a-by) *noun* (*plural* **lullabies**) a soothing song to put a baby to sleep.

lumbago (lum-bay-go) *noun* a severe pain in the lower part of the back.
[Latin *lumbus* the loin]

lumbar (lum-ba) *adjective*
Anatomy of or relating to the lower half of the back.

lumber[1] *noun* timber.
• **lumber** *verb* (*informal*) to burden with something useless or unpleasant: *He lumbered me with the task of firing all our workers.*

lumber[2] *verb* to move about heavily or clumsily.

lumberjack *noun* a person whose job is cutting down trees and bringing them out of the forest.

lumber room *noun* a room for storing junk, old furniture, etc.

luminary (loo-min-ree) *noun* (*plural* **luminaries**) a highly educated and respected person.

luminescence (loo-mi-ness-'nce) *noun* Physics the emission of light from some cause other than high temperature, for example by chemical action, radioactivity or phosphorescence.
Word Family **luminesce** *verb*; **luminescent** *adjective*.

luminous (loo-mi-nus) *adjective*
1 giving off light.
2 bright and full of light.
Word Family **luminously** *adverb*; **luminosity** (loo-mi-noss-i-tee) *noun* the state or quality of being luminous.

lump[1] *noun*
1 a solid, usually small, mass of no particular shape: *a lump of clay.*
2 (*informal*) a stupid or clumsy person.
• **lump** *verb*
Phrase **lump together** to put together in one lump or group without discrimination: *He lumped us all together as time-wasters.*
• **lump** *adjective* in the form of a lump or lumps: *lump sugar.*
Word Family **lumpy** *adjective* (**lumpier; lumpiest**) full of lumps or covered with lumps; **lumpily** *adverb*; **lumpiness** *noun*; **lumpish** *adjective* 1 like a lump. 2 stupid or clumsy.

lump[2] *verb*
Phrase **lump it** (*informal*) to endure or put up with something: *Well, I'm going and you can like it or lump it.*

lump sum *noun* a single substantial sum of money.

lunacy (loo-na-see) *noun*
1 insanity.

2 (*plural* **lunacies**) an act of insanity.
[Latin *luna* the moon, formerly believed to
cause insanity]

lunar (loo-na) *adjective*
1 of or relating to the moon.
2 measured by the moon's revolutions.

lunatic (loo-na tik) *adjective*
of or relating to lunacy: *another of her
lunatic schemes.* □ *a lunatic asylum.*
• **lunatic** *noun* a person who is insane.

> The word **lunatic** came into English
> via Old French *lunatique* from Latin
> *lunaticus*. This was derived from *luna*,
> the Latin word for 'moon', the
> connection being that certain types of
> mental illness were thought to be
> related to phases of the moon.
> Nowadays *lunatic* is used of someone
> who behaves eccentrically or
> irresponsibly. It is considered offensive
> to use it of the mentally ill.

lunatic fringe *noun*
the more extreme or eccentric members of
a community or movement.

lunch *noun* (*plural* **lunches**)
the second meal of the day, usually taken
about 1 p.m.
Phrase **out to lunch** (*informal*) not
normal or sane.
• **lunch** *verb*.

luncheon (lun-ch'n) *noun*
(*dated or formal*) a lunch.

luncheon meat *noun*
a food made of chopped pork and cereal,
usually sold in a tin.

luncheon voucher *noun*
short form is **LV** a piece of paper that can
be exchanged for a meal, sometimes given
by employers to their workers.

lung *noun*
Anatomy either of two large spongy organs
in the chest cavity, which absorb oxygen
from the air and release waste carbon
dioxide into it.

lunge¹ (lunj) *noun*
a sudden forward movement, such as a
thrust with a bayonet, etc.
• **lunge** *verb*.
[French *allonger* to lengthen or extend]

lunge² *noun*
a long rope used to guide a horse in
training or exercise.

lupin (loo-pin) *noun*
a garden plant with brightly coloured
flowers in long tapering spikes.
[from Latin]

lurch¹ *noun* (*plural* **lurches**)
a sudden rolling or swaying to one side:
The ship gave a terrible lurch.
• **lurch** *verb*.

lurch² *noun*
Phrase **leave someone in the lurch** to
leave a person who is helpless or in
difficulties.

lure *noun*
anything which attracts or entices, such as
a worm used to attract fish.
• **lure** *verb* to attract or entice.

Lurex (lyoor-eks) *noun*
(*trademark*) a cloth containing shiny
metallic thread.

lurgy (lerg-ee) *noun* (*plural* **lurgies**)
(*informal*) an illness.

lurid (loo-rid) *adjective*
1 sensational or shockingly vivid: *The
papers delighted in all the lurid details of the
murder.*
2 lit up by an unnatural reddish glare: *a
lurid patch of sky above the burning factory.*
[Latin *luridus* pale yellow, ghastly]

lurk *verb*
to loiter in a secretive or furtive manner.
*Figurative A faint doubt still lurked in the
back of my mind.*

luscious (lush-us) *adjective*
delicious.
Word Family **lusciously** *adverb*;
lusciousness *noun*.

lush¹ *adjective*
luxuriant.
Word Family **lushly** *adverb*; **lushness**
noun.

lush² *noun* (*plural* **lushes**)
American (*informal*) a drunkard.

lust *noun*
any strong desire, especially a powerful
sexual desire.
Word Family **lust** *verb*; **lustful** *adjective*;
lustfully *adverb*; **lustfulness** *noun*.

lustre (lust-er) *noun* (*American* **luster**)
the soft reflected light playing over a
surface: *the lustre of pearls.*
Word Family **lustrous** (lus-trus)
adjective.
[Latin *lustrare* to illumine]

lusty *adjective* (**lustier**; **lustiest**)
vigorous or hearty.
Word Family **lustily** *adverb*; **lustiness**
noun.

lute *noun*
Music a fretted instrument whose strings
are plucked with the fingers, popular in
the Middle Ages.

Lutheran (loo-tha-r'n) *noun*
Protestantism a member of the Protestant
Church founded on the doctrine of
salvation by faith alone.
Word Family **Lutheran** *adjective*;
Lutheranism *noun*.
[after *Martin Luther*, 1483-1546, its
German founder]

luxuriant (lug-*zhoor*-ee-ent) *adjective*
growing thickly and abundantly.
Word Family **luxuriantly** *adverb*;
luxuriance *noun*.

luxury (luk-sha-ree) *noun* (*plural*
luxuries)
1 a state of great sumptuousness or
comfort, surrounded by things which are
rare, expensive, or extremely gratifying.
2 something which is pleasing or elegant,
but not really necessary: *Their budget allows
few luxuries.*
Word Family **luxurious** (lug-*zhoor*-ee-
us) *adjective* characterized by luxury;
luxuriously *adverb*; **luxuriousness** *noun*;
luxuriate (lug-*zhoor*-ee-ayt) *verb* to
indulge oneself.
[Latin *luxuria* excess, extravagance]

lychee (lie-chee) *noun* also **litchi**
a small Chinese fruit with a firm shell and
a soft jelly-like middle.

lychgate *noun*
the roofed gateway of a churchyard where
the coffin can rest before a funeral service.
[Old English *lic* corpse]

Lycra (lie-kra) *noun*
(*trademark*) an elastic material used
especially in sports clothing.

lying[1] the present participle of **lie**[1].

lying[2] the present participle of **lie**[2].

lynch *verb*
to condemn and kill a person by mob
action, without legal authority.
[first employed as a form of rough justice
by *Captain William Lynch*, an American
magistrate, about 1780]

lynchpin ⇨ LINCHPIN.

lynx *noun* (*plural* **lynxes**)
any of various wildcats with a short tail
and tufted ears.
Word Family **lynx-eyed** *adjective* sharp-
sighted.
[Greek]

lyre (lire) *noun*
Music a stringed instrument of ancient
Greece, consisting of two long curved
arms meeting in a soundbox at the base.
[from Greek]

lyric (lirr-ik) *noun*
1 *Poetry* a short poem that has the form
and musical quality of a song, and that
gives direct expression to the poet's
thoughts and feelings.
2 (**lyrics**) the words of a popular song.
• **lyric** *adjective*.

lyrical (lirr-i-k'l) *adjective*
1 of or relating to a lyric.
2 poetic and enthusiastic: *The salesman
grew quite lyrical about his company's
products.*
Word Family **lyrically** *adverb*.

lyricist (lirr-i-sist) *noun* a person who
writes the words for a song.

lysergic acid diethylamide (lie-ser-jik
ass-id die-eth-il-**ay**-mide) *noun*
short form is **LSD** an illegal drug
producing hallucinations.

Mm

ma'am (mahm) *noun*
madam.

mac *noun* also **mack**
(*informal*) a mackintosh.

macabre (ma-**kah**-bra) *adjective*
ghastly, horrible or gruesome.
[French]

macadam (ma-**kad**-'m) *noun*
the crushed rock or stone used in layers to
make roads.
[after *J. L. McAdam*, 1756-1836, a
Scottish surveyor]

macadamia (mak-a-**day**-mee-a) *noun*
the round edible nut of a tree that grows in
the Australian rainforest.
[after *J. Macadam*, 1827-1865, an
Australian chemist]

macaroni *noun*
a pasta shaped like short hollow tubes.
[Italian]

macaroon *noun*
a sweet crisp cake made with coconut or
almonds.
[Italian]

macaw (ma-**kaw**) *noun*
a large long-tailed South American parrot,
with brightly coloured feathers and a
harsh voice.
[Portuguese]

mace[1] *noun*
1 a club-like weapon, usually with a spiked
metal head.
2 a staff carried by an official as a symbol
of office.

mace[2] *noun*
a spice made from the dried outer
covering of nutmeg.

macerate (**mass**-a-rate) *verb*
to soak something in order to soften it.
Word Family **maceration** (mass-a-**ray**-
sh'n) *noun*.
[Latin *maceratus* softened]

Mach (mark *or* mak) *noun* also called
Mach number.
Physics the ratio of the speed of a body to
the speed of sound in the medium through
which it is travelling. At Mach 1 the body
is moving at the speed of sound.
[after *Ernst Mach*, 1836-1916, an Austrian
physicist]

machete (ma-**shet**-ee) *noun*
a large heavy knife with a broad blade,
used for chopping or as a weapon.
[Spanish]

Machiavellian (mak-ee-a-**vel**-ee-an)
adjective
having no scruples to obtain what one
wants, especially in politics.
[after *Niccolò Machiavelli*, 1469-1527, an
Italian writer on political theory]

machinate (**mak**-in-ate *or* **mash**-in-ate)
verb
to scheme or plot, usually in an evil way.
Word Family **machination** (mak-in-**ay**-
sh'n *or* mash-in-**ay**-sh'n) *noun* 1 the act of
plotting. 2 a plot or scheme.
[Latin *machinari* to contrive]

machine (ma-**sheen**) *noun*
1 a mechanical device which performs a
certain function: *a sewing machine*.
2 a group of people working efficiently as a
system: *The government machine functions
smoothly.*
Word Family **machine** *verb* to make with
a machine; **machinery** *noun* 1 the parts
of a machine. 2 any or all machines;
machinist *noun* a person who operates a
machine.
[Greek *mekhané* a contrivance]

machine code *noun*
Computers a language in the binary
number system which can be understood
directly by a computer.

machine gun *noun*
an automatic weapon capable of rapid
continuous fire.

machine-readable *adjective*
able to be directly processed by computer:
machine-readable data.

machine tool *noun*
a lathe or other power-operated tool for
shaping, planing, drilling or milling metal,
wood or plastics.

machismo (ma-**chiz**-mo *or* ma-**kiz**-mo)
noun
the urge that a man has to show how
strong or virile he is.
[Spanish]

Mach number ⇨ MACH.

macho (**match**-o) *adjective*
displaying machismo.

mack ⇨ MAC.

mackerel *noun* (*plural* **mackerel** or
mackerels)
an edible fish with wavy markings.

mackerel sky *noun* (*plural* **mackerel
skies**)
ripples of high cirrus cloud in patterns
resembling a mackerel's back.

mackintosh *noun* (*plural* **mackintoshes**)
also **macintosh** (*plural* **macintoshes**)
a raincoat made of cotton treated with
waterproof rubber.
[after *C. Macintosh*, 1766-1843, a Scottish
chemist, who invented it]

macramé (ma-**krah**-may) *noun*
1 the knotting of thread or cord in
patterns.
2 the decorative work made in this way.
[Turkish *magrama* towel]

macrobiotic (mak-ro-by-**ot**-ik) *adjective*
relating to a diet consisting of a high
proportion of organically grown fruit,
vegetables and grain, and a small amount
of meat, eggs, etc., said to make for a long
life.
[Greek *makros* long + *bios* life]

macrocosm (**mak**-ro-kozm) *noun*
the world or universe as a whole.
[Greek *makros* large + *kosmos* world]

mad *adjective* (**madder; maddest**)
1 insane.
2 foolish: *mad ideas*.
3 (*informal*) excited, chaotic: *a mad rush for
seats*.
4 (*informal*) enthusiastic: *She's mad about
netball*.
5 (*informal*) furious.
Word Family **madden** *verb* to make mad;
madness *noun* 1 the state of being mad.
2 mad behaviour; **madly** *adverb*.

madam (**mad**-'m) *noun*
1 a polite form of address to a woman.
2 a woman in charge of a brothel.
[French *ma dame* my lady]

Madame (ma-**dahm**) *noun* (*plural*
Mesdames) (may-**dahm**)
a title for a married woman, in a French-
speaking country.
[French *ma dame* my lady]

madcap *adjective*
crazy or reckless.

mad cow disease *noun*
(*informal*) bovine spongiform
encephalopathy.

madder *noun*
a strong red or reddish-orange dye
obtained from the root of a European
plant.

made the past tense and past participle of
make.

Mademoiselle (mad-'m-wa-**zel**) *noun*
(*plural* **Mesdemoiselles**) (may-d'm-wa-
zel)
a title for an unmarried woman in a
French-speaking country.
[French]

madly ⇨ MAD.

madness ⇨ MAD.

Madonna *noun*
1 the Virgin Mary.
2 a picture or statue of the Virgin Mary.
[Italian *ma donna* my lady]

madrigal (**mad**-ri-g'l) *noun*
an unaccompanied song for several voices
singing two or more melodies together,
from the 16th century or 17th century.

maelstrom (**male**-strom) *noun*
1 a great or violent whirlpool.
2 a violent force or whirl of events: *the
maelstrom of war*.
[Dutch]

maestro (**my**-stro) *noun* (*plural* **maestri**
(**my**-stree) or **maestros**)
a master of any art, especially an eminent
musician or conductor.
[Italian, master]

Mae West *noun*
(*informal dated*) an inflatable life jacket.
[after *Mae West*, 1892-1980, a film star
with a full figure]

Mafia *noun*
1 *History* a secret nationalist society in
French-ruled Sicily which degenerated
into a collection of hired thugs specializing
in blackmail, 'protection' rackets and
murder, and believed to still exist.
2 a gang of political or other conspirators
or suspected conspirators.
Word Family **Mafioso** *noun* (*plural*
Mafiosi) a Mafia member.
[Sicilian dialect, bragging, boldness]

magazine (mag-a-**zeen**) *noun*
1 a publication appearing at regular
intervals, of more specialized interest than
a newspaper.
2 the part of a gun where cartridges are
stored.

3 a place where arms and explosives are
stored.
[Arabic *makhzan* storehouse]

magenta (ma-**jen**-ta) *noun*
a brilliant reddish-purple colour.
• **magenta** *adjective*.
[a dye of this colour was discovered in
1859, the year of a battle at *Magenta*,
northern Italy]

maggot *noun*
the larva of a fly, usually living in decaying
matter.
Word Family **maggoty** *adjective* infested
with maggots.

magi
the plural of **magus**.

magic *noun*
1 the attempted use of supernatural forces
and practices to change or influence
normal events.
2 conjuring.
3 a mysterious power: *We were caught up in
the magic of the music.*
Word Family **magic, magical** *adjective*
of or like magic; **magician** (ma-**jish**-'n)
noun a person who practises magic;
magically *adverb*.
[from Greek from old Persian]

magic carpet *noun*
a carpet which is supposed to fly through
the air, taking one anywhere one wants.
[possessed by King Solomon (according
to the Koran) and also featured in 'The
Arabian Nights']

magic lantern *noun*
an old type of slide projector.

magic mushroom *noun*
(*informal*) a type of toadstool which causes
hallucinations when eaten.

magistrate (**maj**-iss-trate) *noun*
a person appointed to administer justice in
a magistrate's court, either as an unpaid
justice of the peace or as a salaried
(stipendiary) magistrate.
Word Family **magisterial** (maj-iss-**teer**-
i-al) *adjective* 1 of or like a magistrate.
2 imperious, domineering; **magistracy**
(**maj**-iss-tra-see) *noun* (*plural*
magistracies) 1 the position of a
magistrate. 2 magistrates considered as a
group.
[Latin *magister* master]

magistrate's court *noun*
a local court, with powers to try minor
cases (summary jurisdiction), to hold
preliminary inquiries into more serious
cases which may go to a higher court, and
to license publicans, etc.

magma *noun*
Geology the molten rock layer between the
inner solid core of the earth and the
mantle. Compare LAVA.

magnanimous (mag-**nan**-i-mus) *adjective*
generous, forgiving or free from pettiness.
Word Family **magnanimity** (mag-na-
nim-i-tee) *noun* generosity;
magnanimously *adverb*.
[Latin *magnus* great + *animus* spirit]

magnate (**mag**-nayt) *noun*
a person who has power, especially due to
property, wealth or position.
[Latin *magnus* great]

magnesia (mag-**nee**-zi-a) *noun*
a tasteless white powder used in medicine
as an antacid and laxative.

magnesium (mag-**nee**-zi-um) *noun*
a light metal which burns with a very
bright white flame. It is used in lightweight
alloys and many chemical processes and is
essential to form chlorophyll.
[after *Magnesia*, a metal-bearing region in
Greece]

magnet *noun*
1 a piece of metal, usually iron, which
attracts other iron objects, and aligns itself
north and south when suspended.
2 a person, place or thing that attracts
people.
Word Family **magnetize, magnetise**
verb to make into a magnet.
[same root as *magnesium*]

magnetic (mag-**net**-ik) *adjective*
1 *Physics* having a crystal structure such
that, if placed in an electric field, it
becomes magnetized, either permanently
(**ferromagnetic**) or only as long as it
remains in the electric field
(**electromagnetic**).
2 of or relating to such forces: *a magnetic
compass*.
3 attractive: *a magnetic personality*.
Word Family **magnetically** *adverb*;
magnetism (**mag**-nit-izm) *noun*.

magnetic field *noun*
a field of force around a magnet's poles or
around a wire carrying an electric current.

magnetic north ⇨ NORTH (definition 2).

magnetic tape ⇨ TAPE (definition 2).

magneto (mag-**nee**-to) *noun*
an electrical generator using magnets,
especially one used to provide ignition in
an internal-combustion engine.

magnificent (mag-**niff**-i-s'nt) *adjective*
splendid or very fine.
Word Family **magnificence** *noun*;
magnificently *adverb*.
[Latin *magnificus* grand, on a large scale]

magnify (mag-ni-fie) *verb* (**magnifies;**
magnifying; magnified)
1 to make something appear larger: *A
microscope magnifies objects.*
2 an old word meaning 'to praise'.
Word Family **magnifier** *noun* a person
or thing that magnifies; **magnification**
(mag-ni-fi-**kay**-sh'n) *noun* 1 the act of
magnifying. 2 the power to magnify. 3 a
magnified copy or reproduction.

magnitude *noun*
1 size or extent.
2 importance.
3 *Astronomy* a measure of the apparent
brightness of a star.
4 *Maths* the absolute value of a number.
5 *Maths* the length of a vector.
[Latin *magnitudo* greatness]

magnolia *noun*
a shrub or tree with large pink or white
waxy flowers, widely cultivated for
ornament.
[after *P. Magnol*, 1638-1715, a French
botanist]

magnum *noun*
a large wine bottle holding approximately
1½ litres.

magnum opus *noun* (*plural* **magnum**
opuses or **magnum opera**)
a person's greatest achievement, especially
a literary work.
[Latin, big work]

magpie *noun*
1 a large black and white bird related to
the crow and noted for its chattering and
for stealing miscellaneous objects.
2 a chatterbox.
3 a random collector of miscellaneous
objects.

magus (**may**-gus) *noun* (*plural* **magi**)
(**may**-jie)
1 an ancient priest, astrologer or wise man.
2 (**the Magi**) *Christianity* the three wise
men from the East who came to pay
homage to the infant Jesus.
[Persian]

maharaja (mah-ha-**rah**-ja) *noun* also
maharajah
a title for certain ruling princes in India.
[Sanskrit *maha* great + *raja* king]

maharani (mah-ha-**rah**-nee) *noun* also
maharanee
the wife or widow of a maharaja.
[Sanskrit *maha* great + *rani* queen]

mah-jong (mah-**jong**) *noun* also **mah-**
jongg
a Chinese game for four people, played
with pieces or tiles marked with suits or
families.
[Mandarin Chinese]

mahogany (ma-**hog**-a-nee) *noun*
1 a tropical tree with a hard reddish-brown
wood, used for furniture.
2 a reddish-brown colour.
• **mahogany** *adjective*.

maid *noun*
1 a female servant.
2 an old or poetic word for a girl or young
woman.
old maid a woman who is not married
and is thought to be too old to marry.

maiden *noun*
1 an old or poetic word for a girl or young
woman.
2 short form of **maiden over** *Cricket* an
over in which no runs are scored.
• **maiden** *adjective*
1 virginal or unmarried.
2 first: *his maiden speech in parliament.*
□ *the ship's maiden voyage.*
Word Family **maidenly** *adjective*;
maidenhood *noun*.

maidenhair *noun* also called **maidenhair**
fern.
a fern with fine stalks and delicate fronds.

maidenhead *noun*
an old word for the hymen.

maiden name *noun*
the surname that a girl has when she is
born.

mail¹ *noun*
1 letters, parcels, etc. sent by post.
2 *Computers* email.
• **mail** *verb*
1 to send by post.
2 *Computers* to email.

mail² *noun*
flexible armour made of metal rings, chain
or small plates.

mail order *noun*
a system of buying goods by post.

maim *verb*
to cripple or injure severely.

main *adjective*
chief or most important: *the main thing to
remember.*

main *noun*

1 the principal pipe or cable in a gas or electrical system.

2 an old or poetic word for the open ocean: *They sailed the Spanish Main.*

Phrase in the main mostly.

Word Family mainly *adverb* chiefly.

mainframe *noun*

a fast powerful computer used by large organizations.

mainland *noun*

the principal land mass, as distinguished from islands.

mainline *verb*

(*informal*) to inject a narcotic drug directly into the vein.

mainsail (main-sail *or* main-s'l) *noun*

Nautical the principal sail hoisted from the tallest mast on a ship.

mainspring *noun*

1 the principal spring of a clock, watch, etc.

2 the chief motivating force.

mainstay *noun*

1 the chief support.

2 *Nautical* the rope which secures the mainmast forward.

mainstream *noun*

the main trend in thought, fashion, etc.

maintain *verb*

1 to preserve or continue: *They tried to maintain a good relationship.*

2 to keep in good order: *maintaining the school grounds.*

3 to affirm or assert: *He maintained that he was totally innocent.*

Word Family maintainer *noun*; maintainable *adjective.*

[Latin *manu* in the hand + *tenere* to hold]

maintenance (mane-t'n-ançe) *noun*

1 the act or process of maintaining.

2 a means of support, such as the money paid by one partner in a marriage to the other after separation.

maisonette (may-z'n-et) *noun*

a self-contained flat, usually occupying more than one floor of a house.

[French, small house]

maître d'hôtel (may-tra doe-tel) *noun*

(*plural* maîtres d'hôtel) (may-tra doe-tel) also maître d' (may-tra dee) (*plural* maître d's)

1 a head waiter.

2 a hotel manager.

[French, master of the house]

The term **maître d'hôtel** is a French expression that English has taken over without changing its form. France was long considered to have the best restaurants and the best chefs in the world. Thus many cooking terms have been adopted directly into English, as in *au gratin*, which describes a dish cooked with a browned topping, and many menus in expensive restaurants list and describe their dishes in French.

maize *noun*

a cereal plant with heads thickly packed with large succulent yellow grain.

[from Cuban Spanish]

majesty (maj-ess-tee) *noun* (*plural* majesties)

1 regal grandeur and dignity: *The procession continued with pomp and majesty.*

2 supreme or royal authority.

3 (Majesty) a form of address for a monarch: *Your Majesty.*

Word Family majestic (ma-jest-ik) *adjective* having great dignity; majestically *adverb.*

majolica (ma-yol-i-ka *or* ma-jol-i-ka) *noun* also maiolica

a variety of Italian earthenware with an opaque glaze and rich colours.

[from Italian name of *Majorca*, from where it was imported]

major (may-ja) *noun*

1 *Army* a commissioned officer ranking between captain and lieutenant colonel.

2 *American* a main subject of study at certain universities.

major *adjective*

1 greater or more important: *The major part of my money goes on rent.* □ *He is a major artist of our century.*

2 *Music* relating to the more normal of the two chief arrangements of the semitones in a key or scale. Compare MINOR *adjective* (definition 2.)

major *verb* to specialize in a subject at certain universities.

[Latin, greater]

major-domo *noun*

a butler or steward in charge of an important household.

[Spanish *mayor-domo* chief household official]

major general *noun*

Army a commissioned officer ranking between brigadier and lieutenant general.

majority (ma-**jorr**-i-tee) *noun* (*plural* **majorities**)
1 the greater part or number: *The majority of students work hard.*
2 the difference between the votes for one party or candidate in an election and another party or candidate: *Labour had a huge majority.*
3 the age at which one is legally an adult.

make *verb* (**makes; making; made**)
1 to create, form or bring into existence: *I made a pie.*
2 to cause to be done, performed, etc.: *What makes it move?*
3 to cause to be or become: *He made me angry.*
4 to appoint: *They made her Queen.*
5 to force to do something: *You can't make me go.*
6 to estimate to be: *What time do you make it?*
7 to agree on: *We made a date for Saturday.*
8 to earn: *She made a fortune.*
9 to become, prove to be: *He would make a fine doctor.*
10 to achieve selection for: *Did you make the team?*
11 (*especially American*) to get to the rank of: *She might make captain.*
12 to bring success to: *That scene made the film for me.*
13 to deliver: *He made a speech.*
14 to put in order: *Make your bed.*
15 to total: *That makes ten altogether.*
16 to reach, arrive at: *We hope to make Edinburgh by lunchtime.*
Phrases **make do** to manage, get by. **make for 1** to move towards. **2** to help to create: *A friendly boss makes for a happy workplace.* **make it** to achieve one's goal. **make of** to reckon to be, judge: *What did you make of her speech?* **make off with** to steal. **make out 1** to decipher, understand. **2** to write: *He made out a cheque for £50.* **3** to suggest: *Are you making me out to be an idiot?* **4** to get on: *How is she making out in her new job?* **5** *American* (of two people) to pet or make love. **make over** to transform or remodel. **make up 1** to comprise or be comprised of. **2** to put together. **3** to invent. **4** to supply, give: *He had to make up the time he had wasted.* **5** to become friends again. **6** to apply make-up to. **make up to** to try to gain the favour of: *She's always making up to the teachers.*
• **make** *noun*
1 the way or style in which something is made.

2 a brand.
Phrase **on the make** seeking to gain something.
Word Family **maker** *noun*.

makeover *noun*
a complete transformation or remodelling, particularly of a person's appearance.

makeshift *adjective*
serving as a temporary substitute or alternative: *We made a makeshift shelter for the night.*

make-up *noun*
1 a product used on the face, e.g. lipstick or eyeshadow.
2 somebody's personality or characteristics.

makeweight *noun*
a small quantity added to make up a deficiency.

making *noun*
1 the process of creating something.
2 (**makings**) qualities that are needed for something: *He has the makings of a great dancer.*
Phrase **be the making of someone** to be the cause of someone's success or advancement.

malacca (ma-**lak**-a) *noun*
a brown cane walking stick made from the stem of a palm tree.
[after *Malacca*, a district in Malaysia]

maladjusted (mal-a-**jus**-tid) *adjective*
badly adjusted, especially unable to adapt to one's surroundings or form relationships.
Word Family **maladjustment** *noun* the condition of being maladjusted.

maladministration *noun*
(*formal*) bad management.

maladroit (mal-a-**droyt**) *adjective*
clumsy or awkward.
Word Family **maladroitly** *adverb*; **maladroitness** *noun*.

malady (**mal**-a-dee) *noun* (*plural* **maladies**)
a disorder or disease.

malaise (mal-**aze**) *noun*
a general feeling of unexplained discomfort or weakness.
[French *mal* bad + *aise* ease]

malapropism (**mal**-a-prop-izm) *noun*
the inappropriate or unsuitable use of words: *It is a malapropism to say 'credible' when you mean 'credulous'.*
[from *Mrs Malaprop*, a character in Sheridan's play 'The Rivals']

malaria (ma-**lair**-ee-a) *noun*
a recurrent disease transmitted by
mosquitoes and causing fevers and chills.
Word Family **malarial** *adjective*.
[Italian *mala* bad + *aria* air]

malarkey *noun*
(*informal*) nonsense.

malcontent (**mal**-kon-tent) *noun*
a person who is discontented.
● **malcontent** *adjective*.

male *noun*
1 a person of the sex which generates, but
does not give birth to, children; a man or
boy.
2 an animal of this sex.
3 *Biology* the parts of a plant which
fertilize the female parts.
● **male** *adjective*
1 of or characteristic of a male.
2 designed to fit into a corresponding part:
a male plug.

male chauvinist (male **sho**-va-nist) *noun*
a man who believes that men are superior
to women, and acts in a prejudiced way
towards them.

malediction (mal-a-**dik**-sh'n) *noun*
a curse.

malefactor (**mal**-i-fak-ta) *noun*
(*formal*) a criminal or wrongdoer.

malevolent (ma-**lev**-a-l'nt) *adjective*
showing ill will or wishing harm to others.
Word Family **malevolently** *adverb*;
malevolence *noun*.
[Latin *malé* badly + *volens* willing]

malfeasance (mal-**fee**-zence) *noun*
Law an unlawful act.

malformed *adjective*
badly formed or shaped.
Word Family **malformation** *noun*.

malfunction *noun*
a failure of a machine.
● **malfunction** *verb* (of a machine or part)
to fail.

malice (**mal**-iss) *noun*
a desire or intention to hurt or cause
suffering.

malicious (ma-**lish**-us) *adjective*
full of or showing malice.
Word Family **maliciously** *adverb*;
maliciousness *noun*.
[Latin *malitia* badness]

malign (ma-**line**) *verb*
to slander or speak ill of someone.
● **malign** *adjective* causing evil or injury.

Word Family **malignly** *adverb*;
maligner *noun* a person who maligns;
malignity (ma-**lig**-ni-tee) *noun* ill will.
[Latin *malignus* ill-natured]

malignant (ma-**lig**-nant) *adjective*
1 feeling or showing extreme ill will.
2 *Medicine* tending to regrow and cause
damage to tissue in the body: *The tumour
was malignant*. Compare BENIGN
(definition 2).
Word Family **malignantly** *adverb*;
malignancy *noun*.

malinger (ma-**ling**-ga) *verb*
to pretend to be ill, especially in order to
escape work.
Word Family **malingerer** *noun*.

mall (mal *or* maul *or* mol) *noun*
an enclosed shopping area.

mallard *noun* (*plural* **mallard** *or*
mallards)
the common European wild duck. The
female has brown plumage and the male
has a dark green head.

malleable (**mal**-ee-a-b'l) *adjective*
1 able to be hammered into thin sheets or
rolled into shape: *Silver is malleable*.
Compare DUCTILE (definition 1).
2 easily influenced.
Word Family **malleability** (mal-ee-a-
bill-i-tee) *noun*.
[Latin *malleus* a hammer]

mallet *noun*
1 a hammer, especially one with a wooden
head.
2 a wooden stick with a long handle, used
to strike the ball in croquet.

malnutrition (mal-new-**trish**-'n) *noun*
poor nutrition due to a lack of the correct
foods, especially vitamins or protein.

malodorous (mal-o-der-us) *adjective*
having an unpleasant smell.

malpractice (mal-**prak**-tis) *noun*
improper conduct, especially by a
professional person.

malt (mawlt) *noun*
a germinated grain, often barley, used in
brewing and distillation.

maltreat (mal-**treet**) *verb*
to treat badly or cruelly.
Word Family **maltreatment** *noun*.

mama *noun* also **mamma**
(*especially American*) mother.

mamba *noun*
a deadly poisonous African tree snake.
[Zulu]

mambo *noun*
a dance of Latin American origin.
[Haitian]

mammal *noun*
a member of the group of vertebrates
whose young feed on milk from the
mother's breast.
Word Family **mammalian** (mam-**ay**-
lee-an) *adjective*.
[Latin *mamma* breast]

mammary (**mam**-a-ree) *adjective*
of or relating to the breast.
[Latin *mamma* breast]

mammary gland *noun*
the milk-producing gland in females.

mammogram (**mam**-a-gram) *noun*
an X-ray taken of the breasts for early
detection of cancer.
Word Family **mammography** (ma-
mog-ra-fee) *noun*.

Mammon *noun*
wealth or riches.
[after *Mammon*, wealth and greed
personified in the Bible as a false god]

mammoth *noun*
an extinct elephant.
• **mammoth** *adjective* huge.

man *noun* (*plural* **men**)
1 an adult male human being.
2 people in general: *Man is destroying the
environment.*
3 a boyfriend or partner: *She's got a new
man.*
4 one of the pieces used in playing certain
games such as chess.
Phrases **man about town** a person with
an active social life. **man of the world** a
person of wide experience. **the man in
the street** a person supposed to represent
the most common point of view. **to a man**
without exception.
• **man** *verb* (**mans**; **manning**; **manned**)
to supply with people, especially for
defence: *Man the pumps!*

The word **man** has given rise to a great
deal of controversy. It used to be
completely acceptable to use *man*
meaning 'mankind', as in *Man destroyed
the environment* or 'a human being', as
in *No man is completely honest.* Many
people now prefer to use terms which
represent women as well as men, such
as *humankind, people, person, human
being, human race,* etc.

manacle (**man**-a-k'l) *noun*
a shackle or handcuff.

• **manacle** *verb* to restrain with manacles.
[Latin *manicula* little hand]

manage (**man**-ij) *verb*
1 to control or handle something properly
or successfully: *Can you manage that horse?*
2 to succeed in doing something: *She
managed to sell her car for a good price.*
Word Family **manageable** *adjective*.

management *noun*
1 the act or manner of managing: *Her
management of the children is excellent.*
2 executive skill or ability: *The young
woman was trained in management.*
3 a person or group in charge of a
business: *Take your complaint to the
management.*

manager *noun*
a person who manages, especially
someone in charge of a business or team.

manageress *noun* (*plural*
manageresses)
a woman who manages something,
especially a business.

managerial (man-a-**jeer**-i-al) *adjective*
of or like a manager: *She was given some
managerial responsibility.*

managing director *noun*
a person who manages a company.

mañana (man-**yah**-na) *noun*
tomorrow.
[Spanish]

mandala (**man**-da-la *or* man-**dah**-la) *noun*
a sacred or magical diagram, often a
circle representing the universe, used for
meditation, etc.
[Sanskrit]

mandarin[1] *noun*
a small sweet orange citrus fruit.

mandarin[2] *noun*
1 *History* a member of any of the nine
ranks of public officials during the
Chinese Empire.
2 (**Mandarin**) the language upon which
the official language of China is based.
3 a high-ranking civil servant.

mandate *noun*
1 a command or order.
2 the instruction given by an electorate to
its representative, expressed by the result
of an election: *The winning party may
consider itself to have a mandate from the
people to carry out its policies.*
3 the commission given to one nation to
administer the government and affairs of a
territory, colony, etc.
[Latin *mandatus* commanded]

mandatory (**man**-da-tree) *adjective*
compulsory.

mandible *noun*
1 the bottom part of a bird's beak.
2 *Anatomy* the lower movable jawbone.
Word Family **mandibular** (man-**dib**-
yoo-la) *adjective*.
[Latin *mandere* to chew]

mandir (**mun**-deer) *noun*
a Hindu temple.
[Hindi]

mandolin (man-da-**lin**) *noun*
1 a musical instrument similar to the lute,
having four pairs of metal strings plucked
with a plectrum.
2 also **mandoline** a kitchen utensil used
for slicing vegetables.
Word Family **mandolinist** *noun*.
[from Italian]

mandrake *noun*
a narcotic herb.
[Greek *mandragoras*]

mandrel *noun*
a shaft or spindle in a lathe, used to
support pieces being worked on.

mandrill *noun*
a large West African baboon with a beard
and mane. The male has blue and scarlet
markings on its face and buttocks.

mane *noun*
1 the long hair on the neck of animals such
as horses, lions, etc.
2 a person's long or thick hair.

manful *adjective*
brave and determined.
Word Family **manfully** *adverb*.

mange (*rhymes with* strange) *noun*
a skin disease due to parasitic mites,
causing scab-like sores and loss of hair,
usually in animals.

manger (**mane**-ja) *noun*
a box or trough from which cattle or
horses feed.

mangetout (**monzh**-too) *noun* (*plural*
mangetout or **mangetouts**) (**monzh**-
too)
a variety of peas with thin flat edible pods.
[French, eat all]

mangle[1] *verb*
to cut or damage something badly.
*Figurative He mangled his speech on
television* (= ruined through mistakes).

mangle[2] *noun*
a device which squeezes water out of
clothes and other laundry by pressing
them between rollers.

mango *noun* (*plural* **mangoes** or **mangos**)
an oval yellowish-red tropical fruit with
orange flesh.
[Tamil]

mangold *noun*
a large variety of beet, cultivated for cattle
food.
[German *Mangold* beet]

mangrove *noun*
a low tree with exposed roots, usually
found in tropical tidal swamps.

mangy (**mane**-jee) *adjective* also **mangey**
(**mangier; mangiest**)
1 suffering from mange.
2 shabby.

manhandle *verb*
to handle roughly.

manhole *noun*
a hole, usually with a cover, through which
a person may enter a boiler, sewer, etc.

manhood *noun*
the state or time of being a man.

man-hour *noun*
an hour of work done by one person, used
as an industrial time unit.

mania (**may**-nee-a) *noun*
1 an uncontrollable and often violent form
of insanity.
2 a great excitement or enthusiasm.

maniac (**may**-nee-ak) *noun*
someone who behaves in a wild or violent
way.
Word Family **maniacal** (ma-**nie**-a-k'l)
adjective of or characteristic of mania.

manic *adjective*
1 of or produced by a mania.
2 wildly excited.
Word Family **manically** *adverb*.

manic depression *noun*
a mental disorder marked by alternate
moods of excitement and depression.
Word Family **manic-depressive** *noun*,
adjective.

manicure *verb*
to treat or care for the hands and
fingernails.
Word Family **manicure** *noun*;
manicurist *noun* a person who
manicures.
[Latin *manus* hand + *cura* care]

manifest (**man**-i-fest) *adjective*
plain or obvious: *He told a manifest lie*.
• **manifest** *verb* to show clearly: *His guilt
was manifested in court*.
• **manifest** *noun* Commerce a list of cargo.
Word Family **manifestly** *adverb*.
[Latin *manifestus* palpable, plain]

manifestation (man-i-fes-**tay**-sh'n) *noun*
1 the act of manifesting.
2 a sign or indication: *His house is a manifestation of his wealth.*

manifesto *noun*
a statement, e.g. by a political party, which explains actions, intentions or policies.

manifold (**man**-i-fold) *adjective*
many and various: *She performs manifold duties at work.*
• **manifold** *noun* a pipe or chamber with a number of inlets or outlets, such as one used for conducting air and fuel into, or exhaust gases out of, an internal-combustion engine.

manikin (**man**-i-kin) *noun* also **mannikin**
1 a very small man.
2 a tailor's dummy.

Manila (ma-**nil**-a) *noun* also **Manilla**
a strong, light brown paper used to make envelopes, folders, etc.
[made of hemp from *Manila*, Philippines]

manipulate (ma-**nip**-yoo-late) *verb*
1 to handle, use or manage something skilfully: *learning to manipulate tools.*
2 to influence someone cleverly.
Word Family **manipulation** (ma-nip-yoo-**lay**-sh'n) *noun*; **manipulator** *noun*.

mankind *noun*
all living people.

manly *adjective* (**manlier**; **manliest**)
having the qualities thought to be appropriate to a man, such as bravery and strength.
Word Family **manliness** *noun*.

manna *noun*
anything valuable which is received unexpectedly.
[Hebrew, of the bread God rained from heaven upon the famished Israelites in the desert, according to the account in the Bible, Exodus 16]

mannequin (**man**-i-kin) *noun*
a dummy in a shop window.
[French]

manner *noun*
1 the way in which something happens or is done.
2 a way of speaking or behaving.
3 a type, sort: *Every manner of dog could be seen at the show.*
4 (**manners**) ways of behaving, especially polite or socially acceptable ways.
Word Family **mannered** *adjective*
1 having a particular sort of manners:

a bad-mannered child. 2 having artificial mannerisms; **mannerly** *adjective* polite.

mannerism (**man**-a-rizm) *noun*
a distinctive habit or way of behaving.

mannikin ⇨ MANIKIN.

mannish *adjective*
like a man: *a mannish woman.*

manoeuvre (ma-**noo**-va) *noun* (*American* **maneuver**)
1 a planned and organized move or series of moves.
2 a skilful plan.
3 (**manoeuvres**) an exercise using troops.
Word Family **manoeuvre** *verb* (**manoeuvres**; **manoeuvring**; **manoeuvred**).
[French]

man-of-war *noun* (*plural* **men-of-war**) also **man-o'-war** (*plural* **men-o'-war**)
1 a warship.
2 a marine animal. ⇨ PORTUGUESE MAN-OF-WAR.

manometer (ma-**nom**-i-ta) *noun*
an instrument used to measure the pressure of a gas or a liquid.
[Greek *manos* thin + METER]

manor *noun*
1 *Medieval history* the house and lands of a feudal lord.
2 a large country house with land.
Word Family **manorial** (ma-**naw**-ree-al) *adjective*.

manpower *noun*
power as measured by the number of people available or required.

manqué (**mong**-kay) *adjective*
unsuccessful or unfulfilled: *The theatre critic was really an actor manqué.*
[French, failed]

mansard *noun*
a roof in which the angle of the slope changes halfway, the lower half being steeper than the upper.

manse *noun*
the home of a church minister, especially in Scotland.

mansion (**man**-sh'n) *noun*
a large elaborate house usually with extensive grounds around it.
[from Latin]

manslaughter (**man**-slaw-ta) *noun*
the crime of unintentionally killing a person. Compare MURDER (definition 1).

mantelpiece *noun* also **mantlepiece**
a structure above and around a fireplace, usually with a projecting shelf.

mantilla *noun*
a lace headscarf, attached to a comb and falling over the shoulders, worn by women in Spain.
[Spanish, small mantle]

mantis (**man**-tiss) *noun* (*plural* **mantis** or **mantises**) also called **praying mantis**.
any of a group of large flesh-eating insects which hold their forelegs together as if in prayer.

mantle *noun*
1 an old word for a woman's cloak.
2 something which covers or conceals: *a mantle of fog.*
3 *Geology* the layer of solid rock between the earth's crust and the magma.
4 also called **gas mantle**. a fine network placed over a gas flame and heated by the flame so that it becomes white-hot and produces brilliant light.

mantra *noun*
a Hindu or Buddhist sacred sound or chant.

manual (**man**-yew-al) *adjective*
1 of or done with the hands: *manual labour.*
2 using human rather than mechanical or automatic power: *manual gears in a car.*
• **manual** *noun* a book providing information or instruction.
Word Family **manually** *adverb.*
[Latin *manus* hand]

manufacture (man-yoo-**fak**-cher) *verb*
1 to make or produce goods, etc., especially by an industrial process.
2 to invent: *She manufactured an excuse so that she could miss the meeting.*
Word Family **manufacture** *noun* the making or producing of goods;
manufacturer *noun*.
[Latin *manus* by hand + *factus* made]

manumit (man-yoo-**mit**) *verb*
(**manumits; manumitting; manumitted**)
to release a slave.

manure (man-**yoor**) *noun*
the excrement of animals put in the soil to fertilize it.
Word Family **manure** *verb* to add manure to.

manuscript (**man**-yoo-skript) *noun*
a handwritten or typed copy of an article, book, report, etc., before it is printed.
[Latin *manus* hand + *scriptum* writing]

Manx cat *noun*
a short-haired tailless cat with long hind legs.
[*Manx*, of the Isle of Man]

many *adjective* (**more; most**)
a large number of: *Many people have their own homes.*
• **many** *noun* (used with plural verb) a large number: *Many were killed.*
Phrase **how many?** what number?

map *noun*
a drawing which shows part or all of the earth's surface, looked at from above.
Phrase **put something on the map** to make something, e.g. a town, well known.
Word Family **map** *verb* (**maps; mapping; mapped**) 1 to make or put on a map. 2 to sketch a plan of something.

maple *noun*
a tree or shrub with sap which yields syrup, e.g. the sugar maple or the field maple.

maple syrup *noun*
a sweet thick syrup made from the sap of maple trees.

mar *verb* (**mars; marring; marred**)
to spoil or damage.

maraca (ma-**rakk**-a) *noun*
a percussion instrument consisting of a gourd filled with dried seeds, stones, etc.

marathon *noun*
1 a long-distance race, especially a foot race of about 26 miles, or 42 km.
2 any long test or competition of endurance.
• **marathon** *adjective* long and difficult: *Getting the house decorated was a marathon effort.*
[from the running of a messenger to Athens to tell of the Greek victory at the *Battle of Marathon* in 490 B.C.]

maraud (ma-**rawd**) *verb*
to raid in search of plunder.
Word Family **marauder** *noun*.
[French, vagabond]

marble *noun*
1 a form of hard limestone, usually veined or mottled, which is cut and polished for use in buildings, statues, etc.
2 a small ball of stone or glass, which is used in a children's game.
3 (**marbles**) a game played with these small balls.
Word Family **marble** *verb* to colour or stain something like marble; **marble** *adjective* of or like marble; **marbling** *noun* marble-like decoration.

marcasite (**mar**-ka-site) *noun*
Geology a brass-coloured mineral consisting of iron pyrites, used for jewellery.

march *verb*
1 to walk with measured and regular steps, like soldiers.
2 to cause to march: *The prisoners were marched to their cells.*
• **march** *noun* (*plural* **marches**)
1 the act of marching.
2 a piece of music to accompany marching.
Phrase **steal a march** to gain or take an advantage.
[French *marcher* to walk]

March *noun*
the third month of the year, after February and before April.
[after the ancient Roman god *Mars*]

marching orders *plural noun*
(*informal*) instructions to leave.

marchioness (mar-sha-**ness**) *noun* (*plural* **marchionesses**)
1 a female marquess.
2 the wife or widow of a marquess.

mare[1] (*rhymes with* air) *noun*
a female horse or pony.

mare[2] (**mar**-ray) *noun* (*plural* **maria**) (**mah**-ree-a)
a large dark plain on the moon.
[Latin, sea]

margarine (mar-ja-**reen**) *noun*
a substitute for butter made from vegetable oils or animal fats.

margin (**mar**-jin) *noun*
1 the space between writing and the edge of a page.
2 any edge.
3 *Commerce* the difference between the cost and the selling price.
4 an amount: *She won by a narrow margin.*

marginal *adjective*
1 of or situated on a margin: *marginal notes.*
2 closely contested: *a marginal seat in the election.*
Word Family **marginalize, marginalise** *verb* to treat as unimportant or of lesser importance; **marginally** *adverb*.
[from Latin]

marigold (**marr**-i-gold) *noun*
a garden plant with bright yellow or orange flowers.

marijuana (marr-i-**wah**-na) *noun* also **marihuana**
cannabis, especially as smoked in cigarettes.

marimba *noun*
an African musical instrument similar to a large xylophone.

marina (ma-**reen**-a) *noun*
a harbour for small boats and yachts.
[Italian]

marinade (marr-i-nayd) *noun*
a seasoned liquid in which food is soaked before cooking to increase the flavour and make it more tender.
[Spanish *marinada* pickle]

marinate (**marr**-i-nate) *verb*
to soak meat or other food in a marinade.

marine (ma-**reen**) *adjective*
1 existing in or produced by the sea: *marine life.*
2 of or relating to the sea or shipping, etc.: *marine navigation.*
• **marine** *noun* a soldier who serves at sea as well as on land.
[Latin *marinus* of the sea]

mariner (**marr**-i-na) *noun*
an old or poetic word for a sailor.

marionette (marr-i-a-**net**) *noun*
a puppet moved by strings.

marital (**marr**-i-t'l) *adjective*
of or relating to marriage.
[Latin *maritus* matrimonial]

maritime (**marr**-i-time) *adjective*
of or relating to the sea or ships.

marjoram (**mar**-ja-r'm) *noun*
a herb with small purplish-white flowers, used in cooking.

mark[1] *noun*
1 a small damaged area that shows up against a background, e.g. a spot or a stain.
2 something that shows a position or point.
3 a symbol: *an exclamation mark.*
4 a stage: *We had reached the halfway mark.*
5 a score, e.g. in a test.
6 a target: *The arrow hit the mark.*
7 *Rugby football* a clean catch of the ball by a player, leading to a free kick.
Phrases **leave one's mark** to have a distinct effect; **make one's mark** to be successful; **on your marks** *Athletics* take your starting positions.
• **mark** *verb*
1 to put a mark or sign on: *The farmer marked all his sheep.*

2 to read and judge a piece of work or a test.
3 *Sport* to stay close to an opponent.
4 *Rugby football* to make a mark.
5 to do something to show that something special has happened: *They marked the new millennium by planting a tree.*
6 to pay attention to: *You just mark my words!*
Phrases **mark down** to reduce the price of. **mark off** to separate by a line. **mark out** to single someone out for something. **mark up 1** to increase the price of. **2** to mark with symbols or notes.

mark² *noun*
the basic unit of money in Germany.

marked *adjective*
very noticeable.
Word Family **markedly** (**mark**-id-lce) *adverb.*

marker *noun*
1 a thing used to mark something.
2 a thick felt-tip pen.
3 a person who marks.

market *noun*
1 an area where people meet to buy and sell goods, especially food.
2 an institution or group of people involved in trade, exchange, etc.: *the stock market.*
3 the demand for a product.
4 the people who are likely to buy a product.
Phrases **corner the market** to control the supply of something. **in the market for** wanting to buy. **on the market** for sale. **play the market** to speculate on the stock exchange.
• **market** *verb* to sell or promote.
Word Family **marketable** *adjective* fit or easy to sell; **marketing** *noun.*

market garden *noun*
land or a garden on which fruit or vegetables are grown for sale.

market opportunity *noun* (*plural* **market opportunities**)
an opportunity to sell a new product or to sell an existing product to a different group of people.

market research *noun*
Commerce the systematic investigation of what is the likely market for a product, how well a product is known, etc.

marking *noun*
a mark or series of marks, e.g. the patterns on an animal's skin.

marksman *noun* (*plural* **marksmen**)
a person who shoots firearms accurately.
Word Family **marksmanship** *noun* the art of accurate shooting.

marl *noun*
a deposit of clay and calcium carbonate, formerly used as a fertilizer.

marlin *noun*
a large strong fish with a spear-like snout.
[from MARLINSPIKE, whose shape it resembles]

marlinspike *noun* also **marlinespike**
Nautical a heavy metal pin used to separate strands of rope in splicing.
[from Dutch]

marmalade *noun*
a preserve made from oranges or other citrus fruit.
[Greek *melimelon* honey apple]

marmoset (**mar**-ma-zet) *noun*
a small monkey with soft woolly fur and a bushy tail, found in tropical America.
[Old French *marmouset* grotesque little figure]

marmot (**mar**-m't) *noun*
a small burrowing rodent which resembles a squirrel, found in the Alps and other mountains of Europe, and recognizable by its piercing scream.

maroon¹ (ma-**roon**) *noun*
a moderate brownish-red colour.
Word Family **maroon** *adjective.*
[French *marron* chestnut]

maroon² *verb*
to isolate or strand, as after a shipwreck: *marooned on a desert island.*

marquee (mar-**kee**) *noun*
a large tent or tent-like canopy used for entertaining outdoors.

marquess (**mar**-kwis) *noun* (*plural* **marquesses**)
a person who ranks between a duke and an earl.

marquetry (**mark**-i-tree) *noun* also **marquetery; marqueterie**
inlaid work of coloured woods or other materials, especially in furniture.

marquis (**mar**-kwis) *noun* (*plural* **marquises**)
1 a foreign title equivalent to marquess.
2 a marquess.

marriage *noun*
1 a formal agreement between a man and a woman to live together according to the customs of their religion or society.
2 a union: *the marriage of true minds.*

Word Family **marriageable** *adjective*
suitable for marriage.

marrow *noun*
1 also called **bone marrow**. *Anatomy* the
soft tissue in which blood cells are formed,
and which fills the hollow spaces within
bones.
2 a large green gourd, usually cooked and
eaten as a vegetable.

marrowbone *noun*
a bone containing edible fatty tissue.

marry *verb* (**marries; marrying;
married**)
1 to join or be joined in marriage.
2 (of a priest or civil official) to join as
husband and wife.

Mars *noun*
Astronomy the planet in the solar system
fourth from the sun.
[after the ancient Roman god *Mars*]

Marsala (mar-**sah**-la) *noun*
a sweet dark fortified wine.
[first made in *Marsala*, Sicily]

marsh *noun* (*plural* **marshes**)
a swamp.
Word Family **marshy** *adjective*
(**marshier; marshiest**).

marshal *verb* (**marshals; marshalling;
marshalled**)
1 to arrange in an orderly manner: *The
troops were marshalled for the parade.*
2 to lead or conduct.
• **marshal** *noun*
1 a person who marshals or organizes.
2 the highest-ranking officer in some
armed forces.
3 *American* an officer appointed to carry
out court orders.

marshal of the RAF *noun* (*plural*
marshals of the RAF)
Air force a commissioned officer of the
highest rank.

marsh gas *noun*
methane.

marshmallow *noun*
a soft spongy sweet made with gelatin,
sugar and flavouring.

marsupial (mar-**soo**-pee-ul) *noun*
a member of an order of mammals which
produce living young in a very immature
state, the development of the offspring
being completed in a pouch on the
mother's abdomen.
[Greek *marsipos* a purse or bag]

mart *noun*
a market.

marten (**mar**-tin) *noun*
a slender furry mammal like a weasel
which lives in conifer woods and eats flesh.
They are hunted for their golden or dark
brown fur.

martial (**mar**-sh'l) *adjective*
of or relating to war or the armed forces.

martial arts *plural noun*
fighting techniques which have developed
to the level of an art, e.g. karate and judo.

martial law *noun*
a temporary government of a country by
military rule and the suspension of civil
law.

Martian (**mar**-sh'n) *adjective*
of or relating to Mars.
• **Martian** *noun* a person or creature
believed to come from Mars.

martin *noun*
a house martin or related bird.

martinet (mar-tin-**et**) *noun*
a person who enforces strict discipline.
[after *Jean Martinet*, a French army officer
in the 17th century]

martingale *noun*
a forked strap passing between a horse's
forelegs from the girth to the bridle, used
to keep its head down.

martyr (**mar**-ta) *noun*
1 a person who is willing to die or suffer
for his or her religion or beliefs.
2 someone who is willing to put up with
inconvenience or pain in order to gain pity
or praise.
Word Family **martyr** *verb* 1 to kill as a
martyr. 2 to make a martyr of;
martyrdom *noun* the suffering or death
of a martyr.
[Greek, a witness]

marvel *verb* (**marvels; marvelling;
marvelled**)
to wonder or be very surprised.
• **marvel** *noun* something which is
marvellous.

marvellous (**mar**-va-lus) *adjective*
astonishing or wonderful: *He's a marvellous
cook.*
Word Family **marvellously** *adverb*;
marvellousness *noun*.

Marxism (**mark**-sizm) *noun*
a political and economic theory which
states that the struggle between social
classes determines historical change, and
must lead inevitably to the replacement of
capitalism by communism.
Word Family **Marxist** *adjective, noun*.

[after *Karl Marx*, 1818-1883, a German political philosopher]

marzipan *noun*
a rich sugary paste made from ground almonds, sugar and egg whites.

mascara (mass-**kar**-a) *noun*
a coloured substance applied to the eyelashes to make them darker or thicker. [Spanish, mask]

mascarpone (mass-ka-**po**-nay *or* mass-ka-**po**-nee) *noun*
a kind of soft mild Italian cream cheese.

mascot *noun*
a person, animal or object believed to bring good luck.

masculine (**mass**-kew-lin) *adjective*
1 of or relating to the male sex.
2 having the qualities said to be appropriate to males.
3 *Grammar* ⇨ GENDER (definition 1).
Word Family **masculinity** (mass-kew-lin-i-tee) *noun*.

mash *noun* (*plural* **mashes**)
1 a soft pulpy mass.
2 a soaked or boiled mixture of grains, which is fed to livestock.
3 (*informal*) mashed potatoes.
● **mash** *verb* to crush or beat to a mash.

masher *noun*
an instrument used for mashing: *a potato masher.*

masjid (**muss**-jid) *noun*
a mosque.
[Arabic]

mask *noun*
1 a covering for the face, worn for protection, disguise, etc.
2 a disguise or pretence: *a mask of friendliness.*
● **mask** *verb* to hide or disguise.

masochism (**mass**-a-kizm) *noun*
a pleasure, especially sexual pleasure, in one's own suffering, pain or humiliation. Compare SADISM.
Word Family **masochist** *noun* a person who indulges in masochism; **masochistic** (mass-a-**kist**-ik) *adjective*; **masochistically** *adverb*.
[after *Leopold von Sacher-Masoch*, 1836-1895, an Austrian novelist who described this condition]

mason *noun*
1 a person who works with or builds in stone or brick.
2 (**Mason**) a Freemason.

Word Family **masonic** (ma-**son**-ik) *adjective*.

masonry (**may**-s'n-ree) *noun*
1 stonework or brickwork.
2 the trade or skill of a mason.

masque (mahsk) *noun*
a form of entertainment popular in England in the 16th and 17th centuries, which consisted of songs, dances, poetry and mime.

masquerade (mass-ka-**rade**) *noun*
1 a pretence or false appearance.
2 a social function at which masks and disguises are worn.
Word Family **masquerade** *verb*; **masquerader** *noun*.
[Spanish *mascara* a mask]

mass *noun* (*plural* **masses**)
1 a large body or amount: *An iceberg is a floating mass of ice.*
2 a large number of people or things.
3 a bulk: *the sheer mass of the mountain.*
4 (**the mass**) the main part: *The mass of the spectators sat in the open.*
5 (**the masses**) the ordinary people.
6 *Physics* the fundamental quantity describing the ratio of the force acting on an accelerating body to the acceleration produced by that force. ⇨ WEIGHT *noun* (definition 2).
● **mass** *verb* to form or gather into a mass.

Mass *noun* (*plural* **Masses**)
1 the celebration of the Eucharist.
2 a musical setting of some of the fixed portions of the Mass.

massacre (**mass**-a-ka) *noun*
the merciless killing of large numbers of people or animals.
● **massacre** *verb* (**massacres; massacring; massacred**).
[French]

massage (**mass**-arzh) *noun*
the rubbing and kneading of the muscles and joints of the body to relieve stiffness, etc.
● **massage** *verb*
1 to give a massage to.
2 to rub in.
3 to manipulate figures or data in order to make them seem more acceptable.
Word Family **masseur** (mass-**er**) *noun* a person who gives massages, especially a man; **masseuse** (mass-**erz**) *noun* a woman who gives massages.

massage parlour *noun*
a place where massages are given.

massif (mass-**eef**) *noun*
a compact part of a mountain range, rising into peaks towards the summit.
[French]

massive *adjective*
1 very large, heavy and solid: *a massive oak table.*
2 very large or severe: *They had got into massive debt.*
Word Family **massively** *adverb*;
massiveness *noun*.

mass number *noun*
Physics the total number of protons and neutrons in the nucleus of an atom.
Compare ATOMIC NUMBER.

mass-produce *verb*
to make goods in very large quantities by standardized processes.
Word Family **mass production** *noun*.

mast¹ (mahst) *noun*
an upright pole, especially one rising from the deck or the keel of a boat for carrying flags, radio aerials, sails, etc.

mast² *noun*
beech nuts, acorns, chestnuts, etc., the food of free-range pigs.

mastectomy (mass-**tek**-ta-mee) *noun*
(*plural* **mastectomies**)
a surgical operation to remove a breast.
[Greek *mastos* breast + *ektomé* a cutting out]

master (*rhymes with* faster) *noun*
1 a man or boy who owns a dog, cat, etc.: *Lassie always came when her master whistled.*
2 a person who is highly skilled: *a master of disguise.*
3 a great artist.
4 someone who has power or control.
5 a male teacher.
6 a title for a boy.
7 *Nautical* the person in charge of a merchant ship.
8 an original recording, etc. from which copies are made.
● **master** *verb*
1 to become skilled in: *He mastered French after three months in Paris.*
2 to control: *She mastered her anger.*
● **master** *adjective*
1 principal or main: *the master bedroom.*
2 very skilful: *a master joiner.*
[Latin *magister*]

master-at-arms *noun* (*plural* **masters-at-arms**)
Navy a warrant officer appointed as a police officer on a ship.

masterful *adjective*
1 domineering: *a masterful personality.*
2 highly skilled: *a masterful display of acrobatic grace.*
Word Family **masterfully** *adverb*;
masterfulness *noun*.

master key *noun*
a skeleton key.

masterly (**mah**-sta-lee) *adjective*
showing the skill of a master: *a masterly performance.*

mastermind *verb*
to plan and direct an activity at the highest level: *She masterminded the bombing campaign.*
● **mastermind** *noun*.

master of ceremonies *noun* (*plural* **masters of ceremonies**)
a person who is in charge of the ceremonial side of a formal occasion, e.g. the person who announces speakers at a banquet.

masterpiece *noun*
a very great work of art, or the best work of a given person: *Some people regard 'Hamlet' as Shakespeare's masterpiece.*

master plan *noun*
an overall plan.

mastery (**mah**-sta-ree) *noun*
1 the skill or knowledge of a master: *his mastery of the technique.*
2 the upper hand: *her complete mastery of the situation.*

masthead *noun*
1 the top of a mast, especially the tallest mast.
2 the title of a newspaper or magazine, printed at the top of the front page or contents page.

masticate *verb*
to chew.
Word Family **mastication** *noun*.
[Greek *mastikhan* to gnash the teeth]

mastiff *noun*
a large heavy dog with short hair and drooping ears.

mastitis (mass-**tie**-tis) *noun*
a bacterial inflammation in the breast or udder.
[Greek *mastos* breast + *-itis*]

mastodon (**mass**-ta-don) *noun*
an extinct elephant-like mammal.

mastoid (**mass**-toyd) *noun* also called **mastoid process**.
a part of the skull behind the ear.
● **mastoid** *adjective*.
[Greek *mastoeides* breast-shaped]

masturbate (**mass**-ta-bate) *verb*
to stimulate the sexual organs, especially
one's own, to give sexual pleasure.
Word Family masturbation (mass-ta-
bay-sh'n) *noun*; **masturbatory** *adjective*;
masturbate *noun*.
[from Latin]

mat¹ *noun*
1 a piece of heavy fabric or rug-like
material, used as a floor covering.
2 a piece of cork, fabric, etc. placed under
ornaments or hot dishes.
3 *Computers* a mouse mat.
4 a tangled mass: *a mat of weeds.*

mat² ⇨ MATT.

matador *noun*
a bullfighter on foot who taunts the bull
with a cape and tries to kill it with a sword.
Compare PICADOR.
[Spanish]

match¹ *noun* (*plural* **matches**)
1 a short stick of wood with a head made
of phosphorus, etc. which ignites when
rubbed on certain surfaces.
2 the wick used to fire a cannon, etc.

match² *noun* (*plural* **matches**)
1 an official competition or game: *a cricket
match.*
2 a person or thing that is exactly like or
combines well with another: *The two
colours were a good match.*
3 a person or thing that is equal to another
in strength, skill, etc.: *He had met his
match.*
• **match** *verb*
1 to go well with: *His tie matched his shirt.*
2 to be equal to: *You'll never match her for
quick thinking.*
3 to put in competition with: *He was
matched against last year's winner in the
final.*
Word Family **matchless** *adjective*
without equal.

matchlock *noun*
a musket fired by lighting the gunpowder
with a slow-burning match.

matchmaker *noun*
a person who arranges marriages.

match point *noun*
Sport the final point needed to win a
contest.

matchwood *noun*
small pieces or splinters of wood: *The
storm reduced the house to matchwood.*

mate¹ *noun*
1 (*informal*) a friend.
2 a fellow worker: *the builder's mate.*

3 a bird or animal that joins with another
to produce young.
4 *Nautical* an officer next in rank below the
master of a merchant ship.
• **mate** *verb* to join in a pair or match,
especially to pair animals for producing
offspring.

mate² ⇨ CHECKMATE (definition 1).

mater (**may**-ta) *noun*
(*dated informal*) mother.
[Latin, mother]

material (ma-**teer**-i-ul) *noun*
1 the substance of which something is
made: *radioactive material.*
2 fabric.
3 ideas or information: *The episode provided
plenty of material for a story.*
4 (*usually* **materials**) the substances
needed to make something: *building
materials.*
5 (*usually* **materials**) the equipment
needed to do an activity: *drawing materials.*
• **material** *adjective*
1 relating to the body or bodily needs.
2 important: *She was a material witness in
the case.*
Word Family **materially** *adverb*
1 considerably. 2 in terms of money,
possessions, etc.

materialism *noun*
1 a way of living in which possessions and
self-interest are valued more than anything
else.
2 *Philosophy* the belief that all beings and
events can be explained by physical laws.
Word Family **materialist** *noun*
materialistic (ma-teer-i-a-**list**-ik)
adjective; **materialistically** *adverb*.

materialize, materialise *verb*
1 to give or take on a bodily or visible
form: *Three figures materialized out of the
fog.*
2 to happen, come into effect: *The tax cuts
never materialized.*
Word Family **materialization** *noun*.

maternal (ma-**ter**-n'l) *adjective*
1 of or like a mother: *maternal love.*
2 related through a mother: *my maternal
grandfather.*
Word Family **maternally** *adverb*.
[Latin *mater* mother]

maternity (ma-**tern**-i-tee) *noun*
the state of being a mother.
Word Family **maternity** *adjective*
relating to pregnancy or childbirth.

math *noun*
American maths.

maths *noun*
short form of **mathematics** the study of logical relationships involving numbers, shapes, functions and sets.
Word Family **mathematical** (math-a-**mat**-i-k'l) *adjective* 1 of or relating to maths. 2 having the precision or exactness of maths; **mathematician** (math-a-ma-**tish**-'n) *noun* a person who is trained or skilled in maths; **mathematically** *adverb*.

matinee (**mat**-in-ay) *noun*
an afternoon performance of a play, film, ballet, etc.
[French *matin* morning]

matins *plural noun* also **mattins**
(*used with singular verb*) *Christianity* the service for morning prayer in the Church of England.
[Latin *matutinus* of or in the morning]

matriarch (**may**-tree-ark) *noun*
a woman who is the leader or head of a family, group, etc.
Word Family **matriarchal** (may-tree-**ark**-'l) *adjective*; **matriarchy** *noun* (*plural* **matriarchies**) a social system in which a woman is the head of the family.
[Latin *mater* mother + Greek *arkhos* leader]

matricide (**mat**-ri-side) *noun*
1 *Law* the crime of killing one's mother.
2 *Law* the person who does this.
Word Family **matricidal** (mat-ri-**side**-'l) *adjective*.
[Latin *mater* mother + *caedere* to kill]

matriculate (ma-**trik**-yoo-late) *verb*
to be accepted as qualified to enter a university.
Word Family **matriculation** (ma-trik-yoo-**lay**-sh'n) *noun*.
[Latin *matrix* a public register or roll]

matrilineal (mat-ri-**lin**-i-ul) *adjective*
of or based on descent through the mother's family.
Word Family **matrilineally** *adverb*.
[Latin *mater* mother + *linea* a line]

matrimony (**mat**-rim-a-nee) *noun*
marriage.
Word Family **matrimonial** (mat-ri-mo-nee-ul) *adjective*.
[from Latin]

matrix (**may**-triks) *noun* (*plural* **matrices** (**may**-tri-seez) or **matrixes**)
1 *Maths* an ordered array of numbers or variables, as used for computer programming.
2 a mould in which type is cast.

3 rock in which gems, fossils, metals, etc. are embedded.
[Latin, a female animal, a womb]

matron (**may**-tr'n) *noun*
1 a married woman or widow, especially one who is dignified and respectable.
2 a person in charge of the nursing staff in a hospital.
3 a woman who looks after the children at a boarding school if they are ill.
Word Family **matronly** *adjective* of or like a matron.

matron of honour *noun* (*plural* **matrons of honour**)
a married woman who attends the bride at a wedding.

matt *adjective* also **matte; mat**
not shiny.
[French *mat*]

matted *adjective*
tangled.

matter *noun*
1 physical substance, solid, liquid or gas, which exists in time and space and is affected by gravity.
2 a situation: *a matter of life and death*.
3 (**the matter**) the problem: *What's the matter with him?*
4 articles: *printed matter*.
Phrases **a matter of** a question of: *It was only a matter of time until they were discovered*. **a matter of course** a natural event or outcome. **as a matter of fact** in fact. **no matter** 1 regardless of: *No matter what she did, the cat wouldn't come down.* 2 never mind.
• **matter** *verb* to be important.
[Latin *materia* materials, theme]

matter-of-fact *adjective*
practical or unimaginative.
Word Family **matter-of-factly** *adverb*.

matting *noun*
a coarse woven fabric used for floor coverings.

mattins ⇨ MATINS.

mattock *noun*
a tool similar to a pick with a broad blade, used for loosening soil, digging, etc.

mattress *noun* (*plural* **mattresses**)
a long flat bag filled with a soft substance and used on or as a bed.
[from Arabic]

mature (mat-**yoor**) *adjective*
1 fully grown or developed.
2 responsible and sensible: *a mature decision*.

3 fully ripe: *mature Cheddar*.
Word Family mature *verb* **1** to come or bring to full development. **2** (of a bill, dividends, etc.) to become payable; **maturely** *adverb*; **maturity** (mat-**yoor**-i-tee) *noun* the state of being mature; **maturation** (mat-yoo-**ray**-sh'n) *noun* the process of maturing.
[Latin *maturus* ripe, early]

matzo (**mat**-sa) *noun* (*plural* **matzos** or **matzoth** (**mat**-sote)) also **matzoh; matzah**
a dry biscuit of unleavened bread that Jews traditionally eat at Passover.

maudlin (**mawd**-lin) *adjective*
sentimental in a melancholy or weak way.

The word **maudlin** derives from *Magdalene*. Its pronunciation, indeed, is the same as that given to colleges in Oxford and Cambridge, spelt *Magdalen* and *Magdalene* respectively. *Magdalene* has its origins in Mary Magdalene, Mary of Magdala, on the Sea of Galilee. According to the Bible she was present at Christ's crucifixion and was the first to meet him after he had risen from the dead. She is described as tearful and many paintings show her weeping. *Maudlin*, through Middle English *maudelen*, has come to mean 'sentimentally melancholy' or even 'drunkenly sentimental'.

maul (mawl) *verb*
to handle roughly: *The bear mauled the zookeeper*.
[Latin *malleus* hammer]

Maundy Thursday (mawn-dee **therz**-day) *noun*
Christianity the Thursday before Easter, commemorating the Last Supper.

mausoleum (maw-sa-**lee**-um) *noun* (*plural* **mausolea** (maw-sa-**lee**-a) or **mausoleums**)
a magnificent tomb.
[after the tomb of *Mausolus*, a king of Caria who died in 353 B.C.]

mauve (*rhymes with* stove) *noun*
a light pinkish-purple colour.
• **mauve** *adjective*.

maverick *noun*
1 a person who has unorthodox or dissident views.
2 *American* an unbranded or orphaned animal, especially a calf.
[after *S. Maverick*, 1803-1870, a Texas rancher who did not brand his cattle]

mawkish *adjective*
sentimental in a sickly way.
Word Family mawkishly *adverb*; **mawkishness** *noun*.

maxi *noun*
a skirt, dress, etc. which reaches to the ankle or just above it.

maxilla (mak-**sill**-a) *noun* (*plural* **maxillae**) (mak-**sill**-ee)
Anatomy either of the two bones of the skull between the eyes and the teeth, forming the upper jaw.
Word Family maxillary *adjective*.
[Latin, jaw]

maxim *noun*
a short saying expressing a general rule of conduct, as in *waste not, want not*.

maximize, maximise *verb*
to increase to the greatest possible extent: *moving the furniture to maximize the space in the room*.

maximum *noun* (*plural* **maxima** or **maximums**)
the greatest amount that is actual, possible or allowable: *We can invite a maximum of 25 people*. Compare MINIMUM.
Word Family maximal *adjective*.
[Latin *maximus* greatest]

may[1] *verb* (**might**)
an auxiliary verb indicating:
1 permission: *You may leave now*.
2 possibility: *That story may be totally wrong*.
3 a hope: *May you live a long and happy life*.

may[2] ⇨ HAWTHORN.

May *noun*
the fifth month of the year, after April and before June.
[after the Roman goddess *Maia*]

maybe *adverb*
perhaps.

Mayday *noun*
an international radio distress call used by ships and aeroplanes.
[French *m'aidez* help me]

May Day *noun*
1 a spring festival held on 1 May.
2 a workers' international celebration on that day.

mayfly *noun* (*plural* **mayflies**)
a fly which lives close to water and lives for one day only.
[they first appear in *May*]

mayhem (**may**-hem) *noun*
1 violence, chaos: *There was mayhem at the football match*.

2 an old word for the crime of injuring someone.
[Old French, maim]

mayn't contraction
a short form of **may not**: *They mayn't have noticed.*

mayonnaise (may-on-**aze**) noun
a thick creamy sauce made from eggs, vinegar, oil and seasonings, used with salads.
[French]

mayor noun
the chief executive or ceremonial head of a city, borough, etc. In the City of London and in some large British cities the mayor may be called the **Lord Mayor**.
Word Family **mayoralty** (mare-ul-tee) *noun* the office of mayor.
[Latin *major* greater]

mayoress noun (*plural* **mayoresses**)
1 the wife of a mayor.
2 a woman who is a mayor.

maypole noun
a pole decorated with ribbons and flowers which is danced around on May Day.

maze noun
a complicated network of passages, paths, etc. in which it is difficult to find one's way.

mazurka (ma-**zer**-ka) noun
a lively Polish dance.

me[1] pronoun (*plural* **us**)
the objective form of **I**: *He hit me.* □ *Give the book to me.* □ *Open the door, it's me.*

> **!** Note that *Between you and me* is correct and *Between you and I* is not. This is because the preposition *between* must be followed by the objective form of the pronoun (*me*). People sometimes confuse examples like this with those where the subjective form (*I*) is correct, as in *You and I have to share a room.*

me[2] noun also **mi**
Music a note in the scale. ⇨ DOH.

mead[1] noun
an old or poetic word for a meadow.

mead[2] noun
an alcoholic drink made by fermenting honey and water.

meadow (**med**-oh) noun
an area of grassy land, especially near a river, used for grazing or hay.

meagre (**mee**-ga) adjective
poor in quality or quantity: *meagre portions.*
[Middle English *megre* lean]

meal[1] noun
1 any of the usual daily eating times: *Breakfast was his favourite meal.*
2 the food eaten at one of these times.

meal[2] noun
an edible grain or pulse which is ground but is less fine than flour.

mealy-mouthed adjective
avoiding the use of plain or direct words.

mean[1] verb (**means; meaning; meant**)
1 to have as an intention or purpose: *Is this meant to be a joke?*
2 to signify: *What does this word mean?*
3 to have as a result: *Having to get a new car meant that we couldn't have a holiday.*

mean[2] adjective
1 unkind, selfish or small-minded: *a mean trick.*
2 miserly: *She is wealthy but mean.*
3 vicious: *The horse had a mean streak.*
4 poor or inferior: *a small mean hovel.*
5 (*informal*) very good: *He's a mean swimmer.*
Word Family **meanly** *adverb*; **meanness** *noun.*

mean[3] noun
1 anything which is halfway between two extremes.
2 *Maths* the sum of several quantities divided by the number of quantities: *The mean of 1, 2 and 9 is (1 + 2 + 9) ÷ 3 = 4.*
• **mean** *adjective* being in the middle position: *the mean monthly temperature.*

meander (mee-**and**-a) verb
to wander aimlessly or on a winding course.
• **meander** *noun* a broad curve in a river.
[from *Meander*, the Greek name for the River Mendereh in Turkey]

meaning noun
that which is intended or expressed: *What is the meaning of this word?*

meaningful adjective
full of meaning: *She gave me a meaningful look.*
Word Family **meaningfully** *adverb.*

meaningless adjective
1 having no meaning: *meaningless scribbles.*
2 having no relevance or point: *The offer was meaningless without the money to back it up.*
Word Family **meaninglessness** *noun.*

means plural noun
1 a method by which something is done or obtained: *a means of transport.* □ *He had no means of contacting her.*

2 wealth or resources: *a woman of private means.*
Phrases **by all means** certainly. **by no means** not at all.

means test *noun*
a check on someone's financial situation to see whether he or she is entitled to a benefit.

meant (ment) the past tense and past participle of **mean¹**.

meantime *noun*
Phrase **in the meantime** meanwhile.

meanwhile *adverb*
1 during the time in between: *They would arrive at noon; meanwhile, he tidied the house.*
2 at the same time: *Meanwhile, back at the ranch, our hero was in trouble.*

measles (mee-z'lz) *plural noun*
(*used with singular verb*) an infectious viral disease, usually in children, causing small red spots on the skin.

measly (meez-lee) *adjective* (**measlier; measliest**)
(*informal*) miserably small: *After all that work he only gave us a measly 20 pence.*

measure (*rhymes with* treasure) *verb*
1 to find the measurements of.
2 to be a certain size, height, etc.: *The room measured 3 m by 2 m.*
Phrase **measure up to** to be adequate for.
• **measure** *noun*
1 an action or proposal: *new safety measures.*
2 a unit of quantity, weight, etc.: *A kilometre is a measure of length.*
3 a ruler, tape, etc, used for measuring.
4 rhythm or metre in poetry.
5 a sign of the extent of something: *His gift was a measure of his generosity.*
Phrase **for good measure** as an extra act or precaution.
[Latin *mensura*]

measurement *noun*
1 the act of measuring.
2 the dimension of something measured.
3 a unit or system of measuring.

meat *noun*
the edible flesh of an animal.

meaty *adjective* (**meatier; meatiest**)
1 of or resembling meat.
2 full of ideas or substance: *a meaty book.*

mechanic (mik-an-ik) *noun*
a person skilled in the maintenance, repair, use or construction of machinery.
[Greek *mekhanikos* ingenious, inventive]

mechanical (mik-an-i-k'l) *adjective*
1 of, like or relating to machinery or mechanics: *a mechanical toy.* □ *He studied mechanical engineering.*
2 unthinking, automatic: *She gave mechanical answers to his questions.*
Word Family **mechanically** *adverb*.

mechanical advantage *noun*
a mathematical formula concerning the use of a mechanism to achieve an improved output.

mechanics (mik-an-iks) *plural noun*
1 (*used with singular verb*) the science of machinery.
2 (*used with singular verb*) the study of the effects of forces on objects.
3 the way in which something works or operates: *the mechanics of government.*

mechanism (mek-a-nizm) *noun*
1 a piece of machinery.
2 any structure which operates by various parts working together: *The human body is a delicate mechanism.*
3 the internal parts and workings of a structure: *the mechanism of a watch.*

mechanize, mechanise (mek-a-nize) *verb*
to introduce machinery into: *mechanized industries.*
Word Family **mechanization** (mek-a-nigh-zay-sh'n) *noun*.

medal *noun*
a small metal disc with a design commemorating a person or event, or given as an award.
Word Family **medallist** *noun* a person who has received a medal.
[Greek *metallon* metal]

medallion (mid-al-y'n) *noun*
1 a metal disc like a medal, worn round the neck as a piece of jewellery.
2 a circular ornamental design on furniture, etc.

meddle *verb*
to interfere in other people's affairs without being asked to do so.
Word Family **meddlesome** *adjective*; **meddler** *noun*.
[Old French *medler* to mix]

media (mee-di-a) *plural noun*
1 a plural of **medium**.
2 all the sources by which news, etc. may be relayed, such as radio, television and newspapers: *The story was greatly exaggerated by the media.*

! The word *media*, strictly speaking, is a plural noun which must be used with a plural verb. However, when *media* means 'sources of news', it is increasingly being treated as a collective noun, like *crew*, which can be used with a singular or plural verb.

mediaeval ⇨ MEDIEVAL.

medial (mee-di-ul) *adjective*
in the middle.

median (mee-di-an) *noun*
1 *Statistics* the value above which half the cases under consideration fall and below which the other half fall.
2 *Maths* the middle number in a list of numbers arranged in order.
3 *Maths* a straight line from the vertex of a triangle bisecting the opposite side.
Word Family **median** *adjective* in or through the middle.
[Latin *medianus* in the middle]

mediate (mee-di-ate) *verb*
to bring about an agreement between opposing sides by acting as a go-between.
Word Family **mediation** (mee-di-ay-sh'n) *noun* the act of mediating; **mediator** *noun* a person who mediates.

medic *noun*
(*informal*) a doctor, medical student or medical orderly.

medical (med-i-k'l) *adjective*
of or relating to the science or practice of healing, especially by using drugs rather than surgery.
• **medical** *noun* a medical examination or check-up.
Word Family **medically** *adverb*.

medication (med-i-kay-sh'n) *noun*
a substance given to cure, heal or relieve the symptoms of a disease.
Word Family **medicated** (med-i-kay-tid) *adjective* containing medicine: *medicated shampoo*.
[Latin *medicare* to cure]

medicine (med-i-sin) *noun*
1 a substance used to treat a disease, preserve health, etc.
2 the study of diseases and ways of maintaining and restoring health.
Word Family **medicinal** (med-iss-i-nal) *adjective* of or like medicine.

medicine ball *noun*
a heavy ball thrown from one person to another for exercise.

medicine man *noun* (*plural* **medicine men**)
a witch doctor.

medieval (med-i-ee-v'l) *adjective* also **mediaeval**
of or relating to the Middle Ages.
[Latin *medius* middle + *aevum* age]

mediocre (mee-di-o-ka) *adjective*
of second-rate or only average quality: *The food was mediocre.*
Word Family **mediocrity** (mee-di-ok-ra-tee) *noun* (*plural* **mediocrities**)
1 the quality of being mediocre.
2 a person of mediocre abilities.
[Latin *mediocris* middling, average]

meditate (med-i-tate) *verb*
to reflect or think deeply or seriously: *meditate on creation.*
Word Family **meditation** (med-i-tay-sh'n) *noun* 1 the act of meditating. 2 deep thought; **meditative** (med-it-a-tiv) *adjective* fond of or characterized by meditation; **meditatively** *adverb*.
[from Latin]

medium (mee-di-um) *noun* (*plural* **media**) (mee-di-a)
1 a means by which something is done: *My favourite medium for sculpture is stone, but in painting I prefer oil.*
2 an intermediate thing through which something moves: *Air is the medium of sound.*
3 *Biology* a nutrient material on which micro-organisms may be grown.
4 (*plural* **mediums**) *Occult* a person through whom spirits are said to be able to communicate.
• **medium** *adjective* average in size or quality: *a man of medium height.*
[Latin *medius* middle]

medium wave *noun*
a radio wave having a wavelength of between 300 kHz and 3 MHz, used in medium-range radio broadcasting.
Compare LONG WAVE; SHORT WAVE.

medley (med-lee) *noun*
1 a mixture of things, such as a piece of music combining several different tunes, etc.
2 a race in which the swimmer performs several different strokes in order.

medulla (mid-ull-a) *noun*
Biology the soft inner part of a structure, especially a kidney.
[Latin, pith, marrow]

medusa (mi-**dew**-sa) *noun* (*plural*
medusae (mi-**dew**-zee *or* mi-**dew**-see) *or*
medusas)
a jellyfish or similar organism.
[Greek *Medousa* a Gorgon whose hair
consisted of snakes]

meek *adjective*
humble, patient or gentle.
Word Family **meekly** *adverb*; **meekness**
noun.

meerschaum (**meer**-shawm *or* **meer**-
sh'm) *noun*
1 a white clay mineral (hydrous
magnesium silicate) used for carving and
especially for pipe bowls.
2 a tobacco pipe with a bowl made of
meerschaum.
[German, sea-foam]

meet *verb* (**meets; meeting; met**)
1 to come face to face with: *I met her in
town.*
2 to come into contact with: *The sounds of
music met her ears.*
3 to experience or come across: *He'd never
met such hostility before.*
4 to pay the cost of.
5 to fulfil: *It didn't meet my expectations.*
□ *You have to meet our entrance requirements.*
6 to join: *The roads meet at the corner.*
Phrase **meet with** to receive: *Does it meet
with your approval?*
• **meet** *noun Sport* a meeting for
competition or enjoyment, such as a hunt.

meeting *noun*
1 a contact or coming together: *a meeting
of rivers.*
2 an assembly or gathering of people.

megabyte *noun*
Computers a unit of computer data or
storage space equal to 1 048 576 bytes.
abbrev. Mb; MB.

megalithic (meg-a-**lith**-ik) *adjective*
being built of large stones.
Word Family **megalith** (**meg**-a-lith)
noun a large stone.
[*mega-* + Greek *lithos* stone]

megalomania (meg-a-lo-**may**-ni-a) *noun*
Psychology a mental disorder in which the
patient thinks he or she is a person of
extreme importance.
Word Family **megalomaniac** *noun*
1 a person suffering from megalomania.
2 a person who constantly seeks power
and personal glory.
[Greek *megalé* great + MANIA]

megaphone (**meg**-a-fone) *noun*
a hand-held device which magnifies
sounds so that they can be heard from a
long distance.
[*mega-* + Greek *phoné* sound]

megaton (**meg**-a-tun) *noun*
a unit for measuring the explosive force of
a nuclear weapon by comparing it to the
mass of trinitrotoluene (TNT) which
would produce the same explosion. A 10-
megaton hydrogen bomb would have the
same explosive force as 10 000 000 metric
tons of TNT. Compare KILOTON.

melancholy (**mel**-'n-koll-ee) *adjective*
sad, gloomy or depressing: *The funeral was
a melancholy occasion.*
Word Family **melancholy** *noun* sadness
or depression; **melancholic** (mel-'n-**koll**-
ik) *adjective*.

> The word **melancholy** means,
> etymologically, 'black bile'. According
> to medieval medical theory there were
> four humours which determined the
> state of the mind and body. These were
> phlegm, blood, choler and black bile.
> An even balance of these made for a
> well-adjusted person but the
> dominance of one determined a
> person's health and mood. Excess of
> black bile was thought to cause
> depression or *melancholy*.

melange (may-**lonzh**) *noun*
a mixture.
[French]

melanin (**mell**-a-nin) *noun*
a dark pigment in the skin, hair, etc.

melanoma (mel-an-**oh**-ma) *noun*
a malignant tumour which develops from
cells containing dark pigments, especially
in the skin.

melatonin (mell-at-**oh**-nin) *noun*
a hormone. ⇨ PINEAL GLAND.

meld *verb*
to merge or blend.
[from M(elt) + (w)ELD]

melee (**mel**-ay) *noun*
a confused fight or struggle.
[French]

mellifluous (mel-**if**-loo-us) *adjective*
sweet-sounding: *a mellifluous voice.*
[Late Latin *mellifluus* flowing with honey]

mellow *adjective*
1 rich and soft in sound or colour.
2 genial, easygoing: *My father has become
mellow in his old age.* □ *The wine made me
mellow.*
• **mellow** *verb* to make or become mellow.

melodrama (**mel**-o-drah-ma) *noun*
1 a play based on an exaggerated or sensational plot and characters.
2 sensational behaviour or events.
Word Family **melodramatic** (mel-o-dra-**mat**-ik) *adjective* of or like a melodrama: *She gave a melodramatic account of her trip*; **melodramatics** *plural noun* melodramatic behaviour.

melody (**mel**-a-dee) *noun* (*plural* **melodies**)
a sequence of notes that make up a pleasant tune.
Word Family **melodic** (mil-**od**-ik) *adjective* of or relating to a melody or melodies; **melodious** (mel-**o**-dee-us) *adjective* tuneful or producing a pleasant sound; **melodiously** *adverb*.
[Greek *meloidia* singing]

melon *noun*
a large juicy fruit with many seeds.
[Greek, apple]

melt *verb*
1 to make or become liquid through heating.
2 to soften or become tender: *My heart melted when I saw the kitten.*
3 to disappear or blend: *The figure melted into the darkness.*

meltdown *noun*
1 the failure of the cooling system of a nuclear reactor which causes the nuclear fuel to overheat and melt, and may result in the release of radioactive material into the atmosphere.
2 a sudden disastrous failure with far-reaching effects, such as a stock-market crash.

melting point *noun*
the temperature at which a solid substance becomes a liquid.

melting pot *noun*
a mixture of various elements, colours, ideas, etc.: *With all its different ethnic groups, London is a real melting pot.*

member *noun*
1 a person who is included in a group, society, etc.
2 (**Member**) a representative in Parliament.
3 a part of a structural whole.
4 *Maths* an element of a set.

Member of Parliament *noun* (*plural* **Members of Parliament**)
someone elected by the people in a constituency to be their representative in Parliament.

membership *noun*
1 being a member: *Do you want to renew your membership?*
2 the number of members: *The club has a total membership of 300.*
[Latin *membrum* limb]

membrane *noun*
Biology a soft thin sheet of tissue which covers and separates organs and structures in an animal or plant.
Word Family **membranous** (**mem**-bra-nus) *adjective* of or like a membrane.
[Latin *membrana* skin, parchment]

memento (mim-**en**-toe) *noun* (*plural* **mementos** or **mementoes**)
something to remind one of an event or person.
[Latin, remember!]

memo (**mem**-o) *noun*
(*informal*) a memorandum.

memoirs (**mem**-wahz) *plural noun*
an autobiography.
[French]

memorable (**mem**-a-ra-b'l) *adjective*
notable or worthy of being remembered: *His 70th birthday was a memorable occasion.*

memorandum (mem-a-**ran**-dum) *noun* (*plural* **memoranda** or **memorandums**)
1 a note made of something to be remembered.
2 a record or written statement of a business or other transaction.
[Latin *memorandus* that is to be remembered]

memorial (mim-**aw**-ri-ul) *noun*
something intended to preserve the memory of a person, event, etc., such as a monument.
• **memorial** *adjective* preserving the memory of a person or thing: *A memorial service was held for the dead soldiers.*

memorize, memorise (**mem**-a-rize) *verb*
to learn by heart.

memory (**mem**-a-ree) *noun* (*plural* **memories**)
1 the ability of the mind to recall things.
2 something that is remembered: *My earliest memory is of running away from school.*
3 the part of a computer in which information is stored.
[Latin *memor* remembering]

men
the plural of **man**.

menace (**men**-iss) *noun*
a threat or danger: *the menace of speeding cars.*
• **menace** *verb* to threaten.

ménage (may-**nahzh**) *noun*
a family or the household.
[French]

ménage à trois (may-nahzh a **trwa**) *noun*
(*plural* **ménages à trois**) (may-nahzh a **trwa**)
the living together of a husband, wife and the lover of either the husband or the wife.
[French]

menagerie (min-**aj**-a-ree) *noun*
a collection of wild or strange animals, as in a circus.
[French]

mend *verb*
1 to repair or get something back into working condition.
2 to reform: *You must mend your ways.*
• **mend** *noun* a repair.

mendacious (men-**day**-shus) *adjective*
untruthful: *a mendacious person.*
Word Family **mendacity** (men-**dass**-i-tee) *noun.*
[Latin *mendax* untruthful]

mendicant *noun*
1 a beggar.
2 a religious person, such as a monk, who lives by begging.
[Latin *mendicans* begging]

menhir (**men**-heer) *noun*
a prehistoric standing stone.

menial (**mee**-ni-ul) *adjective*
not needing much skill: *menial jobs.*
Word Family **menial** *noun* a person whose job is unskilled and unglamorous.

meninges (min-**in**-jeez) *plural noun*
(*singular* **meninx**) (**mee**-ninks)
Anatomy the membranes that cover the brain and spinal cord.

meningitis (men-in-**jie**-tis) *noun*
a serious illness caused by an inflammation of the meninges, resulting in headache, vomiting, fever and a stiff neck.
[Greek *meninx* membrane + *-itis*]

meniscus (min-**isk**-us) *noun* (*plural* **menisci**) (min-**iss**-eye)
Physics the curved upper surface of a liquid in a container, caused by capillarity.
[Greek *meniskos* crescent]

men-of-war
the plural of **man-of-war**.

menopause (**men**-o-pawz) *noun*
the time of life during which a woman's menstrual cycle ceases permanently.
[Greek *menos* of a month + *pausis* cessation]

menorah (min-**aw**-ra) *noun*
Judaism a candelabrum with seven or eight branches which is used in ceremonies.
[Hebrew]

menses (**men**-seez) *plural noun*
the blood and tissue lining the uterus which is discharged during menstruation.

menstruation (men-stroo-**ay**-sh'n) *noun*
the act of discharging blood and tissue from the uterus, occurring about once every four weeks in any woman who is not pregnant and has not reached the menopause.
Word Family **menstrual** (**men**-stroo-ul) *adjective*; **menstruate** (**men**-stroo-ayt) *verb.*
[Latin *menstruus* monthly]

mensuration (men-sha-**ray**-sh'n) *noun*
the study of the procedures for measuring and calculating lengths, areas and volumes.
Word Family **mensurable** (**men**-sha-ra-b'l) *adjective* able to be measured; **mensural** (**men**-sha-r'l) *adjective* relating to measure.
[Latin *mensura* a measure]

mental *adjective*
1 of or relating to the mind: *a mental illness.*
2 done in the head, not on paper: *mental arithmetic.*
3 (*informal*) mad.
Word Family **mentally** *adverb.*
[Latin *mentis* of a mind]

mental age *noun*
a measure of development in intelligence expressed in terms of the age at which an average person reaches such a level.

mentality (men-**tal**-i-tee) *noun* (*plural* **mentalities**)
1 an attitude or way of thinking: *a warlike mentality.*
2 intellectual capacity.

menthol *noun*
a colourless alcohol found in peppermint oil and used in perfumes, cigarettes, cooking and medicine.
Word Family **mentholated** *adjective* containing menthol.

mention (**men**-sh'n) *verb*
to refer to briefly.
Phrase **not to mention** in addition to.
• **mention** *noun*

1 a reference or allusion.
2 a brief notice or recognition.
[Latin *mentio* a calling to mind]

mentor *noun*
a person who advises and helps an
inexperienced person.
[after *Mentor*, who advised Ulysses' son
during his father's absence]

menu (**men**-yoo) *noun*
1 a list of dishes available in a restaurant.
2 the dishes served at a meal.
3 *Computers* a list of the information and
programs provided by a particular
computer.
[French, a detailed list]

meow ⇨ MIAOW.

mercantile (**mer**-k'n-tile) *adjective*
of or relating to merchants, trade or
commerce.
Word Family **mercantilism** *noun* an old
economic theory that a state ought to
amass gold, by boosting exports,
restricting imports and prohibiting the
export of gold.
[Latin *mercans* trading]

mercenary (**mer**-s'n-ree) *adjective*
acting merely for gain.
• **mercenary** *noun* (*plural* **mercenaries**)
a professional soldier serving in a foreign
army.
[Latin *mercenarius* hired for pay]

merchandise (**mer**-ch'n-dice *or* **mer**-
ch'n-dize) *noun*
1 goods bought and sold for profit.
2 goods, e.g. toys and T-shirts, which are
linked to a film, television programme,
pop group, etc.: '*Star Wars*' *merchandise*.

merchant *noun*
1 an old word for a person who buys and
sells goods.
2 a wholesale trader, especially in exports
and imports.
3 *American* a shopkeeper.
• **merchant** *adjective* of or relating to
trade.
[Latin *mercans* trading]

merchant bank *noun*
a bank which specializes in financing
international trade, handling bills of
exchange and other commercial business.
Word Family **merchant banker** *noun*.

merchantman *noun* (*plural*
merchantmen)
a trading ship.

merchant navy *noun*
a country's ships engaged in commerce.

merciful *adjective*
having or showing mercy.
Word Family **mercifully** *adverb* 1 in a
merciful manner. 2 thankfully.

merciless *adjective*
showing no mercy.
Word Family **mercilessly** *adverb*;
mercilessness *noun*.

mercurial (mer-**kyoor**-i-ul) *adjective*
quick and changeable in nature.

mercury (**mer**-kyor-ree) *noun*
1 a metal which is a liquid at normal
temperatures and is used in alloys and
thermometers.
2 (**Mercury**) *Roman mythology* the god of
trade, and a messenger of the gods.
3 (**Mercury**) *Astronomy* the planet in the
solar system closest to the sun.
[so named because alchemists used the
symbol of the planet *Mercury* for the
metal]

mercy (**mer**-see) *noun* (*plural* **mercies**)
1 kindness or compassion, such as is
shown by withholding or reducing a
punishment.
2 a piece of good fortune: *We must be
thankful for small mercies.*
Phrase **at the mercy of** *The rudderless
ship was at the mercy of every large wave*
(= helpless before).
[Latin *merces* reward (later, pity)]

mercy killing *noun*
euthanasia.

mere *adjective*
nothing more than: *They won by a mere two
points.*
Word Family **merely** *adverb* only or
simply: *I was merely asking.*

meretricious (merr-i-**trish**-us) *adjective*
attractive in a showy or false way: *This
novel has attracted attention only because of
the meretricious gimmicks it employs.*
[Latin *meretricius* pertaining to prostitutes]

merganser (mer-**gan**-za *or* mer-**gan**-sa)
noun
a fish-eating duck with a serrated spike-
like bill.
[Latin *mergus* diver + *anser* goose]

merge (merj) *verb*
to blend with or be absorbed by something
larger: *The twilight merged gradually into
darkness.*
Word Family **merger** *noun* the act of
merging, such as the combination of two
or more business companies into one.

meridian (ma-**rid**-ee-an) *noun*
Geography a line of longitude. Compare
PARALLEL *noun* (definition 2).

meringue (ma-**rang**) *noun*
a mixture of sugar and beaten egg whites,
baked slowly and used as a base or
topping, e.g. for fruit or cream.
[French]

merino (ma-**ree**-no) *noun*
1 a sheep with long fine wool, originally
bred in Spain.
2 a soft yarn or fabric, originally one made
from the wool of a merino.
[Spanish]

merit *noun*
1 worth, excellence or superior quality:
There isn't much merit in his proposals.
2 a good point: *We could see the merits of her
plan.*
• **merit** *verb* to be worthy of: *This merits
further discussion.*
Word Family **merited** *adjective* deserved.
[Latin *meritum* deserved, earned]

meritocracy (merr-i-**tok**-ra-see) *noun*
(*plural* **meritocracies**)
1 a government made up of people who
have been chosen according to merit.
2 a society with this type of government.

meritorious (merr-i-**taw**-ri-us) *adjective*
worthy of merit or reward.

mermaid *noun*
an imaginary creature supposed to live in
the sea, having a woman's body and a
fish's tail.
[Middle English *mere* lake or pond + MAID]

merry *adjective* (**merrier; merriest**)
1 cheerful.
2 festive: *a merry Christmas.*
3 (*informal*) slightly drunk.
Word Family **merriment** *noun* any
laughter or gaiety; **merrily** *adverb*.

merry-go-round *noun* also called
roundabout.
a revolving machine fitted with moving
horses, etc. on which children ride at fairs.

mesa (**may**-sa) *noun*
a high rocky plateau with steeply sloping
sides.
[Latin *mensa* table]

mescaline (**mes**-ka-lin *or* mes-ka-lean)
noun also **mescalin** (**mes**-ka-lin)
a drug made from a Mexican cactus and
used to produce hallucinations.

Mesdames
the plural of **Madame; Mrs.**

Mesdemoiselles
the plural of **Mademoiselle.**

mesh *verb*
1 to entangle or fit closely together.
2 (of gears) to engage.
• **mesh** *noun* (*plural* **meshes**)
1 the open spaces or threads of a net or
sieve.
*Figurative He was trapped fast in the
meshes of a political intrigue* (– snares,
entanglements).
2 a knitted or woven fabric with open
spaces between the threads.

mesmerize, mesmerise (**mez**-ma-rize)
verb
1 to hypnotize.
2 to fascinate or spellbind: *We sat there
mesmerized by the beauty of the ballet.*
Word Family **mesmerism** *noun* an old
word for **hypnotism; mesmerist** *noun* an
old word for a **hypnotist; mesmeric**
(mez-**merr**-ik) *adjective* hypnotic;
mesmerically *adverb*.
[after F. A. Mesmer, 1734–1815, an
Austrian doctor]

Mesolithic ⇨ STONE AGE.

meson (**mee**-zon *or* **mez**-on) *noun*
Physics any of a group of unstable
elementary particles produced by cosmic
rays.
[Greek, middle (as intermediate in mass
between proton and electron)]

Mesozoic (mess-o-**zo**-ik *or* mez-o-**zo**-ik)
noun
a geological era which extended from
about 225 million years ago to about 65
million years ago. During this era
dinosaurs appeared and gymnosperms
and angiosperms were the dominant
plants. Towards the end of the era
mammals appeared.
[Greek *mesos* middle + *zoion* animal]

mess *noun* (*plural* **messes**)
1 a dirty, untidy or confused condition:
His desk was in a mess.
2 a difficult or awkward situation.
3 a room where officers, etc. in the armed
forces eat.
• **mess** *verb* to make dirty or untidy.
Phrases **mess about, mess around**
1 to behave in a silly way. 2 to spend time
aimlessly. **mess up 1** to make untidy.
2 to spoil: *He had messed up his chance to
star in the play.*
Word Family **messy** *adjective* (**messier;
messiest**); **messily** *adverb*; **messiness**
noun.

message (**mess**-ij) *noun*
1 a piece of information, etc. sent from one person or group to another: *send a message on a mobile phone*.
2 a moral or point: *a story with a message*.
Word Family **messenger** *noun* a person who carries a message or goes on an errand.

Messiah (miss-**eye**-a) *noun*
1 *Judaism* the expected deliverer of the Jewish people.
2 *Christianity* Jesus Christ.
Word Family **messianic** (mess-i-**an**-ik) *adjective*.
[Hebrew *mashiah* the anointed]

Messrs
the plural of **Mr**.

met the past tense and past participle of **meet**.

metabolism (mi-**tab**-a-lizm) *noun*
Biology the chemical processes occurring in an organism or cell, including the build-up of simple substances into complex substances and the breakdown of complex substances into simple ones.
Word Family **metabolic** (met-a-**bol**-ik) *adjective*; **metabolize, metabolise** (mi-**tab**-a-lize) *verb* to subject to metabolism.
[Greek *metabolé* change]

metacarpus (met-a-**karp**-us) *noun* (*plural* **metacarpi**) (met-a-**karp**-eye)
Anatomy the five bones in each hand joining the thumb and fingers to the wrist.
[*meta*- + Greek *karpos* wrist]

metal *noun*
Chemistry any of those elements which tend to be ductile and malleable, conduct heat and electricity and form positive ions, e.g. silver, copper or tin.
Word Family **metal, metallic** (mit-al-ik) *adjective*; **metallically** *adverb*.
[Greek *metallon* a mine]

metalloid ⇨ SEMIMETAL.

metallurgy (mit-**al**-a-jee) *noun*
the study of metals, their extraction from ores, their properties and uses.
Word Family **metallurgist** *noun* a person skilled or trained in metallurgy; **metallurgic** (met-a-**ler**-jik), **metallurgical** *adjective* relating to metallurgy; **metallurgically** *adverb*.
[METAL + Greek *ergon* work]

metamorphic (met-a-**mor**-fik) *adjective*
Geology relating to rocks which have had their structure altered by changes in temperature and pressure.
Word Family **metamorphism** *noun*.

metamorphosis (met-a-**mor**-fa-sis) *noun* (*plural* **metamorphoses**) (met-a-**mor**-fa-seez)
a change or transformation, e.g. that of a caterpillar into a butterfly or of a tadpole into a frog.
Word Family **metamorphose** (met-a-**mor**-foze) *verb*.
[*meta*- + Greek *morphé* shape + *-osis*]

metaphor (**met**-a-for) *noun*
a figure of speech in which one thing is identified with another, e.g. *He was a tower of strength during the crisis*. Compare SIMILE.
Word Family **metaphorical** (met-a-**forr**-i-k'l), **metaphoric** *adjective*; **metaphorically** *adverb*.
[Greek *metapherein* to transfer]

metaphysical (met-a-**fizz**-i-k'l) *adjective*
of or relating to the study of questions which cannot be answered in factual terms: *Science may tell us how the universe works but why it exists at all is a metaphysical question*.
Word Family **metaphysics** *noun*.
[Greek *ta meta ta physika* the works after the Physics (in Aristotle's collected works, those on metaphysics happened to be so placed)]

metastasis (mit-**as**-ta-sis) *noun* (*plural* **metastases**) (mit-**as**-ta-seez)
Medicine the transfer of a disease or its manifestations from one part of the body to another, as can occur in cancer.
Word Family **metastasize, metastasise** *verb*.
[*meta*- + Greek *stasis* a standing still]

metatarsus (met-a-**tar**-sus) *noun* (*plural* **metatarsi**) (met-a-**tar**-sigh)
Anatomy the five bones in each foot joining the toes to the ankle.
[*meta*- + Greek *tarsos* flat of the foot]

metathesis (mit-**ath**-a-sis) *noun* (*plural* **metatheses**) (mit-**ath**-a-seez)
the changing of the order of letters, sounds or syllables in a word: *Middle English 'bridd' became Modern English 'bird' by metathesis*.
[*meta*- + Greek *thesis* a putting]

mete (meet) *verb*
to deal out or allot: *The courts are supposed to mete out justice*.

meteor (**mee**-tee-or) *noun* also called **falling star; shooting star**.
Astronomy a small solid body from space which usually burns up on entering the earth's atmosphere. One which reaches the earth's surface is called a **meteorite**.
[Greek *meteoros* high in the air]

meteoric (mee-ti-**orr**-ik) *adjective*
1 of or relating to a meteor.
2 swift, brilliant: *a meteoric rise to power*.
Word Family **meteorically** *adverb*.

meteorology (mee-ti-a-**rol**-a-jee) *noun*
the study of weather, and the processes in
the atmosphere which affect it.
Word Family **meteorologist** *noun* a
person trained in meteorology;
meteorological (mee-ti-a-ra-**loj**-i-k'l)
adjective; **meteorologically** *adverb*.

meter *noun*
an instrument used to measure something:
a gas meter.
• **meter** *verb* to measure with or register
on a meter.
[from METE]

methane (**mee**-thane) *noun*
a colourless inflammable gas (formula
CH_4), the first member of the paraffin
series, formed from decaying organic
matter and occurring in coal gas and
natural gas.

methinks *verb* (**methought**)
an old word meaning 'it seems to me'.

method *noun*
a way of doing something, especially an
orderly or systematic way: *new teaching
methods*.
Word Family **methodical** (mith-**odd**-
i-k'l) *adjective* done or acting according
to an orderly method; **methodically**
adverb.
[Greek *methodos* a pursuit (of knowledge)]

Methodist *noun* also called **Wesleyan**.
Christianity a member of a revivalist
movement based on the ideas of John and
Charles Wesley, 18th-century preachers.
Word Family **Methodist** *adjective*;
Methodism *noun*.
[from their methodical rules of prayer and
fasting]

methodology (meth-a-**doll**-a-jee) *noun*
(*plural* **methodologies**)
the study of the methods used in a
particular subject.
Word Family **methodological** (meth-a-
da-**loj**-i-k'l) *adjective*.

meths *noun*
(*informal*) methylated spirit.

methyl (**mee**-thile *or* **meth**-ile *or* **mee**-
thil) *adjective*
Chemistry of or relating to organic
compounds or radicals containing the
univalent (CH_3) group.
Word Family **methanol** (**meth**-'n-ol)
noun the alcohol based on a methyl group.
[Greek *methy* wine + *hylé* wood]

methylated spirit *noun* also **methylated
spirits**
a mixture, mainly methyl alcohol, dyed
and rendered poisonous, used as a fuel
and solvent.

meticulous (mi-**tik**-yoo-lus) *adjective*
extremely or excessively careful and
precise about details.
Word Family **meticulously** *adverb*;
meticulousness *noun*.

> The word **meticulous** is often used as
> a compliment to someone who is
> careful and conscientious. However, in
> the 19th century it meant 'over-
> concerned with details, over-careful'
> and nowadays this is still a possible
> meaning. Its original meaning in the
> 17th century was 'timid' or 'fearful'.

métier (**met**-yay) *noun*
a person's trade or line of work, interest,
etc., especially the work for which
someone is particularly suited.
[French]

metonymy (mit-**on**-i-mee) *noun*
the use of a word to replace or suggest
another to which it is in some way related,
*e.g. The pen (= the power of literature) is
mightier than the sword* (= force).
[meta- + Greek *onyma* name]

metre¹ (**mee**-ta) *noun* (*American* **meter**)
the base SI unit of length equal to 100 cm
or about 39 inches. *abbrev.* m.
Word Family **metric** (**met**-rik) *adjective*
of or relating to the metre or the system of
measurement based on it.
[Greek *metron* measure]

metre² *noun*
a measured rhythm or pattern of stresses
in poetry.
Word Family **metric** (**met**-rik),
metrical *adjective* 1 of or relating to
metre. 2 composed in verse not prose;
metrically *adverb*.

metrication *noun*
the process of changing from British or
imperial units to SI units.

metric system *noun*
the measuring system based on the metre,
litre and gram.

metric ton *noun* also **metric tonne**
a unit of mass equal to 1000 kg.

metro *noun*
an underground railway system in certain
cities, notably Paris.
[French abbreviation of *métropolitaine*]

metronome (**met**-ra-nome) *noun*
Music a device for sounding an adjustable number of beats per minute.
[Greek *metron* a measure + *nomos* law]

metropolis (mi-**trop**-a-lis) *noun* (*plural* **metropolises**)
a large city, especially a capital city.
[Greek, mother state]

metropolitan (met-ra-**pol**-i-t'n) *adjective*
relating to a large city.

mettle *noun*
spirit or courage.
Phrase **on one's mettle** incited to do one's best.
Word Family **mettlesome** *adjective* spirited or courageous.
[from METAL]

mew *verb*
to make the sound of a cat or seagull.
• **mew** *noun*.

mewl *verb*
to cry feebly like a child.

mews *noun* (*plural* **mews**)
a group of stables built around an alley or court, now often converted into private flats.
[originally of the *Royal Mews* at Charing Cross, London]

Mexican wave *noun*
a ripple effect in a crowd caused by successive sections of spectators standing up and waving and then sitting down.
[first publicized in the soccer World Cup in Mexico in 1986]

mezuzah (miz-**oo**-za) *noun* (*plural* **mezuzahs** or **mezuzoth** (miz-**oo**-zote))
a scroll containing a section from the Torah placed in a case and attached to the doorpost of a Jewish home as a sign of faith.
[Hebrew, doorpost]

mezzanine (**mez**-a-neen *or* **met**-sa-neen) *noun*
a storey, usually in the form of a balcony or platform, between two main storeys of a building.
[Italian *mezzano* middle]

mezzo (**met**-so) *noun* also called **mezzo-soprano**.
a woman with a singing voice between soprano and contralto.
[Italian]

mezzotint (**met**-so-tint) *noun*
Art a print made by an engraving process in which the plate is roughened all over with a toothed rocker and the burr partly

or wholly scraped away to give half-tones and highlights.
[Italian, half-tint]

mi ⇨ ME².

miaow (mee-**ow**) *noun* also **meow**
the sound made by a cat.
• **miaow** *verb*.

miasma (mee-**az**-ma *or* my-**az**-ma) *noun*
1 a poetic word for swamp mists, once thought to cause malaria.
2 a bad atmosphere.
[Greek, pollution]

mica (**my**-ka) *noun*
a flaky, often transparent mineral, mainly composed of complex silicates of aluminium and potassium, widely used in electrical apparatus owing to its very high electrical resistance and melting point.
[Latin, a crumb]

mice
the plural of **mouse**.

mickey *noun*
Phrase **take the mickey out of** to tease or mock.

microanalysis (my-kro-a-**nal**-i-sis) *noun*
Chemistry a form of analysis using minute quantities of chemicals.

microbe (**my**-krobe) *noun*
a micro-organism.

microbiology (my-kro-by-**ol**-a-jee) *noun*
the study of micro-organisms.
Word Family **microbiological** (my-kro-by-a-**loj**-ik-'l) *adjective*; **microbiologist** *noun*.

microchip (**my**-kro-chip) *noun* also called **chip**.
a tiny piece of silicon printed with electronic circuits, used in a computer.

microclimate *noun*
the climate in a small area, environment or habitat.

microcomputer *noun*
a small computer, usually used in the home or at school.

microcosm (**my**-kro-kozm) *noun*
a system in which everything is on a small scale.
[*micro-* + Greek *kosmos* universe]

microdot (**my**-kro-dot) *noun*
1 *Photography* a microfilm which has been further reduced until it is the size of a printed or typed dot, used by spies, etc.
2 a small amount of the drug LSD.

microelectronics (my-kro-ill-ek-**tron**-iks) *plural noun* (*used with singular verb*) the design and manufacture of integrated circuits, used in spacecraft, missiles, aircraft, radar and desktop computers.

microfiche (**my**-kro-feesh) *noun*
a sheet of microfilm which contains many pages of text used for storing newspapers, library catalogues, etc.

microfilm *noun*
Photography very small pictures taken of documents, etc. to be kept as a record.
• **microfilm** *verb*.

micrometer (my-**krom**-it-a) *noun*
an instrument used to measure small lengths, adjusted by a finely threaded screw on which there is a graduated scale.
Word Family **micrometry** *noun* the method or art of measuring with a micrometer.

micron (**my**-kron) *noun*
one millionth of a metre (10^{-6} m).

micro-organism *noun*
any very small organism which can only be seen with a microscope, e.g. a virus or a bacterium.

microphone *noun*
a device which changes sound waves into electrical waves to be transmitted or recorded.
[*micro-* + Greek *phoné* sound]

microprocessor *noun*
Computers a chip imprinted with all the circuitry of the central processing unit.

microscope (**my**-kra-skope) *noun*
an optical instrument for viewing objects too small to be seen with the naked eye.
Word Family **microscopic** (my-kra-**skop**-ik) *adjective* **1** of or relating to the microscope. **2** extremely tiny;
microscopy (my-**kross**-ka-pee) *noun* the use of a microscope.
[*micro-* + Greek *skopein* to look at]

microsurgery (my-kro-**sir**-ja-ree) *noun*
a type of surgery performed on very small parts of the body such as blood vessels, nerve fibres, etc.

microwave (**my**-kro-wave) *noun*
1 *Physics* an electromagnetic wave with a very high frequency, used in television, radar, etc. and including ultra high frequency and super high frequency waves.
2 a microwave oven.
• **microwave** *verb* to cook in a microwave oven.

microwave oven *noun*
an oven which cooks extremely quickly by microwaves rather than by radiant heat.

micturate (**mik**-tyoor-ate) *verb*
(*formal*) to urinate.
Word Family **micturition** (mik-tyoor-**ish**'n) *noun*.
[from Latin]

mid *adjective*
in the middle of.

midday (mid-**day**) *noun*
noon, or the middle of the day.

midden *noun*
Archaeology a mound of kitchen wastes, shells, pots, etc.

middle *noun*
1 the point or part that is at an equal distance from the edges or extremes: *The chair is in the middle of the room.* □ *Ring me in the middle of the week.*
2 (*informal*) the waist.
• **middle** *adjective*
1 at a middle point.
2 average or medium.

middle-aged *adjective*
aged between 45 and 60, approximately.

Middle Ages *plural noun*
the period from about the 5th to the 15th century, approximately from the end of the Western Roman Empire to the Renaissance.

middle class *noun*
the social class generally considered to consist of those in businesses or professions.
• **middle-class** *adjective*.

Middle East *noun*
the countries from the eastern shores of the Aegean and Mediterranean Seas to Iran.

Middle English *noun*
the English language from approximately 1150 to 1470.

middleman *noun* (*plural* **middlemen**)
1 a trader, such as a wholesaler, who buys goods from a manufacturer and sells them to a retailer.
2 a person who acts as a go-between or intermediate agent.

middle-of-the-road *adjective*
moderate.

middle school *noun*
a school for children who are aged about nine to 12 or 13.

middleweight *noun*
a weight division in boxing, equal to about 75 kg or 158 lb.

middling *adjective*
medium: *a town of middling size.*

midge *noun*
a small fly with two wings. They can be found near water and marshy places.

midget (mij-it) *noun*
a very small person.

midi *noun*
a skirt, dress, etc. between mini and maxi which reaches to the calf.

midland *noun*
1 the inner or middle part of a country.
2 (**the Midlands**) the central counties of England.

midnight *noun*
the middle of the night, 12 a.m.
Phrase **burn the midnight oil** to work late into the night.

midpoint *noun*
a point halfway between the beginning and end of a line, etc.

midriff *noun*
the middle part of the body between the chest and the waist.

midshipman *noun* (*plural* **midshipmen**)
Navy the lowest commissioned officer, between warrant officer and sub-lieutenant.

midst *noun*
an old or poetic word meaning 'the middle'.
Phrase **in our midst** among us.

midsummer *noun*
1 the middle of summer.
2 the summer solstice, about 21 June, the longest day.

Midsummer Day *noun* also **Midsummer's Day**
24 June, a quarter day.

midway *adjective, adverb*
in or to the middle of something.

midwife *noun* (*plural* **midwives**)
a person trained to assist a mother during childbirth.
Word Family **midwifery** (mid-**wiff**-a-ree) *noun* the practice of being a midwife.

mien (meen) *noun*
a person's appearance or expression: *a sorrowful mien.*

miffed *adjective*
(*informal*) offended.

might¹ *verb*
1 the past tense of **may¹**.
2 used instead of **may** as a polite form: *Might I speak to you for a moment?*
3 used instead of **may** to express a less probable condition: *We might win if we are very lucky.*
Word Family **mightn't** *contraction* a short form of **might not**.

might² *noun*
great strength or capacity: *The army has the might to repel the invaders.*
Phrase **with might and main** with all one's strength and ability.

mighty *adjective* (**mightier; mightiest**)
1 powerful: *a mighty ruler.*
2 (*informal*) great or huge: *a mighty mountain range.*
• **mighty** *adverb* (*especially American informal*) very: *You seem mighty pleased with yourself.*
Word Family **mightily** *adverb* extremely; **mightiness** *noun.*

migraine (**mee**-grane *or* **my**-grane) *noun*
a periodic, severely painful headache, usually on only one side of the head and often accompanied by nausea or vomiting and blurred vision.
[Greek *hemikrania* a pain on one side of the head]

migrate (my-**grate** *or* **my**-grate) *verb*
1 (of birds or animals) to move periodically from one area to another.
2 (of a person) to move permanently to a new area or country; to emigrate or immigrate.
Word Family **migrant** (**my**-gr'nt) *noun* a person, bird, etc. that migrates; **migration** (my-**gray**-sh'n) *noun* the act of migrating; **migratory** (**my**-gra-tree *or* my-**gray**-ta-ree) *adjective* having the habit of migrating.

mikado (mik-**ah**-do) *noun*
History a title for the emperor of Japan.
[Japanese, exalted gate, meaning the gate of the emperor's palace]

mike *noun*
(*informal*) a microphone.

mild (*rhymes with* child) *adjective*
1 moderate or temperate: *mild weather.*
2 not sharp or strong: *a mild cheese.*
• **mild** *noun* a beer with a sweeter milder taste than bitter, though often just as strong.
Word Family **mildly** *adverb* gently or moderately; **mildness** *noun.*

mildew (**mill**-dew) *noun*
a plant disease caused by a fungus producing a powdery growth on a surface.

mile *noun*
1 also called **statute mile**. a unit of length equal to 1760 yards or 1·609 km.
2 (**miles**) (*informal*) a great distance or amount.
[Latin *mille* 1000 paces (nearly one mile)]

mileage (**my**·lij) *noun* also **milage**
1 the total number of miles travelled: *This car has a low mileage.*
2 (*informal*) usefulness: *There might be some mileage in advertising in the local shop.*

mileometer ⇨ MILOMETER.

milepost *noun*
(*especially American*) a milestone.

milestone *noun*
1 a stone at the side of a road showing the distance from a town or city.
2 an important event or stage.

milieu (mil-**yer**) *noun* (*plural* **milieux** or **milieus**) (mil·**yer** *or* mil·**yerz**)
someone's environment or surroundings.
[French]

militant *adjective*
aggressive or eager to fight.
Word Family **militant** *noun* a person who shows militant qualities; **militancy** *noun*; **militantly** *adverb*.

militarism (**mil**-it-a-rizm) *noun*
a belief in the use of military power to solve political problems.
Word Family **militarist** *noun* a supporter of militarism; **militaristic** (mil·it·a·**rist**·ik) *adjective*.

military (**mill**-i-tree) *adjective*
of or relating to soldiers, the armed forces, war, etc.
• **military** *noun* (**the military**) the armed forces.

militate (**mil**-i-tate) *verb*
to operate or have effect: *The weather militated against our plans to go away for the weekend.*
[Latin *militare* to soldier]

> ⚠ Do not confuse *militate* with MITIGATE.

militia (mil-**ish**-a) *noun*
a group of trained citizens called to fight in an emergency.
[Latin *militis* of a soldier]

milk *noun*
1 *Biology* the white liquid produced in the mammary glands of female mammals to feed their young, and, in the case of cows and some other animals, used for food or as a source of dairy products.
2 a liquid resembling this, such as latex from a tree or liquid in a coconut.
• **milk** *verb* to extract milk from a cow, etc. *Figurative They milked him of all his information* (= drew or extracted from).

milk bar *noun*
a bar where milk drinks, ice cream, etc. are sold.

milk float *noun* also called **float**.
an electric delivery vehicle used by milkmen.

milkmaid *noun*
an old word for a girl or woman who milks cows.

milkman *noun* (*plural* **milkmen**)
a man who delivers milk to houses.

Milk of Magnesia *noun*
(*trademark*) magnesium hydroxide (formula $Mg(OH)_2$) in water, used as a laxative or antacid.

milkshake *noun*
a sweet drink made by vigorously mixing a syrup flavouring with milk.

milksop *noun*
a person who is weak or timid.

milk tooth *noun* (*plural* **milk teeth**)
any of the temporary teeth in young humans and other mammals, later replaced by permanent teeth.

milky *adjective* (**milkier; milkiest**)
1 of or like milk: *milky tea*.
2 cloudy: *a milky liquid*.

Milky Way *noun*
Astronomy the bright band in the night sky formed by the stars of our galaxy.

mill *noun*
1 a building in which grain is ground.
2 a building with machinery in which a product is manufactured.
3 a device for grinding or crushing: *a pepper mill*.
• **mill** *verb*
1 to grind or treat in or as if in a mill.
2 to add fine notches to the edge of a coin when minting.
Phrase **mill about, mill around** to move around in a confused or aimless way.
[Latin *mola* millstone]

millennium (mil-**en**-i-um) *noun* (*plural* **millennia** or **millenniums**)
1 a period of 1000 years.
2 *Christianity* a future period of universal happiness based on a biblical prophecy.

Word Family **millennial** *adjective*.
[Latin *mille* thousand + *annus* year]

> ⚠ Note the spelling of *millennium*: it
> has two *l*'s and two *n*'s.

millennium bug *noun*
a computer problem caused by software
being unable to deal with dates from the
year 2000 onwards.

miller *noun*
the owner or operator of a mill, especially
a flour mill.

millet *noun*
a cereal plant with small edible grains.

millibar *noun*
a metric unit of pressure used in
meteorology, equal to 100 pascal.
[*milli-* + Greek *baros* weight]

milligram *noun* also **milligramme**
a unit of mass equal to one-thousandth of
a gram. *abbrev.* mg.

millilitre *noun* (*American* **milliliter**)
a unit of volume for liquids equal to one-
thousandth of a litre. *abbrev.* ml.

millimetre *noun* (*American* **millimeter**)
a unit of length equal to one-thousandth
of a metre. *abbrev.* mm.

milliner *noun*
a person who makes or sells hats for
women.
[originally a dealer in goods from *Milan*]

million *noun* (*plural* **millions** or **million**)
a cardinal number, the symbol 1 000 000
or 10^6.
Word Family **million** *adjective*;
millionth *noun*, *adjective*.

millionaire (mill-y'n-**air**) *noun*
a person who has a million pounds,
dollars, etc.
[from French]

millipede (**mill**-i-peed) *noun*
a long arthropod with a body made up of
many segments. They move slowly and eat
plants.
[Latin *mille* thousand + *pedis* of a foot]

millstone *noun*
1 either of the pair of circular stones
between which grain is ground.
2 a burden.

milometer (my-**lom**-i-ta) *noun* also
mileometer
an instrument in a vehicle that shows how
many miles the vehicle has travelled.

milt *noun*
the spermatozoa from a male fish.
Compare ROE[1].

mime *noun*
a form of entertainment consisting of
scenes performed using only actions or
gestures.
• **mime** *verb*
1 to act in a mime.
2 to imitate a person or action without
using words.
[from Greek]

mimesis (mi-**mee**-sis *or* my-**mee**-sis) *noun*
imitation.
Word Family **mimetic** (mi-**met**-ik)
adjective.
[Greek]

mimic *verb* (**mimics; mimicking;
mimicked**)
to imitate a person's speech or manner.
Word Family **mimic** *noun* a person or
thing that mimics; **mimicry** *noun* the act
or an instance of mimicking.

mimosa (mim-o-za *or* mim-o-sa) *noun*
1 an Australian tree with yellow flowers.
2 a tree or shrub with sensitive leaves.

minaret *noun*
a tall spire on a mosque, with balconies
from which people are called to prayer.
[Arabic *manarat* lighthouse]

minatory (**min**-a-tree) *adjective*
threatening or menacing.
[Latin *minari* to threaten]

mince *verb*
1 to cut into small pieces.
2 to walk in an affected way.
• **mince** *noun* finely chopped meat.
Word Family **mincingly** *adverb*
affectedly.

mincemeat *noun*
a mixture of suet, apples, raisins, sultanas,
peel, etc. used in mince pies.
Phrase **make mincemeat of** to defeat or
destroy thoroughly.

mince pie *noun*
a small covered tart made with a filling of
mincemeat.

mind (*rhymes with* find) *noun*
1 the faculty which thinks, reasons,
remembers, etc.
2 a person considered in relation to this
faculty: *the greatest mind of our age*.
3 what a person thinks, feels, etc.: *He
doesn't know his own mind.* □ *to change one's
mind.*
Phrases **cross one's mind** to come to
one as an idea. **have a good mind to** to
be inclined to. **in one's mind's eye** in
one's imagination. **of the same mind** of
the same opinion. **out of one's mind** not

thinking properly, mad. **put one's mind to, set one's mind to** to concentrate on. **speak one's mind** to say what one really thinks.

• **mind** *verb*

1 to pay attention to or take care of: *Will you mind the house while I'm away?* □ *Mind your manners, young man.*

2 to feel troubled or upset by: *Do you mind if I smoke?*

Phrases **mind one's own business** to keep out of other people's affairs. **mind you** please note or understand that: *Mind you, I wouldn't invite them again.*

Word Family **mindful** *adjective* attentive or careful; **mindless** *adjective* senseless or careless.

minder *noun*
(*informal*) a person employed to look after someone or something or to act as a bodyguard.

mind-reading *noun*
telepathy.
Word Family **mind-reader** *noun*.

mine¹ *possessive pronoun* (*plural* **ours**)
belonging to me: *That book is mine.*

mine² *noun*

1 a hole dug in the ground to take out minerals, gems, etc.
Figurative She is a mine of information (= rich source).

2 an explosive device placed in a concealed position to destroy enemy troops, ships, etc.

• **mine** *verb*

1 to extract ore, etc. from the ground.

2 to dig.

3 to lay military mines: *The enemy mined the entrance to the harbour.*

minefield *noun*

1 *Military* an area of land or water where mines have been laid.

2 a situation in which one needs to be careful.

miner *noun*
a person who works in a mine, especially a coal mine.

mineral (**min**-a-r'l) *noun*
a substance, such as quartz, with a definite chemical composition and a constant structure, found in the earth's surface.
Word Family **mineral** *adjective* **1** of or relating to minerals. **2** containing minerals; **mineralize, mineralise** *verb* to make into or add minerals to.

mineralogy (min-a-**ral**-a-jee) *noun*
the study of minerals, a branch of geology.

Word Family **mineralogist** *noun*;
mineralogical (min-er-a-**loj**-i-k'l) *adjective*.

mineral water *noun*
water naturally or artificially containing dissolved mineral salts or gases.

minestrone (min-i-**stro**-nee) *noun*
a thick vegetable soup, highly seasoned and served with grated cheese.
[Italian]

minesweeper *noun*
a ship equipped to remove mines from the water.

mingle *verb*
to mix or become mixed or blended: *The shouts of the children mingled with the noise of the traffic.*

mingy (**min**-jee) *adjective* (**mingier; mingiest**)
(*informal*) mean or stingy.
[M(ean) + (st)INGY]

mini *noun*
(*informal*) a thing which is small, especially a short skirt.

miniature (**min**-i-cher) *noun*
any small-scale copy or representation, such as a very small painting.
Word Family **miniaturize, miniaturise** *verb* to make small or on a small scale.

minibus *noun*
a vehicle which is smaller than a bus and usually has seats for about ten or twelve passengers.

minicomputer *noun*
a medium-sized computer used for general office and commercial applications.

minim *noun*
Music a note with half the time value of a semibreve.
[Latin *minimus* smallest]

minimal *adjective*
being the smallest or least possible: *He showed minimal interest in his work.*

minimize, minimise *verb*
to reduce to the smallest possible amount: *The rain has minimized the chances of a pleasant weekend.*

minimum *noun* (*plural* **minima** or **minimums**)
the least amount: *The minimum I could accept for my car is £100.* Compare MAXIMUM.
[Latin, least]

minion (**min**-y'n) *noun*
a servant or follower of an important
person.

minister *noun*
1 *Parliament* a member of either House of
Parliament who is the political head of a
government department.
2 *Parliament* any of various other members
of government, e.g. junior ministers,
ministers without portfolio, etc.
3 a diplomatic representative.
4 *Christianity* a member of the clergy.
• **minister** *verb* to give service or aid: *The
nurse ministered to his broken arm.*

> The word **minister** means,
> etymologically, 'servant', having come
> into English via Old French Latin
> *minister* (attendant). This in turn was
> derived from Latin *minus* meaning
> 'less'. The meaning of *minister* in
> English moved from 'servant' to
> 'church attendant' to 'member of the
> clergy'. The political meaning of the
> word arises from a political minister
> being a servant of the Crown.

ministerial (min-i-**steer**-i-ul) *adjective*
of or relating to a minister or ministry.

ministry (**min**-i-stree) *noun* (*plural*
ministries)
1 *Parliament* the department under the
charge of a minister.
2 *Christianity* the clergy.
3 *Christianity* the profession or duties of a
minister.
4 the act of ministering.

mink *noun* (*plural* **mink** or **minks**)
1 a small stoat-like mammal with a long
pointed nose, highly prized for its shiny
brown fur.
2 the fur of this animal.

minnow *noun*
a small silvery freshwater fish.

minor (**my**-na) *adjective*
1 smaller or less important: *a minor poet.*
□ *one or two minor objections.*
2 *Music* relating to one of two particular
arrangements of the semitones in a key or
scale. Compare MAJOR *adjective* (definition
2).
• **minor** *noun* a person who has not
reached the legal age of adulthood.
[Latin, less]

minority (my-**norr**-i-tee) *noun* (*plural*
minorities)
1 the lesser part or number: *Only a
minority of the shops were open on Sundays.*

2 a group of people in a society, e.g. an
ethnic or religious group.
3 the state or time of being under full legal
age.

minster *noun*
Christianity a large church, especially one
that originally belonged to a monastery.
[Greek *monasterion* monastery]

minstrel *noun*
a travelling musician and singer in
medieval Europe.

mint[1] *noun*
1 a pleasant-smelling herb used in
cooking.
2 a sweet flavoured with peppermint.
[Greek *minthé*]

mint[2] *noun*
1 a place where coins are made.
2 (*informal*) a vast amount of money: *He's
worth a mint.*
• **mint** *verb* to make coins.
• **mint** *adjective* unused, or in the
condition in which it was issued: *a mint
stamp.*
[Latin *moneta* money]

minuet (min-yoo-**et**) *noun*
1 a stately court dance from France.
2 the music for such a dance.
[Old French *menuet* very small]

minus (**my**-nus) *preposition*
1 reduced by: *2 minus 1 equals 1.*
2 below zero by: *It was minus 20 degrees last
night.*
3 (*informal*) without: *He returned home
minus his umbrella.*
• **minus** *adjective* below zero: *a minus
number.*
• **minus** *noun* (*plural* **minuses**)
1 the minus sign.
2 (*informal*) a disadvantage: *Her lack of
punctuality is rather a minus.*
[Latin, less]

minuscule (**min**-a-skewl) *adjective*
very small, especially of print or writing.
[Latin *minusculus* rather small]

minus sign *noun*
a symbol (–), used to show subtraction or
a value that is less than zero.

minute[1] (**min**-it) *noun*
1 a unit of time equal to 60 seconds or
one-sixtieth of an hour.
2 (*informal*) a short time.
3 one-sixtieth of a degree.
Phrases **this minute** immediately. **up to
the minute** most recent or modern.
[Latin *minutus* little]

minute² (my-**newt**) *adjective*
1 very small: *a minute insect.*
2 very precise or exact: *minute detail.*
Word Family minutely *adverb*;
minuteness *noun*.

minutes (**min**-its) *plural noun*
the official record of what is said at a
meeting.
Word Family minute *verb* to record the
things said at a meeting.

minutiae (my-**new**-shee-ee) *plural noun*
also **minutia** (my-**new**-shee-a)
small or unimportant details.

minx *noun* (*plural* **minxes**)
an impudent or flirtatious girl.

miracle (**mirr**-a-k'l) *noun*
1 an event which is believed to have a
supernatural or divine cause.
2 any wonderful or surprising event.

miraculous (mir-**ak**-yoo-lus) *adjective*
of or like a miracle.
Word Family miraculously *adverb*;
miraculousness *noun*.
[Latin *miraculum* a marvel]

mirage (mirr-ahzh *or* mirr-**ahzh**) *noun*
an optical phenomenon due to
atmospheric conditions which creates the
illusion of water or the reflected images of
distant objects.
[French *mirer* to look in a mirror]

mire *noun*
swampy ground or mud.

mirror (**mirr**-a) *noun*
a reflecting surface, usually glass with a
metal backing.
*Figurative This newspaper is a mirror of
society* (= true reflection).
• **mirror** *verb* to reflect in or like a mirror:
*The lake mirrored the snow-capped
mountains.*

mirth *noun*
1 merriment or rejoicing.
2 laughter, e.g. at something absurd.
Word Family mirthful *adjective*;
mirthless *adjective*.

misadventure *noun*
1 also called **death by misadventure**.
Law death caused accidentally, without
any harm being intended.
2 an accident.

misalliance (miss-a-**lie**-ance) *noun*
an unsuitable alliance or marriage.

misanthrope (**miz**-'n-thrope *or* **miss**-'n-
thrope) *noun* also **misanthropist** (miz-
an-thra-pist *or* miss-**an**-thra-pist)
a person who hates or distrusts people in
general.
Word Family misanthropic (miz-'n-
throp-ic *or* miss-'n-**throp**-ik) *adjective*;
misanthropy (miz-**an**-thra-pee *or* miss-
an-thra-pee) *noun*.
[Greek *misos* hatred + *anthropos* man]

misapply *verb* (**misapplies**;
misapplying; **misapplied**)
to use wrongly.

misapprehension (miss-ap-ri-**hen**-sh'n)
noun
a misunderstanding.

misappropriate (miss-a-**pro**-pree-ayt)
verb
to use in a wrongful way, especially
someone else's money.
Word Family misappropriation (miss-
a-pro-pree-**ay**-sh'n) *noun*.

misbehave *verb*
to behave badly.
Word Family misbehaviour *noun*
(*American* **misbehavior**)

miscarriage *noun*
the premature delivery of a foetus that is
too undeveloped to survive.
Phrase **miscarriage of justice** a failure
to arrive at a just result.

miscarry *verb* (**miscarries**;
miscarrying, **miscarried**)
to have a miscarriage.

miscellaneous (miss-a-**lay**-nee-us)
adjective
consisting of things of different or various
kinds.
Word Family miscellany (mi-**sell**-a-nee)
noun (*plural* **miscellanies**) a mixed
collection, especially of articles in a book.
[Latin *miscellanea* a hash of chopped meat]

mischance *noun*
bad luck or an unlucky event.

mischief (**mis**-chif) *noun*
1 playful conduct which teases or irritates.
2 injury or harm: *The storm did great
mischief to the trees.*

mischievous (**mis**-cha-vus) *adjective*
1 fond of mischief.
2 causing mischief.
Word Family mischievously *adverb*;
mischievousness *noun*.

miscible (**miss**-a-b'l) *adjective*
Chemistry able to be mixed in any proportions to form an even homogeneous substance.
Word Family **miscibility** (miss-i-**bill**-i-tee) *noun*.
[Latin *miscere* to mix]

misconception *noun*
an idea or opinion based on a mistake.

misconduct (mis-**kon**-dukt) *noun*
1 wrong or unlawful behaviour.
2 bad or unlawful management, as by an official.
Word Family **misconduct** (mis-kon-**dukt**) *verb*.

misconstrue *verb* (**misconstrues;**
misconstruing; misconstrued)
to misunderstand or misinterpret.

miscount (**miss**-count) *noun*
a wrong count, especially of votes.
• **miscount** (miss-**count**) *verb*.

miscreant (**mis**-kree-ant) *noun*
a villainous or criminal person.
[Old French, unbeliever, heretic]

misdeed *noun*
a crime or wicked action.

misdemeanour (miss-di-**mee**-na) *noun*
(*American* **misdemeanor**)
1 a minor crime.
2 any misbehaviour.

miser (**my**-za) *noun*
a person who is greedy for or mean with money.
Word Family **miserly** *adjective;*
miserliness *noun*.
[Latin, wretched]

miserable (**miz**-a-ra-b'l) *adjective*
1 very unhappy or uncomfortable.
2 very small: *She gave me a miserable portion of chips.*
Word Family **miserably** *adverb*.

misery (**miz**-a-ree) *noun* (*plural* **miseries**)
1 extreme unhappiness or distress.
2 something which causes unhappiness or distress.

misfire *verb*
(of a gun) to fail to fire.

misfit *noun*
a person or thing that fits badly, especially a person who cannot adapt to his or her environment.

misfortune *noun*
bad luck, such as an unlucky accident.

misgiving *noun*
a feeling of doubt, fear or worry.

misguided *adjective*
based on bad judgement or reasoning.

mishandle *verb*
to handle or treat badly.

mishap (**mis**-hap) *noun*
an unlucky accident, usually a minor one.

mishmash *noun*
a jumble.

misinform *verb*
to give wrong or misleading information.
Word Family **misinformation** *noun*.

misinterpret *verb*
to explain or understand wrongly.
Word Family **misinterpretation** *noun*.

misjudge *verb*
to form a wrong or unjust opinion of a person, event, etc.
Word Family **misjudgement** *noun*.

mislay *verb* (**mislays; mislaying;**
mislaid)
to lose something temporarily by forgetting where it was put.

mislead *verb* (**misleads; misleading;**
misled)
to lead astray.
Word Family **misleadingly** *adverb*.

mismanagement *noun*
incompetent or dishonest management.
Word Family **mismanage** *verb*.

misnomer (mis-**no**-mer) *noun*
1 a name wrongly applied to a person or thing.
2 the act of naming something wrongly.
[*mis-* + Latin *nomen* a name]

miso (**mee**-so) *noun*
a thick brown salty paste made from soya beans, used to flavour soup and savoury dishes.
[Japanese]

misogyny (miss-**oj**-a-nee) *noun*
a hatred of women.
Word Family **misogynist** *noun*.
[Greek *misos* hatred + *gyné* woman]

misplace *verb*
to put something in a wrong place.

misprint *noun*
a mistake in printing.

mispronounce *verb*
to pronounce a word incorrectly.
Word Family **mispronunciation** *noun*.

misquote *verb*
to quote incorrectly.
Word Family **misquotation** *noun*.

misrepresent *verb*
to give a false or misleading account, description, etc. of.
Word Family misrepresentation *noun*.

misrule *noun*
bad rule or government.

miss¹ *verb*
1 to fail to do or perform some action: *I missed the ball.* □ *He missed his appointment.*
2 to feel regret at the absence of someone or something: *missing her family.*
Phrase miss out to omit or be omitted from something.
• **miss** *noun* (*plural* **misses**) a failure to perform some action.

miss² *noun* (*plural* **misses**)
1 (**Miss**) a title used before the name of an unmarried woman.
2 a young unmarried woman.

missal *noun*
Roman Catholicism a book containing the services of the Eucharist for the year.
[Latin *missa* Mass]

misshapen (mis-**shay**-p'n) *adjective*
unnaturally or badly shaped.

missile *noun*
an object, usually a weapon, which is thrown, fired or ejected.
[Latin *missilis* that may be thrown]

missing *adjective*
absent, lacking or lost.

missing link *noun*
a hypothetical animal supposed to have formed the link in evolution between apes and humans.

mission (mish-'n) *noun*
1 an assignment for a particular purpose, e.g. military or diplomatic, usually in a foreign country: *The pilots were briefed for their dangerous mission.*
2 the person or people sent on such an assignment.
3 an organization or centre for religious and charitable work, especially overseas.
4 a vocation: *He felt that his mission in life was to fight alcoholism.*
[Latin *missio* a sending]

missionary (mish-'n-ree) *noun* (*plural* **missionaries**)
a priest or other person sent overseas to spread the teaching of a religion.
Word Family missionary *adjective* connected with or engaged on a mission.

missive *noun*
(*formal*) a letter or written message.

misspell *verb* (**misspells; misspelling; misspelt** or **misspelled**)
to spell a word incorrectly.

misspend *verb* (**misspends; misspending; misspent**)
to waste or squander something, such as money or time.

missus *noun* (*plural* **missuses**) also **missis** (*plural* **missises**)
(*informal*) a wife: *not a word to the missus!*

mist *noun*
1 a light fog.
2 condensed vapour in the form of fine drops of liquid: *a mist of hairspray.*
3 a blur: *a mist of tears.*
• **mist** *verb* to become covered with mist.

mistake *noun*
a wrong idea or action: *It was a mistake to leave my umbrella behind.* □ *I made a mistake in my addition and got the wrong answer.*
• **mistake** *verb* (**mistakes; mistaking; mistook; mistaken**)
1 to understand wrongly: *I mistook the meaning of her words.*
2 to believe to be someone or something else: *He always mistakes me for my twin brother.*

mistaken *adjective*
wrong, not true.
Word Family mistakenly *adverb*.

mister *noun*
a title for a man. *abbrev.* Mr.

mistime *verb*
to time something wrongly.

mistletoe (miss-'l-toe) *noun*
a plant which is parasitic on trees, with green leaves and white berries.

mistreat *verb*
to treat badly or wrongly.
Word Family mistreatment *noun*.

mistress *noun* (*plural* **mistresses**)
1 a woman or girl who owns a dog, cat, etc.: *The puppy followed his mistress everywhere.*
2 a woman who has power or control.
3 a female teacher.
4 a woman who is having a sexual relationship with another woman's husband.
5 a woman who is highly skilled.
6 (**Mistress**) an old word for **Mrs**.

mistrial (miss-**try**-al) *noun*
Law a trial which is declared invalid due to an error in proceedings.

mistrust *noun*
doubt, lack of trust.

Word Family **mistrust** *verb;* **mistrustful**
adjective; **mistrustfully** *adverb;*
mistrustfulness *noun.*

misty *adjective* (**mistier; mistiest**)
1 covered with mist.
2 full of mist.
3 faint or blurred.
Word Family **mistily** *adverb;* **mistiness**
noun.

misunderstand *verb* (**misunderstands;**
misunderstanding; misunderstood)
to understand wrongly.
Word Family **misunderstanding** *noun*
1 a failure to understand.
2 a disagreement: *The landlord and I had a*
misunderstanding about the rent.

misuse (miss-**yooz**) *verb*
1 to use something for the wrong purpose
or in the wrong way.
2 to maltreat.
● **misuse** (miss-**yooss**) *noun.*

mite[1] *noun*
a small arachnid.

mite[2] *noun*
a small child.
Phrase **a mite** somewhat.

mitigate (**mitt**-i-gate) *verb*
to make less intense or severe: *The design of*
the building mitigated the effects of the
earthquake.
Word Family **mitigation** (mitt-i-**gay**-
sh'n) *noun.*
[Latin *mitigare* to make mild]

> ⚠ Do not confuse *mitigate* with
> *militate. Militate* means 'to have a
> powerful influence against something',
> as in *Circumstances militated against our*
> *plans for a holiday.*

mitre (**my**-ta) *noun*
1 *Christianity* the tall headdress worn by a
bishop during certain ceremonies.
2 also called **mitre joint**. a joint made by
cutting the ends of two pieces at identical
angles and fixing the cut faces together.
[Greek *mitra* turban]

mitt *noun*
1 a type of glove which does not fully cover
the fingers.
2 a mitten.
3 also called **baseball mitt**. a large thick
glove worn to catch a baseball.
4 (*informal*) a hand.

mitten *noun*
a glove that covers the thumb separately
and the other four fingers together.

mix *verb*
1 to put things together so that the various
parts are blended or no longer fully
distinct: *Mix the ingredients thoroughly.*
□ *Several age groups were mixed in one class.*
2 to combine various sounds on one
soundtrack.
3 to talk to other people, e.g. at a party.
Phrase **mix up 1** *He mixed up our names*
(= confused). **2** *Don't get mixed up in*
politics (= involved).
● **mix** *noun* (*plural* **mixes**)
1 a mixture.
2 a prepared set of ingredients for cooking:
a cake mix.
[from Latin]

mixed *adjective*
1 consisting of several different things:
mixed vegetables.
2 for males and females: *a mixed hospital*
ward.

mixed blessing *noun*
an event which has disadvantages as well
as advantages.

mixed marriage *noun*
a marriage between people of different
religions or ethnic groups.

mixed number *noun*
a number containing an integer and a
common fraction, e.g. $3\frac{1}{2}$.

mixed-up *adjective*
(*informal*) emotionally or psychologically
confused.

mixer *noun*
1 a machine for mixing: *a cake mixer.*
2 a drink, such as lemonade, that can be
mixed with alcohol.

mixture *noun*
1 a combination of different things,
elements, qualities, etc.: *This stew is a*
mixture of meat and vegetables.
2 *Chemistry* two or more pure substances
(elements or compounds) which are
mixed but not chemically combined.
Solutions and colloids are types of
mixture.

mix-up *noun*
(*informal*) a confused mistake.

mizzen *noun* also **mizen**
1 also called **mizzenmast**. *Nautical* the
mast nearer the stern.
2 also called **mizzensail**. *Nautical* the sail
on this mast.

mnemonic (nim-**on**-ik) *noun*
a short verse or phrase which helps one to
remember: *'I' before 'e' except after 'c' is a*

*mnemonic for spelling words such as 'believe'
and 'deceive'.*
Word Family mnemonic *adjective*
assisting the memory.
[Greek *mnemonikos* for the memory]

moa (**mo**-a) *noun*
a large extinct flightless bird of New
Zealand, similar to an emu or ostrich.
[Maori]

moan *noun*
1 a long low sound of pain or pleasure.
2 a sound similar to this: *the moan of the
wind.*
3 (*informal*) a grumble: *He always has a
moan about the traffic.*
● **moan** *verb*.

moat *noun*
a pit or ditch, usually filled with water, dug
around a building, e.g. a castle, to defend
it.

mob *noun*
a large group of people or animals,
especially a disorderly or uncontrollable
crowd.
● **mob** *verb* (**mobs; mobbing; mobbed**)
to crowd around in great numbers: *The
screaming girls mobbed the film star.*
Word Family mobster *noun* (*informal*) a
criminal.
[Latin *mob(ile vulgus)* fickle crowd]

mob cap *noun*
a woman's old-fashioned soft round cap
for indoor wear, drawn in or gathered at
the base.

mobile (**mo**-bile) *adjective*
moving or able to be moved easily: *a mobile
crane.*
● **mobile** *noun*
1 a hanging structure or sculpture with
freely moving balanced parts.
2 a mobile phone.
[Latin *mobilis* easy to move]

mobile phone *noun* also called **mobile
telephone.**
a small portable telephone.

mobility (mo-**bill**-i-tee) *noun*
the quality of being mobile.

mobilize, mobilise (**mo**-bil-ize) *verb*
1 to prepare armed forces for war.
2 to organize people or things to get a job
done.
Word Family mobilization (mo-bil-eye-
zay-sh'n) *noun*.

moccasin (**mok**-a-sin) *noun*
a very soft leather shoe, first worn by
Native Americans.

mocha (**mok**-a) *noun*
1 the flavour of chocolate and coffee
combined.
2 a high-quality Arabian coffee.
[exported through the Red Sea port of
Mocha]

mock *verb*
to ridicule or make fun of a person or
thing.
Phrase mock up to build a model to test
or study a proposed device, apparatus, etc.
● **mock** *adjective* not real or genuine: *a
mock battle.*
Word Family mocking *adjective*;
mockingly *adverb*; **mock-up** *noun*.

mockery *noun*
ridicule.

mockingbird *noun*
a type of American songbird which mimics
sounds.

mod *adjective*
(*informal*) modern or fashionably up to
date.
[shortening of MODERN]

mode *noun*
1 a way in which something appears or is
done: *She has a strange mode of dress.*
2 a fashion or style.
3 *Music* a scale.
4 *Maths* the number in a set which occurs
most frequently: *The mode of 1, 2, 4, 4 is 4.*
Word Family modal (**mo**-d'l) *adjective*;
modality (mo-**dal**-i-tee) *noun* (*plural*
modalities) a method of procedure.
[Latin *modus* a measure, manner]

model *noun*
1 a representation of something, usually in
miniature, used as a basis or design for
copy, construction, etc.: *a model of the
proposed urban development.*
2 a person who is a perfect example: *She is
a model of honesty.*
3 a specific design: *the latest model of the
car.*
4 a person who poses for a painter, etc.
5 a person employed to wear and display
clothes.
● **model** *verb* (**models; modelling;
modelled**)
1 to act as a model.
2 to form or shape.
3 to copy: *He models himself on his father.*
4 to use a spreadsheet or other computer
software to explore the effect of changing
something, e.g. aspects of a design.
Word Family model *adjective*;
modelling *noun*.
[Latin *modulus* a small measure]

modem (mo-dem) *noun*
a device which converts data from one
computer into a form which can be
transmitted along telephone lines to
another computer.
[MO(dulator) + DEM(odulator)]

moderate (mod-a-rit) *adjective*
1 not great or excessive: *a moderate income.*
2 having political views that are not too
right-wing or left-wing.
• **moderate** *noun* a person who has
moderate ideas.
• **moderate** (mod-a-rate) *verb*
1 to make or become less extreme.
2 to check exam papers to make sure that
the grades are consistent.
Word Family **moderately** *adverb.*
[Latin *moderari* to set bounds to]

moderation (mod-a-ray-sh'n) *noun*
1 the quality of being moderate: *She shows
moderation in her eating.*
2 the act of moderating.

moderator *noun*
1 a person or thing that moderates.
2 a minister in charge of meetings of
certain religious bodies, e.g. the
Presbyterian General Assembly.

modern *adjective*
of or characteristic of the present or most
recent times: *modern history.* □ *a modern
building.*
• **modern** *noun* a person of modern ideas
or opinions.
Word Family **modernity** (mod-**ern**-i-
tee) *noun* the quality of being modern.
[Latin *modo* lately]

modernism *noun*
support for modern methods or ideas.
Word Family **modernist** *noun* a person
who supports modern ideas; **modernist**,
modernistic *adjective.*

modernize, modernise *verb*
to make or become modern.
Word Family **modernization** *noun.*

modest (mod-ist) *adjective*
1 not vain or boastful: *She is a genius but
she's very modest about it.*
2 moderate in amount, appearance, etc.:
He has modest needs.
3 not revealing too much of the body: *a
modest skirt that covered her knees.*
Word Family **modestly** *adverb.*
[Latin *modestus* restrained, sober]

modesty (mod-i-stee) *noun*
the quality of being modest.

modicum (mod-i-k'm) *noun*
a small quantity or portion.
[Latin *modicus* of middling size]

modify (mod-i-fie) *verb* (**modifies;
modifying; modified**)
1 to make or become somewhat different
in form, character, etc.: *The car was
modified to take unleaded fuel.*
2 to revise by making less extreme,
uncompromising, etc.: *to modify one's
views.*
3 *Grammar* to describe, limit or
characterize the meaning of.
Word Family **modifier** *noun* a person or
thing that modifies; **modification** (mod-i-
fi-**kay**-sh'n) *noun.*

modish (mo-dish) *adjective*
fashionable.
Word Family **modishly** *adverb*;
modishness *noun.*

modulate (mod-yoo-late) *verb*
1 to change or regulate, e.g. the tone of
voice.
2 *Music* to move from one key to another.
Word Family **modulator** *noun* a person
or thing that modulates.
[Latin *modulari*]

modulation (mod-yoo-**lay**-sh'n) *noun*
1 the act of modulating.
2 the state of being modulated.

module (mod-yool) *noun*
1 a component made of standardized size
so that it can be combined with others in
building, furniture, electronics, etc.
2 a unit or section of an educational
course treating a specific topic.
Word Family **modular** (mod-yoo-la)
adjective.

modus operandi (mo-dus op-a-**ran**-dee)
noun (*plural* **modi operandi**) (mo-dee
op-a-**ran**-dee)
a method or plan of operating or working.
[Latin]

modus vivendi (mo-dus vi-**ven**-dee) *noun*
(*plural* **modi vivendi**) (mo-dee vi-**ven**-dee)
1 a compromise or temporary agreement
made between the parties in a dispute.
2 a mode of living.
[Latin]

mogul *noun*
(*informal*) an important or powerful
person.
[after Grand *Mogul*, the European name
for the Indian emperors who ruled at
Delhi]

mohair *noun*
1 the fleece of an Angora goat.
2 a fabric made from this.
[from Arabic]

moiety (moy-a-tee) *noun* (*plural* **moieties**)
(*formal*) a portion, especially a half.

moire (mwah) *noun* also **moiré** (mwah-ray)
silk that has a rippled pattern because it has been treated in a special way.
[French, mohair]

moist *adjective*
slightly wet.
Word Family **moisten** (moy-s'n) *verb* to make moist; **moistly** *adverb*; **moistness** *noun*.

moisture *noun*
liquid or vapour, especially water vapour, which makes something moist.

moisturize, moisturise *verb*
to give or restore moisture to.
Word Family **moisturizer** *noun* something that moisturizes, especially a cream or liquid used on the skin.

molar[1] (mole-a) *noun* also **molar tooth**
Anatomy any of the twelve square teeth at the back of the mouth.
• **molar** *adjective*.
[Latin *mola* millstone]

molar[2] *adjective*
Chemistry of or relating to a mole or measurement in moles.

molasses *noun*
1 the syrup obtained from raw sugar.
2 *American* golden syrup.
[from Portuguese]

mole[1] *noun*
Anatomy a small dark often slightly raised spot on the skin.

mole[2] *noun*
1 a small insect-eating mammal that lives underground.
2 a spy.

mole[3] *noun*
1 *Chemistry* the amount of a substance which contains the same number of particles as there are carbon atoms in 12 g of carbon.
2 *Chemistry* the base SI unit of amount of substance. *abbrev.* mol.
[German *Mol* molecule]

mole[4] *noun*
a pier or breakwater.
[Latin *mola* a mass]

molecular (mo-lek-yoo-la) *adjective*
of, caused by or consisting of molecules.

molecular biology *noun*
the study of the structure and function of the large molecules found in living cells.

molecule (mol-i-kewl) *noun*
Chemistry a stable group of atoms held together by weak attractive forces between electrons in neighbouring atoms; the smallest structural unit into which a chemical substance can be divided and still have the properties of that substance.
[Latin *moles* a mass]

molehill *noun*
a small mound of earth raised up by burrowing moles.

moleskin *noun*
1 the fur of a mole.
2 a strong cotton fabric.

molest (mo-lest) *verb*
to interfere with so as to annoy or injure.
Word Family **molester** *noun*; **molestation** (mol-est-ay-sh'n) *noun*.
[Latin *molestus* irksome]

moll *noun*
1 (*informal*) the girlfriend of a gangster.
2 (*informal*) a prostitute.
[diminutive of *Mary*]

mollify (mol-i-fie) *verb* (**mollifies; mollifying; mollified**)
to calm down or appease.
Word Family **mollification** (mol-i-fi-kay-sh'n) *noun*.
[Latin *mollis* soft + *facere* to make]

mollusc *noun* (*American* **mollusk**)
a soft invertebrate, usually with a shell, such as an oyster or snail.
[Latin *mollis* soft]

mollycoddle *verb*
to pamper or coddle.

Molotov cocktail *noun*
a home-made bomb consisting of a bottle filled with petrol or paraffin, and a wick.
[after *V. M. Molotov*, 1890-1986, a Russian statesman]

molten *adjective*
turned to liquid by heating: *molten rock*.

moment *noun*
1 a short space of time: *Wait a moment.*
2 a particular point of time: *I cannot speak to you at this moment.*
3 (*formal*) importance: *The new discovery is of great moment.*
4 *Physics* a tendency to produce motion, especially about an axis.
5 *Physics* the product of a physical quantity and its distance from an axis.
Phrase **moment of truth** a moment when a person is put to a great test.

momentary (mo-men-tree) *adjective*
lasting only a moment: *a momentary glimpse.*
Word Family **momentarily** *adverb* for a moment.

momentous (mo-**men**-tus) *adjective*
very important or likely to have serious consequences.
Word Family **momentously** *adverb*; **momentousness** *noun*.

momentum (mo-**men**-t'm) *noun* (*plural* **momenta**)
1 *Physics* the moving force or energy of an object, calculated by multiplying its mass by its velocity.
2 the ability or tendency of something to develop faster and faster: *The campaign gained momentum after the TV programme.*
[Latin, movement]

monarch (**mon**-ark) *noun*
a hereditary leader of a country, such as a king or queen, often with powers limited by a constitution or parliament.
Word Family **monarchic** (mon-**ark**-ik) *adjective* also **monarchal** of, like or befitting a monarch.
[Greek *monos* alone + *arkhein* to rule]

monarchism (**mon**-a-kizm) *noun*
1 the principles of government by a monarch.
2 support or favour for such principles.
Word Family **monarchist** *noun* a supporter of monarchism.

monarchy (**mon**-a-kee) *noun* (*plural* **monarchies**)
government or a country ruled by a monarch.

monastery (**mon**-a-stree) *noun* (*plural* **monasteries**)
1 a community of monks.
2 the buildings in which they live.

monastic (mo-**nas**-tik) *adjective*
of or characteristic of monks or a monastery.
Word Family **monastic** *noun* a monk; **monasticism** (mon-**ass**-ti-sizm) *noun* the monastic system or way of life.
[Greek *monazein* to live alone]

Monday *noun*
the second day of the week, after Sunday and before Tuesday.
[Old English *monen* moon + *daeg* day]

monetarism (**mun**-i-ta-rizm) *noun*
an economic policy based on the belief that only control of the money supply will decrease inflation and improve the economy generally.

money (**mun**-ee) *noun* (*plural* **moneys** or **monies**)
coins or notes used as a medium of exchange.
Phrases **for my money** *For my money I think the plan won't work* (= in my opinion). **in the money** rich. **money for jam, money for old rope** money that is very easily come by.
Word Family **monetary** (**mun**-i-tree) *adjective* of or relating to money, currency or finance; **moneyed** *adjective* wealthy.

> The word **money** came into English from Old French *moneie* but its origins lie in *Moneta*, a name applied to the Roman goddess Juno. It was also applied to her temple in Rome, which contained a place for making coins, a mint. *Moneta* became the word for 'a mint' and then a word for a coin that was minted.

moneybags *plural noun*
(*informal*) a very wealthy person.

money-grubber *noun*
(*informal*) a person who is greedy for money.

money order *noun*
an order for the equivalent of money deposited at one post office to be paid out at another post office to a person named.

money-spinner *noun*
something which is very profitable.

mongolism (**mong**-g'l-izm) *noun*
an old word for Down's syndrome.

mongoose *noun* (*plural* **mongooses**)
a small ferret-like mammal found in Africa and Asia, noted for its ability to kill poisonous snakes.
[Indian *mangus*]

mongrel (**mung**-gr'l) *noun*
a dog of mixed breed.
Word Family **mongrel** *adjective*.

monitor (**mon**-it-a) *noun*
1 a device used to control or check something: *a baby monitor.*
2 a pupil appointed to perform certain duties in a class or school: *a blackboard monitor.*
3 a television screen in a studio for checking each stage of a programme being broadcast.
4 a screen attached to a computer.
5 also called **monitor lizard**. a large flesh-eating lizard with a slender head and long tail, found in Australia, Africa and Asia.

• **monitor** *verb* to check, observe or
supervise.
Word Family **monitorial** (mon-i-taw-
ri-ul) *adjective*.
[Latin, a reminder, adviser]

monk (munk) *noun*
a male member of a religious order living
under vows, often apart from the secular
world.
Word Family **monkhood** *noun* the
condition or following of a monk.
[Greek *monakhos* solitary]

monkey (munk-ee) *noun*
a small primate, such as the marmoset,
rhesus monkey, etc., found in tropical
regions. After the ape, it is the closest to
humans in evolutionary development.
Compare APE.
Phrase **make a monkey of** to make a
fool of.
• **monkey** *verb* to play or fool around.

monkey business *noun*
(*informal*) trickery or underhand dealing.

monkey nut *noun*
a peanut.

monkey puzzle *noun*
a type of large pine tree originally from
Chile.
[so named because it would puzzle a
monkey if it tried to climb this tree]

monkey wrench *noun*
an adjustable spanner.

mono *adjective*
monophonic.

monochrome (mon-a-krome) *noun*
1 a painting or drawing in tones of one
colour.
2 a black and white photograph.
Word Family **monochromatic** (mon-a-
kro-**mat**-ik) *adjective*.
[*mono-* + Greek *khroma* colour]

monocle (mon-a-k'l) *noun*
a single lens held in front of the eye by the
angle between the nose and the eyebrow.
[*mono-* + Latin *oculus* eye]

monogamy (mon-og-a-mee) *noun*
the custom of having one husband or wife
at a time. Compare POLYGAMY.
Word Family **monogamist** *noun*;
monogamous *adjective*.
[*mono-* + Greek *gamos* marriage]

monogram *noun*
a design consisting of several letters
combined, such as a person's initials.
[*mono-* + Greek *gramma* something
written]

monograph *noun*
an account of one particular subject.
Word Family **monographic** *adjective*.

monolith *noun*
1 a single block of stone or rock of
considerable size, such as Cleopatra's
Needle.
2 a large organization seen as something
uniform or unyielding.
Word Family **monolithic** (mon-a-**lith**-
ik) *adjective*
1 of or like a monolith.
2 massive and uniform: *No individual
freedom was allowed in the monolithic state.*
[*mono-* + Greek *lithos* a stone]

monologue (mon-a-log) *noun*
a speech, especially a long speech, made
by one person, e.g. in a play.
[*mono-* + Greek *logos* a word]

monomania (mon-a-may-ni-a) *noun*
an exaggerated obsession with a single
thing or subject.
Word Family **monomaniac** *noun*.

monomer (mon-o-mer) *noun*
Chemistry any of the small molecules that
join to form a polymer.

mononucleosis (mon-o-new-klee-o-sis)
noun
a blood disorder which can be associated
with glandular fever.

monophonic (mon-a-fon-ik) *adjective*
of or relating to sound reproduction
through one sound source. Compare
QUADRAPHONIC; STEREOPHONIC.
[*mono-* + Greek *phoné* a sound]

monoplane *noun*
an aeroplane with one pair of wings.

monopolize, monopolise (mon-op-a-
lize) *verb*
to have or exercise a monopoly: *She
monopolized all his attention.*
Word Family **monopolizer** *noun* a
person who monopolizes;
monopolization (mon-op-a-lie-**zay**-
sh'n) *noun*.

monopoly (mon-**op**-a-lee) *noun* (*plural*
monopolies)
an exclusive control over or right to
something.
Word Family **monopolistic** (mon-op-a-
list-ik) *adjective*.
[*mono-* + Greek *polein* to sell]

monorail *noun*
a railway with carriages running on a
single rail.

monosodium glutamate (mon-o-so-dee-um **gloo**-ta-mate) *noun*
a white crystalline solid, soluble in water, used to intensify the flavour of foods.

monostable (**mon**-o-stay-b'l) *adjective*
Electronics having one stable state: *a monostable circuit.*

monosyllable (**mon**-o-sill-a-b'l) *noun*
a word of one syllable.
Word Family **monosyllabic** (mon-o-sil-**ab**-ik) *adjective* using or composed of a monosyllable or monosyllables: *a monosyllabic reply.*

monotheism (**mon**-o-thee-izm) *noun*
the belief that there is only one God or supreme being. Compare POLYTHEISM.
Word Family **monotheist** *noun;*
monotheistic (mon-o-thee-**ist**-ik) *adjective.*
[*mono-* + Greek *theos* a god]

monotone *noun*
a sound that does not change in tone or pitch.

monotony (mon-**ot**-a-nee) *noun*
a wearisome sameness or a lack of variety: *He was tired of the monotony of his job.*
Word Family **monotonous** *adjective* lacking variety or interest: *a flat monotonous landscape.* **monotonously** *adverb;* **monotonousness** *noun.*
[*mono-* + Greek *tonos* tone]

monotreme (**mon**-a-treem) *noun*
the most primitive type of mammal, such as the platypus or echidna, found only in Australia and New Guinea. Like birds, they lay eggs and have a common opening at the posterior end for the genital, digestive and urinary tracts.
[*mono-* + Greek *trema* hole]

Monotype *noun*
(*Printing trademark*) a typesetting machine which sets single letters.

Monseigneur (mon-sen-**yer**) *noun* (*plural* **Messeigneurs**) (may-sen-**yer**)
a French title of honour for princes, bishops, etc.
[French *mon* my + *seigneur* lord]

Monsieur (m'ss-**yer**) *noun* (*plural* **Messieurs**) (mess-**yer**)
the French title for a man.

Monsignor (mon-**seen**-ya *or* mon-seen-**yor**) *noun* (*plural* **Monsignori**) (mon-seen-**yor**-i)
Roman Catholicism an honorary title for certain officials.
[Italian]

monsoon *noun*
1 a seasonal wind of the Indian Ocean and southern Asia, usually blowing from the south-west in summer and from the north-east in winter.
2 the season of the south-west monsoon which brings heavy rain.
[Arabic *mawsim* fixed season]

monster *noun*
1 a large frightening imaginary animal.
2 a person or thing of abnormal shape or size.
3 a cruel or wicked person.
Word Family **monster** *adjective* huge.
[Latin *monstrum* a wonder]

monstrous (**mon**-strus) *adjective*
1 huge and frightening.
2 very bad, shocking: *a monstrous crime.*
Word Family **monstrosity** (mon-**stross**-i-tee) *noun* (*plural* **monstrosities**) 1 the state of being monstrous. 2 something which is monstrous or like a monster; **monstrously** *adverb;* **monstrousness** *noun.*

montage (mon-**tahzh** *or* mon-tah*zh*) *noun*
the arrangement of several pictures or designs together or on top of each other.
[French, a putting together]

month (munth) *noun*
each of the twelve parts into which the calendar year is divided.

monthly *adjective, adverb*
1 of or occurring once a month.
2 of or occurring every month.
3 lasting for a month: *a monthly ticket.*
• **monthly** *noun* (*plural* **monthlies**) a magazine or publication produced once a month.

monument *noun*
1 a building or structure, such as a statue, built in memory of a person or event.
2 a thing that serves as an important example or reminder.
[Latin *monere* to remind]

monumental (mon-yoo-**men**-t'l) *adjective*
1 huge, colossal or imposing: *a monumental achievement.*
2 of or like a monument.
Word Family **monumentally** *adverb* hugely.

moo *verb* (**moos; mooing; mooed**)
to make the deep sound that a cow makes.
• **moo** *noun.*

mooch *verb*
(*informal*) to loiter or lounge about.

mood¹ *noun*
1 a state of mind or feeling: *He was in a good mood.*
2 a sulky or angry state of mind.

mood² *noun*
Grammar the change of form in a verb to express the manner in which the statement is made.
imperative mood the mood used to express a command, e.g. *Buy this book now.*
indicative mood the mood used to state a simple fact or ask a question, e.g. *The boy rode a bicycle.*
subjunctive mood the mood used to express doubt or supposition, e.g. *If he should come, I would be very surprised.*

moody *adjective* (**moodier; moodiest**)
having frequent changes of mood, especially having sulky moods.
Word Family **moodily** *adverb*; **moodiness** *noun*.

moon *noun*
1 (*often* **Moon**) *Astronomy* the natural satellite of the earth.
2 *Astronomy* any natural satellite of another planet.
Phrase **once in a blue moon** very seldom.
• **moon** *verb*
1 to wander about or gaze dreamily.
2 (*informal*) to show one's bare buttocks as a rude gesture.

moonbeam *noun*
a ray of moonlight.

moonlight *noun*
the light of the moon.

moonlighter *noun*
a person who works in a second job, especially at night.
Word Family **moonlight** *verb* (**moonlights; moonlighting; moonlighted**) to do a second job: *moonlighting as a taxi driver.*

moonshine *noun*
1 any nonsensical talk or ideas.
2 (*especially American informal*) illegally distilled or smuggled liquor.

moon shot *noun*
the launching of a rocket to the moon.

moonstone *noun*
Geology a translucent sometimes milky feldspar mineral, used as a gem.

moonstruck *adjective*
dazed or mad, supposedly due to the moon's influence.

moor¹ *noun*
an open wild area of land covered with coarse grasses and other low vegetation.

moor² *verb*
to fix a boat in position by ropes, weights, etc.
Word Family **moorage** *noun* 1 the state of being moored. 2 a place for mooring; **mooring** *noun* also **moorings** 1 a place where a boat can be moored. 2 ropes, anchors, etc. used for mooring.

moorhen *noun*
a small stout blackish waterbird with a red and yellow beak.

moose *noun* (*plural* **moose**)
American an elk.

moot (*rhymes with* boot) *verb*
to raise a question, etc. for discussion.
• **moot** *noun*
1 *Law* a meeting of law students in order to gain practice by discussing imaginary cases.
2 *History* a meeting for debate in Anglo-Saxon England.
Word Family **moot** *adjective* doubtful or open to debate: *a moot point.*
[Old English *gemot* a meeting]

mop *noun*
1 a loose bunch of cloth or yarn attached to a long handle and used for cleaning floors, etc.
2 an unruly mass of hair.
• **mop** *verb* (**mops; mopping; mopped**)
to clean or wipe with or as if with a mop: *He mopped the sweat from his brow.*
Phrase **mop up** to clear a captured area of any remaining enemy troops.

mope *verb*
to be listless or dejected

moped (mo-ped) *noun*
a bicycle equipped with a motor.
[MO(tor) + PED(als)]

moquette (mok-et) *noun*
a thick velvety fabric used for carpets and upholstery.
[French]

moraine (ma-**rane**) *noun*
Geography the fragments of rock material transported and deposited by a glacier, usually forming a ridge or mound.
[French]

moral (*rhymes with* coral) *noun*
1 a lesson taught by the example set in a story or fable.
2 (**morals**) principles concerning right and wrong.

• **moral** *adjective*
1 relating to principles of right and wrong: *Abortion raises moral questions.*
2 acting in a way that is considered right: *a moral person.*
Word Family morally *adverb;* **moralist** *noun* a person who teaches or encourages moral behaviour; **moralistic** (morr-a-**list**-ik) *adjective.*
[Latin *mores* customs, morals]

morale (ma-**rahl**) *noun*
the confidence, zeal, cheerfulness, etc. of a person or group of people: *The troops lost the battle because of low morale.*
[from French]

morality (mo-**rall**-i-tee) *noun (plural* **moralities**)
1 good or virtuous conduct.
2 a system or code of morals.
3 moral character or quality.

moralize, moralise (**morr**-a-lize) *verb*
to speak or write on moral questions, especially in a self-righteous way.
Word Family moralizer *noun;* **moralizingly** *adverb;* **moralization** (morr-a-lie-**zay**-sh'n) *noun.*

moral support *noun*
psychological support.

moral victory *noun (plural* **moral victories**)
a defeat, but one which is morally satisfying.

morass (ma-**rass**) *noun (plural* **morasses**)
1 a bog or area of soft wet land.
2 a complex situation.

moratorium (morr-a-**taw**-ri-um) *noun* (*plural* **moratoriums** or **moratoria**)
a temporary halt or delay, such as a legal authorization to delay payment of a debt.
[Latin *morari* to delay]

morbid *adjective*
1 gloomy or mentally unwholesome.
2 of or caused by disease.
Word Family morbidly *adverb;* **morbidness, morbidity** (mor-**bid**-i-tee) *noun.*
[Latin *morbus* disease]

mordant *adjective*
biting or sarcastic: *mordant wit.*
Word Family mordantly *adverb;* **mordancy** *noun.*
[Latin *mordere* to bite]

more *adjective*
greater in amount, quantity, etc.: *I'd like to do more painting.* □ *There has been more fighting.*
• **more** *adverb*

1 to a greater extent or degree: *The film was more frightening than we expected.*
2 again.
Phrase **more or less** approximately.

moreover *adverb*
besides.

mores (**maw**-rayz *or* **maw**-reez) *plural noun*
the accepted moral customs of a group or society.
[Latin]

morganatic (mor-ga-**nat**-ik) *adjective*
relating to a marriage between a person of high rank and a person of lower rank in which the spouse and children do not share or inherit the rank or property of the person of higher rank.

morgue (morg) *noun*
a place where dead bodies are kept for identification.

The word **morgue** is an alternative for 'mortuary', probably more common in American English than in British English. It takes its name from *Le Morgue*, the name of a Paris mortuary.

moribund *adjective*
close to death or extinction.
[from Latin]

morn *noun*
a poetic word for morning.

morning *noun*
the beginning or the early part of the day, before noon.

morning glory *noun (plural* **morning glories**)
a climbing plant with trumpet-shaped, usually blue, flowers.

morning sickness *noun*
nausea experienced in the early months of pregnancy.

morning star *noun*
a planet seen in the east before sunrise, especially Venus.

morocco (ma-**rok**-o) *noun*
a fine leather made from goatskins.
[first made in *Morocco*, Africa]

moron (**maw**-ron) *noun*
(*informal*) a stupid person.
Word Family moronic (maw-**ron**-ik) *adjective.*
[Greek *moros* foolish]

morose *adjective*
gloomily bad-tempered or unsociable.
Word Family morosely *adverb;* **moroseness** *noun.*
[Latin *morosus* peevish]

morpheme (**more**-feem) *noun*
the smallest meaningful unit of language,
forming part or all of a word: *The
morphemes 'un-', 'fair' and '-ness' make up
the word 'unfairness'.*

morphine (**more**-feen) *noun*
a bitter substance which is the most
important narcotic in opium, used to
relieve pain and as a narcotic.
[after *Morpheus*, the ancient Greek god of
dreams]

morphology (mor-**fol**-a-jee) *noun* (*plural*
morphologies)
the study of the shape, form and structure
of anything, such as biological or
geographical forms.
Word Family **morphologist** *noun*;
morphological (mor-fa-**loj**-i-k'l) *adjective.*
[Greek *morphé* shape + *-logy*]

morris dance *noun*
a traditional folk dance in fancy dress,
associated with May Day.
[alteration of *Moorish dance*]

morrow *noun*
an old word meaning 'the next day': *on the
morrow.*

Morse *noun* also **Morse code**
a method of signalling, using a
combination of short and long pulses
(called dots and dashes) for each letter of
the alphabet.
[after *Samuel Morse*, 1791-1872, American
inventor of the telegraph system]

morsel *noun*
a small piece or amount.
[Latin *morsum* bite]

mortal¹ (**more**-t'l) *adjective*
1 subject to death: *All men are mortal.*
2 causing death: *The soldier received a
mortal wound.*
• **mortal** *noun* a human being.
Word Family **mortally** *adverb.*
[Latin *mortis* of death]

mortality (more-**tal**-i-tee) *noun* (*plural*
mortalities)
1 the condition of being mortal or having
to die.
2 any death or loss of life.
3 also called **mortality rate**. the number
of deaths in a particular place or period, or
from a particular cause.

mortar¹ (**more**-ta) *noun*
1 a heavy bowl in which substances may be
crushed with a pestle.
2 a portable cannon with a short barrel,
firing shells or bombs at a steep angle.

mortar² *noun*
a mixture of cement or lime, sand and
water which sets hard and is used for
joining bricks, etc. Compare CONCRETE.

mortar board *noun*
a stiff square black cap, often part of
formal university clothing.

mortgage (**mor**-gij) *noun*
a loan given to someone by a bank or
building society so that he or she can buy a
property, e.g. a house. The bank or
building society can take back the
property if the money is not repaid.
• **mortgage** *verb* to use property as a way
of guaranteeing a loan.
Word Family **mortgagor** (mor-ga-**jaw**)
noun a person borrowing money to buy a
property; **mortgagee** (mor-ga-**jee**) *noun* a
lender, e.g. a bank or building society.
[French *mort* dead + *gage* pledge]

mortician (mor-**tish**-'n) *noun*
(*especially American*) an undertaker.

mortify (**mor**-ti-fie) *verb* (**mortifies;**
mortifying; mortified)
to make someone feel humiliated or
ashamed.
Word Family **mortifyingly** *adverb*;
mortification (mor-ti-fi-**kay**-sh'n) *noun*

mortise (**mor**-tiss) *noun* also **mortice**
a deep rectangular hole or slot in a surface,
into which a matching tapered end (a
tenon), is fitted to form a joint.
• **mortise** *verb*
1 to join by or as if by a mortise.
2 to cut a mortise in.

mortuary (**mor**-tew-ree) *noun* (*plural*
mortuaries)
a place where bodies are kept before
burial.
[Latin *mortuus* dead]

mosaic (mo-**zay**-ik) *noun*
1 a decoration consisting of small pieces of
coloured glass, stone, etc. applied to a
surface to form a design.
2 any similar form or pattern.
• **mosaic** *adjective.*
[Greek *mouseios* of the Muses]

Moslem ⇨ MUSLIM.

mosque (mosk) *noun*
a Muslim house of worship.

mosquito (moss-**kee**-toe) *noun* (*plural*
mosquitoes)
a fly with scaly wings which can transmit
diseases such as malaria and yellow fever.
The female has a long proboscis for
sucking blood.
[Spanish, little fly]

mosquito net *noun*
a net for keeping out mosquitoes.

moss *noun* (*plural* **mosses**)
a small green plant with very small leaves and root-like filaments, growing in damp places.
Word Family **mossy** *adjective* (**mossier; mossiest**) like or overgrown with moss.

most *adjective*
greatest in amount, quantity, etc.: *I did the most work.*
• **most** *adverb* to the greatest extent: *the most useful tool.*
• **most** *noun* nearly all: *We saw most of the show.*
Phrases **at the most** *He can stay until midnight at the most* (= as a maximum).
make the most of to use to the best advantage.
Word Family **mostly** *adverb* **1** almost completely. **2** generally.

mote *noun*
a particle of dust.

motel (mo-**tel**) *noun*
a hotel which provides accommodation for motorists.

motet (mo-**tet**) *noun*
a piece of sacred music, usually for unaccompanied voices.

moth *noun*
any of a group of usually nocturnal insects, similar to butterflies but with longer antennae and often with duller colouring.

mothball *noun*
a small ball made of naphthalene or camphor, used in cupboards, etc. to repel moths.

moth-eaten *adjective*
old and shabby, as though eaten by moths.

mother (**mu**-*tha*) *noun*
1 a female parent.
2 (**Mother**) the head of a female religious community.
• **mother** *adjective* being or like a mother: *a mother hen.*
• **mother** *verb*
1 to be the mother of.
2 to care for as a mother.
Word Family **motherly** *adjective*; **motherliness** *noun*; **motherhood** *noun* the state of being a mother.

mother-in-law *noun* (*plural* **mothers-in-law**)
the mother of one's husband or wife.

motherland *noun*
a person's native country.

mother-of-pearl *noun*
the shiny rainbow-coloured lining of certain shells, especially the pearl oyster, commonly used to make ornaments.

Mother Superior *noun*
the head of a convent.

mother tongue *noun*
a person's native language.

motif (mo-**teef**) *noun*
a repeated theme, subject or figure, e.g. in a design.
[French]

motion (mo-sh'n) *noun*
1 movement or the process of moving: *The clouds were in constant motion.*
2 a formal proposal at a meeting, etc.
3 *Medicine* a bowel action or faeces.
Phrase **go through the motions** to do something in an insincere or incomplete manner.
• **motion** *verb* to direct or gesture: *He motioned us to be quiet.*
Word Family **motionless** *adjective* still.
[from Latin]

motion picture *noun*
(*especially American*) a film, such as is shown in a cinema.

motive (mo-tiv) *noun*
something which causes a person to act in a particular way: *a motive for murder.*
• **motive** *adjective* of or causing motion: *Feet are the motive organs of most animals.*
Word Family **motivate** *verb* to provide with a motive or motives; **motivation** (mo-ti-**vay**-sh'n) *noun*.

mot juste (mo *zhoost*) *noun* (*plural* **mots justes**) (mo *zhoost*)
a word which expresses the exact meaning of something.
[French, exact word]

motley *adjective*
made up of very different parts: *a motley crowd.*

motor *noun*
a device which receives and converts energy, especially electricity, in order to drive machinery.
• **motor** *adjective*
1 operated by or used in a motor: *a motor vehicle.*
2 causing motion: *A motor nerve excites muscle movement.*
• **motor** *verb* (*informal*) to drive in a motor car.
[Latin, a mover]

motorbike *noun*
a motorcycle.

motor boat *noun*
a boat propelled by means of an engine.

motorcade *noun*
a procession of motor vehicles.
[MOTOR + (caval)CADE]

motor car *noun*
a car.
Word Family **motorist** *noun* a person
who drives a car.

motorcycle *noun*
a motor vehicle similar to a heavy bicycle.
Word Family **motorcyclist** *noun*.

motorize, motorise *verb*
to provide with a motor: *a motorized
wheelchair.*
Word Family **motorization** *noun*.

motor scooter ⇨ SCOOTER (definition 2).

motorway *noun*
a divided highway with several lanes, no
crossroads and limited entry and exit
points, designed to speed up the flow of
traffic.

mottled *adjective*
marked or covered with spots or blotches
of a different colour.

motto *noun (plural* **mottoes** *or* **mottos***)*
a word or sentence which expresses one's
rule or rules of conduct: *His motto was
'Never say die.'*
[Italian, word]

moue (moo) *noun*
a pouting grimace.
[French]

mould¹ (mold) *noun (American* **mold***)*
1 a hollow form into which a liquid is
poured and left to harden into the
required shape.
2 character, nature: *He is an actor in the
same mould as his father.*
● **mould** *verb* to model or form into the
required shape: *She moulded a head from
clay.*

mould² *noun (American* **mold***)*
a growth of minute fungi forming a furry
layer.

moulder *verb (American* **molder***)*
to decay or rot.

moulding *noun (American* **molding***)*
a line of ornamental plaster or woodwork
around a wall, window, etc.

mouldy *adjective* (**mouldier; mouldiest**)
covered with mould.

moult (molt) *verb (American* **molt***)*
(of an animal) to shed feathers, skin, etc.
which are replaced by new growth.

mound *noun*
1 a heap of earth, sand, stones, etc.
2 a natural elevation, such as a hillock or
knoll.

mount¹ *verb*
1 to ascend or climb onto: *He mounted his
horse.*
2 to fix something into a position, setting,
etc.: *to mount photographs in an album.*
3 to increase in amount: *Costs were
mounting rapidly.*
4 to stage or organize: *mounting a production
of 'Oliver!'* □ *mounting a campaign.*
● **mount** *noun*
1 a support, etc. on which something is
mounted.
2 a horse for riding.

mount² *noun*
a mountain: *Mount Kilimanjaro.*

mountain *noun*
1 an area of very high land rising to a
summit.
2 a large heap or pile.
[Latin *montis* of a mountain]

mountain ash *noun (plural* **mountain
ashes***)* ⇨ ROWAN.

mountain bike *noun*
a bicycle with thick deep-treaded tyres and
multiple gears, designed for riding on
mountainous or rough terrain.

mountaineer *noun*
a mountain climber.
Word Family **mountaineering** *noun*.

mountain lion *noun*
American a puma.

mountainous *adjective*
1 full of mountains.
2 huge or very high: *a mountainous pile of
rubbish.*

mountebank (mount-i-bank) *noun*
a quack or trickster.
[Italian *monta in banco* mount on a bench,
referring to a bench on which such a
person could be seen by an audience]

mourn (morn) *verb*
to grieve or feel sorrow, especially after
someone has died.
Word Family **mourner** *noun* a person
who mourns or attends a funeral;
mourning *noun* 1 sorrow. 2 the outward
signs of bereavement or grief, e.g. the
wearing of black clothes.

mournful *adjective*
exhibiting, expressing or feeling deep
sorrow.
Word Family **mournfully** *adverb*;
mournfulness *noun*.

mouse *noun* (*plural* **mice**)
1 a small rodent with a long hairless tail.
2 a shy or timid person.
3 (*plural* **mouses** or **mice**) a small box
connected to a computer, which can be
moved about a desk to control a cursor on
a screen and to enable the operator to
enter commands without keying.
[Latin *mus*]

mousetrap *noun*
1 a spring trap to catch mice, often baited
with cheese.
2 (*informal*) cheese which one considers is
only fit to be used in such a trap.

mousse (moose) *noun*
1 a light fluffy dish made with cream, eggs,
gelatin and flavouring, usually served
chilled: *chocolate mousse.* □ *salmon mousse.*
2 a foam or gel for cosmetic use.
[French, froth]

moustache (muss-**tahsh**) *noun* (*American*
mustache)
the hair on the face which grows above the
upper lip.
[Greek *mystakos* of the upper lip]

mousy *adjective* (**mousier**; **mousiest**) *also*
mousey
1 resembling a mouse in colour, etc.
2 timid.

mouth *noun*
1 *Biology* the opening through which food
is taken in.
2 an opening or entrance: *the mouth of a
cave.*
3 something which has the shape, position
or function of a mouth: *the mouth of a river.*
Phrase **down in the mouth** unhappy or
depressed.
● **mouth** (mou*th*) *verb*
1 to form words silently with the mouth.
2 to declaim or speak pompously.

mouth organ *noun* ⇨ HARMONICA.

mouthpiece *noun*
1 the part of something, such as a musical
instrument, which is placed near or in the
mouth.
2 someone who speaks for another person
or a company.

mouth-to-mouth resuscitation *noun*
a method of artificial respiration in which
one person breathes into the mouth of
another.

mouth-watering *adjective*
appetizing.

movable (moo-va-b'l) *adjective* also
moveable
1 able to be moved.
2 varying in date: *Easter is a movable feast.*
Word Family **movables** *plural noun*
personal property that can be moved from
the house, especially furniture.

move (moov) *verb*
1 to change place or position: *The branches
of the tree moved gently in the wind.*
2 to move to a new house.
3 to prompt: *What on earth moved you to do
it?*
4 to arouse, especially feelings of pity or
compassion: *We were moved by her sad
story.*
5 to make a formal proposal, suggestion,
etc.
● **move** *noun*
1 a movement: *One move and I'll shoot you.*
2 a turn in a game: *It's your move.*
Phrases **get a move on** hurry up! **make
a move** *It's time we made a move* (= began
to act). **on the move 1** *The troops are on the
move* (= moving). **2** *We had to have lunch
on the move* (= while moving).
[from Latin]

movement *noun*
1 the act, process or result of moving.
2 (**movements**) actions, activities: *I've
been following your movements.*
3 the organization of a group of people for
a special goal: *the anti-smoking movement.*
4 *Music* a main division of a symphony,
etc.

movie *noun*
(*especially American*) a film.
[shortening of *moving picture*]

moving *adjective*
1 in motion.
2 arousing pity, compassion, etc.
Word Family **movingly** *adverb*.

moving staircase *noun*
an escalator.

mow (mo) *verb* (**mows**; **mowing**; **mowed**;
mowed or **mown**)
to cut down grass, etc. with a scythe or
machine.
Phrase **mow down** to destroy or kill by
gunfire or by knocking down with a
vehicle.
Word Family **mower** *noun* a person or
device that mows.

mozzarella (mot-sa-**rel**-a) *noun*
a firm white Italian curd cheese.
[Italian *mozzare* to cut off]

Mr (**mis**-ta) *noun* (*plural* **Messrs**) (**mess**-'z)
a title for a man.

Mrs (**mi**-siz) *noun* (*plural* **Mesdames**) (**may**-**dahm**)
the title used before the name of a married woman.

Ms (m'z *or* miz) *noun*
the title used instead of 'Mrs' or 'Miss', especially when the woman's marital status is not known or is not relevant.

much *adjective* (**more**; **most**)
great in amount, size, etc.: *Did you have much trouble finding the shop?*
Phrase **much of a muchness** very similar.
• **much** *noun* a great amount or quantity: *Much of the work was difficult.*
• **much** *adverb*
1 greatly.
2 approximately.
Phrase **make much of** 1 *I didn't make much of the film* (= understand). 2 *You make too much of such a small thing* (= attach much importance to).

mucilage (**mew**-si-lij) *noun*
a sticky substance, such as glue.
Word Family **mucilaginous** (**mew**-si-**laj**-in-us) *adjective* sticky.
[Latin *mucus* nasal mucus]

muck *noun*
1 manure or dirt.
2 rubbish.
Phrases **muck about, muck around** to loaf or fool around. **muck out** to remove manure or dirt from stables, etc. **muck up** to spoil or ruin.
Word Family **mucky** *adjective* (**muckier**; **muckiest**) messy or dirty.

muckraking *noun*
finding out scandal or secrets in order to embarrass or discredit someone famous.

mucous membrane (**mew**-kus **mem**-brane) *noun*
Anatomy a lubricating membrane lining internal surfaces such as the nose and throat.

mucus (**mew**-kus) *noun*
a thick slimy secretion of a mucous membrane.
Word Family **mucous** *adjective*.
[Latin]

mud *noun*
soft wet earth.
Phrases **as clear as mud** not clear at all. **one's name is mud** one is in disgrace.

muddle *verb*
to confuse or mix up.

Phrases **muddle along, muddle through** to manage to cope, usually without organized planning.
• **muddle** *noun* a jumbled or confused state: *My mind is in a muddle.*
Word Family **muddler** *noun*.

muddle-headed *adjective*
vague or confused.

muddy *adjective* (**muddier**; **muddiest**)
1 covered with mud.
2 not clear or bright.
• **muddy** *verb* (**muddies**; **muddying**; **muddied**)
1 to make muddy.
2 to make less clear.

mudguard *noun*
a metal or plastic guard preventing mud or water being thrown outwards from the wheels of a vehicle.

mud pack *noun*
a face pack made from clay.

muesli (**mewz**-lee) *noun*
a breakfast food of cereals, nuts and dried fruits.
[Swiss German]

muezzin (moo-**ez**-in) *noun*
a caller who summons Muslims to prayers.
[Arabic *m'adhdhin* to call]

muff[1] *noun*
a cylindrical fur bag with open ends, used to keep the hands warm.

muff[2] *verb*
(*informal*) to bungle or do something clumsily.

muffin *noun*
1 a flat round spongy yeast cake, eaten toasted and buttered.
2 *American* a small cake: *blueberry muffins.*

muffle *verb*
1 to wrap or cover closely, as for warmth, etc.
2 to prevent or deaden sound by covering, wrapping, etc.: *muffled footsteps.*

muffler *noun*
1 a thick scarf.
2 something which muffles, such as a device fitted to a musical instrument.
3 *American* a silencer on an exhaust.

mufti (**muff**-ti) *noun*
civilian clothes worn by someone who usually wears a uniform.

mug *noun*
1 a large cup with a handle, used without a saucer.
2 (*informal*) a person who is easily fooled.
3 (*informal*) the face.

• **mug** *verb* (**mugs; mugging; mugged**)
(*informal*) to attack violently, usually in
order to rob: *The old man was mugged in the
dark alley.*
Word Family mugger *noun* a person who
mugs someone.

muggy *adjective* (**muggier; muggiest**)
humid and oppressive: *a muggy day.*

Muhammad (mu-**ham**-ad) *noun*
Islam the name of the final Prophet.

mulatto (mew-**lat**-o) *noun* (*plural*
mulattoes or **mulattos**)
a person who has one white and one black
parent.

mulberry *noun* (*plural* **mulberries**)
1 a tree, the leaves of which are fed to
silkworms.
2 its purple or white berry, similar to a
blackberry.
3 a dark reddish-purple colour.
Word Family mulberry *adjective.*

mulch *noun* (*plural* **mulches**)
a mixture of peat, leaves, straw, etc. spread
on gardens to protect plants or improve
the soil.
• **mulch** *verb* to spread or cover with a
mulch.

mulct *verb*
(*formal*) to deprive a person of something
by trickery.
[Latin *multare* to punish]

mule *noun*
1 the offspring of a male donkey and a
female horse. Compare HINNY.
2 a stubborn person.
3 also called **spinning mule**. a machine
that spins cotton.
Word Family muleteer (mew-li-**teer**)
noun a driver of mules; **mulish** *adjective*
stubborn.
[from Latin]

mull *verb*
to ponder or reflect: *I'll mull over what you
said.*

mulled wine *noun*
wine that has been heated with spices and
sugar.

mullet *noun*
any of a group of small edible fish.

mulligatawny *noun*
a spicy soup.
[Tamil, pepper-water]

mullion (**mull**-y'n) *noun*
an upright strip, often of wood or stone,
which divides windows or sections of
panelling.

multicoloured *adjective* (*American*
multicolored) also **multicolour**
(*American* **multicolor**)
having many colours.

multicultural *adjective*
relating to or consisting of people from
different cultural or ethnic groups.
Word Family multiculturalism *noun;*
multiculturally *adverb.*

multifaceted (mul-ti-**fass**-i-tid) *adjective*
having many aspects.

multifarious (mul-ti-**fair**-i-us) *adjective*
having many different parts, forms, etc.

multigrade *noun*
a motor oil which retains the same
thickness over a wide range of
temperatures.

multilateral *adjective*
having three or more parties taking part:
a multilateral agreement.

multilingual (mul-ti-**ling**-gw'l) *adjective*
1 able to speak three or more languages
fluently.
2 in several languages.

multimedia *noun*
the use of several media, e.g. text,
graphics, sound and video, to provide
information.
• **multimedia** *adjective.*

multimillionaire *noun*
a person who has at least two million
pounds, dollars, etc.

multinational (mult-i-**nash**-a-n'l)
adjective
operating within several countries.
• **multinational** *noun* a company
operating in several countries.

multiple *adjective*
having many parts, elements, etc.: *a multiple
fracture of the arm.*
• **multiple** *noun Maths* a number formed
by multiplying one number by any integer
4, 6 and *8 are multiples of 2.*

multiple-choice *adjective*
(of a question) followed by several possible
answers from which the correct one must
be chosen.

multiple sclerosis ⇨ SCLEROSIS
(definition 2).

multiplicity (mul-ti-**pliss**-i-tee) *noun*
(*plural* **multiplicities**)
a large number or variety.

multiply verb (**multiplies; multiplying; multiplied**)
1 to increase in number, amount, etc.: *Her debts have multiplied during the past year.*
2 *Maths* to repeat a number a given number of times in order to find the total: *2 multiplied by 4 (2 × 4 or 2 + 2 + 2 + 2) equals 8.*
Word Family **multiplication** noun; **multiplier** noun 1 a person or thing that multiplies 2 *Maths* the number by which another is multiplied.

multi-storey adjective
having many storeys: *a multi-storey car park.*

multitude (mul-ti-tewd) noun
a great number of people or things.
Word Family **multitudinous** (mul-ti-tew-di-nus) adjective.
[from Latin]

num¹ noun
(*informal*) a mother.

num² adjective
Phrase **keep mum** keep quiet: *Keep mum about what we did.*
• **mum** noun
Phrase **mum's the word** say nothing about it!

mumble verb
to mutter or speak indistinctly.
Word Family **mumble** noun; **mumblingly** adverb.

mumbo-jumbo noun
(*informal*) any meaningless speech or ritual.

> **Mumbo Jumbo** was said by traveller Mungo Park to be a deity worshipped by the Mandingo tribes of West Sudan. *Mama dyamba*, the African name of the god, was a grotesque idol who inspired great unthinking awe and fear. *Mumbo-jumbo* nowadays is used of high-sounding or complicated meaningless nonsense.

mummer noun
an old word for an actor in a traditional English folk play, especially in medieval times.

mummify (mum-i-fie) verb (**mummifies; mummifying; mummified**)
to make a dead body into a mummy by embalming.
Word Family **mummification** (mum-i-fi-**kay**-sh'n) noun.

mummy¹ noun (*plural* **mummies**)
(*informal*) a mother.

mummy² noun (*plural* **mummies**)
a dead body preserved by embalming or other methods, especially in ancient Egypt.
[Arabic *mum* embalming wax]

mumps plural noun
(*used with singular verb*) an infectious viral disease causing swelling of the face due to inflammation of the salivary glands.

munch verb
to chew steadily, vigorously and noisily.

mundane adjective
1 ordinary, unexciting: *a mundane job.*
2 of or relating to the world or earth.
[Latin *mundus* world]

mung bean noun
the edible green or yellow seeds of a variety of East Asian bean plant, which is the source of bean sprouts.
[Hindi]

municipal (mew-**niss**-i-p'l) adjective
of or relating to the local government of a town or city: *municipal elections.*

municipality (mew-niss-i-**pal**-i-tee) noun (*plural* **municipalities**)
a district with its own local government, such as a town or city.
[Latin *municipium*]

munificent (mew-**niff**-i-s'nt) adjective
extremely generous.
Word Family **munificently** adverb; **munificence** noun.
[Latin *munus* gift + *faciens* making]

munitions (mew-**nish**-'nz) plural noun
military stores, such as ammunition and weapons.
Word Family **munition** verb to provide with munitions.
[Latin *munitionis* of a fortification]

mural (**myoor** al) noun
a painting on a wall or ceiling.
[Latin *murus* wall]

murder noun
1 the deliberate killing of a person. Compare MANSLAUGHTER.
2 (*informal*) something extremely difficult or unpleasant: *It was murder trying to park my car near the football ground.*
• **murder** verb to kill deliberately.
Word Family **murderer** noun a person who has murdered someone; **murderess** noun a woman who has murdered someone; **murderous** adjective 1 capable of or intending to commit murder.
2 deadly.

murky *adjective* (**murkier; murkiest**)
dark or gloomy.
Word Family **murk** *noun* darkness;
murkiness *noun*.

murmur *verb*
1 to make a low continuous sound: *The
leaves murmured in the breeze.*
2 to speak very softly.
• **murmur** *noun*
1 the act or sound of murmuring: *a
murmur of disapproval.*
2 a murmuring of the heart revealed by a
stethoscope and indicating an
abnormality.
[Greek *mormyrein* to roar (of water)]

murti (**moor**-tee) *noun*
Hinduism the image or deity which is used
as a focus for worship.
[Sanskrit, embodiment]

muscat *noun*
1 a musk-flavoured grape.
2 a sweet white wine made from muscat
grapes.

muscatel (mus-ka-**tel**) *noun*
1 a muscat grape.
2 a raisin made from a muscat grape.
3 a sweet wine made from muscat grapes.

muscle (**muss**-'l) *noun*
Anatomy a tissue made up of bundles of
small fibres that contract to produce body
movement.
• **muscle** *verb* (*informal*) to force one's
way: *He muscled his way into a position of
power.*
[Latin *musculus* little mouse (from the
shape of some muscles)]

muscular (**musk**-yoo-la) *adjective*
1 of or affected by a muscle or muscles.
2 strong.
Word Family **muscularity** (musk-yoo-
larr-i-tee) *noun*.

muscular dystrophy *noun*
a genetic disease producing progressive
deterioration of the muscles.

muse (mewz) *verb*
to meditate or think deeply.
Word Family **musingly** *adverb*.

Muse *noun*
1 *Greek mythology* any of the nine
goddesses of the arts, e.g. of tragedy, song,
etc.
2 (**muse**) creative power.
[Greek *Mousa*]

museum (mew-**zee**-um) *noun*
a building for storing and exhibiting
objects of artistic, scientific or historical
interest.
[Greek *Mouseion* the abode of the Muses]

museum piece *noun*
a person or thing considered to be out of
date.

mush *noun* (*plural* **mushes**)
1 a thick soft mass: *The food had turned to
mush on her plate.*
2 something which is sickly sentimental.
Word Family **mushy** *adjective* (**mushier;
mushiest**); **mushiness** *noun*.

mushroom *noun*
1 an umbrella-shaped fungus, especially
an edible variety.
2 a pinkish-brown colour.
• **mushroom** *verb*
1 to spread or grow quickly: *new housing
developments mushrooming everywhere.*
2 to have or take on the shape of a
mushroom.
3 to gather mushrooms.

music (**mew**-zik) *noun*
1 a combination of sounds which express
ideas or emotions by the use of rhythm,
melody, etc.
2 the printed score of a musical
composition.
Phrase **face the music** to accept the
unpleasant consequences of one's actions.
[Greek *mousike* (*tekhné*) (art) of the
Muses]

musical *adjective*
1 of or producing music: *a musical
instrument.*
2 full of harmony or melody: *a musical
voice.*
3 fond of or skilled in music: *He is very
musical.*
• **musical** *noun* a play or film in which
songs are important.
Word Family **musically** *adverb*.

musical box *noun* (*plural* **musical boxes**)
a box with a mechanism which produces
tunes.

music centre *noun*
a radio, cassette player, compact disc
player and sometimes a turntable,
combined in one unit.

music hall *noun*
a theatre for variety entertainment.

musician (mew-**zish**-'n) *noun*
a person skilled or trained in music,
especially someone who plays an
instrument professionally.
Word Family **musicianship** *noun* skilful
musical performance.

musicology (mew-zi-**kol**-a-jee) *noun*
the study of the theory and history of
music.
Word Family **musicologist** *noun*.

musingly ⇨ MUSE.

musk *noun*
a strong-smelling powdery substance obtained from an Asian deer and used in perfumes.
Word Family **musky** *adjective* (**muskier; muskiest**).

musket *noun*
an early type of firearm fired from the shoulder.
Word Family **musketeer** (mus-ka-**teer**) *noun* a soldier armed with a musket.

musk melon *noun*
a yellow or green melon with a rough skin.
[the name is puzzling, as it has no taste or smell of musk]

musk ox *noun*
a large ox with a shaggy brownish-black coat, found in northern Canada and Greenland.

muskrat *noun*
a rat-like aquatic North American mammal with a musky smell. It is valued for its dark brown fur.

Muslim (**muz**-lim *or* **muz**-lim) *noun* also **Moslem**
a follower of Islam.
Word Family **Muslim** *adjective*.

muslin (**muz**-lin) *noun*
a fine cotton fabric.
[first made in *Mosul*, Iraq]

musquash *noun*
an old word for a muskrat.

muss *verb*
(*especially American informal*) to disarrange or rumple.

mussel *noun*
a black aquatic mollusc with two hinged shells.

must[1] *verb*
an auxiliary verb indicating obligation or necessity: *You must leave before midnight.*
• **must** *noun* (*informal*) something which is necessary: *Don't miss that film, it's a must!*

must[2] *noun*
wine before it has fermented.
[Latin *mustus* new (wine)]

must[3] *noun*
mould or staleness.
Word Family **musty** *adjective* (**mustier; mustiest**) stale.

mustang *noun*
a small wild horse of the western plains of North America, descended from Spanish stock.
[Spanish *mestengo* wild]

mustard *noun*
a paste made from the sharp hot seeds of certain plants, used in cooking or eaten with cold meat.

mustard gas *noun*
an oily liquid causing burns, blindness and death, used in chemical warfare.

muster *verb*
to summon or assemble: *to muster troops.*
□ *to muster all one's strength.*
• **muster** *noun* a gathering of troops.
Phrase **pass muster** to measure up to a required standard.
[Latin *monstrare* to show]

mustn't (**muss**-n't) *contraction*
a short form of **must not**: *You mustn't be late.*

must've *contraction*
a short form of **must have**: *She must've missed the train.*

> ! *Of* is sometimes incorrectly used instead of *'ve*: *You must have* or *must've* (not *must of*) *known.*

mutable (**mew**-ta-b'l) *adjective*
liable to change.
Word Family **mutability** (mew-ta-**bill**-i-tee) *noun*.

mutation (mew-**tay**-sh'n) *noun*
1 a change or alteration.
2 *Biology* a sudden change in a gene, chromosome structure or chromosome number, which, if it occurs in a gamete, may result in an individual with different features that can be passed on to the next generation.
Word Family **mutate** (mew-**tate**) *verb* to change; **mutant** *adjective* changing; **mutant** *noun*.
[Latin *mutare* to change]

mute *adjective*
1 not speaking or not able to speak.
2 silent: *The 'b' in 'doubt' is mute.*
• **mute** *noun*
1 (*dated*) a person who is unable to speak or make sounds.
2 *Music* a device, e.g. a clamp or pad, used to soften the sound of an instrument.
Word Family **mute** *verb* to soften or reduce the sound of; **muted** *adjective* soft, subdued; **mutely** *adverb*; **muteness** *noun*.
[from Latin]

mutilate (**mew**-ti-late) *verb*
to injure, disfigure or maim severely.
Word Family **mutilator** *noun* something which mutilates; **mutilation** (mew-ti-**lay**-sh'n) *noun*.
[from Latin]

mutiny (mew-ta-nee) *noun* (*plural* **mutinies**)
an open rebellion against authority, especially by soldiers or sailors against their officers.
• **mutiny** *verb* (**mutinies; mutinying; mutinied**) to rebel, to take part in a mutiny.
Word Family **mutinous** *adjective* rebellious; **mutineer** (mew-ta-**near**) *noun*.

mutt *noun*
1 (*informal*) a dog.
2 (*informal*) a foolish person.
[shortening of *muttonhead*]

mutter *verb*
to speak indistinctly or in a low voice.
• **mutter** *noun*.

mutton *noun*
the meat of a fully grown sheep.

mutton chop whiskers *plural noun*
a man's sideburns shaped like a chop, narrow at the top and wider at the bottom.

mutual (mew-tew-ul) *adjective*
shared or exchanged between two or more people or parties: *She and I have a mutual respect.*
Word Family **mutually** *adverb*; **mutuality** (mew-tew-**al**-i-tee) *noun*.
[Latin *mutuus* interchangeable]

Muzak (**mew**-zak) *noun*
(*trademark*) continuous taped music played in public places, e.g. shops or lifts.

muzzle *noun*
1 the open end of a gun, from which the bullet is discharged.
2 the snout of an animal.
3 an arrangement of straps, etc. put on an animal's mouth to prevent it from biting or eating.
• **muzzle** *verb* to put a muzzle on an animal.

muzzy *adjective* (**muzzier; muzziest**)
dazed or confused.
Word Family **muzzily** *adverb*; **muzziness** *noun*.

my *possessive adjective* (*plural* **our**)
belonging to me: *It is my book.*

myalgic encephalomyelitis (my-al-jik en-sef-al-o-my-el-**eye**-tiss) ⇨ CHRONIC FATIGUE SYNDROME.

mycology (my-**kol**-a-jee) *noun*
the study of fungi, a branch of botany.
Word Family **mycologist** *noun*.

mynah (**my**-na) *noun* also **myna**; also called **mynah bird**.
a bird from Asia or Australasia which mimics human speech, and is related to the starling.
[Hindi]

myopia (my-o-pee-a) *noun*
short-sightedness.
Word Family **myopic** (my-**op**-ik) *adjective*.
[Greek *myein* to shut + *ops* eye]

myriad (**mirr**-i-ad) *noun*
a poetic word for a very great number.
Word Family **myriad** *adjective* consisting of vast numbers.
[Greek *myrioi* ten thousand]

myrrh (*rhymes with* fur) *noun*
a fragrant resin obtained from a shrub and used for incense and perfume.
[from Greek]

myrtle (*rhymes with* turtle) *noun*
an evergreen shrub with black berries and fragrant white flowers.

myself *pronoun*
1 the reflexive form of **I**: *I washed myself.*
2 the emphatic form of **I**: *I did it myself.*
3 my normal or usual self: *I am not myself today.*

mysterious (mis-**teer**-i-us) *adjective*
puzzling, obscure or full of mystery: *a mysterious murder.*
Word Family **mysteriously** *adverb*.

mystery (**mist**-a-ree) *noun* (*plural* **mysteries**)
1 something that is puzzling, unknown or unexplained: *His disappearance is a mystery.*
2 a book, play or film about the solving of a crime.
3 (**mysteries**) ancient religions to which chosen followers were admitted by secret rites.
[Greek *mysterion* a secret doctrine]

mysticism (**mist**-i-sizm) *noun*
a belief in or practice of direct spiritual contact with divine things through contemplation or psychic experience.
Word Family **mystic** (**mist**-ik) *noun* a person who practises mysticism; **mystic**, **mystical** *adjective* 1 of hidden or mysteriously symbolic meaning: *ancient mystic ceremonies.* 2 of or relating to mysticism or mystics.
[Greek *mystes* an initiate]

mystify (**mist**-i-fie) *verb* (**mystifies; mystifying; mystified**)
to puzzle or bewilder: *She was mystified by his strange behaviour.*

Word Family **mystification** (mist-i-fi-kay-sh'n) *noun*.

mystique (mis-**teek**) *noun*
1 a mysterious or fascinating quality or power.
2 the secrets of an art or craft, known only to its practitioners.
[French]

myth (mith) *noun*
1 a traditional tale, usually about supernatural beings or events, sometimes used as an explanation of natural events.
2 a fictitious person or thing.
3 a popular belief: *the myth that women are worse drivers than men.*

Word Family **mythical** *adjective* 1 of or relating to myths. 2 imaginary or fictitious.
[Greek *mythos* a story]

mythology (mith-**ol**-a-jee) *noun* (*plural* **mythologies**)
a collection of myths, especially the myths of a particular religion or culture.
Word Family **mythological** *adjective* 1 of myths or mythology. 2 unreal; **mythologist** *noun*.

myxomatosis (mik-sa-ma-**toe**-sis) *noun*
an infectious viral disease in rabbits.
[Greek *myxa* mucus + *-oma* a tumour + *-osis*]

Nn

naan ⇨ NAN.

nab *verb* (**nabs; nabbing; nabbed**)
(*informal*) to catch or arrest.

nabob (**nay**-bob) *noun*
(*formerly*) any wealthy person, originally a British person who became rich in India.
[Arabic *na'ib* deputy]

nacho (**natch**-oh) *noun*
a piece of tortilla covered with melted cheese, chopped peppers, etc.
[Mexican Spanish]

nacre (**nay**-ka) *noun*
mother-of-pearl.
Word Family **nacreous** (**nay**-kree-us) *adjective* **1** of or relating to nacre. **2** (of minerals) having a lustre like nacre.

nadir (**nay**-deer) *noun*
Astronomy the lowest point on the celestial sphere, opposite the zenith.
Figurative The nadir of the king's fortunes came when he was deposed and humiliated (= the lowest point).
[Arabic]

naff *adjective*
(*informal*) lacking in style or taste.

nag¹ *verb* (**nags; nagging; nagged**)
1 to irritate by constant fault-finding, complaints or requests.
2 to cause discomfort or pain: *Financial worries nagged at her all day.*
• **nag** *noun* a person who nags.
Word Family **naggingly** *adverb*; **nagger** *noun*.

nag² *noun*
(*informal*) a horse, especially an old or worthless one.

nail *noun*
1 a metal pin with a flat head, usually used to join two or more objects together.
2 *Anatomy* a tough horny growth strengthening the upper tip of the fingers and toes.
Phrases **hit the nail on the head** to say exactly the right thing. **pay cash on the nail** (*informal*) to pay immediately in cash.

• **nail** *verb* to fasten something with nails.
Figurative Terror nailed him to the spot (= fixed firmly). □ The inspector was determined to nail the cat burglar (= catch, arrest).

nail bomb *noun*
a bomb containing nails, designed to cause widespread damage and injury.

naive (nie-**eev**) *adjective* also **naïve**
unaffectedly or unsophisticatedly simple and artless.
Word Family **naively** *adverb*; **naivety** (nie-**ee**-va-tee) *noun*.
[French]

naked (**nay**-kid) *adjective*
having no clothing or covering: *naked hills stripped of vegetation.* □ The naked wound gaped open.
Figurative Snowfields lay before us as far as the naked eye could see (= unassisted by optical instruments). □ Few people want to hear the naked truth about themselves (= plain, blunt).
Word Family **nakedly** *adverb*; **nakedness** *noun*.

namby-pamby *adjective*
sentimental or insipid: *a namby-pamby mother's boy.*

name *noun*
the word by which a person or thing is known.
Figurative She called him all the names she could think of (= insulting terms). □ He has a good name in business circles (= reputation). □ His show was full of big names (= famous people).
Phrases **in the name of** by the authority of: *Open in the name of the law.* **take someone's name in vain** to use someone's name disrespectfully: *How dare you take my father's name in vain!* **to one's name** belonging to one: *I haven't got a penny to my name.*
• **name** *verb*
1 to give a name to: *I name this child John.*
2 to state the correct name of: *Can you name all the states in America?*
3 to specify: *Shall we name the day of our wedding?*
Phrase **name and shame** to state the names of people or organizations so that they have to take responsibility for their actions.

name-dropper *noun*
a person who talks about well-known people as if they were personal friends, in order to impress others.

nameless *adjective*
  1 not having a name: *a nameless grave*.
  2 not named or specified: *a certain person,
  who shall remain nameless*.
  Word Family **namelessly** *adverb*;
  namelessness *noun*.

namely *adverb*
  that is to say: *the UK's two largest cities,
  namely, London and Birmingham*.

namesake *noun*
  a person having the same name as another.

nan *noun* also **naan**
  a flat oval-shaped bread, usually eaten
  with Indian food.
  [Hindi]

nanny *noun* (*plural* **nannies**)
  a person who is trained to look after
  children as a job.

nanny goat *noun*
  a female goat. Compare BILLY GOAT.

nanny state *noun*
  a government regarded as patronizing and
  interfering.

nap[1] *verb* (**naps**; **napping**; **napped**)
  1 to have a short sleep.
  2 to be off one's guard: *That remark caught
  me napping*.
  • **nap** *noun* a short sleep.

nap[2] *noun*
  a surface on a fabric, made by raising all
  the short fibres in it and then cutting and
  smoothing them.
  • **nap** *verb* (**naps**; **napping**; **napped**) to
  raise a nap on.

napalm (nay-pahm) *noun*
  a jelly-like incendiary substance mixed
  with petrol, used in bombs, flame-
  throwers, etc.

nape *noun*
  Anatomy the back of the neck.

napery (nay-pa-ree) *noun*
  an old word meaning 'household linen'.

napkin *noun*
  1 short form of **table napkin** a serviette.
  2 (*dated*) a nappy.

nappy *noun* (*plural* **nappies**)
  short form of **napkin** a piece of towel or
  an absorbent paper pad, worn by a baby
  underneath or instead of pants.

narcissism (nar-sis-izm) *noun*
  an extreme self-love.
  Word Family **narcissist** *noun*;
  narcissistic (nar-si-**sis**-tik) *adjective*.

narcissus (nar-**siss**-us) *noun* (*plural*
  narcissi (nar-**siss**-eye) or **narcissuses**)
  any of a group of flowers including
  jonquils and daffodils.

> The word **narcissus** takes its name
> from a legend. The story is that a
> handsome Greek youth fell in love with
> his own reflection in a pool. Unable to
> take hold of the beautiful creature that
> he thought he could see in the water, he
> pined away and died, leaving a flower in
> his place. The story also gives us the
> word *narcissism*, a feeling of excessive
> admiration for oneself.

narcosis (nar-ko-sis) *noun*
  Medicine the state of being sleepy or
  drowsy due to some external cause, such
  as gases, drugs, etc.
  [Greek *narkosis* a benumbing]

narcotic (nar-kot-ik) *noun*
  a substance which is often habit-forming
  and dulls the senses, relieves pain or
  induces sleep. In large amounts it
  produces complete insensibility.
  • **narcotic** *adjective* producing narcosis.

nark *noun*
  (*informal*) a person who spies, especially
  for the police.
  • **nark** *verb* (*informal*) to nag or irritate.
  Word Family **narky** *adjective* (*informal*)
  irritated.
  [Romany *nak* a nose]

narrate (na-**rate**) *verb*
  to tell the story of an event, experience,
  etc.
  Word Family **narrative** (**narr**-a-tiv)
  noun 1 a recounting of events, experiences,
  etc. 2 the subject matter of a narrative;
  narrator *noun*; **narration** *noun* 1 a
  narrative. 2 the act or process of
  narrating.
  [Latin *narrare* to make known]

narrow *adjective*
  not broad or wide: *a narrow corridor*.
  Figurative He's really a very narrow person
  (= limited in views or sympathies). □ *a
  narrow escape* (= close).
  • **narrow** *verb* to make or become
  narrower: *The path narrows near the hedge*.
  *Figurative They narrowed down the list of
  suspects to two or three* (= limited or
  restricted).
  Word Family **narrowly** *adverb*;
  narrowness *noun*.

narrow-minded *adjective*
  prejudiced or intolerant.

Word Family **narrow-mindedly** *adverb*;
narrow-mindedness *noun*.

narwhal (**nar**-wul) *noun*
an aquatic mammal found in the Arctic,
the male having a long tusk extending
from the upper jaw.

nasal (**nay**-z'l) *adjective*
1 of or relating to the nose.
2 *Language* of or relating to the making of
sounds through the nose, in letters such as
m, *n* or *ng*.
• **nasal** *noun* a nasal speech sound.
Word Family **nasally** *adverb*.
[Latin *nasus* nose]

nascent (**nass**-ent *or* **nay**-sunt) *adjective*
(*formal*) beginning to exist, grow or
develop: *a nascent idea.*
[Latin *nascens* being born]

nasturtium (na-**ster**-sh'm) *noun*
any of a group of garden plants with showy
yellow, red or orange flowers and large
edible leaves.
[Latin *nasturcium* cress]

nasty (**nah**-stee) *adjective* (**nastier**;
nastiest)
1 disagreeable or unpleasant: *There is a
nasty stain on the carpet.* □ *He really is a
nasty little boy.*
2 rather severe: *He came home from school
with a nasty cut on his leg.*
Word Family **nastily** *adverb*; **nastiness**
noun.

natal (**nay**-t'l) *adjective*
(*formal*) of or relating to a person's birth.
[Latin *natus* born]

nation (**nay**-sh'n) *noun*
a large group of people united by some or
all factors such as history, government,
race, language or geography.
Word Family **national** (**nash**-a-n'l)
adjective of or relating to a nation;
national *noun* a citizen of a particular
nation: *She's a French national.*
[Latin *natio* birth, a race]

national anthem *noun*
a song adopted by a country to express
patriotism and loyalty.

national curriculum *noun*
the curriculum of study prescribed for
state schools in England and Wales.

national debt *noun*
the total debt of a government, consisting
of government stocks, National Savings
and all other loans.

nationalism (**nash**-na-lizm) *noun*
1 a sense of national unity.

2 a political movement to assert the right
of one's country to full independence.
Compare INTERNATIONALISM.
Word Family **nationalist** *noun*;
nationalistic (nash-na-**list**-ik) *adjective*.

nationality (nash-a-**nall**-a-tee) *noun*
(*plural* **nationalities**)
1 the fact of belonging to or being born in
a particular country.
2 the status of belonging to a nation by
birth or naturalization.
3 a nation or people: *the various
nationalities of Africa.*

nationalize, nationalise (**nash**-na-lize)
verb
to make privately owned land, industries,
etc. the property of the nation.
Word Family **nationalization** (nash-na-
lie-**zay**-sh'n) *noun*.

nationally *adverb*
on a national scale.

national park *noun*
an area of land set aside by a government
to preserve the natural features, wildlife,
etc. of the area for public enjoyment.

national service *noun*
any compulsory military training or
service for young people.

nationhood *noun*
the state of being a nation.

nationwide *adjective, adverb*
happening in all parts of a country:
a nationwide strike. □ *The film opens
nationwide on Friday.*

native (**nay**-tiv) *adjective*
1 relating to the place where one was born:
This is my native country.
2 (*sometimes* **Native**) belonging to a race
regarded as the original inhabitants of a
country: *a Native American.*
3 occurring naturally: *the plants native to
these parts.*
4 belonging by birth: *English is my native
tongue.*
5 natural, inborn: *Her native intelligence has
never really been tapped.*
• **native** *noun*
1 a person who is born in a particular
place: *I am a native of Ireland.*
2 one of the original inhabitants of a
country. This term is often considered
offensive.
3 a plant or animal occurring naturally in a
region or country.
[Latin *nativus* born, natural, inborn]

nativity (na-**tivv**-i-tee) *noun* (*plural*
nativities)
1 (**Nativity**) *Christianity* the birth of
Christ or the festival commemorating this.
2 an old word for **birth**.

natter *verb*
(*informal*) to chatter or gossip.
• **natter** *noun* (*informal*) a chat.

natty *adjective* (**nattier; nattiest**)
(*informal*) neat or trim.
Word Family **nattily** *adverb*.

natural (**natch**-a-r'l) *adjective*
1 existing in or produced by nature: *a
natural ability.* □ *He died of natural causes.*
2 concerned with nature: *natural history.*
3 in accordance with circumstances, etc.:
*An accident was the natural result of such
carelessness.*
4 based on instinct: *Anger is a natural
response to provocation.*
5 illegitimate: *a natural son.*
6 lifelike, unaffected: *It was a natural piece
of acting.*
7 *Music* (of a note) neither sharp nor flat.
8 *Music* (of a horn, etc.) not having valves
or keys and so producing the notes
dictated by the length of the tube.
natural hazard a natural risk or source of
danger which threatens people, e.g. the
risk caused by living in an earthquake
zone.
natural increase the growth of a
population calculated by subtracting the
death rate from the birth rate.
• **natural**
1 a person or thing that is naturally suited
or qualified: *She's a natural for the part.*
2 *Music* a note that is not affected by either
a sharp or flat.
3 *Music* a symbol placed before a note
cancelling the effect of a previous sharp or
flat.
4 *Music* (on a keyboard instrument) a
white key.

natural gas *noun*
a mixture of hydrocarbon gases, usually
containing methane, found under the
earth or seabed near oil deposits and used
as fuel and in making organic compounds.

natural history *noun*
the study of animal or plant life.

naturalism (**natch**-er-a-lizm) *noun*
1 *Art, Literature* a form of realism.
2 *Philosophy* the belief that all things occur
naturally and are unrelated to external or
divine forces.

naturalist *noun*
a person who studies natural history,
especially in the natural environment
rather than in a laboratory, e.g. a zoologist
or a botanist.

naturalistic *adjective*
1 of or in accordance with nature.
2 of or relating to natural history or
naturalists.

naturalized, naturalised *adjective*
having become, by law, a citizen of another
country, with all the rights of a person of
that nationality.
Word Family **naturalization** (natch-er-
al-eye-**zay**-sh'n) *noun*; **naturalize** *verb*.

naturally *adverb*
1 in a natural manner: *Even though you will
be nervous, try to act naturally.*
2 of course: *Naturally, I would have nothing
to do with such an offer.*
3 by nature: *He is naturally obedient and
courteous.*

naturalness *noun*
the state of being natural.
[from Latin]

natural philosophy *noun*
an old term for the physical sciences,
especially physics.

natural rubber ⇨ **rubber**¹ (definition 1).

natural science *noun*
the study of natural or physical objects,
e.g. chemistry, physics or geology.

natural selection *noun* also called
survival of the fittest.
Biology Darwin's theory that only those
plants and animals which are best adapted
to their environment survive to breed,
and so, through inheritance, their
characteristics become established in
future generations. This process is the
main agent of evolutionary change.
⇨ DARWINISM.

nature (**nay**-cher) *noun*
1 the essential character of something: *the
nature of a chemical compound.* □ *He has a
forgiving nature.*
2 (*often* **Nature**) the material world and all
things contained in it except those made
by man.
3 (*often* **Nature**) all the forces at work
throughout the material world: *Scientists
may study the laws of nature.*
4 sort: *I didn't intend anything of that nature
by my remarks.*
Phrase **in the nature of** like: *A bonus is
something in the nature of a reward.*
[Latin *natura* blood relationship, quality,
disposition, the world]

naturism ⇨ NUDISM.

naturopathy (nay-cher-**opp**-a-thee) *noun*
a method of treating disease which uses
herbal remedies, vitamins, etc. to assist the
body's own natural healing forces.
Word Family **naturopath** (**nay**-cher-a-
path) *noun*; **naturopathic** (nay-cher-a-
path-ik) *adjective*.

naught (nawt) *noun*
an old word for **nothing**. Compare
NOUGHT.
Phrase **set at naught** to consider as
being of no importance.

naughty (**naw**-tee) *adjective* (**naughtier;
naughtiest**)
1 disobedient or full of mischief: *They were
naughty children.*
2 (*informal*) improper: *a naughty word.*
Word Family **naughtily** *adverb*;
naughtiness *noun*.

nausea (**naw**-si-a) *noun*
1 a feeling of sickness in the stomach,
often followed by vomiting.
2 a feeling of extreme disgust or loathing.
Word Family **nauseate** *verb* to cause
nausea in; **nauseous** (**naw**-si-us) *adjective*
causing or feeling nausea.
[Greek *nausia* seasickness]

nautical (**naw**-ti-k'l) *adjective*
of or relating to sailors, ships or
navigation.
Word Family **nautically** *adverb*.
[Greek *nautes* sailor]

nautilus (**naw**-ti-lus) *noun* (*plural*
nautiluses or **nautili** (**naw**-ti-lie))
any of a group of aquatic molluscs related
to the cuttlefish, having a spiral
chambered shell with pearly walls.
[Greek *nautilos* sailor]

naval (**nay**-v'l) *adjective*
1 of or relating to a navy: *naval affairs.*
2 having a navy: *the great naval powers.*
[Latin *navalis* relating to a ship]

nave¹ *noun*
the main body of a church between the
aisles, stretching from the entrance to the
chancel.

nave² *noun*
the hub or central part of a wheel.

navel *noun* also called **belly button**
(*informal*); **umbilicus** (*formal*).
Anatomy the small pit in the centre of the
abdomen left by the breaking of the
umbilical cord at birth.

navigate (**navv**-i-gate) *verb*
1 to guide the direction and speed of a
ship, aeroplane, etc.
2 to sail through or over: *The canal cannot
be navigated by large ships.*
Word Family **navigation** (navv-i-**gay**-
sh'n) *noun* the act or art of navigating;
navigational *adjective*; **navigable** (**navv**-
i-ga-b'l) *adjective* (of waters, vessels, etc.)
capable of being navigated; **navigability**
(navv-i-ga-**bill**-i-tee) *noun*.
[Latin *navis* ship + *agere* to drive]

navigator *noun*
1 a person who practises, or is skilled in,
navigation.
2 an old word for a sea explorer.

navvy *noun* (*plural* **navvies**)
(*dated*) a labourer who makes roads,
railways, etc.

navy (**nay**-vee) *noun* (*plural* **navies**)
the part of the armed forces of a country
that is organized for fighting at sea.
[Latin *navis* a ship]

navy blue *noun*
short form is **navy** a dark blackish-blue
colour.

nawab (na-**wahb**) *noun*
(*formerly*) a deputy governor in India.
[Arabic *na'ib* deputy]

nay *adverb*
an old word for **no**.

Nazi (**naht**-see) *noun*
a member of the National Socialist Party
in Germany which, led by Adolf Hitler,
gained political control of the country in
1933.
Word Family **Nazism** (**naht**-sizm) *noun*.
[German N_A(*tionalso*)z_I(*alist*)]

Neanderthal (nee-**and**-a-tahl) *noun*
an extinct species of human being.
[the remains were first found at
Neanderthal, a valley in Germany]

neap tide ⇨ TIDE *noun* (definition 1).

near *adverb, preposition, adjective*
at, within or to a short distance: *They live
quite near.* □ *Stand near me.*
Figurative He is a very near and dear
friend (= intimate). □ *It's odd discovering a
near relative you never knew you had*
(= closely related).
• **near** *verb* to come within a short
distance: *He leapt ashore as the boat neared
the jetty.*
Word Family **nearly** *adverb* 1 all but: *He
nearly perished from hunger.* 2 not distantly,
as in space, time, condition, etc.: *His story
approximated very nearly to the facts.*

Phrase **not nearly** *That's not nearly enough money to live on for a week* (= far from); **nearness** *noun*.

nearby *adjective, adverb*
not far away.

near miss *noun* (*plural* **near misses**)
1 something that just fails to hit the target.
2 a situation in which two aircraft narrowly miss a mid-air collision.

nearside *noun*
1 the left-hand side of a vehicle where traffic drives on the left. Compare OFFSIDE *noun* (definition 1).
2 the left side of a horse. Compare OFFSIDE *noun* (definition 2).
[originally the side from which one mounts a horse]

near-sighted *adjective*
short-sighted.
Word Family **near-sightedly** *adverb*; **near-sightedness** *noun*.

neat[1] *adjective*
1 tidy or orderly: *a neat desk*.
2 clever: *a neat trick*.
3 undiluted or unadulterated: *He drinks neat gin*.
4 *American* (*informal*) excellent.
Word Family **neatly** *adverb*; **neatness** *noun*; **neaten** *verb*.
[Latin *nitidus* shining]

neat[2] *noun* (*plural* **neats** or **neat**)
an old word for a member of the cattle family.

neath *preposition*
a poetic word for **beneath**.

neb *noun*
1 *Scottish* a nose.
2 the beak of a bird.

nebula (neb-yoo-la) *noun* (*plural* **nebulae**) (neb-yoo-lee)
Astronomy a cloudy luminous or dark patch consisting of gas and dust in the night sky. Most nebulae are the birthplaces of stars.
Word Family **nebular** *adjective*.
[Latin]

nebulizer, nebuliser *noun*
a device which produces a fine spray of a medicinal liquid for inhaling.

nebulous (neb-yoo-lus) *adjective*
1 vague or unclear.
2 *Astronomy* cloudy.
Word Family **nebulously** *adverb*; **nebulousness** *noun*.

necessary (ness-is-ree) *adjective*
indispensable or unavoidable: *Food is necessary for life*.
● **necessary** *noun* (*plural* **necessaries**) (*usually* **necessaries**) a necessary thing: *Food and clothing are necessaries of existence*.
Word Family **necessarily** *adverb*.

necessitate (nis-ess-a-tate) *verb*
to make something necessary: *His sudden collapse necessitated calling an ambulance*.

necessity (nis-ess-i-tee) *noun* (*plural* **necessities**)
1 something that is necessary: *Food is a necessity for life*.
2 the fact of being necessary: *We all agree on the necessity of eating well-balanced meals*.
3 any circumstances that compel a person to do something: *Necessity forced him to steal*.
[Latin *necesse* needful]

neck *noun*
1 *Anatomy* the part of the body that connects the head to the shoulders.
2 the part of a garment covering or extending around the neck.
3 something which has the shape, position or function of a neck: *the neck of a bottle*.
□ *the neck of a violin*.
Phrase **neck and neck** (of two or more people, teams, etc.) level in a race, competition, struggle, etc. **neck of the woods** (*informal*) a particular area or region. **stick one's neck out** to act, express an opinion, etc. in such a way as to expose oneself to danger, criticism or hostility.
● **neck** *verb* (*informal*) to hug and kiss amorously.

necklace *noun*
an ornament for the neck, often a string of beads, pearls or jewels.

necromancy (nek-ro-man-see) *noun*
1 in ancient times, a method of divination by summoning up the dead to ask them about the future.
2 (by confusion of *necro-* with *negro-*) black magic.
Word Family **necromancer** *noun*; **necromantic** (nek-ro-**man**-tik) *adjective*.
[Greek *nekros* a corpse + *manteia* divination]

necropolis (nek-**ropp**-a-lis) *noun* (*plural* **necropolises**)
an ancient cemetery.
[Greek *nekros* corpse + *polis* city]

necrosis (nek-ro-sis) *noun*
Biology the death of a tissue.

Word Family necrotic (nek-**rot**-ik)
adjective.
[Greek *nekrosis* a killing]

nectar *noun*
1 *Biology* the sugary substance that attracts
insects and is produced by many flowers.
2 *Ancient mythology* the drink of the gods.
[Greek]

nectarine (**nek**-ta-rin *or* **nek**-ta-reen)
noun
a small fruit with a smooth red and yellow
skin, resembling a peach but with a firmer
texture.
[from NECTAR]

née (nay) *adjective*
born, used to indicate a married woman's
maiden name: *Mrs Browning, née Barrett.*
[French]

need *noun*
1 a want, requirement or necessity: *He
acted promptly to meet the needs of the
situation.* □ *There's no need to worry.*
2 a situation or time of difficulty: *We would
all try and help a friend in need.*
• **need** *verb*
1 to be in need of: *We all need love.* □ *Does
he need any help?*
2 to be obliged: *You need not go home yet.*
Word Family needful *adjective* (*formal*)
necessary; **needless** *adjective* unnecessary;
needlessly *adverb;* **needn't** *contraction* a
short form of **need not**.

needle *noun*
1 a small slender steel object used for
sewing, pointed at one end and with a hole
at the other for carrying thread.
2 *Medicine* a hypodermic needle.
3 something which has the shape of a
needle: *a pine needle.*
4 *Audio* ⇨ STYLUS.
Phrase **needle in a haystack** something
unlikely to be found: *It was like looking for a
needle in a haystack.*
• **needle** *verb* (*informal*) to tease or annoy.

needlepoint *noun*
an embroidery stitch in which small
stitches cover the whole canvas to
resemble tapestry.

needlewoman *noun* (*plural*
needlewomen)
a woman skilled in needlework.

needlework *noun*
any sewing or embroidery.

needs *adverb*
Phrase **must needs** to have to do
something of necessity.

needy *adjective* (**needier; neediest**)
very poor.
Word Family neediness *noun.*

ne'er (nair) *adverb*
a poetic word for **never**.

ne'er-do-well *noun*
a worthless person.

nefarious (nif-**air**-i-us) *adjective*
(*formal*) very wicked.
Word Family nefariously *adverb;*
nefariousness *noun.*
[Latin *nefarius* impious]

negate (nig-**ate**) *verb*
1 to make ineffective or futile: *His efforts to
help them were negated by their distrust.*
2 to contradict or prove untrue: *Later
evidence negated my theory.*
Word Family negation (nig-**ay**-sh'n)
noun 1 the act of negating. 2 a denial or
negative statement. 3 the absence or
opposite of something.

negative (**negg**-a-tiv) *adjective*
1 expressing denial or refusal: *He gave a
negative answer to my question.*
Figurative *a negative chest X-ray*
(= showing no sign of disease). □ *Negative
criticism is useless* (= not helpful or
constructive).
2 *Maths* relating to a quantity less than
zero: *–3 is a negative number.*
3 *Electricity* having an excess of electrons.
• **negative** *noun*
1 something which is negative.
2 *Photography* an image on a developed
film in which the dark parts are light and
the light parts dark. Compare POSITIVE
noun (definition 2).
Word Family negatively *adverb;*
negativeness, negativity (neg-a-**tivv**-i-
tee) *noun;* **negativism** (**neg**-a-tiv-izm)
noun the quality of denying or being
negative in ideas or behaviour; **negativist**
noun.
[Latin *negare* to deny]

neglect (nig-**lekt**) *verb*
to ignore, disregard or leave uncared for:
She neglected her duties.
Word Family neglect *noun;* **neglectful**
adjective; **neglectfully** *adverb;*
neglectfulness *noun.*
[Latin *neglectus* unheeded]

negligee (**neg**-li-zhay) *noun*
a woman's dressing gown of very thin
fabric.
[French]

negligent (neg-li-j'nt) *adjective*
(*formal*) taking too little care: *The accident happened because he was negligent.*
Word Family **negligently** *adverb*;
negligence *noun* **1** failure to take proper care. **2** an instance of this.

negligible (neg-li-ja-b'l) *adjective*
unimportant or very little: *a negligible sum of money.*
Word Family **negligibly** *adverb*.

negotiate (nig-oh-shee-ate) *verb*
1 to bargain or confer with others to reach mutual agreement.
2 to succeed in getting over or past: *The hurdler successfully negotiated all the jumps.*
Word Family **negotiation** (nig-oh-shee-ay-sh'n) *noun* mutual discussion and bargaining; **negotiable** (nig-oh-sha-b'l) *adjective* **1** able to be negotiated: *The salary for the job is negotiable.* **2** *Commerce* (of a cheque) able to be transferred from one person to another; **negotiability** (nig-oh-sha-**bill**-i-tee) *noun*.
[Latin *negotium* business]

Negro (nee-gro) *noun* (*plural* **Negroes**)
one of a race of dark-skinned people, originally from Africa.
Word Family **Negroid** *adjective* like or relating to a Negro or the Negro race;
Negress *noun* (*plural* **Negresses**) a female Negro.
[Spanish, black]

> **Negro** is a term that is considered offensive nowadays. The preferred term is *black* or *Afro-Caribbean* in Britain, or *African American* in America.

neigh (nay) *noun*
the cry of a horse.
• **neigh** *verb*.

neighbour (nay-ba) *noun* (*American* **neighbor**)
1 a person who lives next door or close to another.
2 any person or thing that is near another: *France and Spain are neighbours.*
• **neighbour** *verb* to live or be situated near.
Word Family **neighbourly** *adjective* friendly and helpful: *neighbourly advice*;
neighbourhood *noun* **1** a district or locality: *This is a wealthy neighbourhood.*
2 the people living in a particular district: *Do you want the whole neighbourhood to hear?*

neighbourhood watch *noun* (*plural* **neighbourhood watches**)
an association formed by residents in a district in conjunction with the police, intended to reduce or prevent local crime by people being vigilant and security-conscious.

neither (nigh-*th*a or nee-*th*a) *adjective, pronoun, adverb*
not one or the other of two things: *Neither twin is well-behaved.*

> **!** In formal English, *neither ... nor* should be followed by a singular verb (*Neither James nor Sarah was present*) unless at least one of the alternatives referred to is plural (*Neither accommodation nor refreshments were provided*). Note that *neither* is followed by *nor*, not *or*.

nelson *noun*
Wrestling a hold in which one arm (**half-nelson**) or both arms (**full nelson**) are placed under the opponent's armpit from behind, and then up onto the back of his or her neck.

nemesis (nemm-a-sis) *noun* (*plural* **nemeses** (nemm-a-seez)
1 retribution by fate for wrongdoing.
2 (**Nemesis**) *Greek mythology* the goddess who allotted good and bad fortune and saw to it that great good fortune was offset by subsequent disaster.
[Greek *nemein* to give what is due]

Neolithic ⇨ STONE AGE.
[neo- + Greek *lithos* a stone]

neologism (nee-oll-a-jizm) *noun*
1 (*formal*) a new word or phrase.
2 the introduction of new words or phrases.
Word Family **neologize, neologise** *verb*;
neologist *noun*.
[neo- + Greek *logos* a word]

neon (nee-on) *noun*
a colourless odourless inert gas found in tiny amounts in the earth's atmosphere and used in some electric lights.

neophyte (nee-a-fite) *noun*
(*formal*) a person who has newly entered a religious faith or order.
[neo- + Greek *phytos* planted]

neoplasm *noun*
an abnormal growth of tissue in the body.

nephew (nef-yoo) *noun*
1 a son of one's brother or sister.
2 a son of one's husband's or wife's brother or sister. Compare NIECE.
[Latin *nepos* descendant]

nephritis (nif-**rye**-tis) *noun*
a group of diseases causing the kidneys to function inefficiently.
Word Family **nephritic** (nif-**ritt**-ik) *adjective*.
[Greek *nephros* kidney + -*itis*]

nepotism (**nepp**-a-tizm) *noun*
undue favour shown to relatives, e.g. by giving them jobs, etc.
Word Family **nepotist** *noun*.
[Latin *nepos* a descendant]

Neptune *noun*
Astronomy the planet in the solar system eighth from the sun.
[after *Neptune*, the Roman god of the sea]

nerd *noun*
(*informal*) a stupid, boring or socially inept person.

nerve *noun*
1 a cord-like bundle of nerve cells.
2 courage or self-possession: *It took nerve to climb that mountain.*
3 (*informal*) impudence or impertinence: *What a nerve to insult me like that!*
4 (**nerves**) nervousness: *She suffers from nerves.*
Phrases **get on someone's nerves** (*informal*) to irritate or annoy someone.
lose one's nerve suddenly to lose one's self-confidence.
• **nerve** *verb* to give strength or courage to.
Word Family **nerveless** *adjective*
1 without feeling. 2 confident. 3 *Biology* without nerves.
[Latin *nervus* a sinew]

nerve cell *noun* also called **neuron; neurone**.
Anatomy a long single cell within the body of an animal which sends messages from one part of the body to another.

nerve centre *noun*
Anatomy a place where a number of nerves join together, such as a plexus, the brain or the spinal cord.

nerve-racking *adjective* also **nerve-wracking**
extremely frightening and stressful.

nervous *adjective*
1 uneasy or afraid of something: *I feel nervous in the dark.*
2 highly excitable: *a nervous girl who laughs hysterically at nothing at all.*
3 *Psychology* of or relating to the nerves and disorders of the nerves or personality.
Word Family **nervously** *adverb*;
nervousness *noun*.

nervous breakdown *noun*
any of various psychiatric disorders resulting in loss of emotional control.

nervous system *noun*
the system of nerve cells and fibres which transmits impulses between parts of the body.
autonomic nervous system the part of the nervous system which controls the unconscious activities of the heart, intestines, glands, etc.
central nervous system the brain and spinal cord, which act as the body's switchboard for incoming messages and outgoing commands.
peripheral nervous system the network of nerves all over the body.

nervy *adjective* (**nervier; nerviest**)
nervous or tense.

nescience (**ness**-i-ence) *noun*
a poetic word for *ignorance*.
Word Family **nescient** *adjective*.

ness *noun* (*plural* **nesses**)
an old word for a headland or cape.

nest *noun*
1 a structure made by birds for hatching and rearing their young.
2 the breeding place of an animal or insect.
3 a group of articles designed to fit within each other when not in use, such as tables.
Phrase **feather one's nest** to make things comfortable for oneself.
• **nest** *verb*.

nest egg *noun*
a sum of money saved for emergencies, etc.

nestle (**ness**-'l) *verb*
1 to settle down comfortably: *He nestled down in the armchair.*
2 to cuddle: *The old lady nestled the baby in her arms.*

nestling (**nest**-ling) *noun*
a bird too young to leave the nest.

net[1] *noun*
1 a lace-like mesh of thread, wire, etc.: *a fishing net.*
2 *Sport* a barrier made of net that is stretched across the width of a court over which a ball, shuttlecock, etc. must be hit.
3 *Sport* an area covered with net into which a ball must be hit, thrown or kicked.
4 (**Net**) ⇨ INTERNET.
5 a flat two-dimensional layout of something that can be folded into a three-dimensional shape, e.g. a box.

• **net** *verb* (**nets; netting; netted**) to catch in or cover with a net.
Word Family **netting** *noun* net fabric.

net² *adjective* also **nett**
remaining after deductions: *What is your net income?* Compare GROSS *adjective* (definition 4).
Figurative What was the net result of the argument? (= final).
• **net** *verb* (**nets; netting; netted**) to gain or clear, e.g. a profit.

netball *noun*
a game closely resembling basketball but differing in rules, size of court, etc.

nether (**neth**-er) *adjective*
(*dated*) lower or under.

nettle *noun*
any of a group of small wild plants with stinging hairs.
• **nettle** *verb* to irritate or provoke.

nettlerash *noun*
hives.

net weight *noun*
the weight of something without its container.

network *noun*
1 any net-like or interconnected system of lines, passages, filaments, etc.
2 an agency providing ready-made radio or television programmes.
3 a chain or system of interconnected operations, systems, things, etc., such as computers.
4 a group of people with similar careers, background, etc., who keep in regular communication with each other, usually for their mutual personal benefit.
• **network** *verb*
1 to cover with a network.
2 to broadcast simultaneously over a network of radio or television stations
3 to link together systems, things, etc., particularly computer systems so that data, software, etc., can be shared.
4 to keep in regular contact with a group of people of similar careers, background, etc., usually for personal benefit, such as career advancement.

neural (**new**-r'l) *adjective*
of or relating to nerve cells.
[Greek *neuron* a nerve]

neuralgia (new-**ral**-ja) *noun*
a pain along a nerve.
Word Family **neuralgic** *adjective*.
[Greek *neuron* a nerve + *algos* pain]

neuritis (new-**rye**-tis) *noun*
Medicine an inflammation of a nerve.
[Greek *neuron* a nerve + -*itis*]

neurology (new-**rol**-a-jee) *noun*
the study of the nervous systems and their diseases.
Word Family **neurologist** *noun*;
neurological (new-ra-**loj**-i-k'l) *adjective*.

neuron (**new**-ron) *noun* also **neurone** (**new**-rone) ⇨ NERVE CELL.

neurosis (new-**roh**-sis) *noun* (*plural* **neuroses**) (new-**roh**-seez)
Psychology an emotional disorder marked by extreme anxiety, obsession or hysteria.

neurosurgery (new-roh-**serj**-a-ree) *noun*
the branch of medicine concerned with surgery of the nerves.
Word Family **neurosurgeon** (new-roh-serj-'n) *noun*; **neurosurgical** *adjective*.

neurotic (new-**rott**-ik) *adjective*
suffering from a neurosis.
Figurative The neurotic old man kept 17 cats in his room (= obsessive, eccentric).
• **neurotic** *noun* a neurotic person.
Word Family **neurotically** *adverb*;
neuroticism (new-**rot**-iss-izm) *noun*.

neuter (**new**-ta) *adjective*
1 having no sexual organs.
2 having underdeveloped sexual organs.
3 *Grammar* ⇨ GENDER (definition 1).
• **neuter** *noun* a castrated animal.
• **neuter** *verb* to remove the reproductive organs of: *My cat has been neutered.*
[Latin, neither]

neutral (**new**-tr'l) *adjective*
1 not taking part in an argument, dispute, etc.
2 of no definite colour, characteristics, etc.: *The carpet is a neutral colour so that it won't clash with the curtains.*
3 *Electricity* having no electric charge.
4 *Chemistry* neither acidic nor alkaline, but containing equal numbers of hydrogen and hydroxyl ions and having a pH of 7.
• **neutral** *noun*
1 a neutral person, country or thing.
2 the position of disengaged gears in a motor vehicle.
Word Family **neutrality** (new-**trall**-i-tee) *noun* the state of being neutral;
neutralize, neutralise *verb* 1 to make neutral. 2 to make ineffective;
neutralization (new-tral-eye-**zay**-sh'n) *noun*; **neutrally** *adverb*.

neutron (**new**-tron) *noun*
Physics an elementary particle with the same mass as a proton, but no charge. Any

variation in the number of neutrons in an atom gives rise to isotopes. Compare PROTON.

neutron bomb *noun*
a nuclear weapon which produces a large number of neutrons, designed to kill people and animals without extensive destruction of property.

névé (**nevv**-ay) *noun*
the mixture of compressed snow and ice which forms the beginning of a glacier.

never *adverb*
1 not ever or at no time: *I've never seen him before.*
2 not at all: *Never fear.*

nevermore *adverb*
a poetic word meaning 'never again'.

never-never *noun*
Phrase on the never-never (*informal*) using the system of hire purchase.

nevertheless *adverb*
all the same; in spite of that.

new *adjective*
1 of recent origin, make or existence: *A new style of dress has been created.*
2 previously unknown: *A new planet has been discovered.*
3 not previously used: *Start each chapter on a new sheet of paper.*
Phrase new to unfamiliar with: *He makes mistakes because he is new to the work.*
● **new** *adverb* lately or recently: *new-found vigour.*
Word Family **newly** *adverb* 1 recently or lately: *the newly appointed mayor.* 2 afresh: *The garage had been newly painted;* **newness** *noun.*

New Age *noun*
a cultural movement which rejects modern Western-style values and culture in favour of alternative medicine, health foods, environmentalism, spiritualism and astrology.

New Age traveller ⇨ TRAVELLER (definition 3).

newcomer *noun*
a person who has recently arrived in a place.

newel *noun*
a pillar at the top or bottom of a staircase, supporting the handrail.

newfangled *adjective*
needlessly or undesirably novel.

newly-wed *noun*
a person who has recently got married.

new man *noun* (*plural* **new men**)
a man who has modern attitudes towards his home and family, and helps with the housework and the children, etc.

new moon *noun*
Astronomy the moon when it is between the sun and the earth and only a small crescent is visible.

news *plural noun*
1 (*used with singular verb*) a report of events as given each day by newspapers, radio, etc.
2 (*used with singular verb*) information which was not known before: *That's news to me.*

newsagent *noun*
a person who sells newspapers, magazines, stationery, etc.

newscast *noun*
a broadcast of the news on radio or television.
Word Family **newscaster** *noun.*

newsflash *noun* (*plural* **newsflashes**)
a special announcement of a single important item of news.

newsgroup *noun*
a group of Internet users who communicate with each other on a topic of shared interest.

newsletter *noun*
a printed letter giving news or details about a group or society.

newspaper *noun*
1 a publication, usually daily or weekly, printed on large sheets of paper, which describes and comments on news and contains features and advertisements.
2 the organization publishing this.

newspeak *noun*
a style of official language designed to conceal the truth and confuse.
[from G. Orwell's *1984*]

newsprint *noun*
the paper on which newspapers are printed.

newsreader *noun*
a person who reads the news bulletin on radio or television.

newsreel *noun*
a short film of the news.

newsworthy *adjective*
important enough to be announced as news.

newsy *adjective* (**newsier; newsiest**)
(*informal*) full of news.

newt *noun*
any of various small-tailed amphibians related to the salamanders.

New Testament *noun*
Religion the second part of the Bible, produced in the time of the early Christian Church. Compare OLD TESTAMENT.

newton *noun*
Physics the SI unit of force, which is equal to the force required to give a mass of one kilogram an acceleration of one metre per second squared. *abbrev.* N.
[after *Sir Isaac Newton, 1642-1727,* a British physicist and mathematician]

New World *noun*
North and South America. Compare OLD WORLD.

new year *noun*
1 the year approaching or just begun.
2 (**New Year**) a new calendar year, beginning on the first day of January.

next *adjective, adverb*
immediately following: *We shall see you next week.* □ *It's my turn next.*
• **next** *noun* the next person or thing: *The next to arrive was Big Louie.*
Phrases next to 1 *The shop is next to the school* (= beside). **2** *Next to vanilla, he likes chocolate ice cream best* (= after). **next to nothing** very little.

next door *adverb, adjective*
living in or occupying the adjoining house, building, etc.: *Who lives next door to you?*

nexus *noun* (*plural* **nexuses**)
a connecting principle or link.
[Latin]

niacin (**nigh**-a-sin) *noun*
an acid which is part of the vitamin B complex, found in fresh meat and yeast.

nib *noun*
the writing point of a pen.

nibble *verb*
to take small bites: *She nibbled the chocolate.*
Figurative *to nibble at an offer* (= show interest).
• **nibble** *noun.*

nibs *noun*
Phrase his nibs (*informal*) an arrogant man.

Nicam (**nigh**-kam) *noun* also **NICAM**
a digital television system which produces high-quality stereo sound.

nice *adjective*
1 pleasant, pleasing, agreeable, etc.: *It's a nice day.* □ *It's nice of you to say that.*

Figurative *That is not a nice way to behave* (= proper).
2 subtle, precise or accurate: *He made a nice distinction between the technical terms.*
Word Family nicely *adverb;* **niceness** *noun.*

> The word **nice** is frequently used by all of us – indeed *too* frequently, because we use it to save us thinking of another adjective of approval. *Nice*, however, has undergone changes of meaning. Before 'pleasant' it meant 'particular' or 'fastidious', as in *nice manners*, or 'subtle' or 'discriminating', as in *a nice distinction*. The latter meaning is still quite common. Before this, *nice* meant 'delicate' or 'shy' and before that 'wanton'. In fact, *nice* originally meant 'foolish' or 'stupid', its original source being *nescius*, meaning 'ignorant'.

nicety (**nice**-a-tee) *noun* (*plural* **niceties**)
1 a refinement or elegance: *She uses the niceties of the language.*
2 accuracy: *She argued her case with great nicety.*
Phrase to a nicety *She described his character to a nicety* (= precisely).

niche (neesh *or* nitch) *noun*
1 a shallow recess in a wall for ornaments, etc.
2 *Biology* a position or function of an organism in a community of plants and animals.
Figurative *He found a niche in the vast organization* (= suitable and comfortable position).
[Latin *nidus* nest]

nick *verb*
1 to indent or make a notch in something
2 (*informal*) to capture or arrest.
3 (*informal*) to steal.
• **nick** *noun*
1 a notch or groove.
2 (*informal*) a prison.
Phrases in good nick (*informal*) in good condition. **in the nick of time** only just in time.

nickel *noun*
1 a magnetic metal used in coins and alloys and for protective plating.
2 *American* a five-cent coin.

nickel silver *noun* also called **German silver.**
an alloy of copper, zinc and nickel, usually electroplated for use in tableware.

nick-nack ⇨ KNICK-KNACK.

nickname noun
a name used familiarly in place of or in addition to the proper name of a person, place, etc.
● **nickname** verb.

nicotine (**nick**-a-teen) noun
a poisonous alkaloid found in tobacco.
[introduced to France by *Jacques Nicot* in 1560]

niece (neece) noun
1 a daughter of one's brother or sister.
2 a daughter of one's husband's or wife's brother or sister. Compare NEPHEW.

nifty adjective (**niftier; niftiest**)
(*informal*) neat, smart or stylish.

niggardly adjective
stingy or miserly.
Word Family **niggard** noun a person who is stingy; **niggardliness** noun.

niggle verb
to annoy or irritate by constant criticism, etc.
● **niggle** noun a trifling complaint.
Word Family **niggler** noun.

nigh adverb, adjective
an old word meaning 'near' or 'nearly': *The end of the world is nigh*.

night noun
the period of dark between two successive days, being between sunset and sunrise.

nightbird ⇨ NIGHT OWL.

nightcap noun
1 *History* a cap worn in bed.
2 a hot or alcoholic drink taken just before going to bed.

nightclothes plural noun
clothes that are worn in bed, such as pyjamas.

nightclub noun
a place providing food, drink and entertainment between nightfall and morning.
Word Family **nightclubbing** noun.

nightdress noun (*plural* **nightdresses**)
short form is **nightie** (*informal*) a woman's loose dress for sleeping in.

nightfall noun
the coming of night.

nightingale noun
a small brown woodland warbler related to the thrush, the male of which sings night and day until the eggs are hatched.
[NIGHT + Old English *galan* to sing]

nightjar noun
any of various brown plump birds with a loud distinctive song at night.

nightlife noun
the entertainments provided in towns at night, such as nightclubs, casinos, etc.

nightly adjective
1 of or occurring at night.
2 occurring every night.
● **nightly** adverb every night.

nightmare noun
a frightening dream.
Figurative *Driving through the blizzard was a nightmare* (= frightening experience).
Word Family **nightmarish** adjective.
[NIGHT + Old English *mare* an evil spirit supposed to suffocate people during sleep]

night owl noun also **nightbird**
(*informal*) a person who stays up late at night.

nightshade ⇨ BELLADONNA.

nightshirt noun
a long loose shirt worn in bed.

nightwatchman noun (*plural* **nightwatchmen**)
a person employed to guard property, etc. during the night.

nihilism (**nigh**-a-lizm) noun
a total rejection of all existing principles, values and institutions.
Word Family **nihilist** noun; **nihilistic** (nigh-a-**list**-ik) adjective.
[Latin *nihil* nothing + -*ism*]

nil noun
nothing.

nimble adjective
quick and easy in movement: *nimble fingers*. □ *a nimble brain*.
Word Family **nimbly** adverb; **nimbleness** noun.

nimbus noun (*plural* **nimbi** (**nim**-bye) or **nimbuses**)
1 a rain cloud.
2 a halo.
[Latin *nimbus* a thunder cloud]

Nimby noun (*plural* **Nimbies**)
a person who takes the attitude 'Not In My BackYard' when objecting to unpleasant things, such as a nuclear waste dump, being placed near his or her home, the implication being that such things are acceptable elsewhere.

nincompoop noun
(*dated*) a very foolish person.

nine *noun*
a cardinal number, the symbol 9 in Arabic numerals, IX in Roman numerals.
Word Family **nine** *adjective*; **ninth** *adjective, noun.*

ninepins *plural noun*
(*used with singular verb*) the game of skittles.

nineteen *noun*
a cardinal number, the symbol 19 in Arabic numerals, XIX in Roman numerals.
Word Family **nineteen** *adjective*; **nineteenth** *adjective, noun.*

nineteenth hole *noun*
Golf the bar in the clubhouse.

ninety *noun* (*plural* **nineties**)
1 a cardinal number, the symbol 90 in Arabic numerals, XC in Roman numerals.
2 (**nineties**) the numbers 90 to 99 in a series, such as the years within a century.
Word Family **ninety** *adjective*; **ninetieth** *adjective, noun.*

ninja *noun*
a Japanese spy or assassin trained in stealth and martial arts.
[Japanese, a spy]

ninny *noun* (*plural* **ninnies**)
(*informal*) a very foolish or simple person.

nip[1] *verb* (**nips; nipping; nipped**)
1 to squeeze.
2 to remove by squeezing: *He nipped off the withered leaves.*
3 to sting or cause pain, as cold does.
Word Family **nip** *noun*; **nippy** *adjective* (**nippier; nippiest**) sharp and stinging, e.g. cold weather.

nip[2] *noun*
a small quantity of alcoholic spirits: *A nip of brandy put me right.*

nipper *noun*
1 (*informal*) a small child.
2 a person or thing that nips, such as a crab's claw.

nipple *noun*
1 also called **teat**. *Anatomy* the small projection on the end of the breast or mammary gland through which a baby mammal sucks its mother's milk.
2 also called **teat**. *Anatomy* a similar but functionless projection on male mammals.
3 something which has the shape or function of a nipple, such as the small valve through which grease may be supplied to a bearing.

Nirvana (neer-vah-na) *noun*
Buddhism an indescribable state of enlightenment or bliss, where individual identity is lost in complete freedom from concern about oneself or the external world.
[Sanskrit, extinction]

Nissen hut *noun*
a prefabricated semicircular building made of timber and galvanized iron.
[invented by *Colonel P. N. Nissen*, 1871-1930, an army engineer]

nit *noun*
1 the egg or young form of the louse or other parasitic insect.
2 (*informal*) a stupid person.

nit-picking *noun*
(*informal*) fussing over trivial details, especially fault-finding.
Word Family **nit-picker** *noun*; **nit-pick** *verb.*

nitrate (**nigh**-trate) *noun*
1 *Chemistry* any compound containing the univalent $(NO_3)^-$ ion.
2 a fertilizer containing potassium nitrate and sodium nitrate.
[Greek *nitron* washing soda]

nitric acid (nigh-trik **ass**-id) *noun*
a strong colourless corrosive acid. It attacks most metals and many other substances and is widely used in industry.

nitrite (**nigh**-trite) *noun*
Chemistry any compound containing the univalent $(NO_2)^-$ ion.

nitrogen (**nigh**-tra-j'n) *noun*
a colourless odourless chemically inactive gas forming about 78 per cent of the earth's atmosphere. It is an essential part of protein and is used in fertilizers, explosives and dyes.
Word Family **nitrogenous** (nigh-**troj**-a-nus) *adjective.*

nitroglycerine (nigh-tro-gliss-a-reen) *noun*
Chemistry a pale yellow dense oily liquid (formula $C_3H_5(NO_3)_3$), used as an explosive.

nitrous oxide ⇨ LAUGHING GAS.

nitty-gritty *noun*
(*informal*) the basic facts, details, etc.

nitwit *noun*
(*informal*) a slow-witted person.

nix *noun*
(*informal*) nothing.
[alteration of German *nichts*]

no¹ adverb
1 used to express dissent or refusal: *'May I go out?' – 'No, you may not.'*
2 used to emphasize a previous negative or qualify a previous statement: *No, not even in Paris did I see so many beautiful dresses.*
3 used with a comparative to indicate negation: *She is no prettier than Sue.*
• **no** noun (plural **noes**)
1 a denial or refusal: *She got a definite no to her request.*
2 a negative vote or voter.

no² adjective
1 not any: *There is no food left.*
2 used to imply the opposite: *He is no fool.*

nob noun
1 (*informal*) a person of wealth or social distinction.
2 (*informal*) the head.

nobble verb
1 (*informal*) to tamper with a racehorse, especially by drugging it.
2 (*informal*) to catch someone you want to speak to.
Word Family **nobbler** noun.

nobility (no-**bill**-i-tee) noun (plural **nobilities**)
1 an excellence of mind or character.
2 the peers, baronets and knights and their wives and children.

noble adjective
1 of high hereditary rank.
2 showing high character or qualities: *a noble sacrifice.*
3 imposing or stately: *a noble monument.*
4 *Chemistry* chemically inactive, and not corroded or easily attacked by chemical agents.
• **noble** noun a member of the nobility.
Word Family **nobly** adverb.
[Latin *nobilis* known, famous]

nobleman noun (plural **noblemen**)
a male member of the nobility.
Word Family **noblewoman** noun (plural **noblewomen**).

noblesse oblige (no-bless o-**bleezh**) noun
the obligations, such as honourable behaviour, associated with high rank or position.
[French *noblesse* nobility + *oblige* obliges]

nobody pronoun
no person.
• **nobody** noun (plural **nobodies**) a person of no importance.

nocturnal (nok-**ter**-n'l) adjective
relating to or active in the night-time: *A nocturnal animal is awake at night.*
Compare DIURNAL (definition 2).
Word Family **nocturnally** adverb.
[Latin *noctis* of the night]

nocturne (nok-tern) noun
a short gentle piece of music, especially for the piano.
[French]

nod verb (**nods; nodding; nodded**)
to bow the head briefly, usually to express agreement, greeting, etc.
Figurative He nodded off for a few moments by the fire (= dozed). □ *The plants were nodding in the breeze* (= swaying, bending).
• **nod** noun.

node noun
1 a knot or knob, such as a joint on a stem from which a leaf grows.
2 a point at which two things intersect.
Word Family **nodal** adjective.
[Latin *nodus* a knot]

nodule (**nod**-yool) noun
a knob or small rounded lump.
Word Family **nodular** adjective.

Noel (no-**el**) noun also **Noël**
Christmas.
[Latin *natalis* a birthday]

noggin noun
1 (*informal*) the head.
2 (*informal*) a glass of beer.

noise (*rhymes with* boys) noun
1 any sound, especially when loud or confused: *deafening noises.*
2 *Electronics* any unwanted electrical disturbance which obscures or reduces the clarity or quality of a signal.
Word Family **noisy** adjective (**noisier; noisiest**) making or full of noise; **noisily** adverb; **noisiness** noun; **noiseless** adjective; **noiselessly** adverb; **noiselessness** noun.

nomad (**no**-mad) noun
1 any of a group of people who move from place to place to find food, etc. according to the seasons.
2 any person who wanders or moves about.
Word Family **nomadic** (no-**madd**-ik) adjective; **nomadically** adverb.
[Greek *nomas, nomados* roaming about for pasture]

no-man's-land noun
1 the area between two opposing armies.
2 any unclaimed or disputed area.

nom de plume (nom da **ploom**) *noun*
(*plural* **noms de plume**) (nom da **ploom**)
a pen name.
[French *nom* name + *de plume* of pen]

nomenclature (no-**men**-kla-cher) *noun*
a system of names used in a particular
subject.
[from Latin]

nominal (**nom**-i-n'l) *adjective*
1 existing in name only: *a nominal ruler of a
country.*
2 small in relation to the real value: *We only
pay a nominal rent, as the house belongs to my
parents.*
3 *Grammar* of or relating to a noun or
name.
Word Family **nominally** *adverb.*
[Latin *nominis* of a name]

nominate (**nom**-i-nate) *verb*
1 to put forward or suggest a person as
suitable for appointment or election.
2 to name: *Which film would you nominate
as the best?*
Word Family **nomination** (nom-i-**nay**-
sh'n) *noun* 1 the act of nominating. 2 the
state of being nominated; **nominator**
noun; **nominee** (nom-i-**nee**) *noun* a
person who is nominated.

nominative case (**nom**-in-a-tiv case)
noun
a grammatical case expressing the subject
of a verb.

nonagenarian (nonn-a-j'n-**air**-i-an) *noun*
a person who is over 90 but less than 100
years old.
[Latin *nonageni* 90 each]

nonagon (**nonn**-a-g'n) *noun*
any closed plane figure with nine straight
sides.
[Latin *nonus* ninth + Greek *gonia* a corner]

non-aligned *adjective*
not taking part in an alliance, etc.
Word Family **non-alignment** *noun.*

nonce *noun*
Phrase **for the nonce** for the present.
[Middle English *for then anes* for the one
(purpose)]

nonchalant (**non**-sha-l'nt) *adjective*
unconcerned, cool or indifferent.
Word Family **nonchalantly** *adverb;*
nonchalance *noun.*
[French]

non-combatant (non-**kom**-ba-t'nt) *noun*
a person who is not involved in fighting,
such as a medical officer or chaplain in the
armed forces.

non-commissioned officer *noun*
a member of the armed forces appointed
to a position of authority but subject to the
command of officers. *abbrev.* NCO.

non-committal *adjective*
not committing oneself to a particular
view, course of action, etc.
Word Family **non-committally** *adverb.*

non compos mentis (non kom-poss
men-tis) *adjective*
not sane or responsible for one's actions.
[Latin, not in control of the mind]

nonconformist *noun*
1 a person who does not conform.
2 (**Nonconformist**) a member of a
Protestant Church which became
separated from the established Church of
England in the 17th century, e.g. a
Methodist or Baptist.
Word Family **nonconformity** *noun* a
lack of conformity or agreement.

nondescript (**non**-da-skript) *adjective*
of no particular type or sort: *It was such a
nondescript dress that I don't remember what
colour it was.*

none (nun) *pronoun*
1 not any: *That is none of your business.*
2 (*used with singular or plural verb*) not one:
None of them would help.
• **none** *adverb* not at all; in no way: *He was
none the worse for the experience.*

nonentity (non-**en**-ta-tee) *noun* (*plural*
nonentities)
a person or thing of no importance.

nonetheless (nun-*the*-**less**) *adverb*
nevertheless.

non-ferrous metal *noun*
1 a metallic compound which contains no
iron.
2 any metal other than iron or steel.

non-fiction *noun*
any factual prose writing
• **non-fiction** *adjective* also **non-fictional**
not imagined or made-up.

non-intervention *noun*
a failure or refusal to intervene or
interfere, especially of one country with
the affairs of another.

nonplus *verb* (**nonplusses; nonplussing;
nonplussed**)
to puzzle or perplex completely.
[Latin *non plus* no further]

non-proliferation *noun*
the halting of the spread of nuclear
weapons among non-nuclear powers by
common agreement.

nonsense *noun*
1 something which is absurd or makes no sense.
2 senseless or foolish conduct.
Word Family **nonsensical** (non-**sen**-si-k'l) *adjective*.

non sequitur (non **sek**-wi-ta) *noun*
a conclusion that does not follow from the basic statements or assumptions.
[Latin, it does not follow]

noodle[1] *noun*
a pasta in long narrow pieces used in soup or with a sauce.
[German *Nudel*]

noodle[2] *noun*
1 (*dated informal*) the head.
2 (*dated informal*) a simpleton.

nook (nook) *noun*
1 a secluded corner.
2 a small recess.

noon *noun*
midday.

no one *pronoun*
nobody.

noontide *noun*
a poetic word for midday.

noose *noun*
a loop, as in a lasso, with a knot which tightens when the rope is pulled.

nor *conjunction*
1 used to connect negative alternatives: *She is neither brilliant nor stupid.*
2 used to emphasize a negative such as *not*, *never*, etc.: *Never did I meet such an idiot, nor do I wish to.*

norm *noun*
1 a model or standard.
2 the average behaviour or performance for a group of people.
Word Family **normative** *adjective* corresponding with the norm.
[Latin *norma* a carpenter's square]

normal *adjective*
1 conforming to a usual or typical pattern: *Such behaviour is normal in young children.*
2 *Maths* being at right angles.
• **normal** *noun* anything normal.
Word Family **normally** *adverb* usually; **normality** (nor-**mal**-i-tee), **normalcy** *noun*.

normalize, normalise *verb*
to make normal.
Word Family **normalization** (nor-m'l-eye-**zay**-sh'n) *noun*.

Norman *adjective*
History relating to the kings of England from 1066 to 1154.

north *noun*
1 the direction along the meridian to the left of the position where the sun rises.
2 also called **magnetic north**. the cardinal point of the compass at 90° to the left of east and opposite south.
Word Family **north** *adjective*, *adverb*.

north-east *noun*
1 the point or direction midway between north and east.
2 a region in this direction.
• **north-east** *adjective*, *adverb*
1 in or towards the north-east.
2 coming from the north-east.
Word Family **north-easterly, north-eastern** *adjective* from or towards the north-east; **north-easterly, north-easter** *noun* a wind coming from the north-east.

northerly *adjective*
(of a direction, course, etc.) from or towards the north: *We set off on a northerly course.*
• **northerly** *noun* (*plural* **northerlies**) a wind coming from the north.
• **northerly** *adverb*.

northern *adjective*
(of a place) situated in the north: *the northern edge of the desert.*
Word Family **northernmost** *adjective* furthest north.

Northern Lights *plural noun*
the aurora borealis.

North Star ⇨ POLE STAR.

northward *adjective*
towards the north.
Word Family **northwards, northward** *adverb*.

north-west *noun*
1 the point or direction midway between north and west.
2 a region in this direction.
• **north-west** *adjective*, *adverb*
1 in or towards the north-west.
2 coming from the north-west.
Word Family **north-westerly, north-western** *adjective* from or towards the north-west; **north-westerly, north-wester** *noun* a wind coming from the north-west.

nose (noze) *noun*
1 *Anatomy* the organ of smell, through which air is taken in.

2 something which has the shape or position of a nose: *the nose of an aeroplane.*
3 the sense of smell.
Figurative That reporter has a keen nose for a good story (= ability to detect or discover). □ *Please keep your nose out of our business* (= prying, interference).
Phrases **by a nose** by a very short distance. **keep one's nose to the grindstone** to continue working hard. **look down one's nose at** to treat or regard with disdain. **pay through the nose** to pay too much. **put someone's nose out of joint** (*informal*) to upset the feelings or pride of someone. **turn up one's nose at** (*informal*) to be ungrateful to or contemptuous of.
● **nose** *verb*
1 to touch or examine with the nose: *The horse nosed the boy's hand.*
2 to sniff or smell.
Figurative The car nosed forward slowly in the heavy traffic (= moved). □ *Don't nose into other people's affairs* (= pry).

nosebag *noun*
a bag containing dry feed, held near a horse's mouth by straps around its head.

nosedive *noun*
a sudden downward plunge, especially a dive in which an aircraft is pointed almost straight down.
Word Family **nosedive** *verb.*

nosegay *noun*
a small bunch of flowers.

nose job *noun*
(*informal*) a cosmetic-surgery operation on the nose.

nosey ⇨ NOSY.

nosh *verb*
(*informal*) to eat, especially a snack or titbit.
● **nosh** *noun* (*informal*) food.
[Yiddish]

no-show *noun*
(*informal*) a person who reserves a table in a restaurant or seats in a theatre but fails either to appear or to cancel.

nostalgia (noss-**tal**-ja) *noun*
a longing for people, places or things which are past or distant.
Word Family **nostalgic** *adjective*;
nostalgically *adverb.*
[Greek *nostos* a return home + *algos* pain]

nostril *noun*
either of the two openings in the nose through which air is breathed.

nostrum *noun*
1 a medicine, especially a false one.
2 a pet scheme or plan for improvement.
[Latin, our own thing]

nosy *adjective* (**nosier; nosiest**) also **nosey**
(*informal*) inquisitive or meddlesome.
Word Family **nosily** *adverb*; **nosiness** *noun.*

nosy parker *noun*
(*informal*) an inquisitive person.

not *adverb*
a word expressing denial, refusal or prohibition: *That is not true!*

nota bene (no-ta **ben**-ay)
(*formal*) used as an instruction, 'note well'.
[Latin]

notable (**no**-ta-b'l) *adjective*
1 worthy of notice.
2 distinguished: *a notable artist.*
● **notable** *noun* an important person.
Word Family **notably** *adverb*; **notability** (no-ta-**bill**-a-tee) *noun.*

notary *noun* (*plural* **notaries**) also **notary public**
an official authorized to certify contracts and take affidavits, depositions, etc.
[from Latin]

notation (no-**tay**-sh'n) *noun*
1 a system of symbols to represent numbers, quantities, etc., as is used in arithmetic, algebra and music.
2 a note or record of something.
Word Family **notate** *verb*; **notational** *adjective.*

notch *noun* (*plural* **notches**)
a V-shaped cut in a surface, sometimes used as a record or to keep count.
Figurative Her remark cut him down several notches (= degrees, steps)
● **notch** *verb*
1 to cut a notch.
2 to score.

note *noun*
1 a short written or printed record, used for reference or as a reminder, an informal message, etc.
2 a piece of paper currency: *a five-pound note.*
3 *Music* a single sound: *a low note.*
4 *Music* the written symbol of a sound: *The first note is a minim.*
5 *Music* a key on a piano, organ, etc.
6 any musical or expressive sound: *The notes of a magpie's call are very distinctive.*
7 importance or significance: *Did anything of note happen while I was away?*

8 heed or notice: *Please take note of the revised timetable.*
9 tone or feeling: *There was a note of warning in the doctor's voice.*
Phrases **strike a false note** to do or say something inappropriate or which betrays insincerity. **strike the right note** to do or say the appropriate thing.
• **note** *verb*
1 to watch or notice carefully: *Note the way Monet uses colour here.*
2 to make a note of: *Note the date on your calendar.*
Word Family noted *adjective* famous.
[Latin *nota* a sign, mark, note]

notepaper *noun*
sheets of paper used for writing letters.

noteworthy *adjective*
worthy of notice or recognition.
Word Family noteworthiness *noun*.

nothing (**nuth**-ing) *noun*
1 no thing: *This carton has nothing in it, so throw it away.*
2 nought: *Four minus four equals nothing.*
Figurative *There is nothing on television tonight* (= not anything interesting or important). □ *She shows nothing of her former enjoyment of life* (= no trace or part).
Phrases **make nothing of 1** *I could make nothing of her hysterical speech* (= not understand). **2** *They all tried kindly to make nothing of my clumsiness* (= treat lightly).
next to nothing very little. **nothing doing!** (*informal*) certainly not! **nothing for it** no other possible course of action: *There was nothing for it but to jump.*
nothing in something no truth or profit in something: *Why should you help? There's nothing in it for you.*
• **nothing** *adverb* not at all.
Word Family nothingness *noun* **1** the state of being nothing. **2** emptiness or worthlessness.

notice (**no**-tiss) *noun*
1 attention or awareness: *It has come to my notice that you have been arriving late.*
2 a written or printed announcement.
3 a review: *The new play received very good notices after its opening.*
4 a formal announcement of intention, especially to leave a job: *to give notice.*
• **notice** *verb* to be aware of or pay attention to: *Did you notice the man wearing pink shoes?*
Word Family noticeable *adjective* **1** able to be seen. **2** significant; **noticeably** *adverb*.
[Latin *notitia* a being known]

notifiable disease *noun*
a serious infectious disease which must be reported to the health authorities, e.g. smallpox or diphtheria.

notify (**no**-ti-fie) *verb* (**notifies; notifying; notified**)
to inform or make known to: *Please notify the police if you have seen this car.*
Word Family notification (no-ti-fi-**kay**-sh'n) *noun* a written notice.

notion (**no**-sh'n) *noun*
1 a general idea or feeling: *I have a strange notion that we have been here before.*
2 an opinion or belief: *Her notions about marriage are very old-fashioned.*
[from Latin]

notorious (no-**taw**-ree-us) *adjective*
widely known, especially in an unfavourable way.
Word Family notoriously *adverb*; **notoriety** (no-ta-**rye**-a-tee) *noun* the quality of being famous or notorious.
[Latin *notus* known]

notwithstanding *preposition*
(*formal*) in spite of: *Notwithstanding their warnings, she went out alone.*
• **notwithstanding** *adverb* nevertheless: *We continued on our way notwithstanding.*

nougat (**noo**-gah) *noun*
a chewy sweet with nuts.
[French]

nought (nawt) *noun*
zero, the symbol 0. Compare NAUGHT.

noughts and crosses *plural noun*
(*used with singular verb*) a game for two people using noughts and crosses as symbols, in which each player tries to build the first row of three of his or her symbols within a square consisting of nine smaller squares.

noun *noun*
a word which refers to a person, animal, place, thing or idea: *In the sentence 'Cats are furry', 'cats' is a noun.*

nourish (**nurr**-ish) *verb*
1 to feed or sustain with food.
2 to cherish or promote.
Word Family nourishing *adjective*; **nourishment** *noun*.

nous (*rhymes with* mouse) *noun*
(*informal*) common sense.
[Greek, mind]

nouveaux riches (noo-vo **reesh**) *plural noun*
people who have newly become rich.
[French]

nouvelle cuisine (noo-vel kwi-**zeen**)
noun
a style of cooking in which freshness of
ingredients, simplicity and presentation
play a major part and elaborate sauces and
rich ingredients are rejected.
[French, new cooking]

nova *noun* (*plural* **novae** (**no**-vee) *or*
novas)
a faint star which, after an internal
explosion, displays a tremendous increase
in radiation, but only for a few days or
weeks.
[Latin *novus* new]

novel¹ (**nov**-'l) *noun*
a long prose narrative of imaginary people
and events.
Word Family **novelist** *noun* a person who
writes novels; **novelistic** (nov-'l-**ist**-ik)
adjective of or like a novel.

novel² *adjective*
new, unusual or different.
[Latin *novus* new]

novella (n'-**vell**-a) *noun*
a short novel.

novelty *noun* (*plural* **novelties**)
1 the quality of being novel or new: *the
novelty of snow in summer.*
2 anything which is novel: *Eating with
chopsticks was a novelty.*
3 a small inexpensive toy or article.

November *noun*
the eleventh month of the year, after
October and before December.
[Latin, the ninth month of the Roman
calendar]

novice (**nov**-is) *noun*
a person who is new to some activity,
religious order, etc.
[Latin *novicius* newly arrived]

novitiate (no-**vish**-l-it) *noun* also
noviciate
1 a novice or beginner.
2 the state or period of being a novice.

now *adverb*
1 at this time or moment: *What sort of work
are you doing now?*
2 at once: *Please stop that noise now.*
3 at that time: *The rain was now falling more
heavily than ever.*
4 as a result: *Now we may never see him
again.*
Phrases **just now** *It arrived just now in the
post* (= very recently). **now and again,
now and then** occasionally.
• **now** *conjunction* since: *Now that you
mention it, I do remember that car.*

Word Family **nowadays** *adverb* at the
present time.

nowhere *adverb*
not anywhere.
Phrase **get nowhere** to achieve nothing.
• **nowhere** *noun* an unknown or non-
existent place.

noxious (**nok**-shus) *adjective*
harmful.
Word Family **noxiously** *adverb*;
noxiousness *noun*.
[from Latin]

nozzle *noun*
a projecting spout or end through which
something is poured or discharged, such
as a fitting on the end of a pipe or hose.

nth (enth) *adjective*
Maths relating to a general term, in an
unspecified position in a series.
Phrase **to the nth degree** to the utmost
or greatest extent.

nuance (**new**-onss) *noun*
a slight or subtle shade or variation, e.g. in
colour or meaning.
[French]

nub *noun*
1 a knob or lump.
2 (*informal*) the point or gist of anything:
Let us get to the real nub of our discussion.

nubile (**new**-bile) *adjective*
(of a young woman) physically mature and
attractive.
[Latin *nubere* (of a woman) to be married
to]

nuclear (**new**-klee-a) *adjective*
1 relating to, involving or powered by
nuclear energy.
2 having nuclear weapons: *Is India a
nuclear power?*
3 of or forming a nucleus: *a nuclear family.*
4 of or relating to the nucleus of an atom:
nuclear physics.

nuclear energy *noun* also called **atomic
energy**
1 the immensely powerful force, the nature
of which is unknown, required to keep
charged protons and neutrons densely
packed in an atom's nucleus.
2 this force released in nuclear fission or
nuclear fusion.

nuclear family *noun* (*plural* **nuclear
families**)
a family unit consisting of husband, wife
and children only. Compare EXTENDED
FAMILY.

nuclear fission *noun*
short form is **fission** the splitting of the
nucleus of an atom of a heavy element, e.g.
a uranium isotope, producing enormous
energy which is controlled in nuclear
reactors for peaceful uses or uncontrolled
for atom bombs.

nuclear fuel *noun*
any of the elements used in producing
nuclear power, e.g. uranium or plutonium.

nuclear fusion *noun*
short form is **fusion** the fusion of two
nuclei of a light element, e.g. hydrogen, to
form one nucleus of a heavier element, e.g.
helium, releasing vast amounts of energy
(more than that produced by fission), used
in the hydrogen bomb but not yet
controllable for peaceful use.

nuclear power *noun*
1 the product of nuclear fission controlled
in a nuclear reactor for peaceful uses.
2 a country which possesses nuclear
weapons.
Word Family **nuclear-powered**
adjective.

nuclear reactor *noun* also called **atomic
pile**.
any of various widely differing systems for
damping down the energy released in
nuclear fission so that it can be used in
generating electricity, propelling ships, etc.

nuclear waste *noun*
harmful radioactive products formed
when nuclear energy is produced.

nuclear weapon *noun*
1 a tactical or short-range weapon, e.g. an
atom bomb or a ship-launched or
vehicle-launched missile with a small
warhead in which the explosive force is
derived from nuclear fission.
2 a strategic or long-range weapon, e.g. a
missile launched from an aircraft,
submarine or land-based silo, or a
hydrogen bomb, in which the explosive
force is derived from nuclear fusion
triggered off by a nuclear-fission
detonator, or from nuclear fission alone.

nuclear winter *noun*
a period of extremely low temperatures
and darkness that it has been suggested
would follow a nuclear explosion.

nucleic acid (new-klee-ik **ass**-id *or* new-
klay-ik **ass**-id)
Biology a long-chain molecule found in all
living things and forming chromosomes.

nucleon (new-klee-on) *noun*
Physics a proton or neutron.

nucleus (new-klee-us) *noun* (*plural* **nuclei**
(new-klee-eye) *or* **nucleuses**)
1 a central part around which other things
are grouped.
*Figurative The resigning members formed
the nucleus of a new progressive party*
(= basis, foundation).
2 *Physics* the heavy positively charged core
of an atom, made up of protons and
(except in hydrogen) neutrons.
3 *Biology* a body within a cell that contains
the chromosomes and which is essential
for the life of most plant and animal cells.
[Latin, kernel]

nude (newd) *adjective*
naked.
• **nude** *noun* a naked human figure or a
drawing, painting or photograph of one.
Word Family **nudity** (new-di-tee) *noun*.
[from Latin]

nudism *noun* also called **naturism**.
the practice of going nude in places
reserved for this purpose.
Word Family **nudist** *noun*.

nudge *verb*
to push gently, especially with the elbow,
in order to attract attention, etc.
• **nudge** *noun*.

nugatory (new-ga-tree) *adjective*
1 (*formal*) having no value or worth.
2 (*formal*) having no power or effect.
[Latin *nugae* trifles]

nugget *noun*
a small lump or mass, especially of a
precious metal such as gold.

nuisance (new-s'nce) *noun*
a person or thing that is annoying,
troublesome or inconvenient.

nuisance call *noun*
an unwanted telephone call, often from
someone who hangs up without speaking
or from someone who makes abusive or
obscene remarks.

nuke (newk) *noun*
(*informal*) a nuclear device.
• **nuke** *verb*
1 (*informal*) to attack or destroy with
nuclear weapons.
2 (*informal*) to destroy.

null *adjective*
1 having no effect, force or significance.
2 non-existent.
Phrase **null and void** having no legal
force.
Word Family **nullify** *verb* (**nullifies;
nullifying; nullified**) to make or declare

null; **nullification** (null-i-fi-**kay**-sh'n)
noun the state of being null or ineffective.
[Latin *nullus* none]

numb (num) *adjective*
unable to feel or move: *Her fingers were
numb with cold.* □ *We were numb with shock
at the news.*
Word Family numb *verb*; **numbly**
adverb; **numbness** *noun*.

number *noun*
1 any of a series of symbols or figures
indicating quantity or position in a series:
Choose a number over ten. □ *an odd number.*
2 a particular number given to a person or
thing to fix place, establish identity, etc.:
a telephone number.
3 a quantity, total or amount: *The number
of deaths is estimated at 35.*
*Figurative Numbers of spectators were
injured* (= many, a large quantity). □ *We lost
the vote because we didn't have the numbers*
(= greater quantity).
4 a single part in a series, such as an item
in a programme, an issue of a magazine,
etc.
Phrases **any number of** a large but
indefinite quantity of. **without number**
too many to be counted.
• **number** *verb*
1 to add up to: *His true friends do not
number very many.*
2 to add, note or give a number to, in turn
or one by one.
*Figurative He was numbered among the few
survivors* (= included). □ *The doctors say
that the days of his life are numbered*
(= limited).
Word Family numberless *adjective*
1 countless. 2 without a number.
[Latin *numerus*]

number cruncher *noun*
(*informal*) a person whose work involves
dealing with numbers, e.g. a statistician.

number one *noun*
1 (*informal*) oneself: *He always looks after
number one.*
2 *Nautical* the first lieutenant.

number plate *noun* also called
registration plate.
a plate with numbers and letters on it to
identify the motor vehicle carrying it.

number theory *noun*
Maths the study of integers and their
interrelationships.

numbskull *noun* also **numskull**
(*informal*) a stupid person.

numeral (**new**-ma-r'l) *noun*
a letter, figure or word expressing a
number: *The Roman numeral for two is II.*
• **numeral** *adjective* of or expressing a
number.

numerate (**new**-ma-rit) *adjective*
able to do arithmetic or maths.
Word Family numeracy *noun* the state
of being numerate.

numerator *noun*
Maths the part of a fraction above the line,
such as 3 in $\frac{3}{4}$. Compare DENOMINATOR.

numerical (new-**merr**-i-k'l)
1 relating to a number or series of
numbers: *Please put your pages in numerical
order.*
2 of or expressed in a number or numbers:
7 is a numerical symbol.
Word Family numerically *adverb*.

numerology (new-ma-**roll**-a-jee) *noun*
the study of numbers, such as a person's
birth date, to discover their supposed
influence on events.
Word Family numerologist *noun*.

numerous (**new**-ma-rus) *adjective*
forming or having a great number.
Word Family numerously *adverb*.

numinous (**new**-min-us) *adjective*
(*formal*) spiritually or religiously inspired
or inspiring.
[Latin *numinis* of divine power]

numismatics (new-miz-**matt**-iks) *plural
noun*
(*used with singular verb*) the science or
study of coins and medals.
Word Family numismatic *adjective*;
numismatist (new-**miz**-ma-tist) *noun*.
[Greek *nomismata* currency]

numskull ⇨ NUMBSKULL.

nun *noun*
Christianity a female member of a religious
order living under vows, often apart from
the secular world.

nuncio (**nun**-si-o) *noun*
Roman Catholicism a diplomatic
representative of the Pope.
[Latin *nuntius* messenger]

nunnery *noun* (*plural* **nunneries**)
an old word for a convent.

nuptials (**nup**-sh'lz) *plural noun*
(*dated*) a marriage ceremony or wedding.
Word Family nuptial *adjective*.
[Latin *nuptiae* a wedding]

nurse *noun*
1 a person trained to care for the sick,
young children, etc.

2 any person or thing that encourages growth, development, etc.
• **nurse** *verb*
1 to work as a nurse.
2 to care for or look after.
3 to breastfeed.
4 to hold gently: *He nursed his sore leg.*
5 to have a feeling secretly: *Do not nurse any grudges.*
Word Family nursing *noun.*
[Latin *nutricius* that nourishes]

nursemaid *noun*
an old word for a woman employed to take care of children.

nursery *noun* (*plural* **nurseries**)
1 a place where children are looked after.
2 a room in a house for children to sleep and play.
3 a place where plants are grown for sale, experimentation, etc.
Word Family nurseryman *noun* (*plural* **nurserymen**) a person who owns or works in a plant nursery.

nursery rhyme *noun*
a short traditional poem or song for children.

nursery school ⇨ KINDERGARTEN.

nursery slope *noun*
a gentle ski slope suitable for beginners.

nursing home *noun*
a private residential home which provides medical care by qualified staff for elderly people.

nursing officer *noun*
a senior nurse with administrative duties.

nurture (**ner**-cher) *verb*
(*formal*) to feed or nourish.
Figurative *The new law nurtured a feeling of public resentment* (= promoted).
• **nurture** *noun*
1 food or nourishment.
2 training or upbringing.

nut *noun*
1 a dry fruit enclosed in a hard shell: *cashew nuts.*
2 a piece of metal with a hole in the centre for screwing onto the end of a bolt.
3 also **nutcase** (*informal*) a person who is eccentric or insane.
4 (*informal*) the head.
Phrases a hard nut to crack (*informal*) a difficult person or problem. **nuts and bolts** (*informal*) 1 the basic essential details. 2 the working parts of a machine.

• **nut** *verb* (**nuts; nutting; nutted**)
(*informal*) to hit in the face with one's head.

nutcracker *noun*
an implement for breaking the hard outer shell of a nut.

nut loaf *noun* (*plural* **nut loaves**)
a vegetarian dish made from nuts, vegetables and herbs.

nutmeg *noun*
a sweet spice made from the dried berry of a tropical tree and used in cooking.
[NUT + Latin *muscus* musk]

nutria ⇨ COYPU.

nutrient (**new**-tri-ent) *noun*
a substance which nourishes, especially as an ingredient in food: *The mother's milk is rich in nutrients.*

nutriment (**new**-tra-m'nt) *noun*
(*formal*) anything which nourishes, sustains or promotes growth.

nutrition (new-**trish**-'n) *noun*
1 the act of nourishing, especially the ingestion, digestion and assimilation of food materials by an organism.
2 food.
3 the study of nutrients.
Word Family nutritious *adjective* giving a high degree of nourishment;
nutritiously *adverb*; **nutritive** (**new**-tra-tiv) *adjective* 1 providing nourishment.
2 relating to nutrition; **nutritional** *adjective*; **nutritionally** *adverb*;
nutritionist *noun*.

nuts *adjective*
(*informal*) mad.

nutshell *noun*
the hard shell of a nut.
Phrase in a nutshell in brief, concisely.

nutter *noun*
(*informal*) a person who is eccentric or insane.

nutty *adjective* (**nuttier; nuttiest**)
1 like a nut, especially in taste.
2 (*informal*) mad or eccentric.

nuzzle *verb*
1 to push against or burrow with the nose.
2 to cuddle or snuggle.
• **nuzzle** *noun*.

nylon *noun*
1 any of a large class of polymers that have recurring amide groups along the chain of the molecule. Thread made from nylon is

used to make a variety of products, such as yarn, fabric and fishing line.
2 (**nylons**) stockings made of nylon.

nymph (nimf) *noun*
1 *Mythology* any of various beautiful young goddesses who inhabited the sea, woods, meadows, etc.
2 *Biology* a young wingless sexually immature form in the development of certain insects.
[from Greek]

nymphomania (nim-fa-**may**-nee-a) *noun Psychology* an abnormally strong sexual desire in women. Compare SATYRIASIS.
Word Family nymphomaniac *noun*, *adjective*.

Oo

oaf *noun*
a stupid or clumsy person.
Word Family **oafish** *adjective*; **oafishly**
adverb; **oafishness** *noun*.

oak *noun*
any of a group of large trees which
produce acorns and a fine hard wood.
Word Family **oaken** *adjective* an old word
meaning 'made of oak'.

oak apple *noun*
an apple-shaped abnormal growth formed
by a type of wasp on oak-tree branches.

oakum (o-kum) *noun*
loose fibre, such as jute or hemp, formerly
used for filling joints.

oar (or) *noun*
a long thin piece of wood with a flat blade
at one end, fitted into a rowlock and used
to row a boat.
Phrase **put one's oar in** (*informal*) to
interfere.
Word Family **oared** *adjective*; **oarsman**
(*plural* **oarsmen**) *noun* a person who rows
a boat.

oasis (o-ay-sis) *noun* (*plural* **oases**) (o-ay-
seez)
1 an area in a desert made fertile by water
from a spring or a stream.
2 a haven of peace amidst turmoil.
[Greek]

oast *noun*
an oven for drying hops and malt.

oast house *noun*
a building containing an oast.

oat *noun*
(*usually* **oats**) a cereal plant cultivated for
its edible seed.
Phrase **sow one's wild oats** to indulge in
wild behaviour while young.

oath *noun*
1 a formal promise made in the name of a
god or holy person.
2 an irreverent or blasphemous
expression.

oatmeal *noun*
ground oats, used to make porridge, etc.

obdurate (ob-dew-rit) *adjective*
1 hard-hearted or stubborn.
2 refusing to repent.
Word Family **obduracy, obdurateness**
noun.
[from Latin]

obedient (a-bee-di-unt) *adjective*
willing to obey.
Word Family **obediently** *adverb*;
obedience *noun* 1 the state of being
obedient. 2 the act of obeying.

obeisance (a-bay-s'nce) *noun*
a bow or curtsy expressing respect.
[French, obedience, allegiance]

obelisk (obb-a-lisk) *noun*
a tapering stone column with four sides
and a pyramidal top, common as an
ancient Egyptian monument.
[Greek *obeliskos* a pointed instrument]

obese (o-beece) *adjective*
excessively fat.
Word Family **obesity** *noun*.
[Latin *obesus* having overeaten]

obey (o-bay) *verb*
1 to do as commanded or instructed: *You
must obey your parents.*
2 to act according to: *You must obey your
intuition.*

obfuscate (ob-fa-skate) *verb*
(*formal*) to obscure or confuse.
Word Family **obfuscation** (ob-fa-skay-
sh'n) *noun*.
[Latin *ob* very + *fuscus* murky]

obituary (a-bit-yoo-ree) *noun* (*plural*
obituaries)
a notice of a death of a person, sometimes
with an article about his or her life.
[Latin *obitus* death]

object (ob-jekt) *noun*
1 anything which can be seen, touched or
perceived by any of the senses.
2 a person or thing to which attention,
thought, action, etc. is directed: *She hated
being an object of pity.* □ *The object of the
meeting is to elect a president.*
3 *Grammar* the person or thing affected by
the action of a verb: *In the sentence 'I like
cats', 'cats' is the object.* ⇨ DIRECT OBJECT;
INDIRECT OBJECT.
● **object** (ob-jekt) *verb* to disapprove of,
dislike, feel or argue against: *I object to your
coming in without knocking first.*
Word Family **objector** *noun*.
[Latin *objectus* thrown in the way]

objection (ob-**jek**-sh'n) *noun*
1 something said or offered in opposition, disagreement or disapproval: *He raised an objection to the decision.*
2 a reason for such disagreement.
3 dislike.

objectionable (ob-**jek**-sh'n-a-b'l) *adjective*
unpleasant or offensive: *an objectionable person.*
Word Family **objectionably** *adverb*.

objective (ob-**jek**-tiv) *adjective*
1 not influenced by personal feelings or opinions: *an objective criticism.*
2 relating to something material, as distinct from thoughts, feelings, etc.: *the objective universe.*
3 *Grammar* of the case of nouns and pronouns that is used after a preposition or for the object of a transitive verb: *'Her' is the objective form of the pronoun 'she'.*
• **objective** *noun* something which is aimed at or striven for: *The main objective of the war was to recapture lost land.*
Word Family **objectively** *adverb*;
objectivity (ob-jek-**tivv**-i-tee) *noun* **1** the quality of being objective. **2** visible or external reality.

object lesson *noun*
an example or illustration of a moral, principle, etc.: *The exclusion of the boy was an object lesson to the other students.*

objet d'art (ob-**zhay dar**) *noun* (*plural* **objets d'art**) (ub-**zhay dar**)
an object valued for its artistic worth.
[French *objet* object + *d'art* of art]

oblate *adjective*
(of something nearly spherical) flattened at top and bottom, like the earth.

oblation (a-**blay**-sh'n) *noun*
a religious or charitable offering.
Word Family **oblatory** (**ob**-la-tree) *adjective*.
[Latin *oblatus* offered]

obligated (**ob**-li-ga-tid) *adjective*
morally or legally bound: *You are obligated to pay this fine.*
• **obligate** (**ob**-li-git) *adjective Biology* (of an organism) restricted to a particular type of life: *an obligate parasite.*

obligation (ob-li-**gay**-sh'n) *noun*
1 something which one is or feels obliged, required, etc. to do: *She felt an obligation not to smoke in the waiting room.*
2 a debt, especially of gratitude: *I am under an obligation to you for all your kindness.*
[Latin *ob* down + *ligare* to bind]

obligatory (ob-**ligg**-a-tree) *adjective*
required or compulsory: *Attendance at the meeting is obligatory.*
Word Family **obligatorily** *adverb*.

oblige *verb*
1 to be or make compulsory: *Students are obliged to attend all lessons.*
2 to place under a debt of gratitude: *I am obliged to you for all your help.*
3 to do a favour for: *The singer obliged the audience with another song.*
Word Family **obliging** *adjective* helpful, polite or kind; **obligingly** *adverb*;
obligingness *noun*.

oblique (a-**bleek**) *adjective*
1 slanting or sloping.
2 not straight or direct.
Figurative His oblique answers irritated the interviewer and the audience (= indirect, evasive).
3 *Biology* (of a leaf, etc.) having unequal sides.
Word Family **obliquely** *adverb*;
obliqueness *noun*; **obliquity** (a-**blik**-wit-ee) *noun* **1** a departure from correct conduct or sound judgement. **2** the state of being oblique.
[from Latin]

obliterate (a-**blitt** a-rate) *verb*
to destroy or remove all traces of something: *Heavy rain had obliterated any footprints at the murder scene.*
Word Family **obliteration** (a-blitt-a-ray-sh'n) *noun*.
[Latin *ob* over + *littera* a letter]

oblivion (a-**blivv**-i-un) *noun*
1 the state of being forgotten.
2 forgetfulness or disregard.
[from Latin]

oblivious (a-**blivv**-us) *adjective*
regardless or unaware: *He seems oblivious to her faults.*
Word Family **obliviously** *adverb*;
obliviousness *noun*.

oblong *adjective*
elongated, especially having a longer length than width.
• **oblong** *noun* a rectangle, usually having a longer length than width.
[from Latin]

obloquy (**ob**-la-kwee) *noun*
1 abuse, blame or reproach.
2 disgrace or subjection to abuse.
[Latin *ob* against + *loqui* to speak]

obnoxious (ob-**nok**-shus) *adjective*
offensive or unpleasant.

oboe *noun*

Music a double-reed wooden wind instrument consisting of a slender conical tube.

Word Family oboist *noun* a person who plays the oboe.

[French]

> The **oboe** gets its name from its high pitch. The old form of the word was *hautboy* from French *hautbois*, for *haut* (high) and *bois* (wood). In time *hautboy* was affected by Italian to become *oboe*.

obscene (ob-**seen**) *adjective*
indecent or morally offensive.

Word Family obscenely *adverb*; **obscenity** (ob-**senn**-i-tee) *noun* (*plural* **obscenities**) 1 the quality of being obscene. 2 anything which is obscene or offensive.

[from Latin]

obscure (ob-**skyoor**) *adjective*
1 dim or hard to see: *an obscure shape in the shadows.*
2 hard to understand: *The meaning of the book is too obscure for me.*
3 not well known: *The stranger had an obscure, mysterious past.*
• **obscure** *verb* to make dark or unclear.

Word Family obscurely *adverb*; **obscurity** *noun* 1 the state of being obscure. 2 darkness.

[from Latin]

obsequies (**ob**-si-kwiz) *plural noun* (*formal*) a funeral ceremony.

obsequious (ob-**see**-kwi-us) *adjective*
servile or excessively humble.

Word Family obsequiously *adverb*; **obsequiousness** *noun.*

[from Latin]

observance (ob-**zer**-v'nce) *noun*
1 the act of obeying or following a law, custom, etc.: *Observance of the law is enforced by the police.*
2 a particular procedure, custom or ceremony: *a day of religious observance.*

observant (ob-**zer**-v'nt) *adjective*
1 alert or quick to notice: *It was very observant of you to notice that spelling mistake.*
2 obeying laws or religious rules.

observation (ob-za-**vay**-sh'n) *noun*
1 the act of observing or watching: *close observation of detail.*

2 a remark or comment.
3 any information or record gained by observing or watching: *weather observation.*

Word Family observational *adjective.*

observatory (ob-**zerv**-a-tree) *noun* (*plural* **observatories**)
a room or building fitted with apparatus for observing stars, weather, etc., usually equipped with telescopes.

observe (ob-**zerv**) *verb*
1 to watch or look at: *Observe carefully how they do it.* □ *I only came to observe the meeting, not take part.*
2 to pay tribute to, celebrate: *Do you observe Christmas in your country?*
3 to obey: *You must observe the road laws.*
4 to comment or remark: *'That's beautiful,' she observed.*

Word Family observer *noun* a person who observes, especially as distinct from taking part; **observable** *adjective* able to be seen or noticed; **observably** *adverb.*

[Latin *ob* before + *servare* to keep]

obsess *verb*
to occupy or dominate the thoughts or feelings continually: *He is becoming obsessed with cleanliness.*

Word Family obsessed *adjective*; **obsessive** *adjective* tending to obsess; **obsession** (ob-**sesh**-'n) *noun* 1 something which obsesses or haunts. 2 the state of being obsessed or haunted; **obsessional** *adjective*; **obsessive** *adjective*; **obsessively** *adverb.*

[Latin *obsessus* besieged]

obsidian *noun*
Geology a black natural glass produced in small amounts by volcanoes, much used in early times for weapons and tools.

obsolescent (ob-sa-**less**-'nt) *adjective*
becoming obsolete.

Word Family obsolescence *noun.*

obsolete (**ob**-sa-leet) *adjective*
out of date or no longer used.

[Latin *obsoletus* worn out]

obstacle (**ob**-sti-k'l) *noun*
something which stands in the way or obstructs.

obstetrics (ob-**stet**-riks) *plural noun* (*used with singular verb*) the study and care of women before, during and after childbirth.

Word Family obstetric *adjective*; **obstetrician** (ob-sta-**trish**-'n) *noun.*

[Latin *obstetrix* one who stands by]

Word Family obnoxiously *adverb*; **obnoxiousness** *noun.*

[Latin *ob* exposed to + *noxa* harm]

obstinate (ob-sti-nit) *adjective*
1 stubborn: *She persisted with her obstinate refusal.*
2 difficult to manage, control, etc.: *It is impossible to handle such an obstinate horse.*
Word Family obstinately *adverb*; **obstinacy** (ob-sti-na-see) *noun*.
[Latin *obstinans* persisting in]

obstreperous (ab-strep-a-rus) *adjective* unruly or noisily resisting control.

obstruct *verb*
to block, close up or make difficult to proceed, pass, etc.: *The fallen rocks obstructed our path.* □ *The Opposition members tried to obstruct the legislation.*
Word Family obstruction *noun* 1 the act of obstructing or hindering. 2 anything which obstructs or blocks; **obstructive** *adjective*; **obstructiveness** *noun*.
[Latin *ob* in the way + *structus* built]

obtain *verb*
to come to possess, especially as a result of effort or asking: *Did you obtain permission to ride the horse?*
Word Family obtainable *adjective*.
[Latin *obtinere* to keep firm hold on]

obtrude *verb*
to intrude or push oneself forward.
Word Family obtrusion (ob-troo-zh'n) *noun*; **obtrusive** *adjective*; **obtrusively** *adverb*.
[Latin *ob* in the way + *trudere* to thrust]

obtuse (ob-tewce) *adjective*
1 not sharp or acute.
Figurative His obtuse answers to such simple questions embarrassed us (= stupid, unintelligent).
2 (of an angle) being greater than 90° but less than 180°.
Word Family obtusely *adverb*; **obtuseness** *noun*.
[Latin *ob* towards + *tusus* blunted]

> ! Do not confuse *obtuse* with
> ABSTRUSE.

obverse *adjective*
facing towards the observer.
● **obverse** *noun*
1 a matching or duplicate part, situation, etc.
2 the main face of a coin, medal or postage stamp. Compare REVERSE *noun* (definition 2).
Word Family obversely *adverb*.

obviate (ob-vee-ate) *verb*
to get rid of or prevent difficulties, objections, etc.
Word Family obviation (ob-vee-ay-sh'n) *noun*.
[Late Latin *obviare* to stand in the way of]

obvious *adjective*
easily seen or understood.
Word Family obviously *adverb*; **obviousness** *noun*.
[Latin *obvius* in the way]

ocarina (ok-a-reen-a) *noun*
a toy musical instrument with holes covered by the fingers and a flute-like tone.
[Italian *oca* goose (as it is the size and shape of a goose's egg)]

occasion (a-kay-zh'n) *noun*
1 a particular time: *We have met on several occasions.*
2 a special or important event, time, etc.: *on the occasion of your wedding.*
Figurative I would like to meet her if the occasion arises (= opportunity).
3 (*formal*) the cause or reason for some action or result: *What was the occasion of his dismissal from the job?*
Phrase **rise to the occasion** to show oneself able to deal with matters.
● **occasion** *verb* to cause or bring about.
[Latin *occasio* a happening]

occasional (a-kay-zh'n-al) *adjective*
1 happening from time to time: *Occasional rain fell, but it did not stop the match.*
2 designed for special but not regular use: *The Poet Laureate writes occasional verse for royal or national events.*
Word Family occasionally *adverb* now and then.

Occident (ok-si-d'nt) *noun*
a poetic word for the countries of the West, especially Europe and America. Compare ORIENT.
Word Family occidental (ok-si-den-t'l) *adjective*; **Occidental** *noun* an inhabitant of Europe or America.
[Latin *occidens* the west, sunset]

occlude (a-klood) *verb*
1 to close, obstruct or block up.
2 *Chemistry* (of a solid) to absorb and retain gases.
Word Family occlusive *adjective*.
[from Latin]

occluded front *noun* ⇨ FRONT *noun*.

occlusion (a-kloo-zh'n) *noun*
1 the state of being occluded, e.g. the contact between teeth when the jaws are closed.
2 *Weather* an occluded front.

occult (**ok**-ult *or* o-**kult**) *adjective*
1 mysterious, supernatural or beyond the scope of human knowledge: *Spiritualism is an occult science.*
2 secret or esoteric.
• **occult** *noun* occult science, study or practice.
Word Family occultism *noun* the study of the occult; **occultist** *noun.*
[Latin *occultus* hidden]

occupant (**ok**-yoo-p'nt) *noun*
a person who occupies a place, position or building.
Word Family occupancy *noun* 1 the fact of being an occupant. 2 the act or time of occupying.

occupation (ok-yoo-**pay**-sh'n) *noun*
1 a regular activity, especially a person's employment or job.
2 the act or time of occupying: *The people resisted the occupation of their country by the enemy.*
3 the state of being occupied: *Occupation with the task took all his attention.*
Word Family occupational *adjective* relating to an occupation or activity; **occupationally** *adverb.*

occupational hazard *noun*
a risk attached to a particular occupation.

occupational therapy *noun*
Medicine a type of therapy designed to assist recovery from illness or injury by exercising the mind and muscles with handicrafts, painting, etc.
Word Family occupational therapist *noun.*

occupy (**ok**-yoo-pie) *verb* (**occupies; occupying; occupied**)
1 to fill or take up: *Gardening occupies much of my spare time.*
2 to live or have an established place in: *Nobody has occupied that house for many years.*
Figurative The President occupies a position of great responsibility (= has). □ *She was so occupied with writing that she did not hear the doorbell* (= busy).
3 to take possession or control by invasion, military conquest, etc.
Word Family occupier *noun.*
[from Latin]

occur (a-**ker**) *verb* (**occurs; occurring; occurred**)
to happen or take place: *The accident occurred yesterday.*
Phrase **occur to** to suggest itself to: *It did not occur to me that the restaurant would be closed.*

occurrence (a-**kurr**-ence) *noun*
1 an event or incident.
2 the act of happening or occurring: *Measures were taken to prevent the occurrence of further accidents.*
[Latin *occurrere* to run towards]

ocean (o-**shun**) *noun*
1 the very large area of salt water which covers about 71 per cent of the earth's surface.
2 a major division of this: *the Pacific Ocean.*
3 a very large area or amount: *an ocean of faces in the crowd.*
Word Family oceanic (o-shee-**an**-ik) *adjective* of or relating to the ocean.
[from Latin]

oceanography (o-shun-**og**-ra-fee) *noun*
the study of oceans and ocean beds, a branch of geography.
Word Family oceanographer *noun;* **oceanographic** (o-shun-a-**graf**-ik) *adjective.*

ocelot (**oss**-a-lot) *noun*
a small leopard-like mammal found in Central and South America.
[Amerindian]

oche (**oh**-kee) *noun*
Darts the line behind which a player stands when throwing a dart.

ochre (*rhymes with* poker) *noun* (*American* **ocher**)
1 any of various types of earth, ranging from pale yellow to reddish-brown, used as pigments.
2 a pale yellowish-brown colour.
Word Family ochre *adjective.*
[Greek *okhros* pale yellow]

o'clock *adverb*
used to give the exact hour when stating the time: *It's now two o'clock.*
[shortening of *of the clock*]

octagon *noun*
any closed plane figure with eight straight sides.
Word Family octagonal (ok-**tag**-a-n'l) *adjective.*
[*octa-* + Greek *gonia* a corner]

octahedron (ok-ta-**hee**-dr'n) *noun* (*plural* **octahedra** or **octahedrons**)
a solid or hollow body with eight plane faces.
Word Family octahedral *adjective.*
[*octa-* + Greek *hedra* a seat]

octane *noun*
a simple hydrocarbon with eight carbon atoms (formula C_8H_{18}).

octane number *noun*
a measure of the anti-knock properties of a fuel which help to stop premature combustion in an engine.

octant *noun*
a sector equal to one-eighth of a circle or one-eighth of the circumference of a circle.

octave (ok-tiv) *noun*
1 *Music* an interval of eight steps. The frequency of any note is half that of the same note one octave higher.
2 also **octet** *Poetry* a stanza with eight lines.

octavo (ok-tah-vo) *noun*
a paper size achieved by folding a sheet into eight.

octet *noun*
1 a group of eight musicians.
2 a musical composition for eight musicians or instruments.
3 *Poetry* ⇨ OCTAVE (definition 2).
4 any group of eight people or things.

October *noun*
the tenth month of the year, after September and before November.
[Latin, the eighth month of the Roman calendar]

octogenarian (ok-ta-j'n-air-i-an) *noun*
a person who is over 80 but less than 90 years old.
[Latin *octogeni* eighty each]

octopus *noun* (*plural* **octopuses**)
a marine animal that has a soft body and eight long tentacles with suckers.
[*octo-* + Greek *pous* foot]

ocular (ok-yoo-la) *adjective*
of or relating to the eye.
● **ocular** *noun* the eyepiece of an optical instrument.

oculist (ok-yoo-list) *noun*
a doctor who treats diseases of the eye.
[Latin *oculus* eye]

odd *adjective*
1 puzzlingly different from the usual or normal.
2 *Maths* (of a number) having a remainder of one when divided by two, e.g. 3, 5, etc.
Compare EVEN *adjective* (definition 4).
3 extra or additional: *three pounds and a few odd pence.*
4 not matching: *odd socks.*
5 not fixed, occasional: *He does gardening and odd jobs around the house.*
6 about: *There were fifty-odd people at the lecture.*

Word Family **oddly** *adverb*; **oddness** *noun*; **oddity** *noun* (*plural* **oddities**) a person or thing that is odd.

oddment *noun*
an object or part which is left over or is part of an incomplete set: *oddments of dressmaking fabric.*

odds *plural noun*
1 the difference between the money placed on a bet and the money that would be received as winning payment.
2 chances or possibilities: *What are the odds that the lost child will be found?*
3 the chances of winning or losing: *She's fighting against fearful odds.*
Phrase **be at odds** to disagree or quarrel.

odds and ends *plural noun*
any remaining or miscellaneous bits.

odds-on *adjective*
(*informal*) almost certain.

ode *noun*
a usually dignified lyric poem addressed to someone or something.
[Greek]

odious (o-dee-us) *adjective*
hateful or repulsive.
Word Family **odiously** *adverb*; **odiousness** *noun* repulsiveness; **odium** *noun* 1 an intense hatred or disgust.
2 reproach or discredit connected with something hateful.
[Latin *odium* dislike]

odometer (o-dom-it-a) *noun*
(*especially American*) an instrument for measuring the distance travelled by a vehicle.

odontology (odd-on-tol-a-jee) *noun*
the science or study of the anatomy, growth and diseases of teeth.
Word Family **odontologist** *noun*; **odontological** (odd-on-ta-loj-i-k'l) *adjective*.
[Greek *odontos* of a tooth + *-logy*]

odour (o-da) *noun* (*American* **odor**)
a smell or scent.
Word Family **odorous** *adjective* having an odour, especially a pleasant one; **odourless** *adjective*.
[from Latin]

odyssey (od-i-see) *noun*
a long wandering or series of wanderings.
[after *Odysseus*, a hero in Greek mythology who wandered for ten years]

oedema (id-ee-ma) *noun* also called **dropsy**.
Anatomy an excess of fluid in the tissues.
[Greek *oidema* a swelling]

Oedipus complex (ee-di-pus kom-pleks)
noun (plural **Oedipus complexes**)
Psychology the complex of emotions said
by the psychologist Sigmund Freud to
occur when a boy adores his mother so
much that he becomes jealous of and
hostile to his father, often unconsciously.
[after Oedipus, a king of Thebes in Greek
mythology, who unknowingly killed his
father and married his mother]

o'er adverb, preposition
an old word for **over**.

oesophagus (ee-soff-a-gus) noun (plural
oesophagi (ee-soff-a-gye) or
oesophaguses) (American **esophagus**)
Anatomy a muscular tube connecting the
mouth to the stomach, through which
food passes.

oestrogen (ees-tra-jen) noun (American
estrogen)
a female sex hormone secreted in
mammals by the ovaries, which controls
part of the reproductive cycle.

oestrus (ees-trus) noun (American **estrus**)
the period of increased sexual urge during
the menstrual cycle.

of (ov) preposition
1 a word used to indicate material or
contents: a piece of wood. □ a box of washing
powder.
2 a word used to indicate distance or
separation: a few kilometres west of here.
3 a word used to indicate inclusion or
possession: a cousin of ours.
4 a word used to indicate origin,
production or source: the sonnets of
Shakespeare.
5 a word used to indicate cause: The dog
died of grief.
6 a word used to indicate identity or name:
the city of Edinburgh.
7 a word used to indicate possession of a
quality: He is a man of fine taste.
8 about or concerning: Let's talk of a
happier event.

off preposition
1 away from: The vase fell off the desk. □ He
is off work until he recovers completely.
2 leading out of: The shop is in a lane off
King Street.
3 from or with what is provided: The
survivors had lived off the island's fruits for
many months.
4 less than: All goods are selling for £2 off the
usual price.
5 not up to the usual standard of: The
champion seemed to be off his game today.

6 (informal) abstaining from: I am off cakes
until I lose weight.
• **off** adverb
1 so as to be no longer in place, attached
or in contact: He took off his coat. □ Please
switch off the lights before you leave.
2 away: He drove off quickly. □ Christmas is
only a month off.
3 free from work: Our employees get five
weeks off a year.
4 completely, successfully: This spray will
kill off all insect pests.
Phrases be off (informal) to leave: We
must be off before it gets dark. **on and off,
off and on** intermittently.
• **off** adjective
1 disconnected: The TV is off.
2 cancelled: The match is off because of rain.
3 no longer available: The menu included
mackerel, but the waiter told us it was off.
4 bad: This milk is off.
5 Cricket being on the same side of the
field as the batsman's bat: fielding on the off
side. Compare LEG.
• **off** noun
1 (informal) the start of a race or journey:
ready for the off.
2 Cricket the off side.

offal noun
the intestines, heart, kidneys, liver, etc. of
an animal, often eaten for their nutritional
value.

offbeat adjective
(informal) unconventional.

off-chance noun
a remote possibility.

off-colour adjective (American **off-color**)
1 (informal) slightly unwell.
2 slightly indecent: an off-colour joke.

offcut noun
a piece of waste material remaining after a
large piece of the material has been
trimmed down.

offence (a-fence) noun (American
offense)
1 a crime or transgression: It is an offence to
smoke in this theatre.
2 the state of being offended: He took
offence at what I said.
3 something which offends: The rubbish tip
is an offence to the neighbourhood.
4 the act of attacking: weapons of offence.

offend (a-fend) verb
to hurt or cause resentment: Her abrupt
manner offends many people.
Word Family offended adjective.
[Latin offendere to strike against]

offender *noun*
a person who offends, especially one who breaks the law.

offensive (a-fen-siv) *adjective*
1 offending the mind or feelings.
2 relating to an attack or aggression.
• **offensive** *noun* an attacking position or action.
Word Family **offensively** *adverb*; **offensiveness** *noun*.

offer *verb*
to put forward for acceptance or rejection: *She offered a suggestion.* □ *How much will you offer for the house?*
• **offer** *noun*.
[Latin *offerre* to bring before]

offering *noun*
anything offered or given.

offertory (off-a-tree) *noun* (*plural* **offertories**)
an offering, such as the collection of money taken during a church service.

offhand *adjective*
disdainful or abrupt in manner: *Her offhand refusal irritated me.*
• **offhand** *adverb* without previous thought or consideration: *Do you know offhand how many people will be there?*

office (off-iss) *noun*
1 a room or building where administrative work, professional duties, etc. are carried out.
2 the staff working in such a place.
3 the duty, function or position of a particular person: *He holds the office of secretary to the football club.*
4 a department or branch of an organization: *a post office.* □ *the ticket office.*
5 a religious service or set of prayers, etc.
[Latin *opificium* work]

officer (off-i-sa) *noun*
a person having a position of rank and authority, e.g. in the armed forces or the police force.

official (a-fish-'l) *adjective*
1 of, relating to, or authorized by a recognized authority: *The President has official powers.* □ *This is the first official report.*
2 formal or ceremonious: *An official dinner was held for the Prince.*
• **official** *noun* a person who holds a position, especially in a large organization.
Word Family **officially** *adverb*.

officialdom (a-fish-'l-dum) *noun*
1 all officials.

2 the practices or policies characteristic of officials.

officialese (a-fish-a-leez) *noun*
a style of writing or speaking said to be characteristic of officials and considered to be too complicated or difficult to understand.

officiate (a-fish-i-ate) *verb*
to carry out special duties, such as performing the office of a priest or minister, taking charge of a meeting, etc.
Word Family **officiator** *noun*.

officious (a-fish-us) *adjective*
giving unwanted advice or instruction.
Word Family **officiously** *adverb*; **officiousness** *noun*.

offie *noun* also **offy** (*plural* **offies**)
(*informal*) an off-licence.

offing *noun*
Phrase **in the offing** likely to occur.

off-key *adjective*
sung or played in the wrong key.

off-licence *noun*
a shop where alcohol is sold to be drunk elsewhere.

off-line *adjective, adverb*
Computers not connected to a computer or to the Internet: *I'm working off-line at the moment.* Compare ONLINE.

offload *verb*
to unload.

off-peak *adjective*
not at its maximum degree of activity, etc.

off-piste (off-peest) *adjective, adverb*
Skiing away from designated ski runs.

off-putting *adjective*
(*informal*) discouraging or disconcerting.

off-road *adjective*
for driving on rocky terrain.

off season *noun*
the time of year that is not the most popular for something.

offset *verb* (**offsets**; **offsetting**; **offset**)
to compensate for or balance out: *The company's small profit could not offset the losses.*
• **offset** *noun*
1 something that compensates.
2 a method of printing in which the image is transferred from the plate onto paper by a rubber-covered cylinder.

offshoot *noun*
1 something that branches out or originates from a particular source, such as a shoot from the main stem of a plant.
2 a by-product.

offshore *adjective, adverb*
1 at a distance from the shore.
2 off or away from the shore: *An offshore breeze blew the raft out to sea.*

offside *adjective, adverb*
Sport being so placed in front of the opponents' goal that one is not allowed to touch the ball.
• **offside** *noun*
1 the right-hand side of a vehicle where traffic drives on the left. Compare NEARSIDE (definition 1).
2 the right side of a horse. Compare NEARSIDE (definition 2).

offspring *noun* (*plural* **offspring**)
a descendant of an animal or plant.

off-the-record *adjective*
not intended to be made public.

off-white *noun*
a yellowish or greyish-white colour.

offy ⇨ OFFIE.

oft *adverb*
an old word for **often**.

often (**off-'n**) *adverb*
frequently.

ogle *verb* (**o-g'l**)
to stare at, especially in an amorous or lecherous way.
Word Family **ogler** *noun.*

ogre (**o-ga**) *noun*
1 a man-eating mythological giant.
2 a person who is cruel, unpleasant or frightening.
Word Family **ogreish, ogrish** (**o-grish**) *adjective*; **ogress** *noun* (*plural* **ogresses**) a female ogre.

ohm (**ome**) *noun*
the SI unit of electric resistance.
[after *G. S. Ohm*, 1787–1854, a German physicist]

oil *noun*
1 any of a large group of substances which are liquid at 20° C, insoluble in water but soluble in organic solvents, and used to make a wide variety of products, such as ointments, fuel, lubricants, etc.
2 any similar substance.
3 an oil paint.
4 an oil painting.
Phrase **pour oil on troubled waters** to calm or pacify.
• **oil** *verb* to smear or lubricate with oil.

oilcake *noun*
a mass of linseed or cottonseed after the oil has been extracted, used as fodder for cattle or as a fertilizer.

oilcloth *noun*
any fabric made waterproof by using oil.

oilfield *noun*
any area where oil is found.

oil-fired *adjective*
(of a central-heating system) fuelled by oil.

oil of turpentine ⇨ TURPENTINE (definition 2).

oil paint *noun* also **oil colour**
a mixture of pigment and oil for painting.

oil painting *noun*
a work produced with oil paints.
Phrase **be no oil painting** (*informal*) not to be particularly attractive.

oilskin *noun*
1 a fabric treated with oil to make it waterproof, used for fishermen's clothes, etc.
2 (*usually* **oilskins**) any piece of clothing made from this fabric.

oily *adjective* (**oilier; oiliest**)
1 of, like or covered with oil.
2 too smooth or fawning in speech or manner.

ointment *noun*
any substance, such as a paste, cream or liquid, usually medicated, applied to the skin.

OK (**o-kay**) *adjective, adverb* also **okay**
(*informal*) all right; correct.
• **OK** *verb* (**OK's; OK'ing; OK'd**)
(*informal*) to endorse or approve something.
• **OK** *noun* (*informal*) an approval or endorsement.

> **OK** is of uncertain origin. It seems most likely that it was short for *orl korrekt*, a humorous American spelling of *all correct*. In 1840, a year after *OK* became established, it was used as an election slogan by American presidential candidate Martin Van Buren, whose nickname was *Old Kinderhook*, *OK* for short, after his birthplace of Kinderhook in New York State.

okra *noun* also called **ladies' fingers**.
a tall West African herb, the pods of which are used as a vegetable.

old *adjective*
1 having existed or lived for a relatively long time: *He was an old man of 98 when he died.*
Figurative an old head on young shoulders
(= mature, sensible). □ *I met an old school*

friend yesterday (= former). □ *He always uses the same old excuse* (= familiar, worn-out).

2 having a specified age: *She could read when she was three years old.*

3 dear or cherished through long association: *good old Tim.* □ *the old country.*

Phrase of old of former times: *We studied the kings of old.*

> [!] *Old* has two sets of comparative and superlative forms: *older/oldest*, which are used of people or things (*the oldest house in the village*), and *elder/eldest*, which are used only of people, especially family members (*his eldest sister*). ⇨ ELDER[1].

old boy *noun*
a male former member of a particular school: *I am going to an old boys' reunion.*

old boy network *noun*
favouritism, e.g. in filling a vacancy, due to the tendency of old boys of the same school to help each other, possibly to the detriment of others or of efficiency.

olden *adjective*
a poetic word for **old**.

old-fashioned *adjective*
out of date or no longer fashionable.

old girl *noun*
a female former member of a particular school.

old hat *adjective*
(*informal*) old-fashioned.

old master *noun*
1 any of the leading or distinguished early European painters, especially from the 15th to the 18th centuries.
2 a painting by such an artist.

old school tie *noun*
1 a tie indicating a man's former public school.
2 the alleged traditionalism and clannishness of the wearers of these.

old stager *noun*
a person with long experience in a particular activity, occupation, etc.

Old Testament *noun*
Religion the first part of the Bible, containing the Jewish scriptures. Compare NEW TESTAMENT.

old-timer *noun*
(*informal*) a person who has lived, resided, been a member, etc. for a very long time.

old wives' tale *noun*
a traditional superstitious belief.

Old World *noun*
the countries in Europe, western Asia and north Africa. Compare NEW WORLD.

oleaginous (o-lee-**aj**-i-nus) *adjective*
oily or greasy.
[Latin *oleum* oil]

oleander (o-lee-**un**-da) *noun*
any of a group of large poisonous evergreen shrubs with delicate white or pink flowers.

olfactory (ol-**fak**-ta-ree) *adjective*
of or relating to the sense of smell.
[Latin *olfacere* to smell]

oligarchy (**oll**-i-gar-kee) *noun* (*plural* **oligarchies**)
1 a government in which a small group of people has power.
2 a country with this form of government.
Word Family oligarchic (oll-i-**gar**-kik), **oligarchical** *adjective*; **oligarch** *noun*.
[Greek *oligos* few + *arkhos* a leader]

olive (**oll**-iv) *noun*
1 a small green or black oval fruit with a stone, usually pickled or crushed for its oil.
2 a deep brownish-green colour.
● **olive** *adjective* of or having the colour olive.
[from Latin]

olive branch *noun* (*plural* **olive branches**)
something offered as a symbol of peace.

olive oil *noun*
oil obtained from olives, widely used in cooking.

olivine (**oll**-iv-een) *noun*
Geology a dense common mineral (magnesium silicate), occurring in olive green masses in basic igneous rocks.

Olympian (a-**lim**-pi-an) *noun*
1 *Greek mythology* one of the gods, believed to live on Mount Olympus.
2 a person who is calm, aloof and disdainful.
3 a competitor in the Olympic Games.
Word Family olympian *adjective*.

Olympic Games *plural noun* also **Olympics**
(*used with singular or plural verb*) a series of international sports events held every four years in a different country, originally held at Olympia in Ancient Greece.

ombudsman (**om**-budz-man) *noun* (*plural* **ombudsmen**)
a government official appointed to investigate complaints by individuals against the government or civil service.
[Swedish, legal representative]

omega (o-migg-a) *noun*
1 the 24th and last letter of the Greek alphabet.
2 the end of anything. Compare ALPHA.

omelette (om-let) *noun* (*American* **omelet**)
a dish of eggs beaten and lightly fried, often eaten with a filling.

omen (o-men) *noun*
a sign of a coming event, often regarded as a threat or warning: *a bad omen*.
[Latin]

ominous (omm-i-nus) *adjective*
threatening or suggesting evil.
Word Family **ominously** *adverb*.

omit (a-mit) *verb* (**omits; omitting; omitted**)
to leave out or fail to do something.
Word Family **omission** (a-**mish**-'n) *noun*.
[from Latin]

omnibus (om-ni-bus) *noun* (*plural* **omnibuses**)
1 a single book containing several works on a particular topic or by one author.
2 (*dated*) a bus.
• **omnibus** *adjective* (of an edition of a television or radio programme) comprising two or more previously broadcast episodes.
[Latin, for all]

omnipotent (om-**nipp**-a-t'nt) *adjective*
having great or unlimited power.
Word Family **omnipotence** *noun*.

omnipresent (om-ni-**prezz**-'nt) *adjective*
present in all places at the same time.
Word Family **omnipresence** *noun*.

omniscient (om-**niss**-i-ent) *adjective*
having unlimited knowledge.
Word Family **omnisciently** *adverb*; **omniscience** *noun*.
[*omni*- + Latin *sciens* knowledge]

omnivorous (om-**nivv**-a-rus) *adjective*
of or relating to an organism which eats all types of food, especially an animal which can eat both meat and vegetation.
Word Family **omnivore** (**om**-ni-vor) *noun*.
[*omni*- + Latin *vorare* to devour]

on *preposition*
1 a word used to indicate support or contact: *the book on the desk.* □ *The child scribbled on the wall.* □ *a scar on her face.*
2 a word used to indicate time or occasion: *on Monday.* □ *They greeted me on my arrival home.*

3 about or concerning: *a discussion on conservation.*
4 a word used to indicate association or activity: *to sit on a jury.* □ *to go on holiday.*
□ *She is on her best behaviour.*
5 a word used to indicate direction: *on the left.*
6 a word used to indicate basis or reason: *I have it on good authority that he is dead.*
7 a word used to indicate proximity: *a town on the river.*
8 a word used to indicate state, process, etc.: *The car was on fire.*
9 a word used to indicate means of conveyance: *We went on foot.*
• **on** *adverb*
1 in place, attached to or in contact with a place or person: *She put her coat on.*
2 in continued activity: *They worked on till midnight.*
3 further, onwards: *We hurried on.*
4 towards: *We looked on while they worked.*
5 (of an electrical appliance) so as to be functioning: *Turn the radio on.*
Phrases **on and off, off and on** intermittently. **on and on** without stopping.
• **on** *adjective*
1 operating: *The heating is on.*
2 (of an event) happening. *Is anything on tomorrow?*
3 *Cricket* being on the same side of the field as the batsman's legs.
Phrase **be on to** (*informal*) to be aware of or informed about.

once (wunce) *adverb*
1 formerly: *a once powerful nation.*
2 at a single time: *once a week.*
Phrases **once and for all** finally and decisively. **once upon a time** long ago.
• **once** *noun* a single occasion: *Once is enough.*
Phrases **all at once** suddenly. **at once**
1 immediately. 2 at the same time.
• **once** *conjunction* when, as soon as.

once-over *noun*
(*informal*) a quick or superficial inspection.

oncology (on-**koll**-a-jee) *noun*
the study of cancer.
Word Family **oncologist** *noun*; **oncological** (on-ko-**loj**-i-k'l) *adjective*.

oncoming (on-kumm-ing) *adjective*
approaching: *oncoming traffic.*

one (wun) *noun*
1 a cardinal number, the symbol 1 in Arabic numerals, I in Roman numerals.

2 a single person or thing: *Please give me one of those.*
Phrases one and all everybody. **one by one** singly and in succession.

• **one** *adjective*
1 being an individual, unit or object.
2 being a particular instance of a number: *one member of a group.* □ *one evening last week.*
Figurative One Fred Brown was chosen (= a certain). □ *We will meet again one day* (= some future).
Phrase all one all the same.

• **one** *pronoun*
1 a particular person or thing: *She's the only musical one in the family.*
2 a person: *He is not one to be easily frightened.* □ *One cannot always find time for reading.*

> ⚠ Both *one* and *you* can be used to mean 'people in general', as in *One should look after one's health* and *You never know what's in store for you*, but *one* is more formal.

one-armed bandit *noun*
(*informal*) a fruit machine.

one-horse *adjective*
(*informal*) small or unimportant: *a one-horse town.*

oneness (**wun-**ness) *noun*
agreement or unity of thought, purpose, etc.

one-off *adjective*
1 (*informal*) happening only once.
2 (*informal*) made or designed for one person or one occasion only.
• **one-off** *noun* (*informal*) something that happens or is made only once.

onerous (**o-**na-rus *or* **onn-**a-rus) *adjective*
heavy or burdensome.
Word Family onerously *adverb*; **onerousness** *noun*.
[Latin *oneris* of a burden]

oneself *pronoun*
1 the reflexive form of **one**: *to wash oneself.*
2 the emphatic form of **one**: *In those days one did it oneself.*
3 one's normal or usual self.

one-sided *adjective*
1 considering only one aspect of a matter: *a one-sided view of the situation.*
2 very unequal: *a one-sided fight.*
3 having or occurring on only one side.

one-time *adjective*
former: *a one-time friend.*

one-track *adjective*
1 having a single track.

2 (*informal*) restricted to one subject: *a one-track mind.*

one-upmanship *noun*
(*informal*) the art of slyly disconcerting others in order to appear superior, e.g. by competitive name-dropping.
[invented by Stephen Potter, 1952]

ongoing *adjective*
progressing, continuing.

onion (**un-**y'n) *noun*
a small to medium-sized brown or white bulb which has a strong taste or smell and is used as a vegetable.

online *adjective, adverb*
Computers connected to a computer or to the Internet: *You'll have to go online to register.* Compare OFF-LINE.

onlooker *noun*
a spectator.

only (*rhymes with* lonely) *adjective*
1 being the single one in a class or group: *He is the only millionaire I know.*
2 without brothers or sisters: *She is an only child.*

• **only** *adverb*
1 without anyone or anything else: *Only Peter was late.*
2 no more than: *The baby can only crawl* □ *She is only ten years old.*

• **only** *conjunction* except: *I like the car, only it is too expensive.*

> ⚠ Strictly speaking, *only* should come immediately before the word or phrase it qualifies, as in *I eat only fruit on Mondays* (= I eat nothing but fruit on Mondays) and *I eat fruit only on Mondays* (= I don't eat fruit except on Mondays).

onomatopoeia (on-a-mat-ta-**pee-**a) *noun*
the formation of a word whose sound suggests its meaning, as in 'coo', 'hiss', 'buzz', etc.
Word Family onomatopoeic (on-a-mat-ta-**pee-**ik) *adjective*.
[Greek *onoma* name + *poiein* to make]

onrush *noun* (*plural* **onrushes**)
a strong forward rush.

onset *noun*
1 a beginning: *At the onset of rain the players left the field.*
2 (*dated*) an attack.

onside *adjective, adverb*
Sport not offside.

onslaught (**on-**slawt) *noun*
an attack, especially a fierce or violent one.

on to *preposition* also **onto**
used to indicate movement towards the surface or top of something: *The child climbed on to the stool.*

> **!** Although *on to* is increasingly written as one word with the meaning as in *He drove onto the pavement*, it should remain as two words where *on* and *to* have separate meanings, as in *He drove on to the station* (= He continued driving until he reached the station).

ontology (on-**toll**-a-jee) *noun*
Philosophy the study of being or existence.
Word Family ontological (on-ta-**loj**-i-k'l) *adjective*; **ontologist** *noun*.
[Greek *on, ontos* being + *-logy*]

onus (o-nus) *noun* (*plural* **onuses**)
a burden or responsibility.
[Latin]

onward *adjective*
advancing ahead or forwards.
Word Family onwards, onward *adverb*.

onyx (**on**-iks) *noun*
Geology a type of chalcedony with coloured bands, often used in ornaments.
[Greek]

oodles *plural noun*
(*informal*) a large quantity.

ooze[1] *verb*
to flow or leak out slowly.
Word Family oozy *adjective* 1 oozing moisture. 2 damp with moisture.

ooze[2] *noun*
1 *Geography* the very fine mud found on the bottom of the ocean.
2 any mud or slime.
Word Family oozy *adjective*.

opal (o-pul) *noun*
Geology a naturally occurring hydrated amorphous form of silica, often iridescent and used as a gem.

opalescent (opa-**less**-'nt) *adjective*
having a shimmer of colours like that of opal.
Word Family opalescence *noun*.

opaque (o-**pake**) *adjective*
1 not able to be seen through.
2 not transmitting or reflecting light.
3 obscure or difficult to understand.
Word Family opaquely *adverb*; **opacity** (o-**pass**-i-tee), **opaqueness** *noun*.
[Latin *opacus* shady, dark]

op art *noun*
a style of painting or sculpture which gives the impression of movement due to optical effects.
[OP(tical) + ART]

open *adjective*
1 allowing unobstructed entrance and exit: *The sheep wandered out of the open gate.*
2 not closed, covered or enclosed: *an open jar.* □ *the open countryside.*
3 not decided or specified: *With no clues, it was an open verdict.* □ *Fill this open cheque in for any amount you wish.*
4 not limited or restricted: *open season.*
Figurative *Is the job you advertised still open?* (= available). □ *The shop is often open on Sundays* (= ready for business). □ *I admire his open manner* (= candid, unreserved). □ *Her behaviour leaves her open to attack* (= liable, susceptible) □ *I have almost decided what to do, but I am still open to suggestions* (= receptive). □ *Open newspapers lay all over the floor* (= unfolded, spread out).
● **open** *verb*
1 to become or cause to become open.
2 to unwrap: *She opened her birthday present.*
3 to have an outlet: *The rooms open on to the veranda.*
● **open** *noun* any unenclosed area: *We spent the day in the open.*

open-and-shut *adjective*
obvious or easily decided: *an open-and-shut case of murder.*

opencast mining *noun*
mining from the surface rather than from shafts.

open day *noun*
a day on which visitors are invited to look around a school, hospital, etc.

open-ended *adjective*
being organized so as to allow for various possibilities: *an open-ended agreement.*

opener *noun*
a person or device that opens.

open-handed *adjective*
generous.
Word Family open-handedly *adverb*; **open-handedness** *noun*.

open-hearted *adjective*
1 frank or unreserved.
2 kind.
Word Family open-heartedness *noun*.

open house *noun*
1 the fact of offering hospitality to all friends or visitors.
2 a social event at which such hospitality exists.

opening *noun*
1 a beginning or first movement, such as the first performance of a play, etc.
2 an open space: *A small, narrow opening led into the secret passage.*
3 a vacancy or opportunity: *We have an opening for an ambitious worker.*
• **opening** *adjective* first or beginning: *opening night.*

openly *adverb*
without hiding anything.

open-minded *adjective*
unprejudiced and willing to consider new ideas, arguments, etc.
Word Family **open-mindedly** *adverb*; **open-mindedness** *noun.*

open-mouthed *adjective*
gaping with astonishment.

open-plan *adjective*
(of offices, etc.) having few interior walls.

open sandwich *noun (plural* **open sandwiches**)
a slice of bread with a topping, but no top slice of bread.

open secret *noun*
a matter which is supposed to be secret but is in fact generally known.

open shop *noun*
a workplace where non-union labour can be employed. Compare CLOSED SHOP.

open verdict *noun*
Law a verdict that an unknown person has committed a crime or that a cause for a violent death is not specified.

opera[1] (**opp**-er-a) *noun*
1 a play which is set to music.
2 a performance of such a play.
Word Family **operatic** (opp-a-**rat**-ik) *adjective.*
[Latin, labour]

opera[2]
a plural of **opus**.

operable (**op**-er-a-b'l) *adjective*
1 able to be used or put into practice.
2 *Medicine* capable of being cured or removed by surgical operation.

opera glasses *plural noun*
a small pair of binoculars for use in a theatre.

operate (**op**-a-rate) *verb*
1 to function: *This computer operates much faster than the human brain.*
2 to use or control the functioning of: *He operates the switchboard.*
3 *Medicine* to cut a body to remove or repair part of it.
[Latin *operari* to work]

operation (op-a-**ray**-sh'n) *noun*
1 the act or method of operating: *Your operation of the machine shows you are well trained.*
2 the state of being operative: *The machine is out of operation.*
3 a course or process of work, activity, etc., such as a planned military attack.
Word Family **operational** *adjective*
1 relating to operations. 2 fit for use.

operative (**op**-ra-tiv) *adjective*
1 operating or in effect: *The law became operative last week.*
2 efficient: *First we must try to formulate an operative plan.*
3 most significant: *Compromise has been the operative word during the discussions.*
4 of or relating to surgical operations.
• **operative** *noun* a worker.

operator (**op**-a-ray-ta) *noun*
1 a person who operates a mechanical device.
2 (*informal*) a shrewd, often unscrupulous person.

operetta (op-a-**rett**-a) *noun*
a short and simple form of opera, usually amusing.

ophthalmic (off **thal**-mik) *adjective*
of or relating to the eye.

ophthalmic optician *noun*
a person qualified to prescribe lenses for spectacles, who also makes, sells or dispenses the complete spectacles.

ophthalmologist (off-thal-**moll** a-jist) *noun*
a doctor who treats disorders and diseases of the eye.
Word Family **ophthalmology** *noun.*
[Greek *ophthalmos* eye + *-logy*]

opiate (**o**-pee-it) *noun*
1 any substance made from opium.
2 any substance causing dullness or a feeling of inactivity.

opine (a-**pine**) *verb*
(*formal*) to hold or express an opinion.

opinion (a-**pin**-y'n) *noun*
a belief, attitude or viewpoint: *What is your opinion of modern art?* □ *The lawyer advised me to seek a second opinion.*

opinionated *adjective*
dogmatic or obstinately maintaining one's opinions.

opinion poll *noun* also **poll**
a survey of public opinion, particularly voting intentions before an election.

opium (o-pee-um) *noun*
the juice of certain poppies, containing morphine and other substances, used in medicine to relieve pain, induce sleep, etc. [Greek *opos* juice]

opossum *noun*
a small tree-dwelling marsupial found in North and South America and noted for its habit of feigning death when in danger.

opponent (a-**po**-nent) *noun*
a person who is on the opposite side in a contest, argument, etc. [Latin *opponere* to place against]

opportune (op-a-**tewn**) *adjective*
favourable or convenient: *Wait for the most opportune moment.*
Word Family **opportunely** *adverb.*
[from Latin]

opportunism (op-a-**tew**-nizm) *noun*
the policy of taking advantage of situations, often involving the sacrifice of principles.
Word Family **opportunist** *noun;* **opportunistic** (op-a-tew-**nist**-ik) *adjective;* **opportunistically** *adverb.*

opportunity (op-a-**tew**-ni-tee) *noun*
(*plural* **opportunities**)
1 a favourable or suitable time.
2 a chance.

oppose *verb*
1 to resist or be against: *Some people opposed the introduction of daylight-saving time.*
2 to set against or put forward as a contrast: *Love is opposed to hate.*
Word Family **opposed** *adjective;* **opposing** *adjective.*

opposite (**op**-a-zit) *adjective*
1 placed or situated directly facing a person or object: *She sat at the opposite end of the table to me.*
2 entirely different: *the opposite direction.*
• **opposite** *noun* something which is opposite: *North and south are opposites.*
• **opposite** *adverb* on the opposite side: *the house opposite.*
• **opposite** *preposition* on the opposite side from: *We live opposite the hotel.*
[Latin *oppositus* placed against]

opposite number *noun*
a person who holds a corresponding position in another situation.

opposition (op-a-**zish**-'n) *noun*
1 the state of being opposed: *We all voted in opposition to the new rule.*
2 (**the Opposition**) *Parliament* the party or parties outside the ruling party who

criticize and try to amend government decisions.

oppress *verb*
1 to treat cruelly or unjustly.
2 to weigh down: *He was oppressed with worries.*
Word Family **oppression** *noun;* **oppressor** *noun.*
[Latin *oppressus* pressed down]

oppressive *adjective*
1 unjustly cruel.
2 physically or mentally distressing: *oppressive heat.*
Word Family **oppressively** *adverb;* **oppressiveness** *noun.*

opprobrium (ap-**pro**-bree-um) *noun*
1 any disgrace arising from shameful conduct.
2 a cause of this.
Word Family **opprobrious** *adjective.*
[Latin, a reproach, a scandal]

oppugn (a-**pewn**) *verb*
an old word meaning 'to argue against or call into question'.
[Latin *oppugnare* to fight against]

opt *verb*
to make a choice: *I opted to stay on at school for another year.*
Phrase **opt out** 1 to choose not to be involved. 2 (of schools or hospitals) to choose not to be run by a local authority.
[Latin *optare* to wish for]

optical *adjective*
1 also **optic** of or relating to the eye or the function of sight.
2 designed to assist vision: *an optical lens.*
[Greek *optos* seen]

optical fibre *noun*
a thin strand of glass through which light is transmitted.

optician (op-**tish**-'n) *noun*
a person who makes or sells optical instruments, especially spectacles.

optic nerve *noun*
Anatomy the nerve that carries visual messages from the eyes to the brain.

optics *plural noun*
(*used with singular verb*) the study of light and vision, a branch of physics.

optimism (**op**-ti-mizm) *noun*
1 a tendency to look on the favourable or bright side of things.
2 *Philosophy* the belief that the universe is organized for the good of all, and must certainly improve. Compare PESSIMISM (definition 2).

Word Family optimist *noun*; **optimistic** (op-ti-**mist**-ik) *adjective* tending to take a hopeful or favourable view of things; **optimistically** *adverb*.
[Latin *optimus* best]

optimize, optimise (**op**-ti-mize) *verb* to make the best use of.

optimum (**op**-ti-mum) *adjective* also **optimal** the best or most favourable.

option (**op**-sh'n) *noun*
1 the right or power to choose: *I had no option but to accept their offer.*
2 the act of choosing.
3 anything which is or may be chosen: *There are only two options open to us.*
4 the right to buy or sell something within a certain time on the stated terms.
Word Family optional *adjective* open to choice; **optionally** *adverb*.
[Latin *optare* to wish for]

optometry (op-**tom**-a-tree) *noun* the practice or profession of testing the eyes for defects in vision, so that suitable spectacles can be prescribed.
Word Family optometrist *noun*.

opulent (**op**-yoo-l'nt) *adjective* rich or abundant, especially in wealth.
Word Family opulence *noun*
[from Latin]

opus (**o**-pus) *noun* (*plural* **opuses** or **opera** (**op**-er-a))
1 a written work, especially a musical composition.
2 *Music* one of the compositions of a composer, numbered according to the order of publication.
[Latin]

or *conjunction*
1 used to connect alternatives: *to be or not to be.* □ *Either that dog goes, or I go.*
2 used to connect synonyms or related words, phrases, etc.: *a pound, or 100 pence.*
3 used to suggest uncertainty or approximation: *There were 20 or 30 people at the meeting.*

oracle (**orr**-i-k'l) *noun*
1 *Ancient religion* a shrine where questions were asked of gods or goddesses.
2 *Ancient religion* a deity's response to a question, or the person giving it.
3 any statement or person considered to have infallible authority or wisdom.
Word Family oracular (o-**rak**-yoo-lar) *adjective*.
[Latin *oraculum* an utterance]

oral (**or**-ul) *adjective*
1 spoken, as distinct from written.
2 of, used in or taken through the mouth: *oral medicine.*
• **oral** *noun* a spoken examination.
Word Family orally *adverb*.
[Latin *oris* of the mouth]

orange (**orr**-inj) *noun*
1 a reddish-yellow colour, the colour between red and yellow in the spectrum.
2 a round medium-sized citrus fruit with an orange rind.
• **orange** *adjective* of or having the colour orange.
[Persian *narang*]

orangeade (orr-inj-**aid**) *noun* a drink containing orange juice or flavoured with orange, often carbonated.

orange blossom *noun* the white scented flowers of the orange tree, traditionally carried by brides.

orang-utan (or-**rang** oo-tang) *noun* also **orang-utang** a large ape with reddish-brown hair found in the forests of Borneo and Sumatra.
[Malay]

> The word **orang-utan** is Malay for 'wild man' and probably reached English via Dutch. The term possibly first referred to tribes who lived in the forests, but it was taken by European travellers to refer to the large red-haired ape inhabiting the same forests.

oration (or-**ay**-sh'n) *noun* a formal speech.
Word Family orator (**orr**-a-ta) *noun*; **oratorical** (orr-a-**torr**-i-k'l) *adjective*.
[Latin *orare* to speak, to plead a case]

oratorio (orr-a-**taw**-ri-o) *noun* a long musical composition written as a drama for singers and orchestra, usually with a religious theme.
[Italian]

oratory[1] (**orr**-a-tree) *noun* the art of eloquence or public speaking.

oratory[2] *noun* (*plural* **oratories**) *Christianity* a small chapel or room used for private worship.

orb *noun*
1 a circle or sphere, such as the sun or the moon.
2 a poetic word for the sun or an eye.

orbit *noun*
1 *Astronomy* the path of a planet around the sun, or of a satellite around a planet.

2 any similar curved path of one body around another, such as that of an electron around the nucleus of an atom.
Figurative The orbit of the country's power extended across the world (= range of influence).
3 *Anatomy* ➪ EYE SOCKET.
● **orbit** *verb* to move or travel in an orbit.
Word Family **orbital** *adjective*.
[Latin *orbis* a circle]

orchard (or-ch'd) *noun*
1 an area of land planted with fruit trees.
2 the trees grown in such an area.
[Latin *hortus* a garden + YARD[2]]

orchestra (ork-ist-ra) *noun*
1 a large group of musicians playing woodwind, brass, percussion and string instruments.
2 the space in a theatre reserved for musicians, usually immediately in front of and below the stage.
Word Family **orchestrate** *verb* to write or arrange music for an orchestra; **orchestration** (ork-i-**stray**-sh'n) *noun*; **orchestral** (or-**kest**-r'l) *adjective*.
[Greek *orkhestra* the space where the chorus danced during a play]

orchid (or-kid) *noun*
any of a group of plants with brightly coloured luxurious flowers.
[Latin *orchis* testicle]

ordain *verb*
1 *Christianity* to appoint as a bishop, priest or deacon.
2 to solemnly order or decide.
[Latin *ordinis* of an order]

ordeal *noun*
1 any severe or distressing experience: *The interview was an ordeal for the nervous applicant.*
2 a primitive form of trial which tested the effect of fire, etc. on the accused person.

order *noun*
1 a direction or command, especially one given officially or with authority.
2 a system or arrangement of things in relation to each other or in a series: *alphabetical order.* □ *a new political and social order.*
3 a state or condition: *The house is in good order.*
4 a proper or right condition: *The car is out of order.* □ *The troops couldn't keep order.*
5 a request to supply or provide: *He placed an order for a car.*
6 something requested or supplied: *Your order is ready.*
7 *Biology* the group below 'class' used in the classification of animals and plants.
8 *Religion* a group of people living under a common religious rule, e.g. in a monastery.
9 *Religion* any of the ranks of clergy.
10 (*formal*) level or degree: *Her bravery is of the highest order.*
Phrases **in order** *Is it in order for the meeting to end earlier?* (= suitable, acceptable). **in order that, in order to** so that. **of the order of** approximately. **on order** having been ordered but not yet delivered. **out of order** broken down; not working. **to order** *a coat made to order* (= to the buyer's instructions).
● **order** *verb*
1 to give or make an order.
2 to put in order.
Phrase **order about** to instruct or direct in a domineering manner.

orderly *adjective*
1 arranged in a tidy or systematic way.
2 obedient or well-behaved: *an orderly crowd.*
● **orderly** *noun* (*plural* **orderlies**)
1 a person who does non-medical work in a hospital.
2 a soldier acting as an officer's messenger.
Word Family **orderliness** *noun*.

ordinal[1] *adjective*
relating to an order.
● **ordinal** *noun* an ordinal number.

ordinal[2] *noun*
Religion a book of instructions or procedures for certain services or ceremonies.

ordinal number *noun*
Maths a number indicating order, e.g. 1st, 2nd, 3rd, etc. Compare CARDINAL NUMBER.

ordinance *noun*
(*formal*) an official command, law or rule.

ordinary (or-din-ree) *adjective*
1 normal or usual: *Change into your ordinary clothes.*
2 average or not outstanding: *The meal was quite ordinary.*
● **ordinary** *noun*
Phrase **out of the ordinary** unusual: *This talented singer is quite out of the ordinary.*
Word Family **ordinarily** (or-din-a-ra-lee) *adverb* 1 usually. 2 in the ordinary way; **ordinariness** *noun*.

ordinary seaman *noun* (*plural* **ordinary seamen**)
Navy a sailor of the lowest rank.

ordinate (or-da-n't) *noun*
Maths the vertical distance of a point from the origin of a graph; the *y*-coordinate. Compare ABSCISSA.

ordination (or-di-**nay**-sh'n) *noun*
1 the act or ceremony of ordaining.
2 the fact of being ordained.

ordnance *noun*
any military equipment, especially artillery.

Ordnance Survey *noun*
the government civil department which carries out surveys of the whole country and produces detailed maps.
[originally carried out by the army's Board of *Ordnance*]

Ordovician (or-da-**vish**-ee-an) ➪ PALAEOZOIC.

ordure (**ord**-yoor) *noun*
dung.
[Latin *horridus* uncouth, frightful]

ore *noun*
a mineral or mixture of minerals containing a metal or non-metal in sufficient amounts to be profitable if mined.

oregano (orr-i-**gah**-no) *noun*
a sweet-smelling herb related to mint, used in cooking.
[Spanish]

organ *noun*
1 *Music* a keyboard instrument in which notes are sounded by wind blown through pipes by means of bellows or electric power.
2 *Anatomy* any part of an organism, consisting of one or more kinds of tissue, that forms a structural and functional unit, such as a kidney, a leaf, etc.
3 a means of publicizing (especially political) opinion, e.g. a periodical: *This journal is the chief organ of the extreme right wing.*
[Greek *organon* an instrument, a tool]

organdie (**or**-gan-dee) *noun*
a very fine stiff muslin, used for dresses, curtains, etc.

organelle (or-ga-**nel**) *noun*
Biology a tiny structure within a biological cell which carries out a specific function.

organ-grinder *noun*
a street musician who plays a small organ by turning a handle.

organic (or-**gann**-ik) *adjective*
1 of or relating to living organisms.
2 relating to the organ or organs of an animal or plant.
3 (of disease) affecting the structure of an organ.
4 of or produced by the use of natural fertilizers such as compost, as distinct from manufactured ones: *organic vegetables.*
5 *Chemistry* of or relating to a class of compounds containing carbon combined with hydrogen and often with oxygen, nitrogen and other elements. The molecules are often very large and complex, containing large numbers of carbon atoms in chains and rings. Compare INORGANIC (definition 2).
6 organized or arranged systematically: *an organic whole.*
Word Family **organically** *adverb.*

organism (**or**-ga-nizm) *noun*
1 *Biology* any living thing; an animal or plant.
2 any system or organization with dependent parts.

organist *noun*
Music a person who plays the organ.

organization, organisation (or-gan-eye-**zay**-sh'n) *noun*
1 the act of organizing: *The organization of accommodation should be done before the tour.*
2 the state of being organized: *There is not enough organization in your method.*
3 a number of people or groups joined and organized for some purpose: *a charitable organization.*
Word Family **organizational** *adjective*; **organizationally** *adverb.*

organize, organise (**or**-ga-nize) *verb*
to bring or put together as a whole: *We must organize a demonstration.*
Word Family **organized** *adjective*; **organizer** *noun.*

organza (or-**gan**-za) *noun*
a thin stiff fabric made from silk or nylon mixed with cotton.

orgasm (**or**-gazm) *noun*
the climax of excitement in sexual activity.
Word Family **orgasmic** (or-**gaz**-mik) *adjective.*
[Greek *organ* to swell or to be excited]

orgy (**or**-jee) *noun* (*plural* **orgies**)
1 a wild, drunken or immoral festivity or celebration.
2 any excessively indulgent or uncontrolled activity.

Word Family **orgiastic** (or-jee-**ast**-ik) *adjective*.

[Greek *orgia* secret rites, the mysteries]

oriel (**or**-ee-ul) *noun*
a bay window high in a building.

Orient (**or**-ee-unt) *noun*
a poetic word for the countries of Asia, especially eastern Asia. Compare OCCIDENT.

Word Family **oriental, Oriental** (or-ee-**en**-t'l) *adjective* of or characteristic of the Orient; **oriental** *noun* (*usually* **Oriental**) an offensive word for an inhabitant of Asia.

[Latin *oriens* the east, sunrise]

orientate (**or**-ee-un-tate) *verb also* **orient** (**or**-ee-ent)
to place or face in a particular position or direction.

Figurative She is not orientated to her new life (= adjusted, adapted).

Word Family **orientation** (or-ee-un-**tay**-sh'n) *noun* 1 the act of orientating. 2 the state of being orientated: *The house's orientation is to the north.*

orienteering *noun*
a sport of cross-country running over a set course.

orifice (**or**-i-fiss) *noun*
an opening or hole.

[Latin *oris* of the mouth + *facere* to make]

origami (orr-i-**gah**-mee) *noun*
the art of folding paper into decorative shapes, e.g. animals and flowers.

[Japanese *ori* a folding + *kami* paper]

origin (**or**-i-jin) *noun*
1 something from which anything else starts, issues or is derived: *What is the origin of that folk song?*
2 a beginning or first stage: *The origin of the war dates back several years.*
Figurative The politician did not hide the fact of his humble origins (= birth, parentage).
3 *Maths* the point where two or more axes meet.

[Latin *originis* of the source]

original (a-**rij**-i-n'l) *adjective*
1 relating or belonging to the origin or beginning of something: *This Victorian house still has its original features.*
2 being the first, from which a copy, translation, etc. is made: *Do you still have the original photo?*
3 new, unusual or different: *She dresses in very original clothes.*
4 creative, individual or inventive in thought or action.
• **original** *noun*
1 something which is original, as distinct from a copy or imitation.
2 the person or thing represented in a painting, piece of writing, etc.
3 an eccentric or individual person.

Word Family **originality** (a-rij-i-**nal**-i-tee) *noun*; **originally** *adverb* 1 at first. 2 from the beginning.

original sin ⇨ SIN.

originate (a-**rij**-i-nate) *verb*
1 to bring into being: *Who originated the annual reunion?*
2 to begin or arise: *Their quarrel originated from a silly disagreement.*

Word Family **origination** (a-rij-i-**nay**-sh'n) *noun*; **originator** *noun*.

oriole (**or**-ee-ole) *noun*
any of a family of bright yellowish-green and black birds, mostly in America.

[Latin *aureus* golden]

orison (**or**-i-z'n) *noun*
an old word for a prayer.

ormolu (**or**-ma-loo) *noun*
an alloy of copper, zinc and tin which resembles gold and is used to decorate furniture, clocks, etc.

[French *or moulu* ground gold]

ornament (**or**-na-m'nt) *noun*
an object or detail used to add beauty or decoration.
• **ornament** (**or**-na-ment) *verb*
1 to provide with ornaments.
2 to increase the beauty of.

Word Family **ornamental** (or-na-**men**-t'l) *adjective*; **ornamentation** (or-na-men-**tay**-sh'n) *noun*.

[Latin *ornare* to equip, adorn]

ornate (or-**nate**) *adjective*
elaborately decorated.

Word Family **ornately** *adverb*; **ornateness** *noun*.

ornithology (or-ni-**tholl**-a-jee) *noun*
the study of birds.

Word Family **ornithological** (or-nith-a-**loj**-i-k'l) *adjective*; **ornithologist** *noun*.

[Greek *ornithos* of a bird + *-logy*]

orotund (**orr**-a-tund) *adjective*
1 (of a voice or words) clear and rich in tone.
2 (of speech) pompous.

[Latin *ore rotundo* with round mouth]

orphan (**or**-f'n) *noun*
a child whose parents are dead.

Word Family orphan *verb*; **orphanage**
(**or**-fa-nij) *noun* an institution where
orphans are cared for.
[Greek *orphanos* bereaved]

orris *noun*
a fragrant powder obtained by grinding
the root of a variety of iris, used in
perfumes.
[from IRIS]

orthodontics (or-tho-**don**-tiks) *plural
noun*
(*used with singular verb*) the art of
straightening irregular teeth, a branch of
dentistry.
Word Family orthodontic *adjective*;
orthodontist *noun*.
[Greek *orthos* straight + *odontos* of a tooth]

orthodox (**orth**-a-doks) *adjective*
1 conventional or conforming to accepted
standards: *The barrister's intimidating
methods during the trial were not considered
orthodox.*
2 correct or traditional in religious
doctrine or practice.
Word Family orthodoxly *adverb*;
orthodoxy *noun*.
[Greek *orthos* straight + *doxa* an opinion]

Orthodox Church *noun* also called
Eastern Orthodox Church.
a body of Christian Churches of Greek or
Slavic origin.

orthographic projection (or-tho-graf-ik
pro-**jek**-sh'n) *noun*
a way of drawing the detail of a three-
dimensional object in two dimensions by
showing square-on views.

orthography (or-**thog**-ra-fee) *noun*
the study or use of correct spelling.
[Greek *orthos* straight + *graphein* to write]

orthopaedics (or-tha-**pee**-diks) *plural
noun* (*American* **orthopedics**)
(*used with singular verb*) the treatment of
deformities of the bones, especially in
children, a branch of surgery.
Word Family orthopaedic *adjective*;
orthopaedist *noun*.
[Greek *orthos* straight + *paidos* of a child]

oryx (**orr**-iks) *noun* (*plural* **oryxes**)
any of various desert antelopes of Africa
and Arabia with long ringed horns.
[Greek]

Oscar *noun*
(*trademark*) any of several small gold
statuettes awarded annually in America for
outstanding achievement in making or
acting in films.

oscillate (**oss**-i-late) *verb*
to move or swing backwards and forwards,
as a pendulum does.
Figurative *He oscillates between wanting to
be a doctor and an architect* (= wavers,
fluctuates).
Word Family oscillator *noun*;
oscillation (oss-i-**lay**-sh'n) *noun* 1 the act
of oscillating. 2 a single swing or
movement of a body; **oscillatory** (o-**sill**-
a-tree) *adjective*.
[Latin *oscillare* to swing]

oscilloscope (as-**sill**-a-skope) *noun*
Physics a device which makes the shape of
a wave visible on a cathode ray tube.
[Latin *oscillare* to swing + Greek *skopein* to
look at]

osculate (**oss**-kew-late) *verb*
1 *Maths* (of curves or surfaces) to come
into close contact.
2 (*humorous*) to kiss.
Word Family osculation (oss-kew-**lay**-
sh'n) *noun*; **osculatory** (**oss**-kew-la-tree)
adjective.
[from Latin]

osier (**o**-zee-a) *noun*
1 any of a group of willows, the branches
of which are used for wickerwork.
2 a willow twig.

osmosis (oz-**mo**-sis) *noun*
1 *Biology, Chemistry* the percolation and
intermixture of fluids separated by a
porous membrane.
2 a gradual absorption or assimilation.
Word Family osmotic (oz-**mott**-ik)
adjective; **osmotically** *adverb*.
[Greek *osmos* push + *-osis*]

osprey (**oss**-pree or **oss**-pray) *noun*
a large eagle-like bird which plunges feet
first into the water to catch fish.
[Latin *ossifragus* bone-breaking]

osseous (**oss**-i-us) *adjective*
made of or resembling bone.

ossify (**oss**-i-fie) *verb* (**ossifies**; **ossifying**;
ossified)
to change into or harden like bone.
Figurative *The old man's attitudes have
ossified* (= become fixed or set).
Word Family ossification (oss-i-fi-**kay**-
sh'n) *noun*.
[Latin *ossis* of a bone + *facere* to make]

ostensible (oss-**ten**-si-b'l) *adjective*
professed or supposed: *Few people believed
her ostensible reason for going overseas.*
Word Family ostensibly *adverb*.
[Latin *ostendere* to stretch out, exhibit]

ostentation (oss-ten-**tay**-sh'n) *noun*
a showy display intended to impress
others.
Word Family ostentatious *adjective*;
ostentatiously *adverb*.

osteoarthritis (oss-ti-o-arth-**rye**-tis) *noun*
a degenerative arthritic disease mainly of
old age, usually located in the shoulder,
knee, hip or spine.
[Greek *osteon* bone + ARTHRITIS]

osteomyelitis (oss-ti-o-my-a-**lie**-tis) *noun*
a bacterial disease of the bones causing
pain and fever.
[Greek *osteon* bone + *myelos* marrow +
-itis]

osteopathy (oss-ti-**op**-a-thee) *noun*
the treatment of disease by manipulation
of parts of the body, especially the spine,
based on the belief that many diseases are
chiefly due to misplacement of bones.
Word Family osteopath (**oss**-ti-o-path)
noun a person who practises osteopathy.
[Greek *osteon* bone + *pathos* suffering]

osteoporosis (oss-ti-o-per-**o**-sis) *noun*
the development of brittle bones due to a
calcium deficiency.

ostler (**oss**-la) *noun* also **hostler**
an old word for a person who looks after
horses at an inn.
[from earlier *hostler*, from HOSTEL(er)]

ostracize, ostracise (**oss**-tra-size) *verb*
to exclude or banish from one's company,
friendship, country, etc.
Word Family ostracism (**oss**-tra-sizm)
noun.

> The word **ostracize** comes from the
> Greek word for a fragment of pottery,
> *ostrakon*. In ancient Greece, when there
> was a proposal to banish someone as a
> danger to the state, a vote would be
> taken. Those in favour of the exile
> would write the person's name on a
> piece of broken pottery; if enough
> pieces were inscribed, the exile would
> take place and last ten years.

ostrich *noun* (*plural* **ostriches**)
a long-legged two-toed flightless bird
found in Africa and Arabia, the largest bird
in existence.
[Greek *strouthion*]

other (*rhymes with* mother) *adjective*
1 different from the one named or implied:
Her house is at the other end of the street.
2 remaining: *Where are the other members of
the team?*
3 extra, more: *He needs one other person.*

Phrase **the other day (week, etc.)** *The
other day I saw an old friend* (= a few days
ago).
• **other** *pronoun* the other one: *I'll have this
room and you take the other.*
Figurative *We will get there some time or
other* (= another).

otherwise *adverb*
1 under different circumstances:
Otherwise, I would stay and help.
2 differently: *I wanted to come, but John felt
otherwise.*
3 in other respects: *He can no longer play
football but leads an otherwise active life.*

other-worldly *adjective*
1 of or characteristic of another, imaginary
or mystical, world.
2 impractical or remote from reality.
Word Family other-worldliness *noun*.

otiose (**o**-tee-ohss *or* **o**-shee-ohss) *adjective*
1 superfluous or useless.
2 an old word meaning **idle**.
[Latin *otiosus* at leisure, unemployed]

otter *noun*
any of a group of furry aquatic mammals
with webbed feet and a long tail.

ottoman *noun*
1 a silk or rayon fabric with long parallel
ridges.
2 an upholstered seat or divan without
back or arms.
3 a cushioned footstool.
[after *Othman*, the founder of the Turkish
Empire]

ouch *interjection*
an exclamation expressing sudden pain.

ought (awt) *verb*
1 an auxiliary verb indicating duty or
obligation: *You ought to visit your parents
more often.*
2 an auxiliary verb indicating probability:
We ought to be there soon at this speed.
3 an auxiliary verb indicating desirability:
*You ought to see the paintings in the National
Gallery.*
Word Family oughtn't *contraction* a short
form of **ought not**: *You oughtn't to say such
things about your brother!*

> [!] The negative form of *ought* is *ought
> not* (or *oughtn't*), not *didn't ought*.

Ouija board (**wee**-ja bord) *noun*
(*trademark*) a board marked with letters,
words and symbols, over which a pointer
moves and spells out words, supposedly
telepathically.

ounce¹ *noun*

1 a unit of mass in the avoirdupois system, equal to one sixteenth of a pound or about 28 grams. *abbrev.* oz.

2 a unit of mass in the apothecaries' and troy systems equal to about 31 grams. *abbrev.* oz.

3 a very small amount: *Don't you have even an ounce of intelligence?*

ounce² ⇨ SNOW LEOPARD.

our *possessive adjective* (*singular* **my**) belonging to us: *They are our bikes.*

ours *possessive pronoun* (*singular* **mine**) belonging to us: *The books are ours.*

> ! Note that there is no apostrophe in *ours*.

ourself *pronoun*

(*informal*) ourselves: *We tell ourself we're doing the right thing.*

> ! *Ourself* is sometimes used instead of *ourselves* when *we* is used to mean 'people in general', but some people think this is wrong.

ourselves *pronoun*

1 the reflexive form of **we**: *We washed ourselves.*

2 the emphatic form of **we**: *We did it ourselves.*

oust *verb*

to expel or eject.

out *adverb*

1 away from or not in a particular place, position, state, etc.: *She ran out a moment ago.* □ *This phone is out of order.* **Figurative** *Stretch out your hand* (= away from you). □ *They are giving out free tickets over there* (= away). □ *Short skirts went out last year!* (= out of fashion). □ *The miners are out for more pay* (= on strike).

2 to an end, conclusion or extinction: *My shoes have worn out.*

3 into view or evidence: *The sun came out.*

4 into existence: *An epidemic broke out.*

5 fully or completely: *Empty out that bucket and bring it here.* □ *The bride was decked out in white.*

Phrases all out *He has gone all out to finish the job in time* (= exerted himself to the utmost). **out of 1** *Six out of ten voted for the proposal* (= from amongst). **2** *That chair is made out of fibreglass* (= from). **3** *He did it out of spite* (= owing to, because of). **out to** *He is out to get elected this time* (= trying to, determined to).

● **out** *adjective*

1 wrong or inaccurate: *Your guess was out by a long way.*

2 not at home or at work: *I'm afraid she's out.*

3 unconscious: *The boxer was out for two minutes.*

4 *Sport* (of a ball) outside the boundary lines of a court, field, etc.

5 *Sport* (of a player or team) removed from play by being caught, etc.

6 (of a flower) open.

7 finished or over: *We will be there before the day is out.*

Phrase out of without: *We are out of eggs again.*

● **out** *verb* (*informal*) to make someone's homosexuality public.

> ! The use of *out* instead of *out of*, as in *The boy stared out the window*, is not acceptable in formal English.

out and out *adjective*

thorough or complete.

outback *noun*

a remote and sparsely inhabited inland region, especially in Australia.

outbalance *verb*

to outweigh.

outbid *verb* (**outbids; outbidding; outbid**)

to bid higher than.

outboard motor *noun*

an internal-combustion engine with a propeller, clamped to the back of a boat.

outbreak *noun*

a breaking out or eruption, e.g. of a disease, etc.

Figurative *There were angry outbreaks after the new taxes were announced* (= public disturbances, riots).

outbuilding *noun*

any building, such as a barn, close to or adjoining a larger one.

outburst *noun*

a sudden and violent bursting or pouring out: *Her outburst of anger stunned us all into silence.*

outcast *noun*

a person who is rejected or homeless.

● **outcast** *adjective* rejected.

outclass *verb*

to be ahead of or do better than: *The winner of the race easily outclassed the other runners.*

outcome *noun*

the result or consequence: *What was the outcome of your argument?*

outcrop *noun*
something which projects or protrudes: *a rocky outcrop.*

outcry *noun* (*plural* **outcries**)
1 a protest or expression of indignation: *There was a public outcry at the strictness of the new law.*
2 a loud cry or noise.

outdated *adjective*
no longer fashionable.

outdistance *verb*
to leave far behind.

outdo (out-**doo**) *verb* (**outdoes; outdoing; outdid; outdone**)
to do better than.

outdoor *adjective*
in the open air.

outdoors *adverb*
outside or in the open air.
• **outdoors** *noun.*

outer *adjective*
further out: *The outer circle of spectators found it difficult to see.*
Word Family **outermost** *adjective* furthest out.

outer space ⇨ SPACE (definition **3**).

outfield *noun*
Sport an outer part of the field, such as the area beyond the bases in baseball or furthest from the batsman in cricket.
Word Family **outfielder** *noun* a player in the outfield.

outfit *noun*
1 the clothes worn by a particular person at one time, usually including shoes and other accessories.
2 (*informal*) a group or organization: *Their company is quite a big outfit now.*
3 the equipment needed for a particular task: *an explorer's outfit.*
Word Family **outfit** *verb* (**outfits; outfitting; outfitted**); **outfitter** *noun* **1** a person who sells clothes. **2** a person who supplies equipment.

outflank *verb*
to move round and behind the flank of enemy forces.
Figurative He outflanked his opponent quite easily (= got the better of).

outgoing *adjective*
1 friendly or extroverted.
2 departing: *an outgoing chairman.*

outgoings *plural noun*
expenditure.

outgrow *verb* (**outgrows; outgrowing; outgrew; outgrown**)
1 to grow too large for something: *He has outgrown all his clothes.*
2 to leave behind due to development or the passing of time: *She outgrew her moodiness.*

outgrowth *noun*
1 something which grows outwards or protrudes: *A horn is an outgrowth on the head of a bull.*
2 a natural result or development.

outhouse (out-house) *noun*
an outbuilding.

outing *noun*
1 a short pleasure trip.
2 (*informal*) the act of making someone's homosexuality public.

outlandish *adjective*
1 noticeably odd or outrageous: *Her outlandish behaviour horrified many people.*
2 an old word for 'remote' or 'strange': *So he went to some outlandish country, I forget where.*
Word Family **outlandishly** *adverb*; **outlandishness** *noun.*

outlast *verb*
to last longer than.

outlaw *noun*
a person, especially a criminal, who defies the law and is deprived of legal rights or protection.
• **outlaw** *verb*
1 to forbid or prohibit.
2 to exclude from the benefits of the law.
Word Family **outlawry** *noun.*

outlay *noun*
1 money spent.
2 the spending of money.

outlet *noun*
1 an opening or passage through which something goes out or is released: *A power point is an outlet for electricity.* □ *Writing poetry is a useful outlet for emotional tension.*
2 an agency for selling or distributing goods: *That shop is an outlet for home-made cakes and jams.*

outline *noun*
1 a line representing the outer boundary of something: *The outline of the trees was obscured by the fog.*
2 a drawing consisting only of simple lines.
Figurative The introduction gives an outline of the plot (= summary, account).
• **outline** *verb* to draw or give an outline of.

outlive (out-**liv**) *verb*
to live longer than.

outlook *noun*
1 an attitude or point of view: *Her outlook has changed since her overseas trip.*
2 the future: *The outlook was bleak for the impoverished family.*
3 a view: *This room has a beautiful outlook on the sea.*

outlying *adjective*
distant or remote.

outmanoeuvre (out-ma-**noo**-va) *verb* (*American* **outmaneuver**)
to get the better of with superior tactics or manoeuvres.

outmoded (out-**mo**-ded) *adjective*
obsolete or old-fashioned.

outnumber (out-**num**-ba) *verb*
to exceed in number.

out-of-body experience *noun*
a feeling of being outside one's body and floating above it.

out of date *adjective*
old-fashioned or useless.

out of doors *adverb*
outside, in the open air.

out of the way *adjective*
secluded or remote: *It is very peaceful and out of the way here.*

outpatient *noun* ⇨ PATIENT *noun*.

outplay (out-**play**) *verb*
to play better than.

outpost *noun*
1 a position or station at some distance from the main body of troops.
2 a distant or remote settlement.

outpouring *noun*
a flowing or pouring out.

output *noun*
1 the act of producing.
2 a product or the amount produced: *Our output has doubled in the last week.*
● **output** *verb* (**outputs; outputting; output** or **outputted**) (of a computer) to produce or display data.

outrage *noun*
1 an extreme act of violence or cruelty.
2 something which offends, shocks or insults: *His frank remarks were an outrage to her pride.*
Word Family **outrage** *verb* to shock or offend; **outrageous** (out-**ray**-jus) *adjective* unacceptable, offensive or shocking; **outrageously** *adverb*; **outrageousness** *noun*.

outré (oo-**tray**) *adjective*
eccentric or outrageous.
[French *outre* beyond]

outrider *noun*
a person, especially a motorcyclist, who rides beside or ahead of a vehicle as an escort, etc.

outrigger *noun*
1 a framework projecting from the side of a boat or canoe, to which floats are attached to prevent capsizing.
2 any projecting frame or support.

outright (out-**rite**) *adjective*
1 complete or absolute: *an outright criminal.*
2 clear or unqualified: *the outright winner.*
● **outright** (out-**rite**) *adverb*
1 completely.
2 openly: *He lied outright.*
3 at once: *The blow killed him outright.*

outrun *verb* (**outruns; outrunning; outran; outrun**)
to run faster than.

outset *noun*
the beginning.

outshine *verb* (**outshines; outshining; outshone**)
to be excellent or more splendid than.

outside *noun*
1 the outer side, edge or part: *The outside of the house needs painting.*
2 the external appearance: *From the outside it looked like a very simple matter.*
Phrase **at the outside** at the most: *There were 50 people at the outside.*
● **outside** *adjective*
1 from, being or occurring on the outside: *the outside lane of traffic.*
Figurative Her attitudes were affected by outside influences (= other, not personal).
□ *There is an outside chance that the favourite will be defeated* (= unlikely, remote).
2 extreme or greatest: *The outside price I can pay is £200.*
● **outside** *adverb, preposition*
1 on, to or into the outside: *He stood in the cell and gazed outside.*
2 in, to or into the open air: *May we go outside and play?*
3 (*informal*) excluding: *There are four in the family, outside myself.*

> **!** The use of *outside of*, meaning 'outside' or 'apart from', is thought by many people to be unacceptable in formal British English: *There is a taxi outside* (not *outside of*) *the house.*

outside broadcast *noun*
a television or radio programme recorded
in a location away from the studio.

outsider *noun*
1 a person who does not belong to a
particular group, etc.
2 a competitor, especially a horse in a race,
considered unlikely to win.

outsize *adjective* also **outsized**
unusually large.
● **outsize** *noun* an unusual size, especially
a larger one.

outskirts *plural noun*
the outer districts.

outsmart *verb*
to be too clever for.

outspoken *adjective*
frank or unreserved: *She is known for her
outspoken opinions.*
Word Family **outspokenly** *adverb*;
outspokenness *noun*.

outstanding *adjective*
1 great or prominent: *The play was an
outstanding success.* □ *This medal is for
outstanding bravery.*
2 still existing, unpaid or unsettled:
outstanding debts.
Word Family **outstandingly** *adverb*.

outstay *verb*
to stay longer than.

outstretched *adjective*
extended or stretched out: *He welcomed her
with outstretched arms.*

outstrip *verb* (**outstrips; outstripping;
outstripped**)
1 to do better than.
2 to go faster than.

out-take *noun*
a part cut out of a film or television
programme before it is shown publicly.

outvote *verb*
to defeat in voting.

outward *adjective*
1 of or towards the outside: *an outward
voyage.*
2 evident, apparent or visible: *He gave no
outward sign of fear although he felt sick with
terror.*
Word Family **outwards, outward** *adverb*
out or towards the outside: *The cyclone
moved outwards to the sea;* **outwardly**
adverb in relation to the outward
appearance.

outwear *verb* (**outwears; outwearing;
outwore; outworn**)
to last or wear longer than.

Word Family **outworn** *adjective* 1 out-of-
date. 2 exhausted or worn out.

outweigh (out-**way**) *verb*
to have greater value or importance than.

outwit *verb* (**outwits; outwitting;
outwitted**)
to get the better of someone by superior
cleverness or cunning.

ova
the plural of **ovum**.

oval (o-vul) *adjective*
egg-shaped.
● **oval** *noun*
1 an oval shape or design: *a pattern of ovals.*
2 an oval field or track for sports, athletics,
etc.

ovary (o-va-ree) *noun* (*plural* **ovaries**)
Anatomy either of the two small solid
bodies on each side of the uterus,
producing the ova and the sex hormones.
Word Family **ovarian** (o-**vair**-i-an)
adjective.
[Latin *ovum* egg]

ovation (o-**vay**-sh'n) *noun*
enthusiastic applause.
[Latin *ovatio* rejoicing]

oven (**uvv**-'n) *noun*
an enclosed chamber, usually in a cooker,
in which food or other objects are cooked,
heated or dried.

ovenproof *adjective*
safe for use in an oven.

ovenware *noun*
any heat-resistant dishes in which food can
be cooked in the oven.

over *preposition*
1 above: *The sun rose over the hill.* □ *Over 20
people arrived late.* □ *She always chooses
mystery stories over romances.*
Figurative Who will rule over the country?
(= in control of).
2 on or on top of: *Put this rug over your legs.*
□ *She has a strange influence over you.*
3 through or throughout: *Over the years he
has grown grey.* □ *We'll discuss it over dinner.*
□ *Show her over the house.*
4 on or to the other side of: *Walk over the
bridge.*
5 about or concerning: *They argue over
money all the time.*
Phrase **over and above** *We had to pay for
accommodation over and above the fares*
(= as well as).
● **over** *adverb*
1 over the top or edge: *Her hand shook and
the coffee spilt over.*

2 at or to the place indicated or implied: *She's over in France for a month.* □ *Come over and see us at home.*

3 to a fallen position: *Don't knock that cup over.*

4 to the other side: *Flip the pancake over.*

5 remaining: *I did not have any money left over.*

6 all through: *He has travelled the world over.*

7 again: *I have asked you ten times over!*
Phrases all over 1 everywhere: *I looked all over for him.* **2** finished: *The game is all over now.* **over against 1** next to, in front of: *Stand over against the wall.* **2** in contrast to.

● **over** *noun* Cricket a group of six successive deliveries by one bowler from one end of the pitch.

over-abundance *noun*
an excessive supply.
Word Family over-abundant *adjective*; **over-abundantly** *adverb*.

overact (o-ver-**akt**)*verb*
to act in an exaggerated manner.

overactive (o-ver-**akt**-iv) *adjective*
too active or energetic.
Word Family overactivity (o-ver-ak-**tiv**-i-tee) *noun*.

over age *adjective*
beyond the proper or required age.

overall *adjective, adverb*
1 from one end or limit to the other: *the overall dimensions of the land.*
2 including everything: *the overall cost of the renovations.*
● **overall** *noun*
1 (**overalls**) a pair of long trousers with a flap covering the chest.
2 a loose-fitting garment, such as a smock, worn to protect ordinary clothes.

overarm *adjective*
Sport (of a stroke or throw) made with the arm raised above the shoulder, moving forward and down. Compare UNDERARM (definition **2**).

overate the past tense of **overeat**.

overawe *verb*
to overcome with awe.
Word Family overawed *adjective*.

overbalance *verb*
to lose one's balance or fall over.

overbearing *adjective*
arrogant or dictatorial in manner.
Word Family overbearingly *adverb*.

overblown *adjective*
1 swollen or inflated: *overblown pride.*
2 too fully open: *an overblown rose.*

overboard *adverb*
over the side of a boat into the water.
Phrase go overboard (*informal*) to be excessively enthusiastic.

overburden *verb*
to load too heavily.

overcast *adjective*
1 (of the sky) covered by cloud.
2 dark or gloomy.
● **overcast** *verb* (**overcasts; overcasting; overcast**)
1 to make cloudy or dark.
2 to sew over the edge of fabric, especially to prevent fraying.

overcharge *verb*
1 to ask too high a price.
2 to put too much electric charge into a battery.

overcoat *noun*
a coat worn over normal clothing.

overcome *verb* (**overcomes; overcoming; overcame; overcome**)
1 to defeat or be too strong for: *You must overcome your silly fears.*
2 to make weak: *We were overcome with helpless laughter.*

overcompensate (o-ver-**kom**-p'n-sayt) *verb*
to compensate to an exaggerated degree.
Word Family overcompensation (o-ver-kom-p'n-**say**-sh'n) *noun*.

overconfident *adjective*
too confident
Word Family overconfidence *noun*.

overcrowd *verb*
to crowd or fill too much.
Word Family overcrowding *noun*.

overdo (over-**doo**) *verb* (**overdoes; overdoing; overdid; overdone**)
1 to do or use to excess.
2 to cook too much: *This steak has been overdone.*

overdose *noun*
an excessive dose, especially of a drug.
● **overdose** *verb*.

overdraft *noun*
an amount of money drawn out by a customer beyond the amount in his or her bank account.

overdraw *verb* (**overdraws; overdrawing; overdrew; overdrawn**)
to draw out money beyond the amount in one's bank account.

overdressed *adjective*
dressed in too formal or elaborate a manner.
Word Family **overdress** *verb*.

overdrive *noun*
an extra higher gear which can be switched on in a car to give a higher top speed without increased engine revolutions, thus saving petrol consumption and engine wear.

overdue *adjective*
1 late: *Your rent is overdue by six months.*
2 too long awaited: *That amendment of the law was long overdue.*

overeat *verb* (**overeats; overeating; overate; overeaten**)
to eat too much.
Word Family **overeating** *noun*.

over-elaborate (o-ver-ee-**lab**-a-rit) *adjective* too elaborate or ornate.
• **over-elaborate** (o-ver-ee-**lab**-a-rate) *verb* to describe in too much detail.

overestimate *verb*
1 to estimate too great an amount.
2 to give too high a value to.
Word Family **overestimation** (o-ver-est-i-**may**-sh'n) *noun*.

overexpose *verb*
to expose too much or for too long.
Word Family **overexposure** *noun*.

overflow *verb*
to flow or spill over: *The bath overflowed on to the floor.*
Figurative His heart overflowed with joy (= was filled beyond capacity).
• **overflow** *noun*
1 the act of overflowing.
2 something which is overflowing.
3 an outlet for overflowing water.

overgrazing *noun*
the process whereby grazing animals eat more vegetation than the land can support. Overgrazing often leads to soil erosion.

overgrow *verb* (**overgrows; overgrowing; overgrew; overgrown**)
to cover with growth.
Word Family **overgrowth** *noun*.

overhang (o-ver-hang) *verb* (**overhangs; overhanging; overhung**)
to hang or extend over.
Figurative A sense of danger overhung their adventure (= surrounded, threatened).
Word Family **overhang** (o-ver-hang) *noun* something which projects or hangs over, such as part of a balcony.

overhaul (o-ver-**hawl**) *verb*
1 to examine, take apart and repair.
2 to overtake.
• **overhaul** *noun*.

overhead *adjective*
situated or moving above the head: *The overhead cables shook in the breeze.*
• **overhead** *adverb* over one's head or in the air: *The jet flew silently high overhead.*

overhead projector *noun*
a projector that projects slides on to a screen by means of an overhead mirror.

overheads *plural noun*
the general costs of running a business, such as rent, electricity, etc.

overhear *verb* (**overhears; overhearing; overheard**)
to hear something spoken to another person.

overindulge (o-ver-in-**dulj**) *verb*
to indulge excessively.
Word Family **overindulgence** *noun*; **overindulgent** *adjective*.

overjoyed *adjective*
highly delighted.

overkill *noun*
1 the capacity of weapons, especially nuclear, to destroy infinitely more than is needed to achieve victory.
2 unnecessary excess.

> The word **overkill** is now more common in its figurative sense of 'any unnecessary excess' than it is in its original meaning of 'excessive physical destruction'. This is true of several technical expressions that have recently come into English, e.g. *meltdown*.

overladen (o-ver-**lay**-d'n) *adjective*
overloaded.

overland *adjective*
across or by land: *an overland tour across Europe to Asia.*
Word Family **overland** *adverb*.

overlap *verb* (**overlaps; overlapping; overlapped**)
to fold or lie over part of something else.
Figurative Many of our interests overlap (= coincide, correspond).

overlay (o-ver-lay) *verb* (**overlays; overlaying; overlaid**)
to cover with, lay on or spread on.
• **overlay** (o-ver-lay) *noun* a layer on or over something, for decoration, protection, etc.

overleaf *adverb*
on the other side of the page.

overload *verb*
to give too large or heavy a load to.

overlook *verb*
1 to fail to see: *You have overlooked several mistakes.*
2 to ignore or disregard: *We will overlook your rudeness this once.*
3 to have a view of: *Your room overlooks the garden.*

overlord *noun*
a person having supreme power or authority.

overly *adverb*
excessively.

overmaster *verb*
a poetic word meaning 'to overpower'.

overmuch *adverb*
very much: *I don't like her overmuch.*

overnight *adverb, adjective*
during or throughout the night: *Please stay with us overnight.*
Figurative *She grew up overnight* (= very quickly).

overplay *verb*
to act or emphasize too much.
Phrase **overplay one's hand** to spoil one's chances because of overconfidence: *He overplayed his hand when he threatened to resign if they did not agree.*

overpower *verb*
to master or subdue by superior strength: *Police soon overpowered the unarmed attacker.*
Figurative *Fear overpowered her at the sight of the burglar* (= made helpless or weak).
Word Family **overpowering** *adjective.*

overran the past tense of **overrun**.

overrate *verb*
to value too highly.
Word Family **overrated** *adjective.*

overreach *verb*
1 to exert oneself or do too much.
2 to reach beyond the aim or target.

overreact *verb*
to react with excessive emotion.
Word Family **overreaction** *noun.*

override *verb* (**overrides; overriding; overrode; overridden**)
1 to disregard or go against: *He overrode all advice and sold his shares.*
2 to have dominance over: *The director's decision will override all others.*
Word Family **overriding** *adjective.*

overripe *adjective*
too ripe.

overrule *verb*
to decide against or refuse to allow: *The judge overruled the barrister's objections.*

overrun *verb* (**overruns; overrunning; overran; overrun**)
1 to run beyond: *The play overran the scheduled time.*
2 to defeat or take possession of: *The country was overrun by foreign troops.*
3 to spread or swarm over: *Those weeds will overrun the garden soon.*
● **overrun** *noun.*

overseas *adverb*
across or beyond the sea: *Have you ever travelled overseas?*
● **overseas** *adjective, noun.*

oversee *verb* (**oversees; overseeing; oversaw; overseen**)
to supervise or watch over, especially over work or workers.
Word Family **overseer** *noun.*

overshadow *verb*
to cast a shadow over.
Figurative *Her quiet personality is overshadowed by her brother's boisterousness* (= made insignificant).

overshoes *plural noun*
waterproof covers worn over ordinary shoes for protection.

overshoot *verb* (**overshoots; overshooting; overshot**)
to go over or past: *The plane overshot the runway as it landed and hit some trees.* □ *The torpedo overshot its mark.*

oversight *noun*
1 a failure to notice or do: *Not locking the door was an oversight on my part.*
2 supervision.

oversized *adjective* also **oversize**
larger than usual.

oversleep *verb* (**oversleeps; oversleeping; overslept**)
to sleep too long or beyond the usual time.

overspend *verb* (**overspends; overspending; overspent**)
to spend more than is necessary or can be afforded.

overspill *noun*
something which spills over or out.
Figurative *Satellite towns were built to provide for the city's overspill* (= extra population).

overstate (over-**stayt**) *verb*
to exaggerate when stating.

Word Family **overstatement** (o-ver-stayt-m'nt) *noun.*

overstay *verb*
to stay beyond the fixed or expected time of.

overstep *verb* (**oversteps; overstepping; overstepped**)
to pass over or beyond.

overstock *verb*
to have or establish too great a stock or supply.

overt *adjective*
open or unconcealed: *The review was an overt attack on the author.*
Word Family **overtly** *adverb.*

overtake *verb* (**overtakes; overtaking; overtook; overtaken**)
1 to catch up with or pass.
2 to come upon unexpectedly: *A storm overtook us as we reached the top of the mountain.*

overtax *verb*
to impose too high a tax.
Figurative *They overtaxed themselves by the long walk* (= exhausted).

overthrow (o-ver-throw) *verb* (**overthrows; overthrowing; overthrew; overthrown**)
1 to defeat or destroy: *The government was overthrown by the revolution.*
2 to throw further than intended.
Word Family **overthrow** (o-ver-throw) *noun.*

overtime *noun*
1 any extra work done by an employee outside the regular working hours.
2 the payment received for this work, usually at least one and a half times the normal wage.
• **overtime** *adverb.*

overtone *noun*
1 an additional or suggested meaning: *Despite his smile, his voice carried an overtone of malice.*
2 *Music* ⇨ HARMONIC.

overtook the past tense of **overtake**.

overture (o-ver-cher) *noun*
1 an orchestral introduction to an opera or ballet.
2 an opening or introductory part, especially a proposal or offer.

overturn *verb*
1 to turn over or upside down.
2 to defeat or conquer.
• **overturn** *noun.*

overview *noun*
a general view or outline of something.

overweening *adjective*
extreme or exaggerated: *We were angered by his overweening vanity.*
Word Family **overweeningly** *adverb.*

overweight (o-ver-wate) *adjective*
over the normal or required weight.

overwhelm *verb*
1 to overcome completely: *She was overwhelmed with grief at the death of her dog.*
2 to submerge or cover: *The town was overwhelmed by the flood.*
Word Family **overwhelming** *adjective;* **overwhelmingly** *adverb.*

overwork *verb*
to work or cause to work too hard.
Figurative *She tends to overwork her jokes to a boring degree* (= use too often or too much).

overwrought (o-ver-rawt) *adjective*
extremely nervous or excited.

oviparous (o-vipp-er-us) *adjective*
Biology (of an animal) producing eggs which mature and hatch after leaving the body of the mother, as in birds.
Word Family **oviparity** (o-vi-parr-i-tee) *noun.*
[Latin *ovum* egg + *parere* to bring forth]

ovulate (ov-yoo-late) *verb*
Biology to release eggs from an ovary.
Word Family **ovulation** (ov-yew-lay-sh'n) *noun.*

ovum (o-vum) *noun* (*plural* **ova**)
Biology the female reproductive cell.
[Latin, egg]

owe (o) *verb*
to have a duty to do or provide: *You owe me a pound that I lent you last week.* □ *I owe you an apology for my rudeness.*

owing to *preposition*
on account of: *Owing to rain the match was postponed.*

> [!] On the use of *owing to* and *due to*
> ⇨ DUE.

owl (*rhymes with* fowl) *noun*
any of a group of nocturnal birds with a broad flat head, large eyes, and a short hooked beak.
Word Family **owlet** *noun* a young owl; **owlish** *adjective* solemn like an owl; **owlishly** *adverb.*

own (*rhymes with* bone) *verb*
1 to have as one's possession.
2 (*formal*) to acknowledge or admit: *I own that you have proved me wrong.*

Phrase **own up** to confess: *You must own up if you did break the window.*

• **own** *adjective* belonging to the person or thing indicated: *Is that your own car?*

• **own** *noun*

Phrases **come into one's own** to obtain one's rightful position, etc. **get one's own back** to get revenge. **of one's own** *You should save up for a car of your own* (= belonging to yourself). **on one's own** 1 *I went to the cinema on my own* (= alone). 2 *You are on your own in this matter* (= responsible, alone, independent).

Word Family **owner** *noun*; **ownership** *noun.*

own goal *noun*
Football a goal scored when a player accidentally puts the ball in his or her team's own goal.

ox *noun* (*plural* **oxen**)
1 an old word for a castrated bull used for draught work.
2 (**oxen**) male or female draught cattle.

oxbow (oks-bo) *noun*
1 a bow-shaped piece of wood placed around the neck of an ox as part of a harness.
2 a horseshoe-shaped bend in a river that has become cut off from the main flow.
oxbow lake a curved lake formed from an oxbow (definition 2).

oxidant (ok-si-d'nt) *noun*
the substance which supplies the oxygen in an oxidation reaction, especially for the burning process in a rocket engine.

oxidation (ok-si-**day**-sh'n) *noun* also **oxidization, oxidisation** (ok-si-die-**zay**-sh'n)
1 *Chemistry* the combination of a substance with oxygen.
2 *Chemistry* the loss of hydrogen from a substance.
3 *Chemistry* the loss of an electron from an atom or ion.
Word Family **oxidize** *verb*; **oxidizer** *noun.*

oxide *noun*
Chemistry any simple compound containing oxygen and one other element.

oxtail *noun*
the skinned tail of an ox, used in soups or stews.

oxyacetylene burner (ok-si-a-**set**-a-leen **burn**-er) *noun*
a device for producing an extremely hot flame by burning a mixture of oxygen and acetylene in a special jet, used for welding and metal cutting.

oxygen (ok-si-j'n) *noun*
a colourless odourless gas, the most abundant in the earth's crust, forming about 21 per cent of the earth's atmosphere. It is essential for combustion and living tissues and is used in welding and metal cutting.
Word Family **oxygenate** (ok-si-j'n-ate) *verb* to treat, supply or combine with oxygen; **oxygenation** (ok-si-j'n-ay-sh'n) *noun.*

oyez (o-yes) *interjection*
hear! listen! (formerly uttered by a town crier or court official).
[Old French]

oyster *noun*
any of a group of edible bivalve marine molluscs, often cultivated for food or for the pearls produced by some forms.
[Greek *ostreon*]

oystercatcher *noun*
a large black-and-white bird of seashores and estuaries, with a long orange bill.

ozone (o-zone) *noun*
1 *Chemistry* a poisonous form of oxygen (formula O_3), a bluish gas with a sharp smell produced when oxygen is acted on by an electric discharge such as lightning, and present in the atmosphere. It is a strong oxidizing agent and is used as a bleach.
2 (*informal*) invigorating fresh air.

ozone-friendly *adjective*
not containing chemicals which damage the ozone layer.

ozone hole *noun*
an area of the ozone layer in which there has been a reduction in ozone because of atmospheric pollution or a build-up of CFCs.

ozone layer *noun*
a region in the outer stratosphere where much of the atmospheric ozone is concentrated.
[Greek *ozein* to smell]

Pp

paan (pahn) *noun* also **pan**
betel leaves and other ingredients, chewed in India and other parts of Asia.
[Hindi]

pace¹ *noun*
1 the rate or speed of movement: *Our neighbours live life at a hectic pace.*
2 a single step: *Take one pace forward.*
3 a gait of a horse.
Phrase **put someone through his** or **her paces** to test the abilities of a person.
● **pace** *verb*
1 to cover by paces: *He paced the floor anxiously.*
2 to measure by paces: *She paced out the distance from the house to the back fence.*
3 to set the pace for.
4 (of a horse) to move with a gait in which the two legs on one side move together.
[from Latin]

pace² (**pay**-see) *preposition*
(used to express polite disagreement) with due respect to: *And, pace Henry Ford, history is not bunk!*
[Latin, with your peace (that is, if the person mentioned will not be offended)]

pacemaker *noun*
1 a person, animal or group that sets the pace, e.g. in a race or competition.
2 *Medicine* a small electronic machine implanted into a patient and producing an electric current to control the heart rate.

pacer *noun*
1 a pacemaker.
2 (*especially American*) a horse whose natural gait is a pace, or one which is bred and trained for pacing.

pacha ⇨ PASHA.

pachyderm (**pak**-i-derm) *noun*
any of a group of large thick-skinned animals, such as the elephant, hippopotamus or rhinoceros.
[Greek *pakhys* thick + *derma* skin]

pacifism *noun*
the belief that all war and violence is wrong.
Word Family **pacifist** *noun*.

pacify (pa-si-fie) *verb* (**pacifies; pacifying; pacified**)
to calm or make peaceful: *It is difficult to pacify a crying baby.*
Word Family **pacification** *noun*; **pacific** *adjective* peaceable; **pacifier** *noun* 1 a person or thing that pacifies. 2 *American* a dummy for a baby.
[Latin *pacis* of peace + *facere* to make]

pack *noun*
1 a bundle or parcel of things tied up for carrying: *a train of mules carrying packs.*
2 a light bag, often with a stiffened frame, for carrying on the back.
3 a set of 52 playing cards.
4 a group of animals which hunt together: *a pack of wolves.*
5 a group of people or things: *a pack of thieves.*
6 (**Pack**) a group of Cubs or Brownies.
7 *Rugby* all the forwards of a team, especially when acting together.
● **pack** *verb*
1 to put things into a box, bundle, suitcase, etc.: *Have you packed for your holiday yet?*
2 to crush or crowd together: *People packed into the store for the sale.*
3 to put soft material around or into something, to prevent damage, loss or leakage: *glassware packed in cotton.* □ *to pack an open wound.*
Phrases **pack it in** (*informal*) to give it up, stop it: *I'm so sick of this job I feel like packing it in.* **pack someone off, send someone packing** to send someone away unceremoniously or in a hurry. **pack up** to break down, fail: *My car has packed up.*
Word Family **packed** *adjective*; **packer** *noun* a person or machine that packs things.

package (**pak**-ij) *noun*
1 a bundle or parcel.
2 a group of things taken together.
Word Family **package** *verb*; **packaging** *noun* the wrapping used to protect a product.

package deal *noun*
a deal which includes a number of items and has to be accepted as a whole, the less favourable items along with the favourable ones.

package tour *noun*
a holiday which is completely arranged beforehand by the organizer.

pack drill *noun*
Army an extra drill, wearing full kit, imposed as a punishment.

packet *noun*
1 a small parcel or bundle: *a packet of letters.*
2 (*dated*) *Nautical* a ferry.
3 (*informal*) a large sum of money: *He lost a packet at the races.*

packhorse *noun*
a horse used to carry goods.

pack ice *noun*
a mass of large pieces of ice floating in the sea.

pact *noun*
an agreement.
[Latin *pactum* agreed]

pad¹ *noun*
1 a soft cushion-like mass, used for comfort, protection, stuffing, etc.: *shoulder pads.* □ *shin pads.*
2 *Biology* the soft fleshy underpart of the feet of dogs, foxes, etc.
3 a pile of sheets of paper held together at one edge, especially for writing letters or notes.
4 (*informal*) a house or flat.
• **pad** *verb* (**pads; padding; padded**) to fill with something soft: *He padded the seat of the chair with foam rubber.*
Phrase **pad out** *She padded out her essay with long descriptions* (= made it longer).

pad² *verb* (**pads; padding; padded**)
to walk or move softly: *The lion padded towards us.*

paddle¹ *noun*
1 a short stiff piece of wood with a flat blade at one end, held in the hand without a rowlock, to propel a boat or canoe.
2 something which has the shape or function of a paddle, such as a broad flat board on a paddle wheel or mill wheel.
• **paddle** *verb* to propel a canoe with a paddle.

paddle² *verb*
to dabble or play in or as if in shallow water.

paddle steamer *noun* also **paddle boat**
a boat propelled by a steam engine, which turns one or more large paddle wheels through the water.

paddle wheel *noun*
a large wheel with paddles on its circumference, used instead of a propeller to propel a boat.

paddock *noun*
1 a small field used as a pasture.
2 *Sport* an area in which horses or cars are brought together before a race starts.

paddy¹ *noun* (*plural* **paddies**) also **paddy field**
a piece of land which is flooded for growing rice.
[Malay *padi* rice]

paddy² *noun* (*plural* **paddies**)
(*informal*) a rage.

padlock *noun*
a detachable lock hanging by a curved bar that is hinged at one end and snapped shut at the other.
• **padlock** *verb.*

padre (**pah**-dray) *noun*
Military a chaplain.
[Latin *pater* father]

paean (**pee**-an) *noun*
a song of praise, joy or triumph.

paederasty ⇨ PEDERASTY.

paediatrics (pee-di-**at**-riks) *plural noun* (*American* **pediatrics**)
(*used with singular verb*) the study and treatment of diseases in children.
Word Family **paediatric** *adjective*;
paediatrician (pee-di-a-**trish**-'n) *noun* a doctor who specializes in the diseases of children.
[Greek *paidos* of a child + *iatros* healer]

paedophilia (peed-o-**fil**-i-a) *noun*
sexual attraction to children.
Word Family **paedophiliac** *adjective*;
paedophile *noun* someone who is sexually attracted to children.

paella (pie-**yel**-a) *noun*
a Spanish dish made of rice, meat, seafood and vegetables, and flavoured with saffron.
[Spanish]

paeony ⇨ PEONY.

pagan (**pay**-g'n) *noun*
someone who believes in a religion that is not one of the main religions of the world.
Word Family **paganism** *noun* the beliefs or practices of pagans.
[Latin *paganus* a civilian, because pagans were not considered 'soldiers of Christ']

page¹ *noun*
1 a sheet of paper in a book, etc.
2 one side of a sheet of paper.
3 *Computers* a section of text, etc. fitting on a screen.
• **page** *verb* to go through the pages of a book, etc.

page² noun
1 *Medieval history* a boy servant or attendant to a person of rank.
2 a pageboy.
• **page** *verb* to seek a person either by having his or her name called or by contacting him or her on a pager.
[Greek *paidion* a small child]

pageant (paj-'nt) *noun*
an elaborate public spectacle, especially one where there is a procession in costume.
Word Family **pageantry** *noun* a splendid display.

pageboy *noun*
1 also **page** a young boy attending the bride at a wedding.
2 also **page** a bellboy.
3 a hairstyle in which the hair is long, smooth and turned under at the bottom.

pager (pay-ja) *noun* also called **beeper**.
a portable electronic device which uses a high-pitched sound to contact or convey instructions to the person carrying it.

pagination (paj-i-**nay**-sh'n) *noun*
the numbering of the pages in a book.
Word Family **paginate** *verb*.

pagoda (pag-o-da) *noun*
an ornate Hindu or Buddhist temple in the shape of a pyramid or tower.

paid the past tense and past participle of **pay**.

pail *noun*
a bucket.

paillasse ⇨ PALLIASSE.

pain *noun*
1 physical or mental suffering: *stomach pains*. □ *the pain of seeing their home destroyed*.
2 (*informal*) an annoying person or task.
Phrase **on pain of** *The traitor was banished from his homeland on pain of death if he ever returned* (= with the punishment of).
Word Family **pain** *verb* to cause pain to; **painful** *adjective* 1 hurting. 2 causing pain; **painfully** *adverb*; **painless** *adjective*; **painlessly** *adverb*.
[Latin *poena* penalty]

painstaking *adjective*
extremely careful.
Word Family **painstakingly** *adverb*.

paint *noun*
a liquid containing a pigment in suspension, which hardens to form an opaque coating when applied to a surface.
• **paint** *verb*
1 to cover or decorate with, or as if with, paint.
2 to make pictures with paint: *He paints small landscapes*.
3 to represent or depict in paint: *I asked her to paint me*.
4 to give a description of: *a novel painting a graphic picture of the horrors of war*.
5 *Computers* to use a graphics program to draw or colour.
Word Family **painting** *noun* 1 a picture made with paints. 2 the act or work of a person who paints.
[Latin *pingere*]

painter¹ *noun*
1 an artist who paints pictures.
2 a person whose work is covering or decorating walls, houses, etc. with paint.

painter² *noun*
Nautical a rope used to tie up a small boat.
[from Old French]

pair *noun*
1 a set of two people or things that are the same or go together: *a pair of shoes*.
2 a single thing consisting of two parts that cannot be used separately: *a pair of glasses*.
• **pair** *verb*
1 to arrange in pairs.
2 to form a pair or pairs.
[Latin *paria* equal things]

paisley (**paze**-lee) *noun*
a very elaborate and colourful pattern made up of small curved shapes.
[from a soft woollen fabric with this pattern, first made in *Paisley*, Scotland]

pakora (pa-**kor**-a) *noun*
an Indian savoury snack consisting of diced vegetables or meat dipped in a spiced batter and deep-fried.
[Hindi]

pal *noun*
(*informal*) a friend or comrade.
Word Family **pally** *adjective* (**pallier**; **palliest**) friendly.
[Romany, brother]

palace (**pal**-is) *noun*
a large elaborate building used as the official home of a monarch or bishop.
[Latin *Palatium* the Palatine Hill, Rome, on which the palace of the Emperor Augustus stood]

paladin (**pal**-a-din) *noun*
Medieval history a knightly hero or champion.
[Latin *palatinus* of the palace]

Palaeocene (pal-i-o-seen) *noun*
(*American* **Paleocene**)
Geology relating to a geological era which
was the earliest epoch of the Tertiary
period. During this era mammals were
developing.
[*palaeo-* + Greek *kainos* new]

Palaeolithic (*American* **Paleolithic**) ⇨
STONE AGE.

palaeontology (pal-i-on-**tol**-a-ji) *noun*
(*American* **paleontology**)
the study of fossils.
Word Family palaeontological (pal-i-
on-ta-**loj**-ik-al) *adjective*; **palaeontologist**
noun.
[*palaeo-* + Greek *onta* things + *-logy*]

Palaeozoic (pal-i-o-**zo**-ik) *noun*
(*American* **Paleozoic**)
a geological era which extended from
about 570 million years ago to 225 million
years ago and contains the **Cambrian,**
Ordovician, Silurian, Devonian,
Carboniferous and **Permian** periods.
During this era green plants became
abundant and the first land vertebrates
appeared.
• **Palaeozoic** *adjective*.
[*palaeo-* + Greek *zoion* animal]

palanquin (pal-'n-**keen**) *noun* also
palankeen
a box-like vehicle, carried by means of
poles resting on people's shoulders; used
in India and other Eastern countries.
[from Portuguese, from Sanskrit]

palatable (pal-a-ta-b'l) *adjective*
1 agreeable to taste: *a palatable meal.*
2 acceptable, congenial: *He didn't find the
idea at all palatable.*

palate (**pal**-it) *noun*
1 *Anatomy* the roof of the mouth, hard at
the front and soft at the rear.
2 the sense of taste: *She has a sophisticated
palate.*
*Figurative Romantic novels just do not suit
my palate* (= liking, mental taste).
3 the flavour of wine or beer.
Word Family palatal *adjective*.
[from Latin]

palatial (pal-**ay**-sh'l) *adjective*
of or like a palace.

palaver (pa-**lah**-va) *noun*
1 (*informal*) fuss or bother.
2 (*informal dated*) a parley or conference.
[Pidgin English from Portuguese *palavra* a
word]

palazzo (pa-**lat**-so) *noun* (*plural* **palazzos**
or **palazzi** (pa-**lat**-see))
a palace or large building, especially in
Italy.

pale[1] *adjective*
1 without much colour: *a pale complexion.*
□ *a pale moon.*
2 feeble, faint: *only a pale version of what it
used to be.*
Word Family pale *verb* 1 to turn pale.
2 to become less significant; **palely** *adverb*;
paleness *noun*.
[Latin *pallidus*]

pale[2] *noun*
a stake, often pointed at the top, used for
fences.
Phrase **beyond the pale** socially or
morally unacceptable.
[Latin *palus*]

paleface *noun*
a name for a white person, supposed to be
used by Native Americans.

palette (**pal**-it) *noun*
1 *Art* a board on which a painter mixes
colours.
2 *Art* the range of colours used by a
particular painter.
[Latin *pala* a spade]

palette knife *noun* (*plural* **palette knives**)
1 a thin flexible blade used by painters for
mixing colours, and applying or removing
paint from a surface.
2 a long flexible spatula used in the
kitchen, e.g. to lift cakes.

palindrome *noun*
a word or words which are spelt the same
backwards as they are forwards: *The word
'level' and the sentence 'Was it a cat I saw?'
are palindromes.*
[Greek *palindromos* a running back again]

paling (**pay**-ling) *noun*
a fence of stakes.

palisade (pal-i-**sade**) *noun*
a fence made of upright stakes or metal
railings, used as a defence, etc.

pall[1] (pawl) *noun*
1 a cloth spread over a coffin.
2 a cloud of something: *a heavy pall of
smoke.*
[Latin *pallium* covering, cloak]

pall[2] *verb*
to become boring or less enjoyable: *After a
while the flight began to pall.*
[from APPAL]

pall-bearer *noun*
a person helping to carry the coffin at a funeral.

pallet¹ *noun*
1 a bed or mattress of straw.
2 a rough bed.
[French *paille* straw]

pallet² *noun*
1 a flat blade with a handle, used by potters for shaping or mixing clay, etc.
2 a movable platform for the storage or transportation of goods, especially one designed to be lifted by a forklift truck.
3 *Art* a palette.
[from PALETTE]

palliasse (pal-i-ass) *noun* also **paillasse**
a mattress filled with straw.
[French *paille* straw]

palliate (pal-i-ate) *verb*
1 *Medicine* to ease or relieve the symptoms of a disease without curing it.
2 to make something appear less serious: *In his speech to the jury the lawyer tried to palliate his client's offence.*
Word Family **palliation** *noun*; **palliative** *adjective* serving to palliate; **palliative** *noun* something which palliates, e.g. a medicine.
[Latin *palliatus* covered with a cloak]

pallid *adjective*
pale or wan: *the pallid complexion of a sickly child.*
Word Family **pallidly** *adverb*; **pallidness** *noun*.
[from Latin]

pallor *noun*
an unnatural paleness, caused by illness, fear, death, etc.

pally ⇨ PAL.

palm¹ (pahm) *noun*
the inner surface of the hand between the wrist and the fingers.
Phrases **grease someone's palm** to bribe someone. **have an itching palm** to be greedy for money, especially to be always ready to receive a bribe. **have someone in the palm of one's hand** to have influence over someone.
• **palm** *verb* to conceal in the hand: *The conjuror palmed the coin and the audience thought it had vanished into thin air.*
Phrase **palm off** to dispose of something unwanted by getting someone else to accept it, especially by fraudulent means.
[from Latin]

palm² *noun*
1 also called **palm tree**. a mainly tropical or subtropical tree, usually tall and branchless and with a crown of long leaves: *a date palm.*
2 a leaf or branch of a palm as a symbol of victory.
[from Latin]

palmate (pal-mate) *adjective*
having the shape of an open palm: *a palmate leaf.*

palmcorder *noun*
a small camcorder which can be held easily in the hand.

palmistry (pah-mis-tree) *noun*
the study of lines on the palm of a hand, as a way of discovering a person's character or destiny.
Word Family **palmist** *noun* a person who practises palmistry.

Palm Sunday *noun*
Christianity the Sunday before Easter, commemorating the entry of Christ into Jerusalem when he was acknowledged by people waving palms.

palmtop *noun*
a small computer that can be held in the palm of the hand.

palomino (pal-a-mee-no) *noun*
a breed of golden or tan horses, with a white mane and tail, originally bred in America.
[Spanish, like a dove]

palpable (pal-pa-b'l) *adjective*
1 able to be touched or felt.
2 obvious: *a palpable lie.*
Word Family **palpably** *adverb*.
[Latin *palpare* to feel]

palpate *verb*
Medicine to examine by touching or feeling.

palpitate *verb*
1 (of the heart) to beat unnaturally fast, e.g. from exertion, fear, illness, etc.
2 to tremble or quiver: *His body palpitated with terror.*
Word Family **palpitation** *noun*.
[Latin *palpitare* to throb]

palsy (pawl-zee *or* pol-zee) *noun*
(dated) paralysis.
Word Family **palsied** *adjective*.
[from PARALYSIS]

paltry (pawl-tree) *adjective* (**paltrier**; **paltriest**)
trifling or almost worthless: *a paltry sum.*
Word Family **paltriness** *noun*.

pampas *noun*
(*used with singular or plural verb*) large areas of grassland in South America.
[Spanish, plains]

pampas grass *noun* (*plural* **pampas grasses**)
a tall South American grass with large feathery flowers.

pamper *verb*
to treat very indulgently: *He pampered her when she was ill.* □ *Pamper yourself with this luxurious bubble bath!*

pamphlet (pam-flit) *noun*
1 a booklet in paper covers, especially one dealing with a question of current interest: *a political pamphlet.*
2 a leaflet.
Word Family **pamphleteer** (pam-flit-eer) *noun* a person who writes pamphlets.

pan¹ *noun*
1 a round metal vessel, usually shallow, used for cooking, etc.
2 anything which has the shape of a pan, such as the dishes on a pair of scales.
3 *Geography* a depression in the ground: *a salt pan.*
4 a steel drum.
● **pan** *verb* (**pans; panning; panned**)
1 (*informal*) to dismiss as worthless or criticize severely: *The critic panned the new film.*
2 to wash sand, gravel, etc. in a pan to separate out gold that is in it.
Phrase **pan out** *How did your plans for the trip pan out?* (= turn out).

pan² *noun* ⇨ PAAN.

pan³ *verb* (**pans; panning; panned**)
Film to swing a camera around horizontally from a fixed position, so as to cover a wide area, etc.
[shortening of PANORAMA]

Pan *noun*
Greek mythology the god of flocks and herds. He has the upper body of a man and the ears, horns and legs of a goat.

panacea (pan-a-see-a) *noun*
a universal remedy.
[*pan-* + Greek *akes* remedy]

panache (pan-ash) *noun*
1 style: *Everything he does, he does with panache.*
2 a plume or bunch of feathers, especially one worn as an ornament on a helmet.
[French]

panama (pa-na-mah) *noun*
a hat with a broad brim, originally made from the plaited leaves of a palm tree.
[after *Panama*, in Central America]

panatella (pan-a-tell-a) *noun*
a long thin cigar.
[Spanish, a long thin biscuit]

pancake *noun*
1 very thin cake cooked in a pan, from a batter made with eggs, milk and flour.
2 *Beauty* a solid cake of make-up which combines foundation and powder.

panchromatic (pan-kro-mat-ik) *adjective*
Photography (of a black-and-white film) sensitive to light of all colours.
[*pan-* + Greek *khromatos* of a colour]

pancreas (pan-kree-us) *noun* (*plural* **pancreases**)
Anatomy a gland lying under the stomach. It secretes the hormone insulin and produces digestive juices which pass into the duodenum.
Word Family **pancreatic** (pan-kree-at-ik) *adjective.*
[*pan-* + Greek *kreas* flesh]

panda *noun* also called **giant panda**.
a large white bear-like mammal, with black legs and black around the eyes; it feeds on bamboo, fish and small rodents and is found in the mountains of China and Tibet.
[a Nepalese name]

pandemic *adjective*
affecting people over a wide area.
Compare EPIDEMIC.

pandemonium (pan-di-mo-nee-um) *noun*
1 uproar.
2 *Mythology* the place where all demons or evil spirits live.
[from *pan-* + Greek *daimon* demon]

pander *verb*
to indulge or gratify someone's wishes: *pandering to her every whim.*
[after *Pandarus*, a character in the old tale of Troilus and Cressida]

Pandora's box *noun*
Greek mythology a box containing all the evils which Pandora (the equivalent of Eve) opened, letting them escape to plague us ever since.
Phrase **open a Pandora's box** to uncover previously hidden problems by starting something, e.g. a process or investigation.

pane *noun*
a single sheet of glass.

panegyric ⇨ EULOGY.

panel (pan-'l) *noun*
1 a separate part of a door, ceiling, etc., usually raised above or sunk below the surrounding area.
2 a broad strip of cloth set into a piece of clothing and usually of a different colour.
3 a thin flat piece of wood, etc., such as one on which a picture is painted.
4 a group of people gathered together to take part in a discussion, judge a contest, etc.: *a panel of jurors*.
5 the part of a machine on which controls or instruments are mounted.
Word Family **panelled** *adjective* (*American* **paneled**) furnished or decorated with panels; **panelling** *noun* wood or other material made into panels; **panellist** *noun* a member of a panel.
[Latin *pannus* a piece of cloth]

pang *noun*
a sudden short sharp pain or feeling: *pangs of hunger*. □ *a pang of regret*.

panhandle *verb*
(*American informal*) to beg.
Word Family **panhandler** *noun*.

panic *noun*
1 sudden fear, especially fear that causes desperate behaviour: *There was a general panic when the theatre caught fire.* □ *I got into a real panic when I thought I was drowning.*
2 (*informal*) a mad rush to do something.
Word Family **panic** *verb* (**panics; panicking; panicked**) to affect with or be stricken by panic; **panicky** *adjective*
1 liable to panic. 2 in a state of panic.
[Greek *Panikos* caused by the god Pan, who was believed to be the cause of sudden or groundless fear]

panjandrum (pan-**jan**-dr'm) *noun*
a person who is, or claims to be, very important.

> The word **panjandrum** was invented by the actor and playwright Samuel Foote in the 17th century in a list of meaningless words made up to test the memory of actor Charles Macklin, who claimed that he could memorize and repeat anything said to him. *Panjandrum* came to mean 'a pompous, self-important person' in the 19th century.

pannier *noun*
a basket, especially one of a pair carried across the back of an animal, motorcycle, etc.
[Latin *panarium* a basket for bread]

pannikin *noun*
a small metal cup.

panoply (pan-a-plee) *noun* (*plural* **panoplies**)
an impressive or splendid display or collection.
[Greek *panoplia* full armour]

panorama (pan-a-**rah**-ma) *noun*
1 an unbroken view over a wide area.
2 a comprehensive survey, e.g. of a topic.
Word Family **panoramic** (pan-a-**ram**-ik) *adjective*.
[*pan-* + Greek *horama* a view]

pansy (**pan**-zee) *noun* (*plural* **pansies**)
1 a small plant, often cultivated for its brightly coloured flowers.
2 (*dated informal*) an offensive word for an effeminate man.
[French *pensée* a thought]

pant *verb*
1 to breathe hard and quickly, from exertion or excitement.
2 to yearn: *panting for revenge*.
3 (of the heart) a poetic word meaning 'to throb with emotion'.
Word Family **pant** *noun*; **pantingly** *adverb*.

pantaloons *plural noun*
trousers, especially baggy ones that are gathered at the ankle.
[after *Pantaloon*, a stock character in old Italian comedies]

pantechnicon (pan-**tek**-ni-kon) *noun*
(*dated*) a large furniture removal van.
[the name of an old furniture repository in London]

pantheism (**pan**-thee-izm) *noun*
the belief that God and the universe are the same.
Word Family **pantheist** *noun* a person who believes in pantheism; **pantheistic** (pan-thee-**iss**-tik) *adjective*.
[*pan-* + Greek *theos* god]

pantheon (**pan**-thee-on) *noun*
1 all the gods of a particular mythology.
2 a temple dedicated to all the gods.

panther *noun*
1 a leopard, especially a black leopard.
2 *American* a jaguar or puma.
[Greek]

panties *plural noun*
(*informal*) knickers.

pantomime *noun*
a form of entertainment, traditionally performed at Christmas, usually based on

a fairy tale with modern songs or comedy added.
[Greek *pantos* of all + MIME]

pantry *noun* (*plural* **pantries**)
a larder.
[Old French *panetier* a servant in charge of bread]

pants *plural noun*
1 underpants.
2 *American* trousers.

pantyhose *plural noun* also **pantihose**
American tights.

panzer *noun*
a German unit of troops using armoured vehicles.
[German, suit of armour]

pap¹ *noun*
soft food, such as bread soaked in milk, eaten by babies and invalids.

pap² *noun*
an old word for a teat or nipple.

papa (pa-**par** *or* **par**-pa) *noun*
(*American or dated*) one's father.

papacy (**pay**-pa-see) *noun* (*plural* **papacies**)
Roman Catholicism the rank, office or period of a pope.
[Medieval Latin *papa* pope]

papal (**pay**-p'l) *adjective*
of or relating to a pope or the papacy.

paparazzi (pa-pa-**rat**-si) *plural noun* (*singular* **paparazzo**) (pa-pa-**rat**-so)
press photographers who pursue the famous, hoping to get photographs that they can sell.
[Italian]

papaya (pa-**pie**-ya) *noun* also called **pawpaw**.
a tropical fruit with orange flesh and black seeds.

paper *noun*
1 a substance, often made from wood pulp, consisting of thin sheets used for writing on, wrapping, etc.
2 a piece or sheet of this substance.
3 a newspaper.
4 (**papers**) documents of identity.
5 an essay or article.
6 a written examination.
7 a government report.
Phrase **on paper** in theory: *Your plan sounds fine on paper, but will it work in practice?*
• **paper** *verb* to cover, line or decorate with paper, e.g. a wall or shelf.

• **paper** *adjective* made or consisting of paper: *a paper bag.*
Figurative *All this company ever makes is paper profits* (= existing only in the accounting books).
Word Family **papery** *adjective* thin or flimsy like paper.
[Latin *papyrus*]

paperback *noun*
a book bound with a flexible paper cover. Compare HARDBACK.

paperchase *noun*
a cross-country run following a trail of scraps of paper.

paper clip *noun*
a metal or plastic clasp for holding loose papers together.

paperhanger *noun*
a professional hanger of wallpaper.

paperknife *noun* (*plural* **paperknives**)
a knife-like instrument for opening letters.

paper tape *noun*
Computers a strip of paper punched with holes representing information. Paper tape was used as a way of feeding information into older computers.

paper tiger *noun*
a person or thing that appears strong but is really weak.

paperweight (**pay**-pa-wate) *noun*
a small heavy object placed on top of loose papers to keep them in place.

paperwork *noun*
written, clerical or administrative work, especially as part of one's normal occupation.

papier mâché (pap-ee-ay **mash**-ay) *noun*
a mixture of mashed paper, usually newspaper soaked in water and glue. It can be used to make simple models, trays, boxes, etc. and is often lacquered, gilded and painted.
[French *mâché* chewed + *papier* paper]

papilla (pa-**pil**-a) *noun* (*plural* **papillae**) (pa-**pil**-ee)
Anatomy a nipple or small nipple-like structure, such as a taste bud or a hair root.
Word Family **papillary** *adjective.*
[Latin]

papilloma (pap-i-lo-ma) *noun* (*plural* **papillomas** or **papillomata** (pap-i-lo-ma-ta))
a small skin tumour, such as a wart or corn.
[Latin *papilla* nipple + *-oma* tumour]

papist (**pay**-pist) *noun*
1 a Roman Catholic.
2 *History* a supporter of the papacy.
Word Family papism *noun*.

papoose *noun*
an offensive word for a Native American baby or young child.

paprika (pa-**pree**-ka *or* **pap**-ri-ka) *noun*
a red spice made from sweet peppers.
[Hungarian]

papyrus (pa-**pie**-rus) *noun* (*plural* **papyri**
(pa-**pie**-rye *or* pa-**pie**-ree) *or* **papyruses**)
1 a material used for writing on by ancient civilizations, especially the Egyptians, made from soaked, dried and compressed strips of the stem of a water plant.
2 the tall aquatic plant used for this.
[Greek *papyros*]

par *noun*
1 *Golf* the average number of strokes that a first-class player, making no mistakes, should take for each hole or a number of holes.
2 *Commerce* the nominal or face value of a stock or share, rather than the market value.
Phrases **above par** above the average or normal amount, degree, condition, etc.
below par, under par below the average or normal amount, degree, condition, etc.
on a par with equal in amount, quality, etc. to.
[Latin, equal]

parable (**pa**-ra-b'l) *noun*
a short story which illustrates a moral or lesson.
[Greek *parabolé* comparison]

parabola (pa-**rab**-a-la) *noun*
Maths a symmetrical plane curve formed when a cone is cut by a plane parallel to the side.

parachute (**pa**-ra-shoot) *noun*
an umbrella-shaped canopy of lightweight fabric which permits a person or cargo to drop safely to the ground from a height owing to air filling the canopy and retarding its downward fall.
Word Family parachute *verb* to descend or land by parachute; **parachutist** *noun*.
[French *parer* to prevent or avoid + *chute* fall]

Paraclete (**pa**-ra-kleet) *noun*
Christianity the Holy Spirit.
[Greek *parakletos* an advocate]

parade (pa-**rade**) *noun*
1 a ceremonial procession, as held on a special occasion.

2 an orderly assembly of troops for inspection or display.
3 a display, exhibition: *making a parade of his abilities.*
4 a row of shops, a promenade or a public square.
● **parade** *verb.*
[French, a show]

parade ground *noun*
a place where troops assemble for inspection and parade.

paradigm (**pa**-ra-dime) *noun*
1 a pattern or example.
2 a table of the principal parts of irregular verbs, etc.
[Greek *paradeigma* showing side by side]

paradise (**pa**-ra-dice) *noun*
1 heaven.
2 (**Paradise**) the Garden of Eden.
3 a place of extreme beauty or delight.
[ancient Persian, an enclosed garden]

paradox (**pa**-ra-doks) *noun* (*plural* **paradoxes**)
1 a statement which appears to contradict itself, often made intentionally to emphasize a point.
2 a person or situation that is puzzling because of contradictory qualities.
Word Family paradoxical (pa-ra-**dok**-si-k'l) *adjective* of or like a paradox; **paradoxically** *adverb.*
[*para-* + Greek *doxa* opinion]

paraffin (**pa**-ra-fin) *noun*
1 also **paraffin wax** a waxy substance produced in the distillation of petroleum, used in sealing and candles.
2 also **paraffin oil; liquid paraffin** a mixture of hydrocarbons produced during the distillation of petroleum, used for domestic heating and lighting, as a solvent, and in jet engines.
[Latin *parum* little + *affinis* related (as being unreactive)]

paragliding *noun*
a sport in which someone glides down from a height using a rectangular parachute.
Word Family paraglide *verb*; **paraglider** *noun.*

paragon (**pa**-ra-g'n) *noun*
a model of excellence: *My daughter is a paragon of good behaviour.*
[Italian *paragone* touchstone]

paragraph (**pa**-ra-grahf) *noun*
a group of sentences placed together because they have a common idea,

beginning on a new line of the page and
sometimes having an indent.
• **paragraph** verb to divide into
paragraphs.
[para- + Greek graphein to write]

parakeet (parr-a-keet) noun also
parrakeet
a small brightly coloured parrot with a
long tail.

parallax (pa-ra-laks) noun
Physics the apparent change in the position
or direction of an object due to the
observer changing his or her position.
Word Family parallactic adjective.
[Greek parallaxis change]

parallel (pa-ra-lel) adjective
1 Maths (of lines, planes and surfaces) the
same distance apart and never meeting, no
matter how far they are extended.
2 similar, having the same direction or
tendency: The two friends had parallel
careers.
3 Computers involving the performance of
operations at the same time.
• **parallel** noun
1 a similarity or comparison. There are
obvious parallels between the two countries.
□ The brilliance of this novel is without
parallel.
2 Geography a line of latitude. Compare
MERIDIAN.
• **parallel** verb (**parallels; paralleling;
paralleled**)
1 to be parallel to.
2 to compare.
[Greek parallelos side by side]

parallelogram (pa-ra-lell-a-gram) noun
any quadrilateral with opposite sides equal
and parallel.

Paralympics (pa-ra-lim piks) plural noun
(used with singular or plural verb) a series of
international sports events for disabled
athletes, organized like the Olympic
Games.
[para(plegic) + (O)lympics]

paralyse (pa-ra-lize) verb (American
paralyze)
1 to affect with paralysis: Her legs were
paralysed after the accident.
2 to be unable to move temporarily: He
was paralysed with terror.
3 to cause disruption to: The strikes
paralysed the city.

paralysis (pa-ral-a-sis) noun (plural
paralyses) (pa-ral-a-seez)
1 Medicine the loss of voluntary movement
of the muscles.

2 a stoppage, inability to function.
[Greek para on one side + lysis a
loosening]

paralytic (pa-ra-lit-ik) adjective
1 of or affected with paralysis.
2 (informal) extremely drunk.
• **paralytic** noun a person affected with
paralysis of the entire body.

paramecium (pa-ra-mee-si-um) noun
(plural **paramecia**)
a microscopic freshwater animal with hair-
like threads on its outer surface which help
it move.
[Greek paramekes oval]

paramedic (pa-ra-med-ik) noun
someone who has been trained to give
medical help, especially in an emergency.

parameter (pa-ram-i-ta) noun
1 a limit: You must work within these
parameters.
2 Maths a variable, e.g. in a mathematical
expression, upon which other variables are
dependent.
3 a characteristic of a statistical population
that can be measured.

paramilitary adjective
having a military structure or organization
which is supplementary to the regular
armed forces.
• **paramilitary** noun (plural
paramilitaries) a person who belongs to
a paramilitary organization.

paramount (pa-ra mount) adjective
superior or supreme: of paramount
importance.

paramour (pa-ra-mor) noun
an old word for a lover, especially the lover
of a married person.

paranoia (pa-ra-noy-a) noun
a mental disorder marked by the
unjustified belief that one is being
persecuted, usually accompanied by
megalomania and insane distrust.
Word Family paranoid adjective of,
relating to or affected by paranoia;
paranoid noun a person with paranoia.
[Greek, derangement]

paranormal adjective
not able to be explained by normal
scientific laws: Telepathy is a paranormal
means of communication.

parapet noun
1 a low wall around the edge of a balcony
or the top of a building.
2 a low defensive wall or bank in front of a
trench or other fortification.

paraphernalia (pa-ra-fa-**nay**-lee-a) *plural noun*
miscellaneous belongings or equipment.
[Greek]

> The word **paraphernalia** originally
> referred to the part of a woman's
> property that was not her dowry. On
> marriage, a dowry became the property
> of a woman's husband but the rest of it,
> the *paraphernalia*, remained her own.
> *Paraphernalia* ultimately comes from
> Greek *parapherna* from *para* (beside)
> and *pherné* (dowry).

paraphrase (**pa**-ra-fraze) *verb*
to reword a piece of writing to make it
shorter or clearer.
• **paraphrase** *noun*.

paraplegic (pa-ra-**plee**-jik) *adjective*
having both legs paralysed.
Word Family **paraplegia** *noun*;
paraplegic *noun* a person who is
paraplegic.
[*para-* + Greek *plegia* a stroke]

parapsychology (pa-ra-sigh-**koll**-a-jee)
noun
the study of psychological phenomena
which cannot be scientifically explained,
e.g. clairvoyance, telepathy, seeing ghosts.
Word Family **parapsychological** (pa-
ra-sigh-ka-**loj**-i-k'l) *adjective*.

parasailing *noun*
a sport in which someone glides with an
open parachute while being towed by a
motor boat.

parascending *noun*
the sport of paragliding or parasailing.

parasite (**pa**-ra-site) *noun*
1 *Biology* an organism which can obtain
food only by living in or on another
organism.
2 a person who relies on other people and
gives nothing in return.
Word Family **parasitic** (pa-ra-**sit**-ik)
adjective of, relating to or like a parasite;
parasitically *adverb*; **parasitism** *noun*.
[Greek *parasitos* dinner guest]

parasitology (pa-ra-sigh-**tol**-a-jee) *noun*
the study of parasites, a branch of biology.
Word Family **parasitologist** *noun*.

parasol *noun*
a light umbrella made of cloth or stiffened
paper, for protection from sunlight.
[Latin *para* guard against + *sol* sun]

paratha (pa-**rah**-ta) *noun*
an Indian unleavened bread made from
layers of very thin dough.
[Hindi]

paratrooper *noun*
a soldier trained and equipped to
parachute from aircraft, especially in order
to fight behind enemy lines.
Word Family **paratroops** *plural noun*
paratroopers.

par avion (par av-**yon**) *adverb*
by airmail.
[French, by aeroplane]

parboil *verb*
to boil food until it is partly cooked.
[PAR(t) + BOIL, confused with French
parbouillir to boil thoroughly]

parcel (**par**-s'l) *noun*
1 an object or a collection of objects
wrapped up to be carried or posted.
2 a piece or amount of something: *a parcel
of land*.
• **parcel** *verb* (**parcels; parcelling;
parcelled**)
1 to make up into a parcel.
2 to divide up or distribute something.
[Latin *particula* a small part]

parch *verb*
to make hot and dry: *The desert winds
parched the weary pilgrims*.

parched *adjective*
(*informal*) very thirsty.

parchment *noun*
1 the skin of animals prepared as a surface
for writing.
2 a paper resembling parchment.

pardon *verb*
1 to forgive or excuse.
2 *Law* to release a person from a penalty or
from liability for a crime.
• **pardon** *noun*
1 the act of forgiving or being forgiven for
something.
2 *Law* the releasing of a convicted person
from punishment for a crime.
3 *History, Religion* an indulgence.
• **pardon** *interjection* used to ask someone
to repeat what he or she has said.
Word Family **pardonable** *adjective* able
or worthy to be pardoned.

pardoner *noun*
History a person appointed to sell religious
pardons for sins.

pare *verb*
1 to cut or trim the edges of: *paring the rind
off the cheese*.
2 to reduce: *paring down one's expenses*.

paregoric (pa-ra-**gorr**-ik) *noun*
a soothing medicine, such as one formerly
used to check diarrhoea.

parent (**pair**-ent) *noun*
1 a mother or father.
2 an animal or plant which produces other animals or plants.
• **parent** *verb* to be or act as the parent of.
Word Family **parental** (pa-**ren**-t'l) *adjective* of or like a parent: *parental love*; **parenthood, parenting** *noun*.
[Latin *pariens* bringing forth young]

parentage (**pair**-en-tij) *noun*
origin or descent: *a man of noble parentage.*

parent company *noun* (*plural* **parent companies**)
a company which owns or manages one or more other companies.

parenthesis (pa-**ren**-tha-sis) *noun* (*plural* **parentheses**) (pa-**ren**-tha-seez)
1 a word or words inserted into a sentence or passage as a separate comment, usually placed in brackets or between dashes or commas.
2 brackets used for this purpose.
⇨ BRACKET (definition 2).
Word Family **parenthetic** (pa-ren-**thet**-ik) *adjective*.
[Greek, putting in beside]

par excellence (par ck-sa-**lonce**) *adjective*
superior to all others: *a cook par excellence.*
[French]

parfait (**par**-fay) *noun*
a rich frozen dessert of egg, fruit and whipped cream.
[French, perfect]

pariah (pa-**rye**-a) *noun*
a person or animal that is despised; an outcast.
[Tamil, a drummer]

parietal bone (pa-**rye**-a-t'l bone) *noun*
Anatomy either of two bones forming the upper sides and roof of the skull.
[Latin *paries* a partition]

parings (**pair**-ingz) *plural noun*
thin strips cut from the edge or outside of something: *nail parings.*

parish (**pa**-rish) *noun* (*plural* **parishes**)
1 a district with its own church and clergy.
2 a local government area based on this.
[Greek *paroikesis* a neighbourhood]

parishioner (pa-**rish**-on-a) *noun*
a person who lives in a parish.

parity (**pa**-ri-tee) *noun*
(*formal*) equality: *Everyone in this school receives parity of treatment.*
[Latin *par* equal]

park *noun*
1 an area of open land, usually with trees, etc., set aside for public recreational use.
2 the land surrounding a country house.
• **park** *verb*
1 to leave a vehicle in a particular place.
2 (*informal*) to leave something somewhere: *Can I park my books on this chair?*

parka *noun*
a warm anorak with a hood which is often trimmed with fur.
[Eskimo]

Parkinson's disease *noun* also **Parkinsonism**
a progressive nervous disorder resulting in tremor, muscular rigidity, partial paralysis and weakness.
[after *J. Parkinson*, 1755-1824, a British doctor]

Parkinson's law *noun*
a humorous law stating that 'work expands so as to fill the time available for its completion'.
[invented in 1958 by *C. N. Parkinson*, 1909-1993, a British historian]

parkland *noun* also **parklands**
an area of grass with scattered trees.

parlance *noun*
a way of speaking: *in legal parlance.*
[Old French, speaking]

parley (**par**-lee) *noun*
a conference, especially with an enemy to discuss terms.
• **parley** *verb*.

parliament (**par**-la-m'nt) *noun*
1 an assembly of elected representatives from all parts of a country that meets to make laws, advise the government, control taxation and expenditure, etc.
2 (**Parliament**) in Britain, the House of Commons and House of Lords, the two Houses of Parliament.
Word Family **parliamentary** *adjective* of or relating to a parliament.
[Old French *parlement* talking]

parliamentarian (par-la-men-**tair**-i-an) *noun*
a member of a parliament, especially someone who is experienced in parliamentary debate and procedure.
Word Family **parliamentarianism** *noun* the supporting of a parliamentary system of government.

parlour (**par**-la) *noun* (*American* **parlor**)
1 (*dated*) a living room or room where visitors are entertained.

2 (*especially American*) a particular type of business or shop: *a beauty parlour.*

parlous (par-lus) *adjective*
an old word meaning 'dangerous, very bad': *Things are in a parlous state.*
[alteration of *perilous*]

Parmesan (par-ma-**zan**) *noun*
an Italian hard cheese with a strong smell.
[Italian *Parmigiano* from Parma]

parochial (pa-**ro**-kee-ul) *adjective*
1 of or relating to a parish: *The clergyman's parochial duties took up much of his time.*
2 narrow in outlook.
Word Family **parochially** *adverb*;
parochialism *noun.*

parody (pa-ra-dee) *noun* (*plural*
parodies)
a humorous imitation of a serious piece of writing.
● **parody** *verb* (**parodies; parodying; parodied**).
[*para-* + Greek *oidé* an ode]

parole (pa-**role**) *noun*
Law the early release of a prisoner on a promise of good behaviour. Compare
PROBATION.
● **parole** *verb* to release a prisoner on parole.
[French, word (of honour)]

paroxysm (pa-rok-sizm) *noun*
a sudden uncontrolled fit of pain, coughing, laughter, anger, etc.
[Greek *paroxysmos* irritation]

parquet (par-kay *or* par-kee) *noun*
flooring made from small pieces of wood laid in a pattern.
Word Family **parquetry** (par-ka-tree) *noun* inlaid and patterned woodwork.
[French, floor]

parrakeet ⇨ PARAKEET.

parricide (pa-rih-side) *noun*
1 *Law* the crime of killing either of one's parents or a close relative.
2 *Law* a person who does this.
[Latin *pater* father or *parens* parent + *caedere* to kill]

parrot *noun*
a brightly coloured tropical bird with a hooked bill and fleshy tongue. Some parrots have a gift for mimicry.
● **parrot** *verb* to imitate or repeat words like a parrot: *Having no original ideas, he parrots what others say.*

parry *verb* (**parries; parrying; parried**)
to evade or deflect: *She parried her opponent's sword thrust.* □ *He parried the reporter's questions.*
● **parry** *noun* (*plural* **parries**).

parse (parz) *verb*
Grammar to give a word its grammatical description.

parsec (par-sek) *noun*
a unit of length used in astronomy and equal to about 3·25 light years or $3·08 \times 10^{16}$ metres.
[PAR(allax) + SEC(ond)]

parsimonious (par-si-**mo**-nee-us)
adjective
extremely frugal, miserly or stingy.
Word Family **parsimoniously** *adverb*;
parsimony (par-sim-a-nee) *noun.*
[from Latin]

parsley (par-slee) *noun*
a garden plant with green crinkled leaves used for flavouring and to decorate food.

parsnip *noun*
a white fleshy cone-shaped root used as a vegetable.

parson *noun*
a vicar, rector or other clergyman.

parsonage (par-sa-nij) *noun*
the residence of a parson.
[Latin *persona* a person]

parson's nose *noun*
(*informal*) the fatty tail of cooked chicken or other poultry.

part *noun*
1 a piece or portion of a whole: *A part of this book is missing.* □ *I need some new parts for my car.*
2 a role in a play: *He has learnt his part.*
3 *Music* the music for a particular voice or instrument: *a choral work for eight parts.*
4 (**parts**) (*informal*) areas, lands: *travelling in foreign parts.*
5 (**parts**) an old word meaning 'abilities': *a man of many parts.*
Phrases **for the most part** mostly. **in part** to some extent. **part and parcel** a necessary part. **take part** to join in or participate. **take someone's part** to support or defend: *She always takes her sister's part in arguments.* **take something in good part** to take no offence.
● **part** *verb*
1 to move things so that they are no longer together: *I'll part you two if you don't stop talking!* □ *She'll never part with her teddy bear.*
2 to make a parting in the hair.

Word Family **part, partly** *adverb* in part;
part *adjective* being partly composed of.
[from Latin]

partake *verb* (**partakes; partaking,
partook; partaken**)
(*formal*) to take part or share in
something: *Will you partake of dinner with
us?*

parterre (par-**tair**) *noun*
a formal arrangement of lawns, paths and
flower beds as part of a larger garden.
[French]

parthenogenesis (par-tha-no-**jen**-i-sis)
noun
Biology the development of an ovum
without fertilization occurring.
[Greek *parthenos* virgin + GENESIS]

partial (**par**-sh'l) *adjective*
1 not total or complete: *The meeting was
only a partial success.*
2 biased or prejudiced: *It's useless having
the dispute decided by a partial judge.*
3 fond of: *He's very partial to marmalade
sandwiches.*
Word Family **partially** *adverb*;
partiality (par-shee-**al**-i-tee) *noun*.

participate (par-**tiss**-i-pate) *verb*
to have a role or share in: *She doesn't often
participate in class discussions.*
Word Family **participant, participator**
noun a person who participates;
participation *noun* the act of
participating.
[Latin *partis* of a part + *capere* to take]

participle (par-**tiss**-i-p'l) *noun*
Grammar a word formed from a verb and
used as a verb, noun or adjective.
past participle a participle expressing an
action or state which is already completed:
*In 'after the show had finished', 'finished' is a
past participle.*
present participle a participle expressing
an action or state which is happening at
this moment. *In 'while opening the door',
'opening' is a present participle.*

particle (**par**-ti-k'l) *noun*
1 a very small piece of material: *Particles of
food can get trapped in the teeth and lead to
decay.*
2 *Physics* a tiny distinct object, e.g. a
molecule, atom or subatomic particle.
[from Latin]

particoloured *adjective* (*American
particolored*)
having different colours in different parts.

particular (par-**tik**-yoo-la) *adjective*
1 relating to one person, group or thing
rather than to all: *We will make an exception
in your particular case.*
2 special: *She is a particular friend of mine.*
3 careful or attentive to details: *He is very
particular about what he eats.*
• **particular** *noun* a point: *You are correct
in every particular.*
Phrase **in particular** especially: *In
particular I think the photography in the film
was excellent.*
Word Family **particularly** *adverb*
especially.

parting *noun*
1 a leave-taking or departure.
2 a dividing line down the head, where the
hair is brushed to left and right.
3 a division or separation.
• **parting** *adjective* said, done, etc. on
parting: *She never forgot his parting words.*

partisan (**par**-ti-zan *or* par-ti-**zan**) *noun*
1 a supporter of a person, party or cause.
2 a member of a military force, but not
part of a regular army, fighting for the
liberation of a country.
Word Family **partisan** *adjective* biased.
[Italian *partigiano*]

partition (par-**ti**-sh'n) *noun*
1 a separation or division of a whole into
parts: *The partition of his farm into building
sites made him a wealthy man.*
2 something that divides or separates,
especially a wall or screen dividing a room.
• **partition** *verb* to divide or separate into
parts.

partner *noun*
1 a person who shares an activity with
another: *a dancing partner.*
2 a person on the same team as another at
tennis, cards, etc.
3 a husband or wife, or a member of a
couple who have been together for a long
time.
• **partner** *verb* to be or act as someone's
partner.

partnership *noun*
the state or condition of being a partner:
The brothers own the business in partnership.
□ *The batsmen had a cricket partnership of
120 runs.*

part of speech *noun* (*plural* **parts of
speech**)
a class of words, e.g. noun or adjective,
that has a particular function in a
sentence.

partook the past tense of **partake**.

partridge *noun* (*plural* **partridge** or **partridges**)
a plump brown game bird.

part song *noun*
a song with parts for several voices.

part-time *adjective, adverb*
(of work or an interest) which does not take up the full working hours in a week.
Word Family **part-timer** *noun*.

parturition (par-tyor-**ish**-'n) *noun*
(*formal*) childbirth.
Word Family **parturient** (par-**tyor**-ri-ent) *adjective* giving or about to give birth.

party *noun* (*plural* **parties**)
1 a social gathering, especially a private one.
2 a group of people with the same beliefs and policies, usually in opposition to others: *a political party*.
3 a group of people doing something together: *a rescue party*.
4 a person or group on one side in an argument, discussion, etc.
• **party** *verb* (**parties; partying; partied**) (*informal*) to attend or enjoy oneself at a party: *partying until late*.
• **party** *adjective*
1 of or relating to a party: *a party hat*.
2 of or relating to something shared: *properties joined by a party wall*.

party line *noun*
1 the official ideas or policies of a political party.
2 a telephone line shared by more than one household, each having a separate telephone.

parvenu (**par**-va-new) *noun*
a person who has risen above his or her original status through the sudden attainment of wealth or position.
[French, arrived]

parvovirus (**par**-vo-vie-rus) *noun* (*plural* **parvoviruses**)
any of a group of very small viruses which contain DNA and are the causes of various animal diseases.

pascal *noun*
the SI unit of pressure. *abbrev.* Pa.
[after *Blaise Pascal, 1623-1662, a French mathematician and philosopher*]

paschal (**pas**-k'l *or* **pars**-k'l) *adjective*
Judaism, Christianity of or relating to Passover or Easter.

pas de deux (pah da **der**) *noun* (*plural* **pas de deux**) (pah da **der**)
Ballet a dance or part of a dance for two.
[French, step of two]

pasha *noun* also **pacha**
a title added after the names of generals and governors under the old Turkish Empire, and retained in some countries after its collapse.
[Turkish, chief]

pashmina (push-**mee**-na) *noun*
a fine material made from the wool of Indian goats, or a shawl made from this.
[Persian]

pass[1] (pahs) *verb*
1 to go by: *The days passed quickly.*
2 to give or transfer something from one person or position to another: *Pass me the butter.*
3 to go past, overtake: *She needed to pass two other runners to win.*
4 to exceed: *We never passed 30 miles per hour.*
5 to spend time: *We passed the weekend playing games.*
6 to come to an end: *All good things must pass.*
7 to get through an examination, course, etc.
8 to say that someone has been successful in an examination, course, etc.
9 to approve a law or proposal.
10 to utter, pronounce: *passing judgement.*
11 to excrete: *passing urine.*
12 to fail to bid, take one's turn, etc.
Phrases **come to pass** to happen. **pass away** to die. **pass off 1** to take place. **2** to misrepresent as: *He tried to pass himself off as a doctor.* **pass out** to faint. **pass over** to ignore or overlook. **pass up** to refuse or reject: *She passed up the chance to go skiing.*
• **pass** *noun* (*plural* **passes**)
1 an act of passing, especially an act of transferring a ball from one player to another in a team game.
2 a success in an examination.
3 a ticket allowing free entrance, travel, etc.: *a bus pass.*
4 a stage, especially a bad one: *Things have come to a terrible pass.*
5 (*informal*) an amorous advance: *He made a pass at her, but she turned him down.*

> ⚠️ Note that the past tense and past participle of the verb *pass* is *passed*, as in *I passed him on the way home.* The word *past* is an adjective, noun and preposition, as in *I walked past him on the way home.*

pass² *noun* (*plural* **passes**)
a narrow route through mountains.

passable *adjective*
1 acceptable: *a passable knowledge of Spanish.*
2 able to be walked or driven on or along.
Word Family **passably** *adverb* fairly or moderately.

passage (pa-sij) *noun*
1 the act of passing: *the passage of time.*
2 a corridor.
3 an extract from a written work or piece of music.
4 a journey across the sea from one port to another, or a journey by air.
5 the right to pass through or across someone's land, etc.
[Latin *passus* a pace]

passbook *noun*
a book in which a record of payments to a bank or building society is kept.

passé (pass-ay) *adjective*
old-fashioned or out of date.
[French, passed]

passenger (pas-in-ja) *noun*
a person who travels in a vehicle who is not a driver, pilot or member of the crew.

passer-by *noun* (*plural* **passers-by**)
a person who happens to be passing something.

passing *noun*
the act of going by: *the passing of the long summer days.*
• **passing** *adjective* brief or cursory.

passion (*rhymes with* fashion) *noun*
1 emotion or feeling which is very strong and compelling, such as love, hate, anger, hope, grief, etc.
2 a strong enthusiasm for someone or something: *He has a passion for poetry.*
3 (**Passion**) *Christianity* the sufferings of Christ, especially at the crucifixion.
4 (**Passion**) *Christianity* a musical setting or enactment of Christ's sufferings.
[Latin *passio* suffering]

passionate (pash-a-n't) *adjective*
showing passion or caused by passion:
a passionate supporter of animal rights.
□ *a passionate embrace.*
Word Family **passionately** *adverb.*

passion fruit *noun*
a small round purple fruit with a tough skin and many small seeds, growing on a vine.

passive (pas-iv) *adjective*
1 accepting what happens, submissive.

2 *Chemistry* (especially of a metal surface) inactive.
3 *Grammar* ⇨ VOICE *noun* (definition 4).
Word Family **passively** *adverb*;
passiveness, passivity (pa-**siv**-i-tee) *noun.*

passive smoking *noun*
the involuntary inhalation of tobacco smoke from the cigarettes of other people.

Passover (**pah**-so-ver) *noun* also **Pesach**
a Jewish spring festival commemorating the Exodus from Egypt.

passport *noun*
an official document which identifies a person wishing to travel in foreign countries. Compare VISA.
[PASS + PORT]

password *noun*
a secret word or phrase permitting a person using it to pass guards or sentries.

past *adjective*
1 having occurred at a time before the present: *I have been ill for the past week.*
2 *Grammar* (of a verb form) used when referring to something that has already happened: *the past tense.*
• **past** *noun*
1 any time before the present: *History is a study of the past.*
2 the events in a person's earlier life or experiences: *How can I trust you when I know nothing about your past?*
3 *Grammar* a past tense or form.
• **past** *preposition*
1 after in time: *It is past 6 p.m.* □ *She is well past 70.*
2 beyond or further than: *The shop is past the corner.*

> [!] Do not confuse *past* with *passed*
> (⇨ PASS¹).

pasta (**pas**-ter) *noun*
a dough of flour and eggs which has been cut into various shapes, e.g. spaghetti or macaroni, cooked and eaten with a sauce.
[Italian]

paste *noun*
1 a mixture, e.g. of flour and water, used for sticking paper, etc.
2 any soft smooth preparation: *toothpaste.*
□ *fish paste.*
3 a bright glassy substance used to make artificial gems.
• **paste** *verb* to fasten or stick something using paste, glue, etc.
[Greek *pasté* barley soup]

pasteboard *noun*
a flat board made of lots of sheets of paper stuck together.

pastel (pas-t'l) *noun*
1 a soft delicate hue.
2 a crayon made of chalk, pigments, etc.
3 a picture drawn with pastels.
• **pastel** *adjective*.
[from PASTA]

pastern (pas-turn) *noun*
the part of a horse's foot between the fetlock and the hoof.

pasteurize, pasteurise (pass-cha-rize or pas-cha-rize) *verb*
to reduce the number of micro-organisms present in a liquid such as milk, by heating but not boiling.
Word Family **pasteurization** *noun*.
[after *Louis Pasteur*, 1822-1895, a French chemist]

pastiche (pas-teesh) *noun*
a work of art which imitates or borrows from the work or style of other artists.
[Italian *pasta* paste]

pastille (pas-til) *noun*
a small flavoured sweet or lozenge.
[Latin *pastilla* a small loaf]

pastime (pahs-time) *noun*
an amusement, hobby or sport that helps time pass pleasantly.

past master *noun*
an expert or person with long experience.

pastor *noun*
Christianity a minister in charge of a congregation.
[Latin, shepherd]

pastoral *adjective*
1 used as pasture or for grazing, etc.:
pastoral land. Compare ARABLE.
2 of or characteristic of the country or country life: *a pastoral poem*.
3 of or relating to spiritual guidance, e.g. by a member of the clergy.
4 of or relating to the responsibility of school staff for the general care of their pupils.
• **pastoral** *noun* a work of art dealing with shepherds or country life.
Word Family **pastorally** *adverb*;
pastoralism *noun*.

pastorale (pas-ta-rahl) *noun* (*plural* **pastorales** or **pastorali** (pas-ta-rah-lee))
Music a choral or orchestral work depicting or concerning pastoral life.

past participle ⇨ PARTICIPLE.

pastry (pay-stree) *noun* (*plural* **pastries**)
1 dough, especially when used as the base or crust of a pie.
2 a tart or small cake made with pastry.

pasture (pahs-cher) *noun*
an area covered with grass used or suitable for grazing cattle, etc.
• **pasture** *verb* to put livestock on a pasture to graze.
[from Latin]

pasty[1] (pay-stee) *adjective* (**pastier; pastiest**)
1 of or like paste.
2 pale and sickly: *a pasty complexion*.

pasty[2] (pas-tee) *noun* (*plural* **pasties**)
an envelope of pastry filled with meat and vegetables and cooked.

pat[1] *verb* (**pats; patting; patted**)
to touch or strike lightly, especially with the open hand or with something flat:
Wash your hands if you've been patting the dog. □ *He patted down the earth after planting the seedlings.*
Phrase **pat someone on the back** to congratulate someone.
• **pat** *noun*
1 a light strike or touch.
2 a small mass of something, especially butter.

pat[2] *adjective*
glib or facile: *Your answer was just a little too pat.*
• **pat** *adverb* exactly or aptly.
Phrase **have something off pat** to know something by heart.

patch *noun* (*plural* **patches**)
1 a piece of fabric used to cover holes in clothing, etc.
2 a covering for a wound: *an eyepatch*.
3 a piece of material which releases a medicine or drug into the body.
4 (*informal*) a time: *going through a bad patch*.
5 a small piece of land: *a vegetable patch*.
6 an area of something that is different from the surrounding parts: *a darker patch on the carpet*.
7 *Computers* an extra piece of code downloaded to correct or improve a program.
Phrase **not a patch on** (*informal*) not nearly as good as.
• **patch** *verb* to mend or repair with a patch.
Phrase **patch up 1** to repair simply or quickly. **2** to settle a quarrel.

patchouli (pa-choo-lee) *noun*
the oil of an Asian plant, used as a perfume.

patchwork *noun*
1 a form of needlework in which small pieces of fabric are sewn together.
2 anything formed from different pieces: *His book is a patchwork of old and new ideas.*

patchy *adjective* (**patchier; patchiest**)
of uneven quality: *Your work is rather patchy.*

pate *noun*
an old word for the head.

pâté (**pa**-tay) *noun*
a savoury paste made from finely chopped meat or fish and herbs.
[French]

pâté de foie gras (pa-tay da fwah **grah**) *noun*
short form is **foie gras** a savoury paste with a rich taste, made from goose liver.
[French]

patella (pa-**tell**-a) *noun* (*plural* **patellae** (pa-**tel**-ee)
Anatomy the kneecap.
[Latin, a plate]

patent (**pay**-t'nt *or* **pat**-'nt) *noun*
the official right given to an inventor to make or sell his or her invention for a certain time without it being copied.
• **patent** (**pay**-t'nt) *adjective*
1 plain or obvious: *a patent lie.*
2 having or protected by a patent.
Word Family **patent** *verb* to obtain a patent for; **patently** *adverb* plainly or obviously.
[Latin *patens* lying open]

patent leather *noun*
a leather coated with a hard glossy surface, used for shoes and handbags.

pater (**pay**-ta) *noun*
(*informal dated*) father.
[Latin]

paternal (pa-**ter**-nal) *adjective*
1 of or like a father: *He treats us in a paternal way.*
2 related on the father's side: *my paternal grandmother.*
Word Family **paternally** *adverb.*

paternalism (pa-**ter**-na-lizm) *noun*
the principle of treating those over whom one has control in the same way that a father treats his children.
Word Family **paternalistic** (pa-ter-na-lis-tik) *adjective*; **paternalistically** *adverb.*

paternity (pa-**ter**-ni-tee) *noun*
1 the state of being a father.
2 a relationship to or derivation from a father: *Her paternity is unknown.*

paternity suit *noun*
Law a case in which a woman tries to prove that a certain man is the father of her child.

path *noun*
1 a track or way for walking.
2 the track in which something moves: *the path of the earth around the sun.*

pathetic (pa-**thet**-ik) *adjective*
1 causing pity or sympathy: *The starving child was a pathetic sight.*
2 (*informal*) miserably weak or inadequate.
Word Family **pathetically** *adverb.*

pathogen (**path**-a-j'n) *noun*
an organism that can cause disease, e.g. a virus or micro-organism.
Word Family **pathogenic** (pa-tha-**jen**-ik) *adjective* producing disease.
[*patho-* + *-gen*]

pathological (pa-tha-**loj**-i-k'l) *adjective* (*American* **pathologic**)
1 due to or involving disease.
2 (*informal*) compulsive: *a pathological liar.*
3 of or relating to pathology.
Word Family **pathologically** *adverb.*

pathology (pa-**thol**-a-jee) *noun*
1 the study of diseases and their causes and effects.
2 *Medicine* the conditions and progress of a disease.
Word Family **pathologist** *noun* a person who studies diseases.

pathos (**pay**-thos) *noun*
a quality in music, literature, etc. which creates a feeling of sadness or pity.
Compare BATHOS.
[Greek]

pathway *noun*
a path.

patience (**pay**-sh'nce) *noun*
1 the ability to endure something or to wait calmly and uncomplainingly.
2 *Cards* a game for a single player.

patient (**pay**-sh'nt) *adjective*
having or showing patience.
• **patient** *noun* a person being treated by a doctor or in a hospital. An **inpatient** stays at the hospital during treatment and an **outpatient** goes home between treatments.
Word Family **patiently** *adverb.*
[Latin *patiens* experiencing suffering]

patina *noun*
1 the greenish surface on old bronze, caused by oxidation.
2 a sheen which develops on a surface over time.
[Latin, a dish]

patio (**pat**-i-o) *noun*
a paved area or courtyard adjoining a house.
[Spanish]

patisserie (pa-**tee**-ser-ee *or* pa-**tiss**-er-ee) *noun*
1 a shop selling pastries and cakes.
2 pastries and cakes.

patois (**pat**-wah) *noun* (*plural* **patois** (**pat**-wahz))
a regional dialect of a language.
[French]

patriarch (**pay**-tree-ark) *noun*
1 a man who is the leader or head of a family, tribe, etc.
2 *Christianity* a principal bishop or head of an Orthodox Church.
3 an early Israelite leader such as Abraham, Isaac or Jacob.
Word Family **patriarchal** *adjective*; **patriarchy** *noun* (*plural* **patriarchies**) a social system in which a man is the head of the family.
[*patri-* + Greek *arkhos* a leader]

patrician (pa-**tri**-sh'n) *noun*
a nobleman.
• **patrician** *adjective*.
[from Latin]

patricide (**pat**-ri-side) *noun*
1 *Law* the crime of killing one's father.
2 *Law* the person who does this.
[*patri-* + Latin *caedere* to kill]

patrimony (**pat**-ri-ma-nee) *noun* (*plural* **patrimonies**)
1 property inherited from one's father or male ancestors.
2 the property of a church, etc.
Word Family **patrimonial** (pat-ri-**mo**-nee-ul) *adjective*.
[from Latin]

patriot (**pat**-ree-ot *or* **pay**-tree-ot) *noun*
a person who is willing to defend and support his or her country.
Word Family **patriotic** *adjective*; **patriotically** *adverb*; **patriotism** *noun*.
[Greek *patris* fatherland]

patrol (pa-**trole**) *verb* (**patrols**; **patrolling**; **patrolled**)
to inspect or guard an area.
• **patrol** *noun*
1 the act of patrolling: *a quick patrol of the grounds*.
2 a group of persons whose job is to patrol.
[German]

The word **patrol** came into English from German, which acquired it from Old French *patrouiller*, meaning 'to tramp round in the mud of a military camp when on guard duty'. This was an alteration of *patouiller* (to walk in mud), from *patte* (paw).

patron (**pay**-tr'n) *noun*
1 a person who gives support or protection, especially financial help.
2 a client or customer.
[Latin *patronus* legal defender]

patronage (**pat**-ra-nij *or* **pay**-tra-nij) *noun*
1 the support or encouragement given by a patron: *Your shop offers such shoddy service, I am taking my patronage elsewhere*.
2 the right or power to grant jobs, offices or privileges.
3 a patronizing manner.

patronize, patronise (**pat**-ra-nize) *verb*
1 to treat someone as inferior or less intelligent: *He explained what the word meant but he patronized me by using simplified language*.
2 to be a customer of: *She patronized the local butcher's shop*.
Word Family **patronizing** *adjective*; **patronizingly** *adverb*.

patron saint *noun*
a saint who is regarded as giving special protection to a country, profession, etc.: *St Andrew is the patron saint of Scotland*.

patronymic (pat-ra-**nim**-ik) *noun*
a name formed from the name of a father or ancestor, e.g. *Johnson* (son of John).
[Greek *pater* father + *onyma* name]

patten *noun*
History a shoe or sandal with an elevated sole to protect the feet from mud.

patter¹ *noun*
a series of light tapping sounds: *the patter of raindrops*.
• **patter** *verb* to make such sounds.

patter² *noun*
1 fast, clever and often meaningless words or speech used to keep one's attention, such as those used by a salesperson or a comedian.
2 the special speech or phrases of a group or class of people.

pattern *noun*
1 a decorative design.
2 a design or system of markings: *the pattern of footsteps in the snow*.
3 a guide or model: *Cut the cloth according to the paper pattern*.

4 a system or order.

5 *Geography* the way natural or human features occur or are arranged: *changing weather patterns.*

• **pattern** *verb*

1 to decorate something with a pattern.

2 to take as a pattern: *I shall pattern my life on the lives of the great artists.*

patty *noun* (*plural* **patties**)
a small pie.

paucity (paw-si-tee) *noun*
(*formal*) scarcity: *There is a paucity of doctors in our town.*
[Latin *paucus* few]

paunch (pawnch) *noun* (*plural* **paunches**)
a large protruding stomach.
Word Family paunchy *adjective*;
paunchiness *noun*.
[Latin *pantices* the bowels]

pauper (paw-pa) *noun*
a very poor person.
[Latin]

pause (pawz) *noun*

1 a short or temporary stop.

2 *Music* a sign (⌢), used to indicate that a note or rest is to be held for longer than usual.

• **pause** *verb* to hesitate or stop briefly: *I paused before knocking because I was afraid of disturbing him.*
[from Greek]

pavane (pa-vahn *or* pa-van) *noun* also
pavan (pav-an)
a slow dignified court dance from Spain.

pave *verb*
to cover a road, footpath, etc. with stones, bricks, concrete or bitumen.
[Latin *pavire* to beat down]

pavement *noun*

1 a raised paved path at the side of a road.

2 *American* a road surface.

pavilion (pa-vil-y'n) *noun*

1 a building or other shelter, used for entertainment, exhibitions, etc.

2 a large tent for temporary exhibitions. etc.

3 a building containing changing rooms, etc. at a sports ground.
[Latin *papilio* tent]

pavlova (pav-low-va) *noun*
a dessert of fruit and cream on a meringue base.
[after *Anna Pavlova*, 1885-1931, a Russian ballerina]

paw *noun*

1 the foot of an animal, usually with claws or nails.

2 (*informal*) a hand.

• **paw** *verb*

1 to strike or scrape with, or as if with, a paw.

2 (*informal*) to touch or handle.

pawl *noun*
a pivoted bar or tooth that fits into a cogwheel or ratchet, to move it forwards or to prevent it moving backwards.

pawn¹ *verb*
to deposit personal property with a pawnbroker as security for a loan.
• **pawn** *noun.*
Phrase **in pawn** being pawned.

pawn² *noun*

1 *Chess* a small piece which can move forward two squares on the first move and then one square at a time, but which captures diagonally.

2 a person who is used as the tool of another: *I was only a pawn in his plan.*
[Medieval Latin *pedo* foot soldier]

pawnbroker *noun*
a person who lends money at interest on goods that are left with him or her.
Word Family pawnshop *noun.*

pawpaw ⇨ PAPAYA.

pay *verb* (**pays**; **paying**; **paid**)

1 to give money or other compensation for goods, labour or services.

2 to be profitable: *It pays to be honest.*

3 to suffer because of something: *You'll pay for that remark.*

4 to make a visit or a call.
Phrases **pay back 1** to return a debt. **2** to avenge an injury or insult. **pay off** *I paid off the debt* (= paid in full). **put paid to** *The rain put paid to our plans for an enjoyable weekend* (= put an end to).

• **pay** *noun* a sum of money given for work or services.
Word Family payment *noun* **1** the act of paying. **2** a sum of money paid or to be paid; **payee** *noun* a recipient of a payment, especially the person to whom a cheque is made out.
[Latin *pacare* to appease]

payable *adjective*
owed or due: *The rent is payable at the end of the month.*

paying guest *noun*
a boarder or lodger.

payload *noun*

1 the part of a cargo which earns income.

2 *Aerospace* the people, equipment or satellites which are carried by a spacecraft.
3 *Military* the warhead of a missile.

paymaster *noun*
1 a person in charge of paying wages or salaries.
2 a person who pays someone to do something.

pay-off *noun*
1 (*informal*) a final settlement, especially a financial one.
2 (*informal*) a consequence.

payola (pay-o-la) *noun*
(*especially American*) bribery given to persuade someone to promote something, e.g. on a radio show.

payroll *noun*
a list of a company's employees and the amounts to be paid to each.

pea *noun*
a small round green vegetable growing in pods.

peace *noun*
freedom from war, strife or disturbance: *We all hope for a lasting peace between the nations.* □ *I am at peace with myself.*
Phrases **hold one's peace** to keep silent.
keep the peace to remain peaceful, or persuade others to do so.
[Latin *pacis* of peace]

peaceable *adjective*
1 not quarrelsome.
2 peaceful.
Word Family **peaceably** *adverb*.

peace dividend *noun*
a supposed saving in a country's defence budget brought about, for example, by international disarmament negotiations.

peaceful *adjective*
1 calm.
2 of or relating to peace: *resolving disputes by peaceful means.*
Word Family **peacefully** *adverb*;
peacefulness *noun*.

peacekeeping *noun*
the maintenance of law and order, especially by the presence of an armed force.

peach¹ *noun* (*plural* **peaches**)
1 a medium-sized round fruit with a large stone, juicy yellowish-orange flesh and a downy skin.
2 a light pinkish-yellow colour.
3 (*informal*) an admired or beautiful person or thing.

Word Family **peach** *adjective*; **peachy** *adjective* (**peachier; peachiest**) **1** like a peach in colour or appearance.
2 (*informal*) wonderful or excellent.
[Greek *Persikon* Persian apple]

peach² *verb*
Phrase **peach on someone** to inform against a friend or accomplice.
[shortening of IMPEACH]

peacock *noun*
a male bird noted for its large and brightly coloured tail.

peafowl *noun*
a peacock or a peahen.

peahen *noun*
a female peafowl. Peahens have shorter tails than peacocks and are not as brightly coloured.

peak *noun*
1 a pointed part or top.
2 the stiff brim of a cap.
3 a mountain, especially a pointed one.
4 the highest point of something: *the peak of success.*
● **peak** *verb*
1 to reach a point.
2 *Maths* to reach a highest point: *A distribution peaks around the modal value.*
● **peak** *adjective* relating to the time when something reaches its maximum degree: *Avoid the city centre at peak times.*

peaky *adjective* (**peakier; peakiest**)
(*informal*) pale and thin: *The illness had left her looking peaky.*

peal *noun*
1 a prolonged loud resonant sound: *a peal of bells.* □ *a peal of thunder.*
2 a set of bells tuned to one another.
3 a tune rung on a set of bells.
● **peal** *verb*.

peanut *noun*
1 a small oily edible nut that grows underground.
2 (**peanuts**) (*informal*) a very small amount of money.

pear (*rhymes with* air) *noun*
a medium-sized green, yellow or brown fruit which is usually round at the base and tapering towards the stem.

pearl (perl) *noun*
1 the hard silver or bluish-white pellet formed as a deposit around any foreign object in an oyster shell and valued as a gem.
2 a very pale pinkish- or bluish-grey.
Phrase **cast pearls before swine** to

utter words of wisdom beyond the comprehension of one's audience.

pearl barley *noun*
barley ground into small round grains, for use in soups, etc.

pearly *adjective* (**pearlier; pearliest**)
like a pearl.

peasant (pez-ant) *noun*
1 a farm labourer or small farmer.
2 (*informal*) an ignorant or unsophisticated person.
Word Family **peasantry** *noun* peasants considered as a group.
[Latin *paganus* a villager]

pease (peez) *plural noun*
an old word for peas: *pease pudding*.

pea-shooter *noun*
a tube through which dried peas are blown at a target.

pea-souper *noun*
(*informal*) an extremely thick fog.

peat *noun*
soil composed of accumulated vegetable matter, occurring at the early stage of coal formation, found in swamps and used as fuel when dried.
Word Family **peaty** *adjective*.

pebble *noun*
a small rounded stone.
Word Family **pebbly, pebbled** *adjective*.

pecan (pee-k'n *or* pi-**kan** *or* pi-**kahn**) *noun*
a large oval edible nut that grows in North America on the hickory tree.
[American Indian]

peccadillo (pek-a-**dil**-o) *noun* (*plural* **peccadilloes** *or* **peccadillos**)
a small sin or fault.
[Spanish *pecadillo* little sin]

peccary (**pek**-a-ree) *noun* (*plural* **peccaries**)
a South American mammal like a wild pig.

peck[1] *verb*
1 (of a bird) to strike with the beak, especially repeatedly.
2 to kiss quickly or lightly.
Phrase **peck at** to eat food unenthusiastically.
• **peck** *noun*
1 a stroke with the beak.
2 a hasty kiss.

peck[2] *noun*
a unit of volume for grain, etc. equal to two gallons or $\frac{1}{4}$ of a bushel.

pecker *noun*
Phrase **keep one's pecker up** (*informal*) to stay cheerful.

pecking order *noun* also **peck order**
a system of rank or privilege in a group.
[as first noticed among domestic fowls]

peckish *adjective*
(*informal*) hungry.

pectin *noun*
an organic acid found in some ripe fruit, such as apples, used as a setting agent in marmalade, fruit jellies, etc.

pectoral (**pek**-ta-r'l) *adjective*
of or relating to the breast or the front of the chest.
• **pectoral** *noun* a muscle covering the front of the ribcage.
[Latin *pectoris* of the breast]

peculiar (pik-**yoo**-lee-a) *adjective*
1 strange, odd or unusual.
2 (*formal*) special, particular: *This novel has a peculiar value for our purposes.*
Phrase **peculiar to** belonging characteristically to: *Each age has certain habits peculiar to itself.*
Word Family **peculiarly** *adverb*.
[Latin *peculiaris* one's own (private property)]

peculiarity (pi-kyoo-li-**arr**-i-tee) *noun* (*plural* **peculiarities**)
1 something which is peculiar: *The book is a peculiarity among novels of that time.*
2 the quality of being peculiar: *We had noticed the peculiarity of her behaviour.*

pecuniary (pik-**yoo**-ni-a-ree) *adjective*
relating to or consisting of money: *I have a small pecuniary interest in the company.*
[Latin *pecunia* property, money]

pedagogue (**ped**-a-gog) *noun*
(*formal*) a teacher.
Word Family **pedagogy** (**ped**-a-goj-i) *noun* the science or art of teaching; **pedagogic** (ped-a-**goj**-ik), **pedagogical** *adjective*.
[Greek *paidagogos* a slave who escorted a boy to school]

pedal *noun*
a lever worked by the foot, e.g. on a bicycle, an organ or a sewing machine.
• **pedal** *verb* (**pedals; pedalling; pedalled**).
[Latin *pedis* of the foot]

pedant (**ped**-ant) *noun*
a person who makes an unnecessary or tiresome display of his or her learning, especially concerning petty details.
Word Family **pedantic** (ped-**an**-tik) *adjective*; **pedantically** *adverb*; **pedantry** (**ped**-an-tree) *noun* an unnecessary display of learning concerned with small details.

peddle *verb*
to carry from place to place in order to sell: *to peddle goods from door to door.*
Figurative *newspapers peddling scandal* (= spreading).

peddler ⇨ PEDLAR.

pederasty (ped-a-ras-tee) *noun* also **paederasty**
a sexual relationship between a man and a boy.
Word Family **pederast** *noun.*
[Greek *paidos* of a child + *erastes* lover]

pedestal (ped-i-stal) *noun*
a support for a statue, vase, column, etc.
Phrase **put someone on a pedestal** to idealize someone or admire him or her greatly.

pedestrian (pid-es-tri-an) *noun*
a person who travels on foot.
• **pedestrian** *adjective*
1 of or for pedestrians: *a pedestrian crossing.* □ *a pedestrian precinct.*
2 dull, unimaginative: *She writes in a very pedestrian manner.*
[Latin *pedester* on foot]

pedicel (ped-i-sel) *noun*
Botany a small stalk or stalk-like part.

pedicure (ped-i-cure) *noun*
a cosmetic treatment for the feet and toenails.
[Latin *pedis* of a foot + *cura* cure]

pedigree (ped-i-gree) *noun*
1 an ancestry or line of descent, e.g. of a dog.
2 a person's ancestry.
3 the origin or history of something or someone.
Word Family **pedigreed** *adjective* having a list of pure-bred ancestors.

pediment (ped-i-ment) *noun*
a triangular section of a building above a portico in classical architecture.

pedlar *noun* also **peddler**
1 a person who goes from house to house selling goods.
2 a person who sells drugs or other illegal items.

peduncle (pi-dun-k'l) *noun*
Botany the stalk of a flower or fruit.

pee *verb* (**pees; peeing; peed**)
(*informal*) to urinate.
• **pee** *noun.*

peek *verb*
to peep or peer.
• **peek** *noun.*

peel *noun*
the skin of a fruit or vegetable.
• **peel** *verb*
1 to remove the skin, rind, bark, etc. of: *to peel an orange.*
2 (of a surface) to lose part of its upper layer in strips or flakes: *My face peeled after a day in the sun.*
Phrase **peel off** to strip off clothing.
Word Family **peelings** *plural noun* the rind or skin peeled from a fruit or vegetable; **peeler** *noun* a device for removing peel.

peen *noun* also **pein**
a blunt or rounded end of a hammer head, opposite the face.

peep¹ *noun*
a short quick look, especially when furtive or prying.
• **peep** *verb* to take a peep at.
Figurative *The sun peeped out from behind a cloud* (= came partly into view).
Word Family **peeper** *noun* 1 a prying or spying person. 2 (**peepers**) (*informal*) the eyes.

peep² *noun*
the weak shrill cry of young birds, mice, etc.
Figurative *I don't want to hear a peep out of you for at least an hour* (= slightest noise).
• **peep** *verb* to make a peep.

peeping Tom *noun*
a voyeur.

> **Peeping Tom** was the name of an 11th-century tailor who disobeyed the rule that no one was to look at Lady Godiva as she rode naked through the town of Coventry. Her husband, the Earl of Mercia, said that if she did this he would remove certain taxes from his tenants.

peer¹ *noun*
1 a person of the same ability, age, etc. as another: *She is popular with her peers.*
2 a person of the rank of duke, marquess, earl, viscount or baron.
Word Family **peerage** *noun* 1 the rank or dignity of a peer. 2 (**the peerage**) the peers of a country collectively. 3 a book giving a list of the peers of a country.
[Latin *par* equal]

peer² *verb*
to look closely, in an attempt to see clearly: *I peered at the building through the fog.*

peeress *noun* (*plural* **peeresses**)
1 a woman who is a peer.
2 the wife or widow of a peer.

peer group *noun*
a group of people of the same age, ability, etc.

peerless *adjective*
having no equal: *the peerless beauty of Italian marble.*

peevish *adjective*
irritable.
Word Family **peevishly** *adverb*; **peevishness** *noun*; **peeve** *verb* (*informal*) to make peevish.

peewit ⇨ LAPWING.

peg *noun*
a piece of wood, metal or plastic, used for fastening, hanging, etc.: *a clothes peg.* □ *a tent peg.*
Phrases **a square peg in a round hole** a person who does not fit in well in a job, social situation, etc. **off the peg** (of clothes) ready-made, not made for a particular customer. **take someone down a peg or two** to humiliate or humble someone.
• **peg** *verb* (**pegs**; **pegging**; **pegged**)
1 to fasten with pegs: *I pegged the washing out.*
2 to mark with pegs.
3 *Commerce* to keep prices or wages at a set level as an official policy.
Phrases **peg away at** (*informal*) to keep on working at. **peg out** (*informal*) to die.

pegboard *noun*
a board with holes in which pegs, hooks, etc. can be inserted.

peg leg *noun*
(*informal*) an artificial leg, especially a wooden one.

peignoir (**pane**-wah) *noun*
a woman's dressing gown.
[French]

pein ⇨ PEEN.

pejorative (pi-**jorr**-a-tiv) *adjective*
derogatory or disparaging: *Some people would say that the word 'authoress' is rather pejorative.*
Word Family **pejoratively** *adverb*.
[Latin *pejor* worse]

Pekinese (pee-kin-**eez**) *noun* (*plural* **Pekinese**) also **Pekingese** (*plural* **Pekingese**)
a breed of small snub-nosed long-haired dogs.
[originally from *Peking*, China]

pelagic (pel-**aj**-ik) *adjective*
of or relating to the ocean.
[Greek *pelagikos* pertaining to the sea]

pelican *noun*
a large white seabird with a long pouched bill from which the young feed.
[Greek *pelekan*]

pelisse (pil-**eece**) *noun*
a woman's long outdoor cloak with arm openings, originally lined or trimmed with fur.
[Latin *pelliceus* made of fur]

pellagra (pe-**lag**-ra *or* pe-**lay**-gra) *noun*
a disease causing skin rashes, diarrhoea and mental problems.
[Latin *pellis* skin + Greek *agra* seizure]

pellet (**pel**-it) *noun*
1 a small round ball, e.g. of bread, paper, etc.
2 a small bullet or piece of shot.

pellicle *noun*
a thin skin or membrane.

pell-mell *adverb, adjective*
in a disorderly or hasty manner.

pellucid (pi-**lyoo**-sid *or* pi-**loo**-sid) *adjective*
1 allowing light to pass through.
2 clear: *a pellucid explanation.*
Word Family **pellucidly** *adverb*.
[Latin *pellucidus* shining through, very bright]

pelmet *noun*
a narrow board or piece of cloth placed along the top of a window to hide the curtain rail.

pelota (pi-**lot**-a *or* pi-**loh**-ta) *noun*
a ball game of Basque or Spanish origin played in a long walled court by two or four players with wicker baskets attached to their wrists.
[Spanish, ball]

pelt¹ *verb*
1 to throw violently: *The boys were pelting snowballs at each other.*
2 to hurry: *She came pelting past me.*
Phrase **pelt down** to rain, hail or snow hard.
• **pelt** *noun*
Phrase **at full pelt** at full speed.

pelt² *noun*
the skin of an animal, especially one treated to make clothes.

pelvis *noun* (*plural* **pelvises**)
Anatomy the strong bony framework formed by the two hip bones and the sacrum.
Word Family **pelvic** *adjective*.
[Latin, basin]

pen¹ *noun*
an instrument for writing or drawing with ink.
• **pen** *verb* (**pens; penning; penned**) to write with a pen: *to pen a letter*.
[Latin *penna* feather]

pen² *noun*
a small enclosure for domestic animals.
• **pen** *verb* (**pens; penning; penned**) to put in a pen.

penal (**pee-**n'l) *adjective*
of, relating to or used for punishment: *a penal colony*.
[Latin *poena* penalty]

penalize, penalise (pee-na-lize) *verb*
to subject to a penalty: *A foul is penalized in most sports.* □ *The courts penalize those who break the law.*
Word Family **penalization** *noun*.

penalty (pen-al-tee) *noun* (*plural* **penalties**)
1 a thing which is imposed to punish an infringement of rules or laws: *The penalty for speeding may be a fine.*
2 also **penalty kick** *Sport* a free kick awarded to a team because of a foul.
Phrase **under penalty of, on penalty of** *Do not touch this money, on penalty of death* (= with death as the penalty).

penance (pen-ence) *noun*
a task or punishment accepted by a person as an expression of repentance, especially one given by a priest.

pence
a plural of **penny**.

penchant (pon-shon) *noun*
a taste or liking: *a penchant for good wines*.
[French *pencher* to incline or lean]

pencil (pen-sil) *noun*
an instrument for writing or drawing, consisting of a wooden cover and a thin central rod of graphite or other material.
• **pencil** *verb* (**pencils; pencilling; pencilled**) to write, draw or mark with a pencil.
[Latin *penicillum* paintbrush]

pencil skirt *noun*
a very narrow and straight skirt.

pendant *noun*
a necklace made from an object hanging on a chain.
• **pendant** *adjective* pendent.
[Latin *pendens* hanging]

pendent *adjective*
hanging.

pending *adjective*
1 awaiting decision: *pending cases*.
2 going to happen: *pending tax cuts*.
• **pending** *preposition* until: *I am not allowed to comment pending the publication of the report.*

pendulous (pen-dew-lus) *adjective*
hanging loosely so as to swing freely.
Word Family **pendulously** *adverb*.

pendulum (pen-dew-lum) *noun*
a weight suspended so that it will move to and fro freely, especially such a device used for controlling the mechanism of a clock.

penetrate (pen-i-trate) *verb*
to get into or through: *A piece of flying glass penetrated the spectator's leg.*
Word Family **penetrating** *adjective* easily heard: *a penetrating voice*; **penetratingly** *adverb*; **penetration** *noun* 1 the act of penetrating. 2 sharpness of intellect; **penetrable** (pen-i-tra-b'l) *adjective* able to be penetrated; **penetrative** (pen-i-tra-tiv) *adjective* tending to penetrate.
[Latin *penitus* in the inside]

penfriend *noun* also **pen pal**
a person, usually living in another country, with whom one exchanges letters.

penguin (peng-gwin) *noun*
a flightless seabird with webbed feet and flipper-like wings, living in the southern hemisphere.

penicillin (pen-i-sill-in) *noun*
an antibiotic which is widely used to treat bacterial infections.

peninsula (pi-nin-syoo-la) *noun*
a piece of land almost surrounded by water and joined by a narrow neck to the mainland.
Word Family **peninsular** *adjective*.
[Latin *paene* almost + *insula* island]

penis (pee-nis) *noun* (*plural* **penises**)
Anatomy the male organ used for sexual intercourse and urination.
Word Family **penile** (pee-nile) *adjective*.
[Latin, tail]

penitent (pen-i-tent) *adjective*
showing remorse for doing wrong and a readiness to make amends.
Word Family **penitent** *noun* a person who is penitent; **penitently** *adverb*; **penitence** *noun*; **penitential** (pen-i-ten-sh'l) *adjective*.
[Latin *poenitens* being sorry]

penitentiary (pen-i-ten-sha-ree) *noun* (*plural* **penitentiaries**)
American a prison.

penknife noun (plural **penknives**)
a small knife with a folding blade.

penmanship noun
the art of handwriting.

pen name noun
a pseudonym adopted by an author:
*Charlotte Brontë used the pen name Currer
Bell.*

pennant noun
a long triangular flag, used as a signal on
naval vessels, or as a banner, souvenir, etc.

penne (**pen**-ay *or* **pen**-ee) noun
a type of pasta in the form of short wide
tubes.

penniless adjective
without any money.

penny noun (plural **pence** or **pennies**)
1 a coin equal to one hundredth of a
pound.
2 (*American informal*) a one-cent coin.
Phrases **a pretty penny** (*informal*) a lot
of money. **spend a penny** (*informal*) to
urinate. **the penny has dropped** the
explanation or remark has been
understood.

penny-farthing noun
an early type of bicycle with a large front
wheel and a small rear wheel.

pennyweight noun
a unit of mass, equal to 24 grains or one-
twentieth of an ounce troy.

penology (pee-**nol**-a-jee) noun
the science that deals with the prevention
and punishment of crime, and the
management of prisons.
Word Family **penologist** noun.
[Latin *poena* penalty + *-logy*]

pen pal ⇨ PENFRIEND.

pen-pusher noun
(*informal*) a person whose job involves a
lot of boring writing.

pensile adjective
hanging: *a pensile nest.*

pension¹ (**pen**-sh'n) noun
a regular payment of money by a
government or company to someone who
has retired or is unable to work.
• **pension** verb.
Phrase **pension off** to cause to retire on a
pension.
[Latin *pensionis* of a payment]

pension² (**pon**-syon) noun
a small hotel or guest house in a European
country.

pensioner noun
a person who receives a pension, especially
an old-age pension.

pensive (**pen**-siv) adjective
thoughtful in a serious or sad way.
Word Family **pensively** adverb;
pensiveness noun.
[Latin *pensare* to ponder]

pentagon noun
1 any closed plane figure with five straight
sides.
2 (**the Pentagon**) the five-sided building
which houses the offices of the American
Defence Department.
Word Family **pentagonal** (pen-**tag**-a-
n'l) adjective.
[*penta-* + Greek *gonia* corner]

pentagram noun
a five-pointed star, used as a symbol in
magic.
[*penta-* + Greek *gramma* something
written]

pentahedron (pen-ta-**hee**-dron) noun
(*plural* **pentahedrons** or **pentahedra**)
any solid shape with five plane faces.

pentathlon (pen-**tath**-lon) noun
Athletics a contest in which athletes aim
for the highest total score in five separate
events.
[*penta-* + Greek *athlon* contest]

Pentecost (**pen**-ti-kost) noun
1 *Judaism* the Jewish festival of Shavuoth,
seven weeks after Passover.
2 *Christianity* a celebration of the coming
of the Holy Spirit to the followers of
Christ at this feast. Compare WHITSUN.
[Greek]

penthouse (**pent**-howss) noun
a room or flat on the top storey of a tall
building, especially a luxurious room or
flat.

pent-up adjective
kept in, confined: *His pent-up fury exploded
in violence.*

penultimate (pi-**nult**-i-mit) adjective
next to last: *November is the penultimate
month of the year.*
[Latin *paene* almost + *ultimus* last]

penumbra (pi-**num**-bra) noun (*plural*
penumbras or **penumbrae** (pi-**num**-
bree))
Physics the outer, less dark region of
shadow cast by an object, especially a part
of the earth or moon during an eclipse.
Compare UMBRA.
Word Family **penumbral** adjective.
[Latin *paene* almost + *umbra* shade or
shadow]

penurious (pen-**yor**-i-us) *adjective*
1 (*formal*) extremely poor.
2 (*formal*) mean with money.
Word Family **penuriously** *adverb*;
penuriousness *noun*.

penury (**pen**-yor-ee) *noun*
extreme poverty.
[Latin *penuria* want or scarcity]

peon (**pee**-on *or* **pay**-on) *noun*
a labourer or servant in South America.
[Spanish]

peony (**pee**-a-nee) *noun* (*plural* **peonies**)
also **paeony** (*plural* **paeonies**)
a garden plant with large showy flowers.

people (**pee**-p'l) *plural noun*
1 humans in general.
2 (**the people**) the citizens of a country.
3 relatives: *Come and meet my people.*
4 (*plural* **peoples**) (*used with singular or
plural verb*) the members of a group or
nation: *desert peoples.*
• **people** *verb* to populate, fill with people.
[Latin *populus*]

> [!] The word *person* has two plural
> forms: *people* and *persons*. *People* is
> much more common, as in *There are
> four people in my family*; *persons* is mainly
> used in formal language, as in *This lift
> can carry up to 14 persons.*

pep *noun*
(*informal*) vigour or energy.
• **pep** *verb* (**peps**; **pepping**; **pepped**)
Phrase **pep up** to give vigour to.
[shortening of PEPPER]

pepper *noun*
1 a spice made from dried peppercorns.
2 a long or bell-shaped red, yellow, orange
or green fruit, eaten raw or cooked. Some
peppers have a hot taste.
• **pepper** *verb*
1 to season or sprinkle with pepper.
*Figurative John's face is peppered with
freckles* (= thickly sprinkled).
2 to pelt with small objects.
Word Family **peppery** *adjective* 1 like or
full of pepper. 2 irritable.

pepper-and-salt *adjective*
consisting of a fine mixture of black and
white flecks: *a pepper-and-salt beard.*

peppercorn *noun*
the dried berry-like fruit from a type of
vine.

peppercorn rent *noun*
a very low or nominal rent.

peppermint *noun*
1 the strong-smelling leaves of a plant,

or an oil made from them, used as a
flavouring.
2 a sweet with this flavour.

pepperoni (pep-a-**roh**-nee) *noun* also
peperoni
pork and beef sausage seasoned with
pepper.

pepsin *noun*
Biology an enzyme, secreted by the
stomach, that breaks down proteins.
[Greek *pepsis* digestion]

pep talk *noun*
(*informal*) a talk intended to stimulate or
inspire someone.

peptic *adjective*
of or relating to digestion.

per *preposition*
for each: *There is one biscuit per person.*
[Latin]

peradventure *adverb*
an old word meaning 'perhaps'.
[French *par* by + *aventure* chance]

perambulate (pi-**ram**-byoo-late) *verb*
(*formal*) to walk about or stroll.
Word Family **perambulation** *noun*.
[*per-* + Latin *ambulare* to walk]

perambulator *noun*
(*dated*) a pram.

per annum *adverb*
for each year: *He earns £20 000 per annum.*
[Latin]

per capita *adverb*, *adjective* also **per caput**
(per **ca**-put)
for each person: *the per capita income of a
country.*

perceive (per-**seev**) *verb*
to become aware of, especially through the
sense of sight or the mind: *She hadn't
perceived that the old man had fallen asleep.*
[Latin *percipere* to grasp]

per cent (per **sent**) *adverb*
by, for or in every hundred: $\frac{3}{100}$ *is 3 per cent
and is written 3%.*
[*per-* + Latin *centum* one hundred]

percentage (per-**sen**-tij) *noun*
1 a rate per hundred: *'What percentage of
children walk to school?' – 'About 30 per cent.'*
2 a part or proportion: *A large percentage of
the food is wasted.*

perceptible (per-**sep**-ti-b'l) *adjective*
able to be perceived: *There was no
perceptible movement.*
Word Family **perceptibly** *adverb*;
perceptibility *noun*.

perception (per-**sep**-sh'n) *noun*
1 the ability to perceive something.
2 the perceiving of something.
3 understanding or insight: *They have no perception of what my life is like.*

perceptive (per-**sep**-tiv) *adjective*
good at observing or noticing things.
Word Family **perceptively** *adverb*; **perceptiveness** *noun*.

perceptual (per-**sep**-tew-'l) *adjective*
of or relating to perception.
Word Family **perceptually** *adverb*.

perch[1] *noun* (*plural* **perches**)
anything on which a bird may rest.
Figurative From his perch up in the treetop he could see a long way (= high position).
• **perch** *verb* to come to rest or alight: *A canary perched on his shoulder.*
Figurative a chalet perched on the top of a mountain (= sitting high up).
[Latin *pertica* measuring rod]

perch[2] *noun* (*plural* **perch** or **perches**)
a small scaly fish, the freshwater varieties of which are used as food.
[Greek *perké*]

perch[3] *noun* (*plural* **perches**)
1 (*formerly*) also called **rod**; **pole**. a unit of length equal to $5\frac{1}{2}$ yards, or about 5·029 m.
2 (*formerly*) a unit of area equal to $30\frac{1}{4}$ square yards, or about 25·29 m².

perchance (per-**chance**) *adverb*
an old word meaning 'perhaps'.
[French *par* by + *chance* chance]

percipient (per-**sip**-i-ent) *adjective*
perceptive: *a percipient remark.*
Word Family **percipience** *noun*.

percolate (**per**-ka-late) *verb*
to filter a liquid through a substance, especially when part of the substance dissolves in the liquid.
Figurative Freud's ideas have percolated through to every level of society (= filtered, circulated).
Word Family **percolation** (per-ka-**lay**-sh'n) *noun*.
[from Latin]

percolator *noun*
a coffee pot in which boiling water filters through ground coffee.

percussion (per-**kush**-'n) *noun*
1 *Music* the playing of an instrument which produces sound by being struck or shaken.
2 *Music* the section of an orchestra having these instruments.
3 (*formal*) the forceful striking of one thing against another.

Word Family **percussive** *adjective* of or relating to percussion; **percussionist** *noun* a person who plays a percussion instrument.
[from Latin]

percussion cap *noun*
a small metallic cap or cup containing an explosive substance which sets off the main charge in a gun.

perdition (per-**dish**-'n) *noun*
Christianity a state of eternal damnation.
[Latin *perditio* an act of destroying]

peregrination (perr-i-gri-**nay**-sh'n) *noun*
an old word meaning 'a travelling from one place to another, a journey'.
[Latin *peregrinari* to live or travel abroad]

peregrine (**perr**-i-grin) *noun*
a large grey falcon which swoops on its prey in a fast vertical dive, and lives on cliffs and crags.
[Latin *peregrinus* foreign (as caught during migration)]

peremptory (per-**emp**-ta-ree) *adjective*
insisting on obedience, imperious: *He spoke in a peremptory tone.*
Word Family **peremptorily** *adverb*; **peremptoriness** *noun*.
[Latin *peremptus* destroyed, cut off]

perennial (per-**renn**-ial) *adjective*
1 continuing throughout the whole year.
2 *Biology* living for several years: *a perennial plant.*
3 lasting for a long time.
• **perennial** *noun* a plant that lives for several years.
[*per-* + Latin *annus* a year]

perestroika (per-i-**stroy**-ka) *noun*
History the restructuring and reform of the economic and political system of the former Soviet Union under Mikhail Gorbachev in the late 1980s.
[Russian]

perfect (**per**-fikt) *adjective*
1 having all the necessary qualities, parts, etc.: *a perfect circle.*
2 faultless, without defect: *the perfect solution.*
3 complete: *perfect strangers.*
• **perfect** (per-**fekt**) *verb*
1 to make perfect: *to perfect a technique.*
2 to bring to completion.
Word Family **perfectly** *adverb*.
[Latin *perfectus* made thoroughly]

perfection (per-**fek**-sh'n) *noun*
1 the state or quality of being perfect.
2 the act or process of making something perfect.

3 a perfect person or thing.
Word Family **perfectionist** *noun* a person who is not happy unless something is perfect.

perfidy (**per**-fi-dee) *noun*
a poetic word for treachery, especially a deliberate breaking of faith or trust.
Word Family **perfidious** (per-**fid**-i-us) *adjective*; **perfidiously** *adverb*; **perfidiousness** *noun*.
[Latin *perfidia* faithlessness]

perforate (**per**-fa-rate) *verb*
to make a hole or holes through, e.g. to make a row of tiny holes in paper so that part may be torn off.
Word Family **perforation** *noun* **1** the act of perforating. **2** a hole or holes.
[from Latin]

perforce (per-**force**) *adverb*
(*formal*) of necessity.

perform *verb*
1 to carry out or through: *to perform an action*. □ *to perform a rite*.
2 to act, sing, dance, etc. in front of an audience.
Word Family **performer** *noun*.

performance (per-**for**-m'nce) *noun*
1 the act of performing: *She's lazy in the performance of her work*.
2 a deed or accomplishment: *Coming top was a splendid performance*.
3 (*informal*) a fuss or bother: *Getting the suitcases packed was a bit of a performance*.
4 the functioning or capabilities of a machine, manufactured product, etc.: *performance criteria*. □ *performance testing*.

perfume (**per**-fewm) *noun*
1 a liquid obtained from flowers or chemicals which gives a pleasant smell as it evaporates.
2 an agreeable smell.
• **perfume** (per-**fewm** *or* per-fewm) *verb*
to fill or scent with perfume.
Word Family **perfumer** *noun* a person who makes or sells perfumes; **perfumery** *noun* (*plural* **perfumeries**) **1** the art or business of making perfumes. **2** a place where perfumes are made or sold.
[*per-* + Latin *fuma* smoke]

perfunctory (per-**funk**-ta-ree) *adjective*
performed as a duty, but without interest or care: *He gave a perfunctory greeting, then ignored us*.
Word Family **perfunctorily** *adverb*; **perfunctoriness** *noun*.
[Latin *perfunctorius* done in a superficial way]

pergola (**per**-ga-la) *noun*
an arrangement of small columns or posts supporting a horizontal trellis over which vines or other plants may be grown.
[Latin *pergula* a balcony, arcade]

perhaps *adverb*
possibly.

pericardium (pe-ri-**kar**-di-um) *noun*
(*plural* **pericardia**) (pe-ri-**kar**-di-a)
Anatomy the membranous sac enclosing the heart.
[*peri-* + Greek *kardia* heart]

peridotite (pe-ri-da-tite) *noun*
a green or brown rock, composed mainly of olivine.
Word Family **peridot** *noun* a pale green gemstone.

perigee (pe-ri-jee) *noun*
Astronomy the point in the orbit of the moon, a planet or an artificial satellite when it is closest to the earth. Compare APOGEE.
[*peri-* + Greek *ge* earth]

peril *noun*
any serious danger: *I felt my life was in peril*. □ *to risk the perils of the sea*.
Phrase **at one's peril** at one's own risk.
Word Family **perilous** *adjective*; **perilously** *adverb*; **perilousness** *noun*.
[Latin *periculum* danger]

perimeter (pi-**rim**-i-ta) *noun*
1 the outside edge of any closed plane figure or area.
2 the length of the boundary of any plane figure.
[*peri-* + Greek *metron* a measure]

perineum (pe-ri-**nee**-um) *noun* (*plural* **perinea**) (pe-ri-**nee**-a)
Anatomy the region of the body between the anus and the urogenital organs.
Word Family **perineal** *adjective*.

period (**peer**-i-od) *noun*
1 a portion of time: *a period of rest*. □ *a period of history*.
2 the time taken for a school lesson.
3 a portion of geological time: *the Jurassic period*.
4 the monthly flow of blood that a woman has when she menstruates.
5 *American* a full stop.
Word Family **period** *adjective* of or from a particular historical period: *figures in period dress*; **periodic** (peer-i-**od**-ik) *adjective* occurring or happening at intervals; **periodically** *adverb*.
[Greek *periodos* a going around]

periodical (peer-i-**od**-i-k'l) *noun*
a magazine.
• **periodical** *adjective*
1 issued at regularly recurring intervals.
2 periodic.

periodic table *noun*
Chemistry an arrangement of the chemical
elements in order of their atomic
numbers, demonstrating the law that
elements having similar properties occur
at regular intervals and fall into groups of
related elements.

peripatetic (perr-i-pa-**tet**-ik) *adjective*
1 wandering from place to place.
2 working in different places: *a peripatetic
piano teacher.*
[*peri-* + Greek *patein* to walk up and
down]

peripheral nervous system ⇨ NERVOUS
SYSTEM.

periphery (pi-**rif**-a-ree) *noun* (*plural*
peripheries)
the outside boundary or surface of
something.
Word Family **peripheral** *adjective*
1 relating to, situated in, or forming the
periphery. 2 of minor importance;
peripheral *noun Computers* a device
connected to a computer, such as a disk
drive or printer; **peripherally** *adverb*.
[Greek *periphereia* circumference]

periphrasis (pi-**rif**-ra-sis) *noun* (*plural*
periphrases (pi-**rif**-ra-seez))
a roundabout way of saying something:
*'The finny denizens of the deep' is a
periphrasis for 'fish'*
[*peri-* + Greek *phrasis* speech]

periscope (**pe**-ri-skope) *noun*
an instrument consisting of mirrors and a
tube which allows the viewer to see things
which are above him or her or otherwise
out of sight; used in submarines, etc.
Word Family **periscopic** (pe-ri-**skop**-ik)
adjective.
[*peri-* + Greek *skopein* to look]

perish *verb*
1 to die: *to perish in the desert.*
2 to rot or decay: *Many fruits perish quickly
in summer.*
3 to be destroyed or ruined.
Word Family **perishable** *adjective* liable
to spoil or decay; **perishability** (pe-rish-
a-**bil**-i-tee) *noun*; **perisher** *noun*
(*informal*) an annoying person; **perishing**
adjective (*informal*) freezing cold;
perishingly *adverb*.

peristalsis (pe-ri-**stal**-sis) *noun*
Biology the alternate constriction and
dilation of muscular tubes, especially the
intestine, which causes the contents of the
tube to move in a definite direction.
[*peri-* + Greek *stalsis* compression]

peristyle (**pe**-ri-stile) *noun*
Architecture a row of columns surrounding
a temple or court.
[*peri-* + Greek *stylos* a column]

peritoneum (pe-ri-ta-**nee**-um) *noun*
(*plural* **peritoneums** or **peritonea**)
Anatomy the membrane lining the
abdominal cavity and covering the organs
within it.
[*peri-* + Greek *tonos* stretched]

peritonitis (pe-ri-ta-**nie**-tis) *noun*
inflammation of the lining of the
abdomen.

periwig *noun*
a wig of a kind formerly worn by men and
women, and still worn by judges and
barristers.

periwinkle[1] *noun*
a winkle.

periwinkle[2] *noun*
a creeping evergreen plant with blue
flowers.

perjury (**per**-ja-ree) *noun* (*plural*
perjuries)
Law making a statement under oath which
one knows to be untrue.
Word Family **perjure** *verb*; **perjurer**
noun.
[Latin *perjurare* to break one's oath]

perk[1] *verb*
Phrase **perk up** to recover interest and
liveliness: *She perked up when we told her the
good news.*
Word Family **perky** *adjective* (**perkier**,
perkiest) 1 lively. 2 cheeky; **perkily**
adverb; **perkiness** *noun*.

perk[2] *noun*
(*informal*) a benefit arising from one's job,
e.g. the use of a car.
[shortening of PERQUISITE]

perm[1] *noun* also **permanent wave**
a method of treating hair with chemicals
to give it a curl which lasts for several
months.
• **perm** *verb*.

perm[2] *noun*
(*informal*) short form of **permutation**
a multiple forecast on a football pool
coupon, in the form of a mathematical
combination.

permafrost *noun*
ground which is permanently frozen, often to a great depth.

permanent *adjective*
lasting or intended to last.
Word Family **permanently** *adverb*;
permanence *noun* the condition or quality of being permanent.
[Latin *permanens* persisting, enduring]

permeable (per-me-a-b'l) *adjective*
allowing water, air, etc. to pass through: *a permeable membrane.* □ *Permeable rocks allow water to pass through pores and cracks.*
Compare IMPERMEABLE.
Word Family **permeability** (per-mi-a-**bill**-i-tee) *noun*.
[from Latin]

permeate (**per**-me-ate) *verb*
to spread throughout something: *He said that racist attitudes had permeated society.*
Word Family **permeation** *noun*.

Permian ⇨ PALAEOZOIC.

permission (per-**mish**-'n) *noun*
the act of permitting: *You have my permission to leave the room.*
Word Family **permissible** *adjective* allowable; **permissibly** *adverb*; **permissibility** *noun*.

permissive (per-**miss**-iv) *adjective*
allowing people freedom of choice and expression, especially in moral and sexual matters: *a permissive society.*
Word Family **permissively** *adverb*; **permissiveness** *noun*.

permit (per-**mit**) *verb* (**permits; permitting; permitted**)
1 to give permission to: *Will you permit me to introduce myself?*
2 to give permission for: *Smoking is not permitted.*
3 to make possible: *The vents permit gases to escape.*
• **permit** (**per**-mit) *noun* a written order, such as a licence, granting permission to do something: *a travel permit.*
[Latin *permittere* to allow to go through]

permutation (per-mew-**tay**-sh'n) *noun*
1 a way in which things can be arranged or put in order.
2 *Maths* the act of changing the order of sequence of elements in a series, especially the making of all possible changes in a sequence: *The permutations of the series 'xyz' are 'xzy', 'zxy', 'zyx', 'yxz' and 'yzx'.*
3 *Maths* any of these arrangements by itself, such as *xyz.* Compare COMBINATION (definition 3).

4 ⇨ PERM².
Word Family **permutate** *verb*.
[Latin *permutare* to change completely]

pernicious (per-**nish**-us) *adjective*
extremely harmful, especially in a subtle way: *the pernicious effects of watching violent videos.*
Word Family **perniciously** *adverb*; **perniciousness** *noun*.
[Latin *perniciosus* destructive]

pernickety (per-**nik**-a-tee) *adjective* (*informal*) fussy.

peroration (pe-ra-**ray**-sh'n) *noun*
the conclusion of a speech or essay which emphasizes the most important points again.
[from Latin]

peroxide *noun*
a substance (hydrogen peroxide) used to bleach or lighten the colour of hair.

perpendicular (perp-en-**dik**-yoo-la) *adjective*
1 *Maths* being at right angles to a line or plane.
2 vertical or upright.
Word Family **perpendicularity** (perp-en-dik-yoo-**larr**-i-tee) *noun*; **perpendicular** *noun* a perpendicular line, plane or position; **perpendicularly** *adverb*.
[Latin *perpendiculum* a plummet]

perpetrate (**per**-pa-trate) *verb*
to carry out a crime or harmful act.
Word Family **perpetrator** *noun*; **perpetration** *noun*.
[Latin *perpetrare* to accomplish]

perpetual (per-**pet**-yew-'l) *adjective*
1 lasting for ever: *perpetual motion.*
Figurative There's been a perpetual stream of phone calls all morning (= continuous, incessant).
2 blooming all or nearly all the year: *perpetual carnations.*
Word Family **perpetually** *adverb*; **perpetuate** (per-**pet**-yoo-ate) *verb* to make last for ever; **perpetuation** *noun*.
[Latin *perpetuus* uninterrupted]

perpetual motion *noun*
the motion of a hypothetical device which would continue for ever without further application of energy.

perpetuity (per-pi-**tew**-i-tee) *noun* (*plural* **perpetuities**)
1 the state of being perpetual.
2 a fixed income paid annually for a lifetime, usually a form of insurance.
Phrase **in perpetuity** for ever.

perplex (per-**pleks**) *verb*
to bewilder or confuse.
Word Family **perplexed** *adjective*
puzzled; **perplexing** *adjective* bewildering;
perplexingly *adverb*.
[Latin *perplexus* entangled]

perquisite (per-kwi-zit) *noun*
(*formal*) ⇨ PERK².
[Latin *perquisitum* sought for]

perry *noun* (*plural* **perries**)
a cider made with pears instead of apples.
[Latin *pirum* pear]

per se (per **say**) *adverb*
by or in itself: *There wasn't anything wrong
with it per se – I just didn't like it.*
[Latin]

persecute (per-sa-kewt) *verb*
to persist in ill-treatment or harassment of
someone.
Word Family **persecution** (per-sa-kew-
sh'n) *noun*; **persecutor** *noun*.
[Latin *persequi* to pursue]

persevere (per-si-**veer**) *verb*
to keep on doing something despite
difficulties or obstacles: *She persevered with
the book and began to find it interesting.*
Word Family **perseveringly** *adverb*;
perseverance *noun* the act or habit of
persevering.
[from Latin]

persiflage (per-si-flah*zh*) *noun*
(*formal*) light-hearted or mocking speech.
[French]

persimmon (per-**sim**-'n) *noun*
a plum-like reddish-orange fruit which
only becomes sweet when fully ripe.

persist (per-sist) *verb*
1 to continue firmly in some course of
action, state, etc. despite opposition or
difficulties
2 to last: *The bruise persisted for two weeks.*
Word Family **persistence, persistency**
noun 1 the action or fact of persisting: *the
persistence of a cold.* 2 the quality of being
persistent: *He has incredible persistence;*
persistent *adjective*; **persistently** *adverb*.
[from Latin]

person *noun* (*plural* **people** or **persons**)
1 a human being.
*Figurative He's matured to become a person
in his own right* (= individual personality).
2 (*formal*) the body: *He received several
blows about his person.*
3 *Grammar* any of three forms taken by a
pronoun or verb, to indicate the person
speaking (**first person**), the person who is

spoken to (**second person**), or the person
being spoken about (**third person**).
Phrase **in person** *She came in person to
deliver the news* (= herself).

> **!** On the plurals of *person* ⇨ PEOPLE.

persona (per-**so**-na) *noun* (*plural*
personas or **personae** (per-so-nee))
1 the image a person presents, or hopes to
present, to the world.
2 a character in a drama, novel, etc.
[Latin, an actor's mask]

personable (per-s'n-a-b'l) *adjective*
attractive or pleasing in personal
appearance and manner.
Word Family **personably** *adverb*.

personage (per-sa-nij) *noun*
a person, especially an important person.

persona grata (per-so-na **grah**-ta) *noun*
(*plural* **personae gratae**) (per-so-nee
grah-tee)
someone who is acceptable.
[Latin]

personal *adjective*
1 of or for a particular person: *a personal
letter.* □ *a personal favour.*
2 involving the presence of someone: *a
personal appearance.*
3 private: *asking questions about her personal
life.*
4 attacking, offensive: *personal remarks.*
5 of or relating to the body: *personal
cleanliness.*

personal computer *noun*
a small computer used for word-
processing or computer games.

personal identification number *noun*
short form is **PIN** a secret number used
with a plastic card to operate an automatic
teller machine.

personality (per-sa-**nal**-i-tee) *noun* (*plural*
personalities)
1 the qualities in a person which make him
or her individual and unique.
2 a celebrity: *a TV personality.*
3 the qualities that make someone
popular: *She has lots of personality.*

personalize, personalise *verb*
to make personal: *He personalized his
stationery by having his address printed on it.*
□ *Can we discuss the problem of bullying
without personalizing it?*

personally *adverb*
1 in person: *I personally interviewed each
applicant.*

2 used to give one's own feelings about something: *Personally, I don't care for caviar.*
3 as a person: *We like him personally, we just don't like his style of living.*
4 as though intended for or directed towards oneself: *Don't take her abruptness personally, it's just her manner.*

personal organizer, personal organiser *noun*
1 a loose-leaf file in a wallet holding a diary, appointments book, address book and notebook.
2 a pocket-sized computerized device that stores information about dates, addresses, etc.

personal stereo *noun*
a very small audio cassette or compact disc player with lightweight headphones, carried on a belt or in a pocket.

persona non grata (per-so-na non **grah**-ta) *noun* (*plural* **personae non gratae**) (per-so-nee non **grah**-tee)
an unwelcome or unacceptable person.
[Latin]

personify (per-**sonn**-i-fie) *verb* (**personifies; personifying; personified**)
1 to give human characteristics to abstract ideas, animals, objects, etc.: *Love is personified in the saying 'Love is blind'.*
2 to embody: *She personifies grief.*
Word Family **personification** (per-sonn-if-i-**kay**-sh'n) *noun.*

personnel (per-sa-**nel**) *noun*
all the people employed in a particular business or work.

perspective (per-**spek**-tiv) *noun*
1 the technique of achieving the illusion of space and depth on a flat surface, e.g. in a painting or drawing.
2 a particular way of looking at something: *Try to see things from my perspective.* □ *a different perspective on life.*
Phrase **in perspective** in a true or proper proportion.
[Latin *perspectus* looked through]

Perspex *noun*
(*trademark*) a colourless transparent plastic which softens when heated and is widely used as a substitute for glass.

perspicacious (per-spi-**kay**-shus) *adjective*
quick at understanding or grasping things.
Word Family **perspicaciously** *adverb*; **perspicacity** (per-spi-**kass**-i-tee) *noun.*
[Latin *perspicax* seeing clearly]

perspire *verb*
to sweat.
Word Family **perspiration** *noun* **1** the act or process of perspiring. **2** sweat.
[Latin *perspirare* to breathe through]

persuade (per-**swade**) *verb*
to make willing to do or believe by arguing, urging, etc.: *We couldn't persuade him to stay.* □ *She persuaded me I was wrong.*
Word Family **persuadable, persuasible** *adjective* able to be persuaded; **persuasive** *adjective* able to persuade; **persuasively** *adverb*; **persuasiveness** *noun.*
[from Latin]

persuasion (per-**sway**-zh'n) *noun*
1 the act of persuading: *No persuasion could move him from his course.*
2 the power of persuading: *Her argument lacks persuasion.*
3 a firm belief or conviction.
4 a religious system or belief.

pert *adjective*
1 bold or impudent: *a pert answer.*
2 jaunty: *a pert little hat.*
Word Family **pertly** *adverb*; **pertness** *noun.*

pertain (per-**tane**) *verb*
1 (*formal*) to relate: *files pertaining to the investigation.*
2 (*formal*) to belong: *the house and all the land pertaining to it.*
[Latin *pertinere* to reach, relate to]

pertinacious (per-ti-**nay**-shus) *adjective*
(*formal*) holding firmly or determinedly to a purpose, course of action, idea, etc.
Word Family **pertinaciously** *adverb*; **pertinaciousness, pertinacity** (per-ti-**nass**-i-tee) *noun.*
[Latin *pertinax* very tenacious]

pertinent *adjective*
relevant or to the point: *a pertinent remark.*
Word Family **pertinently** *adverb*; **pertinence** *noun.*

perturb (per-**terb**) *verb*
to disturb greatly: *The anonymous telephone calls were perturbing.*
Word Family **perturbation** *noun* **1** anxiety or lack of composure. **2** a cause of anxiety.
[Latin *perturbare* to throw into confusion]

peruke (pe-**ruke**) *noun*
an old word for a wig.
[from Italian]

peruse (pe-**rooz**) *verb*
(*formal*) to examine, especially with care or thoroughly: *I shall peruse the prospectus at my leisure.*

Word Family perusal noun the act of perusing.

pervade (per-**vade**) verb
to spread throughout: *A smell of damp pervaded the old house.*
Word Family pervasive adjective tending to pervade: *the pervasive sense of doom;* **pervasively** adverb; **pervasiveness** noun.
[from Latin]

perverse (per-**verse**) adjective
1 wilful or wayward: *a perverse refusal to obey.*
2 against expectations or what is thought to be good or proper.
3 morally wrong.
Word Family perversely adverb; **perverseness** noun; **perversity** (per-ver-si-tee) noun (plural **perversities**) 1 the quality of being perverse. 2 an instance of being perverse.
[Latin *perversus* askew, distorted]

perversion (per-**ver**-zh'n) noun
1 the act of perverting.
2 unusual or unacceptable behaviour, especially in relation to sex.

pervert (per-**vert**) verb
1 to turn from the right course or the truth: *The lawyer tried to pervert the course of justice.* □ *to pervert the mind of a child.* □ *The report perverts the true meaning of the statistics.*
2 to change to unusual or unacceptable behaviour, especially in relation to sex.
• **pervert** (**per**-vert) noun a sexually perverted person.

pervious adjective
allowing penetration: *Sandy soil is pervious to water.*
Word Family perviousness noun.
[per- + Latin *via* a way]

Pesach (**pay**-sahkh) noun ⇒ PASSOVER.
[from Hebrew]

peseta (pe-**say**-ta) noun
the basic unit of money in Spain.

pesky adjective (**peskier; peskiest**) (informal) annoying.

peso (**pay**-so) noun
the basic unit of money in various South American and Central American countries.
[Spanish, weight]

pessary (**pess**-a-ree) noun (plural **pessaries**)
1 *Medicine* an object placed in the vagina to support the uterus after it has been displaced.
2 *Medicine* a contraceptive device inserted into the vagina to block the cervix.

3 *Medicine* a vaginal suppository.
[Greek *pessos* an oval stone]

pessimism (**pess**-i-mizm) noun
1 the tendency to take a gloomy view of things.
2 *Philosophy* the belief that the universe is evil by nature and that it cannot improve. Compare OPTIMISM (definition 2).
Word Family pessimist noun; **pessimistic** adjective; **pessimistically** adverb.

> The word **pessimism** was first used in English to mean 'the worst possible state'. The sense of 'expecting the worst' did not develop until later. The word came into English from French and has its origins in Latin *pessimus* (worst).

pest noun
1 an annoying or harmful insect or other animal, such as a locust.
2 (informal) a nuisance: *My little sister can be a pest.*
[Latin *pestis* plague or disease]

pester verb
to annoy, especially with repeated questions or interruptions.
[Old French *empestrer* to hobble a horse]

pesticide (**pes**-ti-side) noun
a substance which is used to destroy pests.
[PEST + Latin *caedere* to kill]

pestiferous (pes-**tif**-er-us) adjective
troublesome or annoying.
Word Family pestiferously adverb.
[PEST + Latin *ferre* to bring]

pestilence (**pes**-ti-l'nce) noun
an old word for a deadly epidemic disease.
Word Family pestilential (pes-ti-len-sh'l) adjective 1 of or relating to pestilence. 2 carrying disease. 3 (informal) troublesome or annoying.

pestilent adjective
1 (formal) harmful to life: *The pestilent disease raged unchecked.*
2 an old word meaning 'harmful to peace, morals, etc.': *the pestilent effects of war.*
[Latin *pestilens* unhealthy]

pestle (rhymes with wrestle) noun
a baton-shaped utensil for crushing substances in a mortar.
[Latin *pistillum*]

pet¹ noun
1 an animal that is kept and cared for affectionately.
2 a favourite person or thing.

• **pet** *verb* (**pets; petting; petted**) to fondle or pat.

• **pet** *adjective*
1 kept as a pet: *a pet rabbit.*
2 relating to pets: *pet care.* □ *A pet shop.*
3 favourite: *She has a pet theory about why he is so aggressive.*
4 particular: *his pet hate.*

pet² *noun*
a fit or state of sulking or bad temper.

petal *noun*
one of the usually brightly-coloured outer parts of a flower, forming the corolla.
[Greek *petalon* a leaf]

peter (**pee**-ta) *verb*
Phrase **peter out** to lessen slowly and then disappear altogether.

petite (pi-**teet**) *adjective*
small and delicate: *a petite woman.*
[French, little]

petition (pi-**ti**-sh'n) *noun*
a request, especially one presented formally to a person or people in authority.

• **petition** *verb* to request by or as if by a petition: *I shall petition the court for damages.*
Word Family **petitionary** *adjective* of or like a petition; **petitioner** *noun* a person who petitions.
[from Latin]

petrel *noun*
any of various small long-winged usually black and white seabirds.

Petri dish (**pet**-ri dish) *noun*
a small shallow dish with a loose cover, used for growing micro-organisms.
[after *Julius Petri*, 1852-1921, a German bacteriologist]

petrify (**pet**-ri-fie) *verb* (**petrifies; petrifying; petrified**)
1 to make or become rigid or paralysed: *petrified with fear.*
2 to turn into stone: *petrified trees.*
Word Family **petrification, petrifaction** *noun.*
[Latin *petra* rock, from Greek]

petrochemical (pet-ro-**kem**-i-k'l) *noun*
a chemical substance derived from petroleum or natural gas.

• **petrochemical** *adjective.*

petrol *noun*
a complex mixture of hydrocarbons and special additives, used as a fuel and a solvent.

petroleum (pi-**tro**-lee-um) *noun*
an oily naturally occurring liquid which is a source of petrol, oils and waxes and is used as the basis for many compounds.
[Latin *petra* rock, from Greek + Latin *oleum* oil]

petroleum jelly *noun*
a semi-solid mixture obtained from petroleum, used as a basis for ointments, protective dressings, etc.

petrology (pi-**trol**-a-jee) *noun*
the study of the composition and structure of rocks.
[Greek *petra* rock + -*logy*]

petrol station ⇒ SERVICE STATION.

petticoat *noun*
a thin skirt or dress made of cotton, silk or nylon, worn under clothes.

petty *adjective* (**pettier; pettiest**)
1 unimportant: *petty details.*
2 mean or ungenerous: *petty criticism.*
Word Family **pettily** *adverb*; **pettiness** *noun.*
[French *petit* small]

petty cash *noun*
a sum of money set aside for minor expenses, e.g. in an office.

petty officer *noun*
Navy a non-commissioned officer ranking between leading rating and chief petty officer.

petulant (**pet**-yoo-l'nt) *adjective*
sulky.
Word Family **petulantly** *adverb*; **petulance** *noun.*
[Latin *petulans* pert, impudent]

petunia (pi-**tyoo**-ni-a) *noun*
a garden plant with brightly coloured trumpet-shaped flowers.

pew *noun*
1 a heavy wooden bench with a back, used in churches.
2 (*informal*) a seat: *Take a pew.*

pewter *noun*
an alloy of tin and copper with a little antimony, used for making drinking vessels and utensils.

peyote (pay-o-tee) *noun*
1 mescal, a Mexican cactus from which mescaline is derived.
2 a hallucinogenic drug made from the root of this plant.

phaeton (fay-t'n) *noun*
History a light open four-wheeled carriage, usually drawn by two horses.
[in Greek mythology *Phaeton* drove the chariot of the sun]

phalanx (fal-anks) *noun*
1 (*plural* **phalanxes**) a group of soldiers in close formation.
2 (*plural* **phalanges**) (fa-**lan**-jeez) *Anatomy* a bone in the finger or toe.
[Greek]

phallus (fal-us) *noun* (*plural* **phalluses** or **philli** (fa-lie *or* fa-lee))
1 the penis.
2 an image of the penis used as a symbol of strength and fertility in some religions.
Word Family **phallic** *adjective*.
[from Greek]

phantasm (fan-tazm) *noun*
a poetic word for an illusion or apparition, e.g. a ghost.
Word Family **phantasmal** (fan-**taz**-m'l), **phantasmic** *adjective*.
[from Greek]

phantasmagoria (fan-taz-ma-**gaw**-ri-a *or* fan-taz-ma-**gorr**-i-a) *noun*
a changing series of images or appearances, as in a dream.
Word Family **phantasmagorical** (fan-taz-ma-**gorr**-i-k'l) *adjective*.
[from Greek]

phantom (fan-t'm) *noun*
1 a ghost or apparition.
2 an image in a dream or the mind.
• **phantom** *adjective* ghostly or unreal.
[from Greek]

pharaoh (fair-oh) *noun*
an ancient Egyptian ruler.
Word Family **pharaonic** (fair-ay-**on**-ik) *adjective*.

Pharisee (farr-i-see) *noun*
a hypocritical or self-righteous person.
[after the *Pharisees*, an ancient Jewish sect concerned with strict obedience to tradition and the laws]

pharmacology (far-ma-**kol**-a-jee) *noun*
the study of drugs and their effects.
Word Family **pharmacologist** *noun*.

pharmacy (far-ma-see) *noun* (*plural* **pharmacies**)
1 a shop where medicines are prepared, dispensed and sold.
2 the study and practice of preparing medicines.
Word Family **pharmacist** (far-ma-sist) *noun* a person trained to prepare and dispense medicines; **pharmaceutical**

(far-ma-**syoo**-ti-k'l) *adjective* of or relating to medicines.
[Greek *pharmakon* a drug]

pharynx (farr-inks) *noun* (*plural* **pharynges**) (fa-rin-jeez)
Anatomy the wide air passage which connects the nose to the throat.
[Greek]

phase (faze) *noun*
1 a stage of development or change: *the adolescent phase.* □ *the phases of the moon.*
2 *Physics* any specified point on, or section of, a wave or other periodic phenomenon.
Phrase **in phase** (of two similar wave patterns) having corresponding phases occurring simultaneously.
• **phase** *verb*
Phrases **phase something in** to introduce something gradually: *to phase in a new method.* **phase something out** to take something out of use gradually.
[Greek *phasis* appearance]

pheasant (fe-z'nt) *noun*
a large long-tailed game bird. The male has brightly coloured feathers.
[Greek *phasianos*]

phenomenon (fin-om-i-non) *noun* (*plural* **phenomena**)
1 something which can be seen and observed directly.
2 a remarkable or extraordinary person, object or event.
Word Family **phenomenal** *adjective*
1 remarkable or extraordinary. 2 of or being a phenomenon; **phenomenally** *adverb*.
[Greek *phainomenon* appearing]

> **!** Note that *phenomena* is the plural form of *phenomenon* and should not be used where the singular form is required, as in *This is an interesting phenomenon.*

phew (few) *interjection*
(*informal*) an exclamation of disgust, relief, surprise, etc.

phial (file) *noun*
a small glass container for storing liquids, e.g. medicines.
[Greek *phialé* a pan]

philander (fil-and-a) *verb*
(of a man) to flirt or have a number of casual affairs.
Word Family **philanderer** *noun*.
[Greek *philein* to love + *andros* of a man]

philanthropy (fil-an-thro-pee) *noun*
a love of humanity, especially as shown by acts of goodness or kindness.

Word Family philanthropist noun;
philanthropic (fill-an-**throp**-ik) adjective.
[Greek philein to love + anthropos man]

philately (fil-**at**-a-lee) noun
the study and collection of postage
stamps.
Word Family philatelist noun;
philatelic (fil-a-**tel**-ik) adjective.
[Greek philein to love + ateleia tax
exemption (that is, tax has already been
paid by buying the stamp)]

philharmonic (fil-har-**mon**-ik) adjective
'devoted to music', mostly used in the
names of orchestras.

philippic (fil-**lip**-ik) noun
a poetic word for a bitter or attacking
speech.
[from the orations delivered by
Demosthenes, an Athenian orator, against
King Philip of Macedon in the 4th century
B.C.]

philistine (**fil**-iss-tine) noun
a person who lacks or dislikes culture and
refinement.
Word Family philistinism noun.
[after the Philistines, the people who did
battle with Saul and David in biblical
history, unfairly branded as uncivilized]

philology (fil-**ol**-a-jee) noun
the study of language, especially of ancient
languages and texts.
Word Family philologist noun;
philological (fil-a-**loj**-i-k'l) adjective.
[Greek philein to love + logos a word]

philosopher (fil-**oss**-a-fer) noun
someone who studies philosophy.

philosopher's stone noun
an imaginary substance, long sought by
alchemists, which would change base
metals into gold.

philosophy (fil-**oss**-a-fee) noun (plural
philosophies)
1 the pursuit of wisdom and knowledge,
e.g. about the purpose of life.
2 the study of the principles of a particular
subject, such as science or history.
3 a basic theory or principle: His philosophy
was to live life to the full.
**Word Family philosophize,
philosophise** verb to think or form
theories about; **philosophical** (fil-a-**sof**-i-
k'l), **philosophic** adjective 1 of or relating
to philosophy: a philosophical theory.
2 calm and rational: We'll have to be
philosophical about our bad luck;
philosophically adverb.
[Greek philein to love + sophia wisdom]

philtre (**fil**-ta) noun (American **philter**)
a drink or drug believed to have magic
powers, especially to inspire love.
[Greek philtron love charm]

phlegm (flem) noun
the thick mucus of the throat, brought up
by coughing when one has a cold, etc.
[Greek phlegma inflammation]

phlegmatic (fleg-**mat**-ik) adjective
unemotional or not easily excited.

phloem (**flo**-em) noun
Biology the cells in plants conducting food
downwards from their leaves.
[Greek phloos bark]

phlox (floks) noun (plural **phlox** or
phloxes)
a plant with colourful flowers, often grown
in borders.
[Greek, flame]

phobia (**fo**-bee-a) noun
an irrational fear of some object or
situation.
Word Family phobic adjective.
[Greek, fear]

phoenix (**fee**-niks) noun
Egyptian mythology a beautiful bird, the
only one of its kind, believed to live for
500 years and then to burn itself on a pyre
and to rise again from the ashes as a young
bird.

phone[1] (fone) noun
a telephone.
• **phone** verb.

phone[2] noun
Language a speech sound.
[Greek, sound]

phonecard noun
a card which can be used instead of coins
to pay for telephone calls from certain
public kiosks.

phonetics (fo-**net**-iks) plural noun
(used with singular verb) Language the study
of sounds in language or speech.
Word Family phonetic adjective;
phonetically adverb.

> **Phonetic symbols** are used to
> represent speech sounds or
> pronunciation. The International
> Phonetic Alphabet (IPA) has a unique
> symbol for each human speech sound
> and is thus useful in the learning of
> foreign languages. It is also used in
> many dictionaries in the pronunciation
> guides. Phonetic symbols are quite
> difficult to understand at first, so this
> dictionary uses ordinary letters of the
> alphabet in its pronunciation guides.

phoney (fo-nee) *adjective* (**phonier;
phoniest**) also **phony**
(*informal*) false or counterfeit.
• **phoney** *noun* (*plural* **phoneys** or
phonies) also **phony** a false person or
thing.

phonics (fon-iks) *plural noun*
(*used with singular verb*) a method of
teaching reading by using common
sounds.
Word Family **phonic** *adjective*.

phonograph (fo-no-grahf) *noun*
1 an early type of gramophone.
2 *American* a record player.
[Greek *phoné* sound + *graphein* to write]

phonology (fon-ol-a-jee) *noun*
the science or study of the way in which
sounds are made into words.
[Greek *phoné* + -*logy*]

phosphate (fos-fate) *noun*
Chemistry any compound containing the
trivalent (PO_4)$^{3-}$ ion, as in most fertilizers.

phosphorescence (fos-fa-res-'nce) *noun*
1 the property of being luminous at
temperatures below white heat, e.g. from
exposure to light.
2 the luminous appearance produced.
Word Family **phosphorescent** *adjective*;
phosphoresce *verb*.

phosphorus (fos-fa-rus) *noun*
a non-metal that can be found in different
forms. It is an essential part of protein, and
is used in fertilizers, detergents and
matches.
Word Family **phosphoric** (fos-**forr**-ik)
adjective.
[Greek *phosphoros* bringing light]

photo (fo-toe) *noun*
(*informal*) a photograph.

photocall → PHOTO OPPORTUNITY.

photochemical (fo-toe-**kem**-i-k'l)
adjective
of or relating to chemical reactions that are
affected by light.
Word Family **photochemistry** *noun*.

photocopy (fo-toe-kop-ee) *noun* (*plural*
photocopies)
a photographic copy made by a machine
which copies documents onto sensitized
paper.
Word Family **photocopier** *noun* a
machine which makes photocopies;
photocopy *verb* (**photocopies**;
photocopying; photocopied).

photoelectric cell (fo-toe-il-**ek**-trik sel)
noun
Electronics a cell which produces electricity
when exposed to light.

photo finish *noun* (*plural* **photo finishes**)
a race in which the competitors finish so
close together that a photograph is needed
to decide the winner.

photofit *noun*
a picture of a face made up of several
different photographs, used especially by
the police to get a likeness of a criminal.

photogenic (fo-toe-**jen**-ik *or* fo-toe-**jee**-
nik) *adjective*
appearing attractive in photographs.
[*photo*- + -*gen*]

photograph (fo-ta-grahf) *noun*
an image produced by the chemical effect
of light on a light-sensitive surface such as
film.
Word Family **photographic** (fo-ta-**graf**-
ik) *adjective* 1 of or relating to
photography. 2 having the accuracy or
detail of a photograph: *a photographic
memory*; **photograph** *verb*.
[*photo*- + Greek *graphein* to write]

photography (fo-**tog**-ra-fee) *noun*
the art or process of taking photographs.
Word Family **photographer** *noun*.

photogravure (fo-toe-grav-**yoor**) *noun*
an image made by transferring a
photographic negative to a metal plate and
etching it in.

photometer (fo-**tom**-it-a) *noun*
an instrument for measuring the intensity
of light.

photon (fo-ton) *noun*
Physics a quantum of electromagnetic
radiation.

photo opportunity *noun* (*plural* **photo
opportunities**) also called **photocall**
an event organized for photographers to
take publicity photographs of a famous
person.

photosensitive (fo-toe-**sen**-sa-tiv)
adjective
sensitive to or changed by light.

Photostat (fo-toe-stat) *noun*
(*trademark*) a photocopier, or a copy made
by it.
• **photostat** *verb* (**photostats;
photostatting; photostatted**).

photosynthesis (fo-toe-**sin**-tha-sis) *noun*
Biology the process by which green plants
make carbohydrates from water and

carbon dioxide using the energy that is absorbed by chlorophyll from sunlight.
Word Family **photosynthetic** (fo-toe-sin-**thet**-ik) *adjective*.

phrasal verb (fray-z'l **verb**) *noun*
Grammar a phrase made up of a verb and an adverb or a preposition: *'Throw out' and 'look after' are phrasal verbs.*

phrase (fraze) *noun*
1 a group of words forming a unit within a sentence, usually excluding a verb.
2 a meaningful group of words, such as a short saying.
3 *Music* a small group of notes forming a unit in a melody.
• **phrase** *verb*
1 to express in words.
2 *Music* to group or mark off notes in a phrase.
[Greek *phrasis* speech]

phrase book *noun*
a book of common sentences translated into one or more languages, for use by travellers.

phraseology (fray-zee-**oll**-a-jee) *noun*
the choice and arrangement of words and phrases in expressing ideas.

phrenology (fri-**nol**-a-jee) *noun*
the judging of a person's character or intelligence from the shape of the skull.
Word Family **phrenologist** *noun*.
[Greek *phren* mind + *-logy*]

pH value *noun*
Chemistry a number used to express degrees of acidity or alkalinity in solutions. The **pH scale** runs from 1 (strong acid), through 7 (neutral), to 14 (strong alkali).

phyllo ⇨ FILO.

phylum (**fie**-lum) *noun* (*plural* **phyla**)
Biology one of the large groups used in the classification of animals.
[Greek *phylon* race]

physical (**fiz**-i-k'l) *adjective*
1 of or relating to the body.
2 of or relating to natural or material things: *physical geography.* □ *the physical characteristics of the product.*
3 relating to physics.
Word Family **physically** *adverb*.

physical education *noun*
the teaching of sports and gymnastics.

physical geography *noun*
the geography of natural features, patterns and processes. Compare HUMAN GEOGRAPHY.

physical sciences *plural noun*
the sciences concerned with natural objects that are not alive, including physics, geology and chemistry.

physician (fi-**zish**-'n) *noun*
a doctor of medicine, especially a specialist in medicine as opposed to surgery.

physics (**fiz**-iks) *plural noun*
(*used with singular verb*) the study of the natural laws and properties of matter and energy which are not restricted to living things.
Word Family **physicist** (**fiz**-i-sist) *noun*.
[Greek *physikos* natural]

physio *noun*
(*informal*) a physiotherapist.

physiognomy (fiz-i-**on**-a-mee) *noun*
(*plural* **physiognomies**)
someone's facial features, thought of as revealing his or her character or ethnic group.
[Greek *physis* nature + *gnomon* judge]

physiology (fiz-i-**oll**-a-jee) *noun*
1 the study of the function of various parts of living things. Compare ANATOMY (definition 2).
2 the way that a part of the body or a living thing functions: *the physiology of the heart.*
Word Family **physiologist** *noun*;
physiological (fiz-i-a-**loj**-i-k'l) *adjective*;
physiologically *adverb*.
[Greek *physis* nature + *-logy*]

physiotherapy (fiz-i-oh-**therr**-a-pee) *noun*
the treatment of bodily disorders by physical means, such as exercises or massages.
Word Family **physiotherapist** *noun*.

physique (fiz-**eek**) *noun*
the physical build of a person: *a muscular physique.*

pi (pie) *noun*
Maths the symbol π (3·141592....), which is the ratio of the circumference of a circle to its diameter.
[name of the Greek letter]

pianissimo (pee-a-**niss**-i-mo) *adverb*, *adjective*
Music very soft or very softly.
[Italian]

piano[1] (pee-**an**-o) *noun*
Music a large keyboard instrument in which metal strings are struck by felt-covered hammers.
grand piano a piano which has horizontal strings.

upright piano a piano which has vertical strings.
Word Family **pianist** (**pee**-a-nist) *noun* a person who plays the piano.

piano² (**pyah**-no) *adverb, adjective*
Music soft or softly.
[Italian]

piano accordion *noun*
an accordion with a piano-like keyboard and chord stops.

Pianola (pee-an-**ole**-a) *noun*
(*trademark*) a piano with a mechanism which allows it to be played automatically from punched paper rolls.

piazza (pee-**at**-sa) *noun*
a public square or a marketplace.
[Italian]

pica (**pie**-ka) *noun*
Printing a unit of type size and line length equal to 12 points, about 4 mm.

picador (**pik**-a-dor) *noun*
a bullfighter on horseback who uses a lance to taunt the bull. Compare MATADOR.
[Spanish *picar* to pierce]

picaresque (pik-a-**resk**) *adjective*
of or relating to literature which tells the story of a rogue or knave in a series of episodes.
[Spanish *picaro* rogue]

piccalilli (pik-a-**lil**-ee) *noun* (*plural* **piccalillies** or **piccalillis**)
a pickle made up of vegetables, mustard and hot spices.

piccolo (**pik**-a-lo) *noun*
Music a small high-pitched flute.
[Italian, small]

pick¹ *verb*
1 to pull off a flower or fruit while it is still growing.
2 to choose or select: *Pick a biscuit from the tin.*
3 to touch, remove or irritate something with a pointed instrument, finger, etc.: *Don't pick off that scab.* □ *She picked her teeth with a cocktail stick.*
4 to pluck the strings of an instrument such as a guitar.
5 to open with a pointed instrument: *picking a lock.*
6 to steal from: *picking someone's pocket.*
7 to start: *He tried to pick a fight with me.*
Phrases **pick at** to eat only a little of: *picking at her food.* **pick off** to shoot from a distance, especially one person or thing out of a group. **pick on** to blame or criticize continually. **pick out 1** to distinguish. **2** to choose. **3** to give a

highlight or contrast to: *His name was picked out in bold red letters.* **pick up 1** to lift or carry. **2** to collect. **3** to start talking to someone with the intention of having a sexual relationship. **4** to get or learn something. **5** to improve or increase. **6** to catch something, e.g. an infection. **7** to receive a signal or sound.
• **pick** *noun*
1 a choice, or a turn to choose.
2 (**the pick**) (*informal*) the best thing or person out of a group: *He always had the pick of the girls at school.*

pick² *noun* also **pickaxe** (*American* **pickax**)
a tool with a wooden handle and an iron head which is curved and pointed at both ends for breaking hard soil, rock, etc.

picket *noun*
1 a group of people stationed at a factory gate, etc. to persuade employees not to go to work during a strike.
2 a pointed post forming part of a fence.
• **picket** *verb* to stand outside as a picket: *picketing the car factory.*

pickings *plural noun*
1 remnants or leftovers selected as worth saving.
2 profits made by dishonest means.

pickle *noun*
1 a vegetable or other food preserved in vinegar and spices.
2 the liquid, such as brine, in which food is preserved.
3 *American* a pickled cucumber.
4 (*informal*) a predicament.
• **pickle** *verb* to store or preserve in a pickle.
Word Family **pickled** *adjective*
1 preserved in a pickle: *pickled onions.*
2 (*informal*) drunk.

pick-me-up *noun*
(*informal*) something, especially a drink, taken to improve and revive a person's mood or health.

pickpocket *noun*
a person who steals from people's pockets, handbags, etc.

pickup *noun*
1 also **pickup truck** a van with low sides.
2 an improvement: *a pickup in the economy.*
3 a device consisting of a movable arm, with a head containing the stylus, which will pick up the sounds recorded on a spinning record when placed in contact with it.

4 a device on a guitar that converts the vibrations of the strings into electrical signals.

picnic *noun*
1 an outing on which one takes food to eat outdoors.
2 the meal eaten on such an outing.
Word Family picnic *verb* (**picnics; picnicking; picnicked**); **picnicker** *noun*.
[from French]

pictograph (**pik**-to-grahf) *noun* also **pictogram**
a sign or symbol in the form of a picture.

pictorial (pik-**taw**-ri-ul) *adjective*
of, like or illustrated by pictures.
Word Family pictorially *adverb*.

picture (**pik**-cher) *noun*
1 a representation of objects, people, scenes, etc. on a flat surface, such as a painting, sketch, photograph, etc.
2 a film, such as is shown in a cinema.
3 (**the pictures**) the cinema.
4 an impression that one gets from a description: *We don't yet know the full picture.* □ *They painted a graphic picture of life in the camps.*
Phrases **in the picture** understanding or having been informed about something. **look a picture** to be a beautiful sight. **the picture of** the embodiment of: *looking the picture of misery.*
• **picture** *verb*
1 to show in a picture.
2 to imagine: *I couldn't picture him winning.*
[Latin *pictura* a painting]

picturesque (pik-cher-**esk**) *adjective*
1 charming or attractive to look at: *The countryside was dotted with picturesque villages.*
2 strikingly vivid or graphic: *using picturesque phrases.*
Word Family picturesquely *adverb*.

picture window *noun*
a very large window, especially one facing a pleasant view.

pidgin (**pij**-in) *noun*
a simple form of a language used when people speaking different languages need to communicate.
[Chinese, alteration of *business*]

pie *noun*
a baked dish which contains a sweet or savoury filling, usually covered with a crust of pastry.

piebald *adjective*
having patches of different colours, especially black and white: *a piebald horse.*
Compare SKEWBALD *adjective*.
• **piebald** *noun* a piebald horse.
[(mag)PIE + BALD]

piece (peece) *noun*
1 a portion or fragment: *a piece of wood.* □ *an interesting piece of news.*
2 an item that is part of a set: *a chess piece.*
3 a composition: *learning a new piano piece.*
4 a coin: *a 10p piece.*
Phrases **go to pieces** to lose control, e.g. because one is nervous. **piece of work** (*informal*) a person of a specified kind: *She's a selfish piece of work.* **say one's piece** to give one's opinion.
• **piece** *verb* to make by putting or joining things: *He tried to piece together the broken plate.* □ *We pieced together the clues.*

pièce de résistance (pee-ess de ray-**zis**-tonce) *noun*
the best or most important part in a selection of things, such as a dish at a meal or a work of art at an exhibition.
[French]

piecemeal *adverb, adjective*
gradually or piece by piece.

piece of eight *noun* (*plural* **pieces of eight**)
(*formerly*) a Spanish coin.

piecework *noun*
work that is paid by the number of jobs done rather than by the time they take.

pie chart *noun*
a circular graph divided into wedge-shaped segments in proportion to the relative quantities.

pied (pide) *adjective*
having patches of two or more colours.

pied-à-terre (pyay-da-**tair**) *noun* (*plural* **pieds-à-terre**) (pyay-da-**tair**)
a flat or house kept for occasional use.
[French *pied* foot + *à terre* on the ground]

pier (peer) *noun*
1 a structure built from the land into water, used as a landing place for boats.
2 an upright support or pillar of brick or stone, used in building walls, etc.

pierce *verb*
1 to penetrate or make a hole in: *A thorn pierced the skin of my arm.*
2 to affect or cut through sharply: *Her screams pierced the air.* □ *His story pierced her heart.*
Word Family piercing *adjective* 1 very cold. 2 high-pitched. 3 astute or sharp.

pietà (py-ay-ta) *noun*
Art a painting or a sculpture of the Virgin Mary mourning over the dead body of Christ.
[Italian, pity]

piety (pie-a-tee) *noun*
the quality of being devoutly religious: *an old woman known for her piety.*
[Latin *pietas* dutiful conduct]

piezoelectricity (pic-ee-zo-il-ek-**triss**-i-tee) *noun*
the property of some crystals, e.g. quartz, of acquiring opposite electrical charges on opposing faces when put under pressure; used in generating ultrasonic waves, etc.
[Greek *piezein* to press + ELECTRICITY]

piffle *noun*
(*informal*) nonsense.
Word Family **piffling** *adjective* (*informal*) unimportant.

pig *noun*
1 a domesticated mammal with short legs, bristly hair, a curly tail and a snout.
2 a similar wild animal.
3 (*informal*) a greedy, dirty or disagreeable person.
4 a block or mould of metal, especially iron or lead.
Phrase **make a pig's ear of** (*informal*) to mess up, ruin.

pigeon (pij-in) *noun*
1 any of a family of fast-flying birds with a compact body, small head and short legs.
2 (*informal, especially American*) a person who is tricked or deceived.

pigeonhole *noun*
one of a number of small open boxes above a desk or on a wall in which papers, letters, etc. are kept.
• **pigeonhole** *verb*
1 to place in a pigeonhole.
2 to put in a category, especially one that is too narrow: *She had been pigeonholed as a presenter of cookery programmes.*

pigeon-toed *adjective*
having the toes or feet turned inwards.

piggery *noun* (*plural* **piggeries**)
a farm where pigs are kept.

piggish *adjective*
like a pig, especially in being greedy or disagreeable.
Word Family **piggishly** *adverb*; **piggishness** *noun*.

piggy *adjective*
like a pig: *piggy eyes.*

piggyback *noun*
a ride on someone's back.

piggy bank *noun*
a small money box, especially one shaped like a pig.

pig-headed *adjective*
stubborn or obstinate.

pig iron *noun*
an impure form of iron obtained from blast furnaces.

piglet *noun*
a young pig.

pigment *noun*
1 the substance that gives animal or plant tissue its colour.
2 a substance used for colouring or painting.
Word Family **pigmentation** *noun* the amount or arrangement of colouring in something.
[from Latin]

pigmy ⇨ PYGMY.

pig-sticking *noun*
the sport of hunting wild boars with knives, spears and dogs, on horseback.

pigsty *noun* (*plural* **pigsties**)
1 an enclosed pen for pigs.
2 a very dirty or untidy place.

pigtail *noun*
a single braid or plait of hair hanging down from the side or back of the head.

pike¹ *noun* (*plural* **pike**)
any of a group of large slender vicious freshwater fish with long snouts.

pike² *noun*
a spear with a pointed metal head.

pikelet *noun*
a thin crumpet.
[from Welsh]

pilaster (pil-ast-a) *noun*
a square strip or column attached to a wall.

pilchard (pil-ch'd) *noun*
a small oily fish related to the herring.

pile¹ *noun*
1 a number of things lying on top of each other.
2 (*informal*) a large quantity or amount.
• **pile** *verb* to form into or make a pile.
Phrases **piled with** covered in piles of: *a desk piled with books.* **pile into** to get into in a disorderly way: *We all piled into the car.* **pile up** to form a pile, increase.
[Latin *pila* a pillar]

pile² noun
a large post of wood, concrete or steel, set upright in the ground to support a floor in a house, bridge, wall, etc.
[Latin *pilum* a javelin]

pile³ noun
a raised surface on fabric, e.g. on a carpet, made of upright loops of yarn or fibre.
[Latin *pilus* a hair]

piledriver noun
a machine for forcing piles into the ground.

piles *plural noun* ⇨ HAEMORRHOIDS.

pile-up noun
1 (*informal*) a collision, especially between cars.
2 (*informal*) a collecting or increasing, e.g. of things to be done.

pilfer verb
to steal, especially things of little value.
Word Family **pilferage** *noun* petty theft; **pilferer** *noun*.

pilgrim noun
a person who travels a long distance to a shrine, etc. as an act of devotion.
Word Family **pilgrimage** *noun* a journey made by a pilgrim.
[Latin *peregrinus* foreigner]

pill noun
1 a small tablet of medicine.
2 (**the Pill**) a pill taken regularly as a contraceptive.

pillage (pill-ij) *verb*
to rob or plunder violently, especially in war.
Word Family **pillage** *noun* the act of pillaging; **pillager** *noun*.

pillar noun
1 a column.
2 a person or thing which supports or preserves: *He is a pillar of society.*
Phrase **from pillar to post** hither and thither, from one predicament or place to another.
[Latin *pila*]

pillar box noun (*plural* **pillar boxes**)
a large red public postbox.

pillbox noun (*plural* **pillboxes**)
1 a small box for holding pills.
2 a small cylindrical brimless hat.
3 *Military* a small low concrete fortification.

pillion noun
a seat for an extra passenger behind the driver on a motorcycle.

pillory (pill-a-ree) *noun* (*plural* **pillories**)
History a device forcing a person to stand upright with his or her head and hands locked through a wooden frame, used for public punishment or ridicule.
• **pillory** *verb* (**pillories; pillorying; pilloried**)
1 to put in a pillory.
2 to ridicule publicly.

pillow noun
a bag filled with soft material such as feathers, used as a support for the head, especially in bed.

pillowcase noun also **pillowslip**
a cloth bag used to cover a pillow.

pilot noun
1 a person who controls an aircraft.
2 *Nautical* a person who guides a ship through a difficult area of water, e.g. the entrance to a busy port.
3 something used as an experiment or to test a future project, such as a sample film for a television series.
• **pilot** *verb*
1 to steer, guide or conduct.
2 to test.

pilot light noun
a small flame kept burning continuously and used to light a large burner, e.g. in a gas cooker or a boiler.

pilot officer noun
Air force a commissioned officer ranking between warrant officer and flying officer.

pimento (pi-**men**-toe) *noun*
1 ⇨ PIMENTO.
2 (*especially West Indian*) allspice.

pimiento (pim-i-**en**-toe *or* pim-**yen**-toe) *noun* also **pimento**
a sweet red pepper.
[Spanish *pimienta* pepper]

pimp noun
a person who obtains customers for a prostitute.
• **pimp** *verb*.

pimpernel (**pimp**-a-nel) *noun*
a small wild plant with scarlet flowers.

pimple noun
a small swelling on the skin, usually containing pus.
Word Family **pimply** *adjective* having many pimples.

pin noun
1 a small piece of wire or metal for fastening or joining, such as a safety pin.
2 a badge or brooch.
3 a wooden or metal pole or peg.

4 (**pins**) (*informal*) legs: *He was unsteady on his pins.*

● **pin** *verb* (**pins; pinning; pinned**)
1 to fasten or attach with a pin or pins.
2 to hold firmly: *They pinned me against a wall.*
3 ⇨ UNDERPIN (definition 1).
Phrase **pin down** to get a definite commitment or decision from.

pinafore *noun*
1 also **pinafore dress** a dress without sleeves, worn over a blouse or jumper.
2 an apron.

pinball *noun* also called **bagatelle**.
a game played on a sloping board with a ball which scores points by hitting objects.

pince-nez (pance-**nay**) *noun*
(*used with singular or plural verb*) a pair of spectacles held on the nose by a clip.
[French *pincer* to pinch + *nez* nose]

pincer *noun*
1 *Biology* the prehensile claw of an arthropod such as a crab.
2 (**pincers**) a tool with a pair of jaws for pulling nails out of wood, etc.

pinch *verb*
1 to squeeze tightly, especially between the thumb and finger: *She pinched his arm.* □ *I pinched my finger in the door.*
2 (*informal*) to steal.
● **pinch** *noun* (*plural* **pinches**)
1 a squeeze.
2 a very small amount, such as that held between the finger and thumb: *a pinch of salt.*
Phrases **at a pinch** if absolutely necessary. **feel the pinch** to have financial difficulties.
[Latin *punctus* pricked]

pinched *adjective*
(of the face or lips) thin and drawn from worry, pain, etc.

pincushion *noun*
a small cushion into which sewing pins are stuck and kept.

pine¹ *noun* also **pine tree**
any of a group of evergreen trees with cones and usually long needle-like leaves, used for timber.
[from Latin]

pine² *verb*
1 to long greatly: *The prisoner pined for his freedom.*
2 to become weak and waste away: *He pined away from sickness and starvation.*
[Latin *poena* punishment]

pineal gland (pin-ee'l gland) *noun* also **pineal body**
Anatomy a gland in the brain that secretes a hormone called **melatonin**, which inhibits the formation of melanin.
[Latin *pinea* pine cone (in shape)]

pineapple *noun*
a large fruit with a tough brown prickly skin and juicy yellow flesh.

> The word **pineapple** originally meant 'pine cone'. The name was transferred to the tropical fruit because of its external resemblance to a pine cone.

ping *verb*
to make a short high-pitched ringing sound.
● **ping** *noun*.

ping-pong *noun*
(*informal*) table tennis.

pinion¹ (pin-y'n) *noun*
a small wheel with cogs, which engages a larger similar wheel, bar, etc.

pinion² *noun*
the end of a bird's wing.
● **pinion** *verb*
1 to tie or fasten a person's arms to prevent movement.
2 to cut or bind a bird's wing to prevent it flying.

pink¹ *noun*
a pale red colour.
Phrase **in the pink** feeling very well.
● **pink** *adjective*
1 having the colour pink.
2 (*informal*) having moderately left-wing political views.
3 connected with homosexuals: *the pink economy.*

pink² *verb*
to cut with a zigzag or notched pattern, especially to cut the raw edge of fabric in this way to prevent fraying.

pink³ *verb*
(of a vehicle engine) to rattle or knock because of the fuel-air mixture in the cylinders combusting too quickly.

pinking shears *plural noun*
a pair of scissors with notched blades for giving fabric a zigzag edge.

pin money *noun*
a small sum of money set aside for incidental expenses.

pinnacle (pin-a-k'l) *noun*
a high pointed part or structure, such as a mountain peak.

Figurative She reached the pinnacle of
success (= highest point or position).

pinnate *adjective*
shaped like the vanes of a feather: *a pinnate
leaf*.
[Latin *pinna* feather]

pinochle (**pee**-nok-'l) *noun*
a card game played by two to four people
with a special pack of 48 cards.

pinpoint *verb*
to find or describe exactly: *Can you
pinpoint precisely where you lost the money?*
• **pinpoint** *adjective* extremely precise:
with pinpoint accuracy.

pins and needles *plural noun*
a tingling sensation in a limb after
numbness.

pinstripe *noun*
a very narrow stripe on a fabric.

pint *noun*
1 a unit of volume for liquids equal to $\frac{1}{8}$ of
a gallon, or 0·568 litre. *abbrev.* pt.
2 *American* a unit of volume for liquids
equal to $\frac{1}{8}$ of a gallon, or 0·473 litre.
3 (*informal*) a pint of beer.

pint-sized *adjective*
(*informal*) small.

pin-up *noun*
1 a picture of an attractive or well-known
person pinned up on a wall by an admirer.
2 a person who is attractive and famous.

pinworm *noun*
a small parasitic worm found in the
intestines of vertebrates.

pioneer (pie-a-**neer**) *noun*
1 a person who first enters, explores or
settles a new region.
2 an innovator: *Picasso was a pioneer of
modern art*.
• **pioneer** *verb*
1 to explore or settle for the first time.
2 to discover or open the way for: *She
pioneered this treatment for autistic children*.

pious (**pie**-us) *adjective*
1 having respect for religion or a god.
2 virtuous in a hypocritical way.
3 unlikely to come true: *pious hopes*.
Word Family **piously** *adverb*; **piousness**
noun.
[Latin *pius* dutiful]

pip[1] *noun*
a small seed found in fleshy fruit such as
apples or grapes.

pip[2] *noun*
1 any of various marks or spots on dice,
playing cards or dominoes.

2 *Army* one of the stars indicating rank,
worn on the shoulder of an officer's
uniform.

pip[3] *noun*
a short high-pitched sound, such as a time
signal heard on a radio.

pip[4] *verb* (**pips; pipping; pipped**)
(*informal*) to defeat in a competition by a
small margin.
Phrase **pip someone at the post** to
defeat someone right at the end, e.g. of a
race.

pipe *noun*
1 a hollow tube or cylinder for carrying
fluids, etc.
2 an object consisting of a hollow tube
with a small bowl at one end, used for
smoking tobacco.
3 *Music* a hollow cylinder or cone in which
air vibrates, as in an organ or wind
instrument.
4 *Music* a simple wind instrument
consisting of a tube with holes.
5 (**pipes**) *Music* bagpipes.
• **pipe** *verb*
1 to carry by means of pipes.
2 to play on a musical pipe.
3 to speak, call or sound in a shrill or high-
pitched tone.
4 to trim a piece of clothing with piping.
Phrases **pipe down** (*informal*) to keep
quiet. **pipe up** to speak up or interrupt
shrilly.
[Latin *pipare* to chirp]

pipe dream *noun*
a dream or hope which is far-fetched or
unlikely to be fulfilled.

pipeline *noun*
a length of pipe connecting two places,
especially one conveying oil or gas.
Phrase **in the pipeline** in the course of
being supplied, produced, etc.

piper *noun*
a person who plays a pipe or the bagpipes.

pipette (pip-**et**) *noun*
a slender graduated tube, usually open
at both ends, used in laboratories for
measuring and transferring small volumes
of liquids.
[French]

piping (**pie**-ping) *noun*
1 a system of pipes, e.g. for plumbing.
2 the material used to make pipes.
3 thin lines of icing or cream as
decoration.
4 a thin rolled strip of fabric used as
trimming on clothing.

5 playing a pipe or pipes.
Phrase **piping hot** very hot: *piping hot soup.*

pipit *noun*
a small bird similar to the lark.

pippin *noun*
a type of large apple.

pipsqueak *noun*
(*informal*) a small or insignificant person.

piquant (pee-k'nt *or* pee-kont) *adjective*
1 pleasantly sharp or spicy in taste or flavour.
2 stimulating or interesting.
Word Family **piquantly** *adverb*;
piquancy *noun*.
[French, pricking, stinging]

pique (peek) *noun*
a feeling of resentment or irritation due to hurt pride, vanity, etc.
• **pique** *verb*
1 to cause irritation or vexation.
2 to stimulate or arouse: *Our curiosity was piqued by their secretive whispering.*
[French *piquer* to prick or sting]

piqué (pee-kay) *noun*
a fabric woven with a raised, corded or quilted pattern.

piquet (pee-ket) *noun*
a card game for two people, played with a pack of 32 cards.

piranha (pi-**rahn**-a *or* pi-**rahn**-ya) *noun*
a small vicious South American freshwater fish, which attacks in groups and is dangerous to humans and other animals.
[Portuguese *pira* fish + *sainha* tooth]

pirate (pie-rit) *noun*
1 a person who plunders, robs or commits illegal acts of violence at sea or along the coast.
2 any person who uses the work of someone else without permission, especially in breach of copyright or patent.
Word Family **pirate** *verb*; **piracy** *noun*
the practice of being a pirate; **piratical**
(pie-**rat**-i-k'l) *adjective.*
[Greek *peirates*]

pirate radio *noun*
a radio station which broadcasts on an unauthorized wavelength.

pirouette (pirr-oo-et) *noun*
a spinning step done on one foot, especially on the tips of the toes, as in dancing.
• **pirouette** *verb.*
[French, whirl]

Pisces (pie-seez) *noun*
Astrology a group of stars, the twelfth sign of the Zodiac; the sign of the Fish or Fishes.
[Latin]

pish *interjection*
(*dated*) an exclamation of contempt.

piss *verb*
(*informal*) to urinate.
Phrase **piss off** (*informal*) go away.
Word Family **piss** *noun* (*informal*).

pissed *adjective*
(*informal*) drunk.

pistachio (pis-**tah**-shi-o *or* pis-**tat**-sho)
noun
the nut of a small Mediterranean tree, with a hard shell and an edible green kernel.
[from Persian]

pistil *noun*
Biology a flower's female organs; the stigma, style and ovary.
Word Family **pistillate** (**pist**-il-it)
adjective having pistils.
[Latin *pistillum* a pestle]

pistol *noun*
a small gun designed to be held and fired with one hand.

piston *noun*
a cylinder with an attached rod which is driven back and forth by pressure, e.g. in an internal-combustion engine.

piston ring *noun*
a ring, usually of metal, which makes a seal between a piston and cylinder.

pit *noun*
1 a hole in the ground.
2 a hole or hollow filled with a particular substance: *a sandpit.*
3 *Mining* a mine for coals or minerals.
4 a hollow or depression in a surface.
5 the part of a theatre where an orchestra sits.
6 an area beside a racetrack where cars can be repaired or refuelled during a race.
• **pit** *verb* (**pits; pitting; pitted**)
1 to mark with holes or hollows: *a face pitted with scars.*
2 to set in opposition or competition: *to pit your wits against someone.*

pita ⇨ PITTA.

pit-a-pat *noun* also **pitapat**
a movement or sound of quick light taps.

pit bull terrier *noun*
a breed of bull terrier originally bred for dogfighting.

pitch¹ noun (plural **pitches**)
1 the highness or lowness of a sound or musical note.
2 the angle of slope of something, e.g. a roof.
3 a level: *Excitement had reached a high pitch.*
4 *Sport* an area marked out for an outdoor team game.
5 *Cricket* the playing area between the wickets.
6 words used to try to persuade someone: *a sales pitch.*
7 a place where someone has a stall.
8 an act or movement of rocking or swaying.
• **pitch** verb
1 to throw, fling or toss.
2 to fall or plunge.
3 *Baseball* to throw the ball for someone who is batting.
4 to set or aim: *She pitched her talk at the right level for the children.*
5 to put up or set up: *They pitched the tent by a stream.*
6 to rock lengthwise: *The ship pitched in the rough seas.*
Phrases pitch in (*informal*) to join in or contribute. **pitch up** (*informal*) to turn up, arrive.

pitch² noun
a thick black sticky substance obtained from the distillation of tar or turpentine and used for waterproofing.

pitchblende (**pitch**-blend) noun
a brownish-black mineral which is the main ore of uranium.
[PITCH² + German *Blende* zinc sulphide]

pitched battle noun
a battle that has been arranged beforehand, rather than one that happens by chance.

pitcher¹ noun
a large jar with a spout and a handle, used for pouring liquids.

pitcher² noun
Baseball the player who throws the ball to the batter.

pitchfork noun
a large heavy garden fork for pitching hay, turning soil, etc.

pitch pipe noun
Music a small pipe sounded to give a standard pitch or note when tuning an instrument or getting the correct pitch for the voice.

piteous (**pit**-i-us) adjective
inspiring pity or compassion.
***Word Family* piteously** adverb;
piteousness noun.

pitfall noun
a trap or hidden danger.

pith noun
1 the soft spongy substance between the flesh and rind of a citrus fruit.
2 *Biology* the spongy cellular tissue in a plant stem or branch.
3 the essence, basic part of something.
4 force or vigour.
• **pith** verb to remove the pith from.

pithead (**pit**-hed) noun
Mining the top of a shaft.

pith helmet noun
a light dome-shaped hat made from the dried pith of an Indian plant, used to keep off the sun.

pithy adjective (**pithier; pithiest**)
1 containing pith.
2 full of force or vigour: *pithy language.*
***Word Family* pithily** adverb; **pithiness** noun.

pitiable (**pit**-i-a-b'l) adjective
1 deserving pity.
2 inspiring or deserving contempt.
***Word Family* pitiably** adverb;
pitiableness noun.

pitiful adjective
1 inspiring pity.
2 inadequate: *She made a pitiful attempt to break the window.*
***Word Family* pitifully** adverb;
pitifulness noun.

pitiless adjective
showing no pity or mercy.
***Word Family* pitilessly** adverb;
pitilessness noun.

piton (**pee**-ton) noun
a heavy metal pin with a hole at one end, used by mountaineers for setting into a rock to pass a rope through it.
[French, eye bolt]

pitta (**pit**-a) noun also **pita**
a type of bread made in flat oval-shaped cakes, split open and filled, e.g. with meat and vegetables.

pittance noun
a very small or inadequate amount, especially of money or income.

pitter-patter noun
a rapid series of light beats or taps.
• **pitter-patter** adverb.

pituitary (pi-**tyoo**-it-a-ree) *noun* (*plural* **pituitaries**) *also* **pituitary gland; pituitary body**
a pea-sized gland at the base of the brain which secretes hormones that control growth and the functioning of other glands.
[Latin *pituita* slime, phlegm]

pity *noun*
1 a feeling of sympathy or sorrow inspired by the suffering, misfortune, etc. of someone else.
2 something which causes pity, sorrow or regret: *What a pity that it is raining.*
• **pity** *verb* (**pities; pitying; pitied**).
[Latin *pietas* dutiful conduct]

pivot *noun*
1 a part or point about which something turns.
2 something on which other things depend.
Word Family **pivot** *verb* to turn on or as if on a pivot; **pivotal** *adjective*.

pixel *noun*
one of the tiny points of light that make up a picture on a TV screen or computer monitor.
[short for *picture element*]

pixie *noun* (*plural* **pixies**) *also* **pixy**
a supernatural creature with a human shape, usually with pointed ears and a pointed hat.

pizza (**peet** sa) *noun*
a pie-like food consisting of a flat dough covered with ingredients such as tomato, cheese, olives, sausage, etc.
[Italian, pie]

pizzazz (piz-**az**) *noun also* **pizazz; pzazz**
(*informal*) a flamboyant theatrical style.

pizzeria (peet-sa-**ree**-a *or* pit sa-**ree**-a) *noun*
a place where pizzas are made or eaten.
[Italian]

pizzicato (pit-si kah-toe) *adjective, adverb*
Music played by plucking the strings of bowed instruments with the finger.
[Italian *pizzicare* to pinch]

placard (**plak**-ard) *noun*
a poster or notice for public display.

placate (pla-**kate** *or* **plak**-ate *or* **play**-kate) *verb*
to pacify or make calm.
Word Family **placatory** (pla-**kay**-ta-ree) *adjective* intending to placate; **placatingly** *adverb*.
[from Latin]

place *noun*
1 a particular area of space: *You've put those books in the wrong place.* □ *We forgot to lay a place for her at the table.*
2 a vacancy: *There were no more places on the course.*
3 a position: *I know what I'd do if I were in your place.* □ *someone's place in society.*
4 *Maths* the position of a digit in a number: *calculated to four decimal places.*
5 a name for a short street or court: *24, Fairfield Place.*
6 (*informal*) someone's home: *You can stay at my place.*
7 a point that someone has reached in a book: *I've lost my place now!*
Phrases **go places** 1 to travel. 2 to be successful. **in place of** instead of. **out of place** 1 out of the correct position.
2 unsuitable, not appropriate. **put someone in his** or **her place** to humiliate or humble someone. **take place** to happen.
• **place** *verb*
1 to put or fix in a particular place. *I placed the book on the desk.* □ *Place your trust in me.*
2 to make an order, bet, etc.
3 to make a telephone call.
4 to identify or remember: *He couldn't quite place her*
[Greek *plateia* (*hodos*) broad (way)]

placebo (pla-**see**-bo) *noun*
a harmless pharmacologically inactive substance administered instead of a drug to a patient in the course of drug trials or for psychological purposes.
[Latin]

The word **placebo** means 'I shall please' in Latin and was adopted into English because it illustrated the idea that a particular medicine 'pleased' the patient even though it had no physiological effect.

placement *noun*
1 a temporary job, e.g to gain work experience.
2 placing or being placed.

placenta (pla-**sen**-ta) *noun* (*plural* **placentas** *or* **placentae** (pla-**sen**-tee))
Anatomy a spongy organ formed within the uterus during pregnancy so that food and oxygen from the mother's blood supply can reach the fetus, and waste products from the fetus can be eliminated.
Word Family **placental** *adjective*.
[Greek *plakountos* of a flat cake]

placid (**plas**-id) *adjective*
calm or composed.
Word Family placidly *adverb*; **placidity**
(pla-**sid**-i-tee) *noun*.
[from Latin]

placket *noun*
an overlapping piece covering the
fastenings or pocket on a piece of clothing.

plagiarist (**play**-ja-rist) *noun*
a person who copies or takes someone
else's work or ideas and pretends they are
his or her own.
Word Family plagiarism *noun*;
plagiarize, plagiarise *verb* to copy.
[Latin *plagiarius* kidnapper]

plague (playg) *noun*
1 an infectious epidemic disease, especially
bubonic or pneumonic plague.
2 a sudden invasion or arrival of large
numbers of insects or animals that do
damage.
• **plague** *verb* to trouble, annoy or bother:
*The police have been plagued with complaints
about the noise.*
[Latin *plaga* a blow, a wound]

plaice (place) *noun* (*plural* **plaice**)
a type of flatfish with bright orange spots,
used as food.
[Greek *platys* broad]

plaid (plad) *noun*
1 woollen cloth with a tartan design.
2 a piece of this worn over the shoulder by
someone in Scottish Highland costume.
[Gaelic]

plain *adjective*
1 not decorated, simple: *a plain blue skirt.*
2 without lines or markings: *plain paper.*
3 ordinary, not very attractive: *a plain
child.*
4 easily understood: *The meaning was
plain.*
5 frank, open: *I believe in plain speaking.*
6 absolute: *It was plain madness to try.*
• **plain** *noun*
1 an area of low flat land.
2 a simple stitch in knitting.
Word Family plainly, plain *adverb* **1** in a
simple or plain manner. **2** clearly or
obviously; **plainness** *noun*.
[Latin *planus* level, clear]

plain chocolate *noun*
dark chocolate that has a slightly bitter
taste.

plain clothes *plural noun*
ordinary clothes as distinct from a
uniform.

plain flour *noun*
flour that does not contain baking powder.

plain sailing *noun*
an easy or unobstructed course, progress,
etc.

plainsong *noun*
a form of chant used in early church
music, using a single melody line with no
additional parts or accompaniment.

plaintiff *noun*
Law a person who starts a case against
someone in a court. Compare DEFENDANT.
[Latin *plangere* to lament]

plaintive *adjective*
expressing sorrow, sadness or melancholy:
a plaintive smile.
Word Family plaintively *adverb*;
plaintiveness *noun*.

plait (plat) *noun*
a length of something, e.g. hair, divided
into three strands and intertwined.
• **plait** *verb*.
[Latin *plicatus* folded]

plan *noun*
1 an action, method or programme
worked out beforehand: *a plan of attack.*
□ *holiday plans.*
2 a drawing showing the structure or
arrangement of something; a diagram: *a
plan of the house.* □ *a town plan.*
• **plan** *verb* (**plans; planning; planned**)
1 to form or decide on a plan for: *to plan a
campaign.*
2 to draw or devise a plan for: *The garden
was planned by a landscape architect.*
3 to have as a plan: *He planned to catch the
last bus.*
Word Family planner *noun*.

plane¹ *noun*
1 a flat or level surface.
2 a level, e.g. of existence: *living on a
different plane.*
3 an aeroplane.
• **plane** *verb*
1 to glide.
2 to travel on top of the water rather than
through it, e.g. as is done by a speedboat,
waterskier, etc.
• **plane** *adjective* flat.

plane² *noun*
a tool with a blade slotted through a
smooth surface, for shaping or smoothing
the surface of wood, etc.
• **plane** *verb*.
[Latin *planus* level]

plane³ *noun also* **plane tree**
a tall tree with large broad leaves and flaky bark.
[Greek *platanos*]

plane figure *noun*
Geometry any figure whose parts all lie on the same plane.

planet (plan-it) *noun*
1 *Astronomy* any body that does not produce light and revolves around a star, especially the nine planets of our solar system. Compare SATELLITE (definition 1).
2 *Astrology* any of the seven heavenly bodies, consisting of Mercury, Venus, the moon, the sun, Mars, Jupiter and Saturn, believed to influence personality and events in conjunction with the stars.
Word Family **planetary** *adjective*.
[Greek *planetes* wanderer]

planetarium (plan-i-tair-i-um) *noun*
(*plural* **planetariums** or **planetaria** (plan-i-**tair**-i-a))
a building with a hemispherical ceiling on which the positions and movements of the stars and planets can be displayed by a projector.

planetoid ⇨ ASTEROID.

plank *noun*
a long flat piece of cut timber.
Phrase **walk the plank** to be forced to walk to one's death from a plank extended over the water from a ship's side.
Word Family **planking** *noun*.
[from Latin]

plankton *noun*
Biology the marine or freshwater microscopic animals and plants that drift with the surrounding water.
[Greek *plagktos* wandering]

plant *noun*
1 a living organism that is usually unable to move about but is usually able to make its own food from chemical elements. Compare ANIMAL (definition 1).
2 a small plant, such as a herb, which has no permanent woody stem, as distinct from a tree or shrub.
3 the buildings or equipment for a particular industry or mechanical system: *an electrical plant*.
4 a person placed in a certain situation as a spy, decoy, etc.
5 something used to trick, swindle or mislead.
• **plant** *verb*
1 to place a seed, cutting, tree, etc. in the ground so that it will grow.

2 to place or put firmly: *He planted his suitcase on the platform.*
3 to put a bomb somewhere.
4 to establish or introduce an idea, a doubt, etc.
5 to place someone as a spy, etc.
6 to hide something to get someone into trouble: *He said they had planted drugs in his flat.*
[Latin *planta* a shoot, sprig]

Plantagenet (plan-taj-i-nit) *noun*
a member of the royal house in England from 1154 to 1399.

plantain¹ (plan-tin or plan-tane) *noun*
a tropical tree with long green fruit, similar to a banana but less sweet, eaten as a vegetable.

plantain² *noun*
a weed with broad leaves and long spikes of small greenish flowers.
[Latin *planta* sole of the foot (from the shape of the leaves)]

plantation (plan-tay-sh'n) *noun*
1 a large farm, especially in tropical regions, where a cash crop such as coffee, sugar, bananas, etc. is grown.
2 a group of planted trees.

planter *noun*
1 the owner or manager of a plantation.
2 a container for a growing plant.
3 a machine or tool for planting or sowing seeds, or a person who plants.

plaque (plak) *noun*
1 a flat ornamental disc or tablet hung on a wall.
2 a sticky film which forms on teeth and which can cause gum disease.
[French]

plasma (plaz-ma) *noun*
1 the liquid part of unclotted blood in which cells are suspended. Compare SERUM (definition 1).
2 also **plasm** *Biology* cytoplasm or protoplasm.
3 *Physics* an intensely hot gas that has been completely broken up into positive ions and electrons.
Word Family **plasmatic** (plaz-**mat**-ik), **plasmic** *adjective*.
[Greek, something shaped]

plaster *noun*
1 a mixture of lime and sand or similar substances, used to cover brickwork, etc. inside or outside a house.
2 also **plaster of Paris** a white powder, calcium sulphate, obtained by heating gypsum. It swells and hardens when mixed

with water and is used for making moulds, etc.

3 ⇨ STICKING PLASTER.

• **plaster** *verb*

1 to apply or cover with plaster.

2 to spread or cover with something: *buses plastered with advertisements.* □ *wet hair plastered to his head.*

Word Family plasterer *noun*; **plastered** *adjective* (*informal*) drunk.

[Greek *emplastos* daubed over]

plastic *noun*

1 *Chemistry* any of a complex group of substances which can be shaped when soft and then hardened.

2 (*informal*) credit cards as opposed to cash: *I'll have to pay with plastic.*

• **plastic** *adjective*

1 made of plastic: *a plastic bag.*

2 able to be moulded or shaped: *Clay is a plastic substance.*

Word Family plasticity (plas-**tiss**-i-tee) *noun*; **plasticize, plasticise** *verb* to make or become plastic.

[Greek *plastikos* moulded]

plastic bullet *noun*

a bullet made from a plastic substance, used to control rioters.

Plasticine (**plas**-ti-seen) *noun* (*trademark*) a plastic modelling compound, obtainable in many colours.

plastic surgery *noun*

surgery which is concerned with remodelling, repairing or restoring the appearance of external parts of the body.

Word Family plastic surgeon *noun.*

plastid *noun*

Biology any of various small bodies found in the cytoplasm of plant cells.

plate *noun*

1 a shallow dish, usually circular in shape, used for food.

2 items made from gold or silver, e.g. utensils.

3 a dish or trophy made of gold or silver, given as a prize.

4 a thin flat smooth sheet or piece of something.

5 *Geology* a large section of the earth's crust. The movement of plates causes earthquakes and fold mountains.

6 *Baseball* a base, especially the base where the batter stands.

7 a sheet or surface used in printing, engraving, photography, etc.

8 *a print* produced from such a surface, especially an illustration taking up a full page of a book.

Phrases **on a plate** with no effort required: *The match was given to them on a plate.* **on one's plate** needing to be dealt with, taking up one's time: *He had too much on his plate.*

• **plate** *verb*

1 to coat with a thin layer or film of metal: *The nickel was plated with silver.*

2 to cover with metal plates or armour.

Word Family plating *noun* a thin coating or layer, e.g. on metal.

[Greek *platys* flat]

plateau (**plat**-o) *noun* (*plural* **plateaus** or **plateaux** (**plat**-oze))

1 *Geography* a large fairly flat area of highland.

2 any fairly steady or stable period or condition.

[French]

plate glass *noun*

a thick glass used for windows, doors, etc.

platelet *noun*

Biology any of the many small irregularly shaped fragments in blood, necessary for forming blood clots.

platform *noun*

1 any raised floor or horizontal surface.

2 the raised surface next to a railway line where passengers can stand.

3 *Politics* the policies or principles of a party, usually declared publicly before an election.

4 *Computers* a type of computer hardware, or an operating system.

platinum (**plat**-i-num) *noun*

1 a ductile malleable metal resistant to heat and acids. It is used in alloys, electrical contacts, scientific apparatus and jewellery.

2 a metallic greyish-white or silvery colour.

• **platinum** *adjective*.

[Spanish *plata* silver]

platitude (**plat**-i-tewd) *noun*

an unoriginal remark or statement, especially one meant to sound wise or refreshing.

platonic (pla-**tonn**-ik) *adjective*

spiritual as distinct from sexual or sensual: *platonic love.*

Word Family platonically *adverb.*

[after *Plato*, an ancient Greek philosopher who advocated ideal love]

platoon (pla-**toon**) *noun*

Military a part of a company, usually consisting of two or more sections.

[French *peloton* little group]

platter *noun*
a large shallow dish for serving food, etc.

platypus (plat-i-p'ss) *noun* (*plural* **platypuses**) also called **duck-billed platypus**.
a brown furry egg-laying Australian mammal living in rivers and lagoons and growing to about 65 cm long, with webbed feet and a leathery duck-like snout.
[Greek *platys* flat + *pous* foot]

plaudits (plaw-dits) *plural noun*
enthusiastic applause or praise.
[Latin *plaudere* to applaud]

plausible (plaw-zi-b'l) *adjective*
seeming worthy of belief or acceptance: *His alibi sounded quite plausible to the jury.*

play *verb*
1 to take part in a game, a sport or an amusement: *playing tennis.* □ *playing a trick on someone.*
2 to toy or tamper with something: *She's always playing with her hair.* □ *Don't play with those switches.*
3 to compete against: *Who are Man United playing this week?*
4 to move or lay down a card, playing piece, etc.
5 to produce, or be able to produce, music on an instrument: *She played the piano.*
6 to perform a part in a film, play, etc.
7 to cause a compact disc, tape, video, computer game, etc. to operate.
8 to move in a light and quick way: *sunlight playing on the coloured glass.*
Phrases **play along** to pretend to cooperate. **play fast and loose** to behave in an irresponsible or fickle way: *playing fast and loose with someone's affections.* **play it cool** to try to seem unconcerned. **play on** to make use of: *He played on her generous nature.* **play something down** to pretend that something is not important. **play up** to be naughty. **play up to** to try to win the favour of.
• **play** *noun*
1 any activity done for pleasure: *Play is very important for children.*
2 fun or joking.
3 a work written to be acted, especially in a theatre: *the plays of Shakespeare.*
4 *Sport* the state of a ball being in use in a game: *The ball went out of play.*
5 a move in a sport or game.
6 free movement or activity: *There was too much play in the steering wheel.*
7 quick irregular movement: *the play of sunlight on water.*

play-act *verb*
to act or pretend.

playback *noun*
the reproducing or replaying of recorded images or sounds.

playbill *noun*
a programme or poster for a theatrical performance.

playboy *noun*
a carefree and usually wealthy man devoted to the pleasures of a social or sophisticated life.

player *noun*
1 a person who plays, especially someone taking part in a game or sport.
2 (*dated*) an actor.
3 a machine for playing cassettes, videos, CDs, etc.

playful *adjective*
1 joking or light-hearted: *a playful fight.*
2 full of fun or high spirits: *playful puppies.*
Word Family playfully *adverb*;
playfulness *noun.*

playground *noun*
an area of land with swings, slides or other facilities for children to play with.

playgroup *noun*
a group or class for pre-school children which is organized by parents.

playhouse *noun*
1 a theatre.
2 a toy house that children can play in.

playing card ⇨ CARD¹ (definition 3).

playing field *noun*
a field where team games can be played.

playmate *noun*
a person or friend with whom one plays.

play-off *noun*
a game or match played to decide a draw.

plaything *noun*
a toy.

playwright (play-rite) *noun*
a person who writes plays.

plaza *noun*
1 an open area or public square in a city.
2 *American* a shopping mall.
[Spanish, place]

plea (plee) *noun*
1 a request or entreaty: *a plea for peace.*
2 *Law* a statement, especially in answer to a charge: *She changed her plea to guilty.*
3 an excuse.

plead (pleed) *verb*
to make a plea: *The accused man pleaded insanity.* □ *I pleaded with him not to go.*

pleasant (plez-'nt) *adjective*
1 enjoyable or pleasing.
2 friendly, considerate.
Word Family **pleasantly** *adverb*;
pleasantness *noun*.

pleasantry (plez-'n-tree) *noun* (*plural*
pleasantries)
a joke or polite remark.

please *verb*
1 to be agreeable or give satisfaction to:
The king's speech did not please the crowd.
2 to wish: *Do as you please.*
Phrase **please oneself** to do whatever
one wants.
• **please** *adverb* used as a polite form of
request or question, or to accept
something: *Please can I come?* □ *Two sugars,
please.*
Word Family **pleased** *adjective* feeling
happiness or satisfaction; **pleasing**
adjective; **pleasingly** *adverb*.
[Latin *placere*]

pleasure (*rhymes with* treasure) *noun*
a satisfying or pleasant experience: *It is a
pleasure to see you.* □ *Wine is one of the
pleasures of life.*
Word Family **pleasurable** *adjective*
pleasing; **pleasurably** *adverb*.

pleat (pleet) *noun*
a fold made by doubling cloth on itself,
and sewing or pressing it in place.
Word Family **pleat** *verb*; **pleated**
adjective.
[alteration of PLAIT]

pleb *noun*
(*informal*) an offensive word for a person
from the lower classes of society.

plebeian (pli-bee-an) *noun*
1 *History* a common person in ancient
Rome.
2 a person from the lower classes of
society.
• **plebeian** *adjective*.
[Latin *plebeius* belonging to the common
people]

plebiscite (pleb-i-sit) *noun*
a referendum.
[Latin *plebis* of the people + *scitum* a
decree]

plectrum *noun* (*plural* **plectrums** or
plectra)
a small piece of plastic, wood or metal,
used to pluck a stringed instrument.
[Greek *plektron*]

pledge *noun*
1 a vow or promise: *a pledge of loyalty.*

2 *Law* something given as security for a
loan or debt.
3 something given as a token: *This ring is a
pledge of my friendship.*
Phrase **take the pledge** to promise to
give up drinking alcohol.
• **pledge** *verb* to give or make a pledge.

plenary (plee-na-ree) *adjective*
1 complete or absolute: *plenary authority.*
2 attended by all qualified members: *a
plenary meeting.*
[Latin *plenus* full]

plenipotentiary (plen-i-pa-ten-sha-ree)
noun (*plural* **plenipotentiaries**)
a person who can make decisions on
behalf of his or her government, e.g. an
ambassador.
• **plenipotentiary** *adjective* having full
authority.
[Latin *plenus* full + *potentia* power]

plenitude (plen-i-tewd) *noun*
(*formal*) an abundance or the condition of
abundance.

plenteous (plen-ti-us) *adjective*
a poetic word meaning 'plentiful,
abundant'.
Word Family **plenteously** *adverb*;
plenteousness *noun*.

plenty *pronoun*
a large enough amount: *plenty of time.*
• **plenty** *noun* a situation in which there is
an abundance: *in times of plenty.*
• **plenty** *adverb* (*informal*) fully: *I'm plenty
warm enough, thanks.*
Word Family **plentiful** *adjective* existing
in plenty, abundant; **plentifully** *adverb*.
[Latin *plenitas* fullness]

plethora (pleth-a-ra) *noun*
an excess: *a plethora of new Internet
companies.*
[Latin]

> The word **plethora** came into English
> directly from the Latin, which was
> derived from Greek *plethoré* (fullness).
> Both in Latin and at first in English it
> was used in medicine to mean 'an
> excess of blood or other bodily fluids'.
> In English it later came to refer to an
> excess or a surplus of any kind.

pleura (plor-a) *noun* (*plural* **pleurae**)
(plor-ee)
Anatomy either of two delicate membranes
covering each lung in mammals, folded
back to form a lining of the chest wall.
Word Family **pleural** *adjective*.
[Greek, ribs]

pleurisy (plor-i-see) *noun*
an inflammation of the pleura, sometimes accompanying other diseases such as tuberculosis, measles or scarlet fever.

plexus *noun* (*plural* **plexus** or **plexuses**)
Anatomy a junction or network of several major nerves or blood vessels.
[Latin, interwoven]

pliable (ply-a-b'l) *adjective*
flexible or easily bent.
Figurative She will do what you ask because she's so pliable (= easily influenced).
Word Family **pliably** *adverb*; **pliability** (ply-a-bill-i-tee) *noun*.
[French *plier* to fold or bend]

pliant *adjective*
pliable.
Word Family **pliantly** *adverb*; **pliancy** *noun*.

pliers (ply-erz) *plural noun*
a small metal tool with long jaws for holding small objects, bending wire, etc.

plight[1] *noun*
a dangerous or difficult situation.

plight[2] *verb*
an old word meaning 'to pledge or promise loyalty or faithfulness'.

plimsoll *noun* also **plimsole**
a light sports shoe with a rubber sole.

Plimsoll line *noun* also **Plimsoll mark**
a mark painted on the outside of the hull of a ship to show how deeply it may sit in the water when loaded.
[after *S. Plimsoll*, 1824–1898, an English politician]

plinth *noun*
the lowest part of the base of a column, statue, wall, etc.
[Greek *plinthos* squared stone]

plod *verb* (**plods**; **plodding**; **plodded**)
1 to walk slowly and heavily.
2 to work slowly at something dull.
Word Family **plodder** *noun*; **ploddingly** *adverb*.

plonk[1] *verb*
(*informal*) to drop heavily or suddenly.
• **plonk** *noun* the act or sound of dropping heavily.

plonk[2] *noun*
(*informal*) cheap wine.

plonker *noun*
(*informal*) a stupid person.

plop *verb* (**plops**; **plopping**; **plopped**)
to drop with a dull quiet sound.
• **plop** *noun* a quiet falling sound.

plot *noun*
1 a secret plan, often with an unlawful purpose.
2 the main story of a novel, play, etc.
3 a small piece of ground for building or gardening.
• **plot** *verb* (**plots**; **plotting**; **plotted**)
1 to plan secretly: *The prisoners plotted their escape.*
2 to mark or draw on a map, chart, plan, graph, etc.: *We plotted the route taken by the explorers.* □ *Plot these points on your graph.*
Word Family **plotter** *noun*.

plough (*rhymes with* cow) *noun* (*American* **plow**)
a farming implement for cutting or turning soil.
• **plough** *verb*
1 to turn soil with a plough.
2 (of a ship) to travel through water.
3 (of a vehicle) to move fast with no control: *The racing car ploughed into the barrier.*
4 to invest or reinvest: *We ploughed the profits back into the company.*

ploughshare *noun*
the broad blade of a plough.

plover (pluv-a) *noun*
a wading bird with long legs and a short beak, found on seashores and moors.
[Latin *pluvia* rain]

ploy *noun*
a ruse or tricky manoeuvre.

pluck *verb*
1 to grasp and pull out: *plucking your eyebrows.* □ *plucking the feathers from a chicken.*
2 *Music* to sound the strings of an instrument by pulling them with the fingers or a plectrum.
Phrase **pluck up** *He was unable to pluck up enough courage* (= summon).
• **pluck** *noun* courage, spirit or resolution: *She's full of pluck and daring.*
Word Family **plucky** *adjective* (**pluckier**; **pluckiest**) brave; **pluckily** *adverb*; **pluckiness** *noun*.

plug *noun*
1 a piece of metal, rubber, etc. used to stop up a hole, e.g. in a bath.
2 anything which acts as a wedge or stopper, such as the mass of solidified rock in the vent of a volcano.
3 a device which, when inserted in a socket, connects with a supply of electric current.
4 (*informal*) an electric socket.

5 a piece of tobacco, especially one used for chewing.
6 (*informal*) a piece of favourable publicity: *The author gave her new book a plug on the show.*
• **plug** *verb* (**plugs; plugging; plugged**)
1 to stop up with or insert a plug.
2 (*informal*) to give favourable publicity to something.
3 (*informal*) to shoot or hit someone.
Phrases **plug away** to work hard and consistently. **plug in** to connect an electrical device to a socket.

plum *noun*
a small round juicy fruit, usually red, yellow or purple in colour.
Phrase **have a plum in one's mouth** to have an upper-class voice.
[Latin *prunum*]

plumage (**ploo**-mij) *noun*
the feathers on a bird.

plumb (plum) *verb*
1 to find the depth of water.
2 to check an upright surface, e.g. a wall, to make sure it is vertical.
• **plumb** *noun* a weight attached to a line, used to measure the depth of water or check a vertical line on an upright surface.
• **plumb** *adverb*
1 (*informal*) exactly or vertically.
2 *American* absolutely: *He's plumb crazy.*
[Latin *plumbum* lead]

plumber (**plum**-a) *noun*
a person who installs or repairs pipes, etc. for water and drainage systems.
Word Family **plumb in** *verb* to install a bath, washing machine, etc. by connecting its pipes to the water supply: *to plumb in a dishwasher.*

plumbing *noun*
1 the work of a plumber.
2 the system of pipes, drains, etc. in a building.

plumb line *noun*
a length of cord with a plumb on the end of it.

plum duff *noun*
a boiled suet pudding with currants or raisins.
[*duff* as for DOUGH]

plume (ploom) *noun*
a feather, especially a large one.
[from Latin]

plummet *verb*
to drop downwards suddenly and quickly: *The eagle plummeted from the heavens.*

plummy *adjective* (**plummier; plummiest**)
1 like a plum.
2 (*informal*) having a rich mellow tone, as if upper-class: *a plummy voice.*
3 (*informal*) choice, desirable.

plump[1] *adjective*
rounded and rather fat.
Word Family **plump** *verb* to make or become plump: *She plumped up the pillows;* **plumpness** *noun.*

plump[2] *verb*
to drop or fall heavily: *He plumped down his heavy load.*
Phrase **plump for** to choose: *Which candidate did you plump for?*

plum pudding *noun*
a rich steamed or boiled pudding made with dried fruits and spices, eaten especially at Christmas.

plum tomato *noun* (*plural* **plum tomatoes**)
a variety of tomato that is oval in shape.

plunder *verb*
to steal from or rob, especially violently.
• **plunder** *noun* goods which are stolen or gained illegally.

plunge (plunj) *verb*
1 to put or thrust forcibly and suddenly: *He plunged his hand into the water.*
2 to fall quickly and sharply: *The car plunged off the cliff.*
• **plunge** *noun*
1 the act of plunging.
2 a leap or dive.
Phrase **take the plunge** (*informal*) to decide to start a course of action, despite the risks involved.

plunge pool *noun*
Geography a deep pool under a waterfall caused by erosion.

plunger (**plun**-jer) *noun*
1 something which plunges, such as a piston.
2 a device consisting of a rubber suction cup and rod, used to clear drains.

plunk *verb*
1 (*informal*) to pluck or twang the strings of a musical instrument.
2 (*informal, especially American*) to set down heavily.
• **plunk** *noun* the act or sound of plunking.

plural (**plor**-al) *adjective*
of, consisting of or expressing more than one.
• **plural** *noun* a plural number, form or word: *The plural of 'mouse' is 'mice'.*
[Latin *pluris* of more]

pluralism (plor-a-lizm) *noun*
1 the retention of their own customs and beliefs by the racial or religious minorities of a country.
2 the sharing of power by a number of political parties.
3 *Christianity* the holding of more than one benefice at a time.
Word Family pluralist *noun, adjective*; **pluralistic** *adjective*.

plurality (plor-**al**-i-tee) *noun*
1 the state of being plural.
2 *American* the obtaining of more votes in an election than any other rival candidate, without obtaining an absolute majority.

plus *preposition*
also or in addition to: *4 plus 2 equals 6.*
• **plus** *adjective*
1 above zero, positive.
2 at least: *They sold the house for half a million plus.*
• **plus** *noun* (*plural* **pluses**)
1 the plus sign.
2 (*informal*) an advantage: *The fact that she doesn't smoke is a big plus.*
[Latin]

plus fours *plural noun*
short loose trousers drawn into a band below the knee, worn especially by golfers.
[so called because they overlap below the knee by four inches]

plush *adjective*
(*informal*) richly luxurious and expensive.
• **plush** *noun* a thick fabric of silk, wool, etc., with a less dense pile than velvet.

plus sign *noun*
a symbol (+), used to show addition or a value that is greater than zero.

Pluto (**ploo**-toe) *noun*
Astronomy the planet in the solar system furthest from the sun.
[after *Pluto*, another name for Hades, god of the underworld in Greek mythology]

plutocracy (ploo-**tok**-ra-see) *noun* (*plural* **plutocracies**)
1 the exercise of power by the rich.
2 a state or society governed by the rich.
3 the rich viewed as a ruling class.
Word Family plutocrat (**ploot**-a-krat) *noun* a very rich and influential person; **plutocratic** (ploot-a-**krat**-ik) *adjective*.
[Greek *ploutos* wealth + *kratia* rule]

plutonic (ploo-**tonn**-ik) *adjective*
Geology relating to igneous rocks such as granite formed deep below the earth's surface.

Word Family pluton *noun* a body of plutonic rock.
[after PLUTO]

plutonium (ploo-**toe**-nee-um) *noun*
a man-made radioactive metal, discovered while the atomic bomb was being made and later used in nuclear weapons.
[after PLUTO, being next after the metal neptunium as Pluto is next after Neptune]

pluvial (**ploo**-vi-ul) *adjective*
Geology of or caused by rain.

ply[1] *verb* (**plies; plying; plied**)
1 to work with a tool: *plying a needle.*
2 to work at a trade.
3 to go regularly from one place to another, as a ferry does.
4 to provide with food or drink continuously.
5 to ask someone many questions.

ply[2] *noun* (*plural* **plies**)
1 a strand of yarn.
2 a thickness or layer of wood, etc.

plywood *noun*
a building material made of several thin sheets of wood glued together.

pneumatic (new-**mat**-ik) *adjective*
operated by or filled with compressed air or other gases: *a pneumatic drill.*
[Greek *pneumatos* of a wind]

pneumoconiosis (new-ma-koe-nee-o-sis) *noun*
the progressive damage to the lungs of miners caused by inhaling coal or metal dust.
[Greek *pneumon* lung + *konia* dust + *-osis*]

pneumonia (new-**mone**-ya) *noun*
an inflammation of the lungs, caused by bacterial infection.
Word Family pneumonic (new-**mon**-ik) *adjective*.
[Greek *pneumon* a lung]

poach[1] *verb*
1 to steal game or fish from someone's land.
2 to take in an unfair or secret way: *poaching customers.*
Word Family poacher *noun* a person who poaches.

poach[2] *verb*
to cook in simmering water: *poached eggs.*
Word Family poacher *noun* a pan or device for poaching.

pock *noun*
a pockmark.

pocket *noun*
1 a small bag set into clothing for carrying money, etc.
2 a pocket-like or enclosed cavity, area or position: *the pockets on a snooker table.*
3 a small isolated area of something: *pockets of fighting.*
Phrases one's pocket one's finances: *My pocket won't stand another spending spree.*
out of pocket having lost money.
• **pocket** *verb* to put or enclose in a pocket: *I pocketed the money.* □ *The snooker player pocketed the ball.*

pocketbook *noun*
1 a notebook.
2 *American* a wallet, purse or handbag.

pocket knife *noun* (*plural* **pocket knives**)
a penknife.

pocket money *noun*
a sum of money for personal expenses, such as is given regularly to a child by a parent.

pockmark *noun* also **pock**
a mark or scar left by a spot or pustule.
• **pockmark** *verb.*

pod *noun*
a long two-sided container of seeds such as peas.
• **pod** *verb* (**pods; podding; podded**)
1 to produce pods.
2 to shell peas, etc.

podgy (**poj**-ee) *adjective* (**podgier; podgiest**)
(*informal*) plump, chubby.
Word Family podginess *noun.*

podium (**po**-dee-um) *noun* (*plural* **podiums** or **podia**)
a small platform used by the conductor of an orchestra, someone making a speech, etc.
[Greek *podis* of a foot]

podzol *noun* also **podsol**
a poor acidic forest soil found in cold areas, with a greyish-white upper layer and a brownish lower layer.
[Russian]

poem (**po**-im) *noun*
a composition arranged in lines, usually with a particular rhythm and sometimes with rhymes.

poesy (**po**-i-zee *or* **po**-i-see) *noun*
an old word for poetry.

poet (**po**-it) *noun*
a person who writes poems.

poetic (po-**et**-ik) *adjective* also **poetical**
1 of or relating to poets or poetry.
2 having the feeling, form or character of a poem.
Word Family poetically *adverb*; **poetess** *noun* (*plural* **poetesses**) a female poet.
[from Greek]

poetic justice *noun*
ideal justice, in which all good actions are rewarded and all evil ones are punished.

poetic licence *noun*
the liberty taken by a poet or writer to ignore normal literary forms, such as rhyme, or to ignore facts and logic, in order to create a better effect.

Poet Laureate (po-it **lorr**-i-at) *noun* (*plural* **Poets Laureate**)
a poet appointed to the royal household who writes poems on special royal and national occasions.

poetry *noun*
1 text arranged in lines, usually with a particular rhythm and sometimes with rhymes.
2 the composing of such text.

pogo stick *noun*
a toy for jumping up and down on, consisting of a stick on a spring, with rests for the feet near the bottom.
Word Family pogo *verb* (**pogoes; pogoing; pogoed**) to jump up and down on or as if on a pogo stick.

pogrom *noun*
an organized massacre of people belonging to an ethnic group, such as the Jews in Russia.
[Russian, destruction]

poignant (**poyn**-y'nt) *adjective*
deeply moving or distressing.
Word Family poignantly *adverb*; **poignancy** *noun.*
[Old French, pricking]

poinsettia (poyn-**set**-i-a) *noun*
a Mexican plant with bright scarlet bracts which look like flowers.
[after J. R. Poinsett, 1799-1851, an American diplomat]

point *noun*
1 a sharp tapering end or part, e.g. of a needle.
2 something which has the shape or position of a point, such as a headland.
3 an exact spot or position: *a point on a map.* □ *a point in time.*
4 a purpose: *What's the point of continuing?*
5 a detail: *We need to discuss a few points.*
6 the most important idea: *Just get to the point.*

7 a quality: *He mentioned some of her good points.*
8 a unit of scoring in games such as football, cards, etc.
9 a degree or position on a scale of measurement: *the boiling point of water.*
□ *The stock market rose 12 points.* □ *the points of the compass.*
10 a position directly in front of: *held at the point of a gun.*
11 *Maths* a basic element of space which determines position.
12 *Maths* a decimal point.
13 *Grammar* a full stop.
14 *Cricket* a fielding position on the offside, near and facing the batsman.
15 any of the contacts controlling the flow of current in a circuit.
16 (**points**) *Railways* a device for shifting vehicles from one line to another.
17 *Printing* a unit of measurement for type sizes, one-twelfth of an em.
Phrases **beside the point** not relevant.
labour the point to treat something at excessive length. **make a point of** to do or undertake deliberately: *He made a point of being friendly to everybody.* **on the point of** just about to. **point of no return** the point at which one has gone too far to be able to turn back. **to the point** apt or relevant.
● **point** *verb*
1 to direct or indicate the direction of: *Don't point your finger at me.* □ *The needle pointed north.*
2 (of a hunting dog) to stand stiffly with its nose in the direction of game.
3 to finish off the joints in stone and brickwork with mortar or cement.
Phrase **point out** to draw attention to.
[Latin *punctum* a puncture]

point-blank *adjective*
1 aimed or fired at very close range.
2 blunt, without explanation: *a point-blank refusal.*
● **point-blank** *adverb*.

point duty *noun*
the controlling of traffic at a junction or intersection, e.g. by a police officer.

pointed *adjective*
1 having a sharp point or end.
2 having a clear meaning: *As I rushed in, she made a pointed remark about people being late.*
Word Family **pointedly** *adverb*; **pointedness** *noun*.

pointer *noun*
1 a person or thing that points.

2 a hint or suggestion.
3 a large breed of dog with long legs and smooth hair, trained to point when scenting game.

pointillism (**pwan**-ti-lizm) *noun*
Art a painting method in which small, closely spaced dots of colour are used, which are blended by the eye to form intermediate colours.
Word Family **pointillist** *noun, adjective*.
[French *pointiller* to mark with points]

pointless *adjective*
without sense or purpose: *That was a pointless remark.*
Word Family **pointlessly** *adverb*; **pointlessness** *noun*.

point of order *noun* (*plural* **points of order**)
a question as to whether the procedure of a meeting, debate, etc. is according to the rules.

point of view *noun* (*plural* **points of view**)
an attitude or position from which things are considered.

point-to-point *noun*
a meet for steeplechase racing held by a hunt at the end of the hunting season.

poise *noun*
1 balance or steadiness, as in movement: *She walks with poise.*
2 gracious dignity or self-possession.
● **poise** *verb* to be or make balanced or suspended: *The cat was poised and ready to pounce.*
Figurative *The country was poised on the brink of war.*
Word Family **poised** *adjective* dignified and self-assured.

poison *noun*
1 a substance which harms or destroys life.
2 a harmful or destructive influence: *the poison of hatred.*
● **poison** *verb*
1 to give poison to.
2 to be harmful or destructive to: *a friendship poisoned by jealousy.*
[Latin]

> **Poison** is, etymologically, just something you drink, being ultimately derived from Latin *potio* (I drink), the source also of English *potion*. It then came to mean 'a poisonous drink' and then simply 'poison', whether it was a drink or not.

poisonous *adjective*
1 containing poison.
2 malicious.
Word Family **poisonously** *adverb*.

poison pen letter *noun*
an anonymous letter which is intended to hurt, e.g. by a revelation.

poke *verb*
to jab or thrust: *He poked me in the ribs with his finger*. □ *I poked my head out of the window to have a look.*
• **poke** *noun* a jab or thrust.

poker[1] *noun*
a metal rod for stirring a fire.

poker[2] *noun*
a card game played by two or more people, with bets progressively increased by those who stay in. The player who bluffs the others into thinking he or she has the best hand (or who even actually has it) scoops the jackpot.
[possibly from German *Pochspiel* bragging game]

poker dice *plural noun*
a set of dice which have marks representing the six highest playing cards instead of numbers.

poker face *noun*
an expressionless face, like that of an experienced poker player.
Word Family **poker-faced** *adjective*.

poky (po-kee) *adjective* (**pokier; pokiest**)
also **pokey**
small and confined: *a poky room in a cheap hotel.*

polar *adjective*
of or relating to a pole, such as the poles of the earth, a magnet, etc.
Figurative The twins are polar opposites in all their likes and dislikes (= complete).

polar bear ⇨ BEAR[2].

polarity (po-**larr**-i-tee) *noun* (*plural* **polarities**)
1 the possession of two poles.
2 the possession of two directly opposite or contrary tendencies, qualities, etc.

polarize, polarise *verb*
1 to divide into two contrasting groups.
2 *Physics* to cause to acquire polarity.
Word Family **polarization** *noun*; **polarizer** *noun*.

Polaroid (**pole**-a-royd) *noun*
(*trademark*) a thin film of plastic that produces polarized light, used in cameras, sunglasses, etc.

polder *noun*
an area of low land reclaimed from the sea and protected by dykes, especially in the Netherlands.

pole[1] *noun*
1 a long rounded piece of wood or metal.
2 ⇨ PERCH[3] (definition 1).
Phrase **up the pole** 1 mad. 2 *Irish* pregnant.
• **pole** *verb* to propel with a pole.

pole[2] *noun*
1 *Geography* either of the northernmost or southernmost points of the earth's axis.
2 *Physics* either of two points where opposite quantities or forces appear to be concentrated: *the poles of a battery*. □ *the poles of a magnet.*
Phrase **poles apart** *Our views on most things are poles apart* (= widely different, completely opposite).
[Greek *polos* pivot, axis, sky]

poleaxe *noun* (*American* **poleax**)
1 a large axe used in warfare.
2 a combined axe and hammer for felling or stunning animals.
• **poleaxe** *verb*
1 to fell with a poleaxe.
2 to give a terrible shock to.

polecat (**pole**-kat) *noun*
1 a small flesh-eating mammal with a very unpleasant smell, related to the weasel and found in Europe and Asia.
2 *American* a skunk.

polemic (pol-**em**-ik) *noun*
1 an argument, dispute or controversy.
2 also **polemics** the art or practice of controversial arguing.
Word Family **polemic, polemical** *adjective*; **polemically** *adverb*.
[Greek *polemikos* warlike]

polenta *noun*
maize flour, used to make a paste or dough which is cooked as part of an Italian dish.
[Italian]

Pole Star *noun* also called **North Star**.
Astronomy a star situated close to the North Pole of the heavens, formerly used as a guide by sailors.

pole vault *noun*
Athletics a contest in which competitors jump as high as they can over a raised bar, with the help of a long pole.
Word Family **pole-vault** *verb*; **pole-vaulter** *noun*.

police (pol-**eece**) *noun*
1 (*used with plural verb*) an organized group of officials appointed to enforce a

country's laws and prevent and detect crime.

2 (*used with plural verb*) the members of such a force.

Word Family **police** *verb* to keep order with or as if with police; **policeman** *noun* (*plural* **policemen**) a male member of a police force; **policewoman** *noun* (*plural* **policewomen**) a female member of a police force; **police officer** *noun* a member of a police force.

police state *noun*
a state in which political dissent is stamped out by secret police.

policy¹ (poll-i-see) *noun* (*plural* **policies**)
a plan or course of action or procedure: *a business policy.* □ *a country's foreign policy.*

policy² *noun* (*plural* **policies**)
a document stating the conditions of insurance.

Word Family **policyholder** *noun* the person insured by an insurance policy.

polio (pole-ee-o) *noun*
short form of **poliomyelitis** an infectious viral disease of the spinal cord, causing paralysis of muscles.
[shortening of *poliomyelitis*, from Greek *polios* grey + *myelos* marrow + *-itis*]

polish (pul-ish) *verb*
1 to make or become smooth and shining: *He polished his shoes.*
2 to improve, add finishing touches to: *She polished her speech.*
Phrase **polish off** to finish quickly, dispose of: *They soon polished off the sandwiches.*
● **polish** *noun* (*plural* **polishes**)
1 a substance used to make a surface smooth and glossy: *shoe polish.*
2 the act of polishing: *I gave the car a final polish.*
3 smoothness, glossiness.
4 refinement or elegance.
Word Family **polished** *adjective*; **polisher** *noun*.

politburo (poll-it-byor-oh) *noun*
Politics the leading committee in a communist party, which decides on policy.

polite *adjective*
1 displaying good manners or consideration toward others: *a polite request.*
2 refined, cultured: *in polite society.*
Word Family **politely** *adverb*; **politeness** *noun*.
[Latin *politus* polished]

politic (poll-itik) *adjective*
(*formal*) wise or sensible: *It is politic not to anger one's boss.*

political *adjective*
1 relating to the government.
2 interested in or involved in politics.
Word Family **politically** *adverb*.

political correctness *noun*
the use of language and action that does not discriminate against particular people in society, or put them at a disadvantage.
Word Family **politically correct** *adjective*.

political science *noun*
the study of governments, political affairs and political principles.
Word Family **political scientist** *noun* a person trained or skilled in political science.

politician (pol-i-**tish**-an) *noun*
a person who is professionally involved in politics, especially an MP.

politics (pol-i-tiks) *plural noun*
1 (*used with singular verb*) the matters connected with the government or organization of a country or group of countries.
2 someone's political opinions or beliefs.
3 scheming for power or advancement: *office politics.*
Word Family **politicize, politicise** (po-lit-i-size) *verb* to become or cause to become aware of politics and political issues.
[Greek *politikos* of citizens]

polity (pol-i-tee) *noun* (*plural* **polities**)
1 a particular system of government, e.g. a republic, federation or empire.
2 a community organized as a state.

polka (pol-ka *or* pole-ka) *noun*
1 a fast dance in which couples move around the room in large circles.
2 the music for such a dance.

polka dot *noun*
a dot repeated to make a pattern on a fabric, etc.

poll (pole) *noun*
1 the voting in or results of an election.
2 ⇨ OPINION POLL.
● **poll** *verb*
1 to receive votes: *Our candidate polled the highest number of votes.*
2 to vote at an election.
3 to take a survey of opinion.

pollard (pol-'d) *verb*
to cut back the branches of a tree so that

it will produce denser foliage when it regrows.
• **pollard** *noun* a pollarded tree.

pollen *noun*
Biology the fine yellow powder found in flowers, each grain being a male reproductive cell.
[Latin, fine flour]

pollen count *noun*
a measure of the pollen in the air.

pollinate *verb*
to transfer pollen from an anther of a flower to a stigma.
Word Family **pollination** *noun*.

polling booth *noun*
a cubicle in which voters can mark their election votes in secrecy.

pollster (**pole**-sta) *noun*
a person who conducts or examines opinion polls.

poll tax *noun* (*plural* **poll taxes**)
a tax that each adult has to pay, regardless of income.

pollution (pol-**oo**-sh'n) *noun*
1 the act of making dirty or impure.
2 the spoiling of the environment or atmosphere by human or industrial waste, noise, etc.
Word Family **pollute** *verb*; **polluter** *noun*; **pollutant** *noun* a substance causing pollution.
[Latin *pollutus* defiled]

polo (**pole**-o) *noun*
a game similar to hockey, played on horseback using long-handled mallets and a small wooden ball.
[Tibetan, ball]

polonaise (pol-a-**naze**) *noun*
1 a slow dance from Poland which includes promenades for couples.
2 the music for such a dance.
[French, Polish]

polo neck *noun* also called **roll neck**.
a raised collar which folds over in one piece, on a jumper or shirt.
Word Family **polo-necked** *adjective*.

polo shirt *noun*
a casual cotton shirt with short sleeves and buttons at the neck.

poltergeist (pol-ta-**guyst**) *noun*
a mischievous ghost believed to be the cause of disturbing noises and petty destructiveness in a house.
[German *poltern* to make a noise + *Geist* ghost]

poltroon (pol-**troon**) *noun*
an old word for a coward.
[perhaps Italian *poltro* sluggard]

polychromatic (pol-i-kro-**mat**-ik) *adjective*
being of many colours.
[*poly-* + Greek *khromatos* of colour]

polyester (pol-i-**ess**-ta) *noun*
Chemistry any of a class of complex organic compounds used in making synthetic resins, plastics and (mixed with other fibres) in many crease-resistant fabrics.

polyethylene ⇨ POLYTHENE.

polygamy (pol-**ig**-a-mee) *noun*
the custom of having several spouses or mates at one time. Compare MONOGAMY.
Word Family **polygamist** *noun* a person who practises or advocates polygamy; **polygamous** *adjective*; **polygamously** *adverb*.
[*poly-* + Greek *gamos* marriage]

polyglot (**pol**-i-glot) *noun*
a person who knows several different languages.
[*poly-* + Greek *glotta* tongue]

polygon (**pol**-i-g'n) *noun*
Geometry a closed plane figure with three or more straight sides, especially one with at least five sides.
Word Family **polygonal** (pol-**ig**-a-n'l) *adjective*.
[*poly-* + Greek *gonia* corner]

polyhedron (pol-i-**he**-dr'n) *noun* (*plural* **polyhedrons** or **polyhedra**)
Geometry a solid figure with many plane faces.
Word Family **polyhedral** *adjective*.
[*poly-* + Greek *hedra* a base]

polymer (**pol**-im-a) *noun*
Chemistry a compound composed of one or more large molecules which are formed from repeated units of smaller molecules (monomers).

polymerization, polymerisation (pol-im-a-rye-**zay**-sh'n) *noun*
Chemistry the process in which small molecules join to form a large molecule or polymer.

polymorphism (pol-i-**mor**-fizm) *noun*
Biology the existence within a species of several distinct forms of individuals.
Word Family **polymorphous**, **polymorphic** *adjective*; **polymorph** *noun* an organism exhibiting polymorphism.
[*poly-* + Greek *morphé* form]

polynomial (pol-i-**no**-mee-al) *noun*
Maths an algebraic expression with many
terms, all with positive integer indices, e.g.
$3x^5 + 4x^2 - 1$.

polyp (**pol**-ip) *noun*
1 *Zoology* a form of aquatic invertebrate
animal, e.g. a sea anemone, that is fixed to
one spot, such as the many small
organisms of which coral is composed.
2 *Medicine* a growth on a mucous surface,
e.g. in the nose.
[*poly-* + Greek *pous* foot]

polyphonic (pol-i-**fon**-ik) *adjective*
Music having two or more simultaneous
voices or parts, each with an individual
melody, but all harmonizing.
[*poly-* + Greek *phoné* sound]

polypropylene (pol-i-**pro**-pa-leen) *noun*
a colourless transparent plastic which is a
polymer of propylene, with similar
properties to polythene but much
stronger; used in lightweight upholstery
fabrics.

polystyrene (pol-i-**sty**-reen) *noun*
a colourless solid, softening when heated,
which is a polymer of styrene. It is a good
electrical insulator.

polysyllabic (pol-i-sil-**ab**-ik) *adjective*
having more than one syllable.

polytechnic (pol-i-**tek**-nik) *noun*
a college at which students can study for
qualifications or degrees, especially in
vocational subjects. After 1992 British
polytechnics were allowed to call
themselves universities.
[*poly-* + Greek *tekhné* an art]

polytheism (**pol**-i-thee-izm) *noun*
the belief in more than one god or many
gods. Compare MONOTHEISM.
Word Family **polytheist** *noun* a person
who believes in more than one god,
polytheistic (pol-i-thee-**ist**-ik) *adjective*.
[*poly-* + Greek *theos* a god]

polythene (**pol**-a-theen) *also called*
polyethylene.
Chemistry a tough waxy transparent plastic
which is a polymer of ethylene, used as
insulation and as a protective wrapping in
packaging.

polyunsaturated (pol-i-un-**satch**-a-rayt-
id) *adjective*
Chemistry lacking hydrogen bonds at
several points in the chain of carbon
atoms: *polyunsaturated fat.*
Word Family **polyunsaturates** *plural
noun* polyunsaturated fats or oils.

polyvinyl acetate (pol-i-vie-n'l **ass**-a-
tate) *noun*
short form is **PVA** a colourless solid,
softening when heated, used in adhesives,
inks, lacquers and fabrics.

polyvinyl chloride (pol-i-vie-n'l **klaw**-
ride) *noun*
short form is **PVC** a colourless solid,
softening when heated, having a good
resistance to water, alkalis, acids, and
alcohol, and used in making many
domestic and industrial articles, including
upholstery fabrics.

pomade (pom-**aid** *or* pom-**ahd**) *noun*
a perfumed ointment applied to the head
and scalp.
• **pomade** *verb*.

pomander (pa-**man**-da *or* pom-'n-da)
noun
1 a perforated spherical container for pot-
pourri.
2 an orange with cloves stuck into it.
[Old French *pomme d'ambre* apple of
amber]

pome (pohm) *noun*
Botany a fleshy fruit such as an apple,
pear, etc., which has seeds but no stone.
[Latin *pomum* apple]

pomegranate (**pom**-i-gran-it) *noun*
a medium-sized round red fruit with a
tough skin and many seeds in the edible
acid flesh.
[Old French *pome granate* many-seeded
fruit]

pommel (**pum**-el) *noun*
1 the front part of a saddle, which curves
upwards.
2 a rounded end on a handle of a sword or
dagger.
• **pommel** *verb* (**pommels,
pommelling; pommelled**) to pummel.

Pommy *noun* (*plural* **Pommies**) *also*
Pommie
Australian (*informal*) a British person,
especially an immigrant.
[probably a play on the words *immigrant*
and *pomegranate*]

pomp *noun*
stately or ceremonious splendour or
display: *The coronation was conducted with
great pomp.*
[Greek *pompé* a solemn procession]

pompom *noun also* **pompon**
a small ball of coloured wool used as a
trimming on hats, etc.
[French, topknot]

pompous (**pom**-pus) *adjective*
full of self-importance or an exaggerated
sense of one's dignity.
Word Family **pompously** *adverb*;
pompousness, pomposity (pom-**poss**-i-
tee) *noun* the quality of being pompous.

ponce *noun*
1 (*informal*) a man who lives off the
earnings of a prostitute.
2 an offensive word for a man who is
effeminate.
• **ponce** *verb* to live off the earnings of a
prostitute.
Phrase **ponce about, ponce around**
(*informal*) to act in an affected way.

poncho *noun*
a blanket-like cloak with a hole in the
middle for the head to go through.
[Amerindian]

pond *noun*
a small often man-made area of water,
surrounded by land.
[from POUND³]

ponder *verb*
to consider deeply or carefully.
[Latin *pendere* to weigh]

ponderous *adjective*
1 slow and clumsy because of heaviness.
2 dull, tedious: *He writes in a very
ponderous fashion.*
Word Family **ponderously** *adverb*;
ponderousness *noun*.

pong *noun*
(*informal*) an unpleasant smell.
• **pong** *verb*.

pontiff *noun*
the Pope.
Word Family **pontifical** (pon-**tif**-i-k'l)
adjective 1 of or relating to the Pope or
papacy. 2 pompous; **pontifically** *adverb*.
[Latin *pontifex* a high priest]

pontificate (pon-**tif**-i-kate) *verb*
to speak pompously or with an
exaggerated sense of authority.

pontoon¹ (pon-**toon**) *noun*
a boat or floating tank, used to support
bridges, piers or other structures on water.
[from Latin]

pontoon² *noun* also called **blackjack;
vingt-et-un**.
Cards a game played against the banker
where the winner is the player whose
points are closest to, but not more than,
21.

pony *noun* (*plural* **ponies**)
1 a small horse, especially one less than 15
hands in height.
2 (*informal*) 25 pounds sterling.

ponytail *noun*
a hairstyle in which a long bunch of hair is
pulled back and tied so as to hang like a
horse's tail.

poodle *noun*
one of a breed of curly-haired dogs,
usually elaborately trimmed and clipped.
[German *Pudelhund*]

poof *noun* also **poofter; pouf**
(*informal*) an offensive word for a man
who is effeminate or homosexual.

pooh *interjection* also **poo**
(*informal*) an exclamation of disgust or
contempt.
• **pooh** *noun* also **poo** (*informal*)
excrement, or an act of defecating.
• **pooh** *verb* also **poo** (*informal*) to
defecate.

pooh-pooh *verb*
(*informal*) to dismiss contemptuously.

pooja ⇨ PUJA.

pool¹ *noun*
1 a small area of still liquid.
2 a still deep part in an area of water.
3 a swimming pool.
• **pool** *verb* to form a pool.

pool² *noun*
1 a common fund, supply or service.
2 the stakes played for in certain games.
3 a form of billiards for several players,
each having a ball of a different colour.
Compare SNOOKER *noun*.
4 (**pools**) also called **football pools**. an
organized form of gambling based on the
results of football matches.
• **pool** *verb* to put things together for
common advantage: *Three of us pooled our
savings to buy an old car.*

poop¹ *noun* also **poop deck**
a short deck built over the main deck at
the stern of a ship.
[Latin *puppis* the stern]

poop² *verb*
(*American informal*) to tire or exhaust: *I
was pooped after the long walk.*

poor (por) *adjective*
1 having very little money, property or
resources.
2 showing poverty: *a poor cottage.*
3 lacking something needed: *poor soil.*
□ *in poor health.* □ *a poor excuse.*

4 unfortunate: *That poor little bird has hurt its wing.*
Word Family **poorly** *adjective* in poor health; **poorly** *adverb* badly: *poorly planned*; **poorness** *noun*.
[Latin *pauper*]

poor box *noun* (*plural* **poor boxes**)
History a box in a church, courtroom, etc. in which money could be placed for distribution to poor people.

poorhouse *noun*
History a workhouse.

pop[1] *verb* (**pops**; **popping**; **popped**)
1 to make a short quick explosive sound: *The champagne cork popped loudly.*
2 to move, come or go suddenly or unexpectedly: *A rabbit popped up from its hole.*
3 to put quickly: *He popped the book straight into his bag.*
4 (of eyes) to stare, bulge.
Phrase **pop off** (*informal*) to die.
• **pop** *noun*
1 a short quick explosive sound.
2 (*informal*) any effervescent soft drink: *a glass of pop.*

pop[2] *noun* also called **pop music**.
commercially produced music with a strong beat, liked especially by young people.
• **pop** *adjective*.

popadom, popadum ⇨ POPPADOM.

pop art *noun*
a style of modern art using images of the everyday commercial world, such as advertising slogans, comic strips, etc.
[from POP(ular) + ART]

popcorn *noun*
the burst puffed kernels of maize after they have been heated, eaten either salted or sweetened as a snack.

pope *noun*
(**the Pope**) the bishop of Rome as the head of the Roman Catholic Church.
[Greek *pappas* father]

popery *noun*
1 the papal system.
2 ceremonies and teachings associated with Roman Catholicism.

pop-eyed *adjective*
(*informal*) having bulging or staring eyes.

popinjay *noun*
(*dated*) a conceited foppish person.
[Spanish *papagayo* a parrot]

popish (**po**-pish) *adjective*
Roman Catholic.

poplar *noun*
a tall quick-growing deciduous tree used for timber.
[Latin *populus*]

poplin *noun*
a woven fabric of cotton, and often polyester, with a corded surface.

pop music ⇨ POP[2].

poppadom (**pop**-a-dum) *noun* also **poppadom; popadom; poppadum; poppadum**
a round crisp wafer-thin bread made from lentils, usually eaten with Indian food.
[Hindi]

poppet *noun*
(*informal*) a term of endearment for a child.

poppy *noun* (*plural* **poppies**)
a plant with showy flowers, one variety of which is the source of opium.
[Latin *papaver*]

poppycock *noun*
(*dated informal*) nonsense.

populace (**pop**-yoo-lis) *noun*
the general public.

popular (**pop**-yoo-la) *adjective*
1 having widespread approval, favour or appreciation: *She's very popular.*
2 of, from or representing the people, especially the general population: *a popular revolutionary government.*
3 general, widespread or common: *popular superstitions.*
Word Family **popularity** (pop-yoo-**lar**-i-tee) *noun* the condition of being widely admired or liked; **popularly** *adverb*; **popularize, popularise** *verb* to make popular or interesting; **popularization** *noun*; **popularizer** *noun* a person who makes something popular or interesting.

popular front *noun*
Politics the joining of communist, socialist or other parties in a democratic or revolutionary movement, as against capitalism or fascism.

populate (**pop**-yoo-late) *verb*
1 to supply with inhabitants or a population.
2 to inhabit.

population (pop-yoo-**lay**-sh'n) *noun*
1 all the people, organisms or individuals of one biological species living in a certain region.
2 the act or process of populating.
3 *Maths* the total group of individuals, scores, etc. from which a sample is taken.

population density *noun*
the number of people in a given area,
usually measured in people per km².
[Latin *populus* people]

populist *noun*
a politician who campaigns for ordinary
people against an elite, big business, the
Establishment, etc.

populous (**pop**-yoo-lus) *adjective*
having a large population.
Word Family **populously** *adverb*;
populousness *noun*.

porcelain (**por**-sa-lin) *noun*
1 a type of pottery that is hard, white and
non-porous, made by firing clay at an
extremely high temperature.
2 cups, plates, ornaments, etc. made from
this.

porch *noun* (*plural* **porches**)
a roofed doorway or entrance to a
building.
[Latin *porticus* colonnade]

porcupine (**pork**-yoo-pine) *noun*
a large rodent covered with long protective
spines.
[Old French *porc* pig + *espin* spiny]

pore¹ *verb*
to study or look at closely and carefully:
He pored over the map.

pore² *noun*
a very small opening in a surface,
especially the skin, for absorbing or
emitting liquid, etc.
[Greek *poros* a passage]

pork *noun*
the flesh of a pig.
[Latin *porcus* pig]

porker *noun*
a young pig fattened for food.

porky *adjective* (**porkier**; **porkiest**)
(*informal*) fat.

pornography (por-**nog**-ra-fee) *noun*
short form is **porn** pictures or writing
produced to cause sexual excitement.
Word Family **pornographer** *noun*;
pornographic (por-no-**graf**-ik) *adjective*.
[Greek *pornographos* writing about
prostitutes]

porous (**paw**-rus) *adjective*
having pores which allow the passage of
gas or liquid: *porous rock*.
Word Family **porousness**, **porosity**
(paw-**ross**-i-tee) *noun*.

porphyry (**porf**-i-ree) *noun* (*plural*
porphyries)
Geology an igneous rock which has large
crystals scattered in a fine-grained
material.
[Latin *porphyrites* purple stone]

porpoise (**por**-pus *or* **por**-poice) *noun*
a small whale with a short round snout
and a triangular fin.
[Latin *porcus* pig + *piscis* fish]

porridge *noun*
a food made by boiling oatmeal and milk
or water to a thick paste.
[French]

> The word **porridge** is a development
> of *pottage*, a stew or soup. This in turn
> came from Old French *potage*,
> something cooked in a *pot* (a pot).

port¹ *noun*
a town with a harbour where ships load
and unload cargo.
Phrase **port of call** a place which is
briefly visited.
[Latin *portus*]

port² *noun*
the left side of a boat or aeroplane when
looking towards the front. Compare
STARBOARD.

port³ *noun* also **port wine**
a sweet fortified red wine.
[first shipped from *Oporto*, a city in
Portugal]

port⁴ *noun*
1 a porthole.
2 an opening for steam, liquid or gas to
pass through.
3 *Computers* a socket for a device: *a printer
port*.
[Latin *porta* a passage, gate]

portable *adjective*
able to be carried or moved easily: *a
portable television set*.
● **portable** *noun* something which is
portable.
[Latin *portare* to carry]

portal *noun*
1 a doorway or entrance, especially a large
or imposing one.
2 *Computers* an Internet site showing a lot
of links to other sites.

portal vein *noun*
Anatomy the large vein carrying blood rich
in digested food from the stomach and
intestines to the liver.

portcullis (port-**kull**-is) *noun* (*plural* **portcullises**)

a strong grating which can be let down to close a gateway to a castle or other fortified place.

[Old French *porte* door + *coleice* sliding]

portend (por **tend**) *verb*

to be an omen or warning of: *The black clouds portend a storm.*

portent (**por**-tent) *noun*

an indication or omen, especially of a disaster.

Word Family **portentous** (por-**ten**-tus) *adjective* 1 having the character of a portent. 2 solemn.

[Latin *portendere* to predict]

porter[1] *noun*

1 a person employed to carry luggage, e.g. in a railway station or hotel.

2 a person employed by a hospital to move equipment and patients around.

3 a dark brown beer containing malt which has been dried at a high temperature.

porter[2] *noun*

an employee in charge of the entrance to a block of flats, a hotel, etc.

porterhouse steak *noun*

a choice piece of upper cut of beef sirloin.

portfolio *noun*

1 a large thin flat case for carrying papers, letters or documents.

2 a selection of someone's work, e.g. drawings, chosen as a demonstration of his or her ability.

3 *Politics* the office or duties of a government minister.

[Italian *portare* to carry + *fogli* sheets or leaves]

porthole (**port**-hole) *noun*

a small circular window in the side of a ship to let in light and air.

portico (**por**-tik-o) *noun* (*plural* **porticoes** or **porticos**)

a roof supported by columns, forming an entrance to a building.

[Latin *porticus* colonnade]

portion (**por**-sh'n) *noun*

1 a section of a whole.

2 a share or allotment.

• **portion** *verb* to divide.

[from Latin]

portly *adjective* (**portlier**; **portliest**)

rather stout: *a portly gentleman.*

Word Family **portliness** *noun.*

portmanteau (port-**mant**-o) *noun* (*plural* **portmanteaus** or **portmanteaux** (port-**mant**-oze))

a large oblong piece of luggage which opens into two equal sections.

[French *porter* to carry + *manteau* a coat]

portmanteau word *noun*

a word coined by telescoping two words together: *The word 'chortle' is a portmanteau word formed from 'chuckle' and 'snort'.*

portrait (**por**-trit) *noun*

1 a painting, drawing or photograph of a person, usually showing the face.

2 a description, especially of a person.

3 a format where the sides of the page are larger than the top. Compare LANDSCAPE.

Word Family **portraiture** *noun* the art of making portraits; **portraitist** *noun.*

[Latin *protractus* revealed]

portray (por-**tray**) *verb*

to make a picture of or describe: *The painting portrayed a Mediterranean landscape.* □ *The book portrayed her as a lonely woman.*

Word Family **portrayal** *noun.*

Portuguese man-of-war *noun* (*plural* **Portuguese men-of-war**)

a marine animal related to the jellyfish, with a sail-like crest and a very painful sting.

port wine ⇨ PORT[3].

pose (poze) *verb*

1 to take up or hold a position, e.g. in front of a camera.

2 to represent oneself to others: *He poses as a connoisseur of wine.*

3 to act in an affected or pretentious way.

4 to put forward: *The examiner posed several difficult questions.*

5 to cause: *Lack of seating posed quite a problem at the play.*

• **pose** *noun*

1 a position or posture of the body: *Please make your pose more relaxed.*

2 an attitude or way of behaving, especially one designed to give a false impression: *She seems shy and vulnerable, but it is only a pose.*

Poseidon (poss-**eye**-d'n) *noun*

Greek mythology the god of the sea, identified with the Roman god Neptune.

poser[1] *noun*

a person who poses.

poser[2] *noun*

a puzzling problem or question.

poseur (po-zer) *noun*
a person who behaves in an affected manner to try to impress people.
[French]

posh *adjective*
(*informal*) stylish, high-class or upper-class: *a posh hotel.* □ *posh clothes.* □ *a posh accent.*
Word Family **poshness** *noun*.

> The word **posh** probably comes from a slang word meaning 'a dandy', although various other ideas have been put forward. These include the suggestion that it is based on the initials of *port out starboard home*, referring to the cooler and more expensive side of British ships which rich people preferred when travelling to and from India.

posit (poz-it) *verb*
to lay down or assume as a fact or as a basis for argument.
[Latin *positus* placed]

position (po-zi-sh'n) *noun*
1 the place where something is or belongs: *This car is parked in the wrong position.*
2 the way in which something is placed or arranged: *She had to sit in a cramped position.*
3 a situation: *The theft put the manager in a difficult position.*
4 a job: *We have several positions vacant.*
5 a point of view: *He wasn't willing to change his position on the issue.*
• **position** *verb* to put in a particular or correct position: *The general positioned his troops along the road.*

position vector *noun*
Maths a vector which represents the position of a point relative to an origin.

positive (poz-i-tiv) *adjective*
1 expressing agreement, acceptance or certainty: *a positive reply to the invitation.*
2 allowing no doubt or question: *The police have found positive proof of the murderer's identity.*
3 optimistic or hopeful: *positive thinking.*
4 *Maths* relating to a quantity greater than zero: *3 is a positive number.*
5 *Grammar* ⇨ DEGREE (definition 6).
6 *Electricity* having a deficiency of electrons.
• **positive** *noun*
1 something which is positive.
2 *Photography* an image on a developed film, in which the light and dark areas appear as photographed. Compare NEGATIVE *noun* (definition 2).

Word Family **positively** *adverb*; **positiveness** *noun*.

positive discrimination *noun*
a deliberate bias towards people who are usually discriminated against on the grounds of race, sex, etc.

positron *noun*
Physics a particle having the same mass as an electron and an opposite charge.
[POSIT(ive) + (elect)RON]

posse (poss-ee) *noun*
1 *American* (*formerly*) a force of men called in to help an officer of the law in an emergency.
2 (*informal*) a group of people.
[shortening of Medieval Latin *posse comitatus* county force]

possess (po-zess) *verb*
1 to hold, keep or control as one's own: *Do you possess many books?*
2 (*formal*) to take over, dominate: *Rage possessed her at the sight of such cruelty.*
Word Family **possessor** *noun*; **possessed** *adjective* obsessed or strongly affected, e.g. by a supernatural force.
[from Latin]

possession (po-zesh-'n) *noun*
1 the act of possessing.
2 the state of being possessed.
3 anything which is possessed: *That ring is my most valuable possession.*

possessive (po-zess-iv) *adjective*
1 wanting to possess someone totally: *She is very possessive and won't let him even speak to other women.*
2 unwilling to share things.
3 *Grammar* indicating or relating to possession: '*His*' is a possessive pronoun.
Word Family **possessively** *adverb*; **possessiveness** *noun*.

posset (poss-it) *noun*
a spiced drink made of hot milk curdled with wine or spirits.

possible *adjective*
1 capable of being, being done or happening: *It is possible to go to the moon.*
2 able or likely to be true: *It is possible that she swam that far.*
Word Family **possibly** *adverb*; **possibility** (poss-i-bil-i-tee) *noun* (*plural* **possibilities**) 1 the fact of being possible. 2 something that is possible.

possum *noun*
1 an Australasian marsupial which lives in trees and has a long tail.
2 *American* an opossum.

Phrase **play possum** to pretend to be unaware, asleep or dead.

post¹ *noun*
1 an upright piece of wood or metal used as a support, etc.
2 a starting post or winning post for a race.
• **post** *verb*
1 to stick or display: *Post no advertisements on this wall.*
2 to announce, declare or publish: *Five sailors were posted as missing after the storm.*
[Latin *postis* a doorpost]

post² *noun*
1 the system of sending, collecting and delivering letters and parcels, usually organized by a government department or a large company.
2 letters or parcels distributed in this way.
• **post** *verb* to send or place something for delivery by post.
Phrase **keep someone posted** to keep someone informed.
Word Family **postal** *adjective*.
[Latin *positus* placed]

post³ *noun*
1 a position or appointment.
2 the position where a sentry is stationed.
• **post** *verb* to appoint or station to a place or position: *Two guards were posted behind the bank.* □ *The solicitor was posted to the Hong Kong office.*

postage (poast-ij) *noun*
the cost of sending letters, etc. by post.

postage stamp *noun*
a small printed label attached to an envelope or parcel as evidence that postage has been paid.

postal order *noun*
a type of money order, in various fixed denominations, bought and cashable at any post office.

postbox *noun* (*plural* **postboxes**)
a fixed container into which letters are posted, to be sorted and delivered by the post office.

postcard *noun*
a card, usually with a picture on one side, which can be sent by post without an envelope.

postcode *noun*
a system by which districts or towns are given a code number in order to speed the sorting of the post.

post-date *verb*
1 to write a future date on: *to post-date a cheque.*
2 to come after in time: *The skeleton post-dates the building of the church.*

poster *noun*
a large printed sheet of paper or card, often illustrated, used as an announcement or advertisement, or for decoration.

poste restante (poast ress-**tont**) *noun*
a department in a post office where letters are kept until collected.
[French, post remaining]

posterior (pos-**teer**-i-a) *adjective*
1 relating to or situated at the rear or behind. Compare ANTERIOR (definition 1).
2 (*formal*) coming later in time or position.
• **posterior** *noun* the buttocks.
[Latin, following after]

posterity (pos-**terr**-i-tee) *noun*
the future time or future generations.

postgraduate (poast-**grad**-yew-it) *adjective*
(of study) beyond the level of a first degree.
• **postgraduate** *noun* a person engaged in such study. Compare GRADUATE.

post-haste *adverb*
as fast as possible: *I'll do it post-haste.*

posthumous (pos-tew-mus) *adjective*
occurring, continuing or given after one's death: *The soldier received a posthumous award for bravery.*
Word Family **posthumously** *adverb*.
[Latin *postumus* last (confused with *humus* ground, grave)]

postilion (pos-**til**-y'n) *noun* also **postillion**
a person who rides one of the horses which is pulling a carriage, to help guide the team.

Post-it *noun*
(*trademark*) a small piece of paper with an adhesive edge for sticking to a surface. It can be removed without damaging the surface, and is used for leaving messages and reminders.

postman *noun* (*plural* **postmen**)
a man employed by a post office to carry and deliver the post.

postmark *noun*
a mark stamped on an envelope over the postage stamp, usually showing when and where the letter was posted.
• **postmark** *verb*.

postmaster *noun*
the official in charge of a post office.

post meridiem (poast me-**rid**-i-em)
adverb
the time after midday. *abbrev.* p.m.
Compare ANTE MERIDIEM.
[Latin, after midday]

postmistress *noun* (*plural*
postmistresses)
a woman in charge of a post office.

post-mortem *noun*
1 also called **autopsy**. an inspection and
dissection of a body after death to
determine the cause of death.
2 an inquiry or examination carried out
after an event.
[Latin, after death]

post-natal *adjective*
of or happening in the period immediately
after birth. Compare ANTENATAL.

post office *noun*
1 the company or department of
government responsible for a country's
postal and telecommunication services.
2 an office or building in which letters, etc.
are received, sorted and sent out, stamps
are sold, etc.

post-operative *adjective*
of or relating to the time or events after a
surgical operation.

postpone *verb*
to cause to occur at a date later than
planned or expected: *We had to postpone the
wedding because of the bride's accident.*
Word Family **postponement** *noun*.
[*post-* + Latin *ponere* to place]

postscript *noun*
1 a sentence, note or paragraph added at
the end of a letter, after the signature.
2 something additional, an extra part.
[*post-* + Latin *scriptum* written]

post-traumatic stress disorder *noun*
a psychological disorder involving anxiety,
depression or withdrawal occurring after a
traumatic experience e.g. an accident.

postulant (**pos**-tew-l'nt) *noun*
a candidate for admission to a religious
order.

postulate (**pos**-tew-late) *verb*
to assume without proof, especially as the
basis of an argument.
Word Family **postulate** *noun* something
which is postulated, such as a principle;
postulation *noun* the act of postulating.
[Latin *postulatus* claimed]

posture (**pos**-cher) *noun*
1 the arrangement or position of the body:
an awkward posture. □ *These exercises will
improve your posture.*
2 an attitude towards something: *a defiant
posture.*
[from Latin]

postviral syndrome *noun* also **postviral
fatigue syndrome**
myalgic encephalomyelitis occurring after
someone has had a viral infection.

postwoman *noun* (*plural* **postwomen**)
a woman employed by a post office to
carry and deliver the post.

posy (**po**-zee) *noun* (*plural* **posies**)
a small bunch of flowers.

pot¹ *noun*
1 a round deep container: *a cooking pot.*
□ *a flowerpot.*
2 (*dated*) a potty.
3 (*informal*) a pot belly.
4 a common fund shared by several
people, such as the total amount of money
bet by all the players for one hand of cards.
Phrase **go to pot** (*informal*) to lessen in
or lose quality, etc.: *The housework went to
pot while I was ill.*
● **pot** *verb* (**pots; potting; potted**)
1 to place or plant in a pot.
2 to preserve food in a pot: *potted shrimps.*
3 to make items out of pottery.
4 (*informal*) to shoot.
5 *Billiards, Snooker* to hit a ball into a
pocket.

pot² *noun* (*informal*) cannabis.

potable (**poe**-ta-b'l) *adjective*
suitable for drinking.
[Latin *potare* to drink]

potash *noun*
either potassium carbonate or potassium
hydroxide, both of which are strongly
alkaline.
[as it was first obtained by evaporating
leached *ashes* in a *pot*]

potassium (pot-**ass**-i-um) *noun*
a soft strongly reactive metal. Its
compounds are essential to life and are
used as fertilizers and in liquid soaps.
Word Family **potassic** *adjective*.
[as it was first discovered in *potash*]

potato *noun* (*plural* **potatoes**)
a medium-sized white tuber growing
under the ground and used as a vegetable.
[Haitian *batata* sweet potato]

potato crisp ⇨ CRISP.

pot belly *noun* (*plural* **pot bellies**)
a large abdomen.
Word Family pot-bellied *adjective*.

potboiler *noun*
(*informal*) a work of literature or art
produced quickly for financial gain.
[as this was done to keep the *pot
boiling*, that is to get food]

potent (po-t'nt) *adjective*
1 full of power or strength: *a potent remedy*.
2 having the ability to perform sexual
intercourse, not impotent.
Word Family potency *noun* the quality of
being potent or powerful; **potently** *adverb*.
[Latin *potens* capable]

potentate (po-t'n-tate) *noun*
a person with great power, such as a ruler
or dictator.

potential (po-ten-sh'l) *adjective*
possible future: *a potential champion
swimmer*.
• **potential** *noun*
1 a likely ability or capacity: *She already
shows great potential as a singer.* □ *This room
has great potential.*
2 *Electricity* the amount of electric charge
on a body with respect to earth, which is
considered to have zero potential.
Word Family potentially *adverb*;
potentiality (po-ten-shi-**al**-i-tee) *noun* a
possibility.

potential difference *noun*
Electricity the difference in potential
between two bodies. If they are connected
together, electric charge will flow between
them.

potential energy *noun*
Physics the energy a body possesses
because of its position in an electric,
magnetic or gravitational field, or because
of how its parts are arranged. Compare
KINETIC ENERGY.

pothole (pot-hole) *noun*
1 a hole, e.g. in a road surface.
2 an underground cavern, especially one
eroded in limestone by underground
streams.
Word Family potholing *noun* the
exploration of potholes; **potholer** *noun*.

potion (poe-sh'n) *noun*
a liquid with medicinal or magical effects.

pot luck *noun*
a random or chance choice: *We couldn't
book seats in advance, so we took pot luck.*

pot-pourri (po-poo-ree) *noun*
1 a mixture of dried petals with herbs or
spices, kept for its fragrant scent.
2 any mixture of unrelated or
miscellaneous things.
[French *pot* pot + *pourri* rotten, originally
meaning a stew made with different
meats]

pot roast *noun*
a large piece of meat which is cooked
slowly in a small amount of water in a
covered pot, often with vegetables.
Word Family pot-roast *verb*.

potsherd (pot-sherd) *noun*
a fragment of pottery, such as is found in
an archaeological excavation.

pot shot *noun*
a wild or random shot.

pottage (pot-ij) *noun*
soup or stew.

potted *adjective*
1 preserved in a pot.
2 shortened or condensed: *a potted history
of the town*.

potter[1] *verb*
1 to move or act slowly or aimlessly.
2 to pass time in a relaxed manner.

potter[2] *noun*
a person who makes pottery.

potter's wheel *noun*
a rotating metal or wooden disc on which
a potter shapes clay.

pottery *noun* (*plural* **potteries**)
1 the art or business of making cups,
ornaments, etc. by shaping and firing clay.
2 cups, bowls, etc. made of pottery.
3 a place or factory where pottery is made.

potty[1] *adjective* (**pottier; pottiest**)
1 (*informal*) mad or foolish: *His whingeing
drove me potty*.
2 (*informal*) very keen: *She's potty about
pigs*.
Word Family pottiness *noun*.

potty[2] *noun* (*plural* **potties**)
(*informal*) a bowl with a handle, for use as
a toilet, especially by very young children.

pouch *noun* (*plural* **pouches**)
1 a small bag to hold miscellaneous small
items.
2 a loose or sagging fold of skin under the
eye.
3 *Biology* a pocket-like part of an animal,
especially one used to carry the young of a
marsupial.

pouf *noun*
1 ⇨ POOF.
2 ⇨ POUFFE.

pouffe (*rhymes with* roof) *noun* also **pouf**
a large thick cushion used as a seat.
[French]

poulterer (pole-ta-ra) *noun*
a person who sells poultry.

poultice (pole-tis) *noun*
a soft warm moist dressing, applied to
sores or inflamed parts of the body for
relief.
• **poultice** *verb* to apply a poultice to.
[Latin *pultis* of pottage]

poultry (pole-tree) *noun*
chickens, turkeys, ducks and geese.
[Latin *pullus* chicken]

pounce (*rhymes with* bounce) *verb*
to spring at or seize suddenly: *The cat
pounced on the trembling mouse.*
• **pounce** *noun* a sudden spring or swoop.

pound¹ *verb*
1 to beat or strike heavily and repeatedly:
He pounded desperately on the door.
2 to crush: *Pound the nuts with a rolling pin.*
3 to run heavily or noisily: *The children
pounded along the corridor.*
4 to throb: *My heart was pounding.*

pound² *noun*
1 a unit of mass in the avoirdupois system,
equal to 16 ounces, or about 0·454 kg.
abbrev. lb.
2 a unit of mass in the apothecaries' and
troy systems equal to about 0·373 kg.
abbrev. lb.
3 also **pound sterling** the basic unit of
money in the UK.
4 the basic unit of money in Egypt, Syria,
Cyprus and certain other countries.
[Latin *pondo* a pound weight]

pound³ *noun*
1 a place where stray animals are confined.
2 a place where confiscated goods, e.g.
cars which have been towed away, are
kept.

pour (*rhymes with* door) *verb*
1 to cause to flow or stream: *Pour that milk
into a cup.*
2 to flow strongly: *The flooding river poured
over its banks.*
3 to rain heavily: *It's pouring, so take your
coat.*

pout (*rhymes with* out) *verb*
to push out the lips in a disappointed or
sullen expression.
• **pout** *noun.*

poverty (pov-a-tee) *noun*
1 the state of having little or no money or
resources except for the most basic needs.

2 the state of voluntarily giving up
personal possessions and income, as in
certain religious orders.
3 (*formal*) a shortage or lack: *a poverty of
imagination.*
[Latin *paupertas*]

powder *noun*
1 very fine particles of a substance which
has been crushed, ground, etc.
2 any of various substances prepared in
this form: *talcum powder.*
3 gunpowder.
• **powder** *verb*
1 to crush or reduce to powder.
2 to apply or cover with powder: *The
actress powdered her cheeks.*
Word Family powdery *adjective* of, like
or covered with powder.
[Latin *pulvis* dust]

powder blue *noun*
a pale greyish-blue colour.

powder monkey *noun*
History a ship's boy who took gunpowder
to the guns.

powder puff *noun*
a soft pad of cotton wool or fabric for
putting powder on the face or body.

powder room *noun*
a women's cloakroom and toilet in a
restaurant or other public building.

power *noun*
1 the ability to act or do: *Most birds have
the power of flight.* □ *I'll do all in my power to
help.*
2 great force, might or superiority: *political
power.*
3 energy available for doing work, such as
that supplied by machinery as distinct
from humans or animals.
4 *Physics* mechanical or electrical energy:
horsepower.
5 *Maths* ⇨ EXPONENT (definition 2).
Phrase **the powers that be** those in the
positions of power.
• **power** *verb* to provide with the means of
operation or activity: *The machines are all
powered by electricity.*

powerboat *noun*
a fast motor boat which moves on the
surface of the water rather than through it.

powerful *adjective*
having, producing or exerting power:
a powerful man. □ *a powerful computer.*
Word Family powerfully *adverb*;
powerfulness *noun.*

powerless *adjective*
having no power: *I was powerless to stop them fighting.*
Word Family powerlessly *adverb*;
powerlessness *noun.*

power of attorney *noun*
a legal authority given by one person to another, to act on his or her behalf.

power station *noun*
a place where electrical power is generated.

powwow *noun*
1 a ceremony among Native Americans.
2 (*informal*) any meeting or conference.

pox *noun* (*plural* **poxes**)
1 a viral disease that produces pimples filled with pus which can leave pockmarks: *chickenpox.*
2 (**the pox**) *History* smallpox.
3 (**the pox**) (*informal*) syphilis.

practicable (**prak**-tik-a-b'l) *adjective*
able to be done or put into practice: *Think of a practicable plan.*
Word Family practicably *adverb*;
practicability (prak-tik-a-**bill**-i-tee) *noun.*

practical *adjective*
1 relating to or resulting from practice, action or use: *Does your invention have any practical value?* □ *Do you have any practical experience in this field?*
2 taking a realistic approach: *You can count on Ruth to be practical.*
3 good at manual jobs.
4 virtual: *a practical certainty.*
Word Family practically *adverb* 1 in a practical manner. 2 nearly or almost;
practicality *noun* (*plural* **practicalities**).
[Greek *praktikos* fit for action]

practical joke *noun*
a trick played on someone for fun.

practice (**prak**-tis) *noun*
1 repeated effort or experience to improve a skill: *It takes years of practice to play golf well.*
2 action or performance: *How will your plan turn out in practice?*
3 the usual or customary way in which something is done: *It is the practice in some countries to marry young.*
4 the business of a professional person: *a doctor's practice.*
Phrase **out of practice** below one's usual form from lack of recent practice.

> **!** Do not confuse the noun *practice*, as in *football practice*, with the verb *practise*, as in *to practise the piano*. The noun ends in *ce* and the verb ends in *se* (like *licence/license* and *advice/advise*). In American English both the noun and the verb are spelt *practice*.

practise (**prak**-tis) *verb* (American **practice**)
1 to work at repeatedly to improve a skill: *practising the piano.*
2 to make a habit of: *He tries to practise being truthful at all times.*
3 to conduct or exercise a profession, etc.: *She practises medicine at the clinic.*
4 to live by the rules of a religion: *He is not a practising Catholic.*
Word Family practised *adjective*
experienced or skilful.

> **!** Do not confuse *practise* with PRACTICE.

practitioner (prak-**tish**-'n-a) *noun*
a person who practises a profession: *A doctor is a medical practitioner.*

praeternatural ⇨ PRETERNATURAL.

pragmatic (prag-**mat**-ik) *adjective*
matter-of-fact, concerned with practical ideas and results: *a pragmatic approach.*
Word Family pragmatism (**prag**-ma-tizm) *noun* 1 the quality of being pragmatic. 2 *Philosophy* the belief that the truth or merit of an idea should be judged by its practical results; **pragmatist** *noun* a pragmatic person; **pragmatically** *adverb*
[Greek *pragmatikos* relating to fact]

prairie (**prair**-ee) *noun*
a large area of grassland in North America.
[Latin *pratum* meadow]

prairie dog *noun*
a burrowing squirrel with a short tail, found in the open plains of North America.

praise (praze) *verb*
1 to express approval or admiration of: *The teacher praised my handwriting.*
2 to worship: *praising God.*
● **praise** *noun*
1 admiration or approval which is offered or expressed.
2 worship.
Word Family praiseworthy *adjective*
admirable.
[Latin *pretium* value]

pram *noun*
a comfortable four-wheeled carriage for a
baby.
[shortening of PERAMBULATOR]

prance *verb*
to walk or move with a springing or
bounding movement.
Word Family **prance** *noun*; **prancingly**
adverb.

prang *noun*
(*informal*) a crash, especially a minor car
crash.
● **prang** *verb*.

prank *noun*
a playful trick.
Word Family **prankster** *noun* a person
who plays pranks.

prate *verb*
to talk long and foolishly.

prattle *verb*
to talk quickly or chatter childishly.
● **prattle** *noun* childish talk.

prawn *noun*
a shrimp-like aquatic animal.

pray *verb*
1 to address a god or saint as an act of
worship or entreaty: *He prayed for a
miracle.*
2 to wish or hope for something.

prayer (*rhymes with* hair) *noun*
1 the act of praying: *He closed his eyes in
prayer.*
2 an address to a god or saint: *a prayer of
thanks.*
3 a wish or hope.
Phrase **not have a prayer** (*informal*) not
to have any chance at all.
[Latin *precari* to entreat]

praying mantis ⇨ MANTIS.

preach *verb*
1 to deliver a sermon.
2 to teach or proclaim in support of an
action or idea: *She preaches moderation as a
way of life.*
[Latin *praedicare* to proclaim]

preacher *noun*
a person who preaches, especially a
Christian minister.

preamble (pree-**am**-b'l *or* **pree**-am-b'l)
noun
an introductory statement, especially at
the beginning of a book or document.
[*pre-* + Latin *ambulare* to walk]

pre-arrange *verb*
to arrange beforehand.
Word Family **pre-arrangement** *noun*.

Precambrian (pree-**cam**-bri-an) *adjective*
relating to a geological period which
ended about 570 million years ago.

precarious (pri-**kair**-i-us) *adjective*
uncertain, insecure or unsafe: *He had a
precarious position on top of the ladder.*
Word Family **precariously** *adverb*;
precariousness *noun*.
[Latin]

> The word **precarious** derives from
> Latin *precarius*, meaning 'obtained by
> asking or praying'. In English it was
> originally a legal term, meaning
> 'dependent on another's will or favour'.
> Since this was obviously an uncertain
> situation, the word came to mean
> 'chancy' and then 'risky'.

precast (pree-**kahst**) *adjective*
Building shaped or constructed before
being placed in position: *precast concrete.*

precaution (pri-**kaw**-sh'n) *noun*
1 care taken in advance to guard against
something undesirable: *Lock the house as a
precaution against thieves.*
2 (**precautions**) (*informal*) the use of
some form of contraception.
Word Family **precautionary** *adjective*.
[*pre-* + Latin *cautus* on guard]

precede (pree-**seed**) *verb*
to come or go before: *Spring precedes
summer.*

> [!] Do not confuse *precede* with
> *proceed*. *Proceed* means 'to start' or
> 'to continue', as in *He proceeded to
> explain how it worked.*

precedence (**press**-i-d'nce) *noun*
the right to precede or go first: *You will
have to wait because I have precedence.*

precedent (**press**-i-d'nt) *noun*
a case or action which serves as a guide or
justification in later cases: *If I don't punish
you it will set a precedent, and others will want
to be let off too.*
[*pre-* + Latin *cedens* going]

precept (**pree**-sept) *noun*
a moral instruction or rule of action: *The
precept not to kill is common to most religions.*
Word Family **preceptive** *adjective*.

precinct (**pree**-sinkt) *noun*
1 the area immediately around any place,
such as the grounds of a church or the
environs of a town.
2 an area restricted for a particular group
or activity: *a shopping precinct.*
3 *American* a police or electoral district.
[Latin *praecinctum* an enclosure]

precious (**presh**-us) *adjective*
1 extremely valuable: *A diamond is a precious stone.*
2 much loved or treasured: *Every moment we spend together is precious.*
• **precious** *adverb*
Phrase precious little very little: *We have precious little time left.*
Word Family preciously *adverb*; **preciousness** *noun*.
[Latin *pretium* price]

precipice (**press**-i-piss) *noun*
a very steep edge of a cliff.
[Latin *praeceps* headlong]

precipitant (pri-**sip**-i-t'nt) *noun*
Chemistry a substance causing precipitation.

precipitate (pri-**sip**-i-tate) *verb*
1 to make something happen more quickly: *Swearing at the boss precipitated his dismissal.* □ *The border clash precipitated the two countries into war.*
2 (of water vapour) to condense and fall as rain, hail, dew, etc.
3 *Chemistry* to separate a solid from a solution.
• **precipitate** (pri-**sip**-i-t't) *adjective*
extremely fast or sudden: *moving with precipitate speed.* □ *Are you sure your decision is not too precipitate?*
• **precipitate** (pri-**sip**-i-t't or pri-**sip**-i-tate) *noun Chemistry* an insoluble substance formed from a solution as a result of a chemical reaction.
Word Family precipitately *adverb*.

precipitation (pri-sip-i-**tay**-sh'n) *noun*
1 *Chemistry* the action or process of precipitating.
2 *Weather* any condensed moisture, such as rain or dew.
3 *Weather* the total amount of rain, snow, sleet and hail which falls at a location during a given period.

precipitous (pri-**sip**-it-us) *adjective*
extremely steep, like a precipice.

precis (**pray**-see) *noun* (*plural* **precis**) (**pray**-seez)
a summary.
• **precis** *verb* to summarize, e.g. a piece of writing.
[French]

precise (pri-**sice**) *adjective*
1 accurate: *Give me precise directions how to get there.*
2 taking care over details: *She couldn't stand his precise ways.*
3 exact: *at that precise moment.*

Word Family precisely *adverb*.
[Latin *praecisus* cut short]

precision (pri-**sizh**-'n) *noun*
accuracy: *She remembered the details with precision.*

preclude (pri-**klood**) *verb*
(of a previous action, etc.) to exclude or make impossible as a consequence: *The suicide note precluded the possibility of murder.*
Word Family preclusive *adjective*; **preclusion** *noun*.
[*pre-* + Latin *claudere* to shut]

precocious (pri-**ko**-shus) *adjective*
developed very early, especially in relation to others of the same age.
Word Family precociously *adverb*; **precociousness, precocity** (pre-**koss**-i-tee) *noun*.
[Latin *praecox* ripe before its time]

preconceived (pree-kon-**seevd**) *adjective*
formed in advance: *He had a preconceived idea of what the job would be like.*
Word Family preconception (pree-kon-**sep**-sh'n) *noun* a preconceived idea or opinion.

precondition *noun*
a condition or requirement that must be fulfilled before a certain result is obtained.

precursor (pri-**ker**-sa) *noun*
a person or thing that precedes: *This law is a precursor of many more reforms.*
Word Family precursory *adjective*
preceding or introductory.
[*pre-* + Latin *currere* to run]

pre-date *verb*
to precede in time: *This civilization pre-dates that one.*

predator (**pred**-a-ta) *noun*
1 *Biology* a carnivorous animal that hunts and eats other animals.
2 a person who uses other people.
Word Family predatory *adjective* of or like a predator.
[Latin *praeda* booty, plunder]

predecease (pree-di-**seece**) *verb*
(*formal*) to die before: *Most parents predecease their children.*

predecessor (**pree**-di-sess-a) *noun*
1 a previous holder of a position: *My predecessor retired after 40 years in office.*
2 any person or thing that precedes, such as an ancestor.
[*pre-* + Latin *decessor* a retiring official]

predestination (pree-des-ti-**nay**-sh'n)
noun
Christianity the act of God deciding the outcome of all events or actions before they occur, including whether a person is to go to heaven.

predestine (pree-**des**-tin) *verb*
to ordain or decree beforehand: *The plan was predestined to succeed.*

predetermine (pree-di-**ter**-min) *verb*
to decide beforehand: *We followed a predetermined plan.*
Word Family **predetermination** *noun.*

predicament (pri-**dik**-a-m'nt) *noun*
a difficult or unpleasant situation.

predicate (**pred**-i-kit) *noun*
Grammar a group of words in a sentence telling something about the subject: *In 'The girl wore a red hat', 'wore a red hat' is the predicate.*
• **predicate** (**pred**-i-kate) *verb* to declare or assert.
Word Family **predication** *noun;* **predicative** (pri-**dik**-a-tiv) *adjective.*
[Latin *praedicare* to proclaim]

predict (pri-**dikt**) *verb*
to say in advance that something will happen: *The forecast predicted rain.*
Word Family **prediction** (pri-**dik**-sh'n) *noun* 1 the act of predicting. 2 an instance of this: *Her prediction of her results was correct;* **predictable** *adjective;* **predictability** *noun.*
[*pre-* + Latin *dicere* to say]

predilection (pree-di-**lek**-sh'n) *noun*
a preference or liking.
[*pre-* + Latin *dilectus* chosen]

predispose (pree-dis-**poze**) *verb*
to render subject or liable: *Old age predisposed her to illness.*
Word Family **predisposition** *noun.*

predominate (pri-**dom**-i-nate) *verb*
to be strongest in power or influence: *The desire for revenge predominated as a motive for murder.*
Word Family **predominant** *adjective*
1 being the strongest or main element of something: *Red is the predominant colour in the design.* 2 having the most power or influence: *It is the predominant political party in the country;* **predominantly** *adverb;* **predominance** *noun.*

pre-eminent *adjective*
most distinguished or superior: *The professor is the pre-eminent scholar of the decade.*

Word Family **pre-eminently** *adverb;* **pre-eminence** *noun.*
[*pre-* + Latin *eminere* to stand out]

pre-empt *verb*
1 to do something in order to stop something happening: *She pre-empted his tantrum by offering him an apple.*
2 to buy or obtain something before others have the chance.
3 *Cards* to make a bid in bridge high enough to prevent the opposition bidding.
Word Family **pre-emptive** *adjective* intended to pre-empt; **pre-emption** *noun* the act or right of pre-empting.
[*pre-* + Latin *emptus* bought]

preen *verb*
1 (of a bird) to smooth its feathers with its beak.
2 (of a person) to arrange the hair or clothes with great care and attention.
3 to pride or congratulate oneself.

pre-exist *verb*
1 to exist beforehand.
2 to exist in a previous life or form.
Word Family **pre-existent** *adjective;* **pre-existence** *noun.*

prefab (**pree**-fab) *noun*
(*informal*) a prefabricated house or other building.

prefabricate (pree-**fab**-ri-kate) *verb*
to build parts in a factory so that they can be assembled elsewhere.
Word Family **prefabrication** *noun.*

preface (**pref**-us) *noun*
the explanatory notes by the author at the beginning of a book, giving details such as the origin, scope and reason for the book. Compare FOREWORD.
• **preface** *verb* to introduce.
Word Family **prefatory** (**pref**-a-tree) *adjective* of or like a preface.
[Latin *praefatio* a saying beforehand]

prefect (**pree**-fekt) *noun*
1 a senior pupil with authority to help keep order in a school.
2 any person appointed to supervise or govern, such as a provincial governor in ancient Rome or a district administrator in modern France.
Word Family **prefecture** *noun* 1 the office or term of office of a prefect. 2 an administrative area in France, etc.
[Latin *praefectus* overseer]

prefer *verb* (**prefers; preferring; preferred**)
1 to like better: *Do you prefer tea or coffee?*

2 (*formal*) to put forward or submit: *to prefer a legal charge.*
Word Family preferable (**pref**-ra-b'l) *adjective* better or more desirable: *Tuesday would be preferable;* **preferably** *adverb;* **preferability** *noun.*
[Latin *praeferre* to carry or place before]

preference (**pref**-r'nce) *noun*
1 the act of preferring: *I stated my preference for tea.*
2 something which is preferred: *My preference was tea.*
3 an advantage or favour, such as granted by one country to another in trade.

preferential (pref-a-**rcn**-sh'l) *adjective* showing or giving preference: *One pupil seemed to be getting preferential treatment.*

preferment (pre-**fer**-m'nt) *noun* appointment or promotion: *His preferment to archbishop took ten years.*

prefix *noun* (*plural* **prefixes**)
Grammar one or more syllables attached to the beginning of a word to form another word.

pregnant *adjective*
1 having a fetus in the womb.
2 significant: *a pregnant pause.*
Word Family pregnancy *noun* (*plural* **pregnancies**) the state or a time of being pregnant.
[*pre*- + Latin *gnasci* to be born]

prehensile (pri-**hen**-sile) *adjective* adapted for grasping or holding: *A possum clings to branches with its prehensile tail.*
[*pre*- + Latin *hensus* grasped]

prehistoric (pree-his-**torr**-ik) *adjective* before recorded history.

prejudge *verb* to form an opinion before hearing all the evidence.
Word Family prejudgement, **prejudgment** *noun.*

prejudice (**prej**-oo-dis) *noun*
1 an opinion formed without reason, knowledge or experience: *He has a prejudice against Australians.*
2 *Law* harm or injury that may result from an action: *The prisoner was treated without prejudice to his rights.*
• **prejudice** *verb*
1 to affect with a prejudice: *His speech prejudiced me in his favour.*
2 to affect unfavourably: *to prejudice an issue.*
Word Family prejudicial (prej-oo-**dish**-'l) *adjective* causing prejudice or disadvantage.

prelate (**prel**-'t) *noun*
(*formal*) a bishop or archbishop.
Word Family prelacy *noun* (*plural* **prelacies**) **1** the system of church government by prelates. **2** a prelate's office or rank.
[Latin *praelatus* borne in front]

preliminary (pri-**lim**-in-ree) *adjective* introductory or preparatory: *First I shall make a preliminary statement.*
• **preliminary** *noun* (*plural* **preliminaries**) anything which is preliminary.
[*pre*- + Latin *liminis* of a threshold]

prelude (**prel**-yood) *noun*
1 something which introduces or prepares for a later, more important event.
2 *Music* an introductory piece, such as an overture.
[*pre*- + Latin *ludere* to play]

premature (**prem**-a-cher) *adjective* occurring before the proper or usual time: *a premature baby.*
Word Family prematurely *adverb;* **prematurate** *noun.*

premeditate (pree-**med**-i-tate) *verb* to consider or plan beforehand: *The jury found that the killing was not premeditated.*
Word Family premeditation *noun.*

premier (**prem**-i-a *or* **pree**-mi-a) *noun* a leader of government; a Prime Minister.
• **premier** *adjective* chief or most important: *the premier league.*
Word Family premiership *noun* the position or term of office of a premier.
[French, first]

premiere (prem-i-**air**) *noun* the first public performance of a play, film, etc.
[French, first]

premise (**prem**-is) *noun* also **premiss** (*plural* **premisses**)
a proposition or assumption which is used as the basis for an argument or a conclusion.

premises (**prem**-iss-iz) *plural noun* a building and its grounds: *No dogs are allowed on the premises.*

premium (**pree**-mi-um) *noun*
1 the amount of money paid for an insurance policy, loan, etc.
2 a bonus or extra amount, such as the amount by which shares are selling above their established value.
Phrases at a premium 1 at a high price.
2 in high demand. **put a premium on,** **place a premium on** to value

particularly: *He places a premium on careful driving.*
[Latin *praemium* booty, reward]

Premium Bond *noun*
a British government bond that instead of earning interest is entered into monthly draws for cash prizes.

premolar ⇨ BICUSPID.

premonition (prem-a-**ni**-sh'n) *noun*
a feeling that something is to occur.
Word Family premonitory (pree-**mon**-a-tree) *adjective*.
[*pre-* + Latin *monere* to advise]

prenatal (pree-**nay**-t'l) *adjective*
relating to the time before birth.

prenuptial agreement (pree-nup-sh'l er-**gree**-ment) *noun*
an agreement between a couple who are about to marry detailing how their money and possessions will be split up if they divorce.

preoccupy (pree-**ok**-yoo-pie) *verb*
(**preoccupies; preoccupying; preoccupied**)
to take up all one's attention: *preoccupied with financial worries.*
Word Family preoccupation (pree-ok-yoo-**pay**-sh'n) *noun* **1** the state of being preoccupied. **2** something which preoccupies.

preordain *verb*
to ordain or decree beforehand.

prep *noun*
(*informal*) homework, or a period of time assigned for homework.

preparation (prep-a-**ray**-sh'n) *noun*
1 the act or process of preparing: *Preparations for the voyage were under way.*
2 something which is prepared: *a herbal preparation for insomnia.*

preparatory (pre-**parr**-a-tree) *adjective*
serving to prepare: *to make a few preparatory arrangements.*

preparatory school *noun*
an independent primary school which prepares children aged between seven and thirteen for public school.

prepare *verb*
to make or get ready: *I prepared myself for the interview.* □ *Will you prepare lunch?*
Phrase be prepared to do something to be willing to do something: *He wasn't prepared to put up with that sort of behaviour.*
Word Family preparedness *noun*.
[*pre-* + Latin *parare* to make ready]

prepay *verb* (**prepays; prepaying; prepaid**)
to pay in advance: *A year's Internet access has been prepaid.*
Word Family prepayment *noun*.

preponderant (pri-**pon**-da-r'nt) *adjective*
superior in size, numbers, power, etc.
Word Family preponderance *noun*;
preponderantly *adverb*; **preponderate** *verb*.

preposition (prep-a-**zish**-'n) *noun*
Grammar a word used before a noun or pronoun which shows how it relates to another word in the sentence: *In the sentence 'I walked through the forest', 'through' is a preposition.*
Word Family prepositional *adjective*.

prepossessing (pree-po-**zess**-ing) *adjective*
looking attractive or appealing: *a prepossessing child.*

preposterous (pri-**pos**-ta-rus) *adjective*
totally unreasonable or absurd.
Word Family preposterously *adverb*;
preposterousness *noun*.
[Latin *praeposterus* inverted]

prep school *noun*
a preparatory school.

prepuce ⇨ FORESKIN.

prequel (**pree**-kw'l) *noun*
a story or film which shows what happened before one which had been published or released earlier. Compare SEQUEL.

prerequisite (pree-**rek**-wi-zit) *noun*
something that is required as a special qualification or condition.
● **prerequisite** *adjective*.

prerogative (pri-**rog**-a-tiv) *noun*
a special right or privilege, especially of a ruler or leader.
[Latin *praerogativa* the right of voting first]

presage (**press**-ij *or* pri-**sage**) *verb*
1 to be an omen or warning of something.
2 an old word meaning 'to predict'.
● **presage** (**press**-ij) *noun* an omen or a warning.

presbyter (**prez**-bi-ter) *noun*
1 (*formerly*) a Christian minister or Church elder.
2 (*formal*) a minister under a bishop in episcopal Churches.
[Greek *presbyteros* elder]

Presbyterianism (prez-bi-**teer**-i-an-izm)
noun
1 a form of Church government based on representative groups of ministers and elders.
2 the beliefs of Churches which are governed in this way.
Word Family **Presbyterian** *noun* a member of such a Church.

presbytery (**prez**-bi-tree) *noun* (*plural* **presbyteries**)
1 a body of Church elders.
2 *Roman Catholicism* the home of a priest.
3 the eastern part of the chancel in a church.

pre-school *adjective*
relating to the time before a child starts studying at school.

prescient (**press**-i-ent) *adjective*
having foresight or a knowledge of something before it occurs.
Word Family **prescience** *noun*;
presciently *adverb*.
[*pre-* + Latin *sciens* knowing]

prescribe *verb*
to order or recommend: *I don't prescribe any particular method.* □ *The doctor prescribed several months' rest.*
[*pre-* + Latin *scribere* to write]

> ! Do not confuse *prescribe* with *proscribe*. *Proscribe* means 'to condemn or forbid', the opposite of *prescribe*. A *prescribed method* is one which you should use, whereas a *proscribed method* is one which you must not use.

prescription *noun*
something which is prescribed, such as a written instruction from a doctor for the preparation of a medicine or remedy.

prescriptive *adjective*
giving orders or directions.

presence (**prez** 'nce) *noun*
1 the state of being in or at a particular place: *Her presence unnerved him.* □ *Do not laugh in his presence.*
2 an appearance, air: *She has a distinctive presence.*
3 a supernatural or spiritual being: *We were aware of a presence in the room.*
Phrase **presence of mind** the ability to be alert, calm and efficient, especially in a crisis.

present¹ (**prez**-'nt) *adjective*
1 being or occurring here or now: *the present time.*
2 being in the place referred to: *Were you present at the meeting?*

3 *Grammar* (of a verb form) used when referring to something that is happening now: *the present tense.*
● **present** *noun*
1 the present time.
2 *Grammar* a present tense or form.

present² *noun*
something which is given freely, as a token of friendship, affection, etc.
● **present** (pri-**zent**) *verb*
1 to give or award: *He was presented with first prize.*
2 to introduce someone formally: *May I present my parents?*
3 to cause: *This presents a problem.*
4 to put on a show, exhibition, etc.
5 to be the presenter of a programme, e.g. on television.
Phrases **present arms** (of a soldier) to hold a rifle vertically in front of the body in salute. **present oneself** to appear to other people.

presentable (pri-**zen**-ta-b'l) *adjective*
fit to be seen by other people.
Word Family **presentably** *adverb*.

presentation (prez-'n-**tay**-sh'n) *noun*
1 the act of presenting something.
2 something which is given, e.g. an award.
3 a talk, demonstration, or performance.

presenter (pri-**zen**-ta) *noun*
somebody who introduces a television or radio programme.

presentiment (pri-**zent**-i-m'nt) *noun*
a premonition.
[*pre-* + Latin *sentire* to perceive]

presently *adverb*
1 soon.
2 at the present time.

present participle ⇨ PARTICIPLE.

preservative (pri-**zer**-va-tiv) *noun*
a chemical agent added to foods, etc. to make them last longer.

preserve (pri-**zerv**) *verb*
1 to keep whole, safe or in existence: *He found it difficult to preserve his dignity in such a ridiculous situation.*
2 to prepare food, etc. so that it will not decay.
● **preserve** *noun*
1 something which is preserved, especially fruit cooked with sugar: *apricot preserve.*
2 an area or place set aside for a special group or purpose, especially one in which wildlife is bred or kept for hunting.

preside (pri-**zide**) *verb*
to control, direct or have authority over:
*The Speaker presides over meetings in
Parliament.*

president (**prez**-i-d'nt) *noun*
1 the elected leader of a republic, e.g. as in
France or America.
2 a person chosen or elected to preside
over a group, meeting, etc.: *the president of
a company.*
Word Family **presidential** (prez-i-**den**-
sh'l) *adjective*; **presidency** *noun* (*plural*
presidencies) the office or term of a
president.

press¹ *verb*
1 to apply or put steady weight or force on:
She pressed the doorbell impatiently.
2 to make flat by applying weight: *to press
flowers.*
3 to clasp, squeeze: *He pressed my hand.*
4 to urge, insist: *They are pressing for the
introduction of reforms.*
5 to iron: *This shirt needs pressing.*
Phrase **pressed for** *We cannot stay as we
are very pressed for time* (= short of).
• **press** *noun* (*plural* **presses**)
1 newspapers, magazines and other
printed publications: *the importance of
having a free press.*
2 (**the press**) (*used with singular or plural
verb*) journalists and people who write for
magazines, etc.
3 any of various machines or devices
which press, squeeze, etc.: *a garlic press.*
4 any of various machines for printing on
paper.
5 a business engaged in printing and
publishing books, etc.
6 a place where printing is carried out.
7 the act of pressing: *He gave her hand a
quick press.*
8 a pressing or crowding together: *She
became caught in the press of tourists.*
[Latin *pressus* squeezed]

press² *verb*
History to force into service, especially in
the navy, etc.

press conference *noun*
a meeting at which information is given to
journalists by a politician or celebrity.

press gang *noun*
History a group of men appointed to seize
or force other men to join the army, navy,
etc.
• **press-gang** *verb.*

pressie ⇨ PREZZIE.

pressing *adjective*
urgent: *a pressing need to sneeze.*
Word Family **pressingly** *adverb.*

press release *noun*
a statement or announcement given to the
press for publication.

press stud *noun*
a small metal fastener used on clothing,
consisting of two parts pressed together.

press-up *noun*
an exercise in which a person lies face
down on the floor and keeps the body
rigid while raising it to the full extent of
the arms and then lowering it.

pressure (**presh**-er) *noun*
1 the act of applying weight or force.
2 a measure of the force acting on a given
area.
3 persuasion, influence: *They put pressure
on me to make me change my mind.*
4 demands: *the pressure of work.*
5 *Weather* ⇨ ATMOSPHERIC PRESSURE.
• **pressure** *verb* to use influence or force
on.

pressure cooker *noun*
a strong metal vessel in which food can be
rapidly cooked in steam, at above normal
boiling temperature.

pressure group *noun*
a group or organization which tries to
influence others in order to promote its
own interests or aims.

pressurize, pressurise (**presh**-a-rize)
verb
1 to maintain the normal air pressure in an
enclosed space, especially in an aeroplane.
2 to compress a gas or liquid to a greater
than normal pressure.
Word Family **pressurization** *noun.*

prestidigitation (pres-ti-dij-i-**tay**-sh'n)
noun
(*formal*) sleight of hand.
[Latin *praesto* ready + *digitus* finger]

prestige (press-**teezh**) *noun*
importance, influence or good reputation
gained through achievement, success or
position.
Word Family **prestigious** (press-**tij**-us)
adjective of or producing prestige.
[Latin *praestigiae* an illusion, from
praestringere to dull the sight, to dazzle]

presto¹ *adverb, adjective*
Music fast.
[Italian]

presto² ⇨ HEY PRESTO.

prestressed (pree-**strest**) *adjective*
made stronger by introducing internal
stresses in order to counteract stresses
resulting from applied loads: *prestressed
concrete.*

presumably (priz-**yoo**-ma-blee) *adverb*
probably.

presume (pri-**zyoom**) *verb*
1 to assume to be true in the absence of
proof to the contrary: *I presume that this
photo is of your mother.*
2 to be arrogant enough to do something:
I would not presume to contradict her.
[Latin *praesumere* to forestall]

presumption (pri-**zump**-sh'n) *noun*
1 the act of presuming.
2 supposition or strong probability.
3 a daring or offensive boldness.
Word Family **presumptive** *adjective*
based on presumption; **presumptuous**
adjective offensively bold.

presuppose (pree-sup-**oze**) *verb*
to assume or suppose beforehand.
Word Family **presupposition** *noun.*

pretence *noun* (*American* **pretense**)
1 the act of pretending or acting falsely.
2 a false or deceptive display or expression.
a pretence of anger.
3 a claim: *I make no pretence to being a good
cook.*

pretend *verb*
1 to play a part or act in order to deceive:
I'm sure she's only pretending to be sick.
2 to make-believe. *They pretended they were
elephants.*
Phrase **pretend to** to lay claim to: *She
pretends to a great knowledge of wine.*
Word Family **pretend** *adjective*
(*informal*) not real, make-believe: *a pretend
camera;* **pretender** *noun* 1 a person who
pretends. 2 a person claiming rights to be
a monarch.
[Latin *praetendere* to tender (an excuse or
pretext)]

pretension (pri-**ten**-sh'n) *noun*
1 a claim.
2 a false or exaggerated opinion,
assumption or estimate: *She has no
pretensions about being beautiful.*

pretentious (pri-**ten**-shus) *adjective*
trying to appear impressive or important:
*I'd be embarrassed to ride in such a
pretentious car.*
Word Family **pretentiousness** *noun;*
pretentiously *adverb.*

preternatural (pree-ta-**natch**-a-r'l)
adjective also **praeternatural**
not normal or usual.
[Latin *praeter* beyond, contrary to +
NATURE]

pretext (**pree**-tekst) *noun*
a false reason or purpose given: *She went to
see what the new neighbours were like on the
pretext of taking them a cake.*
[Latin *praetextus* woven before, alleged as
excuse]

pretty (**prit**-ee) *adjective* (**prettier;
prettiest**)
delicately pleasing in appearance: *a pretty
face.*
Phrase **cost a pretty penny** (*informal*) to
cost a lot of money.
• **pretty** *adverb* (*informal*) reasonably or
moderately: *She paints pretty well for a
beginner.*
Phrase **be sitting pretty** (*informal*) to be
in an advantageous situation.
Word Family **prettily** *adverb* in a
charming or pretty manner; **prettiness**
noun; **prettify** *verb* (**prettifies;
prettifying; prettified**) to make pretty.

> **Pretty** is an example of a word whose
> meaning has moved far from its origins.
> It derives from Old English *praetig*
> (clever, wily), which came from Old
> English *praett* (a trick or wile). From
> this it came to mean 'clever' in a
> positive sense, then 'cleverly made', and
> then 'beautiful'.

pretzel *noun*
a small crisp salted biscuit in the form of a
knot or stick.
[German]

prevail (pri-**vale**) *verb*
1 to triumph or succeed: *Justice prevailed
and the robbers were caught*
2 to be widespread or dominant: *light rains
prevailing in the afternoon.*
Phrase **prevail upon** to persuade or
influence: *I prevailed upon him to change his
mind.*
[*pre-* + Latin *valere* to have power]

prevalent (**prev**-a-l'nt) *adjective*
widespread or common: *That view is
prevalent in society.*
Word Family **prevalence** *noun;*
prevalently *adverb.*

prevaricate (pri-**varr**-i-kate) *verb*
to speak or act evasively.
Word Family **prevaricator** *noun* a
person who prevaricates; **prevarication**
noun.
[Latin *praevaricari* to walk crookedly]

prevent (pri-vent) *verb*
to stop or keep from taking place: *It was difficult to prevent a fight.*
Word Family **prevention** *noun*; **preventive, preventative** *adjective* serving to prevent; **preventive, preventative** *noun* something which prevents, such as a drug used to prevent disease.
[*pre-* + Latin *ventus* come]

preview (pree-vew) *noun*
a viewing beforehand, especially of a film, etc. before it is released to the public.
• **preview** *verb* to show or be shown beforehand.

previous (pree-vi-us) *adjective*
1 earlier or former: *I think we were introduced on a previous occasion.*
2 (*informal*) too hasty, premature: *His judgement was shown to be a bit previous.*
Word Family **previously** *adverb*.
[Latin *praevius* going before]

prey (pray) *noun*
1 an animal hunted and killed by another animal for food.
2 a victim: *Tourists were the unsuspecting prey of local shopkeepers.*
• **prey** *verb*
Phrase **prey on, prey upon 1** to hunt for prey: *owls preying on mice.* **2** to have a troublesome or destructive effect: *thoughts preying on her mind.*
[Latin *praeda* plunder]

prezzie (prez-ee) *noun* also **pressie**
(*informal*) a present.

price *noun*
1 the amount of money, etc. for which something is bought, sold or acquired.
2 something which occurs as a necessary part of something else: *Misery is the price of war.*
Phrases **at a price** *She won his confidence but at a price* (= at a high cost to herself).
at any price *I will not go at any price* (= no matter what).
Word Family **price** *verb* to fix the price of; **priceless** *adjective* **1** beyond value: *priceless rubies.* **2** (*informal*) extremely funny or absurd: *The look on his face was priceless!*
[Latin *pretium*]

pricey *adjective* (**pricier; priciest**) also **pricy**
(*informal*) expensive.

prick *verb*
1 to make a small hole or mark with a sharp point.

2 to stir emotionally: *Her conscience was pricked by the appeal for aid for the refugees.*
Phrase **prick up one's ears** to be on the alert and listen carefully.
• **prick** *noun*
1 the act of pricking.
2 the pain or sensation caused by pricking: *He felt a sharp prick.*
3 a hole or mark made by pricking.

prickle *noun*
1 a small sharp point or thorn.
2 a pricking or sharp tingling sensation.
• **prickle** *verb* to cause or have a sharp tingling sensation.

prickly *adjective* (**pricklier; prickliest**)
1 covered with prickles.
2 having or causing a pricking sensation.
3 easily angered or upset.
4 difficult, awkward: *a prickly subject.*
Word Family **prickliness** *noun*.

prickly pear *noun*
a cactus with pear-shaped prickly edible fruit.

pride *noun*
1 a feeling of pleasure or satisfaction due to something one owns, has done, has achieved, etc.: *She felt great pride on receiving the award.*
2 something which causes such a feeling: *That child is their pride and joy.*
3 conceit or an exaggerated opinion of oneself: *His pride and arrogance lost him many friends.*
4 a poetic word meaning 'the best or most thriving condition': *in the pride of her youth.*
5 a group of lions.
Phrase **pride of place** the most important position: *I put his photo in pride of place on the mantelpiece.*
• **pride** *verb*
Phrase **pride oneself on** to take pride in.

priest (preest) *noun*
1 *Christianity* a minister in the Catholic, Orthodox or Anglican Church who has authority to perform the sacraments.
2 *Religion* a person who performs certain acts or rituals in non-Christian religions.
Word Family **priesthood** *noun* **1** the office or duties of a priest. **2** the body of priests in a particular religion; **priestly** *adjective* of or like a priest; **priestliness** *noun*.
[from PRESBYTER]

priestess *noun* (*plural* **priestesses**)
Religion a woman who is a priest of a non-Christian religion.

prig *noun*
a self-righteous person.
Word Family **priggish** *adjective*;
priggishly *adverb*; **priggishness** *noun*.

prim *adjective*
1 precise, especially in a formal or affected manner.
2 demure or prudish.
Word Family **primly** *adverb*; **primness** *noun*.

primacy (**pry**-ma-see) *noun*
1 the state of being first or most important.
2 *Christianity* the office of primate.

prima donna (pree-ma **don**-a) *noun*
1 also called **diva**. the principal female singer in an opera company.
2 a temperamental or theatrical person.
[Italian, first lady]

primaeval ⇨ PRIMEVAL.

prima facie (pry-ma **fay**-shi-ee) *adjective, adverb*
Law at first sight.
[Latin *primus* first + *facies* face]

primal (**pry**-m'l) *adjective*
first, original or basic: *primal urges*.

primarily (**prime**-ra-lee *or* pry-**merr**-i-lee) *adverb*
mainly.

primary (**pry**-ma-ree) *adjective*
1 chief, principal: *the primary cause of heart disease*.
2 first, original: *a primary school*.
3 relating to activity which produces resources from the earth, e.g. farming, forestry, mining, etc.: *primary industry*.
□ *primary goods*. Compare SECONDARY (definition 2); TERTIARY (definition 2).
• **primary** *noun* (*plural* **primaries**)
American a preliminary election held in each state to select candidates for the later election of the President.

primary colour *noun*
any colour having no trace of another colour: red, yellow, green and blue, plus the pair black and white. Compare SECONDARY COLOUR.

primary school *noun*
a school for children up to about eleven years old.

primate[1] (**pry**-mate) *noun*
Zoology any mammal of the group which includes humans, monkeys, apes and lemurs.

primate[2] (**pry**-mate *or* **pry**-mit) *noun*
Christianity a chief bishop or archbishop in a group of dioceses or a whole country.

prime[1] *adjective*
1 first in rank or importance: *the prime minister*.
2 excellent: *prime cuts of meat*.
• **prime** *noun*
1 the most flourishing or perfect stage or condition: *in the prime of his youth*.
2 a prime number.

prime[2] *verb*
1 to prepare or make ready for a particular purpose: *First prime the window with an undercoat*.
2 to prepare for a situation by giving information to: *The witness had been primed before she gave evidence*.

prime minister *noun*
the minister leading the government.

prime mover *noun*
1 the originator or chief promoter of a scheme of action.
2 the initial source of power, e.g. a windmill or stationary engine.

prime number *noun*
Maths a positive integer that is exactly divisible only by itself and one: *Prime numbers include 5, 7 and 11*.

primer[1] (**pry**-ma) *noun*
a simple book of instruction or learning.

primer[2] *noun*
1 an undercoat of paint, varnish, etc. on a surface.
2 a part of a cartridge containing a substance which explodes when struck by the firing pin, thus firing the main powder charge.

prime time *noun*
the time at which the largest audience for a television or radio programme is expected.

primeval (pry-**mee**-v'l) *adjective* also **primaeval**
of or relating to prehistoric times.
Word Family **primevally** *adverb*.
[Latin *primus* first + *aevum* age]

primitive (**prim**-i-tiv) *adjective*
1 being the earliest stage or form of something: *a primitive writing system*.
2 having undergone little cultural or technological development: *primitive peoples*.
3 simple, crude: *a primitive shelter*.

4 *Art* being in a simple or self-taught style.
Word Family **primitive** noun a person or thing that is primitive; **primitively** adverb; **primitiveness** noun.

primogeniture (pry-ma-**jen**-i-cher) noun
1 the fact of being the firstborn child.
2 a rule or tradition saying that property is to be inherited by the firstborn child.
[Latin *primo* at first + *genitus* born]

primordial (prime-**ord**-i-ul) adjective
original or first in time.

primp verb
to make fussy adjustments, e.g. to one's clothes.

primrose noun
1 any of a group of small spring plants with pale yellow flowers.
2 a pale yellow colour.
Phrase **primrose path** a life of pleasure.
• **primrose** adjective.
[Late Latin *prima rosa* first rose]

Primus (**pry**-mus) noun (plural **Primuses**)
(*trademark*) a portable stove which burns vaporized oil.

prince noun
1 a male member of a royal family, usually one other than the monarch.
2 the ruler of a small state or territory in a monarchy or empire.
Word Family **princely** adjective **1** of or worthy of a prince. **2** generous; **princedom** noun **1** the rank or status of a prince. **2** a principality.
[Latin *princeps* first or principal]

princess noun (plural **princesses**)
1 a female member of a royal family, usually one other than the monarch.
2 the wife or widow of a prince.
3 a female ruler of a small state or territory in a monarchy or empire.

principal (**prin**-si-p'l) adjective
first in rank or importance.
• **principal** noun
1 the head or leading official of a school, college or other organization.
2 a person with the leading part or position, as in one section of an orchestra, a play, etc.
3 a sum of money lent, borrowed or invested, on which interest is paid.
4 *Law* any person who employs another as an agent.
Word Family **principally** adverb.

! The words *principal* and *principle* sound the same but have different spellings and meanings. *Principal* ends in *al* and is an adjective or noun referring to the most important person or thing (*the principal routes out of the city; He is the new principal of the school*); *principle* ends in *le* and is only a noun, meaning 'a policy or standard' (*She has no principles*).

principality (prin-si-**pal**-i-tee) noun (plural **principalities**)
a state ruled by a prince.

principle (**prin**-si-p'l) noun
1 a basic truth, law or policy: *the principles of maths.* □ *He acts according to the principle of an eye for an eye.*
2 any standard or rule of right or moral behaviour: *He is a scoundrel and has no principles at all.*
Phrases **in principle** in theory: *I agree in principle but not in practice.* **on principle** as a matter of moral policy: *I had to refuse on principle.*

! Do not confuse *principle* with PRINCIPAL.

prink verb
Phrase **prink oneself** to dress up or adorn oneself fussily.

print noun
1 a mark made on a surface by pressure: *a footprint.*
2 an engraving or etching produced from a metal plate.
3 a cotton fabric with a design on it.
4 any printed matter.
5 *Photography* a picture developed when light-sensitive paper is exposed to light through a negative.
Phrases **in print** (of a book) available for purchase: *Is the book still in print?* **out of print** (of a book) no longer available for purchase.
• **print** verb
1 to press a mark, design, picture, etc. on to a surface.
2 to produce in inked, typed form: *They print two million copies of this newspaper every day.* □ *I printed out her e-mail.*
3 to write with separated letters: *Print your name at the top of the form.*
4 *Photography* to produce a print.
Word Family **printable** adjective suitable to be printed or published.

printed circuit ⇨ CIRCUIT.

printer *noun*
1 a person or company whose business is to produce printed material.
2 a device which prints, especially one attached to a computer.

printing *noun*
the act or process of producing printed matter, especially books, etc.

printout *noun*
Computers the information or results delivered in printed form by a computer.

prior[1] (**pry**-or) *adjective*
preceding in time, order, importance, etc.: *She couldn't go because she had a prior engagement.*
Phrase prior to before: *Prior to that, he had lived in Wales.*
[Latin]

prior[2] *noun*
1 *Christianity* a person in an abbey ranking below an abbot.
2 *Christianity* a person in charge of a friary.

prioress *noun* (*plural* **prioresses**)
1 *Christianity* a woman in charge of a nunnery.
2 *Christianity* a woman in an abbey ranking below an abbess.

priority (pry-**orr**-i-tee) *noun* (*plural* **priorities**)
1 the state of being first in an established order of importance.
2 the right to such a position: *His age gives him priority over us.*
Word Family prioritize, prioritise *verb* to arrange in order of relative importance.

priory *noun* (*plural* **priories**)
a monastery or nunnery in the charge of a prior or prioress.

prise (prize) *verb* (*American* **prize**)
to raise or force with a lever.
[French, a grip]

prism (prizm) *noun*
a solid or hollow body with similar equal and parallel ends. The faces of a prism are usually parallelograms.
Word Family prismatic (priz-**mat**-ik) *adjective*.
[Greek *prisma* something sawn]

prison (**pri**-z'n) *noun*
a building where convicted criminals are kept.

prisoner *noun*
1 a person who is kept in captivity, custody or a prison.
2 a person who is restrained or restrained.
[Latin *prensus* caught]

prissy *adjective* (**prissier; prissiest**)
prim or prudish.
Word Family prissily *adverb*; **prissiness** *noun*.

pristine (**pris**-teen *or* **pris**-tine) *adjective*
1 in an original state or condition: *a pristine edition of a book.*
2 undamaged or as new: *in pristine condition.*
[Latin *pristinus* former, earlier]

prithee (**prith**-ee) *interjection*
an old word meaning 'please'.
[shortening of *I pray thee*]

private (**pry**-vit) *adjective*
1 not seen, used or shared by others: *a private discussion between the leaders.* □ *private information.*
2 personal or belonging to oneself: *He didn't tell her his most private worries.*
3 used or controlled by individuals, rather than the public or the government: *a private clinic.* □ *A private detective is not a member of the police force.*
• **private** *noun Army* a soldier of the lowest rank.
Word Family privately *adverb*; **privacy** (**priv**-a-see *or* **pry**-va-see) *noun* 1 the state of being private or secluded. 2 secrecy.
[from Latin]

private enterprise *noun*
any privately owned business or businesses, as distinct from those owned or controlled by the government.

privateer (pry-va-**teer**) *noun*
1 a privately owned ship instructed to attack the ships and cargo of an enemy during war.
2 the commander or a crew member of such a ship.

private eye *noun*
(*informal*) a private detective.

private means *plural noun*
an income not from wages or salary but from property or investments.

private practice *noun*
that part of a professional business in which individual clients are charged fees for services rendered; a term used especially of a doctor's work outside the National Health Service.

private school *noun*
a school that is run by a private or religious organization which charges a fee for attendance.

privation (pry-**vay**-sh'n) *noun*
a lack of necessities or comforts: *War led to serious privation and poverty.*
[Latin *privatus* deprived]

privative (**priv**-a-tiv) *adjective*
1 lacking something, e.g. a quality.
2 *Grammar* giving a negative meaning to a word: *The 'a' in 'amoral' is a privative prefix.*

privatize, privatise (**pry**-v't-ize) *verb*
to remove from public or state ownership.
Word Family **privatization** *noun*.

privet (**priv**-it) *noun*
an evergreen shrub with small white flowers, sometimes used for garden hedges.

privilege (**priv**-i-lij) *noun*
1 a right, advantage or opportunity granted to a particular person or group: *I had the privilege of leading the procession.*
2 the principle of allowing or enjoying such rights or benefits: *A society with social classes is based on privilege.*
• **privilege** *verb* (*formal*) to grant a privilege to.
[Latin *privus* one's own + *legis* of law]

privy (**priv**-ee) *adjective*
Phrase **privy to** taking part in something private or secret: *Only a few villagers were privy to the plot.*
• **privy** *noun* (*plural* **privies**) an outside toilet.
Word Family **privily** *adverb* secretly.
[from PRIVATE]

privy purse *noun*
the amount of money allowed by parliament for private use by the monarch.

prize *noun*
1 something offered or given as a reward for success, victory, etc.
2 something captured or seized: *The pirates' prize was a chest of jewellery.*
• **prize** *adjective*
1 offered or given as a prize: *prize money.*
2 worthy of or having received a prize: *our prize bull.*
• **prize** *verb* to value highly: *I prize these books above all my possessions.*

pro¹ *noun*
an argument, or person, in favour of something.
Phrase **the pros and cons** facts, arguments, etc. for and against something.
• **pro** *preposition* in favour of.
[Latin, for]

pro² *noun*
(*informal*) a professional.
• **pro** *adjective* professional.

pro³ *noun*
(*informal*) a prostitute.

proactive *adjective*
creating or controlling a situation by taking the initiative or being ready to take the initiative: *a proactive approach to crime prevention.*

probability (prob-a-**bil**-i-tee) *noun* (*plural* **probabilities**)
1 the state of being probable.
2 a probable condition, event, etc.: *There is a probability that the train will be late.*
3 *Maths* a measure of chance expressed as the ratio of the number of favourable outcomes to the total number of outcomes.
Phrase **in all probability** very likely.

probable (**prob**-a-b'l) *adjective*
likely to happen or be true.
Word Family **probably** *adverb*.
[Latin *probabilis* commendable, credible]

probate (**pro**-bate) *noun*
1 *Law* the formal procedure for establishing the validity of a will.
2 *Law* the document showing this.
[Latin *probatus* proved]

probation (pro-**bay**-sh'n) *noun*
1 a trial period, e.g. for a new employee.
2 *Law* the system of allowing criminals to remain free, instead of being imprisoned, on a promise to behave well in the future. Compare PAROLE.
Word Family **probationary** *adjective*; **probationer** *noun* a person undergoing probation. **probation officer** *noun* a person appointed to supervise the behaviour of criminals on probation.

probe *noun*
1 a slender instrument used to explore wounds, etc.
2 an investigation.
3 ⇨ SPACE PROBE.
• **probe** *verb* to investigate or examine.
[Latin *probare* to test]

probity (**pro**-bit-ee) *noun*
integrity or honesty.
[Latin *probus* good]

problem *noun*
1 a difficult question, situation, person, etc.
2 a question proposed for solution or discussion.
Word Family **problematic** (prob-la-**mat**-ik), **problematical** *adjective* uncertain; **problematically** *adverb*.
[Greek *problema* a defence, excuse, questioning]

proboscis (pro-**boss**-iss) *noun* (*plural*
proboscess (pro-**boss**-eez) or
proboscides (pro-**boss**-i-deez) or
proboscises (pro-**boss**-iss-iz))
a trunk-like growth from the head, such as
that on elephants and some insects.
[Greek, a means of providing food]

procedure (pro-**seed**-yer) *noun*
the method or manner of acting or
proceeding: *Is there a set procedure for this
job?*
Word Family procedural *adjective*.

proceed (pro-**seed**) *verb*
1 to begin something: *The surgeon
proceeded to insert the tube.*
2 to continue, carry on: *When the light is
green, the cars can proceed.*
[Latin *procedere* to advance]

> [!] Do not confuse *proceed* with
> PRECEDE.

proceedings *plural noun*
1 legal steps.
2 something that has a set procedure.
3 a record of the activities of a club,
society, etc.

proceeds (pro-seedz) *plural noun*
the money obtained from a sale or other
transaction.

process (pro-sess) *noun* (*plural*
processes)
1 a series of actions or changes for a
particular purpose: *the process of refining
sugar.* □ *the process of digestion.* □ *the process
of erosion by a river.* □ *Packing the crockery
into boxes was a slow process.*
2 *Biology* a natural outgrowth from an
organ.
Phrase **in the process of** in the course
of: *a building in the process of construction.*
• **process** *verb*
1 to treat something in a particular way,
especially to preserve it or change it:
processed cheese.
2 to deal with somebody according to a
procedure.
3 *Computers* to carry out operations on
data.

procession (pro-**sesh**-'n) *noun*
1 a line or group of people, vehicles, etc.
moving along in an orderly way.
2 the act of moving in orderly sequence:
the procession of the seasons.
Word Family processional *adjective* of or
for a procession.

proclaim (pro-**klame**) *verb*
to announce or make known, especially
publicly or officially.

Word Family proclamation (prok-la-
may-sh'n) *noun*.
[Latin *proclamare* to shout out]

proclivity (pro-**kliv**-i-tee) *noun* (*plural*
proclivities)
(*formal*) a natural tendency or disposition:
She has a proclivity to criticize.
[Latin *proclivis* steep, inclined]

procrastinate (pro-**kras**-ti-nate) *verb*
to put off doing something.
Word Family procrastination *noun*;
procrastinator *noun* a person who
procrastinates.
[*pro-* + Latin *crastinus* of tomorrow]

procreate (pro-kree-ate) *verb*
to produce offspring.
Word Family procreation *noun*.
[from Latin]

proctor *noun*
an official in some universities, especially
one responsible for discipline among
undergraduates.
[Latin *praecurator* an administrator]

procure (pro-**kyor**) *verb*
1 to obtain, especially by care or effort: *I
managed to procure a rare edition of the novel.*
2 to obtain a prostitute for the use of
someone else.
Word Family procurement *noun*;
procurer *noun* a person who procures,
especially prostitutes; **procurable**
adjective.
[Latin *procurare* to take charge of]

prod *verb* (**prods; prodding; prodded**)
1 to poke or push with a pointed object.
2 to urge, persuade.
• **prod** *noun*
1 a pointed instrument used for prodding.
2 a poke with or as if with a prod.
3 a reminder.

prodigal (**prod**-i-g'l) *adjective*
1 recklessly wasteful.
2 giving profusely.
• **prodigal** *noun* a person who is
extravagant or wasteful.
Word Family prodigally *adverb*;
prodigality (prod-i-**gal**-i-tee) *noun*.
[Latin *prodigus* lavish]

prodigious (prod-**ij**-us) *adjective*
enormous: *a prodigious sum of money.*
Word Family prodigiously *adverb*.

prodigy (**prod**-i-jee) *noun* (*plural*
prodigies)
1 a person, especially a child, with
extraordinary abilities.
2 something wonderful.
[Latin *prodigium* a marvellous portent]

produce (pro-**dewce**) *verb*
1 to bring forth: *The rabbit produced five offspring.* □ *Many novelists produce a new book every year.* □ *Their defence lawyer produced some new evidence.*
2 to make or manufacture: *a factory producing doors and windows.*
3 to show, exhibit: *We had to produce our tickets.*
4 to organize a play, concert, etc.
• **produce** (**prod**-yooce) *noun* something produced, especially agricultural or natural products.
[Latin *producere* to bring forward]

producer (pro-**dew**-sa) *noun*
1 a person or thing that produces.
2 the person who organizes the business side of a play or film. Compare DIRECTOR.
3 *Biology* an organism which produces its own food by the process of photosynthesis.

product (**prod**-ukt) *noun*
1 something which is produced.
2 *Maths* the result of multiplication. Compare QUOTIENT.
3 *Chemistry* an element or compound which is formed in a chemical reaction.
product analysis close examination of a product.

production (pro-**duk**-sh'n) *noun*
1 the act of producing.
2 something which is produced, e.g. a particular play or film.
3 the total amount produced.
production process the way in which a product is made.

productive (pro-**duk**-tiv) *adjective*
1 producing readily or abundantly: *productive soil.*
2 profitable or useful: *a productive meeting.*
Word Family productively *adverb*; **productiveness** *noun*.

productivity (prod-uk-**tiv**-i-tee) *noun*
1 the effectiveness with which something is produced.
2 the ability to produce something.

profane *adjective*
1 having or showing a lack of reverence for God or sacred things.
2 secular.
3 blasphemous: *profane language.*
Word Family profanely *adverb*; **profaner** *noun*.
[Latin *profanus* outside the temple]

profanity *noun* (*plural* **profanities**)
1 profane conduct or language.
2 a swear word.

profess *verb*
1 to claim: *I don't profess to be an expert.* □ *He professed extreme disappointment.*
2 to affirm faith in a religion.
[Latin *professus* frankly declared]

profession (pro-**fesh**-'n) *noun*
1 an occupation, especially one requiring advanced education and special training: *He is a dentist by profession.*
2 all the people engaged in such an occupation: *the dental profession.*
3 a statement or declaration of belief, feeling, etc.: *His professions of love only made her blush.*

professional (pro-**fesh**-a-n'l) *adjective*
1 of or relating to a profession: *a professional couple.* □ *We need professional advice.*
2 doing something for payment or as a full-time occupation: *a professional footballer.*
3 maintaining appropriate standards: *He has a very professional manner.*
Word Family professional *noun* a professional person; **professionally** *adverb*; **professionalism** *noun* professional skill or qualities.

professor (pro-**fess**-a) *noun*
a university teacher of the highest rank.
Word Family professorial (prof-a-**saw**-ree-ul) *adjective* of or characteristic of a professor.

proffer *verb*
to offer for acceptance: *She proffered her cheek for me to kiss.*

proficient (pro-**fish**-'nt) *adjective*
skilled or expert in something: *a proficient swimmer.*
Word Family proficiently *adverb*; **proficiency** *noun*.

profile (**pro**-file) *noun*
1 an outline showing the side view of a person's face.
2 a drawing of a vertical section through something, such as a building, soil, etc.
3 a study or article about a person, published in a newspaper, etc.
4 the extent to which someone or something attracts attention.
Phrase keep a low profile to try to remain unnoticed.
• **profile** *verb*.

profit (**prof**-it) *noun*
1 financial gain, especially the amount remaining after expenses, cost of production, etc. have been deducted.
2 advantage, benefit.

Word Family **profit** *verb* to gain or be of benefit; **profitable** *adjective* yielding profit; **profitably** *adverb*.
[Latin *proficere* to gain advantage]

profiteer (prof-i-**teer**) *noun*
a person who seeks or makes excessive profits, especially by taking advantage of a general shortage.
Word Family **profiteer** *verb*;
profiteering *noun*.

profiterole (pra-**fit**-a-roll) *noun*
a small ball of cooked choux pastry filled with cream and covered with chocolate sauce.
[French, small profit]

profit-sharing *noun*
the sharing of profits between employers and employees, in addition to salaries and wages.

profligate (**prof**-li-git) *adjective*
1 recklessly extravagant.
2 shamelessly immoral.
Word Family **profligate** *noun* a profligate person; **profligacy** *noun*.
[Latin *profligatus* debased]

profound *adjective*
1 very great: *profound changes in the system.*
2 severe: *profound deafness.*
3 showing great understanding or knowledge.
Word Family **profoundly** *adverb*;
profundity (pro-**fund**-i-tee) *noun*.
[Latin *profundus* deep]

profuse (pro-**fewce**) *adjective*
abundant, often to excess: *profuse apologies.*
Word Family **profusely** *adverb*;
profusion (pro-**few**-zh'n) *noun*.
[Latin *profusus* poured forth]

progenitor (pro-**jen**-i-ta) *noun*
1 a direct ancestor.
2 the originator of something: *the progenitor of post-Impressionism.*

progeny (**proj**-a-nee) *noun*
(*used with singular or plural verb*) offspring.

progesterone (pro-**jest**-a-rone) *noun*
Biology a hormone secreted by the ovaries of mammals and producing changes before and during pregnancy.

prognosis (prog-**no**-sis) *noun* (*plural* **prognoses**) (prog-**no**-seez)
a forecast or prediction, especially of the probable course and outcome of a disease.
Word Family **prognostic** *adjective*.
[Greek, perceiving beforehand]

prognosticate (prog-**nos**-ti-kate) *verb*
to prophesy.

Word Family **prognosticator** *noun*;
prognostication (prog-nos-ti-**kay**-sh'n) *noun*.

program (**pro**-gram) *noun*
Computers a series of instructions for a computer.
• **program** *verb* (**programs**;
programming; **programmed**) to provide instructions for a computer.
Word Family **programmer** *noun* a person who prepares computer programs.

> [!] On the spellings *program* and *programme* ⇨ PROGRAMME.

programme (**pro**-gram) *noun* (*American* **program**)
1 a list of items, events, etc., e.g. for a concert or theatrical performance.
2 a radio or television show.
3 a list or set of things to be done: *a programme of environmental reforms.*
Word Family **programme** *verb* to organize or include in a programme;
programmer *noun*.
[Greek *programma* a public notice]

> [!] **Programme** is an example of a word with alternative spellings. The spelling *programme* is the usual British form and *program* the American form. When applied to computers, however, *program* is used in both British and American English.

progress (**pro**-gress) *noun*
1 movement in a desired direction.
2 growth or development.
Phrase **in progress** under way, taking place: *The meeting is in progress.*
Word Family **progress** (pro-**gress**) *verb*;
progression (pro-**gresh**-'n) *noun* 1 the act of progressing. 2 *Maths* a sequence of numbers; **progressional** *adjective*.
[Latin *progressus* advanced]

progressive (pro-**gress**-iv) *adjective*
1 favouring improvement, change, etc.: *progressive politics.*
2 progressing or advancing by stages: *progressive paralysis.*
3 consisting of continuous movement or changes: *a progressive waltz.*
Word Family **progressively** *adverb*;
progressiveness *noun*.

prohibit (pro-**hib**-it) *verb*
1 to forbid by authority: *Smoking is prohibited on this train.*
2 to prevent: *Having a baby prohibited her from taking the job.*
[Latin *prohibere* to hinder]

> [!] Do not confuse *prohibit* with
> INHIBIT.

prohibition (pro-hib-**ish**-'n) *noun*
1 the act of prohibiting.
2 a law that prohibits.
3 (**Prohibition**) a time when the manufacture and sale of alcoholic drinks is illegal, especially the years 1920-1933 in America.
Word Family **prohibitionist** *noun* a person who favours prohibition of alcoholic drinks.

project (**proj**-ekt) *noun*
1 a scheme that is contemplated, devised or planned for the future.
2 a piece of work, involving research, given to a student or group of students.
• **project** (pro-**jekt**) *verb*
1 to protrude: *The shelf projected from the wall.*
2 to plan or intend: *housing developments projected for the next decade.*
3 to throw: *The ball was projected into the air.* □ *You have to learn to project your voice.*
4 *Psychology* to unknowingly attribute one's own attitudes, etc. to others.
5 to get across, communicate: *She does not project her ideas very well.*
6 to show an image on a surface using light: *The slides were projected onto the wall.*
[Latin *projectus* thrown forwards]

projectile *noun*
1 an object fired from a gun by means of an explosive charge, such as a bullet, shell, etc.
2 something thrown.

projection (pro-**jek**-sh'n) *noun*
1 the act of projecting: *Her voice projection is excellent.*
2 something which protrudes: *a projection of rock on the side of a mountain.*
3 *Geography* a system of lines drawn on a plane surface, as in a map, representing the meridians of longitude and parallels of latitude, upon which the surface of the earth, or some portion of it, can be depicted.

projector (pro-**jek**-ta) *noun*
a device throwing still or moving photographic images onto a screen.
Word Family **projectionist** *noun* a person who operates a projector.

prolapse (pro-laps) *noun*
Medicine the downward movement of an organ from its normal position.
Word Family **prolapse** (pro-**laps**) *verb*.
[Latin *prolapsus* slipped forward]

proletariat (pro-la-**tair**-i-at) *noun*
the working class or the people who do not own property.
Word Family **proletarian** *adjective*, *noun*.
[from Latin]

proliferate (pro-**lif**-a-rate) *verb*
to increase or reproduce in large quantities.
Word Family **proliferation** *noun*.
[Latin *proles* offspring + *ferre* to bear]

prolific (pro-**lif**-ik) *adjective*
producing abundantly: *a prolific writer.*
[Latin *proles* offspring + *facere* to make]

prolix (**pro**-liks) *adjective*
lengthy or boring, in speaking or writing.
Word Family **prolixity** (pro-**lik**-si-tee) *noun*; **prolixly** *adverb*.

prologue (**pro**-log) *noun*
1 the introductory part of a play, book, etc. Compare EPILOGUE.
2 an act or event which introduces.
[*pro-* + Greek *logos* speech]

prolong (pro-**long**) *verb*
to make longer in time.
Word Family **prolonged** *adjective*.

prom *noun*
1 (*informal*) a promenade concert.
2 ⇨ PROMENADE (definition 1).
3 *American* a formal dance held for a class at a school or college.

promenade (prom-i-**nahd**) *noun*
1 also **prom** a public place for walking, especially along a seafront.
2 a leisurely walk.
• **promenade** *verb*.
[French *se promener* to walk]

promenade concert *noun*
Music a concert of classical music at which the audience stands or walks around.

promethium (pro-**mee**-thi-um) *noun*
a radioactive metal.

prominent (**prom**-i-nent) *adjective*
1 standing out so as to be easily seen: *the most prominent peak in the range.*
2 important, well-known: *a prominent politician.*
Word Family **prominently** *adverb*; **prominence** *noun* 1 the state of being prominent. 2 something which is prominent.
[from Latin]

promiscuous (prom-**iss**-kew-us) *adjective*
having an indiscriminate number of casual sexual relationships.
Word Family **promiscuity** (prom-iss-**kew**-i-tee) *noun*; **promiscuously** *adverb*.
[from Latin]

promise (**prom**-iss) *noun*
1 an assurance that something will be done.
2 an indication or likelihood of future success: *She shows promise.*
Word Family **promise** *verb* 1 to make an assurance. 2 to indicate; **promising** *adjective* indicating future success.

promissory note *noun*
a written and signed promise to pay a person a sum of money on a certain date or on demand.

promontory (**prom**-en-tree) *noun* (*plural* **promontories**)
a headland.

promote *verb*
1 to encourage, aid: *This tonic will promote the growth of new hair.*
2 to publicize: *a campaign to promote road safety.* □ *posters promoting a new band.*
3 to raise in position, rank, etc.: *She was promoted to team captain.*
Word Family **promotion** (pro-mo-sh'n) *noun*; **promotional** *adjective*; **promoter** *noun* a person who promotes, especially one who provides the capital for an enterprise.
[Latin *promovere* to move forwards]

prompt *adjective*
1 quick: *a prompt reply.*
2 on time: *He is always prompt with his payments.*
● **prompt** *verb*
1 to cause or inspire to action: *His speech prompted me to vote for him.*
2 to give help or suggestions.
3 *Theatre* to remind an actor when he or she forgets the lines.
Word Family **promptly** *adverb*; **promptness, promptitude** *noun*; **prompt** *noun* something which prompts; **prompt, prompter** *noun* a person who prompts.
[Latin *promptus* brought out]

promulgate (**prom**-'l-gate) *verb*
to declare or make known openly: *to promulgate a law.*
Word Family **promulgation** *noun*; **promulgator** *noun* a person who promulgates.
[from Latin]

prone *adjective*
1 tending or liable to: *He is prone to accidents.*
2 lying flat or still, especially face downwards.
Word Family **proneness** *noun*.
[Latin *pronus* leaning forward]

prong *noun*
a sharply pointed part, such as a division of a fork.

pronoun (**pro**-nown) *noun*
a word used instead of a noun to refer to someone or something already mentioned.

pronounce *verb*
1 to make the sounds of a word or phrase: *How do you pronounce 'phlegm'?*
2 to say: *You do not pronounce the 'p' in 'pterodactyl'.*
3 to state or declare: *The judge pronounced the death sentence.*
Word Family **pronounceable** *adjective*; **pronouncement** *noun* 1 a statement.
2 the act of pronouncing; **pronouncer** *noun*; **pronunciation** (pro-nun-see-**ay**-sh'n) *noun* the manner of pronouncing words.
[Latin *pronuntiare* to announce]

pronounced *adjective*
strongly marked or distinct: *a pronounced limp.*
Word Family **pronouncedly** *adverb*.

pronto *adverb*
(*informal*) quickly.
[Spanish]

proof *noun*
1 evidence which establishes that something is true.
2 the act of proving something.
3 a trial or test: *The proof of the pudding is in the eating.*
4 *Photography* a temporary print, often made directly from the film without being enlarged.
5 the strength of an alcoholic liquor.
6 *Printing* a trial impression of a section of type, engraving, etc. made for the purpose of correction.
● **proof** *adjective* fully resistant: *waterproof.*
[Latin *probare* to test]

proof-read *verb* (**proof-reads; proof-reading; proof-read**)
to read a manuscript or printer's proof in order to find and mark any mistakes.
Word Family **proof-reader** *noun*.

proof spirit *noun*
a standard mixture of alcohol and water which contains 57·10 per cent alcohol by volume.

prop[1] *verb* (**props; propping; propped**)
to support or rest: *Prop that chair against the door to keep it open.*
● **prop** *noun*
1 a beam or other rigid support.
2 any person or thing serving as a support.

prop² noun
Theatre any object used in a play, film, etc. apart from the scenery.
[shortening of PROPERTY]

propaganda (prop-a-**gan**-da) noun
opinions, principles, etc., especially biased or false ones, spread or publicized to persuade, change or reform.
Word Family **propagandist** noun; **propagandize, propagandise** verb.

propagate (**prop**-a-gate) verb
1 (of an organism) to multiply or cause to multiply.
2 to send out or spread: *They have been propagating their ideas.*
Word Family **propagation** noun; **propagator** noun.
[Latin *propagare* to spread]

propane (**pro**-pane) noun
Chemistry a colourless inflammable gas used as a fuel.

propanol (**pro**-pa-nol) noun
Chemistry a colourless liquid alcohol used as a solvent.

propel (pro-**pel**) verb (**propels; propelling; propelled**)
to drive or push forward: *The spacecraft is propelled by a rocket.*
Figurative The song propelled him to stardom.
Word Family **propellent** adjective
capable of propelling.

propellant (pro-**pell**-ant) noun
anything used to provide force or thrust, such as an explosive in a gun or compressed gas in an aerosol container.

propeller noun
a device consisting of rotating blades which propels a ship, aircraft, etc.

propelling pencil noun
a pencil with a replaceable lead, the length of which is adjusted by moving the outer case.

propensity (pra-**pen**-si-tee) noun (plural **propensities**)
a natural tendency: *She has a propensity to drop things.*

proper (**prop**-a) adjective
1 genuine, real: *It wasn't a proper meal, just a snack.*
2 used to show that something is definitely considered to have a particular identity: *We came out of the suburbs and into the city proper.*
3 suitable or appropriate: *the proper clothes to wear to a wedding.*
4 respectable: *He's very proper.*

Word Family **properly** adverb.
[Latin *proprius* one's own]

proper fraction ⇨ COMMON FRACTION.

proper noun noun
the name of a person, place or thing which is written with a capital letter: *Sarah, February and Manchester are proper nouns.*

property (**prop**-a-tee) noun (plural **properties**)
1 a person's possessions.
2 a piece of land owned by a person.
3 an essential quality of something: *What are the properties of a gas?*
[from Latin]

prophecy (**prof**-a-see) noun (plural **prophecies**)
1 a prediction.
2 the ability to predict the future: *the gift of prophecy.*

prophesy (**prof**-a-sigh) verb (**prophesies; prophesying; prophesied**) to make a prophecy.
[*pro-* + Greek *phanai* to speak]

prophet (**prof**-it) noun
1 a religious teacher claiming divine inspiration and authority.
2 a person who predicts future events.
[Greek]

> The word **prophet**, etymologically, means 'one who speaks for another'. It is derived via Old French and Latin from Greek *prophétés*, from *pro-* (for) and *phétés* (speaker). It frequently referred to someone who spoke on behalf of the gods to humans, or who interpreted their will. The religious meaning is a development of this and the meaning of 'foreteller of the future' is a further development.

prophetic (prof-**et**-ik) adjective
1 of or relating to a prophet.
2 of or having the nature of a prophecy: *a prophetic dream.*
Word Family **prophetical** adjective; **prophetically** adverb.

prophylactic (prof-i-**lak**-tik) noun
1 something, such as a medicine, which prevents something.
2 (*especially American*) a condom.
Word Family **prophylactic** adjective; **prophylaxis** (prof-i-**lak**-sis) noun the prevention of disease.
[Greek *prophylaktikos* guarding against]

propinquity (pro-**pink**-wi-tee) *noun*
a nearness, e.g. in place, relationship, etc.:
*Her friendship with her neighbour was due to
propinquity rather than common interests.*
[Latin *propinquus* near]

propitiate (pro-**pish**-i-ate) *verb*
to pacify or win over: *He tried to propitiate
his angry wife with flowers.*
Word Family **propitiation** *noun*;
propitiatory *adjective*.
[from Latin]

propitious (pro-**pish**-us) *adjective*
favourable: *The accident was hardly a
propitious start to the day.*

prop jet ⇨ TURBOPROP.

proponent (pro-**po**-nent) *noun*
a person who supports or argues for a
particular cause.
[*pro-* + Latin *ponere* to put]

proportion (pro-**por**-sh'n) *noun*
1 the comparative relationship of size,
quantity, etc. between things or parts:
*What is the proportion of yeast to flour in this
loaf?*
2 a correct or balanced relationship: *The
size of the house is not in proportion to the
garden.*
3 a part: *A large proportion of the class failed
the exam.*
4 (**proportions**) size: *an inheritance of
huge proportions.*
5 *Maths* a statement of equality of two
ratios: *1 and 2 are in proportion to 5 and 10
because the ratio of the first pair (1:2) equals
the ratio of the second (5:10).*
Word Family **proportional** *adjective*
relative or corresponding; **proportionally**
adverb; **proportionate** *adjective* in correct
proportion; **proportionately** *adverb*.
[Latin *proportio* symmetry]

proportional representation *noun*
Politics an electoral system where each
party receives the same percentage of seats
in parliament as it receives of the total
vote.

propose (pro-**poze**) *verb*
1 to put forward, offer or suggest: *to
propose a new law.*
2 to make an offer of marriage.
Word Family **proposal** *noun* 1 an offer,
especially of marriage. 2 something which
is proposed, such as a scheme or plan;
proposer *noun*.
[from Latin]

proposition (prop-a-zi-sh'n) *noun*
1 something which is proposed or
suggested.

2 *Logic, Maths* a statement to be proved or
demonstrated.
Word Family **proposition** *verb*
(*informal*) to make a proposition,
especially to suggest sexual intercourse;
propositional *adjective*.

propound *verb*
(*formal*) to propose or suggest.

proprietary (pro-**pry**-a-tree) *adjective*
1 relating to an owner or ownership.
2 made and sold under a trade name:
proprietary brands of painkiller.

proprietor (pro-**pry**-a-tor) *noun*
an owner, especially of a business.
Word Family **proprietorial** (pro-pry-a-
taw-ree'l) *adjective*.

proprietress *noun* (*plural*
proprietresses)
a woman who owns a business.
[Latin *proprius* one's own]

propriety (pro-**pry**-a-tee) *noun* (*plural*
proprieties)
1 behaviour in accordance with accepted
or established standards.
2 the state of being right or appropriate.
3 (**proprieties**) the rules of correct
behaviour.

propulsion (pro-**pul**-sh'n) *noun*
1 the act of propelling or driving forward.
2 a propelling force.

propylene (**pro**-pill-een) *noun*
Chemistry a colourless inflammable gas.

pro rata (pro **rah**-ta *or* pro **ray**-ta)
adjective, adverb
in proportion.
[Latin, according to the rate]

prorogue (pro-**roag**) *verb*
to end a session of parliament.
Word Family **prorogation** (pro-ro-**gay**-
sh'n) *noun*.
[Latin *prorogare* to prolong]

prosaic (pro-**zay**-ik) *adjective*
dull or unimaginative.
Word Family **prosaically** *adverb*;
prosaicness *noun*.
[from PROSE]

proscenium (pro-**see**-ni-um) *noun* (*plural*
prosceniums or **proscenia**)
Theatre the front of a stage, especially the
curtain and its framework.
[Greek *proskenion* before the stage]

proscribe (pro-**skribe**) *verb*
to condemn or forbid.
Word Family **proscription** (pro-**skrip**-
sh'n) *noun*; **proscriptive** *adjective*.
[Latin *proscribere* to outlaw]

> ⚠️ Do not confuse *proscribe* with PRESCRIBE.

prose (proze) *noun*
writing or speech with no formal rhythm or pattern, as distinct from poetry.
[Latin *prosa* straightforward]

prosecute (**pross**-i-kewt) *verb*
to take legal action against.
[Latin *prosecutus* pursued]

prosecution (pross-i-**kew**-sh'n) *noun*
1 the act of prosecuting.
2 the lawyer or lawyers appointed to prosecute.

prosecutor *noun*
a person who prosecutes, especially a public official appointed to prosecute accused people.

proselyte (**pross**-i-lite) *noun*
a person converted to another belief, opinion or religion.
Word Family **proselytize, proselytise** (**pross**-ill-i-tize) *verb* to make a proselyte.
[Greek *proselytos* a newcomer]

prosody (**pross**-a-dee) *noun*
1 the theories or principles of writing or analysing the structure of verse.
2 the patterns of rhythm and sound in verse.
[Greek *prosoidia* accentuation]

prospect (**pross**-pekt) *noun*
1 a future possibility or chance: *There is little prospect of the weather improving.*
2 (**prospects**) chances for success.
3 (*formal*) an extended view or outlook: *There is a beautiful prospect from the window.*
4 *Mining* a mineral deposit or an indication of a possible deposit.
• **prospect** *verb* to search for valuable minerals.
Word Family **prospector** *noun* a person who searches for valuable minerals.

prospective (**pross**-**pek**-tiv) *adjective*
expected or likely in the future: *an open evening for prospective parents.*
Word Family **prospectively** *adverb*.

prospectus *noun* (*plural* **prospectuses**)
a printed booklet describing a school or university or advertising something.
[Latin, a distant view]

prosper *verb*
to flourish or be successful: *The company prospered under the new director.*
Word Family **prosperity** (pross-**pe**-ri-tee) *noun* success or wealth; **prosperous** *adjective* successful or wealthy: *Over the years he became a prosperous businessman;*

prosperously *adverb*; **prosperousness** *noun*.
[Latin *prosperus* as one hoped]

prostate gland *noun*
Anatomy a gland found at the top of the urethra in the male reproductive system. It produces part of the fluid in which the sperms swim.
[Greek *prostates* standing before]

prosthesis (pross-**thee**-sis) *noun* (*plural* **prostheses**) (pros-**thee**-seez)
an artificial device used to build up or replace a damaged or missing part of the body, e.g. an artificial leg.
Word Family **prosthetic** (pross-**thet**-ik) *adjective*.
[Greek, an addition]

prostitute *noun*
a person who engages in sexual activity for payment.
Word Family **prostitute** *verb* to use one's abilities unworthily; **prostitution** *noun*.
[Latin *prostitutus* exposed for sale]

prostrate (**pross**-trate) *adjective*
1 lying face down: *The worshippers were prostrate before the altar.*
2 overcome: *prostrate with grief.*
Word Family **prostrate** (pross-**trate**) *verb* to cast oneself down, in adoration or pleading; **prostration** *noun* 1 the act of prostrating. 2 extreme weakness or helplessness.
[Latin *prostratus* thrown to the ground]

protagonist (pro-**tag**-a-nist) *noun*
1 the main character in a story or play.
2 a person who leads, supports or represents a cause, etc.: *a protagonist of women's rights.*
[Greek *protos* first + *agonistes* contestant]

protean (pro-ti-an *or* pro-tee-an) *adjective*
readily changing, variable.
[after *Proteus*, a sea god in Greek mythology who could assume different forms]

protect *verb*
to keep or guard from harm, attack, etc.
Word Family **protective** *adjective* intending or serving to protect; **protectively** *adverb*; **protector** *noun* a person or thing that protects.
[from Latin]

protection (pro-**tek**-sh'n) *noun*
1 the act of protecting.
2 the state of being protected.
3 an economic system of protecting industry and agriculture from foreign competition by placing a tax on imports.

4 money paid to criminals in exchange for a promise of safety from their violence.
Word Family **protectionism** *noun* the theory of economic protection; **protectionist** *noun, adjective*.

protectorate (pro-**tek**-ta-rit) *noun* a country protected and partly controlled by another. Compare COLONY (definition 1).

protégé (**prot**-izh-ay *or* **pro**-tizh-ay) *noun* a person given helpful protection, support or favour by someone else.
Word Family **protégée** *noun* a female protégé.
[French, protected]

protein (**pro**-teen) *noun* any of a group of complex organic compounds containing carbon, hydrogen, oxygen and nitrogen, composed of amino acid chains and essential for all living things.
[Greek *proteios* primary]

pro tem *adjective, adverb* for the present.
[shortening of Latin *pro tempore*]

protest (pro-**test**) *verb*
1 to express disapproval or objection: *I must protest at such rudeness.*
2 to declare or affirm: *She continued to protest her innocence.*
• **protest** (**pro**-test) *noun* an expression or display of disapproval, etc.
Phrase **under protest** although complaining or objecting: *He agreed under protest.*
Word Family **protester** *noun*; **protestingly** *adverb*; **protestation** (prot-ess-**tay**-sh'n) *noun*.
[*pro-* + Latin *testari* to assert]

Protestant (**prot**-is-t'nt) *noun* *Christianity* a member of any of the Churches which separated from the Roman Catholic Church from the 16th century onwards.
Word Family **Protestantism** *noun* **1** the religion or principles of a Protestant. **2** all Protestant Churches.

protocol (**pro**-ta-kol) *noun* the customs and rules relating to ceremonies and other official occasions.
[Greek *protokollon* the summary of the contents of a manuscript]

proton (**pro**-ton) *noun* *Physics* a stable positively charged elementary particle, equivalent to a hydrogen ion and a part of all atomic nuclei. Compare NEUTRON.
[Greek, first thing]

protoplasm (**pro**-toe-plazm) *noun* *Biology* the living substance of a cell, consisting of the nucleus and cytoplasm.
[*proto-* + PLASM]

prototype (**pro**-toe-tipe) *noun* the first example of a type, from which other forms are developed or further refined.

Protozoa (pro-toe-**zo**-a) *plural noun* a large group of microscopic animals with one cell and at least one nucleus.
Word Family **protozoon** (pro-toe-**zo**-on) *noun*.
[*proto-* + Greek *zoion* animal]

protract *verb* to lengthen or extend in time: *Let's not protract this silly argument.*
Word Family **protraction** *noun*.
[*pro-* + Latin *tractus* dragged]

protractor *noun* a flat instrument with a graduated scale, used for measuring angles.

protrude *verb* to push or jut out: *Her lower lip protruded sulkily.*
Word Family **protrusion** (pro-**troo**-zh'n) *noun*.
[from Latin]

protuberance (pro-**tew**-ba-r'nce) *noun*
1 something which projects or protrudes.
2 the state of protruding.
Word Family **protuberant** *adjective* bulging.
[*pro-* + Latin *tuber* a swelling]

proud *adjective*
1 feeling or showing pride or satisfaction, especially in oneself or one's possessions.
2 inspiring pride or self-satisfaction: *This is a proud moment for us.*
Phrase **do someone proud 1** to be a source of credit to someone. **2** to entertain someone lavishly.
Word Family **proudly** *adverb*.
[Latin *prodesse* to do good]

prove (proov) *verb* (**proves; proving; proved; proved** *or* **proven**)
1 to show to be true or genuine: *You must prove your accusation.*
2 to turn out to be: *It proved to be a terrible mistake.*
3 *Cooking* to cause yeast dough to rise in a warm place before baking.
4 *Law* to obtain probate of a will.
[Latin *probare* to test]

provenance (**prov**-a-nence) *noun* the place where something comes from: *the provenance of an old painting.*
[French]

provender (**prov**-in-da) *noun*
1 dry food, such as hay or oats, used for livestock.
2 food.
[Latin *praebenda* food allowance]

proverb (**prov**-erb) *noun*
a short saying, usually containing a useful or well-known belief or truth, e.g. 'All's well that ends well'.
Word Family **proverbial** (pro-**ver**-bi-ul) *adjective* 1 expressed in a proverb or proverbs. 2 widely known or referred to; **proverbially** *adverb*.
[from Latin]

provide *verb*
1 to supply or make available: *The school will provide exercise books.*
2 to make preparations or arrangements: *We didn't provide for the possibility of such a long delay.*
Word Family **provider** *noun* a person who provides, especially one whose income supports a family.
[Latin *providere* to foresee]

provided *conjunction*
on the condition: *You may come, provided that you don't talk.*

providence (**prov**-i-d'nce) *noun*
1 *Christianity* the care or protection provided by God.
2 (**Providence**) *Christianity* God.
3 careful or economical management.
Word Family **providential** (prov-i-**den**-sh'l) *adjective* as if guided by providence, fortunate or opportune; **providentially** *adverb*.

provident (**prov**-i-d'nt) *adjective*
1 providing for the future.
2 economical or thrifty.
Word Family **providently** *adverb*.

providing *conjunction*
provided that: *We will have a picnic providing the weather stays fine.*

province (**prov**-ince) *noun*
1 an administrative division or unit of a country.
2 (**the provinces**) the parts of a country outside the capital.
3 someone's sphere of knowledge or authority: *That problem is outside my province.*
[Latin *provincia* sphere of administration]

provincial (pro-**vin**-sh'l) *adjective*
1 of or belonging to a province or provinces: *a provincial newspaper.*
2 narrow-minded: *provincial attitudes.*
• **provincial** *noun*

1 a person who comes from a province or the provinces.
2 *Christianity* the head of a religious order in a region.

provision (pra-**vi**-*zh*'n) *noun*
1 the act of supplying or providing: *Let us organize the provision of food for the party.*
2 preparation: *Have you made any provision for a change in the weather?*
3 (**provisions**) supplies, especially of food.
4 a condition inserted into a document or agreement.
• **provision** *verb* to supply with food.

provisional *adjective*
1 provided for the present only: *New drivers are given a provisional permit for three years.*
2 possible or conditional.
Word Family **provisionally** *adverb*.

proviso (pro-**vie**-zo) *noun*
a condition or limitation, e.g. in a document or agreement: *I will pay in advance, with the proviso that I may be given a refund if necessary.*
Word Family **provisory** *adjective*.
[Latin, it being provided]

provoke *verb*
1 to stir or stimulate to action, emotion, etc.: *The decision provoked an outcry from local people.*
2 to deliberately annoy: *I found her very provoking.*
Word Family **provocation** (prov-a-**kay**-sh'n) *noun*; **provocative** (pro-**vok**-a-tiv) *adjective* 1 stimulating, especially in a sexual way: *a provocative pose.* 2 irritating; **provocatively** *adverb*.
[Latin *provocare* to call forth, challenge]

provost (**prov**-ust) *noun*
1 an old title retained by certain university and church officials.
2 *Scottish* the chairman of a town council and the town's chief official.
[Latin *praepositus* placed over]

prow (*rhymes with* cow) *noun*
the pointed front part of a boat; the bow.
[Greek *proira*]

prowess *noun*
outstanding skill or courage.

prowl *verb*
to move about furtively or secretively, especially in search of something.
Word Family **prowler** *noun* a person who prowls; **prowl** *noun* an act of prowling: *out on the prowl.*

proximal (prok-si-m'l) *adjective*
towards the centre of the body or point of attachment to a limb, etc. Compare DISTAL.

proximity (prok-sim-i-tee) *noun*
nearness or closeness.
Word Family **proximate** (prok-si-mit) *adjective* 1 close or closely related. 2 approximate.
[Latin *proximus* nearest]

proxy (prok-see) *noun* (*plural* **proxies**)
1 the authority to act for another person. 2 a person authorized to act for another.

prude *noun*
a person who finds sex and nudity shocking.
Word Family **prudish** (proo-dish) *adjective*; **prudishly** *adverb*; **prudishness, prudery** *noun*.
[French]

prudent (proo-d'nt) *adjective*
acting with caution, foresight or discretion; mindful of consequences: *It was not prudent of you to mention her name.*
Word Family **prudently** *adverb*; **prudence** *noun*; **prudential** (proo-den-sh'l) *adjective* having or showing good sense, especially business sense.
[from Latin]

prune¹ *noun*
a purplish-black dried plum.
[Greek *prounon* plum]

prune² *verb*
1 to cut branches or parts off plants, especially to promote later growth. 2 to reduce, cut down: *We must prune our expenses.*
[*pro-* + Latin *rotundus* round]

prurient (proor-i-ent) *adjective*
obsessed by sexual or erotic thoughts, desires, etc.
Word Family **prurience** *noun*.
[Latin *pruriens* itching]

Prussian blue *noun*
a deep greenish-blue colour or pigment.

prussic acid *noun*
an old word for hydrocyanic acid, a deadly poison.
[as it was first obtained from *Prussian* blue]

pry¹ *verb* (**pries; prying; pried**)
to look or ask with excessive curiosity.
Word Family **prying** *adjective*; **pryingly** *adverb*.

pry² *verb* (**pries; prying; pried**)
(*especially American*) to prise or lever.

psalm (sahm) *noun*
a sacred song or hymn.
Word Family **psalmist** *noun* a person who writes psalms.
[Greek *psalmos* a song sung to the harp]

psephology (se-foll-a-jee) *noun*
the analysis of election results and voting habits.
[Greek *psephos* a pebble (used in voting) + *-logy*]

pseudonym (syoo-d'-nim) *noun*
an invented name, especially one adopted by an author.
[*pseudo-* + Greek *onyma* name]

psittacosis (sit-a-ko-sis) *noun*
an infectious viral disease of birds, easily transmitted to humans and causing fever and coughing.
[Greek *psittakos* a parrot + *-osis*]

psych (sike) *verb* also **psyche**
1 (*informal*) to motivate others using psychological techniques, to improve performance in a competition, etc. 2 (*informal*) to encourage oneself to perform better using similar techniques: *Chloe psyched herself up for her last throw of the day.*
Phrase **psych out** to make an opponent worried or unsure by appearing very confident.

psyche (sigh-kee) *noun*
the soul, spirit or mind.
[Greek, breath, life]

psychedelic (sigh-ka-dell-ik) *adjective*
1 relating to drugs which lead to greatly increased consciousness, sensitivity or perception. 2 having vivid or luminous colours and shapes.
[PSYCHE + Greek *deloein* to reveal]

psychiatry (sigh-kie-a-tree) *noun*
the branch of medicine which deals with the diagnosis and treatment of mental disorders. Compare PSYCHOLOGY (definition 1).
Word Family **psychiatrist** *noun*; **psychiatric** (sigh-kee-at-rik) *adjective*.
[PSYCHE + Greek *iatros* healer]

psychic (sigh-kik) *adjective*
1 having supernatural or extrasensory powers. 2 relating to or produced by such powers. 3 relating to the mind or self.
Word Family **psychical** *adjective*; **psychically** *adverb*.

psychoanalysis (sigh-ko-a-**nall**-a-sis)
noun also called **analysis**.
a method of treatment in psychotherapy,
concerned with the role of unconscious
motives in behaviour.
Word Family **psychoanalyse** *verb*;
psychoanalyst *noun*.

psychology (sigh-**koll**-a-jee) *noun*
1 the branch of science which studies
consciousness and behaviour. Compare
PSYCHIATRY.
2 the actual mental processes of a
particular person or group.
Word Family **psychologist** *noun* a
person trained in psychology;
psychological (sigh-ko-**loj**-i-k'l) *adjective*
relating to psychology or the mind;
psychologically *adverb*.
[*psycho-* + *-logy*]

psychopath (**sigh**-ko-path) *noun*
a person with a chronic mental disorder
which can lead to abnormal or violent
behaviour.
Word Family **psychopathic** *adjective*.

psychopathology (sigh-ko-pa-**tholl**-a-
jee) *noun*
the investigation, understanding and
treatment of mental disorders.
[*psycho-* + Greek *pathos* suffering + *-logy*]

psychosis (sigh-**ko**-sis) *noun* (*plural*
psychoses) (sigh-**ko**-seez)
a severe mental disorder in which the
perception of reality is distorted, e.g.
schizophrenia.
Word Family **psychotic** (sigh-**kot**-ik)
adjective.
[*psycho-* + *-osis*]

psychosomatic (sigh-ko-so-**mat**-ik)
adjective
caused or affected by the patient's mental
or emotional condition, rather than
physical factors: *a psychosomatic illness*.
[*psycho-* + Greek *somatos* of a body]

psychotherapy (sigh-ko-**therr**-a-pee)
noun
the treatment of mental disorders using
psychological methods.

ptarmigan (**tar**-mi-g'n) *noun*
a grouse that lives at high altitudes.
[Gaelic]

pterodactyl (terr-a-**dak**-til) *noun*
a large flying reptile of the late Jurassic
period, with a bird-like head. Each wing
consisted of a flap of skin extending from
the body to the long outer finger.
[Greek *pteron* wing + *daktylos* finger]

ptomaine (**toe**-mane) *noun*
(*dated*) *Chemistry* any of several alkaloids
found in putrefying flesh and vegetation,
formerly believed to cause food poisoning.
[Greek *ptoma* corpse]

ptyalin (**tie**-a-lin) *noun*
Biology an enzyme found in saliva,
converting starch into sugar as the first
stage of digestion.
[Greek *ptyalon* spittle]

pub *noun*
a building where alcoholic drinks are
served.

puberty (**pew**-ba-tee) *noun*
the period of developing sexual maturity,
ending when an individual is able to
produce an offspring.
[Latin *puber* adult]

pubes (**pew**-beez) *noun* (*plural* **pubes**)
(**pew**-beez)
Anatomy the region where the legs join the
trunk, covered with hair after puberty.
[Latin]

pubescence (pew-**bess**-'nce) *noun*
1 the time of puberty.
2 *Biology* soft fine hair, e.g. on the stem of
a plant.
Word Family **pubescent** *adjective*.

pubic (**pew**-bik) *adjective*
of or relating to the pubis or pubes.

pubis (**pew**-bis) *noun* (*plural* **pubes**)
(**pew**-beez)
Anatomy the arch of bone in the front of
the region where the legs join the trunk.

public *adjective*
1 of or for all the people of a place or
country: *public transport*.
2 open to any or all people: *a public
meeting*.
• **public** *noun* the people belonging to a
particular community or country.
Phrase **in public** openly, in front of other
people.
Word Family **publicly** *adverb*.
[Latin *publicus* of the people]

publican *noun*
a person who runs or owns a pub.
[Latin]

> The word **publican** originally meant 'a
> tax collector'. It was derived from Latin
> *publicanus*, a person who collected
> public revenues and received a
> percentage of them (from *publicum*
> 'public revenue').

publication (pub-li-**kay**-sh'n) *noun*
1 anything which is published, such as a
book or magazine.

2 the act of publishing: *He prepared his novel for publication.*

public convenience ⇨ CONVENIENCE (definition 4).

public enemy *noun* (*plural* **public enemies**)
a notorious wanted criminal.

public house *noun*
(*formal*) a pub.

publicity (pub-**liss**-i-tee) *noun*
1 the bringing of something to the attention of the public by advertising, news items, etc.
2 the public notice or attention resulting from this.
Word Family **publicize, publicise** (**pub**-li-size) *verb* to advertise or give publicity to.

public prosecutor *noun*
the law officer who conducts criminal prosecutions in cases of importance or great difficulty.

public relations *plural noun*
the practice or techniques of establishing a favourable image or relationship for a company, government, etc. with the community.

public school *noun*
1 in Britain, a private secondary school, financed by fees and endowments.
2 *American* a school maintained at public expense.

public servant *noun*
someone who works for the state, or for local government.

public-spirited *adjective*
eager to act in the interests of the public.

publish *verb*
1 to organize the printing of a book, magazine, newspaper, etc. for distribution to the public.
2 to make something known, e.g. by printing it.
Word Family **publisher** *noun* a person or company that publishes books, etc.

puce (pewce) *noun*
a dark purplish-brown colour.
● **puce** *adjective.*
[Latin *pulicis* of a flea]

puck *noun*
the flat rubber disc used instead of a ball in ice hockey.

pucker *verb*
to wrinkle.
● **pucker** *noun* a wrinkle.

puckish *adjective*
mischievous or impish.
[after *Puck*, a mischievous elf]

pudding *noun*
1 a dessert made from flour, milk and eggs, usually with added flavouring or fruit.
2 any dessert.
3 a sweet or savoury dish made with flour or suet: *steak and kidney pudding.*

puddle *noun*
a small pool of liquid, especially muddy rainwater.

pudgy *adjective* (**pudgier; pudgiest**)
(*informal*) rather fat.

pueblo (**pweb**-lo) *noun*
a village or settlement, especially a settlement of Native Americans, e.g. in New Mexico or Arizona.
[Spanish, people]

puerile (**pyor**-ile) *adjective*
foolishly childish or trivial.
[Latin *puer* a boy]

puff *noun*
1 a short quick release of breath, air, smoke, etc.: *a puff of wind.*
2 any soft rounded mass or part.
● **puff** *verb*
1 to make puffs: *She puffed after running uphill.* □ *He puffed smoke into my face.*
2 to smoke a pipe or cigarette.
Phrase **puff up** to swell or become inflated.
Word Family **puffed** *adjective* out of breath.

puffball *noun*
a type of fungus with a ball-like body which releases a cloud of spores when broken.

puffin *noun*
a type of auk with a large head and brightly coloured bill.

puff pastry *noun*
a light and flaky pastry.

puffy *adjective* (**puffier; puffiest**)
1 swollen or distended: *Her face became puffy after she was stung.*
2 softly rounded.

pug *noun*
any of a breed of dogs with a flat wrinkled face, short hair and a tightly curled tail.

pugilist (**pew**-ji-list) *noun*
(*dated*) a boxer.
Word Family **pugilistic** (pew-ji-**lis**-tik) *adjective*; **pugilism** *noun.*
[Latin *pugil*]

pugnacious (pug-**nay**-shus) *adjective*
quarrelsome or aggressive.
Word Family **pugnaciously** *adverb*;
pugnacity (pug-**nass**-i-tee) *noun*.
[Latin *pugna* fight]

pug nose *noun*
a short upturned nose.
Word Family **pug-nosed** *adjective*.

puja (**poo**-jah) *noun* also **pooja**
Hinduism a form of worship in the home
or temple.
[Sanskrit]

puke *verb*
(*informal*) to vomit.
● **puke** *noun*.

pukka *adjective* also **pukkah**
1 (*informal*) genuine or sound.
2 (*informal*) excellent.
[Hindi, cooked, ripe]

puling (**pew**-ling) *adjective*
a poetic word meaning 'crying,
whimpering'.

pull (*rhymes with* wool) *verb*
1 to bring towards or after oneself or in a
particular direction: *a horse pulling a cart.*
2 to strain a muscle or ligament.
3 to move: *The car pulled out in front of me.*
□ *She shouted as the bus began to pull away.*
4 to inhale, e.g. on a cigarette.
5 (*informal*) to draw out a weapon: *He
pulled a knife on me.*
6 to attract an audience, customers, etc.
7 (*informal*) to attract a sexual partner.
Phrases **pull oneself together** to recover
self-control. **pull over** to move to one side
of the road and stop. **pull something off**
to succeed in doing something. **pull up**
1 to stop. 2 to reprimand or rebuke.
● **pull** *noun*
1 an act of pulling: *She gave the rope a pull.*
2 an injury to a muscle or ligament.
3 something that forces or compels.
4 the act of drawing in liquid or smoke
into the mouth.
5 ⇨ HOOK *noun* (definition 3).

pullet (**pull**-it) *noun*
a young hen.
[Latin *pullus* a chicken]

pulley (**pull**-ee) *noun*
a wheel or system of wheels with grooves
in the rim for ropes or chains, used to lift
weights, apply force, etc.

Pullman *noun*
a very comfortable railway carriage or
train.
[designed by *George Pullman*, 1831-1897,
an American industrialist]

pullover *noun*
a knitted piece of clothing with sleeves,
pulled on over the head to cover the upper
part of the body.

pulmonary (**pul**-m'n-ree) *adjective*
of or relating to the lungs.
[Latin *pulmonis* of a lung]

pulp *noun*
1 *Biology* the fleshy part of a fruit.
2 any soft moist mass of a substance.
3 a soft wet mass of rags or wood which is
treated to be made into paper.
● **pulp** *verb* to make into or become pulp:
*Old newspapers are often pulped and
reprocessed.*

pulpit (**pull**-pit) *noun*
a stone or timber platform with a desk,
reached by steps and used for preaching
sermons in church.
[Latin *pulpitum* a stage]

pulsar *noun*
Astronomy a star which emits enormously
powerful radio signals in very regular
pulses. Pulsars have many bizarre features
indicative of some final stage in stellar
evolution.
[PULS(ating) + (st)AR]

pulsate (pul-**sate**) *verb*
to expand and contract regularly, as the
heart or an artery does.
Word Family **pulsation** *noun* 1 the act of
pulsating. 2 a single throb or vibration.
[Latin *pulsare* to batter]

pulse[1] *noun*
1 *Biology* the rhythmic movement in the
arteries caused by the beating of the heart
as it pumps the blood through them.
2 a single throb.
3 any strong rhythm: *the pulse of city life.*
● **pulse** *verb* to throb, especially strongly.

pulse[2] *noun*
the edible seeds of plants such as peas,
beans and lentils.

pulverize, pulverise *verb*
1 to grind or crush a substance into a
powder.
2 (*informal*) to defeat utterly: *The boxer
pulverized his opponent.*
[Latin *pulveris* of powder]

puma (**pew**-ma) *noun*
a flesh-eating American mammal of the
cat family, with a tawny coat.

pumice (**pum**-is) *noun*
a light porous volcanic rock used as an
abrasive.
[from Latin]

pummel (pum-'l) *verb* (**pummels;
pummelling; pummelled**)
to hit or beat repeatedly with the fists.

pump[1] *noun*
any of various devices for moving a liquid
or a gas through a pipe: *a petrol pump.*
• **pump** *verb*
1 to transfer or supply with or as if with a
pump: *She pumped air into the tyres.*
2 to move vigorously up and down: *He
pumped my hand gratefully.*
3 (*informal*) to try to get information from
someone by asking questions.

pump[2] *noun*
1 a light dancing shoe made of satin or
shiny leather.
2 a plimsoll.

pumpernickel *noun*
a dark rye bread.
[German]

pumpkin *noun*
a large fruit with firm orange flesh.

pun *noun*
a clever or humorous play on the meanings
of words which sound or look similar, as in
Hilaire Belloc's suggested epitaph for
himself: 'His sins were scarlet but his
books were read'.
• **pun** *verb* (**puns; punning; punned**) to
make a pun or puns.

punch[1] *verb*
to hit hard with the fist.
• **punch** *noun* (*plural* **punches**)
1 a blow with the fist.
2 (*informal*) effect, force: *a speech with quite
a lot of punch.*

punch[2] *noun* (*plural* **punches**)
a tool or machine for cutting holes,
stamping designs, etc.
• **punch** *verb* to pierce or stamp with or as
if with a punch.

punch[3] *noun* (*plural* **punches**)
a spiced drink made with a combination of
water, fruit juices, wine or spirits, spices,
etc.

punchbag *noun*
a heavy suspended stuffed bag, punched
by boxers in training.

punch-drunk *adjective*
1 suffering from a form of brain damage
due to repeated blows on the head.
2 dazed.

punched card *noun* also **punchcard**
a card punched with holes representing
information, formerly used to program
computers.

punchline *noun*
the final line or sentence of a joke, on
which the whole joke depends.

punch-up *noun*
(*informal*) a fight.

punctilious (punk-**till**-i-us) *adjective*
very careful about small details.
[Latin *puntiglio* a little point]

punctual (punk-tew-'l) *adjective*
prompt or arriving at the correct time: *He
is always punctual.*
Word Family punctually *adverb* on time;
punctuality (punk-tew-**al**-i-tee) *noun.*

punctuate (**punk**-tew-ate) *verb*
1 to divide a sentence or paragraph with
marks, such as full stops and commas, to
make the meaning clearer.
2 to interrupt: *He punctuated his speech with
short silences.*

punctuation (punk-tew-**ay**-sh'n) *noun*
1 the marks used to punctuate sentences:
The punctuation is wrong.
2 the use of punctuation marks: *She's good
at punctuation and spelling.*
[Latin *punctum* a point]

punctuation mark *noun*
a sign such as a comma, question mark or
apostrophe, used to punctuate a sentence.

puncture (**punk**-cher) *noun*
a small hole made by a sharp object: *a
puncture in a tyre.*
• **puncture** *verb* to prick or pierce
something with a sharp object: *The doctor
punctured the skin with a needle.*

pundit *noun*
an expert.
[Hindi *pandit* learned]

pungent (**pun**-j'nt) *adjective*
1 sharp or biting in taste or smell: *a
pungent curry.*
2 sharp, severe: *pungent criticism.*
Word Family pungently *adverb*;
pungency *noun.*
[Latin *pungens* pricking]

punish *verb*
1 to make a person suffer pain or loss as a
penalty for wrongdoing.
2 to treat roughly: *The fighter punished his
opponent.*
Word Family punishable *adjective* liable
to punishment: *a crime punishable by death.*
[Latin *poena* penalty]

punishment *noun*
1 the act of punishing.
2 a penalty: *a punishment to fit the crime.*

punitive (**pew**-ni-tiv) *adjective*
inflicting or serving as punishment:
punitive action.

punk *noun*
1 also **punk rock** a type of loud aggressive
pop music.
2 also **punk rocker** a person who listens
to or plays punk music.
3 (*informal, especially American*) a
worthless person or petty criminal.

punnet (**pun**-it) *noun*
a small basket, such as those used to hold
strawberries.

punt[1] *noun*
a narrow flat-bottomed boat which is
moved along by pushing a long pole
against the bottom of the river, etc.
• **punt** *verb.*

punt[2] *noun*
Rugby, American Football a kick in which
the ball is dropped and kicked before it
reaches the ground.
• **punt** *verb.*

punt[3] *verb*
(*informal*) to gamble or bet, especially on
horse races.
Word Family **punt** *noun* (*informal*) a bet;
punter *noun* 1 (*informal*) a person who
punts. 2 (*informal*) a client, customer.

punt[4] (punt) *noun*
the basic unit of money in the Republic of
Ireland.

puny (**pew**-nee) *adjective* (**punier;**
puniest)
small and weak.

pup *noun*
a puppy.

pupa (**pew**-pa) *noun* (*plural* **pupae**) (**pew**-
pee)
the resting stage between larva and adult
in some insects, during which great
developmental changes occur.
Word Family **pupate** (pew-**pate**) *verb* to
become a pupa; **pupation** *noun.*
[Latin, doll]

pupil[1] (**pew**-pil) *noun*
a person who is learning, especially in a
school.
[Latin *pupus* boy]

pupil[2] *noun*
Anatomy the clear area in the front of the
eye, appearing as a black hole.

puppet (**pup**-it) *noun*
1 a hollow doll worn on the hand with its
head and arms moved by the operator's
fingers.

2 a marionette.
3 a person controlled or manipulated by
another.
Word Family **puppeteer** *noun* a person
who manipulates puppets; **puppetry**
noun.

puppy *noun* (*plural* **puppies**)
a young dog.

puppy fat *noun*
the fatness or plumpness of a child's body,
usually only lasting until adolescence.

puppy love *noun*
intense love or infatuation, especially as
felt by a young person.

purblind *adjective*
partially blind.

purchase (**per**-chis) *verb*
(*formal*) to buy.
• **purchase** *noun*
1 the act of buying: *the purchase of goods by
post.*
2 something which is bought.
Word Family **purchaser** *noun.*

purdah *noun*
1 *Hinduism, Islam* a curtain or screen
hiding women from the sight of men.
2 *Hinduism, Islam* the system of such
seclusion.
[Persian]

pure *adjective*
1 unmixed with any other substance: *pure
orange juice.*
2 abstract or theoretical: *pure maths.*
Compare APPLIED.
3 innocent: *the pure mind of a child.*
4 complete: *It was pure fabrication.*
Word Family **purely** *adverb;* **pureness**
noun.
[Latin *purus*]

purée (**pyor**-ay) *noun*
Cooking any fruit or vegetables mashed or
sieved to a smooth cream.
• **purée** *verb* (**purées; puréeing;**
puréed).
[French, strained]

purgative (**per**-ga-tiv) *adjective*
purging or cleansing, especially of the
bowels.
• **purgative** *noun* a laxative.

purgatory (**per**-ga-tree) *noun* (*plural*
purgatories)
1 *Roman Catholicism* a place or condition
in which it is believed that the souls of
dead people are purified.
2 torment or anguish.

Word Family **purgatorial** (per-ga-**taw**-ri-ul) *adjective* **1** of or like purgatory.
2 cleansing.
[Latin *purgare* to cleanse]

purge (perj) *verb*
1 to rid of something unwanted: *to purge someone of their guilt.*
2 to remove unwanted people from something, e.g. a political party.
3 to remove by cleansing or purifying.
• **purge** *noun*
1 an act of purging.
2 *History* the removal of political opponents by force.

puri (**pu**-ree) *noun*
a round piece of unleavened bread that is deep-fried and eaten with Indian food.
[Hindi]

purify (pyor-i-fie) *verb* (**purifies; purifying; purified**)
to make pure.
Word Family **purification** *noun.*

purist (pyor-ist) *noun*
a person who insists on following the traditional rules, especially those of language and style.
Word Family **purism** *noun.*

puritan (pyor-i-t'n) *noun*
a person who is excessively strict in regard to morals, religion, etc.
Word Family **puritanical** (pyor-i-tan-i-k'l) *adjective*; **puritanically** *adverb.*
[after the *Puritans*, the Dissenters (later Nonconformists) who separated from the Church of England in Cromwell's time]

purity (pyor-i-tee) *noun*
the state of being pure.

purl[1] *verb*
a poetic word meaning 'to flow or ripple with a murmuring sound'.
• **purl** *noun* the sound of this.

purl[2] *noun*
a stitch made by putting the needle through the front of the stitch from right to left.
• **purl** *verb.*

purlieus (**perl**-yooz) *plural noun*
(*formal*) the outskirts or environs.
[Old French *pourallee* beating the bounds (confused with *lieu* place)]

purlin *noun*
Building a beam which crosses rafters and supports roofing material.

purloin (per-**loyn**) *verb*
(*formal*) to steal.

purple *noun*
a reddish-violet colour.

• **purple** *adjective* of the colour purple.
[Greek *porphyra* a shellfish used in dyeing things purple]

purple prose *noun*
ornate, elaborate prose.

purport (per-**port**) *verb*
to claim to be or do something, especially falsely: *The note purported to come from the solicitor.*
• **purport** (**per**-put) *noun* the gist or meaning of something: *What was the purport of his speech?*

purpose (**per**-pus) *noun*
something which forms the basis or reason for some action, event, etc.: *What is the purpose of your visit?*
Phrases **on purpose** deliberately. **to little purpose** with little or no result or effect. **to the purpose** (*formal*) relevant.
• **purpose** *verb* (*formal*) to have as a purpose.
[Latin *propositus* put forward]

purposeful *adjective*
1 determined or resolute.
2 having a purpose.
Word Family **purposefully** *adverb*; **purposefulness** *noun.*

purposely *adverb*
on purpose, deliberately.

purr *verb*
to make a low vibrating sound, as a cat does in pleasure or satisfaction: *The engine purred smoothly.*
• **purr** *noun.*

purse *noun*
1 a small bag for carrying money, etc.
2 *American* a handbag.
3 finances, funds.
4 a sum of money given as a prize.
Phrase **hold the purse strings** to control the use of money.
• **purse** *verb* to draw into folds or wrinkles: *He pursed his lips.*
[Greek *byrsa* leather]

purser *noun*
Nautical a ship's officer in charge of accounts.

pursuance (per-**syoo**-ence) *noun*
(*formal*) the carrying out of something: *in the pursuance of her duties.*

pursuant *adjective*
Phrase **pursuant to** (*formal*) in accordance or agreement with.

pursue (pers-**yoo**) *verb*
1 to go after in order to catch up with, capture or kill.

2 to seek: *pursuing happiness*.
3 to carry on, continue: *The police are pursuing their enquiries*.
[Latin *persecutus* followed to the end]

pursuit *noun*
1 the act of pursuing: *We are in pursuit of the thieves*.
2 an activity or hobby: *She enjoys fishing and other outdoor pursuits*.

purulent (**pyor**-a-l'nt) *adjective*
containing or forming pus.
[Latin *puris* of pus]

purvey (per-**vay**) *verb*
(*formal*) to supply or provide, especially food.
Word Family **purveyor** *noun* a person who purveys; **purveyance** *noun* the act of purveying.

pus *noun*
a thick yellowish-white substance containing dead bacteria and white blood cells, produced in abscesses, pimples, boils, etc.
[Latin]

push (push) *verb*
1 to move by force away from oneself: *pushing a car uphill*.
2 to force a way: *The army pushed into new territory*.
3 to urge: *She was pushed into applying for the job*.
4 to demand: *doctors pushing for shorter working hours*.
5 (*informal*) to promote: *pushing a new product*.
6 (*informal*) to sell an illegal drug.
Phrases **be pushed for** to be short of: *We're pushed for time*. **be pushing** to be approaching: *He's pushing 30*. **push in** to go in front of someone in a queue. **push off** to move away or leave. **push on** to continue or proceed.
• **push** *noun* (*plural* **pushes**)
1 the act of pushing.
2 an effort.
3 energy, drive.
Phrase **at a push** (*informal*) if absolutely necessary.

pushbike *noun*
(*informal*) a bicycle.

pushchair *noun*
a chair on wheels in which a baby or small child can be pushed along.

pusher *noun*
a person or thing that pushes, especially a person who sells drugs illegally.

pushover *noun*
1 (*informal*) anything which is done very easily.
2 (*informal*) a person, team, etc. that is easily defeated.

pushrod *noun*
a rod which is moved by the camshaft to operate the valves in an internal-combustion engine.

pushy *adjective* (**pushier; pushiest**)
assertive or ambitious.
Word Family **pushily** *adverb*; **pushiness** *noun*.

pusillanimous (pew-si-**lan**-i-mus) *adjective*
cowardly or timid.
Word Family **pusillanimously** *adverb*; **pusillanimity** (pew-sill-a-**nim**-i-tee) *noun*.
[Latin *pusillus* petty + *animus* spirit]

puss¹ *noun* (*plural* **pusses**)
(*informal*) a cat.

puss² *noun* (*plural* **pusses**)
(*American informal, Irish or Scottish*) the face.

pussy *noun* (*plural* **pussies**)
(*informal*) a cat.

pussyfoot *verb*
to act cautiously or timidly.

pussy willow *noun*
a willow with silky catkins.

pustule (**pust**-yool) *noun*
a small swelling in the skin containing pus.

put (put) *noun* (**puts; putting; put**)
1 to move something to a particular position: *Let's put the picture here.* □ *Put that gun down.* □ *She put some of the money in the bank.*
2 to make someone do or experience something: *He was put to death at dawn.* □ *I'll put you to work in the garden.* □ *You've put me to a lot of trouble.*
3 to express: *Please put your request in writing.*
4 to estimate: *I put the crowd at 3000.*
5 to bet: *Did you put any money on the winner?*
6 to apply: *to put something to good use.*
7 *Sport* to throw a shot or weight.
8 to ask: *She put several questions to him.*
9 to suggest: *I'll put the idea to him later.*
10 to move, go out: *The boat put out to sea.*
Phrases **put about 1** to circulate a rumour, etc. **2** (of a ship) to change direction. **put across** to communicate. **put aside, put by** to save or store up. **put down 1** to suppress. **2** to attribute: *I put*

her actions down to shyness. **3** to kill an animal because it is very ill or weak. **4** to criticize or belittle: *She's always putting me down.* **put it to** to suggest something to: *I put it to you that the government has not spent enough money on hospitals.* **put off 1** to postpone: *The meeting was put off until tomorrow.* **2** to make less enthusiastic: *The smell put me off the meal.* **put on 1** to assume: *She put on a French accent.* □ *He put on a sulky expression.* **2** to stage: *We're putting on a play this summer.* **put out 1** to cause a fire, cigarette, etc. to stop burning. **2** to inconvenience: *I hope our visit hasn't put you out.* **put up 1** to provide: *She will put up the money.* **2** to provide somewhere for someone to sleep: *We can put you up.* **3** to erect: *to put up a building.* **put someone up to something** to persuade someone to do something wrong or mischievous. **put up with** to tolerate.
● **put** *noun* a throw, especially a weight or shot.

putative (pew-ta-tiv) *adjective*
(*formal*) supposed or reputed: *the putative mother of the child.*

put-down *noun*
(*informal*) a remark that is intended to humiliate someone.

putrefy (pew-tri-fie) *verb* (**putrefies, putrefying; putrefied**)
to rot or decay.
Word Family putrefaction (pew-tri-fak-sh'n) *noun.*

putrid (pew-trid) *adjective*
rotten, decayed or foul-smelling.
[from Latin]

putsch (putch) *noun* (*plural* **putsches**)
a coup d'état.
[Swiss German, a thrust, blow]

putt (*rhymes with* hut) *verb*
Golf to strike the ball towards the hole when on the green.
Word Family putt *noun;* **putter** *noun* a straight iron-headed club used for putting.

putting green ⇨ GREEN *noun*
(definition 2).

putty (putt-ee) *noun* (*plural* **putties**)
a soft easily moulded mixture, usually of linseed oil and ground chalk, used to secure window panes, fill holes, etc.

put-up job *noun*
(*informal*) a secretly planned deception.

puzzle *noun*
1 a toy or game which requires skill to solve, such as a crossword or jigsaw.

2 a person or thing that is hard to understand.
● **puzzle** *verb*
1 to be or cause to be unable to understand: *Her strange behaviour puzzles me.*
2 to think deeply and work something out: *He was puzzling over what to do.*
Word Family puzzlement *noun* the state of being puzzled; **puzzler** *noun* a difficult question or problem; **puzzling** *adjective;* **puzzlingly** *adverb.*

pygmy (pig-mee) *noun* (*plural* **pygmies**)
also **pigmy** (*plural* **pigmies**)
1 a member of a race of people in equatorial Africa who are of very short stature.
2 any very small person or thing.
● *adjective* very small.
[Greek]

> The word **pygmy** derives from Greek *pugmé* (a fist). *Pugmé* then came to mean 'a measure of length equal to the distance from the elbow to the knuckles'. From this was formed *pugmaios*, meaning 'small in stature, dwarfish'. From the late 19th century, the name was applied to certain peoples of equatorial Africa.

pyjamas (pa-jah-mas) *plural noun*
(*American* **pajamas**)
a loose jacket and trousers for sleeping in.
[Urdu, leg clothes]

pylon (pie-lon) *noun*
a high tower or similar structure, especially one with a steel framework for carrying overhead cables.
[Greek, gateway]

pyramid (pirr-a-mid) *noun*
1 a solid or hollow body on a square base with sloping triangular faces which meet at the apex.
2 any structure, arrangement, etc. with this form.
Word Family pyramidal (pi-ram-i-d'l) *adjective.*
[Greek, probably from Egyptian]

pyre (pire) *noun*
a large pile of firewood, especially for burning a dead body.
[Greek *pyr* fire]

pyrethrin (pie-ree-thrin) *noun*
Chemistry a white powder used as a contact insecticide.

pyretic (pie-**ret**-ik) *adjective*
of, relating to or producing fever.

Pyrex (**pie**-reks) *noun*
(*trademark*) a heat-resistant glassware used
for cooking.

pyridoxine (pirr-ee-**dok**-sin) *noun*
vitamin B₆.

pyrites (pie-**rye**-teez) *noun* also called
iron pyrites; pyrite.
a mineral consisting of iron disulphide,
often golden in colour. ⇨ FOOL'S GOLD.
[Greek, of fire]

pyromania *noun*
an obsessive wish to set fire to things.
[Greek *pyros* fire + MANIA]

pyrotechnics (pie-ro-**tek**-niks) *plural
noun*
1 fireworks.
2 a spectacular display.
Word Family **pyrotechnic** *adjective*.

pyrrhic victory (pirr-ik **vik**-ta-ree) *noun*
(*plural* **pyrrhic victories**)
a victory gained at a great cost.
[after *Pyrrhus*, who defeated the
Romans in a battle in 279 B.C. but lost
many men]

Pythagoras' theorem (pie-thag-'r-'s
theer-um) *noun*
a theorem in geometry, according to which
the square of the length of the hypotenuse
of a right-angled triangle equals the sum
of the squares of the lengths of the other
two sides.
[*Pythagoras*, c. 580–c. 500 B.C. Greek
philosopher and mathematician]

python (**pie**-th'n) *noun*
a large non-venomous snake found mostly
in Africa and western Asia. Pythons coil
around and crush their victims.
[after *Python*, a huge monster in Greek
mythology]

pzazz ⇨ PIZZAZZ.

Qq

quack¹ *verb*
to make the loud harsh cry of a duck.
• **quack** *noun*.

quack² *noun*
1 a person who pretends dishonestly to be competent in a skill, especially in medicine.
2 (*informal*) any medical doctor.
Word Family **quack** *adjective*; **quackery** *noun*.

quad (kwod) *noun*
1 (*informal*) a quadrangle.
2 (*informal*) a quadruplet.

quad bike *noun*
a motorcycle with four large wheels for off-road use.

quadrangle (kwod-rang-'gl) *noun*
1 a closed plane figure with four straight sides, especially a square or rectangle.
2 a square open space surrounded by buildings.
Word Family **quadrangular** (kwod-rang-gew-la) *adjective*.
[*quadri-* + ANGLE¹]

quadrant (kwod-r'nt) *noun*
1 a sector equal to a quarter of a circle, or a quarter of the circumference.
2 something with the shape of a quarter of a circle.
3 an instrument formerly used to measure angles of altitude in astronomy, navigation, etc.
[Latin *quadrans* a fourth part]

quadraphonic (kwod-ra-fonn-ik) *adjective*
of or relating to sound reproduction through four distinct sound sources.
Compare MONOPHONIC; STEREOPHONIC.
[*quadri-* + Greek *phoné* sound]

quadratic equation (kwod-rat-ik ik-way-zh'n) *noun*
Maths an equation that contains a square of an unknown quantity and no powers of degree 3 or higher, such as $x^2 - 36 = 0$.

quadrilateral (kwod-ri-latt-a-r'l) *noun*
any closed plane figure with four straight sides.
• **quadrilateral** *adjective* having four sides.
[*quadri-* + Latin *lateris* of a side]

quadrille (kwod-ril) *noun*
1 a dance for four couples, or the music for such a dance.
2 a card game fashionable in the 18th century.
[French]

quadriplegic (kwod-ri-plee-jik) *adjective*
having the arms and legs paralysed.
Word Family **quadriplegic** *noun* a person who is quadriplegic; **quadriplegia** *noun*.
[*quadri-* + Greek *plegé* a stroke]

quadruped (kwod-roo-ped) *noun*
any animal with four feet.
[*quadri-* + Latin *pedis* of a foot]

quadruple (kwod-roo-p'l) *adjective*
1 consisting of four parts.
2 being four times as big.
Word Family **quadruple** *verb*; **quadruple** *noun*.

quadruplet (kwod-roo-plit) *noun*
any of four offspring born at one birth.

quaff (kwof) *verb*
to drink at one go, or in large gulps.

quagmire (kwag-mire *or* kwog-mire) *noun*
an area of soft muddy ground.

quail¹ *noun*
a small sandy-coloured game bird related to the partridge.

quail² *verb*
to feel or show fear.

quaint *adjective*
1 old-fashioned in an attractive way: *a quaint little old lady*.
2 curiously strange or unusual.
Word Family **quaintly** *adverb*; **quaintness** *noun*.

quake *verb*
to shake or tremble *He quaked with fear*.
• **quake** *noun*
1 (*informal*) an earthquake.
2 a shaking or trembling.

Quaker *noun*
a member of the **Society of Friends**, a Christian sect rejecting formal belief, etc. and emphasizing simple personal experience of divine revelation.
Word Family **Quaker, Quakerish** *adjective*; **Quakerism** *noun*.

[from George Fox's bidding to a magistrate to '*quake* at the word of the Lord']

qualification (kwoll-i-fi-**kay**-sh'n) *noun*
1 a quality, accomplishment, etc. which makes a person suitable for a particular position or job.
2 the act of qualifying: *her qualification of the statement.*
3 something which qualifies or modifies.
[Latin *qualitas* quality + *facere* to make]

qualify (**kwoll**-i-fie) *verb* (**qualifies; qualifying; qualified**)
1 to have the qualities or training necessary for something: *He is 70 so he qualifies for the old age pension.* □ *She qualified as a doctor after six years of studying.*
2 to modify or limit: *Adverbs qualify verbs.* □ *Please qualify your statement.*
Word Family **qualified** *adjective*; **qualifier** *noun*.

quality (**kwoll**-i-tee) *noun* (*plural* **qualities**)
1 a characteristic.
2 character with respect to excellence: *Meat of the highest quality is very expensive.* □ *quality of manufacture.*
Word Family **qualitative** (**kwoll**-it-a-tiv) *adjective* of or concerning quality or characteristics; **qualitatively** *adverb*.
[Latin]

quality assurance *noun*
maintaining standards of excellence in manufactured products.

quality of life *noun*
the well-being of a person or population. Factors which affect one's quality of life include income, health, housing, personal relationships and culture.

quality time *noun*
a period of time in which a person concentrates his or her full attention on a person or thing; often used of time spent by parents with their children.

qualm (kwahm) *noun*
1 a sudden misgiving or apprehensive feeling.
2 a pang of conscience.

quandary (**kwon**-da-ree) *noun* (*plural* **quandaries**)
a state of uncertainty or perplexity.

quango (**kwang**-go) *noun*
a body of people appointed by a government to be responsible for a particular area of public interest.

[*qu*(*asi*-) + A(utonomous) + N(on) + G(overnmental) + O(rganization)]

quantify (**kwont**-i-fie) *verb* (**quantifies; quantifying; quantified**)
to express as a quantity.
Word Family **quantifiable** *adjective*.
[Latin *quantus* how much + *facere* to make]

quantity (**kwon**-ti-tee) *noun* (*plural* **quantities**)
1 a particular or indefinite amount of something.
2 a considerable amount: *If you find gold in quantity you will soon be rich.*
Word Family **quantitative** (**kwon**-ti-ta-tiv) *adjective* of or concerning quantity.
[from Latin]

quantity surveyor *noun*
a person who estimates the quantities and costs of materials required for the construction of a building.

quantum (**kwon**-t'm) *noun* (*plural* **quanta**)
1 a total quantity or amount.
2 a share or portion.
3 *Physics* the fundamental unit of quantity for the energy of atoms or parts of atoms.
⇨ QUANTUM THEORY.

quantum leap *noun*
1 *Physics* a sudden change in an atom, electron, etc. from one energy level to another.
2 (*informal*) any sudden major advance in one's understanding.
3 (*informal*) any sudden major change.

quantum theory *noun*
Physics the theory that the energy of electromagnetic waves (e.g. light) is emitted or absorbed not continuously but in separate packets (quanta), the size of which is determined by the frequency of the radiation.

quarantine (**kworr**-'n-teen) *noun*
1 a period of isolation imposed on people, animals or plants thought to have an infectious disease.
2 a government system maintained at ports, etc. to prevent the spread of disease brought in from overseas.
• **quarantine** *verb* to put in or subject to quarantine.
[Italian *quarantina* 40 days (the original period of isolation)]

quark¹ (kwark) *noun*
Physics any of three hypothetical elementary particles suggested to be the basis of all other elementary particles.

[from a phrase in James Joyce's *Finnegans Wake*, 1939, 'Three *quarks* for Muster Mark']

quark² (kwark) *noun*
soft cheese made from skimmed milk.
[German *Quark* curds]

quarrel (**kworr-'l**) *noun*
1 an angry argument.
2 a cause for argument or complaint: *What is your quarrel with the plan?*
Word Family **quarrel** *verb* (**quarrels; quarrelling; quarrelled**); **quarrelsome** *adjective* tending to quarrel.
[Latin *querella* a complaint]

quarry¹ (**kworr-ee**) *noun* (*plural* **quarries**)
a large pit, formed as a result of stone, etc. being extracted by digging and blasting.
• **quarry** *verb* (**quarries; quarrying; quarried**)
1 to obtain stone from a quarry.
2 to dig a quarry.

quarry² (**kworr-ee**) *noun* (*plural* **quarries**)
a person or animal that is hunted or pursued.

quart (kwort) *noun*
1 a unit of volume for liquids equal to 2 pints, or about 1·13 litres.
2 *American* a unit of volume for liquids equal to two American pints, or about 0·94 litres.
[Latin *quartus* fourth]

quarter (**kwor-ta**) *noun*
1 any of four equal parts into which something is divided.
2 a period of 15 minutes: *I waited a quarter of an hour.* □ *It's a quarter past three.*
3 a part of a town: *He lives in the Latin quarter of Paris.*
4 a source: *From what quarter is your information?*
5 (in fighting) mercy: *They showed no quarter to their captives.*
6 *American* a 25-cent coin.
7 a unit of mass equal to 28 pounds, about 12·6 kg.
8 (**quarters**) lodgings, rooms: *the officers' quarters.*
9 (**quarters**) the hindquarters of a horse.
Phrase **close quarters** a close position or contact.
• **quarter** *verb*
1 to divide into four equal parts.
2 *Military* to billet troops.
• **quarter** *adjective*.

quarterback *noun*
American football a player who directs attacking play.

quarter day *noun*
one of the four days in the year when rents become payable and quarterly tenancies end or commence.

quarterdeck *noun*
the part of a ship's upper deck near the stern, used especially by officers.

quarter-final *noun*
the last competitions or matches played before a semi-final.

quarterly (**kwor-ta-lee**) *adjective*
1 of or occurring once in three months.
2 every three months.
• **quarterly** *noun* (*plural* **quarterlies**)
a magazine published four times a year.
• **quarterly** *adverb*.

quartermaster *noun*
1 *Army* the officer in charge of stores, rations, allocation of quarters, etc.
2 *Navy* the petty officer in charge of steering, taking soundings, signalling, etc.

quarter note *noun*
American a crotchet.

quarter sessions *plural noun*
criminal courts formerly sitting at least quarterly; now superseded by the Crown Courts.

quarterstaff (**kwor-ta-stahf**) *noun*
Medieval history a long heavy pole with an iron tip, used by villagers as a weapon and in fencing contests.

quartet (**kwor-tet**) *noun*
1 a group of four musicians.
2 a musical composition for four musicians or instruments.
3 any group of four people or things.

quartile (**kwor-tile**) *noun*
Maths a value which divides a distribution into four groups of equal frequency.

quarto (**kwor-toe**) *noun*
a traditional size of paper about 254 mm x 203 mm

quartz (kworts) *noun*
a very common mineral, silicon dioxide (formula SiO_2), used in glass-making, abrasives, electronics, etc. ⇨ AMETHYST; CHALCEDONY.
[German]

quartz clock *noun*
an extremely precise clock deriving its accuracy from the constant frequency of the vibrations of a quartz crystal.

quasar (**kway**-zar) *noun*
Astronomy a small, very distant, star-like source of intense radio energy emitted at much longer intervals than those of a pulsar.
[*quas*(*i*-) + (stell)AR (radio source)]

quash (kwosh) *verb*
1 to suppress completely.
2 *Law* to cancel a decision.

Quaternary (kwa-**tern**-a-ree) *noun*
Geology a geological period which began about 1·5 million years ago.
● **quaternary** *adjective*
1 consisting of four.
2 arranged in fours.
3 (**Quaternary**) of or produced in the geological Quaternary.

quatrain (**kwot**-rane) *noun*
Poetry a stanza with four lines.

quaver (**kway**-va) *verb*
to shake or tremble.
● **quaver** *noun*
1 a sound that quavers.
2 *Music* a note with half of the time value of a crotchet.
Word Family **quavering, quavery**
adjective trembling.

quay (kee) *noun*
a wharf.

quayside (**kee**-side) *noun*
a wharf and the area around it.

queasy *adjective* (**queasier; queasiest**)
1 feeling nausea.
2 easily disturbed, shocked or made uncomfortable.
Word Family **queasily** *adverb*;
queasiness *noun*.

queen *noun*
1 a female ruler of a country, usually inheriting her position.
2 the wife of a king.
3 *Cards* a playing card with a picture of a queen, having a value just below a king.
4 *Chess* the most powerful piece, which can move any number of squares in any direction.
5 a fertile female ant, bee, etc.
6 (*informal*) a male homosexual.
● **queen** *verb*
Phrase **queen it** to act in an imperious or overbearing manner.
Word Family **queenly** *adverb, adjective*.

queen mother *noun*
the widow of a king, who is also the mother of a reigning monarch.

Queen's Bench *noun*
(when monarch is a man **King's Bench**) a division of the High Court which deals with common-law cases such as damages, debt, breach of contract, etc.

Queen's Counsel *noun* also called **Silk**.
(when monarch is a man **King's Counsel**) *Law* a barrister of at least ten years' standing, appointed as such by the Lord Chancellor and entitled to wear a silk gown in court.

Queen's English *noun*
(when monarch is a man **King's English**) a standard form of written and spoken English considered to be correct and desirable.

Queen's evidence *noun*
(when monarch is a man **King's evidence**) *Law* any evidence given by an accomplice in a crime against others who took part.

queen-sized *adjective* also **queen-size**
(of beds) larger than usual but smaller than king-sized.

queer *adjective*
1 strange or unusual: *He has some queer ideas.*
2 suspicious: *We could hear queer noises in the garden.*
3 an old word meaning 'faint, unwell': *The hot weather has made me feel queer.*
4 (*informal*) an offensive word meaning 'homosexual'.
Phrase **in Queer Street** (*informal*) in debt.
● **queer** *noun* (*informal*) an offensive word for a homosexual.
● **queer** *verb* (*informal*) to spoil or ruin.
Word Family **queerly** *adverb*; **queerness** *noun*.

quell *verb*
to suppress or subdue.

quench *verb*
1 to put out fire, flames, etc.
2 to cool hot metal, etc. by plunging it in oil or water.
Figurative to quench one's thirst (= satisfy). □ *His anger was quenched by her mild, loving words* (= ended).
Word Family **quenchable** *adjective*.

quern *noun*
a hand-operated mill used for grinding corn.

querulous (**kwer**-oo-lus) *adjective*
complaining.

Word Family **querulously** *adverb*;
querulousness *noun*.
[Latin]

query (**kweer**-ee) *noun* (*plural* **queries**)
1 a question or inquiry.
2 ⇨ QUESTION MARK.
Word Family **query** *verb* (**queries**;
querying; **queried**)
[Latin *quaere* ask!]

quest *noun*
a search or pursuit: *a quest for gold*.
Word Family **quest** *verb* to search.
[Latin *quaesitus* searched for]

question (**kwes**-ch'n) *noun*
1 a sentence which asks something.
2 a problem or subject for discussion,
investigation, etc.
3 debate or dispute: *Your argument is open
to question*.
Phrases **a question of** a matter of: *It is
simply a question of turning up on time*.
beyond question without a doubt. **call
into question** to challenge or cast doubt
upon. **in question** under consideration.
out of the question impossible. **pop the
question** (*informal*) to propose marriage.
Word Family **question** *verb*,
questionable *adjective* open to question;
questionably *adverb*; **questioning**
adjective implying a question: *He gave me a
questioning look*; **questioningly** *adverb*.
[Latin *quaestio* a seeking]

question mark *noun* also called **query**;
interrogation mark.
a punctuation mark (?), used when asking
a question or expressing doubt.

questionnaire (kwes-ch'n-**air**) *noun*
a set of questions, usually printed on a
form, designed to obtain a person's
opinion or gather information for a survey,
statistics, etc.
[French]

queue (kew) *noun*
1 a line of people, vehicles, etc. awaiting
their turn.
2 an old word for a single plait or pigtail of
hair worn hanging down behind.
Phrase **jump the queue** to get
something ahead of one's proper turn.
• **queue** *verb* to form a line.
[French, tail]

quibble *verb*
to make petty distinctions or argue about
unimportant details.
• **quibble** *noun*.

The word **quibble** is thought to have
come from an obsolete word *quib*,
which was derived from *quibus* (to
whom or by whom), from Latin *qui*.
Quibus was frequently found in legal
documents written in Latin, indicating
that many questions were being asked
on points of law – lawyers were
quibbling.

quiche (keesh) *noun*
a tart with a savoury filling of cheese, eggs,
etc.

quick *adjective*
1 moving rapidly.
2 being done in a short time: *a quick meal*.
3 understanding or learning with speed:
He is quick at figures.
4 (of one's temper) impatient.
• **quick** *noun*
1 the tender skin under the nails.
2 an old word meaning 'living people': *the
quick and the dead*.
Phrase **cut to the quick** to hurt or upset
deeply.
Word Family **quickly** *adverb*; **quickness**
noun.

quicken *verb*
1 to make or become more rapid.
2 to excite or stimulate feelings, etc.

quickie *noun*
(*informal*) something made or done very
quickly.

quicklime *noun* also called **unslaked
lime**.
a white substance, calcium oxide (formula
CaO), formed by heating limestone and
used to make mortar or cement.

quicksand *noun* also **quicksands** *plural
noun*
an area of wet sand which yields to
pressure and tends to suck down any
object resting on its surface.

quicksilver *noun*
an old word for **mercury**.

quickstep *noun*
a fast ballroom dance.

quid *noun* (*plural* **quid**)
(*informal*) one pound in money: *Can you
lend me five quid?*

quid pro quo *noun*
one thing in return for another.
[Latin]

quiescent (kwee-**ess**-'nt) *adjective*
inactive or at rest.
Word Family **quiescently** *adverb*;
quiescence *noun*.
[Latin]

quiet (kwy-et) *adjective*
having little or no sound or movement.
Figurative *a quiet afternoon reading*
(= peaceful, tranquil). □ *The quiet colours
added warmth to the room* (= not bright).
• **quiet** *noun* peace or freedom from
disturbance.
Phrase **on the quiet** (*informal*) secretly.
Word Family **quiet, quieten** *verb*;
quietly *adverb*; **quietness** *noun*; **quietude**
noun the state of being calm or still.
[Latin *quietus* at rest]

> [!] Do not confuse *quiet* with *quite*.
> *Quiet* has two syllables and means
> 'having little sound'; *quite* has one
> syllable and means 'completely' or
> 'fairly'.

quill *noun*
1 the hard base of a feather where it is
attached to the bird.
2 a feather used as a pen for writing.
3 one of the spines on a hedgehog or
porcupine.

quilt *noun*
1 a bedspread with padding which is
stitched into place between two layers of
fabric.
2 any bedspread.
• **quilt** *verb* to pad and stitch fabric into a
quilt or quilt-like form.
Word Family **quilted** *adjective*.

quin *noun*
(*informal*) a quintuplet.

quince *noun*
a yellow pear-shaped fruit with an acid
taste, used in jams and jellies.

quinine (kwin-een) *noun*
a bitter colourless drug, formerly used in
medicine to treat and prevent malaria.

quinsy (kwin-zee) *noun*
an abscess which causes swelling of the
tonsils.
[Greek *kynagkhē*]

quintessence (kwin-tess-'nce) *noun*
1 the most essential part of a thing.
2 a pure or perfect example: *She is the
quintessence of beauty.*
Word Family **quintessential** (kwin-ti-
sen-sh'l) *adjective*; **quintessentially**
adverb.
[Medieval Latin *quinta essentia* the fifth
element, of which the heavenly bodies
were supposed to consist]

quintet (kwin-tet) *noun*
1 a group of five musicians.
2 a musical composition for five musicians
or instruments.

3 any group of five people or things.
[Latin *quintus* fifth]

quintuplet (kwin-tyoo-plit) *noun*
any of five offspring born at one birth.

quip *noun*
a witty or sarcastic remark.
Word Family **quip** *verb* (**quips**;
quipping; **quipped**).

quire *noun*
a measure of paper containing 24 or 25
sheets.

quirk *noun*
1 a peculiarity of manner or action.
2 a sudden twist or turn.
Word Family **quirky** *adjective* (**quirkier**;
quirkiest); **quirkiness** *noun*.

quisling (kwiz-ling) *noun*
a person who works with an enemy
occupying his or her country.
[after *V. Quisling*, 1887-1945, a Norwegian
army major who helped the Germans in
the Second World War]

quit *verb* (**quits**; **quitting**; **quitted** or
quit)
1 to leave or go away.
2 (*informal*) to stop: *Quit talking and do
some work.*
Word Family **quitter** *noun* (*informal*) a
person who gives up easily.

quite *adverb*
1 completely or entirely: *He has quite
recovered.*
2 *American* actually or really: *I find the job
quite a bore.*
3 (*informal*) to some extent: *She is quite
pretty, but not beautiful.*

> [!] Do not confuse *quite* with QUIET.

quits *adjective*
equal by paying or retaliating.
Phrase **call it quits** to end or give up a
contest, quarrel, etc.

quiver[1] (kwivv-a) *verb*
to tremble.
Word Family **quiver** *noun*; **quivering**,
quivery *adjective*.

quiver[2] *noun*
a container for arrows.

quixotic (kwik-sott-ik) *adjective*
extravagantly romantic or idealistic.
[after *Don Quixote*, a chivalrous but
impractical hero in a romantic novel by
the Spanish writer Cervantes]

quiz *verb* (**quizzes**; **quizzing**; **quizzed**)
to question closely.
• **quiz** *noun* (*plural* **quizzes**)

1 a test, especially of general knowledge.
2 a questioning.

quizzical *adjective*
suggesting puzzlement.
Word Family **quizzically** *adverb*.

quoin (koyn) *noun*
Architecture a projecting brick or stone at
the corner of a building.

quoit (koyt *or* kwoyt) *noun*
1 a flat ring made of rope or iron.
2 (**quoits**) (*used with singular verb*) a game
in which such rings are aimed and thrown
around a peg.

Quorn *noun*
(*trademark*) a kind of vegetarian meat
substitute derived from a small edible
fungus.

quorum *noun*
the least number of people needed to
make a formal meeting valid, e.g. in
parliament or a club.
Word Family **quorate** *adjective* having
enough people present to make a quorum.
[Latin, of whom (from a legal phrase)]

quota (kwo-ta) *noun*
1 a share, allocation: *What is your quota of
work?*
2 the maximum amount of a product that
can be produced, imported or exported:
farmers complaining about their milk quotas.
3 the fixed number of a group allowed to
do something, e.g. immigrants coming
into a country to live and work.
[Latin *quot?* how many?]

quotation (kwo-**tay**-sh'n) *noun*
1 the act of quoting.
2 also **quote** the passage that is quoted:
a famous quotation from Shakespeare.
3 also **quote** a statement of the estimated
cost of something.

quotation marks ⇨ SPEECH MARKS.

quote *verb*
1 to repeat or copy exactly the writing or
speech of another person, usually with
acknowledgement.
2 to refer to for proof: *I could quote many
more examples.*
3 to state a price of goods or services: *Our
builder quoted £50 for the repair.*
• **quote** *noun*
1 a quotation.
2 (**quotes**) ⇨ SPEECH MARKS.

quoth (*rhymes with* both) *verb*
an old word meaning 'said'.

quotidian (kwo-**tidd**-i-an) *adjective*
daily.
[Latin]

quotient (kwo-sh'nt) *noun*
Maths the result of division. Compare
PRODUCT.
[Latin *quotiens?* how many times?]

Qur'an (ku-**rahn**) also **Quran** ⇨ KORAN.

qwerty (**kwur**-tee) *adjective*
(of a keyboard) laid out in the standard
English-language style, with *q,w,e,r,t,*
and *y* being the first six keys in the first
row of letters.

Rr

rabbi (**rab**-eye) *noun*
a Jewish teacher of the Law, especially the ordained spiritual leader of a synagogue.
Word Family **rabbinic** (ra-**bin**-ik), **rabbinical** *adjective*.
[Hebrew, my master]

rabbit *noun*
1 any of various small long-eared grass-eating mammals, often kept and bred as pets.
2 the flesh or fur of this animal.
● **rabbit** *verb*
1 to hunt for rabbits.
2 (*informal*) to chatter.

rabbit warren ⇨ WARREN.

rabble *noun*
a disorderly crowd.

rabble-rouser *noun*
a person who tries to stir up mobs by arousing prejudices and passions.

Rabelaisian (rab-a-**lay**-*zh*'n) *adjective*
characterized by bawdy and boisterous humour.
[after *F. Rabelais*, 1494?-1553, a French satirist]

rabid (**rab**-id *or* **ray**-bid) *adjective*
1 extreme, e.g. in opinion, etc.: *a rabid conservative*.
2 having rabies.

rabies (**ray**-beez) *noun*
an infectious viral disease of dogs, cats, etc. that may be transmitted to humans if bitten, causing convulsions, delirium, frothing at the mouth and a terror of water.
[Latin, madness, rage]

raccoon (ra-**koon**) *noun* also **racoon**
a small flesh-eating American mammal with a bushy tail ringed with black and white.

race[1] *noun*
1 a competition of speed.
2 (**the races**) a series of such competitions, especially between horses.

3 a competition to achieve something: *the race for the presidency*.
4 a swift current of water.
5 a channel carrying water.
● **race** *verb*
1 to compete in a race.
2 to move or cause to move, operate, etc. at a high speed.
Word Family **racer** *noun* a person or thing that races.

race[2] *noun*
1 a group of people having common ancestors and with similar physical characteristics.
2 any group which shares some distinctive features: *the human race*.
3 *Biology* ⇨ SUBSPECIES.
Word Family **racial** (**ray**-sh'l) *adjective*; **racially** *adverb*.

racecourse *noun* also **racetrack**
a place where races, especially horse races, are held.

racily ⇨ RACY.

raciness ⇨ RACY.

racism (**ray**-sizm) *noun* also **racialism**
any discrimination based on the supposed differences between races.
Word Family **racist, racialist** *noun*, *adjective*.

rack[1] *noun*
1 a framework or shelf: *a luggage rack*.
2 a bar with teeth on one side, which engages with the teeth of a pinion, etc.
3 (**the rack**) *History* a device for torture which stretched the body.
Phrase **on the rack** suffering severely.
● **rack** *verb* also **wrack** to cause to suffer distress: *She was racked with pain*.

rack[2] *noun* also **wrack**
Phrase **rack and ruin** a state of neglect and collapse.

rack[3] *noun*
a cut of lamb, veal, etc. from the neck of the animal.

racket[1] *noun*
1 a loud noise or uproar.
2 any scheme or activity to make money illegally or by exploitation.
Word Family **racketeer** (rack-a-**teer**) *noun* a person engaged in an illegal racket.

racket[2] *noun* also **racquet**
a long-handled bat with interlaced strings, used for hitting the ball in tennis, squash, etc.

The word **racket** meaning 'bat' was originally, and is still sometimes, spelt *racquet*, derived from French *raquette*, which originally meant 'palm of the hand'. This in turn was derived from Arabic *raha* (palm). It is not etymologically related to *racket* meaning 'noise', whose origin is uncertain, but which was possibly formed in imitation of the sound of a *racket*.

rack rent *noun*
an extortionate rent.

raconteur (rack-on-**ter**) *noun*
a person skilled in telling stories or anecdotes.
[French]

racoon ⇨ RACCOON.

racy (**ray**-see) *adjective* (**racier; raciest**)
1 spirited or vivid.
2 suggestive, risqué: *racy jokes*.
Word Family **racily** *adverb*; **raciness**
noun.

rad *noun*
a unit of dosage for radiation.

radar (**ray**-dar) *noun*
a device used to track or locate objects which are out of sight, by measuring the time, etc. for a microwave to return from the object.
[RA(dio) + D(etection) + A(nd) + R(anging)]

radar gun *noun*
a piece of equipment held by a police officer to check the speed of vehicles going past.

radial (**ray**-dee-al) *adjective*
1 having or arranged like rays or radii.
2 *Anatomy* of or relating to the radius of the forearm.
• **radial** *noun*
short form of **radial-ply tyre** a thin-walled pneumatic tyre with a reinforced tread and fabric running across the line of the tyre.
[Latin *radius* a wheel spoke, a ray]

radian (**ray**-dee-an) *noun*
the SI unit of a plane angle, equal to $(180/\pi)°$, which is the angle made at the centre of a circle by an arc the same length as the radius.

radiant (**ray**-dee-ant) *adjective*
1 emitting or consisting of heat, light or other radiation.
2 bright or lit up: *a radiant smile*.

Word Family **radiantly** *adverb*;
radiance *noun*.
[Latin *radians* emitting beams]

radiate (**ray**-dee-ate) *verb*
1 to spread out like rays from a centre.
2 to give off rays, waves or particles.
Figurative She absolutely radiates health
(= has an obvious air of).
Word Family **radiation** (ray-dee-ay-sh'n) *noun* 1 the act of radiating. 2 *Physics* any rays, energy or particles which are radiated. 3 *Physics* any transfer of energy which moves outwards in all directions.

radiation sickness *noun*
a disease due to exposure to large doses of radioactive matter or radiation, causing diarrhoea, anaemia and haemorrhaging.

radiator (**ray**-dee-ay-ta) *noun*
1 any of various heating appliances: *the radiators in the central heating system*.
2 a device for cooling liquids consisting of fine tubes through which the liquid flows, being cooled by air passed over the tubes: *a car radiator*.
3 a person or thing that radiates.

radical (**rad**-i-k'l) *adjective*
1 favouring basic social or political change: *His radical ideas upset his conservative parents*.
2 fundamental: *The plan failed because of a radical fault*.
3 *Maths* of or relating to a root.
4 *Biology* of or arising from the root or the base of the stem of a plant.
• **radical** *noun*
1 a person who holds political beliefs which favour fundamental reform.
2 *Chemistry* an atom or group of atoms which acts as a unit in a chemical reaction and is incapable of existing independently beyond the reaction.
Word Family **radically** *adverb*.
[Latin *radicis* of a root]

radicchio (ra-**deek**-ee-o) *noun*
a type of chicory with reddish-purple leaves with white veins, used in salads.
[Italian]

radii
a plural of **radius**.

radio (**ray**-dee-o) *noun*
1 the use of electromagnetic waves to send sounds or pictures without wires.
2 the broadcasting of programmes by radio: *I don't listen to the radio much*.
3 a piece of equipment for receiving broadcast programmes.

4 a piece of equipment for sending and receiving messages: *a police officer's radio.*
• **radio** *verb* to send a message by radio.
[Latin *radius* a wheel spoke, a ray]

radioactivity (ray-dee-o-ak-**tiv**-i-tee) *noun*
1 *Physics* the property of some atomic nuclei to break down into simpler nuclei and release alpha particles, beta particles, neutrinos or gamma rays.
2 *Physics* particles that emit radiation.
Word Family **radioactive** (ray-dee-o-**ak**-tiv) *adjective* emitting radiation.

radio astronomy *noun*
the use of radio telescopes to pick up stellar radiations, thus making it possible to map regions of space which are inaccessible to optical instruments and leading to the discovery of quasars, pulsars, etc.

radiocarbon dating ⇨ CARBON DATING.

radiogram (ray-dee-o-gram) *noun*
an instrument consisting of a radio and a record-player, popular in the 1950s.

radiography (ray-dee-**og**-ra-fee) *noun*
the production of pictures and images, especially of the interior of the body, using X-rays or other radioactive rays.
Word Family **radiographer** *noun.*

radio ham ⇨ HAM² (definition 2).

radiological (ray-dee-o-**loj**-i-k'l) *adjective*
1 of or relating to radioactive substances.
2 of or relating to radiology.

radiology (ray-dee-**oll**-a-jee) *noun*
the study of X-rays and their uses in medicine.
Word Family **radiologist** *noun.*

radio telescope *noun*
Astronomy a device for picking up and focusing radio signals from objects in space.

radiotherapy (ray-dee-o-**therr**-a-pee) *noun*
the treatment of disease, especially cancer, using X-rays or other radioactive substances.
Word Family **radiotherapist** *noun.*

radio wave *noun*
any electromagnetic wave suitable for carrying sounds or pictures through the air from a transmitter to a receiver.

radish (**rad**-ish) *noun* (*plural* **radishes**)
a small red-skinned root used as a vegetable, usually eaten raw.

radium (**ray**-dee-um) *noun*
a rare, naturally occurring, radioactive metal used in the treatment of cancer.
[Latin *radius* a ray]

radius (**ray**-dee-us) *noun* (*plural* **radii** (**ray**-dee-eye) or **radiuses**)
1 *Maths* a straight line drawn from the centre of a circle to any point on its circumference, or from the centre of a sphere to its surface.
2 *Maths* the length of such a line.
Figurative *They searched within a ten-kilometre radius of the city* (= range, distance).
3 *Anatomy* the shorter of the two long bones in a human forearm or foreleg.

radon (**ray**-don) *noun*
a rare radioactive inert gas.

raffia (**raf**-ee-a) *noun*
a fibre obtained from a palm tree and used to make baskets, hats, etc.
[Malagasy]

raffish *adjective*
disreputable.

raffle *noun*
a form of lottery where the winners receive objects as prizes, usually held to raise money for a charity, etc.
• **raffle** *verb* to dispose of in a raffle.

raft¹ (rahft) *noun*
a floating platform used for moving people or goods over water, or moored for use by divers, etc.

raft² *noun*
a large number or amount.

rafter (**rahft**-a) *noun*
a timber support in a roof.

rag¹ *noun*
1 a scrap of fabric, especially one that is old or torn.
2 (**rags**) any old or torn clothes.
3 (*informal*) a newspaper or magazine, especially one considered to be of poor quality.
4 a piece of music in ragtime.
glad rags (*informal*) fine clothes.

rag² *verb* (**rags; ragging; ragged**)
to tease or play jokes on.
• **rag** *noun* (*dated*) a prank, especially one played by students.

ragamuffin *noun*
a ragged or dirty person, especially a child.

rag-and-bone man *noun* (*plural* **rag-and-bone men**)
a man who goes round collecting old clothes, etc.

rag doll *noun*
a doll made out of cloth.

rage *noun*
1 violent anger.

2 (*dated*) a craze.
***Phrase* be all the rage** (*informal*) to be very fashionable.
● **rage** *verb*
1 to act or speak in rage.
2 to proceed with great violence or intensity: *The fire raged out of control.*

ragged (**rag**-id) *adjective*
1 tattered or wearing tattered clothes.
2 having rough or sharp projections.
***Phrase* run someone ragged** to exhaust someone.
***Word Family* raggedly** *adverb*;
raggedness *noun*.

raglan *adjective*
(of a sleeve) continuing up to the neck and joining the piece of clothing by two diagonal seams.
[after *Lord Raglan*, 1788-1855, a British field marshal]

ragout (rag-oo) *noun*
a well-seasoned meat and vegetable stew.
[from French]

ragtime *noun*
a style of jazz with a syncopated rhythm, first popular in America in about 1900

rag trade *noun*
(*informal*) the clothes-manufacturing trade.

ragwort *noun*
a herbal weed with yellow daisy-like flowers.

raid *noun*
a sudden surprise attack.
***Word Family* raid** *verb*; **raider** *noun*.

rail[1] *noun*
1 a horizontal bar of metal or wood used as a support, in a fence, etc.
2 either of two steel girders on which a train, tram, etc. travels.
3 the railway: *We travelled by rail to Newcastle.*
***Phrase* go off the rails** (*informal*) to start to behave in an odd or unacceptable way.

rail[2] *verb*
***Phrase* rail against, rail at** to complain strongly about or to.

railcard *noun*
a special card bought in order to get discounts on train fares.

railing *noun*
(*often* **railings**) a barrier made of rails.

raillery (**ray**-la-ree) *noun*
any good-natured teasing or ridicule in conversation.

railroad *noun*
American a railway.
● **railroad** *verb*
***Phrase* railroad someone into something** to put pressure on someone so that he or she does something without thinking it through properly.

railway *noun*
1 a pair of parallel steel rails, or a system of such rails, designed to carry trains.
2 a company or organization which owns or operates such a system.

raiment (**ray**-m'nt) *noun*
an old word for clothes.

rain *noun*
1 *Weather* drops of water which fall to the ground from the clouds: *The rain fell all night.*
2 a shower of such drops: *There was a heavy rain overnight.*
3 anything falling thickly: *A rain of blows came down on his head.*
***Phrase* be as right as rain** to be perfectly all right.
● **rain** *verb* to fall as or like rain.

rainbow *noun*
1 an arc of the colours of the spectrum, especially one seen in the sky, due to the reflection and refraction of light in drops of water.
2 any similar arc of colours.

rain check *noun*
(*especially American informal*) a postponement, especially of accepting an invitation.
[from *rain check* a ticket for future use given to sporting spectators when an event is postponed owing to rain]

raincoat *noun*
a waterproof coat.

rainfall *noun*
1 the total amount of rain, snow, etc. which falls at a location during a given period.
2 a shower of rain.

rainforest *noun*
the dense evergreen forest found in areas of very high rainfall, especially the tropical rainforest in equatorial regions.

rainy *adjective* (**rainier; rainiest**)
wet with or bringing rain.
***Phrase* a rainy day** a time of need in the future.

raise (raze) *verb*
1 to move to a higher position: *It is not known exactly how they raised the stones at Stonehenge.*

2 to build: *A monument was raised in his honour.*

3 to increase: *Her boss raised her salary.*

4 to improve: *Hassan's encouragement raised our spirits.*

5 to collect together: *We helped to raise money for the flood victims.*

6 to bring up: *It's time you got married and raised a family.*

7 to make heard or thought about: *They raised several objections.*

8 to make contact with by telephone or radio.

9 *Cards* to make a higher bid than: *I'll raise you £10.*

• **raise** *noun*

1 a lifting.

2 *American* a pay rise.

> ❗ Do not confuse the verb *raise* with *rise*. Both mean 'to move from a lower to a higher position', but *raise* has an object and *rise* does not. In other words, one *raises* something (*Sam raised his hand*), but something *rises* (*A hand rose somewhere at the back of the classroom*).

raisin (**ray**-z'n) *noun*
a dried grape.

raising agent *noun*
an ingredient which makes food rise.

raison d'être (ray-zon **det**-ra)
the chief purpose or justification for the existence of something.
[French]

raj (rahj) *noun*
Indian history British rule in India before India gained independence in 1947.
[Hindi, reign]

raja (**rah**-ja) *noun* also **rajah**
a title for a ruler in India.
[Hindi]

rake[1] *noun*

1 a long-handled tool with a comb-like row of teeth for levelling earth, gathering grass, etc.

2 an act of raking.

• **rake** *verb*

1 to gather or remove with, or as if with, a rake.

2 to search or attack with a sweeping movement: *His eyes raked the crowd.*

☐ *Gunfire raked the ship.*

Phrases **rake it in** (*informal*) to make a lot of money. **rake up 1** to collect together with difficulty. **2** to talk about something from the past that would be better left alone.

rake[2] *noun*
an old word for a self-indulgent or immoral man, especially one in fashionable or sophisticated society.

rake-off *noun*
(*informal*) a commission or share of profits, especially if dishonest or illegal.

rakish (**ray**-kish) *adjective*

1 jaunty or smart: *a rakish hat.*

2 like a sophisticated person or rake.
Word Family **rakishly** *adverb*;
rakishness *noun*.

rally *verb* (**rallies; rallying; rallied**)

1 to bring or come together for a common purpose: *to rally support for a cause.*

2 to recover strength: *The pound rallied towards the close of trading.*

Phrase **rally round** to give support or assistance to.

• **rally** *noun* (*plural* **rallies**)

1 a mass meeting, especially one to promote a cause.

2 *Commerce* a rise in price and trading after a decline.

3 *Tennis* an exchange of strokes between players before a point is scored.

4 a race for cars which involves navigating and driving over a long or difficult course.

ram *noun*

1 a male sheep.

2 any of various devices for battering, crushing or forcing.

• **ram** *verb* (**rams; ramming; rammed**)
to strike or force with heavy blows.
Figurative He rammed his hat on
(= pushed firmly).

Ramadan (**ram**-a-dan *or* ram-a-**dan**)
noun also **Ramadhan** (**ram**-a-zan)
the ninth month of the Muslim year, when no food or drink may be taken during daylight.

ramble *verb*

1 to walk in a wandering or aimless manner.

2 (of a plant) to wind irregularly.
Phrase **ramble on** to talk in a disjointed way.
Word Family **ramble** *noun* a leisurely walk; **rambler** *noun* a person or thing that rambles, such as a climbing rose.

Ramboesque (ram-bo-**esk**) *adjective*
tough, aggressive and violent.
[*Rambo*, hero of adventure films]

ramekin (**ram**-a-kin) *noun*
a small deep dish in which food is baked or served.

ramification (ram-i-fi-**kay**-sh'n) *noun*
  1 the act of branching out or dividing.
  2 (**ramifications**) consequences: *This
  decision will have widespread ramifications.*
  [Latin *ramus* a branch + *facere* to make]

ramp *noun*
  a sloping surface connecting two different
  levels.
  [French *ramper* to creep or crawl]

rampage (ram-**page**) *verb*
  to act or move about violently or furiously.
  • **rampage** (**ram**-page) *noun* any violent
  or wild action or behaviour.

rampant *adjective*
  1 wild or uncontrolled: *rampant weeds.*
  2 *Heraldry* (of an animal) rearing up on its
  hind legs.

rampart *noun*
  an earth mound, usually with a wall on it,
  built for protection.

ram raid *noun*
  a shop robbery carried out by driving a
  vehicle through the windows or security
  gates.
  Word Family **ram-raider** *noun.*

ramrod *noun*
  a long rod formerly used for ramming the
  charge down the barrel of a muzzle-
  loading gun.
  • **ramrod** *adjective* stiff or severe.

ramshackle *adjective*
  badly made or liable to collapse:
  a ramshackle old house.

ran the past tense of **run**.

ranch *noun* (*plural* **ranches**)
  a large farm, especially one for cattle
  Word Family **ranch** *verb* to own or
  manage a ranch; **rancher** *noun* a person
  who owns or works on a ranch.
  [Spanish *rancho* a group of people who eat
  together]

rancid (**ran**-sid) *adjective*
  (of oily foods) unpleasantly stale.
  Word Family **rancidity** (ran-**sid**-i-tee)
  noun.
  [Latin *rancidus* stinking]

rancour (**ran**-ka) *noun* (*American* **rancor**)
  a bitter resentment or hatred.
  Word Family **rancorous** *adjective*;
  rancorously *adverb.*

rand *noun*
  the basic unit of money in South Africa.
  [Afrikaans, edge]

random *adjective*
  having no definite order, aim or method.
  • **random** *noun*

Phrase **at random** in an unmethodical
way.
  Word Family **randomly** *adverb*;
  randomness *noun*; **randomize**,
  randomise *verb.*
  [Old French *randir* to gallop]

random-access memory *noun*
  short form is **RAM** *Computers* a temporary
  memory which stores and recalls
  information in any order or sequence.
  Information can be altered, but unless it is
  saved the memory is lost when the
  computer is switched off. Compare READ-
  ONLY MEMORY.

randy *adjective* (**randier; randiest**)
  (*informal*) sexually aroused.

rang the past tense of **ring**[2].

range *noun*
  1 the limits between which something may
  exist, occur or vary: *a range of prices.* □ *the
  range of his singing voice.*
  2 a set of items of a similar type: *a new
  range of skincare products.*
  3 a line or group of mountains.
  4 an area on which shooting takes place:
  a rifle range.
  5 the distance to which something is
  effective or will operate: *hearing range.*
  □ *the range of an aircraft.*
  6 *American* a large area of open land for
  grazing, hunting, etc.
  7 a stove which has a flat surface with coils
  or plates for cooking, an oven, etc.
  • **range** *verb*
  1 to vary between: *Prices range from £10 to
  £10 000.*
  2 to put or arrange.
  3 to move or travel through.
  Word Family **ranger** *noun* a warden who
  patrols and guards a forest, etc.

rangefinder *noun*
  any of various devices for determining the
  distance of an object, such as that used in
  focusing a camera.

rangy (**rane**-jee) *adjective* (**rangier;
  rangiest**)
  having slender long legs.

rani (**rah**-nee) *noun* also **ranee**
  1 the wife of a raja, king or prince in India,
  etc.
  2 a reigning queen or princess in India.
  [Hindi]

rank[1] *noun*
  1 a position in society or any group or
  organization: *a poet of the highest rank.*
  □ *the rank of general.*

2 a high position, place or status: *He is a man of rank in the literary world.*
3 (*usually* **ranks**) a row, line or series: *Ranks of bright flowers lined the garden.*
4 (**ranks**) the people who are members of an organization: *She left the party's ranks to form an independent movement.*
5 (**the ranks**) ordinary soldiers, as distinct from officers, etc.
Phrase **pull rank** to use one's high position to achieve one's aim.
• **rank** *verb*
1 to have or hold a particular position.
2 to arrange or place in a row.

rank² *adjective*
1 (of plants) growing strongly or vigorously.
2 having an unpleasant or offensive smell.
3 unmistakable: *rank bad manners.*
Word Family **rankly** *adverb*; **rankness** *noun.*

rank and file *noun*
the main body of an organization, as distinct from its leaders.

rankle *verb*
to cause or continue to cause irritation, bitterness or unpleasantness: *After a time their cruel remarks began to rankle.*

ransack *verb*
to search vigorously or violently, especially in order to rob or plunder.

> The word **ransack** means, etymologically, 'to search a house'. It is derived from the 13th-century Old Norse *rannsaka*, formed from *rann* (house) and *saka* (search). *Ransack* is related to *ramshackle*, which comes from an obsolete word *ranshackle*, formed from *ransack*.

ransom *noun*
the money demanded by criminals for the release of a person captured or detained.
• **ransom** *verb*
1 to free by paying a ransom.
2 to release after receiving a ransom.
[Latin *redemptio* redemption]

rant *verb*
to talk wildly or violently.
• **rant** *noun.*

rap *verb* (**raps; rapping; rapped**)
1 to hit or knock sharply, quickly or lightly.
2 to perform rap music.
Phrase **rap out** to say sharply.
• **rap** *noun*
1 a sharp quick knock or blow.
2 the sound it makes.
3 (*informal*) punishment or blame.

4 *Music* a type of music which involves a rapid rhythmical chanting to an instrumental backing.

rapacious (ra-**pay**-shus) *adjective*
excessively or unpleasantly greedy.
Word Family **rapacity** (ra-**pas**-i-tee), **rapaciousness** *noun*; **rapaciously** *adverb.*
[Latin *rapax* grasping]

rape¹ *noun*
1 the crime of having sexual intercourse with a person without his or her consent.
2 abusive or improper treatment of a place.
Word Family **rape** *verb*; **rapist** (**ray**-pist) *noun.*
[Latin *rapere* to seize or carry off]

rape² *noun*
a plant with yellow flowers, grown as food for livestock and for the oil of its seeds.
[Latin *rapum* turnip]

rapid (**ra**-pid) *adjective*
with great speed.
• **rapid** *noun* (*usually* **rapids**) the swiftly moving part of a river where it flows over or between rocks, or down a steep slope.
Word Family **rapidly** *adverb*; **rapidity** (ra-**pid**-i-tee), **rapidness** *noun.*
[from Latin]

rapier (**ray**-pee-a) *noun*
a sword with a long straight blade, used chiefly for thrusting.

rapine (**ray**-pine) *noun*
an old word for plunder.

rapport (ra-**por**) *noun*
a feeling of understanding or sympathy.
[French]

rapprochement (ra-**prosh**-mon) *noun*
the re-establishing of a friendly relationship.
[French *rapprocher* to bring closer]

rapscallion (rap-**skal**-y'n) *noun*
an old word for a rogue or rascal.

rapt *adjective*
1 deeply absorbed or fascinated.
2 full of emotion or delight.
[Latin *raptus* seized]

rapture (**rap**-cher) *noun*
extreme delight or joy.
Phrase **in raptures** full of delight or enthusiasm.
Word Family **rapturous** *adjective*; **rapturously** *adverb*; **rapturousness** *noun.*

rare¹ (*rhymes with* air) *adjective*
1 not occurring often: *a rare disease.*

2 (of air) of low density or pressure.
Word Family rareness *noun*; **rarely**
adverb; **rarity** (rair-i-tee) *noun* **1** (*plural*
rarities) something which is rare. **2** the
state of being rare.
[Latin *rarus* thin, not dense]

rare² *adjective*
(of red meat) lightly cooked.

rarefied *adjective*
1 very subtle.
2 ⇨ RARE¹ (definition 2).

raring *adjective*
(*informal*) very eager to set off or start on
something: *Everyone was raring to go.*

rascal (rahs-k'l) *noun*
a mischievous or dishonest person.
Word Family rascally *adjective, adverb.*

rase ⇨ RAZE.

rash¹ *adjective*
done hastily and without caution.
Word Family rashly *adverb*; **rashness**
noun.
[Middle English *rasch* nimble]

rash² *noun*
1 any reddening of the skin.
2 a sudden outbreak: *There has been a rash
of bombings throughout the country.*

rasher *noun*
a thin slice of bacon.

rasp (rahsp) *verb*
1 to scrape or rub roughly.
2 to make a harsh scraping sound.
● **rasp** *noun*
1 the act or sound of rasping.
2 a file with a coarse pointed surface.

raspberry (rahz-b'r-ee) *noun* (*plural*
raspberries)
1 a small juicy edible red berry growing on
a bush.
2 a dark reddish purple colour.
3 (*informal*) a harsh noise made with the
tongue and lips to express contempt, etc.
● **raspberry** *adjective.*

Rastafarian (ras-ti-fair-ee-an) *noun* also
Rasta (*informal*)
a member of the religious and political
movement, largely Jamaican, which
believes Ras Tafari, the former Emperor of
Ethiopia, Haile Selassie, to be the
Messiah.
Word Family Rastafarianism *noun.*

rat *noun*
1 any of various common rodents, larger
than mice, with long hairless tails.
2 (*informal*) a sneaky or contemptible
person.

***Phrase* smell a rat** (*informal*) to be or
become suspicious.
● **rat** *verb* (**rats; ratting; ratted**)
***Phrase* rat on someone** (*informal*) to
betray or desert someone.

ratatouille (rat-at-oo-ee) *noun*
a vegetable stew.

ratchet *noun*
a device consisting of a toothed wheel with
a catch which allows it to move in only one
direction.

rate *noun*
1 a measured amount in relation to a unit
or fixed quantity of something else:
travelling at the rate of 60 kilometres an hour.
2 the speed at which something happens:
We were losing height at a frightening rate.
3 a price: *What is your hourly rate?*
4 (**rates**) a tax on land and buildings
imposed by local governments and used for
local services, such as street lighting, etc.
***Phrases* at any rate** anyway: *Come for a
short time at any rate.* **at this rate, at that
rate** if things continue like this or that.
● **rate** *verb*
1 to estimate the value or quality of: *How
do you rate him as a singer?*
2 (*informal*) to think of as good at
something.
3 (*informal*) to deserve: *Such a small matter
would not rate a mention in the newspaper.*
Word Family rateable, ratable (ray-ta-
b'l) *adjective* **1** able to be estimated.
2 liable to payment of rates.
[Latin *ratus* reckoned]

rate of exchange *noun* also called
exchange rate.
the ratio used, or the price quoted, in
exchanging one currency for another, e.g.
from pounds sterling to American dollars.

ratepayer *noun*
a person who pays rates.

rather (*rhymes with* father) *adverb*
1 preferably or more willingly: *I would
rather not come with you.*
2 to a certain degree: *I rather like her,
though I'm not sure why.*
3 with more truth or accuracy: *It's raining,
or rather it rained earlier.*

> The word **rather** was originally a
> comparative form of the adjective *rathe*.
> *Rathe* meant 'quick', so *rather* meant
> 'quicker'. Both were derived from Old
> English, *rathe* from *hraeth* and *rather*
> from *hrathor*.

ratify (**rat**-i-fie) *verb* (**ratifies; ratifying; ratified**)
to approve or confirm, especially formally or officially: *Russia has ratified the nuclear arms agreement.*
Word Family **ratification** (rat-i-fi-**kay**-sh'n) *noun.*

rating (**ray**-ting) *noun*
1 a measured position relative to others: *His popularity rating is at an all-time low.*
2 *Navy* any non-commissioned sailor.
3 (**the ratings**) the figures which show how many people watch or listen to broadcast programmes.

ratio (**ray**-she-o) *noun*
1 a comparison or proportion of the value, quantity, etc. of two things: *What is the ratio of girls to boys in the sixth form?*
2 *Maths* the relative size of two numbers or quantities *2:3 is the ratio of 2 to 3 and means $\frac{2}{3}$.*
[Latin, a reckoning]

ration (**rash**-'n) *noun*
a fixed amount permitted or supplied, especially of food.
• **ration** *verb* to restrict to limited amounts.
Word Family **rationing** *noun.*

rational (**rash**-n'l) *adjective*
1 using sense, reason or logic: *a rational argument.*
2 able to think or reason: *We are rational animals.*
3 *Maths* relating to a number that can be expressed as a ratio of two integers. Compare IRRATIONAL (definition 3).
Word Family **rationally** *adverb;* **rationality** (rash-a-**nal**-i-tee) *noun.*

rationale (rash-a-**nahl**) *noun*
1 the basic reasons for or logic of something.
2 a statement or explanation of reasons.

rationalize, rationalise (**rash**-'n-a-lize) *verb*
1 to invent an acceptable explanation to justify behaviour.
2 to introduce new or efficient methods into a business, etc.
Word Family **rationalization** (rash-'n-a-lie-**zay**-sh'n) *noun.*

rat pack *noun*
(*informal*) journalists and photographers, thought of as aggressively anxious to get a news story.

rat race *noun*
(*informal*) the unscrupulous competitive struggle for success, social status, etc.

rat run *noun*
(*informal*) a minor road made unusually busy by rush-hour traffic avoiding congested major roads.

rattan (ra-**tan**) *noun*
any of a group of tropical climbing palms, the branches of which are used for wickerwork.
[Malay]

rattle *verb*
1 to make a rapid series of short sharp sounds.
2 to move with such sounds: *The train rattled over the bridge.*
3 (*informal*) to fluster or confuse: *Don't let the police rattle you.*
Phrases **rattle off** (*informal*) to say quickly: *He rattled off a list of things to buy.*
rattle on (*informal*) to talk rapidly about unimportant things.
• **rattle** *noun*
1 a rapid series of short sharp sounds.
2 any of various devices designed to make such a sound, such as a child's toy.
Word Family **rattly** *adjective* making or tending to make a rattling sound.

rattler *noun*
(*informal*) a rattlesnake.

rattlesnake *noun*
any of a group of poisonous American snakes related to the viper, but with a tail made of horny loosely connected joints which make a rattling sound when the snake is angry.

rattletrap *noun*
a shaky or rickety object, especially an old car.

ratty *adjective* (**rattier; rattiest**)
1 of or like a rat.
2 (*informal*) irritable.
Word Family **rattily** *adverb;* **rattiness** *noun.*

raucous (**raw**-kus) *adjective*
hoarsely or harshly loud.
Word Family **raucously** *adverb;* **raucousness** *noun.*
[from Latin]

ravage (**rav**-ij) *verb*
to spoil, ruin or destroy.
Word Family **ravages** *plural noun* extreme destruction.

rave *verb*
1 to talk wildly or incoherently.
2 to talk or write very enthusiastically.
• **rave** *noun*
1 (*informal*) a wild party.

2 a very large organized party, often in a warehouse, where the participants take part in very fast athletic dances.
• **rave** *adjective* (*informal*) wildly enthusiastic.

raven (**ray-v'n**) *noun*
a large bird related to the crow, with shiny black feathers.
• **raven** *adjective* shiny and black.

ravenous (**rav-'n-us**) *adjective*
extremely hungry.
Word Family ravenously *adverb*; **ravenousness** *noun*.

ravine (ra-**veen**) *noun*
a long, narrow and deep valley.

raving *adjective*
wildly excited or incoherent.
• **raving** *adverb*
Phrase raving mad (*informal*) completely mad.

ravioli (rav-ee-o-lee) *plural noun*
envelopes of pasta filled with chopped meat, etc. and usually served with a tomato sauce.
[Italian]

ravish (**rav-ish**) *verb*
1 a literary word meaning 'to seize and take by force'.
2 to rape.
Word Family ravishing *adjective* enchanting or delightful; **ravishingly** *adverb*; **ravishment** *noun*.
[Latin *rapere* to seize]

raw *adjective*
1 (of food) not cooked.
2 (of a substance) not prepared, treated or refined: *raw sugar*.
3 (of data) not yet organized.
4 (of skin) red and badly grazed.
5 (of nerves) extremely sensitive.
6 (of emotions) extremely strong.
7 (of weather) harsh and cold.
• **raw** *noun*
Phrase in the raw 1 not refined.
2 naked.
Word Family rawly *adverb*; **rawness** *noun*.

raw materials *plural noun*
the materials used in manufacturing, especially in their natural state before processing.

ray¹ *noun*
1 a narrow line: *a ray of sunlight*.
Figurative *There is not even a ray of hope* (= a slight indication).
2 *Physics* a straight line along which a wave travels.

3 *Maths* an infinite straight line which starts from a given point.
4 *Biology* any of the arms of a starfish.
[Latin *radius*]

ray² *noun*
any of various fish, with gills on the lower surface of their flattened bodies, e.g. the skate.
[Latin *raia*]

ray³ *noun* also **re**
Music a note in the scale. ⇨ DOH.

rayon *noun*
any of various synthetic fibres made from cellulose.

raze *verb* also **rase**
to demolish or destroy completely.

razor (**ray-za**) *noun*
any of various sharp cutting instruments, used especially to shave hair, etc.
[Latin *rasus* scraped]

razzmatazz *noun*
(*informal*) any noisy activity or display.

re¹ (ray *or* ree) *preposition*
concerning or with reference to.
[Latin]

re² ⇨ RAY³.

reach *verb*
1 to get to: *We reached Glasgow at midnight.*
2 to put or stretch out or towards: *She reached into her bag for her purse.*
3 to go as far as in length, height, or size: *The dress reaches her ankles.*
4 *Nautical* to sail across the wind.
• **reach** *noun* (*plural* **reaches**)
1 the act of reaching or stretching.
2 the distance which something can reach or by which it can be reached: *within close reach of the shops.*
3 a continuous area or expanse: *They flew low over a vast reach of desert.*
4 the part of a river, channel, etc. between its curves.
5 *Nautical* the distance travelled between tacks in a sailing boat.

react (ree-**akt**) *verb*
1 to act in return or opposition to something earlier: *Teenagers often react against a strict upbringing.*
2 *Chemistry* to take part in a reaction.

reaction (ree-**ak**-sh'n) *noun*
1 an action or effect produced by or in response to another.
2 *Physics* a force produced by an object which is equal and opposite to a force applied to the object.

3 *Chemistry* the interaction of two or more substances, resulting in chemical changes in them.
4 a tendency to conservatism and opposition to progress, reform, etc., especially in politics.
Word Family **reactionary** *adjective* extremely conservative or opposed to progress; **reactionary** *noun* (*plural* **reactionaries**).

reactivate (ree-ak-tiv-ate) *verb* to cause something to start again.

reactive (ree-**ak**-tiv) *adjective*
1 tending or likely to react.
2 *Chemistry* readily entering into a reaction.

reactor (ree-ak-ter) *noun*
1 a person or thing that reacts.
2 *Electricity* a device used to introduce opposition to the flow of alternating electric current.
3 *Physics* a nuclear reactor.

read *verb* (**reads; reading; read** (red))
1 to look at, understand or say aloud written words: *Read me the first paragraph.*
2 to look at a figure as a measuring instrument.
3 (of a piece of writing or a measuring instrument) to contain the words or figures: *The speedometer read 85 miles an hour.*
4 (of a piece of writing) to give a particular impression: *The story reads like a child's school essay.*
5 to interpret: *I read her gesture as a warning to keep quiet.*
6 to study at university: *She's at Oxford, reading English.*
Phrases **read up on** to read a lot about: *I'll have to read up on the company before I go to the interview.* **take something as read** to assume something: *We'll take it as read that our parents will all object to this scheme.*
Word Family **read** *noun* the act of reading; **reading** *noun* **1** the activity of reading. **2** an interpretation: *my reading of the situation.* **3** an occasion when something is read to a lot of people: *a poetry reading.* **4** a figure shown on a measuring instrument; **readable** *adjective* **1** easy or interesting to read. **2** able to be read or deciphered; **readability** *noun*.

reader *noun*
1 a person who reads.
2 a book for instruction or practice in reading.

3 (**Reader**) a university lecturer next in rank below a professor, usually one who has done special research.
Word Family **readership** *noun* **1** all the readers of some publication, especially a regular one. **2** (**Readership**) the position or duties of a Reader.

readjust (ree-a-**just**) *verb* to adjust or arrange again.
Word Family **readjustment** *noun*.

readmit (ree-ad-**mit**) *verb* (**readmits; readmitting; readmitted**) to admit or let in again.
Word Family **readmittance, readmission** *noun*.

read-only memory *noun* short form is **ROM** *Computers* a permanent memory which is built into the central processing unit and can be accessed but not altered. Compare RANDOM-ACCESS MEMORY.

ready (**red**-ee) *adjective* (**readier; readiest**)
1 equipped or arranged for action or use: *Is dinner ready yet?*
2 willing: *She is always ready to help.*
3 spontaneous and quick: *a ready wit.*
• **ready** *noun* (*plural* **readies**) (*informal*) money.
Phrase **at the ready** ready for action.
Word Family **readily** *adverb*; **readiness** *noun*.

ready-made *adjective*
1 made to a standard size or pattern rather than for a particular person or thing: *a ready-made suit.* □ *ready-made components.*
2 suitable and available: *Here's a ready-made opportunity for making money.*

reafforestation ⇨ REFORESTATION.

reagent (ree-ay-j'nt) *noun* any substance used in a chemical reaction.

real *adjective*
1 existing as fact, especially in nature or the universe: *I used to think the Tooth Fairy was real.*
2 true, as distinct from apparent or imagined: *real love.*
3 not artificial or false: *real diamonds.*
Word Family **real** *adverb* (*informal*) very; **realness** *noun*; **really** (**reel**-ee) *adverb* **1** truly. **2** indeed.
[Latin *res* a thing]

real ale *noun* a beer made by traditional methods that is not fizzy.

real estate *noun*
any immovable property, such as land or a house.

realism (ree-a-lizm) *noun*
1 a tendency to be practical and sensible or to see things as they really are.
2 the portrayal of accurate or realistic detail, e.g. in a painting, book, film, etc.
Word Family **realist** *noun, adjective*.

realistic (ree-a-**lis**-tik) *adjective*
1 having a practical or sensible attitude to life, etc.
2 representing or showing something as it is in life or fact: *a realistic portrait*.
Word Family **realistically** *adverb*.

reality (ree-al-i-tee) *noun* (*plural* **realities**)
1 the state of being real.
2 something which is real or exists in fact: *Her dream of success had become a reality*.
Phrase **in reality** in truth.

realize, realise (ree-a-lize) *verb*
1 to understand clearly or fully: *Do you realize what you have done?*
2 to make real or a fact: *He trained hard to realize his ambition of playing in the orchestra*.
3 (*formal*) to sell for: *The house realized a high price at the auction*.
4 to exchange for money: *She decided to realize her shares to help pay her debts*.
Word Family **realization** (ree-a-lie-**zay**-sh'n) *noun*; **realizable** *adjective*.

really ⋄ REAL.

realm (relm) *noun*
a kingdom.

real tennis *noun* also **royal tennis**
the earliest form of tennis, played over a sagging net in a specially constructed walled court.
[Old French *real* royal]

ream[1] *noun*
1 a measure of paper consisting of 500 sheets.
2 (**reams**) a large amount of something.

ream[2] *verb*
to finish or shape a hole or opening.

reap *verb*
1 to cut and harvest grain.
2 to gain: *She reaped the benefits of hard work*.
Word Family **reaper** *noun* a person or machine that reaps.
Phrase **the Grim Reaper** Death, thought of as a sinister cloaked figure with a scythe.

reappear (ree-a-peer) *verb*
to appear again.
Word Family **reappearance** *noun*.

reapply (ree-a-ply) *verb* (**reapplies; reapplying; reapplied**)
to apply again.
Word Family **reapplication** (ree-ap-li-kay-sh'n) *noun*.

reappraisal (ree-a-**pray**-z'l) *noun*
a new examination and judgement.
Word Family **reappraise** *verb*.

rear[1] *noun*
the back part of something: *The entrance is at the rear of the shop*.
Word Family **rear** *adjective*; **rearward, rearwards** *adjective, adverb* in or towards the rear.

rear[2] *verb*
1 to care for and support a child or young animal until adulthood.
2 (of a horse) to rise on its hind legs, so that its body is nearly vertical.
3 to lift up: *The spectre of famine reared its ugly head*.

rear admiral *noun*
Navy a commissioned officer ranking between commodore and vice admiral.

rearguard *noun*
the part of an army, etc. prepared to meet any sudden attack from the rear.

rearm (ree-**arm**) *verb*
to arm again, especially with new or better equipment.
Word Family **rearmament** *noun*.

rearrange (ree-a-range) *verb*
to arrange in a different way.
Word Family **rearrangement** *noun*.

reason (**ree**-z'n) *noun*
1 a motive for doing or believing something: *What are your reasons for choosing this university?*
2 the mind or intellect.
3 sanity or good sense: *Have you lost your reason?*
Phrases **it stands to reason** it is obvious. **within reason** within sensible limits.
• **reason** *verb* to think or draw conclusions which follow naturally and in correct sequence from the original statements or assumptions.
Phrase **reason with someone** to persuade someone with arguments.
Word Family **reasoned** *adjective* logically argued or thought out.
[Latin *rationis* of a calculation]

reasonable (ree-z'n-a-b'l) *adjective*
1 having or showing reason or common
sense: *Your plan sounds quite reasonable.*
2 fairly good: *She paid a reasonable price for
the shoes.*
Word Family **reasonably** *adverb*;
reasonableness *noun*.

reasoning (ree-z'n-ing) *noun*
the process of thinking or drawing correct
conclusions: *Her powers of reasoning are
amazing.*

reassess (ree-a-sess) *verb*
to assess again.
Word Family **reassessment** *noun*.

reassure (ree-a-shor) *verb*
to restore the confidence of: *He was afraid
at first but I reassured him with my
arguments.*
Word Family **reassurance** *noun*;
reassuringly *adverb*.

rebate (ree-bate) *noun*
a sum of money which is returned, such as
a discount or a tax refund.
[*re-* + ABATE]

rebel (rebb-'l) *noun*
a person who resists or defies authority.
• **rebel** (ri-bell) *verb* (**rebels**; **rebelling**;
rebelled) to openly resist authority.
[*re-* + Latin *bellum* war]

rebellion (ri-bell-y'n) *noun*
the act of rebelling, especially an organized
armed resistance to the established
government in a country.

rebellious (ri-bell-yus) *adjective*
1 of or relating to rebels or rebellion.
2 defiant or disposed to rebel.
Word Family **rebelliously** *adverb*;
rebelliousness *noun*.

rebirth *noun*
a new or second birth.

reboot *verb*
Computers to boot again: *First reboot your
system.*

reborn *adjective*
born again.

rebound (ree-bound) *verb*
to bounce or spring back after hitting
something: *The ball rebounded from the wall
and broke a window.*
• **rebound** (ree-bound) *noun* a bouncing
or springing back.
Phrase **on the rebound** as a reaction:
*She married him on the rebound after an
unhappy relationship.*

rebuff (ri-buff) *verb*
to refuse or reject something coldly and
abruptly: *She rebuffed my offer of help.*
• **rebuff** *noun* a repulse, rejection or
defeat.
[*re-* + Italian *buffo* a puff]

rebuke *verb*
to criticize sharply.
• **rebuke** *noun*.
[Old French *rebuchier* to fell trees]

rebus (ree-bus) *noun* (*plural* **rebuses**)
a game in which words must be guessed
from pictures which represent the sounds.

rebut (ri-but) *verb* (**rebuts**; **rebutting**;
rebutted)
to prove something wrong by using
argument and evidence.
Word Family **rebuttal** *noun* 1 the act of
rebutting. 2 the evidence used in
rebutting.

recalcitrant (ri-kal-si-tr'nt) *adjective*
rebellious or actively disobedient.
[Latin *recalcitrare* to kick back]

recall (ri-kawl) *verb*
1 to bring back to mind: *I couldn't recall her
name.*
2 to summon back: *The king recalled his
foreign ambassadors.*
• **recall** (ree-kawl) *noun* the act of
recalling.

recant (ri-kant) *verb*
to formally withdraw or give up a
statement or belief.
Word Family **recantation** (ree-kan-tay-
sh'n) *noun*.
[*re-* + Latin *cantare* to sing]

recap *verb* (**recaps**; **recapping**;
recapped)
(*informal*) to recapitulate.
• **recap** *noun*.

recapitulate (ree-ka-pit-yoo-late) *verb*
to stress again or summarize the main
points at the end of a speech, etc.
Word Family **recapitulation** (ree-ka-pit-
yoo-lay-sh'n) *noun*.
[*re-* + Latin *capitulum* a small head]

recce ⇨ RECONNAISSANCE.

recede (ri-seed) *verb*
1 to move back or to a more distant
position: *We were able to cross when the tide
receded.*
2 to slope backwards: *a receding chin.*
[Latin *recedere* to go back]

receipt (ri-seet) *noun*
1 a written statement acknowledging
payment.

2 the action of receiving something.
[Latin *receptus* recovered]

receive (ri-**seev**) *verb*
1 to get into one's hand or possession: *I received a letter this morning.*
2 to undergo or experience: *patients receiving chemotherapy.*
3 to welcome formally: *The Duchess received her guests in the drawing room.*
4 to pick up: *The ship was not receiving our signals.*
5 to accept as a member: *He was received into the Catholic Church.*

receiver *noun*
1 a person who receives something.
2 any device which receives electromagnetic waves and reproduces them as sound or pictures: *a telephone receiver.*
3 *Law* a person appointed by a court to take charge of a bankrupt business or a property which is involved in a dispute.
Word Family **receivership** *noun Law* the state of being in the hands of a receiver.

recent (**ree**-s'nt) *adjective*
having appeared or happened not long ago: *a recent illness.*
Word Family **recently** *adverb*; **recentness** *noun*
[from Latin]

receptacle (ri-**sep**-ti-k'l) *noun*
anything that holds or contains something.

reception (ri-**sep**-sh'n) *noun*
1 the act or manner of receiving: *My theory met with a cold reception.*
2 the area where people are greeted, e.g. in a hotel.
3 a formal occasion held by a person or group: *a wedding reception.*
4 *Radio* the signals received on a radio or television receiver.

receptionist (ri-**sep**-sh'n-ist) *noun*
a person employed to receive guests, visitors or clients in an office or hotel.

receptive (ri-**sep**-tiv) *adjective*
able to take in or receive something, especially when necessary.
Word Family **receptiveness** *noun.*

recess (ri-**sess** *or* **ree**-sess) *noun* (*plural* **recesses**)
1 a part or space that is set back from the main wall or line.
2 the hidden central part of something: *She lived deep in the recesses of the forest.*
3 a period of time when work stops, e.g. in parliament.

Word Family **recessed** *adjective* set back in a recess.

recession (ri-**sesh**-'n) *noun*
1 the act of receding or withdrawing.
2 a decline in commercial and industrial activity, less severe than a depression.
[Latin *recessus* gone back]

recessive (ri-**sess**-iv) *adjective*
1 tending to recede or go back.
2 *Biology* of or relating to a hereditary character that only shows itself when genes are inherited from both parents. Compare DOMINANT.

recharge *verb*
to charge with electricity again.
Word Family **rechargeable** *adjective.*

recherché (ra-**shair**-shay) *adjective*
too carefully chosen or far-fetched.
[French]

recipe (**ress**-i-pee) *noun*
a list of ingredients and instructions for preparing food, etc.
Figurative What's your recipe for success? (= formula).
[Latin, take!]

recipient (ri-**sip**-ee-ent) *noun*
a person or thing that receives.

reciprocal (ri-**sip**-ra-k'l) *adjective*
mutual: *The two countries have a reciprocal trade agreement.*
• **reciprocal** *noun Maths* a quantity produced by dividing 1 by a given number: *The reciprocal of of 3 is $\frac{1}{3}$.*
Word Family **reciprocally** *adverb.*

reciprocate (ri-**sip**-ra-kate) *verb*
1 to give in return: *She told him she loved him, but he felt unable to reciprocate.*
2 to give and receive mutually.
3 (of a mechanical part) to move in a straight line first in one direction and then in the opposite direction. *reciprocating motion.*
Word Family **reciprocation** (ri-sip-ra-**kay**-sh'n) *noun.*
[Latin *reciprocare* to move back and forth]

reciprocity (ress-i-**pross**-i-tee) *noun*
the practice or principle of reciprocating, especially relating to formal agreements between countries.

recital (ri-**sigh**-t'l) *noun*
1 a performance given by one or two musicians, etc.
2 a detailed account: *He gave a recital of the places he'd visited.*

recite (ri-**site**) *verb*
to say from memory: *Ashraf recited some verses from the Koran.*
Word Family **recitation** (re-si-**tay**-sh'n) *noun*.
[Latin *recitare* read aloud]

reckless *adjective*
unthinkingly careless or rash: *The accident was caused by reckless driving.*
Word Family **recklessly** *adverb*; **recklessness** *noun*.

reckon *verb*
1 to count or calculate.
2 (*informal*) to have the opinion that: *I reckon it will rain later.*
Phrases **reckon on** to rely on: *We can't reckon on their support.* **reckon with 1** to deal with: *Don't threaten her again, or you'll have us to reckon with!* 2 to take seriously: *We hadn't reckoned with his friends in high places.*

reckoning *noun*
a calculation: *By my reckoning we're 30 points behind them.*
day of reckoning a time when something must be atoned for or accounted for.

reclaim *verb*
to make something productive or useful again: *The swamp was reclaimed by draining.*
Word Family **reclaimable** *adjective*; **reclamation** (rek-la-**may**-sh'n) *noun* the act or process of reclaiming.

recline *verb*
to lean back in a resting position.
[Latin *reclinare* to bend back]

recluse (ri-**klooss**) *noun*
a person who lives apart from others.
Word Family **reclusive** *adjective*.
[Latin *reclusus* shut up]

recognize, recognise (**rek**-'g-nize) *verb*
1 to identify again: *Do you recognize this tune?*
2 to accept something as true or valid: *Some countries do not recognize the governments of other countries.*
Word Family **recognition** (rek-'g-**nish**-'n) *noun* 1 the act of recognizing. 2 the state of being recognized: *In recognition of your services, accept this gift;* **recognizable** *adjective;* **recognizably** *adverb.*
[Latin *recognoscere* to call to mind again]

recoil (ri-**koil**) *verb*
to jump or spring back: *The gun recoiled and injured his shoulder.* □ *She recoiled from the dead body in disgust.*
● **recoil** (**ree**-koil) *noun* the act of recoiling, such as the backward movement

of a gun when it is fired.
[*re-* + Latin *culus* buttocks]

recollect (rek-a-**lekt**) *verb*
to remember.
Word Family **recollection** *noun* 1 the act or power of recollecting. 2 something that is recollected.

recommence (ree-ka-**mence**) *verb*
to begin again.
Word Family **recommencement** *noun*.

recommend (rek-a-**mend**) *verb*
to present something as worthwhile or advisable: *I can recommend this book.*
□ *I recommend that you see an optician.*
Word Family **recommendation** (rek-a-men-**day**-sh'n) *noun*.

recompense (**rek**-'m-pence) *verb*
(*formal*) to repay or make compensation: *I will recompense you for all your trouble.*
● **recompense** *noun* repayment or compensation.

reconcile (**rek**-'n-sile) *verb*
to bring or come into a state of harmony or agreement: *The enemies reconciled their differences after the fight.* □ *How does this statement reconcile with what you said yesterday?*
Word Family **reconciliation** (rek-'n-sill-ee-**ay**-sh'n) *noun;* **reconcilable** *adjective* able to be reconciled.
[*re-* + CONCILIATE]

recondite (**rek**-'n-dite) *adjective*
dealing with obscure or little-known matters.
[Latin *reconditus* hidden]

recondition (ree-k'n-**dish**-'n) *verb*
to repair or overhaul.

reconnaissance (ri-**kon**-i-sance) *noun*
short form is **recce** (**rek**-ee)
1 *Military* any air or ground operation designed to assess the position, strength and movements of the enemy.
2 any preliminary study or survey.
[French, recognition]

reconnoitre (rek-a-**noy**-ta) *verb* (*American* **reconnoiter**)
to make a reconnaissance.

reconsider (ree-k'n-**sid**-a) *verb*
to consider again, especially with a view to changing a decision.
Word Family **reconsideration** (ree-k'n-sid-a-**ray**-sh'n) *noun*.

reconstitute (ree-**kon**-sti-tewt) *verb*
to make up or put together again.
Word Family **reconstitution** (ree-kon-sti-**tew**-sh'n) *noun*.

reconstruct *verb*
1 to construct again.
2 to recreate or re-enact past events.
Word Family **reconstruction** *noun*.

record (ri-**kord**) *verb*
1 to register or set down in writing, on tape, in a computer, etc.: *The concert was recorded for television.*
2 to state officially.
● **record** (**rek**-ord) *noun*
1 a written account: *A record is kept of all court cases.*
2 the best rate or amount so far achieved: *His time for the race is a new record.*
3 facts known about the past of a person, company, etc.: *This airline has a good safety record.*
4 a criminal past: *He's got a record as long as your arm.*
5 a thin plastic plate with a continuous groove in each side for recording and reproducing sounds.
Phrases **off the record** unofficial, not to be published. **on record** recorded: *This is the fastest time on record.*
[Latin *recordari* to remember]

recorder (ri-**kor**-da) *noun*
1 a person or thing that records.
2 *Music* any of a family of simple wind instruments without reeds.

recording *noun*
a record of sounds, music, etc., on tape, CD, etc.

record player *noun*
a machine that reproduces the sounds on a record.

recount[1] (ri-**kownt**) *verb*
to relate or give an account of.

recount[2] (ree-**kownt**) *verb*
to count again.
● **recount** (ree-**kownt**) *noun*.

recoup (ri-**koop**) *verb*
to recover or receive compensation for.

recourse (ri-**korse**) *noun*
Phrase **have recourse to** to seek help from.
[Latin *recursus* a retreat]

recover (ri-**kuvv**-a) *verb*
1 to get back again: *The police recovered the stolen goods.* □ *She soon recovered her sense of humour.*
2 to return to a healthy or normal situation: *I've recovered from my illness.*
Word Family **recovery** *noun* (*plural* **recoveries**) the act of recovering: *grateful for the recovery of the stolen goods.*
[Latin *recuperare*]

re-cover (ree-**kuvv**-a) *verb*
to cover again.

recreate (ree-kree-**ate**) *verb*
to create again.
Word Family **recreation** (ree-kree-**ay**-sh'n) *noun*.

recreation (rek-ree-**ay**-sh'n) *noun*
1 any relaxing pastime, hobby, amusement, etc.
2 the relaxation produced by such pastimes.
Word Family **recreational** *adjective*.

recrimination (ri-krim-i-**nay**-sh'n) *noun*
a state of affairs when people blame each other for something.
[*re-* + Latin *criminis* of an accusation]

recruit (ri-**kroot**) *verb*
to enlist people for service or membership in a group or society or in the armed forces.
● **recruit** *noun* a new or recently enlisted member, especially of the armed services.

The word **recruit** means, etymologically, 'something which grows again'. The Latin verb *recrescere* (to regrow) became *recroître* in French, with the same meaning. The feminine form of the past participle of *recroître* was *recrue* (regrown) in standard French but *recrute* in the dialect of north-east France. In the 17th century this came to mean 'new growth' and then 'a new levy of troops'.

rectal *adjective*
Anatomy of or relating to the rectum.

rectangle (**rek**-tang-g'l) *noun*
a quadrilateral which has four right angles and usually adjacent sides of unequal length.
Word Family **rectangular** (rek-**tang**-gew-la) *adjective*.
[Latin *rectus* straight + ANGLE]

rectify (**rek**-ti-fic) *verb* (**rectifies**, **rectifying**; **rectified**)
to remedy or put right.
Word Family **rectification** (rek-ti-fi-**kay**-sh'n) *noun*.

rectitude (**rek**-ti-tewd) *noun*
rightness of thought or conduct.

rector *noun*
1 *Christianity* a clergyman in charge of a parish.
2 the head of certain universities and colleges.
Word Family **rectory** *noun* (*plural* **rectories**) the house of a rector.
[Latin, a controller]

rectum *noun*
Anatomy the end portion of the colon, connected to the anus.
[Latin, straight (intestine)]

recumbent (ri-**kum**-b'nt) *adjective*
lying down or reclining.
Word Family **recumbently** *adverb*; **recumbency** *noun*.
[from Latin]

recuperate (ri-**koo**-pa-rate) *verb*
to recover, especially from ill health.
Word Family **recuperative** (ri-**koo**-per-a-tiv) *adjective* of or helping recovery; **recuperation** (ri-koo-per-**ay**-sh'n) *noun*.
[from Latin]

recur (ri-**ker**) *verb* (**recurs; recurring; recurred**)
to repeat, return or occur again: *She suffers from recurring back trouble.*
Word Family **recurrence** (ree-**kurr**-'nce) *noun* the act or process of recurring; **recurrent** *adjective*.
[Latin *recurrere* to run back]

recurring decimal *noun*
a decimal fraction that recurs to infinity, e.g. $3 \cdot 3333 \ldots$

recycle (ree-**sigh**-k'l) *verb*
to put waste products through a process of purification or conversion to make something useful.
Word Family **recyclability** (ree-sigh-kla-**bill**-i-tee) *noun*; **recyclable** *adjective*.

red *noun*
1 a primary colour like that of fresh blood; the colour next to orange at the end of the spectrum.
2 (*informal*) a person with left-wing political views.
Phrases **in the red** in debt. Compare IN THE BLACK under BLACK *noun*. **see red** (*informal*) to become extremely angry.
Word Family **red** *adjective* (**redder; reddest**); **redden** *verb* to make or become red; **reddish** *adjective* slightly red.

red admiral *noun*
a type of butterfly.

red blood cell *noun*
any of the tiny disc-like cells in the blood of vertebrates, containing haemoglobin and carrying oxygen through the body.

red-blooded *adjective*
vigorous or virile.

red-brick *adjective*
(of a university) founded in the late 19th century or in the early 20th century.

red carpet *noun*
a strip of red carpet for important people to walk on.

redcoat *noun*
History a British soldier, named after the scarlet jackets worn by the regiments.

Red Cross *noun*
the international organization which looks after victims of war and large-scale natural disasters, such as earthquakes. In Muslim countries the organization is called the **Red Crescent**.

red deer *noun* (*plural* **red deer**)
a reddish-brown deer whose males have large antlers.

redden ⇨ RED.

reddish ⇨ RED.

redeem (ri-**deem**) *verb*
1 to get back by payment, etc.
2 (**redeem oneself**) to compensate or make amends: *She managed to redeem herself with a brief apology.*
3 *Religion* to deliver from sin or its consequences by means of a sacrifice, etc.
4 to fulfil a promise, pledge, etc.
Word Family **redeemable** *adjective* able to be redeemed; **redeemer** *noun* a person who redeems.

redemption (ri-**demp**-sh'n) *noun*
the act of redeeming or the state of being redeemed: *He returned from confession assured of his redemption.*
[Latin *redemptus* bought back]

red ensign ⇨ ENSIGN.

redeploy (ree-di-**ploy**) *verb*
to reorganize troops, etc. so as to use them more effectively.
Word Family **redeployment** *noun*.

redevelop (ree-di-**vel**-up) *verb*
to develop again: *The slum area was redeveloped into a modern housing estate.*
Word Family **redeveloper** *noun* a person or company that redevelops; **redevelopment** *noun*.

red-faced *adjective*
having a red face, especially due to embarrassment.

red flag *noun*
1 a symbol of socialism or revolution.
2 a red banner used as a signal of danger.

red-handed *adjective, adverb*
in the act of committing a crime or misdeed.

redhead *noun*
a person, especially a woman, with red hair.

red herring *noun*
something irrelevant, introduced to distract attention.
[from the use, in the past, of a dried fish in training hounds]

red-hot *adjective*
1 extremely hot, or glowing red with heat.
2 (*informal*) very exciting: *a red-hot tip for a horse in the next race.*

red-letter day *noun*
a memorable occasion.
[from the custom of marking festivals in red on Church calendars]

red-light district *noun*
an area sometimes indicated by red lights, with prostitutes, brothels, etc.

redolent (**red**-a-l'nt) *adjective*
having a strong smell, especially one that is reminiscent of something.
Figurative dark caverns redolent of mystery (= suggestive).
[from Latin]

redouble (ree-**dubb**-'l) *verb*
to double or increase greatly.

redoubt (ri-**dowt**) *noun*
a small fort in a system of fortifications surrounded by or joined to others by a parapet.
[Latin *reductus* retired]

redoubtable *adjective*
worthy of great respect.
[re- + Latin *dubitare* to doubt]

redound *verb*
Phrase **redound to** (*formal*) (of an action) to contribute to the credit of: *The whole affair redounded greatly to his credit.*
[Latin *redundare* to surge back]

redress (ri-**dress**) *noun*
the setting right of what is wrong.
• **redress** *verb*.

re-dress (ree-**dress**) *verb*
to dress again.

red shift *noun*
the apparent shift of a spectrum of light or other electromagnetic radiation to longer wavelengths, due to the extreme speed at which the source of the light is receding from the earth. Galaxies in every direction have red shift, indicating that they are all receding and suggesting that the universe is expanding.

redskin *noun*
(*dated informal*) a Native American. This term is now considered offensive.

red tape *noun*
excessive attention to rules and regulations.
Word Family **red-tape** *adjective*.
[from the *red tape* used to tie up documents]

reduce (ri-**dewce**) *verb*
1 to lower in degree, size, number, etc.: *My parents actually reduced my pocket money by £1!*
2 to boil a liquid so that it becomes thicker.
3 *Maths* to change a fraction into its simplest form.
Phrase **reduce something to** to bring something into a particular state, condition, etc.: *The fire reduced the house to ashes.*
Word Family **reduction** (ri-**duk**-sh'n) *noun* 1 the act of reducing. 2 the amount by which something is reduced: *a ten per cent reduction on all goods in the sale.*
3 *Chemistry* the addition of electrons to or the removal of oxygen from an atom, ion or molecule; **reducible** *adjective* able to be reduced.
[Latin *reducere* to bring back]

redundant (ri-**dun**-d'nt) *adjective*
1 unemployed: *My uncle has been made redundant.*
2 unnecessary or excessive.
Word Family **redundantly** *adverb*; **redundancy** *noun* (*plural* **redundancies**).
[Latin *redundantia* an overflow]

redwood (**red**-wud) *noun*
a very tall Californian tree (a sequoia), usually 60–100 m in height.

reed *noun*
1 any of various tall grasses, usually growing in marshy areas, or the stalk of such a grass.
2 *Music* (in some wind instruments) a small piece of cane or metal, fixed at one end inside the mouthpiece, while the other end vibrates freely, or any instrument fitted with such a device.
Word Family **reedy** *adjective* (**reedier**; **reediest**) 1 full of reeds. 2 having a tone like that of a reed instrument; **reediness** *noun*.

reef¹ *noun*
1 *Geography* a line or group of rocks or coral near the surface of the sea, sometimes visible at low tide.

2 *Mining* a vein.

barrier reef a coral reef which rises from
deep water, with a wide deep lagoon
between it and the coast.

reef² *noun*
Nautical a part of a sail rolled and tied
down to lessen the area exposed to the
wind.
• **reef** *verb* to reduce the size of a sail.

reefer¹ *noun*
Nautical a person who reefs.

reefer² *noun*
(*informal*) a cigarette containing cannabis.

reef knot *noun*
a flat knot which does not slip.

reek *verb*
1 to smell strongly and unpleasantly.
2 (*dated*) to give off steam, smoke, etc.
Phrase **reek of** to suggest strongly.
• **reek** *noun*.

reel *noun*
1 any of various devices on which a fishing
line, cable, etc. can be wound.
2 a quantity of something wound on such
a device: *I bought two reels of wire.*
3 a lively Scottish dance, or the music for
it.
• **reel** *verb*
1 to draw with a reel or by winding.
2 to stagger or sway under a blow, shock,
etc.
Figurative His brain reeled with the shock
(= whirled).
Phrase **reel off** to recite fluently: *She
reeled off the list of party guests.*

re-elect *verb*
to elect again.

re-enact *verb*
to enact or act out again.

reeve *noun*
Medieval history a bailiff.

ref *noun*
(*Sports informal*) a referee.

refectory (ri-**fek**-ta-ree) *noun* (*plural*
refectories)
a dining room, usually in a school or
monastery.
[Latin *refectus* refreshed]

refer (ri-**fer**) *verb* (**refers; referring;
referred**)
1 to speak of: *It is all over now, so please do
not refer to it again.*
2 to consult: *I referred to my notes before
answering the question.*

Phrase **refer to** to direct to a source of
information, help, etc.: *She referred me to
her boss.*
Word Family **referral** *noun* the act of
referring.
[*re-* + Latin *ferre* to bring]

referee (ref-a-**ree**) *noun*
1 *Sports* a person who makes sure that the
rules are obeyed in a game.
2 a person who provides information
about someone's character or abilities.
• **referee** *verb* (**referees; refereeing;
refereed**) to act as a referee in a sports
event.

reference (**ref**-r'nce) *noun*
1 the act of referring: *I made no reference to
the incident in my report.*
2 a written statement concerning the
character, abilities, etc. of a person.
3 a number that guides one to a particular
piece of information: *a map reference.*
Phrase **with reference to** concerning.

referendum (ref-a-**ren**-dum) *noun* (*plural*
referendums or **referenda**)
the making of a political decision by asking
each person in a country to vote on it.

refill (ree-**fill**) *verb*
to fill again.
• **refill** (**ree**-fill) *noun* a replacement for
the used contents of a container.
Word Family **refillable** *adjective*.

refine (ri-**fine**) *verb*
1 to make something pure or clean: *a plant
for refining petroleum.*
2 to make small changes in order to
improve: *The scientists have refined their
experimental techniques.*
Word Family **refiner** *noun* a person who
refines; **refined** *adjective* elegant and
sophisticated: *a lady of refined taste.*

refinement *noun*
1 a small improvement.
2 the quality of being elegant and
sophisticated.
3 the process of refining.

refinery (ri-**fie**-na-ree) *noun* (*plural*
refineries)
a place where something is refined, such as
petroleum or sugar.

reflation (ree-**flay**-sh'n) *noun*
Economics measures taken to increase
demand for goods and services,
introduced after a recession to restore the
economy to a stable position.
Word Family **reflate** *verb*.

reflect (ri-**flekt**) *verb*
1 to throw back light, sound, etc. from a surface.
2 to be a sign of: *The mood of the town reflects public anxiety about government reforms.*
3 (*formal*) to think carefully: *Just reflect for a moment on what you are proposing.*
Phrase **reflect well on, reflect badly on** to cause people to have a good or bad impression of.
Word Family **reflection** *noun*; **reflective** *adjective*; **reflectively** *adverb*; **reflector** *noun* a substance or device that reflects light, sound, etc.
[Latin *reflectere* to bend back]

reflex (**ree**-fleks) *noun* (*plural* **reflexes**)
an involuntary or immediate movement, such as sneezing, in response to a stimulus.
• **reflex** *adjective* occurring in or as a reaction.

reflex angle *noun*
Maths an angle between 180° and 360°.

reflexive (ri-**flek**-siv) *adjective*
Grammar of a pronoun or verb referring back to the subject of the sentence: *'I washed myself' is a reflexive verb and 'myself' is a reflexive pronoun.*
Word Family **reflexively** *adverb*.

reflexology (ree-flek-**sol**-a-jee) *noun*
a form of therapy used in alternative medicine which involves massaging the soles of the feet.
Word Family **reflexologist** *noun*.

reforestation (ree-forr-i-**stay**-sh'n) *noun* also **reafforestation** (ree-a-forr-i-stay-sh'n)
the replanting of trees in a forest area.

reform (ri-**form**) *verb*
to improve by changing, for example by giving up a bad habit.
Word Family **reform** *noun* an improvement or amendment: *the reform of the Corn Laws*; **reformer** *noun*.

re-form (ree-**form**) *verb*
to form again.

reformat *verb* (**reformats; reformatting; reformatted**)
Computers to give a new format to.

reformation (reff-a-**may**-sh'n) *noun*
1 the act of reforming or the state of being reformed.
2 (**the Reformation**) *History* the religious movement which began in Europe in the 16th century to reform the Roman Catholic Church, and led to the formation of the Protestant Churches.

reformatory (ri-**form**-a-tree) *adjective*
serving or designed to reform.
• **reformatory** *noun* (*plural* **reformatories**) also **reform school**
History an institution where children convicted of crimes were held in detention.

refraction (ri-**frak**-sh'n) *noun*
Physics the change in direction of an oblique wave when it passes from one medium to another, e.g. a ray of light is bent as it passes from air into glass.
Word Family **refract** *verb* to deflect by refraction; **refractive** *adjective*; **refractiveness** *noun*.
[re- + Latin *fractus* broken]

refrain¹ (ri-**frane**) *verb*
to keep oneself from doing or saying something: *I refrained from shouting at the children.*
[re- + Latin *frenum* a bridle]

refrain² *noun*
a phrase or verse recurring at intervals in a song or poem.
[re- + Latin *fringere* to break]

refresh (ri-**fresh**) *verb*
to revive or make fresh, for example by rest, food, etc.
Word Family **refresher** *noun* a person or thing that refreshes; **refreshing** *adjective* capable of refreshing; **refreshingly** *adverb*.

refresher course *noun*
a course of instruction to bring doctors, teachers, etc. up to date with recent developments in their field.

refreshment *noun*
something which refreshes, such as food or drink for a light meal.

refrigerate (ri-**frij**-a-rate) *verb*
to make or keep cool or cold.
Word Family **refrigeration** (ri-frij-a-ray-sh'n) *noun*.

refrigerator (ri-**frij**-a-ray-ta) *noun* also **fridge**
an appliance consisting of an enclosed space which can be kept at a constantly low temperature, used for storing foods, medicines, etc.

> [!] Note the spelling of *refrigerator*: it does not have a *d* in it, unlike *fridge*.

refuel (ree-**fewl**) *verb* (**refuels; refuelling; refuelled**)
to supply again with fuel.

refuge (ref-yooj) *noun*
shelter or protection from danger, trouble, etc.
[Latin *refugere* to run away from]

refugee (ref-yoo-jee) *noun*
a person who has fled from his or her home or country because of some danger or disaster, such as a flood, war, dictatorship, etc.

refund (ree-fund) *verb*
to give back, especially money.
• **refund** (ree-fund) *noun*.
Word Family **refundable** *adjective*.

refurbish (ree-fur-bish) *verb*
to renovate or make clean.
Word Family **refurbishment** *noun*.

refuse[1] (ri-fewz) *verb*
to say one will not do, accept, give, allow, etc.: *My parents refused to let me go on the trip.*
Word Family **refusal** *noun*.

refuse[2] (ref-yooce) *noun*
anything discarded as worthless or useless.

refute (ri-fewt) *verb*
to prove a statement to be false.
Word Family **refutable** *adjective* able to be refuted; **refutation** (ref-yew-tay-sh'n) *noun*.
[Latin *refutare* to check]

regain (ri-gane) *verb*
1 to get back again: *After the illness it took a month for her to regain her strength.*
2 a literary word meaning 'to reach again'.

regal (ree-g'l) *adjective*
1 of or relating to a monarch.
2 dignified and stately.
Word Family **regally** *adverb*; **regality** (ree-gal-i-tee) *noun*.
[from Latin]

regale (ri-gale) *verb*
to entertain, especially with good food or drink.
[from French]

regalia (ri-gale-ya) *plural noun*
(*used with singular or plural verb*) the insignia, decorations or emblems of a powerful position, especially that of a monarch.

regard (ri-gard) *verb*
1 to think of in a particular way: *She is regarded as the best student in the school.*
2 to look at in a specific way: *She regarded him with a hostile stare.*
• **regard** *noun*
1 any concern or attention: *He seems to have no regard for my wishes.*

2 esteem or respect.
3 a long steady look.
4 (**regards**) sentiments of affection, esteem, etc.: *Please give my regards to your parents.*
Phrases **as regards, in regard to, with regard to** about or concerning. **in this regard** in connection with this.
Word Family **regardless** *adjective* without care, consideration or thought for; **regarding** *preposition* about: *a document regarding your uncle's will.*

regatta (ri-gat-a) *noun*
a gathering of boats at which contests or races are held.
[Italian *regata* a gondola race]

regenerate (ree-jen-a-rate) *verb*
1 to construct or create again.
2 *Biology* to grow again a part of an organism that has been removed.
Word Family **regenerative** (ree-jen-er-a-tiv) *adjective*; **regeneration** (ree-jen-a-ray-sh'n) *noun*.

regent (ree-j'nt) *noun*
a person who carries out the duties of a monarch who is too young, ill, etc. to rule.
Word Family **regency** *noun* (*plural* **regencies**) 1 the office of a regent.
2 a period of regency, especially (**the Regency**) that of the future George IV, 1811-1820; **Regency** *adjective* relating to the style of architecture, furniture, etc. which was fashionable in Britain in the early 19th century.
[Latin *regens* guiding, controlling]

reggae (reg-ay) *noun*
a highly stylized form of popular music originating in Jamaica in the West Indies in the 1970s.

regicide (rej-i-side) *noun*
Law the crime of killing a monarch, or the person who does this.
[Latin *regis* of a king + *caedere* to kill]

regime (ray-zheem) *noun*
1 a system of government, especially an authoritarian one.
2 a particular government.
3 a regimen.
[French]

regimen (rej-i-m'n) *noun*
Medicine a balanced programme of careful diet and exercise intended to maintain or restore good health.
[Latin, guidance]

regiment (rej-i-m'nt) *noun*
Military an army unit consisting of two or more battalions.

• **regiment** (rej-i-ment) *verb* to subject to strict discipline.
Word Family regimentation (rej-i-men-tay-sh'n) *noun*; **regimental** (rej-i-men-t'l) *adjective*.

region (ree-j'n) *noun*
1 *Geography* an area with similar features which distinguish it from another area: *the mountainous regions of Spain.* □ *an administrative region.*
2 a part of the body: *in the chest region.*
Phrase in the region of approximately.
Word Family regional *adjective* relating to a particular region; **regionally** *adverb*.
[from Latin]

register (rej-ist-a) *noun*
1 a formal or official list of items, names, etc., or a book for such entries.
2 the range of a voice or instrument.
3 *Linguistics* a range of language relating to particular circumstances or contexts, e.g. formal or informal.
4 ⇨ CASH REGISTER.
• **register** *verb*
1 to enter in a register.
2 to indicate on a scale, etc.
3 to indicate: *She registered no signs of stress or worry.*
4 to make an impression: *He told me his name but it didn't register.*
5 to pay extra for a letter, etc. at a post office to ensure safe delivery.
Word Family registration (rej-i-stray-sh'n) *noun*.
[Latin *regestus* recorded]

register office *noun* also **registry office**
an office where births, marriages and deaths are recorded and civil marriages take place.

registrar (rej-i-strar *or* rej-i-strar) *noun*
1 an official who keeps records.
2 an important administrator at a college.
3 a doctor in a hospital who is training to be a specialist.

registration plate ⇨ NUMBER PLATE.

registry (rej-i-stree) *noun* (*plural* **registries**)
a place where registers are kept.

regression (ri-gresh-'n) *noun*
1 backward movement.
2 a return to an earlier or less mature level of development.
Word Family regress *verb*; **regressive** *adjective*; **regressively** *adverb*.
[from Latin]

regret *verb* (**regrets**; **regretting**; **regretted**)
to feel sorry, dissatisfied or distressed, especially about something one has done or said.
• **regret** *noun*
1 a feeling of loss, repentance or sorrow, e.g. for a missed opportunity.
2 (**regrets**) a formal expression of disappointment, e.g. when declining an invitation.
Word Family regrettable *adjective*; **regrettably** *adverb*; **regretful** *adjective* full of regret; **regretfully** *adverb*; **regretfulness** *noun*.
[Old French *regreter* to bewail]

regular (reg-yoo-la) *adjective*
1 happening or done repeatedly at similar intervals: *Her breathing was now regular.*
2 orderly or symmetrical: *a regular shape.*
3 normal, usual or customary: *my regular duties.*
4 also called **weak**. *Grammar* (of a verb) having the most common changes of form for each tense, usually by means of endings, as in *talk* (present), *talked* (past) and *talked* (past participle). Compare IRREGULAR (definition 2).
• **regular** *noun*
1 a member of the permanent armed forces.
2 (*informal*) a regular customer or visitor.
Word Family regularly *adverb*; **regularity** (reg-yoo-larr-i-tee) *noun*; **regularize, regularise** *verb* to make regular.
[Latin *regula* a rule]

regulate (reg-yoo-late) *verb*
1 to control by a rule, method, etc.
2 to adjust to a standard, e.g. for accuracy.
Word Family regulator *noun* a person or device that regulates; **regulative, regulatory** *adjective*.

regulation (reg-yoo-lay-sh'n) *noun*
1 a rule or law designed to control behaviour or actions: *The soldier said it was against regulations.*
2 the act of regulating or the state of being regulated.

regurgitate (ri-gerj-i-tate) *verb*
to bring undigested food back into the mouth.
Word Family regurgitation (ri-gerj-i-tay-sh'n) *noun*.
[*re-* + Latin *gurgitis* of a flood]

rehabilitate (ree-h'-bill-i-tate) *verb*
to restore to a state of health, well-being or usefulness.

Word Family rehabilitation (ree-h'-bill-i-**tay**-sh'n) *noun*.

rehash (ree-**hash**) *verb*
to work into a new or different form.
• **rehash** (**ree**-hash) *noun* (*plural* **rehashes**).

rehearsal (ri-**her**-s'l) *noun*
a practice or trial performance before an event, especially of a play, film, etc. before it is performed in public.
dress rehearsal the last full rehearsal of a play, etc., with costumes, lights and music, before the first performance.

rehearse (ri-**herce**) *verb*
to practise a play, part, etc. to prepare for a public performance.

> The word **rehearse** came into English from Old French *rehercer*, meaning 'to repeat', which is what it first meant in English also. It was formed from the verb *hercer* (to harrow), from the noun *herce* (harrow). A harrow is an agricultural implement for raking, so when people rehearsed something they were raking over it again or repeating it.

reign (rane) *noun*
1 the length of time for which a monarch rules.
2 the length of time when a particular power or influence is dominant: *a reign of fear*.
• **reign** *verb*
1 to have the power or title of a monarch.
2 to be dominant or in control.
[Latin *regnum* monarchy]

reimburse (ree-im-**berce**) *verb*
to repay or make a refund for money spent or lost.
Word Family reimbursement *noun*.

rein (rane) *noun*
(*usually* **reins**) a long strip of leather on a bridle, passing from the bit to the rider's hands, used to control and guide a horse.
Phrases **give free rein to** to allow complete freedom to. **keep a tight rein on** to control closely.
• **rein** *verb* to check, control or restrain.

reincarnation (ree-in-kar-**nay**-sh'n) *noun*
1 the act of being born again after one's death, into a new body.
2 the actual form taken on by the reborn soul.
Word Family reincarnate (ree-in-**kar**-nate) *verb*.

reindeer (**rane**-deer) *noun* (*plural* **reindeer**)
a large northern European deer, with branched antlers.

reinforce (ree-in-**force**) *verb*
to make stronger or more effective, especially by adding extra pieces, support, etc.
Word Family reinforcement *noun* **1** the act of reinforcing: *the reinforcement of an argument with facts*. **2** (*often* **reinforcements**) something used to add strength or support, such as extra troops sent to help in a battle.

reinforced concrete *noun*
concrete with metal in it to make it stronger.

reinstate (ree-in-**state**) *verb*
to put back in a former position, state, etc.
Word Family reinstatement *noun*.

reiterate (ree-**it**-a-rate) *verb*
to repeat.
Word Family reiteration (ree-it-a-**ray**-sh'n) *noun*.

reject (ri-**jekt**) *verb*
1 to refuse to accept or use: *She rejected all the advice she received.*
2 to throw away.
• **reject** (**ree**-jekt) *noun* something which is rejected, refused or discarded.
Word Family rejection *noun*.
[Latin *rejectus* thrown back]

rejig *verb* (**rejigs; rejigging; rejigged**)
(*informal*) to rearrange: *I managed to rejig my diary to fit in the appointment.*

rejoice (ri-**joice**) *verb*
to be glad or joyful.
Word Family rejoicing *noun*, *adjective*.

rejoin[1] (ree-**join**) *verb*
to join or come together with again: *We rejoined the meeting.*

rejoin[2] (ri-**join**) *verb*
to answer or reply.
Word Family rejoinder *noun* an answer or response.

rejuvenate (ri-**joo**-vi-nate) *verb*
to make young or new again.
Word Family rejuvenation (ri-joo-vi-**nay**-sh'n) *noun*.
[*re-* + Latin *juvenis* young]

rekey (ree-**kee**) *verb*
Computers to put into a computer again: *We had to rekey the data.*

rekindle (ree-**kin**-d'l) *verb*
to kindle or stir up again.

relaid the past tense and past participle of
relay[2].

relapse (ri-**laps**) *verb*
to fall or slip back to a former, usually
worse, condition.
• **relapse** (**ree**-laps) *noun*.
[from Latin]

relate *verb*
1 to tell or describe: *The explorer related his
adventures.*
2 to show a connection between.
Phrase **relate to 1** to be concerned with:
What does your complaint relate to, exactly?
2 to have an understanding of another
person's attitudes or of a situation: *'I can't
discuss anything with my parents.' – 'Yes, I can
relate to that!'*
[Latin *relatus* brought back]

related *adjective*
connected: *drug-related problems.*
Phrase **be related** to be members of the
same family: *You two look very alike – are
you related?*

relation (ri-**lay**-sh'n) *noun*
1 a relative: *She is a distant relation of my
mother's.*
2 a connection or association between
people or things: *These notes bear no relation
to the finished poem.*
3 (**relations**) the way people or groups
feel or behave towards each other:
*Relations between us and the French are
rather strained at the moment.*
4 the act of telling or narrating.
Word Family **relationship** *noun* a
connection or association.

relative (**rell**-a-tiv) *adjective*
existing or considered only in comparison
or connection with something else: *They
live in relative luxury.*
• **relative** *noun* a person who is related to
another.
Word Family **relatively** *adverb*
comparatively.

relative clause *noun*
Grammar a clause which gives further
information about a noun or pronoun,
often beginning with a **relative pronoun**
such as *who, whom, whose, which* or *that*: *In
the sentence 'The woman who saw the
accident refused to give evidence', 'who saw
the accident' is a relative clause.*

relax (ri-**laks**) *verb*
1 to make or become less formal, tense,
etc.: *Please sit down and relax.*

2 to make or become looser, less strict or
firm: *As time went by, his employers relaxed
the rules.*
[*re-* + Latin *laxus* loose]

relaxation (ree-lak-**say**-sh'n) *noun*
1 an activity or diversion which provides
relief, enjoyment or rest: *Gardening is my
greatest relaxation.*
2 a loosening or relaxing.

relay[1] (**ree**-lay) *noun*
1 a group or set of people who take the
place of others, such as a shift of workers.
2 *Sport* a race whose distance is divided
into four or more parts, each of which is
run or swum by one member of a team.
3 *Electricity* a device which is controlled by
electric currents in one circuit so that it
acts as a switch in another circuit.
• **relay** (**ree**-lay *or* ri-**lay**) *verb* (**relays;
relaying; relayed**) to pass by or
as if by relay: *Please relay this message to her.*

relay[2] (**ree**-lay) *verb* (**relays; relaying;
relaid**)
to lay again: *We relaid the patio.*

release *verb*
1 to set free or let go: *He was released from
prison a week ago.*
2 to issue to the public: *The government has
released a public statement.*
• **release** *noun*
1 a freeing or setting free: *a release from
pain.*
2 something which sets free or releases:
She found shouting a great release for tension.
3 the issue of something for public
exhibition, use, purchase, etc.: *the release of
his new film.* □ *The band's latest release was
an instant hit.*

relegate (**rell**-a-gate) *verb*
to send to a particular place, condition,
etc., especially an inferior one: *My team
was relegated to a lower division.*
Word Family **relegation** (rell-a-**gay**-
sh'n) *noun*.
[Latin *relegare* to send into retirement]

relent (ri-**lent**) *verb*
to become less severe or unyielding: *My
dad finally relented and let us go to the party.*
Word Family **relentless** *adjective*
1 without pity. **2** steady or persistent;
relentlessly *adverb*; **relentlessness** *noun*.
[*re-* + Latin *lentus* flexible]

relevant (**rell**-a-v'nt) *adjective*
connected to the matter being discussed.
Word Family **relevance, relevancy**
noun; **relevantly** *adverb*.

reliable (ri-**lie**-a-b'l) *adjective*
able to be relied or depended on: *I can prove that the witness is not reliable.*
Word Family reliably *adverb*; **reliability** (ri-lie-a-**bill**-i-tee) *noun*.

reliant (ri-**lie**-'nt) *adjective*
Phrase reliant on dependent on.
Word Family reliance *noun*.

relic (**rell**-ik) *noun*
1 something which has survived from a past time and serves as a reminder.
2 something kept as an object of religious worship, especially some part or personal reminder of a holy person.
[Latin *reliquiae* leavings]

relief (ri-**leef**) *noun*
1 a lessening or removal of pain, anxiety, etc.: *It was a great relief to see her son was safe.*
2 something which provides help or comfort: *The government promised to send relief to the flood victims.*
3 a person who replaces another at a task: *The watchman waited for his relief to arrive.*
4 the projecting of a part or figure from its background or a surface, such as a sculptured figure from a wall, or a work, design, etc. done in this way.
5 *Geography* the shape and height of the earth's surface.
[*re-* + Latin *levis* light (in weight)]

relief map *noun*
Geography a map that shows the height and shape of the land using contours or shading.

relieve (ri-**leev**) *verb*
1 to bring relief or ease to: *Nothing could relieve her distress.*
2 to replace another person at a task: *I'm being relieved at 4 p.m.*
Phrases relieve oneself to urinate.
relieve someone of something to remove something from someone: *She was relieved of her duties while her employers investigated the theft.*

relieved *adjective*
feeling better because a cause of anxiety has been removed: *Meena was relieved that they were safe.*

religion (ri-**lij**-'n) *noun*
1 any of various systems of belief or worship concerned with the spiritual or inner nature of human beings and usually a superhuman power recognized as creator or controller.

2 any practice, matter, etc. treated with devotion or keen conscientiousness: *Tidiness is a religion with her.*
[Latin *religio* scrupulousness or obligation]

religious (re-**lij**-us) *adjective*
1 of or relating to religion: *a religious belief.*
2 faithful to one's religion: *She's very religious.*
Word Family religiously *adverb*; **religiousness** *noun*; **religiosity** (re-lij-ee-**oss**-i-tee) *noun* the state of being religious to an extreme degree.

relinquish (ri-**link**-wish) *verb*
to let go, surrender or give up.
Word Family relinquishment *noun*.
[Latin *relinquere* to leave behind]

reliquary (**rell**-i-kwa-ree) *noun* (*plural* **reliquaries**)
a container for religious relics.

relish (**rell**-ish) *noun* (*plural* **relishes**)
1 an appreciation, pleasure or enjoyment: *He watched his enemy's downfall with relish.*
2 a savoury substance, such as a pickle or sauce, added to a meal.
• **relish** *verb* to take pleasure in or enjoy: *She relished the thought of getting revenge.*

relive (ree-**liv**) *verb*
to live or experience again.

relocate (ree-lo-**kate**) *verb*
to establish or become established in a new place.
Word Family relocation (ree-lo-**kay**-sh'n) *noun*.

reluctant (ri-**luk**-t'nt) *adjective*
unwilling: *My father was obviously reluctant to lend me his car.*
Word Family reluctantly *adverb*; **reluctance** *noun*.
[*re-* + Latin *luctans* struggling]

rely (ri-**lie**) *verb* (**relies; relying; relied**)
Phrase rely on, rely upon to have trust or confidence in: *I'm relying on you.*

remain *verb*
1 to stay or continue: *Remain in your seats.* □ *He remained calm during the crisis.*
2 to be left: *A lot of work remains to be done.*
[from Latin]

remainder *noun*
the part which is left: *If you take 6 from 10 the remainder is 4.*

remains *plural noun*
1 any parts left over after destruction, use, etc.: *the remains of a bombed city.* □ *the remains of dinner.*
2 a dead body: *The victim's remains have not been identified.*

remake (ree-make) *verb* (**remakes;
remaking; remade**)
to make or construct again.
• **remake** (ree-make) *noun* something
which is made again, especially a film.

remand (ri-**mahnd**) *verb*
Law to hold an accused person to await
further trial.
• **remand** *noun*
Phrase **be on remand** to be in prison
before one's trial has begun.
[*re-* + Latin *mandare* to commit]

remark (ri-**mark**) *verb*
1 to say casually.
2 an old word meaning 'to notice'.
• **remark** *noun*
1 a comment or casual expression: *I
thought that was an odd remark.*
2 the act of commenting or noticing: *The
event was scarcely worthy of remark.*
Word Family **remarkable** *adjective*
unusual or worthy of remark; **remarkably**
adverb.

remarry *verb* (**remarries; remarrying;
remarried**)
to marry again after widowhood or
divorce.
Word Family **remarriage** *noun.*

remedial (ri-**mee-dee-ul**) *adjective*
1 providing a remedy: *to take remedial
action to change the situation.*
2 intended to correct or improve, as with
special extra help: *remedial teaching.*

remedy (**rem-a-dee**) *noun* (*plural*
remedies)
anything which heals, removes or relieves
pain, fault, etc.
• **remedy** *verb* (**remedies; remedying;
remedied**) to fix or put right.
Word Family **remediable** (ri-mee-dee-
a-b'l) *adjective* able to be cured or fixed.
[from Latin]

remember *verb*
to keep in or bring back to the mind: *Please
remember to bring your coat.* □ *I can't
remember his name.*
Phrase **remember someone to
someone** to take greetings from one
person to another: *Please remember me to
your parents.*
[*re-* + Latin *memor* mindful]

remembrance (ri-**mem-br'nce**) *noun*
1 the act of remembering.
2 a token or souvenir, especially one given
to serve as a reminder.

remind *verb*
to cause to remember: *Remind me to phone
Grant when we get home.*
Word Family **reminder** *noun* something
which causes one to remember.

reminisce (rem-i-**niss**) *verb*
to remember and enjoy or describe past
experiences, events, etc.
• **reminiscence** *noun*
1 the act of reminiscing.
2 (*usually* **reminiscences**) a person's
description of past experiences.
[from Latin]

reminiscent *adjective*
Phrase **reminiscent of** inspiring
memories of.

remiss (ri-**miss**) *adjective*
careless or neglectful.
Word Family **remissness** *noun.*
[Latin *remissus* sent back, slackened]

remission (ri-**mish-'n**) *noun*
1 a pardon, release or forgiveness: *the
remission of sins.*
2 a lessening in strength or intensity: *The
cancer is in remission.*

remit (ri-**mit**) *verb* (**remits; remitting;
remitted**)
1 (*formal*) to pardon, release from.
2 (*formal*) to send: *remit money.*
3 (*formal*) to lessen in strength or
intensity.
• **remit** (ree-mit) *noun* (*formal*) an
official set of duties and responsibilities:
That is not within the remit of the committee.

remittance *noun*
(*formal*) money or payment sent or given.
[Latin *remittere* to let go back]

remnant *noun*
a remaining part, quantity or fragment.

remonstrate (rem-'n-**strate**) *verb*
to say in protest or objection.
Word Family **remonstration** (rem-'n-
stray-sh'n), **remonstrance** (ri-**mon-
str'nce**) *noun.*
[*re-* + Latin *monstrare* to show]

remorse *noun*
a feeling of sincere and painful regret or
sorrow for one's misdeeds.
Word Family **remorseful** *adjective*;
remorsefully *adverb*; **remorsefulness**
noun; **remorseless** *adjective* without pity
or remorse; **remorselessly** *adverb*;
remorselessness *noun.*
[*re-* + Latin *morsus* bitten]

remote *adjective*
1 far away or distant: *a remote town.* □ *the
remote past.*

2 (of a person) cold and unfriendly.
3 (of a chance, idea, etc.) slight: *a remote possibility*.
Word Family **remotely** *adverb*;
remoteness *noun*.
[Latin *remotus* removed]

remote control *noun*
1 the control of a machine, etc. by electrical or radio signals at a distance.
2 a device for controlling things from a distance.

remould (ree-**mold**) *verb* (*American* **remold**)
to mould or shape again, e.g. by adding new rubber walls, etc. to a used tyre.
• **remould** (ree-**mold**) *noun* a tyre which has been remoulded.

remove (ri-**moov**) *verb*
1 to take off or away: *Remove your shoes before entering*.
2 to dismiss: *The security man was immediately removed from his post*.
• **remove** *noun*
1 the distance by which things are separated: *This party is a far remove from last year's celebrations*.
2 *Education* a class in some schools.
Word Family **removable** *adjective*;
removal (ri-**moo**-v'l) *noun* 1 the act of removing. 2 an act of moving house, office, etc.
[Latin *removere* to put away]

remunerate (ri-**mew**-na-rate) *verb*
to pay, reward or compensate.
Word Family **remuneration** (ri-mew-na-**ray**-sh'n) *noun*; **remunerative** (ri-**mew**-ner-a-tiv) *adjective* profitable.
[*re-* + Latin *muneris* of a gift]

Renaissance (ri-**nay**-sonce) *noun*
1 the revival of classical learning and art in Europe from the 14th century to the 16th century.
2 (**renaissance**) any revival or rebirth.
[French, rebirth]

renal (**ree**-n'l) *adjective*
Anatomy of or relating to the kidneys.
[Latin *ren* kidney]

rename (ree-**name**) *verb*
to give a new name to.

renascent (ri-**nay**-s'nt) *adjective*
being renewed or growing again.

rend *verb* (**rends; rending; rent**)
a literary word meaning 'to split or tear apart violently'.

render *verb*
1 to provide, give or make available: *to render assistance*.

2 to cause to be: *This news rendered him speechless*.
3 to represent or depict.
4 *Building* to coat a wall with a layer of plaster or mortar.
[Latin *reddere* to give back]

rendezvous (**ron**-day-voo) *noun* (*plural* **rendezvous**) (**ron**-day-vooz)
1 an arranged meeting.
2 a meeting place.
• **rendezvous** *verb*.
[French *rendez-vous* present yourself]

rendition (ren-**dish**-'n) *noun*
a rendering, performance or interpretation.

renegade (**ren**-a-gade) *noun*
a person who leaves or betrays a party, belief or cause.
[Spanish *renegado* renounced]

renege (ri-**nayg** *or* ri-**neeg**) *verb*
to fail to carry out one's word or promise.
[*re-* + Latin *negare* to deny]

renegotiate (ree-ni-**go**-shee-ate) *verb*
to negotiate or revise a contract or agreement again.

renew (ri-**new**) *verb*
1 to begin again or make new: *They soon renewed their friendship*.
2 to extend: *We will renew the lease for another year*.
Word Family **renewable** *adjective* 1 able or due to be renewed. 2 (of energy, resources, etc.) unable to be used up: *The wind is a renewable source of energy*;
renewal *noun*.

rennet *noun*
a substance obtained from the inner lining of a calf's stomach and used to curdle milk, e.g. in making cheese.

renounce (ri-**nounce**) *verb*
to reject or disown: *His son has renounced all claim to the inheritance*.
Word Family **renunciation** (ri-nun-see-**ay**-sh'n) *noun*.
[*re-* + Latin *nuntiare* to announce]

renovate (**ren**-a-vate) *verb*
to repair to the original condition: *They are renovating an old house*.
Word Family **renovation** (ren-a-**vay**-sh'n) *noun* 1 the act of renovating.
2 (**renovations**) the changes or repairs made; **renovator** *noun*.
[*re-* + Latin *novus* new]

renown (ree-**noun**) *noun*
fame.
Word Family **renowned** *adjective*.
[*re-* + Latin *nomen* a name]

rent¹ *noun*
the payment made by one person or group in return for the use or occupation of a property which belongs to another.
Word Family **rent** *verb* to give or obtain use or occupation of property in exchange for payment.

rent² *noun*
a tear or rip.

rent³ the past tense and past participle of **rend**.

rental *noun*
the amount received or paid as rent.
• **rental** *adjective*
1 of rent.
2 available for renting.

renunciation ⇨ RENOUNCE.

reoccupy (ree-**ok**-yoo-pie) *verb*
(**reoccupies; reoccupying; reoccupied**)
to occupy or live in again.

reopen (ree-o-pen) *verb*
to open or begin again: *His words reopened an old wound.*

reorganize, reorganise (ree-**or**-ga-nize) *verb*
to organize again.
Word Family **reorganization** (ree-or-ga-nigh-**zay**-sh'n) *noun*.

rep ⇨ SALES REPRESENTATIVE.

repaid the past tense and past participle of **repay**.

repair¹ (ri-**pair**) *verb*
to put back into good or whole condition.
Word Family **repair** *noun* 1 the work or process of repairing. 2 the condition due to repairing; **repairable, reparable** (**rep**-ra-b'l) *adjective*; **repairer** *noun*.
[*re-* + Latin *parare* to make ready]

repair² *verb*
an old word meaning 'to go or take oneself'.
[Old French *reparer* to return to one's own country]

reparation (rep-a-**ray**-sh'n) *noun*
1 the act of making amends or compensating.
2 something done or given as compensation.

repartee (rep-ar-**tee**) *noun*
conversation made up of quick or witty exchanges.
[French *repartir* to reply promptly]

repast (ri-**pahst**) *noun*
(*formal*) a meal.
[*re-* + Latin *pastus* fed]

repatriate (ree-**pat**-ree-ate) *verb*
to send back a person, such as a refugee or prisoner of war, to his or her own country.
Word Family **repatriation** (ree-pat-ree-ay-sh'n) *noun*.
[*re-* + Latin *patria* native land]

repay (ree-**pay**) *verb* (**repays; repaying; repaid**)
to pay back: *She finally managed to repay the loan.*
Word Family **repayment** *noun*.

repeal *verb*
to cancel or withdraw: *Parliament has now repealed the law.*
• **repeal** *noun*.
[Old French *rapeler* to call back]

repeat *verb*
1 to say or do again: *Repeat the poem until you know it by heart.*
2 to tell to any other person: *Please never repeat what I have just told you.*
• **repeat** *noun*
1 the act of repeating.
2 something which is repeated, such as a television programme.
Word Family **repeated** *adjective* done or said again and again; **repeatedly** *adverb*; **repetition** (rep-a-**tish**-'n) *noun* 1 the act of repeating. 2 something repeated.
[*re-* + Latin *petere* to seek]

repel (ri-**pel**) *verb* (**repels; repelling; repelled**)
1 to turn back or force away: *to repel an invading army.*
2 to be distasteful to: *His greasy hair repelled her.*
3 (of a substance) not to mix with: *Oil will repel water.*
4 *Physics* to push apart: *Two objects with the same magnetic poles will repel one another.*
Word Family **repellence, repellency** *noun*.
[*re-* + Latin *pellere* to drive]

repellent (ri-**pell**-'nt) *noun*
something which repels, especially a substance or solution used to repel insects, etc.
• **repellent** *adjective*
1 able to repel or keep off.
2 distasteful or revolting.

repent (ri-**pent**) *verb*
to feel sorry or remorseful, especially with the intention to improve or reform: *The priest told him to repent.*
Word Family **repentance** *noun*; **repentant** *adjective*.
[*re-* + Latin *paenitere* to regret]

repercussion (ree-pa-**kush**-'n) *noun*
(*usually* **repercussions**) an indirect result
or effect of some action, event, etc.,
especially if unexpected or unpleasant.
[*re-* + Latin *percussus* struck]

repertoire (**rep**-a-twah) *noun*
the range of works, parts or pieces
presented by a performer or company.
[French]

repertory (**rep**-a-tree) *noun*
the system by which a group of actors
presents a number of different plays for a
limited time.

repetition ⇨ REPEAT.

repetitious (rep-a-**tish**-us) *adjective*
tending to repeat, especially in a needless
way.
Word Family **repetitiousness** *noun*.

repetitive (ri-**pet**-at-iv) *adjective*
of or tending to repeat.
Word Family **repetitively** *adverb*.

rephrase *verb*
to express in different words.

replace (ri-**place**) *verb*
1 to put back in place or position: *Please
replace books on their correct shelves.*
2 to take the place of: *No one could ever
replace her first love.*
Word Family **replacement** *noun*.

replay (ree-**play**) *verb*
to play over again: *The match will have to be
replayed.*
• **replay** (**ree**-play) *noun*.

replenish (ri-**plen**-ish) *verb*
to supply or fill again.
Word Family **replenishment** *noun*.
[*re-* + Latin *plenus* full]

replete (ri-**pleet**) *adjective*
(*formal*) well supplied or filled.
Word Family **repletion** *noun*.
[Latin *repletus* filled]

replica (**rep**-li-ka) *noun*
a copy or reproduction, especially of a
work of art.
Word Family **replicate** *verb* to make an
exact copy of; **replication** (rep-li-**kay**-
sh'n) *noun*.
[Italian]

reply (ri-**ply**) *verb* (**replies; replying;
replied**)
to say or do something in return: *Have you
replied to her email yet?*
• **reply** *noun* (*plural* **replies**) a statement
or action made or given in return.
[Latin *replicare* to repeat]

report *noun*
1 an account of a particular subject: *a news
report on the famine in Ethiopia.*
2 a description by a teacher of a student's
progress.
3 a loud bang or explosion.
• **report** *verb*
1 to give an account, statement or
description of: *His speech was reported in the
newspapers.*
2 to make a complaint or charge against:
*She reported her noisy neighbours to the
police.*
3 to present oneself: *You should report for
work at noon.*
[Latin *reportare* to bring back]

reported speech ⇨ INDIRECT SPEECH.

reporter *noun*
1 a person employed to collect and report
or write about news, current events, etc.
2 a person appointed to take notes or
report on official proceedings, etc.: *a court
reporter.*

repose¹ (ri-**poze**) *noun*
1 rest or relaxation.
2 a calm confidence.
Word Family **repose** *verb* 1 to lie on
something. 2 to be resting or peaceful;
reposeful *adjective* calm; **reposefully**
adverb.
[*re-* + Latin *pausa* a pause]

repose² *verb*
Phrase **repose something in** (*formal*) to
place or put, usually one's faith, trust or
confidence, in.
[*re-* + Latin *positus* placed]

repository (ri-**poz**-i-tree) *noun* (*plural*
repositories)
a place where things are deposited or
stored.

repossess (ree-po-**zess**) *verb*
to take back possession of: *The hire
company have repossessed the car.*
Word Family **repossession** *noun*.

reprehensible (rep-ri-**hen**-si-b'l) *adjective*
deserving blame or criticism.
Word Family **reprehensibly** *adverb*.
[*re-* + Latin *prehensus* seized]

represent (rep-ri-**zent**) *verb*
1 to speak officially for: *I represent the
defendant in this case, Your Honour.*
2 to be a sign meaning: *These marks
represent different musical notes.*
3 to portray: *The newspapers represent her as
an evil, scheming woman, but we liked her.*

Word Family representative *noun* a
person who acts for or instead of another
or others: *Who is your legal representative?*
□ *I got a job as a sales representative;*
representative *adjective* **1** serving to
represent. **2** typical.

representation (rep-ri-zen-**tay**-sh'n)
noun
1 the act of representing: *His representation
of the facts was rather misleading.*
2 the state of being represented: *The
women demanded equal representation in
parliament.*
3 something which represents or depicts,
such as a statue.
4 (**representations**) statements made on
behalf of a person, group, etc.

repress (ri-**press**) *verb*
to hold back or restrain: *She could not
repress a smile.*
Word Family repression (ri-**presh**-'n)
noun; **repressive** *adjective* tending to
repress.
[Latin *repressus* checked]

reprieve (ri-**preev**) *verb*
to postpone, suspend or cancel the
punishment of.
• **reprieve** *noun*
1 the postponement, etc. of a punishment.
2 a temporary relief or release.

reprimand (**rep**-ri-mahnd) *verb*
to rebuke sharply, usually publicly.
• **reprimand** *noun.*
[Latin *reprimanda* that should be
repressed]

reprint (ree-**print**) *verb*
to print again.
• **reprint** (**ree**-print) *noun* anything which
has been printed again, such as a new,
unchanged edition of a book.

reprisal (ri-**pry**-z'l) *noun*
an attack, punishment, injury, etc. made in
retaliation for some injury.

reprise (ri-**preez**) *noun*
the repeating of a sequence of musical
notes.

reproach *verb*
to express disapproval, usually about a
personal matter and intending to cause a
feeling of shame.
Word Family reproach *noun* (*plural*
reproaches); **reproachful** *adjective*
expressing blame; **reproachfully** *adverb;*
reproachfulness *noun.*

The word **reproach** is related to
approach. Both go back in origin to
Latin *prope* (near), *reproach* having
come into English from Old French
reprochier. The idea was that someone
who had done wrong would be brought
'near' to their misdeed or wrongdoing
and held to blame.

reprobate (**rep**-ra-bate) *noun*
a person without principles or morals.
[Latin *reprobatus* disapproved of]

reprocess *verb*
to treat specially in order to use again:
reprocessed nuclear fuel.

reproduce (ree-pro-**dewce**) *verb*
1 to have or give birth to offspring.
2 to produce an identical or very similar
form of: *Other scientists have not been able to
reproduce her experimental results.*
Word Family reproduction (ree-pro-
duck-sh'n) *noun* **1** the act of reproducing.
2 something which is produced again or in
an identical form: *an excellent reproduction
of a Monet on the wall;* **reproductive**
adjective **1** of or relating to reproduction.
2 able to reproduce; **reproducible**
adjective able to be reproduced.

reprogram *verb* (**reprograms;**
reprogramming; reprogrammed)
Computers to program again.

reprove (ri-**proov**) *verb*
to scold or express disapproval.
Word Family reproof, reproval *noun*
1 the act of reproving. **2** an expression of
disapproval, etc.; **reproving** *adjective;*
reprovingly *adverb.*

reptile *noun*
1 any of a group of cold-blooded air-
breathing animals, such as the snake,
turtle, etc., having a backbone and usually
scales or tough horny skin.
2 (*informal*) a sly or treacherous person.
Word Family reptilian (rep-**till**-ee-an)
adjective.
[Latin *reptilis* creeping]

republic (ri-**pub**-lik) *noun*
a country without a monarch, especially
one with a single elected leader.
Word Family republican *adjective*
1 relating to a republic. **2** in favour of a
republic as the form of government;
republican *noun* a person who favours a
republic as the form of government;
republicanism *noun.*
[Latin *res publica* public concern]

repudiate (ri-**pew**-dee-ate) *verb*
to refuse to accept, recognize or own.
Word Family **repudiation** (ri-pew-dee-ay-sh'n) *noun*.
[Latin *repudium* divorce]

repugnant *adjective*
offensive or distasteful.
Word Family **repugnance** *noun* an extreme dislike or distaste.
[Latin *repugnans* fighting against]

repulse (ri-**pulse**) *verb*
1 to drive back or resist: *Our troops have repulsed the enemy.*
2 to cause to feel disgust: *His greasy hair repulsed her.*
Word Family **repulse** *noun* a rejection; **repulsion** (ri-**pulsh**-'n) *noun* 1 the act of repulsing or repelling. 2 a feeling of disgust.
[Latin *repulsus* repelled]

repulsive *adjective*
causing extreme distaste or dislike: *a repulsive smell.*

reputable (**rep**-yoo-ta-b'l) *adjective*
having a good reputation.
Word Family **reputably** *adverb*; **reputability** (rep-yoo-ta-**bill**-i-tee) *noun*.

reputation (rep-yoo-**tay**-sh'n) *noun*
the general opinion concerning the character or qualities of a person or thing: *This restaurant has an excellent reputation locally.*
[Latin *reputare* to think over]

repute (ri-**pewt**) *noun*
fame or reputation, especially favourable reputation.
● **repute** *verb*
Phrase **be reputed to be** to be considered by many people to be.
Word Family **reputedly** *adverb*.

request (ri-**kwest**) *verb*
(*formal*) to ask for.
● **request** *noun*
1 the act of asking: *a polite request for silence.*
2 something which is asked for.
[Latin *requisitus* searched for]

request stop *noun*
a bus stop at which people can get off only if they have first pressed the bell to ask for the bus to stop.

requiem (**rek**-wee-em) *noun*
1 *Roman Catholicism* a mass celebrated for the peace of the dead.
2 any ceremony, composition, etc. for the dead.
[Latin *requies* rest]

require (ri-**kwire**) *verb*
to need: *All visitors require permission to enter.*
Phrase **require someone to do something** to make it compulsory for someone to do something: *The new law requires schools to test students at the age of ten.*
Word Family **requirement** *noun* something which is required or obligatory.
[Latin *requirere* to search for]

requisite (**rek**-wi-zit) *adjective*
(*formal*) necessary or required.
● **requisite** *noun* a requirement.

requisition (rek-wi-**zish**-'n) *noun*
1 a formal demand or request.
2 the act of demanding or requesting.
● **requisition** *verb* to take over or demand for use, especially for official or military purposes.

reredos (**reer**-doss) *noun* (*plural* **reredoses**)
a screen or wall behind the altar in a church.
[REAR + French *dos* back]

rerun (**ree**-run) *noun*
a film or programme which is repeated, e.g. on television, etc.
● **rerun** (ree-**run**) *verb* (**reruns; rerunning; reran; rerun**).

resat the past tense and past participle of **resit**.

rescind (ri-**sind**) *verb*
to cancel or withdraw formally.
[Latin *rescindere* to cut back]

rescue (**resk**-yoo) *verb*
to free from danger, imprisonment or unpleasantness.
Word Family **rescue** *noun* the act of rescuing; **rescuer** *noun*.

research (ri-**serch**) *noun* (*plural* **researches**)
careful or systematic work to find out facts, information, etc.
● **research** *verb* to investigate thoroughly.
Word Family **researcher** *noun*.

research fellow ⇨ FELLOW (definition 4).

resemble (ri-**zem**-b'l) *verb*
to be or appear like or similar to: *She resembles her grandmother.*
Word Family **resemblance** *noun* 1 the fact of resembling. 2 the degree or amount to which something resembles another: *There is little resemblance between the two languages.*
[*re-* + Latin *similis* like]

resent (ri-zent) *verb*
to feel an indignant or angry dislike for.
Word Family **resentment** *noun*;
resentful *adjective*; **resentfully** *adverb*;
resentfulness *noun*.
[re- + Latin *sentire* to feel]

reservation (rezz-a-vay-sh'n) *noun*
1 an arrangement to keep something aside
for someone: *Her husband had made a
reservation at her favourite restaurant.*
2 a slight doubt: *I still have a few
reservations about our agreement.*
3 an area of public land set aside for a
particular purpose, especially for the use
of native or aboriginal peoples.

reserve (ri-zerv) *verb*
1 to arrange for someone to keep
something aside: *I've reserved us a table at
Antonio's.*
2 to keep back or save: *These seats are
reserved for the school governors.*
• **reserve** *noun*
1 (*often* **reserves**) something which is
kept, saved or set aside: *a reserve of food.*
2 an area of land kept aside for animals or
for a group of people: *a nature reserve.*
3 a quality of aloofness and unwillingness
to express emotions or opinions.
4 *Sport* an extra member of a team who is
prepared to replace any player unable to
take part in or continue a game.
5 the part of the armed forces not
belonging to the regular forces of the
country but called to active service in time
of war.
Phrase **in reserve** set aside: *I kept a few
Easter eggs in reserve in case any other
children visited us.*
[re- + Latin *servare* to keep]

reserved *adjective*
not forthcoming with reactions, opinions,
etc.: *Amy seemed rather reserved on this
occasion.*
Word Family **reservedly** (ri-zer-vid-lee)
adverb; **reservedness** (ri-zer-vid-niss)
noun.

reservoir (rezz-a-vwah) *noun*
1 a place or container for storing water.
2 any container for a fluid.
3 a supply or store: *He has a vast reservoir
of knowledge.*
[French]

reset (ree-set) *verb* (**resets; resetting;
reset**)
to set again: *Reset the clock.*

reshuffle (ree-shuff-'l) *verb*
to change the jobs of a set of people
around: *The Prime Minister is expected to
reshuffle her Cabinet in the spring.*
• **reshuffle** (ree-shuff-'l) *noun.*

reside (ri-zide) *verb*
(*formal*) to have one's place or home for a
particular time: *She now resides in Italy.*
Word Family **residence** (rezz-i-d'nce)
noun 1 the place in which one lives. 2 a
large house. 3 the act of residing.

resident (rezz-i-d'nt) *noun*
1 a person who lives in a particular place.
2 *Medicine* a doctor who lives in a hospital,
often during his or her first year as a
qualified doctor.
3 *Biology* any animal which does not
migrate.
Word Family **resident** *adjective* 1 living
or dwelling. 2 living in the place of
one's work; **residency** *noun* (*plural*
residencies) the fact or time of residing,
especially of a medical resident;
residential (rezz-i-den-sh'l) *adjective*
of or used for residence.
[re- + Latin *sedens* sitting]

residual (ri-zid-yew-'l) *adjective*
left over or remaining.

residue (rezz-i-dew) *noun*
something which remains or is left over:
What is that residue in the test tube?
[Latin *residuus* remaining]

resign (ri-zine) *verb*
to give up a job, etc.
Phrase **be resigned to** to accept
reluctantly: *I am resigned to the fact that we
may not win.*
Word Family **resignation** (rezz-ig-nay-
sh'n) *noun* 1 the act of resigning one's
position or job, or a statement of this.
2 the state of being submissive or
unresisting; **resignedly** (ri-zine-id-lee)
adverb in a way that shows reluctant
acceptance of something.
[Latin *resignare* to unseal, cancel]

resilient (ri-zill-y'nt) *adjective*
1 (of a substance) elastic or springing
back.
2 (of a person) quick to recover: *Her
resilient nature helped her to get better quickly.*
Word Family **resilience, resiliency**
noun the quality of being resilient;
resiliently *adverb*.
[re- + Latin *salire* to jump]

resin (rezz-in) *noun*
Chemistry any of a class of substances
which are insoluble in water but soluble in

organic solvents and are used as polishes and lacquers.
Word Family **resinous** *adjective* resembling or containing resin.
[from Latin]

resist (ri-**zist**) *verb*
1 to fight or act against: *Try to resist temptation.*
2 to stop oneself from doing or producing: *We could not resist a smile at his antics.*
Word Family **resister** *noun*; **resistive** *adjective* able or working to resist; **resistor** *noun* an electronic component which resists electricity.
[re- + Latin *sistere* to stand fast]

resistance *noun*
1 the act or power of resisting or opposing: *This medicine will increase your resistance to infection.*
2 *Electricity* the tendency of all substances to resist the flow of electric current and to convert it into heat.
3 *Electricity* a measure of the opposition to the flow of electric current. It is the ratio of voltage to current.
4 (*often* **Resistance**) the secret organizations in an enemy-occupied country, which continue to work for liberation.
Phrase **the line of least resistance** the easiest and least troublesome way.
Word Family **resistant** *adjective* able or working to resist.

resit *verb* (**resits; resitting; resat**) to take (an exam) again because one has failed previously.

resolute (**rezz**-a-loot) *adjective* firmly determined.
Word Family **resolutely** *adverb*; **resoluteness** *noun*.

resolution (rezz-a-**loo**-sh'n) *noun*
1 a firm decision or determination: *I've made a resolution not to swear any more.*
2 a formal statement of a decision or proposal: *The chairman read out the resolution so that it could be voted on.*
3 a solution or answer: *The resolution of this problem is going to be difficult.*
4 the act or process of separating into parts.

resolve (ri-**zolv**) *verb*
1 to fix or decide firmly: *I resolved never to do it again.*
2 to deal with, solve or settle: *We must resolve the issue now.*
● **resolve** *noun* firm determination.
[Latin *resolvere* to untie]

resonance (**rezz**-a-nance) *noun* the prolonging, vibrating or re-echoing of sound.
Word Family **resonant** *adjective* of, producing or showing resonance; **resonantly** *adverb*; **resonate** *verb* to resound or re-echo.
[re- + Latin *sonare* to sound]

resort (ri-**zort**) *verb*
Phrase **resort to** to make use of for help, etc.: *We were forced to resort to walking during the bus drivers' strike.*
● **resort** *noun*
1 a place visited or used often: *a popular tourist resort.*
2 the act of resorting: *We must try to win without resort to violence.*
last resort a person or thing used when all else has failed.

resound (ri-**zound**) *verb* to echo or ring again, especially loudly.
Word Family **resounding** *adjective*
1 echoing or ringing. 2 very great: *The play has been a resounding success*; **resoundingly** *adverb*.

resource (ri-**sorce** *or* ri-**zorce**) *noun*
1 (*usually* **resources**) a source or supply: *His resources of energy were running out.*
2 (**resources**) reserves of potential wealth in the form of goods, raw materials, etc.: *a nation rich in natural resources.*
3 (*formal*) skill or ability, especially in dealing with difficulties, etc.: *a man of great resource.*
Word Family **resourceful** *adjective* skilful or efficient at dealing with problems; **resourcefully** *adverb*; **resourcefulness** *noun*.
[re- + Latin *surrectus* risen]

respect *noun*
1 an appreciation of a person's worth or qualities: *We have great respect for him as a leader.* □ *Please show your mother more respect.*
2 a detail or aspect: *Our opinions differ in many respects.*
3 (**respects**) (*formal*) best wishes for someone's health and well-being.
Phrase **in respect of, with respect to** (*formal*) in connection with: *He writes with respect to your visit next month.*
Word Family **respect** *verb* to feel or show respect, consideration, etc. for; **respectable** *adjective* 1 of an acceptable moral or social standard, reputation, etc.: *This doesn't look like a respectable neighbourhood.* 2 fairly good: *She inherited a respectable sum*; **respectably** *adverb*;

respectability (ree-spek-ta-**bill**-i-tee)
noun; **respectful** *adjective* feeling or
showing respect; **respectfully** *adverb*;
respectfulness *noun*.
[Latin *respectus* consideration, regard]

respective *adjective*
particular or individual: *What are the
respective merits of the two towns?*
Word Family respectively *adverb*.

respiration (resp-i-**ray**-sh'n) *noun*
1 the action of breathing.
2 a single breath.
3 *Biology* the process by which oxygen and
carbohydrates are incorporated into an
organism and carbon dioxide and water
are given off.
Word Family respire (ri-**spire**) *verb* to
breathe; **respiratory** (re-**spirr**-a-tree)
adjective of or used for respiration.
[*re-* + Latin *spirare* to breathe]

respirator (**resp**-i-ray-ta) *noun*
1 a machine to induce artificial
respiration.
2 ⇨ GAS MASK.

respite (**resp**-ite *or* **resp**-it) *noun*
a brief or temporary rest, delay or relief:
*The rain provided a little respite from the
intense heat.*

resplendent (ri-**splen**-d'nt) *adjective*
splendid or shining brilliantly.
Word Family resplendency,
resplendence *noun*; **resplendently**
adverb.
[*re-* + Latin *splendens* shining]

respond (ri-**spond**) *verb*
to speak or act in return: *She responded to
the joke with a smile.*
[*re-* + Latin *spondere* to pledge]

respondent *noun*
1 *Law* the defendant in a court case,
especially in a divorce case.
2 a person who responds, e.g. to a
questionnaire.

response *noun*
1 the act of responding.
2 something said or done in return.
Word Family responsive *adjective* readily
responding or reacting; **responsively**
adverb; **responsiveness** *noun*.

responsible (ri-**spon**-si-b'l) *adjective*
1 having to look after, manage, take blame
on behalf of, etc.: *Parents are responsible for
their children while in this play area.*
2 deserving of blame or credit for
something: *After the accident the police
looked for the person responsible.*

3 involving the making of important
decisions: *She has a very responsible position
in the company.*
4 sensible and reliable: *She is a very
responsible child for her age.*
Word Family responsibility (ri-spon-si-
bill-i-tee) *noun* (*plural* **responsibilities**)
1 the state of being responsible. 2 a person
or thing for which one is responsible;
responsibly *adverb* in a responsible or
reliable manner.

rest¹ *noun*
1 a stopping of or relief from activity,
work, etc.: *Let's have a rest when we get
round the next bend.* □ *The ball came to rest
just a few centimetres from the hole.*
2 a freedom from worry, disturbance, etc.:
Please put her mind at rest.
3 a pause, such as a silence between
musical notes or a break in a line of poetry.
4 a device or object which supports: *an
armrest.*
Phrase lay to rest, put to rest 1 to bury.
2 to suppress or put down.
● **rest** *verb*
1 to have a rest: *She rested for a few
moments.*
2 to put for support: *I rested my leg on the
table.*
3 (of a person) to lie buried.
Phrases let something rest not to
continue investigating or interfering with
something: *The police decided to let the
matter rest.* **rest on, rest upon** to depend
on. **rest with** (of a decision, etc.) to be the
responsibility of.

rest² *noun*
Phrase the rest (used with singular or
plural verb) the part or amount which
remains or is left over: *I gave the dog the rest
of the cake.* □ *John went home and the rest of
us stayed there till midnight.*
● **rest** *verb* to remain or continue to be.

restate (ree-**state**) *verb*
to state again or in a different way.
Word Family restatement *noun*.

restaurant (**rest**-a-ront) *noun*
a place where meals are bought, served
and eaten.
Word Family restaurateur (rest-a-ra-
ter) *noun* a person who owns or manages a
restaurant.

The word **restaurant** was adopted into
English from French. The French word
restaurant comes from the verb *restaurer*
meaning 'to restore', being a place
where travellers could be restored when
hungry and thirsty. Note that there is
no *n* in *restaurateur*, the name for a
person who runs a *restaurant*.

restful *adjective*
1 giving rest.
2 quiet or peaceful.
Word Family **restfully** *adverb*;
restfulness *noun*.

rest home *noun*
a place where old or ill people live and
receive specialist care.

restitution (rest-i-**tew**-sh'n) *noun*
a restoring of or compensation for loss,
damage, expense, etc.
[from Latin]

restive (**rest**-iv) *adjective*
impatiently discontented or irritated: *The
crowd became restive waiting for the game to
begin.*
Word Family **restively** *adverb*;
restiveness *noun*.

restless *adjective*
not able to rest, relax or remain quiet:
a restless sleeper.
Word Family **restlessly** *adverb*;
restlessness *noun*.

restore (ri-**stor**) *verb*
1 to bring back: *The police tried to restore
order after the riot.*
2 to put back into an original condition:
She restores old paintings for a living.
3 (*formal*) to give back.
Word Family **restoration** (rest-a-**ray**-
sh'n) *noun* 1 the act of restoring: *The
restoration of old houses to their original
condition.* 2 something which has been
returned to its original condition. 3 (**the
Restoration**) *History* the period after the
return of Charles II in 1660; **restorer**
noun; **restorative** *adjective* able to renew
or restore; **restorative** *noun*.
[from Latin]

restrain *verb*
to hold back.
Word Family **restraint** *noun* 1 the act of
restraining. 2 an action, influence, etc.
which restrains or restricts. 3 self-control:
*I think I showed great restraint in not telling
him what I thought of him!*

restrict *verb*
to keep within limits, etc.: *Please restrict
your questions to the main topic.*
Word Family **restriction** *noun*;
restrictive *adjective* tending or used to
restrict; **restricted** *adjective* (of an area,
etc.) for the use of authorized or chosen
people only.
[Latin *restrictus* tightened]

restroom *noun*
(*especially American*) a toilet in a public
building.

result (ri-**zult**) *noun*
1 something which is caused by or arises
from an action, condition, etc.: *His attitude
is a result of a very unhappy childhood.*
2 *Maths* a quantity or answer obtained by
calculation.
3 the outcome of a game, contest, exam,
etc.
Phrase **get a result** (*informal*) to be
successful.
● **result** *verb* to exist or occur because of:
His loss of energy results from his poor diet.
Phrase **result in** to have as a
consequence: *The tragedy resulted in the
stadium being permanently closed.*
Word Family **resultant** *adjective*
following as a result.
[Latin *resultare* to rebound]

resume (ri-**zewm**) *verb*
1 to begin or take up again: *We will resume
this lesson tomorrow.*
2 to occupy or take again: *Please resume
your seats for the speech.*
Word Family **resumption** (ri-**zump**-
sh'n) *noun*.
[from Latin]

résumé (**rez**-yoo-may) *noun*
1 a summary.
2 (*American*) a curriculum vitae.
[French]

resurgent (ri-**sir**-j'nt) *adjective*
rising or returning again.
Word Family **resurgence** *noun*.
[from Latin]

resurrect (rezz-a-**rekt**) *verb*
to bring back to life.
Figurative *They tried to resurrect their old
friendship* (= resume).
Word Family **resurrection** (rez-a-
rek-sh'n) *noun* 1 the act of coming back
to life. 2 any revival or return. 3 (**the
Resurrection**) *Christianity* the rising
of Christ from the tomb, on the third
day after the Crucifixion. 4 (**the
Resurrection**) *Christianity* the rising of
the dead on the Day of Judgement.

resuscitate (ri-**suss**-i-tate) *verb*
to revive, especially from collapse or
unconsciousness.
Word Family **resuscitator** *noun*
something which resuscitates, especially a
machine for this purpose; **resuscitation**
(ri-suss-i-**tay**-sh'n) *noun*.
[*re-* + Latin *suscitare* to stir up]

retail *noun*
the selling of goods to the general public,
usually in small quantities. Compare
WHOLESALE *noun*.

• **retail** *verb* to sell or be sold directly to individuals: *products retailing at less than £100.*
Word Family **retail** *adverb*; **retailer** *noun* a person or shop that deals in retail.
[Old French *retaille* a piece cut off]

retail price *noun*
the price which a product sells for in the shops.

retain (ri-**tane**) *verb*
to continue to hold, do, use, etc.: *She retained her dignity despite the embarrassing mistake.*
[from Latin]

retainer *noun*
1 a servant, especially a personal one.
2 a device for holding a part in place.
3 a fee paid to reserve the services of a professional, such as a lawyer.

retaliate (ri-**tal**-ee-ate) *verb*
to repay an injury, wrong, etc. with another: *Her brother retaliated with a few embarrassing remarks of his own.*
Word Family **retaliation** (ri-tal-ee-**ay**-sh'n) *noun*; **retaliatory** (ri-**tal**-ee-a-tree), **retaliative** *adjective*.
[re- + Latin *talis* such]

retard (ri-**tard**) *verb*
to slow down or delay the progress of.
Word Family **retardation** (ree-tar-**day**-sh'n) *noun* 1 the state of being retarded or the act of retarding. 2 also called **deceleration**. *Physics* the rate of decrease of velocity; **retarder, retardant** *noun*.
[re- + Latin *tardus* slow]

retch (retch) *verb*
to try to vomit.
• **retch** *noun* (*plural* **retches**).
[Old English *hraca* a clearing of the throat]

retention (ri-**ten**-sh'n) *noun*
1 the act or power of retaining.
2 the capacity for retaining

retentive (ri-**ten**-tiv) *adjective*
having the ability to retain.
Word Family **retentiveness** *noun*.

rethink (ree-**think**) *verb* (**rethinks**; **rethinking**; **rethought**)
to reconsider.
• **rethink** (ree-**think**) *noun*.

reticent (**ret**-i-s'nt) *adjective*
not communicative.
Word Family **reticently** *adverb*; **reticence** *noun*.
[Latin *reticens* keeping silent]

retina (**ret**-in-a) *noun* (*plural* **retinas** or **retinae** (**ret**-i-nee))
Anatomy the inner lining at the back of the eye, containing the light-sensitive cells.
Word Family **retinal** *adjective*.
[Latin *rete* a net]

retinue (**ret**-i-new) *noun*
a group of attendants accompanying an important person.
[French, retained]

retire *verb*
1 to give up work permanently.
2 (*formal*) to go away or withdraw to another place, as for rest, etc.
Word Family **retirement** *noun*.
[from French]

retiring *adjective*
shy or reserved.

retort[1] *verb*
to reply to an argument, accusation, etc. with another one, usually quickly and sharply.
• **retort** *noun*.

retort[2] *noun*
1 *Chemistry* a bulb-shaped glass vessel with a long neck sloping downwards from the top, used in distillation.
2 *Chemistry* any vessel in which chemical reactions take place in industrial processes.
[Latin *retortus* twisted back]

retouch (ree-**tutch**) *verb*
to improve or correct by adding new details, etc.: *We'll have to retouch these photos.*

retrace *verb*
to go back over: *We retraced our steps to look for the keys.*

retract *verb*
to withdraw or take back: *The tortoise retracted its head.* □ *I insist that you retract your statement.*
Word Family **retractable** *adjective*; **retraction** *noun* 1 the act or power of retracting. 2 a withdrawal; **retractor** *noun* a person or thing that retracts.
[from Latin]

retread (ree-**tred**) *noun*
a tyre which is restored or renewed by moulding a new rubber tread onto it.
• **retread** (ree-**tred**) *verb* (**retreads**; **retreading**; **retreaded**) to restore a tyre in this way.

retreat *noun*
1 the act of withdrawing to safety, etc., such as the forced withdrawal of a military force.

2 a place which is quiet, safe or peaceful: *a holiday retreat*.
3 a period of seclusion or retirement: *She's gone on a religious retreat*.
● **retreat** *verb* to go back or withdraw.
[Latin *retrahere* to draw back]

retrial (ree-trile) *noun*
a second trial.

retribution (ret-ri-bew-sh'n) *noun*
a repayment, especially in the form of punishment.
Word Family **retributive** (ri-trib-yoo-tiv) *adjective* relating to or involving retribution.
[*re-* + Latin *tribuere* to assign]

retrieve (ri-treev) *verb*
to bring back or recover: *The dog retrieved the birds we had shot.* □ *We had to call in a computer expert to retrieve the files we had lost.*
Word Family **retriever** *noun* something which retrieves, such as a breed of dog trained to retrieve game; **retrieve, retrieval** *noun* recovery.
[Old French *retrover* to find again]

retroactive (ret-ro-ak-tiv) *adjective*
(of a law, etc.) having retrospective effect.
Word Family **retroactively** *adverb*.

retrograde *adjective*
moving backwards, especially to an earlier or less developed condition.
[*retro-* + Latin *gradus* a step]

retrogress *verb*
to move backwards, especially to an earlier or worse condition.
Word Family **retrogressive** *adjective*; **retrogression** *noun*.

retrorocket *noun*
a rocket motor attached to a spacecraft, fired in the direction in which the spacecraft is travelling in order to slow it down.

retrospect (ret-ro-spekt) *noun*
Phrase **in retrospect** when subsequently considered.
Word Family **retrospective** (ret-ro-spekt-iv) *adjective* **1** looking back or to the past. **2** (of a law, etc.) having effect from a past date.
[*retro-* + Latin *spectus* looked]

retsina (ret-see-na) *noun*
a strong Greek white wine.

return *verb*
1 to come or go back: *At last I returned home.*

2 to cause something to come or go back: *Sharma asked me to return the books he had lent me.*
3 to elect: *Our town returned a Labour MP for the first time.*
4 (of an investment) to produce as profit.
● **return** *noun*
1 the act of returning: *I phoned her immediately upon my return to England.*
2 something which is returned, such as an unwanted ticket for a play.
3 also **return ticket** a ticket for travelling to a place and back again.
4 profit: *What return did you get on your investment?*
5 an official statement: *She filled in her tax return.*
6 also **return key** *Computers* a key which moves the point at which text can be introduced down to the next line.
Phrases **by return** by the next post.
many happy returns used as a greeting to people on their birthday.
Word Family **returnable** *adjective* able to be returned.

returning officer *noun*
the official who supervises an election and announces the result.

return match *noun* (*plural* **return matches**)
a game played again between the same opponents so that the loser has a chance of challenging the winner.

reunion (ree-yoon-y'n) *noun*
the act of being reunited, especially the meeting of people after a separation.

reunite (ree-yoo-nite) *verb*
to unite or bring together again.

rev *verb* (**revs; revving; revved**)
(*informal*) to increase engine speed quickly.
● **rev** *noun* an engine revolution.

revamp *verb*
to renovate or repair.

reveal *verb*
1 to make known: *Don't reveal my secret to anyone.*
2 to allow to be seen: *The door swung open to reveal a terrible scene.*
Word Family **revealing** *adjective*; **revealingly** *adverb*.
[Latin *revelare* to unveil]

reveille (ri-vall-ee) *noun*
Military the bugle call or drum roll signalling soldiers to get up in the morning. Compare LAST POST.
[French *réveillez* wake up]

revel (rev-'l) *verb* (**revels; revelling; revelled**)
to celebrate merrily and noisily.
Phrase **revel in** to take great pleasure or delight in.
Word Family **revels** *plural noun* merrymaking; **revelry** *noun* (*plural* **revelries**) merrymaking.
[French *reveler* to rebel or make a noise]

revelation (rev-a-lay-sh'n) *noun*
1 the act of revealing: *We were shocked by the revelation of his secret.*
2 something that is revealed: *His attitude was a revelation to us.*

revenge (ri-venj) *noun*
any repayment for a wrong or injury: *She swore to get revenge on her attacker.*
● **revenge** *verb*
Phrase **revenge oneself on, be revenged on** literary expressions meaning 'to get revenge for a wrong or injury done to one'.
Word Family **revengeful** *adjective*; **revengefully** *adverb*; **revengefulness** *noun*.
[re- + Latin *vindicare* to lay claim to]

| ! | Do not confuse *revenge* with AVENGE. |

revenue (rev-a-new) *noun*
any income, especially that received by a government from taxation.
[French, returned]

reverberate (ri-ver-ba-rate) *verb*
to sound or echo again and again: *His screams reverberated in the tunnel.*
Word Family **reverberation** (ri-ver-ba-ray-sh'n) *noun*.
[re- + Latin *verber* a lash]

revere (ri-veer) *verb*
to treat or regard with deep respect.
Word Family **reverence** (rev-a-r'nce) *noun* 1 a feeling of deep respect and awe.
2 (**Reverence**) *Christianity* a title of respect for a clergyman of high rank: *Thank you, Your Reverence*; **reverent, reverential** (rev-a-ren-sh'l) *adjective* feeling, showing or characterized by reverence; **reverently, reverentially** *adverb*.
[re- + Latin *vereri* to feel awe]

Reverend (rev-a-r'nd) *adjective*
Christianity a title of respect for a clergyman: *the Reverend William Hudson.*
● **reverend** *noun* (*informal*) a clergyman.

reverie (rev-a-ree) *noun*
1 quiet pleasant dreaminess.
2 a daydream.
[French *rêver* to dream]

reverse *adjective*
opposite in order, direction, position or character: *the reverse side of the paper.*
● **reverse** *noun*
1 the opposite of something: *The reverse of what he says is true.*
2 the back of a coin, medal or postage stamp. Compare OBVERSE *noun* (definition 2).
3 also **reverse gear** *Mechanics* a gear that enables a car to move backwards.
4 a setback: *Our plans suffered a major reverse.*
● **reverse** *verb* to turn in or into an opposite direction, order, position or character: *She reversed the car into the parking space.*
Word Family **reversal** *noun* the act or an instance of reversing: *The new system was a reversal of the usual procedure.*
[Latin *reversus* turned round]

reversible *adjective*
able to be reversed: *a reversible jacket.*

revert *verb*
1 to return to a former state, condition, subject, etc.: *When he left prison he quickly reverted to his old ways.*
2 *Law* to return to the original owner.
Word Family **reversion** *noun*.

review (ri-vew) *noun*
1 a survey or examination: *a review of the year's political events.* □ *The general carried out a review of his troops.*
2 a short critical article about a new book, film, play, art exhibition, etc.
3 a magazine which contains articles examining current events, books, etc.
● **review** *verb*
1 to make, write or publish a review.
2 to look at again: *The government has promised to review its transport policy.*
Word Family **reviewer** *noun* a person who reviews books, films, etc.

revile *verb*
to insult or abuse.
[Old French *reviler* to despise]

revise (ri-vize) *verb*
1 to alter or change: *I have revised my opinion.*
2 to read or study again, especially before an examination.
Word Family **revision** (ri-vizh-'n) *noun*
1 the act or process of revising: *I did a month's intensive revision before the exams.*
2 something which is revised, such as a new edition of a book.
[re- + Latin *visere* scrutinize]

revitalize, revitalise (ree-**vie**-ta-lize) *verb*
to put new life or energy into.
Word Family **revitalization** (ree-vie-ta-lie-**zay**-sh'n) *noun*.

revive *verb*
to bring back to life or existence: *The lifeguard couldn't revive the swimmer.* □ *Their government revived an old law.*
Word Family **revival** (re-**vie**-v'l) *noun*
1 the act of reviving. **2** a reawakening of religious interest; **revivalist** *noun*, *adjective*; **revivalism** *noun*.
[*re-* + Latin *vivus* alive]

revivify (ree-**viv**-i-fie) *verb* (**revivifies**; **revivifying**; **revivified**)
to give new life to.

revoke *verb*
to withdraw: *The head teacher immediately revoked all sixth-form privileges.*
[*re-* + Latin *vocare* to call]

revolt *noun*
the act of resisting authority, especially as a protest against oppression.
• **revolt** *verb*
1 to rise in rebellion against authority. **2** to cause to be disgusted or horrified.
Word Family **revolting** *adjective*; **revoltingly** *adverb*.

revolution (rev-a-**loo**-sh'n) *noun*
1 a complete change, such as that caused by the overthrow of a government or political system.
2 the act or process of rotating or revolving: *the revolution of the earth around the sun.*
3 a single turn or rotation.
Word Family **revolutionize, revolutionise** *verb* to bring about a revolution or radical change.

revolutionary (rev-a-**loo**-sh'n-ree) *noun* (*plural* **revolutionaries**)
a person favouring or taking part in a revolution.
• **revolutionary** *adjective* of, like or characterized by revolution.

revolve *verb*
to turn or cause to turn around something: *The earth revolves around the sun.*
[*re-* + Latin *volvere* to roll]

revolver *noun*
a pistol which has a revolving cylinder with a number of chambers so that the bullets can be fired in succession.

revue (ri-**vew**) *noun*
a form of entertainment consisting of a series of short acts and songs which usually satirize people and events.
[French, review]

revulsion (ri-**vul**-sh'n) *noun*
a violent reaction of disgust: *She couldn't hide her revulsion.*
[Latin *revulsio* a plucking away]

reward *noun*
something offered or given in return for service or merit.
Word Family **reward** *verb* to give a reward to; **rewarding** *adjective* satisfying; **rewardingly** *adverb*.

rewind (ree-**wined**) *verb* (**rewinds**; **rewinding**; **rewound**)
1 to wind again.
2 to wind back.

rewire *verb*
to provide with new wiring.

reword *verb*
to put into other words.

rhapsody (**rap**-sa-dee) *noun* (*plural* **rhapsodies**)
1 a feeling or expression of great enthusiasm or delight.
2 *Music* a short piece of romantic music.
Word Family **rhapsodical** (rap-**sod**-i-k'l) *adjective* of or like a rhapsody; **rhapsodize, rhapsodise** *verb*.
[Greek *rhapsoidos* one who strings songs together]

rheostat (**ree**-o-stat) *noun*
a variable electrical resistor, such as a dimmer for theatrical lighting.
[Greek *rheos* stream + *statos* stationary]

rhesus factor *noun*
Biology a substance usually present in the red blood cells of humans and higher animals.

rhesus negative *adjective*
Biology lacking the rhesus factor in the blood.

rhesus positive *adjective*
Biology containing the rhesus factor in the blood.

rhetoric (**ret**-a-rik) *noun*
1 the art of using words persuasively.
2 insincere or artificial words.
Word Family **rhetorical** (ri-**torr**-i-k'l) *adjective* **1** of or characteristic of rhetoric. **2** artificial or exaggerated in language: *This essay is empty and rhetorical*; **rhetorically** *adverb*.
[from Greek]

rhetorical question *noun*
a question that is asked for effect rather than to get an answer, e.g. 'How should I know?'

rheumatic fever (roo-mat-ik **fee**-va)
the after-effects of a bacterial infection, especially in children, which causes fever and joint pains and affects the lining of the heart.

rheumatism (**roo**-ma-tizm) *noun*
any of various diseases linked by the presence of pain and stiffness in joints and muscles, including arthritis and gout.
Word Family **rheumatic** (roo-**mat**-ik) *adjective* also **rheumatoid** (**roo**-ma-toyd) of, relating to or affected by rheumatism.

rheumatoid arthritis *noun*
a disease affecting the joints of fingers and toes which progressively stiffen.

> The word **rheumatism** is related to *rheum*, a watery discharge from the nose and the eyes of the kind you get when you have a cold. The connection is that in former times pains in the joints were thought to be caused by similar watery discharges within the body.

rhinestone (**rine**-stone) *noun*
a colourless imitation gem, usually imitating a diamond, made out of paste or glass.
[a translation of French *caillou du Rhin*]

rhinoceros (rye-**noss**-er-us) *noun* (*plural* **rhinoceros** or **rhinoceroses**)
short form is **rhino** a large thick-skinned mammal with one or two horns on its snout, found on the plains of Africa and Asia.
[Greek *rhinos* nose + *keras* horn]

rhizome (**rye**-zome) *noun*
Biology an underground stem which is an organ of vegetative reproduction.
[from Greek]

rhododendron (ro-da-**den**-dr'n) *noun*
any of a group of shrubs with large clusters of flowers.
[Greek *rhodon* rose + *dendron* tree]

rhomboid (**rom**-boyd) *noun*
a parallelogram with adjacent sides unequal and without any right angles.
● **rhomboid** *adjective*.
[RHOMBUS + *-oid*]

rhombus (**rom**-bus) *noun* (*plural* **rhombuses** or **rhombi** (**rom**-bye))
a quadrilateral which has equal parallel sides but no right angles.
Word Family **rhombic** *adjective*.

rhubarb (**roo**-barb) *noun*
1 the thick long red stalks of a garden vegetable, usually eaten cooked as a dessert.
2 (*informal*) a confused noise (from stage extras repeating this word to imitate the hubbub of a crowd).
[Greek *rha* rhubarb + *barbaros* foreign]

rhyme (rime) *noun*
1 a word that ends with the same sound as another: *'Fight', 'delight' and 'write' are rhymes.*
2 a verse or poem in which the last words of each line are rhymes.
Phrase **without rhyme or reason** without any logic: *Her behaviour seems completely without rhyme or reason.*
● **rhyme** *verb*
1 (of words or lines of verse) to end with the same sound: *'Break' rhymes with 'take'.*
2 to make or write rhymes or verses.
[Greek *rhythmos* rhythm]

rhyming slang *noun*
a form of slang where the last word of a phrase rhymes with the word which is really meant, such as *apples and pears* used to mean 'stairs'.

rhythm (**rith**-'m) *noun*
any regular or recurrent pattern: *interesting drum rhythms.* □ *the rhythm of the seasons.*
Word Family **rhythmical** (rith-**mik**-'l), **rhythmic** *adjective* having a marked rhythm; **rhythmically** *adverb*.
[from Greek]

rhythm and blues *noun*
a style of popular music combining modern elements with the traditional blues style.

ria (**ree**-a) *noun*
an inlet of the sea formed when a river valley was drowned. Compare FJORD.
[Spanish]

rib *noun*
1 *Anatomy* any of the slender bones forming a cage around the heart and lungs.
2 something which has the shape or function of a rib, such as the vein of a leaf or a curved timber in a ship's frame.
● **rib** *verb* (**ribs**; **ribbing**; **ribbed**)
(*informal*) to tease gently.
Phrase **be ribbed** to be marked with ridges.

ribald (**rib**-'ld) *adjective*
irreverent and coarsely humorous.
Word Family **ribaldry** *noun* ribald speech or behaviour.

ribbing *noun*
1 an arrangement of ribs or rib-like parts, such as a ship's framework.
2 a raised pattern made by knitting.

ribbon *noun*
1 a thin band of fabric, used for tying things or for decoration.
2 anything that is long and thin like a ribbon: *a ribbon of flowerbed along the fence.*
Phrase **cut something to ribbons, tear something to ribbons** to damage something so that it hangs in shreds: *My coat was torn to ribbons.*

riboflavin (ry-bo-**flay**-vin) *noun*
vitamin B₂.

rice *noun*
a cereal plant with white seeds that are an important food, often grown in water in warmer climates.
[Greek *oryza*]

ricepaper *noun*
a very thin edible paper made from a Chinese shrub, used in oriental painting and in baking.

rich *adjective*
1 having great wealth, resources or possessions.
2 strong in taste, colour, smell, sound, etc.
3 expensive or elaborate in dress, jewellery, decoration, etc.: *the rich tapestries on the walls.*
4 (of land, soil, etc.) producing abundantly.
5 (*informal*) (of a remark) unreasonable and rather amusing: *He said I was selfish – that's rich, coming from him!*
Phrase **rich in** containing a lot of: *foods that are rich in protein.*
Word Family **richly** *adverb* 1 in a rich manner: *He was richly dressed.* 2 fully: *She lost her job – a fate she richly deserved.*
richness *noun*; **riches** *plural noun* wealth.

Richter scale (**rick**-ta scale) *noun*
a scale which measures the strength of earthquakes on the basis of the energy released.
[after *C. F. Richter*, 1900-1985, an American seismologist]

rick¹ *noun*
a stack of hay or straw, usually thatched or covered for protection.

rick² *verb*
to strain the muscles or ligaments of the neck, back, etc.
• **rick** *noun*.

rickets *plural noun*
a disease due to a lack of vitamin D in the diet, causing deformed bones.

rickety (**rik**-a-tee) *adjective*
shaky or tottering: *The rickety table finally collapsed.*
Word Family **ricketiness** *noun.*

rickshaw *noun*
a small two-wheeled vehicle with a canopy, pulled by one or more men and used in Asia to carry goods or passengers.
[Japanese *jinrikisha* man-power-vehicle]

ricochet (**rik**-a-shay) *verb* (**ricochets; ricocheting; ricocheted**)
(of a stone, bullet, etc.) to skip or rebound one or more times from the surface which it hits.
• **ricochet** *noun* a rebound.
[French]

ricotta *noun*
a soft Italian cheese.
[Italian, cooked twice]

rid *verb* (**rids; ridding; rid** or (*dated*) **ridded**)
to make free: *At last my mind was rid of worries.*
Phrase **get rid of** to dispose of: *You should get rid of those old trainers!*

riddance *noun*
a removal or clearing away.
Phrase **good riddance** an expression of relief that a person or thing has gone.

riddle¹ *noun*
1 a puzzle using words.
2 any puzzling person or thing.

riddle² *verb*
to make many holes in something: *The gangster's corpse was riddled with bullets.*
[Middle English *riddil* sieve]

ride *verb* (**rides; riding; rode; ridden**)
1 to sit on a horse, bicycle, etc. and drive it forward.
2 to be carried as a passenger, e.g. in a vehicle or on someone's back.
3 to float or move as if by riding: *The ship rode at anchor.* □ *The eagle rode the wind.*
Phrases **let something ride** (*informal*) to allow something to go unmentioned or unpunished: *It's such a small mistake you can let it ride.* **ride high** to feel happy and successful: *Yasmin is riding high at the moment.* **ride on** to depend on: *He needed to do well at this interview – a lot was riding on it.* **ride out** to remain strong despite a problem, and survive it: *Sit back and ride out the scandal.*

• **ride** *noun* a trip on horseback, on a bicycle, in a car, etc.
Phrase **take someone for a ride** (*informal*) to deceive someone for one's own advantage.

rider *noun*
1 a person who rides.
2 an extra provision or condition.

ridge (rij) *noun*
1 a long narrow area of raised land.
2 any long raised line where two sloping sides meet, e.g. along a roof or the backbone of an animal.
3 *Weather* an area of high pressure extending from a high.

ridicule (**rid**-i-kewl) *verb*
to scoff at or make fun of: *The others ridiculed my suggestion.*
• **ridicule** *noun* words intended to make people laugh at or feel contempt for a person or thing.
[from Latin]

ridiculous (ri-**dik**-yoo-lus) *adjective*
absurd, preposterous or laughable.
Word Family **ridiculously** *adverb*; **ridiculousness** *noun*.

rife *adjective*
(especially of something unpleasant) widespread or common.

riff *noun*
Music a melodic phrase played repeatedly as background or used as the main theme in jazz, etc.

riffle *verb*
also **riffle through** to turn quickly: *I riffled through the documents.*

riff-raff *noun*
any low or worthless people.

rifle[1] (**rye**-f'l) *noun*
a gun that is fired from the shoulder and has spiral grooves, called **rifling**, cut inside the barrel to make the bullet spin and so give greater accuracy.

rifle[2] *verb*
1 to search through in order to find or steal something.
2 to steal.

rift *noun*
1 a split or opening: *a rift in the cliff face.*
2 a disagreement: *a rift between the two friends.*

rift valley *noun*
Geography a valley formed by land sinking between two parallel faults.

rig *noun*
1 *Nautical* the arrangement of masts, spars and sails on a boat.
2 the equipment for some purpose, such as the drilling apparatus, derricks, etc. for mining.
3 (*informal*) dress or costume.
• **rig** *verb* (**rigs**; **rigging**; **rigged**)
1 to fit a ship with masts, sails, etc.
2 to manipulate or control dishonestly: *The election was rigged.*
Phrases **rig someone out in** to dress someone in. **rig up** to make or assemble quickly.
Word Family **rigger** *noun*.

rigging *noun*
Nautical the ropes, lines and stays used on or above the deck of a boat.

right *adjective*
1 of or relating to the side of a person or thing which is towards the east when the subject is facing north: *She writes with her right hand.*
2 in accordance with what is considered morally good, correct, true, honourable, etc.: *It's not right to treat an animal like that.*
3 true, correct or accurate: *Have you got the right time?*
4 *Politics* of or relating to the right wing.
5 (*informal*) complete: *Well, you're a right idiot, aren't you?*
6 (**Right**) (used in front of certain titles) very: *the Right Honourable Mr Justice Robbins.*
• **right** *noun*
1 that which is morally right: *At this age a child can't tell the difference between right and wrong.*
2 a just claim or title: *I have a right to be here.*
3 (**the right**) anything on or towards the right side
4 (**the Right**) *Politics* all individuals and groups with a conservative outlook.
5 a hit given with the right fist.
Phrases **by rights** in all fairness or justice. **in the right** having truth, justice, etc. on one's side. **put to rights, set to rights** to put things into their correct or proper place.
• **right** *adverb*
1 on or to the right side: *Move right a little.*
2 straight or directly: *Let's get right to the point.*
3 completely or all the way: *The car turned right over.*
4 correctly or properly: *I can't do a thing right today!*

Phrase **right away** immediately: *I'll come right away.*

• **right** *verb*
1 to set upright again.
2 to correct: *These wrongs must be righted.*
Word Family **rightly** *adverb* **1** in a morally right manner. **2** correctly or properly. **3** (*informal*) exactly: *I don't rightly know;* **rightness** *noun*.

right angle *noun*
Maths an angle of 90°, which is one quarter of a circle.
Word Family **right-angled** *adjective*.

righteous (**rite**-yus) *adjective*
virtuous or just.
Word Family **righteously** *adverb*; **righteousness** *noun*.

rightful *adjective*
proper or correct: *Let the judge decide who is the rightful owner of the land.*
Word Family **rightfully** *adverb*; **rightfulness** *noun*.

right-hand *adjective*
1 on, of or relating to the direction of right: *the right-hand side.*
2 (of a person) being of the most help possible: *This is Harris, my right-hand man.*

right-handed *adjective*
1 preferring to use the right hand.
2 being done with or adapted to the right hand.
Word Family **right-handedly** *adverb*; **right-handedness** *noun*; **right-hander** *noun*.

rightist *noun*
Politics a person who supports the views of the right wing.
• **rightist** *adjective*.

rightly ⇨ RIGHT.

rightness ⇨ RIGHT.

right of way *noun*
1 the right of a person to pass over the land of another, or the piece of land over which passage is made.
2 the right of a vehicle or vessel to proceed ahead of another.

right-wing *adjective*
Politics conservative: *Mike joined the Communist Party in rebellion against his father's right-wing attitudes.*

• **right wing** *noun* the most conservative section of a political party or group, usually meaning (in a parliamentary democracy) extremists in conservative parties and moderates in socialist parties.
Word Family **right-winger** *noun*.

rigid (**rij**-id) *adjective*
1 stiff or unbending.
2 strict and not able to be changed: *a rigid system of discipline.*
Word Family **rigidly** *adverb*; **rigidity** (ri-**jid**-it-ee) *noun*.
[from Latin]

rigmarole (**rig**-ma-role) *noun*
any long or complicated process.

rigor mortis (rig-a **mor**-tis) *noun*
Medicine the stiffening of a body after death.
[Latin, stiffness of death]

rigorous (**rig**-a-rus) *adjective*
strict, exacting or demanding: *Athletes have to do rigorous training.*
Word Family **rigorously** *adverb*; **rigorousness** *noun*.

rigour (**rig**-a) *noun* (*American* **rigor**)
severity or harshness: *the rigour of a long winter.*
[Latin *rigor* stiffness, coldness, strictness]

rile *verb*
(*informal*) to irritate or annoy.

rill *noun*
a very small stream.

rim *noun*
the outer edge or margin, especially of a curved or circular object, such as a wheel or cup.
• **rim** *verb* (**rims**; **rimming**; **rimmed**) to provide with a rim or border.

rime[1] *noun, verb*
an old spelling of **rhyme**.

rime[2] *noun*
a deposit of ice formed by water droplets of fog or drizzle as they settle and freeze.
Compare FROST; HOAR FROST.

rind (*rhymes with* find) *noun*
a hard outer skin, especially of bacon, fruit or cheese.
[Old English, bark]

ring[1] *noun*
1 a circular band, especially one of precious metal worn on the finger.
2 a space or area, often enclosed and circular in shape, used for a particular purpose: *a circus ring.* □ *a boxing ring.*
3 a circular apparatus on a cooker for emitting heat: *a gas ring.*
4 (*informal*) an exclusive group of persons acting privately or illegally: *a smuggling ring.*
Phrase **run rings round** (*informal*) to surpass easily or be superior to.
• **ring** *verb* (**rings**; **ringing**; **ringed**)

1 to encircle or surround with a ring.
2 to put a band round the leg of a bird in order to follow its movements.

ring² *verb* (**rings; ringing; rang; rung**)
1 to give forth a clear sound when vibrating: *The doorbell rang.* □ *Is that the phone ringing?*
2 to be filled with sound: *Our ears were ringing for some time after the explosion.*
3 to cause a bell to sound, especially in order to summon: *Lord Emsworth rang for his butler.*
4 to make a telephone call to: *I'll ring you later.*
5 (of words) to give a feeling of having a particular quality: *Her reasons for not coming didn't really ring true.*
Phrases **ring off** to end a telephone conversation. **ring out** to make a loud ringing noise. **ring up 1** to telephone. **2** to record an amount on a cash register.
● **ring** *noun*
1 an act of ringing.
2 a sound of ringing.
3 a loud clear sound.
4 (*informal*) a telephone call: *I'll give you a ring.*
5 a quality suggested by something: *Her story had the ring of truth about it.*

ringer *noun*
1 a person or thing that rings: *bell ringers.*
2 (*informal*) a double of or substitute for a person or thing.

ring finger *noun*
the third finger of the hand, on which a wedding ring is often worn.

ringleader *noun*
a person who leads others, especially in improper or illegal activities.

ringlet *noun*
a long spiral curl of hair.

ringmaster *noun*
the person in charge of the performances in the ring of a circus.

ring pull *noun*
a metal ring on the top of a can which is pulled back to open it.

ring road *noun*
a road linking different suburbs without passing through the city centre.

ringside *noun*
the seats or area closest to and surrounding a boxing or similar ring.

ringside seat *noun*
any place providing a very good close view.

ringworm *noun*
a fungal infection of the skin, often on the scalp, causing an itchy circular rash.

rink *noun*
1 also **ice rink** a smooth artificial surface of ice for ice hockey, curling, or ice-skating.
2 any flat surface for roller-skating.

rinse *verb*
1 to wash lightly.
2 to remove soap, etc. with water.
● **rinse** *noun*
1 the act of rinsing.
2 a liquid used for rinsing the mouth.
3 a hair-colouring which lasts only until the hair is washed.

riot (**rye**-ot) *noun*
1 a wild disturbance created by a large number of people.
2 a brilliant display of colours, etc.
3 (*informal*) a person or thing that causes great amusement, enthusiasm, etc.
Phrases **read the Riot Act** (*informal*) to censure or reprimand severely. **run riot**
1 to act with wild recklessness. **2** to grow wildly.
Word Family **riot** *verb*; **rioter** *noun*; **riotous** *adjective*; **riotously** *adverb*.

rip¹ *verb* (**rips; ripping; ripped**)
1 to cut or tear roughly: *I'm ripped my trousers on the fence.*
2 to be torn or cut apart: *His trousers had ripped.*
Phrases **let rip** (*informal*) to speak or behave in a very emotional way. **let something rip** (*informal*) to cause a vehicle to move along extremely fast: *He put his foot on the accelerator and really let her rip.* **rip someone off** (*informal*) to want or get far too much money from someone for something: *£40 for that? He's really ripped you off!* **rip something off** (*informal*) to steal something.
● **rip** *noun* a cut or tear.

rip² *noun*
a stretch of rough water at sea or in a river.

ripcord *noun*
a control cord which opens a parachute.

ripe *adjective*
1 (of fruit or crops) mature or fully developed: *a ripe apple.*
2 (of a person's age) advanced.
3 (of a time) suitable for action: *The time is ripe for revolution.*
4 (*informal*) (of language) rude.
Word Family **ripen** *verb*; **ripely** *adverb*; **ripeness** *noun*.

rip-off *noun*
(*informal*) an article that is not worth anything like the price being asked for it: *He wants £40 for a ticket? What a rip-off!*

riposte (ri-**posst**) *noun*
1 *Fencing* a thrust made by a fencer after parrying an opponent's attack.
2 a quick sharp reply or action.
• **riposte** *verb*.
[from Italian]

ripping *adjective*
(*dated informal*) excellent.

ripple *noun*
1 a small wave on a surface, especially water.
2 any sound or movement like that of water flowing in ripples: *a ripple of laughter.*
Word Family ripple *verb*; **ripply** *adjective*.

rip-roaring *adjective*
1 (*informal*) wild and noisy.
2 (*informal*) absolute or total: *a rip-roaring success.*

rise (rize) *verb* (**rises; rising; rose; risen**)
1 to move into a standing position: *He rose and bowed.*
2 to move from a lower to a higher position, rank, amount, etc.: *House prices are still rising.* □ *She rose within the company to become Sales Manager.*
3 (of a mountain, building, etc.) to stand above the surroundings: *A skyscraper rose above the school.*
4 (of a river) to have its source.
5 (of the sun, etc.) to appear in the sky.
6 also **rise up** to rebel or revolt: *The army rose against the government.*
7 (of bread, cakes, etc.) to swell from the action of yeast or heat.
8 a literary word meaning 'to get up in the morning'.
9 (of an official body) to adjourn: *The court will rise.*
Phrases **rise above** to refuse to become emotionally upset by: *Don't let his insults get to you – rise above it all!* **rise to** 1 to become upset by and respond angrily to: *He goaded her, trying to get her to rise to his remarks.* 2 to produce a particularly good response to: *Neil rose to the challenge.*
• **rise** *noun*
1 the act of rising.
2 an elevated place, such as a small hill.
3 an increase in salary or wages: *I asked my boss for a rise.*
4 the height of each step in a flight of stairs.

Phrases **get a rise out of, take a rise out of** (*informal*) to try to get an emotional reaction from: *I only said it to get a rise out of him.* **give rise to** to cause or produce.

> [!] Do not confuse *rise* with RAISE.

riser *noun*
Phrase **early riser, late riser** someone who gets up early or late in the morning.

risible (**riz**-a-b'l) *adjective*
causing laughter.
Word Family risibility (riz-a-**bill**-i-tee) *noun*.
[from Latin]

risk *noun*
1 the possibility of suffering harm, loss, etc.: *tips to minimize the risk of a heart attack.*
2 any property or person causing a risk: *This building is a fire risk.*
Phrase **run a risk, take a risk** to expose oneself to a risk.
Word Family risk *verb* to expose to risk; **risky** *adjective* (**riskier; riskiest**); **riskily** *adverb*; **riskiness** *noun*.
[Italian *riscare* to run into danger]

risk assessment *noun*
the process of identifying hazards and working out ways to eliminate them, e.g. in manufacturing industry.

risotto *noun*
a dish of rice, meat and onions.
[Italian *riso* rice]

risqué (riss-**kay**, **riss**-kay *or* **ree**-skay) *adjective*
daringly close to indecency: *a risqué joke.*
[French]

rissole *noun*
a mixture of minced meat or vegetables, often coated in breadcrumbs before frying.
[French]

rite *noun*
a formal religious or solemn ceremony.
Phrase **the last rites** the final ceremonies for someone who is dying.
[from Latin]

ritual (**rit**-yew-'l) *noun*
a formal or ceremonial action.
Word Family ritual *adjective* of or relating to a rite or rites; **ritualistic** (rit-yew-'l-**ist**-ik) *adjective* of or similar to a ritual; **ritualistically** *adverb*.

ritzy *adjective* (**ritzier; ritziest**)
(*informal*) luxurious or elegant.
[after the *Ritz*, a luxurious hotel in London]

rival (rye-v'l) *noun*
a person who competes against another.
Word Family **rival** *adjective*; **rival** *verb*
(**rivals**; **rivalling**; **rivalled**); **rivalry** *noun*
(*plural* **rivalries**) competition.
[Latin *rivales* those living near the same
stream]

riven (rivv-'n) *adjective*
an old word meaning 'split apart'.
[past participle of old verb to *rive*]

river (rivv-a) *noun*
1 a large permanent flow of water in a
natural channel with banks, which flows
into the sea, a lake, etc.
2 any flow: *a river of blood*.
[Latin *riparius* of river banks]

river basin *noun* ⇨ DRAINAGE BASIN.

rivet (rivv-it) *noun*
a pin with a head, used to fix metal plates
together by placing it through a hole and
flattening the end opposite the head.
Word Family **rivet** *verb* 1 to fasten with a
rivet or rivets. 2 to engross or hold firmly:
a riveting tale; **riveter** *noun*.

rivulet (rivv-yoo-let) *noun*
a very small river.

roach *noun* (*plural* **roach**)
a common freshwater fish.

road *noun*
a prepared surface or route for the
movement of vehicles, people, etc.
*Figurative It was a long and difficult road
to peace* (= way, course).
Phrase **one for the road** (*informal*) a last
alcoholic drink before leaving.

roadblock *noun*
a barrier placed across a road by police,
soldiers, etc. to control or inspect passing
traffic.

road hog *noun*
(*informal*) a motorist who drives in a
selfish way.

roadie *noun*
(*informal*) a person who accompanies a
touring band, setting up their equipment,
etc.

road rage *noun*
extreme anger caused by the behaviour of
another driver: *a serious road rage incident
on the M5*.

roadshow *noun*
any of a series of shows broadcast on TV
or on the radio from different sites around
a country or an area.

roadway *noun*
a road.

roadworthy *adjective*
(of a motor vehicle) fit to be used on the
roads.
Word Family **roadworthiness** *noun*.

roam (*rhymes with* home) *verb*
to move or travel without purpose or plan.
Word Family **roam** *noun*; **roamer** *noun* a
person who roams.

roan *noun*
a horse of a plain colour with white hairs
sprinkled throughout.

roar (ror) *verb*
1 to make a loud deep sound, especially in
excitement, anger, etc.
2 (of a vehicle) to move fast, making a loud
sound: *The motorbike roared past us*.
• **roar** *noun*.

roaring *adjective*
1 (*informal*) complete: *a roaring success*.
2 (*informal*) brisk: *Mrs Evans was doing a
roaring trade in her home-made cakes*.

roast (*rhymes with* most) *verb*
1 to cook food by using dry heat, e.g. in an
oven.
2 to make or become hot: *I'm roasting!*
3 (*informal*) to criticize severely.
• **roast** *noun*
1 a meal of roasted meat and vegetables.
2 a piece of meat which may be cooked by
roasting.

rob *verb* (**robs**; **robbing**; **robbed**)
to take something that belongs to someone
else, especially by force or threat of
violence.
Phrase **rob someone of something** to
deprive someone of something.
Word Family **robber** *noun* a person who
robs; **robbery** *noun* (*plural* **robberies**).
[Old French *robe* booty]

robe *noun*
1 a gown.
2 any long loose piece of clothing, such as
a dressing gown.
• **robe** *verb*.

robin *noun*
a little brown bird with a bright orange
breast.

robot (ro-bot) *noun*
1 a machine in the shape of a human
being.
2 (*informal*) a person who thinks or acts
like a machine.
Word Family **robotic** (ro-bot-ik)
adjective of or relating to robots; **robotics**
plural noun (*used with singular verb*) the
science concerned with the design and
building of robots.

The word **robot** is Czech in origin. It comes from *robota*, Czech for 'forced labour', and became internationally popular through Karel Čapek's play *R.U.R.* (Rossum's Universal Robots), published in 1920. His *robots* were mechanical people designed to perform menial tasks.

robust (ro-bust) *adjective*
strong and vigorous.
Word Family **robustly** *adverb*;
robustness *noun*.
[Latin *robur* an oak]

roc *noun*
(in stories) a gigantic bird.

rock¹ *noun*
1 a large mass of stone: *rocks and boulders on the beach.*
2 *Geology* a mass of mineral matter of varying composition: *a layer of volcanic rock.*
3 a hard sweet made in long sticks: *peppermint rock.*
4 a firm foundation or support.
5 (*informal*) any large gem, especially a diamond.
6 (*informal*) a small piece of crack cocaine.
Phrase **on the rocks** (*informal*) 1 in a state of disaster. 2 (of drinks) served with ice, but with no water added.

rock² *verb*
1 to sway back and forth or from side to side.
2 to cause a lot of distress to: *I was rocked by the news of his death.*
3 (*informal*) to dance to or play rock music.
• **rock** *noun*
1 the act of rocking.
2 also **rock music** a form of popular music which has developed from rock and roll and pop music.
3 rock and roll.

rock and roll *noun* also **rock 'n' roll**
a form of popular music originating during the 1950s and characterized by a strong beat, a repetitious melody and rhythm, and an exaggerated style of singing.

rock bottom *noun*
the lowest level possible.
Word Family **rock-bottom** *adjective*.

rock cake *noun*
a small hard cake containing currants.

rocker *noun*
1 (*informal*) a rocking chair.

2 one of the curved pieces on which a cradle or rocking chair rocks.
Phrase **off one's rocker** (*informal*) mad or crazy.

rockery *noun* (*plural* **rockeries**) also **rock garden**
a garden with earth and rocks amongst which plants are set.

rocket *noun*
1 a structure, usually shaped like a cylinder, which moves by expelling burning gases.
2 a firework that rises into the air and then explodes.
3 (*informal*) a reprimand.
• **rocket** *verb*
1 to move like a rocket.
2 to increase rapidly.

rocketry *noun*
the study of rockets, their design, development and flight.

rocking chair *noun*
a chair mounted on rockers which allow it to swing back and forth.

rocking horse *noun*
a toy horse, set on rockers, for children to ride.

rock music ⇨ ROCK² (definition 2).

rock 'n' roll ⇨ ROCK AND ROLL.

rock pool *noun*
a small pool of water trapped among rocks on a shore: *looking for crabs in the rock pools.*

rock salt *noun*
common salt, sodium chloride, occurring in large rock-like masses.

rocky¹ *adjective* (**rockier; rockiest**)
1 containing or consisting of rocks.
2 firm or hard like a rock.
Word Family **rockiness** *noun*.

rocky² *adjective* (**rockier; rockiest**)
shaky or inclined to rock.

rococo *noun*
an 18th-century style of art and architecture developed from, and more exaggerated than, the baroque, characterized by shell motifs, scrolls and curves in general.
[French *rocaille* shell-work]

rod *noun*
1 a stick or pole made of wood, metal, etc.
2 ⇨ PERCH³ (definition 1).
Phrase **make a rod for one's own back** to do something which will later cause trouble for oneself.

rode the past tense of **ride**.

rodent (ro-d'nt) *noun*
any of a large group of gnawing animals
such as beavers, squirrels, mice, etc.
[Latin *rodens* gnawing]

rodeo (ro-dee-oh *or* ro-**day**-oh) *noun*
1 a series of competitions covering
different aspects of a cowboy's skill,
usually for entertainment.
2 a cattle muster.
[Spanish *rodear* to go round]

roe[1] *noun*
the eggs of a female fish. Compare MILT.

roe[2] *noun* (*plural* **roe** or **roes**) also **roe
deer**
a small agile deer, the male of which has
three-pointed antlers.

roebuck *noun*
a male roe deer.

rogue *noun*
1 a dishonest person.
2 a playfully mischievous person.
Word Family **roguish** *adjective*;
roguishly *adverb*; **roguery, roguishness**
noun.

rogue elephant *noun*
an elephant which has left or been cast out
from the herd, notorious for savagery.

roister (**roy**-sta) *verb*
an old word meaning 'to act in a
boisterous manner'.
[Latin *rusticus* a peasant]

role *noun*
1 the character represented by an actor in
a play, film, etc.: *I play the role of Juliet's
nurse.*
2 a person's job or function. *What is a
teacher's role?*

role model *noun*
a person whose behaviour is admired by
someone else, who may then copy it.

role playing *noun* also **role play**
the playing of imaginary parts, especially
for educational or therapeutic purposes.

roll (role) *verb*
1 to move by turning over and over: *The
ball rolled along the floor.* □ *Sarah rolled the
dice.*
2 to move or be moved on wheels: *The car
rolled backwards.*
3 (of a vehicle or vessel) to lean first one
way and then the other: *The ship rolled and
lurched in the rough seas.*
4 (of waves, clouds, etc.) to flow forward.
5 (of time) to pass: *The years rolled by.*

6 also **roll up** to wind into a cylindrical or
ball shape: *I rolled the string into a ball.*
7 also **roll out** to flatten with something
heavy: *He rolled the icing out.*
8 (of a noise) to echo with a deep sound:
The thunder rolled.
9 to pronounce with a trill: *You need to roll
your r's more when you speak French.*
10 (of a machine) to operate.
Phrases **be rolling in it** (*informal*) to be
extremely rich. **roll in** 1 to arrive in large
quantities: *The money rolled in.* 2 to arrive
late but unconcerned: *Wayne finally rolled
in at 10 a.m.* **roll out** to spread out or
unroll. **roll up** 1 to form into a roll.
2 (*informal*) to arrive or gather round.
• **roll** *noun*
1 something rolled up in cylindrical form:
a roll of film.
2 a list containing the names of people in a
class, group, etc.
3 a very small loaf of bread that is baked
into various shapes.
4 the act or an instance of rolling: *a sailor
who walks with a roll.* □ *a roll of drums.*
Phrase **be on a roll** (*informal*) to be
having a lot of success at the moment.
[Latin *rotulus* a small wheel]

roll-call (**role**-cawl) *noun*
the calling of a list of names of soldiers,
students, etc. to determine those present.

roller *noun*
1 a person or thing that rolls.
2 a long wave coming in towards the shore.
3 a cylindrical device for winding,
spreading or crushing something.
4 also called **curler**. a small roll of plastic
or metal around which the hair is wrapped
to set it into curls or waves.

Rollerblade *noun*
(*trademark*) an in-line skate.
Word Family **rollerblade** *verb*;
rollerblader *noun*.

roller coaster *noun* also called **big
dipper**.
an open-car railway with sharp turns and
steep slopes, ridden for amusement at
fairs, etc.

roller skate *noun*
one of a pair of boots running on small
wheels, used on a smooth hard surface.
Word Family **roller-skate** *verb*; **roller
skater** *noun*.

rollicking[1] *adjective*
behaving or moving in a carefree manner.

rollicking[2] *noun* also **rollocking**
(*informal*) a severe telling-off.

rolling *adjective*
(of land) looking like waves: *the rolling hills.*

rolling pin *noun*
a cylinder, often wooden, with a handle at each end, for flattening dough or pastry.

rolling stock *noun*
the wheeled vehicles of a railway, such as locomotives, carriages, etc.

roll neck ⇨ POLO NECK.

roll-on *noun*
a bottle of deodorant that has a rotating ball in its neck for application.

rollover *noun*
(in a lottery) an occasion when the prize money from a previous occasion is available in addition to the usual prize money.

roll-top desk *noun*
a desk fitted with a lid which can be rolled up or down.

roll-up *noun*
(*informal*) a cigarette made by the smoker from loose tobacco and paper wraps.

roly-poly *adjective*
plump.

roman (**ro-m'n**) *noun*
the usual style of upright printing, such as this is. Compare ITALIC.

Roman alphabet *noun*
the alphabet used for writing western European and other languages.

Roman Catholic *noun*
Religion a member of the Western or Roman Church, a Christian denomination with the Pope as its supreme head.
Word Family **Roman Catholicism** *noun* the faith, practices, etc. of Roman Catholics; **Roman Catholic** *adjective* of or relating to Roman Catholicism.

romance (**ro-mance** *or* **ro-mance**) *noun*
1 a story about love.
2 the pleasant atmosphere experienced by people who are in love: *She was thrilled by the romance of the occasion.*
3 a love affair.
4 a story about unusual or exciting adventures, or the quality of adventure found in such stories.
Word Family **romantic** *adjective* of or relating to romance or a story about romance; **romantic** *noun* a person who enjoys romance; **romantically** *adverb*; **romanticism** *noun* romantic spirit or style; **romanticize, romanticise** *verb* to make romantic.

Romanesque *noun*
a style of architecture of the 10th, 11th and 12th centuries which made much use of vaulting and thick pillars.

Roman law *noun*
a system of law based on that of ancient Rome, which forms the basis of civil law in many countries.

Roman nose *noun*
a nose with a high bridge.

Roman numerals *plural noun*
the letters used in the ancient Roman system of counting, now used in more formal contexts such as for dates on monuments. The common basic symbols are I (= 1), V (= 5), X (= 10), L (= 50), C (= 100), D (= 500) and M (= 1000). These symbols are used in combinations to represent other numbers, as in IX = 9; XI =11; XLII = 42; LXIV = 64.

Romany (**ro-ma-nee**) *adjective*
of the gipsies, their language and culture.
• **Romany** *noun* (*plural* **Romanies**) a gipsy.
[Romany *rom* a man]

romp *verb*
to play or frolic boisterously.
Phrase **romp home** (*informal*) to win a race, etc. easily.
• **romp** *noun*.

rompers *plural noun* also **romper suit**
a one-piece suit for a baby.

rood *noun*
1 a large cross or crucifix in a church, usually set into a screen.
2 *Christianity* an old word for the cross on which Christ died.

roof *noun*
1 a protective structure placed over a building and supported by the walls, usually made of tiles, iron or timber.
2 something resembling or serving as a roof, such as the top of a car, etc.
Phrases **go through the roof** 1 also **hit the roof** (*informal*) to become very angry.
2 (of figures, prices, etc.) to reach very high levels.
Word Family **roof** *verb* to provide or cover with a roof; **roofer** *noun*; **roofless** *adjective*.

roofing *noun*
the materials used to make a roof, such as iron, slate or tiles.

roof rack *noun*
a metal frame placed on the roof of a car to carry bulky goods.

rook¹ (*rhymes with* book) *noun*
a black crow with a bare face, which nests in colonies.

rook² *noun* also called **castle**.
Chess a piece that can move any number of squares horizontally or vertically.
[Persian *rukh*]

rookery *noun* (*plural* **rookeries**)
a breeding place for rooks or other birds or animals, such as penguins and seals.

rookie *noun*
(*informal*) a new recruit in the army, police, etc.

room *noun*
1 any of the various areas into which a house is divided by the walls.
2 the people present in such an area: *The whole room was silent.*
3 (**rooms**) lodgings.
4 the space occupied by or available for something: *The boxes took up a lot of room.*
5 scope, opportunity: *Your work leaves plenty of room for improvement.*
● **room** *verb*
Phrase **room with** to share a room with.

rooming house *noun*
a boarding house.

room-mate *noun*
a person with whom one shares a room.

room service *noun*
the serving of food or drink to a guest in his or her room in a hotel, etc.

roomy *adjective* (**roomier**; **roomiest**)
spacious or large.
Word Family **roomily** *adverb*;
roominess *noun*.

roost *noun*
a perch upon which hens or other birds rest, or a place containing such perches.
● **roost** *verb* (of a bird or bat) to rest on a roost, especially for the night.

rooster *noun*
a male domestic fowl.

root¹ *noun*
1 *Biology* the part of a plant which grows down into the soil, fixing it and absorbing water and minerals from the soil.
2 something which has the position or function of a root.
3 the fundamental or essential part: *Let's try to get to the root of the problem.*
4 (**roots**) the condition or feeling of belonging to a place, society, etc.
5 *Maths* a number which, when multiplied by itself a certain number of times, results

in a given number: *3 is the square root of 9 (3 × 3), written √9.*
6 *Grammar* a word, or part of a word, on which all other forms of that word are based: *'Dance' is the root of 'dancer' and 'dancing'.*
● **root** *verb*
1 to send out roots and begin to grow.
2 to become fixed or established.
Phrase **root out** to find and eliminate.

root² *verb*
to dig with or as if with the snout or nose.
Phrase **root for** (*informal*) to shout encouragement to: *Which team are you rooting for?*

root beer *noun*
an American drink made from the juices of various roots and herbs.

root vegetable *noun*
a vegetable whose edible part grows under the ground, e.g. the potato or carrot.

rope *noun*
1 a strong twisted cord made from strands of hemp, nylon, etc.
2 (**the ropes**) (*informal*) the methods or procedures: *It took me a few weeks to learn the ropes.*
● **rope** *verb* to catch a horse, cow, etc. with a rope.
Phrases **rope in**, **rope into** (*informal*) to persuade to join in an activity: *I was roped in to wash the dishes.* **rope off** to enclose with a rope: *The main arena was roped off.*

ropy *adjective* (**ropier**; **ropiest**) also **ropey**
1 (*informal*) of poor quality.
2 (*informal*) in poor health.
Word Family **ropiness** *noun*.

rosary (ro-za-ree) *noun* (*plural* **rosaries**)
Roman Catholicism a string of beads used to count when reciting a certain series of prayers.

rose¹ (roze) *noun*
1 any of a group of garden shrubs with prickly stems and showy, sometimes fragrant, flowers.
2 a pinkish-red colour.
3 an ornamental plate or moulding surrounding a fitting such as a door knob.
4 a nozzle, cap, etc. with many holes in it, attached to a pipe or hose to spray water.
Phrase **be coming up roses** (*informal*) to be developing in a very successful way.
[from Latin]

rose² the past tense of **rise**.

rosé (ro-zay) *noun*
a pink wine.
[French]

roseate (ro-zee-it) *adjective*
a literary word meaning 'rosy'.

rosemary *noun*
a shrub with fragrant leaves that are used as a herb.

> **Rosemary** was originally *rosmarine*, in English, being derived from Latin *rosmarinum*, from *ros* (dew) and *marinus* (of the sea). It was called *sea dew* because it grew near the sea. In English the *marine* part of *rosmarine* in time became confused with the Christian name Mary, associated with the Virgin Mary, hence *rosemary*.

rosette (ro-zet) *noun*
a rose-shaped arrangement of ribbons or other materials, used for decoration.

rose water *noun*
a pleasant-smelling water made from rose petals.

rose window *noun*
a round window divided into sections.

Rosh Hashana (rosh ha-**shah**-na) *noun*
also **Rosh Hashanah**
the Jewish New Year.
[Hebrew]

rosin (roz-in) *noun*
a yellowish solid resin obtained from the distillation of turpentine, used in varnishes, soaps and soldering fluxes.

roster *noun*
a list of names, especially one showing periods of duty.
● **roster** *verb* to put on a roster.

rostrum *noun* (*plural* **rostrums** or **rostra**)
1 a raised platform for a conductor of an orchestra, a speaker, etc. to stand on.
2 a movable platform, such as one used for a TV camera.
[Latin]

rosy (ro-zee) *adjective* (**rosier; rosiest**)
1 pink or pinkish-red.
2 promising: *The future looks rosy for you.*
Word Family **rosily** *adverb;* **rosiness** *noun.*

rot *verb* (**rots; rotting; rotted**)
to become bad or decomposed.
● **rot** *noun*
1 the process of rotting, or the state of being rotten.
2 (*informal*) nonsense.

rotary (ro-ta-ree) *adjective*
of or involving rotation, especially on an axis.

rotate (ro-**tate**) *verb*
1 to turn or spin on an axis.
2 to alternate in sequence: *to rotate crops.*
[Latin *rota* a wheel]

rotation (ro-**tay**-sh'n) *noun*
1 the act of rotating.
2 the spinning of a planet or star on its axis, or one complete spin.

rote *noun*
Phrase **by rote** in a mechanical way, without understanding or thinking of the meaning.

rotisserie (ro-**tiss**-a-ree) *noun*
1 a revolving skewer on which meat, poultry, etc. is cooked over heat.
2 a restaurant where such a device is used.
[French, roasting place]

rotor *noun*
1 a rotating part of a machine.
2 a system of rotating blades used to lift and control helicopters.

rotten *adjective*
1 bad or decomposed.
2 corrupt.
3 unfortunate: *What rotten luck!*
● **rotten** *adverb* (*informal*) very much: *She spoils him rotten.*
Word Family **rottenly** *adverb;* **rottenness** *noun.*

rotter *noun*
(*dated informal*) a thoroughly worthless or objectionable person.

Rottweiler (rot-vie-ler) *noun*
a German breed of tall strongly-built black and tan dog with a short coat.

rotund (ro-**tund**) *adjective*
plump or rounded.
Word Family **rotundity** (ro-**tun**-di-tee), **rotundness** *noun;* **rotundly** *adverb.*
[Latin *rotundus* round]

rotunda (ro-**tun**-da) *noun*
a round building, usually with a dome.

rouble (roo-b'l) *noun* also **ruble**
the basic unit of money in Russia and some other former republics of the Soviet Union.

roué (roo-ay) *noun*
an ageing and dissolute man.
[French, (deserving to be) broken on the wheel]

rouge (roozh) *noun*
a red cream or powder used to colour the cheeks.
● **rouge** *verb.*
[French, red]

rough (ruf) *adjective*
1 having an uneven surface; not smooth: *rough ground.*
2 (of weather or waves) violent: *The rough seas made us seasick.*
3 imperfectly finished, polished, refined, etc.: *She made a rough draft of her speech.* □ *a rough diamond.*
4 (of a voice) harsh.
5 (of behaviour) not gentle: *his rough treatment of his children.*
6 (*informal*) unfair and difficult to cope with: *It seems a bit rough to make her wash all the dishes for 20 people!*
Phrase **rough and ready** crude but effective.
● **rough** *noun*
Golf any uncleared part of the golf course, especially with long grass or trees.
Phrase **in rough** in a quick form, without much detail.
● **rough** *verb*
Phrases **rough in, rough out** to shape or sketch in a rough or incomplete form. **rough it** to live without the ordinary comforts, etc., e.g. while camping. **rough someone up** (*informal*) to treat someone in a rough or violent way.
Word Family **roughly** *adverb*; **roughen** *verb*; **roughness** *noun*.

roughage (ruff-ij) *noun*
the coarser parts of food which are of little nutritive value, but aid digestion.

rough and tumble *noun*
a scuffle.

rough diamond *noun*
a coarse or unrefined person with likable qualities.

roughneck *noun*
(*informal*) a rough rowdy person.

roughshod *adjective*
Phrase **ride roughshod over** to dominate or treat without consideration.

roulette (roo-**let**) *noun*
a game in which one bets on where a small ball will come to rest on a revolving wheel with numbered divisions. ⇨ RUSSIAN ROULETTE.
[French, little wheel]

round *adjective*
1 shaped like a ball, ring or circle.
2 curved or without angles: *a round face.*
3 (of a number) given to the nearest whole number: *That comes to £151.25 – call it £150, in round figures.*
● **round** *noun*

1 a complete course, succession or series: *She was bored with the usual round of Christmas parties.*
2 (*sometimes* **rounds**) a course of usual actions, duties, etc.: *The consultant did his round of the wards.*
3 a single section of a contest: *He got knocked out in the second round.*
4 ammunition for a single shot from a gun.
5 a set of drinks for each person in a group, usually paid for in turn: *Whose round is it?*
6 *Music* a song in which each voice copies the last, at the same pitch or in octaves.
7 a slice of bread, or a sandwich made with two slices of bread.
Phrase **round of applause** a period of clapping: *Let's give the kids another round of applause.*
● **round** *verb*
1 to make or become round.
2 to go or pass round: *The ship rounded the Cape of Good Hope.*
Phrases **round off** to complete or perfect. **round on** to make a sudden attack on. **round up** to collect up: *The teachers rounded up all their pupils and got them onto the coach.*
● **round** *adverb*
1 on every side of a place: *They swarmed round.*
2 here and there: *We had a look round for the keys.*
3 throughout: *The park is open all the year round.*
4 in a circle: *The hands of the clock aren't going round.*
● **round** *preposition*
1 encircling: *Tie the string round the parcel.*
2 on every side of: *all round us.*
3 near: *Do you live round here?*
Word Family **roundness** *noun*; **rounded** *adjective* made round.
[Latin *rotundus*]

roundabout *noun*
1 an intersection laid out so that traffic moves in one direction around a central structure.
2 a revolving piece of playground equipment for children.
3 ⇨ MERRY-GO-ROUND.
● **roundabout** *adjective* indirect.

rounders *plural noun*
(*used with singular verb*) a game similar to baseball, usually played by children with a small soft ball and a bat.

roundly *adverb*
thoroughly or bluntly.

round trip *noun*
a journey to a place and back again.

round-up *noun*
a collecting together, especially of cattle or other animals.

rouse (*rhymes with* cows) *verb*
1 to stir out of a state of sleep, inactivity, apathy, etc.
2 to stir to anger, action, etc.
Word Family **rousing** *adjective*; **rousingly** *adverb*.

rout (*rhymes with* out) *noun*
Military a disorderly retreat after an overwhelming defeat.
• **rout** *verb* to defeat utterly.

route (root) *noun*
the way taken or planned for travel.
• **route** *verb*.

route march *noun* (*plural* **route marches**)
a long march by soldiers during training.

routine (roo-**teen**) *noun*
a fixed or usual way of doing something.
• **routine** *adjective* like or according to a routine: *It's just a routine operation these days.*
Word Family **routinely** *adverb*.
[French]

roux (roo) *noun* (*plural* **roux**) (roo)
a mixture of flour and butter heated to form a binding element in sauces and soups.
[French, browned]

rove *verb*
to wander freely or aimlessly.
Word Family **rover** *noun*.

row[1] (ro) *noun*
1 an arrangement of people or objects arranged beside or behind each other.
2 a line of seats facing in the same direction, e.g. in a theatre.

row[2] (ro) *verb*
to propel a boat with oars.
Word Family **row** *noun* a trip in a rowing boat; **rower** *noun* a person who rows.

row[3] (*rhymes with* cow) *noun*
1 a noisy quarrel.
2 a loud noise.
• **row** *verb* to have a quarrel.

rowan *noun* also called **mountain ash**.
a small tree with red berries.

rowdy *adjective* (**rowdier; rowdiest**)
rough, loud and disorderly.
Word Family **rowdily** *adverb*; **rowdiness** *noun*.

rowing boat *noun*
a boat propelled by oars.

rowlock (**rol**-uk) *noun*
a U-shaped device attached to the side of a boat to hold an oar in place.

royal *adjective*
1 of or relating to a monarch.
2 suitable for a monarch: *His mother gave us a royal welcome.*
Word Family **royal** *noun* (*informal*) a member of a royal family; **royally** *adverb*.
[Latin *regalis*]

royal blue *noun*
a deep blue colour.

royalist *noun*
(*sometimes* **Royalist**) any supporter of monarchy.

royal jelly *noun*
a substance made by bees and fed to the young larvae that are to become queen bees.

royal tennis ➪ REAL TENNIS.

royalty *noun* (*plural* **royalties**)
1 monarchs and their families considered as a group.
2 the power, status or dignity of a monarch.
3 a share paid to an inventor, author, etc. out of the proceeds from the sale or performance of his or her work.

rub *verb* (**rubs; rubbing; rubbed**)
1 to move something over a surface with pressure or friction, especially to clean, smooth, polish, etc.
2 to become or cause to become chafed or irritated: *My new shoes are rubbing horribly.*
Phrases **rub down** 1 to rub smooth, etc.
2 to massage, dry or clean by rubbing. **rub it in** (*informal*) to make someone uncomfortable by continuing to talk about something embarrassing. **rub off** 1 to remove by or as if by rubbing. 2 to transfer or be transferred. **rub out** 1 to remove by rubbing: *rub out the pencil marks.* 2 (*informal*) to kill.
• **rub** *noun*
1 the act of rubbing.
2 an obstacle or difficulty.

rubber[1] *noun*
1 an elastic solid obtained from the sap of a tropical tree (called **indiarubber** or **natural rubber**), or man-made (called **synthetic rubber**), usually combined with other substances, such as sulphur, when made into articles. ➪ VULCANIZE.

2 also called **eraser**. a piece of rubber or synthetic material used to remove pencil or pen marks.
Word Family **rubbery** *adjective* like rubber; **rubberiness** *noun*.
[from RUB]

rubber² *noun*
1 *Cards* the best of three games of bridge, etc.
2 any tournament consisting of a series of separate games.

rubber band *noun* also called **elastic band**.
a thin loop of elastic rubber used for holding objects, etc. together.

rubber stamp *noun*
1 a small rubber device with raised figures for printing dates, etc.
2 (*informal*) a person or group that gives immediate or unthinking approval.
Word Family **rubber-stamp** *verb*.

rubbing *noun*
a reproduction or print made by rubbing, especially using a dark crayon on paper placed over a raised design, e.g. of church brass.

rubbish *noun*
1 any waste or worthless material.
2 nonsense: *You're talking utter rubbish.*
• **rubbish** *verb* (*informal*) to criticize as being worthless.
• **rubbish** *adjective* (*informal*) very poor in quality.
Word Family **rubbishy** *adjective* (*informal*) worthless.

rubble *noun*
any fragments of broken rock or masonry.

rubella → GERMAN MEASLES.

rubicund (roo-bi-kund) *adjective*
having a healthy rosy complexion.
[Latin *rubicundus* red]

ruble → ROUBLE.

rubric (roo-brik) *noun*
any title or instruction inserted in a book, etc.
[Latin *rubrica* red earth, title of a law (written with red ochre)]

ruby (roo-bee) *noun* (*plural* **rubies**)
1 a red crystalline variety of corundum used as a gemstone.
2 a rich deep red colour.
Word Family **ruby** *adjective*.
[Latin *rubeus* red]

ruck *verb*
(of cloth) to crease or wrinkle.
• **ruck** *noun*.

rucksack (ruk-sack *or* ruuk-sack) *noun*
a bag with a supporting frame, used especially by young travellers.
[German *Rücken* back + SACK]

ruckus *noun* (*plural* **ruckuses**)
a noisy and confused situation.

ructions *plural noun*
(*informal*) a row or disturbance.

rudd *noun* (*plural* **rudd**)
a freshwater fish of the carp family.

rudder *noun*
a flat structure hinged to the stern of a boat or the tail of an aeroplane and used for steering.
Word Family **rudderless** *adjective*.

ruddy *adjective* (**ruddier; ruddiest**)
1 reddish in colour: *a ruddy complexion.*
2 (*dated informal*) damned: *You're a ruddy lunatic.*
Word Family **ruddiness** *noun*.

rude *adjective*
1 impolite, disrespectful or discourteous.
2 referring to sex in an improper way: *a rude joke.*
3 rough or crude: *a rude shelter.*
Word Family **rudely** *adverb*; **rudeness** *noun*.
[Latin *rudis* in the natural state]

rudiments (roo-di-m'nts) *plural noun*
the elementary principles of a subject or skill: *My father taught me the rudiments of algebra.*
Word Family **rudimentary** (roo-di-men-ta-ree) *adjective* **1** elementary.
2 undeveloped: *Flightless birds have rudimentary wings.*
[Latin *rudimentum* a first attempt]

rue (roo) *verb* (**rues; rueing** *or* **ruing; rued**)
to regret or think about bitterly: *I rue the day we met.*
Word Family **rueful** *adjective* sorry or regretful: *a rueful smile*; **ruefully** *adverb*; **ruefulness** *noun*.

ruff *noun*
1 a collar drawn into stiff regular folds, popular in the 16th century.
2 a ring of differently marked hair or feathers around the neck of an animal or bird.

ruffian *noun*
a violent or rough person.
[from Italian]

ruffle *verb*
to disturb the smoothness of something: *The parrot ruffled its feathers in annoyance.*

• **ruffle** *noun* a strip of cloth drawn together to form a frill, e.g. on a shirt.

rug *noun*
1 a small thick carpet.
2 a thick warm blanket: *a travelling rug.*

rugby *noun* also **rugby football** (*formal*)
a type of football played with an oval ball which can be handled. There are two forms of the game: **rugby league**, with 13 players in a side, and **rugby union**, with 15.
[invented at *Rugby* School]

rugged (**rug**-id) *adjective*
1 rough, uneven or rocky: *a rugged range of mountains.* □ *a rugged weather-beaten face.*
2 sturdy: *She's succeeded through rugged determination.*
Word Family ruggedly *adverb*;
ruggedness *noun.*

rugger *noun*
(*informal*) rugby.

ruin (**roo**-in) *noun*
1 a state of collapse or decay: *The old castle fell into ruin.*
2 something that has collapsed or is destroyed: *The castle is now a ruin.*
3 one's downfall: *Gambling will be the ruin of him.*
Phrase **in ruins** in a state of ruin.
• **ruin** *verb*
1 to bring to ruin: *The rain ruined the harvest.* □ *You'll ruin your shoes if you wear them in the mud.*
2 to lose all one's money, possessions, etc.: *The family was ruined during the depression.*
Word Family ruinous (**roo**-in-us) *adjective* 1 causing ruin: *a ruinous war.* 2 in ruins; **ruinously** *adverb*; **ruinousness** *noun*; **ruination** (roo-in-**ay**-sh'n) *noun.*
[Latin *ruina* a tumbling down]

rule *noun*
1 a principle or code of behaviour or action: *Do you know the rules of the game?*
2 authority or control: *Australia was once under British rule.*
3 a ruler for measuring, etc.
Phrase **as a rule** usually.
• **rule** *verb*
1 to control or direct: *The king ruled for 40 years.*
2 to declare officially: *The court ruled the will invalid.*
3 to draw lines with a ruler.
Phrase **rule out** to dismiss as an option: *We can rule out the possibility of murder.*
[Latin *regula* a straight stick]

rule of thumb *noun*
any practical method or procedure based on experience rather than on theory.

ruler *noun*
1 a person who rules, especially a monarch.
2 a strip of wood, plastic, etc. with a straight edge for ruling lines, measuring, etc.

ruling *noun*
an authoritative judgement or decision, such as one given by a court.

rum[1] *noun*
a strong liquor made from molasses or sugar cane.

rum[2] *adjective* (**rummer**; **rummest**)
(*dated informal*) odd or strange.

rumba *noun*
a ballroom dance from Cuba with a complex rhythm, or the music for such a dance.
[American Spanish]

rumble *verb*
1 to make a low continuous heavy sound, like that of distant thunder.
2 to move with this sound: *The heavy carts rumbled across the cobblestones.*
3 (*informal*) to detect or uncover: *I think the teachers have rumbled our plan.*
Word Family rumble *noun*; **rumbling** *adjective.*

ruminant (**roo**-mi-nant) *noun*
any mammal that returns partly digested food to the mouth to be re-chewed, e.g. the cow.

ruminate (**roo**-mi-nate) *verb*
1 (of a person) to meditate or ponder.
2 (of an animal) to chew the cud.
Word Family rumination (roo-mi-**nay**-sh'n) *noun*; **ruminative** (**roo**-min-a-tiv) *adjective*; **ruminatively** *adverb.*

rummage (**rum**-ij) *verb*
to look for something, especially by moving things around: *She rummaged through the drawers of the desk for a pencil.*
• **rummage** *noun.*

> The word **rummage** has nautical connections. It has its origins in Old French *arrumage*, a noun formed from the verb *arrumer*, meaning 'to stow in a ship's hold'. The searching would originally have been restricted to the searching of ships' holds.

rummage sale *noun*
(*especially American*) a sale of used articles to raise money for charity.

rummy *noun*
a card game for two or more players.

rumour (**roo**-ma) *noun* (*American* **rumor**)
an unconfirmed story or report in
circulation: *There's a rumour that you are
going away.*
• **rumour** *verb*
Phrase **be rumoured** to be circulated as
a rumour: *It is rumoured that you're going to
Africa.*
[Latin *rumor* a noise]

rump *noun*
1 the fleshy hind parts of most mammals,
equivalent to the buttocks in a human
being.
2 a cut of beef from this area.
3 any lesser or unimportant parts or
remnants.

rumple *verb*
to crush or crumple.

rumpus *noun* (*plural* **rumpuses**)
a noisy uproar or disturbance.

run *verb* (**runs; running; ran; run**)
1 to move quickly on foot: *The children ran
to their mother.*
2 to pass or move quickly: *He ran his eyes
over the page.*
3 (*informal*) to take someone in a vehicle:
Hop in – I'll run you to the station.
4 to flow or cause to flow: *Run the hot water
first.*
5 (of a dye or a colour) to spread because
of being wet.
6 to move or operate: *This engine runs
quietly.* □ *I run this business myself.* □ *Trains
run every half-hour.*
7 to continue or extend: *The fence runs
round the property.* □ *The play ran for six
weeks.* □ *My tastes don't run to champagne.*
8 to pass into a particular state: *Our stock
of coffee is running low.* □ *The crowd suddenly
ran riot.*
9 to be a candidate: *He may run for
President.*
10 (of a delicate fabric) to ladder.
11 to print: *The magazine is running a series
of articles on stress.*
12 to smuggle: *arrested for gun-running.*
Phrases **run across** to meet
unexpectedly. **run away** to escape. **run
away with** to win easily: *Najma will run
away with the science prize!* **run down 1** (of
a clock, etc.) to slow down and stop. 2 to
knock down while in a car, etc. 3 to speak
unkindly about: *Try not to run your sister
down all the time.* **run in 1** to operate
carefully to bring to full working
condition: *I'm driving slowly because I'm

still running the car in.* 2 (*informal*) to
arrest. **run into 1** to meet unexpectedly.
2 to amount to: *The final cost ran into six
figures.* **run off 1** to escape. 2 to print. **run
out 1** to be used up. 2 *Cricket* to put a
batsman out by hitting the wicket with the
ball while the batsman is still running. **run
out on** to desert or abandon. **run over**
1 to knock down with a vehicle and injure
or kill. 2 to review quickly: *Let's just run
over that scene again.* **run short** to be
nearly all used up. **run through 1** to stab
deeply: *Robin Hood ran him through with his
sword.* 2 to review quickly. **run up 1** to
amass: *I'd run up an enormous bill.* 2 to
make quickly on a machine: *My mum ran
me up a Roman toga for the party.* 3 to raise
a flag. **run up against** to meet with: *Her
plan ran up against bitter opposition.*
• **run** *noun*
1 the act of running: *Let's go for a run in the
park.* □ *The play had a six-week run.*
2 an excursion or journey: *She took us for a
run in the car.*
3 a course or track: *a ski run.*
4 an enclosed area for animals or birds:
a chicken run.
5 *Sport* the score unit in cricket, baseball,
etc.
6 a sequence: *You've just had a run of bad
luck.*
7 *Cards* a sequence of cards of the same
suit.
8 (**the run of**) the usual type of: *He was
different from the general run of salesmen.*
9 (**the run of**) the freedom to use: *I'll give
you the run of the house while I'm away.*
10 a sudden heavy demand: *There's been a
run on these sweets today.*
11 ⇨ LADDER (definition 2).
12 (**the runs**) (*informal*) diarrhoea.
Phrases **in the long run** ultimately. **in
the short run** considering only the
immediate effects. **on the run 1** escaped
and in hiding. 2 retreating: *Now we have
the enemy forces on the run.*

runabout *noun*
a small car, used for short journeys.

runaround *noun*
Phrase **give someone the runaround** to
avoid giving someone a truthful answer.

runaway *adjective*
1 escaped or fugitive: *a runaway horse.*
2 uncontrollable: *runaway inflation.*
• **runaway** *noun*.

rundown *noun*
a brief review or summary.
• **run-down** *adjective*

1 in a poor or dilapidated condition: *a run-down old house*.
2 rather tired and unwell.

rune (roon) *noun*
any of the characters of an alphabet formerly used in Scandinavian and Anglo-Saxon inscriptions.
Word Family **runic** *adjective*.
[Old English *run* a mystery]

rung[1] the past participle of **ring**[2].

rung[2] *noun*
a crosspiece set in a ladder or between the legs of a chair for support.
[Old English *hrung* a pole]

run-in *noun*
(*informal*) a disagreement.

runnel *noun*
1 a small stream.
2 a small channel for water.

runner *noun*
1 a person or thing that runs.
2 a messenger or agent for an employer.
3 the part by which something moves or glides along, such as strips of wood on the edges of a drawer or the blade on an ice skate.
4 a long narrow carpet extending along a hallway.
5 *Biology* a slender stem that grows along the ground and may produce roots.
Phrase **do a runner** (*informal*) to leave hastily to avoid something.

runner bean *noun*
a plant with large green edible pods which are cooked after stringing and slicing.

runner-up *noun* (*plural* **runners-up**)
a competitor who comes second in a competition.

running *noun*
1 the activity of a runner.
2 the way something is organized: *My son has taken over the running of the business*.
Phrases **in the running** having a chance of success. **make the running** to set the pace. **out of the running** having no chance of success.
● **running** *adjective*
1 of or relating to a person or thing that runs: *running water*.
2 continuous: *She gave us a running commentary on what was happening outside*.
3 consecutive: *My brother stayed out late for three nights running*.
Phrase **in running order** (of a machine) working properly.

running board *noun*
a narrow ledge beneath the doors on the side of a vehicle, to assist people getting in or out.

running mate *noun*
American the less important candidate on an electoral ticket, such as the person running for vice-president.

running stitch *noun* (*plural* **running stitches**)
Needlework a small continuous stitch.

runny *adjective* (**runnier; runniest**)
1 liquid or flowing: *runny butter*.
2 discharging a fluid: *a runny nose*.

run-of-the-mill *adjective*
ordinary or mediocre.

runt *noun*
1 an undersized animal, especially the smallest in a litter.
2 (*informal*) an undersized person.

run-through *noun*
a rehearsal.

run-up *noun*
1 the period immediately before an event: *during the run-up to the election*.
2 *Sports* a brief burst of fast running before a jump, throw, etc.

runway *noun*
a cleared, usually concrete, strip of ground for aeroplanes to take off from and land on.

rupee (roo-pee) *noun*
the basic unit of money in India, Pakistan and certain other countries.
[Hindi]

rupture (**rup**-cher) *verb*
to break or burst: *She ruptured a blood vessel*.
● **rupture** *noun*
1 a breaking or bursting.
2 ⇨ HERNIA.
[Latin *ruptus* broken]

rural (**roo**-r'l) *adjective*
of or relating to the country or countryside: *a peaceful rural scene*.
Compare URBAN.
[Latin *ruris* of the countryside]

ruse (rooz) *noun*
a trick or deceitful scheme.

rush[1] *verb*
1 to go or move quickly and forcefully: *I rushed home from school*.
2 to do something very quickly: *Never rush a job like this*.
3 to make someone act more quickly: *Don't rush me!*

4 to move quickly towards and attack: *We'll have to rush the security guard.*

• **rush** *noun* (*plural* **rushes**)
1 any rapid or forceful movement: *There was a mad rush for seats.*
2 a need to hurry: *Wait a minute – there's no rush!*
3 a sudden heavy demand: *There's been a rush on ice creams today.*
4 (**rushes**) *Film* the first proofs of a motion picture.
5 a sudden strong feeling of pleasure or excitement.
• **rush** *adjective* requiring speed: *a rush delivery.*

rush² *noun* (*plural* **rushes**)
any of various slender leafless marsh plants used in weaving baskets, etc.

rush hour *noun*
one of the busy times of day for traffic, when people travel between home and work.

rusk *noun*
a crisp dry biscuit, given to babies to help them when teething.

russet *noun*
1 a reddish-brown colour.
2 a type of apple.
• **russet** *adjective.*
[Latin *russus* red]

Russian roulette *noun*
a suicidal game of chance in which a revolver loaded with a bullet in only one of its chambers is held to one's head and the trigger pulled.

rust *noun*
1 *Chemistry* a flaky reddish-brown coating of iron oxide, which forms on iron or steel when it is exposed to air and moisture.
2 a reddish-brown or orange colour.
• **rust** *verb* to corrode or develop rust.
Word Family **rustiness** *noun.*

rust bucket *noun*
(*informal*) a vehicle that is old and falling to pieces.

rustic (**rust**-ik) *adjective*
1 rural.

2 (of a piece of furniture, etc.) made of rough branches.
• **rustic** *noun* a country person, especially an unsophisticated one.
Word Family **rustically** *adverb;* **rusticity** (rust-**iss**-i-tee) *noun.*
[from Latin]

rustle (**russ**-'l) *verb*
1 to make soft quiet sounds, like things rubbing gently together: *The leaves rustled in the wind.*
2 to move with such a sound: *A deer rustled through the undergrowth.*
3 to steal cattle, etc.
Phrase **rustle up** (*informal*) to manage to find: *I expect I could rustle up a bit of supper.*
Word Family **rustle** *noun* a rustling sound; **rustler** *noun.*

rusty *adjective* (**rustier; rustiest**)
1 affected with rust.
2 having the colour of rust.
3 (of a skill) weak through lack of practice: *My French is a little rusty.*

rut¹ *noun*
1 a narrow furrow in the ground, especially one made by the wheels of a vehicle.
2 a fixed way of life: *I'm afraid I'm getting into a bit of a rut.*
Word Family **rutted** *adjective.*

rut² *noun*
a period of recurring sexual excitement in animals such as sheep and goats.
• **rut** *verb* (**ruts; rutting; rutted**) to be affected by rut.
[Latin *rugitus* bellowing]

ruthless (**rooth**-liss) *adjective*
pitiless or merciless.
Word Family **ruthlessly** *adverb;* **ruthlessness** *noun.*

rye *noun*
1 a cereal plant used to make flour and whisky, and as food for cattle.
2 a whisky distilled from rye.

rye bread *noun*
a dark bread made with flour from rye.

Ss

sabbath *noun*
1 (*often* **Sabbath**) *Religion* the seventh day of the week, Saturday, kept as a day of rest by Jews and certain Christian sects.
2 (*often* **Sabbath**) *Religion* the first day of the week, Sunday, kept by Christians as a day of rest in celebration of Christ's resurrection.
3 a secret meeting of witches held at night.
[Hebrew *shabath* to rest]

sabbatical (sa-**bat**-i-k'l) *adjective*
1 of or relating to the sabbath.
2 of or relating to a period of rest.
• **sabbatical** *noun* a year or other period of time when an employed person, especially a university teacher, is freed from duties for travel, study, etc.
[under Mosaic law land was left untilled (fallow) every seventh year]

sable *noun*
1 a small ferret-like mammal of North America, Europe and Asia.
2 the fur of this animal.
• **sable** *adjective*
1 made of sable.
2 black.

sabotage (**sabb**-a-tah*zh*) *noun*
any deliberate destruction or obstruction, e.g. of machinery or installations during wartime or during an industrial dispute.
Word Family **sabotage** *verb*; **saboteur** (sabb-a-**ter**) *noun* a person who commits sabotage.

> The word **sabotage** comes from the French word *sabot* (clog). The connection between *sabotage* and *sabot* is thought to be the French verb *saboter*, 'to walk noisily and clumsily in clogs', which came to mean 'to work clumsily' and then 'to destroy tools and machinery deliberately'.

sabre (**say**-ba) *noun* (*American* **saber**)
1 a heavy sword with a slightly curved blade, having one cutting edge, used by cavalry.

2 a light fencing sword with a flexible tapering blunt-edged blade and a semicircular guard.
[from Hungarian]

sabre-rattling *noun*
a provocative or warning display of military strength.

sabre-toothed tiger *noun*
a long-extinct large tiger with big upper front teeth.

sac *noun*
a small bag-like part of an animal or plant, often containing fluid.
[French]

saccharin (**sakk**-a-rin) *noun*
Chemistry a crystalline solid which is about 400 times sweeter than cane sugar and is used as a sugar substitute in cases of diabetes or obesity.
Word Family **saccharine** (**sakk**-a-rine *or* **sakk**-a-reen) *adjective* cloyingly sweet: *a saccharine smile*.
[Greek *sakkharon* sugar]

sacerdotal (sass-a-**doe**-t'l *or* sakk-a-**doe**-t'l) *adjective*
of or relating to priests.
[Latin *sacerdotis* of a priest]

sachet (**sash**-ay) *noun*
a small sealed envelope or bag containing perfume, shampoo, etc.
[French]

sack¹ *noun*
1 a large strong bag, usually made of hessian, for carrying coal, potatoes, etc.
2 (*informal*) dismissal from employment: *He threatened to give me the sack.*
Phrase **hit the sack** (*informal*) to go to bed.
• **sack** *verb*
1 to put into sacks.
2 (*informal*) to dismiss from employment.
[Greek *sakkos*]

sack² *verb*
to loot or plunder after capture: *to sack a city.*
Word Family **sack** *noun*.
[French *mettre à sac* to put to the sack]

sack³ *noun*
an old word for various strong wines, originally from Spain and the Canary Islands.
[French *vin sec* dry wine]

sackcloth *noun*
a coarse fabric.
Phrase **in sackcloth and ashes** extremely repentant.

sacking noun
1 any coarse fabric used for sacks, such as hessian.
2 (*informal*) dismissal from employment.

sack race noun
a race in which each contestant jumps forward with his or her legs in a sack.

sacra
the plural of **sacrum**.

sacrament (sak-ra-m'nt) noun
1 *Christianity* a ceremony or rite such as baptism or the Eucharist, believed to confer grace on believers who participate.
2 any sacred or solemn event or undertaking.
Word Family **sacramental** (sak-ra-**men**-t'l) adjective.
[Church Latin *sacramentum* a mystery]

sacred (say-krid) adjective
dedicated to a god or religious purpose.
Figurative This statue is sacred to her memory (= reverently dedicated). □ the sacred memory of the king (= revered).
Word Family **sacredly** adverb; **sacredness** noun.
[Latin *sacer* holy]

sacred cow noun
a person or thing that escapes critical examination because of popular esteem, high repute, etc.
[from the Hindu belief that the *cow* is holy]

sacrifice (sak-ri-fice) noun
1 the giving up of something one values for the sake of something considered more important.
2 something which is lost or given up in this way.
3 the offering of something to a deity.
4 something which is offered to a deity.
Word Family **sacrifice** verb; **sacrificial** (sak-ri-**fish**-'l) adjective; **sacrificially** adverb.
[from Latin]

sacrilege (sak-ri-lij) noun
any injury to or disrespectful treatment of anything regarded as sacred.
Word Family **sacrilegious** (sak-ri-lij-us) adjective; **sacrilegiously** adverb.
[Latin *sacra* sacred things + *legere* to steal]

sacristan (sak-ris-t'n) noun
a sexton.
[Latin *sacrare* to regard as holy]

sacristy (sak-ris-tee) noun (*plural* **sacristies**) ⇨ VESTRY.

sacrosanct (sak-ro-sankt) adjective
extremely sacred or inviolable.
[Latin *sacro* by a sacred rite + *sanctus* made holy]

sacrum (say-krum) noun (*plural* **sacra**)
Anatomy a bone in the lower back, consisting of five vertebrae fused together.
[Latin *os sacrum* sacred bone (as used in sacrifices)]

sad adjective (**sadder; saddest**)
1 sorrowful or unhappy.
2 causing or expressing sorrow.
3 (*informal*) pitifully inadequate: *a sad attempt.*
Word Family **sadly** adverb; **sadness** noun; **sadden** verb.

saddle noun
1 a padded leather seat for a rider on the back of a horse or similar animal.
2 a similar seat on a bicycle, etc.
3 something which has the shape or position of a saddle, such as a hollow ridge between two mountain peaks.
4 a cut of lamb taken from the upper back of the animal.
Phrase **in the saddle** in control.
● **saddle** verb to put a saddle on a horse, etc.
Figurative She was saddled with all the responsibilities during his absence (= loaded, left).

saddlebag noun
a bag buckled to, or hung over, a saddle, used for carrying things.

saddlery (sad-la-ree) noun (*plural* **saddleries**)
1 saddles, bridles and related equipment for horses.
2 a shop or business which deals in such equipment.
Word Family **saddler** noun a person who makes or sells saddlery.

sadism (say-dizm) noun
a pleasure, especially sexual pleasure, in causing suffering, pain or humiliation to another person. Compare MASOCHISM.
Word Family **sadist** noun; **sadistic** (sa-**diss**-tik) adjective; **sadistically** adverb.
[after the *Marquis de Sade*, 1740-1814, a French novelist notorious for a mixture of sex and cruelty in his books]

sadomasochism (say-doe-**mass**-a-kizm) noun
a liking for both sadism and masochism.

safari (sa-**far**-ee) *noun*
1 an expedition, especially for hunting.
2 the people, animals, etc. forming such an expedition.
[Arabic *safara* to travel]

safari park *noun*
a large park where wild animals are kept in the open and which visitors can drive through.

safe *adjective*
1 free from danger, injury or risk: *Keep the jewels in a safe place.* □ *We arrived safe and sound.*
2 unable to do any further harm: *He's safe in jail now.*
Figurative He is a safe player (= cautious).
• **safe** *noun* a strong metal box, usually with a complex lock or combination, in which money and other valuables are kept.
Word Family **safely** *adverb*.
[Latin *salvus*]

safe conduct *noun*
1 a document which ensures safe passage through an area, especially in wartime.
2 the privilege of so passing.

safe deposit *noun*
a room or building fitted with safes, etc. for storing valuable articles.

safeguard (**safe**-gard) *noun*
a protective measure or device.
• **safeguard** *verb* to protect.

safe keeping *noun*
protection.

safe sex *noun*
sexual activity during which precautions are taken to avoid the spread of sexually transmitted diseases, especially Aids.

safety *noun*
the state of being safe.

safety belt ⇨ SEAT BELT.

safety catch *noun* (*plural* **safety catches**)
a locking device to prevent a gun being fired accidentally.

safety glass *noun*
any of various forms of specially strengthened glass, such as two panes joined by a layer of plastic, which is designed not to shatter.

safety match *noun* (*plural* **safety matches**)
a match designed to light only on contact with special surfaces.

safety net *noun*
1 a net in a circus to catch a trapeze artist or tightrope walker if he or she falls.

2 something that affords protection against danger or misfortune.

safety pin *noun*
a pin with a rounded guard in which the point is held.

safety razor *noun*
a razor blade with a protective guard.

safflower *noun*
a thistle-like plant with large reddish-orange flowers used as a dye, as a source of oil and in medicine.

saffron *noun*
1 the dried orange-coloured stigmas of a variety of crocus, used whole or powdered to colour or flavour food.
2 a deep yellowish-orange colour.
[from Arabic]

sag *verb* (**sags; sagging; sagged**)
to sink or bend downwards, especially in the middle, due to weight or pressure.
Figurative Her shoulders sagged after the busy day (= drooped).
Word Family **sag** *noun*.

saga (**sah**-ga) *noun*
1 a medieval Icelandic epic written in prose.
2 a novel that traces a family's fortunes through several generations.
3 any long story or description: *He told the saga of his journey across Asia.*
[Old Norse, narrative]

sagacious (sa-**gay**-shus) *adjective*
showing keen judgement and common sense.
Word Family **sagaciously** *adverb*; **sagacity** (sa-**gass**-i-tee) *noun*.
[Latin *sagax*]

sage[1] *noun*
a herb with strongly flavoured greyish-green leaves.
[Latin *salvia* a healing plant]

sage[2] *noun*
an extremely wise person.
• **sage** *adjective* wise.
Word Family **sagely** *adverb*; **sageness** *noun*.
[Latin *sapere* to be wise]

sage green *noun*
a greyish-green colour.

saggy *adjective* (**saggier; saggiest**)
tending to sag or droop.

Sagittarius (saj-i-**tair**-i-us) *noun*
Astrology a group of stars, the ninth sign of the Zodiac; the sign of the Archer.
[Latin *sagitta* an arrow]

sago (**say**-go) *noun*
a starchy rice-like substance obtained from plants, used in puddings and soups.
[Malay]

sahib (sahb *or* **sah**-ib) *noun*
a polite form of address used by Indians to a man.
[Arabic, friend]

said (sed) *adjective*
named or mentioned already: *the said witness.*
• **said** *verb* the past tense and past participle of **say**.

sail *noun*
1 a piece of fabric, originally canvas, fastened to a mast so that it catches the wind and propels a boat.
2 something which has the shape, position or function of a sail: *the sails of a windmill.*
3 a trip in a sailing boat or ship: *We went for a sail before the storm.*
Phrase **set sail** to start a trip or voyage.
• **sail** *verb*
1 to move across the surface of water by the action of wind on a sail or sails.
2 to travel by water: *We sailed to Cape Town in a luxury ship.*
Figurative A bullet sailed past her ear (= moved rapidly). □ *She sailed angrily out of the room* (= moved with dignity).
3 to manage a sailing boat.
Phrases **sail into** (*informal*) to go boldly or aggressively into action. **sail through** (*informal*) to succeed with ease in an examination, etc.
Word Family **sailing** *noun.*

sailboard *noun*
a board with a sail attached, used for windsurfing.
Word Family **sailboarder** *noun;* **sailboarding** *noun.*

sailcloth *noun*
1 a strong canvas used for sails, etc.
2 a lightweight canvas used to make clothes, etc.

sailfish *noun* (*plural* **sailfish** *or* **sailfishes**)
any of a group of large fast-swimming fish related to the marlin, having a high sail-like dorsal fin.

sailor *noun*
a member of the crew of any boat or ship.

sailplane *noun*
a glider with very long wings intended for sustained flying.

saint *noun*
1 *Christianity* any person of exceptional holiness, formally recognized and venerated by the Church.
2 any very holy or unselfish person.
Word Family **saintly** *adjective;* **saintliness** *noun;* **sainthood** *noun.*
[Latin *sanctus* holy]

St Bernard *noun*
any of a breed of very large heavy wavy-haired dogs.
[originally used by monks in the monastery of *St Bernard* in the Swiss Alps to search for lost travellers]

St John's wort *noun*
a herbaceous plant with yellow flowers.

saint's day *noun*
a Church feast day in memory of a saint.

St Vitus's dance ⇨ CHOREA.

saith (seth)
an old third person singular present tense of **say**.

sake[1] *noun*
1 benefit, cause or interest: *Please do it for my sake.*
2 purpose, motive or end: *for the sake of argument.*

sake[2] (**sah**-ki) *noun*
a Japanese alcoholic drink made of fermented rice.
[Japanese]

salaam (sa-**lahm**) *noun*
a word or bow given in greeting, especially amongst Muslims.
Word Family **salaam** *verb.*
[Arabic *salam* peace]

salacious (sa-**lay**-shus) *adjective*
lustful or erotic.
Word Family **salaciously** *adverb;* **salaciousness** *noun.*
[from Latin]

salad *noun*
a dish of cold raw vegetables, meat, fruit, etc., usually served with a dressing.
[Latin *sal* salt]

salad days *plural noun*
days of youthful inexperience.

salamander (**sall**-a-man-da) *noun*
any of a group of amphibians whose larvae usually live in the water although the adults live on land.
[from Greek]

salami (sa-**lah**-mee) *noun*
a spicy sausage, often containing garlic.
[Italian]

salary (sall-a-ree) *noun* (*plural* **salaries**)
a regular payment to an employee, usually
monthly.
Word Family **salaried** *adjective* earning
or yielding a salary.
[Latin *salarium* money paid to Roman
soldiers to buy salt]

sale *noun*
1 the act of selling.
2 the exchange of anything, especially
goods, for money.
3 a special disposal of goods at reduced
prices.

saleable *adjective*
subject to or suitable for sale.
Word Family **saleability** (sale-a-**bill**-i-
tee) *noun*.

salesman *noun* (*plural* **salesmen**)
a man engaged in selling either to
customers in a shop or to shops.

salesmanship *noun*
the art of persuading people to buy goods.

salesperson *noun* (*plural* **salespersons**
or **salespeople**)
a salesman or saleswoman.

sales representative *noun*
short form is **rep** a person engaged in
selling a firm's goods to shops, etc.

sales tax *noun* (*plural* **sales taxes**)
a tax added to the retail price of certain
articles.

saleswoman *noun* (*plural* **saleswomen**)
a woman engaged in selling either to
customers in a shop or to shops.

salient (**say**-li-'nt) *adjective*
1 striking or prominent.
2 jutting out.
• **salient** *noun* a part of a fortification,
trench or battle line that projects towards
the enemy.
Word Family **saliently** *adverb*; **salience,
saliency** *noun*.
[Latin *saliens* leaping]

saline (**say**-line) *adjective*
of or containing salt.
Word Family **salinity** (sa-**lin**-i-tee) *noun*.
[Latin *sal* salt]

saliva (sa-**lie**-va) *noun*
the fluid, containing ptyalin, secreted by
glands in the mouth and beginning the
digestion of food.
Word Family **salivary** (sa-**lie**-va-ree)
adjective; **salivate** (**sall**-i-vate) *verb* to
produce saliva; **salivation** (sall-i-**vay**-
sh'n) *noun*.
[from Latin]

sallow *adjective*
(of the complexion) yellowish or sickly.
Word Family **sallowness** *noun*.

sally *noun* (*plural* **sallies**)
1 a sudden sortie by besieged troops
against the enemy.
2 an excursion or a burst of activity.
3 a quick or witty remark.
Word Family **sally** *verb* (**sallies;
sallying; sallied**).
[Latin *salire* to leap]

salmon (**sam**-'n) *noun* (*plural* **salmon** or
salmons)
1 any of a large group of highly prized fish
with pink flesh, which live in the sea but go
up rivers to spawn.
2 a light pinkish-orange colour.

salmonella (sal-ma-**nell**-a) *noun*
a group of bacteria, many of which may
cause diseases, including typhoid and food
poisoning.
[after *D. E. Salmon*, 1861-1914, an
American veterinary surgeon]

salmon trout *noun* (*plural* **salmon trout**)
also called **sea trout**.
a variety of trout which lives at sea but
comes up rivers to spawn.

salon *noun*
1 a building or room used for a particular,
usually fashionable, business: *a beauty
salon*.
2 a private meeting between selected
guests, such as artists or politicians, first
held in France in the 18th century by
wealthy women.
3 an exhibition of modern art.
[French, drawing room]

saloon *noun*
1 a ship's cabin, originally one for first-
class passengers.
2 a closed car of standard size with a
separate boot.
3 *American* a place where alcoholic drinks
are sold to be drunk on the premises.
[from Latin]

saloon bar *noun*
the most elegant bar in a pub, more
expensive than the public bar.

salopettes *plural noun*
quilted or padded trousers with shoulder
straps, worn for skiing.

salsa *noun*
1 a type of Latin American dance music.
2 a dance performed to salsa music.
3 a spicy Mexican tomato sauce.

salsify (**sal**-si-fee) *noun*
a winter root vegetable which tastes rather like asparagus; there are white and black varieties.
[from Italian]

salt (sawlt) *noun*
1 a white compound, sodium chloride (formula NaCl), widely used to flavour and preserve food.
2 *Chemistry* a compound formed by the action of an acid on a metal or base.
3 (**salts**) any of a group of salts used as laxatives.
4 (**salts**) smelling salts.
5 (*informal*) a sailor, especially an experienced one.
Phrases **salt of the earth** the best type of people. **take with a pinch of salt** to believe with reservation. **worth one's salt** deserving one's pay, reward or position.
• **salt** *verb*
1 to add salt in order to season or preserve food.
2 (*informal*) to introduce rich ore into a mine, etc. to give a false impression of value.
Word Family **salt, salty** *adjective* (**saltier, saltiest**) containing or tasting of salt; **saltily** *adverb*; **saltiness** *noun*.
[Latin *sal*]

salt cellar *noun*
a small, often decorative, container for sprinkling salt.

salt marsh *noun* (*plural* **salt marshes**)
1 a coastal marsh which is sometimes covered by seawater.
2 an inland marsh in a dry area where the water contains much salt.

salt pan *noun*
a hollow from which water has evaporated, leaving a layer of salt.

saltpetre (sawlt-**pee**-ta) *noun* (*American* **saltpeter**)
potassium nitrate, a white crystalline solid used in medicine, for pickling meat and in gunpowder.
[Latin *sal* salt + *petra* a rock]

salubrious (sa-**loo**-bri-us) *adjective*
good for one's health.
Word Family **salubriously** *adverb*; **salubriousness, salubrity** (sa-**loo**-bri-tee) *noun*.
[Latin *salubris*]

saluki (sa-**loo**-kee) *noun*
any of a breed of tall slender dogs related to the greyhound and having a tawny coat.
[from Arabic]

salutary (**sal**-yoo-tree) *adjective*
1 promoting some beneficial purpose.
2 an old word meaning 'good for one's health'.
[Latin *salutis* of health]

salutation (sal-yoo-**tay**-sh'n) *noun*
a greeting.

salute (sa-**loot**) *verb*
1 *Military* to make a gesture of respect or acknowledgement by raising the right hand to the cap or forehead, firing artillery, etc.
2 to greet.
Word Family **salute** *noun*.
[Latin *salutare* to wish health to]

salvage (**sal**-vij) *noun*
1 the act of saving a ship from shipwreck, goods from a fire, etc.
2 the property saved.
• **salvage** *verb* to save from loss or destruction.

salvation (sal-**vay**-sh'n) *noun*
1 preservation or deliverance from sin, evil or difficulty.
2 a means or cause of such deliverance.
[Latin *salvare* to save]

Salvation Army *noun*
Christianity a religious organization founded by William Booth in 1865, with a military structure and concerned with a general revival of religion, helping the poor, etc.
Word Family **Salvationist** *noun, adjective*.

salve[1] *noun*
something which soothes, such as an ointment.
Word Family **salve** *verb* to soothe.

salve[2] *verb*
an old word meaning 'to salvage'.

salver *noun*
a tray, usually of silver.
[from French]

salvo *noun* (*plural* **salvos** or **salvoes**)
1 the firing of guns together or in succession, especially as a salute.
2 any sudden outburst, e.g. of applause.
[Italian *salva* salutation]

sal volatile (sal va-**latt**-il-ee) *noun*
ammonium carbonate, an aromatic solution used as smelling salts.
[Latin, volatile salt]

Samaritan (sa-**marr**-i-tan) *noun* also **good Samaritan**
a person who helps another who is in trouble.
[from the biblical parable of the *Good Samaritan*, Luke 10:33]

samba *noun*
a ballroom dance from Brazil.

same *adjective, pronoun*
corresponding or unchanged: (as an adjective) *He gets up at the same time every morning.* □ (as a pronoun) *Tom ordered lobster and I asked for the same.*
Phrase **all the same, just the same** despite all that.

sameness *noun*
1 the state of being the same: *There is a marked sameness about your cooking lately.*
2 lack of variety: *the monotonous sameness of the desert scenery.*

samizdat (**sam**-iz-dat) *noun*
1 in the former Soviet Union, the illegal printing and distribution of literature not by the government.
2 the literature itself.

samosa (sa-**moh**-sa) *noun*
a small triangle of pastry filled with spiced minced meat or vegetables and deep-fried.
[Hindi]

samovar (**sam**-a-var) *noun*
a metal urn for heating water, especially to make tea.
[Russian *samo* self + *varit* boil]

Samoyed (**sam**-a-yedd *or* sa-**moy**-edd) *noun*
one of a breed of white long-haired dogs, originally from Asia.
[Russian]

sampan *noun*
a small flat-bottomed boat with a small roof of mats, used in China and nearby countries.
[Chinese]

sample (**sahm**-p'l) *noun*
a part of something which shows the quality or character of the whole: *Taste a sample of the cheese before you buy it.*
• **sample** *verb* to test something by taking a sample: *Would you like to sample the cheese?*
[Old French *essample* example]

sampler (**sahm**-pla) *noun*
1 a person or thing that samples.
2 a piece of cloth with various designs embroidered on it, to demonstrate skill in needlework.

sampling *noun*
1 the process of taking a random sample.
2 the process of taking a piece of recorded music and reusing it as part of another recording.

samurai (**sam**-yoo-rye) *noun*
History a member of the Japanese military class.

Sanatan Dharma (san-at-an **dar**-ma) *noun*
Hinduism.
[Sanskrit, the eternal way]

sanatorium (san-a-**taw**-ri-um) *noun* (*plural* **sanatoriums** *or* **sanatoria**)
a place for people convalescing after an illness or operation, originally a place for tuberculosis patients in a favourable climate.
[Latin *sanare* to make healthy]

sanctify (**sank**-ti-fie) *verb* (**sanctifies; sanctifying; sanctified**)
to make holy or sacred.
Word Family **sanctification** (sank-ti-fi-**kay**-sh'n) *noun.*
[Latin *sanctus* holy + *facere* to make]

sanctimonious (sank-ti-**mo**-nee-us) *adjective*
hypocritical, pretending to be holy or saintly.
Word Family **sanctimoniously** *adverb*; **sanctimoniousness, sanctimony** (**sank**-ti-ma-nee) *noun.*
[Latin *sanctimonia* sacredness]

sanction (**sank**-sh'n) *noun*
1 permission granted by authority: *You may only travel in restricted areas with official sanction.*
Figurative *This ancient ceremony has the sanction of centuries* (= approval).
2 any punishment or threat provided as a way of enforcing a law: *Trade sanctions were applied against the illegal regime.*
• **sanction** *verb* to approve or authorize.
[Latin *sanctio* a law dealing with penalties for contravention]

sanctity (**sank**-ti-tee) *noun*
holiness or sacredness.

sanctuary (**sank**-tew-ree) *noun* (*plural* **sanctuaries**)
1 an especially sacred or holy place, such as the area around the altar in a Christian church.
2 protection or refuge.
3 any place which provides protection, such as a reserve for wildlife.
[Latin *sanctus* holy]

sanctum *noun*
a holy or private place.

sand *noun*
the fine loose particles of decomposed and weathered rocks, finer than gravel but coarser than silt.

• **sand** *verb*
1 to smooth or polish with sand or sandpaper.
2 to sprinkle with sand or add sand to.

sandal *noun*
any of various light shoes with a leather, wooden or plastic sole and straps enclosing the foot.
Word Family **sandalled** *adjective*.
[Greek *sandalion*]

sandalwood *noun*
the fragrant central wood of certain Asian trees, used for carving, as a dye and for incense.

sandbag *noun*
a bag filled with sand, used to make protective walls in wartime trenches, during a flood, etc., or as ballast.

sandbank *noun*
a ridge of sand in the sea or a river, often uncovered at low tide.

sandbar *noun*
a bar of sand formed in the sea or a river by the action of tides or currents.

sandblast *verb*
to clean metal or other hard surfaces with a blast of air containing sand or grit.

sand dune ⇨ DUNE.

sander *noun*
a person or thing that sands.

sandfly *noun* (*plural* **sandflies**)
any of a group of small bloodsucking flies similar to mosquitoes, which may transmit diseases.

sandglass *noun* (*plural* **sandglasses**)
an hourglass.

sandhopper *noun*
a hopping flea-like insect found on beaches.

sandman *noun*
in fairy tales, a man who puts children to sleep by putting sand in their eyes.

sandpaper *noun*
a sheet of heavy paper coated with sand or a similar substance and used as an abrasive.
Word Family **sandpaper** *verb* to smooth or polish with sandpaper.

sandpiper *noun*
a bird related to the snipe and plover, which lives on the seashore and makes a piping sound.

sandpit *noun*
a hollow filled with sand, set in a garden or park, in which children play.

sandshoe *noun*
a light canvas shoe with a rubber or hemp sole, for beachwear.

sandstone *noun*
a sedimentary rock formed of layers of sand laid down and held together by silica, lime, etc.

sandwich *noun*
1 two pieces of bread with a filling between.
2 something which has the shape or arrangement of a sandwich.
• **sandwich** *verb* to squeeze something between two other things: *The lady was sandwiched between two fat men in the train.*

> The word **sandwich** is eponymous. In other words, it is named after a person, the person being John Montagu, fourth Earl of Sandwich (1718-1792). The idea of putting meat between two pieces of bread is older than that but it was the Earl who popularized it. He was a compulsive gambler and was reluctant to leave the gambling table to eat; he therefore had quantities of cold beef between slices of toast brought to him.

sandwich board *noun*
one of a pair of boards bearing advertisements, etc. carried on a person's back and chest.

sandwich course *noun*
an educational course with alternating periods of study and work.

sandy *adjective* (**sandier; sandiest**)
1 having or containing sand.
2 (of hair) of a yellowish-orange colour.
Word Family **sandiness** *noun*.

sane *adjective*
having a normal mental condition.
Figurative That is a very sane idea (= sensible).
Word Family **sanely** *adverb*.
[Latin *sanus* healthy]

sang the past tense of **sing**

sangfroid (song-**frwah**) *noun*
self-control or cool-headedness.
[French *sang* blood + *froid* cold]

sanguinary (sang-gwin-ree) *adjective*
1 causing much bloodshed: *a sanguinary war.*
2 bloodthirsty.

sanguine (sang-gwin) *adjective*
1 hopeful or optimistic.
2 (of a complexion) red.

Word Family **sanguinely** *adverb*;
sanguineness *noun*.
[Latin *sanguinis* of blood]

sanitary (**san**-i-tree) *adjective*
1 clean and healthy, especially with regard
to precautions against disease.
2 of or relating to health.
[Latin *sanitatis* of health]

sanitary protection *noun*
sanitary towels and tampons.

sanitary towel *noun* (*American* **sanitary
napkin**)
an absorbent pad worn by a woman to
absorb menstrual blood.

sanitation (san-i-**tay**-sh'n) *noun*
1 the use or practice of sanitary methods.
2 a drainage or sewerage system.

sanitize, sanitise *verb*
1 to make more hygienic.
2 to make something unpleasant more
acceptable.

sanity (**san**-i-tee) *noun*
the fact or quality of being sane.

sank the past tense of **sink**.

Santa Claus (**san**-ta klawz) *noun*
the legendary person bringing presents to
children at Christmas.
[Dutch-American, *St Nicholas*]

sap¹ *noun*
1 the fluid in a plant.
2 (*informal*) a fool.

sap² *noun*
Military a deep trench or tunnel dug to
approach or undermine enemy
fortifications.
• **sap** *verb* (**saps**; **sapping**; **sapped**)
to undermine or weaken.
[Italian *zappa* a spade]

sapient (**say**-pi-'nt) *adjective*
(*formal*) wise.
Word Family **sapiently** *adverb*; **sapience**
noun.
[Latin *sapiens* being wise]

sapling *noun*
a young tree.

sapper *noun*
a soldier in the engineering or survey
corps of an army.

sapphire (**saff**-ire) *noun*
1 a blue variety of corundum, used as a
gem and for watch bearings.
2 a deep blue colour.
[Greek *sappheiros* lapis lazuli]

sappy *adjective* (**sappier**; **sappiest**)
1 (*American informal*) foolish.
2 full of sap.

saprophyte (**sap**-ro-fite) *noun*
Biology an organism, such as certain fungi
and bacteria, which lives on dead organic
matter.
[Greek *sapros* putrid + *phyton* a plant]

saraband (**sarr**-a-band) *noun* also
sarabande
Music a slow dance from Spain, often part
of a suite.
[Spanish *zarabanda*]

sarcastic *adjective*
using harsh bitter words intended to hurt
or insult, especially in an exaggerated or
ironical way.
Word Family **sarcastically** *adverb*;
sarcasm (**sar**-kazm) *noun* 1 the quality of
being sarcastic. 2 sarcastic speech.
[Greek *sarkazein* to tear flesh]

sarcoma (sar-**koh**-ma) *noun* (*plural*
sarcomas or **sarcomata**)
Medicine a type of malignant tumour.

sarcophagus (sar-**koff**-a-gus) *noun*
(*plural* **sarcophagi**) (sar-**koff**-a-guy or
sar-**koff**-a-jie)
a stone coffin.
[Greek *sarkos* of flesh + *phagein* to eat]

sardine (sar-**deen**) *noun*
any of a group of small edible fish related
to the pilchard, often preserved in oil and
canned.
[Greek *Sardo* Sardinia]

sardonic (sar-**don**-ik) *adjective*
gloomily scornful or mocking, especially
of oneself.
Word Family **sardonically** *adverb*.
[Greek *sardanios* scornful laughter]

sari (**sar**-ee) *noun*
a long Indian dress, consisting of a piece of
material wound around the body with one
end over the shoulder. Compare SARONG.
[Hindi]

sarnie *noun*
(*informal*) a sandwich.

sarong (sa-**rong**) *noun*
a skirt consisting of a piece of material
wound around the lower half of the body
and tucked in at the waist, worn by Asian
men and women. Compare SARI.
[Malay, a sheath]

sarsaparilla (sar-spa-**rill**-a) *noun*
1 the dried root of certain tropical
climbing plants of the lily family, used in
medicine and to flavour food or drink.
2 a soft drink flavoured with this.
[Spanish *zarza* bramble + *parilla* little
vine]

sartorial (sar-**taw**-ri-'l) *adjective*
relating to men's clothing or tailoring.
Word Family sartorially *adverb*.
[Latin *sartor* mender of old clothes]

sartorius (sar-**taw**-ri-us) *noun*
Anatomy the longest muscle in the body,
which stretches from the upper hip across
the thigh to the tibia and controls leg
movement.

sash¹ *noun* (*plural* **sashes**)
a wide strip of cloth worn around the waist
or over the shoulder, for decoration or as
part of a uniform.
[Arabic *shash* turban]

sash² *noun* (*plural* **sashes**)
the separate frame which supports the
glass in a window, often sliding or hinged.

sashimi (sa-**shim**-ee) *noun*
a Japanese dish of small pieces of raw fish
with soy sauce.
[Japanese]

sash window *noun*
a window which slides up and down on a
rope (the **sash cord**), which is attached to
weights acting as a counterbalance.

sassafras *noun*
a deciduous American tree from which oil
for perfume is obtained.
[Spanish]

Sassenach (**sass**-a-nakh) *noun*
a Scottish person's name for an English
person.
[Gaelic, Saxon]

sat the past tense and past participle of **sit**.

Satan (**say**-t'n) *noun*
the devil.
Word Family satanism *noun* worship of
the devil; **satanist** *noun*.
[Hebrew *shatan* adversary]

satanic (sa-**tan**-ik) *adjective*
of Satan, very wicked or evil.
Word Family satanically *adverb*.

satay (**sat**-ay) *noun* also **saté**
a south-east Asian dish consisting of pieces
of spiced barbecued meat or vegetables
cooked on a skewer and usually served
with a peanut sauce.
[Malay]

satchel *noun*
a light leather or canvas bag with a
shoulder strap, e.g. for carrying books.
[Latin *sacellus* little sack]

sate *verb*
to satisfy fully: *My appetite was sated after
the huge meal.*

sateen (sa-**teen**) *noun*
a cotton fabric with a satin-like shine.

satellite (**sat**-a-lite) *noun*
1 any body that revolves around another of
greater mass, including artificial bodies
launched into orbit by human beings.
Compare PLANET (definition 1).
2 a town or country dependent on or
controlled by another.
Word Family satellite *adjective*.
[Latin *satellus* a bodyguard]

satellite dish *noun* (*plural* **satellite
dishes**)
a concave dish-shaped aerial for receiving
broadcasting signals transmitted by
satellite.

satellite television *noun*
the transmission of television programmes
via an artificial satellite, to subscribers
paying a fee and having the appropriate
satellite dish.

satiate (**say**-shi-ate) *verb*
to satisfy to excess.
Word Family satiation (say-shi-**ay**-sh'n)
noun; **satiable** *adjective*; **satiety** (sa-**tie**-a-
tee) *noun* the state of being satiated.
[Latin *satiare* to glut]

satin (**sat**-in) *noun*
a smooth shiny fabric, usually woven from
rayon or silk.
Word Family satiny *adjective* 1 of or like
satin. 2 smooth.
[from the Arabic name of a Chinese town]

satinette *noun* also **satinet**
a type of satin containing cotton.

satin stitch *noun* (*plural* **satin stitches**)
an embroidery stitch consisting of very
close parallel stitches.

satinwood *noun*
the hard light-coloured wood of an Asian
tree, used for making furniture.

satire *noun*
1 the use of mocking or exaggerated
humour to ridicule faults and vices.
2 a piece of writing, song, etc. which does
this.
Word Family satirical (sa-**tirr**-i-k'l),
satiric *adjective* 1 of, like or containing
satire: *a satirical book.* 2 using or fond of
satire: *a satirical author*; **satirically** *adverb*;
satirist (**sat**-a-rist) *noun* a writer of
satires; **satirize, satirise** (**sat**-a-rize) *verb*
to attack or describe in a satire: *This book
satirizes the clergy.*
[Latin *satura* a medley]

satisfaction (sat-iss-**fak**-sh'n) *noun*
1 the act of satisfying: *The satisfaction of his demands was almost impossible.*
2 the state of being satisfied: *I felt satisfaction after my horse won.*
3 something that satisfies: *Your daughter must be a great satisfaction to you.*
Figurative I demand satisfaction for that insult (= reparation, payment).
[Latin *satis* enough + *facere* to make]

satisfactory (sat-iss-**fak**-ta-ree) *adjective*
giving satisfaction, as by meeting the required standard: *Did you find your rooms satisfactory?*
Word Family satisfactorily *adverb*;
satisfactoriness *noun*.

satisfy (**sat**-is-fie) *verb* (**satisfies;
satisfying; satisfied**)
to make happy by supplying needs or demands: *Did my answer satisfy your curiosity?*
Figurative How can I satisfy you that I'm telling the truth? (= convince). □ *I finally satisfied my debt* (= repaid in full).
Word Family satisfied *adjective*;
satisfying *adjective*; **satisfyingly** *adverb*.

satrap *noun*
a subordinate ruler, e.g. of a province.
Word Family satrapy (**sat**-ra-pee) *noun*
(*plural* **satrapies**) the territory ruled by a satrap.
[Persian, district chief]

satsuma (sat-**soo**-ma) *noun*
a type of tangerine with a loose skin.
[after the former Japanese province of *Satsuma*]

saturate (**satch**-a-rate) *verb*
1 to wet thoroughly: *Rain saturated the dry earth.*
2 *Chemistry* to cause a substance to absorb as much as possible of another substance.
Word Family saturated *adjective*.

saturation (satch-a-**ray**-sh'n) *noun*
1 the act of saturating.
2 the state of being saturated.
3 *Weather* the condition of the atmosphere when it can store no more water vapour and any excess moisture will condense as droplets or crystals.
[Latin *saturare* to glut]

saturation point *noun*
the point at which a substance can absorb no more of another substance.

Saturday *noun*
the seventh day of the week, after Friday.
[after the planet *Saturn*]

Saturn *noun*
1 *Roman mythology* the god of fertility and agriculture.
2 *Astronomy* the planet in the solar system sixth from the sun, and surrounded by three rings, one inside the other, probably from a broken-up satellite.

saturnine (**sat**-a-nine) *adjective*
gloomy or morose.
[as if born under the influence of Saturn]

satyr (**sat**-a) *noun*
1 *Greek mythology* a god of the woods, with the body of a man and the ears, horns, tail and legs of a goat or horse, identified with the Roman gods called fauns.
2 a man with a very strong sexual desire.
[from Greek]

satyriasis (sat-a-**rye**-a-sis) *noun*
Psychology an abnormally strong sexual desire in men. Compare NYMPHOMANIA.

sauce (*rhymes with* horse) *noun*
1 a sweet or savoury liquid, usually thickened, served with food to give it extra flavour.
2 (*informal*) impudence or impertinence.
Word Family sauce *verb*; **saucy** *adjective*
(**saucier; sauciest**) (*informal*)
impertinent; **saucily** *adverb*; **sauciness** *noun*.
[Latin *salsus* salted, flavoured]

sauce boat *noun*
a long narrow dish for serving sauce at table.

saucepan *noun*
a round deep metal cooking pot with a detachable lid and a handle.

saucer (**saw**-sa) *noun*
1 a shallow curved dish on which a cup stands.
2 something which has the shape of a saucer, such as a wide shallow depression in land.
[Old French *saussiere* sauce boat]

sauerkraut (**sour**-krowt) *noun*
pickled shredded cabbage.
[German *sauer* sour + *Kraut* cabbage]

sauna (**saw**-na) *noun*
a closed room filled with steam as a form of bath, originally from Finland.

saunter (**sawn**-ta) *verb*
to stroll or wander slowly.
● **saunter** *noun*
1 a leisurely stroll.
2 a leisurely pace.

sausage (**soss**-ij) *noun*
minced meat, such as pork or beef, mixed
with spices, etc. and packed into a
cylindrical skin.
[same root as SAUCE]

sausage roll *noun*
a small lump or cylinder of sausage meat
enclosed in pastry and baked.

sauté (**so**-tay) *verb* (**sautés; sautéing;
sautéed** or **sautéd**)
to cook lightly in a small amount of fat.
• **sauté** *noun* a dish of lightly fried food.
[French]

Sauternes (so-**tern**) *noun*
a rich sweet white wine.

savage (**savv**-ij) *adjective*
1 wild, untamed or uncivilized.
2 fierce or vicious: *a savage glare.*
• **savage** *verb* to maul or injure viciously:
The swimmer was savaged by a shark.
• **savage** *noun* a wild or uncivilized
person.
Word Family **savagery** (savv-ij-ree)
noun 1 the state of being savage: *The
primitive tribe lived in a condition of
savagery.* 2 savage behaviour: *The cruel
king treated his subjects with savagery;*
savagely *adverb;* **savageness** *noun.*
[Latin *silvaticus* of the woods]

savannah (sa-**van**-a) *noun* also **savanna**
a region, usually bordering equatorial
rainforests, which has a wet and a dry
season and a vegetation of grass and
scattered trees.
[Old Spanish *zavana*]

savant (**savv**-'nt) *noun*
a person of great learning or intelligence.
[French, knowing]

save[1] *verb*
1 to rescue or keep safe from danger, harm
or loss: *I was saved from drowning.*
Figurative to save time (= not waste).
2 to keep for future use: *She saved her
money for a holiday.*
• **save** *noun* the act of saving.
Word Family **saver** *noun.*
[Latin *salvus* safe]

save[2] *preposition*
(*formal*) except: *Everyone may leave save
you two.*

saveloy (**savv**-a-loy) *noun*
a highly seasoned dry sausage.
[Italian *cervello* brain (as originally made
of pig's brains)]

saving (**say**-ving) *noun*
1 something which is saved: *The bargain
price means a saving of £10.*

2 (**savings**) any money which has been
saved.
• **saving** *adjective* rescuing or redeeming.
• **saving** *preposition* except.

saving grace *noun*
one good quality which makes up for all
the bad ones: *Her one saving grace is her
loyalty to her friends.*

saviour (**save**-yer) *noun* (*American* **savior**)
1 a person who rescues or saves.
2 (**Saviour**) *Christianity* God or Christ.

savoir-faire (sav-wah-**fair**) *noun*
knowledge of how to act correctly or
tactfully in any situation.
[French *savoir* to know + *faire* to do]

savour (**say**-ver) *noun* (*American* **savor**)
taste, smell or flavour.
• **savour** *verb*
1 to give a savour to: *The chillies savoured
the whole dish.*
2 to enjoy, especially the taste or flavour of
something: *He savoured the spicy cheese.*
Phrase **savour of** to suggest or smack of:
Your behaviour savours of rudeness.
[Latin *sapor* flavour]

savoury (**say**-va-ree) *noun* (*plural*
savouries) (*American* **savory**)
any small tasty food, such as an appetizer
or a course at the beginning or end of a
meal.
• **savoury** *adjective*
1 sharp or spiced, not sweet: *a savoury
biscuit.*
2 having an appetizing taste or smell.
Word Family **savouriness** *noun.*

savoy *noun*
a winter cabbage with wrinkled leaves and
a compact head.
[originally from *Savoy*, France]

savvy *verb* (**savvies; savvying; savvied**)
(*informal*) to understand.
• **savvy** *noun* (*informal*) understanding or
common sense.
[Spanish *sabe* do you know?]

saw[1] *noun*
a tool with a sharp-toothed blade for
cutting, usually by pulling it back and
forth across a surface.
• **saw** *verb* (**saws; sawing; sawed; sawn**
or **sawed**)
1 to use or cut with a saw.
2 to move as though using a saw: *He sawed
the air with his hands.*

saw[2] the past tense of **see**[1].

saw[3] *noun*
a saying such as a proverb or a maxim.

sawbones *noun* (*plural* **sawbones**)
(*dated informal*) a surgeon.

sawdust *noun*
the fine powder or shavings produced by
cutting or sawing wood.

sawfish *noun* (*plural* **sawfish** or
sawfishes)
any of a group of shark-like rays with a
large ridged snout resembling a saw.

sawmill *noun*
a place where logs are cut into boards, etc.

sawn a past participle of **saw**[1].

sawyer *noun*
a person whose occupation is sawing
wood.

Saxe-Coburg-Gotha (sacks-koh-berg-
go-tha) *noun*
the name of the British royal family 1901-
1917.

saxhorn *noun*
a brass musical instrument similar to a
cornet.

saxifrage (saks-i-frayj) *noun*
any of a very large and varied group of
rock plants with tufted leaves.
[Latin *saxum* rock + *frangere* to break]

saxophone (saks-a-fone) *noun*
Music any of a family of wind instruments
with a single reed and a metal body.
Word Family **saxophonist** (sak-**soff**-a-
nist) *noun*.
[after *A. Sax*, 1814-1894, its Belgian
inventor]

say *verb* (**says**; **saying**; **said**)
to speak or express in words.
Figurative I can't say who is right or wrong
(= state with certainty). □ *I'll meet you at,
say, 6 p.m.* (= possibly, approximately).
Phrases **go without saying** *It goes
without saying that you are absolutely correct*
(= is obvious). **that is to say** *in four days'
time, that is to say next Saturday* (= in other
words).
● **say** *noun*
1 what a person has to say: *Have you
finished your say?*
2 the right to take part in decisions, etc.:
a say in the running of the country.
3 a person's turn to speak: *Be quiet, it's my
say now.*

saying *noun*
something said, usually a short well-
known phrase or sentence expressing a
truth, etc.

say-so *noun*
(*informal*) command or authority: *On
whose say-so are you acting?*

scab *noun*
1 the crust that forms over a wound or
sore as it heals.
2 (*informal*) ⇨ BLACKLEG (definition 1).
Word Family **scabby** *adjective*;
scabbiness *noun*.

scabbard (skab-'d) *noun*
a sheath or cover for the blade of a sword,
dagger, etc., usually worn on the belt.

scabies (skay-beez) *noun*
an infectious skin disease caused by mites
burrowing into the skin.
[Latin *scabere* to scratch]

scaffold *noun*
1 a raised platform on which criminals
were formerly executed.
2 any raised framework, such as
scaffolding.

scaffolding (skaff-'l-ding) *noun*
a temporary platform of pipes, posts and
boards, used especially when constructing,
cleaning or repairing a building.

scalar (skay-lar) *adjective*
being a quantity which has only
magnitude and no direction: *Mass and time
are scalar quantities.*
Word Family **scalar** *noun*.

scald (skawld) *verb*
1 to burn or hurt with hot liquid or steam.
2 to heat to just below boiling point.
● **scald** *noun* a burn caused by hot liquid,
steam, etc.
Word Family **scalding** *adjective*.

scale[1] *noun*
1 *Biology* any of the thin flat pieces
forming the skin covering of certain
animals, such as fish and snakes.
2 any small flat flake or piece, e.g. on a
plant.
● **scale** *verb*
1 to remove the scales from: *Please scale
this fish.*
2 to come off in flakes or scales: *The paint
scaled from the wall.*

scale[2] *noun*
1 (*usually* **scales**) a balance or device for
weighing.
2 a pan or dish on a balance.
Phrase **tip the scales, turn the scales**
*The arrival of reinforcements tipped the scales
in our favour* (= influenced events).

scale[3] *noun*
1 a sequence of points at regular intervals
used for measuring, as on a thermometer.
2 *Music* a succession of notes ascending or
descending according to fixed intervals,

especially such a series beginning on a particular note.
3 any arrangement in steps or degrees: *the decimal scale.* □ *a wage scale.*
4 the relative or proportional size or standard of something: *What scale is this map?* □ *Their house is on a modest scale.*
• **scale** *verb*
1 to climb up or over something.
2 to vary in amount according to a fixed scale: *We must scale down our expenses.*
Word Family **scalable** *adjective.*
[Latin *scalae* a ladder]

scalene (skay-leen) *adjective*
(of a triangle) having three unequal sides.

scallion (skal-y'n) *noun*
American an onion, such as a spring onion, which does not develop an enlarged bulb.

scallop (skoll-op) *noun also* **scollop**
1 an edible shellfish consisting of twin shells with ribbed edges held by a muscle.
2 the large fan-shaped shell of a scallop, or a dish of similar shape, used for cooking and serving food.
3 a wavy edge, e.g. on pastry, fabric or a garment.
Word Family **scallop** *verb.*

scally *noun* (*plural* **scallies**)
(*informal*) a roguish or mildly criminal person.

scallywag *noun*
(*informal*) a naughty or mischievous young person.

scalp *noun*
1 *Anatomy* the skin covering the human cranium, usually hair-covered.
2 this covering cut from the head of an enemy and used as a token of victory.
3 any token of victory.
• **scalp** *verb* to cut the scalp from.
Word Family **scalper** *noun.*

scalpel *noun*
a small light knife used in surgical operations and dissections.
[Latin *scalpellum* little chisel]

scaly (skay-lee) *adjective* (**scalier**; **scaliest**)
1 covered with scales: *the scaly skin of a lizard.*
2 (of a person's skin) dry and flaky.
Word Family **scaliness** *noun.*

scam *noun*
(*informal*) a fraudulent scheme.

scamp *noun*
a mischievous or idle person.

scamper *verb*
to run or move lightly and quickly.
Word Family **scamper** *noun.*

scampi (skam-pee) *noun*
large prawns, usually fried in batter or breadcrumbs.
[Italian]

scan *verb* (**scans**; **scanning**; **scanned**)
1 to examine closely: *He scanned her face for a sign of feeling.*
2 to sweep broadly across: *The radio telescope scanned the skies.*
Figurative I *only scanned the newspaper this morning* (= glanced at).
3 to obtain an image of an internal part of the body for diagnosis of illness, e.g. using X-rays or ultrasonic waves.
4 to examine stored computer data usually to retrieve information.
5 *Poetry* to analyse the metre of lines.
Word Family **scan** *noun*; **scanner** *noun*
1 a person or thing that scans, e.g. a device used to obtain an image of an internal part of the body in medical diagnosis. **2** a device used to convert printed text or pictures into a form which can be stored or processed by a computer.

scandal (skan-d'l) *noun*
1 a shameful or disgraceful action or situation: *It is a scandal that the innocent person was imprisoned.*
2 sensational or malicious gossip: *Have you heard the scandal about Mrs Smith and the milkman?*
3 a person whose conduct brings disgrace: *He is a scandal to the profession.*
Word Family **scandalize**, **scandalise** *verb* to shock.
[Greek *skandalon* a stumbling block]

scandalous *adjective*
causing or full of scandal: *It is a scandalous rumour, and not based on truth.*
Figurative His *behaviour is scandalous* (= shocking, disgraceful).
Word Family **scandalously** *adverb.*

scansion (skan-sh'n) *noun*
Poetry the analysis of the metre of lines.

scant *adjective*
very little or barely enough: *She paid scant attention to my advice.*

scantling *noun*
a narrow board or beam.

scanty *adjective* (**scantier**; **scantiest**)
scant or inadequate: *The poor rain meant only a scanty harvest.*
Word Family **scantily** *adverb*;
scantiness *noun.*

scapegoat *noun*
a person blamed or punished for things others have done.
[after the ancient Jewish practice of symbolically placing the people's sins onto a goat which was then driven away into the wilderness]

scapula (**skap**-yoo-la) *noun* (*plural* **scapulae** (**skap**-yoo-lee) or **scapulas**)
also called **shoulder blade**.
Anatomy either of two large triangular bones behind the shoulder.
Word Family **scapular** *adjective*.
[Latin]

scar[1] *noun*
a mark left by a healed cut or wound, e.g. on the human skin or on a plant where a leaf was once attached.
Figurative Your gossip left a scar on my reputation (= blemish).
• **scar** *verb* (**scars; scarring; scarred**) to mark with a scar or scars: *The bombs scarred the countryside with giant craters.*
[Greek *eskhara* a scab]

scar[2] *noun*
a steep rocky place or cliff.

scarab (**skarr**-ab) *noun*
1 a type of beetle considered sacred by the ancient Egyptians.
2 an image or carving in the shape of a scarab.
[from Greek]

scarce (skairce) *adjective*
in short supply: *Tomatoes were scarce during the floods.*
Phrase **make oneself scarce** to leave a place or keep out of the way.
Word Family **scarcely** *adverb* barely or hardly: *There were scarcely 25 people at the meeting*; **scarcity** (**skair**-si-tee) *noun* (*plural* **scarcities**) shortness of supply: *The scarcity of tomatoes was caused by the floods*; **scarceness** *noun*.
[Latin *excerptus* picked out]

scare *verb*
to frighten.
• **scare** *noun* a feeling of fear or alarm: *You gave me quite a scare.* □ *After the cyclone there was a scare of cholera.*
Word Family **scared** *adjective*.

scarecrow *noun*
an object, usually a figure of a man in old clothes, set up to scare birds away from a crop.

scarf[1] *noun* (*plural* **scarves** or **scarfs**)
a strip or square of cloth worn around the head or neck.
Word Family **scarf** *verb*.

scarf[2] *noun* (*plural* **scarfs**)
a joint made by fitting two tapered pieces together.

scarify (**skarr**-i-fie) *verb* (**scarifies; scarifying; scarified**)
1 to scratch or break the surface of.
2 to criticize severely.
Word Family **scarification** (skarr-if-i-**kay**-sh'n) *noun*.

scarlet *noun*
a vivid reddish-orange colour.
Word Family **scarlet** *adjective*.

scarlet fever *noun* also called **scarlatina** (skar-la-**tee**-na).
an infectious bacterial disease causing tonsillitis and a red rash.

scarp *noun*
a steep slope or ridge of rock.
[from Italian]

scarper *verb*
(*informal*) to run away, especially after having done something wrong.
[rhyming slang *Scapa Flow* = go]

scarves
a plural of **scarf**[1].

scary (**skair**-i) *adjective* (**scarier; scariest**)
(*informal*) frightening.

scat *interjection*
(*informal*) go away!
[shortening of SCATTER]

scathing (**skay**-thing) *adjective*
severely critical or scornful: *a scathing review of a bad film.*
Word Family **scathingly** *adverb*.

scatology (ska-**tol**-a-jee) *noun*
the continual use in literature of images of human waste, etc.
Word Family **scatological** (skat-a-**loj**-i-k'l) *adjective*.
[Greek *skatos* of dung + -*logy*]

scatter *verb*
to send, move or distribute in many different directions: *We scattered the seed on the ploughed land.* □ *The crowd scattered when it heard the sirens.*
Word Family **scattering** *noun* a scattered number or quantity.

scatterbrain *noun*
a person who cannot remember or concentrate on things.
Word Family **scatterbrained** *adjective*.

scatter diagram *noun*
a graph with points plotted along two coordinate axes, e.g. 0x and 0y, to indicate

any relationship between the variables *x* and *y*.

scatty *adjective* (**scattier; scattiest**) (*informal*) scatterbrained or silly.

scavenger (skavv-in-ja) *noun*
any person or animal that searches for or lives on decaying or discarded material.
***Word Family* scavenge** *verb* to search for or amongst, especially for discarded matter which may be used, etc.

scenario (sin-**ar**-i-o) *noun*
a detailed outline of the plot of a play, film, ballet or opera.
***Word Family* scenarist** *noun* a writer of scenarios.
[Italian]

scene (seen) *noun*
1 a place or area where action occurs: *the scene of the crime.*
2 a view: *This painting is a scene of Paris.*
3 an incident or outburst: *There was a terrible scene when I came home late.*
4 (*informal*) world, sphere of influence: *The music scene is always changing.*
5 a minor division of an act in a play, etc., usually with a fixed setting.
***Phrases* behind the scenes** privately or secretly. **on the scene** present: *Were you on the scene at the time?*

> The word **scene** came into English from Latin *scena*, which was derived from the Greek *skené*. It originally meant a 'tent' or 'booth'. Plays were presented in such booths and the word *skené* came to mean a backdrop for a play.

scenery (**seen**-a-ree) *noun*
1 the natural features of a landscape: *impressive mountain scenery.*
2 the structures and props used to decorate a stage during a play, film, etc.

scenic (**seen**-ik) *adjective*
of or having fine or impressive scenery.
***Word Family* scenically** *adverb.*

scent (sent) *noun*
1 a perfume.
2 a smell that is left in passing, such as one that can be followed by an animal.
3 the sense of smell: *Dogs hunt by scent.*
• **scent** *verb*
1 to detect by or as if by smelling: *The dogs scented a rabbit.* □ *to scent trouble.*
2 to make fragrant with scent: *The flowers scented the whole house.*
***Word Family* scented** *adjective.*
[Latin *sentire* to perceive]

sceptic (skep-tik) *noun* (*American* **skeptic**)
a person who doubts the truth of a claim, theory or belief.
***Word Family* sceptical** *adjective* unwilling to believe without questioning or doubting; **sceptically** *adverb*; **scepticism** (**skep**-ti-sizm) *noun* an attitude of doubt or disbelief.
[Greek *skeptikos* thoughtful]

sceptre (**sep**-ta) *noun* (*American* **scepter**)
a rod, often highly decorated, carried by a ruler as a symbol of power.
[Greek *skeptron* a staff]

schedule (**shed**-yool *or* **sked**-yool) *noun*
1 a timetable of events, duties, appointments, etc.
2 a written list or table of classifications, etc.: *a schedule of poisons.*
• **schedule** *verb* to arrange or put in a schedule: *You are scheduled to give a speech after the dinner.*
[Greek *skhedé* a papyrus strip]

schema (**skee**-ma) *noun* (*plural* **schemata**) (**skee**-ma-ta)
a diagram, plan, chart or scheme.
***Word Family* schematic** (skee-**mat**-ik) *adjective*; **schematically** *adverb.*

schematize, schematise (**skee**-ma-tize) *verb*
to arrange or organize according to a plan or scheme.

scheme (skeem) *noun*
any plan designed to accomplish something.
Figurative a colour scheme (= system, arrangement).
• **scheme** *verb* to plan or plot, especially dishonestly.
***Word Family* schemer** *noun.*
[Greek *skhema* form]

scherzo (**skert**-so) *noun*
a lively rhythmic piece of music, often the second or third movement of a sonata or symphony.
[Italian, sport or jest]

schilling (**shill**-ing) *noun*
the basic unit of money in Austria.

schism (sizm *or* skizm) *noun*
the splitting of a group or organization into opposing parties.
***Word Family* schismatic** (siz-**mat**-ik) *adjective* of or guilty of schism.
[Greek *skhisma* a cleft]

schist (shist) *noun*
Geology a medium-grained metamorphic rock, often with a glistening appearance, which splits unevenly into flaky sheets.
[Greek *skhistos* split]

schizoid (skits-oyd) *adjective*
resembling or tending towards schizophrenia.
• **schizoid** *noun* a schizoid person.
[schiz(ophrenia) + -oid]

schizophrenia (skits-o-free-ni-a) *noun*
any of a wide group of psychoses characterized by the inability to act or think realistically, sometimes marked by delusions and withdrawal into a private world.
Word Family **schizophrenic** (skits-o-fren-ik) *noun* a person suffering from schizophrenia; **schizophrenic** *adjective*.
[Greek *skhizein* to split + *phren* mind]

schmaltz (shmawlts) *noun*
(*informal*) excessive sentimentality, especially in art, music, etc.
Word Family **schmaltzy** *adjective* (**schmaltzier; schmaltziest**).
[Yiddish, lard, grease]

schmuck (shmuk) *noun*
(*American informal*) a fool.
[Yiddish]

schnapps *noun*
a strong alcoholic drink made from potatoes.
[German]

scholar (skoll-a) *noun*
1 a person specializing in a field of study.
2 a pupil or student, especially one who has won an award.
Word Family **scholarly** *adjective* 1 of or like a scholar. 2 showing knowledge or careful study: *a scholarly text*; **scholarliness** *noun*.

scholarship (skoll-a-ship) *noun*
1 a sum of money given to a student to continue his or her studies.
2 knowledge or skill gained by advanced study: *The professor was a man of great scholarship*.

scholastic (skol-ass-tik) *adjective*
of schools or learning: *What is your scholastic record?*
• **scholastic** *noun* a scholarly or pedantic person.
Word Family **scholasticism** (skol-ass-ti-sizm) *noun*.

school¹ (skool) *noun*
1 an institution for training or instruction, especially one for children.

2 the body of people attending such an institution.
3 any regular course of lessons or meetings for instruction.
Figurative There's no school today (= lessons).
4 a university or college faculty.
5 a group of people who have a common style or method: *the Heidelberg school of painters*.
• **school** *verb* to train or instruct: *I'll school you in the art of singing*.
Word Family **schooling** *noun* education.
[Greek *skholé* leisure, disputation, school]

school² *noun*
a large group of fish swimming together.
[same root as SHOAL¹]

schoolboy *noun*
a boy who attends school.

schoolgirl *noun*
a girl who attends school.

school run *noun*
the daily routine of transporting children to and from school.

schooner (skoo-na) *noun*
1 a ship with two or more masts, all fore-and-aft rigged. Compare SHIP *noun* (definition 3).
2 a larger than normal glass for sherry or beer.

sciatica (sigh-at-i-ka) *noun*
a pain in the area of the hip and thigh, sometimes due to pressure on a nerve.
Word Family **sciatic** *adjective*.
[Greek *iskhion* hip joint]

science (sigh-'nce) *noun*
1 a particular body of knowledge obtained by systematic observation and testing.
2 the systematic study or methods used to obtain this knowledge.
3 a branch of knowledge or study, such as chemistry or botany, concerned with the investigation of natural or physical substances, facts, laws, etc.
Word Family **scientist** *noun* a person skilled or trained in science.
[Latin *sciens* knowing]

science fiction *noun*
any fiction, often set in the future, that uses scientific facts or theories in an imaginative way.

science park *noun*
an area where scientific research and development is carried out.

scientific (sigh-'n-tiff-ik) *adjective*
1 of or relating to science: *scientific instruments*.

2 of or according to the principles or methods of science: *a scientific mind.*
Word Family scientifically *adverb.*

sci-fi *noun*
(*informal*) science fiction.

scimitar (**simm**-i-ta) *noun*
a sword with a curved blade and one cutting edge, formerly used by Turkish and Persian soldiers.

scintillating (**sin**-ti-lay-ting) *adjective*
1 sparkling or flashing.
2 witty.
Word Family scintillate *verb;*
scintillation (sin-ti-**lay**-sh'n) *noun;*
scintilla (sin-**till**-a) *noun* a spark or trace.
[Latin *scintilla* a spark]

scion (**sigh**-on) *noun*
1 a young member of a family.
2 a shoot of a plant with one or more buds, especially one used for grafting.

scissors (**sizz**-erz) *plural noun*
1 an instrument consisting of two sharp blades with handles, joined at the centre so that they may open and close for cutting.
2 any position or movement which resembles the opening and closing of scissors.
[Latin *scissus* cut]

sclerosis (skle-**ro**-sis) *noun*
1 a hardening or thickening of a tissue.
2 also **multiple sclerosis** a disease causing progressive deterioration of the nervous system.
[Greek *skleroun* to harden + -*osis*]

scoff[1] *verb*
to deride or treat with contempt: *He scoffed at my fears.*
Word Family scoff *noun* **a jeer; scoffer** *noun;* **scoffingly** *adverb.*

scoff[2] *verb*
(*informal*) to eat greedily and quickly.

scold *verb*
to criticize or find fault angrily
• **scold** *noun* an old word for a person who scolds.

scollop ⇨ SCALLOP.

scone (skon) *noun*
a small light round cake, usually eaten with butter.

scoop *noun*
1 a utensil with a shovel or cup-like holder at one end for lifting loose or soft substances such as sugar or ice cream.
2 (*informal*) an important news item which a reporter or publisher obtains before anyone else.

• **scoop** *verb*
1 to lift with or as if with a scoop: *Scoop the coal onto the fire.* □ *He scooped the papers up in his arms.*
2 (*informal*) to obtain a newspaper scoop.

scoop neck *noun*
a wide curved neck on a woman's dress or top.

scoot *verb*
1 (*informal*) to move very quickly.
2 (*informal*) to run away.

scooter *noun*
1 a two-wheeled vehicle, used by children, with a flat board to stand on and an upright support for a handlebar.
2 also **motor scooter** a light motorcycle with small wheels.
• **scooter** *verb* to use or go on a scooter.

scope *noun*
the space which something exists within, covers or is limited to: *He has a wide scope of knowledge.*
Figurative *There is little scope for promotion in that job* (= opportunity).
[Greek *skopos* a target]

scorch *verb*
to burn slightly: *I've scorched my shirt with the iron.*
Figurative *We scorched along at 200 km an hour* (= raced, sped).
• **scorch** *noun* (*plural* **scorches**) a slight burn.
Word Family scorcher *noun* 1 a person or thing that scorches. 2 (*informal*) a very hot day; **scorching** *adjective;* **scorchingly** *adverb.*

scorched earth *noun*
the process of destroying things which could be useful to an invading army, e.g. by burning crops.

score *noun*
1 the points won by a player or team.
Figurative *Add up the bill and I'll pay the score* (= total).
2 a line or scratch.
3 any written music, especially for a group of players or singers, showing the parts for each instrument or voice printed one under the other.
4 the background music of a film, etc.
5 a group of twenty: *fourscore years* (= eighty).
6 (**scores**) very many: *Scores of lives were lost.*
7 (*informal*) the state of progress: *What's the score on the new space programme?*
8 a matter: *Settle your mind on that score.*

• **score** *verb*
1 to win points in a game.
Figurative She scored a great success with her poetry (= gained).
2 to keep a record of points won.
3 to be worth in points: *Red aces score twenty.*
4 to mark or cut with lines, notches or scratches: *The lashes of the whip scored the slave's back.*
5 to arrange music for an orchestra or other group.
Phrase **score off** *You couldn't resist the opportunity to score off her* (= gain an advantage over).
Word Family **scorer** *noun.*

scoria (skaw-ri-a) *noun*
a very porous dark rock formed from fragments of lava that have been blown out of a volcano and quickly cooled.
[Greek, refuse]

scorn *noun*
extreme lack of respect.
• **scorn** *verb*
1 to feel or show scorn for: *She scorns all politicians.*
2 to reject with scorn: *I scorned his offer to help.*
Word Family **scornful** *adjective* full of scorn; **scornfully** *adverb.*

Scorpio *noun*
Astrology a group of stars, the eighth sign of the Zodiac; the sign of the Scorpion.

scorpion *noun*
an arachnid, usually found in warm climates, having a long narrow tail with a poison gland.
[from Greek]

scotch *verb*
1 to put an end to: *I'll have to scotch that rumour.*
2 an old word meaning 'to maim or cripple'.

Scotch *noun* (*plural* **Scotches**)
short form of **Scotch whisky** a whisky distilled in Scotland from barley and malt.

Scotch mist *noun*
a very fine light drizzle.

scot-free *adjective*
completely free from any penalty or harm.
[from an old word, *scot*, tax or payment]

scoundrel *noun*
a wicked or dishonourable person.

scour¹ (*rhymes with* power) *verb*
1 to clean or polish by hard rubbing: *Scour the saucepans.*
2 to remove dirt, grease, etc.: *to scour wool.*

Figurative The storm scoured a gully in the hillside (= cleared out).
3 (of cattle, etc.) to have diarrhoea.
• **scour** *noun* the act of scouring.
Word Family **scourer** *noun* a person or thing that scours, especially a pad for cleaning saucepans, etc.

scour² *verb*
to search thoroughly and energetically: *She scoured the city looking for work.*

scourge (skerj) *noun*
a whip used for punishment.
Figurative War is a scourge of civilization (= affliction, source of suffering).
• **scourge** *verb*
1 to whip.
2 to cause suffering to.

scout *noun*
1 a person sent out to gain information.
2 (**Scout**) a member of the Scout Association, a youth organization which emphasizes self-reliance and proficiency in a wide range of activities.
• **scout** *verb* to act as a scout.
Figurative Scout around for some coffee (= hunt).

scowl *noun*
an angry or bad-tempered expression.
• **scowl** *verb* to have or make a scowl.

scrabble *verb*
1 to scrape or claw.
2 to struggle to possess or obtain.
• **scrabble** *noun*
1 a scramble or scratching.
2 (**Scrabble**) (*trademark*) a word game for two to four players.

scrag *noun*
1 (*informal*) a skinny person or animal.
2 the butcher's name for the thin part of the neck, especially in mutton.
Word Family **scraggy** *adjective* (**scraggier; scraggiest**) thin and bony.

scram *interjection*
(*informal*) go away!

scramble *verb*
1 to move, crawl or climb hurriedly.
Figurative Children scrambled for the spilt sweets (= struggled, scuffled).
2 to mix or put together confusedly.
3 *Radio* to send a jumbled signal which can only be translated by a special receiver.
• **scramble** *noun*
1 a confused or wild struggle, scuffle, etc.: *There was a violent scramble to get the last two seats.*
2 a motorcycle race over rough ground.

Word Family **scrambler** *noun* a device for scrambling radiotelephone messages.

scrambled egg *noun*
eggs beaten with milk and butter and cooked gently.

scrap[1] *noun*
1 a small piece or fragment, especially a remnant.
2 anything useless or unwanted.
3 scrap metal.
4 (**scraps**) leftover food.
• **scrap** *verb* (**scraps; scrapping; scrapped**)
1 to discard as useless or unwanted: *Let's scrap that idea and start again.*
2 to make into scrap.

scrap[2] *noun*
(*informal*) a fight or argument.

scrapbook *noun*
a book with blank pages in which press cuttings, pictures, etc. are pasted.

scrape *verb*
to rub or scratch, especially in order to remove an outer layer: *Do not peel or scrape the potatoes before cooking.*
Phrases **scrape through** *Peter scraped through his exams* (– only just succeeded in). **scrape together, scrape up** *I managed to scrape together enough money for a ticket* (= collect with difficulty).
• **scrape** *noun*
1 the act of scraping.
2 a sound or mark made by scraping.
3 (*informal*) a fight.
4 (*informal*) a difficult or embarrassing situation.
Word Family **scraper** *noun* something which scrapes, especially a device used for this purpose; **scraping** *noun* 1 the act or sound of rubbing or scratching.
2 (**scrapings**) any pieces or parts which are scraped.

scrapie *noun*
a disease of the central nervous system in sheep, related to BSE in cattle.

scrap metal *noun*
any pieces of metal which can be used or processed again.

scrappy *adjective* (**scrappier; scrappiest**)
like or made up of scraps or fragments.
Figurative The plumber did a very scrappy job fixing the pipes (= careless).
Word Family **scrappily** *adverb*.

scratch *verb*
1 to mark, cut or tear with something sharp or rough: *Be careful those thorns don't scratch you.*

2 to rub with a grating sound or effect, e.g. with the fingernails to relieve itching.
3 to erase or cross off: *Your name has been scratched from our records.*
Figurative Several horses have been scratched from the race (= withdrawn).
Phrase **scratch the surface** *This new book on the Roman Empire only scratches the surface of such a big subject* (= covers superficially).
• **scratch** *noun* (*plural* **scratches**)
1 the act of scratching: *The dog had a vigorous scratch at its fleas.*
2 a mark left by scratching.
3 *Sport* a score, time or starting position with no handicap added or subtracted.
Phrases **from scratch** *Tell me your story again from scratch* (= from the beginning).
up to scratch *His playing has not been up to scratch because of his injury* (= at a good enough standard).
• **scratch** *adjective*
1 chosen at random: *a scratch search party assembled at once.*
2 *Sport* without a handicap in a competition or race.
Word Family **scratcher** *noun*;
scratching *noun*; **scratchy** *adjective* (**scratchier; scratchiest**) 1 making a scratching noise or movement. 2 uneven or disorganized; **scratchily** *adverb*;
scratchiness *noun*.

scratch card *noun*
a card having a section covered with a coating which can be scratched away to reveal whether a prize has been won.

scrawl *verb*
to write hastily or carelessly.
Word Family **scrawl** *noun*; **scrawly** *adjective*.

scrawny *adjective* (**scrawnier; scrawniest**)
thin or bony.
Word Family **scrawniness** *noun*.

scream *verb*
to make a loud, sharp or violent cry or sound: *The child screamed in pain.*
Figurative Bright colours would scream in such a small room (= be very conspicuous).
• **scream** *noun*
1 a loud piercing sound or cry.
2 (*informal*) a person or thing that is very funny.
Word Family **screamingly** *adverb*
extremely: *screamingly funny.*

scree *noun*
a wide expanse of small stones piled up on a mountain slope, which slide away underfoot.

screech *verb*
to make a harsh shrill cry or sound.
Word Family **screech** *noun* (*plural* **screeches**); **screechy** *adjective* (**screechier; screechiest**).

screed *noun*
1 a long speech or piece of writing.
2 *Building* a strip of wood or plaster used for levelling the plaster on a surface.
3 *Building* a finishing layer of plaster or concrete.

screen *noun*
1 something which divides, protects, hides or shelters, especially any of various covered frames, etc.
2 a smooth surface on which slides, films, etc. may be projected.
3 (*informal*) films or the profession of acting in films: *Humphrey Bogart was a star of the screen for many years.*
4 the fluorescent end of the picture tube in a television set, where electric currents are changed into pictures.
• **screen** *verb*
1 to hide, protect or shelter: *Clouds screened the sun from our sight.*
Figurative *All applicants for the job were screened by the committee* (= checked closely).
2 to show on a screen: *The society is screening a travel film tonight.*
Word Family **screening** *noun*.

screenplay *noun*
a detailed script of a film, usually including technical descriptions such as camera positions, etc.

screen-printing *noun*
a method of printing by squeezing ink through a stretched fabric screen, prepared by blocking off non-printing areas with a stencil.

screen saver *noun*
Computers a program with a moving pattern, used to protect the screen.

screenwriter *noun*
a person who writes screenplays.
Word Family **screenwriting** *noun*.

screw *noun*
1 a metal pin with a head and a spiral thread around its length, used to fasten wood, metal, etc. together.
2 a twisting or turning movement of or like a screw: *Give that lid another screw.*

3 something twisted in such a way: *a screw of paper.*
4 a propeller.
5 (*informal*) a prison warder.
6 (*informal*) salary or wages.
Phrases **have a screw loose** (*informal*) to be mad or eccentric. **put the screws on** (*informal*) to use force or pressure, especially in order to persuade.
• **screw** *verb*
1 to attach, fasten or tighten by means of a screw: *Screw down the lid of the box.*
2 to twist into position: *Screw the cap on the jar.*
Figurative *She screwed her face into a grimace of pain* (= contorted). □ *He screwed up the letter and threw it away* (= pressed and twisted into a ball). □ *He screwed up his courage and asked for a holiday* (= gathered, forced).

screwball *noun*
(*American informal*) an eccentric person.
Word Family **screwball** *adjective*.

screwdriver *noun*
1 a tool with a narrow shaped end which fits into the slot in the head of a screw and is turned to drive it into or withdraw it from a surface.
2 an alcoholic drink made with vodka and orange juice.

screw thread *noun* ⇨ THREAD *noun* (definition 3).

screw top *noun*
a lid that can be screwed on to the top of a bottle or jar.

screwy *adjective* (**screwier; screwiest**)
(*informal*) mad or peculiar.

scribble *verb*
1 to write or draw carelessly.
2 to make meaningless marks or lines.
• **scribble** *noun* any careless handwriting or written work.
Word Family **scribbler** *noun*.
[Latin *scribere* to write]

scribe[1] *noun*
1 *History* a person employed to make copies of manuscripts, etc.
2 *History* a teacher of Jewish laws or keeper of Jewish records.
Word Family **scribal** *adjective*.

scribe[2] *verb*
to mark or score something with a pointed instrument.
• **scribe** *noun* a pointed instrument for marking things.

scrimmage (**skrim**-ij) *noun*
a rough or disorganized struggle.

Word Family scrimmage *verb*.
[alteration of SKIRMISH]

scrimp *verb*
to skimp or be frugal: *She scrimps on food so that she can buy more clothes.*

scrip *noun*
a provisional document entitling the holder to a share in the stock of a business company.
[abbreviation of *subscription receipt*]

script *noun*
1 handwriting: *She has a clear legible script.*
2 a copy of the text of a play, film, etc. used by an actor or director, e.g. for rehearsing.

scripture (skrip-cher) *noun* also **scriptures**
any sacred writing or book regarded as a religious authority, such as the Christian Bible.
Word Family scriptural *adjective* of or according to scripture; **scripturally** *adverb*.
[Latin *scriptus* written]

scroll (skrole) *noun*
1 a roll of paper, especially parchment, used for writing, etc.
2 something which has a coiled or partly rolled form, such as a decoration on a column, etc.
• **scroll** *verb Computers* to move through text on the screen, e.g. by moving the cursor up or down.

Scrooge (skrooj) *noun*
a miserly or mean person.
[after *Ebenezer Scrooge*, a miserly old man in Charles Dickens' *A Christmas Carol*]

scrotum (skro-tum) *noun* (*plural* **scrota** or **scrotums**)
Anatomy the sac in males which hangs between the legs and contains the testes.
[Latin]

scrounge *verb*
(*informal*) to beg, borrow or gather, especially by wheedling.
Word Family scrounger *noun*.

scrub[1] *verb* (**scrubs; scrubbing; scrubbed**)
1 to rub vigorously in order to clean.
2 (*informal*) to remove or cancel: *He was scrubbed from the team.*
Word Family scrub *noun*.

scrub[2] *noun*
an area covered with low trees or bushes.

scrubby *adjective* (**scrubbier; scrubbiest**)
1 covered with scrub or undergrowth.
2 inferior, shabby or wretched.

scruff *noun*
the back of the neck.

scruffy *adjective* (**scruffier; scruffiest**)
untidy or dirty.
Word Family scruffily *adverb*; **scruffiness** *noun*.
[alteration of *scurfy*]

scrum *noun*
1 a stage in a rugby game at which the opposing forwards pack down and push against one another.
2 the players who take part in the scrum.

scrummage (skrum-ij) *noun*
1 a rugby scrum.
2 a struggle or fight.
Word Family scrummage *verb*.
[alteration of SKIRMISH]

scrumptious (skrump-shus) *adjective*
(*informal*) delicious or splendid.

scrumpy *noun*
a potent dry cider that is famous in south-west England.
[dialect *scrump* a small apple]

scrunchy *noun* (*plural* **scrunchies**) also **scrunchie**
a fabric-covered elastic band used to fasten the hair in a ponytail.

scruple (skroo-p'l) *noun*
1 (*usually* **scruples**) a hesitation or objection due to conscience or moral principles.
2 a unit of mass in the apothecaries' system, equal to 20 grains, about 1·3 g.
Word Family scruple *verb* to have scruples; **scrupulous** (skroo-pew-lus) *adjective* 1 precise or carefully exact: *She copied the text with scrupulous care.* 2 having a conscience or moral principles; **scrupulously** *adverb*; **scrupulousness** *noun*.
[Latin *scrupulus* a rough pebble, an uneasy feeling]

scrutineer (skroo-ti-neer) *noun*
a person who checks that votes have been correctly made and counted in an election.

scrutinize, scrutinise (skroo-ti-nize) *verb*
to examine closely or carefully.
Word Family scrutiny *noun* (*plural* **scrutinies**).

scuba (skoo-ba) *noun*
an aqualung.
[from s(elf) + c(ontained) + u(nderwater) + b(reathing) + a(pparatus)]

The word **scuba** is a kind of abbreviation since it is composed of the initial letters of the words which it stands for. However, since the letters form an actual pronounceable word, rather than simply being a series of letters like *BBC*, it is not an abbreviation but an acronym. Acronyms are becoming increasingly common in English. *Aids* is one of the most well known of these.

scud *verb* (**scuds; scudding; scudded**)
to move or race along swiftly.
Word Family scud *noun*.

Scud missile *noun*
a long-range surface-to-surface missile designed to carry nuclear and other warheads, used by Iraq in the Gulf War.
[NATO code name]

scuff *verb*
1 to scrape or shuffle when walking.
2 to mark or wear away by use.
• **scuff** *noun*
1 the act or sound of scuffing.
2 a mark made by scuffing.

scuffle *verb*
1 to struggle or fight confusedly.
2 to scamper noisily.
• **scuffle** *noun*
1 a confused struggle.
2 a scuffling noise.

scull *noun*
1 *Rowing* a racing boat for one person with a pair of oars.
2 *Rowing* either of a pair of oars used by one person.
Word Family scull *verb*; **sculler** *noun*.

scullery (skull-a-ree) *noun* (*plural* **sculleries**)
a small room for kitchen work such as washing up.
[Latin *scutella* a salver]

scullion (skull-y'n) *noun*
an old word for a kitchen servant.
[Old French *escouillon* a dishcloth]

sculpture (skulp-cher) *noun*
1 the modelling, carving or constructing of three-dimensional objects.
2 any object or objects created in this way.
Word Family sculpt, sculpture *verb* to carve or make a sculpture; **sculptor, sculptress** *noun* a person who practises sculpture; **sculptural** *adjective*; **sculpturally** *adverb*; **sculpturesque** *adjective* having the qualities of a sculpture.

scum *noun*
1 a layer of impure or waste matter on a liquid.
2 (*informal*) someone or something worthless or vile.
• **scum** *verb* (**scums; scumming; scummed**)
1 to become covered with scum.
2 to remove scum.
Word Family scummy *adjective* (**scummier; scummiest**) 1 covered with scum. 2 (*informal*) worthless.

scupper *noun*
an opening in the side of a ship at deck level to let water drain away.
• **scupper** *verb* to sink a ship deliberately.
Figurative *The announcement scuppered our plans* (= thwarted).

scurf *noun*
dandruff or any scaly crust formed on a surface.

scurrilous *adjective*
1 outrageously abusive.
2 coarsely jocular.
Word Family scurrilously *adverb*; **scurrility** (skurr-ill-i-tee), **scurrilousness** *noun*.

scurry *verb* (**scurries; scurrying; scurried**)
to move or rush quickly.
• **scurry** *noun* a rushing noise or movement.

scurvy *noun*
a disease due to a lack of vitamin C in the diet, causing swollen gums, anaemia and bruising.
• **scurvy** *adjective* (**scurvier; scurviest**) an old word meaning 'mean or contemptible'.
Word Family scurvily *adverb*.

scuttle[1] *noun*
a coal scuttle.

scuttle[2] *verb*
to run or move hurriedly.
Word Family scuttle *noun*.

scuttle[3] *noun*
a small rectangular opening with a movable cover in a ship's deck or side.
• **scuttle** *verb* to sink a ship by cutting holes in its sides or bottom.

scythe (si*the*) *noun*
a long-handled farm tool with a long thin slightly curved blade for reaping grass, etc. Compare SICKLE.
• **scythe** *verb* to cut with a scythe.

sea *noun*
1 an area of an ocean, often surrounded by land.
2 the ocean.
Figurative A sea of faces was turned towards the stage (= large expanse or mass).
3 *Astronomy* any of the smooth featureless areas on the moon, formerly believed to contain water.
Phrase **at sea** *I'm all at sea with maths* (= puzzled, bewildered).

sea anchor *noun*
a device, usually a canvas cone held open at the wider end, trailed behind a ship to slow and steady it.

sea anemone *noun*
a non-mobile marine animal having a circular body with a ring of tentacles to trap food from the water.

seabird *noun*
any bird, such as the seagull or the albatross, which is usually found around the coast or sea.

seaboard *noun*
the coastline or land near the sea.

sea cow ⇨ DUGONG.

sea dog *noun*
a sailor with many years of experience.

sea elephant *noun*
a large seal with a trunk-like nose, found in Arctic and Antarctic waters.

seafarer (see-fair-a) *noun*
a sailor or traveller on the sea.
Word Family **seafaring** *adjective* travelling by or working at sea.

seafood *noun*
shellfish used as food.

seafront *noun*
any land or road which borders the very edge of the sea.

seagoing *adjective*
built for or travelling at sea.

seagull ⇨ GULL¹.

sea horse *noun*
any of a group of small fish with a long tail and a beaked head.

seakale *noun*
a winter vegetable, the blanched shoots of which have a delicate flavour.

seal¹ *noun*
1 a device, such as a stamp or ring, with a raised engraved mark which is impressed onto wax or a similar surface.
2 the impression made by such a device, especially as a token attached to a document to indicate authenticity, consent, etc.
Figurative This product has the company's seal of approval (= pledge).
3 any thing or substance which closes, fixes or prevents leakage, exposure, etc.
Phrases **set the seal on** to approve or confirm. **under seal** (*formal*) having an official seal.
● **seal** *verb*
1 to fix or close with or as if with a seal: *Seal all the envelopes.*
2 to close so as to be airtight: *Seal the jars of jam after cooling.*
Figurative The nations sealed the cultural agreement (= confirmed, approved). □ *The accident sealed her fate* (= fixed firmly).
[Latin *sigilla*]

seal² *noun*
any of various large fish-eating marine mammals with a sleek furry body.

sealant *noun*
any substance, such as liquid or wax, used to seal or protect a surface.

sea legs *plural noun*
(*informal*) the ability to walk steadily on a ship or not become seasick.

sealer¹ *noun*
1 a coat of paint, varnish, etc. used to seal a surface.
2 a person or device that attaches or impresses seals onto a surface.

sealer² *noun*
a person or boat taking part in hunting seals.

sea level *noun*
the height of the sea, especially when it is halfway between high and low tide.

sealing wax *noun*
a resinous substance, originally of beeswax, melted and used to seal envelopes, packages and documents.

sea lion *noun*
any of various large seals with prominent ears, found in the Pacific Ocean.

seam *noun*
1 a line of sewing joining two pieces of cloth.
2 any line, ridge, etc., especially one which joins edges.
3 a comparatively thin stratum, such as a coal stratum.
● **seam** *verb*
1 to join with a seam.
2 to become wrinkled, cracked or lined.
Word Family **seamless** *adjective* having no seams or gaps.

seaman noun (plural **seamen**)
a member of a ship's crew other than an officer.
Word Family **seamanship** noun the theory, practice or skill of handling a ship.

sea mile noun
a unit of length equal to about 1·9 km.

seamstress noun (plural **seamstresses**)
a woman whose work is sewing.

seamy adjective (**seamier; seamiest**)
sordid, wretched or depressing.

seance (say-onss) noun
a meeting to communicate with spirits.
[French *séance* a sitting]

seaplane noun
any aeroplane able to take off or land on water, such as an amphibian or a flying boat.

sear verb
1 to burn or scorch: *The flames seared her eyebrows.*
2 to cause to dry up or wither: *The grass was seared by the summer sun.*
3 to brown and seal the surface of meat by briefly applying very intense heat.

search (serch) verb
1 to look carefully or thoroughly in order to find something.
2 to frisk a person or ransack a house when looking for stolen goods, weapons, contraband, etc.
Phrase **search me!** (*informal*) I don't know.
• **search** noun (plural **searches**) the act of searching or examining.
Word Family **searching** adjective thorough; **searchingly** adverb.

searchlight noun
a very strong electric light with a reflector, mounted so that it can be turned in any direction.

search warrant noun
a written authority issued by a magistrate for the police to search premises where it is suspected that stolen goods, wanted persons, etc. may be found.

searing adjective
very intense: *a searing pain.*

seascape noun
a view or picture of the sea.

seashore noun
the land along the sea, especially the ground covered and uncovered by the tide.

seasick adjective
suffering nausea caused by the movement of a ship at sea.
Word Family **seasickness** noun.

seaside noun
the land along the seashore, especially towns or suburbs used as resorts.

season (see-z'n) noun
1 one of the natural climatic divisions of the year, of which there are four (spring, summer, autumn, winter) in temperate areas.
2 a part of the year with a particular type of weather: *the wet season.*
3 a time of year distinguished by a particular activity, crop, etc.: *the football season.*
4 (**the season**) the time of year when a number of traditional upper-class social activities take place.
Phrases **in season 1** available for eating, etc. **2** at the right time. **3** (of animals) on heat. **out of season 1** not available for eating, etc. **2** at the wrong time.
• **season** verb
1 to improve the flavour of food by adding spices or herbs.
Figurative The discussion was seasoned with angry words (= given life or interest).
2 to dry, harden and treat timber.
Figurative He was now a seasoned soldier of many battles (= experienced).
Word Family **seasonal** adjective relating to or occurring in a particular season; **seasonally** adverb; **seasonable** adjective at the suitable or correct time; **seasonably** adverb; **seasonableness** noun.
[Latin *satio* a sowing, planting]

seasonal affective disorder noun
a state of tiredness and depression occurring only during the winter months.

seasoning (seez-ning) noun
1 any spices, herbs or flavourings used to season food.
2 the process of drying and hardening timber.

season ticket noun
a ticket which may be used for an unlimited number of journeys, performances, etc. over a particular period, bought at a reduced rate.

seat noun
1 something on which one sits, especially a chair, etc.
2 the buttocks.
3 the part of a garment covering the buttocks: *the seat of his pants.*
4 the base or bottom of anything.

Figurative Our city is the seat of local government (= centre, location). □ *In the old days a rich man would divide his time between his town house and his country seat* (= house and estate).
5 a manner of sitting: *She has a very relaxed seat on a horse.*
• **seat** *verb* to place in or on a seat: *Please seat yourselves for dinner.*
Figurative This hall seats 700 people (= has seats or room for). □ *The fears were deeply seated in his mind* (= fixed).

seat belt *noun* also called **safety belt**.
a harness in a car, aircraft, etc. to keep an occupant in his or her seat in rough conditions, in a crash, etc.

seating *noun*
the number or arrangement of seats.

sea trout ➪ SALMON TROUT.

sea urchin *noun*
any of a group of spiny marine animals with a spherical shape and a shell made up of many calcareous discs.

sea wall *noun*
a wall or embankment to prevent the sea eroding the land.

seaward *adjective*
situated or facing towards the sea: *The house has a seaward aspect.*
Word Family seawards, seaward *adverb* towards the sea from land.

seaway *noun*
a ship's route or progress at sea.

seaweed *noun*
any plant growing in salt water.

seaworthy *adjective*
(of a ship) strong enough and suitably equipped for going to sea.
Word Family seaworthiness *noun.*

sebaceous glands (si-**bay**-shus glandz) *plural noun*
Anatomy any of numerous small glands in the skin, usually near hair, which secrete oils.
[Latin *sebum* grease]

sec *noun*
(*informal*) a second: *Wait a sec.*

secant (**see**-kant) *noun*
1 *Maths* the reciprocal of cosine. *abbrev.* sec.
2 any straight line that cuts a curve.
[Latin *secans* cutting]

secateurs (sek-a-**terz** *or* **sek**-a-terz) *plural noun*
a small pair of shears with short curved crossed blades for pruning trees, etc.
[French]

secede (si-**seed**) *verb*
to withdraw officially from a federation, organization or group.
Word Family secession (si-**sesh**-'n) *noun* the act of seceding; **secessionist** *noun* a person who secedes or favours secession.
[from Latin]

seclude (si-**klood**) *verb*
to keep apart from the company of others: *He secluded himself in a mountain retreat to meditate.*
Word Family secluded *adjective* 1 living apart from others. 2 protected from view or disturbance; **seclusion** (si-**kloo**-*zh*'n) *noun* 1 the act of secluding. 2 solitude or retirement.
[from Latin]

second¹ (**sek**-'nd) *adjective*
1 being number two in order or a series.
Figurative You won't get a second chance (= another).
2 *Music* relating to the performing of a lower-pitched part and sometimes being lesser in rank: *the second violins.*
• **second** *noun*
1 the base SI unit of time, equal to one-sixtieth of a minute. *abbrev.* s.
2 a person or thing that is second.
3 a person who aids or assists another person: *A duellist's second is his representative.*
4 (**seconds**) (*informal*) a second helping.
5 (**seconds**) (*informal*) a second course.
6 (*usually* **seconds**) any products which are damaged or marked, offered for sale at a reduced price.
7 a unit of plane angle equal to one-sixtieth of a minute.
• **second** *verb*
1 to assist or back up.
2 to give support to a suggestion or nomination.
Word Family second *adverb* in second place.
[Latin *secundus* following, next]

second² (si-**kond**) *verb*
to transfer a person temporarily to another post, position or responsibility.
Word Family secondment *noun.*

secondary (**sek**-'n-dree) *adjective*
1 coming second in time, place, importance, etc.
Figurative That's only a matter of secondary importance now (= minor). □ *A historian should avoid relying too much on secondary sources* (= not primary or original).

2 relating to activity which manufactures things: *secondary industry*. □ *secondary goods*. Compare PRIMARY *adjective* (definition **3**); TERTIARY (definition **2**).

secondary colour *noun*
any colour produced by mixing two primary colours, such as orange, which is a mixture of red and yellow. Compare PRIMARY COLOUR.

secondary school *noun*
a school for children over the age of about eleven years old.

second childhood *noun*
feebleness of mind due to being senile.

second cousin ⇨ COUSIN.

seconder (sek-'nd-a) *noun*
a person who seconds a suggestion or nomination.

second-hand *adjective*
having been previously owned or used.
Figurative The essay was filled with second-hand ideas (= not original).
Word Family **second-hand** *adverb*.

second lieutenant *noun*
Army a commissioned officer ranking between warrant officer and lieutenant.

secondly *adverb*
in second place in a series or in importance.

second nature *noun*
a habit which a person has practised for so long that it has become a fixed part of his or her character.

second person ⇨ PERSON (definition **3**).

second-rate *adjective*
inferior or only of average quality.
Word Family **second-rater** *noun*.

second sight *noun*
clairvoyance.

second string *noun*
Phrase **have a second string to one's bow** to have an alternative course of action ready.

second wind *noun*
Phrase **get one's second wind** to recover after exhaustion or great effort.

secret (see-krit) *adjective*
1 kept from the knowledge of others: *The diplomats were conducting secret negotiations.* □ *a secret society.*
2 secretive.
● **secret** *noun*
1 something which is secret or hidden.
2 a hidden reason or cause: *The secret of his success is hard work.*

Word Family **secrecy** (see-kra-see) *noun*
1 the state of being secret or hidden.
2 lack of frankness or openness.
[Latin *secretus* put apart, separated]

> [!] Do not confuse *secret* with *secrete*. *Secrete* means 'to conceal', as in *He secreted the gun in his inside pocket*.

secret agent *noun*
a spy.

secretaire (sek-ra-**tair**) *noun*
a writing desk with drawers.

secretariat (sek-ra-**tair**-i-at) *noun*
1 the administrative officials of a government or other large organization, such as the United Nations.
2 their offices.

secretary (**sek**-ra-tree) *noun* (*plural* **secretaries**)
1 a person who writes letters, keeps records, etc. for another person or an organization.
2 an administrative assistant to a government minister, ambassador, etc.
Word Family **secretarial** (sek-ra-**tair**-i-'l) *adjective*; **secretaryship** *noun*.

> The word **secretary** is connected with *secret*. It is derived from Latin *secretarius*, someone who was in someone else's confidence and shared secrets, *secretus* being the Latin for 'secret'. The idea is still present today in the term 'confidential secretary'.

secretary bird *noun*
a long-legged African bird over 1 m long, which eats reptiles.
[from its crest, like a quill pen]

Secretary General *noun* (*plural* **Secretaries General**)
the head of a secretariat.

Secretary of State *noun* (*plural* **Secretaries of State**)
a person who is in charge of a government department: *the Secretary of State for Foreign Affairs.*

secrete (si-**kreet**) *verb*
1 *Biology* to produce a secretion.
2 to hide or conceal: *to secrete one's cigarettes under the mattress.*

> [!] Do not confuse *secrete* with SECRET.

secretion (si-**kree**-sh'n) *noun*
1 *Biology* the process of passing the products of a cell from inside to outside the cell membrane.

2 *Biology* the products so passed.
Word Family **secretory** (si-**kree**-ta-ree) *adjective*.
[Latin *secretio* a separating]

secretive (**see**-kra-tiv) *adjective*
inclined to secrecy.
Word Family **secretively** *adverb*;
secretiveness *noun*.

secretly *adverb*
in a clandestine manner.

secret service *noun*
a secret government organization whose
duties may include spying, counter-
spying, code breaking, subversion in
enemy territory, surveillance of dissidents,
psychological warfare, etc.

sect *noun*
a group of people sharing the same
religious beliefs. Compare CULT.
Word Family **sectarian** (sek-**tair**-i-an)
adjective **1** relating to a particular sect.
2 concerned for or relating to the interests
of one's own group: *Sectarian squabbles
divided the country into hostile camps*;
sectarian *noun* a member of a sect;
sectarianism *noun*.
[Latin *sectus* cut]

section (**sek**-sh'n) *noun*
1 a distinct or separate part or division:
This section of the book is boring. □ *A military
section is a part of a platoon.*
2 a cross section.
3 a very thin slice of tissue for microscopic
study.
• **section** *verb* to cut into sections.
Word Family **sectional** *adjective* **1** made
of sections. **2** concerned with or interested
in one's own area or group, especially to
the exclusion of others; **sectionally**
adverb; **sectionalism** *noun* sectional
interests or bias.

sector (**sek**-ta) *noun*
1 *Maths* the part of a circle between two
radii and the included arc.
2 any field or part of a field of activity: *The
Prime Minister antagonized the business
sector by his statements.*

secular (**sek**-yoo-la) *adjective*
1 worldly or material rather than spiritual
or religious: *A secular attitude prevails in this
age.*
2 not relating to or dealing with religion:
secular education.
3 not living inside monasteries: *the secular
clergy.*
Word Family **secularly** *adverb*;
secularism *noun* the belief that morality,

public education or civil policy should not
be based on religion; **secularist** *noun*;
secularize, secularise *verb* to make
secular; **secularization** (sek-yoo-la-rye-
zay-sh'n) *noun*.
[Latin *saeculum* a generation, the spirit of
the age]

secure (sik-**yoor**) *adjective*
1 free from danger or anxiety: *a secure
hiding place.* □ *to feel secure about one's
future.*
2 well fastened or not likely to fall, give
way, fail, etc.: *Is that ladder secure?*
*Figurative Our victory in the competition is
secure* (= certain, sure).
• **secure** *verb* to make secure.
*Figurative I have secured good seats for the
concert* (= obtained). □ *The creditor requires
something to secure the loan* (= cover the risk
of).
Word Family **securely** *adverb*;
secureness *noun*; **security** *noun* (*plural
securities*) **1** something which protects or
makes safe. **2** protective measures taken
against theft, spying, etc. **3** something
given as a pledge that a person will fulfil a
promise or undertaking. **4** a certificate of
ownership, e.g. a bond, stock or share.
[Latin *se-* apart + *cura* care]

sedan (si-**dan**) *noun*
1 short form of **sedan chair** a vehicle for a
person, consisting of an enclosed chair
carried on poles by two people.
2 also called **saloon**. *American* a large
closed car for four or more people.

sedate (si-**date**) *adjective*
composed or calm: *to live a life of sedate
retirement.*
• **sedate** *verb* to administer a sedative to.
Word Family **sedately** *adverb*;
sedateness *noun*; **sedation** *noun* **1** the
state of being sedated. **2** the act of
sedating.
[Latin *sedatus* settled]

sedative (**sedd**-a-tiv) *noun* also called
depressant.
Medicine any substance that temporarily
decreases the function of part or all of the
body and is used to relieve anxiety, pain,
etc. Compare STIMULANT.
• **sedative** *adjective* having a soothing or
calming effect.

sedentary (**sed**-'n-tree) *adjective*
1 done sitting down: *Writing is a sedentary
occupation.*
2 taking or requiring little exercise: *to lead
a sedentary life.*

3 *Biology* (of animals) moving little or fixed to one spot.
Word Family sedentariness *noun*.
[Latin *sedens* sitting]

Seder (**say**-der) *noun*
Judaism a home-based ceremonial meal during Pesach, at which the Exodus from Egypt is recounted.
[Hebrew, order, procedure]

sedge *noun*
any of a group of grass-like plants, usually growing in swampy areas.

sediment (**sedd**-i-m'nt) *noun*
1 the material which settles to the bottom of a liquid.
2 *Geology* any mineral or organic matter deposited by wind, ice or water.
Word Family sedimentation (sedd-i-men-**tay**-sh'n) *noun*; **sedimentary** (sedd-i-**men**-tree) *adjective* **1** of or relating to sediment. **2** *Geology* relating to rocks, such as sandstone and limestone, formed from the compression of sediment, e.g. soil, sand and salt, over millions of years.
[Latin *sedere* to sit]

sedition (si-**dish**-'n) *noun*
the act of trying to promote rebellion or revolt against the government.
Word Family seditious *adjective*;
seditiously *adverb*.
[Latin *seditio* a going apart]

seduce (si-**dewce**) *verb*
1 to persuade to have sexual intercourse.
2 to lead into wrongdoing: *He has seduced me into bad habits.*
Word Family seduction (si-**duk**-sh'n) *noun* **1** the act of seducing. **2** something which seduces; **seductive** *adjective* **1** sexually attractive. **2** tending to seduce; **seductively** *adverb*; **seductiveness** *noun*; **seducer** *noun*; **seductress** *noun*.

sedulous (**sed**-yew-lus) *adjective*
diligent or persevering: *Tim worked with sedulous attention to detail.*
Word Family sedulously *adverb*.
[Latin]

see¹ *verb* (**sees**; **seeing**; **saw**; **seen**)
1 to perceive through the eyes.
2 to experience: *He travelled the world to see a bit of life.*
3 to appreciate or understand: *Do you see the error of your ways now?*
4 (*informal*) to make sure: *Please see that you do the job properly.*
5 to consider or regard: *I see some things very differently from my parents.*
6 to imagine: *I just can't see her as vice-president of the company.*

7 to attend: *My secretary sees to that side of the business.*
8 to find out: *See who that is at the door.*
9 to visit: *I went to see your aunt today.*
10 to receive: *The manager will see you shortly.*
11 to escort: *Let me see you to the door.*
Phrases see about 1 to take care of or attend to. **2** to consider or deliberate over: *We'll have to see about that request, young man.* **see out** *She's determined to see the job out* (= continue until completion). **see over** *I'd like to see over the factory* (= inspect). **see through 1** *We saw through his disguise* (= were not deceived by). **2** *I need something to see me through the sleepless nights* (= help, support).

see² ⇨ DIOCESE.
[Latin *sedes* a seat]

seed *noun*
1 *Biology* the mature fruit of a plant containing an embryo ready for germination.
Figurative The seeds of revolt lay in the harsh laws (= beginnings).
2 semen or sperm.
3 offspring: *And the seed of Abraham shall be mighty in the land.*
4 *Tennis* a player classified according to skill and distributed in a tournament so as not to meet other skilled players in the early matches.
Phrase go to seed, run to seed 1 to come to the stage of yielding seed. **2** to deteriorate.
● **seed** *verb*
1 to plant seed in the soil.
2 to remove the seeds from fruit or plants.
3 to produce or shed seeds.
4 *Weather* to scatter fine particles of material in a cloud to encourage large droplets or ice crystals to form and make rain.
5 *Tennis* to classify.
Word Family seedless *adjective*.

seedbed *noun*
a small area of soil prepared for the growing of seeds.
Figurative This place is a seedbed of rebels and anarchists (= source, place of origin).

seed cake *noun*
a cake flavoured with caraway seed.

seeder *noun*
1 a machine which plants seeds.
2 a machine which removes seeds from fruit, etc.

seedling *noun*
a young plant.

seed pearl noun
a very small pearl, less than 0·25 grain in weight.

seedy adjective (**seedier**; **seediest**)
1 shabbily disreputable.
2 (informal) physically unwell.
Word Family **seedily** adverb; **seediness** noun.

seeing conjunction
considering or in view of the fact: *Seeing he is two hours late, we should not expect him this evening.*

seek verb (**seeks**; **seeking**; **sought**)
to try to find or obtain: *He sought his fortune in the city.* □ *I shall seek to persuade him by flattery.*
Phrase **be sought after** to be in demand.
Word Family **seeker** noun.

seem verb
to appear: *The old man seemed to hear voices.* □ *It seems best to leave now.*
Word Family **seeming** adjective apparent; **seemingly** adverb.

seemly adjective
(of conduct, etc.) fitting or becoming: *Belching in church is not considered seemly behaviour.*

seen the past participle of **see**[1].

seep verb
(of a liquid) to pass slowly through or out of.
Figurative New ideas seep gradually into circulation (= pass, enter).
Word Family **seepage** noun 1 the act of seeping. 2 the liquid that seeps or leaks out.

seer noun
a person reputed to be able to see into the future.

seersucker noun
a lightweight fabric with a regularly crinkled surface, made of various fibres.
[Persian *shir o shakkar* milk and sugar]

see-saw noun
1 a plank fastened in the middle so that each of the two ends, on which a child sits, moves up and down in turn.
2 the act of moving up and down or back and forth.
3 an up-and-down or back-and-forth movement.
Word Family **see-saw** verb, adjective.

seethe (see*th*) verb
(of a liquid) to bubble and foam as if boiling: *The flood waters seethed around lampposts and doorways.*

Figurative The troops seethed with rebellion (= were in a state of agitation).

segment (seg-m'nt) noun
1 a part into which something naturally divides: *the segments of an orange.*
2 *Maths* the part of a circle or sphere cut off by a line or plane.
3 *Maths* a finite part of a line.
• **segment** (seg-**ment**) verb to divide into segments.
Word Family **segmental, segmentary** adjective; **segmentation** (seg-m'n-**tay**-sh'n) noun 1 the act of dividing into segments. 2 the state of being divided into segments.
[from Latin]

segregate (seg-ra-gate) verb
to separate people or groups from each other. Compare INTEGRATE.
Word Family **segregation** (seg-ra-**gay**-sh'n) noun 1 the act of segregating. 2 the state of being segregated. 3 a policy, law or process of separating one racial, ethnic or religious group from the main body of society; **segregationist** noun a person who advocates segregation.
[Latin *se-* apart + *gregis* of the flock]

seigneur (sane-**yer**) noun
Medieval history the superior party in a feudal contract, such as a nobleman who rented out sections of his estate in exchange for military service, etc. Compare VASSAL.
Word Family **seigneurial** adjective.
[from Old French, from Latin *senior*]

seismic (**size**-mik) adjective
of, relating to or caused by earthquakes.
Word Family **seismology** (size-**moll**-a-jee) noun the science of earthquake phenomena; **seismologist** noun.
[Greek *seismos* an earthquake]

seismograph (**size**-mo-grahf) noun
an instrument for measuring the vibrations caused by earthquakes.

seize (seez) verb
1 to lay hold of firmly: *He seized her by the arm.* □ *His mind seized upon the idea that he was a genius.*
Figurative The mob was seized by a blind urge to burn and kill (= possessed). □ *Never fail to seize an opportunity* (= take advantage of).
2 to bind or become jammed: *The engine overheated and seized.*
Word Family **seizure** (**see**-zha) noun 1 the act of seizing. 2 a fit.

seldom *adverb*
not often.

select (si-**lekt**) *verb*
to choose.

● **select** *adjective* specially chosen: *a select crew of sailors.* □ *Wilson's select brand of chocolates.*
Word Family selection *noun* 1 a choice: *Will you please make your selection?*
2 something which has been selected: *Take your selections to the nearest cash register.* 3 a range of things to choose from: *We have a very wide selection of shirts.* 4 *Biology* the choosing of certain animals or plants for purposes of reproduction. This may occur naturally or may be artificially guided by human beings, as in the breeding of cattle, etc.; **selective** *adjective* 1 having the power to select. 2 fastidious or exclusive; **selector** *noun.*
[Latin *se-* apart + *lectus* picked]

selenography (sell-a-**nog**-ra-fee) *noun*
the study of the physical features of the moon.
[Greek *selené* moon + *graphein* to write]

selenology (sell-a-**noll**-a-jee) *noun*
the branch of astronomy dealing with the moon.

self *noun* (*plural* **selves**)
1 one's own person.
Figurative When he's tired his better self disappears (= nature, character).
□ *Whatever she does she does for reasons of self* (= selfishness, personal interest).
2 the ego.
Word Family self *pronoun.*

self-absorbed *adjective*
preoccupied with one's own thoughts, interests, etc.
Word Family self-absorption *noun.*

self-addressed *adjective*
addressed to oneself: *a self-addressed envelope.*

self-aggrandizement, self-aggrandisement *noun*
an increase in one's own power, prestige, wealth, etc., usually achieved aggressively.

self-appointed *adjective*
acting or speaking as if having authority, without having been requested or authorized to do so: *a self-appointed spokesman.*

self-assertive *adjective*
insisting on one's own wishes, opinions, importance, etc.
Word Family self-assertion *noun.*

self-assured *adjective*
confident in one's own abilities, etc., especially to an extreme degree.
Word Family self-assurance *noun.*

self-aware *adjective*
aware of one's own nature, weaknesses and abilities.
Word Family self-awareness *noun.*

self-centred *adjective* (*American* **self-centered**)
selfish or excessively concerned with oneself.
Word Family self-centredness *noun.*

self-confidence *noun*
belief in one's own abilities, worth, judgement, etc.
Word Family self-confident *adjective;* **self-confidently** *adverb.*

self-conscious *adjective*
1 excessively conscious of how one appears to other people.
2 conscious of one's own self, existence, thoughts, etc.
Word Family self-consciously *adverb;* **self-consciousness** *noun.*

self-contained *adjective*
1 (of a flat or house) having its own bathroom, kitchen, etc., so that sharing is not necessary.
2 reserved or disposed to say little.
3 self-possessed or calm.

self-control *noun*
control of one's self, feelings, actions, etc.
Word Family self-controlled *adjective.*

self-deception *noun*
the fact or act of deceiving oneself.

self-defeating *adjective*
(of an action, plan, etc.) having inherent defects which prevent its successful achievement, conclusion, etc.

self-defence *noun* (*American* **self-defense**)
the defence of one's person, property, etc., especially when involving the use of physical force.

self-denial *noun*
the denial of one's own desires.
Word Family self-denying *adjective.*

self-discipline *noun*
the discipline or training of oneself, especially for self-improvement.

self-effacement *noun*
the act or habit of not drawing attention to oneself, especially through modesty or timidity.
Word Family self-effacing *adjective.*

self-employed *adjective*
earning one's income from one's own business, skills, etc., and not receiving a salary or wages from an employer.

self-esteem *noun*
a good opinion of oneself.

self-evident *adjective*
obviously true and therefore requiring no proof or explanation.
Word Family **self-evidently** *adverb.*

self-explanatory *adjective*
obvious.

self-expression *noun*
the expression of one's own personality in art or in one's behaviour.

self-help *noun*
the practice of achieving things through one's own efforts.

selfhood *noun*
the state of being an individual person.

self-image *noun*
one's own idea of one's appearance or personality.

self-important *adjective*
having an exaggerated idea of one's own importance.
Word Family **self-importantly** *adverb*; **self-importance** *noun.*

self-improvement *noun*
an improvement of one's skills, status, etc. by one's own efforts.

self-indulgent *adjective*
indulging one's own desires, passions, etc. with little regard for the welfare of others.
Word Family **self-indulgently** *adverb*; **self-indulgence** *noun.*

self-interest *noun*
personal advantage or interest.
Word Family **self-interested** *adjective.*

selfish *adjective*
caring too much for oneself and too little for others.
Word Family **selfishly** *adverb*; **selfishness** *noun.*

selfless *adjective*
unselfish.
Word Family **selflessly** *adverb*; **selflessness** *noun.*

self-loading *adjective*
(of a firearm) reloading automatically.

self-love *noun*
selfishness or egotism.

self-made *adjective*
having achieved success unaided.

self-opinionated *adjective*
1 conceited.
2 obstinate in one's opinions.

self-pity *noun*
excessive pity for oneself.
Word Family **self-pitying** *adjective.*

self-portrait *noun*
an artist's portrait of himself or herself.

self-possessed *adjective*
having or showing control of one's feelings, behaviour, etc.
Word Family **self-possession** *noun.*

self-raising flour *noun*
flour containing a substance, such as baking powder, to make it rise.

self-realization, self-realisation *noun*
the full development of one's capabilities.

self-reliance *noun*
a reliance on one's own resources.
Word Family **self-reliant** *adjective.*

self-respect *noun*
a respect or esteem for one's own character and conduct.
Word Family **self-respecting** *adjective.*

self-restraint *noun*
self-control.

self-righteous *adjective*
piously sure of one's own righteousness or virtue.
Word Family **self-righteously** *adverb*; **self-righteousness** *noun.*

self-sacrifice *noun*
the sacrifice of one's own interests, desires, etc. for the sake of some other person, principle, etc.
Word Family **self-sacrificing** *adjective.*

selfsame *adjective*
the very same: *Is that the selfsame John Smith I was talking about before?*

self-satisfied *adjective*
feeling satisfied with oneself.
Word Family **self-satisfaction** *noun.*

self-seeking *adjective*
pursuing or seeking one's own interests.
Word Family **self-seeker** *noun.*

self-service *adjective*
(of a restaurant, shop, etc.) in which customers help themselves to goods, food, etc. and pay at a till or checkout.

self-starter *noun*
1 a self-motivated person.
2 (*dated*) a device which starts an internal-combustion engine without cranking by hand.

self-styled *adjective*
(of a name, etc.) applied to oneself,
especially undeservedly.

self-sufficient *adjective*
able to provide or manage for oneself
without aid.
Word Family **self-sufficiency** *noun.*

self-willed *adjective*
obstinate.

sell *verb* (**sells; selling; sold**)
1 to exchange for money or its equivalent.
2 to offer for sale or deal in, e.g. for one's
livelihood: *He sells used cars.*
3 to attract buyers: *The bright package sells
this soap powder.*
Figurative *I'm not sold on the idea*
(= convinced, caused to accept).
Phrases **sell off** to sell at a reduced price.
sell out 1 to dispose of completely by
selling. **2** to betray. **sell someone short**
to underestimate or belittle someone's
worth or abilities. **sell up** to sell all of
one's goods or property.
Word Family **sell** *noun.*

sell-by date *noun*
a date marked on food packaging by which
it is recommended the product should be
sold.

seller *noun*
1 a person who sells.
2 something considered in terms of its
sales potential: *All the books in this series are
good sellers.*

Sellotape *noun*
(*trademark*) an adhesive tape.

> **Sellotape** is such a common everyday
> thing that few people realize that it
> should be spelt with a capital letter
> because it is a trademark. There are
> many words like this in English: *Filofax*,
> *Jacuzzi*, for example, and even *Catseyes*,
> glass reflectors marking traffic lanes at
> night. Some of them become so
> common that other parts of speech are
> formed from them. Thus we speak of
> *hoovering* a room, *sellotaping* a parcel
> and *xeroxing* a document.

seltzer (**selt**-sa) *noun*
an effervescent mineral water.
[originally from *Selters* a German spa]

selvedge (**sel**-vij) *noun* also called **selvage**
the edge of a length of fabric, wallpaper,
etc., sewn or finished so that it will not pull
undone.
[SELF + EDGE]

selves
the plural of **self**.

semantics (si-**man**-tiks) *plural noun*
(*used with singular verb*) the science or
study of the meanings of words, especially
in relation to their historical change.
Word Family **semantic** *adjective.*
[Greek *semantikos* significant]

semaphore (**semm**-a-for) *noun*
a method of signalling, using flags or a
mechanical device with arms, where
different positions represent the letters of
the alphabet.
[Greek *sema* sign + *phoros* bearing]

semblance *noun*
an outward appearance: *The deserted house
had a semblance of decay.*
Figurative *Not a semblance of guilt showed
in his face* (= trace).
[Latin *simulare* to make like]

semen (**see**-m'n) *noun* also called
seminal fluid.
Biology the combined secretions of the
male reproductive organs, including the
testes and prostate gland, which forms the
fluid expelled from the penis in
ejaculation.
[Latin, seed]

semester (si-**mest**-a) *noun*
either of the two halves into which the
teaching year at a university, college, etc.
may be divided, especially in America.
[Latin *sex* six + *mensis* a month]

semi *noun*
(*informal*) a semi-detached house.

semi-annual (semm-i-**an**-yew-'l) *adjective*
1 occurring twice a year.
2 lasting for half a year.

semi-automatic (semm-i-aw-t'-**matt**-ik)
adjective
1 partly automatic.
2 (of a firearm) loading automatically but
requiring a separate pull of the trigger at
each shot.

semibreve *noun*
Music a note with the time value of two
minims or four crotchets.

semicircle (**semm**-i-sir-k'l) *noun*
1 a half of a circle.
2 something which has this shape.
Word Family **semicircular** (semm-i-**sir**-kew-la) *adjective.*

semicolon (semm-i-**kole**-on) *noun*
a punctuation mark (;), used in a sentence
to separate clauses or introduce a pause
longer than that of a comma: *He failed his*

exams; therefore he can't go to university this year. Compare COLON.

semiconductor *noun*
Electronics any of a class of crystals, such as silicon and germanium, with conductivity ranging from nil at −200°C to poor at normal temperatures and good when heated or when impurities are added (as in transistors). They are used in electronic and microelectronic circuits and photoelectric cells.

semi-conscious (semm-i-**kon**-shus) *adjective*
not fully conscious.

semi-detached *adjective*
(of a pair of houses) detached from other buildings but sharing a common wall.

semi-final (semm-i-**fie**-n'l) *noun*
the last competition or match played before a final game in a series.
Word Family **semi-finalist** *noun* a person or team that competes in a semi-final.

semimetal *noun* also called **metalloid.**
Chemistry any element, such as arsenic, showing some properties of a metal and some properties of a non-metal.

seminal (**semm**-i-n'l) *adjective*
1 *Biology* of or relating to semen.
2 of or relating to a seed.
3 having possibilities of future development.
[Latin *seminis* of seed]

seminal fluid ⇨ SEMEN.

seminar (**semm**-i-nar) *noun*
a class or group discussion usually for advanced study or research.
[Latin *seminarium* a seedbed]

seminary (**semm**-in-ree) *noun* (*plural* **seminaries**)
1 *Christianity* a training college for priests.
2 (*formerly*) a private school, especially one for girls.

semi-precious (semm-i-**presh**-us) *adjective*
having some value as a gem but not classified as precious, e.g. amethyst.

semi-skilled *adjective*
partly skilled or trained for work.

semi-skimmed *adjective*
(of milk) with some of the cream removed.

semitone *noun*
Music the smallest interval used in European music. On the piano this represents the interval between one note and the next, whether it is white or black.

semolina (semm-a-**lee**-na) *noun*
the hard parts of wheat grain left after making flour, used to make puddings, etc.
[Italian *semolino* little bran]

Semtex *noun*
(*trademark*) a pliable plastic explosive.

senate *noun*
1 the upper house of the American Congress and some other legislatures.
2 the supreme council of state in ancient Rome.
3 the governing body of some universities.
Word Family **senator** *noun* a member of the senate; **senatorial** (senn-a-**taw**-ri-'l) *adjective*.
[Latin *senatus* from *senex* old man]

send *verb* (**sends; sending; sent**)
to cause to go or be carried: *to send a letter.*
□ *The bowler sent down a fast ball.*
Figurative (*dated informal*) *This music really sends me* (= excites, inspires).
Phrases **send down 1** to expel from a university. **2** (*informal*) to imprison: *The judge sent him down for five years.* **send for** to ask or demand to appear. **send up** (*informal*) to mock or mimic.

send-off *noun*
(*informal*) a friendly gathering for a person who is leaving.

send-up *noun*
(*informal*) a mockery or satire.

senescent (si-**ness**-'nt) *adjective*
(*formal*) growing old.
Word Family **senescence** *noun*.
[from Latin]

senile (**see**-nile) *adjective*
1 of or relating to old age.
2 lacking mental or physical health due to old age.
Word Family **senility** (si-**nill**-i-tee) *noun*.

senior (**seen**-ya) *adjective*
1 being more advanced in years, rank, standing, etc.
2 (**Senior**) used by the father when father and son have the same name: *Sammy Davis Senior.*
• **senior** *noun* a person who is more advanced in years, rank, standing, etc.
[Latin, an elder, older]

seniority (seen-i-**orr**-i-tee) *noun*
1 the state of being senior.
2 precedence of position, especially by reason of age or long service.

señor (sen-**yor**) *noun*
the Spanish title for a man.

señora (sen-**yor**-a) *noun*
the Spanish title for a married woman.

señorita (sen-yor-**eet**-a) *noun*
the Spanish title for an unmarried woman.

sensation (sen-**say**-sh'n) *noun*
1 any perception through the senses.
Figurative I had the sensation that someone was watching me (= impression, idea).
2 a state of great interest and excitement:
The pop group caused a sensation.
3 an event, person, etc. causing such interest and excitement.
Word Family **sensational** *adjective*;
sensationally *adverb*.

sensationalism (sen-**say**-sh'n-a-lizm)
noun
the deliberate use of startling or thrilling methods in writing, politics, etc.
Word Family **sensationalist** *noun*.

sense *noun*
1 any of the faculties of sight, hearing, smell, taste and touch.
2 a feeling or perception: *There was a sense of menace in his voice.*
Figurative She has no sense of humour (= appreciation).
3 practical judgement.
4 sound mental faculties.
5 the meaning of a word, statement, etc.:
In what sense are you using the word?
6 *Maths* the direction of a vector.
Phrases **in a sense** to a certain extent.
make sense to be intelligible or acceptable. **make sense of** to understand.
• **sense** *verb* to be or become aware of:
I sensed someone was looking at me.
[from Latin]

senseless *adjective*
1 unconscious: *He was knocked senseless in the fight.*
2 stupid or foolish: *Being rude to the policeman was a senseless thing to do.*
3 lacking meaning: *His senseless speech confused all of us.*
Word Family **senselessly** *adverb*;
senselessness *noun*.

sensibility (sen-sa-**bill**-i-tee) *noun* (*plural* **sensibilities**)
1 the ability to feel or perceive.
2 a keen perception or sensitivity.
3 (**sensibilities**) emotions or feelings.

sensible (sen-sa-b'l) *adjective*
1 having or showing good sense.
2 able to be perceived by the senses.
3 conscious: *I was stunned but still sensible.*
Figurative He is sensible of the danger of his situation (= aware).

Word Family **sensibly** *adverb*;
sensibleness *noun*.

sensitive (**sen**-sa-tiv) *adjective*
1 affected by stimuli or impressions.
2 easily offended or hurt: *She is very sensitive about being so tall.*
3 able to measure finely and exactly: *a sensitive thermometer.*
Word Family **sensitively** *adverb*;
sensitivity (sen-sa-**tivv**-i-tee) *noun* (*plural* **sensitivities**); **sensitiveness** *noun*.

sensitize, sensitise (**sen**-sa-tize) *verb*
to make sensitive, e.g. to make a photographic film sensitive to light.
Word Family **sensitization** (sen-sa-tie-zay-sh'n) *noun*.

sensor *noun*
an instrument or device which reacts to heat, light, etc.

sensory (**sen**-sa-ree) *adjective*
of or relating to the senses or sensation:
sensory qualities.

sensual (**sence**-yew-'l) *adjective*
1 relating to or affecting the senses.
2 sexy or erotic.
Word Family **sensually** *adverb*;
sensuality (sence-yoo-**al**-i-tee) *noun*;
sensualist *noun* a person who seeks sensual pleasure; **sensualism** *noun*.

sensuous (**sence**-yew-us) *adjective*
affecting or giving pleasure to the senses.
Word Family **sensuously** *adverb*;
sensuousness *noun*.

sent the past tense and past participle of **send**.

sentence *noun*
1 *Grammar* a group of words that express a complete meaning. Sentences begin with a capital letter and end with a full stop, question mark or exclamation mark.
2 *Law* the decision of a court, stating the punishment a convicted person is to receive.
3 *Law* the punishment itself.
• **sentence** *verb* to condemn to punishment.
[Latin *sententia* opinion]

sententious (sen-**ten**-shus) *adjective*
1 given to pompous moralizing.
2 self-righteous.
Word Family **sententiously** *adverb*;
sententiousness *noun*.
[from Latin]

sentient (**sen**-sh'nt) *adjective*
perceiving by the senses.
Word Family **sentiently** *adverb*;
sentience *noun*.
[Latin *sentiens* feeling]

sentiment (sen-ti-m'nt) *noun*
1 any attitudes based on tender or emotional feelings rather than reason.
2 an opinion or attitude: *What are your sentiments on the subject?*
3 the emotional meaning of something.
[Latin *sentire* to feel]

sentimental (sen-ti-men-t'l) *adjective*
having, causing or appealing to tender or romantic feelings: *We all cried during the sentimental film.*
Word Family **sentimentalize, sentimentalise** *verb* 1 to indulge in sentiment. 2 to make sentimental; **sentimentally** *adverb*; **sentimentality** (sen-ti-men-**tal**-i-tee) *noun*.

sentinel *noun*
a sentry.
[from Italian]

sentry *noun* (*plural* **sentries**)
a soldier placed to keep watch and warn of attacks.

sepal (see-p'l) *noun*
Biology one of the small green leaf-like outer parts of a flower, forming the calyx and found under the petals and surrounding a bud.
[from SEP(arate) + (pet)AL]

separable (sepp-er-a-b'l) *adjective*
capable of being separated.
Word Family **separably** *adverb*, **separability** (sepp-er-a-bil-i-tee) *noun*.

separate (sepp-a-rate) *verb*
1 to remove parts so that they are no longer together: *Separate the milk from the cream.*
2 to distinguish between: *You must separate right and wrong in your own mind.*
3 to part company
4 to stop living together.
• **separate** (sepp-a-rit) *adjective* not shared or joined: *We sleep in separate rooms.*
□ *List each separate item.*
Word Family **separately** *adverb*; **separation** (sepp-a-ray-sh'n) *noun* the act or fact of separating; **separateness** *noun*.
[Latin *se-* apart + *parare* to make ready]

> ⚠ Note the spelling of *separate*: the middle syllable is *par* (as in *part*), not *per*.

separatist (sepp-er-a-tist) *noun*
a person who wants political or religious independence.
Word Family **separatism** *noun*.

sepia (seep-i-a) *noun*
1 a brown pigment obtained from an ink-like secretion of various cuttlefish.

2 a deep brown colour.
[Greek, cuttlefish]

sepsis *noun*
the presence of pathogenic organisms or their poisons in the blood or tissues.
[Greek, going rotten]

September *noun*
the ninth month of the year, after August and before October.
[Latin, the seventh month of the Roman calendar]

septet *noun*
any group of seven people or things.
[Latin *septem* seven]

septic *adjective*
of or causing sepsis or infection.

septicaemia (sep-ti-see-mi-a) *noun*
(*American* **septicemia**)
an infection originating in a wound, in which the organisms breed in the blood.
[Greek *septikos* rotten + *haima* blood]

septic tank *noun*
a tank in which sewage is broken down by the action of bacteria.

septuagenarian (sep-tew-a-j'n-**air**-i-an) *noun*
a person who is over 70 but less than 80 years old.
[Latin *septuagent* seventy each]

septum *noun* (*plural* **septa**)
Biology a wall separating parts of a structure in an animal or plant.
[Latin, a fence]

sepulchre (sepp-ul-ka) *noun* (*American* **sepulcher**)
a tomb or burial vault.
Word Family **sepulchral** (si-**pul**-kr'l) *adjective* 1 of or for a tomb. 2 (of a voice) deep and hollow.
[Latin *sepultus* buried]

sequel (see-kw'l) *noun*
something following, a consequence.
Compare PREQUEL.

sequence (see-kw'nce) *noun*
1 the following of one thing after another.
2 the order in which one or more things follow each other: *We arranged the words in alphabetical sequence.*
Figurative A strange sequence of events led to my adventure (= continuous or connected series).
Word Family **sequential** (see-kwen-sh'l) *adjective*; **sequentially** *adverb*.
[Latin *sequens* following]

sequester (si-**kwest**-a) *verb*
1 to remove or withdraw into solitude or retirement.
2 also **sequestrate** *Law* to hold or confiscate, etc.
Word Family **sequestration** (see-kwi-**stray**-sh'n) *noun*.
[Latin, a trustee]

sequin (**see**-kwin) *noun*
a small coloured shining disc, used to decorate clothes, etc.
[from Italian]

sequoia (see-**kwoy**-a) *noun*
either of two species of very tall evergreen trees native to California, one of which is the redwood.
[named after a Native American chief]

sera
a plural of **serum**.

seraglio (ser-**rah**-li-o) *noun*
the part of a Muslim house in which the females live.
[Italian]

seraph (**serr**-af) *noun* (*plural* **seraphim** (**serr**-a-fim) or **seraphs**)
an angel of the highest rank.
Word Family **seraphic** *adjective* angelic: *a seraphic smile*.
[Hebrew]

serenade (serr-a-**nade**) *noun*
music of the kind originally sung or played beneath a loved one's window in the evening.
Word Family **serenade** *verb*.
[from Italian from Latin *serenus* cloudless + *serus* late]

serendipity (serr-en-**dip**-i-tee) *noun*
the faculty of making unexpected but desirable discoveries.

> The word **serendipity** was coined by the British author Horace Walpole in 1754. He wrote a fairy tale called *The Three Princes of Serendip*, whose main characters were always making accidental and fortunate discoveries. *Serendip* is an ancient name of Sri Lanka.

serene (s'-**reen**) *adjective*
calm and tranquil.
Word Family **serenely** *adverb*; **serenity** (s'-**renn**-i-tee) *noun*.
[from Latin]

serf *noun*
Medieval history a labourer forced to work on the land for a feudal lord.
Word Family **serfdom** *noun*.
[Latin *servus* a slave]

serge *noun*
a very durable worsted or woollen fabric, used for clothing.

sergeant (**sar**-j'nt) *noun*
1 *Air force* a non-commissioned officer ranking between a corporal and warrant officer.
2 *Army* a non-commissioned officer ranking between a corporal and warrant officer.
3 a police officer ranking between a constable and an inspector.
[Latin *servientis* of a servant]

sergeant major *noun*
Army a warrant officer.

serial (**seer**-i-al) *noun*
1 a story which is presented in parts, e.g. week by week in a magazine or on television or radio.
2 a publication issued in successive numbered parts.
• **serial** *adjective* of or arranged in a series.
Word Family **serially** *adverb*; **serialize**, **serialise** *verb* to publish or broadcast in the form of a serial; **serialization** (seer-i-a-lie-**zay**-sh'n) *noun*.

> [!] Do not confuse *serial* with CEREAL.

sericulture (**serr**-i-kul-cher) *noun*
the breeding of silkworms to produce silk.
[Latin *sericum* silk + CULTURE]

series (**seer**-eez) *noun* (*plural* **series**)
any ordered arrangement of a number of related things, events, etc.
[Latin, a row, a chain]

serif *noun*
Printing the curved or projecting ends on the main stroke of a letter, e.g. those at the top and bottom of M.

serious (**seer**-i-us) *adjective*
1 thoughtful or solemn: *Her serious face told us something was wrong.*
2 important: *This is a serious decision.*
3 critical: *a serious illness.*
4 sincere or meaning what one says: *Stop teasing and be serious for once.*
5 (*informal*) worth taking seriously, considerable: *serious money.*
Word Family **seriously** *adverb*; **seriousness** *noun*.
[from Latin]

sermon *noun*
a speech on a religious or moral subject, especially one based on the Bible and spoken from a church pulpit.
Word Family **sermonize, sermonise** *verb* to preach or lecture.
[Latin *sermonis* of a talk]

serpent *noun*
1 a snake.
2 *Music* an old serpent-shaped wind instrument with a deep tone.
[Latin *serpere* to creep]

serpentine (ser-pen-tine) *adjective*
1 of or like a serpent.
2 twisting and turning like a snake: *the serpentine meanderings of the river.*

serrated (si-ray-tid) *adjective*
having a sharply notched or grooved edge, e.g. as a saw.
Word Family **serration** *noun* 1 the act of making serrated. 2 a serrated notch or edge.
[from Latin]

serried *adjective*
an old word meaning 'pressed close together': *the serried ranks of troops.*
[French *serré* closed]

serum (seer-um) *noun* (*plural* **sera** or **serums**)
1 the pale yellow liquid part of blood, after the cells and the parts which cause clotting have been removed. Compare PLASMA (definition 1).
2 this substance obtained from immunized animals and used for medical purposes as antiserum.
[Latin, whey]

servant *noun*
1 a person who works in the household of another, such as a maid.
2 a person employed by the government: *a civil servant.*

serve *verb*
1 to perform work or duties for: *I served the king for 40 years.* □ *How long did you serve in the army?*
Figurative This box will serve as a table (= act, suffice). □ *The bull served the cow* (= mated with).
2 to provide with or deal out goods, etc.: *She serves in a milk bar.* □ *May I serve dinner now?*
Figurative I was served with a summons to appear in court (= presented).
3 *Sport* in racket games, to hit the ball or shuttlecock into play.
Phrases **serve someone right** *Your punishment serves you right for telling fibs* (= is just or deserved). **serve time** to spend time in prison.
• **serve** *noun* ⇨ SERVICE *noun* (definition 10).
[Latin *servus* a slave]

server *noun*
1 a person who serves.
2 something used to serve food, etc., such as a special tray or a salad spoon.
3 *Computers* a computer or program which controls access to a service in a network.

service (ser-viss) *noun*
1 the act of helping or serving: *I gave good service to the king.* □ *Does this shop give quick service?*
2 the providing of some facility required by the public: *a bus service.*
3 the act of checking and repairing equipment and machinery: *My car needs a service.*
4 *Religion* a meeting for worship.
5 *Religion* the form of such a meeting: *the marriage service.*
6 a set of objects used for a special purpose: *a tea service.*
7 a government department or the people in it: *the diplomatic service.*
8 (**services**) the armed forces.
9 (**services**) activities in employment: *They dispensed with his services.*
10 also **serve** *Sport* the act of serving the ball or shuttlecock.
Phrases **at your service** *I am always at your service* (= ready to help). **be of service** *Can I be of service to you?* (= be helpful).
• **service** *verb*
1 to maintain or repair machinery, etc.
2 (of a male animal) to mate with.
• **service** *adjective*
1 relating to servants or tradesmen: *Please use the service entrance.*
2 relating to the armed forces: *service uniforms.*

serviceable (ser-viss-a-b'l) *adjective*
able to give good service, especially by being strong and durable: *Active children need serviceable clothes.*
Word Family **serviceably** *adverb*; **serviceability** (ser-viss-a-bill-i-tee) *noun.*

service charge *noun*
a percentage or a sum of money added to a bill to pay for service given.

service line ⇨ BASELINE.

serviceman *noun* (*plural* **servicemen**)
a member of the armed forces.

service road *noun*
a road parallel to a main road, used to provide access to buildings without interrupting the main traffic.

service station *noun* also called **petrol station**.
a place where petrol, oil, etc. is sold, and where motor vehicles may be repaired.

servicewoman *noun* (*plural* **servicewomen**)
a female member of the armed forces.

serviette (ser-vi-**et**) *noun* also called **table napkin**.
a piece of cloth or paper used at a meal to protect the clothes, wipe the lips, etc.
[Old French]

servile (**ser**-vile) *adjective*
fawning: *She paid no attention to his servile flattery.*
Word Family **servilely** *adverb*; **servility** (ser-**vill**-i-tee) *noun*.

serving *noun*
a portion of food.

servitor (**ser**-vi-ter) *noun*
an old word for a servant or attendant.

servitude (**ser**-vi-tewd) *noun*
compulsory labour: *penal servitude on Devil's Island.*
Figurative The peasants struggled for centuries under the servitude of greedy landowners (= control).

servomechanism (**ser**-vo-mekk-a-nizm) *noun*
short form is **servo** a device to control speed, position, direction, voltage, etc. of a mechanism using electrical, hydraulic, etc. power governed by feedback to correct deviations. Applications include power-assisted steering, automatic pilots, etc.

servomotor *noun*
a motor supplying power to a servomechanism.

sesame (**sess**-a-mee) *noun*
the seeds from a tropical plant, used in bread, sweets and cakes or as a spice.
[Greek]

sessile *adjective*
1 *Biology* of part of a plant without a stalk or a support.
2 *Biology* of animals which are permanently in one place, such as an oyster.
[Latin *sessilis* sitting down]

session (**sesh**-'n) *noun*
1 the meeting together of a court, group or organization.
2 a period in the life of a parliament, from its opening to its prorogation, when it goes into recess.

3 any single meeting for a particular purpose: *The orchestra has two practice sessions weekly.*
Word Family **sessional** *adjective*.

sestet ⇨ SEXTET (definitions 1, 2).

set *verb* (**sets**; **setting**; **set**, definition 5 **setted**)
1 to put: *Set the chairs around the table.* □ *Set a limit to your spending.* □ *Set your mind at rest.*
Figurative His behaviour sets a fine example (= presents). □ *Which books are set for study?* (= prescribed). □ *Please set the table* (= put cutlery and crockery on). □ *Set the alarm before going to bed* (= adjust).
2 to become hard or firm: *The ice cream set quickly in the freezer.*
3 to give a fixed position or shape to: *The gem was set in gold.* □ *I washed and set my hair in rollers.*
4 to start: *The book set me thinking.* □ *His father set him up in business.*
5 to divide pupils into sets, to teach a subject in sets.
6 (of the sun, moon, etc.) to sink below the horizon.
Phrases **set in** *The cold weather has set in early this year* (= begun). **set off 1** *He set off for Canada* (= departed). **2** *The black jumper sets off your pearls* (= shows to advantage). **set on, set upon 1** *The thugs set on the old man* (= suddenly attacked). **2** *He is set on being a doctor* (= determined on). **set out 1** *She set out to become boss* (= aimed). **2** *Set out your request in writing* (= state). **set up 1** *Don't set yourself up as an expert* (= claim to be). **2** (*informal*) *The murderer set up his victim for the kill* (= trapped).
● **set** *noun*
1 a number of things which together form a complete collection: *a set of dinner plates.*
Figurative He's a member of the artistic set (= group of people, clique).
2 the way in which something stands or is placed: *the determined set of his jaw.*
3 an apparatus which receives radio signals, etc.: *a television set.*
4 the scenery used to represent a particular place during a play or film.
5 an area where filming takes place.
6 a group of students of a similar ability in a particular subject who are taught together.
7 *Tennis* a division of the match where one player has won at least six games and is two games ahead of his or her opponent.
8 *Maths* a collection of distinct elements considered together as a single unit.

● **set** *adjective* fixed: *a set smile*. □ *Meet me at a set time*. □ *Have you read the set texts?*

setback *noun*
a reverse or check to progress: *Farming suffered a setback during the drought.*

set square *noun*
a flat instrument in the shape of a right-angled triangle, used for architectural drawing, etc.

settee *noun*
a sofa.

setter *noun*
any of various large long-haired gun dogs, which stand rigid when scenting game.

set theory *noun*
Maths the study of sets and their construction, algebra and interrelationships.

setting *noun*
1 that in which something is set: *The diamond was in a gold setting*. □ *The play's setting was ancient Rome.*
Figurative The lake is a wonderful setting for a restaurant (= environment).
2 the arrangement of cutlery, mats, glasses, etc. on a table, especially for one person.

settle *verb*
1 to agree: *We finally settled on where to spend our holiday.*
Figurative Who'll settle the bill? (= pay).
2 to go and live in a new place: *Colonists settled on the coast of the new continent.*
3 to sink down or rest: *The mud settled on the river bottom.*
4 to cause to sink down or rest: *This drink will settle your stomach.*
Figurative Are you settling into your new job quickly? (= adapting).
5 to bestow property on someone by gift or legal deed, especially on a wife at marriage
Word Family settled *adjective* fixed or unchanging.

settlement *noun*
1 the act of settling: *Settlement of the argument took months*. □ *Settlement of the new continent was rapid.*
Figurative Please find enclosed the full settlement (= payment).
2 a group of houses and other buildings, especially in a new or sparsely populated area.

settler *noun*
a person who settles, especially in a new country or area.

set-up *noun*
an arrangement.

seven *noun*
a cardinal number, the symbol 7 in Arabic numerals, VII in Roman numerals.
Word Family seven *adjective*; **seventh** *noun, adjective.*

seventeen *noun*
a cardinal number, the symbol 17 in Arabic numerals, XVII in Roman numerals.
Word Family seventeen *adjective*; **seventeenth** *noun, adjective.*

seventy *noun (plural* **seventies)**
1 a cardinal number, the symbol 70 in Arabic numerals, LXX in Roman numerals.
2 (**seventies**) the numbers 70 to 79 in a series, such as the years in a century.
Word Family seventy *adjective*; **seventieth** *noun, adjective.*

sever (sevv-a) *verb*
to cut as though by a sharp blow.
Figurative He severed all ties with his ex-girlfriend (= broke off).
Word Family severance *noun* the act of severing, dividing or breaking off: *a severance of diplomatic relations.*
[Latin *separare*]

several *adjective*
more than two or three, but not a great number.
Figurative After the conference, the speakers returned to their several countries (= individual, respective).
● **several** *pronoun* some or a few.
Word Family severally *adverb* respectively or individually.

severance pay *noun*
the money paid to an employee by his or her employer to compensate for the loss of his or her job.

severe (s'-veer) *adjective*
1 stern or strict: *Don't be too severe with the child.*
2 serious: *Is the illness severe?*
Word Family severely *adverb*; **severity** (s'-verr-i-tee) *noun* sternness: *the severity of the long winter.*
[from Latin]

sew (so) *verb* (**sews; sewing; sewed; sewn** or **sewed**)
to join, mend, decorate or make with a needle and thread, either by hand or machine.

sewage (soo-ij) *noun*
waste matter carried in sewers.

sewage farm *noun*
a place where sewage is treated to make it harmless.

sewer¹ (soo-a) *noun*
a pipe, usually underground, for carrying human waste, etc. from buildings.
Word Family **sewerage** *noun* 1 the removal of waste matter by sewers. 2 a system of sewers.

sewer² (so-a) *noun*
a person who sews.

sewing (so-ing) *noun*
any work being sewn.

sewing machine *noun*
a machine for stitching fabric.

sewn a past participle of **sew**.

sex *noun* (*plural* **sexes**)
1 the character of being male or female.
2 the differences between males and females.
3 sexual intercourse or other sexual activity: *The film is full of sex.*
• **sex** *verb* to ascertain the sex of.
Word Family **sexed** *adjective* having a certain degree of sexuality; **sexless** *adjective* 1 neither male nor female.
2 (*informal*) having no sex appeal.
[Latin *secus* a division]

sex appeal *noun*
the quality of being sexually attractive.

sex chromosome *noun*
a chromosome which carries sex-determining factors. In humans the **X chromosome** carries female factors and the **Y chromosome** carries male factors. Males have one X and one Y chromosome, and females have two X chromosomes.

sexism *noun*
1 an attitude which stereotypes people according to their sex.
2 any discrimination based on the supposed differences between the sexes.
Word Family **sexist** *noun* a person who discriminates between people on the basis of their sex; **sexist** *adjective*.

sextant *noun*
an instrument for measuring the angle of altitude of planets and stars, used in determining latitude and longitude.
[Latin *sextantis* of the sixth part (as it has an arc of 60°)]

sextet *noun*
1 also **sestet** a group of six musicians.
2 also **sestet** a musical composition for six musicians or instruments.
3 any group of six people or things.

sexton *noun*
Christianity an official in charge of a church building and its contents.

sextuplet (seks-tew-plit) *noun*
any of six offspring born at one birth.

sexual (seks-yew-'l) *adjective*
1 of or relating to sex or the sexes.
2 suggesting or involving sex.
Word Family **sexually** *adverb*; **sexuality** (seks-yoo-al-i-tee) *noun* 1 the fact of being sexy. 2 sexual preference.

sexual harassment *noun*
persistent and unwelcome sexual remarks, looks and actions directed at someone, especially in a place of work.

sexual intercourse *noun*
the inserting of the male's erect penis into the female's vagina, followed by ejaculation.

sexy *adjective* (**sexier; sexiest**)
1 sexually attractive or exciting.
2 (*informal*) exciting, interesting or trendy: *sexy sports cars.*
Word Family **sexily** *adverb*; **sexiness** *noun*.

sforzando (sfort-san-doe) *adjective*, *adverb*
Music playing a note or chord loudly and with special emphasis.
[Italian]

Shabbat (shab-at) *noun*
Judaism the sabbath.
[Hebrew]

shabby *adjective* (**shabbier; shabbiest**)
in a poor, used or worn-out condition: *a shabby old coat.*
Figurative Your treatment of her was rather shabby (= mean, contemptible).
Word Family **shabbily** *adverb*; **shabbiness** *noun*.

shack *noun*
a small hut or house, usually roughly built or in poor condition.
• **shack** *verb*
Phrase **shack up** (*informal*) *Come and shack up at my house* (= stay, live).

shackle *noun*
an iron ring to lock round a prisoner's wrist or ankle.
Figurative I am bound by the shackles of politeness (= restraints).
Word Family **shackle** *verb*.

shaddock *noun*
the large yellow thick-skinned edible fruit of a Polynesian citrus tree.

shade noun

1 the comparative darkness and coolness caused by cutting off the sun's rays: *the shade of a tree.*
Figurative *Her brilliant wit put me in the shade* (= state of insignificance).
2 a variety of a particular colour.
Figurative *There is only a shade of difference between their ages* (= slight amount).
3 anything, such as a window blind, used for protection against light, heat, etc.
4 a lampshade.
5 a ghost or spirit of the dead.
• **shade** *verb*
1 to protect or cover from direct light or heat.
2 to draw or paint light and dark sections in a sketch, etc.
Word Family shading *noun Art* the lines, etc. in a drawing or painting which indicate the degree of darkness or light.

shadow noun

1 a dark shape or image of something, cast on a surface when the light is intercepted.
2 any dark area: *shadows under the eyes.*
Figurative *Poor countries live in the shadow of starvation* (= constant fear). □ *He is only a shadow of his former self* (= faintly similar image). □ *not a shadow of a doubt* (= trace).
3 (*informal*) a person who follows another closely.
• **shadow** *verb*
1 to cast shade or shadow.
2 (*informal*) to follow a person closely.
• **shadow** *adjective* imitating the actions, organization, etc. of something: *the Opposition's shadow Cabinet is ready to take office if the Government resigns.*
Word Family shadowy *adjective* 1 having or casting a shadow. 2 faint or vague.

shadow-boxing noun

the act of boxing with an imaginary opponent, for practice, exercise, etc.

shady (shay-dee) adjective (shadier; shadiest)

1 having or giving shade.
2 (*informal*) of doubtful honesty or character: *a shady business deal.*
Word Family shadily *adverb*; **shadiness** *noun*.

shaft noun

1 the long slender stem of a tool or weapon, as of an arrow or axe.
2 something resembling this in shape, such as the length of a column or a ray of sunlight.
3 a well-like passage or enclosed space: *a mine shaft.* □ *a lift shaft.*

shag[1] noun

1 a mass of rough matted hair, wool, etc.
2 a fabric with long woollen pile on one side.
3 a coarse-cut tobacco.
Word Family shaggy *adjective* (**shaggier; shaggiest**) roughly matted or unkempt; **shagginess** *noun*.

shag[2] ⇨ CORMORANT.

shaggy-dog story noun (plural shaggy-dog stories)

a long, complicated and amusing but pointless joke or story.

shagreen (sha-green) noun

a rough untanned leather made from the skin of a horse, shark or seal and usually dyed green.

shah noun

a title for the King of Iran.
[Persian]

shake verb (shakes; shaking; shook; shaken)

1 to move from side to side or to and fro with short sharp quick movements: *Take the rug outside and shake it.* □ *Shake the bottle before using.* □ *The whole house shook in the gale.*
Figurative *The bad news shook me* (= affected violently).
2 to waver or tremble: *Her voice shook with emotion.*
Phrases shake off to get rid of or escape.
shake up *We must shake things up in this office* (= liven up).
• **shake** *noun*
1 a shaking movement: *Give the bottle a good shake.*
2 a drink made by shaking the ingredients together: *a milk shake.*
Phrases no great shakes (*informal*) not very good. **two shakes** (*informal*) a moment.

shako (shay-ko) noun

a cylindrical hat with a peak at the front and a plume, worn by soldiers.
[Hungarian, peaked]

shaky (shay-kee) adjective (shakier; shakiest)

unsteady or unsafe.
Word Family shakily *adverb*; **shakiness** *noun*.

shale noun

Geology a soft slate-like rock formed of compacted layers of mud and clay.

shall verb (**should**)
an auxiliary verb indicating the future tense: *I shall go there tomorrow*.

shallot (sha-**lot**) *noun*
a small onion-like bulb which divides into smaller sections and is used as a vegetable, etc.

shallow (**shall**-o) *adjective*
of little depth: *shallow water*. □ *shallow arguments*.
• **shallow** *noun* (*usually* **shallows**) a shallow part of a body of water.
Word Family **shallowly** *adverb*; **shallowness** *noun*.

sham *noun*
a pretence: *His illness was only a sham*.
• **sham** *verb* (**shams; shamming; shammed**) to pretend.

shaman (**shah**-man) *noun*
a medicine man and priest who works with the supernatural.
Word Family **shamanism** *noun*.
[Russian]

shamble *verb*
to shuffle or walk clumsily.
Word Family **shamble** *noun* a shambling walk.

shambles *noun*
a state of confused muddle or disorder.
Word Family **shambolic** (sham-**bol**-ik) *adjective*.

> The word **shambles** has its origin in *shamble* (a meat table or meat stall), where meat would be laid out at market. The plural of the word then came to mean 'a meat market' and, by association, 'a slaughterhouse'. It then began to be used figuratively to mean 'a scene of bloodshed' and it was not until the early 20th century that it came to mean 'a scene of disorder'.

shame *noun*
1 pain or embarrassment caused by dishonourable or foolish behaviour: *I blushed with shame after telling such a lie*.
2 modesty: *Have you no shame?*
3 a pity: *What a shame!*
Phrase **put to shame** *Her skill at maths puts me to shame* (= disgraces).
• **shame** *verb*
1 to disgrace or make ashamed.
2 to force or compel through shame: *My actions shamed me into apologizing*.
Word Family **shameful** *adjective* causing or bringing shame or disgrace; **shamefully** *adverb*; **shamefulness** *noun*; **shameless** *adjective* immodest or lacking

in shame; **shamelessly** *adverb*; **shamelessness** *noun*.

shamefaced *adjective*
showing shame.
Word Family **shamefacedly** *adverb*.

shampoo *noun*
1 a soap or detergent used for washing hair or carpets.
2 a wash using such a soap.
Word Family **shampoo** *verb*.
[Hindi]

shamrock *noun*
a small clover-like plant with three leaves on each stem, the national emblem of Ireland.
[Irish, little clover]

shandy *noun* (*plural* **shandies**)
a drink made by mixing beer with lemonade or ginger beer.

shanghai (shang-**high**) *verb*
to force a person to join a ship's crew by means of alcohol, drugs or violence.
[after *Shanghai*, China]

Shangri-La (shang-gri-**lah**) *noun*
a paradise on earth.
[after a hidden paradise in *Lost Horizon* by James Hilton]

shank *noun*
1 the part of the leg between the knee and the ankle.
2 a cut of meat from the lower leg of an animal.
3 the main straight part of an anchor, key, spoon, etc.

Shanks's pony *noun*
Phrase **on Shanks's pony** (*informal*) on foot.

shan't *contraction*
a short form of **shall not**: *I shan't give up easily*.

shantung *noun*
a fabric with a rough surface, woven from coarse silk.
[after *Shantung*, a province in China]

shanty[1] *noun* (*plural* **shanties**)
a shack.

shanty[2] *noun* (*plural* **shanties**)
a sailor's song with a strong rhythm.
[French *chanter* to sing]

shanty town *noun*
an area of a town where houses are built of poor quality materials, often by the residents themselves, and have poor access to services such as water, electricity, etc.

shape *noun*
an external line or outline: *That cloud has the shape of a camel.*
Figurative The garden is in poor shape (= condition).
Phrases **lick into shape** *The sergeant swore he would lick the new recruits into shape* (= put into proper form or condition).
take shape *Our plans slowly took shape* (= took on definite form, developed).
● **shape** *verb* to make or fashion: *He shaped the wood into a broom handle.*
Phrase **shape up** *The new recruits are shaping up well* (= developing).
Word Family **shapeless** *adjective* having no regular or definite shape; **shapelessly** *adverb*; **shapelessness** *noun*; **shapely** *adjective* (**shapelier; shapeliest**) having a pleasing or attractive shape; **shapeliness** *noun*.

shape poem *noun*
a poem in which the layout of the words reflects an aspect of the subject.

shard *noun* also **sherd**
a fragment, especially of broken pottery.

share[1] *(rhymes with* air) *noun*
1 a part divided out: *Each will have to do his share of the work.*
2 *Commerce* a part of the capital of a company, returning to the holder a proportion of the profits.
● **share** *verb* to give or receive a part of something: *Share these sweets with your friends.*

share[2] *noun*
a ploughshare.

sharecropper *noun*
American a farmer who pays a share of the crop as rent.

shareholder *noun*
a person who owns shares in a company.

shark *noun*
1 any of a group of large, powerful and often dangerous marine fish, the most primitive jaw-bearing vertebrates.
2 (*informal*) a cheat or swindler.

sharp *adjective*
1 having a fine cutting or piercing edge or point: *a sharp sword.* □ *a sharp pencil.*
Figurative That corner is too sharp (= abrupt). □ *I now saw the sharp outline* (= distinct). □ *His retort was sharp* (= harsh, biting). □ *Keep a sharp lookout* (= alert). □ *I call that sharp practice* (= dishonest).

2 *Music* being raised in pitch by a semitone. Compare FLAT[1] *adjective* (definition 4).
● **sharp** *adverb* suddenly: *The horse pulled up sharp.*
Figurative Come at noon sharp (= punctually).
● **sharp** *noun*
1 *Music* a sharp note.
2 *Music* the symbol (#) indicating this.
3 (*informal*) a cheat: *a card sharp.*
Word Family **sharply** *adverb*; **sharpness** *noun*.

sharpen *verb*
to make or become sharp or sharper.
Word Family **sharpener** *noun* a person or thing that sharpens, such as a device for sharpening pencils.

sharper *noun*
(*informal*) a swindler or trickster.

sharpshooter *noun*
a person skilled at shooting.

sharp-tongued *adjective*
speaking harshly or bitterly.

sharp-witted *adjective*
being mentally quick or alert.

shashlik (**shahsh**-lik) *noun* also **shashlick**
a shish kebab.

shatter *verb*
to break violently into fragments: *The bullet shattered the glass.*
Figurative I'm shattered to hear the terrible news (= extremely distressed).
Word Family **shattering** *adjective*.

shave *verb*
1 to remove hair from the face, legs, etc. with a razor.
2 to remove in layers or thin slices: *to shave wood.*
Figurative The car shaved the fence (= scraped).
● **shave** *noun* the act of shaving, especially of the face.
Figurative That was a close shave (= narrow escape).
Word Family **shavings** *plural noun* thin slices of wood, etc. shaved off.

shaver *noun*
1 an electric razor.
2 (*dated informal*) a youngster.

shawl *noun*
a large piece of soft fabric worn around the shoulders or wrapped around a baby.

she *pronoun* (*plural* **they**)
1 the third person singular nominative pronoun, used to indicate a female: *She ate the cake.* ⇨ HE; HER; HERS.
2 used traditionally of certain objects and institutions, such as ships and nations: *The ship looked splendid as she sailed into the bay.*
3 used as a noun: *Is the cat a she?*
4 used in combination to indicate a female: *a she-goat.*

sheaf *noun* (*plural* **sheaves**)
1 a small bundle of cut cereal plants.
2 any small bundle: *a sheaf of papers.*

shear *verb* (**shears; shearing; sheared; shorn** or **sheared**)
1 to cut the wool or hair off: *to shear sheep.*
Figurative The king was shorn of his powers (= stripped).
2 (of metals, etc.) to crack or break off through strain or fatigue.
Word Family **shearer** *noun* a person who shears, especially one who shears sheep.

shears *plural noun*
a pair of large scissors with long heavy blades.

shearwater *noun*
any of various kinds of ocean birds which skim the waves on long narrow stiff wings and visit land only to breed.

sheath (sheeth) *noun*
1 a case for the blade of a knife, etc.
2 any closely fitting covering on part of an animal or plant.
3 a condom.

sheathe (shee*th*) *verb*
1 to replace a knife, etc. in its sheath.
2 to cover with a protective layer: *to sheathe a roof with copper.*
Word Family **sheathing** *noun* a protective cover or sheath.

sheath knife *noun* (*plural* **sheath knives**)
a knife having a fixed blade fitting into a sheath.

sheave *verb*
to gather or bind into a sheaf or sheaves.

sheaves
the plural of **sheaf**.

shed¹ *noun*
a simple building for storage, etc.

shed² *verb* (**sheds; shedding; shed**)
to lose or let fall: *The cattle had shed their winter coats.*
Phrase **shed blood** to injure or kill.

she'd *contraction*
a short form of **she had** or **she would**: *She'd lost her purse.*

sheen *noun*
a shining or glossy brightness.
Word Family **sheeny** *adjective* (**sheenier; sheeniest**) shiny.

sheep *noun* (*plural* **sheep**)
1 any of various wild or domesticated grass-eating mammals, valued for their wool and flesh.
2 a meek or timid person.

sheep dip *noun*
a solution in which sheep are immersed to destroy bacteria, parasites, etc.

sheepdog *noun*
any of various breeds of dog trained to guard and control sheep.

sheepish *adjective*
embarrassed or timid.
Word Family **sheepishly** *adverb*; **sheepishness** *noun*.

sheepshank *noun*
a knot used to shorten a piece of rope.

sheer¹ *adjective*
1 fine and transparent: *sheer silk.*
2 pure or absolute: *She laughed for sheer joy.*
3 steep: *sheer cliffs.*
Word Family **sheer, sheerly** *adverb*; **sheerness** *noun*.

sheer² *verb*
to swerve or turn aside.

sheet¹ *noun*
1 a large rectangle of cloth, usually cotton, used in pairs on a bed, one to cover the mattress and the other to cover the person in bed.
2 any thin piece or mass: *a sheet of paper.*
Figurative A sheet of flame swept across the field (= broad expanse).
• **sheet** *verb* to provide or cover with a sheet or sheets.
Word Family **sheeting** *noun* any material used to make sheets.

sheet² *noun*
Nautical a rope used to adjust and control a sail.
• **sheet** *verb* to secure or extend by means of a sheet or sheets.

sheet anchor *noun*
1 *Nautical* a large anchor used in an emergency.
2 a dependable person or resource.

sheet bend *noun*
a knot used to join one piece of rope to another.

sheet lightning *noun*
the diffused light from a flash within a cloud, or the reflection of a distant flash.

sheikh (shake *or* sheek) *noun* also **sheik**
a Muslim chief or leader.
Word Family **sheikhdom** *noun* a country
or state ruled by a sheikh.
[Arabic *shaikh* old man]

sheila (**shee**-la) *noun*
(*Australian informal*) a girl or woman.

shekel (**shek**-'l) *noun*
1 the basic unit of money in Israel.
2 (**shekels**) (*informal*) money.
[from *shekel*, an ancient Babylonian coin]

shelf *noun* (*plural* **shelves**)
1 a piece of wood, etc. fixed to a wall or as
part of a cupboard, for supporting objects.
2 a ledge on a cliff face.
3 a continental shelf.
Phrase **on the shelf 1** not in use. **2** not
married or not likely to be married.

shelf life *noun* (*plural* **shelf lives**)
the length of time that a product remains
fresh, usable, safe to eat, etc.

shell *noun*
1 the hard covering or case of some
animals, such as mussels, snails, etc.
2 any outer covering, usually hard: *an
eggshell*
*Figurative Only the shell of the house
remained after the fire* (= framework). □ *It
was difficult to penetrate her shell* (= reserve,
shyness).
3 any of various projectiles containing an
explosive charge and designed to explode
in the air or upon impact.
4 a cartridge.
5 *Science* a class of electron orbits in an
atom, all of which have the same energy.
6 *Rowing* a light narrow racing boat with a
smooth hull.
• **shell** *verb*
1 to remove the shell of: *Shell the eggs.*
2 to fire shells or explosives at.

she'll *contraction*
a short form of **she will**: *She'll be ten in
November.*

shellac (shel-**ak**) *noun*
a yellowish resin produced by an insect of
India and Thailand, used as a varnish and
for electrical insulation.
• **shellac** *verb* (**shellacs**; **shellacking**;
shellacked) to coat with shellac.

shellfire *noun*
the firing of shells or explosives.

shellfish *noun* (*plural* **shellfish**)
an aquatic animal, such as an oyster, with
a shell or hard outer covering.

shellproof *adjective*
able to survive the effects of explosive
shells.

shell shock ⇨ COMBAT FATIGUE.

shell suit *noun*
a double-layered track suit with a
showerproof outer nylon layer and a soft
cotton inner layer, the outer layer usually
being brightly coloured with panels of
different colours.

shelter *noun*
a place or structure which provides
protection, covering or safety.
• **shelter** *verb* to find or provide with a
shelter.

shelve[1] *verb*
1 to place on a shelf or shelves.
*Figurative The plans were shelved for
another year* (= put aside, postponed).
2 to provide with a shelf or shelves.

shelve[2] *verb*
to slope gradually.

shelves
the plural of **shelf**.

shemozzle (shi-**mozz**-'l) *noun*
(*informal*) a state of disturbance or
confusion.
[Yiddish]

shenanigans (shi-**nan**-i-g'nz) *plural noun*
(*informal*) trickery or nonsense.

shepherd (**shepp**-'d) *noun*
1 a person who guards or herds sheep.
2 a person who protects or cares for a
group.
• **shepherd** *verb* to protect, guard or
watch over.
Word Family **shepherdess** *noun* a female
shepherd.

shepherd's pie *noun* also called **cottage
pie**.
a dish of minced meat covered with a layer
of mashed potato and baked.

sherbet *noun*
a sweet fizzy powder used in drinks and
sweets.
[Arabic *sharab* a drink]

sherd ⇨ SHARD.

sheriff (**sherr**-if) *noun*
1 *American* an officer appointed to enforce
the law in a county.
2 an honorary official appointed by the
Crown to carry out judicial and electoral
functions, which vary in different parts of
the country.
3 in Scotland, a judge in the sheriff court.
[from SHIRE + REEVE]

sheriff court *noun*
in Scotland, a court where many civil actions and less serious criminal actions are heard.

sherry *noun* (*plural* **sherries**)
1 a sweet or dry fortified Spanish wine.
2 a similar wine made elsewhere.
[*Xeres* (now Jerez) in Spain]

she's *contraction*
a short form of **she is** or **she has**: *She's my sister.* □ *She's got a new boyfriend.*

Shetland pony *noun* (*plural* **Shetland ponies**)
any of a breed of very small strong ponies.
[originally from the *Shetland Islands*]

shiatsu (shee-**at**-soo) *noun*
acupressure.
[Japanese]

shibboleth (**shibb**-a-leth) *noun*
a catchphrase, tenet or social trick selected as a test of loyalty to a political party, conformity to a social group, etc.

> The word **shibboleth** comes from the Old Testament of the Bible. It meant first 'an ear of corn' and then 'a stream', but it was not its meaning but its pronunciation that was important. The Gileadites used it as a test word to find out if the people that were challenged were Ephraimites, enemies of the Gileadites. The Ephraimites could not pronounce *sh* and would say 'Sibboleth', so giving themselves away.

shield (sheeld) *noun*
1 any of various types of defensive armour carried in the hand or on the arm.
2 something used to protect, hide or defend: *He wanted a shield against poverty in old age.*
• **shield** *verb* to protect or hide.

shift *verb*
to move from one place or position to another: *Shift the logs into the yard.*
• **shift** *noun*
1 a movement or change to another place, position, etc.
2 a period of working time, especially in a factory, etc.
3 the employees who work during this time.
4 a simple dress, usually sleeveless.

shift key *noun*
a typewriter lever or computer key which adjusts the machine to type capital letters.

shiftless *adjective*
lazy, inefficient or lacking purpose.

Word Family **shiftlessly** *adverb*; **shiftlessness** *noun*.

shifty *adjective* (**shiftier; shiftiest**)
sly or furtive.
Word Family **shiftily** *adverb*; **shiftiness** *noun*.

shiitake (shi-**tah**-kay) *noun*
a kind of dark brown mushroom with pale beige gills used in oriental cooking.
[Japanese]

shillelagh (shill-**ay**-lee) *noun*
an Irish cudgel made of blackthorn or oak.
[after *Shillelagh*, County Wicklow]

shilling *noun*
(*formerly*) an old British coin equal to five pence.

shilly-shally *verb* (**shilly-shallies; shilly-shallying; shilly-shallied**)
to hesitate or remain undecided.
[from older *shill I? shall I?*]

shim *noun*
a thin strip of metal, plastic, etc., placed between two close surfaces to fill a gap.
• **shim** *verb* (**shims; shimming; shimmed**) to insert a shim or shims.

shimmer *verb*
to shine with a faintly flickering light.
• **shimmer** *noun* a faint flickering light.

shin *noun*
1 *Anatomy* the front of the leg between the knee and the ankle.
2 a cut of beef containing the lower front leg of the animal.
• **shin** *verb* (**shins; shinning; shinned**) to climb by gripping with the arms and legs.

shindig *noun*
(*informal*) a party, especially a noisy one.

shindy *noun* (*plural* **shindies**)
(*informal*) a brawl or noise.

shine *verb* (**shines; shining; shone** or **shined**, definition 3 **shined**)
1 to give out light or brightness.
Figurative He shines in all his subjects (= is excellent or outstanding).
2 to aim or point the light of: *Shine that torch over here.*
3 to polish: *I must shine my shoes.*
• **shine** *noun*
1 light or brightness.
Figurative Come rain or shine (= fair weather).
2 the act of cleaning: *Give those forks a shine.*
Phrase **take a shine to** (*informal*) to like or fancy immediately.

shiner *noun*
(*informal*) a black eye.

shingle[1] *noun*
1 a thin oblong piece of wood used in overlapping rows to form a roof or as wall cladding.
2 a tapered haircut.
Word Family **shingle** *verb*.

shingle[2] *noun*
large and small rounded stones, especially on a beach.
Word Family **shingly** *adjective*.

shingles *plural noun*
(*used with singular verb*) a viral infection of the nerves causing severe pain and a rash of blisters, often round the waist.
[Latin *cingulum* a girdle]

shinty *noun*
a simplified version of hockey played in Scotland.

shiny (shy-nee) *adjective* (**shinier; shiniest**)
bright or glossy.

ship *noun*
1 a large seagoing vessel, other than a coastal trader.
2 a warship, other than a submarine.
3 *History* a square-rigged sailing vessel with more than two masts. Compare SCHOONER (definition 1).
Phrases **jump ship** (of a sailor) to leave a ship without permission. **when one's ship comes in** when one has become rich.
• **ship** *verb* (**ships; shipping; shipped**)
1 to send or transport by ship, rail, etc.
2 (*informal*) to send: *He was shipped off to school at an early age.*
Word Family **shipping** *noun* 1 the act or business of sending goods by sea. 2 any or all ships.

shipboard *noun*
Phrase **on shipboard** aboard ship.

shipment *noun*
1 the shipping of goods.
2 the goods shipped.

shipshape *adjective*
neatly arranged or in order.

shipwreck (ship-rek) *noun*
1 the destruction of a ship, as by a storm, etc.
2 the wrecked remains of a ship.
Figurative She saw the disaster as the shipwreck of her hopes (= ruin, failure).
Word Family **shipwreck** *verb*.

shipyard *noun*
an area where ships are built or repaired.

shire *noun*
an old word for a county.

shire horse *noun*
a large and powerful draught horse.
[bred in the Shires, that is the Midlands]

shirk *verb*
to avoid or put off, especially work, duty, etc.
Word Family **shirker** *noun*.
[German *Schurke* scoundrel or parasite]

shirr *verb*
to gather fabric into parallel folds by stitching or elastic.
Word Family **shirring** *noun* an arrangement of shirred folds.

shirt (*rhymes with* hurt) *noun*
a light piece of clothing, usually reaching to the waist or hips, having sleeves and a collar and fastened down the front.
Figurative He bet his shirt on the favourite for the race (= total supply of money).
Phrase **keep one's shirt on** (*informal*) to refrain from being angry or impatient.

shirty *adjective* (**shirtier; shirtiest**)
(*informal*) annoyed or irritated.

shish kebab *noun* (shish ki-bab)
short form is **kebab** small pieces of seasoned meat grilled on a skewer, usually with vegetables.
[Turkish *sis* skewer + *kebap* roast meat]

shiver[1] (shivv-a) *verb*
to shake or tremble, as from cold, fear, etc.
Word Family **shiver** *noun*; **shivery** *adjective* shaking or trembling.

shiver[2] *noun*
a sliver or fragment.

shoal[1] *noun*
1 a group of fish.
2 (*informal*) any large group of people or things.

shoal[2] *noun*
a sandbank on the bed of the sea, a river, etc, creating an area of shallow water.
• **shoal** *verb* to make or become shallow.

shock[1] *noun*
1 a sudden violent impact or disturbance.
2 *Medicine* a sudden nervous collapse caused by severe physical injury or emotional disturbance.
3 something which causes a mental or physical disturbance: *His death was a great shock to us all.*
• **shock** *verb* to strike or affect with great surprise, horror or disgust: *The news shocked the world.*
Word Family **shocking** *adjective*

1 causing horror or disgust. 2 (*informal*) very bad.

shock² *noun*
a thick bushy mass: *a shock of red hair*.

shock absorber *noun*
any of a variety of devices used to absorb impact, especially those used on a motor vehicle to prevent excessive movement of the suspension.

shocker *noun*
(*informal*) something which is shocking, unpleasant or disagreeable.

shockproof *adjective*
able to survive damage caused by shocks.

shock therapy *noun* also called **shock treatment**.
a method of treating certain mental disorders, by giving shocks to the brain with electricity.

shock troops *plural noun*
any troops trained to begin an assault.

shock wave *noun*
Physics a very narrow region of high pressure and temperature caused by an explosion or by a body moving faster than the speed of sound.

shoddy *adjective* (**shoddier; shoddiest**)
badly or cheaply made: *a shoddy imitation gold bracelet*.
Word Family **shoddily** *adverb*; **shoddiness** *noun*.

shoe (shoo) *noun*
1 any of various strong coverings for the foot, usually of leather and reaching to the ankle.
2 something which has the shape, position or function of a shoe: *a horseshoe*.
3 *Building* a metal holder which supports the end of a beam or joist.
4 *Engineering* the part of a brake that is pressed against a wheel or drum to produce the friction necessary for braking.
Phrase **in someone's shoes** *I'm glad I'm not in your shoes* (= in the position you are in).
• **shoe** *verb* (**shoes; shoeing; shod**)
1 to provide or fit with shoes.
2 to cover or protect with a wooden or metal guard.

shoehorn *noun*
a spoon-shaped piece of horn or metal used to ease on a shoe.

shoestring *noun*
Phrase **on a shoestring** (*informal*) with a small or inadequate sum of money.
Word Family **shoestring** *adjective*.

shoe tree *noun*
an implement inserted into a shoe to help it keep its shape or stretch it.

shone a past tense and past participle of **shine**.

shoo *interjection*
go away!
Word Family **shoo** *verb*.

shook the past tense of **shake**.

shoot (*rhymes with* boot) *verb* (**shoots; shooting; shot**)
1 to fire or discharge a missile from a weapon.
Figurative He shot out his leg to trip her (= moved or sent quickly). □ *Make sure that you shoot the bolt back* (= slide). □ *The player shot towards the goal area* (= aimed or sent the ball). □ *The model's dress was shot with gold* (= marked, streaked).
2 to wound or kill with a bullet from a weapon: *Police shot the hijacker*.
3 (*informal*) to inject with a drug.
4 to photograph or film.
5 (of a plant) to put out new growths.
Phrases **shoot one's mouth off** (*informal*) to talk wildly or indiscreetly.
shoot through (*Australian informal*) to go away, especially quickly and unexpectedly.
shoot up *You have really shot up since I last saw you* (= grown quickly).
• **shoot** *noun*
1 an act of shooting.
2 an outing or contest for shooting: *a duck shoot*.
3 a new or young growth on a plant.
Word Family **shooter** *noun*; **shooting** *noun* an incident involving the firing of bullets.

shooting box *noun* (*plural* **shooting boxes**)
a lodge used by hunters during the shooting season.

shooting gallery *noun* (*plural* **shooting galleries**)
an enclosed or indoor area with targets, used for shooting practice, competitions, etc.

shooting star ⇨ METEOR.

shooting stick *noun*
a walking stick with a small folding seat at one end, used by people watching sports.

shoot-out *noun*
(*informal*) a decisive gun battle often ending in death.

shop *noun*
1 a place where goods are sold.

2 a place where work is carried out: *a workshop*.
Phrases **set up shop** to establish a business or similar activity. **talk shop** to talk about one's business or work.
• **shop** *verb* (**shops; shopping; shopped**)
1 to visit shops in order to inspect or buy.
Figurative They say he is shopping around for a wife (= looking, searching).
2 (*informal*) to inform on.
3 (*informal*) to put in prison.
Word Family **shopper** *noun*; **shopping** *noun* 1 the act of buying at shops. 2 the goods bought.

shop floor *noun*
1 workers, especially factory workers.
2 the part of a factory where machines, workers, etc. are situated.

shopkeeper *noun*
a person who owns or manages a shop.

shoplifter *noun*
a person who steals goods from a shop.
Word Family **shoplift** *verb*; **shoplifting** *noun*.

shopping mall *noun*
(*especially American*) an enclosed shopping area.

shop-soiled *adjective* also **shopworn**
dirtied or damaged due to being displayed or handled in a shop.

shop steward *noun*
a trade union official appointed to represent the workers in a particular factory or place of work.

shopwalker *noun*
a person employed in a department store to direct customers, detect shoplifters, etc.

shore[1] *noun*
the area along the edge of a sea, lake, river, etc.

shore[2] *noun*
a wooden support, usually for a wall, with one end fixed to the ground and the top fixed to the wall.
Word Family **shore** *verb* to prop up or support.

shoreline *noun*
the line at which the sea meets land.

shorn a past participle of **shear**.

short *adjective*
not long or tall: *a short distance.* □ *a short man.*
Figurative Rations are in short supply (= scanty, low in amount). □ *Do not be so short with your mother* (= rudely abrupt).

Phrases **make short work of** to finish, etc. quickly. **nothing short of** *The decision was nothing short of madness* (= real, absolute). **short for** *TV is short for television* (= a shorter form of). **short of** *I am short of money this month* (= lacking in).
• **short** *adverb*
1 abruptly or suddenly: *The horse stopped short.*
2 before reaching: *The bombs fell short of the mark.*
• **short** *noun*
1 something which is short, such as a short film shown before the feature film at a cinema.
2 (**shorts**) a pair of short trousers usually reaching to somewhere between the thigh and the knee.
3 (**shorts**) *American* underpants.
4 *Electricity* a short circuit.
Phrase **in short** *In short, this is my suggestion* (= briefly).
• **short** *verb Electricity* to short-circuit.

shortage (**short**-ij) *noun*
an insufficient amount.

short back and sides *noun*
a conservative short hairstyle.

shortbread (**short**-bred) *noun*
a thick crumbly biscuit made with flour, sugar and butter.

short-change *verb*
1 to give less change than is due.
2 to cheat or deceive.

short circuit *noun*
Electricity a fault in an electric circuit, in which two points of different voltage become connected, causing the current to flow directly between them rather than through the complete circuit.
Word Family **short-circuit** *verb*
1 *Electricity* to suffer a short circuit or cause a short circuit in. 2 to bypass or circumvent.

shortcoming (**short**-kumm-ing) *noun*
a flaw or weakness: *The plan has some obvious shortcomings which must be corrected.*

short cut *noun*
a quicker way.

shorten *verb*
to make or become shorter.

shortening *noun*
any fat, such as butter or lard, used in cakes or pastry.

shorthand noun
a method of rapid writing by using symbols instead of words and phrases. Compare LONGHAND.

short-handed adjective
not having enough workers, helpers, etc.

shortlist noun
a list of the most likely candidates, chosen from a larger group of applicants.
Word Family **shortlist** verb.

shortly adverb
1 soon.
2 briefly or abruptly.

shortness noun
the quality of being short.

short-range adjective
having a limited extent in distance or time.

short-sighted adjective
not able to see far.
Figurative The short-sighted plan had failed by the end of the year (= lacking concern for the future).
Word Family **short-sightedly** adverb; **short-sightedness** noun.

short-tempered adjective
irritable or easily made angry.

short-term adjective
existing or developing within a short time.

short ton ⇨ TON (definition 2).

short wave noun
a radio wave having a wavelength of less than 100 m and a frequency of less than 30 MHz. Compare LONG WAVE; MEDIUM WAVE.

short-winded adjective
becoming out of breath easily.

shot¹ noun
1 the firing or discharge of a weapon, especially a gun.
Figurative The golfer drove a brilliant shot down the fairway (= hit, stroke). □ Have a shot at this puzzle (= try, attempt). □ The vet gave the dog a tetanus shot (= injection). □ Her parting shot was a cynical laugh (= reply, remark). □ The colour returned to her face after a shot of brandy (= drink).
2 a pellet, bullet, etc. discharged from a weapon.
3 any or all such pellets.
4 a marksman: He is a very good shot.
5 (informal) a photograph.
6 Athletics the heavy iron ball thrown in the contest of putting the shot.
Phrases **big shot** (informal) an important person. **like a shot** (informal) at once: She accepted the exciting invitation like a shot.

shot in the arm (informal) something which brings back energy, interest, etc.
shot in the dark a wild guess.

shot² adjective
woven so that different or changing colours are visible: shot silk.
• **shot** verb the past tense and past participle of **shoot**.

shotgun noun
a sporting gun having one or two barrels with a smooth bore, used to fire small shot or pellets.

shotgun wedding noun
(informal) a wedding occurring, or hastened, because the bride is pregnant.

should (rhymes with good) verb
1 the past tense of **shall**.
2 used to indicate duty or necessity: You should apologize for your rudeness.
3 used to indicate likelihood: They should get there before dark.

shoulder (**shole**-da) noun
1 Anatomy the upper part of the body between the arm and the neck.
2 the corresponding part of an animal.
3 a cut of meat from this part.
4 the part of a garment covering the shoulders: This coat has padded shoulders.
5 something shaped like a shoulder: a shoulder of rock.
Phrases **give someone the cold shoulder** to snub someone. **rub shoulders with** to meet or associate with. **straight from the shoulder** (of a reprimand, etc.) direct and frank.
• **shoulder** verb
1 to push with the shoulder or shoulders.
2 to carry or take on the shoulders.
Figurative The company will shoulder your travelling expenses (= carry, bear).

shoulder blade ⇨ SCAPULA.

shouldn't contraction
a short form of **should not**: You shouldn't fight with your sister.

should've contraction
a short form of **should have**: I should've saved some of my pocket money.

> [!] Of is sometimes incorrectly used instead of 've: They should have or should've (not should of) listened.

shout verb
to call or cry out loudly.
Phrase **shout down** to silence by talking or shouting more loudly than.
Word Family **shout** noun.

shove (shuv) verb
to push rudely or roughly.

Phrase shove off (*informal*) to go away or leave.
Word Family shove *noun*.

shovel (shuv-'l) *noun*
a long-handled tool with a broad scooped blade for moving things, such as soil, coal, etc.
• **shovel** *verb* (**shovels; shovelling; shovelled**)
1 to lift or move with a shovel.
2 to put or lift in large quantities or with great speed.
Word Family shoveller *noun*.

show (sho) *verb* (**shows; showing; showed; shown** or **showed**)
to cause or allow to be seen: *Show me the book that you mentioned.*
Figurative *Can you show the gentleman out?* (= conduct). □ *The clock showed midnight* (= registered). □ *I'll show you how to do it* (= instruct).
Phrases show off *He showed off his new car* (= exhibited for attention or approval).
show up 1 *The argument showed up her ignorance* (= made obvious, revealed).
2 *He did not show up at the office until lunch time* (= arrive).
• **show** *noun*
1 the act of showing.
2 a public performance or exhibition: *a cattle show.* □ *There's a new show on at the local theatre.*
Figurative *That company is quite a big show now* (= organization, undertaking). □ *Her fright was all show* (= pretence).
Phrases good show! splendid! **show of hands** a vote taken, especially by counting raised hands. **steal the show** *She stole the show with her exciting speech* (= won the most attention or popularity).

showbiz *noun*
(*informal*) show business.

show business *noun*
all forms of public entertainment, such as plays, films, etc.

showcase *noun*
1 a glass cabinet for displaying objects.
2 a situation, place, etc. by or in which something is shown at its best.

showdown *noun*
1 a final revelation of intentions, hostility, etc.
2 an open trial of strength.

shower (*rhymes with* flower) *noun*
1 a brief fall of rain, snow, etc.

Figurative *A shower of sparks shot from the soldering iron* (= fall, scattering). □ *He was met with a shower of abuse* (= stream, flow).
2 a bathroom fitting usually mounted above head height, consisting of a nozzle with small holes to spray the water.
3 the room or area containing this.
4 the act of washing oneself using such equipment.
5 *American* a party for a prospective bride or mother.
• **shower** *verb*
1 to fall in or as if in a shower.
2 to wash under a shower.
Word Family showery *adjective*.

showgirl *noun*
a chorus girl, especially in a musical, nightclub, etc.

showing *noun*
an exhibition, display or performance.

showjumping *noun*
a horseriding competition in which a series of obstacles must be jumped in a certain order.

showman *noun* (*plural* **showmen**)
1 a man who owns or exhibits a show.
2 a person who has a flair for doing things in a dramatic or entertaining way.
Word Family showmanship *noun*.

shown a past participle of **show**.

show-off *noun*
(*informal*) a person who ostentatiously displays skill or wealth.

showplace *noun*
1 a building exhibited to the public because of its beauty, interest, etc.
2 any impressive building: *The architect's home was a real showplace.*

showroom *noun*
a room used for displaying goods.

show trial *noun*
History a mock trial of political opponents.

showy *adjective* (**showier; showiest**)
1 making a brilliant or impressive display: *a plant with large showy flowers.*
2 ostentatious or making a vulgar display: *a showy dress.*
Word Family showily *adverb*; **showiness** *noun*.

shoyu (sho-yoo) *noun*
a Japanese soy sauce.
[Japanese]

shrank the past tense of **shrink**.

shrapnel *noun*
1 the fragments from an exploding shell.

2 a type of shell designed to explode in the air and send fragments in all directions. [invented by *H. Shrapnel*, 1761-1842, a British army officer]

shred *noun*
a small narrow strip cut or torn off: *The cat tore my slippers to shreds.*
Figurative There's not a shred of evidence to support your story (= piece, particle).
• **shred** *verb* (**shreds; shredding; shredded**) to reduce to shreds.
Word Family **shredder** *noun*.

shrew *noun*
1 a mouse-like insect-eating mammal with a pointed snout.
2 a bad-tempered scolding woman.
Word Family **shrewish** *adjective*.

shrewd (shrood) *adjective*
clever or showing good judgement, often in a sharp way: *a shrewd businessman.*
Word Family **shrewdly** *adverb*; **shrewdness** *noun*.

> The word **shrewd** is now quite a complimentary term, but it originally meant 'wicked' or 'malignant', derived from Middle English *shrewed*. This probably came from an early meaning of *shrew*, 'a wicked malignant man' (not 'scolding woman', which came to be the modern meaning). There is, however, a possibility that *shrewd* came from an obsolete verb meaning 'to curse'.

shriek (shreek) *noun*
a loud shrill cry: *I heard a shriek from the bushes.*
• **shriek** *verb*
1 to utter a shriek.
2 to utter with or in a shriek.
Word Family **shrieker** *noun*.

shrift *noun*
an old word for the absolution granted by a priest.
Phrase **short shrift** *Her request was given short shrift by the busy official* (= hasty or unsympathetic treatment).

shrike *noun*
any of various birds with a strong hooked beak which impale their prey on thorns.

shrill *adjective*
high-pitched and piercing: *a shrill whistle.*
• **shrill** *verb*
1 to make a shrill sound.
2 to utter in a shrill voice.
Word Family **shrilly** (shril-lee) *adverb*; **shrillness** *noun*.

shrimp *noun* (*plural* **shrimp** or **shrimps**)
1 any of a group of small edible marine shellfish, considered a delicacy.
2 (*informal*) a very small or thin person, especially a child.

shrine *noun*
1 a tomb or casket containing sacred remains, such as those of a saint.
2 any building or place considered sacred because of its historic or religious associations.
[Latin *scrinium* a box]

shrink *verb* (**shrinks; shrinking; shrank; shrunk** or **shrunken**)
1 to become or make smaller: *Some fabrics shrink in hot water.*
2 to draw back or recoil: *The frightened child shrank back against the hedge.*
Figurative The authorities shrank from taking such extreme steps (= held back in reluctance).
• **shrink** *noun* (*informal*) a psychiatrist.
Word Family **shrinkable** *adjective*; **shrinkage** *noun* **1** the act or fact of shrinking: *This fabric is subject to shrinkage.* **2** the amount or degree of shrinking: *The shrinkage of this garment was excessive.*

shrink wrap *noun*
a thin transparent protective plastic film wrapped tightly round a product for sale.
Word Family **shrink-wrapped** *adjective*.

shrive *verb* (**shrives; shriving; shrove; shriven**)
Christianity an old word meaning 'to give absolution to'.

shrivel (shriv-'l) *verb* (**shrivels; shrivelling; shrivelled**)
to shrink or become dry.

shroud (*rhymes with* loud) *noun*
1 a cloth in which a dead person is wrapped for burial.
2 *Nautical* a wire or rope leading from the top of a mast to either side of a ship.
• **shroud** *verb* to clothe in a shroud.
Figurative The whole affair is shrouded in mystery (= covered, hidden).

Shrove Tuesday *noun*
the day before the beginning of Lent.

shrub *noun*
a woody perennial plant, smaller than a tree and lacking a main trunk.
Word Family **shrubby** *adjective*; **shrubbery** *noun* (*plural* **shrubberies**)
1 a place planted with shrubs. **2** any or all shrubs.

shrug *verb* (**shrugs; shrugging; shrugged**)

to lift and lower the shoulders as an expression of disbelief, indifference, perplexity, disdain, etc.

Phrase **shrug off 1** *She shrugged off their insults with a laugh* (= let pass, paid no attention to). **2** *He could not shrug off his pursuers* (= escape, get rid of).

Word Family **shrug** *noun* **1** the act of shrugging. **2** a woman's lightweight garment covering the shoulders and arms.

shrunk a past participle of **shrink**.

shrunken a past participle of **shrink**.

shucks *interjection*

American an exclamation of disappointment, annoyance or disgust.

shudder *verb*

to shiver violently with cold, fear, etc.
Word Family **shudder** *noun*; **shudderingly** *adverb*.

shuffle *verb*

1 to walk with dragging or scraping steps. **2** *Cards* to mix the cards in a pack so as to change their order, especially before dealing.

Figurative *He was shuffled from one job to another* (= moved about). □ *She always shuffles if asked a direct question* (= acts evasively).

Phrase **shuffle off** to shrug off.
Word Family **shuffle** *noun*.

shuffleboard *noun*

1 a board or table game in which discs or coins are driven towards squares in order to score.
2 a similar game on a large scale played on a ship's deck.

shun *verb* (**shuns; shunning; shunned**)

to avoid consistently or deliberately: *He shuns all publicity.*

shunt *verb*

1 to turn or move aside or onto another course: *The discussion got shunted off into trivialities.*

Figurative *The teacher was shunted from one school to another* (= shifted, transferred).
2 *Railways* to sort and marshal trains.
• **shunt** *noun*

1 the act of shunting.
2 *Electricity* a low resistance alternative path for a portion of an electric current.
Word Family **shunter** *noun*.

shush *verb*

to ask for quiet, especially by making the sound 'shh'.
• **shush** *interjection* hush.

shut *verb* (**shuts; shutting; shut**)

1 to move something into position so as to block an opening: *Please shut the window.* □ *Shut the valve on the pipeline.*
2 to secure by fastening doors, windows, etc.: *He always shuts the shop himself.*
3 to bring together or fold: *I can't shut my umbrella.*
4 to cease normal operations: *The cinema was shut for two weeks while the roof was repaired.*

Phrases **shut down 1** to secure by lowering a lid, cover, etc. **2** to cease operating for a time, e.g. a factory, machine, etc. **shut off 1** to stop the flow of water, electricity, etc. **2** to isolate. **shut up 1** to confine or imprison. **2** (*informal*) to stop talking. **3** to secure by fastening windows, doors, etc.

shutdown *noun*

the closing of a factory or other place of work.

shut-eye *noun*

(*informal*) sleep.

shutter *noun*

1 a hinged cover for a window.
2 *Photography* a device on a camera which opens and shuts to allow light to pass through the lens onto the film.
• **shutter** *verb* to provide or close with shutters.

shuttle *noun*

a device on a loom, used for passing the threads of the weft to and fro between the threads of the warp.
• **shuttle** *verb* to move rapidly to and fro: *The ants shuttled back and forth moving the breadcrumbs into their nest.*
[Old English *seytel* dart, arrow]

shuttlecock *noun*

a piece of cork or plastic stuck with feathers and used instead of a ball in certain games such as badminton.

shuttle service *noun*

a transport system, usually making frequent trips back and forth over a short distance, e.g. in an emergency.

shy[1] *adjective*

1 lacking confidence when with others.
2 easily startled or frightened.
Figurative *I'm a bit shy of investing in stocks and shares* (= wary, cautious).
3 (*informal*) short or lacking: *I'm a bit shy of funds at the moment.*
Phrase **fight shy of** to avoid.
• **shy** *verb* (**shies; shying; shied**)

1 (of a horse) to jump suddenly sideways, usually in fright.
2 to draw back, as from doubt or caution: *Never bully a client or he'll shy away from the deal.*
Word Family shy *noun* (*plural* **shies**).

shy² *verb* (**shies; shying; shied**)
to throw, especially with a swift sideways motion: *We shied stones across the lake.*
Word Family shy *noun* (*plural* **shies**) **1** a sudden swift throw. **2** a coconut shy.

shyster (shy-ster) *noun*
(*informal*) a person who conducts business in an unscrupulous or unethical way.

Siamese cat (sigh-a-meez **cat**) *noun*
one of several breeds of short-haired cats, having a light grey or fawn coat with darker ears, face, paws and tail.

Siamese twins (sigh-a-meez **twinz**)
plural noun
a set of twins joined together at some part of the body.

sibilant (sib-i-l'nt) *adjective*
hissing.
• **sibilant** *noun Language* a sibilant sound, as in *less, past,* etc.
Word Family sibilance *noun.*

sibling *noun*
a brother or sister.

sibyl (sib-il) *noun*
Mythology a prophetess.

sic *adverb*
so or thus: inserted in brackets after a word or phrase, etc. to show that it appears in this form in the original.
[Latin]

sick *adjective*
1 ill or affected by disease.
Figurative I'm sick of working today
(= tired, weary). □ *His constant arrogance makes me sick* (= disgusted).
2 vomiting or feeling like vomiting: *Sea trips always make me sick.*
3 of or for sick people: *a sick ward.*
4 mentally disturbed.
5 morbid or macabre: *No more sick jokes, please.*
• **sick** *noun* (*informal*) vomit.
Word Family sicken *verb* to make or become sick; **sickening** *adjective* disgusting or revolting; **sickeningly** *adverb*; **sickness** *noun* **1** the state of being sick. **2** a particular disease. **3** a feeling of being sick. **4** a sick feeling in the stomach.

sickle *noun*
a short-handled tool with a curved blade for cutting, trimming plants, etc. Compare SCYTHE.

sickly (sik-lee) *adjective* (**sicklier; sickliest**)
1 not strong or healthy: *a sickly child.*
2 of, caused by or associated with sickness: *a sickly pallor.*
3 being too sweet or rich: *sickly sweet tea.*
□ *sickly sentimentality.*
Word Family sickliness *noun.*

side *noun*
1 a surface of an object, especially a surface joining a top and a bottom: *the side of a hill.* □ *the sides of a crate.*
2 either of the two surfaces of a piece of paper, cloth, etc.: *Do not write on both sides of the page.*
3 any of the straight lines that make up a two-dimensional shape: *A triangle has three sides.*
4 a half or part: *Which side of your body is the pain on?* □ *The east side of the city is the business sector.*
5 one of two or more opposing groups, sets of opinion, etc.: *Whose side are you on?*
□ *Everyone has ignored my side of the question.*
6 the space immediately next to a person or thing: *I stood at his side.*
7 a line of descent: *On my mother's side of the family everyone was tall and fair.*
8 (*informal*) a supercilious or pretentious manner: *It's no good putting on side with me.*
9 *Billiards* a spin given to a ball by striking it on one side.
10 half a carcass: *a side of bacon.*
Phrases **get on the right side of** to have or achieve the approval of. **get on the wrong side of** to incur the displeasure of.
on the side (*informal*) **1** as a sideline.
2 secretly.
• **side** *adjective*
1 at or on one side: *a side door.*
2 from or to one side: *a side glance.*
Figurative Don't get confused by side issues
(= secondary, incidental).
• **side** *verb*
Phrases **side against** to set oneself against. **side with** to support or take the part of.

side arms *plural noun*
any weapons worn at the side, such as swords, bayonets, etc.

sideboard *noun*
1 a piece of furniture with a flat top, drawers and cupboards, for storing tableware or serving food.
2 (**sideboards**) ⇨ SIDEBURNS.

sideburns *plural noun* also called **sideboards**.
the hair growing down the side of a man's face in front of his ears.

sidecar *noun*
a one-wheeled compartment for a passenger, attached to the side of a motorcycle.

side dish *noun* (*plural* **side dishes**)
a dish served to accompany the main dish of a course.

side effect *noun*
any effect produced in addition to those intended, e.g. by a drug.

sidekick *noun*
(*informal*) a close associate or friend.

sidelight *noun*
1 a light at or coming from the side.
Figurative The book contains some interesting sidelights on Napoleon's private life (= incidental details).
2 a window in the side of a building, at the side of a door, another window, etc.
3 a car's parking or subsidiary front light.

sideline *noun*
1 any activity pursued in addition to one's regular business or work.
2 a subsidiary line of merchandise.
3 (**sidelines**) *Sport* the area beyond the boundary lines.
4 (**sidelines**) *Sport* the place where the spectators sit.
Phrase **from the sidelines** from the point of view of a spectator or outsider.

sidelong *adjective, adverb*
directed to one side. *a sidelong glance.*

sidereal (sigh-**deer**-i-al) *adjective*
of or relative to the stars.

sidereal day *noun*
Astronomy the time taken for the earth to rotate once on its axis, measured relative to a star. Compare DAY (definition 4); SOLAR DAY.

side saddle *noun*
a saddle designed for women wearing long skirts, in which both of the rider's legs are on the same side, usually the left side, of the horse.
• **side-saddle** *adverb* seated on or as if on a side saddle.

sideshow *noun*
a small show or exhibition associated with a fair, circus, etc.

sidesman *noun* (*plural* **sidesmen**)
a churchwarden's assistant who acts as usher and takes the collection.

side-splitting *adjective*
extremely funny.
Word Family **side-splittingly** *adverb*.

sidestep *verb* (**sidesteps; sidestepping; sidestepped**)
1 to step out of the way of: *to sidestep a puddle.*
2 to avoid: *You are always trying to sidestep your responsibilities.*
Word Family **sidestep** *noun*.

side street *noun*
a street leading off a main street.

sidestroke *noun*
a swimming style in which the swimmer lies on his or her side, while each arm pulls alternately and the legs kick.

sidetrack *verb*
to distract or divert from the main issue or course.

sidewalk *noun*
American a pavement.

sidewall *noun*
one of the side surfaces of a tyre.

sideways *adjective, adverb*
1 towards or from one side.
2 with one side towards the front.

siding (**side**-ing) *noun*
Railways a length of track running off a main line, used for parking, loading and marshalling trains.

sidle *verb*
to move sideways, especially in a furtive manner.

siege (seej) *noun*
the surrounding of a fortified place by a military force intent on capturing it.
Phrase **lay siege to** to besiege.
[Latin *sedere* to sit]

sierra (see-**err**-a) *noun*
a range of hills or mountains with sharp peaks.
[Spanish, a saw]

siesta (see-**ess**-ta) *noun*
a rest or short sleep, especially one taken after the midday meal.
[Spanish, from Latin *sexta* (*hora*) sixth hour]

sieve (siv) *noun*
a round container made of wire mesh or finely perforated metal, used for straining or sifting.
• **sieve** *verb* to put or force through a sieve.

sift *verb*
1 to separate fine particles from coarse ones using a sieve.
Figurative *The detective carefully sifted all the evidence* (= sorted through).
2 to scatter with a sieve: *Sift the sugar over the plums.*
Figurative *The snow sifted gently down* (= fell in fine particles).
Word Family **sifter** *noun*.

sigh *verb*
to give out a deep long audible breath, as in weariness, sorrow, relief, etc.
Figurative *The homesick lad sighs continually for home* (= yearns).
Word Family **sigh** *noun*.

sight *noun*
1 the ability to see: *to lose one's sight.*
2 the act or fact of seeing.
3 the range or field of one's vision: *in sight of land.*
4 something which is seen: *A beautiful sight lay before us.*
5 (**sights**) something worth seeing: *to see the sights of New York.*
6 (*informal*) a lot: *The party was a sight better than we expected.*
7 something odd or unattractive to see: *He looked a sight in the tattered old coat.*
Phrases **lose sight of** to fail to keep in view. **on sight 1** as soon as seen. **2** on being presented: *a sterling draft payable on sight.* **sight unseen** without having seen the thing in question.
• **sight** *verb*
1 to get a glimpse or view of: *to sight a school of whales.*
2 to take a sight or observation with an instrument.
3 to take aim with a gun, etc.
Word Family **sighted** *adjective* not blind; **sighting** *noun* an occasion when something or someone is seen; **sightless** *adjective* blind; **sightly** *adjective* pleasing to see; **sightliness** *noun*.

sight-read *verb*
Music to play or sing from written music without previous practice or rehearsal.

sightseeing *noun*
the act of visiting places and things of interest, especially as a tourist.
Word Family **sightseer** *noun*.

sign (sine) *noun*
1 something that points to the existence or likelihood of something: *He gave no sign that suicide was on his mind.* □ *Dark clouds are a sign of rain.*
2 an action or gesture intended to convey an idea, information, etc.: *He made a sign with his finger that warned us to keep quiet.*
3 a board or poster serving to display information or advertise.
4 a conventional symbol or figure which stands for a word, mathematical operation, division of the zodiac, etc.
Figurative *He disappeared without a sign* (= indication).
• **sign** *verb*
1 to write one's signature on.
Figurative *The team has just signed a new player* (= hired by written contract).
2 to communicate by a sign: *He signed to me to follow him up the stairs.*
3 to communicate using sign language.
Phrases **sign off** to cease broadcasting, etc. **sign on 1** to register as unemployed. **2** to be hired or employed by a contract. **3** to begin broadcasting, etc. **sign up** to enlist, e.g. in the armed forces.
Word Family **signer** *noun*; **signing** *noun*.
[Latin *signum* a mark, token]

signal (sig-n'l) *noun*
1 any action, message, device, etc. used to convey a warning, order, or information: *a railway signal.* □ *Give the signal to begin.*
2 *Electricity* a wave, sound, etc. which transmits information.
• **signal** *verb* (**signals; signalling; signalled**)
1 to make a signal to.
2 to make known by signals or signs: *Her face signalled her distress.*
• **signal** *adjective*
1 conspicuous or notable: *a signal victory for our side.*
2 used to signal: *a signal fire burning on the hilltop.*
Word Family **signaller** *noun*; **signally** *adverb* notably.

signatory (sig-na-tree) *noun* (*plural* **signatories**)
a person or nation that has signed a treaty or other document.

signature (sig-na-cher) *noun*
1 a person's name as signed by himself or herself.
2 the act of signing a document.
3 *Music* a sign used to indicate key or tempo.

signature tune *noun*
a piece of music always played with a particular programme, etc. to identify it.

signboard (**sine**-bord) *noun*
a board or hoarding bearing writing, advertisements, etc.

signet (**sig**-nit) *noun*
a small seal, impressed on a document to authenticate it.

signet ring *noun*
a ring in which initials or a seal are set.

significant (sig-**niff**-i-k'nt) *adjective*
1 notable: *a significant victory.*
2 full of meaning: *a significant glance.*
Word Family **significantly** *adverb*;
significance *noun*.

signify (**sig**-ni-fie) *verb* (**signifies**;
signifying; **signified**)
1 to be a sign of: *Raised eyebrows signify surprise.*
2 to make known by signs: *He signified his approval by nodding his head.*
3 to matter: *What does it signify if they do not believe us?*
Word Family **signification** (sig-niff-i-**kay**-sh'n) *noun* 1 the act of signifying.
2 what is signified.
[Latin *significare* show by signs]

sign language *noun*
the use of certain gestures as a method of communication with and between deaf people.

signor (seen-**yor**) *noun* (*plural* **signori**)
(seen-**yor**-ee)
the Italian title for a man.

signora (seen-**yor**-a) *noun* (*plural* **signore**) (seen-**yor**-ay)
the Italian title for a married woman.

signorina (seen-ya-**ree**-na) *noun* (*plural* **signorine**) (seen-ya-**ree**-nay)
the Italian title for an unmarried woman.

signpost *noun*
1 a post bearing a sign which points out a particular place, direction, etc.
2 any indication, sign or clue.

signwriter *noun*
a person who designs and produces signs, notices, etc.
Word Family **signwriting** *noun*.

Sikhism (**seek**-izm) *noun*
a monotheistic religion of Indian origin whose members believe in the teachings of the ten Gurus and the holy book known as the Guru Granth Sahib.
Word Family **Sikh** *noun, adjective*.
[Hindi *Sikh* disciple]

silage (**sigh**-lij) *noun*
fodder for farm animals, made from green plants preserved in a silo.

silence (**sigh**-l'nce) *noun*
1 the absence of sound: *the silence of an underground cave.*
2 the state or fact of being silent: *He was reduced to silence by the teacher's anger.*
Figurative I *shall have to swear you to silence about this matter* (= secrecy).
• **silence** *verb* to make silent or bring to silence.
Figurative His *convincing explanation silenced all our doubts* (= put an end to).
[from Latin]

silencer (**sigh**-l'n-sa) *noun*
a device attached to a gun, car exhaust system, etc. to reduce noise.

silent (**sigh**-l'nt) *adjective*
1 making no sound or noise.
2 taciturn, reticent: *He's one of the strong silent types.*
3 having no soundtrack: *She was a star of the silent movies.*
4 not pronounced: *The word 'pneumonia' has a silent 'p'.*
Word Family **silently** *adverb*.

silent majority *noun*
those who do not agitate, demonstrate or campaign and whose views are therefore liable to be forgotten.

silent partner ⇨ SLEEPING PARTNER.

silhouette (sill-oo-et) *noun*
1 a portrait in profile, showing an outline only, usually black on white.
2 the outline of a solid figure seen against a contrasting background.
Word Family **silhouette** *verb*.

The word **silhouette** takes its name from Étienne de *Silhouette* (1709-1767), a French Minister of Finance. His connection with it is not clear. A *silhouette*, being an outline only, was considerably cheaper than a portrait and, apparently, Silhouette was famous for his meanness. However, he may simply have been the creator of such pictures.

silica (**sill**-i-ka) *noun*
silicon dioxide (formula SiO_2), a hard white mineral occurring in many forms, such as quartz.
Word Family **siliceous** (sill-**ish**-us) *adjective* containing, resembling or consisting of silica.
[Latin *silicis* a flint]

silicon (**sill**-i-kon) *noun*
a very common non-metal. Widely
occurring as silica, it is used in glass,
silicones and alloys.

silicon chip *noun*
a microchip.

silicone (**sill**-i-kone) *noun*
Chemistry any of a group of complex
polymers of carbon and silicon, used as
lubricants, resins and lacquers.

silicosis (sill-i-**ko**-sis) *noun*
a disease of the lungs caused by inhaling
siliceous particles in stone dust, etc.

silk *noun*
1 a fine soft fibre obtained from the
cocoon of a silkworm, used to make yarn
or fabric.
2 any substance resembling silk, such as
the fibres on an ear of corn.
3 ⇨ QUEEN'S COUNSEL.
4 (**silks**) a jockey's racing clothes, usually
in the horse owner's registered colours.
Word Family **silky** *adjective* (**silkier**;
silkiest) smooth, soft and glossy like silk;
silkily *adverb*; **silkiness** *noun*; **silken**
adjective 1 made of silk. 2 silky.
[Latin *sericum*]

silk screen *noun*
a printing process in which the ink is
pressed through a stencil in the form of
specially prepared fine material, originally
silk.

silkworm *noun*
a caterpillar which spins a soft cocoon of
fine silk threads.

sill *noun*
1 a horizontal piece of wood or stone
across the bottom of a door, window, etc.
2 *Geology* a sheet of lava which has
solidified between layers of other rock.

silly *adjective* (**sillier**; **silliest**)
1 showing a lack of good sense.
Figurative The blow knocked me silly
(= stunned, dazed).
2 *Cricket* (of a fielding position) very close
to the batsman.
• **silly** *noun* (*plural* **sillies**) a silly person.
[Middle English *sely* happy]

silly season *noun*
the summer holiday season when
journalists short of copy traditionally fill
newspapers, television news programmes,
etc. with exaggerated or sensationalized
accounts of trivial events.

silo (**sigh**-lo) *noun*
1 a large tower-like building in which grain
or fodder is stored.

2 an underground launching place for
ballistic missiles.
[Greek *siros* a pit to keep grain in]

silt *noun*
a fine deposit laid down by a river when it
floods.
• **silt** *verb*
Phrase **silt up** to fill or become filled with
silt.

Silurian (sile-**yoor**-i-an) ⇨ PALAEOZOIC.
[Latin *Silures* a Welsh tribe]

silvan ⇨ SYLVAN.

silver *noun*
1 a ductile malleable metal, a good
conductor of heat and electricity. It is used
for making mirrors, coins and ornaments
and its light-sensitive compounds are used
in photography.
2 a lustrous white or whitish-grey colour.
3 any objects, such as coins, cutlery, etc.,
which are made of silver.
4 a silver medal.
• **silver** *adjective*
1 of, made of or containing silver.
2 having the colour of silver.
*Figurative The silver notes of a soprano
voice* (= clear and ringing). □ *The orator
had a silver tongue* (= eloquent,
persuasive).
• **silver** *verb*
1 to coat or plate with silver or a silver-like
substance.
2 to become the colour of silver.

silver birch *noun* (*plural* **silver birches**)
the common birch, which has silvery white
bark that sheds in layers.

silverfish *noun* (*plural* **silverfish** or
silverfishes)
a primitive wingless insect which feeds on
paper, sugar, starch, etc.

silver foil ⇨ ALUMINIUM FOIL.

silver jubilee *noun*
the 25th anniversary of an important
event.

silver medal *noun*
a medal made of silver or silver in colour
awarded to the person or team coming
second in a race or competition.

silver plate *noun*
a thin silver veneer applied to another
metal surface.
Word Family **silver-plate** *verb*.

silverside *noun*
the upper side of a round of beef.

silversmith *noun*
a person who makes and repairs articles of silver.

silverware *noun*
any articles, such as candlesticks, etc., which are made of silver.

silver wedding *noun*
a 25th wedding anniversary.

silvery (silv-a-ree) *adjective*
1 covered with or containing silver.
2 having the colour or lustre of silver.
3 having a soft clear ringing sound.
Word Family **silveriness** *noun*.

simian (simm-i-an) *adjective*
of or relating to apes or monkeys.
[Greek *simos* snub-nosed]

similar (simm-i-la) *adjective*
1 close or related in appearance, nature, etc.
2 *Maths* relating to figures with equal angles and proportional sides.
Word Family **similarly** *adverb*;
similarity (simm-i-**larr**-i-tee) *noun*
(*plural* **similarities**) 1 the state of being similar. 2 a point of likeness.

simile (simm-i-lee) *noun*
a figure of speech in which two unlike things are compared, e.g. *He chattered like a magpie*. Compare METAPHOR.
[Latin *similis* like]

similitude (sim-ill-i-tewd) *noun*
similarity.

simmer *verb*
1 to cook gently just below boiling point.
2 to be filled with suppressed emotion.
Phrase **simmer down** (*informal*) to become calm or calmer.
Word Family **simmer** *noun*.

simony (sigh-ma-nee) *noun*
the buying and selling of church offices.
[after *Simon Magus*, who tried to buy apostolic powers]

simper *verb*
to smile in a silly or self-conscious way.
Word Family **simper** *noun*; **simperingly** *adverb*.

simple *adjective*
1 easy: *It was a simple test and everyone passed.*
2 having one part only: *a simple leaf.*
Figurative His simple style of writing is very popular (= not elaborate, unaffected).
□ *a simple cottage* (= not complicated).
□ *a simple cold* (= ordinary). □ *You must think I'm simple if you expect me to believe that* (= ignorant, silly).

Word Family **simplicity** (sim-**pliss**-i-tee), **simpleness** *noun*; **simplify** (sim-pli-fie) *verb* (**simplifies; simplifying; simplified**) to make simple or more simple; **simplification** (sim-pliff-i-**kay**-sh'n) *noun*.
[from Latin]

simple interest *noun* ➪ INTEREST *noun*.

simple-minded *adjective*
1 artless or unsophisticated.
2 mentally deficient.

simpleton (sim-p'l-t'n) *noun*
a silly or ignorant person.

simplistic *adjective*
adopting an over-simple or unsophisticated approach to a complex problem.
Word Family **simplistically** *adverb*.

simply *adverb*
1 in a simple manner: *The catering was done simply but quite adequately.*
2 merely or only: *It is simply a question of money.*
3 absolutely: *It is simply ridiculous to try such a scheme.*

simulate (sim-yoo-late) *verb*
to imitate: *We simulated real conditions for the experiment.* □ *Computers can be used to simulate real life.*
Figurative She simulated enthusiasm (= pretended).
Word Family **simulation** (sim-yoo-**lay**-sh'n) *noun*; **simulator** *noun*.
[Latin *similis* like]

simulcast (sim-'l-kahst) *noun*
a programme broadcast on radio and television at the same time.
Word Family **simulcast** *verb*.
[from SIMUL(taneous broad)CAST]

simultaneous (sim-'l-**tay**-ni-us) *adjective*
happening, existing or done at the same time.
Word Family **simultaneously** *adverb*; **simultaneousness, simultaneity** (sim-'l-ta-**nee**-i-tee) *noun*.
[Latin *simul* at the same time]

sin *noun*
an offence or fault, especially against moral or religious laws.
Phrases **live in sin** (*informal*) (of an unmarried couple) to live together.
original sin *Christianity* the natural tendency of human beings to commit sin, considered to be the inherited result of Adam's disobedience.
Word Family **sin** *verb* (**sins; sinning; sinned**).

since *adverb*
1 between a particular past time and the present: *He went overseas and I have not heard from him since.*
2 in the past: *I had long since forgotten our quarrel.*
Phrase ever since from then until now.
• **since** *preposition* after or during the time after: *We have been working since daybreak.*
• **since** *conjunction*
1 in the period following the time when: *He has not written since he went overseas.*
2 because: *Since it is late I shall go home now.*

sincere (sin-**seer**) *adjective*
(of feelings, behaviour, etc.) free from pretence, deceit, etc.
Word Family sincerely *adverb*; **sincerity** (sin-**serr**-i-tee) *noun.*
[Latin *sincerus* clean, untainted]

sine (sine) *noun*
Maths the ratio of the side opposite an angle of a right-angled triangle to the hypotenuse. *abbrev.* sin.

sinecure (**sigh**-ni-kyoor) *noun*
a position or office which requires little or no work but yields profitable returns.
[Latin *sine cura* without a care]

sine die (sin-i **dee**-ay) *adverb*
Law with no date announced for reassembly or resumption: *The court adjourned sine die.*
[Latin, without a day (mentioned)]

sine qua non (sin-i kwah **non**) *noun*
something which is essential.
[Latin, without which not]

sinew (**sin**-yoo) *noun*
a tendon.
Word Family sinewy *adjective* muscular.

sinfonia *noun*
Music a symphony.

sinful *adjective*
wrong or wrongful.
Word Family sinfully *adverb*; **sinfulness** *noun.*

sing *verb* (**sings; singing; sang; sung**)
1 to make musical sounds with the voice.
2 to make a humming or buzzing sound: *My ears are singing.*
3 to proclaim enthusiastically: *to sing someone's praises.*
4 (*informal*) to inform against: *The robber was worried that his accomplice might sing to the police.*
Phrase sing out (*informal*) to shout.
Word Family singer *noun.*

singe (sinj) *verb* (**singes; singeing; singed**)
to burn slightly.
Word Family singe *noun.*

single *adjective*
separate or being one only: *Not a single person arrived.* □ *Every single seat was empty.*
Figurative *A single man desires lodgings* (= unmarried). □ *The room contained two single beds* (= for one person). □ *She bought a single ticket for London* (= for one trip or direction only).
• **single** *verb*
Phrase single out to choose or pick out from others.
• **single** *noun*
1 a single thing, e.g. a hit for one run at cricket or a one-way rail ticket.
2 a room in a hotel, etc. for one person.
3 a record with one song on each side.
4 (**singles**) *Sport* a game of tennis, etc. between two players.
[from Latin]

single-breasted *adjective*
(of a coat) having flaps fastened with one row of buttons. Compare DOUBLE-BREASTED.

single file *noun* also called **Indian file**.
a line of people or things arranged one behind the other.

single-handed *adjective*
1 working or done alone or unaided.
2 having or requiring the use of only one hand or person.
Word Family single-handedly *adverb.*

single market *noun*
a free trade association of countries, e.g. those of the EU, allowing unrestricted movement of goods, capital and personnel.

single-minded *adjective*
devoted exclusively to one cause, interest, etc.
Word Family single-mindedly *adverb*; **single-mindedness** *noun.*

singleness *noun*
the state of being single.

single parent *noun*
a person who is bringing up a child on his or her own.

singlet *noun*
a short-sleeved or sleeveless garment with a round neck, worn as a shirt or vest.

singleton *noun*
something occurring singly, especially a playing card which is the only one of a suit in a hand.

singly adverb
1 one by one.
2 by oneself.

sing-song adjective
having a regular, often monotonous, rising and falling rhythm, intonation, etc.
• **sing-song** noun (informal) an informal gathering at which everyone sings.

singular (sing-gew-ln) adjective
1 extraordinary, strange or remarkable: The Christmas party was a singular success.
2 Grammar (of a word) expressing only one: In the sentence 'I went to buy a book', the noun 'book' is singular.
Word Family singularly adverb; **singularity** (sing-gew-larr-i-tee) noun.
[Latin singularis alone, unique]

sinister (sinn-ist-a) adjective
suggesting or threatening evil.
[Latin, on the left, ill-omened]

sink verb (sinks; sinking; sank; sunk or sunken)
1 to go or cause to go below the surface or to the bottom of a liquid, etc.
2 to fall slowly: She sank weakly to her knees.
Figurative The sick man sank fast (= became weaker). □ Her face sank at the news (= became depressed).
3 Sport to hit the ball directly into the hole, etc.: to sink a putt.
Figurative to sink a well (= drill, dig).
□ He sank his money into the worthless shares (= invested).
Phrase sink in to be understood.
• **sink** noun a basin, usually connected to a water supply and drain, and often set into a worktop, used for washing dishes, etc.
Word Family sinkable adjective.

sinker noun
a weight attached to a fishing line or net to make it sink in the water.

sinkhole noun also called **swallow hole**.
a hole formed in soluble rock by the action of water, which conducts surface water to an underground passage.

sinner noun
a person who sins.

sinuous (sin-yew-us) adjective
having many bends or curves.
Figurative sinuous arm movements (= supple).
Word Family sinuously adverb.
[from Latin]

sinus (sigh-nus) noun (plural **sinuses**)
Anatomy any cavity within a bone, especially one of those within the nose and face.
[Latin, a curve, a fold]

sinusitis (sigh-na-sigh-tiss) noun
an inflammation, often chronic, of the sinuses.
[SINUS + -itis]

sip verb (sips; sipping; sipped)
to drink a little at a time.
Word Family sip noun.

siphon (sigh-f'n) noun also **syphon**
1 a piece of tube through which a liquid may flow up over the wall of its container and down to a lower level by atmospheric pressure.
2 a soda siphon.
• **siphon** verb
1 to pass through a siphon.
2 to draw off or remove from a larger source.
[Greek, a pipe]

sippet noun
an old word for a small bit, especially a small piece of toasted or fried bread dipped in soup, etc.

sir noun
1 a respectful form of address used to a man.
2 (**Sir**) a title for a knight, etc.

sire (rhymes with fire) noun
1 the male parent, especially of horses and dogs.
2 a form of address formerly used to a monarch.
• **sire** verb (of a male) to produce offspring.

siren (sigh-r'n) noun
1 any of various devices, e.g. on an ambulance, which produce a loud wailing sound.
2 any alluring or seductive woman.
[from the Sirens, a group of sea nymphs in Greek mythology who lured sailors to shipwreck by their sweet singing]

sirloin noun
a choice cut of beef from the upper part of the loin.
[French sur over + LOIN]

sirocco noun
a dry dusty wind from the Sahara which picks up humidity over the Mediterranean and brings hot enervating rainy weather to southern Europe.
[Italian scirocco]

sisal (*sigh*-z'l) *noun*
a fibre made from the stems of a cactus-like plant and used for ropes.
[from *Sisal*, a port of Yucatan, Mexico]

sissy *noun* (*plural* **sissies**) also **cissy**
an effeminate or cowardly man or boy.
[from SISTER]

sister *noun*
1 a daughter of the same parents as another child.
2 any female who has a close bond with another.
3 a woman belonging to a religious order.
4 a senior nurse.
Word Family **sisterly** *adjective*;
sisterhood, sisterliness *noun*.

sister-in-law *noun* (*plural* **sisters-in-law**)
1 the sister of one's husband or wife.
2 the wife of one's brother or brother-in-law.

sit *verb* (**sits; sitting; sat**)
1 to rest with the body supported upon the buttocks.
Figurative When the artist's model was sick I sat for him (= posed). □ *The bird was sitting on a branch* (= perching).
2 to cause to sit: *I sat the child in the chair.*
3 to be in session: *Parliament sat every day last week.*
4 to babysit.
5 to fit or hang: *This skirt does not sit properly.*
6 to enter as a candidate: *Did you sit for the exam?*
Phrases **be sitting pretty** (*informal*) to be established in comfort or at an advantage. **sit back** to take no action. **sit down** to sit after standing. **sit in on** to take part in as an observer or visitor. **sit on** (*informal*) 1 to snub. 2 to delay: *to sit on a project.* **sit out 1** to stay until the end of. 2 to take no part: *I sat out while they danced.* **sit tight** (*informal*) to bide one's time. **sit up 1** to raise oneself from a lying or slouched position. 2 to remain awake or out of bed. 3 to become interested and alert.

sitar (*sit*-ar) *noun*
a guitar-like Indian musical instrument with a main set of strings and a second group which provides resonance.

sitcom *noun*
(*informal*) a regular television or radio comedy series involving the same set of characters.

sit-down strike *noun*
a strike in which those taking part refuse either to work or leave their place of employment, etc. until their demands are satisfied.

site *noun*
the physical position of something, such as a town.
● **site** *verb* to locate or place.
[Latin *situs* situated]

sit-in *noun*
an organized passive protest in which workers or demonstrators sit down in a place normally prohibited to them and refuse to move.

sitter *noun*
1 a person who sits.
2 a babysitter.
3 (*informal*) something which is easily accomplished.

sitting *noun*
1 a period of remaining seated, for example when posing for a portrait.
2 a session of a parliament, court, etc.

sitting duck *noun*
(*informal*) a person who is an easy target or victim.

sitting room *noun*
a living room.

sitting tenant *noun*
a tenant in occupation of premises when their ownership changes.

situate (*sit*-yoo-ate) *verb*
1 to give a particular place to: *The museum is situated in the main square.*
2 to place in a particular condition or circumstances: *How are you situated financially?*

situation (sit-yoo-*ay*-sh'n) *noun*
1 a location: *The situation of the new house is very beautiful.*
2 a state of affairs: *The present situation could easily lead to war.*
3 a job: *I am applying for a situation with the bank.*

> The word **situation** in the sense of 'a state of affairs' is frequently overused, as in *the political situation, the financial situation.* Some people, being interviewed on television, will use the word several times even in the same sentence. It is often used unnecessarily, as in *We are in a war situation* or *A strike situation developed.* ⇨ CLICHÉ.

sit-up *noun*
an abdominal exercise in which one raises one's upper body from a supine position without using the arms for leverage.

SI unit *noun*
a unit of the International System of units, in which the units for all quantities are interrelated and derived from seven base units, namely: metre, kilogram, second, ampere, kelvin, mole and candela.
[French S(ystème) + I(nternational d') + UNIT(és)]

six *noun (plural* **sixes***)*
1 a cardinal number, the symbol 6 in Arabic numerals, VI in Roman numerals.
2 *Cricket* a score of six runs, obtained by a batsman hitting the ball over the boundary of the field without it bouncing.
Phrase **at sixes and sevens** in disorder or confusion.
Word Family **six** *adjective;* **sixth** *noun, adjective.*

sixpence *noun*
(*formerly*) an old British coin equal to 2.5 pence.

six-shooter *noun*
a revolver with six chambers.

sixteen *noun*
a cardinal number, the symbol 16 in Arabic numerals, XVI in Roman numerals.
Word Family **sixteen** *adjective;* **sixteenth** *adjective, noun.*

sixth form *noun*
the students of a secondary school who are studying for A levels.

sixth sense *noun*
intuition or perception beyond the five senses.

sixty *noun (plural* **sixties***)*
1 a cardinal number, the symbol 60 in Arabic numerals, LX in Roman numerals.
2 (**sixties**) the numbers 60 to 69 in a series, such as the years in a century.
Phrase **the sixty-four thousand dollar question** the crucial or most difficult question, originally in a quiz programme.
Word Family **sixty** *adjective;* **sixtieth** *adjective, noun.*

size¹ *noun*
1 the amount of space taken up by something: *What size is the garden?*
Figurative He is more concerned with size than quality (= largeness).
2 any of the measured categories into which manufactured articles are divided: *What size are your shoes?*

3 the actual condition: *That is about the size of the matter.*
• **size** *verb* to make or sort according to size.
Phrase **size up** to form a judgement or opinion about.

size² *noun*
any of various glues or starches used for mixing paints, sealing surfaces, etc.
• **size** *verb* to coat or treat with size.

sizeable (**size-a-b'l**) *adjective* also **sizable**
of considerable size: *He has a sizeable fortune.*
Word Family **sizeably** *adverb.*

sizzle *verb*
1 to make a hissing sound, as in frying or burning.
2 (*informal*) to be very hot.
• **sizzle** *noun* the sound of sizzling.
Word Family **sizzler** *noun.*

sjambok (**sham-bok**) *noun*
a whip made from rhinoceros hide.
[Afrikaans]

skate¹ *noun*
a device consisting of an edged blade, wheels, etc. attached to the underside of a shoe or boot for moving over a smooth surface: *an ice skate.*
• **skate** *verb* to glide over ice or other smooth surfaces wearing a pair of skates.
Phrase **skate over, skate round** to avoid in conversation, etc.
Word Family **skater** *noun.*

skate² *noun*
any of a group of flat edible fish of the ray family, with a blunt tail and a pointed snout.

skateboard *noun*
a flat board with wheels on which the rider stands or crouches to travel at speed, particularly on sloping surfaces.
Word Family **skateboarder** *noun;* **skateboarding** *noun.*
[SKATE + BOARD]

skedaddle (**ski dud-'l**) *verb*
(*informal*) to run away.

skein (**skane**) *noun*
a length of thread or yarn wound into a coil.

skeleton (**skell-i-t'n**) *noun*
1 *Anatomy* the framework of bones of the body.
2 any supporting framework.
Figurative The author prepared a rough skeleton of his next book (= outline).
3 (*informal*) a very thin or bony person or animal.

Phrase **skeleton in the cupboard** a fact which is kept secret because it may cause shame or embarrassment.

• **skeleton** *adjective* forming a nucleus: *a skeleton staff*.

Word Family **skeletal** (skell-i-t'l) *adjective*.

[Greek *skeletos* dried up]

skeleton key *noun* also called **master key**.

a key which fits various locks which usually require separate keys.

sketch *noun* (*plural* **sketches**)

1 a hastily or roughly drawn picture, etc., especially a preliminary one giving an outline but no details.

2 any rough or brief outline, e.g. of a story, incident or plan.

3 a short comic play, etc.

Word Family **sketch** *verb*; **sketchy** *adjective* (**sketchier**; **sketchiest**) 1 giving only outlines. 2 incomplete or superficial; **sketchily** *adverb*; **sketchiness** *noun*.

[Greek *skhedios* impromptu]

skew *adjective*

having an oblique direction or position.

Word Family **skew** *verb* to move or cause to move at an angle.

skewbald (skew-bawld) *adjective*

(of a horse) having patches of different colours, especially brown and white. Compare PIEBALD *adjective*.

• **skewbald** *noun* a skewbald animal, especially a horse.

skewer *noun*

a long pin of wood or metal, especially one put through meat during cooking to hold it in shape, etc.

Word Family **skewer** *verb*.

ski (skee) *noun*

a long narrow strip of wood, metal or plastic turned up at the front and attached to a boot, etc. for travelling over snow or water.

• **ski** *verb* to travel on or use skis.

Word Family **skier** *noun*.

[Norwegian]

skid *verb* (**skids**; **skidding**; **skidded**)

to slide or slip sideways due to loss of traction, e.g. when a vehicle turns a corner.

• **skid** *noun*

1 the act of skidding over a surface.

2 a runner on the underpart of some aircraft.

Phrase **on the skids** (*informal*) on the way to ruin or disaster.

skidpan *noun*

a prepared slippery surface on which motorists are taught to control skids.

skiff *noun*

a light racing boat for one sculler.

skiffle *noun*

a style of music based on American folk songs and played on a variety of instruments.

ski lift *noun*

any form of rope, tow or lift to take skiers up a mountain, such as a T-bar, which supports a skier while his or her skis run over the snow.

skill *noun*

an ability to do something well, due to knowledge, practice, training, etc.

Word Family **skilful** (*American* **skillful**) *adjective* having or showing skill; **skilfully** *adverb*; **skilfulness** *noun*; **skilled** *adjective* trained or experienced.

skillet *noun*

1 a frying pan.

2 (*formerly*) a long-handled saucepan on legs.

skilly *noun*

a thin oatmeal broth flavoured with meat: *Officers' wives have puddings and pies, but soldiers' wives have skilly.*

skim *verb* (**skims**; **skimming**; **skimmed**)

1 to move or glide lightly over or along a surface.

Figurative *She skimmed over her essay before handing it to the teacher* (= read superficially).

2 to remove any floating matter from a liquid with a spoon, etc.

Word Family **skimmer** *noun* a person or thing that skims, such as a ladle-like utensil with holes, used to skim fat, etc. from liquids.

skimmed milk *noun*

milk from which the cream has been removed.

skimp *verb*

1 to use sparingly or be frugal.

2 to do hastily or inattentively.

Word Family **skimpy** *adjective* (**skimpier**; **skimpiest**) 1 not big enough. 2 mean; **skimpily** *adverb*; **skimpiness** *noun*.

skin *noun*

1 the external covering of an animal body, fruit, etc.

2 any layer or coating on a surface: *A skin formed on the boiling milk.*

Phrases **by the skin of one's teeth** narrowly. **get under one's skin** (*informal*) to have an irresistible or infuriating effect on. **jump out of one's skin** to be very frightened or surprised. **save one's skin** to escape harm. **skin and bone** emaciated.

• **skin** *verb* (**skins**; **skinning**; **skinned**)
1 to remove skin from: *to skin a rabbit*.
2 to cut or injure the skin or surface of: *to fall and skin one's knee*.
3 (*informal*) to strip of money or belongings.

skin-deep *adjective*
slight or superficial.

skin-diver *noun*
a person equipped with an aqualung, etc. for swimming under water.
Word Family **skin-dive** *verb*.

skinflint *noun*
(*informal*) a mean or extremely frugal person.

skinny *adjective* (**skinnier**; **skinniest**)
very thin.

skint *adjective*
(*informal*) with no money at all.
[alteration of *skinned*]

skintight *adjective*
(of a garment) fitting as tightly as skin.

skip¹ *verb* (**skips**; **skipping**; **skipped**)
to jump lightly, as over a skipping rope.
Figurative Please don't *skip the interesting parts* (= leave out). □ *The robbers had skipped the country* (= left hastily). □ *He skipped through the first few pages* (= passed without attention to details).
Word Family **skip** *noun*.

skip² *noun*
a container for transporting materials in building or mining operations.

ski-plane *noun*
an aeroplane fitted with skis to enable it to land on snow or ice.

skipper¹ *noun*
(*informal*) a captain or leader.

skipper² *noun*
a person or thing that skips.

skipping rope *noun*
a rope which one or more people hold, swinging it in a loop and jumping over it.

skirmish (**skerm**-ish) *noun* (*plural* **skirmishes**)
a minor, especially an unexpected, encounter with enemy forces.

skirt *noun*
1 a piece of clothing which wraps round the lower half of the body.
2 a cut of meat taken from below the fillet, used in steak pies, etc.
3 (*informal*) a girl or woman.
• **skirt** *verb*
1 to lie on or along the border of: *Our land skirts the river*.
2 to pass or go around: *We skirted the city to avoid the traffic*.

skirting *noun* also **skirting board**
a protective strip of wood set round the base of a wall where it joins the floor.

skit *noun*
a short play or piece of writing which makes fun of a person or event.

skittish *adjective*
1 (of a horse) nervous.
2 (of a woman) flirtatious or frivolous.
Word Family **skittishly** *adverb*; **skittishness** *noun*.

skittle *verb*
to knock over or send flying.
• **skittle** *noun*
1 a wooden pin used in a game resembling tenpin bowling
2 (**skittles**) (*used with singular verb*) a bowling game in which such pins are used.

skivvy *noun* (*plural* **skivvies**)
(*informal*) a female servant, especially one doing heavy work.

skua *noun*
any of various hawk-like seabirds which chase other birds until they disgorge their catch of fish.

skulduggery *noun*
any mean dishonesty or trickery.

skulk *verb*
to move about stealthily, sneak away, lurk or shirk.

skull *noun*
1 *Anatomy* the framework of fused bones forming the head of animals.
2 (*informal*) the head considered as the source of intelligence, etc.

skull and crossbones *noun*
a representation of the human skull above two crossed bones, formerly used by pirates as a symbol of death.

skullcap *noun*
a small close-fitting cap.

skunk *noun*
1 a small black North American mammal with a white stripe down its back, noted

for the strong-smelling liquid it ejects when in danger.

2 (*informal*) a thoroughly contemptible person.

sky *noun* (*plural* **skies**)
the upper air, seen as blue when there are no clouds.
Phrases **the sky's the limit** there is no limit. **to the skies** highly, extravagantly: *The critics praised his new play to the skies.*
● **sky** *verb* (**skies; skying; skied**)
(*informal*) to strike or raise high into the air.

skydiving *noun*
the sport of jumping from an aircraft, and only opening the parachute late in descent.
Word Family **skydive** *verb*; **skydiver** *noun.*

sky-high *adjective, adverb*
very high.

skyjack *verb*
to hijack an aeroplane.
● **skyjack** *noun* an instance of skyjacking.

skylark¹ *noun*
a lark which sings a sustained high-pitched song in flight.

skylark² *verb*
to frolic boisterously or in high spirits.

skylight *noun*
an opening in a roof, often with glass set into it, to let in light.

skyline *noun*
1 the boundary line between earth and sky; the apparent horizon.
2 the outline of something seen against the sky.

skyrocket *noun*
a firework in the shape of a rocket.
● **skyrocket** *verb* (*informal*) to rise quickly and suddenly: *Prices skyrocketed.*

skyscraper *noun*
a tall multi-storey building.

skyward *adjective*
directed or tending towards the sky.
Word Family **skywards, skyward** *adverb.*

skywriting *noun*
writing made in the sky by smoke released from an aeroplane.

slab *noun*
1 a broad flat piece of stone, wood, etc.
2 a thick slice: *For lunch we had slabs of bread with jam.*

slack¹ *adjective*
1 (of rope, etc.) not tense or taut.
2 (of a tide, wind, etc.) sluggish.
Figurative She was scolded for producing such slack work (= careless, lazy). □ *Trade was slack after the Christmas rush* (= dull, inactive).
● **slack** *noun*
1 a loose or slack part or portion of something, such as a rope, sail, etc.
2 a period of little activity.
● **slack** *verb*
1 to slacken or relax.
2 (*informal*) to shirk a duty, etc.
Word Family **slackly** *adverb*; **slackness** *noun.*

slack² *noun*
the fine refuse of coal.

slacken *verb*
1 to loosen: *Slacken the rope or it will break.*
2 to make or become less active, intense, etc.: *Slacken speed so that I can catch up.*

slacker *noun*
(*informal*) a lazy person.

slacks *plural noun*
(*dated*) trousers.

slag *noun*
1 any non-metallic residue obtained during the smelting of metal ores.
2 *Geology* the scoria from a volcano.
● **slag** *verb* (**slags; slagging; slagged**)
(*informal*) to insult or criticize.

slag heap *noun* a mound of waste matter from mining or a similar process.

slain the past participle of **slay.**

slake *verb*
1 to satisfy or partly satisfy a desire, thirst, etc.
2 to add water to lime to form calcium hydroxide (**slaked lime**).

slalom (**slah**-l'm) *noun*
the art of racing in and out of a line of posts or other obstacles, as in skiing. [Norwegian, sloping track]

slam¹ *verb* (**slams; slamming; slammed**)
1 to shut violently and noisily: *She slammed the door.*
2 to put or knock down violently and noisily: *She slammed the books onto the table.*
3 to criticize severely: *The critics slammed my new book.*
● **slam** *noun* a violent and noisy closing or impact.

slam² *noun*
Cards the winning of all the tricks (a **grand slam**) or all but one (a **small slam**) at whist, bridge, etc.

slam dunk *noun*
in basketball, an instance of shooting the ball forcefully through the basket.

slander *noun*
Law a false spoken statement against another person. Compare LIBEL.
Word Family slander *verb*; **slanderer** *noun*; **slanderous** *adjective*; **slanderously** *adverb*.

slang *noun*
words that are used very informally, usually by a particular group of people, as distinct from formal language. Compare COLLOQUIAL.
Word Family slangy *adjective* (**slangier; slangiest**).

slanging match *noun* (*plural* **slanging matches**)
an exchange of insults or abuse.

slant (slahnt) *verb*
to slope or lean at an angle: *My writing slants forwards.*
Figurative *The story was slanted to make him appear guilty* (= distorted).
● **slant** *noun* a lean or slope: *the slant of a roof.*
Figurative *The news gave a new slant to the situation* (= point of view, aspect).

slap *verb* (**slaps; slapping; slapped**)
1 to strike or smack, especially with the open hand: *He slapped my face.*
2 to put down loudly and forcefully: *He slapped his wallet onto the counter.*
● **slap** *noun*
1 a smart blow or smack.
2 the sound of such a blow.
Phrases slap in the face a rebuff or disappointment. **slap on the back** congratulations.
● **slap** *adverb*
1 exactly: *slap in the middle of the road.*
2 straight: *It hit me slap on the head.*

slap bang *adverb*
(*informal*) suddenly or violently.

slapdash *adjective, adverb*
in a careless or hasty manner.

slap-happy *adjective*
(*informal*) cheerfully carefree or irresponsible.

slapstick *noun*
any form of entertainment based on practical jokes or loud and boisterous play-acting, e.g. between two circus clowns.

slap-up *adjective*
(*informal*) first-class: *a slap-up meal.*

slash *verb*
to cut with long sweeping strokes: *The chair has been slashed with a knife.*
Figurative *The new government slashed taxes* (= greatly reduced).
● **slash** *noun* (*plural* **slashes**)
1 a sweeping stroke or cut.
2 a gash made by such a stroke.

slat *noun*
a long thin narrow piece of wood, metal, etc., such as those used in Venetian blinds.

slate *noun*
1 *Geology* a hard grey fine-grained rock, formed from compressed mudstone, which splits easily into sheets.
2 a thin sheet of slate used in overlapping rows to form a roof, or formerly to write on.
3 a dark bluish-grey colour.
Phrases clean slate a good record. **put on the slate** to record an amount for future payment.
● **slate** *verb* to cover with slates.
Figurative *Why do the critics always slate my novels?* (= criticize severely).

slattern *noun*
an old word for a dirty or untidy girl or woman.
Word Family slatternly *adjective*.

slaughter (slaw-ta) *noun*
the killing of animals, especially for food.
Figurative *The slaughter of civilians in a war is tragic* (= brutal killing).
● **slaughter** *verb*
1 to kill and cut up animals for food.
2 to massacre.
Figurative *We slaughtered our opponents in the game* (= thoroughly defeated).
Word Family slaughterous *adjective* brutal or destructive.

slaughterhouse *noun*
an abattoir.

slave *noun*
1 a person who is owned by another for whom he or she works without pay, rights, etc.
2 a person who is completely dominated by or in the power of another person, influence, etc: *a slave to fashion.*
● **slave** *verb* to work very hard: *He slaved all night on his essay.*
Word Family slaver *noun* 1 a person who owns or deals in slaves. 2 a ship used to

transport slaves; **slavery** *noun* 1 the condition of being a slave. 2 the practice of keeping slaves.

slave-driver *noun*
1 a person who makes people work very hard.
2 an overseer of slaves.

slaver (**slavv**-a) *verb*
to slobber or dribble.
***Word Family* slaver** *noun* saliva.

slavish (**slay**-vish) *adjective*
of or like a slave: *Slavish obedience to his every command.*
***Word Family* slavishly** *adverb*;
slavishness *noun*.

slay *verb* (**slays; slaying; slew; slain**)
an old word meaning 'to kill or destroy'.

sleazy *adjective* (**sleazier; sleaziest**)
shabby, dirty or sordid.
***Word Family* sleaze** *noun* (*informal*)
immoral or dishonest behaviour.

sled *noun*
a sledge, often used for transporting loads.

sledge *noun*
1 a vehicle mounted on runners, used over snow and ice and drawn by huskies, etc.
2 a smaller version of this to take one or two people, used in the pastime of sliding down snowy slopes.
***Word Family* sledge** *verb*.

sledgehammer *noun*
a large heavy hammer.

sleek *adjective*
1 soft, smooth and glossy.
2 (of a person) well-fed or well-groomed.
Figurative The new boss is a little too sleek in his manners (= suave).
• **sleek** *verb* to smooth or make sleek.
***Word Family* sleekly** *adverb*; **sleekness** *noun*.

sleep *noun*
the condition or period during which the mind and body rest, and voluntary movements and full consciousness are suspended.
• **sleep** *verb* (**sleeps; sleeping; slept**) to rest or repose in sleep.
Figurative This hotel sleeps 60 people (= has beds for). □ *I shall sleep in the open tonight* (= pass the night).
Phrases **put to sleep** to kill painlessly:
The vet put the sick dog to sleep. **sleep on** to think about for a while, especially overnight: *I'll sleep on the problem.* **sleep with** to have sexual intercourse with.

sleeper *noun*
1 a person or animal that sleeps.
2 a railway carriage with sleeping accommodation.
3 a beam or slab forming part of the foundation for railway tracks.
4 a ring worn in the ear after it has been pierced, to prevent the hole closing.

sleepily *adverb*
in a sleepy manner.

sleepiness *noun*
the state of being sleepy.

sleeping bag *noun*
a long bag, often waterproof, for sleeping outdoors, etc.

sleeping partner *noun* also called **silent partner**.
a person who puts money into a business but takes no active part in it.

sleeping pill *noun*
any tablet taken to induce sleep.

sleeping sickness *noun*
a tropical African disease transmitted to human beings by the tsetse fly, causing increasing lethargy and, if untreated, death. Compare SLEEPY SICKNESS.

sleepless *adjective*
1 without sleep.
2 unable to sleep.
***Word Family* sleeplessly** *adverb*;
sleeplessness *noun*.

sleepover *noun*
an occasion when someone has a friend or friends to stay the night at his or her house.

sleepwalker *noun*
a person who walks or performs other activities while asleep.
***Word Family* sleepwalk** *verb*.

sleepy *adjective* (**sleepier; sleepiest**)
ready or wishing to sleep.
Figurative This is a sleepy little town (= quiet).

sleepyhead *noun*
(*informal*) a sleepy or inattentive person.

sleepy sickness *noun*
a viral, sometimes epidemic, form of encephalitis, marked by extreme lethargy, which may be followed by partial or complete recovery or may lead on to Parkinson's disease. Compare SLEEPING SICKNESS.

sleet *noun*
a mixture of falling rain and snow.
***Word Family* sleet** *verb*.

sleeve *noun*
1 the part of a piece of clothing which encloses all or part of the arm.
2 something, such as the protective cover for a record, which fits over or encloses another thing.
Word Family **sleeveless** *adjective.*

sleigh (slay) *noun*
1 a light sledge drawn by one or more horses.
2 any of the various light sledges used in winter sports, e.g. the bobsleigh.
Word Family **sleigh** *verb.*

sleight of hand (slite 'v **hand**) *noun* also called **legerdemain.**
conjuring tricks, such as making cards disappear, pulling rabbits out of hats, etc.
[*sleight* = slyness]

slender *adjective*
attractively thin: *the slender stem of a wine glass.*
Figurative I only had a slender chance of winning (= small).
Word Family **slenderly** *adverb;* **slenderness** *noun.*

slept the past tense and past participle of **sleep.**

sleuth (slooth) *noun*
(*informal*) a detective or investigator.
[Icelandic *slodh* track]

slew[1] the past tense of **slay.**

slew[2] *verb*
to twist or swerve round, especially without moving from one place.

slice *noun*
1 a thin, flat and wide piece cut off from something: *a slice of bread.*
2 any piece or portion: *a slice of good luck.*
3 any tool or utensil with a broad flat blade: *a fish slice.*
4 *Sport* a stroke which causes the ball to spin away from the desired direction, e.g. to the right of a right-handed player. Compare HOOK (definition 3).
• **slice** *verb*
1 to cut up into slices.
Figurative The boat sliced through the waves (= cut).
2 *Sport* to hit a slice.

slick[1] *adjective*
suave: *the slick talk of a salesman.*
Figurative (*informal*) *That new suit looks slick* (= smart). □ *a slick business deal* (= shrewd, clever).
• **slick** *noun* a smooth or slippery area, such as a film of oil on water.

Word Family **slickly** *adverb;* **slickness** *noun.*

slick[2] *verb*
to make sleek or smooth: *to slick one's hair with oil.*

slicker *noun*
1 (*informal*) a slick person.
2 a person who is rather too smartly dressed.
3 a city slicker.

slide *verb* (**slides; sliding; slid**)
to move smoothly over a polished or slippery surface: *The car slid on the icy road.*
Figurative She slid out of the back door (= went quickly or quietly, without fuss). □ *He slid into bad habits* (= passed gradually). □ *He had let things slide* (= deteriorate, fall into neglect).
• **slide** *noun*
1 a sliding movement.
2 a structure with a smooth sloping surface down which children can slide.
3 also called **transparency.** *Photography* a positive image on film, usually in colour and projected on to a screen.
4 a small oblong piece of glass on which objects are placed for study under a microscope.
5 something which slides, such as a clasp worn in the hair, a movable part in a musical instrument, etc.

slide rule *noun*
a device for calculations, consisting of two or more logarithmic scales which slide past each other on a rule.

sliding scale *noun*
a scale of prices, wages, etc. which may be varied in relation to other factors such as taxes or cost of living.

slight *adjective*
1 small in amount, importance, etc.: *a slight increase in salary.*
2 slender or frail-looking: *a young girl of slight build.*
Phrase **in the slightest** *I'm not worried in the slightest* (= at all).
• **slight** *verb* to snub or ignore: *He felt slighted because I had no time for a chat.*
• **slight** *noun* a snub or rebuff.
Word Family **slightly** *adverb* 1 to a small degree. 2 slenderly; **slightness** *noun;* **slighting** *adjective* insulting; **slightingly** *adverb.*

slim *adjective* (**slimmer; slimmest**)
(of a person) not stout or heavy.

Figurative Your slim excuse isn't convincing (= poor, insufficient). □ *a slim chance* (= small).

• **slim** *verb* (**slims; slimming; slimmed**) to lose weight by dieting, etc.

Word Family **slimly** *adverb*; **slimness** *noun*; **slimmer** *noun*.

> The word **slim** is now complimentary when used of people, but originally it meant 'small, meagre' or even 'inferior', being derived from Middle Dutch *slim*, meaning 'slanting, awry, crooked'. The sense of 'unfortunately small' survives when it is applied to words such as *chance* or *hope*.

slime *noun*
1 soft sticky oozing mud.
2 any thick sticky fluid.

slimy (**sly-mee**) *adjective* (**slimier; slimiest**)
of, like or covered in slime.
Figurative He's only a slimy flatterer (= unpleasantly servile).
Word Family **slimily** *adverb*; **sliminess** *noun*.

sling *noun*
1 a loop or band by which something is suspended, such as the bandage supporting a broken arm.
2 a strap with a string attached to each end from which a stone is hurled by whirling it round the head and releasing one of the strings.

• **sling** *verb* (**slings; slinging; slung**)
1 to hurl or fling: *Stop slinging stones.*
2 to arrange or support something so that it swings loosely: *He slung the bag over his shoulder.*

slink *verb* (**slinks; slinking; slunk**)
to move in a secret, guilty or ashamed manner.

slinky *adjective* (**slinkier; slinkiest**)
(*informal*) slender and flowing.

slip¹ *verb* (**slips; slipping; slipped**)
1 to lose one's balance or foothold: *I slipped and fell from the tree.*
2 to fall or escape by not being held firmly: *The glass slipped from my hand.* □ *The dog slipped its leash.*
3 to move smoothly and gently: *The boat slipped through the water.*
Figurative Let's slip away from the party (= go quickly or quietly, without fuss). □ *She slipped a note into my hand* (= put quietly). □ *The stock market slipped* (= declined).

Phrases **let slip** to reveal unintentionally: *Now you've let slip the secret.* **slip up** to be careless or make a mistake.

• **slip** *noun*
1 the act of slipping.
2 a mistake, especially a careless one.
3 a thin skirt or dress made of nylon, cotton or silk, worn under clothes.
4 *Cricket* a fielding position on the off-side close to and behind the wicket.
Phrases **give someone the slip** (*informal*) to escape from someone. **slip of the tongue** something said or mentioned accidentally.

slip² *noun*
1 a strip or narrow piece of wood, paper, etc.: *a bank deposit slip.*
2 a part of a plant suitable for grafting or planting.
Phrase **slip of a** *He's only a slip of a boy* (= slim or young).

slip knot (**slip-not**) *noun*
a knot which can slide along the piece of rope round which it is tied.

slipped disc *noun*
a painful condition caused by a disc between the spinal vertebrae becoming displaced and pressing on adjacent nerves.

slipper *noun*
a loose light shoe for wearing in the house.

slippery *adjective*
smooth and wet so as to cause slipping: *I could not hold the slippery fish.*
Figurative He's a slippery rascal (= untrustworthy).
Word Family **slipperiness** *noun*.

slip road *noun*
a road that gives access to a main road or motorway.

slipshod *adjective*
careless or untidy.

slipstream *noun*
the flow of air directly behind a moving vehicle.

slip-up *noun*
(*informal*) a mistake.

slipway *noun*
a ramp, from the shore into the water, from which boats may be launched or repaired.

slit *noun*
a long narrow cut or opening.

• **slit** *verb* (**slits; slitting; slit**) to make a long cut or opening: *She slit open the letter with a paperknife.*

slither (slith-a) *verb*
to slide or slip unsteadily or awkwardly.
Word Family **slither** *noun*.

sliver (slivv-a) *noun*
a small thin piece broken or split off from
a larger piece.
• **sliver** *verb* to cut or break off in slivers.

Sloane *noun* also **Sloane Ranger**
a young upper-class person, usually a
woman, who dresses expensively but
informally and has the conventional tastes
of the rest of her group. Compare HOORAY
HENRY.
[*Sloane Square* in London]

slob *noun*
(*informal*) an uncouth untidy person.

slobber *verb*
to let saliva, etc. run from the mouth.
• **slobber** *noun* saliva.
Word Family **slobbery** *adjective*
1 unpleasantly wet. 2 slobbering.

sloe *noun*
the small astringent black plum of the
blackthorn.

sloe-eyed *adjective*
having attractively oval-shaped dark eyes.

sloe gin *noun*
a liqueur made by steeping sloes in gin.

slog *verb* (**slogs; slogging; slogged**)
1 (*informal*) to work hard and steadily.
2 (*informal*) to trudge or walk heavily.
3 (*informal*) to hit hard.
• **slog** *noun*
1 (*informal*) hard work.
2 (*informal*) a strong heavy blow.
Word Family **slogger** *noun*.

slogan (slo-g'n) *noun*
a distinctive and easily remembered
phrase, used to advertise a product,
political party, etc.
[Gaelic *sluagh* army + *gairm* cry]

slo-mo *noun*
short form of **slow motion**.

sloop *noun*
a yacht with one mast, a mainsail and one
foresail.
[from Dutch]

slop *verb* (**slops; slopping; slopped**)
to spill or splash.
• **slop** *noun* (*often* **slops**) any dirty water
or other liquid waste from a kitchen, etc.

slope *verb*
to lean or be at an angle: *The roof slopes
downwards.*
Phrase **slope arms** to move a rifle from
ground to shoulder in military drill.

• **slope** *noun*
1 a sloping line.
2 the degree of deviation of a line from the
horizontal.
3 (*often* **slopes**) an area of rising or falling
ground: *mountain slopes.*

sloppy *adjective* (**sloppier; sloppiest**)
1 wet, muddy or slushy.
2 (*informal*) careless or untidy.
3 (*informal*) foolishly sentimental.
Word Family **sloppily** *adverb*;
sloppiness *noun*.

sloppy joe *noun*
(*informal*) a loose thick jumper.

slosh *verb*
1 to splash about in mud or slush.
2 (*informal*) to hit heavily.
• **slosh** *noun* (*informal*) a heavy blow.

slot *noun*
a narrow groove or opening into which
something is put or fitted.
*Figurative The programme is scheduled for
the midday time slot* (= particular position).
• **slot** *verb* (**slots; slotting; slotted**) to
make a slot or slots in or for.

sloth *noun*
1 laziness.
2 a slow-moving South American
mammal, noted for hanging upside down
from tree branches.
Word Family **slothful** *adjective*;
slothfully *adverb*; **slothfulness** *noun*.
[from SLOW]

slot machine *noun*
any coin-operated machine.

slouch (*rhymes with* ouch) *verb*
to sit, stand or move with a lazy drooping
posture.
• **slouch** *noun* (*plural* **slouches**)
1 a slouching posture.
2 (*informal*) a slovenly performer.

slough[1] (*rhymes with* cow) *noun*
a swamp or a marshy area.

slough[2] (sluff) *verb*
to shed or cast off: *Snakes slough their outer
layer of skin.*
• **slough** *noun* a layer of dead skin or
tissue.

slovenly (sluv-'n-lee) *adjective*
dirty, careless or untidy in dress, habits,
etc.
Word Family **sloven** *noun* an old word
for a slovenly person; **slovenliness** *noun*.
[Dutch *slof* careless]

slow (sloh) *adjective*
1 taking a comparatively long time: *a slow train.* □ *I'm a slow reader.*
Figurative The clock is slow (= behind the correct time). □ *The slow child had trouble reading* (= not quick to learn). □ *We left the party early as it was so slow* (= dull, uninteresting). □ *Cook the meat in a slow oven* (= only warm).
2 *Sport* (of a field, court, etc.) tending to make movement slow because the surface is wet.
• **slow** *verb* to make or become slow or slower.
Word Family **slowly** *adverb*; **slowness** *noun*.

slowcoach *noun* (*plural* **slowcoaches**) (*informal*) a person who is slow.

slow motion *noun*
the showing of film in which the images move slowly, having been photographed at a greater number of frames per second than normal or being projected more slowly than normal.

slow-worm *noun* also called **blindworm**. a snake-like lizard without legs.

sludge (sluj) *noun*
1 thick oozing mud or mire.
2 any mud-like substance or deposit.

slug¹ *noun*
1 a slimy snail-like animal without a shell.
2 a small metal bullet.
3 (*informal*) a serving of alcohol.

slug² *verb* (**slugs; slugging; slugged**) (*informal*) to hit very hard, especially with the fist.
• **slug** *noun* (*informal*) a heavy blow with the fist.

sluggard *noun*
a lazy or slow-moving person.

sluggish *adjective*
moving or acting slowly and without energy.
Word Family **sluggishly** *adverb*; **sluggishness** *noun*.

sluice (slooss) *noun*
1 short form of **sluiceway** a channel which carries or controls a flow of water.
2 a gate or valve used to control such a flow.
• **sluice** *verb* to send a stream of water out, over or through.

slum *noun*
1 a dirty, poor and overcrowded section of a city.
2 a squalid building, house, etc.

• **slum** *verb* (**slums; slumming; slummed**)
1 to go visiting in a slum area.
2 (*informal*) to live at a low or degraded level.
Word Family **slummy** *adjective*.

slumber *verb*
a poetic word meaning 'to sleep'.
• **slumber** *noun* a poetic word for sleep, especially deep sleep.
Word Family **slumberous, slumbrous** *adjective* 1 sleepy. 2 causing sleep.

slump *verb*
1 to fall or drop heavily: *He slumped exhausted into a chair.* □ *Prices slumped.*
2 to droop limply: *slumped over a book.*
• **slump** *noun* a heavy or sudden fall.

slung the past tense and past participle of **sling**.

slunk the past tense and past participle of **slink**.

slur *verb* (**slurs; slurring; slurred**) to pronounce words indistinctly by running them together.
• **slur** *noun*
1 the act of slurring: *He spoke with a slur.*
2 a suggestion of disgrace; a stain: *It's a slur on my good name.*
3 *Music* a curved line over two or more notes, indicating that they should be played together smoothly.

slurp *verb*
(*informal*) to eat or drink noisily.

slurry *noun* (*plural* **slurries**)
a thin watery mixture, especially of cement or manure.

slush *noun*
1 a mixture of melting snow, ice and mud.
2 any soft or watery substance.
3 (*informal*) silly or sentimental talk, writing, etc.
Word Family **slushy** *adjective*; **slushiness** *noun*.

slush fund *noun*
a secret fund of money used to bribe officials, especially so as to gain orders and favours for an organization.

slut *noun*
a slovenly or immoral woman.
Word Family **sluttish** *adjective*.

sly *adjective*
1 secretive and cunning: *a sly pickpocket.*
2 playful or mischievous: *sly humour.*
Phrase **on the sly** secretly.
Word Family **slyly** *adverb*; **slyness** *noun*.

smack¹ *verb*
to strike sharply, especially with the palm of the hand.
Phrase **smack one's lips** to make a loud sharp sound with the lips, e.g. in enjoyment or anticipation.
• **smack** *noun*
1 a sharp quick stroke or blow.
2 a smacking of the lips.
3 (*informal*) a loud kiss.
Phrase **smack in the eye** (*informal*) a rebuff.
• **smack** *adverb* suddenly or sharply: *The car ran smack into a tree.*

smack² *verb*
to have a trace or suggestion: *Your behaviour smacks of insolence.*
• **smack** *noun* a slight flavour or trace.

smack³ *noun*
a small sailing boat, especially one used for fishing.

smack⁴ *noun*
(*informal*) heroin.

smacker *noun*
1 (*informal*) a loud kiss.
2 (*informal*) a pound or dollar.

small (*rhymes with* ball) *adjective*
1 not large or great in size, amount, etc.: *a small house.* □ *There's still one small problem.*
2 doing things on a limited scale: *a small shopkeeper.* □ *He's only a small eater.*
Figurative You have a small mind (= mean, petty). □ *Caught in the act of stealing, she felt really small* (= ashamed, humble).
• **small** *noun*
Phrase **the small of the back** (of the body) the lower middle part of the back.
• **small** *adverb* into small pieces.
Word Family **smallness** *noun*; **smallish** *adjective* rather small.

small arms *plural noun*
any firearms which can be carried.

small change *noun*
coins of low value.

small fry *plural noun*
young or insignificant people or things.

smallholding *noun*
a small farm.
Word Family **smallholder** *noun*.

small hours *plural noun*
the early hours of the morning.

small intestine ⇨ INTESTINE.

small-minded *adjective*
selfish or petty.

smallpox *noun*
an infectious viral disease causing blisters which often form permanent pockmarks.

small print *noun*
(*informal*) the numerous restrictive and exclusive clauses printed on a contract, e.g. of insurance, often in small close-set type which is difficult to read.

smalls *plural noun*
(*informal*) underwear.

small-scale *adjective*
of small size or scope: *a small-scale model of the solar system.* □ *a small-scale business venture.*

small slam ⇨ SLAM².

small talk *noun*
unimportant chatter.

small-time *adjective*
(*informal*) petty or unimportant: *a small-time hoodlum.*

smalt (smawlt) *noun*
a form of blue glass made by blending silica with cobalt oxide.

smarmy *adjective* (**smarmier**; **smarmiest**)
(*informal*) unpleasantly flattering.
Word Family **smarminess** *noun*.

smart *adjective*
1 clever or bright: *That's a smart little lad.*
Figurative a smart remark (= cleverly rude). □ *a smart businessman* (= shrewd).
2 lively: *We set off at a smart pace.*
3 elegantly neat or fashionable: *a smart outfit.* □ *She belongs to a very smart set.*
4 stinging or severe: *a smart slap.*
5 (of a device, material, etc.) capable of apparently intelligent actions: *Smart textiles react to heat and light.*
• **smart** *verb* to cause or feel a stinging pain: *This cut smarts.*
Figurative He smarted under the stinging rebuke (= felt hurt and distressed).
• **smart** *noun*
1 a sharp stinging pain.
2 acute mental distress.
Word Family **smartly** *adverb*; **smartness** *noun*; **smarten** *verb* also **smarten up 1** to make or become more trim and neat in appearance. **2** to make brisker or more vigorous.

smart alec *noun* also **smart aleck**
(*informal*) a conceited know-all.

smart card *noun*
a plastic card resembling a bank card with a microprocessor embedded in it, used in conjunction with an electronic card reader

to authorize financial transactions, such as the automatic transfer of funds between bank accounts, designed to combat fraud.

smash *verb*
1 to break violently, especially into pieces: *The windscreen was smashed in the accident.* *Figurative All my illusions about work were smashed* (= destroyed, shattered).
2 to rush violently or crash: *The car smashed into the wall.*
3 *Sport* to hit the ball with a hard fast overarm stroke.
• **smash** *noun* (*plural* **smashes**)
1 the act or sound of smashing: *The tea tray fell with an awful smash.*
2 (*informal*) a smash hit.
• **smash** *adverb* with a smashing movement or sound: *He ran smash into the brick wall.*
Word Family **smashing** *adjective* (*informal*) very good; **smashingly** *adverb*; **smasher** *noun* 1 (*informal*) a smashing blow or crash. 2 (*informal*) a strikingly good-looking person. 3 (*informal*) a smash hit.

smash-and-grab *noun*
a very swift robbery performed by breaking a shop window, grabbing the goods and running off.

smash hit *noun*
(*informal*) something which is an immediate and great success.

smattering *noun* also **smatter**
a superficial or incomplete knowledge of something.

smear *verb*
1 to spread with a sticky or greasy substance.
2 to smudge: *Do not smear the drawing.*
3 to damage someone's reputation.
• **smear** *noun*
1 a mark made by or as if by smearing.
2 slander or libel: *a smear campaign.*
3 something which is smeared, such as a small amount of a substance examined on a microscopic slide.

smear test *noun*
a test for the early detection of cervical cancer involving a smear taken from the lining of the cervix.

smell *verb* (**smells; smelling; smelt** or **smelled**)
1 to perceive by means of the nose. *Figurative I smell trouble* (= anticipate).
2 to be perceived by the nose as: *The roses smell sweet.*

3 to be perceived by the nose as offensive: *You smell!*
Phrases **smell of** *The plan smells of crime* (= suggests). **smell out** *A good reporter can smell out stories* (= find, search out).
• **smell** *noun*
1 the sense of smelling.
2 the quality of something which may be smelt: *Certain flowers have no smell.* *Figurative It all had the smell of a trick* (= suggestion).
3 the act of smelling: *May I have a smell of your perfume?*
Word Family **smelly** *adjective* (**smellier; smelliest**) having an offensive smell; **smelliness** *noun*.

smelling salts *plural noun*
(*formerly*) any substance, consisting mainly of ammonium carbonate, sniffed to cure faintness, headache, etc.

smelt[1] *verb*
to extract a metal from its ores by heating, melting, etc.

smelt[2] *noun* (*plural* **smelt** or **smelts**)
a small round fish of the salmon family with a delicate flavour.

smidgen (**smij-'n**) *noun*
(*informal*) a small amount.

smile *verb*
to express pleasure, amusement, kindliness, scorn, etc. by curving the corners of the mouth upwards.
Figurative The gods smile upon the brave (= look with approval or kindness).
Word Family **smile** *noun*; **smilingly** *adverb*.

smirch *verb*
to soil, stain or dirty.
Figurative The violent attacks smirched the city's reputation (= disgraced).
Word Family **smirch** *noun*.

smirk *verb*
to smile in an affected, silly or self-satisfied way.
Word Family **smirk** *noun*.

smite *verb* (**smites; smiting; smote; smitten**)
an old word meaning to strike or hit hard: *He smote his attacker with a cudgel.*
Figurative The town was smitten with plague (= affected severely). □ *I think he is rather smitten with her* (= in love).

smith *noun*
a person who works with metals, especially a blacksmith.

smithereens (smith-a-**reenz**) *plural noun*
(*informal*) small bits and pieces: *smashed to smithereens*.

smithy (**smith**-ee) *noun* (*plural* **smithies**)
a blacksmith's workshop.

smitten the past participle of **smite**.

smock *noun*
1 a loose dress or blouse, especially one decorated with smocking.
2 a loose dress or apron worn to protect clothes.
Word Family **smocking** *noun* a style of needlework in which the fabric is gathered with small stitches to form a decorative pattern of folds; **smock** *verb*.

smog *noun*
fog contaminated by pollution.
Word Family **smoggy** *adjective*
(**smoggier**; **smoggiest**).
[SM(oke) + (f)OG]

smoke *noun*
1 the suspension of fine solid particles in a gas, given off by burning substances.
2 (*informal*) the act of taking in and breathing out the smoke from a cigarette, etc.
3 (*informal*) a cigarette, etc.
Phrase **go up in smoke** 1 to be burnt up completely. 2 to end in failure.
● **smoke** *verb*
1 to give off smoke.
2 to inhale and exhale the smoke of a cigarette, etc.
3 to preserve and flavour food by drying it in smoke.
Phrase **smoke out** 1 to drive out from concealment with smoke. 2 to bring to public view or awareness.
Word Family **smokeless** *adjective*;
smoker *noun* 1 a person or thing that smokes. 2 Railways a railway compartment or carriage in which smoking is allowed.

smoke bomb *noun*
a bomb which sends out clouds of smoke, used for concealment or in theatrical productions.

smokeless zone *noun*
an area where it is illegal to burn fuels which produce smoke.

smokescreen *noun*
1 a dense smoke made to conceal military operations from enemy observation.
2 anything used to conceal the truth: *He threw up a smokescreen of excuses*.

smokestack *noun*
a chimney or funnel, e.g. on a factory or steamboat, through which smoke, gases, etc. are discharged.

smoking jacket *noun*
a man's loose soft jacket, often made of silk or velvet, formerly worn after dinner.

smoky *adjective* (**smokier**; **smokiest**)
1 full of or giving off much smoke.
2 having the taste or colour of smoke.
Word Family **smokily** *adverb*;
smokiness *noun*.

smooch *verb*
(*informal*) to kiss and cuddle.
Word Family **smooch** *noun*.

smooth (smooth) *adjective*
having a surface without irregularities:
a smooth table top. □ *smooth seas*.
Figurative a smooth ride (= free from bumps and jolts). □ *I don't like his smooth manners* (= suave). □ *This old whisky is very smooth* (= free from sharpness or harshness of taste). □ *Add the milk to the flour and stir to a smooth paste* (= without lumps). □ *The skater traced out a smooth curve* (= easy and uninterrupted).
● **smooth** *verb* to make or become smooth: *He smoothed out the crumpled paper*.
Figurative to smooth the way (= remove difficulties or hindrances from). □ *She tried to smooth my ruffled feelings* (= calm down).
Phrase **smooth over** He's always trying to smooth over the difficulties (= cover up, gloss over).
● **smooth** *noun* something which is smooth.
Word Family **smoothly** *adverb*;
smoothness *noun*.

smoothie (smoo-thee) *noun*
1 (*informal*) a glib soft-spoken plausible rogue.
2 a thick drink made by liquidizing fruit in a blender with milk, yogurt or fruit juice.

smooth-spoken *adjective*
smooth-tongued.

smooth-tongued *adjective*
glib and plausible: *a smooth-tongued rascal*.

smorgasbord (**smorg**-uz-bord) *noun*
a meal with many different dishes, usually cold meats and salads, to which diners help themselves.
[Swedish *smorgas* sandwich + *bord* table]

smote the past tense of **smite**.

smother (rhymes with mother) *verb*
to stifle or suffocate: *The baby was smothered by his pillow*.

Figurative He smothered his anger
(= suppressed). □ *He smothered himself in a
coat and scarf* (= thickly covered or
wrapped).

smoulder (**smole**-da) *verb* (*American*
smolder)
to burn and smoke without flame: *The
embers smouldered in the grate.*
Figurative Her eyes smouldered with rage
(= showed suppressed feelings).
□ *Rebellion smouldered in the hearts of the
soldiers* (= existed inwardly).
Word Family **smoulder** *noun.*

smudge *noun*
a dirty, blotted or blurred mark: *There's a
smudge on your forehead.* □ *The castle was
just a smudge on the horizon.*
● **smudge** *verb*
1 to make a smudge or smudges on.
2 to become blurred or blotted.
Word Family **smudgy** *adjective;*
smudgily *adverb;* **smudginess** *noun.*

smug *adjective* (**smugger; smuggest**)
self-satisfied.
Word Family **smugly** *adverb;* **smugness**
noun.

smuggle *verb*
to bring goods into a country without
paying customs duty on them.
Figurative She smuggled a file into the
prison (= got secretly).
Word Family **smuggler** *noun.*

smut *noun*
1 a piece of soot or dirt.
2 a black dirty mark.
3 any indecent language or writing.
4 a fungal disease of plants, especially
cereals, causing a black powdery surface.
Word Family **smutty** *adjective*
(**smuttier; smuttiest**) 1 grimy or dirty.
2 indecent or obscene; **smuttily** *adverb;*
smuttiness *noun.*

snack *noun*
a small meal or refreshment.
● **snack** *verb* to eat a snack rather than a
full meal.

A **snack** was originally 'a bite' or 'a
snap' of the kind given by dogs. It was
borrowed from Middle Dutch *snacken*
(to bite). Its present meaning, as a
noun, dates from the 18th century and,
as a verb, from the later part of the 20th
century.

snaffle *noun*
a jointed bit for a horse.
● **snaffle** *verb* (*informal*) to steal or
appropriate.

snag *noun*
1 a sharp or jagged projection, especially
one below the surface of water.
Figurative There's been a snag in our plans
(= unexpected or hidden difficulty).
2 a small hole or ladder in a piece of
clothing, caused by catching it on a sharp
object.
● **snag** *verb* (**snags; snagging; snagged**)
to get caught by or as if by a snag: *I've
snagged my tights.* □ *The boat was snagged
fast.*

snail *noun*
a slimy air-breathing gastropod with a
single, often spirally coiled, external shell.
Phrase **at a snail's pace** very slowly.

snail mail *noun*
(*informal*) the ordinary postal system, as
opposed to email.

snake *noun*
1 any of various slender scaly legless
reptiles without eardrums or movable
eyelids, and having the two halves of the
lower jaw connected by elastic fibres.
2 a treacherous person.
Phrase **snake in the grass** an insidious
or hidden enemy.
● **snake** *verb* to move, wind or curve like a
snake.
Word Family **snaky** *adjective* (**snakier;
snakiest**) 1 of or like a snake. 2 (*informal*)
ungrateful or treacherous.

snake charmer *noun*
a person who controls a snake by means of
rhythmic music and bodily movements.

snakes and ladders *plural noun*
(*used with singular verb*) a children's board
game in which a dice is thrown to
determine progress round the board, up
ladders or down snakes.

snap *verb* (**snaps; snapping; snapped**)
1 to make or cause to make a sudden
sharp sound: *He snapped his fingers to
attract the waiter's attention.*
Figurative He snapped the lid shut crossly
(= closed with a snap). □ *He snapped to
attention as the general passed him* (= moved
quickly).
2 to break suddenly with a sharp sound:
A twig snapped under her foot.
Figurative Her self-control finally snapped
under the continual taunting (= gave way).
3 to make a sudden quick bite or snatch:
The dog snapped at my ankles.
Figurative She snapped angrily in reply
(= spoke sharply).
4 to take a photograph of.

***Phrases* snap out of it** (*informal*) to recover from a mood quickly. **snap up** *You should snap up this bargain* (= seize quickly).

• **snap** *noun*
1 a sudden sharp sound: *The rope broke with a snap.*
2 a sudden sharp breaking.
3 a quick sudden bite or snatch.
4 a quick sharp speech.
5 a catch or clasp: *We had to break the snap to get the box open.*
6 a thin crisp biscuit: *a ginger snap.*
7 *Weather* ⇨ COLD SNAP.
8 *Cards* a simple game in which each player thows cards onto a pile aiming to win by being first to notice two consecutive cards of equal value.
9 a snapshot.

• **snap** *adjective* made or done hastily or without considering: *a snap decision.*
***Word Family* snappish** *adjective* 1 apt to snap. 2 impatient or irritable; **snappishly** *adverb*; **snappishness** *noun*.

snapdragon *noun*
a plant with showy spikes of brightly coloured flowers.

snappy *adjective* (**snappier; snappiest**)
1 (*informal*) impatient or irritable: *Don't get snappy with me.*
2 (*informal*) quick or lively in action. *She walks along at a very snappy pace.*
3 (*informal*) neat and smart: *Flight attendants wear snappy uniforms.*
***Phrase* make it snappy** (*informal*) to hurry up.
***Word Family* snappily** *adverb*; **snappiness** *noun*.

snapshot *noun*
a quickly taken or informal photograph.

snare¹ (*rhymes with* air) *noun*
1 a device, usually a noose, for trapping animals.
2 anything which catches or traps unexpectedly.
• **snare** *verb* to catch in a snare.

snare² *noun*
any of the strings or wires stretched across the skin of a small double-headed drum to increase reverberation.

snark *noun*
any of a variety of imaginary creatures, some of which have feathers and bite and others have whiskers and scratch.
[invented by Lewis Carroll in a narrative poem, 1876]

snarl¹ *verb*
1 to make a harsh angry growl: *The dog snarled at the strangers.*
2 to speak in an angry, resentful or quarrelsome manner: *He just snarled at her from behind his paper.*
***Word Family* snarl** *noun*; **snarly** *adjective* (**snarlier; snarliest**).

snarl² *noun*
a tangle: *a traffic snarl.* □ *Try to pull a comb through these snarls!*
Figurative *He tried to sort out a snarl which had arisen at work* (= complication).
***Word Family* snarl** *verb*.

snarl-up *noun*
(*informal*) a confusion or mix-up.

snatch *verb*
to seize suddenly: *He snatched his car keys and ran.*
Figurative *They snatched victory at the last minute* (= obtained by prompt action).
***Phrase* snatch at 1** to try to seize. **2** to take eagerly.
• **snatch** *noun* (*plural* **snatches**)
1 the act of snatching: *He made a snatch at my sandwich.*
2 a small fragment: *I can only remember snatches of the melody.*
3 a brief period of time: *to sleep in snatches.*
***Word Family* snatchy** *adjective* done or occurring in snatches; **snatcher** *noun*.

snazzy *adjective* (**snazzier; snazziest**)
(*informal*) very smart or well-dressed.

sneak *verb*
1 to move or act in a furtive way: *He sneaked down the hall to the kitchen.*
2 to do or act secretly or stealthily: *Sneak a look through the keyhole.*
3 (*informal*) to tell tales: *It's just like him to sneak on us to the teacher.*
• **sneak** *noun* (*informal*) a telltale.
***Word Family* sneaking** *adjective* 1 acting in an underhand way. 2 secret or unavowed: *I think she feels a sneaking sympathy for him.* 3 growing insidiously: *a sneaking suspicion*; **sneaky** *adjective* (**sneakier; sneakiest**) mean, tricky, cowardly or contemptible; **sneakily** *adverb*; **sneakiness** *noun*.

sneaker *noun*
1 a light canvas shoe with a rubber sole.
2 a person who sneaks about.

sneer *verb*
to show contempt by a curl of the lips, scornful words, etc.
• **sneer** *noun* a sneering remark or expression.

Word Family **sneerer** *noun* a person who sneers; **sneering** *adjective*; **sneeringly** *adverb*.

sneeze *verb*
to expel air through the nose and mouth in a sudden explosive action.
Phrase **not to be sneezed at** (*informal*) not to be dismissed lightly.
• **sneeze** *noun* the act or sound of sneezing.
Word Family **sneezer** *noun*.

snick *noun*
1 a small cut: *He made a snick in the wood with his penknife.*
2 a click: *The door closed behind us with a snick.*
3 *Sport* a hit which deflects the ball sideways.
Word Family **snick** *verb*.

snicker *noun*
1 a long soft snorting neigh.
2 a snigger.
Word Family **snicker** *verb*.

snide *adjective*
slyly nasty or derogatory: *snide remarks.*
Word Family **snidely** *adverb*.

sniff *verb*
1 to draw into the nose in short audible breaths: *to sniff snuff.*
2 to smell by sniffing: *He sniffed the wine before he tasted it.*
Phrases **sniff around** *The police have been sniffing around* (= looking, investigating). **sniff at** *They sniffed at her modern ideas* (= expressed contempt for). **sniff out** *He could sniff out trouble like nobody else I knew* (= detect).
• **sniff** *noun*
1 the act or sound of sniffing.
2 something which is inhaled by sniffing.
Word Family **sniffer** *noun*; **sniffy** *adjective* (**sniffier**; **sniffiest**) (*informal*) scornful or disdainful.

sniffer dog *noun*
(*informal*) a dog that is trained by the police, etc. to sniff out drugs.

sniffle *verb*
to sniff repeatedly.
Word Family **sniffle** *noun*.

snigger *noun*
a half-suppressed or smothered laugh, usually expressing derision, disrespect, etc.
Word Family **snigger** *verb*.

snip *verb* (**snips**; **snipping**; **snipped**)
to cut with a small quick stroke or strokes: *to snip a person's fringe.*
• **snip** *noun*

1 the act or sound of snipping: *With a few quick snips she pruned the bush.*
2 a small cut: *Make a snip here for the buttonhole.*
3 a small piece snipped off.
4 (*informal*) a bargain.
5 (**snips**) small shears for cutting metal.

snipe *noun*
1 a long-billed marsh bird, often shot as game.
2 a shot, etc. fired from a concealed position.
• **snipe** *verb*
1 to fire shots from a concealed position.
2 to make nasty or critical remarks.
Word Family **sniper** *noun*.

snippet *noun*
a small piece or amount.

snitch[1] *verb*
(*informal*) to steal.

snitch[2] *verb*
(*informal*) to turn informer.
Word Family **snitcher** *noun*.

snivel (sniv-'l) *verb* (**snivels**; **snivelling**; **snivelled**)
1 to weep and sniff.
2 to complain in a tearful or whining way.
3 to have mucus running from the nose.
Word Family **snivel** *noun* the act of snivelling; **sniveller** *noun*.
[Old English *snofl* mucus]

snob *noun*
a person who sets too high a value on social standing and wealth, seeking to imitate or associate with those he or she believes to be superior and despising those regarded as inferior.
Word Family **snobbery, snobbishness** *noun* the state or quality of being a snob; **snobbish** *adjective* of or like a snob; **snobbishly** *adverb*.

snog *verb* (**snogs**; **snogging**; **snogged**)
(*informal*) to kiss and cuddle.

snood (*rhymes with* food) *noun*
an old-fashioned net-like hat holding the hair at the back of the head.

snook *noun*
a gesture of contempt made with thumb to nose and outstretched fingers: *He cocked a snook at me.*

snooker *noun*
a game similar to billiards, using 22 balls of different colours, which are hit into the pockets in various orders. Compare POOL[2] *noun* (definition 3).
• **snooker** *verb* (*informal*) to prevent a person from achieving some aim, etc.

snoop *verb*
(*informal*) to prowl or pry.
Word Family snooper, snoop *noun* a
person who snoops; **snoopy** *adjective*
(**snoopier; snoopiest**).

snoot *noun*
(*informal*) the nose.

snooty (snoo-tee) *adjective* (**snootier;
snootiest**)
(*informal*) haughty or snobbish.

snooze *verb*
(*informal*) to doze.
Word Family snooze *noun*.

snooze button *noun*
a button on an alarm clock used to set the
alarm to repeat after a short time.

snore *verb*
to breathe during sleep with a harsh rough
sound.
Word Family snore *noun*; **snorer** *noun*.

snorkel *noun*
a breathing tube held in the mouth and
projecting upwards, so that a swimmer
may breathe when just under water.
Word Family snorkel *verb* (**snorkels;
snorkelling; snorkelled**) to swim under
water with a snorkel.
[German *Schnorkel*]

snort *verb*
1 to force breath through the nostrils with
a loud harsh sound.
2 to let out a loud burst of laughter.
3 to express contempt, indignation, etc.
with a snort.
Word Family snort *noun* 1 the act or
sound of snorting. 2 (*informal*) a small
drink of alcohol.

snot *noun*
1 (*informal*) mucus from the nose.
2 (*informal*) a contemptible person.
Word Family snotty *adjective* (**snottier;
snottiest**) 1 dirty. 2 (*informal*) conceited
or arrogant.

snout (*rhymes with* out) *noun*
1 the nose of an animal, often including
the jaws.
2 something which has the shape, position
or function of a snout.

snow (sno) *noun*
1 the delicate ice crystals formed in clouds
from water vapour below freezing point,
which join together and fall to the ground
as flakes.
2 white spots on a television screen,
caused by interference or weak signals.
• **snow** *verb* to fall as snow: *It has been
snowing.*

Figurative Letters and telegrams snowed in
all day for her birthday (= poured).
Phrases **be snowed in, be snowed up** to
be shut in by snow. **snowed under**
1 covered with snow. 2 overwhelmed: *We
are snowed under with work.*

snowball *noun*
a ball of snow pressed together to be
thrown.
Word Family snowball *verb* 1 to throw
snowballs at. 2 to grow larger in continual
stages.

snowboard *noun*
a board used for sliding down a snow-
covered slope.
• **snowboard** *verb* to slide down a snow-
covered slope on a snowboard.
Word Family snowboarder *noun*;
snowboarding *noun*.

snowdrift *noun*
a bank or heap of deep snow blown by the
wind.

snowdrop *noun*
a small early spring plant with white
flowers, growing from a bulb.

snowfall *noun*
1 a fall of snow.
2 the amount of snow which has fallen at a
particular time or place.

snowfield *noun*
an area of permanent snow.

snowflake *noun*
a crystal of snow.

snow goose *noun* (*plural* **snow geese**)
a pure white goose with black wing tips.

snow leopard *noun* also called **ounce**.
a long-haired leopard found in the
mountains of Asia.

snowline *noun*
the height on a mountain above which
there is always snow.

snowman *noun* (*plural* **snowmen**)
the shape of a man, made in snow.

snowmobile (snow-mo-beel) *noun*
a small motorized vehicle with short skis at
the front and a caterpillar track at the rear,
used to travel over snow.

snowplough *noun* (*American* **snowplow**)
a device attached to the front of a vehicle
and used to push snow aside.

snowshoe *noun*
a device, similar to a tennis racket,
consisting of a network of thongs in a
wooden frame and attached to boots for
walking over soft snow.

snowy *adjective* (**snowier; snowiest**)
1 white as snow.
2 covered with snow.

snub *verb* (**snubs; snubbing; snubbed**)
to treat a person with contempt or coolness, especially by ignoring him or her.
• **snub** *noun* contemptuous words or behaviour.

snub-nosed *adjective*
having a short turned-up nose.

snuff¹ *noun*
a form of powdered tobacco taken into the nose by sniffing.
• **snuff** *verb* to sniff or snort: *The dog snuffed at the tree.* □ *He snuffed and coughed.*

snuff² *verb*
to extinguish a candle.
Phrase **snuff it** (*informal*) to die.
• **snuff** *noun* the burnt part of a candle wick.
Word Family **snuffer** *noun* an instrument for snuffing candles.

snuffle *verb*
1 to breathe or sniff noisily, as with a cold.
2 to speak through the nose or with a nasal tone.
Word Family **snuffle** *noun*; **snuffly** *adjective* (**snufflier; snuffliest**).

snuff movie *noun*
(*informal*) an illegal film involving the actual torture and killing of someone, as opposed to a dramatized episode involving an actor.

snug *adjective* (**snugger; snuggest**)
1 cosy: *a snug corner beside the fire.*
2 close-fitting: *a snug waistcoat.*
Word Family **snugly** *adverb*; **snugness** *noun*.

snuggle *verb*
to cuddle up or more closely, for warmth, comfort, affection, etc.

so¹ *adverb*
1 just as said, directed, suggested or implied: *Hold your arm out so.* □ *He said he would succeed, and he did so.*
2 in the same way: *Keith says we should go, and I think so too.*
3 then: *Home we went, and so to bed.*
4 to an indicated or suggested degree or extent: *I didn't realize the plains stretched so far.*
5 very or extremely: *You are so helpful.*
6 to a definite but unspecified extent or degree: *I can only stay for a day or so.*
7 most certainly or indeed: *Midnight? So it is!*

8 therefore: *The camel was thirsty, so we gave it a drink.*
9 true: *That is just not so.*
10 according to the truth of what has been sworn or asserted: *so help me God.*
11 apparently: *So you don't have an alibi.*
Phrases **and so on, and so forth** et cetera. **just so** *He always wants to have everything just so* (= in perfect order). **so as** *I'll work late tonight so as to catch up* (= with the purpose of). **so much for** *So much for your hopes of wealth and power* (= that's the end of). **so that 1** *He shunned society, so that people thought he was dead* (= with the result that). **2** *Write to me so that I know how you are* (= in order that). **so what!** (*informal*) what does that matter.
• **so** *conjunction*
1 in order that: *Be quiet so you don't wake the baby.*
2 therefore: *They were expensive, so use them sparingly.*
• **so** *interjection* used to indicate realization of a fact, situation, etc.: *So! You've been lying to me again.*

so² ⇨ SOH.

soak *verb*
to remain or allow to remain in a liquid until saturated.
Figurative *Water was soaking through the roof of the tent* (= seeping). □ *The news has not soaked in yet* (= been taken in).
□ *Blotting paper soaks up ink* (= draws, dries). □ *She soaks herself in romantic novels* (= involves eagerly).
• **soak** *noun*
1 the act of soaking: *Give the sheets a good soak.*
2 (*informal*) a drunkard.

so-and-so *noun*
1 a person or thing that is not definitely named.
2 (*informal*) a mean or nasty person.

soap *noun*
1 a substance made from a mixture of natural oils and fats with an alkali, used for washing.
2 (*informal*) a soap opera.
• **soap** *verb* to rub or cover with soap.
Word Family **soapy** *adjective* (**soapier; soapiest**); **soapily** *adverb*; **soapiness** *noun*.

soapbox *noun* (*plural* **soapboxes**)
a place or means, originally an improvised platform, used to make a speech, express one's opinions, etc.

soap opera *noun*
a radio or television serial depicting the everyday lives of a group of characters. [of the type originally sponsored by advertisers of soap, detergents, etc.]

soapstone *noun*
Geology a soft stone with a greasy feeling, usually a variety of talc and used for table tops, hearths, etc.

soar *verb*
1 to rise or fly upwards, like a bird. *Figurative The mountain soars into the clouds* (= ascends). □ *Her heart soared with delight* (= was inspired).
2 to glide at a great height.
Word Family **soarer** *noun*; **soaring** *adjective*.

sob *verb* (**sobs; sobbing; sobbed**)
1 to weep with loud or shaking catches of the breath.
2 to make a similar sound: *The wind sobbed in the trees.*
● **sob** *noun* a sobbing sound.

sober (so-ba) *adjective*
1 not drunk.
2 serious: *a sober young student.*
Figurative All employees should wear sober clothes (= plain, not elaborate). □ *He made a sober decision concerning his career* (= rational, sensible).
● **sober** *verb* to make or become sober.
Word Family **soberly** *adverb*; **soberness** *noun*.
[from Latin]

sobriety (so-**bry**-a-tee) *noun*
1 the state of being sober.
2 seriousness.

sobriquet (so-bri-kay) *noun* also **soubriquet**
a nickname.
[French]

sob story *noun* (*plural* **sob stories**)
a story intended to inspire sentiment or pity, especially one used as an excuse.

so-called *adjective*
known by this term, often incorrectly: *He was deserted by all his so-called friends.*

soccer *noun*
a type of football played with a spherical ball which must not be handled except by the goalkeeper, and having eleven players in a side.
[shortening of *Association football*]

sociable (so-sha-b'l) *adjective*
friendly or enjoying the company of others.
Word Family **sociably** *adverb*; **sociability** (so-sha-**bill**-it-ee) *noun*.

social (so-sh'l) *adjective*
1 living or tending to live in a community rather than alone: *Bees are social insects.*
2 of or relating to life within a society: *Democracy is a social and political theory.*
Figurative She is part of a social clique (= wealthy and worldly). □ *The politician attended several social functions in the district* (= organized for friendly gathering).
● **social** *noun* a party or friendly gathering.
Word Family **socially** *adverb*; **sociality** (so-shee-**al**-i-tee) *noun* the state of being social or sociable, especially the tendency to form communities.
[Latin *socius* a partner or acting jointly]

social class *noun* (*plural* **social classes**)
a group of people in a society, classified by their sharing of similar occupations, incomes and social and political attitudes and forming part of a hierarchy.

social climber *noun*
a person who tries to move into a higher social class.

socialism (so-sha-lizm) *noun*
a social theory or system based on public control and ownership of the means of production and distribution of goods.
Word Family **socialist** *noun*; **socialist**, **socialistic** (so-sha-**list**-ik) *adjective*.

socialite (so-sha-lite) *noun*
a person who moves in rich or fashionable circles.

socialize, socialise (so-sha-lize) *verb*
1 to make someone ready for life in a community, e.g. by acquiring accepted behaviour patterns.
2 to establish or organize according to socialism: *socialized medicine.*
3 (*informal*) to take part in social activities.
Word Family **socialization** (so-sha-lie-zay-sh'n) *noun*.

social science *noun* also **social studies**
the study of subjects such as economics, sociology, politics, etc. which relate to people within a society.

social security *noun*
the financial care provided by a government for the elderly, the sick and the unemployed.

social service *noun*
1 the organized work of people trained to improve social conditions.
2 (**social services**) social welfare.

social worker *noun*
a person trained to take part in social welfare, giving advice to individuals in

need and working to improve conditions for poor people, etc.
Word Family social work *noun*.

society (so-*sigh*-a-tee) *noun* (*plural* **societies**)
1 human beings considered collectively as a group or community: *21st-century society*.
2 a relatively settled group of people or animals who have some degree of organization and cooperation.
3 the structure, institutions, culture, way of life, etc. of such a group: *Western society has reached a turning point*.
4 wealthy and privileged people and their interrelationships.
5 a group of people associated by their occupation or interests: *a society of engineers*. □ *a debating society*.
Figurative *He enjoyed their society immensely* (= companionship, company).

Society of Friends ⇨ QUAKER.

sociology (so-see-*ol*-a-jee) *noun*
the study of social behaviour, especially in relation to the development or changing of societies and social institutions.
Word Family sociologist *noun*; **sociological** (so-see-a-*loj*-i-k'l) *adjective*.

sock¹ *noun*
a short stocking, usually of nylon, cotton or wool and reaching to the ankle or knee.
Phrase pull one's socks up (*informal*) to try to improve.

sock² *verb*
(*informal*) to hit.
Word Family sock *noun*.

socket *noun*
a hollow part or opening, especially one into which something fits: *an eye socket*.

sod¹ *noun*
1 a piece of grassy soil or turf.
2 the ground, especially grass-covered earth.

sod² *noun*
(*informal*) a disagreeable person.
[short form of *sodomite*]

soda (*so*-da) *noun*
1 soda water.
2 any simple sodium compound.
3 *American* a soft drink.
[from Arabic]

soda siphon *noun*
a bottle containing soda water under pressure which can be dispensed by opening a valve.

soda water *noun*
carbonated water.

sodden *adjective*
completely soaked or wet.

sodium (so-dee-um) *noun*
a strongly reactive metal. Its compounds are very abundant, especially **sodium chloride** (common salt).

sodomy (*sod*-a-mee) *noun*
sexual intercourse using the anal opening, especially when performed between males.
Word Family sodomite *noun*.

> **Sodomy** is named after the ancient Palestinian city of *Sodom*. Along with Gomorrah, it traditionally represents depravity and was destroyed by God for its wickedness.

sofa *noun*
a long upholstered seat, with a back and armrests.

sofa bed *noun*
a sofa that converts into a bed.

soft *adjective*
1 not firm, hard or stiff: *the soft skin of a baby*.
Figurative *Her soft voice lulled us to sleep* (= pleasant, smooth). □ *His soft glance was sympathetic* (= tender). □ *You must not be soft with the students* (= weak). □ *The soft lights gave the room an intimate atmosphere* (= not bright or harsh). □ (*informal*) *His father got a soft job for him* (= easy).
□ (*informal*) *I think he's a bit soft in the head* (= simple, foolish).
2 *Physics* (of radiation) having low penetrating power.
3 (of water) relatively free of mineral salts that prevent the lathering of soap.
4 (of the sounds *c* and *g*) pronounced as in *cent* and *gem*.
Phrase have a soft spot for to like or be fond of.
Word Family soften (*soff*-'n) *verb* to make or become soft or softer; **softener** *noun*.

soft drink *noun*
any non-alcoholic drink.

soft drug *noun*
any drug which is considered to be non-addictive. Compare HARD DRUG.

soft-focus *adjective*
Photography slightly and intentionally out of focus, to achieve a romantic effect.

soft furnishings *plural noun*
the fabrics used for decorating rooms in a house, such as curtains, bedcovers and carpets.

soft goods *plural noun*
products such as fabrics, etc.

soft-headed *adjective*
foolish.
Word Family **soft-headedness** *noun.*

soft-hearted *adjective*
ready to feel or show sympathy, pity, etc.
Word Family **soft-heartedness** *noun.*

softie *noun* also **softy** (*plural* **softies**)
(*informal*) a person who is weak or easily
upset.

softly *adverb*
in a soft manner.

softness *noun*
the quality of being soft.

soft-pedal *verb* (**soft-pedals; soft-
pedalling; soft-pedalled**)
to put little emphasis on.
Word Family **soft pedal** *noun* a pedal,
especially on a piano, which is used to
lessen the volume of the sound.

soft sell *noun*
gentle persuasive salesmanship. Compare
HARD SELL.

soft soap *noun*
(*informal*) flattery, especially to gain
something.
Word Family **soft-soap** *verb* to flatter.

software *noun*
computer programs, etc. Compare
HARDWARE (definition 1).

softwood *noun*
the wood from coniferous trees, such as
pine. Compare HARDWOOD.

softy ⇨ SOFTIE.

soggy *adjective* (**soggier; soggiest**)
wet through.
Word Family **sogginess** *noun.*

soh *noun* also **so**
Music a note in the scale. ⇨ DOH.

soi-disant (swa-dee-**zon**) *adjective*
self-styled, would-be or professed.
[French, oneself saying]

soigné (swann-**yay**) *adjective* (*feminine
form* **soignée**)
very well-groomed.
[French, taken care of]

soil¹ *noun*
1 the top layer of the earth's surface, in
which plants will grow. It contains organic
matter, inorganic matter and living
organisms.
2 a particular type of this earth: *sandy soil*.

Figurative *They returned to their native soil*
(= country).
soil erosion the removal of soil from the
land by water or wind.

soil² *verb*
to make dirty: *Try not to soil your new shirt.*
Figurative *His reputation was soiled by the
rumours.*

soirée (swah-**ray**) *noun*
a small evening party.
[French *soir* evening]

sojourn (**soj**-ern) *verb*
to stay temporarily.
• **sojourn** *noun* a stay.

solace (**soll**-iss) *noun*
1 the giving of comfort in sorrow or
trouble.
2 something which gives comfort, relief,
etc.: *Drink was her only solace.*
Word Family **solace** *verb.*

solar (**sole**-a) *adjective*
1 of or relating to the sun.
2 using or operated by energy from the
sun: *solar power.*
[Latin *sol* sun]

solar day *noun*
Astronomy the time taken for the earth to
rotate once on its axis, measured relative
to the sun. Compare DAY (definition 4);
SIDEREAL DAY.

solar energy *noun*
energy from the sun's rays which may be
used as a source of power, e.g. to heat
water.

solar flare *noun*
Astronomy a brief high-temperature
outburst seen as a bright area in the sun's
atmosphere, apparently occurring with
sunspots.

solarium (so-**lair**-i-um) *noun*
a room or area exposed to the sun's rays,
as in a hospital, etc.

solar plexus *noun*
1 an important centre of the autonomous
nervous system situated behind the
stomach.
2 (*informal*) the vulnerable front of the
stomach just below the ribs.

solar power *noun*
power derived from solar energy.

solar system *noun*
1 *Astronomy* the nine planets, the periodic
comets and the asteroids moving in
elliptical orbits around the sun.
2 *Astronomy* any group of planets orbiting
around a star.

sola topi *noun*
a thick pith helmet, formerly worn by
Europeans in the tropics as protection
against sunstroke.
[Hindi]

sold the past tense and past participle of
sell.

solder (sole-da) *noun*
any of various alloys used, when molten,
for joining metals.
• **solder** *verb* to join with or as if with a
solder.
[Latin *solidare* to make firm]

soldering iron *noun*
a tool used for applying solder.

soldier (sole-jer) *noun*
a person serving in an army.
• **soldier** *verb* to act or serve as or like a
soldier.
Word Family **soldierly** *adjective* of or
characteristic of a soldier; **soldiery** *noun*
1 soldiers considered as a group. 2 the
profession of being a soldier.

soldier of fortune *noun* (*plural* **soldiers
of fortune**)
a person who will serve in an army
wherever there is adventure or personal
gain.

sole¹ *adjective*
being the only one: *I am the sole owner of
this house.*
Word Family **solely** *adverb*.

sole² *noun*
1 *Anatomy* the under surface of the foot.
2 the bottom surface of a shoe, boot, etc.,
excluding the heel.
3 anything which has the position or
function of a sole: *She rested the sole of her
golf club on the grass.*
• **sole** *verb* to fit a shoe, etc. with a sole.

sole³ *noun*
any of a group of small edible flatfish with
a hooked snout.

solecism (soll-a-sizm) *noun*
1 the ungrammatical use of language.
2 a social gaffe.
[Greek *soloikos* speaking incorrectly]

solemn (soll-'m) *adjective*
1 very grave: *a solemn warning.*
2 full of dignity or ceremony: *This is a
solemn occasion.*
Figurative a solemn vow of chastity
(= religious, sacred).
Word Family **solemnly** *adverb*;
solemnness *noun*; **solemnity** (so-**lem**-ni-
tee) *noun* (*plural* **solemnities**) 1 the state
of being solemn. 2 (*often* **solemnities**) a

formal or solemn ceremony, procedure,
etc.
[Latin *sollemnis* annual, customary]

solemnize, solemnise (soll-'m-nize)
verb
to perform or celebrate, especially with a
formal ceremony: *to solemnize a marriage.*
Word Family **solemnization** (soll-'m-
nye-**zay**-sh'n) *noun*.

solenoid (soll-i-noyd) *noun*
an electrical conductor consisting of
tightly wound coils, through which an
electric current is passed to produce a
magnetic field.
[Greek *solen* a tube + *-oid*]

solicit (so-liss-it) *verb*
1 to seek or request, especially in a formal
or persistent manner.
2 (of a prostitute, etc.) to approach and
offer sexual services to.
Word Family **solicitation** (so-liss-i-**tay**-
sh'n) *noun*.

solicitor (so-**liss**-it-a) *noun*
Law a lawyer who advises clients and gives
facts and opinions to barristers on cases to
be tried in the higher courts. Compare
BARRISTER; LAWYER.
[Latin *sollicitus* worrying]

solicitous (so-**liss**-i-tus) *adjective*
full of anxiety or concern: *a solicitous care
for the sick child.*
Word Family **solicitously** *adverb*;
solicitude *noun*.

solid *adjective*
1 having a definite shape and volume: *Ice is
water in its solid state.*
2 having the inside filled, especially with
the same substance throughout: *a solid gold
ring.*
Figurative They built a solid wall of stones
(= closely packed). □ *an athlete's solid
muscles* (= strong). □ *This job will take
a solid day's work* (= full, entire). □ *We
were swayed by her solid argument*
(= convincing). □ *a solid and respected leader*
(= responsible, reliable). □ *It was a solid
vote in favour of the idea* (= united).
3 three-dimensional: *a solid figure.*
• **solid** *noun Physics* something which is
solid, especially that which maintains its
shape unless forcefully changed. Compare
GAS *noun* (definition 1); LIQUID *noun*.
Word Family **solidly** *adverb*; **solidness,
solidity** (soll-**id**-i-tee) *noun*.
[Latin *solidus* compact]

solidarity (soll-i-**darr**-i-tee) *noun*
a unity or agreement in interests, opinions, relationships, etc.

solidify (soll-**id**-i-fie) *verb* (**solidifies; solidifying; solidified**)
1 to make solid, hard or compact.
2 to make strong: *We must solidify our position.*
Word Family **solidification** (soll-id-if-i-**kay**-sh'n) *noun*.

solid-state *adjective*
(of electronic devices) consisting of solid components such as semiconductors, transistors, etc.
solid-state physics the study of the physical properties of solids.

soliloquy (so-**lill**-a-kwee) *noun* (*plural* **soliloquies**)
1 talking to oneself.
2 a speech made by a character in a play when alone on the stage.
Word Family **soliloquize, soliloquise** (so-**lill**-a-kwize) *verb* to talk to oneself.
[Latin *solus* alone + *loqui* to speak]

solipsism (soll-ip-sizm) *noun*
Philosophy the belief that only the self or ego exists or can be known.
Word Family **solipsist** *noun*.

solitaire (soll-i-tair) *noun*
1 a board game for one played with marbles or pegs, the object being to end with one peg remaining, preferably in the centre.
2 (*especially American*) patience (the card game).
3 a ring containing a single gem.
[French]

solitary (soll-i-tree) *adjective*
single: *a solitary lighthouse to guide the ships.*
Figurative He felt afraid in such a solitary area (= lonely, secluded).
• **solitary** *noun* (*plural* **solitaries**)
1 a person who lives alone.
2 solitary confinement.
Word Family **solitariness** *noun*.
[Latin *solitarius* alone]

solitary confinement *noun*
the keeping of a prisoner in a cell by himself or herself.

solitude (soll-i-tewd) *noun*
1 the state of being alone.
2 a lonely life or place.

solo *noun*
1 something designed for or performed by one person, such as a song or piece of music for one person.

2 a flight in which the pilot, usually a learner pilot, is not accompanied by an instructor.
3 *Cards* a game based on whist, in which one player plays against the rest.
• **solo** *adjective* performed or performing alone.
Word Family **solo** *adverb*; **soloist** (so-lo-ist) *noun* a person, especially a musician, who performs a solo.
[Latin *solus* alone]

solstice (sol-stiss) *noun*
either of two times, about 21 June or 22 December, when the sun is at the greatest distance from the equator and the longest or shortest day occurs.
Word Family **solstitial** (sol-stish-'l) *adjective*.
[Latin *sol* sun + *sistere* to stand still]

soluble *adjective*
1 capable of being dissolved, especially in water: *Salt is soluble in water.* □ *soluble aspirin.*
2 also **solvable** able to be solved or explained: *This puzzle is easily soluble.*
Word Family **solubility** (sol-yoo-**bill**-i-tee) *noun* 1 the ability to be dissolved.
2 *Chemistry* the extent to which one substance will dissolve in another at a given temperature.

solute (sol-yoot) *noun*
Chemistry a substance which dissolves in another to form a solution: *In a solution of salt in water, salt is the solute.* Compare SOLVENT.
• **solute** *adjective* dissolved.

solution (so-loo-sh'n) *noun*
1 an explanation: *We cannot find a solution to this problem.*
2 the method or process of solving or explaining a problem.
3 *Chemistry* a homogeneous mixture of the molecules of two or more substances with different molecular structures. This usually refers to solids in liquids, but includes gases in liquids, liquids in liquids, gases in solids and solids in solids.
[Latin *solutus* untied, loosened]

solvable ⇨ SOLUBLE (definition 2).
Word Family **solvability** (sol-va-**bill**-i-tee) *noun*.

solve *verb*
to find an answer or explanation for.
[Latin *solvere* to untie]

solvent *adjective*
1 having money, especially enough to pay one's debts.

2 able to dissolve other substances.
● **solvent** *noun Chemistry* a substance, usually liquid, able to dissolve other substances in it: *In a solution of salt in water, water is the solvent.* Compare SOLUTE.
Word Family **solvency** *noun* the ability to pay one's debts.

solvent abuse *noun*
the use of various forms of solvent, such as glue, as an inhalant.

sombre (**som**-ba) *adjective* (*American* **somber**)
dark, especially in a gloomy or dull way.
Figurative Her *sombre expression made us stop laughing* (= serious, gloomy).
Word Family **sombrely** *adverb*; **sombreness** *noun*.
[*sub-* + Latin *umbra* shade]

sombrero (som-**brair**-o) *noun*
a pointed hat with a very wide upturned brim, as is worn in Mexico and south-west America.
[from Spanish *sombra* shade]

some (sum) *adjective*
not indicating a particular one, type, number, etc.: *Some day you will understand.* □ *Some children were late.*
Figurative He *remained silent for some time* (= a fairly long). □ *That was certainly some feat* (= a remarkable).
● **some** *pronoun* an indefinite number of people or things: *Some were seen to leave early.*

somebody (**sum**-b'd-ee) *pronoun*
some person: *I saw somebody who looks like you.*
Word Family **somebody** *noun* (*plural* **somebodies**) a person of importance.

somehow *adverb*
in a way which is not known or understood: *Somehow I'll get my revenge.*
Figurative I *think somehow that he won't try it* (= for no definite reason).

someone *pronoun*
somebody.

somersault (**summ**-a-sawlt) *noun*
a complete circular roll of the body head over heels, either forwards or backwards.
Figurative Her *first feelings had undergone a somersault* (= complete reversal).
Word Family **somersault** *verb*.
[Old French *sombre saut* leap over]

something *pronoun*
a thing which is not specified: *I've got something to show you.*

sometime *adverb*
at a time not stated, especially in the future: *We will arrive sometime after lunch.*
● **sometime** *adjective* former: *a sometime director of our company.*

sometimes *adverb*
at times.

somewhat *adverb*
to a certain degree: *She is somewhat foolish.*

somewhere *adverb*
in, at or to a place not stated or known: *I know that she is somewhere in the garden.*
Figurative They *left somewhere between six and seven o'clock* (= sometime).

somnambulism (som-**nam**-bew-lizm) *noun*
the habit or practice of sleepwalking.
Word Family **somnambulist** *noun* a sleepwalker.
[Latin *somnus* sleep + *ambulare* to walk]

somnolent (**som**-na-l'nt) *adjective*
sleepy.
Word Family **somnolently** *adverb*; **somnolence** *noun*.
[Latin *somnus* sleep]

son (sun) *noun*
1 a male child in relation to his parents.
2 any male descendant.
3 a male person strongly influenced by or involved with something: *sons of the soil.*
4 a familiar term of address to a younger man from an older person.

sonar (**so**-nar) *noun*
an electronic device or system using echoes from underwater sound waves for directing submarines, mines, shoals of fish, etc.
[SO(und¹) + N(avigation) + A(nd) + R(anging)]

sonata (sonn-**ah**-ta) *noun*
Music an instrumental composition in three or four distinct and often contrasting movements.
[Italian, sounded]

sonatina (sonn-a-**tee**-na) *noun*
a short or simplified sonata.

song *noun*
1 a musical composition with words.
2 any musical or melodious sound: *the song of a bird.*
Phrase **for a song** I *bought these old chairs for a song because they are damaged* (= very cheaply).
Word Family **songster** *noun* 1 a singer.
2 a bird which sings; **songstress** *noun* a female singer.

songbird *noun*
a bird which sings.

sonic (**sonn**-ik) *adjective*
relating to sound: *a sonic boom*.
[Latin *sonus* sound]

sonic barrier ⇨ SOUND BARRIER.

sonic boom *noun*
a loud explosive sound caused by an
aircraft or missile moving faster than the
speed of sound.

son-in-law *noun* (*plural* **sons-in-law**)
the husband of one's daughter.

sonnet *noun*
a poem of 14 lines, normally with ten
syllables per line and a formal rhyme
scheme.

sonny (**sun**-ee) *noun*
(*informal*) a familiar or affectionate term
of address to a little boy.

sonorous (**sonn**-a-rus) *adjective*
having a deep full sound: *Her sonorous
snores woke me.*
Word Family **sonorously** *adverb*;
sonorousness, sonority (sa-**norr**-i-tee)
noun.
[Latin *sonor* sound]

soon *adverb*
in the near future: *Write to me soon.*
Figurative *The rainy season came too soon
this year* (= early).
Phrases **as soon** *I would as soon not come*
(= willingly, in preference). **as soon as** *As
soon as she spoke, the crowd cheered*
(= immediately).

soot *noun*
a black, usually powdery, substance
formed by the incomplete burning of
carbon fuels. It contains carbon plus many
other substances, including sulphur and
hydrocarbons.
Word Family **sooty** *adjective* (**sootier;
sootiest**) **1** covered with soot. **2** black or
dark; **sootiness** *noun*.

sooth (*rhymes with* tooth) *noun*
an old word for truth or fact.

soothe (sooth) *verb*
to bring ease or comfort to.
Word Family **soothingly** *adverb*.

soothsayer *noun*
a prophet or fortune-teller.

sop *noun*
1 something given to appease or pacify
another.
2 something, such as a piece of bread,
which is soaked or dipped in a liquid.

• **sop** *verb* (**sops; sopping; sopped**) to
absorb or soak.

sophism (**soff**-izm) *noun*
sophistry.

sophisticated (so-**fist**-i-kay-tid) *adjective*
1 fine, refined or cultured: *She has a
sophisticated taste in music.*
2 worldly or having lost natural innocence
or simplicity through education,
experience, etc.
3 technologically advanced, complex: *This
is a very sophisticated device.*
Word Family **sophistication** (so-fist-i-
kay-sh'n) *noun*.

> The word **sophisticated** has had a
> change of meaning since its origin. It is
> now frequently a complimentary term
> but it originally meant 'adulterated' or
> 'corrupted'. Borrowed via Latin from
> Greek, it is derived from *sophistés*,
> meaning 'an expert', but is also the
> name for a member of a school of
> Greek philosophers (*Sophists*) who
> came to be known for their dishonest
> reasoning in arguments.

sophistry (**soff**-iss-tree) *noun* (*plural*
sophistries)
1 the use of false, tricky or deceptive
arguments.
2 such an argument.
Word Family **sophist** *noun*
[Greek *sophizein* to make wise]

sophomore (**soff**-a-mor) *noun*
American a student in his or her second
year at college.

soporific (sopp-a-**riff**-ik) *adjective*
of or producing sleep.
[Latin *sopor* deep sleep + *facere* to make]

sopping *adjective*
soaked or drenched.

soppy *adjective* (**soppier; soppiest**)
(*informal*) sloppily sentimental.

soprano (so-**prah**-no) *noun*
1 the highest singing voice in women and
boys.
2 any instrument having this range.
[Italian *sopra* above]

sorbet (**sor**-bay) *noun*
a fruit-flavoured frozen dessert.
[French]

sorcerer (**sor**-sa-ra) *noun*
a person who practises magic, especially
witchcraft.
Word Family **sorceress** *noun* a female
sorcerer; **sorcery** *noun* magic, especially
witchcraft.

sordid *adjective*
1 mean, selfish and ignoble: *sordid deeds of cheats and swindlers.*
2 wretched, filthy and shabby: *a sordid slum.*
Word Family **sordidly** *adverb*; **sordidness** *noun*.
[Latin *sordidus* dirty]

sore *adjective*
physically tender or painful.
Figurative That subject is a sore point with her (= annoying, irritating). □ *Don't get sore at me* (= annoyed, irritated). □ *I'm in sore need of money* (= great).
● **sore** *noun*
1 a place on the body which is sore, inflamed or injured.
2 a cause of distress, irritation, etc.
Word Family **sorely** *adverb*; **soreness** *noun*.

sorghum (sor-gum) *noun*
a cereal grass grown in warm climates, used as a grain and a source of syrup or treacle.

sorority (so-**rorr**-i-tee) *noun* (*plural* **sororities**)
American a society of female students. Compare FRATERNITY (definition 2).
[Latin *soror* sister]

sorrel[1] *noun*
1 a reddish-brown colour.
2 a horse of this colour.

sorrel[2] *noun*
a plant similar to spinach, having smaller sour-tasting leaves.

sorrow *noun*
1 unhappiness or regret due to loss, etc.
2 something which causes such feelings: *His death was a great sorrow to us.*
● **sorrow** *verb* to feel unhappiness or regret.
Word Family **sorrowful** *adjective* feeling or causing sorrow; **sorrowfully** *adverb*.

sorry *adjective* (**sorrier**; **sorriest**)
1 feeling regret, sympathy, etc.: *I'm sorry for my rudeness.* □ *I'm sorry to hear you've been ill.*
2 miserable or pitiful: *The old camel was in a sorry condition.*

sort *noun*
1 a particular kind or type: *What sort of music do you like?* □ *I said nothing of the sort.*
2 (*informal*) a person: *She's a decent sort.*
Phrases **of sorts, of a sort** *Food of sorts was provided* (= of a mediocre or poor kind). **out of sorts** not in one's normal or best health or condition. **sort of** (*informal*) to some extent.
● **sort** *verb* to arrange or separate into groups or sorts: *Sort these eggs into their sizes.*
Phrase **sort out** 1 to separate into groups or categories. 2 to solve a problem.
3 (*informal*) to deal sternly with a person who is causing trouble.
Word Family **sorter** *noun* a person or thing that sorts, such as a post-office employee who sorts letters.

sortie (sor-tee) *noun*
a raid or attack made against a besieging enemy.
[French *sortir* to go out]

SOS (ess-o-**ess**) *noun*
a distress signal or call for help.
[S(ave) + O(ur) + S(ouls)]

so-so *adjective*
(*informal*) neither good nor bad.
Word Family **so-so** *adverb*.

sot *noun*
a drunkard.
[French]

sotto voce (sott-o **vo**-chay)
in a low voice.
[Italian, under the voice]

sou (soo) *noun*
(*informal*) a very small sum of money: *not a sou.*
[an old French coin of little value]

soubrette (soo-**bret**) *noun*
a pert or coquettish young woman, especially such a character in an opera or play.
[French]

soubriquet ⇨ SOBRIQUET.

soufflé (soo-flay) *noun*
a light fluffy baked dish made of savoury or sweet ingredients with beaten egg whites.
[French, puffed]

sough (*rhymes with* cow) *verb*
(of the wind, waves, etc.) to make a sighing or murmuring sound.
● **sough** *noun* a soughing sound.

sought the past tense and past participle of **seek**.

soul (sole) *noun*
1 the non-physical, spiritual or emotional centre of a person.
2 the soul as the element which survives death.
Figurative There wasn't a soul in sight (= person). □ *She's the soul of wit*

(= embodiment). □ *She was the life and soul of the party* (= enlivening element).
3 the nobler feelings or instincts: *He has no soul.*
4 also **soul music** a type of black American music combining elements of gospel, jazz and rhythm and blues.
Phrase **sell one's soul for** *I'd sell my soul for a cup of tea* (= go to any lengths to get).

soul-destroying *adjective*
unendurably monotonous or tedious; demoralizing.

soul food *noun*
the kind of food, for example chitterlings, yams and ham hocks, traditionally eaten by black Americans.

soulful *adjective*
having or showing deep feeling: *soulful eyes.*
Word Family **soulfully** *adverb*; **soulfulness** *noun*.

soulless (sole-liss) *adjective*
heartless or unfeeling.

soulmate *noun*
a perfect companion and partner in life.

soul music ⇨ SOUL (definition 4).

sound¹ *noun*
any vibrations in the air which are detectable by the ear: *the sound of music.*
Figurative I don't like the sound of the news (= implications).
● **sound** *verb*
1 to make or give out a sound: *The trumpets sounded.*
2 to cause to make a sound: *Sound the bells.*
3 to give a certain impression: *Your story sounds odd.*
Phrase **sound off 1** to speak angrily or dogmatically. **2** to boast.
Word Family **soundless** *adjective*; **soundlessly** *adverb*.
[Latin *sonare* to make a noise]

sound² *adjective*
1 in good or healthy condition: *sound teeth.*
2 reasonable or reliable: *sound advice.*
3 (*informal*) excellent.
Figurative I gave him a sound thrashing (= thorough).
Word Family **soundly** *adverb*; **soundness** *noun*.

sound³ *verb*
to test or measure the depth of water, etc., e.g. by dropping a weighted line.
Phrase **sound someone out** to discover or try to discover someone's views by means of indirect questions, etc.

● **sound** *noun* something used for sounding, such as a slender instrument used to probe tubes or cavities in the body.
[*sub-* + Latin *unda* a wave]

sound⁴ *noun*
1 *Geography* a narrow channel of water, such as a strait.
2 *Geography* an inlet of the sea.

soundalike *noun*
a person who sounds like another.

sound barrier *noun* also called **sonic barrier**.
the rapid increase in drag as an aeroplane reaches the speed of sound.

sound bite *noun*
a short punchy phrase or sentence extracted from a speech or interview, often used by the media.

soundbox *noun* (*plural* **soundboxes**)
the hollow part of a stringed instrument which increases the resonance.

sound effects *plural noun*
any sounds other than speech or music, used on radio or film, such as the noise of trains, traffic, etc.

sounding board *noun*
1 also **soundboard** a wooden board on a stringed instrument which increases and improves the sound by vibrating when the strings are struck.
2 a person or thing used to give wider publicity to plans, theories, etc.: *He is acting as the minister's sounding board.*

soundproof *adjective*
not able to be penetrated by sound.
● **soundproof** *verb* to make soundproof.

soundtrack *noun*
1 a magnetic or other strip attached to a film on which sounds are recorded to be played through a loudspeaker.
2 a recording made on this.

sound wave *noun*
Physics a wave by which sound is transmitted.

soup (soop) *noun*
a liquid food made from meat, fish or vegetables and usually served hot.
Phrase **in the soup** (*informal*) in trouble.
● **soup** *verb*
Phrase **soup up** (*informal*) to modify a car engine to make it more powerful, especially by fitting a supercharger.

soupçon (soop-son) *noun*
a very small trace or amount.
[French, suspicion]

soup kitchen *noun*
a place where soup or other food is served to poor people.

sour *adjective*
1 having a sharp acid taste, as of vinegar or unripe fruit.
2 bad-tempered, surly: *She had a sour expression.*
• **sour** *verb* to make or become sour.
Word Family **sourly** *adverb*; **sourness** *noun*.

source (*rhymes with* horse) *noun*
any place or thing from which something comes or starts: *Where is the source of the river? □ My news is from a reliable source.*
[from Latin]

sour cream *noun*
cream artificially soured by the addition of bacteria.

sour grapes *plural noun*
the act of criticizing or pretending to despise something which one cannot have for oneself.
[from a fable by Aesop in which the fox pretended that the grapes he couldn't reach were sour]

souse (*rhymes with* mouse) *verb*
1 to throw into or drench with water.
2 to pickle something, usually fish.
Figurative (*informal*) *I feel slightly soused* (= drunk).

soutane (soo-**tahn**) *noun*
Roman Catholicism a priest's cassock.
[Italian *sotto* under]

south *noun*
1 the direction along the meridian to the right of the position where the sun rises.
2 the cardinal point of the compass at 90° to the right of east and opposite north.
Word Family **south** *adjective, adverb*.

south-east *noun*
1 the point or direction midway between south and east.
2 a region in this direction.
• **south-east** *adjective, adverb*
1 in or towards the south-east.
2 coming from the south-east.
Word Family **south-easterly, south-eastern** *adjective* from or towards the south-east; **south-easterly, southeaster** *noun* a wind coming from the south-east.

southerly (**suth**-a-lee) *adjective*
(of a direction, course, etc.) from or towards the south: *We set off on a southerly course.*
• **southerly** *noun* (*plural* **southerlies**) a wind coming from the south.
• **southerly** *adverb*.

southern (**suth**-ern) *adjective*
(of a place) situated in the south: *the southern edge of the desert.*
Word Family **southernmost** *adjective* furthest south.

Southern Lights *plural noun*
the aurora australis.

southward *adjective*
towards the south.
Word Family **southwards, southward** *adverb*.

south-west *noun*
1 the point or direction midway between south and west.
2 a region in this direction.
• **south-west** *adjective, adverb*
1 in or towards the south-west.
2 coming from the south-west.
Word Family **south-westerly, south-western** *adjective* from or towards the south-west; **south-westerly, south-wester** *noun* a wind coming from the south-west.

souvenir (soo-va-**neer**) *noun*
an object given or kept as a memento.
[French *se souvenir* to remember]

sou'wester (sow-**west**-a) *noun*
a waterproof hat with a downturned brim long enough to cover a collar at the back.

sovereign (**sov**-rin) *noun*
a king or queen.
• **sovereign** *adjective* having supreme rank, power or authority.
Figurative The colony fought to become a sovereign state (= independent).
Word Family **sovereignty** *noun* the status or power of a sovereign or sovereign state.

soviet (**so**-vee-et) *noun*
the local governing council in the former Soviet Union.

sow[1] (so) *verb* (**sows; sowing; sowed; sown**)
to plant or scatter seed, etc. so that it will grow.
Figurative You are sowing discontent among the people (= introducing, spreading).
Word Family **sower** *noun*.

sow[2] (*rhymes with* cow) *noun*
an adult female pig.

soya bean *noun* also **soy bean**
the nutritious seed of an Asian plant, used as food and as a source of oil.
[from Chinese, salted beans oil]

soy sauce *noun* also **soya sauce**
a salty brown sauce made by pickling
fermented soya beans, used for flavouring
in oriental cooking.

sozzled *adjective*
(*informal*) drunk.

spa *noun*
1 a mineral spring.
2 a health resort where there is a mineral
spring.
[after *Spa*, a resort town in Belgium]

space *noun*
1 that in which all objects exist and move.
2 a portion of this: *How much space will this
table take up?*
3 also **outer space** the part of the universe
beyond the earth's atmosphere.
4 an area or extent of a surface: *Fill in the
blank spaces on the form.*
5 an extent of time: *a space of half an hour.*
• **space** *verb* to fix, divide or separate into
spaces or intervals: *Space your words further
apart.*
Phrase **be spaced out** (*informal*) to be
disorientated, having taken or as if having
taken drugs.
Word Family **spacing** *noun*.
[from Latin]

space age *noun*
the era when space travel began.
Word Family **space-age** *adjective* very
modern or futuristic.

space bar *noun*
a key on a typewriter or a computer
keyboard used to insert a space.

space capsule *noun*
a container for instruments or astronauts,
which may be sent into space and
recovered on its return.

spacecraft *noun* (*plural* **spacecraft** or
spacecrafts)
a vehicle designed to travel outside the
earth's atmosphere.

space heater *noun*
a heater designed to heat the whole of an
enclosed area such as a single room.

spaceman *noun* (*plural* **spacemen**)
1 an astronaut.
2 a being who lives in outer space.

space probe *noun*
a spacecraft which sends information back
to earth on conditions in space.

spaceship *noun*
a manned spacecraft.

space shuttle *noun*
a reusable rocket-propelled spacecraft
used to transport people and equipment
between earth and a satellite.

space station *noun*
a manned spacecraft or satellite in semi-
permanent orbit.

spacesuit *noun*
a protective garment worn by astronauts,
which can withstand high or low
temperatures, radiation, etc. and carries its
own oxygen supply.

spacious (**spay**-shus) *adjective*
occupying or providing much space:
a comfortable spacious house.
Word Family **spaciously** *adverb*;
spaciousness *noun*.

spade¹ *noun*
a long-handled tool with a broad flat blade
for digging.
Phrase **call a spade a spade** to speak
plainly.

spade² *noun*
1 *Cards* a black figure like an inverted
heart on a playing card.
2 a playing card with this figure.
3 (**spades**) the suit with this figure.

spadework *noun*
any hard work needed at the start of
something.

spaghetti (spag-**ett**-i) *noun*
pasta made into long strings.
[Italian, little cords]

spaghetti western *noun*
(*informal*) a film about cowboys, etc. made
in Europe by an Italian director.

spake an old past tense of **speak**.

Spam *noun*
(*trademark*) a tinned pressed meat
mixture, mainly ham.
[SP(iced) + (h)AM]

spam *noun*
messages, especially irrelevant or unasked-
for ones, sent to many people on the
Internet.
• **spam** *verb* (**spams**; **spamming**;
spammed) to send a message to many
people on the Internet.

span *noun*
1 the distance between two edges or
extremes of something, such as the tips of
a pair of wings or two supports of a bridge.
2 the full reach or extent of anything: *a life
span of 60 years.*

• **span** *verb* (**spans; spanning; spanned**)
to extend over or across: *A bridge spanned the river.*

spangle *noun*
1 a small thin disc of shining metal, used to decorate dresses, etc.
2 any bright or glittering part, piece, etc.
• **spangle** *verb* to decorate or glitter with spangles.
Word Family **spangly** *adjective*.

spaniel (**span**-y'l) *noun*
any of various small long-haired gun dogs. [Latin *Hispania* Spain]

spank *verb*
to slap the buttocks with the open hand, etc.
• **spank** *noun* a smart or a resounding slap.

spanking *noun*
a slapping on the buttocks, especially as a punishment.
• **spanking** *adjective*
1 brisk or rapid: *a spanking pace.*
2 (*informal*) very fine or excellent: *in spanking health.*
• **spanking** *adverb* (*informal*) very: *a spanking new car.*

spanner *noun*
a metal bar with jaws or a hole at its end for turning a bolt, nut, pipe, etc.
Phrase **spanner in the works** (*informal*) something which disrupts, confuses or obstructs.
[German *spannen* to tighten up]

spar[1] *noun*
any strong pole such as a mast or a boom supporting a ship's sails.

spar[2] *verb* (**spars; sparring; sparred**)
1 to strike or box with light punches, e.g. for exercise or practice.
2 (*informal*) to argue or dispute.
Word Family **spar** *noun*.

spar[3] *noun*
Geology any of various lustrous and easily cleavable crystalline minerals.

spare *adjective*
1 extra: *I've no spare time.* □ *a spare tyre.*
2 small or meagre: *a spare diet.*
• **spare** *verb*
1 to refrain from hurting, damaging, destroying, etc.: *The judge spared the man's life.*
2 to dispense or part with from a supply: *Can you spare me a dollar?*
3 to use economically: *Spare the butter as there's not much left.*
Figurative No expense was spared (= denied).

• **spare** *noun*
1 something extra or in reserve: *This tyre is a spare.*
2 *Tenpin bowling* a score obtained by knocking over all ten pins in two successive shots. Compare STRIKE *noun* (definition 4).
Word Family **sparely** *adverb*; **spareness** *noun*.

spare rib *noun*
(*usually* **spare ribs**) a cut of meat, especially pork, containing a front rib with little fat on it.

sparing (**spair**-ing) *adjective*
careful or economical: *She's sparing in her use of money.*
Word Family **sparingly** *adverb*.

spark *noun*
1 a tiny glowing particle, especially one thrown out by a fire or produced by striking flint and metal.
2 a brief electrical discharge usually with a visible flash, and some sound.
Figurative Bill didn't show much spark at the party (= liveliness). □ *He hasn't a spark of kindness in him* (= slight bit).
• **spark** *verb*
1 to produce or throw out sparks.
2 (of an ignition system) to start functioning correctly.
Figurative He tried to spark some interest (= stimulate).
Phrase **spark off** *The speech sparked off a riot* (= started).

sparkle *verb*
to send out or shine with sparks or little gleams of light.
Figurative The hostess sparkled with wit (= was brilliant).
• **sparkle** *noun* a small spark or gleam.
Figurative She was full of sparkle (= liveliness, brilliance).
Word Family **sparkling** *adjective*; **sparkly** *adjective*.

sparkler *noun*
1 a taper-like firework that gives off small sparks and is held in the hand.
2 (*informal*) a diamond.

spark plug *noun* also **sparking plug**
a device screwed into the combustion chamber of an internal-combustion engine, used to ignite the fuel by an electric spark.

sparrow *noun*
a small brown bird related to the finch.

sparrowhawk *noun*
a long-legged short-winged bird related to the falcon and preying on other birds.

sparse *adjective*
thin or thinly scattered: *a sparse beard.*
□ *The sparse population in a desert.*
Word Family sparsely *adverb*;
sparseness, sparsity *noun.*
[Latin *sparsus* scattered]

Spartan *adjective*
sternly austere or disciplined.
Word Family Spartan *noun.*

> **Spartan** is the adjective from *Sparta* –
> an ancient Greek city noted for the
> military skills, courage and discipline of
> its inhabitants. They were also noted for
> the plainness of their diet and lifestyle,
> and it is this last quality that we refer to
> today when we speak of someone living
> in *Spartan* conditions.

spasm *noun*
a sudden involuntary movement of the muscles.
Figurative *He only works in spasms*
(= short sudden bursts).
Word Family spasmodic (spaz-**mod**-ik)
adjective done or occurring in short
irregular bursts; **spasmodically** *adverb.*
[from Greek]

spastic *adjective*
suffering from continuous or
uncontrollable muscle spasms, as in
cerebral palsy.
• **spastic** *noun* a person who is spastic.
Word Family spastically *adverb.*

spat[1] a past tense and past participle of
spit[1].

spat[2] *noun*
(*usually* **spats**) a pair of stiff cloth covers
enclosing the ankle and the top part of a
shoe.

spat[3] *noun*
a petty quarrel.

spatchcock *noun*
a very small chicken which is split open,
skewered flat and grilled.

spate *noun*
a sudden flood or rush: *a spate of business
activity before Christmas.*

spatial (spay-sh'l) *adjective*
1 of or relating to space or spaces: *the
painting's spatial qualities.*
2 existing or occurring in space.
Word Family spatially *adverb*; **spatiality**
(spay-shee-**al**-i-tee) *noun.*

spatter *verb*
to splash or sprinkle in many directions:
*The bus spattered mud all over my new
trousers.*
• **spatter** *noun*
1 a shower or sprinkling.
2 a splash or spot of something spattered.

spatula (spat-yoo-la) *noun*
a tool with a flat blade for lifting, mixing or
spreading food, etc.
[Latin]

spavin (spavv-in) *noun*
any of a group of diseases of horses
causing enlargement of the hock joint.

spawn *noun*
1 *Biology* the mass of egg cells emitted by
fish and other aquatic organisms.
2 *Biology* the thread-like matter from
which mushrooms, etc. grow.
• **spawn** *verb* to produce or shed spawn.
Figurative *High prices spawned discontent
and riots* (= caused).

spay *verb*
to remove the ovaries of a female animal to
prevent it having offspring. Compare
CASTRATE; STERILIZE (definition 1).
[Old French *espeer* to cut with a sword]

speak *verb* (**speaks; speaking; spoke** or
(*old form*) **spake; spoken**)
1 to utter or pronounce words in an
ordinary voice: *Can your baby speak yet?*
2 to converse with someone: *She wants to
speak to you.*
3 to express: *He's speaking the truth.*
4 to lecture: *She spoke for four hours to a
packed hall.*
5 to know and be able to use a language:
Do you speak Spanish?
Phrases so to speak as one might say.
speak for 1 *This speaks well for his ability*
(= is evidence of). **2** *I shall speak for you in
court* (= act on behalf of). **3** *This chair is
spoken for* (= reserved). **speaking likeness**
a real or lifelike resemblance. **speak out** to
express one's views boldly. **to speak of**
Nothing exciting happened to speak of
(= worth mentioning).
Word Family speaking *noun, adjective.*

speakeasy *noun* (*plural* **speakeasies**)
American a place where alcoholic drinks
were sold illegally, especially during
Prohibition.

speaker *noun*
1 a person who speaks, especially one who
addresses a meeting, etc.
2 *Audio* a loudspeaker.

3 (**Speaker**) *Parliament* a member of the House of Commons elected to control its meeting.

speaking clock *noun*
a telephone service which gives the time to the nearest second, announced by recorded tape.

spear *noun*
a weapon with a sharp pointed blade mounted on a long pole.
• **spear** *verb* to pierce or wound with or as with a spear.

speargrass *noun*
a tall grass with upright stiff sharp leaves.

speargun *noun*
an underwater gun that fires a barbed spear, powered by springs or compressed air.

spearhead *noun*
1 the sharply pointed head of a spear.
2 a person or thing that leads an attack, etc.
Word Family **spearhead** *verb*.

spearmint *noun*
a variety of mint with small purplish flowers, yielding an aromatic oil used as a flavouring.

spec *noun*
Phrase **on spec** (*informal*) as a risk or gamble.
[short form of *speculation*]

special (**spesh-**'l) *adjective*
1 of a distinct kind: *This is a special holiday train.* □ *Did you come here for any special purpose?*
2 belonging exclusively to a particular person or thing: *The special features of our leasing arrangements.*
3 not ordinary or usual: *dining out on a special occasion.*
4 exceptionally good: *He is a very special friend.*
• **special** *noun* something which is special, such as a special edition of a newspaper.
[Latin *specialis* individual]

special constable *noun*
a part-time auxiliary policeman.

special correspondent *noun*
a journalist commissioned to report on a particular field of interest or a specific event.

special effects *plural noun*
sound effects and visual effects created for a film by computer graphics, etc.

specialist *noun*
a person who studies or is skilled in one particular subject or branch of a subject: *a skin specialist.*
Word Family **specialism** *noun*.

speciality (spesh-i-**al**-i-tee) *noun* (*plural* **specialities**) also **specialty**
1 something which is special or distinct.
2 an activity or product particularly dealt with by a person or business: *The chef's speciality is curried beef.*

specialize, specialise (**spesh**-a-lize) *verb*
1 to follow a special line of study or activity: *She specializes in foreign languages.*
2 *Biology* to adapt for a particular purpose: *A fish's gills are specialized to allow it to breathe in water.*
Word Family **specialization** (spesh-a-lie-**zay**-sh'n) *noun*.

special licence *noun*
a licence to marry without following all the normal legal procedure.

specially *adverb*
particularly.

special needs *plural noun*
the educational needs of those with physical, emotional, behavioural or learning difficulties.

special offer *noun*
an article offered at or as if at a reduced price.

special school *noun*
a school for children with special needs.

specialty (**spesh**-'l-tee) *noun* (*plural* **specialties**) ⇨ SPECIALITY.

specie (**spee**-shee) *noun*
coin or coined money.

species (**spee**-sheez *or* **spee**-shiz) *noun* (*plural* **species**)
1 *Biology* the group below genus, used in the classification of animals or plants. It indicates a group of individuals able to breed among themselves but not with members of another such group.
2 a distinct group or sort.
[Latin, outward appearance]

specific (sp'-**siff**-ik) *adjective*
precise or particular: *a specific description.*
• **specific** *noun* something that is specific, such as a remedy for a particular disease.
Word Family **specifically** *adverb*.

specification (spess-if-i-**kay**-sh'n) *noun*
1 the act of specifying.

2 a statement of details and instructions, such as the dimensions and materials to be used for a building.

specify (spess-i-fie) *verb* (**specifies;
specifying; specified**)
to mention specifically or definitely: *Please specify your time of arrival.*

specimen (spess-i-m'n) *noun*
a single part or thing taken as typical or representative: *This painting is a specimen of the work I do.*
Figurative He's a very strange specimen (= person).
[Latin, visible evidence]

specious (spee-shus) *adjective*
deceptively good, correct or pleasing: *a specious argument.*
Word Family **speciously** *adverb;*
speciousness *noun.*
[Latin *speciosus* showy]

speck *noun*
a very small spot or particle.
Word Family **specked** *adjective* marked with specks.

speckle *noun*
a small mark or spot.
• **speckle** *verb* to mark with speckles.

specs *plural noun*
(*informal*) spectacles.

spectacle (spek-ti-k'l) *noun*
1 anything viewed or seen: *The sunset was a fine spectacle.*
2 an impressive or large-scale public show or display.
3 (**spectacles**) ⇨ GLASSES.
Phrase **make a spectacle of oneself** to draw attention to oneself by unseemly dress or behaviour.
[from Latin]

spectacular (spek-tak-yoo-la) *adjective*
making an impressive sight: *a spectacular display of fireworks.*
• **spectacular** *noun* a film, etc. which is lavishly produced, relying on crowd scenes, elaborate scenic effects, etc. rather than subtlety of plot or characters.
Word Family **spectacularly** *adverb.*

spectator (spek-tay-ta) *noun*
a person who watches or looks on.

spectral *adjective*
1 of or like a spectre.
2 of or relating to a spectrum.

spectre (spek-ta) *noun* (*American*
specter)
a ghost or apparition.
[from Latin]

spectrum *noun* (*plural* **spectra**)
1 *Physics* the series of bands produced when a wave is split up into its component frequencies. White light forms bands of red, orange, yellow, green, blue, indigo and violet.
2 a range of ideas, beliefs, etc.
[Latin, image]

speculate (spek-yoo-late) *verb*
1 to meditate or reflect on a given subject.
2 to form hypotheses or opinions on the basis of little or no evidence.
3 to undertake risky business or investments in the hope of making a large profit.
Word Family **speculator** *noun* a person who speculates; **speculative** (spek yoo-la-tiv) *adjective*; **speculation** (spek-yoo-lay-sh'n) *noun.*
[Latin *specula* a lookout, watchtower]

speculum (spek-yoo-lum) *noun* (*plural*
specula)
1 a mirror or reflector, especially one of polished metal.
2 *Medicine* an instrument used to inspect an inaccessible part of the body.
3 *Biology* a brightly coloured area on the wing of certain birds.
[Latin]

speech *noun* (*plural* **speeches**)
1 the power or act of speaking.
2 a spoken address, usually formal.
3 a person's manner of speaking: *Her speech is slow and difficult to hear.*
4 the language or dialect of a region, country, etc.
Word Family **speechless** *adjective* characterized by absence or loss of speech; **speechlessly** *adverb*; **speechlessness** *noun.*

speech marks *plural noun* also called
**inverted commas; quotation marks;
quotes.**
punctuation marks (' ') or (" "), used to enclose direct speech, quotations, titles, etc.: *'Is it raining?' she asked.*

speech therapy *noun*
treatment of speech and language problems.
Word Family **speech therapist** *noun.*

speed *noun*
1 swiftness in moving, travelling, etc.
2 *Physics* the rate of change of linear displacement, regardless of direction. Compare VELOCITY (definition 1).
3 (*informal*) any of various strong amphetamines.

4 *Photography* a measure of the exposure required by an emulsion.
Phrase **at full speed** as fast as possible.
● **speed** *verb* (**speeds; speeding; speeded** or **sped**)
1 to move or cause to move swiftly: *He sped past.*
2 to increase the rate of progress: *We must speed up production.*
3 to drive a motor vehicle faster than the speed limit.
Word Family **speeder** *noun*.

speedboat *noun*
a small fast motor boat.

speed limit *noun*
1 the maximum legal speed at which a vehicle may travel in a particular area.
2 the regulation which orders this.

speedometer (spee-**domm**-it-a) *noun*
an instrument for measuring the speed of, and distance travelled in, a vehicle.

speed trap *noun*
any of various devices, such as radar, etc., used by police to verify the speed of motor vehicles.

speedway *noun*
a racetrack for motorcycles.

speedy *adjective* (**speedier; speediest**)
very quick or prompt.
Word Family **speedily** *adverb*; **speediness** *noun*.

speleology (spee-li-**oll**-a-jee) *noun*
the study and exploration of caves.
Word Family **speleologist** *noun*; **speleological** (spee-li-a-**lojj**-i-k'l) *adjective*.
[Greek *spelaion* cave + *-logy*]

spell[1] *verb* (**spells; spelling; spelt** or **spelled**)
1 to name or write the letters of a word, etc., correctly.
2 (of letters) to form: *C-a-t spells 'cat'.*
3 to signify: *The storm spelt disaster for the rowing boat.*
Phrase **spell out 1** to read slowly or laboriously. **2** to explain in detail.
Word Family **speller** *noun* **1** a person who spells. **2** a spelling textbook; **spelling** *noun*.

spell[2] *noun*
1 a word or words believed to have magic power.
2 any strong influence.

spell[3] *noun*
1 a short period of time: *She went away for a spell.*
2 a period of weather: *a hot spell.*

3 a short turn of work: *I took a spell at the wheel so that the driver could rest.*
4 a fit: *a coughing spell.*
Word Family **spell** *verb* to give a period of rest to.

spellbound *adjective*
entranced.

spellchecker *noun*
a computer program which checks the spelling in a text file.

spencer (**spen**-sa) *noun*
a knitted woollen jacket.

spend *verb* (**spends; spending; spent**)
1 to pay out money, etc.: *I spent £50 at the supermarket.*
Figurative *The storm had spent its fury* (= used up, exhausted).
2 to make use of time, etc.: *We spent the weekend in the country.*
Word Family **spender** *noun*; **spent** *adjective*.
[Latin *dispendere* to weigh out]

spendthrift *noun*
a person who is extravagant or wasteful with money or possessions.

sperm *noun* (*plural* **sperm** or **sperms**)
1 a spermatozoon.
2 semen.
Word Family **spermatic** (sper-**mat**-ik) *adjective*.
[Greek *sperma* seed]

spermaceti (sperm-a-**see**-ti *or* sperm-a-**sett**-i) *noun*
a waxy substance obtained from the oil of certain whales and used in ointments and cosmetics.
[SPERM + Greek *ketos* whale]

spermatozoon (sperm-a-ta-**zoh**-on) *noun* (*plural* **spermatozoa**)
Biology a male reproductive cell.
[Greek *spermatos* of seed + *zoion* animal]

spew *verb*
(*informal*) to vomit.
Figurative *The factory spews all its waste into the river* (= discharges).

sphagnum (**sfag**-num) *noun*
any of a group of mosses growing in damp areas and building up into layers of peat.
[from Greek]

sphere (sfeer) *noun*
1 a three-dimensional circular figure with all points on its surface equidistant from its centre, e.g. the moon or a tennis ball.
2 an environment or field of activity, etc.: *My social sphere is rather limited.*

Word Family spherical (sferr-i-k'l)
adjective having the rounded shape of a
sphere.
[Greek *sphaira* a ball]

sphincter (sfink-ta) *noun*
Anatomy a ring of muscle, such as the
anus, surrounding an opening or tube
within the body and able to close it.
[Greek *sphingein* to throttle]

sphinx *noun* (*plural* **sphinxes**)
1 *Egyptian mythology* a wingless monster
with the head of a man and the body of a
lion.
2 *Greek mythology* a winged monster with
the head and breasts of a woman and the
body of a lion, who killed those who could
not solve its riddles.
3 an enigmatic person.
[Greek *sphingein* to throttle]

spice *noun*
1 a substance from a plant, such as pepper,
etc., which is used to add flavour to food.
2 something that is interesting or adds
flavour: *Variety is the spice of life.*
Word Family spice *verb*; **spicy** *adjective*
(**spicier; spiciest**) **1** of, like or containing
spice. **2** scandalous or sensational; **spicily**
adverb; **spiciness** *noun*.
[Late Latin *spocies* merchandise]

spick and span *adjective*
very neat and clean.

spider *noun*
Biology any of various wingless eight-
legged arthropods which usually spin
webs, having the head and thorax fused
together but separated from the abdomen.
Word Family spidery *adjective* long and
thin.

spiel (shpeel *or* speel) *noun*
(*informal*) any glib or plausible talk, such
as a salesman's prepared speech.
[German, play]

spigot (spigg-'t) *noun*
a device for stopping the hole in a barrel,
etc.

spike¹ *noun*
1 a strong pointed piece of metal, etc.
2 a sharp metal projection on the sole of a
running shoe.
3 (**spikes**) a pair of shoes with such
projections, worn by athletes, etc.
• **spike** *verb*
1 to impale or injure with a spike.
2 to put an end to: *His reappearance spiked
all rumours about his death.*
3 (*informal*) to add alcohol to.

Word Family spiky *adjective* (**spikier;
spikiest**) **1** like or having a spike or spikes.
2 (*informal*) easily irritated.

spike² *noun*
1 an ear of grain.
2 a long cluster of stalkless or nearly
stalkless flowers.
[from Latin]

spill¹ *verb* (**spills; spilling; spilt** *or*
spilled)
1 to run or fall out, or to cause to run or
fall out, as from a container.
Figurative *Much blood was spilt in the
battle* (= shed). □ *He was spilt from his horse
at the first jump* (= caused to fall).
2 *Nautical* to let the wind out of the sails.
3 (*informal*) to tell or disclose: *Who spilt
the story to the newspapers?*
• **spill** *noun* the act of spilling.
Word Family spillage *noun*.

spill² *noun*
a piece of wood or paper used to light
candles, etc.

spillway *noun*
an overflow channel on a dam, reservoir,
etc.

spin *verb* (**spins; spinning; spun**)
1 to make yarn by twisting and winding
fibres into a long thread.
2 (of spiders, etc.) to form a thread, web,
etc. by giving out a sticky substance.
3 to rotate rapidly: *She spun the coin on the
table.*
4 to tell a story: *to spin a tale.*
Phrase spin out to draw out or make last.
• **spin** *noun* a rapid rotating movement.
Figurative *Her head was in a spin due to all
the excitement* (= confused state). □ *Let's
take the car for a spin* (= short journey).
□ *The plane went into a spin*
(= continuously spinning descent).
Phrase in a flat spin (*informal*) in a state
of great confusion or panic.

spina bifida (spy-na **biff**-i-da) *noun*
a disabling congenital condition in which
the spinal meninges protrude through
their bony coverings.
[Latin *spina* spine + *bifidus* split in two]

spinach (spin-itch) *noun*
a green leafy vegetable.
[from Persian]

spinal (spy-n'l) *adjective*
of or relating to a spine, especially the
backbone.

spinal cord *noun*
Anatomy a cylinder of nerve tissue extending from the base of the brain down the inside of the bones of the back.

spindle *noun*
1 a rod onto which thread or yarn is wound for spinning or sewing.
2 any of various rods or thin shafts which revolve or serve as an axis for larger revolving parts, e.g. in a lathe.

spindly *adjective* (**spindlier; spindliest**)
long and thin.

spin doctor *noun*
(*informal*) a political spokesperson employed to convey a favourable interpretation of events to journalists.

spin-dry *verb* (**spin-dries; spin-drying; spin-dried**)
to extract most of the water from wet clothes by spinning them rapidly in a machine.
Word Family **spin dryer** *noun* a machine for spin-drying clothes.

spine *noun*
1 also called **backbone**. *Anatomy* a series of bones enclosing and protecting the spinal cord and supporting the other bones of the skeleton.
2 a ridge, e.g. of ground, rock, etc.
3 a pointed projection on an animal or plant, such as a quill or thorn.
4 the part of a cover of a book which holds the pages together.
[from Latin]

spine-chilling *adjective*
making one fearfully apprehensive.
Word Family **spine-chiller** *noun* a book, play or film designed to make one fearful.

spineless *adjective*
1 lacking moral courage or resolution.
2 lacking a spine or spines.
Word Family **spinelessly** *adverb*; **spinelessness** *noun*.

spinet (spin-**et**) *noun*
Music a small wing-shaped type of harpsichord, now seldom played.
[Latin *spina* spine (as the strings were plucked by quills)]

spinnaker (spin-a-ka) *noun*
Nautical a very large ballooning jib sail hoisted when racing before the wind.
[from *Sphinx*, the first yacht to use one]

spinner *noun*
a person or thing that spins, such as a fishing lure which rotates rapidly in the water.

spinneret (spin-a-**ret**) *noun*
an organ in an insect or spider which produces the thread for a cocoon or web.

spinney (**spin**-ee) *noun*
a small dense group of trees or shrubs.
[from Latin]

spinning jenny *noun* (*plural* **spinning jennies**)
short form is **jenny** an early spinning machine which had several spindles, so that more than one yarn could be spun at one time.

spinning mule ⇨ MULE (definition 3).

spinning top ⇨ TOP².

spinning wheel *noun*
any of various machines for spinning flax or wool, consisting of a spindle driven by a wheel which is worked by a foot treadle.

spin-off *noun*
an incidental benefit in another field resulting from research and development in a particular field: *Pocket calculators are a spin-off from space research*.

spinster *noun*
an unmarried woman.
Word Family **spinsterhood** *noun*.
[Middle English, one who spins]

> The word **spinster** is now mostly used either in a legal context as in *spinster of this parish* or in a deliberately derogatory way, as in *just an old spinster*. *Unmarried woman* or *single woman* are much more acceptable terms while *bachelor girl* is sometimes used informally or humorously.

spiny *adjective* (**spinier; spiniest**)
(of animals and plants) having or resembling spines.

spiracle (**spy**-ra-k'l) *noun*
Biology a small hole for exchange of gases during respiration, found in insects, fish and some other animals.
[from Latin]

spiral (**spy**-r'l) *noun*
1 a continuous curve moving round a fixed point at a steadily increasing or decreasing distance, as in a coiled rope.
2 a continuous curve winding round a central axis but continually changing plane, as in the thread of a screw.
3 a continuously quickening increase or decrease: *a wage spiral*.
• **spiral** *adjective* having the shape or form of a spiral: *a spiral staircase*.

• **spiral** *verb* (**spirals; spiralling; spiralled**) to have a spiral shape or movement.
Word Family **spirally** *adverb*.

spire *noun*
1 an upright tapering structure on top of a church tower or other building.
2 the top part or point of something which tapers upwards.
[Greek *speira* a coil]

spirit *noun*
1 the soul.
2 any supernatural or divine being, such as a ghost, fairy, etc.
3 the essential part of a person's feelings, emotions, character, etc.: *The hard life had broken her spirit.*
4 (**spirits**) the state of one's mind, feelings, etc.: *to be in high spirits.*
Figurative The university was filled with the spirit of revolution (= inspiring force).
□ *He is well liked for his intelligence and spirit* (= liveliness, courage). □ *Try to join in the spirit of Christmas* (= dominant mood).
□ *I could only grasp the spirit of her letter* (= general meaning). □ *All players have a strong team spirit* (= loyalty).
5 (usually **spirits**) any strong distilled alcoholic liquor.
6 *Medicine* a solution of a substance in alcohol.
• **spirit** *verb* (**spirits; spiriting; spirited**) to carry off secretly or mysteriously.
Word Family **spirited** *adjective* 1 having liveliness or courage. 2 relating to a person's mood or emotional state: *a high-spirited young man*; **spiritedly** *adverb*; **spiritedness** *noun*; **spiritless** *adjective*.
[Latin *spiritus* breathing]

spirit level *noun*
an instrument for finding a true horizontal level, by means of a bubble of air which floats in a tube of alcohol set in a frame.

spirits of salt *noun*
an old term for a solution of hydrochloric acid in water.

spiritual (**spirr**-i-tew-'l) *adjective*
1 of or relating to the soul rather than the physical body.
2 of or relating to supernatural beings.
3 of or relating to religious or sacred things.
• **spiritual** *noun* a religious folk song which originated among black Americans.
Word Family **spiritually** *adverb*; **spirituality** (spirr-i-tew-**al**-i-tee) *noun*.

spiritualism (**spirr**-i-tew-'l-izm) *noun*
1 the belief that spirits of the dead can be contacted by the living.
2 the practices, such as seances, associated with such a belief.
Word Family **spiritualist** *noun*.

spit¹ *verb* (**spits; spitting; spat** or **spit**)
1 to eject from the mouth, especially to eject saliva: *I spat out the tablet.*
Figurative He spat out his words (= uttered violently).
2 (of rain or snow) to fall in light scattered drops.
3 to make a noise as if spitting: *The wood fire hissed and spat.*
Phrase **spit it out** (*informal*) to speak.
• **spit** *noun*
1 saliva.
2 the act of spitting.
3 (*informal*) a spitting image.

spit² *noun*
1 a pointed revolving rod for roasting food over a grill or fire.
2 *Geography* a low narrow tongue of land which grows outwards from the shore across a bay or inlet. Spits are formed by longshore drift. Compare BAR *noun* (definition 9).
• **spit** *verb* (**spits; spitting; spitted**) to pierce or stab with or as if with a spit.

spit and polish *noun*
a careful cleaning, as of military equipment, etc.

spite *noun*
a malicious urge or desire to hurt, humiliate or annoy.
Phrase **in spite of** *I will do it in spite of your advice* (= regardless of).
• **spite** *verb* to annoy or thwart because of spite.
Word Family **spiteful** *adjective*; **spitefully** *adverb*; **spitefulness** *noun*.
[from DESPITE]

spitfire *noun*
a person who has a fiery temper.

spitting image *noun*
(*informal*) the close likeness or counterpart of a person, etc.

spittle *noun*
saliva.

spittoon *noun*
a vessel or bowl for spitting into.

spiv *noun*
(*informal*) a black-market dealer or petty criminal, especially one who dresses in a vulgar or flashy way and does no regular work.

splash *verb*

1 to wet or soil with drops of water, mud, etc.

2 (of a liquid) to fly about and fall in drops.

3 to make a noise similar to that made by splashing.

Figurative *The news was splashed across the front page of the newspaper* (= displayed very prominently).

Phrase **splash out** (*informal*) to spend money lavishly.

• **splash** *noun* (*plural* **splashes**)

1 the act or sound of splashing.

2 a quantity of liquid splashed around or on something.

3 a mark or spot caused by something splashed.

Figurative *a splash of colour* (= patch, small area). □ *The extravagant party made a big splash* (= sensation).

Word Family **splashy** *adjective* (**splashier**; **splashiest**).

[alteration of *plash*]

splashdown *noun*

the landing of a spacecraft in the sea following its flight.

splatter *verb*

to splash.

splay *verb*

to spread out or extend.

• **splay** *adjective* spread out.

[shortening of DISPLAY]

splay-footed *adjective*

having broad flat feet which turn outwards.

spleen *noun*

1 *Anatomy* the large red organ which lies between the stomach and the left kidney; it produces lymph cells and stores red blood cells.

2 bad temper or spite: *He always vents his spleen on his poor wife.*

Word Family **splenetic** (splin-**ett**-ik) *adjective*.

[from Greek]

splendid *adjective*

1 superb or brilliant: *a splendid sunset.*

2 (*informal*) very satisfactory: *What a splendid end to the story.*

Word Family **splendidly** *adverb*; **splendidness** *noun*; **splendiferous** (splen-**diff**-er-us) *adjective* (*informal*) splendid.

[Latin *splendidus* shining]

splendour (**splend**-er) *noun* (*American* **splendor**)

1 a superb or brilliant appearance, colouring, etc.: *the splendour and display of the royal visit.*

2 glory or distinction: *the splendour of ancient Rome.*

splice *verb*

1 to join two parts or pieces, e.g. of rope or wood, by interweaving, overlapping, etc.

2 (*informal*) to join in marriage.

• **splice** *noun* a joint made by splicing.

spline *noun*

1 a strip of metal which fits into and locks with matching slots, e.g. in a shaft and wheel.

2 one of the slots into which a spline fits.

splint *noun*

a thin piece of wood, metal, etc. used to keep an injured or diseased bone or joint fixed in a desirable position.

• **splint** *verb* to secure in position by means of a splint or splints.

splinter *noun*

a sharp slender piece of wood, metal, glass, etc. split or broken off from a main body.

• **splinter** *verb* to split or break into splinters.

Word Family **splintery** *adjective*.

splinter group *noun*

a group of members of an organization who separate from the others, especially after a disagreement.

split *verb* (**splits**; **splitting**; **split**)

1 to break or divide, especially from one end to the other.

2 to divide or separate in any way: *The substance was split into its elements.* □ *Opinions were split over the matter.*

3 to burst or rip: *He split his trousers as he sat down.*

4 (*informal*) to leave.

Phrases **split on** (*informal*) *The criminal split on his mates* (= betrayed, divulged secrets about). **split one's sides** (*informal*) to laugh heartily. **split the difference** to reach agreement by both sides compromising an equal amount. **split up 1** to share or divide up. **2** to part or become separated.

• **split** *noun*

1 a crack caused by splitting.

Figurative *a split within the committee* (= sharp division of opinion).

2 (*informal*) a share: *Here's your split of the loot.*

3 (**splits**) the spreading of one's legs along the floor so that they form a straight line at right angles to or in the plane of the body.
4 a dish made from sliced fruit and ice cream covered with nuts and syrup: *a banana split.*
Word Family **splitting** *adjective* (of a headache) severe.

split infinitive *noun*
a simple infinitive, e.g. *to leave,* with a word dividing it, e.g. *to hurriedly leave.*

split-level *adjective*
(of a building, etc.) having certain floors slightly above or below the main storey level.

split pea *noun*
a dried pea, cut in half, used in soups and as a vegetable.

split personality *noun* (*plural* **split personalities**)
1 a tendency to behave in conflicting ways.
2 (*informal*) schizophrenia.

split pin *noun*
a fastener which is made from a strip of metal folded in half so that it may be passed through a hole and the ends bent apart to hold it in place.

split ring *noun*
a ring, such as a key ring, with a movable opening through which objects may be inserted.

split-second *adjective*
1 performed with great precision.
2 achieved immediately: *a split-second decision.*
Word Family **split second** *noun* a very short time.

splotch *noun* (*plural* **splotches**) also **splodge**
a large messy spot, stain, etc.
Word Family **splotch** *verb*; **splotchy** *adjective* (**splotchier; splotchiest**).

splurge *noun*
(*informal*) an extravagant display or indulgence: *We had a splurge and went to an expensive restaurant.*
Word Family **splurge** *verb.*

splutter *verb*
1 to speak confusedly or with a spitting sound, e.g. from excitement or embarrassment.
2 to spit drops of liquid noisily.
Word Family **splutter** *noun*; **splutterer** *noun.*

spoil *verb* (**spoils; spoiling; spoilt** or **spoiled**)
1 to damage the quality, value or usefulness of: *The rain spoilt our holiday.* □ *Rust will spoil those scissors.*
2 to harm or damage the character or nature of by excessive indulgence: *That child is spoilt by his grandparents.*
3 (of food, etc.) to go bad.
Phrase **be spoiling for** *You could see the gang was spoiling for a fight* (= eager for).
● **spoil** *noun* (*usually* **spoils**) the booty or plunder taken in war, robbery, etc.
Figurative the spoils of public office (= profits, advantages).
Word Family **spoilage** *noun* **1** the act of spoiling. **2** something which is spoilt; **spoiler** *noun.*
[Latin *spolium* plunder]

spoilsport *noun*
a person who ruins the enjoyment of others.

spoke[1] the past tense of **speak.**

spoke[2] *noun*
1 any of the rods which connect the hub of a wheel to the rim.
2 any similar rod, e.g. on an umbrella.
3 a rung of a ladder.
Phrase **put a spoke in someone's wheel** to interfere with someone's plans.

spoken the past participle of **speak.**

spokesman *noun* (*plural* **spokesmen**)
a person, especially a man, who speaks on behalf of another person or other people.

spokesperson *noun* (*plural* **spokespersons** or **spokespeople**)
a person who speaks on behalf of another person or other people.

spokeswoman *noun* (*plural* **spokeswomen**)
a woman who speaks on behalf of another person or other people.

spoliation (spo-lee-ay-sh'n) *noun*
the act of plundering or spoiling.

sponge (spunj) *noun*
1 a non-mobile aquatic animal consisting of many cells arranged in a porous structure.
2 the light absorbent skeleton of this animal, or a synthetic imitation, used for washing, bathing, etc.
3 something which has the texture or qualities of a sponge, such as a light fluffy cake.
Phrase **throw in the sponge** to admit defeat or failure.
● **sponge** *verb*

1 to wash, wipe, clean or absorb with a sponge.

2 (*informal*) to live at the expense of others: *He's always sponging off his relatives.*
Word Family sponger *noun*; **spongy** *adjective* (**spongier; spongiest**) soft or absorbent like a sponge.
[from Greek]

sponsor *noun*

1 a person, such as a godfather, who takes responsibility for another.

2 a person who proposes or supports something: *Who was the sponsor for the divorce reform bill?*

3 a person, business, etc. that finances or helps to finance a sport, cultural event, broadcast, etc., usually in return for advertising facilities.

4 a person who agrees to pay a sum of money to a charity if another person performs a particular feat.
• **sponsor** *verb* to act as sponsor for.
Word Family sponsorship *noun*.
[Latin]

spontaneous (spon-**tay**-nee-us) *adjective* occurring or produced naturally and not caused by external forces: *spontaneous combustion.*
Figurative *a spontaneous laugh* (= not rehearsed, impulsive).
Word Family spontaneously *adverb*; **spontaneity** (spon-ta-**nay**-a-tee) *noun*.
[Latin *sponte* voluntarily]

spontaneous generation *noun* also called **abiogenesis**.
Biology the incorrect theory that living things can be produced from non-living matter. Compare BIOGENESIS.

spoof *noun*
(*informal*) a parody or hoax.

spook *noun*
a ghost.
Word Family spooky *adjective* (**spookier; spookiest**) eerie or suggestive of spooks.

spool *noun*
a cylindrical device onto which tape, thread, etc. is wound for use.

spoon *noun*

1 any kitchen utensil with a handle and small bowl-shaped end used for eating, measuring, serving, etc.

2 something which has the shape or function of a spoon.
• **spoon** *verb*

1 to lift or carry with or as if with a spoon.

2 *Sport* to hit a ball high into the air.

3 (*informal*) to act in a playfully amorous way.
Word Family spoonful *noun*.

spoonbill *noun*
a wading bird related to the ibis, having a long flat beak with a spoon-like end.

spoonerism (**spoon**-a-rizm) *noun*
an unintentional changing of the order of sounds in words, as in *The teacher accused him of tasting two worms* (= wasting two terms).
[after *W. A. Spooner*, 1844-1930, a British clergyman noted for such slips]

spoon-fed *adjective*

1 fed food with a spoon.

2 looked after too carefully.

spoor *noun*
the tracks left by wild animals.

sporadic (spa-**radd**-ik) *adjective*
occurring or appearing at only occasional intervals in time or space: *We heard sporadic firing all afternoon.* □ *sporadic outcrops of granite.*
Word Family sporadically *adverb*.
[Greek *sporas* scattered (seed)]

spore *noun*
Biology a reproductive cell or group of cells which separates from the parent before it begins to develop.
[Greek *spora* a sowing]

sporran *noun*
a pouch made of leather and fur hung at the front of a belt as part of Scottish Highland costume for men.
[Gaelic]

sport *noun*

1 any activity for exercise or enjoyment involving physical skill and organized with a set form, rules, etc.
Figurative *We made great sport of her shyness* (= fun, mockery). □ *We had quite good sport* (= shooting, hunting, etc.).

2 (**sports**) an athletic competition between several teams.

3 (*informal*) a person considered in relation to his or her attitudes or fairness in competition, difficult situations, etc.: *She's a good sport and doesn't mind a bit of teasing.*
• **sport** *verb*

1 to play or frolic: *Lambs sported in the fields.*

2 to display, wear or carry ostentatiously: *He was sporting a bright red scarf.*
Word Family sporting *adjective* 1 used for or connected with sport. 2 fair or honourable, especially in competition;

sportingly *adverb*; **sportive** *adjective*
playful or jokey; **sportively** *adverb*;
sportiveness *noun*.
[shortening of DISPORT]

sporting chance *noun*
a reasonable chance, given luck.

sports car *noun*
a high-powered low-built car, usually with
two seats and a removable or soft folding
roof.

sports jacket *noun* also called **sports
coat**.
a man's casual jacket made of tweed or
checked fabric.

sportsman *noun* (*plural* **sportsmen**)
1 a man who takes part in sport.
2 a man who is fair and honourable in
competition, etc.

sportsmanship *noun*
the behaviour or qualities considered
appropriate to a competitor or person
taking part in sport.

sportsperson *noun* (*plural*
sportspersons or **sportspeople**)
1 a person who takes part in sport.
2 a person who is fair and honourable in
competition, etc.

sportswear *noun*
clothes worn for sport or for casual wear.

sportswoman *noun* (*plural*
sportswomen)
1 a woman who takes part in sport.
2 a woman who is fair and honourable in
competition, etc.

sporty *adjective* (**sportier**; **sportiest**)
1 interested or showing talent in sports.
2 (of a car) fast and stylish.

spot *noun*
1 a round, usually small, mark on a
surface, having a different colour from its
surroundings: *a white dress with blue spots*.
2 any mark on a surface, such as a stain,
pimple, etc.
*Figurative Just a spot of milk in my tea,
please* (= little bit).
3 a place: *This seems like a good spot to fish.*
*Figurative I'm in rather a difficult spot at
the moment* (= predicament).
4 a spotlight.
***Phrases* hit the spot** to provide what is
necessary or satisfying. **knock spots off** to
outdo or defeat easily. **on the spot 1** *We
will mend shoes on the spot* (= here, at once).
2 *That tricky question put her on the spot*
(= in a difficult or embarrassing situation).
● **spot** *verb* (**spots**; **spotting**; **spotted**)

1 to mark or stain with spots: *Her hands
were spotted with paint.*
2 to find or discover: *Can you spot any
mistakes on this page?*
3 *Billiards* to place the ball on any of the
various spots marked on the table.
***Word Family* spotless** *adjective* very
clean; **spotlessly** *adverb*; **spotlessness**
noun; **spotted** *adjective*.

spot check *noun*
an unannounced and random
examination: *Police are conducting spot
checks on cars in the area.*

spotlight *noun*
a light with a strong narrow beam, as used
in a theatre.
*Figurative Shy people dislike being in the
spotlight* (= public attention or notice).
***Word Family* spotlight** *verb* (**spotlights;
spotlighting; spotlighted** or **spotlit**).

spot on *adjective*
(*informal*) absolutely correct or accurate.

spotter *noun*
a person or thing that spots, especially one
that looks for and reports something:
a talent spotter.

spotty *adjective* (**spottier**; **spottiest**)
1 marked with spots.
2 uneven or irregular.

spot-weld *verb*
to weld in one place by pressing electrical
conductors to either side of two pieces of
metal and briefly applying a high electric
current.

spouse (*rhymes with* mouse *or* cows) *noun*
one's husband or wife.
[Latin *sponsus* betrothed]

spout *noun*
1 a pipe or tube, usually with a lip-like
end, for pouring.
2 a stream or gush of liquid discharged
under pressure.
***Phrase* up the spout** (*informal*) *His
business is completely up the spout because of
wage increases* (= ruined).
● **spout** *verb*
1 to pour out in gushes.
2 (*informal*) to utter pompously: *He loves
spouting pieces of Greek verse.*

sprain *verb*
to twist or strain a part of the body
without breaking it.
● **sprain** *noun* a twisting or straining
without actual breakage.

sprang the past tense of **spring**.

sprat *noun*
a small edible marine fish, related to the herring.
Phrase **sprat to catch a mackerel** a small favour or concession made in hopes of a far larger one in return.

sprawl *verb*
to stretch out in a careless or ungraceful manner: *Stop sprawling in your chair.*
Figurative The suburbs sprawled across the countryside (= spread out, straggled).
• **sprawl** *noun* an ungraceful or irregular stretch or extent.

spray¹ *noun*
1 a liquid blown or forced through the air as fine drops.
Figurative Bonnie and Clyde were met with a spray of bullets (= fine shower, scattering).
2 any of various devices which force out a shower of fine particles or drops: *a perfume spray.*
• **spray** *verb*
1 to apply a liquid as a spray.
2 to move or fall as a spray.
Word Family **sprayer** *noun.*

spray² *noun*
1 a small fine branch with leaves, flowers, berries, etc., often used for decoration.
2 a design or ornament with this form.

spray gun *noun*
a gun-shaped device using compressed air to spray liquids, such as paint, insecticides, etc., evenly over an area.

spread (spred) *verb* (**spreads; spreading; spread**)
1 to make or become larger, wider or further apart: *The eagle spread his wings.*
□ *Spread the map out on the table.*
2 to distribute or extend over an area, especially evenly: *Spread the butter on the bread.* □ *The payments are spread over 12 months.* □ *The disease spread throughout the country.*
Figurative The news spread rapidly (= was made widely known). □ *Spread your clothes out to dry by the fire* (= lay).
• **spread** *noun*
1 the act of spreading: *He watched the slow spread of the eagle's wings.*
2 the amount by which something spreads: *The aircraft's wings had a spread of 30 m.*
3 something which spreads, covers or is spread: *a bedspread.* □ *cheese spread.*
4 something which extends or stretches: *We could see a wide spread of forest ahead.*

5 two pages which face each other in a book, magazine, etc.
6 a story, advertisement, etc. which extends across all or part of two such pages.
7 (*informal*) a feast: *The dinner they provided was a real spread.*
Word Family **spreader** *noun.*

spreadeagled *adjective* also **spreadeagle**
with the arms and legs stretched out.
Word Family **spreadeagle** *verb.*

spreadsheet *noun*
a type of computer software which produces a document with rows and columns in which numbers or words can be entered, and which can automatically perform calculations and other tasks.

spree *noun*
a period of indulgence or excess in some activity: *a shopping spree.*

> The word **spree** means 'a bout of indulgence'. The indulgence originally took the form of having a good time drinking and eating and then was extended to shopping. In recent times it has taken on more sinister overtones with terms such as *shooting spree*, totally indiscriminate shooting and killing. The origin of *spree* is not certain, but it is thought to have connections with Scots *spreath*, meaning 'a cattle raid' or 'foray'.

sprig *noun*
a twig or small branch, often used for decoration: *a sprig of holly.*

sprightly (**sprite**-lee) *adjective*
(**sprightlier; sprightliest**)
full of life or nimble energy.
Word Family **sprightliness** *noun.*

spring *verb* (**springs; springing; sprang; sprung**)
1 to rise or move lightly and suddenly.
Figurative Angry words sprang to her lips (= rushed, came quickly). □ *We sprang the dinner party as a surprise* (= produced unexpectedly). □ *The boat has sprung another leak* (= developed). □ *The feud sprang from a misunderstanding* (= arose, originated). □ (*informal*) *His friends intend to spring him from prison* (= cause to escape).
2 to make or become bent: *These old floorboards have sprung.*
• **spring** *noun*
1 the act of springing: *a tiger's spring at its prey.*

2 any of various devices made from twisted, bent or layered metal which regains its shape after force has been applied, such as a spiral spring in a sofa.
3 a springing quality, force or movement: *Her walk has no spring or liveliness in it.*
4 the season between winter and summer, in which plants start to grow.
5 a natural flow or stream of water from under the ground: *This river starts at a mountain spring.*
6 the source of something.
Word Family **springer** *noun* **1** a person or thing that springs. **2** any of various breeds of short-haired spaniels.

springbok *noun*
a small South African antelope.
[Afrikaans, SPRING + BUCK[1]]

spring chicken *noun*
(*informal*) a young or inexperienced person: *The new geography teacher is no spring chicken.*

spring-clean *verb*
to clean or tidy thoroughly, especially as an annual clean-up of the whole house in the spring.
Word Family **spring-cleaning** *noun*

spring fever *noun*
a feeling of listlessness or restless desire, often experienced at the beginning of spring.

spring onion *noun*
an onion with a small bulb and long green shoots, often eaten raw.

spring roll *noun*
a Chinese dish consisting of a thin pancake rolled up and stuffed with a savoury mixture and fried.

spring tide ⇨ TIDE *noun* (definition 1).

springy *adjective* (**springier; springiest**)
tending to spring, bounce or rebound.
Word Family **springiness** *noun*.

sprinkle *verb*
to scatter or fall in drops or small particles.
Figurative Her conversation was sprinkled with little laughs (= interrupted at intervals).
● **sprinkle** *noun*
1 a light fall of drops.
2 a small quantity.
Word Family **sprinkler** *noun* something which sprinkles, especially a device with a nozzle which scatters drops of water over a garden, etc.; **sprinkling** *noun* a light small shower or scattering.

sprint *verb*
to run or race at full speed, especially over a short distance.
● **sprint** *noun* a short race at top speed.
Word Family **sprinter** *noun*.

sprite *noun*
Folklore a fairy.

sprocket *noun*
any of the pointed teeth on a wheel, which fit into the links of a chain, as on a bicycle.

sprog *noun*
(*informal*) a child.

sprout *verb*
to begin to grow or develop.
● **sprout** *noun*
1 a young growth or shoot.
2 a Brussels sprout.

spruce[1] *noun*
any of a group of evergreen fir trees with cones and short angular needle-like leaves arranged densely round a twig.
[Old English *Pruce* Prussia]

spruce[2] *adjective*
neat and smart, especially in one's dress.
Phrase **spruce oneself up** to make oneself neat and smart.

sprung the past participle of **spring**.

spry *adjective*
nimble or sprightly.
Word Family **spryly** *adverb*; **spryness** *noun*.

spud *noun*
1 (*informal*) a potato.
2 a small spade with a narrow blade or prongs, for digging up weeds, etc.

spume (spewm) *noun*
a poetic word for foam or froth.
Word Family **spume** *verb*; **spumy** *adjective* frothy.
[from Latin]

spun the past tense and past participle of **spin**.

spunk *noun*
(*informal*) courage.
Word Family **spunky** *adjective* (**spunkier; spunkiest**).

spur *noun*
1 a sharp metal projection strapped to the heel of a rider's boot to urge the horse on.
Figurative The prize was a spur to the competitors (= stimulus, inspiration).
2 a projecting part, such as a ridge on the side of a hill or a horny growth on the leg of certain birds or animals.
3 a short or undeveloped branch on a tree.

Phrase **on the spur of the moment**
suddenly or spontaneously.
• **spur** *verb* (**spurs; spurring; spurred**)
to prick or strike with a spur: *The
huntsman spurred his horse.*
Figurative Fear spurred her to greater efforts
(= inspired).

spurious (**spew**-ri-us) *adjective*
false or counterfeit.
Word Family **spuriously** *adverb*;
spuriousness *noun*.
[from Latin]

spurn *verb*
to treat or reject with scorn or contempt.

spurt *noun*
a sudden flow or outpouring: *a spurt of
water from the burst pipe.*
*Figurative His last spurt to the line won him
the race* (= burst of energy). □ *In a spurt of
jealousy he killed his lover* (= outburst).
Word Family **spurt** *verb*.

sputnik *noun*
any of the early artificial satellites used by
the former Soviet Union for space
research.
[Russian, travelling companion]

sputter *verb*
to spit or splash in an explosive manner.
*Figurative She sputtered with rage at their
rudeness* (= stammered, spluttered).
Word Family **sputter** *noun*.

sputum (**spew**-t'm) *noun*
spittle or phlegm.
[Latin]

spy *noun* (*plural* **spies**)
1 a person sent to gather information
secretly in enemy or what is potentially
enemy territory.
2 a person employed to watch and report
secretly on the activities of others.
• **spy** *verb* (**spies; spying; spied**)
1 to act as a spy.
2 to catch sight of or see.

squab (skwob) *noun*
1 a young pigeon.
2 a soft cushion.

squabble (**skwob**-'l) *noun*
a trivial argument.
Word Family **squabble** *verb*.

squad (skwod) *noun*
any small group selected for a particular
purpose, such as a group of soldiers.
[Old French *esquadre* a square]

squad car *noun*
a police patrol car.

squadron (**skwod**-r'n) *noun*
1 a group of warships on a particular
mission.
2 a unit of the air force, cavalry or tank
regiments.
[Italian *squadra* square]

squadron leader *noun*
Air force a commissioned officer ranking
between flight lieutenant and wing
commander.

squalid (**skwoll**-id) *adjective*
1 depressingly or miserably dirty.
2 degraded.
Word Family **squalidly** *adverb*;
squalidness *noun*.
[Latin *squalidus* rough, unkempt]

squall¹ (skwawl) *noun*
1 a sudden gust of strong wind.
2 a noisy disturbance or fight.
Word Family **squally** *adjective*.

squall² *verb*
to scream or cry out harshly.
Word Family **squall** *noun*.

squalor (**skwoll**-a) *noun*
depressing or wretched conditions.

squamous (**skway**-mus) *adjective*
Biology covered with or consisting of
scales.
[Latin]

squander (**skwon**-da) *verb*
to spend or use wastefully: *Do not squander
your spare hours.*
Word Family **squanderer** *noun*.

square *noun*
1 a quadrilateral having equal sides and
four right angles.
2 something which has this shape, such as
any of the divisions on a chessboard, etc.
3 *Maths* the second power of a number:
The square of 2, written 2^2, is $2 \times 2 = 4$.
4 an open area in a town or city, usually
bordered by buildings or streets, and
planted with trees, etc.
5 (*informal*) a person considered to be
dully conservative or old-fashioned.
6 a unit of area in buildings equal to 100
square feet or $9 \cdot 3 \, m^2$.
Phrase **back to square one** (*informal*)
back to where one started, so one has to
begin again.
• **square** *verb*
1 to make into a square or similar shape.
*Figurative His story does not square with
yours* (= agree). □ *He squared his shoulders
and stood to attention* (= straightened, made
level). □ *You must square your debts first*
(= pay, settle).

2 *Maths* to multiply a number by itself.
Phrases square up *The company has
squared up all its overdue accounts*
(= settled). **square up to** *She must square
up to these responsibilities* (= face bravely).
• **square** *adjective*
1 having four sides and four right angles:
a square box.
Figurative Our accounts are square now
(= settled). □ *We must have a square answer*
(= honest, straightforward). □ *(informal)
This is the first square meal I've had for a
week* (= good, substantial). □ *The players
finished with their scores square* (= equal).
2 being in the form of a right angle:
a square corner.
3 presenting a measured unit of area
equivalent to a square with sides of the
specified length: *a square metre.*
4 *(informal)* dull, conservative or old-
fashioned.
• **square** *adverb*
1 in a square form or at right angles.
2 *(informal)* honestly or directly.
Word Family **squarely** *adverb.*
[from Latin]

square-bashing *noun*
(informal) army drill on the barracks
square.

square dance *noun*
a dance by couples arranged in a square or
other set pattern, and who follow
instructions by a caller in order to make a
pattern.

square-rigged *adjective*
Nautical having square sails set on
horizontal yards across the length of the
ship.

square root *noun*
Maths the number which, when multiplied
by itself, equals the given number: *4 is the
square root of 16.*

squash[1] (skwosh) *verb*
to press or beat, especially into a flat mass.
*Figurative The rebellion was squashed by
government troops* (= stopped, put down).
• **squash** *noun* (*plural* **squashes**)
1 the act or sound of squashing: *The plums
made a soft squash as they fell.*
2 something which is squashed or pressed.
3 also **squash rackets** a game played by
two or four players in a walled court, with
rackets and a small rubber ball.
4 a drink made with fruit juice or cordial
as a base.
5 a crowd or crowded gathering.

Word Family **squashy** *adjective*
(**squashier; squashiest**) soft and easily
squashed.
[alteration of QUASH]

squash[2] (skwosh) *noun* (*plural* **squashes**)
an edible vegetable similar to a marrow.

squat (skwot) *verb* (**squats; squatting;
squatted**)
1 to sit on one's heels or in a crouching
position.
2 to settle on an area of public land before
acquiring a legal right to it.
3 to enter an unoccupied house and live
there without paying rent.
• **squat** *noun*
1 the act of squatting.
2 the position when squatting.
• **squat** *adjective* (**squatter; squattest**)
short and thick.
Word Family **squatter** *noun* a person
who squats.

squaw *noun*
an offensive word for a North American
Indian woman.

squawk *verb*
(of a bird) to utter a harsh cry, e.g. when
frightened.
*Figurative (informal) Buyers are
squawking about increased prices*
(= protesting angrily or noisily).
Word Family **squawk** *noun.*

squeak *verb*
to make a short high-pitched sound
*Figurative He just squeaked through the
entrance exam* (= achieved by a small
margin).
• **squeak** *noun*
1 the act or sound of squeaking.
2 *(informal)* an escape: *That was a narrow
squeak!*
Word Family **squeaky** *adjective*
(**squeakier; squeakiest**) making squeaks;
squeakily *adverb*; **squeakiness** *noun.*

squeaky clean *adjective*
1 *(informal)* (of hair) washed so clean that
it squeaks.
2 *(informal)* totally without blame, above
reproach: *a squeaky clean politician.*

squeal *verb*
to make a long loud high-pitched cry or
sound.
*Figurative (informal) The traitor has
squealed to the police* (= turned informer).
• **squeal** *noun* a squealing sound.
Word Family **squealer** *noun.*

squeamish *adjective*
easily sickened or shocked.
Word Family **squeamishly** *adverb*;
squeamishness *noun.*

squeeze *verb*

1 to press firmly: *He squeezed her hand in sympathy.*
Figurative Can we all squeeze into the back seat? (= fit or force by pressure). □ *The bank is squeezing us to repay the loan* (= urging, putting pressure on).
2 to extract by pressing: *Squeeze the juice from three lemons.* □ *He tried to squeeze a confession out of me.*
• **squeeze** *noun* the act of squeezing: *a squeeze of the hand.*
Figurative We managed to get into the bus, but it was a tight squeeze (= crush, squash). □ *Add a squeeze of lemon* (= small amount). □ *a financial squeeze* (= time of restriction or difficulty).
Word Family **squeezer** *noun* something which squeezes, especially a device for extracting juice from fruits.

squelch *verb*
to make a splashing sucking sound.
Figurative His sharp retort squelched her (= made quiet or subdued).
Word Family **squelch** *noun* (*plural* **squelches**).

squib *noun*
a small firework which sparkles and then explodes.
Phrase **damp squib** an effort which fails miserably.

squid *noun*
any of a group of edible cephalopods with ten arms, some spanning 15 m.

squidgy *adjective* (**squidgier; squidgiest**)
(*informal*) soft and squashy.

squiggle *noun*
a wiggly or careless mark in drawing or writing.

squint *verb*
1 to look with the eyes partly closed or screwed up: *to squint against the sun's glare.*
2 to be cross-eyed.
Word Family **squint** *noun*.

squire *noun*
1 a country gentleman, used as an unofficial title for the owner of a manor house, etc.
2 also **esquire** *Medieval history* a young nobleman serving as attendant to a knight, as training for his own knighthood.
• **squire** *verb* (of a man) to escort or accompany a woman.

squirm *verb*
to wriggle or twist the body about.

Figurative We squirmed under his angry scrutiny (= felt embarrassed or uncomfortable).
Word Family **squirm** *noun*; **squirmy** *adjective*.

squirrel *noun*
1 any of various small rodents with grey or reddish-brown fur and a bushy tail, usually living in trees.
2 the fur of such an animal.
[Greek *skiouros* from *skia* shade + *oura* tail]

squirt *verb*
to discharge liquid in a quick stream: *Squirt water on the fire.*
• **squirt** *noun*
1 the act of squirting.
2 a thin fast stream of liquid.
3 (*informal*) a small or insignificant person, especially if impudent or presumptuous.

squish *noun*
a squashing sound.
Word Family **squish** *verb* to squash; **squishy** *adjective* (**squishier; squishiest**).

stab *verb* (**stabs; stabbing; stabbed**)
to pierce or wound with or as if with a knife: *stabbed by a robber.*
Figurative She was stabbed by feelings of guilt (= affected sharply).
• **stab** *noun*
1 the act of stabbing.
2 a thrust made with or as if with a pointed weapon.
3 a wound caused by stabbing.
Figurative He felt a stab of remorse (= painful feeling). □ (*informal*) *At least have a stab at the answer!* (= attempt, guess).
Phrase **stab in the back** a betrayal or unfair attack.
Word Family **stabbing** *noun*.

stabilize, stabilise (stay-bi-lize) *verb*
to make stable or level: *The government is trying to stabilize prices.*
Word Family **stabilization** (stay-bill-eye-**zay**-sh'n) *noun*; **stabilizer** *noun*
1 something which stabilizes, such as a substance used to control or limit chemical changes in other substances, etc.
2 any of various systems which stabilize a ship in rough seas. 3 (**stabilizers**) a pair of small wheels fitted either side of a child's bicycle to give support.

stable¹ *noun*
1 a building in which horses are kept.
2 all the horses owned by one person or establishment: *a racing stable.*

Figurative The speakers obviously belong to the same political stable (= group organization).

• **stable** *verb* to put or keep in a stable.
Word Family stabling *noun* **1** any or all stables. **2** accommodation for horses in a stable.
[from Latin]

stable² *adjective*
1 steady and not likely to fall or collapse: *That bridge does not look very stable.*
Figurative We need a reliable stable character for this position (= well-balanced, dependable). □ *They have built up a stable relationship* (= lasting).
2 *Chemistry* not easily decomposed.
Word Family stability (sta-**bill**-i-tee) *noun*; **stably** *adverb*.

staccato (sta-**kah**-toe) *adjective*
Music short and abrupt.
Word Family staccato *adverb*.
[Italian, detached]

stack *noun*
1 a large pile, often arranged in layers: *a haystack.*
2 a number of things grouped together.
Figurative (*informal*) *I have a stack of things to do today* (= great number).
3 a single chimney or flue.
4 a group of chimneys.
5 *Geography* a pillar of rock left standing in the sea after erosion has cut it off from the land.
• **stack** *verb*
1 to place or arrange in a stack: *Stack those chairs in the corner.*
2 to arrange so as to give oneself an advantage: *He stacked the rally with his own supporters.*

stadium (stay-dee-um) *noun* (*plural* **stadiums** or **stadia**)
a sports ground surrounded by raised banks of seats for spectators.

> The word **stadium** came into English through Latin *stadium.* Many English words directly derived from Latin used always to retain the form of plural that existed in Latin – thus *stadia* (plural of *stadium*), *hippopotami* (plural of *hippopotamus*) and *rostra* (plural of *rostrum*). Nowadays the plural form with *s* is increasingly common.

staff (stahf) *noun*
1 a group of people working together under a manager or other authority in an organization, business, etc.: *the staff of a hospital.*

2 a rod, pole or stick used as a weapon, flagpole, etc.
Figurative Food is the staff of life (= sustainer, supporter).
3 also **stave** *Music* the framework of lines and spaces on which music is written.
• **staff** *verb* to provide an office, etc. with workers.

staff nurse *noun*
a nurse ranking just below sister or charge nurse.

staff officer *noun*
Military a commissioned officer directly responsible to, and issuing the orders of, a commander.

staff sergeant *noun*
Army a non-commissioned officer ranking between sergeant and warrant officer.

stag *noun*
1 a male deer, especially a red deer.
2 (*informal*) a man, especially one at a party, etc. without a woman.
• **stag** *adjective* (of a party, etc.) excluding women.

stage *noun*
1 the platform or area, usually raised, on which actors perform, especially in a theatre.
Figurative The stage was set for war (= scene, atmosphere).
2 any raised floor or platform, such as a scaffolding.
3 the profession of acting: *He is training to go on the stage.*
4 the theatre: *a work written for the stage.*
5 a single step in a progress, development, series, etc.: *The first stage of our research is complete.* □ *the larval stage of an insect.*
6 a main bus stop.
7 a section of a bus route.
8 a powered section of a rocket vehicle, which is ejected after firing.
Phrase **hold the stage** to be the centre of attention.
• **stage** *verb* to put or exhibit on or as if on a stage.
Figurative The workers have staged a massive strike (= arranged and carried out).

stagecoach *noun* (*plural* **stagecoaches**)
an enclosed carriage with the driver's seat outside at the front, once used to carry passengers, mail, etc. over a set route.

stage door *noun*
an outside door for performers, etc. to enter the backstage area of a theatre.

stage fright *noun*
any nervousness caused by being in front of an audience, especially for the first time.

stage manager *noun*
Theatre a person appointed to organize and control the rehearsals and performance of a play.

stage-struck *adjective*
fascinated by or eager to have a career in acting or the theatre.

stage whisper *noun*
a loud or exaggerated whisper, such as one from an actor intended to be heard by the audience.

stagflation (stag-**flay**-sh'n) *noun*
high inflation along with high unemployment and stagnant demand for goods.

stagger *verb*
1 to walk or move unsteadily: *She staggered with exhaustion.*
Figurative We were staggered by the brilliant results (= amazed, overwhelmed).
2 to arrange in alternating or overlapping periods or intervals: *Employees should stagger their lunch breaks so that the office is never empty.*
● **stagger** *noun*
1 the act of staggering.
2 (**staggers**) (*used with singular verb*) any of various diseases affecting horses, cattle, etc., causing blindness and staggering movements.
Word Family **staggering** *adjective*; **staggeringly** *adverb*.

staging (**stay**-jing) *noun*
1 the act of putting on a play.
2 a temporary platform or structure, usually raised.

stagnant *adjective*
1 not flowing.
2 stale or foul due to lack of movement: *a stagnant pool.*
Figurative They found the local art scene quite stagnant (= lifeless, inactive).
Word Family **stagnantly** *adverb*; **stagnation** (stag-**nay**-sh'n) *noun*; **stagnate** (stag-**nayt**) *verb*.
[Latin *stagnum* a pool]

stag night *noun*
a social gathering for men only, held shortly before the wedding of one member of the group. Compare HEN NIGHT.

stagy (**stay**-jee) *adjective* (**stagier**; **stagiest**)
theatrical, especially in an artificial way.
Word Family **staginess** *noun*.

staid *adjective*
serious and sedate, especially in a tedious way.
Word Family **staidly** *adverb*; **staidness** *noun*.
[alteration of *stayed*]

stain *noun*
1 a discoloured area or mark produced or left by a substance: *Coffee stains are difficult to get rid of.*
Figurative The crime left a serious stain on his reputation (= bad mark).
2 a liquid dye, consisting of colour dissolved in water or spirit, which soaks into and colours a surface.
● **stain** *verb*
1 to make a stain on.
2 to colour with a liquid dye.
3 to corrupt or bring blame upon.
Word Family **stainer** *noun*; **stainless** *adjective*.

stained glass *noun*
a decorative form of glass, usually coloured with metallic oxides, used in church windows, etc.

stainless steel *noun*
any of a group of alloys of iron and chromium which are very resistant to corrosion and are used for making utensils, etc.

stair *noun*
1 any of a series of steps leading from one level of a building to another.
2 (**stairs**) a series of such steps.
Phrase **below stairs** the servants' quarters, in the basement.

staircase *noun* also called **stairway**.
a series of fixed steps and its framework, etc., between two levels in a building.

stairwell *noun*
the opening around which a staircase is built.

stake[1] *noun*
a pointed stick or post, usually of wood or metal, driven into the ground as a support, marker, etc.
● **stake** *verb*
1 to mark a position or boundary with a stake or stakes: *to stake off the garden.*
2 to support or secure with or to a stake: *You should stake those tomato plants.*

stake[2] *noun*
1 (*often* **stakes**) the money or any other thing promised as payment for a bet.
2 (**stakes**) the prize for a competition: *The stakes for the race were £1000.*

3 interest or involvement: *He has a personal stake in this matter.*
Phrase at stake *There is too much at stake for us to fail* (= being risked, involved).
• **stake** *verb* to offer money or any other thing as part of a bet.

stalactite (**stal**-ak-tite) *noun*
Geology any tapering mass of calcium carbonate formed by dripping water, hanging from the roof of a cave, etc. Compare STALAGMITE.
[Greek *stalaktos* dripping]

stalagmite (**stal**-ag-mite) *noun*
Geology any mass of calcium carbonate rock deposited on the floor of a cave, usually projecting upwards. Compare STALACTITE.
[Greek *stalagma* a dripping]

stale *adjective*
not fresh: *stale bread.* □ *a stale old joke.*
• **stale** *verb* to make or become stale.
Word Family stalely *adverb*; **staleness** *noun.*

stalemate *noun*
1 *Chess* a position where neither player can move without putting his or her king in check, resulting in a draw
2 any deadlock.
• **stalemate** *verb* to bring into a stalemate.

stalk¹ (stawk) *noun*
the stem of a plant, flower, leaf, fruit, etc.

stalk² *verb*
1 to approach or follow stealthily: *The cat stalked the mouse.*
2 to harass someone in an obsessive and frightening way.
3 to walk slowly and stiffly: *He stalked off in a huff.*
Word Family stalk *noun*; **stalker** *noun.*

stalking horse *noun*
1 a horse or dummy horse behind which a hunter hides.
2 something used to hide one's real intentions.

stall¹ (*rhymes with* ball) *noun*
1 a compartment of a cowshed or stable for one animal.
2 a bench or table used to display goods for sale, e.g. in a market.
3 a small open-fronted shop: *a newspaper stall.*
4 (**stalls**) the seats on the ground floor of a theatre.
5 any of the fixed seats used by the choir or clergy in a church.
• **stall** *verb*
1 to put or keep animals in a stall.

2 (of a motor) to stop running owing to insufficient power, speed, etc.
3 (of an aircraft) to lose flying speed and plummet out of control.

stall² *verb*
to act evasively or deceptively: *Stop stalling and answer the question.*
Word Family stall *noun.*

stallion (**stal**-y'n) *noun*
a male horse, especially one used for breeding.

stalwart (**stawl**-w't) *adjective*
1 strongly and stoutly built.
2 firm and steadfast: *My stalwart supporters will never desert me.*
• **stalwart** *noun* a stalwart person.

stamen (**stay**-m'n) *noun*
Biology the organ of a flower which produces pollen, consisting of the filament and the anther.
Word Family staminate (**stam**-in-it) *adjective.*
[Latin, the warp]

stamina (**stam**-in-a) *noun*
strength and the power to endure.

stammer *noun*
1 a stutter.
2 any hesitation in speech.
Word Family stammer *verb*; **stammerer** *noun*; **stammering** *adjective*; **stammeringly** *adverb.*

stamp *noun*
1 the act of bringing the foot down forcefully: *He gave a stamp of impatience.*
2 a postage stamp.
3 any device used to impress a shape, design or mark.
4 the design, etc. made by such a device.
Figurative The story has the stamp of truth (= distinctive mark).
5 a device used to cut or crush.
• **stamp** *verb*
1 to put one's foot down forcefully.
2 to walk with heavy or violent steps: *He stamped across the room.*
3 to mark with a design, shape, etc. by means of pressure.
Figurative Stamp this on your memory (= mark firmly). □ *Your actions stamp you as a coward* (= mark, distinguish).
4 to stick a postage stamp on a letter, etc.
Phrase stamp out to end or destroy something by force.

stamp duty *noun*
a tax charged by the government on certain legal documents, payment being

shown by sticking a stamp on the document.

stampede (stam-**peed**) *noun*
a sudden uncontrolled rush by a large group of horses, cattle or people.
• **stampede** *verb* to rush or cause to rush in a stampede.

stamping ground *noun*
(*informal*) a place habitually frequented by a person or animal.

stance *noun*
Sport the positioning of the body when making a stroke at golf, cricket, fencing, etc.
Figurative She has adopted a firm stance on Women's Lib (= attitude, standpoint).
[Italian *stanza* a standing place]

stanch *verb* ⇨ STAUNCH *verb*.

stanchion (stan-sh'n) *noun*
any upright post or support, e.g. in the steel framework of a building.

stand *verb* (**stands; standing; stood**)
1 to take or keep an upright position on the feet: *Everyone stood when the princess entered.*
Figurative Stand and deliver (= halt, stop). □ *The pony stands 14 hands high* (= measures).
2 to be or put in an upright position: *Stand the bottle on the table.*
3 to be or remain in a certain condition, situation or position: *The shop stood on the corner of a busy street.* □ *You stand convicted of treason.* □ *How much money do you stand to win?* □ *She stood firm in her beliefs.*
4 to undergo: *You must stand trial.*
5 to tolerate: *I can't stand the noise.*
6 to be a candidate: *She stood for parliament.*
7 (*informal*) to pay for: *She stood us a meal in a restaurant.*
Phrases as it stands *I shall buy the car as it stands* (= in its present state). **stand alone** *As a boxer he stands alone* (= has no equal). **stand by 1** *Stand by for further orders* (= wait and be ready). 2 *She stood by me when I was in trouble* (= supported). 3 *You'll have to stand by our agreement* (= stick to). **stand down 1** *The candidate stood down from the contest* (= withdrew). 2 *The factory stood down 50 workers* (= suspended). **stand for 1** *I won't stand for your nonsense* (= tolerate). 2 *What does this hieroglyph stand for?* (= serve to designate or express). **stand in** *We need someone to stand in for Andrew while he's away* (= be a substitute). **stand off 1** to keep at a distance. 2 to suspend from

work. **stand on** *I stand on my rights* (= insist on). **stand out 1** *She stands out from her friends* (= is noticeably different). 2 *They are still standing out for more money* (= insisting on). **stand over 1** to remain near and watch. 2 (*informal*) to intimidate: *I refuse to let them stand over me like that.* **stand someone up** (*informal*) to fail to keep an appointment with someone. **stand up** to stand, especially after sitting. **stand up for** to defend or support. **stand up to 1** *The table won't stand up to rough treatment* (= remain in good condition during). 2 *Stand up to him and his insults* (= oppose, resist).
• **stand** *noun*
1 a position taken: *She took a stand by the door.* □ *What's your stand on censorship?*
Figurative We made a stand against the enemy (= defence, resistance).
2 a halt or stop: *The battle came to a stand.*
3 a platform or other structure for people to watch sports, etc.
4 a piece of furniture or other support on or in which something is placed: *an umbrella stand.*
5 a small stall or shop: *a news-stand.*
6 an area or building at a trade fair, etc.: *the Spanish stand at the exhibition.*
7 a place where vehicles wait to be hired: *a taxi stand.*

standard *noun*
1 a level, especially of achievement or excellence: *What standard have you reached in school?* □ *We expect high standards of behaviour.*
2 *Commerce* a monetary system based on a certain commodity: *the gold standard.*
3 an established measure of extent, quantity, value, etc.: *There are no standards of comparison.*
4 an image or a symbol on a flag used as an emblem for a nation or an army.
Figurative This song is an old standard (= popular piece).
• **standard** *adjective*
1 of recognized or established authority: *a standard text.* □ *Speak in standard English.*
2 accepted or normal: *a standard shoe size.* □ *Follow the standard procedure.*

standard assessment task *noun*
a test to assess the progress of school pupils as part of the national curriculum.

standard deviation *Maths* ⇨ DEVIATION (definition 4).

standard form *noun*
Maths the form of numbers written $A \times 10^n$, where A is less than 10 and greater

than or equal to 1, and *n* is an integer: *4 ×
10³ is 4000 written in standard form.*

Standard Grade *noun*
Scottish an examination equivalent to the
GCSE in England and Wales.

standardize, standardise *verb*
to make of a standard size, shape, quality,
etc.
Word Family standardization (stand-
er-die-**zay**-sh'n) *noun*.

standard lamp *noun*
a tall lamp set on an upright support
whose base rests on the floor.

standard of living *noun* (*plural*
standards of living)
Economics the level of incomes,
possessions, consumption, etc. of a nation,
group, family, etc.: *Most people expect their
standard of living to improve year by year.*

standard time *noun*
the time officially adopted for the whole or
part of a country, usually the time of some
nearby meridian.

standby *noun* (*plural* **standbys**)
1 something kept for emergency use.
2 last-minute allocation of unclaimed
airline seats.
Word Family standby *adjective*.

stand-in *noun*
a substitute.

standing *noun*
1 reputation or status: *a family of good
standing.*
2 existence or duration: *a dispute of long
standing.*
• **standing** *adjective*
1 continuing or permanent; *a standing
dispute.* □ *a standing order for the morning
newspaper.*
2 done **in** or from an upright position:
a standing jump.
3 stagnant: *standing water.*

standing order *noun*
1 an order to a bank to make periodic
payments to a specified person or
organization until further notice.
2 any of various rules for the procedures
during a meeting, especially in a
parliament.

stand-off *noun*
a situation in which neither of two
opposing parties is prepared to make a
move until the other does.

stand-offish *adjective*
(*informal*) aloof or reserved.

Word Family stand-offishly *adverb*;
stand-offishness *noun*.

standpipe *noun*
a vertical pipe directly tapping a water
main, used as a hydrant or for communal
water supply when domestic supplies are
cut off in a drought, etc.

standpoint *noun*
an attitude or point of view.

standstill *noun*
a halt or stop: *The strike brought public
transport to a standstill.*

stand-up *adjective*
1 (of comedy or a comedian) involving
telling jokes solo in front of an audience.
2 (of a fight or argument) confrontational
and unrestrained.

stank a past tense of **stink**.

stannous *adjective*
Chemistry of or relating to compounds of
tin in which tin has a valency of two.

stanza *noun*
one of a series of generally uniform groups
of lines into which a poem may be divided.
[Italian]

staphylococcus (staf-i-lo-**kokk**-us) *noun*
(*plural* **staphylococci**) (staf-i-lo-**koks**-
eye)
any of a group of round bacteria occurring
in clusters and which may cause infections
such as boils.
[Greek *staphylé* bunch of grapes + *kokkos* a
berry]

staple¹ *noun*
a U-shaped piece of wire or metal pressed
into a surface to hold something in
position, e.g. an electric cable, or to fasten
things together, e.g. sheets of paper.
• **staple** *verb* to secure or fasten with a
staple.
Word Family stapler *noun* any of various
machines for driving staples into a surface.

staple² *noun*
1 the chief commodity produced or used
in a country or a region.
2 the main constituent of something.
3 a particular length and degree of
fineness of fibre in wool, etc.
• **staple** *adjective* chief or most important.

star *noun*
1 *Astronomy* any large body like the sun,
intensely hot and producing its own
energy by nuclear reactions.
2 a figure, shape or design with points
around it, suggesting a star in shape.

3 a heavenly body regarded as influencing a person's life, etc.

4 (**stars**) a horoscope.

5 a famous or very talented person, such as a leading actor or sportsperson.

• **star** verb (**stars; starring; starred**)

1 to mark with or as if with a star or stars.

2 to have or present in the lead role: *The film stars Brad Pitt.*

3 to be in the lead role: *The captain starred in the match.*

Word Family star adjective 1 brilliant or distinguished. 2 chief.

starboard noun

the right side of a boat or aeroplane when looking towards the front. Compare PORT².

starch noun (plural **starches**)

1 the common carbohydrate formed by green plants and stored in seeds, tubers, etc.

2 a preparation of this substance, used to stiffen linen, etc.

Figurative *His manner was full of starch* (= stiffness, formality).

3 a food rich in starch.

• **starch** verb to stiffen with starch.

Word Family starchy adjective (**starchier; starchiest**); **starchily** adverb; **starchiness** noun.

star-crossed adjective

a poetic word meaning 'having consistent bad luck, as if due to the influence of the stars'.

stardom noun

the status of a star or famous person.

stardust noun

a dreamy romantic quality.

stare verb

to look fixedly.

Phrase stare down, stare out to look fixedly at someone until he or she looks away.

• **stare** noun a fixed look.

starfish noun (plural **starfish** or **starfishes**)

a marine animal with a star-shaped body.

starfruit noun also called **carambola**.

the greenish-yellow fruit, star-shaped in cross section, of the carambola tree, native to South-East Asia.

stark adjective

1 harsh or severely desolate: *a stark landscape.*

2 complete or utter: *Your idea is stark madness.*

• **stark** adverb utterly or absolutely: *stark naked.*

Word Family starkly adverb.

starkers adjective

(*informal*) completely naked.

starlet noun

(*informal*) a young actress who is publicized as a future star.

starling noun

a bird having black plumage with a purple or green sheen and brown spots, which mimics sounds and makes a chattering noise.

starry adjective (**starrier; starriest**)

1 lit by or shining like stars.

2 (*informal*) of, like or relating to stars.

starry-eyed adjective

fanciful or romantically impractical.

start verb

1 to come or bring into being, activity or operation: *Start work immediately.* □ *I can't start the car on cold mornings.* □ *It is starting to rain.*

Figurative *We started for Egypt* (= left). □ *My horse started in the third race* (= took part).

2 to make a sudden involuntary movement, as from surprise, fright, pain, etc.

• **start** noun

1 the act of starting: *Make a start on your work.* □ *She gave a start at the loud bang.*

2 the place where something starts: *Competitors should assemble at the start.*

Figurative *The start of the film was boring* (= first part).

3 a lead or advantage, such as one given to weaker competitors at the beginning of a race.

Phrase for a start as a first step.

starter noun

1 a person or thing that starts, such as the first course of a meal.

2 any competitor in a race or contest.

3 a person who gives the signal for a race to start.

4 short form of **starter motor** a small motor used to start an internal-combustion engine.

Phrase under starter's orders (of racehorses) all ready and waiting for the signal to start.

starter home noun

a modest home intended for first-time buyers.

starting block noun

Athletics either of a pair of angled blocks fixed to the track to give a sprinter a foothold when making a crouching start.

starting gate *noun*
a set of stalls which open simultaneously at the start of a horse race, etc.

starting price *noun*
the betting odds on a horse, etc., at the time when a race starts.

startle *verb*
to alarm or surprise suddenly.
Word Family **startled** *adjective*;
startling *adjective*; **startlingly** *adverb*.

starve *verb*
1 to suffer or die from hunger.
2 to cause suffering or death from hunger:
The army starved the rebels by cutting off their supplies.
Word Family **starving** *adjective*;
starvation (star-**vay**-sh'n) *noun*;
starveling *noun* an old word for a starving person or animal.

stash *verb*
(*informal*) to hide or store away.
● **stash** *noun* (*plural* **stashes**) (*informal*) a secret store of something, e.g. drugs.

stasis (**stay**-sis) *noun*
(*formal*) a state or condition in which there is no progress or movement.
[Greek]

state *noun*
1 the circumstances of a person or thing:
The house was in a filthy state. □ *How's your state of health?*
Figurative The sick man was in quite a state (= tense, nervous or excited frame of mind).
2 the form of something: *The ice was melting to a liquid state.*
3 a country.
4 (*sometimes* **State**) a division of a country for the purposes of local government: *the southern states of America.*
5 (*usually* **State**) a country's civil government or administration: *The police force is controlled by the State.*
Phrase **in state** with great dignity and honour.
● **state** *verb* to set forth clearly and specifically: *The barrister stated his client's case.*
Word Family **statehood** *noun* the fact or status of being a state; **statecraft** *noun* the art of government and diplomacy.
[from ESTATE and STATUS]

stateless *adjective*
having lost the citizenship of one country without acquiring that of another.

stately *adjective* (**statelier**; **stateliest**)
majestic or dignified.
Word Family **stateliness** *noun*.

stately home *noun*
a large house which belongs or belonged to an upper-class family, especially one which members of the public may pay to visit.

statement *noun*
1 a declaration.
2 a report showing the amount of money owed or in credit in an account.

state-of-the-art *adjective*
using the latest techniques and equipment: *state-of-the-art technology.*

stateroom *noun*
1 a first-class cabin on a passenger ship.
2 a large room in a palace or public building, for formal occasions.

state school *noun*
a school organized and financed by local authorities and government.

statesman *noun* (*plural* **statesmen**)
a respected political leader or head of state.
Word Family **statesmanlike** *adjective* wise or diplomatic; **statesmanship** *noun*;
stateswoman *noun* (*plural* **stateswomen**)

static (**statt**-ik) *adjective*
not active, moving or changing.
● **static** *noun*
1 a discharge of electricity in the atmosphere which causes a radio or television receiver to crackle.
2 any stationary electric charges, such as those produced when brushing one's hair.
Word Family **statically** *adverb*.
[Greek *statikos* standing]

station (**stay**-sh'n) *noun*
1 a place or position occupied or equipped for a particular job: *Take your action stations.* □ *a police station.*
Figurative He had ideas above his station (= social rank).
2 a stopping place on a railway, bus route, etc.
3 the buildings, etc. at such a stopping place.
4 *Australian, New Zealand* a very large farm for raising cattle or sheep, usually in the outback.
● **station** *verb* to put at or in a certain place: *Sentries were stationed at each gate.*
[Latin *statio* a standing still]

stationary (**stay**-sh'n-ree) *adjective*
1 not moving: *a stationary tram.*
2 not movable: *a stationary crane.*

! The words *stationary* and *stationery* sound the same but have different spellings and meanings. *Stationary* ends in *ary* and is an adjective meaning 'not moving'; *stationery* ends in *ery* and is a noun meaning 'writing materials'.

stationery (stay-sh'n-ree) *noun*
writing paper and related materials such as pens, pencils, etc.
Word Family **stationer** *noun* a person who sells stationery.

! Do not confuse *stationery* with STATIONARY.

The word **stationer** was adopted into English from Latin *stationarius*, 'a trader with a permanent stall' (from *statio* meaning 'standing still'). Permanent stalls were rare, many tradesmen being itinerant, but exceptions were the bookstalls licensed by the universities, so *stationer* came to mean 'a bookseller's'. In the middle of the 17th century it came to mean 'a seller of paper, pens, etc.'

stationmaster *noun*
a person in charge of a railway station.

station wagon *noun*
American an estate car.

statistics (sta-**tist**-iks) *plural noun*
1 (*used with singular verb*) the collection and analysis of facts and data in the form of numbers.
2 the facts and data themselves.
vital statistics (*informal*) a woman's measurements at the bust, waist and hips.
Word Family **statistical** *adjective*;
statistically *adverb*; **statistician** (stat-ist-**ish**-'n) *noun* an expert in, or compiler of, statistics.

statue (**stat**-yoo) *noun*
a free-standing sculpture of a human or animal figure.
Word Family **statuary** (**stat**-yoo-a-ree) *noun* statues collectively; **statuette** (stat-yoo-**et**) *noun* a small statue.
[from Latin]

statuesque (stat-yoo-**esk**) *adjective*
like a statue in stature, dignity, beauty, etc.

stature (**stat**-yoor) *noun*
the height of something, especially of a person.
Figurative a person of his stature in the music world (= achievement, importance).
[from Latin]

status (**stay**-tus) *noun* (*plural* **statuses**)
a person's or group's social, professional or legal position in relation to others.
[Latin, posture, position]

status quo (stay-tus **kwo**) *noun*
the existing condition or state of things.
[Latin, state in which]

status symbol *noun*
a possession, such as an expensive car, which is considered to indicate the owner's wealth, social position, etc.

statute (**stat**-yoot) *noun*
a law made by Act of Parliament.
Word Family **statutory** (**stat**-yoo-tree) *adjective* 1 of or like a statute. 2 fixed, done or required by statute: *Is death the statutory penalty for murder?*; **statutorily** *adverb*.
[Latin *statutus* set up]

statute mile ⇨ MILE (definition 1).

staunch (stawnch) *adjective*
firmly loyal or steadfast: *She's a staunch supporter of law reform.*
● **staunch** *verb* also **stanch** to stop the flow of a liquid, especially of blood from a wound.
Word Family **staunchly** *adverb*;
staunchness *noun*.
[Old French *estanche* watertight, reliable]

stave *noun*
1 any of the thin curved pieces of wood forming the sides of a barrel.
2 a rung of a chair, ladder, etc.
3 a rod or pole.
4 *Music* ⇨ STAFF *noun* (definition 3).
● **stave** *verb* (**staves**; **staving**; **staved** or **stove**) to crush inwards or make a hole in.
Phrase **stave off** *It was impossible to stave off disaster* (= delay, ward off).
[from STAFF]

stay¹ *verb*
1 to continue to be in a place or condition: *Stay in bed for a few days.*
2 to stop, check or delay: *This snack will stay your hunger.*
3 to reside on a temporary basis: *Where are you staying while you're in town?*
Figurative I will stay the night (= reside for the duration of).
4 to be able to endure or continue: *He will not stay the course.*
Phrase **stay up** not to go to bed until later than usual.
● **stay** *noun*
1 a halt, stop or period of staying: *He had a short stay in Paris.*
2 a postponement: *A stay of execution was granted to the condemned prisoner.*

3 (**stays**) (*formerly*) a corset stiffened with bones.

stay² *noun*
a brace or other structure to prevent movement, such as a rope supporting a ship's mast.

stead (sted) *noun*
place: *I couldn't go, but sent another in my stead.*
Phrase stand in good stead *This money will stand you in good stead* (= be useful to).

steadfast (sted-fahst) *adjective*
firm, steady or unwavering: *steadfast loyalty.* □ *a steadfast gaze.*
Word Family steadfastly *adverb*; **steadfastness** *noun.*

steady (stedd-ee) *adjective* (**steadier; steadiest**)
1 not likely to fall over, topple, wobble, etc.: *Is this ladder steady?*
Figurative *You need steady nerves for this job* (= not easily disturbed or upset).
2 constant or regular: *a steady breeze.*
□ *He's a good steady worker.*
● **steady** *adverb* in a steady manner.
Phrase go steady (*informal*) to go out regularly with one girlfriend or boyfriend.
● **steady** *verb* (**steadies; steadying; steadied**) to make or become steady.
Word Family steadily *adverb*, **steadiness** *noun*; **steadier** *noun.*

steak (stake) *noun*
a thick slice of meat, usually beef, which is grilled, fried, etc.

steal *verb* (**steals; stealing; stole; stolen**)
1 to take something that belongs to someone else without their knowledge or permission.
Figurative *The kitten stole his heart* (= won). □ *I stole a few minutes' sleep* (= took secretly).
2 to move quietly or secretly: *I stole into the house at midnight.*

stealth (stelth) *noun*
quiet secrecy or cunning.
Word Family stealthy *adjective* (**stealthier; stealthiest**); **stealthily** *adverb*; **stealthiness** *noun.*

steam *noun*
1 water in the form of gas or vapour, caused by boiling.
2 (*informal*) energy or power.
Phrase let off steam, blow off steam (*informal*) to release suppressed energy or feeling.
● **steam** *verb*
1 to give off steam: *The kettle is steaming.*

2 to become covered with condensed water vapour: *The kitchen windows are all steamed up.*
3 to cook, soften, clean, etc. using steam.
4 to move, work, etc. under the power of steam: *The ship steamed into port.*

steamboat ⇨ STEAMSHIP.

steamed up *adjective*
(*informal*) angry or excited.

steam engine *noun*
any engine worked by the force of steam.

steamer *noun*
1 ⇨ STEAMSHIP.
2 a container in which things are steamed, especially food.

steam iron *noun*
an iron which releases steam onto clothes, etc. to make them easier to iron.

steamroller *noun*
a heavy vehicle with large rollers for levelling roads, etc., formerly powered by a steam engine.

steamship *noun* also called **steamboat; steamer.**
a ship driven by a steam engine.

steamy *adjective* (**steamier; steamiest**)
1 of, covered with or full of steam.
2 passionate: *steamy love scenes.*

steed *noun*
an old word for a horse.
[Old English *steda* a stud horse]

steel *noun*
1 any of a large group of hard alloys of iron, carbon and various other elements.
2 something made of steel, such as a sword or a rod for sharpening knives.
3 a steel-like quality or nature: *There was steel in his voice.*
● **steel** *verb* to make hard, determined, etc.: *Steel yourself against fear.*
● **steel** *adjective* of, containing or like steel.
Word Family steely *adjective* (**steelier; steeliest**) of or like steel in colour, hardness or strength.

steel band *noun*
a West Indian band playing percussion instruments made from steel oildrums, etc.

steel wool *noun*
a pad made of steel shavings and used for scraping or cleaning.

steelyard *noun*
a weighing device consisting of an arm with a movable counterpoise at one end and a hook at the other to hold the object being weighed.

steep¹ *adjective*
1 (of a slope) rising or falling sharply:
a steep flight of stairs.
2 (*informal*) unreasonable or excessive:
The price is too steep.
● **steep** *noun* a steep slope or place.
Word Family **steepen** *verb* to make or
become steep or steeper; **steeply** *adverb*;
steepness *noun*.

steep² *verb*
to soak thoroughly: *Steep the meat in claret
before cooking.*
Phrase **steeped in** *He sat there, steeped in
misery* (= saturated with).

steeple *noun*
the tower and spire on top of a church.

steeplechase *noun*
a horse race over ditches, hedges, etc. on a
racetrack or across country.
Word Family **steeplechaser** *noun* a
participant in a steeplechase.
[so called because the goal of the race was
originally a distant church steeple]

steeplejack *noun*
a person who climbs steeples, tall
chimneys, etc. to do repairs.

steer¹ *verb*
to guide or direct the course of something,
such as a vehicle.
*Figurative She steers a path between
conservatism and reform* (= takes).
Phrase **steer clear of** to avoid.
Word Family **steering** *noun*.

steer² ⇨ BULLOCK.

steerage *noun*
(in a passenger ship) the accommodation
allotted to the passengers who travel at the
cheapest rate.
[originally the part of the ship containing
the steering gear]

steersman *noun* (*plural* **steersmen**)
a person who steers a ship.

stein (stine) *noun*
an earthenware mug, especially one for
drinking beer.
[German, stone]

stele *noun*
1 (**stee**-lee) *Archaeology* a stone column or
upright slab, inscribed or carved with
decoration.
2 (steel) *Biology* the central core of
vascular tissue in the stem or root of a
plant.
[Greek]

stellar *adjective*
1 of or relating to a star.

2 (*informal*) excellent, outstanding.
[from Latin]

stellate *adjective*
having the shape of a star.

stem¹ *noun*
1 *Biology* the part of a plant which is
normally above ground and carries the
leaves and buds.
2 something resembling the stem of a
plant: *the stem of a pipe.* □ *the stem of a wine
glass.*
3 *Grammar* the main part of a word to
which affixes are attached.
4 the forward part of a ship: *from stem to
stern.*
● **stem** *verb* (**stems; stemming;
stemmed**) to originate or develop: *His
fear of dogs stems from an attack in his
childhood.*

stem² *verb* (**stems; stemming;
stemmed**)
to stop or hold back a flow, movement, etc.

stem ginger *noun*
crystallized ginger pieces.

stench *noun* (*plural* **stenches**)
an offensive smell.

stencil (**sten**-sil) *noun*
a sheet of paper or other material with a
pattern cut into it which may be
reproduced on a surface on which the
stencil is placed, by applying ink or paint
to the areas left uncovered by the stencil.
Word Family **stencil** *verb* (**stencils;
stencilling; stencilled**).

Sten gun *noun*
a sub-machine gun.
[named from the British inventors' initials
R. V. Shepherd and *H. J. Turpin* + EN(FIELD),
on the model of BREN GUN]

stenographer (sten-**og**-ra-fa) *noun*
American a person who specializes in
taking dictation in shorthand.
Word Family **stenography** *noun* the art
of writing in shorthand; **stenographic**
(sten-o-**graff**-ik) *adjective*.
[Greek *stenos* narrow + *graphein* to write]

stentorian (sten-**taw**-ri-an) *adjective*
very loud or powerful in sound: *His
stentorian voice could be heard everywhere in
the large hall.*
[after *Stentor,* a herald in Greek mythology
who had a very loud voice]

step *noun*
1 a movement made by lifting the foot and
setting it down in another place, e.g. in
walking, running or dancing.

2 the distance covered by such a movement: *He moved back a step when I shouted at him.*
3 the sound of such a movement: *I heard a step on the gravel.*
4 a ledge-like support for the foot in ascending or descending: *I had to climb many steps to reach the observation platform.*
5 (**steps**) course: *I retraced my steps to look for my lost ring.*
Figurative The first steps towards peace (= moves).
Phrases **in step** 1 at the same pace, and usually with the same foot movements, as others. 2 in harmony or conformity. **out of step** 1 at a different pace or with different foot movements from others.
2 not in harmony or conformity. **step by step** carefully or gradually; one stage at a time: *The manual takes you step by step through the process of creating a database.*
Word Family **step-by-step** *adjective*.
take steps to start a course of action.
watch one's step to take care.
● **step** *verb* (**steps; stepping; stepped**)
1 to move by taking a step or steps: *He stepped back when I shouted.*
Figurative Please step this way (= come, walk).
2 to put or press the foot down: *I stepped on a piece of glass.*
3 to measure by pacing: *He stepped out the 100 m length.*
Phrases **step down** 1 to decrease: *When sales increased the advertising campaign was stepped down.* 2 to resign: *After the scandal the mayor decided to step down.* 3 (of a transformer) to decrease voltage. **step in** to intervene or become involved. **step on it** (*informal*) to hurry. **step up** 1 to increase: *Because the goods were not selling, the advertising campaign was stepped up.*
2 (of a transformer) to increase voltage.

step aerobics *plural noun*
(used with singular verb) a form of aerobics involving stepping onto and off a portable step.

stepchild *noun* (*plural* **stepchildren**)
a husband's or wife's child from a previous marriage.
Word Family **stepdaughter** *noun*; **stepson** *noun*.

stepladder *noun*
a ladder with a hinged support to keep it upright.

step-parent *noun*
a person who marries one's father or mother.
Word Family **stepfather** *noun*; **stepmother** *noun*.

steppe (step) *noun*
a wide plain, the climate of which generally allows grass but not trees to grow.
[Russian]

stepping stone *noun*
1 a stone which provides a place to step, e.g. over a stream.
2 a means of advancing or rising.

stereo (sterr-i-o *or* steer-i-o) *noun*
an instrument for stereophonic sound reproduction.
● **stereo** *adjective* stereophonic.

stereophonic (sterr-i-o-**fonn**-ik) *adjective*
of or relating to sound reproduction through two distinct sound sources.
Compare MONOPHONIC; QUADRAPHONIC.
[Greek *stereos* solid + *phoné* a sound]

stereoscope (sterr-i-o-skope) *noun*
a device which blends two pictures taken from slightly different points of view into one image which has an impression of relief and solidity.
Word Family **stereoscopy** (sterr-i-osk-a-pee) *noun*; **stereoscopic** (sterr-i-o-skopp-ik) *adjective*.
[Greek *stereos* solid + *skopein* to look at]

stereotype (sterr-i-o-tipe) *noun*
a person or thing considered to represent a set or conventional type.
Word Family **stereotype** *verb*; **stereotypical** (sterr-i-o-tip-ik-'l) *adjective*.
[Greek *stereos* solid + *typos* impression]

sterile (sterr-ile) *adjective*
1 *Biology* being unable to reproduce.
2 *Biology* being free from living micro-organisms.
Word Family **sterility** (st'-**rill**-i-tee) *noun*.
[from Latin]

sterilize, sterilise (sterr-i-lize) *verb*
1 to make infertile, usually by an operation on the Fallopian tubes in females or on the vas deferens in males. Compare CASTRATE; SPAY.
2 to destroy the micro-organisms in something, usually by bringing it to a high temperature.
Word Family **sterilization** (sterr-i-lie-zay-sh'n) *noun*; **sterilizer** *noun*.

sterling *noun*
the British currency with the pound as its basic unit.
● **sterling** *adjective*
1 of or relating to sterling: *a sterling draft.*
2 excellent: *a man of sterling character.*
[probably from Old English *steorling* a coin with a star on it]

sterling silver *noun*
an alloy of 92·5 per cent silver and 7·5 per cent copper, used as a standard for silver in jewellery, cutlery, etc.

stern¹ *adjective*
1 grave or harsh: *We received a stern reprimand for breaking the rules.*
2 demanding and enforcing obedience: *a stern teacher.*
Word Family **sternly** *adverb*; **sternness** *noun*.

stern² *noun*
1 *Nautical* the back end of a boat. Compare BOW³.
2 the back of anything.

sternum *noun* (*plural* **sternums** or **sterna**) also called **breastbone**.
Anatomy a flat bone in the front of the chest, joined to the ribs.
[Greek *sternon* chest, breast]

steroid (**steer**-oyd *or* **sterr**-oyd) *noun*
any of a large group of fat-soluble organic compounds widely distributed in nature and including the sex hormones.
[Greek *stereos* stiff + *-oid*]

stertorous (**stert**-a-rus) *adjective*
(of breathing) characterized or accompanied by a snoring sound.
Word Family **stertorously** *adverb*.
[Latin *stertere* to snore]

stethoscope (**steth**-a-skope) *noun*
Medicine an instrument used for listening to the sounds of the heart and lungs.
[Greek *stethos* breast + *skopein* to look at]

Stetson *noun*
(*trademark*) a man's hat with a wide crown and brim.
[invented by *J. B. Stetson*, 1830-1906, an American hatmaker]

stevedore (**steev**-a-dor) *noun*
a person who supervises the loading or unloading of ships.
[Spanish *estivador* from Latin *stipare* to pack tight]

stew *verb*
1 to cook slowly by simmering in liquid.
2 (*informal*) to fret or worry.
● **stew** *noun*
1 a combination of meat and vegetables, or fish, cooked slowly in liquid.
2 (*informal*) a state of agitation or uneasiness.

steward *noun*
1 a person who waits on passengers in a ship, aeroplane, train, etc.
2 a person who organizes, arranges or manages, e.g. the details of a race meeting, etc.
Word Family **stewardess** *noun* a female steward; **stewardship** *noun*.

Stewart ⇨ STUART.

stick¹ *noun*
1 a long slender piece of wood, especially a branch or stem from a tree, etc.
2 something resembling this: *a walking stick.* □ *a hockey stick.*
Figurative I only possess a few sticks of furniture (= pieces).
3 a joystick.
4 (**sticks**) (*informal*) an area far from a city or town.
Phrases **in a cleft stick** in an impossible position or dilemma. **the wrong end of the stick** a complete misunderstanding of facts, etc.

stick² *verb* (**sticks; sticking; stuck**)
1 to pierce, puncture or penetrate with a pointed instrument: *to stick a skewer into meat.*
2 to attach or fasten with or as if with adhesive: *to stick a stamp on an envelope.*
Figurative The thought of their suffering *stuck in my mind* (= stayed, remained fixed). □ *I stuck to my promise despite the difficulties* (= held faithfully).
3 (*informal*) to put or place in a particular position: *He stuck his hands in his pockets.* □ *Please stick the kettle on the stove.*
4 to be at or come to a standstill: *We got stuck in the peak-hour traffic.*
Figurative I am completely *stuck by this question* (= puzzled, confused).
Phrases **stick at** to persevere with. **stick it out** to persevere to the end. **stick out** 1 to protrude. 2 to be very obvious. **stick out for** to continue to demand: *We shall stick out for better working conditions.* **stick up** 1 to protrude vertically. 2 (*informal*) to rob, especially at gunpoint. **stick up for** to speak or act in defence of. **stuck with** (*informal*) unable to get out of: *Well, I asked for the job and now I'm stuck with it.*

sticker *noun*
1 an adhesive label.
2 (*informal*) a person who sticks at things.

sticking plaster *noun*
short form is **plaster** an adhesive dressing for covering and protecting minor wounds.

stick insect *noun*
any of a group of insects with long slender twig-like bodies.

stick-in-the-mud *noun*
(*informal*) an unadventurous person who is opposed to new ideas, novelty, etc.

stickleback *noun*
any of a group of small freshwater fish with one or more spines on their backs.

stickler *noun*
a person who insists on something unyieldingly: *He is a stickler for accuracy.*

stick-up *noun*
(*informal*) a robbery, especially at gunpoint.

sticky *adjective* (**stickier; stickiest**)
1 tending to stick or adhere.
Figurative I don't like this sticky weather (= humid).
2 (*informal*) difficult or awkward: *a sticky problem.*

stiff *adjective*
1 not easily bent or changed in shape: *a stiff piece of cardboard.*
2 hard to stir, move, work, etc.: *The new car had stiff gears.* □ *I had stiff muscles after the long walk.*
Figurative The teacher set a stiff examination and most students failed (= difficult). □ *The prince gave a stiff bow* (= ceremonious). □ *After the accident I needed a stiff drink* (= strong). □ *The judge gave him a stiff sentence* (= severe).
• **stiff** *adverb*
1 in or to a rigid state: *The animal was frozen stiff.*
2 extremely or completely: *I was bored stiff by the dull lecture.*
• **stiff** *noun* (*informal*) a dead body.
Word Family **stiffly** *adverb*; **stiffness** *noun*; **stiffen** *verb*; **stiffener** *noun*.

stiff-necked *adjective*
perversely obstinate.

stifle (sty-f'l) *verb*
1 to suffocate.
2 to suppress: *She stifled a yawn.*
Figurative He stifled his children by excessive discipline (= repressed).
Word Family **stifling** *adjective* suffocating; **stiflingly** *adverb*.

stigma *noun*
1 a mark of disgrace or reproach: *The stigma of divorce is disappearing in most countries.*
2 *Biology* the end of the style of a flower, which receives the pollen.
Word Family **stigmatic** (stig-**mat**-ik) *adjective*; **stigmatize, stigmatise** *verb* to characterize as disgraceful.

The word **stigma** does not nowadays refer to a physical mark but it is derived from the Greek meaning of a mark made on the skin by a sharp implement. In the plural, *stigmata*, it was used of the marks made on Christ's hands and feet by the nails with which he was fastened to the cross.

stigmata (stig-**mah**-tu) *plural noun*
marks on certain people believed to be a supernatural replica of the wounds received by Christ on the cross.

stile *noun*
1 a group of steps on both sides of a fence allowing people to climb over.
2 a turnstile.

stiletto (still-**ett**-o) *noun*
1 a stiletto heel.
2 a dagger with a slender tapering blade.
[Latin *stilus* pointed instrument]

stiletto heel *noun*
a high heel on a woman's shoe which tapers to an extremely small base.

still[1] *adjective*
1 free from movement.
2 free from disturbance or commotion: *a still night.*
3 silent.
Figurative The still small voice of conscience (= hushed, subdued).
4 relating to a single or static photograph.
5 not effervescent: *We ordered a still wine.*
• **still** *noun*
1 a single photograph, especially one showing a scene from a film.
2 silence or calm.
• **still** *adverb*
1 free from movement.
2 now as before: *She is still away.*
3 in the future as in the past: *Now and then questions will still be asked about the murder.*
4 in increasing amount or degree: *Still warmer weather is forecast.*
5 nevertheless: *She has many clothes and still wants more.*
• **still** *verb*
1 to make or become still.
2 to calm.
Word Family **stillness** *noun*.

still[2] *noun*
a machine used for distilling a liquid, especially alcohol.

stillborn *adjective*
born dead.
Word Family **stillbirth** *noun*.

still life noun (plural **still lifes**)
a painting or drawing of a collection of inanimate objects, such as fruit, bottles, etc.

stilt noun
1 either of two long poles with supports for the feet, used for walking high above the ground.
2 a heavy pole used with others to support a house, etc. above the ground, especially near water.

stilted adjective
stiffly or unnaturally formal.
Word Family **stiltedly** adverb; **stiltedness** noun.

stimulant (stim-yoo-l'nt) noun
Medicine any substance, such as caffeine, which temporarily quickens the functioning of some processes. Compare SEDATIVE.

stimulate (stim-yoo-late) verb
to rouse to action or increased activity.
Word Family **stimulating** adjective; **stimulation** (stim-yoo-lay-sh'n) noun.

stimulus (stim-yoo-lus) noun (plural **stimuli**) (stim-yoo-lie)
1 something which causes a response.
2 an incentive.
[Latin, a goad]

sting verb (**stings; stinging; stung**)
1 to pierce with or as if with a sharply pointed structure or organ: *I was stung by a bee.*
2 to cause a sharp pain.
Figurative She was stung by his cruel remarks (= caused to suffer acutely).
□ *That stung him into action* (= stimulated).
3 (informal) to obtain money from: *He stung me for £10.*
• **sting** noun
1 the act of stinging.
2 a wound or pain caused by or as if by stinging.
3 a keen stimulus or spur.
4 *Biology* any sharp organ for piercing or injecting poison, used in attack or defence by an organism.
Phrase **sting in the tail** *He offered me a new job but – and this was the sting in the tail – at lower pay* (= unpleasant aspect mentioned last).
Word Family **stinger** noun; **stinging** adjective.

stingray noun
any of a group of fish of the ray family having a flat disc-like body with a long narrow tail, usually ending in three poisonous spines.

stingy (stin-jee) adjective (**stingier; stingiest**)
1 (informal) reluctant to give or spend money.
2 (informal) scanty or meagre: *We paid a lot of money but only got a stingy meal.*
Word Family **stinginess** noun.

stink verb (**stinks; stinking; stank** or **stunk; stunk**)
1 to emit a strong offensive smell.
2 (informal) to be highly offensive.
Figurative The whole affair stinks of corruption (= is strongly suggestive).
• **stink** noun
1 a strong offensive smell.
2 (informal) a scandal or fuss.
Word Family **stinky** adjective (**stinkier; stinkiest**).

stinker noun
1 (informal) a person or thing that stinks.
2 (informal) a disgusting or objectionable person.
3 (informal) something which is difficult or unpleasant.

stinking adjective
(informal) highly offensive.

stint noun
an amount or period of work to be done: *We all did a stint in the garden.*
• **stint** verb
1 to limit or restrict.
2 to be sparing or frugal: *Don't stint on the butter.*

stipe noun
Biology a stalk or similar support.
[Latin *stipes* a tree trunk]

stipend (sty-pend) noun
a fixed or regular payment, especially a clergyman's salary.
Word Family **stipendiary** (sty-pen-dee-a-ree) adjective 1 receiving a stipend.
2 relating to a stipend.
[Latin *stipendium* tax, pay]

stipple verb
to engrave, paint or draw with dots.
[Dutch *stippen* to prick]

stipulate (stip-yoo-late) verb
to specify or promise in an agreement: *I stipulate that I will only attend the meeting if you pay my expenses.*
Word Family **stipulation** (stip-yoo-lay-sh'n) noun.
[from Latin]

stir verb (**stirs; stirring; stirred**)
1 to mix by circular movements.

2 to move or cause to move, especially slightly: *The breeze stirred the leaves.*

3 to rouse or be roused: *The story stirred my imagination.* □ *Pity stirred in his heart when he heard our story.*

Figurative (*informal*) *Don't listen to him, he's only stirring* (= being provocative).

• **stir** *noun*

1 the act of stirring: *Give the paint a stir.*

2 a commotion.

Word Family **stirring** *adjective* rousing, exciting; **stirringly** *adverb*; **stirrer** *noun* a person or thing that stirs, especially a person who stirs up trouble or difficulty.

stir-fry *verb* (**stir-fries; stir-frying; stir-fried**)

to cook quickly small pieces of food such as mixed vegetables by stirring together while frying over a high heat.

Word Family **stir-fry** *noun* (*plural* **stir-fries**).

stirrup *noun*

1 either of two loops, usually made of metal, hanging from a horse's saddle on straps and into which the rider places his or her feet for support and balance.

2 any of various similar supports.

[Old English *stigan* to climb + ROPE]

stirrup cup *noun*

a parting drink.

[originally given to a guest mounted and ready to depart]

stitch *noun* (*plural* **stitches**)

1 one complete movement of the needle in knitting, sewing, crocheting, etc.

2 the loop of cotton, wool, etc. left by the movement of a needle.

Figurative (*informal*) *She went swimming without a stitch on* (= piece of clothing)

3 a particular method used in sewing, etc.

4 a sudden sharp pain in the side, e.g. one felt after strenuous exercise.

Phrase **in stitches** *He had us in stitches with his stories* (= laughing uproariously).

• **stitch** *verb* to fasten, join or ornament with stitches.

Word Family **stitching** *noun*.

stoat ⇨ ERMINE (definition 1).

stock *noun*

1 the complete supply of goods kept by a merchant, etc.

2 a supply accumulated for future use.

3 livestock.

4 (*usually* **stocks**) *Commerce* government gilt-edged securities, i.e. money lent to the government at a fixed rate of interest.

5 (*usually* **stocks**) *Commerce* a company's fully paid-up capital not divided into shares.

6 a line of ancestry: *a girl who comes from Scottish stock.*

7 a plant from which cuttings are obtained, or onto which a graft is made.

8 the clear liquid obtained by boiling bones, meat or vegetables, used as a base for soups or sauces.

9 (**stocks**) a heavy wooden frame locking a person by the ankles, formerly used as a public punishment.

10 (**stocks**) the frame on which a ship rests during construction.

11 a stiff wide cravat.

12 a supporting structure or handle of a gun, plough, whip, etc.

13 a plant with brightly coloured fragrant flowers.

Phrases **in stock** (of manufactured goods) available. **out of stock** (of manufactured goods) temporarily unavailable. **take stock 1** to make a list of stock in hand. **2** to make an estimate of prospects, resources, etc.

• **stock** *adjective*

1 kept readily available for sale or use.

2 commonplace: *a stock reply to that question.*

3 of or relating to stock: *a stock clerk.*

• **stock** *verb*

1 to provide with stock.

2 to have as a supply or stock.

stockade (stok-ade) *noun*

a fortification or enclosure consisting of a wall of posts set in the ground.

stockbroker *noun*

a member of a stock exchange, who buys and sells stocks and shares on behalf of his clients for a commission.

Word Family **stockbrokerage, stockbroking** *noun*.

stockbroker belt *noun*

an affluent suburban residential area.

stock car *noun*

an old car used in special races where competitors aim to collide with, and knock aside, the other cars.

stock cube *noun*

a cube consisting of dried meat, vegetable or fish extract, used to make stock.

stock exchange *noun*

1 a place where stocks or shares may be bought and sold.

2 an association of dealers in stocks and shares.

stockholder *noun*
American a shareholder.

stocking *noun*
1 a closely fitting light piece of clothing worn on the foot and leg.
2 something that has the shape of a stocking.
Word Family **stockinged** *adjective*.

stock-in-trade *noun*
1 the stock of a merchant, store, etc.
2 the resources, ability or speciality of a company, person, etc.

stockist *noun*
a retailer who sells a particular type of goods.

stockman *noun* (*plural* **stockmen**)
a person who works on a sheep or cattle station.

stock market *noun*
1 a stock exchange.
2 the business transactions in a stock exchange.

stockpile *verb*
to accumulate raw materials, arms, etc. for future use.
• **stockpile** *noun* a supply of goods or materials.

stock-still *adverb*
absolutely motionless.

stocktaking *noun*
1 the examining, valuing and listing of all stock held in a warehouse, shop, factory, etc., usually done once a year.
2 a reappraisal or reassessment of one's position, progress, etc.

stocky *adjective* (**stockier; stockiest**)
solidly built.
Word Family **stockily** *adverb*; **stockiness** *noun*.

stockyard *noun*
an enclosed area for keeping cattle, etc. for a short time, before selling, slaughtering or shipment.

stodgy *adjective* (**stodgier; stodgiest**)
1 (*informal*) (of food) heavy and solid.
2 (*informal*) dull or uninteresting.
Word Family **stodgily** *adverb*; **stodge, stodginess** *noun*.

stoep (stoop) *noun*
South African a raised veranda in front of a house.
[Afrikaans, step]

stoical (sto-ik-'l) *adjective* also **stoic**
1 showing fortitude, self-control or imperturbability in adversity.

2 indifferent to or unaffected by pleasure, pain, etc.
Word Family **stoic** *noun*; **stoically** *adverb*; **stoicism** (sto-i-sizm) *noun* the belief or practice of being stoical.
[Greek *stoa* the porch in Athens where Zeno taught this philosophy of life]

stoichiometry (stoy-ki-**omm**-a-tree) *noun*
the branch of chemistry studying the quantities of chemical elements or compounds involved in chemical reactions.
Word Family **stoichiometric** (stoy-ki-a-**met**-rik) *adjective*.
[Greek *stoikheion* a component part + *metron* a measure]

stoke *verb*
to stir or feed a fire.

stoker ⇨ FIREMAN (definition 2).

stole[1] the past tense of **steal**.

stole[2] *noun*
1 a wide strip of fabric or fur, worn by women round the shoulders.
2 a long strip of silk, etc. hung over the shoulders and reaching beneath the knees, worn by Christian priests while administering the sacraments.
[Greek *stolé* clothing]

stolen the past participle of **steal**.

stolid (stoll-id) *adjective*
having or showing little emotion or perception.
Word Family **stolidly** *adverb*; **stolidity** (sto-**lid**-i-tee) *noun*.
[Latin *stolidus* dull]

stoma (sto-ma) *noun* (*plural* **stomas** or **stomata**) (sto-ma-ta)
Biology a pore on the surface of a plant, usually on the lower surface of a leaf, allowing the movement of gases in and out of the plant.
[Greek, mouth]

stomach (stum-'k) *noun*
1 *Anatomy* a thick-walled bag between the oesophagus and the duodenum, where food is mixed with gastric juices and digestion begins.
2 (*informal*) the abdomen.
3 an appetite for food.
Figurative I had no stomach for their jokes (= liking).
• **stomach** *verb* to endure or tolerate.
[Greek *stomakhos* gullet]

stomach pump *noun*
a small pump used to withdraw the
contents of the stomach through a long
tube passed down the oesophagus.

stomp *verb*
(*informal*) to stamp.
• **stomp** *noun*
1 the act or sound of stamping.
2 a dance, including stamping of the feet,
performed to jazz-type music.
[alteration of STAMP]

stone *noun*
1 the hard non-metallic substance of
which rock is composed.
2 a small piece of rock.
3 a particular type of rock: *sandstone.*
4 something which resembles a stone:
a hailstone.
5 a piece of stone designed for a particular
purpose: *a tombstone.*
6 a gem.
7 a unit of mass in the avoirdupois system,
equal to 14lb or about 6·35 kg. *abbrev.* st.
8 the hard central seed of many fruits,
such as peaches, apricots, etc.
9 also called **calculus**. *Medicine* a solid
body formed in an organ, such as the
kidney, gall bladder, etc.
10 a light grey colour.
Phrase **leave no stone unturned** to try
every means.
• **stone** *verb*
1 to remove the stones from fruit, etc.
2 to throw stones at.

Stone Age *noun*
the long period in the development of the
human race when weapons and tools were
first made from stone, before the use of
metals was discovered. The earliest part
was called the **Palaeolithic**, the middle
period was called the **Mesolithic**, and the
later part was called the **Neolithic**.

stoned *adjective*
(*informal*) very drunk or under the
influence of a drug such as marijuana.

stone-dead *adjective*
completely dead.

stone-deaf *adjective*
completely deaf.

stonemason *noun*
1 a person who cuts stone and prepares it
for use.
2 a builder in stone.
3 a person who carves inscriptions on
stone.

stone's throw *noun*
a short distance.

stonewall *verb*
1 to obstruct, e.g. the passage of a
parliamentary bill.
2 *Cricket* to bat defensively, aiming to stay
in rather than score.

stoneware *noun*
1 a type of pottery that is stronger and
heavier than earthenware, made by firing
clay at higher temperatures so that it
becomes non-porous.
2 cups, plates, etc. made from this.

stonewashed *adjective*
(of denim clothing) having a faded effect
achieved by being washed with small
stones.

stony (**sto-nee**) *adjective* (**stonier;
stoniest**)
1 full of stones.
2 hard like stone.
*Figurative He met my request with a stony
silence* (= hard-hearted, unmoved).

stony broke *adjective*
(*informal*) having no money at all.

stood the past tense and past participle of
stand.

stooge *noun*
1 the partner in a comedy duo who is the
butt of the comedian's jokes.
2 (*informal*) a person who acts as or is the
tool or dupe of another.
3 (*informal*) a person placed or stationed
for the purposes of spying or informing on
others: *a police stooge.*
• **stooge** *verb* to act as a stooge.

stool *noun*
1 a movable seat without armrests or a
back, usually for one person.
2 a portable support for the feet or knees:
a prayer stool.
3 *Medicine* a piece of faeces.
Phrase **fall between two stools** to fail to
choose between two alternatives due to
hesitation or indecision.

stool pigeon *noun*
(*informal*) a decoy or informer.

stoop¹ *verb*
1 to bend the head and shoulders forward.
*Figurative I would never stoop so low as to
beg* (= descend). □ *He would never stoop to
listen to a mere buying clerk* (= condescend).
2 (of a hawk) to swoop on prey.
• **stoop** *noun*.

stoop² *noun*
American a small porch or platform at the
entrance to a house.

stop *verb* (**stops; stopping; stopped**)
  1 to put to an end the motion or progress of, or to cease moving or making progress: *Please stop the car here.* □ *You can't stop me coming if I want to.* □ *The bank stopped payment on the forged cheque.* □ *I shall stop at nothing to get my way.*
  Figurative (*informal*) *I'll stop at home, if it's all the same to you* (= stay).
  2 to fill or cover an opening, hole, etc.: *Stop that leak with a bung.*
  3 *Music* to place a finger on a string so that only part of it may vibrate.
  4 *Music* to alter pitch in a wind instrument by opening or closing a device (a **stop**).
  5 to fill a tooth cavity.
  Phrase **stop by, stop off, stop over** to visit briefly, especially on the way to somewhere else.
  • **stop** *noun*
  1 the act of stopping: *We drove all the way without one stop.*
  2 the state of being stopped: *We must bring this business to a stop.*
  3 the place where something stops: *a bus stop.*
  4 something which stops: *a doorstop.* □ *Plug the bottle with a stop.* □ *An organ stop allows the sounding of particular sets of pipes.*

stopcock *noun*
  a valve in a pipe to control the flow of liquids.

stope *noun*
  Mining an underground opening with access from the shaft, etc., especially used for extracting ore from a vertical or steeply inclined vein.

stopgap *noun*
  a temporary substitute.

stop light *noun*
  a red light at a road junction, etc., indicating that a vehicle facing it must stop.

stopover *noun*
  a temporary stay in the course of a journey, etc.

stoppage (stop-ij) *noun*
  1 the act of stopping.
  2 an obstruction.

stoppage time ⇨ INJURY TIME.

stopper *noun*
  any plug or cork used to block a hole.
  Word Family **stopper** *verb*.

stop press *noun*
  a column for news inserted in a newspaper just before it is printed.

stopwatch *noun* (*plural* **stopwatches**)
  an accurate watch with a hand or hands which may be started and stopped at any instant, used for timing races, etc. to a fraction of a second.

storage heater *noun*
  a domestic room heater filled with bricks warmed by electricity at off-peak periods and at cheaper rates.

store *noun*
  1 a quantity or supply of something which has been kept or saved: *I've got a store of cold beer in the fridge.*
  2 (**stores**) goods kept or supplied for a purpose: *military stores.*
  3 a place where goods are kept.
  4 a shop, often a large one.
  Phrases **in store** *There's a surprise in store for you tonight* (= coming). **set store by** *I don't set much store by astrologers' predictions* (= value, have regard for).
  • **store** *verb*
  1 to collect and keep for future use: *to store coal for the winter.*
  2 to put away or deposit for keeping.
  Figurative His mind is well stored with all kinds of facts (= stocked).
  Word Family **storage** *noun* **1** the act of storing. **2** the space for storing goods. **3** a charge for storing; **storekeeper** *noun*.

store card *noun*
  a credit card for use only in a particular store or chain of stores.

storehouse *noun*
  a building in which things are stored.
  Figurative His mind is a storehouse of information (= source of supply).

storey (stor-ee) *noun* (*American* **story**)
  any of the levels of a building.

stork *noun*
  a large black and white wading bird with long legs, neck and bill.

storm *noun*
  1 a disturbance of the atmosphere by very strong winds, with rain, snow, etc.
  2 a heavy fall of rain, hail, or snow.
  3 a heavy or violent fall or outburst: *a storm of arrows.* □ *a storm of tears.*
  Phrases **storm in a teacup** a great fuss over a minor matter. **take by storm 1** to capture by a sudden and violent military assault. **2** to captivate completely: *The singer took the town by storm.*
  • **storm** *verb*
  1 to rain, hail, snow or blow hard: *It stormed all night.*

Figurative He stormed out of the room
(= went angrily and violently). □ *She
stormed at them to leave her alone* (= said
angrily).
2 *Military* to capture a place by a sudden
and violent attack.
Word Family stormy *adjective*
(**stormier; stormiest**) 1 affected by
storms. 2 violent; **stormily** *adverb*;
storminess *noun*.

storm petrel *noun*
a very small black seabird with a white
rump, which follows ships and whose
appearance was thought to announce a
coming storm.

storm trooper *noun*
a member of troops trained for violent
attacks.

stormy petrel *noun*
1 (*dated*) a storm petrel.
2 a person who foreshadows or seems to
attract trouble, e.g. by rebelling against
accepted ideas, practices, etc.

story *noun* (*plural* **stories**)
1 a narrative, usually fictitious, intended to
entertain a reader or hearer.
2 the main narrative or events of a novel,
poem, etc.
3 a journalist's account of an event: *He
expects us to print his story on a flower show!*
4 the subject matter of a journalist's
account.
5 (*informal*) a lie: *That's all a story about
Santa Claus.*
6 (*informal*) an excuse: *So that's your story,
young man!*
Phrase **a likely story!** a sarcastic
expression of disbelief.
[Greek *historia* a finding out, a narrative]

storyboard *noun*
a plan for a visual production or an activity
which shows the plot or the main events
through a series of pictures.

storybook *adjective*
romantic or like a children's story: *She lives
in a storybook world of knights and princesses.*

storyline *noun*
the plot of a film, book, play, etc.

stout *adjective*
1 rather fat or bulky in figure: *He's grown
rather stout.*
Figurative A castle must be built with stout
walls (= strongly made).
2 brave, bold or stubborn: *They made a
stout defence of their lands.*
• **stout** *noun* a dark beer flavoured with
roasted malt.

Word Family stoutly *adverb*; **stoutness**
noun.

The word **stout** has two modern
meanings. *Stout* meaning 'large' or 'fat'
is now more common, but *stout* in the
sense of 'brave' as in *stout fighter* is
older, having come from Old French
estout (bold). Brave and successful
fighters would usually be assumed to be
of powerful physique, hence the
development of the meaning 'large'.

stout-hearted *adjective*
courageous or resolute.
Word Family stout-heartedly *adverb*;
stout-heartedness *noun*.

stove[1] *noun*
a closed apparatus for cooking or heating,
that uses gas or electricity or in which
coke, wood, etc. is burnt.

stove[2] a past tense and past participle of
stave.

stovepipe *noun*
a pipe carrying smoke from a stove to a
chimney.

stow (sto) *verb*
to pack or place: *The goods were stowed
below deck.*
Phrase **stow away** to hide oneself on a
ship, aeroplane, etc. to get a free trip.
Word Family stowage (**stu-ij**) *noun* 1 the
act or manner of stowing. 2 the state of
being stowed. 3 space for stowing goods.
4 the goods stowed. 5 the charge for
stowing goods.
[shortening of BESTOW]

stowaway *noun*
a person who stows away on a ship,
aeroplane, etc.

straddle *verb*
1 to stand or sit with one leg or part on
either side of something: *to straddle a horse.*
□ *The bridge straddles the river.*
2 to have the legs wide apart: *He sat with
his legs straddled.*

strafe *verb*
Military to fire on ground troops, etc. from
the air with machine guns.
Word Family strafe *noun*.
[German *strafen* to punish]

straggle *verb*
1 to stray or lag behind the main group.
2 to grow, spread, etc. in an irregular or
rambling manner: *tendrils of ivy straggling
all over the place.*
Word Family straggler *noun*; **straggly**
adjective (**stragglier; straggliest**).

straight (strate) *adjective*
1 extending uniformly in one direction without a bend or curve: *a straight line.* □ *She has straight black hair.*
2 level or symmetrical: *Are the pictures straight?*
3 tidy or in proper order: *I have to get my business affairs straight before my holiday.* **Figurative** *You must get your facts straight* (= correct).
4 honest or open: *He isn't straight in his business dealings.* □ *Please give us a straight answer.*
5 (of an alcoholic drink) neat: *a straight whisky.*
6 *Theatre* of or relating to a serious play or film, as distinct from a comedy or musical.
7 (*informal*) heterosexual.
● **straight** *adverb* in a straight line or way. **Figurative** *Come straight home* (= directly). □ *She put him straight about who was in charge* (= right, clear).
Phrases go straight to lead an honest life, especially after having been a criminal. **straight away, straight off** immediately. **straight out** directly: *I told him straight out what I thought of him.*
● **straight** *noun*
1 the condition of being straight.
2 a straight part, especially of a race course.
3 *Cards* a hand having all consecutive cards.
Phrase the straight and narrow *After a dissolute youth Gordon kept to the straight and narrow for the rest of his life* (= religious or moral rectitude).
Word Family straightly *adverb*; **straightness** *noun.*

straighten *verb*
to make or become straight.
Phrases straighten out to set right or restore order to. **straighten up** to make tidy.
Word Family straightener *noun.*

straightforward *adjective*
1 open, honest or without evasion: *a straightforward explanation.*
2 easy or simple: *a dictionary written in straightforward language.*
Word Family straightforwardly *adverb*; **straightforwardness** *noun.*

strain¹ *verb*
1 to draw tight or stretch: *The rope was strained by the weight.*
2 to pull hard: *The dog strained at its lead.*
3 to make extreme or excessive demands on: *He strained his ears to try and hear.*
□ *The hurdler strained and damaged a muscle.*
4 to pour through a filter, etc. to separate liquid from solid matter.
● **strain** *noun*
1 a straining force, weight or effort.
2 an injury caused by too great an effort.
3 *Science* the change in shape of a body as a result of some external force. Compare STRESS *noun* (definition 3).
4 (*usually* **strains**) musical sounds or a tune: *the distant strains of a street organ.*
Word Family strained *adjective* 1 tense.
2 forced; **strainer** *noun* 1 a device which strains. 2 a main post in a wire fence.
[Latin *stringere* to draw tight]

strain² *noun*
1 a race or stock: *He comes from a hardy peasant strain.*
2 inherited quality or character: *It's the peasant strain in him that gives him his determination.*
3 *Biology* a group of animals or plants bred from a certain species or variety.

strait *noun*
1 a narrow strip of water between two pieces of land.
2 (**straits**) a situation of great difficulty, need or distress: *When the father died the family was left in financial straits.*
[Latin *strictus* tightened]

straitened *adjective*
Phrase in straitened circumstances short of money.

straitjacket *noun*
a tight canvas jacket for restraining the arms of violent patients or prisoners.

strait-laced *adjective*
very strict or prudish in behaviour, etc.

strand¹ *noun*
a single fibre, thread, hair, string of yarn, etc.

strand² *noun*
a poetic word for the shore of a lake or sea.
● **strand** *verb*
1 to drive a ship aground.
2 to leave someone helpless or in difficulties.
Word Family stranded *adjective.*

strange *adjective*
1 odd or unusual: *What a strange thing to do.*
2 not previously known: *We moved to a strange area.* □ *That particular moth is strange to me.*
Word Family strangely *adverb*; **strangeness** *noun.*
[Latin *extraneus* foreign]

stranger (**strane**-jer) *noun*
1 a person one has not known, seen or heard of before.
2 a person who is new to a place: *I am a stranger to your city.*
Figurative *He is no stranger to suffering* (= person unacquainted with).

strangle *verb*
to choke to death: *He strangled the old lady with his bare hands.*
Figurative *He tried to strangle a sob* (= stifle, suppress). □ *The flowers had been strangled by the lush growth* (= choked).
Word Family strangled *adjective;*
strangler *noun* a person who murders by strangling his or her victims; **strangles** *plural noun* (*used with singular verb*) an infectious disease of horses causing blockages in the air passages.
[Greek *strangalē* a halter]

stranglehold *noun*
1 a wrestling hold by which one chokes one's opponent.
2 anything that prevents or restricts free movement, development, etc.

strangulate (**strang**-gyoo-late) *verb*
1 to strangle.
2 to interfere with the blood supply to some part of the body.
Word Family strangulation (strang-gyoo-**lay**-sh'n) *noun.*

strap *noun*
1 a strip of leather or other flexible material for supporting, fastening or holding things together: *Fasten the straps on your pack.*
2 something which has the shape or function of a strap, such as a metal or leather loop in a train for a standing passenger to grip.
• **strap** *verb* (**straps; strapping; strapped**)
1 to fasten with a strap.
2 to beat with a strap.
Word Family strapless *adjective;*
strappy *adjective.*
[from STROP]

straphanger *noun*
(*informal*) a standing passenger in a bus, train, tram, etc., who holds a strap for support.

strapline *noun*
a small headline in a newspaper above the main headline.

strapping *adjective*
tall, strong and healthy.

stratagem (**stratt**-a-jem) *noun*
a plan or trick, especially one for deceiving the enemy.
[Greek *stratagema* generalship]

> [!] Either *stratagem* or *strategy* can be used of a plan, but a *stratagem* is usually a cunning trick, whereas a *strategy* is a well-thought-out policy. Only *strategy* can be used of large-scale planning, as in *The general is a master of military strategy.*

strategy (**stratt**-a-jee) *noun* (*plural* **strategies**)
1 planning or management on a large scale, e.g. a military campaign.
2 a plan to achieve a long-term goal.
Word Family strategic (stra-**tee**-jik) *adjective* 1 of or relating to strategy. 2 (of weapons, bombing, etc.) intended or used to injure the whole economy or offensive power of an enemy. Compare TACTICAL; **strategically** *adverb;* **strategist** (**stratt**-a-jist) *noun* a person who is expert in strategy.
[Greek *strategos* a general]

> [!] Do not confuse *strategy* with STRATAGEM.

stratify (**stratt**-i-fie) *verb* (**stratifies; stratifying; stratified**)
1 to form in layers.
2 to form social groups at different levels determined by class, status, etc.
Word Family stratification (stratt-if-i-**kay**-sh'n) *noun.*

stratosphere (**stratt**-a-sfeer) *noun*
the upper layers of the atmosphere above the troposphere, beginning about 20 km from the earth's surface. Compare TROPOSPHERE.
[STRATUM + SPHERE]

stratum (**strah**-tum) *noun* (*plural* **strata**)
1 a horizontal layer of any material, especially a layer of sedimentary rock, usually one of several parallel layers.
2 any level or grade.
[Latin, strewn]

> [!] Note that *strata* is the plural form of *stratum* and should not be used where the singular form is required, as in *a different social stratum.*

stratus (**strah**-tus) *noun*
a layer or sheet of cloud.

straw *noun*
1 a collection of coarse stems and leaves of cereal plants, usually dried, cut and used for bedding. Compare HAY.

2 a natural or artificial fibre resembling straw, used for making hats, etc.

3 a hollow tube for sucking up liquids.

4 a trifle: *I don't care a straw for him.*

***Phrases* catch at straws, clutch at straws** to try anything in a desperate situation. **last straw** an added burden, task, etc. which makes a situation intolerable. **straw in the wind** a hint or sign of things to come, showing which way the wind is blowing.

strawberry *noun* (*plural* **strawberries**)
a red fleshy edible berry with a sweet taste.

straw poll *noun*
an unofficial vote to give an indication of the general trend of opinion.

stray *verb*
to wander or lose one's way.

• **stray** *noun* a domestic animal that has strayed.

• **stray** *adjective*

1 lost or out of place.

2 scattered or occasional.

[from ASTRAY]

streak *noun*

1 a long thin line or mark: *There's a streak of dirt on your forehead.*

Figurative There's a streak of cruelty in you (= trace). □ *Let's hope for a streak of good luck now* (= spell, period).

2 *Geology* the colour of a finely powdered mineral.

***Phrase* streak of lightning** *He disappeared like a streak of lightning* (= very fast indeed).

• **streak** *verb*

1 to mark with a streak or streaks.

2 to move at great speed: *The runner streaked past the finishing line.*

3 (*informal*) to run naked through a public place.

***Word Family* streaky** *adjective* (**streakier; streakiest**); **streakily** *adverb*; **streakiness** *noun*; **streaker** *noun* (*informal*) a person who runs naked through a public place.

stream *noun*

1 a small river.

2 a steady flow of water or other liquid: *the Gulf Stream.*

3 a steady flow or emission: *The spotlight sent a stream of light onto the stage.* □ *A stream of abuse fell from his lips.*

Figurative The stream of opinion is against you (= drift, run).

• **stream** *verb*

1 to flow in or as if in a stream: *Water streamed down the window.* □ *The crowd streamed through the stadium gates.*

2 to divide students into classes according to their ability, or the subjects they are studying.

***Word Family* streaming** *noun, adjective.*

streamer *noun*

1 a long narrow strip of material: *Her bonnet was decorated with streamers.*

2 *Newspapers* a headline that runs across a full page.

streamlined *adjective*

1 (of a car, boat, etc.) having a shape designed to offer the least possible resistance to air or water.

2 made more efficient, modern, etc.

***Word Family* streamline** *verb.*

street *noun*

1 a road in an urban area, usually lined with houses, shops, etc.

2 (*informal*) the people living in a street: *The whole street protested about the increased rates.*

***Phrases* not in the same street** (*informal*) not to be classed with. **streets ahead** (*informal*) far ahead. **up one's street** (*informal*) within one's field of skill, interest, etc.

• **street** *adjective* relating to the fashionable urban youth subculture: *street fashions.*

[Latin (*via*) *strata* a paved (way)]

streetcar *noun*
American a tram.

street cred *noun* also **street credibility**

1 (*informal*) popular acceptance, especially among urban young people.

2 (*informal*) a familiarity with contemporary style and fashion.

streetwalker *noun*
a prostitute who seeks customers in the street.

streetwise *adjective*
(*informal*) good at surviving and coping with life, especially in an urban and often poor environment.

strength *noun*

1 bodily or muscular power: *Samson was a man of great strength.*

2 the capacity to resist or sustain stress: *The strength of the steel in the main girders is crucial.* □ *strength of character.*

Figurative Strength of numbers favours our side (= superiority). □ *The normal strength of the regiment is 3000 men* (= number).

□ *What's the strength of this rumour I heard?* (= reliability).
3 degree of intensity: *What strength do you like your coffee?* □ *What strength of colour there is in that painting!*
Phrases **from strength** *I am negotiating from strength* (= from a strong bargaining position). **on the strength of** *I went to visit the art gallery on the strength of your recommendation* (= on the basis of).
Word Family **strengthen** *verb* to make or become strong or stronger; **strengthener** *noun*.

strenuous (stren-yew-us) *adjective*
requiring great effort or exertion: *a strenuous hike through the hills.* □ *a strenuous appeal for funds.*
Word Family **strenuously** *adverb*; **strenuousness** *noun*.
[Latin *strenuus* vigorous]

streptococcus (strep-toe-**kokk**-us) *noun* (*plural* **streptococci**) (strep-toe-**koks**-eye)
a group of round bacteria which occur in pairs or chains and may cause disease, such as throat infections, in human beings.
[Greek *streptos* twisted + *kokkos* a berry]

streptomycin (strep-toe-**my**-sin) *noun*
an antibiotic used mainly in the treatment of tuberculosis.
[Greek *streptos* twisted + *mykes* fungus]

stress *noun* (*plural* **stresses**)
1 special weight or significance: *The school lays great stress on discipline.*
2 the extra force placed on a word or syllable: *In the word 'window' the stress is on the first syllable.*
3 *Science* the force per unit of area applied to a body. Compare STRAIN[1] *noun* (definition 3).
4 emotional or intellectual pressure or tension: *The court case placed him under a great deal of stress.*
● **stress** *verb*
1 to lay stress on.
2 to subject to mechanical stress.
Word Family **stressful** *adjective*.
[Latin *strictus* tightened]

stretch *verb*
to make or become longer, wider, larger, tighter, etc. by pulling: *He stretched the new shoes to make them pinch less.* □ *She stretched the skin of the drum.*
Figurative *The blow stretched him out on the floor* (= laid at full length). □ *He stretches the truth a bit* (= distorts, exaggerates). □ *Her continual chatter stretched my patience to the limit* (= strained). □ *The hills stretch*

for *miles* (= continue). □ *She stretched out a hand* (= reached). □ *He got up from a cramped position and stretched* (= extended his body and limbs).
Phrase **stretch a point** to make concessions.
● **stretch** *noun* (*plural* **stretches**)
1 the act of stretching: *He gave a stretch and got up.* □ *It takes quite a stretch of the imagination to believe that.*
2 a continuous length, distance, period, etc.: *a stretch of shallow water.* □ *There was a considerable stretch when I couldn't get work.*
3 (*informal*) a term in prison.
4 *Horse racing* either of the two straight parts of a race course, especially the part between the last turn and the finishing post.
Phrase **at full stretch** to the utmost of one's powers.
Word Family **stretchy** *adjective* (**stretchier**; **stretchiest**).

stretcher *noun*
1 a piece of material supported by two long poles, used to carry sick or injured people.
2 a wooden frame over which canvas or other fabric may be held taut.

strew *verb* (**strews**; **strewing**; **strewed**; **strewn** or **strewed**)
to spread about loosely or randomly: *They strewed her path with rose petals.* □ *Papers were strewn about all over the floor.*

striated (stry-**ay**-tid) *adjective*
marked with fine grooves or furrows: *A glacier will often leave a mass of striated rocks behind it.*
Word Family **striation** *noun*.
[from Latin]

stricken *adjective*
1 afflicted or affected by: *the fever-stricken town.*
2 deeply affected by emotion, especially fear, despair, etc.

strict *adjective*
1 demanding obedience: *a strict teacher.*
2 harsh: *strict discipline.*
3 exact: *My watch doesn't keep very strict time.*
Figurative *I am telling you this in strict confidence* (= absolute, complete). □ *He's a very strict Catholic* (= devout, closely conforming). □ *Keep a strict eye on the children while I'm away* (= close, careful).
Word Family **strictly** *adverb*; **strictness** *noun*.
[Latin *strictus* tightened]

stricture (**strik**-cher) *noun*
1 severe criticism: *to pass strictures on the quality of my work.*
2 *Medicine* a narrowing in a duct or vessel, causing an obstruction.

stride *verb* (**strides; striding; strode; stridden**)
1 to walk with long steps.
2 to sit or stand with one leg on each side of: *to stride a stile.*
• **stride** *noun*
1 a long step.
2 the space covered in such a step.
Phrases **make rapid strides** to make quick progress. **take in one's stride** to do or respond to without difficulty or extra effort.
Word Family **strider** *noun.*

strident (**stry**-d'nt) *adjective*
(of a sound) shrill and harsh.
Word Family **stridently** *adverb*; **stridency** *noun.*
[Latin *stridens* grating, hissing]

strife *noun*
angry fighting or quarrelling.

strike *verb* (**strikes; striking; struck**)
1 to give a blow to or with: *I struck him on the chin.*
2 to come or cause to come into violent contact with: *The ship struck a reef.*
Figurative The cattle raiders struck at dusk (= attacked). □ *Strike that remark from the record* (= remove). □ *He tried to strike a match in the wind* (= ignite). □ *The clock struck four* (= announced by chiming). □ *At midday a shaft of light strikes the unknown soldier's tomb* (= falls upon). □ *The news struck me speechless* (= rendered). □ *An idea suddenly struck him* (= occurred to). □ *Does he strike you as an honest man?* (= impress). □ *The ham actor struck a pose* (= assumed). □ *We managed to strike some kind of an agreement* (= make).
3 to stop work as a protest or in order to gain something: *The workers are striking for better conditions.*
4 to mint a coin, medal, etc.
5 *Nautical* to lower or take down a sail.
6 to take root: *I don't thing the cuttings will strike in this cold weather.*
Phrases **strike home** to deal an effective or telling blow. **strike out** to set out: *The shipwrecked sailor struck out for the distant shore.* **strike up** to begin or form: *We immediately struck up a conversation.* **struck on** (*informal*) infatuated with.
• **strike** *noun*

1 the act of striking: *a bombing strike by enemy aircraft.*
2 the stopping of work as a threat or protest: *The entire workforce went on strike.*
3 *Baseball* an unsuccessful attempt to hit a pitched ball.
4 *Tenpin bowling* a score obtained by knocking over all ten pins in one shot. Compare SPARE *noun* (definition **2**).
5 a discovery of oil, ore, etc. in a well or mine.
Word Family **striker** *noun* **1** a football player whose main role is to score goals. **2** a worker who is on strike. **3** something which strikes, such as the hammer of a bell, etc. **4** *Tennis* the player who faces the server; **striking** *adjective* **1** attractive or impressive. **2** on strike; **strikingly** *adverb.*

> The word **strike** in the sense of 'stopping work as a protest' is thought to be nautical in origin; to *strike sail* meant to lower a sail and so stop sailing. Thus to *strike tools* meant to lay them down and stop working. This sense came into the language in the latter part of the 18th century.

strike-breaker *noun*
a person who helps to break up a strike by taking a striker's job.

Strimmer *noun*
(*trademark*) a kind of machine for cutting grass, especially in areas inaccessible to an ordinary lawnmower, using a filament or length of strong cord that rotates rapidly within a protective guard.

Strine *noun*
(*informal*) Australian English.
[the supposed Australian pronunciation of the word *Australian*]

string *noun*
1 a long slender flexible material, usually made of fibres twisted together and used for tying.
2 something which has the shape or function of a string: *the string of a bean.*
3 a set of objects threaded together: *a string of pearls.*
Figurative The speaker had to answer a string of questions (= series, collection). □ *He was seeking a relationship with no strings attached* (= conditions).
4 *Music* a tightly stretched length of catgut or wire which produces a note when made to vibrate.
5 (**strings**) *Music* any instruments having such strings, especially those of the violin family.

Phrases **keep on a string** to have under one's control. **pull strings** to use influence and social contacts to gain something.

• **string** *verb* (**strings; stringing; strung**)
1 to furnish with or as if with strings.
2 to remove the strings of beans, etc.
3 to thread: *Stringing the beads on the thread was tedious work.*
Figurative The streets were strung with lanterns (= adorned, hung).
Phrases **string along** (*informal*) to lead on. **string along with** (*informal*) to cooperate with. **string out 1** *The horses were strung out all over the field* (= spread out). *2 He strung the discussion out because he had time to waste* (= prolonged). **string up** (*informal*) to hang.
Word Family **stringed** *adjective*; **stringer** *noun* 1 a device which removes bean strings. 2 a horizontal timber beam, used as a support, etc.; **stringy** *adjective* (**stringier; stringiest**) 1 containing tough fibre. 2 wiry or sinewy; **stringiness** *noun.*

stringent (strin-j'nt) *adjective*
imposing rigorous standards of performance or obedience: *stringent laws.* □ *stringent discipline.*
Figurative He presented a very stringent argument for his proposal (= convincing, forcible).
Word Family **stringently** *adverb*; **stringency** *noun.*
[Latin *stringens* drawing tight]

string quartet *noun*
a group of four musicians playing two violins, a viola and a cello.

strip *verb* (**strips; stripping; stripped**)
1 to take the covering from something: *They stripped the trees of bark.* □ *They stripped the paint from the walls.*
Figurative The suspects were stripped and searched (= undressed). □ *The wind stripped all the leaves from the boughs* (= removed, took off).
2 to tear the thread or teeth from a screw or gear.
• **strip** *noun*
1 a long narrow piece: *a strip of cloth.* □ *a strip of land.*
2 (*informal*) a striptease.
Phrase **tear someone off a strip, tear a strip off someone** to criticize or reprimand someone harshly.

strip cartoon *noun*
a story told, or information conveyed, in a series of small drawings, often with the dialogue encased in balloons emerging from the mouths of the characters depicted.

stripe *noun*
1 a long narrow piece or section, different in colour, texture, etc. from the rest of a surface or thing.
2 *Military* a piece of cloth worn on a uniform to indicate rank, etc.
3 an old word for a blow struck with a whip or rod, as in punishment: *He was sentenced to 100 stripes.*
• **stripe** *verb* to mark with a stripe or stripes.
Word Family **striped**, **stripy** *adjective.*

strip lighting *noun*
a form of lighting consisting of long fluorescent tubes or glass strips containing a filament.

stripling *noun*
an old word for a young man who is not yet fully grown.

stripper *noun*
1 an entertainer who performs a striptease.
2 a machine or solvent which strips.

striptease *noun*
a form of entertainment performed to music, in which a person gradually undresses.
Word Family **stripteaser** *noun.*

strive *verb* (**strives; striving; strove; striven** (strivv-'n))
to try hard: *He strove for success.*
Figurative The swimmer strove against the current (= fought).

stroboscope (stro-ba-skope) *noun*
1 a device used to make moving objects appear stationary, e.g. by regularly interrupting vision, using intermittent lighting, etc.
2 a lamp which flashes coloured lights intermittently on stage or on a dance floor.
Word Family **stroboscopic** (stro-ba-skopp-ik) *adjective*; **strobe** *noun* 1 a stroboscope. 2 stroboscopic light.
[Greek *strobos* whirling + *skopein* to look at]

strode the past tense of **stride**.

stroke *noun*
1 a blow or act of striking, e.g. of an axe, lightning, a clock, etc.
Figurative She arrived on the stroke of eleven (= exact moment).

2 a single movement of the hand, arm, etc. by which something is made or done.

3 a mark made by one movement of a pen, pencil, brush, etc.

Figurative That was a stroke of luck (= piece). □ *It was a stroke of genius to solve that problem* (= brilliant or sudden act).

4 *Medicine* a sudden loss of consciousness and paralysis due to a blockage in a blood vessel that supplies blood to part of the brain.

5 any of a series of alternating movements between two extreme positions, such as one made by the pistons of a car engine.

6 *Rowing* the oarsman nearest the stern of the boat, who sets the pace for the crew.

7 *Sport* a way of hitting a ball: *Her opponent replied with a powerful backhand stroke.*

• **stroke** *verb*

1 to pass the hand over gently or caressingly.

2 *Rowing* to act as stroke.

stroll (strole) *verb*
to walk in a leisurely or casual manner.
Word Family **stroll** *noun;* **stroller** *noun.*

strong *adjective*

1 powerful: *Hercules was a very strong man.* □ *Have a cup of strong coffee.*
Figurative He proved strong against temptation (= firm). □ *He's strong in languages* (= very competent). □ *The battalion dug itself into a strong position* (= easy to defend). □ *The government used strong measures to stop the riots* (= harsh, extreme). □ *She used strong language* (= forceful, bad).

2 distinct or marked: *a strong contrast in their attitudes.*

3 lasting, durable: *Walking boots have to be made of strong leather.*

• **strong** *adverb*

1 in a strong manner: *He's still going strong at 90.*

2 in numbers: *Their army is 200 000 strong.*
Word Family **strongly** *adverb.*

strong-arm *adjective*
(*informal*) depending on physical force: *The police had to use strong-arm tactics to disperse the demonstrators.*

strongbox *noun* (*plural* **strongboxes**)
a metal box for keeping money or valuables.

stronghold *noun*

1 a fortress.

2 a place where an attitude, belief, etc. is strong.

strongman *noun* (*plural* **strongmen**)
an entertainer who performs feats of strength.

strong-minded *adjective*
having a vigorous determined will or mind: *She's being very strong-minded about her diet.*

strongpoint *noun*
a special aptitude or quality: *Writing is not my strongpoint.*

strongroom *noun*
a room in a bank for valuable articles, etc., built to resist fire and theft.

strontium *noun*
a reactive metal similar to calcium and whose compounds are used in fireworks. Radioactive strontium-90 is produced in atomic explosions.
[after *Strontian* in Scotland]

strop[1] *noun*
a device, usually leather, with an abrasive surface for sharpening implements, such as razors.
Word Family **strop** *verb* (**strops; stropping; stropped**) to sharpen on a strop.

strop[2] *noun*
(*informal*) an angry mood, bad temper.

strophe (stro-fee) *noun*
Poetry a stanza, especially the first of a pair of alternating forms.
[Greek, turning]

stroppy *adjective* (**stroppier; stroppiest**)
(*informal*) angry or complaining.

strove the past tense of **strive**.

struck the past tense and past participle of **strike**.

structure (struk-cher) *noun*

1 the way something is put together: *to study the structure of a single cell.*

2 something which is constructed, such as a bridge, building, etc.

• **structure** *verb* to arrange something in an organized system.
Word Family **structural** *adjective* of or essential to a structure; **structurally** *adverb.*
[from Latin]

strudel (stroo-d'l) *noun*
a cake made from very thin flaky pastry filled with fruit.
[German]

struggle *verb*

1 to make violent physical efforts: *The policeman struggled with the drunken spectator.*

2 to work very hard at a task or problem:
They struggled for a living.
3 to proceed with great effort: *They
struggled through the dense undergrowth.*
• **struggle** *noun*
1 the act of struggling: *The policeman could
not restrain the spectator without a struggle.*
2 a great effort: *the struggle for liberty.*
Word Family **struggler** *noun.*

strum *verb* (**strums; strumming;
strummed**)
1 to sound the strings of a guitar, etc. by a
downward finger movement.
2 to idly play a stringed musical instrument.
Word Family **strum** *noun.*

strumpet *noun*
an old word for a prostitute.

strung the past tense and past participle of
string.

strut[1] *verb* (**struts; strutting; strutted**)
to walk in a stiff-legged pompous manner.
• **strut** *noun* a strutting way of walking.

strut[2] *noun*
a supporting part of a structure which
takes the pressure or weight along its
length.

strychnine (**strik-neen**) *noun*
a white crystalline poison which may be
used in small quantities to stimulate the
nervous system.
[Greek *strykhnos* nightshade]

Stuart (**stew-'t**) *noun* also **Stewart**
a member of the royal family in Scotland
from 1371 to 1714 and in England from
1603 to 1649 and from 1660 to 1714.

stub *noun*
1 the short blunt end of something which
has been worn down, used up, cut, etc.: *the
stub of a cigar.*
2 also called **counterfoil**. *Commerce* the
portion of a cheque remaining in a
chequebook, on which the details are
recorded.
• **stub** *verb* (**stubs; stubbing; stubbed**)
to strike against something: *to stub one's toe
on the leg of the bed.*
Phrase **stub out** to extinguish a cigarette,
etc. by crushing the lighted end against a
surface.

stubble *noun*
1 the cut stalks of cereal plants left in the
ground after a harvest.
2 anything resembling stubble, such as the
unshaven growth of beard on a face.
Word Family **stubbled, stubbly**
adjective.
[Latin *stipula* straw]

stubborn (**stub-'n**) *adjective*
1 inflexible in intention or opinion: *her
stubborn refusal.*
2 difficult to manage, control, etc.: *a
stubborn horse.*
Word Family **stubbornly** *adverb*;
stubbornness *noun.*

stubby *adjective* (**stubbier; stubbiest**)
short and thick: *stubby fingers.*
Word Family **stubbily** *adverb*;
stubbiness *noun.*

stucco (**stuk-o**) *noun*
a type of plaster used on walls or other
surfaces to form a rough knobbled
surface.
• **stucco** *verb* to cover with stucco.
[Italian]

stuck the past tense and past participle of
stick[2].

stuck-up *adjective*
(*informal*) conceited or superior.

stud[1] *noun*
1 a small metal button for fastening shirt
collars, etc.
2 a large-headed nail or knob projecting
from a surface, especially as a decoration.
3 a threaded rod or bolt without a head.
4 an upright post or support, e.g. in the
framework of a wall or house.
• **stud** *verb* (**studs; studding; studded**)
to set or decorate with or as if with studs:
a shield studded with jewels.

stud[2] *noun*
1 a collection of horses for racing, hunting,
breeding, etc.
2 a stallion or other male animal kept for
breeding.
3 (*informal*) a sexually active and virile
man.
Word Family **stud book** *noun* a register
of horses' pedigrees.

stud[3] *noun*
stud poker.

student (**stew-d'nt**) *noun*
1 a person who studies at a school or other
institution.
2 any person who studies: *a student of
Hebrew.*
Word Family **studentship** *noun* 1 the
state or condition of being a student. 2 a
scholarship for a student.
[Latin *studens* being zealous]

studied (**stud-id**) *adjective*
1 not spontaneous or natural: *a studied
smile.*
2 deliberate: *a studied insult.*

studio (stew-dee-o) *noun*
1 the workroom of an artist, photographer, etc.
2 a room or building with equipment for broadcasting, making films, etc.
[Italian]

studio flat *noun*
a small flat with one main room.

studious (stew-dee-us) *adjective*
1 devoted to study: *a studious pupil.*
2 painstaking: *definitions written with studious care.*
Word Family **studiously** *adverb.*

stud poker *noun*
Cards a form of poker in which some rounds of cards are dealt face up.

study (stud-ee) *noun* (*plural* **studies**)
1 the process of acquiring knowledge through reading, investigation or thinking.
2 a branch of knowledge or something that is to be studied: *He is engaged on several archaeological studies now.*
Figurative She sank into a deep study (= reverie, state of thought). □ *He has several distinguished studies to his credit* (= publications, reports). □ *His face was a real study* (= something worth seeing).
3 a room for studying, reading or writing.
4 a work, such as a musical composition for one instrument, which is produced as a technical or preliminary exercise.
• **study** *verb* (**studies; studying; studied**) to engage in or conduct a study or studies.
Figurative We're studying your suggestions carefully (= examining).

stuff *verb*
1 to cram or fill tightly: *We stuffed the cushion with down.*
Figurative My nose is all stuffed up (= blocked). □ *She stuffed herself at the feast* (= ate too much).
2 to fill meat, poultry, vegetables, etc. with a highly seasoned mixture.
3 to fill the empty carcass of an animal, etc. with material in order to make it appear lifelike for display purposes.
Phrase **get stuffed!** (*informal*) go away! shut up!
• **stuff** *noun*
1 the material out of which something is made: *He's just not the stuff a leader is made of.*
2 material or substance of any indefinite kind: *Just give me some stuff to rub on it when it aches.*
Figurative (*informal*) You can just pack up your stuff and go (= belongings).

□ (*informal*) You can cut out the rough stuff (= actions, language). □ (*informal*) We've hired a man there who really knows his stuff (= trade, profession).
Phrases **do one's stuff** (*informal*) to do what is expected of one or show what one can do. **stuff and nonsense** foolish talk, ideas, writing, etc.
[Greek *styphein* to draw together]

stuffed shirt *noun*
(*informal*) a pompous or pretentious person.

stuffing *noun*
any material used to fill or pack something, such as a mixture of seasoned breadcrumbs, etc. used to stuff poultry, etc. before cooking.
Phrase **knock the stuffing out of** (*informal*) to weaken or defeat.

stuffy *adjective* (**stuffier; stuffiest**)
1 (of a room, etc.) poorly ventilated.
Figurative stuffy old textbooks (= dull, lacking interest).
2 blocked: *a stuffy nose.*
3 prim or easily shocked: *my stuffy old relations.*
Word Family **stuffily** *adverb*; **stuffiness** *noun.*

stultify (stult-i-fie) *verb* (**stultifies; stultifying; stultified**)
to make useless or futile.
Word Family **stultification** (stult-if-i-kay-sh'n) *noun.*
[Latin *stultus* foolish + *facere* to make]

stumble *verb*
1 to trip and almost fall.
2 to walk or proceed in an unsteady or blundering way.
Figurative He stumbled badly in his estimate of the cost of the project (= blundered, made a mistake). □ *He stumbled upon the new drug in the course of other research* (= came accidentally or unexpectedly).
Word Family **stumble** *noun*; **stumblingly** *adverb*; **stumbler** *noun.*

stumbling block *noun*
an obstacle or hindrance.

stump *noun*
1 the part of a tree remaining after the tree has fallen or been cut down.
2 anything remaining after the main part has been cut off, worn down, etc.: *the stump of a leg.*
3 *Cricket* any of the three upright wooden pegs (called the leg, middle and off stumps) set at either end of the pitch.

• **stump** *verb*
1 to walk heavily or clumsily: *He stumped up the stairs in a huff.*
2 to baffle or leave at a loss: *The last question stumped all the candidates.*
3 *American* to travel through a district making political speeches.
4 *Cricket* to dismiss the batsman by knocking the bails off with the ball while he or she is out of the crease attempting a stroke.
Phrase **stump up** *(informal)* to pay up.
Word Family **stumper** *noun (informal)* a puzzling question; **stumpy** *adjective* short and thick; **stumpily** *adverb*; **stumpiness** *noun*.

stun *verb* (**stuns**; **stunning**; **stunned**)
to knock unconscious or nearly unconscious by a blow, shock, etc.
Word Family **stunning** *adjective (informal)* strikingly attractive; **stunningly** *adverb*; **stunner** *noun (informal)*
1 a strikingly attractive person or thing.
2 a person or thing that stuns.

stung the past tense and past participle of **sting**.

stunk a past tense and the past participle of **stink**.

stunt[1] *verb*
to hinder the growth or development of: *The cold winters have stunted the trees.*
Word Family **stunted** *adjective*; **stuntedness** *noun*.

stunt[2] *noun*
1 a bold, daring or unusual feat.
2 an action meant to attract attention, etc.: *It was an advertising stunt.*

stuntman *noun (plural* **stuntmen***)*
a person paid to perform stunts, especially as a substitute for an actor in dangerous scenes.

stupefy (stew-pi-fie) *verb* (**stupefies**; **stupefying**; **stupefied**)
to make stupid or senseless: *He was completely stupefied with drink.*
Word Family **stupefying** *adjective*

stupendous (stew-**pend**-us) *adjective*
1 amazing or astounding: *The Grand Canyon is a stupendous sight.*
2 immense: *I have a stupendous amount of work to get through.*
Word Family **stupendously** *adverb*; **stupendousness** *noun*.

stupid (stew-pid) *adjective*
1 slow to apprehend or understand: *He's too stupid to understand your question.*

2 unthinking, silly: *That was a stupid thing to say.*
3 *(informal)* boring, uninteresting: *I really hate this stupid job.*
Word Family **stupidly** *adverb*; **stupidity** (stew-**pidd**-i-tee) *noun* dullness or lack of intelligence.
[Latin *stupidus* struck senseless]

stupor (stew-pa) *noun*
a state of apathy and drowsiness.
Word Family **stuporous** *adjective*.
[Latin, numbness]

sturdy *adjective* (**sturdier**; **sturdiest**)
strong or robust: *children's sturdy little legs.*
□ *sturdy common sense.*
Word Family **sturdily** *adverb*; **sturdiness** *noun*.

> The word **sturdy** may be related to 'a thrush' and a drunken one at that. The word came into English from Old French *estourdi* (stunned, dazed), whose origins may go back to *turdus*, Latin for 'a thrush'. In Roman times the thrush was a symbol of drunkenness, perhaps because it feasted on fermenting grapes. *Estourdi* came to mean 'violent' in Old French and this meaning passed into English where it later became 'robust'.

sturgeon (ster-j'n) *noun*
any of a group of large edible fish found in the northern hemisphere, used as a source of caviar.

stutter *noun*
a speech defect in which sounds are repeated, or found difficult to say, often accompanied by facial contortions and uncontrollable pauses.
Word Family **stutter** *verb*; **stutterer** *noun*; **stuttering** *noun*; **stutteringly** *adverb*.

sty[1] *noun (plural* **sties***)*
1 a pigsty.
2 any filthy place.

sty[2] *noun (plural* **sties***)* also **stye**
a small swelling on the edge of an eyelid.

style *noun*
1 the particular manner in which something appears, is done, etc.: *a hairstyle.* □ *He won in fine style.* □ *The author writes in a natural style.*
Figurative Live in style while the money lasts (= an elegant manner).
2 the combination of characteristics that distinguish a period of art, etc.: *the Gothic style.*

3 *Biology* the slender upper part of the carpel of a flower.

● **style** *verb*
1 to give a title or name to: *He styled himself Emperor of the World*.
2 to design or give a style to: *She cut and styled his hair*.
Word Family stylish *adjective* elegant or fashionable; **stylishly** *adverb*; **stylishness** *noun*; **stylistic** *adjective* of or relating to style; **stylistically** *adverb*; **stylize, stylise** *verb* to represent or treat in accordance with a principle of design or style rather than as it is in nature: *Most Egyptian sculpture is highly stylized*; **stylization** (stile-eye-**zay**-sh'n) *noun*.
[Latin *stilus* a writing instrument, a way of writing]

stylist (stile-ist) *noun*
1 a person who designs or creates styles in hairdressing, etc.
2 a person, especially a writer, who cultivates a good style.

stylus (sty-lus) *noun* (*plural* **styli** (sty-lie) *or* **styluses**)
1 also called **needle**. a very fine sapphire or diamond which follows the groove in a gramophone record and transmits the resulting vibrations to the cartridge.
2 a pointed implement for writing or engraving.

stymie (sty-mee) *verb* (**stymies**; **stymying** *or* **stymieing**; **stymied**)
1 *Golf* to play a ball to a position between the opponent's ball and the hole, thus preventing him or her, under the old rules, from making a direct putt.
2 to block or thwart: *Her ambition was stymied by opposition from the family*.

styrene (sty-reen) *noun*
a colourless oily liquid obtained from petroleum and used to make polystyrene.

Styrofoam (sty-ro-fome) *noun* (*trademark*) a lightweight firm polystyrene plastic used for packaging, insulation, etc.

suave (swahv) *adjective*
(of a man) elegant and charming, sometimes excessively so.
Word Family suavely *adverb*; **suavity, suaveness** *noun*.
[Latin *suavis* pleasant]

subaltern (sub-'l-tern) *noun*
Military an army officer below the rank of captain.

subatomic (sub-a-**tomm**-ik) *adjective* consisting of particles smaller than, or forming part of, an atom.

subcommittee *noun*
a committee appointed from a larger committee.

subconscious (sub-**kon**-shus) *adjective* (of mental processes) outside the immediate field of consciousness, but able to be recalled to conscious awareness under hypnosis, etc.
Word Family subconscious *noun*; **subconsciously** *adverb*.

subcontinent *noun*
a land mass which is part of a continent, e.g. the Indian subcontinent.

subcontract (sub-**kon**-trakt) *noun* an arrangement by which a person who has agreed to do a job makes a contract with some other person to do part or all of the job for him or her.
Word Family subcontract (sub-k'n-**trakt**) *verb*; **subcontractor** *noun*.

subculture *noun*
a separate system of behaviour or beliefs existing within a larger culture or society.

subcutaneous (sub-kew-**tay**-ni-us) *adjective*
under the skin.
[*sub-* + Latin *cutis* skin]

subdivide *verb*
to divide again or into smaller parts: *to subdivide land for a housing estate*.
Word Family subdivision *noun*
1 another or further division. 2 a part, such as a piece of land, resulting from subdividing. 3 an area of land, etc. composed of subdivided lots.

subdue (sub-**dew**) *verb*
1 to conquer or overcome: *I subdued my fears and stepped out into the dark*.
2 to soften or tone down: *Curtains will subdue the harshness of the light in this room*.
Word Family subdued *adjective*.

sub-heading *noun* also **sub-head**
1 a heading given to a section of an article, etc.
2 a second or lesser part of a main title.

subhuman *adjective*
1 of an order of beings that is lower than the human.
2 (of a person's behaviour) disgusting or uncivilized.

subjacent (sub-**jay**-s'nt) *adjective* located beneath or at a lower level.

subject (sub-jikt) *noun*
1 a topic or main theme: *The subject of my talk will be collecting antiques.* □ *orchestral variations on a musical subject*.

2 a person or thing that is the object of experiment, testing, etc.: *We need 100 subjects for a psychological test.*
3 *Grammar* the word or phrase in a sentence about which something is said: *In the sentence 'The old lady is ill', 'the old lady' is the subject.*
4 the thing represented in or the model for a painting, sculpture, etc.
5 a person who owes allegiance to a sovereign or a government: *a British subject.*
6 any area of knowledge which may be studied.
• **subject** (sub-**jekt**) *verb*
1 to bring under some power or influence: *The Moors subjected all Spain to their rule.*
2 to cause to undergo or experience: *to subject a patient to massive doses of radiation.*
• **subject** (sub-**jikt**) *adjective*
1 under the power of another: *a subject nation.*
2 open or exposed to: *The decision is subject to appeal.*
3 dependent upon: *Subject to the council's approval, the tree-planting ceremony will go on*
Word Family **subjection** (sub-**jek**-sh'n) *noun*.
[*sub-* + Latin *jactus* thrown]

subjective (sub-**jek**-tiv) *adjective*
1 influenced by one's personal interests, emotions or prejudices: *to take a subjective view of things.*
2 taking place solely within the mind.
3 *Grammar* of the case of nouns and pronouns that is used for the subject of a sentence.

sub judice (sub joo-di-see) *adjective*
Law before, or about to come before, a court.
[Latin, under the *judge*]

subjugate (**sub**-joo-gate) *verb*
to conquer or bring under control: *to subjugate a nation.* □ *to subjugate one's passions.*
Word Family **subjugation** (sub-joo-**gay**-sh'n) *noun*.
[*sub-* + Latin *jugum* a yoke]

subjunctive (sub-**junk**-tiv) *adjective*
Grammar in the subjunctive mood.
subjunctive mood ⇨ MOOD².
• **subjunctive** *noun*
1 the subjunctive mood.
2 a verb in the subjunctive mood.
[*sub-* + Latin *junctus* joined]

sublet (sub-**let**) *verb* (**sublets; subletting; sublet**) also **sublease**
to rent out to another person property that one is already renting.

sub-lieutenant *noun*
Navy an officer ranking between midshipman and lieutenant.

sublimate (**sub**-li-mate) *verb*
1 *Psychology* to redirect a socially unacceptable impulse into some other more acceptable activity.
2 *Chemistry, Physics* to sublime.
• **sublimate** (**sub**-li-mit) *noun* the material obtained when a substance is sublimed, especially when regarded as purified by the process.
Word Family **sublimation** (sub-li-**may**-sh'n) *noun*.
[Latin *sublimare* to lift up]

sublime (sub-**lime**) *adjective*
1 lofty or noble: *sublime music.* □ *sublime mountain scenery.*
2 perfect, complete: *We tried to regain that sublime moment of happiness.*
• **sublime** *verb Chemistry, Physics* to cause a solid substance to convert to a gas, and then to solidify again without passing through a liquid phase, by the application of heat or pressure.
Word Family **sublimely** *adverb*; **sublimity** (sub-**limm**-i-tee), **sublimeness** *noun*.
[Latin *sublimis* uplifted]

subliminal (sub-**limm**-i-n'l) *adjective*
Psychology perceived below the threshold of consciousness, such as an image or stimulus of too low an intensity for one to become clearly conscious of it.
Word Family **subliminally** *adverb*.
[*sub-* + Latin *liminis* of a threshold]

sub-machine gun *noun*
a light automatic weapon fired from the shoulder or the hip.

submarine (**sub**-ma-reen) *noun*
a ship designed and equipped to travel and operate both on and below water.
• **submarine** *adjective* beneath the surface of the sea: *submarine plants.*
Word Family **submariner** (sub-**marr**-in-a) *noun*.
[*sub-* + Latin *marinus* of the sea]

submerge (sub-**merj**) *verb* also **submerse**
to plunge under water or some other liquid: *The sandbank is submerged at high tide.* □ *The submarine submerged.*

Word Family **submergence,
submersion** (sub-**mer**-sh'n) *noun*;
submerged *adjective Biology* growing
under water; **submersible** *adjective*.
[*sub-* + Latin *mergere* to dip]

submit (sub-**mit**) *verb* (**submits;
submitting; submitted**)
1 to surrender to the will or authority of
another: *The defeated troops agreed to submit
to the enemy's terms.*
2 to present for the consideration,
judgement, approval, etc. of another: *to
submit a manuscript to a publisher.*
*Figurative I submit that the punishment is
unfair* (= suggest).
Word Family **submission** (sub-**mish**-'n)
noun **1** the act of submitting: *a willing
submission to punishment.* **2** the state of
having submitted: *Submission was written
all over his face.* **3** something which is
submitted: *a written submission from each
applicant;* **submissive** (sub-**miss**-iv)
adjective **1** willing or inclined to submit: *a
submissive child.* **2** marked by or indicating
submission: *a submissive answer;*
submissively *adverb;* **submissiveness**
noun.
[*sub-* + Latin *mittere* to send]

subnormal *adjective*
below the average: *subnormal temperatures
for this time of year.*
Word Family **subnormality** (sub-nor-
mal-i-tee) *noun.*

subordinate (sub-**or**-di-nit) *adjective*
1 belonging to a lower rank or status.
2 secondary: *That's only of subordinate
importance.*
3 *Grammar* of a clause or phrase which
adds to the meaning of another, but makes
no sense by itself: *In the sentence 'He visited
his sister, who was in hospital', 'who was in
hospital' is the subordinate clause.*
4 *Grammar* of a conjunction which
introduces a subordinate clause or phrase,
e.g. *because, since, if, as* and *whether.*
• **subordinate** (sub-**or**-di-nate) *verb* to
make subordinate: *You must learn to
subordinate your unruly temper.*
• **subordinate** (sub-**or**-di-nit) *noun* a
subordinate person or thing.
Word Family **subordinately** *adverb;*
subordination (sub-or-di-**nay**-sh'n)
noun.
[*sub-* + Latin *ordinare* to set in order]

suborn (sub-**orn**) *verb*
to persuade a person to commit an illegal
act, especially perjury.

Word Family **subornation** (sub-a-**nay**-
sh'n) *noun.*
[Latin *subornare* to supply secretly]

sub-plot *noun*
a secondary plot in a book, film or play.

subpoena (sa-**pee**-na) *noun*
Law a court document which summons a
person to appear in court as a witness.
• **subpoena** *verb* (**subpoenas;
subpoenaing; subpoenaed** or
subpoena'd) to serve or summon with a
subpoena.
[Latin, under penalty (first words of the
document)]

subpolar *adjective*
between the polar and the cool temperate
regions, having long cold winters, low
rainfall and coniferous forests.

sub rosa (sub **ro**-za) *adverb*
confidentially or in secret.
[Latin, under the rose, which was the
symbol of Horus, the Egyptian god of
silence]

subroutine *noun* also called **subprogram**.
Computers a set of instructions used to
perform a single task which can be
repeated.

subscribe *verb*
1 to undertake to receive and pay for a
certain number of issues of a periodical,
tickets to concerts, etc.
2 to express agreement or approval:
I heartily subscribe to that theory.
3 to promise or contribute a sum of
money: *Will you subscribe to the new
government loan?*
4 to sign one's name at the end of a
document, especially as a sign of
agreement, approval, acceptance, etc.
Word Family **subscriber** *noun* **1** a
person who subscribes to a periodical, etc.
2 a person who rents a telephone;
subscription (sub-**skrip**-sh'n) *noun* **1** the
act of subscribing. **2** something which is
subscribed, such as money.
[*sub-* + Latin *scribere* to write]

subscriber trunk dialling *noun*
short form is **STD** a direct system for
making long-distance telephone calls, in
which the subscriber dials the number
himself or herself.

subscript *noun*
a character printed lower than the other
characters, such as the 2 in CO_2.
[*sub-* + Latin *scriptus* written]

subsequent (**sub**-si-kw'nt) *adjective*
following or coming after or later:
*Subsequent developments changed our first
opinion of the case.*
[*sub-* + Latin *sequens* following]

subsequently *adverb*
later or afterwards: *She subsequently
changed her mind.*

> ! Do not confuse *subsequently* with
> CONSEQUENTLY.

subserve (sub-**serv**) *verb*
(*formal*) to be useful in forwarding or
promoting: *The secondary plot subserves the
main plot.*

subservient (sub-**serv**-i-ent) *adjective*
servile or tamely submissive.
***Word Family* subserviently** *adverb*;
subservience *noun*.

subset *noun*
Maths a set of elements contained within
another set (the superset).

subside (sub-**side**) *verb*
1 to sink to a lower level or the bottom:
The surrounding land had subsided.
2 to abate, quieten down: *The storm of
applause subsided.*
***Word Family* subsidence** (sub-**sigh**-
d'nce *or* sub-si-d'nce) *noun*.
[*sub-* + Latin *sidere* to settle]

subsidiary (sub-**sid**-ee-a-ree) *adjective*
of secondary or subordinate importance.
• **subsidiary** *noun* (*plural* **subsidiaries**)
1 a subsidiary person or thing.
2 *Commerce* a company which has more
than half its shares owned by another
company.
***Word Family* subsidiarity** (sub-sid-ee-
arr-i-tee) *noun* the principle of granting
political power to individual members or
smaller groups within a large organization.
[Latin *subsidium* aid]

subsidy (**sub**-si-dee) *noun* (*plural*
subsidies)
1 any financial assistance given by one
government or individual to another.
2 government funds used to keep down
the price of food, rent, etc.
***Word Family* subsidize, subsidise** *verb*
to give a subsidy to; **subsidization** (sub-
si-die-**zay**-sh'n) *noun*; **subsidizer** *noun* a
person or group that subsidizes.

subsist (sub-**sist**) *verb*
to continue in existence or keep alive:
Human beings cannot subsist without water.
□ *Superstition still subsists in our scientific
age.*
[*sub-* + Latin *sistere* to stand]

subsistence *noun*
1 the act or fact of keeping alive: *What is
your means of subsistence?*
2 a means of keeping alive: *Selling matches
is her subsistence.*
subsistence farming farming which
provides only enough food for the farmer
and his or her family to live on. Compare
COMMERCIAL FARMING under COMMERCIAL
adjective.
subsistence level a standard of living
only just sufficient to sustain life.

subsoil *noun*
the layer between the soil and bedrock,
which has less organic material and is less
fertile than soil.

subsonic (sub-**sonn**-ik) *adjective*
1 moving slower than the speed of sound.
2 below the limits of human hearing.
[*sub-* + Latin *sonus* sound]

subspecies (**sub**-spee-sheez *or* sub-spee-
shiz) *noun* (*plural* **subspecies**) also called
race.
Biology a subdivision of a species,
sometimes used in the classification of
animals and plants.

substance *noun*
1 what a thing consists of: *Ice, water and
steam are the same substance in different
states.*
2 a particular kind of this: *Oil is a greasy
substance.*
3 an object itself, as distinct from its
properties.
Figurative Skip the details, and give me the
substance of what he said (= main or
essential part). □ *Broth has almost no
substance to it* (= body). □ *Her mother is a
woman of substance* (= wealth).
[from Latin]

sub-standard *adjective*
inadequate or not meeting an established
standard: *sub-standard housing.*

substantial (sub-**stan**-sh'l) *adjective*
1 of or consisting of substance.
2 of considerable size, importance, value
or amount: *a substantial rise in salary.* □ *We
need a more substantial reason.*
3 *Philosophy* of or relating to objects rather
than events.
***Word Family* substantially** *adverb*;
substantiality (sub-stan-shi-**al**-i-tee)
noun.

substantiate (sub-**stan**-shi-ate) *verb*
to provide proof for: *Can you substantiate
your claims?*
***Word Family* substantiation** (sub-stan-
shi-**ay**-sh'n) *noun*.

substantive (sub-st'n-tiv) *adjective*
1 having an independent existence.
2 essential or basic.
3 (of military rank) permanent.
• **substantive** *noun Grammar* a noun.
Word Family **substantively** *adverb*.

substation (sub-stay-sh'n) *noun*
an auxiliary station, etc., especially one for
transforming, distributing or converting
electric current in a system.

substitute (sub-sti-tewt) *noun*
a person or thing that acts or stands in
place of another.
• **substitute** *verb* to put a person or thing
in the place of another: *Yogurt can be
substituted for cream in this recipe.*
Word Family **substitution** (sub-sti-tew-
sh'n) *noun*.
[*sub-* + Latin *statuere* to set]

substratum (sub-strah-tum) *noun* (*plural*
substrata) (sub-strah-ta)
a layer beneath another, such as an
underlayer of earth, rock or subsoil.
*Figurative There is a substratum of truth in
what you say* (= an underlying basis).

substructure *noun*
the foundations, especially of a structure
such as a building or bridge.
Word Family **substructural** *adjective*.

subsume (sub-syoom) *verb*
to place in a larger group or category.
[*sub-* + Latin *sumere* to take]

subsystem *noun*
a system which works within another
system.

subtenant (sub-ten-'nt) *noun*
a person who rents a house, land, etc. from
a tenant.
Word Family **subtenancy** *noun*.

subtend *verb*
Maths to be opposite to: *The chord subtends
an arc.*
[*sub-* + Latin *tendere* to stretch]

subterfuge (sub-ta-fewj) *noun*
an underhand method used to escape or
avoid an awkward situation, etc.
[Latin *subter* underneath + *fugere* to flee]

subterranean (sub-ta-ray-ni-'n) *adjective*
underground.
[*sub-* + Latin *terra* earth]

subtext *noun*
an underlying message in writing or
speech.

subtitle *noun*
1 any of the short sentences shown on the
screen during a foreign film to translate
the soundtrack.

2 a second or alternative title of a book,
poem, etc., often serving as an explanation
of the first.
• **subtitle** *verb* to give a subtitle or
subtitles to.

subtle (sutt-'l) *adjective*
fine, slight or delicate, so as to be difficult
to detect, etc.: *subtle perfume.* □ *a subtle
distinction.*
*Figurative She has a subtle understanding
of the problem* (= penetrating, acute).
□ *a subtle smile* (= faint).
Word Family **subtly** *adverb*; **subtleness**
noun; **subtlety** (sutt-'l-tee) *noun* (*plural*
subtleties) 1 the state of being subtle.
2 something which is subtle, such as a fine
distinction or shade of meaning.
[Latin *subtilis* fine-woven]

subtopia *noun*
the sprawl of suburbs that surrounds the
modern city.
[SUB(urb) + (U)TOPIA]

subtotal *noun*
the total of part of a set of figures.

subtract *verb*
to take away, especially one quantity from
another.
Word Family **subtraction** (sub-trak-
sh'n) *noun* the act of subtracting,
especially as a problem in arithmetic.
[*sub-* + Latin *tractus* dragged]

subtropical *adjective*
of or occurring in the regions near the
tropics.

suburb (sub-erb) *noun*
1 an area of a city with its own shops and
services, but not always a local
government division.
2 (**suburbs**) the outer areas of a town or
city, where land is usually mainly used for
housing.
Word Family **suburban** *adjective* (sub-
er-b'n) 1 relating to a suburb or suburbs.
2 conventional or narrow-minded;
suburbanite *noun*; **suburbia** (sub-er-bi-
a) *noun* 1 the suburbs. 2 the style of life in
the suburbs.
[*sub-* + Latin *urbs* city]

subvention (sub-ven-sh'n) *noun*
an official gift of money to an institution,
etc., e.g. by a government.
[*sub-* + Latin *venire* to come]

subversive (sub-ver-siv) *adjective*
tending or intending to weaken, destroy or
overthrow: *a subversive revolutionary.*
• **subversive** *noun* a subversive person.

Word Family **subversion** (sub-**ver**-sh'n) *noun*; **subvert** *verb* to overthrow or destroy.
[*sub-* + Latin *versus* turned]

subway *noun*
1 a passage or tunnel under a road, for use by pedestrians.
2 (*especially American*) an underground railway.

succeed (suk-**seed**) *verb*
1 to achieve the desired or intended result.
2 to come after in time, position, etc.: *Who will succeed the king when he dies?*
Word Family **succeeding** *adjective*.
[Latin *succedere* to go upwards]

success (suk-**sess**) *noun* (*plural* **successes**)
1 the achievement of what is attempted, intended or desired: *Did you have success with your plan?*
Figurative She has achieved worldwide success as an author (= fame, prosperity).
2 a person or thing that succeeds: *His birthday party was a great success.*
Word Family **successful** *adjective*
1 having or achieving the desired or intended result. 2 having gained wealth, fame or prosperity; **successfully** *adverb*.

succession (suk-**sesh**-'n) *noun*
1 the act of following in order or a series: *Her succession to the throne was at a late age.*
2 a line or series of people or things: *a succession of visitors.*
Word Family **successor** *noun* a person or thing that follows another, especially in a position, office, etc.

successive (suk-**sess**-iv) *adjective*
following, especially in an uninterrupted order: *It rained for four successive days.*
Word Family **successively** *adverb*.

> ⚠ Do not confuse *successive* with CONSECUTIVE.

succinct (suk-**sinkt**) *adjective*
clearly expressed in a few words.
Word Family **succinctly** *adverb*; **succinctness** *noun*.
[Latin *succinctus* girded up]

succour (**sukk**-a) *noun* (*American* **succor**)
help or relief.
Word Family **succour** *verb*.
[Latin *succurrere* to run to the aid of]

succulent (**suk**-yoo-l'nt) *adjective*
1 rich, delicious: *a succulent roast.*
2 fleshy and full of juice: *A cactus has succulent stems.*
[Latin *succus* juice]

succumb (s'-**kumm**) *verb*
to give in or give up: *Do not succumb to temptation!*
[Latin *succumbere* to fall under]

such *adjective*
1 of this or that kind: *I haven't read such an interesting novel for years.*
Figurative Nuts, dried fruits and all such foods (= similar). □ *She really is such a telltale* (= so great or extreme).
2 being as indicated or mentioned already: *Such are the facts of the matter.*
Phrases **as such** *Fame, as such, no longer appeals to him* (= in itself). **such and such** *It was at such and such a time* (= particular but not indicated). **such as 1** *I love all old houses such as this one* (= similar to). 2 *Do you need anything, such as fruit or vegetables?* (= for example).
Word Family **suchlike** *adjective* of a similar kind.

> ⚠ *Such as* should come directly before a noun phrase, without a preposition in between, as in *treatment such as vaccination* (not *treatment such as by vaccination*).

suck *verb*
1 to hold and moisten or absorb in the mouth: *to suck sweets.*
2 to draw up or in: *The vacuum cleaner sucks up dirt.*
Phrases **suck in** (*informal*) *Don't be sucked in by her innocent smile* (= deceived) **suck up to** (*informal*) *He's always sucking up to the teacher* (= flattering).
• **suck** *noun* the act or sound of sucking.

sucker *noun*
1 a person or device that sucks.
2 (*informal*) a person who is easily tricked or deceived.
3 a shoot arising from an underground stem or root.

suckling pig *noun*
a very young pig, especially one used for roasting.

suckle *verb*
to take or allow to take milk at the breast.
Word Family **suckling** *noun* a young mammal which has not yet been weaned.

sucrose (**soo**-kroze) *noun* also called **cane sugar**.
a crystalline carbohydrate found in sugar cane, sugar beet, etc. and used as a sweetener, preservative, etc.
[French *sucre* sugar]

suction (**suk**-sh'n) *noun*
1 the act or force of sucking.

2 *Physics* the process of removing, or attempting to remove, gas from an enclosed space.
[Latin *suctus* sucked]

sudden *adjective*
done or occurring quickly and usually unexpectedly: *a sudden storm*.
Word Family suddenly *adverb*; **suddenness** *noun*.

sudden infant death syndrome ⇨ COT DEATH.

suds *plural noun*
soapy water.
Word Family sudsy *adjective*.

> The word **suds** is probably derived from Middle Dutch *sudse*, meaning 'a marsh or swamp', and was used with this meaning in the East Anglian dialect of English. Swamp water often has a scum on it which would have given rise to the 'bubbles' of its present meaning.

sue (soo) *verb*
to bring legal action against.

suede (swade) *noun*
a leather with a soft surface, made from skins with the flesh side napped.
[French *Suède* Sweden]

suet (soo-it) *noun*
the fat from the kidneys and loin of sheep and cattle, used in boiled puddings.

suffer *verb*
to feel bad or unpleasant effects: *He's suffering from a cold.* □ *The country suffered from bad government.*
Figurative *The family has suffered great hardship* (= experienced). □ *I will not suffer such foolishness* (= tolerate, put up with).
Word Family sufferer *noun*; **suffering** *noun*.
[Latin *suffere* to bear up under]

sufferance *noun*
the ability to bear pain, distress, etc.
Phrase on sufferance *He is only here on sufferance* (= reluctantly tolerated).

suffice *verb*
to be enough or adequate: *Don't add too much salt – a teaspoonful should suffice.*

sufficient (sa-**fish**-'nt) *adjective*
as much as is needed.
Word Family sufficiently *adverb*; **sufficiency** *noun* (*plural* **sufficiencies**) a sufficient supply or amount.

suffix *noun* (*plural* **suffixes**)
Grammar a syllable or group of syllables attached to the end of a word to form another word.

suffocate (**suff**-a-kate) *verb*
1 to die or cause to die due to insufficient oxygen.
2 to cause discomfort or difficulty in breathing due to lack of fresh air.
Word Family suffocation (suff-a-**kay**-sh'n) *noun*; **suffocatingly** *adverb*.
[Latin *suffocare* to choke]

suffragan (**suff**-ra-g'n) *noun*
an assistant bishop.

suffrage (**suff**-rij) *noun*
1 a vote.
2 the right to vote in political elections.
Word Family suffragist *noun* a person in favour of extending the right to vote, especially a peaceful campaigner for suffrage for women; **suffragette** (suff-ra-**jet**) *noun* a woman who fought for suffrage for women, especially in the first part of the 20th century.
[from Latin]

suffuse (suf-**yooz**) *verb*
to spread over the surface of: *A blush suffused her cheeks.*
Word Family suffusion *noun*.
[Latin *suffusus* poured over]

sugar (**shug**-a) *noun*
a granular substance obtained from sugar cane or sugar beet.
● **sugar** *verb* to add, coat or mix with sugar.
Word Family sugary *adjective*
1 containing or resembling sugar.
2 pleasant to an excessive degree.
[Arabic *sukkar*]

sugar beet *noun*
a variety of beet with white roots.

sugar cane *noun*
a tall tropical grass with thick segmented stems.

sugar daddy *noun* (*plural* **sugar daddies**)
(*informal*) a wealthy older man who gives money or gifts to a young woman.

suggest (sa-**jest**) *verb*
to offer or put forward to be considered or acted upon: *Let me suggest a better method.*
Figurative *This painting suggests many things to me* (= calls to mind). □ *Are you suggesting I'm a liar?* (= saying).
Word Family suggestion (sa-**jess**-ch'n) *noun* **1** the act of suggesting. **2** something which is suggested: *That's a stupid suggestion!* **3** a slight trace: *There was just a*

suggestion of mockery in her laugh. **4** the process by which one thought, action, etc. leads to or is associated with another.
5 *Psychology* the process of getting others to accept one's ideas without using force;
suggestive *adjective* tending to suggest, especially something indecent;
suggestively *adverb*; **suggestiveness** *noun*; **suggestible** *adjective* easily influenced by suggestion.
[Latin *suggestus* supplied]

suicide (soo-i-side) *noun*
1 the act of deliberately killing oneself: *to commit suicide.*
Figurative It's suicide to invest all your money in that company (= ruin inflicted on oneself).
2 a person who deliberately kills himself or herself.
Word Family **suicidal** (soo-i-sy-d'l) *adjective* **1** of or likely to commit or lead to suicide. **2** dangerously foolish; **suicidally** *adverb.*
[Latin *sui* of oneself + *caedere* to kill]

suit (*rhymes with* boot) *noun*
1 a set of clothes worn together, such as a skirt or trousers with a matching jacket, usually of the same colour or material.
2 an outfit for a particular purpose: *a bathing suit.*
3 *Cards* any of the four sets (clubs, diamonds, hearts or spades) of 13 cards which make up a pack.
4 any legal action taken by one person against another in a court.
5 the act of wooing.
Phrase **follow suit 1** *Cards* to play a card of the same suit as one led. **2** to follow an example.
● **suit** *verb* to be acceptable, appropriate or adequate to: *I hope this room will suit you.*
Figurative You must suit your clothes to the occasion (= make suitable).
Phrase **suit oneself** *He suits himself about what food he eats* (= does as he chooses).

suitable (soo-ta-b'l) *adjective*
correct, adequate or pleasing for a particular event, situation, etc.: *I'm afraid your qualifications are not suitable for the job.*
□ *Those jeans are not suitable for work.*
Word Family **suitably** *adverb*;
suitability (soo-ta-bill-i-tee), **suitableness** *noun.*

suitcase *noun*
a bag with a stiffened frame, or of rigid material such as leather, for carrying clothes, etc., when travelling.

suite (sweet) *noun*
1 a group of connected or related things forming a set or series: *an opera suite.*
□ *a suite of hotel rooms.* □ *a bathroom suite.*
2 a group of attendants or followers.

suitor (soo-ta) *noun*
a person wooing a woman.

sulk *verb*
to be silent in a gloomy or resentful manner.
● **sulk** *noun*
1 (*usually* **sulks**) a fit of sulking.
2 a person who sulks.

sulky *adjective* (**sulkier**; **sulkiest**)
resentfully silent or angry.
Word Family **sulkily** *adverb.*

sullen *adjective*
sulky, especially in a persistent or unpleasant manner.
Word Family **sullenly** *adverb*;
sullenness *noun.*

sully *verb* (**sullies**; **sullying**; **sullied**)
to stain, spoil or make dirty.

sulphur (sull-fa) *noun* (*American* **sulfur**)
a yellow non-metal forming allotropes. It is essential for living tissue and is used in making gunpowder, matches, sulphuric acid and for vulcanizing rubber.
Word Family **sulphurous** *adjective* **1** of or containing sulphur. **2** fiery; **sulphuric** (sulf-yoor-ik) *adjective* of or containing sulphur.
[from Latin]

sulphur dioxide *noun*
a colourless suffocating gas, used in various industrial processes.

sulphuric acid *noun*
Chemistry a colourless oily liquid, which is an acid of sulphur and is used in many industrial processes.

sultan *noun*
the ruler of a Muslim city or country.
Word Family **sultanate** *noun* a country or state ruled by a sultan.
[Arabic]

sultana (sul-tah-na) *noun*
1 a small sweet seedless raisin.
2 the wife, concubine or close female relative of a sultan.

sultry *adjective* (**sultrier**; **sultriest**)
1 hot, moist and oppressive: *a sultry tropical climate.*
2 sensual: *a sultry Spanish dancer.*
Word Family **sultrily** *adverb*; **sultriness** *noun.*

sum *noun*
1 the amount obtained by adding: *What is the sum of 7 and 13?*
Figurative And is that the sum of your complaints? (= whole amount or number).
2 a simple arithmetical problem of addition, division, multiplication, etc.
3 an amount of money: *She inherited a huge sum from her father.*
• **sum** *verb* (**sums; summing; summed**)
to add together.
Phrase **sum up 1** to make or give a summary of. **2** to assess or describe: *It is difficult to sum up such a temperamental person.*
[Latin *summa* the main thing]

sumac (**soo-**mak) *noun* also **sumach**
1 a small tree which has brightly coloured leaves in autumn.
2 a mixture of the dried and powdered leaves of certain plants used as dyes, for tanning, etc.
[from Arabic]

summary (**sum-**a-ree) *noun* (*plural* **summaries**)
a short statement of important points or details.
• **summary** *adjective*
1 concise or brief.
2 quick.
Word Family **summarily** *adverb;* **summariness** *noun;* **summarize, summarise** *verb* to be or make a summary of.

summation (sum-**ay**-sh'n) *noun*
1 a summary, especially as a concluding statement.
2 the act of adding.

summer *noun*
1 the season between spring and autumn, in which the weather is warmest.
2 (*usually* **summers**) a poetic word for a year: *a young woman of 20 summers.*
• **summer** *verb* to spend the summer.
Word Family **summery** *adjective* like or suitable for summer.

summer house *noun*
a simple building providing shade in a garden or park.

summer school *noun*
a course of teaching or lectures held at a university or school during the summer holidays.

summer time *noun*
a system of putting the clock forward one or more hours, usually in summer, to increase the number of hours of daylight in the working day.

summit *noun*
1 the highest point or top: *the summit of a hill.*
2 (*informal*) a meeting between leaders, especially from powerful countries.
[Latin *summus* highest]

summon *verb*
to send for or ask to appear: *Sir Richard summoned the cook.*
Figurative You must summon all your courage (= gather together). □ *The garrison was summoned to surrender* (= called upon).
[Latin *summonere* to give a hint to]

summons *noun* (*plural* **summonses**)
1 *Law* an order or notice to appear in court.
2 any call or command.
• **summons** *verb* to issue or present with a summons.

sumo (**soo-**mo) *noun*
a type of Japanese wrestling between very heavy contestants.
[Japanese]

sump *noun*
1 a metal pan fastened to the underside of an engine crankcase, usually forming a reservoir for lubricating oil.
2 a pit or well in which water collects, especially at the bottom of a mineshaft.

sumptuary (**sump-**tew-a-ree) *adjective*
relating to expense or spending.

sumptuous (**sump-**tew-us) *adjective*
suggesting or involving great expense: *a sumptuous meal at the best restaurant.*
Word Family **sumptuously** *adverb;* **sumptuousness** *noun.*
[from Latin]

sun *noun*
1 *Astronomy* the star around which the earth and the other eight planets of the solar system revolve.
2 the energy, especially heat and light, radiated by the sun: *Go out and play in the sun.*
Phrase **under the sun** the richest person under the sun (= anywhere).
• **sun** *verb* (**suns; sunning; sunned**) to expose to the sun, especially in order to warm, dry or colour.

sunbathe *verb*
to expose the body to the sun's rays, especially in order to acquire a suntan.
Word Family **sunbather** *noun.*

sunbeam *noun*
a ray of sunlight.

sunbed *noun*
a piece of equipment with rows of ultraviolet lights used to acquire an artificial suntan.

sunblock *noun*
a cream for providing the skin with complete protection from the sun's rays.

sunburn *noun*
a reddening or blistering of the skin caused by too much exposure to the sun's rays.
Word Family **sunburnt, sunburned** *adjective*.

sundae (**sun-day**) *noun*
a serving of ice cream with fruit and sauce, often topped with chopped nuts and whipped cream.

Sunday *noun*
the first day of the week, before Monday.
Phrase **a month of Sundays** *I have not seen her in a month of Sundays* (= a very long time).

Sunday best *noun*
(*informal*) a person's best clothes.

Sunday school *noun*
Christianity a class for religious instruction held on a Sunday.

sun deck *noun*
a passenger ship's top deck.

sunder *verb*
a poetic word meaning 'to part or separate'.

sundial (**sun-dile**) *noun*
an instrument with a flat base and upright rod which indicates the time by the position of the shadow cast by the rod on the base.

sundown *noun*
(*especially American*) sunset.

sundry (**sun-dree**) *adjective*
various or miscellaneous.
Phrase **all and sundry** *everybody*.
Word Family **sundries** *plural noun* various small items.

sun-dry *verb* (**sun-dries; sun-drying, sun-dried**)
to dry out in the sun: *sun-dried tomatoes*.

sunflower *noun*
a tall garden plant having large yellow daisy-like flowers with blackish-brown centres. The seeds are used as a source of oil.

sung the past participle of **sing**.

sunglasses *plural noun*
a pair of spectacles with tinted lenses, worn to protect the eyes from the glare and invisible rays of the sun.

sunk a past participle of **sink**.

sunken *adjective*
lying below the surface of the ground, etc.: *a sunken bath*.
Figurative Her sunken cheeks told of the weeks of starvation (= deeply recessed).
• **sunken** *verb* a past participle of **sink**.

sunlamp *noun*
1 an appliance which gives off ultraviolet rays to produce an artificial suntan or for skin treatment.
2 a very bright light with parabolic mirrors, used in making films.

sunlight *noun*
the light from the sun.
Word Family **sunlit** *adjective*.

sunny *adjective* (**sunnier; sunniest**)
1 full of sunlight.
2 cheerful.
Word Family **sunnily** *adverb*; **sunniness** *noun*.

sunrise *noun*
1 the rising of the sun above the horizon in the morning.
2 the time at which this occurs.

sunroof *noun*
a section in the roof of a motor vehicle, which may be opened to allow the sun and fresh air to enter.

sunscreen *noun*
a cream for providing the skin with protection from the sun's rays.

sunset *noun*
1 the passing of the sun below the horizon in the evening.
2 the time at which this occurs.

sunshade *noun*
something used as protection from the sun's rays, such as a parasol, blind, etc.

sunshine *noun*
the direct light or brightness of the sun.

sunspot *noun*
Astronomy any dark patch on the surface of the sun, usually associated with turbulent motion such as magnetic storms.

sunstroke *noun*
heatstroke.

sunsuit *noun*
a light piece of clothing, such as shorts or a skirt with a top, often in one piece.

suntan *noun*
a brownness of the skin achieved by
exposure to the sun's rays.
Word Family **suntanned** *adjective*.

sunup *noun*
(*especially American*) sunrise.

sun visor *noun*
short form is **visor** a hinged flap mounted
above the windscreen of a motor vehicle
and used to protect the driver's eyes from
the sun.

sup¹ *verb* (**sups; supping; supped**)
an old word meaning 'to entertain with, or
eat, supper'.

sup² *verb* (**sups; supping; supped**)
to eat or drink in sips or small mouthfuls.

super (soo-per) *adjective*
(*informal*) extremely pleasing or excellent.
● **super** *noun* (*informal*) a superintendent.

superable (soo-pra-b'l) *adjective*
able to be overcome: *a superable risk*.

superabundance (soo-per-a-**bun**-d'nce)
noun
an amount which is more than enough or
too great.
Word Family **superabundant** *adjective*.

superannuation (soo-per-an-yoo-**ay**-
sh'n) *noun*
a pension or allowance paid to an
employee after retirement, usually one
towards which he or she has contributed.
Word Family **superannuate** (soo-per-
an-yoo-ate) *verb* to allow an employee to
retire and receive superannuation.
[*super-* + Latin *annus* a year]

superb (soo-**perb**) *adjective*
magnificent.
Word Family **superbly** *adverb*;
superbness *noun*.
[Latin *superbus* haughty, splendid]

supercargo *noun* (*plural* **supercargoes**
or **supercargos**)
an agent in a merchant ship, in charge of
its cargo and of all commercial
transactions.

supercharge *verb*
to fill or supply with a large amount of
something.

supercilious (soo-per-**sill**-i-us) *adjective*
disdainful or contemptuous: *the
supercilious snob*.
Word Family **superciliously** *adverb*;
superciliousness *noun*.

> The word **supercilious** comes from
> Latin *supercilium*, meaning 'an
> eyebrow', from *super* (above) and *cilium*
> (an eyelid). Raising the eyebrows is a
> sign of disdain or haughtiness, hence
> the present meaning.

super-duper *adjective*
(*informal*) very good, fine, pleasing, etc.

superego (soo-per-ee-go) *noun*
Psychology that part of the personality
which absorbs the moral codes of society,
similar to the conscience.

supererogation (soo-per-err-a-**gay**-sh'n)
noun
Christianity the doing of more than is
required by duty or obligation: *works of
supererogation*.
[*super-* + Latin *erogare* to pay out]

superficial (soo-per-**fish**-'l) *adjective*
of or on the surface: *The cut was only
superficial*.
Figurative *My understanding of physics is
very superficial* (= not deep or thorough).
Word Family **superficiality** (soo-per-
fish-i-**al**-i-tee) *noun*; **superficially** *adverb*.
[Latin *superficies* the upper side]

superfluid (soo-per-floo-id) *noun*
Physics a fluid which flows without friction
and has a very high thermal conductivity.
Word Family **superfluidity** (soo-per-
floo-**id**-i-tee) *noun*.

superfluous (soo-**per**-floo-us) *adjective*
more than is needed: *As I have one car
another would be superfluous*.
Word Family **superfluously** *adverb*;
superfluousness *noun*; **superfluity** (soo-
per-**floo**-a-tee) *noun* (*plural*
superfluities) **1** the fact of being
superfluous. **2** the amount by which
something is superfluous.
[Latin *superfluus* overflowing]

superglue *noun*
a type of very strong quick-setting glue.

supergrass *noun* (*plural* **supergrasses**)
(*informal*) a person who informs on a large
group of people to the police.

superhero *noun* (*plural* **superheroes**)
a fictional crime-fighter with superhuman
powers.

superhuman *adjective*
exceeding ordinary human power,
achievement, etc.: *We needed a superhuman
effort to finish the job in time*.

superimpose (soo-per-im-**poze**) *verb*
to put on top of something else: *A map of the UK was superimposed on the map of France to show their relative sizes.*
Word Family **superimposition** (soo-per-im-pa-**zish**-'n) *noun*.

superintend (soo-per-in-**tend**) *verb*
to supervise.
Word Family **superintendent** *noun*
1 a supervisor. 2 a police officer above the rank of inspector; **superintendence** *noun*.

superior (soo-**peer**-i-a) *adjective*
1 high or higher in order, degree, rank, etc.: *He is my superior officer.*
Figurative The enemy defeated us with superior numbers (= greater). □ *He gave a superior smile* (= supercilious).
2 of a high quality: *a superior product.*
3 situated above or on top: *The 2 in 10² is a superior number.*
4 *Astronomy* of or relating to planets in our solar system which are further from the sun than the earth.
• **superior** *noun* a person or thing that is superior.
Word Family **superiority** (soo-peer-i-**orr**-i-tee) *noun*.
[Latin]

superiority complex *noun* (*plural* **superiority complexes**)
(*informal*) an exaggerated idea of one's own worth.

superlative (soo-**per**-la-tiv) *adjective*
1 of the highest degree or quality: *This job calls for superlative skill.*
2 *Grammar* ⇨ DEGREE (definition 6).
• **superlative** *noun* a word in the superlative degree.
Figurative The critics greeted the film with a fanfare of superlatives (= extreme or exaggerated expressions).
Word Family **superlatively** *adverb*.
[*super-* + Latin *latus* carried]

superman *noun* (*plural* **supermen**)
a man of more than ordinary human powers.

supermarket *noun*
a large self-service shop selling food and other domestic goods.

supermodel *noun*
a very famous and highly paid fashion model.

supernatural (soo-per-**natch**-a-r'l) *adjective*
1 not belonging to the natural world: *Ghosts are supernatural beings.*
2 greater than what is normal or usual: *She has a supernatural ability to remember things.*
• **supernatural** *noun* (**the supernatural**) supernatural beings, forces, etc.
Word Family **supernaturally** *adverb*.

supernova (soo-per-**no**-va) *noun* (*plural* **supernovae** (soo-per-**no**-vee) or **supernovas**)
a star which suddenly becomes much brighter when activity in the core ceases and the star collapses, leading to a massive explosion which throws the star's outer layer off into space.
[a misleading term, as it has no relation to a *nova*]

supernumerary (soo-per-**new**-mer-a-ree) *adjective*
in excess of or additional to the usual number.
• **supernumerary** *noun* (*plural* **supernumeraries**) an extra person or thing.

superpower *noun*
an extremely powerful and influential country.

superscript *noun*
a character printed higher than the other characters, such as the 3 in 5³.

supersede (soo-per-**seed**) *verb*
to replace with something more powerful, modern, effective, etc.: *The new car supersedes all previous models.*
[Latin *supersedere* sit above]

> ❗ Note the spelling of *supersede*: it ends in *sede*, not *cede*.

superset *noun*
Maths a set of elements which contains another set (the subset).

supersonic (soo-per-**sonn**-ik) *adjective*
relating to bodies moving faster than the speed of sound.
[*super-* + Latin *sonus* sound]

superstar *noun*
a very famous person, such as an actor, singer or sportsperson.

superstition (soo-per-**stish** 'n) *noun*
1 an irrational fear of mysterious or unknown things.
2 a belief or practice based on faith in magic or chance.
Word Family **superstitious** *adjective*
1 of, like or resulting from superstition.
2 believing in superstition: *I'm not superstitious about walking under ladders;* **superstitiously** *adverb*; **superstitiousness** *noun*.
[Latin *superstitio* an unreasonable belief or fear]

superstore *noun*
a very large supermarket usually built outside a town or city.

superstructure (soo-per-struk-cher) *noun*
1 the parts of a structure which rest on the foundations, especially if above ground level.
2 any structure built on something else, such as the parts of a ship above the deck.

supertanker *noun*
a very large ship built with tanks for transporting liquid goods such as oil.

supervene (soo-per-veen) *verb*
to come or follow as a change or interruption: *Rain supervened and the picnic was postponed.*
Word Family **supervention** (soo-per-ven-sh'n) *noun*.
[*super-* + Latin *venire* to come]

supervise (soo-per-vize) *verb*
to direct or manage work, workers, etc.
Word Family **supervisor** *noun*;
supervisory *adjective*; **supervision** (soo-per-vizh-'n) *noun*.
[*super-* + Latin *visus* seen]

superwoman *noun* (*plural* **superwomen**)
(*informal*) a woman of more than ordinary human powers.

supine (syoo-pine *or* soo-pine) *adjective*
1 lying flat on the back.
2 lazy or inactive.
Word Family **supinely** *adverb*.
[Latin *supinus* face upwards]

supper *noun*
1 a late-night snack.
2 the main evening meal.

supplant (sa-plahnt) *verb*
to replace, especially by strategy, etc.:
The dictator was supplanted by an elected government.
[Latin *supplantare* to trip up]

supple *adjective*
easily bent or bending: *The gymnast had supple limbs.*
Figurative *She has a supple mind* (= adaptable, quick).
Word Family **suppleness** *noun*.
[Latin *supplex* kneeling in supplication]

supplement (sup-li-m'nt) *noun*
1 something added to improve or complete: *a supplement of technical terms at the back of the book.*
2 an extra part of a newspaper, etc.:
a literary supplement.
• **supplement** (sup-li-ment) *verb* to complete or add to: *She must supplement her income by working on Saturdays.*

Word Family **supplementary** (sup-li-ment-a-ree) *adjective* 1 added or extra.
2 *Maths* relating to either of two angles which total 180°; **supplementation** (sup-li-m'n-tay-sh'n) *noun*.
[from Latin]

suppliant (sup-li-ant) *noun*
a person who asks for something humbly.
• **suppliant** *adjective* asking humbly.

supplicate (sup-li-kate) *verb*
to ask or entreat humbly and earnestly.
Word Family **supplicant** *noun* a person who supplicates; **supplicatory** *adjective*;
supplication (sup-li-kay-sh'n) *noun*.
[Latin *supplicare* to bend, kneel]

supply (sa-ply) *verb* (**supplies;
supplying; supplied**)
to give or make available: *The chickens supply us with all the eggs we need.*
Figurative *Will this supply your needs?* (= satisfy).
• **supply** *noun* (*plural* **supplies**)
1 the act of supplying.
2 an amount that is supplied: *We'll have a fresh supply of caviar tomorrow.*
3 (**supplies**) any stores, such as materials used by the armed forces.
4 *Commerce* the quantity of goods and services available to consumers.
5 a grant made by parliament for government expenses.
Word Family **supplier** *noun*.

supply-side economics *plural noun*
(*used with singular verb*) an economic policy based on the belief that supply creates demand.

supply teacher *noun*
a teacher who substitutes for other teachers while they are on sick leave, maternity leave, etc.

support *verb*
1 to hold up or add strength to: *Tall columns supported the roof.* □ *Support your theory with evidence.*
Figurative *He supports the local football team* (= gives loyalty, belief or aid to).
□ *She supports ten children* (= provides for).
□ *I can't support bad language* (= tolerate).
2 to have a secondary role to: *The film was supported by some cartoons.*
• **support** *noun*
1 the act of supporting: *Can I rely on your support?*
2 the state of being supported.
3 a person or thing that supports: *She's the main support of her family.* □ *The supports of the bridge collapsed.*

Word Family **supportable** *adjective*;
supporter *noun* a person or thing that
supports, such as a person who favours
and encourages a football team, etc.;
supportive *adjective* giving support and
encouragement.
[Latin *supportare* to carry up to]

suppose (sa-**poze**) *verb*
to take as a fact or likelihood: *I suppose his
advice is sensible.*
Figurative *Am I supposed to clean up?*
(= meant). □ *A belief in flying saucers
supposes the existence of life on other planets*
(= implies).
Word Family **supposing** *conjunction* in
the case that; **supposed** *adjective* accepted
as probable: *This is the supposed site of an
ancient city;* **supposedly** (sa-**poze**-id-lee)
adverb; **supposition** (sup-a-**zish**-'n) *noun*
1 the act of supposing. **2** something
guessed or supposed.
[Latin *suppositus* placed under]

suppository (sa-**pozz**-i-tree) *noun* (*plural*
suppositories)
a solid mass of medicine inserted into the
rectum or vagina, where it dissolves.

suppress *verb*
1 to end or abolish: *The army suppressed the
rebellion.* □ *The slave trade was suppressed by
parliament.*
2 to prevent something being seen, known,
etc.: *The government suppressed news of the
scandal.*
Word Family **suppressive** *adjective;*
suppression (sa-**presh**-'n) *noun,*
suppressor *noun.*
[Latin *suppressus* pressed down]

suppurate (**sup**-yoo-rate) *verb*
to form or discharge pus.
Word Family **suppuration** (sup-yoo-
ray-sh'n) *noun.*
[from Latin]

supremacist (soo-**premma**-sist) *noun*
a person who believes that his or her own
race or group is superior or supreme.
Word Family **supremacism** *noun.*

supreme (soo-**preem**) *adjective*
1 of highest rank or authority: *The dictator
had supreme power.*
2 utmost or greatest: *I have supreme
confidence in you.*
Word Family **supremacy** (soo-**premm**-
a-see) *noun* supreme power or authority;
supremely *adverb.*
[Latin *supremus* topmost]

supreme court *noun*
the highest court of justice.

supremo (soo-**pree**-mo) *noun*
(*informal*) a person with supreme power.
[Spanish]

surcharge *noun*
1 an extra charge.
2 a mark overprinted on a postage stamp
showing a new value.
Word Family **surcharge** *verb.*

surd *noun*
Maths a quantity not capable of being
expressed as a rational number, such as
$\sqrt{3}$.
[from Latin]

sure (shore) *adjective*
1 convinced or free from doubt: *Are you
sure of your facts?*
Figurative *She is sure to be late* (= bound).
□ *Be sure to lock the door* (= careful).
2 solid, tested or reliable: *sure ground.* □ *Is
there a sure cure for a hangover?*
● **sure** *adverb* (*informal*) really or
undoubtedly: *You sure were lucky.*
Phrases **make sure** to guarantee or make
certain. **sure enough** in fact: *I said you'd
win, and sure enough you did.*
Word Family **surely** *adverb* **1** almost
without doubt: *It will surely rain tomorrow.*
2 steadily: *He worked slowly but surely.* **3** it
is to be hoped or believed that: *Surely you
wouldn't do that!;* **sureness** *noun.*
[Latin *securus* carefree]

sure-footed *adjective*
not likely to slip or stumble.

surety (**shoor**-a-tee) *noun* (*plural*
sureties)
a person who agrees to be responsible for
someone else's debts or behaviour.

surf *noun*
the waves, especially large ones, which
break on the shore into foamy water.
● **surf** *verb*
1 to bathe in or ride on surf.
2 (*informal*) to browse on the Internet.

surface (**ser**-fis) *noun*
1 the outside or outer boundary of
something: *Most glass has a smooth surface.*
□ *A cube has six surfaces.*
2 the top level: *The ship sank beneath the
sea's surface.*
Figurative *Beneath the surface he's a nice
guy* (= outward appearance).
● **surface** *verb*
1 to rise to the surface.
2 to give a surface to: *The road was surfaced
with tar.*
[French]

surface mail *noun*
the carrying of post by land or sea.
Compare AIRMAIL.

surface tension *noun*
Physics the tendency of a liquid surface to
contract due to unbalanced molecular
forces at or near the surface.

surfboard *noun*
a narrow board on which a person
balances to ride to shore on the crest of a
wave.

surfeit (ser-fit) *noun*
1 too much of something.
2 nausea or disgust due to having had too
much.
Word Family **surfeit** *verb*.

surfing *noun*
the sport of swimming in or riding a
surfboard on surf.
Word Family **surfer** *noun*.

surge (serj) *verb*
to rush or swell strongly like rolling waves.
• **surge** *noun* an onrush of strong forward
or upward movement.
[Latin *surgere* to rise]

surgeon (ser-j'n) *noun*
a doctor who performs operations.

surgery (ser-ja-ree) *noun* (*plural*
surgeries)
1 the art of treating diseases, injuries, etc.
by operations, appliances, etc.
2 the branch of medicine using this
treatment.
3 any operation done by a surgeon.
4 the room or building in which a doctor,
dentist, etc. treats patients.
Word Family **surgical** *adjective*;
surgically *adverb*.
[Greek *kheirourgia* handiwork]

surgical spirit *noun*
methylated spirits, used in surgery for
disinfecting and cleansing.

surly *adjective* (**surlier**; **surliest**)
rude, bad-tempered or unfriendly.
Word Family **surlily** *adverb*; **surliness**
noun.

surmise (ser-mize) *verb*
to guess.
Word Family **surmise** *noun*.

surmount (ser-mount) *verb*
1 to get over, across or on top of: *It was
difficult to surmount the obstacle.*
2 to be or have on top: *A steeple surmounted
the tower.*
Word Family **surmountable** *adjective*.

surname *noun*
the name of one's family.

surpass *verb*
to be better or greater than: *Your new book
surpasses all your earlier ones.*

surplice (ser-pliss) *noun*
a loose white linen robe with wide sleeves,
as worn by clergy during religious services.

surplus (ser-pl'ss) *noun* (*plural*
surpluses)
that which is left above what is used or
needed: *The good harvest resulted in a
surplus of grain.*

surprise (ser-prize) *noun*
1 something sudden or unexpected: *What
a pleasant surprise to see you again.*
2 the feeling of shock or wonder caused by
this: *He almost fainted with surprise.*
Phrase **take by surprise** *Your early
arrival took us by surprise* (= caught
unprepared).
• **surprise** *verb*
1 to give a feeling of surprise to: *Her
unkind remark surprised me.*
2 to face or come upon suddenly and
without warning: *I surprised him in the act
of stealing fruit.*
Word Family **surprising** *adjective*;
surprisingly *adverb*.

surrealism (ser-rear-lizm) *noun*
a 20th-century movement in art and
literature seeking to reveal the inner world
of fantasy and dreams by using distorted
images.
Word Family **surrealist** *adjective, noun*;
surreal, **surrealistic** (ser-rear-list-ik)
adjective; **surrealistically** *adverb*.

surrender (ser-ren-da) *verb*
to deliver something or oneself up to the
control or power of someone or something
else: *The besieged troops refused to surrender.*
□ *She was forced to surrender her passport.*
□ *Don't surrender yourself to despair.*
Word Family **surrender** *noun*.

surreptitious (surr-ip-tish-us) *adjective*
secret or stealthy: *She stole a surreptitious
glance at him.*
Word Family **surreptitiously** *adverb*;
surreptitiousness *noun*.
[Latin *surreptitius* snatched away secretly]

surrogate (surr-a-git) *noun*
1 a substitute.
2 a deputy.
Word Family **surrogacy** *noun* (*plural*
surrogacies).
[Latin *surrogare* to propose as substitute]

surrogate mother noun
a woman who bears a child on behalf of
another woman.

surround verb
to enclose or extend completely around:
The house is surrounded by trees. □ *We
surrounded the thief so that he was trapped.*
• **surround** noun
1 a border that surrounds.
2 (**surrounds**) surroundings.
Word Family **surroundings** *plural noun*
everything around a person, thing or
place: *Where can I see lions in their natural
surroundings?*

surtax noun (*plural* **surtaxes**)
an additional tax, especially one on any
personal income which exceeds a specified
amount.

surveillance (ser-**vay**-l'nce) noun
a close watch or guard.
[French]

survey (ser-**vay**) verb
1 to take an overall view: *You can survey the
whole town from this lookout.*
2 to collect sample opinions, etc. in order
to estimate the general situation.
3 to plot or measure boundaries, positions,
etc. on land.
• **survey** (**ser**-vay) noun
1 a general view or examination: *a survey
of public opinion.*
2 a record or report of this.
3 the act of surveying land.
4 a map or record of this.
Word Family **surveyor** noun.

survive (ser-**vive**) verb
to continue to live or exist after something:
Everyone survived the earthquake.
Word Family **survivor** noun; **survival**
noun the act of surviving; **survival of the
fittest** ⇨ NATURAL SELECTION.

susceptible (sa-**sept**-i-b'l) adjective
likely to experience or be affected by: *The
old lady was highly susceptible to rheumatism.*
Word Family **susceptibly** adverb;
susceptibility (sa-sept-i-**bill**-i-tee) noun
(*plural* **susceptibilities**) 1 the capacity or
tendency to be affected by something: *His
susceptibility to flattery is obvious.*
2 (**susceptibilities**) a person's sensitive
feelings.
[Latin *suscipere* to catch]

sushi (**soo**-shee) noun
a Japanese dish of cakes of boiled rice
topped with raw fish.
[Japanese]

suspect (sa-**spekt**) verb
1 to think something likely or possible:
I suspect it will rain soon.
2 to consider guilty without actual or
adequate proof: *I suspect her of arson.*
Figurative *I suspect his motives* (= doubt,
distrust).
• **suspect** (**suss**-pekt) noun a person
suspected of a crime or misdemeanour.
• **suspect** (**suss**-pekt) adjective open to
suspicion.
[Latin *suspectus* looked up at]

suspend verb
to attach from above: *The light bulb was
suspended from the ceiling.*
Figurative Dust was suspended in the hot
still air (= held stationary). □ *You may
suspend payment for a month* (= defer,
postpone). □ *The football player was
suspended for three matches* (= debarred).

suspended animation noun
a trance-like state.

suspended sentence noun
a sentence of imprisonment not
implemented provided the offender is of
good behaviour over a specified period.

suspenders plural noun
1 strips of elastic attached to a belt or
girdle, with a fastener for holding up
stockings.
2 *American* braces.

suspense noun
a state of anxious uncertainty: *The film kept
us in suspense about the murderer's identity.*
Word Family **suspenseful** adjective.
[Latin *suspensus* hung up]

suspension (sa-**spen**-sh'n) noun
1 the act of suspending: *The tribunal's
suspension of our best player is disastrous.*
2 the state of being suspended: *He is under
suspension from school.*
3 the springs, shock absorbers, etc.
connecting the wheels or axles of a vehicle
to the chassis or body.

suspension bridge noun
a bridge hung from steel cables, supported
by towers and anchored at either side.

suspicion (sa-**spish**-'n) noun
1 a feeling that something is likely or
possible: *I had a suspicion you'd be late.*
2 a feeling that someone is guilty.
Figurative *I have suspicions about your
motives* (= doubts, distrusts). □ *There was a
suspicion of garlic in the soup* (= suggestion
or slight taste).

Word Family suspicious *adjective* feeling or causing suspicion; **suspiciously** *adverb*; **suspiciousness** *noun*.
[from Latin]

suss *verb*
(*informal*) to work out or understand: *I soon had the problem sussed.*

sustain *verb*
1 to support or bear the weight of: *Will this table sustain the load?*
Figurative *It's hard to sustain a conversation with her* (= maintain). □ *The court sustained my claim* (= upheld).
2 to suffer or undergo: *The victim sustained a broken arm.*
Word Family sustainable *adjective* capable of being sustained at a steady level without exhausting natural resources or damaging the environment: *sustainable development*; **sustainably** *adverb*; **sustainability** (sa-stay-na-**bill**-i-tee) *noun*.
[from Latin]

sustenance (**suss**-ta-n'nce) *noun*
1 food or other means of sustaining life.
2 the act of sustaining.

sutra (**soo**-tra) *noun*
any of various writings on ritual, spiritual, philosophical or scientific subjects in various Eastern religions, such as Buddhism.
[Sanskrit, thread, rule]

suttee (sa-**tee**) *noun*
(*formerly*) a Hindu custom in which a widow was required to burn herself to death on her husband's funeral pyre.

suture (**soo**-cher) *noun*
1 *Medicine* the joining of the edges of a cut or wound by stitching.
2 *Medicine* the thread, wire or material used to do this.
[from Latin]

svelte (svelt) *adjective*
slender and graceful.
[French]

swab (swob) *noun*
1 *Medicine* a small piece of cotton wool used to wipe away fluids, apply medication or take samples of bodily secretions for analysis.
2 *Medicine* the sample so taken.
3 a large mop used to clean floors, etc.
● **swab** *verb* (**swabs; swabbing; swabbed**)
1 to clean with or as if with a swab.
2 to take specimens with a swab.

swaddle (swod-'l) *verb*
to wrap or bind with long strips of cloth.

swag *noun*
1 *Australian* a roll or bundle containing the possessions of a bush traveller, miner, etc.
2 (*informal*) stolen goods.
Word Family swagman *noun* (*plural* **swagmen**) *Australian* 1 a tramp. 2 a man who carries a swag.

swagger *verb*
to walk or strut proudly or smugly.
Word Family swagger *noun*; **swaggeringly** *adverb*.

swain *noun*
an old word for a young rustic lover.
[Old English, swineherd]

swallow[1] (*rhymes with* follow) *verb*
1 to take food, etc. into the stomach through the throat.
2 to move the throat muscles to do, or as if doing, this.
Figurative *The clouds swallowed the mountain completely* (= enveloped, made disappear). □ *It was an insult I could not swallow* (= accept). □ *Swallow your fears and follow us* (= suppress).
● **swallow** *noun*
1 the act of swallowing.
2 the amount swallowed at one time.

swallow[2] *noun*
any of various long-winged graceful migrating birds which catch insects while flying.

swallow dive *noun*
a dive performed with the arms extended until near the water.

swallow hole ⇨ SINKHOLE.

swam the past tense of **swim**.

swami (**swah**-mee) *noun*
Hinduism a title for a religious teacher.
[Hindi, master]

swamp (swomp) *noun*
an area of soft permanently wet ground, often with coarse grasses.
● **swamp** *verb* to flood or soak with water.
Figurative *The firm was swamped with orders* (= overwhelmed).
Word Family swampy *adjective* (**swampier; swampiest**).

swan (swon) *noun*
a large graceful bird of the duck family with a long slender neck.

swanky *adjective* (**swankier; swankiest**)
(*informal*) smart or stylish.

swansong *noun*
the last work or creation of an artist, etc. before his or her death.
[from the legend that a dying swan sings sweetly]

swap (swop) *verb* (**swaps; swapping; swapped**) also **swop**
to exchange one thing for another.
Word Family **swap** *noun*.

sward (swawd) *noun*
short form of **greensward**, an old word for a lawn.

swarm¹ *noun*
1 a large group of bees or other insects moving together.
2 any large group of people or things in motion.
• **swarm** *verb* to move in large numbers: *Crowds swarmed to the beach in the hot weather.*
Figurative The beaches were swarming with swimmers (= abounding).

swarm² *verb*
to climb a rope, etc. by clasping it with the hands and legs and pulling oneself up.

swarthy (swor-thee) *adjective* (**swarthier; swarthiest**)
having a dark complexion.
Word Family **swarthiness** *noun*.

> The word **swarthy** is derived from Old English *sweart*, meaning 'black'. It has connections with words in several of the other Germanic languages – *schwarz* in German, *zwart* in Dutch, *svart* in Swedish and *sort* in Danish.

swash (swosh) *noun*
Geography The movement of waves up a beach. Compare BACKWASH.

swashbuckler (swosh-buk-la) *noun*
a daring or showy swordsman.
Word Family **swashbuckling** *adjective*.

swastika (swost-ikk-a) *noun*
an ancient symbol comprising a regular cross with its arms extended and bent at right angles in a clockwise direction, and adopted by the Nazi Party as its symbol.
[Sanskrit *svasti* well-being]

swat (swot) *verb* (**swats; swatting; swatted**)
to hit flies, etc. with a sharp blow.
• **swat** *noun* a sharp blow.

swatch (swotch) *noun* (*plural* **swatches**)
a small sample of a fabric.

swathe (swayth) *noun*
a row of grass or grain cut by a scythe or machine.

Figurative The police charge cut a swathe through the crowd (= path, broad strip).
• **swathe** *verb* to wrap or bind in or as if in bandages: *The baby was absolutely swathed in clothes.*

sway *verb*
1 to swing or cause to swing from side to side: *She was swaying from exhaustion.* □ *A breath of wind swayed the trees.*
2 to influence or exert control over: *The passionate speech swayed the voters.*
• **sway** *noun*
1 a swaying motion.
2 any rule, control or influence.

swayback *noun*
a sagging back, especially in horses, caused by an excessive bend in the backbone.
Word Family **sway-backed** *adjective*.

swear (swair) *verb* (**swears; swearing; swore; sworn**)
1 to promise or declare solemnly: *He swore he'd be on time.*
2 *Law* to take or cause to take an oath to tell the truth.
3 to curse or utter blasphemous or obscene oaths.
Phrases **swear by** (*informal*) *He swears by that remedy* (= has complete confidence in). **swear in** *The President was sworn in at an official ceremony* (= admitted to office by taking an oath). **swear off** (*informal*) *He's sworn off alcohol for life* (= promised to give up). **sworn enemies** irreconcilable enemies. **sworn friends** devoted friends.
Word Family **swearer** *noun*; **swearword** *noun* a word used as a curse or a blasphemous or obscene oath.

sweat (swet) *verb*
1 also **perspire** to excrete a watery substance through the pores in an attempt to reduce body temperature.
Figurative The damp concrete wall was sweating moisture (= giving off in droplets).
2 (*informal*) to work very hard. *I really sweated over that assignment.*
3 (*informal*) to worry or suffer: *He made me sweat for three weeks before he told me the job was mine.*
Phrase **sweat it out** (*informal*) to wait anxiously or helplessly.
• **sweat** *noun*
1 the salty fluid secreted through the sweat glands.
2 the act or state of sweating: *He brought the horse back in a sweat.*
3 (*informal*) a state of impatience or worry: *There's no need to get into a sweat.*

Phrase **no sweat** (*informal*) no difficulty at all.

Word Family **sweated** *adjective* employed in hard work for low wages: *Sweated labour was rife in 19th-century Britain*; **sweaty** *adjective* (**sweatier; sweatiest**); **sweatily** *adverb*; **sweatiness** *noun*.

sweater (swett-a) *noun*
a knitted jumper.

sweatshirt *noun*
a loose collarless jumper worn by athletes, etc.

sweatshop (swet-shop) *noun*
a factory or workshop where employees work very long hours, often in unpleasant conditions and for low wages.

swede *noun*
a large root vegetable with yellow flesh related to the turnip.

sweep *verb* (**sweeps; sweeping; swept**)
to clean or clear with or as if with a broom: *He swept the floor.* □ *The king promised to sweep the seas of pirates.*
Figurative Her dress swept the floor as she walked (= touched lightly). □ *His eyes swept over the page* (= passed quickly). □ *The floods swept away houses and trees* (= carried). □ *The road sweeps along the coast* (= extends, follows).
• **sweep** *noun*
1 the act of sweeping: *Give the room a sweep.*
Figurative With a sweep of his arm he cleared his desk (= long stroke or movement). □ *We surveyed the long sweep of coastline* (= unbroken stretch). □ *Listen to the sweep of the wind over the plains* (= uninterrupted movement).
2 a person who cleans soot, etc. from chimneys.
3 short form of **sweepstake** a form of gambling, usually on the result of a horse race, where tickets representing all the horses are sold and the money paid in becomes the prize money for the winners.
Phrase **make a clean sweep of** to get rid of or reorganize completely.
Word Family **sweeping** *adjective* 1 of wide range: *a sweeping generalization.* 2 decisive: *a sweeping victory*; **sweeper** *noun*; **sweepingly** *adverb*.

sweet *adjective*
1 having the pleasant taste of sugar: *I don't like my coffee too sweet.*
2 pleasant to the senses, feelings or mind: *the sweet sounds of birds singing.*
3 having or showing a pleasant disposition: *She is a sweet girl.*

Phrases **keep someone sweet** (*informal*) to stay in favour with someone. **sweet on** (*informal*) fond of.
• **sweet** *noun*
1 a small piece of food which contains a large amount of sugar, such as a chocolate, toffee, etc.
2 dessert.
Word Family **sweetly** *adverb*; **sweetness** *noun*; **sweeten** *verb* to make sweet; **sweetener** *noun* something that sweetens.

sweet-and-sour *adjective*
having both a sweet and a sour or sharp flavour: *sweet-and-sour chicken.*

sweetbread *noun*
the pancreas of an animal, usually calf or lamb.

sweetcorn *noun*
the small yellow kernels of maize, especially when removed from the cob and eaten as a vegetable.

sweetheart (sweet-hart) *noun*
1 a lover.
2 a term of endearment: *Good night, sweetheart.*

sweetmeat *noun*
an old word for any sweet food.

sweet pea *noun*
a climbing garden plant of the pea family with fragrant colourful flowers.

sweet potato *noun* (*plural* **sweet potatoes**)
the edible root of a vine.

sweet tooth *noun* (*plural* **sweet tooths**) (*informal*) a great liking for sweet foods.

sweet william (sweet **will**-y'm) *noun*
a garden plant with coloured flowers which form in dense rounded clusters.

swell *verb* (**swells; swelling; swelled; swelled or swollen**)
1 to become or cause to become greater in size, force, intensity, etc.: *The wood swelled after being saturated in the rain.* □ *The noise swelled until it was unbearable.*
2 to cause to protrude: *The wind swelled the sails.*
• **swell** *noun*
1 the act of swelling: *There was a swell in the music.*
2 the condition of being enlarged in size, force, etc.
3 a regular undulating movement of the surface of the sea.
4 (*dated*) a distinguished person, or one very fashionably dressed: *He was all dressed up and looking like a swell.*

• **swell** *adjective*

1 (*dated informal*) fashionable or stylish: *a swell hotel*.

2 (*American informal*) excellent or first-rate: *What a swell idea!*

Word Family **swelling** *noun* **1** a swollen part: *I'm worried about this swelling on my knee.* **2** an increase in size.

swelter *verb*

to suffer from oppressive heat: *I always swelter during summer.*

Word Family **sweltering** *adjective*

1 suffering from oppressive heat.

2 oppressively hot and humid; **swelteringly** *adverb*.

swept the past tense and past participle of **sweep**.

swerve *verb*

to turn aside suddenly or sharply from a course or purpose.

Word Family **swerve** *noun*.

swift *adjective*

1 moving or performing movements in a brief time: *We caught a swift train.* □ *Her swift fingers moved across the loom.*

2 prompt or ready: *He's always been very swift to anger.*

• **swift** *noun* any of various small fast-flying birds similar to the swallow.

Word Family **swiftly** *adverb*; **swiftness** *noun*.

swig *verb* (**swigs; swigging; swigged**) (*informal*) to take a deep drink.

Word Family **swig** *noun*.

swill *noun*

1 a rinse: *Give the barrel a good swill out with water.*

2 a mixture of liquid and solid food, especially as a food for pigs.

• **swill** *verb*

1 to drink greedily or excessively.

2 to rinse.

swim *verb* (**swims; swimming; swam; swum**)

1 to move or cause to move through water by movements of the arms, legs, fins, etc.: *Everyone should learn to swim.* □ *He swam across the flooded river.*

Figurative *I don't like my meat to be swimming in gravy* (= immersed, floating). □ *His eyes were swimming with tears* (= overflowing).

2 to seem to whirl: *The room swam before his eyes.* □ *My head is swimming and I feel sick.*

Phrase **swim with the stream, swim with the tide** to follow the fashion or majority.

• **swim** *noun* the act of swimming.

Phrase **in the swim** actively taking part in social activities, current affairs, etc.

Word Family **swimmer** *noun*; **swimming** *noun*; **swimmingly** *adverb* easily or with great success.

swim bladder *noun*

a bladder containing gas, present in the abdomen of fish.

swimming costume *noun*

short form is **costume** a swimsuit.

swimsuit *noun*

a piece of clothing worn when bathing.

swindle *verb*

to cheat someone out of money or property.

Word Family **swindle** *noun*; **swindler** *noun*.

[from German]

swine *noun*

1 (*plural* **swine**) (*formal*) a pig.

2 (*plural* **swine** or **swines**) (*informal*) a brutish, unpleasant or greedy person.

Word Family **swinish** *adjective*; **swinishly** *adverb*.

swing *verb* (**swings; swinging; swung**)

1 to move or cause to move back and forth in a regular motion, usually suspended from above: *The pendulum swung evenly.* □ *He swung his arms as he walked.*

Figurative *He swings from one opinion to another* (= fluctuates).

2 to pivot: *A gate swings on its hinges.*

3 to move or cause to move in a circular or sweeping motion: *He swung his sword above his head.* □ *The car swung round the corner.*

4 (*informal*) to complete successfully: *I'm trying to swing a big deal with the oil company.*

5 (*informal*) to be lively and modern: *I want to go somewhere that really swings.*

• **swing** *noun*

1 a swinging movement: *a golfer's swing.*

2 a seat suspended from above, on which children swing to and fro.

3 a ride on such a swing.

4 a swinging gait or rhythmic movement: *a rollicking old song that goes with a swing.*

5 *Music* a form of dance music popular after 1935, based on jazz rhythms.

Phrases **get into the swing of** (*informal*) to become familiar with or active in something. **go with a swing** (*informal*) to be lively. **in full swing** in full operation: *Production will be in full swing by April.*

Word Family **swinger** *noun* **1** a person or thing that swings. **2** (*informal*) a lively modern person; **swinging** *adjective* (*informal*) lively or modern.

swing bridge *noun*
a bridge, part of which is pivoted in the centre and may be turned horizontally, to allow boats, etc. to pass.

swingeing (**swinn**-jing) *adjective*
severe, drastic: *swingeing cuts in the country's defence budget.*

swing-wing *adjective*
(of an aeroplane) having the wings pivoted at the fuselage so that they may be swept back to varying degrees to suit the aeroplane's speed.

swipe *noun*
a long sweeping blow or stroke: *The batsman made a swipe at the ball.*
• **swipe** *verb*
1 to hit with a sweeping blow.
2 to steal.
3 to pass a credit card, debit card, etc. through an electronic reader.

swirl *verb*
to move or cause to move in a twisting or whirling motion: *The leaves swirled around.*
Word Family **swirl** *noun;* **swirly** *adjective.*

swish *verb*
1 to move through the air with a hissing or whistling sound: *The horse swished its tail.*
2 (of clothes) to rustle.
• **swish** *noun* (*plural* **swishes**) a swishing sound or movement.
• **swish** *adjective* (*informal*) smart or fashionable.

switch *noun* (*plural* **switches**)
1 any device for opening, closing or directing an electric circuit.
2 (**switches**) *Railways* a device for shifting vehicles from one line to another.
3 a turning, shifting or changing: *a switch of voters' preferences.*
4 a long separate tress of hair fastened together at one end and used to add to a hairstyle.
5 a flexible rod or cane, used for whipping.
• **switch** *verb*
1 to connect or disconnect by a switch: *Switch off that fan.*
2 to shift, change or divert: *Let's switch the conversation to something else.* □ *The train was switched to another track.*
3 to exchange: *Let's switch rooms for a week.*
4 to swing or lash: *The cow switched her tail.*
Word Family **switcher** *noun.*

switchback *noun*
1 an undulating road.
2 a roller coaster.

3 a zigzag railway or road climbing a steep incline.

switchblade *noun*
a knife with a spring-loaded retractable blade which is released when a switch is pressed.

switchboard *noun*
Electricity a panel containing switches for connecting and disconnecting electrical circuits, e.g. in a telephone exchange.

swivel (**swiv**-'l) *noun*
a link, pivot or other fitting which allows one section of two attached parts to turn independently of the other, e.g. in a **swivel chair**, where the seat revolves without revolving the base.
• **swivel** *verb* (**swivels; swivelling; swivelled**) to turn on or as if on a swivel.

swizz *noun* (*plural* **swizzes**) also **swiz**
1 (*informal*) a disappointment.
2 (*informal*) deception or fraud.

swizzle stick *noun*
a small stick used to make fizzy drinks less or more fizzy.

swollen (**swole**-en) a past participle of **swell**.

swollen-headed *adjective*
(*informal*) having an excessively high opinion of oneself.

swoon *verb*
to faint.
Word Family **swoon** *noun.*

swoop *verb*
1 to descend suddenly: *The eagle swooped down on the rabbit.*
2 to take or seize suddenly: *He swooped up his trophy and marched out of the room.*
• **swoop** *noun* a swooping movement.
Phrase **at one fell swoop** all at once.

swop *verb* (**swops; swopping; swopped**)
⇨ SWAP.

sword (sord) *noun*
a weapon with a long sharp blade and a handle.
Phrases **cross swords** to disagree violently. **put to the sword** to massacre.
Word Family **swordsman** *noun* (*plural* **swordsmen**) a man who is trained or skilled in the use of a sword; **swordsmanship** *noun.*

swordfish *noun* (*plural* **swordfish** or **swordfishes**)
any of a group of large edible marine fish with the upper jaw elongated into a sword-like weapon.

swore the past tense of **swear**.

sworn the past participle of **swear**.

swot *verb* (**swots; swotting; swotted**)
(*informal*) to study hard, especially for
examinations.
Phrase **swot up** (*informal*) to learn or
memorize.
• **swot** *noun* (*informal*) a person who
studies hard.
[alteration of SWEAT]

swum the past participle of **swim**.

swung the past tense and past participle of
swing.

sybarite (**sibb**-a-rite) *noun*
a person who is fond of luxury and
pleasure.
Word Family **sybaritic** (sibb-a-**ritt**-ik)
adjective.
[after *Sybaris* in southern Italy, noted in
ancient times for luxury]

sycamore (**sikk**-a-mor) *noun*
a variety of European maple tree.
[Greek *sykon* fig + *moron* mulberry]

sycophant (**sikk**-a-fant) *noun*
a servile flatterer.
Word Family **sycophantic** (sikk-a-**fan**-
tik) *adjective*; **sycophancy** (**sikk**-a-fan-
see) *noun*.
[Greek *sykophantes* an informer]

syllable (**sill**-a-b'l) *noun*
Language the smallest unit of speech,
consisting of a vowel sound with or
without one or more consonant sounds:
The word 'asleep' contains two syllables.
Word Family **syllabic** (si-**lab**-ik)
adjective of, relating to or consisting of a
syllable or syllables.
[Greek *syllabé* something held together]

syllabus (**sill**-a-bus) *noun* (*plural*
syllabuses or **syllabi** (**sill**-a-bye))
the set programme of a course of study.
[Greek *sittyba* a label]

syllogism (**sill**-a-jizm) *noun*
Logic an argument with two premises from
which a conclusion is drawn, e.g. *All birds
have feathers; seagulls are birds; therefore
seagulls have feathers.*
Word Family **syllogistic** (sill-a-**jist**-ik)
adjective; **syllogistically** *adverb*.
[Greek *syn*- together + *logizesthai* to
reason]

sylph (silf) *noun*
1 a spirit of the air.
2 a slender graceful young woman.
Word Family **sylph-like** *adjective*.
[from Greek]

sylvan (**sil**-v'n) *adjective* also **silvan**
a poetic word meaning 'of or relating to
woods or forests'.

symbiosis (sim-bi-**oh**-siss) *noun* (*plural*
symbioses) (sim-bi-**oh**-seez)
Biology the living together of two types of
organisms for their mutual benefit.
Word Family **symbiotic** (sim-bi-**ott**-ik)
adjective; **symbiotically** *adverb*.
[Greek]

symbol (**sim**-b'l) *noun*
something which is used to suggest or
represent something else: *A dove is a
symbol of peace.*
Word Family **symbolic** (sim-**bol**-ik)
adjective; **symbolically** *adverb*;
symbolize, symbolise *verb* 1 to be a
symbol of. 2 to represent by a symbol or
symbols.
[Greek *symbolon* a token]

symbolism (**sim**-ba-lizm) *noun*
1 the use of symbols to denote
relationships, objects, emotions, etc. as in
art and literature.
2 the symbolic meaning or significance of
something.

symmetry (**simm**-a-tree) *noun* (*plural*
symmetries)
1 an exact correspondence between the
opposite halves of a figure, form, line,
pattern, etc., on either side of an axis or
centre.
2 a balance or proportion between parts of
a whole, e.g. in a painting or sculpture.
Word Family **symmetrical** (si-**met**-ri-
k'l) *adjective*; **symmetrically** *adverb*.
[*sym*- + Greek *metron* a measure]

sympathy (**sim**-pa-thee) *noun* (*plural*
sympathies)
1 the capacity for sharing the feelings of
others.
2 a feeling or expression of pity, etc. for
another person's distress or suffering.
Figurative We are in sympathy on many of
the issues (= agreement).
Word Family **sympathetic** (sim-pa-
thett-ik) *adjective*; **sympathetically**
adverb; **sympathize, sympathise** *verb* to
feel or express sympathy; **sympathizer**
noun.
[*sym*- + Greek *pathos* feeling]

symphonic poem ⇨ TONE POEM.

symphony (**sim**-fa-nee) *noun* (*plural*
symphonies)
1 *Music* a long serious orchestral
composition, usually having four
movements.

2 (*informal*) a symphony orchestra.
Word Family symphonic (sim-**fon**-ik)
adjective of or having the character of a
symphony.
[*sym-* + Greek *phoné* sound]

symphony orchestra *noun*
a large orchestra designed to play
symphonies.

symposium (sim-**po**-zee-um) *noun* (*plural*
symposia (sim-**po**-zee-a) or
symposiums)
1 a meeting to discuss a particular topic.
2 a collection of writings by different
authors on the same subject.

> The word **symposium** in English
> suggests a formal occasion where
> people take it in turn to give talks on a
> specific topic. However, it is derived
> from the Greek *sumposion*, which was a
> much jollier occasion, being a gathering
> at which participants enjoyed drinks as
> well as exchanging views.

symptom (**simp**-t'm) *noun*
1 *Medicine* an observable change in bodily
or mental condition that indicates the
presence of disease.
2 a sign of the existence of something: *The
riots were an obvious symptom of social
unrest.*
Word Family symptomatic (simp-ta-
mat-ik) *adjective* serving as a symptom;
symptomatically *adverb*.
[from Greek]

synagogue (**sin**-a-gog) *noun*
1 a regular assembly of Jews for worship
and religious instruction.
2 a building where such an assembly is
held.
[Greek *synagogé* a meeting]

synchromesh (**sink**-ro-mesh) *noun*
a system used in the gearbox of a motor
vehicle, in which the gears are made to
spin at the same speed before being
engaged.
[SYNCHRO(nized) + MESH]

synchronize, synchronise (**sink**-ra-
nize) *verb*
1 to occur at the same time: *His arrival
synchronized with my departure.*
2 to make agree in time: *They synchronized
their watches.*
3 to move or take place at the same rate or
exactly together: *The soundtrack was not
synchronized with the picture.*
Word Family synchronization (sink-ra-
nigh-**zay**-sh'n) *noun*.

synchronized swimming *noun*
a competitive sport in which teams of
swimmers perform complicated
synchronized movements to music.

synchronous (**sink**-ra-nus) *adjective*
occurring at the same time or in the same
phase.
Word Family synchronously *adverb*.
[*syn-* + Greek *khronos* time]

synchronous orbit *noun*
the orbit of a satellite which causes the
satellite to stay over one spot on the earth.

syncopate (**sink**-o-pate) *verb*
Music to place the stress on beats that are
normally unstressed.
Word Family syncopation (sink-o-**pay**-
sh'n) *noun*.
[*syn-* + Greek *koptein* to cut off]

syndicate (**sin**-di-kit) *noun*
a combination of individuals or companies
to carry out a project, usually commercial,
such as a newspaper organization which
sells news or an article to several
publications at once.
Word Family syndicate (**sin**-di-kate)
verb; **syndication** (sin-di-**kay**-sh'n) *noun*.
[*syn-* + Greek *diké* justice]

syndrome (**sin**-drome) *noun*
1 a set of symptoms and signs typically
found together and associated with a
particular disease or psychological
disorder.
2 a distinctive pattern of behaviour.
[Greek *syndromé* a running together]

synergy (**sin**-a-jee) *noun* (*plural*
synergies) also **synergism**
the joint action of two substances,
organisms, organizations, etc. to achieve
an effect of which each is incapable alone.
[Greek *synergos* working together]

synod (**sin**-od) *noun*
a council, especially of clergy to conduct
church business.
[Greek *synodos* an assembly]

synonym (**sin**-a-nim) *noun*
a word with the same or a similar meaning
to another: *Happy is a synonym of glad.*
Compare ANTONYM.
[*syn-* + Greek *onyma* name]

synonymous (si-**nonn**-i-mus) *adjective*
expressing or suggesting the same idea:
These two words are synonymous. □ *Our
company's name is synonymous with good
value.*
Word Family synonymously *adverb*.

synopsis (si-**nop**-sis) *noun* (*plural* **synopses**) (si-**nop**-seez)
a summary, especially of the plot of a novel, play, etc.
[Greek, a general view]

syntax (**sin**-taks) *noun*
Grammar the arrangement and interrelationships of words in phrases and sentences.
Word Family **syntactic** (sin-**tak**-tik), **syntactical** *adjective*.
[syn- + Greek *tassein* to arrange]

synthesis (**sin**-tha-sis) *noun* (*plural* **syntheses**) (**sin**-tha-seez)
the combination of parts or elements into a complex whole. Compare ANALYSIS (definition 1).
Word Family **synthesize, synthesise** *verb* to make up by combining parts or elements.
[Greek]

synthesizer, synthesiser (**sin**-tha-size-a) *noun*
an electronic instrument consisting of a keyboard which is programmed by a computer to make music.

synthetic (sin-**thett**-ik) *adjective*
1 artificially made: *synthetic fabrics*.
2 not genuine: *his synthetic charm*.
3 produced by synthesis.
synthetic rubber ⇨ RUBBER[1] (definition 1).
Word Family **synthetically** *adverb*.

syphilis (**siff**-i-lis) *noun*
a sexually transmitted disease which develops in stages and, if untreated, can eventually affect many parts of the body.
Word Family **syphilitic** (siff-i-**lit**-ik) *adjective* relating to or affected with syphilis; **syphilitic** *noun* a person suffering from syphilis.
[the name of a character in a Latin poem (1530) who was a victim of it]

syphon ⇨ SIPHON.

syringe (si-**rinj**) *noun*
Medicine a hollow tube with a piston which can be fitted onto a hypodermic needle and used to inject fluids into, or withdraw them from, the body.

• **syringe** *verb* to cleanse or inject by means of a syringe.
[Greek *syringos* a (musical) pipe]

syrup (**sirr**-up) *noun*
a thick sweet liquid made by boiling sugar, water and often flavouring.
Word Family **syrupy** *adjective*.
[Arabic *sharab* a drink]

system (**siss**-t'm) *noun*
1 a group of things or parts forming a whole: *a railway system*. □ *the digestive system*.
2 an organized group of ideas, principles, beliefs, etc.: *a system of philosophy*. □ *a system of government*.
Figurative There's no system in the way he works (= organized basis). □ *a new system of marking exams* (= procedure). □ *Your whole system is run-down and you need a holiday* (= body).
3 (**the System**) (*informal*) the network of established institutions which controls a country, regarded as suppressing any attempt to change it.
Word Family **systematic** (siss-ta-**mat**-ik) *adjective* 1 according to a system: *a systematic search*. 2 arranged in a system; **systematically** *adverb*; **systematize, systematise** *verb* to arrange in or according to a system; **systematization** (siss-t'm-a-tie-**zay**-sh'n) *noun*.
[Greek *systema* a setting together]

systemic (siss-**temm**-ik *or* siss-**teem**-ik) *adjective*
of or relating to a system as a whole.

systems analysis *noun*
the use of mathematics to predict future behaviour in various circumstances of complex groups of related objects or people. It is of value in planning or designing automation, transport systems, ballistic missiles, etc.
Word Family **systems analyst** *noun*.

systole (**siss**-ta-lee) *noun*
Biology the rhythmical contraction phase of the heartbeat. Compare DIASTOLE.
Word Family **systolic** (siss-**tol**-ik) *adjective*.
[Greek]

Tt

ta *interjection*
(*informal*) thank you.

tab *noun*
1 a small flap or loop on a garment, etc.
2 (*especially American informal*) a bill, e.g. in a restaurant.
3 *American* a ring pull.
Phrase **keep tabs on** to keep a check on.

tabard (tab-'d) *noun*
a piece of clothing made from a front and back piece, with no sleeves.

Tabasco *noun*
(*trademark*) a very hot sauce made from capsicums.
[name of a Mexican state]

tabby *noun* (*plural* **tabbies**)
a cat with a striped or brindled coat.

tabernacle (tab-a-nak-'l) *noun*
1 *Religion* a place of worship.
2 *Roman Catholicism* an ornamental recess or cabinet for consecrated bread and wine at the Eucharist.
[Latin *tabernaculum* tent, booth]

table *noun*
1 a piece of furniture which has a flat top and is supported by legs.
2 an orderly arrangement of data, usually shown in rows and columns.
3 the sequential listing of the multiples of a number: *the seven times table*.
Phrase **turn the tables** to cause a complete reversal of circumstances.
• **table** *verb* Parliament to place a resolution, proposal, etc. on the table for discussion.
[Latin *tabula* a plank]

tableau (tab-lo) *noun* (*plural* **tableaux**)
(**tab**-loze)
a colourful scene, e.g. one represented by a group of actors in period costume.
[French]

tablecloth *noun*
a cloth used to protect or decorate a table.

table d'hôte (tah-bla **dote**) *noun*
a restaurant meal at a fixed price and offering no or limited choice of dishes. Compare À LA CARTE.
[French, the host's (choice of) food]

tableland *noun*
a large fairly flat area of highland, a plateau.

table napkin ⇨ SERVIETTE.

tablespoon *noun*
a large oval spoon used to serve or measure food.
Word Family **tablespoonful** *noun*.

tablet (**tab**-l't) *noun*
1 a small round solid preparation containing a medicine, etc.
2 a piece of soap.
3 a slab of stone, etc. bearing an inscription.

table tennis *noun*
an indoor game played on a table using small cork or wooden bats and a light plastic ball.

tableware *noun*
the crockery and cutlery used at meals.

tabloid (**tab**-loyd) *noun*
a small newspaper which usually emphasizes pictures and popular features. Compare BROADSHEET (definition 2).

taboo (ta-**boo**) *noun* also **tabu**
a social or religious custom banning something from being used or talked about.
• **taboo** *adjective*
1 banned by social custom.
2 sacred and therefore not used, talked about, etc.
[Tongan]

tabor (**tay**-ba) *noun*
Music a small drum struck with the fingers.
[Persian *tabira* a drum]

tabular (**tab**-yoo-la) *adjective*
1 arranged as a table or list.
2 having the form of a table or tablet.

tabulate (**tab**-yoo-late) *verb*
to arrange information in a table.
Word Family **tabulation** (tab-yoo-**lay**-sh'n) *noun*.

tachometer (ta-**kom**-i-ta) *noun*
an instrument used to measure the rate at which an engine is turning.
[Greek *takhos* speed + *-meter*]

tacit (**tass**-it) *adjective*
implied but not spoken.
Word Family **tacitly** *adverb*.
[Latin *tacitus* silent]

taciturn (**tass**-i-tern) *adjective*
saying very little.
Word Family **taciturnly** *adverb*;
taciturnity (tass-i-**ter**-ni-tee) *noun*.

tack[1] *noun*
1 a short sharp nail with a large flat head.
2 a long loose stitch used to fasten seams in preparation for more thorough sewing.
3 *Nautical* the direction in which a sailing boat is moving.
4 an approach or course of action: *This has not worked so let's try a different tack.*
Phrase **get down to brass tacks** to think about practical details or realities.
● **tack** *verb*
1 to fasten or attach with a tack.
2 to sew with long loose stitches.
3 to sail a boat in a series of zigzags.
Phrase **tack on** to add.

tack[2] *noun*
all the equipment used for horse riding, e.g. saddles and bridles.

tackle *noun*
1 any equipment, especially the rods, reels, etc. used in fishing.
2 a system of ropes, pulley blocks and hooks used for lifting.
3 the act of tackling, e.g. in football.
● **tackle** *verb*
1 to try to seize and pull down by force.
2 to try to deal with.
3 to speak to someone about a problem or difficult situation.

tacky[1] *adjective* (**tackier; tackiest**)
sticky or slightly adhesive to the touch.
Word Family **tackiness** *noun*.

tacky[2] *adjective* (**tackier; tackiest**)
(*informal*) lacking in taste or quality.
Word Family **tackily** *adverb*; **tackiness** *noun*.

taco (**tak**-o *or* **tah**-ko) *noun*
a Mexican dish consisting of a tortilla folded and filled with spiced meat or chicken.
[Mexican Spanish]

tact *noun*
the ability to appreciate the delicate or difficult nature of a situation and handle it without giving offence.
Word Family **tactful** *adjective* showing tact; **tactfully** *adverb*; **tactless** *adjective* lacking tact; **tactlessly** *adverb*; **tactlessness** *noun*.
[Latin *tactus* sense of touch]

tactic (**tak**-tik) *noun*
1 a plan or procedure for achieving a desired end.

2 (**tactics**) the art of organizing armed forces and operations in a war.
[Greek *taktos* arranged]

tactical *adjective*
intended or used to achieve small-scale local objectives: *tactical bombing*. Compare STRATEGIC (definition 2) under STRATEGY.
Word Family **tactically** *adverb*.

tactical vote *noun*
a vote for the person who is most likely to defeat the candidate whom one least wants to win, especially when one's ideal candidate has no chance of winning.

tactician (tak-**tish**-'n) *noun*
a person experienced in using tactics in the army, etc.

tactile (**tak**-tile) *adjective*
1 of or relating to the sense of touch.
2 able to be felt through touch.
[Latin *tactus* touched]

tadpole *noun*
the stage after the egg in the development of a frog before the growth of forelimbs and when it still has a tail.
[Middle English *tadde* toad + *poll* head]

tae kwon do (tie kwon **doh**) *noun*
a Korean martial art that is similar to karate.
[Korean]

taffeta (**taff**-i-ta) *noun*
a thin smooth fabric of shot silk, nylon, etc. that is rather stiff.
[from Persian]

tag[1] *noun*
1 a strip of paper, metal, etc. attached to something as a label.
2 a word applied as characteristic of a person.
3 an often quoted phrase, especially one from another language.
4 the hard part at the end of a cord, shoelace, etc.
5 an electronic device attached to something or someone, such as a criminal, so that their whereabouts can be monitored by computer.
● **tag** *verb* (**tags; tagging; tagged**)
1 to attach a tag to.
2 (*informal*) to follow closely.

tag[2] *noun*
a children's game in which one person chases the other players until he or she touches someone who then becomes the chaser.
● **tag** *verb* (**tags; tagging; tagged**).

tagliatelle (tal-yi-a-**tel**-i) *noun*
a form of pasta made in narrow strips.
[Italian]

tahini (ta-**hee**-ni) *noun* also **tahina** (ta-**hee**-na)
a thick paste made from sesame seeds, used in Middle Eastern cooking.
[Arabic]

t'ai chi ch'uan (tie chee **chwahn**) *noun* also **t'ai chi**
a Chinese martial art and system of physical exercises using slow controlled movements.
[Chinese]

tail *noun*
1 the hind part of an animal, especially when elongated and extending beyond the main part of the body.
2 something which has the shape or position of a tail: *the tail of a comet*.
3 the bottom or concluding part of anything: *The story had a sting in its tail*.
4 (**tails**) the side of a coin which does not bear the image of a head.
5 the lower hanging part of a shirt or coat.
6 (**tails**) (*informal*) a tailcoat, or a suit with a tailcoat.
7 (*especially American informal*) the buttocks.
8 (*informal*) a person secretly following and watching someone.
Phrase **turn tail** to run away.
● **tail** *verb* (*informal*) to follow and watch someone.
Phrase **tail off** to decrease gradually.

tailback *noun*
a long line of stationary or slow-moving vehicles caused by an obstruction in the road or heavy traffic.

tailcoat *noun*
a man's coat with a short front and two long tapering flaps at the back, worn on formal occasions.

tailgate *noun* also called **tailboard**.
a door or gate at the rear of an estate car, truck, etc., which may be folded open for loading or unloading the vehicle.

tailings *plural noun*
the waste material removed during the processing of mineral ores.

tailless *adjective*
having no tail.

tail light *noun* also called **tail lamp**.
a red light at the back of a motor vehicle.

tailor *noun*
a person who makes clothes, especially for men.
● **tailor** *verb*
1 to make, adapt or fit clothes.

2 to adjust, adapt or make for a specific purpose: *The author had tailored the book for an American market*.
[French *tailler* to cut]

tailor-made *adjective*
1 made by a tailor: *a tailor-made suit*.
2 designed for a particular need.

tailspin *noun*
the steep spinning descent of a stalled aircraft.

tailwind *noun*
a wind blowing in the same direction as a vehicle is travelling, thus increasing its speed. Compare HEADWIND.

taint *verb*
1 to affect slightly with something undesirable.
2 to pollute or spoil.
● **taint** *noun*.

take *verb* (**takes; taking; took; taken**)
1 to get into one's hands, possession or control: *Take this hammer*. □ *The army took the city*.
2 to catch: *You took me by surprise*. □ *She was taken ill last week*.
3 to bring or receive into some relation with oneself: *She was forced to take lodgers*. □ *It's time he took a wife*.
4 to adopt: *The god took the shape of a bull*. □ *The nun took a vow of silence*.
5 to admit or let in: *The boat was taking water fast*. □ *The car takes six passengers*.
6 to feel: *She seems to take pleasure in being nasty*.
7 to lead, carry or cause to go to another place: *The bus will take you to the city*. □ *Who took you to the ball?*
8 to perform, do, etc.: *We took a walk*. □ *Take careful aim*. □ *He took revenge*.
9 to understand or interpret: *Now, don't take this the wrong way*.
10 to win: *She took first prize*.
11 to require: *That takes courage*.
12 to accept: *She had taken a bribe*.
13 to begin to grow or germinate: *The seedlings took*.
14 to subtract: *If you take 3 from 6 you have 3 left*.
15 to consume: *You must take your medicine*.
16 to be taught a particular subject, or be examined in it: *I'm taking French and German*.
17 to consider: *I took him to be an honest man*.
Phrases **have what it takes** to have the qualities required for success, etc. **take after** to inherit from or resemble in

appearance, etc. **take against** to begin to dislike. **take down** to write down. **take in** 1 to provide lodging for. 2 to make a piece of clothing smaller. 3 to include. 4 to understand. 5 to trick or deceive. **take it** to assume: *You're coming too, I take it?* **take it or leave it** you can accept it or not, it is immaterial to me. **take off** 1 to stop working, etc. for: *Why don't you take an hour off?* 2 to leave the ground. 3 to imitate or mimic. **take on** 1 to hire. 2 to undertake to do something. 3 to start a fight with. **take out** 1 to remove or extract. 2 to obtain: *He took out a patent on his invention.* 3 to accompany or escort. 4 to vent one's anger, etc. **take over** to assume or acquire control. **take to** to become attracted to: *They took to each other right away.* **take up** 1 to raise or lift. 2 to make a piece of clothing shorter or smaller. 3 to begin or begin again. 4 to use or occupy: *The fridge takes up a lot of space.* 5 to accept: *to take up a cause.* □ *to take up an option.* **take up with** to begin an association, etc. with.

• **take** *noun*
1 the amount of something taken: *Today's take in the shop was £500.*
2 a scene filmed without stopping the camera.
Word Family **taker** *noun* a person who takes, especially one who accepts a bet, offer, etc.

takeaway *noun*
1 a restaurant or shop selling food which customers eat off the premises: *a Chinese takeaway.*
2 a meal from such a restaurant or shop.

take-home pay *noun*
the actual money received by an employee, after tax and other payments have been taken out.

take-off *noun*
1 the act of leaving the ground, especially by an aircraft.
2 a satirical imitation: *Everyone laughed at Rupia's take-off of the science teacher.*

takeover *noun*
an assuming of control, ownership, etc.

takings *plural noun*
money received by a shop, stall, etc.

talc *noun*
1 *Geology* a soft pale greenish-grey mineral (hydrous magnesium silicate), used as a lubricant or in talcum powder.
2 ⇨ TALCUM POWDER.
[from Persian]

talcum powder *noun*
short form is **talc** a form of the mineral talc that has been purified and perfumed, used on the skin to dry and soothe it.

tale *noun*
1 a story.
2 a deliberate lie.

talent *noun*
1 a natural or acquired ability, especially an outstanding one.
2 talented people: *The company is looking for new talent.*
Word Family **talented** *adjective* having talent; **talentless** *adjective*.
[Greek *talanton* a sum of money (through the biblical phrase 'hiding one's talents')]

talent scout *noun*
a person appointed to find and employ people who appear to have talent.

talisman (**tal-iz-man**) *noun*
an object worn because it is supposed to work wonders or bring good luck, due to its possessing and transmitting magic powers.
[Greek *telesma* a consecrated object]

talk (**tawk**) *verb*
1 to say things or communicate by words: *We talked about her trip.*
2 to gossip: *People will talk if we are seen together.*
3 to discuss: *Let's talk business.*
4 to persuade: *She talked me into having my hair cut.*
5 (*informal*) to criticize: *You can't talk after what you've done.*
Phrases **talk back** to answer impudently. **talk big** to boast. **talk down to** to speak condescendingly to. **talk over** to discuss.

• **talk** *noun*
1 a conversation.
2 a lecture or speech: *a talk on wild flowers.*
3 the subject of conversation: *the talk of the town.*
4 (**talks**) formal discussions.
Word Family **talker** *noun*.

talkative *adjective*
inclined to talk a great deal.
Word Family **talkatively** *adverb*; **talkativeness** *noun*.

talking-to *noun*
(*informal*) a scolding.

tall *adjective*
1 of more than average height.
2 having a height as specified: *How tall is your sister?*
3 unlikely, exaggerated: *a tall story.*
Word Family **tallness** *noun*.

tallboy *noun*
a tall chest of drawers mounted on short legs.

tallow (tal-o) *noun*
the melted fat of animals, especially cattle and sheep, used to make candles, soap, etc.

tally *noun* (*plural* **tallies**)
1 a score or account.
2 also **tally stick** (*formerly*) a stick on which notches were made to keep a count or score.
• **tally** *verb* (**tallies; tallying; tallied**)
1 to reckon or count.
2 to agree or correspond: *Do their answers tally?*

tally-ho *interjection*
a hunting cry signalling to hounds that a fox has been sighted.
[from French]

Talmud (tal-mud) *noun*
Judaism the books of traditional Jewish ceremonial and civil laws.
[Hebrew *talmudh* instruction]

talon (tal-on) *noun*
a claw, especially of a bird of prey.
[Latin *talus* ankle]

Tamagotchi (tam-a-goch-ee) *noun*
(*trademark*) an electronic toy representing a creature which the owner must look after as if it were a pet.

tamarind *noun*
1 a tropical tree used for timber.
2 the large edible fruit of this tree, consisting of a long pod with seeds and acid-tasting flesh.
[Arabic *tamr-hindi* Indian date]

tambour *noun*
1 a drum.
2 a frame consisting of two hoops to keep a section of material firm while embroidery is being worked.
[same root as TABOR]

tambourine (tam-ba-reen) *noun*
Music a small flat one-sided drum with small metal plates set in the side, which is hit or shaken to produce sound.

tame *adjective*
1 domesticated, not dangerous: *tame animals.*
2 lacking in excitement, dull: *a tame ending.*
Word Family **tame** *verb;* **tamer** *noun* a person who tames animals; **tamely** *adverb;* **tameness** *noun.*

tameable *adjective* also **tamable**
able to be tamed.

tam-o'-shanter (tam-a-shan-ta) *noun*
a soft round cap similar to a beret, worn in Scotland.

tamp *verb*
to press down or pack closer by firm repeated blows: *Tamp down the earth around the base of the seedlings.*

tamper *verb*
to interfere or meddle.
[alteration of TEMPER]

tampon *noun*
1 a plug of soft material placed in the vagina to absorb blood during menstruation.
2 *Medicine* a plug of absorbent material used to stop a wound or absorb blood, etc.
[French]

tan *verb* (**tans; tanning; tanned**)
1 to make a hide into leather, usually by soaking in any of a variety of substances, such as oak bark.
2 to brown a person's skin in the sun.
3 (*dated informal*) to beat or thrash.
• **tan** *noun*
1 a light reddish-brown colour.
2 the brown colour imparted to the skin by the sun's rays.
Word Family **tan** *adjective.*

tandem *noun*
a bicycle for two people, with two seats and sets of pedals.
Phrase **in tandem** together, or one behind the other.
• **tandem** *adverb* one behind the other.

> **Tandem** is Latin for 'at length' meaning 'eventually'. Someone in the 18th century jokingly called a carriage with two horses, one behind the other, a *tandem* as a play on the words 'at length'. In the late 19th century the name *tandem* was transferred to a bicycle with two seats, one behind the other.

tandoori (tan-doo-ri) *noun*
an Indian method of cooking meat, chicken or vegetables on a spit over charcoal in a clay oven, called a tandoor.
[Hindi]

tang *noun*
a sharp distinctive taste, flavour or smell.

tangent (tan-j'nt) *noun*
1 *Maths* any straight line touching a curve.
2 *Maths* a ratio of the length of the side

opposite an angle to the adjacent side of a right-angled triangle. *abbrev.* tan.
3 a sudden change of course.
Word Family **tangential** (tan-**jen**-sh'l) *adjective* 1 relating to a tangent. 2 only partially relevant.
[Latin *tangens* touching]

tangerine (tan-ja-**reen**) *noun*
1 a small orange citrus fruit with a loose skin.
2 a reddish-orange colour.
• **tangerine** *adjective*.
[after *Tangiers*, Morocco]

tangible (**tanj**-i-b'l) *adjective*
1 real or definite: *We need tangible evidence, not just theories.*
2 capable of being touched.
Word Family **tangibly** *adverb*;
tangibility (tanj-i-**bill**-i-tee), **tangibleness** *noun*.

tangle *verb*
1 to intertwine in a confused mass: *The wool became tangled as the cat played with it.*
2 (*informal*) to become involved in an argument or fight: *That's the last time I tangle with her!*
• **tangle** *noun*.

tango *noun*
1 a ballroom dance of Spanish-American origin with varied steps and turns.
2 the music for such a dance

tangram *noun*
a Chinese puzzle consisting of a square cut into seven pieces which can then be used to make other shapes.

tangy *adjective* (**tangier; tangiest**)
having a sharp distinctive flavour or smell.

tank *noun*
1 a large container for holding a liquid or gas.
2 a heavily armoured military vehicle with tracks and a powerful gun.

tanka (**tank**-a) *noun*
a Japanese poem based on haiku but having two additional lines usually with seven syllables each.
[Japanese *tan* short + *ka* song]

tankard *noun*
a large glass or pewter drinking vessel with a handle, sometimes having a hinged lid.

tanker *noun*
a ship, aircraft or road vehicle designed to carry liquid, such as oil, in bulk.

tanner[1] *noun*
a person who tans animal hides.

tanner[2] *noun*
(*formerly*) an informal word for an old British coin equal to 2·5 pence, no longer used.

tannery *noun* (*plural* **tanneries**)
a place where hides and skins are made into leather.

tannin *noun*
any of a group of complex substances found in plants and used in the making of ink and leather.

Tannoy *noun*
(*trademark*) a system used to make public announcements.

tantalize, tantalise *verb*
to tease or torment with or as if with something which is desired but out of reach.
Word Family **tantalizingly** *adverb*;
tantalization *noun*; **tantalizer** *noun*.
[after *Tantalus* in Greek mythology, who was punished by being made to stand in water which receded when he tried to drink, and under fruit-laden boughs which he could not reach]

tantalus *noun* (*plural* **tantaluses**)
a lockable stand for decanters.
[as for TANTALIZE]

tantamount *adjective*
equivalent in effect, value, force, etc.: *His manner was tantamount to rudeness.*
[Italian *tanto montare* to amount to so much]

tantrum *noun*
a sudden violent fit of bad temper.

Tao (*rhymes with* cow) *noun*
the Chinese philosophy of a principle which underlies the universe and which shows a way of behaving that is in harmony with the natural order.
Word Family **Taoism** *noun*; **Taoist** *noun, adjective*.
[Chinese]

tap[1] *verb* (**taps; tapping; tapped**)
to strike gently.
• **tap** *noun*
1 a gentle blow.
2 the sound this makes.
3 tap dancing.
4 (**taps**) ⇒ LAST POST.

tap[2] *noun*
1 a device for controlling the flow of a liquid or gas from a pipe, etc.
2 a plug for a cask, etc.
3 a tool for cutting an internal screw thread.

4 a device used to listen to someone's conversations.
Phrase on tap 1 ready to be drawn off and served, such as beer in a cask. 2 ready for immediate use.
• tap *verb* (taps; tapping; tapped)
1 to draw a liquid or gas from a container, etc.
2 to open the outlets of: *to tap a water main.*
3 to provide with a plug, etc.
4 to use or draw upon: *The reporter tapped all her usual news sources.*
5 to listen to secretly: *to tap a phone conversation.*
6 to make an internal screw thread.

tapas *plural noun*
light snacks or appetizers, eaten as part of Spanish cuisine, often with drinks.
[Spanish]

tap dance *noun*
a style of dancing in which metal heel and toe plates are attached to the shoes to produce tapping sounds.
Word Family tap-dance *verb*; tap dancer *noun*; tap-dancing *noun*.

tape *noun*
1 a narrow strip of fabric, paper, etc.
2 also **magnetic tape** a plastic ribbon coated with a magnetic substance and used to record sounds or pictures.
3 a string, etc. stretched across the finishing line in a race and broken by the winning contestant.
• tape *verb*
1 to record on tape.
2 to tie up or bind with tape.

tape deck *noun*
a piece of equipment on which audio tapes can be played.

tape measure *noun*
a long thin strip of fabric or metal, with measurements marked on it.

taper *verb*
to make or become gradually narrower at one end: *The blade tapered to a sharp point.*
Phrase taper off to become gradually less.
• taper *noun*
1 a long wick covered with wax, used to light candles or gas.
2 a slender candle.

tape recorder *noun*
a device using magnetic tape wound from one spool to another to record and reproduce sound.

Word Family tape recording *noun* a magnetic tape on which sound has been recorded; tape-record *verb*.

tapestry (tap-a-stree) *noun* (*plural* tapestries)
a fabric on which coloured threads are woven or stitched by hand to make a design.
[French *tapis* carpet]

tapeworm *noun*
a long flat worm that lives as a parasite in the intestine of some mammals, including human beings.

tapioca (tap-i-o-ka) *noun*
a granular substance made by drying cassava starch, used in puddings and soups.

tapir (tay-pa *or* tay-peer) *noun*
a large pig-like mammal with short legs and a long fleshy nose, found in South America and Malaysia.

tappet *noun*
a projecting part in a machine or engine which regularly comes into contact with another part, from or to which movement is passed.

taproot *noun*
Biology the main root of a plant, which gives off lateral roots: *A carrot is a taproot.*

tar¹ *noun*
1 a dark viscid substance obtained from the distillation of coal, wood, etc.
2 a similar substance formed when tobacco is burnt.
• tar *verb* (tars; tarring; tarred) to smear or cover with tar.
Phrase tar and feather to smear a person with tar and feathers as a form of punishment or ridicule.

tar² *noun*
(*dated informal*) a sailor.
[short form of TARPAULIN]

taramasalata (tarr-a-ma-sa-lah-ta) *noun* also **tarama** (tarr-a-ma)
a Greek appetizer consisting of a pinkish paste made from the roe of grey mullet or smoked cod.
[Modern Greek]

tarantella (ta-ren-tell-a) *noun* also **tarantelle** (ta-ren-tell)
1 a fast Italian dance usually for two people.
2 the music for such a dance.
[the dance was formerly believed to be a remedy for the bite of a *tarantula*]

tarantula (ta-**rant**-yoo-la) *noun*
1 a large hairy spider of America.
2 a large wolf spider of southern Europe.
[after *Taranto*, Italy]

tardy *adjective* (**tardier; tardiest**)
late or slow.
Word Family tardily *adverb*; **tardiness**
noun.
[from Latin]

tare¹ (tair) *noun*
the weight of a container, motor vehicle,
etc. without its load or contents.

tare² *noun*
a plant of the vetch family.

target *noun*
1 a board marked with circles or numbers
which people aim at in archery or
shooting.
2 an objective which someone is trying to
reach: *a target of 30 cars produced per week.*
□ *My target is to get grade A.*
3 a group of people aimed at: *target market.*
□ *target audience.*
• **target** *verb*
1 to make a target of: *targeting young people.*
2 to aim or direct: *targeting the benefits at
the poorest families.*

tariff *noun*
1 a customs duty imposed by a
government, especially on imported
goods.
2 a list of prices or charges, e.g. in a hotel.
[Arabic *tarif* notification]

tarmac (**tar**-mak) *noun*
1 ⇨ ASPHALT.
2 a road, airport runway etc. made of
asphalt.
[short form of *tarmacadam*, TAR +
MACADAM]

tarn *noun*
a small mountain lake.

tarnish *verb*
1 to make or become dull or discoloured:
*The metal had tarnished as a result of
oxidation.*
2 to spoil or make less respected: *The crime
tarnished the school's reputation.*
• **tarnish** *noun*.

tarot (*rhymes with* barrow) *noun*
a pack of 78 cards used to predict future
events.
[French]

tarpaulin (tar-**paw**-lin) *noun*
a large piece of tarred canvas or other
waterproof fabric used as a protective
covering.

tarpon *noun*
a huge game fish found in warm Atlantic
and Pacific waters.
[from Dutch]

tarragon (**tarr**-a-gon) *noun*
a herb with narrow green leaves used in
cooking.

tarry¹ (*rhymes with* marry) *verb* (**tarries;
tarrying; tarried**)
an old word meaning 'to wait or linger'.

tarry² (**tah**-ree) *adjective* (**tarrier;
tarriest**)
like or smeared with tar.

tarsal bone ⇨ ANKLE.

tarsier *noun*
a very small monkey-like primate with
large round eyes, found in the islands of
south-east Asia.

tarsus *noun* (*plural* **tarsi**) (**tar**-sie *or* **tar**-
si)
Anatomy the group of bones which join the
leg to the foot.

tart¹ *adjective*
1 sharp or sour in taste.
2 bitter or sarcastic: *a tart reply.*
Word Family tartly *adverb*; **tartness**
noun.

tart² *noun*
a sweet or savoury pie, especially a sweet
one without a top crust.

tart³ *noun*
(*informal*) an offensive word for a
prostitute or a woman who is
promiscuous.
• **tart** *verb*
Phrase tart up to decorate or make
attractive, especially cheaply.

tartan *noun*
a woollen woven fabric with checks of
different colours and sizes, associated with
different Scottish clans and localities.

tartar¹ (**tar**-ta) *noun*
1 a hard substance deposited on the teeth
from the saliva.
2 a deposit, impure potassium hydrogen
tartrate, formed when wine ferments.

tartar² *noun*
a savage or cruel person.
[after the *Tartars*, the Mongolian
tribesmen who conquered Asia and
eastern Europe under Genghis Khan in
the Middle Ages]

tartare sauce *noun* also **tartar sauce**
a cold sauce of mayonnaise, onions,
gherkins and capers, eaten with fish.

task *noun*
a piece of work, especially a difficult one.
Phrase **take to task** to blame or reprimand.

task force *noun*
1 *Military* a temporary joining of battalions or units under one commander for a particular operation.
2 a team or group formed for a particular task.

taskmaster *noun*
a person who assigns work, especially hard or heavy work, to others.

Tasmanian devil (taz-may-ni-an **dev**-il) *noun*
a marsupial with a big head, strong jaws and dark fur, found in Tasmania.

tassel *noun*
a knot of threads or cords with the ends left hanging, used for decoration.

taste *noun*
1 the sensation produced when food, etc. is put in the mouth or on the tongue.
2 the sense by which this is perceived.
3 a discernment or understanding of what is excellent or appropriate, in art, dress, manners, etc.
4 a small amount or mouthful: *Have a taste of this soup.*
5 a brief sample or experience: *a taste of working in an office.*
6 a liking: *She developed a taste for historical novels.*
• **taste** *verb*
1 to try or have some of a food or drink: *Do you want to taste the wine?*
2 to have a particular flavour: *These sandwiches taste of onion.*
3 to experience: *The dog had tasted freedom.*
Word Family **taster** *noun* someone who tastes food or drink, especially a person who tests it for quality.

taste bud *noun*
Anatomy any of numerous small structures inside the mouth, particularly on the tongue, which together form the organ of taste.

tasteful *adjective*
showing good taste, judgement or discernment: *His home had been decorated in a tasteful style.*
Word Family **tastefully** *adverb*; **tastefulness** *noun*.

tasteless *adjective*
1 having little or no flavour.
2 showing a lack of taste, judgement or discernment: *a tasteless remark.*

Word Family **tastelessly** *adverb*; **tastelessness** *noun*.

tasty (**tay**-stee) *adjective* (**tastier; tastiest**)
1 having a pleasing taste: *a tasty soup.*
2 (*informal*) attractive: *a new boy band with a tasty lead singer.*
Word Family **tastily** *adverb*; **tastiness** *noun*.

tattered *adjective*
torn or made up of tatters.

tatters *plural noun*
torn pieces of cloth, paper, etc.
Phrase **in tatters 1** torn, ragged. **2** ruined: *His career was in tatters.*

tatting *noun*
handmade lace made by knotting cotton or linen thread with a shuttle.

tattle *verb*
to gossip or reveal secrets.
Word Family **tattle** *noun*; **tattler** *noun*.

tattoo¹ *noun*
a permanent design put on the body by pricking the skin and marking it with dyes.
Word Family **tattoo** *verb*; **tattooist**, **tattooer** *noun*.
[Polynesian]

tattoo² *noun*
1 a rhythmic beating, tapping, etc., such as drum taps signalling troops to retire to their quarters in the evening.
2 a public military display of marching or music.
[Dutch *taptoe* close the tap (of beer casks)]

tatty *adjective* (**tattier; tattiest**)
(*informal*) shabby or tattered: *a tatty old coat.*

taught (tawt) the past tense and past participle of **teach**.

taunt (tawnt) *verb*
to provoke or make angry by insult, mockery, etc.
• **taunt** *noun* a taunting remark or action.
[French *tant pour tant* tit for tat]

Taurus (**taw**-rus) *noun*
Astrology a group of stars, the second sign of the Zodiac; the sign of the Bull.
[Latin]

taut (tawt) *adjective*
tightly pulled or strained, tense: *The rope was taut.* □ *My nerves were taut.*
Word Family **tautly** *adverb*; **tautness** *noun*; **tauten** *verb* to make or become tightly stretched.

tautology (taw-**tol**-a-jee) *noun* (*plural*
tautologies)
the needless use or repetition of a word or
idea in a sentence, which does not make
the meaning any clearer: *To say that
something is a 'free gift' is tautology.*
Word Family tautological (taw-ta-**loj**-i-
k'l) *adjective*.
[Greek *tautos* the same + *logos* word]

tavern *noun*
an old word for an inn or pub.
[from Latin]

taw *noun*
1 a large marble.
2 a game of marbles.

tawdry (taw-dree) *adjective* (**tawdrier;
tawdriest**)
cheap and gaudy.
Word Family tawdrily *adverb*;
tawdriness *noun*.
[short form of *tawdry lace*, which was an
alteration of *St Audrey's lace*, from *Audrey*,
a name for the patron saint of Ely where
cheap lace was sold at a fair]

tawny *noun*
a yellowish-brown colour.
● **tawny** *adjective* (**tawnier; tawniest**).
Word Family tawniness *noun*.

tax *noun* (*plural* **taxes**)
1 a sum of money claimed by a
government for its support and paid by
citizens on income and property or on
purchases.
2 a burden or oppressive strain: *a tax on
someone's patience.*
● **tax** *verb*
1 to claim tax from.
2 to pay the tax for a vehicle.
3 to make great demands on: *The race
taxed his strength.*
Word Family taxable *adjective* subject to
tax; **taxation** *noun* 1 the system of taxes.
2 money paid in tax.
[Latin *taxare* to estimate]

taxi (**tak**-see) *noun*
a car which may be hired with its driver; it
is usually fitted with a device (called a
taximeter) which calculates and indicates
the fare due.
● **taxi** *verb* (**taxies; taxiing** or **taxying;
taxied**) (of an aeroplane) to move slowly
along the ground before take-off or after
landing.
[French *taxe* a tariff]

taxidermy (**tak**-si-derm-i) *noun*
the art of preserving and stuffing animal
skins.

Word Family taxidermist *noun*.
[Greek *taxis* arrangement + *derma* skin]

taxonomy (tak-**sonn**-a-mee) *noun* (*plural*
taxonomies)
a process or system of classification.
Word Family taxonomic (tak-sa-**nom**-
ik) *adjective*.
[Greek *taxis* arrangement + *nomos* law]

T-bar *noun*
a type of ski lift.

T-bone *noun*
a cut of beef from the loin of the animal,
containing a T-shaped bone.

te (tee) *noun*
Music a note in the scale. ⇨ DOH.

tea *noun*
1 the dried leaves of an Asian shrub.
2 a drink made from these leaves brewed
in water.
3 a similar drink made by brewing: *herbal
tea.*
4 a meal taken in the late afternoon or
early evening.
[Chinese *ch'a*]

tea bag *noun*
a small paper or cloth packet containing
tea leaves, placed in boiling water to make
tea.

tea break *noun*
a rest from work to have tea, coffee, etc.,
usually in the middle of the morning or
afternoon.

teacake *noun*
a round currant bun, often toasted, sliced
in half and buttered.

teach *verb* (**teaches; teaching; taught**)
1 to impart knowledge, especially by
lessons: *Can you teach me how to juggle?*
□ *He teaches sixth-formers.*
2 to communicate the knowledge of: *She
teaches maths.*
3 to train.
4 to cause someone to learn by experience:
That will teach you not to touch nettles!
Word Family teacher *noun* a person who
teaches or instructs, especially one trained
to do so in a school, etc.; **teaching** *noun*
1 the work or profession of a teacher.
2 something which is taught.

> **!** Do not confuse *teach* with LEARN.

tea chest *noun*
a large wooden box in which tea is stored
or carried.

tea cloth *noun*
a tea towel.

teacup *noun*
a small cup for drinking tea.

teak *noun*
a large Asian tree with hard durable wood which is used for shipbuilding and making furniture.

teal *noun* (*plural* **teal** or **teals**)
a small freshwater duck.

team *noun*
1 an organized group of people doing something together, especially playing sport against another such group: *a football team.*
2 two or more horses harnessed together to pull a plough, etc.
● **team** *verb*
Phrase **team up** to work together.
Word Family **teammate** *noun* a person belonging to the same team as another.

teamwork *noun*
any combined effort or organized cooperation between a group of people.

teapot *noun*
a round pot, usually of china or metal, with a spout, lid and handle, in which tea is made or served.

tear¹ (teer) *noun*
a drop of salty fluid produced in glands in the eye, moistening the eye and usually released as a result of emotion.
Phrase **in tears** weeping.
Word Family **tearful** *adjective* 1 weeping or shedding tears. 2 causing tears; **tearfully** *adverb*; **tearfulness** *noun.*

tear² (tair) *verb* (**tears; tearing; tore; torn**)
1 to pull apart with force or violence: *He tore the page in two.*
2 to make an opening in by catching or pulling at violently: *The branch tore her shirt.*
3 to damage by stretching too much: *She had torn a ligament in her leg.*
4 to disrupt: *a country torn by fighting.*
5 (*informal*) to race or rush: *They tore down the road.*
Phrases **tear down** to destroy or demolish. **tear into** to attack without restraint. **tear oneself away** to leave even though one is very keen to stay. **tear up** to pull into pieces. **torn between** unable to choose between.
● **tear** *noun*
1 the act of tearing.
2 an opening caused by pulling apart.

tearaway (tair-a-way) *noun*
a person who is wildly uncontrollable.

tear gas (teer gas) *noun*
gas that strongly irritates and brings tears to the eyes, usually distributed as vapour or smoke.

tearing (tair-ing) *adjective*
violent or headlong: *a tearing hurry.*

tear jerker (teer jer-ker) *noun*
(*informal*) a film, play, story, etc. which is very sentimental.

tea room *noun*
a shop or restaurant where tea, etc. is served.

tease (teez) *verb*
1 to annoy, make fun of or raise the hopes of in a playful manner.
2 to separate fibres of wool, hair, etc. by pulling gently or combing.
Phrase **tease out** to find out information or the truth by searching through other information.
● **tease** *noun*
1 (*informal*) a person or thing that teases, puzzles or annoys.
2 (*informal*) the act of teasing.
Word Family **teasingly** *adverb.*

teasel (tee-z'l) *noun* also **teazel; teazle**
a plant with prickly leaves, stems and heads formerly dried and used to raise the nap of fabrics.

teaser *noun*
1 someone who teases.
2 (*informal*) a puzzle or difficult question.

tea set *noun*
the cups, saucers, plates, etc., usually with a matching pattern, used for serving tea.

teaspoon *noun*
a small oval-shaped spoon used for stirring tea, coffee, etc. and measuring quantities.

teat *noun*
1 *Anatomy* ⇨ NIPPLE.
2 the nipple-shaped mouthpiece of a baby's bottle.

tea towel *noun*
a cloth for drying dishes.

tea tree *noun* also **ti tree**
an Australasian shrub or tree with leaves that can be used for tea.

tea tree oil *noun*
an oil obtained from the tea tree, used as an antiseptic.

teazel ⇨ TEASEL.

teazle ⇨ TEASEL.

tech (tek) *noun*
(*informal*) a technical college.

technetium (tek-**nee**-shi-um) *noun*
a radioactive metal, the first element to be
made artificially, formed as a fission
product of uranium.
[Greek *tekhnetos* artificial]

technical (**tek**-ni-k'l) *adjective*
1 relating or belonging to technology or a
particular trade, science, etc.: *Building is a
technical skill.*
2 having specialized skill or knowledge,
especially scientific or mechanical: *a
technical adviser to the project.*
3 relating to the working of machines: *We
have a technical hitch.*
4 theoretical: *The suspect was released
because of a technical loophole.*
Word Family technically *adverb*.
[Greek *tekhnikos* skilful, workmanlike]

technical college *noun*
a college which provides courses in
technology, commerce, art, etc.

technicality (tek-ni-**kal**-i-tee) *noun* (*plural*
technicalities)
1 the fact of being technical.
2 a petty distinction, especially one based
only on theory.

technical knockout *noun*
Boxing a victory based on the referee's
decision to stop the fight because one
boxer is considered unable to continue.

technician (tek-**nish**-'n) *noun*
a person skilled in a particular process or
method, especially one requiring special
mechanical or scientific training.

Technicolor (**tek**-ni-kull-a) *noun*
(*trademark*) a process of making colour
films by superimposing the three primary
colours to produce a final colour print.

technique (tek-**neek**) *noun*
the particular method or procedure for
doing something: *The champion has an
unusual swimming technique.*

technocracy (tek-**nok**-ra-see) *noun*
(*plural* **technocracies**)
a government or social system based on
the organization of industry, etc. by
technical experts.
Word Family technocrat (**tek**-na-krat)
noun a member or supporter of a
technocracy.
[Greek *tekhné* art + *kratia* rule]

technology (tek-**noll**-a-jee) *noun* (*plural*
technologies)
the study of the application of science and
scientific knowledge, especially to
industry.

Word Family technological (tek-na-**loj**-
i-k'l) *adjective* relating to or resulting from
science or technology; **technologist** *noun*.
[Greek *tekhné* art + -*logy*]

techy ⇨ TETCHY.

tectonic (tek-**tonn**-ik) *adjective*
Geography relating to the structure of the
earth's crust or the processes within it.
tectonic plate any of the large pieces of
which the earth's crust is made. Tectonic
plates are constantly moving; where they
meet, earthquakes and volcanoes are
usually found.
[Greek *tekton* carpenter, builder]

teddy *noun* (*plural* **teddies**) also called
teddy bear.
a stuffed toy bear.

> The word **teddy** was named after
> President Theodore Roosevelt of
> America (1858-1919), whose nickname
> was *Teddy*. He was a keen bear-hunter
> and after a story about him sparing the
> life of a cub in Mississippi appeared
> in the press and in cartoons, a
> manufacturer began to make stuffed
> toy bears and got permission to call
> them *teddy bears.*

tedious (**tee**-di-us) *adjective*
tiresome or uninteresting, especially if
long: *a tedious speech.*
Word Family tediously *adverb*;
tediousness, tedium (**tee**-di-um) *noun*.
[Latin *taedium* weariness]

tee *noun*
1 *Golf* a level area of ground from which
the player first hits the ball for each hole.
2 *Golf* a wooden or plastic peg on which
the ball is placed for the first stroke.
● **tee** *verb* (**tees; teeing; teed**) *Golf* to
place the ball on a tee.
Phrases tee off to hit a golf ball from the
tee. **tee up** to place a golf ball on the tee.

teem¹ *verb*
to swarm or be full: *The playground teemed
with shouting children.*

teem² *verb*
to rain heavily.

teenager *noun*
a person who is over twelve but less than
20 years old.
Word Family teenage *adjective*; **teens**
plural noun the years of being a teenager.

teeny *adjective* (**teenier; teeniest**)
(*informal*) tiny.

teeny-bopper *noun*
(*informal*) a young teenager who is wildly enthusiastic about pop music and fashion.

teepee ⇨ TEPEE.

tee shirt ⇨ T-SHIRT.

teeter *verb*
to totter or wobble: *The glass teetered on the very edge of the table.*

teeth
the plural of **tooth**.

teethe (tee*th*) *verb*
to develop teeth.

teething ring *noun*
a hard circular disc on which babies may bite during teething.

teething troubles *plural noun* also called **teething problems**.
problems in the early stages of a project, etc.

teetotaller (tee-toe-t'l-a) *noun*
a person who abstains completely from alcoholic drinks.
Word Family **teetotal** *adjective*.
[*t-total* (emphatic repetition of *t*)]

Teflon *noun*
(*trademark*) a tough waxy plastic used in bearings and in articles requiring a non-adhesive chemically resistant surface, such as non-stick frying pans.

tektite *noun*
a small black glassy object thought to be formed from a meteorite impact.
[Greek *tektos* molten]

telecast (tel-i-kahst) *noun*
a television broadcast.
• **telecast** *verb* (**telecasts; telecasting; telecast; telecast** or **telecasted**).

telecommunications *plural noun*
(*used with singular verb*) the science or technology of communicating sounds, signals or pictures by wire or radio.
[*tele-* + COMMUNICATION]

teleconference *noun*
a conference held between people physically separated but communicating by computer links, video and telephone.

telegram (tel-i-gram) *noun*
a message sent by telegraph.

telegraph (tel-i-grahf) *noun*
a method, device or system for sending messages from a transmitter to a receiver, usually along electrical wires.
Word Family **telegraph** *verb* to send a message by telegraph; **telegraphy**
(tel-**eg**-ra-fee) *noun* the process of communicating by telegraph;
telegrapher *noun*; **telegraphic** (tel-i-**graff**-ik) *adjective*; **telegraphically** *adverb*.
[*tele-* + Greek *graphein* to write]

telekinesis (tel-i-kie-**nee**-sis *or* tel-i-kin-**ee**-sis) *noun*
the apparent movement of objects without physical means, as in levitation.
[*tele-* + Greek *kinesis* movement]

telemeter (tel-i-mee-ta *or* ti-**lem**-i-ta) *noun*
a device for recording information about something distant, such as the instruments on a space capsule which transmit measurements by radio from space back to earth.

teleology (tel-i-**oll**-a-jee) *noun*
the belief that events occur because they have a particular purpose.
Word Family **teleological** (tel-i-o-**loj**-i-k'l) *adjective*.
[Greek *teleos* end + -*logy*]

telepathy (ti-**lep**-ath-ee) *noun*
the communication of one person's thoughts to another, without using normal methods of communication.
Word Family **telepathic** (tel-i-**path**-ik) *adjective*.
[*tele-* + Greek *pathos* feeling]

telephone (tel-i-fone) *noun*
1 an apparatus for sending or receiving voice messages, usually along electrical wires.
2 the method or system of doing this.
• **telephone** *verb*
1 to speak to or contact by telephone.
2 to make a telephone call.
[*tele-* + Greek *phoné* a sound]

telephone box *noun* (*plural* **telephone boxes**)
an upright structure containing a public telephone.

telephone exchange *noun* also called **exchange**.
the equipment used to connect telephone lines when a call is made.

telephonist (ti-**leff**-a-nist) *noun*
a person who operates a telephone switchboard.

telephoto lens (tel-i-fo-to **lenz**) *noun* (*plural* **telephoto lenses**)
Photography a lens with a narrow viewing angle like a telescope, used for photographing distant objects.

teleprinter (tel-i-prin-ta) *noun*
a device similar to a typewriter, which
sends or receives messages by telegraph.

Teleprompter *noun*
American (*trademark*) an Autocue.

telescope (tel-i-skope) *noun*
an instrument that is used to make distant
objects appear nearer and larger.
• **telescope** *verb*
1 to slide together so that one part fits
inside another, as in a small telescope.
2 to condense or shorten: *The survey
telescopes her life's work into a few pages.*
Word Family **telescopic** (tel-i-**skop**-ik)
adjective.
[*tele-* + Greek *skopein* to look at]

teleshopping *noun*
a system of shopping conducted from
home using a computer and a telephone.

teletext (tel-i-tekst) *noun*
a system of broadcasting information (e.g.
news or weather forecasts) by printed text
which can be received on a modified
television set.

televangelist (tel-i-**vanj**-i-list) *noun* also
tele-evangelist
(*especially American*) an evangelical
preacher who uses television to preach his
or her message.

televise (tel-i-vize) *verb*
to make, send or receive pictures by
television.
[*tele-* + Latin *visus* seen]

television (tel-i-vizh-'n) *noun* short form
is **TV**
1 the use of cables or radio to send
pictures to a place where they are
reproduced by a receiver.
2 also **television set** an apparatus for
receiving these pictures.

teleworking *noun*
working from home using a computer and
a telephone to keep in touch with clients
and a central office.

telex *noun* (*plural* **telexes**)
1 a system of sending printed messages
using teleprinters.
2 a message sent or received using this
system.
[TEL(eprinter) + EX(change)]

tell *verb* (**tells**; **telling**; **told**)
1 to make known or give information,
especially by speaking: *Tell me your name.*
□ *She told me the news.*
2 to utter: *Don't tell lies.*
3 to order or instruct: *I told you to be quiet.*

4 to determine: *I couldn't tell whether she
was enjoying herself.*
5 to distinguish: *I can't tell which twin is
which.*
Phrases **all told** in all, in total. **tell off** to
scold severely. **tell on** to inform against.

teller *noun*
1 a person who tells: *the teller of a tale.*
2 a person who receives or pays out money
at a bank, etc.

telling *adjective*
impressive or effective: *a telling argument.*
Word Family **tellingly** *adverb.*

telltale *noun*
a person who reveals secrets or informs on
others.
• **telltale** *adjective* unconsciously
revealing.

telly *noun* (*plural* **tellies**)
(*informal*) television.

temerity (ti-**merr**-i-tee) *noun*
reckless boldness.
[from Latin]

temp *noun*
(*informal*) someone who works somewhere
temporarily, especially in an office.

temper *noun*
1 a particular state of mind: *a good temper.*
2 composure of mind: *He lost his temper.*
3 an angry mood: *She's always in a temper
on Mondays.*
4 a degree of hardness or elasticity of steel.
• **temper** *verb*
1 to soften or modify: *Temper your rashness
with common sense.*
2 *Metallurgy* to heat and then cool steel
quickly to bring it to the proper degree of
hardness.

tempera (tem-per-a) *noun*
1 a fast-drying paint, originally mixed with
egg yolk, but now mixed with other similar
substances.
2 a method of painting using this.
[Italian]

temperament (tem-pra m'nt) *noun*
the emotional nature of a person: *The shy
boy had a nervous temperament.*
Word Family **temperamental** (tem-
pra-**men**-t'l) *adjective* having quickly
changing moods, ideas, etc.;
temperamentally *adverb.*
[Latin *temperamentum* moderation]

temperance *noun*
total abstinence from alcoholic drink.

temperate (tem-pr't) *adjective*
1 moderate: *a temperate climate.*

2 relating to parts of the earth between the tropics and the Arctic and Antarctic Circles, with a clearly defined winter and summer: *the temperate zone.*
Word Family temperately *adverb;* **temperateness** *noun.*
[Latin *temperatus* kept within due measure]

temperature (tem-pri-cher) *noun*
1 a measure of how hot or cold something is.
2 an excessive degree of heat in the body: *She's in bed with a temperature.*

tempest *noun*
a violent storm.
Word Family tempestuous (tem-**pess**-tew-us) *adjective* violent, stormy or turbulent: *tempestuous weather.* □ *a tempestuous period of history;* **tempestuously** *adverb;* **tempestuousness** *noun.*
[Latin *tempestas* a season, (stormy) weather]

template (tem-plit *or* tem-playt) *noun*
also **templet**
1 a thin plate of metal, plastic, etc. used as a guide or gauge for cutting something out or in mechanical work.
2 something used as a model.

temple¹ *noun*
a building used for worship.
[Latin *templum* a place set apart]

temple² *noun*
Anatomy the area on the side of the head, just next to the eye.

tempo *noun* (*plural* **tempos** *or* **tempi** (tem-pee))
speed or pace: *Play the music at a brisk tempo.*
[Latin *tempus* time]

temporal (tem-pa-r'l) *adjective*
1 of or relating to time.
2 of or relating to the present physical world as distinct from eternal or spiritual things.
Word Family temporally *adverb.*
[Latin *temporis* of time]

temporal bone *noun*
Anatomy either of two bones just above the ears, forming the side of the skull.
[Latin *temporis* of the temple]

temporary (tem-pra-ree) *adjective*
intended or lasting for a short time only.
Word Family temporarily *adverb;* **temporariness** *noun;* **temporary** *noun* (*plural* **temporaries**) short form

(*informal*) is **temp** a person in a temporary job.

temporize, temporise *verb*
to be indecisive or evasive to gain time.

tempt *verb*
to persuade or try to persuade someone to do something regarded as against his or her right or proper judgement.
Word Family temptation (temp-**tay**-sh'n) *noun* 1 the act of tempting. 2 the state of being tempted: *I yielded to temptation.* 3 something which tempts or attracts: *The money was too great a temptation to resist;* **tempter** *noun* a person who tempts, especially to do wrong; **temptress** *noun* (*plural* **temptresses**) a female tempter.
[Latin *temptare* to test by probing]

ten *noun*
a cardinal number, the symbol 10 in Arabic numerals, X in Roman numerals.
Word Family ten *adjective;* **tenth** *noun, adjective.*

tenable (ten-a-b'l) *adjective*
able to be held or maintained: *The job is tenable for twelve months.* □ *New evidence makes your theory less tenable.*
Word Family tenability (ten-a-**bill**-i-tee) *noun.*
[French *tenir* to hold]

tenacious (ti-**nay**-shus) *adjective*
sticking or holding on firmly and persistently.
Word Family tenaciously *adverb;* **tenacity** (ti-**nass**-i-tee), **tenaciousness** *noun.*
[Latin *tenax* holding fast]

tenant (ten-'nt) *noun*
a person who rents a house, land, etc.
Word Family tenancy (ten-'n-see) *noun* (*plural* **tenancies**) 1 the holding or use of property as a tenant. 2 the period of a tenant's occupancy.
[Latin *tenens* holding]

tench *noun* (*plural* **tench**)
a freshwater fish resembling the carp.

Ten Commandments *plural noun*
Judaism, Christianity the laws summarizing duties to God and fellow human beings, delivered to Moses on Mount Sinai and set down in the Bible (Exodus 20:1-17).

tend¹ *verb*
1 to have a bias towards doing something: *She tends to swear when she is angry.*
2 to have a certain attitude or characteristic: *I tend to agree with you.* □ *Puddings tend to be sweet.*
[Latin *tendere* to stretch]

tend² *verb*
to mind or attend to.
[from ATTEND]

tendency (ten-d'n-see) *noun* (*plural*
tendencies)
a movement, leaning or bias towards doing
something: *He has a tendency to mumble.*

tendentious (ten-**den**-shus) *adjective*
1 having a definite bias or underlying
purpose.
2 not impartial.
Word Family **tendentiously** *adverb*;
tendentiousness *noun*.

tender¹ *adjective*
1 not hard or tough: *tender meat.*
2 gentle, affectionate: *tender kisses.*
3 sensitive, painful: *Her knee was still tender.*
4 young: *at the tender age of three.*
Word Family **tenderly** *adverb*;
tenderness *noun*.
[Latin *tener*]

tender² *verb*
to offer or present formally: *I tendered my
resignation.*
• **tender** *noun* an offer, especially one to
provide goods or services, which includes
detailed estimates of the total cost: *We
called for tenders to build the bridge.*
[Old French *tendre* to stretch]

tender³ *noun*
1 a person who looks after or tends:
a bartender.
2 something which attends or supplies,
such as a small wagon carrying fuel and
water for a locomotive.
[from ATTEND or TEND]

tender-hearted *adjective*
easily moved to pity or sympathy.
Word Family **tender-heartedness** *noun*.

tenderize, tenderise (tend-a-rize) *verb*
to beat or add chemicals to meat to make
it tender.

tendon *noun*
Anatomy a dense cord of tissue joining a
muscle to a bone.
[Greek *tenon*]

tendril *noun*
1 *Biology* a slender specialized leaf or stem
used by climbing plants to attach
themselves to a support.
2 a thin lock or curl of hair.
[Latin *tener* tender]

tenement (ten-a-m'nt) *noun*
a large house or building divided into flats.
[Latin *tenere* to hold]

tenet (ten-et) *noun*
a belief, principle or doctrine.
[Latin, he holds]

tenner *noun*
(*informal*) a ten-pound note.

tennis *noun*
a ball game for two or four people played
on a court divided by a central net over
which the ball is hit with rackets.
[Old French *tenez!* receive!]

tennis elbow *noun*
a pain in the elbow joint due to excessive
or unaccustomed movement of the arm or
wrist, as in playing tennis.

tenon ⇨ MORTISE.

tenon saw *noun*
a short saw used for cutting accurate
angles.

tenor¹ (ten-a) *noun*
1 *Music* the adult male singing voice
between countertenor and baritone.
2 *Music* an instrument having the second
or third lowest pitch in its family: *a tenor
recorder.*

tenor² *noun*
the general sense or meaning of
something. *Don't report the whole speech,
just give us the tenor of it.*

tenpin bowling *noun*
a game in which a ball is rolled along a
long track in an attempt to knock over the
bottle-shaped objects, called **tenpins**,
arranged in a triangle at the other end.

tense¹ *adjective*
1 tightly stretched or strained.
2 nervous and unable to relax: *She was
tense for days before the job interview.*
Word Family **tense** *verb* to make or
become stiff or tense; **tensely** *adverb*;
tenseness *noun*.
[Latin *tensus* stretched]

tense² *noun*
Grammar the way a verb changes its
endings to show the time at which an
action takes place.

tensile *adjective*
1 of or relating to tension.
2 capable of being stretched.

tension (ten-sh'n) *noun*
1 the state or degree of being tense: *the
tension of a guitar string.*
2 a strained state, e.g. between people.
3 *Physics* a force which tends to stretch a
body.

tent *noun*
a shelter, usually made of waterproof canvas or plastic, held up by poles and with the sides pinned to the ground with ropes and pegs.
[Latin *tensus* stretched]

tentacle (tent-i-k'l) *noun*
a long flexible outgrowth on an organism, e.g. an octopus, used as an organ of touch or attachment.

tentative (tent-a-tiv) *adjective*
1 provisional or experimental: *The agreement is only tentative.*
2 hesitant: *The baby took a few tentative steps.*
Word Family tentatively *adverb*; **tentativeness** *noun*.

tenterhooks *plural noun*
Phrase on tenterhooks in a state of suspense.
[from *tenter*, a frame on which fabric is stretched on hooks to dry]

tenuous (ten-yew-us) *adjective*
1 weak or flimsy: *The old man only had a tenuous hold on life.*
2 fine, delicate: *tenuous clouds.*
Word Family tenuously *adverb*; **tenuousness** *noun*.
[Latin *tenuis* thin]

tenure (ten-yoor) *noun*
the holding or possession of something: *The tenure of office of chairman is twelve months.* □ *She signed the lease and now has tenure of the house.*
[Latin *tenere* to hold]

tepee (tee-pee) *noun* also **teepee; tipi**
a tent of animal hides or bark used by some American Indians.

tepid (tep-id) *adjective*
moderately warm.
Word Family tepidly *adverb*; **tepidity** (tep-**id**-i-tee), **tepidness** *noun*.
[from Latin]

tequila (tek-ee-la) *noun*
a Mexican alcoholic drink made from a cactus-like plant.

tercentenary (ter-sen-**tee**-na-ree) *noun*
(*plural* **tercentenaries**)
a 300th anniversary.
Word Family tercentennial (ter-sen-**ten**-i-al) *adjective*.
[Latin *ter* thrice + CENTENARY]

term *noun*
1 a fixed or definite period of time: *a school term.* □ *serving a term of imprisonment.*
2 a condition: *The treaty was signed when its terms were finally agreed on.*

3 a word or phrase: *Legal terms are sometimes hard to understand.* □ *She speaks of you in warm terms.*
4 (**terms**) a particular relationship: *on good terms with his neighbours.* □ *They are not on speaking terms now.*
Phrases come to terms to become accustomed: *He had come to terms with his deafness.* **in terms of** as expressed by, in the language of.
• **term** *verb* to name or call: *I'd term your behaviour sheer vandalism.*
Word Family termly *adjective, adverb*
once a term: *a termly maths test.*
[Latin *terminus* a boundary]

termagant (term-a-gant) *noun*
a noisy quarrelsome woman.

> The word **termagant** is now used of women but it came into English in reference to men. In medieval times, miracle or mystery plays were popular and these had several stock characters; one of these was called *Termagant*, a violent, blustering, imaginary Muslim deity.

terminable (term-in-a-b'l) *adjective*
able to be terminated.

terminal *noun*
1 a building at a bus terminal, airport, etc.
2 *Electricity* either of the points at which electric current enters or leaves an electrical device.
3 *Computers* a display unit and keyboard connected to a computer.
• **terminal** *adjective*
1 of, situated or occurring at the end: *The twig had small terminal buds.*
2 likely to lead to death: *terminal cancer.*

terminate *verb*
to end: *The bus terminates here.* □ *I am terminating your contract.*
[Latin *terminare* to set bounds to]

termination (term-i-**nay**-sh'n) *noun*
1 the act of ending.
2 the state of being ended.
3 the place where something ends.

terminology (term-i-**noll**-a-jee) *noun*
(*plural* **terminologies**)
the special words used in a particular field of study.

terminus *noun* (*plural* **terminuses** or **termini** (term-i-nie))
the end of anything, especially either of the ends of a railway line, bus or air route, etc.
[Latin]

termite *noun*
any of a group of soft-bodied tropical insects, not related to ants, which cause damage to wooden buildings, furniture, etc.
[Latin *tarmes* a woodworm]

tern *noun*
a seabird related to the gull, having a slender body, long wings and graceful flight.

ternary (**tern**-a-ree) *adjective*
formed from or consisting of three.
[Latin *term* three each]

terotechnology (terr-o-tek-**nol**-a-jee) *noun*
the branch of technology which relates to the efficient operation and maintenance of machinery and equipment.
[Greek *tereo* to watch]

terrace (**terr**-us) *noun*
1 an open outdoor living area, usually paved, connected to a house.
2 one of a series of raised strips of land with vertical or sloping banks which rise one above the other, e.g. one of a series cut into a hillside and used for growing crops.
3 a row of joined houses.
• **terrace** *verb* to form or provide with a terrace or terraces.
[Italian *terrazza*]

terracotta (terr-a-**kot**-a) *noun*
1 a type of pottery, usually reddish in colour and unglazed, fired to low temperatures.
2 a small sculpture in this material.
3 a strong reddish-brown colour.
• **terracotta** *adjective*.
[Italian, baked earth]

terra firma (terr-a **fir**-ma) *noun*
dry land.
[Latin, solid earth]

terrain (terr-**ane**) *noun*
the shape or physical features of the land surface: *rough terrain*.

terrapin (**terr**-a-pin) *noun*
any of a group of freshwater edible North American turtles.
[Amerindian]

terrazzo (terr-**at**-so) *noun*
a floor covering made of small pieces of polished stone set into concrete.
[Italian]

terrestrial (t'-**rest**-ri-'l) *adjective*
of or relating to the earth or land.
[from Latin]

terrible *adjective*
1 very bad or serious: *He died in terrible agony.* □ *She was accused of terrible crimes.*
2 causing terror: *The thing gave a terrible howl.*
Word Family terribly *adverb* 1 in a terrible manner: *He upset me terribly.*
2 very: *I'm terribly late.*

terrier *noun*
any of various breeds of small dog, originally bred to pursue game into its hole or burrow: *a fox terrier.* □ *a wire-haired terrier.*
[Latin *terra* earth]

terrific (t'-**rif**-ik) *adjective*
1 terrible or terrifying: *a terrific storm.*
2 (*informal*) very good: *a terrific book.*
Word Family terrifically *adverb*.

terrify (**terr**-i-fie) *verb* (**terrifies;**
terrifying; terrified)
to fill with terror or make extremely afraid: *The baby was terrified by the fireworks.*

territorial (terr-i-**taw**-ri-'l) *adjective*
relating to land or territory: *Cats are territorial animals.*

territorial waters *plural noun*
the area of sea around the coast of a country and controlled by it.

territory (**terr**-i-tree) *noun* (*plural* **territories**)
1 any land, region or district.
2 the land under the control of a state or ruler.
3 (**Territory**) a region administered by the central government of its own or another country, but having some degree of autonomy.
4 the area which an animal claims as its own and will defend against intruders.
[from Latin]

terror *noun*
1 intense or extreme fear: *The trapped animal bristled with terror.*
2 (*informal*) a nuisance: *My sister is a real terror.*
[Latin]

terrorism (**terr**-a-rizm) *noun*
the use of violence or threats to generate fear, especially for political purposes.
Word Family terrorist *noun* a person who uses or favours the use of terrorism.

terrorize, terrorise (**terr**-a-rize) *verb*
to fill with terror.
Word Family terrorization (terr-a-rie-zay-sh'n) *noun*.

terse *adjective*
short and to the point.

Word Family **tersely** *adverb;* **terseness**
noun.
[Latin *tersus* polished]

tertiary (**tersh-a-ree**) *adjective*
1 third.
2 relating to activity which provides
services to people, e.g. health or
education: *tertiary industry.* □ *tertiary
occupations.* Compare PRIMARY *adjective*
(definition 3); SECONDARY (definition 2).
• **Tertiary** *noun* a geological period which
extended from about 65 million years ago
to about 1·5 million years ago.
[Latin *tertius* third]

tertiary education *noun*
education beyond the level received at
school, e.g. at a college or university.

Terylene (**terr-a-leen**) *noun*
(*trademark*) a synthetic polyester fibre used
in clothing, etc.

tessellate (**tess-a-layt**) *verb*
Maths (of shapes) to fit together in a
repeating pattern without any gaps or
overlapping.
Word Family **tessellated** *adjective;*
tessellation (tess-a-**lay-sh'n**) *noun.*
[from Latin]

test *noun*
1 a trial or procedure to determine quality,
ability, composition, etc.: *an intelligence
test.* □ *a blood test for disease.*
2 *Sport* a test match.
• **test** *verb.*
[Latin *testa* a pot in which metals were
tested]

testament *noun*
1 *Law* a will.
2 (**Testament**) either of the collections of
books which form the Bible, the Old
Testament and the New Testament.
[from Latin]

testate (**test-ate**) *adjective*
Law having left a valid will. Compare
INTESTATE.

testator (test-**ay**-ter) *noun*
a person who has made a will.

test case *noun*
Law a case which establishes a precedent
which can be referred to later in similar
cases.

tester *noun*
a person or thing that tests.

testicle (**test-i-k'l**) *noun*
Anatomy either of two rounded organs in
male mammals, suspended below the
trunk in the scrotum, producing sperm.

testify (**test-i-fie**) *verb* (**testifies;
testifying; testified**)
1 to give evidence: *The witness testified that
he saw the crime.*
2 to serve as evidence: *The murder weapon
testifies to your guilt.*
[Latin *testis* a witness + *facere* to make]

testimonial (test-i-**mo-nee-'l**)
noun
1 a written statement testifying to the
quality of someone or something.
2 something done or given as a mark of
esteem, appreciation, etc.
[Latin *testimonium* evidence]

testimony (**test-i-m'-nee**) *noun* (*plural*
testimonies)
1 a statement or evidence, such as that
given in a court of law.
2 something that is evidence or proof.

testis *noun* (*plural* **testes**) (**test-eez**)
an organ that produces sperm, especially a
testicle.
[Latin]

test match *noun* (*plural* **test matches**)
Sport a match between teams representing
two countries, especially in cricket or
rugby.

testosterone (test-**ost**-a-rone) *noun*
the hormone made in the testes of
animals, producing male secondary sexual
characteristics.

test pilot *noun*
a pilot who flies newly designed aircraft in
order to test their qualities, performance,
etc.

test tube *noun*
a hollow cylinder of thin glass, closed at
one end and used in chemical tests.

test-tube baby *noun* (*plural* **test-tube
babies**)
(*informal*) a baby whose conception is
produced scientifically outside the
mother's body.

testy *adjective* (**testier; testiest**)
irritable or impatient.
Word Family **testily** *adverb;* **testiness**
noun.

tetanus (**tet-a-nus**) *noun*
an infectious bacterial disease, sometimes
fatal, which affects the nervous system,
causing severe muscle spasms.
[Greek *tetanos* a spasm]

tetchy *adjective* (**tetchier; tetchiest**) also
techy (**techier; techiest**)
irritable.
Word Family **tetchily** *adverb;* **tetchiness**
noun.

tête-à-tête (tate-ah-**tate** *or* tet-a-**tet**) *noun*
a private conversation, usually between
two people.
[French, head to head]

tether (**teth**-a) *noun*
a rope or chain by which an animal is tied
to a tree, fence, etc. to limit its movements.
Phrase **at the end of one's tether** at the
end of one's patience or endurance.
● **tether** *verb*.

tetracycline (tet-ra-**sigh**-kleen *or* tet-ra-
sigh-klin) *noun*
any of a group of drugs used as antibiotics
to overcome bacterial infections.

tetrahedron (tet-ra-**hee**-dr'n *or* tet-ra-
hed-r'n) *noun* (*plural* **tetrahedrons** *or*
tetrahedra)
a solid or hollow body with four triangular
faces; a triangular pyramid.
Word Family **tetrahedral** *adjective*.
[*tetra-* + Greek *hedra* a base]

tetralogy (tet-**rall**-a-jee) *noun* (*plural*
tetralogies)
a series of four related plays, operas,
literary compositions, etc.
[*tetra-* + *-logy*]

text *noun*
1 the actual words of something written or
printed.
2 the main body of words in a book,
magazine or newspaper, excluding
footnotes, index, etc.
3 a short extract or quotation used as the
subject of a lecture, sermon, etc.
Word Family **textual** (**teks**-tew-'l)
adjective.
[Latin *textus* literary style]

textbook *noun*
a book giving instruction and information
in a subject.

textile *noun*
a fabric which is made by weaving,
knitting, bonding or other methods.
textile technology the study of how
textile products are designed and made.

texture (**teks**-cher) *noun*
the composition or structure of a
substance, especially as conveyed to the
sense of touch.
Word Family **textural** *adjective*;
texturally *adverb*.
[Latin *textus* woven]

textured vegetable protein *noun*
a vegetable substance made from soya
beans, used as a meat substitute.

thalidomide (tha-**lid**-a-mide) *noun*
a drug formerly used as a sedative until it
was found to damage a fetus if taken
during pregnancy.

thallus *noun* (*plural* **thalli**) (**thall**-eye *or*
thall-ee)
Biology a simple vegetative plant body
which is not divided into root, stem and
leaf.
[Greek *thallos* young shoot, twig]

than *preposition, conjunction*
introducing the second part of a
comparison: *I am older than you.*

thane *noun*
History a person who held land in
exchange for military service.

thank *verb*
to express thanks to.

thankful *adjective*
1 pleased, relieved: *She was thankful that no
one had been hurt.*
2 showing gratitude: *The villagers offered up
a thankful prayer when the rains finally
came.*
Word Family **thankfully** *adverb*;
thankfulness *noun*.

thankless *adjective*
1 not appreciated: *Housework is a thankless
task.*
2 not feeling or showing gratitude.
Word Family **thanklessly** *adverb*;
thanklessness *noun*.

thanks *plural noun*
a grateful acknowledgement of a favour,
gift, etc.
Phrase **thanks to** as a result or
consequence of.
● **thanks** *interjection* thank you.

thanksgiving *noun*
1 the grateful acknowledgement of favours
or benefits, especially to God.
2 (**Thanksgiving**) a day of holiday
celebrated in America to give thanks to
God.

thank you *interjection*
an expression of gratitude.
● **thank you** *noun*.

that *pronoun* (*plural* **those**)
1 a demonstrative pronoun used to
indicate the person, place, thing, etc.
present or just mentioned.
2 a demonstrative pronoun used to
indicate the person, place, thing, etc.
further removed or less obvious: *that red
chair over there!*
3 a relative pronoun used to introduce a
clause: *There is the man that I saw.*

4 something: *There is that about the man which intrigues me.*
Phrases **at that** *She won, and won easily at that* (= as well). **that is** in clarification or example. **that's that** that is the finish of the matter. **with that** *and with that she burst into tears* (= immediately afterwards).
• **that** *conjunction*
1 used to introduce a clause stating a fact, wish, reason, etc.: *I thought that I was late.*
2 used to introduce a sentence or clause expressing desire, surprise, etc.: *That it should come to this!*
Word Family **that** *adjective*; **that'll** *contraction* a short form of **that will**; **that's** *contraction* a short form of **that is.**

thatch *noun (plural **thatches**)*
a roof covering made from straw, reeds, etc.
• **thatch** *verb* to cover a roof with thatch.

thaw *verb*
1 to melt.
2 (of weather) to become warm enough to melt ice and snow.
3 to become friendlier.
• **thaw** *noun*
1 the process of thawing.
2 a period during which ice and snow melt.

the¹ *article*
Grammar the definite article. See ARTICLE (definition 2).

the² *adverb*
(used to modify an adjective or adverb in the comparative degree) to that extent: *the sooner the better.*

theatre (thee-a-ta) *noun (American **theater**)*
1 a building where plays, ballet or opera are performed on a stage.
2 any similar room or place where particular actions are performed: *a lecture theatre.* □ *an operating theatre.*
3 the world or profession of actors, playwrights, etc.
4 any dramatic writing or performance.
5 (*especially American*) a cinema.
6 a place of action: *the theatre of war.*
[Greek *theatron* seeing place]

theatrical (thee-at-ri-k'l) *adjective*
1 of or relating to the theatre.
2 exaggerated or artificial.
Word Family **theatricals** *plural noun* dramatic performances, especially as given by amateurs; **theatrically** *adverb.*

thee (thee) *pronoun*
an old word meaning 'you' (singular).

theft *noun*
the act of stealing.

their *possessive adjective (singular **her**, **his** or **its**)*
belonging to them: *It is their cake.*

> [!] The words *their*, *there* and *they're* sound the same but have different spellings and meanings. *Their* means 'of them' (*their house*); *there* means 'in or to that place' (*the house over there*); *they're* is a short form of *they are* (*They're in the house*). ⇨ THEY.

theirs *possessive pronoun (singular **hers**, **his** or **its**)*
belonging to them: *The cake is theirs.*

> [!] Note that there is no apostrophe in *theirs.*

theism (thee-izm) *noun*
a belief in a supernaturally revealed God, especially one with whom a personal relationship is possible, and in Providence. Compare DEISM.
Word Family **theist** *noun*; **theistic** (thee-ist-ik) *adjective.*
[Greek *theos* a god]

them *pronoun (singular **her**, **him** or **it**)*
the objective form of **they**: *We hit them.*
□ *Give the cake to them.*

> [!] ⇨ THEY.

theme *noun*
a central topic, basis or idea which is expressed, expanded, etc., as in a speech, essay or musical composition: *What is the main theme of the book?*
Word Family **thematic** (thee-mat-ik) *adjective.*
[from Greek]

theme park *noun*
an amusement park in which the structures and settings are all related to a specific theme.

themself *pronoun*
(*informal*) themselves: *Everyone can help themself.*

> [!] *Themself* is sometimes used instead of *themselves* (or *himself* or *herself*) to refer to a person of unspecified sex, but many people think this is wrong. ⇨ THEY.

themselves *pronoun*
1 the reflexive form of **they**: *They washed themselves.*
2 the emphatic form of **they**: *They did it themselves.*

3 having their normal or usual selves: *For many weeks after the accident they were not themselves.*

then *adverb*
1 at another time in the past or future: *I was happier then.*
2 next in time, space or order: *I stayed in Hong Kong first and then went to Singapore.*
3 in that case; accordingly.
4 in addition: *and then you must remember to buy some vegetables.*
Phrases **but then** but on the other hand. **then and there**, **there and then** at once, on the spot.
● **then** *adjective* being so at that time: *the then President.*
● **then** *noun* that time: *Since then he has not looked back.*

thence (*thence*) *adverb*
1 from that time or place.
2 for that reason.
Word Family **thenceforth**, **thenceforward** *adverb* old or poetic words meaning 'from that time or place onward'.

theocracy (thee-**ok**-ra-see) *noun* (*plural* **theocracies**)
1 a system of government in which the established Church has political power.
2 a government by a god, either directly or through a class of priests.
Word Family **theocratic** (thee-o-**krat**-ik) *adjective.*
[Greek *theos* a god + *kratia* rule]

theodolite (thee-**odd**-a-lite) *noun*
a surveyor's instrument resembling a small telescope, used for measuring horizontal and vertical angles.

theology (thee-**oll**-a-jee) *noun*
the study of divinity or religious doctrines, such as the characteristics of a god or gods in relation to people and the universe.
Word Family **theological** (thee-a-**loj**-i-k'l) *adjective*; **theologically** *adverb*; **theologian** (thee-a-**lo**-j'n) *noun* a person teaching or having knowledge of theology.
[Greek *theos* a god + *-logy*]

theorem (**theer**-um) *noun*
1 a general proposition the truth of which is demonstrable by argument.
2 *Maths* a general law in the form of an equation or formula, e.g. in algebra, used as a basis for further operations.
[Greek *theorema* speculation]

theoretical (thee-a-**ret**-i-k'l) *adjective*
1 relating to theory: *theoretical knowledge.*

2 based on theory: *It's a theoretical possibility.*
Word Family **theoretically** *adverb.*

theoretician (thee-a-ret-**ish**-'n) *noun*
a person who deals with the theoretical side of a subject.

theorist *noun*
a theoretician.

theorize, theorise *verb*
to form a theory or theories about something.

theory (**theer**-ee) *noun* (*plural* **theories**)
1 a systematically organized group of general propositions used to analyse, predict or explain facts or events.
2 an explanation of the principles of a subject, such as art, as distinct from the practice of it.
3 a conjecture or opinion: *That's your theory, but I disagree.*
[Greek *theoros* a spectator]

theosophy (thee-**oss**-a-fee) *noun*
any religious or philosophical system of thought claiming direct knowledge of divine or supernatural things.
Word Family **theosophist** *noun*; **theosophical** (thee-o-**sof**-i-k'l) *adjective.*
[Greek *theos* a god + *sophia* wisdom]

therapy (**therr**-a-pee) *noun* (*plural* **therapies**)
1 the treatment of disease or physical disorders.
2 the psychological treatment of problems of the mind.
Word Family **therapist** *noun* a person trained to practise therapy; **therapeutic** (therr-a-**pew**-tik) *adjective* **1** relating to the treatment or curing of disease. **2** having the power to heal or cure.
[from Greek]

there *adverb*
1 in or at that place: *The book is there, where I left it.*
2 to, into or towards that place: *Let's go there now.*
3 at a particular point of time, action, etc.: *She paused there and asked if we understood.*
● **there** *interjection* an exclamation of satisfaction, encouragement, etc.: *There! I've finished!*

> ❗ Do not confuse *there* with THEIR.

thereabouts *adverb* also **thereabout**
near that place, time, number, etc.: *at 7 p.m. or thereabouts.*

thereafter *adverb*
(*formal*) from a particular time onwards.

thereby *adverb*
(*formal*) by that means: *She fell and thereby lost the race.*

therefore *adverb*
for that reason.

therein *adverb*
(*formal*) in that place, matter, etc.

thereof *adverb*
(*formal*) of, from or relating to that.

thereon *adverb*
(*formal*) on or upon that.

there's *contraction*
a short form of **there is** or **there has**: *There's no need to cry.*

thereto *adverb*
(*formal*) to that place, subject, etc.

thereupon *adverb*
(*formal*) immediately after, especially as a result.

therm *noun*
a unit of energy, equal to 100 000 British thermal units.
[Greek *thermé* heat]

thermal *adjective*
1 of or relating to heat or temperature.
2 providing good insulation: *a thermal vest.*
• **thermal** *noun* a rising current of warm air.
Word Family **thermally** *adverb.*

thermal expansion *noun*
the expansion of a solid as its temperature increases.

thermal power *noun*
electricity produced by burning fossil fuels.

thermionic valve *noun*
Electronics a radio valve which contains a heated cathode.

thermistor (ther-**mist**-a) *noun*
Electricity a small device whose electrical resistance varies with temperature.
[THERM(al) + (res)ISTOR]

thermocouple (ther-mo-kup-'l) *noun*
Electronics a device consisting of two different conductors joined at each end, used for measuring temperature. An electric current is generated if the temperature of one junction changes with respect to the other.

thermodynamics (ther-mo-die-**nam**-iks) *plural noun*
(*used with singular verb*) the branch of physics studying the relationships between heat and work and the conversion of one to another.

Word Family **thermodynamic**, **thermodynamical** *adjective*; **thermodynamically** *adverb.*

thermometer (ther-**mom**-it-a) *noun*
an instrument used to measure temperature.

thermonuclear (ther-mo-**new**-kleer) *adjective*
Physics using a nuclear reaction which occurs only at high temperature, such as nuclear fusion: *a thermonuclear missile.*

thermoplastic *noun*
any of a group of plastics with properties which allow them to be re-formed after initial shaping.

Thermos *noun* (*plural* **Thermoses**)
(*trademark*) a double-walled container with a vacuum between, usually of silvered glass or stainless steel, used to keep substances at a constant temperature.

thermosetting plastic *noun*
any of a group of plastics which cannot be reheated and re-formed into new shapes after initial moulding.

thermosphere (ther-mo-sfeer) *noun*
the outer regions of the earth's atmosphere where the temperature continues to increase towards the sun.

thermostat *noun*
any of various devices used to control temperature.
Word Family **thermostatic** (ther-mo-**stat**-ik) *adjective*; **thermostatically** *adverb.*
[Greek *thermé* heat + *statos* stationary]

thesaurus (tha-**saw**-rus) *noun* (*plural* **thesauruses** or **thesauri** (tha-**saw**-rie))
a book of words and phrases grouped according to meaning.
[Greek *thesauros* treasure]

these
the plural of **this**.

thesis (**thee**-sis) *noun* (*plural* **theses** (**thee**-seez))
a statement or theory, especially a long original work presented by a student for a postgraduate degree.
[Greek, putting]

thespian (**thes**-pi-an) *adjective*
of or relating to drama, especially tragedy.
• **thespian** *noun* an actor.
[after *Thespis*, a Greek poet in the 6th century B.C.]

thew *noun* also **thews**
a poetic word for muscle, or physical strength.

they (thay) *pronoun* (*singular* **he**, **it** or **she**)
1 the third person plural nominative pronoun, used to indicate people or things: *They ate the cake.* ⇨ THEIR; THEIRS; THEM.
2 used to indicate people in general: *They say he is guilty.*
Word Family they'd *contraction* a short form of **they had** or **they would**; **they'll** *contraction* a short form of **they will**; **they're** *contraction* a short form of **they are**; **they've** *contraction* a short form of **they have**.

> ! Do not confuse *they're* with THEIR.

> ! *They, them, their*, etc. are sometimes used to refer to a person of unspecified sex, as in *Everyone should do their best* (instead of *his best* or *his or her best*), but some people think this is wrong.

thiamine (thigh-a-min) *noun* also
thiamin
vitamin B₁.

thick *adjective*
1 having relatively great extent from one surface or side to its opposite: *a thick wall in a castle.*
2 measuring in this dimension: *a wall 1 m thick.*
3 closely packed: *thick undergrowth.*
4 heavy: *a thick jumper.*
5 filled: *The room was thick with smoke.*
6 dense: *thick fog.*
7 having a firm consistency: *thick paint.*
8 (*informal*) stupid.
9 very pronounced: *a thick Scottish accent.*
10 (*informal*) intimate: *as thick as thieves.*
• **thick** *noun* (**the thick**) the most active or intense part: *I was caught in the thick of the crowd.*
Phrase through thick and thin under all circumstances.
Word Family thickly *adverb*; **thickness** *noun* (*plural* **thicknesses**); **thicken** *verb*
1 to make or become thick or thicker.
2 to make or grow more intense or complex; **thickening** *noun* **1** a thickened part or place. **2** something used to thicken.

thicket *noun*
a small group of shrubs or trees growing very close together.

thickset *adjective*
having a short stocky body.

thief (theef) *noun* (*plural* **thieves**) (theevz)
a person who steals, especially secretly and without force.

thieve (theev) *verb*
to steal.
Word Family thievery (thee-va-ree) *noun*; **thievish** *adjective*.

thigh *noun*
Anatomy the upper part of the leg or hind limb.

thimble *noun*
a small metal or plastic cap used to protect the end of the finger when sewing.
Word Family thimbleful *noun* a very small quantity.

thin *adjective* (**thinner**; **thinnest**)
1 having relatively little extent from one surface or side to its opposite: *The thin ice cracked under her weight.*
2 not great in diameter or cross section: *a thin wire.*
3 lacking in substance, especially because worn: *thin socks.*
4 not fleshy or fat: *a thin face.*
5 sparse: *thin vegetation.*
6 liquid: *thin paint.*
7 weak, inadequate: *a thin excuse.* □ *thin evidence.*
Word Family thinly *adverb*; **thinness** *noun*; **thin** *verb* (**thins**; **thinning**; **thinned**) to make or become thin or thinner.

thine (thine) *possessive pronoun*
an old word meaning 'yours' (singular).

thing *noun*
1 a material object lacking life or consciousness.
2 something which cannot be described or named exactly: *It had a thing on the end like a tassel.*
3 (**things**) possessions or belongings: *I packed a few things and left.*
4 (**things**) the general state of affairs: *How are things?*
5 a person: *You poor thing!*
6 an aspect or area: *One thing about the situation was not considered.*
Phrases do one's own thing to do what one likes or does best. **have a thing about** to have an unaccountable attitude or feeling about. **make a thing of** to turn into a major issue. **one of those things** an event which was unavoidable.

think *verb* (**thinks**; **thinking**; **thought**)
1 to use the mind to form ideas, judgement, etc.
2 to consider: *They're thinking about moving to the country.*
3 to have an opinion: *What did you think of the book?*

4 to remember: *I couldn't think what I'd done with my keys.*
5 to believe: *She thought I was joking.*
Phrases **think big** to have great ambitions. **think twice** to consider with great care.
Word Family **thinker** *noun*; **think** *noun* (*informal*) an act of thinking; **thinking** *noun* opinion, conclusions.

think tank *noun*
a government organization or private company which tries to forecast economic or other trends and give advice on long-term policies.

thinner *noun*
a liquid added to a substance to dilute it, such as turpentine added to paint.

third *adjective*
1 being number three in a series.
2 being one out of every three: *We get paid every third week.*
● **third** *noun*
1 any of three equal parts into which something is divided.
2 a person or thing that is number three in a series.
Word Family **thirdly** *adverb*.

third degree *noun*
the prolonged or intense questioning of someone or the use of violence to obtain information, etc.

third party *adjective*
relating to a policy which insures against liability or damage to another person or his or her property in a motor accident.
● **third party** *noun* any person other than the principals involved in an agreement, etc.

third person ⇨ PERSON (definition 3).

third-rate *adjective*
distinctly inferior.

Third World *noun*
the countries of the world that are outside the main industrial economies of Europe, America, Asia and Australasia.

thirst *noun*
1 a dryness of the mouth and throat leading to a desire to drink liquid.
2 a strong desire: *a thirst for adventure.*
Word Family **thirst** *verb*.

thirsty *adjective* (**thirstier; thirstiest**)
1 needing liquid or moisture.
2 eager for something: *The crowd were thirsty for details.*
Word Family **thirstily** *adverb*;
thirstiness *noun*.

thirteen *noun*
a cardinal number, the symbol 13 in Arabic numerals, XIII in Roman numerals.
Word Family **thirteen** *adjective*;
thirteenth *adjective, noun*.

thirty *noun* (*plural* **thirties**)
1 a cardinal number, the symbol 30 in Arabic numerals, XXX in Roman numerals.
2 (**thirties**) the numbers 30 to 39 in a series, such as the years in a century.
Word Family **thirty** *adjective*; **thirtieth** *adjective, noun*.

this (*this*) *pronoun* (*plural* **these**) (*theez*)
1 a demonstrative pronoun used to indicate the person, place, thing, etc. present, nearby or just mentioned.
2 a demonstrative pronoun used to indicate the person, place, thing, etc. nearer or more obvious: *This chair is nicer than that one over there.*
● **this** *adjective, adverb*.

thistle (**thiss**-'l) *noun*
a wild plant with prickly leaves and fluffy flowers.

thistledown *noun*
the fluff of a thistle flower, which carries the seeds.

thither (**thith**-er) *adverb*
an old or poetic word meaning 'to or towards that place or point'.

thong *noun*
1 a narrow strip of leather used for fastening things, etc.
2 a pair of underpants or a swimming costume in a very skimpy style like a G-string.

thorax (**thor**-aks) *noun* (*plural* **thoraxes** or **thoraces** (**thor**-a-seez))
1 the upper part of the trunk of a mammal between the neck and abdomen, containing the heart and lungs.
2 a corresponding part in birds, reptiles, fish, insects, etc.
Word Family **thoracic** (thor-**ass**-ik) *adjective*.
[Greek]

thorn *noun*
a small sharp outgrowth on a plant.
Phrase **thorn in one's side** a source of annoyance or discomfort.

thorny *adjective* (**thornier; thorniest**)
1 having many thorns.
2 difficult or complex: *a thorny issue.*

thorough (**thurr**-a) *adjective*
1 full, perfect or complete: *Give the back of your neck a thorough scrubbing.*
2 working methodically and leaving nothing incomplete.
Word Family **thoroughly** *adverb*; **thoroughness** *noun*.

thoroughbred *noun*
any of a breed of racehorses bred from English and Arabian stock.
● **thoroughbred** *adjective* of pure stock or breed.

thoroughfare *noun*
a road or route.

thoroughgoing *adjective*
1 methodical, detailed.
2 complete.

those
the plural of **that**.

thou (thou) *pronoun*
an old word meaning 'you' (singular).

though (tho) *conjunction*
1 in spite of the fact that: *I disagree, though I see your point.*
2 if: *Act as though you didn't hear.*
● **though** *adverb* however.

thought[1] (thawt) *noun*
1 the act or process of thinking: *She sat in thought.*
2 the result of thinking: *a clever thought.*
3 care, concern: *She left the gate open, with no thought for the consequences.*
4 the ideas or way of thinking of a particular time, place, group, etc.
Phrases **have second thoughts** to reconsider and change one's mind.
on second thoughts after some consideration. **without a second thought** without much consideration.

thought[2] the past tense and past participle of **think**.

thoughtful *adjective*
1 showing or full of thought: *a thoughtful suggestion.*
2 attentive or careful, especially towards others.
Word Family **thoughtfully** *adverb*; **thoughtfulness** *noun*.

thoughtless *adjective*
1 showing little or no thought: *a thoughtless answer.*
2 selfish or inconsiderate.
Word Family **thoughtlessly** *adverb*; **thoughtlessness** *noun*.

thousand *noun* (*plural* **thousands** or **thousand**)
a cardinal number, the symbol 1000 in Arabic numerals, M in Roman numerals.
Word Family **thousand** *adjective*; **thousandth** *adjective, noun*.

thrall (thrawl) *noun*
a slave.
Phrase **in thrall to** under the power of.
Word Family **thraldom** *noun* slavery.

thrash *verb*
1 to beat soundly, especially as punishment.
2 to move violently: *He thrashed about in the water.*
3 (*informal*) to defeat easily.
Phrase **thrash out** to solve or decide by discussion.
[alteration of THRESH]

thread (thred) *noun*
1 a long fine piece of a spun substance.
2 something with the shape of a thread, such as a thin line of colour, etc.
3 also **screw thread** a spiral ridge cut around the length of a bolt or screw.
● **thread** *verb*
1 to pass a thread through.
2 to move in a twisting or winding way: *She threaded her way through the crowd.*
3 to cut a thread on or in a bolt, hole, etc.

threadbare *adjective*
very worn or thin: *a threadbare carpet.*

threadworm *noun*
a thread-like worm found in the human intestine, usually in children.

threat (thret) *noun*
1 a statement of intention to hurt or punish, especially in order to force someone to do something: *She only paid the money under threat of violence.*
2 someone or something likely to be harmful, dangerous, etc.
3 the possibility of something dangerous or bad: *a threat of rain.*

threaten *verb*
1 to utter a threat against: *She threatened me with dismissal unless I behaved.*
2 to put at risk: *The school was threatened with closure.* □ *His career as a footballer was threatened by the knee injury.*

three *noun*
a cardinal number, the symbol 3 in Arabic numerals, III in Roman numerals.

three-dimensional (three-di-**men**-sh'n-al) *adjective*
1 having or appearing to have the dimension of depth.

2 realistic: *The book's main characters are three-dimensional.*

three-legged race *noun*
a running race in which pairs of competitors have their adjacent legs tied together.

three-point landing *noun*
a landing in which all three sets of wheels of an aeroplane touch the ground at the same time, considered a perfect landing.

three-point turn *noun*
a turning of a car in a narrow road in three moves.

threnody (thren-a-dee) *noun* (*plural* **threnodies**)
a funeral dirge.
[Greek *threnos* wailing + *oidé* an ode]

thresh *verb*
to separate the seeds of a cereal plant from the chaff.

thresher *noun*
a person or thing that threshes, especially a flail or machine.

threshold (thresh-hold) *noun*
1 the entrance to a building, especially the stone, etc. laid in front of a door.
2 the lowest level at which a stimulus will produce an effect: *the threshold of consciousness.*
3 the beginning of something: *on the threshold of a new career.*

threw the past tense of **throw.**

thrice *adverb*
an old or poetic word meaning 'three times'.

thrift *noun*
careful or economical use, especially of money.
Word Family **thrifty** *adjective* (**thriftier**; **thriftiest**) using thrift; **thriftily** *adverb*; **thriftiness** *noun*.

thrift shop *noun* also called **thrift store.**
American a shop which sells second-hand clothes and whose proceeds usually go to charity.

thrill *noun*
1 a nervous tremor or tingle of great excitement: *It gave him a thrill to ride the camel.*
2 an experience causing this: *It's a thrill to meet you.*
• **thrill** *verb* to feel or cause a thrill in: *Winning the race thrilled me.*

thriller *noun*
a book, play or film dealing with exciting or mysterious events.

thrips *noun* (*plural* **thrips**) also **thrip**
a very small sap-sucking insect which may be destructive to cereals and fruit trees.
[Greek, woodworm]

thrive *verb* (**thrives; thriving; thrived** or **throve; thrived** or **thriven**)
to grow strong and healthy: *The garden cannot thrive in this drought.*

throat *noun*
1 the oesophagus.
2 the front part of the neck.
Phrases **jump down someone's throat** to criticize someone severely. **stick in someone's throat** to be hard to accept.

throaty *adjective* (**throatier; throatiest**)
1 hoarse.
2 produced deep in the throat.
Word Family **throatily** *adverb*; **throatiness** *noun*.

throb *verb* (**throbs; throbbing; throbbed**)
1 to beat with a strong or rapid rhythm.
2 to pulsate, e.g. with pain: *My head was throbbing.*
• **throb** *noun* a strong beat or rhythm.

throes *plural noun*
violent pains or convulsions: *The wounded person was in his death throes.*
Phrase **in the throes of** 1 in violent struggle with. 2 in the process of.

thrombosis (throm-bo-sis) *noun* (*plural* **thromboses**) (throm-bo-seez)
the formation of a stationary clot which develops inside a blood vessel and blocks the flow of blood.
[Greek *thrombos* a lump + *-osis*]

throne *noun*
1 a raised ornamental chair used on important occasions, e.g. by a monarch.
2 sovereign power or authority: *The republicans sought abolition of the throne.*
[Greek *thronos* a high seat]

throng *noun*
a crowd: *Throngs of people watched the procession.*
• **throng** *verb* to crowd: *Thousands thronged to the beaches last summer.*

throttle *verb*
1 to choke or strangle.
2 to reduce the speed of an engine.
• **throttle** *noun* a device in the carburettor of an internal-combustion engine, connected to the accelerator pedal, which controls engine speed.

through (throo) *preposition*
1 in one side and out the other: *Climb through the window.* □ *The road goes through the jungle.*
2 between: *Tarzan swinging through the trees.*
3 from beginning to end: *You talked through the whole speech.* □ *Look through the book for the answer.*
4 due to or because of: *She succeeded through hard work.*
5 *American* up to and including: *Monday through Friday.*
• **through** *adverb*
1 from side to side or beginning to end: *Let us pass through.* □ *She slept the night through.*
2 at or to the end or all the way: *Are you through with this book?* □ *The train goes through to Perth.*
3 connected by telephone: *I'll put you through to the manager.*
• **through** *adjective*

throughflow *noun*
Geography the movement of water through the soil.

throughout (throo-**out**) *preposition*
1 in or to every part: *Search throughout the countryside.*
2 from the beginning to the end of: *She slept throughout the film.*
• **throughout** *adverb*
1 in every part: *The house has carpet throughout.*
2 at all times: *The baby cried throughout.*

throve a past tense of **thrive**.

throw *verb* (**throws; throwing; threw; thrown**)
1 to send forcibly through the air, especially by a movement of the arm: *Don't throw stones at the dog.*
2 to put as if by throwing: *Throw him into prison.* □ *We were thrown into confusion.*
3 to aim: *She threw a punch at him.*
4 to disconcert: *The answer threw him completely.*
5 to project or cast: *to throw a shadow.* □ *to throw your voice.*
6 to have: *She always throws a tantrum when she doesn't get her own way.*
7 (*informal*) to give: *He throws great parties.*
8 to make on a potter's wheel.
Phrases **throw away** *You've thrown away a wonderful opportunity* (= wasted). **throw in** *We paid for the coach tour and the meals were thrown in* (= included free of charge). **throw off** to free oneself from. **throw out** 1 *They threw out the proposal* (= did not

accept or keep). 2 *He threw out a hint* (= uttered casually). 3 *The noise threw me out in my counting* (= caused to make a mistake). **throw up** 1 to vomit.
2 to abandon.
• **throw** *noun*
1 the act of throwing: *She returned the ball with a fine throw.* □ *a throw of the dice.*
2 a light cover for furniture.

throwaway *adjective*
1 intended to be thrown away after use.
2 uttered casually with apparent disregard for effect: *a throwaway remark.*

throwback *noun*
1 a reversion to an ancestral type or character.
2 an example of this.

thrush¹ *noun* (*plural* **thrushes**)
a brown songbird with a spotted breast.

thrush² *noun*
a fungal disease of mucous membranes, especially in the mouth of a child.

thrust *verb* (**thrusts; thrusting; thrust**)
to push suddenly or forcibly: *He thrust the sword into his opponent's heart.* □ *The girl thrust her way through the crowd.*
• **thrust** *noun* the act of thrusting: *a sword thrust.* □ *the forward thrust of a jet engine.*

thud *noun*
a dull sound, as of a heavy blow or fall.
• **thud** *verb* (**thuds; thudding; thudded**)
to strike or fall with a thud.

thug *noun*
a brutal violent ruffian or criminal.
Word Family **thuggish** *adjective*; **thuggery** *noun*.

> The word **thug** is derived from Hindi where it means 'a robber' or 'a swindler'. In India it came to be applied to members of a religious sect who robbed and strangled people. *Thug* was adopted into English in the early 19th century meaning 'a violent brutal person'.

thulium (**thew**-li-um) *noun*
a rare metal.

thumb (thum) *noun*
1 *Anatomy* the short thick digit set apart from the fingers.
2 the part of a glove, etc. covering the thumb.
Phrases **all thumbs** clumsy or awkward. **thumbs down** an expression of disapproval. **thumbs up** an expression of approval or triumph. **under someone's**

thumb under someone's power or influence.

• **thumb** *verb*
1 to turn pages, etc. over quickly: *I thumbed through the catalogue.*
2 (of a hitch-hiker) to solicit a free ride.
Phrase **thumb one's nose** to express defiance or contempt.

thumbnail sketch *noun* (*plural* **thumbnail sketches**)
a brief concise description.

thumbscrew *noun*
1 an instrument of torture designed to crush one or both thumbs.
2 a screw which can be twisted into a surface by the thumb and finger.

thump *verb*
to beat heavily, especially with a thick dull sound.

• **thump** *noun*
1 a heavy strike or blow.
2 the dull sound of this.

thunder *noun*
1 the loud noise produced when the heat from lightning causes the air to expand suddenly.
2 any loud noise.
Phrase **steal someone's thunder** to steal the credit of someone else's ideas, inventions, policy, etc.

• **thunder** *verb*
1 to make thunder.
2 to speak or act loudly or violently: *She thundered on the door with her fists.*
Word Family **thunderous, thundery** *adjective;* **thunderously** *adverb.*

thunderbolt *noun*
a flash of lightning accompanied by thunder.

thunderclap *noun*
a crash of thunder.

thunderstorm *noun*
a storm in which strong upward air currents generate static electricity, producing thunder and lightning.

thunderstruck *adjective*
amazed or astounded.

Thursday *noun*
the fifth day of the week, after Wednesday and before Friday.
[after *Thor*, the ancient Scandinavian god of thunder]

thus (*th*us) *adverb*
1 (*formal*) in this way: *Watch me and do it thus.*
2 (*formal*) consequently: *Thus, after all the evidence, I must be right.*

thwack *verb*
to whack.
• **thwack** *noun.*

thwart (thwort) *verb*
to prevent something being done successfully: *The police thwarted the attempted bank robbery.*
• **thwart** *noun* a seat across a small boat.

thy (*th*y) *possessive adjective*
an old word meaning 'your' (singular).

thyme (time) *noun*
a low shrub with fragrant leaves used in cooking.
[from Greek]

thymus (**thigh**-mus) *noun* (*plural* **thymi**) (**thigh**-my)
Anatomy a gland, large in children but very small in adults, situated near the base of the neck.
[Greek *thymos* the soul]

thyroid *noun* also **thyroid gland**
Anatomy a gland in the lower neck, secreting hormones which control the metabolic rate of the body.
[Greek *thyreoeides* shield-shaped, oblong]

thyself *pronoun*
an old word meaning 'yourself'.

tiara (tee-**ar**-a) *noun*
a semicircular band of jewels, etc. worn as a head ornament.
[Greek]

tibia (**tib**-i-a) *noun* (*plural* **tibiae**) (**tib**-i-ee)
Anatomy the thicker of the two long bones of the lower leg.
[Latin]

tic *noun*
a twitch, especially of the facial muscles.
[French]

tick¹ *noun*
1 a light recurring click or beat, as of a clock or watch.
2 (*informal*) a moment.
3 a small written mark to show that something is correct, noted, etc.
• **tick** *verb* to make a tick or ticks: *The time bomb ticked away quietly.* □ *The customer ticked her list.*
Phrases **make someone tick** to make someone behave in a particular way. **tick off** to scold. **tick over** (of an engine) to run slowly and quietly in neutral.

tick² *noun*
a blood-sucking arachnid, often parasitic on mammals.

tick³ *noun*
  Phrase on tick on credit: *All their furniture was bought on tick.*
  [short form of *ticket*]

ticker *noun*
  1 (*informal*) a watch.
  2 (*informal*) the heart.

ticker tape *noun*
  the long strips of paper on which a tape machine prints information.
  ticker tape parade a parade in which ticker tape, streamers, etc. are thrown from windows.

ticket *noun*
  1 a small piece of cardboard or paper indicating that its owner is entitled to something: *a train ticket.* □ *a theatre ticket.*
  2 a tag or label showing price, etc.
  3 a fine or summons for a traffic offence: *a parking ticket.*
  4 (*especially American*) the list of candidates from any one party in an election.

ticking *noun*
  a strong cotton fabric used for covering mattresses, pillows, etc.

tickle *verb*
  1 to excite the nerves by lightly touching sensitive parts of the skin.
  2 to amuse or please: *The children were tickled by the antics of the clowns.*
  Phrase tickled pink greatly amused or pleased.
  • **tickle** *noun.*

ticklish *adjective*
  1 sensitive to tickling.
  2 needing delicate care or handling: *Are you able to handle such a ticklish situation?*

tidal (**tide**-al) *adjective*
  of or relating to the tide.

tidal basin *noun*
  Geography an area in which the water level rises and falls with the tide.

tidal wave *noun*
  a large destructive wave produced by an earthquake at sea.

tiddly *adjective* (**tiddlier; tiddliest**)
  (*informal*) slightly drunk.

tiddlywinks *plural noun* (*American* **tiddledywinks**)
  (*used with singular verb*) a game in which small discs must be flicked into a cup.

tide *noun*
  1 the rise and fall of the surface of the sea, caused by the gravitational pull of the sun and moon; the sea floods in to **high tide**

and ebbs out to **low tide** twice a day; the maximum and minimum range between the two occur twice a month, at **spring tide** and **neap tide** respectively.
  2 a stream or current, e.g. of public opinion.
  • **tide** *verb*
  Phrase tide over *Lend me some money to tide me over until I get paid* (= support).

tidemark *noun*
  1 the line of wrack and flotsam which marks the highest point of recent tides.
  2 a similar mark in a dirty bath.

tidings (**tide**-ingz) *plural noun*
  a poetic word for news or information.

tidy *adjective* (**tidier; tidiest**)
  1 having everything in its right place.
  2 in the habit of arranging things in their right place.
  3 (*informal*) large: *a tidy sum of money.*
  • **tidy** *verb* (**tidies; tidying; tidied**).

tie *verb* (**ties; tying; tied**)
  1 to fasten or attach by string, rope, etc.: *Tie the prisoner's hands.* □ *Tie this label to your case.*
  2 to form by interlacing, etc.: *to tie a knot.*
  3 to connect: *We are trying to tie him to the crime.*
  4 to score equally in a contest.
  Phrases tie in with to connect or agree with. **tie up 1** *She's tied up every night this week* (= occupied, busy). **2** *The agreement was finally tied up* (= concluded, settled). **3** *The strike tied up shipping for a month* (= hindered). **4** *He was tied up with the scandal* (= connected).
  • **tie** *noun*
  1 something which ties or connects: *a tie of friendship.*
  2 a strip of cloth, usually of cotton, silk or wool, worn around the neck under a collar and knotted at the front.
  3 an equality of votes, points, etc. between contestants.

tied house *noun*
  a pub owned by a brewery, whose brands it sells in preference to others. Compare FREE HOUSE.

tie-dye *verb* (**tie-dyes; tie-dyeing; tie-dyed**)
  to dye fabric or clothes by tying them in patterns of knots before applying the dye, so that the knotted areas are not coloured.

tier (**teer**) *noun*
  a row or level, especially one of a series rising one above or behind the other, as of seats in a theatre.

tie-up *noun*
an association or connection.

tiff *noun*
(*informal*) a slight quarrel.

tiger (**tie**-ga) *noun*
a large flesh-eating Asian mammal of the cat family, having a tawny coat with black stripes.
[from Greek]

tight *adjective*
1 fastened or fixed firmly.
2 fitting closely: *tight shoes.*
3 firm: *a tight grip.*
4 impervious to water, air, etc: *Is the boat watertight?*
5 stretched: *a tight elastic band.*
6 limited: *a tight space.* □ *a tight schedule.*
7 (*informal*) stingy.
8 (*informal*) drunk.
Word Family **tight, tightly** *adverb*; **tightness** *noun*; **tighten** *verb* to make or become tight.

tight-fisted *adjective*
(*informal*) miserly or stingy.

tight-lipped *adjective*
saying little or nothing.

tightrope *noun*
a rope or wire stretched high above the ground, on which an acrobat walks or performs tricks.

tights *plural noun*
a piece of clothing covering the bottom, legs and feet, made of nylon or wool.

tigress (**tie**-gress) *noun* (*plural* **tigresses**)
a female tiger.

tilde (**til**-da) *noun Language* ⇨ ACCENT.
[Spanish]

tile *noun*
1 a sheet, usually of baked clay, used in overlapping rows to form a roof, or glazed on one side and used to cover floors, walls, etc.
2 a flat piece used in certain games.
Phrase **on the tiles** on a spree.
Word Family **tile** *verb* to cover with tiles; **tiler** *noun* a person who lays tiles.

till[1] *preposition, conjunction*
until.

> [!] *Till* and *until* mean the same, but *till* is slightly more informal.

till[2] *verb*
to plough or cultivate the soil.

till[3] *noun*
a cash register or drawer for money.

tiller[1] *noun*
Nautical the handle attached to the top of a rudder for steering.

tiller[2] *noun*
a plough or implement for tilling.

tilt *verb*
1 to put in or move into a sloping position: *If you tilt the table the plates will fall off.*
2 to joust.
● **tilt** *noun*
1 the act of tilting.
2 a tilting position: *The table was at a tilt.*
Phrase **at full tilt** at top speed.

timber *noun*
1 wood which has been cut and treated, used in building, making furniture, etc.
2 the trees used for this.

timberline *noun*
(*especially American*) the treeline.

timbre (**tam**-br') *noun*
the characteristic quality of a sound produced by a particular voice or instrument.
[French]

time *noun*
1 the fact or concept of continuous existence.
2 a system of measuring or dividing this: *Greenwich Mean Time.*
3 a portion or measure of this, especially as a definite moment or period: *What time is it?* □ *Have you got time to help me?*
4 an instance: *How many times do I have to tell you?*
5 (**times**) used to indicate multiplication: *five times five.*
6 an experience: *We had a good time.*
7 a while: *She lived in France for a time.*
8 (*informal*) a prison sentence: *doing time for a burglary.*
9 the closing time of a pub.
10 *Music* the basic rhythmical patterns.
11 *Music* the length of a particular note.
Phrases **at the same time** *I'll give you my permission, but at the same time I think you're being foolish* (= nevertheless). **at times, from time to time** occasionally. **behind the times** old-fashioned. **have no time for** to be unable to tolerate. **in good time 1** *The pain will go away in good time* (= eventually). **2** *We arrived in good time and got the best seats* (= early). **in no time** very quickly. **in time 1** in the same rhythm. **2** early enough. **3** eventually. **mark time 1** to march on the spot. **2** to wait. **on time** punctually. **pass the time of day** to exchange brief greetings. **play for time** to manoeuvre to gain extra time.

race against time to try hard to finish in time. **take one's time** to act in a leisurely way.

• **time** *verb*
1 to record or measure the time of something: *The race was timed on a stopwatch.*
2 to arrange or choose the moment for: *We timed our holidays to coincide with the good weather.*

time-and-motion study *noun* (*plural* **time-and-motion studies**)
the analysis of work methods, to improve efficiency or increase production in a business.

time bomb *noun*
a bomb containing a mechanism that will cause it to explode at a set time.

time-honoured *adjective*
respected because of tradition or long use: *a time-honoured custom.*

timekeeper *noun*
a person or thing that keeps time, such as an official who times races in a sporting contest.

time lag *noun* also **lag**
the period of time between two events, etc.

time-lapse *adjective*
denoting the process of taking a series of photographs over a long period of time to record a particular event, such as the gradual opening of a flower bud.

timeless *adjective*
relating to no particular time: *a timeless fairy story.*

timely *adjective*
occurring at the right or favourable time: *a timely rescue.*
Word Family **timeliness** *noun.*

time off *noun*
time away from work or study.

time out *noun*
1 (*especially American*) rest time.
2 a short period spent on one's own, e.g. by a child who has been misbehaving.

timepiece *noun*
an instrument used to measure and show time, e.g. a clock or watch.

timer *noun*
a mechanism for activating a device at a time that has been set.

timescale *noun*
the time over which something happens.

time-sharing *noun*
a method of joint ownership of a holiday property where each owner is entitled to

use the property for a specified amount of time each year.
Word Family **timeshare** *noun.*

time sheet *noun*
a card or sheet of paper on which an employee's time of arrival and departure, or the actual hours worked, is recorded.

time signature *noun*
Music the sign at the beginning of a work to indicate the type and number of beats in each bar.

timetable *noun*
a list or table showing the times of particular events: *a train timetable.* □ *a lecture timetable.*
• **timetable** *verb* to set a timetable for any activity.

time-worn *adjective*
showing the effects of deterioration or age, long use, etc.

timid *adjective*
easily frightened or made nervous.
Word Family **timidly** *adverb*; **timidity** (tim-**id**-i-tee), **timidness** *noun.*
[from Latin]

timing (**time**-ing) *noun*
the art or process of establishing or maintaining the correct and most effective time, speed, sequence, etc.: *The timing of her jokes is always perfect.* □ *The timing in this engine is not quite right.*

timorous (**tim**-a-rus) *adjective*
timid or full of fear.
Word Family **timorously** *adverb*; **timorousness** *noun.*
[Latin *timor* fear]

timpani (**timp**-a-nee) *plural noun* also **tympani**
kettledrums.
Word Family **timpanist** *noun* a person who plays the timpani.
[Italian]

tin *noun*
1 a malleable ductile metal used in protective coating and alloys.
2 a container made from tin or tinplate, especially one which is sealed: *a tin of soup.*
3 an unsealed metal container, used for storing, baking, etc.
Word Family **tin** *verb* (**tins**; **tinning**; **tinned**) to cover with or pack in tins; **tin** *adjective* made of tin.

tincture (**tink**-cher) *noun*
1 a solution of a medicine in alcohol.
2 a slight trace.
3 *Heraldry* any of the colours, metals or furs used in coats of arms.
[Latin *tinctura* dyeing]

tinder *noun*
dry twigs, etc. used to start a fire.

tine *noun*
a prong or other projecting point.

tinea (**tin**-i-a) *noun*
ringworm.
[Latin, gnawing worm]

tinfoil ⇨ ALUMINIUM FOIL.

tinge (tinj) *verb*
to give a slight colour, taste or smell to:
black hair tinged with grey. □ *air tinged with
smoke.*
• **tinge** *noun.*
[Latin *tingere* to dye]

tingle *verb*
to feel a slight pricking or prickling: *Her
face tingled with cold.*
• **tingle** *noun.*

tinker *noun*
1 a person who travels about mending pots
and pans, etc.
2 an offensive word for a gypsy or traveller.
• **tinker** *verb* to fiddle or experiment: *He
tinkered with the computer for a while.*

> The word **tinker** is of uncertain origin.
> It was perhaps imitative of the noise
> someone makes when working with
> pots and pans or it may have meant
> someone who worked with *tin.*

tinkle *noun*
1 a light high-pitched ringing sound.
2 (*informal*) a telephone call: *Give me a
tinkle this afternoon.*
• **tinkle** *verb.*

tinnitus (tin-**eye**-tus *or* **tin**-a-tus) *noun*
ringing in the ears.
[Latin *tinnire* to ring]

tinny *adjective*
1 having a metallic sound.
2 made of thin metal.
3 having a metallic taste.
Word Family **tinnily** *adverb;* **tinniness**
noun.

tinplate *noun*
sheet steel or iron coated with a layer of
tin.

tinpot *adjective*
(*informal*) inferior or worthless: *a tinpot
government.*

tinsel *noun*
1 a glittering metallic substance used in
thin strips, threads or sheets for
decoration, e.g. on a Christmas tree.
2 superficial glamour.

tinsmith *noun*
a person who makes or repairs tin or metal
goods.

tint *noun*
1 a variety of a particular colour.
2 any slight or pale colour, such as a
temporary hair dye.
• **tint** *verb.*
[Latin *tinctus* dyed]

tiny (**tie**-nee) *adjective* (**tinier; tiniest**)
very small.

tip¹ *noun*
1 a tapered end or top: *a fingertip.*
2 a piece or part at the end of something:
a filter tip on a cigarette.
Phrase **on the tip of one's tongue** about
to be remembered or spoken.
• **tip** *verb* (**tips; tipping; tipped**)
1 to provide with a tip.
2 to decorate or mark the tip of.

tip² *verb* (**tips; tipping; tipped**)
1 to move or cause to move to a slanting
position: *The bucket tipped dangerously but
stayed upright.*
2 to empty out by tipping: *He tipped the
crumbs into the bin.*
3 to strike with a light glancing blow.
• **tip** *noun*
1 the act of tipping.
2 a rubbish dump.

tip³ *noun*
1 a small gift of money, e.g. to a waiter or
porter to show appreciation for service.
2 a private hint or piece of information
given as a guide: *a betting tip.*
• **tip** *verb* (**tips; tipping; tipped**) to give a
tip to.
Phrase **tip off** *He tipped off the police about
the robbery* (= warned or informed in
advance).
Word Family **tip-off** *noun* a hint given as
a warning. **tipster** *noun* a person who
provides tips, especially as an occupation
or business.

tipi ⇨ TEPEE.

tipple *verb*
to drink alcohol often or excessively.
Word Family **tipple** *noun* (*informal*)
alcohol; **tippler** *noun* a person who
tipples.

tipsy *adjective* (**tipsier; tipsiest**)
slightly drunk.
Word Family **tipsily** *adverb;* **tipsiness**
noun.

tiptoe *verb* (**tiptoes; tiptoeing; tiptoed**)
to walk very quietly on or as if on the tips
of the toes.

tip-top *adjective*
excellent or best.

tirade (tie-**rade** *or* ti-**rade**) *noun*
a long speech, especially a violently angry
or critical one.
[Italian *tirata* a volley]

tiramisu (ti-ra-mi-**soo**) *noun*
an Italian dessert of sponge cake flavoured
with coffee, mascarpone and brandy or
liqueur.
[Italian]

tire *verb*
1 to use up or lessen the energy or strength
of: *Don't tire yourself playing.*
2 to lose patience or interest: *We soon tired
of the boring game.*
Word Family **tired** *adjective*; **tiredly**
adverb; **tiredness** *noun*.

tireless *adjective*
never becoming tired.
Word Family **tirelessly** *adverb*;
tirelessness *noun*.

tiresome *adjective*
irritating or annoying.

tiro ⇨ TYRO.

'tis (tiz) *contraction*
a poetic short form of **it is**.

tisane (tiz-**an**) *noun*
a herbal tea
[French]

tissue (**tish**-oo) *noun*
1 *Biology* an organized group of similar
cells in an organism, such as bone,
cartilage, etc.
2 a thin soft paper handkerchief.
3 tissue paper.
Phrase **tissue of lies** a carefully
constructed series of lies.

tissue paper *noun*
very thin soft paper used for wrapping,
protecting, etc.

tit *noun*
any of a group of small birds, such as the
blue tit or tomtit.

titan (**tie**-t'n) *noun*
a person of great strength, size or
importance.
Word Family **titanic** (tie-**tan**-ik) *adjective*
very large or strong.
[after the *Titans*, a family of twelve gods
and goddesses of Greek mythology who
ruled Olympus until overthrown by Zeus]

titbit *noun* (*American* **tidbit**)
a small choice piece, e.g. of food.

tithe (tithe) *noun*
one tenth, especially one tenth of one's
farm produce, taken as a tax to support
the clergy, etc.
• **tithe** *verb* to demand a tithe.

Titian (**tish**-'n) *adjective*
of a reddish-brown colour: *Titian hair.*
[after *Titian*, c. 1488-1576, an Italian
painter who often used this colour to paint
hair]

titillate (**tit**-i-late) *verb*
to excite or tease pleasantly.
Word Family **titillation** (tit-i-**lay**-sh'n)
noun.

titivate (**tit**-i-vate) *verb*
(*informal*) to decorate or make smart.
Word Family **titivation** (tit-i-**vay**-sh'n)
noun.

title (**tie**-t'l) *noun*
1 a word or words giving the distinctive
name of a book, play, painting, etc.
2 a form of address which indicates a
person's occupation, rank, social position,
etc.
3 a claim to be the champion of a sport:
the world heavyweight title.
4 *Law* a deed or document which proves a
person's right of possession, control, etc.,
especially of land or property.
Word Family **titled** *adjective*; **title** *verb*.

ti tree ⇨ TEA TREE.

titter *verb*
to laugh or giggle in a nervous or half-
restrained way.
• **titter** *noun*.

tittle-tattle *noun*
gossip or foolish chatter.
• **tittle-tattle** *verb*.

titular (**tit**-yoo-la) *adjective*
1 of, being or having a title.
2 holding a position in name but not in
fact: *the titular head of the government.*

tizzy *noun* (*plural* **tizzies**) also **tizz** (*plural*
tizzes)
(*informal*) a state of nervous confusion or
excitement.

to *preposition*
a word used to indicate the following:
1 movement in the direction of: *from
London to Singapore.*
2 limit: *prizes to the value of £100.* □ *open
from 1 p.m. to 6 p.m.*
3 aim or intention: *Let's go to see a film.*
4 attachment or contact: *Stick to your view.*
□ *Apply paint to the wall.*

5 addition or accompaniment: *Garlic gives flavour to this soup.*
6 comparison or contrast: *at right angles to the wall.*
7 result: *He tore it to pieces.*
8 relation or reference: *She claims her right to the pension.*
9 before: *ten to five.*
10 in: *How many metres to one kilometre?*
11 special use before a verb in its infinitive form: *to see.*
● **to** *adverb* into a particular position, especially closed: *Pull that door to behind you.*
Phrase **to and fro** backwards and forwards.

> ⚠ The words *to, too* and *two* sound the same but have different spellings and meanings. *To* is a preposition (*I went to France*); *too* means 'also' or 'excessively' (*It's too late*); *two* is a number (*two kittens*).

toad *noun*
any of a group of amphibians resembling the frog but with drier and more warty skins.

toad-in-the-hole *noun*
a batter pudding containing sausages.

toadstool *noun*
any of various fleshy fungi, other than mushrooms, with a stalk and umbrella-like cap, some of which are poisonous.

toady *verb* (**toadies; toadying; toadied**)
to flatter in a servile fashion.
● **toady** *noun* (*plural* **toadies**).

toast *noun*
1 a slice of bread browned on both sides under a grill or in a toaster so that it becomes crisp.
2 an act of drinking in honour of someone: *We drank a toast to the happy couple.*
3 a person who is praised or celebrated: *The writer was the toast of the literary world.*
● **toast** *verb*
1 to cook or brown in a toaster or under a grill.
2 to warm oneself, e.g. by a fire.
3 to drink in honour of.

toaster *noun*
an electrical device for toasting bread.

toastmaster *noun*
a person who proposes toasts and introduces speakers at formal dinners.

toastmistress *noun* (*plural* **toastmistresses**)
a woman who proposes toasts and introduces speakers at formal dinners.

tobacco (t'-**bak**-o) *noun*
1 the dried leaves of a tropical plant which are prepared for smoking, chewing or as snuff.
2 the plant itself.
Word Family **tobacconist** *noun* a person who sells tobacco, cigarettes, etc.
[from Spanish]

toboggan (t'-**bog**-'n) *noun*
a light vehicle on runners used for sliding downhill on snow.
● **toboggan** *verb* to use or ride on a toboggan.
[Canadian French]

toby jug *noun*
a large drinking mug in the shape of a stout old man wearing a three-cornered hat.
[after *Toby Philpot*, a legendary drinker of fabulous capacity]

toccata (tok-**ah**-ta) *noun*
Music a brilliant piece of instrumental music designed to display the soloist's technique.
[Italian, touched]

tocsin (**tok**-sin) *noun*
an old word for a bell rung as a signal of alarm.
[French]

today *adverb*
on this or the present day.
● **today** *noun*.

toddle *verb*
to walk with short unsteady steps.
Word Family **toddler** *noun* a very young child.

toddy *noun* (*plural* **toddies**)
a hot alcoholic drink made from spirits, hot water and spices.

to-do *noun*
(*informal*) a fuss.

toe *noun*
1 any of the ten end parts of the feet.
2 the part of a shoe or piece of clothing covering a toe or toes.
Phrases **on one's toes** ready and alert.
tread on someone's toes to offend someone. **turn up one's toes** to die.
● **toe** *verb* (**toes; toeing; toed**) to touch or kick with the toes.
Phrase **toe the line** to obey or conform.

toehold *noun*
a small ledge, etc. which may support the toe in climbing.
Figurative The promotion gave him a toehold in management.

toff *noun*
(*informal*) a rich or upper-class person.

toffee *noun*
a sweet made by boiling sugar or treacle with butter and other ingredients.

toffee apple *noun*
a toffee-coated apple on a stick.

toffee-nosed *adjective*
(*informal*) snobbish, supercilious.

tofu (toe-foo) *noun* also called **bean curd**.
a soft solid substance obtained from soya beans, used in Asian and vegetarian dishes.

toga (toe-ga) *noun*
a long loose robe worn in ancient Rome.

together *adverb*
1 in or as one group, etc.: *Let's go there together.* □ *He weighs more than all of us together.*
2 so as to be joined, near or in contact: *Stick the two parts together.*
3 to a closer relationship: *The shared danger brought them together.*
4 in harmony or cooperation: *We will work together.*
Word Family **togetherness** *noun* a feeling of harmony, closeness or friendship.

toggle *noun*
a fastener consisting of a rod or pin mounted at its centre and passed through a loop or eye of rope, cable, etc., e.g. on a duffel coat.

togs *plural noun*
(*informal*) clothes.

toil *verb*
1 to work hard or continuously.
2 to proceed with difficulty: *The hikers toiled up the last steep slope.*
• **toil** *noun*.

toile (twahl) *noun*
a fine stiff linen fabric.

toilet (toy-let) *noun*
1 a bowl-like receptacle for urination and defecation, fitted with a device to flush it clean with water and connected by a pipe to the drains.
2 a room or similar structure containing such an apparatus.
3 the process of washing, dressing or grooming oneself.
[French *toilette* a cloth]

toiletries *plural noun*
articles or cosmetics used in washing, dressing or grooming oneself.

toilet water *noun*
a perfume diluted with alcohol.

toilworn *adjective*
a poetic word meaning 'showing the effects of hard work'.

token (toe-k'n) *noun*
1 something which represents or indicates a feeling, fact, etc.: *a token of affection.*
2 a symbol or sign.
3 a voucher exchangeable in shops for goods, e.g. books: *a gift token.*
4 a stamped piece of metal or plastic used in place of coins in some machines.
Phrase **by the same token** similarly, moreover or incidentally.
• **token** *adjective* done as a minimal gesture only: *You only have to make a token payment to become a member.*

tokenism (toe-k'n-izm) *noun*
the policy of making only nominal concessions to a demand, such as employing one woman in an all-male firm.

told the past tense and past participle of **tell**.

tolerable *adjective*
1 able to be tolerated or endured.
2 reasonable.
Word Family **tolerably** *adverb*.

tolerance (tol-a-r'nce) *noun*
1 the ability to endure or put up with difficulties, etc.
2 the quality or practice of accepting or being fair towards beliefs, customs, etc. which are different from one's own: *religious tolerance.*
3 a permitted variation from a standard quality, dimension, etc.
Word Family **tolerant** *adjective* showing or feeling tolerance; **tolerantly** *adverb*.

tolerate (tol-a-rate) *verb*
1 to allow or bear the existence or practice of without opposition: *I will not tolerate such rudeness.*
2 to accept: *The government tolerates the many religious groups.*
Word Family **toleration** (tol-a-ray-sh'n) *noun*.
[Latin *tolerare* to endure]

toll[1] (*rhymes with* roll) *verb*
1 (of a bell) to sound or cause to sound with slow regular rings.
2 to announce by ringing a bell in such a way: *to toll an alarm.*
• **toll** *noun*.

toll[2] *noun*
1 a charge made for the use of a road, bridge, etc.

2 the number of people or things killed, injured, lost, etc. in an accident or disaster.

toll gate *noun*
a gate or barrier across a road at which a toll is collected.

tom *noun*
a male animal: *a tomcat.*

tomahawk (tom-a-hawk) *noun*
a small axe, such as that used as a weapon by American Indians.

tomato *noun* (*plural* **tomatoes**)
a medium-sized fleshy red fruit with many pips, used as a vegetable or in salads.
[from Nahuatl]

tomb (toom) *noun*
a grave or vault for the dead.
Word Family **tombstone** *noun* an inscribed stone set above a grave.
[from Greek]

tombola (tom-bo-la) *noun*
a game played at a fête, with a drum containing numbered tickets, some of which win prizes.

tomboy *noun*
a rough or boisterous young girl.

tome *noun*
a large book.
[from Greek]

tomfoolery (tom-fool-a-ree) *noun*
foolish behaviour.

Tommy *noun* (*plural* **Tommies**)
(*informal*) a British soldier.
[after *Thomas Atkins*, a fictitious name used in sample forms for army privates]

tommy gun *noun*
(*informal*) a type of sub-machine gun.
[after *J. T. Thompson*, 1860-1940, an American army officer]

tommyrot *noun*
(*dated informal*) nonsense.

tomorrow (t'-morr-o) *noun*
the day after today.
• **tomorrow** *adverb.*

tomtit *noun*
a small bird of the tit family, especially a blue tit.

tom-tom *noun*
a small drum, especially one beaten with the hands.

ton (tun) *noun*
1 also called **long ton**. a unit of mass equal to 2240 lb avoirdupois, about 1020 kg.

2 also called **short ton**. (*especially American*) a unit of mass equal to 2000 lb avoirdupois, about 907 kg.
3 also **tonne** a metric ton.
4 (*informal*) a large number or quantity.
5 (*informal*) a speed of 100 miles per hour.

tonal (toe-n'l) *adjective*
relating to tone or tonality, especially in music.

tonality (toe-nal-i-tee) *noun* (*plural* **tonalities**)
a balance or harmony in a system, e.g. of the colours of a painting, or the keys used in a musical composition.

tone *noun*
1 a sound, especially one with a particular quality, length, etc.: *the clear tones of a church bell.*
2 a quality: *a furious tone of voice.*
3 a feeling or mood: *a light-hearted tone to the meeting.*
4 *Music* the interval which equals two semitones.
5 a shade or hue, or any slight variation in a colour: *tones of blue and green.*
6 *Medicine* the usual firmness in the muscles of a healthy body.
• **tone** *verb* to give a particular tone or quality to.
Phrases **tone down** *Please try to tone down your language* (= soften, moderate).
tone up *Exercises will tone up your muscles* (= make firm or strong). **tone with** *That furniture tones with the modern house* (= harmonizes).
[Greek *tonos* tension]

tone-deaf *adjective*
not able to hear the difference in pitch in musical notes.

tone poem *noun* also called **symphonic poem**.
a piece of orchestral music which tries to represent the mood of a particular poem, the sounds of nature in a particular setting, etc.

toner *noun*
1 a liquid applied to the skin to reduce oiliness.
2 a powder used instead of ink in a copying machine or printer.

tongs *plural noun*
a device with two hinged or sprung arms, for picking up or holding something.

tongue (tung) *noun*
1 *Anatomy* the mobile muscular organ in the mouth of vertebrate animals. In mammals it is the organ of taste, and in

human beings it is also the main organ of speech.

2 the tongue of an animal, especially the lamb or ox, used as food.

3 something which has the shape, position or function of a tongue, such as the hanging piece inside a bell, or the flap of material under the laces or fastening of a shoe.

4 a language: *French is his native tongue.*

5 a manner of speaking: *She has a cruel tongue.*

Phrases **hold one's tongue** to be quiet. **tongue in cheek, with tongue in cheek** mockingly or ironically. **with one's tongue hanging out** thirsty (like a dog) or greedily waiting for something.

• **tongue** *verb* (**tongues; tonguing; tongued**)

1 to sound a wind instrument with the tongue.

2 to touch with the tongue.

tongue and groove *noun*

a joint made by cutting a narrow groove along the edge of one piece of wood, into which the matching tapered edge (called the **tongue**) of another piece is fitted, especially in floorboards, etc.

tongue-lashing *noun*

a scolding.

tongue-tied *adjective*

unable to speak, especially due to shyness or embarrassment.

tongue-twister *noun*

a word or words difficult to say quickly.

tonic *noun*

1 something, especially a medicine, which invigorates.

2 *Music* the first note of a scale.

3 tonic water.

• **tonic** *adjective Music* of or based on the tonic.

[Greek *tonos* tension, musical pitch]

tonic water *noun*

a non-alcoholic carbonated water containing quinine, often mixed with spirits.

tonight *noun*

the present or coming night.

• **tonight** *adverb.*

tonnage (**tun**-ij) *noun*

the amount of space in which a ship can carry goods.

tonne (tun) *noun*

a metric ton.

tonsil *noun*

Anatomy either of two masses of connected lymph nodes, forming a ring where the mouth and nose open into the throat.

[from Latin]

tonsillectomy (ton-sil-**ekt**-a-mee) *noun* (*plural* **tonsillectomies**)

an operation to remove the tonsils.

[TONSIL + Greek *ektomé* a cutting out]

tonsillitis (ton-sil-**eye**-tis) *noun*

an inflammation of the tonsils, common in children, which may require removal of the tonsils.

[TONSIL + *-itis*]

tonsorial (ton-**saw**-ri-'l) *adjective* (*formal*) relating to hairdressing.

tonsure (**ton**-sher) *noun*

1 the shaving of the head, or part of the head, especially that of a monk.

2 the part of the head which is shaved.

• **tonsured** *adjective.*

[Latin *tonsura* shearing]

tontine (**ton**-teen) *noun*

a scheme under which several friends buy a joint annuity, the share of each one who dies being divided among the rest until the last survivor inherits all.

[after *Lorenzo Tonti*, the 17th-century Italian originator]

too *adverb*

1 also: *Are you coming too?*

2 used to indicate excess: *The box is too heavy to lift.*

Phrase **only too** *I'm only too glad to help* (= extremely).

> ⚠ Do not confuse *too* with TO.

took the past tense of **take**.

tool *noun*

any of various hand-held objects or instruments which help in performing work.

• **tool** *verb* to shape or decorate with a tool.

toot *verb*

1 to blow a horn, whistle, trumpet, etc.

2 (of a horn, whistle, etc.) to sound.

• **toot** *noun.*

tooth *noun* (*plural* **teeth**)

1 *Anatomy* any of the hard enamel-covered parts attached in rows to the jaws, used for chewing and biting.

2 any tooth-like part or projection, as on a comb, saw, rake, etc.

Phrases **get one's teeth into** to tackle something vigorously. **in the teeth of** despite, in direct opposition to. **long in the tooth** old. **set someone's teeth on edge** to annoy or irritate someone. **tooth and nail** fiercely.
Word Family **toothless** *adjective*; **toothy** *adjective* (**toothier; toothiest**) having or showing prominent teeth; **toothsome** *adjective* pleasant-tasting.

toothpaste *noun*
a flavoured paste used for cleaning the teeth.

toothpick *noun*
a small stick used to remove food, etc. from between the teeth.

top[1] *noun*
1 the highest or uppermost place, surface or position: *Climb to the top of the hill.* □ *Start at the top of the page.*
2 a person or thing that has the highest place or position: *She is top of the class.*
3 the highest point, pitch or degree: *She screamed at the top of her voice.* □ *A car in top is in the highest gear.*
4 a lid or covering: *Put the top back on the bottle.*
5 a piece of clothing which covers the upper part of the body: *My new suit has green trousers with a matching top.*
Phrases **blow one's top** to lose one's temper. **on top of** *I can't handle any more problems on top of all my others (= as well as).*
• **top** *verb* (**tops; topping; topped**)
1 to be or provide a top for: *The building was topped by a tower.*
2 to reach the top or above the top of: *The sun topped the horizon.* □ *His record topped the charts.*
3 *Sport* to hit the ball above its centre so that it moves only a short distance.
4 to surpass: *She topped my story with an even funnier one.*
Phrases **top off** to finish off: *a cake topped off with a cherry.* **top up** to fill up a partly filled container.

top[2] *noun* also **spinning top**
a toy which spins when set in motion.
Phrase **sleep like a top** to sleep soundly.

topaz (toe-paz) *noun* (*plural* **topazes**)
Geology a mineral of varying transparent shades, such as pale blue or golden brown, used as a gem.
[from Greek]

top brass *noun* ⇨ BRASS (definition 5).

topcoat *noun*
an overcoat.

top dog *noun*
(*informal*) the person in the highest or strongest position in a particular field.

top drawer *noun*
(*informal*) the best or highest level of society.
• **top drawer** *adjective*.

tope *verb*
an old or poetic word meaning 'to drink alcohol habitually or to excess'.
Word Family **toper** *noun*.

top flight *adjective*
first-rate or superior.

top hat *noun*
a man's tall silk hat worn on ceremonial occasions.

topi (toe-pee) *noun* also **topee**
a pith helmet.
[from Hindi]

topic *noun*
something forming the matter for discussion, conversation, etc.
[Greek *topos* a commonplace]

topical *adjective*
of current or local interest.
Word Family **topically** *adverb*; **topicality** (top-i-kal-i-tee) *noun*.

topknot (top-not) *noun*
a knot or tuft of hair on the top of the head.

topless *adjective*
without a top, especially showing the breasts: *a topless dancer.*

top-notch *adjective*
(*informal*) first-rate.

topography (top-og-ra-fee) *noun*
Geography a detailed description or representation of the natural and artificial features of an area.
Word Family **topographical** (top-a-graf-i-k'l) *adjective*; **topographically** *adverb*.
[Greek *topos* place + *graphein* to write]

topology *noun*
Maths the study of those properties of shapes which remain the same when changed by bending, stretching, etc.
Word Family **topological** *adjective*; **topologically** *adverb*.
[Greek *topos* a place + -*logy*]

topping *noun*
something added on top: *pizza toppings*.

topple *verb*
to waver unsteadily and tumble down.

top secret *adjective*
extremely secret.

topside *noun*
a boneless cut of beef from the thigh of the animal.

topsy-turvy *adjective, adverb*
1 upside down.
2 in confusion.

toque (toke) *noun*
a small hat, usually with a narrow turned-up brim.
[French]

tor *noun*
a small rocky hill or peak.

Torah (taw-rah *or* taw-**rah**) *noun*
Judaism the law of God, written in the first five books of the Old Testament.
[Hebrew, instruction]

torch *noun (plural* **torches)**
1 a small electric lamp powered by batteries.
2 a hand-held light of any burning substance.
Phrase **carry a torch for** to suffer unrequited love for.
• **torch** *verb (informal)* to set fire to: *The rioters torched several parked cars.*

tore the past tense of **tear**².

toreador (torr-i-a-dor *or* torr-i-a-**dor**) *noun*
a bullfighter.
[Spanish *toro* bull]

torment (tor-ment) *noun*
1 great suffering, worry, etc.: *the torments of toothache*.
2 a cause of such suffering: *That child is a torment to his parents.*
• **torment** (tor-**ment**) *verb* to cause torment to, especially in a persistent manner: *Stop tormenting her with your silly questions.*
Word Family **tormentor** *noun*.
[Latin *tormentum* a torture rack]

torn the past participle of **tear**².

tornado (tor-nay-doe) *noun (plural* **tornadoes** *or* **tornados)**
a small, fast-moving and very intense cyclone with a strong upward spiral of air. Tornadoes are formed over hot surfaces when the air is moist and unstable.

The word **tornado** is thought to derive from Spanish *tronada* (thunderstorm), from *tronar* (to thunder). It became confused with *tornar* (to turn) and so became *tornado*. First used in English for a violent storm, it soon came to be applied to a whirlwind. In America another word for a *tornado* is a *twister*.

torpedo (tor-pee-doe) *noun (plural* **torpedoes)**
a self-propelled underwater missile, used to destroy ships and fired from a submarine or low-flying aircraft.
• **torpedo** *verb* (**torpedoes; torpedoing; torpedoed)** to attack or destroy with a torpedo.
[Latin, the electric ray]

torpid *adjective*
inactive, dull and uninterested.
Word Family **torpidly** *adverb*; **torpidity** (tor-**pid**-i-tee) *noun*.
[Latin *torpidus* numb]

torpor (tor-pa) *noun*
1 a state of physical or mental inactivity.
2 the state of dormancy.
[Latin]

torque (tork) *noun*
Physics the force which tends to cause rotation.
[Latin *torquere* to twist]

torrent *noun*
a violent rushing stream.
Word Family **torrential** (torr-en-sh'l) *adjective* of or like a torrent.
[from Latin]

torrid *adjective*
1 extremely hot or scorching.
2 passionate.
Word Family **torridly** *adverb*; **torridity** (torr-id-i-tee) *noun*.
[Latin *torridus* parched]

torsion (tor-sh'n) *noun*
a twisting force along the axis of a body.
Word Family **torsional** *adjective*; **torsionally** *adverb*.
[Latin *tortus* twisted]

torso *noun*
1 the human figure without the head, arms and legs.
2 a sculpture of this.
[Italian]

tort *noun*
Law a careless act causing harm to another person which may lead to a claim for damages.
[French, wrong]

tortilla (tor-**tee**-ya) *noun*
a thin pancake made of maize flour eaten in Mexican cookery. ⇨ ENCHILADA.
[Spanish, *little cake*]

tortoise (**tor**-tus *or* **tor**-toyz) *noun*
a reptile, usually living on land, with its body enclosed in a thick shell into which the legs and head can be withdrawn. Compare TURTLE (definition 1).

tortoiseshell *noun*
1 the horny outer shell of a turtle, usually yellow and brown, used in the making of decorative combs, etc.
2 a long-haired domestic cat, usually a female, with a yellowish and black coat.
3 an orange, yellow and black butterfly.

tortuous (**tor**-tew-us) *adjective*
1 twisting, winding or crooked: *a tortuous path down the sides of a canyon.*
2 very long and complicated: *tortuous logic.*
Word Family **tortuously** *adverb;*
tortuousness *noun.*
[Latin *tortuosus* full of turns and twists]

torture (**torch**-er) *noun*
1 the inflicting of extreme pain.
2 the pain and suffering so inflicted.
• **torture** *verb* to subject to torture.
Word Family **torturer** *noun;* **torturous** *adjective.*
[Latin *tortus* twisted]

Tory *noun* (*plural* **Tories**)
1 *History* a member of the British political party which supported the monarchy and the established order of the Church and State. Compare WHIG.
2 a member or supporter of the modern Conservative Party.
Word Family **Tory** *adjective;* **Toryism** *noun.*
[originally used of Irish outlaws]

toss *verb*
1 to throw into or through the air: *Toss me the newspaper.* □ *The horse tossed its head in fear.*
2 to throw a coin into the air to decide something on the way it lands.
3 to turn: *Toss the pasta in the sauce.*
Phrase **toss up** to decide something by tossing a coin.
Word Family **toss** *noun* (*plural* **tosses**); **toss-up** *noun* 1 (*informal*) the tossing of a coin. 2 (*informal*) an even chance.

tot¹ *noun*
1 a small child.
2 a small portion of alcoholic drink.

tot² *verb* (**tots; totting; totted**)
Phrase **tot up** to add up.
[shortening of TOTAL]

total (**toe**-t'l) *noun*
the sum or whole of something.
• **total** *adjective*
1 full or whole.
2 complete or absolute: *It was a total failure.*
• **total** *verb* (**totals; totalling; totalled**)
1 to add up to.
2 to find the total of.
Word Family **totally** *adverb;* **totality** (toe-**tal**-i-tee) *noun* the whole of something.
[Latin *totus* the whole]

total internal reflection *noun*
the process in which light rays pass through a dense substance, e.g. a glass block, and are reflected from its inner surface back into the substance.

totalitarianism (toe-tal-i-**tair**-i-an-izm) *noun*
a political system based on the absolute power of a single party or dictator.
Word Family **totalitarian** *adjective, noun.*

totalizator, totalisator (tote-a-lie-zay-ta) *noun* also **totalizer**
an organized system of betting in which winners share the total amount bet on the race, less a percentage for costs and taxes.

tote¹ *verb*
(*especially American informal*) to carry.

tote² *noun*
(*informal*) a system of betting based on the totalizator.

totem (**toe**-t'm) *noun*
an animal, plant or object used by a tribe or clan as an emblem.
Word Family **totemic** (toe-**tem**-ik) *adjective;* **totemism** *noun.*
[Amerindian]

totem pole *noun*
a pole on which totems have been carved.

totter *verb*
to move or sway unsteadily.
Word Family **totter** *noun;* **tottery** *adjective.*

toucan (**too**-k'n) *noun*
a large tropical American fruit-eating bird with a huge beak.

touch (tuch) *verb*
1 to bring the hand, finger, etc. lightly into contact with: *Touch the paint and see if it's still wet.*
2 to affect with pity: *The sad story touched his heart.*
3 to have anything to do with: *He won't touch that job.*

4 to compare with: *You can't touch him for genius.*
Phrases touch down 1 *Rugby* to score a try. **2** (of an aircraft) to land. **touch off** to cause or start: *The rumour touched off widespread panic.* **touch on** to mention briefly. **touch up** to add the final details to.
• **touch** *noun* (*plural* **touches**)
1 the act of touching.
2 the state of being in communication, etc.: *We keep in touch by letter.*
3 a trace: *There was a touch of bitterness in her voice.*
4 the feeling caused by touching: *The marble had a smooth touch.*
5 the sense giving such feeling: *It was cold to the touch.*
6 a style or manner of touching: *The pianist had a delicate touch.*
Word Family **touchable** *adjective*; **touchdown** *noun* 1 *Rugby* the scoring of a try. 2 the moment that an aircraft lands.

touch-and-go *adjective*
uncertain, risky.

touché (too-**shay**) *interjection*
used to acknowledge a good point or retort.
[French, touched, a call made by a fencer to acknowledge a hit by an opponent]

touching (tuch-ing) *adjective*
arousing pity or sympathy.
Word Family **touchingly** *adverb*.

touchpaper (tuch-pay-pa) *noun*
a strip of paper containing potassium nitrate, which makes it smoulder slowly. It is used as a fuse for fireworks and explosives.

touchstone (tuch-stone) *noun*
1 a black stone on which gold or silver is rubbed to test its purity.
2 a test of quality.

touch-type (tuch-tipe) *verb*
to type without looking at the keys.

touchy (tuch-ee) *adjective* (**touchier, touchiest**)
easily provoked or offended.
Word Family **touchily** *adverb*; **touchiness** *noun*.

tough (tuf) *adjective*
1 not easily cut, broken or worn out: *The steak is too tough to chew.* □ *The seed has a tough outer layer.*
2 difficult, trying or severe: *I couldn't answer her tough questions.*
3 rough: *a tough character.*

Word Family **toughen** *verb* to make or become tough or tougher; **toughly** *adverb*; **toughness** *noun*.

toupee (too-pay) *noun* also **toupet** (too-pay *or* too-pit)
a small wig or hairpiece worn to cover a bald patch.
[French *toupet*]

tour (toor) *noun*
1 a journey in which a number of places are visited.
2 *Military* a period of duty in a place.
• **tour** *verb*.
[Greek *tornos* a circle]

tour de force (toor de force) *noun* (*plural* **tours de force**) (**toor** de force)
a feat of skill or sustained effort.
[French]

touring car *noun*
an open car designed to take several passengers and their luggage.

tourist *noun*
a person who travels for sightseeing and pleasure.
Word Family **tourism** *noun*.

tourist class *noun*
the cheapest class, e.g. in an aeroplane.

tournament (torn-a-m'nt) *noun*
1 a competition or series of contests in sport, chess, etc.
2 *History* a contest between knights on horseback armed with blunted weapons.

tournedos (toor-na-doe) *noun* (*plural* **tournedos**) (**toor**-na-doze)
a cut of meat from the middle of the fillet.
[French *tourner* to turn + *dos* back]

tourney *noun*
a tournament for knights on horseback.

tourniquet (toor-ni-kay) *noun*
a device used to prevent bleeding by compressing the blood vessels.
[French]

tousled (towz-'ld) *adjective*
unkempt or disordered: *tousled hair.*
Word Family **tousle** *verb*.

tout (rhymes with out) *verb*
1 to pester possible customers with one's goods or services: *men touting Cup Final tickets.*
2 to obtain and sell information, especially regarding horse races.
3 to try to gain something in a persistent manner: *touting for favour.*
• **tout** *noun* a person who touts: *a ticket tout.*

tow¹ (toe) *verb*
to drag or pull by a rope or chain.
• **tow** *noun* the act of towing.
Phrase **in tow** *She arrived with the whole family in tow* (= following).
Word Family **towage** *noun* a charge made for towing.

tow² *noun*
the fibre of flax, hemp, etc., prepared for spinning.

towards *preposition* also **toward**
1 in the direction of: *She turned towards the door.*
2 near: *It was towards midnight when he left.*
3 as a contribution to: *Here is some money towards a new car.*
4 concerning or in relation to: *What is your attitude towards compulsory sport?*

towel *noun*
a thick cotton cloth for drying oneself or things.
Phrase **throw in the towel** to give up or admit defeat.
Word Family **towel** *verb* (**towels; towelling; towelled**) to dry with a towel; **towelling** *noun* an absorbent fabric used for towels, beach clothes, etc.

tower (*rhymes with* flower) *noun*
a tall narrow building or structure, sometimes forming part of another building.
Phrase **tower of strength** a source of comfort or support.
• **tower** *verb* to rise to a great height.
Phrase **tower over** to rise above or surpass.

towering *adjective*
1 tall or lofty: *a towering skyscraper.*
2 extremely violent or intense: *a towering rage.*

tow-headed (toe-hed-id) *adjective*
having pale yellow or untidy hair.

town *noun*
1 a distinct densely populated area, with some degree of self-government.
2 the business or commercial centre of such an area, in contrast to the suburbs.
Phrases **go to town** to act with wild enthusiasm. **on the town** seeking entertainment in a town. **paint the town red** to celebrate wildly.

town hall *noun*
a building consisting of local government offices and often a large hall for public meetings, etc.

town house *noun*
a tall house, usually part of a terrace.

townie *noun* also **townee**
(*informal*) a town-bred person, as distinct from someone who lives in the country.

town planning *noun*
the planning of buildings, services, roads, etc. for a new town or for the extension or improvement of an existing town.

township *noun*
1 a small town.
2 *South African* an area outside a large town occupied by black people, especially one formerly set aside for them under the system of apartheid.

toxaemia (tok-see-mee-a) *noun* (*American* **toxemia**)
a form of blood poisoning.
Word Family **toxaemic** *adjective.*

toxic (tok-sik) *adjective*
1 poisonous.
2 relating to or caused by poison.
Word Family **toxically** *adverb*; **toxicity** (tok-**sis**-i-tee) *noun*; **toxicology** (tok-si-**kol**-a-jee) *noun* the study of poisons.
[Greek *toxikon pharmakon* arrow poison, from *toxa* arrows]

toxin (tok-sin) *noun*
a poison, especially one produced by living things, such as bacteria.

toy *noun*
an object made to play with.
• **toy** *verb*
1 to consider in a casual manner: *She toyed with the idea of going to London.*
2 to treat or handle lightly or idly: *He toyed with a pencil as he spoke.*

trace¹ *noun*
1 a sign or evidence of something having existed, happened or been present: *The wanted man has disappeared without a trace.*
2 a very small amount: *You have a trace of grey in your hair.*
• **trace** *verb*
1 to follow the course of: *We traced the river to its source.*
2 to draw by reproducing outlines on a transparent sheet placed on top of the original.
3 to find or locate: *The agency traces missing persons.*
[Latin *tractus* a dragging, drawing]

trace² *noun*
either of the two straps or chains running from each side of a horse's collar to the load or carriage being pulled.
Phrase **kick over the traces** to rebel.

trace element *noun*
a chemical element which is essential for normal animal and plant growth but is only needed in very small amounts.

tracer *noun*
1 a person or thing that traces.
2 ammunition containing a chemical which leaves a trail of smoke or fire, used to check the aim of an automatic weapon.

tracery (**trace**-a-ree) *noun* (*plural* **traceries**)
1 a decorative pattern of branch-like bars, e.g. on a window.
2 any similar pattern or network.

trachea (tra-**kee**-a *or* **tray**-kee-a) *noun* (*plural* **tracheas** *or* **tracheae** (tra-**kee**-ee *or* **tray**-kee-ee)) also called **windpipe**.
the tube of joined cartilage rings forming the air passage from the larynx to the lungs.
Word Family **tracheal** (**tray**-kee-'l) *adjective*.
[Greek *trakheia* (*arteria*) rough (artery)]

tracing (**trace**-ing) *noun*
a traced copy of something.

track *noun*
1 a rough road made by frequent use.
2 a mark or series of marks left by something that has passed.
3 any line or course of movement, such as the flight path of an aircraft.
4 a course laid out for a particular purpose.
5 an endless ribbed band of metal passing around the wheels of a vehicle such as a tank.
6 *Music* a section of a tape, compact disc or record containing one song or piece of music.
Phrases **cover one's tracks** to conceal what one has done, where one has been, etc. **in one's tracks** where one is standing. **keep track of** to follow the course or progress of. **lose track of** to fail to stay in touch with. **make tracks** to depart. **off the beaten track** secluded. **on the wrong track** pursuing the wrong course in investigation, reasoning, etc.
● **track** *verb*
1 to follow the tracks of: *We tracked the animal to its den.*
2 *Film* (of a camera) to move in any direction while filming.
Phrase **track down** to search for and find.
Word Family **tracker** *noun* a person or thing that tracks.

track events *plural noun*
Athletics events on a running track, e.g. races.

track record *noun*
a history of achievements in any area of endeavour: *The company has a bad track record on environmental issues.*

tracksuit *noun*
a warm outfit worn by athletes when training, between events, etc. or as leisure wear.

tract¹ *noun*
1 a large area of land.
2 *Anatomy* a group or system of parts, organs, etc. with a related function: *the digestive tract.*

tract² *noun*
a pamphlet containing information, such as those distributed by a religious group.

tractable (**trak**-ta-b'l) *adjective*
easily managed or dealt with: *a tractable problem.*
Word Family **tractably** *adverb*; **tractability** (trak-ta-**bil**-i-tee) *noun*.
[from Latin]

traction (**trak**-sh'n) *noun*
the act or power of drawing or pulling, e.g. by a railway engine.
Phrase **in traction** *Medicine* being raised and supported, usually with a straining pressure applied by a pulley-like device, e.g. for a broken leg
[Latin *tractus* drawn]

traction engine *noun*
an early form of tractor, very large and usually steam-powered, for hauling very heavy loads.

tractor *noun*
a motor vehicle, especially one with heavy tyres, used for pulling machinery or heavy loads.

trad *adjective*
(*informal*) traditional: *trad jazz.*

trade *noun*
1 the business or process of buying, selling or exchanging goods.
2 the people involved in a particular business: *Discounts are available only to the trade.*
3 (*especially American*) a swap.
4 an occupation, especially one which involves skilled mechanical or manual work as distinct from a profession.
5 a trade wind.
● **trade** *verb*
1 to engage in the business of buying, selling or exchanging goods.
2 to exchange.

Phrases **trade in** to give as part payment for something being bought, exchanged, etc. **trade on** *He will try to trade on your weaknesses* (= take advantage of, make use of).
Word Family **trader** *noun* 1 a person who buys, sells or exchanges. 2 a ship used for trade.

trademark *noun*
a registered name or mark officially used by a manufacturer to identify a particular product and distinguish it from others.

trade name *noun*
1 the name under which a business operates or an article is sold.
2 the name for an article, business process, etc. used in a trade, but not an official trademark.

trade price *noun*
the price paid for goods by a retailer to a wholesaler, or by members of the same trade.

tradesman *noun* (*plural* **tradesmen**)
a person involved in a trade, especially one who sells or delivers goods.

trade union *noun* also **trades union**
an organized group of workers providing aid and protection, especially in relation to wages and conditions of work, for all the workers in an industry.
Word Family **trade unionist** a member or supporter of a trade union; **trade unionism** *noun*.

trade wind *noun*
a north-east or south-east wind blowing fairly regularly from the subtropics towards the equator.

trading post *noun*
a general store in a sparsely populated region.

trading stamp *noun*
a stamp given by a retailer to a customer making a purchase, which can be collected and exchanged for goods.

tradition (tra-**dish**-’n) *noun*
1 the passing down of customs, culture, beliefs, etc. from generation to generation.
2 something which is passed on in this way.

traditional *adjective*
1 based on or existing due to tradition: *a traditional folk tune*.
2 based on the style of jazz music developed in the early 20th century, consisting of improvised instrumental music: *traditional jazz*.
Word Family **traditionally** *adverb*.
[Latin *traditio* a handing on]

traditionalist *noun*
someone who believes in upholding tradition.
Word Family **traditionalism** *noun*.

traduce (tra-**dewce**) *verb*
to slander or speak maliciously of.
[Latin *traducere* to disgrace publicly]

traffic *noun*
1 the passing or movement of vehicles or people along a route.
2 the vehicles or people moving.
3 the transporting of people or goods for sale, etc. by land, sea or air.
4 illegal trade: *the traffic of drugs*.
5 an old word for dealings or communication.
● **traffic** *verb* (**traffics; trafficking; trafficked**) to take part in illegal business.
[from Italian]

traffic cone ⇨ CONE (definition 4).

tragedy (**traj**-a-dee) *noun* (*plural* **tragedies**)
1 a story or play with a serious theme, which usually ends with death or defeat. Compare COMEDY (definition 1).
2 any event which is disastrous, fatal or dreadful.
Word Family **tragedian** (tra-**jee**-di-an) *noun* a person who writes or acts in tragedies; **tragedienne** (tra-jee-di-**en**) *noun* a woman who acts in tragedies.

The word **tragedy** is, etymologically, probably connected with goats, coming ultimately from Greek *tragoidia*, from *tragos* (goat) and *oide* (song). It is thought that in Greek drama there may once have been a chorus which dressed up as goat-like deities or satyrs.

tragic (**traj**-ik) *adjective*
1 characteristic of or relating to tragedy: *a tragic ending*.
2 dreadful, sad: *the tragic death of a young boxer*.
Word Family **tragically** *adverb*.

tragicomedy (traj-i-**kom**-a-dee) *noun* (*plural* **tragicomedies**)
1 a play or novel based on a combination of tragedy and comedy.
2 an event or situation which is both serious and funny.
Word Family **tragicomic** *adjective*.

trail *verb*
1 to drag or allow to drag along the ground, etc.
2 to follow slowly: *He trailed behind them with his sore leg*.

3 to grow along and hang down: *a trailing vine*.

4 to fade away: *His voice trailed away as he realized we weren't listening*.

5 to move in a straggling way: *A small group trailed along the beach*.

6 to be behind or losing: *The team were trailing by three goals at half-time*.

7 to follow the path or movements of: *to trail a suspect*.

8 to advertise with a trailer.

• **trail** *noun*

1 a track, mark or series of marks left behind by something which has passed: *A trail of blood led to the door.* □ *The invaders left a trail of destruction.*

2 a track or scent: *The hounds quickly found the deer's trail*.

3 a path or track made through a remote area, etc.

[Latin *tragula* dragnet]

trail bike *noun*
a motorcycle designed for use on rough terrain.

trailblazer *noun*
a person who is an innovator or a leader in a particular field.

trailer *noun*

1 a short sequence of scenes from a feature film, television programme, etc., used as an advertisement.

2 a person or thing that trails, especially a small vehicle drawn by another.

3 *American* a caravan.

train *noun*

1 a set of railway vehicles connected to a locomotive engine.

2 a line or series of vehicles, people, etc.: *The President was followed by a train of bodyguards.* □ *a strange train of events*.

3 something which is drawn behind or follows, such as a long back part of a skirt, etc.

• **train** *verb*

1 to instruct or educate for a particular skill, occupation, etc.

2 to practise or exercise to keep fit: *The players train every evening*.

3 to cause to grow: *Train the ivy up the wall*.

4 to aim or point: *He trained the gun on the man's head*.

Word Family **trainer** *noun* a person who trains others; **trainee** (tray-**nee**) *noun* a person being trained; **trainers** *plural noun* sports shoes worn for running, jogging, other sports or leisure wear; **training** *noun*.

[Latin *trahere* to drag]

traipse *verb*
to walk or travel about, especially in an aimless or weary manner.

trait (tray *or* trate) *noun*
a feature or quality which distinguishes or sets apart.

[French]

traitor (tray-ta) *noun*
a person who betrays his or her country, another person or a belief.

Word Family **traitorous** *adjective* disloyal or treacherous; **traitorously** *adverb*.

[from Latin]

trajectory *noun* (*plural* **trajectories**)
the path, especially a curve, traced by a moving object, etc.: *the trajectory of a bullet*.

[*trans-* + Latin *jacere* to throw]

tram *noun*

1 also **tramcar** a passenger vehicle running on rails in the street and usually powered by electricity from an overhead wire.

2 *Mining* a truck for carrying coal.

trammels *plural noun*
a poetic word for restrictions.

Word Family **trammel** *verb* (**trammels**; **trammelling**; **trammelled**) to hinder or restrict.

tramp *verb*

1 to walk with steady or heavy steps.

2 to walk a long way, especially reluctantly.

• **tramp** *noun*

1 a person with no fixed home and usually little or no money, who travels about on foot.

2 a heavy firm step or tread.

3 a long walk or hike.

4 (*especially American informal*) a promiscuous woman.

trample *verb*
to tread on heavily or crushingly.

Figurative *He trampled on her feelings with cruel taunts* (= treated harshly).

trampoline (tram-pa-leen) *noun*
a canvas sheet held taut by springs in a frame above the floor, used for bouncing and other acrobatic tricks.

• **trampoline** *verb*.

[Italian *trampoli* stilts]

tramway *noun*
the system of tracks or cables for a tram.

trance *noun*

1 a half-conscious or hypnotized state.

2 a dazed or mentally absorbed state.

3 a type of electronic dance music.

[Latin *transire* to pass over]

tranquil (**trank**-wil) *adjective*
free from agitation or disturbance: *a tranquil sleep*.
Word Family **tranquillity** (trank-**wil**-i-tee) *noun* calmness or peace; **tranquilly** *adverb*.
[from Latin]

tranquillize, tranquillise *verb* (*American* **tranquilize**)
to make or become calm, especially by the use of a drug.
Word Family **tranquillizer** *noun* a drug which has a calming effect, a sedative.

transaction (tran-**zak**-sh'n) *noun*
1 a piece of business, such as the sale of some object.
2 (**transactions**) the written records of a society, etc.
Word Family **transact** *verb* to carry out or conduct business.
[Latin *transactus* settled]

transceiver (tran-**see**-va) *noun*
a radio set able to transmit and receive radio waves.
[TRANS(mitter) + (re)CEIVER]

transcend (tran-**send**) *verb*
1 to be or go beyond or above: *The result transcended our wildest hopes*.
2 to be or do better than.
Word Famil **transcendent** *adjective* going beyond ordinary limits;
transcendence *noun*; **transcendently** *adverb*.
[Latin *transcendere* to climb over or beyond]

transcendental (tran-sen-**den**-t'l) *adjective*
1 being or going completely beyond normal human experience, belief or knowledge.
2 very abstract, obscure or visionary.
Word Family **transcendentally** *adverb*.

transcendentalism (tran-sen-**den**-ta-lizm) *noun*
a branch of philosophy concerned with abstract ideas or intuition rather than physical experience.
Word Family **transcendentalist** *noun*, *adjective*.

Transcendental Meditation *noun*
the attempted achievement of peace of mind by oriental methods of meditation taught by gurus.

transcendental number *noun*
Maths a number, e.g. π, which does not satisfy any algebraic equation with rational coefficients.

transcribe *verb*
1 to express, record or make a copy of in writing.
2 *Music* to rewrite a composition for an instrument other than the one for which it was originally written.
Word Family **transcript** *noun* a written copy or record, especially an official record of a court case; **transcription** *noun* 1 the act of transcribing. 2 a written copy or reproduction. 3 a musical composition which has been transcribed.
[Latin *transcribere* to copy]

transducer (tranz-**dew**-ser *or* trahnz-**dew**-ser) *noun*
a device which changes one form of energy into another, e.g. sound into electrical energy in a microphone.
[Latin *transducere* to lead across]

transect *verb*
to cut across.
[from Latin]

transept *noun*
the side parts in a cross-shaped church.
[*trans*- + Latin *saeptum* enclosure]

transfer (trans-**fer**) *verb* (**transfers; transferring; transferred**)
to take or move from one place, person, etc. to another: *He transferred his savings to another bank*.
• **transfer** (**trans**-fer) *noun*
1 the act of transferring.
2 something which is transferred, such as a design which is removed from paper and pressed onto a surface.
Word Family **transferrer** *noun* a person or thing that transfers; **transference** (trans-fa-r'nce) *noun* the act of transferring.
[*trans*- + Latin *ferre* to carry]

transfiguration (tranz-fig-a-**ray**-sh'n) *noun*
a complete change to a beautiful state.
Word Family **transfigure** (tranz-**fig**-a) *verb* to make more beautiful or spiritual.

transfix *verb*
1 to make unable to move: *She was transfixed by the dreadful sight*.
2 to pierce through and fix: *He transfixed the king with his sword*.

transform *verb*
1 to change in form, nature or character: *Experience had transformed her into a wiser person.*
2 *Electricity* to change the magnitude of an alternating current.

transformation *noun*
a change in form, condition, etc.

transformer *noun*
a device which changes the magnitude of an alternating current.

transfusion (tranz-**few**-zh'n) *noun*
the transferring of a liquid from one container to another, especially transferring blood from the veins or arteries of one person or animal to another.
Word Family **transfuse** *verb*.

transgress *verb*
to go beyond a limit, etc., especially a limit set by law.
Word Family **transgression** *noun* a crime or sin.
[*trans-* + Latin *gressus* gone]

tranship ⇨ TRANS-SHIP.

transhumance (tranz-**hew**-m'nce *or* trahnz-**hew**-m'nce) *noun*
the seasonal movement of cattle, especially from the Alps in summer to the valleys in winter.
[French from *trans-* + Latin *humus* ground]

transient (**tran**-zi-ent *or* **trahn**-zi-ent) *adjective*
not lasting or remaining: *He only left a transient impression.*
Word Family **transience** *noun*; **transiently** *adverb*; **transient** *noun* a person who remains for only a short time, such as a guest in a hotel.
[Latin *transiens* going across]

transistor *noun*
1 *Electronics* a semiconductor device capable of amplification and having three or more electrodes.
2 short form of **transistor radio** a small radio using such devices.
Word Family **transistorize**, **transistorise** *verb*.
[TRANS(fer) + (res)ISTOR]

transit (**tran**-zit) *noun*
1 the act of passing across or through, e.g. the movement of people or goods from one place to another.
2 *Astronomy* the passage of a planet or star across the meridian of a particular place.

3 *Astronomy* the passage of a satellite in front of its primary, such as Venus in front of the sun.
[from Latin]

transition (tran-**zish**-'n) *noun*
a passing or changing from one position or condition to another.
Word Family **transitional**, **transitionary** *adjective* of or during a transition; **transitionally** *adverb*.

transitive *adjective*
Grammar (of a verb) needing a direct object to complete its meaning. The verb *buy* is transitive, because it needs a direct object, as in *The boy bought a book.*
Compare INTRANSITIVE.

transitory *adjective*
not lasting or permanent: *a transitory illness.*

translate (tranz-**late** *or* trahnz-**late**) *verb*
1 to express the sense or meaning of something in another language.
2 to change or convert: *His energy was translated into a violent outburst.*
Word Family **translator** *noun*.
[*trans-* + Latin *latus* carried]

translation *noun*
1 the putting of words into another language.
2 a version, passage, etc. which has been or is to be translated.
3 the act of translating.
4 *Maths* motion in which all points in a body move in parallel paths.

transliterate *verb*
to change letters or words into corresponding characters of another alphabet or language: *Greek π is transliterated as English p.*
Word Family **transliteration** *noun*.
[*trans-* + Latin *littera* a letter]

translucent (tranz-**loo**-s'nt *or* trahnz-**loo**-s'nt) *adjective*
allowing light to pass through imperfectly so that objects cannot be seen distinctly.
Compare TRANSLUCENT (definition 1).
Word Family **translucently** *adverb*; **translucence**, **translucency** *noun*.
[Latin *translucens* shining through]

transmigrate *verb*
(of the soul) to be reborn in another body.
Word Family **transmigration** *noun*; **transmigratory** *adjective*.

transmission *noun*
1 the act or process of transmitting, such as the sending of electromagnetic waves from a transmitter to a receiver.

2 the transfer of motion from one part of a machine to another.

3 any device for doing this, such as the gearbox, differential, etc. of a motor vehicle.

transmit *verb* (**transmits; transmitting; transmitted**)

1 to pass on: *to transmit radio messages.* □ *Metal transmits heat.*

2 to spread or communicate: *The disease is transmitted by fleas.*

[*trans-* + Latin *mittere* to send]

transmitter *noun*
a device which generates and transmits electromagnetic waves to be picked up by a receiver.

transmogrify *verb* (**transmogrifies; transmogrifying; transmogrified**)
to change into a different form as if by magic.

transmutation *noun*

1 the act of changing from one form, substance or state to another, especially the theoretical changing of one biological species into another.

2 the conversion of base metals into silver or gold attempted by alchemists.

Word Family **transmute** *verb* to change from one form or state into another; **transmutable** *adjective*.

transom *noun*

1 a flat beam forming part of the stern of a boat.

2 a horizontal strip, often of wood or stone, which divides a window, etc.

3 also **transom window** a small window set above a door or big window.

transparency *noun* (*plural* **transparencies**)

1 the quality of being transparent.

2 *Photography* ⇨ SLIDE *noun* (definition 3).

transparent *adjective*

1 allowing light to pass through so that objects on the other side may be seen clearly. Compare TRANSLUCENT.

2 obvious, easily seen.

Word Family **transparently** *adverb*.

[*trans-* + Latin *parere* to appear]

transpire (tran-**spire**) *verb*

1 to become known: *It transpired that the witness had not told the truth.*

2 to happen.

3 (of a plant) to give off water vapour through its leaves into the air.

Word Family **transpiration** (tran-spi-**ray**-sh'n) *noun*.

[*trans-* + Latin *spirare* to breathe]

transplant (trans-**plahnt** *or* trahns-**plahnt**) *verb*
to remove something, such as a tree, body part, etc., from one place and put it in another.

● **transplant** (**trans**-plahnt *or* **trahns**-plahnt) *noun*

1 the process of transplanting.

2 something which is transplanted.

Word Family **transplantable** *adjective*.

transport *verb*

1 to carry from one place to another.

2 to strongly move or affect: *She was transported by the beauty of the opera.*

3 to send to a prison colony: *Thieves used to be transported to Australia.*

● **transport** *noun*

1 a system for carrying passengers or goods.

2 a vehicle used for this.

3 (**transports**) a state of rapture or intense excitement.

Word Family **transportation** (tran-spor-**tay**-sh'n) *noun* 1 the act of transporting. 2 a vehicle used for or as a means of transport.

[*trans-* + Latin *portare* to carry]

transpose *verb*

1 to change or reverse the order or position of.

2 *Maths* to move a term from one side of an equation to the other, involving a change of sign.

3 *Music* to write or play a melody in a key other than the original one.

Word Family **transposition, transposal** *noun*.

[*trans-* + Latin *positus* placed]

trans-ship *verb* (**trans-ships; trans-shipping; trans-shipped**) also **tranship** (**tranships; transhipping; transhipped**)
to transfer goods from one ship or other kind of transport to another.

transverse *adjective*
lying across.

Word Family **transversely** *adverb*.

[*trans-* + Latin *versus* turned]

transvestite *noun*
a person who dresses in the clothing of the opposite sex.

Word Family **transvestism** *noun*.

trap *noun*

1 a device for catching animals, such as a cage with a door that snaps shut when the animal enters it.

2 anything used to catch or trick, especially unexpectedly.

3 a device which collects or prevents the passage of fluids, liquids, etc.
4 a light two-wheeled passenger vehicle, pulled by a pony.
5 (*informal*) the mouth.
6 a device which flings objects, such as clay pigeons, into the air to be shot at.
• **trap** *verb* (**traps**; **trapping**; **trapped**)
1 to catch in or as if in a trap.
2 to seal off or confine.

trapdoor *noun*
a hinged or sliding door in a floor, roof, etc.

trapeze (tra-**peez**) *noun*
1 also **flying trapeze** a short bar, with a long rope attached to each end, which is hung above the ground and used by acrobats and gymnasts.
2 *Nautical* a harness attached to a sailing boat by a wire and worn by a member of the crew, enabling him or her to lean out from the boat.

trapezium (tra-**pee**-zi-um) *noun* (*plural* **trapeziums** or **trapezia**)
a quadrilateral with two sides parallel.

trapper *noun*
a person who traps animals for their flesh or fur.

trappings *plural noun*
clothes or equipment, especially if ornamental or ceremonial: *He was photographed in all the trappings of his office, including a plumed helmet.*

trap shooting *noun*
the sport of shooting at birds or clay pigeons hurled into the air by a trap.

trash *noun*
1 (*especially American*) rubbish.
2 (*especially American*) a person or thing considered worthless or contemptible.
Word Family **trashy** *adjective* (**trashier**; **trashiest**) worthless; **trashily** *adverb*; **trashiness** *noun*.

trash can *noun*
American a dustbin.

trattoria (trat-a-**ree**-a) *noun*
an Italian restaurant.

trauma (**traw**-ma or **trow**-ma) *noun*
(*plural* **traumas** or **traumata**)
1 *Medicine* an injury.
2 an emotional shock.
Word Family **traumatic** (traw-**mat**-ik) *adjective* 1 relating to or produced by a trauma. 2 like a trauma; **traumatically** *adverb*; **traumatize, traumatise** *verb*.
[Greek, wound]

travail (tra-**vale**) *noun* also **travails**
a poetic word for work or effort.
• **travail** *verb*.
[Old French]

travel *verb* (**travels**; **travelling**; **travelled**)
1 to go from one place to another, especially over a considerable distance.
2 to move: *Light travels more quickly than sound.*
• **travel** *noun*
1 the act of travelling: *a book about travel.*
2 the distance moved by a part in a machine.

travel agency *noun* (*plural* **travel agencies**)
an agency which books flights, passages, hotels, package tours, etc. for travellers.

travel bureau *noun* (*plural* **travel bureaus** or **travel bureaux**)
a travel agency.

traveller *noun* (*American* **traveler**)
1 a person who travels.
2 a gypsy.
3 also **New Age traveller** someone who has New Age values and travels around, living in different places.

traveller's cheque *noun*
a cheque issued by a bank, etc. and signed by the bearer, which can be cashed anywhere if signed again in the presence of the payer.

travelling salesman *noun* (*plural* **travelling salesmen**)
a person who travels from place to place to sell goods or obtain orders for them.

travelogue (**trav**-a-log) *noun*
a film or book which describes travel, foreign countries, etc.
[TRAVEL + Greek *logos* speech]

traverse *verb*
1 to go across, along or through: *to traverse a paddock.*
2 *Law* to deny formally.
3 *Mountaineering* to climb in a horizontal or diagonal direction.
Word Family **traverse** *noun* 1 the act of traversing. 2 something which crosses, such as an intersecting line; **traversable** *adjective*.
[*trans-* + Latin *versus* turned]

travesty (**trav**-a-stee) *noun* (*plural* **travesties**)
an exaggerated ridiculous imitation, often as a form of comedy.
• **travesty** (**travesties**; **travestying**; **travestied**) *verb* to ridicule or make a travesty of.
[French *travesti* having changed clothes, disguised]

trawl *verb*
1 to fish by dragging a net along the seabed.
2 to search thoroughly.
• **trawl** *noun*
1 a strong net used for trawling.
2 an act of trawling: *a trawl through the archives.*
Word Family **trawler** *noun* a fishing boat used for trawling.

tray *noun*
a flat object of metal, wood or plastic, often with a raised rim, for holding or carrying articles.

treacherous (trech-a-rus) *adjective*
1 betraying trust or faith.
2 not to be trusted or relied on: *a treacherous smile.*
Word Family **treacherously** *adverb*; **treacherousness, treachery** *noun.*

treacle (tree-k'l) *noun*
a dark syrup obtained while refining sugar.
Word Family **treacly** *adjective.*

> The word **treacle** came into English through Old French *triacle* via Latin from Greek *theriake*. This was short for *antidotos theriake*, 'an antidote to poisonous or wild animals', *therion* meaning 'a wild animal'. In English it at first meant the same as in Greek, but it later came to mean 'medicine' generally. When the practice of sweetening medicines to disguise their unpleasant taste began, the resulting syrup was known as *treacle*.

tread (tred) *verb* (**treads; treading; trod; trodden** or **trod**)
1 to walk or walk on.
2 to make by treading: *The cattle trod a path to the waterhole.*
• **tread** *noun*
1 the act, manner or sound of treading.
2 the part of a tyre that touches the road, usually patterned to improve its grip.
3 the part of a step or stair on which the foot is placed.

treadle (tred-'l) *noun*
a lever worked by foot, e.g. on a sewing machine.

treadmill *noun*
1 a machine worked by the weight of people or animals moving a wheel.
2 an exercise machine that has a moving belt on which one walks or runs.
3 any job or way of life which is boring or repetitive.

treason (tree-z'n) *noun* also **high treason**
Law an act of disloyalty to or betrayal of one's country or monarch.
Word Family **treasonable** *adjective* of or involving treason; **treasonably** *adverb*; **treasonous** *adjective.*

treasure (trezh-a) *noun*
accumulated wealth, especially in the form of gems, precious metals, etc.
Figurative Our last gardener was a real treasure (= highly valued person).
• **treasure** *verb* to retain carefully or cherish: *I shall treasure the memory of this day.*
[Greek *thesauros*]

treasurer (trezh-a-ra) *noun*
a person who is in charge of the money of a society, company, city or government.

treasure trove *noun*
1 *Law (formerly)* any treasure, of unknown ownership, found hidden in the earth.
2 a valuable source: *This book is a treasure trove of fascinating information.*
[Old French *tresor* treasure + *trové* found]

treasury (trezh-a-ree) *noun* (*plural* **treasuries**)
1 a place where private or public funds are received, kept and paid out.
2 (**Treasury**) the department of a government that controls such functions.
3 a collection of valuable things: *the Golden Treasury of English Poets.*

Treasury bill *noun*
a bill of exchange issued by a government to get short-term finance.

treat (treet) *verb*
1 to act or behave in a specific way towards: *He treated her with consideration.*
2 to handle or deal with: *The author treats the subject very sensitively.*
3 to give medical care to: *He is being treated for leukaemia.*
4 to pay for on someone's behalf: *We treated Suresh to a birthday lunch.*
5 to subject to a chemical or physical process: *The fabric has been treated to resist shrinkage.*
• **treat** *noun* something which gives unusual pleasure, especially if unexpected: *It was a treat for the children to go to the zoo.*
Phrase **one's treat** an act of paying: *This is going to be my treat.*
[Latin *tractare* to handle]

treatise (tree-tiss or tree-tiz) *noun*
a long detailed systematic book or essay on a subject.

treaty (tree-tee) *noun* (*plural* **treaties**)
1 a formal agreement between two or more nations.
2 the document containing such an agreement.

treble¹ (treb-'l) *adjective*
being three times as big or having three parts.
• **treble** *noun* something three times as big or having three parts.
• **treble** *verb* to multiply by three.
[Latin *triplus* triple]

treble² *noun*
1 a high-pitched singing voice.
2 an instrument having this range: *a treble recorder.*

treble chance *noun*
a football pool competition with prizes for selecting eight drawn, but not scoreless, matches.
[the name refers to the (originally three, now four) possible scores for each selection]

treble clef ⇨ CLEF.

tree *noun*
1 a perennial plant having a single self-supporting woody trunk, often of considerable height, with branches and foliage developing at some distance from the ground.
2 something having the shape of a tree: *a family tree.*

treeline *noun*
the height on a mountain above which trees do not grow.

treen *noun*
small wooden articles of domestic use made by people of earlier generations.
[an old word for *wooden*, from TREE]

trefoil (tref-oil *or* tree-foil) *noun*
1 a plant similar to clover, with yellow flowers.
2 an architectural ornament resembling a three-leafed clover in shape.
[*tri-* + Latin *folium* leaf]

trek *verb* (**treks; trekking; trekked**)
to travel, especially arduously or in the bush.
• **trek** *noun.*
[Afrikaans]

trellis *noun* (*plural* **trellises**)
a light frame of crossed wooden or metal strips, used for supporting climbing plants, etc.

trematode (trem-a-tode) *noun*
a flatworm that is an internal parasite.
[Greek *trematodes* perforated]

tremble *verb*
1 (of a person) to shake involuntarily, e.g. from fear, cold, etc.
2 to feel anxiety: *I tremble to think what your father will do when he hears the news.*
3 to vibrate.
Word Family **tremble** *noun*;
tremblingly *adverb.*
[Latin *tremulus* trembling]

tremendous (tre-men-dus) *adjective*
1 enormous or very great: *A boulder of tremendous size blocked our path.*
2 (*informal*) wonderful: *It was a tremendous concert.*
Word Family **tremendously** *adverb*;
tremendousness *noun.*
[Latin *tremendus* dreadful or fearful]

tremolo (trem-a-lo) *noun*
Music a wavering effect produced by the voice or an instrument.
[Italian]

tremor (trem-a) *noun*
1 a shaking: *There was a nervous tremor in her voice.*
2 *Geography* a shaking of the earth's surface caused by an earthquake: *an earth tremor.*
[Latin]

tremulous (trem-yoo-lus) *adjective*
1 trembling.
2 timid or fearful.
Word Family **tremulously** *adverb*;
tremulousness *noun.*
[from Latin]

trench *noun* (*plural* **trenches**)
a long narrow hole dug in the ground, especially one used to protect soldiers from gunfire, etc.: *Her great-uncle died in the trenches in the First World War.*

trenchant (tren-ch'nt) *adjective*
incisive or keen: *He has a trenchant wit.*
Word Family **trenchantly** *adverb*;
trenchancy *noun.*
[Old French *tranchier* to cut]

trench coat *noun*
a thick raincoat tied with a belt.

trencher *noun*
a wooden plate, formerly used for serving food.
Word Family **trencherman** *noun* (*plural* **trenchermen**) a person with a healthy appetite.

trend *noun*
1 a general movement or tendency: *The modern trend is towards self-government.*
2 a fashion.

trendy *adjective* (**trendier; trendiest**)
(*informal*) fashionable.
Word Family trendily *adverb*;
trendiness *noun*.

trepan (tri-**pan**) *noun*
a trephine.
• **trepan** *verb* (**trepans; trepanning;
trepanned**)
to make a hole in a skull with a trepan.

trephine (tri-**fine** *or* tri-**feen**) *noun*
Medicine a special saw for making circular
holes, used by surgeons to make a hole in a
skull during an operation.
• **trephine** *verb*.

trepidation (trep-i-**day**-sh'n) *noun*
a state of alarm or agitation.
[from Latin]

trespass *verb*
1 *Law* to enter or go on to a person's
property without permission.
2 an old or poetic word meaning 'to do
wrong': *as we forgive them that trespass
against us*.
3 to take advantage of: *I didn't want to
trespass on his hospitality*.
Word Family trespass *noun* (*plural*
trespasses); **trespasser** *noun* a person
who trespasses on another's property.
[Old French *trespasser* to pass over]

tress *noun* (*plural* **tresses**)
a long lock or curl of hair.

trestle (**tres**-'l) *noun*
a supporting structure, usually a beam
with a pair of slanted legs at each end.

trestle table *noun*
a table made of a board or boards laid
across trestles.

triad (**try**-ad) *noun*
1 a group of three persons or things.
2 *Music* any three notes played together.

trial (**trile**) *noun*
1 *Law* the examination of evidence,
followed by a decision on the guilt or
innocence of a person, made by a judge or
jury.
2 a test, e.g. of performance or endurance.
3 something that tests someone: *one of life's
little trials*.
Phrase trial and error a process of
investigation, experimentation, etc. in
which various theories, methods, etc. are
tried until a successful one is found.

triangle (**try**-ang-g'l) *noun*
1 a closed plane figure with three straight
sides.

2 *Music* an instrument consisting of a thin
steel bar bent into a triangle and hit with a
small steel rod.
Word Family triangular (try-**ang**-gew-
la) *adjective* of, shaped like or bounded by
a triangle.
[*tri-* + Latin *angulus* corner]

triathlon (try-**ath**-lon) *noun*
Athletics a contest in which athletes aim for
the highest total score in three separate
events.
[*tri-* + Greek *athlon* contest]

tribe *noun*
1 an independent social group claiming or
occupying a particular territory, and
sharing a common ancestry, leadership or
customs.
2 *Biology* the group between family and
genus, sometimes used in the classification
of animals and plants.
Word Family tribal *adjective*; **tribesman**
noun (*plural* **tribesmen**); **tribeswoman**
noun (*plural* **tribeswomen**).
[from Latin]

tribulation (trib-yoo-**lay**-sh'n) *noun*
1 severe trouble or grief.
2 something that is a cause of this.
[Latin *tribulare* to oppress]

tribunal (try-**bew**-n'l) *noun*
a person or group appointed to hear and
settle disputes.

tribune (**trib**-yoon) *noun*
1 *Ancient history* an elected Roman
magistrate whose duties included
protection of the lower classes.
2 *Ancient history* any of six officers of a
legion, each in command for two months
of the year.
3 a popular leader.
Word Family tribuneship *noun* the
office of a tribune.

tributary (**trib**-yoo-tree) *noun* (*plural*
tributaries)
1 *Geography* a river or stream which flows
into a larger one.
2 (*formerly*) a person or country paying
tribute to another.

tribute (**trib**-yoot) *noun*
1 an acknowledgement of respect,
gratitude, admiration, etc.
2 (*formerly*) a payment demanded by one
nation or ruler from another for
protection, etc.
[Latin *tributus* assigned]

trice *noun*
Phrase in a trice in a very short period of
time.

tricentenary (try-sen-**tee**-na-ree) *noun*
(*plural* **tricentenaries**)
a 300th anniversary.
Word Family tricentennial (try-sen-
ten-i-al) *adjective*.

triceps (**try**-seps) *noun* (*plural* **triceps**)
Anatomy the large muscle at the back of
the upper arm which branches into three
parts and controls movement of the
forearm.
[Latin, three-headed]

trick *noun*
1 an action or device designed to deceive,
outwit or gain an advantage: *The phone call
was a trick to lure her out of the house.*
2 an illusion: *I thought the statue had moved
but it was just a trick of the light.*
3 a mannerism: *He has an odd trick of
stroking the side of his nose.*
4 *Cards* all the cards which are involved
and may be won in one round.
Phrase do the trick *That should do the
trick* (= achieve the desired result).
● **trick** *verb* to deceive or cheat by a trick
or tricks.
Word Family trickery *noun* the practice
of tricks; **trickster** *noun* a person who
habitually tricks people; **tricky** *adjective*
(**trickier; trickiest**) 1 given to or
characterized by trickery. 2 requiring skill
or difficult to handle; **trickily** *adverb*;
trickiness *noun*.

trickle *verb*
(of a liquid) to flow or cause to flow in a
thin stream or in drops.
Figurative *At peak hour the cars just trickle
through the city* (= move slowly).
● **trickle** *noun*.

tricolour (**trik**-a-la *or* **try**-kull-a) *noun*
(*American* **tricolor**)
a flag having three colours, especially the
French flag.
Word Family tricolour, tricoloured
adjective having three colours.

tricycle (**try**-sik-'l) *noun*
a vehicle resembling a bicycle with one
wheel at the front and two at the back.

trident (**try**-d'nt) *noun*
a three-pronged fork, especially as the
emblem of Poseidon (Neptune) or
Britannia.
[*tri-* + Latin *dentis* of a tooth]

triennial (try-**enn**-i-al) *adjective*
lasting for or occurring every three years.
Word Family triennially *adverb*.
[*tri-* + Latin *annus* year]

triennium *noun* (*plural* **triennia** or
trienniums)
a period of three years.

trifle (**try**-f'l) *noun*
1 a dessert made from sponge cake, fruit,
cream and custard.
2 a thing of little value or importance:
Don't get upset over trifles.
3 a small amount: *The jacket was a trifle
short.*
● **trifle** *verb*
Phrase trifle with to treat as if
unimportant: *to trifle with someone's
affections.*

trifling (**try**-fling) *adjective*
unimportant.

trigger *noun*
1 any of various mechanisms which release
a spring: *the trigger of a gun.*
2 something that sets something off.
● **trigger** *verb* to start or set off: *The
explosion triggered off a series of secondary
explosions.* □ *The film triggered memories of
her childhood.*

trigger-happy *adjective*
inclined to shoot or act at the slightest
provocation.

trigonometry (trig a **nom** a tree) *noun*
a branch of maths studying the
relationships between angles and sides of
triangles and other figures.
Word Family trigonometric (trig-a-no-
met-rik), **trigonometrical** *adjective*.
[Greek *trigonos* three-cornered + *metron* a
measure]

trilateral (try-**lat**-a-r'l) *adjective*
having three sides.
[*tri-* + Latin *lateris* of a side]

trilby *noun* (*plural* **trilbies**)
a soft felt hat with a dent in the crown.

> Trilby comes from the name Trilby
> O'Ferrall, the heroine of George
> Maurier's novel *Trilby* (1894). In the
> stage version of the novel, she wore a
> soft felt hat with an indented crown.

trilinear (try-**lin**-i-a) *adjective*
of, relating to or bounded by three lines.

trilingual (try-**ling**-gw'l) *adjective*
using or speaking three languages.

trill *noun*
1 a quavering or tremulous sound, such as
that made by certain birds.
2 *Music* a very fast alternation of two notes
either a tone or a semitone apart.
● **trill** *verb*.

trillion (**tril**-y'n) *noun* (*plural* **trillions** or **trillion**)
a cardinal number, traditionally 1 000 000 000 000 000 000 or 10^{18} (a million million million), but the American usage, 1 000 000 000 000 or 10^{12} (a million million), is now very common. Compare BILLION.

trilogy (**tril**-a-jee) *noun* (*plural* **trilogies**)
a series of three related novels or plays, each complete by itself, but having the same general subject or characters.
[*tri-* + *-logy*]

trim *verb* (**trims; trimming; trimmed**)
1 to make neat or tidy by clipping or pruning: *He trimmed his beard.*
2 to remove by cutting: *to trim away the loose threads.*
3 to ornament or decorate: *The hat was trimmed with feathers.*
4 *Nautical* to adjust the sails to suit the wind.
5 *Nautical* to distribute cargo or ballast so that a ship is balanced.
• **trim** *noun*
1 a haircut which neatens the appearance of the hair without altering the style.
2 ornamentation or material used for decorating, such as the upholstery and other fittings of a car.
3 a state of good order or fitness: *Everything was in good trim.* □ *The boxer was in fighting trim.*
Word Family **trim** *adjective* (**trimmer; trimmest**) in good or neat order; **trimmer** *noun* a person or thing that trims; **trimly** *adverb*; **trimness** *noun*.

trimaran (**try**-ma-ran) *noun*
a boat or raft with three hulls which are parallel and joined above the water. Compare CATAMARAN.
[*tri-* + (cata)MARAN]

trimester (try-**mest**-a) *noun*
a period or term of three months.
[*tri-* + Latin *mensis* month]

trimming *noun*
1 something that is added for ornament or to give a finished effect.
2 a piece that is cut off or removed by trimming.
3 (**trimmings**) (*informal*) any extras or accessories: *We had roast beef with all the trimmings.*

trinitrotoluene (try-nite-ro-**tol**-yoo-een) *noun*
short form is **TNT** a pale yellow crystalline solid which is a powerful explosive. It is safe to handle as it requires a detonator and is used in bombs and other weapons.

trinity (**trin**-i-tee) *noun* (*plural* **trinities**)
1 (**Trinity**) *Christianity* the three persons of the Godhead: the Father, the Son and the Holy Spirit, being one God.
2 any group of three.
[Latin *trinitas* a triad]

trinket *noun*
a small ornamental article, e.g. a piece of jewellery, usually of little value.

trinomial (try-**no**-mee-'l) *adjective*
Maths of or relating to an expression containing three terms, e.g. $x + 2y - z$.
[*tri-* + Greek *nomos* a part]

trio (**tree**-o) *noun*
1 a group of three people or things.
2 a group of three musicians.
3 a musical composition for three musicians or instruments.
4 the middle section of a minuet, march, etc.
[Italian]

triode (**try**-ode) *noun*
Electricity a valve with three electrodes, an anode, a cathode and a grid.
[*tri-* + (electr)ODE]

trip *verb* (**trips; tripping; tripped**)
1 to catch one's foot and almost fall: *I tripped over the step.*
2 to cause to almost fall: *I put out my foot and tripped him.*
3 to move quickly or with short light steps.
4 (*informal*) to take or experience the effects of a hallucinogenic substance, such as lysergic acid diethylamide (LSD).
5 to release or be released: *This lever trips the catch and the door swings open.*
Phrase **trip up 1** to make or cause to make a mistake. **2** to catch in a mistake.
• **trip** *noun*
1 a journey, especially one for pleasure.
2 (*informal*) the effects of a hallucinogenic drug.

tripartite (try-**par**-tite) *adjective*
being divided into, or composed of, three parts.

tripe *noun*
1 the flat white stomach of cattle, often cooked.
2 (*informal*) nonsense.

triplane (**try**-plane) *noun*
an aeroplane with three pairs of wings, one above another.

triple *adjective*
being three times as big or having three parts.

• **triple** *verb* to make or become three
times as many or as large.
• **triple** *noun* a group or set of three.
[from Latin]

triple jump *noun*
Athletics a contest in which competitors
must get as far as possible by making a
hop, a step and a jump in a continuous
movement.

triplet *noun*
1 any of three offspring born at one birth.
2 *Poetry* a group of three rhyming lines.
3 *Music* a group of three equal notes
performed in the time of two.

triplicate (**trip**-li-kit) *adjective*
consisting of three identical parts or
examples.
[*tri-* + Latin *plicare* to fold]

tripod (**try**-pod) *noun*
a stool or stand with three legs, as is used
to support a camera.
[*tri-* + Greek *podos* of a foot]

tripper *noun*
(*informal*) a person on an excursion.

triptych (**trip**-tik) *noun*
a series of altar paintings on three panels
side by side. Compare DIPTYCH.
[Greek *triptykhos* three-folded]

trireme (**try**-reem) *noun*
Ancient history a war galley with three
banks of oars, one above another.
[*tri-* + Latin *remus* an oar]

trisect (try-**sekt**) *verb*
to divide into three, usually equal, parts.

trite *adjective*
commonplace or lacking originality: *a trite
remark*.
Word Family **tritely** *adverb*; **triteness**
noun.
[Latin *tritus* worn with use]

triumph (**try**-umf) *noun*
1 a victory or success.
2 a feeling of joy because of a victory.
Word Family **triumph** *verb*; **triumphal**
(try-**um**-f'l) *adjective* of, relating to or in
the nature of a triumph; **triumphant**
(try-**um**-f'nt) *adjective* 1 victorious.
2 exultant because of a victory or success;
triumphantly *adverb*.
[Latin *triumphus* a victory parade]

triumvir (try-**um**-va *or* **try**-um-va) *noun*
(*plural* **triumvirs** *or* **triumviri** (try-um-
vi-rie *or* **try**-um-vi-rie))
Ancient history any of three men who
shared joint administrative authority in
Rome.
[Latin *trium virorum* of three men]

triumvirate (try-**um**-va-rit) *noun*
1 the position or term of office of a
triumvir.
2 any group of three people who together
exercise authority or control.

trivet *noun*
a low metal stand on legs, used to support
a pot or kettle over a fire.
[Latin *tripes* three-footed]

trivial (**triv**-i-al) *adjective*
insignificant or of trifling value: *a trivial
objection*.
Word Family **trivially** *adverb*; **triviality**
(triv-i-**al**-i-tee) *noun* (*plural* **trivialities**)
1 the state or quality of being trivial. 2 a
trivial matter, event, idea, etc.; **trivia**
(**triv**-i-a) *plural noun* insignificant or
unimportant matters.
[Latin *trivialis* commonplace]

trod the past tense and a past participle of
tread.

trodden a past participle of **tread**.

troglodyte (**trog**-la-dite) *noun*
a cave-dweller.
[Greek *troglodytes*]

troika (**troy**-ka) *noun*
a Russian vehicle drawn by a team of three
horses running abreast.
[Russian *troie* three]

troll *noun*
Scandinavian mythology a supernatural
being, sometimes believed to be a giant
and sometimes a mischievous dwarf.

trolley *noun*
1 a large metal basket on wheels, used in a
supermarket.
2 a frame on wheels, used for pushing
luggage, e.g. at a station or airport.
3 a small table on wheels, used for carrying
food to the table.
4 a trolleybus.
5 a trolley car.

trolleybus *noun* (*plural* **trolleybuses**)
a bus powered by electricity from two
overhead wires.

trolley car *noun*
American a tram.

trollop (**troll**-up) *noun*
an immoral woman.

trombone *noun*
Music a brass wind instrument in which a
slide is moved to lengthen or shorten the
tube.
Word Family **trombonist** *noun*.
[Italian *tromba* trumpet]

troop *noun*
1 an assembled company: *A troop of admirers followed him everywhere.*
2 (**troops**) *Military* soldiers.
3 *Military* a tactical unit of cavalry.
• **troop** *verb* to come, go or gather as a troop: *The children trooped out of school.*

trooper *noun*
1 a soldier in the cavalry or armoured corps.
2 *American* a police officer.
Phrase **swear like a trooper** to use very bad language.

trophy (**tro-fee**) *noun* (*plural* **trophies**)
1 a prize, especially for the winner of a sporting competition.
2 something kept in memory of a victory: *He took his enemy's sword for a trophy.*

tropical *adjective*
of, relating to or occurring in the tropics.

tropical cyclone *noun*
an area of intense low pressure formed over warm tropical oceans, having strong circular winds revolving around a calmer central area and bringing heavy rain and stormy seas. A tropical cyclone is known as a **hurricane** in the Caribbean and eastern states of America, a **typhoon** in the western North Pacific and a **cyclone** in the Bay of Bengal and around Australia.

tropic of Cancer *noun*
a line of latitude 23° 30' north of the equator, the northernmost point at which the sun can be overhead.

tropic of Capricorn *noun*
a line of latitude 23° 30' south of the equator, the southernmost point at which the sun can be overhead.

tropics *plural noun*
the area of the earth lying either side of the region of the equator, between the tropics of Cancer and Capricorn.
[Greek *tropé* a turning (as the sun appears to turn back after reaching these points)]

tropism (**tro-pizm** *or* **trop-izm**) *noun*
Biology the involuntary response of an organism to an external stimulus. The orientation of the leaves of certain plants towards the sun is a tropism.
[Greek *tropé* turning]

troposphere (**trop-a-sfeer** *or* **tro-pa-sfeer**) *noun*
the lower layers of the atmosphere below the stratosphere, up to about 6-10 km from the earth's surface. Compare STRATOSPHERE.
[Greek *tropos* turning + SPHERE]

trot *noun*
1 a gait of a horse between a walk and canter, in which the legs move in diagonal pairs.
2 a running or jogging gait using quick short steps.
• **trot** *verb* (**trots; trotting; trotted**) to move or run at a trot.
Phrase **trot out** to produce or bring out.

troth (**troath** *or* **troth**) *noun*
1 an old word for faithfulness or loyalty.
2 an old word for truth.

Trotskyism *noun*
the principles of the Russian revolutionary Leon Trotsky, who advocated world revolution to establish socialism.
Word Family **Trotskyist, Trotskyite** *noun, adjective.*

trotter *noun*
1 the foot of an animal, especially the pig or sheep.
2 a horse bred or trained for trotting races.

trotting *noun*
racing for horses pulling two-wheeled vehicles called sulkies.

troubadour (**troo-ba-dor**) *noun*
a travelling musician and singer, especially in medieval France.
[Old French, finder, inventor, composer]

trouble (*rhymes with* **bubble**) *verb*
1 to cause worry or anxiety, etc.: *My son's violent behaviour troubles me.*
2 to disturb: *I'm sorry to trouble you.*
3 to make the effort to do something: *Don't trouble to meet me at the station.*
• **trouble** *noun*
1 worry, anxiety or misfortune.
2 a person or thing causing this.
3 unrest: *industrial trouble.*
Phrase **in trouble** in a position likely to bring hardship or punishment.
Word Family **troublesome** *adjective* causing trouble.
[Latin *turbidus* crowded, disturbed]

troubleshooter *noun*
a person who finds and eliminates causes of trouble.

trough (**trof**) *noun*
1 an open box-like container used for feeding or watering animals, washing ore, etc.
2 *Weather* an area of low pressure extending from a low.
3 a long narrow channel, e.g. the hollow between successive ocean waves.

trounce *verb*
1 to beat or defeat severely.
2 to punish or reprimand.

troupe (troop) *noun*
a group of actors or performers, especially ones who travel about.
[French, troop]

trouper *noun*
1 a member of a troupe.
2 a loyal and hard-working person.

trousers *plural noun*
a piece of clothing covering the lower half of the body, enclosing each leg separately.
• **trouser** *adjective* of trousers: *trouser pockets.*

trousseau (troo-so) *noun* (*plural* **trousseaus** or **trousseaux**) (troo-soze)
the clothes and household items which a bride brings with her on marriage.
[French *trousse* bundle]

trout *noun* (*plural* **trout** or **trouts**)
a freshwater fish related to the salmon and highly esteemed as sport and food.

trow (tro) *verb*
an old word meaning 'to think or believe'.

trowel (*rhymes with* towel) *noun*
1 a tool with a short handle and a flat blade for spreading mortar.
2 a small tool with a curved blade for gardening.

troy *noun*
a system of units of mass for precious metals and gems in which one pound equals 12 ounces. The units are the grain, pennyweight, ounce and pound.
Compare AVOIRDUPOIS.

truant (troo-ant) *noun*
a pupil who stays away from school without permission.
Phrase **play truant** to be a truant.
Word Family **truant** *adjective* wandering; **truancy** (troo-an-see) *noun;* **truant** *verb.*

truce *noun*
an agreement to stop fighting for a period of time.

truck[1] *noun*
1 a motor vehicle for carrying heavy loads.
2 any wheeled structure for moving heavy goods, such as a railway wagon.
• **truck** *verb* (*especially American*) to transport goods by truck.

truck[2] *noun*
American garden produce grown for the market: *truck farming.*
Phrase **have no truck with, want no truck with** to have or want no dealings with.

truculent (truk-yoo-l'nt) *adjective*
aggressive or belligerent.

Word Family **truculence** *noun;* **truculently** *adverb.*
[Latin *trux* fierce]

trudge *verb*
to walk heavily or wearily.
• **trudge** *noun.*

true (troo) *adjective*
1 corresponding to the actual state of things: *It was an unlikely story but he insisted it was true.*
2 not artificial or counterfeit: *true love.*
3 accurate: *a true reading.*
4 loyal or faithful: *a true and trusted follower.*
5 related to the earth's axis rather than the magnetic poles: *true north.*
• **true** *adverb* in a true or truthful manner.
Phrase **come true** to happen in reality.

true-blue *adjective*
loyal to the Conservative Party.

truffle *noun*
1 an underground fungus, considered a delicacy.
2 a round chocolate and cocoa sweet.
[Latin *tubera*]

trug *noun*
a shallow wooden basket used in gardening to collect produce.

truism (troo-izm) *noun*
an obvious or self-evident truth.

truly (troo-lee) *adverb*
1 truthfully: *She speaks truly.*
2 undeniably: *a truly superb meal.*

trump *noun*
1 (**trumps**) *Cards* the chosen suit, all of whose cards outrank any others during a particular hand.
2 *Cards* a card in this suit.
3 a powerful or decisive stroke, resource, etc.
4 (*dated informal*) an admirable person.
Phrase **turn up trumps, come up trumps** to turn out better or more helpful than one expected.
• **trump** *verb*
1 *Cards* to play a trump.
2 *Cards* to win a trick or outrank another card by playing a trump.
Phrase **trump up** *The police trumped up charges against the innocent man* (= invented dishonestly).
[from TRIUMPH]

trumpet *noun*
1 *Music* a high-pitched brass wind instrument with a flared bell-shaped end.
2 something which has the shape of a trumpet.

3 the cry of an elephant.
Phrase **blow one's own trumpet** to praise oneself.
● **trumpet** *verb*
1 to blow a trumpet.
2 to make a trumpet-like sound.
3 to proclaim: *They trumpeted the news all over town.*
Word Family **trumpeter** *noun* a person who plays the trumpet.

truncated *adjective*
shortened by having a part or end cut off.
Word Family **truncate** *verb*.
[Latin *truncare* to mutilate, lop off]

truncheon (**trun-ch'n**) *noun*
a police officer's short club or baton.
[Latin *truncus* a tree trunk]

trundle *verb*
to move or roll along, especially something which is heavy or awkward.

trunk *noun*
1 the main stem of a tree excluding the roots and branches.
2 *Anatomy* the main part of the body excluding the head, neck, arms and legs.
3 a large box with a hinged lid, for carrying or storing clothes, etc.
4 the long flexible snout of an elephant.
5 *American* the boot of a car.
● **trunk** *adjective*
1 (*dated*) relating to a telephone line connecting two distant exchanges: *a trunk call*.
2 relating to a main line or artery: *a trunk road*.
[from Latin]

trunks *plural noun*
men's shorts worn for swimming or as underpants.

truss *noun* (*plural* **trusses**)
1 a framework constructed so that all the forces on its parts are either tensions or compressions, used to support bridges, roofs, etc.
2 a padded belt worn to support a hernia.
3 a bundle, e.g. of hay, etc.
● **truss** *verb*
1 to tie up or bind.
2 to support with a truss or trusses.

trust *noun*
1 a firm belief in something: *I have full trust in your ability to succeed.*
2 responsibility: *a position of trust.*
3 *Law* a relationship between two people whereby property is held by one person for the benefit of the other.

4 *Commerce* a group of firms formed to control prices, production, etc. but otherwise independent of each other.
Phrase **on trust** *You'll have to take my word on trust* (= without proof).
● **trust** *verb*
1 to have or place trust in: *I don't trust his promises.* □ *Can I trust you not to reveal the secret?*
2 to hope: *I trust you'll have a pleasant journey.*
Word Family **trusting, trustful** *adjective* having ready trust or confidence; **trustingly** *adverb*; **trustingness** *noun*.

trustee *noun*
1 *Law* a person appointed to take care of the business affairs of an institution, company, etc.
2 *Law* a person who holds property for the benefit of another.
Word Family **trusteeship** *noun*.

trustworthy *adjective*
able to be trusted.
Word Family **trustworthily** *adverb*; **trustworthiness** *noun*.

trusty *adjective* (**trustier; trustiest**)
faithful or reliable: *his trusty sword.*
● **trusty** *noun* (*plural* **trusties**) a trusted prisoner.

truth (**trooth**) *noun*
1 that which is true: *Are you telling the truth?*
2 the quality or state of being true: *There is no truth in the rumour.*
3 something which has been verified or cannot be disputed: *a scientific truth.*
Phrase **in truth** in fact or reality.
Word Family **truthful** *adjective* 1 telling the truth. 2 true; **truthfully** *adverb*; **truthfulness** *noun*.

truth drug *noun*
a drug which is administered to a person under investigation, said to render the person more likely to blurt out the truth.

try *verb* (**tries; trying; tried**)
1 to attempt: *Try to speak quietly.*
2 to test: *Try the soup and see whether you like it.*
3 *Law* to determine the guilt or innocence of a person during a trial.
4 to strain: *You're trying my patience.*
Phrases **try on** to put on clothes, etc. to see if they fit or look good. **try out** to test or experiment with.
● **try** *noun* (*plural* **tries**)
1 an attempt, endeavour or effort.
2 *Rugby* the act of carrying the ball over the opposing team's goal line and touching

the ground with it. The scoring side then tries to score a goal from a place kick.

trying *adjective*
annoying or irritating: *She needed to relax after a trying day at the office.*

tryst (trist) *noun*
a poetic word for an appointment or meeting between lovers.
[Old French *triste* a waiting place (a hunting term)]

tsar (zar *or* tsar) *noun* also **czar; tzar**
1 *History* an emperor in Russia from 1547 to 1917.
2 a person in charge of something: *The government are going to appoint a drug tsar.*
Word Family tsarist *noun* a supporter of a tsar or government by tsars.
[Russian, from Latin *Caesar*]

tsarina (zar-**ee**-na *or* tsar-**ee**-na) *noun* also **czarina; tzarina**
History an empress in Russia from 1547 to 1917.

tsetse (**tset**-si *or* **tet**-si) *noun* also **tsetse fly** (*plural* **tsetse flies**)
an African blood-sucking fly which may transmit sleeping sickness to people and various serious diseases to cattle.

T-shirt *noun* also **tee shirt**
a light cotton shirt with short sleeves and no collar.
[from its shape when spread out]

T-square *noun*
a T-shaped ruler used for drawing right angles.

tsunami (tsoo-**nah**-mee) *noun*
a large tidal wave caused by an earthquake under the sea.
[Japanese *tsu* harbour + *nami* wave]

tub *noun*
1 any large low open vessel made of metal, wood, etc., used for washing, growing plants, etc.
2 a small plastic container, e.g. for ice cream or margarine.
3 (*informal*) an old or slow boat.

tuba (**tew**-ba) *noun*
Music a low-pitched brass wind instrument.
[Latin]

tubby *adjective* (**tubbier; tubbiest**)
(*informal*) short, round and fat.
Word Family tubbiness *noun.*

tube *noun*
1 an extended hollow cylinder made from glass, metal, rubber, etc.

2 something which has the shape of this, such as some organs of the human body: *the bronchial tubes.*
3 a soft metal container with a screw cap at one end: *a tube of toothpaste.*
4 (*informal*) the London underground railway system.
5 (*informal*) an underground train.
6 an electrical valve: *a television tube.*
Word Family tubing (**tube**-ing) *noun* any material in the form of a tube; **tubular** (**tube**-yoo-la) *adjective* having, consisting of or shaped like a tube.
[from Latin]

tuber (**tew**-ba) *noun*
Biology the swollen end of an underground stem, such as a potato, containing a store of food and acting as an organ of vegetative reproduction.
Word Family tuberous *adjective* of, like or producing tubers.
[Latin, bump or swelling]

tuberculosis (tew-ber-kew-**lo**-sis) *noun*
a bacterial disease often affecting the lungs, causing a swelling (called a **tubercle**) in the affected tissue.
Word Family tubercular (tew-**ber**-kew-la), **tuberculous** *adjective.*
[Latin *tuberculum* a small swelling + *-osis*]

tuberose (**tew**-ba-roze) *noun*
a Mexican garden plant with spikes of fragrant cream flowers growing from a bulb.
[Latin *tuberosus* swollen]

tuck *verb*
1 to fold under or push in the loose edge or end of: *Tuck the blankets under the mattress.* □ *Tuck in your shirt.*
2 to make tucks in, by folding and stitching.
Phrases tuck away to hide: *a cottage tucked away in the forest.* **tuck in, tuck into** to eat heartily.
● **tuck** *noun*
1 *Needlework* a fold in cloth that is stitched into place.
2 (*informal*) an operation to remove fat: *a tummy tuck.*
3 (*informal*) food eaten as a snack at school: *a tuck shop.*

Tudor (**tew**-der) *noun*
a member of the royal house in England from 1485 to 1603.

Tuesday *noun*
the third day of the week, after Monday and before Wednesday.
[named after the ancient German god *Tiw*, identified with Mars]

tuff *noun*
Geology a rock formed by compacted layers of ash from a volcano.
[from Latin]

tuft *noun*
a bunch of feathers, hair, grass, etc. growing or held together at the base.
Word Family **tufted, tufty** *adjective* containing tufts.

tug *verb* (**tugs; tugging; tugged**)
to pull or pull at forcefully: *She tugged my sleeve.*
• **tug** *noun*
1 the act of tugging: *Give the rope a hard tug.*
2 also **tugboat** a small boat with a powerful engine used to tow and manoeuvre other ships.

tug of war *noun*
a competition between two teams, in which each holds an end of a rope, the aim being for one team to pull the other across a central line.

tuition (tew-*ish*-'n) *noun*
the teaching or instruction of students.
[Latin *tuitio* a looking after]

tulip (*tew*-lip) *noun*
a garden plant with single cup-shaped flowers growing from a bulb.
[Turkish *tulbend* turban]

tulle (tewl) *noun*
a thin net-like fabric used for veils and dresses.
[originally made in *Tulle*, France]

tumble *verb*
to roll or fall over or down: *The clumsy boy tumbled off the chair.*
Phrase **tumble to** *At last she tumbled to his real meaning* (= understood).
• **tumble** *noun*
1 a fall.
2 a confused state or heap.

tumbledown *adjective*
dilapidated: *a tumbledown shack.*

tumble-dryer *noun*
a machine for drying laundry by spinning it in hot air.
Word Family **tumble-dry** *verb* (**tumble-dries; tumble-drying; tumble-dried**).

tumbler *noun*
1 a flat-bottomed drinking glass.
2 a person who performs somersaults and other tricks.
3 any of the parts of a lock which move when the key is turned.
4 a tumble-dryer.

tumbril *noun* also **tumbrel**
a cart which may be tilted backwards to empty its load.
[French *tomber* to fall]

tumescent (tew-*mess*-'nt) *adjective*
swelling or swollen.
Word Family **tumescence** *noun*.
[from Latin]

tumid (*tew*-mid) *adjective*
swollen or bulging.
Word Family **tumidity** (tew-*mid*-i-tee) *noun*.
[from Latin]

tummy *noun* (*plural* **tummies**)
(*informal*) the stomach.

tumour (*tew*-ma) *noun* (*American* **tumor**)
an abnormal swelling in the body, which may be benign or malignant.
[from Latin]

tumult (*tew*-mult) *noun*
1 a commotion or disturbance made by a crowd.
2 a confused state: *Her mind was in a tumult.*
Word Family **tumultuous** (tew-*mul*-tew-us) *adjective* 1 noisy. 2 disturbed; **tumultuously** *adverb*.
[from Latin]

tumulus (*tew*-mew-lus) *noun* (*plural* **tumuli**) (*tew*-mew-lie *or* *tew*-mew-lee)
a prehistoric barrow.
[Latin, a mound]

tun *noun*
a large cask for wine or beer.

tuna (*tew*-na) *noun* (*plural* **tuna** *or* **tunas**) also called **tunny**.
a large edible marine fish with a distinctive pink flesh.
[Greek *thynnos*]

tundra *noun*
the treeless lands close to the North Pole where little grows except mosses, grass and lichens. There are long severe winters and the subsoil is permanently frozen.
[Russian]

tune *noun*
a rhythmic series or arrangement of musical sounds, e.g. of a song.
Phrases **call the tune** to control or give orders. **change one's tune** to change one's ideas or behaviour. **in tune** *Can you sing in tune?* (= in harmony or correct pitch). **out of tune** *This old piano is out of tune* (= not in harmony or correct pitch). **to the tune of** to the amount of: *She was in debt to the tune of £200.*

• **tune** *verb* to adjust a musical instrument, radio, car engine, etc. to get the correct pitch, resonance or performance.
Phrases **tune in** to locate a particular station or programme by adjusting the controls of a radio. **tune up** *The orchestra were already tuning up as we took our seats* (= getting in tune).
Word Family **tuneful** *adjective* having or full of tune; **tunefully** *adverb*; **tunefulness** *noun*.
[alteration of TONE]

tuner *noun*
1 a person or thing that tunes: *a piano tuner.*
2 *Radio* the part of a receiver which selects signals for amplifying, thus determining performance.

tungsten *noun*
a malleable ductile metal used for electric light filaments and cutting tools.
[Swedish *tung* heavy + *sten* stone]

tunic (**tew**-nik) *noun*
1 a short loose sleeveless dress, often with a belt.
2 a coat or jacket worn as part of a police or military uniform.
[from Latin]

tuning fork *noun*
a two-pronged metal object which vibrates at a set pitch when struck. It is used to check the pitch of musical instruments and voices.

tunnel *noun*
an underground passage, especially an artificial one.
• **tunnel** *verb* (**tunnels, tunnelling, tunnelled**) to make a tunnel.

tunnel vision *noun*
1 lack of peripheral vision.
2 (*informal*) narrow-mindedness, seeing only one point of view.

tunny *noun* (*plural* **tunnies**)
a tuna.

tuppence ⇨ TWOPENCE.

turban *noun*
a head covering consisting of a long strip of cloth wound around the head, worn by Muslim and Sikh men.
[Turkish *tulbend*]

turbid (**ter**-bid) *adjective*
1 not clear or transparent: *The turbid river was full of silt.*
2 confused: *turbid thoughts.*

Word Family **turbidly** *adverb*; **turbidity** (ter-**bid**-i-tee) *noun*.
[Latin *turbidus* crowded, disturbed]

turbine (**ter**-bine *or* **ter**-bin) *noun*
a motor in which the shaft is turned by the action of a fluid, such as gas, steam or water, passing over blades set in a wheel.
[Latin *turbinis* of a spinning top]

turbojet *noun*
a jet engine with a turbine-driven compressor.

turboprop *noun* also called **prop jet**.
1 a jet engine which produces thrust by a propeller connected to the turbine shaft.
2 an aircraft driven by one or more such engines.

turbot *noun* (*plural* **turbot** *or* **turbots**)
a very large flatfish, highly valued as food and having similarities to brill and halibut.
[French]

turbulent (**ter**-bew-l'nt) *adjective*
violent, unruly or uncontrolled: *the turbulent waters of a whirlpool.*
Word Family **turbulence** *noun* 1 a turbulent state. 2 *Weather* the irregular movements of air near the ground and in air currents; **turbulently** *adverb*.
[from Latin]

tureen (tew-**reen** *or* ta-**reen**) *noun*
a deep round dish with a lid, for serving soup.
[French *terrine*]

turf *noun* (*plural* **turfs** *or* **turves**)
1 the layer of earth containing grass and its matted roots.
2 a piece of this.
3 (**the turf**) horse racing.
• **turf** *verb* to cover with turf.
Phrase **turf out** to throw out.

turf accountant *noun*
(*formal*) a bookmaker.

turgid (**ter**-jid) *adjective*
1 pretentious or pompous: *turgid prose.*
2 swollen.
Word Family **turgidly** *adverb*; **turgidity** (ter-**jid**-i-tee) *noun*.
[Latin *turgidus* swollen]

turkey (**ter**-kee) *noun*
a large edible fowl, both wild and domesticated, originally from North America.
Phrases **cold turkey** the effects of sudden withdrawal from an addictive drug, such as heroin. **talk turkey** to talk seriously.

The word **turkey** was originally applied to the guineafowl because this bird was imported into Europe from Africa by the Portuguese, through Turkey. When the bird we now call *turkey* was introduced from America to Britain, it became known as this because it reminded people of the original *turkey*.

Turkish bath *noun*
1 a steam bath followed by a wash and massage.
2 a building where this is available.

turmeric (**term**-a-rik) *noun*
the yellow powdered root of an Indian plant, used as a spice, a dye and in medicine.

turmoil *noun*
a state of great commotion or agitation: *The government was in turmoil over the scandal.*

turn *verb*
1 to move or cause to move around an axis or centre: *The wheels turned as the car rolled forward.*
2 to change or cause to change direction, position, etc. by moving through a part of a circle: *Turn the corner.* □ *He turned his head to see.*
3 to change so that the upper side becomes the lower: *Turn the pancakes before they burn.* □ *Turn the page carefully.*
4 to move or orientate to a particular or new position: *Turn to page 63.* □ *Turn your thoughts to the future.*
5 to become or cause to become: *She turned red with rage.* □ *The twins turn three tomorrow.* □ *The witch turned the prince into a frog.*
6 to shape or form, as on a lathe.
7 (of leaves) to change colour in the autumn.
8 to go bad: *The milk has turned.*
9 to spin: *My head was turning.*
10 to resort: *I turned to her for help.* □ *She turned to drink.*
11 to sicken: *to turn someone's stomach.*
Phrases **turn against** to become or cause to become hostile towards. **turn away** to refuse help or admittance to. **turn down 1** to lessen in volume, flow, etc. **2** to refuse or reject. **turn in 1** to go to bed. **2** to hand over to the police, etc.: *The escaped prisoner turned himself in.* **turn off 1** to diverge or divert. **2** to repulse or bore. **turn on 1** to attack suddenly. **2** to excite. **turn out 1** to switch off: *Turn out the lights.* **2** to make or manufacture. **3** to empty: *Turn out your pockets.* **4** to assemble or

muster: *The troops turned out at reveille.*
5 to equip or outfit. **turn over 1** to ponder or meditate. **2** (of an engine) to start. **3** to hand over. **turn up 1** to happen. **2** to arrive. **3** to find or be found.
● **turn** *noun*
1 a turning movement: *Give the key a hard turn.*
2 a change in direction, condition, etc.: *There were many turns in the road.* □ *His health took a turn for the worse.*
3 the place at which something turns: *Take the second turn left.*
4 the time at or during which something occurs in rotation: *Wait for your turn.*
5 an action which affects someone: *She did me a good turn.*
6 *Theatre* an act.
7 (*informal*) a shock: *The news gave me quite a turn.*
Phrases **at every turn** constantly. **on the turn** turning or about to turn or change. **take turns** to alternate. **to a turn** to just the right degree: *The sausages were done to a turn.* **turn and turn about** alternately.
[Greek *tornos* a lathe]

turncoat *noun*
a renegade.

turning *noun*
the place where a road turns, especially at a fork or junction.

turnip *noun*
a white round root used as a vegetable.

turnkey (**tern**-kee) *noun*
an old word for a jailer.

turn-off *noun*
a road, path, etc. branching off a main road.

turnout *noun*
a gathering of people at an event.

turnover *noun*
1 the total amount of money received from the sale of goods in a certain period of time.
2 the rate at which goods, money, employees, etc. are replaced.
3 a semicircular pie made by folding one half of the crust over the other.

turnpike *noun*
1 *History* a road on which a toll must be paid.
2 *American* a motorway on which a toll must be paid.

turnstile *noun*
a revolving gateway admitting one person at a time, used for counting and

controlling the people entering a sports ground, etc.

turntable *noun*
1 the part of a record player on which the record sits and revolves.
2 *Railways* a section of a railway line set on a disc, which may be rotated to transfer railway vehicles onto other lines.

turn-up *noun*
1 a fold of material turned up on the outside of a trouser leg.
2 (*informal*) an unexpected or lucky result or event.

turpentine (**ter**-pen-tine) *noun*
1 a mixture of oil and resin produced by pine trees, used to make rosin and oil of turpentine.
2 also **oil of turpentine** an inflammable oil distilled from this, used for mixing or thinning oil paints, etc.
[Greek *terebinthos* a tree yielding turpentine]

turpitude (**ter**-pi-tewd) *noun*
(*formal*) wickedness or depravity.
[Latin *turpis* ugly, filthy]

turps *noun*
(*informal*) oil of turpentine.

turquoise (**ter**-kwoyz *or* **ter**-kwahz) *noun*
1 *Geology* a hard blue or blue-green mineral used as a gem.
2 a bright greenish-blue colour.
• **turquoise** *adjective*.

turret *noun*
1 a small tower, often decorative.
2 a revolving heavily armoured structure containing large guns, e.g. in a warship or on a tank.
[Latin *turris* a tower]

turtle *noun*
1 an aquatic reptile having a shell and living in the sea or fresh water, with legs modified for swimming. Compare TORTOISE.
2 *Computers* a cursor which can be given instructions to move in a particular direction on a screen.
Phrase **turn turtle** to capsize.

turtle dove *noun*
a type of small long-tailed dove noted for its gentle coo.
[Latin *turtur*]

turtleneck *noun*
a high tight round neck on a sweater.

turves
a plural of **turf**.

tusk *noun*
a long protruding tooth found in some mammals, such as the elephant and walrus.
Word Family **tusker** *noun* an animal with tusks.

tussle *verb*
to fight or struggle roughly.
• **tussle** *noun*.

tussock *noun*
a thick clump of grass.

tut *interjection*
an exclamation expressing rebuke or disapproval.

tutelage (**tew**-ta-lij) *noun*
1 guardianship.
2 instruction, teaching.

tutelary (**tew**-ta-la-ree) *adjective*
of or serving as a guardian or protector.

tutor (**tew**-ta) *noun*
1 a private teacher, especially of a single pupil or very small class.
2 a college or university teacher who supervises the work and welfare of undergraduates taking a particular degree course.
Word Family **tutor** *verb*; **tutorship** *noun* the position of a tutor.
[Latin, guardian]

tutorial (tew-**taw**-ri-al) *noun*
a period of instruction with a university tutor.

tut-tut *interjection*
an exclamation expressing rebuke or disapproval.

tutu (**too**-too) *noun*
a short frilly flared skirt made of tulle, worn by female ballet dancers.
[French]

tuxedo (tuk-**see**-do) *noun* (*plural* **tuxedos** *or* **tuxedoes**)
short form is **tux** (*especially American*) a dinner jacket.
[after a New York club]

twaddle (*rhymes with* doddle) *noun*
(*informal*) meaningless or foolish talk or writing.

twain *noun*
an old word for two.

twang *verb*
to make a sharp vibrating sound, e.g. by plucking the string of a musical instrument.
• **twang** *noun*
1 a twanging sound.
2 a sharp nasal sound in the human voice.

tweak *verb*
1 to pinch or twist: *He tweaked the child's nose.*
2 (*informal*) to make slight adjustments to.
• **tweak** *noun*.

twee *adjective*
affectedly sentimental or quaint.

tweed *noun*
1 a coarse heavy woollen fabric with a rough surface, which comes in a variety of weaves and colours.
2 (**tweeds**) clothes made of this fabric. [alteration of TWILL (confused with the River *Tweed*)]

tweet *verb*
to chirp.
• **tweet** *noun*.

tweeter *noun*
a loudspeaker designed for high frequencies. Compare WOOFER.

tweezers *plural noun*
a small implement with two arms, used for plucking hairs or picking up small objects, etc.

twelve *noun*
a cardinal number, the symbol 12 in Arabic numerals, XII in Roman numerals.
Word Family **twelve** *adjective*; **twelfth** *noun, adjective*.

twenty *noun* (*plural* **twenties**)
1 a cardinal number, the symbol 20 in Arabic numerals, XX in Roman numerals.
2 (**twenties**) the numbers 20 to 29 in a series, such as the years in a century.
Word Family **twenty** *adjective*; **twentieth** *noun, adjective*.

twerp *noun*
(*informal*) a stupid or dislikable person.

twice *adverb*
two times.

twiddle *verb*
to twist or turn idly or aimlessly: *to twiddle the knobs on a radio.*

twig[1] *noun*
a small shoot at the end of a branch or stem.

twig[2] *verb* (**twigs; twigging; twigged**)
(*informal*) to understand: *He finally twigged what was going on.*

twilight (**twy**-lite) *noun*
1 the period of reduced light either after sunset or before sunrise.
2 a period or condition after full development, glory, etc.: *the twilight of someone's life.*

twill *noun*
a woven fabric with the threads forming parallel diagonal lines.

twin *noun*
1 either of two offspring born at one birth.
2 either of a pair of identical or similar things.
fraternal twins twins which develop from two fertilized ova, so each twin has distinct hereditary characteristics.
identical twins twins which develop from a single fertilized ovum which splits into two, so each twin has identical hereditary characteristics.
• **twin** *verb* (**twins; twinning; twinned**) to link, especially to link towns in two different countries as twin towns.

twine *noun*
a strong thread made by twisting two or more strands together.
• **twine** *verb* to twist or wind together or around.

twinge (twinj) *noun*
a sudden sharp pain.
• **twinge** *verb*.

twinkle *verb*
to sparkle with a flickering light.
• **twinkle** *noun* a sparkle or brightness.
Phrase **in a twinkling, in the twinkling of an eye** in an instant.

twinset *noun*
a cardigan and jumper of the same material and colour, worn as a matching pair.

twirl *verb*
to turn round and round, especially quickly.
• **twirl** *noun*
1 an act of twirling.
2 something in a twirling shape.
[TW(ist) + (wh)IRL]

twist *verb*
1 to turn or wind strands or threads together.
2 to turn the two ends of something in opposite directions.
3 to turn sharply: *She fell and twisted her ankle.*
4 to wind: *a twisting path.*
5 to give a different meaning to: *The newspaper twisted her words.*
6 to dance the twist.
• **twist** *noun*
1 a twisting action or motion.
2 a bend or curve.

3 an unexpected development: *a film with a twist at the end*.
4 a new way of presenting something.
5 a dance consisting of twisting movements of the body.

twisted *adjective*
abnormal in an unhealthy way: *a twisted sense of humour*.

twister *noun*
American a tornado.

twit *noun*
(*informal*) a fool.

twitch *noun* (*plural* **twitches**)
1 a short jerky movement of a muscle or part of the body.
2 a short sudden pull.
• **twitch** *verb*.

twitter *verb*
1 to make light chirping sounds.
2 to chatter nervously.
• **twitter** *noun*
1 the act or sound of twittering.
2 a state of nervous excitement.
Word Family **twittery** *adjective*.

two (too) *noun*
a cardinal number, the symbol 2 in Arabic numerals, II in Roman numerals.
Phrase **put two and two together** to draw an obvious conclusion.
• **two** *adjective*.

> **!** Do not confuse *two* with TO.

two-bit *adjective*
(*especially American informal*) small-time: *a two-bit gangster*.

two-dimensional *adjective*
having length and breadth but not depth.

two-faced *adjective*
deceitful or hypocritical.

twopence (tup-'nce) *noun* also **tuppence**
1 a sum of money to the value of two pennies.
2 (*informal*) a bit: *She doesn't care twopence about him*.

two-step *noun*
a ballroom dance of sliding steps.

two-stroke *adjective*
of or relating to an internal-combustion engine in which the fuel is taken into the cylinder, compressed, burnt and released into the exhaust in two successive strokes of the piston. Compare FOUR-STROKE.

two-time *verb*
(*informal*) to be unfaithful to a partner.
Word Family **two-timer** *noun*.

tycoon (tie-koon) *noun*
a very wealthy or powerful person in business.

> The word **tycoon** came into English from Japanese. The Japanese word for 'military commander' was *taikun*, literally 'great ruler'. This in turn was derived from Chinese *taijun*. English acquired it as 'high-ranking person' in the 1850s but the sense of 'powerful person in business' did not come in until after the First World War.

tying the present participle of **tie**.

tympani ⇨ TIMPANI.

tympanum (tim-pa-num) *noun* (*plural* **tympanums** or **tympana**)
1 *Anatomy* the eardrum.
2 *Architecture* the recessed space of a pediment or arch above a doorway, etc.
Word Family **tympanic** (tim-**pan**-ik) *adjective*.
[Greek *tympanon* a drum]

type *noun*
1 a group or grouping with common characteristics.
2 a person or thing in such a group: *a type of cheese*. □ *He's the strong silent type*.
3 a piece or pieces of metal cast with the imprint of a letter, figure, etc.
4 printed characters: *a headline in huge type*.
• **type** *verb* to produce words by pressing the keys of a typewriter or computer keyboard.
[Greek *typos* something impressed]

typecast *verb* (**typecasts**; **typecasting**; **typecast**)
to persist in giving an actor the same kind of role: *He was afraid of being typecast as a villain*.

typeface *noun*
Printing a design of type.

typescript *noun*
any typed material.

typeset *verb* (**typesets**; **typesetting**; **typeset**)
to arrange type for printing.
Word Family **typesetter** *noun*.

typewriter (tipe-rite-a) *noun*
a machine with a keyboard which produces printed characters by pressing each letter or symbol separately onto paper through an inked ribbon.
Word Family **typewritten** *adjective*.

typhoid (tie-foyd) *noun* also **typhoid fever**
an infectious bacterial disease spread by contaminated food and water, causing severe intestinal disorders.
[TYPHUS + -*oid*]

typhoon (tie-**foon**) ⇨ TROPICAL CYCLONE.
[Chinese *tai* big + *feng* wind]

typhus (tie-fus) *noun*
an infectious viral disease transmitted by lice or mites, causing fever, weakness and a rash.
[Greek *typhos* a vapour]

typical (tip-i-k'l) *adjective*
conforming to a particular type or character: *It is typical of you to be late.*
Word Family **typically** *adverb.*

typify (tip-i-fie) *verb* (**typifies; typifying; typified**)
to be a typical example of: *He typifies the English country gentleman.*

typist (tie-pist) *noun*
a person who uses a typewriter.

typography (tie-**pog**-ra-fee) *noun*
the art or process of designing the printed layout of a book, magazine, etc.
Word Family **typographic** (tie-po-**graf**-ik), **typographical** *adjective.*

typology (tie-**pol**-a-jee) *noun* (*plural* **typologies**)
the study of types, e.g. in a system of classification.

tyrannosaur (ti-**ran**-a-saw or tie-**ran**-a-saw) *noun* also **tyrannosaurus**
a very large carnivorous dinosaur which walked erect on its hind limbs and had small front limbs resembling claws.

tyranny (tirr-a-nee) *noun* (*plural* **tyrannies**)
1 the rule of a tyrant.
2 any cruel or unjust use of power: *the tyranny of a harsh father's discipline.*
Word Family **tyrannical** (ti-**ran**-i-k'l), **tyrannous** (tirr-a-nus) *adjective;* **tyrannically** *adverb;* **tyrannize, tyrannise** *verb* to rule or oppress with power exercised cruelly or absolutely.
[from Greek]

tyrant (tie-r'nt) *noun*
a ruler who exercises absolute power cruelly and oppressively.

tyre *noun* (*American* **tire**)
a band of hollow inflated rubber around the rim of a wheel to grip the road and cushion vibration.

tyro (tie-ro) *noun* also **tiro**
a beginner or learner.

tzar ⇨ TSAR.

tzarina ⇨ TSARINA.

tzatziki (tsat-**see**-kee) *noun*
a Greek dish eaten as a dip, consisting of yoghurt and finely chopped cucumber, flavoured with garlic and mint.

Uu

ubiquitous (yoo-**bik**-wi-tus) *adjective*
being everywhere at the same time.
Word Family **ubiquitously** *adverb*;
ubiquitousness, ubiquity (yoo-**bik**-wi-tee) *noun*.
[Latin *ubique* everywhere]

U-boat *noun*
a German submarine.
[German *Untersee* undersea + BOAT]

udder *noun*
a mammary gland, especially when having more than one teat, as on a cow.

ugly (**ug**-lee) *adjective* (**uglier; ugliest**)
unpleasant in appearance.
Figurative an ugly temper (= unpleasant, bad).
Word Family **ugliness** *noun*.

ugly duckling *noun*
an unremarkable child who grows up to be clever or handsome.
[from a Hans Andersen fairy tale]

ukulele (yoo-ka-**lay**-lee) *noun*
Music a small guitar-like instrument with four strings.
[Hawaiian]

ulcer (**ul**-sa) *noun*
an open sore, usually occurring on the skin or on the inner surface of an organ, such as the stomach.
Word Family **ulcerous** *adjective* 1 like an ulcer. 2 affected with ulcers; **ulcerate** *verb* to make or become ulcerous; **ulceration** (ul-sa-**ray**-sh'n) *noun* 1 the forming of an ulcer. 2 an ulcer.

ulna *noun* (*plural* **ulnae** (**ul**-nee) or **ulnas**)
Anatomy the longer of the two bones of the forearm or forelimb.
[Latin]

ulster *noun*
a long loose overcoat.

ulterior (ul-**teer**-ee-a) *adjective*
concealed and not evident or expressed: *I think she must have an ulterior motive.*
[Latin]

ultimate (**ul**-ti-mit) *adjective*
1 final or fundamental: *Death is man's ultimate fate.*
2 the maximum or greatest possible: *the ultimate accolade.*
Word Family **ultimately** *adverb* finally or at last.
[Latin *ultimus* last]

ultimatum (ul-ti-**may**-t'm *or* ul-ti-**mah**-t'm) *noun* (*plural* **ultimatums** or **ultimata**)
a final proposal in a discussion, refusal of which causes negotiation to end and other action to be taken.

ultra-high frequency *noun*
short form is **UHF** *Radio* a high frequency of radio wave used for television and some kinds of radar.

ultramarine (ul-tra-ma-**reen**) *noun*
a brilliant pure blue colour or pigment.
• **ultramarine** *adjective.*
[*ultra-* + Latin *marinus* of the sea (as originally obtained from the lapis lazuli which came from 'beyond the sea')]

ultrasonic (ul-tra-**son**-ik) *adjective*
Physics (of waves) having such a high frequency that they are not within the range of normal human hearing.
Word Family **ultrasonically** *adverb.*
[*ultra-* + Latin *sonus* a sound]

ultrasound *noun*
Medicine the use of ultrasonic waves to form images of or detect abnormalities in body tissue.

ultraviolet ⇨ LIGHT[1] *noun* (definition 3).

umbilical cord (um-**bill**-i-k'l kord) *noun*
Anatomy a cord-like structure containing a network of blood vessels connecting the bloodstream of an unborn child to that of its mother through the placenta.

umbilicus ⇨ NAVEL.

umbra *noun* (*plural* **umbras** or **umbrae** (**um**-bree))
Physics the darker part at the centre of a shadow. Compare PENUMBRA.
[Latin, shade]

umbrage (**um**-brij) *noun*
Phrase **take umbrage** to take offence.

umbrella *noun*
1 a folding circular frame with a stick and handle, covered in a waterproof material and used for protection from the rain.
2 a protective force: *acting under the umbrella of the UN.*
• **umbrella** *adjective* including many parts: *an umbrella organization.*
[Italian *ombrella* a little shade]

umlaut *Language* ⇨ ACCENT.

umpire *noun*
a person appointed to judge or make decisions on rules during a competition or game.
• **umpire** *verb*.

umpteen *adjective*
(*informal*) of an indefinite, but usually large, number.
Word Family **umpteenth** *adjective*.

'un *pronoun*
(*informal*) one: *the big 'un that got away.*

unable *adjective*
not able to do something.

unaccompanied *adjective*
not accompanied: *unaccompanied singing.*

unaccountable *adjective*
1 impossible to find an explanation for.
2 not responsible.
Word Family **unaccountably** *adverb*; **unaccountability** *noun*.

unaccounted for *adjective*
not explained or taken into account.

unaccustomed *adjective*
not accustomed: *unaccustomed to public speaking.*

unadulterated *adjective*
1 complete: *His speech was pure unadulterated rubbish.*
2 having no alien substances added.

unaffected *adjective*
1 not showing any effects.
2 genuine or free from affectedness.
Word Family **unaffectedly** *adverb*; **unaffectedness** *noun*.

unalloyed *adjective*
pure or unmixed.

unanimous (yoo-**nan**-i-mus) *adjective*
in or demonstrating complete agreement.
Word Family **unanimously** *adverb*; **unanimity** (yoo-na-**nim**-i-tee), **unanimousness** *noun*.
[Latin *unus* one + *animus* mind]

unappealing *adjective*
not attractive: *The prospect of a visit from my mother was unappealing.*

unapproachable *adjective*
1 (of a place) not able to be approached or reached.
2 (of a person) haughty or not encouraging friendliness.
Word Family **unapproachably** *adverb*; **unapproachability** *noun*.

unarmed *adjective*
not carrying weapons.

unassuming *adjective*
modest.
Word Family **unassumingly** *adverb*; **unassumingness** *noun*.

unattached *adjective*
1 not attached.
2 not engaged or married.

unattended *adjective*
1 not accompanied.
2 not taken care of: *His wounds were left unattended.*

unauthorized, unauthorised *adjective*
not having authority or permission.

unavailing *adjective*
producing no effect; unsuccessful.

unaware *adjective*
not conscious or aware of something.
Word Family **unawares, unaware** *adverb* unexpectedly: *We crept up on him unawares.*

unbalanced *adjective*
1 not balanced.
2 mentally disturbed or lacking soundness of judgement.
Word Family **unbalance** *verb*.

unbearable *adjective*
not able to be tolerated or endured.
Word Family **unbearably** *adverb*; **unbearableness** *noun*.

unbeatable *adjective*
not able to be surpassed or beaten.

unbecoming (un-bi-**kumm**-ing) *adjective*
1 improper or unsuitable.
2 not attractive.
Word Family **unbecomingly** *adverb*; **unbecomingness** *noun*.

unbeknown (un-bi-**nohn**) *adjective* also **unbeknownst** (un-bi-**nohnst**)
Phrase **unbeknown to** unknown to: *Unbeknown to her, he was already married.*

unbelievable *adjective*
1 not likely to be true.
2 amazing: *She ran the race in an unbelievable three minutes!*
Word Family **unbelievably** *adverb*.

unbeliever *noun*
a person who does not believe, especially in some religious doctrine.

unbend *verb* (**unbends; unbending; unbent**)
1 to relax or become less formal.
2 to straighten or release from a bent position or form.

unbending *adjective*
inflexible and severe.

unbidden *adjective*
not invited: *Strange thoughts came unbidden to his mind.*

unbridled *adjective*
without restraint: *his unbridled lust.*

unbroken *adjective*
1 not broken: *His record for the high jump remains unbroken.*
2 continuous, without interruption.
3 (of a horse) not yet broken in.

unburden *verb*
to free from or get rid of a burden.
Phrase **unburden oneself** to tell someone one's problems or feelings.

unbuttoned *adjective*
1 having the buttons undone.
2 (*informal*) relaxed or informal.
Word Family **unbutton** *verb*.

uncalled for *adjective*
not justified and not necessary.

uncanny *adjective* (**uncannier; uncanniest**)
strange or unnatural.
Word Family **uncannily** *adverb*;
uncanniness *noun*.

unceasing *adjective*
continuous.
Word Family **unceasingly** *adverb*.

unceremonious (un-serr-i-**mo**-nee-us)
adjective
abrupt and brusque: *He made an unceremonious exit through the window.*
Word Family **unceremoniously** *adverb*;
unceremoniousness *noun*.

uncertain *adjective*
1 not certainly known or able to be relied on: *an uncertain temper.*
2 not sure: *She seemed uncertain how to reply.*
Word Family **uncertainly** *adverb*;
uncertainty *noun* (*plural* **uncertainties**).

uncharacteristic *adjective*
not typical.
Word Family **uncharacteristically** *adverb*.

uncharitable *adjective*
1 unforgiving.
2 miserly.
Word Family **uncharitably** *adverb*.

unchecked *adjective*
(of something unwanted) not controlled:
The weeds spread unchecked through the gardens.

uncivil (un-**siv**-'l) *adjective*
rude or discourteous.
Word Family **uncivilly** *adverb*.

uncle *noun*
1 a brother of a parent.
2 the husband of an aunt.
3 (*informal*) used as a title for a male friend of a child's parents: *Say hello to Uncle Peter.*
[Latin *avunculus* maternal uncle]

Uncle Sam *noun*
(*informal*) America or its government.

> The expression **Uncle Sam** owes its existence to the fact that the initial letters of the United States are *US*. In the early 19th century, soldiers stamping 'US' on government supplies and looking for ways to amuse themselves thought of *Uncle Sam* as a lengthened form of *US*.

uncomfortable (un-**kumf**-ta-b'l) *adjective*
1 causing discomfort: *an uncomfortable chair.*
2 in a state of discomfort: *He made me feel uncomfortable.*
Word Family **uncomfortably** *adverb*;
uncomfortableness *noun*.

uncommon *adjective*
not usual.
Word Family **uncommonly** *adverb*
(*dated*) remarkably.

uncompromising (un-**kom**-pra-my-zing)
adjective
not allowing any compromise: *He took an uncompromising stand on the issue.*
Word Family **uncompromisingly** *adverb*.

unconcerned (un-k'n-**sernd**) *adjective*
having or showing no concern: *He seemed unconcerned about his future.*
Word Family **unconcernedly** *adverb*.

unconditional (un-k'n-**dish**-'n-al)
adjective
without any conditions attached: *an unconditional surrender.*
Word Family **unconditionally** *adverb*.

unconscionable (un-**kon**-sh'n-a-b'l)
adjective
not in accordance with what is right or reasonable.
Word Family **unconscionably** *adverb*.

unconscious (un-**kon**-shus) *adjective*
1 not conscious: *The unconscious boxer was carried off.*
2 *Psychology* of or relating to mental processes that take place below consciousness.
• **unconscious** *noun Psychology* the system of mental processes of which a

person cannot become directly conscious, but which is capable of influencing conscious processes and behaviour.
Word Family unconsciously *adverb*.

unconsidered *adjective*
1 not given due thought.
2 disregarded: *unconsidered trifles*.

unconstitutional (un-kon-sti-**tew**-sh'n-al) *adjective*
not in accordance with the political constitution of a country.
Word Family unconstitutionally *adverb*.

unconventional *adjective*
not based on or obeying accepted or traditional views and standards.

uncool *adjective*
(*informal*) not acceptable or pleasing.

uncouple *verb*
1 to disconnect.
2 to release dogs paired together.

uncouth (un-**kooth**) *adjective*
uncultured, awkward or ungraceful.
Word Family uncouthness *noun*.
[*un-* + Old English *cuth* known]

uncover (un-**kuv**-a) *verb*
1 to remove the cover from.
2 to reveal or disclose.

uncritical *adjective*
not discriminating or critically perceptive.
Word Family uncritically *adverb*.

unction (**unk**-sh'n) *noun*
Religion the act of anointing with oil.
extreme unction the religious sacrament of anointing a dying person with oil.
[from Latin]

unctuous (**unk**-chew-us) *adjective*
earnest in an exaggerated or insincere way.
Word Family unctuously *adverb*;
unctuousness *noun*.
[Latin *unctus* greasy]

undaunted (un-**dawn**-tid) *adjective*
not discouraged or dismayed.

undead *plural noun*
(**the undead**) in fiction, beings that are dead but still move around, especially vampires.

undecided (un-di-**side**-id) *adjective*
1 not having been decided: *Their fate is still undecided.*
2 not having made up one's mind: *We were undecided as to how to achieve this.*

undemanding *adjective*
(of a task) not difficult.

under *preposition*
1 below: *We sat under the trees.*

2 less than: *Children under five are not admitted.*
3 lower in rank than: *A captain is under a major.*
4 affected or influenced by: *Everything is under control.* □ *Under the new law, the council must provide housing for you.*
5 in the process of: *The matter is under consideration.*
6 contained in the group of or below the heading of: *Look under 'diet' in the encyclopedia.*
Phrases **under the name of** using the name: *He travelled under the name of Hawkins.* **under way 1** *Nautical* (of a ship) having started on her way. **2** in progress: *The meeting had only been under way for a few minutes when the lights failed.*
• **under** *adverb*.

underachieve *verb*
to perform below the accepted standard, especially of one's own ability.

under age *adjective*
not yet old enough to do particular activities legally, e.g. drink alcohol in a pub.

underarm *adjective*
1 under the arm.
2 *Sport* (of a stroke or throw) made with the arm moving forward and up. Compare OVERARM.

underbelly *noun* (*plural* **underbellies**)
1 the lower part of the belly.
2 any similarly unprotected part.

undercarriage *noun*
1 the wheeled part of an aircraft's structure that supports it on the ground.
2 a supporting framework, e.g. of a motor vehicle.

underclass *noun*
the least privileged section of society, the members of which fall outside the usual social scale and suffer from poverty, homelessness, social disadvantage, etc.

underclothes ⇨ UNDERWEAR.

undercoat *noun*
the paint applied to a surface as a base before the main colour or layer is put on.

undercover *adjective*
secret: *an undercover agent.*
• **undercover** *adverb*.

undercurrent *noun*
1 also called **undertow**. a current below another current or a surface.
2 a hidden tendency: *There's an undercurrent of bitterness in his jokes about women.*

undercut *verb* (**undercuts;**
undercutting; undercut)
1 to offer goods or services at a lower price
than one's competitors.
2 *Sport* to hit a ball from underneath,
causing a backspin.
• **undercut** *noun*.

underdeveloped (un-der-di-**vell**-upt)
adjective
1 (of a country) not highly industrialized.
2 *Photography* not sufficiently developed,
so that there is a lack of contrast.
3 not adequately or normally developed:
an underdeveloped body.
Word Family **underdevelop** *verb*.

underdog *noun*
a person or team that loses or is expected
to lose a struggle, contest, etc.

underdone (un-der-**dun**) *adjective*
(of meat, vegetables, etc.) too lightly
cooked.

underestimate (un-der-**est**-im-ayt)
verb
to form too low an estimate of: *They*
underestimated the cost of the project.
• **underestimate** (un-der-**est**-im-'t)
noun.

underexpose *verb*
Photography to expose a film to light for
too short a time.
Word Family **underexposure** *noun*.

underfelt *noun*
a layer of felt laid beneath a carpet.

underfoot *adverb*
beneath the feet.
Figurative I'm sick of the children being
underfoot all day.

undergarment *noun*
a piece of underwear.

undergo *verb* (**undergoes; undergoing;**
underwent; undergone)
to experience or be subjected to: *She will*
have to undergo surgery yet again.

undergraduate (un-der-**grad**-yew-it)
noun
a university student who is studying for his
or her first degree.
• **undergraduate** *adjective*.

underground *adjective, adverb*
1 below the surface of the earth.
2 secret, subversive or not generally
known: *an underground movement.*
• **underground** *noun*
1 a movement or organization which is
secret or outside the established or
accepted society, etc., such as nationalist

groups during the Second World War who
worked to overthrow occupying enemy
forces.
2 a railway system running through
underground tunnels.

undergrowth *noun*
the small trees and plants which grow
below and among larger trees.

underhand *adjective* also **underhanded**
1 devious or sly.
2 *Sport* underarm.

underlay *noun*
a layer of fabric laid beneath a carpet.

underline *verb*
1 to draw a line under.
2 to emphasize: *He thumped the desk to*
underline his point.

underling *noun*
a subordinate.

underlying *adjective*
1 basic or fundamental: *the underlying*
reasons for the split in the party.
2 hidden or implicit: *an underlying note of*
sarcasm.

undermine *verb*
1 to make an excavation beneath,
especially as a means of weakening a
foundation.
2 to destroy gradually: *Their constant*
teasing undermined her confidence.

underneath *adverb, preposition*
beneath or below.
Word Family **underneath** *adjective*
lower; **underneath** *noun* a lower part or
surface.

underpants *plural noun*
a pair of light short trousers worn next to
the skin, especially by men or boys.

underpass *noun* (*plural* **underpasses**)
a passage under a roadway, usually for
pedestrians and sometimes for traffic.

underpin *verb* (**underpins;**
underpinning; underpinned)
1 also **pin** *Building* to support a wall, etc.
with props.
2 to support: *Careful research underpinned*
her theory.
Word Family **underpinning** *noun*.

underplay *noun*
1 to perform with restraint.
2 to make something seem of less
importance than it actually is.

underprivileged *adjective*
with less than the usual rights and
opportunities in society, because of
poverty, etc.

underrate (un-der-**rate**) *verb*
to underestimate: *Never underrate your opponent.*

undersea *adjective*
existing, carried on or adapted for use beneath the surface of the sea.

undersecretary *noun* (*plural* **undersecretaries**)
a junior minister in a government department.

undersell *verb* (**undersells; underselling; undersold**)
to sell something at a lower price than one's competitors.

undershoot *verb* (**undershoots; undershooting; undershot**)
(of an aeroplane, missile, etc.) to land short of the runway, target, etc.

underside *noun*
the lower side of something.

undersized *adjective*
being less than the normal size.

understand *verb* (**understands; understanding; understood**)
1 to appreciate the meaning, significance, nature or explanation of: *I don't understand this diagram.* □ *You can understand why he was upset.*
2 to have been told: *I understand that the funeral took place yesterday.*
Word Family **understandable** *adjective* capable of being understood; **understandably** *adverb*.

understanding *noun*
1 the ability or power to understand: *She has a clear understanding of the problem.*
2 sympathy: *All he was asking for was a little understanding.*
3 an agreement: *We came to a friendly understanding.*
Phrase **on the understanding that** on the condition that.

understate *verb*
to declare to be smaller or less important than is actually so.
Word Family **understatement** *noun*.

understudy *noun* (*plural* **understudies**)
a person prepared to take over an important role in a play, ballet, etc. if the performer is unable to appear.
Word Family **understudy** *verb* (**understudies; understudying; understudied**).

undertake *verb* (**undertakes; undertaking; undertook; undertaken**)
1 to attempt.

2 to decide or agree to do: *He rashly undertook to finish the job by Tuesday.*
Word Family **undertaking** *noun* 1 a task or enterprise which one has decided or agreed to do.
2 a promise or guarantee: *He gave me a solemn undertaking that he would give up drink.*

undertaker *noun*
a person whose business it is to arrange for the burial of the dead.

under-the-counter *adjective*
(of goods) kept hidden to be disposed of in some illegal way, such as on the black market.

undertone *noun*
1 a low quiet voice.
2 an underlying quality: *There's an undertone of sadness in his humour.*

undertow ⇨ UNDERCURRENT (definition 1).

undervalue *verb*
to put too low a value on.

underwater *adjective*
being, occurring or used below the surface of a body of water.
• **underwater** *adverb*.

underwear *noun* also called **underclothes**.
any clothing worn near to the skin under trousers, dresses, etc.

underweight (un-der-**wate**) *adjective*
having less than normal, required or accepted weight.

underwent the past tense of **undergo**.

underworld *noun*
1 the criminal world of a society.
2 *Mythology* Hades, where the spirits of the dead go.

underwrite *verb* (**underwrites; underwriting; underwrote; underwritten**)
to guarantee or assume responsibility for, e.g. by signing an insurance policy.
Word Family **underwriter** *noun*.

undesirable *adjective*
unpleasant or objectionable.
• **undesirable** *noun* an objectionable person.

undetermined *adjective*
not established or certain: *a word of undetermined meaning.*

undeveloped (un-di-**vell**-upt) *adjective*
1 not fully grown.
2 not developed: *an undeveloped roll of film.*
3 (of land) not built on.

undid the past tense of **undo**.

undies (**un**-deez) *plural noun*
(*informal*) underwear.

undiscriminating *adjective*
not knowing good from bad, or not
bothering to distinguish between them;
uncritical.

undisguised *adjective*
(of a feeling) without an attempt at
concealment: *her undisguised joy at his
downfall.*

undistinguished (un-dis-**ting**-gwisht)
adjective
not outstanding or distinctive.

undivided *adjective*
complete: *This job requires my undivided
attention.*

undo (un-**doo**) *verb* (**undoes; undoing;
undid; undone**)
1 to unfasten and open.
2 to reverse the effects of: *You have undone
all my good work.*
Word Family **undoing** *noun* ruin, or the
cause of ruin: *Drink was her undoing.*

undoubted (un-**dow**-tid) *adjective*
accepted as beyond question.
Word Family **undoubtedly** *adverb.*

undress *verb*
to remove clothing.
Word Family **undress** *noun* a state of
having few or no clothes on; **undressed**
adjective 1 not clothed. 2 (of leather, etc.)
not treated or prepared.

undue *adjective*
excessive or extreme.
Word Family **unduly** *adverb.*

undulate (**un**-dew-late) *verb*
to move or cause to move like a wave or
waves.
Word Family **undulation** (un-dew-**lay**-
sh'n) *noun* a wave-like part, motion, form,
outline, etc.
[Latin *unda* a wave]

undying *adjective*
(of an emotion) everlasting.

unearth *verb*
to dig up or uncover.

unearthly *adjective*
1 supernatural or ghostly: *an unearthly
scream.*
2 (*informal*) unreasonably early: *Why did
you wake me at this unearthly hour?*

uneasy *adjective* (**uneasier; uneasiest**)
uncomfortable or anxiously restless.

Word Family **uneasily** *adverb*;
uneasiness, unease *noun.*

uneconomical *adjective* also
uneconomic
wasteful or unprofitable.

unemployment *noun*
1 the lack of a job or jobs: *the difficulty of
coping with unemployment.*
2 the number of people who cannot get a
job: *Unemployment rose at the end of the
year.*
Word Family **unemployed** *adjective*;
unemployable *adjective.*

unending *adjective*
1 everlasting.
2 continual.
Word Family **unendingly** *adverb.*

unenlightened *adjective*
not adequately informed or instructed.

unenterprising *adjective*
not showing much initiative.

unenviable *adjective*
difficult or unpleasant: *I had the
unenviable task of telling her that her dog had
died.*

unequal *adjective*
not equal: *coins of unequal value.*
Phrase **unequal to** not having enough
ability for: *He felt unequal to the task.*
Word Family **unequalled** *adjective.*

unequivocal (un-i-**kwiv**-a-k'l) *adjective*
plain, clear or without ambiguity.
Word Family **unequivocally** *adverb.*

unerring *adjective*
without error or well-aimed.
Word Family **unerringly** *adverb.*

unethical *adjective*
contrary to a moral code, especially of
professional conduct.
Word Family **unethically** *adverb.*

uneven *adjective*
1 not level or flat: *uneven ground.*
2 not equal or balanced: *an uneven contest.*
3 irregular: *a book of uneven quality.*
Word Family **unevenly** *adverb*;
unevenness *noun.*

uneventful *adjective*
(of an occasion or period of time) having
nothing exciting or unusual happening.

unexceptionable (un-ek-**sep**-sh'n-a-b'l)
adjective
not able to be criticized or objected to.

unexceptional (un-ek-**sep**-sh'n-al)
adjective
usual or ordinary.

unexpected *adjective*
coming without warning.
Word Family **unexpectedly** *adverb*;
unexpectedness *noun*.

unexposed *adjective*
(of photographic film) unused.

unfailing *adjective*
continuous or dependable: *He seemed to
have an unfailing supply of jokes.*
Word Family **unfailingly** *adverb*.

unfair *adjective*
not fair or just.
Word Family **unfairly** *adverb*;
unfairness *noun*.

unfaithful *adjective*
1 not loyal or true to a promise, duty, or
other person.
2 having sex with a person other than
one's usual partner.
Word Family **unfaithfully** *adverb*;
unfaithfulness *noun*.

unfamiliar *adjective*
not previously or familiarly known:
Apologizing was unfamiliar territory to Luke.
Phrase **unfamiliar with** not knowing
about.
Word Family **unfamiliarity** *noun*.

unfathomable *adjective*
not able to be comprehended.

unfazed *adjective*
(*informal*) not at all disconcerted or upset.

unfeeling *adjective*
not sensitive or sympathetic.
Word Family **unfeelingly** *adverb*.

unfettered *adjective*
not restrained or restricted.

unfit *adjective*
1 not physically fit.
2 not suitable: *This water is unfit for human
consumption.*
Word Family **unfitness** *noun*.

unflappable *adjective*
not easily upset.

unfold *verb*
1 to open or spread out: *Suresh unfolded the
map.*
2 to make or become known or visible: *The
landscape unfolded before us.*

unforeseen *adjective*
not expected or predicted.
Word Family **unforeseeable** *adjective*.

unforgettable *adjective*
never likely to be forgotten.
Word Family **unforgettably** *adverb*.

unforgivable *adjective*
(of an action) not able to be forgiven.

unforgiving *adjective*
1 not willing to forgive.
2 (of land or weather) extremely bleak and
harsh.

unfortunate *adjective*
1 not lucky.
2 regrettable: *He made an unfortunate
decision to resign.*
Word Family **unfortunately** *adverb*.

unfounded *adjective*
without any basis in fact: *her totally
unfounded accusations against an innocent
person.*

unfriendly *adjective* (**unfriendlier;
unfriendliest**)
not friendly.
Word Family **unfriendliness** *noun*.

unfrock ⇨ DEFROCK.

unfulfilled *adjective*
1 (of aims, wishes, etc.) not achieved: *Her
ambitions are still unfulfilled.*
2 (of a person) not feeling satisfied with
one's life and achievements.
Word Family **unfulfilling** *adjective*.

unfurl *verb*
to open or spread out something that is
rolled up: *He unfurled the flag.*

ungainly *adjective* (**ungainlier;
ungainliest**)
clumsy or awkward.
Word Family **ungainliness** *noun*.

ungodly *adjective* (**ungodlier;
ungodliest**)
1 sinful or irreligious.
2 (*informal*) outrageous: *Why are we getting
up at this ungodly hour?*
Word Family **ungodliness** *noun*.

ungovernable *adjective*
uncontrollable: *an ungovernable temper.*

ungracious (un-**gray**-shus) *adjective*
not gracious or courteous.
Word Family **ungraciously** *adverb*;
ungraciousness *noun*.

unguarded *adjective*
1 not guarded.
2 thoughtless or not discreet: *He gave
himself away in an unguarded moment.*
Word Family **unguardedly** *adverb*;
unguardedness *noun*.

unguent (un-**gw'nt**) *noun*
a soft creamy paste, such as an ointment or
lubricant.
[from Latin]

unhand *verb*
an old word meaning 'to release' or 'to let go of'.

unhappy *adjective* (**unhappier; unhappiest**)
1 not happy.
2 (*formal*) not lucky: *an unhappy accident*.
Word Family **unhappily** *adverb*; **unhappiness** *noun*.

unhealthy *adjective* (**unhealthier; unhealthiest**)
1 not healthy.
2 dangerous to health: *an unhealthy drain*.
3 indicating poor health: *an unhealthy complexion*.
Word Family **unhealthily** *adverb*; **unhealthiness** *noun*.

unheard of *adjective*
never known or heard of before.

unheralded *adjective*
1 not announced in advance.
2 not expected.

unhinge (un-**hinj**) *verb*
1 to remove from the hinges.
2 to upset or unbalance: *His mind is unhinged*.

unholy *adjective* (**unholier; unholiest**)
1 wicked or sinful.
2 (*informal*) outrageous.

uni *noun*
(*informal*) university.

unicameral (yoo-ni-**kam**-a-r'l) *adjective*
(of a parliament) having one chamber or house only. Compare BICAMERAL.

unicellular (yoo-ni-**sel**-yoo-la) *adjective*
consisting of one cell.

unicorn (**yoo**-ni-korn) *noun*
Mythology a creature similar to a horse, with one long horn in the centre of its forehead.
[*uni-* + Latin *cornu* a horn]

unicycle (yoo-ni-**sigh**-k'l) *noun*
a vehicle with a single wheel propelled by pedals, used e.g. by acrobats.

unidentified flying object *noun*
short form is **UFO** any object which is detected in the sky but which cannot be identified.

uniform (**yoo**-ni-form) *noun*
the clothes worn by members of a particular group or institution, used to distinguish or identify them.
• **uniform** *adjective* not varying in form, quality, character, etc.: *Mix the ingredients to a uniform thickness*.

Word Family **uniformed** *adjective* wearing a uniform; **uniformly** *adverb* in a uniform way; **uniformity** (yoo-ni-**for**-mi-tee) *noun* sameness.
[*uni-* + Latin *forma* form]

unify (**yoo**-ni-fie) *verb* (**unifies; unifying; unified**)
to make into one.
Word Family **unification** (yoo-ni-fi-**kay**-sh'n) *noun*.
[*uni-* + Latin *facere* to make]

unilateral (yoo-ni-**lat**-a-r'l) *adjective*
of, on or by one side only: *a unilateral declaration of independence*.
Word Family **unilaterally** *adverb*.
[*uni-* + Latin *lateris* of a side]

unimaginable (un-im-**aj**-in-a-b'l) *adjective*
not able to be imagined or comprehended.
Word Family **unimaginably** *adverb*.

unimpaired *adjective*
not damaged.

unimpeachable *adjective*
that cannot be questioned or doubted: *unimpeachable conduct*.

uninhibited *adjective*
free from restraints or inhibitions.
Word Family **uninhibitedly** *adverb*; **uninhibitedness** *noun*.

uninspiring *adjective* also **uninspired**
dull or dreary.

unintelligent *adjective*
lacking intelligence.
Word Family **unintelligently** *adverb*.

unintelligible *adjective*
not able to be understood.
Word Family **unintelligibly** *adverb*.

uninterested *adjective*
having or showing no interest or concern.
Word Family **uninterestedly** *adverb*.

⚠ Do not confuse *uninterested* with DISINTERESTED.

uninteresting *adjective*
not interesting.
Word Family **uninterestingly** *adverb*.

union (**yoo**-nee-un) *noun*
1 a trade union.
2 the act of uniting into one: *the union of colonies into a single state*.
3 a combination formed by uniting.
4 a social organization for students in a college or university.
5 *Maths* the set of elements containing all the elements of two given sets and no others.
[Latin *unio* unity]

unionist (yoo-nee-un-ist) *noun*
1 a person who supports union.
2 a member of a trade union.

unique (yoo-**neek**) *adjective*
1 being the only one of its kind.
2 (*informal*) remarkable and special.
Word Family **uniquely** *adverb*;
uniqueness *noun*.

> ! The main meaning of *unique* is
> 'being the only one of its kind'.
> Words such as *rather* and *very* should
> not be used with *unique* in this sense.

unisex *adjective*
of, for or not distinguishing between both
sexes: *a unisex hairdresser*.

unison (yoo-ni-sun) *noun*
a speaking or sounding together or
simultaneously: *The class recited the poem in
unison.*
[*uni-* + Latin *sonus* a sound]

unit (yoo-nit) *noun*
1 any person, thing or group considered as
a single thing but forming part of a larger
group or whole: *We need some more storage
units in the kitchen.* □ *in command of a unit
of soldiers.*
2 a quantity or amount used as a standard
of measurement: *The litre is a unit of
volume.*
3 the smallest whole number (1).
[Latin *unus* one]

Unitarian (yoo-nit-**air**-ee-un) *noun*
Religion a member of the denomination
that rejects the Trinity, original sin,
atonement, eternal punishment, etc.
Word Family **Unitarianism** *noun*.

unitary (yoo-ni-tree) *adjective*
1 of or like a unit or units.
2 of or characterized by unity.
unitary ratio *Maths* the ratio 1 : *n*,
where *n* is a whole number.

unite (yoo-**nite**) *verb*
to combine together: *The states united to
form a single country.*
Word Family **unity** (yoo-ni-tee) *noun* the
state of being united, especially into a
complete or harmonious whole; **unitedly**
adverb.
[from Latin]

univalve (yoo-ni-valv) *noun*
a mollusc with only one part to its shell.
Compare BIVALVE.

universal (yoo-ni-ver-s'l) *adjective*
of, by, including or affecting all: *universal
agreement.*
● **universal** *noun* something which is
universal, such as an unchanging quality, a
common pattern of behaviour, etc.

Word Family **universally** *adverb*;
universality (yoo-ni-ver-**sall**-i-tee) *noun*.

universe (yoo-ni-verce) *noun*
1 all the space, matter and energy which is
thought to exist.
2 a particular set of surroundings: *He was
the centre of her universe.*
[Latin *universus* all together]

university (yoo-ni-**ver**-si-tee) *noun* (*plural*
universities)
1 an institution for teaching at a more
advanced level than a school, which
awards degrees to its students and also
offers facilities for postgraduate research.
2 the members of a university considered
as a group.

unjust *adjective*
not fair or just.
Word Family **unjustly** *adverb*;
unjustness *noun*.

unjustified *adjective*
not justified.
Word Family **unjustifiable** *adjective*;
unjustifiably *adverb*.

unkempt *adjective*
untidy or neglected.
[*un-* + Medieval English *kempt* combed]

unkind *adjective*
not kind; harsh.
Word Family **unkindly** *adverb*;
unkindness *noun*.

unknown *adjective*
not known.
● **unknown** *noun*
1 (**the unknown**) anything mysterious or
beyond normal experience: *a journey into
the unknown.*
2 *Maths* an unknown quantity.

unlawful *adjective*
relating to an act or relationship which the
law forbids.
Word Family **unlawfully** *adverb*.

unleaded *adjective*
(of petrol) containing a reduced amount
of lead in order to reduce pollution of the
atmosphere.

unleash *verb*
to release or let loose.

unleavened (un-**levv**-'nd) *adjective*
(of bread) made without yeast.

unless *conjunction*
except on the condition that: *You'll catch
cold unless you dress warmly.*

unlettered *adjective*
illiterate or not educated.

unlike *adjective*
not like or alike.
• **unlike** *preposition* not typical of: *It is unlike you to be so rude.*

unlikely *adjective* (**unlikelier; unlikeliest**)
not likely or probable.
Word Family **unlikelihood, unlikeliness** *noun.*

unlimited *adjective*
having no limits or restrictions.

unload *verb*
1 to remove the load from: *The ship was quickly unloaded.*
2 to remove ammunition or a film from: *I unloaded my camera.*
3 (*informal*) to get rid of.

unlooked for *adjective*
not expected or foreseen.

unloose *verb*
to let loose or free.

unlucky *adjective* (**unluckier; unluckiest**)
1 having bad luck: *That was very unlucky!*
2 bringing bad luck: *It is said to be unlucky to walk under a ladder.*
3 resulting from bad luck.
Word Family **unluckily** *adverb.*

unmanageable (un-**man**-ij-a-b'l) *adjective*
impossible to handle or control properly.

unmanly *adjective*
cowardly or not manly.

unmask *verb*
to reveal the true character of : *The traitor was finally unmasked.*

unmatched *adjective*
not matched or equalled.

unmentionable (un-**men**-sh'n-a-b'l) *adjective*
not fit or worthy to be mentioned.

unmistakable *adjective* also **unmistakeable**
about which no mistake is possible.
Word Family **unmistakably** *adverb.*

unmitigated *adjective*
very great or absolute.

unmoved (un-**moovd**) *adjective*
not moved or affected: *He was unmoved by their pleas.*

unnatural *adjective*
not natural or normal.
Word Family **unnaturally** *adverb;* **unnaturalness** *noun.*

unnecessary (un-**ness**-is-ree *or* un-**ness**-a-serr-ee) *adjective*
not necessary or more than is necessary.
Word Family **unnecessarily** *adverb.*

unnerve *verb*
to deprive of nerve, courage or self-control.
Word Family **unnerving** *adjective;* **unnervingly** *adverb.*

unnumbered *adjective*
1 not marked with a number: *unnumbered pages.*
2 countless.

unobtrusive (un-ob-**troo**-siv) *adjective*
not attracting attention.
Word Family **unobtrusively** *adverb;* **unobtrusiveness** *noun.*

unofficial *adjective*
not official.
Word Family **unofficially** *adverb.*

unorthodox *adjective*
not orthodox, conventional or approved: *unorthodox teaching methods.*
Word Family **unorthodoxy** *noun.*

unpack *verb*
1 to remove the contents of a suitcase, etc.
2 to take out of a suitcase, etc.: *She unpacked her nightdresses.*
3 *Computers* to convert into an easier form that takes up more space on a disk.

unpalatable (un-**pal**-it-a-b'l) *adjective*
1 unpleasant to eat or drink.
2 distasteful: *the unpalatable truth.*

unparalleled *adjective*
having no parallel or equal.

unparliamentary *adjective*
not in accordance with parliamentary procedure.

unperturbed *adjective*
not concerned or upset.

unpick *verb*
to undo the stitches of.

unpleasant (un-**plezz**-'nt) *adjective*
not pleasant.
Word Family **unpleasantly** *adverb;* **unpleasantness** *noun.*

unplug *verb* (**unplugs; unplugging; unplugged**)
1 to disconnect an electrical appliance.
2 to unblock.

unplumbed (un-**plumd**) *adjective*
of unknown depth.

unpopular (un-**pop**-yoo-la) *adjective*
not popular.
Word Family **unpopularity** (un-pop-yoo-**larr**-i-tee) *noun;* **unpopularly** *adverb.*

unprecedented (un-**press**-id-ent-id) *adjective*
without precedent.

unpredictable *adjective*
not able to be predicted: *an unpredictable temper.*
Word Family **unpredictably** *adverb;* **unpredictability** *noun.*

unpremeditated *adjective*
not planned or decided on in advance.

unpretentious *adjective*
quiet and modest.

unprincipled (un-**prin**-sip-'ld) *adjective*
without moral principles or scruples.

unprintable *adjective*
not considered fit to be printed.

unprofessional *adjective*
not in accordance with the standards of a particular profession.
Word Family **unprofessionally** *adverb.*

unprofitable *adjective*
showing no profit or advantage.
Word Family **unprofitably** *adverb.*

unprotected *adjective*
1 not protected.
2 (of sex) done without using a condom.

unproven (un-**proo**-v'n *or* un-**proh**-v'n) *adjective* also **unproved** (un-**proovd**)
1 not proved.
2 not yet tested.

unprovoked *adjective*
without provocation.

unqualified *adjective*
1 having insufficient qualifications.
2 total or absolute: *an unqualified success.*

unquestionable *adjective*
not able to be doubted.

unquestioned *adjective*
accepted without challenge or dispute.

unquestioning (un-**kwes**-ch'n-ing) *adjective*
done or believed without question or protest: *his unquestioning obedience to God.*
Word Family **unquestioningly** *adverb.*

unquiet *adjective*
a poetic word for restless or uneasy.

unravel *verb* (**unravels; unravelling; unravelled**)
to pull apart or separate the threads of.
Figurative I felt I was beginning to unravel the mystery.

unread (un-**red**) *adjective*
not read.
Word Family **unreadable** (un-**reed**-a-b'l) *adjective* 1 not worth reading as it is too badly written to be read with pleasure.
2 illegible.

unreal *adjective*
1 imaginary: *unreal fears.*
2 not true to life: *an unreal portrayal of the industry.*
3 (*informal*) amazing; incredible.
Word Family **unreality** *noun.*

unrealized, unrealised *adjective*
1 not fulfilled: *unrealized ambitions.*
2 not changed into money: *unrealized assets.*

unreasonable *adjective*
not reasonable; excessive.
Word Family **unreasonably** *adverb;* **unreasonableness** *noun.*

unreasoning *adjective*
not using or guided by reason.

unregenerate *adjective*
(*formal*) not having repented or reformed.

unrelated *adjective*
1 having no connection or relationship.
2 untold.

unrelenting *adjective*
1 remaining harsh or severe.
2 maintaining a constant rate or speed.
Word Family **unrelentingly** *adjective.*

unreliable (un-ri-**lie**-a-b'l) *adjective*
not to be relied or depended upon.
Word Family **unreliably** *adverb;* **unreliability** (un-ri-lie-a-**bill**-i-tee) *noun.*

unrelieved *adjective*
not varied or made less monotonous.

unremarkable *adjective*
ordinary.
Word Family **unremarkably** *adverb.*

unremarked *adjective*
without being noticed.

unremitting *adjective*
not stopping or relaxing.
Word Family **unremittingly** *adverb.*

unrepentant *adjective*
not repentant.
Word Family **unrepentantly** *adverb.*

unrequited (un-ri-**kwy**-tid) *adjective*
not returned or reciprocated.

unreserved *adjective*
1 full or complete: *unreserved support.*
2 frank.
3 not booked or reserved in advance.
Word Family **unreservedly** *adverb.*

unresolved *adjective*
(of a problem, etc.) not decided or solved.

unrest *noun*
strong restlessness or dissatisfaction.

unrivalled *adjective*
having no rival or equal.

unroll *verb*
to open or spread out.

unruffled *adjective*
calm and undisturbed.

unruly (un-**roo**-lee) *adjective* (**unrulier; unruliest**)
uncontrollable and noisy.
Word Family **unruliness** *noun*.

unsaddle *verb*
1 to take the saddle from.
2 to throw out of the saddle.

unsaid (un-**sed**) *verb*
not said or expressed.

unsatisfactory *adjective*
not satisfactory: *Your work is of an unsatisfactory standard.*
Word Family **unsatisfactorily** *adverb*;
unsatisfactoriness *noun*.

unsavoury *adjective* (*American* **unsavory**)
unpleasant or distasteful.
Word Family **unsavouriness** *noun*.

unscathed (un-**skaythd**) *adjective*
unhurt or unharmed.

unschooled *adjective*
1 not trained or educated.
2 uncontrolled.

unscrew *verb*
1 to remove or be removed by turning.
2 to unfasten by turning or removing a screw or screws.

unscrupulous (un-**skroo**-pew-lus) *adjective*
having no conscience or scruples.
Word Family **unscrupulously** *adverb*;
unscrupulousness *noun*.

unseal *verb*
to break or remove the seal of
Word Family **unsealed** *adjective* not sealed or closed.

unseasonable *adjective*
1 not in or characteristic of the proper season.
2 ill-timed.
Word Family **unseasonably** *adverb*

unseasoned *adjective*
not seasoned.

unseat *verb*
1 to throw or remove from a seat or saddle.
2 to depose from an official position.

unsecured *adjective*
1 not made secure or fastened.
2 (of a mortgage, loan, etc.) not covered by assets.

unseemly *adjective*
not proper.
Word Family **unseemliness** *noun*.

unseen *adjective*
1 not seen or evident.
2 invisible.
● **unseen** *noun* a passage not previously seen, set for translation in examinations, etc.

unsettle *verb*
1 to change or move from a settled condition.
2 to make troubled, anxious or uncertain.
Word Family **unsettled** *adjective*.

unshackle *verb*
to free from or as if from shackles.

unshakeable *adjective* also **unshakable**
(of opinions, beliefs, etc.) not easily changed or shaken.
Word Family **unshakeably** *adverb*;
unshakeability *noun*; **unshaken** *adjective*.

unsheathe *verb*
to remove a sword, etc. from a sheath or scabbard.

unshriven *adjective*
Roman Catholicism not having confessed or received the last sacrament.

unsightly *adjective*
not pleasant to look at: *Her room was an unsightly mess.*
Word Family **unsightliness** *noun*.

unskilled *adjective*
(of a worker) having or needing no special training for his or her job.
Word Family **unskilful** (*American* **unskillful**) *adjective*.

unslaked limo ⇨ QUICKLIME.

unsociable (un-so-sha-b'l) *adjective*
not inclined to seek the company of others.
Word Family **unsociably** *adverb*;
unsociability (un-so-sha-**bill**-i-tee) *noun*.

unsocial hours *plural noun*
hours worked outside the normal working day.

unsolicited *adjective*
not requested: *unsolicited advice.*

unsophisticated (un-sof-**iss**-tik ay-tid) *adjective*
1 not showing much knowledge of the world and people's behaviour.
2 simple or basic.

unsound *adjective*
1 not safe or trustworthy.
2 (of a person) not completely reliable or sane: *A doctor declared him to be of unsound mind.*
Word Family **unsoundly** *adverb*;
unsoundness *noun*.

unsparing *adjective*
holding nothing back.

unspeakable *adjective*
1 extremely bad: *an unspeakable crime.*
2 not capable of expression in words: *She was filled with an unspeakable joy.*
Word Family **unspeakably** *adverb.*

unstable *adjective*
1 not stable: *an unstable structure.* □ *His character is unstable.*
2 *Chemistry* (of certain compounds) readily decomposing into other compounds.

unsteady *adjective* (**unsteadier; unsteadiest**)
1 not stable: *You look a bit unsteady on top of that ladder.*
2 uneven or wavering: *steering an unsteady course.*
Word Family **unsteadily** *adverb;* **unsteadiness** *noun.*

unstick *verb* (**unsticks; unsticking; unstuck**)
to free, e.g. one thing which is stuck to another.
Phrase **come unstuck** (*informal*) to end in disaster or defeat.

unstinting *adjective*
given without holding anything back.
Word Family **unstintingly** *adverb.*

unstressed *adjective*
1 not under stress or strain.
2 *Language* not stressed or accented.

unstudied *adjective*
1 not planned or premeditated.
2 natural or not affected: *an unstudied grace.*

unsuitable *adjective*
not appropriate: *parents who feel the film is unsuitable for their children.*

unsuited (un-**soo**-tid) *adjective*
1 not suited: *unsuited for that purpose.*
2 incompatible.

unsung *adjective*
not celebrated in or as if in song: *an unsung hero.*

unsure (un-**shor**) *adjective*
1 lacking confidence or assurance.
2 not certain: *The outcome is still unsure.*

unswerving *adjective*
not altering direction; constant.

untangle *verb*
1 to free from tangles.
2 to clear up or straighten out: *untangle a problem.*

untapped *adjective*
not drawn from: *the untapped resources of the human brain.*

untenable *adjective*
not able to be defended or maintained: *Her theories are quite untenable.*

unthinkable *adjective*
1 not imaginable.
2 outrageous or out of the question: *That's unthinkable!*

unthinking *adjective*
lacking thoughtfulness, care or attention.
Word Family **unthinkingly** *adverb.*

untidy *adjective* (**untidier; untidiest**)
not tidy or neat.
Word Family **untidily** *adverb;* **untidiness** *noun.*

untie *verb* (**unties; untying; untied**)
1 to loosen or unknot.
2 to free from something that binds or restrains.

until *preposition*
1 up to the time of: *Let's wait until tomorrow.*
2 before: *They didn't get home until midnight.*
● **until** *conjunction*
1 to the time when: *I'll stay here until I die.*
2 before: *I couldn't leave until the boss left.*

> ❗ On the use of *until* and *till* ⇨ TILL[1].

untimely *adjective*
1 premature: *his untimely death.*
2 badly timed.

unto *preposition*
an old word for **to.**

untold *adjective*
1 not told or revealed: *an untold secret.*
2 incapable of being counted or numbered: *Untold thousands perished.*

untouchable (un-**tuch**-a-b'l) *adjective*
not able to be touched or affected.
● **untouchable** *noun* a Hindu who does not belong to any of the main Hindu castes. The term is now considered offensive.

untoward *adjective*
inappropriate or undesirable: *an untoward remark.*
Word Family **untowardness** *noun.*

untried *adjective*
1 not tested: *the raw untried recruits.*
2 not tried in a court of law.

untrue *adjective*
1 contrary to fact: *an untrue assertion.*
2 unfaithful or disloyal.

untruth *noun*
1 a lie.
2 falseness.
Word Family untruthful *adjective*;
untruthfully *adverb*; **untruthfulness**
noun.

untutored (un-**tew**-t'd) *adjective*
not taught or instructed.

untying the present participle of **untie**.

unused *adjective*
1 (un-**yoozd**) not yet used.
2 (un-**yoost**) not accustomed: *I am unused
to such rudeness.*

unusual *adjective*
not usual, common or ordinary.
Word Family unusually *adverb*;
unusualness *noun*.

unutterable *adjective*
1 not able to be expressed: *unutterable bliss.*
2 not able to be pronounced.
Word Family unutterably *adverb*.

unvarnished *adjective*
straightforward, plain or simple: *the
unvarnished truth.*

unveil (un-**vale**) *verb*
1 to remove a veil from.
2 to reveal publicly.

unvoiced *adjective*
Language uttered without vibration of the
vocal cords. ⇨ VOICE *verb* (definition 2).

unwaged *adjective*
not receiving a wage or salary.

unwarranted *adjective*
not justified: *an unwarranted intrusion into
my private life.*
Word Family unwarrantedly *adverb*.

unwell *adjective*
not well or healthy.

unwholesome (un-**hole**-sum) *adjective*
1 harmful to health or morals.
2 unhealthy.

unwieldy (un-**weel**-dee) *adjective*
(**unwieldier**; **unwieldiest**)
difficult to move or manage, because of
great size, awkward shape, etc.
Word Family unwieldiness *noun*.

unwilling *adjective*
reluctant.
Word Family unwillingly *adverb*;
unwillingness *noun*.

unwind *verb* (**unwinds**; **unwinding**;
unwound)
1 to undo something wound up: *I unwound
about five metres of rope.*

2 to relax: *It takes me a couple of hours to
unwind after work.*

unwise *adjective*
not sensible.
Word Family unwisely *adverb*.

unwitting *adjective*
not intended: *an unwitting insult.*
Word Family unwittingly *adverb*.

unwonted *adjective*
not usual, habitual or regular.

unworkable *adjective*
not capable of being put into operation:
Her plan is completely unworkable.

unworldly *adverb*
not motivated by materialistic values or
interests.
Word Family unworldliness *noun*.

unworthy *adjective* (**unworthier**;
unworthiest)
not worthy: *He is unworthy of high office.*

unwound the past tense and past
participle of **unwind**.

unwrap *verb* (**unwraps**; **unwrapping**;
unwrapped)
to remove the wrapping from.

unwritten law *noun*
a law, custom or rule which is generally
assumed or agreed upon rather than
officially recorded.

up *adverb, preposition, adjective*
1 from a lower to a higher level, position,
etc.: *I'm in my room – come on up.* □ *Turn
the TV up.*
2 in a higher place: *She's up in her room.*
3 into a particular condition: *He folded the
map up.*
4 in or to the north: *We're moving up to
Liverpool*
5 along: *They hiked up the valley*
6 out of bed: *Isn't Helen up yet?*
7 (of time) finished: *Your half-hour is up!*
8 (*informal*) happy.
9 (*informal*) wrong: *Something is up with the
machine.*
Phrases be all up (*informal*) to be at an
end: *It's all up – the police are here.* **be up
against** (*informal*) to be faced with: *He
sensed he was up against a lot of opposition.*
be up and running to be operating.
be up for (*informal*) to be prepared to try:
*I'm going to enter the London marathon. Are
you up for it?* **be up on** to know a lot about.
be up to 1 to be doing: *What are you kids
up to?* **2** to be capable of doing: *I'm not
really up to a shopping trip today.* **be up to
someone** to be someone's responsibility
or choice: *It's up to you to make a success of*

this job. **up to 1** as far as: *She was up to her neck in mud.* **2** no more than: *This bus holds up to 45 people.* **what's up?** (*informal*) what is the matter?

• **up** *verb* (**ups; upping; upped**) to raise: *I upped my offer.*
Phrase up and do something (*informal*) to do something unexpected: *He upped and fled before the wedding had begun.*

• **up** *noun* (*informal*) a rise or an ascent: *the ups and downs of life.*
Phrase on the up and up (*informal*) achieving success.

up-and-coming *adjective*
promising or becoming successful: *an up-and-coming young businessman.*

upbeat *adjective*
(*informal*) cheerful and optimistic.

upbraid *verb*
to scold severely.

upbringing *noun*
the rearing and training received during childhood.

upcoming *adjective*
forthcoming.

upcountry *adjective*
remote from the coast, the lowlands or the border: *an upcountry settlement.*
Word Family upcountry *adverb.*

update *verb*
to make up to date.
• **update** *noun.*

upend *verb*
to stand or place on end.

upfront *adjective*
1 (*informal*) frank and open.
2 paid in advance or at the beginning of a financial arrangement: *money upfront.*
Word Family up front *adverb* **1** at the front. **2** (of a payment) in advance.

upgrade *verb*
to raise to a higher position, rank or standard: *I think it's time we upgraded our computer.*
• **upgrade** *noun.*

upheaval *noun*
a violent disturbance or change.

uphill *adjective*
1 going up a hill or slope: *an uphill climb.*
2 difficult: *You'll have an uphill job to convince him.*
• **uphill** *adverb.*

uphold *verb* (**upholds; upholding; upheld**)
to maintain or give support to: *A higher court upheld the judge's decision.*
Word Family upholder *noun.*

upholster *verb*
to provide chairs, etc. with stuffing, springs, cushions and coverings.
Word Family upholsterer *noun;*
upholstery *noun* **1** the fabrics, etc. used in upholstering. **2** the art or business of upholstering.
[Medieval English *uphold* to keep in repair]

upkeep *noun*
1 the maintenance of an establishment, machine, etc.
2 the cost of such maintenance.

upland *noun* also **uplands**
an area of high land.

uplift *verb*
1 to raise up.
2 to raise spiritually or mentally.
• **uplift** *noun.*

uplighter *noun*
a lamp that throws light upwards.

upmarket *adjective, adverb*
superior in quality and style: *The restaurant has gone upmarket.*

upon *preposition*
on.

upper[1] *adjective*
1 higher than something else: *peers and other members of the upper classes.*
2 (of a surface) facing upwards.
• **upper** *noun* the part of a shoe that covers the top of the foot.
Phrase on one's uppers (*informal*) badly in need of money.

upper[2] *noun*
(*informal*) a stimulant drug, especially amphetamine. Compare DOWNER (definition 2).

upper case *noun*
Printing capital letters, e.g. A, B, C.
Compare LOWER CASE.

upper circle *noun*
the section of seats above the dress circle in a theatre.

upper class *noun*
the aristocracy.
• **upper-class** *adjective.*

upper crust *noun*
(*informal*) the aristocracy or very wealthy class.

uppercut *noun*
Boxing a heavy punch to the head, made by swinging the arm upwards with the elbow bent.

upper house *noun* also **upper chamber**
the higher of the two houses of a
parliament, in the UK the House of Lords.
Compare LOWER HOUSE.

uppermost *adjective*
highest in place, rank, authority, etc.
• **uppermost** *adverb*.

uppish *adjective* also **uppity**
(*informal*) inclined to be snobbish or
arrogant.
Word Family **uppishly** *adverb*;
uppishness *noun*.

upright *adjective*
1 being in a vertical position.
2 honest or honourable: *an upright and
decent man*.
• **upright** *noun* an object standing
vertical, such as a piece of timber used as a
support.
• **upright** *adverb* in a vertical position or
direction: *Stand upright!*

upright piano ⇨ PIANO[1].

uprising *noun*
an act of popular resistance or protest: *The
new corn tax led to uprisings in the provinces.*

upriver *adjective, adverb*
at or to a place nearer the source of a river.

uproar *noun*
a state of noisy excitement and confusion:
The meeting ended in an uproar.
Word Family **uproarious** *adjective*
1 loud, noisy and boisterous. 2 very funny;
uproariously *adverb*.

uproot *verb*
to tear or pull up by the roots: *The high
winds uprooted an ancient oak tree.*
*Figurative The war uprooted millions of
citizens.*

uprush *noun* (*plural* **uprushes**)
a sudden or violent upward movement,
flow, etc,: *He felt an uprush of hatred possess
him.*

upset (up-set) *verb* (**upsets; upsetting;
upset**)
1 to knock or tip over: *He upset the cup of
tea in his lap.*
2 to disturb, disorder or defeat: *The news
upset me considerably.* □ *a very upsetting
incident.*
• **upset** (up-set) *noun* a disturbance or
disorder, especially an unexpected one:
a stomach upset.
• **upset** (up-set) *adjective.*

upshot *noun*
the final outcome.

upside (up-side) *noun*
the positive or advantageous side of
something.

upside down *adjective*
1 with the upper side down.
2 in disorder.
• **upside down** *adverb* in or to an upside
down position.

upstage *verb*
1 *Theatre* to distract the attention of the
audience from another actor by
manoeuvring him or her to the back of
the stage.
2 to distract attention or interest from
another person to oneself.
• **upstage** *adverb, adjective* to or relating to
the back or furthest part of the stage in a
theatre.

upstairs *adjective*
of or relating to an upper floor or floors.
• **upstairs** *adverb*
1 up the stairs: *She walked upstairs.*
2 in, to or on an upper floor.
3 to or in a higher rank or office.
Phrase **kick someone upstairs**
(*informal*) to remove someone by
promoting him or her, especially to a
position of less power.
• **upstairs** *noun* an upper storey.

upstanding *adjective*
1 honest or upright: *an upstanding citizen.*
2 (*formal*) standing erect: *Let us be
upstanding to drink the toast.*

upstart *noun*
a person who has an arrogant self-
confidence, often due to achieving wealth
or importance very quickly.
• **upstart** *adjective.*

upstate *noun*
American the section of a state lying north
of the principal city or away from the
coast.
• **upstate** *adverb.*

upstream *adverb, adjective*
to or at the upper part of a stream, against
the direction of the current.

upsurge (up-serj) *noun*
a surge upwards.

upswing *noun*
a swinging or movement upwards.

uptake *noun*
1 the act of taking advantage of an offer,
etc.
2 the act of understanding or
comprehending: *He's a bit slow on the
uptake.*

uptight *adjective*
(*informal*) tense, annoyed or anxious.

up to date *adjective*
containing the latest information,
improvements, etc.: *an up-to-date atlas.*

up-to-the-minute *adjective*
incorporating the very latest news,
information, etc.: *an up-to-the-minute sports
report.*

upturn *verb*
to turn up or over.
• **upturn** *noun* an improvement or upward
turn, e.g. in prices, business, etc.

upward *adjective*
moving or directed up.
Word Family **upwards, upward** *adverb*
towards a higher place or level: *The hikers
climbed upwards for what seemed like an age;*
upwards of more than; in excess of.

upwind (up-**winned**) *adverb, adjective*
in the direction from which the wind is
blowing.

uranium (yoo-**ray**-nee-um) *noun*
a radioactive metal occurring in two
isotopes, one of which is used in nuclear
reactors and formed the basis of the first
atomic bombs.
[after URANUS]

Uranus (**yoo**-r'n-us *or* yoo-**ray**-nus) *noun*
Astronomy the planet in the solar system
seventh from the sun.
[after *Uranus*, god of the sky in Greek
mythology]

urban *adjective*
of or relating to cities and large towns.
Compare RURAL.
Word Family **urbanize, urbanise** *verb*
to make or become urban in character or
nature; **urbanization** *noun* the growth of
towns and cities as more and more people
live in them.

> The words **urban** and *urbane* have
> come into English by different routes
> but from the same word. *Urban* came
> straight from Latin *urbanus*, from *urbo*,
> meaning 'a city'; *urbane* came from Old
> French *urbaine*, also derived from Latin
> *urbo*.

urbane (er-**bane**) *adjective*
sophisticated, refined or smoothly polite.
Word Family **urbanely** *adverb*; **urbanity**
(er-**ban**-i-tee) *noun* the quality of being
urbane.
[Latin *urbanus* a city-dweller, courteous]

urban guerrilla *noun*
a terrorist who specializes in sporadic acts
of bombing, kidnapping or assassination
in cities.

urban myth *noun*
a short story about something unusual in
everyday life, told by many people but not
likely to be true.

urban renewal *noun*
the rebuilding of slum areas in a city,
based on extensive planning for social and
physical needs.

urchin (**er**-chin) *noun*
1 a small mischievous shabbily dressed
child: *a street urchin.*
2 *Biology* a sea urchin.
[Latin *hericius* hedgehog]

urea (yoo-**ree**-ta) *noun*
Biology the main nitrogenous product
excreted by mammals, some fish, etc.
[Greek *ouron* urine]

ureter (yoo-**ree**-ta) *noun*
Anatomy either of two tubes through
which the urine, collected in the kidneys,
passes to be stored in the bladder.
[from Greek]

urethra (yoo-**ree**-thra) *noun*
Anatomy the tube through which urine is
emptied from the bladder.
[from Greek]

urge (erj) *verb*
to push or drive forward with force,
threats, etc.: *With whip and spur he urged
the horse on.*
Figurative He urged me to buy some
insurance (= tried to persuade).
• **urge** *noun* a strong desire: *the sexual urge.*

urgent (**er**-j'nt) *adjective*
1 requiring immediate attention or action:
*There were several urgent messages to be dealt
with.*
2 insistent: *She made her request in an urgent
whisper.*
Word Family **urgently** *adverb*; **urgency**
noun.
[Latin *urgens* pressing onwards]

urinal (yoo-**rye**-n'l *or* yoo-**rin**-'l) *noun*
a fixture into which men can urinate.

urinate (**yoo**-ri-nate) *verb*
to pass urine.
Word Family **urination** (yoo-ri-**nay**-
sh'n) *noun.*

urine (**yoo**-rin) *noun*
a fluid secreted by the kidneys and
excreted from the body as a waste.

Word Family **urinary** *adjective* of,
relating to or involved in the production
and excretion of urine.
[from Latin]

urn (ern) *noun*
1 a vase, usually with a base or stem, used
for storing the ashes of the dead.
2 a large metal container in which tea or
coffee can be made or kept hot.
[from Latin]

urticaria ⇨ HIVES.

us *pronoun* (*singular* **me**)
the objective form of **we**: *He told us
everything.* □ *Give the books to us.*

usage (yoo-sij) *noun*
1 the way of treating or using a person or
thing.
2 customary or habitual practice.
3 the actual way in which words, etc. are
used in a language.
4 a particular written or verbal expression.

use (yooz) *verb*
1 to bring or put into action or service: *We
use the front room as a study.*
2 to take advantage of: *He's just using you to
get business for his company.*
3 (*informal*) to take illegal drugs.
Phrases **used to** (yoost too) 1 did
formerly or regularly in the past: *This
building used to be a cinema.* □ *I used to go
riding every weekend.* 2 accustomed to:
You'll soon get used to your new school. **use
up** to consume something entirely: *We've
used up all the fuel.*
• **use** (yooce) *noun*
1 the act of using: *Make good use of your
time.*
2 the purpose for which something is used:
A dictionary has many uses.
3 the right or ability to use something: *I've
lost the use of one eye.*
4 the way or manner of using: *the correct
use of a telescope.*
5 the need or occasion to use: *Do you have
any further use for this book?*
Phrase **have no use for** (*informal*) to
dislike or find irritating.
Word Family **usable, useable** (yooz-a-
b'l) *adjective* available for use or in a
condition to be used; **useful** (yooce-ful)
adjective serving a use or purpose: *a useful
gadget;* **usefully** *adverb;* **usefulness** *noun;*
useless (yooce-liss) *adjective* 1 not serving
any beneficial purpose. 2 (*informal*) not
skilled: *I'm useless at maths;* **uselessly**
adverb; **uselessness** *noun.*
[from Latin]

> ⚠ The negative form of *used to* is
> *used not to,* as in *I used not to like
> coffee.* The form *didn't use to* is also
> acceptable in informal English, but
> *didn't used to* is wrong.

used (yoozd) *adjective*
having been used already or owned by
someone else: *a used car.*

user *noun*
1 a person who uses something: *First
put your user name into the computer.*
2 a person who takes advantage of
others.
3 (*informal*) a person who takes illegal
drugs.

user-friendly *adjective*
reasonably easy to use or understand.
Word Family **user-friendliness** *noun.*

usher *noun*
1 a person who escorts others to their seats
in a cinema, church, etc.
2 an official in a law court who maintains
order.
• **usher** *verb* to escort or conduct.
Word Family **usherette** (ush-a-ret) *noun*
a female usher in a cinema or theatre.
[Latin *ostiarius* doorman]

usual (yoo-zhoo-'l) *adjective*
expected because of past experience or
occurrence: *She arrived at the usual time.*
• **usual** *noun*
Phrase **the usual, one's usual** (*informal*)
the drink that one normally drinks.
Word Family **usually** *adverb.*

usurp (yoo-zerp *or* yoo-serp) *verb*
to seize wrongfully or by force something
belonging to another, such as power or
property.
Word Family **usurper** *noun;* **usurpation**
(yoo-zer-pay-sh'n) *noun.*
[from Latin]

usury (yoo-zha-ree) *noun*
1 the business of lending money, especially
at a rate of interest which is high or above
the legal rate.
2 this rate of interest.
Word Family **usurer** *noun;* **usurious**
(yoo-zhoor-ee-us) *adjective.*
[from Latin]

utensil (yoo-ten-sil) *noun*
any instrument, container or tool serving
some useful purpose: *kitchen utensils.*
[Latin *utensilis* fit for use]

uterus (yoo-ta-rus) *noun* (*plural* **uteri**
(yoo-ta-rye) *or* **uteruses**) also called
womb.

Anatomy the thick-walled organ lying in the pelvic cavity in females, in which the young grow between fertilization and birth.

utilitarian (yoo-till-i-**tair**-ee-an) *adjective*
1 useful rather than beautiful.
2 *Philosophy* believing that all actions should be aimed at the greatest happiness for the greatest number of people.
Word Family **utilitarian** *noun* a believer in utilitarian principles; **utilitarianism** *noun.*

utility (yoo-**till**-i-tee) *noun* (*plural* **utilities**)
1 the quality of being useful.
2 something which is useful.
3 a government-owned organization which supplies basic needs, such as water, electricity, gas, etc.
[Latin *utilis* useful]

utility room *noun*
a room containing a sink, a washing machine and other useful household appliances.

utilize, utilise (**yoo**-ti-lize) *verb*
to make use of.
Word Family **utilizable** *adjective*; **utilizer** *noun*; **utilization** (yoo-ti-lie-**zay**-sh'n) *noun.*

utmost *adjective* also **uttermost**
the greatest possible: *You must exercise the utmost care.*

Word Family **utmost** *noun* the most possible: *She had done her utmost to make the room comfortable.*

Utopia (yoo-**toe**-pee-a) *noun*
any perfect place or situation.
Word Family **utopian** *adjective* excellent but impractical; **utopian** *noun* an idealistic but impractical reformer; **utopianism** *noun.*
[after *Utopia*, a book by Sir Thomas More, 1478-1535, describing an island of political and social perfection]

utter[1] *verb*
to express audibly: *The mouse uttered a squeak.*
Word Family **utterance** *noun* 1 the act of uttering. 2 something which is uttered or expressed.

utter[2] *adjective*
total: *They lived in utter misery.*
Word Family **utterly** *adverb.*

U-turn *noun*
1 a turn to completely reverse the direction of travel of a vehicle.
2 a complete reversal of direction of opinion, policy, etc.

uvula (**yoo**-vew-la) *noun*
Anatomy the small conical mass of tissue hanging above the back of the tongue.
Word Family **uvular** *adjective.*
[Latin, a small grape]

vac *noun*
(*informal*) a vacation.

vacant (vay-k'nt) *adjective*
not occupied: *Are these seats vacant?*
Word Family vacancy *noun* 1 the state or
condition of being vacant. 2 (*plural*
vacancies) a space, position or place
which is vacant: *a vacancy for a secretary in
our office*; **vacantly** *adverb*; **vacate** (vay-
kate *or* va-**kate**) *verb* to leave or give up:
The landlord insisted we vacate the house.
[Latin *vacans* being empty]

vacation (vay-**kay**-sh'n *or* va-**kay**-sh'n)
noun
1 a holiday.
2 the period between terms at universities
and law-courts.
3 the act of vacating.
[Latin *vacatio* freedom]

vaccinate (vak-si-nate) *verb*
to administer a vaccine.
Word Family vaccination (vak-si-**nay**-
sh'n) *noun*.

vaccine (vak-seen) *noun*
a modified infective agent such as a virus,
which gives immunity to a disease, often
by introducing a mild form of the disease.

The word **vaccine** is derived from
Latin *vaccinus*, from *vacca* (cow). At the
end of the 18th century, a British
doctor, Edward Jenner, discovered that
milkmaids who had suffered from
cowpox, a mild type of smallpox, did
not get smallpox. He argued that
inoculation with the cowpox virus
would make the inoculated person
form antibodies that would be effective
against the smallpox virus. The
inoculation with the cowpox virus was
called *vaccination* and the material
inoculated came to be called *vaccine*.
Later, *vaccination* techniques were used
in the treatment of other diseases.

vacillate (vass-i-late) *verb*
to waver.

Word Family vacillation (vass-i-**lay**-
sh'n) *noun*.
[from Latin]

vacuole (vak-yoo-ole) *noun*
Biology a space in cell protoplasm
containing air, fluid or partially digested
food.

vacuous (vak-yew-us) *adjective*
empty or blank: *a dull vacuous stare into
space.*
Word Family vacuously *adverb*.
[Latin *vacuus* empty]

vacuum (vak-yoom) *noun*
1 a space entirely void of matter.
2 *Physics* an enclosed space from which air
and all other gases have been removed.
3 (*informal*) a vacuum cleaner.
Phrase in a vacuum without being
affected by other ideas or actions going on
at the same time.
• **vacuum** *verb* to clean with a vacuum
cleaner.
[Latin]

vacuum cleaner *noun*
an electrical appliance which sucks up dirt
and dust.

vacuum flask *noun*
(*dated*) a Thermos flask.

vacuum-packed *adjective*
(of a food product) sealed in packaging
from which the air has been removed, in
order to maintain freshness for longer.

vagabond (vag-a-bond) *noun*
1 a person who wanders from place to
place, especially because he or she has no
home.
2 an idle or worthless person.
[Latin *vagari* to wander]

vagary (vay-ga-ree) *noun* (*plural*
vagaries)
an extravagant whim or fancy.

vagina (va-jie-na) *noun* (*plural* **vaginas** *or*
vaginae (va-jie-nee))
Anatomy the tube which connects the
uterus to the vulva in female mammals.
Word Family vaginal *adjective*.
[Latin, a sheath]

vagrant (vay-gr'nt) *noun*
a tramp.
Word Family vagrant *adjective*
wandering or with no home; **vagrancy**
noun.

vague (vaig) *adjective*
1 not clear or distinct: *a vague shadowy
figure in the fog.* □ *a vague memory.*

2 vacant or without a clear expression: *a vague stare*.
Word Family **vaguely** *adverb*; **vagueness** *noun*.
[Latin *vagus* wandering]

vain *adjective*
1 too proud of one's looks, abilities, etc.
2 futile or useless: *a vain attempt to try to stop the flood*.
Phrase **in vain** to no use or effect.
Word Family **vainly** *adverb*; **vanity** *noun*
1 excessive pride or desire for praise.
2 the quality of being worthless or futile.
[Latin *vanus* empty]

vainglorious *adjective*
a literary word meaning 'boastful'.

valance (**val**-ence) *noun* also **valence**
a decorative strip of cloth put round the edge of a bed frame, over the top of a window, etc.

vale *noun*
an old word for a valley.

valediction (val-a-**dik**-sh'n) *noun*
(*formal*) a farewell, especially as expressed in speech or writing.
Word Family **valedictory** *adjective*; **valedictory** *noun* (*plural* **valedictories**) a farewell speech.
[Latin *vale* goodbye + *dicere* to say]

valency (**vay**-l'n-see) *noun* (*plural* **valencies**) also **valence**
Chemistry the combining power of an atom, equal to the number of hydrogen atoms which an atom will combine with or replace, e.g. the valency of oxygen is two, so it combines with two atoms of hydrogen to form water, H_2O.
[Latin *valens* being strong]

valentine (**val**-'n-tine) *noun*
1 a token of love or friendship sent to a person on 14 February (St Valentine's Day), which is set aside for this tradition.
2 the person to whom the token is sent.

valet (**val**-et or val-**ay**) *noun*
1 a male servant who attends his employer personally.
2 a hotel employee who cleans the guests' clothes, etc.
[French]

valiant (val-ee-unt) *adjective*
brave.
Word Family **valiantly** *adverb*.

valid *adjective*
1 having full or official force or effect: *This ticket is only valid for one person*.
2 sound or reasonable: *valid criticism*.

Word Family **validly** *adverb*; **validity** (va-**lid**-i-tee) *noun*; **validate** *verb* to make valid.
[Latin *validus* strong]

valise (va-**leez**) *noun*
a small travelling bag or case, carried in the hand.
[French]

Valium (**val**-ee-um) *noun*
(*trademark*) *Medicine* the drug diazepam.

valley *noun*
a low stretch of land between hills or higher land, often with a river flowing through it.
[from Latin]

valour (**val**-a) *noun* (*American* **valor**)
heroic courage.
Word Family **valorous** *adjective*.
[Latin *valere* to be strong]

value (**val**-yoo) *noun*
1 what something is worth in money: *The value of our house increased last year*.
2 the fact of being useful or desirable: *I don't think there would be much value in making her go against her will*.
3 (**values**) any ideals, goals or standards upon which actions or beliefs are based.
• **value** *verb*
1 to estimate the value of.
2 to regard highly: *I value your friendship*.
Word Family **valuable** (**val**-yoo-b'l) *adjective* of great value: *a valuable lesson to learn*; **valuables** *plural noun* objects which have financial value; **valuer** *noun* a person who estimates values; **valuation** (val-yoo-**ay**-sh'n) *noun* 1 the process of deciding the value of something. 2 an estimated value.
[Latin *valere* to be worth]

value added tax *noun*
short form is **VAT** a tax on the value added to an article at each stage of manufacture.

value judgement *noun*
a personal assessment of quality, merit, etc., as contrasted with an objective assessment or statement of facts.

valve *noun*
1 any of various devices controlling or regulating the flow of fluids or gases in a pipe or tube.
2 *Biology* one of the parts of a shell.
[Latin *valva* a door]

vamoose *verb*
(*informal*) to leave in a hurry.
[Spanish *vamos* let us go]

vamp noun
a seductive woman who uses her physical charms to exploit men.
[shortening of *vampire*]

vampire noun
1 *Folklore* an unnatural evil being or revived corpse, believed to leave its grave at night and suck the blood of the living.
2 also **vampire bat** a tropical American bat which feeds on the blood of animals.
[Hungarian]

van[1] noun
a covered vehicle, often large, for carrying goods, etc.: *a removal van*.
[shortening of *caravan*]

van[2] ⇨ VANGUARD.

van[3] noun *Tennis* ⇨ ADVANTAGE noun (definition 2).

vanadium (va-**nay**-dee-um) noun
a metal used to toughen steel.

vandal noun
a person who destroys or defaces things on purpose.
Word Family **vandalism** noun; **vandalize, vandalise** verb.
[after the *Vandals*, a Germanic tribe which sacked Rome in A.D. 455]

vane noun
a blade or flat surface fixed to a rotating axis, as in a windmill.

vanguard (**van**-gard) noun also **van**
1 the leading part of a military force, providing warning and protection.
2 the forefront of a trend or movement.
[French *avant* before + *garde* guard]

vanilla noun
an extract from a pod-like fruit, widely used as a flavouring in cooking.
[Spanish *vainilla* pod]

vanish verb
1 to disappear completely, especially quickly.
2 *Maths* to become zero.
[Latin *evanescere* to evanesce]

vanishing cream noun
a white cream which is absorbed when put on the face, used formerly as a base for powder, etc.

vanity ⇨ VAIN.

vanity case noun
a fitted travelling case for cosmetics, hairbrushes, etc.

vanity unit noun
a washbasin with cupboards under it.

vanquish (**van**-kwish) verb
to conquer or defeat.
[from Latin]

vantage point (**vahn**-tij poynt) noun
a position giving a wide or clear view.

vapid (**vap**-id) adjective
flat, dull or tasteless.
Word Family **vapidly** adverb; **vapidity** (va-**pid**-i-tee) noun.
[from Latin]

vaporize, vaporise (**vay**-pa-rize) verb
to change into vapour.
Word Family **vaporizer** noun a thing which vaporizes, such as a perfume spray; **vaporization** (vay-pa-rye-**zay**-sh'n) noun.

vapour (**vay**-pa) noun (*American* **vapor**)
1 a gaseous substance, such as mist, to which some substances may be reduced by heat.
2 (**the vapours**) an old word for low spirits or faintness.
[from Latin]

vapour trail noun
the condensation trail left by a high-flying aeroplane.

variable (**vair**-ee-a-b'l) adjective
changing or changeable: *Britain's variable weather is impossible to predict.*
• **variable** noun
1 something liable to change.
2 *Maths* a symbol for any member of a set of numbers.
Word Family **variably** adverb; **variability** (vair-ee-a-**bill**-i-tee), **variableness** noun.
[from Latin]

variance (**vair**-ee-ence) noun
difference or disagreement: *Explain the variance between your two statements.*
Word Family **variant** adjective alternative or different; **variant** noun something variant, such as a different spelling of the same word.

variation (vair-ee-**ay**-sh'n) noun
1 a change from the normal or a standard: *variations in temperature.*
2 *Music* one of a set of versions of a given theme, differing in key, tempo, orchestration, etc.

varicose (**varr**-i-kohss) adjective
(of veins) enlarged or swollen.
[Latin *varicis* of a dilated vein]

varied (**vair**-eed) adjective
including many different features: *The work is very varied.*

variegate (**vair**-ee-a-gate) *verb*
to mark with different colours or patches.
Word Family **variegation** (vair-ee-a-gay-sh'n) *noun*.

variety (va-**rye**-a-tee) *noun* (*plural* **varieties**)
1 the quality of being different or varied: *I want a job with variety, not dull routine.*
2 a different kind, sort or form: *They sell 37 varieties of ice cream.*
3 a number or collection of different things: *She disagreed for a variety of reasons.*
4 a form of entertainment consisting of songs, dances and comedy acts.

various (**vair**-ee-us) *adjective*
1 different: *The skirt is available in various colours.*
2 more than one: *Various meetings were being held.*
Word Family **variously** *adverb*.
[from Latin]

varlet *noun*
an old word for a scoundrel.

varmint *noun*
(*American informal*) an annoying person or animal.

varnish *noun* (*plural* **varnishes**)
1 a substance consisting of a resin dissolved in a solvent, which dries and leaves a glossy transparent finish when applied to a surface.
2 the result of applying this: *You've got a good varnish on that table.*
• **varnish** *verb* to apply varnish to.
[French *vernis*]

varsity (**var**-si-tee) *noun*
(*dated informal*) a university.

vary (**vair**-ee) *verb* (**varies; varying; varied**)
1 to change or alter: *The quality of our product never varies.*
2 to introduce new or different forms to: *You should vary your diet.*

vascular (**vass**-kew-la) *adjective*
Biology relating to or consisting of vessels which conduct fluids.
[Latin *vasculum* a small vessel]

vase (vahz) *noun*
an ornamental container for flowers.
[Latin *vasum* a vessel]

vasectomy (va-**sek**-ta-mee) *noun* (*plural* **vasectomies**)
an operation to cut or remove part of the tube in the testicle which transports semen to the penis.
[Latin *vas* a vessel + Greek *ektomé* a cutting out]

Vaseline (**vass**-a-leen) *noun*
(*trademark*) a yellow or whitish form of petroleum jelly, used as an ointment, etc.

vassal *noun*
Medieval history a person subject to a feudal contract, such as a peasant given a piece of land from a nobleman's estate in exchange for military service, etc.
Compare SEIGNEUR.
Word Family **vassalage** *noun*.

vast (vahst) *adjective*
of very great size or extent: *a vast desert.*
□ *vast sums of money.*
Word Family **vastly** *adverb*; **vastness** *noun*.
[Latin *vastus* empty, desert]

vat *noun*
a large container for liquids.

vaudeville (**vaw**-da-vil) *noun*
American music hall or variety entertainment.
[after *Vau de Vire*, a Normandy valley where satirical songs were popular]

vault[1] (vawlt) *noun*
1 an underground room or chamber, such as a burial place under a church, or a room for storing valuable objects in a bank.
2 an arched roof.
[Latin *volutus* turned over]

vault[2] *verb*
to spring or leap over something, using the hands or a pole as support.
Word Family **vault** *noun*; **vaulter** *noun*.

vaunt (vawnt) *verb*
to boast about.
[Latin *vanitas* vanity]

veal *noun*
the flesh of a calf.
[Latin *vitellus* calf]

vector *noun*
1 *Maths* a quantity which has both magnitude and direction.
2 *Biology* any organism transmitting parasites from one host to the next, such as a malaria-carrying mosquito.
[Latin, a carrier]

veer *verb*
to change course or direction suddenly.
[Dutch]

veg (*rhymes with* ledge) *plural noun*
(*informal*) vegetables.

vegan (**vee**-g'n) *noun*
a strict vegetarian who eats no animal products.

vegetable (vej-ta-b'l) *noun*
1 a plant or part of a plant that is used as food.
2 (*informal*) a person who is incapable of independent thought or movement, usually because of brain damage after an accident.
[Latin *vegetare* to animate]

vegetable oil *noun*
any of various oils obtained from the fruit or seeds of plants.

vegetarian (vej-a-**tair**-ce-un) *noun*
a person who eats vegetable foods only, usually with the exception of eggs and dairy produce, but not meat or fish.
Word Family **vegetarian** *adjective*;
vegetarianism *noun*.

vegetate (vej-a-tate) *verb*
to live in an unthinking or inactive way.

vegetation (vej-a-**tay**-sh'n) *noun*
the plant life in a place.

vegetative (vej-it-a-tiv) *adjective* also
vegetive
1 of vegetation or vegetable growth.
2 *Medicine* existing but not showing any signs of brain activity.

veggie *noun*
(*informal*) a vegetarian.

vehement (vee-u-m'nt) *adjective*
having or showing strong or passionate feeling.
Word Family **vehemently** *adverb*;
vehemence *noun*.
[from Latin]

vehicle (vee-i-k'l) *noun*
1 any device for moving or carrying, especially one on wheels.
2 any medium for carrying or communicating: *The director used the film as a vehicle for his political ideas.*
Word Family **vehicular** (vee-**hik**-yoo-la) *adjective*.
[Latin *vehere* to carry]

veil (vale) *noun*
1 a fine piece of cloth, often transparent, worn on the head and hanging over the face or shoulders.
2 anything that hides or disguises: *a veil of mist.*
Phrase **take the veil** to become a nun.
• **veil** *verb* to cover or conceal with or as with a veil.
[Latin *velum* a curtain]

vein (vane) *noun*
1 *Anatomy* any of the thin-walled tubes carrying blood back from the tissues of the body to the heart. Compare ARTERY (definition 1); CAPILLARY.
2 a vein-like part or support, as in a leaf or an insect's wing.
3 also called **lode; reef**. *Geology* a strip of minerals along a joint or fault line in rocks.
4 any streak or marking.
5 a small amount of a particular quality: *a vein of humour running through the novel.*
[from Latin]

Velcro *noun*
(*trademark*) a special fabric in double strips used for fastening things together, having hundreds of tiny hooks on one surface and loops on the other.

veld (velt) *noun* also **veldt**
open grassland in southern Africa.
[Afrikaans, field]

vellum *noun*
a smooth parchment, usually made from calfskin.
[Latin *vitulus* a calf]

velocity (ve-**loss**-i-tee) *noun* (*plural* **velocities**)
1 *Physics* the vector quantity describing the rate of change in the displacement of an object in both magnitude and direction, including **linear velocity**, expressed in metres per second and **angular velocity**, expressed in radians per second. Compare SPEED *noun* (definition 2).
2 (*informal*) speed.
[Latin *velox* swift]

velour (vil-**oor**) *noun* also **velours** (vil-**oor**)
a fabric with a velvet-like pile.
[French, velvet]

velvet *noun*
1 a silk, cotton or fibre fabric with a soft short thick pile.
2 something which is soft or smooth like this fabric.
3 the covering, which is rich in blood vessels, on developing antlers in deer.
Word Family **velvety** *adjective*.
[Latin *villus* shaggy hair]

velveteen (vell-va-teen) *noun*
an imitation velvet made from cotton.

venal (vee-n'l) *adjective*
(*formal*) corrupt or easily corruptible.
[Latin *venalis* for sale]

vendetta *noun*
1 a sustained campaign of relentless hostility.
2 a feud in which the family of a murdered person takes revenge on the murderer or the murderer's family.
[Italian, vengeance]

vending machine *noun*
a coin-operated machine dispensing small articles for sale, such as cigarettes, soft drinks, etc.

vendor *noun*
a person who sells something.
Word Family **vend** *verb*.
[from Latin]

veneer (vin-**ear**) *noun*
a thin layer of wood, plastic, etc. used to cover a surface.
Figurative Under his veneer of meekness he's a vicious person (= appearance).
• **veneer** *verb* to apply a veneer to.
[Old French *fournir* to furnish]

venerate (**ven**-a-rate) *verb*
to treat with great respect or reverence.
Word Family **veneration** (ven-a-**ray**-sh'n) *noun* 1 the act of venerating. 2 a feeling of deep respect; **venerable** (**ven**-a-ra-b'l) *adjective* worthy of being venerated; **venerability** (ven-'ra-**bill**-i-tee) *noun*.
[from Latin]

venereal disease (vin-**ear**-ee-al diz-eez) *noun*
any disease transmitted by sexual intercourse.
[Latin *veneris* of sexual love, from Venus, see APHRODITE]

venetian blind *noun*
a window blind with overlapping slats which can be opened, closed, or raised by pulling a cord.
[from *Venice*]

vengeance (**ven**-j'nce) *noun*
revenge or retribution.
Phrase **with a vengeance** to excess: *The water started pouring in again, with a vengeance.*
[Latin *vindicare* to claim]

vengeful *adjective*
having or showing a desire for revenge.
Word Family **vengefully** *adverb*; **vengefulness** *noun*.

venial (**vee**-nee-ul) *adjective*
(*formal*) (of a fault or sin) forgivable or excusable.
Word Family **veniality** (vee-nee-**al**-i-tee) *noun*.
[from Latin]

venison *noun*
the flesh of a deer.
[Latin *venatio* hunting]

venom *noun*
1 a poison made by certain animals, such as snakes, and transmitted to victims by a bite or sting.
2 great spite or bitterness.
Word Family **venomous** (**ven**-a-mus) *adjective* 1 having the ability to make venom. 2 full of spite or bitterness; **venomously** *adverb*; **venomousness** *noun*.
[from Latin]

venous (**vee**-nus) *adjective*
of or relating to veins or the blood carried in them.

vent *noun*
1 any opening serving as an outlet, such as one allowing air or smoke to escape from a room, or gases, lava and ash from a volcano.
2 a slit in the back or sides of a coat or skirt.
Phrase **give vent to** to express or utter.
• **vent** *verb* to find or provide an outlet for: *She vented her anger on the unfortunate bystanders.*
[Old French *fente* a slit]

ventilate (**ven**-ti-late) *verb*
to provide with or circulate fresh air.
Word Family **ventilator** *noun* something which ventilates, such as a device in the wall of a building; **ventilation** (ven-ti-**lay**-sh'n) *noun* 1 the act of ventilating. 2 a device or means for ventilating.
[Latin *ventilare* to fan]

ventral *adjective*
of or relating to the abdomen.
[from Latin]

ventricle (**ven**-tri-k'l) *noun*
1 *Anatomy* either of the two pumping chambers of the heart.
2 *Anatomy* any of four cavities in the brain.
[Latin *ventriculus* little belly]

ventriloquist (ven-**trill**-a-kwist) *noun*
a person producing sounds or voices which seem to come from another source.
Word Family **ventriloquism** *noun*.

> The word **ventriloquist** is etymologically related to the stomach. It is a form of Late Latin *ventriloquus*, formed from *venter* (stomach) and *loqui* (to speak). Originally it referred literally to the supposed practice of speaking from the stomach, this being thought to be a sign of being possessed by the devil. Later it came to be used for the art of producing vocal sounds that seem to come from another source.

venture *noun*
any undertaking involving some risk.
• **venture** *verb* to risk.
Figurative Might I venture a suggestion?
(= dare to offer).
Word Family **venturesome** *adjective*
willing to take risks.
[shortening of ADVENTURE]

venue (ven-yoo) *noun*
the place where an event, action, etc. takes
place.
[French]

Venus (vee-nus) *noun*
Astronomy the planet in the solar system
next to the earth and second from the sun.
[after *Venus*, the goddess of love, beauty,
fertility, etc. in Roman mythology]

veracity (vir-ass-i-tee) *noun*
truth or truthfulness.
Word Family **veracious** (vir-ay-shus)
adjective; **veraciously** *adverb*.
[from Latin]

veranda (vir-an-da) *noun* also **verandah**
an open area with a floor and roof,
attached to the outside of a building.
[Hindi]

verb *noun*
a word which shows what a person or
thing is doing, thinking, or feeling or what
state they are in, such as come, has, or
smiled.

verbal *adjective*
1 of, relating to or expressed in words.
2 *Grammar* of or relating to verbs.
3 (*informal*) oral: *a verbal agreement*.
Word Family **verbally** *adverb*;
verbalize, verbalise *verb* 1 to express in
words. *They verbalized their discontent.*
2 *Maths* to write a numeral as a word or
words, e.g. to write 20 as *twenty*.

verbatim (ver-bay-tim) *adjective, adverb*
using exactly the same words.

verbiage (ver-bee-ij) *noun*
too many useless words.

verbose (*rhymes with* gross) *adjective*
using too many unnecessary words.
Word Family **verbosely** *adverb*;
verbosity (ver-boss-i-tee) *noun*.

verdant *adjective*
fresh or green with vegetation.
[Latin *viridans* green]

verdict *noun*
a judgement or decision, especially that of
a jury in a court case.
Phrase **return a verdict** (of a jury) to
give a verdict.
[Latin *vere* true + *dictus* said]

verdigris (ver-di-gree *or* ver-di-greece)
noun
a greenish-blue pigment formed on copper
or brass by the action of acetic acid.
[Old French *vert de Grèce* Greek green]

verdure (verd-ya) *noun*
the fresh greenness of vegetation, or the
vegetation itself.

verge (verj) *noun*
an edge, margin or border, such as a strip
of grass beside a road.
Phrase **be on the verge of** to be very
close to something or just about to do
something: *He was on the verge of tears*.
• **verge** *verb*
Phrase **verge on** to be almost: *Her
attitude verged on rudeness*.
[Latin *virga* a rod]

verger (ver-ja) *noun*
Christianity a person who takes care of the
interior of a church.
[Latin *virga* a rod (of office)]

verify (verr-i-fie) *verb* (**verifies;
verifying; verified**)
to confirm the truth or accuracy of: *The
police can verify your alibi by asking your
witnesses*.
Word Family **verification** (verr-i-fi-kay-
sh'n) *noun* 1 the act of verifying. 2 proof
or confirmation; **verifiable** *adjective*.
[Latin *verus* true + *facere* to make]

verily *adverb*
an old word meaning 'truly or indeed'.

verisimilitude (verr-i-si-mill-i-tewd) *noun*
an appearance or semblance of truth.

veritable (verr-i-ta-b'l) *adjective*
real or unquestionable.
Word Family **veritably** *adverb*.

vermicelli (ver-mi-chell-ee) *plural noun*
pasta in long thin threads.
[Italian, little worms]

vermilion (ver-mill-y'n) *noun* also
vermillion
a vivid red to reddish-orange colour.

vermin *plural noun*
1 any harmful or objectionable small
animals or parasitic insects, for example
rats or lice.
2 any obnoxious people.
Word Family **verminous** *adjective*.
[Latin *vermis* worm]

vermouth (ver-muth) *noun*
a red or white wine flavoured with herbs
which can have a sweet or dry taste.
[German *Wermuth* wormwood]

vernacular (ver-**nak**-yoo-la) *noun*
the native language of a country or nation,
especially its colloquial form.
• **vernacular** *adjective*
1 relating to the native language.
2 popular or informal.

vernal *adjective*
of, occurring in or appropriate to spring.
[Latin *ver* spring]

verruca (vir-**oo**-ka) *noun* (*plural*
verrucae (vir-**oo**-kee *or* vir-**oo**-see) *or*
verrucas)
a wart on the sole of the foot.

versatile (**ver**-sa-tile) *adjective*
having many abilities or functions: *a
versatile little gadget.*
Word Family versatility (ver-sa-**till**-i-
tee) *noun*; **versatilely** *adverb*.
[Latin *versatilis* capable of turning]

verse *noun*
1 a division of a poem, similar to a
paragraph in prose.
2 a poem or poems.
3 a short division of a chapter in the Bible.
blank verse poetry which does not
rhyme, but has a regular rhythm.
free verse poetry which has neither
rhyme nor regular rhythm.
[Latin *versus* a line (of writing)]

versed *adjective*
Phrase **versed in something** skilled or
experienced at something.
[Latin *versatus* engaged in]

version (**ver**-zh'n) *noun*
1 an account or description from a single
point of view: *Don't believe his version of the
accident.*
2 an adaptation or variation: *the film
version of a novel.*
[Latin *versus* turned]

versus *preposition*
against.
[Latin]

vertebra (**ver**-ta-bra) *noun* (*plural*
vertebrae (**ver**-ta-bree)
any of the chain of bones that form the
spine or backbone.
Word Family vertebral *adjective*.
[Latin]

vertebrate (**ver**-ta-brit) *noun*
any animal with a backbone, e.g. a
mammal or a reptile. Compare
INVERTEBRATE.

vertex *noun* (*plural* **vertices** (**ver**-ti-seez)
or **vertexes**)
1 *Maths* the highest point, such as the apex
of a pyramid.

2 *Maths* a point where two or more lines or
three or more planes intersect.
[Latin, top of the head]

vertical *adjective*
at right angles to the plane of the horizon.
Compare HORIZONTAL.
Word Family vertical *noun* a vertical
line, plane or position; **vertically** *adverb*.

vertigo *noun*
dizziness and loss of balance.
[Latin, whirling]

verve *noun*
enthusiasm, energy or vigour.

very *adverb*
1 to a high degree.
2 used to intensify or emphasize: *a cloth of
the very best quality.* □ *the very next day.*
• **very** *adjective*
1 actual or exact: *Those were her very words.*
2 mere: *The very thought frightens me.*
[Latin *verus* true]

very high frequency *noun*
short form is **VHF** *Radio* the frequency
used in short-range radio, relatively free
from interference.

Very light (**verr**-ee lite *or* **veer**-ee lite)
a coloured flare used as a signal.
[invented by *E. M. Very*, 1847-1910]

vespers *plural noun*
(*used with singular verb*) *Christianity* a
service held in the evening.
[Latin *vespera* evening]

vessel *noun*
1 a ship or large boat.
2 any container for liquids, etc.
3 *Anatomy* a tube or duct in the body,
which carries some fluid, especially blood.
[Latin *vascellum* small vase]

vest *noun*
1 a light collarless shirt without sleeves,
worn as underwear.
2 a similar piece of clothing worn as
protection: *a bulletproof vest.*
3 *American* a waistcoat.

vestal virgin *noun*
in ancient Rome, a woman who vowed to
live a life of chastity.
[after *Vesta*, the Roman goddess of the
hearth]

vested interest *noun*
a personal interest in making sure
something happens.

vestibule (**vest**-i-bewl) *noun*
(*formal*) an entrance hall or lobby.

vestige (**vest**-ij) *noun*
a mark or trace of something that once existed: *Not a vestige of the castle remained.*
Word Family vestigial (vest-**ij**-'l) *adjective.*
[Latin *vestigium* footprint]

vestment *noun*
a ceremonial robe, especially one worn by the clergy during religious services.

vestry *noun* (*plural* **vestries**) also called **sacristy**.
Christianity the part of a church where the sacred vessels, robes, etc. are kept.

vet *verb* (**vets**; **vetting**; **vetted**)
to check carefully.
• **vet** *noun* (*informal*) a veterinary surgeon.

vetch *noun* (*plural* **vetches**)
any of various plants of the bean family.
[from Latin]

veteran (**vet**-a-run) *noun*
a person who has had long service or experience: *a war veteran.*
• **veteran** *adjective* (of a motor vehicle) built before 1918. Compare VINTAGE *adjective* (definition 3).
[Latin *vetus* old]

veterinarian (vet-er-i-**nair**-ee-an) *noun*
American a veterinary surgeon.

veterinary (**vet**-er-in-tree) *adjective*
relating to medical or surgical treatment of animals.
[Latin *veterina* draught cattle]

veterinary surgeon *noun*
a person qualified to perform veterinary treatment.

veto (**vee**-toe) *noun* (*plural* **vetoes**)
the right or power to prevent or reject something, often by a vote, or the exercise of this.
• **veto** *verb.*
[Latin, I forbid]

vex *verb*
to trouble, worry or annoy.
Word Family vexation *noun* the act of vexing or the state of being vexed.
[Latin *vexare* to jostle]

via (**vie**-a) *preposition*
1 by way of: *The shortest route is via Stockport.*
2 by means of: *I got into computing via my interest in the Internet.*
[Latin, way]

viable (**vie**-a-b'l) *adjective*
1 practicable or workable: *His plan does not seem viable.*

2 *Biology* being able to live and grow independently.
Word Family viably *adverb*; **viability** (vie-a-**bill**-i-tee) *noun.*
[French from Latin *vita* life]

viaduct (**vie**-a-dukt) *noun*
a long bridge, especially one of arched masonry spanning a valley.
[Latin *via* way + *ductus* brought]

vial (vile) *noun*
a small thin glass medicine container.

vibes (viebz) *plural noun*
(*informal*) feelings experienced or communicated.
[VIB(ration)]

vibrant (**vie**-br'nt) *adjective*
1 lively and energetic.
2 (of colour or sound) rich or strong.
Word Family vibrantly *adverb*; **vibrancy** *noun.*
[Latin *vibrare* to tremble]

vibrate (**vie**-brate) *verb*
1 to throb or shake.
2 (of sounds) to sound or resound.
Word Family vibration (vie-**bray**-sh'n) *noun* 1 the act of vibrating. 2 a vibrating movement; **vibratory** (**vibe**-ra-tree), **vibrational** *adjective*; **vibrator** *noun* something which vibrates or causes vibration.

vibrato (vi-**brah**-toe) *noun*
Music the rapid alternation of two notes close in pitch.
[Italian]

vicar (**vikk**-a) *noun*
1 *Protestantism* a member of the clergy of the Church of England in charge of a parish.
2 *Roman Catholicism* a representative: *The Pope is considered the vicar of Christ.*
Word Family vicarage *noun* the home of a vicar.
[Latin *vicarius* taking another's place]

vicarious (vie-**kair**-ee-us) *adjective*
1 done, received or undergone on behalf of someone else.
2 imagined through the experience of another: *vicarious pleasure.*
Word Family vicariously *adverb*; **vicariousness** *noun.*
[Latin *vicarius* substituted]

vice[1] *noun*
1 a bad habit: *Smoking isn't one of my vices.*
2 immoral conduct.
[Latin *vitium* a blemish]

vice² *noun*
 any of various instruments with two jaws
 which can be tightened to hold an object.
 [Italian *vite* a screw]

vice admiral *noun*
 Navy a commissioned officer ranking
 between rear admiral and admiral.

vice chancellor *noun*
 the chief administrative officer of a
 university.

viceroy (**vice**-roy) *noun*
 a person, such as a governor, appointed to
 rule as a representative of a monarch.
 Word Family **viceregal** (vice-**ree**-g'l)
 adjective.
 [*vice* + French *roi* king]

vice versa (vice **ver**-sa *or* vie-sa **ver**-sa)
 adverb
 the opposite is also true.
 [Latin]

vicinity (viss-**in**-i-tee) *noun*
 1 the area near or around a place.
 2 (*dated*) closeness or proximity.
 [Latin *vicus* a row of houses]

vicious (**vish**-us) *adjective*
 1 fierce: *a vicious dog*.
 2 evil, spiteful or malicious: *a vicious lie*.
 Word Family **viciously** *adverb*;
 viciousness *noun*.
 [Latin *vitiosus* bad]

vicious circle *noun*
 a situation in which a difficulty only leads
 to further problems or difficulties and
 eventually back to the first: *Higher wages
 produce inflation and inflation produces
 higher wage claims, so it's a vicious circle*.

vicissitude (viss-**iss**-i-tewd) *noun*
 a change or variation, especially in one's
 fortune in life.

victim *noun*
 a person or thing that suffers harm or
 injury: *She was the victim of a vicious attack*.
 [Latin *victima* beast for sacrifice]

victimize, victimise *verb*
 to punish selectively or unfairly.
 Word Family **victimization** *noun*.

victory (**vik**-ta-ree) *noun* (*plural* **victories**)
 success against an opponent, etc., or an
 instance of this.
 Word Family **victor** *noun* a person or
 thing that achieves victory; **victorious**
 (vik-**taw**-ree-us) *adjective*; **victoriously**
 adverb.
 [from Latin]

victuals (**vitt**-'lz) *plural noun*
 any food prepared for eating.
 [Latin *victus* food]

video *noun*
 1 also called **video recorder**. a machine
 that records vision and sound signals, used
 for recording and playing back films,
 television programmes, etc.
 2 also called **videotape**. a tape on which a
 film, etc. is recorded: *Have we got a blank
 video?*
 3 a film, etc. recorded on a tape: *This is a
 great video!*
 • **video** *verb* to record (a television
 programme, etc.) on a video.

video cassette recorder *noun*
 short form is **VCR** (*formal*) a video
 recorder.

videoconferencing *noun*
 communications in sound and vision
 between people in different places, using
 cameras and microphones attached to
 computers and high-speed telephone
 lines.

video game *noun*
 a game played by electronically
 manipulating graphic symbols on a visual
 display unit.

video nasty *noun* (*plural* **video nasties**)
 a video film depicting scenes of violence
 and cruelty, horror or pornography.

videophone *noun*
 a telephone equipped to send and receive
 audio and visual signals so the users can
 see as well as hear each other.

video recorder ⇒ VIDEO *noun*
 (definition 1).

videotape ⇒ VIDEO *noun* (definition 2).

vie *verb* (**vies; vying; vied**)
 to compete or contend.

view *noun*
 1 sight or vision, or the range of this: *A car
 sped into view*.
 2 a sight of land, countryside, etc., or a
 picture of this: *We had a good view of the
 harbour from our window*.
 3 a particular way of thinking about
 something: *What are your views on
 marriage?*
 Phrases **a dim view** an unfavourable
 opinion. **in view of** on account of: *In view
 of the bad weather we'll stay in the museum*.
 on view in a place for public inspection.
 with a view to with the intention of: *She
 bought the car solely with a view to selling it at
 a profit*.
 • **view** *verb*
 1 to see or look at.
 2 to regard or consider.
 Word Family **viewable** *adjective*.
 [French *vu* seen]

viewer *noun*
1 a person that views: *a survey of the programme's viewers.*
2 a small device for lighting or magnifying photographic slides.

viewfinder *noun*
Photography a small window in a camera through which the subject can be viewed.

viewpoint *noun*
1 a place from which one can see something.
2 an opinion.

vigil (**vij**-il) *noun*
1 the act of staying awake at night, especially to keep watch.
2 a watch kept in this way.
[Latin *vigilia* wakefulness]

vigilant (**vij**-il-'nt) *adjective*
keenly attentive or watchful.
Word Family **vigilantly** *adverb*;
vigilance *noun*.
[Latin *vigilans* keeping awake]

vigilante (vij-il-**an**-tee) *noun*
a member of an unauthorized and usually extreme group who seek justice by their own means.
[Spanish, vigilant]

vignette (vin-**yet**) *noun*
1 a decorative design or small illustration without a clear-cut border.
2 a short graceful literary description.
[French]

vigour (**vigg**-a) *noun* (*American* **vigor**)
energetic strength or force.
Word Family **vigorous** *adjective*;
vigorously *adverb*
[from Latin]

vile *adjective*
repulsive or disgusting.
Word Family **vilely** *adverb*; **vileness** *noun*.
[Latin *vilis* cheap]

vilify (**vill**-i-fie) *verb* (**vilifies; vilifying; vilified**)
to speak maliciously of.
Word Family **vilification** (vill-i-fi-**kay**-sh'n) *noun*.
[Latin *vilis* cheap + *facere* to make]

villa *noun*
1 a house, especially a large one which one rents for a holiday abroad.
2 in ancient Rome, a large house with a farm attached.
[Latin]

village (**vill**-ij) *noun*
1 a populated area in the countryside which is smaller than a town.
2 its inhabitants.
Word Family **villager** *noun* an inhabitant of a village.
[Latin *villa* a country house or farm]

villain (**vill**-un) *noun*
an evil or wicked person.
Word Family **villainous** *adjective* wicked or evil; **villainy** *noun* 1 evil conduct.
2 (*plural* **villainies**) (*dated*) an evil act.

villein (**vill**-un) *noun*
Medieval history a serf.
[Latin *villanus* a farmer]

vim *noun*
(*informal*) energy.
[from Latin]

vinaigrette (vin-i-**gret**) *noun*
a dressing for salads, etc. made of oil, vinegar and seasoning.
[French]

vindicate (**vin**-di-kate) *verb*
to clear from suspicion, blame, criticism, etc.
Word Family **vindication** (vin-di-**kay**-sh'n) *noun* 1 the act of vindicating. 2 a defence or justification.
[Latin *vindicare* to lay claim]

vindictive (vin-**dik**-tiv) *adjective*
vengeful or spiteful.
Word Family **vindictively** *adverb*;
vindictiveness *noun*.
[Latin *vindicta* vengeance]

vine *noun*
1 a grapevine.
2 any plant that trails or climbs by winding its slender stem round a support.
[from Latin]

vinegar (**vin**-i-ga) *noun*
a sour liquid obtained by fermenting wine, beer, etc. and used for flavouring, pickling, etc.
Word Family **vinegary** *adjective*.
[French *vin* wine + *aigre* sour]

vineyard (**vin**-yard) *noun*
a plantation of grapevines.

vingt-et-un (vant-ay-**uhn**) ⇨ PONTOON[2].
[French, twenty-one]

vino (**vee**-no) *noun*
(*informal*) wine.

vintage (**vin**-tij) *noun*
the grape harvest, especially that obtained in one year from a particular area.
• **vintage** *adjective*

1 (of wine) made or harvested during a particularly good year.
2 showing all the best characteristics of a person or thing: *a new song that is actually vintage Michael Jackson*.
3 (of a motor vehicle) built between 1918 and 1930. Compare VETERAN *adjective*.

> The word **vintage** came into English from Old French *vendage*, which in turn is derived from Latin *vindemia* (grape gathering). *Vintage* was at first used to mean the grape crop itself and then also came to mean the crop of a particular year. It then came to be applied also to the crop, and so to the wine, of a particularly good year. It is also used figuratively of things other than grapes or wine.

vintner *noun*
a person who deals in or sells wines.

vinyl (**vie**-nil) *noun*
a type of strong plastic: *vinyl flooring*.
Phrase **on vinyl** on record, in contrast to CDs, etc.

viol (vile) *noun*
a medieval stringed instrument from which the violin, etc. developed.

viola (vee-**ole**-a) *noun*
Music a stringed instrument played with a bow, slightly larger and having a lower pitch than a violin.

violate (**vie**-a-late) *verb*
1 to break a law, promise, agreement, etc.: *The ceasefire agreement was violated again*.
2 to treat with great disrespect: *to violate a grave*.
3 (*dated*) to rape.
Word Family **violator** *noun*; **violation** (vie-a-**lay**-sh'n) *noun*.
[Latin *violare* to do violent harm to]

violent (**vie**-a-l'nt) *adjective*
1 involving aggression and force: *a violent crime*.
2 (of a person) liable to hurt others.
3 having or showing great strength or power: *a violent storm*. □ *a violent headache*.
Word Family **violence** (**vie**-a-l'nce) *noun* **1** violent behaviour. **2** strength or intensity: *The violence of his feelings astonished her*; **violently** *adverb*.

violet (**vie**-a-let) *noun*
1 a small plant with fragrant dark purple flowers.
2 a deep bluish-red colour, the colour next to indigo at the end of the spectrum.
shrinking violet (*informal*) a timid or retiring person.

● **violet** *adjective*.
[from Latin]

violin (vie-a-**lin**) *noun*
Music a stringed high-pitched instrument held horizontally between the chin and the neck and played with a bow.
Word Family **violinist** *noun*.
[Italian from Latin *vitulari* to make merry]

violoncello ⇨ CELLO.

viper *noun*
1 any of a group of thick-bodied poisonous snakes found in Europe, Africa and Asia, especially the adder.
2 a treacherous or malicious person.
[from Latin]

virago (vir-**ah**-go) *noun*
a sharp-tongued bad-tempered woman.
[Latin, a woman soldier]

viral ⇨ VIRUS.

virgin (**ver**-jin) *noun*
a person who has not had sexual intercourse.
Phrases **the Virgin Birth** *Christianity* the doctrine of the miraculous conception of Christ by the Virgin Mary through the power of the Holy Spirit and without the agency of a human father. **the Virgin Mary** *Christianity* Mary, the mother of Christ.

● **virgin** *adjective*
1 being a virgin.
2 a literary word meaning 'pure and untouched': *The virgin snow lay all about*.
3 (of olive oil) obtained from the first pressing of the olives, without the use of heat, and therefore especially fine.
Word Family **virginal** *adjective* of, like or as pure as a virgin; **virginity** (ver-**jin**-i-tee) *noun* the state or condition of being a virgin.
[from Latin]

virginal *noun*
Music a small oblong type of harpsichord.

Virgo (**ver**-go) *noun*
Astrology a group of stars, the sixth sign of the Zodiac, the sign of the Virgin.
[Latin]

virile (**vir**-ile) *adjective*
having or showing vigorous strength.
Word Family **virility** (vi-**rill**-i-tee) *noun* the state or quality of being virile.
[Latin *virilis* like a man]

virology (vie-**rol**-a-jee) *noun*
the study of viruses.
Word Family **virologist** *noun*.

virtual (ver-tew-ul) *adjective*
1 being something in effect but not in actual name or form: *The accountant had so much power that he was the virtual head of the company.*
2 *Computers* appearing to exist in three dimensions, due to software: *walking through a virtual garden.*
Word Family **virtually** *adverb* 1 nearly.
2 *Computers* using virtual reality programming.

virtual reality *noun*
a computer-simulated environment which gives the operator the impression of actually being in the environment and being able to interact with it, by means of special equipment, such as goggles or a joystick, used, for example, in video games.

virtue (ver-tew) *noun*
1 the quality of moral goodness or excellence.
2 a particular kind of moral excellence: *Patience is a virtue.*
3 advantage; merit: *The virtue of his plan lies in its simplicity.*
4 an old word for chastity.
Phrases **by virtue of** because of. **make a virtue of necessity** to get the best advantage out of doing what one is forced to do anyway.
Word Family **virtuous** *adjective*; **virtuously** *adverb*; **virtuousness** *noun*.
[Latin *virtus* courage, moral excellence]

virtuoso (ver-tew-oh-so) *noun* (*plural* **virtuosi** (ver-tew-oh-see) or **virtuosos**)
a person who displays masterly or dazzling skill in the arts, especially in music.
Word Family **virtuosity** (ver-tew-oss-i-tee) *noun* the skill of a virtuoso.
[Italian, skilful]

virulent (virr-a-l'nt) *adjective*
1 (of a disease, etc.) causing severe effects.
2 extremely bitter and aggressive: *virulent abuse.*
Word Family **virulently** *adverb*; **virulence** *noun* the quality of being virulent.
[Latin *virulentus* poisonous (wound)]

virus (vie-rus) *noun* (*plural* **viruses**)
1 a tiny agent, too small to be seen with a microscope, which can only multiply within a living cell and may cause disease.
2 (*informal*) an illness caused by a virus.
3 also called **computer virus**. *Computers* a set of instructions secretly put or sent into a computer in order to damage or destroy the data it contains.

Word Family **viral** (vie-rul) *adjective* of, like or caused by a virus.
[Latin, poison]

visa (vee-za) *noun*
an official permit from a foreign country allowing a person to visit. Compare PASSPORT.
[Latin, seen]

visage (viz-ij) *noun*
a person's face or facial expression.
[Latin *visus* seen]

vis-à-vis (veez-a-vee) *preposition*
in relation to: *Her position vis-à-vis the coming election was unclear.*
[French]

viscera (viss-er-a) *plural noun*
all the soft inner organs in the cavities of the body, such as the lungs, stomach, heart, etc.
Word Family **visceral** *adjective* arising from deep emotion, intuition, etc.
[Latin]

viscose (vis-kohss) *noun*
1 *Chemistry* a liquid prepared from cellulose, used for making rayon, cellulose film for transparent wrappings, etc.
2 rayon made with viscose.

viscount (vie-count) *noun*
a nobleman ranking between an earl and a baron.
Word Family **viscountess** *noun* (*plural* **viscountesses**) 1 a female viscount. 2 the wife of a viscount; **viscountcy, viscounty** *noun*.
[Latin *vice* in place of + COUNT]

viscous (visk-us) *adjective*
sticky and having the consistency of heavy syrup or glue.
Word Family **viscously** *adverb*; **viscousness, viscosity** (vis-koss-i-tee) *noun*.

visible (viz-i-b'l) *adjective*
able to be seen.
Word Family **visibility** (viz-i-bill-i-tee) *noun* the distance at which things are visible: *The plane crashed because visibility was down to 45m;* **visibly** *adverb*
[Latin *visus* seen]

vision (vizh-'n) *noun*
1 the power of seeing.
2 imagination regarding the future: *Our leaders lack political vision.*
3 an apparition or prophetic dream.
4 something seen, actually or in the imagination: *I switched on the TV but got no vision, only sound.*
5 a thing of unusual beauty.

Word Family **visionary** (vizh-'n-ree)
adjective **1** showing imagination about
the future. **2** relating to dreams, etc.
3 impractical; **visionary** *noun* (*plural*
visionaries) **1** a person who has visions.
2 an impractical or idealistic dreamer.

visit (viz-it) *verb*
to go or come to see: *Have you visited the
exhibition yet?* □ *visit a website.*
Phrase **visit something on someone** an
old expression meaning 'to make someone
suffer something'.
Word Family **visit** *noun*; **visitor** *noun* a
person or thing that visits.
[from Latin]

visitation (viz-i-tay-sh'n) *noun*
a visit, especially one of official inspection.

visor (vie-za) *noun* also **vizor**
1 the movable part of a helmet which
protects the face.
2 ⇨ SUN VISOR.

vista *noun*
1 a view, especially one seen through an
opening or along a passage.
2 a mental image: *New vistas of sunny work-
free days opened up in his mind.*
[Italian, sight]

visual (viz-yew-al) *adjective*
of or involving the sense of sight: *The
teacher used maps and other visual aids to
illustrate her point.*
Word Family **visualize, visualise** *verb* to
form a mental image of: *Try to visualize the
scene;* **visualization** (viz-yew-al-eye-**zay**-
sh'n) *noun*; **visually** *adverb*.

visual display unit *noun*
short form is **VDU** *Computers* a screen
which displays information.

vital (vie-t'1) *adjective*
1 essential: *Control of pollution is vital for the
survival of our environment.*
2 of, relating to or necessary for life: *The
heart is one of the vital organs.*
3 full of energy and enthusiasm for life:
She was a vital happy girl before the accident.
4 an old word meaning 'causing ruin or
death'.
Word Family **vitally** *adverb*.
[Latin *vita* life]

vitality (vie-tal-i-tee) *noun*
vigorousness of mind or body: *The wrong
eating habits soon lead to a loss of vitality.*

vital statistics ⇨ STATISTICS.

vitamin (vit-a-min *or* vie-ta-min) *noun*
Biology an organic dietary compound
essential for the life and growth of
organisms, but which does not supply

energy and is only needed in very small
amounts.
vitamin A a vitamin found in fruit and
vegetables which is essential for growth.
Deficiency may cause night blindness and
dry skin.
vitamin A₂ a compound very similar to
vitamin A, found in the liver of freshwater
fish.
vitamin B complex an important group
of water-soluble vitamins, including
vitamin B₁, vitamin B₂, etc.
vitamin B₁ also called **thiamine**. a
vitamin found in liver and cereal grains.
Deficiency may cause beri-beri.
vitamin B₂ also called **riboflavin**. a
vitamin found in liver and milk.
Deficiency may cause inflammation of the
lips and tongue.
vitamin B₆ also called **pyridoxine**. a
vitamin found in yeast, wheat, corn, liver,
etc. Deficiency may cause convulsions and
irritability.
vitamin C also called **ascorbic acid**. a
vitamin found in citrus fruits, vegetables,
etc. Deficiency may cause scurvy.
vitamin D a group of fat-soluble vitamins
found in milk and the liver of fish.
Deficiency may cause rickets.
vitamin E a vitamin found in wheatgerm
oil that promotes fertility in mammals and
helps prevent miscarriages.
vitamin K₁ a vitamin found in vegetables,
rice, etc., which promotes clotting of the
blood.
vitamin P a water-soluble vitamin found
in citrus fruits and paprika. It is essential
for growth of cell walls and capillaries.
[Latin *vita* life + *amino*]

vitreous (vit-ree-us) *adjective*
glassy or resembling glass.

vitreous humour *noun*
Anatomy the transparent jelly-like
substance which fills the eyeball behind
the lens. Compare AQUEOUS HUMOUR.
[Latin *vitrum* glass]

vitrify (vit-ri-fie) *verb* (**vitrifies;
vitrifying; vitrified**)
to turn into glass.
Word Family **vitrification** (vit-ri-fi-**kay**-
sh'n) *noun*.
[Latin *vitrum* glass + *facere* to make]

vitriol (vit-ree-ol) *noun*
1 *Chemistry* any of various compounds of
sulphuric acid.
2 biting criticism; malice.
Word Family **vitriolic** (vit-ree-**ol**-ik)
adjective.
[Latin *vitrum* glass]

vituperation (vi-tew-pa-**ray**-sh'n) *noun*
bitter abuse or censure.
Word Family **vituperative** (vi-**tew**-pa-ra-tiv) *adjective* abusive.
[from Latin]

viva *noun*
short form of **viva voce** (vie-va **vo**-chee)
an oral examination.
[Latin, with the living voice]

vivacious (viv-**ay**-shus) *adjective*
full of life and spirits.
Word Family **vivaciously** *adverb*;
vivaciousness, vivacity (viv-**ass**-i-tee)
noun.
[Latin *vivax* long-lived, brisk]

vivid *adjective*
1 intense: *the vivid blues of the lagoons.*
2 lively and strong: *You certainly have a vivid imagination.*
Word Family **vividly** *adverb*; **vividness**
noun.
[Latin *vividus* full of life]

viviparous (viv-**ip**-a-rus) *adjective*
of or relating to animals of which the
young are born live and fully formed.
[Latin *vivus* alive + *parus* bringing forth]

vivisection (viv-i-**sek**-sh'n) *noun*
the act of dissecting a living body, such as
a cat, dog, etc., for medical research.
Word Family **vivisectionist** *noun*;
vivisect (vi-vi-sekt) *verb*.
[Latin *vivus* alive + *sectus* cut]

vixen (**vik**-s'n) *noun*
1 a female fox.
2 a vicious or bad-tempered woman.

viz *adverb*
namely.
[old abbreviation of Latin *videlicet* from
Latin *videre* to see + *licet* it is permissible]

vizier (vi-**zeer** or **viz**-ee-a) *noun*
a high Muslim official.
[Arabic *wazir*]

vizor ⇨ **visor.**

vocabulary (vo-**kab**-yoo-la-ree) *noun*
(*plural* **vocabularies**)
1 the whole range of words known and
used by a person or group: *Your nine-year-
old has an excellent vocabulary.*
2 a list of common words in a foreign
language or book, with translations.
[Latin *vocabulum* a name]

vocal (**vo**-k'l) *adjective*
1 of or spoken by the voice.
2 expressing oneself loudly or frankly.
3 (of a piece of music) with an
accompanying song.

Word Family **vocals** *plural noun* the
words of a piece of music; **vocally** *adverb*;
vocalist *noun* a singer; **vocalize, vocalise**
verb to utter or make vocal.
[Latin *vocis* of a voice]

vocal cords *plural noun*
Anatomy the two folds of membrane in the
larynx which vibrate and produce sound
when air is passed over them.

vocation (vo-**kay**-sh'n) *noun*
a profession or occupation, especially one
to which a person is particularly drawn or
suited: *She has a vocation for nursing.*
Word Family **vocational** *adjective* of or
relating to a vocation.
[Latin *vocare* to call]

vocational guidance *noun*
professional help offered to students, etc.
to help them choose a career.

vociferous (vo-**siff**-er-us) *adjective*
vehement or making a loud outcry.
Word Family **vociferously** *adverb*;
vociferousness *noun*.
[Latin *vocis* of a voice + *ferre* to carry]

vodka *noun*
a strong liquor made from rye, corn or
potatoes, originally made in Russia.
[Russian *voda* water]

vogue *noun*
the current fashion, style, etc.

voice *noun*
1 the sounds made by a human being in
speaking or singing: *in a quiet voice.*
2 the power of speaking or singing: *She's
lost her voice.*
3 an opinion, or the right to hold an
opinion: *You have no voice in this matter.*
4 *Grammar* the change in the form of a
verb to show whether a person or thing
performs the action (**active voice**), or is
acted upon (**passive voice**): '*The shop sells
books*' is in the *active voice*;'*Books are sold by
the shop*' is in the *passive voice.*
Phrase **give voice to** to express or utter.
• **voice** *verb*
1 to express.
2 *Language* to utter with vibration of the
vocal cords: *In 'this' the 'th' is voiced and in
'thin' it is unvoiced.*
Word Family **voiceless** *adjective* 1 having
no voice. 2 *Language* (of sounds) made
without using the vocal cords, as in the
letters *s* or *f*.
[from Latin]

voice box ⇨ LARYNX.

voicemail *noun*
a system that electronically stores telephone messages so that they can be accessed later.

voice-over *noun*
the commentary of an unseen speaker recorded on a film's soundtrack.

void *noun*
empty space.
Figurative an aching void in one's heart (= feeling of emptiness or loneliness).
• **void** *adjective*
1 having no legal effect: *The court declared the contract void.*
2 containing no matter.
• **void** *verb* to make void.

voile *noun*
a soft semi-transparent fabric used for dresses, etc.
[French, a veil]

volatile (vol-a-tile) *adjective*
1 changing rapidly or readily from one mood, idea or state to another.
2 *Chemistry* having a low boiling point, and so easily changing from a liquid into a vapour.
Word Family **volatility** (vol-a-**till**-i-tee) *noun.*
[Latin *volatilis* flying, fleeing]

vol-au-vent (vol-oh-von) *noun*
puff pastry filled with chicken, fish, etc. and a sauce.
[French, a puff of wind]

volcano (vol-**kay**-no) *noun (plural* **volcanoes** *or* **volcanos**)
a cone-shaped hill or mountain formed from lava and ash, which has erupted from beneath the earth's crust.
Word Family **volcanic** (vol-**kan**-ik) *adjective.*
[after *Vulcan* the ancient Roman god of fire]

vole *noun*
any of various small rodents resembling rats and mice, but having a heavier body and a shorter tail.
[Scandinavian, a field]

volition (vo-**lish**-'n) *noun*
the act or power of using one's own will: *I did it of my own volition.*
[Latin *volo* I wish]

volley (vol-ee) *noun*
1 the simultaneous firing of a number of weapons.
Figurative a volley of oaths (= string).
2 *Sport* a hitting of the ball before it has touched the ground.

• **volley** *verb.*
[French *volée* flight]

volleyball *noun*
1 a game for two teams played on a court with a high net, the aim being to stop the ball touching the ground by hitting it over the net by hand.
2 the ball used in this game.

volt (*rhymes with* bolt) *noun*
the SI unit of electric potential difference.
abbrev. V.
[after *Alessandro Volta*, 1745-1827, an Italian physicist]

voltage (vole-tij *or* vol-tij) *noun*
Electricity the potential difference expressed in volts.

voltameter (vol-**tam**-it-a) *noun*
Electricity an instrument for measuring an electric current by means of the amount of metal deposited or gas liberated from an electrolyte in a given time by the passage of the current.

volte-face (volt-**fahss**) *noun*
a sudden reversal of position.
[Italian *voltare* to turn + *faccia* the face]

voltmeter *noun*
Electricity an instrument used to measure potential difference in volts.

voluble (vol-yoo-b'l) *adjective*
talking or able to talk easily or readily.
Word Family **volubly** *adverb*; **volubility** (vol-yoo-**bill**-i-tee) *noun.*
[Latin *volubilis* revolving]

volume (vol-yoom) *noun*
1 the amount of space a body takes up.
2 a quantity or amount, especially a large quantity: *The volume of business we do is steadily increasing.*
3 a book, especially one of a set of books.
4 (of sounds) the loudness.
Phrase **speak volumes** to express clearly without words: *His guilty expression spoke volumes.*

> The word **volume** is derived from Old French *volum*, from Latin *volumen*, itself derived from *volvere* (to roll). The connection with 'roll' is that books were originally written on rolls of parchment or papyrus. In time, *volume* came to be particularly associated with a *big* book, from which, later, the idea of size developed.

voluminous (vol-yoo-min-us) *adjective*
of great size, extent, etc.: *the queen's voluminous skirts.*

voluntary (vol-'n-tree) *adjective*
1 done or acting of one's own free choice, without being compelled or motivated by hopes of reward: *I made a voluntary statement to the police.*
2 supported by voluntary contributions: *The Red Cross is a voluntary organization.*
3 (of actions of the body) occurring through conscious control.
• **voluntary** *noun* (*plural* **voluntaries**) *Music* an organ solo played as the congregation enters or leaves the church. *Word Family* **voluntarily** (vol-'n-**tair**-i-lee) *adverb*.
[Latin *voluntas* a wish]

volunteer (vol-un-**teer**) *noun*
a person who offers to do something of his or her own free will, such as a soldier who is not conscripted or a worker who is not paid.
• **volunteer** *verb*
1 to offer voluntarily: *He volunteered his help on the day of the party.*
2 to come forward as a volunteer.

voluptuous (vol-**up**-tew-us) *adjective*
luxuriously sensuous or sensual. *Word Family* **voluptuously** *adverb*; **voluptuousness** *noun*.
[Latin *voluptas* pleasure]

vomit *verb*
to bring up the contents of the stomach through the mouth; to be sick. *Figurative The volcano vomited lava high into the air* (= ejected forcibly).
• **vomit** *noun* the matter ejected when vomiting.

voodoo *noun* also called **hoodoo**.
1 the practices of some people of the West Indies, especially Haiti, involving sorcery and witchcraft.
2 a charm or fetish used in such practices. *Word Family* **voodooism** *noun*,
[Creole]

voracious (vo-ray-shus) *adjective*
very greedy: *a voracious appetite.*
Figurative a voracious reader (= eager and untiring).
Word Family **voraciously** *adverb*; **voraciousness**, **voracity** (vo-**rass**-i-tee) *noun*.
[Latin *vorax* devouring]

vortex (**vor**-teks) *noun* (*plural* **vortexes** or **vortices** (**vor**-ti-seez))
a whirling mass of water, air, etc., such as a whirlpool or whirlwind.
[Latin]

votary (vo-ta-ree) *noun* (*plural* **votaries**)
1 a person who has chosen to be bound by a vow, such as a monk or nun.
2 any devoted follower.
[Latin *votus* vowed]

vote *noun*
1 an expression of preference for a candidate, proposal, etc.: *We had a vote on it.*
2 the total amount of these considered together: *She needs to capture the immigrant vote.*
3 (**the vote**) the right to express a choice in an election: *The suffragettes demanded the vote for women.*
• **vote** *verb*
1 to cast a vote: *I voted for Hislop.*
2 (*informal*) to express an opinion or a wish: *The children voted the trip a great success.* □ *I vote we ask him to wash up.*
Phrase **vote in, vote out** to appoint or dismiss by voting: *Londoners voted him in as mayor in 2000.*
Word Family **voter** *noun* a person who votes or has the right to vote.
[Latin *votum* a vow]

votive (vo-tiv) *adjective*
given or done in fulfilment of a vow.

vouch *verb*
Phrase **vouch for** to guarantee: *I can vouch for the truth of his story.*

voucher (vow-cha) *noun*
1 a document or form which may be used in place of cash to buy certain items.
2 a receipt.

vouchsafe *verb*
(*formal*) to grant graciously or condescendingly.

vow *noun*
a solemn promise or declaration: *marriage vows.*
• **vow** *verb* to make a vow.

vowel *noun*
1 *Language* a sound made without blockage of the breath.
2 *Language* the letters which express these sounds, being a, e, i, o and u. Compare CONSONANT.

voyage (**voy**-ij) *noun*
a journey, especially in a ship. *Word Family* **voyage** *verb* to go on a voyage; **voyager** *noun*.

voyeur (voy-er) *noun*
1 a person who gains sexual pleasure by looking at pictures, watching others undressing, etc.

2 a person who enjoys watching the distress in other people's lives.
Word Family **voyeuristic** (voy-er-**ist**-ik) *adjective*; **voyeurism** *noun*.
[French, looker]

vulcanize, vulcanise (vulk-a-nize) *verb*
Chemistry to heat rubber with sulphur to increase its elasticity and durability, e.g. for car tyres.
Word Family **vulcanization** (vulk-a-nigh-**zay**-sh'n) *noun*.
[after *Vulcan*, the ancient Roman god of fire]

vulgar *adjective*
1 showing a lack of good taste and manners, especially because of dealing with sex: *vulgar jokes*.
2 (*dated*) unrefined or of the common people.
Word Family **vulgarity** (vul-**garr**-i-tee) *noun* **1** the quality or character of being vulgar. **2** (*plural* **vulgarities**) a vulgar word or gesture, etc.; **vulgarly** *adverb*.
[Latin *vulgus* the masses, the people, the public]

vulgar fraction ⇨ COMMON FRACTION.

vulnerable (**vul**-ner-a-b'l) *adjective*
capable of being hurt, damaged or attacked: *She is very vulnerable to criticism.*
☐ *The troops were in a vulnerable position.*
Word Family **vulnerably** *adverb*; **vulnerability** (vul-ner-a-**bill**-i-tee) *noun* (*plural* **vulnerabilities**).
[Latin *vulneris* of a wound]

vulpine (**vulp**-ine) *adjective*
of or like foxes.
[Latin *vulpes* fox]

vulture (**vulch**-er) *noun*
1 a large scavenging bird of prey.
2 a greedy ruthless person who preys on the misfortunes of others.
[from Latin]

vulva *noun*
Anatomy the area immediately around the clitoris and the openings of the urethra and vagina in females.
[Latin]

vying the present participle of **vie**.

wacky adjective (**wackier; wackiest**)
also **whacky** (**whackier; whackiest**)
(*informal*) crazy: *a wacky idea.*

wad (wod) *noun*
1 any soft mass, e.g. of fabric.
2 any paper, banknotes, etc. folded or rolled together.
• **wad** *verb* (**wads; wadding; wadded**)
1 to make into a wad.
2 to line or stuff with something soft.

wadding *noun*
any soft substance used for padding.

waddle (*rhymes with* toddle) *verb*
to walk with short swaying steps.
• **waddle** *noun.*

wade *verb*
to walk through any substance, such as water, mud, etc., which makes progress difficult.
Figurative I waded through the boring book (= proceeded with difficulty).

wader *noun*
1 a long-legged bird which wades in water looking for food.
2 (**waders**) waterproof boots reaching to the top of the legs.

wadi (**wah**-di *or* **wod**-i) *noun* also **wady**
(*plural* **wadies**)
a desert watercourse which carries water only after heavy rain.
[Arabic]

wafer *noun*
1 a thin flat sheet or slice.
2 a sweet thin biscuit.
3 *Christianity* a thin disc of unleavened bread used in the Eucharist.

waffle¹ (wof-'l) *noun*
a flat cake made from batter cooked in a special mould.

waffle² *noun*
(*informal*) any vague or nonsensical speech or writing.
• **waffle** *verb.*

waft (woft *or* wahft) *verb*
to carry or float gently, especially through the air: *The voices wafted up from the street below.*
• **waft** *noun*
1 a wafting movement.
2 a sound or smell carried through the air.

wag¹ *verb* (**wags; wagging; wagged**)
to move from side to side or up and down, especially quickly.
• **wag** *noun* a wagging movement.

wag² *noun*
a person who makes jokes.
Word Family **waggish** *adjective* full of jokes or mischief.

wage *noun*
1 (*often* **wages**) a payment to an employee, usually on an hourly or weekly rate.
2 (**wages**) (*used with singular verb*) a result: *The wages of sin is death.*
• **wage** *verb* to engage in: *to wage war.*

wager (*rhymes with* major) *noun*
a bet.
• **wager** *verb*

waggle *verb*
(*informal*) to wag with quick short movements.

wagon *noun* also **waggon**
a vehicle with four wheels, e.g. one pulled by a horse, used for carrying loads.
Phrase **on the wagon** (*informal*)
abstaining from alcoholic drink.

wagtail *noun*
a small bird with a slender body and a long narrow tail which is habitually wagged up and down.

waif *noun*
a homeless neglected person, especially a child.

wail *verb*
to make a long high mournful cry.
• **wail** *noun.*

wain *noun*
an old word for a cart or wagon.

wainscot *noun*
a piece of wooden panelling at the foot of the walls of a room.

wainwright *noun*
a person who makes wagons.

waist *noun*
1 *Anatomy* the slender part of the human body between the ribs and hips.
2 the part of something, especially a dress, covering the waist.

waistcoat *noun*
a closely fitting sleeveless jacket reaching to the waist, sometimes worn under a jacket.

wait *verb*
1 to stay or rest in expectation: *Wait here till I return.* □ *You'll have to wait your turn.*
2 to remain neglected for a time: *Is this urgent or can it wait?*
Phrases **wait on, wait upon** to serve or attend personally, e.g. at table or in a shop.
wait up to stay awake at night in expectation.
• **wait** *noun* the act or time of waiting: *a long wait for the bus.*
Phrase **lie in wait** to wait in ambush.

waiter *noun*
a man who serves people in a restaurant.

waiting list *noun*
a list of people who are in a queue, e.g. for a surgical operation.

waiting room *noun*
a room where people wait, e.g. at a hospital or station.

waitress *noun* (*plural* **waitresses**)
a woman who serves people in a restaurant.

waive (wave) *verb*
to give up or not insist on: *The eldest son waived his right to inherit his father's title.*
Word Family **waiver** *noun* the intentional relinquishing of a right.

> ❗ Note the spelling of *waive*, meaning 'not to insist on': it has an *i* in the middle, unlike the more common word *wave*, meaning 'a surging movement', 'to move to and fro', etc.

wake¹ *verb* (**wakes; waking; woke; woken**)
to rouse from sleep: *I woke late.* □ *Don't wake the baby.*
Phrases **wake up** to wake. **wake up to** to become aware of: *We finally woke up to the fact that he was leaving.*
• **wake** *noun*
1 a watch, especially one at night before or after a funeral.
2 (**wakes**) in some parts of Northern England, workers' holidays.

wake² *noun*
the pattern of disturbed water left behind a moving ship.
Phrase **in the wake of** following or as a result of.

wakeful *adjective*
1 unable to sleep.

2 vigilant: *He deluded himself that he was surrounded by ever-wakeful enemies.*
Word Family **wakefully** *adverb*; **wakefulness** *noun*.

waken *verb*
to rouse from sleep.
Figurative How can I waken your interest? (= excite).

wale *noun*
a ridge or raised line in a fabric, especially in knitting.

walk (wawk) *verb*
1 to go or proceed on foot at a moderate pace.
2 (of a horse) to go at the slowest gait, with two feet always on the ground at any time.
Phrases **walk off with 1** to steal. **2** to win easily. **walk out** to go on strike. **walk out on** to abandon or desert.
• **walk** *noun*
1 the act of walking.
2 a place, distance or time of walking.
3 a manner of walking: *What an odd walk he has.*
4 the slowest gait of a horse.
Phrase **walk of life** *She met people from all walks of life* (= occupations, activities).

walkabout *noun*
1 *Aboriginal* a period of wandering.
2 an informal stroll by someone important through the crowd.

walkie-talkie *noun*
a light radio device which combines a transmitter and receiver and which can be carried and operated while moving.

walking stick *noun*
a narrow stick, carried or used as a support when walking.

Walkman *noun* (*plural* **Walkmans** or **Walkmen**)
(*trademark*) a type of small portable stereo unit consisting of cassette player, radio and earphones.

walk-on *adjective*
coming on stage briefly but not speaking: *a walk-on part.*

walkout *noun*
a walking out or leaving as an act of protest, e.g. in a strike.

walkover *noun*
an unopposed or easy victory.

wall *noun*
1 a solid upright structure used for supporting, surrounding or dividing: *The brick walls of a house.* □ *a defensive wall surrounding the city.*

2 something resembling a wall in shape or solidity: *a wall of fire*. □ *a wall of prejudice*.
3 *Biology* the outside layer surrounding an organ or cell.
• **wall** *verb* to enclose, shut off or divide with or as with a wall.
[Latin *vallum* a rampart]

wallaby (woll-a-bee) *noun* (*plural* **wallabies**)
an Australian marsupial, similar to a kangaroo but smaller and furrier.
[Aboriginal]

wallet (woll-it) *noun*
a small folding holder for paper money, stamps, etc. carried in the pocket.

wallflower *noun*
1 a plant with sweet-scented flowers.
2 (*informal*) someone left without a partner at a dance.

wallop (woll-up) *verb*
1 (*informal*) to strike heavily.
2 (*informal*) to defeat soundly.
Word Family **wallop** *noun* a forceful blow or impact; **walloping** *noun* a thrashing.

wallow (woll-oh) *verb*
to roll about: *The children wallowed happily in the snow.*
Figurative *The rich man wallowed in luxury* (= indulged fully).

wallpaper *noun*
paper, usually with a decorative pattern, for covering interior walls.
• **wallpaper** *verb*.

wall-to-wall *adjective*
covering the whole floor: *a wall-to-wall carpet.*

walnut (wawl-nut) *noun*
1 the edible wrinkled kernel of a large and handsome deciduous tree.
2 the wood of this tree, used to make furniture.

walrus (wawl-russ) *noun* (*plural* **walruses**)
an arctic marine mammal related to the seal, having two long tusks.

waltz (wawlss *or* wolss) *noun* (*plural* **waltzes**)
1 a ballroom dance in which partners revolve in a one-two-three rhythm.
2 the music for such a dance in triple time.
• **waltz** *verb*
1 to dance a waltz.
2 to move lightly and quickly.
Figurative *He waltzed off with first prize* (= took easily).
[German *walzen* to revolve]

wan (*rhymes with* on) *adjective*
pale or sickly.
Word Family **wanly** *adverb*.

wand (wond) *noun*
1 a stick, such as one used by a conjuror performing magic tricks.
2 a rod or staff used as a symbol of authority on ceremonial occasions.

wander (wond-a) *verb*
1 to move or roam aimlessly or casually.
2 to leave the right path or direction.
Word Family **wander** *noun* a casual walk or stroll; **wanderer** *noun*.

wanderlust *noun*
a strong urge to travel or roam about.
[German]

wane *verb*
1 *Astronomy* to decrease in size, as the moon's face does in changing from full to new moon. Compare WAX².
2 to decrease in power or intensity: *Her popularity had waned.*
• **wane** *noun*
Phrase **on the wane** decreasing.

wangle *verb*
(*informal*) to accomplish, especially by scheming or indirect methods: *He was trying to wangle an invitation to the party.*

want (wont) *verb*
1 to desire: *I want a new bike.* □ *Do you want another drink?*
2 to require to see or speak to: *Mum wants you.*
3 to be sought by the police: *He is a wanted man.*
4 (*informal*) to need: *Your hair wants cutting.*
Phrase **want for** *She never wants for money* (= is short of).
• **want** *noun*
1 the state of wanting: *The garden is in want of water.*
2 something wanted: *Money is not his most important want.*
3 lack: *I took this job for want of anything better.*

wanting *adjective*
1 lacking or deficient.
2 (*informal*) simple-minded: *I think he's a bit wanting.*

wanton (won-t'n) *adjective*
1 pointless or unprovoked: *wanton cruelty.*
2 unrestrained or wild: *wanton profusion.*
Word Family **wantonly** *adverb*; **wantonness** *noun*.

war (wor) *noun*
1 the use of armed forces in conflict, especially between countries.
2 any conflict: *a propaganda war*.
● **war** *verb* (**wars; warring; warred**) to engage in a war.

warble (worb-'l) *verb*
to sing with trills or vibrations.

warbler *noun*
a person or thing that warbles, especially any of various types of bird.

ward (*rhymes with* ford) *noun*
1 a district, especially an electoral district, of a town or city.
2 *Law* any person under the care of a guardian.
3 any of the separate divisions of a large building, e.g. in a hospital.
● **ward** *verb*
Phrase **ward off** to avert or repel.
Word Family **wardship** *noun* care or custody.

warden (wor-d'n) *noun*
a person having control or superintendence over: *a hostel warden*.

warder (wor-da) *noun*
a guard or officer in a prison.

wardrobe (wor-drobe) *noun*
1 a large cupboard for storing and hanging clothes, etc.
2 any collection of clothes.

wardroom *noun*
Nautical the room where officers eat.

ware¹ (*rhymes with* care) *noun*
1 manufactured goods of a specified type: *silverware.* □ *hardware*.
2 (**wares**) any articles for sale.

ware² *verb* also **'ware**
beware.

warehouse *noun*
a large building where goods are stored, such as one in which a wholesaler keeps stock.

warehouse party *noun* (*plural* **warehouse parties**)
a large party involving music and dancing, held in a warehouse or other large building. The details are often kept secret until the last moment to avoid police intervention, because they are held without permission.

warfare (wor-fair) *noun*
war.

war game *noun*
1 a training exercise for soldiers, etc.

2 a game based on a situation involving conflict, used as a test of initiative, personality, etc.

warhead *noun*
the front part of a self-propelled missile, containing the explosive charge.

warily ⇨ WARY.

wariness ⇨ WARY.

warlike *adjective*
1 hostile.
2 ready for war.

warlock (wor-lock) *noun*
a man who is a witch.

warlord *noun*
the military leader of a region.

warm (*rhymes with* form) *adjective*
1 moderately hot.
2 involving lively or enthusiastic feeling: *a warm welcome*.
3 containing orange or red tones: *warm colours*.
4 made of thick material: *a warm jumper*.
● **warm** *verb* to make or become warm or warmer.
Phrase **warm up** to practise or do exercises before a game, performance, etc.
Word Family **warmly** *adverb*; **warmth** *noun* 1 moderate heat. 2 affection or enthusiasm.

warm-blooded *adjective*
Biology having a constant body temperature: *Birds and mammals are warm-blooded*. Compare COLD-BLOODED (definition 2).

warm front ⇨ FRONT *noun*.

warm-hearted *adjective*
cordial or sympathetic.
Word Family **warm-heartedly** *adverb*.

warming pan *noun*
a pan with a long handle, filled with hot coals, etc., formerly used to warm a bed.

warmonger (wor-mung-ga) *noun*
a person eager for or provoking war.

warn (*rhymes with* corn) *verb*
to inform in advance, especially of possible unpleasant consequences: *I warn you not to be late or I'll be angry*.
Word Family **warning** *noun*; **warningly** *adverb*.

war of attrition *noun* (*plural* **wars of attrition**)
a war in which the victorious side is the side that can hold out the longest.

warp (wawp) *verb*
to twist or bend out of shape.

Figurative Don't listen to his warped ideas (= distorted, biased).

• **warp** *noun*
1 a bend, twist or distortion.
2 the yarn placed lengthwise in a loom to form the basis of a fabric. Compare WEFT.

warpath *noun*
Phrase **on the warpath** very angry.

warrant (*rhymes with* torrent) *noun*
1 *Law* a document giving authority: *a warrant of arrest.* □ *a death warrant.*
2 a justification or authorization: *You've got no warrant for such an accusation.*

• **warrant** *verb*
1 to authorize.
2 to justify.
3 to guarantee.

warrant officer *noun*
a rank of officer in the armed forces, below a commissioned officer and above an NCO.
[appointed by Secretary of State's *warrant*]

warranty (**worr**-'n-tee) *noun* (*plural* **warranties**)
a guarantee, e.g. one given by a manufacturer when a product is bought.

warren (**worr**-'n) *noun* also called **rabbit warren**.
an area where rabbits breed and abound.

warrior (**worr**-ee-a) *noun*
a soldier or fighter.

warship *noun*
a ship equipped to take part in battles.

wart (wawt) *noun*
a small hard swelling on the skin, caused by a viral infection.
Phrase **warts and all** not omitting defects and blemishes.

warthog (**wawt**-hog) *noun*
a large African wild pig with two large tusks and warty growths on the face.

wartime *noun*
a time when a war is being fought. *She grew up in wartime.*

wary (**ware**-ee) *adjective* (**warier, wariest**)
careful or guarded.
Word Family **warily** *adverb;* **wariness** *noun.*

was (woz) the first and third person singular past tense of **be**.

wash (*rhymes with* posh) *verb*
1 to clean with water or other liquid.
2 to cover or wet with a liquid, e.g. in order to separate gold from gravel.
3 to flow: *The waves washed against the cliff.*
4 to carry with a flow: *The river washed away the hillside.*
5 (*informal*) to convince: *Your excuse won't wash, I'm afraid.*
Phrases **wash down** 1 to wash thoroughly. 2 to swallow food with the aid of liquid. **wash up** to wash dishes, cutlery, etc. after a meal.

• **wash** *noun* (*plural* **washes**)
1 an act or instance of washing: *Give your hair a good wash.*
2 any clothes, etc. washed or to be washed.
3 any liquid with which something is washed: *whitewash.*
4 the pattern of disturbed water made by a moving boat.
5 *Geography* a formation of alluvial deposits.
6 *Art* a very thin watery pigment spread over a surface.
Phrase **come out in the wash** to come out all right in the end.
Word Family **washable** *adjective.*

washboard *noun*
1 a board or frame with a ridged surface on which clothes may be rubbed while washing them.
2 such a device scratched or scraped as a musical accompaniment in jazz, etc.

washed out *adjective*
1 pale or faded.
2 exhausted.
3 abandoned owing to rain: *The sports meeting was washed out.*

washed-up *adjective*
(*informal*) ruined or finished.

washer *noun*
1 a person or thing that washes.
2 a flat circular piece of metal, rubber or leather with a hole in the centre, used with a nut and bolt to give tension or to seal a joint.

washing *noun*
1 the act of washing.
2 clothes, etc. washed or to be washed.

washing machine *noun*
a machine in which clothes, sheets, etc. can be washed.

washing-up *noun*
dishes, cutlery, etc. to be washed after a meal.

washout *noun*
(*informal*) a failure or fiasco.

washroom *noun*
American a room with toilets, basins, etc., especially one in a large building.

washstand *noun*
a support for a bowl and jug formerly used for washing the hands and face.

wasn't *contraction*
a short form of **was not**: *She wasn't anywhere to be seen.*

wasp (wosp) *noun*
a stinging insect which lives in a colony, often having a striped black and yellow body and a narrow waist.

waspish (woss-pish) *adjective*
irritable or given to spiteful stinging remarks.
Word Family **waspishly** *adverb*.

wassail (woss-ail *or* woss-al *or* wass-ail) *noun*
1 an old word for a drink such as mulled wine, served on festive occasions.
2 an old word for a drinking celebration.
• **wassail** *verb*
1 to drink and make merry.
2 to sing Christmas carols from house to house.
[from Old Norse *ves heil* be healthy]

wast (wost) an old form of the second person singular past tense of **be**.

waste *verb*
1 to use unnecessarily or without purpose: *She wastes money.*
2 to fail to use: *He wasted the perfect opportunity.*
3 to become or make thin and weak: *a wasting disease.* □ *She was wasting away.*
• **waste** *noun*
1 the act of wasting: *a waste of time.*
2 something which is not or cannot be used, e.g. refuse, desert, unproductive land, etc.
Phrase **lay waste** to destroy or devastate.
• **waste** *adjective*
1 desolate: *the waste spaces of the world.*
2 no longer wanted or useful: *waste paper.*
Word Family **wastage** *noun* loss due to waste, etc.; **wasteful** *adjective*; **wastefully** *adverb*; **wastefulness** *noun*.
[Latin *vastus* empty]

wasteland *noun*
an area of land which is not used for building, planting, etc.

watch (wotch) *verb*
1 to look at or look out attentively.
2 to mind or guard: *Can you watch my bag for me?*
3 to be careful about: *Watch the step!*
Phrase **watch over** to guard or protect.
• **watch** *noun* (*plural* **watches**)

1 the act of watching: *Keep a watch on the time.*
2 a period of time for watching or keeping guard, especially on a ship.
3 a small clock designed to be worn or carried.
Word Family **watchful** *adjective* alert; **watchfully** *adverb*; **watchfulness** *noun*.

watchdog *noun*
1 a dog kept to guard property.
2 someone responsible for making sure that people buying or using a service are treated fairly.

watchmaker *noun*
a person who makes and repairs watches.

watchman *noun* (*plural* **watchmen**)
a person who keeps watch, e.g. at night in an empty factory.

watchword *noun*
a short phrase summarizing a guiding principle: *The company's watchword is 'Safety first'.*
[originally a password]

water (waw-ta) *noun*
1 *Chemistry* hydrogen oxide (formula H_2O), a liquid without any taste, odour or colour.
2 (*sometimes* **waters**) the water or liquid of a river, sea, mineral spring, tide etc.
3 any liquid secretion, especially urine.
4 a solution of a substance in water: *rosewater.*
5 the degree of transparency or brilliance of a diamond or other gem.
Phrases **hold water** to prove sound or valid. **in deep water** in trouble. **in hot water** in trouble. **like water** very freely: *He spends money like water.* **throw cold water on** to discourage. **tread water** to float in a vertical position by moving one's arms and legs in the water. **water under the bridge** in the past and unable to be remedied: *All that is water under the bridge.*
• **water** *verb*
1 to wet with water.
2 to supply with water.
3 to dilute with water.
4 (of the eyes or mouth) to secrete or fill with water: *The smoke made his eyes water.*
Phrase **watered down** less vivid or weakened.

waterbed *noun*
a bed consisting of a plastic or rubber mattress filled with water and set into a frame.

water boatman *noun* (*plural* **water boatmen**)
a long-legged insect which skims over the surface of fresh water.

water buffalo *noun* (*plural* **water buffalo** or **water buffaloes**)
a large buffalo of tropical Asia, often domesticated as a work animal.

water cannon *noun* (*plural* **water cannon** or **water cannons**)
a device for projecting powerful jets of water, used in quelling riots, etc.

water chestnut *noun*
the edible nut-like fruit of an aquatic plant, used in Chinese cooking.

water closet *noun*
(*dated*) a toilet.

watercolour *noun* (*American* **watercolor**)
1 a pigment mixed with water.
2 a painting done with such pigment.
3 the art or method of using such pigments.

watercourse *noun*
1 a stream or river.
2 the bed of a stream or river.

watercress *noun*
a herb with pungent leaves which are used in salads and soups.

water cycle *noun*
the constant movement of water between the land, the sea, and the atmosphere.

water diviner *noun*
a person who tries to find water or minerals under the earth, often using a Y-shaped stick called a divining rod.

waterfall *noun*
a steep fall or flow of water from a height.

waterfront *noun*
the part of a town or city that lies next to a body of water.

water gas *noun* (*plural* **water gases**)
Chemistry a gas made by passing steam over red-hot coke, used as a fuel.

water hammer *noun*
a pressure wave created by suddenly turning off a tap in a domestic water system, and causing a pipe to vibrate with a thump against a wall, floorboard, etc.

waterhen *noun*
a moorhen or a similar bird.

waterhole *noun*
a well, spring or hollow where water collects naturally, especially such a place where animals come to drink.

wateriness ⇨ WATERY.

watering can *noun*
a plastic or metal container with a long spout, used for watering plants.

water lily *noun* (*plural* **water lilies**)
a plant which grows from rhizomes in the mud at the bottom of ponds, etc., having large flat leaves and big flowers which float on the surface of the water.

waterline *noun*
the level reached by the water on the side of a boat.

waterlogged *adjective*
excessively filled or saturated with water.

watermark *noun*
a mark or design in paper, visible when held to the light, indicating its quality, authenticity, etc.

watermelon *noun*
a very large green fruit with a hard skin and juicy red flesh with many pips.

water pipe ⇨ HOOKAH.

water pistol *noun*
a toy gun which sprays water.

water polo *noun*
a game played in a swimming pool in which each team tries to throw the ball into the opponent's goal.

waterproof *adjective*
permitting no water to enter or pass through.
• **waterproof** *verb*.

watershed *noun*
1 *Geography* a boundary or divide between areas drained by different river systems.
Figurative The event is a historical *watershed* (= dividing point).
2 a time after which adult television programmes can be broadcast.
[a translation of German *Wasserscheide* water boundary]

waterski *verb* (**waterskis; waterskiing** or **waterski-ing; waterskied**)
to skim over water on skis while being towed by a motor boat.
Word Family **waterski** *noun*; **waterskier** *noun*.

water softener *noun*
a substance added to hard water to counteract the effect of its mineral content, or a device used for this.

waterspout *noun*
Weather a whirling funnel-shaped mass of cloud and water, formed at sea.

water table *noun*
the level of water in the ground. Below it soil and rocks are saturated with water.

watertight *adjective*
made so that water cannot enter or leak through.
Figurative She had a watertight excuse (= foolproof).

water tower *noun*
a large tank raised above the ground to regulate the flow and give pressure to a town's water system.

waterway *noun*
a navigable canal or river.

waterwheel *noun*
a wheel which is turned by the force of water striking the blades or buckets attached to it.

water wings *plural noun*
floats worn on the arms by people learning to swim.

waterworks *plural noun*
1 the system of buildings and structures by which water is provided for a town, etc.
2 (*informal*) the urinary system.
3 (*informal*) tears.

watery *adjective*
1 of or like water.
2 containing much or too much water.
3 pale or weak.
Word Family **wateriness** *noun*.

watt (wot) *noun*
the SI unit of power. *abbrev.* W.
Word Family **wattage** *noun* the amount of electrical power expressed in watts.
[after *James Watt*, 1736-1819, a Scottish inventor]

wattle¹ (*rhymes with* bottle) *noun*
1 the branches of trees intertwined with twigs to make fencing.
2 any of the Australian acacias.

wattle² *noun*
a fold of skin, often brightly coloured, hanging from the throat of a turkey or other bird.

waul (wawl) *verb*
to give a long piercing cry.

wave *noun*
1 a ridge or swell moving on the surface of a body of water, e.g. on the sea.
2 a surging or swelling movement: *A wave of relief passed over him.*
Figurative A fresh wave of infantry came into the attack (= surging mass).
3 a change in temperature passing over a large area: *a heatwave.*

4 an up-and-down or to-and-fro movement: *a wave of the hand.*
5 a rising curve or series of curves.
6 *Physics* a regular progressive vibration by which energy is transmitted through a medium without any net movement of the medium itself.
• **wave** *verb*
1 to move in a wave or waves.
2 to indicate by waving the hand: *She waved me to a seat.*
3 (of hair) to curl slightly.

> [!] Do not confuse *wave* with WAIVE.

waveband *noun*
the range of frequencies allocated for particular purposes or to broadcasting or other telecommunication stations.

wavelength *noun*
Physics the distance in a wave between two points of equal phase. In waves at sea, the wavelength is the distance between two successive crests. In electromagnetic radiation the wavelength is in inverse proportion to the frequency.

waver *verb*
1 to sway to and fro.
2 to be undecided or uncertain.
Word Family **waveringly** *adverb*.

wavy *adjective* (**wavier; waviest**)
having waves: *wavy hair.* □ *a wavy line.*
Word Family **wavily** *adverb*; **waviness** *noun*.

wax¹ *noun* (*plural* **waxes**)
any of a variety of solid non-greasy organic substances with a low melting point.
Word Family **wax** *verb* 1 to cover or polish with wax. 2 to remove hair by applying wax and then pulling it off: *to wax one's legs.*

wax² *verb*
Astronomy to increase in size, as the moon's face does in changing from new moon to full moon. Compare WANE (definition 1).

waxed paper *noun*
paper made waterproof by a coating of wax.

waxen *adjective*
smooth and pale.

waxwork *noun*
1 a model of the human figure in wax.
2 (**waxworks**) an exhibition of such models.

waxy *adjective* (**waxier; waxiest**)
resembling wax in colour or consistency.
Word Family **waxiness** *noun*.

way noun

1 a course of action or proceeding: *Don't do it that way.*

2 a route: *I can't find the way out.*

3 a direction: *Which way is north?*

4 a distance: *It was a long way.*

5 (*informal*) a particular area: *He lives round our way.*

6 room, space: *Make way!*

7 a habit, custom: *her strange ways.* □ *It's just his way.*

8 a respect: *a good candidate in many ways.*

9 a state of health, condition: *He's in a bad way.*

10 a solution: *There must be a way.*

Phrases **by way of** as: *We had pizza by way of a treat.* **go out of one's way** to make a special effort: *He went out of his way to make us welcome.* **have a way with** to be skilful in dealing with. **in a way** to a certain extent. **look the other way** to connive at or pretend not to have seen something. **no way!** (*informal*) it is absolutely impossible.

wayfarer noun

a poetic word for a traveller, especially one on foot.

Word Family **wayfaring** noun.

waylay verb (**waylays; waylaying; waylaid**)

to lie in ambush for and attack suddenly.

way-out adjective

(*informal*) very unusual, eccentric or excellent.

wayward (way-w'd) adjective

wanting one's own way: *a wayward child.*

Word Family **waywardness** noun.

we pronoun (*singular* **I**)

1 the first person plural nominative pronoun, used to represent the speaker and one or more others: *We bought the books.* ⇨ OUR; OURS; US.

2 used by a monarch or by an editor when referring to himself or herself in formal speech or writing: *We are not amused.*

weak adjective

1 not strong: *I was feeling weak after my illness.* □ *a weak link in the chain.* □ *a weak king.* □ *weak tea.*

2 *Grammar* ⇨ REGULAR adjective (definition 4).

Word Family **weaken** verb to make or become weak or weaker; **weakly** adverb.

weak-kneed (week-**need**) adjective

1 weak, e.g. from fear.

2 easily frightened.

weakling noun

a feeble person or animal.

weakness noun (*plural* **weaknesses**)

1 the state or quality of being weak.

2 a slight fault, weak point.

3 a liking: *a weakness for cute kittens.*

weal¹ noun also **wheal**

a raised mark on the skin caused by a blow.

weal² noun

(*formal*) well-being.

wealth (welth) noun

any goods, assets, currency or property which have value.

Figurative The painter uses a wealth of bright colours (= abundance).

wealthy adjective (**wealthier; wealthiest**)

having a great deal of money, assets, etc.

Word Family **wealthily** adverb.

wean verb

1 to introduce a child or other mammal to food other than its mother's milk.

2 to gradually turn away from: *to wean someone off cigarettes.*

weapon (wep-'n) noun

any instrument used for fighting.

Word Family **weaponry** noun any or all weapons.

wear (wair) verb (**wears; wearing; wore; worn**)

1 to have or carry on the body, face, etc.: *She wears glasses.* □ *He wore a frown.*

2 to impair or be impaired by use, exposure to the elements, etc.: *Some rocks wear more quickly than others.*

3 to make or become by constant use, exposure, etc.: *He wore a hole in his sock.* □ *My patience is wearing thin.*

Phrases **wear off** (of a drug, etc.) to lose its effect. **wear on** (of time) to pass gradually or tediously. **wear out 1** to make or become unusable through constant use. 2 to exhaust.

● **wear** noun

1 the act of wearing.

2 damage or loss of quality from use: *There's quite a bit of wear on that front tyre.*

3 things to wear: *beach wear.*

Phrases **fair wear and tear** no more than the normal damage from usage. **the worse for wear 1** damaged by use: *My shoes are a bit the worse for wear.* 2 not looking one's (or its) best.

Word Family **wearer** noun; **wearable** adjective; **wearing** adjective tiring.

weary (weer-ee) *adjective* (**wearier; weariest**)
very tired.
Word Family weary *verb* (**wearies; wearying; wearied**); **wearily** *adverb*; **weariness** *noun*; **wearisome** *adjective* causing fatigue.

weasel (weez-'l) *noun*
1 a small flesh-eating mammal with reddish-brown fur.
2 (*informal*) a cunning sneaky person.

weather (*rhymes with* feather) *noun*
the state of the atmosphere at a given place and time, described by temperature, rainfall, wind, etc., or the day-to-day changes in this.
Phrases **make heavy weather of** to make difficulties for oneself in doing something. **under the weather** not feeling very well.
• **weather** *verb*
1 to go or come through safely: *The ship weathered the storm.* □ *The company weathered the crisis.*
2 to expose to the weather.
3 to show the effects of exposure to the weather.
4 *Geology* (of rocks) to be broken down through the effects of rain, frost, heat and wind: *Granite weathers slowly.*

weather-beaten *adjective*
1 seasoned or hardened by exposure to the weather.
2 damaged or showing the ill effects of exposure to the weather.

weatherboard *noun*
a thin plank of wood used in overlapping rows to cover the outside walls of a house.

weather forecast *noun*
an announcement predicting the weather.

weathervane *noun*
a device consisting of a pole with a piece of metal, often in the shape of a rooster, which spins in the wind and indicates its direction.

weave[1] (weev) *verb* (**weaves; weaving; wove; woven** or **wove**)
1 to intertwine threads, etc. to make a fabric: *to weave a rug.*
2 to put together different elements to make a story.
Word Family weave *noun* the style of weaving; **weaver** *noun*.

weave[2] *verb* (**weaves; weaving; weaved**)
to move in a twisting and turning path: *The car was weaving across the motorway.*

web *noun*
1 anything made of interlaced threads: *a spider's web.*
2 any complex network: *a web of roads across the country.*
3 *Biology* a piece of skin joining two digits on the foot of some animals and birds which swim, such as ducks.
4 (**Web**) the World Wide Web.
Word Family webbed *adjective*.

webbing *noun*
a strong woven fabric made from hemp, cotton, etc. and used in upholstery.

web browser *noun*
a program that allows the user to download and display documents on the Internet.

weber (vay-ba) *noun*
the derived SI unit of magnetic flux.

web site *noun*
a collection of related documents or pages on the Internet: *The school is setting up its own web site.*

we'd *contraction*
a short form of **we had, we would** or **we should**: *We'd had an early lunch.* □ *We'd rather stay at home.*

wedding *noun*
a marriage ceremony.
Word Family wed *verb* (**weds; wedding; wedded** or **wed**).
[Old English *weddian* to pledge]

wedge *noun*
1 any solid triangular or tapered implement or piece used to split a piece of wood or to fix something firmly.
2 something which has the shape or function of a wedge: *a wedge of pie.*
3 *Golf* a club with a wedge-shaped base, used to lift the ball out of sand, etc.
• **wedge** *verb*
1 to fix in place with a wedge.
2 to split with a wedge.
3 to crowd or force into a narrow space: *We were tightly wedged into the lift.*

wedlock *noun*
the state of marriage.

Wednesday (wenz-day) *noun*
the fourth day of the week, after Tuesday and before Thursday.
[named after the ancient German god *Woden*]

wee *adjective* (**weer; weest**)
(*especially Scottish*) tiny.

weed *noun*
1 a wild plant growing where it is not wanted.
2 (*informal*) a thin unhealthy-looking person.
• **weed** *verb* to remove weeds.
Phrase **weed out** to remove, especially something which is undesirable or unwanted.

weedy *adjective* (**weedier; weediest**)
1 full of weeds.
2 (*informal*) thin and weak.
Word Family **weediness** *noun*.

week *noun*
1 a period of seven days.
2 the period of time devoted to work during a week: *She works a 35-hour week.*

weekday *noun*
any day of the week except Saturday or Sunday.

weekend *noun*
Saturday and Sunday.

weekly *adjective*
of, done or occurring once a week or every week.
• **weekly** *noun* (*plural* **weeklies**) a newspaper or periodical published once a week.
• **weekly** *adverb* once a week.

weeny *adjective* (**weenier; weeniest**) (*informal*) very small.

weep *verb* (**weeps; weeping; wept**)
1 to shed tears.
2 to drip liquid: *a weeping wound.*

weepie *noun* also **weepy** (*plural* **weepies**) (*informal*) a film or book that makes one cry.

weeping willow *noun*
a willow with trailing branches reaching to the ground.

weepy *adjective* (**weepier; weepiest**) (*informal*) inclined to weep.
• **weepy** *noun* ⇨ WEEPIE.

weevil *noun*
any of a group of beetles with elongated heads which eat grain, nuts, etc.
Word Family **weevily** *adjective* infested with weevils.

weft *noun*
the yarn that is interlaced horizontally between the warp on a loom. Compare WARP *noun* (definition 2).

weigh (way) *verb*
1 to find the weight of.
2 to have weight: *I weigh more than my sister.*

3 to consider: *weighing a decision carefully.*
4 to burden: *weighed down by guilt.*
5 to count: *The testimony weighed heavily against him.*
Phrases **weigh in** (of a boxer or jockey) to be weighed before or after a competition. **weigh up** to consider: *weighing up her options.*
Word Family **weigh-in** *noun*.

weighbridge *noun*
a platform onto which a motor vehicle may be driven to measure its weight when loaded up.

weight (wate) *noun*
1 the amount or degree of heaviness of something.
2 *Physics* the force of gravitational attraction between two bodies, especially that between any massive body and the earth. ⇨ CENTRE OF GRAVITY; GRAVITY; MASS *noun* (definition 6).
3 a solid object used as a standard in weighing.
4 an object used to hold something in place or down: *a paperweight.*
5 an object used in weightlifting, such as a dumbbell.
6 importance: *a matter of some weight.*
Phrases **carry weight** to have influence or importance. **pull one's weight** to do one's full share. **throw one's weight around** to exercise one's authority more than is necessary.
• **weight** *verb*
1 to add weight to.
2 to attach importance to.
Word Family **weightless** *adjective* experiencing little or no gravitational pull; **weightlessness** *noun*.

weighting *noun*
1 an adjustment made to compensate for something.
2 an extra allowance to reflect the higher cost of living in certain areas.

weightlifting *noun*
the sport of lifting barbells, etc.
Word Family **weightlifter** *noun*.

weighty *adjective* (**weightier; weightiest**)
1 heavy.
2 serious or important.
Word Family **weightily** *adverb*; **weightiness** *noun*.

weir (weer) *noun*
a dam across a watercourse, over which the water may flow.

weird (weerd) *adjective*
1 supernatural: *A weird light surrounded the headless horseman.*
2 (*informal*) odd or strange: *a weird hairstyle.*
Word Family **weirdly** *adverb*; **weirdness** *noun.*

welch ⇨ WELSH.

welcome (**well**-kum) *adjective*
1 gladly received or admitted: *a welcome guest.* □ *a welcome letter.*
2 free to use, take, etc.: *You're welcome to come too.*
Phrase **you're welcome** a conventional response to 'thank you'.
Word Family **welcome** *noun*; **welcome** *verb* to give a welcome to; **welcome** *interjection.*

weld *verb*
1 to join metals, plastics, etc. by applying heat and melting them together.
2 to unite closely or intimately.
Word Family **weld** *noun*; **welder** *noun.*

welfare (**well**-fair) *noun*
1 a state of well-being, either physical or mental.
2 aid given to those in need.

welfare state *noun*
a state in which the government assumes primary responsibility for the social welfare of its members, e.g. through unemployment benefits, health insurance, etc.

welkin *noun*
a poetic word for the sky or heaven.
[Old English *wolcen* a cloud]

well¹ *adverb* (**better**; **best**)
1 satisfactorily, commendably or favourably: *Did you do well in the test?*
2 in comfort: *They live well.*
3 thoroughly: *Clean your teeth well.*
4 to a great extent: *We are well behind America in space research.*
5 (*informal*) very: *He thinks he's well hard.*
6 probably: *That may well be true.*
Phrases **as well 1** *He's trimmed his beard, and cut his hair as well* (= in addition, besides). **2** *He might as well have given it away* (= with equal effect). **just as well**
1 preferable. 2 *It was just as well you came in time* (= lucky). **very well 1** *I can't very well refuse him a favour* (= with reason or propriety). **2** *You know very well you can't do that* (= undeniably). **3** *Very well, leave me alone to shiver in the cold* (= all right, certainly).
● **well** *adjective*

1 in good health: *I feel well.*
2 in a satisfactory state.
3 advisable or prudent: *It would be well not to swim immediately after eating.*
● **well** *interjection*
1 an exclamation expressing surprise, indignation, etc.
2 an exclamation used to cover a pause, begin a speech, etc.

> **!** On the use of *well* as an adverb ⇨ GOOD.

well² *noun*
1 a hole drilled in the earth, to obtain water, oil or gas.
2 something which has the shape or function of a well: *an inkwell.*
● **well** *verb* to rise or flow up like water in a spring: *Her eyes welled with tears.*

we'll *contraction*
a short form of **we will** or **we shall**: *We'll be back soon.*

well advised *adjective*
sensible.

well appointed *adjective*
properly equipped, furnished, etc.

well-being *noun*
the state of being healthy, happy or prosperous.

well earned *adjective*
thoroughly deserved.

well-heeled *adjective*
(*informal*) wealthy.

wellington *noun* also called **wellington boot.**
a waterproof plastic or rubber boot reaching to the knee.

> **Wellingtons** are named after the first Duke of Wellington, who won fame for his military campaigns during the Napoleonic Wars, particularly for his generalship at the Battle of Waterloo, where Napoleon was defeated. Other articles of clothing were named after him, but only *wellington boots* have survived to modern times.

well meaning *adjective* also **well meant**
intending to be useful or helpful.

well-nigh *adverb*
a poetic word meaning 'almost'.

well off *adjective*
1 wealthy.
2 in fortunate circumstances.

wellspring *noun*
a poetic word for the source of a spring.

well-to-do *adjective*
wealthy.

well turned *adjective*
1 pleasingly expressed: *a well turned compliment.*
2 nicely formed: *a well turned ankle.*

well worn *adjective*
worn through use: *a well worn carpet.*
□ *a well worn saying.*

welsh *verb* also **welch**
to evade paying: *to welsh on a bet.*
Word Family **welsher** *noun.*

Welsh corgi ⇨ CORGI.

Welsh rarebit *noun* also called **Welsh rabbit**.
melted seasoned cheese on toast.

welt *noun*
1 a stripe raised on the skin by a blow.
2 a strip of cloth or covered cord sewn into a seam to strengthen it.
3 the strip of leather attaching the upper and sole of a shoe.
• **welt** *verb* to furnish with a welt or welts.

welter *noun*
a confusion or medley, e.g. of thoughts.
• **welter** *verb* to lie or wallow in a liquid.

welterweight *noun*
a weight division in boxing, not more than 67 kg for amateurs and professionals.

wench *noun* (*plural* **wenches**)
an old or jocular word for a girl or young woman, e.g. a farm girl or servant.

wend *verb*
an old word for **go**: *to wend one's way home.*

went the past tense of **go**.

wept the past tense and past participle of **weep**.

were the plural and second person singular past tense of **be**.

we're *contraction*
a short form of **we are**: *We're home!*

weren't *contraction*
a short form of **were not**: *They weren't there.*

werewolf (**wair**-wolf *or* **weer**-wolf) *noun* (*plural* **werewolves**)
Folklore a person who is able to turn into a wolf.
[Old English *wer* man + WOLF]

wert an old form of the second person singular past tense of **be**.

Wesleyan ⇨ METHODIST.

west *noun*
1 the direction of the sun at sunset.

2 the cardinal point of the compass at 90° to the left of north and opposite east.
3 (**the West**) Europe and North America.
4 (**the West**) (*formerly*) the non-communist countries of Europe, North America, etc.
Word Family **west** *adjective, adverb.*

westerly (**west**-a-lee) *adjective*
(of a direction, course, etc.) from or towards the west: *We set off on a westerly course.*
• **westerly** *noun* (*plural* **westerlies**) a wind coming from the west.
• **westerly** *adverb.*

western *adjective*
(of a place) situated in the west.
• **western** *noun* a film or book about frontier America, cowboys, etc.
Word Family **westernmost** *adjective* furthest west.

westward (**west**-w'd) *adjective*
towards the west.
Word Family **westwards, westward** *adverb.*

wet *adjective* (**wetter; wettest**)
1 covered or soaked with water or some other liquid.
2 still in a liquid state: *wet paint.*
3 having a rainy climate.
4 (*informal*) allowing the consumption of alcohol: *a wet state.*
5 (*informal*) stupid or feeble.
• **wet** *verb* (**wets; wetting; wet** *or* **wetted**) to make wet.
• **wet** *noun*
1 moisture.
2 rainy weather.
3 (*informal*) a feeble person.

wet blanket *noun*
(*informal*) a person who has a discouraging or depressing effect.

wet dream *noun*
a sexually exciting dream which is accompanied by an ejaculation of semen during sleep.

wether (*rhymes with feather*) *noun*
a castrated ram.

wet nurse *noun*
(*especially formerly*) a woman hired to breastfeed another woman's child.

wetsuit *noun*
a piece of clothing made of rubber, covering the whole body, worn by divers. It does not prevent water getting in, but restricts the flow, maintaining a warm layer of water around the wearer.

we've *contraction*
a short form of **we have**: *Guess where we've been!*

whack *noun*
1 (*informal*) a sharp resounding stroke or blow.
2 (*informal*) the noise made by such a blow.
3 (*informal*) an attempt.
4 (*informal*) a part or share.
• **whack** *verb* (*informal*) to strike sharply.

whacking *adjective*
(*informal*) very big.

whacky ⇨ WACKY.

whale (wale) *noun*
any of a group of very large marine mammals found in all oceans and hunted for their oil, bone and flesh.
Phrase **a whale of a time** a great time.
Word Family **whale** *verb* to hunt whales; **whaling** *noun*.

whaleboat *noun*
(*formerly*) a long boat pointed at both ends, used for hunting whales.

whalebone *noun*
the horny plates hanging from the upper jaw of toothless whales.

whaler *noun*
a ship used for hunting whales.

wham (wam) *verb* (**whams; whamming; whammed**)
to hit or strike with a loud sound.

wharf (worf) *noun* (*plural* **wharves** or **wharfs**)
a permanent landing place where ships are loaded and unloaded.

wharfage *noun*
1 the storage of goods on a wharf.
2 the charge for the use of a wharf.

what (wot) *pronoun*
1 which particular thing?: *What shall we order to eat?*
2 of which kind or character?: *What is this plant?*
3 of how much value, significance, etc.?: *What is money to a dying man?*
4 that which or the thing that: *This is what I think.*
Phrases **and what have you** and anything else that there may be. **what about?** *What about going to the theatre?* (= what do you say to the idea of). **what for?** why? **what of it?** what does it matter? **what's what** the true position.
• **what** *adjective* which one or ones of a number?: *What dress shall I wear?*
• **what** *adverb* how?: *What does it matter?*
Word Family **what'll** *contraction* a short

form of **what will; what's** *contraction* a short form of **what is** or **what has**.

whatever *pronoun*
1 everything or anything that: *Do whatever you like.*
2 no matter what: *Go whatever happens.*
• **whatever** *adjective*.

> ! On *what ever* and *whatever* ⇨ EVER.

whatsoever *adverb*
at all: *She had no luck whatsoever.*

wheal ⇨ WEAL[1].

wheat (weet) *noun*
a cereal plant used to make flour.
Word Family **wheaten** *adjective*.

wheedle (wee-d'l) *verb*
to persuade or obtain by flattery, etc.
Word Family **wheedler** *noun*; **wheedling** *adjective*.

wheel (weel) *noun*
1 any circular construction which turns on a central axis.
2 something resembling a wheel in construction or movement, such as the steering device on a vehicle.
3 an old instrument of torture, consisting of a circular frame on which a person was stretched, while his or her limbs were broken by beating.
Phrases **at the wheel** 1 driving a vehicle.
2 in control or command. **wheels within wheels** complicated motives and influences.
• **wheel** *verb*
1 to revolve or rotate.
2 to turn or whirl around.
Word Family **wheeled** *adjective*.

wheelbarrow *noun*
a vehicle, usually with a single wheel at one end and handles at the other, used in gardening or building.

wheelbase *noun*
the distance between the front and rear axles of a vehicle.

wheelchair *noun*
a chair with wheels which may be operated by hand or mechanically, used by an invalid or disabled person.

wheel clamp *noun*
a clamp locked to the wheel of an illegally parked car to immobilize it until the required fine is paid.

wheeler-dealer *noun* also called **wheeler and dealer**.
a shrewd or cunning schemer or trader.
Word Family **wheeler-dealing** *noun*.

wheelwright (weel-rite) *noun*
a person who makes or repairs wheels, wheeled carriages, etc.

wheeze (weez) *verb*
to breathe with difficulty, producing a whistling sound.
Word Family wheeze *noun*; wheezy *adjective* (wheezier; wheeziest); wheezily *adverb*; wheeziness *noun*.

whelk (welk) *noun*
a mollusc with a spiral shell, used as food.

whelp (welp) *noun*
an old word for the young of a dog, wolf, or similar mammal.

when (wen) *adverb*
at what time?: *When will breakfast be ready?*
• **when** *conjunction*
1 then at that time: *We were about to leave when there was a knock at the door.*
2 at what time: *You must learn when to be quiet.*
3 at any time: *I get annoyed when I am kept waiting.*
4 while or whereas: *She sat down when she should have remained standing.*
• **when** *pronoun* what or which time?: *Since when have you been in charge?*
Word Family when'll *contraction* a short form of **when will**; when's *contraction* a short form of **when is**.

whence (wenss) *adverb, conjunction*
an old word meaning from what place, source, origin, etc: *He asked me whence I came.*

whenever *conjunction*
at any time that: *Leave whenever you like.*

> [!] On **when ever** and **whenever**
> ⇨ EVER.

where (wair) *adverb*
1 at or in what place?: *Where is it?* □ *Where did you hear that?*
2 to what place?: *Where are you going now?*
• **where** *conjunction*
1 in or at what place, position, etc.: *Find out where the leak is.*
2 in or at the place, position, etc. in which: *My purse is not where I left it.*
3 to which or any place that: *You may wander where you wish.*
• **where** *pronoun*
1 the place in which: *This is where I lost it.*
2 what place?: *from where?*

whereabouts *adverb*
in, at or near what location?
• **whereabouts** *noun*.

whereas *conjunction*
1 while on the contrary: *He was late, whereas I was early.*
2 it being the case that.

whereby *adverb*
by which: *She blushed, whereby I guessed she was lying.*

wherefore *adverb, conjunction*
an old word meaning 'for what purpose or reason?'

where's *contraction*
a short form of **where is**: *Where's Dad?*

whereupon *conjunction*
after which: *The mouse ran out, whereupon the cat pounced.*

wherever *adverb, conjunction*
in, at or to whatever place.

> [!] On **where ever** and **wherever**
> ⇨ EVER.

wherewithal *noun*
the necessary money, etc. for something.

whet (wet) *verb* (whets; whetting; whetted)
1 to sharpen a knife, etc. by grinding.
2 to stimulate, heighten: *to whet one's appetite.*

whether (weth-a) *conjunction*
1 if it is so that: *Tell me whether you are considering my proposal.*
2 either: *Whether by luck or skill, she got the right answer.*

whetstone (wet-stone) *noun*
a fine abrasive stone used for sharpening tools, etc.

whew (few) *interjection*
an exclamation of relief, amazement, etc.

whey (way) *noun*
the milk serum which separates as a watery liquid from curd when it coagulates, e.g. when cheese is made.

which (witch) *adjective*
1 used to ask for information about a particular one or ones: *Which kitten do you like best?*
2 being previously mentioned: *four hours, during which time we slept.*
• **which** *pronoun*
1 a thing, person, event, etc. previously mentioned or implied: *The missing book, which has a red cover, is mine.*
2 any one: *Choose which you'd like.*
3 a thing or circumstance that: *and, which is worse, he lost his passport.*

whichever *pronoun*
1 any one or ones: *Take whichever you want.*

2 no matter which: *Whichever you choose, people will criticize your choice.*

> ! On *which ever* and *whichever* ⇨ EVER.

whiff (wif) *noun*
1 a faint odour carried in the air.
2 (*informal*) an unpleasant odour.
3 a puff of air, smoke, etc.
4 a trace: *a whiff of danger.*
Word Family **whiff** *verb*.

Whig (wig) *noun*
History a member of the British political party which supported the superiority of Parliament over the monarchy. Compare TORY (definition 1).
[from Scottish *whiggamore*, a nickname for rebels who supported the Roundheads, from *whig* to drive + MARE]

while (wile) *noun*
a period of time: *a while ago.*
Phrases **once in a while** occasionally. **the while** *We have been searching the woods and all the while you were sitting here* (= during this time). **worth one's while** worth one's time, effort, etc.
• **while** *conjunction*
1 during or in the time that: *While you are here I shall bake a cake.*
2 although: *While I am flattered by the offer, I can't marry you.*
• **while** *verb*
Phrase **while away** to spend time pleasantly or idly: *to while away the day.*

whilst *conjunction*
while.

whim (wim) *noun*
a sudden fancy or desire.

whimper (wim-pa) *verb*
to cry with low broken sounds.
Word Family **whimper** *noun*;
whimperer *noun* a person who whimpers.

whimsical (wim-zi-k'l) *adjective*
1 having fanciful or odd ideas.
2 quaint or quaintly funny.
Word Family **whimsically** *adverb*;
whimsy, whimsey *noun* quaint or fanciful ideas, behaviour, etc.

whine (wine) *verb*
1 to make a low complaining cry or sound.
2 to complain in an annoying way.
Word Family **whine** *noun*; **whiny** *adjective* (**whinier; whiniest**); **whiner** *noun*.

whinge (winj) *verb*
(*informal*) to complain in an annoying way.

whinny (win-ee) *verb* (**whinnies; whinnying; whinnied**)
(of a horse) to neigh.
• **whinny** *noun* (*plural* **whinnies**).

whip (wip) *verb* (**whips; whipping; whipped**)
1 to strike or beat with quick repeated strokes.
2 to flog as punishment.
3 (*informal*) to defeat, e.g. in a match.
4 to move or turn quickly: *He whipped round as the door opened.*
5 (*informal*) to steal.
6 to wind string or cord around the end of a rope, etc. to prevent fraying.
Phrase **whip up 1** to arouse to fury, etc.: *to whip up an audience.* **2** to create quickly: *He whipped up a splendid lunch for us.*
• **whip** *noun*
1 a flexible cord or leather lash with a rigid handle for striking or beating.
2 *Parliament* an elected officer from a political party, who organizes members to attend debates, etc.
3 *Parliament* the instruction of a whip to attend a debate.
Word Family **whipper** *noun* a person who whips; **whipping** *noun*.

whip hand *noun*
the position of control or advantage: *Who has the whip hand in the relationship?*

whiplash *noun*
1 the lash of a whip.
2 a sudden jerking movement, especially of the head in a car accident.

whippersnapper (wip-a-snap-a) *noun*
(*informal*) an insignificant person who tries to appear important.

whippet (wip-it) *noun*
any of a small breed of racing dogs like a small greyhound.

whipping boy *noun*
a person who is made to suffer or take the blame for someone else.

whippoorwill (wip-a-will) *noun*
a small brownish North American nightjar.
[imitating its cry]

whip-round *noun*
(*informal*) an appeal among a group for contributions of money for a charitable purpose, etc.

whirl (werl) *verb*
1 to spin or cause to spin rapidly.
2 to have the sensation of turning around rapidly: *The room whirled before her.*
• **whirl** *noun*

1 the act of whirling.
2 a whirling movement.
3 a state of hurried or confused activity.

whirlpool *noun*
a circular eddy in water, produced by two currents meeting, etc.

whirlwind *noun*
a small nearly vertical column of air rotating rapidly about a central area of low pressure.
Figurative The house was a whirlwind before the party (= place of frenzied activity).

whirr (wer) *verb also* **whir** (**whirrs; whirring; whirred**)
to move quickly with a vibrating or buzzing sound.
• **whirr** *noun*.

whisk (wisk) *verb*
1 to move quickly and lightly: *She whisked into the office without knocking.*
2 to mix or beat with a whisk.
• **whisk** *noun* a light wire utensil for beating or mixing eggs, cream, etc.

whisker *noun*
1 (**whiskers**) hair growing on the cheek of a man.
2 a long stiff bristly hair growing around the mouth of cats, rats, etc.

whisky (wiss-kee) *noun* (*plural* **whiskies**)
(*American and Irish* **whiskey**)
a strong liquor made from grain.
[Gaelic *usquebaugh* water of life]

whisper (wiss-pa) *verb*
1 to speak very softly.
2 a poetic word meaning 'to rustle': *the leaves whispering in the breeze.*
Word Family **whisper** *noun*; **whisperer** *noun* a person who whispers.

whist (wist) *noun*
Cards a game for four people playing in pairs, each pair trying to win more tricks than the other.

whistle (wiss-'l) *verb*
1 to produce a clear musical sound by forcing air through the teeth or lips.
2 to move with a whistling sound: *The arrow whistled past his ear.*
• **whistle** *noun*
1 a sound produced by or as if by whistling.
2 any instrument which produces whistling sounds.
Word Family **whistler** *noun*.

whit (wit) *noun*
a bit: *I'm not a whit better off than I was before.*

white (wite) *noun*
1 the lightest achromatic colour, the opposite of black.
2 something which has this colour, such as the part of an egg surrounding the yolk or the part of an eye surrounding the pupil.
3 a person with a light skin.
4 white clothes: *dressed in white.*
5 (**whites**) white cricket or tennis clothes.
• **white** *adjective*
1 of the colour white.
2 light and clear in colour: *white wine.*
3 pale: *His face was white.*
4 containing milk: *white coffee.*
5 white in colour, refined: *white rice.*
6 having a light skin.
Word Family **whiteness** *noun*.

whitebait *noun*
the fry of herring, sprat or pilchard, cooked and eaten whole.

white blood cell *noun*
any of the cells in the blood of vertebrates which cannot carry oxygen, including those that fight disease, etc.

white-collar worker *noun*
a person employed in professional or office work, and receiving a salary. Compare BLUE-COLLAR WORKER.

white elephant *noun*
something which is annoyingly useless or expensive to keep.

The phrase **white elephant** comes from a story about a certain king of Siam who used to present *white elephants* to courtiers who had displeased him. *White elephants* were very highly thought of, so they had to be extremely well taken care of and the cost of keeping them was such that the courtiers would be ruined.

white ensign ⇒ ENSIGN.

white feather *noun*
a white feather given as a symbol of cowardice.

white flag *noun*
any symbol or sign of surrender, usually a white flag.

white gold *noun*
any of a group of white alloys, containing gold and various other metals, such as platinum, used in jewellery.

white goods *plural noun*
electrical goods, such as washing machines, refrigerators, etc., traditionally painted white.

white horses *plural noun*
the small white-crested waves whipped up by a moderate breeze at sea.

white-hot *adjective*
extremely hot, so that a bright white light is given off.
Word Family **white heat** *noun* the temperature or state of a substance which is white-hot.

white knight *noun*
a person who comes to someone else's rescue, particularly a company that comes to the rescue of a company facing a takeover bid from an unwelcome source.

white lead (wite **led**) *noun*
a white powder, lead carbonate mixed with lead hydroxide, used in paint pigments.

white lie *noun*
a harmless or excusable lie, usually told with good intentions.

white light *noun*
Physics the light which contains all the wavelengths of the visible spectrum.

white metal *noun*
any of a group of alloys containing tin or lead, used for bearings, etc.

whiten *verb*
to make or become white.

White Paper *noun*
an official report produced by the government on a particular subject.

white tie *noun*
1 a white bow tie worn by a man in full evening dress.
2 full evening dress.

whitewash *noun*
1 any of several preparations, such as lime and water, used to paint surfaces white.
2 anything used to disguise or cover faults, etc.
3 a victory such as one in which a team loses every game in a series.
• **whitewash** *verb*.

whither *adverb, conjunction*
an old or poetic word meaning 'where'.

whiting¹ (**wye**-ting) *noun* (*plural* **whiting**)
a small edible fish with white flesh.

whiting² *noun*
a prepared form of pure white chalk used for whitewashing.

whitish *adjective*
close to white in colour.

whitlow (**wit**-lo) *noun*
a deep bacterial infection in the tip of a finger causing an abscess.
[WHITE + FLAW]

Whitsun *noun* also **Whitsuntide**
Christianity the festival, held seven weeks after Easter, commemorating the coming of the Holy Spirit to the followers of Christ. Compare PENTECOST (definition 2).
[*Whit* as for *white*, from the white dresses worn by converts at this festival in the early days of the Church]

whittle (**wit**-'l) *verb*
to carve by cutting off small pieces with a knife.
Figurative How can we whittle down the cost of the trip? (= cut, reduce).

whizz *verb* also **whiz** (**whizzes; whizzing; whizzed**)
1 to make a hissing or whirring sound, as of something moving quickly through the air.
2 to move with such a sound: *The car whizzed past us.*
• **whizz** *noun* (*plural* **whizzes**)
1 also **whiz** a whizzing sound or movement.
2 also **wiz** (*informal*) a person who is extremely skilled or clever: *a whizz at maths.*

whizz-kid *noun* also **whiz-kid**
(*informal*) a successful or clever young person.

who (hoo) *pronoun*
1 which person or persons?: *Who told you that?*
2 used as a relative pronoun referring to a person already mentioned: *Is that the teacher who makes films?*
Phrase **know who's who** to know which are the people who have power, influence and importance.

> [!] *Who* is now often used in cases where *whom* is grammatically correct, as in *the girl who* [or *whom*] *I met on holiday*, especially in informal spoken English. However, *whom* is still used after a preposition, as in *The person to whom the letter was addressed.*

whoa (wo) *interjection* also **wo**
(usually used to stop a horse or other animal) stop!

who'd *contraction*
a short form of **who had** or **who would**: *Who'd left the door open?* □ *Who'd like to come?*

whodunnit (hoo-**dun**-it) *noun* (*American* **whodunit**)
(*informal*) a detective story.

whoever *pronoun*
any person who: *Whoever wins this race will be the champion.*

> ⚠ On *who ever* and *whoever* ⇨ EVER.

whole (hole) *adjective*
1 containing all its parts: *a whole set of plates.*
2 being in one piece: *The saucer is whole but the cup has a broken handle.*
3 entire: *I didn't see the whole film.*
• **whole** *noun* a whole thing or amount.
Phrases **as a whole** considering all things together. **on the whole** generally.
Word Family **wholeness** *noun*.

wholefood *noun* also **wholefoods**
food which has had a minimum of processing, such as brown rice, which still contains the bran and the germ.

wholehearted (hole-**har**-tid) *adjective*
sincere or unqualified.
Word Family **wholeheartedly** *adverb*; **wholeheartedness** *noun*.

wholemeal *adjective*
being made with complete wheat grains: *wholemeal bread.*

whole number *noun*
a number without a fraction, such as 1, 2, 3, 4, etc.

wholesale *noun*
the selling of goods, usually in large quantities, to retailers, etc., as distinct from the general public. Compare RETAIL *noun*.
• **wholesale** *adjective*
1 relating to or engaged in wholesale.
2 massive, indiscriminate: *the wholesale dismissal of employees.*
Word Family **wholesale** *verb* to sell by wholesale; **wholesaler** *noun*.

wholesome (hole-sum) *adjective*
good for one's health: *a wholesome breakfast.*
Word Family **wholesomely** *adverb*; **wholesomeness** *noun*.

wholewheat *noun*
whole grains of wheat.

who'll *contraction*
a short form of **who will**: *Who'll take the dog out?*

wholly (hole-ee) *adverb*
to the fullest or whole amount, etc.: *I wholly agree with you.*

whom (hoom) *pronoun*
the objective case of **who**: *With whom do you wish to speak?*

> ⚠ On **whom** and **who** ⇨ WHO.

whomever *pronoun*
(*formal*) the objective case of **whoever**.

whomsoever *pronoun*
(*formal*) the objective case of **whosoever**.

whoop (hoop *or* woop) *noun*
a hooting shout or cry: *a whoop of laughter.*
• **whoop** *verb*
1 to make a hooting sound.
2 to make the harsh gasping sound characteristic of whooping cough.
Phrase **whoop it up** to have a lively or boisterous time.

whoopee (wup-ee) *interjection*
(*informal*) a shout of excitement or enthusiasm.

whooping cough (**hoop**-ing koff) *noun*
an infectious bacterial disease, usually in children, causing severe fits of coughing.

whoops (woops) *interjection* also called **whoops-a-daisy.**
an exclamation of dismay, surprise etc.

whoosh (woosh) *noun* also **woosh**
a loud rushing or swishing sound, as of water or air.
• **whoosh** *verb* also **woosh**.

whop (wop) *verb* (**whops; whopping; whopped**)
(*informal*) to hit.

whopper *noun*
1 (*informal*) a very big person or thing.
2 (*informal*) an outrageous lie.

whopping *adjective*
(*informal*) very big.

whore (hor) *noun*
a prostitute or promiscuous woman.
• **whore** *verb* to act as or associate with a whore or whores.

whorl (worl *or* werl) *noun*
1 a circular arrangement of like parts, e.g. in leaves, lines on a fingerprint, etc.
2 anything with the shape of a spiral or coil.
Word Family **whorled** *adjective* having or consisting of whorls.

whortleberry ⇨ BILBERRY.

who's *contraction*
a short form of **who is** or **who has**: *Who's at the door?* □ *Who's got my pen?*

> ⚠ Do not confuse *who's* with *whose*, the possessive case of the pronoun *who*, as in *Whose is this pen?*

whose (hooz) *possessive pronoun*
the possessive case of **who**: *He is the one whose car was stolen.*

[!] Do not confuse *whose* with WHO'S.

whosoever *pronoun*
(*formal*) whoever.

why (wye) *adverb*
1 for what reason or purpose?: *Why did you do that?*
2 the reason for which: *That is why I don't want to go.*
• **why** *interjection* an exclamation of surprise, pleasure, etc.
• **why** *noun* a cause or reason.

wick *noun*
a piece of cord, cotton or other material in a candle or lamp through which the fuel soaks up to the flame.
Phrase **get on someone's wick** to annoy someone intensely.

wicked (**wick**-id) *adjective*
1 evil or sinful.
2 mischievous: *a wicked smile.*
3 (*informal*) excellent, wonderful.
Word Family **wickedly** *adverb*; **wickedness** *noun*.

wicker *noun*
thin pliable twigs that can be woven into baskets or furniture.
• **wicker** *adjective* made of wicker: *a wicker basket.*

wickerwork *noun*
plaited or woven twigs, or an article made from these.

wicket *noun*
1 *Cricket* either of the two sets of three stumps joined across the top by the bails, at which the bowler aims the ball.
2 *Cricket* the pitch or playing area: *The ball bounced little because the wicket was wet.*
3 *Cricket* the dismissing of a batsman.
4 a small door or gate, especially one next to or part of a larger one.
sticky wicket (*informal*) a difficult situation.

wicketkeeper *noun*
Cricket the fielder who stands directly behind the stumps at the batsman's end, to stop all the bowled balls that pass the batsman.

wide *adjective*
1 being large from side to side: *a wide river.*
2 having a particular measurement from one side to the other: *16 cm wide.*
3 fully open: *wide eyes.*
4 varied: *a wide range of products.*
5 too far to one side: *a wide ball.*
• **wide** *adverb*

1 to a wide extent: *Open your mouth wide.*
2 aside: *His first shot went wide.*
3 over a great distance: *to travel far and wide.*
• **wide** *noun Cricket* a ball bowled outside the batsman's reach.
Word Family **widely** *adverb*; **wideness** *noun*; **widen** *verb* to make or become wide or wider.

wide-angle lens *noun* (*plural* **wide-angle lenses**)
Photography a lens which allows a wider angle of view than an ordinary lens, used in taking photographs of buildings, etc.

wide awake *adjective*
completely awake.

wide-eyed *adjective*
with the eyes wide open, especially due to innocence, amazement, etc.

widespread (**wide**-spred) *adjective*
existing or scattered over a wide area or in many places, people, etc.

widgeon ⇨ WIGEON.

widow *noun*
1 a woman who has not remarried after her husband has died.
2 a woman whose husband neglects her in favour of a sport or other activity: *a golf widow.*
Word Family **widow** *verb* to make into a widow; **widowhood** *noun* the state or time of being a widow.

widower *noun*
a man who has not remarried after his wife has died.

widow's mite *noun*
a small gift of money from a person who cannot really afford to give it.

widow's peak *noun*
a hairline forming a V-shaped point in the middle of the forehead.

widow's weeds *plural noun*
the black clothes which a widow in mourning wears.

width *noun*
1 the measurement of something from side to side.
2 something with a particular measurement from side to side: *a width of fabric.*

wield (weeld) *verb*
1 to handle or manage the action of: *to wield a sword.*
2 to have, exercise: *Political parties wield great power.*

wife noun (plural **wives**)
the female partner in a marriage.
old wives' tale an ignorant superstition or
travesty of scientific fact.
Word Family wifely adjective of or
considered appropriate to a wife.

wig noun
a covering for the head, made of real or
artificial hair.
[shortening of periwig]

wigeon (wij-'n) noun also **widgeon**
any of various freshwater ducks.

wiggle verb
to move or cause to move with quick
movements from side to side: He wiggled
his ears.
Word Family wiggle noun a wiggling
movement, line, etc.; **wiggly** adjective
wiggling or waving.

wigwam noun
a dwelling formerly made by some North
American Indian peoples, consisting of
bark or animal skins stretched over a
round framework of poles.

wild (rhymes with child) adjective
1 living, growing or existing in a natural or
uncultivated state: wild animals. □ a wild
herb.
2 uncontrolled, violent: wild fighting.
3 not civilized: wild tribes.
4 unlikely or unconsidered: a wild guess.
5 (informal) very enthusiastic: I'm not wild
about the idea.
6 (informal) very angry: Mum was wild
when she found out.
7 disordered: wild curly hair.
Word Family wild noun (usually **wilds**)
an uncultivated or uninhabited area;
wildly adverb; **wildness** noun.

wild card noun
a playing card which has a value chosen by
the person who holds it.

wildcat noun
1 a small wild cat which is thought to be
the ancestor of the domestic cat.
2 a bobcat or similar mammal.
3 someone with a hot temper.

wildcat strike noun
an unofficial strike.

wildebeest ⇨ GNU.

wilderness noun (plural **wildernesses**)
any land or area which is uncultivated or
uninhabited.

wildfire noun
Phrase spread like wildfire The exciting
news spread like wildfire (= spread with
great or uncontrollable speed).

wild goose chase noun
a hopeless or useless chase or undertaking.

wildlife noun
wild animals, especially those living in
uncultivated areas.

wildly ⇨ WILD.

wildness ⇨ WILD.

wile noun
a trick or deceitful method.

wilful adjective (American **willful**)
1 deliberate or intentional: He was charged
with wilful murder.
2 stubbornly persistent: Wilful disobedience
must be punished.
Word Family wilfully adverb; **wilfulness**
noun.

wilily ⇨ WILY.

wiliness ⇨ WILY.

will¹ verb (**would**)
an auxiliary verb indicating:
1 future tense: He will come afterwards.
2 command: You will go home at once.
3 willingness: Will you do some shopping for
me?
4 habit: She would work late every night.
5 desire: Do what you will.

will² noun
1 the power or ability to deliberately
decide to choose to act.
2 wish, desire: against someone's will.
3 Law a document providing for the
distribution of a person's property after his
or her death.
Phrases at will The tourists could wander
at will about the friendly city (= at their
pleasure). **have a will of one's own** to
have a strong independence of mind. **with
a will** They started the new work with a will
(= eagerly, willingly).
• **will** verb
1 to bequeath in a will.
2 to decide or influence by using the will.
3 to order or command.

willies plural noun
(informal) a feeling of uneasiness, fear or
dislike: The house gave her the willies.

willing adjective
1 ready or happy to do something: Are you
willing to drive?
2 given, done, etc. freely.
Word Family willingly adverb;
willingness noun.

will-o'-the-wisp noun

1 a small flickering light often seen in swamp areas, once believed to lead travellers off their path.
2 something which is misleading or elusive.
[originally *Will with the wisp* (of lighted hay)]

willow noun

a tree or shrub, often with slender drooping branches and strong light wood used for weaving and making cricket bats.
Word Family **willowy** *adjective* tall and gracefully slender.

will power noun

mental strength or control over one's wishes, actions, etc.: *You need great will power to remain on a diet.*

willy-nilly adverb

1 whether it is desired or not.
2 in a haphazard or disorganized way.
[alteration of *will I, nill I* (*nill* = won't)]

wilt verb

to become or cause to become limp and drooping: *The flowers wilted in the hot sun.*

wily (wye-lee) adjective (wilier; wiliest)

cunning or full of deceitful tricks.
Word Family **wilily** *adverb*; **wiliness** *noun*.

wimp noun

(*informal*) a weak, shy or ineffectual person.
• **wimp** *verb*
Phrase **wimp out** to be a coward about something.

wimple noun

a cloth wound around the head to frame the face and wrapped in folds around the neck under the chin, as worn by nuns.

win verb (wins; winning; won)

1 to earn or achieve success, especially when in competition against others: *to win a race.*
2 to be victorious in a battle, war, etc.
3 to receive as a reward for achievement or success: *to win first prize.*
Phrase **win over** to gain the favour or approval of: *Her gentle nature soon won him over.*
Word Family **win** *noun* the act of winning; **winner** *noun*.

wince verb

to flinch in pain, etc.
• **wince** *noun*.

winceyette (win-see-et) noun

a soft cotton fabric used for pyjamas, etc.

winch noun (plural winches)

1 a lifting or pulling device, often having several gearwheels attached to it.
2 the crank handle used on such a device.
• **winch** *verb* to hoist or pull by means of a winch.

wind¹ (rhymes with tinned) noun

1 a movement of air, especially along the earth's surface.
2 breath: *I had run out of wind.*
3 a build-up of gases produced in the stomach.
4 the scent of an animal carried in the air.
5 *Music* (*usually* **winds**) wind instruments.
Phrases **get wind of** *The newspapers soon got wind of the scandal* (= became aware of, sensed). **sail close to the wind 1** to sail as directly against the wind as possible. **2** to get close to the limits of decency or honesty. **see how the wind blows** to test public or others' opinion. **take the wind out of someone's sails** to outmanoeuvre someone, especially by anticipating and frustrating his or her plans.
• **wind** *verb* (**winds; winding; winded**)
1 to cause to have trouble breathing: *The punch winded me.*
2 to pat on the back after feeding: *to wind a baby.*
Word Family **winded** *adjective* temporarily out of breath.

wind² (rhymes with find) verb (winds; winding; wound)

1 to follow a course of turns and bends: *a lazy, winding river.*
2 to wrap around in rolls or coils: *Wind the reins around that branch.*
3 to adjust a mechanical device by turning a key, etc.
4 to haul or hoist by turning a handle, etc.: *Wind that fish in carefully.*
5 to move backwards or forwards on a spool, etc.: *to wind a video tape.*
Phrase **wind up 1** to end up: *You'll wind up on the streets.* **2** (*informal*) to tease or annoy. **3** to bring to an end.
Word Family **wind** *noun* a winding movement or course; **winder** *noun* a thing that winds.

windbag noun

(*informal*) a person who talks continually, usually about uninteresting or unimportant matters.

windbreak noun

a line of trees or a screen giving shelter from the wind.

windcheater *noun*
a short jacket of windproof and rainproof material, gathered in at the wrists and waist.

wind chill *noun*
the added effect of wind, e.g. during winter weather.

windfall *noun*
1 an unexpected piece of good luck, especially money.
2 something blown down by the wind, especially a ripe apple.

wind instrument *noun*
Music an instrument, such as a flute, in which sound is produced by the vibration of air in a tube.

windjammer *noun*
1 a large sailing ship.
2 *American* a windcheater.

windlass *noun* (*plural* **windlasses**)
any of various devices for lifting objects, usually consisting of a rope or chain wound around a drum, which is fitted with a crank handle.

windmill *noun*
any of various wind-driven machines with large vanes fixed onto an axle, used to grind grain, pump water, etc.

window *noun*
1 an opening in a wall to let in light, etc., usually consisting of a movable frame, into which glass is set.
2 the framework, glass or fittings in such an opening.
3 something which has the appearance or function of a window, such as the transparent part of an envelope through which an address may be read.
4 *Computers* a rectangular area of a display screen that can be manipulated separately from the rest of the screen.
5 an interval of time during which conditions are appropriate for something to be accomplished. *a window of opportunity*.
6 a period of free time in an appointments diary or schedule.

window box *noun* (*plural* **window boxes**)
a container for growing plants, placed on or outside the sill of a window.

window dressing *noun*
1 the art of arranging goods in a shop window to attract customers.
2 the presenting of something in its most attractive or appealing form, usually to disguise its less favourable qualities.

windowpane *noun*
a pane of glass in a window.

window seat *noun*
a seat set beneath the sill of a window in an alcove, etc.

window-shop *verb* (**window-shops; window-shopping; window-shopped**)
to look at goods in the windows of shops, rather than buying anything.
Word Family **window-shopper** *noun*.

window sill *noun*
a ledge at the bottom of a window.

windpipe ⇨ TRACHEA.

windscreen *noun* (*American* **windshield**)
a window of safety glass at the front of a motor vehicle.

windscreen wiper *noun*
a device with rubber blades for removing rain, snow, etc. from the windscreen of a vehicle.

windsock *noun*
a device for indicating wind direction at airports, etc., consisting of an open sleeve flown from a pole.

Windsor (win-zer) *noun*
the official name of the British royal family from 1917.

windsurfing *noun* also called **boardsailing.**
the sport of riding on water using a surfboard steered and propelled by a sail.
Word Family **windsurf** *verb*; **windsurfer** *noun*.

windswept *adjective*
exposed to or blown by the wind.

wind tunnel *noun*
a machine for testing aeroplane parts or models by generating a strong airstream in a tunnel.

windward *adjective*
of or facing the direction from which the wind is blowing. Compare LEEWARD.
• **windward** *adverb* towards the wind or the direction from which it is blowing.
• **windward** *noun* the direction from which the wind is blowing.

windy *adjective* (**windier; windiest**)
1 accompanied by wind.
2 of, like or exposed to wind.
3 suffering from or causing flatulence.

wine *noun*
1 a red or white alcoholic beverage made from grape skins and the fermented juice of grapes.
2 a similar drink made from the juice of other fruits, such as berries.
3 also called **wine red.** a dark red colour.

• **wine** *adjective* of or having the colour wine.
• **wine** *verb*
Phrase **wine and dine** to have or treat to dinner and drinks.

winery *noun* (*plural* **wineries**)
a place where wine is made.

wineskin *noun*
a container for wine, made from the skin of an animal.

wing *noun*
1 an organ of flight, consisting of a modified forelimb in animals, and a flat movable structure in insects, etc.
2 something which has the shape or function of a wing, such as the long flat horizontal parts on either side of an aeroplane.
3 something which has the position of a wing, such as a section of a building which projects from the main part or the backstage areas on either side of the stage in a theatre.
4 a folding or hinged part.
5 a distinct section or group within a political party, organization, etc.: *the right wing*.
6 the part of a motor vehicle above the wheel.
7 *Sport* (in football, hockey, etc.) the area along the edges of the field.
8 *Military* a part of an army protecting the main force from attack on the flank.
9 a tactical unit in the air force, consisting of several squadrons.
10 (**wings**) the emblem worn by a qualified pilot.
Phrases **in the wings** waiting in readiness in the background. **on the wing** flying. **take wing** to fly away. **under one's wing** in one's care.
• **wing** *verb*
1 to move as if on wings.
2 to wound in a wing, limb or other minor part.

wing commander *noun*
Air force a commissioned officer ranking between squadron leader and group captain.

winger *noun*
a player positioned on the wing in football, hockey, etc.

wing nut *noun*
a nut with two wing-like projections which enable it to be turned by the thumb and forefinger.

wingspan *noun* also called **wingspread**.
the distance between the tips of the wings of an aeroplane, bird, etc.

wink *verb*
1 to open and close one eye quickly, often as a signal.
2 to flash: *lights winking in the fog*.
Phrase **wink at** *The police will wink at minor offences* (= pretend not to see).
• **wink** *noun* a winking movement or action, especially of an eye.
forty winks a short sleep.
Phrase **not sleep a wink** not to sleep at all.

winkle *noun*
a small mollusc with a spiral shell.

winner ⇨ WIN.

winning *adjective*
1 successful: *the winning team*.
2 charming or disarming: *a winning smile*.

winnings *plural noun*
money that has been won, e.g. in a card game.

winnow *verb*
to separate grain from chaff, etc. using a current of air.
Figurative The jury must winnow the truth from all the evidence (= sort, separate).

wino (**wine-o**) *noun*
(*informal*) an alcoholic.
[from WINE]

winsome (**win-sum**) *adjective*
charming or attractive.
[Old English *wyn* joy + SOME]

winter *noun*
the season between autumn and spring, when it is cold and snow sometimes falls.
Word Family **winter** *verb* to spend the winter.

wintergreen *noun*
a plant from which a pleasant-smelling oil is derived for use in perfumes and as a flavouring in toothpaste.

wintry *adjective* (**wintrier; wintriest**) also **wintery**
like or characteristic of winter: *a wintry landscape*.

wipe *verb*
to rub or pass over lightly with a cloth, etc., in order to clean or dry: *I wiped the baby's face*.
Phrase **wipe out 1** to destroy completely. **2** (of a surfer) to lose balance and fall or jump off the surfboard.
Word Family **wipe** *noun* the act of wiping; **wiper** *noun* something used for

wiping or cleaning, such as a windscreen wiper, etc.

wire *noun*
1 a long thin piece of metal, usually round in cross section and having many uses, e.g. for conducting electricity, as fencing material, etc.
2 (*informal*) a telegram.
Phrase **get one's wires crossed** to talk at cross purposes.
• **wire** *verb*
1 to provide or fasten with a wire or wires: *A champagne cork is wired in place.*
2 to fit with a system of wires to provide electricity.
3 (*especially American informal*) to send a telegram, etc.
Word Family **wiring** *noun* a system of wires providing electricity, e.g. for lighting.

wire-haired *adjective*
having stiff wiry hair.

wireless *noun* (*plural* **wirelesses**)
1 (*dated*) also called **wireless set**. a radio set.
2 (*dated*) the use of radio signals for broadcasting or telegraphy.
• **wireless** *adjective*
1 (*dated*) using radio signals for broadcasting or telegraphy.
2 not having or using wires.

wiretapper *noun*
a person who listens to or records telephone conversations.
Word Family **wiretap** *verb* (**wiretaps**; **wiretapping**; **wiretapped**).

wiry (**wire**-ee) *adjective* (**wirier**; **wiriest**)
1 resembling wire in shape, stiffness, etc.
2 slender but strong: *He has a wiry build.*

wisdom (**wiz**-d'm) *noun*
1 good judgement or understanding of what is right, true, etc.
2 learning or knowledge acquired by study, experience, etc.

wisdom tooth *noun* (*plural* **wisdom teeth**)
the last molar at either end of the upper and lower jaws in humans.

wise (**wize**) *adjective*
having or showing wisdom: *a wise old professor.* □ *Is it wise to go out in the storm?*
Phrase **wise to** aware of: *After a few days they were wise to his methods.*
• **wise** *verb*
Phrase **wise up** to make or become aware, informed, etc.
Word Family **wisely** *adverb*.

wiseacre (**wize**-ay-ka) *noun*
a know-all.

wisecrack *noun*
(*informal*) a smart or flippant remark.
• **wisecrack** *verb*.

wish *verb*
1 to want or long for: *I wish it would stop raining.*
2 to express a desire, as if for magical results: *What did you wish for as you blew out the candles?*
3 to ask for something to be done.
4 to express a hope, etc.: *I wished her goodnight.*
Phrase **wish something on** to hope that something will happen to.
• **wish** *noun* (*plural* **wishes**)
1 a desire or longing: *a wish for peace.*
2 something which is wanted: *What is your wish?*
3 a word or words which express a wish, especially as a polite greeting, etc.: *Give my best wishes to your parents.*

wishbone *noun*
a forked bone in front of the breast of some birds.

wishful *adjective*
hoping or longing.
Word Family **wishfully** *adverb*.

wishful thinking *noun*
a hopeful confidence that what one wishes for will occur or is the case.

wishy-washy *adjective*
lacking strength or substance.

wisp *noun*
1 a small fine bunch of strands, etc.: *a wisp of hair.*
2 a person who is small, frail or thin.
Word Family **wispy** *adjective* (**wispier**; **wispiest**) in wisps or resembling a wisp.

wist the past tense and past participle of **wit**[2].

wisteria (wiss-**teer**-ee-a) *noun* also **wistaria** (wiss-**tair**-ee-a)
any of various climbing plants with compound leaves and blue, purple or white flowers.
[after *C.Wistar*, 1761-1818, an American anatomist]

wistful *adjective*
expressing sadness, regret or disappointed hope.
Word Family **wistfully** *adverb*; **wistfulness** *noun*.

wit[1] *noun*
1 a clever ability to perceive, connect or express ideas, etc. especially in a fresh, unexpected and amusing way.
2 an example of such an ability in speech or writing.
3 a person with such a talent.
4 (**wits**) acute mental powers, especially sanity or good sense.
Phrases **at one's wits' end** thwarted and not knowing what to do next. **have one's wits about one** to be alert to what is happening. **live by one's wits** to make a living by haphazard exploitation and sharp practice. **out of one's wits** *The explosion scared them out of their wits* (= to an extreme degree).

wit[2] *verb* (**wot; witting; wist**)
an old word for **know**.
Phrase **to wit** that is to say.

witch *noun* (*plural* **witches**)
1 a woman who practises magic, especially one who uses black magic.
2 (*informal*) any ugly or evil old woman.
3 a fascinating or bewitching woman.

witchcraft *noun*
the art or influence of magic, especially for evil purposes.

witch doctor *noun*
a magician believed to have the power of healing.

witchery *noun*
1 the practice of magic.
2 a fascinating power.

witch hazel *noun* also **wych hazel**
1 a winter-flowering garden shrub.
2 an astringent liquid prepared from this shrub, used on bruises, inflammations, etc.

witch-hunt *noun*
an emotional campaign, usually political, to find or investigate people considered to be unorthodox or disloyal.

witching hour *noun*
midnight.

with *preposition*
1 used to indicate company: *Come with me.*
2 used to indicate connection: *Mix the flour with the butter.*
3 used to indicate manner or means: *Cut the bread with this knife.*
4 used to indicate opposition: *arguing with his father.*
5 used to indicate result or effect: *He mellowed with age.*
6 used to indicate agreement: *We're with you on that.*

7 used to indicate separation: *to part with something.*
8 in the same direction as: *swimming with the current.*
9 having or possessing: *the girl with green eyes.*
10 at the same time as: *She gets up with the dawn.*
11 in the possession of: *Leave your coat with me.*
12 concerning: *I am furious with her.*
13 in proportion to: *Prices rose with the increasing shortage of goods.*

withdraw *verb* (**withdraws; withdrawing; withdrew; withdrawn**)
1 to take out: *I'd like to withdraw ten pounds.*
2 to take back or away; to remove: *She withdrew her hand.*
3 to leave: *The soldiers withdrew.*
4 to go somewhere quieter.
5 to stop taking an addictive drug.

withdrawal *noun*
1 the act of withdrawing, such as the removal of a drug or other habit-forming substance from a person's experience.
2 an amount of money, etc. which is withdrawn.

withdrawn *adjective*
reserved or lost in one's own thoughts.

wither *verb*
to make or become faded, dry and shrunken: *The leaves withered and fell from the tree.*

withering *adjective*
scornful: *a withering look.*

withers *plural noun*
the highest part of the back behind the shoulders of a horse, donkey, etc.

withhold *verb* (**withholds; withholding; withheld**)
to hold back or refuse to give: *Police withheld the victim's name for several days.*

within *preposition*
1 in or into: *within the house.*
2 according to the limits of: *to live within one's means.*
3 not further than: *Their house is within shouting distance of ours.*
• **within** *adverb*.

with it *adjective*
(*informal*) fashionably up to date.

without *preposition*
1 not having: *The strike left us without transport.*
2 not accompanied by: *I saw Joey without his mother.*
3 an old or poetic word meaning 'outside'.

withstand *verb* (**withstands;**
withstanding; withstood)
to resist or oppose successfully: *The*
reinforced windows will withstand great
pressure.

witless *adjective*
foolish.
Word Family **witlessly** *adverb;*
witlessness *noun.*

witness *noun* (*plural* **witnesses**)
1 a person who is present at, sees or hears
something: *This man was a witness to the*
attack.
2 *Law* a person who makes a statement or
gives evidence, especially in a court case.
3 *Law* a person who signs a document as a
declaration or agreement to its validity.
Phrase **bear witness** to be or give
evidence.
• **witness** *verb* to be or perform the duties
of a witness.

witness box *noun* (*plural* **witness boxes**)
(*American* **witness stand**)
the enclosed area in a courtroom, where a
witness stands to give evidence.

witter *verb*
(*informal*) to talk on and on about
unimportant things: *He was wittering on*
about the traffic.

witticism (wit-i-sizm) *noun*
a witty comment.

wittingly *adverb*
knowingly or deliberately.

witty *adjective* (**wittier; wittiest**)
possessing or showing wit.
Word Family **wittily** *adverb;* **wittiness**
noun.

wives
the plural of **wife**.

wiz ⇨ WHIZZ *noun* (definition 2).

wizard *noun*
1 a magician or sorcerer.
2 a very clever or skilled person: *a wizard*
at chess.
Word Family **wizardry** (wiz-'d ree)
noun 1 magic or witchcraft. 2 great
cleverness or skill in a particular area, or
something showing this: *technical wizardry.*
[Middle English, wise one]

wizened (wiz-'nd) *adjective*
withered or shrivelled.

wo ⇨ WHOA.

woad *noun*
a plant with yellow flowers and leaves
formerly used to make a blue dye.

wobble *verb*
1 to move or cause to move unsteadily
from side to side: *Anisa wobbled the loose*
tooth until it came out.
2 (of the voice) to tremble.
Word Family **wobble** *noun;* **wobbly**
adjective (**wobblier; wobbliest**) unsteady;
wobbliness *noun.*

woe *noun*
1 a poetic word meaning 'sorrow or
misery'.
2 (**woes**) troubles.
Phrase **woe betide** *Woe betide you if you*
fail (= trouble will come to).

woebegone (wo-bee-gon) *adjective*
looking unhappy or miserable.

woeful *adjective*
1 unhappy: *a woeful experience.*
2 deplorable or worthy of pity: *She shows a*
woeful lack of intelligence.
Word Family **woefully** *adverb;*
woefulness *noun.*

wok *noun*
a frying pan with a curved base like a
bowl, used in Chinese cookery.

woke the past tense of **wake**[1].

woken the past participle of **wake**[1].

wolf *noun* (*plural* **wolves**)
a mammal like a large dog, which hunts in
packs and is found in the northern parts of
Europe, Asia and America.
Phrases **cry wolf** to give false alarms.
keep the wolf from the door to keep
away poverty or hunger. **wolf in sheep's**
clothing a person who appears harmless
but in fact has hostile or malicious
intentions.
• **wolf** *verb* to eat ravenously: *He wolfed his*
dinner and left.
Word Family **wolfish** *adjective;* **wolfishly**
adverb.

wolfhound *noun*
a large breed of dog, originally bred to
hunt wolves.

wolfram (wul-fr'm) *noun*
tungsten or its ore.
[German]

wolf spider *noun*
a fast spider that jumps on its prey.

wolf whistle *noun*
a loud whistle used as a sign of admiration.
Word Family **wolf-whistle** *verb.*

wolverine (wul-va-reen) *noun*
a common burrowing rodent with a thick
body and short legs, found in northern
forests.

woman (**wum**-'n) *noun* (*plural* **women**)
(**wim**-in)
an adult female human being.
Word Family **womanly** *adjective* having
the qualities considered to be appropriate
to a woman; **womanliness** *noun*;
womanhood *noun* the state of being a
woman.
[Old English *wife-man*]

womanish *adjective*
1 a rather offensive word meaning 'suitable
for a woman'.
2 effeminate: *He has a womanish walk.*

womanize, womanise *verb*
(of a man) to have numerous casual affairs
with women.
Word Family **womanizer** *noun.*

womb (*rhymes with* room) ⇨ UTERUS.

wombat *noun*
any of a group of heavily built, burrowing
and grazing marsupials of Australia.
[Aboriginal]

women's movement *noun*
an international movement aimed at
increasing the rights and status of women.

won (wun) the past tense and past
participle of **win**.

wonder (**wun**-da) *verb*
1 to feel curiosity or doubt: *I wonder if he is
as rich as people say he is.*
2 to have a feeling of awe or admiration:
I wonder at his bravery.
• **wonder** *noun*
1 something which causes awe or
admiration: *one of the wonders of the ancient
world.*
2 the emotion excited by such a thing:
*I was filled with wonder when they landed
on the moon.*
3 a strange or surprising person, thing or
event: *It's a wonder she survived the accident.*
Word Family **wonderingly** *adverb*;
wonderment *noun* awe.

wonderful (**wun**-da-f'l) *adjective*
extremely good or fine.
Word Family **wonderfully** *adverb.*

wonderland (**wun**-da-land) *noun*
1 a marvellous imaginary place.
2 a marvellous real place: *Austria is a
winter wonderland for skiers.*

wondrous (**wun**-drus) *adjective*
a poetic word meaning 'inspiring awe or
admiration'.

wonky *adjective* (**wonkier; wonkiest**)
1 (*informal*) crooked.
2 (*informal*) shaky or wobbly.

wont (woant) *adjective*
an old or poetic word meaning
'accustomed': *He is wont to smoke after a
meal.*
Word Family **wont** *noun* a habit; **wonted**
adjective habitual.

won't *contraction*
a short form of **will not**: *I won't tell you
again.*

woo *verb* (**woos; wooing; wooed**)
1 to seek the affection of, especially with
intent to marry.
2 to seek to achieve: *to woo fame.*
3 to invite by one's own actions: *to woo
disaster by dangerous living.*
Word Family **wooer** *noun* a person who
woos.

wood *noun*
1 the hard fibrous substance of tree trunks
or branches.
2 this substance cut down for use in
carpentry, building, etc.
3 (*often* **woods**) an area of land covered
with trees, usually less dense than a forest.
4 *Golf* any wooden-headed club, mainly
used over long distances and each
numbered according to the angle of the
head to the handle. Compare IRON *noun*
(definition 4).
Phrases **out of the wood, out of the
woods** having overcome the most difficult
or dangerous part of something. **touch
wood** a superstitious action or interjection
after expressing a hope. **unable to see the
wood for the trees** unable to distinguish
the important points of a problem, etc.
from the mass of detail.
Word Family **wood** *adjective* 1 made of or
using wood. 2 living in the woods;
wooded *adjective* having trees or woods.

woodcock *noun* (*plural* **woodcock**)
a plump game bird related to the snipe.

woodcut *noun*
a print made from an engraved wooden
block.

wooden *adjective*
1 made or consisting of wood.
2 stiff, clumsy: *wooden actors.*
Word Family **woodenly** *adverb.*

wooden spoon *noun*
a booby prize.

woodiness ⇨ WOODY.

woodland *noun* also **woodlands**
an area of land covered in trees.

woodlouse *noun* (*plural* **woodlice**)
a small land crustacean living in damp
shady places, e.g. under stones.

woodpecker *noun*
a bird which uses its beak to drill holes in tree trunks and extract insects with its long tongue.

woodwind *noun*
1 *Music* the wind instruments, such as the flutes, clarinets, etc.
2 *Music* the section of an orchestra having these instruments.

woodwork *noun*
1 making things with wood.
2 the wooden fittings in a building

woodworm *noun*
the larva of a species of furniture beetle, which bores its way through cracks in furniture and leaves a circular exit hole.

woody *adjective* (**woodier; woodiest**)
1 covered with trees, wooded.
2 made of or like wood.
Word Family **woodiness** *noun*.

wooer ⇨ WOO.

woof¹ *noun*
a dog's bark.
• **woof** *verb*.

woof² *noun*
the weft in weaving.

woofer *noun*
a loudspeaker designed for low frequencies. Compare TWEETER.

wool *noun*
1 the soft curly hair of sheep, used to make yarn or fibre.
2 the yarn, used for knitting, weaving, etc., or fabric produced from this hair.
3 any similar material: *cotton wool*.
Phrase **pull the wool over someone's eyes** to deceive or delude someone.

wool-gathering *noun*
indulgence in fanciful daydreams.

woollen *adjective* (*American* **woolen**)
made of wool.

woollens *plural noun*
knitted clothing made of wool.

woolly *adjective* (**woollier; woolliest**) (*American* **wooly**)
1 consisting of, covered with or resembling wool.
2 confused or indistinct: *I only have a woolly idea of what she was trying to say.*

woosh ⇨ WHOOSH.

woozy (woo-zee) *adjective* (**woozier; wooziest**)
(*informal*) dazed or unsteady.

word (*rhymes with* bird) *noun*
1 the basic unit of language, a combination of sounds having a complete meaning.
2 an utterance, remark or expression: *a word of warning*.
3 speech or talk: *May I have a word with you?*
4 (**words**) the sounds spoken or sung in a song, etc.
5 (**words**) a quarrel: *They had had words the day before and glared angrily at each other on the bus.*
6 a promise or assurance: *I'll keep your secret, I give you my word.*
7 a command: *Just give the word!*
8 news: *We had received word of an army in the south.*
Phrases **in so many words** explicitly. **play on words** a pun. **put in a good word for someone** to recommend someone. **put words in someone's mouth** to say, incorrectly, that someone said something. **take someone at his** or **her word** to act on the assumption that someone means what he or she says. **take the words out of someone's mouth** to say exactly what someone else was about to say. **the last word** 1 the closing remark in an argument, etc. 2 the very latest or most fashionable thing.
Word Family **word** *verb* to express in words; **wording** *noun* the words in which something is expressed.

word-perfect *adjective*
being able to recite something, e.g. a part in a play, word for word.

word-processing *noun*
the input, editing, storage and retrieval of written material using a computer.
Word Family **word processor** *noun* a computer which can be used in word-processing.

wordy (wer-dee) *adjective* (**wordier; wordiest**)
expressed in or using more words than are necessary.
Word Family **wordily** *adverb*; **wordiness** *noun*.

wore the past tense of **wear**.

work (werk) *noun*
1 effort directed towards making or doing something.
2 something produced by effort: *a work of art*.
3 an undertaking.
4 what a person does to earn a living.
5 (**works**) a factory, building, etc. where something is manufactured: *the steel works*.
6 *Physics* a scalar quantity equal to the force on a body multiplied by the distance it moves in the direction of the force.

7 (**works**) the main parts of any machine, e.g. a clock.
Phrases **have one's work cut out to** have a difficult task. **set to work** to begin. **the works** the whole lot.

• **work** *verb*
1 to engage in work.
2 to operate: *to work a machine.* □ *This machine won't work.*
3 to prove successful: *The plan had worked.*
4 to mould: *He worked the clay until it was soft.*
5 to cultivate: *to work the land.*
6 to cause, bring about: *to work a miracle.*
7 to move gradually: *She worked her way to the front.* □ *The button had worked loose.*
8 to bring into a particular state: *to work oneself into a rage.*
Phrases **work out 1** to solve a problem. **2** to train or practise, especially as an athlete. **work up 1** to excite or arouse. **2** to increase in intensity, etc.
Word Family **workable** *adjective*
1 practicable or feasible. **2** suitable for being worked.

workaholic *noun*
(*informal*) a person who feels compelled to work very hard and for very long hours, as if addicted to his or her job.

worker (**wer**-ka) *noun*
1 a person who works, especially one doing manual labour.
2 *Biology* a sterile female which, among social insects, does the work of the colony.

work-harden *verb*
to make a material, especially a metal, harder or stronger by working it.

workhouse *noun*
History the parish institution to which paupers were sent to work under harsh conditions.

working (**wer**-king) *adjective*
1 employed.
2 capable of being used: *a working model.*

working class *noun* (*plural* **working classes**)
those who work in skilled trades or as manual labourers.
• **working class** *adjective*.

working drawing *noun*
a drawing which contains all the information needed to make a product.

workman *noun* (*plural* **workmen**)
a worker, especially a manual or industrial worker.
Word Family **workmanship** *noun* **1** the art, skill or technique of a worker. **2** the

quality of a worker's skill or art;
workmanlike *adjective* efficient or skilled.

workout *noun*
a practice or period of training.

workshop *noun*
1 a room or building where work, especially mechanical work, is done.
2 an organized meeting of people with the same interests or skills, to practise together or exchange ideas: *a theatre workshop.*

world (werld) *noun*
1 the earth or globe.
2 a particular section of the earth: *the western world.*
3 a particular section of the earth's inhabitants: *the animal world.*
4 one's life: *Her world fell apart.*
5 a sphere, realm: *the world of dreams.*
6 another planet.
Phrases **bring into the world** to bear or deliver a child. **come into the world** to be born. **in the world** *What in the world made you say that?* (= conceivable thing). **of the world** worldly. **on top of the world** extremely delighted or elated. **out of this world** marvellous or fabulous. **think the world of** to have a high opinion of.

world-beater *noun*
an exceptionally good person or thing.

world-class *adjective*
of highest or international quality.

worldly (**werld**-lee) *adjective* (**worldlier; worldliest**)
1 not religious or spiritual.
2 sophisticated or experienced in the ways of the world.
Word Family **worldliness** *noun.*

worldly-wise *adjective*
experienced and not easily shocked.

world music *noun*
a variety of popular music incorporating elements from various national or ethnic styles, especially those from developing countries.

world war *noun*
a war involving countries in many different parts of the world, especially the First World War (1914-1918) and the Second World War (1939-1945).

worldwide *adjective*
extending throughout the world.

World Wide Web *noun*
a system of information on the Internet that people with computers can use.

worm (werm) *noun*
1 any of various creeping animals with soft bodies and no limbs, often living in the ground or as parasites.
2 (*informal*) a contemptible person.
3 (**worms**) the presence of parasitic worms in the intestines.
4 *Engineering* a coarse thread cut on a shaft, e.g. on the gear of a motor vehicle.
● **worm** *verb*
1 to move like a worm.
Figurative He wormed the secret out of her (= got by devious means).
2 to free from intestinal worms: *to worm a cat.*

wormwood *noun*
a bitter-tasting plant used to make vermouth and in medicines.

worn *adjective*
1 impaired by wear or use.
2 very tired or weary.
● **worn** *verb* the past participle of **wear**.

worn out *adjective*
1 used until no longer effective or valuable.
2 utterly exhausted.

worry (*rhymes with* hurry) *verb* (**worries; worrying; worried**)
1 to feel or cause to feel uneasy or slightly fearful.
2 to pull, bite or tear at repeatedly.
● **worry** *noun* (*plural* **worries**)
1 the state of being worried.
2 a person or thing that causes someone to be worried.
Word Family **worrier** *noun*.

The word **worry** is connected with German *würgen* (to choke or strangle). It then came to mean 'to harass or annoy in a physical manner' – in the way that dogs worry sheep. The modern sense of 'cause concern to' or 'disturb' developed from that and in turn led to the sense of 'feel uneasy or fearful' as in *Try not to worry.*

worry beads *plural noun*
a string of beads played with for relaxation or distraction.

worse (werse) *adjective*
the comparative of **bad**.
Word Family **worse** *adverb*; **worsen** *verb* to make or become worse.

worship (wer-ship) *noun*
1 the act of revering or honouring a god, etc., especially by ceremonies, rites or services.

2 a high regard or love for a person or thing.
3 (**Worship**) a form of address, as in Your Worship, used to a magistrate or mayor.
Word Family **worship** *verb* (**worships; worshipping; worshipped**);
worshipper *noun*; **worshipful** *adjective* feeling or showing worship, adoration, etc.

worst (werst) *adjective*
the superlative of **bad**.
● **worst** *noun*
Phrase **if the worst comes to the worst** if events turn out in the worst possible way.
Word Family **worst** *adverb*; **worst** *verb* to defeat: *to be worsted in an argument.*

worsted (wuss-tid) *noun*
1 a firmly twisted yarn used for weaving, etc.
2 a woollen fabric made from this yarn, with a firm smooth surface.
[after *Worstead* in Norfolk, where once made]

worth (werth) *noun*
1 the quality of something which makes it valuable, desirable, deserving of respect, etc.
2 the value of something.
● **worth** *adjective*
1 deserving of: *a place worth a visit.*
2 having a value of: *worth a million dollars.*
Phrase **for all one is worth** (*informal*) with all one's might: *She pushed for all she was worth.*
Word Family **worthless** *adjective* having no use, value, importance, etc.; **worthlessness** *noun*.

worthwhile (werth-wile) *adjective*
sufficiently rewarding to justify one's time, attention, work, trouble, etc.

worthy (wer-thee) *adjective* (**worthier, worthiest**)
having worth, merit or value: *a worthy cause.*
Phrase **worthy of** *a person worthy of respect* (= who should be given).
Word Family **worthy** *noun* (*plural* **worthies**) an eminent person; **worthily** *adverb*; **worthiness** *noun*.

wot the first and third person singular present tense of **wit**[2].

would (*rhymes with* good) the past and conditional tense of **will**[1].

would-be *adjective*
intending or hoping to be: *a would-be film star.*

wouldn't *contraction*
a short form of **would not**: *Wouldn't you like to go?*

would've *contraction*
a short form of **would have**: *I would've phoned first, but I was in a hurry.*

> [!] *Of* is sometimes incorrectly used instead of *'ve*: *If you'd tried harder, you would have* or *would've* (not *would of*) *succeeded.*

wound¹ (woond) *noun*
any injury, usually one caused by external violence rather than due to a disease.
• **wound** *verb* to inflict a wound or wounds.

wound² (*rhymes with* round) the past tense and past participle of **wind**².

wove the past tense and a past participle of **weave**¹.

woven a past participle of **weave**¹.

wrack¹ *verb* ⇨ RACK¹ *verb*.

wrack² *noun* ⇨ RACK² *noun*.

wrack³ (rack) *noun*
a coarse brown seaweed.

wraith (rayth) *noun*
an apparition, especially one of a person seen just before or after a death.

wrangle (rang-g'l) *verb*
to quarrel.
• **wrangle** *noun*.

wrap (rap) *verb* (**wraps**; **wrapping**; **wrapped**)
1 to cover or enclose, e.g. with paper, etc.
2 to clasp, fold or coil about something.
Figurative She was wrapped in thought (= immersed).
Phrase **wrap up** to finish or settle.
• **wrap** *noun* a shawl, rug, etc. to keep one warm.
Word Family **wrapper** *noun* something in which an object is wrapped or covered.

wrath (roth) *noun*
violent or resentful anger.
Word Family **wrathful** *adjective* a poetic word meaning 'full of anger'; **wrathfully** *adverb*; **wrathfulness** *noun*.

wreak (reek) *verb*
1 to cause damage, etc. or inflict vengeance.
2 an old word meaning 'to avenge'.

wreath (reeth) *noun*
a circular band of flowers, leaves, etc. sent to a funeral, put on a grave, etc.

wreathe (reeth) *verb*
to encircle or adorn with or as if with a wreath.

Figurative Her face was wreathed in smiles (= enveloped).

wreck (rek) *verb*
1 to destroy, especially accidentally: *The ship was wrecked when it hit the rocks.*
2 to damage or spoil.
• **wreck** *noun*
1 the remains of something that has been wrecked.
2 a person in a poor mental or physical state.
Word Family **wreckage** (rek-ij) *noun* the remains of something which has been wrecked; **wrecker** *noun*.

wren (ren) *noun*
a tiny songbird with an erect tail.

wrench (rench) *verb*
1 to twist suddenly and forcibly.
2 to twist and sprain.
• **wrench** *noun* (*plural* **wrenches**)
1 a sudden violent twist.
2 a tool like a spanner, which can be adjusted to grip a nut or bolt.

wrest (rest) *verb*
to take away by force: *I wrested the knife from him.*

wrestle (ress-'l) *verb*
to struggle with and try to throw an opponent to the ground.
Figurative He wrestled with the problem all night (= struggled, tried to deal).
Word Family **wrestling** *noun* a contest between two opponents who wrestle as a sport; **wrestler** *noun*.

wretch (retch) *noun* (*plural* **wretches**)
1 an unfortunate or unhappy person.
2 (*informal*) a despicable person.

wretched (retch-id) *adjective*
1 miserable.
2 contemptible or despicable: *What a wretched thing to do.*
Word Family **wretchedly** *adverb*; **wretchedness** *noun*.

wriggle (rig-'l) *verb*
1 to twist or turn the body with winding motions.
2 to move by such motions.
Phrase **wriggle out of** *How did she wriggle out of the washing-up?* (= manage to avoid).
Word Family **wriggle** *noun*; **wriggly** *adjective*; **wriggler** *noun*.

wright (rite) *noun*
an old word for a builder or maker, now only used in compound words: *a playwright.*

wring (ring) *verb* (**wrings; wringing; wrung**)
1 to twist and squeeze.
2 to remove liquid, etc. by twisting and squeezing: *He wrung out the towels.*
3 to cause pain or distress to: *to wring someone's heart.*
Phrases **wringing wet** very wet indeed.
wring something out of *He managed to wring an apology out of the company* (= get with difficulty).
Word Family **wring** noun.

wringer *noun*
a mangle.

wrinkle (ring-k'l) *noun*
a small furrow or ridge on a normally smooth surface.
Word Family **wrinkle** verb; **wrinkly** adjective (**wrinklier; wrinkliest**).

wrist (rist) *noun*
1 *Anatomy* the movable part between the forearm and the hand, made up of eight small bones, called carpal bones.
2 something covering the wrist.

wristlet *noun*
a band worn around the wrist for decoration, etc.

wristpin *noun* also called **wrist**.
a pin joining the piston to the connecting rod of an internal-combustion engine.

writ (rit) *noun*
Law a court order, for a person to do, or refrain from doing, a particular act.

write (rite) *verb* (**writes; writing; wrote; written**)
1 to form letters, words, etc. on a surface using a pen, pencil or similar instrument.
2 to compose or produce a poem, book, letter, piece of music, etc.
3 to fill in: *writing a cheque.*
4 to write a letter to someone: *She doesn't write very often.*
Phrases **the writing on the wall** signs of trouble coming (a biblical reference).
write off to consider as a complete loss.
Word Family **write-off** noun. **write up** to review or write about something in a newspaper, etc. *Word Family* **write-up** noun.
Word Family **writer** noun a person who writes, especially for a living; **writing** noun 1 the act of a person who writes.
2 anything which is written.

writhe (rithe) *verb*
to twist or squirm, for example because of pain or discomfort.

writing frame *noun*
a template for a piece of writing to be done as a school exercise, often taking the form of opening phrases of paragraphs and sometimes suggested vocabulary.

wrong (rong) *adjective*
1 not correct in action, opinion, method, etc.: *a wrong answer.* □ *a wrong turn.*
2 not in accordance with what is considered good, correct, true, etc.: *It is wrong to steal.*
3 inappropriate, unsuitable: *Did I say the wrong thing?*
4 in a bad condition: *Something is wrong with the machine.*
• **wrong** *noun* something which is wrong, such as an injury or unjust act.
Phrase **in the wrong** guilty or in error.
• **wrong** *verb* to treat unfairly or unjustly.
Word Family **wrongly, wrong** adverb; **wrongful** adjective illegal, unfair; **wrongfully** adverb; **wrongfulness** noun.

wrongdoer *noun*
a person who does wrong.
Word Family **wrongdoing** noun wrong behaviour or action, such as a crime.

wrong-headed *adjective*
misguided and stubborn.

wrote the past tense of **write**.

wroth (roth) *adjective*
an old word meaning 'angry or wrathful'.

wrought (rawt) *adjective*
shaped by hammering, etc.
[from *wrought*, the old past tense and past participle of WORK]

wrought iron *noun*
the purest commercial form of iron containing very little carbon and easily worked and welded.

wrung the past tense and past participle of **wring**.

wry (rye) *adjective*
1 bitterly or ironically humorous.
2 slightly twisted.
Word Family **wryly** adverb; **wryness** noun.

wudu (woo-doo) *noun*
ablution performed by Muslims before prayer.
[Arabic]

wych hazel ⇨ WITCH HAZEL.

X chromosome ⇨ SEX CHROMOSOME.

xenon (zen-on) *noun*
a rare colourless inert gas found in the earth's atmosphere and used in some electric lights.

xenophobia (zenn-a-**fo**-bee-a) *noun*
an irrational dislike of foreigners.
Word Family **xenophobic** *adjective*; **xenophobe** (**zen**-a-fobe) *noun*.
[Greek *xenos* foreign + PHOBIA]

xerophyte (**zeer**-a-fite) *noun*
a plant which is adapted for growth under extremely dry conditions.
Word Family **xerophytic** (zeer-a-**fit**-ik) *adjective*.
[*xero-* + Greek *phyton* a plant]

Xerox (**zeer**-roks) *noun*
(*trademark*) a system of printing in which carbon powder sticks to paper that has been electrically charged.
• **xerox** *verb*.

Xmas (**kriss**-muss *or* **eks**-muss) *noun*
(*plural* **Xmases**)
(*informal*) Christmas.

X-ray *noun*
1 a form of electromagnetic radiation of wavelength shorter than ultraviolet, between 10^{-11} nm and 10^{-10} nm, able to penetrate wood, flesh and, in varying degrees, metal.
2 a photograph of the interior of a solid substance, especially a part of the body, by a machine using X-rays which can show up fractures, tumours, a barium meal in the intestines, etc.
X-ray therapy the destruction of cancer cells, etc. by X-rays.
• **X-ray** *verb* to examine by means of an X-ray.

xylem (**zye**-l'm) *noun*
Biology the cells conducting water in plants. The xylem helps to form the woody part of the stem.
[Greek *xylon* wood]

xylophone (**zye**-la-fone) *noun*
Music a percussion instrument consisting of tuned wooden bars struck with small hand-held hammers.
Word Family **xylophonic** (zye-la-**fonn**-ik) *adjective*; **xylophonist** (zye-**loff**-a-nist) *noun*.
[Greek *xylon* wood + *phoné* sound]

yabby *noun* (*plural* **yabbies**)
a small freshwater crayfish.

yacht (yot) *noun*
a boat used for cruising or racing and propelled by sails or an engine.
Word Family yacht *verb*; **yachtsman** *noun* (*plural* **yachtsmen**); **yachtswoman** *noun* (*plural* **yachtswomen**).
[Dutch]

yackety-yak *noun*
(*informal*) any prolonged empty or pointless talk.

yahoo (yah-hoo) *noun*
(*informal*) an uncouth person.
[after a tribe of vulgar brutes in *Gulliver's Travels* by Jonathan Swift, 1726]

yak¹ *noun*
a large ox-like humped mammal with long hair, found in the mountains of Tibet, and often kept as a work animal.
[Tibetan]

yak² *verb* (**yaks**; **yakking**; **yakked**)
(*informal*) to chatter constantly.
Word Family yak *noun*.

Yale lock *noun*
(*trademark*) a lock with a cylinder mechanism into which a specially grooved key is placed to release the barrel and open the lock.
[after *Linus Yale*, 1821-1868, an American locksmith]

yam *noun*
a tropical edible starchy root.

yang *noun*
one of the two complementary forces in Chinese philosophy, representing the creative, active and positive aspects of the universe. Compare YIN.
[Chinese, male genitals, sun, positive]

yank *verb*
(*informal*) to pull with a sudden jerking motion: *He yanked the bag out of my hands and ran off down the street.*
• **yank** *noun*.

Yank *noun* also **Yankee**
(*informal*) an American, especially one from New England or a northern State.
[either Dutch *Janke* little John, or Amerindian pronunciation of *English*]

yap *verb* (**yaps**; **yapping**; **yapped**)
to bark sharply.
Figurative No one listened as the children *yapped* (= talked noisily or foolishly).
• **yap** *noun*.

yard¹ *noun*
a unit of length equal to 3 feet or about 0·914 m. *abbrev.* yd.

yard² *noun*
1 an enclosed area adjoining a building or surrounded by buildings.
2 an enclosed area used for a specific purpose: *a shipyard*.
3 *American* a garden.

yardarm *noun*
either end of a long cylindrical spar which is attached crosswise to a mast.

yardstick *noun*
any standard of measurement.

yarmulke (yar-mul-ka) *noun* also **yarmulka**
a skullcap worn by Jewish men.

yarn *noun*
1 a thread made by twisting fibres together, used for weaving, knitting, etc.
2 (*informal*) a chat or conversation.
3 (*informal*) a long story, especially about unlikely events.

yashmak *noun*
a veil worn in public by some Muslim women.
[Arabic]

yaw *verb*
Nautical to deviate temporarily from a straight course.

yawl *noun*
Nautical a two-masted yacht with a mizzen mast whose sail extends beyond the stern.

yawn *verb*
to open the mouth involuntarily with a deep intake of breath, usually from drowsiness or boredom.
Figurative The hole yawned before us (= opened wide).
Word Family yawn *noun*; **yawning** *adjective*.

yaws *plural noun*
(*used with singular verb*) an infectious tropical skin disease, resembling syphilis.

Y chromosome ⇨ SEX CHROMOSOME.

ye¹ (yee) *pronoun*
an old word for **you** (singular or plural).

ye² (yee) *article*
an old word for **the**.
[*the* was first written with a *thorn* (þ),
subsequently replaced by *y* and
then by *th*]

yea (yay) *adverb*
an old word for **yes**.

yeah (yair) *interjection*
(*informal*) yes.

year *noun*
1 a period of 365¼ days, the period during
which the earth makes one revolution
around the sun.
2 a period of twelve months on the
Gregorian calendar.
3 any period of twelve months, e.g. from
March to March.
4 *Astronomy* the period during which any
planet makes one revolution round the
sun.
5 all or part of a twelve-month period
devoted to a specific purpose: *the academic
year*.
6 a set of students in the same class or at
the same level of study: *She's in the year
above me.*
7 (**years**) age, especially old age: *Out of
respect for his years, we stood up.*
8 (**years**) (*informal*) a long time: *I've
waited years for this!*
calendar year 1 a year of 365 days
starting on 1 January and ending on
31 December. 2 a leap year.
leap year a year of 366 days, the extra day
being 29 February.
Phrase **year in, year out** occurring
continuously.
Word Family **yearly** *adjective, adverb* 1 of
or occurring once a year or every year.
2 valid for a year: *I travel on a yearly ticket.*

yearbook *noun*
a book issued once a year giving
information about that year, especially
statistics and reports of business and
trade.

yearling *noun*
a horse, cow, etc. that is one year old.

yearn (yern) *verb*
to have a strong desire.
Word Family **yearning** *noun*;
yearningly *adverb*.

yeast *noun*
1 a fungus with one cell which usually
multiplies by budding. Some varieties are

used to produce fermentation when
making beer, etc.
2 a preparation consisting of living yeast
cells, compressed or powdered, used as a
raising agent in baking.
Word Family **yeasty** *adjective* (**yeastier;
yeastiest**).

yell *verb*
to scream with fright, surprise, etc.
• **yell** *noun*.

yellow *noun*
1 a primary colour like that of butter.
2 the colour between orange and green in
the spectrum.
• **yellow** *adjective*
1 of or relating to the colour yellow.
2 (*informal*) cowardly.
• **yellow** *verb* to become yellow, often with
age.
Word Family **yellowish, yellowy**
adjective somewhat yellow.

yellow fever *noun*
an infectious viral disease transmitted by
mosquitoes, causing fever, aching limbs
and jaundice.

Yellow Pages *plural noun*
(*trademark*) a telephone directory which
classifies business subscribers according to
trade, etc.

yellow streak
(*informal*) a certain amount of cowardice.

yelp *verb*
to give a quick sharp cry or bark.
• **yelp** *noun*.

yen¹ *noun* (*plural* **yen**)
the basic unit of money in Japan.

yen² *noun*
(*informal*) a desire or longing: *I have a yen
to visit Mexico.*

yeoman (yo-man) *noun* (*plural* **yeomen**)
1 *History* a farmer who cultivated his own
land.
2 *History* an attendant, especially one in a
royal household.
3 *Navy* a petty officer in the navy who
supervises signalling by flag, semaphore,
etc.
[probably for YOUNG MAN]

Yeoman of the Guard *noun* (*plural*
Yeomen of the Guard) also called
beefeater.
a member of the bodyguard of the royal
household, now with only ceremonial
duties.

yeoman service *noun*
honest hard work.

yes *adverb*
1 used to express assent or affirmation: *Yes, you may go now.*
2 used to emphasize a previous statement: *I went, yes, I really went.*
● **yes** *noun* (*plural* **yeses** or **yesses**)
1 an affirmative reply: *We were pleased that his answer was a firm yes.*
2 a positive vote or voter: *Less than 50 per cent of the referendum votes were yeses.*

yes-man *noun* (*plural* **yes-men**)
(*informal*) a person who always agrees.

yesterday *noun*
1 the day before today: *Yesterday was sunny.*
2 the time recently past: *That's yesterday's news.*
● **yesterday** *adverb* on the day before today: *I did it yesterday.*

yet *adverb*
1 at this time; now: *Don't leave yet, wait a few more minutes.*
2 up to this point in time: *He has not yet left.*
3 in the time remaining; still: *There is yet time to change your decision.*
4 in addition: *Let us try yet again.*
Phrase **as yet** up to the present time.
■ **yet** *conjunction* nevertheless: *He's young, yet very wise.*

yeti (**yet**-ee) *noun* also called **Abominable Snowman**.
a large hairy creature alleged to have been sighted on rare occasions high above the Himalayan snowline.
[Tibetan]

yew *noun*
an exceptionally long-lived evergreen tree, associated with churchyards and the longbow.

yield (yeeld) *verb*
1 to produce or give forth: *The farm yielded a good wheat crop.* □ *The bonds yield ten per cent interest.*
2 to submit: *They yielded to the enemy and lost the battle.* □ *I yielded to their persuasion.*
● **yield** *noun*
1 the act of yielding.
2 the amount yielded.
3 something which is yielded, such as a crop.

yin *noun*
one of the two complementary forces in Chinese philosophy, representing the receptive, passive and negative aspects of the universe. Compare YANG.
[Chinese, feminine, moon, shade]

yippee *interjection*
an exclamation of joy, pleasure, etc.

ylang-ylang (ee-lang **ee**-lang) *noun*
a sweet-smelling essential oil obtained from a tropical flower and used in aromatherapy.

yob *noun* also **yobbo**
(*informal*) a young hooligan.
[*boy* spelt backwards]

yodel (**yo**-d'l) *noun*
1 a style of singing, partly falsetto, popular in the Austrian and Swiss mountains.
2 a song sung in this style.
Word Family **yodel** *verb* (**yodels; yodelling; yodelled**); **yodeller** *noun*.
[from German]

yoga (**yo**-ga) *noun*
any of the forms of mental, physical or moral discipline practised in Indian religion to achieve spiritual union with the Absolute.
hatha yoga the form of yoga taught in the West, primarily concerned with physical well-being and peace of mind.
[Sanskrit, union]

yogi (**yo**-gee) *noun*
a person practising or teaching yoga.

yogurt (**yo**-gert *or* **yogg**-ert) *noun* also **yoghurt; yoghourt**
a thick liquid made from fermented milk.
[Turkish]

yoke *noun*
1 a crossbar with two U-shaped pieces which are placed around the necks of a pair of horses, oxen, etc.
2 a pair of animals joined by such a device.
3 something resembling a yoke, such as a frame worn over the shoulders to carry buckets, etc.
Figurative *The slaves finally threw off their yoke of bondage* (= burden).
4 a shaped part of a garment, usually below the neck, from which the rest of the garment hangs.
● **yoke** *verb*.

yokel (**yo**-k'l) *noun*
a country bumpkin.

yolk (yoke) *noun*
the yellow centre of an egg.

Yom Kippur (yom **kip**-er *or* yom kip-**oor**)
noun
Judaism the Day of Atonement, a fast day
occurring on the tenth day after Rosh
Hashana.
[Hebrew]

yomp *verb*
(*informal*) (of a soldier) to march over
rough ground with a lot of equipment.

yon *adjective, adverb*
a poetic word for **yonder**.

yonder *adjective*
an old word meaning 'being at an
indicated distance, usually within sight':
yonder fields.
• **yonder** *adverb* an old word meaning
'over there'.

yonks *plural noun*
(*informal*) a long time: *I haven't been to the
cinema for yonks*.

yore *noun*
Phrase **of yore** of long ago: *in days of
yore*.

York *noun*
the royal house in England from 1461 to
1485.

yorker *noun*
Cricket a bowled ball which pitches
underneath the batsman's bat.
[introduced by *Yorkshire* bowlers]

Yorkshire pudding *noun*
baked batter traditionally eaten with roast
beef.

you (yoo) *pronoun*
1 the second person singular or plural
nominative pronoun, used to indicate the
person or persons addressed by the
speaker: *You have dropped your pen*.
2 the second person singular or plural
objective pronoun: *I gave you the book*.
□ *I gave the book to you*. ⇨ YOUR; YOURS.
Figurative That dress simply isn't you
(= suitable for or typical of).
3 one: *You would think the government could
do better than that*.
Word Family **you'd** *contraction* a short
form of **you had** or **you would**; **you'll**
contraction a short form of **you will**;
you're *contraction* a short form of **you
are**; **you've** *contraction* a short form of
you have.

> [!] ⇨ ONE; YOUR.

young (yung) *adjective*
1 being in the early stage of life or
development: *a young man*. □ *a young
country*.

2 seeming less old or experienced than
most people of one's age: *She has a rather
young attitude*.
• **young** *plural noun*
1 young people: *The young have all their
lives before them*.
2 (of animals) offspring: *a bird and its
young*.
Phrase **with young** (of animals)
pregnant.

young offender *noun*
Law a person aged 14 to 17 who has
committed a crime.

youngster (yung-sta) *noun*
a child or young person.

your (yor) *possessive adjective*
1 belonging to you: *It is your book*.
2 (*informal*) used to indicate all members
of a group: *Your typical shop assistant does
not earn much*.

> [!] Do not confuse *your* with *you're*, a
> short form of *you are*, as in *You're
> my best friend*.

yours *possessive pronoun*
belonging to you: *The book is yours*.

> [!] Note that there is no apostrophe
> in *yours*.

yourself *pronoun* (*plural* **yourselves**)
1 the reflexive form of **you**: *You've cut
yourself*. □ *Give yourselves a treat!*
2 the emphatic form of **you**: *You did it
yourself*.
3 your normal or usual self: *For many weeks
after the accident you were not yourself*.

youth (yooth) *noun*
1 the condition or quality of being young.
2 an early stage of development or
existence.
3 young people considered as a group: *the
youth of today*.
4 a young person, especially a male.
Word Family **youthful** *adjective*;
youthfully *adverb*; **youthfulness** *noun*.

youth club *noun*
a place where young people can meet and
socialize.

youth hostel *noun*
a place that provides cheap rooms for
young people who are travelling around a
country.

yowl *verb*
to howl or wail.
• **yowl** *noun*.

yo-yo *verb* (**yo-yoes**; **yo-yoing**; **yo-yoed**)
1 to move rapidly up and down.
2 to fluctuate frequently or be very
unsettled.

Yo-yo (yo-yo) *noun*
(*trademark*) a round toy containing string round its grooved centre, so that it spins up and down as the string winds and unwinds.

yuck *interjection* also **yuk**
(*informal*) used to express disgust.

yule *noun* also **Yuletide**
an old word for **Christmas**.

yummy *adjective* (**yummier; yummiest**)
(*informal*) delicious or delightful: *a yummy chocolate cake.*

yuppie *noun* also **yuppy** (*plural* **yuppies**)
(*informal*) a young ambitious and successful person.
[Y(oung) + U(rban) (or (U)pwardly mobile) + P(rofessional)]

Zz

zakat (za-**kaht**) *noun* also **zakah** (za-**kah**)
Islam an obligatory requirement to give a portion of one's wealth annually for charitable and other purposes.
[Arabic, almsgiving]

zany (**zay**-nee) *adjective* (**zanier**; **zaniest**)
clownish or comical.
[Italian *Gianni* John]

zap *verb* (**zaps**; **zapping**; **zapped**)
1 (*informal*) to hit or shoot.
2 (*informal*) to do or make quickly.
3 (*informal*) to change television channels rapidly by remote control.
● **zap** *noun*.

zeal *noun*
eagerness or enthusiasm.
Word Family **zealous** (**zell**-us) *adjective* eager or enthusiastic; **zealously** *adverb*; **zealousness** *noun*; **zealot** (**zell**-ot) *noun* 1 an eager or enthusiastic person. 2 a fanatic.
[from Greek]

zebra *noun*
an African mammal resembling a donkey with black-and-white stripes.
[Congolese]

zebra crossing *noun*
a pedestrian crossing marked by broad white stripes.

zebu (**zee**-boo) *noun* also called **Brahmin**.
an ox-like Asian or African mammal with a hump on its shoulders, sometimes kept as a work animal.
[French]

Zen *noun*
a form of Buddhism based on exclusive reliance on individual intuition as a means to sudden enlightenment, rejecting metaphysical speculation.
[Japanese]

zenith (**zenn**-ith) *noun*
Astronomy the highest point on the celestial sphere, being vertically above the observer and opposite the nadir.

Figurative Becoming manager was the zenith of her career (= culmination, highest point).
[Arabic]

zephyr (**zeff**-a) *noun*
a poetic word for a gentle breeze.
[Greek *zephyros* the west wind]

Zeppelin (**zep**-'l-in) *noun*
History an airship.
[after *Count Ferdinand von Zeppelin*, 1838-1917, a German general and aeronautical engineer]

zero (**zeer**-o) *noun*
1 a cardinal number, the symbol 0 in the Arabic system, but not represented in the Roman system.
2 the point on an instrument such as a thermometer, between the positive and the negative values.
Figurative After Christmas, my bank balance was zero (= nil).
● **zero** *verb* (**zeroes**; **zeroing**; **zeroed**)
Phrase **zero in** to approach a target, etc. accurately.
[Arabic]

zero hour *noun*
the time set for any planned move or activity to begin.

zero tolerance *noun*
strict enforcement of the law; especially on such crimes as drug offences and domestic violence.

zest *noun*
1 any great enjoyment or gusto: *She approached the task with zest.*
2 something which adds extra taste or enjoyment: *The wine gave zest to the meal.*
3 a piece of citrus rind used as a flavouring.
Word Family **zestful** *adjective*; **zestfully** *adverb*; **zestfulness** *noun*.
[French *zeste* orange peel]

zidovudine (zid-**ovv**-yoo-den) *noun*
Medicine an antiviral drug used to treat people with HIV.

zigzag *noun*
a line or path which turns sharply right and left.
● **zigzag** *verb* (**zigzags**; **zigzagging**; **zigzagged**) to move in a zigzag.
Word Family **zigzag** *adjective*, *adverb*.

zilch *noun*
(*informal, especially American*) nothing.

zillion (**zill**-y'n) *noun*
(*informal*) a very large but unspecified number: *zillions of pounds.*

Zimmer *noun* also **Zimmer frame**
(*trademark*) a walking frame for elderly or
infirm people.

zinc (zink) *noun*
a metal used in alloys, especially brass,
and as a protective coating.
[German]

zing *noun*
(*informal*) vitality or enthusiasm.

zinnia *noun*
any of a group of annual garden plants
with brightly coloured flowers.
[after *J. Zinn*, 1727-1759, a German
botanist]

Zionist (zye-on-ist) *noun*
a member of a movement originally aimed
at re-establishing a Jewish state in
Palestine (then Turkish) and now
concerned with the development of Israel.
Word Family **Zionism** *noun*.
[after *Zion*, a hill in Jerusalem on which
Solomon's Temple was built]

zip *noun*
1 a long narrow fastener consisting of two
rows of interlocking teeth which can be
joined or separated by a small bar pulled
between them.
2 (*informal*) energy or liveliness.
• **zip** *verb* (**zips; zipping; zipped**)
1 to fasten with a zip.
2 to move quickly or energetically.
Word Family **zippy** *adjective* (**zippier;
zippiest**) lively or energetic.

zip code *noun*
American a postcode.

zipper *noun*
(*especially American*) a zip.

zircon (zer-k'n) *noun*
a hard mineral of zirconium, used in
industry and as a gem.
[Greek]

zirconium (zer-ko-nee-um) *noun*
a hard silver-coloured metal which is very
resistant to corrosion.
[Latin]

zither (*zith*-a) *noun*
a flat musical instrument with many
strings, usually placed on a horizontal
surface to be played.
[from Greek]

zloty (zlott-ee) *noun* (*plural* **zloty** or **zlotys**
or **zloties**)
the basic unit of money in Poland.

zodiac (zo-dee-ak) *noun*
1 *Astrology* a part of the heavens forming
an imaginary band, extending about 8° on
either side of the sun's apparent path and
containing the path of the main planets. It

is divided into twelve parts (each called a
house) and each is given the name of a
particular group of stars.
2 *Astrology* a circular diagram of this.
[Greek *zoidion* a sculpture of an animal]

zombie *noun*
1 a dead body supposed to be brought to
life by witchcraft.
2 (*informal*) a person who lacks animation,
intelligence, independent ideas, etc.
[Bantu *Zombi* a West African snake god]

zone *noun*
any area distinguished in some way from
other areas: *a military zone.* □ *a residential
zone.* □ *the geographical zones of the earth.*
• **zone** *verb* to divide into zones.
Word Family **zonal** *adjective*.
[Greek *zoné* a girdle]

zonked *adjective*
(*informal*) drunk or drugged.

zoo *noun*
an area in which many types of live
animals are kept and exhibited to the
public.
[short form of *zoological gardens*]

zoology (zoo-**oll**-a-jee *or* zo-**oll**-a-jee)
noun
the study of animals.
Word Family **zoologist** *noun*; **zoological**
(zoo-a-**lojj**-i-k'l *or* zo-a-**lojj**-i-k'l) *adjective*;
zoologically, *adverb*.
[Greek *zoion* an animal + -*logy*]

zoom *verb*
1 to move quickly and sharply: *The aircraft
zoomed into the clouds.*
2 *Photography* to make the subject being
filmed appear to come closer or move
away by using a zoom lens.
• **zoom** *noun*.

zoom lens *noun* (*plural* **zoom lenses**)
a camera lens which can continuously
change the size of an image and still
remain in focus.

zoomorphic (zoo-a-**morf**-ik *or* zo-a-
morf-ik) *adjective*
using animal forms or shapes, e.g. in a
design.
Word Family **zoomorphism** *noun*.

zounds (zowndz) *interjection*
an old word used as an exclamation of
surprise, anger, etc.
[shortening of *God's wounds*]

zucchini (zoo-kee-nee) *noun* (*plural*
zucchini or **zucchinis**)
(*especially American*) a courgette.
[Italian, little gourds]

REFERENCE SECTION

CONTENTS

REFERENCE SECTION

CONTENTS

Abbreviations and Acronyms

A ampere(s)
AA 1. Alcoholics Anonymous
2. Automobile Association
A & E accident and emergency
abbrev. abbreviated; abbreviation
ABTA Association of British Travel Agents (acronym)
AC alternating current
a/c account
.ac.uk UK academic institution (in Internet address)
A.D. in the year of the Lord (Latin, Anno Domini), used in dates
ADP automatic data processing
ADSL asymmetric digital subscriber line
AGM annual general meeting
AH in the year of the Hegira (Latin, anno Hegirae), used in the Muslim system of dating years, numbered from the occurrence of the Hegira
AI 1. Amnesty International
2. artificial insemination 3. artificial intelligence
AID artificial insemination by donor
Aids acquired immune deficiency syndrome (acronym)
AIH artificial insemination by husband
aka also known as
A level advanced level (examination)
AM amplitude modulation
a.m. before noon (Latin, ante meridiem)
amp 1. ampere(s) 2. (*informal*) amplifier
ANC African National Congress
anon. anonymous
AOB any other business
AOR adult-oriented rock
APEX Advance Purchase Excursion (acronym)
approx. approximate
APR annualized percentage rate
APS Advanced Photo System
APT advanced passenger train
asap as soon as possible
ASCII American Standard Code for Information Interchange (acronym)
ASDL asymmetric digital subscriber line
AS level advanced subsidiary level (examination)
ASSR Autonomous Soviet Socialist Republic
ATB all-terrain bike
ATC Air Traffic Control
ATM automated teller machine
ATV all-terrain vehicle
AV Authorized Version (of the Bible)
AWOL absent without leave (acronym)

BA 1. Bachelor of Arts 2. British Airways
BAFTA British Association of Film and Television Arts (acronym)
B & B bed and breakfast
Bart. baronet
BASIC Beginners' All-purpose Symbolic Instruction Code (acronym), computing language program using common English terms
BB 1. Boys' Brigade 2. (of pencils) double black
BBC British Broadcasting Corporation
B.C. before Christ, used in dates
BCG Bacillus Calmette-Guérin, antituberculosis vaccine
BD Bachelor of Divinity
BDS Bachelor of Dental Surgery
BEd Bachelor of Education
b.f. brought forward
bhp brake horsepower
BLT bacon, lettuce and tomato
BM British Museum
BMA British Medical Association
BMX bicycle motocross
BO (*informal*) body odour
BP 1. blood pressure 2. British Pharmacopoeia
bp boiling point
B.Sc. Bachelor of Science
BSE bovine spongiform encephalopathy
BSI British Standards Institution
BST British Summer Time
BT British Telecommunications
B2B business to business
B2C business to consumer
bu bushel

C 1. Celsius 2. Centigrade 3. 100 (Roman numeral) 4. coulomb
c about (Latin, circa)
CA chartered accountant
ca about (Latin, circa)
CAB Citizens' Advice Bureau
CAD computer-aided design
CADCAM computer-aided design, computer-aided manufacturing
CAL computer-aided/assisted learning
Cal large calorie
cal small calorie
CAM computer-aided manufacturing
CAP Common Agricultural Policy
CAT scanner ⇨ **CT scanner**
CB 1. Citizens' Band 2. Companion (of the Order) of the Bath
CBE Commander (of the Order) of the British Empire
CBI Confederation of British Industry

cc 1. carbon copy/copies 2. cubic centimetre(s)
CCP critical control point
CCTV closed-circuit television
CD 1. compact disc 2. diplomatic corps (French, *corps diplomatique*)
cd candela
CDI compact disc interactive
CD-ROM compact disc read-only memory
CDT craft, design, technology
cf. compare (Latin, *confer*)
c.f. carried forward
CFC chlorofluorocarbon
CFE College of Further Education
cgs centimetre-gram-second
CH Companion of Honour
ChB Bachelor of Surgery (Latin, *Chirurgiae Baccalaureus*)
CIA Central Intelligence Agency
CID Criminal Investigation Department
CIM computer-integrated manufacture
CIS Commonwealth of Independent States
CJD Creutzfeldt-Jakob disease
cl centilitre(s)
cm centimetre(s)
CND Campaign for Nuclear Disarmament
CO Commanding Officer
Co. Company
c/o care of
COBOL COmmon Business Oriented Language
COD cash on delivery
C of E Church of England
.com commercial organization (in Internet address)
cont. continued
cos cosine
cosec cosecant
cot cotangent
.co.uk UK commercial organization (in Internet address)
CPU central processing unit
CRT cathode ray tube
CSE Certificate of Secondary Education
CTC City Technology College
CT scanner computerized tomography scanner
CV curriculum vitae
cwt. hundredweight

D 500 (Roman numeral)
DA 1. Diploma in Art 2. District Attorney
DAT digital audio tape
DATV digitally assisted television
dB decibel(s)
DBE Dame Commander (of the Order) of the British Empire
DBS direct broadcasting satellite
DC direct current

DCM Distinguished Conduct Medal
DD Doctor of Divinity
DDT dichlorodiphenyltrichloroethane (insecticide)
DE Department of Employment
DF Defender of the Faith
DFC Distinguished Flying Cross
DFE Department for Education
DfEE Department for Education and Employment
DFM Distinguished Flying Medal
DG 1. by the grace of God (Latin, *Dei gratia*) 2. thanks be to God (Latin, *Deo gratias*)
DipEd Diploma in Education
DIY do-it-yourself
DJ 1. dinner jacket 2. disc jockey
DMA direct memory access
DNA deoxyribonucleic acid
DOA dead on arrival
DOE Department of the Environment
DoH Department of Health
DOS disk operating system (acronym)
DoT Department of Transport
DP data processing
DPhil Doctor of Philosophy
DPP Director of Public Prosecutions
Dr Doctor
DSM Distinguished Medal
DSS Department of Social Security
DTI Department of Trade and Industry
DTP desktop publishing
DTs delirium tremens
DV God willing (Latin, *Deo volente*)
DVD 1. digital versatile disk 2. digital video disc

E 1. East 2. electronic 3. Ecstasy
ECG electrocardiogram/electrocardiograph
ECT electroconvulsive therapy
EDP electronic data processing
EEG electroencephalogram/electroencephalograph
EFL English as a Foreign Language
EFTA European Free Trade Association (acronym)
EFTPOS electronic funds transfer at point of sale (acronym)
e.g. for example (Latin, *exempli gratia*)
ELT English Language Teaching
EMF 1. electromotive force 2. European Monetary Fund
EMS European Monetary System
EMU European Monetary Union
ENT ear, nose and throat
EPNS electroplated nickel silver
ER Queen Elizabeth (Latin, *Elizabeth Regina*)
ERM Exchange Rate Mechanism

Ernie electronic random number indicator equipment (acronym for equipment used in selecting winning premium bonds)
ESL English as a Second Language
ESP extrasensory perception
Esq. Esquire
ET extraterrestrial
ETA estimated time of arrival
etc. et cetera
EU European Union

F Fahrenheit
FA Football Association
FAQ frequently asked question
FBI Federal Bureau of Investigation
FCO Foreign and Commonwealth Office
FE further education
FIFA (French) Fédération Internationale de Football Association (acronym for the governing body of international soccer)
FM frequency modulation
FO Foreign Office
FoE Friends of the Earth
fp freezing point
FPA Family Planning Association
FRCP Fellow of the Royal College of Physicians
FRCS Fellow of the Royal College of Surgeons
FRCVS Fellow of the Royal College of Veterinary Surgeons
FRS Fellow of the Royal Society
ft foot/feet
FT Index Financial Times Index

G constant of gravitation
g 1. acceleration due to gravity 2. gram(s)
gal. gallon(s)
GATT General Agreement on Tariffs and Trade (acronym)
GB 1. Great Britain 2. Girls' Brigade
Gb/GB gigabyte(s)
GBH grievous bodily harm
GC George Cross
GCE General Certificate of Education
GCSE General Certificate of Secondary Education
GDP gross domestic product
GHQ general headquarters
GI soldier in the US army (Government Issue)
GIGO garbage in, garbage out
GM 1. genetically modified 2. George Medal
GMC General Medical Council
GMT Greenwich Mean Time
GNB Good News Bible
GNP gross national product

GNVQ General National Vocational Qualification
GOC General Officer Commanding
.gov.uk UK government (in Internet address)
GP general practitioner
GPO General Post Office
GPS global positioning system
GT (Italian) gran turismo, a high-performance hard-roofed sports car

H (of pencils) hard
ha hectare(s)
HACCP hazard analysis and critical control point
HDTV high-density television
HEP hydroelectric power
HF high frequency
HIV human immunodeficiency virus
HM Her/His Majesty
HMG Her/His Majesty's Government
HMI Her/His Majesty's Inspector
HMS Her/His Majesty's Ship
HMSO Her/His Majesty's Stationery Office
HNC Higher National Certificate
HND Higher National Diploma
HO head office
HP hire purchase
hp horsepower
HQ headquarters
HR human resources
hr hour(s)
HRH Her/His Royal Highness
HRT hormone replacement therapy
HST high-speed train
HTML hypertext markup language
HTTP hypertext transfer protocol
Hz hertz

I 1 (Roman numeral)
IAP Internet Access Provider
IATA International Air Transport Association (acronym)
IBA Independent Broadcasting Authority
ibid. in the same place (Latin, ibidem)
ICBM intercontinental ballistic missile
ICI Imperial Chemical Industries
ICT information and communications technology
ICU intensive care unit
ID identification
i.e. that is (Latin, id est)
IHS Jesus (first three letters of the name in Greek)
IMF International Monetary Fund
in. inch(es)
info (*informal*) information

INRI Jesus of Nazareth, King of the Jews (Latin, Iesus Nazarenus Rex Iudaeorum)
I/O input/output
IOC International Olympic Committee
IOU I owe you
IP Internet Protocol
IPA International Phonetic Alphabet
IQ intelligence quotient
IRA Irish Republican Army
ISA Individual Savings Account (acronym)
ISBN International Standard Book Number
ISDN Integrated Services Digital Network
ISP Internet Service Provider
IT information technology
ITA Initial Teaching Alphabet
ITN Independent Television News
ITV Independent Television
IUD intra-uterine device
IV intravenous
IVF in vitro fertilization

J joule(s)
JC Jesus Christ
JCB a type of construction machine (from the initials of Joseph Cyril Bamford, the manufacturer; trademark)
JFK John Fitzgerald Kennedy, US president (1961-1963)
JP Justice of the Peace
JPEG Joint Photographic Experts Group

K 1. 1000 2. kelvin(s)
Kb/KB kilobyte(s)
KBE Knight (Commander of the Order) of the British Empire
kcal kilocalorie(s)
KCB Knight Commander (of the Order) of the Bath
KG Knight (of the Order) of the Garter
kg kilogram(s)
KGB Soviet secret police (Russian, Komitet Gosudarstvennoi Bezopasnosti = State Security Committee)
kHz kilohertz
kJ kilojoule(s)
km kilometre(s)
KO knockout
kph kilometres per hour
KT Knight of the (Order of the) Thistle
kW kilowatt
kWh kilowatt-hour(s)

L 1. 50 (Roman numeral) 2. learner driver
l litre(s)
LAN local area network
lat. latitude
lb pound(s) (Latin, libra)
LBO leveraged buyout

lbw leg before wicket
lc lower case
LCD liquid crystal display
LEA Local Education Authority
LED light-emitting diode
LEDC less economically developed country
LF low frequency
LGV large goods vehicle
l.h. left hand
LLB Bachelor of Laws
loc. cit. in the place mentioned (Latin, loco citato)
long. longitude
LP long-playing (gramophone record)
LPG liquid petroleum gas
LRP lead replacement petrol
LSD lysergic acid diethylamide
LSE London School of Economics
Ltd Limited
LV luncheon voucher
LW long wave

M 1. 1000 (Roman numeral) 2. motorway
m metre(s)
MA Master of Arts
MB Bachelor of Medicine
Mb/MB megabyte(s)
MBE Member (of the Order) of the British Empire
MC Master of Ceremonies
MCC Marylebone Cricket Club
MCP male chauvinist pig
MD managing director
MDMA methylenedioxymethamphetamine (the drug Ecstasy)
ME myalgic encephalomyelitis
MEd Master of Education
Med Mediterranean
MEDC more economically developed country
MEP Member of the European Parliament
Messrs plural of Mr (French, Messieurs)
Met 1. meteorological 2. metropolitan
MF medium frequency
mg milligram(s)
MHz megahertz
MI5 Military Intelligence, Section 5
min. minute(s)
MIRV multiple independently targeted re-entry vehicle (acronym)
misc. miscellaneous
ml millilitre(s)
MLR minimum lending rate
MM Military Medal
mm millimetre(s)
MMR measles, mumps and rubella (combined vaccine against these)
MO 1. Medical Officer 2. modus operandi

MOD Ministry of Defence
mod cons (*informal*) modern conveniences
MOH Medical Officer of Health
mol mole
MOR middle-of-the-road (of music)
MORI Market and Opinion Research Institute (acronym)
MOT Ministry of Transport, now Department of Transport
MP 1. Member of Parliament 2. Military Police
MPEG Motion Pictures Experts Group
mph miles per hour
MP3 Motion Picture Experts Group 1, Audio Layer 3
MPV multi-purpose vehicle
Mr Mister
MRC Medical Research Council
Mrs title used before the name of a married woman (Mistress)
MS 1. manuscript 2. multiple sclerosis
Ms title substituted for Miss or Mrs
MSc Master of Science
MSG monosodium glutamate
MSP Member of the Scottish Parliament
Mt Mount
MV 1. megavolt(s) 2. motor vessel
MW 1. medium wave 2. megawatt(s)

N 1. North 2. newton
n/a 1. not applicable 2. not available
NAAFI Navy, Army and Air Force Institutes (acronym)
NASA National Aeronautics and Space Administration (acronym)
NATO North Atlantic Treaty Organization (acronym)
NB note well (Latin, nota bene)
NCO non-commissioned officer
NE north-east
NEB New English Bible
NEC National Executive Committee
NGO non-governmental organization
NHS National Health Service
NI National Insurance
NIC newly industrialized country
Nicam/NICAM near instantaneous companded audio multiplex (a technique for coding audio signals into digital form) (acronym)
Nimby not in my back yard (acronym)
NIV New International Version (of the Bible)
nm nanometre(s)
NMR nuclear magnetic resonance
No. number
np new paragraph
NSB National Savings Bank

NSPCC National Society for the Prevention of Cruelty to Children
NT 1. National Trust 2. New Testament
NTP normal temperature and pressure
NVQ National Vocational Qualification
NW north-west

OAP old-age pensioner
OAU Organization of African Unity
OBE Officer (of the Order) of the British Empire
obs. obsolete
OC Officer Commanding
OD overdose
OECD Organization for Economic Co-operation and Development
OED Oxford English Dictionary
OFT Office of Fair Trading
OHMS On Her/His Majesty's Service
OHP overhead projector
O level ordinary level (examination)
OM Order of Merit
o.n.o. or nearest offer
OP organophosphate
op. 1. operation 2. opus
o.p. out of print
OPEC Organization of Petroleum-Exporting Countries (acronym)
OR 1. operational research 2. other ranks
OS 1. Ordnance Survey 2. out of stock 3. outsize
OT Old Testament
OTC Officers' Training Corps
OTT (*informal*) over the top
OXFAM Oxford Committee for Famine Relief (acronym)
Oz (*informal*) Australia
oz ounce(s)

P parking
p 1. page 2. penny/pence
PA 1. personal assistant 2. public address 3. Press Association
Pa pascal
p.a. per year (Latin, per annum)
p. & p. postage and packing
para. paragraph
PAYE pay as you earn
PC 1. personal computer 2. police constable 3. politically correct
p.c. 1. per cent 2. postcard
pdq (*informal*) pretty damn quick
PDSA People's Dispensary for Sick Animals
PE physical education
PER Professional Employment Register
PFI private finance initiative
PG parental guidance
PGA Professional Golfers' Association

pH potential of hydrogen, a measure of acidity/alkalinity

PhD Doctor of Philosophy

PIN personal identification number (acronym)

plc public limited company

PM 1. post-mortem 2. Prime Minister

p.m. after noon (Latin, post meridiem)

PMS premenstrual syndrome

PMT premenstrual tension

PO 1. postal order 2. Post Office

POP Point of Presence

POS point of sale

POW prisoner of war

pp on behalf of (Latin, per procurationem)

PPE philosophy, politics and economics

PPS 1. Parliamentary Private Secretary 2. a second postscript

PR 1. proportional representation 2. public relations

PS 1. postscript 2. Private Secretary

Ps psalm

PSBR public sector borrowing requirement

PSHE personal, social and health education

PSV public service vehicle

pt pint

PTA parent-teacher association

Pte Private

PTO please turn over

PVA polyvinyl acetate

PVC polyvinyl chloride

PVS 1. persistent vegetative state 2. postviral syndrome

PW policewoman

QB Queen's Bench

QC Queen's Counsel

QED which was to be shown or proved (Latin, quod erat demonstrandum)

qt quart(s)

quango quasi-autonomous non-governmental organization (acronym)

qv see (Latin, quod vide)

R 1. Queen/King (Latin, Rex/Regina) 2. River

RA Royal Academy

RAC Royal Automobile Club

RADA Royal Academy of Dramatic Art (acronym)

RAF Royal Air Force

RAM random-access memory (acronym)

R & D research and development

RC 1. Red Cross 2. Roman Catholic

RCM Royal College of Music

RCN Royal College of Nursing

RCP Royal College of Physicians

RCS 1. Royal College of Science 2. Royal College of Surgeons

RD refer to drawer

RE religious education

ref. reference

regt regiment

REM rapid eye movement

rep 1. repertory 2. representative

ret. retired

Rev./Revd Reverend

rev. revolution

r.f. radio frequency

RGN Registered General Nurse

RGS Royal Geographical Society

r.h. right hand

Rh factor rhesus factor

RIBA Royal Institute of Architects

RIP rest in peace (Latin, requiescat in pace)

RMA Royal Military Academy

RN Royal Navy

RNA ribonucleic acid

RNIB Royal National Institute for the Blind

RNLI Royal National Lifeboat Institution

ROM read-only memory (acronym)

RP received pronunciation

RPI retail price index

rpm revolutions per minute

RRP recommended retail price

RSA Royal Scottish Academy

RSM Regimental Sergeant Major

RSPB Royal Society for the Protection of Birds

RSPCA Royal Society for the Prevention of Cruelty to Animals

RSVP please reply (French, répondez s'il vous plaît)

Rt Hon Right Honourable

Rt Rev Right Reverend

RU Rugby Union

RUC Royal Ulster Constabulary

S South

s second(s)

SA 1. Salvation Army 2. South Africa 3. South America

SAD seasonal affective disorder

sae stamped addressed envelope

SALT Strategic Arms Limitation Talks (acronym)

SAM surface-to-air missile (acronym)

SAS Special Air Service

SAT standard assessment task

SAYE save as you earn

SDI Strategic Defense Initiative

SDP Social Democratic Party

SE south-east

sec 1. second(s) 2. secant

SF science fiction

Sgt Sergeant

SI international system of units (French, Système International)
SIDS sudden infant death syndrome
sin sine
SLR single-lens reflex (of a camera)
SM Sergeant Major
SMG Scottish Media Group
SPQR the senate and people of Rome (Latin, Senatus Populusque Romanus)
Sqn squadron
SRN State Registered Nurse
SS 1. Saints 2. (German) Schutzstaffel, protection squad, a paramilitary organization within the Nazi party 3. steamship
SSM surface-to-surface missile
St Saint
st stone
STD 1. sexually transmitted disease 2. subscriber trunk dialling
stg sterling
STOL short take-off and landing (of aircraft)
STV Scottish Television
SW south-west

t ton(s)
TA Territorial Army
tan tangent
T & E (*informal*) tired and emotional, slightly drunk
TAVR Territorial and Army Volunteer Reserve
TB tuberculosis
TCP trichlorophenylmethyliodisalicyl (trademark)
TCP/IP transmission control protocol/Internet protocol
tech (*informal*) technical college
TEFL teaching (of) English as a foreign language (acronym)
temp temporary worker
TESL teaching (of) English as a second language
TKO technical knockout
TLC tender loving care
TM transcendental meditation
TNT trinitrotoluene, an explosive
TRAM transverse rectus abdominus myocutaneus
TT 1. teetotal 2. Tourist Trophy 3. tuberculin-tested
TUC Trades Union Congress
TV television
TVEI Technical and Vocational Educational Initiative
TVP textured vegetable protein

U universal
UCAS Universities and Colleges Admissions Service (acronym)

UDI unilateral declaration of independence
UEFA Union of European Football Associations (acronym)
UFO unidentified flying object
UGC University Grants Committee
UHF ultra-high frequency
UHT ultra heat treated
UK United Kingdom
UN United Nations
UNESCO United Nations Educational, Scientific and Cultural Association (acronym)
UNICEF United Nations Children's Fund, formerly United Nations International Children's Emergency Fund (acronym)
UP United Press
URL uniform resource locator
US United States
USA United States of America
USSR Union of Soviet Socialist Republics, now CIS
UV ultraviolet

V 1. 5 (Roman numeral) 2. volt(s)
V and A Victoria and Albert Museum
VAT value added tax
VC Victoria Cross
VCR video cassette recorder
VD venereal disease
VDU visual display unit
VE Day Victory in Europe Day, 8 May 1945
VHF very high frequency
VHS video home system
VIP very important person
VJ Day Victory over Japan Day, 15 August 1945
VPL visible panty line
VR virtual reality
VS veterinary surgeon
VSOP very special old pale (brandy)
VTOL vertical take-off and landing (of aircraft)
VTR videotape recorder

W 1. watt 2. West
WAAC Women's Army Auxiliary Corps
WAAF Women's Auxiliary Air Force
WAN wide-area network
WAP wireless application protocol (acronym)
WASP White Anglo-Saxon Protestant (acronym)
WBA World Boxing Association
WBC World Boxing Council
WC water closet
WEA Workers' Educational Association
WHO World Health Organization
WI 1. West Indies 2. Women's Institute

WIMP windows, icons, mice and pull-down menus/pointers (acronym)
WO 1. War Office 2. Warrant Officer
WORM write once; read many (times) (acronym)
WP 1. word processing 2. word processor
WPC woman police constable
wpm words per minute
WRAC Women's Royal Army Corps
WRAF Women's Royal Air Force
WRNS Women's Royal Naval Service
WRVS Women's Royal Voluntary Service
WTO World Trade Organization
WWF 1. Worldwide Fund for Nature 2. World Wrestling Federation

WWW World Wide Web
WYSIWYG what you see is what you get (acronym)

X 10 (Roman numeral)

yd yard(s)
YHA Youth Hostels Association
YMCA Young Men's Christian Association
yr year(s)
YTS Youth Training Scheme
Y2K the year 2000
YWCA Young Women's Christian Association

Grammatical Terms

adjective
Adjectives help to make the meaning of nouns or pronouns fuller or more precise. Adjectives which come before a noun are called **attributive** adjectives: *my new CD; a skilful player*. Adjectives which come after the verb and are used as a complement are **predicative** adjectives: *She is brilliant. The chocolates were delicious*. An adjective can appear as a **comparative** or **superlative**. Some adjectives use **-er** and **-est** endings to express these contrasts: *smaller, smallest*. Others use **more** and **most**: *more beautiful, most beautiful*.

adverb
Adverbs help to make the meanings of verbs, adjectives or other adverbs fuller or more precise. Adverbs generally answer the questions: when, why, where, how?: *I saw her yesterday; I saw her there; I saw her briefly*. Adverbs formed from adjectives are often formed by adding the suffix *-ly*. An adverb phrase can be one or more adverbs: *He spoke really quietly*. Some adverb phrases contain no adverbs. They just work as an adverb in the sentence: *I lost my purse at the bowling alley; I lost my purse this afternoon*. These types of construction are called **adverbials**.
See also **adverbial**.

adverbial
Adverbials provide information about other parts of a sentence. Adverbials generally answer the questions: where, when, how, why?: *My Gran lives in a flat; I go there often; I go by train; I go because she tells me funny stories*. There are various types of adverbial, e.g. 1. adverb phrase: *She ran very fast*. 2. prepositional phrase: *We sat in the garden*. 3. some nouns and noun phrases: *Jack came to see me this morning*. 4. a subordinate clause: *I jumped when the phone rang*.

article
An article, which is a type of **determiner**, is a word used before nouns or noun phrases. The **definite article**, *the*, specifies a particular person or thing: *the gym; the head teacher*. The **indefinite articles**, *a* and *an*, do not specify a particular person or thing: *a footballer; an exciting film. A* is used before a consonant, and *an* before a vowel or a silent *h*: *a house; an apple; an hour*.

Some people use *an* before an *h* which is not silent, but this is considered old-fashioned: *an hotel*.
See also **determiner**.

clause
A clause is a group of words which makes sense and normally contains a verb: *I gave the dress to Louise*. Sentences may contain one or more clauses: *Ryan plays football/but his brother plays rugby. I don't understand/why you said that*. In complex sentences the **main clause** is the clause which could stand as a sentence on its own: *She left home when she was sixteen*. Subordinate clauses cannot stand alone and make sense. They depend on the main clause to complete their meaning: *I know what he said; They arrived before she left; He can go if he likes*. A **relative clause** is a type of subordinate clause which begins with a relative pronoun and which gives more information about a noun in the main clause. There are two types of relative clauses: **restrictive** and **non-restrictive**. A restrictive clause gives information which is essential in pinpointing the noun it relates to, and is not separated from the main clause by a comma or commas: *Professional footballers who play for top clubs earn lots of money*. A non-restrictive clause gives additional information about the noun it relates to without restricting its meaning and is separated from the main clause by a comma or commas: *Professional footballers, who have short careers, should prepare for the future*.
See also **pronoun** and **sentence**.

complement
The complement adds to the meaning of another clause element – either the subject (the **subject complement**) or the object (the **object complement**). The subject complement usually follows the subject and verb: *He is a teacher*. The object complement usually follows the direct object: *He made me happy*. A complement can be: 1. a noun phrase: *She is an engineer*. 2. an adjective phrase: *The sky was bright blue*. 3. a pronoun: *Where is that?* 4. a subordinate clause: *That is what I said*.

conjunction
Conjunctions are words which join other words, phrases and clauses together. There

are two types: **co-ordinating conjunctions** and **subordinating conjunctions**. Co-ordinating conjunctions link words, phrases or clauses of equal status: *bread **and** butter; She lives in London **but** she was born in Liverpool.* Subordinating conjunctions link subordinate or dependent clauses to the main clause of a sentence: *They enjoyed the picnic **although** it was raining; She left **before** the end of the concert.*

determiner

A determiner is a word used before a noun or noun phrase to tell you something about it. Determiners include: **definite** and **indefinite articles**: *the, a, an;* **demonstratives**: *this, that, these, those;* **quantifiers**: *each, every, few, many, some, several.* Demonstratives distinguish between people or things. *This* and *those* are used for someone or something that is closer, and *that* and *those* for someone or something that is further away: *I like **this** picture better than **that** one; **These** books are mine and **those** ones on the table are Najma's.* Quantifiers indicate the number or quantity of people or things: ***every** day of the week; **some** people; **several** times.*
See also **article**.

direct speech

Direct speech refers to the exact words used by a speaker. When reporting direct speech the speaker's words are placed inside speech marks (also known as inverted commas or quotation marks): *'What are you doing?' the teacher asked.* Each new piece of speech should start with a capital letter even if it is not the first word in a sentence: *'Nothing,' the children replied.* Each piece of speech should end with a full stop, question mark, exclamation mark or comma before the speech marks: *'If you don't hurry up,' the teacher said, 'you will be late!'*
See also **indirect speech** and **speech marks**.

exclamation
See **interjection**.

indirect speech

Indirect speech reports what someone has said without using the exact words. It is also known as reported speech. Speech marks (or inverted commas or quotation marks) are not used: *They said that we were going to be late; She replied that we would be there in time.*
See also **direct speech**.

interjection

An interjection is a word or phrase used to express a feeling or reaction such as happiness, pain, admiration or gratitude: *Ouch!; Cool!; Thank you!* Interjections are also known as exclamations.

modifier

A modifier is a word or phrase which affects the meaning of another word or phrase. Modifiers are divided into **premodifiers**, which precede the word modified: *a **green** dress; **beautiful old brick** houses; a **very obviously happy young** man;* and **postmodifiers**, which follow the word modified: *people **of Spanish descent**; miserable **to the point of despair**; the man **in the grey suit**.*

noun

Nouns refer to people, places, things and ideas. Nouns can be divided into different groups: 1. **countable** or **uncountable**. Countable nouns can be counted and so have a plural: *cat, table.* Uncountable nouns cannot be counted and do not have a plural: *information, health.* 2. **concrete** or **abstract**. Concrete nouns refer to things you can touch, taste, hear, see or smell: *table, orange.* Abstract nouns refer to thoughts, feelings and ideas which cannot be touched: *beauty, safety.* 3. **proper** or **common**. Proper nouns are names of people, places, months, days: *Victoria, Tuesday.* Common nouns are all other nouns. A **noun phrase** has a noun which acts at the centre or beginning of the phrase: *Amy is **my sister**. She likes **coffee cake with chocolate icing**.*
See also **phrase**.

object

The object is the person or thing which is affected by the action of a verb. In sentences the object usually comes after the verb: *I love **you**; The neighbours don't like **him**; He decided to vote against **her**.* There are two types of object: **direct object** and **indirect object**. The direct object is the person or thing which is directly affected by the action of the verb: *The boys broke **the window**.* The indirect object refers to the person or thing which receives the action: *She gave **him** the book.*

phrase

A phrase is a single word or group of words which makes sense but not full sense on its own. A phrase does not contain a complete verb and must be seen in relation to the rest of the sentence: *He climbed **over the wall**; The ship was **a very long way off**; She ate **carrot cake**.* Phrases are categorized according to the function of the phrase in a sentence: 1. **noun phrase**: *I like **ice cream**; I like **chocolate and vanilla ice cream with nuts**; Luke is **my brother**.* 2. **verb phrase**: *I like **ice cream**; I **would have liked to eat** all the ice cream.* 3. **adverb phrase**: *She moved **quickly**; He spoke **rather slowly**; He lived in the red house **at the top of the hill**.* 4. **adjective phrase**: *This dress is **pretty**; She was **sad to the point of despair**.*

prefix
A prefix is one or more syllables attached to the beginning of a word to form another word. Common prefixes include: *anti-, auto-, bio-, contra-, dis-, extra-, for-, in-, inter-, mega-, mini-, multi-, non-, out-, post-, re-, super-, trans-, un-, under-*. English prefixes are formed from a variety of source languages including Old English, Old French, Latin and Greek.

preposition
A preposition shows how two parts of a sentence are related to each other: *We ate **in** a restaurant; They climbed **up** the stairs; We walked **across** the field.* **Complex prepositions** contain more than one word: *He lost his job **because of** poor timekeeping; They acted **in accordance with** official instructions.*

pronoun
Pronouns are used in place of nouns and noun phrases. There are various kinds:
1. **personal pronouns**: *I, me, we, us, you, he, she, it, him, her, they, them*: *She is going to a sleepover tonight.* 2. **possessive pronouns**: *my, your, her, their, mine, yours, hers, theirs*: *His car is broken; The red car is **mine**.* 3. **demonstrative pronouns**: *this, that, these, those*: *I chose **that** myself.* 4. **interrogative pronouns**: *who, whom, whose, which, what*: ***Who** is that?; **Which** is yours?* 5. **relative pronouns**: *who, whose, whom, which, that*: *She doesn't like the woman **who** lives next door; That is the boy **whose** father is ill.* 6. **distributive pronouns**: *each, either, both, all, neither*: *We asked her parents but **neither** of them wanted to come.* 7. **reflexive pronouns**: *myself, yourself, itself, ourselves*: *Behave **yourself**!* 8. **indefinite pronouns**: *anyone, everything, everyone, someone, something, no one, nothing*:

Someone has stolen my purse. 9. **reciprocal pronouns**: *each other, one another*: *They grew to hate **each other**.*

sentence
A sentence is a group of words which express a complete meaning. Sentences begin with a capital letter and end with a full stop, question mark or exclamation mark. There are four different kinds of sentence: 1. **statement**: *I've got a new car.* 2. **question**: *Do you like my new car?* 3. **directive**: *Show me your new car!* 4. **exclamation**: *What a great car!* Every full statement sentence contains a subject and a verb: *He loves my new car.* (*He* is the subject and *loves* is the verb.) Sentences can also be divided up according to their structure:
1. **simple sentences** have a single clause: *She bought a new dress.* 2. **compound sentences** have more than one clause linked by *and*, *but* or *or*: *They have sold their house and they are going to live abroad.* 3. **complex sentences** have a main clause and one or more subordinate clauses: *They will have to go by car as there is no train service.*
See also **clause**.

subject
The subject of a sentence or clause tells us what it is about. In statement sentences it usually comes before the verb: *I like chocolate; Alun, Claire and Emma are going to Spain; The old lady is ill; Where you live is important.* In questions the subject comes before, after or in the middle of the verb: *You don't eat meat?; Is she happy?; Are you coming?*

suffix
A suffix is a syllable or group of syllables attached to the end of a word to form another word. Common suffixes include: *-able, -dom, -ee, -ent, -ese, -fold, -free, -friendly, -hood, -ible, -ish, -ism, -itis, -ize/ise, -let, -man, -ness, -ship, -wards, -wise, -woman, -worthy*. English suffixes are formed from a variety of source languages, such as Old English, Old French, Latin and Greek.

tense
Tense refers to the way a verb changes its endings to show the time at which an action takes place. There are two tense forms in English: 1. **present tense**: *We **walk** to school; The world **is** round.* 2. **past tense**: *She **failed** her exam; I **swam** every day.* There is no future tense ending in English. English

expresses future time by a variety of means, e.g. the use of *will* and *shall*: *They will get the results tomorrow*. **Aspect** refers to whether the action of the verb is complete or in progress: **perfective** or **progressive** (or continuous). The perfective aspect is constructed using the auxiliary verb *have*. It occurs in the present: *I have lived in London all my life*. It also occurs in the past: *I was sad that I had never met him*. The progressive aspect uses *be* along with the *-ing* form of the main verb to express an event in progress at a given time: *They are singing*; *They were singing*; *They have been singing*; *They had been singing*.

verb

A verb shows what somebody or something is doing, thinking or feeling or what state they are in: *He ran home*; *They are very happy*. Verbs are usually essential to any sentence. It is difficult to write a full sentence without a verb. Most verbs have these forms: **base** *sing*; **infinitive** *to sing*; **present form** *sings*; **present participle** *singing*; **past form** *sang*; **past participle** *sung*. **Auxiliary verbs** are special verbs which help other verbs to form tenses and voices and to form negatives and questions. Primary auxiliary verbs are *be*, *have* and *do*: *I have been walking*; *I don't want to go home*.

Modal auxiliary verbs are *may*, *might*, *can*, *could*, *shall*, *should*, *will*, *would*, *must*: *We might go to the beach*; *You must come to my party*. Verbs can be divided into various categories, e.g. 1. **transitive** and **intransitive**: Transitives are verbs which have an object: *He sold second-hand clothes*. Intransitives do not have an object. They can stand alone and make sense: *I have been swimming*. 2. **finite** and **non-finite**. Finite verbs have different tenses and change their forms to match the subject of the sentence. *She misses her mother*; *I miss my mother*; *He missed his mother*. Non-finite verbs do not have a subject and have no variation for tense. Most verbs have a non-finite form. *The keys are missing*; *The boy was missing*; *Are you missing me?*

voice

Voice refers to the change in the form of a verb to show whether a person or thing performs the action (**active voice**) or is acted upon (**passive voice**). The active consists of a main verb or verb phrase: *Beckham scored the first goal*; *Ben will write the report*. The passive consists of a form of the verb *be* plus a past participle: *The first goal was scored by Beckham*; *The report will be written by Ben*.

Punctuation

apostrophe
There are two uses for the apostrophe: 1. to show that something belongs to someone, that is, to show possession. When something belongs to just one person the apostrophe is placed before the **s**: *Asif's pen*. If the word is a plural ending in **s** the apostrophe should follow the **s**: *my parents' car*. 2. to show when letters have been missed out: *I'm (I am)*; *We haven't (We have not)*.

brackets
Brackets are also known as parentheses. They are used in pairs to show that the words enclosed are separated off from the rest of the sentence without affecting its structure: *Ms Jakobsson (the music teacher) comes in three days a week.*

capital letters
Capital letters are used for: 1. the first letter in a sentence: *This is fun.* 2. the first letters of names of people, places, days of the week, months of the year and public and religious holidays and festivals: *Laura*; *Christmas*. 3. the pronoun *I*. 4. the first letters of titles of books, films and TV programmes: *Men in Black*; *Brookside*. 5. some abbreviations: *BBC*. 6. trade names: *Nintendo*.

colon
A colon is used 1. to introduce a clause which explains the preceding clause: *I've done something terrible: I've broken the neighbours' window.* 2. to introduce a list: *The ingredients are as follows: chicken, lemon juice, garlic, olive oil and oregano.*

comma
Commas are used to show pauses in sentences and to make our writing easier to read. When lists are used within sentences, they are much easier to read if the items are separated by commas: *He played tennis, cricket, football, rugby and golf when he was younger.* Commas are used to enclose information which doesn't belong to the main part of the sentence: *The car driver, a 22-year-old father of two, escaped unhurt*; *The corner shop, which sells groceries and newspapers, is closed on Wednesday afternoons.* Commas are sometimes used to divide two clauses in a sentence, especially if the first clause introduces the main clause and is rather long: *If the train doesn't arrive within the next hour, we're going to be late.*

dash
Dashes can be used: 1. to show that the words between them are separated off from the rest of the sentence as though they were in brackets: *She introduced her husband – a tall, rather shy-looking man – to her colleagues.* 2. to indicate a change of subject: *I'm making the tea – what was that noise?* 3. to introduce a statement which explains or expands on what has just been said: *The burglars took everything – jewellery, CD player, television, video, PC and a valuable painting.*

ellipsis
An ellipsis is used to show that a word or words are omitted from a statement: *One, two, three... ninety-nine, one hundred.*

exclamation mark
An exclamation mark is used to end a sentence which is an interjection or exclamation: *Be quiet!*

full stop
The main use of a full stop is to end a sentence which is not a question or interjection: *The sun is shining.* Full stops are also used in abbreviations to show that a single letter or a group of letters stand for a word: *S. Park* for *Stephen Park*; *Capt.* for *Captain*. Full stops were at one time used in many abbreviations but they are often now omitted: *BBC*; *Dr*; *Mr*. The full stop is also used in decimals: *6.5 litres*, and in times: *5.40 p.m.*

hyphen
Hyphens are used 1. between the elements of a compound word: *back-up*. 2. to split a word at the end of a line in printed text.

inverted commas
See **speech marks**.

parentheses
See **brackets**.

question mark
A question mark is used to end a sentence which is a question: *Have you done your homework?*

quotation marks
See **speech marks**.

semicolon

Semicolons are used to separate main clauses that are connected in sense or to show pauses in sentences which are longer than those shown by commas: *You couldn't expect it to last very long; it was too cheap.*

speech marks

Speech marks are also known as inverted commas or quotation marks. They are used: 1. to enclose direct speech: *'The shop is closed,' she said.* 2. to enclose a direct quotation from another source: *'full of scorpions is my mind, dear wife'* (*Macbeth*). 3. to enclose titles of articles, chapters in books, single short poems, songs, etc.: *She read Keats' poem 'Ode to a Nightingale'.* In most modern books single speech marks are used. In school you are often taught to use double speech marks. It doesn't matter which you choose as long as you are consistent throughout a single piece of work. If you need to use two sets of speech marks, most people use double within single: *'I want you all to sing "Happy Birthday" when I bring in the cake,' said Beth.* See also **direct speech**.

Prefixes

a- not or without: *asymmetrical*; *anarchy*.

ab- off, from or away from: *abnormal*.

ac- ⇨ AD-.

ad- in the direction of, towards or in addition: *accolade*; *advent*; *affinity*; *aggression*; *allegiance*; *announce*; *approach*; *arrange*; *assault*; *attack*.

aero- aircraft: *aerodrome*.

af- ⇨ AD-.

ag- ⇨ AD-.

al- ⇨ AD-.

ambi- both: *ambidextrous*.

amphi- on both or all sides: *amphitheatre*.

an-¹ ⇨ A-.

an-² ⇨ AD-.

ante- before: *antecedent*.

anthropo- human beings: *anthropology*.

anti- against, opposite or opposed to: *antibiotic*.

ap- ⇨ AD-.

ar- ⇨ AD-.

arch- first or chief: *archbishop*.

as- ⇨ AD-.

astro- stars or outer space: *astrophysics*.

at- ⇨ AD-.

atto- one million million millionth: *attotesla*.

auto- self: *autobiography*.

be- about or all over: *bedraggled*.

bene- well: *beneficial*.

bi- two or twice: *biennial*.

biblio- a book: *bibliography*.

bio- life or living things: *biology*.

by- secondary or incidental: *bypass*.

centi- one hundredth: *centimetre*.

cine- motion: *cinematography*.

circum- movement around or on all sides: *circumnavigate*.

co- together or associated: *cooperate*.

col- ⇨ COM-.

com- with or jointly: *compare*; *collaborate*; *connect*; *corrupt*.

con- ⇨ COM-.

contra- against or opposite: *contraception*.

cor- ⇨ COM-.

counter- opposite or in reply to: *counteract*.

cyber- the Internet or virtual reality: *cybercafé*.

de- 1. the opposite of: *decode*. 2. down: *depress*. 3. away or off: *deport*. 4. completely: *despoil*.

deca- ten: *decahedron*.

deci- one tenth: *decilitre*.

demi- half: *demigod*.

di- two or double: *dilemma*.

dia- 1. through: *diarrhoea*. 2. across: *diagonal*.

dis- 1. not or without: *distrust*. 2. reversal or removal: *discard*. 3. apart: *disintegrate*.

dodeca- twelve: *dodecahedron*.

duo- two: *duologue*.

e- electronic: *email*.

eco- ecology or the environment: *ecosystem*.

electro- electricity: *electromotive*.

em- ⇨ EN-.

en- 1. in or into: *engulf*; *embed*. 2. to make or cause to be: *enable*; *empower*.

endo- internal: *endocrine gland*.

epi- on, to or against: *epicentre*.

equi- equal: *equilibrium*.

Euro- 1. European: *Eurodollar*. 2. European Union: *Euro-sceptic*.

ex- 1. out of or away from: *expel*. 2. thoroughly: *exasperate*. 3. former: *ex-husband*.

extra- outside or beyond: *extraordinary*.

femto- one thousand million millionth: *femtosecond*.

fore- before in time or position: *foresee*.

gastro- stomach: *gastroenteritis*.

geo- the earth: *geology*.

giga- one thousand million: *gigahertz*.

haemo- blood: *haemophilia*.

hecto- one hundred: *hectolitre*.

helio- sun: *heliocentric*.

hemi- half: *hemisphere*.

hepta- seven: *heptagon*.

hetero- other or different: *heterosexual*.

hexa- six: *hexagon*.

homo- the same: *homosexual*.

hydro- water: *hydroelectric*.

hyper- excessively or higher than normal: *hyperactive*.

hypo- under: *hypothermia*.

il- ⇨ IN-².

im- ⇨ IN-².

in-¹ in or into: *include*.

in-² not, lacking or without: *invariable*; *illegal*; *impossible*; *irregular*.

infra- below: *infrastructure*.

inter- 1. between or among: *interbreed*. 2. reciprocally or mutually: *interact*.

intra- within: *intravenous*.

ir- ⇨ IN-².

iso- equal: *isobar*.

kilo- one thousand: *kilometre*.

mal- bad or wrongful: *maltreat*.

matri- mother: *matriarch*.

mega- 1. great: *megastar*. 2. one million: *megatonne*.

meta- 1. altered: *metamorphosis*. 2. behind or after: *metacarpal*.

micro- 1. very small: *microfilm*. 2. one millionth: *microfarad*.

mid- middle: *midway*.

milli- one thousandth: *millimetre*.

mini- small: *minibus*.

mis- mistaken or wrongly: *misunderstand*.

mono- one or single: *monosyllable*.

multi- many: *multistorey*.

nano- one thousand millionth: *nanosecond*.

neo- new: *neologism*.

neuro- nerves: *neurosurgery*.

non- not: *nonconformist*.

ob- against: *objection*.

octa- eight: *octagon; octopus*.

octo- ⇨ OCTA-.

omni- all: *omnipresent*.

out- 1. more or greater than: *outdo*. 2. external: *outhouse*.

over- 1. too or too much: *overweight*. 2. position above or across: *overhead*. 3. movement to a lower or reversed position: *overturn*.

palaeo- old or ancient: *Palaeocene*.

pan- all: *panchromatic*.

para- 1. near or beside: *paramilitary*. 2. beyond: *paranormal*.

patho- disease or suffering: *pathology*.

patri- father: *patriarch*.

penta- five: *pentagon*.

per- through or throughout: *pervade*.

peri- around or about: *perimeter*.

phono- sound: *phonology*.

photo- light: *photosensitive*.

physio- physical: *physiotherapy*.

pico- one million millionth: *picofarad*.

poly- many: *polyglot*.

post- behind or after: *posthumous*.

pre- before: *prearrange*.

pro- 1. in favour of: *pro-British; pro-life*. 2. forward: *proceed*.

proto- first: *prototype*.

pseudo- false or pretended: *pseudonym*.

psycho- psyche: *psychology*.

quadri- four: *quadrilateral*.

quasi- as if: *quasi-victory*.

re- 1. repetition: *recur*. 2. return or movement backwards: *retreat*.

retro- backwards: *retrospect*.

self- oneself: *self-control*.

semi- half: *semicircle*.

sept- seven: *septuagenarian*.

sex- six: *sextet*.

Sino- Chinese: *Sino-Tibetan*.

socio- social or society: *socio-economic*.

step- a relationship resulting from the remarriage of a parent: *stepmother*.

sub- 1. near: *subtropical*. 2. under: *submarine*. 3. further: *subdivide*.

super- 1. above or outside: *superstructure*. 2. superior in size or quality: *superman*. 3. an extreme or greater than usual degree: *supercharge*.

sym- ⇨ SYN-.

syn- together: *synchronize; symmetry*.

techno- technology: *technophobe*.

tele- distant: *telescope*.

tera- one million million: *terahertz*.

tetra- four: *tetrahedron*.

thermo- heat: *thermostat*.

trans- across: *transverse*.

tri- three: *triangle*.

ultra- 1. beyond: *ultrasonic*. 2. extremely: *ultraconservative*.

un- 1. not: *unable*. 2. the opposite or absence of something: *undesirability*. 3. the reversal of an action: *unbutton*.

under- 1. below or beneath: *underwear*. 2. not sufficiently: *underdeveloped*.

uni- one or single: *unicorn*.

vice- deputy: *vice-president*.

xeno- strange or foreign: *xenophobia*.

xero- dry: *xerophyte*.

Suffixes

-able 1. able to be: *obtainable*; *visible*.
2. worthy of: *likeable*; *contemptible*.

-aholic ⇨ -OHOLIC.

-an belonging to: *American*.

-ana a collection of material relating to a particular subject: *Victoriana*.

-archy rule or government: *matriarchy*.

-ase an enzyme: *amylase*.

-cide killing or killer: *suicide*.

-dom 1. a domain: *kingdom*. 2. a collection of people: *officialdom*. 3. a condition: *boredom*.

-ee a person who undergoes or receives something: *employee*.

-en[1] made of or resembling: *golden*.

-en[2] the plural of certain nouns: *children*.

-er[1] 1. a person or thing that performs an action: *sprinter*. 2. a person from a particular place: *New Yorker*.

-er[2] 1. the comparative degree of an adjective: *brighter*. 2. the comparative degree of an adverb: *sooner*.

-ese a language or style of language: *Chinese*.

-ess the feminine form of certain nouns: *countess*.

-est 1. the superlative degree of an adjective: *brightest*. 2. the superlative degree of an adverb: *soonest*.

-ette 1. something small: *cigarette*. 2. the feminine form of certain nouns: *usherette*.

-fold multiplied by: *twofold*.

-free 1. not containing: *sugar-free*. 2. not involving: *cruelty-free*.

-friendly 1. helpful to: *user-friendly*. 2. not harmful to: *environment-friendly*.

-gate a scandal: *Irangate*.

-gen producing: *hydrogen*.

-gon a plane figure with a certain number of sides: *hexagon*.

-hood a state, condition or character: *adulthood*.

-ible ⇨ -ABLE.

-ish 1. belonging to: *British*. 2. like: *childish*. 3. somewhat: *reddish*. 4. about: *fiftyish*.

-ism 1. an action or process: *terrorism*. 2. a characteristic: *Anglicism*. 3. a doctrine or theory: *socialism*. 4. discrimination on the grounds of: *racism*.

-ist 1. a person who does something: *artist*. 2. discriminating or a person who discriminates on the grounds of: *sexist*.

-ite a person associated with a place, doctrine, etc.: *Thatcherite*.

-itis inflammation: *tonsillitis*.

-ive 1. showing a tendency: *active*. 2. performing a function: *preservative*.

-ize, -ise 1. to perform an action or policy: *apologize*. 2. to cause to become something: *legalize*.

-less without: *friendless*.

-let something small: *booklet*.

-like resembling: *childlike*.

-logist a person who is skilled or trained in something: *psychologist*.

-logy the science or study of: *mythology*.

-ly 1. forming an adverb from an adjective: *sadly*. 2. like: *ghostly*. 3. per: *monthly*.

-mania extreme enthusiasm or desire for something: *megalomania*.

-meter an instrument which measures: *barometer*.

-metre a metre: *kilometre*.

-ness a quality or state: *darkness*.

-oholic addiction: *alcoholic*; *workaholic*.

-oid similar or something similar: *humanoid*.

-or a person or thing that performs an action: *governor*.

-ory[1] having a function or tendency: *compulsory*.

-ory[2] a person or thing used for a particular purpose: *observatory*.

-osis a process, condition or state: *metamorphosis*.

-path 1. a person who practises a kind of medical treatment: *homeopath*. 2. a person suffering from a disease: *psychopath*.

-pathy 1. feeling: *sympathy*. 2. medical treatment: *homeopathy*.

-person (used to avoid sex discrimination) a person: *salesperson*.

-phile a person who likes something: *bibliophile*.

-phobia fear or dislike: *claustrophobia*.

-phone sound: *telephone*.

-proof insulated from or not affected by: *fireproof*.

-ship condition, office, skill, etc.: *friendship*.

-th forming ordinal numbers: *sixth*.

-ward in a particular direction: *upward*.

-wards in a particular direction: *northwards*.

-wise 1. in a particular direction or position: *lengthwise*. 2. with reference to: *workwise*.

-worthy worthy of: *trustworthy*.

English Words Borrowed from Other Languages

This list gives examples of words that English has taken from a wide range of languages.

Language	Word
Afrikaans	apartheid
	trek
Arabic	alcohol
	assassin
	cotton
	mattress
	sash
	syrup
	zero
Bantu	banjo
	chimpanzee
	zombie
Chinese	gung-ho
	ketchup
	kowtow
	tai chi
	tea
	typhoon
Czech	robot
Dutch	boss
	coleslaw
	easel
	tattoo
	yacht
French	abattoir
	aide
	aperitif
	aplomb
	au gratin
	avalanche
	avant-garde
	baton
	bistro
	bouquet
	bureau
	bureaucracy
	café
	cigarette
	cliché
	envelope
	exchequer
	garage
	limousine
	meringue
	money
	morgue
	mousse
	oboe
	porridge
	racket
	rehearse
	restaurant

Language	Word
French cont.	routine
	rummage
	sabotage
	serviette
	souvenir
	suede
German	blitz
	delicatessen
	flak
	lager
	patrol
	poltergeist
	snorkel
	spanner
	zinc
Greek	antelope
	apocalypse
	charisma
	cosmetic
	cosmos
	drama
	hierarchy
	hysteria
	lantern
	martyr
	oasis
	paraphernalia
	pathos
	prophet
	stigma
	symposium
	tragedy
	trauma
Haitian	barbecue
Hebrew	jubilee
Hindi	bangle
	Blighty
	bungalow
	chapatti
	chintz
	chutney
	cot
	cushy
	dekko
	dinghy
	dungarees
	gymkhana
	jungle
	kedgeree
	loot
	pundit
	shampoo

Language	Word
Hindi *cont.*	thug
	veranda
Icelandic	berserk
	geyser
Irish Gaelic	hubbub
Italian	ditto
	fiasco
	ghetto
	gusto
	influenza
	lava
	malaria
	paparazzi
	pasta
	pizza
	portfolio
	replica
	soprano
	spaghetti
	studio
	torso
	umbrella
	vendetta
Japanese	judo
	karaoke
	karate
	sushi
	tycoon
Latin	ad hoc
	album
	alibi
	area
	arena
	candidate
	cemetery
	circus
	confetti
	dictator
	emancipate
	fraternal
	omnibus
	placebo
	plethora
	precarious

Language	Word
Latin *cont.*	publican
	quibble
	recruit
	secretary
	stadium
	stationer
	status quo
	tandem
	urban
	vaccine
	vacuum
	ventriloquist
Malay	amok
	bamboo
	gong
	orang-utan
	sarong
Norwegian	ski
Old Norse	ransack
Persian	caravan
	sherbert
Portuguese	albatross
Russian	glasnost
	intelligentsia
	perestroika
	steppe
	vodka
Sanskrit	lilac
Spanish	bonanza
	canyon
	cargo
	guerrilla
	incommunicado
	mosquito
	oregano
	patio
	tobacco
	tornado
	tortilla
Swedish	ombudsman
Tamil	catamaran
	curry
Turkish	kiosk
	tulip
	yogurt
Welsh	corgi
	flannel

Common Spellings

Common spelling	Other spellings

1 Vowel sounds

hat	pla*i*t, meringue
gate	train, gaol, gauge, hay, break, weight, convey, vein
past	calm, hard, heart, draught, clerk
ten	many, heavy, says, said, heifer, friend, guest, burial, leopard
pair	care, mayor, prayer, wear, there, their
see	gleam, aeon, quay, conceive, thief, even, magazine, key, amoeba, trio, people
hill	physics, women, business, building, England, sieve
ear	peer, pier, weird, mere, serious
bite	light, sky, lie, guy, height, eye, aisle
not	yacht, trough, wand, knowledge, cauliflower
so	bureau, sew, boat, yeoman, brooch, slow, although, owe, hoe
or	wall, saw, August, caught, door, board, sought, court
shoot	drew, move, crude, suit, true, shoe, through, manoeuvre, you, ewe, queue, feud
oil	boy, buoy
crowd	loud, bough, sauerkraut
cup	love, does, trouble, blood
put	book, wolf, worsted, could
fern	burn, err, were, first, myrtle, learn, masseur, journey, worm
away, fath**er**, mot**or**	soldier, probable, several, colour, metre, glorious

2 Consonant sounds

ball	rabbit
chair	hatch, righteous, institution, digestion
done	ladder, filled
find	philosophy, rough, cuff
give	ghost, guard, exist
help	who
jug	ridge, tragic, exaggerate, procedure, grandeur
cat	acclaim, question, ache, sack, kite, barque, biscuit, scholarship, box
let, ill	
man	summer, comb, solemn, paradigm
nose	knife, gnu, planning, pneumonia, mnemonic
sing	sink, meringue
paint	stopped
rain	rhythm, write, carry
sound	ceiling, ice, promise, scent, boss, psalm
shout	sugar, schedule, ocean, machine, special, conscience, execution, passion, expansion
table	thyme, ptomaine, lottery
thin	
there	lathe
vent	of, Stephen
weather	question, choir, whether
yellow	unite, euphemism, ewe
zero	was, scissors, xenophobia
mirage	treasure, decision

THE PERIODIC TABLE

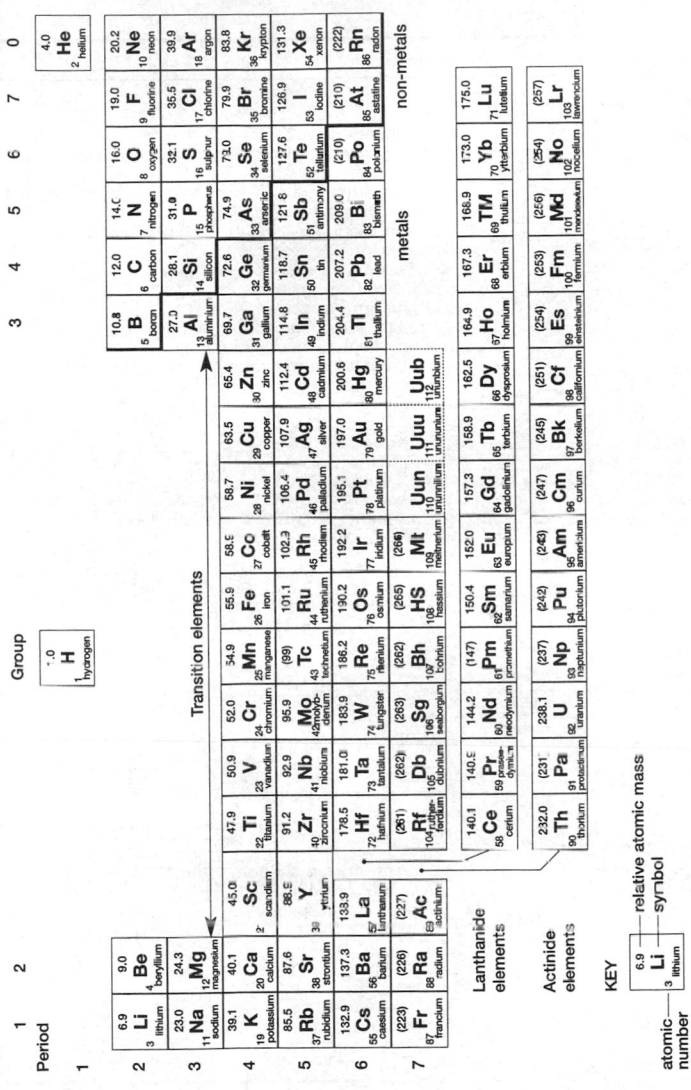

headword —

predicate (**pred**-i-kit) *noun*
Grammar a group of words in a sentence telling something about the subject: *In 'The girl wore a red hat', 'wore a red hat' is the predicate.*
● **predicate** (**pred**-i-kate) *verb* to declare or assert.
Word Family predication *noun*; **predicative** (pri-**dik**-a-tiv) *adjective*.
[Latin *praedicare* to proclaim]

clear guide to pronunciation and stress

etymology

prefer *verb* (**prefers; preferring; preferred**)
1 to like better: *Do you prefer tea or coffee?*
2 (*formal*) to put forward or submit: *to prefer a legal charge.*
Word Family preferable (**pref**-ra-b'l) *adjective* better or more desirable: *Tuesday would be preferable;* **preferably** *adverb;* **preferability** *noun*.
[Latin *praeferre* to carry or place before]

irregular spellings and parts of verb

clearly separated definitions

directly related words

prelude (**prel**-yood) *noun*
1 something which introduces or prepares for a later, more important event.
2 *Music* an introductory piece, such as an overture.
[*pre-* + Latin *ludere* to play]

word used in special field

principal (**prin**-si-p'l) *adjective*
first in rank or importance.
● **principal** *noun*
1 the head or leading official of a school, college or other organization.
2 a person with the leading part or position, as in one section of an orchestra, a play, etc.
3 a sum of money lent, borrowed or invested, on which interest is paid.
4 *Law* any person who employs another as an agent.
Word Family principally *adverb*.

same word as different part of speech

> [!] The words *principal* and *principle* sound the same but have different spellings and meanings. *Principal* ends in *al* and is an adjective or noun referring to the most important person or thing (*the principal routes out of the city; He is the new principal of the school*); *principle* ends in *le* and is only a noun, meaning 'a policy or standard' (*She has no principles*).

common error